P9-DBL-025

The SOURCE

A Guidebook of American Genealogy

The

SOURCE

A Guidebook of American Genealogy

Edited by Arlene Eakle and Johni Cerny

Published by
Ancestry Publishing Company
Salt Lake City, Utah
1984

Library of Congress
Catalog Card Number 84-70206

ISBN Number 0-916489-00-0

First Printing 1984
10 9 8 7 6 5 4

Printed in the United States of America.

CONTENTS

Foreword .... **ix**
P. William Filby

Preface .... **xi**
Arlene H. Eakle, Johni Cerny

Introduction to Genealogical Records and Techniques **1**
Richard W. Price, William Thorndale, Arlene H. Eakle

Categories of Source Materials
- Archives, Libraries, and Other Repositories
- Microform Materials
- Original Manuscripts and Photocopied Books
- Printed Histories and Compiled Sources

Choosing How-To Genealogy Books
Bibliography of How-To Publications
- Bibliographies
- General Series

State-by-State List
Finding Aids
- Guides and Inventories
- Institutional and Private Collections
- Periodicals, Books, and Book Dealers
- Finding Books
- Access to and Use of Indexes

Geography and History
- Maps, Atlases, and Locality Collections
- Migration and Settlement Patterns
- County Boundaries and Boundary Changes

Census Indexes and Spelling Variants
William Thorndale

- The Historical Dimension

Special Research Skills
- Notekeeping and Analysis of Data
- Fraudulent Pedigrees

Legalities
- Proper Documentation
- Rights of Privacy
- Freedom of Information
- Copyright

PART I. MAJOR RECORD SOURCES

1. Family and Home Sources, Family Traditions, and Oral Histories **30**
Richard W. Dougherty

Birth Records
Marriage Records
Death Records
Other Family Sources
Oral History
Bibliography

2. Vital Records and Cemetery Research **48**
Johni Cerny

Births and Deaths in Public Records
Problems with Vital Records
Finding Aids

Cemetery Records
Arlene H. Eakle

Types of Cemeteries
Types of Records
Research Preparation
Searching a Cemetery
Reading the Stones
Special Problems with Stones
Recording Cemetery Data
Bibliography

3. Marriage and Divorce Records **74**
Johni Cerny

Jurisdictions
Types of Marriage Records
Locating Marriage Records
Special Problems in Using Marriage Records

Divorce
Divorce Records
Locating Divorce Records

4. Census Records **90**
Arlene H. Eakle

Problems in Census Use
Suggestions for Microfilm Searches
Federal Censuses
Special Federal Schedules
State and Local Census Schedules, 1623-1918
Bibliography of Census Finding Aids, Tools, and Related Sources

5. Church Records in the United States **130**
Richard W. Dougherty

Immigrant churches
Types of Church Records
Church Records Projects

Locating Church Records
Research Suggestions

Denomination Archives, Repositories, and Recordkeeping Practices
Bibliography of Finding Aids

6. American Court Records.................150
Arlene H. Eakle

Importance of Courts in American Society
Legal Terms
Court Procedure
Sample Civil Case
Sample Criminal Case
Sample Equity Case
Court Records
How to Search Court Records
Probate
Special Court Proceedings
Bibliography

7. Land and Tax Records.....................216
William Thorndale

Deeds
State-Land States
Public-Domain States
Military Bounty Land
Taxes
Use of Land Records
Summary of State Land Records

8. Military Records...........................254
Johni Cerny

Service Records
Records of Veterans' Benefits
State Military Records
Selected Bibliography of American Military Records

9. Institutional Records......................300
Johni Cerny

Prison Records
Mortuary Records
Coroners' Records
School Records
Orphanage Records
Hospital and Medical Records
Bibliography

10. Business and Employment Records......326
Kory L. Meyerink

Colonial Business and Employment Records
Early American Business and Employment Records, 1780-1870
Modern American Business and Employment Records, 1870-Present
Locating Modern Records
Defunct Businesses
Railroad Employees
Bibliography
Appendix 1: Old Trades and Occupations
Appendix 2: Life Insurance Companies Commencing Business Prior to 1876 and in Active Operation in 1942
Appendix 3: United States Labor Union Records
Appendix 4: Index of Companies Profiled in *Everybody's Business, An Almanac,* 1981

United States Companies Ranked by *Fortune:* An Address List
Elaine Barton, Compiler
Appendix 5: 500 Top United States Companies
Appendix 6: Fifty Largest Life Insurance Companies
Appendix 7: Fifty Largest Transportation Companies
Appendix 8: Fifty Largest Retailing Companies
Appendix 9: Fifty Largest Utilities
Appendix 10: Fifty Largest Commercial Banking Companies
Appendix 11: Forty-five Largest Diversified Service Companies
Appendix 12: Fifty Largest Diversified Financial Companies

How to Find Business and Employment Records
Arlene H. Eakle

Finding Aids
Colleges and Universities
U.S. Government Personnel
Research Hints

PART II. PUBLISHED GENEALOGICAL SOURCES

11. City Directories and Their Cousins..386
Gordon Lewis Remington

General Problems with Directories
City and Telephone Directories
County and Regional Directories
Professional Directories
College-Related Directories
Religious Directories
Post Office and Street Directories
Bibliography

12. Newspapers..................................406
Loretto Dennis Szucs

How to Find Newspapers
United States Newspaper Project
How to Search Newspapers
Religious Newspapers
Foreign Language Newspapers
Current Newspapers
Indexes
Bibliography
How-To's and Anayltical Studies
Directories
Bibliographical Studies
State-by-State Bibliography
Ethnic, Religious, Foreign-Language, Occupational and Specialty Newspapers
General Indexes and Abstracts
State-by-State Indexes and Abstracts
Special Indexes

13. Genealogical Tools and Indexes........428
Kory L. Meyerink

Indexes Generated by the Church of Jesus Christ of Latter-day Saints
Family History and Genealogy Indexes and Bibliographies
Local Histories Indexes and Tools
Periodical Indexes
Indexes to Records
Regional Indexes
Other Name Indexes
Directories of Genealogists
Bibliography of Additional Research Aids

14. Compiled Biographies......................444
Jimmy B. Parker

Types of Biographies
Evaluation of Biographies
Finding Aids
Bibliography of General Biographical Compilations

PART III. SPECIAL RESOURCES

15. Tracking Immigrant Origins............452
Arlene H. Eakle

Emigration/Immigration Records
The Process of Americanization
Research Approaches
European/British Sources
Nationality Reference Directory
General Bibliographies
Immigration and Reprint Series
Immigrant Registers
National Source Papers
Specialty Genealogical Periodicals
Special Research Aids
Genealogical Society of Utah Microfilm Collections
Finding Aids
Country-by-Country Summary of Aids

16. Sources for Urban Ancestors............518
Loretto Dennis Szucs and David S. Weber

City Records
Neighborhood Sources
Ethnic Sources
Settlements
Other Urban Sources
Municipal Archives and Libraries
Selected Bibliography of Urban Sources
Urban Research Archives, Sources, and Guides
Urban Jurisdictions not Subject to County Authority

17. Records Relating to Native American Research: The Five Civilized Tribes 534
George J. Nixon

Records Relating to the Five Civilized Tribes, Federal Archives and Records Center, Fort Worth, Texas
Records Relating to the Five Civilized Tribes, National Archives, Washington, D.C.
Non-Federal Records
Records Relating to the Five Civilized Tribes, Oklahoma Historical Society
Case Studies
Bibliography
Appendix 1: Bureau of Indian Affairs Field Office Records

18. Genealogical and Historical Sources in the Spanish and Mexican Southwest....................................558
George J. Nixon

Records under Spanish Sovereignty and Mexican National Government
Records of New Mexico under Spanish Sovereignty and Mexican National Government
Records of Arizona under Spanish Sovereignty and Mexican National Government
Records of California under Spanish Sovereignty and Mexican National Government
Repositories
Bibliography of Guides, Inventories, and Catalogs

19. Black Ancestral Research................578
Johni Cerny

Federal Census Schedules
Military Records
Freedmen's Bureau and Related Records
Records of Slaves and Slavery
The Underground Railroad 1786-1860
Anti-Slavery Groups and Their Records
Registry of Black Ancestry
Bibliography

20. Asian Americans: Sources for Ancestral Research....................596
Spencer J. Palmer

Ethnic Groups in the United States
Tracing Asian Ancestry in the United States
Genealogical Sources in Asia
Bibliography of Asian-American Materials in United States Libraries

21. Jewish-American Research.............602
Johni Cerny

Jewish Synagogue Records in America
Congregational and Jewish Community Histories
Locating the Immigrant Ancestral Home
Jewish Ancestral Research Outside the United States
Tracing Victims and Survivors of the Holocaust
Printed Genealogies and Family Histories
Bibliography
German-Jewish Records on Microfilm
Polish-Jewish Records on Microfilm
Hungarian-Jewish Records on Microfilm

22. The Computer and the Genealogist..650
Wade C. Starks

The Computer Database
Using the Data
Hardware
Computer Glossary

Bibliography of Computer Databases and Information Sources
Wilma Adkins, Compiler

Reading List

23. Hereditary and Lineage Society Records..............................670
Grahame Thomas Smallwood, Jr.

"War" Societies
Early Settler and Ship Societies
Colonial Societies
Nationality (Ethnic) Societies
Religious Societies
Royal and Baronial Societies
Family Societies and Organizations
Location of Lineage Society Source Material
Comments for the Serious Lineage Society Researcher

List of Contributors..............................690

Appendix A: Regional Federal Archives and Records Centers..........................692

Appendix B: State Historical Archives and Record Depositories.....................693

Appendix C: Historical Societies and Agencies in the United States............694

Appendix D: Genealogical Society of Utah and Branches........................696

Appendix E: Selected Research Libraries..702

Appendix F: "Where to Write for Vital Records: Births, Deaths, Marriages, and Divorces,"
DHHS Publication No. (PHA) 82-1142.............703

Appendix G: Genealogical Societies of the United States..............................716

Appendix H: Genealogy Book Publishers..741

Glossary..742

Bibliographic Index..............................750

Subject Index..760

FOREWORD

As a bibliographer of genealogy I am constantly shown new manuals "guaranteed to help genealogists." They are almost invariably by one writer who attempts to cover all aspects; and while the compiler may be a leading authority on certain points, it is most unlikely that he or she can have the authority demanded for other aspects. There are a few manuals which are notable exceptions, but these are now showing signs of age and the bibliographies are hopelessly out of date. This is also true of such classics as Val Greenwood, *Researcher's Guide to American Genealogy*. The time is ripe for a completely new manual, current in all aspects, particularly in booklists and in discussions.

Salt Lake City, long a center of genealogy with outstanding collections and genealogists, has several who are recognized as leading authorities, generally in one subject. I have studied the text of *THE SOURCE,* and I was astonished at the knowledge shown by the sixteen authors of the four sections. Every problem is authoritatively examined and discussed, and in clear language researchers are told the solution—where the records are, how to secure them, how to use them, and how to do further research. Each subject has up-to-date bibliographies (I noted several references for December 1983); and most important of all, each compiler has listed many articles from magazines. So often we examine bibliographies and find to our disappointment that they contain only books, whereas an article of twenty pages often tells succinctly as much as a book of 200 pages. I have always advocated the inclusion of articles in any bibliography which is intended to convey to the user all that is available in any given subject.

Since immigration and naturalization are my specialties I took Arlene Eakle's study and found that, in spite of my absorption with the subject for some years, there was much that I did not know and that the bibliography was surely one of the best in existence. In particular, she has ferreted out many articles from comparatively unknown journals. These will be of inestimable value to researchers. Although I am no authority in many other subjects, each is written similarly and contains book and article lists. I am confident that what has been done on immigration has been equaled in other subjects.

Normally, it would be expected that certain subjects would get slighter treatment or might be omitted, but in this work there are a few subjects never seen in manuals, such as urban ancestral research, useful for its study of neighborhood libraries, newspapers, or vital records. City directories and business and employment records are given full treatment. In all, this is the best work of its kind attempted—certainly during my life in the field started some twenty-five years ago. I cannot conceive of any question not covered and answered for genealogists of all levels of skill and experience. Students, teachers, librarians, and historians in other fields will also find much of interest and use.

P. William Filby

PREFACE

THE SOURCE: A Guidebook of American Genealogy fills a need that has long been recognized by the genealogical community. In one volume, it identifies, locates, and interprets all of the basic manuscript, microfilm, and published record groups currently available for genealogical research between the beginnings of European colonization in America and 1910. This date was selected because it is the last federal census available for research under the restrictions of state and federal privacy laws.

Admittedly these chapters are representative rather than comprehensive in their use of examples. The much-needed chapter on sources for Indian research uses the Five Civilized Tribes and their records as illustrations of the types of resources available. The chapter on tracing immigrant ancestors to their overseas point of origin concentrates on British-Germanic emigration. Such choices were desirable in view of the areas of expertise of each author, the current needs of active genealogists as reflected in a 1983 survey conducted by the Genealogical Institute (Salt Lake City), and the space limitations for the volume.

Much of the information presented is, however, available here for the first time. Johni Cerny's analysis of prison records is a first. Elaine Barton has, for the first time, correlated manuscript collections in the Library of Congress's *National Union Catalogue of Manuscript Collections* (NUCMC) with the Fortune 500 and other major groups of United States businesses—a majority of them extending well back into the nineteenth century. No other in-one-place chart exists describing federal and state censuses available state by state with locations and finding aids. Other sections unique to this volume are William Thorndale's state-by-state description of documents of first title, essential for those tracing colonial ancestors; Arlene Eakle's research strategies for discovering locations of personnel records of noncurrent business firms and searching both sides of the Atlantic when seeking immigrant origins; Gordon Remington's comparative table linking directories available for cities with populations of 10,000 or more in the unindexed 1860-70 censuses; and Loretto D. Szucs's exhaustive list of finding aids for American newspapers, among others.

Our goal throughout has been to make these record sources usable by both the novice and the professional. Each record group is examined by source, record types, scope and quality of data provided, special problems in use, specific locations, and finding aids. Each chapter contains examples of the use of the sources by working genealogists. Maps and illustrations drawn from actual documents are selected to familiarize beginners with the formats they can expect when they go for the first time to a courthouse or thread their first reel of microfilm on the reader. Each chapter begins with a record-by-record grid showing what information you can expect to find on, say, a marriage license in Chapter 3, These grids also show which record types include signatures (essential for distinguishing between two persons of the same name), photographs, Social Security numbers, other relatives whose names are often unknown to the researcher, and the actual number of children a woman had.

An overview-summary chart, also at the beginning of each chapter, asks, "Can You Use This Chapter?" and discusses the types of records, the period of time during which they were kept, and some of the clues in your research that can alert you to the usefulness of these records. A glossary introduces unfamiliar terms, while seven appendixes give instant access to the addresses of federal records centers, state archives and historical societies, branch libraries of the Genealogical Society of Utah, genealogical societies in the United States, vital records centers in each state, and publishers that specialize in genealogical works. Every effort has been made to make the subject index comprehensive and analytical, with notes, bibliographies, and reading lists referenced in a separate Bibliography Index.

In short, *THE SOURCE* has been designed with the user in mind. Not only does it attempt to be a comprehensive reference work, it is also a guide to the research process that will help you plan research tasks more efficiently, evaluate findings more carefully, and construct pedigrees more accurately.

It is not, however, a how-to book. That function is filled by our companion volume, *Ancestry's Guide to Research* (Salt Lake City: Ancestry Publishing, 1984), a 300-page handy-sized paperback that uses a case-study approach with documents to teach research processes, information collection procedures, and—most crucially—the evaluation of evidence at tough research points.

The Source, needless to say, represents the combined efforts of many genealogists, all of whom, at one point or another, surpassed what could be considered reasonable expectations to meet the goals of comprehensiveness, thoroughness, and accuracy. The cooperation of the authors throughout has been exemplary. Many of them were asked to perform weekend miracles, not once but often. The professionalism and personal cordiality of personnel at the Genealogical Library of the Church of Jesus Christ of Latter-day Saints (often referred to as the Genealogical Society of Utah) has been unequalled throughout as they assisted with suggestions, encouragement, and permission to draw on its vast collection of printed and microfilmed sources for examples and illustrations. The National Archives and Records Service's printed guides and microfilm holdings have come a close second in usefulness.

We owe particular thanks to our colleagues in specialized areas, many of whom willingly critiqued early drafts of different chapters. Among them are Robert C. Anderson, Fellow of the American Society of Genealogists (FASG), formerly of Belchertown, Massachusetts (New England section of Chapter 7, "Land and Tax Records"); Colin James of Denver, Colorado (Chapter 6, "Court and Probate Records"); P. William Filby, Fellow of the Society of Genealogists, London (FSG) and compiler of the massive six-volume *Passenger and Immigration Lists Index, 1538-1900* (Chapter 15, "Tracking Immigrant Origins"); Hugh T. Law, European reference specialist, Genealogical Society of Utah (Chapter 15, "Tracking Immigrant Origins"); Paul Andereck, editor of *Genealogical Computing* (Chapter 22, "The Computer and the Genealogist"); Rabbi Malcolm H. Stern, genealogist for the American Jewish Archives (Chapter

21, "Jewish-American Records"); and George K. Schweitzer, Alumni Distinguished Professor at the University of Tennessee (Chapter 11, "City Directories and Their Cousins"). We have been grateful for their suggestions; but a work of this magnitude cannot hope to escape some errors of fact and/or interpretation. For these, we alone bear responsibility.

In addition, the commitment to excellence could not have been maintained if it had not been shared by the publisher John Sittner, who personally managed the project, the staff coordinators: first Sandra Western and then Robert Welsh; word processors Camille Kiger and Shirlene Franzen; Lavina Fielding Anderson and her staff at Editing, Inc., Larry and Nan Mead of Mead Graphics (Denver), Steve Newman and Robert Passey of Newman Passey Design (Salt Lake City), and Scott Mulvay and his staff at Mor Media Typesetting (Ogden).

INTRODUCTION TO GENEALOGICAL RECORDS AND TECHNIQUES

Richard W. Price, William Thorndale, and Arlene H. Eakle

This book exists for one reason—to give you, the researcher, a solid introduction to the major American record types from their beginnings up to 1910. It strikes a balance between the general survey and the specialized study, bringing into one volume material that is not available elsewhere, each chapter written by an expert on that record type who is either a practicing genealogist or an academic researcher.

You must realize that compiling a family history or genealogy requires more than a study of census, church, probate, land, and vital records. Hundreds of other tools exist, and you need to be able to locate, gain access to them, and understand their composition.

In most cases such vital statistics as birth, marriage, and death dates are not readily available, if at all, until the mid-nineteenth or even the twentieth centuries. Therefore, requesting "genealogical" information from a record repository on a given individual will usually yield nothing. Asking for historical information on a given individual, such as his or her name in a list of the sick, those fighting in a battle or working on a canal, will be more fruitful. You must be a detective in your research—creative, innovative, patient, and persistent in seeking answers.

Before anything else, you need to understand where to find records, how to use repositories, what the genealogical process is, and the geographical, historical, and legal implications of the research process.

Categories of Source Materials

Archives, Libraries, and Other Repositories

More than 30,000 libraries and historical societies exist in the United States. These, as well as courthouses and other archives, are the major places you will find records once you have plumbed the sources in your home and those of relatives. As a researcher you must know how to find and use these repositories. Public records and historical documents are preserved in an archive. *Archives* can also refer to the documents actually held in the repository.

You might immediately think of major repositories such as the National Archives, Genealogical Society of Utah, New England Historic Genealogical Library, or Newberry Library. However, repositories in every county and virtually every city in the country have records valuable to the genealogist. The local library is a good place to begin your search. The county courthouse in the county of interest would also be a high priority. Most libraries have books listing other repositories where important genealogical records are kept. These include:

Akey, Denise S., ed. *Encyclopedia of Associations*. 17th ed. Detroit: Gale Research Company, 1983.

Craig, Tracey Linton, comp. and ed. *Directory of Historical Societies and Agencies in the United States and Canada*. 12th ed. Nashville: American Association for State and Local History, 1982.

Filby, P. William, comp. *American and British Genealogy and Heraldry: A Selected List of Books*. 3rd ed. Boston: New England Historic Genealogical Society, 1983.

Hamer, Philip M., ed. *A Guide to Archives and Manuscripts in the United States*. New Haven: Yale University Press, 1961.

Library of Congress. *National Union Catalog of Manuscript Collections*. Washington, D.C.: Library of Congress, 1975.

National Register Company. *The Official Museum Directory*. Skokie, Ill.: Standard Rates and Data, 1983. Published annually.

Young, Margaret L., and Harold C. Young, eds. *Directory of Special Libraries and Information Centers*. 6th ed. Detroit: Gale Research Company, 1981.

To determine what libraries are available in a given locality, consult Jacques Cattell Press, *American Library Directory* (New York: R. R. Bowker Company, 1983). A new edition of this volume is printed biannually. This directory includes all libraries in the United States, its possessions, and Canada. Some 30,000 libraries are described as well as library agencies, libraries for the deaf and blind, and interlibrary loan systems.

The libraries listed in *American Library Directory* are categorized alphabetically, first by state, then by city, then by name of the institution. With each listing is the address, telephone number, name of directors, year founded, number of volumes, names of special collections, and branches and bookmobiles available. Copies are available at your public library.

When you use resources in any repository you should follow some basic rules. Original documents, often found in county court houses and public record centers, need to be handled with great care. Pencil, rather than pen, should be used to protect the original record from damage. It is also easier to make corrections in your notes with pencil.

Great care should be taken with transcribed or printed records. Human error is always possible when a record is copied. Whenever possible, use an original record or microform of an original record so that items omitted or recorded incorrectly in transcribed records are not missed.

People in a local library or courthouse who work regularly with the records in the area where an ancestor resided may be aware of indexes and collections of records that are not available elsewhere.

When you enter a library or archive you must understand its cataloging system and know how to locate its holdings. If a guide has been published, acquaint yourself with it before visiting the repository. (Guides and inventories are discussed below.) Catalogs in most repositories are similar, yet each has peculiarities. Traditional systems use three-by-five card files which categorize all books, manuscripts, serials, and maps under at least three different headings: author, title, or subject. Genealogical libraries usually add a fourth for locality. More modern facilities have the same classifications but are converting their card systems to microform or computer. When computer terminals are used, written instructions are usually supplied. If you input an error (phrase your request incorrectly), the Cathode Ray Tube (CRT) will flash up an explanation of what to do to make corrections.

Once a desired record is found in a catalog, it will usually be classified under the Library of Congress (LC) or Dewey Decimal classification systems (call number). A basic knowledge of these systems will help in using any library. Most libraries in the United States use the Dewey system or an adaptation of it. Larger libraries, especially those with concentrated collections on specific topics find the Library of Congress system easier, since new books often come with Library of Congress cards preprinted.

The Dewey Decimal system is based on ten major subject divisions, each further broken into subdivisions through the use of Arabic numbers and decimals. Every classification is based on a three-digit number. If the topic is a more minute subdivision of the main subject, additional digits are added after a decimal point.

The Library of Congress classification system also classifies according to subject but utilizes the letters of the alphabet. Knowledge of either of these classification systems is helpful but will not substitute for using the library catalog. Browsing the shelves is an easy way to find what books are available for a given locality, but it is also risky since important materials will be classified under different categories. You may overlook oversize books, often kept in separate locations; and as more and more records are collected on microform, browsing will not help you effectively determine what records are available in a given repository.

In addition to the basic letter or numbering systems of the Library of Congress and Dewey systems, each book is assigned at least one Cutter number, named, like Dewey, for the librarian who devised it. This number, usually appears directly below the subject class number, and in the Dewey system, uses the first one or two letters (depending on the name) of the author's surname, followed by a number assigned to that particular author. When an author has written more than one book, the first letter(s) of the first word of the book title will follow so the books can be shelved alphabetically. For example, in Val Greenwood's *The Researcher's Guide to American Genealogy*, the Cutter number would be something like G859r. The "G" stands for Greenwood, "859" is the number assigned to this author, and the "r" is the first letter in the title of the book, (*The*, *A*, or *An* never count).

The Library of Congress system also frequently uses Cutter numbers to indicate things other than author, and a book may often have two Cutter numbers (seldom more) – one for the author, and one for something else. The Genealogical Society of Utah has modified its Cutter numbers to refer to record category rather than author. See Norman E. Wright and David H. Pratt, *Genealogical Research Essentials* (Salt Lake City: Bookcraft, 1967), Chapter 5.

Microfilm and microfiche records, more and more prevalent, especially in genealogical repositories, are often classified separately from the Dewey or Library of Congress systems and can be explained with a flier or by a reference consultant at the repository. Their call numbers may be recorded in a separate register. Whenever a given record cannot be found or if the system used by a library or archive is not clear, never hesitate to ask for assistance. Hours can be saved by a short chat with a consultant.

In addition to the references already cited, these may be helpful:

Iredale, David. *Enjoying Archives: What They Are, Where to Find Them, How to Use Them*. Newton Abbot, England: David & Charles, 1973.

Kaminkow, Marion J., ed. *United States Local Histories in the Library of Congress: A Bibliography*. Baltimore: Magna Carta Book Company, 1975.

Wagner, Anthony Richard. *English Genealogy*. 2nd ed. Oxford: Clarendon Press, 1972.

See also the "How-to Books" section below. Most methods books describe how to use libraries effectively.

Microform Materials

As time passes and pedigrees are extended, the number of records you need grows voluminously. You would need to spend a lifetime travelling from town to town in a county, from county to county in a given state, and on to other states and countries to find all the records necessary to compile a pedigree. The development of the microform in the past fifty years has been invaluable in making this myriad of record sources accessible.

Microform is a generic term for any information, communication, or storage medium containing images too small to be read without magnification. The most common microforms found in genealogical and historical archives are the 35mm or 16mm reels of microfilm. The microfiche, a sheet of microfilm containing multiple micro-images in a two-dimensional grid pattern of rows and columns, is also coming into greater use in all main libraries. Old library card files are changing to microfiche card catalogues. Newspapers and telephone directories are also commonly found on microfiche as is the Genealogical Society of Utah's International Genealogical Index.

Other types of microform include ultrafiche, a microfiche that reduces the size of the original ninety times or more, whereas microfilm and fiche reduce only twelve to twenty-four times. Ultrafiche makes possible extremely high-storage density and may be the microform of the future. Micro-opaque cards are like microfiche, but have different images on each side of the card, enabling them to hold twice as much data as microfiche. Cassette and cartridge microforms are also being used in many storage systems and may become more common to the genealogist with time. All of these systems can be duplicated quickly and inexpensively and will undoubtedly be invaluable to archivists and family historians in coming years.

Libraries which have microform holdings also have reading machines to use these tools. Instruction booklets or directions from the librarian can help you learn to use these records quickly.

Microform has made a tremendous impact on record storage. For example, the sheer size and volume of newspapers makes it difficult to have them bound and made accessible to the public. Because they are printed on cheap high-acid paper they are also a problem to store and constant use of such original records would also damage them irreversibly in time. Such registers could never be replaced if lost or stolen so any method to preserve them and make them accessible to the public is desirable. Furthermore, smaller libraries with neither the funding nor the storage space for such records, need sources that are inexpensive and take little space.

Microfilm, the first type of microform to be used extensively, has saved for archives many records that have subsequently been burned, stolen, or otherwise lost. The National Archives would have lost valuable letters from the U.S. Attorney General's files in 1962 had not a Stanford University professor microfilmed the bulk of the folders a short time before their disappearance. Today, many archives systematically store valuable items in vaults and make microform duplicates available for use.

Although most family historians would prefer to use the original record, most repositories don't give them a choice. Microforms are used to preserve older materials in danger of deterioration, reduce theft and mutilation, save shelving space, reduce circulation costs, make cataloging more economical, and make original records available to numerous repositories, thus reducing costs of travel to gain access to records.

Microfilm usually reproduces bound volumes of records like printed books, recorded deeds, marriage registers, and other documents recorded in bound volumes. Loose papers such as certificates, case files, petitions, and correspondence may not be filmed because it is too costly to unfold each document individually for filming, then refold it for storage. The bulk of these records will be found in file boxes in courthouse attics and inadequately protected storage areas.

Except in the case of private institutions, most microform records can be acquired through interlibrary loan from major repositories and libraries throughout the United States and in some foreign countries. In addition to the catalogs which most major repositories hold for their own collections, Ardis Voegelin-Carleton, *Guide to Microforms in Print, Incorporating International Microforms in Print* (Westport, Conn.: Microform Review Inc., 1980), helps to determine what records are available in microform.

Happily, some repositories allow open access to the shelves of microfilm or microfiche, eliminating the filling out of forms, waiting in lines to order desired records, and waiting for attendants to produce the records you want.

Here are some sources that will help you read further into the miniaturized marvels of microform.

Ashby, Peter. *Microform Publishing.* Boston: Butterworth Inc., 1979.

Bahr, Alice Harrison. *Microforms: The Librarians' View, 1978-79.* White Plains, N.Y.: Knowledge Industry Publications, Inc., 1980.

Ballou, Hubbard W., ed. *1973 Supplement to the Guide to Microreproduction Equipment.* New York: Vance Weaver Compositions, Inc., 1973.

Gabriel, Michael R., and Dorothy P. Ladd. *The Microform Revolution in Libraries.* Foundations in Library and Information Science, edited by Robert D. Stueart, vol. 3. Greenwich, Conn.: Jai Press Inc., 1980.

Kish, Joseph L., Jr. *Micrographics: A User's Manual.* New York: John Wiley & Sons, Inc., 1980.

Meckler, Alan Marshall. *Micropublishing: A History of Scholarly Micropublishing in America, 1938-1980.* Contributions in Librarianship and Information Science, edited by Paul Wasserman, no. 40. Westport, Conn.: Greenwood Press, 1982.

Nixon, Hargrave, Devans, and Doyle. *Admissibility in Evidence of Microfilm Records.* Rochester, New York: Eastman Kodak Company, 1971.

Professional Librarian Series. *The Professional Librarian's Reader in Library Automation and Technology.* White Plains, New York: Knowledge Industry Publications, Inc., 1980.

Saffady, William. *Micrographics.* Littleton, Colo.: Libraries Unlimited, Inc., 1978.

Original Manuscripts and Photocopied Books

The most valuable record to you as a researcher is the one prepared at the time an event occurred, preferably by an eyewitness or by someone connected closely to the event at hand. This is a primary source. Records that are made at a later date or from secondhand knowledge are commonly referred to as secondary sources. Original manuscripts such as church and court records, generally handwritten, are the type of records found basically in archival collections. Public libraries seldom have such manuscripts, although they often will have microform copies of such records, which, if photoreproduced correctly, are as valuable as the original manuscript itself.

The *National Union Catalog of Manuscript Collections* (Washington, D.C.: Library of Congress, 1962 is a multi-volume set of books listing all known major manuscript collections in reposi tories in the United States. This catalog (commonly referred to as NUCMC) categorizes the collections by title, physical description, location, or main entry or name of person/family/corporate body around which the collection was formed with a brief annotation of the contents.

NUCMC intends to bring scholars and manuscripts together. No limitations are placed on the time, place or origin, or nature of the collections recorded. It is categorized by subject and indexed in various ways. One section lists thousands of genealogies alphabetically by surname; other sections include church records, court records, land records, and other references vital to the genealogist.

The *Directory of Archives and Manuscript Repositories in the United States* (Washington, D.C.: National Historical Publications and Records Commission, 1978) gives details about archives that hold collections listed in NUCMC, as well as numerous other repositories valuable to the genealogist. Public libraries' holdings and ethnic collections are specifically referenced. Although not a complete listing of all groups of archives and manuscripts in all depositories, it does guide a searcher in finding the particular groups of archives or manuscripts that contain the information he desires. This directory is arranged alphabetically by state and subsequently by city and institutional name within the city. Preceding each state entry is a description of its program for local government records. This volume updates Hamer.

Philip M. Hamer, *A Guide to Archives and Manuscripts in the United States* (New Haven: Yale University Press, 1961) is a resource similar to the above *Directory.* As an illustration, Hamer describes the Chicago's renowned Newberry Library this way:

> The Newberry Library, at 60 West Walton Pl. Chicago, has over 4 million pages of material dated from 800 A.D. to the present day. It covers material relating to world history and literature, including a Medieval and Renaissance collection, material on Indians including Creek, Cherokee and others. Original manuscripts relating to the Philippines, Spain, Cuba, Mexico, Matamoros, and many states in the Union are included. Details of these papers, their authors, time period covered and content are included in the *Guide.*

Since Hamer also describes microfilm holdings, his work contains important information not found in other directories. University Microfilms (300 Zeeb Road, Box 1467, Ann Arbor, MI 48106) makes available to the public virtually all dissertations and theses produced at American universities in xerox or microform copy. It also has a large genealogical and local history collection, and over 100,000 out-of-print books which can be ordered at a reasonable price, and some 13,000 periodicals are available in paper copy or microform. Hence, by contacting University Microfilms, you can read virtually any book, dissertation, or periodical that has ever been published in the United States, and many foreign records. University Microfilms absorbed Microfilm Corporation of America's genealogy program in 1983. It will send, at no cost, a copy of its *Genealogy and Local History Catalogue* on request. Questions can also be answered by telephone at (800) 521-0600 ext. 293.

Another valuable source of manuscripts is edited by B. R. Crick and Miriam Alman, *A Guide to Manuscripts Relating to America in Great Britain and Ireland* (Oxford: Oxford University Press, 1961). This can be especially useful if you're seeking information about individuals who have migrated from Great Britain and Ireland to the Americas.

Countless copies of these manuscripts are available in microform or xerox copies in libraries and other repositories across the country. Although you may not always be allowed to check out genealogical books at libraries or order them through interlibrary loan, usually you can order many necessary records through this process. Most university and public libraries belong to the system of interlibrary loans and borrow works from each other for their patrons. For example, the United States censuses from 1790 through 1910 are available on loan to any bona fide library, genealogical or historical society through a private contractor who deals with the National Archives. The fee for borrowing one microfilm (as of 1984) is $2.25. The needed census can be kept at the repository for seven calendar days, then returned. To order the microfilms, including Soundexes (name indexes) for 1880, 1900, and 1910 censuses, write to DDD Company, Census Microfilm Rental Program, Box 2940, Hyattsville, MD 20784. They will supply the repository with literature and order forms for the needed records.

Printed Histories and Compiled Sources

As you conduct your research, second only to home and family sources are printed histories, genealogies, and other compiled sources. If you don't consult the records relating to a given family before beginning research, you may be duplicating a search. Comb through all secondary records before undertaking original research. Here are some books which will help you find what has already been published.

Marion J. Kaminkow, ed., *Genealogies in the Library of Congress: A Bibliography* 2 vols. (Baltimore: Magna Carta Book Company, 1972) and its supplement published in 1977 brings up to date similar printed works published in 1910 and 1919 and 1954 under the title *American and English Genealogies in the Library of Congress*. These newer versions include not only English and American genealogies but also Canadian, Irish, Welsh, Scottish, Australian, Latin American, Polish, German, Dutch, Scandinavian, French, Spanish, Italian, Portuguese, and Asian sources. It includes all the entries from the Family Name Index, the sixty-drawer card catalog located in the Local History and Genealogy Room of the Library of Congress. These cards refer both to printed books and to genealogies that exist only in typescript and manuscript. These indexes place together family names which are pronounced alike, or almost alike, even though there are differences in spelling. A particularly helpful service is that the bibliography includes Library of Congress call numbers so that you can order a desired book through interlibrary loan or through University Microfilms if it is not locally available.

An important supplement is M. J. Kaminkow, *A Complement to Genealogies in the Library of Congress* (Baltimore: Magna Carta Book Company, 1981). The *Complement* also lists holdings of other libraries with genealogical collections and includes foreign genealogies and unpublished genealogies.

These tools tell you about specific family histories. Some of the older, out-of-print genealogies are being reproduced in microform so that smaller or more recently established genealogical libraries can acquire them easily. If you examine the same book in more than one library, you may find different marginal corrections, additions, appendixes, and the like by the author or a member of the family. It is unlikely, however, that unpublished material will be found anywhere except in one library.

Another important record is Miranda C. Herbert and Barbara McNeil, eds., *Biography and Genealogy Master Index* (Detroit: Gale Research Company, 1980). This is a consolidated index to more than 3,200,000 biographical sketches in over 350 current and retrospective biographical dictionaries. It helps determine which edition of which publication to consult and includes over 350 publications. It is particularly useful to smaller libraries, as it tells which sources may have information about an individual. It covers biographical dictionaries, subject encyclopedias, and volumes of literary criticism. It emphasizes the United States but includes some Canadian, British, African, Far East, and Australasian biographies as well. For more details on published biographies, see Chapter 14, "Compiled Biographies," and Chapter 13, "Genealogical Tools and Indexes."

Compiled sources, such as printed genealogies, come in as wide a variety as there are surnames. Carefully check for types of sources listed in these records, as well as the quantity and quality of the source materials used. In a printed genealogy you might find that virtually every name, date, and place is documented by footnotes to a primary source or other valid record. Such a record will save you countless hours. If you question the links made between generations, consult the source as cited to prove or disprove your conclusions. Such perfectly cited histories are not common but they *are* available and should be sought.

At the other end of the spectrum is the family history, perhaps of four or five hundred pages, which may include all descendants of an immigrant ancestor from 1600 to the 1900s. It looks like a goldmine, but be wary if it contains no source material or references telling where the information originated. In addition, there may be no introduction or discussion of the preparation of the volume, and as the book was published in the nineteenth century, the author can not be contacted. Think of it as a map but spot-check extensively against original sources. If it doesn't have a high degree of accuracy, then resist the temptation to use it.

As you can see, you must develop a critical outlook on all materials prepared by others on a given family. A trained genealogist can tell in a few minutes the quality of the record under investigation. Most printed sources can be used as valuable tools in extending a pedigree, but care must be taken in trusting the contents of any compiled genealogy.

Choosing How-to Genealogy Books

Since each pedigree problem is different enough to take the researcher into sources unique to that problem, each writer brings a different insight and experience to genealogy. For this reason, we suggest that you use more than one how-to book. If there are three articles on researching New Jersey ancestry, compare all of them for coverage.

Some books offer a comprehensive treatment of each topic. Some include brief comments only. Reading promotional literature may not enlighten you either, for books are often sold as comprehensive when they include a major focus only, omitting all topics that do not fit the focus.

A how-to book is most helpful when it is easy to follow and which you can refer back to as your research progresses. Here are some tests of usefulness:

1. Does it have a preface or introduction describing the purpose of the book and identifying the audience it is especially designed for? A statement about what is included and what is omitted is also helpful.
2. See if there is an index or a detailed table of contents. What is the level of detail? A careful subject index is a necessity for any reference book more than fifty pages in length. Sometimes a detailed table of contents can serve almost the same purpose if major headings and subheads for each section are included.
3. Does the author describe the content of his/her sources in both original and printed form? Are indexes and finding aids cited? Are addresses included for obscure items? Are suggestions for further reading given so you can learn more if your interest is keen? A good how-to book will instruct you on techniques and sources and then send you off to try them out on your own, carefully fortified with references to tools which make searching easier and with examples of how other genealogists have used that information. In this way, you can begin at once and increase your own expertise as you search.
4. Try reading a paragraph or two. What reading level is expected? Are unfamiliar words defined in parentheses, footnotes, or a glossary? Are step-by-step instructions clear and easy to follow? With clear examples, you will feel, "Aha! I can do this!" If you are a beginner, you will need a step-by-step guide with clear, *easy-to-follow* instructions that are well illustrated, involve you directly in the action, and stress the *how* rather than the *who* or the *what*.

Harriet Stryker-Rodda, *How to Climb Your Family Tree* (1977; reprint ed., Baltimore: Genealogical Publishing Co., 1983) is such a beginner's book. It is short (144 pages), informal, and personal. It describes the basic record categories and what they contain with carefully selected extracts. It also includes sample extract sheets.

For a beginner, collection of data is an important stage of the research process. *How to Climb Your Family Tree* covers this first stage adequately. It does not, however, tell how to fit the information together nor how to resolve problems of identity, where more than one person of the same name exist at the same time in the same place.

Two other books published about the same time are Suzanne Hilton, *Who Do You Think You Are? Digging for Your Family Roots* (New York: New American Library, 1976) and Bill R. Linder, *How to Trace Your Family Tree: A Basic Guide to Genealogy* (New York:

Everest House, 1978). These books are more complete and cover the whole research process in simple, effective, and interesting ways.

Table 1 is an evaluation grid showing the contents of each of these three beginners' books. As you can see, each is valuable in its own way, bringing you the author's specific experiences and insights. Knowing what each contains, you can choose the one most likely to fit your present research needs.

Suzanne Hilton's book may seem to be the best buy – it covers more topics in more pages and costs less. However, it treats each topic in less detail than Harriet Stryker-Rodda's book, which covers less material and spends more time on each source. Bill Linder's book emphasizes record keeping and family cooperative effort. The one you choose, as a beginner, will be the one that appeals to you or fits your specific needs.

For more experienced researchers who need greater depth of treatment, a variety of how-to books are available. The charts in Table 2 and Table 3 are adapted and updated from the *APG Newsletter* 3 (Jan.-Feb. 1981): 8-11 and 6 (Jan. 1984), both special how-to issues published by the Association of Professional Genealogists, Box 11601, Salt Lake City, UT 84147. Table 2 deals with various research techniques you will find in different methodology books. Table 3 deals with source materials and their genealogical applications. Full publication information follows the tables. Each table will help you choose the books and articles most likely to cover the topics you need. How-to guides for tracing immigrants into their places of birth are listed in Chapter 15, "Tracking Immigrant Origins."

The bibliography lists how-to and source guides for specific geographical areas. It is arranged by state for easy reference. Names and addresses for publishers of these materials can be found in Appendix H of this volume.

Askin, Jayne, with Bob Oskam. *Search: A Handbook for Adoptees and Birthparents*. New York: Harper & Row, 1982. 313 pp. Emphasis is on twentieth-century research with some excellent research strategies for accessing and using modern records. Includes descriptions of sources not included in other methods books.

Beard, Timothy F. *How to Find Your Family Roots*. New York: McGraw Hill, 1977. 1,005 pp. About half of the 1,005 pages is a comprehensive guide to names and addresses of record repositories throughout the world.

Bremer, Ronald A. *Compendium of Historical Sources: The How and Where of American Genealogy*. Salt Lake City: Butterfly Publishing, Inc., 1983. 1,003 pp. Available from Ronald A.

Table 1

Important Elements In a How-To Book

A. Suzanne Hilton, *Who Do You Think You Are? Digging for Your Family Roots* (New York: New American Library, 1976), paperback, 194 pp. $1.75.

B. Bill R. Linder, *How to Trace Your Family History: A Basic Guide to Genealogy* (New York: Everest House 1978), hardcover, 187 pp. $6.95.

C. Harriett Stryker-Rodda, *How to Climb Your Family Tree: Genealogy for Beginners* (1977; Baltimore: Genealogical Publishing Co., 1983), paperback, 144 pp. $6.95.

Ideas Treated:	A.	B.	C.
Beginning with self	●	●	●
Family records	●	●	●
Oral interviews	●	●	●
Importance of grandparents		●	
Contacting relatives	●	●	
Family organizations	●	●	
Personal history	●	●	
Family traditions			●
Names, spellings	●	●	
Relationships	●	●	
Handwriting		●	
Recordkeeping	●	●	●
Sample forms	●	●	●
Calculating dates	●	●	●
Documenting genealogy	●	●	●
Using libraries	●	●	●
Periodicals	●	●	●
Using indexes	●		
Geography, history	●	●	●
Heraldry	●	●	
Abstracting data		●	●
Evaluating sources	●	●	
Church sources	●	●	●
Cemeteries	●		●
Deeds, mortages	●	●	●
Probate records	●	●	●
Census records	●	●	●
Military records	●	●	●
Court records	●	●	
Naturalizations	●	●	
Passenger lists	●	●	
Vital records	●	●	●
Names and addresses	●		
Photographs	●		
Adoptees	●		
Divorces	●		
Ethnic ancestors	●		
Prisoners	●		
Drug addicts	●		
Black genealogy	●	●	
Immigrants	●	●	●
Writing your history	●	●	
Sharing research	●	●	
Recommended readings	●	●	
Hiring a professional	●	●	
Genealogy as a career	●	●	

Table 2
Techniques Covered

Authors

	Askin	*Beard*	*Bremer*	*Brown*	*Cerny, Eakle*	*Dixon, Flack*	*Doane, Bell*	*Draznin*	*Greenwood*	*Harland*	*Helmbold*	*Jacobus*	*Jaussi, Chaston*	*Jones, Eakle, Christensen*	*Rubincam, ed.*	*Smith, ed.*	*Westin*	*Williams*	*Wright*	*Zabriskie*
Adoptees	●	●	●	●												●	●			
Advertising in newspapers	●													●						
Alternatives to writing a family history																				
Arranging a genealogy					●		●	●										●		
Bibliography	●	●	●		●	●	●	●	●		●		●	●		●	●	●	●	●
Calendars, dating		●	●		●		●		●	●	●		●	●	●	●		●		●
Case studies				●	●							●				●			●	●
Compiled genealogies and histories		●		●			●		●	●		●	●	●	●					
Correspondence	●		●		●	●		●	●		●		●	●	●				●	●
Ethnic research	●	●	●	●			●	●							●	●			●	
Evaluating evidence			●		●	●		●	●	●	●	●	●	●	●				●	●
Family tradition	●		●		●		●		●		●	●		●	●			●	●	
Finding aids and guides	●		●		●		●		●					●	●	●		●		
Glossary of terms			●		●				●				●					●		●
Heraldry		●		●			●										●	●		
Home sources		●			●	●	●				●	●	●	●	●		●	●	●	
How to Begin	●		●	●	●	●		●		●			●	●	●	●		●	●	●
How to form a family organization													●	●			●			
How to hire a genealogist	●		●	●	●		●					●	●	●			●			●
How to plan research					●				●	●	●			●						●
How to use indexes, tools					●		●		●					●		●		●	●	
How to use a library	●	●	●		●		●	●	●		●	●	●	●		●	●	●	●	●
Immigrant ancestors		●	●	●	●		●	●	●		●				●		●	●	●	
Index	●		●		●		●	●	●	●	●	●	●	●		●		●		●
Interviewing relatives	●	●		●	●	●	●	●			●		●	●			●			●
Notekeeping			●	●	●		●	●	●	●	●		●	●		●	●	●	●	●
Numbering charts, forms		●			●		●	●					●						●	●
Placing ancestors in historical context			●		●	●			●	●		●		●				●		●
Publishing a history							●			●					●					●
References for further study, readings	●		●	●	●	●			●				●	●		●		●	●	●
Relationships			●	●	●		●					●	●	●					●	●
Research ethics	●				●			●		●		●		●				●		●
Sources–use and contents	●	●	●	●	●	●	●	●	●	●	●	●	●	●	●	●	●	●	●	●
Special lists		●	●		●		●		●				●	●		●	●	●	●	
Step-by-step approach					●						●		●	●						●
Surnames, names			●	●	●		●		●			●	●	●	●		●	●		
Use of maps		●		●										●				●		
Writing family history				●		●		●				●				●	●	●		

Table 3

Sources Covered

Authors

	Askin	Beard	Bremer	Brown	Cerny, Eakle	Dixon, Flack	Doane, Bell	Draznin	Greenwood	Harland	Helmbold	Jacobus	Jaussi, Chaston	Jones, Eakle, Christensen	Rubincam, ed.	Smith, ed.	Westin	Williams	Wright	Zabriskie
Afro-American (black)		●			●		●	●							●	●	●			
Asian-American					●			●								●	●			
Biographical sources		●			●				●		●			●	●					
Business/Employment	●			●	●															
Cemetery records	●	●	●	●	●	●	●	●	●	●	●				●	●	●		●	
Census	●	●	●	●	●		●	●	●	●	●				●	●	●	●	●	
Church records	●	●	●		●	●	●	●	●	●	●	●	●		●	●	●	●	●	
City directories	●	●			●															
Computer databases			●		●														●	
Court, probate	●	●	●		●		●	●	●	●	●	●				●		●	●	
Hispanic-American					●			●								●	●			
Home sources	●	●	●	●	●	●		●			●	●	●	●	●		●	●	●	
Immigration sources		●	●	●	●		●	●	●		●		●		●		●	●	●	
Indian: *See* Native American																				
Institutional records	●	●	●		●				●					●	●			●		
Jewish research		●			●		●	●							●		●			
Land records	●	●	●	●	●		●	●	●	●	●				●	●		●	●	
Legalities	●				●							●								
Marriage	●	●			●		●		●	●						●	●	●		
Military records	●		●		●		●		●	●	●				●	●	●	●	●	
Native American research		●			●		●	●			●					●	●		●	
Newspapers	●	●			●		●	●	●		●	●		●		●				
Patriotic/lineage societies		●	●	●	●						●				●		●			
Repositories (names, addresses)	●	●	●	●		●	●	●									●			
Urban ancestors research					●															
Vital records	●	●	●	●	●	●	●	●	●	●	●	●			●	●	●	●	●	
Special techniques																				
Autobiography						●										●				
Handwriting					●				●		●			●	●					
Oral history					●	●	●							●	●	●			●	
Photograph analysis					●															
Psychohistory	●				●												●			
Quantification/statistics					●											●				

Bremer, Box 16422, Salt Lake City, UT 84116. Useful odd facts—the sort of information Ron Bremer is famous for: reconstructing military records lost by fire, census forms with headings reproduced directly from original enumeration sheets, county name changes and multiple courthouses, property qualifications for voting in the American colonies, and names and addresses for thousands of record and information agencies.

Brown, Norman. *The Trace Your Roots Workbook*. New York: Grosset & Dunlap, 1978. Title is misleading. It is *not* a workbook.

Cerny, Johni, and Arlene H. Eakle. *Ancestry's Guide to Research*. Salt Lake City: Ancestry Publishing Co., 1984. 300 pp. Uses real genealogical cases to demonstrate research techniques and analysis of evidence. Chapters on tracing ancestors with common names, immigrants, ancestors with military backgrounds, women, and "typical" American cases.

Dixon, Janice T., and Dora D. Flack. *Preserving Your Past*. Garden City, N.Y.: Doubleday & Co., 1977. 334 pp. Guide for *writing* autobiography, personal history, and family history.

Doane, Gilbert H., and James C. Bell. *Searching for Your Ancestors*. 5th ed. Minneapolis: University of Minnesota Press, 1980. 270 pp. Bell has prepared a family history record book (work manual) to accompany it. Replaces classic third edition. Substantial changes in fifth edition. Where both are available, the genealogist will find both valuable.

Draznin, Yaffa. *The Family Historian's Handbook*. New York: Jove Publications, 1978. Based on her personal experiences. Focuses on Jewish and ethnic family history.

Greenwood, Val D. *The Researcher's Guide to American Genealogy*. Baltimore: Genealogical Publishing Company, 1973. 535 pp. American research with a strong legal flavor, comprehensive chapters on probate records and land records. Used by National Genealogical Society as official text for home study.

Harland, Derek. *Genealogical Research Standards*. Salt Lake City: Bookcraft, 1963. 404 pp. How to evaluate sources, data, and evidence. Excellent study even though with LDS emphasis.

Helmbold, F. Wilbur. *Tracing Your Ancestry*. Birmingham: Oxmoor House, 1976. 210 pp. Concise step-by-step guide.

Jacobus, Donald Lines. *Genealogy as a Pastime and a Profession*. 2nd ed. Baltimore: Genealogical Book Company, 1968. Emphasizes the need for professionalism in genealogy.

Jaussi, Laureen, and Gloria Chaston. *Fundamentals of Genealogical Research*. 3rd ed. Salt Lake City: Deseret Book Company, 1977. A basic how-to book. Introduces the records held by the Genealogical Society of Utah and how to use them.

Jones, Vincent L., Arlene H. Eakle, and Mildred H. Christensen. *Family History for Fun and Profit*. Salt Lake City: The Genealogical Institute, 1972. 326 pp. Originally issued as *Genealogical Research: A Jurisdictional Approach*. Comprehensive text on the research process, including notekeeping procedures.

Rubincam, Milton, ed. *Genealogical Research: Methods and Sources*. 2 vols. Washington, D.C.: American Society of Genealogists, 1980-83. These volumes provide state-by-state advice, sources for materials.

Smith, Jessie Carney, ed. *Ethnic Genealogy: A Research Guide*. Foreword by Alex Haley. Westport, Conn.: Greenwood Press, 1983. 440 pp. Includes chapters by James D. Walker (National Archives), Roger Scanland (Genealogical Society of Utah), Jimmy B. Parker (American Indians), Charles L. Blockson (blacks), Greg Gubler (Asian-American), Lyman De Platt (Hispanic records), and others.

Westin, Jeane Eddy. *Finding Your Roots*. Los Angeles: J. P. Tarcher, Inc., 1977. 243 pp. A basic guide which has had much influence on the general public.

Williams, Ethel W. *Know Your Ancestors*. Rutland, Vt.: Charles E. Tuttle Company, 1960. 313 pp. Emphasizes American research, sources, and regional help.

Wright, Norman E. *Preserving Your American Heritage: A Guide to Family and Local History*. Provo, Utah: Brigham Young University Press, 1981. 285 pp. Originally issued in 1974 under the title *Building an American Pedigree*. There are some substantial differences in the updated text, including changes in illustrations and maps. Check both editions where available.

Zabriski, George O. *Climbing Our Family Tree Systematically*. Salt Lake City: Parliament Press, 1969. This volume emphasizes methods and techniques for research.

The very newest of the how-to books described in these tables is Johni Cerny and Arlene H. Eakle, *Ancestry's Guide to Research* (Salt Lake City: Ancestry Publishing Co., 1984) a companion volume to *The Source*. The beginner will appreciate this new volume because it describes research techniques in an easy-to-follow step-by-step format, giving numerous examples of how to trace specific ancestors and drawing on a rich cache of genealogy cases to illustrate research strategies. How do you get the records you need if you live in outback Kansas or far-west Nebraska? How do you trace a common surname like Smith, or Jones, or Brown? How do you fit the family all together when there are no family Bibles or household census enumerations to tell you who fits where? How do you join the DAR when you can't find your ancestor in current lineage books? How do you determine if your ancestor really was Irish?

Bibliography of How-to Publications

Bibliographies

Filby, P. William. *American and British Genealogy and Heraldry: A Selected List of Books*. 3rd ed. Boston: New England Historic Genealogical Society, 1983.

Soliday, Gerald L., ed., et al. *History of the Family and Kinship: A Select International Bibliography*. Millwood, N.Y.: Kraus International Publications, 1980.

Trask, David F. and Robert W. Pomeroy, Ill. *The Craft of Public History: An Annotated Select Bibliography*. Westport, Conn.: Greenwood Press, 1983. Chapter 5: Genealogy and Family History.

General Series

Clint, Florence. Area Keys Series. Available from Keyline Publishers, Inc., Box 98, Elizabeth, CO 80107.

Colorado Area Key, 2nd ed., 1978.

Boulder, Colorado Area Key, 1969.

Ohio Area Key, 1977.

New York: A Guide to the Genealogical Records of the State of New York, 1979. An excellent reference.

Pennsylvania Area Key, 1970. There are separate keys for each county of Pennsylvania except Philadelphia (1974).

Genealogical Society of Utah. Research Aids. Available at 50 East North Temple, Salt Lake City, UT 84150 or General Church Distribution Center, 1999 West 1700 South, Salt Lake City, UT 84104. *World Conference on Records Papers*, 1969. Individual papers are $1.25 each. Order form and list of papers available on request. *World Conference on Records*, 1980, papers available individually at $1 per copy, by regional volume at $4.20 per volume, or for the whole conference, 13 volumes for $48. Some presentations are available on cassette tape as well. Order form and list of papers available on request. Genealogical Research Papers. North America. Series B: 1, *Genealogical Records in the United States*, 1978. $1.30; 3, *Major Genealogical Records of the Indians of the United States*, n.d., $1.30; 4, *Records of the State of New York*, n.d., $3.50.

Handy Tip Guides. Logan, Utah: Everton Publishers, 1982.
New England. 24 pp.
Ohio. 33 pp.
Southern States. 36 pp.
Early Pennsylvania. 14 pp.
New York. 24 pp.

McCay, Mrs. Betty L. (deceased). *McCay's Genealogy Aids*. Copies are available in many research libraries.
Sources for Genealogical Searching in Illinois. 1970.
Sources for Genealogical Searching in Indiana. 1973.
Sources for Genealogical Searching in Kentucky. 1973.
Sources for Genealogical Searching in Maryland. 1972.
Sources for Genealogical Searching in North Carolina. 1969.
Sources for Genealogical Searching in Ohio. 1973.
Sources for Genealogical Searching in Pennsylvania. 1973.
Sources for Genealogical Searching in Tennessee. 1970.
Sources for Genealogical Searching in Virginia and West Virginia. 1971.

National Genealogical Society Special Publications. Available at 1921 Sunderland Place, N.W., Washington, DC 20036.

14. *General Aids to Genealogical Research*, 1957:

Carter, Clarence E. "Territorial Papers as a Source for the Genealogist."
Grover, Wayne C. "Genealogy and American Scholarship."
Helman, Frances Strong. "Trailing Ancestors Through Pennsylvania."
Owen, Thomas M., Jr. "How the National Archives Can Aid Genealogists."
Rubincam, Milton. "Pitfalls in Genealogical Research."
Shull, Tressie Nash. "County Atlases for Genealogical Use."
Tolles, Frederick B. "William Wade Hinshaw Index to Quaker Meeting Records."

15. *Special Aids to Genealogical Research on Southern Families.* 1957.

Burns, Annie Walker. "Aids to Genealogical Research in Kentucky."
Bryan, Mary Givens. "Genealogical Research in Georgia."
Dorman, John Frederick. "Some Sources for Genealogical Research in Kentucky."
Hardin, Bayliss E. "Genealogical Research in Kentucky."
Wakefield, Roberta P. "Genealogical Source Material in South Carolina."

16. *Special Aids to Genealogical Research in Northeastern and Central States.* 1957.

Dickoré, Marie. "Genealogical Records in the Cincinnati, Ohio Area."
Fox, William L. "New England in Northeastern Ohio."
Gleason, Margaret. "Genealogical Material in the State Historical Society of Wisconsin."
Johnson, William Perry. "The Quaker Records of Indiana."
McCracken, George E. "Genealogical Sources in Iowa Archives."
Stephenson, Jean. "The Connecticut Settlement of Nova Scotia to the Revolution."

Par-Fam Heritage Enterprises. Box 102, West Bountiful, UT 84087. Research Series pamphlets:

No. 1 *Guide to Genealogical Research in Pennsylvania.*
No. 2 *Guide to Genealogical Research in Virginia.*
No. 3 *Guide to Genealogical Research in New Jersey.*
No. 4 *Guide to Genealogical Research in New York.*
No. 5 *Guide to Genealogical Research in Ohio.*
No. 6 *Guide to Genealogical Research in West Virginia.*
No. 7 *Guide to Genealogical Research in Kentucky.*
No. 8 *Guide to Genealogical Research in North Carolina.*

Midwest

Cox, E. Evelyn. *Ancestree Climbing in the Midwest.* Owensboro, Ky.: McDowell Publications, 1982. pp. 116. Illinois, Indiana, Iowa, Kansas, Missouri, Nebraska.

Doane, Gilbert H. "Vermont, A Stumbling Block in Midwestern Genealogy." *Indiana Magazine of History,* 1938. pp. 14-33.

St. Louis Genealogical Society. *Tracing Family Trees in Eleven States.* Brentwood, Mo.: Members of St. Louis Genealogical Society Regional Workshop, 1970.

New England

Connecticut Society of Genealogists. *Family History in the Northeast.* 2 vols. Hartford: Hartford '83, 1983. Available at Box 435, Glastonbury, CT 06033. Papers presented at Hartford 1983 include all New England states, New York, and New Jersey.

Crandall, Ralph A., ed. *Genealogical Research in New England.* Baltimore: Genealogical Publishing Company, 1983. Includes articles on each New England state reprinted from *New England Historic and Genealogical Register.*

Denis, Michael J. *Genealogical Researching in New England.* 1981. 62 pp.

Wright, Norman Edgar. *Genealogy in America. Vol. 1: Massachusetts, Connecticut, Maine,* Salt Lake City, Utah: Deseret Book Co., 1968. pp. 299.

A Genealogist's Handbook for New England Research. New England Library Association Bibliography Committee, 1981. 129 pp.

Alabama

Webb, M. F. "Alabama: Its Development and Records." *National Genealogical Society Quarterly* 57 (1969): 3-12.

Alaska

Hales, David A. "Uncle Joe Went North! Or How to Find Your Illustrious, Illusive Alaskan Ancestors." *Genealogy Digest* June 1983, pp. 11-15.

Arkansas

Thwing, V. *Researching Arkansas History.* Little Rock: Rose Publishing Co., 1980. Includes genealogy.

California

Barton, Noel R. "Genealogical Research in the Records of the California Spanish Missions." *Genealogical Journal,* 4 (March 1975): 13-33.

Parker, J. Carlyle. *Sources of California: From Padrone to Voter Registration.* Salt Lake City: Genealogical Society of Utah, 1969.

Sanders, Patricia. *Searching in California.* Costa Mesa, Calif.: ISC Publications, 1982. 175 pp.

Connecticut

Barlow, C. W. *Sources for Genealogical Searching in Connecticut and Massachusetts.* Syracuse: Central New York Genealogical Society, 1973.

Case, Marjorie E. "Connecticut Resources for Genealogical Research." *National Genealogical Society Quarterly* 36 (1948): 1-4.

Kemp, Thomas Jay. *Connecticut Researcher's Handbook.* Detroit, Mich.: Gale Research Co., 1981. 755 pp.

Sperry, Kip. *Connecticut Sources for Family Historians and Genealogists.* Logan, Utah: Everton Publishers, 1980. 112 pp.

Delaware

DeValinger, Leon, Jr. "Delaware Records for Genealogical Research." *National Genealogical Society Quarterly* 35 (1947): 1-3.

Fields, D. "Genealogical Source Material in the Historical Society of Delaware," *Pennsylvania Genealogical Magazine* 28 (1973): 86-93.

Florida

Robie, Diane C. *Searching in Florida: A Reference Guide to Public and Private Records.* Costa Mesa, Calif.: ISC Publications, 1982. 135 pp. Available from Everton Publishers, Box 368, Logan, UT 84321.

Georgia

Adams, Marilyn. *Georgia Local and Family History Sources in Print.* Clarkston, Ga.: Heritage Research, n.d. Available from Heritage Research, Box 742, Clarkston, GA 30021.

Davis, Robert Scott, Jr. *Research in Georgia.* Easley, S.C.: Southern Historical Press, 1981. 269 pp.

Hathaway, Beverly West. *Primer for Georgia Genealogical Research.* West Jordan, Utah: Allstates Research Co., Inc., 1973. 27 pp.

Hawes, Lilla Mills. "Early Georgia and its Genealogical Records." *Georgia Genealogical Society Quarterly* 1967-68, no. 4, pp. 806-10.

Hawaii

Cole, William A., and Elwin W. Jensen. "Israel in the Pacific: A Genealogical Text for Polynesia." Salt Lake City, Utah: Polynesian Dept. of Genealogical Society of Utah, 1961.

Nordyke, Eleanor C., and Y. Scott Matsumoto. "The Japanese in Hawaii: A Historical and Demographic Perspective." *Hawaiian*

Journal of History 11 (1977): 162-74.

Ohai, Jean. *Chinese Genealogy and Family Book Guide: Hawaii and Chinese Sources*. Honolulu: Hawaii Chinese History Center, 1975. 14 pp. Excellent reference.

Illinois

Evancich, Sherry A. *Genealogical Research Aids in Cook County, Illinois*. 1982. 36 pp. Available from S. A. Evancich, R.R. 1, Box 43, Tinley Park, IL 60477.

O'Hara, Margaret. *Finding Your Chicago Ancestor*. 1979. 72 pp. Available at 3950 N. Bell, Chicago, IL 60681.

Szucs, Loretto D. *Cook County Research: Not an Impossible Dream*. Decatur, Ill.: Illinois State Genealogical Society, 1981. 13 pp. New edition in preparation.

Vogel, V.J. "Tracing Ancestry in Illinois," *Tree Searcher* , 1973.

Volkel, Lowell M., and Marjorie Smith. *How to Research a Family with Illinois Roots*. Indianapolis, Ind.: Ye Olde Genealogie Shoppe, 1977. 44 pp.

Indiana

Miller, C. L. *Aids for Genealogical Searching in Indiana*. Detroit: Detroit Society for Genealogical Research, 1970.

Newhard, Malinda E. E. *A Guide to Genealogical Records in Indiana*. 2nd ed. rev. N.p.: For the author, 1981. 140 pp.

Iowa

McCracken, George E. "Genealogical Resources in the Iowa Archives." *National Genealogical Society Quarterly* 41 (1951): 67-69.

Kentucky

Beckner, Lucien. "Some Kentucky Genealogical Sources." *Indiana History Bulletin* (1940): 117-23.

Burns, Annie Walker. "Aids to Genealogical Research in Kentucky." *National Genealogical Society Quarterly* 38 (1950): 74-76.

Dorman, John Frederick. "Some Sources for Kentucky Genealogical Research." *National Genealogical Society Quarterly* 42 (1954): 1-6.

Gammon, William J. "Kentucky Records." *National Genealogical Society Quarterly* 3 (1914-15): 9-10.

Hardin, Bayless E. "Genealogical Research in Kentucky." *National Genealogical Society Quarterly* 37 (1949): 65-70.

Hathaway, Beverly West. *Inventory of County Records of Kentucky*. West Jordan, Utah: Allstates Research Co., Inc., n.d.

____________. *Kentucky Genealogical Research Sources*. West Jordan, Utah: Allstates Research Co., Inc., 1974. 156 pp.

Hinds, Charles F. "Kentucky Records: How to Use Them and Where They are Located." *National Genealogical Society Quarterly* 59 (1971): 3-7.

McDowell, Sam, and M. L. Cook. *Kentucky Genealogical Sources*. Owensboro, Ky.: McDowell Publications, n.d. 354 pp.

Schweitzer, George K. *Kentucky Genealogical Research*. Knoxville, Tenn.: George K. Schweitzer, 1981. 154 pp.

Maine

Fisher, Carleton E. "Research in Maine." *National Genealogical Society Quarterly* 55 (1967): 83-88.

Maryland

Meyer, Mary K. *Genealogical Research in Maryland: A Guide*. Baltimore: Maryland Historical Society, 1972. 83 pp.

Massachusetts

Barlow, C. W. *Sources for Genealogical Searching in Connecticut and Massachusetts*. Syracuse: Central New York Genealogical Society, 1973.

Powell, Sumner Chilton. *Puritan Village*. Garden City, N.Y.: Doubleday & Co., Inc., 1965. 258 pp.

Michigan

Anderson, Alloa, and Polly Bender. *Genealogy in Michigan – What, When, Where*. Ann Arbor: Genealogical Society of Washtenaw County, Mich., 1978. 44 pp.

Minnesota

Pope, Wiley R. *Tracing Your Ancestors in Minnesota: French and Canadian, A Brief Outline*. St. Paul, Minn.: Pope Families Association, 1979.

____________, and Alissa L. Wiener. *Tracing Your Ancestors in Minnesota: A Guide to Sources*. St. Paul, Minn.: Minnesota Family Trees, 1980. 228 pp.

____________, et al. *Tracing Your Ancestors in Minnesota: South Central Minnesota*. St. Paul, Minn.: Minnesota Family Trees, 1981. 126 pp.

Missouri

Anderson, Robert D. "Research in Missouri." *Journal of Genealogy* 3 (Sept. 1978): 14-31.

Parkin, Robert E. *Parkin's Guide to Tracing Your Family Tree in Missouri*. St. Louis, Mo.: Genealogical Research and Productions, 1979. 248 pp.

Williams, J. H., and B. H. Williams. *Resources for Genealogical Research in Missouri*. Warrensburg, Mo.: For the authors, 1969.

Montana

Richards, Dennis L. *Montana's Genealogical Records*. Detroit, Mich.: Gale Research Co., 1981. 363 pp.

Nebraska

Glynn, Joseph M. *Guide to Nebraska Genealogy*. Newton, Mass.: Nebraska Family History Society, n.d.

Nebraska State Genealogical Society. *County Guides*. 1980. Available from Platte Valley Books, Box 756, Alliance, NE 69301. A separate guide for each county.

Nevada

Jensen, E. G., and B. M. Olsen. *Nevada Records*. San Leandro, Calif.: For the author, 1965.

New Hampshire

Towle, Laird C. and Ann N. Brown. *Guide to Genealogical Research in New Hampshire*. 2nd ed. Bowie Md.: Prince George's County Genealogical Society, 1983. 98 pp.

New Jersey

Genealogical Society of New Jersey. *Genealogical Research: A Guide to Source Materials in the Archives and History Bureau of the New Jersey State Library*. Genealogical Society of New Jersey for State of New Jersey Department of Education, 1971.

Marsh, Warren L. "Researching in New Jersey," *Connecticut Nutmegger* 8 (1976): 483-98.

Rankin, Russell B. "Genealogical Sources in New Jersey," *Genealogical Magazine of New Jersey* 8 (1932): 1-11, 23-27; 9 (1933): 49-56, 73-74.

Stryker-Rodda, Kenn. "Genealogical Spade Work in the Garden State." *New Jersey Historical Society Proceedings*, April 1961, pp. 264-81.

____________. "Limits of 18th Century Sources in New York and New Jersey." *Families* 11 (1972): 116.

__________. *New Jersey: Digging for Ancestors in the Garden State*. Detroit: Detroit Society for Genealogical Research, Inc., 1970. 35 pp.

__________. "New Jersey Records: A Genealogical Haystack Full of Needles." *Pennsylvania Genealogical Magazine*, 1965, pp. 3-14.

__________. "That Genealogical Quagmire: New Jersey." *National Genealogical Society Quarterly*, 1960, pp. 59-71.

New York

Barch, D. C. *Some References for Genealogical Searching in New York State*. Detroit: Detroit Society for Genealogical Research, 1960.

Christoph, Peter R. "Hunting Forebears in the Mohawk Valley." *Families* 19 (1980): 265-76.

Horn, Field. *Genealogical Guide to Saratoga County*. 1980. 16 pp.

Seversmith, Herbert F., and Kenn Stryker-Rodda. *Long Island Genealogical Source Material: A Bibliography*. Washington, D.C.: National Genealogical Society Quarterly, 1962. 121 pp.

North Carolina

Campbell, Wanda S. "Bladen County, N.C.: Its History and Records." *North Carolina Genealogical Society Journal* 2 (1976): 85-88.

Draughon, Wallace R., and William Perry Johnson. *North Carolina Genealogical Reference*. Durham, N.C.: The Seeman Printery, 1966. 571 pp.

Hurr, Doris S. "Resources for Local History and Genealogy in North Carolina Public Libraries." *North Carolina Genealogical Society Journal* No. 1, 1975, pp. 1-3.

Leary, Helen F. M., and Maurice R. Stirewalt. *North Carolina Research Genealogy and Local History*. Raleigh, N.C.: North Carolina Genealogical Society, 1980. 633 pp.

Ohio

Bell, Carol Willsey. *Ohio Genealogical Guide*. 2nd ed. Youngstown, Ohio: For the author, 1979. 164 pp. See also Flavell, Carol Willsey.

Colket, Meredith B., Jr. "Genealogical Material Relating to the Western Reserve." *National Genealogical Society Quarterly* 59 (1971): 281-82.

Dickoré, Marie. "Genealogical Resources in the Cincinnati, Ohio Area." *National Genealogical Society Quarterly* 43 (1955): 1-5.

Douthit, Ruth Long. *Ohio Resources for Genealogists with Some References for Genealogical Searching in Ohio*. 2nd ed. Detroit, Mich.: Detroit Society for Genealogical Research, Inc., 1960. 136 pp.

Flavell Carol Willsey. *Ohio Genealogical Periodical Index. A County Guide*. 2nd ed. Indianapolis, Ind.: Ye Olde Genealogie Shoppe, 1979. 69 pp.

__________. "Research at the Ohio Historical Society." *Genealogists' Journal* no. 6, 1977, pp. 55-58.

Khouw, P., et al. *County by County in Ohio Genealogy*. Columbus: State Library of Ohio, 1978.

Main, Florence. *Ohio Genealogical Records*. Cleveland: Western Reserve Historical Society, 1968.

Oregon

Duniway, D. C. *Have You an Oregon Ancestor?* Salem, Ore.: Oregon State Library, 1962.

Genealogical Forum of Portland. "Genealogical Research in Oregon." *National Genealogical Society Quarterly*, 1959.

Pennsylvania

Bell, Raymond Martin. *Searching in Western Pennsylvania*. Detroit: Detroit Society for Genealogical Research, Inc., 1968. 35 pp.

Dructor, Robert M. *A Guide to Genealogical Sources at the Pennsylvania State Archives*. Harrisburg, Penn.: For the archives, 1980. 129 pp.

Helman, Frances Strong. "Trailing Ancestors Through Pennsylvania." *National Genealogical Society Quarterly*, no. 39, 1951, pp. 1-8.

Hoenstine, Floyd G. *Guide to Genealogical and Historical Research in Pennsylvania*. Knightstown, Ind.: The Bookmark, 1973. 439 pp.

Pennsylvania Line: A Research Guide to Pennsylvania Genealogy and Local History. 3rd ed., Laughlintown, Penn.: Southwest Pennsylvania Genealogical Services, 1983. 225 pp.

Western Pennsylvania Genealogical Society Quarterly Magazine 8 (May 1982): number 32, a special issue on genealogical resources for Pennsylvania.

Rhode Island

Fiske, Jane Fletcher. "Genealogical Research in Rhode Island." *The New England Historical and Genealogical Register* 136 (1982): 173-219. Excellent.

South Carolina

Cote, Richard N. *The Genealogists' Guide to Charleston County, SC*. Greenville, S.C.: A. Press, Inc., 1981. 45 pp.

__________. *South Carolina Family and Local History: A Bibliography*. Charleston, S.C.: Southern Historical Press, n.d. 600 pp.

Frazier, Mrs. Evelyn. *Hunting Your Ancestors in South Carolina: A Guide for Amateur Genealogists*. Walterboro, S.C.: Florentine Press, 1969. 23 pp.

Holcomb, Brent H. *A Brief Guide to South Carolina Genealogical Research and Records*. Greenville, S.C.: A. Press, Inc. 1979.

Tennessee

Hailey, N. *Guide to Genealogical Research in Tennessee*. Owensboro, Ky.: Cook and McDowell, 1979.

Hathaway, Beverly West. *Genealogy Research Sources in Tennessee*. West Jordan, Utah: Allstates Research Co., n.d.

Schweitzer, Dr. George K. *Tennessee Genealogical Research*. Knoxville, Tenn.: Dr. George K. Schweitzer, n.d. 130 pp.

Sistler, Byron, and Barbara Sistler. *The Yellow Pages: Sources and Suggestions for Searching in Tennessee*. Nashville: Byron Sistler and Associates, 1976. 36 pp.

Texas

Winfrey, G. "Gone to Texas: Sources for Genealogical Research." *Stirpes* 9 (1969): 87-95.

Utah

Fotheringham, Ila Jean. *Genealogical Sources for Utah and LDS Church Survey and Research*. n.p. 1968. 32 pp.

Jaussi, Laureen R., and Gloria Duncan Chaston. *Fundamentals of Genealogical Research*. 3rd ed. Salt Lake City, Utah: Deseret Book Co., 1977. 243 pp.

__________. *Genealogical Records of Utah*. Salt Lake City, Utah: Deseret Book Co., 1974. 312 pp.

Virginia

Allen, Roy C., and Victoria Allen Fleming. *Virginia State, County, and City Records*. Arlington, Va.: National Genealogy Service, 1981. 6 pp.

Clay, Robert Young. *Virginia Genealogical Resources*. Detroit:

Detroit Society for Genealogical Research, Inc., 1980. 57 pp.

Martin, Donald J. "In the Beginning All America Was Virginia." *Journal of Genealogy,* Feb. 1979, pp. 23-36. Excellent combination of narrative how-to and selected bibliography.

Schweitzer, George K. *Virginia Genealogical Research*. Knoxville, Tenn.: George K. Schweitzer, 1982. 187 pp.

Virginia Genealogy, A Guide to Resources in the University of Virginia Library. Charlottesville, Va.: University Press of Virginia, 1983. 75 pp.

Washington

Eckert, Timothy E. *Genealogical Resources in Washington State*. Olympia: Secretary of State Division of Archives, 1983.

West Virginia

Shetler, C. *Guide to Study of West Virginia History*. Morgantown, W.V.: University of West Virginia, 1960. Includes genealogy.

Stinson, Helen S. *A Handbook for Genealogical Research in West Virginia*. South Charleston, W.V.: Kanawha Valley Genealogical Society, 1981. 323 pp.

Wisconsin

Gleason, Margaret. "Genealogical Materials at the State Historical Society of Wisconsin." *National Genealogical Society Quarterly* 43 (1955): 131-32.

____________. *Printed Resources for Genealogical Searching in Wisconsin: A Selective Bibliography*. Detroit: Detroit Society for Genealogical Research, 1964.

Ryan, Carol Ward. *Searching for Your Wisconsin Ancestors in the Wisconsin Libraries*. Green Bay, Wis.: n.p., 1979.

Finding Aids

Guides and Inventories

Many libraries, historical societies, and archives prepare inventories of their holdings and guides to collections. These guides can help you locate the very records you came to that archive to use. When printed, these can help you to prepare in advance what you will need to study at a given depository or to hire an agent to search the records needed.

These guides are an important support to card catalogs in many libraries. A table or shelf at the entrance of an archive or library usually has lists of serials and periodicals, histories/genealogies on microfiche, census collections, and directories available. You may miss important records if you don't use these tools when you begin your work at the depository. These guides will list the holdings of the library with call numbers and sometimes a description of the record. They may also contain collections and call numbers not recorded in the main card catalog.

One of the finest examples of a thorough guide to genealogy is Helen F. M. Leary and Maurice R. Stirewalt, eds., *North Carolina Research: Genealogy and Local History* (Raleigh: The North Carolina Genealogical Society, 1980). This detailed volume describes every aspect of research that might be undertaken for a North Carolina problem. The editors first list research techniques, then describe the libraries, archives, and manuscript collections in North Carolina. City, county, and state records are discussed, covering not only the typical church and court records, but details on tax, school, election, corporation, and business sources as well.

V. Irons and P. C. Brennan, eds., *Descriptive Inventory of the Archives of the State of Illinois* (Springfield: Illinois State Archives, 1978) is a thorough inventory describing available sources in that state. This book does not contain any genealogical instruction but is strictly an inventory and description of available resources. It describes in detail the territorial records, constitutional officers, state institutions such as schools for deaf, soldiers' and widows' homes, and state and mental hospitals. It also lists the collections of records from state departments of agriculture, finance, labor, health, welfare, and many others. Education, military, medical, commerce, and bank records are also noted. A vast collection of records relating to Abraham Lincoln are cataloged with locations and descriptions.

Institutional and Private Collections

In addition to libraries, historical societies and archives, many institutional and private collections are valuable for your research. Some of these collections are held by heraldic and patriotic societies. Denise S. Akey, *Encyclopedia of Associations* (Detroit: Gale Research Company, 1983) lists many of these organizations. The name of the society, such as "General Society of Mayflower Descendant," with the address, telephone, membership numbers requirements, and annual meetings are noted. We are told, for example, that the Mayflower Society conducts research into descendants of the *Mayflower* Pilgrims, maintains a library on Pilgrim history and genealogy, and publishes the *Mayflower Quarterly*. For more information on such lineage societies, see Chapter 23, "Patriotic and Lineage Societies."

Margaret L. Young and Harold C. Young, *Directory of Special Libraries and Information Centers* (Detroit: Gale Research Company, 1981) is another tool for finding such collections. It lists special libraries and includes major sections on genealogical, historical, religious, and newspaper centers. They are classified by location and indexed by topic.

Countless university, school, church, and other private collections of records exist throughout the country. Some have guides and inventories telling what their collections hold. For example, the University of Pittsburgh library has special collections in the Archives of Industrial Society and Hillman Library. See Archives of Industrial Society, *A Descriptive Checklist of Acquisitions, 1963-68* (Pittsburgh: University of Pittsburgh Libraries, 1969). This repository collects and preserves records about the development of industrial society, with emphasis on Pittsburgh and Western Pennsylvania. Records relate to the Civil War resistance movement, Allegheny County borough records, church records, diaries, and private family papers and letters for Pennsylvania families. By consulting its guide, *A Descriptive Checklist of Acquisitions,* you can see if the collection has something important on the family you are studying.

Kathleen Jacklin, ed., *Collection of Regional History and the University Archives* (Ithaca, N.Y.: Cornell University Libraries, 1974) is a thorough inventory of the vast collection of records at the Cornell University Libraries—more than seven million manuscripts relating to central and western New York. West Virginia University has a similar collection of great value but has no guide to its holdings. In order to determine what records are available, you must visit the university.

Innumerable sources are available in every state to help you. Items which appear to be simply local history can become invaluable genealogical tools. Expecting archivists and librarians to make the searches, however, is inappropriate and can be discouraging. For example, two archival collections in Syracuse, New York, relate to canal building and travel in New York State. When a colleague wrote one of these archives, the Canal Museum (Weighlock Building, Erie Boulevard East, Syracuse, NY 13202), she was told: "We get a lot of genealogy questions at the Canal Museum Library and are unfortunately not able to be of any help in most of the requests. Our library does not have much material that is of use to genealogical researchers." The letter added: "We have an index of people identified as working or traveling on the canal documented in our collections, but our success rate of finding information for our geneological [*sic*] researchers is very poor." With the letter was a two-page guide to canal holdings in general, other repositories in New York with canal materials, and search procedures for specific canal boats.[1] The museum houses over 900,000 manuscripts; only a few are indexed. The archivist, with limited time and resources to make searches, has prepared the two-page guide to help genealogists *go somewhere else*. And the letter is correct in a sense for this archive has no births or marriages, and few deaths – the traditional definition of "genealogical information." A personal visit to the museum, with enough time alloted to search the manuscripts preceded by a letter advising the archivist of your arrival and specific interests can be fruitful. Those documents do contain references to ancestors – canal boat itineraries, survey maps, correspondence and bills of lading, newspaper clippings, passenger lists, bonds, manifests, time sheets and wage rolls, boat permits, damage claims, payrolls, land papers, lotteries, stock certificates, promises to pay, and other records.

The two-page guide is also a tool for planning searches in the other repositories mentioned. Equipped with the search procedure for canal boats, the genealogist can search canal records with some hope of success and without encroaching unreasonably on the archivist's time.

Other private collections have obvious benefit to the genealogist. Since this book was largely written by Utah genealogists, it draws heavily on the invaluable resources of the Genealogical Society of Utah, an appendage of the Church of Jesus Christ of Latter-day Saints. This society has the largest collection of genealogical materials in the world. Virtually every type of genealogical and historical resource in published and microform version is available at this depository. Extensive collections of periodicals are included with the vital, court, church, and civil records. Heavy emphasis is placed on American, Canadian, British, and European collections. Central and South American church and civil records have been microfilmed as well. The goal is to collect all possible records relating to people of the past in all countries of the world, and the society's ambitious international microfilming program continues to add new collections daily.

The Genealogical Society, although operated by a private institution, is open to the public. Over 460 branch libraries throughout the world have facilities for borrowing microfilm copies of all records held by the Genealogical Society. One of the most valuable research tools of the society is its International Genealogical Index (IGI), which indexes births and marriages from vital records throughout the United States, Canada, and Europe and includes some 68 million names. Although no complete inventory has been published for this institution's collection, the branch libraries have copies of its catalogues and holdings. A partial list of the American collection is Mary J. Brown, *Handy Index to the Holdings of the Genealogical Society of Utah*, 2nd ed. (Logan, Utah: Everton Publishers, 1982), and Arlene H. Eakle and L. Ray Gunn, *Finding Aids to the Microfilmed Manuscript Collection of the Genealogical Society of Utah: Descriptive Inventory of the New York Collection* (Salt Lake City: University of Utah Press, 1980).

The Huntington Library in San Marino, California, has a collection of more than five million items of original manuscript and published material dealing with British history and literature from the eleventh century to 1837, American history and literature to 1900, Spanish explorations, the colonial-Revolutionary period, the Civil War, the westward movement, and California. The Huntington Library is a private library open to qualified researchers. Some of its collections are available on microfilm in other repositories. Various inventories of their holdings have been published, but no complete guide has yet been prepared.

Many churches have important collections of historical and church records. (See Chapter 5, "Church Records in the United States.") The Historical Foundation of the Presbyterian and Reformed Churches in Montreat, North Carolina, has records of churches throughout the world, especially those in the southern United States. Presbyterian organizations in North and South America, Europe, the Orient, Africa, and Mexico house their records in this archive.

The Southern Baptist Convention houses its records at the Dargan-Carver Library in Nashville, Tennessee. Materials pertaining to the history, biography, doctrine, life, and work of Baptists are held there. Records of over 2,000 Baptist churches and associations in the United States, Mexico, Brazil, Argentina, Nigeria, and other foreign countries are also there.

The American Jewish Historical Society in New York City has hundreds of boxes of manuscripts relating chiefly to the history of the Jews in America from 1590 to the present. They include papers of individuals covering activities of their later years, attorneys' papers, synagogue records, family papers, records of the Jewish Child Care Association of New York, and many other records relating to Jewish history. A useful reference is Consortium Book, *The Directory of Religious Organizations in the United States,* 2nd ed. (Falls Church, Va.: McGrath Publishing Company, 1982).

Names of similar associations are cited in the directories in the section on "Archives and Libraries" at the beginning of the Introduction.

Periodicals, Books, and Book Dealers

Genealogical periodicals should be used regularly in research. Hundreds of societies publish monthly, quarterly, or annual periodicals or newsletters. They deal with a given city, county, state, or region, with specific surnames, or with selected topics. To determine what publications are available for a given area of interest see J. Konrad, ed., *A Directory of Genealogical Periodicals,* 3rd ed. (Monroe Falls, Ohio: Summit Publications, 1979). It provides as comprehensive a list as possible, including over 1,100 genealogical periodicals, and is indexed in various categories. It can be acquired, if not available in a local library, through Summit Publications, Box 222, Munroe Falls, OH 44262.

Sources of Serials, 2nd ed. (New York: R. R. Bowker Company, 1981) is another important tool for locating periodicals. This is an international serials authority file, listing titles and publishers of nearly 100,000 currently available serials. It includes copyright and copy availability policy, indicating what you can photocopy as well as how to go about gaining permission for photocopying. (See the section on "Legalities" in this introduction for more information on copyrights.) The titles and annotation are categorized by author and by publisher and are indexed by title of the periodical.

Several surname indexes for families included in many of these periodicals will speed your search. Although none of these indexes includes every name in the serials they index, nor do they index all major genealogical periodicals, they can still save a great deal of research time.

Munsell's *Index to American Genealogies,* 5th ed. (1900) indexes genealogical and historical magazines published through 1900 with a supplement to 1908. Donald Lines Jacobus, *Index to Genealogical Periodicals,* 3 vols., begins about 1900 and includes periodicals published through 1951. A new edition of Jacobus's valuable work is available from Carl Boyer, III, Box 333, Newhall, CA 91322. Boyer has completely revised the index in a format easier to use with a place-name and topic index added. *Annual Index to Genealogical Periodicals and Family Histories* covers 1952-61. The *Genealogical Periodical Annual Index* (GPAI) has been prepared to cover periodicals from 1962 to the present.

When you find an article published after 1978 and the desired periodical is not available locally, see if Original Article Text Service (OATS) includes it in its 7,000-plus journals. If so, OATS can put the needed article in the mail within forty-eight hours of request. OATS's booklet, "Source Publications for Original Article Text Service," lists the journals included as well as details as to how to order copies, available from:

Institute for Scientific Information
3501 Market Street
University City Science Center
Philadelphia, PA 19104
(215) 386-0100

For articles published prior to 1978, contact the Copyright

Clearance Center as discussed in the "Legalities" section. Articles from a specific journal can also be borrowed through the interlibrary loan system. Article reprints from 13,000 periodicals are also available from University Microfilms, 300 Zeeb Road, Box 1467, Ann Arbor, MI 48106, (800) 521-0600. UMI has back issues for about 7,000 titles.

Most publications have four major types of articles: how to use a particular source or do research in a given area; multi-generation pedigrees, historical articles on migration patterns, the effect of the Civil War on families of Indiana, etc.; and extracts of hidden source material like family Bibles, cemetery inscriptions, church records, tax lists, and apprenticeship, voting, divorce, and vital records.

To give you some idea of the coverage of major genealogical periodicals, here are ten of the most respected journals, surveyed for content from 1978 through 1983.[2]

1. *The American Genealogist*, 1232 39th Street, Des Moines, IA 50311, $10 membership, no advertising, no affiliated association. Quarterly. This magazine contains over 60 percent genealogies of American families. A few English, Canadian, and other foreign pedigrees are included but they have some connection with the United States. About 20 percent of the articles are extracts of sources with the remainder being "how-to" articles or historical articles. Foreign topics are discussed in relation to American immigrants or relatives.

2. *The Detroit Society for Genealogical Research Magazine*, Detroit Society for Genealogical Research Inc., Burton Historical Collection, Detroit Public Library, 5201 Woodward Avenue, Detroit, MI 48202, $15 membership. About 60 percent of the articles are extracts from sources dealing with Michigan and surrounding states/provinces. Family history material for Pennsylvania, New Jersey, and other states whose pedigrees tie in with Michigan families are also plentiful. Book reviews and queries are included.

3. *The Genealogical Helper*, Box 368, Logan, UT 84321, 3223 South Main Street, Nibley, UT 84321, $15.50 for six bimonthly issues, mostly advertising, affiliated with Everton Publishers. This is not a scholarly publication, has virtually no published genealogies, and a few "how-to" and historical articles. But it is invaluable to the genealogist. Over 100 pages in each issue are filled with advertisements of missing ancestors, surnames being worked with, county histories and genealogies being published as well as numerous lists, finding aids, collections, services, forms to use, computer services, etc. Its list of advertising by professional genealogists is current, whereas many of the lists of accredited, certified, and registered genealogists include professionals who do not actively serve clients. The *Helper* is published by computer and every name and topic is indexed in each issue.

4. The *Genealogical Journal*, Box 1144, Salt Lake City, UT 84110, $20. Quarterly. Published by the Utah Genealogical Association. This publication is 95 percent how-to articles with some book reviews. It has very little coverage of Utah records and emphasizes American and European research. Many of the articles are written by professional genealogists or employees of the Genealogical Society of Utah.

5. *The Genealogist*, Box 1058, Rockefeller Center Station, New York, NY 10185, $25 one year, $45 two years, affiliated with Association for the Promotion of Scholarship in Genealogy, Ltd. Semi-annual. This periodical aims at collecting scholarly, well-documented articles of interest to the serious genealogist. Its primary articles are genealogies of prominent families anywhere in the world with some "how-to" and historical articles and book reviews. It encourages new scholars with a prize of $100 for the best article to be submitted for publication between 1 January 1983 and 31 December 1984 by a person who has not had any work previously published in one of the leading genealogical publications.

6. *Genealogists' Magazine*, 37 Harrington Gardens, London SW7 4JX, England, $28 membership, affiliated with Society of Genealogists. Quarterly. Although this magazine is primarily British, it is important to American genealogists doing research on British origins, by far the largest source of American ancestors. It includes "how-to" and historical articles mainly, with an occasional celebrity pedigree (Princess Diana). Excellent articles on English source material and "how-to" articles for many countries are valuable for those doing research relating to France, Canada, United States, Scotland, Ireland, Australia, or New Zealand. Book reviews are also included, along with queries and advertising.

7. *National Genealogical Society Quarterly*, 1921 Sunderland Place, N.W., Washington, DC 20036, $25 membership, affiliated with National Genealogical Society. Quarterly. Over 40 percent of the material is "how-to" and historical articles dealing with sources for all parts of the United States. The remainder of the content is split equally between printing manuscript sources and genealogies of prominent American and British families. It also covers ethnic groups in the United States, book reviews, advertising, and "Genealogical Gleanings" in England.

8. *The New England Historical and Genealogical Register*, 101 Newbury Street, Boston, MA 02116, $20, affiliated with New England Historic Genealogical Society. The majority of articles are genealogies of New England families. Probably because most New England records are in print there are few extracts of sources or "how-to" articles although services include valuable book reviews, queries ($5 to members), lists of recent books, and advertisements. A cumulative index is nearly ready for publication.

9. *The New York Genealogical and Biographical Record*,, 122 E. 58th Street, New York, NY 10022, $15, affiliated with New York Genealogical and Biographical Society. The main articles deal with New York genealogies and family histories. Numerous shorter articles include printed extracts of sources and "how-to" articles dealing with New York research techniques. It also carries reviews, advertising, and "Genealogical Exchange," a query section.

10. *The Virginia Genealogist*, Box 4883, Washington, D.C. 20008, $15. Quarterly. This journal prints mostly extracts of source material and genealogies relating to Virginia with special emphasis on English families of the colonial period. Queries and reviews are also published.

Here are some resources to consult on genealogical periodicals.

Eakle, Arlene H., ed. "Get More Genealogical Data for the Time and Money You Spend on Research." *Research News*, vol. 1, 2 (Sept. 1983); Salt Lake City: Family History World, 1983.

Genealogical Society of Utah, *Periodicals and Serials list 1979 Edition*. Salt Lake City: Genealogical Department, Church of Jesus Christ of Latter-day Saints, 1979.

Institute for Scientific Information, *Need a Journal Article Fast? Turn to Original Article Test Service*. (Pamphlet) Philadelphia: Institute for Scientific Information, 1982.

Mayhew, Catherine M., comp., and Laird C. Towle, ed. *Genealogical Periodical Annual Index*. 18 vols. Bowie, Md.: Heritage Books Inc., 1982.

Munsell Publishers. *Index to American Genealogist*, 5th ed. Detroit: Gale Research Co., 1966.

R. R. Bowker Company. *Sources of Serials*. 2nd ed. (New York: R. R. Bowker Company, 1981).

Xerox University Microfilms. *Mass Communications: A Catalog of Dissertations, Theses, Books, and Serials*. Ann Arbor, Mich.: Xerox University Microfilms, 1975.

Finding Books

Another important tool, as discussed in the "Printed Histories" section of the introduction, includes published books of family and local history. When you cannot locate a desired book in your local library, try interlibrary loan.

University Microfilms of Ann Arbor, Michigan, offers a service to anyone interested in acquiring copies of masters' theses or Ph.D. dissertations from all universities in the United States and in most foreign countries. They will also microfilm or photocopy manuscript or typed records in libraries throughout the country. For example, Newberry Library in Chicago has the only known copy of a 300-page typescript genealogy of the Caywood family. You can, with permission of the author or copyright holder, obtain a xerox or microfilm copy of the record from University Microfilms. It will also supply copies of out-of-print books in the public domain or with permission from the author. This program is titled Books on Demand.

To determine what resources are available through University Microfilms use Xerox University Microfilms, *Mass Communications: A Catalog of Dissertations, Theses, Books and Serials* (Ann Arbor, Mich.: Xerox University Microfilms, 1975). To request information from University Microfilms, contact:

Dissertations Publishing
University Microfilms International
300 N. Zeeb Road
Ann Arbor, MI 48106
(800) 521-3042

The cost for ordering dissertations is $35. Copies of other books run 25 cents per page.

Used book stores are a third resource to help locate a missing volume. They are located in many cities; but those below specialize in genealogical materials.

Jonathan Sheppard Books
Box 2020
ESP Station
Albany, NY 12220

Genealogists Bookshelf
343 E. 85th Street
Box 468
New York, NY 10028

Tuttle Antiquarian Books
Box 541
Rutland, VT 05701

By contacting one of these book dealers, it is possible to locate and purchase copies of out-of-print books. A listing of other antiquarian book dealers is included in the January 1983 newsletter of the Association of Professional Genealogists (Box 11601, Salt Lake City, Utah 84147). These catalogs are available from the above cited dealers for $1.

Access to and Use of Indexes

Historical and genealogical societies, individuals, and professional companies constantly compile indexes. Using them will save untold hours. Indexes, card files, or computerized listings may include tombstone inscriptions, obituaries, marriage records, censuses, mortuary, passenger and immigration lists, and many more sources. Many are printed but others are available only at the library or archive where the indexed records are housed.

You may get some free help by asking a state archive by mail to check its indexes for a given individual and requesting the fee for a copy of the original document. This way you can verify that the individual appears on the desired record. When writing to any depository or society include a self-addressed, stamped envelope to speed the reply and help insure an answer.

Most local libraries have valuable indexes. Some are of top quality with good detail; others might only list a surname and page number, relatively useless when dealing with a heavily populated area and a common surname. Quality as well as quantity of entries is very important.

When reviewing a source of vital records, a county history, or census book, you must check not only the back of the volume but the beginning and even a center section of the book to be certain that you do not miss an index. Sometimes an introduction to an index explains how names are listed, for there are different methods of alphabetizing the same set of surnames. Are *Mc* names listed separately or as if spelled *Mac?*

Consider the possibility, as well, of variant spellings of surnames. Some indexes group all spelling variants together; others are strictly alphabetical. Even when spelling variants are listed together, you need to be creative in determining other spellings of the same name which have not been cataloged together. Remember that names were often Americanized after immigrants arrived from foreign countries. Both the original spellings and common Anglicized spellings must be considered. If a name has multiple syllables, check for each syllable. If an ancestor has two given names, check for both. Johann Heinrich might be listed under Johann, John, Heinrich, and/or Henry. Refer to the section on "Spelling Variants" in this introduction for an elaboration on these principles. See also Chapter 13, "Genealogical Tools and Indexes."

An example of differences in indexes is the International Genealogical Index of the Genealogical Society of Utah. The 1978 edition attempted to categorize all spellings of a surname together. The 1981 edition separated them into exact spellings. Using these tools requires considerable difference in research techniques.

Geography and History

Maps, Atlases, and Locality Collections

Every genealogist must learn to identify place-names and geographical jurisdictions. If a census says John Smith was born in Mississippi about 1813 and another census says Alabama, you need to know that Alabama was part of Mississippi Territory until 1817. Perhaps a death certificate says the person was born in Yellow Bush, Mississippi, and there is no such town. A look at Mississippi place-names should eventually suggest Yalobusha County as a possibility. What do you do when a person is listed in nearby counties in three successive censuses and yet no deeds or other records suggest moves? Perhaps the county lines changed and the person did not move at all.

Three possible changes can happen singly or in any combination: generations change, people move, and jurisdictions and place-names change. A new John Smith in a county or New England town could be a young man just come of age, a newcomer recently arrived, or a long-settled resident shifted into the county or town by a boundary change.

Maps, atlases, and gazetteers are therefore necessary tools for any genealogist. Maps may be either topographical or historical, though either can show cultural features such as the town and creek names that are so important to genealogical research. Sheet maps can be harder to use than books and manuscripts. They are hard to photocopy because they are large; libraries find them inconvenient to store and retrieve: and their titles may be uninformative. Faced with a score of maps, each listed in the catalog as "Map of Connecticut," you may be tempted to forget the whole thing. Looking at two hundred pages of bibliography on pre-1900 Connecticut maps is usually not very enlightening unless the editor helps with detailed descriptive notes on map contents. This is not to discourage you from using maps, only to warn that frustration with map titles is normal. If you have access to appropriate maps, by all means develop the patience to use them.

Every genealogist doing much United States research should own a good atlas such as the current edition of the low-cost, softcover Rand McNally *Road Atlas*. It is extremely important to find on the map each place-name in a research problem and to see how that place relates to nearby rivers, mountains, valleys, large towns and cities, sea and lake ports, and adjoining states. See Norman J. W. Thrower, "The County Atlases of the United States," *Surveying and Mapping* 21 (1961): 365-73, for parts of the United States with county atlases available.

In one family research project, a person was known to have lived in three towns, one each in Missouri, Kansas, and Nebraska.

Research on state and county records for each of these towns would be easy without consulting an atlas. Many researchers do this all the time, but it is a bad habit. A check *first* in an atlas showed that the three towns were in adjoining counties where the states came together. In fact, the three towns were within ten miles of each other. Suddenly the research problem reduced itself from the vague project of doing three states into a township-sized problem that happened – inconveniently, it must be admitted – to straddle three state lines. No strange, long-distance "migration" pattern between states was involved at all.

The small scale of a road atlas eliminates hamlets and most creeks. The Rand McNally *Commercial Atlas*, found in nearly all U.S. public libraries, is a common atlas of somewhat larger scale. For maps of much larger scales there are the U.S. Geological Survey (USGS) maps, which have the advantage of showing just about any named cluster of houses but the disadvantage of being loose sheets without place-name indexes. However, many states and even counties have place-name lists which can be used in conjunction with the USGS maps. Several national gazetteers were published in the last century listing many small towns now nonexistent or renamed. To see what exists, use the catalogs of research libraries and also Richard B. Sealock, et al., *Bibliography of Place-Name Literature: United States and Canada* (Chicago, Ill: American Library Association, 1982). Modern towns can be sought in *Bullinger's Postal and Shipper's Guide to the United States and Canada* (Westwood, N.J.: Bullinger's, 1982).

The USGS publishes several series of maps in different scales designed to fit together to cover the whole United States. Scales are expressed as proportions such as 1:24,000, 1:500,000, etc., meaning the map reproduces a real feature at 1/24,000th or 1/500,000th of actual size. To use Virginia as an example, there are 1:1,000,000 and 1:500,000 single sheets of the whole state in black and white that show towns, rivers, swamps, railroads, and county lines.

The 1:250,000 is a topographical series in color showing the above-mentioned features as well as elevations, thus revealing mountain and valley systems. Topographical maps try to show what an area would look like if you were floating above, looking down. Topographical maps of the Appalachian Mountains will quickly show genealogists why roads, and therefore people, went in some directions and rarely in others. The 1:250,000 series is excellent if you want to cover a large region in a good topographical scale. It takes fourteen sheets to cover Virginia in this scale, but these maps include portions of the neighboring states, covering most of Maryland and half of Delaware.

The 1:24,000 is the large-scale topographical map that hikers often buy. This scale is especially suited for drawing land-grant tracts as explained in Chapter 7, "Land and Tax Records." It zeroes in when you want a neighborhood in large scale and shows such specific features as cemeteries and mills. It takes about 808 sheets in 1:24,000 to cover Virginia.

The USGS maps are authoritative and inexpensive. To receive a free index to scales and series available for any state, write to the Eastern Distribution Branch, USGS, 1200 South Eads Street, Arlington, VA 22202. You will also buy maps for areas east of the Mississippi River, including Minnesota, from this address. For USGS maps covering areas west of the Mississippi, including Louisiana, order from the Western Distribution Branch, USGS, Box 25286, Federal Center, Denver, CO 80225.

The USGS also has many specialty maps such as metropolitan areas, national parks, battlefields, and historical site maps. Inquire about your special needs at the Arlington branch. Also consult local university and major research libraries for USGS and other maps.

The USGS has a National Cartographic Information Center, 507 National Center, Reston, VA 22092. This center will help you with more exotic items such as aerial photographs, colored Landsat maps, and color separates of topographical maps which might be used for clearer printed maps in a book you plan to publish. These technical matters are of no concern to most genealogists, but knowing the Cartographic Information Center exists may help some. In summary, the Arlington and Denver branches handle routine maps, the Reston center more technical matters. Each supplies free catalogs of its products. Also, some large cities have local USGS map sales offices.

The Reston center has extremely useful microfilms of out-of-print USGS topographic maps. These are black-and-white microfilms of the 1:24,000 series (and occasional other scales), with each state's maps filmed in alphabetical order by the names of the sheets. It takes six reels to cover Virginia. For the genealogist who expects to do very extensive, even massive, research in a particular state, or perhaps specialize in professional work in one state, these reels are much less expensive and far easier to store than a full set of 1:24,000 topographical sheets of the state.

Historical maps are not so uniform or easily described as topographical maps, nor can they be so conveniently purchased. *Historical* refers to maps designed to present historical information such as colonial roads, migration routes, former county boundaries, and land grant bounds, and also to maps now so old they preserve historical information, such as nineteenth-century county and land ownership maps or property tax maps. The surest way to see the best maps for an area is to visit a major research library specializing in that area. Here are ten titles that should also help pinpoint map and atlas titles and collections:

American Geographical Society. *Index to Maps in Books and Periodicals*. Boston, Mass.: G. K. Hall, 1968, 10 vols., plus 1st and 2nd supplements (1971, 1976). 2 vols.

Bancroft Library. *The Bancroft Library, University of California, Berkeley: Index to Printed Maps*. Boston, Mass.: G. K. Hall, 1964.

Carrington, David K., and Richard W. Stephenson. *Map Collections in the United States and Canada: A Directory*. New York: Special Libraries Association, 1978.

William L. Clements Library. *Research Catalog of Maps of America to 1860 in the William L. Clements Library*. 4 vols., Boston Mass.: G. K. Hall, 1973.

Department of the Interior. *Catalog of the United States Geological Survey Library*. Boston, Mass.: G. K. Hall, 1964. 25 vols., plus 1st and 2nd supplements (1972, 1974). 15 vols.

Hargett, Janet L. *List of Selected Maps of States and Territories* Washington, D.C.: National Archives, 1971.

LeGear, Clara Egli. *United States Atlases: A List of National, State, County, City, and Regional Atlases in the Library of Congress*. 2 vols. Washington, D.C.: Library of Congress, 1953.

Library of Congress. *The Bibliography of Cartography*. Boston, Mass.: G. K. Hall, 1973. 5 vols., plus 1st supplement (1979), 2 vols.

Newberry Library. *Checklist of Printed Maps of the Middle West to 1900*. 11 vols. Boston, Mass.: G. K. Hall, 1980.

New York Public Library, Research Libraries. *Dictionary Catalog of the Map Division*. 10 vols. Boston, Mass.: G. K. Hall, 1971.

Anyone who enjoys keeping current on geography and cartography publications can do so by reading the quarterly *Bulletin* of the Special Libraries Association, Geography and Map Division.

An estimated two million maps in the National Archives are briefly described in the *Guide to Genealogical Research in the National Archives* (Washington, D.C.: National Archives Trust Fund 1982), pp. 255-62. If you want a copy made of a particular old map, inquire of the cartographic department. Also, the Library of Congress has a vast map collection in its Geography and Map Division, which will make reproductions.

Migration and Settlement Patterns

Migration routes in American history are very important to the genealogist, but there are many exceptions to the typical routes. The wise researcher will resort to a good history such as Ray Allen Billington and Martin Ridge, *Westward Expansion* (New York: Macmillan, 1982). Several historical atlases compiled to help historians and, specifically, genealogists are:

Adams, James Truslow, with Kenneth T. Jackson. Rev. ed. *Atlas of American History*. New York: Scribner's, 1978. Includes fifty-one more maps than the 1943 edition.

Cappon, Lester J., et al. *Atlas of Early American History: The Revolutionary Era, 1760-1790*. Princeton, N.J.: Princeton University Press, 1976.

Kirkham, E. Kay. *A Genealogical and Historical Atlas of the United States of America*. N.p., 1976.

Jackson, Richard H. *Historical and Genealogical Atlas of North America: Volume 1; United States East of the Mississippi*. Provo, Utah: Gentech, 1974. No subsequent volumes.

Paullin, Charles O., and John K. Wright. *Atlas of the Historical Geography of the United States*. Washington, D.C.: Carnegie Institution of Washington and the American Geographical Society of New York, 1932.

County Boundaries and Boundary Changes

A problem nearly all genealogists doing American research must face is understanding county and New England town boundaries. Both usually went through several area changes before reaching stable, modern bounds. Unfortunately, no complete list of all present and defunct United States counties exists nor do many states have compilations mapping the evolutions of county lines. In fact, even as of 1983 no bibliography exists for the books, articles, theses, and monographs on county boundary changes. Many states have various discussions on the subject, from outstanding books for California, Indiana, and New Jersey, through listings of laws on boundary changes without maps, as for Virginia and North Carolina, to no comprehensive work on the subject at all, as with Arkansas and Florida. See Arlene H. Eakle, ed., "Mapping Family History," *Research News* 2 (Dec. 1983); Salt Lake City: Family History World, 1983, for a preliminary list of studies available.

The three standard listings of counties in the United States are George B. Everton, Sr., *The Handy Book for Genealogists* (Logan, Utah: Everton Publishers, 1981); Ronald V. Jackson et al., *Encyclopedia of Local History and Genealogy: U.S. Counties* (Bountiful, Utah: Accelerated Indexing Systems, 1977); and Joseph Nathan Kane, *The American Counties: Origins of Names, Dates of Creation and Organization Data, and Published Sources* (Metuchen, N.J.: Scarecrow Press, 1972). Everton and Jackson omit many defunct counties; Kane lists only surviving modern counties.

The Newberry Library in Chicago attempted to plot all county boundary changes on computer so any boundary for any *day* from 1607 could be retrieved if known. Only fourteen states were completed—New Jersey, Delaware, Maryland, Pennsylvania, the five states north of the Ohio River, Missouri, Iowa, Minnesota, and the two Dakotas. There are plans to publish some of these maps.

Dollarhide Systems is publishing *Map Guide to the U.S. Federal Censuses, 1790-1920,* a project promising to map all county boundaries for each census for each state. The project hopes to complete all states east of the Mississippi River by 1984. For what is available, send a SASE to The Dollarhide Systems, Box 5282, Bellingham, WA 98227. Again, unfortunately, this *Map Guide* will not solve the ultimate need for detailed maps showing all county boundary changes from their creation dates, though it will show boundaries at ten-year intervals.

Two sets of such decennial boundary maps are already available. The U.S. Department of Agriculture made a set of maps, 1840-1940, eastern and western U.S. sheets, for each year. Stephen S. Birdsall and John W. Florin did *A Series of County Outline Maps of the Southeastern United States for the Period 1790-1860* (Chapel Hill: Department of Geography, University of North Carolina, 1973). Both the USDA and North Carolina series suffer from using a very small scale which makes them crudely accurate but with numerous obvious errors, especially for early years of newly created states and territories. Thus, American researchers must make do for the present with very inadequate tools when trying to determine the changes in county boundaries.

Spelling Variants

Aside from a few oral interviews, most of a genealogist's searches are for written names. If those written names are not spelled as expected, you could pass over them and miss crucial evidence. "Stephenson" along the Scottish border could be pronounced "Ste'enson," so Stinson is a natural variation. Likewise, would you recognize McHuron and Mehurin as the same name? Tom Dooley of ballad fame was a Confederate soldier from North Carolina whose more common spelling was Dula.

Such spelling problems are complicated further because a Dutch Reformed minister in colonial New York and a Mexican official in Texas in the early 1830s would naturally tend to spell foreign names according to Dutch or Spanish phonetics, just as Dutch and Spanish surnames were made to look and sound more English by English-speaking clerks.

All the best research ingenuity could be wasted if the researcher working on O'Connor or Hollaway does not also check, among other spellings, Connor or Allaway. To explain something of such spelling variants and also their relationship to census indexes, this article is edited and reprinted with permission from the *Association of Professional Genealogists (APG) Newsletter* 4 (1982), no. 5.

CENSUS INDEXES AND SPELLING VARIANTS

William Thorndale

An index to the 1840 Georgia census consistently transcribes the old long-short double "s" as "p", so Jesse Moss could come out as Jepe Mop. Some of the O's in the Soundex for the 1900 Illinois census are mistakenly not filmed by the National Archives. In one computer-sorted index, some New England entries get published in an index for a Southern state. A recent article in *Prologue* finds the 1900 Soundex index so inaccurate that the author favors using city directories keyed to street maps as superior to Soundex.[1]

Such problems aside, just how accurate are state-wide census indexes? What are we to make of an 1850 census index that can list a person named Xzlly Mzfgin—yes, Xzlly Mxfgin.[2] Is this a botched entry or maybe just a drollery of a bored typist? What are the chances that the average index will correctly produce the names of the census?

In the only detailed analysis of which I am aware, a researcher claimed an index for the 1800 New York census failed to produce 7 percent of the Clinton County entries. The author, after trying flights of spelling fancy, could not find 56 of the 799 Clinton entries.[3] This seems to confirm the impression of regular users that such indexes are handy but not very accurate. I wonder. A Salt Lake professional once complained to me that the 1800 North Carolina index produced by Accelerated Indexing Systems (AIS) was so bad that it missed all the Fespermans known to be in the state and listed in the census. It did, but this professional might have thought of looking under Fisperman.

There are actually two questions here: what percentage of entries are actually in the index somewhere, and what percentage are entered in spellings reasonable enough for the user to find?

Looking for Fesperman under all forms of the first vowel – Fasp..., Fesp ..., etc., seems an elementary duty of the users and thus the index is accurate if Fesperman happens to be listed as Fisperman or Fosperman.

In comparing two 1850 indexes for Arkansas against an index for Fulton County, I found that over 97 percent of county entries were in each state index.[4] In checking a small part of the Frederick County, Maryland, census of 1850 against the AIS Maryland 1850 index, the figure was over 99 percent.[5]

In the first case, the card catalog showed that Fulton County, Arkansas, had an every-name transcription of the 1850 census, and this was used as the authoritative list against which to measure two different state-wide indexes. Having such a county listing provides an independent opinion of what the census entries actually are and frees the evaluator of the state indexes from having to judge his readings of the manuscript census against those of the indexers of those state indexes. The county transcription was photocopied and then every "Fulton" entry in each state index was located and marked on the county transcript. (The state indexes, of course, only list heads of households plus differing surnames within the households.)

Upon analysis, one state index produced 433 of the 444 entries in the county transcript, and the other (AIS) produced 435 of 444. These are 97.5 percent and 98.0 percent coverage. Every "Fulton" entry in both state indexes was located in the county transcript, which implies the county transcript is complete. The two state indexes *together* included 442 of the 444 names, for 99.5 percent coverage.

Mary Hitselberger and John Philip Dern spent over six years making duplicate transcriptions of the 1850 census of Frederick County, Maryland. They published a joint transcript, each thus providing an independent check on the other's work. Their massive transcript was honored as the best publication of Maryland genealogical source records in 1978-79.[6] I checked the AIS 1850 Maryland index against all A to D entries found in the Hitselberger-Dern transcript for Petersville District. I found at least 140 of the 141 target entries were in the AIS index – 99.3 percent – "at least" because I would not be surprised if the one entry not found is really there somewhere in the AIS index. From this example and the Fulton example, I conclude tentatively that persons indexing censuses rarely omit entries.

The problem is not omissions so much as misreadings. Had I done this analysis "backwards" – taken a county transcript and looked up each name in the state index – I would have found fewer entries because some misreadings in the state censuses are so bad that some may be effectively lost. Examples from Fulton County are as follows, the county transcript version first: Sweat/Soveat/Loveat, Rarinnes?/Rammer?/Ramnes, Crow/Corn, Steakley/Starkley, Harris?/ Parris, Tindel/Lindels, Hattey/Hatley, Cromwell/Carrell, Chamtes?/ Chamie, Whetstine/Whitshire, Kates/Keetes, Stuart/Thiart, Wrapp/ Weapp, Younge/Yonige, Mainer/Miner, Yarberry/Tarberry, Leymons/Seymons, Norman/Newman, Joseph/Josiah, Stirrit/Stinnet/Stirvet, Wrice/Weice/Wice, Murphrey/Hurphrey, and Skiver/Skinner.

Which of these are so unexpected as to be lost is a subjective evaluation; but, ignoring the spelling variants an alert researcher should catch, I would estimate that perhaps ten entries are so unexpected as to be essentially unfindable with any reasonable effort. This being so, the two Arkansas state indexes are at least 95 percent complete and accurate.

The Frederick County example produces these differences between the Hitselberger-Dern transcript and the AIS index: Lawson/Lanson, Buttle/Butler, Allen/Allne and Crampton/Carmpton (transposed letters) Bligh/Blish, Delauder/Delander, Duvall/Duball, Barger/Banger, Diek/ Drake, Burnison/Bumison, and Cartee/Carter.

If we estimate that ten entries would be hidden, this gives (when added to the one entry not found in the AIS Index) an accuracy of 92.2 percent for the AIS Index. In sum, from my examples and the Clinton County, New York, case already published, the average state index probably has an effective accuracy of 92 percent to 95 percent. Of course, where the original census is in a semi-legible handwriting or the microfilm is very faint or unreadable, then the index will be grossly less accurate.

This estimate of 92 percent to 95 percent effective accuracy assumes the researcher uses some imagination in how names might be hidden in the index, which raises the matter of spelling variants. These spelling variations arise from how people spelled their names, and how census enumerators and indexers wrote those names. Since spelling variations are much noted in genealogical publications, I will not dwell on most of the possible sources of error but would like to briefly summarize some categories just because we genealogists can never be reminded enough that we are not hunting for people but for ***written words***.

1. Calligraphic look-alikes: Daniel/David, Nathan/Mathew, Ball/Bell/Boll/Bull, Sanderdale/Lauderdale.
2. Phonetic equivalents: Lydecker/Litaker, Myatt/Maillotte, de la Hunte/Dillahunty, Hansel/Ansel, St. Cyr/Sincere, Ratton/Wroughton, Vanlandingham/Flannagen.
3. Translation equivalents: Calbfleisch/Veal, Rubsamen/Turnip seed.
4. Truncates: Fitzgerald/Gerald/Jurrell, O'Sullivan/Sully!!, Haythornthwaite/Haythorn, Strohmaier/Maier, de Villeponteaux/Pontoux.
5. Spelling irregularities: Cowper pronounced as Cooper, Coke pronounced as Cook, Featherstonehaughs pronounced (so it is said) Fanshaw. This category brings to mind the limerick:

A young man called Cholmondeley Calquhoun
Kept as a pet a babolquhoun.
  His mother said, "Cholmondeley,
  Do you think it quite colmondeley
To feed your babolquhoun with a spolquhoun?"

To be alert to examples in these five classes requires mostly experience; they are tricky. But there is another category of spelling variants systematic enough to provide mechanical rules when searching census indexes.

Consider the Apache Kid. His native name has been variously anglicized as Haskaybaynayntayl, Oskabennantelz, and Eskibinadel.[7] Isolating the consonantal bones gives:

Haskay-bay-nay-ntayl	(H)	sk	b	n	ntl
Oska-ben-nan-telz		sk	bn	nn	tlz
Es-ki-bi-nadel		s-k	b	n	ndl

The U.S. Census Bureau's surname list in *A Century of Population Growth* (1909), pages 227-70, is well-known. This compilation lists all surnames with at least one hundred persons given in the surviving 1790 U.S. census – not one hundred heads of households, but surnames totaling at least one hundred persons in the households, so that ten Nettle households averaging ten persons each would qualify. The list provides a very broad survey of U.S. surnames in 1790. Excluding 263 surnames with only one spelling, there remain 3398 surnames in 19,788 spelling variants. All these were analyzed for spelling patterns, as the following examples illustrate:

L	igh	t		Ea	s	l	ey	W	a	t	s	o	n	
L	eigh	t		Ea	se	l	y	W	a	t	s	e	n	
L	ei	t	z	E	s	l	y	W	a	t	st	o	n	
L	igh	te		E	s	l	ey	W	a	tt	s	o	n	s
L	igh	t	s	I	s	l	ey	Wh	a	t	s	o	n	
L	i	te						W	o	t	s	o	n	

The interchangeability of letters and sound groups was tallied as shown in Table A and converted to percentages in the column at the right.

A letter may behave differently at the beginning of a name from

Table A
Spelling/Sound Patterns in Surnames

A Century of Population Growth, U.S. Census Bureau, (Washington, DC, 1909), pp. 227-270, lists all surnames in the 1790 U.S. census having at least 100 persons (whites). Of the 3661 surnames with a total of 20,051 spelling variants, 263 have only one spelling, leaving 3398 surnames totaling 19,788 multiple spellings. An analysis of these nearly 20,000 spellings produces the following major spelling/sound patterns. In phonetics, the / / indicates a phoneme or distinct sound. A simplified version of the International Phonetic Alphabet is followed, but some of the specialized symbols are not used.

Letter	Sound	Initial	Internal	Percentages*
a	various	A Ai/Ay Au E	vowel	A91.0% Ai/Ay4.5 Au1.5 E1.5
b	/b/	B	b bb	B100.0; b87.3 bb11.6
c	none			see /s/ and /k/
	/ch/	Ch	ch tch dg	actually /t/+/sh/; Ch100.0; ch48.0 tch42.7 dg3.2
d	/d/	D	d dd t	D100.0; d88.6 dd5.3 t5.1
e	various	E Ea I Ei	vowel	E78.1 Ea17.2 I2.6 Ei1.2
f	/f/	F Ph	f ff ph gh v	F93.8 Ph6.2; f53.5 ff29.0 ph8.5 gh2.4 v1.8; (Pfeiffer/Pifer not included in above percentages)
g	/g/	G	g gg gh k/ck	G99.6 Gh0.4; g72.1 gg18.6 gh5.1 k/ck2.4
h	/h/	H, dropped	h, dropped	H100.0; h internally often dropped
i	various	I E U	vowel	I70.1 E28.6 U1.2
j	/j/	J G	g dg j d gg	J87.0 G13.0; g46.1 dg32.1 j12.2 d2.9 gg2.0; actually /j/=/d/+/zh/
k	/k/	C K Ch	k ck c ch x	C66.6 K32.2 Ch1.1; k36.7 ck32.1 c16.6 ch7.8 x3.4
l	/l/	L	l ll	L99.6; l:70.4 ll:25.9 (much of remaining % is l+d forms)
m	/m/	M	m mm mb mp n	M100.0; m85.0 mm8.1 mb3.3 mp1.6 n1.4
n	/n/	N Kn	n nn ng nd nt	N85.7 Kn14.3; n83.2 nn6.2 ng5.3 nd3.1 nt1.5
o	various	O Oa U	vowel	O90.1 Oa7.3 U2.1
p	/p/	P	p pp b pb	P100.0; p76.2 pp11.5 b1.3 pb1.1
q	/kw/	Qu	qu k	Qu100.0; qu rare and often /k/; "q" actually = /k/+/w/
r	/r/	R Rh	r rr, semi-vowel	R97.2 Rh2.6 (also Wr); as semi-vowel r·er·re etc. often interchangeable with vowels
s	/s/	S C	s ss z st	S97.4 C0.9; s71.4 ss10.2 z5.4 st2.9 (in 1.7% no letter appears)
	/sh/	Sh Sch	sh ch	Sh90.3 Sch8.4; sh82.0 ch6.3
t	/t/ & /th/	T Th	t tt th d	T86.7 Th13.3; t58.8 tt17.4 th9.9 d2.3
u	various	U	vowel	U100.0
v	/v/	V	v f	V100.0; v92.1 f1.2
w	/w/	W Wh	w wh r, vowel	W84.3 Wh15.2 (R0.5); internally as consonant and vowel
x	/k/+/s/	-		included under /k/ with "s" ignored
y	/y/	Y Yh	y, vowel	Y97.4 Yh1.3
z	/z/	Z	see /s/	Z100.0

*Percentages sometimes are significantly short of totaling 100% because only the major interchanageable letters are shown.

how it operates inside the name. An obvious example would be that a double *g* is common within a surname but English does not use an initial double *G*. Conversely, an initial *N* is replaced by *Kn* 14.3 percent of the time, but essentially never does the *Kn* appear inside surnames as the *n* sound (except possibly the initial sound of a "subword" such as Maryknoll).

The genealogical researcher should think in terms of phonemic units. *Lancaster* is really L+vowels+n/nn/nd/nt+k/ck/c/ck/ch+..., the dots indicating that the rest of the surname is probably not important for position in the index. Since experience teaches that the capital *L* and the capital *S* often look alike, the researcher might be wise to search for L/S+vowel++n/nn/nd/nt+k/ck/c/ch+....

The key rule here is to search for all forms of the first vowel –*automatically*. Trying to remember the various ways to spell Witherspoon is complicated, likely impossible, distracting, and unnecessary. The conversion table suggests instead that a search for W/Wh+vowels+t/tt/th/d+...should put the researcher in the right parts of the index to encounter the various spelling variants of Witherspoon. Anyone who has done research on this surname knows that the first vowel appears as Wa..., We..., Wi..., Wo..., Wu..., and Wy... (plus all Wh...forms) with fluid abandon.

Also note:

1. Surnames beginning with a vowel or *H* should be sought under all vowels plus *H*, at least at the beginning of research, until one becomes familiar with spelling variants that do not seem *ever* to appear.

2. *H* slips in and out of words in disconcerting fashion–Allard/Alhurd–; be especially alert to put an *h* after plausible initial letters–Whood, Ghorman, Champbell.

3. *R* is a semi-vowel within words and occasionally appears in unexpected places in a pattern not clear to me.

4. Learn to think in terms of word elements (syllables), e.g., Al+borrow, Black+more, Sweet+land, since between such elements may appear extra letters such as a vowel, *s*, *r*, and *h*. Thus, Lowman/Loreman, Jackson/Jackison, Carlysle/Carslile.

5. Letter transpositions are sometimes fairly standardized, such as Smi*ht* and All*ne*, in computerized indexes, caused by one hand getting ahead of the other on the keyboard.

6. The best strategy is to search *all* entries under an initial letter, such as reading every *B* surname when seeking all Blighs; in fact, if this strategy were used for the Frederick County example given above, every one of the eleven entries misplaced by AIS would have been found and the AIS index would have had about a 99 percent accuracy.

One of the most depressing situations I experience as a professional genealogist is giving suggestions to people doing their own research. These people come to the great Salt Lake library all excited to solve a stonewall problem, and they ask for my suggestions (paid consultations). I try to emphasize how important spelling variants are to such problems and practically plead for these researchers to *always check all forms of the first vowel* when searching census indexes. A few days later, they are failing and discouraged because the names are not in the census indexes. So out of curiosity I look and there they are under some spelling variation, usually because of a different initial letter or first vowel, or maybe they are hidden by an *h* as the second letter, which throws the surname into an unexpected place in the index. Occasionally, the problem is the computer's placement of names due to spacing. That is, *MacDonald* and *Mac Donald* can be different surnames in an AIS index, just as Arnold,David (no space after the comma) will be listed *after* Arnold, Z. I hope I have made myself clear: an enormous amount of genealogical research fails because people do not take simple precautions in searching for spelling variants.

If most state census indexes are at least 92 percent to 95 percent accurate, then the bad name such indexes have is probably only partly merited. I suspect many of the complaints about an index not having a name are really the fault of the user. If you are looking for Fesperman, simple prudence says you will look under F/Ph/Pf+ vowels+s/ss/z/st+p..., and if the index puts it under Fisperman, so what?

Notes

1. Keith R. Shlesinger, "An 'Urban Finding Aid': for the Federal Census," *Prologue* 13 (1981): 251-62.

2. Accelerated Indexing Systems, *Maryland 1850 Census Index* (Bountiful, Utah: AIS, 1976).

3. David Kendall Martin, "New York 1800 Census Index," *American Genealogist* 54 (1978): 53-54.

4. Mrs. Leister E. Presley, *Arkansas Census 1850 Surname Index* (Searcy, Ark., By the author, 1974); Accelerated Indexing Systems, *Arkansas 1850 Census Index,* (Bountiful, Utah: AIS, 1976).

5. Mary Fitzhugh Hitselberger and John Philip Dern, *Bridge in Time: The Complete 1850 Census of Frederick County, Maryland* (Redwood City, Calif.: Monocacy Book Co., 1978); Accelerated Indexing Systems, *Maryland 1850 Census Index,* (Bountiful, Utah: AIS, 1976).

6. "News Item," *Maryland Magazine of Genealogy* 2 (1979): 67, 84.

7. Dan L. Thrapp, *Al Sieber, Chief of Scouts* (Norman: University of Oklahoma Press, 1964), p. 322.

The Historical Dimension

As a genealogist, you need to know the history behind your ancestors, to understand the historical seas in which they swam. For instance, it is possible to trace Southern families in the years between the Revolution and Civil War as they went from one area of newly opened Indian lands to the next. Understanding which Indian lands were opened for settlement could start with the technical listing by Charles C. Royce, *Indian Cessions in the United States* (1900; reprint ed., New York: Arno Press, 1971) From there you could go to local histories.

A great many examples could be marshalled to prove the importance of understanding history. If an ancestor was a Methodist circuit rider, you want to know what that means. Could circuit riders be married? How long were they assigned to one particular circuit? Just what and how large was a "circuit"? Where and in what sorts of Methodist records would one look for records on a circuit rider? What is the difference between a circuit rider, a regular Methodist preacher, and a lay exhorter?

Assume the immigrant ancestor whose British origins are unlocated arrived in a colony about 1690 and was soon appointed as the crown's legal officer for a county. What sort of legal education would such a person likely have? Could he be a lawyer in the colonies without having gone to the London Inns of Court? Was there any other school in England that trained lawyers? Would a degree from Cambridge or Oxford be sufficient? What was the Scottish or Irish equivalent of these English schools and would study in them permit practicing law in the colonies? Could one be a lawyer in 1700 just from apprenticing to a practicing lawyer? Would such an apprentice-trained lawyer likely be chosen King's Counsel? Is trying to use this legal background even a plausible way to hunt for the man's British birthplace?

Suppose a family tradition says ancestress Mary Jones was born a Catholic but was adopted by Quakers after the French and Indian War when she was eight years old in 1763. Would it help to know that adoption did not exist under colonial law and that the earliest adoption law in the United States seems to have been the 1851 Massachusetts law? Perhaps this "adoption" was really a guardianship? If her parents were Catholic, were there laws supressing the Catholic Church about 1763 and would there have ever been a Catholic Church register naming Mary? Was it illegal to practice Catholicism in New York in 1763 but legal in Pennsylvania?

Obviously, the list could continue. Obviously, a genealogist needs this information. Equally obviously, it is easy to put off doing background research because it is hard to locate a convenient book or article detailing what you want to know about Catholic life in the colonies in 1763. A good local library is an obvious boon, though the interlibrary loan of history books is practical. Helpfully, many college libraries offer borrowing privileges for nonstudents for a quarterly or yearly fee.

Finding the history book or article you need is a hit-and-miss affair that is called developing a bibliography. Even the most expert historian or genealogist suffers from the frustrations of trying to learn what has been published. Take these normal frustrations in stride. Certain finding aids will help.

The bibliographic *Harvard Guide to American History,* Frank Freidel, ed. (Cambridge, Mass.: Belknap Press of Harvard University Press, 1974), 2 vols., is a good place to begin. It leads the user directly to specific history titles by topics. A great many specialty bibliographies may be listed in Theodore Besterman, *A World Bibliography of Bibliographies,* 5 vols. (Lausanne, Switzerland: Societas Bibliographica, 1965).

American associations compile yearly bibliographies, and the two major services are *America: History and Life* and *Writings on American History,* also online at university library computer-search centers. If *C.R.I.S.: The Combined Retrospective Index Set to Journals in History, 1838-1974* by Annadel N. Wile et al. (Washington, D.C.: Carrollton Press, 1977), 11 vols., is available, it should be checked for articles. Many state bibliographies also exist either in book form or as yearly bibliographies in state historical journals. If you are concentrating on a particular area and have access to the back issues of historical journals devoted to that area, first seek a cumulative index to the periodical and, if there is none, run through the title pages of each issue to see what was published. Also check the titles in the book review section.

If this all seems a scattergun way to do things, you're right. But this is the way it is done. There is usually no one-step service for building the good bibliography you want. And without that technical knowledge of the world of your ancestors, you stand a much smaller chance of solving lineage problems.

Special Research Skills

Notekeeping and Analysis of Data

A good notekeeping system makes preserving and analyzing information easier. How you keep notes is not important so long as the material found is preserved in an efficient and careful way, easily understandable to you or to others. It is remarkable how quickly you can forget the meaning of even your own notes! Most researchers can tell you a personal horror story of neglecting to copy a vital fact or its source and then spending years searching for it again.

Every genealogist should find some notekeeping system that is comfortable to use. No one system is correct, though writing on only one side of the notepaper is probably as near a universal rule as there is. Experts differ widely on how to keep notes, so do not be intimidated into using something you do not like. The extremes in notekeeping systems are these:

Family Group Sheets. To summarize what is known about a couple and their children, the researcher usually uses a family group sheet, with spaces for names, parents, dates, places of events, children spouses, sources, and other information to help identify members of one particular family. But the Family Group Sheet (FGS) Notekeeping System goes a step further and uses FGSs to keep the actual notes. One FGS is used for each source entry. Thus, a man and his family described in a Revolutionary War pension file are copied onto FGS's as shown in Figure 1. Sources are checked in the corner and the extract is complete. Likewise a family located in a Federal census gets its own FGS copied like the first family. The same approach is used for censuses, deeds, wills, newspaper obituaries, and other records. Each family entry from one source is copied onto its own separate source FGS so the sheets can be sorted any way the researcher desires.

This system makes it easier to compile summary family group sheets with everything known about the couple. After extensive research all the FGS sheets for censuses, probates, deeds, Bibles, newspapers, printed biographies, and anything else used are combined and sorted into groups, such as by head of household. Bringing together all the sheets for one name makes it easy to see if they seem to represent one man or more than one. This system also requires indepth evaluation of each record as it is searched. The process of placing information into a set format is an analytic one. Clues for follow-up and discrepancies in dates, spellings, or places of origin, obvious during the extraction process, can be forgotten or overlooked later.

Users of this FGS system also like the freedom of sorting and resorting the notes. The great disadvantage of the system is that it scatters the information found in one source. It is often important to see again how many Wetzels were in the 1850 Randolph County census and who is shown next to each other. Once the FGS source sheets have been sorted into families, this information is destroyed and can only be reconstituted by resorting the individual sheets to bring together all the 1850 Randolph County census entries.

Tablet Notes. Just the opposite from the FGS notekeeping system is recording information on blank pages such as lined yellow legal (8½ x 14") or letter-size (8½ x 11") tablets. You write page 1 on the first sheet, copy as Source 1 the source citation and the desired data, and then skip a line and copy Source 2 with citation and data, etc., etc. Each sheet is filled and numbered. If you read first a census, then a county history, then a probate volume, your notes are in that sequence. This system has the advantage of using a minimum of paper and thus reducing the amount of paper stored. It also preserves *unaltered* what was found. If you want to refresh your memory on how many Wetzels were in the 1850 Randolph County census and who was enumerated next to whom, you can see it just as you copied it in Source 73. The copied notes are unedited, meaning that you do not change, add to, or alter the information. Once the data is copied from a source, it is left alone. If you wish to add a comment or question to yourself, it is done in the margin or in brackets after the entry as an annotation. This should be true of any notekeeping system; it is just clearer with the tablet system because not even the order of the sources copied can be altered. For purposes of analysis you will probably compile family group sheets synthesizing the raw data from the tablet notes. The disadvantage of the tablet system is that it requires much reading and re-reading of jumbled notes and a good memory for scattered pieces of information.

The family group sheet system and the tablet system are the extremes, presented here to set the outer limits of two approaches. Most researchers compromise. Some copy each source on a separate blank page or form. Thus, all the Wetzels in Randolph County are copied onto an 1850 census form (or forms). Then all the 1860 entries are copied on a new form or blank page. This preserves the grouping of all the 1850 Wetzels and yet allows some sorting of the notes. It combines both systems described above. Again, however, a compiled family group sheet is made for each couple and their children for purposes of analysis. The copied notes are thus kept separate from the working conclusions of who goes where in the lineage.

Notekeeping techniques vary. Some researchers use different printed forms to help them; others consider forms a bother to obtain and carry around. Two forms are popular for keeping track of copied information: the research log and the correspondence log. Examples of both are in Chapter 1 on home sources and oral history. The research log, also called a calendar, is a running list of sources checked and an annotation to see if source X turned anything up. The log shows all sources checked and acts as a table of contents to the research notes. The correspondence log lists all the letters you send and receive, with perhaps a number key written on those letters so they can be stored and easily retrieved. The correspondence log tells you if you did or did not answer Cousin Mary Jones or if it has really been six months since you sent to

Figure 1. Samples from the FGS Notekeeping System: Research Calendar, family group sheets for Peter Greenlee, Reuben and Nancy Johnson, Reuben Johnson, and Nancy Greenlee Johnson, and Peter Greenlee.

HUSBAND Reuben Johnson
Birth/Chr. ______ Place ______
Marriage 20 Nov 1788 Place Wilkes Co., North Carolina
Death 26 Jan 1833 Place ______
Burial ______ Place ______
Father ______ Mother ______

Doc. No. 14 Search No. 25 Family Line ______
Home ______ Institution ______ Township ______
Parish ______ County ______ Municipal ______
Local ______ District ______ State NC National ______
Personal Papers ______ Census ______ Financial ______ Interview ______
Family Records ______ Land ______ License ______ Corresp. ______

Widow
WIFE Nancy Johnson
Birth/Chr. ______
Death ______
Burial ______
Father ______

CHILDREN
1
2
3
4
5
6
7
8

EVALUATIVE COMMENTS:

HUSBAND Reuben Johnson
Birth/Chr. ______ Place ______
Marriage ______ Place North Carolina
Death ______ Place ______
Burial ______ Place ______
Father ______ Mother ______

moved to South Carolina with Peter Greenlee, the two families lived on same plantation.

Doc. No. 15 Search No. 25 Family Line ______
Home ______ Institution ______ Township ______
Parish ______ County ______ Municipal ______
Local ______ District ______ State NC National ______
Personal Papers ______ Census ______ Financial ______ Interview ______
Family Records ______ Land ______ License ______ Corresp. ______
Pedigree ______ Probate ______ Church ______ Original ✓
History ______ Court ______ Employment ______ Copy ✓

Sister
WIFE Nancy Johnson ne[e]
Birth/Chr. ______
Death ______
Burial ______
Father Peter Greenlee

CHILDREN
1
2
3
4
5
6
7
8

EVALUATIVE COMMENTS:

Father
HUSBAND Peter Greenlee
Birth/Chr. ______ Place ______
Marriage ______ Place ______
Death Ca. 40 years ago Place ______
Burial ______ Place ______
Father ______ Mother ______

Mother
WIFE
Birth/Chr. ______ Place ______
Death 1 Dec 1842 Place ______
Burial ______ Place ______
Father ______ Mother ______

Doc. No. 15 Search No. 25 Family Line ______
Home ______ Institution ______ Township ______
Parish ______ County ______ Municipal ______
Local ______ District ______ State ______ National ______
Personal Papers ______ Census ______ Financial ______ Interview ______
Family Records ______ Land ______ License ______ Corresp. ______
Pedigree ______ Probate ______ Church ______ Original ✓
History ______ Court ______ Employment ______ Copy ✓
Biography ______ Tax ______ Cemetery ______ Manuscript ✓
MSS Colls ______ Military ✓ School ______ Printed ______
Coat of Arms ______ Poor Relief ______ Newspaper ______ Handwritten ______
Oral History ______ Birth ______ Profession ______ Typed ______
Periodical ______ Marriage ______ Estate ______ Extract ______
Membership ______ Death ______ Insurance ______ Legible ______
Election ______ Shipping ______ Language ______
Sworn statement, Margaret Burroughs
Rev. War pension file, W 10156
Call No. GS 971,428 Volume ______ Page ______
Doc. Dated [1844] Date Recorded ______
Date of Search ______ Proofread for Accuracy ______

CHILDREN	BIRTH (Date and Place)	MARRIAGE (Spouse, Date and Place)	DEATH (Date and Place)	BURIAL (Date and Place)
1 Nancy Johnson nee Greenlee, sister		Reuben Johnson		
2 Margaret Burroughs age 6 when Nancy married				

RESEARCH CALENDAR

RECORDED BY: ______

DOC. NO.	S NO.	LOC NO.	DATE OF SEARCH	SOURCE: Description, Condition, How Searched	COMMENTS AND FOLLOW-UP	LOCALITY	JURISDICTION	PERIOD OF TIME	SURNAMES OR NAMES	RESULTS
14- 15	25		1 Feb 1984	Revolutionary War pension file, National Archives, W10156. Microfilm Copy, Genealogical Society of Utah 971,428.	Did Nancy's father Peter Greenlee also serve in the war? Check to see.			1843-44	Reuben Johnson-fgs	
				Alphabetical under "J." Widow's pension granted to Nancy Johnson.						

Salt Lake City, UT 84101

HUSBAND Peter Greenlee
Birth/Chr. ______ Place ______
Marriage ______ Place ______
Death Ca. 1804 Place prob. South Carolina
Burial ______ Place ______
Father ______ Mother ______

WIFE
Birth/Chr. ______ Place ______
Death 1 Dec 1842 Place prob. South Carolina
Burial ______ Place ______
Father ______ Mother ______

Doc. No. 14-15 Search No. 25 Family Line ______
Home ______ Institution ______ Township ______
Parish ______ County ______ Municipal ______
Local ______ District ______ State ______ National ______
Personal Papers ______ Census ______ Financial ______ Interview ______
Family Records ______ Land ______ License ______ Corresp. ______
Pedigree ______ Probate ______ Church ______ Original ✓
History ______ Court ______ Employment ______ Copy ✓
Biography ______ Tax ______ Cemetery ______ Manuscript ✓
MSS Colls ______ Military ✓ School ______ Printed ______
Coat of Arms ______ Poor Relief ______ Newspaper ______ Handwritten ______
Oral History ______ Birth ______ Profession ______ Typed ______
Periodical ______ Marriage ______ Estate ______ Extract ______
Membership ______ Death ______ Insurance ______ Legible ______
Election ______ Shipping ______ Language ______
Summary Sheet, Rev. War pension file, W10156
Call No. GS 971,428 Volume ______ Page ______
Doc. Dated 1843-44 Date Recorded ______
Date of Search ______ Proofread for Accuracy ______

W. South Temple • Salt Lake City, UT 84101

CHILDREN*	BIRTH (Date and Place)	MARRIAGE (Spouse, Date and Place)	DEATH (Date and Place)	BURIAL (Date and Place)
1 Nancy Greenlee		20 Nov 1788 Wilkes Co. NC Reuben Johnson		
2 Margaret Greenlee	Ca. 1782	Burroughs		
3				
4				
5				
6				
7				
8				

EVALUATIVE COMMENTS:
* Probably other children in this family, at least 12 years between births of Nancy and Margaret.

Family History World • 57 W. South Temple • Salt Lake City, UT 84101

New York City for a birth certificate.

Much more could be said about refinements and variations on note keeping systems, but the major point to remember here is that you must settle on some comfortable system of notekeeping that preserves the information gleaned in your research and enables you to go back to the exact source for any particular fact. Abstracting information is something learned from experience rather than how-to books. The rule is to take the time to copy all pertinent information. You learn to recognize "all pertinent information" from experience.

Competent research cannot be undertaken in a disorganized fashion. Plan ahead to use all sources available. First, survey the published and unpublished records pertaining to your subject. Rank the records available according to their priority in the research process. Records most likely to solve your problems should be consulted first. Of course, you must consider the physical location of important records. While accessible records are most easily consulted, you will probably save time by waiting until you can make a field trip or receive a response to correspondence.

From the beginning you must understand exactly what you want to learn and then use the records most likely to produce such results. Basic genealogical research steps need to be outlined. First, start from the known and go to the unknown. Choosing an illustrious patriot such as Patrick Henry when your own name is John Henry and striving to build a descending pedigree to link yourself with him is almost always fruitless and can be extremely time-consuming. Documented facts about parents and grandparents should be used to begin extending a pedigree back in time. If the line does in fact go back to Patrick, fine; but if he is not the ancestor, all of the records in the world cannot make the link a reality.

A well-seasoned genealogist is best distinguished by his/her ability to analyze record sources. Anyone can extract names from appropriate records; but if you can't identify relationships and find meaning in these extractions, the records are basically useless. *All genealogical conclusions must be based on accurately recorded, carefully documented, and exhaustively analyzed records.* No possible clues should be ignored, no stone left unturned. Because of the ample record sources available – the chapters which follow will impress even experts – there is no reason to put a pedigree together without convincing proof.

A second important point is that you need explicit proof for saying that any two records apply to the same person. Far too many pedigrees have been compiled erroneously because the compiler found, for example, a birth record for a John Smith twenty-five years prior to the marriage of another John Smith in Allegheny County, Pennsylvania. Because he would have been approximately twenty-five years old when wed, he seems to be the correct John Smith. Wrong. He may well be; but without analysis of other records and the family situation you cannot responsibly make such a conclusion.

An excellent discussion of the analytical process and evaluation of evidence can be found in the companion to this volume, Johni Cerny and Arlene H. Eakle, *Ancestry's Guide to Research* (Salt Lake City: Ancestry Publishing Co., 1984), and the old but still very sound Derek Harland, *Genealogical Research Standards* (Salt Lake City: Bookcraft, Inc., 1970), Chapters 2-4. A helpful essay is Robert C. Anderson and Neil D. Thompson, "Evaluating Evidence: The Test of a Good Genealogist," paper presented at Third Annual Conference in the States, National Genealogical Society, Fort Worth, Texas, 16 April 1983; also available on cassette tape from Triad Productions, Box 486, Delavan, IL 61734.

Fraudulent Pedigrees

Supplying phony noble ancestries for the newly rich has been a profitable business for thousands of years. Just as there have been forgeries in art and letters, so there have been forgeries in genealogy. The motive is often obscure, as when English antiquarian William Stukeley in the eighteenth century fabricated a pedigree for Robin Hood.[3]

The line between wishful thinking, inadequate research, and incompetence on the one hand and outright fraud on the other may be fuzzy, but American researchers should realize that some genealogical work is simply invented, often to fill a void in the records. Because descent from early frontier heroes is socially prestigious and such pioneers rarely left personal accounts of their lives, they are often a target for fraudulent connections. The fraudulant Horn Papers still contaminate early genealogical research on southwestern Pennsylvania (though volume 3 on land grants is reliable).[4] In 1959 the *Tennessee Historical Quarterly* printed a diary dating from the earliest years of white settlement in middle Tennessee but ten years later published accusations that the diary was a fraud, though whether a total fabrication or based on some genuine family papers was then impossible to determine.[5] Colonel Richard Lee, immigrant ancestor of the notable Virginia family, has been a favorite of creative fancy, since his father's name remains unknown. Experts have had to bat down claims to a noble pedigree for the Lees and expose as spurious a Bible entry which supplied the colonel with a birthplace and father.[6]

Enthusiastic but untrained hobbyists have further muddied the waters. The Genealogical Society of Utah's patron section includes a family group sheet of Thomas Gates, supposedly born 1698 in Virginia, which says that his four sons were born 1724-32 in Kanawha County, West Virginia.[7] That there were no white settlers in that area so early could indicate an honest mistake; that the allegedly published sources cited on the sheet cannot be located in the reference catalogs of any major genealogical collection suggests a need for cautious use of this family group sheet – a caution that is echoed by posters in this section of the society's stacks warning that family group sheets submitted by patrons have not been verified.

Some people will also fabricate evidence to join lineage societies. Here is an example described by the editor of the *Stewart Clan Magazine* 22 (1944-45), p. 51:

> Some years ago a woman got hold of a few numbers of the *Stewart Clan Magazine*, picked herself out a soldier and put her Zeke Stewart – it wasn't Zeke – in as a son, and asked us if it wasn't right. We said no; there was no evidence of this soldier ever having had a son Zeke, and Zeke's father was living in Pennsylvania at the time the soldier was living in New Jersey. Nonetheless, the applicant was welcomed into the [lineage society] on this bogus claim, and she cited the *Stewart Clan Magazine* to prove it!

This editor may have been unfair to claim the society "welcomed" the applicant, as if it were a party to the fraud. Such lineage societies have developed increasingly stricter requirements for accurate applications; but there is no protection against fraud camouflaged with phony citations.

Proper Documentation

The word *documentation* has a double meaning: the *data* that proves the point claimed and also the *citing* of that data. To make things clearer, the words *proof* and *citation* will be used here instead of *documentation*. If you invent a child and add it to some family, then the data would be fabricated and unproved, but the citation "Child invented by author" would be correct and acceptable.

While this example is intentionally fanciful, the point is a very important one. Consider this quotation from a genealogical magazine aimed at the hobbyist market:

> My advice to all genealogists is to publish a book as soon as there is enough material to make it worthwhile. The book need not be a fine, leather-bound volume with gilt edges, and the facts in the book do NOT need to be fully documented! I disagree with that old rule of the purists: "publish only what you can prove" – for if you stick with that idea, you may never publish anything. Publish what you have, but label the undocumented portions properly. If you use family legend, be sure to say it is unproved legend.[8]

This is good advice but the statement that "the facts in the book do NOT need to be fully documented!" confuses proof and citations.

No genealogy of any scope can likely *prove* every contention, link, and statement; but it can give sources for each. If the fourth child of a colonial family is only tentatively placed, the author should say so and explain why this has been done. The proof may be shaky but the citation of sources and reasons can still be thoroughly given.

Some people feel they do not need to prove their contentions or give their sources, that for their word to be questioned is an insult. Here is one author's encounter with such a person:

> However, by checking the 'Greer Family' record I found a difference in most of the dates. Usually the year was the same but the day and month could be different. After I found this discrepancy in the two records, I wrote to Mr. Peters for proof of his dates and he answered back with a scathing letter telling me that I had my nerve to question his memory. I did not pursue the matter any further to prove one way or the other of who was right.[9]

Put in this fashion, the idea of being above citing one's sources seems absurd. Yet probably 90 percent of all family histories published in book form in the United States today have few or no citations. Whatever proof lies behind all the information in these books, neither the present reader nor future genealogists will be able to determine from the books themselves. Some have a page or two in the back listing some books and articles checked and even some document collections, but they do not give specific citations for specific statements. If X was born and died in a stated time and place, it does little good to give a page or two in the back on general sources. The user deserves the specific source or sources concerning when X was born and died, and authors ought to be proud to show where they were so industrious as to find these facts. Further, if the author gives specific citations, the user can evaluate such sources and better correspond with the author, thus improving what is known about these people.

Experts debate just how extensive source citations should be. A thorough citing of sources and discussing of conjectures would take more pages than the lineages, so efforts should be taken to keep citations as few and short as good scholarship allows. To see how the experts handle citations, look at some lineage articles in the major American genealogical journals. Three of the best are the *National Genealogical Society Quarterly*, the *New England Historical and Genealogical Register*, and *The Genealogist* (begun in 1980).

Here is the simple system modeled after the footnotes used by historians. The genealogy happens to begin with Isaac[1] Lindsey, so he is indicated in superscript as the first generation.[10]

> Isaac[1] Lindsey was born about 1742, probably in the vicinity of Long Marsh in what is now Clark Co., VA, the son of Abraham Lindsey of the Enoree Settlement, Newberry Co., SC, and Wilkes Co., GA.[1] Isaac saw active service in the Virginia militia during the French and Indian War.[2] According to his grandson's Bible, Isaac married (1) Susannah Smith 4 May 1762.[3] He bought land in Frederick Co., VA, in 1763 and sold it a year later when he moved to South Carolina with his father.[4] After a brief time in Newberry Co., SC he. . .
>
> ---
>
> 1. Laurens Co., SC, Deeds A:294-297; Tryon Co., NC, Deeds 1:45
> 2. *Statutes at Large . . . of All the Laws of Virginia*, William H. Hening, (Richmond, VA: 1820), 7:215-217.
> 3. DAR Lineage Book 80:254; National Society DAR Application #79703, 26 Feb 1910, with Supplement, refers to Bible of Caleb Crane, as cited by Katherine Coker Dalton, great granddaughter of Caleb, who was a grandson of Isaac and Susannah Lindsey. Whereabouts of Bible presently unknown.
> 4. Frederick Co., VA, Deeds 8:239, 9:345; South Carolina Plat 8:489 (not patented), Plat 23:561 and Grant 16:366, Plat 16:371 and Grant 32:310.

The specific footnote style used is up to the author. *The Source* uses the widely accepted *Chicago Manual of Style*, 13th ed., (Chicago: University of Chicago Press, 1983), supplemented on genealogical points by Richard S. Lackey, *Cite Your Sources: A Manual for Documenting Family Histories and Genealogical Records* (New Orleans, La.: Polyanthos, 1980). The important point is to give sources in an economical yet complete way so other researchers can judge the quality of the proof and know where to find the cited sources. If the source is "Personal interview, 12 Feb 1978, with Mable Ann (Alton) Jones, Upper Fairfax, Pierce Co., Wash.," say so. If the information is from a will not seen but given in a published abstract of probates, say that: Halifax Co., N.C., wills 3:377, Edward Montford, 3 Nov. 1801, proved Aug. ct. 1802, as cited in Margaret M. Hofmann, *Genealogical Abstracts of Wills 1758 through 1824, Halifax County, North Carolina* (Weldon, N.C.: Roanoke News Co., 1970), p. 121. Unless you are meeting the requirements of a publisher, it is far more important to be consistent, complete, and efficient than it is to use any given style.

Proofs and citations should present lineages in a family history so the user can easily follow lines down through descendants or back toward the founding ancestors. Here experts agree that the *Register* system, named for the *New England Historical and Genealogical Register* where it was refined and popularized, is best.

The earliest ancestor is designated as number 1, the children as numbers 2, 3, 4, etc. If possible, the lineage begins with the surname immigrant to the United States, so a superscript can be assigned to each generation: Stephen[3] Mahurin (Ebenezer[2], Hugh[1]).

Following is part of Francis H. Huron, "Hugh Mahurin of Taunton Massachusetts," *New England Historical and Genealogical Register* 136 (1982): 27. The author has discussed what is known about Hugh[2], child number 5 of the founding immigrant Hugh[1] Mahurin, and then summarizes Hugh, Jr.'s, children briefly. Only the children's lines further discussed are assigned numbers in the left margin – eleven to fourteen – and these numbers can be easily found further along in the article. The *Register* system is valuable because these numbers are simple to trace down through descendants or back through ancestors.

> Children by first wife Lydia, born at Bridgewater (Mitchell, *History of Bridgewater*, 251; *Bridgewater VRs*, 1:223):
>
> i. *SARAH*[3], b. 9 June 1732; m.. *JOHN MITCHELL* at Bridgewater, 28 Nov. 1751; d. as a widow 17 Oct. 1762 (Mitchell, *History of Bridgewater*, 251, 254; *Bridgewater VRs*, 2:253, 528).
> 11. ii. *HEZEKIAH*, b. 26 Mar. 1734.
> iii. *LUCY*, b. 25 Mar. 1736; d. 7 Feb. 1739 (*Bridgewater VRs*, 2:523).
> 12. iv. *BENJAMIN*, b. 13 July 1739.
> v. *ISAAC*, b. 15 June 1741; presumed to have died prior to 1760 (see discussion in the record for Isaac[3] [14]. No further data regarding Isaac b. 1741 has been discovered).
>
> Children by his second wife Mehetabel, born at Bridgewater (Mitchell, *History of Bridgewater*, 251; *Bridgewater VRs*, 1:223):
>
> 13. vi. *JONATHAN*, b. 23 Apr. 1752.
> vii. *SYLVIA*, b. 17 July 1754; d. single, 23 Dec. 1841 aged 87 (*Bridgewater VRs*, 2:524). Her will left all her estate to Achsa Mehurin, "daughter of my late brother Isaac dec." (Ply. Co. Probates, 84:152).
> 14. viii. *ISAAC*, b. 1760 or 1761, poss. posthumously.

Notice how the citations are handled in this article. Most are incorporated into the text but there are also footnotes such as [14] under child v., Isaac.

The *Register* system can vary slightly in handling the number in the left margin. Some authors assign a number to each child and indicate the continued lines with a + or *. Thus the two variants compared are:

i. Sarah[3]	23. Sarah[3]
11. ii. Hezekiah	+ 24. Hezekiah
iii. Lucy	25. Lucy
12. iv. Benjamin	+ 26. Benjamin
v. Isaac	27. Isaac

One obvious problem of either numbering approach is that newly discovered children cannot be added except by some auxiliary numbering such as 12a or 26a.

Generally such descents from an ancestor follow only his surname lines, i.e., detailing the males lines and dropping the female lines. Since the daughters are as much a part of the family as the sons, this may seem unfair. (One wonders what a book would be like that traced all the female lines and dropped the male!) The reason is usually one of practicality. Tracing every female line *doubles* the new material in each generation. If a Smith brother and sister married a Jones sister and brother in 1750, it seems needless duplication for the Smith family history to detail all the descendants of Sister Smith's marriage to Mr. Jones when the Jones' book would automatically follow her descendants, or at least her Jones-surnamed descendants.

It is quite acceptable for an author to trace every line male and female. It is often done for royal lines, such as all known descendants from George I of England. But tracing only the male-surnamed lines is the usual way because it is less voluminous. Perhaps a good system would be to trace every daughter's children and then drop them; this would include all first cousins in the book.

Most family histories record descendants counting from an early ancestor. Books also run in the opposite direction from a recent individual (often the author), tracing all direct ancestors back in each line as far as possible, i.e., one's parents, grandparents, great-grandparents, etc.

Analyzing data and assigning people to their correct families requires a combination of common sense, a knowledge of history, and a marshalling of sufficient sources. How-to books will give some suggestions, though beyond obvious things such as a plausible chronology, it is very difficult to explain analytical techniques in a brief discussion. One book devoted to the subject is Noel C. Stevenson, *Genealogical Evidence: A Guide to the Standard of Proof Relating to Pedigrees, Ancestry, Heirship and Family History* (Laguna Hills, Calif.: Aegan Park Press, 1979). This book over-emphasizes *legal* standards of proof, but is well worth reading. *Ancestry's Guide to Research,* already mentioned, is the best book available for showing, with examples, how to evaluate evidence and ask the kinds of questions necessary to construct a valid case.

Legalities

Rights of Privacy

Genealogical research into the past involves records of private individuals, families, business entities, and government agencies. Where researching involves records created in or before the nineteenth century, there is seldom a legal conflict concerning rights of privacy versus rights of access.

For records kept by individuals, families, and business entities, access is gained only through consent of those who create and own the records. If you need information kept privately, such as records from a church or family sources, you must obtain special consent. Usually it is not a problem to gain permission to use and even publish such information. If a person presents him/herself to the record keeper at a reasonably convenient time and place, access is usually allowed. Some inexperienced genealogists are demanding when tactfulness, consideration, and willingness to give as well as receive will elicit better cooperation.

Records created by and in the possession of government agencies create a more complex situation. In most states, after a certain period the record becomes public information and access is not restricted. The situation varies from state to state; but typically, if a record was created 75 to 100 years ago, restrictions of access are removed.

If you have a specific question about records in a given state, you should consult *A Summary of Freedom of Information and Privacy Laws of the 50 States*. This booklet details updates and amendments to each state's laws and bills concerning open records, information and criminal systems regulation, privacy study commissions, arrest records, and financial and medical records. The booklet can be acquired through:

Plus Publications, Inc.
2626 Pennsylvania Avenue, N.W.
Washington, DC 20037

These restrictions usually apply to access by individuals other than the person appearing in the record or his/her immediate family or direct descendants. Typically, no restrictions are placed on information about yourself.

Normally the genealogist has little need for government records compiled in the past seventy-five years. You can usually extend a known genealogy back a century using home sources almost exclusively. See Chapter 1.

When you do not have access to family records, it may be necessary to consult modern records created and kept by the government. If an individual is adopted, orphaned, illegitimate, simply separated from close relatives, or undertaking research for another family, then he/she will have to face the realities of the Freedom of Information Act and the Right of Privacy Act of 1974 and the myriad of regulations that have grown from these laws.

This privacy act gives an individual the right to see what a federal agency has kept on him or her except for "classified" material. It also gives freedom from unwarranted publicity and protection from any wrongful intrusion into his/her private life which could cause mental suffering or humiliation.

Some jurisdictions have maintained that this may only be enforced by the person whose right has been infringed and that the individual right of privacy dies with him/her. Other jurisdictions maintain that heirs and personal representatives have the right to bring an action for an unwarranted invasion of the right of the deceased. The Right of Privacy is not an absolute right and is subject to limitations. It is designed to ward off undesired publicity for those whose affairs are of no legitimate concern to the community.

A public officer, by virtue of his/her office, is the legal custodian of all papers, books, and records pertaining to that office. He/she is responsible for their safekeeping and protection against alteration, injury, or mutilation and for their delivery to his/her successor.

However, the right of the general public to have access to public records is recognized both by statute and at the common law. It is generally agreed that you may inspect public records of interest to you or make copies or memoranda thereof when you have proven the necessity and proper purpose for such an inspection and where the disclosure would not be detrimental to the public interest. There is no right of inspection merely to satisfy curiosity or to speculate.

Congress has said the Secretary of Commerce *may*, upon written request, furnish individuals "data for genealogical and other proper purposes." The statute goes on to provide that "in no case shall information furnished under the authority of this section be used to the detriment of the persons to whom such information relates."[11]

Typical state statutes provide that records of public agencies like the Bureau of Vital Statistics, while open to inspection, are subject to regulations of the department. The custodian of the records may permit their inspection when satisfied that the applicant has a "direct, tangible and legitimate interest in the information and record requested."[12]

The court closes most modern adoption records relating to the biological parents. Without a court order rescinding the previous court's action, it is not possible for anyone to have access to information regarding the biological parents of an adoptive child, but laws in each state and circumstance are different. The practice presents a very real problem for the genealogist seeking a true and accurate record. It does not exist when examining ancient records. Most old birth records candidly set forth the facts of birth including illegitimacy where that is the case.

Ordinarily, every person has the right to inspect the records of judicial proceedings, at least after such proceedings are completed and entered on the journal of the court. There is no corresponding right to inspect the records of a pending case, and the court may impound its files in such a case and deny public inspection of them when justice so requires. In addition, inspection may be limited by statute in certain actions such as divorce.

In review, the Privacy Act was established to protect the individual against public access to personal information of a private nature. It was not established to prohibit individuals from learning about their past, their roots, and historical facts about their progenitors. Some states have devised strict laws relating to the disclosure of information, especially in vital records in the twentieth century. Usually access is easier if you show that you want the information for genealogical purposes. In some states when records have been closed, local genealogical societies have lobbied to remove indiscriminate legislation and have usually won. Only in such sensitive areas as adoption and illegitimacies have records been closed completely.

Some additional readings on implications of the privacy laws are:

Allen, Walter C., and Jerome K. Miller, eds., "Current Problems in Copyright," *Library Trends* 32 (Fall 1983). Includes copyright of manuscripts, databases, video and cassette materials, musical works. What libraries can do to protect copyright when requested to make copies. A valuable issue.

Brandon, Dick. "Prepare for Privacy Law." *Boardroom Reports*, 30 June 1977, p. 6.

"Government Snooping–How to Fight Back." *U.S. News and World Report*, 22 Sept. 1975, pp. 21-22.

"How New Privacy Law Protects You." *U.S. News and World Report*. 30 Dec. 1974. pp. 16-17.

Lewis, Linda. "Naked Before the Public." *Seattle Post-Intelligencer Northwest*, 25 Dec. 1977, pp. 8-12.

McClain, Wallis E., ed. *A Summary of Freedom of Information and Privacy Laws of the 50 States*. Access Reports, No. 3. Washington, D.C.: Plus Publications, Inc., 1979.

U S. Department of Justice. "Criminal Justice Information Systems. *Federal Register* 40, no. 98 (20 May 1975): 22114-19.

Winkler, Karen J. "A Question of 'Historical Malpractice'." *Chronicle of Higher Education*, 14 Jan. 1980, p. 3.

Freedom of Information

The Freedom of Information Act of the U.S. government is the counterpart to the Privacy Act. As Americans we not only have the right to *express* ideas and to disclose information, but also the right to *receive* ideas and information. This law provides that records of federal government agencies shall be made available to the public and also outlines the procedures by which private citizens may share these records. Of course, the public use of these records must not infringe on the privacy of the individual(s) involved. Three major principles of this law are:

1. Because access to information is vital in a free society, we cannot tolerate any form of prior restraint other than those very rare instances in which disclosure would directly and adversely affect the nation or the rights of its citizens.

2. Release of specific types of information which would directly intrude on the privacy of the individual, such as divorce proceedings, should not be made available to the public, at least during the life time of individuals involved.

3. The proximity of the person in question to the historic or public event or how near the event was to the current time-period are both important considerations. Something that occurred twenty years ago is quite different from something 100 years ago.

For questions regarding specific problems dealing with Freedom of Information, contact:

Freedom of Information Clearing House
Suite 515
2000 P Street, N.W.
Washington, DC 20036
(202) 785-3704

The Rights of Privacy can be counteracted by the Freedom of Information Act only with federally funded institutions and archives. The Freedom of Information Act does not affect local or state records Some states have their own laws covering these local records. The only local records under the jurisdiction of the act are some federally funded universities and libraries.

When dealing with records closed to the public, consider the options for gaining access to such records. Sources dealing with social welfare cases, such as the insane, are open to psychologists and medical doctors. Legal records are open to attorneys. Business records closed to the public are open to city, county, or state officials. Criminal records are open to the police and the FBI. By employing the services of one of these professionals, you may gain access to records in question, and thus solve a genealogical problem or acquire information for a family history.

Some vital records closed to the public are open to certain groups. In Connecticut, for example, birth, marriage, and death records closed to the public are open to those seeking their ancestry. Illinois state records are open to members of the Daughters of the American Revolution, yet closed to the public. Medical records closed to the public would be open to descendants who could show concern for inheriting a disease from an ancestor described in the record. Ingenuity and ambition may thus gain access to needed records through legal means, even though records are "closed" to the public.

Some helpful readings on this topic are:

Myers, Eleanor, et al. "Freedom of Information." *Tree Talks* 19 (1979); 65-69.

Reitman, Alan. "Freedom of Information and Privacy: The Civil Libertarian's Dilemma." *The American Archivist* 38 (1975): 501-8.

"Utilization of Information and Confidentiality." *National Association of Social Workers, Inc., Newsletter* (Washington State), June 1976.

Copyright

Copyright protects authors, printers, and manuscript holders from having their works "stolen." They, and only they, have the right to reproduce and profit from their work. Without this protection, authors would have little incentive to publish.

Only authors or those deriving their rights through authors can rightfully claim copyright. Mere ownership of a manuscript or copy does not necessarily give the owner the right to copyright. In the case of works made for hire, the employer, and not the employee, is regarded as the author and holder of copyright.

Books, including published works, composite works, directories, catalogs, annual publications, and other materials that appear as a book, pamphlet, or even single page can be copyrighted. Periodicals such as newspapers, magazines, and serial publications appearing under a single title at intervals less than a year, as well as contributions to such periodicals, can be copyrighted. Lectures, oral histories and other recordings, maps, and photographs can also be copyrighted.

The U.S. Copyright Law of 1976, which took effect at the end of 1978, recognizes ownership in original manuscripts as well as printed material. The individual or organization responsible for keeping the record can claim copyright to a given record. The archive housing a manuscript can also claim copyright depending upon the situation. Church records would be claimed by the church in question, with the present minister having jurisdiction of records of the past.

A letter written by an individual in the past belongs, by right, to the individual and all of his/her descendants rather than to the archive holding the letter unless those rights were granted the archive at the time it acquired the document. Legally any descendant of the author could claim copyright privileges and press charges if it is published without authority.

This restriction does not, of course, prevent the responsible use of material by scholars. The Modern Language Association, in a statement that seems to represent views of the academic community, explained:

> It is in the interest of publishers and scholars alike to facilitate and spread the use and to increase the value of all scholarly publications by allowing scholars to quote without prior permission from published sources whatever they legitimately need to make their scholarly writings complete, accurate, and authenticated. We believe the scholar is only obligated to give full credit to the author and publisher of the work quoted, and the further obligation to avoid quoting in such amounts, over and beyond scholarly needs, as to impair or destroy the property rights and financial benefits of their fellow scholars and the original publishers from whose work they are quoting.
>
> Publications issued under our imprints may be quoted without specific prior permission in works of original scholarship for accurate citation of authority or for criticism, review, or evaluation, subject to the conditions listed below.
>
> 1. That appropriate credit be given in the case of each quotation.
> 2. That waiver of the requirement for specific permission does not extend to quotations that are complete units in themselves (i.e. poems, letters, journal articles, complete chapters or sections of books, maps, charts, graphs, tables).
>
> The fact that specific permission for quoting of material may be waived under this agreement does not relieve the quoting author and publisher from the responsibility of determining "fair use" of such material.[13]

The Association of American University Presses, including forty-five university presses signed a "Resolution on Permissions" designed to reduce the red tape when a scholar must cite the works of others. It should be noted that the resolution does not relieve the quoting author or publisher of the obligation to make sure that he is not impairing the financial and other rights of the copyright owner. This resolution basically accepts current, responsible academic practice.

Public records, such as U.S. census records, can be published with no restriction. They are not copyright. If you desire to use a manuscript for publication or for commercial gain, the archive holding the record should be contacted for permission. It should be told that a given record will be published and its permission asked. If the archive grants permission in writing then the author is protected. If the archive does not have the authority to grant such permission but gives permission, then it would bear the responsibility.

Fair use has been defined as the right to use copyrighted materials in a reasonable manner without the author's specific consent. It is one of the most important limitations on the copyright owner's exclusive rights and has been described as the court-developed doctrine that permits teachers, librarians, researchers, scholars, and others to use copyright works without paying the copyright holder.

The 1978 Copyright Law states that "the fair use of a copyrighted work, including such use by reproduction in copies of phono records or by any other means specified by [Section 106], for purposes such as . . . teaching (including multiple copies for classroom use), scholarship, or research, is not an infringement of copyright."[14] In determining whether the use made of a work is "fair," the factors to be considered include: the purpose of the use (commercial? nonprofit? educational?), the nature of the copyrighted work (how unique?), the proportion being used and how important it is to the whole, 10 percent or less is considered reasonable, and the effect of the use upon the potential market for or value of the copyrighted work.

The criteria of fair use are necessarily general. The legislation was intended to provide an appropriate balancing of the rights of creators and the needs of users. The details of this legislation apply only to copying for teachers and students in nonprofit educational institutions and to copying from books and periodicals. Copying which does not fall within these guidelines may nonetheless be permitted under the statutory fair-use criteria.

Under the current law, the term of copyright for records copyrighted prior to 31 December 1976 is twenty-eight years from first publication. After the twenty-eight year period expires, a second copyright period goes into effect for another forty-seven years. For records copyright after 1976, the term is for the life of the author, plus an additional fifty years. For works made for hire and for anonymous and pseudonymous works, the new term is seventy-five years from publication or 100 years from creation, whichever is shorter.

Copyright notices placed in books tell that the record is copyright, who holds the copyright, and what terms may apply to such copyright. An example of a clearly identified copyright comes from Darwin Gross, *Your Right to Know* (Menlo Park, Calif.: IWP Publishing, 1981):

> Copyright 1979 by Darwin Gross. All rights reserved. No part of this book may be reproduced, stored in a retrieval system or transmitted in any form by an electronic, mechanical, photocopying, recording means or otherwise without written permission of the copyright holder.

Every time you reproduce a copyrighted work and do not buy the work, you are cheating the copyright holder out of his/her profit on the purchase price. This new copyright law states that such materials may be photocopied (up to 10 pecent of the total record) without permission or payment of royalties only if the use fulfills purposes such as criticism, news reporting, teaching, scholarship, or research. Research for hire is considered to be commercial use and great care should be taken when copies are made for such purposes. Client research, where the genealogist acts as an extension of the client, is not considered commercial use unless the copies are to be included in a work circulated for commercial gain. Fair and reasonable use still applies.

After reading a copyright notice similar to that cited above, ask yourself:

1. Have I made photocopies of any material in this record and sent it to a friend, relative, or client?
2. Have I made copies (including typewritten) for the use of another person?

If the answer to either of these questions is yes, then the copyright law may have been broken. We recommend that copies of all materials written or created by others and all documents not in family possession used in a family history be cleared with permission from the appropriate owner before publication. A library has no right to make unauthorized photocopies of copyright material outside of the terms of this law. The copyright owner seeks a reasonable royalty and will grant licenses to people to make such copies provided a special fee is paid and written permission received. Because of such problems with xeroxing documents since the new law went into effect, several services have been designed to allow the public to make such copies legally.

The Copyright Clearance Center (CCC). This center offers authors and users of copyrighted materials a centralized service which collects royalty fees for copyright owners from photocopy users. Publications are registered at no cost with CCC. Photocopying permission fees are then established by the author and collected by CCC. Along with the copyright notice in a book, the author includes a notice similar to this:

> This journal is registered with the Copyright Clearance Center. Organizations in the U.S.A. who are also registered with CCC may therefore copy material (beyond the limits permitted by Sections 107 and 108 of the U. S. Copyright Law) subject to payment to CCC of the per-copy fee of $2.00. This consent does not extend to multiple copying for promotional or commercial purposes. Payment should be sent directly to CCC. For all other use, permission should be sought from the Cambridge or New York offices of the Cambridge University Press. Cambridge, England, 1982.

With this service, then, any record registered with CCC can be photocopied legally as long as the per-copy fee is sent to CCC whenever copies are made. CCC then reimburses the copyright holder his percentage of the fees incurred. For further information and a copy of *Publisher's Photo-Copy Fee Catalog* write to:

Copyright Clearance Center, Inc.
21 Congress Street
Salem, MA 01970

Other important CCC publications are *Handbook for Libraries and Other Organizational Users Which Copy from Serials and Separates, Trade Publications and Scholarly Publications* (Salem, Mass.: CCC, 1977). All users who make photocopies and register with CCC report each transaction voluntarily, using standard forms.

R. R. Bowker, Company Serials Bibliography Department, *Sources of Serials: International Serials Publishers and Their Titles with Copyright and Copy Availability Information* (New York: R. R. Bowker Company, 1981) includes with its listing of serials information on the copyright and copy availability policy of each. This enables users to find out if a publisher permits free photocopying of articles, if it provides photocopies for a fee, if it is registered with the CCC, and if it permits free use of the abstracts of their articles.

Most manuscript sources would not be registered with CCC. Permission should be acquired from the appropriate depository or individual to photocopy records beyond normal use.

Institute for Scientific Information. The Institute for Scientific Information (ISI) is presently authorized to provide copies from about 4,000 of the 5,000 scientific, technical, and social science journals that it covers, as well as covering journals in the arts and humanities, a service presently being developed, a total of more than 5,000 journals. ISI's base fee is $7 for an article up to twenty pages plus $1 for each additional ten pages or fraction thereof. An additional $1 is charged if the order does not contain ISI's OATS number for the document, with $1 additional for hotline orders. Another fee is charged for airmail service to other countries. ISI pays a license fee per copy to publishers. It also supports CCC. Turnaround time is forty-eight hours from receipt of order.

Institute for Scientific Information
3501 Market Street
Philadelphia, PA 19104
(215) 386-0100

The other pioneer in the licensed copy-supply field is Xerox University Microfilms (UMI). University Microfilm's traditional business has been to supply microforms of journals (usually roll microfilms of full volumes). This service offers full copies of well over 7,000 journals. It also supplies copies of single articles from about 4,000 journals. It responds to most orders within twenty-four hours and to 95 percent within three days. Copies can be supplied from old as well as recent issues of most journals.

National Technical Information Service. This service supplies government research reports to business and industry. If contact with them would assist with a given query, write at 5285 Port Royal Road, Springfield, Virginia 22150, (703)487-4650.

For further information, as well as data included in government records cited in this chapter's bibliography, one of the best sources for copyright information is Donald F. Johnston, *Copyright Handbook* (New York: R. R. Bowker Company, 1978). Genealogists should be scrupulous about observing copyright restrictions. Cooperation will insure protection in the future for those interested in local and family history.

Here are some additional readings on aspects of the law:

The Chicago Manual of Style. 13th ed. Chicago, University of Chicago Press, 1983. Chapter 4 deals with rights and permissions.

Copyright Clearance Center, Inc. *Photocopy Permissions Services Scholarly Publications*. Salem, Mass.: Copyright Clearance Center, Inc., 1981.

Copyright Office, Library of Congress. *Copyright for Books*. Circular 60. Washington: U.S. Government Printing Office, 1977.

__________. *Copyright for Photographs*. Circular 40J. Washington: U.S. Government Printing Office, 1976.

__________. *General Information on Copyright*. Circular 1. Washington: U.S. Government Printing Office, 1977.

__________. *Highlights of the New Copyright Law*. Circular R99. Washington, D.C.: U.S. Government Printing Office, 1977.

Harwell, Rod and Pat, eds. "Editors' Comments: Copyrights and Photocopying." *The Colonial Genealogist* 4 (1972): 139.

Romney, Joseph B., ed. *A Guide to Oral History and the Law*. Pomona, Calif.: California Polytechnic State University, n.d.

U.S. Office of the Law Revision Counsel of the House of Representatives. *United States Code*, 1976 ed., Supplement 5. Washington: United States Government Printing Office, 1982.

Weil, Ben H. "Authorized Services for Supplying Photocopies and for Collection of Payments for In-House Photocopying Under the New Copyright Law." *The Bowker Annual of Library and Book Trade Information*. New York: R. R. Bowker Company, 1977.

Notes

1. Correspondence and two-page guide printed in "Source Book, 1982," pp. 89-91; available from South Suburban Genealogical and Historical Society, Box 96, South Holland, IL 60473.

2. Richard W. Price. "Genealogical Periodicals," paper presented 4 August 1983, Utah Genealogical Association Annual Convention, Provo, Utah.

3. R. H. Hilton, "The Origins of Robin Hood," *Past and Present*, no. 14 (Nov. 1958), p. 32.

4. Arthur Pierce Middleton and Douglass Adair, "The Mystery of the Horn Papers," *William and Mary Quarterly* 3rd series, 4 (1947): 409-45.

5. J. W. L. Matlock, ed., "The Battle of the Bluff, From the Journal of John Cotton," *Tennessee Historical Quarterly* 18 (1959): 252-65; and Stanley J. Folmsbee, "The Journal of John Cotton, The 'Reluctant Pioneer'—Evidences of its Unreliability," ibid., 28 (1969): 84-94.

6. Walter Lee Sheppard, Jr., "The False Noble Pedigree of Colonel Richard Lee of Virginia," *Virginia Genealogist* 11 (1967): 15-19; Grace McLean Moses, "The Parentage of Colonel Richard Lee the Emigrant," ibid., 13 (1969): 147-58; and Ludwell Lee Montague, "The Problem of Richard Lee's Parentage," ibid., 14 (1970): 51-58.

7. Family group sheet on Thomas Gates (b. 1698), Genealogical Society of Utah, Salt Lake City, Utah.

8. Carl Read, "A Few Words about Publishing Your Book," *Genealogy Digest* 13 (April-June 1982): 2.

9. Ison L. Stephans, *Sills & Cliburn & Pitman* (Provo, Utah: J. Grant Stevenson, 1972), p. 175.

10. William Thorndale, "The Lindseys of Lindseys Bluff," *Lindsay Newsletter: Southern Colonial Branches* 1 (1981): 67, 70.

11. Wilford W. Kirton, "The Great Debate on Availability and Use of Records: Legal Problems on Usage, Duplication, and Dissemination of Records," In *World Conference on Records and Genealogical Seminar* A-4, (Salt Lake City: The Genealogical Society of the Church of Jesus Christ of Latter-day Saints, Inc., 1969).

12. Ibid.

13. "For Members Only: Progress in Permissions?" *MLA: Publication of the Modern Language Association* 77 (1962): iv-v.

14. National Education Association, *The New Copyright Law: Questions Teachers and Librarians Ask* (Washington, D.C.: National Education Association, 1977, pp. 17-18.

PART I
MAJOR RECORD SOURCES

INFORMATION GUIDE

Genealogical Information in the Record Group	*Family Bible*	*Medical Records*	*Diaries*	*Letters*	*Army Discharge*	*Passport*
Surname/name	●	●	●	●	●	●
Date of Birth	●	●	●	●		●
Place of Birth		●	●	●	●	●
Sex		●	●			●
Race/color		●				●
Physical Description			●	●	●	●
Occupation			●	●	●	●
Education			●	●		
Military Service			●	●	●	
Slave Status			●			
Property Owned			●	●		
Religion			●	●		
Citizenship			●			●
Marital Status	●		●	●		
Spouses Name	●		●	●		
Children's Names	●		●	●		
Names of Siblings	●		●	●		
Father's Name	●		●	●		
Mother's Name	●		●	●		
Father's Birthplace			●	●		
Mother's Birthplace			●	●		
Date of Death	●			●		
Cause of Death				●		
Name of Cemetery				●		
Residence		●		●	●	●
Age		●	●	●	●	●
Literacy/signature	●			●		●
Photograph/sketch		●				●
Hereditary Diseases		●	●	●		
Relatives				●		

COULD YOU USE THIS CHAPTER?

Type of Record	*Kept from*	*Clues That You Should Consult These Records*
Birth, marriage, death records, and other documents	All periods	This chapter is for all genealogists. Home sources represent genealogical "known" information directly relevant to your own family. With every new ancestor you identify, you will search again for this data. This chapter will explain the importance of those documents called personal papers kept by family members or preserved in libraries and archive collections after their deaths. Birth certificates, even for people who are still alive, are valuable because they document the places of birth and parents' names in ways that may not be known, even to the family. Baptismal certificates, school records, medical records, marriage records, samplers, family Bibles, journals, letters, newspaper clippings in a family scrapbook, and death certificates are all documents that can be found at home to establish vital information about births, marriages, and deaths. Other important papers are naturalization certificates, military records, passports, photographs, inscribed books, and various business records.
Oral history	About 1800 to present	Although many university libraries have active oral history programs, families have also found tape recordings an excellent way of preserving spontaneous memories of its older members. You can conduct such interviews yourself. Other recordings, if they exist, are also valuable to round out an ancestor's life. Oral interviews, recorded by hand, form the base for some of the most significant historical collections we have—the famed Draper Collection at the State Historical Society of Wisconsin and the Bancroft Collection at the University of California, Berkeley. One of these historians may have interviewed your ancestor long ago and left the interview behind for you to use.

Chapter 1

FAMILY AND HOME SOURCES, FAMILY TRADITIONS, AND ORAL HISTORIES

Richard W. Dougherty

Americans become interested in their ancestry for many reasons. Sometimes that interest stops with momentary curiosity; but for millions, it has developed into a full-scale passion. Some become skilled enough to qualify as professional genealogists. But whether amateur or professional, everyone starts with the same question: "Where do I begin?" This chapter describes that point of beginning: family and home sources, family traditions, and oral history.

The process of genealogical research is better understood when compared to the steps taken by a detective trying to solve a crime. The detective first gathers all known facts and pieces of evidence available from eye-witnesses, individuals who have knowledge of the persons and circumstances involved in the crime, and from material evidence found at the scene of the crime and in places frequented by the victims and suspects. Once the data has been assembled, the detective evaluates the evidence. He moves from the known to the unknown, draws conclusions, designs future inquiries, and tests each item as to its validity.

The genealogist follows much the same procedure. Relatives

Figure 1-1. Birth Certificate of Richard Wellington Dougherty, 28 July 1932, Walworth Co., S.D.; in possession of the author.

PARTMENT OF HEALTH State of South Dakota

STANDARD CERTIFICATE OF BIRTH

Department of Commerce Bureau of the Census

PLACE OF BIRTH—

State File No.

County Walworth State SOUTH DAKOTA Registered No. 267

Township or Village 387385

City Mobridge No. Mobridge Hospital St. Ward

(If birth occurred in a hospital or institution, give its NAME instead of street and number)

Full name of child Richard Wellington Dougherty {If child is not yet named, make supplemental report, as directed

Sex Male | If plural births 4. Twin, triplet, or other 5. Number, in order of birth | 6. Premature Full term x | 7. Legitimate? Yes | 8. Date of birth July 28, 1932 (Month, day, year)

FATHER

Full name James Kenneth Dougherty

Residence (usual place of abode). (If nonresident, give place and State) McIntosh, S.D.

Color or race W 12. Age at last birthday 32 (Years)

Birthplace (city or place) Watertown (State or country) S.D.

14. Trade, profession, or particular kind of work done, as spinner, sawyer, bookkeeper, etc. Salesman

15. Industry or business in which work was done, as silk mill, saw mill, bank, etc.

16. Date (month and year) last engaged in this work , 19 17. Total time (years) spent in this work

MOTHER

18. Full maiden name Marian Elizabeth Pederson

19. Residence (usual place of abode). (If nonresident, give place and State) McIntosh, S.D.

20. Color or race W 21. Age at last birthday 27 (Years)

22. Birthplace (city or place) Benson (State or country) Minn.

OCCUPATION

23. Trade, profession, or particular kind of work done, as housekeeper, typist, nurse, clerk, etc. Housewife

24. Industry or business in which work was done, as own home, lawyer's office, silk mill, etc.

25. Date (month and year) last engaged in this work , 19 26. Total time (years) spent in this work

Number of children of this mother (At time of this birth and including this child) 1 (a) Born alive and now living 1 (b) Born alive but now dead 0 (c) Stillborn 0

If stillborn, period of gestation months or weeks 29. Cause of stillbirth { Before labor During labor

CERTIFICATE OF ATTENDING PHYSICIAN OR MIDWIFE

hereby certify that I attended the birth of this child, who was born alive at 9:05 A m. on the date above stated. (Born alive or stillborn)

When there was no attending physician or midwife, then the father, householder, etc., should make this return. Given name added from supplemental report (Date of) Registrar.

(Signed) [signature], M. D.

or , Midwife

Address Mobridge, S.Dak.

Filed Aug 22-1932 [signature] Registrar.

and others who knew members of the family are the first source of information. You must collect this information and evaluate it for content, reliability, and clues for further research. Then design a plan of research to clarify discrepancies, supplement incomplete information, verify questionable facts, add to the evidence on hand, and extend ancestral lines.

Most beginning researchers are surprised by the sheer amount of information in their own homes or in the possession of relatives.[1] Some of the sources are obvious, but many are unusual and will not be found in every home. Additionally, not all of the information in one document or record will be found in another document of the same kind. A complete examination of each record that could possibly be encountered in the home of the researcher or in the possession of relatives is impossible. This chapter describes the most likely sources and offers a discussion of their content, value, and use.

Birth Records

Birth certificates are one of the best sources of genealogical information even though many states did not issue them until the 1920s or so. In addition to the certificates issued by the state, many hospitals provide a certificate of their own. Figure 1-1, a standard birth certificate from South Dakota, is representative of those compiled and issued by most states.

This particular birth certificate is my own. It illustrates a fundamental point in genealogical research—that any clue is significant. For instance, my birth certificate states that I was born in Mobridge, South Dakota, but that the usual residence of my parents was McIntosh, South Dakota, some sixty-five miles distant. In virtually all situations calling for place of birth, I list Mobridge, not only because it is technically accurate but also because my family moved there when I was three. The only official evidence that the

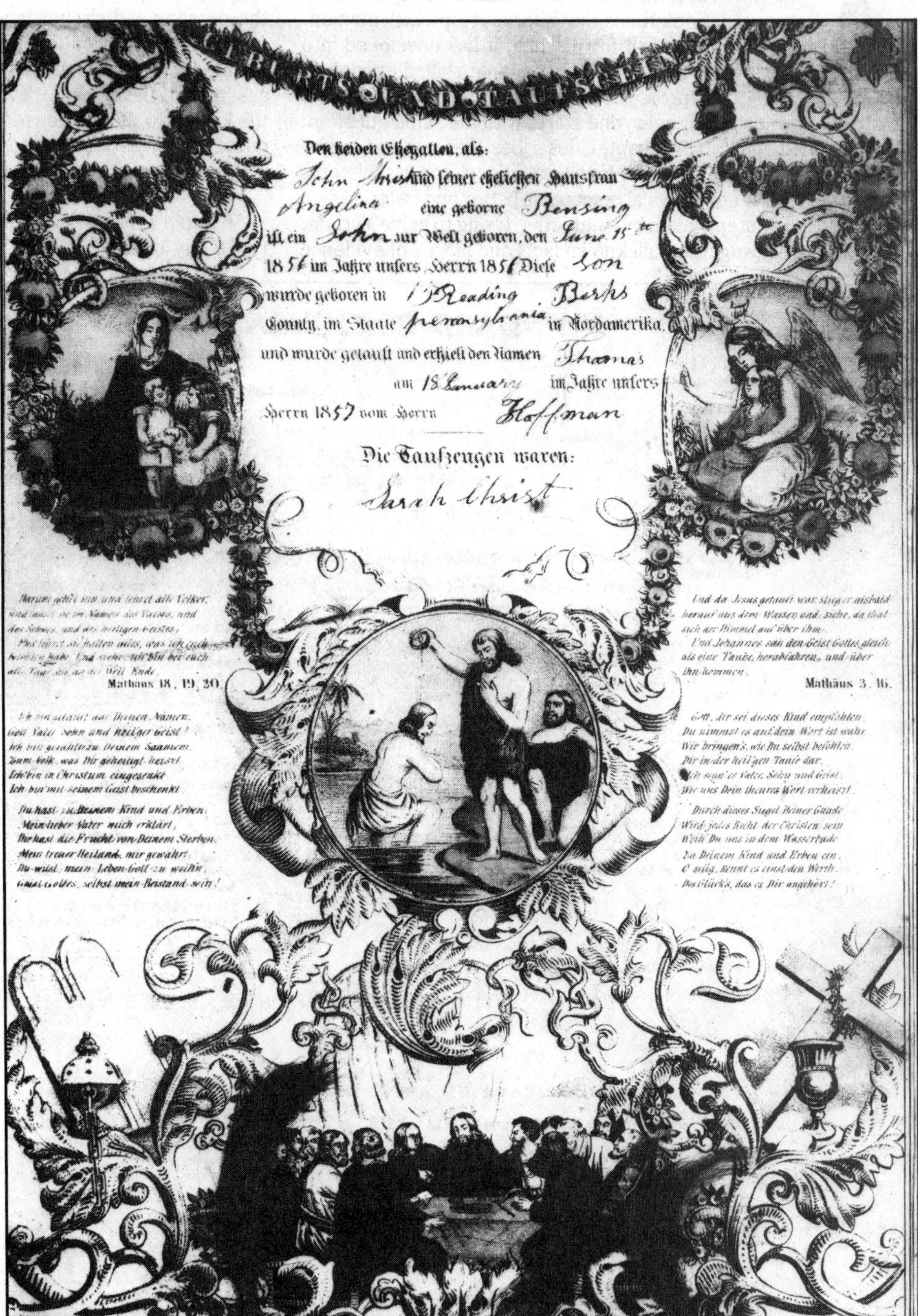

Den beiden Ehegatten, als:
John Christ und seiner ehelichen Hausfrau
Angelina eine geborne Bensing
ist ein John zur Welt geboren, den June 15th
1856 im Jahre unsers Herrn 1856 Diese Son
wurde geboren in 1 Reading Berks
County, im Staate Pennsylvania in Nordamerika,
und wurde getauft und erhielt den Namen Thomas
am 18 January im Jahre unsers
Herrn 1857 vom Herrn Hoffman

Die Taufzeugen waren:
Sarah Christ

Mathäus 18, 19, 20.

Du hast zu Deinem Kind und Erben,
Mein lieber Vater mich erklärt,
Du hast die Frucht von Deinem Sterben,
Mein treuer Heiland, mir gewährt.

Mathäus 3. 16.

Gott, dir sei dieses Kind empfohlen
Du nimmst es auf, dein Wort ist wahr.
Wir bringen's, wie Du selbst befohlen,
Dir in der heil'gen Taufe dar.

Durch dieses Siegel Deiner Gnade
Wird jedes Recht der Christen sein
O selig, kennt es einst den Werth
Des Glück's, das es Dir angehört!

Figure 1-2. Baptismal certificate of Thomas Christ, born 15 June, 1856, (loose document), Reformed Church, Reading, Berks Co., Pa.; original document in Fackenthal Library, Franklin and Marshall College, Lancaster, Penn.; Genealogical Society of Utah (hereafter GS) microfilm 1,290,169.

family actually lived sixty-five miles away is the birth certificate itself.

Although it is not likely that you will find a birth certificate for anyone born before 1900, other documents may provide this information. Many churches baptize or christen infants shortly after birth, and some of those issue baptismal or christening certificates. The information contained in these documents will vary from denomination to denomination and from church to church within a denomination. Figure 1-2 is an example of a *Taufschein* or a baptismal certificate from a German-speaking Reformed Church in Reading, Berks County, Pennsylvania.

Another source of birth information often found in family papers is school records. Report cards, graduation certificates, and yearbooks, in addition to other information, also occasionally yield the precise date of birth. Figure 1-3 illustrates a school record which established the person's eligibility for Social Security benefits, as no birth certificate existed.

Birth dates can also be obtained from medical records in the family's possession. Figure 1-4 is a German vaccination certificate, an *Impfschein,* which states the date of birth of the person vaccinated, the date and place of the vaccination, and that the vaccination was successful.

This particular medical record solved that most difficult of genealogical problems, the place of origin of an immigrant ancestor. Family medical records may also reveal hereditary health problems or conditions.

Figure 1-4. Vaccination record of Olga Dingler, born 1 Jan. 1875; Cassel, Hessen-Naussau, Germany. Public Health Office, 8 Aug. 1875. Used by courtesy of Mrs. Ernest Rathmann, 3453 S. Dadola Drive, Bountiful, UT 84010.

Impfschein.

Impfliste Nr. 14

Impfbezirk Cassel

Olga Dingler

geboren den 1 Januar 1875, wurde am 8 Aug.

1875 zum ersten Male mit Erfolg geimpft.

Durch die Impfung ist der gesetzlichen Pflicht genügt.

Cassel am 8 Aug. 1875

Arzt.

III/2

Figure 1-3. School Record of Marie Moler, 1915-21, Mechanicsburg, Champaign, Ill., courtesy of William Arbuckle, 651 E. 5600 S., Salt Lake City, UT 84107. Used by permission.

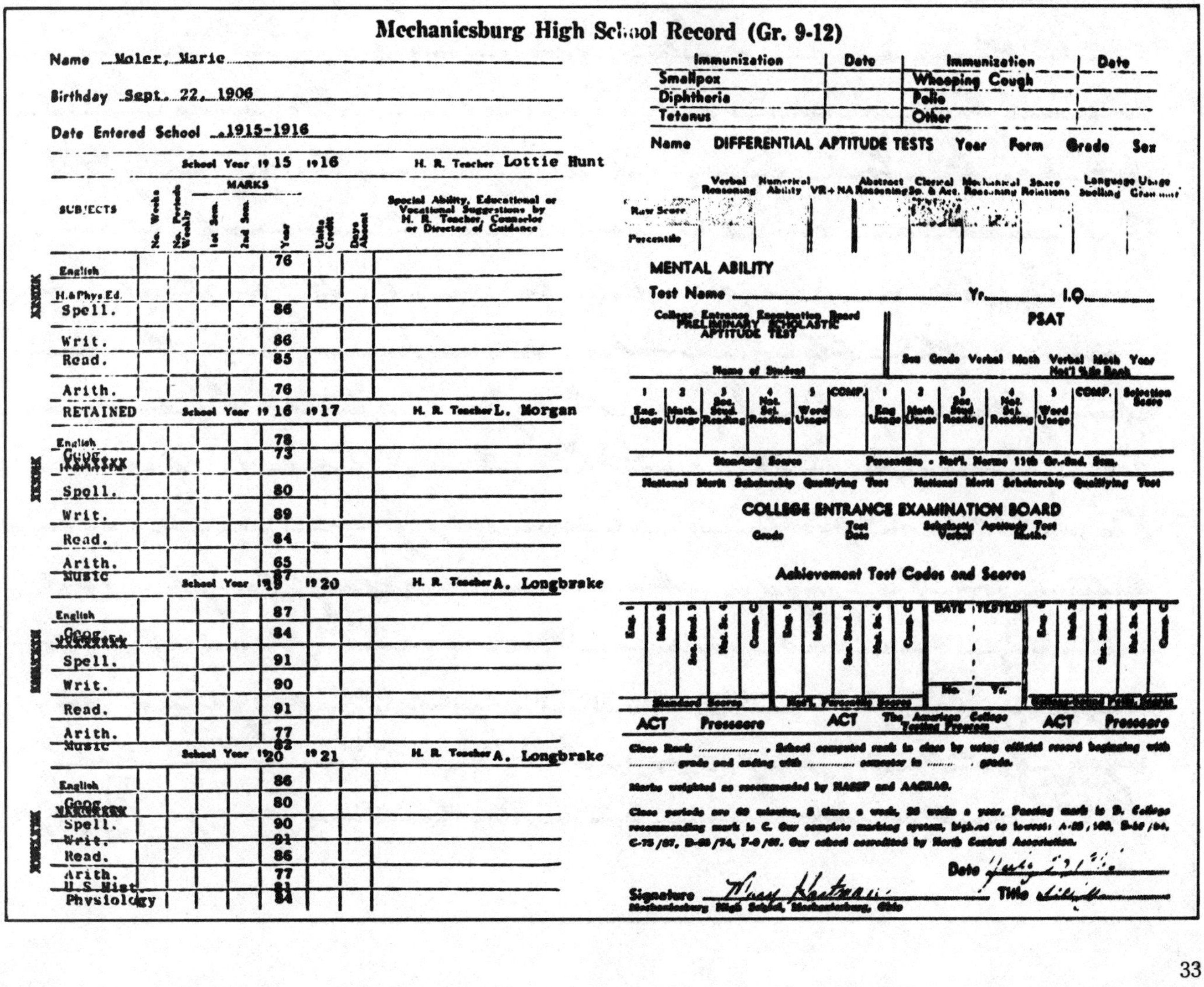

Mechanicsburg High School Record (Gr. 9-12)

Name Moler, Marie

Birthday Sept. 22, 1906

Date Entered School 1915-1916

School Year 1915 1916 H. R. Teacher Lottie Hunt

SUBJECTS	No. Weeks	No. Periods Weekly	MARKS 1st Sem.	2nd Sem.	Year	Units Credit	Days Absent	Special Ability, Educational or Vocational Suggestions by H. R. Teacher, Counselor or Director of Guidance
English					76			
H.&Phys.Ed. Spell.					86			
Writ.					86			
Read.					85			
Arith.					76			

RETAINED School Year 1916 1917 H. R. Teacher L. Morgan

SUBJECTS	No. Weeks	No. Periods Weekly	1st Sem.	2nd Sem.	Year	Units Credit	Days Absent	
English					78			
Geog.					73			
Spell.					80			
Writ.					89			
Read.					84			
Arith.					65			
Music					87			

School Year 1919 1920 H. R. Teacher A. Longbrake

SUBJECTS	No. Weeks	No. Periods Weekly	1st Sem.	2nd Sem.	Year	Units Credit	Days Absent	
English					87			
Geog.					84			
Spell.					91			
Writ.					90			
Read.					91			
Arith.					77			
Music					82			

School Year 1920 1921 H. R. Teacher A. Longbrake

SUBJECTS	No. Weeks	No. Periods Weekly	1st Sem.	2nd Sem.	Year	Units Credit	Days Absent	
English					86			
Geog.					80			
Spell.					90			
Writ.					91			
Read.					86			
Arith.					77			
U.S. Hist.					81			
Physiology					84			

Immunization	Date	Immunization	Date
Smallpox		Whooping Cough	
Diphtheria		Polio	
Tetanus		Other	

Name DIFFERENTIAL APTITUDE TESTS Year Form Grade Sex

	Verbal Reasoning	Numerical Ability	VR + NA	Abstract Reasoning	Clerical Sp. & Acc.	Mechanical Reasoning	Space Relations	Language Usage Spelling	Grammar
Raw Score									
Percentile									

MENTAL ABILITY

Test Name ________ Yr. ______ I.Q. ______

College Entrance Examination Board PRELIMINARY SCHOLASTIC APTITUDE TEST — PSAT

Name of Student — Sex Grade Verbal Math Verbal Math Year

Standard Scores — Percentiles - Nat'l. Norms 11th Gr.-2nd. Sem.

National Merit Scholarship Qualifying Test — National Merit Scholarship Qualifying Test

COLLEGE ENTRANCE EXAMINATION BOARD

Grade Test Date Scholastic Aptitude Test Verbal Math.

Achievement Test Codes and Scores

Standard Scores — Nat'l. Percentile Scores — Date Tested No. Yr.

ACT Prescore ACT The American College Testing Program ACT Prescore

Class Rank .... School computed rank in class by using official record beginning with .... grade and ending with .... semester in .... grade.

Marks weighted as recommended by NASSP and AACRAO.

Class periods are 60 minutes, 5 times a week, 36 weeks a year. Passing mark is D. College recommending mark is C. Our complete marking system, highest to lowest: A-85/100, B-80/84, C-75/87, D-60/74, F-0/59. Our school accredited by North Central Association.

Date [illegible]

Signature [illegible] Title [illegible]

Mechanicsburg High School, Mechanicsburg, Ohio

Figure 1-5. Martha Jane Hannah, 16 June 1860, in possession of Gordon Remington, 163 N. State Street, Apt. 1, Salt Lake City, UT 84103; used by permission.

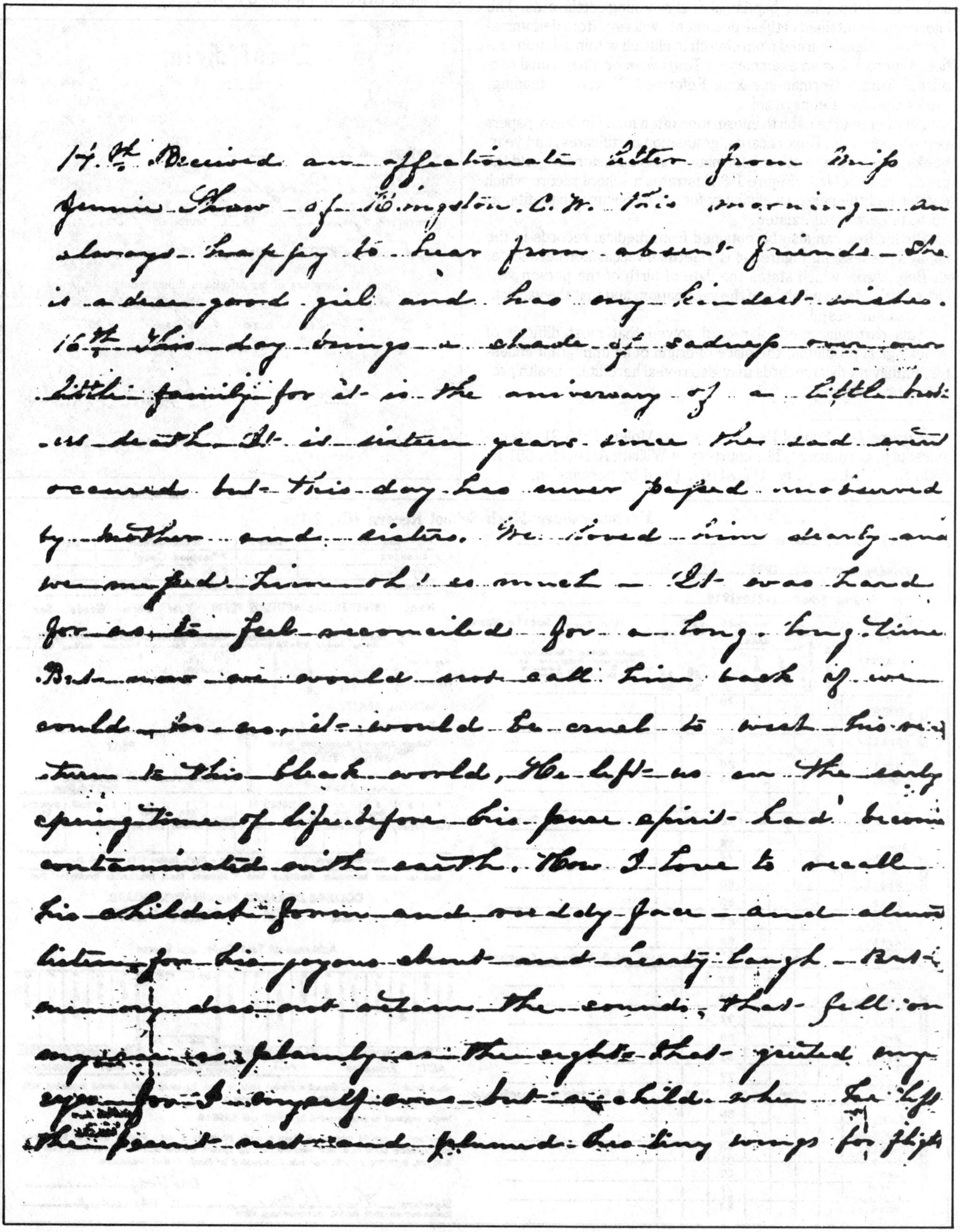

14th Received an affectionate letter from Miss
Jennie Shaw of Kingston C. W. this morning — am
always happy to hear from absent friends — she
is a dear good girl and has my kindest wishes.
16th This day brings a shade of sadness over our
little family for it is the anniversary of a little bro-
-ers death. It is sixteen years since the sad event
occurred but this day has never passed unobserved
by mother and sisters. We loved him dearly and
we missed him oh! so much — It was hard
for us to feel reconciled for a long, long time
But now we would not call him back if we
could for as it would be cruel to wish his re-
turn to this bleak world, He left us in the early
springtime of life before his pure spirit had become
contaminated with earth. How I love to recall
his childish form and ruddy face — and always
listening for his joyous shout and hearty laugh — But
memory does not retain the sounds, that fell on
my ears as plainly as the sights that greeted my
eyes — for I myself was but a child when he left
the parent nest and plumed his tiny wings for flight

As one moves back in time, records produced by the family itself assume even greater importance. Letters, diaries, and Bibles often contain priceless information about births and other family events not recorded elsewhere. For example, a colleague, reading an ancestor's diary (Figure 1-5) for 1860, came across this entry for 16 June: "This day brings a shade of sadness over our little family, for it is the anniversary of a little brother's death. It is sixteen years since this sad event occurred but—this day has never passed unobserved by brother and sisters. . . .He was a dear sensible child for one who had spent but five summers in the school of life." In her entry of 16 June 1861, the diarist again referred to the death anniversary of "brother James." Thus, my colleague learned of a hitherto unknown son who died on 16 June 1844 at the age of five—too young to appear in the 1850 U.S. census. This clue led to the discovery of the Hannah family Bible in the possession of another relative which contained a death entry for "James Hannah, died June the 16th 1844 aged five years three months," and in the birth column, his exact date of birth, 20 March, 1839. Without these family records, James would have been lost to recorded history.

Letters are another source of information about births and other events in the family history, even though they survive less frequently than diaries or Bibles. Figure 1-6 shows two pages of an invaluable letter from Ireland in 1867.

Figure 1-6. John and Eliza Stewart to Thomas Somerville Stewart and Ann Jane Stewart of Philadelphia, Penn., 3 May 1867; in possession of Robert Stewart, 8388 Vickers Street, San Diego, CA 92111; used by permission. Inner pages missing.

At the outset of this genealogical quest, the Stewart family thought their ancestors had emigrated from Scotland. But this letter and others found with it indicated the family was in fact Scotch-Irish from Dungannon, County Tyrone, Ulster. In addition to naming their children, John and Eliza Stewart add some interesting comments about the depopulation of Dungannon in the mid-nineteenth century, from 193 voters in the borough in 1841 to thirteen in 1867.

Birth information can also be found in baby books, birth announcements, hospital records, newspaper clippings, telegrams, photographs, samplers, engraved jewelry, military papers, obituary notices, and naturalization papers.

Naturally, you will not find all of these records for each ancestor or member of the ancestor's family. All that is needed to document a birth is one reference, but as we have seen, it is best to gather as many records as possible.

Marriage Records

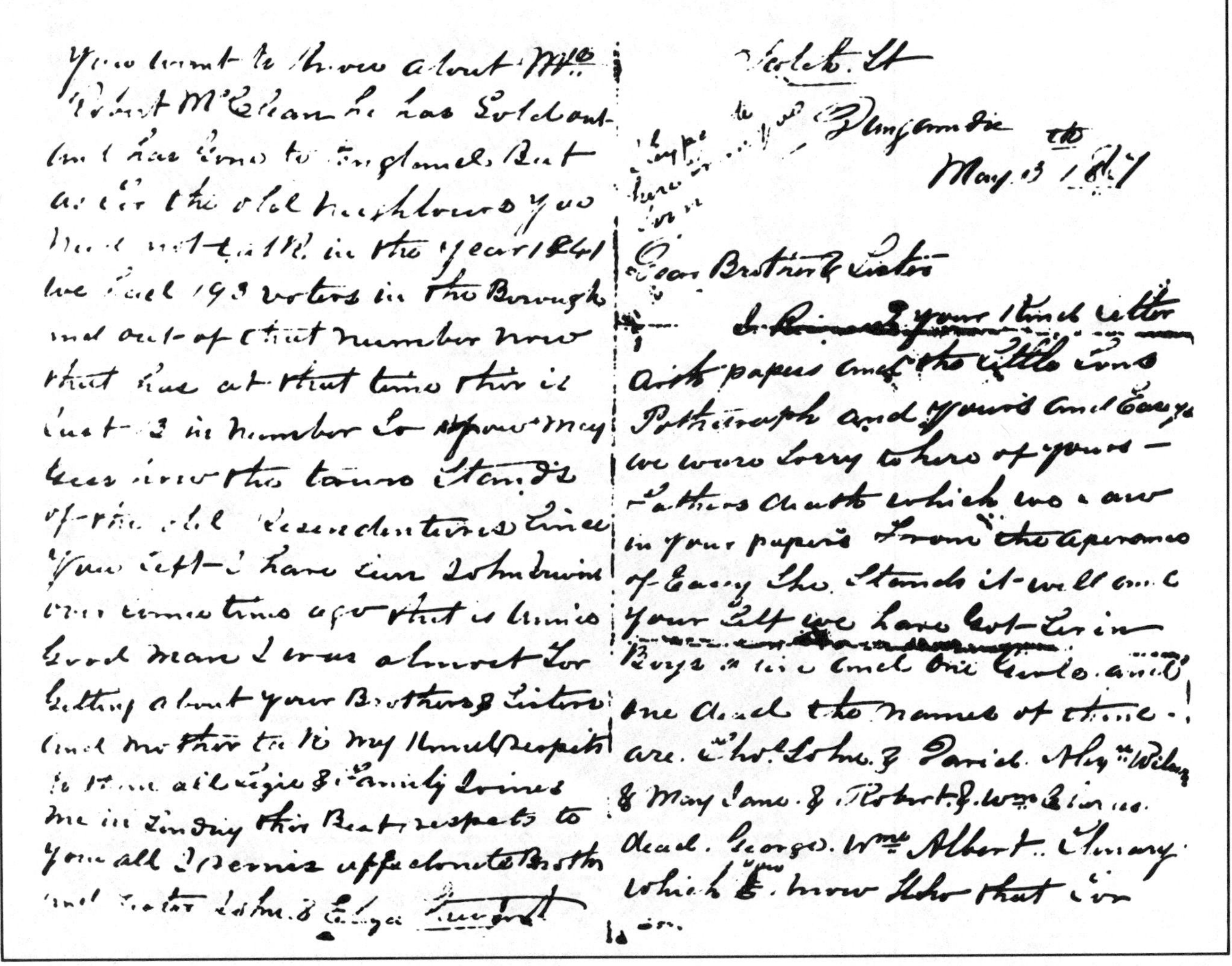

Marriage certificates or licenses are often found in family records. They too differ in content, depending upon the information required by the locality which issued the license. Figure 1-7 shows a marriage license issued in Meigs County, Ohio, in 1900. Despite its ornate decoration, this is a rather bare-bones document. It lists the names of the nuptial pair, a date, and a place. Yet, as with so many family documents, this license points the way to other sources of information. By 1900, Ohio, like many other states, required the prospective bride and groom to fill out a marriage license application, which typically requests place of birth, place of residence, names of parents, etc. And the marriage license return should be signed by the person who performed the marriage. If he was a clergyman, his church marriage register may provide additional genealogical information that is often very valuable. If he was an immigrant, your family may have come with him as part of a religious group migration. In short, marriage documents should be evaluated for the information they may lead to, not only what they contain.

Before marriage licenses were issued, weddings may have been noted in newspaper clippings, military pension records, family Bible records, embroidered samplers, printed wedding announcements, diaries, and other home sources similar to those containing birth information.

Death Records

Death records found among family papers are also valuable sources of genealogical data. The death certificate in Figure 1-8 is fairly typical, but includes the important information of the parents' names, and Peder Pederson's birthdate and birthplace, in this case Norway.

Yet death certificates must be handled with great caution. The information they contain, while usually reliable about time and place of death and burial, can be far off the mark on the names of the parents and the date and place of birth of the deceased. For instance, although Peder's death certificate says he was born in Norway, his obituary, published in the *Willmar Tribune*, Kandiyohi, Minnesota, 18 March 1914, flatly contradicts it by saying he was born in Värmland, Sweden, and brought up in Norway.

This discrepancy simply underscores the fact that family sources must be judged by the same rules of evidence that apply to all genealogical records. In this case, the source of information for the death certificate was Peder's son, while his widow apparently provided the information in the obituary. Census returns, Civil War pension records, and a county history also give Peder's birthplace as Sweden. Since he provided this information while he was still alive, it becomes more reliable than his death certificate.

Another source of death information sometimes found in family record collections is legal notices. Figure 1-9, the notice of a probate hearing, does not give an exact date of death but it gives an acceptable substitute date and thus constitutes a valuable genealogical source.

Death certificates and newspaper obituaries are relatively recent types of death records. As we have seen, letters, diaries, and

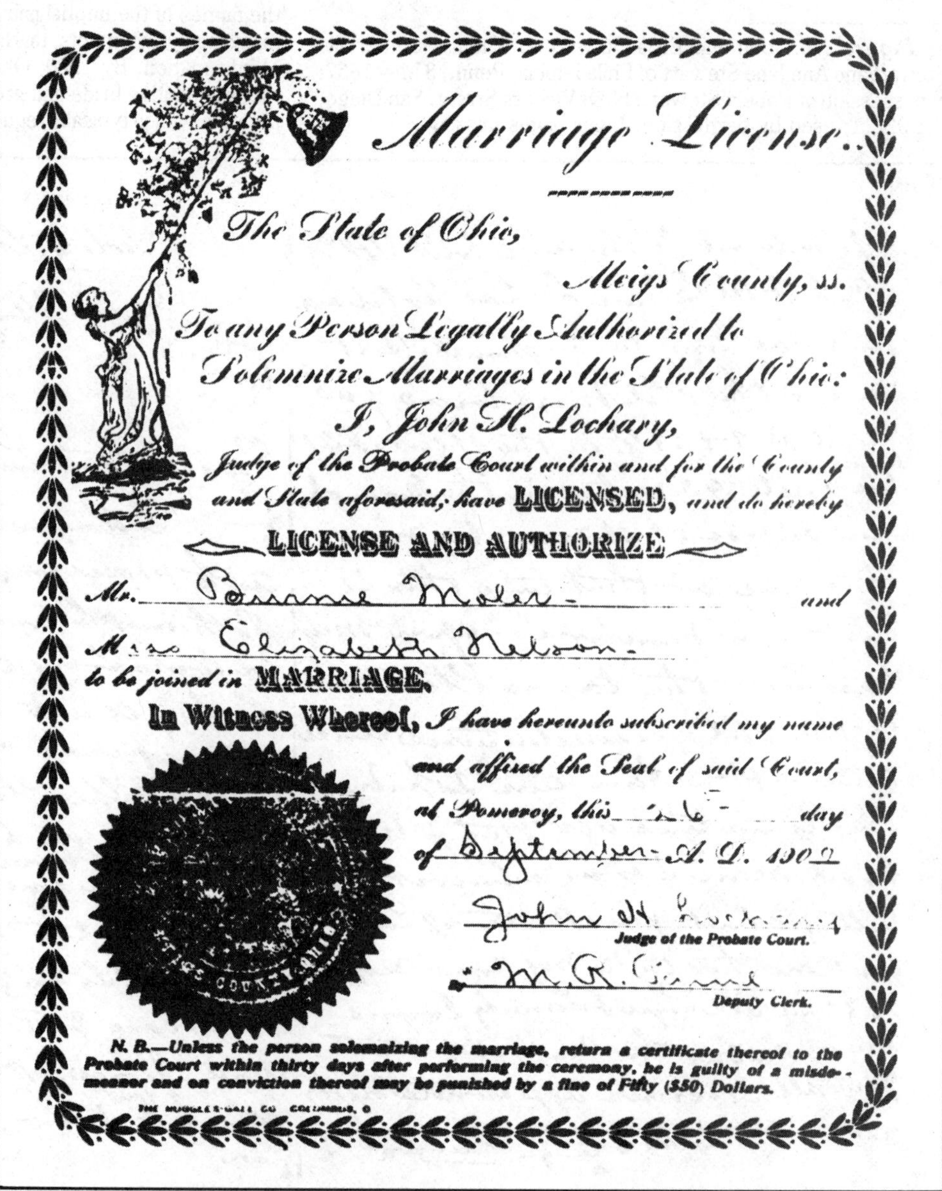

Marriage License.

The State of Ohio,

Meigs County, ss.

To any Person Legally Authorized to Solemnize Marriages in the State of Ohio:

I, John H. Lochary,

Judge of the Probate Court within and for the County and State aforesaid, have LICENSED, and do hereby

LICENSE AND AUTHORIZE

Mr. Burnie Moler and

Miss Elizabeth Nelson.

to be joined in MARRIAGE.

In Witness Whereof, I have hereunto subscribed my name and affixed the Seal of said Court, at Pomeroy, this 26 day of September A. D. 1900

John H. Lochary
Judge of the Probate Court.

M. R. Crane
Deputy Clerk.

N. B.—Unless the person solemnizing the marriage, return a certificate thereof to the Probate Court within thirty days after performing the ceremony, he is guilty of a misdemeanor and on conviction thereof may be punished by a fine of Fifty ($50) Dollars.

THE NUGGLES-GALE CO. COLUMBUS, O.

Figure 1-7. Marriage License of Burnie Moler and Elizabeth Nelson, 26 Sept. 1900, Meigs Co., Ohio; in possession of William Arbuckle. Used by permission.

PLACE OF DEATH

County Kandiyohi
Township Dovre
or Village
or City (No. St., Ward)

STATE OF MINNESOTA
DIVISION OF VITAL STATISTICS
CERTIFICATE OF DEATH

Reg. District No. — No. in Registration Book 5
(Above numbers to be filled in only by local registrar or his deputy.)

[If death occurred in a hospital or institution, give its NAME instead of street and number]

FULL NAME Peder Pederson

PERSONAL AND STATISTICAL PARTICULARS

SEX: Male — Color or Race: White — Single, Married, Widowed, or Divorced (Write the word)

DATE OF BIRTH: Dec 10 1833 (Month) (Day) (Year)

AGE: 80 yrs. 3 mos. 5 ds. — If LESS than 1 day, ... hrs. or ... min.?

OCCUPATION (a) Trade, Profession, or particular kind of work: Farmer
(b) General nature of industry, business, or establishment in which employed (or employer)

BIRTHPLACE (State or country): Norway

PARENTS
Name of Father: Peder Pederson
Birthplace of Father (State or country): Norway
Maiden Name of Mother: Marit Pederson
Birthplace of Mother (State or country): Norway

The above is true to the best of my knowledge
(Informant) John Pederson
(Address) Willmar Minn.

Filed March 20 1914 C.C. Birkeland, Registrar
Address Willmar Minn.

MEDICAL CERTIFICATE OF DEATH

DATE OF DEATH: March 15, 1914 (Month) (Day) (Year)

I HEREBY CERTIFY, That I attended deceased from Feb 26th, 1914, to March 15, 1914, that I last saw him alive on March 8, 1914, and that death occurred, on the date stated above, at 5 p.m.

The CAUSE OF DEATH was as follows:
Mitral regurgitation of heart

(Duration) several months yrs. mos. ds.

Contributory (Secondary) Acute [illegible]
(Duration) 2 months yrs. mos. ds.

(Signed) B. [illegible] Branton, M. D.
3/16 1914 (Address) Willmar Minn

State the Disease Causing Death, or, in deaths from Violent Causes, state (1) Means of Injury; and (2) whether Accidental, Suicidal or Homicidal.

LENGTH OF RESIDENCE (for Hospitals, Institutions, Transients, or Recent Residents)
At place of death ... yrs. ... mos. ... ds. In the State ... yrs. ... mos. ... ds.
Where was disease contracted, if not at place of death?
Former or usual residence

PLACE OF BURIAL OR REMOVAL: Town of Dovre — DATE OF BURIAL: March 18 1914
UNDERTAKER: J. C. Olson — ADDRESS: Willmar Minn

Figure 1-8. Death certificate of Peder Pederson, 15 March 1914, Dovre, Kandiyohi Co., Minn. Copy in possession of the author, issued by the State of Minnesota.

SAIDLER, ESTHER, deceased.—Supplemental citation.—The People of the State of New York, by the grace of God free and independent, to Thomas S. Stewart, A. Wilson Stewart, George Stewart, William Charles Stewart, Mary Jane Hall, Robert Stewart, William Stewart, the heirs and next of kin of Esther Saidler, late of the County of New York, deceased, send greeting:

Whereas Ralph C. Stewart, of the City of Philadelphia, has lately applied to the Surrogate's Court of our County of New York to have a certain instrument in writing, dated August second, 1901, relating to both real and personal property, duly proved as the last will and testament of said Esther Saidler, late of the County of New York, deceased; therefore you and each of you are cited to appear before the Surrogate of our County of New York, at his office in the County of New York, on the 26th day of May, 1903, at half-past ten o'clock in the forenoon of that day, then and there to attend the probate of the said last will and testament.

And such of you as are hereby cited as are under the age of twenty-one years are required to appear by your guardian, if you have one, or if you have none, to appear and apply for one to be appointed, or in the event of your neglect or failure to do so, a guardian will be appointed by the Surrogate to represent and act for you in the proceeding.

In testimony whereof, we have caused the seal of the Surrogate's Court of the said County of New York to be hereunto affixed. Witness, Hon. Frank T. Fitzgerald, a Surrogate of our said County of New York, at said county, the 4th day of April, in the year of our Lord 1903.

[L. S.]

J. FAIRFAX McLAUGHLIN,
Clerk of the Surrogate's Court.

TOWNSEND WANDELL,
Attorney for Proponent,
51 Chambers Street, New York City.

Figure 1-9. Probate notice for the estate of Esther Saidler, *New York Law Journal*, 17 April 1913; courtesy of Robert Stewart.

family Bibles often contain information about deaths in the family. In the nineteenth century, death notices were often sent to members of the family and friends. Figure 1-10 shows such a Scottish funeral notice in 1867.

That John McKinzie was able to afford a printed funeral invitation suggests that he was a man of some means. More typically, the death or funeral notice consisted of a black-bordered letter or card containing a handwritten message.

Space forbids discussion of every source of death information which can be found in the family's possessions. Quilts, samplers, and other types of embroidery work can be extraordinary sources of genealogical data. Where the family no longer has these items, museums and historical societies collect and display them.

Other Family Sources

Of course, family records tell us much more than the bare facts of birth, marriage, and death. For instance, a naturalization certificate such as Figure 1-11 documents an important day in the family history, the day the immigrant ancestor became a full citizen of a new country. In itself, this certificate reveals only the name, country of birth, and former sovereign of the new citizen, along with the date, place, and court where the naturalization took place.

But this certificate suggests a search of other court records. The Highland County Probate Court had preserved the application for citizenship, which contained a wealth of additional genealogical data. Most courts have preserved Declarations of Intention, the so-called "first papers," which often list the immigrant's exact place of birth, and the date and port of arrival, especially after November 1906.

Still another type of document typically found in family records

Figure 1-10. Funeral notice of Grace Bushby McKinzie, 13 April 1867, Craigland's Village; Kirkpatrick Juxta, Scotland, courtesy of William Arbuckle.

Craiglands Village,
KIRKPATRICK JUXTA, 13th April, 1867

Sir,

The favour of your Company to attend the Funeral of GRACE BUSHBY, my Wife, to the place of Interment in the Churchyard of KIRKPATRICK JUXTA, on WEDNESDAY, the 17th Inst., at ONE o'Clock Afternoon, will much oblige,

Sir,

Your most obedient Servant,

JOHN McKINZIE.

Figure 1-11. Naturalization Certificate of John Arbuckle, 2 Oct. 1877, Highland Co., Ohio; in possession of William Arbuckle.

No. 22

UNITED STATES OF AMERICA.

The State of Ohio, Highland County, ss.

To all who shall see these Presents, GREETING:

Know Ye, *That on the* Second *day of* October *Anno Domini* 1867, *at a* **PROBATE COURT,** *held at the Probate Office, in Hillsborough, in and for the County aforesaid and State of Ohio, personally came* John Arbuckle *a native of* Scotland *who produced a Certificate of his intention to be* **NATURALIZED,** *and become* **A CITIZEN OF THE UNITED STATES,** *and also proved to the satisfaction of the Court, that he has behaved as a man of good moral character, attached to the principles of the Constitution of the United States, and well disposed to the good order and happiness of the same. And having fully complied with the Laws of the United States, in relation to the Naturalization of Aliens, the said* John Arbuckle *on being admitted by this Court, took the oath to support the Constitution of the United States of America, and to* **Absolutely and Entirely Renounce and Abjure** *all allegiance and fidelity to every* **Foreign Prince, Potentate, State or Sovereignty** *Whatsoever, and particularly to* Queen Victoria *whose subject he was.*

This is, therefore, to Certify, *That the said* John Arbuckle *...mitted a* **Citizen of the United States.**

...Testimony Whereof, *I have hereunto subscribed my ...e officially, and affixed the seal of said Court, at ...borough, this* 2nd *day of* October *...D. 18*

W J C Norton **Probate Judge.**

are military discharge papers. (See Figure 1-12.)

This personal information, while interesting and specific in itself, pales by comparison with what can be found in military pension records and should always lead to a search among these public documents.

Occasionally, family papers may include a passport. As Figure 1-13 demonstrates, passports often contain an extraordinary amount of genealogical data. This passport of Jean Baptiste Parret, issued in Colmar, Alsace, France in February 1844, lists his age, physical description— right down to the color of his eyebrows— occupation, place of birth, and residence, along with his destination, New York. With such a wealth of information, it was not difficult to locate Jean Baptiste's village of birth, Le Puix, in the Department of Haut Rhin, and his birth entry in the Le Puix civil registers. Thus, the family legend that he had come from Paris was laid to rest.

Passports are rare, but photographs are not. Unfortunately, family photographs seldom name the persons pictured nor list the date. Older relatives can help in identifying persons and approximate dates for such photographs. But some photographs predate the memory of any living human being.

Using a combination of photographs, photographers' registers, and public documents, it is possible to identify precisely who the people in your family photos are. Techniques, examples, and worksheets for this research task are included in Arlene H. Eakle, *Photograph Analysis*, 2nd ed. (Salt Lake City: Family History World, 1984).

The oldest photographs typically found in a family collection are the so-called "tintypes," photographs printed on black lacquered metal, which may date back to the 1850s[2], and nonmetal photographs, which began appearing in the 1860s. Since a professional photographer was required, it was common for the photographer to print the name of his studio and city on the border.

Other photographs often found in family collections are postcards. (See Figure 1-14.) Found in a trunk in Taylor County, Wisconsin, this particular postcard proved crucial in tracing the family line in that it provided a picture of the ancestral village. Although there are several towns by that name in Germany, the reverse side indicated that this village was in the Fichtel Mountains of northeast Bavaria. With this evidence I was able to pinpoint the location of Höchstädt on a large scale map.

16648

Honorable Discharge from The United States Army

This Dis. Recorded
the 25 day of March 1957.
at 2.50 o'clock P. M.
Book 7 Page 320
Recorded March 26, 1957.
C. V. Coffey
Recdr. Champaign County, Ohio
M.S. dep.

TO ALL WHOM IT MAY CONCERN:

This is to Certify, That* Clyde M. Arbuckle
†332323 Sergeant Troop F 4th Cavalry
THE UNITED STATES ARMY, *as a* TESTIMONIAL OF HONEST AND FAITHFUL SERVICE, *is hereby* HONORABLY DISCHARGED *from the military service of the* UNITED STATES *by reason of* ‡ Cir 18 W.D. 1920

Said Clyde M Arbuckle *was born in* Bloomingburg, *in the State of* Ohio

When enlisted he was 21 1/2 *years of age and by occupation a* Baker

He had Blue *eyes,* Brown *hair,* Ruddy *complexion, and was* 5 *feet* 7 *inches in height.*

Given under my hand at San Benito Texas *this* 18th *day of* June, *one thousand nine hundred and* Twenty.

Thos. B. Wyatt
Major 4th Cavalry.
Commanding.

Form No. 525, A. G. O.
Oct. 9-18.

*Insert name, Christian name first; e. g., "John Doe."
†Insert Army serial number, grade, company and regiment or arm or corps or department; e. g., "1,620,302"; "Corporal, Company A, 1st Infantry"; "Sergeant, Quartermaster Corps"; "Sergeant, First Class, Medical Department."
‡If discharged prior to expiration of service, give number, date, and source of order or full description of authority therefor.

Figure 1-12. Discharge Certificate of Clyde M. Arbuckle from the U.S. Army, 18 June 1920, courtesy of William Arbuckle.

After the invention of the Kodak box camera in 1888, thousands of Americans took millions of photographs of each other at work, home, and at play, with home movies and videotapes coming along in the twentieth century. In many respects, the camera has replaced the diary as a record of family history, and identifying photographs properly should have a high priority for a researcher.

Old books in the family's possession may yield unexpected genealogical clues. Figure 1-15 shows the inscription on the flyleaf of a midnineteenth-century Methodist hymnal. Family tradition remembered that Greenberry Wright had lived somewhere in Wisconsin before the Civil War. Ball Prairie had disappeared from the current road map, but by using a Wisconsin gazetteer and the 1850 census, I located Greenberry Wright and his family in the northeastern corner of Winneconne, Winnebago County, where there had once been a hamlet called Ball Prairie.

Other types of records sometimes found in family archives include land, business, and legal records. The will illustrated in Figure 1-16 cleared up a long-standing genealogical mystery. Grace McKenzie, the illegitimate daughter of Agnes McKenzie, had been baptized as the child of her grandparents to conceal the family scandal. But this will revealed her mother's name.

In short, the list of genealogical and historical sources is almost endless. Old Christmas cards, post cards, address books, jewelry, trophies, and artifacts of various sorts can yield valuable and otherwise obscure information. Even furniture may hold a clue. As I write, I am sitting in a captain's chair which once belonged to my Norwegian

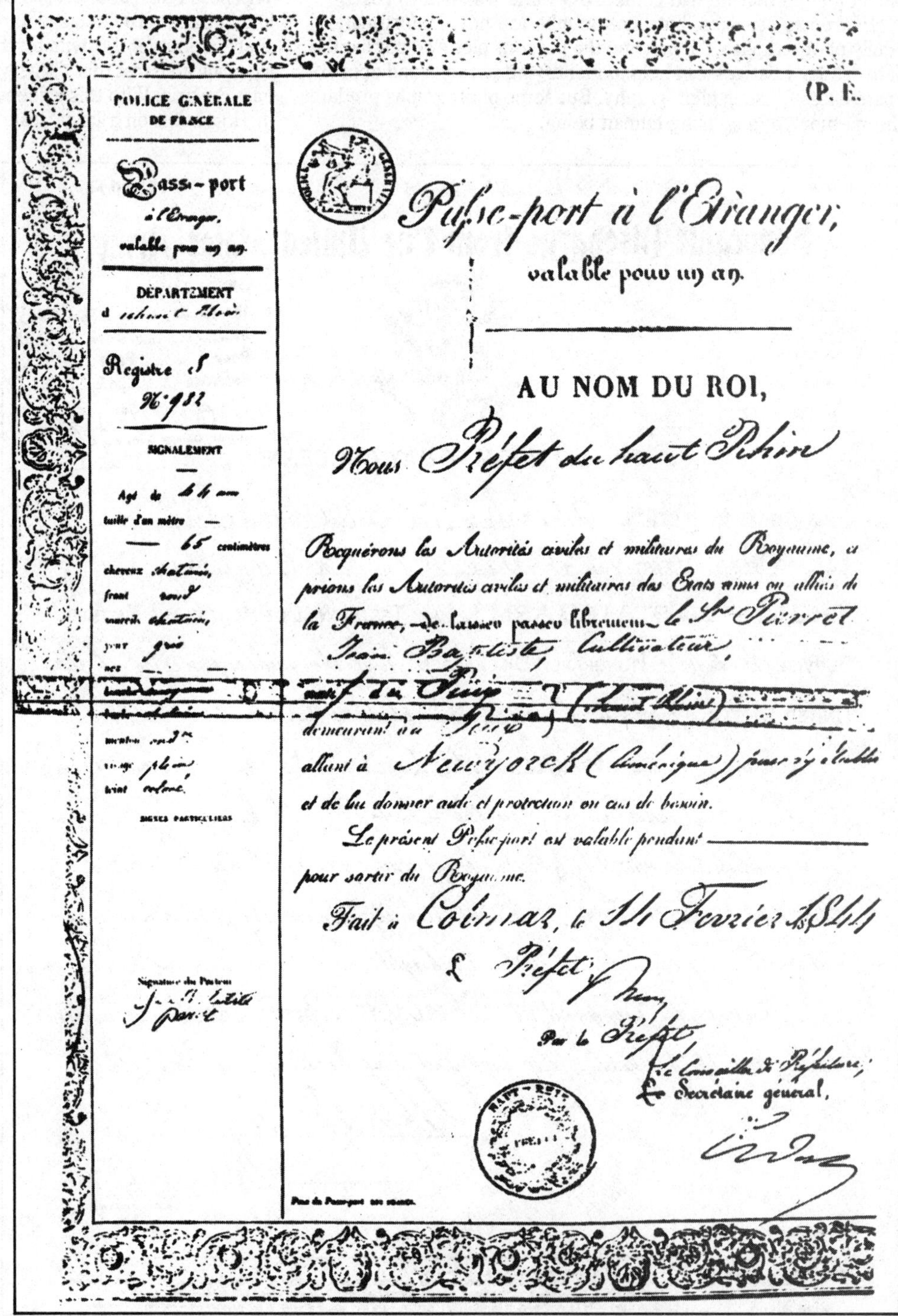

POLICE GÉNÉRALE DE FRANCE

Passe-port à l'Étranger, valable pour un an.

DÉPARTEMENT

Registre

SIGNALEMENT

Signature du Porteur

(P. E.)

Passe-port à l'Étranger; valable pour un an.

AU NOM DU ROI,

Nous Préfet du haut Rhin

Requérons les Autorités civiles et militaires du Royaume, et prions les Autorités civiles et militaires des États amis ou alliés de la France, de laisser passer librement le Sr Parret Jean Baptiste, cultivateur,

demeurant à

allant à Newyorck (Amérique) pour s'y établir

et de lui donner aide et protection en cas de besoin.

Le présent Passe-port est valable pendant

pour sortir du Royaume.

Fait à Colmar, le 14 Février 1844

Le Préfet

Par le Préfet, Le Conseiller de Préfecture, Le Secrétaire général,

Figure 1-13. Passport of Jean Baptiste Parret, Feb. 1844, Colmar, Alsace, France; used courtesy of William Parrett.

Figure 1-14. Postcard from Anna Macht to Babetta Macht, ca 1908, Höchstädt, Oberfranken, Bavaria; in possession of Robert L. Cantin, 418 E. Brook Hollow Drive, Phoenix AZ 85022. Used with permission.

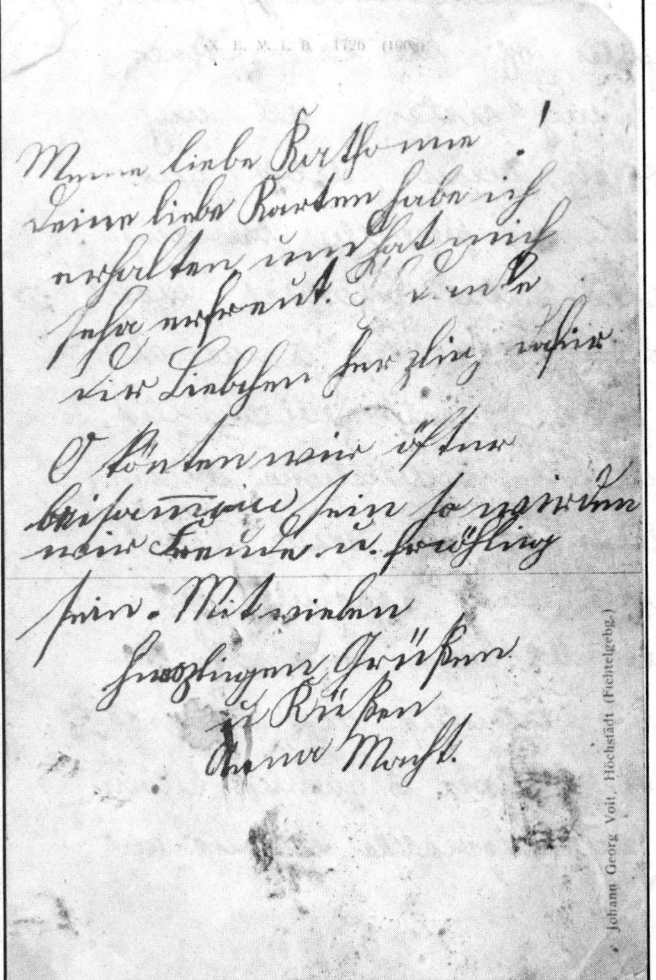

Figure 1-15. Flyleaf inscription of Greenberry Wright, 1851, Methodist hymnal; in possession of the author.

Greenberry Wright's
Book
Ball Prairie
1851

great-grandfather, Lars Brekke. "Clark, Dakota," is stamped in black letters on the underside of the seat, dating the chair to the 1880s; for Dakota Territory achieved statehood in 1889, while Lars settled southeast of Clark in 1881. Ultimately, the limits of home sources for family history are the limits of the genealogist's imagination.

With each new ancestor identified, you will look for "home sources." As you move back in time, the search will often shift from homes of relatives to historical societies and university libraries where personal papers have been deposited, although it is still possible to find eighteenth-century papers in family possession.

Oral History

The memory of a living person, usually the first home source consulted but the most fragile and transitory of all genealogical sources, has drawn a great deal of attention in the last fifteen years or so, with the advent of the professionally prepared and preserved oral history. Oral interviews with older members of the family can provide information and insights into the past available in no other way; yet much time, effort, and money are wasted when oral interviews are conducted without adequate preparation.

In conducting an oral interview for genealogical purposes, you can easily see what data you have and what you still need by using three basic tools: the pedigree chart, the family group sheet, and the research calendar. Figure 1-17 illustrates a standard five-generation pedigree chart, beginning with the client or researcher as person number one, his/her father as person number two, mother as person number three, and so forth. Thus, each person on the chart has a number. All the men have even numbers, while all the women have odd numbers. The pedigree chart provides an organized picture of the generations of direct descent that can be understood at a glance.

The family group sheet (see Figure 1-18) fills in the brothers and sisters of the direct ancestor. Ideally, you should create a family group sheet for each head of a household on the pedigree chart. If you number each sheet corresponding to the pedigree chart, you can quickly locate any individual by generation. Thus the number of Peder Pederson's family group sheet would be 1:12 since he is person number 12 on pedigree chart number 1 displayed in Figure 1-17. Following the same logic, Isaiah Dougherty's family group sheet number would be 1:8. But since James Dougherty, Isaiah's

Figure 1-16. Will of Elizabeth McKenzie, 16 May 1890, Kirkpatrick Juxta Dumfriesshire, Scotland; courtesy of William Arbuckle.

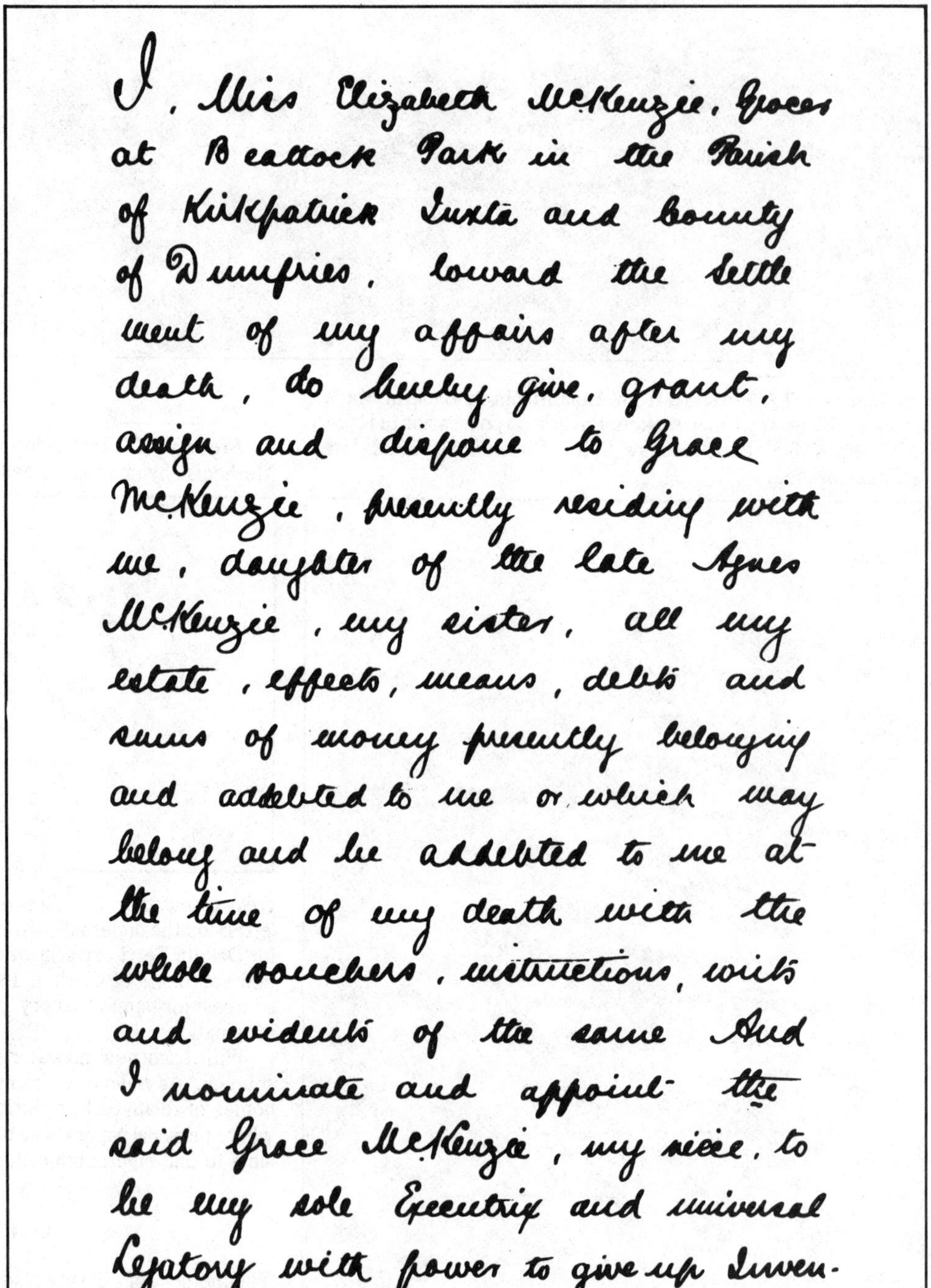

I, Miss Elizabeth McKenzie, Grocer
at Beattock Park in the Parish
of Kirkpatrick Juxta and County
of Dumfries, toward the settle
ment of my affairs after my
death, do hereby give, grant,
assign and dispone to Grace
McKenzie, presently residing with
me, daughter of the late Agnes
McKenzie, my sister, all my
estate, effects, means, debts and
sums of money presently belonging
and addebted to me or which may
belong and be addebted to me at
the time of my death with the
whole vouchers, instructions, writs
and evidents of the same And
I nominate and appoint the
said Grace McKenzie, my niece, to
be my sole Executrix and universal
Legatory with power to give up Inven-
tories of my moveable means and
estate

Figure 1-17. Pedigree of Richard Wellington Dougherty.

PEDIGREE CHART

CHART NO. 1

October 1983
DATE

Richard W. Dougherty
NAME OF PERSON SUBMITTING CHART

862 East 13th South
STREET ADDRESS

Salt Lake City, Utah 84105
CITY STATE

NO. 1 ON THIS CHART IS THE SAME PERSON AS NO. ___ ON CHART NO. ___

1 Richard Wellington/ DOUGHERTY
BORN 28 Jul 1932
WHERE Mooridge, Walworth, South Dakota
WHEN MARRIED
DIED
WHERE

NAME OF HUSBAND OR WIFE

SOURCES OF INFORMATION

2 James Kenneth DOUGHERTY
BORN 12 Jul 1900
WHERE Watertown, Codington, SD
WHEN MARRIED 30 May 1931
DIED
WHERE

3 Marian Elizabeth PEDERSON
BORN 11 Apr 1905
WHERE Benson, Swift, Minnesota
DIED
WHERE

4 James Wellington DOUGHERTY
BORN 31 Oct 1867
WHERE Boston, Norfolk, Ontario
WHEN MARRIED 6 Nov 1895
DIED 20 Mar 1947
WHERE Eau Claire, Eau Claire/ Wisconsin

5 Susie WHITWAM
BORN 14 Jul 1867
WHERE St. Thomas, Elgin, Ont.
DIED 8 Apr 1909
WHERE Watertown, Codington, SD

6 Martin PEDERSON
BORN 8 Sep 1869
WHERE Dovre, Kandiyohi, MN
WHEN MARRIED Jun 1894
DIED 5 Jul 1951
WHERE Eau Claire, Eau Claire/ Wisconsin

7 Betsy BREKKE
BORN 28 Jan 1871
WHERE Pleasant, Winnishiek,/ Iowa
DIED Oct 1956
WHERE Minneapolis, Hennepin, Minnesota

8 Isaiah DOUGHERTY
BORN 19 Aug 1838
WHERE Whitchurch, York, Ont.
WHEN MARRIED 27 Dec 1859
DIED 12 Jul 1896
WHERE Watertown, Codington, SD

9 Sarah MEHARG
BORN 7 Nov 1839
WHERE Hillsboro, Down, Ireland
DIED 1921
WHERE Watertown, Codington, SD

10 Beaumont WHITWAM
BORN 29 Apr 1830
WHERE Golcar, Yorkshire, Eng.
WHEN MARRIED abt 1853
DIED 1 Jan 1892
WHERE Eau Claire, Eau Claire/ Wisconsin

11 Ann POTTICARY
BORN abt 1834
WHERE St. Thomas, Elgin, Ont.
DIED 1919
WHERE Watertown, Codington, SD

12 Peder PEDERSON
BORN 10 Dec 1833
WHERE , Värmland, Sweden
WHEN MARRIED 8 Jun 1867
DIED 15 Mar 1914
WHERE Dovre, Kandiyohi, MN

13 Maren Oleson LÖVBERGET
BORN 13 Mar 1842
WHERE Grue, Solor, Norway
DIED 9 Mar 1926
WHERE Minneapolis, Hennepin, MN

14 Lars Larsson BREKKE
BORN 1847
WHERE Granvin, Hordaland, Nor
WHEN MARRIED 1864
DIED 1931
WHERE Vienna, Clark, SD

15 Sigrid IVARSDATTER
BORN 1846
WHERE Granvin, Hordaland, Nor
DIED
WHERE Vienna, Clark, SD

No.	Name	Cont. on Chart
16	James DOUGHERTY	2
17	Martha	3
18	William MEHARG	4
19	Elizabeth JACOBS	5
20	Christopher WHITWHAM	6
21	Elizabeth BEAUMONT	7
22	Joseph POTTICARY	8
23		
24		
25		
26	Ole Jensen LÖVBERGET	12
27	Kari OLSDATTER	13
28	Lar Larsson BREKKE	14
29	Sigrid Johannesdtr SPILDO	15
30	Ivar JENSSON	16
31	Brita ANVEDSDTR.	17

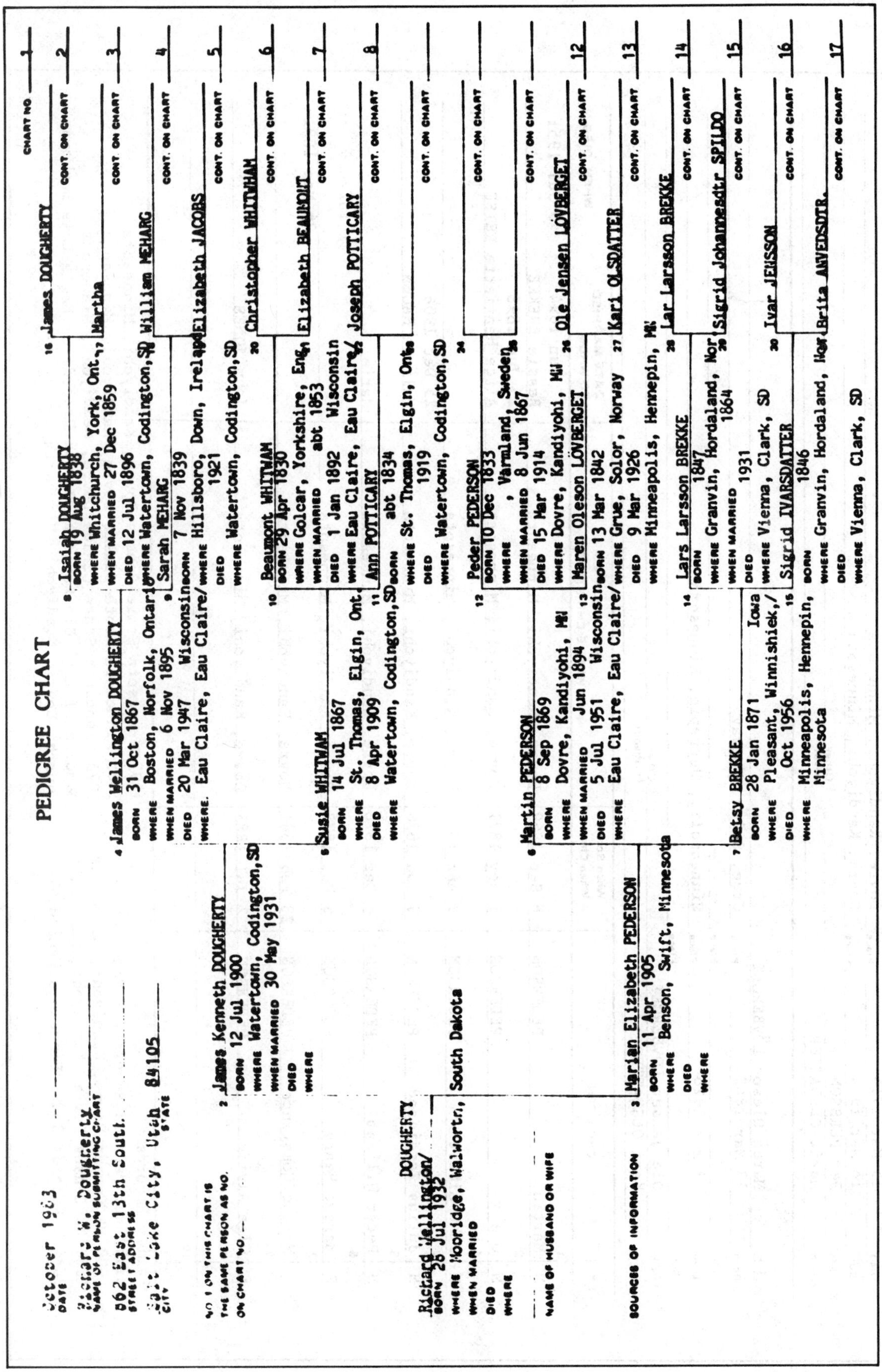

Figure 1-18. Family Group Sheet of Peder Pederson; original in possession of the author.

FAMILY GROUP RECORD

HUS. Peder PEDERSON — Occupation

Born	10 Dec 1832	Place	Södra Finnskoga, Värmland, Sweden
Chr.	11 Dec 1832	Place	Södra Finnskoga, Värmland, Sweden
Marr.	8 Jun 1867	Place	Dahlgren, Carver, Minnesota
Died	15 Mar 1914	Place	Dovre, Kandiyohi, Minnesota
Bur.	18 Mar 1914	Place	Dovre, Kandiyohi, Minnesota
ATHER	Per PERSSON	Other Wives	
THER	Marit OLSDATTER		

WIFE Maren Oleson LÖVBERGET

Born	13 Mar 1842	Place	Grue, Solör, Norway
Chr.		Place	
Died	9 Mar 1926	Place	Minneapolis, Hennepin, Minnesota
Bur.		Place	
ATHER	Ole Jensen LÖVBERGET	Other Husbands	
THER	Kari OLSDATTER		

SEX	CHILDREN		When Born When Chr.	WHERE BORN WHERE CHRISTENED	DATE MARRIED TO WHOM	WHEN DIED
M	1 Martin	PEDERSON	8 Sep 1869	Dovre, Kandiyohi, Minnesota	Jun 1894 Bessie BREKKE	5 Jul 1951
M	2 Ole	PEDERSON	1 Nov 1871	Dovre, Kandiyohi, Minnesota	15 Jun 1898 Alice Henriette REISE	
M	3 John Albert	PEDERSON	9 Apr 1874	Dovre, Kandiyohi, Minnesota		
M	4 Julius Ferdinand	PEDERSON	9 Jun 1876	Dovre, Kandiyohi, Minnesota	25 Dec 1906 Malinda HAGEN	
M	5 Peder William	PEDERSON	6 Dec 1878	Dovre, Kandiyohi, Minnesota	Marie	
F	6 Marcus Henry	PEDERSON	6 Dec 1878	Dovre, Kandiyohi, Minnesota		Infancy
F	7 Marthe Constance	PEDERSON	23 Feb 1881	Dovre, Kandiyohi, Minnesota		26 Mar 1881
F	8 Olga Alvide	PEDERSON	2 Jul 1883	Dovre, Kandiyohi, Minnesota	John JONES	
	9					
	10					

Family Records
Civil War Pension Records of Peder Pederson
1900 US Census Dovre, Kandiyohi, Minnesota
1880 US Census Dovre, Kandiyohi, Minnesota
Parish Records Sodra Finnskoga,Vrmlnd,Sweden
1895 Minnesota State Census Dovre, Kandiyohi, Minnesota
1885 Minnesota State Census Dovre, Kandiyohi, Minnesota
1875 Minnesota State Census Dovre, Kandiyohi, Minnesota
Memoirs of Rev. Ole Paulson; Parish Records of Eagle Lake Lutheran Church, Dovre, Kandiyohi, Minnesota

father, person number 16 on pedigree chart 1, is also person number 1 on pedigree chart 2, his family group sheet number would be 2:1.

Depending upon the amount of data available, you may wish to have a separate file for each family group sheet. (See the introduction to the book for more information on how to organize research materials.) This file, typically a standard-size manila folder, should contain copies of all pertinent documents and correspondence about that particular family. The file should be numbered like the family group sheet, e.g. 1:12. The family group sheet itself should be attached to the right page of the folder where it can be quickly found, not filed loosely among the other documents. The documents and correspondence should be attached to the left page of the folder. The pedigree chart should be filed in your personal folder, i.e., File 1:1

Some genealogists prefer one file per line. This may work perfectly well, especially as you move back in time where the documentation is sparse. But again, the family group sheets should be attached separately.

The exact sources of information for each family group sheet should be listed. Thus, if a problem or question arises, you can quickly consult the primary documents.

This leads us to the third basic record-keeping device, the research calendar. Several types exist. The calendar illustrated in Figure 1-19 was developed by a professional genealogist in Salt Lake City and is used by several genealogical research firms. It summarizes which sources have been checked, the date of the search, and the results. Thus, you are spared the exasperating task of shuffling through a stack of documents trying to determine whether a given source has been checked, doubly exasperating if you are consulting data passed on by someone else.

Once you have organized your data in a comprehensible manner, you are ready to contact your relatives. In the case of the Pederson family, a letter to my aunt produced the names of two of Peder's children who had died in infancy and thus were not listed in his Civil War pension records nor in any of the state and federal census returns. I knew they existed because the 1900 census asked for the number of children a woman bore and the number still living. Thus, by doing some preliminary research, I was able to ask a question which otherwise might not have come up.

If you must correspond, rather than converse with your relatives,

RESEARCH CALENDAR

CLIENT: DOUGHERTY	ACCOUNT NO.:
RESEARCHER: DOUGHERTY	FILE NO.: 1:12

Date	Repository / Call No.	Description of Source	Ind / Cond	Search Objective	Comments	Doc. No.
JUL 1980	GS / 1245305	1900 MINNESOTA SOUNDEX P. 362	Y / G	PEDER PEDERSON + FAMILY	KANDIYOHI CO VOL 27 ED 61 SH 1 LINE 78	
"	" / 1240772	1900 US CENSUS MINNESOTA KANDIYOHI CO DOVRE TWP	Y / G	"		1
"	" / 287,573	1880 MINNESOTA SOUNDEX P. 362	Y / G	"	KANDIYOHI CO SD 3 ED 45	
"	" / 1254624	1880 US CENSUS MINNESOTA KANDIYOHI CO DOVRE TWP	Y / G	"		2
"	" / 565,785	1895 MINNESOTA CENSUS KANDIYOHI CO DOVRE TWP	N / G	"		3
"	" / 565 744	1885 " " " "	N / G	"		4
"	" / 565,723	1875 " " " "	N / G	"		5
"	" / 1000,259	LAWSON, VICTOR. ILLUSTRATED HISTORY OF KANDIYOHI CO. 1905 P 150	PARTIAL / G	"		6
		1870 US CENSUS INDEX MINNESOTA (AIS)	Y	"	NEGATIVE FOR DOVRE TWP. KANDIYOHI CO	

Figure 1-19. Sample Research Calendar on Peder Pederson. Original in possession of the author.

write your questions legibly, or better yet, type them. In addition, I usually enclose a partially filled-out family group sheet and request that the relative fill in whatever blank spaces he or she can.

Telephone interviews can be useful if there is adequate advance notice. A personal interview is generally much better.

In preparing for an oral history interview, select your equipment carefully. The compact size and simplicity of the cassette recorder make it the odds-on favorite. True, you cannot edit a cassette tape; but if necessary, you can transfer it to a reel-to-reel machine whose tapes can be edited.

Once you have decided upon a recorder, learn how to use it with a minimum of distraction. Take along enough tape to record a lengthy interview, extra batteries and other accessories, notepads and pens, and a camera.[3]

As emphasized earlier, learn as much as you can about the family before the interview, so you can ask intelligent questions. Be adaptable. If your situation makes it possible for you to schedule more than one interview with a relative, you might use the first interview to gain general background about the family and build rapport, leaving details for another time. If circumstances dictate only one interview, use discretion and diplomacy in approaching delicate topics. If your relative is obviously uncomfortable, explain your reasons for raising the question. If he or she still hesitates, perhaps you should ask another relative or close friend of the family about the subject.

Avoid leading questions such as "Your brother Ben was born in January 1905, wasn't he?" Such questions tend to influence the answer. Simply ask when brother Ben was born.

Bring along a family group sheet and fill it out during the interview. Schedule a second interview if possible. In the meantime, check out all the leads gained against other documentary and oral evidence. This will make the second interview much more worthwhile.

Finally, evaluate the information you gain. Family traditions can be among the most valuable of genealogical sources. At the same time, they can be very misleading. As a professional genealogist, I spend a great deal of time in the initial stages of a project sorting out fact from fiction in family traditions. My technique is very basic: I document the family history as completely as possible. Sometimes the documents support the family story, and sometimes they do not.

For example, I seldom write to a European parish inquiring about an ancestor if I have only family tradition to go on. My experience has taught me that such inquiries often result in months of delay and ultimately a negative response. Whenever possible, I attempt to document the family story with naturalization papers, church records, obituaries, civil records, and other documents. Occasionally, it is necessary to rely upon unsubstantiated tradition in tracing an immigrant ancestor, but do your utmost to find other sources to support it.

And, of course, every professional genealogist is familiar with at least one client who simply refuses to believe the documentary evidence that explodes his or her family legend. Such people will move from one genealogist to another, spending thousands of dollars in a fruitless attempt to "prove" royal descent or another legend. Such types do not, however, diminish the value of family tradition. They simply represent an extreme element which misuses and distorts a valuable source.

There may also be oral interviews recorded for ancestors and relatives long dead. For example, the famed Draper Manuscript Collection, located in 491 original volumes at the State Historical Society of Wisconsin and on microfilm in more than 300 research libraries across the country, is based on oral interviews with hundreds of people, 1840-91. Reminiscences of frontiersmen, soldiers, travellers, teachers, farmers, and their descendants are recorded by hand in these volumes.[4]

Other historical collections based on oral interviews include the Hubert Howe Bancroft Papers, Bancroft Library, University of California, Berkeley; the Charles Mulks Notebooks, Olin Library, Cornell University, Ithaca, New York; and the Foote Papers, Chautauqua Historical Society, Westfield, New York. These four are a few out of many available for searching. (See Chapter 13, "Genealogical Tools and Indexes," for details on how to find them.) find them.)

Home sources are the first beginning for any search; and usually, they are a fruitful beginning.

Notes

1. Ann I. Mahoney, "You and Your Family as Research Sources," Chapter 4 in American Genealogical Research Institute, *How to Trace Your Family Tree* (New York: Doubleday/Dolphin Books, 1975), pp. 42-53.

2. Georgia Weber, "Home Sources, Family Tradition, Oral Histories," photocopy of typescript, 1983, p. 51; in possession of the publisher.

3. David Weitzman, *Underfoot* (New York: Scribner's, 1976), pp. 21-25.

4. Josephine L. Harper, *A Guide to the Draper Manuscripts* (Madison: State Historical Society of Wisconsin, 1982), and Kip Sperry, "The Draper Manuscripts: A Major Source for the Historian and the Genealogist," *Genealogical Journal* 3 (Sept. 1974): 63-70; 3 (Dec. 1974): 130-35.

Bibliography

Akeret, Robert U. *Photoanalysis*. New York: Simon and Schuster, 1973. Also available in Pocket Books.

Allen, Barbara, and Lynwood Montell. *From Memory to History*. Nashville: American Association for State and Local History, 1981.

Bank, Ann. *First-Person America*. New York: Alfred A. Knopf, 1980.

Baum, Willa K. *Oral History for the Local Historical Society*. Nashville: American Association for State and Local History, 1971.

Bitton, Davis. *Guide to Mormon Diaries and Autobiographies*. Provo, Utah: Brigham Young University Press, 1977.

Colket, Meredith B., Jr. "Family Records Printed During the Colonial Period." *Papers of the Bibliographical Society* 57 (1963): 61-68.

Collier, John, Jr. *Visual Anthropology: Photography as a Research Method*. New York: Holt, Rinehart and Winston, 1972.

Eakle, Arlene H. *Photograph Analysis*. Salt Lake City: Family History World, 1976.

Forbes, Mrs. Harriette M. *New England Diaries, 1602-1800: A Descriptive Catalog of Diaries, Orderly Books, Sea Journals*. Topsfield, Mass.: Privately printed, 1923.

Hartley, William G. *Preparing a Personal History*. Available from Primer Publications, Box 11894, Salt Lake City, UT 84147.

__________. *Diaries and Personal Journals: Why and How*. Available from Primer Publications, Box 11894, Salt Lake City, UT 84147.

Ives, Edward D. *The Tape-Recorded Interview: A Manual for Field Workers in Folklore and Oral History*. Knoxville: University of Tennessee Press, 1980.

Kann, Kenneth. "Reconstructing the History of a Community," *International Journal of Oral History* 2 (Feb. 1981): 4-12.

Kaplin, Louis, et al. *A Bibliography of American Autobiographies*. Madison: University of Wisconsin Press, 1961.

Library of Congress. *Check List of Collections of Personal Papers in Historical Societies, University and Public Libraries, and Other Learned Institutions in the United States*. 1918. Rev. ed., 1924.

Loehr, Rodney C. "Farmers' Diaries: Their Interest and Value as Historical Sources." *Agricultural History* 12 (1938): 313-25.

Mathews, William. *American Diaries: Annotated Bibliography of Those Written Prior to 1861*. Boston: J. S. Canner and Co., 1959.

McPherson, Marion White. "Some Values and Limitations of Oral Histories." *Journal of the History of the Behavioral Sciences* 11 (Jan. 1975): 34-36.

Morrisey, Charles T. "Oral History: More Than Tapes Are Spinning." *Library Journal* 105 (1980): 932-33.

Morrison, Joan, and Charlotte Fox Zabusky. *American Mosiac: The Immigrant Experience in the Words of Those Who Lived it*. New York: E. P. Dutton, 1980.

Norton, Don. "Personal History: A Guide for Transcribing and Editing Oral History." Prepared for Brigham Young University Genealogical Library, 1980.

Pope, Wiley R. *Write It Yourself: A Somewhat Painless Guide to Writing Your Personal History*. Available from Pope Family Association, 718 Sims Avenue, St. Paul., MN 55106.

Robacker, Earl F. "Victorian Wall Mottoes." *Pennsylvania Folklife*. Spring 1974, pp. 2-10.

Romney, Joseph B. *A Guide to Oral History and the Law*. San Luis Obispo: California Polytechnic State University, 1973.

Shumway, Gary L., and William C. Hartley. *An Oral History Primer*. Salt Lake City: Primer Publications, 1973.

Taft, Robert. *Photography and the American Scene: A Social History, 1839-1889*. 1938; reprint ed., Dover Publications, Inc., 1964.

Trout, Mary Jane, and Richard J. Hathaway. "Family Heritage: Children Make Excellent Historians." *Chronicle Magazine of the Historical Society of Michigan* 15 (1979): 23-28.

Webb, Jane. "Keep Your Family's Antiques." *National 4-H News*, Aug.-Sept. 1975, pp. 21-21.

INFORMATION GUIDE

Genealogical Information in the Record Group	*Birth*		*Delayed Birth*		*Death*		*Tombstones*	
	E	*M*	*E*	*M*	*E*	*M*	*E*	*M*
Surname/name	●	●		●	●	●	●	●
Date of Birth	●	●		●			●	●
Place of Birth	●	●		●		●	●	
Sex	●	●		●	●	●		
Race/color	●	●			●	●		
Physical Description								
Occupation		●				●		
Education								
Military Service								
Slave Status	●				●			
Property Owned								
Religion								
Citizenship								
Marital Status								
Spouse's Name								
Children's Names								
Father's Name	●	●		●	●	●	●	●
Mother's Name	●	●		●	●	●	●	●
Father's Birthplace		●		●		●		
Mother's Birthplace		●		●		●		
Date of Death					●	●	●	●
Cause of Death						●		
Name of Cemetery								
Residence		●		●	●	●		
Age				●	●	●	●	●
Literacy/signature				●				
Photograph/sketch								●
Relatives	●			●	●	●		
No. of living children		●					●	
No. of dead children		●					●	
Social Security No.				●		●		
Mortician						●		●
Cemetery						●		

E = Early M = Modern

COULD YOU USE THIS CHAPTER?

Type of Record	*Kept from*	*Clues That You Should Consult These Records*
Birth certificates	Varies from state to state: New England, about 1750; Virginia, 1853; all states by 1917.	Even though state registration of births was not required in all states until the twentieth century, many cities and counties had earlier registration. Church vital records frequently parallel or overlap these civil records. Birth certificates contain a wealth of information besides the person's name, birthdate, and parents. The birthplaces of both parents, their ages, their occupations, the number of other children (both living and deceased), and their address is given. Routinely request a birth certificate for all members for whom one is available, even if you think you know all of the information.
Death certificates	Varies—usually registration of deaths began at the same time as birth registration.	Death certificates, particularly after the turn of the twentieth century have such detailed information that you should get one for all family members for whom you know the county and approximate date of death. A death certificate tells you the names of the individual's parents, the place of death, cause of death, residence at time of death, exact date of death, Social Security number, the name of informant and his/her relationship to the deceased, the funeral home that handled the arrangements, the name of the cemetery or crematory, and the date of burial.
Tombstones	About 1770 to present	If your ancestors are recent immigrants, tombstones may be the only record of the *original* spelling of your surname. Clues for missing maiden names, children under age twelve, military service, occupation, religious affiliation, and places of origin are other bonuses found in cemeteries. Whenever possible, search cemeteries carefully.

Chapter 2

VITAL RECORDS AND CEMETERY RESEARCH

Johni Cerny

Vital records are, as their name suggests, connected with central life events: birth, marriage, and death. Maintained by civil authorities, they are prime sources of genealogical information; but, unfortunately, official vital records are only available for modern times. Marriage records are discussed in detail in Chapter 3, while birth and death records will be considered here. These records, despite their recent creation in the United States, are critically important in genealogical research, often supplying details on family members well back into the nineteenth century.

Births and Deaths in Public Records

Many British and European countries began keeping birth and death records nationally in the nineteenth century. Prior to that time, churches maintained registers of christenings and burials, and colonial settlers in America brought British laws and customs with them. Thus, churches were initially the sole keepers of vital records with ministers in many colonies required by law to report christenings and burials to civil authorities. Some areas consequently will have records of these events in both civil and church records. Eventually, some colonies, primarily those in New England, passed laws requiring local town or county clerks to maintain records of births and deaths. Massachusetts had the most comprehensive laws pertaining to birth and death registration and many of its early records have been published. Figure 2-1 illustrates the published vital records of Rehoboth, Massachusetts.

During the nineteenth century, England and other European countries instituted national registration systems, primarily to compile medical statistics as information on epidemic diseases. The United States did not implement the practice until much later. The majority of the states did not require registration until the first quarter of the twentieth century, and then the responsibility for registering births and deaths was left to the individual states, rather than the federal government, which accounts for both different starting dates and differences in the data called for. The earliest cities to require civil registration were New Orleans 1790, Boston 1848, Philadelphia 1860, Pittsburgh 1870, and Baltimore 1875. Fourteen states also initiated registration prior to 1880:

Delaware	1860
Florida	1865
Hawaii	1850
Iowa	1880
Massachusetts	1841
Michigan	1867
New Hampshire	1840
New Jersey	1878
New York	1880
Rhode Island	1853
Vermont	1770
Virginia	1853
Wisconsin	1876
Washington, D.C.	1871

Declarations of Intentions to Marry

MUNRO Joseph of Swanzey and Anne Goff of Reholoth, Jan. 9, 1741-2.

Elizabeth and Henry West, both of Rehoboth, Aug. 1, 1747.

Sarah and Ichabod Bowen, Jr., both of Rehoboth, June 11, 1757.

Nathaniel of Rehoboth and Ellis Hazard of South Kingetown, R. I., Dec. 13, 1774.

Samuel and Molly Blake, both of Rehoboth, July 8, 1780.

John of Rehoboth and Mary Osborn of Long Island, Aug. 8, 1780.

Waitstill and Asa Daggett, both of Rehoboth, Dec. 27, 1780.

John, Jr., of Rehoboth and Parthania Cornell of Swanzey, June 20, 1782.

Merebah of Swanzey and Joshua Round of Rehoboth, Aug. 24, 1813.

Births

3 90	MUNRO Benjamin, of Benjamin and Mary,	July 18, 1775
8 90	Joseph,	July 21, 1777
3 90	Benjamin,	Aug. 24, 1779
3 90	Allice Allen, of Benjamin and Rahamnah,	Dec. 30, 1803
3 90	Jacob,	March 22, 1805
3 90	Phebe Luther,	Dec. 6, 1806
3 90	Thomas Jefferson,	Jan. 29, 1809
3 90	Margaret Richards,	May 17, 1811
3 168	Hugh, of Hector and Miriam,	Dec. 29, 1765

Deaths

3 364	MUNRO Betty, of Nathan,	Dec. 26, 1758
4 221	Major Nathan, 76 years,	March 6, 1806
8 3	Roanah, widow, 79y 10m 5d,	Jan. 16, 1847
8 12	Charles N., of John N. and Louisanna, 9m 15d,	July 17, 1854
8 16	Ruth, wife of Benjamin, 75 years,	Dec. 22, 1857
3 360	Samuel, of John,	March 23, 1758
11 5	Benjamin, of B. and Mary, 83y 0m 22d,	Sept. 15, 1862

Figure 2-1. James H. Arnold, *Vital Records of Rehoboth, Massachusetts, 1642-1895,* 2 vols. paged continuously (Providence, R.I.: Narragansett Historical Publishing Co., 1897), pp. 479, 688, 854.

The U.S. Department of Health and Human Services periodically compiles "Where to Write for Vital Records – Births, Deaths, Marriages and Divorces," DHHS Publication No. (PHS) 82-1142, which lists, state by state, the dates the records began, the types of records kept, the cost of certified copies, and the address of the records custodian in each state. The 1982 edition of this booklet has been reproduced in Appendix F at the end of the book for your convenience. The fees it lists are subject to frequent increase. Future copies can be obtained from the Government Printing Office, Washington, DC 20402; the current price is $3.50.

Even in areas with early registration laws, enforcement was haphazard, particularly in rural and frontier areas. West Virginia is a good example of the problems in early vital records. The initial law requiring registration was passed by the Virginia legislature to become effective in 1853, when West Virginia was still part of Virginia. The exact extent of citizen compliance is difficult to estimate, but professional genealogists know that many births and deaths were not registered. Oddly enough, a property owner was more likely to register the birth of a slave than the birth of his child since registering a slave was a protection of personal property rights. Sometimes a couple registered one or more children but not all. No doubt the difficulty of traveling long distances over rough terrain had something to do with it.

Of course, even when early vital records are not complete, you should examine them. And of course, a genealogist is not limited to vital records alone for birth and death information. A natural beginning place for research is a survey of the available family records. Family Bibles, family record books, journals, diaries, and letters often include births and deaths of family members. (For an illuminating discussion of the many possible sources of birth information found in an average family, see Chapter 1, "Home Sources.")

During the period when civil authorities did not require vital records, births and deaths were regularly recorded in the family Bible among literate, religious families. These entries often supply the only complete birth and death dates for individuals who were born or died prior to this century, although other forms of family records sometimes contain mention of births and deaths as they occurred. Various groups of the Daughters of the American Revolution have compiled many volumes of family Bible records, frequently including an evaluation of the accuracy and authenticity of the record. The DAR collections are available at the DAR Library in Washington, D.C., and in libraries of state and local DAR groups throughout the nation. (See Appendix E, "Special Libraries." The Genealogical Society of Utah has microfilmed the DAR main collection and many state publications, available through its branch libraries. Brigham Young University Library in Provo, Utah, is indexing every name in the DAR Bible records and diaries for the South. Eventually, this index will be online through computer terminals in major libraries.

Other government or legal documents also contain birth and death information: New England town records, coroners' reports, probate records, land records, mortality schedules, and military records, among others. Other chapters discuss these sources, including family records; thus, their discussion in this chapter will be limited.

Coroners' reports are issued when an inquest is held to investigate unusual or unknown circumstances related to a death. When the inquest is complete, the report includes the causes of death, the autopsy findings, where held, testimony about the circumstances existing at the time of the death, and the findings of the coroner's jury. Coroners' reports are public records available for use by the researcher and may be requested from the state, county, or city coroner's office. Not all deaths of unknown or suspicious nature result in a coroner's inquest; but when there is evidence that an ancestor died in an unusual manner or was murdered, the coroner's records should be examined. There are medical examiners, as coroners are more frequently called today, on city, county, and state levels, and the records may be found on all three levels. (See Chapter 9, "Institutional Records".)

Probate records can also contain birth and death information. The exact date of death may be listed for the individual whose estate is in probate and the names and birthdates of his minor heirs may also be found in the record. These records are usually found in the county probate court or the court having probate jurisdiction in a town or county. They are also public records and are available to the genealogist upon request to the probate clerk. (See Chapter 6, "Court Records.")

Court minutes seem to be a catch-all for miscellaneous items recorded to give them public credibility. For example, John Wills, clerk of the Council for West Jersey, an administrative court, entered a complete list of his brothers and sisters followed by his own children at the end of his minute book, vol. 3 (18 April 1712-6 Feb. 1721/22), just before the index. (See Figure 2-2.) In this way, Clerk Wills made his family vital records a matter of public record.

Occasionally, land and property records contain birth and death information. Sometimes the death date of a person leaving property to heirs appears in a deed executed after his or her death. Birth information is sometimes included in applications for public lands or homesteads filed with the federal government. (See Chapter 7, "Land and Tax Records.")

Mortality schedules were included as part of the decennial (every ten years) census enumerations between 1850 and 1900. These schedules give the name, age, sex, color, occupation, birthplace, month and year of death, cause of death, number of days ill, the attending physician, and other details for persons who died within the year prior to the taking of the census. The 1890 and 1900 mortality schedules were destroyed. To locate those still in existence, see Chapter 4, "Census Records." The Genealogical Society of Utah microfilmed a large number of mortality schedules, available at its Salt Lake City library and at its branch libraries throughout the country.

Military pension files also contain valuable birth and death records. The date and place of birth of the veteran, the birth dates of his children, and the birthdate and birthplace of the veteran and his widow if she received a pension are included in the file in some cases. (See Chapter 8, "Military Records.")

Birth and death records are also found in church records, like parish registers which list christenings, burials, births, and deaths. Some churches took special church census enumerations which are of use to the researcher. Ministers and evangelists kept vital records for their members in personal journals and diaries. Some churches have also established historical societies or departments to collect and maintain official church membership records. The headquarters of the affiliate churches ordinarily maintains the records, but some may be found in local church offices. The researcher should inquire at the local church about the existence and location of the records of interest. (See Chapter 5, "Church Records in the United States.") Personal records for ministers or other church officials can be found by consulting the National Union Catalog of Manuscript Collections (NUCMC). See Chapter 11 for more information on indexes.

Private sources, such as newspapers, morticians' records, hospital and doctor records, business and employment records, and local published histories also contain birth and death information. These records are also discussed in detail in other chapters.

Contents of Birth Records

Early birth records gave little information beyond the name of the child, date and place of birth, and parents' names. Some localities listed only the name of the father. This was particularly true in the early New England town and church records as this example from the town records of Simsbury, Connecticut, shows.

SIMSBURY RECORDS. 119

James the firft Son of James Tullar was Born the firft Day of January A : D : 1737/8

Eli Tullar Son of James Tullar was Born the : 14th Day of february A : D : 1740/41 :

[226] Jerufha the Daughter of Return Holcomb was Born aprill the : 3 : anno : Dom : 1734 :

Stephen the Sone of Return Holcomb was born September the : 23 : A : D : 1736 :

Timothy Cafe the Son of Richard Cafe was born the 2nd Day of February A : D 1759.

Lucy the Daughter of Gillet Adams was born feb : 14th A : D : 1731/2 :

Anne Granger the Daughter of George Granger was born July the : 19th : 1732 :

Rhoda the Daughter of George Grainger was born Aprill : 26th A : D : 1735 :

Simsbury Connecticut Birth, Marriage and Deaths (Hartford: Albert C. Bates, 1898), p. 119.

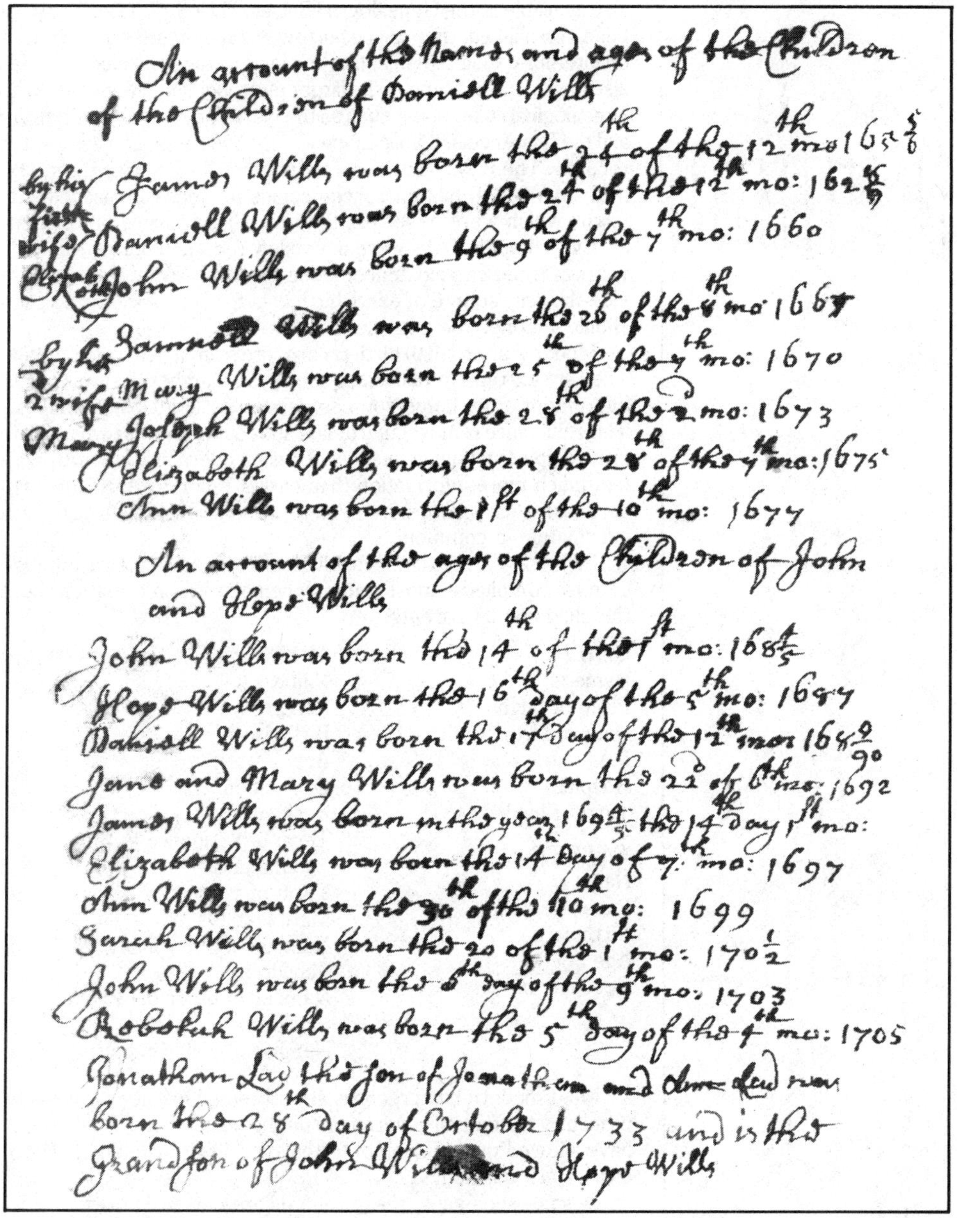

An account of the Names and ages of the Children
of the Children of Daniell Wills
by his first wife — James Wills was born the 24th of the 12 mo 1655/6
Daniell Wills was born the 24th of the 12 mo: 1658/9
Elizabeth — John Wills was born the 9th of the 7th mo: 1660
Samuell Wills was born the 20th of the 8th mo: 1668
by his 2 wife Mary — Mary Wills was born the 5th of the 7th mo: 1670
Joseph Wills was born the 28th of the 2 mo: 1673
Elizabeth Wills was born the 28th of the 7th mo: 1675
Ann Wills was born the 1st of the 10th mo: 1677
An account of the ages of the Children of John
and Hope Wills
John Wills was born the 14th of the 1st mo: 1684/5
Hope Wills was born the 16th day of the 5th mo: 1687
Daniell Wills was born the 17th day of the 12th mo: 1689/90
Jane and Mary Wills was born the 22d of 6th mo: 1692
James Wills was born in the year 1694/5 the 14th day 1st mo:
Elizabeth Wills was born the 14 Day of 7th mo: 1697
Ann Wills was born the 30th of the 10 mo: 1699
Sarah Wills was born the 20 of the 1st mo: 1701/2
John Wills was born the 6th day of the 9th mo: 1703
Rebekah Wills was born the 5th day of the 4th mo: 1705
Jonathan Lad the son of Jonathan and Ann Lad was
born the 28th day of October 1733 and is the
Grandson of John Wills and Hope Wills

Figure 2-2. Listing of John Wills's Siblings and Children in Minutes of the Council of West Jersey, vol. 3, 18 April 1712-6, Feb. 1721-22 following page 138; Rutgers University Library, New Brunswick, NJ 08903; Genealogical Society of Utah (hereafter GS) microfilm 888,812.

Early birth records are also distressingly sparse, with a heavy concentration found in New England only. Church records from the colonial period that can serve as birth records were kept in Pennsylvania, New York, New Jersey, and Virginia, with Virginia trailing far behind the others. The Quaker records for all of the states mentioned above are far superior to most others, providing the exact dates of birth and death of its members. They have been well preserved. Many are included in Willard Wade Hinshaw, *Encyclopedia of American Quaker Genealogy,* 7 vols. (Baltimore: Genealogical Publishing Co., 1969), available in most genealogical libraries in this country. Willard Heiss has expanded coverage for Indiana with seven additional volumes of Quaker entries. These books are also widely available.

By the mid-nineteenth century, birth records in the United States began to include more detailed information. Figure 2-3 is from the birth register of Kanawha County, West Virginia. All Virginia and West Virginia counties used this format beginning in 1853. Some entries in these registers list the mother's maiden name instead of her married name, obviously helpful information in identifying the maternal ancestry of the child.

Early birth records can be obtained from the town or county clerk in the area in which an ancestor was born. These records, too early to fall under the jurisdiction of recent privacy laws, are public records. However, when writing for a birth or death record, state your relationship to the ancestor of interest in case the clerk requires it. Letters should ask for the specific record desired, give the ancestor's full name, and provide as much identifying information as possible, especially when the ancestor has a common surname. The exact birthdate if known or an estimated five-year birth period if not known would be especially valuable. The average fee for birth or death records at the county level is $3. Send this fee with your request. If additional funds are required, the clerk will either request the balance in advance or send the material and ask you to forward the balance. Most jurisdictions will search their records for a five-year period, but few will search further unless specifically requested.

The Genealogical Society of Utah has microfilmed birth records of thousands of towns and counties throughout the United States, concentrating heavily upon the states east of the Mississippi River. These films are available at the Salt Lake City library and upon request through their various branch libraries. (See Appendix D for addresses.) The printed vital records of New England towns are

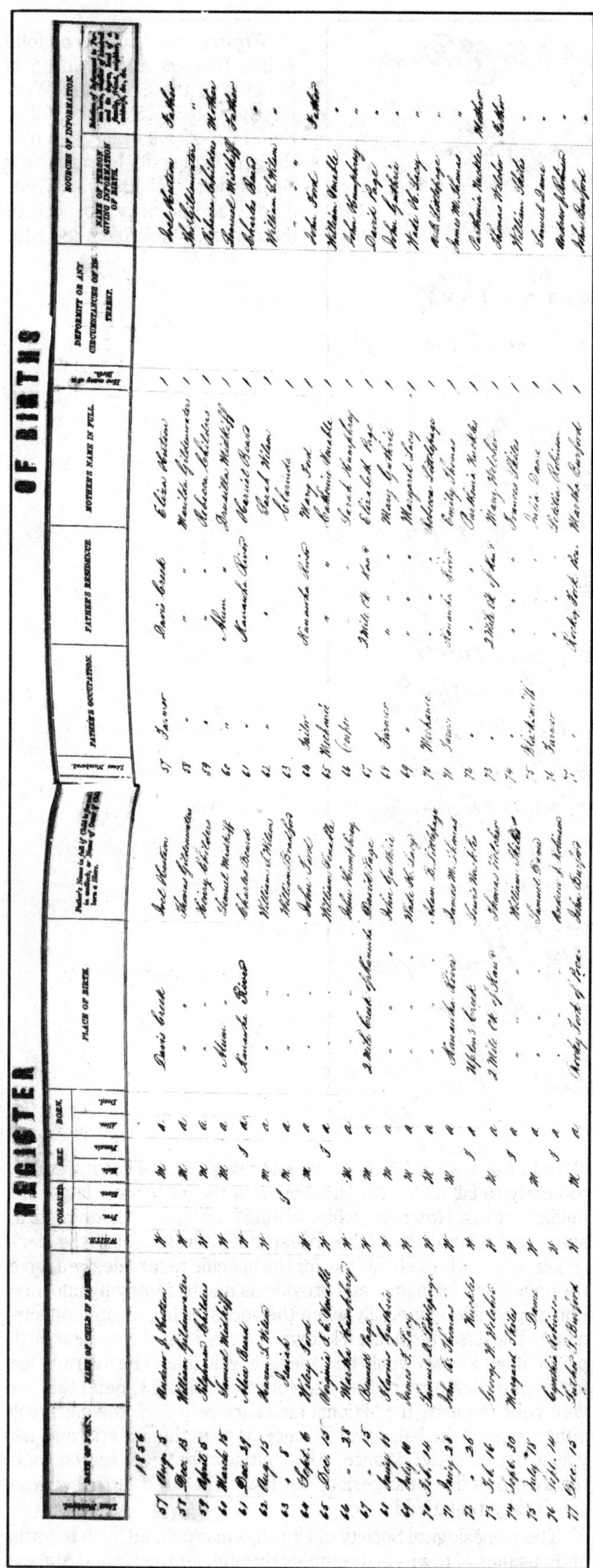
REGISTER OF BIRTHS

Figure 2-3. Register of Births, Kanawha County, West Virginia, 1856; GS 521,891.

also available at the Genealogical Society library. Where they have been microfilmed, they can be borrowed through the branch libraries on interlibrary loan. Many state and local historical society libraries also have copies. Some of the larger metropolitan city libraries with genealogical collections, such as the New York City Public Library and the Los Angeles Public Library, also have copies of these printed records. The Holbrook Research Institute, 57 Locust Street, Oxford, MA 01540 has microfiche copies for those Massachusetts towns which were never printed; price list available on request.

Even though births were not widely recorded during the early years of America's existence, those records in existence may provide the only source of exact birth data for your ancestors. They should routinely be searched.

Modern (after 1910) birth records are maintained by the states. They are extremely valuable; but many researchers, learning birth information from home sources, fail to obtain a birth certificate. This reluctance is most unfortunate and could result in an inaccurate or incomplete family genealogy. These modern birth records contain much more information than earlier records. Although birth certificates vary from state to state, most certificates share much information in common.

Figure 2-4 is my sister's birth certificate – fairly representative of those compiled in most states. It contains this information about the child and its parents:

CHILD
Name
Place of birth
Date of birth
Sex
Hospital
Time of birth

FATHER
Name
Race
Birthplace
Age
Occupation

MOTHER
Name
Race
Birthplace
Age
Occupation
Residence
Term or residence in the community
Term of pregnancy
Marital status
Number of other living children
Number of other deceased children
Number of children born dead

Most modern birth records are protected by the privacy laws passed by the federal government during recent years. Some states have allowed microfilming of births after illegitimate and stillborn entries are masked.

Despite such gaps, these records are obviously useful. Most states require you to complete a request form before they will issue the birth certificate. These forms often ask for more information than you have, but you should fill it out as completely as possible, estimating dates and places as accurately as you can. Some states will search more than a five-year period, while others limit their search to the single year of approximated birth. If the researcher cannot find the record in the year listed, a few states refund the fee. Most do not. Each request should state your relationship to the individual and the purposes for which you will use data. Family history and genealogical research purposes are acceptable reasons in most states. For state addresses, see "Where to Write for Public Records" in Appendix F.

A rarely used form of birth record is the delayed birth certificate. When Social Security benefits were instituted in 1937, individuals claiming benefits had to document their births even if their states had not required birth registration. The 1880 and 1900 federal census enumerations were partially or fully indexed to help provide this documentation. Another method was to file evidence as part of an application for a delayed birth certificate. Figures 2-5 and 2-6 show a petition and delayed certificate from Lake County, Florida. They are representative of the types of records maintained by other states.

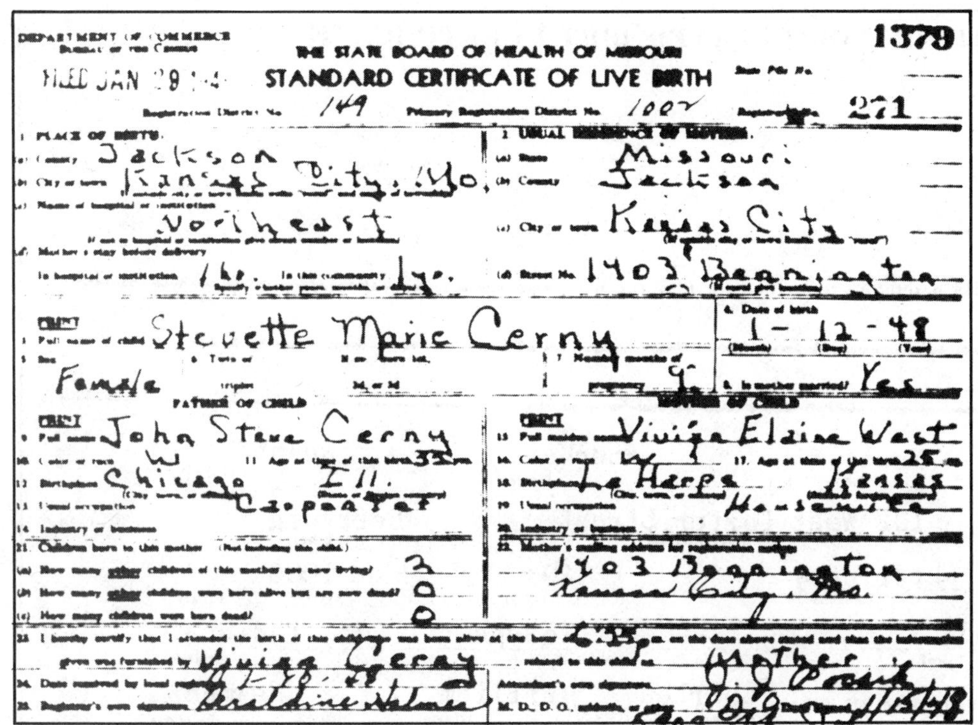
THE STATE BOARD OF HEALTH OF MISSOURI

STANDARD CERTIFICATE OF LIVE BIRTH

1379

FILED JAN 29 1948

Registration District No. 149 Primary Registration District No. 1007 Registrar's No. 271

1. PLACE OF BIRTH: (a) County Jackson (b) City or town Kansas City, Mo. (c) Name of hospital or institution Northeast

2. USUAL RESIDENCE OF MOTHER: (a) State Missouri (b) County Jackson (c) City or town Kansas City (d) Street No. 1403 Bennington

3. Full name of child Stevette Marie Cerny

4. Date of birth 1 - 12 - 48 (Month) (Day) (Year)

5. Sex Female

Is mother married? Yes

FATHER OF CHILD

9. Full name John Steve Cerny

10. Color or race W 11. Age at time of this birth 35 yrs.

12. Birthplace Chicago Ill.

13. Usual occupation Carpenter

MOTHER OF CHILD

15. Full maiden name Vivian Elaine West

16. Color or race W 17. Age at time of this birth 25 yrs.

18. Birthplace La Harpe Kansas

19. Usual occupation Housewife

21. Children born to this mother (Not including this child.)

(a) How many other children of this mother are now living? 3

(b) How many other children were born alive but are now dead? 0

(c) How many children were born dead? 0

22. Mother's mailing address for registration notice: 1403 Bennington, Kansas City, Mo.

23. I hereby certify that I attended the birth of this child who was born alive at the hour 6:35 p.m. on the date above stated and that the information given was furnished by Vivian Cerny related to this child Mother

24. Date received by local registrar 1-23-48

25. Registrar's own signature Bertha ... Holmes

Attendant's own signature J. J. ...

Figure 2-4. Birth Certificate of Stevette Marie Cerny, 12 Jan. 1948, Kansas City, Jackson County, Missouri; copy in possession of the author, Box 417, Salt Lake City, Utah 84110

The individual applying had to submit a petition to the county court stating his/her name, address, birthdate, birthplace; father's name, race, and birthplace; and evidence to support the facts presented. The evidence could be in the form of a baptismal certificate, Bible record, school record, affidavit from the attending physician or midwife, application for an insurance policy, birth certificate of a child, copy of an application for a Social Security account number, or an affidavit from a person having definite knowledge of the facts.

The delayed birth certificate lists vital information abstracted from the supporting evidence. Most states have delayed birth records, some of which are indexed and easily usable. Some delayed birth records have been filed for individuals born as early as 1840. These records are usually filed in the county where the individual applied and not in the county of birth. Though comparatively infrequent, these records provide information about the individual and his/her parents when vital records were not widely kept. The records and testimony used as supporting evidence for the document will lead you to other information sources and also show which relatives were living at the time the certificate was applied for.

Another problem is the family in transition when a baby is born. The family waits just long enough for the mother to recover and then moves to an adjoining town or state where the baby's birth is recorded. In such cases, if you move back in time from the known to the unknown, you will know where the birth was recorded when you may know nothing of where the birth occurred. So check the obvious. See if the birth is recorded after the fact. The resulting document will give you the actual place of birth and you can then make searches there also.

Contents of Death Records

Early death records in the United States provide little more than the name of the deceased, the death date, and the place of death. Burial records contain basically the same information. Occasionally the record will list the name of the spouse of the deceased. These early records appear in town, county, and church records, most extensively in New England where they were kept as late as 1900.

Death records of the nineteenth century are more detailed in many jurisdictions. They often include the name of the deceased, death date, place of death, cause of death, age at the time of death, place of birth, names of parents, place of birth, occupation, name of spouse, name of the person giving the information, and the informant's relationship to the deceased. Race is listed in some records. Some Southern states also note if the deceased was a slave. For example, in Figure 2-7, the published death records of Pulaski County, Virginia, the (S) behind the name of the deceased indicates "slave."

Modern (since 1910) death records, though comparatively recent, are steadily increasing in value. People are living longer, and death records often complete information lacking in the birth record gap between 1885 and 1915 because they provide information about birth as well as death.

Modern death certificates have not been standardized in the United States; but like birth certificates, they basically contain the same types of information. Figure 2-8, a death certificate from Oklahoma, is representative of most modern death certificates. It includes the deceased's name, sex, race, date of death, age at the time of death, place of death, date of birth, place of birth, marital status, name of spouse, Social Security number, occupation, residence, father's name, mother's name, cause of death, and place of burial. Records from other states generally provide the birthplace of the decedent's parents. The Social Security number is not always provided; but when it is, it can be invaluable. Other records, subject to right-of-privacy laws, are accessible if you have the Social Security number.

As any experienced researcher knows, death records are only as accurate as the knowledge of the person providing the information. Many informants will not know the names and/or birthplaces of parents or be fuzzy about birthdates and birthplaces. You should always try to find additional information about parents, birthdates, and birthplaces whenever possible.

Some states will send you a photocopy of the certificate filed at the time of death; some make a transcript of the basic information on a preprinted form, certify it as a true copy, and mail that to you. I strongly suggest that you request a photocopy. Not only does it eliminate the danger of errors in transcription, but it will also give you more data. The clues of cemetery, undertaker, informant, residence at time of death, and other details which take you from the death certificate to other records are found only on the original.

PETITION FOR DELAYED BIRTH CERTIFICATE

In the County Judge's Court,
State of Florida,
County of Lake

County Judge's
File Number 101

Petitioner respectfully says that:

No birth certificate has heretofore been filed for him (or her) ~~and as evidence thereof, petitioner has attached hereto an official statement to that effect from the official custodian of the birth records of the State of ...., being the State of his (or her) birth.~~

Petitioner's full name is Neal (First) Eberhart (Middle) Newman (Last)

His (or her) residence is 102 West Dozier, Street (Street Address) Leesburg (City), Florida

He (or she) was born on February (Month) 20 (Day) 1886 (Year)

at South Bend (City or Town) St. Joseph (County) Indiana (State)

That petitioner's father's name was (or is) Charles (First) William (Middle) Newman (Last)

color or race of father white birthplace of father Clyde, Ohio

maiden name of mother Sylvia (First) Bell (Middle) Eberhart (Last)

color or race of mother white, birthplace of mother Mishawaka, Indiana

and petitioner prays that an order be entered by this court, certifying such facts.

(Signature) Neal Eberhart Newman

If not signed by petitioner,
state relationship to petitioner

Subscribed and sworn to before me this 15th day of November, 1943

(Signed) Marie Lane

(Official Title)

(Seal)

As corroboration of the petitioner's sworn statement of the facts of birth, there may be presented:

Baptismal Certificate
Family Bible.
School Record.
Application for Insurance Policy.
Affidavit from the Attending Physician or Midwife.
Application for Marriage License.
Birth Certificate of Petitioner's Child.
Copy of Application for Social Security Account Number.
Affidavit from Person Having Definite Knowledge of the Facts.

842904

Figure 2-5. Petition for Delayed Birth Certificate of Neal Eberhart Newman, filed 15 Nov. 1943, Lake County, Florida.

DELAYED BIRTH CERTIFICATE

In the County Judge's Court,
State of Florida

State File No.

County of Lake

County Judge's File Number 101

THIS IS TO CERTIFY THAT: It has been made to appear to me that

Neal (First Name) Eberhart (Middle Name) Newman (Last Name) was born on

February (Month) 20 (Day) 1886 (Year)

at South Bend (City or Town) St. Joseph (County) Indiana (State)

to Charles William Newman (Full Name of Father) White (Color or Race)

who was born at Clyde, Ohio (Father's Birthplace) and

Sylvia Bell Eberhart (Full maiden name of Mother) White (Color or Race)

who was born at Mishawaka, Indiana (Mother's Birthplace)

Margin Reserved for Binding

Write on Typewriter, using ... Stamped Signature of Judge Not Acceptable.

Evidence that no birth certificate has heretofore been filed for this person was presented in the form of an affidavit ~~official statement~~ to that effect ~~from the official custodian of the birth records of the State of~~

ABSTRACT OF SUPPORTING EVIDENCE

Affidavit of Mother and older sister show the date and place of birth and parentage as above.

Birth Certificate of applicant's child shows date and place of birth as above.

Application for Fidelity Mutual Life Insurance policy #531253 issued October 8, 1935, shows date and place of birth as above.

...gin Reserved

Given under my hand and seal, at Tavares, Lake County, Florida,

this 16 day of November, 1943.

(Seal)

(Signature) [signature]

County Judge of Lake County.

Figure 2-6. Delayed Birth Certificate of Neal Eberhart Newman, filed 16 Nov. 1943, Tavares, Lake County, Florida

Page 7

	DATE	NAME	SEX	FATHER OR SLAVE OWNER	PLACE	DISEASE OR CAUSE	AGE	BIRTH	OCCUPATION	CONSORT OF OR UNMARRIED	PERSON GIVING INF. OF DEATH
1858											
1.	Mar	NOT NAMED	F	Malvina Hinkle	Pulaski	Cold	2	Mont.			Phebe Hinkle, aunt
2.	Jun	NOT NAMED (S)	F	James Hoge	"	Unknown	3	Pulaski			J. Hoge, master
3.	7-22	SARAH J. HARROLD	F	M. & S. Harrold	"	Scarlet Fever	3-10	"			M. Harrold, father
4.	9-17	CHARLOTTE E. HOGE	F	J. & C. Trollinger	"	Unknown	23	"		J.H. Hoge	J.H. Hoge, husband
5.	12-25	MARY (S)	F	William Hoge	"	Pnumonia	20				Wm. Hoge, master
6.	Oct	LUCINDA HILL	F	A. & S. Odell	"	Consumption	35	"		Harvey Hill	H. Hill, husband
7.	Aug	JOHN H. HILL	M	H. & L. Hill	"	Diarria	11	"			H. Hill, father
8.	Feb	PETER (S)	M	James H. Hoge	"	Old Age	70	"			J.H. Hoge, master
9.	12-22	JAMES S. HOWARD	M	J.D. & A. Howard	"	Dropsey of Heart	13-01-18	"			J.D. Howard, father
10.	4-15	JAMES M. HOLMES	M		"		1-02	"			W. Miller, neighbor
11.	Mar	HARRISON (S)	M	Joseph Graham	"		4				J. Graham, master
12.	Feb	HARRIET (S)	F	Harvey Shepherd	"	Scarlet Fever					H. Shepherd, "
13.	Oct	NOT NAMED (S)	F	Elizabeth Kent	"	Not Known	18				E. Kent, mistress
14.	8-8	MARY F. LITTLE	F	S. & A. Little	"	Scarlet Fever	3-01-25	"			S. Little, father
15.	8-11	WALTER C. LITTLE	M	"	"	"	6-15	"			" "
16.	Oct	NOT NAMED (S)	F	F.A. Morgan	"	Unknown	6	"			Mrs. Morgan, mistress
17.	Oct	NOT NAMED (S)	F	"	"	"	3	"			" "
18.	4-5	SARAH E. MARTIN	F	W. & M. Martin	"	"	3	"			M. Martin, mother
19.	2-22	WILLIAM MARTIN	M	G. & M. Martin	"	Old Age	84	"			Mrs. Shepherd, daughter
20.	12-31	DOLLY ODEL	F	R. & S. Day	"	Unknown	35-06	"		Abram Odel	A. Odel, husband
21.	12-23	RICHARD (S)	M	James M. Pierce	"	Smothered	5	"			Mrs. Pierce, mistress
22.	Jan	BALLARD QUESENBERRY	M	Crockett E. Quesenberry	"	Fever	5	"			C. Quesenberry, father
23.	Feb	MARINDA QUESENBERRY	F	"	"	"	8	"			" "
24.	12-7	JOHN SUTTON	M	Unknown	"	"	64	"	Farmer	Eliz. Sutton	E. Sutton, wife
25.	Mar	ALEX (S)	M	H. Shepherd	"	"	10				H. Shepherd, master
26.	6-24	THOMAS THORTON	M		"	Cholic	54-06	"		Reb. Thorton	R. Thorton, wife
27.		REBECCA THORTON	F		"	Old Age	70	"			" daugh.-in-l
28.	Aug	ELIZABETH VICKERS	F	H. & S. Vickers	"	Scarlet Fever	1-06	"			H. Vickers, father
29.	6-20	JOHN W. WALLACE	M	C. & N. Wallace	"	Unknown	20-11	"			C. Wallace, "
30.	10-1	FRANCIS (S)	F	Edwin Watson	"	Worms	5	"			E. Watson, master
31.	Sep	PANTINA (S)	F	John Wygal	"	Unknown	2	"			J. Wygal, "
32.	Dec	GEORGE W. (S)	M	"	"	Cold	1-06	"			" "
33.	2-5	NOT NAMED	F	J. & M.S. Wygal	"	Infant Cholery	5	"			" father
1859											
34.	6-15	GRAHAM C. ALLISON	M	Wm. & M.A. Allison	"	Typhoid Fever	1-03	"			W. Allison, father
35.	3-23	NOT NAMED	F	F. & M.A. Akers	"	Jaundice	21	"			F. Akers, "
36.	6-13	HETTY ANDERSON	F	J. & E. Carper	"	Infl. Stomach	51-03	"	Housekeeper	Wm. Anderson	W. Anderson, husband
37.	Mar	CHARLES (S)	M	Francis Allison	"	Choaked	3	"			F. Allison, master
38.	Nov	CHARITY (S)	F	"	"	Cold	35				" "
39.	Sep	EASTER (S)	F	"	"	Palsey	40				" "
40.	Jul	WILLIAM (S)	M	Thurman Bullard	"	Whooping Cough	1-01	"			T. Bullard, "
41.	Apr	CAROLINE (S)	F	Chester Bullard	"	Unknown	15				C. Bullard, "
42.	Jun	SARAH (S)	F	"	"	Whooping Cough	2				" "
43.	6-31	NOT NAMED	M	J. & S. Black	"	Unknown	1-15				J. Black, father
44.		REBECCA CARPER	F	I. & H. Carper	"	Cramp	7				I. Carper, "
45.	5-10	JOSEPH W. COCKE	M	T. & M. Cocke	"	Infl. Brain	2-06-21	Mont.			T. Cocke, "
46.	May	GEORGE W. (S)	M	Sebastian W. Cecil	"	Hives	1				S. Cecil, master
47.	Feb	ANDREW DOBBINS	M	Malvina Dobbins	"	Infl. Brai[n]	3	Pulaski			
48.	1-29	ALICE DRAPER	F	J. & J. Draper	"	Pnumonia	76	Wythe			S. Draper, niece

Figure 2-7. Clarita H. Morgan, *Births and Deaths 1853-1871 on Record in Pulaski County Court House, Pulaski, Virginia* (N.p., n.d.), p. 7.

ATTENDING PHYSICIAN
CERTIFICATE OF DEATH
STATE OF OKLAHOMA - DEPARTMENT OF HEALTH

011047
STATE FILE NO.

LOCAL REGISTRAR'S FILE NO. 138

1. DECEASED - NAME: First Charles, Middle Henry, Last West
2. DATE OF DEATH (Month, Day, Year): May 22, 1978
3. SEX: Male
4. RACE (White, Negro, American Indian, Etc.) (Specify): White
5a. AGE Last Birthday (Years): 91
5b. UNDER 1 YEAR Mos. Days
5c. UNDER 1 DAY Hours Min.
6. DATE OF BIRTH (Month, Day, Year): Febr. 27, 1887
7a. COUNTY OF DEATH: Rogers
7b. CITY, TOWN, OR LOCATION OF DEATH: Claremore
7c. INSIDE CITY LIMITS: XX No
7d. HOSPITAL OR OTHER INSTITUTION - NAME (If not in either, give Street and Number): Claremore Health Center
8. STATE OF BIRTH (If not in U.S.A., Name Country)
9. CITIZEN OF WHAT COUNTRY: USA
10. Married / Never Married / Widowed XX / Divorced
11. SURVIVING SPOUSE (If wife, Give Maiden Name)
12. SOCIAL SECURITY NUMBER: 440-20-1707
13a. USUAL OCCUPATION (Give kind of work done during most of working life, even if retired): Building Contractor
13b. KIND OF BUSINESS OR INDUSTRY: Home Builder
14a. RESIDENCE - STATE: Oklahoma
14b. COUNTY: Rogers
14c. CITY, TOWN, OR LOCATION: Claremore
14d. INSIDE CITY LIMITS: XX No
14e. STREET AND NUMBER: 600 S. Choctaw
15. FATHER - NAME: First William, Middle Andrew, Last West
16. MOTHER - MAIDEN NAME: First Laura, Middle, Last Stewart
17a. INFORMANT - NAME
17b. MAILING ADDRESS (Street or R. F. D. No., City or Town, State, Zip)

MEDICAL CERTIFICATION

PART I. DEATH WAS CAUSED BY: (Enter only one cause per line for (a), (b), and (c).) — Approximate Interval Between onset and Death

18. CAUSE OF DEATH — Condition if any, which gave rise to immediate cause(s), stating the underlying cause last
IMMEDIATE CAUSE
(a) Myocardial Infraction Acute
DUE TO OR AS A CONSEQUENCE OF:
(b)
DUE TO OR AS A CONSEQUENCE OF:
(c)

PART II. OTHER SIGNIFICANT CONDITIONS: (Conditions contributing to death but not related to cause given in part 1 (a))
19a. AUTOPSY Yes No
19b. IF YES, Were findings considered in determining cause of death. Yes No

Notice to attending physician: Do not sign this certificate unless you are the physician who attended the deceased for **a natural illness—unrelated to injury or poisoning—to** which the patient has apparently succumbed, provided that death did not occur while deceased was in penal incarceration or during a therapeutic procedure in which death was not reasonably medically expected. For enumeration of deaths subject to investigation and certification by **Medical Examiner**, refer to O.S. Title 63, Sec. 938, or contact office of Chief Medical Examiner in Oklahoma City.

20a. CERTIFICATION - PHYSICIAN: I attended the deceased from 3-15-78 to 5-22-78
20b. And Last saw him/her alive on: 5-22-78
20c. I did/did not view body after death: did
20d. DEATH OCCURRED at 17:30 M at the place, on the date stated, and to the best of my knowledge, due to the cause(s) stated
21a. CERTIFIER - NAME (Type or Print): M. E. Gordon, M. D.
21b. SIGNATURE OF CERTIFIER: [signature]
21c. DATE SIGNED (Month, Day, Year): 5-23-78
21d. MAILING ADDRESS - CERTIFIER: P. O. Box 669, Claremore, Oklahoma 74017
22a. THE DECEDENT was pronounced dead on: 5-22-78
22b. AT 17:30 M
23a. BURIAL, CREMATION, REMOVAL (Specify): Burial
23b. DATE: May 25, 1978
23c. CEMETERY OR CREMATORY - NAME: Welch Cemetery
23d. LOCATION (Crematory or Cemetery) City State: Welch, Oklahoma
24a. FUNERAL HOME - NAME AND ADDRESS (Street or R.F.D. No., City or Town, State, Zip): Claremore Funeral Home, Inc.
24b. FUNERAL DIRECTOR: George F. Raper
25a. LOCAL REGISTRAR SIGNATURE: Claude Johnson, by [signature] Stratton, Dy.
25b. DATE RECD. BY LOCAL REG.: 5-24-78
26. DATE RECEIVED BY STATE REGISTRAR: MAY 25 1978

1907

State Department of Health
State of Oklahoma
OKLAHOMA CITY, OKLAHOMA 73152

ROGER C. PIRRONG
STATE REGISTRAR OF VITAL STATISTICS

CERTIFIED COPY MUST HAVE EMBOSSED SEAL

I hereby certify the foregoing to be a true and correct copy, original of which is on file in this office. In testimony whereof, I have hereunto subscribed my name and caused the official seal to be affixed, at Oklahoma City, Oklahoma, this date.

JAN. 24, 1980

Figure 2-8. Certificate of Death of Charles Henry West, Oklahoma, 22 May 1978, File number 011047; certified copy owned by author, Box 417, Salt Lake City, Utah 84110.

Here's an example. When genealogist Harry L. Carle first requested the death certificate of his grandfather, Harry Chester Lee, he requested a certification of death abstracted from the death register.

STATE OF IOWA. COUNTY REGISTRAR
Vital Statistics

County of Franklin

CERTIFICATION OF DEATH

NAME OF DECEASED Harry Chester Lee Sex Male

Date of Death November 10, 19 40. Place of Death Hampton, Iowa

Date of Birth or Age of Deceased 57 years Date Filed November 1940

Cause of Death Coronary heart disease

I HEREBY CERTIFY that the above information was taken from the Record of Death on file in this office in accordance with the law of Iowa requiring filing of vital records. Recorded in Book 4 Page "L"

Date March 12, 1975 Helen O'Dea
County Registrar and Clerk of District Court

(SEAL) By Carole Dahlman
Deputy Clerk

Certification of Death of Harry Chester Lee, 10 Nov. 1940, Franklin, Iowa; in possession of Harry L. Carle, 8035 168th S.W., Edmonds, WA 98020. This and the subsequent documents are used with permission.

Harry received this certification with a speed message form requesting payment. (See Figure 2-9.) He sent them a check and a request for the original certificate explaining what information he was looking for. Note that it did not need to be certified ("sealed"). The court clerk answered:

HELEN O DEA

Our records do not list all the information you requested. The only additional information we have for Mr. Lee is that the physician was L. E. Hedgecock and the Undertaker was Ray A. Fox

Perhaps the Dept. of Vital Statis tics in Des Moines has it more complete for that year. The address is:

Records & Statistics Div.
Iowa State Dept. of Health
Lucas State Office Building
Des Moines, Iowa 50319

Helen O'Dea
CLERK OF DISTRICT COURT
HAMPTON, IOWA 50441

Note from Helen O'Dea, Clerk of District Court, Hampton, Iowa, to Harry L. Carle.

REORDER MULTISNAP 857-11/5 REPLI-MEMO
TELL IT — VERIFY IT

INSTRUCTIONS TO SENDER: 1. KEEP YELLOW COPY 2. SEND WHITE AND PINK PARTS WITH CARBON TO PERSON ADDRESSED

INSTRUCTIONS TO ADDRESSEE: 1. WRITE REPLY AT BOTTOM 2. DETACH STUB, RETAIN WHITE COPY AND RETURN PINK COPY TO SENDER

To: Harry L. Carle
8035-186th S.W.
Edmonds, Washington 98020

From: FRANKLIN COUNTY
CLERK OF THE DISTRICT COURT
HELEN O'DEA
P. O. BOX 28
HAMPTON, IOWA 50441

SUBJECT: Death certificate — DATE: March 12, 1975 — DEPARTMENT

MESSAGE

Enclosed is the death certificate you requested. The cost of this certificate is $2.00. Please remit this amount to our office as soon as possible. Thank you -

SIGNED Carole Dahlman
Deputy

REPLY — DATE OF REPLY: 17 March 1975

Enclosed is my $2 check and returned Certification of Death (Bk 4, p-L) for Harry Chester Lee, died 10 Nov 1940.

What I need for family records is a copy of the original or complete certificate showing name of physician, mortician, burial, informant and historical vitals. Can you supply that, or similar information? It need not be sealed.

DEPARTMENT — SIGNED Harry L. Carle

ADDRESSEE'S COPY

Figure 2-9. Speed Message between Carole Dahlman, deputy clerk, and Harry L. Carle, 12 and 17 March 1975, original in possession of Harry L. Carle.

When Harry pursued his request to the Des Moines office, he received a photocopy of the original certificate filed with the state. (Figure 2-10.) It was obviously worth the extra correspondence to get this certificate. From it, Harry discovered that Harry Lee had lived in Hampton only six years before his death, that his wife, Sylvia Smith Lee, the informant, was fifty-six years old, that Harry had been born in Chicago, and that he had been a stage worker. It also gave his parents' names and birthplaces, the date and place of burial, the attending physicians' names, and the fact that Harry Lee had suffered from heart disease for about five years before it proved fatal.

Death records are valuable corroborating evidence for family traditions handed down generation after generation without verification. They also help distinguish between two or more persons with the same name. For example, one prominent Texas family gave me its personal files and family sources to produce a family history. Their records included a maternal ancestor named Nettie Green married to Robert Michael. Public records produced a Nettie Green who was also married to a Robert Michael. Thinking they were the same Nettie Green, I extended that family line back two hundred years to the immigrant ancestor. The paternal ancestors were less accommodating; and in the process of identifying them, I requested the death certificate of Nettie's husband. It clearly stated that he had married Nettie Bunting. Furthermore, Robert Albert Michael had always used his middle name. His descendants did not even know that he had a different given name. The marriage records supported the death record—Nettie Bunting was indeed the ancestor—and we bade farewell to two hundred years of the Green family.

Death records, both early and modern, can help you identify others related to the decedent. The information provided in the records is usually given to the authorities by a close relative. If the relative is a married daughter, the record will state her married name. Aunts, uncles, in-laws, cousins, and other relatives are listed as the informant on death records. Each new name is a clue to the identity of other ancestors that should be followed up.

The death record informant may not have been the person who provided vital statistics to the funeral director or to the cemetery sexton. Since the death certificate names both the funeral home and the place of burial, you should check both the mortician's records

I HEREBY CERTIFY THAT THIS IS A TRUE AND CORRECT COPY MADE OF THE ORIGINAL CERTIFICATE ON FILE IN THIS OFFICE IN ACCORDANCE WITH THE LAW OF IOWA REQUIRING FILING OF VITAL RECORDS. THIS RECORD IS NOT VALID IF THIS PHOTOCOPY HAS BEEN ALTERED OR IF IT DOES NOT BEAR THE RAISED SEAL OF THE DEPARTMENT OF HEALTH.

Norman L. Pawlewski
NORMAN L. PAWLEWSKI
STATE REGISTRAR

Carson E. Whitlow
CARSON E. WHITLOW, CHIEF
DIVISION OF RECORDS & STATISTICS DATE APR 15 75

DEPARTMENT OF COMMERCE
Bureau of the Census

IOWA STATE DEPARTMENT OF HEALTH
Division of Vital Statistics
Certificate of Death

State Office No. 35-4-139

1. PLACE OF DEATH:
(a) County Franklin Township Washington
(b) City or Town Hampton
(If outside city or town write RURAL NEAR and give town)
(c) Hospital or Institution: Name and Street Address
(d) Length of stay in Hospital or Inst. (yrs., or mos., or days)
In this community (yrs., or mos., or days) 6 years

2. USUAL RESIDENCE (HOME) OF DECEASED:
For newborn infant give residence of mother
(a) State Iowa (b) County Franklin
(c) City or town Hampton
(If outside city or town limits write RURAL NEAR and give town)
(d) Street No.
(If rural give LOCATION)
(e) If foreign born, how long in U. S. A.? years
3. (b) IF VETERAN, NAME WAR

3. (a) FULL NAME Harry Chester Lee
3. (c) Social Security Account Number 475-23-3422

4. Sex Male
5. Color or Race White
6. (a) Single, married, widowed or divorced Married
6. (b) Name of husband or wife Sylvia Smith
6. (c) If alive, give age 56 years
7. Birth date of deceased (mo., day, yr.) June. 21. 1883
8. Age Years 57 Months 4 Days 19 If less than 1 day hrs. min.
9. Birthplace Chicago, Ill
(Town, county, and state or foreign country)
10. Usual Occupation Stage Worker
11. Industry or business
Father: 12. Name Benjamin Lee
13. Birthplace Peoria, Ill
(City, town or county) (State or foreign country)
Mother: 14. Name B Hinkle
15. Birthplace Glee ford, Ill
(City, town or county) (State or foreign country)
16. (a) Informant's own signature Mrs Sylvia C Lee
(b) Address Hampton, Iowa
17. (a) Burial (b) Date thereof Nov. 13. 40
Burial, cremation, or removal (specify) (Month) (Day) (Year)
(c) Place of burial or cremation Hampton Cemetery
Location Hampton, Iowa
Funeral Director: 18. (a) Signature [signature]
(b) Address Hampton, Ia (c) License No. 2020
Local Registrar: 19. Signature W. T. Wells District 354
Date received Nov. 13 1940 Filed No. 43
Cc. DEC 14 40
(OVER)

MEDICAL CERTIFICATION
20. DATE OF DEATH Nov. 10. 1940 (Month, WRITE OUT) (Day) 19 4/2 P.M. (time)
21. I CERTIFY that death occurred on the date above stated; that I attended deceased from 11/10 1940 to 11/10 1940, and that I saw him alive on 11/10 1940
Immediate cause of death Coronary Heart Disease DURATION 5 yrs?
Due to Hypertension & arteriosclerosis.
Due to
Other conditions
(Include pregnancy within 3 months of death)
OPERATION: Date of
MAJOR FINDINGS: Of operation
Of autopsy
PHYSICIAN Please underline the cause to which the death should be ascribed
22. If death was due to external causes, fill in the following:
ACCIDENT, SUICIDE OR HOMICIDE:
(a) (b) Date of
(Accident, suicide or homicide)
(c) Where did injury occur?
(City or town) (County) (State)
(d) Injured at home, farm, industry, public place (where?)
(e) Injured at work? (Yes or no)
(f) Means of injury
(g) Nature of injury
23. (a) Signature L. E. Hedgecock M.D.
(M. D. or other)
(b) Address Hampton, Iowa
(c) Date signed 11/13/40

Figure 2-10. Certificate of Death of Harry Chester Lee, 15 April 1975, State of Iowa, certified copy owned by Harry L. Carle.

and the sexton's records to confirm the information on the death record and to look for additional information not included in the death certificate. Once you know the exact date of death, you can more easily look for an obituary notice in a local newspaper. Obituaries will usually at least summarize the deceased's life, sometimes including other towns of residence. They may also list all of the living heirs, as well as the names of parents, brothers, and sisters. Tracking backward with these clues, you can look for other members of the family and additional historical information.

In short, you should routinely request birth and death records for ancestors who were born or who died during the period when records are available in that locale. They are rich in genealogical information and may serve to clarify discrepancies in family records.

Problems with Vital Records

Vital records are not without their problems. We have already mentioned the problem of birthdates and places in death records. Many record collections are incomplete, necessitating additional searches in other records to fill the gaps.

Legibility is also a problem in many handwritten records. It may be a good idea to ask for help from someone skilled in reading various types of handwriting when a certificate or register entry is not easily decipherable.

A third problem is that early records may contain a variety of surname spellings—none of them the spelling currently used by branches of the family. Early records clerks, like early census enumerators, spelled people's names as they heard them pronounced. When you are looking for a birth or death record during the earlier periods, consider all possible spellings, especially phonetic spellings, before concluding that no record exists for your ancestor. This is especially important for urban areas where more than one person with the same name is the rule rather than an exception.

A related problem is that records were often indexed many years after they were compiled. The person doing the indexing had to interpret the handwriting in the record just as the researcher must, and his/her skills were not always well developed. The obvious errors in indexes are reading a *T* as an *F*, a *P* as an *R*, and an *L* as an *S*. Take these possibilities into consideration, too, as you try to determine all the possible spellings of a surname.

Additionally, some researchers stop with the index if they can't find their ancestor's name listed. Some indexes have an error rate in excess of 25 percent, meaning that over 25 percent of the individuals in the records were not included in the index. If you know the approximate date of a birth or death, settle down to a page-by-page search before you conclude that your ancestor is not in the records.

One of the real limitations of modern vital records is legally restricted access. Different states regulate in different ways who can have access to vital records and under what circumstances. Some of the new laws attempt to reduce the assumption of a false identity for fraudulent purposes, as, for example, assuming the identity of a deceased person to obtain credit cards to be used for defrauding merchants. Other laws protect the privacy of persons still living. Regardless of the reasons behind such laws, you should find out the laws passed in the states where you will be conducting research. (See the discussion on right-of-privacy laws in the Introduction.)

Finding Aids

There are numerous aids to locating vital records. "Where to Write for Vital Records" (Appendix F) is a good place to begin. Most towns and counties have indexes to birth and death records. Even if they are not complete, they can often facilitate research. Many local historical and genealogical societies have published birth and death records in their periodicals, newsletters, and journals. They too should be examined whenever available. Family members may be able to send photocopies of birth and death records in their possession. It is worth the letter or telephone call to inquire.

Always check for duplicate copies at county, city, town, or state levels. Many counties kept vital records before the state did. Once state registration begins, counties or cities still maintain a register of vital events. In case one set of records is lost or incomplete, you can check the other.

Vital records, despite their comparative modernity, are becoming increasingly useful to the genealogist and will only become more valuable as generations pass. They have limitations and problems, but they can be used effectively to support or disprove existing evidence, to clarify the direction of future research, and to contribute to a more complete genealogy.

Cemetery records and tombstone inscriptions also contain birth and death dates and thus have obvious connections with vital records. The custom of burying the dead in areas set aside for that purpose goes back thousands of years, but the genealogist's interest focuses mainly on historic times in Jewish and Christian communities. The records most commonly found within this group are the church burial registers, sextons' records, cemetery deed and plot registers, burial permit records, grave opening orders, and monument (tombstone) inscriptions.

These records usually supplement standard sources of genealogical information, but sometimes they represent the only information that can be found pertaining to the birth and death of an ancestor. Using these records effectively requires specific knowledge of their content, availability, and location. The Genealogical Institute, under the direction of Arlene H. Eakle, has prepared the most comprehensive work dealing with cemetery records in the United States, *How to Search a Cemetery* (Salt Lake City: The Genealogical Institute, 1974). It has been edited for inclusion in this chapter.

CEMETERY RECORDS

Arlene H. Eakle

Searching cemeteries would repay the extra effort if only for the information they provide about children under the age of twenty-one. In the twentieth century, where the death rate of children runs less than 8 per 1,000 live births, we often fail to realize that the local cemetery may contain the only evidence of some young nineteenth-century lives.

The cemetery is also, sadly enough, sometimes the only real evidence of some women's lives. A woman, hidden in her father's household during her growing years and recorded in pre-1850 censuses as "female 5-10 years of age," may be located under her own name for the first time on her tombstone.

For example, James Bell, born in 1773, was married three times and lost two wives in childbirth. (See Figure 2-11.) His first wife, twenty-five-year-old Sarah, died four hours after giving birth to twins, both of whom survived. His second wife, also named Sarah, died at age seventeen, thirty-five days after giving birth to a namesake daughter who also died thirty-one days later. The third wife, Margaret, died at age sixty-eight. Their son James is buried between his parents in the cemetery of the Old Stone Church in Fort Defiance, Virginia. The family Bible and the cemetery plot are the only records of these women.

Even though colonial stones are often gone or illegible, the surviving stones in a cemetery are an important source for immigrants. Sometimes the only recording of the original surname is on a tombstone, overlooked by a genealogist who was unaware that the family name had been Americanized and thus had missed the original spelling in the alphabetical list. Had the grave plot itself been checked, the person's juxtaposition to known family members would have drawn attention to the difference in the name. The period of time when the largest number of immigrants arrived—1820-1920—coincides with tombstones which have survived.

Types of Cemeteries

The Church Burial Yard

Most churches, until about World War II, were constructed on lots large enough to provide their members with burial facilities. Even old churches in large cities at one time had adjacent burial yards. Some of these still exist; however, the cities grew, memberships increased, real estate values rose, needs for larger burial facilities developed, and burial yards were established in the suburbs while the old plots were used as building sites. Sometimes the graves were moved and sometimes not.

Public or Municipal Cemeteries

Most of the local civil jurisdictions in the United States have some sort of public burial ground. Sometimes they are maintained by the county; however, most of them are village, town, township, or city burial sites. National and state jurisdictions maintain some burial facilities for veterans and their families.

The Family Burial Plot

Still common in rural areas of our country today are family burial grounds. With the enforcement of health codes which require burial permits, the use of licensed morticians, and regulations governing health hazards, such private plots are disappearing. In the nineteenth century or earlier, few rural families did not have a family burial site, usually on the farm first settled by the family in the area. These are the cemeteries most difficult to locate but obviously most valuable for establishing family identity. Today properties on which those cemeteries are located are often in the hands of unrelated persons. Fences are left in disrepair and stones are often overturned, broken, buried, carried away, or otherwise lost. Some are still well preserved and cared for by descendants or local historical societies.

HUSBAND James Bell Esq.
Birth 4 June 1773 Place
Chr. Place
Death 16 Jan 1856 Place
Burial Place Ft. Defiance, Augusta, Va.
Mar. Place
Father Mother

WIFE 1) Sarah of
Birth 1779 Place
Chr. Place
Death 12 Nov 1804 Place
Burial Place Ft. Defiance, Aug. Va.
Father Mother
died at 25 4 hours after birth of twins

Enc # Search # 201 Family Line Bell
Home Institution Township Parish County
Municipal Local ✓ District State National

Personal Papers, Census, Financial, Interview, Family Records, Land, License, Correspondence, Pedigree, Probate, ✓Church, Researcher, History, Court, Employment, ✓Original, Biography, Tax, ✓Cemetery, Trans Copy, MSS Colls, Military, School, Photo Copy, Coat of Arms, Poor Relief, Newspaper, Manuscript, Oral History, Birth, Profession, Printed, Periodical, Marriage, Estate, Extract, Membership, Death, Insurance, ✓Legible, Other, Election, Shipping, Foreign Lang

Old Cemetery, Old Stone Church

DOCUMENT DATED: RECORDED:
Call # Vol. Page Date of Search 4 Mar. 1962

Male or Female	CHILDREN	WHEN BORN Day Mo. Yr.	Buried at: Town	County	State or Country	DIED Day Mo. Yr. Place	MARRIED Date Place To
1	2) wife: Sarah	1779	Ft. Defiance	Aug.	Va.	at 27 13 Dec 1806	35 days after birth of female child
2	female - Sarah Bell	13 Nov 1806	Ft. Defiance	Aug.	Va.	17 Jan 1807	at 66 days
3							
4	3) wife: Margaret	25 Dec 1789	Ft. Defiance	Aug.	Va.	27 Feb 1856	
5	Male - James Bell	1830	Ft. Defiance	Aug.	Va.	29 July 1856	at 26
6							
7							
8							
9							
10							
11	1) 2) and child 3) James James, Esq.						
12							

Figure 2-11. Family Group Sheet of James Bell, Esq., 4 March 1962, in possession of Arlene H. Eakle.

The Commercial Memorial Park

Since World War II, with the development of large, highly transient city populations, a new sort of burial institution has come into being, the commercially owned and operated nonsectarian facility. Few genealogical problems lead to their use at this time.

Types of Records

Written Sources

Entries in the burial registers are chronological as the funerals occurred. If the registrar noted which plot the person was buried in, you can sometimes deduce relationships, a valuable clue since tombstones may have been destroyed or never placed on the grave, women's maiden names are often not recorded, and children may not have been mentioned in previous records.

Church Burial Registers. Churches which have affiliated burial grounds usually maintain records of interments in their burial registers. These records sometimes include the names of other family members, as this register from Killinger's Church shows.[1]

> (62) 1826. Jan.7, Buried Isaac *Lotch*, son of Johannes & Elisabeth Lotch. b. May 20, 1822; bapt. May 10, 1823, by Rev.Hemping. d. Jan. 6, 1826, cause: Gichtern. age: 3 yrs. 8 mos. less 4 days.
>
> Jan.10, Buried Daniel *Deiwler*, in the David's congr. son of Albrecht & Catharina Deiwler. b. Febr. 16, 1771, in Upper Paxton twp.Dauphin county. bapt.by Rev. Mr. Enderlein. married in 1795 to Anna Maria Fissler. They had 11 children, 5 sons & 6 daughters. d. Jan.9,1826, Cause: Hitziges Fieber. age: 54 yrs. 10 mos. 24 days.
>
> Jan.ll, buried in Hoffman's congr. Margaretha *Hoffman*, da.of Johannes & Catharina Herman. b. Nov.7,1753 in Heidelberg twp.Berks county. bapt. & confirmed in Lutheran religion. married Apr. 22, 1772, Johann Nicolaus Hoffman. They had 12 children, 6 sons & 6 daughters. 2 daughters preceded her as also her husband, d. Apr. 28, '14; cause of death: Pilger's Fieber. d. Jan. 9, 1826, survived by 84 grandchildren & 21 great-granchildren. Age: 72 yrs. 2 mos. 2 days.

Finding these registers today presents a problem. They may have been placed in a central church archive or church-affiliated university library;[2] they may have descended through the heirs of the minister or clerk along with other personal effects, or they may be stored in a locked closet or pulpit inside the original meetinghouse. In short, you may have to hunt for them. (See Chapter 5, "Church Records in the United States.")

Sextons' Records. All municipal cemeteries, many large denominational facilities shared by two or more churches in a community, all commercially operated memorial parks, and a few large family burial grounds have offices or official caretakers where you can expect to find a registry of burials called the sexton's book. (See Figure 2-12.) Such records also list the plots available—occupied, owned or unowned—described in sufficient detail for sale and resale. The sexton's record would thus be an accurate record of cemetery deeds and plats.

Cemetery Deeds and Plats. The original cemetery deeds, like the deeds to any real estate, are given to the owner of the plat; however, a recorded copy is retained by the sexton in separate cemetery deed books. Sales, transfers, and bequests of title to this property are duly recorded also. Plats are then prepared for each plot showing the owner of all those buried in that plot. Here is an 1863 example from the Salt Lake City Cemetery:[3]

> This certifies that Edwin Spencer has purchased One half rod of ground in Great Salt Lake Cemetery, known and designated as North Half of Lot 2 in Block 3 in Plat E the payment of which is hereby acknowledged.
>
> And the said Edwin Spencer heirs or assigns are entitled to bury thereon forever, agreeable to the ordinances of said city, which are or shall hereafter be made pertaining thereto.
>
> Given under my hand this First day of Oct. 1863 in Great Salt Lake City, Utah Territory
>
> (Signed) F. A. Mitchell Sexton

Plat Record. In areas before local governments were functioning effectively, graves were dug where convenient with no concept of plots and often without recording the burial. With the platting of cemeteries, selling plots, and registering deeds, attempts were made to record earlier burials. In many instances, the names and burial dates could be obtained but the actual location of the grave was lost. Figure 2-13 shows a plat record reconstructed after burials in the last four decades of the nineteenth century and, for that reason, incomplete.

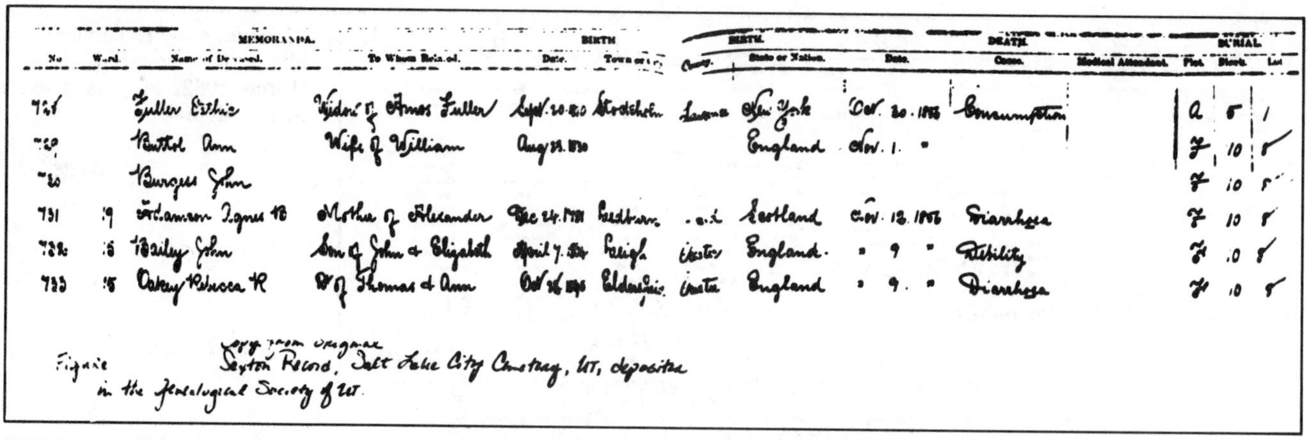

No.	Ward.	Name of Deceased.	To Whom Related.	Birth Date.	Town or City.	County.	State or Nation.	Death Date.	Cause.	Medical Attendant.	Plat.	Block.	Lot.
728		Fuller Esther	Widow of Amos Fuller	Sept. 20. 1800	[illegible]	[illegible]	New York	Oct. 30. 1856	Consumption		a	5	1
729		[illegible] Ann	Wife of William	Aug 28. 1830			England	Nov. 1 "			F	10	8
730		Burgess John									F	10	8
731	19	[illegible] Agnes R	Mother of Alexander	Dec 24. 1781	[illegible]	[illegible]	Scotland	Nov. 13. 1856	Diarrhoea		F	10	8
732	15	Bailey John	Son of John & Elizabeth	April 7. [illegible]	[illegible]	[illegible]	England	" 9 "	Debility		F	10	8
733	15	Oakey Rebecca R	D of Thomas & Ann	Oct 26 [illegible]	[illegible]	[illegible]	England	" 9 "	Diarrhoea		F	10	8

Figure — Copy from original Sexton Record, Salt Lake City Cemetery, UT, deposited in the Genealogical Society of Utah.

Figure 2-12. Sexton's Record, Salt Lake City Cemetery, Utah, 1856, deposited in Genealogical Society of Utah, Salt Lake City.

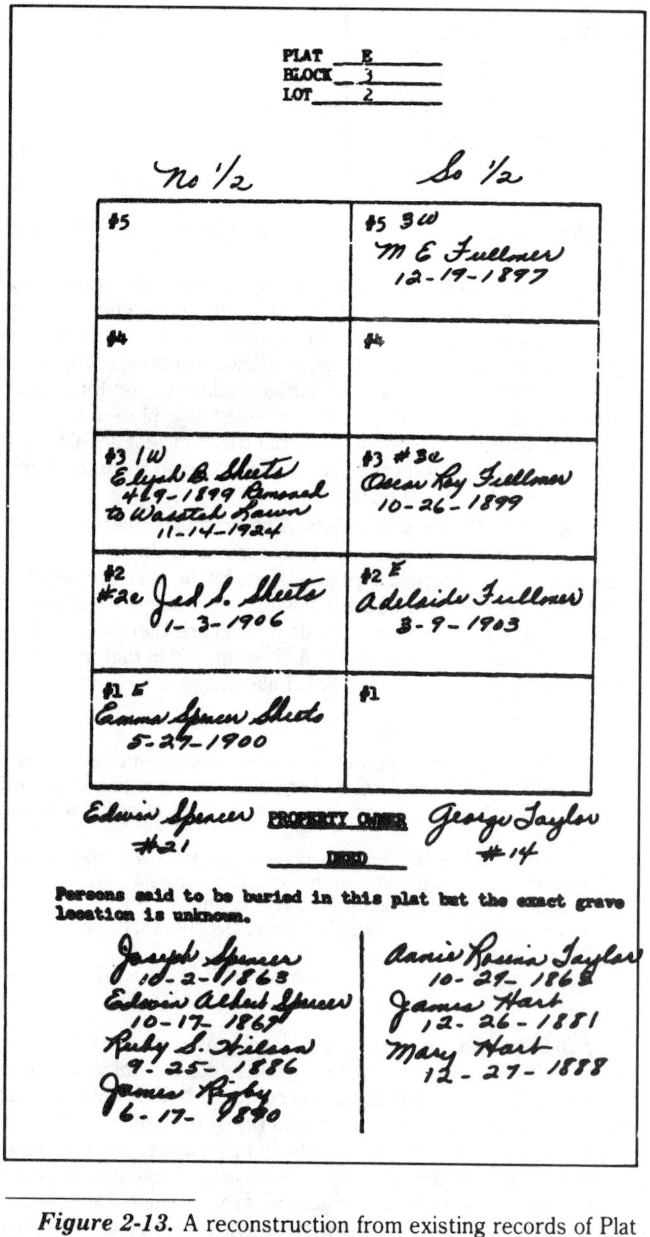

PLAT E
BLOCK 3
LOT 2

No ½	So ½
#5	#5 3W M E Fullmer 12-19-1897
#4	#4
#3 1W Elijah B. Sheets 4-9-1899 Removed to Wasatch Lawn 11-14-1924	#3 #3E Oscar Roy Fullmer 10-26-1899
#2 #2E Jed S. Sheets 1-3-1906	#2 E Adelaide Fullmer 3-9-1903
#1 E Emma Spencer Sheets 5-29-1900	#1

Edwin Spencer #21 — PROPERTY OWNER — George Taylor #14

DEED

Persons said to be buried in this plat but the exact grave location is unknown.

Joseph Spencer 10-2-1863	Annie Rosina Taylor 10-29-1868
Edwin Albert Spencer 10-17-1869	James Hart 12-26-1881
Ruby S. Hilson 9-25-1886	Mary Hart 12-27-1888
James Rigby 6-17-1890	

Figure 2-13. A reconstruction from existing records of Plat E, Block 3, Lot 2, Sexton's Office, Salt Lake City Cemetery.

Burial Permit Records. Since about 1920, state health departments have regulated burials. Today very few jurisdictions permit burials except by licensed morticians who either obtain or determine that someone else has obtained a certified burial permit from the city or county authority. These records constitute another valuable source of burial information. (See Figure 2-14.)

Grave Opening Orders. Most cemeteries preserve a record of all grave openings, whether for burial, postmortem, exhumation, or transfer of body. These records are known as grave opening orders and usually begin about the time of state registration of deaths. The order shown here is for a new grave. We can deduce that Matilda was an adult since children are buried in graves shorter than five feet. Amy Fowler was probably a relative, and a researcher will be able to find the death certificate rapidly since its number is given.

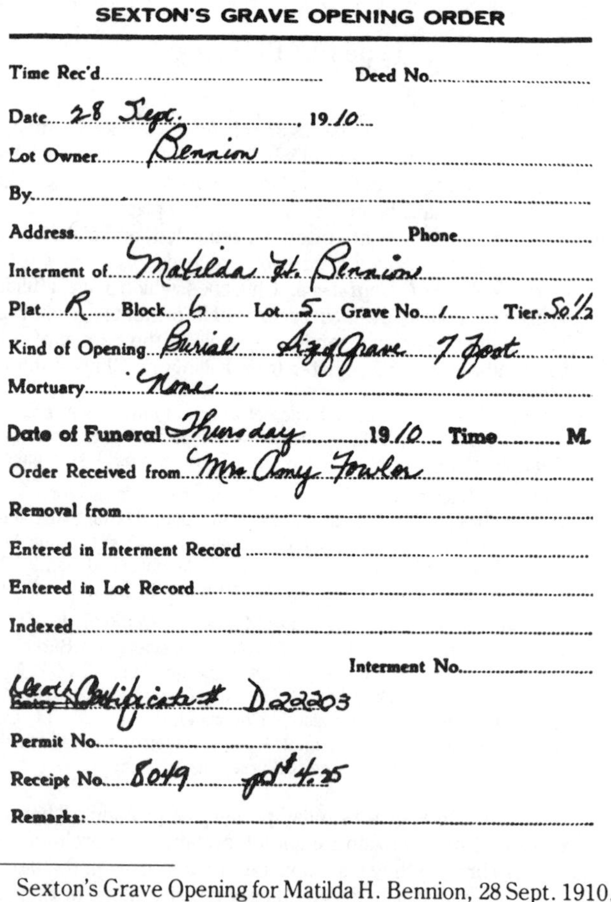

SEXTON'S GRAVE OPENING ORDER

Time Rec'd.......... Deed No..........

Date 28 Sept. 19 10

Lot Owner Bennion

By..........

Address.......... Phone..........

Interment of Matilda H. Bennion

Plat R Block 6 Lot 5 Grave No. 1 Tier So ½

Kind of Opening Burial Size of Grave 7 foot

Mortuary None

Date of Funeral Thursday 19 10 Time .... M.

Order Received from Mrs Amy Fowler

Removal from..........

Entered in Interment Record..........

Entered in Lot Record..........

Indexed..........

Interment No..........

~~Entry No.~~ Death Certificate # D 22203

Permit No..........

Receipt No. 8049 pd $4.25

Remarks:..........

Sexton's Grave Opening for Matilda H. Bennion, 28 Sept. 1910, Salt Lake City Cemetery, Utah.

UTAH DEPARTMENT OF HEALTH

BURIAL ~ TRANSIT PERMIT ______ Death Certificate Number

1. Name of Deceased | 2. Sex | 3. Race
4. Date of Birth | 5. Place of Birth
6. Date of Death | 7. Place of Death
8. Residence
9. Name of Informant
10. Disposition (Burial, Cremation, or Other) | 11. Cemetery
12. Place City County State

A Certificate of Death (or Stillbirth) having been filed according to the laws of Utah permission is hereby given to:

13. Funeral Director | 14. Address | 15. License Number

To dispose of the body as above stated:

16. Embalmer's License Number | 17. Place | 18. Date | 19. Local Registrar

Cemetery or crematory authority shall fill out spaces below:

20. Body was Buried Cremated Other | 21. Date | 22. Cemetery
23. Place City County State | 24. Signature of Person in Charge

Figure 2-14. Burial-Transit Permit, Utah State Department of Health, Division of Vital Statistics.

Family Bibles. While family Bible records are more appropriately classified as home sources, they are also a primary source – sometimes the only one – for private burials. Usually Bibles are still in family hands; however, it has become increasingly popular for local and regional historical societies or other agencies to acquire the personal effects of original settlers and early families of their areas. The National Archives and the Library of Congress in Washington, D.C., also have collections of Bible records sent as evidence in various claims against the United States government. Personnel have pulled these pages from their case files and arranged them in alphabetical order. Lists of the Bible records are available upon request.

Monuments and Memorials

Few experiences in family history offer more intrigue, interest, and even recreation, than searching for monuments and their inscriptions. Even when written records are available and seemingly complete, this source should always be used.

Prominent, influential, and/or affluent families often present special gifts – stained glass windows, altar pieces, sacramental services, confessionals, ornaments, or statues – in the name and memory of their deceased relatives. Small plaques or inscriptions give names, dates, and relationships of those involved in the gift.

Sometimes the family may make contributions in lieu of flowers toward a special trust fund, organization, or project in the memory of a deceased loved one. Records are often maintained of all who contribute, the amount of the contribution, and the date made. Indications of this type of memorial will be found in newspaper accounts, court records, home sources, and the records of the person or institution responsible for the fund or project.

The burial of a loved one in a tomb or raised vault rather than a grave is the custom of some ethnic groups and the practice of some families. These tombs are normally in a special part of the cemetery or in mausoleums expressly for this purpose. The inscriptions found on the tombs themselves are similar to regular monumental inscriptions. The art work associated with the tomb is an important part of the memorial. Burial registers may be stored in a special cupboard inside the tomb.

The ashes of the cremated are usually placed in urns and preserved in vaults at the crematory itself, at the cemetery where other family members are interred, or in the home of a family member. Inscriptions may be etched on a special plaque or label.

Inscriptions on monuments are extremely varied, ranging from a wooden cross rotted into illegibility to a long slab with paragraphs of biography inscribed upon it. Dates of birth and death, place of birth and death (especially when far removed from the place of burial), names of parents, names of spouses, occupation, sometimes brothers and sisters, and special circumstances of life can be found, though not in all cases.

Here are some inscriptions.

- From a cemetery in Manchester, Vermont:

  In Memory of Rufus Munson, who Died Sept. 13th, 1797 in the 35th year of his Age & left a Widow & 4 children the two first letters of thare names is thus:

  C.M: G.M: B.M: P.M:

- From Old Burying Ground, Newport, Rhode Island:

  Wait daughtr of
  William and
  Desire Tripp
  died April 24
  1780 aged 10
  mo 10 days

  Also William
  their son
  died March
  7th 1784 Aged
  22 mo
  Also his Wife's Arm
  Amputated Feby 20th 1786.

- From a cemetery in Norton, Massachusetts:

  In Memory of
  Mr Joseph Hill
  Who Died
  Dec 6, 1826
  Aged 66 years

  My sledge & Hammar ly reclined
  My Bellows too have lost their wind.
  My fire's extinct My forge decayed
  And [in] the dust my vice is laid;
  My iron's spent my coals are gone
  My nails are drove My work is done.

- From a cemetery in Mottville, Michigan:

  Ransom Beardsley
  Died Jan 24 1850
  Aged 56 yr. 7 mo. 21 days
  A Vol. in the War of 1812
  No Pension!

Genealogist should also be aware of indirect evidence which can be supplied in monument art. Art work can express occupations, age, sex, interests, cause of death, religious affiliation, membership in ethnic and fraternal organizations, and philosophies of life. (See Figure 2-15.) These details are rarely recorded by transcribers; but sketches, photographs, and rubbings can preserve these symbolic messages.

In family plots, it is frequently possible to determine family relationships from the relative position of the graves. Usually the dominant couple or parents are in the center with a large stone while children have smaller stones. Positioning of graves can also indicate national origins. Scandinavians seem to position plots with the father in the lower right-hand corner (1), the mother next to him (2), with children and spouses (3-6) placed in order of death clockwise around a large stone bearing the family name.

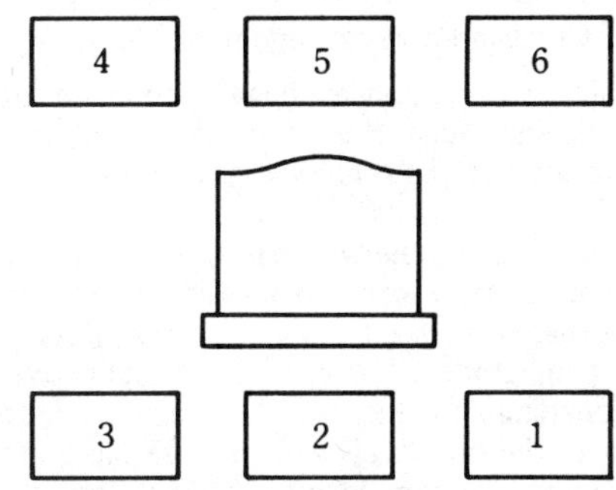

Sketch of Scandinavian grave arrangement.

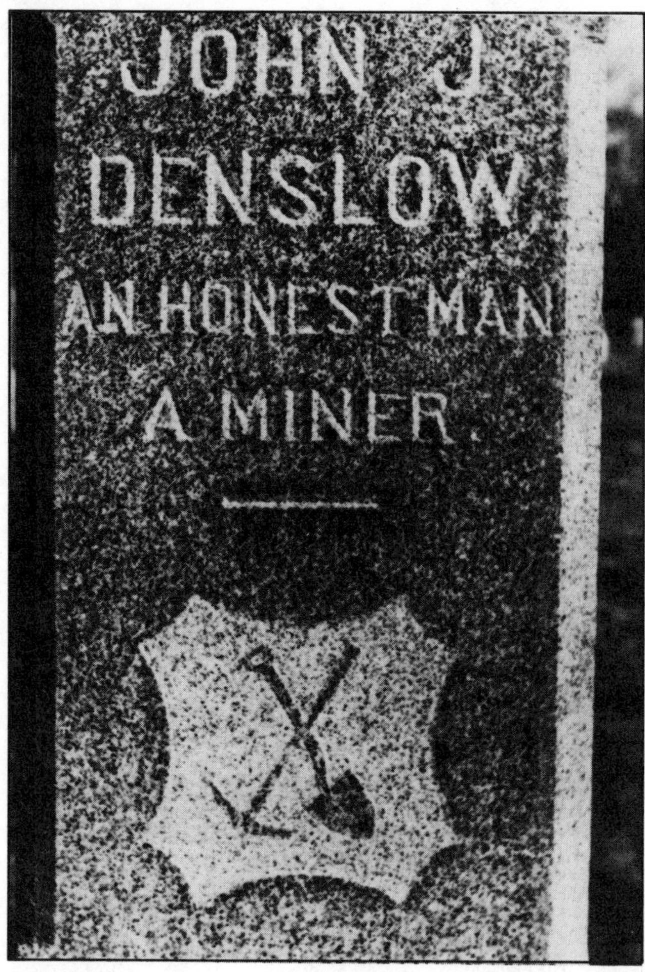

Figure 2-15. Miner's Tombstone, left; Physician's Tombstone, right. Photographs taken 1975, Mt. Olivet Cemetery, Salt Lake City, Utah.

Germans position the family members in a row, in front of the family name stone: father and mother in center, children on either side.

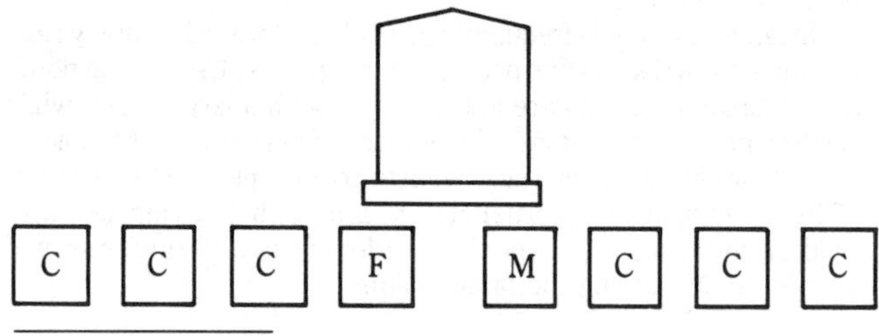

Sketch of German grave arrangement.

About 1850, cemetery planners began recommending positioning as a fashionable sales idea. Plots became even more symmetric, with elaborate aesthetic and practical reasons given to support the symmetry.

The date when the stone was placed on the grave is very important. Obviously one placed two days after the funeral is usually more reliable than one placed fifty years later, although there are exceptions. Tombstones, like cars, have distinctive styles and materials depending upon the year they were made that can provide clues about the time of placement. The illustration in Figure 2-16 will give you a general idea of these styles.

By carefully studying the vintage of the tombstone, the researcher can more accurately determine the validity of its inscription. Modern stones with ancient dates indicate replacement of an earlier stone or considerable time lapse between death and grave marker.

Most older and some new graves sink, leaving a slightly depressed area outlining the dimensions of the grave. If no age or birth date is given, you can determine which graves are those of children and which are adults, by measuring which are over five feet.

Research Preparation

When you search a cemetery, you should arrive with as many clues as you can: surname variants, people who married into your family, maiden names of women on your pedigree, and dates of settlement and migration into and out of the area. Be sure to check land records and county or town histories to learn precisely when and where your first family member settled in that area, when and from where subsequent members of the family arrived in the area, precise property descriptions for graveyards located on family land or nearby farms, land reserved for burial grounds or conveyed to church or township authorities, bequests in wills to maintain a graveyard, location of families in relationship to churches in the area, church affiliations of family members, and the location of families in relationship to cities and villages in the county.

Check death certificates for the names of all cemeteries in which family members are buried. Usually, family members are buried in clusters. Even where surnames may be unfamiliar, consider the probability that persons buried nearby could be related to you. Acquire death certificates for all children of the pedigree ancestor you are seeking.

Check printed cemetery inscriptions. Earning the gratitude of all researchers, county and state genealogical societies, in coopera-

Figure 2-16. Collage of Grave Marker Styles, 1800-present. Photographs taken 1975, City Cemetery, Salt Lake City, Utah.

• **Before 1800:**
Slender, square sandstone or slate slabs with or without elaborate carvings.

• **1830-1910:**
Moderately sculptured stones of white marble and soft gray granite, subject to lichen and weathering.

• **1860-1880:**
Square, towering marble stones often elaborately shaped or with ornate sculpture.

• **1880-present:**
Polished granite or marble, machine-cut, often lying flat on the ground.

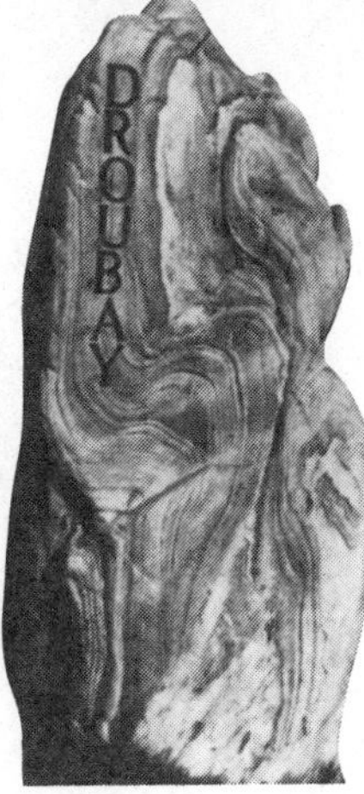

tion with Boy Scout troops, the U.S. Department of Energy, the U.S. Corps of Army Engineers, university and college units, and other interested parties have restored, copied, indexed, and otherwise preserved the information from tombstones. The results are printed in scattered volumes of local proceedings, newsletters, and journals. The printed compilations usually have every-name indexes inexpensively available. The inscriptions are copied by people who know local surnames and who may know where persons are buried for whom there is no stone. The volume will also have a location map showing where the cemeteries are in relation to modern roads. For the names and addresses of local genealogical societies, see Mary K. Meyer, *Directory of Genealogical Societies in the U.S.A. and Canada*. Appendix G contains her 1982 edition for United States societies.

Cemetery Associations

Consult card indexes to inscriptions of cemetery associations where they exist for locations of cemeteries and plots. These can save you hours in search time and provide evidence of family members unknown to you buried nearby. Here are six active in the United States today:

Association for Gravestone Studies
c/o Carol A. Perkins
1233 Cribb Street
Toledo, OH 43612

Membership includes a newsletter, conferences, access to photographic and field notes archives housed at the New England Historic Genealogical Society Library in Boston.

Vermont Old Cemetery Association
Mrs. Ethel Billings, Treas.
R. D. 3
Middlebury, VT 15753

Maine Old Cemetery Association
Dr. Hilda M. Fife, Secy.
6 Sherwood Drive
Eliot, ME 03903

Wisconsin State Old Cemetery Society
F. Winston Luck
4319 N. 70th Street
Milwaukee, WI 53216

Kentucky Cemetery Project
Kentucky Historical Society
300 W. Broadway
Frankfort, KY 40601

Missouri Burial Grounds
Betty Harvey Williams
118 Fairview
Warrensburg, MO 64093

These associations publish newsletters and hints on how to copy tombstone data or how to preserve cemeteries, including funding resources and work assignments. Some publish maps showing locations of cemeteries.

Cemetery Projects

Check cemetery projects in the area of your ancestry. Some are one-man operations, and some are large-scale projects carried out under the supervision of a project director. One such example is the Salt Lake City Cemetery Project funded by the J. E. Wilson Foundation under the direction of Delpha Triptow. Workers handcopied each stone in the large city cemetery, compared the data against the original sexton's records and grave orders, and entered the results into a computer database where it will be sorted, indexed and printed as a competely indexed record of interments and inscriptions.

A complete list of cemetery projects is needed. The difficulty lies in identifying both projects underway and completed cemeteries. A beginning, now badly out of date, is John Stemmons, *Compendium of Cemetery Sources* (Logan, Utah: Everton Publishers, n.d.) available from the publisher, Box 368, Logan, UT 84321. This volume includes call numbers for those in the library of the Genealogical Society of Utah.

Next procure a detailed county or city map where churches and cemeteries are marked. County road maps are usually available through county or state highway departments, assessors' offices, or registrars of deeds. In rural areas, it is also helpful to have a U.S. Geodetic Survey quad map for the area you are researching, for some inactive cemeteries may not be indicated on the current county map. Mark the cemeteries nearest the land holdings or residences of your family members directly on your map.

If this process seems elaborate to you, consider that a county may be 600 square miles in size. You could spend hours driving and asking local residents who may know less than you do about the area and still never locate the cemetery where your ancestors are buried.

In the case of family burial plots, once you are within half a mile of your area, you are dependent upon your own keen observation and the help of local residents. Since the 1930s, increasingly large acreages left untended have succumbed to weeds, brambles, and trees. Some of this land is in the federal land bank. Some has been left by owners who now work in industry. It is not uncommon to find a property owner who is unaware of a burial plot in his woods. The best help may be either oldtimers who have lived in the area for years or young boys who enjoy rabbit and grouse hunting.

Relocated Cemeteries

In areas where the locality has changed from agricultural to urban or industrial, few local people actually know where cemeteries have been relocated, but local historical societies have done much to preserve a record of them.

When a dam is built with subsequent flooding of local areas, or a freeway planned, or an energy reservation set aside, surveys of the local cemeteries are made to determine if any will be disturbed and, if so, where the bodies will be reinterred. These reinterment projects produce a generally careful record of all graves and inscriptions. An effort is made to identify the occupants of unmarked graves using family records, the memories of local residents, and public documents.

These interments are usually recorded on file cards, arranged alphabetically within geographic areas. They are open to the public through mail or telephone requests and the information is usually available without charge or for a nominal copy fee. A good example is the Tennessee Valley Authority, with its thousands of maps, cemetery inscriptions, photographs, and other valuable materials all along the Tennessee River. These materials are available through the TVA Technical Library, 400 Commerce Avenue, E2 B7 Knoxville, TN 37902, (615) 632-4366.

Military cemeteries will also relocate graves. Fort McPherson National Cemetery in Maxwell, Nebraska, opened in 1873 to consolidate twenty-two cemeteries in Colorado, Wyoming, South Dakota, Idaho, and Nebraska. By 1947, the project had been completed. The cemetery is carefully plotted and indexed with control markers throughout the grounds; but even so, there are 584 "unknown" graves. Copies of these records are in the National Archives (Appendix A) and at Fort McPherson, Maxwell, NB 69151.

If churches moved during the years of their existence, they probably have more than one burial place. For example, the old cemetery of the Augusta Stone Church in Fort Defiance, Augusta County, Virginia, is walled and stands behind a screen of trees. The grave of Rachel (Crawford) Berry, born 18 April 1812 and died 23 May 1832, wife of Thornton Berry, lies alone on the side of the hill. One hundred yards away in the Crawford family plot lies her ten-year-old son James. Across the main highway and over a block away lies a new portion adjoining the new Augusta Stone Church. Here we find Thornton Berry, died 11 Dec 1882, age 72.7.2 and his second wife Nancy, died April (year illegible) age 81.1.17, and other members of his family. Had the old portion, which is not visible from the road, been neglected, Thornton's first wife and son would have been missed.

It was fairly common for congregations to split during controversies and for the dissenting unit to build separate facilities—meetinghouse and cemetery—a few miles away. An example is found in Virginia. New Providence congregation broke with Old Providence over the procedure of singing hymns in meetings in the early nineteenth century. As a result there are two churches and two cemeteries located only two miles apart. Sometimes the two congregations reunite at a later time and build still a third meetinghouse, closing down the previous two. Furthermore, because it is common for members of the same family to belong to different churches, you should plan to search all cemeteries in the immediate vicinity of the family home regardless of religious affiliations.

The procedure to follow in locating graves differs somewhat depending upon the size of the cemetery. The sexton's records, when they exist, should be searched first regardless of the size or type of tombstone. Look at the names. In this way you can spot the females with your surnames buried under married names in the plots of other relatives who have surnames unknown to you.

Family cemeteries are usually very small and without sexton's records. You should, therefore, read every tombstone to determine which graves are those of ancestral families.

For very large public, church, and private cemeteries, consult the various kinds of sextons' records to determine when ancestral family members were buried and the exact locations of each one. Then check the master plat or map showing the individual cemetery plats and their smaller subdivisions (sections, blocks, tiers, etc.) to determine the location of graves for the period of time in which you are interested. Some cemeteries provide small replica maps on which you can mark the gravesite in which you are particularly interested as a guide. Figure 2-17 is a typical traffic pattern map.

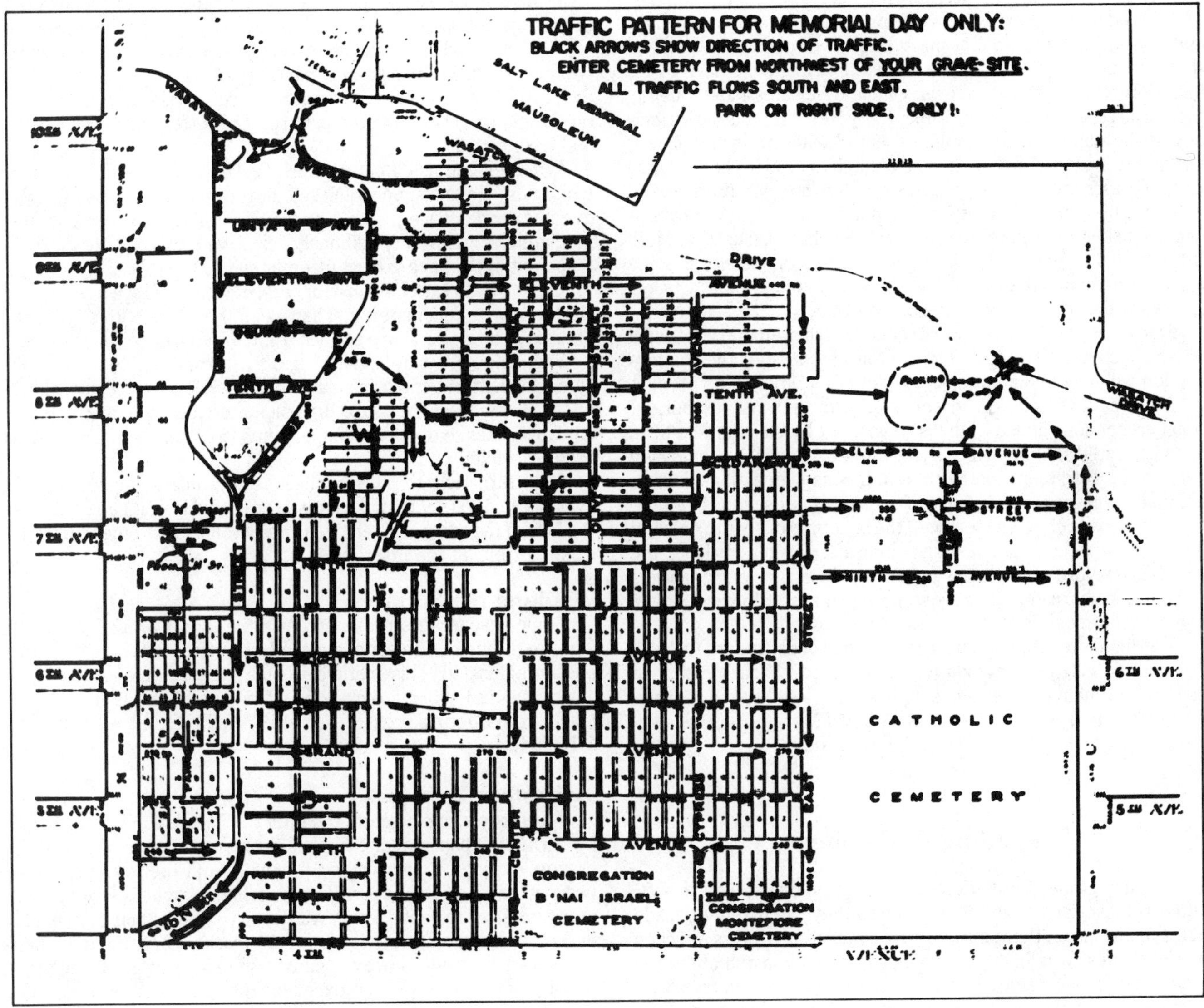

Figure 2-17. Traffic Pattern Map for Salt Lake City Cemetery, no date, from the author's files. New edition printed each year for Memorial Day

Searching a Cemetery

Drive through or walk around the cemetery before examining individual stones. Absorb some of the atmosphere of the setting. Consider the location, the upkeep and condition, size, presence of above-ground burials, fenced-off or enclosed sections, plantings, artwork and statuary, presence of VIP graves, positioning of stones and their relationship to each of the others, and color and material of the stones. These elements provide evidence of ethnic graveyards, the economic base of the community, historical events, lifestyle and outlook of local residents, and other details.

Now zero in on individual stones, looking for naming patterns in the plots. A large name stone in the center with smaller stones around bearing only given names may indicate Swedish origins. If the smaller stones have relationships or initials only, it may indicate German origins.

Note the dates of death. Many headstones with proximate death dates indicate an epidemic, a weather tragedy, a mine accident, or the close of a generation. For example, in the Darling, Minnesota, Swedish cemetery, burials took place starting about 1870. They were the children of the immigrant generation who arrived in Minnesota just before the turn of the century with their parents or were born shortly after arrival here in America.

A Swedish cemetery will have gray, sand, pink, and other warm soft colors. The setting will be uncluttered, with open spaces around the plots and scanty data on the stones. Polish graves have large, heavy black or red stones in rows, with precise dates and frequently the original spellings of the surname. Early New England and Virginia origins show up in ornate carvings of deaths' heads, weeping willows, and all-seeing eyes on stones large enough to include the essential facts and a scriptural verse. These stones are liberally interspersed with flat, biographical stones giving full details of family relationships. Quaker stones are an exact twelve inches high until well into the nineteenth century. Quaker stones with incomplete or missing inscriptions may have been "oversized" monuments that Quaker leaders ordered trimmed to regulation size.

Many cemeteries have special sections of the cemetery set aside for specific kinds of burials. The sexton's records for the paupers section will be found among poor relief or workhouse records; in colored sections, blacks, orientals, and/or Indians are buried; religious sections house Catholic, Jewish, or Muslim burials. In an unconsecrated section of a religious cemetery are those who died without the sacraments of the church. In Masonic sections, burials are made in crypts or wall vaults. Watch for other sections as well.

If you have a choice of seasons, the best time of year to conduct cemetery searches is in the early spring after winter has killed the weeds and before spring briars and grasses begin growing or snakes come out of hibernation. The snow and winter rain will have removed some of the moss from the faces of the stones.

Many cemeteries, particularly abandoned ones, are great places for snakes, chiggers, poison ivy, thorns, etc. Wear protective clothing, including gloves and sturdy shoes. Be alert for animals, uneven ground, and other hazards. A can of Mace or another eye-stinging mist may deter over-enthusiastic dogs.

Reading the Stones

The popular stones for markers in years gone by were often soft. Often old inscriptions are so weathered they can hardly be made out. Furthermore, there may be an accumulation of moss or lichen on the stones. It is highly unprofessional to use harsh abrasives or wire brushes to remove the moss since these measures further damage the inscriptions and are of questionable value even to the immediate user. Numerous other methods do a better job of cleaning the surface of the stone without causing damage. Here are some professionally acceptable techniquesin current use.[4]

Photographing the Stones

While photography provides an exact copy of the stone itself, it may not give you a legible reproduction. Either use a polaroid camera or, if you use a regular camera, always copy the inscription in your notes in case the picture fails.

The American Association for State and Local History (AASLH) recommends using a 35 mm black and white camera with twenty-exposure film, ASA rating, 125. Best results can be obtained when a light meter is used even if the camera has an automatic photocell-controlled lens, since the amount of light hitting the photocell may be different from that hitting the stone. A hazy or slightly overcast day is better than bright sunlight because shadows are at a minimum. For further details see "Cemetery Transcribing: Preparations and Procedures," Technical Leaflet 9, *History News* 26 (May 1971), and "Photographing Tombstones," Technical Leaflet 92, ibid., 32 (Feb. 1977). I have found early morning the best time to photograph tombstones. The early light adds sharpness, and shadows cast on the stone provide a striking contrast between letters (raised or incised) and stone surface.

Prepare the stone to enhance the inscription's legibility. Wash badly discolored stones with a vinegar-saturated sponge or rag. It will remove even the worst moss with little extra rubbing.

If the tombstone is very white, be sure the stone is absolutely dry. Using artist's powdered chalk, available in plastic squeeze containers, puff chalk into the white letters. Clear away excess chalk with a soft three- or four-inch paint brush. Be careful not to get the powder on other parts of the stone as these will appear as smears on the photo. Then take the picture. The letters should be clear and easily read.

Whether you use a polaroid or regular camera, use black and white film. Have a supply of flash bulbs for overcast days or early evening work. Place pictures or film in a tightly covered box immediately. If you want additional copies, take extra photos rather than waiting to have copies made later.

Carry a trash sack for film wrappers, etc. Never leave a cemetery cluttered with this material. Then clean the stone with a solution of three parts water to one part vinegar until all chalk residue is gone.

Sort photos, coat, and dry upon returning home. This will eliminate dust and grit which may otherwise settle on the new damp photo. After the photos are dry, slip into clear four-by-five-inch Kodapak sleeves to prevent fingerprints from handling. Then label them carefully.

An alternative to artist's chalk is styrofoam, inexpensively available in floral shops and variety stores. Rubbing it gently across the face of the stone will remove the moss and leave small particles in the letters of the inscriptions.

Chalking the Surfaces

Some researchers prefer to chalk the stone with white chalk to make the indented inscription stand out against the surface before photographing it. This method is time-consuming and does not always insure legibility. A chalking kit with instructions is available for $5 from Rooting Treasures, 5813 Woodbridge Lane, Midland, MI 48640.

Tombstone Rubbings

For those stones weathered until the inscription is very faint, lay a sheet of paper over the surface and rub a piece of charcoal, crayon, or wax (brown or black) over it until the inscription appears in relief on the paper. Regular white or light-colored paper of any kind in sufficient quantity will do, or you can obtain long sheets of butcher paper from a nearby meat market. See Figure 2-18.

Pellon, the soft nonwoven fabric used for interfacings and linings by dressmakers, is an excellent rubbing material. It can be folded in the bottom of a suitcase for travel and laundered if it gets soiled. It is relatively immune to rain or mildew from moisture or grime on stones where the sun never shines. It comes in various weights and is readily available in fabric shops or departments across

Figure 2-18. Photograph of tombstone rubbing by Adelia Baird, Hardin County, Kentucky, headstone of Susanna Sheets, cemetery unknown.

the nation. In backwoods Mississippi, it is used locally for stiffening sunbonnets. Some genealogists buy it by the bolt at about 46 cents per yard from fabric wholesalers listed in the telephone yellow pages. It comes in white, cream, black, and, on special order, other shades.

Tissue paper is also a versatile rubbing paper under some conditions. If the surface is dry, heavily carved, scratched, or defaced, a careful rubbing with tissue paper will get a good clear image. It is lightweight and can be folded or rolled although it is susceptible to creasing and wrinkling.

Crayola crayons – both regular and jumbo size – come in a wide range of colors. Crayon is a versatile rubbing wax which you can seal into fabric by applying a warm iron. Rubbings can then be washed when they get soiled or pressed if they are creased. However, crayons tend to melt in hot sun or from the heat of your hand, and they chip in extreme cold. They can be ordered from Binney and Smith, Inc., 1100 Church Lane, Box 431, Easton, PA 18042. Rubbing waxes in several colors, including gold and silver, which are more durable and less susceptible to temperature changes, are available from Bracy Brass Rubbing Center, 250 East 100 South, Salt Lake City, UT 84111, (801) 364-4068; and Oldstone Enterprises, 77 Summer Street, Boston, MA 02110. These firms also supply rubbing kits for adults and children including AQABA hemp paper (24" x 36"), waxes, a plastic bag for garbage, a roll of masking tape, a bristle brush for cleaning the surface (do not use the brush!), and an instruction booklet. Waxes and paper are also available in a variety of colors and quantities. Rubbing wax, unlike crayon, cannot be ironed.

Servis Paper Company, 56 Harvester Avenue, Batavia, NY 14020, supplies sensi-copy paper which has a self-carbon effect. You merely rub the paper with a leather belt, rubber ball, or sponge and the image appears. You must be very careful, however, for the paper smears easily.

Special Problems with Stones

Buried and Moved Markers

Markers frequently fall down and are buried under an accumulation of undergrowth and topsoil. When working in poorly kept cemeteries, carry a probe long enough to check the ground eight to ten inches deep. Carefully check fence lines or hedge rows. Fallen markers which cannot be easily replaced are often carried to the side and either propped against the fence or left on the ground. Even though they cannot be readily identified with the appropriate plot, the inscriptions are still valuable.

Duplicate Tombstones

When a new tombstone is prepared for a grave, there is always the possibility that the stone cutter will leave the original stone in place, and you will thus find two stones for the same person. In very old cemeteries, you will also discover some apparent duplicates that are really a headstone and a footstone. A tombstone for the same person may appear in a family cemetery or plot with a second tombstone in the cemetery where the person is actually buried.

Recording Cemetery Data

The more times you copy the inscription, the greater the chance of error. Therefore, take an ample supply of family group worksheets or research notepaper with you and transcribe the data directly on the worksheets or research notepaper to begin with.

Most researchers copy only the direct genealogical data: birthdates, birthplaces, deathdates, parents, husband, or wife. Such a practice, however, can ignore the clues indicated in the selection of epitaphs: church affiliation, survivors, occupations, military service, cause of death, physical descriptions, citizenship, occupation, and migrational patterns. Always reread your notes for accuracy and completeness before you leave the cemetery, checking against the headstone itself.

Comparatively few genealogists also plot the cemetery even though people are usually buried in family units. By drawing a diagram of each plot, you can analyze graves in their relationships to each other: size, location, headstones, etc.

On the back of your worksheets, sketch the tombstones as they appear in the plot; number each one, then list the inscription and description of the stone by the same number on the worksheets. Where family units are definite, record them on the same worksheet as a family; but where there is any question, list each one on a separate sheet and refer by number back to the plot you have drawn for the relationship of each individual grave to the whole plot. Figure 2-19 shows an example from the Lexington Presbyterian Church Cemetery in Lexington, Virginia. The numbers refer to the inscription notes, which made it possible to analyze some family relationships.

Unit 1

1. Margaret McDowell, wife of Robert McDowell, died 14 Feb. 1830, age 70.
2. Robert McDowell, born 10 March 1767, died 2 Aug. 1838. Both stones were, despite the difference in the sketch, identical.

Unit 2

3. Zachariah Johnston, died 7 Jan. 1800, age 57.
4. Ann Johnston, died 25 Aug. 1818, age 77.

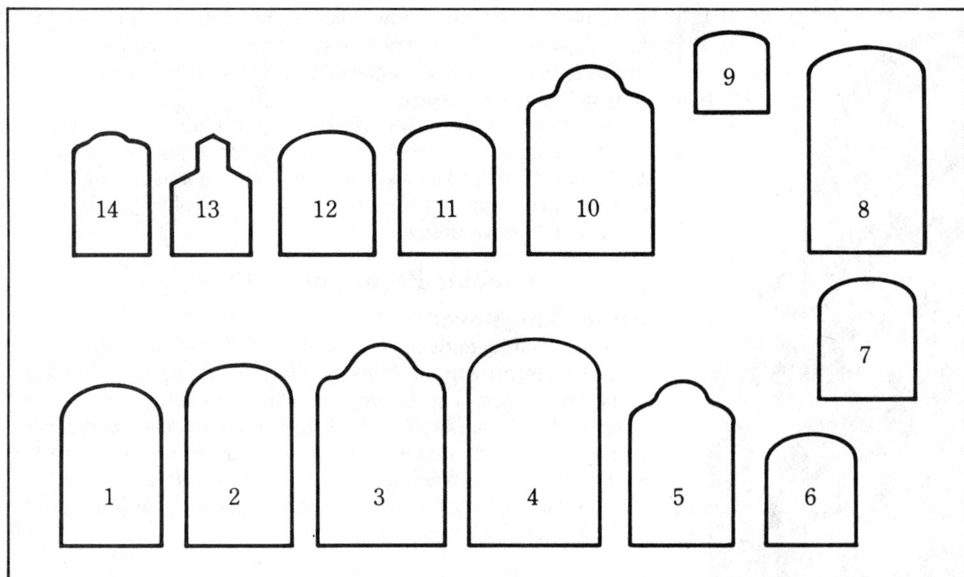

Figure 2-19. Plot of tombstones showing comparative sizes and shapes, Lexington Presbyterian Church Cemetery, Virginia; all of the markers are sandstone with legible inscriptions.

Unit 3

5. Sally W. Johnston, wife of Alexander Johnston, born 29 Jan. 1776, died 30 April 1818, age 43.

6. Zechariah G. Johnston, born 18 June 1807, died 28 June 1815, age 6. This inscription was rather hard to read.

7. A. J., no date, child's grave with no other inscription, probably part of the Johnston family and a grandchild of Zachariah and Ann.

Unit 4

8. Ann, daughter of Susan and Thomas Johnston, born 10 April 1803, died 7 Oct. 1834.

9. William G. Johnston, son of Susan and Thomas Johnston, born 27 Jan. 1819.

10. Susan, daughter of Susan and Thomas Johnston, died 10 April 1832, age 22.

11. Susan Johnston, wife of Thomas Johnston, died 19 Nov. 1857, age 81.

12. Thomas Johnston, born 10 Jan. 1773, died 27 Dec. 1847.

Individual Burials

13. Elizabeth McDowell, "Our Loving Aunt," born 28 Sept. 1796, died 29 May 1861.

14. Rebecca (Our Sister), wife of William C. Lewis, died 2 April 1857, age 57.

In this plat, family groupings are clear in most cases, and certain hypotheses can be made and tested with evidence from other sources.

Even though historical, genealogical, and patriotic societies have performed a valuable and commendable service in preparing compilations of tombstone inscriptions, especially in view of the annual toll taken on grave markers through neglect, highway construction, suburban development, and reclamation projects, these compiled records cannot fully replace the personal search. One great weakness of the compiled source is editorial convention. Alphabetical arrangements, though convenient, obscure family relationships. Figure 2-20 illustrates the real utility of such a plat.

Another weakness of these compilations comes from including only the names, birthdates, deathdates, and relationships. Indirect evidence and clues are omitted because they are too voluminous. In a printed compilation of gravestones in Tinkling Spring Presbyterian Cemetery in Fisherville, Augusta County, Virginia, the alphabetical sequence reads:[5]

Cynthia Johnson
Born 19 Dec 1799
Died 15 Aug 1887
Aged 87 years 7 months and 26 days
Wife of Thomas Johnson

Thomas Johnson
died 19 Dec 1865
Age 75 years, 4 months and 25 days

In the cemetery itself in a lovely wrought-iron fenced enclosure, the graves of Cynthia and Thomas lie surrounded by Cynthia's family: her parents, James and Martha Black; and several of her brothers, sisters, and their families. Nothing in the printed volume connects Cynthia with the Black family.

I confess to a weakness for the emotional impact of searching a graveyard, but the wealth of primary and secondary evidence a cemetery can provide would still justify a search on the least sentimental of grounds. Although the extra time, expense, and inconvenience of on-site searches may deter a genealogist, examining these sources with the same care and thoroughness you would bring to library research pays off.

Notes

1. St. David's Reformed Church, also known as Killinger Church, Death Register Dauphin County, Penn. Microfilm copy of typescript at the Genealogical Society of Utah (hereafter GS), 020,348, item 7.

2. Consult August Suelflow, *Preliminary Guide to Church Records Depositories* (Madison: Society of American Archivists, 1969).

3. Cemetery Deed of Edwin Spencer, 1 Oct. 1863, Certificate 21, Salt Lake City Cemetery Deed Register, sexton's office.

4. These procedures were outlined in a letter to the author by Mrs. Lauretta Russell of San Antonio, Texas, who found this to be the best method of securing clear, accurate copies.

5. Howard M. Wilson, *Tinkling Spring: Headwater of Freedom* (Fisherville, Va.: for the congregation, 1954), Appendix E.

Bibliography

Annese, Domenico. "Construction: Cemetery Design Standards." *Landscape Architecture*, Jan. 1983, pp. 85-87.

Association for Gravestone Studies. *Bibliography of Cemetery Records and Studies*. Available from Carol A. Perkins, 1233 Cribb Street, Toledo, OH 43612.

Barba, Perston A. "Folk Art on Pennsylvania German Tombstones." *Historical Review of Berks County*, Jan. 1955, pp. 43-47.

Barrick, Mac E. "Cumberland County Death Lore." *Pennsylvania Folklife*, Summer 1979, pp. 37-46.

Beable, W. H. *Epitaphs: Graveyard Humor and Eulogy*. 1925; reprint ed., Detroit: Singing Tree Press, 1971.

Benes, Peter. "Abel Webster, Pioneer, Patriot, and Stonecutter." *Historical New Hampshire* 28 (1973): 221-40.

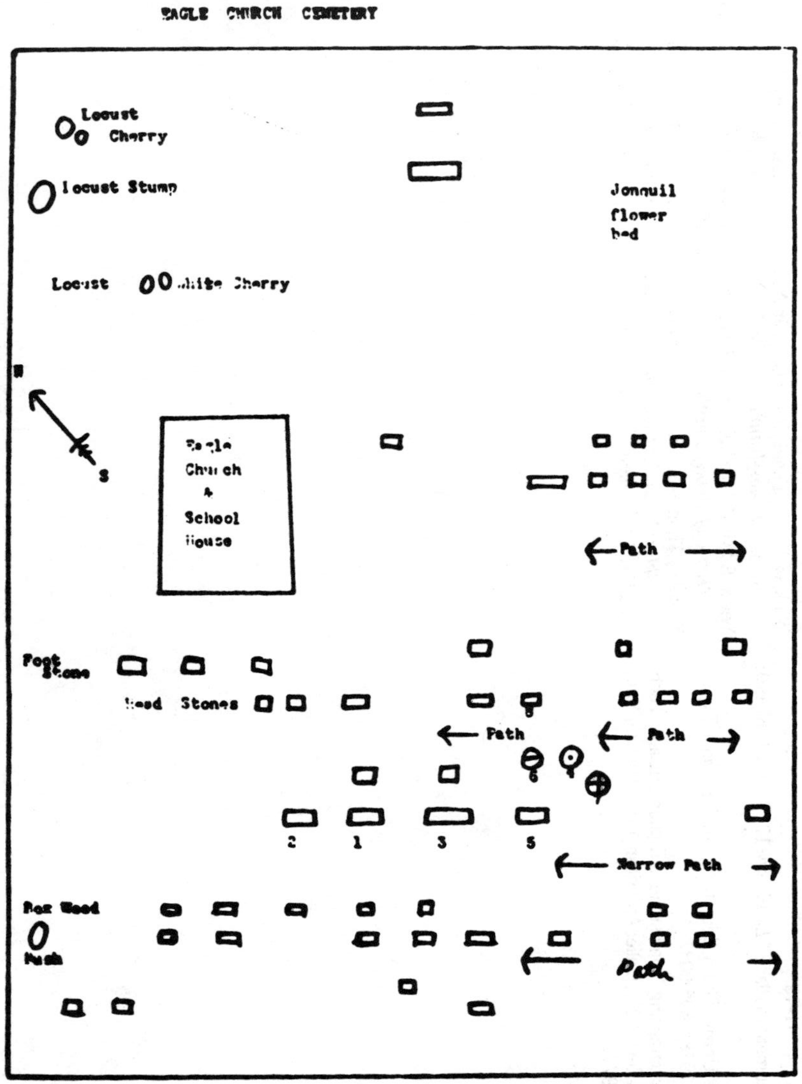

EAGLE CHURCH CEMETERY

Locust Cherry

Locust Stump

Jonquil flower bed

Locust White Cherry

N

S

Eagle Church & School House

Path

Foot Stone

Head Stones

Path

Path

2 1 3 5

Narrow Path

Box Wood

Bush

Path

EAGLE CEMETERY — TOMBSTONES

1. Catherine Eakle wife of John B. Eakle (d) March 14, 1834
   Age 46 years and 3 months
2. Sarah Eakle (d) Jan. 21, 1835
   Age 13 years and 4 months
3. John B. Eakle (d) Nov. 14, 1840— Footstone in place--J. B. E.
   Age 69 years, 9 months and 27 days.
4. Frances Ann wife of G. W. Womeldoff. Stone loose on ground
   (b) Dec. 15, 1819 (d) Feb. 8, 1853
5. James Henry Eakle (Son of C & M. J. Eakle)
   Stone loose on ground
   (d) May 24, 1864 (Says Eakle Bible)
   Age 17 years, 4 months & 9 days.
6. John Kennedy (b) May 9, 1785 (d) March 5, 1862.
   Stone loose on ground
   Age 77
7. M K foot stone (piece) broken short —
   Loose on ground
8. alene Ennedy may be wife of John Kennedy—
   broken headstone on ground.

READABLE TOMBSTONES

The best preserved tombstones with good legible words and dates show that Catherine Eakle, wife of John B. Eakle died March 14, 1834. Sarah Eakle died January 21, 1835 and John B. Eakle died November 14, 1840. In 1956 the six readable stones show death dates from March 14, 1834 to 1864. Yet the fact that 43 limestone and sandstone markers could not be read, certainly indicates that some of them may have been of earlier dates than 1834.

Figure 2-20. Nat G. Barnhart, *History of the United Methodist Church* (Fort Defiance, Va.: For the author, 1973), pp. 21-22.

Bodon, John J. *Rubbings and Textures: A Graphic Technique*. New York: Reinhold Book Corp., n.d.

Bondurant, Lynn, Jr. "Science: A Grave Situation." *The Instructor,* April 1977, pp. 110-14.

Bremer, Ronald A. *The World's Funniest Epitaphs*. Salt Lake City: Ancestral Routes, 1982.

Dethlefson, E. S., and K. Jensen. "Social Commentary from the Cemetery." *Natural History* 86 (1977): 32-39.

Dreyfuss, Henry. *Symbol Source Book: An Authorative Guide to International Graphic Symbols*. New York: McGraw-Hill, 1967. Includes meanings.

Earl, Phil, and Jean Earl. *Basque Aspen Art of the Sierra Nevada: A Bibliography*. Available from Earl Enterprises, Box 13994, Reno, NV 89507.

Eiedesel, Gordon M. "The Geography of Saunders County Rural Cemeteries From 1859." *Nebraska History* 61 (1980): 215-18.

Ellis, Nancy, and Parker Hayden. *Here Lies America*. New York: Hawthorn Books, Inc., 1978.

Firestein, Cecily B. *Rubbing Craft*. New York: Quick Fox, 1977.

Francaviglia. "The Cemetery as an Evolving Cultural Landscape." *Annals, Association of American Geographers* 61 (1973): 501.

Garvin, James L., and Donna-Belle Garvin. "Stephen Webster, Gravestone Maker." *Historical New Hampshire* 29 (1974): 93-104.

Gillespie, Angus K. "Gravestones and Ostentation: A Study of Five Delaware County Cemeteries." *Pennsylvania Folklife,* Winter 1969-70, pp. 34-43.

Gillon, Edmond V., Jr. *Early New England Gravestone Rubbings*. New York: Dover Publications, Inc., 1966.

Grave Matters: Being a Compendium of the Art, History, and the Customs of the Funeral. Available from Highly Specialized Promotions, Inc., 39 Atlantic Avenue, Booklyn, NY 11217, (212) 858-3026.

Habenstein, Robert W., and William M. Lamers. *Funeral Customs the World Over*. Milwaukee: Bulfin Printers, Inc., 1960.

Howett, Catherine. "Living Landscapes for the Dead." *Landscape* 21 (1977): 9-17.

Jack, Phil R. "A Western Pennsylvania Graveyard, 1787-1967." *Pennsylvania Folklife,* Spring 1968, pp. 41-48.

Jackson, J. B. "From Monument to Place." *Landscape* 17 (Winter 1967-68): 22-26.

Jeane, D. Gregory. "The Upland South Cemetery: An American Type." *Popular Culture* 11 (1978): 895-903.

Jones, Mary-Ellen. "Photographing Tombstones: Equipment and Techniques." Technical Leaflet 92. Nashville: American Association for State and Local History, 1977.

Kay, J. H. "Sixty Million Graves: The VA Cemetery Extravaganza." *Nation,* 19 Feb. 1977, pp. 209-12.

Lehner, Ernst. *The Picture Book of Symbols*. New York: William Penn Publishing Company, 1956.

Lindsay, Dean T., and Jeannette H. Lindsay. "Tombstone Photography." *Genealogical Journal* 4 (1975): 103-6.

McDonald, Frank E. "Pennsylvania German Tombstone Art of Lebanon County, Pennsylvania." *Pennsylvania Folklife,* Autumn 1975.

Montell, William Lynwood. *Ghosts Along the Cumberland: Deathlore in the Kentucky Foothills*. Nashville: University of Tennessee, 1968.

Newman, John J. "Cemetery Transcribing: Preparations and Procedures." Technical Leaflet 9. Nashville: American Association for State and Local History, 1971.

Price, Larry W. "Some Results and Implications of a Cemetery Study." *Professional Geographer* 42 (1966): 201-7.

Roberts, Allen D. "Where Are the All-Seeing Eyes?" *Sunstone,* May-June 1978, pp. 22-37.

Roberts, Warren E. "Tools on Tombstones: Some Indian Examples." *Pioneer America,* June 1978, pp. 106-11.

Skinner, Michael Kingsley. *How to Make Rubbings*. New York: Van Nostrand-Reinhold, 1972.

Slater, James A., and Ernest Caulfield. "The Colonial Gravestone Carvings of Obadiah Wheeler." *American Antiquarian Society Proceedings* 84 (1974): 73-104.

"Talking Tombstones," *New York Times Magazine,* 20 Nov. 1977, p. 14.

"Two Cemeteries Are Last Remains of Black Colony of Pleasant Ridge." *Wisconsin Then and Now*. Nov. 1974, pp. 2-3.

Vallentine, John F. "Locating the Correct Cemetery." *Genealogical Journal* 4 (1975): 107-9.

Wallis, Charles L. *American Epitaphs: Grave and Humorous*. New York: Dover Publications, 1975.

Weitzman, David. *Underfoot: An Everyday Guide to Exploring the American Past*. New York: Charles Scribners & Sons, 1976.

Williams, Melvin G. *The Last Word: The Lure and Lore of Early New England Graveyards*. Boston: Oldstone Enterprises, 1979.

Winkler, Louis. "Pennsylvania German Astronomy and Astrology IV: Tombstones." *Pennsylvania Folklife,* Winter 1973, pp. 42-45.

Yeich, Edwin B. "Die Leicht: The Old-Fashioned Country Funeral." *Historical Review of Berks County,* July 1954, pp. 110-11.

Zaniello, Thomas A. "American Gravestone: An Annotated Bibliography." *Folklore Forum: A Communication for Students of Folklore* 9 (Dec. 1979): 115-37. Excellent list of articles in all kinds of publications.

INFORMATION GUIDE

Genealogical Information in the Record Group	*Marriage*	*Divorce*
Surname/name	●	●
Date of Birth	●	
Place of Birth	●	
Sex	●	
Race/color	●	
Physical Description		
Occupation	●	●
Education		
Military Service		●
Slave Status	●	
Property Owned		●
Religion		
Citizenship		
Marital Status	●	●
Spouse's Name	●	●
Children's Names		●
Father's Name	●	
Mother's Name	●	
Father's Birthplace		
Mother's Birthplace		
Date of Death		
Cause of Death		
Name of Cemetery		
Residence	●	●
Age	●	●
Literacy/signature	●	●
Photograph/sketch		
No. of Marriages	●	●
Relatives	●	●

COULD YOU USE THIS CHAPTER?

Type of Record	*Kept from*	*Clues That You Should Consult These Records*
Marriage records	1607 to present	Although the modern marriage license came into existence only in the twentieth century for most states, there have been marriage records from the earliest days of settlement. A variety of jurisdictions were responsible: colonial governors, military and naval personnel, town and county governments, churches, and justices of the peace. Needless to say, not all of these records are currently in the same depository now; but this chapter will describe how to find them and use them. Even more useful is the fact that a variety of marriage records existed before the marriage license as we know it: consent affidavits from parents or guardians for brides and grooms under age; declarations of intent such as banns in churches, "intentions" filed with the town or county clerk, bonds posted by the groom and (sometimes) a male relative of the bride; and marriage contracts. These are in addition to licenses in one form or other and the return—completed and "returned" after the ceremony was performed; and marriage registers kept by those authorized to perform and/or record marriages.
Divorce records	About 1650 to present	Contrary to popular opinion, divorce is not a twentieth-century invention even though the grounds considered acceptable for divorce have varied greatly. Sometimes legislatures granted divorces. At other times (as now) it was a court function. Newspapers frequently are the means for publishing notices of filing of divorce and announcing decrees. County courts have also, at times, had jurisdiction. This chapter will describe the legal background, how to locate the records, and how to use them.

Chapter 3

MARRIAGE AND DIVORCE RECORDS

Johni Cerny

Registering marriages and granting divorces in the United States is a quasi-religious, quasi-legal social function that has been influenced by religious beliefs, custom, and English law since the earliest colonial settlements. The effective genealogist needs a complete understanding of the jurisdictions responsible for maintaining these records, the types of records kept by each jurisdiction, periods in which various types of records were maintained, the circumstances peculiar to each colony and state that created the necessity for registering marriages and divorces, and the factors that produced changes in these registrations.

An additional complication is that the United States, unlike England and some European countries, does not have a national registration program. Instead, marriage registration is the responsibility of the individual states. Futhermore, marriage registration was never uniformly implemented among the states. Prior to state registration requirements, the town in New England and the counties in the remainder of the nation were primary jurisdictions charged with maintaining marriage records. The records ordinarily begin when a town or county is created. There were, however, some states that did not require subordinate jursidictions to keep marriage records until more recent times, such as Pennsylvania and South Carolina.

Jurisdictions

Marriage records in the United States have been, and in some cases still are, kept by churches, ministers, justices of the peace, state boards of health, colonial governors, military and naval personnel, and local (county and town) governments.

State Boards of Health/Bureaus of Vital Statistics

The most important record-keeping agencies for marriages and divorces in the United States today are the state boards of health or bureaus of vital statistics (or some variation of these names). Even though these agencies are primarily state bodies, large cities usually have their own registries. However, they were practically nonexistent until after 1850, and almost no state had such a bureau until after 1830. New Hampshire (1640), Vermont (1770), and Washington, D.C. (1811) were the first; Colorado (1968) was the last. Even when the requirement existed, the laws were seldom enforced. As a result many genealogists are reluctant to spend the time necessary to search for marriage records on file with these agencies during an early period. However, residents of heavily populated cities are not often mentioned in local histories or biographical publications. Quite often they can be found only in major record sources. Thus, it is imperative to search whatever records exist. Appendix F gives a state-by-state list with the dates each began keeping vital records and the address of the responsible agency, a reprint of the U.S. Department of Health, Education, and Welfare Public Health Services booklet entitled *Where to Write for Vital Records—Births, Deaths, Marriages, and Divorces* DHHS Publication (PHS) 82-1142. Addresses and certificate fees change often, future editions can be obtained by sending $3.50 to the Government Printing Office, Washington, D.C. 20001.

Colonial Governors

The earliest marriage records were frequently kept by the office of the colonial governor. While not numerous, many of these records are still in existence, usually in state archives. Some are now in print.

Military and Naval Personnel

Colonial, state, and federal military officers as well as ships' officers (military and civilian) often performed marriages and recorded them in ships' logs, daybooks, and private journals. These records can be found among military records maintained by the federal government or in historical societies, libraries, and museums. (See also Chapter 15, "Tracking Immigrant Origins.")

Town and County Governments

Town clerks in New England and county clerks elsewhere have registered most of the marriages in the United States. Marriage records were kept in New England beginning in the 1600s and in the South in the 1700s. Clerks issued documents granting permission for a couple to marry, and then received notification that the ceremony had taken place from ministers and justices of the peace in the town or county. The remainder of this chapter will discuss in detail the records on file in these town and county jurisdictions.

There is no uniformity in United States marriage records. The researcher should thus become familiar with the laws and customs of each research area and time period. Some jurisdictions required more than one form of document and the information required on different documents often varied. For example, marriage registers in Kentucky usually list the names of the bride and groom, the date and place of the marriage, and the officiating authority. The marriage license, issued as a separate record for the same couple, could add residence, age, place of birth, names of parents, and occupation.

Churches

Churches were among the earliest keepers of marriage records. By 1640 both Virginia and Massachusetts had passed laws requiring ministers to present a record of the marriages they performed to civil officials in the county or parish. Records of marriages in those areas not requiring periodic reporting remained with the minister or the church.

Many churches, especially in the frontier areas, did not keep extensive records, and many records have been lost or destroyed. New England churches, Quaker Monthly Meetings, and the German churches kept and have preserved the most complete records. (See Chapter 5 for a discussion of church records.)

Justices of the Peace

Most states authorized the election or appointment of justices of the peace who could perform marriages. Like ministers, justices were also required to submit a record of the marriages they per-

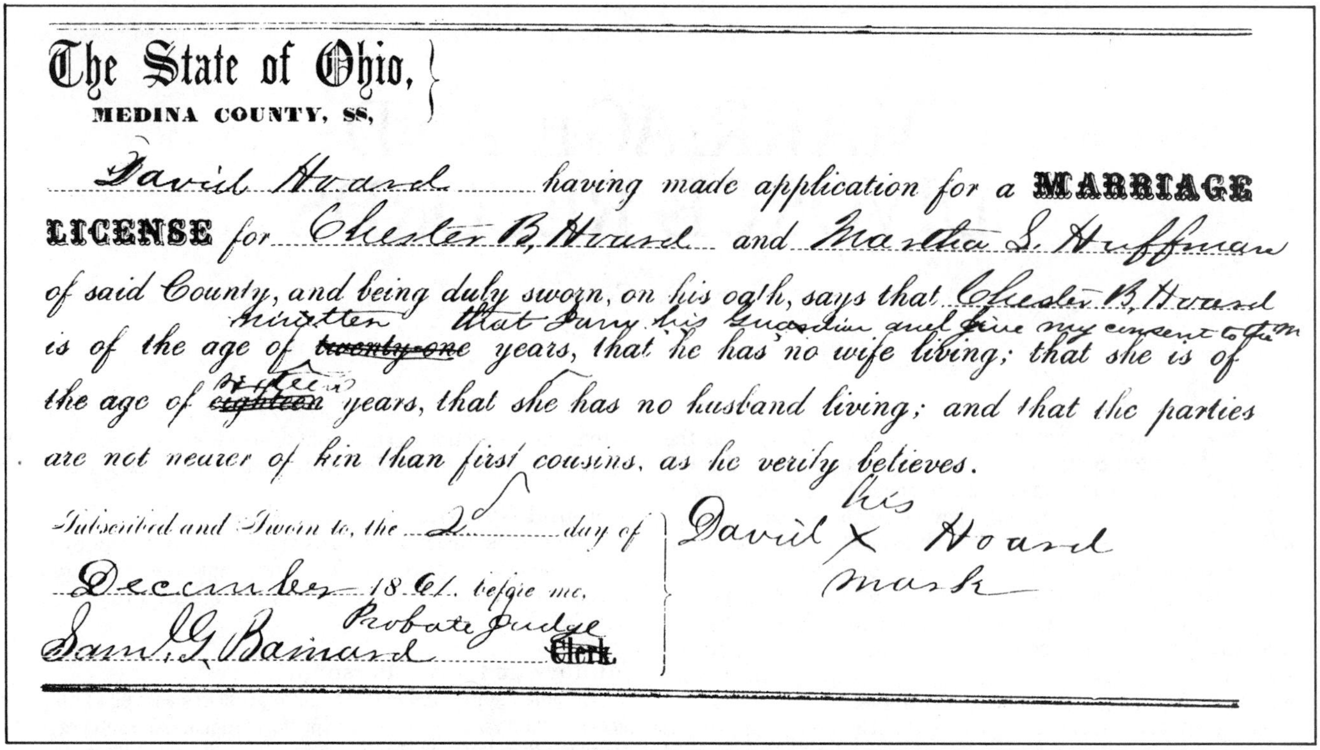

The State of Ohio,
MEDINA COUNTY, ss,

David Hoard having made application for a **MARRIAGE LICENSE** for Chester B. Hoard and Martha S. Huffman of said County, and being duly sworn, on his oath, says that Chester B. Hoard is of the age of ~~twenty-one~~ nineteen years, that he has no wife living; that she is of the age of ~~eighteen~~ sixteen years, that she has no husband living; and that the parties are not nearer of kin than first cousins, as he verily believes. that Dany his guardian and give my consent to them

Subscribed and Sworn to, the 2d day of December 1861. before me.
Saml. G. Barnard Probate Judge ~~Clerk.~~

David his X mark Hoard

Figure 3-1. David Hoard application for marriage license for Chester B. Hoard and Martha S. Huffman, Medina County, Ohio, 2 Dec. 1861, book 1, p. 29; Genealogical Society of Utah (hereafter GS) microfilm 55,536 pt. 3.

formed to civil authorities. Justices also maintained their own registers, often in personal account books where they recorded the fees paid. They sometimes contain marriages and other genealogical information not forwarded to the civil authorities and should not be overlooked by the researcher even when civil records are available. Justices' registers can be found in the care of county clerks, local historical societies, libraries, or descendants of the justices themselves. Several are microfilmed at the Genealogical Society of Utah and some have been published by local genealogical societies.

Types of Marriage Records

Consent Affidavits

The minimum legal age for marriage varies from place to place. While some jurisdictions required consent regardless of age, most demanded consent affidavits from a parent or legal guardian only for those under the minimum age – usually twenty-one for males, eighteen for females. Sometimes a parent or guardian appeared with the underaged person and gave verbal permission. The record will show that the parent was present and was known to the clerk but may not record the name. A detailed, printed consent form was part of the marriage license in a few localities.

The father of the underaged person usually gave consent, especially in the South. When a mother gives consent, the father is likely deceased. When both parents are deceased, the legal guardian will grant permission to marry. If the guardian is related to the person getting married, their relationship may be stated.

Figure 3-1 is an application for a marriage license by David Hoard for Chester B. Hoard and Martha S. Huffman in Medina County, Ohio. He states that he is Chester B. Hoard's guardian, and gives his consent to the marriage.

Consent documents are found in town and county jurisdictions throughout the nation but are more numerous in regions like the South or the frontier which encouraged early marriage.

Declarations of Intent

Declarations of intent to marry have been required in one form or another in all colonies and states during colonial and modern times. The practice may have been abandoned in a particular place for a period of time, only to be reinstated later. There are many types of declarations of intent, both written and oral.

Banns. Publishing banns was a church custom during the colonial period. Banns were usually read in church on three consecutive Sundays (sometimes during public meetings) and, in some areas, were posted in public places as well. Their purpose was to give local residents the opportunity to state why the marriage should not take place. The following is a sample of what might be included in published banns:

> I publishe the Banns of Marriage between Robert Preston of New Haven and Priscilla Fuller of Milford. If any know cause or just impediment why these two persons should not be joined together in Holy Matrimony, ye are to declare it. This is the 1st time asking.
>
> Daniel Stout, Reverend

Intentions. These records were similar to banns but were filed with the town or county clerk. Not generally read aloud, they were posted in public places for a prescribed period of time to give others the opportunity to voice objections to the union.

Many intentions filed in New England have been published. Here is a marriage intention from the Town Records of Beverly, Massachusetts.

Marriage Intentions.

Jofiah Hall of Exeter in the Prouince of new Hampfheir and Mary Woodbery of Beverly their Intention of——— Publifhed March 30th Day 1712

William Grouer and Elizabeth Hull Boath of Beverly their Intention of Marriage publifhed may ye 18th 1712

John Stone Junr of Beverly and Ruth Waldran of Wenham their Intention of Marriage Publifhed May 18th Day 1712

Roger Hafkins and Elizabeth Shaw Boath of Beverly their Intention of Marriage Publifhed auguft 10th 1712

Phillip Piles & Return Ellinwood Boath of Beuerly their Intention of Marriage Publifhed on August 24th 1712

Benjamin Webfter & Ruth Gray Boath of Beuerly there Intention of Marriage publifhed on Nouember 8th 1712
Ifaac Hull Junr & Ann Wood Both of Beuerly their Intention of marriage publifhed on Nouembr 22d 1712
Ebenezer Cleues. & Sarah Stone Boath of Beurley their Intention of Marriage publifhed Nouembr 21ft 1712
Samuel Harris and Sarah Biles boath of Beuerly their Intention of Marriag publifhed Decemb: 5th 1712
Jonathan Ober and Rebeckah ——— their Intention of Marriage publifhed December 28th day 1712
James Afhby and Abigel Reed Both: of Beuerly their Intention of marriage Publifhed april 19th 1713
Samuel Woodbery of Beuerly and hannah Dodge of Salem their Intention of marriage publifhed Auguft 22d 1713
Matthew Butman & Martha Herrick both of Beuerly their Inten-

Augustus A. Galloup, comp., *Early Records of the Town of Beverly, Essex County, Mass.* (Boston: Eben Putnam, 1907), p. 43

Bonds. Marriage bonds were not required by all colonies or states but are found extensively in the South and New England. Bonds were posted prior to the issuing of the required marriage license in some states and were the sole document required in others. Bonds were posted by the groom alone or with a second person, usually the father or the brother of the bride, to defray the costs of litigation in the event the marriage was nullified.

Bonds were posted in the jurisdiction where the marriage was to take place, often in the bride's home county. These bonds, the only marriage records maintained in some jurisdictions, were usually annotated with the marriage date after the ceremony. It was rare for a marriage not to take place within a few days of the posting of the bond even though many bonds do not bear the annotation. Although the missing information could mean that the marriage did not take place, more often it reflects poor record keeping or failure on the part of the justice or minister to report the marriage to local officials. Figure 3-2 is a photocopy of a bond typically found in the South.

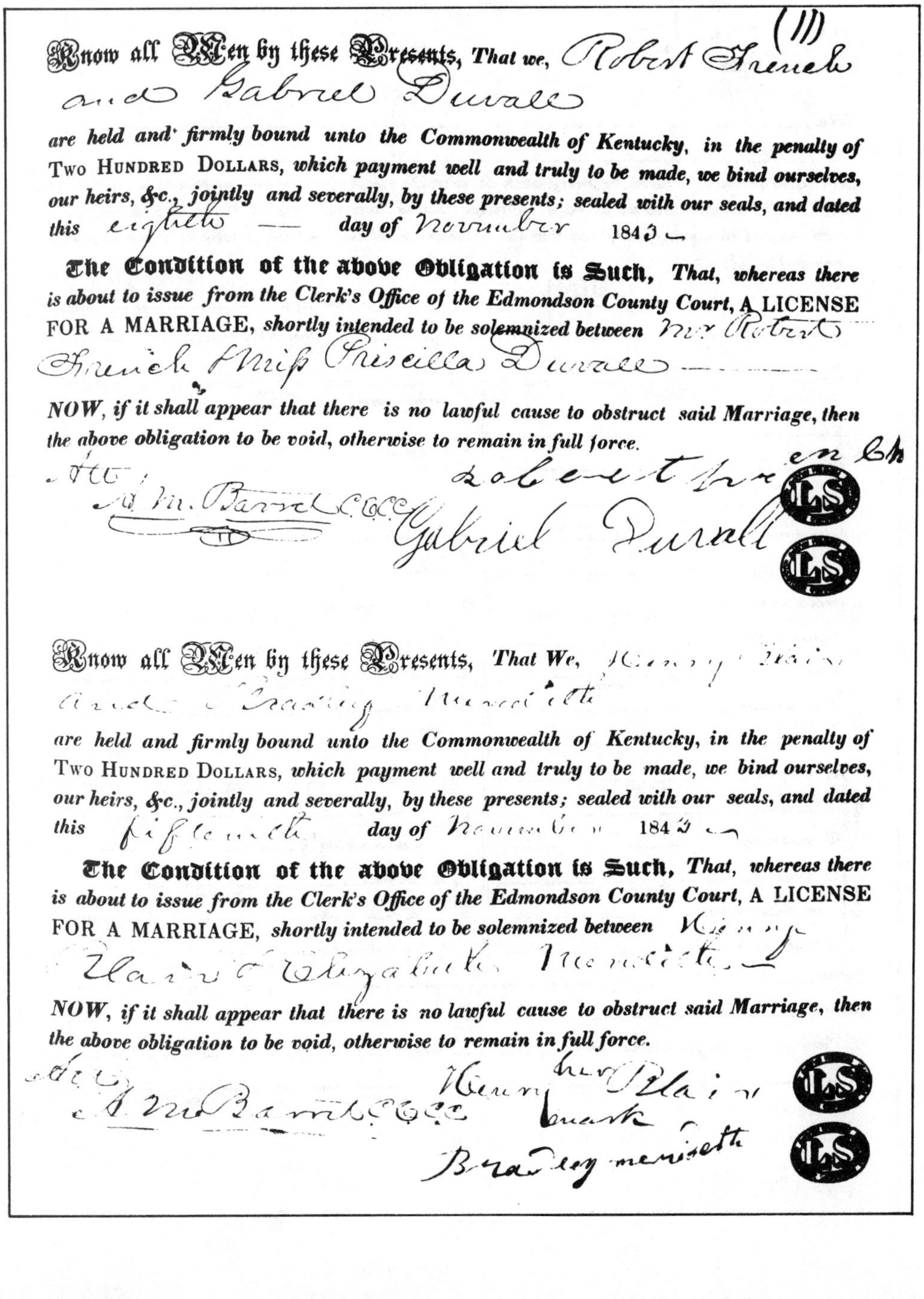

(11)

Know all Men by these Presents, *That we,* Robert French and Gabriel Duvall

are held and firmly bound unto the Commonwealth of Kentucky, in the penalty of TWO HUNDRED DOLLARS, *which payment well and truly to be made, we bind ourselves, our heirs, &c., jointly and severally, by these presents; sealed with our seals, and dated this* eighth *day of* November 1843

The Condition of the above Obligation is Such, *That, whereas there is about to issue from the Clerk's Office of the Edmondson County Court,* A LICENSE FOR A MARRIAGE, *shortly intended to be solemnized between* Mr Robert French & Miss Priscilla Duvall

NOW, if it shall appear that there is no lawful cause to obstruct said Marriage, then the above obligation to be void, otherwise to remain in full force.

Att: A. M. Barret C.C.C. Robert French (L.S.)
Gabriel Duvall (L.S.)

Know all Men by these Presents, *That We,* Henry Blain and Bradley Meniseth

are held and firmly bound unto the Commonwealth of Kentucky, in the penalty of TWO HUNDRED DOLLARS, *which payment well and truly to be made, we bind ourselves, our heirs, &c., jointly and severally, by these presents; sealed with our seals, and dated this* fifteenth *day of* November 1843

The Condition of the above Obligation is Such, *That, whereas there is about to issue from the Clerk's Office of the Edmondson County Court,* A LICENSE FOR A MARRIAGE, *shortly intended to be solemnized between* Henry Blain & Elizabeth Meniseth

NOW, if it shall appear that there is no lawful cause to obstruct said Marriage, then the above obligation to be void, otherwise to remain in full force.

Att: A. M. Barret C.C.C. Henry his mark Blain (L.S.)
Bradley Meniseth (L.S.)

Figure 3-2. Robert French and Priscilla Duvall, Edmundson County, Kentucky, 8 Nov. 1843, Marriage Bonds 1843-58, p. 11; GS 367,211.

Contracts. Marriage contracts are relatively uncommon. They were usually drawn up when one or more of the parties was wealthy or an heir to wealth and wished to protect the inheritance rights of heirs.

Marriage contracts are also found in second marriages. Property left to a widow by her first husband could be protected with a marriage contract. Such documents guarantee the distribution of property to the children of the first husband. Without such a contract, the property inherited at the death of the first husband became the property of the second husband at the time of marriage. He could dispose of that property as he desired, without provision for his stepchildren. Marriage contracts are recorded among marriage records, filed in the court records, or with the deeds.

Louisiana is one state in which marriage contracts were widely used during the colonial period. Under civil law, the French and Spanish used formal marriage contracts to protect their property, regardless of their social position or wealth. The documents are of unequaled value in genealogical research, since they list extended family relationships and often the place of origin of the French immigrant ancestor. The contract between Charles de Lavergne and Marie Joseph Carriere illustrates the superb detail of these documents.

June 16, 1739

CHARLES de LAVERGNE, Lieutenant on half-pay, of this Province of Louisiana, son of Mr. PIERRE de LAVERGNE, Counsellor at Chatelet of Paris, and of Dame ELIZABETH BILLET his father and mother, a native of Paris, Parish of St. Eustache

with

Demoiselle MARIE JOSEPH CARRIERE, minor daughter of the deceased Sieur ANDRE CARRIERE and of Dame MARGUERITTE HARLUT her father and mother, a native of Mobile, Bishopric of Quebec. The named Dame MARGUERITTE HARLUT now wife of Sieur LOUIS

Figure 3-3. Application for License to Marry, State of Utah, County of Utah.

APPLICATION FOR LICENSE TO MARRY

STATE OF UTAH, }ss.
County of Utah

We, ______________________ of ______________________

and ______________________ of ______________________

desiring to procure a license to marry, each do solemnly swear that we are single and unmarried and may lawfully contract and be joined in marriage; that we are not related to each other within the fourth degree of consanguinity and that the following detail data is true, according to our best knowledge and belief:

1. County in which issued ______ UTAH ______. Date issued ______
2. Place of marriage: County ______ City or Town ______ Date of Marriage ______
3. Name and address of person officiating ______ Title ______

GROOM	BRIDE
Full name 4. ______	Maiden name 18. ______
5. Residence: State ______ County ______ City or town ______	19. Residence: State ______ County ______ City or town ______
6. Color or race ______	20. Color or race ______
7. Age last birthday ______ (Years) 8. Birth date ______	21. Age last birthday ______ (Years) 22. Birth date ______
9. Previous marital status ______ (single, widowed, or divorced)	23. Previous marital status ______ (Single, widowed, or divorced)
10. Number of this marriage ______ (1st, 2d, 3d, etc.)	24. Number of this marriage ______ (1st, 2d, 3d, etc.)
11. Birthplace ______ (State or country)	25. Birthplace ______ (State or country)
12. Usual occupation ______	26. Usual occupation ______
13. Industry or business ______	27. Industry or business ______
Father: 14. Birthplace ______ (State or country) A. Name ______ 15. Usual occupation ______	Father: 28. Birthplace ______ (State or country) A. Name ______ 29. Usual occupation ______
Mother: 16. Birthplace ______ (State or country) A. Name - Maiden ______ 17. Usual occupation ______	Mother: 30. Birthplace ______ (State or country) A. Name - Maiden ______ 31. Usual occupation ______

(Signed) ______________________ Male

(Signed) ______________________ Female

Subscribed and sworn to before me this ______ day of ______ 19____

By ______________________ Deputy Clerk ______________________

County Clerk.

TIXERRANT being present.

Consenting for the minor being Sieur JOSEPH CARRIERE her uncle and tutor.

Consenting on the part of the named Sieur de LAVERGNE, Mr. de BIENVILLE, Chevalier of the Royal and Military Order of St. Louis, Governor of this Province, of Louisiana, Mr. de SALMON, Commissioner of the Marines of this Province and Madame his wife, Mr. DIRON DARTAGUETTE, Chevalier of the Royal and Military Order of St. Louis, Commandant at Mobile, Mr. BELLUGA Captain of the King's vessel, Mr. DeVILLER FRANSSURE, Lieutenant, Commander of the King's vessel, Mr. DeMORVILLE also a Lieutenant of the King's vessel, presently of this Colony, his friends and friends of his deceased parents.

And for the named Demoiselle MARIE JOSEPH CARRIERE, Sieur and Dame TIXERRANT her step-father and her mother, Sieur JOSEPH

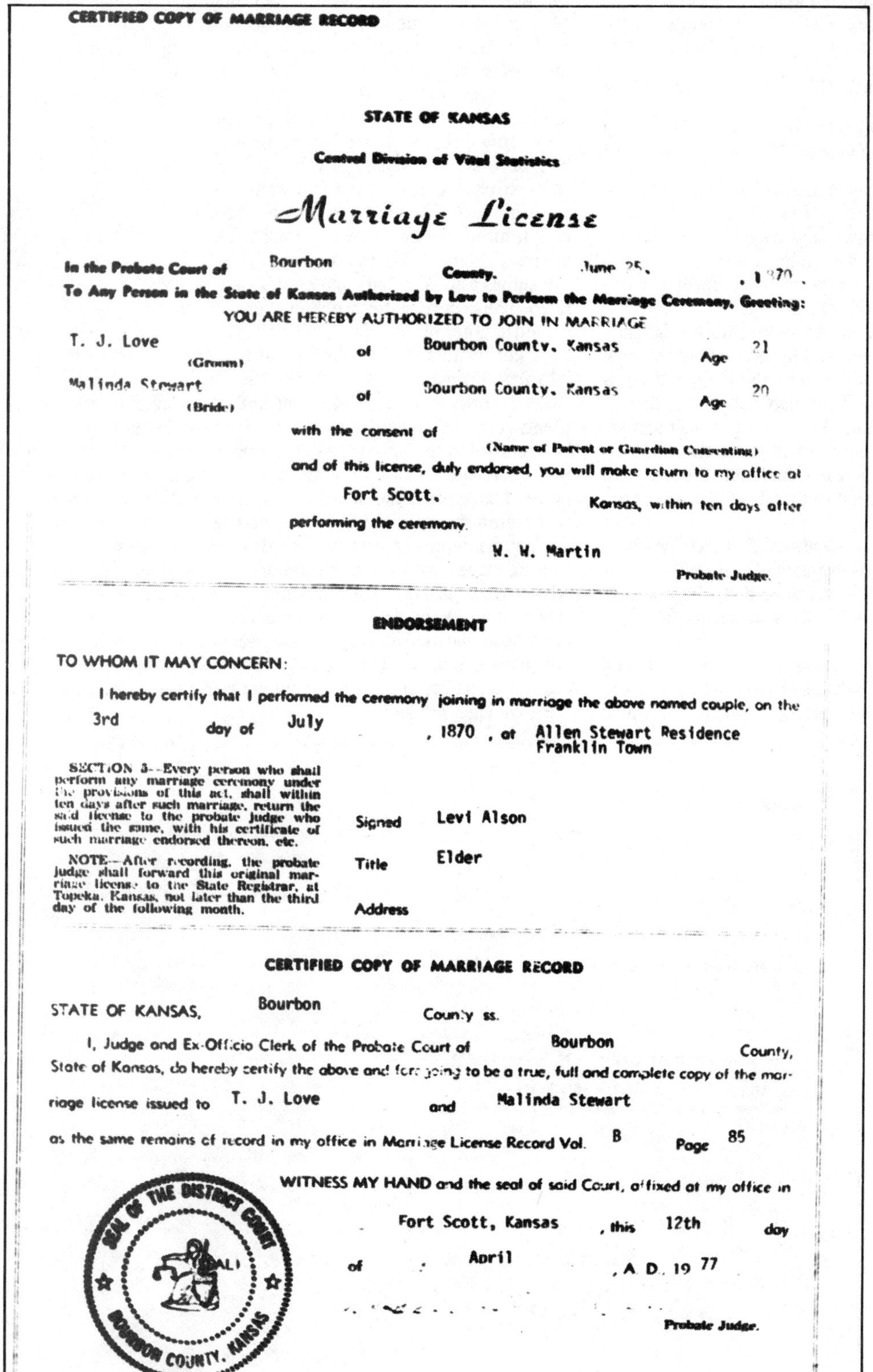

CERTIFIED COPY OF MARRIAGE RECORD

STATE OF KANSAS

Central Division of Vital Statistics

Marriage License

In the Probate Court of Bourbon County. June 25, 1870.

To Any Person in the State of Kansas Authorized by Law to Perform the Marriage Ceremony, Greeting:

YOU ARE HEREBY AUTHORIZED TO JOIN IN MARRIAGE

T. J. Love (Groom) of Bourbon County, Kansas Age 21

Malinda Stewart (Bride) of Bourbon County, Kansas Age 20

with the consent of (Name of Parent or Guardian Consenting)

and of this license, duly endorsed, you will make return to my office at Fort Scott, Kansas, within ten days after performing the ceremony.

W. W. Martin

Probate Judge.

ENDORSEMENT

TO WHOM IT MAY CONCERN:

I hereby certify that I performed the ceremony joining in marriage the above named couple, on the 3rd day of July, 1870, at Allen Stewart Residence Franklin Town

SECTION 3.--Every person who shall perform any marriage ceremony under the provisions of this act, shall within ten days after such marriage, return the said license to the probate judge who issued the same, with his certificate of such marriage endorsed thereon, etc.

NOTE—After recording, the probate judge shall forward this original marriage license to the State Registrar, at Topeka, Kansas, not later than the third day of the following month.

Signed Levi Alson

Title Elder

Address

CERTIFIED COPY OF MARRIAGE RECORD

STATE OF KANSAS, Bourbon County ss.

I, Judge and Ex-Officio Clerk of the Probate Court of Bourbon County, State of Kansas, do hereby certify the above and foregoing to be a true, full and complete copy of the marriage license issued to T. J. Love and Malinda Stewart as the same remains of record in my office in Marriage License Record Vol. B Page 85

WITNESS MY HAND and the seal of said Court, affixed at my office in Fort Scott, Kansas, this 12th day of April, A. D. 19 77

SEAL OF THE DISTRICT COURT (SEAL) BOURBON COUNTY, KANSAS

Probate Judge.

CERTIFIED COPY OF MARRIAGE RECORD

Figure 3-4. T. J. Love marriage license to Malinda Stewart, Bourbon County, Kansas, 25 June 1870, Marriage License Book vol. B, p. 85; certified copy in possession of the author.

CARRIERE her uncle and tutor, Sieur JACQUES CARRIERE also her uncle, Dame FRANCOISE JALLOT widow CARRIERE, Aunt of Demoiselle MARIE MARGUERITTE CARRIERE, her sister, Sieur LOUIS TIXERRANT her brother, Mr. and Madame de LIVAUDAIS her cousin, Mr. and Madame CENDRET, Mr. and Madame deMAZANT also a cousin, Mr. the Chevalier de LOUBOY, of the Royal and Military Order of St. Louis, Mr. de GAUVRY Chevalier of the Royal and Military Order of St. Louis, Captain of the Infantry of the Marines, Mr. D'AUTHERIVE, Chevalier of the Royal and Military Order of St. Louis, Mr. de BELISLE, Mr. BOBE DESCLOSEAUX, comptroller of the Marines, Mr. DUBREUIL VILLARS, contractor for the King's fortifications in this Colony.

This marriage to be solemnized in the Holy Roman Apostolic Catholic Church.

This document collated and entered in the minutes of the Royal Notary, at New Orleans on the 17 of June of 1768. /s/ Garic, Notary.[1]

Marriage Licenses. Marriage licenses are the most common marriage records in the United States. They were issued by the appropriate authority prior to the marriage ceremony and eventually replaced the posting of banns and intentions. Marriage licenses which granted permission for a marriage to be performed were returned to civil authorities after the ceremony.

Applications for marriage licenses were required in some jurisdictions in addition to or in place of bonds. These documents were often filled out by both the bride and groom and contain a large amount of genealogical information. They may list the full names of the bride and groom, their residences, races, ages, birthdates, previous marriages, birthplaces, occupations, and the parents' names, birthplaces (state or country), and occupations. Recent laws require health certificates which attest to the absence of diseases that could be passed on to children.

Marriage applications begin in most locations after the Civil War. Indiana, Wisconsin, and Utah counties maintained them earlier. The application form does not include the marriage date. Figure 3-3, a copy of the marriage application for Utah, is similar to those required in other states.

Marriage licenses come in varying forms. Figure 3-4, a certified copy of a marriage license issued by Kansas and prepared by the probate court in the county where the marriage took place, is much like licenses from most towns or counties. A standard form generally asks for the names of the bride and groom, their residence at the time of application, the date the marriage was performed, the date the license was issued, the place of the marriage, and the person performing the marriage ceremony. In this example, the document states that the marriage took place at the residence of Allen Stewart at Franklin Town, Bourbon County, Kansas. Since the bride is Malinda Stewart, Allen Stewart is probably a relative. (Further research determined that he was, in fact, her father.)

A license from Spencer County, Kentucky (Figure 3-5) illustrates the style of license used during earlier periods in the South. Note that the return after the ceremony is annotated at the bottom of the license in the handwriting of the minister.

Certified copies of marriage records are certified to be correct, but there is a possibility of error in any typescript. It is best to request photocopies when you write the county clerk.

Marriage Certificates. Marriage certificates are given to the couple after the ceremony is completed and are thus usually found in family records. There are some exceptions to this rule. Figure 3-6 shows a book of marriage certificates on file in Medina County, Ohio. These certificates are, however, similar to marriage licenses issued in other places. The bride and groom usually receive a marriage certificate for their family records containing similar historical information, signatures of witnesses, etc.

Marriage Registers and Returns. Colonial and state governments required that marriages performed within their jurisdictions be reported to civil authorities. The town or county clerk then compiled marriage registers, though these registers were rarely complete. Those officiating marriages in the rural areas of the county were often reluctant to travel the distance required to comply with the law. Sometimes ministers' records were lost or destroyed before the marriages were properly reported, and itinerant preachers, who crossed jurisdictional boundaries, rarely registered their marriages at all. A couple sometimes obtained a license, filed a bond, or made application in one jurisdiction and then married in another, but ministers filed returns only in their own counties. Still, marriage returns are the only documents that provide evidence that the marriage actually took place.

Figure 3-5. John S. Summers marriage license to Mary C. Reynolds, Spencer County, Kentucky, 25 Dec. 1863, Marriage Book B, p. 22; GS 482,642, certificate 412.

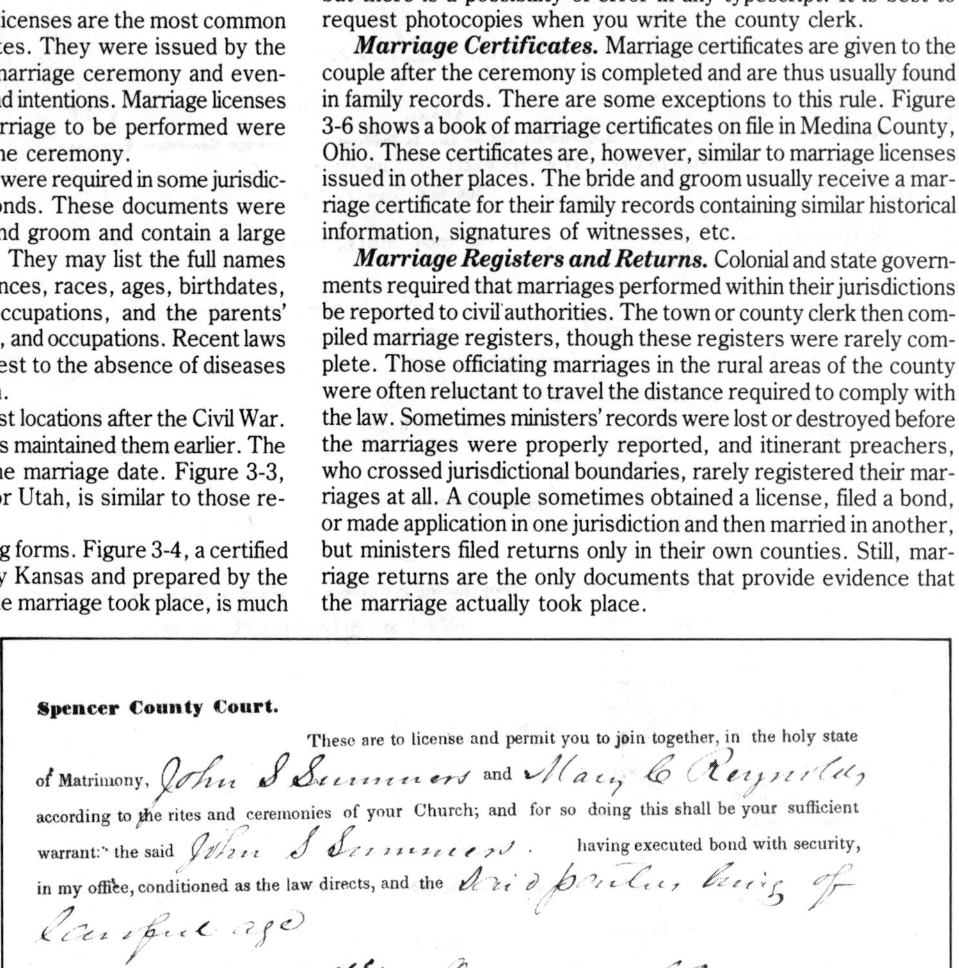

Spencer County Court.

These are to license and permit you to join together, in the holy state of Matrimony, John S Summers and Mary C Reynolds according to the rites and ceremonies of your Church; and for so doing this shall be your sufficient warrant: the said John S Summers having executed bond with security, in my office, conditioned as the law directs, and the bride being of lawful age

GIVEN under my hand, this 25th day of December, 1863

To any Minister of the Gospel, legally authorized to solemnize the rites of Matrimony. Jos. B. Cox clk

Dated 16th day of Febuary 1864 I did sollomnise the rites of Matromony between the above named John S. Summers and Mary E. Reynolds at the house of James Reynolds in Spencer county in presents of William Summett and Mark Summers on the 16th day of Febuary 1864
William Pugh Minister of Methodist E. S church south

14

5 cts U. S. REVENUE STAMP. Cancelled.

MARRIAGE CERTIFICATE.

THE STATE OF OHIO, MEDINA COUNTY, SS.

I hereby Certify, That on the ninth day of January A. D. 1865, I joined together in Marriage, Mr. Charles H. Bennett and Miss Elizabeth Painter

Philander Green Minister.

Filed February 15th 1865 .... Justice of the Peace.

Figure 3-6. Charles H. Bennett marriage certificate to Elizabeth Painter, Medina County, Ohio, 15 Feb. 1865. Book 2, p. 14; GS 55,537 pt. 3.

Marriage registers differ from jurisdiction to jurisdiction. Some required only the names of the couple and the date of the marriage. Registers are normally in chronological order by year, though there can be overlap in registers which were infrequently updated. The Spencer County, Kentucky marriage register shown in Figure 3-7 provides the date of marriage, names of the parties, the person performing the marriage, the place of marriage, the names of witnesses, and the certificate number.

Some registers exist in the absence of licenses. This is true in registers for Virginia and West Virginia after 1853, which provide the marriage date, minister, names of the parties, their ages, places of birth, residences, parents, and occupations. Many of these registers have been transcribed.

Most marriage registers are compiled from written returns submitted by ministers and justices. The lists are copied into the register by a clerk and are thus subject to transcription error. Figure 3-8 is a photocopy of the returns register of Daviess County, Kentucky.

Not all marriage returns were entered into a register. Some were simply noted on the license or bond and others were written on scraps of paper filed loosely in the clerk's office, either in alphabetical order or by the first letter of the groom's surname. Most loose returns have been microfilmed for easier use.

Locating Marriage Records

Marriage records were issued and maintained by town and county jurisdictions before state registration was established. Marriage

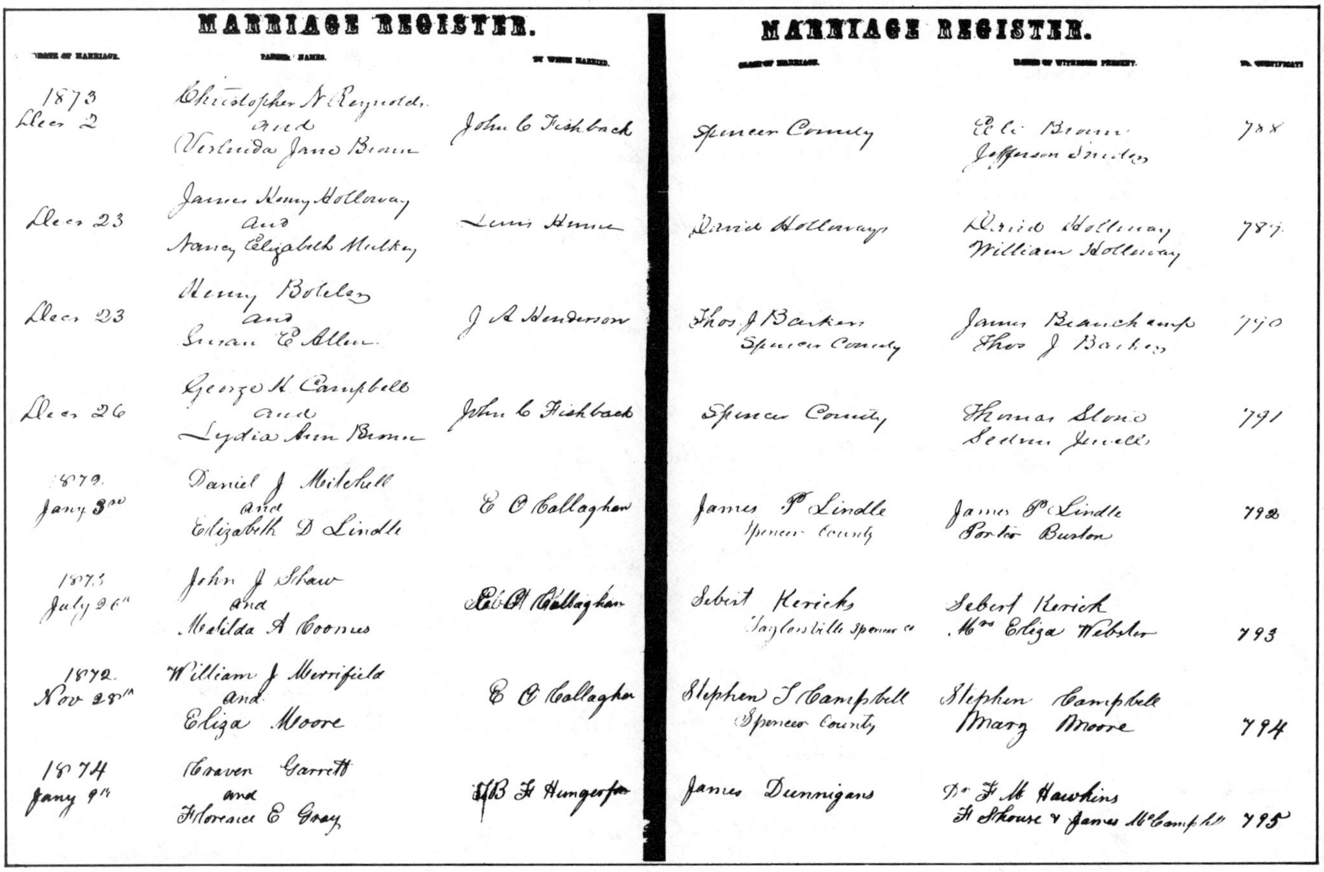

MARRIAGE REGISTER. | **MARRIAGE REGISTER.**

Date of Marriage	Parties' Names	By whom Married	Place of Marriage	Names of Witnesses Present	No. Certificate
1873 Decr 2	Christopher N Reynolds and Verlinda Jane Brown	John C Fishback	Spencer County	Eli Brown, Jefferson Snider	788
Decr 23	James Henry Holloway and Nancy Elizabeth Mulkey	Lewis Hume	David Holloways	David Holloway, William Holloway	789
Decr 23	Henry Boteler and Susan E Allen	J A Henderson	Thos J Barker Spencer County	James Beauchamp, Thos J Barker	790
Decr 26	George K Campbell and Lydia Ann Brown	John C Fishback	Spencer County	Thomas Sloan, Sedum Jewell	791
1874 Jany 3rd	Daniel J Mitchell and Elizabeth D Lindle	E O Callaghan	James P Lindle Spencer County	James P Lindle, Porter Burton	792
1873 July 26th	John J Shaw and Matilda A Coomes	E O Callaghan	Sebert Kericks Taylorsville Spencer Co	Sebert Kerick, Mrs Eliza Webster	793
1872 Nov 28th	William J Merrifield and Eliza Moore	E O Callaghan	Stephen T Campbell Spencer County	Stephen Campbell, Mary Moore	794
1874 Jany 9th	Craven Garrett and Florence E Gray	W B F Hungerford	James Dunnigans	Dr F M Hawkins, H Shouse & James McCamphell	795

Figure 3-7. Spencer County, Kentucky, Marriage Register, 10 April-31 July 1862; GS 482,494.

Figure 3-8. Daviess County, Kentucky, Marriage Returns, GS 582,231.

Date	Parties Names	Return of Marriage
1817		
May 15th	John B Blackwell to Nancy Hollins	A Certificate of the marriage of the parties was returned to me and duly acknowledged as follows "This may Certify I joined together John B Blackwell and Nancy Hollins in the holy state of matrimony this 29 of May 1817 Daniel T Pinkston Minister. Test William R Griffith clerk D County
July 6th	James Hollins to Rachel Taylor	This may Certify that I joined together James Hollins and Rachel Taylor in holy Wedlock this 10th day of July 1817 Daniel T Pinkston Minister. Acknowledged before me William R Griffith clk
Same	William McFarland to Frances Field	not found
July 10th	David Hamilton To Elizabeth Crabtree	I Job Hobbs minister do Certify that I celebrated marriage rites agreeable to a License handed me between Hamilton and Elizabeth Crabtree on the 17th day of July 1817 Job Hobbs. Return. ackd. before me this 8th Jany 1818 William R Griffith Clk
July 21st	James Bartlett to Una Lay	This is to Certify that I joined together the within named James Bartlett and Unci Lay in the holy state of matrimony this 14th of Augt 1817 Daniel T Pinkston Minister. True Copy of the return made on the License to me Test William R Griffith clerk
August 1st	William Sisk to Ann Brown	A Certificate of the marriage of the parties was returned to my office by the minister as follows "This is to Certify that I sollomnized the rites of Matrimony between William Sisk and Ann Brown according to the within Licence I say by me solemnized August 3rd 1817 Thomas Downs minister of the Gospel" Test William R Griffith Clerk DC

records are usually indexed by the surname of the groom, but there are a few jurisdictions that have compiled cross-indexes. Some states are collecting these early marriage records from the local jurisdictions; but since no comprehensive list of these repositories exists, a researcher must write to the town or county first. Addresses, including zip codes for every county and town clerk, can be obtained in the current edition of *Names and Numbers* (New York: John Wiley and Sons, 1978 and subsequent editions).

Genealogical Society of Utah

The Genealogical Society of Utah, operated by the Church of Jesus Christ of Latter-day Saints, has created the world's largest genealogical library, which houses millions of sources, including microfilmed records from most states east of the Mississippi River, and some western states. Filming continues in many counties. The collection is available in its entirety in Salt Lake City, but copies of the films can be obtained on interlibrary loan at branch libraries throughout the United States. (See Appendix D for locations.) This collection includes thousands of original marriage registers and collections of bonds, consents, licenses, and applications. They also have transcribed marriages in book or manuscript form, including Daughters of the American Revolution (DAR) and Works Progress Administration (WPA, part of Roosevelt's New Deal) marriage collections. Where originals and transcripts both exist, it is wise to check both. The transcripts often have cross-indexes to brides, annotations from ministers' journals and account books, newspaper announcements, and even the personal knowledge of the compiler.

Writing for Marriage Records

Researchers without access to the Genealogical Society of Utah's collection can write to the town or county custodian. For a fee, clerks will search the local records and send a copy of the information requested. This process can take a long time, and searches made by clerks are not always thorough. I made three separate requests for a single marriage license to the same county. The clerk wrote back each time saying that there was no record on file. Upon visiting that county myself a few years later, I found the document in less than five minutes. A researcher should make repeated requests or hire an agent to obtain a record when the marriage location is certain.

State boards of vital records and bureaus of vital statistics, because of the recent Right to Privacy Laws, may require you to file a form stating your relationship to the bride and groom and the purpose of the request, but records will usually be provided for family history purposes.

Marriage records can be found in numerous sources. Some counties registered marriages in court records and deed books. Common law marriages, if referred to at all, would be found in court records, which are rarely indexed (unlike deed books) and require substantial research time. However, they should not be overlooked.

Family Records

Family records, such as family Bibles, journals, diaries, and personal histories, also contain marriage documents or references to marriages. Certificates, contracts, and divorce records are also found in personal collections. Some family records have been donated to local historical societies, libraries, universities, or state archives. Manuscripts of unpublished family histories contain valuable genealogical information and are also found in these kinds of libraries, all of which usually have guides to their manuscript collections.

Printed Records

The number of printed volumes of marriage records grows daily as genealogical enthusiasts make their contributions to the field. These volumes are available through libraries, historical and genealogical societies, book sellers, publishers, and private distributors. They vary in usefulness. Some collections improve upon a poor original record by adding details about a couple and their families. However, the quality of the volume always depends on the skill of the transcriber in reading illegible handwriting and damaged records. Since a transcribed copy rarely includes all the information in the original record, you should also look at the original entry whenever possible.

Here is an example of the alphabetized and printed marriage records kept by two brothers who were justices of the peace in Washington County, Pennsylvania, Squires Isaac and Joseph F. Mayes. They married over 3,000 couples, most of whom eloped to their border town from West Virginia and Ohio since Pennsylvania did not require marriage licenses.

DEGARMO, MARTHA
to John Stiger
both of Triadelphia,
Ohio Co., WV
14 January 1871

DEGARMO, MARTHA E.
to Eli Johnston
both of Ohio Co., WV
17 June 1882

. . .

DELANEY, JONATHAN
of Wheeling, Ohio Co., WV
to Rosabella Faulkner
of Belton, Marshall Co., WV
5 November 1865

DELANY, WILLIAM C.
to Mary Virginia Crow
both of Wheeling, Ohio Co., (W)VA
24 August 1862.[2]

Genealogical periodicals published by state and county genealogical societies also include marriage records. Researchers can find large collections of these periodicals in many local libraries or can receive their own copies of such publications by joining the societies.

Newspapers have printed marriage announcements and engagements for decades. These articles often contain such information as the names of the parents of the bride and groom, place of residence after the marriage, and names of those in attendance at the wedding.

Special Problems in Using Marriage Records

An estimated 30 percent of the marriage records in this country are incomplete. Many marriage returns were never submitted to the civil authorities and countless others are lost. Hamilton County, Ohio, which recorded marriages for Cincinnati, is an interesting example. Many records were lost in a courthouse fire. Years later the WPA copied those that survived, mixing applications, licenses, and returns all together, and then indexing them. Local genealogists reconstructed some from ministers' daybooks, original certificates, and newspaper accounts. The DAR also collected marriage records from family and local sources. Since each of these collections came from different sources, the researcher must check them all; and even then, some marriages will not be recorded. Careful checking of all versions becomes important when you realize that Cincinnati, like many American cities, was a Gretna Green (no-questions-asked marriage locale) for couples up and down the Ohio River and from a wide circle of counties in Indiana and Kentucky, as well as Ohio. Therefore, if there is no record in the nearby county where a couple may have lived, chances are good that the entry may be found in the Cincinnati marriage records even though they are incomplete.

Marriage records throughout the United States are often inaccurate. Some information was deliberately falsified by the bride and groom. To reduce their workloads, clerks often entered the date of the marriage at the time the license was issued instead of waiting for the return. Thus, marriage information should be compared with other facts known about an individual. Additional research may be necessary to resolve discrepancies.

Spelling variants are also a problem in marriage records. Many clerks did not ask couples how their names were spelled but made phonetic guesses instead. All possible spellings of a surname should be checked before assuming that a couple is not in a given record.

Many marriage records are virtually illegible due to faded entries, damaged ledger books, poor handwriting, and poorly filmed originals. Published marriage records can assist in clarifying the unreadable entries. If poor filming is the problem, write to the county or town and request a photocopy or certified copy of the original. Sometimes more than one type of marriage record can be obtained.

If a marriage record is not on file for an ancestor, other records can be used to approximate the date. The 1900 Federal Census lists the number of years a couple has been married, and the marriage date can be calculated from that entry. Civil War pension application files contain marriage information. If a veteran's widow filed for the pension, she had to produce proof of the marriage by obtaining an affidavit from the appropriate minister or civil authorities, supplying a copy of the marriage certificate, or sending sworn statements from persons who could testify to the marriage date and place.

For an indepth study of past American marriage customs, see Frank G. Cook, "Marriage Celebration in the Colonies," *Atlantic Monthly* 61 (1888); Mrs. Henry Lowell Cook, "Maids for Wives," *Virginia Magazine of History and Biography* 51 (1943): 71-86; and John E. Semonche, "Common Law Marriage in North Carolina: A Study in Legal History," *American Journal of Legal History* 9 (1965): 320-49.

Good standard histories are Willystine Goodsell, *A History of Marriage and the Family*, rev. ed. (New York: Macmillan, 1934); and George E. Howard, *History of Matrimonial Institutions*, 3 vols. (Chicago: University of Chicago Press, 1904). This is an excellent study of English and American laws and customs. It is arranged by locality and period and has an extensive bibliography of additional references.

DIVORCE

Today one in every three marriages ends in divorce. Divorce was also common in early America as the colonists reacted against the severe divorce tradition inherited from England.[3] Divorce in England at the time of the founding of America was expensive, time-consuming, against Anglican law, and frowned upon socially. The only cause recognized was adultery, and three separate court trials were necessary: (1) a trial before an ecclesiastical court for a divorce from "bed and board" (legal separation), the legal right to live apart as though single but not the right to marry again (an oath or bond was filed promising the parties would not remarry); (2) a suit for damages in a civil court against the spouse's lover; and (3) a petition presented to the House of Lords for a hearing which ended with the grant of an absolute divorce – the dissolution of a legally valid marriage leaving both parties free to remarry.

Prior to 1715, the House of Lords granted only five divorces in the whole British Empire. From 1715 to 1775, sixty were granted; 1776 to 1800, seventy-four; and 1800 to 1850, ninety. Only four of these divorces were granted to women, who had to prove extreme cruelty as well as adultery.[4]

A less expensive but equally elaborate way to dissolve a marriage was to obtain an annulment from the Church of England, which declared the marriage void from the beginning because undue force or fraud had been used or the parties were too closely related by blood, were underage, or one or both parties had been under contract to someone else. Children born to an annulled union were declared illegitimate and could not inherit from their parents unless the church made special exception. Still, many annulments were sought.

American colonists were not anxious to establish ecclesiastical courts in the New World; and American courts, looking to English common law, which lacked divorce procedures, were left without precedent. As a result the divorce law of the U.S. courts is almost totally derived from statute.

In New England where marriage was considered a civil contract, courts granted civil divorces from early times. In the middle colonies – New York, New Jersey, and Pennsylvania – divorces were handled either by the governor and his council or by petition to the Assembly. Adultery or prolonged desertion were the only grounds recognized. In the South, where the Church of England was stronger, few civil divorce laws were in effect until after the Revolution. A married couple could separate by mutual consent, apply for legal recognition of their separation, and petition for alimony. The parties were usually not free to marry again. In all of the original colonies and several of the states, divorce by legislative petition was allowed. As petitions became numerous, however, overburdened legislatures gave this judicial function to the regular courts.

Profound differences still exist from state to state. Each state decides which court will handle the cases – superior court, equity court, probate court, or family or domestic court. The procedure basically allows the judge to decide what is just and equitable in each case within the limits set by the law. Because of this lack of uniformity, a researcher must study the development of divorce in each relevant jurisdiction. (See bibliography on divorce at the end of the chapter.) Table 3-1 outlines which courts supervised divorces in the original colonies, and the states created from colonies of Maine, Vermont, Tennessee, Kentucky, and West Virginia, as well as Ohio, Texas, and Hawaii. The remaining states are discussed in George E. Howard, *History of Matrimonial Institutions*, vols. 2-3 (Chicago: University of Chicago Press, 1904).

Divorce Records

Divorce is a court action recorded in court records: dockets which list plaintiff and defendant and the specific term or day of the court; minute books, which record court judgments and case descriptions (often in terse legal language); and case files, which provide affidavits, lists of children with their ages, property inventories, and other data. The date and place of marriage, ages or birthdates of the couple, birth places, and the grounds for the divorce are usually included. In addition, the record may list the names of other family members, since the children may be in the custody of grandparents, uncles, or close family friends.

Such records may be recorded in volumes with the regular court cases, in separate volumes reserved for divorce cases, or in a series of separate volumes for each kind of record. The examples which follow will introduce the kinds of records which exist.

County Minutes

Charles County, Maryland.

Minutes for 1658-59.

Elizabeth Robins Plt (
Robert Robins Deft (

> Elizabeth Robins petitioneth the court that she may have the privilege to choose an Aturnie to pleade her cause which was granted her and she not finding nor naming any Aturnie the court proceeded and Robert Robins housband to the said Elizabeth Robins taxeth her with adulterie and divers dispositions being read concerning the said buisnes which doe not declare any such thing as she is taxed with by her sayd husband it is thearfor ordered by the Court that the sayd Robert husband to the said Elisabeth his wife that he take the sayd Eliza: his wife againe, & provid for her & her children and further it is ordered that in case the sayd Robert Robins shal make apears by testimonie that shee hath formerlie confessed that the child now in her Arms was not begotten by her sayd housband but by some other that then hee shal not bee charged either to mayntaine her or her Sayd Child.

At a Countie Court held at Humpherie Atwikses the 4th day of June 1658.

The 18th of June 1659 Robert Robins and his wife Elisabeth Robins did come to the office of the Recorder of Charleses Countie and before Josias Fendall Governour and Mr John Hatch and the Clarke of the sayd office did macke this their Particular declaratione which was taken in writing by mee George Thompson Clarke of Charleses Countie which the sayd Robert Robins Caused to bee Recorded:

"I Robert Robins doe hereby disclayme my wife Elizabeth Robins for ever to acknowldege her as my wife and I doe hear oblige myself and everie one from mee never to molest or trouble her any further."

"I Elisabeth Robins doe hereby disclayme my husband Robert Robins for ever to acknowledge him as my husband and I doe hear oblige my selfe and everie one from mee never to Molest or trouble him any further for mayntainance or any other necessaries.

This to bee their owne declaration is affirmed by mee, George Thompson.[5]

This interesting example shows how first the husband tried to gain his freedom by accusing his wife of adultery – the only grounds recognized as valid for divorce or separation in Maryland at this time. When that failed he evidently convinced his wife that the best course was to mutually consent to the separation.

Legislative Act

Connecticut Legislative Resolves and Private Acts, 1837.

Upon the petition of Polly M. Mead of Danbury, Fairfield County, and state of Connecticut, praying a bill of divorce from her husband, Martin Mead of said Danbury, which petition was duly served and returned:

Resolved by the Assembly, that the said Polly M. Mead be, and she is hereby divorced from the said Martin Mead, and is and forever hereafter shall be absolved from all obligations to the said Martin Mead by virtue of said marriage contract, and is hereby declared to all intents and purposes, sole, single, and unmarried.

This entry points to the original petition which may contain case papers and testimony submitted by the parties involved. See Henry S. Cohn, "Connecticut's Divorce Mechanism, 1636-1969," *American Journal of Legal History* 14 (1970): 35-54. Muiti-volume sets of selected abstracts for most of the original colonies have been printed in archives series at government expense and can be found in most large research libraries throughout the United States (See Chapter 6, "Court Records" for a list of these). Abstracts should be used as indexes to the originals.

Civil Divorce

Weber County, Utah. Civil Divorce Case File, 1866:

Christina Anderson (
In the Probate Court County of Weber (
SS for said County (
Special Term July 1866 (
Hon. A. F. Farr, Judge (

Christina Anderson vs. In Divorce Peter Anderson

Now comes the aforesaid Christina Anderson, on this 4th day of July A.D. 1866, and petitions the aforesaid court for a Bill of Divorce against her husband the said Peter Anderson for abuse and maltreatment. Your petitioner for the past two years has lived a very unhappy life with her said husband on account of his conduct towards her, he being quarrelsome in his disposition, and he has in numerous instances shamefully beat her. Your petitioner therefore on these grounds would ask a decree of court dissolving the marriage relations between us.

her
Christina X Anderson
mark

Sworn to and subscribed
this 4th day of July 1866
Walter Thompson
Clerk of Court

Inventory of Belongings

70 acres of land	cooking utensils
1 house & lot (unfenced)	bedding &c
2 cows	30 yards cloth
2 calves	10 tons hay
2 yearlings	50 bushels (approx.) grain raised this year
22 sheep	1 wagon
2 pigs	1 plow
1 yoke oxen	potatoes in the garden
25 bushels wheat due for one cow sold	

Territory of Utah
In the Probate Court for said County
County of Weber
SS Special Term July 4th 1866
Hon. Aaron F. Farr, Judge

Christina Anderson vs. In Divorce – Peter Anderson

The aforesaid cause came up for hearing before the aforesaid court on the day and year above written, upon the petition of the plaintiff. The court having heard the case became satisfied that the parties could not live in happiness as husband and wife and that the petitioner had just grounds for petitioning for a Bill of Divorce against her said husband, Peter Anderson. It was therefore ordered and decreed that the bonds of matrimony theretofore existing between the said Christina Anderson and Peter Anderson be and the same are hereby dissolved.

It was also ordered that the petitioner have the house and lot that the said parties now occupy, ½ of the sheep, ¼ of the grain and vegetables, in the measure raised on the farm the present season, ½ of the bedding and household utensils and any other articles that they may have gathered since their marriage, her wearing apparel and any furniture or other articles she may have brought with her when married.

In testimony whereof I hereunto set my hand and affix the seal of said court the day and year first above written.

Walter Thompson, Clerk.[6]

Early Utah quickly gained the reputation of being a divorce mecca, with its broad grounds for divorce, inexpensive court procedures, and lack of residency requirements. Thus, Christina could obtain a divorce for abuse and maltreatment, grounds which were not allowed in eastern courts. When out-of-state people began arriving to take advantage of this situation, Utah stiffened its residency requirements and lengthened the waiting period.

A second example from a case file shows a pretrial notification:

Cuyahoga County, Ohio, Publication of Divorce, 1933:

Lola Loe v.(Publication of Divorce Lawrence Loe)

Lawrence Loe, whose place of residence is unknown, will take notice that on March 22 the undersigned, Lola Loe, filed her petition against him in the Court of Common Pleas of Cuyahoga County, Ohio, praying for a divorce and relief, on the grounds of gross neglect of duty. Said cause will be for hearing on and after the 26th day of April, 1933.

Lola Loe by Martin H. Blood, Esq., her attorney.[7]

If the location of the defendant had been known, he could have been served with papers by a court official. Instead, the notice was published in the newspapers. During the colonial period, notice would be posted on the town bulletin board at the courthouse, church, or city hall. News notices often ran as long as forty weeks. As communications improved, the time was gradually decreased to three to four weeks.

Some states require a certificate of divorce, with a copy filed at the state bureau of vital statistics. New Hampshire has issued certificates since 1880; other states did not begin this practice until well into the 1930s. Court records are public records, but those issued in the past fifty years are often protected by privacy legislation and permission of the divorced party may be required to get the data. Some states do not have certificates on file but can verify dates and refer queries to the court which has the record.

Table 3-1

Divorce Courts

State	*Legislature**	*Governor, Council*	*Courts*	*Comments*
Massachusetts	1639-1786	1760-1786	Supreme Judicial Court, 1786-1887 Superior Court, 1887 to present, on appeal to Supreme Judicial Court	Includes Plymouth Colony after 1692. Six divorces were granted by General Court of Plymouth Colony (includes Maine until 1820). 1639-92, forty cases 1692-1760, record sketchy 1760-86, ninety-six cases heard by governor and council
Connecticut	1655-1849	to 1711	Superior Court, 1711-present	Legislature, governor and council (Court of Assistants), and Superior Court had concurrent jurisdiction (includes New Haven Colony after 1664). Court of Magistrates granted divorce in New Haven 1648-64. Connecticut courts granted 11 legislative divorces 1655-91 and 390 divorces 1720-88. See Henry S. Cohn, "Connecticut's Divorce Mechanism, 1636-1969," *American Journal of Legal History* 14 (1970): 35-54.
Rhode Island	1650-1851		Court of Trials, 1663-1747	Concurrent jurisdiction. Many divorces granted 1747-90. Supreme Court, 1747-present.
New Hampshire	1766-1791	to 1776	Superior Court, 1791-1855 Supreme Court, 1855-present	Governor and council had primary jurisdiction until 1776; a few legislative divorces.
Vermont			Superior Court, 1779-present	
Maine			Supreme Court, 1821-present	
New York	to 1827	1655-75	Supreme Court, 1787-present	No cases after 1688, because a fire in 1911 severely damaged colonial records. A few legislative divorces before 1827.
New Jersey	to 1844	to 1773	Court of Chancery, 1794-present	Concurrent jurisdiction for legislature and council. A few divorces by mutual consent.
Pennsylvania	to 1847	to 1773	Supreme Court, 1785-1804 Court of Common Pleas, 1804-present	Governor issued most divorces subject to royal veto. Several were disallowed by Royal Council. In 1773, British Parliament forbade royal governors in America to grant divorce. 1776-85 legislative assembly granted all divorces; one hundred from 1817 to 1847.
Delaware	to 1897	to 1773	Superior Court, 1832-present	Twelve legislative divorces, 1848-49; sixty-three in 1889; 102 in 1897.
Maryland	to 1851		Court of Common Pleas, 1842-present	Some separations from bed and board granted by governor and council before 1776. Printed extracts in Mary K. Meyer, *Divorces and Names Changed in Maryland by Act of Legislature, 1634-1854*. (Baltimore: Genealogical Publishing Co., 1972).
Virginia	to 1848		Superior Court of Chancery, 1827-present.	Jury trial. Separation only until 1848. (includes West Virginia until 1863).

West Virginia		Circuit Court, 1863-present	
North Carolina	to 1835	Superior Court, 1814-present	Separation only. Divorces granted by Superior Court were ratified by the general assembly until 1818. Printed extracts in B. Ransom McBride, "Divorces and Separations Granted by Acts of North Carolina Assembly from 1790-1808," *North Carolina Genealogical Society Journal* 3 (1977):43-47 and Haywood Roebuck, "North Carolina Divorce and Alimony Petitions, 1813," *North Carolina Genealogical Society Journal* 1 (1975): 75-90.
South Carolina		1949-present	South Carolina claims that no absolute divorce has ever been granted. Those granted during Reconstruction 1869-70, may have been separations only.
Georgia	1798-1835	Superior Court, 1798-present	Since 1798, Georgia courts could grant absolute divorce only after concurrent verdicts of two separate juries hearing the case at different terms of court. Until 1849 partners who remarried were legally living in bigamy and children were illegitimate. An 1849 general law validated all second marriages, legitimizing children. Litigations and court petitions were required to validate second marriages, 1798-1849. Legislature granted 291 divorces 1798-1835. See"Divorces," *Georgia Genealogical Society Quarterly* 1 (1964-5): 9-19, additions 6 (1970):298. Georgia granted 291 legislative divorces 1793-1833.
Tennessee		Superior Court, 1799-present	
Kentucky	1792-1850	Circuit Court, 1809-present	1842-43 the General Assembly passed a mass divorce law for thirty-seven couples, providing for children, restoring maiden names to women, etc.
Ohio	to 1846	Circuit Court, 1795-1846 Supreme Court, 1804-present	Legislature granted 100 divorces before 1846.
Texas		District Court, 1841-present	
Hawaii		Circuit Court, 1897-present	

*By 1867, 33 of the 37 states had abolished legislative divorce. In 1866 a federal law made legislative divorce illegal.

Locating Divorce Records

Divorce records can be found housed in such diverse places as a well-lighted archives search room, a basement storage vault, or a warehouse. For state-by-state addresses of the depositories of divorce records, see Appendix F, "Where to Write for Vital Records: Birth, Deaths, Marriages, and Divorces."

Legislative divorces continued to be granted in some areas long after the same powers were granted to the regular courts, so a researcher should check the records of assembly and council as well as the court records. Printed volumes can serve as name indexes to the original files.

In addition to the court files, there are two other sources where early divorces are recorded: English Privy Council and Board of Trade minutes and colonial newspapers.

Colonial assemblies were required to submit copies of every law passed to the British government for ratification or veto. Private acts for divorce were included. Sometimes acts of divorce were disallowed by the crown. Since colonial laws were valid and legal until they were disallowed, couples who may even have remarried were sometimes ordered back together after a royal review period which sometimes lasted three to six years. By 1773 the increase in divorces alarmed England, and governors were ordered not to approve any further divorce bills. Hence there were fewer divorces until after the Revolution.

Acts submitted to the crown are recorded in the Colonial Office volumes, available in print in large research libraries. Each volume is individually indexed for all documents abstracted or calendared. Originals are in the Public Record Office, Chancery Lane, London WCZA ILR, England.

Local papers publish legal notices and also lists of divorces granted. Early issues carried notices placed by husbands to warn local tradesmen that they would no longer be responsible for debts incurred by exwives. On occasion wives also placed notices of freedom. (See Chapter 12 for instructions on how to find old newspapers.)

The disposition of property in any divorce case is determined by state statute or by equitable decision of the court.

Alimony is the allowance a woman is entitled to receive from her husband during separation and after divorce. The amount is usually set by the court based on the financial circumstances of the husband and the needs of the wife. In rare instances, a husband may be granted alimony from his wife. Alimony can be paid in monthly or annual installments or as a single lump sum, and usually stops when the spouse remarries. In some jurisdictions, a wife guilty of adultery is denied alimony. In others she receives payment regardless of such circumstances.

In South Carolina, which did not recognize divorce, or states which severely limited the grounds for divorce, courts accepted petitions for alimony to provide for the needs of family members who wished to live apart. In areas in which there were many Shakers, for example, courts addressed the needs of a spouse abandoned when the other spouse joined the celibate group. A woman was given a share of the husband's property and custody of the children. No divorce was granted, and the parties were still legally married, although living apart.

In most jurisdictions, until recently, if the wife was not guilty of adultery, she was entitled to her full dower and one-third of her husband's property at his death, even though a divorce had taken place. Some jurisdictions subtracted from the dower the amount already received in alimony. A husband could claim by right of curtesy one-third of her property.

The court outlines provisions for children of dissolved marriages at the time the divorce is granted. The law generally stipulates that the father must help pay for the upbringing of the children. The amount is determined by the court, based upon the earning ability of the father and the number of children. In cases of nonpayment, the court can order arrears to be made and enforce its decrees, even to the point of garnishing wages if necessary.

The custody of children is usually awarded based upon individual circumstances, although some jurisdictions today permit children above a certain age (eight to fourteen) to choose which parent they wish to live with. Visiting rights may be granted or denied to the other spouse at the discretion of the court.

Divorce Meccas

Certain states (or colonies) gained reputations for easy divorce. Stringent laws in one area led to migration into areas where divorces were easier to obtain. Pennsylvania and New England attracted New Yorkers. Ashtabula County in Ohio, which was readily accessible to New York, Pennsylvania, and Ontario, Canada, granted many divorces to non-Ohio residents. Following the Civil War, Chicago granted 400 divorces in 1868 alone. Utah Territory had no residency requirements until 1878 and even today requires only three months. Indiana had no residency requirements until 1859, and the residency requirements in other states vary widely: twenty-nine states require one year; Delaware, New Jersey, Rhode Island, Tennessee, and Arkansas require two years; Connecticut and Massachusetts require three years; North Carolina and Virginia require six months; Utah three months; Arkansas, Florida, Idaho, Wyoming, and Nevada seem to compete to lower their requirements to attract the divorce trade; Louisiana, New York, Wisconsin, and South Carolina have no specific residency requirement, but the grounds are more stringent in those states.[8]

After the Civil War, the frontier was often the most practical resolution to a bad marriage. Earlier this had been true of immigration to the New World as well. A ride into the sunset by one or both parties was easier and less expensive than petitioning for a legislative divorce. Numerous examples of runaway spouses can be found by reading the ads in early newspapers, a bonus for ancestor hunters.

For additional reading on past divorce laws and customs in the United States, see specialized treatments of colonies and states in: "Divorce in Colonial New York," *New York Historical Society Quarterly* 39 (Oct. 1955): 422; "Early Statutory and Common Law Divorce in North Carolina," *North Carolina Law Review* 604 (1973); "Harding vs. Harding, a 1753 Virginia Divorce," *Kentucky Ancestors* 14 (1978-79): 15-16; Margaret S. Hartman, "Annulments and Divorces in Kentucky." *Kentucky Genealogist* 20 (1978): 60-64, 85-88, 134-37; Guion G. Johnson, *An Evaluation of North Carolina Divorce Law in Antebellum North Carolina: A Social History* (Chapel Hill: University of Carolina Press, 1937); Paul R. Knapp, "Divorce in Washington," *Washington Historical Quarterly* 5 (1914): 121-28; George E. McCracken, "New Jersey Legislative Divorces, 1778-1844," *American Genealogist* 34 (1958): 107-12; and James S. Van Ness, "On Untieing the Knot: The Maryland Legislature and Divorce Petitions," *Maryland Historical Magazine* 67 (1972): 171-75.

Good surveys of American divorce laws are Nelson M. Blake, The *Road to Reno: A History of Divorce in the United States.* (New York: Macmillan, 1972); George E. Howard, *History of Matrimonial Institutions*, vols. 2-3 (Chicago: Chicago University Press, 1904); Gordon Ireland and Jesus de Galindez, *Divorce in the Americas* (New York: Dennis & Co., 1947); and Chester G. Vernier, *American Family Laws*, vol. 2. (Stanford: Stanford University Press, 1931), which covers modern divorce laws most likely to be needed by researchers.

Notes

1. Marriage Contract of Charles de LaVergne and Marie Joseph Carriere in Alice Daly Forsyth and Ghislaine Pleasanton, comps., *Louisiana Marriage Contracts* (New Orleans: Polyanthos Press, 1980), p. 85.

2. Helen L. Harris, CG, Elizabeth J. Wall, and Betty Treat Petrich, comps., *Marriage Records of Squires Isaac and Joseph F. Mayes* (Pittsburgh: n. pub., 1978), p. 59.

3. This section is adapted with permission from *Sources of Birth, Marriage, and Death Prior to 1900* (Salt Lake City: The Genealogical Institute, 1974), pp. 39-50.

4. Nelson M. Blake, *The Road to Reno: A History of Divorce in the United States* (New York: Macmillan, 1972), p. 32.

5. Liber A, p. 4, *Maryland Archives*, (Baltimore: Maryland Historical Society, 1934), vol. 53.

6. Petition for Divorce and Decree of Divorce, Christina Anderson vs. Peter Anderson, "Ancient Civil Divorce Files," 2 Feb. 1859-21 Feb. 1887, 2nd District Court, Utah, Civil Trials Record, H-2, 01.181, Utah State Archives.

7. Copy of original notice filed 22 March 1933, Cuyahoga County Court Clerk, Cleveland, Ohio.

8. See Appendix F.

INFORMATION GUIDE

Genealogical Information in the Record Group	*Population*	*Mortality*	*Veterans*	*Agriculture*	*Manufacturing*	*School*
Surname/name	●	●	●	●	●	●
Date of Birth						●
Place of Birth	●					
Sex	●	●				●
Race/color	●	●				
Physical Description			●			
Occupation	●	●		●	●	
Education	●					
Military Service			●			
Slave Status	●	●				
Property Owned	●			●	●	
Religion						
Citizenship	●					
Marital Status	●	●				
Spouse's Name	●					
Children's Names	●					●
Father's Name						●
Mother's Name						
Father's Birthplace	●					
Mother's Birthplace	●					
Date of Death		●				
Cause of Death		●				
Name of Cemetery						
Residence	●	●	●	●	●	●
Age	●	●	●	●	●	●
Literacy/signature	●					●
Photograph/sketch						
# of living children	●					
Total # of children	●					

COULD YOU USE THIS CHAPTER?

Type of Record	*Kept from*	*Clues That You Should Consult These Records*
Federal Censuses	1790-present	If your ancestors arrived in the United States between 1790 and 1910, search the federal census records (censuses after that date aren't available for research yet, to safeguard the privacy of living persons). You can search for them on a federal census if you know where they lived in any of the ten-year enumerating intervals. Even in areas not yet admitted to the Union, territorial censuses were made and kept. Although these censuses grew more and more detailed as time went on, even the earliest can establish an ancestral household and help you trace it. This chapter tells what each census contains, the indexes and finding aids availabe to use with each.
Special federal censuses	About 1810-1910	From time to time, the government wanted special information: who had died during the previous year, the number of war veterans still living, the number of slaves, the state of the nation's agriculture and manufacturing, social statistics of various kinds, and the Indians who were living on reservations. Not all of these schedules have survived and none of them span the entire century, but they are very helpful on special research problems.
State and local censuses	1623-1935	Many towns, counties, and states took their own censuses to determine, among other things, the number of taxable inhabitants, potential military strength, farming productivity, numbers of school-age children, slaves moving into Northern cities, etc. This chapter tells how to find and use these special censuses.

Chapter 4

CENSUS RECORDS

Arlene H. Eakle

Census, a Latin word, originally meant a count of persons and their property for the purposes of taxation. Its meaning has not varied a great deal over the centuries although it has become more inclusive. This chapter will describe some of the strengths and limitations of censuses, and the information available in federal, state, and local censuses with examples and case studies.

Problems in Census Use

Completeness

Completeness in a census schedule is affected by several important factors, not all of them problems of the enumerator or the time in which the census was taken. First are mistakes of the census taker. Some schedules list persons by initials only; some use nicknames; and some omit places of birth, value of real estate, occupations, and other details. In boarding houses, hotels, and clusters of workers' cottages, the enumerator could easily be unaware of one or two families. He could list the data from his personal knowledge rather than visiting the family or ask neighbors for information, missing newcomers to the area and overlooking families who had moved away.

The purpose of a census is also a limitation. Local and state censuses often focused on one specific group or interest, such as taxable slaves, slaves over sixteen years of age, and slaves under four years and over fifty years of age. This is not a complete tabulation of slaves nor was it intended to be.

Modern technology, for all its benefits, can also cause problems. When census schedules are microfilmed, camera operators have been known to accidentally turn two or more pages at once. Pages can be stuck together or folded over, obscuring other entries. Quality control does not always catch these problems so retakes of the missing data can be made. For example, nine pages were missed during the filming of the 1820 Virginia schedule, now indexed and identified by John Frederick Dorman in *Virginia Genealogist* 18 (1974): 136-39.

Computer tabulation can drop whole districts from a slight surge in electricity or other disturbance during input or printout. Large gaps are discernible, but small ones are easily overlooked. The 1800 census index for Pennsylvania, compiled painstakingly by Gendata Corporation, Salt Lake City, lost one whole county in the merge process. This loss was not discovered until the book appeared in print. It was withdrawn before many copies were sold to an unsuspecting public.

A fourth problem is searching the census. A partial index gives only limited access to the data. For example, the Soundex for the 1880 federal census includes only families with children under the age of ten years, not every family in the census. Military installations, poorhouses, prisons, and other institutions often appear at the end of the schedule with no indication in the contents list of this arrangement. Incorporated cities and local villages are usually enumerated separately from the township in which they are located.[1] Sometimes the township schedule is interrupted to list a city, with little or no warning. Names may be indexed under unknown spelling variants. Even when the census is complete, the method of searching can create incompleteness.

A final problem is "padding the totes," or political considerations behind the census. Frontier areas, anxious for statehood, often added bogus names. In 1857 seven counties in Minnesota had wild population totals, complete with fake names on the schedules.[2] Other instances include San Francisco (1852) where triple entries appear for some names and Utah (1894), where thousands of "gentile" (non-Mormon) names are written on Congressional petitions against statehood. Jurisdictions facing increased taxes might also understate the population to keep the overall per capita tax lower. The 1880 Utah census juggled households to disguise polygamy at a time when federal officials were seeking evidence for the prosecution of those convicted of unlawful cohabitation.

Accuracy

While census records contain some of the most valuable facts we have, they also contain false and misleading data. Census enumerators were not required to consult original records nor even to ask the members of the household themselves to secure their data. They could and did question neighbors, small children, and visiting relatives who gave answers verbally and from memory. Thus, there may be wide variations between the data in one census and that ten years later. The researcher must critically evaluate and corroborate such data with other material to attain any degree of accuracy.

Researchers routinely sigh over the census taker unable to understand the broken English of newly arrived immigrants. In the 1870 census of White Pine County, Nevada, the surname Bremenkampf was recorded "Kamp, Breman" and indexed under K.

Family members themselves may give incorrect data to the census-taker. For example, in the 1880 census for Texas, the five adult children of Isaac and Mary Taylor Lindsey did not agree on their parents' birthplaces. Three thought their father was born in South Carolina, one in Kentucky, and one in Georgia. Guesses about the mother's birthplace included Tennessee, Kentucky, Georgia, South Carolina, and "unknown."[3]

Sometimes even if the data is correctly entered, the format is misleading. For example, a head of household recorded in 1820, 1830, or 1840 may not be the oldest person in the house. It may be a grandparent, a younger brother, or a man with both parents still living at home. Persons given in any age grouping could be servants, visitors, or boarders not related to the family, but the census does not say who they are. Even in 1880, when the relationship is shown for the first time, it applies to heads of household only. Children listed as sons and daughters of the head may be unrelated to the wife.

Watch for duplicate entries. They occur with considerable frequency, and the data do not always support each other. Two enumerators apparently visited the Daniel Davis home in Limestone

County, Texas, for the 1880 census on 21/22 and 25 June. One recorded the two sons as Thomas J. and Edward L. The other put down the names as Thomas and Stanford.[4]

Errors in Printing

Donald L. Jacobus performed a valuable service for all genealogists by comparing the printed 1790 census for Connecticut with the original entries, finding numerous errors. He prefaced his list in the 1923 *New England Historic and Genealogical Register* with the modest disclaimer: "It is not claimed that the corrected readings give the exact spelling of the original, but only that they signify the person who was intended in the original." A similar scan in South Carolina's 1790 census revealed similar spelling and transcription errors.[5]

Branford

Page 92, column 2, *for* Phineas Bench *read* Phineas Beach.

Cheshire

Page 92, column 3, *for* Eneas Andrews *read* Enos Andrews.
for Uriah Benham *read* Uri Benham.
for Lazerus Tuttle *read* Lucius Tuttle.
for Jecobed Tuttle *read* Ichabod Tuttle.
Page 93, column 1, *for* Mineman Hotchkiss *read* Merriman Hotchkiss.
for Bela Hotchkiss, 2nd, *read* Bela Hitchcock, 2nd.
Page 93, column 2, *for* Israel Hotchwick *read* Israel Hotchkiss.
for Rockmary Thompson *read* Roxana Thompson.
for Samuel Durrany *read* Samuel Durand.
for Andrew Durany, 2nd, *read* Andrew Durand, 2nd.
for Samuel Bench *read* Samuel Beach.
for Daniel Hitchcock *read* Dan Hitchcock.
Page 94, column 1, *for* Nathaniel Ford *read* Nathan Ford.
for Elijah Wilmott *read* Elisha Wilmott. (Elijah is correctly listed higher up in this column.)
for Clum Cooke *read* Elam Cooke.

"Partial list of errors in 1790 Census for Connecticut," in *New England Historic Genealogical Register,* 1923, pp. 80-81.

Legibility

Worn and torn pages, faded ink, smeared or bleeding ink, disintegrating paper, words obscured by tightly bound pages, improper focus or lighting for microfilming, poor handwriting, and unfamiliar abbreviations – all of these affect legibility of the census schedules. When a printed page or a microfilm cannot be read, the best solution is to consult the originals. If you are fortunate, the original will be available, but many have either been destroyed by Congressional order, been lost over the course of years, or are too fragile to use.

Suggestions for Microfilm Searches

Because most censuses must be searched on microfilm, here are some suggestions to save time:

1. Become familiar with the surnames in your area so that you can recognize them with only half their letters distinct. Study a county history, a tax list, or a landowner's atlas.
2. Create a "pony" from the actual entries in the census. How does the writer make *a, h, s, p, j,* and other letters which can be misinterpreted? Draft an alphabet with capitals and lower-case letters for comparison. An easy way is to slip a piece of plain paper onto the viewing surface and trace the letters from the page.
3. Use a reader in a darkened room with a strong light to project the image. Slip a colored piece of paper-pink and green are effective-onto the viewing surface.
4. Copy the filmed page, enlarging or reducing the image to make it clearer and sharper. Many microfilm copiers have interchangeable lenses.
5. Review the whole schedule so you don't miss important entries appearing out of place. Record all columns for each entry, even if the information seems unimportant, and *record all members of the household* whether they are familiar or not. In multiple-family dwellings, record all family units living in the building. These families are often related, especially in immigrant settlement areas.
6. Copy the data exactly as it appears in the record. If the given name is abbreviated, copy the abbreviated form. Do not expand it. If the entry is crossed through or changed, copy the entry, the cross-through line, and the changes. Note carefully the last entry on each page. Family units may be split between two pages without a repeat of the surname.
7. Use finding tools and indexes to get into the census quickly, then search the census carefully to get all the data it contains. (See the bibliography of finding aids at the end of the chapter.) If all the data is available, it is possible to block out the pedigree for several generations from this source alone. Then proof can be sought in other records to insure that names in the pedigree really belong there. If you are researching a common name like Brown or Foster, the census can help eliminate those which do not fit so searches in other sources are less time-consuming.

Federal Censuses

Few sources match census records for *specific* information on a family and for useful clues which link those facts to other sources. Because so many indexes and printed schedules of census records are available, they are often used in a hit-and-run fashion. The primary use of census data is to link other documents together. If your family appears in the federal census, also search for that family in county and state records. Table 4-1 gives a summary of the federal census between 1790 and 1910, showing which states participated in which census, comments on the record, and the current location of schedules.

1790-1840

The data in each census schedule from 1790 to 1840 varies from decade to decade. Ages, for example, become more precise. Only the head of household, usually male, is listed by name. If a woman is listed, she is probably a widow or an older child with both parents dead or living in a household where the male adult is elderly or infirm. Here's what you can expect in each decade.

1790	**Name of head of household, number of free white males 16 years and upwards, number of free white males under 16, number of all other free persons, number of slaves, county and sometimes town (or district) of residence**
1800	**Name of head of household; number of free white males and females in age categories: 0-10, 10-16, 16-26, 26-45, 45 and upwards; number of other free persons except Indians not taxed; number of slaves; town (or district) and county of residence**
1810	**Same as 1800**
1820	**Same as 1800 with additional columns for the number of free white males 16-18; number of persons not naturalized; number engaged in agriculture, commercial, or manufacture; number of colored persons (sometimes in age categories); number of other persons except Indians**
1830	**Name of head of household; number of free white males and females in age categories: 0-5, 5-10, 10-15, 15-20, 20-30, 30-40, 40-50, 50-60, 60-70, 70-80, 80-90, 90-100, over 100; number of slaves and free colored persons in age categories; categories for deaf, dumb, and blind persons and aliens; town (or district) and county of residence**

1840	**Same as 1830, with additional columns for Revolutionary War pensioners and ages; number engaged in mining, agriculture, commerce, manufacturing and trade, navigation of the ocean, navigation of canals, lakes, and rivers, learned professions and engineers; number in schools, etc.; number in family over 21 who cannot read and write; number insane**

Genealogical Data Available in Federal Censuses, 1790-1840. Adapted from National Archives Trust Fund Board, *Guide to Genealogical Research in the National Archives* (Washington, D.C.: National Archives Record Service, 1982), p. 20.

You can use 1790-1840 census records to identify what locality to search, distinguish the target family from others of the same name, locate possible relatives with the same name, identify immediate neighbors who may be in-laws, check spelling variations of the surnames, help determine that family groups are complete, and identify blacks. Free men of color will be listed as heads of household by name. Slaves appear in age groupings by name of owner. By combining those age groupings with probate inventories and tax list data, you can determine birth order and names.[6] (See Figure 4-1.)

1850

Each member of the household is listed by name from 1850 on. Table 4-2 summarizes the type of information you can expect in the next eight censuses. It thus becomes possible to identify probable in-law relationships. The 1850 census lists the name of every person whose usual place of abode on June 1850 was in the family, his/her age, sex, and color (white, black, or mulatto); profession, occupation, or trade of each male over fifteen; value of real estate owned; birth state, territory, or country of each person listed; whether married within the year; whether attended school within the year; if over twenty whether unable to read and write; whether deaf, dumb, blind, insane, idiotic, pauper, or convict; town (or district) and county of residence. (Figure 4-2.)

HEADS OF FAMILIES—NEW YORK. 13

ALBANY COUNTY—Continued.

NAME OF HEAD OF FAMILY.	Free white males of 16 years and upward, including heads of families.	Free white males under 16 years.	Free white females, including heads of families.	All other free persons.	Slaves.
ALBANY CITY, FIRST WARD—continued.					
Yates, Peter W	2		8		2
Staats, Henry	3	1	5		2
Radlie, Philip	1		2		2
Hilton, William	1	1	1		
ALBANY CITY, SECOND WARD.					
Cuyler, Jacob	2	3	1		4
Groesbeck, John	2	5	4		1
De Garmo, Bastian	4	1	4		
Rogardus, Jacob	1				
Cavenaugh, William	2	1	3		
Groesbeck, David	2		1		2
Woodruff, Hanlock	2	1	4		2
Hanson, John	2				1
Blucker, Catherine		2	5		3
Beekman, John J	1	1	4		6
Fellows, William	2		1		
Batist, ——*	2			1	
Hagerdy, William	1	2	1		1
Lansing, Jacob	1		1		2
Bradt, Aaron	2	3	1		
Nehemiah, John	1	3	3		
Bradt, John A	1	3	1		
Dunkavy, James	1	1	3		
Barrington, Nicholas	1		3		
Pruyne, Margaret			2		
Muclaroy, Richard	1	1	1		
Devenbagh, Frederick	1	1	3		
Brower, John	1	4	3		
M'Kenney, John	1	1	5		
Groesbeck, Cornelius	1	1	2		
Van Vrankin, Moses R	1	1	3		1
Willitt, Edward, Junr	2		2		(*)
Kennear, James	1	1	2		(*)
Ruby, Conradt	2	1	5		(*)
Park, Henry	1		2		(*)
Davis, Peter	1	1	3		(*)
Sturges, Isaac	1	1	3		(*)
Milligan, James	1		2		(*)
Giles, William	1		1		(*)
Winne, Jacob	1	4	1		(*)
Finch, Isaac	1	1	2		(*)
Van Ness, John	2	2			(*)
Fadon, John	1	4	2		(*)
Hawk, Christopher	1	2	5		(*)
Bulson, John	1		5		(*)
Shaw, Ezra	1	2	4		(*)
Roberts, John	1	1	1		(*)
Amos, Thomas				2	(*)
Stoop, Catherine		1	4		(*)
Visscher, Sarah	1	1	2		(*)
Van Dusen, Aaron	1	1	4		(*)
Fonda, Isaac D	1		2		(*)
Visscher, Tuenis G	1		3		(*)
Johnston, John	1		1		(*)
Driskile, Jeremiah	1	3	1		(*)
Bleeker, Nicholas	1	2	1		(*)
Edgar, Gregg	1		3		(*)
Patrick, James	1		1		(*)
Vanloan, Jacob	1	3	3		(*)
Bleecker, John J	4	2	3	(*)	(*)
Bleeker, Jacob	1			(*)	(*)
Bleeker, Jacob, Junr	1	2	1		4
Cameron, William	1	2	2		
Andrew, John	2	1	1		
Bleeker, John R	1		2		3
Lansing, Gerandus	1		1		5
Bleeker, John N	1	3	6		1
Bleeker, Catelintia	1		4		2
Brower, Cornelius	1	1	4		2
Lyn, Aaron	1	1	3		
Barrington, Lewis	2	2	4		
Magee, John	1		3		
Boyd, John	1	4	2		
Hanson, Albert	1	2	2		
Staats, Barent G	1	1	1		2
Van Zant, John W	1	1	2		
M'Durmot, Michael	2	1	2		
Rider, Barent	1	1	3		
Carson, John	1	4	3		
Fuller, James	1	5	2		
Meggs, Seth	1	1	2		
Pruyn, John F	1		2		6
Merchant, George	3	2	5	1	
Visscher, Matthew	3		2		2
Ten Eyck, Hendrick	1	1	6		3
Jackcum, Jack	1	1		7	
Metcalf, Simon	2	2	4		1
Fonda, Nicholas	1		2		4
Brown William	1	2	4		

NAME OF HEAD OF FAMILY.	Free white males of 16 years and upward, including heads of families.	Free white males under 16 years.	Free white females, including heads of families.	All other free persons.	Slaves.
ALBANY CITY, SECOND WARD—continued.					
M'Farson, Hugh	1	1	1		
Barber, John	3		2		
Watson, Matthew	2	2	2		1
Easterly, Thomas	2	3	4		
Norwood, Mary	1		4		
Fonda, Jacobus	1	1	3		
Bogert, Barent	1	1	5		
Mersales, Gysbert	1		4		2
Cuyler, Philip	1		1		
Hooker, Samuel	3	3	3		
Hanson, John J	1	3	4		
Switz, Cornelius	2	1	3		
Van Schaaick, Cornelius	1	1	1		
Mersailes, John	1		3		
Pruyn, Casparus	3	1	2	1	3
Tiffany, Silvester	3	2	2		1
Whipple, Benjamin	4		5		
Cuyler, Abraham	2		5		5
Ten Eyck, Harmanus	1	2	4		2
Vn Rensselaer, Jeremiah	1		2		3
Vn Schurlyne, Cornelius	2		3		12
Bogert, Abraham	1		1		1
Douglass, Thomas	1	3	4		
Ryan, Patrick	2		2		
M'Gurgy, Edward	1		2		
Dale, William	1	2	2		
Cammeron, John	1	1	1		
Campbell, John	1	1	2		
Haynes, Thomas	1		1		(*)
M'Donald, Donald	1		1		(*)
Bruce, Robert	1		1		(*)
Archer, George	1	1	2		(*)
Andrews, Joseph	1	1	2		(*)
Hannah, Samuel	1		3		(*)
Smith, James	2	1	1		(*)
M'Gourk, James	1		2		(*)
M'Gourk, Robert	1	1	2		(*)
Welch, Joseph	1		1		(*)
Ackerson, James	1		3		(*)
Mersielus, John G	2		5		1
Watson, Alexander	1		1		(*)
Crom, John			1	3	
Burgess, John	1		3		(*)
Mulhance, Peter	1		4		(*)
Ellison, Abraham	1		4		(*)
Lawson, Henry	1	1	1		(*)
Stevenson, Mary			2		(*)
Legrange, Jacobus	1		3		(*)
Cheseham, George	1		3		(*)
M'Cloud, Donald	1	1	4		(*)
Forsight, Alexander	1	3	2		(*)
Barkley, James	1	1	2		(*)
M'Murray, Thomas	1	1	3		(*)
Hendrick, Jacob	1		1		(*)
Ostrander, John	3	1	2	(*)	(*)
Myer, Carol	1		2		
Waggoner, Andrew	1	1	2		
Wilmot, John	1	1	5		
M'Manac, William	1	1	3		
Keating, Garret	2	1	1		
Snyder, Daniel	1		2		
Heath, John	1	3	1		
Staals, Henry	2		1		
Carson, Alexander	1		2		
Bromley, Samuel	1		2		
Horse, George	1		1		
Hay, Alexander	1		3		
M'Mickle, John	3	2	4		
Christie, John	1		1		
Whitney, William	1	2	2		
M'Kown, William	2	4	2		1
Bradt, Daniel	1	2	3		
Truax, John J	1	3	5		
Kagle, Cornelius	1	1	3		
James, John		1		3	
Winne, Killian D	2	1	2		
ALBANY CITY, THIRD WARD.					
Lansing, Abraham A	1	1	4		6
Blair, James	1	1	5		
Sharp, Conradt	1	3	3		
Van Iveren, Rynier	1		2		
Van Duser, Peter	1	2	2		
Young, Peter	1	1	3		
Truax, Isaac	1	1	1		2
Van Arnam, Isaac	1		3		2
Lansing, John, Junr	1	1	4		4
Lansing, Sanders	1		1		2
Walsh, Dudley	1	1			
Ten Broeck, Dirick	1	1	3		6

NAME OF HEAD OF FAMILY.	Free white males of 16 years and upward, including heads of families.	Free white males under 16 years.	Free white females, including heads of families.	All other free persons.	Slaves.
ALBANY CITY, THIRD WARD—continued.					
Stringer, Samuel	2	1	2		2
Lush, Stephen	1	3	3		2
Wendell, * —— H	1	1	3		2
Douw, Volkert A	1		3		4
Lansing, John Jacob	1	1	1		3
Evertson, Bernardus	2	5	4		
lansing, Garrit	1		1		1
lush, Richard	1	1	4		
Graham, John	2		2		
Defrust, Isaac	2	3	3		4
Veeder, Abraham	2	2	1		
Vn Vechten, Teunis T	2	3	3		2
Dexter, Samuel	2		1		
Douw, Peter W	2		1		3
Beekman, Elizabeth	1		2		5
Glen, Cornelius	1		1		5
Caldwell, James	5	3	6		1
Maley, John	2		3		5
Willett, Elbert	2		3		1
Sim, Peter	2	2	2		(*)
Orr, Isabel	1		2		(*)
Waters, David	1				(*)
Hale, Daniel	4	1	3		2
Bloodgood, James	6		2		5
Bower, Barent	1		1		(*)
Roseboom, Eve			3		3
Fonda, David	1	3	5		2
Groesbeck, Garrit	1		2		(*)
Cuyler, John	2				(*)
Kirk, John	1	1	3		(*)
Boyd, John	3	2	1		2
Hunn, Thomas	2		2		
Gansevoort, Harman	1	1	1		7
Gansevoort, Leonard, Junr	1	1	6		(*)
Bleeker, Barent	1		1		(*)
M'Millen, John	1	1	1		(*)
Evertson, Henry	2	1	2		(*)
Yates, Abraham, Junr	2	5	5		(*)
Westerlo, Eilardus	1	1	3		(*)
Gansevoort, Peter	3	1	4		(*)
Ten Broek, John	3	2	4	(*)	(*)
Truax, Henry	1	1	2	(*)	(*)
Glen, Henry	3	1	3		7
Schuyler, Abraham	2		3		9
Cuyler, Jacob, Junr	2	1	1		2
•Wallace, Benjamin	3		2		
Visscher, Nanning H	1		4		
Bisbrown, Thomas	1		1		1
Lansing, Jeremiah	1	2	2		2
Beauman, Charles	1		2		
Visscher, Teunis	1		2		6
Vandebergh, William	2		2		
Van Husen, Cathelina			3		3
Chesney, James	1		4		
Wendell, Barbara			3		5
Bradford, Thomas	1		1		
M'Gibbon, Peter	1	1	6		
Tolbert, William	1	3	3		
Richards, Ezra	1	1	2		
Vander Zee, Walter	1	5	2		
Killburn, York				3	
Ram, John	1		4		
M'Ilargh, John	1		2		1
Van Iveren, Rynier	2		3		5
Ten Broeck, Abraham	1		3		12
Vander Heyden, Jacob	1	2	4		3
Hunn, William	2	2	5		1
Williamson, Timothy	1		1		
Dunbar, William	1	3	3		
Visscher, Garrit T	4		1		1
Icebrase, Hannah		1	2		
M'Ready, William	1	3	7		
Miller, Philip, Junr	1	1	4		1
Van Vronkin, Garrit	1		1		
Gates, John	1	2	3		
Vanderburg, Garrit	1		1		1
Graverato, Henry	2		2		1
Slingerland, Jacob	1		2		
Graham, Theodorus Van Wyck	2	1	3		4
Roff, John	1	1	1		
Bradt, Henry	1		1		
Douw, Catherine		1	3		2
Leonard, Enock	1	1	2		2
Wynkoop, Jacobus	2		3		2
Sharp, Peter	2	2	2		
de frust, Philip	1	1	2		
de frust, Philip, Junr	1		3		
Verplank, William	2		1		2
Winne, Jellis	1	2	3		1
Lansing, Philip	1	2	8		[illegible]

* Illegible.

***Figure 4-1.** 1790 Federal Census, Albany County, New York* (Baltimore: Genealogical Publishing Co., 1971), p. 13. All extant 1790 schedules have been published and reprinted more than once. Copies are readily available in most public and research libraries.

Table 4-1

Summary of Federal Censuses, 1790-1910

An asterisk indicates that the table has been printed. An underline indicates that it is indexed. See Table 4-7 for a summary of censuses that each state conducted. See also Missing Schedules, pp. 124. A fire destroyed nearly all of the 1890 census schedules. 1880 censuses indexed by families with children under ten years of age only.

State	*1790*	*1800*	*1810*	*1820*	*1830*	*1840*	*1850*	*1860*	*1870*	*1880*	*1885*	*1890*	*1900*	*1910*	*Comments*
Alabama				<u>●</u>*	<u>●</u>	<u>●</u>	●	●	●	●			<u>●</u>	<u>●</u>	**1820.** See E. Kay Kirkham, "Personal Names in the Alabama Census Returns of 1820." *Genealogical Journal* 4 (1975): 148-49 for a discussion of completeness; extant tallies printed in *Alabama Historical Quarterly* 6 (1944), from state copy in Department of Archives.
Alaska					●*	●*			●	●			●	●	**1830-40.** Listed in census guides but cannot be verified. May be with Michigan Territory.
Arizona							<u>●</u>	<u>●</u>*	<u>●</u>	●			<u>●</u>	●	**1850-60.** Part of New Mexico Territory.
Arkansas					●	●	●	●	●	●			<u>●</u>	<u>●</u>	**1850-80.** Several counties printed their census schedules. **1860.** Little River County missing.
California							<u>●</u>	●	●	●			<u>●</u>	<u>●</u>	**1850.** Contra Costa, San Francisco, Santa Clara counties missing.
Colorado								●	●	●	●		<u>●</u>	●	**1860.** Included with Kansas.
Connecticut	<u>●</u>*	<u>●</u>*	<u>●</u>	<u>●</u>	<u>●</u>	<u>●</u>	<u>●</u>	●	●	●			<u>●</u>	●	**1790-1850.** Card index to federal census in state archives with microfilm copies available at the National Archives and Genealogical Society of Utah. **1790.** Some two-thirds of Dorchester heads of families missing. See Charles W. Hurst, "The 1790 Census," *Maryland and Delaware Genealogist* 6 (1965): 45.
Delaware		<u>●</u>*	<u>●</u>	<u>●</u>	<u>●</u>	<u>●</u>	<u>●</u>	●	●	●			<u>●</u>	<u>●</u>	**1790.** Missing, reconstructed from tax lists. See Leon de Valinger, *Reconstructed 1790 Census of Delaware* (Washington, D.C.: National Genealogical Society, 1954). 1790 census reportedly found (not confirmed) in Cornell University Library.
District of Columbia	●*	●*	●	●	●	●	●	●	●	●			<u>●</u>	●	**1790.** With Maryland. **1800.** With Delaware.
Florida					●	●	●	●	●	●	●		<u>●</u>	<u>●</u>	
Georgia		●		●*	●*	●*	●*	●	●	●			<u>●</u>	●	**1790-1820.** Department of Archives. Substitutes for *Some Early Tax Digests of Georgia*. (Atlanta: Georgia Department of Archives, 1926), and several volumes of printed land lotteries, **1805-20.** See Missing Schedules, pp. 124. **1800.** Oglethorp County only; original in Department of Archives. **1820.** Franklin, Rabun, Twiggs counties missing. Columbia County missing three districts. See *National Genealogical Society Quarterly* 40 (1971): 118-21. **1850.** Printed county by county. **1890.** Washington County schedule found in files of judge of probate; see "Washington County, Georgia 1890 Census," *Family Puzzlers*, no. 520, 1977; no. 526, 1977; no. 529, 1977.
Hawaii													<u>●</u>	●	
Idaho									●*	●			<u>●</u>	●	
Illinois			●*	●*	●	●*		●*	●	●			<u>●</u>	●	**1810.** Randolph County only. **1825-55.** All censuses, including federal, indexed in "Illinois Early Records Index,"

State	*1790*	*1800*	*1810*	*1820*	*1830*	*1840*	*1850*	*1860*	*1870*	*1880*	*1885*	*1890*	*1900*	*1910*	*Comments*
															manuscript; microfilm copy at Genealogical Society of Utah, 248 reels. **1850.** Printed county by county. Edgar County lists county of birth. **1860-70.** Computer database by Newberry Library and Illinois State Library now in process. **1860.** 31 counties published; see *Illinois State Genealogical Society Quarterly* 14 (1982): 70. **1890.** Tax records for some counties are being transcribed by local genealogical societies to replace missing schedules.
Indiana				●̲	●̲	●̲	●̲	●	●	●			●̲	●	**1820.** Daviess County missing. **1870.** Index announced by Patricia M. Shook, 5033 Holbrook, Anaheim, CA 91807 if interest is high enough.
Iowa						●̲	●̲	●	●	●			●̲	●	
Kansas								●	●	●			●̲	●	
Kentucky			●̲*	●̲	●̲	●̲	●̲	●	●	●			●̲	●	**1790.** Reconstructed from tax lists; see Charles B. Heinemann and Gaius M. Brumbaugh, *"First Census" of Kentucky* (Washington, D.C.: National Genealogical Society, 1940). **1800.** Reconstructed by Garrett G. Clift, *"Second Census" of Kentucky* (Frankfort, n.p., 1954).
Louisiana			●̲*	●̲*	●̲	●̲	●̲	●̲	●	●			●̲	●	
Maine	●̲*	●̲*	●̲	●̲	●̲	●̲	●̲	●	●	●			●̲	●	**1800.** Part of York County missing. **1810.** Part of Oxford County missing. **1820.** Part of Penobscot and Washington counties missing.
Maryland	●̲*	●̲*	●̲	●̲	●̲	●̲	●	●	●	●			●̲	●	**1830.** Montgomery, Prince George's, Saint Mary's, Queen Anne's, and Somerset counties missing.
Massachusetts	●̲*	●̲*	●̲	●̲	●̲	●̲	●̲	●	●	●			●̲	●	**1800.** Part of Suffolk County missing.
Michigan				●̲*	●̲*	●̲	●̲	●	●	●			●̲	●	**1820.** For six counties and Detroit.
Minnesota					●̲	●̲	●̲*	●	●	●			●̲	●	**1870.** Federal copy destroyed by fire. State copy at Minnesota State Historical Society.
Mississippi				●̲*	●̲*	●̲	●̲*	●	●	●			●̲	●	**1830.** Pike County missing. **1860.** Hancock, Sunflower, and Washington counties missing.
Missouri					●̲*	●̲*	●̲*	●	●	●			●̲	●	
Montana								●	●	●			●̲	●̲	**1860.** Included with Nebraska.
Nebraska								●̲	●	●	●		●̲	●	
Nevada								●̲	●	●			●̲	●	**1860.** With Utah.
New Hampshire	●̲*	●̲*	●̲	●̲	●̲	●̲	●̲	●	●	●			●̲	●	**1800.** Part of Rockingham and Strafford counties missing. **1820.** Grafton, part of Rockingham and Strafford counties missing.
New Jersey		●			●̲	●̲	●̲	●	●	●			●̲	●	**1790, 1810, 1820.** All counties missing; see Substitute Censuses, p. 123. **1800.** Cumberland County only; original in Farleigh Dickinson University; microfilm copy at Genealogical Society of Utah. **1860.** Newark Wards 6-8, 10-12, and part of Essex County damaged.
New Mexico							●	●	●	●	●				**1860.** Arizona, Bernalillo, Dona Ana, Rio, Arriba, Santa Ana, and Valencia counties are damaged.
New York		●̲*	●̲*	●	●	●	●	●	●	●	●				**1810.** Cortland, part of Broome county

State	*1790*	*1800*	*1810*	*1820*	*1830*	*1840*	*1850*	*1860*	*1870*	*1880*	*1885*	*1890*	*1900*	*1910*	*Comments*
															missing. **1860.** Chenango and Columbia counties damaged. **1880.** Suffolk County, New York City Wards 21-22 damaged.
North Carolina	●*	●*	●	●*	●	●	●	●	●	●			●̲	●	**1790.** Caswell, Granville, and Orange counties missing. **1810.** Craven, Greene, New Hanover, and Wake counties missing. **1820.** Currituck, Franklin, Martin, Montgomery, Randolph, and Wake counties missing.
North Dakota								●*	●	●	●		●̲	●	
Ohio			●̲*	●̲*	●̲*	●̲	●̲	●̲	●	●			●̲	●̲	**1810.** Washington County only; original at Marietta State College. **1820.** Franklin and Wood counties missing.
Oklahoma								●					●̲	●̲	**1860.** Census of Indian lands west of the Arkansas. **1890.** A card index for the state census is at the state historical society.
Oregon							●̲	●̲*	●̲*	●̲*			●̲	●	**1860-80.** Censuses printed county by county.
Pennsylvania	●̲*	●̲*	●̲	●̲	●̲	●̲	●̲	●	●	●			●̲	●̲	**1800.** Parts of Westmoreland County missing. **1810.** Parts of Bedford, Philadelphia, and Cumberland counties missing. **1820.** Parts of Lancaster and Luzerne counties missing. **1860.** Fayette County missing.
Rhode Island	●̲*	●̲*	●̲	●̲	●̲	●̲	●̲	●̲	●	●			●̲	●	
South Carolina	●̲*	●̲*	●̲	●̲	●̲	●̲	●̲	●̲	●	●			●̲	●̲	**1790.** Section of Lancaster-Kershaw district missing. **1800.** Richland County missing. **1820-50.** Clarendon County missing.
South Dakota								●̲*	●	●	●		●̲	●	
Tennessee			●̲*	●̲*	●̲*	●̲	●̲*	●̲*	●	●*			●̲	●	**1790.** Washington and Mero Districts enumerated 1791; schedules missing; early Tennessee tax lists substituted; see p. 123. **1800.** Abbeville County includes "sojourners," a unique category. **1810.** Rutherford and Grainger counties printed separately; use Pollyanna Creekmore, *Early East Tennessee Tax Lists;* see Substitute Censuses, p. 127. **1820.** Schedules missing for Anderson, Bleasie, Blount, Campbell, Carter, Claiborne, Cocke, Grainger, Greene, Hawkins, Hamilton, Jefferson, Knox, McMinn, Marion, Monroe, Morgan, Rhea, Roane, Sevier, Sullivan, and Washington counties. **1880.** Computer database in process by Byron Sistler & Associates.
Texas							●*	●	●	●			●̲	●	
Utah							●̲*	●̲	●̲	●			●̲	●	**1850-80.** Territorial censuses; originals in LDS Church Historical Department, 50 East North Temple, Salt Lake City, Utah 84150; microfilm copies at Genealogical Society of Utah.
Vermont	●*	●*	●	●	●	●	●	●	●	●			●̲	●	See Holman D. Jordan, Jr., "Value of Census Data in Writing Vermont Town Histories," *Vermont History* 36 (1968): 19-28.
Virginia		●*	●	●	●	●	●	●	●	●			●̲	●	**1790.** Schedules reported found (not confirmed); tax lists substituted; see *Virginia: Records of State Enumerations, 1782-1785* (1908; reprint ed., Baltimore: Genealogical Publishing Co., 1970), and Augusta B. Fothergill and John M. Naugle, *Virginia*

State	1790	1800	1810	1820	1830	1840	1850	1860	1870	1880	1885	1890	1900	1910	Comments
															Tax Payers 1782-1787 (1940; reprint ed., Baltimore: Genealogical Publishing Co., 1971). **1800.** Accomack County only. **1810.** Schedules missing for Grayson, Greenbriar, Halifax, Henley, James City, King William, Louisa, Mecklenburg, Nansemond, Northhampton, Orange, Patrick, Pittsylvania, Russell, and Tazewell counties.
Washington								●*	●*	●			●̲	●	**1860.** Benton, Columbia, San Juan, Snohomish counties missing. **1870.** Benton and Columbia counties missing.
West Virginia									●	●*			●̲	●	See Virginia before **1863,** date of West Virginia's statehood.
Wisconsin						●̲	●̲	●̲	●̲	●			●̲	●̲	**1820-30.** With Michigan; indexes at state historical society are compiled from state copies; thus page references don't match the federal microfilm.
Wyoming									●*	●*			●̲	●	**1860.** With Nebraska. **1870-80.** Manuscript indexes in Wyoming State Archives and Library of Congress.

Figure 4-2. 1850 U.S. Census (Free Schedule), Hamilton Co., Ohio.

SCHEDULE I.—Free Inhabitants in Springfield Township in the County of Ham... of Ohio enumerated by me, on the 17th day of August 1850. Henry ...

Dwelling-houses numbered in the order of visitation	Families numbered in the order of visitation	The Name of every Person whose usual place of abode on the first day of June, 1850, was in this family	Age	Sex	Color	Profession, Occupation, or Trade of each Male Person over 15 years of age	Value of Real Estate owned	Place of Birth, Naming the State, Territory, or Country	Married within the year
1	2	3	4	5	6	7	8	9	10
103	103	Harriet Jane Huffman	23	F				Ohio	
		Milton Huffman	20	M		Farmer		Ohio	
		Elias Huffman	16	M		Farmer		Ohio	
104	104	Israel Shannan	30	M		Laborer		Ireland	
		Margaret Shannan	31	F				Ireland	
		Margaret Shannan	9	F				Ireland	
		Bridget Shannan	4	F				Ireland	
		John Shannan	10/12	M				Ohio	
105	105	John S. Caden	48	M		Laborer		New Jersey	
		Mary Caden	36	F				New Jersey	
		Sarah S. Caden	15	F				Ohio	
		David D. Caden	13	M				Ohio	
		Samuel H. Caden	11	M				Ohio	
		Abigail Caden	9	F				Ohio	
		Eugene Frank Caden	7	M				Ohio	
		Rolandus M. Caden	5	M				Iowa	

Table 4-2

Contents of Census Schedules, 1850-1910.*

(free inhabitants of each household)

	1850	1860	1870	1880	1885	1890	1900	1910
Name and age	Yes	Yes	Yes	Yes	Yes	Yes	Yes	Yes
Name of street and number of house	No	No	No	Yes	Yes	Yes	Yes	Yes
Relationship to head of family	No	No	No	Yes	Yes	Yes	Yes	Yes
Month of birth, if born within the year	No	No	Yes	Yes	Yes	No	Yes	No
Sex, color, birthplace, and occupation	Yes	Yes	Yes	Yes	Yes	Yes	Yes	Yes
Whether naturalized or whether naturalization papers had been taken out	No	No	No	No	No	Yes	Yes	Yes
Number of years in the United States	No	No	No	No	No	Yes	Yes	Yes
Value of personal estate	No	Yes	Yes	No	No	No	No	No
Value of real estate	Yes	Yes	Yes	No	No	No	No	No
Whether home and farm free of mortgage	No	No	No	No	No	Yes	Yes	Yes
Marital status	No	No	No	Yes	Yes	Yes	Yes	Yes
Whether married within the year	Yes	Yes	Yes	Yes	Yes	Yes	No	No
Month of marriage, if married within the year	No	No	Yes	No	No	No	No	No
Whether temporarily or permanently disabled	No	No	No	Yes	Yes	No	No	No
Whether suffering from acute or chronic disease	No	No	No	No	No	Yes	No	No
Whether crippled, maimed, or deformed	No	No	No	Yes	Yes	Yes	No	No
Time unemployed during the census year	No	No	No	Yes	Yes	Yes	Yes	Yes
Whether deaf, dumb, blind, or insane	Yes	Yes	Yes	Yes	Yes	Yes	No	Yes
Whether a pauper	Yes	Yes	No	No	No	Yes	No	No
Whether a prisoner or homeless child	No	No	No	No	No	Yes	No	No
Whether a convict	Yes	Yes	No	No	No	Yes	No	No
Whether able to speak English	No	No	No	No	No	Yes	Yes	Yes
Whether able to read and write and whether attended school within the year	Yes	Yes	Yes	Yes	Yes	Yes	Yes	Yes
Birthplaces of father and mother	No	No	No	Yes	Yes	Yes	Yes	Yes
Whether father or mother of foreign birth	No	No	Yes	Yes	Yes	Yes	Yes	Yes
Number of living children, if a mother	No	No	No	No	No	Yes	Yes	Yes
Whether soldier, sailor, or marine during the Civil War (U.S. or Conf.), or widow of such person	No	No	No	No	No	Yes	Yes	Yes
Number of years in present marriage	No	No	No	No	No	No	Yes	Yes
Number of children born	No	No	No	No	No	No	Yes	Yes
Mother tongue	No	No	No	No	No	No	No	Yes

*National Archives Trust Fund Board, *Guide to Genealogical Research in the National Archives* (Washington D.C.: National Archives Records Service, 1982), p. 21.

With the aid of the 1850 census records, you can plot the migrational routes of family members by their places of birth, deciding which other records to search in that locality. If the family owned real estate, search land and tax records. If a couple was married within the year, search marriages. If the head of house is elderly, search probates. If an unrelated man of marriageable age is present, he might be a potential son-in-law. With this census, you can also identify probable parents of known ancestors, learn principal occupations, discover how much property value this ancestor had, determine which family members died at what ages, and spot remarriages and step-relationships.

Indexes, 1790-1850. All states have been indexed 1790-1850 by father's name or other head of household by Accelerated Indexing Systems, 70 East South Temple, Salt Lake City, UT 84111. Price list available on request. Indexes for 1850 also include everyone in the household with a different surname. Some indexes include every name. The preface to each index will tell who is indexed and how the index was compiled. These indexes are widely available in public and research libraries.

Several states have also been indexed by more than one system. Where more than one index is available, it is a good idea to use both as a check for errors. For example, compare these two indexes for *Hall* in the 1850 Tennessee census.

HALL. RANDOLPH — SUMN 294 16TH DIS
HALL. RANDOLPH. — RUTH 253 MC CRACK
HALL. REBECCA — OVER 063 8TH DIST
HALL. REBECCA — ANDE 024 16TH SUB
HALL. REBECCA — COFF 033 8TH CIVI
HALL. REESE R. — KNOX 235 15TH SUB
HALL. REUBEN. — BEDF 212 20TH CIV
HALL. REUBIN — CANN 391 CRAFTS 5
HALL. RHODA — DAVI 303 2ND SUB
HALL. RHODA — MORG 232 13TH SUB

HALL, Randolph 50, Mary 45, Va Va, Su-10-502
HALL, Randolph 54, Mary 44, Judy A. 27, John R. 13, Abner E. 12, May M. 10, Levander J. 8, Mormon R. 6, Lambert C. 3, Jarmon C. 1, Va Va, Ru-63-505
HALL, Rebecca 55, William 21, T T, Ov-823-120
HALL, Rebecca 45, John 21, Rachel 19, Richard 15, James 10, Rebecca 7, T T, A-52-7
HALL, Reese B. 24, Sarah 20, William Mc. 3, Charles TALIFARRO 12, T NC, K-1596-410
HALL, Rhoda 40, T, Mg-232-583
HALL, Rhoda 70, Albert PAYNE 38, Susan 25, James GRANT 38, Jane 28, Mary 2, LeRoy ARMSTRONG 27, Mary 17, Henry SCHNIDER 24, Ann 20, Romulus 2. Va T. D-332-607

Federal Census Indexing Systems: Accelerated Indexing Systems, Salt Lake City, Utah 1975, and Byron Sistler & Associates, Evanston, Ill., 1975; alphabetically arranged.

Each index thus includes one name that the other omits. Errors, omissions, and differences in page references from index to index occur with some frequency.

1860-1880

Census schedules for 1860 to 1880 chronicle American families during years of immense change. The 1860 census contains the same information as the 1850 enumeration, with a column added for the value of personal estate. With it, you can record the status of an individual family on the eve of the Civil War. Many families would never be as intact or as stable again.

The information about property values for your ancestor's personal estate as well as land is helpful, particularly matched with tax, land, and probate data. Persons of Indian descent not living on reservations are also included.

The 1870 census identifies survivors of the Civil War, including "yours-mine-ours" families and May-December marriages. This census also provides crucial information for Southern research. This is the first census where parents of foreign birth are indicated, a real boon in identifying immigrant ancestors. Immigrants who are naturalized and eligible to vote are identified, suggesting follow-up in court and naturalization sources. This census allows you to verify Chinese, Indian, black, and mulatto descent as well.

The 1880 census (Figure 4-3) adds to the 1870 record by specifying the street and house number in cities; the individual's age at last birthday prior to 1 June 1880; relationship to head of household; illness or disability on the day of the census; marital status; number of months unemployed during census year (1 June 1879-31 May 1880); and the state or country of birth of the father and mother. Children born and people who died after 1 June 1880 were not included even though the enumeration extended a few months after the close of the census year.

With the 1880 census, you can identify the state or country of birth for parents, especially important for tracing movements of immigrant ancestors, supplement birth and marriage records for the census year or even partially replace them where birth and marriage records are not recorded, prove additions to your pedigree, and locate hitherto unknown surnames of married daughters, mothers-in-law, cousins, and other relatives living with the family. This is the first census to state relationship to the head of household, but the wife may not be the mother of the children. This census will also let you begin tracing genetic symptoms and diseases through a family.

Photography became popular by the time of the 1860-80 censuses. If you have unlabeled family photos from this period, with a little detective work, you can combine tax and census information to identify the family members. Tax lists specify gold watches, pianos, carriages, horses, and other personal property which may appear in photographs; with the censuses, you have a cast of characters from which to pick likely candidates.

Indexes 1860-80. Most indexes for 1860 to 1880 censuses cover individual counties only. State-wide indexes for these censuses are summarized in Table 4-3. The addresses of state archives and state historical societies are given in Appendixes B and C.

1880 Soundex. The Soundex is an index in which heads of household and persons of different surnames in the household are listed by letter-and-number code. Consonants in each surname which sound alike have the same code. This throws many spelling variants together. For example, Scherman, Schurman, Sherman, Shireman, and Shurman are indexed together as S655 and will appear on the same roll of film with other surnames such as Sauerman or Sermon.[7] If the name is Kuhne, for example, the index card will be in the "K" segment of the index. The code number for Kuhne, worked out according to the system below, is K 500.

Code Key Letters and Equivalents

1	b,p,f,v
2	c,s,k,g,j,q,x,z
3	d,t
4	l
5	m,n
6	r

The letters *a, e, i, o, u, y, w,* and *h* are not coded. The first letter of a surname is not coded. Every Soundex number must be a three-digit number. A name yielding no code numbers, like Lee, would thus be LOOO; one yielding only one code number would have two zeros added, as Kuhne, coded as K500; and one yielding two code numbers would have one zero added, as Ebell, coded as E140. Only three digits are used, so Ebelson would be coded as E142, not E1425.

When two key letters or equivalents appear together or one key letter immediately follows or precedes an equivalent, the two are coded as one letter, by a single number, as follows: Kelly: K400, Buerck: B620, Lloyd: L300, and Schaefer: S160.

If several surnames have the same code, their cards are arranged alphabetically by given name. Divider cards show most code numbers, but not all. For instance, one divider may be number 350

Page No. 17
Supervisor's Dist. No. 10th
Enumeration Dist. No. 74

Note A.—The Census Year begins June 1, 1879, and ends May 31, 1880.
Note B.—All persons will be included in the Enumeration who were living on the 1st day of June, 1880. No others will. Children BORN SINCE June 1, 1880, will be OMITTED. Members of Families who have DIED SINCE June 1, 1880, will be INCLUDED.
Note C.—Questions Nos. 13, 14, 22 and 23 are not to be asked in respect to persons under 10 years of age.

Received July 24, 18

39

SCHEDULE 1.—Inhabitants in Rochester, in the County of Monroe, State of New York, enumerated by me on the 3rd day of June, 1880.

Horace Jones, Enumerator.

	The Name of each Person whose place of abode, on 1st day of June, 1880, was in this family.	Color	Sex	Age	Relationship of each person to the head of this family	Profession, Occupation or Trade	Place of Birth of this person	Place of Birth of the Father	Place of Birth of the Mother
1	Evangelist Mary	W	F	33		Superior	Canada	Ireland	Ireland
2	Baptiste John	"	"	36		Sister of St Joseph	New York	Ireland	Ireland
3	Margaret Mary	"	"	38		"	Ireland	Ireland	Ireland
4	Delphine Mary	"	"	26		"	Pennsylvania	Ireland	Ireland
5	William Mary	"	"	24		"	New York	Ireland	Ireland
6	Frances Mary	"	"	19		"	Pennsylvania	New York	Maryland
7	O Dellia Mary	"	"	21		"	New York	Ireland	Ireland
8	Herman Mary	"	"	18		"	Canada	Ireland	Ireland
9	James Mary	"	"	60		"	Ireland	Ireland	Ireland
10	Basil Mary	"	"	31		"	Ireland	Ireland	Ireland
11	Monica Mary	"	"	27		"	Canada	Ireland	Ireland
12	Simplicia Mary	"	"	21		"	New York	Ireland	Ireland
13	Gervase Mary	"	"	23		"	Ireland	Ireland	Ireland
14	Barbara Mary	"	"	25		"	Ireland	Ireland	Ireland
15	Allen Catharine	"	"	11	Orphan		New Jersey	Ireland	Ireland
16	Allen Julia	"	"	9			New Jersey		
17	Aldred Jane	"	"	12			New York	Michigan	Michigan
18	Aldred Clara	"	"	10			"	"	"
19	Aldred Rosa	"	"	8					

Figure 4-3. U.S. Census, Monroe County Poorhouse, Rochester, New York, p. 39; Genealogical Society of Utah (hereafter GS) microfilm 43,984, pt. 167.

and the next one 400. Between the two divider cards there may be names coded 353, 350, 360, 365, and 355, but instead of being in numerical order they are interfiled alphabetically by given name. Prefixes to surnames like "van," "Von," "Di," "de," "le," "D," "dela," or "du" are sometimes disregarded in alphabetizing and in coding.

The Soundex also uses an extensive code of abbreviations. See Table 4-4.

Native Americans, Orientals, and Nuns. Names of nuns, American Indians, or Orientals pose special problems. Phonetically spelled Oriental and Indian names were either coded as one continuous name or by what seemed to be a surname. For example, the American Indian name Shinka-Wa-Sa may have been coded as Shinka (S520) or Sa (S000). Check both. Nuns were coded as if "Sister" was the surname, and they appear in each state's Soundex under the code S236, but not necessarily in alphabetical order.

The 1880 Soundex Limits. The 1880 Soundex includes heads of families with children age ten and younger, which somewhat limits its usefulness. Another limitation is the unfortunate omission of over 1,000 cards in the "O" section for the Illinois Soundex. The section is available from Nancy Gibb Frederick, 1208 Maple Avenue, Evanston, IL 60101, for $15.

Use the Soundex to determine surname distribution throughout the state. This can be an important clue, if you don't know which county to search for your family. You can identify family naming patterns since each person living in the family is listed on the Soundex card with relationships stated, find orphaned children living with persons of other surnames, and identify families with grandparents living under the same roof. They are listed on the Soundex card, even though they may not be indexed separately.

1890

Most source guides list the 1890 census as "destroyed." While almost 99 percent of the schedules were so badly damaged in a January 1921 fire in the Commerce Department Building in Washington, D.C., that they were disposed of, significant sections of the population schedule have survived.

This census gives the address, number of families in the house, number of persons in house, and number of persons in family. Then it lists each individual by name; whether a soldier, sailor, or marine during the Civil War and whether Union or Confederate, or whether the widow of a veteran; relationship to head of family; white, black, mulatto, quadroon, octoroon, Chinese, Japanese, or Indian; sex; age; marital status, whether married during year; mother of how many children, number now living, place of birth of the individual and his/her father and mother; if foreign-born, how many years he/she has been in the United States; whether naturalized or in the process of naturalization; profession, trade, or occupation; months unemployed during census year; ability to read and write; ability to speak English; if not, language or dialect spoken; whether suffering from acute or chronic disease, (if so, name of disease and length of time afflicted); whether defective in mind, sight, hearing, or speech, or whether crippled, maimed, or deformed (with name of defect); whether a prisoner, convict, homeless child, or pauper; whether the home is rented or owned by the head or a member of family (if so, whether mortgaged); if head of family is a farmer, if he or a family member rents or owns the farm; and if mortgaged, the post office address of the owner.

The loss of a census with such specific and detailed information

Table 4-3
Indexes to 1860-80 Censuses

State	*1860*	*1870*	*1880*	*Form and Location*
Alabama			●	Manuscripts, Dept. of Archives and History.
Arizona	●	●		Printed.
Colorado	●			Manuscript, state archives.
Illinois	●	●		1860. Card Index (including Chicago) in state library; computer index begun 1982, at the Newberry Library, Chicago. Most counties printed separately.
Indiana		●		1880. Index announced by Patricia M. Shook, 5033 Holbook, Anaheim, CA 92807.
Kansas	●			Manuscript, state historical society.
Minnesota	●			Manuscript, state historical society.
Nebraska	●	●	●	Printed. Available from Platte Valley Books, The Meadows, Box 756, Alliance, NE 69301
New Mexico	●			Printed.
Ohio	●			Printed.
Oklahoma	●			Printed.
Oregon	●		●	Printed county-by-county
Rhode Island	●			Manuscript, state archives.
Tennessee	●			Printed.
Texas	●			Manuscript, Barker History Center, University of Texas, Austin 78712
Washington	●		●	Printed.
Wisconsin	●	●		Card index, state historical society; microfilm copy, Genealogical Society of Utah; card index for Milwaukee, Milwaukee Public Library, 814 West Wisconsin Avenue, Milwaukee, WI 53233.
West Virginia			●	Printed.
Wyoming		●	●	Manuscript, copies in state archives, DAR Library, and Library of Congress.

Printed indexes are usually announced as they are published under book reviews in *Genealogical Helper* (Logan, Utah: Everton Publishers, bimonthly). Most of them are readily available in public and research libraries. The National Archives has announced an updated *Special List 24: Census Schedules*, which will identfy specific publishers and locations for indexes as well as schedules for each census year. Publication of this revised finding aid is expected about 1985.

The Genealogical Society of Utah has begun input of the 1880 Census into its International Genealogical Index (computer database containing some 68 million entries in the 1981 microfiche edition.) When the project is completed, the IGI will include a state-by-state, every-name index to the 1880 census as well. No completion date has been announced for the project.

Table 4-4
Soundex Abbreviations
Relationships to Head of Household

A	Aunt	GF	Grandfather
AdD	Adopted daughter	GGF	Great-grandfather
AdS	Adopted son	GGM	Great-grandmother
At	Attendant	GGGF	Great-great-grandfather
B	Brother	GGGM	Great-great-grandmother
BL	Brother-in-law	GM	Grandmother
Bo	Boarder	GNi	Grandniece
C	Cousin	GS	Grandson
D	Daughter	GU	Great-uncle
DL	Daughter-in-law	Hh	Hired hand
F	Father	I	Inmate
FB	Foster brother	L	Lodger
FF	Foster father	M	Mother
FL	Father-in-law	ML	Mother-in-law
FM	Foster mother	N	Nephew
FSi	Foster sister	Ni	Niece
GA	Great aunt		
GD	Granddaughter		
Nu	Nurse	SM	Stepmother
O	Officer	SML	Stepmother-in-law
P	Patient	SS	Stepson
Pa	Partner (share common abode)	SSi	Stepsister
Pr	Prisoner	SSiL	Stepsister-in-law
Pri	Principal	SSL	Stepson-in-law
Pu	Pupil	Su	Superintendent
R	Roomer	U	Uncle
S	Son	W	Wife
SB	Stepbrother	Wa	Warden
SBL	Stepbrother-in-law		
Se	Servant		
SF	Stepfather		
SFL	Stepfather-in-law		
Si	Sister		
SiL	Sister-in-law		
SL	Son-in-law		

Citizenship Status

A	Alien
NA	Naturalized
PA	First papers filed

is indeed lamentable, but a few schedules – 6,160 legible entries out of a total 62,947,714 persons enumerated[8] – exist:

1. Alabama, Perry County (Perryville Beat No. 11 and Severe Beat No. 8).
2. District of Columbia, Q, Thirteenth, Fourteenth, R,Q, Corcoran, fifteenth, S, R, and Riggs streets, Johnson Avenue, and S Street.
3. Georgia, Muscogee County (Columbus).
4. Illinois, McDonough County, Mound Township.
5. Minnesota, Wright County, Rockford.
6. New Jersey, Hudson County, Jersey City.
7. New York, Westchester County, Eastchester, Suffolk County, Brookhaven Township.
8. North Carolina, Gaston County, South Point Township and River Bend Township; Cleveland County, Township No. 2.
9. Ohio, Hamilton County (Cincinnati) and Clinton County, Wayne Township.
10. South Dakota, Union County, Jefferson Township.
11. Texas, Ellis County, J.P. no. 6, Mountain Peak, and Ovila Precinct; Hood County, Precinct no. 5; Rusk County, Precinct no. 6, and J.P. no. 7; Trinity County, Trinity Town, and Precinct no. 2; Kaufman County, Kaufman.[9]

There is an every-name index to the 1890 census prepared by the National Archives in two rolls, microfilm number M496. It covers all names appearing on the surviving population schedules.

Because the surviving fragments are largely from Western growth areas, they are particularly important for locating unknown family members who have migrated West.

1900

The 1900 census is a significant schedule. For the first time it gives the birth month and year as well as age, the year of immigration to the United States, and the number of children the wife has had, including the number living.

The 1900 census consisted originally of seven schedules with one population schedule for native Americans and one for all other residents. These schedules are reproduced as microfilm publication T623 and are fully described in *1900 Federal Population Census: A Catalog of Microfilm Copies of the Schedules* (Washington, D.C.: Government Printing Office, 1978). Copies are free on request. The discussion which follows is adapted from this valuable catalog. The other schedules – agriculture, manufacturers, mortality, and crime – were not microfilmed but were statistically evaluated and then destroyed.

The population schedules, the most detailed yet, give the name of each person in the household; address; relationship to the head of the household; color or race; sex; month and year of birth; age at last birthday; marital status; the number of years the wife has been married, the total number of children born of that marriage and the number living; places of birth of each individual and the parents of each individual; citizenship; if the individual is foreign born, then the year of immigration and the number of years in the United States; the citizenship status of foreign-born individuals over age twenty-one; occupation; whether the person can read, write, and speak English; whether the home is owned or rented; whether the home is a farm; and whether the home is mortgaged.

1900 Soundex. The Work Projects Administration (WPA) prepared a card index for the 1900 census during the 1930s. Information was abstracted for file cards in three categories: (1) household, (2) individual, and (3) cards for institutions, military posts, naval stations, and United States flag vessels. (Figure 4-4.)

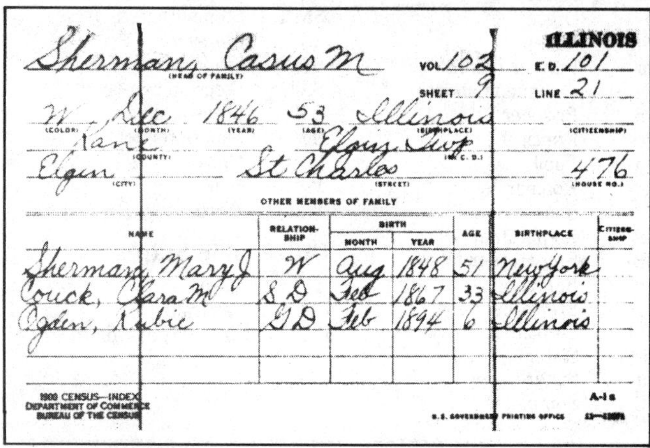

ILLINOIS

Sherman, Casus M (HEAD OF FAMILY) VOL. 102 E.D. 101

SHEET 9 LINE 21

W (COLOR) Dec (MONTH) 1846 (YEAR) 53 (AGE) Illinois (BIRTHPLACE) (CITIZENSHIP)

Kane (COUNTY) Elgin Twp (M.C.D.)

Elgin (CITY) St Charles (STREET) 476 (HOUSE NO.)

OTHER MEMBERS OF FAMILY

NAME	RELATIONSHIP	BIRTH MONTH	BIRTH YEAR	AGE	BIRTHPLACE	CITIZENSHIP
Sherman, Mary J	W	Aug	1848	51	New York	
Couck, Clara M	S D	Feb	1867	33	Illinois	
Ogden, Rubie	G D	Feb	1894	6	Illinois	

1900 CENSUS—INDEX
DEPARTMENT OF COMMERCE
BUREAU OF THE CENSUS

A-1a

U.S. GOVERNMENT PRINTING OFFICE

Figure 4-4. Illinois Soundex household card for Casus M. Sherman in *1900 Federal Population Census: A Catalog of Microfilm Copies of the Schedules* (Washington, D.C.: Government Printing Office, 1978), appendix.

The cards give name, race, month and year of birth, age, citizenship status, place of residence by state and country, civil division, and, where appropriate for urban dwellers, the city name, house number, and street name. The cards also list the volume number, enumeration district number, and page and line numbers of the original schedules from which the information was taken.

1910

The 1910 census schedules record each person's name, relationship to head of household; sex; color or race; age at last birthday; marital status; length of present marriage; if a mother, number of children and number of living children; birthplace, birthplace of parents; if foreign born, year of immigration and citizenship status; language spoken; occupation; type of industry employed in; whether employer, employee, or self-employed; number of weeks unemployed in 1909 if applicable; ability to read and write; if attended daytime school since 1 September 1909; if home is rented or owned; if owned, whether free or mortgaged; if home is a house or a farm; if a veteran of the Union or Confederate army or navy; if blind in both eyes; and if deaf and dumb. The Indian schedule also recorded the tribe and/or band.

No complete index exists for the 1910 census, so a researcher must rely on city directories, county landowners' atlases, enumeration districts, and page-by-page searches of the complete census.[10]

1910 Soundex/Miracode Index. Soundex and Miracode Indexes were created by the Bureau of the Census for twenty-one states. Miracode uses the same phonetic code and abbreviations as the Soundex system; but a Miracode card lists the visitation number assigned by the enumerator, while a Soundex card shows the page and line numbers on the appropriate census schedule. With the exception of Louisiana, which uses both, these states are indexed with either Soundex or Miracode: Alabama, Arkansas, California, Florida, Georgia, Illinois, Kansas, Kentucky, Louisiana, Michigan, Mississippi, Missouri, North Carolina, Ohio, Oklahoma, Pennsylvania, South Carolina, Tennessee, Texas, Virginia, and West Virginia. Both indexing systems give the surname, first name, state and county of residence, city (if applicable), race, age, and place of birth as well as the volume number and enumeration district number of the census schedule from which the information was obtained.

The 1910 Soundex/Miracode is useful for identifying the immigrants who swarmed into California, Illinois, Kansas, Mississippi, Ohio, and Pennsylvania at the turn of the century. This is the first census after this major migration, when families are stable, with United States-born children identified. The index is also helpful for tracing Southern ancestors who moved from the Eastern seaboard into the deep South or Texas. The 1910 census indexed all of the Southern states except Maryland and Delaware.

The 1900-10 censuses are excellent tools for determining dates and places to search for marriage records, birth records of children, deaths of children, and the marriages of children not listed. You can also verify family traditions, identify unknown family members, and link what you know to other sources such as earlier censuses, naturalization records (especially declarations of intent to become citizens), school attendance rolls, property holdings, and employment and occupational records. These records will also verify Civil War service, trace and document ethnic origins, and locate ancestors serving in the armed forces (listed in separate sections of the census).

Special Federal Schedules

In addition to the population schedules, the federal government requested specialized information for administrative decisions. These special schedules are invaluable for genealogy. Each entry is cross-referenced to the population schedule by household number and line.

1885

Under an Act of 3 March 1879, which provided that any state could take an interdecennial census with partial reimbursement by the federal government, Colorado, Florida, Nebraska, and the territories of Dakota and New Mexico (which then included Arizona) returned schedules to the Secretary of the Interior. The schedules are numbered 1, 2, 3, and 5.

Schedule No. 1, inhabitants, lists the number of dwellings and families. It also identifies each inhabitant by the name, color, sex, age, relationship to head of family, marital status, occupation, place of birth, place of birth of parents, literacy, and kind of sickness or disability, if any.

Schedule No. 2, agriculture, gives the name of the farm owner and his tenure, acreage, farm value, expenses, estimated value of farm products, number and kind of livestock, and amount and kind of produce.

Schedule No. 3, products of industry, lists the name of the owning corporation or individual, name of business or products, amount of capital invested, number of employees, wages and hours, number of months in operation during the year, value of materials used, value of products, and amount and type of power used.

Schedule No. 5, mortality, lists the name, age, sex, color, marital status, place of birth, place of birth of parents, and occupation, and gives the cause of death for every person who died within the year ending 31 May 1885.

The schedules are interfiled and arranged alphabetically by state and then by county. Schedules for a number of counties are missing. The National Archives has microfilmed the Colorado (M158, 8 rolls) and Nebraska (M352, 56 rolls) schedules.[11] Originals are in the national archives.

Use the 1885 census to provide data on ancestors living on rapidly growing frontiers: Arizona, Colorado, New Mexico, Nebraska, Florida, and North and South Dakota, locate and document newly arrived immigrants from Europe, and document small businessmen and farmers – many of them immigrants – who were just getting started in their businesses; 1885 is the last manufacturers' schedule available for research. It is our good fortune that it was collected at a critical period in areas where any kind of source is valuable.

Mortality Schedules, 1850-85

Mortality schedules list deaths for the twelve months prior to the census (1 June through 31 May 1849, 1859, 1869, 1879, 1884). Thus, they provide nation-wide, state-by-state death registers. This record predates the recording of vital statistics in most states; and though deaths are underreported (perhaps only 13 percent) they are invaluable. (Figure 4-5.)

Mortality schedules give the dead person's name, sex, age, color (white, black, mulatto; Chinese and Indian added in 1870); free or slave, married or widowed, place of birth (state, territory, or country), month in which the death occurred, profession/occupation/trade, disease or cause of death, and number of days ill. In 1870, the birthplace of parents was added. In 1880, the place where the disease was contracted and how long the deceased was a citizen or resident of the area (fractions mean months when less than one year) are included.

Original schedules are deposited in state archives, in the DAR Library in Washington, D.C., or in the National Archives (NARS). Copies, indexes, and printed schedules are also available in many libraries as Table 4-5 summarizes.

Mortality schedules are useful for tracing and documenting genetic symptoms and diseases and verifying and documenting black, Chinese, and Indian ancestry, although blacks are often omitted especially if they were slaves.[12] By using these schedules to document death dates of family members, you can follow up with focused searches in obituaries, mortuary records, cemeteries, and probates. They will also help you spot migration points and dates and verify the accuracy of information in population schedules.

Veterans' Schedules, 1840, 1890

Revolutionary War pensioners were recorded on the second page (verso) of the 1840 population schedule. It is easy to miss these names, especially in parts of the United States where there were few or no slaves recorded. Slaves were also recorded on page 2 of the schedule. Also, many elderly veterans or their widows were living in the households of married daughters or grandchildren who carried different surnames or who lived in places not yet associated with that family.

By government order, the names of these pensioners were also published in a volume called *A Census of Pensioners for Revolutionary or Military Services* (1841; reprint ed., Baltimore: Genealogical Publishing Co., 1965). The names of some men who had received state or Congressional pensions were inadvertently included with the Revolutionary veterans.[13] The Genealogical

Figure 4-5. Patricia C. Harpole and Mary Nagle, eds., *1850 Mortality Schedule, Minnesota Territorial Census* (St. Paul: Minnesota Historical Society, 1972), p. 100.

Name	Age	Sex	Birthplace	Month of Death	Trade	Disease	Days Ill
Benton County, Sauk Rapids District							
AYR [AYER], Frederick	13	M	Minnesota	August		Affect lungs	[not given]
CRAWFORD, Leonard	1	M	Maine	February		Chronic	"
Ramsey County							
GERVAIS, Pierre	8	M	Minnesota	May		Unknown	42
DONNAR, Magdelin	60	F	Canada	April		Fever	15
BOUVAIS, Antoine	80	M	"	January	Farmer	Pulmonary	30
BIBOT, Zoe	25	F	"	April		Cholera	2
BAPTISTE, John	2	M	"	December		Pulmonary	30
PONCIN, Sophie	7	F	Minnesota	July		Cholera	3
RAMSEY, Alex, Jr.	4	M	Pennsylvania	"		Fever	14
FORBES, W. A.	6/12	M	Minnesota	March		Brain inflammation	21
GLASS, Phoebe	8	F	Wisconsin	February		Burned	2
BARBER, Mary Jane	3	F	Iowa	August		Conjestion	3
Albert	2	M	"	"		"	3
LUMLEY, John	23	M	Ohio	July	Stonemason	Cholera	1
GREEN, James	40	M	Pennsylvania	"	Trader	"	1
GLADDEN, Elijah	35	M	Ohio	"	None	"	5
ROBERT, Francis	25	M	Missouri	December	Trader	Consumption	90
GOODHUE, James, Jr.	2	M	Wisconsin	"		Teething	20

Table 4-5

Mortality Schedule Depositories

An Asterisk indicates publication. Underlining means it has been indexed. For addresses, see Appendix A, National Archives Records Services; Appendix B, State Archives; Appendix D, Genealogical Society of Utah; and Appendix E, Special Libraries. If a state is missing, it means no schedules were taken or have survived.

					State Census Taken With Federal Funds						
	1850	*1860*	*1870*	*1880*	*1885*	*GS*[1]	*DAR*[2]	*NARS*[3] *Micro-Publications*	*State Archives*	*State Historical Society*	*Comments*
Alabama	●	●	●	●					●		
Arkansas			●*	●*		●	●	T655			
Arizona	●̲*	●̲*	●̲*	●̲*		●			●		Printed and indexed; State Department of Archives.
California	●	●	●̲	●			●				DAR has 1870 only.
Colorado			●*	●*	●	●	●	T655			
Connecticut	●	●	●	●		●			●		
Delaware	●	●	●	●					●		
District of Columbia	●̲	●̲	●̲	●̲*			●	T655			
Florida	●	●	●	●	●			●	●		NARS has 1885 only.
Georgia	●̲*	●̲	●̲	●̲		●	●	T655			
Idaho			●*	●*		●				●	
Illinois	●*	●*	●	●				T1156	●		
Indiana	●̲*	●̲	●̲	●̲			●		●		DAR has Jefferson County only.
Iowa	●	●	●	●				T1156		●	
Kansas		●̲*	●̲*	●̲*		●	●	T1130			
Kentucky	●̲*	●̲	●̲	●̲		●	●	T1130			
Louisiana	●̲*	●̲	●̲	●̲		●	●	T655			
Maine	●	●	●	●		●					Originals in Office of Vital Statistics.
Maryland	●̲	●	●	●					●		
Massachusetts	●̲	●	●	●			●	T1204		●	DAR was 1850 only.
Michigan	●̲*	●*	●*	●*			●	T1163	●		
Minnesota	●	●	●			●	●	●		●	NARS has 1870 only.
Mississippi	●*	●	●	●					●		
Missouri	●̲	●̲	●	●			●			●	DAR has 1850-60 only.
Montana		●	●				●	GR6		●	
Nebraska		●*	●*	●*	●		●	T1128		●	NARS has 1885 only
Nevada		●	●				●			●	DAR has 1870 only.
New Hampshire	●	●	●	●		●			●		
New Jersey	●	●	●	●			●	GR21	●		
New Mexico	●	●	●		●					●	NARS has 1885 only.
New York	●	●	●	●			●			●	DAR has 1850 and city of Buffalo only.
North Carolina	●	●	●	●	●		●	GR1	●		
North Dakota		●	●	●*	●	●				●	GS has 1880 only.
Ohio	●*	●		●	●	●		T1159		●	
Oregon	●*	●*	●*	●					●		
Pennsylvania	●	●	●*	●		●	●	T956	●		DAR has Mifflin County only.
Rhode Island	●	●̲	●̲	●̲			●		●		

State	1850	1860	1870	State Census Taken With Federal Funds 1080	1885	GS[1]	DAR[2]	NARS[3] Micro-Publications	State Archives	State Historical Society	Comments
South Dakota		●	●	●	●*	●					GS has 1880 only; NARS has 1885 only.
Tennessee	●	●		●		●	●	T655			GS has 1850-60 only.
Texas	●*	●*	●	●		●		T1134	●		GS has 1850-60 only.
Utah	●	●	●	●		●		T1134			State copy, LDS Historical Department, Salt Lake City, Utah; GS has 1870 only. Originals at Texas State University, Austin, Tx.
Vermont	●*	●*	●	●				GR7	●		NARS has 1870 only.
Virginia	●	●	●	●		●		T1132			State library has 1850, 1870-80; Duke University has 1860; GS has 1870.
Washington		<u>●</u>	<u>●</u>	●			●	T1154			
West Virginia	●*	●*	●*	●*		●			●		
Wisconsin	●	●	●	●			●			●	Milwaukee Public Library has 1860-70; Dar has 1850-70 only.
Wyoming			●	●			●				Originals, State Law Library, Cheyenne, Wyoming.

1. GS: Geneological Society of Utah, Salt Lake City, Utah
2. DAR: Daughters of American Revolution, Washington, D.C.
3. NARS: National Archives and Record Services, Washington, D.C.

Society of Utah indexed the volume, and Genealogical Publishing Company of Baltimore published the index in 1965. These volumes are available in most research libraries. Figure 4-6 shows the pensioners' list for Maine.

> The National Archives has [the surviving] schedules of a special census of Union veterans and widows of veterans in 1890. They are microfilmed on M123, 118 rolls. The schedules are those for Washington, D.C., about half of Kentucky, and Louisiana, Maine, Maryland, Massachusetts, Michigan, Minnesota, Mississippi, Missouri, Montana, Nebraska, Nevada, New Hampshire, New Jersey, New Mexico, New York, North Carolina, North Dakota, Ohio, Oklahoma, and Indian Territories, Oregon, Pennsylvania, Rhode Island, South Carolina, South Dakota, Tennessee, Texas, Utah, U.S. ships and navy yards, Vermont, Virginia, Washington, West Virginia, Wisconsin, and Wyoming. Schedules for other states were destroyed in the same 1921 fire that destroyed the population schedules.
>
> The schedules are arranged by state or territory, thereunder by county, and thereunder by minor subdivision.
>
> Each entry shows the name of a Union veteran of the Civil War, name of his widow, if appropriate; veteran's rank, company, regiment, or vessel; dates of enlistment and discharge and length of service in years, months, and days; post office address; nature of any disability; and remarks.
>
> Unlike the other census records described in this chapter, these schedules are part of the Records of the Veterans Administration, Record Group 15. They are discussed in Evangeline Thurber's "The 1890 Census Records of the Veterans of the Union Army," *National Genealogical Society Quarterly* 34 (March 1946): 7-9.[14]

You can effectively use veterans' schedules to verify military service and specific military unit. Search the state where the ancestor lived in 1890, then follow up in service and pension records. You can also document the surnames of married daughters and grandchildren, locate unknown burial places for Revolutionary War ancestors, and trace Civil War veterans to places of origin.

Slave Schedules, 1850-60

Slaves were enumerated separately during 1850-60 censuses. In most schedules they are listed first, second, third, etc., with age, sex, and color. Some include individual names. The names of owners are recorded. Figure 4-8 is an example of the slave schedule for Kentucky.

Use slave schedules to compare with probate inventories, tax rolls, bills of sale, estate labor registers, and assignment books to identify specific individuals, distinguish between two or more owners with the same name, and locate places of birth for slaves over 100 years of age since the 1860 census usually names these centogenarians.

Agriculture Schedules, 1840-1910

Agriculture schedules are little known and rarely used by genealogists. They are scattered among a variety of archives, where they were deposited by National Archives Records Service in 1918-19. Most are unindexed, and only a few had been microfilmed until recently when the National Archives asked that copies be returned for historical research. The schedules for 1890 were burned and those for 1900-10 were destroyed by Congressional order. See Table 4-6 for the locations of existing schedules.

You can use the agriculture censuses to fill gaps when land and tax records are missing or incomplete; distinguish between men with the same name; document land holdings of ancestors with suitable follow up in deeds, mortgages, tax rolls, and probate inventories; verify and document black sharecroppers and white overseers who may not appear in other records; identify free black men and their property holdings; and trace their movements and economic growth.

Manufacturing Schedules

The first census of manufacturers was taken in 1810. The returns were incomplete, and most of the schedules have been lost except for the few bound with the population schedules. The second, taken in 1820, tabulated the owner's name, the location of his establishment, the number of employees, kind and quantity of machinery, capital invested, articles manufactured, annual production, and general remarks on the business and the demand for its products. The schedules have been arranged alphabetically by county within each state to make research easier. The originals, deposited in the National Archives, in Record Group 29, have been microfilmed in twenty-seven rolls with an index on each roll. These indexes have

Figure 4-6. Revolutionary War Veterans and Military Pensioners of Maine in 1840 in *A Census of Pensioners for Revolutionary or Military Services* (1841; reprinted., Baltimore Genealogical Publishing Co., 1954), p. 1.

CENSUS

OF

PENSIONERS FOR REVOLUTIONARY AND MILITARY SERVICES,

AS

RETURNED UNDER THE ACT FOR TAKING THE SIXTH CENSUS,

IN 1840.

STATE OF MAINE.

Names of pensioners for revolutionary or military services.	Ages.	Names of heads of families with whom pensioners resided June 1, 1840.
YORK COUNTY.		
WATERBOROUGH.		
Noah Ricker	78	Noah Ricker.
Jonathan Knight	77	Simeon C. Knight.
Moses Deshon	76	Moses Deshon.
Abigail Hutchens	87	Abigail Hutchens.
Elizabeth Smith	85	Abner Thing.
Thomas Carpenter	76	Thomas Carpenter.
Sarah McKenney	74	Rufus McKenney.
John Hamilton	75	John Hamilton.
Caleb Lassell	79	Ivory Parcher.
Moses Rhodes	74	Moses Rhodes.
SOUTH BERWICK.		
Mary Chambertin	80	Josiah W. Seaver.
Lydia Jay	92	Ivory Jay.
Henry Beedle	80	Henry Beedle.
Timothy Berdens	76	John Brooks.
Peliliah Stevens	83	John Welch.
Barsham Allen	76	Barsham Allen.
Charles Sargent	86	Charles Sargent.
Lydia Marr	72	Reuben Bennett.
John Hearl	85	John Hearl.
Peace Peirce	69	Samuel Peirce.
Hannah Peirce	81	Hannah Peirce.
Betsey Nasan	81	Betsey Nasan.
Seammon Chadbourn	85	Seammon Chadbourn.
Benjamin Nealey	58	Benjamin Nealey.
WELLS.		
Aaron Warren	83	Walter Warren.
Samuel M. Jefferd	77	Samuel Jefferd.
Mary Gawen	73	James Goodwin.
Joseph Hilton	85	Joseph Hilton.
Miriam Littiefield	85	Joseph Littlefield, 3d.
Daniel Stuart	87	Joseph Stuart.
William Eaton	85	William Eaton.
Abigail Hobbs	72	James Hobbs.
David Hatch	79	David Hatch.
Joseph Williams	90	Moses Williams.
Benjamin Penny	79	Benjamin Penny.
Joseph Wheelwright	88	Joseph Wheelwright.
SANFORD.		
John Hurton	77	John Hurton.
Hepribeth Jacobs.	85	Thedore Jacobs.
Betsey Leavitt	72	Daniel L. Littlefield.
Eunice Goodwin	72	John Lard.
John Quint	79	John Quint.
Samuel Shaw	83	Samuel M. Shaw.
Samuel Shackford	79	Christopher Shackford.
Robert Tripp	76	Robert Tripp.
William Worster	86	Samuel Worster.

Names of pensioners for revolutionary or military services.	Ages.	Names of heads of families with whom pensioners resided June 1, 1840.
YORK COUNTY—Continued.		
SHAPLEIGH.		
Keziah Warren	81	John Pitts.
Jonathan Horn	85	Simon Ross.
Jonathan Ross	91	Gideon Ross.
SACO.		
Stephen Googins	86	Alexander Googins.
John Grace	79	Moses Grace.
Abraham Tyler	77	Abraham Tyler.
PARSONSFIELD.		
Noah Wedgwood	81	Allen Henry.
Levi Chadbourn	82	Levi Chadbourn.
James Brown	83	Edmund Chase.
Jacob Eastman	77	Jacob Eastman.
Josiah Davis	90	Enoch Hale.
Wentworth Lord	84	Wentworth Lord.
William Campnell	80	Nathan Moulton, jr.
George Newbegin	76	George Newbegin.
Thomas Pendexter	58	Thomas Pendexter.
John Stone	82	John Stone.
Thomas Towle	98	Thomas Towle.
Nathan Wiggin	80	Nathan Wiggin.
Jonathan Wingate	82	Lot Wedgwood.
NORTH BERWICK.		
Ichabod Wentworth	52	Ichabod Wentworth.
Absalom Stacpole	88	Absalom Stacpole.
Jacob Allen	82	Jacob Allen.
Simeon Applebee	88	Benjamin Applebee.
Jonathan Hamilton	85	Abraham Henderson.
NEWFIELD.		
Simeon Tibbets	88	Silvester Tibbets.
Ebenezer Colby	81	Ebenezer Colby.
Paul Roberts	78	Nathaniel Roberts.
LYMAN.		
Nathan Raymond	86	Francis Eldreg.
Thomas Murphey	85	Joseph Murphey.
Joshua Gilpatrick	82	Benjamin Goodwin.
Silas Grant	86	Peter Grant.
Jeremiah Roberts	86	Jeremiah Roberts.
Rebecca Ricker	83	George W. Ricker.
Simeon Chadbourn	91	Simeon Chadbourn.
Elizabeth Lord	78	Elizabeth Lord.
John Burbank	88	Reuben Goodwin.
Uriah Hanscomb	59	Felard Davis.
William Clark	88	William Clark.
Amaziah Goodwin	77	James Goodwin.
Isaac Coffin	84	Issaac Coffin.

Figure 4-7. 1890 U.S. Census (Veterans Schedule), Allegeny

[7-741.]

Page No. 1
Supervisor's District No. 3
Enumeration District No. 17

Eleventh Census of the United States.

SPECIAL SCHEDULE.

SURVIVING SOLDIERS, SAILORS, AND MARINES, AND WIDOWS, ETC.

Persons who served in the Army, Navy, and Marine Corps of the United States during the war of the rebellion (who are survivors), and widows of such persons, in Lonaconing**, County of** Allegany**, State of** Maryland**, enumerated in June, 1890.**

Hugh Muir
Enumerator.

	From Schedule No. 1. House No.	From Schedule No. 1. Family No.	Names of Surviving Soldiers, Sailors, and Marines, and Widows.	Rank.	Company.	Name of Regiment or Vessel.	Date of Enlistment.	Date of Discharge.	Length of Service. Yrs.	Length of Service. Mos.	Length of Service. Days.	
	1	2	3	4	5	6	7	8	9			
(1)	7	7	James Atkinson ✓	Corporal	F	10 R P R V cor	15 may 1861	15 June 1864	3	1	+	1
(2)	16	16	John M Gardner ✓	Private Private	A Comp	2 R Md P. H B	August 20 1861	September 28 1864	3	1.	8	2
(3)	168		Joseph Stewart ✓	Private	Comp F	R 10 Pen Vol	July 21 1861	October 31 1862	1	3	10	3
(4)	138		Michael Kenney ✓	Private	A	2 R Md P H B	August 20 1861	September 28 1864				4
(5)	143		Andrew Seuzler ✓	Private	D	R 2d M P H B	September 29 1861	September 29 1864	3	+	+	5
(6)	198		Isaac Cochrane ✓	Private	K	14 Indiana Inf	10 June 1861	10 September 1864	3	2	+	6
(7)	64		John Shearer ✓	Corp.	B	3 west virginia cavalry	12 September 1861	24 September 1864	3	+	12	7
(8)	224		William Whitfield ✓	Private	D	2 Md P H B	September 29 1861	Descharged September 29 1864	3	+	+	8
(9)	85		John Stewart ✓	Sergeant	A	2 Md P.H.B	August 20 1861	Discharged September 28 1864	3	1	8	9
(10)	43		Casper Shade ✓	Private	A	2 Md P.H.B	August 20 1861	September 28 1864	3	1	8	10
(11)	15		Adam McMillan ✓	Private	A	2 Md P.H.B	August 20 1861	September 28 1864	3	1	8	11
(12)	30		James Jonston ✓	Private	A	2 Md P.H.B	August 20 1861	1865	3			12

	Post-Office Address.	Disability Incurred.	Remarks.	
	10	11	12	
1	Lonaconing Md			1
2	Lonaconing Md			2
3	Lonaconing Md	Gun Shott in Cheek		3
4	Lonaconing Md			4
5	Lonaconing Md			5
6	Lonaconing Md	Chronic Diarrhea		6
7	Lonaconing Md			7
8	Lonaconing Md			8
9	Lonaconing Md			9
10	Lonaconing Md			10
11	Lonaconing Md	Chronic Diarrhea		11
12	Lonaconing Md	in Andersonville P 9/12	Got no date of Discharge	12

(19644—200,000.) 240

Table 4-6

Summary of Special Census Schedules, 1850-80

For addresses, see Appendix A, National Archives Records Services; Appendix B, State Archives; Appendix D, Genealogical Society of Utah; and Appendix E, Special Libraries. If only one location is given, all of the schedules are housed there.

State	*Schedule*	*1850*	*1860*	*1870*	*1880*	*Location/Comments*
District of Columbia	Agriculture	●	●	●	●	Duke University, Durham, N.C.
	Manufactures				●	
	Social Statistics	●	●	●	●	
	Industry	●	●	●		
Georgia	Agriculture	●	●	●	●	Duke University
	Social Statistics	●	●	●	●	
	Manufactures	●	●	●	●	
Illinois	Agriculture	●	●	●	●	State Historical Library
	Industry	●	●	●		
	Social Statistics	●	●	●	●	
	Manufactures				●	
Kentucky	Agriculture	●	●	●	●	Duke University
	Industry	●	●	●		
	Social Statistics	●	●	●		
	Manufactures				●	
Louisiana	Agriculture	●	●	●	●	Duke University, Durham, N.C.; copy in state Dept. of Legislature Reference, Baton Rouge, La.
	Social Statistics	●	●	●		
	Manufactures				●	
Maryland	Agriculture	●	●			Hall of Records. Social Statistics schedule for Baltimore City/County only survives.
	Industry	●	●			
	Social Statistics	●				
Massachusetts	Agriculture		●	●		State Archives
	Industry		●	●		State Archives
	Social Statistics		●			State Archives
Minnesota	Agriculture		●	●	●	Minnesota Historical Society
	Manufactures				●	
	Industry		●	●		
	Social Statistics		●	●	●	
Mississippi	Agriculture	●	●	●	●	Dept. of Archives
	Industry	●	●	●		
	Social Statistics	●	●	●		
	Manufactures				●	
Montana	Agriculture			●	●	1870, State Historical Society; 1880 agricultural schedule at Duke University. Other schedules at State Historical Society.
	Social Statistics			●		
	Industry			●		
	Manufactures				●	
Nebraska	Agriculture		●	●	●	National Archives and Records Services
	Social Statistics		●	●	●	
	Industry		●	●		
	Manufactures				●	
Nevada	Agriculture				●	Duke University, Durham, N.C.
North Carolina	Agriculture	●	●	●	●	Dept. of Archives
	Social Statistics	●	●	●	●	
	Industry	●	●	●		
	Manufactures				●	
Pennsylvania	Agriculture	●	●	●	●	National Archives and Records Services
	Social Statistics	●	●	●	●	
	Manufactures	●	●	●	●	
	Industry	●	●	●		
Tennessee	Agriculture	●	●	●	●	Duke University, Durham, N.C.
	Industry	●	●	●		
	Social Statistics	●	●	●		
	Manufactures				●	

State	*Schedule*	*1850*	*1860*	*1870*	*1880*	*Location/Comments*
Texas	Agriculture	•	•	•	•	State Library
	Social Statistics	•	•	•	•	
	Industry	•	•	•		
	Manufactures				•	
Utah	Agriculture	•	•	•	•	Genealogical Society of Utah has a microfilm of the three schedules; originals in LDS Historical Dept.
	Industry	•	•	•		
	Manufactures				•	
	Mining			•		
Vermont	Agriculture	•	•	•		Public Records Commission
	Industry	•	•	•		
Virginia	Slave		•			Duke University, Durham, N.C.
	Agriculture		•			
	Industry		•			
	Social Statistics		•			
Wisconsin	Agriculture	•	•	•	•	Wisconsin State Historical Society
	Social Statistics	•	•	•	•	
	Industry	•	•	•		
	Manufactures				•	
Wyoming	Agriculture				•	Duke University, Durham, N.C.

For those states not included here, check with the state archives or library first. When these schedules were disposed of by the National Archives, state archives were given first rights. Then check with state historical society or state university with historical collections. Addresses can be found in appendixes.

	NAMES OF SLAVE OWNERS.	DESCRIPTION. Number of Slaves.	Age.	Sex.	Colour.	Fugitives from the State.	Number manumitted.	Deaf & dumb, blind, insane, or idiotic.	
	1	2	3	4	5	6	7	8	
1	Saml E. Means	2	5	F	B				1
2		3	3	F	B				2
3		4	1	F	B				3
4	Robert S. McKayder	1	55	F	B				4
5		2	25	F	B				5
6		3	11	F	B				6
7		4	10	F	B				7
8		5	5	F	B				8
9		6	14	M	B				9
10		7	30	M	B				10
11		8	27	M	M				11
12		9	23	M	B				12
13		10	10	M	B				13
14		11	4	M	B				14

Figure 4-8. 1850 U.S. Census (Slave Schedule), District 1, Fayette Co., Kentucky; GS 58,040 pt. 35.

been compiled and printed as National Archives, comp., *Indexes to Manufacturers' Census of 1820: An Edited Printing of the Original Indexes and Information* (reprint ed., Knightstown, Ind.: Bookmark, n.d.).

No manufacturers' schedule was compiled for 1830. None can be located for 1840. From 1850 to 1870, the census was called the Industry Schedule. The 1880 census reverted to the title "manufacturer's schedule." Subsequent years were destroyed by Congressional order. See Table 4-6 for locations.

Social Statistics, 1850-80

Social statistics schedules, compiled from 1850 to 1880, contain three items of specific interest for the genealogist. First, the schedules list cemetery facilities within city boundaries, including maps with cemeteries marked; names, addresses, and general descriptions of all cemeteries; procedures for interment, cemeteries no longer functioning, and the reasons for their closing. Second, the schedules also list trade societies, lodges, clubs, and other groups with addresses, major branches, names of executive officers, and statistics showing members, meetings, and financial worth. The 1880 schedules were printed by the Government Printing Office, and most government documents section of public and university libraries have them.

Third, the schedules list churches with a brief history, a statement of doctrine and policy, and a statistical summary of county-by-county membership. The schedules for 1850-1900 are not listed in the *Preliminary Inventory, 161: Records of the Bureau of the Census in the National Archives* (Washington, D.C.: NARS, 1964). Those for 1906, 1916, and 1926 are printed; the originals were destroyed by order of Congress. Church records are especially helpful when researching immigrants, and the census of social statistics is a finding tool to locate the right group and its records.

The value of special schedules is that they document the lives of small businessmen and merchants who may not appear in land records. When the population schedule gives manufacturing occupations connected with industry, search the manufacturing schedules for more clues. It is also possible to trace the involvement of an ancestor, especially newly arrived immigrants, in a fraternal club, trade society, or other social group.

The information about cemeteries is valuable since many of the small city cemeteries are now abandoned. For example, there is a tiny cemetery in the heart of Greensboro, North Carolina, surrounded by high-rise office buildings and accessible only by a narrow walkway.

Native Americans

Several Indian censuses were taken by the federal government and the Bureau of Indian Affairs. These will be discussed in some detail. Some early Indian populations were tabulated by missionary priests and colonial authorities, but specific examples of these tallies have not been located.

The 1860 and 1870 federal censuses noted only Indians living in non-Indian households. Indians not taxed (living on reservations) and nomad tribesmen in unsettled territories were not counted. So before 1880, these enumerations of Indians are frequently incomplete or inaccurate. Indian origins may not be indicated.

1880 Indian Census. The 1880 Census of Indians, Not-Taxed in four volumes is in NARS Record Group 29.

A special enumeration was taken in 1880 of Indians living near military reservations in Dakota and Washington territories and the state of California. The census included the name of the tribe, the reservation, the agency, and the nearest post office; the number in the household with a description of the dwelling; the Indian name with English translation for each family member; relationship to head of house, marital and tribal status, occupation, health, education, land ownership, and source of subsistence. Some enumerators also added customs and life style.

Volumes 1 and 2 cover Fort Simcoe, Washington; and Tulalip, Washington Territory. Volume 3 covers Fort Yates, Dakota Territory. Volume 4 covers California.

1885-1940 Indian Censuses. The 1885-1940 Indian Census Rolls are microfilmed (692 rolls), NARS M-595. Census enumerations were taken regularly, though not annually, by Indian agents on each reservation from 1885 to 1942. Throughout these rolls are scattered letters written by agents describing why returns were not taken with instructions to enumerators on how to take the census. Vital records are noted in the age columns or appended in separate lists.

In 1978, E. Kay Kirkham, Field Operations, Genealogical Society of Utah, updated and corrected the National Archives listing of Indian bands and tribes in these 692 rolls. He compiled an index for all tribes/bands with Indian agency, National Archives reel number, and Genealogical Society of Utah call number. Tribes are found under several agencies during the period covered by the census, so it is important to study the history of the tribe before beginning research. Copies of this register are available in the Genealogical Society of Utah, American Reference area. Copies can be made on request for use in branch libraries to access the data more easily. There is no master name index to the Indians themselves.

Three copies of the census were made: (1) for the federal government in Washington (now transferred to the National Archives), (2) for the Superintendent of Indian Affairs (BIA), and (3) for the Indian agency. Many Bureau of Indian Affairs copies were destroyed. Some local copies are still in agencies' possession or have been transferred to National Archives Records Service branches. See Table 4-7 for the tribe-by-tribe location of records, then consult Appendix A for the federal archives branch where the National Archives collections are available for searching. For further information on American Indian research, see Chapter 17.

Table 4-7

Indian Censuses, 1840-1942

National Archives microfilm reel numbers are given as NARS 217, etc. Federal Archives Records Centers (FARC) are identified by city. See Appendix A for addresses. See Appendix D for addresses of the Genealogical Society of Utah and its branches.

Tribe	*Reservation/Agency*	*Date of Census*	*Location/Comments*
Apache*	White Mountain	1914	
Assiniboine			*See* Gros Ventre.
Cayuse*	Umatilla	1882	Includes Walla Walla and Umatilla.
Cherokee		1817-19	Those who wished to stay in the East. NARS 217.
		1835	Henderson Roll with index for Cherokees east of Mississippi River in Fort Worth, FARC. See James M. Puckett, Jr., "The Henderson Roll," *Georgia Genealogical Society Quarterly* 6 (1970): 259-80. NARS publication T-496.
		1840	See Homer H. Bradley, II, "The Georgia Cherokee Strip: 1840 U.S. Census," *Georgia Genealogical Society Quarterly* 5 (1969): 1-82.
	Eastern Band, North Carolina	1848	Mullay Roll, NARS 219. Arranged by county, town.
		1851	Silar Roll, Cherokees east of the Mississippi, NARS 219.
		1867	Cherokees residing in the Nations, includes color. Fort Worth, FARC.
	Sequoyah District, Oklahoma Territory	1869-17	Swetland Roll, NARS 219.
		1875-76	Smith Roll
	Cherokee Districts	1880	Schedules 1 (natives) and 3 (rejected claimants) missing for Cooweescoowee. Printed index for Schedules 1-2. Includes Delaware and Shawnee residing in Cherokee districts and orphans roll.
	Cherokee Districts	1883	Schedules: natives, orphans roll, national prison list, supplementary roll of citizens. Fort Worth, FARC.
	Eastern Band	1884	Hester roll, Cherokee citizens. NARC 219.
		1886	Compiled in 1897 from receipt rolls of Cherokee citizens by blood.
	Cherokee Districts	1890	Schedules: natives/adopted orphans under 16, rejected

			claimants, citizenship pending, intruders (whites), residents under permit, blood rolls. Fort Worth, FARC.
	Cherokee Districts	1893	Includes citizens by blood; adoptees; Creek, Shawnee, and Delaware Indians living in the Nations, and intruders (whites). Fort Worth, FARC.
		1893	Freedmen (blacks).
		1894	Compiled in 1897 from 1894 payroll.
	Western Cherokee	1895	Recorded in 1896. Based on 1851 Old Settlers Roll, includes names of heirs for those deceased. Indexed. in NARS publications, 1895. Fort Worth, FARC.
	Eastern Band	1907-8	Churchill Roll, Fort Worth, FARC.
		1909	Fort Worth, FARC.
		1928	
Chickasaw		1837-39	Upshaw roll. Includes muster roll of emigrants 1839. NARS 253.
		1847	Fort Worth, FARC.
	Pickens, Pontotoc Counties	1890	Arranged by town. Includes Choctaws in Chickasaw Nation.
	Pickens, Tishomingo, Pontotoc, Panola countires; 1st and 2nd districts of Choctaw Nation	1896	Includes marriage dates. Fort Worth, FARC.
Chippewa		1848	Prepared for Schoolcraft Roll. Fort Worth, FARC.
	Swan Creek*	1859	
	Black River*	1859	
		1859	Includes Munsee Roll.
	Lake Traverse*	1886	
		1889-1900	Includes supplement and addition rolls. Fort Worth, FARC.
	Turtle Mountain*	1890	
	Michigan	1908	*See* Ottawa.
	White Earth*	1910	
Choctaw	Choctaw Districts	1831	Armstrong Roll. NARS 258.
	Eastern Band	1856	Cooper Roll, Choctaws who remained in the East. NARS 260.
		1860	Genealogical Society of Utah microfilm #2105.
		1874	Used by Dawes Commission for Card Index in 1909, present location unknown.
	1st District; Cedar County	1896	Free inhabitants; slaves and freedmen. Index in 8 vols. Fort Worth, FARC.
	Choctaw Districts; 1st-3rd Districts; Chicksaw District	1896	Indexed, Fort Worth, FARC. Chickasaw District
Creek	Lower Towns*	1832	Recorded in 1833. Parsons/Abbot Roll. Printed as *Senate Exec. Doc. 512,* 23rd Cong., 1st sess. (Serial set, 247)
	Creek Districts of N. Fork, Arkansas, Canadian	1867-69	Freedmen Roll. Confirms all descendants of African descent in Creek Nation. Used by Dawes Commission. Typed copy, Fort Worth, FARC.
		1870	Census of orphans entitled to benefits under 1832 treaty. Arranged by towns. Fort Worth, FARC.
		1895	Arranged by town. Fort Worth, FARC.
	Districts of Coweta, Deep Fork, Eufala, Muscogee, Okmulgee, Wewoka	1895	Alpha index to authenticate rolls of 1890, 1895. Fort Worth, FARC.
Crow		1910*	
	Crow Creek	1942	Kansas City, FARC.
Flathead*		1903-8	
Fox*	Tama, Iowa	1884	
Gros Ventre*		1910	Includes Assiniboine.

Tribe	Agency/Location	Date	Notes
Hopi*	Western Navajo	1918	
Iowa			*See* Santee.
Kansas*		1862	
Kiowa	Oklahoma	1927	Typed carbon copy, Genealogical Society of Utah 970.466/B898c.
Menominee*	Green Bay	1905-07	
Miami*	Indiana	1854	
Mohave*	Camp McDowell	1910	Includes Yuma Apache.
Munsee			*See* Chippewa, Stockbridge.
Navajo*		1915	
Omaha			*See* Santee.
Oneida*	Green Bay	1887	Lists names of ancestors enumerated in 1838.
		1887	Homeless Indians Roll
Ottowa*	Kansas	1848	Part of Schoolcraft Roll.
		1863-64	
		1908	Includes Chippewa (Michigan) descendants of those enrolled in 1870, ancestors listed. Also includes supplement roll.
Oto			*See* Santee.
Pawnee	Nebraska	1860	Genealogical Society of Utah 3624.
Paiute*	Moapa	1920	
	Shivwits	1920	
	Kaibab	1920	
Potawatomie	Rosebud	1942	Kansas City, FARC.
		1943	Kansas City, FARC.
Sac and Fox*	Missouri	1848	Part of Schoolcraft Roll.
	Iowa	1848	Part of Schoolcraft Roll.
Santee	Nemaha	1863-69	Includes mixed-blood Santee, Yankton Sioux, Oto, Omaha, Iowa.
Seminole		1900	4 vols. Arranged by blood bands, includes freedmen. Fort Worth, FARC.
Shawnee*		1888	Orphan roll.
Sioux	Standing Rock	1891-92	Genealogical Society of Utah #494,487. Pencil notes added by Major James McLaughlin for births, deaths, marriages, and migrations.
	Yankton		*See* Santee.
Stockbridge*		1894	Includes Munsee (Wisconsin).
Umatilla			*See* Cayuse.
Uintah		1944	Denver, FARC.
Ute		n.d.	Genealogical Society of Utah #1128.
Walla Walla			*See* Cayuse.
Winnebago*	Wisconsin	1910	
Yuma			*See* Mohave.

*Records in National Archives Records Center, Washington, D.C. See Edward R. Hill, *Preliminary Inventory, 163; Records of the Bureau of Indian Affairs*, 2 vols. (Washington, D.C.: Government Printing Office, 1965).

Table 4-8

Summary of State Census Schedules, 1623-1910

An asterisk indicates that the census has been printed. Underlining indicates that it has been indexed. See also Table 4-1, Summary of Federal Censuses, 1790-1910. The 1885 censuses were conducted with federal funds for Colorado, Florida, Nebraska, New Mexico, North Dakota, and South Dakota.

ALABAMA

Census dates: 1801, 1818, 1821, 1823, 1844, 1855, 1866, 1875, 1907, 1910

Comments: *1907.* Civil War veterans, some counties missing. Microfilm copies at Genealogical Society of Utah.

ALASKA

Census dates: 1872, 1876, 1878, 1881*, 1885*, 1887, 1889, 1890-95*, 1904*, 1905*, 1906-07*

Comments: 1870-1907. Consolidated index by Accelerated Indexing Systems.
1878. Unalaska, Aleutian villages: Belkovsky, Nicholayevsk, Protossoff (also called Morzovog).
1881. Sitka only; printed *House Exec. Doc. 5,* 42nd Cong., 1st sess., serial 2027.
1885. Cape Smyth, Point Barrow; printed *House Exec. Doc. 44,* 48th Cong., 2nd sess., serial 2298.
1890-95. Pribiloff Islands; printed *House Exec. Doc. 92,* pt. 1, 55th Cong. 1st sess., serial 3576.
1904. School Report, Saint George and Saint Paul islands, *Senate Doc. 98,* 59th Cong., 1st sess., serial 4911.
1905. Saint George and Saint Paul islands, same vol. as 1904.
1906-07. Saint George, Saint Paul islands, *Senate Doc. 376,* 60th Cong., 1st sess., serial 5242.

ARIZONA

Census dates: 1790, 1796, 1831, 1864*, 1866*, 1867*, 1869*

Comments: *1790, 1796,* Spanish censuses.
1831. Tucson, Tubac: printed *Copper State Bulletin,* vol. 16.
1866. Pahute, Mohave, Pima, Yuma, Yavapai counties
1867. Mohave, Pima, Yuma counties.
1869. Yavapai County only; originals of 1867-69 censuses in state archives.

ARKANSAS

Census dates: 1821, 1823, 1829, 1838, 1842, 1854

Comments: *1823.* Sheriff census, Arkansas County only.
1829. Pope and Sevier counties missing; Hampstead, Izard, Lafayette, Phillips, and Pulaski counties did not submit names of individuals.

CALIFORNIA

Census dates: 1790,1798,1852, 1855, 1865, 1875, 1885, 1895, 1897, 1905

Comments: *1790.* Spanish census of padrones printed in *Southern California Historical Quarterly,* 67. *1798.* Spanish census in state archives; *1852.* Census copies at DAR Library are indexed. *1856.* See J. Carlyle Parker, *Personal Name Index to 1856 City Directories of California* (Detroit: Gale Research Co., 1979) as a census aid. Several city schedules are also available. See Table 4-10. State censuses were also taken in *1915, 1925, 1935.*

COLORADO

Census dates: 1861, 1866, 1885

Comments: *1885.* Microfilm copy includes agricultural, mortality schedules (a federal enumeration).

CONNECTICUT

Census dates: 1636, 1709*, 1756*, 1762*, 1774*, 1821

Comments: *1709.* Grain census; printed as "Corresponsdence of Gov. George Wyllys," *Connecticut Historical Society Collections,* vol. 21.
1756. Printed in *Connecticut Colony Public Records,* vol. 14, p. 492.
1762. Originals in Public Record Office, London; call number 5/1276/250.
1774. Printed in *Connecticut Colony Public Records,* vol. 14, pp. 485-91.
1821. School census; original in state library, microfilm in Genealogical Society of Utah, #1484, pt. 2.

DELAWARE

Census dates: 1665, 1667, 1669, 1670, 1671, 1672, 1675, 1676, 1677, 1678, 1680, 1681, 1693, 1696, 1697, 1776

Comments: 1665-97. Printed Accelerated Indexing Systems.

DISTRICT OF COLUMBIA

Census dates: 1803, 1807, 1818, 1867, 1878, 1885, 1888, 1894, 1897, 1905-09 (This last census took four years to conduct.)

Comments: Censuses were also taken in 1912-13 (took two years to complete), 1915, 1917, 1919, 1925. The 1885-1925 censuses are police censuses.

FLORIDA

Census dates: 1783, 1786, 1790, 1793, 1814, 1825, 1837, 1845, 1855, 1865, 1868, 1875, 1884, 1895, 1905

Comments:
1790. Spanish census.
1837, 1865, 1875 cannot be found, except Alachua County.
1825. Leon County only; printed *Florida Historical Quarterly* 22 (1945): 34-40.
1868. Leon County only.
1875. Alachua County only.
1783, 1786, 1793. Spanish censuses in private possession; microfilm copy at Genealogical Society of Utah, #1,014,120.
1814. Mosquito Territory; in private possession; microfilm copy at Genealogical Society of Utah, #1,014,120.
1884. Franklin County only.
1784-1820. Spanish censuses of Pensacola, printed.

GEORGIA

Census dates: 1738, 1740, 1750, 1753, 1756, 1810, 1817, 1824, 1829, 1831, 1838, 1845, 1852, 1859

Comments: Public Record Office, London:
1738. C.O. 5/711/16
1740. C.O. 5/711/44.
1750. C.O. 5/643/20.
1756. C.O. 5/645/71.
1753. See E. B. Greene and V. D. Harrington, *American Population Before. . .1790* (New York: n.p., 1932).
1824, 1831. Fragments only.
1838, 1845. Printed Indexes to *State Census Reports*. Some counties missing.

HAWAII

Census dates: 1840-66 (compiled), 1878, 1890, 1896

Comments:
1840-66. Compiled from school censuses, population schedules, tax lists, births and deaths; some in Hawaiian only. Original in state archives; microfilm at Genealogical Society of Utah, 1,990,896, items 1-4.
1866. Original schedule.
1878. Islands of Hawaii, Oahu.
1896. Island of Oahu, Honolulu (enumerated separately).

IDAHO

Census dates: 1863-1878, 1890, 1896

ILLINOIS

Census dates: 1787, 1793, 1818*, 1820, 1825, 1835, 1845, 1855, 1862, 1865

Comments:
1825-55. All manuscripts of censuses, state and national, indexed in *Illinois Early Records Index,* in the state library; microfilmed by Genealogical Society of Utah in 248 reels.
1820. State schedules differ from the national federal census taken the same year; printed in *Collections, Illinois State Historical Society,* vol. 26 (1934).
1825. Edward and Fulton counties only.
1845. Cass, Putnam, and Tazewell counties only.
1862. Military census county-by-county includes men 18-45 years of age. Microfilm copy at Genealogical Society of Utah.
1934. Census of Chicago.

INDIANA

Census dates: 1801, 1807*, 1815*, 1853, 1857, 1859, 1866, 1871, 1877, 1883, 1889, 1895, 1901, 1907

Comments:
1801. Statistics only.
1815. Statistics only. Printed in *Territorial Papers of the U.S.*, vol. 8 (1939).
1853-71. Specific counties only; original schedules in state library.
1877-1919. White males over 21, black males over 21, every 5 years for specific counties only. Originals in state library.
1820-50. White males over 21 tallied every 5 years. Some are statistical only. Originals in state library.
1915. Census also taken.

IOWA

Census dates: 1836*, 1838, 1841, 1844, 1846, 1847, 1849, 1851, 1852, 1853, 1854, 1856, 1859-69, 1873, 1875, 1885, 1881-97, 1895, 1905

Comments:
1838. Van Buren County only.
1844. Keokuk County only.
1846. Louisa, Polk, and Wapello counties only.
1841-49. Every name index, Accelerated Indexing Systems.

1859-69. Statistics only; full description in *Census Data for Iowa,* Des Moines: State Historical Society, 1973.
1881-97. Several cities enumerated. See Table 4-9.
1853. Warren County only.
1856. Personal Name Index to 1856 City Directories of Iowa (Detroit: Gale Research Company, 1979), is a census aid. Censuses taken also in *1915, 1925.*
1925. Gives marriage date for husband and wife.

KANSAS

Census dates: 1855,* 1859, 1865, 1874, 1875, 1885, 1895, 1905
Comments: *1855, 1865.* Card index by Willard C. Heiss, state archives, microfilm copy at Genealogical Society of Utah, #570,188; includes map of election districts.
1859. Davis and Wabaunsee counties; some entries for Riley County with Davis County; printed in *Kansas Kin,* vol. 19 (1981).
1865. Includes military unit, social statistics schedule.
1874. Based on Assessor's Lists.
1875. Includes agricultural schedule.
1885. Includes military census.
Also censuses taken in *1915, 1925.*

KENTUCKY

Census dates: 1792, 1799, 1803, 1807, 1811, 1815, 1819, 1823, 1827, 1831, 1835, 1839, 1843, 1847, 1851, 1859, 1867, 1875, 1883, 1891, 1899
Comments: *1873-1902.* Annual enumerations of males over 21 by tax assessors, printed summaries in *Reports of Kentucky Documents: State Board of Equalization* (Lexington: By order of the State Board, annual.)

LOUISIANA

Census dates: 1699-1732*, 1706*, 1721*, 1722*, 1724*, 1726*, 1731*, 1770-98*, 1774*, 1790, 1799*, 1804*, 1805, 1806, 1807*, 1809*, 1811, 1813*, 1817, 1821, 1825, 1829, 1833, 1837, 1841, 1845, 1853, 1858
Comments: *1699-1732.* French.
1723. Natchez; printed by Winston DeVille, *National Genealogical Society Quarterly* 59 (1971): 94-95.
1774. Attakapos Post only; translated by Winston DeVille et al. (New Orleans: Polyanthos Press, n.d.).
1799. Rapides Post only; translated by Winston DeVille, et al. (New Orleans: Polyanthos Press, n.d.).

MAINE

Census dates: 1652*, 1674*, 1703*, 1711*, 1753*, 1837, 1906
Comments: *1837.* State archives; incomplete.
1906. York County only; printed in *The Saco Register with Old Orchard,* Brunswick: H.E. Mitchell, 1906.

MARYLAND

Census dates: 1683*, 1701, 1704, 1708, 1710*, 1712, 1748-49, 1755, 1758, 1762, 1776*, 1778*
Comments: *1776, 1778.* Oaths of allegiance indexed; contact Bettie Stirling Carothers, 14423 Eddington Dr., Chesterfield, MO 63017.
1708. Public Records Office, London: C.O. 5/716/#54.
1762. C.O. 5/1276/25.
1755. Referenced *Gentleman's Magazine,* vol. 34, p. 261. For colonial censuses see E. G. Greene and V. D. Harrington, *American Population Before. . .1790* (New York: n. pub., 1932).

MASSACHUSETTS

Census dates: 1754, 1764, 1779*, 1783, 1785-86, 1793, 1837, 1855, 1865, 1875, 1885, 1895, 1905
Comments: For colonial censuses, see J. H. Benton, Jr., *Early Census Making in Massachusetts, 1643 to 1765.*
1837. Danvers and Essex counties only.
1912. Essex County only; printed *1912 Register* (Auburn, Maine: Lawton Register Co., 1912).
1915. Statistics only.
Also censuses in *1912, 1915, 1925, 1935, 1945.*

MICHIGAN

Census dates: 1710-1830*, 1796*, 1799, 1806, 1827*, 1834, 1837*, 1841, 1845, 1853, 1854, 1864, 1866, 1874, 1884, 1894
Comments: *1719-1830.* Seventeen early censuses printed in Michigan state censuses cover specific counties only; list of and locations of schedules available from Bentley Historical Library, University of Michigan, 1150 Beal Ave., Ann Arbor, MI 48109.
1796. Printed *National Genealogical Society Quarterly* 64 (1981): 185-94.
Also census for *1935.*

MINNESOTA

Census dates: 1836*, 1849, 1857*, 1865, 1875, 1885, 1895, 1905

Comments: *1836*. Includes Wisconsin, Iowa, and the Dakotas.
1885, 1905. Includes Civil War veterans.
1905. Also includes Spanish-American War veterans.

MISSISSIPPI

Census dates: 1774, 1788, 1789, 1792*, 1801, 1805*, 1808, 1809, 1810*, 1813, 1816*, 1818, 1820, 1822, 1823, 1824, 1825, 1830, 1833, 1837, 1841, 1845, 1853, 1866

Comments: *1801-45*. Abstracts are in Dept. of Archives; microfilm copy in Genealogical Society of Utah, #899,868.
All state censuses 1792-1866 available on microfilm, Genealogical Society of Utah. Some counties have statistical totals only.
1822-24. Birth, death information for heads of households only.
1792. Originals in Spanish; microfilm copy at Genealogical Society of Utah, #899,868.

MISSOURI

Census dates: 1789, 1790, 1796, 1803, 1814, 1817, 1821, 1824, 1828, 1832, 1838, 1844, 1847*, 1852, 1856, 1864, 1868, 1876

Comments: *1847*. Saint Louis only; microfilm copy at Genealogical Society of Utah.
1814-76. Burned in 1911; scattered copies in county possession.
1876. Includes agricultural data; original in state archives; microfilm copy at Genealogical Society of Utah.

MONTANA

Census dates: 1864, 1905

NEBRASKA

Census dates: 1854*, 1855*, 1856*, 1865, 1869, 1885f

Comments: *1865, 1869*. Card index in state archives.
1885. Includes federal agriculture, mortality schedules.

NEVADA

Census dates: 1861, 1863, 1865, 1867, 1875*, 1885, 1895

Comments: Originals in state archives. Indexing project underway.

NEW HAMPSHIRE

Census dates: 1633-99*, 1732*, 1735*, 1767, 1773*, 1774*, 1775, 1786*, 1855, 1865, 1875, 1885, 1895

Comments: *1774*. Public Record Office, London, C.O. 5/938/p. 299.
1767, 1773, 1786. Printed *Provincial Papers of New Hampshire*, vols. 7, 10.
1775. Printed in *New Hampshire Historical Collections*, vol. 1 (1824).
1775. Incomplete.
1855-95. Originals in state archives; microfilm copies at Genealogical Society of Utah.

NEW JERSEY

Census dates: 1693*, 1726, 1737-38, 1745, 1772, 1793*, 1855, 1865, 1875, 1885, 1895, 1905

Comments: *1793*. Compiled from military censuses and tax rolls; see James S. Norton, *New Jersey in 1793*, distributed by Everton Publishers, Box 368, Logan, UT 84321.
1773-1822. Ratables make up *Revolutionary Census of New Jersey* by Kenn Stryker-Rodda (New Orleans: Polyanthos, 1972).
1783. Tax lists on microfilm, DAR Library.
1855, 1865. Some counties missing.
Census also in *1915*.

NEW MEXICO

Census dates: 1790*, 1823*, 1845* 1864, 1865, 1885f, 1895, 1905

Comments: *1790, 1823, 1845*. Translated and edited by Virginia L. Olmstead (Albuquerque: New Mexico Genealogical Society, 1975).

NEW YORK

Census dates: 1663*, 1664*, 1698, 1703, 1712-14, 1723, 1731, 1737, 1746, 1749, 1756, 1771, 1795, 1801, 1804, 1806, 1807, 1814, 1815, 1821, 1825, 1835, 1843, 1845, 1855, 1865, 1875, 1885, 1892, 1905

Comments: *1663-1771*. Printed in Edmund Bailey O'Callagham, *Lists of Inhabitants from the Documentary History of the State of New York* (Baltimore: Genealogical Publishing Co., 1979), includes every-name index.
1703. New York City, printed in *A Century of Population Growth* (Washington, D.C.: Bureau of Census, 1909).

1712-14. Includes census of the poor for New York City; originals New York State Archives among Mayor's Court Minutes 24 May 1713.
1806. Holland Land Company, "Statements of Settlers," Twenty Townships area; microfilm copy at Cornell University Library #1912.
1815. St. Lawrence County only.
1843. Broome County only.
1825-1905. Microfilm copies at Genealogical Society of Utah.
Census also available for 1915, 1925; microfilm copies at Genealogical Society of Utah.

NORTH CAROLINA

Census dates: 1701, 1741-52*, 1784*, 1785*, 1786*, 1787*
Comments: *1784-87*. Compiled by *Alvaretta Register* (Baltimore: Genealogical Publishing Co., 1973); corrects many errors in first edition; see also "1786 Census of North Carolina," *North Carolina Genealogy* 13 (1967): 1996-98.

NORTH DAKOTA

Census dates: 1836*, 1855, 1885, 1905
Comments: *1836-1905*. Originals in state archives.
1885. Includes federal agriculture, population, mortality, and industry schedules; some counties missing; printed in *North Dakota Historical Collections* 4 (1913): 338-48. Also censuses in *1915, 1925*.

OHIO

Census dates: 1790, 1801, 1802, 1807, 1811, 1815, 1819, 1823, 1827, 1831, 1835, 1839, 1843, 1847, 1851, 1855, 1859, 1863, 1867, 1871, 1875, 1879, 1891, 1895, 1899, 1903, 1907
Comments: *1790*. French census.
1863. Census of blacks in 13 counties; Belmont County in "List of Names and Townships in Belmont County, Ohio." *National Genealogical Society Quarterly* 69 (1981): 71-73.
Also censuses in *1911, 1915*.

OKLAHOMA

Census dates: 1890*, 1896, 1902, 1907*
Comments: *1890*. Card index at state historical society.
1907. Seminole County.

OREGON

Census dates: 1842, 1845, 1849, 1852, 1853, 1854, 1855, 1856, 1857, 1858, 1859, 1865, 1885, 1895, 1905
Comments: *1842-59*. Specific counties indexed in state archives; list available on request.

PENNSYLVANIA

Census dates: 1693, 1749, 1763-1807, 1769, 1776
Comments: Possibly *1760*. Philadelphia only; see *William and Mary Quarterly*, 3rd series, 30 (1973): 236.
1763-1807. Septennial censuses of military-age men taken by the assessors. Originals often found with tax rolls in county records; copies sent to state archives.

RHODE ISLAND

Census dates: 1689*, 1708*, 1730, 1747, 1748-49, 1754, 1755, 1776, 1777*, 1782*, 1865, 1875, 1885, 1895, 1905
Comments: *1689*. Bristol Plymouth Colony only; in *New England Historic Genealogical Register* 34 (1880): 404-5.
1708. See *Rhode Island Colonial Record* 4: 59.
1730-49. Referenced E. B. Greene and V. D. Harrington, *American Population Before . . .1790* (New York: n. pub., 1932), p. 66.
1747. Freedmen only.
1755. Public Record Office, London, C.O. 5/1274/118-19.
1777. Includes signers of the Test Act.
1854. Registered voters.
1895. Whereabouts unknown.
Also censuses in *1915, 1925, 1936*.

SOUTH CAROLINA

Census dates: 1670, 1775, 1776, 1869, 1875
Comments: Originals in state archives.

SOUTH DAKOTA

Census dates: 1836*, 1885* (federal), 1895, 1905
Comments: *1885*. Includes federal industry, agriculture, and mortality schedules; some counties missing.
Also censuses in *1915, 1925, 1935*, and *1945*.

TENNESSEE

No state censuses.

TEXAS

Census dates: 1790, 1815, 1819, 1826, 1829*, 1834-35*, 1836*, 1840, 1847, 1848, 1851, 1854-55, 1858, 1867

Comments: *1722-1803*. See Elizabeth Shown Mills, *Natchitoches Colonials: Censuses, Military Rolls, and Tax Lists,* vol 5 in Cane River Creole Series.
1790-1835. Spanish censuses.
1829-36. Printed in *National Genealogical Society Quarterly* 40 (1952); 41 (1953); 42 (1954); 43 (1955); 46 (1956). Reprinted Washington, D.C.: National Genealogical Society, 1962.
1821-45. Compilation of citizenship lists including certificates of entry into Texas; state archives; microfilm copy at Genealogical Society of Utah.
1847, 1848, 1851, 1858. Schedules missing.
1867. Voters list.

UTAH

Census dates: 1852, 1856, 1872, 1896

Comments: *1852*. Includes Mormons at Winter Quarters (Florence, Neb./Council Bluffs, Iowa) in part; schedules scattered among mss. in LDS Church Historical Dept., 50 East North Temple, Salt Lake City, UT 84150.
1856, 1872, 1896. Territorial censuses; originals in LDS Historical Dept.

VERMONT

Census dates: 1623-25, 1634, 1699, 1701, 1703, 1779

Comments: See Holman D. Jordon, Jr., "Value of Census Data in Writing Vermont Town Histories," *Vermont History* 26 (1968): 19-28.

VIRGINIA

Census dates: 1623-25, 1634, 1699, 1701, 1703, 1779

Comments: *1623-25*. Printed J. C. Hotten, *The Original Lists of...Emigrants to American Plantations, 1600-1700* (1874; reprint ed., Baltimore: Genalogical Publishing Co., n.d.).
1634, 1699, 1701. See E. B. Greene and V. D. Harrington, *American Population Before. . .1790* (New York, 1932), pp. 145-48.
1703. See James Oldmixon, *The British Empire in America*, vol. 1 (London, 1741), p. 426.
1779. See William H. Dumont, "A Short Census of Viriginia, 1779," *National Genealogical Society Quarterly* 46 (1958): 163-211.

WASHINGTON

Census dates: 1871, 1883, 1885, 1887, 1889, 1892

Comments: Originals in state archives.

WEST VIRGINIA

No state censuses.

WISCONSIN

Census dates: 1830, 1836*, 1838, 1842, 1846, 1847, 1855, 1865, 1875, 1885, 1895, 1905

Comments: *1836-47*. Schedules for Lafayette and Iowa counties, some for Richland and Jo Daviess counties printed in *Iowa County Heritage*, 2 vols. (Dodgeville, Iowa: Fieldhouse Foundation, 1967).

WYOMING

Census dates: 1905

Comments: *1905*. Indexed by county; originals in state archives; some counties missing. Also censuses in *1915, 1925*, but they are missing.

1898-1906 Indian Census Cards Index. The Indian Census Cards Index was compiled by the Dawes Commission to verify individual rights to tribal allotments for the Five Civilized Tribes (Cherokee, Chickasaw, Choctaw, Creek, and Seminole). To search this index, send the name of the tribe, name of individual, approximate date of birth or death, and location to Chief, Archives Branch, Federal Archives and Records Services, Box 6216, Fort Worth, TX 76115. Copies of the index are available at the Five Civilized Tribes Center, Muskogee, OK 74401, and at the Genealogical Society of Utah.

1910-1939 Indian School Censuses. The Bureau of Indian Affairs took separate Indian School censuses from 1910 to 1939. These include names of all children between six and eighteen years of age, sex, tribe, degree of Indian blood, distance from home to the school, parent or guardian, and attendance during the year. Some schedules are available on microfilm; most are still in original form in the Federal Records Center for the region where the tribe was located. Unlike white census records, these often include the mother's surname.

Indian census records can be used to identify relationships, mothers' full names, aliases, ancestral rights, and inheritances. These census records, however, apply only to Indians registered with the Bureau of Indian Affairs. Many Indian families never enrolled with the government. These persons are recorded in the regular census schedules, usually without evidence of their Indian ties.

Other miscellaneous records document the Indian population. Supplementary rolls list births, deaths, and sometimes marriages. Deduction rolls give deaths or removals from the jurisdiction. Addition rolls include arrivals and births. Allotment rolls list those entitled to payment and the payments received. For a more detailed description of these and other Indian sources, see Chapter 17.

State and Local Census Schedules, 1623-1918

In rapidly growing areas, population counts were sometimes conducted. State censuses were taken between federal censuses in some cases. In others, local censuses were authorized to supply specific data: tallies of school-age children and potential school populations to predict needs for teachers and facilities; censuses of military strength, grain storage, cavalry horse resources, and economic aid needed; city and town enumerations for revenue assessment and urban planning; and lists to monitor blacks moving into northern cities.

Table 4-8 gives a summary of the censuses in each state, the date, comments on them, and their current locations. The vast wealth of data available in these local enumerations can take several forms as the discussion will show.

Local Censuses

Local population schedules usually resemble those of corresponding federal enumerations, but those taken by New York and Boston during the colonial period included details later adopted for federal censuses. Beginning as early as 1703, some cities required that a census be taken of their population. Although these city/town censuses are nowhere near as numerous as the federal population schedules, they are an invaluable source for the genealogist who takes the time to search them. Table 4-9 lists the known extant enumerations of these cities.

An interesting 1776 census was compiled from oaths of allegiance ordered by the new colonial government in Maryland. Several of the lists are arranged in family units like that in Figure 4-9, with ages given for each person – a pattern later used for U.S. federal schedules. This suggests a dual purpose: commitment to the new cause and a count of potential strength – taxables, military age, and

1776 CENSUS OF SUSQUEHANNAH HUNDRED, HARFORD COUNTY, MD.
Taken by Charles Gilbert

Name	Age
Small, Robert	30
Elizabeth	21
John	9mos.
Beacor, George	15
Hare, Patience	11
Small, John	27
Wilson, Andrew	46
Lidiea	36
James	10
Cathron	8
Benjamin	4
Andrew	2
Hallett, John	25
Prigg, Mary	25
Brown, George	14
Eare, Sarah (Widow)	39
Mary	17
Sarah	6
Daniel	3
Rigdon, Charles	27
Molton, Mathew	15
Sulliven, Nathaniel	13
Donovan William	23
Rachel	19
Anos	6mos.
Durbin, Avariller	25
Delila	2
Judd, Daniel	40
Hanah	39
William	17
Daniel	11
Joshua	9
Rachel	8
Ann	6
Elisabeth	3
James	3mos.
Thomson, Edward	45
Jamine	30
Martha	10
Mallon	6
Mary	3
William	1
Sullavin, James	17
Johns, Richard	43

Name	Age
Horton, William	33
Elisabeth	32
William	14
Mary	12
James	10
Sarah	8
Elisabeth	5
Ruth	1
2 negroes	
Cummins, Paul	35
Hannah	27
Samuel	9
James	3
Barns, Joseph	45
Horner, James	29
Mary	28
Elisabeth	7
Thomas	6
Casandrew	4
Mary Gilbert	1
Baker, Jenny Mary	11
2 negroes	
Clarke, Elizabeth	18
Culver, Benjamin	24
1 negro	
Culver, Ann	62
1 negro	
Suillovon, John	27
Margret	18
Coolley, John	21
Rigdon, Sarah	62
Sarah	23
Pritchart, Mary	12
Bedelhall, John	27
5 negroes	
Michael, Belsher	48
Ann	28
John	14
James	13
Bennet	8
Jacob	6
Susannah	4
Daniel	2
William	8mos.
Horten, John	23
4 negroes	

Name	Age
Macantraus, Hugh	24
Feeby	31
Mary	3mos.
Hall, Josias	24
Mecarty, Owing	22
3 negroes	
Choislin, Thomas	41
Young, Thomas	40
Chisholm, Thomas	11
Chisholm, John	7
Hampton, John	85
Ann	84
Mitchel, John	31
Mary	34
Gaberil	19
Elisabeth	6
Rachel	4
Fredrick	1
Purkins, Ritchard	16
Taylor, Ritchard	12
Cortny, Thomas	32
Sarah	27
Jonas	10
John	8
Hollas	6
Semelia	5
Sarah	3
Thomas	2mos.
Brown, James	13
1 negro	
Knight, Jonathan	56
Ellender	46
Holliday, Mary	12
West, Thomas	45
Ann	39
Elisabeth	17
James	14
Thomas	12
Samuel	6
Sarah	6
Mary	3
Isaac	1
Wright, Charles	30
Blackford, Thomas	66

108

Figure 4-9. 1776 Census of Susquehannah Hundred, Barford Co., Maryland, in *1776 Census of Maryland,* published by B. Stirling Carothers, 14423 Eddington Drive, Chesterfield, MO 63017.

Table 4-9

City/Town Schedules

State	Date of Census	City/Town	Location/Comments
Alabama	1935	Alexander City	National Archives Records Service.
		Clanton	
California	1834	Santa Barbara	Spanish originals in Bancroft Library; translation by Marie Northrup, *Southern California Historical Society Quarterly,* vol. 27; all other originals in California State Archives; microfilm copies at the Genealogical Society of Utah.
	1836	Los Angeles	
	1838	Los Angeles	Printed in *Southern California Historical Society Quarterly,* vol. 18 (1936).
	1844	Los Angeles	
	1897	Los Angeles	
	1899	San Diego	
	1902	Oakland	
	1905	Long Beach	
		Santa Monica	
		San Buena Ventura	
	1906	Chico	
		Long Beach	
		San Luis Obispo	
		San Pedro	
	1908	Richmond	
		Kern	
		Long Beach	
		Red Bluff	
	1910	Monrovia	
Hawaii	1878	Islands of Oahu and Hawaii	Originals at Hawaii State Archives; microfilm copy at Genealogical Society of Utah.
	1896	Honolulu	Originals at Hawaii State Archives; microfilm copy at Genealogical Society of Utah.
Illinois	1934	Chicago	Originals in National Archives.
	1936	Crestwood	
	1937	Rock Falls	
		Sterling	
	1938	Lincolnwood	
		Markham	
		Riverside	
Indiana	1857	Hartford	
	1933	Monticello	Originals for 1933 Census in National Archives.
		North Vernon	
		Petersburg	
		Rensselaer	
Iowa	1881	Mason City	Schedules for all Iowa cities in Iowa State Archives.
	1888	Algona	
	1891	Spencer	
		Villisca	
	1892	Carroll	
		Wright	
		Estherville	
		Greene	
		Tama	
	1893	Mystic	
		Hampton	
		Ames	
		Bloomfield	
		Nevada	
		West Union	
	1896	Oelwein	
	1897	New Hampton	

State	Date of Census	City/Town	Location/Comments
Massachusetts	1837	Danvers	
	1845	Boston	Massachusetts State Archives; designed by Lemmel Shattuck, this census was the pattern for the 1850 federal census.
Michigan	1796	Detroit	Printed in *National Genealogical Society Quarterly* 64 (1981): 185-94.
	1820	Detroit	
	1884	Detroit	
Mississippi	1792	Natchez	Originals for all Mississippi cities in state archives.
	1805	Natchez	
	1810	Natchez	
Missouri	1847	Saint Louis	
North Carolina	1932	Hickory	NARS
New York	1703	New York City	Printed in *Century of Population Growth* (Washington, D.C.: Government Printing Office, 1909), pp. 170-80.
Pennsylvania	1749	Philadelphia	See *William and Mary Quarterly*, 3rd series, 30 (1973): 236.
	1760	Philadelphia	See also black censuses, this chapter.
	1769	Philadelphia	
	1933	Johnsonburg	NARS

required protection for women and children. In 1778, a second census tallied those against the Revolution. Included on this second list are Quakers, Mennonites, and others who refused to take oaths, as well as Tories still in the new nation.

School censuses are taken to insure that local facilities and teachers are adequate and to plan for future appropriations. These schedules count the children of school age. Some lists are in family units with parents' names included. Some list children with ages only. See Figure 4-10.

In Figure 4-11, the number of children in each family is given by name of the father. If a woman's name is given, she is probably a widow.

The constable or sheriff census (also called police census) actually had little to do with law enforcement; but the local constable, often under the eye of the sheriff, was the official most often used to accumulate data required for administrative decisions. For example, the governor of Connecticut in 1669-70 required an enumeration of "how many parsons partayn to ech family, and how many boshels of wheat, and of Indian corne, ech famyly hath."

GRAIN IN POSSESSION OF EACH.

A list of the number of psons and of bushells of corn in Windsor[1]

	psons	bush:			
Imp^s Owin Tewder	6	26	John Slater	3	0
J: Miacano		(?)80	Willam buell	4	0
Mr Allin	4	30	George Griswold	8	44
Bath Loomis	9	26	Sarah phelps	10	30
Joseph Loomis	8	30	Willyam parson	3	0
Tho: Loomis	7	30	Mr thomas Allin	6	20
H: Wolcot senor	12	100	Benaiah holcomb	4	8
S: Wolcot	7	20	peeter Browne	8	20
Robert Old	2	½	William Phellpes	5	13
John Porter	12		Timothy Phellpes	8	0
			Timmothe Hall(?)	4	6

List of Families in Windsor with quantity of grain in possession of each in "Correspondence of Governor George Wyllys, 1709," *Connecticut Historical Society Collections*, 21 (1924): 194.

Another sheriff's census was taken by the Committee of Safety and Relief, 16 April 1814, to account for settlers on the Niagara Frontier (Western New York) "victimized during the War of 1812." Money was raised in Albany by voluntary donation to provide aid for these settlers.[15]

Pennsylvania's tax assessors took septennial (seven-year) censuses from 1763 to 1807, listing taxable inhabitants township by township. Occasionally, the list covered males from sixteen to forty-five years only, thus making a militia census. Tax assessors were exempt along with teachers, physicians, provincial/state government leaders, militia captains, and others. Their names will *not* be included on the name lists. Exempt status was set by law.[16]

In areas where a church was established and supported by the civil government, enumerating the population was often the responsibility of church officials. The most common examples come from New England, but others can be found among the church-warden's records in Virginia and South Carolina.

Census of Bristol.

	Wife.	Children.	Servant
Nathaniel Reynolds	1	8	0
Jeremy Osborn	1	1	1
Major Wally	1	5	4
Stephen Bucklin	1	2	1
John Walkley	1	5	2
Jabez Howland	1	4	2
Simon Davis	1	1	1
William Brutton	1	2	0
Thomas Bles go	1	0	2
Joseph Sardy	1	3	0
Sam Smith	1	2	0
Sam. Cobbett	1	0	0
Watching Atherton	1	4	0
Cap. Nathl Byfield	1	2	10
		Black	**1**
John Wilson	1	3	0
Cap. Benjamin Church	1	6	3
Timothy Ingraham	1	0	0

Census of Bristol in Plymouth Colony...1689 in *New England Historical and Genealogical Register* 34 (1880): 404-5.

Figure 4-10. First Monday of August 1821, School census, Glastonbury, Connecticut. Originals in Connecticut State Library, Hartford; GS 1484, p. 2.

The following are the Names of the Persons between the ages of 4 and 16 years in the 2d School district in the first Society in the Town of Glastenbury on the first monday of August 1821

Milla Porter	Sheldon Gaines	Eliza Williams
Mary Cole	Orren Fox	Levrett Case
Sarah Ann Moggat	Roderick Phelps	Alvin House
Charlotte Gillett	Harriot Phelps	Mercy House
Albert Gillett	Harriot Cook	Dolly House
Hopy House	Thadeus Welles	Orren House
Otis Talcott	Anson Williams	Almira Wright
Jerome Jonson	Edwin Welles	Samuel Wright
Polly Talcott	Delia Welles	Sarah Ann Wright
Asa Talcott	Lucy Welles	Amelia Wright
Chester Talcott	Susannah Welles	Lester House
Annah Te Talcott	Mariah Welles	Samuel House 3
Laura E Talcott	James Welles	John House
Abigail S Talcott	Clarricy Welles	Abba Ann Nickelson
Hannah Bell	Abigail Welles	Harriot Nickelson
Elizabeth Plummer	Guy Samson	Israel Smith
Julia Ann Plummer	Martha Ann Samson	Betsey Smith
Isaac W Plummer	Amelia S Samson	Jane Ann Vibbert
Chauncey Talcott	Earl Samson	Almira Vibbert
Adaline Blish	Wm H Linsley	Watson Vibbert
Lucretia Hale Jun	George Wrisle 2d	Caroline Vibbert
Ira B Culver	John Alford Jun	Mary Ann Vibbert
Norman Fox	Oswin Welles	Clarricy Vibbert
Walter Fox	Nancy Welles	Selden House
Charles Fox	John Welles	Dudley House
Harriot Benton	Pelina Price	Camile House
Delina Benton	Almira Price	Almarine Atherton
Elizabeth Benton	Jonathan Price	Lucy S Goodale
George Benton	Julia Ann Price	Laura Goodale
Anna Benton	Abigail Talcott	Lucy Goodale
Emma Gains	Mary Ett Fox	George Jones 2d
Luke Gaines	Linas Fox	
David Gaines 33	Eletia Ann Fox	31
	Laura Ann House	37
	Clarricy House	33
	Abigail House	101
	Lucinda House 37	

I hereby certify that I have carefully enumerated all persons between the ages of four and sixteen within the School district of which I am Committee and do find that on the first Monday of August 1821 there were residing within said district and belonging there to the number of one hundred & one between the ages aforesaid

Solomon Cole School district Committee

On this 30th day of August 1821 personally appeared the above named Committee and made oath to the truth of the above return by him Subscribed

Saml Welles Justice Peace

Samuel Graham	4	John Brown	5
James Brown	4	John Anderson	7
Robt. Armstrong	4	David Brown	2
John McLaughlin	3	Isaac Hughs	3
Thomas Agan	2	James Hughs	1
Sarah Jones	3	John Bingaman	1
Vardamon Hughs	3	James Spalding	1

Figure 4-11. Numeration list of the Pupils belonging to the 6th District in Township no. 6, north of Range no. 9; 25 Jan. 1843 in "Record of Indiana School District," *Indiana Magazine of History* 48 (1952): 191.

As a more modern example, the Church of Jesus Christ of Latter-day Saints enumerated its members in Pottawatomie, Iowa, as part of the Iowa state census ordered in 1847 for all residents. The Church schedules contain the standard information asked for in the Iowa tally, but also include wagons, guns, number of family members ill, aged, or infirm, and oxen/cattle/horses. These data suggest a dual function for the census: to comply with the Iowa law and to prepare for transporting a large body of people westward, a project even then underway. See Figure 4-12. Emigrating companies were enumerated in tens and hundreds before they embarked the organization under which they travelled to Utah. Another census was taken in Utah in 1852. These tallies are valuable because many did not survive the trek across the Great Plains and the Rockies; comparing the two helps clarify mortality figures. Many of the companies Brigham Young sent to colonize the Mormon Corridor before 1872 (Rocky Mountain valleys stretching from Mexico to Canada and from Las Vegas to San Bernardino, California) had summaries made of individuals, professions, state of health, wagons, cattle, and weapons. Many of these schedules are scattered among the collections in the LDS Church Historical Department, 50 East North Temple, Salt Lake City, Utah 84150. More widely known are the twentieth-century census cards (1914-50) which enumerate all LDS families in organized wards available for research on microfilm at the Genealogical Society of Utah. (Figure 4-13)

Still another example is the Holland Land Company Census of 1806. The Holland Land Company had great difficulty getting payments from settlers on their lands in central and western New York. Its census assessed the resources of these settlers, hence their ability to pay. This 1806 data is especially valuable, as many of these people moved on before the 1810 federal census. And for some, it is the only record of their stop in New York.

You may use local censuses to identify children by name who are listed in pre-1850 census schedules by age groupings only. Similarly, these censuses can help you determine the number living in a household as a check for children who die before age twenty-one, and as a check against birth and death records in New England. Use them to verify that an ancestor lived in specific localities when he moved too rapidly to be recorded in other sources, or to identify neighbors who could be in-laws or fellow westward travelers with your ancestor. Combining these local schedules with tax records and other property sources can help distinguish your ancestor from others with similar names.

Black Census Schedules

Northern cities from about 1830 on increasingly felt the need to monitor blacks moving from the South seeking freedom and work. In 1863, in the midst of the Civil War, Ohio called for the number and names of colored persons who had immigrated to Ohio from other states since 1 March 1861, their current township of residence, and their state of origin. Thirteen counties in southeastern Ohio submitted schedules. Hamilton County refused because the numbers were too great and its staff too limited.[17]

1852, June — Emigration Co. Journal p. 29

No	Captain of 1st Ten	No. in Family	Wagons	Oxen	Cows	Mules	Sheep	Horses	men fit for duty	Miscellaneous
1	Thomas Robins	8	2	4	6	"	"	2	1	Dropped from the Capt. ship of disobedience
2	John Tidwell	10	2	7	5	"	8	"	2	
3	Telemachus Rogers	9	2	6	4	"	"	3	1	Appoint Captain in the place of T. Robins.
4	E. Crowel (in pencil)									
5	David Adams	11	1	4	2	"	"	"	1	
6	Richard Lowe	3	1	"	"	"	"	2	1	
7	~~John Trout~~		2							Backed out
8	~~Stephensen M. Trout~~		1							Backed out
9	Henry Howland	7	2	6	2	"	"	2	2	
10	John Heldredge		1	4	6	"	"	"	2	
11	David Ross	8	1	7	2	"	"	"	2	
12	A. D. Boyington	6	1	4	3	"	"	"	1	
	Amount------.	62	13	42	30	"	8	9	13	Amount (p. 27)
	Captain of 2nd Ten									
1	John M. King	8	1	4	4	"	2	"	2	
2	James Mathews	3	1	4	4	"	"	"	1	
3	John Gilespie	2	1	2	4	"	"	"	1	
4	Eleazer King Senr	4	1	6	2	"	"	"	1	
5	Eleazer King Junr.	6	1	4	4	"	"	1	1	
6	~~James Henderson~~		1							Backed out
7	Josuha Gillat	6	1	4	2	"	"	"	1	
8	Robert Forester	3	1	3	4	"	"	"	1	
9	George Howley	3	1	5	1	"	"	"	2	
10	Absolam Yates	4	1	4	2	"	"	"	1	
11	John Merry	6	1	2	4	"	"	"	1	
12	Robert McKell	4	1	4	4	"	"	"	2	Amount
	Amount------	49	11	42	35	"	2	1	14	

Figure 4-12. "Typescript of A Journal of the Emigration Company of Council Point, Pottawatomie Co., Iowa," June 1852, p. 29; GS A979,2/H2be.

Figure 4-13. Joseph W. Pitts Family, Census of [LDS] Church Members 1914; John Frank Pincock Family, Census of [LDS] Church Members 1930; microfilm of original cards: GS 245,155.

1914 CENSUS

Family Name Pitts

Heyburn Ward Boise Stake Address Heyburn Ida.

Date of Census Dec 10. 1914

GIVEN NAMES	AGE	SEX		PRIESTHOOD								SOCIAL RELATION						WHERE BORN						WARD CLERK
		Male	Female	High Priests	Seventies	Elders	Priests	Teachers	Deacons	Members	Children	Single	Married	Divorced	Widowers	Widows	Unknown	Utah	America	Europe	Asia	Islands of Pacific	Unclassified	WARD RECORD NO.
PARENTS 1880																								
Joseph W.	34	1				1							1							1				65
Francis	33		1							1			1					1						66
CHILDREN, OLDEST FIRST																								
Mary Lucille	9		1							1		1							1					194
Evelyn	8		1							1		1						1						195
Kenneth S.	6	1									1	1							1					193
Phylis	1		1								1	1							1					
TOTAL		2	3			1				3	2	4	2					2	3	1				

Census taken by James B. Helliwell

Checked with Ward Record by Mary A. Helliwell acting Ward Clerk

CENSUS OF CHURCH MEMBERS—1930

Sugar WARD FAMILY NAME Pincock

Fremont STAKE ADDRESS Sugar, Idaho

DATE TAKEN July 14, 1930 R. F. D. #1

	SEX Male or Female	P. HOOD MEMBER OR CHILD	WHEN BORN Day	Month	Year	WHERE BORN	SOCIAL RELATION	WARD RECORD NUMBER
Father's Name John Frank	M	E.	15	January	1880	Utah	Married	545-2
Mother's Maiden Name Susie S. Blackford	F	M	22	January	1881	England	Married	546-2
Children's Names—Oldest First Joseph B.	M	T	8	May	1911	Idaho	Single	547-2
Alice	F	M	10	August	1913	Idaho	Single	548-2
Thelma	F	M	4	February	1915	Idaho	Single	549-2
Grace	F	M	10	April	1917	Idaho	Single	550-2
Ruth	F	M	4	January	1919	Idaho	Single	551-2
Grant	M	M	10	April	1922	Idaho	Single	552-2
Paul	M	C	27	May	1924	Idaho	Single	481-2

CENSUS TAKEN BY Eula Haldram

CHECKED WITH WARD RECORD BY Z. Dams WARD CLERK

Philadelphia took three household censuses of its black population: in 1838 and 1856 by the Pennsylvania Abolition Society, and in 1847 by the Society of Friends. In addition to the variables listed in the federal census, the records of 11,600 households contain information describing membership in church, beneficial, and temperance societies; income; education level; school attendance; house, ground, and water rent; how freedom was acquired; and the amount of property brought to Pennsylvania. These superb records constitute the most detailed information we have describing any population group in the mid-nineteenth century and are being computer-processed as part of an urban-immigrant study of blacks in Philadelphia conducted by Temple University.[18]

The National Archives has issued a separate list on "Free Black Heads of Families in the First Census of the U.S., 1790," as Special List 34. This compilation by Debra L. Newman is available free upon request from the National Archives. An expanded version for New York is Alice Eichholz and James M. Rose, comps., *Free Black Heads of Households in the New York State Federal Census, 1790-1830*, Gale Genealogy and Local History Series, Vol. 14 (Detroit: Gale Research Company, 1981).

Missing Censuses

It is commonly reported that the original 1790 census schedules for Delaware, Georgia, Kentucky, New Jersey, Tennessee, and Virginia were burned when the British fired the Capitol during the War of 1812. The story is dramatic and easy to recall—but it is not true. The states retained their own schedules until 1849. Just when they were lost or how, we may never know.

The surviving returns for 1790 are published in *Heads of Families at the First Census of the United States Taken in the Year 1790*, 12 vols., and cover Connecticut, Maine, Maryland, Massachusetts, New Hampshire, New York, North Carolina, Pennsylvania, Rhode Island, South Carolina, and Vermont. These volumes have been reprinted by Genealogical Book Company in Baltimore and can be found in most research libraries.

Concerned genealogists have reconstructed substitute schedules for the missing states using tax lists and following the pattern set by the Bureau of the Census, *Virginia: Records of State Enumerations, 1782-1785*. These substitutions for 1790 schedules include:

- Delaware. Leon deValinger, Jr., *Reconstructed Census*

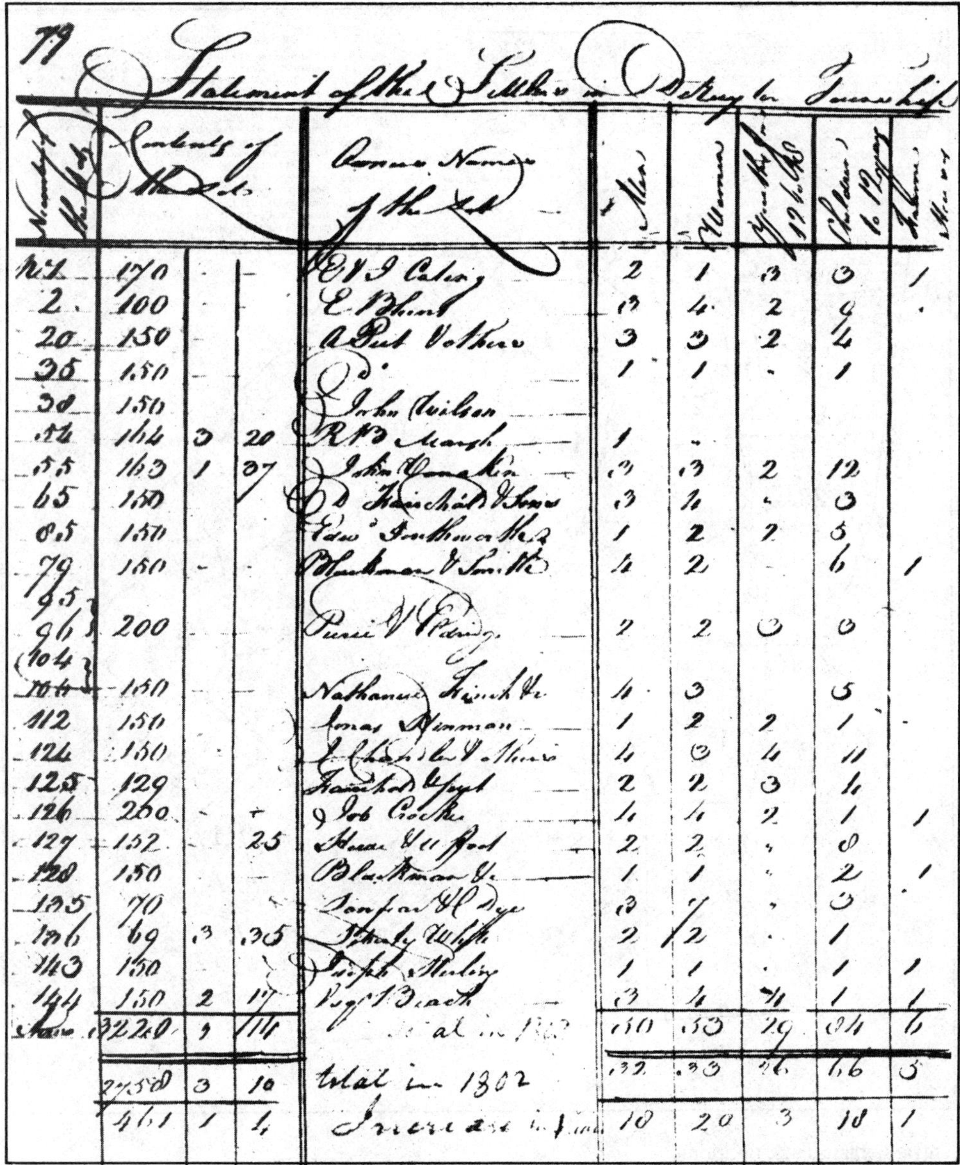

79

Statement of the Settlers in [illegible]

Number of the Lot	Contents of the Lot			Owners Names of the Lot	Men	Women	[illegible]	Children to 16 years	[illegible]
No. 1	170	-	-	[illegible]	2	1	3	0	1
2	100	-		[illegible]	3	4	2	9	
20	150			[illegible]	3	3	2	4	
35	150			do.	1	1	-	1	
30	150			John Wilson					
54	164	3	20	R & D Marsh	1				
55	163	1	37	John [illegible]	3	3	2	12	
65	150			[illegible]	3	4	-	3	
85	150			Edw. [illegible]	1	2	2	5	
79	150	-		[illegible] & Smith	4	2	-	6	1
95, 96, 104	200			[illegible]	2	2	0	0	
104	150			Nathaniel [illegible]	4	3		5	
112	150			Jonas Hinman	1	2	2	1	
124	150			[illegible]	4	0	4	11	
125	129			[illegible]	2	2	3	4	
126	200	-	+	[illegible]	4	4	2	1	1
127	152		25	[illegible]	2	2		8	
128	150			Blackman & [illegible]	1	1		2	1
135	70			[illegible]	3	7		3	
136	69	3	35	[illegible]	2	2		1	
143	150			[illegible]	1	1		1	1
144	150	2	17	[illegible]	3	4	4	1	1
	3220	9	114	Total in 1806	50	53	29	84	6
	2758	3	10	total in 1802	32	33	26	66	5
	461	1	4	Increase in [illegible]	18	20	3	18	1

Figure 4-14. "Statement of Settlers," Holland Land Company Census, 1806, original papers in possession of Central New York Park and Recreation Commission; microfilm copies in Cornell University, Department of Manuscripts and Archives, Ithaca, NY 14853. The facing page includes information about livestock and equipment.

for Delaware (Washington D.C.: National Genealogical Society, 1954).

• Georgia. Georgia Department of Archives and History, *Some Early Tax Digests of Georgia* (Atlanta: Department of Archives, 1926). Also available are several volumes of printed land lotteries, 1805-20, available in most research libraries, and a pamphlet which describes the state's head-right (land bounty for attracting new settlers) and lottery system, including eligibility qualifications. This pamphlet is available upon request from Georgia Department of Archives and History, 330 Capitol Avenue S.W., Atlanta, GA 30334. Lotteries include precise descriptions of qualifications for land ownership for each person drawing land in specific counties created as a result of the land awards. See Map 4-1 showing which years applied to which counties for lotteries.

• Kentucky. Charles B. Heinemann, *"First Census" of Kentucky, 1790* (1940; reprint ed., Baltimore: Genealogical Publishing Co., 1971).

• New Jersey. (1) James S. Norton, *New Jersey in 1793* (based on military census lists and ratables) distributed by Everton Publishers, Box 368, Logan, UT 84321. (2) Kenn Stryker-Rodda, *Revolutionary Census of New Jersey: An Index, Based on Ratables of the Inhabitants during the Periods of the American Revolution* (New Orleans: Polyanthos, 1972). (3) The DAR Library, Washington, D.C., has twenty-four microfilm rolls of New Jersey tax lists for 1783 which can also substitute for 1790 data.

• Tennessee. (1) Pollyanna Creekmore. *Early East Tennessee Tax-payers* (Easley, S.C.: Southern Historical Press, 1980); originally printed in East Tennessee Historical Society Publications beginning 1951. (2) Byron Sistler and Barbara Sistler, *Index to Early Tennessee Tax Lists* (Nashville: Byron Sistler & Associates, 1977).

• Virginia. (1) *Bureau of the Census Records of State Enumerations, 1782-1785* (1908; reprint ed., Baltimore: Genealogical Publishing Company, 1970). (2) Augusta B. Fothergill and John M. Naugle, *Virginia Tax Payers, 1782-1787, Other Than Those Published by the United States Census Bureau* (1940; reprint ed., Baltimore: Genealogical Publishing Co., 1971).

Since substitutes for the 1790 census have been so useful, numerous reconstructions of other missing schedules are also underway.

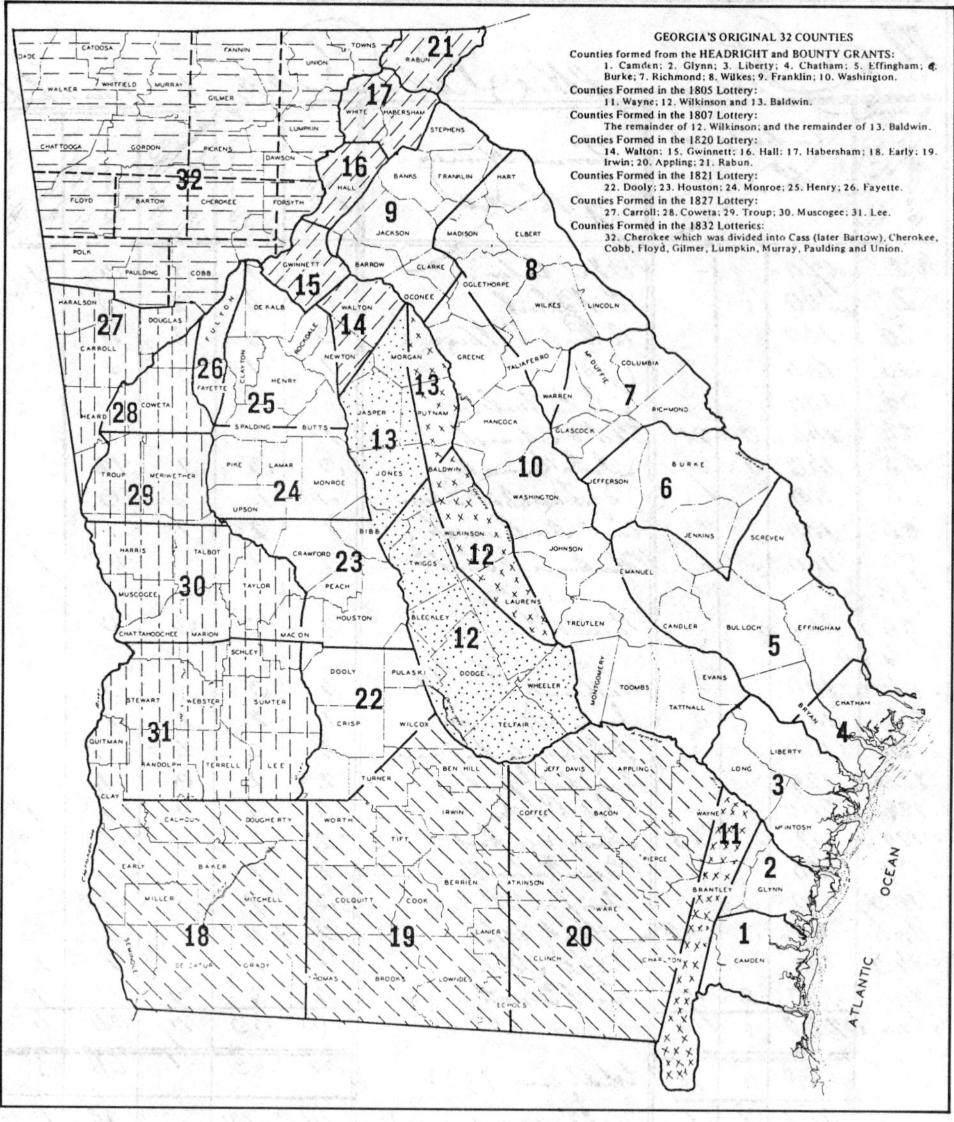

Map 4-1. From Rev. Silas Emmett Lucas, Jr., The Creation of Georgia Counties, 1777-1932; separately published map, copyright 1982. Used with permission.

Tax lists, oaths of allegiance, land entries, militia lists, petitions, road records, and other sources, though never as complete as a census, can go far toward filling the gap left by lost or destroyed census schedules.[19] See Table 4-10, A Checklist of Census Substitutes.

To use substitutes effectively, you must know what specific category of people is included in each source and which ones are left out. Check the glossary and index for references to unfamiliar terms. Most of these records are described in detail in other chapters of this book, and some can be found printed with indexes. Others are still in state archives, awaiting a thorough genealogist to bring their contents to light.

Since three copies of federal censuses were made – the original kept by the county, one copy sent to the state, and the third for the Bureau of the Census, it is possible that some of these copies will turn up in state archives and among collections of university libraries. The thorough genealogist who studies archive inventories carefully and makes it a practice to examine little-used materials can expect to be as successful as the two genealogists researching Farleigh-Dickinson University collections, who recently discovered the 1800 schedule for Cumberland County, New Jersey, and I, who unearthed the 1806 Holland Land Company "Statements of Settlers" in Cornell University Library. There is nothing quite like discovering a record long thought to be missing.

Notes

1. E. Kay Kirkham, *ABC's of American Genealogical Research* (Salt Lake City: Deseret Book Co., 1955), p. 66.

2. "Mythical Cities of Southwestern Minnesota," *Minnesota History* 14 (1933): 243. My thanks to genealogist William Thorndale, Salt Lake City, who called this reference to my attention.

3. Example from files of William Thorndale.

4. 1880 U.S. Census, Limestone County, Texas, pp. 307A, 368B, GS 433,448 and 472, 487.

5. *History of Union County, South Carolina* (Winston-Salem, N.C.: Hunter Publishing Co., 1981), p. 479.

6. My thanks to Wilma Adkins, Lois Knight, and Family History Center Quick-Search of Salt Lake City for the how-to-use sections relating to each census summary.

7. Edited for inclusion from *1900 Federal Population Census: A Catalog of Microfilm Copies of the Schedules* (Washington, D.C.: Government Printing Office, 1978), appendix.

8. *Prologue*, Winter 1972, p. 242.

9. Adapted from *1900 Federal Population Census: A Catalog of Microfilm Copies of the Schedule* (Washington, D.C.: Government Printing Office, 1978), appendix.

10. Ibid., p. 27. The National Archives Records Service Gift Fund, established through the Federation of Genealogical Societies, has announced a 1910 locality atlas for states not yet indexed. The federation suggests

Table 4-10
A Checklist of Census Substitutes

Tax Rolls
____ Poll tax
____ Personal property
____ Real estate
____ 1863 income tax
____ 1798 property tax
____ Assessors' lists
____ Faculty lists
____ Rate lists

Land Records
____ Entries Plats
____ Plat maps
____ Lotteries
____ Processioning lists
____ Perambulations
____ Ground rents
____ Quitrents
____ Debt books
____ Permits to settle
____ Land grant lists
____ Suspended land grants
____ Headright claims
____ Lists of indentured servants
____ Immigrant land allowances
____ Inquisitions
____ Devises' lists
____ Heir lists

Court Records
____ Oaths of allegiance
____ Registers of papists (Roman Catholics)
____ Lists of attornies
____ Lists of constables
____ Lists of jurors
____ Jury pay lists
____ Jury attendance lists
____ Commissions of officials
____ Appointments of justices of the peace
____ Lists of gamekeepers

Road Records
____ Petitions
____ Plats
____ Appointments of road officials

Voters' Records
____ Voters' register
____ Voters' lists
____ Poll books
____ Register of intended voters
____ Register of freemen
____ Lists of freeholders
____ Lists of rejected voters
____ Oaths of office
____ Loyalty oaths
____ Freemen admissions

Militia Records
____ Militia lists
____ Muster rolls
____ Muster-in rolls
____ Muster-out rolls
____ Payrolls
____ Lists of males over age 16
____ Troop returns
____ Enlistments
____ Enrollments
____ Lists of recruits
____ Substitutes
____ Lists of rejected men
____ Wagoners' rolls
____ Casualty lists

Church Records
____ Pew rents
____ Membership lists
____ Rate rolls
____ Collection lists
____ Subscription lists
____ Lists of paupers

School lists
____ Matriculation lists
____ Attendance lists
____ Examination lists
____ Tuition lists
____ Subscription lists
____ Pupil lists
____ Teacher lists

Legislative Records
____ Petitions
____ Memorials

Ships' Records
____ Crew lists
____ Register of seamen
____ Seamens' oaths
____ Seamens' certificates
____ Officers' lists
____ Sick rosters
____ Death registers
____ Casualty lists

Miscellaneous Records
____ Register of prisoners
____ Register of slaves
____ Register of free Negroes
____ Prisoners of war
____ Manumission lists
____ Register of unmarried persons
____ Orphans' register
____ Lists of physicians
____ Lists of midwives
____ Lists of strangers

---

a donation of $1 from each working genealogist, Box 220, Davenport, IA 52805.

11. Katherine H. Davidson and Charlotte M. Ashby, *Preliminary Inventory 161: Records of the Bureau of the Census* (Washington, D.C.: National Archives Record Centers, 1964), p. 109. Schedule 4 is unidentified in this inventory.

12. James Rose and Alice Eichholz, *Black Genesis* (Detroit: Gale Research Company, 1978), p. 26.

13. National Archives Trust Fund Board, *Guide to Genealogical Research in the National Archives* (Washington, D.C.: National Archives Record Service, 1982), p. 126.

14. Ibid., p. 25.

15. See War of 1812 Collection (BOO-15, Boxes 1-5), Buffalo and Erie Historical Society, Buffalo, New York. The relief lists were published in pamphlet form and circulated throughout Western New York by government order. Places of residence, where known, were indicated for each settler.

16. Originals are in the Pennsylvania Historical Commission. Copies will be found in county courthouses and local historical society collections throughout Pennsylvania. Some are written in German.

17. 1863 Ohio State Census (Colored Schedule), originals in Ohio State Archives; Belmont County's returns printed in "List of Names and Townships for Belmont County, Ohio," *National Genealogical Society Quarterly* 69 (1981): 71-73.

18. Project and Sources described in *Journal of Ethnic Studies* 1 (1973): 2-3 and *Historical Methods Newsletter* 9 (March-June 1976): special issue on the Philadelphia Social History Project.

19. Accelerated Indexing Systems has over thirty titles in its Early American Series which include census substitutes. A current list is available on request to AIS, Mezzanine, 70 East South Temple, Salt Lake City, UT 84111. Southern Historical Press, Easley, S.C.; McDowell Publications, Owensboro, Kentucky; and Genealogical Publishing Company, Baltimore, Maryland, issue periodic catalogs with substitute censuses too.

Bibliography of Census Finding Aids, Tools, and Related Sources

The National Archives issues microfilm catalogs listing original census schedules for 1790-1890, 1900, 1910. These are free upon request.

"Analysis of Maryland Census Schedules, 1776-1800." *Maryland and Delaware Genealogist* 18 (1977): 15.

Barrows, Robert C. "The Manuscript Federal Census: Source for a 'New' Local History." *Indiana Magazine of History* 69 (1973): 181-92.

Brewer, Mary M. *Index to Census Schedules in Printed Form, 1969. Supplement, 1970-71.* Describes publications available and where to order them; includes entries not listed in *Directory of Census Information Sources, 1980.* Order from Century Enterprises, Box 607, Huntsville, AL 72740.

Bureau of Business Research. *International Population Census Bibliography.* 7 vols. Austin: University of Texas, 1965-68. Schedules available on microfilm through Research Publications, Box 3903 Amity Station, New Haven, CT 06525.

Census of Pensioners for Revolutionary Services, 1840. (1841; reprint ed., Baltimore: Genealogical Publishing Co., 1965.)

"Confessions of a 1790 Census Enumerator in Morgan District, N.C." *North Carolina Genealogical Society Journal* 4 (1978): 167.

Directory of Census Information Sources, 1980. 4th ed., Munroe Falls, Ohio: Summitt Publications. Sales catalog of printed census publications. Available from publishers at Box 222, Munroe Falls, Ohio 44282.

Fire Insurance Maps in the Library of Congress: Plans of North American Cities and Towns Produced by the Sanborn Map Company. Washington, D.C.: Library of Congress, 1981; and *Union List of Sanborn Fire insurance Maps Held by Institutions in the U.S. and Canada,* 2 vols. Santa Cruz, Calif.: Western Association of Map Libraries, 1976-77. The Sanborn maps describe all houses, farm buildings, and businesses in some 13,000 cities and towns in America (1846-present) with about 750,000 map-sheets. Their precise detail makes it possible to place each household and its members for matching census years in their respective dwellings and business buildings.

Heiss, Willard, "Census Indexes." *Genealogy*, no. 24(1980):1-4.

Ivey, Sandra. "The Wonders of the Federal Census." *Ancestoring II*, 1980, pp. 9-17.

Jordan, Holman D., Jr. "Value of Census Data in the Writing of Vermont Town Histories." *Vermont History* 36 (Winter 1968): 19-24.

Leonard, Mrs. D., comp. *"Who-searches-what-for-how-much": A Directory of Census Research*. Available from the author, 1584 Henry, Des Plaines, IL 60016.

McMillon, Lynn C. "An Index Can Be A Roadblock," *Virginia Genealogist* 21 (1977): 205-6.

Map Guide to the U.S. Federal Censuses. County boundary maps for each census taken, 1790-1910, to which are added modern county boundaries and a summary of which federal schedules survive or are lost for each county and each census. There is a separate set of maps for each state. This series is the result of painstaking research by William Thorndale and William Dollarhide in state laws with each boundary change plotted carefully on the U.S. Geological Survey Base Map of the United States, No. 2B, scale of 1:2,500,000. Maps are available from Dollarhide Systems, Box 5282, Bellingham, WA 98227.

Martin, David K. "The New York 1800 Census Index." *American Genealogist* 54 (1978): 53-54.

Parker, J. Carlyle. *City, County, Town, Township Index to 1850 Federal Census Schedules*. Detroit: Gale Research Company, 1979. Alphabetical list with NARS reel number, Genealogical Society of Utah call number, and specific pages on reel.

Powell, Sumner Chilton. *Puritan Village: The Formation of a New England Town*. Garden City, N.Y.: Doubleday and Company, Inc., 1965.

Ristow, Walter W. "U.S. Fire Insurance and Underwriters Maps, 1852-1968." *Quarterly Journal of Library of Congress* 25 (1968): 194-218.

Schulze, Suzanne. *Population Information in Nineteenth Century Census Volumes*. Phoenix: The Oryx Press, 1984. A critical analysis of all census publications, 1790-1890.

Simon, Roger D. "The City-Building Process: Housing and Services in New Milwaukee Neighborhoods, 1880-1910." *American Philosophical Society Transactions* 68 (1978).

State Census, 1790-1948. Annotated bibliography of state and territorial censuses; useful for laws authorizing censuses. Available from Bookmark, Box 74, Knightstown, IN 46148.

Stemmons, John D. *U. S. Census Compendium*. Logan, Utah: Everton Publishers, 1973. This is a directory of censuses in print, plus tax lists, polls, petitions, and other sources to be used as substitute census data.

Stephenson, Charles. "The Methodology of Historical Census Record Linkage: A User's Guide to the Soundex." *Prologue*, Fall 1980, pp. 151-53. Reprinted from the *Journal of Family History* 5 (1980).

________. "Tracing Those Who Left: Mobility Studies and the Soundex Indexes to the U. S. Census." *Journal of Urban History* 1 (1974): 73-84.

U.S. Bureau of the Census. *A Century of Population Growth, 1790-1900*. 1909; reprint ed., New York City: Johnson Reprints, 1966. Valuable appendix of name variants from 1790 census.

Vallentine, John F. "Census Records and Indexes." *Genealogical Journal* 2 (1973): 133-39; and "Effective Use of Census Indexes in Locating People." *Genealogical Journal* 4 (1975): 51-60. Both articles include tables of state and territorial censuses and their locations, with a state-by-state list of indexes.

Walsh, Leorena S. "The Census Historian as Census Taker: Individual Reconstitution and the Reconstruction of Censuses for a Colonial Chesapeake County." *William and Mary Quarterly*, 3rd series, 38 (1981): 242-60.

Wells, Robert V. *Population of British Colonies in America*. Princeton: University Press, 1975. Survey of colonial censuses including a unique list of schedules located in British archives.

White, Donald W. "Census Making and Local History: In Quest of the People of a Revolutionary Village." *Prologue* Fall 1982, pp. 157-68.

Wood, Ralph V., Jr. "The Census Index Problem," *National Genealogical Society Quarterly* 56 (1968): 188-92.

Enumeration Districts

Where records are unindexed or where transcription errors or variant spellings of a name make it impossible to locate the right entry, enumeration districts may help find the schedules for a given town, civil division, or city ward. See *Census Enumeration District Descriptions (1900)*, microfilm publication T1210, 7 rolls, arranged alphabetically by state and county; and *Census Enumeration District Descriptions (1910)*, microfilm publication T1224, reels 28-40. Districts for other census years are also available on microfilm through the National Archives. Write for descriptive catalog. Procedures for using district descriptions to access census data are outlined in these articles:

Perlmann, Joel. "Using Census Districts in Analysis, Record Linkage, and Sampling." *Journal of Interdisciplinary History* 10 (1979): 284-86.

Schlesinger, Keith R. "An Urban Finding Aid for the Federal Census." *Prologue* 13 (Winter 1981): 251-62; and with Peggy T. Sinko. "Urban Finding Aid for Manuscript Census Searches." *National Genealogical Society Quarterly* 69 (1981): 171-80.

For Census Records Unindexed or Incompletely Indexed

Because of transcription errors or variant spellings of a name, the Soundex may not help you locate an entry. To find the schedules for a given town, civil division, or city ward, find the enumeration district number listed in microfilm publication T1210, *Census Enumeration District Descriptions, 1900*, arranged alphabetically by state and county. Present day boundaries may differ.

The states covered by each roll are: Roll 1: Alabama-Connecticut; Roll 2: Delaware-Illinois; Roll 3: Indian Territory-Kansas; Roll 4: Kentucky-Massachusetts; Roll 5: Michigan-Montana; Roll 6: Nebraska-New York supervisor's districts 1-3; Roll 7: New York supervisor's districts 4-19-Ohio; Roll 8: Oklahoma-Pennsylvania; Roll 9: Rhode Island-Vermont; and Roll 10: Virginia-Wyoming.

For the 1910 enumeration district numbers, see NARS, *Census Enumeration District Descriptions*, rolls 28 through 40 of microfilm publication T1224, assigned within states, counties, and cities and arranged alphabetically by state. Roll 28 covers Alabama through Florida.

Forms, Worksheets

Some genealogists find using a census form to extract data from the originals very useful, for the columns match those in the census. Such forms are produced by:

Ancestry, Inc.
Box 476
Salt Lake City, UT 84111

Dollarhide Systems*
Box 5282
Bellingham, WA 98227

Everton Publishers
Box 368
Logan, UT 84321

Family History Center
Box 11991
Salt Lake City, UT 84147

Family History World
57 West South Temple
Suite 255
Salt Lake City, UT 84101

Genealogical Books in Print
6818 Lois Drive
Springfield, VA 22150

Genealogical Services
7501 Elgar Street
Springfield, VA 22151
1910 forms only

Genealogy Club of America
Box 15861
Salt Lake City, UT 84115

Joyce B. Hensen
2827 Ashland
St. Joseph, MO 64506
1900, 1910 forms only

Sylvia B. Nimmo
6201 Kentucky Road
Omaha, NE 68133

Mrs. Jeff Wade, Jr.*
Bragg City, MO 63827

Western Michigan
Genealogical Society
c/o Grand Rapids Public
Library
Library Plaza
Grand Rapids, MI 49503

*These vendors also have a guide sheet for calculating year of birth from age groupings, 1790-1840.

INFORMATION GUIDE

Genealogical Information in the Record Group	*Baptism*	*Marriage*	*Death*	*Confirmation*	*Biographies*
Surname/name	●	●	●	●	●
Date of Birth	●		●		●
Place of Birth		●	●	●	●
Sex	●	●	●		●
Race/color			●		
Physical Description		●	●		●
Occupation		●	●		●
Education					●
Military Service			●		●
Slave Status	●	●	●		
Property Owned					●
Religion	●	●	●	●	●
Citizenship					
Marital Status		●	●		●
Spouse's Name		●	●		●
Children's Names	●		●		●
Father's Name	●	●		●	●
Mother's Name	●	●			●
Father's Birthplace					●
Mother's Birthplace					●
Date of Death			●		●
Cause of Death			●		●
Name of Cemetery			●		
Residence	●	●	●		●
Age	●	●	●	●	●
Literacy/signature		●			●
Photograph/sketch					●
Relatives	●	●			

COULD YOU USE THIS CHAPTER?

Type of Record	*Kept from*	*Clues That You Should Consult These Records*
Baptism/christening records	Usually from the church's founding	If family tradition links your ancestors with a particular denomination, search its records. An important clue to denominational affiliation is the name of a minister on a marriage return or in a funeral service. Most churches kept their own vital statistics from the time of their founding and, during colonial times and afterwards, were officially charged to be the guardians of such records. This chapter will warn you of pitfalls you might not expect. For instance, groups that practiced adult baptism instead of infant baptism may not record a birthdate at all; if you calculate the birthdate as being very near the baptism date, you may be off by a score of years.
Marriage records	Usually from the church's founding	If your family came from New England, marriage records may be tricky. The early Puritans considered marriage to be a civil contract, not a religious ceremony. Marriages may be noted in civil records only. In contrast, South Carolina did not record civil marriages at either the state or county levels until 1911, so church registers are very important. Where ethnic churches kept their registers in another language besides English, you can usually determine the categories accurately with a little patience and a dictionary.
Death records	Usually from the church's founding	Death records are invaluable when it comes to tracing the European birthplace of an immigrant ancestor, particularly in ethnic churches. Even if you know the ancestor's deathdate, it is valuable to search the church records for other biographical details – especially birthdate and place. If other records can locate your ancestor in a township or county, local histories can tell you what churches flourished in that area.

Chapter 5

CHURCH RECORDS IN THE UNITED STATES

Richard W. Dougherty

Church records rank among the very best genealogical records available. Indeed, before the advent of civil registration of vital statistics, a very late development in many American states, church records rank as the best available.

They are also among the most under-used major records in American genealogy. Part of the reason lies in the proliferation of denominations—literally hundreds of them. Identifying and locating the records of these various churches make professional genealogists hesitate, to say nothing of novices. Yet the task is not impossible. Modern photocopying and indexing techniques make church records more accessible to the genealogist than ever before.

Immigrant Churches

Church records vary a great deal in content and emphasis according to the basic theology and social role of each. However, a useful distinction is the difference between state churches and so-called free churches.

State or established churches in Europe considered every Christian in the state or kingdom to be a member. Free or "gathered" churches emphatically rejected this inclusive view of belonging from birth. Rather, only those who had been "born again" in Christ could be considered true members of his church. The sign of this rebirth in Christ was another baptism (adult baptism) that took primacy over the person's baptism as an infant. For this practice they were called Anabaptists, *rebaptizers* in Latin. The descendants of the Anabaptists include Mennonties, Hutterites, many smaller groups associated with the Pennsylvania Germans, and their British cousins, the Baptists, who form the dominant church in so many parts of America today.

Because Anabaptists saw the most important event in a person's life as his/her rebirth in Christ, not his/her physical birth, their records reflect the difference. In contrast, Lutheran records meticulously record infant births and subsequent parish baptisms. Baptist records are full of valuable historical information about the activities of adult members but do not always deliver accurate birth information.

Of course, theology is not the only factor. In Scandinavia and many German states, the Lutheran Church was the established church. Thus, the pastor was a quasi-public official, who was official recorder of births, deaths, and marriages. Similarly, in England a 1538 Act of Parliament required all ministers of the Church of England to record baptisms, marriages, and burials in their parishes. In 1597, another parliamentary act reinforced the original law, requiring that a duplicate of parish records be sent annually to the bishop of the pertinent diocese, initiating the valuable "bishops' transcripts."

In Scotland, the Netherlands, Switzerland, and certain German states where Calvinism became the established faith, pastors were also official record keepers. Not all German Protestants were Lutherans. In many German states, most notably in Prussia, the state church combined Lutheran and Calvinist elements. This had long-range consequences when German immigrants organized churches in the New World.

In areas of Europe, where Roman Catholicism was the established church, the parish priest was the official recorder of baptisms, marriages, and burials. But he was accountable to more than a local parliament. In 1653, the church's Council of Trent issued a decree requiring proof of baptism before marriage. Subsequent decrees reinforced this edict, notably that of Pope Paul V in 1614, which made parish registers obligatory.

In summary, church record-keeping transcended national and religious boundaries. It was a manifestation of a stage of European civilization which emphasized rationality and bureaucracy. Human memory and oral tradition no longer sufficed. The written record prevailed.

This background is relevant to discussion of American church records since habits, attitudes, and ecclesiastical edicts crossed the ocean with the emigrants. The various immigrant churches, including those which developed in Plymouth Colony in the 1620s, reflected European philosophy and practices. In fact, most of the American colonies promptly established state churches. In New England, the Congregational Church generally held preferred status, while in the southern colonies (Virginia, Georgia, and South Carolina), the Church of England (Protestant Episcopal) became the established church. This was true in Maryland for a time, even though that colony was originally founded as a haven for Roman Catholics. As long as the Dutch controlled New Netherland,now New York, the Dutch Reformed Church served as the established church.

Some of these established churches functioned on a state level until well after the Revolutionary War. But the variety of immigrant groups and religious preferences ultimately defeated all attempts to impose religious uniformity. The Founding Fathers recognized this fact and totally separated church and state nationally when they drew up the Constitution. The wisdom of this decision was verified by the Great Awakening of the late eighteenth and early nineteenth centuries, which shook established churches to the core and guaranteed that American religious life would be fundamentally different from that of the Old World.

The consequence is that Americans possess a tremendous, sometimes bewildering, variety of religious groups, with widely differing record-keeping practices. Nevertheless, we can identify certain basic types of records found at the parish or local level.

Types of Church Records

The first of these are baptism or christening records. These almost always list at least the name of the person baptized and the date of the event. In the case of infant baptisms, the pastor usually recorded parents' names and often their place of residence, particularly if the pastor were serving a circuit rather than a single parish. Quite often the register lists the date of birth or at least the age of the

Figure 5-1. Gertrude Richards, trans. and ed., index by Florence M. Leonard, *Register of the Albemarle Parish Surrey and Sussex [Counties, Virginia], 1739-78* (Richmond: National Society Colonial Dames of America in the Commonwealth of Virginia, 1958), p. 9.

ALBEMARLE PARISH REGISTER 9

Arthur s. of John Burnham and w. Mary; b. June 14; c. Oct 21, 1740; gdpts. William Willie, Arthur Smith, Jean Bennet.

Anne d. of Benja Adams and w. Agnes; b. Sept 29; c. Dec 4, 1740; gdpts.---.

Agnes and Jane, 2 of 3 d. of John Stigal and w. Winnifred; b. Feb 3; c. Feb 4, 1740/1; gdpts.---

Anne d. of Robert Newman and w. Catharine; b. Jan 11; c. March 15, 1740/41; gdpts. Francis Walker, Mary Bobbit, Amy Bobbit.

Amy d. of Charles Hay and w. Sarah; b. Nov 9; c. 1737; gdpts.---.

Amy d. of Charles Mabry and w. Rebecca; b. Dec 9, 1740; c. March 29, 1741; gdpts. Simon Gale, Amy Freeman, Mary Gillum.

()ne d. of Nathl Hawthorn and w. Susanna; b. April 7, c. June 17, 1739; gdpts. Peter Hawthorn, Frances Hawthorn, Eliza Weaver.

Anne d. of Joseph Clarke and w. Margaret; b. July 11, 1740; c. May 4, 1741; gdpts. William Willie, Eliza Willie, Mary Berry.

()y d. of John Weaver and w. Eliza; b. April 15; c. June 28, 1741; gdpts. John Vincent, Mary Shelton, Bridget Tatum.

()y d. of Thomas Musslewite and w. Sarah; b. Sept 4, 1740; c. June 28, 1741; gdpts. John Stigal, Eliza Tatum, Eleanor Smith.

()my d. of Philip Bailey and w. Mary; b. June 19; c. July 19, 1741; gdpts. Alexr Dickens, Lydda Dickens, Mary Shelton.

Arthur s. of Charles Delahay and w. Eliza; b. July 13; c. Sept 13, 1741; gdpts. Henry Freeman, jr, Francis Hutchins, Sarah Ellis.

Amy d. of Abraham Evans and w. Eliza; b. June 19; c. Sept 13, 1741; gdpts. Joshua Rolland, Hannah Bell, Eliza Rolland.

Abigail d. of Thomas Davis and w. Jean; b. Dec 1, 1740; c. Oct 4, 1741; gdpts. Richard King, Mary (), Mary Emmery.

Anne d. of Stephen Pepper and w. Jean; b. Sept 16; c. Nov 12, 1741; gdpts. Richard Pepper, Simon Murphy, Sarah Alsobrook, Susanna Ellis.

Anne d. of Wm Freeman and w. Eliza; b. Dec 28, 1741; c. Jan 24, 1741/2; gdpts. Wm Moss, Susanna Freeman, Anne Sandefour.

() d. of Robert Sandefour and w. Anne; b. Dec 11, 1741; c. Jan 24, 1741/2; Wm Freeman, Susanna Freeman, Eliza Denton.

person being baptized. In addition, many baptismal records list the names of the sponsors or godparents, who are often close relatives of the parents.

Figure 5-1 is a transcription of the christening register of Albemarle (Protestant Episcopal) Parish, Surry and Sussex Counties, Virginia, about 1739-41. These entries predate the change from the Julian to the Gregorian calendar in September 1752. Before then the year began on 25 March. Dates between 1 January and 25 March listed both the current and succeeding year, for example, 5 January 1746/47. Under the present calendar this would be 5 January 1747. The transcriber retained the original double-dating system to avoid confusion.

The rector of Albemarle parish, the Reverend William Willie, was an unusually diligent record keeper; and on page 384 in the same christening register, we find a page of unusual entries. Here are three:

Suky, f.; o. Col Allen; i. --; b. Nov 3, 1774; c. May 14, 1775.

Cuba, f.; o. Mrs Lightfoot; i. --; b. March 31, 1775; c. May 14, 1775.

Ede, f.; o. Capt Thompson; i. --; b. Dec 1774; c. May 14, 1775.

These infants are the children of slaves. The adults listed are not their parents but their owners. Thus, church records can

Baptisms.

No	Names.	Parents.	Birth	When Baptized.
1	Sidney Harry.	Benj. G. & Susan M. Kent.	July 14 – 1867.	December 5 – 1867.
2	Daniel Henry.	Daniel G. & Albenia E. Biser.	March 9 – 1867.	December 26 – 1867.
3	Howard Lee.	William & Sarah Randall.	March 25 – 1867.	January 5 – 1868.
4	Henrietta Jerome.	Benj. & Christiana Reynolds.	March 23 – 1865.	January 5 – 1868.
5	Emma Virginia.	Benj. F. & Jane E. Sweeting.	January 20 – 1868.	March 12 – 1868.

Figure 5-2. Baltimore First English Reformed Church, Baptismal Register, 1867-74, vol. 1, p. 1; Genealogical Society of Utah (hereafter GS) microfilm 940,423.

MARRIAGES.

A record of Marriages Consummated by Me E. P. Ab Anno 1723 Ad Annum &c.

Place of Marriage	Year	Mo.	Day	Names of Parties Married	Places of their abode before Marriage.
Huntington,	1723	Octobr.	31	Epenetus Platt and Sarah Scuddar	Huntington
		Decemr.	18	Jonathan Foster and Elisabeth Chichester	Huntington
	1724	June	1	Daniel Keleg and Unice Jarvis	Norwalk In Connecticot Huntington
			30	Stephen Miller and Sarah Warin	Bedford On ye main Oysterbay
		Decemr.	21	Richard Drage and Mary Coone	Oysterbay.
			22	Samuel Plumbe and Anna Roe	Huntington
	1724/5	Feby.	10	Jonathan Smith and Temperance Whitman	Stamford in Connectcot Huntington.

Figure 5-3. Moses L. Scudder, comp., *Records of the First Church in Huntington, Long Island, 1723-79* (Huntington, N.Y.: For the compiler 1899), p. 61.

sometimes aid the genealogist in the extremely difficult task of tracing blacks before the Civil War.

A second example, Figure 5-2, is taken from the records of the First English Reformed Church of Baltimore, Maryland, about 1867-68.

This register does not contain as much genealogical information as the Albemarle register, which preceded it by 120 years. It lists no sponsors except the parents themselves. This situation, with later church records providing less information than earlier ones, is by no means unique. Five baptisms list only the mother as a parent. This does not necessarily mean that she is widowed or that the child was illegitimate but more probably that she was the only parent who belonged to that church.

The second major type of church records are marriage records. Almost all American denominations have recorded marriages, although there are some interesting exceptions. For instance, the early Puritans viewed marriage as a civil contract. Hence, marriages were performed by a civil magistrate and were not recorded in the church registers.

This was not a typical situation. In most areas, church marriage records predate civil marriage records by many decades and sometimes even centuries. For instance, South Carolina did not record marriages on either county or state levels until 1911. In such a situation, church marriage records acquire greater importance.

Church marriage records differ greatly in content. At times they give nothing more than the names of the bride and groom and the date. Figure 5-3 is a published transcription of records of the First (Congregational) Church in Huntington, Long Island. This record yields an additional dividend to the genealogist because the pastor recorded the previous residences of the couple.

The other extreme is demonstrated by a Roman Catholic marriage register from a parish in South Central Texas shown in Figure 5-4, which records the date of the marriage; the names, ages, residences, birthplaces, and religion of the bride and groom; the occupation of the groom; the place where the ceremony was held; the names and birthplaces of the parents of the nuptial pair; and the name of the officiating priest.

As with most Catholic records, these are in Latin, a custom often cited as an obstacle to their use by genealogists. If so, it is a minor obstacle. Once the records have been put into columnar form, as is the case here, you can decipher the Latin headings using common sense and a Latin word list.

Admittedly, this particular example is unusual, especially in listing the parents' birthplaces. But Catholic, Lutheran, and German Reformed marriage records frequently list the birthplace of the bride and groom. Figure 5-5 shows an alphabetized translation of the records of Saint John's Lutheran Church, Ruma, Illinois.

Church marriage records are useful in locating an immigrant ancestor's birthplace; but in my professional experience, church death registers have been the single most valuable source for tracing an immigrant's place of birth. Originally churches recorded burials rather than deaths, and some churches still do. However, most American church records also list the date of death, and often they record a great deal more.

In one instance, I researched a county history which listed a German immigrant's birthplace as Gubeardstadt, Prussia. I found no such village in any gazetteer. Fortunately, the county history also stated where the family attended church. A letter to the church (then German Evangelical, now United Church of Christ) produced a photocopy of the pertinent page of the death register which noted that this individual was born in Gross Bierstadt, province of Saxony, Prussia. I easily located the village using a standard atlas.

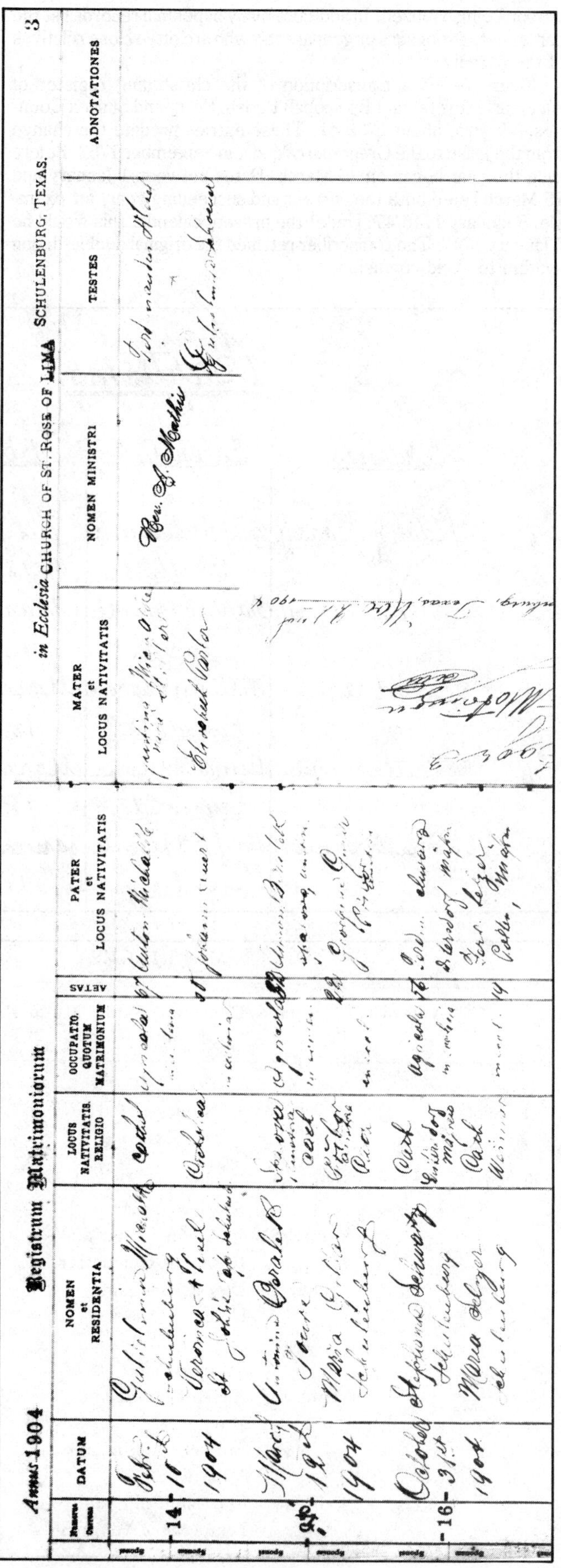
Annus 1904 Registrum Matrimoniorum in Ecclesia CHURCH OF ST. ROSE OF LIMA SCHULENBURG, TEXAS. 3

Numerus Currens	DATUM	NOMEN et RESIDENTIA	LOCUS NATIVITATIS RELIGIO	OCCUPATIO QUOQUE MATRIMONIUM	AETAS	PATER et LOCUS NATIVITATIS	MATER et LOCUS NATIVITATIS	NOMEN MINISTRI	TESTES	ADNOTATIONES

Figure 5-4. Saint Rose of Lima Catholic Church, Schulenberg, Texas Marriage Register, vol. 2, p. 2; GS 025,499.

#245--Lina Schenkel,a child, born at Mascoutah, Ills., living bei Evansville, died 12 März 1879, i. 14 März, aged 13 years, 3 months, 3 days, pages 190-191

#281--Christian Schlimme, widower, born Hannover, living near Ruma, Ills., died 17 Dec 1883, i. 19 Dec 1883, aged 60 years, 11 months, 17 days, pp. 194-195
#364--Heinrich Schlimme, husband, born in Borstel, kingdom of Hannover, Germany, living at Ruma, Ills., died 10 Jan 1900, i. 12 Jan 1900, aged 47 years, 11 months, 26 days--Matthew 24, 44--pages 204-205
#213--Maria Dorothea Schlimme, wife, born in Borstel in Kingdom of Hannover, living at Horse Creek, died 19 May 1877, i. 20 May, aged 47 years, 3 months, 24 days, pages 186-187
#308--Maria Elisabeth Louise Schlimme, a child, born near Ruma, Ills., living near Ruma, Ills., died 26 Oct 1888, i. 27 Oct, aged 12 days, pp. 196-197
#73 --Rosette Maria Carolina Schlimme, a child, living at Horse Creek, died at 11 Sep 1869, i. 12 Sep, aged 7 years, 10 months, 25 days, pages 168-169

#156--Joseph Schmellemeier, husband, born Siegmaringen im Kingdom Würtemberg, living at Evansville, died 19 März 1874, i. 20 März 1874, aged 49 years, 1 month, 4 days, pages 178-179

Figure 5-5. Mrs. Harold Drake, trans. and comp., *Church Records of St. John's Lutheran Church, Ruma, Illinois* (Watseka, Ill.: For the compiler, 1975), p. 16.

While most genealogists are aware of the value of baptismal, marriage, and death records, they sometimes overlook other types of church records which also contain valuable genealogical and historical information. Confirmation records are a case in point. Most how-to books dismiss them as mere name lists, which admittedly is often the case. However, the Scandinavian Lutheran denominations contain voluminous information, as Figure 5-6 shows.

Obviously, a reading knowledge of Norwegian is a more specialized skill than reading Latin, but this basic record is intelligible even without language expertise. I do not have a good command of Norwegian; but with a little common sense and an inexpensive Norwegian-English dictionary, I deciphered the confirmation entries. The first column contains the date of the confirmation; the second column, the name of the confirmed; the third, the age; and the fourth, the name of the parents. The fifth column offers a somewhat greater challenge but, as is often the case, commensurate rewards. It states the place of the baptism. Most of the confirmands were baptized in "this congregation" (***menigheden her***), but Edvart Olson and Karin P. Hausland were baptized in Hjelmedard, Norway. Again, we have the crucial piece of information needed to find the family's place of origin in Europe. The sixth column refers to the degree of "Christian knowledge" possessed by the confirmed. Most received a "good," three received a "very good," and three received "less good." The last column refers to the membership status of the parents of the confirmands. All were members of the congregation but Albret and Anne Olson ("nonmembers") and Ole Olson ("outsider").

Scandinavian-American Lutheran confirmation records is exceptionally good. German-American Lutheran and Reformed confirmation records will often list the date of baptism but not usually the place. Based on my experience, the same generalization can be made about Catholic confirmation records. Most American Protestant denominations, if they perform confirmations at all, merely list the names of the confirmands and the date of the event, marking the young person's entry into full membership in the congregation. Some also give the ages of confirmands yielding more precise estimates of birth data and identities.

Confirmation records lead to another category of church sources, membership records. One type of membership records is communicant lists. While not as valuable to the genealogist as the records already discussed, they can still be of great help in reconstructing a family history. The sudden disappearance of a couple from the communicant lists may signify their departure from the community. The disappearance of one but not the other may indicate death, an important clue if the death records have not survived.

Usually the regular membership list is of greater genealogical value. At times, it too may be only a name list. But by the late nineteenth century, many protestant churches kept fairly good membership records. Figure 5-7 is a page from a membership record of one family in a Methodist Church in Indiana between 1895 and 1927.

The particular value of this record is the information it contains about the movement of its members in and out of the congregation. Some of these "removals" or "dismissals" occurred well after 1910, the date of the latest federal census available to the public. The implications for the genealogist seeking heirs rather than ancestors are obvious. In other words, church records should not be dismissed as irrelevant once civil registration begins in a given state or community.

In addition to the genealogically valuable types of church records discussed here, many other sorts of church records exist: minutes of the church council or vestry, disciplinary records, pew rentals, and family registers, among others. If the ancestor was active in church affairs, such records can be invaluable for reconstructing the family's history in the community and their economic and social status as well.

Church Records Projects

Several projects that make access to church records easier and more effective are listed below. Some are readily available in most research libraries; some access special collections, and you will need to visit the repository or send an agent to search for you.

Pennsylvania German Records

Dr. Frederick S. Weiser, a Lutheran pastor of Pennsylvania Dutch ancestry, has translated, transcribed, and edited most of the Lutheran church registers for colonial Pennsylvania. His translations are meticulous and based on his own personal knowledge of the language and customs of the people. He has also re-translated

Konfirmerede.

No.	Konfirmationsdatum.	Konfirmandens Navn.	Alder (Aar).	Forældrenes Navne.	Hvor döbte.	Kristendoms Kundskab.	Om Forældrene staa i Menigheden.	Anmærkninger.

Figure 5-6. Saint Olaf Lutheran Church, Fayette County, Iowa, Confirmation Register 1884-1910, p. 68; GS 1,034,242.

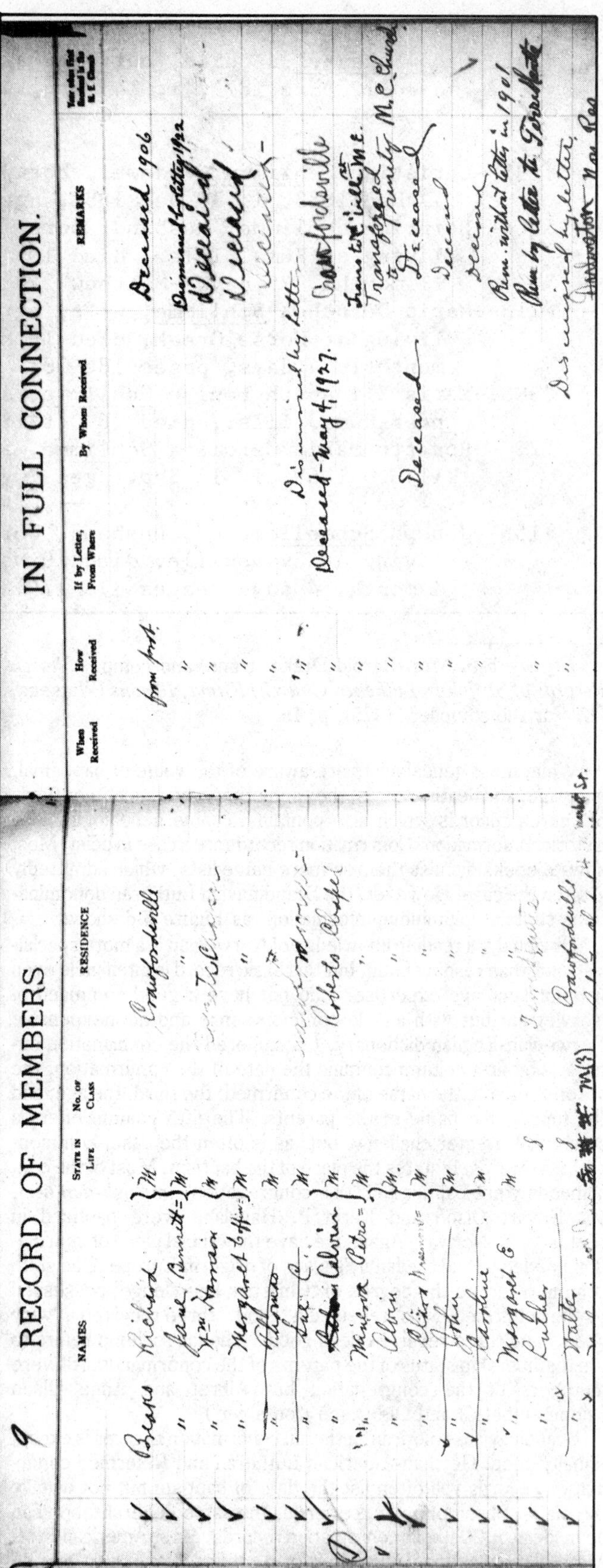

RECORD OF MEMBERS IN FULL CONNECTION.

NAMES	RESIDENCE	STATE IN LIFE	No. of CLASS	When Received	How Received	If by Letter, From Where	By Whom Received	REMARKS	Year when first formed in M. E. Church

Figure 5-7. Roberts Chapel Methodist Episcopal Church, Crawfordsville Circuit, Crawfordsville, Indiana, p. 9; GS 877,714, item 3.

many records originally done by William J. Hinke. Typewritten copies are on deposit in the A. R. Wentz Library, Gettysburg, Pennsylvania, and the Genealogical Society of Utah. Microfilm copies of most are also available through branch libraries.

Pastor Weiser has also compiled a valuable series of *Guides to Central Pennsylvania Lutheran Church Records,* one for each county. These are also available at the two libraries mentioned or you can order copies from Pastor Weiser, New Oxford, PA, (717) 624-4106.

Louisiana Catholic Records

Reverend Donald J. Hebert has translated and transcribed parish records for several Louisiana Parishes. These registers are available in some forty printed volumes to date: *Southwest Louisiana Records,* to 1897, 28 vols., and *Southern Louisiana Records,* to 1895, 9 vols. These volumes are available in many research libraries. Those genealogists who wish to acquire their own copies can order them from Hebert Publications, Box 31, Eunice, LA 70535. Reverend Hebert has also compiled *A Guide to Church Records in Louisiana* (Eunice, La.: For the author, 1975). It covers all denominations.

Western New York Church Records Collection

The Study Center for Early Religious Life in Western New York headquartered at Ithaca College has microfilmed or photocopied 300 collections of church records for that area. The center is no longer in existence, and the records have been deposited in the Regional Collection, Cornell University Library for general use. Because it is a research library, the Cornell staff has only limited personnel to answer queries. Expect some delay in receiving a response. A list of records in the collection is available on request with SASE.

Locating Church Records

Two real difficulties with American church records are, first, locating them, and, second, obtaining access to them. Various denominations have differing policies on public access to their records. See the denomination-by-denomination discussion at the end of this chapter for information on availability.

Determining the church your ancestor attended is the first task. In some families this poses no great problem due to a continuing religious tradition. Even in cases of changing affiliations, the family's Bibles and other papers—baptismal certificates, wedding announcements, etc.—should be searched for clues. County marriage records, if they exist, will often give the name of the clergyman who officiated. If a county history exists, it will usually list the various churches and their clergymen, thus enabling you to identify his denomination.

In large cities the task becomes a bit more complicated, for the county history may not list every clergyman for every church. Fortunately, the city directory will usually list the clergymen and their churches. Larger libraries often possess microfilm copies of city directories dating back to the first half of the nineteenth century.

Of course, the ancestral pair may have been married by the local justice of the peace, which complicates the problem. However, their siblings may have preferred a religious ceremony; and since a wedding customarily takes place in the bride's church, the marriages of the groom's sisters are worth seeking to determine which church his family attended.

The same basic procedure can be followed with the civil death records. The death certificate may list the name of the clergyman who conducted the funeral. If not, it may state the name of the undertaker. If so, a check of a current city or telephone directory may yield the present address of the funeral establishment. A letter to the firm could produce the name of the clergyman, as well as other extremely valuable genealogical information. Specific mortuaries also cater to persons of specific religious affiliations, so ask the mortician directly for this information. If the ancestor was hospitalized before his or her death, hospital records may contain information about religious affiliation and additional genealogical data.

Another approach for determining religious affiliation is the obituary column of the local newspaper. Obituaries vary greatly in quality but usually list the time and place of the funeral and burial.

But what if the ancestor died before civil registration of vital statistics began or before newspapers carried obituaries? As the late Derek Harland put it: "In no other aspect or phase of genealogy is a knowledge of the history or geography of the area in which research is to be carried out more essential than in the study of the church records of the United States."*

Using other types of available records—census returns, land records, and county plat maps—you can pinpoint where the ancestor actually lived, then determine what churches existed in the area. Sometimes the task can be simplified if the area was settled by a single national or ethnic group with a historically dominant religion like Polish (Catholic), Norwegian (Lutheran), or Scottish, (Presbyterian.

However, many European immigrants, even though they came from a country dominated by a state church, chose another religion once they arrived in the United States. For instance, the state church of Sweden was Lutheran, but many Swedes became Baptists or Methodists in America. The Mormons conducted an extremely successful missionary program in Sweden and Denmark in the mid-nineteenth century. Many Germans who immigrated to Pennsylvania in the eighteenth century were not Lutherans but religious dissenters—Amish, Mennonites, or Baptists.

To further complicate things, various German states adopted Calvinism, or a blend of Lutheranism and Calvinism as the state church, among them the Rhenish Palatinate and Prussia. Some immigrant pastors from these areas organized German Reformed or German Evangelical churches in the New World. Today these churches form part of the United Church of Christ. German pastors of Methodist persuasion successfully organized many congregations which are today part of the United Methodist Church.

Generally speaking, immigrants, if they went to church at all, attended a church where their native language was spoken. People needed a community where they could function as equals. Family members often crossed denominational lines to serve as sponsors or witnesses in religious events for friends and relatives. Therefore, try to find all the churches of your ancestor's language group in the area.

In the South, even though it never experienced a major influx of non-English-speaking immigrants in the nineteenth century, church records are crucial for genealogical success, and at the same time, problematic. They are crucial because no other records exist and problematic because they do not always contain needed information. The South was the last area of the United States to establish state-wide civil registration, viewing vital records as the business of the church.

In colonial times the Protestant Episcopal Church was the established church in many southern colonies. In frontier communities, like Augusta County, Virginia, there were more Presbyterians (Scots-Irish) than Protestant Episcopalians or Anglicans (English) so the established parish was manned by Presbyterians and held Presbyterian services. The Augusta Church physically housed the Revolutionary Committee of Safety and even the Virginia Provincial Assembly for a period of time during the break with England. So it is always wise to check the established church records even if your ancestors were known to belong to another faith.

With the advent of the Great Awakening as the eighteenth century closed, that emotional and spiritual declaration of independence so crucial to the formation of the American character, record-keeping tended to lose ground. The date of a person's rebirth in Jesus was

---

*Derek Harland, *Genealogical Research Standards* (Salt Lake City: Bookcraft, 1963), p. 199.

Figure 5-8. Historical Records Survey, Works Project Administration, *Inventory of the Church Archives of New York City: Reformed Church in America* (New York: Historical Records Survey, 1939), p. 14.

- 14 -

NEW YORK CITY CHURCH ARCHIVES

Reformed Church in America Entry A

Reformed Dutch Church, Constitution of the Reformed Dutch church in the United States of America, New York, William Durell, 1793. 354 pp. Edward Tanjore Corwin, D.D., A Digest of Constitutional and Synodical Legislation of the Reformed Church in America, New York, Board of Publications, 1906, pp. 307-12. Charles E. Corwin, Manual of the Reformed Church New York, Board of Publications, 5th ed., 1922, pp. 91-95. Willard Dayton Brown, A History of the Reformed Church in America, New York, Board of Publications, 1928, 140 pp. William Henry Steele Demarest, Notes on the Constitution of the Reformed Church in America, Princeton, N.J. Princeton University Press, 1929. Loc. NN.

MINUTES: General Synod, vol.-1, 1771-1812 (includes minutes of Original and Particular Synods, 1794-99. Minutes of the Coetus, 1738-54. Proceedings of the Conferenti; 1755-67). Vol.-2A, 1813-20, vol.-2B, 1821-26, vol.-3, 1827-31, vol.-4, 1832-36, vol.-5, 1837-41, vol.-6, 1841-45, vol.-7, 1846-49, vol.-8, 1850-55, vol.-9, 1855-60, vol.-10, 1861-65, vol.-11, 1866-69, vol.-12, 1870-73, vol.-13, 1874-77, vol.-14, 1878-81, vol.-15, 1881-85, vol.-16, 1886-89, vol.-17, 1890-93, vol.-18, 1894-97, vol.-19, 1898-1901, vol.-20, 1902-04, vol.-21, 1905-07, vol.-22, 1908-10, vol.-23, 1911-13, vol.-24, 1914-16, vol.-25, 1917-19, vol.-26, 1920-22, vol.-27, 1923-25, vol.-28, 1926-28, vol.-29, 1929-31, vol.-30, 1932-34, vol.-31, 1935-36.

Particular Synod of Albany (Separate yearly booklets kept in cardboard file boxes). Box-1, 1877-1905, box-2, 1906-24, (1909 missing), box-3, 1925-37.

Particular Synod of Chicago (Separate yearly booklets kept in cardboard file boxes), box-1, 1885-86,1887-91,1892-93,1895-1915 (inclusive), box-2, 1916-37.

Particular Synod of Iowa (Seperate yearly booklets kept in cardboard file box). Box-1, 1920-37.

Particular Synod of New Brunswick (In 5 bound vols.), vol.-1, 1869-79, vol.-2, 1880-89, vol.-3, 1900-09, vol.-4, 1910-19, vol.-5, 1920-29. (Seperate yearly booklets kept in cardboard file box). Box-1, 1930-36.

Particular Synod of New York (Separate yearly booklets kept in cardboard file boxes). Box-1, 1850-74, box-2, 1875-99, box-3, 1900-15 (1914 missing), box-4, 1916-29, box-5, 1930-37.

FINANCIAL: Ledgers, 11 vols., 1876-95,1896-1908,1908-19,1919-23, 1924-29,1929-35,1935--; petty ledgers, 1885-89,1889-95,1896-1900,1901-19. General, Cash books, 12 vols., 1869-96,1896-1901,1901-06,1906-11,1911-14, 1914-19,1919-24,1924-37,1937--. Real Estate - Widow's Fund - Disabled Fund, Cash books, 1882-89,1889-95,1895-1922. Journals, 2 vols., 1934-37,1937--. Day Books, 4 vols., 1876-84,1884-93,1893-1904,1904-14. Cancelled Check Stubs, about 50 vols.

Magazine of the Reformed Dutch Church (monthly booklets bound in 4 vols.). Edited by William Craig Brownlee, D.D. Rutgers Press. Printed by Terhune and Letson, New Brunswick, Vol.-1, 1826-27, vol.-2, 1827-28, vol.-3, 1828-29, vol.-4, 1829-30. Vols.-3 and 4. printed by William A. Mercein, 1 Burling Slip, N.Y.

The Mission Field (monthly booklets bound in 23 vols.), 1888-89, 1890-91,1892,1893,1894-95,1896-98,1898-1900,1900-02,1902-04,1904-06,1906-08, 1908-09,1910-11,1911-12,1912-13,1913-14,1914-15,1915-16,1916-17,1917-18,1918-19,1919-20,1921-22.

Christian Intelligencer paper issued weekly - bound in yearly vols. (107 vols.). Issues complete from 1830-1937, with exception of year 1873 which is missing. Printed and published by William A. Mercein, 240 Pearl Street, N.Y.C.

more important than his/her physical birth. And the continuing migration west of settlers made exact record-keeping difficult.

A useful guide through the maze of denominational history in the United States is Frank Mead, *Handbook of American Denominations*, 5th ed. (Nashville: Abingdon Press, 1970). For current information, consult the *Yearbook of American and Canadian Churches* published annually by Abingdon Press under the editorial direction of the National Council of Churches. This extremely useful volume is discussed more fully in the list at the end of this chapter. Another source of information about local church records may be the microfiche catalog of the nearest branch library of the Genealogical Society of Utah, which has made considerable effort to obtain American church records at all levels. As a result, you can often find microfilms or printed transcriptions of local church records of a given township or county in its holdings.

The International Genealogical Index, established by the Genealogical Society of Utah and also available at branch libraries, is rich with American church records: Dutch Reformed records for New York and New Jersey, Lutheran and German Reformed records for Pennsylvania, and Congregational records for the New England states. There is also a smattering of Presbyterian, Quaker, and Roman Catholic sources in the IGI. See Chapter 13, "Genealogical Tools and Indexes," and Chapter 15, " Tracking Immigrant Origins," for how to use the IGI.

In some states, the state historical society has become the official archive for certain denominations. For example, the State Historical Society of Wisconsin is the official archive for the United Church of Christ in that state.

But often the records you need are still in the possession of the local church. If the church is still in existence and the name has not changed, the telephone directory may solve the problem. If the individual church has merged with another one of the same denomination, the yearbook of the denomination should have the name, address, and current pastor of the merged church. If the denomination has merged or split, Mead's *Handbook* can be extremely useful. If the church is defunct, contact another church of the same denomination in the area and inquire about the location of the records. If the denomination requires that the records of defunct churches be sent to a central archive, the local minister may know the address and whom to contact. Another source of information could be the state organization of the denomination.

If you locate the church but the older records are missing, discuss the problem with the current minister. He may know which archive they are stored in. If not, he may know descendants of former pastors who have kept his records, or he can refer you to older members of the congregation well versed in local church history.

Next, contact the local historical or genealogical society. If that does not prove productive, write or visit the denominational archive. Older records of a given church may have been deposited there years before. The state office of the denomination can sometimes help in your quest.

For a complete list of private and state historical libraries, see the current edition of *The Directory of Archives and Manuscript Repositories*, published in 1978 by the National Archives and Records Services. Do not overlook each state's Historical Records Survey of the Work Projects Administration (WPA), undertaken in the later years of the Great Depression (1930s). Among its projects was a compilation of church records on the state and local level—incomplete but still the most comprehensive attempt of its kind ever made. The results were summarized in the *Check List of Historical Records Survey Publications*, published by the WPA in 1943 (reprint ed., Baltimore: Genealogical Publishing Co., 1969). It is essentially a bibliography of research project reports. The individual states in turn published detailed lists showing the church records available on the local level. Figure 5-8 from the *Inventory of the Church Archives of New York City* illustrates the approach generally taken by the survey

A more recent guide to the WPA Historical Records Survey, which covers unpublished material, is Loretta L. Hefner, *The WPA Historical Records Survey: A Guide to the Unpublished Inventories, Indexes, and Transcripts* (Chicago: Society of American Archivists, 1980).

Another, much older guide to unpublished material in church archives is William H. Allison, *Inventory of Unpublished Material for American Religious History in Protestant Church Archives and Other Repositories* (Washington, D.C.: Carnegie Institute, 1910). Some of these archives are still functioning, making the inventory still relevant. A current source of new acquisitions and microfilming projects of church records is the "New Notes" section of *The American Archivist*, the quarterly journal of the Society of American Archivist.

If the records are known to have been destroyed, say in a fire, the personal records of former pastors can sometimes provide an effective substitute. Many clergymen kept their own private record of baptisms, marriages, and funerals at which they officiated. In fact, in areas where no permanent churches existed, the private records of the circuit-riding pastors may be the only records ever made.

The first place to look for these is the denominational archive. But some of these pastoral records have found their way into private or state archives. An extremely useful guide to these private pastoral records and other church records is the *National Union Catalog of Manuscript Collections*. The index and full entry in Figure 5-9 illustrates the type of information provided.

BAPTISTS (Continued)

Kentucky. 70-2356, 72-1858, 72-1871

Massachusetts. 72-15

Mississippi. 72-1569

New York. 71-1439

New York City. 71-13, 71-1439, 71-1440, 72-158

MS 72-1569

Mississippi Baptist church records, 1819-1957. (MS 66-888)

—— Addition, 1837-1968. 6 reels of microfilm (negative)

In Mississippi State University Library (State College, Miss.)

Microfilm of originals which have been returned to owners.

Minute books, lists of church members, histories, constitutions, and other records. Churches represented include Bethel, Wilkinson Co. (1853-93); Liberty, Lauderdale Co. (1845-87); Mt. Pleasant, Chickasaw Co. (1868-1950); Pleasant Ridge, Union Co. (1842-1945); Siloam, Clay Co. (1850-1968); and Toxish, Pontotoc Co. (1837-1967).

Unpublished guide in the library.

Information on literary rights available in the library.

Acquired from various sources.

Additions to this collection are anticipated.

Figure 5-9. Library of Congress, *National Union Catalog of Manuscript Collections* (Washington D.C.: J.W. Edwards, 1972). vol. 11, index and p. 224.

If after all of your efforts, the denomination of your ancestor is still unknown, the local historical or genealogical society can often be of great assistance. If you do not know whether a local society exists, you should consult the current edition of the *Directory of Historical Societies and Agencies in the U. S. and Canada* (updated every five years) or *Meyer's Directory of Genealogical Societies in the USA and Canada*. Since the leadership of such groups can change from year to year, it may require additional effort to identify the current president and his/her mailing address. It is usually worth the effort. I have received very good cooperation from various county historical societies, who will often perform research for a modest fee.

Another possibility is the local public library. In some communities, the public library is the repository of genealogical material, including old church records. Larger public libraries may have a genealogical reference specialist who can assist you. You can usually locate public libraries through directory assistance, but the *American Library Directory* will also list the local library.

But many communities possess neither a local historical society nor a public library. If the town has a weekly newspaper, the editor can sometimes be a good source of local historical information or can refer you to someone who is. The county or town clerk's office may not have sufficient staff to conduct genealogical searches and refers all requests to a local researcher. Often these individuals know a great deal about the local history, including church history.

A vexing situation involving church records can occur when they fall into private hands. Sometimes a clerk of the parish kept the records for so many years that he came to regard them as his personal possessions. More typically, a minister dies and his private records, or those of a defunct church he has served, remain in the possession of his family and never find their way to an archive, public or private. I have been in intermittent pursuit of such a set of minister's records for the past two years. A descendant of the minister recalled having seen her great-grandfather's old records in the house when she was a child. But they had been loaned out to someone in the 1930s to verify a marriage and had apparently never been returned. Perhaps the best way to solve problems of this sort is to visit the area and contact as many relatives and former parishioners of the pastor as possible. If time and money do not permit this approach, you might hire a local researcher well acquainted in the area. This particular problem does not lend itself to easy solutions.

Still another important source of defunct church records is college libraries, particularly denominational colleges. For instance, Swarthmore College, Swarthmore, Pennsylvania, possesses an extremely important collection of Quaker records. The same situation holds true for many other church colleges. In fact, some serve as an official or quasi-official depository for their denomination. *The Yearbook of American and Canadian Churches* contains a list of all church-related colleges with the denominational affiliation noted.

Also, certain private libraries not affiliated with any religious denomination contain a vast amount of genealogical data including church records. The Library of the National Society, Daughters of the American Revolution, in Washington, D.C., is undoubtedly the best known of these. See Appendix E, "Special Libraries."

Finally, a great deal of information on church records appears in genealogical periodicals. The classic index to genealogical periodicals is Donald Lines Jacobus, *Index to Genealogical Periodicals* (1952; reprint ed., Baltimore: Genealogical Publishing Co., 1978). An important complement to that index is the *Genealogical Periodical Annual Index* (GPAI), 1962 to the present.

However, you should not rely on these alone. Local genealogical society periodicals are springing up like mushrooms all over the country. Not all appear in the GPAI index. The local genealogical or historical society in your area of interest may publish a newsletter or quarterly journal. If a given county does not have a genealogical society, one may exist for a multi-county region. Usually, the state historical society tries to acquire and catalog the local genealogical and historical publications in its state.

Research Suggestions

Effective use of church records requires following some basic rules typical of all genealogical research and knowing the particular hazards associated with church records. Be sure to search other available records from the locality. If the church death registers are missing, try the county probate records. Note the names of witnesses at weddings and baptisms and look for your direct ancestors as witnesses. Very important familial relationships can be discovered in this manner. If the congregation is of a particular ethnic group, note the birthplaces of other members as listed in the marriage or death records. Even if your ancestor's place of origin is not given, he/she may have come from the same town or area.

In frontier communities people often attended whatever church or circuit-riding services existed, regardless of affiliation. Thus, a Methodist family may have attended a Baptist church at one time.

Knowing the particular doctrines and discipline of a denomination helps in using the record. If a church did not practice infant baptism, you need to know this or you could make serious errors in calculating birthdates.

Some churches have devised standard forms to reply to requests for information from their records. Some of these date from the 1930s when the primary object was to verify a person's age. Often they do not contain all the information of the record. Hence, you should request *all the information* in the pertinent entry. If you are interested in finding an ancestor's place of birth in Europe, be sure to say so.

Be aware of some of the inherent limitations of church records. Even in churches which practiced infant baptism, a significant amount of time might lapse between the date of a child's birth and baptism. Be wary when it appears that entries have been made some time after the rite occurred. Errors often creep in when this happens.

Particularly problematical are typewritten or printed transcriptions of church records, especially if they have been translated from another language. In spite of the best efforts of the translator or transcriber, mistakes occur. Quite often transcriptions do not contain all of the data in the original entry, including the names of baptismal sponsors or occupations. Sometimes alphabetizing information may hide important clues such as children baptized or a brother and sister marrying the same day. Therefore, make every effort to locate the original record or at least a microfilm copy. Do not let a foreign language deter you. With common sense and a dual-language dictionary you may be able to decipher it. If not, find someone who can. The results may be worth the extra effort.

If the original record is still in the custody of the church, obtaining permission to see it may pose a problem. In several years of genealogical research, I have encountered this situation only once. A Lutheran pastor in Wisconsin felt that his congregational records were too fragile for public use and insisted that he check the records himself, while I watched. His concern was legitimate, as the records clearly needed rebinding. Depending upon the situation, you may suggest that the records could be microfilmed for safekeeping. One genealogist of my acquaintance brought some nineteenth-century church records from Ohio to Salt Lake City to be filmed by the Genealogical Society of Utah, the originals then being returned to the owner. Several states also have microfilming programs.

Historically, Catholic records have been entrusted to the priest alone, and the parish priest still holds that prerogative. The press of pastoral duties has forced many priests to delegate the responsibility for answering genealogical inquiries to the parish secretary or a parish volunteer. More and more Catholic parishes, especially in the eastern states, are now publishing their older records.

When you request data from local church records, do not expect the pastor or the parish secretary to do your genealogical research for you. If your initial inquiry proves unsuccessful, visit the church yourself or hire a local genealogist. Sometimes a church officer can suggest a member of the congregation who has developed genealogical competence. Include a check as well as a self-addressed, stamped envelope with your initial request. Three to five dollars is a reasonable minimum. Send a larger amount if your request covers more than an entry or two. Sometimes a church will return your check. My experience has been that most churches are extremely cooperative, certainly in answering the first inquiry.

DENOMINATION ARCHIVES, REPOSITORIES, AND RECORD-KEEPING PRACTICES

Space forbids an exhaustive treatment of all the denominations. For a complete list, which includes the names and addresses of current officers, see the current edition of the *Yearbook of American and Canadian Churches* (New York and Nashville: Abingdon Press).

Adventist

Inquire at:

Andrews University Library
Berrien Springs, MI 49104

Dr. Linden J. Carter Library
Berkshire Christian College
Lennox, ME 01240

General Conference of Seventh-Day Adventists
6840 Eastern Avenue NW
Washington, DC 20012

Baptist

Encyclopedia of Southern Baptists. 3 vols. Nashville: Broadman, 1958.

Helmbold, F. Wilbur. "Baptist Records for Genealogy and History," *National Genealogical Society Quarterly* 61 (Sept. 1973): 168-78. Contains valuable background and list of record locations, state by state.

____________. "Family History in the Bible Belt: Southern U.S. Church Records." *World Conference on Records: Preserving Our Heritage*, 12-15 Aug. 1980, vol. 3, series 336. Salt Lake City: Church of Jesus Christ of Latter-Day Saints, 1981. Emphasizes Baptist records.

McLaughlin, William G. *New England Dissent, 1630-1833: The Baptists and Separation of Church and State*. 2 vols. Cambridge: Harvard University Press, 1971. Essential reading for genealogists with ancestors who migrated from New England to New York, Pennsylvania, Ohio. Studies individual congregations and records.

Menkus, Belden. "The Baptist Sunday School Board and Its Records," *American Archivist* 24 (1961): 441-44.

Piepkopt, Arthur Carl. "The Primitive Baptists of North America." *Baptist History and Heritage* 7 (Jan. 1972): 33-51.

Starr, Edward Caryl. *A Baptist Bibliography, Being a Register of Printed Material By and About Baptists*. 25 vols. Rochester, N.Y.: American Baptist Historical Society, 1947-76. In progress.

Try to determine the kind of Baptist Church your ancestor might have joined. Narrow your search to a state and county. Begin in the locality, rather than the library, since few records have been published. Use the suggestions made by Wilbur F. Helmbold in the two articles cited.

Realize that today many Baptist archives acquire material for Baptist churches besides their own. Because your ancestor was not a Southern Baptist does not mean the records are not now held by a Southern Baptist archive.

Baptist Major Collections

American Baptist Historical Society
(including Samuel Colgate Baptist Historical Collection)
1106 South Goodman Street
Rochester, NY 14620

This is the major repository for the American Baptist Convention, formerly known as the Northern Baptist Convention.

Andover Newton Theological School
(including Backus Historical Society)
Newton Centre, MA 02159

Baptist Historical Collection
Z. Smith Reynolds Library
Wake Forest University
Winston-Salem, NC 27109

Valuable vertical files for every North Carolina Baptist Church, both extant and extinct and for Baptist ministers. Detailed indexes available.

Bethel Seminary
1480 North Snelling Avenue
St. Paul, MN 55108

Contact this institution about microfilmed records of Swedish Baptist congregations.

Historical Commission
of the Southern Baptist Convention
127 Ninth Avenue North
Nashville, NC 37234

One of the largest collections of original congregation minutes, correspondence, annual reports, missionary records.

Library
Samford University
Birmingham, AL 35209

Can provide information about the various state Baptist repositories.

Seventh Day Baptist Library
Seventh Day Baptist Building
Plainfield, NJ 07060

Has German Baptist collections.

Library
Southern Baptist Theological Seminary
Louisville, KY 40206

Particularly important for Kentucky Baptist records.

Library
Southwestern Baptist Theological Seminary
Fort Worth, TX 76122

Serves as the Texas Baptist repository.

Brethren in Christ Church

Archives of the Brethren in Christ Church
Messiah College
Grantham, PA 17027

Church of Christ, Scientist

The First Church of Christ, Scientist
Archives and Library of the Mother Church
Boston, MA 02115

Church of God

For all bodies under this name, see the current *Yearbook of American and Canadian Churches*.

Church of Jesus Christ of Latter-day Saints (Mormons)

Church of Jesus Christ of Latter-day Saints, Genealogical Department, *LDS Church Records and Research Aids*. Research Paper Series F, No. 1. Salt Lake City: Church of Jesus Christ of Latter-day-Saints, 1978.

Jaussi, Laureen Richardson, and Gloria D. Chaston. *Genealogical Records of Utah*. Salt Lake City: Deseret Book Company, 1974.

__________. *Register of Genealogical Society Call Numbers*. 2 vols. Provo, Utah: Genealogy Tree, 1982. Includes record by record detail for holdings of LDS records.

Records of local Mormon congregations are usually accumulated regularly in Salt Lake City, and four types of records that are of general interest to genealogists are:

1. The International Genealogical Index (IGI), an index to names submitted for processing in LDS temples from 1970 to the present. Many of the names submitted come from historic records. The name index is on microfiche and is arranged alphabetically within a designated geographic region, usually a state. These microfiches are available in all branch libraries of the Genealogical Society of Utah, which has extracted names from many published parish registers, especially in the eastern states. Hence a search of the IGI should prove valuable for anyone pursuing research in eastern church records.

2. The Family Group Record Archives, a microfilmed collection of eight million family group records. Copies are available in all Genealogical Society branch libraries in alphabetical order by the husband's surname followed by his given name(s). This collection is particularly useful for families stemming from New England.

3. The Temple Records Index Bureau (TIB), a collection of more than thirty million cards representing names processed by LDS temples from 1842 through 1969. The TIB is not publically available, but anyone can request a search for individual names. See Chapter 13, "Genealogical Tools and Indexes," for more information on these collections and how to use them.

4. The *International Genealogical Library Catalog*, which lists the holdings of the Genealogical Society library and is available on microfiche at Genealogical Society branch libraries.

Major collections are in:

Genealogical Society of Utah
50 East North Temple
Salt Lake City, UT 84150

LDS Church Archives
Historical Department
50 East North Temple
Salt Lake City, UT 84150
Contains personal journals, letters, and congregational records.

Church of the Brethren

German-American Pietist-Anabaptist background

Bethany Theological Seminary
Butterfield and Meyers Roads
Oak Brook, IL 60521

Brethren Historical Library and Archives
1451 Dundee Avenue
Elgin, IL 60120

Juniata College Library
Huntingdon, PA 16652

Churches of Christ

Harding Graduate School of Religion
Library
1000 Cherry Road
Memphis, TN 38117

Congregational

Greenwood, Val. *The Researcher's Guide to American Genealogy*. Baltimore: Genealogical Publishing Co., 1973, pp. 360-62. Examples of Congregational records.

Walker, Willeston. *The History of the Congregational Churches in the United States*. New York: ACHS, 1894.

So many New England records have been published or microfilmed that it might be most productive to begin with a library search before looking in the locality of interest.

As a result of mergers, schisms, and other historical developments, at least three denominations contain Congregational or former Congregational Churches: Congregational Christian Churches (National Association), Unitarian Universalist Association, and United Church of Christ, which see. Archives of these churches may include old Congregational Church records. The major collection of Congregational records primarily from New England is in:

Congregational Library
14 Beacon Street
Boston, MA 02108
Includes large collection of newspapers, local magazines.

Disciples of Christ

Garrison, W.E. and A.T. DeGroot. *The Disciples of Christ, a History* St. Louis: Bethany Press, 1948.

Major collections are:

Christian Theological Seminary
1000 West 42nd Street
Indianapolis, IN 46208

Culver-Stockton College Library
Canton, MO 63435

The Disciples of Christ Historical Society
Library Archives
1101 Nineteenth Avenue South
Nashville, TN 37212

Lexington Theological Seminary
631 South Limestone
Lexington, KY 40508

Texas Christian University
Mary Couts Burnett Library
Fort Worth, TX 76219

Evangelical Congregational Church

Historical Society of the Evangelical Congregational Church
121 South College Street
Meyerstown, PA 17077

Evangelical Covenant Church of America

Evangelical Covenant Church of America
Archives and Historical Society
5125 North Spaulding Avenue
Chicago, IL 60625

The congregational records of this denomination, originally Swedish-American, have been microfilmed. Write the archive for information.

Evangelical Free Church of America
1515 East 66th Street
Minneapolis, MN 55423

Also Swedish-American in origin, the congregational records of this denomination have also been microfilmed. Write the headquarters for information.

Evangelical United Brethren Church

Sometimes called the "German Methodists," this denomination merged with the United Methodist Church in 1968. The record repository is:

Historical Society
1810 Harvard Building
Dayton, OH 45406

Greek Orthodox

Archives of the Greek Orthodox
Archdiocese of North America
10 East 79th Street
New York, NY 10021

For other Eastern Orthodox church archives, see *Yearbook of American and Canadian Churches.*

Huguenot

(French Protestants of the Reformed Church)

Allen, Cameron. "Records of the Huguenots in the United States, Canada, and the West Indies with Some Mention of Dutch and German Sources," a paper delivered at the World Conference on Records and Genealogical Seminar, 5-8 Aug. 1969, Area F-10, Salt Lake City, sponsored by the Church of Jesus Christ of Latter-day Saints. Much of this material also appears in "Huguenot Migrations," in the American Society of Genealogists, *Genealogical Research: Methods and Sources* (Washington, D.C.: American Society of Genealogists, 1971), vol. 2, pp. 256-90.

Baird, Charles W. *History of the Hugenot Emigration to America.* Baltimore: Genealogical Publishing Company, 1966.

A great deal has been published about Huguenots, including original source material. Beginning with library research may be most productive.

The major collection is in:

Huguenot Historical Society
Box 339
New Palta, NY 12561

Jewish

For a more complete treatment of Jewish records, see Chapter 21.

Kranzler, David. *My Jewish Roots: A Practical Guide to Tracing and Recording Your Genealogy and Family History.* New York: Sepher Hermon Press, 1979.

Kurzweil, Arthur. *From Generation to Generation: How to Trace Your Jewish Genealogy and Personal History.* New York: William Morrow and Company, 1980.

Rottenberg, Dan. *Finding Our Fathers: A Guidebook to Jewish Genealogy.* New York: Random House, 1977. Especially note Chapter 6: "Jewish Sources in America."

Stern, Malcom H. "Church Records of the United States: Jewish Synagogue Records," a paper delivered at the World Conference on Records and Genealogical Seminar, 5-8 Aug. 1969, Salt Lake City, sponsored by the Church of Jesus Christ of Latter-day Saints, Area I, 6 and 7a.

Toledot: The Journal of Jewish Genealogy.

Major collections are in local Jewish historical societies and:

American Jewish Archives
3101 Clifton Avenue
Cincinnati, OH 45220

American Jewish Historical Society
2 Thornton Road
Waltham, MA 02154

Lutheran

Bodensieck, Julius, ed. *The Encyclopedia of the Lutheran Church.* 3 vols. Minneapolis: Augsburg Publishing House, 1965.

Greenwood, Val. *The Researcher's Guide to American Genealogy.* Baltimore: Genealogical Publishing Company, 1973, pp. 373-77. Examples from Lutheran records.

Lueker, Erwin L., ed. *Lutheran Cyclopedia.* St. Louis: Concordia, 1975.

Suelflow, August R. "The Lutheran Family in North America." *World Conference on Records: Preserving our Heritage,* 12-15 Aug. 1980. Salt Lake City: Church of Jesus Christ of Latter-day Saints, 1980, vol. 4, series 368.

____________. "Records of the Lutheran Church in America," a paper delivered at the World Conference on Records, 5-8 Aug. 1969, Salt Lake City, sponsored by the Church of Jesus Christ of Latter- day Saints, Area I, 6 and 7b. Different emphasis from the above; good bibliography.

Lutheran church records rank among the best available and are invaluable for tracing German or Scandinavian ancestors, even though the numerous synods may seem baffling. The three major synods are:

1. The American Lutheran Church was formed in 1960 by a merger of the American Lutheran Church, which was largely Midwestern German-American in background; the Evangelical Lutheran Church, largest of the various Norwegian-American synods; and the United Evangelical Lutheran Church, a Midwestern Danish-American synod headquartered in Nebraska. In 1963, the Lutheran Free Church, a Norwegian-American synod, joined the American Lutheran Church. The American Lutheran Church is microfilming all of its congregational records. About 90 percent of the Norwegian-American Lutheran congregational records have been filmed but not those of the Lutheran Free Church or the Evangelical Lutheran Synod. Since the merger, the records of approximately fifty congregations per year of the formerly German-American and Danish-American groups have been completed. A microfiche catalogue of the microfilmed congregational records is available from the Archives of the American Lutheran Church, Wartburg Theological Seminary, 333 Wartburg Place, Dubuque, IA 52001. The cost of rental is four dollars per roll; however, written permission of the congregation must be received before the microfilm of its records can be released. Robert Wiederaenders, archivist, can grant permission to use records of defunct churches. The archive prefers to loan because it does not have facilities for research.

2. Lutheran Church in America was formed in 1962 by the consolidation of the American Evangelical Lutheran Church (Danish-

American), the Augustana Evangelical Church (Swedish-American), the Finnish Evangelical Lutheran Church (Finnish-American), and the United Lutheran Church in America (German-American, especially strong in the eastern United States.)

The archival holdings of the Lutheran Church in America (LCA) are scattered among several archives reflecting ethnic backgrounds:

Danish-American

Archives of the Lutheran Church
in America
1100 East 55th Street
Chicago, IL 60615

Finnish-American

Finnish-American Historical Archives
Hancock, MI 49930

German-American

Lutheran Archives Center at Philadelphia
7301 Germantown Avenue
Philadelphia, PA 19119

Abdel Ross Wentz Library
Lutheran Theological Seminary
Gettysburg, PA 17325

Both contain significant collections of Pennsylvania German congregational and pastoral records.

Lutheran Southern Seminary
4201 North Main Street
Columbia, SC 29203

Repository for Southern Lutheran church records.

Swedish-American

The congregational records of the Augustana Synod were microfilmed in the 1950s with a grant from the Wallenberg Foundation in Sweden. Since then, microfilming has been completed of other Swedish-American congregations: Evangelical Covenant, Baptist, Methodist, and Evangelical Free Church. Positive copies of the Lutheran records are in the custody of:

Mrs. Lennart Setterdahl
3452 Fourth Street
East Moline, IL 61244

Requests for information searches should be directed to her accompanied by a donation of at least $25. Requests requiring extensive searches would suggest a larger donation. Checks can be made out to the LCA Archives or to Mrs. Setterdahl. She would also be able to supply information about the location of the other denominations.

The LCA Archives in Chicago will not loan copies of the microfilms nor are the records available for on-site use. However, copies of the films can be purchased with the approval of its congregation. Ms Elizabeth Wittman, Associate Archivist, can give permission to use the records of defunct congregations. Microfilm prices depend on the size of the roll and begin at $18. Address all inquiries regarding purchase of Swedish-American Lutheran congregational records to:

Archives of the Lutheran Church in America
1100 East 55th Street
Chicago, IL 60615

Inquiries regarding non-Lutheran Swedish-American church records should be addressed to Mrs. Setterdahl or to the archive of the pertinent denomination.

3. The Lutheran Church-Missouri Synod is concentrated in the Midwest. This church is the most theologically conservative of the three major Lutheran denominations. Largely German in background, it also contains some Slovak Lutheran congregations. It supports the *Concordia Historical Institute*, which publishes a quarterly journal and acts as a clearinghouse for information on locating church records.

Concordia Historical Institute
Department of Archives and History
The Lutheran Church-Missouri Synod
801 De Mun Avenue
St. Louis, MO 63103

The Wisconsin Evangelical Lutheran Church, commonly known as the Wisconsin Synod, maintains an archives at:

Historical Institute of the Wisconsin
Evangelical Lutheran Church
The Wisconsin Evangelical Lutheran
Seminary
11831 North Seminary Drive
Mequon, WI 53092

This denomination is ultra-conservative in its doctrinal position. German-American in background, its congregations are concentrated in the upper Midwest with a scattering elsewhere.

For information about the smaller Lutheran synods, consult August Suelflow's paper, "Records of the Lutheran Church in America," previously cited.

An excellent tool for determining which Lutheran synod the ancestor's church belongs to is the *Lutheran Church Directory for the United States*, published annually by Lutheran Council in the U.S., 315 Park Avenue South, New York, NY 10010. This directory lists the name, address, and synodical affiliation of more than 95 percent of the Lutheran churches in the United States.

Mennonite

The Mennonite Encyclopedia: A Comprehensive Reference Work on the Anabaptist-Mennonite Movement. 4 vols. Hillsboro, Kan.: Mennonite Brethren Publishing House, 1955-59.

Major collections are in:

The Archives of the Mennonite Church
1700 South Main
Goshen, IN 46526

Center for Mennonite Brethren Studies
4824 East Butler
Fresno, CA 93727

Mennonite Historical Library
Bluffton College
Bluffton, OH 45817

Mennonite Library & Archives
Bethel College
North Newton, KS 67117

Simons Historical Library and Archives
Eastern Mennonite College
Harrisonburg, VA 22801

Methodist

General Commission on Archives and History of the United Methodist Church. *The Directory*. Madison, N.J.: United Methodist Church, 1981. Contains a current listing of the Commissions on Archives and History for each Annual Conference in the United States; it is these commissions which are beginning to preserve local church records.

Harmon, Nolan B., ed. *The Encyclopedia of World Methodism*. Prepared and edited under the supervision of the World Methodist Council and the Commission on Archives and History.

Nashville: United Methodist Publishing House, 1974. 2 vols. Locations of archives of some of the smaller Methodist churches are listed under the heading of "Archives." Since the publication date there may have been some changes.

Little, Brooks R. *Methodist Union Catalog of History, Biography, Disciplines, and Hymnals*. Lake Junalaska, N.C.: Association of Methodist Historical Societies, 1967.

Ness, John, Jr. "Church Records of the United States: Methodist Records," a paper delivered at the World Conference on Records and Genealogical Seminar, 5-8 Aug. 1969, Salt Lake City, sponsored by the Church of Jesus Christ of Latter-day Saints, Area I, 4 and 5b.

Williams, Robert H. "Methodist Church Trials in Illinois, 1824-1960," *Methodist History* 1 (1962): 14-32.

Major collections are in:

United Methodist Archives Center
General Commission on Archives and
History of the United Methodist Church
Drew University
Madison, NJ 07940

Moved from Lake Junaluska, North Carolina, in 1982.

Archives of Indiana United Methodism
Roy O. West Library
DePauw University
Greencastle, IN 46153

Much of this collection has been microfilmed and is in the Genealogical Library in Salt Lake City, Utah.

William R. Perkins Library
Manuscript Department
Duke University
Durham, NC 27706

Pitts Theology Library
Emory University
Atlanta, GA 30322

Garrett Evangelical Theological
Seminary Library
2121 Sheridan
Evanston, IL 60201

The Historical Center of the Free
Methodist Church
Winona Lake, IN 46590

Methodist Historical Library
Perkins School of Theology
Southern Methodist University
Dallas, TX 75222

New England Methodist Historical
Society Library
Boston University
School of Theology
745 Commonwealth Avenue
Boston, MA 02215

Pacific School of Religion
Charles Holbrook Library
1798 Scenic Avenue
Berkeley, CA 94709

For Swedish-American Methodist congregational records contact:

Mrs. Lennart Setterdahl
3452 Fourth Street
East Moline, IL 61244

Moravian

Hamilton, Rt. Rev. Kenneth G. "The Resources of the Moravian Church Archives," *Pennsylvania History* 27 (1960): 263-72.

Wallace, Paul A. W. "The Moravian Records," *Indiana Magazine of History* 48 (1952): 141-60.

The Archives of the Moravian Church
1228 Main Street
Bethlehem, PA 18018

Moravian Archives
Southern Provinces of the Moravian Church
Drawer M
Salem Station
Winston-Salem, NC 27108

Moravian Historical Society
Nazareth, PA 18064

Presbyterian

Miller, William B. "Church Records of the United States: Presbyterian," a paper delivered at the World Conference on Records and Genealogical Seminar, 5-8 Aug. 1969, Salt Lake City, sponsored by the Church of Jesus Christ of Latter-day Saints, Area I, 4 and 5c.

Union Catalog of Presbyterian Manuscripts, Presbyterian Library Association, 1964. Lists Presbyterian and Reformed records.

Local church records are generally scattered because no uniform provision was made until relatively recently to preserve local records.

Major collections are in:

Historical Foundation of the Presbyterian
and Reformed Churches
Assembly Drive
Box 847
Montreat, NC 28757

Strongest on Presbyterian Church records in the South. See Thomas H. Spence, Jr. *The Historical Foundation and Its Treasures*. Montreat, N.C.: Historical Foundation, 1960.

McCormick Theological Seminary
McGaw Library
800 West Belden Avenue
Chicago, IL 60614

Presbyterian Historical Society
United Presbyterian Church in the U.S.A.
425 Lombard Street
Philadelphia, PA 19147

This large collection includes the Presbyterian Biographical Index, a card index to periodicals, newspapers, and books for both clergy and laymen.

Princeton Theological Seminary
Speer Library
Mercer Street and Library Place
Princeton, NJ 08540

Protestant Episcopal

Bellamy, V. Nelle. "Church Records of the United States: Protestant Episcopal," a paper delivered at the World Conference on Records and Genealogical Serminar, 5-8 Aug. 1969, Salt Lake City, sponsored by the Church of Jesus Christ of Latter-day Saints, Area I, 6 and 7d. Good explanation; no bibliography.

Greenwood, Val. *The Researcher's Guide to American Genealogy.* Baltimore. Genealogical Publishing Co., 1973, pp. 363-73. Good examples of Protestant Episcopal records.

McQueen, Edith E. "The Commissary in Colonial Maryland," *Maryland Historical Magazine* 25 (1930): 190 ff. The church exercised probate authority in early Maryland.

Oliver, David B. "The Society for the Propagation of the Gospel in the Province of North Carolina," *Proceedings, North Carolina Historical Society*. Beaufort: North Carolina Historical Society 9 (1910).

Painter, Bordon W. *The Anglican Vestry in Colonial America.* New Haven, Conn.: Yale University Press, 1965. The vestry exercised local government functions as well as church administrations. Vestry minutes for most of the Episcopal parishes in Virginia have been printed by the Virginia Historical Society and can be found in many research libraries. These are also available on microfilm through the Genealogical Society of Utah and its branches.

No central depository for Protestant Episcopal records exists. The earliest records are part of the archives of the Church of England with microfilm copies in the Library of Congress and at the University of Texas. Do not overlook the collection at Lambeth Palace Library in London, which includes correspondence, reports, subsidies to settlers, and other materials for colonial congregations and the records of the Society for the Propagation of the Gospel in Foreign Parts, which sponsored several European protestant congregations in America and sent more than 300 missionaries.

Begin searching in the parish first. If the rector doesn't know, often a diocesan registrar or historiographer can indicate where a parish register is located. The current number of *The Episcopal Church Annual* will indicate current names and addresses for parishes and dioceses.

Some records are in secular libraries and archives. Some have been published.

Pentecostal

Oral Roberts University Library
777 South Lewis
Tulsa, OK 74105

Quakers (Society of Friends)

Quaker records rank among the very best available. They form a striking exception to the generalization that "dissenting" church records do not match the quality of "established" church records.

Comfort, William W. "Quaker Marriage Certificates," *Friends Historical Bulletin* 40 (1951): 67-80.

Elliott, Erro T. *Quakers in the American Frontier: History of the Westward Migrations, Settlements, and Developments of Friends on the American Continent.* Richmond, Ind.: Friends United Press, 1969.

Greenwood, Val. *The Researcher's Guide to American Genealogy.* Baltimore: Genealogical Publishing Co., 1973, pp. 377-85.

Heiss, Willard. "American Quaker Records and Family History," *World Conference on Records: Preserving our Heritage*, 12-15 Aug. 1980. Salt Lake City: Church of Jesus Christ of Latter-day Saints, 1969, vol. 4, ser. 350. Besides reviewing the Quaker records, he provides a list of records in print, a bibliography about Quakers, and suggestions for locating the records.

________. "Church Records of the United States: Quaker Records in America: Records with an Extra Dimension," a paper delivered Aug. 1969, Salt Lake City, sponsored by the Church of Jesus Christ of Latter-day Saints. Area I, 6, and 7c. Contains points not discussed in the cited paper.

________, *Guide to Research in Quaker Records in the Midwest.* Indianapolis: Indiana Quaker Records, 1962.

________. *A List of All Friends Meetings That Have Ever Existed in Indiana, 1807-1955.* Indianapolis: John Woolman Press, 1961.

________. *Quakers in the South Carolina Back Country: Wateree and Bush River.* Indianapolis: Quaker Records, 1969.

Hinshaw, William Wade, ed. *Encyclopedia of American Quaker Genealogy.* 6 vols. 1936: reprint ed., Baltimore: Genealogical Publishing Co., 1969.

Jacobsen, Phebe R. *Quaker Records in Maryland,* Annapolis: Hall of Records, 1966.

Jones, Rufus M. *The Quakers in the American Colonies.* New York: Russell and Russell, 1962. Reprint of 1911 edition. Describes original Congregations in each area.

Williams, Ethel W. "Quaker Records" in her *Know Your Ancestors.* Rutland, Vt.: Charles E. Tuttle Co., 1960, pp. 119-37. Less detail on the records themselves than on printed records and locations; strong for Indiana Quakers.

Continued for Indiana by Willard Heiss. *Abstracts of Records of the Society of Friends in Indiana (Volume VII: Encyclopedia of American Quaker Genealogy).* 7 vols. Indianapolis: Indiana Historical Society, 1965-77.

Major collections are in:

Friends Historical Library
(Hicksite Records)
Swarthmore College
Swarthmore, PA 19081

Magill Historical Library
Haverford College
Haverford, PA 19041

Quaker Collection
Guilford College Library
Guilford, NC 27410

Reformed

Dutch

Christian Reformed
Colonial Origins Collection
Calvin College and Seminary
Grand Rapids, MI 49056

General

Holland Society of New York
Manuscript Collection
122 East 58th
New York, NY 10022

Archives of the Reformed Church
in America
New Brunswick Theological Seminary
21 Seminary Place
New Brunswick, NJ 08901

German

See United Church of Christ

For other Reformed churches see *Yearbook of American and Canadian Churches.*

Roman Catholic

Curran, Francis X., S.J. *Catholics in Colonial Law.* Chicago: Loyola University Press, 1965. Discusses legal restrictions, which are also sources useful for identifying Catholics, colony by colony.

Ellis, John Tracy. *Catholics in Colonial America*. Baltimore: Helicon Press, 1963.

Hennesey, James, S. J. "Square Peg in a Round Hole: On Being Roman Catholic in America," *Records of the American Catholic Historical Society of Philadelphia* (1973): 167-95.

McAvoy, Thomas T. "Catholic Archives and Manuscript Collections," *American Archivist* 27 (1964): 409-14.

Vollman, Edward R., S. J. *The Catholic Church in America: An Historical Bibliography*. New York: Scarecrow Press, 1972.

O'Toole, James M. "The Roman Catholic Family in North America: Family History as Viewed Through Catholic Church Records," *World Conference on Records: Preserving our Heritage*, 12-15 Aug. 1980. Salt Lake City: Church of Jesus Christ of Latter-day Saints, 1980, vol. 3, series 317.

Shellem, Rev. John J. "Church Records of the United States: Roman Catholic Sacramental Records," a paper delivered at the World Conference on Records and Genealogical Seminar, 5-8 Aug. 1969, Salt Lake City, sponsored by the Church of Jesus Christ of Latter-day Saints, area I, 4 and 5c. Includes excellent examples.

Start your search in the locality where the ancestral family lived. Inquire at the parish level first and then the diocese. The *Official Catholic Directory*, published annually by P. J. Kenedy & Sons, Box 265, Skokie, IL 60077, provides current addresses for both.

Some old Catholic records have been deposited in local and state historical societies and other secular libraries.

Major collections are in:

Arhives of the University of Notre Dame
South Bend, IN 46624
Archdiocese of New Orleans Records (1576-1865)

Department of Archives and Manuscripts
Catholic University of America
Washington DC 20019

See *Studies in American Church History* published by Catholic University Press for specific accounts and records in various states. Ca. 35 vols.

St. Mary's Seminary and University
Roland Park
Baltimore, MD 21210

Georgetown University
Washington DC 20007

St. Louis University
St. Louis, MO 63103

Salvation Army

Archives and Research Center
Salvation Army
New York, NY 10011

Schwenkfelder

Schwenkfelder Library
Seminary Avenue
Pennsburg, PA 18073

Shakers

Western Reserve Historical Society
History Library
10825 East Boulevard
Cleveland, OH 44106

Unitarian and Universalist

Archives of the Unitarian-Universalist Association
25 Beacon Street
Boston, MA 02108

Harvard University Divinity School
Andover-Harvard Theological Library
Manuscript Department
45 Francis Avenue
Cambridge, MA 02138

Meadville Theological School of
Lombard College
Library
5701 South Woodlawn Avenue
Chicago, IL 60637

United Church of Christ

This church resulted from a merger of the Evangelical and Reformed Church (largely German in background) and the General Council of the Congregational Churches.

Clark, Elmer T. *The Small Sects in America*. New York: Abingdon Press, 1965. Discusses records as well as groups.

Hinke, William J. "German Reformed Church Records in Pennsylvania." *National Genealogical Society Quarterly* 37 (1949): 33-38. Excellent discussion of records.

Rosenberger, Francis C. "German Church Records of the Shenandoah Valley as a Genealogical Source," *Virginia Magazine of History and Biography* 66 (1958): 195-200.

Congregational

Congregational Library
14 Beacon Street
Boston, MA 02108

Divinity Library and University Library
Yale University
New Haven, CT 06520

Hartford Theological Seminary Library
Hartford, CT 06105

Harvard Divinity School Library
Cambridge,MA 02140

Historical Commission of the United Church of Christ
Lancaster Archives
555 West James Street
Lancaster, PA 17603

Evangelical and Reformed

Eden Archives
475 East Lockwood Avenue
Webster Grove, MO 63119

Holds materials from the largely Midwestern Evangelical Synod of North America, a German-American body which merged with the Reformed Church in the United States in 1934 to form the Evangelical and Reformed Church, and later became part of the United Church of Christ.

Evangelical and Reformed Historical Society
Franklin and Marshall College
555 West James Street
Lancaster, PA 17603

Contains a very important collection of early Pennsylvania German Reformed church records.

An extremely useful guide for locating current United Church of Christ (UCC) congregations is *Yearbook United Church of Christ* published annually by UCC, 297 Park Avenue South, New York, NY 10010. Usually a local UCC congregation will have a copy.

Bibliography of Finding Aids

Ganstadt, Edwin Scott. *Historical Atlas of Religions in America*. New York: Harper & Row, 1962. An important research tool.

Pettee, Julia. *List of Churches: Official Forms of the Names for Denominational Bodies with Brief Descriptive and Historical Notes*. Chicago: American Library Association, 1948. Includes names before the many mergers of the ecumenical movement.

Rodda, Dorothy. *Directory of Church Libraries*. Philadelphia: Drexel Press, 1967.

Ruoss, George M. *World Directory of Theological Libraries*. Metuchen, N.J.: Scarecrow Press, 1968.

Sweet, William Warren. *Religion on the American Frontier, 1783- 1840: A Collection of Source Materials*. 4 vols. New York: Cooper Square Publishers, 1964. Covers Baptists, Methodists, Congregationalists, Presbyterians; gives history and reproduces minister journals, letters, and diaries, missionary records, conference minutes.

INFORMATION GUIDE

Genealogical Information in the Record Group	*Court*	*Jury*	*Probate*	*Adoption*	*Vigilante*	*Ku Kluk Klan*
Surname/name	●	●	●	●	●	●
Date of Birth				●		
Place of Birth	●			●	●	●
Sex	●				●	●
Race/color	●					●
Physical Description				●	●	●
Occupation	●	●	●	●	●	●
Education			●	●	●	●
Military Service	●				●	●
Slave Status	●			●	●	●
Property Owned			●	●		●
Religion			●	●		
Citizenship	●	●	●		●	
Marital Status	●		●	●	●	●
Spouse's Name			●	●	●	●
Children's Names			●	●	●	●
Father's Name			●	●		●
Mother's Name			●	●		●
Father's Birthplace						
Mother's Birthplace						
Date of Death	●		●		●	●
Cause of Death	●					●
Name of Cemetery			●			
Residence	●	●	●	●	●	●
Age	●	●	●	●	●	●
Literacy/signature	●	●				●
Photograph/sketch						

COULD YOU USE THIS CHAPTER?

Type of Record	*Kept from*	*Clues That You Should Consult These Records*
Civil, criminal, and equity courts	All periods	"Court day" was a whole-community occasion for gathering, gossipping, and observing the struggles for justice. Courts also had functions long since taken over by government offices, such as issuing licenses, appointing overseers of roads, and other community functions. In short, if court records exist for the area where you have located an ancestor, consult them. Civil, criminal, and equity proceedings are all actions brought – lawsuits between individuals, the state pursuing a charged criminal, or appeal for redress of wrongs. Most case files include lengthy, sometimes verbatim testimony that can round out the data on your ancestors: disclose migration patterns, supply birth or death dates, identify missing maiden names, and distinguish between two people of the same name. Sample cases of each of these three types will acquaint you with legal terminology and "walk you through" so that you can see which actions legally lead to others.
Probate records	All periods	Although only about 50 percent – and sometimes only 25 percent – of property-holding men in a given area made wills, filed them, and had them proved, they can be invaluable in establishing family relationships, death dates, and the marriages of daughters – all of them very difficult to establish in areas where other records are sparse. This chapter will describe how to locate and use wills. Even if a will is not proved, if it can be located in the courthouse records it can supply the same valuable information.
Special courts	Varies in each jurisdiction	Many special courts exist to handle particular legal functions or to fill an administrative gap where other government machinery was not available. Did your ancestors live on a stream or river that emptied into the sea? Perhaps their legal matters were handled by admiralty courts. Was anyone in your family adopted? Different courts handled this function but you can find out, state by state, which records to check. Specific courts were also assigned responsibility for name changes. Courts of claims heard cases from individuals who suffered property loss during wars or engagements with the Indians. An ancestor in the military might appear in court-martial records. Vigilante groups, extra-legal societies, and mining districts set up their own informal systems of justice, consciously based on forms and procedures observed in established courts. Blacks (slaves) and Native Americans also appear in separate courts.

Chapter 6

AMERICAN COURT RECORDS

Arlene H. Eakle

Importance of Courts in American Society

Even today, few people escape mention in court records at some time during their lives as witnesses, litigants, jurors, appointees to office, or as petition signators. However, Americans of a few generations ago also expected to attend their local court proceedings when it was in session. It was a civic duty. Furthermore, they could be fined if they did not.

The predominantly English heritage set a tradition of equitable and just court processes, in which the people had a right to participate actively.[1] A majority of colonists were Englishmen, and they were used to seeking redress in court. With relative freedom from royal supervision in the New World and court enforcement of religious as well as civil laws, American courts tried many matters not subject to court action in other parts of the British Empire and now considered too minor to warrant criminal action. Until the time of the Civil War in many places, criminal prosecutions included gossip, witchcraft, scolding a husband, being publicly disrespectful to the minister, and refusing to attend church services. Indeed, some of these "blue laws" as they were called, are still on the books today, although they are unenforced.[2]

The advantages for the genealogist are considerable. It is not unusual for a single case to involve between seventy-five and a hundred people, naming them all.

Local courts were units of government as well as judicial bodies. They issued licenses to lawyers, physicians, merchants, peddlers, ordinaries (public inns), midwives, ferries, and clergy; regulated apprenticeships; established weights and measures; provided for inspection of goods and services; ordered the destruction of harmful pests and beasts, paid bounties for heads, tails, and skins; oversaw education for orphans and the poor; built housing for the maimed or poor, sometimes in conjunction with the local church; built roads and bridges and oversaw their maintenance; called local militia units to muster; assessed taxes and collected them.[3]

Most of these administrative functions are now filled by county commissions, city councils, and other administrative agencies established for that purpose, each with its own records.

The court also served a social function in bringing a region's people together regularly. Court week, every three months was a festive occasion. Monday morning the courthouse buzzed with activity as people argued about the cases on the docket and gossiped together. Deeds were registered, wills probated, taxes paid, county records audited, elections held, courtships begun, and marriages contracted. Sessions were often juggled to avoid planting and harvest time so most of the people could attend.

On Saturday afternoon, the janitor swept out the courtroom; the judges shook hands all around and prepared to start hearings in adjoining localities the following Monday. In between, the court measured, almost precisely, the moral, physical, spiritual, and economic condition of the people within its jurisdiction. A scolding wife, a quarrelsome neighbor, a Sabbath card-player, the owner of cattle wandering beyond their bounds, a dangerous liberal who freed his slaves and gave them land, an alien (non-English before 1776 or non-American after) applying for citizenship so he could buy a farm; a blind man applying for tax-exempt status – all of these and many, many more "ordinary" citizens appeared in court.

When the courthouse burns, lost records will be reconstructed as far as possible, so that legal business can continue. In short, it is safe to say that even the most modest individuals before World War I in America will appear in court records at least once during their lifetimes.

If court records are so important for genealogical information, why do genealogists hesitate to use them? The answer is simple – they are or appear to be more complicated than census records. Indexes are incomplete, the records seem difficult to decipher, and there are so many of them.

This chapter will acquaint you with legal terms, teach you how to read court material, tell you where to find the records, and describe what you can expect to find in civil, criminal, equity, and probate court records.

Legal Terms

Laws, or the rules of conduct by which society is governed, consist of case law (decisions of the courts based on local custom and common usage or "common law") and statute law (legislative enactment).

The basic law of most states is the common law inherited from England, and based on custom and usage. It is what "seems fair" in a community but is articulated in judicial interpretations, opinions, minutes, and orders. Legislative assemblies enact laws for situations not covered by common law or where a serious disagreement exists about what's "fair." In certain instances, a statute is designed specifically to change or nullify local custom. For example, when a local blue law required closing business houses so employees could attend church, "fairness" worked a hardship on Seventh-day Adventists or Jews since their Sabbath falls on Saturday. Local authorities, by drafting a law making Sunday closing optional, thus changed the custom.

Judicial jurisdiction is the fundamental authority of a court to hear a controversy between parties, to consider the merits of each side, and to render a decision which is binding upon the parties involved.

Original jurisdiction is the authority to commence a case, to hear it for the first time. Civil cases under forty shillings in value were tried first before a justice of the peace in colonial times, and today before small claims courts.

Appellate jurisdiction is the authority to review, upon request, questions of law which arise in the trial of a case. Not all cases can be appealed. The jurisdiction of appeals courts determines the cases acceptable for review.

Exclusive jurisdiction is the sole authority to try a case. Only a federal court can try a case involving citizens of two different states.

Concurrent jurisdiction means that more than one court may try the same case. Litigants choose which court to use.

General jurisdiction is the authority to try almost any case brought before the court except for a few limitations set by law.

Special jurisdiction is the authority to handle specific matters – probate, divorce, military personnel, etc. Often these courts also have exclusive jurisdiction to try their cases.

Limited jurisdiction is the authority of a court to try cases specified by law only or involving less than certain sums of money. Justice of the Peace Courts are limited courts.

The parties in a legal conflict include the plaintiff, who seeks a remedy under the law and starts legal action against the defendant, who must answer the charge. Either party may be represented by legal counsel or power of attorney.

All cases brought before a court of law are called legal actions. There are three main types.

1. Civil actions (person vs. person) arise over injuries done by one individual to the physical being, the property – real or personal – or the reputation of another. Suit is brought to enforce private rights or to seek compensation for injuries. The parties are often encouraged to settle matters out of court. The most common civil actions are torts – property damage, trespass, libel, assault, negligence, and so on.

2. Criminal actions (state or people vs. person) involve the protection of society. This type of case can never be settled out of court, although modern plea-bargaining can reduce or eliminate punishment. Criminal offenses include felonies (murder, robbery, burglary, and rape) and misdemeanors (petty theft, vagrancy, drunkenness, prostitution, and breaking the Sabbath).

The basic difference between civil and criminal actions is visible when you ask, "Does the offense threaten a well-ordered society?" When a man backs his automobile into his neighbor's car, his neighbor can sue for damages. This is a civil case. However, drunk driving threatens anyone on the same road and thus can be prosecuted as a criminal offense.

3. In equity actions, the case is determined by "reasonable justice" and "common good" because legal remedies are inadequate or because enforcing the full letter of the law would be unjust. For example, a man borrows money to buy land. He agrees to repay the money with interest by a specific date or forfeit the land. If he is unable to pay, he could be held to the letter of the law and lose all he has invested. The money owed, however, may be less than the value of the land. The court can order the land sold, pay the money owed, and give the man what remains. This is a fairer solution.

Equity actions usually involve property rights. The remedy of the court could be an order of specific performance – to deliver goods promised, to restore animals to their proper owner, to replace equipment damaged, or to rewrite a document or report. It could be a mandatory injunction to prevent a certain action. It could also be a bill of account for monies spent in a guardianship. Probate, divorce, and adoption are equity actions.

Few jurisdictions have three separate courts, each handling a specific action. Most have one judicial body which handles them all, although it may clearly indicate which hat is worn: "The Court of Rhea County sitting in equity. . ." or "The Criminal Court of Rhea County."

The United States judicial system is a dual one with national (federal) courts whose personnel are appointed by the federal government to adjudicate (try) cases under the United States Constitution or federal statutory law; and a system of state courts whose personnel are elected/appointed to try cases under state constitutions, statutory laws, and local custom. Both systems have two types of courts:

1. Trial courts where cases originate. The jury, or in its absence, the judge, decides what happened and whether, within a given rule of law, the facts constitute guilt or innocence of the accused. Trial courts make up the majority of our system.

2. Appellate courts to which a losing party can appeal for further consideration of the case. These courts may, but usually do not, call witnesses or have juries. The court accepts the evidence of the previous trial presented in the form of a brief or trial resumé, and then reviews points of law where an error has been made in the earlier trial. Some appellate courts also have original jurisdiction.

Figures 6-1, 6-2, and 6-3 show the relationships between trial and appeals courts. They also will introduce the variety of courts you can expect to find as you research your family lines.

Genealogists will encounter many new terms and legal phrases in court records, too many to list here. Standard references are *Black's Law Dictionary*, available in every good public library, county law library, and university or college library. Most college bookstores carry the current edition. Another is William C. Burton, *Legal Thesaurus* (New York: Macmillan, 1981). This special thesaurus is designed for quick recall of nuances and double meanings of words with legal applications. It includes some 5,000 legal terms, definitions of foreign phrases, and a valuable every-word index.

Court Procedures

Court procedures differ slightly from state to state, and three-plus centuries in America have also seen evolution, yet many date from the Middle Ages. On 1 June 1872, federal courts changed their procedural rules to conform to those of the state within which they were located. A walk-through of civil, criminal, and equity actions will define basic words and let you understand what is happening in court minutes and on the dockets.[4]

Starting the Action (Pleadings) in Civil Cases

Every civil case starts suit by issuing a writ of summons, a command which notifies the offender to appear before the court to answer charge. The clerk, upon request of the plaintiff or an attorney, issues the writ under the court's authority.

The court directs the sheriff or constable to serve the writ of summons on the defendant. In most jurisdictions, the defendant must receive it personally; but in a few, the sheriff can leave it with an adult member of the family or with someone in charge at the place of business. In most cases an action cannot proceed until the writ has actually been served. The notable exception is in divorce actions. The writ may be published in newspapers when the defendant is outside of the court's jurisdiction, or when his/her whereabouts are unknown. The usual procedure is for the sheriff to produce the original writ, tell the defendant its contents, and leave him/her a copy. The sheriff will then make out a return, usually on the back of the original writ, stating where, when, and upon whom he has served it, sign it, and return it to the clerk of the court on or before the return day specified in the writ. The writ and the return are filed in the case file or packet as part of the permanent record of the case.

The next step is the filing of the plaintiff's claim. This pleading may be called a statement of claim, a complaint, or a petition. The purpose of the declaration or petition is to explain clearly the plaintiff's reason for taking action so the defendant knows the nature of the claim and so that there is "a cause of action sufficient in law" to justify a judgment in favor of the plaintiff. The declaration and notice are filed with the court clerk, and a copy is served on the defendant or his attorney. In some jurisdictions, only the attorneys exchange pleadings, not filing them with the clerk of the court until they have been completed or until a judgment may be entered.

The defendant then counters with an answer or affidavit of defense admitting or denying the various claims contained in the plaintiff's declaration. It may also present new information bearing on the defense. It is filed with the court clerk, and a copy is served upon the plaintiff or his attorney. If the defendant fails to file an answer within the time allowed by law, the plaintiff is entitled upon motion of the court to enter judgment by default for "failure to file

Figure 6-1

The Colonial Court System, Early to 1775

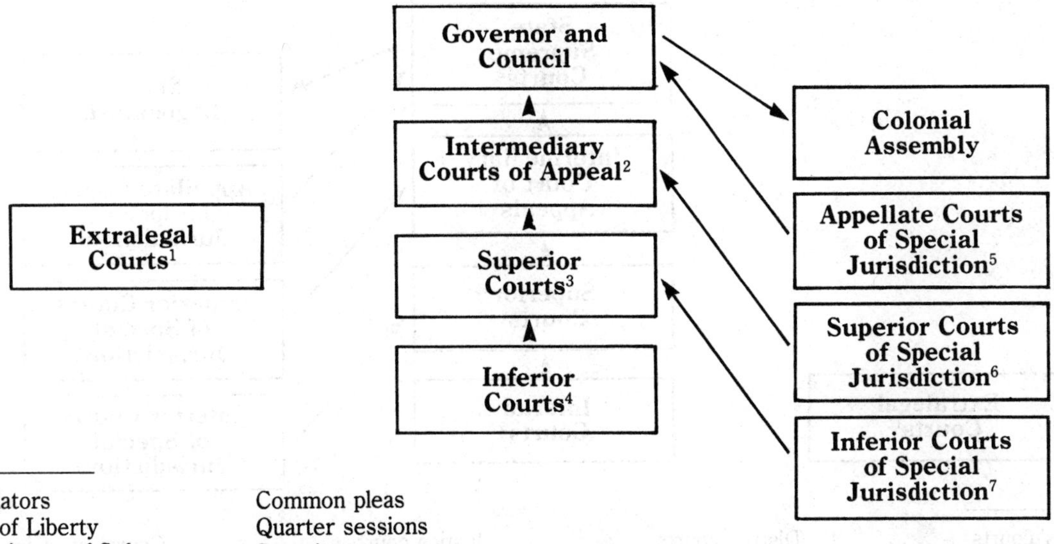

1. Regulators
   Sons of Liberty
   Committees of Safety
   Miners' courts
2. Chief Justice courts
   Court of common rights
   County courts
   Common pleas
   Quarter sessions
   Superior courts
   District courts
   Circuit courts of appeal
   Supreme courts
   Courts of assize
3. District courts
   Circuit courts
   County courts
   Common pleas
   Quarter sessions
   Superior courts
   Recorders' courts
   General sessions
   Civil courts of record
   Criminal courts of record
   Mayors' courts
   Borough courts
4. Mayors' courts
   City courts
   Justice courts
   Municipal courts
   Small claims courts
   Police courts
   Magistrates' courts
   County courts
5. Prerogative courts
   Courts of delegates
6. Chancery courts
   Courts of common right
   Admiralty courts
   Oyer and terminer
   Gaol delivery
   Courts of assize
   Probate courts
   Orphans' courts
   Surrogate courts
   Courts of ordinary
   Courts of exchequer
   Court of claims
   Merchants' courts
   Pie-powder (fair) courts
   Ecclesiastical courts
   Courts martial
   Courts of leftenancy
7. Parish vestry courts
   Courts of examination
   Ships' courts
   Coroners' courts
   Court baron
   Court leet
   Customary courts
   Slave courts
   Courts of conciliation
   Courts of arbitration

and answer." The clerk enters the judgment in the court records, and the court provides for the enforcement of the judgment.

When the declaration and answer have been filed, and if the case has not been judged before, then it is "at issue"—ready for trial before a judge and jury. In many courts, the parties can waive a jury trial and elect to have their case tried before the judge alone. The case is then scheduled on the court's docket.

Most jurisdictions encourage litigating parties to settle their case out of court: it saves time, money, and anger. When it happens, the clerk usually notes it in the court records. Some jurisdictions require that civil cases under a certain amount be brought before a court of arbitration or conciliation before a trial. At this point, there are certain motions which can be entered to delay (stay) judgment. These motions pertain to points of law (legal technicalities). A record of them and their disposition is also part of the case file.

Starting the Action (Pleadings) in Criminal Cases

When a crime has been committed, the offender must be brought, by some legal process, before a tribunal to hear the complaint and take appropriate action. Before the days of organized law enforcement, in any locality, the citizens of a community were responsible to see that offenses were reported and the offenders physically brought to court (presentment). Presentment could be made by a private person, a constable, town watch, selectmen of the town, elected town presenters, grand jurors, government officials, a paid informer, churchwardens, tithingmen, or by the court itself. For example, during the seventeenth century, the English tithing system was established in some colonies for short periods of time. Every male over twelve was enrolled in a tithing (usually ten households), and one was appointed tithingman, responsible to inspect the households under his supervision regularly that "sin and disorder may be prevented and suppressed," to see that everyone attended church on Sunday and kept the day holy, retired at curfew, and did not play cards or engage in other illegal gaming. The tithingman had to report offenders to the court or be fined. Today, the injured person or the state acting for society as a whole, enters its complaint. The court orders the offender to be summoned, usually by means of a warrant or writ of capias issued to some authorized officer (the sheriff, marshall, or other police officer). The officer takes the person named in the writ into custody and usually holds him/her in jail. This officer must produce the accused before the court at a specified time for a hearing. If the detention is legal, the person will be recommitted to jail. If not, he/she will be released on bail to await trial.

Bail is the posting of a bond in a set amount of money to insure that the accused will appear in court. In default of bail, the accused

Figure 6-2

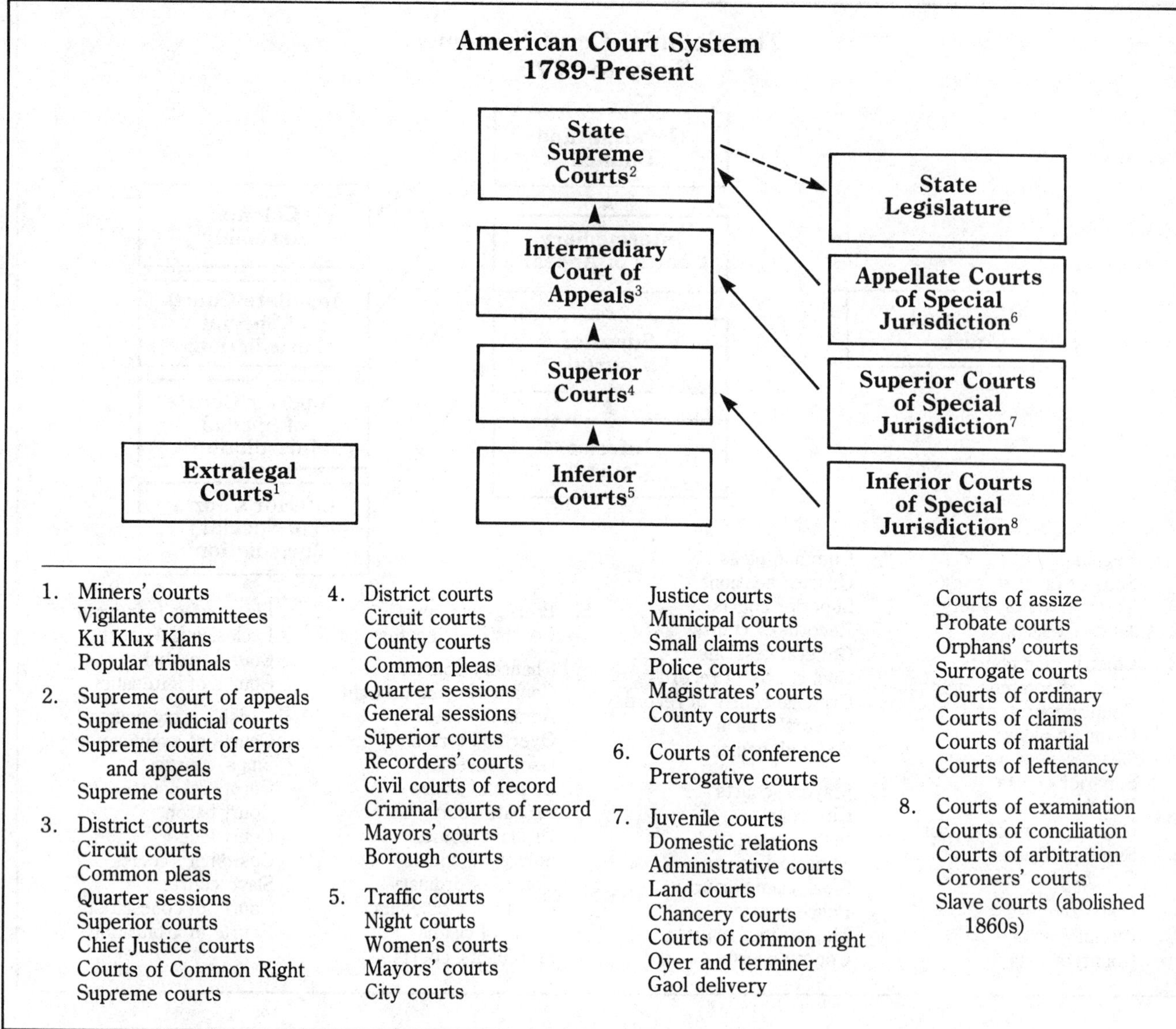

is committed to jail and kept in custody until the case is disposed of by trial or appeal. Capital crimes may have no provisions for bail.

If the crime is minor, the matter may be disposed of by a summary trial before the magistrate without a jury. For example, if the police arrest a vagrant upon the street without a formal complaint having been made, the magistrate decides both facts and law. The amount of the fine or the type of punishment a magistrate may impose is limited by statute.

In most cases, however, the next step is a preliminary hearing held before a magistrate to determine if the evidence against the accused is sufficient to justify holding him/her for trial. Guilt or innocence is not the issue. Witnesses will often be called to testify, and the court in some jurisdictions requires the testimony to be written, attested, and signed by the witnesses.

The magistrate must prepare a copy of the hearing and the case, usually within a limited number of days, to send to the court where the trial is to take place. It contains the name of the defendant, the nature of the charge, the names of the prosecutors and witnesses (sometimes their evidence), the information upon which the arrest was made, and the bail bond.

In the case of murder, the coroner holds an inquest before a jury, which hears evidence and renders a verdict about the cause of death. The coroner then provides a return to the court based upon this semi-judicial investigation. This report is usually presented at the preliminary hearing and becomes a part of the court record.

In some jurisdictions, a grand jury still considers the evidence and renders an indictment based upon the facts presented. In other jurisdictions, the grand jury has been abolished altogether and the indictment is issued by the court, based upon the preliminary hearing or the returns of the magistrate and coroner.

In the next step, the defendant is brought before the court (arraigned) to plead guilty and be sentenced at once without further trial, or not guilty and be bound over for the trial.

Collecting Testimony

At the point when the trial is scheduled, civil and criminal procedures are similar. Witnesses are summoned by subpoena to appear at the trial on behalf of the plaintiff or the defendant. If they must bring documents, the writ describes them. The sheriff, marshall, or constable must serve the subpoena directly on the witness and submit a return to the court. If the witness fails to appear at the time and place specified, a bench warrant is issued on the spot for his/her arrest, and an officer of the court goes out to find the witness.

Figure 6-3

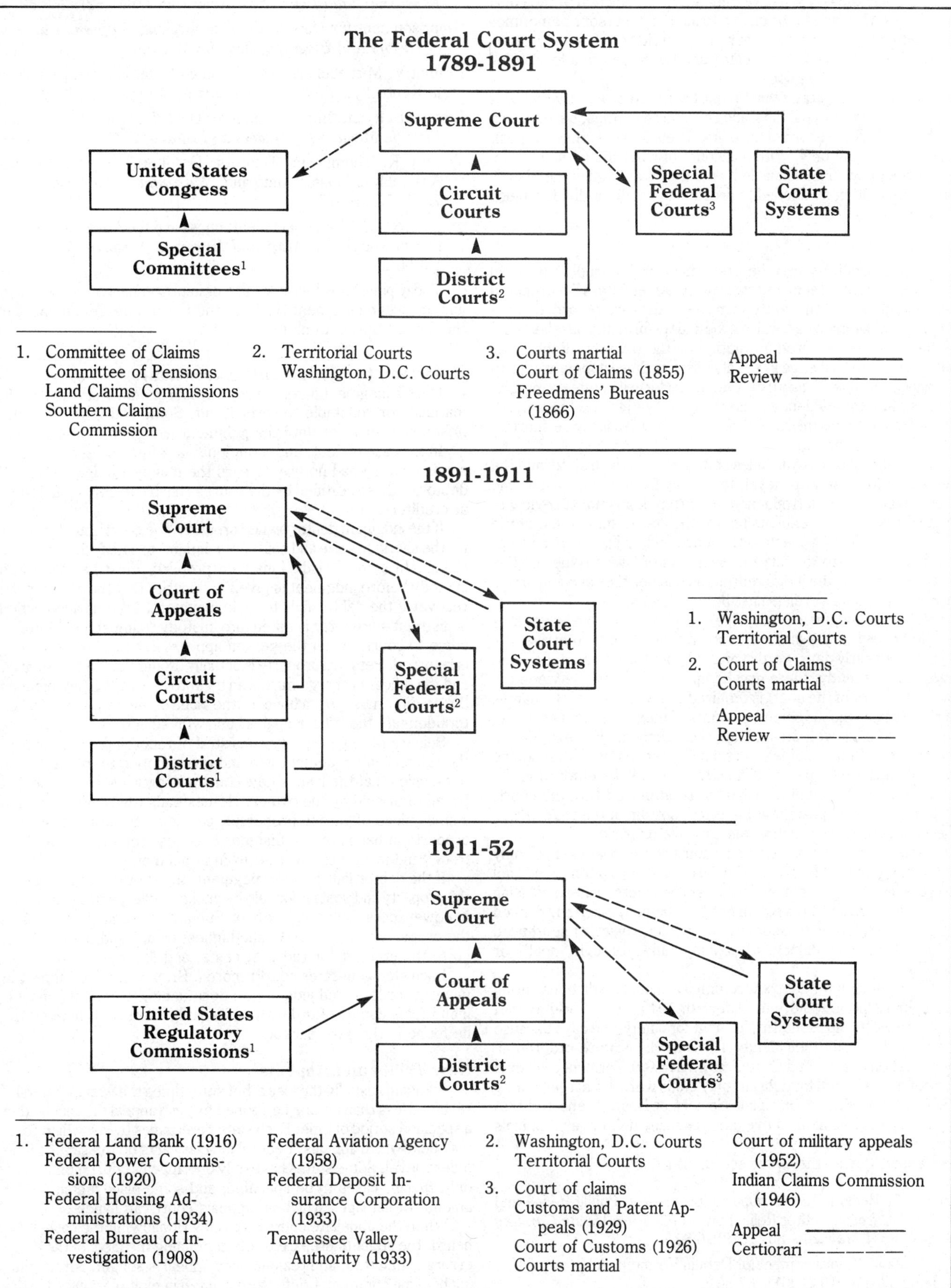
The Federal Court System
1789-1891
Supreme Court
United States Congress
Circuit Courts
Special Federal Courts[3]
State Court Systems
Special Committees[1]
District Courts[2]
1. Committee of Claims
Committee of Pensions
Land Claims Commissions
Southern Claims Commission
2. Territorial Courts
Washington, D.C. Courts
3. Courts martial
Court of Claims (1855)
Freedmens' Bureaus (1866)
Appeal
Review
1891-1911
Supreme Court
Court of Appeals
Circuit Courts
District Courts[1]
State Court Systems
Special Federal Courts[2]
1. Washington, D.C. Courts
Territorial Courts
2. Court of Claims
Courts martial
Appeal
Review
1911-52
Supreme Court
Court of Appeals
District Courts[2]
United States Regulatory Commissions[1]
State Court Systems
Special Federal Courts[3]
1. Federal Land Bank (1916)
Federal Power Commissions (1920)
Federal Housing Administrations (1934)
Federal Bureau of Investigation (1908)
Federal Aviation Agency (1958)
Federal Deposit Insurance Corporation (1933)
Tennessee Valley Authority (1933)
2. Washington, D.C. Courts
Territorial Courts
3. Court of claims
Customs and Patent Appeals (1929)
Court of Customs (1926)
Courts martial
Court of military appeals (1952)
Indian Claims Commission (1946)
Appeal
Certiorari

A representative of the court will interview and take depositions from witnesses who live outside the jurisdiction of the court or who are ill, maimed, or unable to appear in person. Sometimes the testimony consists of answers to written questions (interrogatories) prepared by the court and forwarded to a local court where the witness resides.

These written statements must be attested, and the witness must sign them. Depositions, and any interrogatories, become part of the permanent record of the court. In early cases, these depositions may be the only written account of what the witnesses actually said, especially valuable if an out-of-state family member is providing testimony needed to probate an estate or divide a piece of property.

The Trial

Trial procedures may be prescribed by law and/or by local custom. The jury is selected by drawing names from a list prepared at the beginning of the court term (these lists are recorded in the minutes) or summoning "twelve good and lawful men, housekeepers" as their names appeared in rotation on the tax rolls. Each party has the right to challenge jurors and dismiss those it feels are "prejudicial to the case." The jury is then to perform its duties impartially, based on the evidence presented. Where jury trial is waived, the judge considers the case. A nonjury trial will usually be shorter, with fewer documents.

Presenting the case includes statements by the plaintiff and the defendant (or their attorneys), testimony from the witnesses and cross-examination, introduction of written depositions, review of documents or other exhibits before the court, summation of the case with a parting speech to the judge and/or jury by each side, and instructions to the jury on the points of law at issue. At this point, the jury or the judge retires to consider the case and arrive at a verdict. The verdict must be unanimous.

Rendering judgment is the judge's responsibility. The judge relies on the verdict of the jury or personal deliberations to arrive at a decision. In early days, verdict and judgment were given the same day. More recently, there may be up to ninety days between the two. The clerk of the court is required by law to record the names of the parties, the judgment, amounts of money recovered if any, and the time allowed for meeting the judgment. For example, a money award for damages to crops and fences by a stampeding herd of cattle to be paid within sixty days, will be entered in the court record. A receipt for payment is often filed with the court, and the clerk may paste it at the top or bottom of the page where the judgment is recorded in the case file or packet.

A jail sentence before 1865 was unusual. Local jails served only to hold the accused for trial. Criminal courts were often called gaol delivery because they emptied the jails of prisoners. Instead of "doing time," the convicted person might be whipped, pilloried, ducked in cold water, forced to labor on some public project, or sentenced to pay fines and damages. Capital crimes brought death or banishment.

Imprisonment for debt was common in most jurisdictions during the colonial period and even later. In 1949, two World War II veterans were imprisoned in Vermont for ninety-one days because they could not pay their debts. The state legislature ordered an investigation, which found historically that 4,091 Vermont residents had been imprisoned for debt and only 2,085 were discharged during 1827-29. The Prison Discipline Society of Boston reported that New England jails housed five times as many debtors as criminals during the 1930s.[5]

Consult these studies for specific regions:

Robert A. Becker. "Salus populi supreme lex: Public Peace and South Carolina Debtor Relief Laws, 1763-1788." *South Carolina Historical Magazine* 80 (1979): 65-75.

H. J. Conant. "Imprisonment for Debt in Vermont: A History." *Vermont History* 19 (1951): 67-80.

Robert A. Few. "Imprisonment for Debt in Massachusetts." *Mississippi Valley Historical Review* 48 (1961-62): 252-69.

"Imprisonment for Debt in Colonial Virginia." *Virginia Magazine of History and Biography* 35 (1927): 1-6.

Emmet V. Mittlebeller. "The Decline of Imprisonment for Debt in Kentucky." *Filson Club Quarterly* 49 (1975): 169-89.

Edward L. Ryan. "Imprisonment for Debt: Its Origin and Repeal." *Virginia Magazine of History and Biography* 42 (1934): 53-58.

Tommy R. Thompson. "Debtors, Creditors, and the General Assembly in Colonial Maryland." *Maryland Historical Magazine* 72 (1977): 59-77.

__________. "Personal Indebtedness and the American Revolution in Maryland." *Maryland Historical Magazine* 73 (1978): 13-29.

Today punishment includes fine or imprisonment, or both. "Cruel and unusual punishment" violates the Fourteenth Amendment to the United States Constitution.

Enforcing the Judgment (Execution)

Once a judgment is rendered, the court commands the sheriff, marshall, or constable to carry it out. Some courts ordered imprisonment or labor until the judgment had been met.

In the case of debt, imprisonment was often useless – the person in custody had no way to earn the money. "Judgment-proof" debtors – those certified by the court as unable to pay – could laugh at creditors.

If the judgment debtor owned property, the court issued an order for the sheriff to seize and sell it (attachment) to satisfy the creditor's claims. In some jurisdictions, the property must be taken into custody before judgment is given as security that the creditor can recover if the debtor fails to make payment. A companion action is distraint – property is taken into custody to impel the debtor to come to court. When the person appears in court, the property is returned. Personal property is actually brought to the courthouse, and the officer in charge makes an inventory. In some jurisdictions the creditor must post a bond for the value of the property attached to indemnify the officer against unlawful seizure.

Seizure of real property consisted of recording a writ against the title called a judgment lien and giving notice to the person in possession that the land is now court property and cannot be disposed of or sold by the owner. Homesteads (dwelling house and a small piece of garden property), pensions, bankrupt property, property in hands of guardians or trustees, cemeteries, tools of trade, and insurance are free from attachment.

If the debtor fails to make payment, the sheriff then condemns the property and posts it for sale by publicly advertising on placards, in newspapers, by town crier, or Sunday notice in church. Then the property is auctioned to the highest bidder and the proceeds go to the creditor for redress, costs, and damages.

Each step generates court records. Brief summaries appear in minutes, orders, and judgments; documents, testimony, and exhibits (plus copies of orders), writs, judgments, and notices will be found in the case packets.

New Trials and Appeals

A litigant, usually the loser, but sometimes the winner if he/she received less than he/she petitioned for, can appeal the case within a specified period of time. Each state determines by law which court may hear which appeals. Federal judiciary acts do the same on the federal level. Some states have only one appeals court; some allow only specific cases to be appealed; and some place a limit on the amount of damages which an appeals court can handle.

When the appellate court issues a writ allowing the case to be heard, the litigants prepare briefs containing the facts of the case, errors committed, and reasons why appeal is sought. After printing became common, briefs were printed in multiple copies for the judges, attorneys, litigants, case files, and news media.

New trials or appeals were granted when the judge erred on the admissibility of evidence, the verdict was contrary to the evidence, the verdict was contrary to the law, the judge erred in the charge to the jury, and/or new evidence became available.

When errors occur, the case is tried only on the legal technicalities involved, not on the evidence offered in the trial. The judges consider the matter individually, then collectively, and render their opinions—usually in writing—at a later date.

If the court grants a new trial, the case is sent back to the trial court and the whole cause is retried in accordance with rules laid down by the appeals court.

The two cases that follow are verbatim typescripts of original case papers I retrieved from garbage cans in 1962, Fulton County, Kentucky, where case files were being dumped after they had been microfilmed. As court after court grapples with budget cuts, forced economies, and limited storage space, many files are being culled. Unfortunately, many are not microfilmed nor are funds available to do so.

Genealogists can and should urge that these records be transferred to local historical and genealogical societies. Pottowattamie County, Iowa, transferred court files to the county historical society in 1976 before building a new courthouse. Lancaster County, Pennsylvania, transferred its documents to the Lancaster County Historical Society several years ago, when the county clerk, who was also president of the society, knew the records were in jeopardy and petitioned for custody.

In the sample civil case that follows, only the case papers are included. Order books, minutes, judgments, and the appeal transcript prepared for the circuit court provide more data. However, these eight documents from the case file will familiarize you with typical legal language and procedures. I have added minimal punctuation when needed for clarity.

In this case, Hubbard, a physician, enters a suit against James Brown for medical services rendered but unpaid. Brown is not a resident of Kentucky and owns a horse. The constable serves the summons and attaches the horse. Brown posts bond and takes the horse back. Depositions are ordered in Caddo Parish, Louisiana, possible place of residence of James Brown. The return is on the back.

Brown loses judgment in the county court, appeals the Fulton Circuit Court, posts bond to cover the action, and enters a countersuit against Hubbard.

Sample Civil Case

(On back of document)

55
J N Brown
vs
C Hubbard
To Sept

Executed by obtaining a copy of the within summons to Deft June 24th 1854.

(Signed) R C Pratten S.F.C.

Charles Hubbard vs James Brown
Fulton County Quarterly Court
Kentucky, 1853-54

Plaintiff's Declaration

To the Honorable Lewis Scearce Presiding Judge of Fulton County in Chauncry sitting -

Your complainant states that he has an account against James Brown for $14.50 for medical services rendered by pltft to deft as Physician which is now due, unpaid and in no way satisfied.

Compt further states that said Brown is a non resident of this State and is about to remove all his effects out of this state, and your pltff can have no way of making his debt except out of the property now in this State, which is a horse now in Fulton County and within the Jurisdiction of this Court.

Pltff files his account herewith marked (A) and calls on deft to answer if the same is not just and correct and he asks for process and answer against deft, and for an order directing the Constable to sieze and take into his possession a horse belonging to said Brown and him safely keep till further orders herein unless deft will give Bond with good security conditioned to pay off and satisfy any decree rendered him -

Pltff prays for a decree for the amount of his debt and for all proper relief in the premises -

Atty

Charles Hubbard says the statements of the foregoing Bill am true as he believes -

Sworn to before me this 24th Sept 1853 -

(signed) Lewis Scearce P.J. F.C.C.

(On back of document)

C. Hubbard
vs Bill
Jas Brown
October term Order
of warning vs Brown
and sentinced
January term order travance
and continued

Writ of Summons

The Commonwealth of Kentucky to any Constable of Fulton County—you are commanded to summon Jas Brown to answer a bill in Chancry, filed against him in my office by Charles Hubbard, on the 4th Monday in Oct next, and you are directed to seize and take into your possession a horse belonging to said Brown now in this county, and him safely keep till further order herein unless deft should give Bond with good security conditioned to pay and satisfy any order or decree made in this cause—Given under my hand as Presidy Judge of Fulton County this 24th day of September 1853 -

(signed) Lewis Scearce P.J. F.C.C.

(On back of document)

Oct 8th 1853

Said Brown taken said grey horse and of my possession by Bond which Bond is herein inclosed.

B. F. Easly fs

C. Hubbard
vs
Jas Brown
Contain that 1st day
of Oct 1853
by taking in
my possession
one grey horse
as the property of
James Brown -
b. f. Easly fs

Attachment Bond

Know all men by these presents that we Charles Hubbard and A. D. Kingman are held and firmly bound to James Brown in that just and full sum of Twenty Nine Dollars to which payment well and truly to be made we bind ourselves our heirs to so jointly and severally and firmly by these presents, sealed and dated this 24th of Sept 1853.

The condition of the above obligation is such that whereas the above bound Charles Hubbard is about to sue out an attachment against the said James Brown. Now should the said Charles Hubbard well and truly pay to the said James Brown all such damages and costs so he may sustain by reason of the improper suing out of said attachment then this obligation to be void else to remain in full force and virtue.

Sealed and delivered before me

(signed) Charles Hubbard (seal)
(signed) A. D. Kingman (seal)

(signed) Lewis Scearce P.J. F.C.C.

(On back of document)

C. Hubbard
to (Attachment
(Bond
James Brown

Defendant's Judgement Bond

C. Hubbard—Plaintiff (
against (Bond
James Brown—Defendant (

We undertake and are bound to the plaintiff C Hubbard in the sum of Twenty-Eight Dollars that the defendant James Brown shall perform the Judgement of this court in this action or that the undersigned Joseph A. Fawlkes will have the grey horse attached in this action or his value Seventy five Dollars forth coming and subject to the order of the court for the satisfaction of such Judgement.

Oct 8th 1853 (signed) J. E. Brown
Test (signed) Jos A. Fawlkes
A. F. Easley fs

Notice of Deposition

Charles Hubbard Lis [lawsuit]

Take notice that on the 22nd day of March 1854 at the house of Mrs. Helen Garret in the Parish of Caddo in the State of Louisiana I shall proceed to take the deposition of Miss Mary L. Elgin to be read as evidence in a cause now pending in the Fulton County Quarterly Court wherein you are Plaintiff & James Brown is defendant if said deposition cannot be taken on the 23rd of March, then on the 24th if not on the 24th then on the 28th if not on the 28th then on the 1st of April 1854 and if not completed on that day then from day to day until completed.

(signed) James Brown
for Atty Roulhac

(On back of document)

C. Hubbard
vs (Notice
(Depons.
James Brown

State of Kentucky (Personally appeared before the under-
Fulton County (signed Presiding Judge of the Fulton County Court - Frank Rouchas who makes oath that he did on the 24th day of March 1854 deliver to C. Hubbard in Hickman, Ky a true copy of the within notice Given under my hand March 4th 1854

(signed) Lewis Scearce P.J. F.C.C.

Deposition of Witnesses

This deposition of David Caddis taken on the 24th day of April 1854 at the office of A. D. Kingman in the town of Hickman Ky to be read as evidence in an action pending in the Fulton Quarterly Court wherein Charles Hubbard is plaintiff and James Brown is defendant -

Question by Pltffs Atty. Please state if you know the horse which James Brown had here last fall, and the one attached by Easly in this case.

Ans. Brown said he had bought this mare up in Tennessee and wanted to trade her to a man to get one that match another one he had in a waggon. In a day or two after that he was in my house he could not trade. He said unless he could get a good boot—this was the same horse that was attached by Easly in the case of Hubbard vs Brown — it was of grey color a large fine looking animal.

By Deft. Are you certain [strikeouts omitted] that he claimed the horse as his own property

Ans. He claimed it and said he wished to trade it off or purchase another to match.

By Same. You say it was a mare he spoke to you about so on are you certain it was the same animal which was attached by Easley.

Ans. I cannot say certainly that it was the same animal which was attached by Easly as the attachment was levied at Mr Fowlkes stable when I was not present.

By Same. Did he not also claim a wagon and horse which were in his possession at the same time?

Ans. He did

(signed) David Caddis

Also the deposition of James Wilson taken at the same time, place and for the same purposes -

Question by Pltffs Atty. Please state if you did not hear James Brown say that pltff had rendered medical services to deft in the year 1832 and was or not pltff a practicing physician at the time -

Ans. I did hear him say the plaintiff had rendered him medical services & plaintiff was a physician at the time I carried the Plaintiffs bill to Mr. Brown and when I hand the Dr's Bill to Mr. Brown he Replyed the bill was high but he would settle it and have nothing more to do with Dr. Hubbard.

(signed) James P. Wilson

Also the deposition of Joseph Foowlkes taken by consent at the same time & place to be read as evidence in behalf of the defendant in an action wherein Charles Hubbard is plaintiff & James Brown defendant -

Question by Defendant. Did you or not during the fall of 1853 keep in your stable a large gray horse which was brought there by the defendant Brown & did you not understand from him that the horse was the property of Miss Mary Elgin & was not the property of the same charged to her?

Ans. Mr Brown the defendant arrived at my stable in fall of 1853 reporting himself directly from the eastern part of Texas in the western part of Louisianna. He was riding a large grey geldin which I judged to be about twelve years old. He put him up at my stable and told me he was the property of Miss Mary Elgin. The horse stayed in my stable the greater part of the time Brown stayed here he always spoke of him as Miss Elgins horse told me who she bought him from and how much she gave for him. My stable bill for feeding said horse was made out ajoint Miss Elgin at Mr Brown request. This was the same horse levied on by Mr Easly and placed in my charge by him.

By Pltffs Atty. Are you or not the security of deft Brown for the forthcoming of the property attached in this case?

Ans. I am

(signed) Joseph A. Fowlkes

Also the deposition of Aden Taylor taken at the same time & place on behalf of the defendant.

Question by Defendant. Were you or not keeping stable for Joseph Fowlkes during the fall of 1853 at the time that the defendant James Brown put up the horse attached by Easly & did he or not state that the horse was the property of Miss Mary Elgin & was not the keeping of the same charged to her account.

Answer. I was keeping stable for Joseph Fowlkes in the fall of 1853 – and during that time James Brown put up a horse in the stable which was the horse attached by Easly – Brown stated that the horse was the property of Miss Mary Elgin and the keeping of the horse was charged to her account.

By Same. Did he not put up several other horses at that time which he stated were the property of Miss Mary Elgin & with the paying of which she was also charged?

Ans. Whilst here he put up two other horses and said that they were the property of Miss Elgin and the keeping of them was charged to her account.

By Pltffs Atty. Was you present when Brown told D. Caddis the horses were his property or when he told Thomas Cole they were his?

Ans. I was.

By Deft. Did he or not always assert when in your presence that the horse was the property of Miss Elgin?

Ans. He told me that it was Miss Mary Elgin['s] Horse that she had bought the horse the spring before.

Question. Was or not the horse attached the same horse that the defendant James Brown [unfinished in original].

Ans. It was the same horse.

(signed) Aden Taylor

Also the deposition of Thos Cole taken at the same time, place & for the same purpose in the caption to be read on behalf of pltff -

By Pltffs Atty. Did or not James Brown tell you in the fall of 1853 that he owned a grey horse that he had here in this town & did or not he offer to sell or swap said horse?

Ans. I was in the stable of Fowlks last fall a man named Bevis bartered Brown defts for horse trade and conversed some time about the trade. Brown said his horse cost him from $20 or $30 when he got him either in Texas or Nashville witness dont remember which. The horse Brown offered to Swap was his gray horse. I saw Brown driving the same horse around here sometimes. This was after the time was spoken of between Bevis and Brown.

By Deft. Can you say positive that Brown asserted he had bought the horse or did he claim him as his own property?

Ans. He did not say that he had bought the horse but said he had rode him a long way – and I can not be certain where he said he was from Nashville or Texas.

By Same. Is it not customary for men when acting as agent for others to call the property theirs when trading?

Ans. When I am authorized to issue a horse for motion I think I would call him my horse.

By Pltff. Did or not Brown speak of the horse as his own and did he say he was acting as Agent of any person in the conversation with Bevis?

Ans. He spoke of the horse as being his own. He did not say that he was acting as the agent of any one.

(signed) Thomas Cole

We as Attys for both plaintiff and defendant agree that the foregoing deposition show the said witness exception as to form of taking notice and without certification -

(signed) A. D. Kingman Atty
for plaintiff
(signed) I. R. Breast Atty
for Deft

Examining Fee $3.00
one half to pltff
" " " deft
I U Brewer
Examiner

(On back of document)

Depositions of Thomas Cole & others
to be read in the case of Hubbard vs
Brown -

Filed in open court April 25, 1854
(signed) Lewis Scearce P.J.

Appeal Bond

Know all men by these presents that we James Brown and Jos A. Fowlkes are held and firmly bound to Charles Hubbard in the penal sum of Twenty nine dollars the payment whereof well and truly to be made we bind ourselves our heirs Executors and administrators jointly severally and firmly by these presents sealed with our seals and dated this 16th day of May 1854. The correction of the above obligation is such that whereas the above bound Brown has obtained an appeal to the Fulton Circuit Court from the judgement of the Fulton County Masterly Court rendered at the April term thereof 1854 wherein the said Brown is Deft and the said Charles Hubbard is Pltff now if the said Brown since duly prosecute the said appeal and with effect or shall well and truly satisfy and pay the said Hubbard the amount of his said judgement with interest and costs and all costs and damages which may be awarded so sustained by him the said Brown in case the said judgement is affirmed in while or in part or the said appeal dismissed or discontinued then this obligation shall be void else to remain in full force and virtue.

(seal)
(signed) Jos A. Fowlkes (seal)

(On back of document)

NO 55
Charles Hubbard
vs
James Brown
Appeal by
Deft
Filed May 16th
1854 G S Morris
Sums Issued
June 21st 1854

Writ of Summons

THE COMMONWEALTH OF KENTUCKY
To the Sheriff of Fulton County

You are commanded to summon Charles Hubbard to answer on the first day of the next Sept. term of the Fulton Circuit Court, a petition filed against him in said Court by James Brown and warn him that upon his failing to answer, the petition will be taken for confession, or he will be proceeded against for contempt; and you will make due return of this summons on the first day of the next Sept. term of said Court.

Witness, G. S. Morris Clerk of said Court, this 21st day of June 1854.

(signed) G S Morris

[Note: The testimony in this case is invaluable in tracing the movements of James Brown in Tennessee, Texas, Louisiana, and Kentucky. The testimony given in his behalf constitutes a mini-census of persons who knew him and his movements.]

Sample Criminal Case

The Commonwealth vs. Woodull & c: James
Wiley
George
Hickman County, Kentucky, 1832 Robert
William

Grand Jury Indictment

The Commonwealth of Kentucky, Hickman County and Circuit Set: At a circuit court, holdon for the County and circuit aforesaid, at the Court house of said County, on the second day of April in the year one thousand eight hundred and thirty two before Rezin [Reason] Davage, one of the Circuit Judges, appointed and Commissioned, within said Commonwealth and asigned, and allotted, as the Judge of said Court. The grand jurors of the County and Circuit aforesaid then and there duly emppannelled, sworn and charged, to enquire for said Commonwealth and the body of the County aforesaid in the Court aforesaid in the Commonwealth aforesaid present that Robt Woodall, late of said County, yeoman, William Woodall late of said county, yeoman, James Woodall late of said County, yeoman, Wiley Woodall late of said county, yeoman, and George Woodall late of said county yeoman, not having the fear of God before their eyes but being moved and reduced by the ins[tig]ation of the Devil on the third day of December in year one thousand eight hundred and thirty one, in the county of Hickman and Circuit aforesaid, did with force and arms, feloniously, willfully, and of their [malice] aforethought, make an asault, in and upon one Wilson White, and that the said Robert Woodall, with a certain piece of oak timber of the value of six cents which he the said Robert Woodall in both his hands, then and there had and held, the said Wilson White in and upon the left side of the head of him the said Wilson White, then and there feloniously, willfully, and of his malice aforethought, did strike, giving unto him, the said Wilson White, then and there with the said piece of oak timber, by the stroke aforesaid, in manner aforesaid, in and upon the side of the head of said Wilson White, one mortal wound of the length, of three inches and of the depth of two inches, of which said mortal wound, he the said Wilson White, on and from the said third day of December in the year one thousand eight hundred and thirty one at the County of Hickman and Circuit aforesaid, until the fourth day of December of the same year at three of the clock in the morning of the said fourth day of December at the County of Hickman and Circuit aforesaid, did languish, and languishing did live, on which said fourth day of December at the hour aforesaid of the said year one thousand and eight hundred and thirty one at the County of Hickman and Circuit aforesaid, he the said Wilson White of the mortal wound aforesaid died. And that said William Woodall, James Woodall, Wiley Woodall and George Woodall at the time of committing the felony and murder aforesaid, in manner aforesaid, feloniously, willfully, and of their malice aforethought, were present aiding, abbetting, consorting, supporting and maintaining, the said Robert Woodall in the felony and murder aforesaid in manner and form aforesaid, to do, commit, and perpetrate, and so the jurors aforesaid upon their oath aforesaid, do say, that the said Robert Woodall, William Woodall, James Woodall, Wiley Woodall, and George Woodall, him the said Wilson White, in manner and form aforesaid, feloniously, willfully and of their malice aforethought, did kill and murder, against the statute in that case made and provided, and against the peace and dignity of the Commonwealth of Kentucky.

[signature of attorney not legible]

(On back of document)
We the Jury find the prisoner George Woodall not guilty.
John Campbel
We the Jury find Wiley Woodall not guilty Oct the 2nd 1832.
Wm. Taylor

Commonwealth
v. (Indictment
(for
(Murder
Robert Woodall
William Woodall
James Woodall
Wiley Woodall
and George Woodall

A true bill
George Reese
Foreman
Patterson

[Note: This report follows the completed trial six months later.]

Warrant (Writ of Capias)

THE COMMONWEALTH OF KENTUCKY
To the Sheriff of Hickman County, Greeting:

We command you to take James Woodall, George Woodall, Robert Woodall, Wiley Woodall, and William Woodall if they be found within your bailiwick, and them safely keep, so that you have their bodies before the Judge of Honor[able] Hickman Circuit Court, at the Court House in Clinton, on the first day of the next July term, to answer The Commonwealth of and Indictment found against them by the Grand Jury for murder and have then there this writ.

Witness, Richard Taylor, Jr. Clerk of our said Court, at the courthouse aforesaid, this 18th day of May 1832, and in the 4th year of the Commonwealth.

(signed) Richard Taylor J. C. H.C.C.

(On back of document): Executed on within named James Woodall on the 18th day of June and delivered him into the custody of the jailer on the 19th of said month – George Woodall was found but was so sick prudence forbid moving him – Robert Woodall not found in my bailwick.

(signed) Samuel Gibson, G.H.C.

Commonwealth
vs (
Woodall & C. (Cafs

To July Term
To be executed on James, George and Robert Woodall only.
(signed) Richard Taylor Jr. C.H.C.C.

Jury Summons

James Woodall

The Commonwealth of Kentucky to the Sheriff of Hickman County Greetings: You are hereby commanded to summon and cause to come before the Judge of our Hickman Circuit Court at the Courthouse in the Town of Clinton on the 1st day of the next July Term twelve good and lawful men, housekeepers of your county to pass between the Commonwealth after and James Woodall and his trial for murder who are of no wise a kin to said Woodall and this they shall in no wise omit under the penalty of £100 and have then there this writ witness Richard Taylor Jr Clerk of our said Court at the Courthouse aforesaid this 7th day of June 1832 and in 41st year of the Commonwealth.

(signed) Richard Taylor Jr. C.H.C.C.

(On back of document) [jurors' names]

1. Gabriel David	7. John Johnson
2. Michal Watson	8. Peter Sibert
3. John E. Anderson	9. Asa Vitcherson
4. Porter Brown	10. G. B. Bailey
5. Abraham Watson	11. John Henry
6. Price Edvington	12. Ferral Vincent

Commonwealth
vs. (Venirie
Woodall (facias

To July Term 1832

[Note: This jury summons for James Woodall is repeated for William Wiley, and George, each with a separate list of jurors.]

Summons for Witnesses (Subpoena)

COMMONWEALTH OF KENTUCKY

to the Sheriff of Hickman County, Greetings:

We command you to summon Thomas Griffey, Thomas Wellingham, Robert Tanner, Archibald Appleton, Wright Simpkins, Grey Stone, Benjamin Stacy, Nancy Stacy, John Odeguard, Elijah Bradley, Samuel Sawyer to appear before the Judge of our Circuit Court, at the courthouse of Hickman County, on the 1st day of the October term, to testify and the truth to say, on behalf of the Deft [James Woodall] in a certain matter of controversy in our said court depending and undetermined, wherein The Commonwealth is Plaintiff and [James] Wooddall is Defendant; and this they shall in nowise omit, under the penalty of £100. Witness Richard Taylor Jr. Clerk of our said Court at the court house aforesaid, this 21st day of July 1832, and in the 41st year of the Commonwealth.

(signed) Richard Taylor Jr CHCC

(On back of document)

Executed on all but Tanner and Sawyer.

S. Gibson DS for
Saml Gibson SHC

Wiley Woodall
vs
Commonwealth

To October 1832

[Note: Separate subpoenas were issued for different witnesses ordered to appear on behalf of William, Wiley, and George on July 21 and September 5. We know from the endorsement on back of the indictment above that George and Wiley were judged not guilty. The fate of James, Robert, and William is not stated in the surviving papers. A search in Hickman County newspapers may tell us what happened to them. The court docket lists Commonwealth of Kentucky vs. Woodhull. The case includes seventy-five different residents of Hickman County as witnesses, defendants, clerks, court officers.]

Sample Equity Case

Common equity cases are probate disputes, estate divisions, divorce proceedings, adoptions, dissolution of partnerships, and other cases involving property rights.

The Bill (Declaration or Petition)

The action begins by filing a bill stating the plaintiff's case and praying the chancellor (judge) for relief. The bill must state every fact entitling the plaintiff to relief. Since printing became more common, many courts require these bills to be printed and presented in court as a bound volume.

Filing and Service

The bill is filed with the clerk of the court, and a copy is served on the defendant as prescribed by statute or rules of the court. A proof of service (return) must appear on the back of the record. At this point, the bill may be tested to determine if it is sufficient to entitle the plaintiff to a remedy at equity. This is called a demurrer (meaning to delay or stay).

Answer

The answer, setting up every circumstance the defendant will use, must be filed within the time stated. If there are several defendants, each may file an answer, although one will suffice. If the defendant fails to file or admits all the allegations, judgment by default or decree pro confesse (judgment because of confession) will be given. The case ends here.

Hearings and Proof

Equity trials are generally conducted without a jury. The chancellor has the power to decide both questions of fact as a jury, and questions of law as a judge. The rules of evidence applicable to suits at law also apply, but the proceedings are more direct. Frequently, in cases without serious dispute over the facts, no oral testimony is introduced. The matter is argued to a conclusion upon the allegations set forth in the bill and answer. If proof is necessary, it is usually brief. There are four common methods of presenting proof:

1. Depositions. Obtained by written questions or through oral examination by counsel, summarized and written. Such depositions are valuable where family members have moved from their birthplaces to unknown places for their residences are recorded.
2. Reference to Special Examiners (Masters). This is a convenient method where the facts are complicated or where several hearings are necessary. The chancellor commissions a member of the bar to determine the facts of the case and make a report including testimony and findings on the facts. The chancellor uses the report as a basis for the decree but is not bound to accept the findings of the master.
3. Jury Trial. Generally, equity litigants have no right to a jury trial, though the court may submit questions of fact to a jury if it chooses. The chancellor is not bound by the jury's verdict. In some states, however, the right to a jury trial in chancery cases is given by statute and can only be set aside for reasons which would justify a judge in setting aside a verdict in any law action, as for instance, where the verdict was contrary to the evidence.
4. Hearings before the court itself take place when the trial judge permits litigants or their legal representatives to present oral or written arguments.

Decrees

A decree is the judgment or sentence determining the rights of the parties to the suit. A decree is final when it decides the whole case, reserving no further questions for the future judgment of the court. A decree dismissing a bill or ordering specific performances of a contract would be final. It is interlocutory when it reserves any question for future judicial consideration – for instance, ordering the delivery of property to a receiver or granting a temporary injunction.

A decree in equity is generally easier to enforce than a judgment in law. When the chancellor orders a person to execute a deed, perform a contract, account for trust funds, cancel a mortgage, or any of the various things it may order, the person must comply or be subject to fine or imprisonment. Disobedience to the order is contempt of court. All the machinery of the government, including the army, may be used to enforce a decree of equity.

L. N. Calvert and Wife
vs
Marcus Milners Heirs
Fulton County Circuit Court, Kentucky
and
Kentucky Court of Appeals, 1856-1866

Guardian's Answer

Fulton Circuit Court

L. N. Calvert & wife – pltffs (
against (Answer
Marcus Milners Heirs – Defts (

The answer of A. D. Kingman as Guardian & John B. Milner, the infant heirs [meaning under twenty-one] of Marcus Milner dec'd for answer to pltffs Petition says – that he admits all the alligations of said petition that are in favor of said infants and desires all that are or may be considered prejudical to their interest, and calls for full proof, and asks for full protection of their rights as infants under the laws of the land & that they be dismissed with their costs ye

Sept 11 1856 (signed) A. D. Kingman
Guardian adlitim

[Note: A minor cannot bring suit in a court of law; therefore, a guardian ad litem (in suit) is appointed to serve as litigant in the case. When the case has been terminated, the guardian is released.]

Notice of Deposition

[Note: This notice is usually printed among the legal notices in local papers.]

W. R. Bradley Atty for N. S. Calvert & Wife

Take notice that I shall proceed on the 19th day of Nov 1856 at the residence of Wm Milner in Fulton County Ky to take the deposition of John Milner and others to be read in Evidence on the trial of a suit pending in the Fulton Equity & Criminal Court wherein said Calvert & wife are pltffs and I and others are defendants – and if the taking is not completed on that day, it will be continued from day to day till done.

(signed) Wm Milner -

(On back of document)

Wm Milner
To (
(Notice
(
W. R. Bradley

Executed on W. R. Bradley by delivering to him a true copy of within notice 12 Nov 1856.

P. B. Adams Shf
by F L Morse dept.

Transcript of Case (Brief)

The State of Kentucky (
The Court of Appeals (December 19th 1858

W. Milner et al. Appellant (
against (The Fulton Circuit Court
L. Calvert et al. Appeller (

The Court being sufficiently advised delivered the following opinion herein -

Marcus Millner died in Fulton County in this state leaving an estate in land, slaves etc which was disposed of by his last will between his widow and children.

All of the children except Louisa were of a former marriage and Louisa died soon after the testator, in infancy and without issue – leaving her mother and half brothers and sisters her sole heirs.

This is a contest between the mother of Louisa and the surviving children of the testator as to the mothers rights under the will, and as heir of her deceased child.

Two questions are made: First – what interest she has under the will, and second – In what proportions the mother and half brothers and sisters take the slaves and personalty belonging to the estate of the deceased infant.

The 1st and 9th clauses of the will alone relates to the subject matter in dispute, and must determine the extent of the widows interest as devisees.

They are as follows:

1. I give to my wife Martha the south home quarter – my negro boy Levi and my woman Terry and children to use as she thinks best during her life time, and then to go to my children; and should there be a surplus above her support, the proceeds to be equally divided among my children.

Ninethly, should there be a surplus arising from the farm or tan yard above the support of my family, I desire my Executors to use it to the best advantage for the benefit of my children.

It is concluded that the home quarter and "the farm" are the same; and this controversy is in regard to the "surplus" mentioned in the first clause. Whether the testator intended it as the surplus remaining at the death of the tenant for life, or as the annual surplus to be held by his Executors and used by them for the benefit of his children as it occured as indicated by the nineth clause.

Disregarding the latter clause of the will, no doubt could exist to the meaning of the former. Its language would clearly authorize the view which the court below seems to have taken, and entitled the widow to the surplus whilst she lived giving to the children only what remained at her death. This construction is however in our opinion, not at all allowable in view of the nineth clause of the will, in which the testator clearly indicates a different purpose with regard to such surplus.

Both claims direct that the surplus shall go to the children.

The first is silent as to the character of surplus – whether annual or that remaining at the death of the widow – and also as to the time of enjoyment by the children; but considering the discretion left the widow and the estate conferred upon her, its language would indicate that the testator intended the surplus left at her death. The latter however forbids such an interpretation of the previous clause, because it irrequivocally indicates a very different intention – both as to the character of surplus, and the time off its enjoyment by the children. It shows that he did not mean the surplus remaining at the death of the widow only, but the surplus as it accrued during her life – and also that his children were to have the benefit in their discretion might think most advantageous to them, or, as he says, "to use it to the best advantage".

Our opinion upon this branch of the case, therefore, is, that the widow was only entitled to so much of the rents, and profits of "the farm" or "home quarter" as would support herself and family – that is – the family with her at the death of the testator – including herself – the children of the testator living with her and her servants; and that the Court below erred in adjudging to her and her husband beyond that proposition.

The ruling of the Court is to the proportions in which the mother and half brothers and sisters take as heirs of the deceased infant was obviously correct.

By the Revised Statutes Chapt 30 Sec II, it is provided that "where any person shall die intestate as to his personal estate or any part thereof, the surplus, after payments of funeral expenses, charges of administration, and debts shall pass and be distributed among the same persons and in the same proportions to whom and which real estate directed to descend–except as follows:

"First–the personal estate of an infant shall be distributed as if he had died after full age etc"

Sec 1 of the same Chapter, directs that real estate shall descend, first to children and their descendants, if none, then to the father, if none, then to the mother, brothers and sisters and their descendants etc.

Sec 2 provides that "Collaterals of the half blood shall inherit only half so much as those of the whole blood, or as ascending kindred, when they take with either."

In this case the collaterals are altogether of the last blood–there are none of the whole blood with whom they can take–and the question is, whether they take as brothers and sisters equally with the mother as provided in Sec 1 infra. Restriction imposed by the second section only applies to collaterals of the half blood, when there are collaterals of the whole blood to take with them, and not to a case like the present.

It is difficult to perceive how this position can be maintained in view of the section referred to. It provides not only for cases when there are collaterals of the half and whole blood, but also for such as we are considering.

It limits the shares of collaterals of the half blood to one half in either case–the language, when properly construed, means nothing more nor less than that they shall enherit only half as much as collaterals when they take with them, and the same proportion when they take with ascending kindred.

In this respect, the provision is similar to the 15 Sec of the Act of 1796 -

1. Stat. Law. 564–which declares that "if all be of the half blood, they shall have whole portions only giving the ascendants (if there be any) double portions."

The mother in this case is of the ascending kindred. She is entitled under the 1st Section to take a share equal to a brother or sister of the whole blood–and the chancellor very properly gave her a share double that of either of the collaterals of the half blood.

The judgment is however reversed upon the other ground already indicated, and the cause remanded for further proceedings in conformity with this opinion.

A copy
Att. R. R. Revill C.C.A.

(On back of document)

Milner et al
(
(Co. Opinions
(
Calvert et al

Filed May 31, 1860
John R. McGhee
Clk

Recovered
Fulton

[Note: The case has been appealed by William Milner as executor of the estate of Marcus Milner. A complete resumé of the case as it was presented to the Fulton Circuit Court was prepared by the county clerk containing a brief outline of the facts of the case, the points of law and controversy upon which the appeal is based, and the opinion of the lower court.]

Bill of Costs

S. N. Calvert & Wife Plaintiffs (Fulton Equity Circuit Court
(
(Bill of Costs
(
Milner et al Defendants (To Decs term 1861 & inclusion

Date		Item	Amount	Total
/56 Feb 28	To	Fil Ct^{11} dec^{10} Aty^{10} Sums^{25} 6 Cefs^{60} Ret^{10} oath^{25}	1.40	
" Sep	"	Osdn fil ans^{25} fil^{10} oath^{15} Out Out sy wit my of Byland^{25}	.75	
" "	"	Osdn fr him to be Milners party^{25} Order afy Kin Gad L fr	.25	
" "	"	Infts^{25} One fil In Milner Anst^{25} fil^{10} oath^{15} Out	.75	
" "	"	fit Ans of G ad L^{25} fil^{10} Osd trus fn case	.35	
" "	"	to E Cr Ct^{25} Cent^{25}	.50	4.00
" "	"	Oud apty McGelu Comr^{25} Doct^{10} Ciut^{25}	.60	
/57 Jan	"	Dock^{10} Cuit^{25}	.35	
" Dec	"	One fil Cun^{r} Rept^{25} fil^{10} Ord allowance^{25}	.60	
" "	"	One fil Di ci^{25} fil^{10} at Di ci /56	.35	
" "	"	Owe fr Di ciu to be Recrdur^{25} Recrdng same^{75}	1.00	
" "	"	To Kin Appe Bond^{50} Sup^{25} to Cep^{10}	.85	3.75
		Morris Costs	7.75	
pd by Deft	"	In R McGelu Ex^{r} fr Deposition of In Milner	3.50	
pd by Plts	"	In R McGelu Ex^{r} from Deposition of In R Calvert	3.00	
		McGelu cut (ae paid him)		6.50
	"	Serving notice to take in Milner Dep - PB Adams G Co	.25	.25
	"	To Sheriff for serving 6 copies of Sum 250 Early P C–	3.00	3.00
	"	On McGelu allowance as Com^{r}	10.00	10.00
/60 May	"	One fil Ct of Appl of^{25} one Ruistery Cou^{25} dock^{10} fil^{10}	.70	
	"	Recording175 Curt^{25}	2.00	2.70
/60 Dec	"	Dock^{10} One siz death of Inv B Milner^{25} One cuit^{25}	.60	
	"	Cuit^{25}	.25	
/61 May	"	Dock May/61^{10} Cuit^{25}	.35	
" Dec	"	One cut ______ fr fife to issue on Judge^{25} Dock^{10}	.35	
	"	One submiss of law^{25} Out Surt Death of I B Milner^{25}	.50	
	"	One Qust Milin fr fifu fr 114^{34}/100 Dollars to issue^{25}	.25	
	"	Onthr for said Fifu^{25} fifu^{50} Amt Cost^{25}	1.00	4.10
		Total Costs to Decr/^{61} in claim=		34.30
		state tax		.50
				34.80
		Att fee	5.00	
				5.00
				39.80

[Note: Note particularly the first entry for 60 December, which establishes a family death date. The use of abbreviations is a problem for genealogists unfamiliar with legal terms. *Black's Law Dictionary* will help. Several references to specific court volumes in the document can shorten your searches considerably. For example, Dock 10, Doc$^{t.}$ 10, refer to Dockets, Vol. 10.]

Amendment to Petition

Fulton Circuit Court

L. N. & Martha Calvert Plffs (
Agst (Amd Petition
Wm H. Milner & others Defts (

The Plffs amend their original petition in this they state that Wm Mervin is now the Admr of Decedent Marcus Milner, and that Mary F. Milner has intermarried with I. C. Byland, and that Martha Ann Milner has intermarried with Alexander Burnett.

Wherefore he prays that they be made Defts hereto for proper relief.

L.N. & Martha Calvert

[Note: This valuable document amends the original petition to add two new defendants, the husbands of two of the daughters of Marcus Milner. This writing is in a different penmanship and ink than the rest of the document, and the plaintiffs are cited differently. Thus, although this amendment was filed 20 March 1863, it was probably submitted prior to the appeal, thus placing the marriages not between 1858 and 1863 but rather between 1856 and 1858 while the case was still before the circuit court.]

(On back of the document)

L. N. & Martha Calvert
(
(Amd Pet -
(
Milner Heirs

Filed in Off Court
March 20th 1863
W A Brevard clk

Commissioner's Appointment

State of Kentucky
Fulton Cir Court Sct
March Term March 18th 1864

S. N. Calvert & Wife (Plaintiff
vs (
John Milner Exs & Others (Defendants

It is ordered that John R. McGehee be and he is hereby appointed Commissioner to take proof of Rents and Profits in the above entitled cause and Report to the next term of this court.

Copy Attest

W. A. Brevard Clk

(On back of document)

L N Calvert & Wife
vs
John Milner Exect & others

Not served
Wm Keenin DpC

Judgment Preliminary

Fulton Equity Court

Calvert & Wife (
vs (Judgment preliminary
Milner & wife (

It is ordered that John R McGehee be and he is hereby appointed this courts commissioner – He is instructed to take proof & ascertain the value of the yearly rents and profits of the Tan Yard once owned by Marcus Milner as also the value of the rents & profits of the farm upon the South home quarter where Milner resided at his death, commencing and descriminating in his report from the date of Marcus Milners death up to the date of the removal from the said farm by Calvert and wife. And from that date to the commencement of this suit, and from that date to the next term of this court. He is further instructed to take & ascertain reasonable amount to be allowed to Mrs Calvert for her support taking into view her situation and condition in life and the number of the inmates of her family white & black their age sex and capacity to assist in their own support up to the time of her removal from the farm. But in estimating the assistance she derived from the labor of the slaves she had in her possession – Levy & Terry are not to be estimated as she has the right to their labor in her own right. And also from that time to the next term of this court so far as may be requisite for the support of Mrs Milner & such of the negroes as she may have taken with her from the farm when she removed. Also to take proof and ascertain the age sex and value of the two negroes – Levy – Terry & Child of Terry bequeathed to Mrs. Calvert in the will of her late husband Marcus Milner. The said Commissioner is also instructed to ascertain and report the value of all the personal estate of Marcus Milner decd after payment of debts – the number age sex and value of all the slaves belonging to the estate of said Milner excluding those specifically devised by him – also the yearly hire of said slaves – and whether it is practical so to divide the slaves in kind as to give to the said Mrs Calvert from interest in their equal to a double share out of one sixth of said slaves or whether in his opinion it would most descend to the interest of all concerned that the heirs should pay to the plaintiff Martha if she elects to take the same an amount equal to her portion of the aggregate value of said slaves or whether a sale of any of the slaves would be necessary to a fair decision and if practicable to make division & allott to Mrs Calvert her interest in said slaves and reprt to court & making this division he is instructed to take into the estimate of slaves divided[,] the slaves willed to the plff Mrs Calvert, excluding Mrs Calverts life interest.

(On back of document)

Calvert & Wife Filed Dec 8th 1860
Int O C Gardner Clk
Judgt LHMcDaniels DC
Milner
Recorded

[Note: This document is a type of minute entry recording what has occurred to this point in the case and may signify that no entry has been made in the regular minute book. Reference to other slaves owned by Mrs. Calvert, not part of the estate, is important. If she inherited them from her father, this reference will supply corroborating evidence of relationship.]

Commissioners Report

Fulton Circuit Court

Calvert & Wife (
vs (Commissioners Report
M. Milner & heirs (

Your Commissioners, would beg leave to report as follows – in said case – that he finds the yearly rents & profits of the Tan Yard in Controvercy to be from 1854 to 1866 at $25. per year and the rents of the farm upon south home quarter where sd Milner resided at his death, from 1854 to 1860 to be worth $100. per year and from 1860 to 1866 to be $75. per year. And he would report that it would take to support Mrs. Calvert & the family that resides with her at the death of M. Milner from 1854 to 1866 the sum of $500. per year & in this the labor of the slaves Levi, Terry & her children is not estimated as taken into consideration – That Mrs. Calvert removed from the farm in Nov 1854 and has not returned to it since.

The age of the slaves & their value at date of the order in this case of Levi was 27 years of age his value was $1000. the age of Terry was 40 and her value was $700. Betty was worth $450. Sally worth $700.

The value of the personal effects as come to the hands of Wm Heron as Adms, was in Cash & notes $880. & he has paid out in costs & fee bills the sum of $65. leaving $815. in his hands for distribution.

The number, value, age and sex of all the slaves is found in my report of date Dec 17 1857, now on file in this case. And that's what I regarded them worth at that time, but the slaves Levi, Terry, Sally & Betty, Buck, Fayett were specifically devised by M. Milner in his will and the sd slaves all having left and of no service from about the first of Jany 1862. I cannot now report the value of the same unless they were with their masters where they should be, but I can say that their annual hire from 1854 to end of 1861 to be $825. per year and in this I exclude Levi, Terry, Sally & Betty, Buck & Fayett.

It is not possible to divide sd slaves as they are all now regarded free and worthless to anyone except themselves and not much to them.

Your Commissioners would report that the number of the white family residing with Pltffs Mrs Calvert at the death of M. Milner was seven (vis) Wm[1], Jne[2], B. Martha[3] Fannie[4] Mrs Milner, Thos[5] & Lue[6] Milner all these numbered were children of M. Milner decd.

I further find that the rents of the south home greater & Tan Yard from the profits adduced before me on both sides would not support the widow of M. Milner and the family residing with her at the death of her husband at any time from his death up to the present time. But I find from the evidence offered and introduced before me by the present husband of Mrs. Calvert viz L. N. Calvert that reasonable rents for the South home quarter & Tan Yard would only be $100 per anum. and would not support the widow and her family residing with her at death of M. Milner but that it would take to support the widow and her family residing with her at that time, or at death of M. Milner from 1852 to 1854 the sum of $1000 per year, and from 1854 to 1866 the sum of $600. per year.

All which is respectfully reported to the Court for Approval.

Sept 10th 1866 -

Jne R. McGehee (Com)

Commissioners
fee $25.

[Note: This file does not contain the 1857 report.]

Judgment

Fulton Circuit Court

L. N. & Martha Calvert (
agst (Judgment
Wm Milner & Others (

It appearing from the proscution & filed in the cause that the Defts William Milner, Mary F & I C Byland, Alexander & Martha Burnett & Thomas F Milner, have had the use & Occupation of the Farm and Tan yard willed by Marcus Milner to plff - Martha Milner & new Calvert, since November 1854 & that the same has been worth for rentsuit and that the whole of said rent was not more than sufficient for the support of the said Martha Milner the sum of $100, it is the report adjudged by this Court, that the plaintiffs L N & Martha Calvert, do receive adjudgment against the Defts I.C. Byland, Alexander Burnett and Thomas F Milner for the sum of Sixteen Hundred and fifty dollars with interest on the same from this date at the rate of six per cent per annum, & their costs herein expended for which execution may issue said judgment being for the rent per year at $100, & interest on each years rent as the fill acc.

And the said Mary F Byland & Martha Burnett being firm coverts, no personal judgments can be given against them, but they are ordered to pay to plffs the amount of said judgment interest & cash on or before the first day of the next term of this Court & a payment of said sum of $1650. with interest from this date & costs by them shall be a satisfaction of this judgment, & further orders and proceedings are herein continued –

It is further adjudged that the interest of Mrs. Martha Calvert in the assets in the honor of the Admr of Marcus Milner, Wm Mervin being $815. as reported by Commrs is as heir of her daughter Louisa Twenty six dollars & 60/100 which he is adjudged to pay to her & her husband L N Calvert, but this adjudication is not to effect Mrs. Calverts claim against the former Admrs of M Milner, for assets of said estate pursued with to their honor -

Filed & recorded in open court
Sept 22/66

W A Bevard Clk

Court Records

Most courts in America are courts of record, that is, they are required by law to keep a record of their proceedings. Inferior courts, not required by law to keep a record, usually do so for their own convenience. They need to know what they did and when. Before the days of shorthand and court transcript machines, the clerk received complete written depositions, testimony of witnesses, summons, writs, and often attorneys' arguments so he had a complete record of the essential parts of the case. From these and his own notes, he prepared minutes, orders, and judgments.

While practices vary from court to court and between state and federal courts, you can expect to find the kinds of records summarized in Table 6-1.

In addition to the records in Table 6-1 the court process produces sheriff and constable files, coroners' inquests, jury and jail records, and attorney lists.

Some states file all cases together in one set of volumes, with one set of case files running chronologically by date and number. Other states use a different set for divorces, equity proceedings, and so on. Probate records are almost always separate.

Although the case file is an invaluable collection of testimony and exhibits that may include photographs, marriage certificates, wills, receipts for the division of property in an estate, writs, and subpoenas, it is created only for matters before the court which involve litigants. The administrative activities of the court, such as the binding out of apprentices, the exemption of the elderly from taxes or military service, appointments of road inspectors or militia officers, and memorials for soldiers killed in war are recorded only in the minutes and orders of the court.

Indexes

Indexes to court records are usually incomplete. Some list only the surnames of the litigants (Potts v. Abernathy, 12 81-3, 289), some approach docket-style entries (William Potts, 12, 81, 82, 83, 289) and some index plaintiffs only (William Potts v. Robert Abernathy. Case in Common Pleas: Warrant, 12; deposition, 81-83; report, 289). Since 1900, some courts have prepared typewritten

Table 6-1

Types of Court Records

Record	*Type*	*Bound Volume*	*Filed Papers*	*Loose Papers*	*Case File*
Indexes: (alphabetical)	Plaintiff	●			
	Defendant	●			
	Reverse	●			
	Every name	●			
Dockets: calendar or waiting list of pending cases, in the order they will be considered by the court	Civil	●			
	Criminal	●			
	Equity	●			
	Chancery	●			
	Estate	●			
	Orphans'	●			
	Guardian	●			
	Probate	●			
	Name Change	●			
	Claims	●			
	Insolvents'	●			
	Bankruptcy	●			
	Divorce	●			
	Adoption	●			
	Lunacy	●			
	Reference	●			
	Stet	●			
	Execution	●			
	Appearance	●			
	Appeals	●			
	New actions	●			
Minutes: descriptive entries of all actions taking place in the court process.	Journals	●			
	Register of actions	●			
	Appeal briefs		●		●
Orders: official record of all orders of the judge(s).	Journals	●			
	Writs		●		●
	Summons		●		●
	Warrants		●		●
	Subpoenae		●		●
	Actions	●			
	Indictments		●		●
	Presentments		●		●
	Executions	●			●
	Stays (Demurrers)	●			●
	Injunctions	●			●
	Foreclosures				●
	Attachments				●
	Distraints				●
	Jury lists		●		●
Judgments: final decisions, punishments, and awards made by the court.	Satisfied	●			
	Short	●			
	Equity	●			
	Decrees	●			
	Fines	●			
	Liens	●			
	Verdicts	●			
	Opinions	●			
	Decisions	●			
	Reports		●		
	Appeals		●		●
	Bills of costs		●		●

Record	*Type*	*Bound Volume*	*Filed Papers*	*Loose Papers*	*Case File*
Case Files or Packets: all original papers placed in the hands of the court during a court case.	Civil				●
	Criminal				●
	Equity				●
	Estate				●
	Orphans'				●
	Probate				●
	Chancery				●
	Divorce				●
	Adoption				●
	Claims				●
	Insolvents'				●
	Lunacy				●
	Bankruptcy				●
	Appeals				●
				Bonds	●
				Depositions	●
				Testimony	●
				Declarations	●
				Inventories	●
				Documents	●
				Exhibits	●
				Receipts	●
				Petitions	●
				Affidavits	●
				Pleas	●
				Pleadings	●
				Allegations	●
				Complaints	●
				Inquisitions	●
				Examinations	●
				Promissory notes	●
				Letters	●
				Appraisals	●
				Arbitration reports	●

indexes by plaintiff and defendant, with separate subject indexes for the use of bench and bar. Rarely do these official indexes list jurors, witnesses, attorneys, justices, and other parties mentioned. Administrative court actions are not indexed either. The murder trial, for example, indexed only the Woodall brothers although seventy-five individuals were named in the case file.

During the 1930s, the Works Progress Administration (WPA) organized several court indexing projects using out-of-work school teachers, secretaries, and executives. Projects in West Virginia, Tennessee, Ohio, and other parts of the country have made our search of court records almost painless. The WPA index of the 1823-29 minute dockets of Rhea County, Tennessee, retrieves a Colonel George Gillespie who is not mentioned in the original index. The original index lists a George Gillespie, but the WPA index lists sixty-seven entries for him.

Indexes prepared for genealogical use are still rare, but a notable exception is *The Massachusetts Colonial Court Records Index, 1664-1781,* an every-name card file located at the Massachusetts State Archives, State House, Boston, MA 02133, and available on microfilm copy through the Genealogical Society of Utah (57 reels) and its branches. Figure 6-4 gives reel numbers and index entries.

Dockets

When a judiciary agrees to hear a case, it is placed on the court docket until trial. Abbreviated entries are made on the dockets for all changes in the status or pending action of the case for each term of court until the case is closed, carried over, or settled out of court, or until judgment is rendered. Thus, any time a case is pending, its current status may be determined by examining the docket. Most cases were on docket for at least three or four terms of court.

Most courts maintain several different dockets: criminal, civil, equity (chancery), miscellaneous (condemnations, lunacy commitments, disqualification of voters, adoptions, divorces, tax foreclosures, insolvency, estates, etc.), stets (cases removed from the regular docket because they have been inactive for several years), and claims (claims of creditors against estates and property). A court that maintains separate dockets will usually separate its other records into distinct volumes. Some courts maintain only one court docket for all types of cases. Sometimes duplicate dockets are prepared for judges, attorneys, or court clerks. Many dockets are indexed by plaintiff, by defendant, or by both; naturally such indexes vary a great deal in form.

Dockets may also be called "minute dockets," combining two records into one.

The value of dockets is their use as an index. They are not alphabetically arranged, but reading them is faster than having to read every page. If you are, for example, searching for the surname of Potts, 1813-45, begin with the dockets for the first term of court in 1813. Searching the dockets through twenty-two terms of court to 1 September 1818 you find "William Potts v. Robert Abernathy Crd O" (carried over). This notation tells you that a case involving William Potts has been placed on the docket, but that no judgment has been made. As you search the quarterly dockets you

Massachusetts Court Record's Index

U. S. Film	*Massachusetts...*
543,878	Aa-Anapolis
543,879	Ancaster-Balknam
543,880	Baldwin-Bemus
543,881	Benand-Borstahl
543,882	Bosard-Breau (Braux)
543,883	Breau (Bruse)-Burman
543,884	Burn-Catrill
543,885	Catt-Clark, John
543,886	Clark, John-Cook, David
543,887	Cook, E.-Crowninshield
543,888	Crows-Deareborn
543,889	Deerfield-Dummer, Tho.
543,890	Dummer, William-Equivalent
543,891	Erasmus-Forsyth (Foresight)
543,892	Fort-Garitson
543,893	Garland-Gould, S.
543,898	Gould, T.-Hamlen
543,899	Hamlin-Henchman
543,900	Hender-Howard
543,901	Howchin-Indians (Cuttacquin)
543,902	Indians (Dach)-Indians (Dudley)
543,903	Indians (Eastern)-Johnson, C.
543,904	Jonson, D.-Knight, Robert

U. S. Film	*Massachusetts...*
543,905	Knight, Roger-Leverett, Gov. John
543,906	Leverett, Gov. John-Lynn
543,907	Lynn-Massachusetts, 1742
543,908	Massachussetts, 1742-Monhatoes
543,909	Monhegan-Newton, Thomas
543,910	Newton, Thomas-Oliver, Polly
543,911	Oliver, Rebecca-Pelerine
543,912	Pelham-Pleasant Point
543,913	Pleasure (bark)-Purrington
543,914	Puritan church-Rhode Island, 1665
543,915	Rhode Island, 1668 -Saddlery
543,916	Sady-Selby
543,917	Selden-Smith, John
543,918	Smith, Capt. John-Stoddard, Anthony
543,919	Stoddard, Anthony-Temple, Capt.
543,920	Temple, Col.-Trades (Keepers)
543,921	Trades (Laborers)-Wade, J.
543,922	Wade, L.-Wells
543,982	Wells River-Willey
543,983	Willis-Worcester, 1761
543,984	Worcester, 1761-Z
	Illegible names 1643-1775

Figure 6-4. *Massachusetts Court Record's Index.* Reproduced from *Utah Genealogical Association Newsletter,* first quarter (1980): 3 with permission.

find that the case appeared on the docket and was carried over in December 1818, March 1819, June 1819, September 1819, December 1819, and March 1820.

From these entries you can expect to find information in both the minutes and the orders for each term of court through March 1820 when the case was closed. At this point, most court clerks place all of the miscellaneous papers pertaining to the case into one file labeled with the term of court in which judgment was rendered, the title of the case, and the case number. This case file is now your point of interest, supplementing the minutes and orders. If the court kept judgment records, they too will be arranged chronologically. Thus, you have gained entrance to the minutes, the orders, the judgments, and the case files by using the dockets.

Court Minutes

All actions of the court will be briefly recorded by the clerk in the minutes. Though rarely indexed, minutes are valuable. Where dockets and indexes are missing, minutes will identify terms of court where your ancestors' cases appear. The minutes may not always be complete enough to mention the names of all witnesses and jurors; however, it is far easier to search through unindexed minutes than it is to examine the individual papers filed in each case file for each term of court.

The following extracts are typical of the contents of court minute books:

Chester County Court, Pennsylvania, 1685[6]

Att a Court held att Chester	(John Symcocke Presid^{t}	
for ye County of Chester	(John Blunstone	(
the 1st 3^{d} day in the	(Robert Wade	(
1st Weeke of ye 8th	(George Maris	(Justices
moneth being y^{e}	(Nicholas Newland	(
6th day of y^{e}	(Robert Pile	(
moneth 1685	(Thomas Usher	(

Jeremy Collett Shreife
Robert Eyre Clerke

After Proclimation made The Constables were Called over ffor to bring In thyr Returns & they Returnd All was well and there were new ones Chosen for to serve for this next yeare: John Pennick Constable ffor the Township off Beathell Richard Barnard Constable for Aishtown: William Vestall of Burmingham: John Boyeter off Middelltowne: John worrola off Edgment: Joseph Edge: of Springfield: Daniell Broome of marpoole: of Darby William fflower off Chichester: moris Lewellin of Haverford Allixander Edwards of Radnor Robert Scothern In the Room of Josiah ferne

Josiah Taylor and Mary Williamson was Called to Answer the presentment of the Grand Juery ffor being to ffamilier with each other: they appeare and will Travis it

David Loyd their Majesties Attorny: In that Case

The Petty Juery was Called and attested: Thomas Varnon John Worroclaw: Joseph Baker: Robert Barber: Randall mallin: Robert Varnon William Mallin: James SwaFoord: John Beales: Thomas Green: Thomas Minshall: Robert Carter:

John Barbery being taken up as a runaway was ordered to give in Security not to depart untill Certificate should be brought from his master that he is a free man and untill such time to have lyberty to worke for himselfe

William Johnson made over a deed dated this Instant for fifty Acres of Land lying on the north side of Chester Creeke to Peter Thomas and his heirs for ever he the said Peter Thomas Allowing a Convenient high way through the said land from the house of the said Wm Johnson leading to Chester roade

Jeremy Collett made returne of an Execution granted ye last Court against Henry Renolds for Crowners fees and Constaples Charges &c dated ye 4th 7th moneth 1685 which he levied on an Oxe Appriased at £4 10^{s}

Henry Renolds came into Court and made full Satisfaction for the said Oxe Whereupon the Court Ordered him his Oxe againe

Thomas Usher Presented Henry Renolds for keeping an Ordinary Contrary to Law.

Ordered that William Hues be vewer of Pipe Staves for this County

Robertt Browne came into Courtt & acknowledged himselfe Gilty of Lying with a yonge Woman and haveing ye Carnall knowledge of her Contrary to ye Law in that case made and provided, and Cast himselfe upon ye mercy of ye bench to doe what ye pleased with him; And the Courtt Considering the unlawfull act of unclainess seeing the woman is not be found and ye s^{d} Browne Humbly submiting himselfe & promising for ye future to be carefull & doe soe noe more The Court have been pleased to show him mercey and doe fine him forty shillings to be paid into The sheriff before y^e next Court and to be discharged paying his fees. And Thomas Browne Brother to y^e s^d Robertt, doth Recognize himself in ye sum of Ten pounds for y^e payment of y^e $afores^d$ fine and Charges &c

The Courtt Adjorned for one hour and mett againe. . . .

Orders

Orders of the court are recorded by law in most jurisdictions for future reference. Executions are an important kind of order, often rating a separate volume for recording. They are directed to the sheriff, marshall, or constable to enforce, usually include a brief resumé of the court case and describe the judgment to be carried out. This example is typical:

Springfield Magistrate's Court, 1640

To John Searles of Springfield: These are in his Majesties name to require you presently uppon the receite hereof That you attach the body of John Woodcoke uppon an execution granted to Mr. George Moxon by the jury against the said John Woodcoke for an action of slander: and that you kepe his body in prison or irons untill he shall take some course to satisfie the said execution of £6 13^s 4^d granted by the Jury January 2d 1639. That you use what means you can to put him out to service and labor till he make satisfaction to the said George Moxon for the said £6 13^s 4^d and also to satisfie yourselfe for such charges as you shall be at for the keeping of his person: And when Mr. Moxon and your selfe are satisfied, Then you are to discharge his person out of prison; faile not at your perill.

Springfield this 5 October 1640
Per William Pynchon

Execution October 1, 1640

John Woodcoke not appreainge to give satisfaction to Mr. Moxon accordinge to the liberty tendered to him: Therefore I ordaine the execution as above.[7]

Many items of court business, especially before 1800, have nothing to do with litigation, for courts were administrative bodies as well as courts of law. The following extracts from court minutes and orders will show you the potential value of these records. Walter V. Ball, in an article titled "Family Records from County Court Order Books," notes:

Sometimes it is impossible to trace a family line without checking the county court order books, especially in the absence of any land records. Many of these records are not indexed and must be checked page by page which is a time-consuming task. Most, if not all, of these records have been microfilmed and sent to the state capitals. Unfortunately many of them have been destroyed by fire or otherwise but for anyone having access to them they are a valuable source of information.

My father was born in Tazewell County, Virginia, and as a youth I often heard him say his mother's people, the Cecils, came from Maryland. Several years ago I became interested in genealogy and through research I found so much history that I published a book on the Cecil family. This would not have been possible without reference to the county court order books, and it may be interesting to describe some of the missing links I found in them.

In checking in the Hall of Records, Annapolis, Maryland, I found some reference to William Cecil in the probate records but nothing in the land records. I found that he was in Queen Anne's Parish in Prince George's County and I spent many days checking the court records of that county. The first entry was found in the record of the September, 1696 court, where he was sued for debt of 459 pounds of tobacco. The next entry was so unusual that it is quoted below.

"March, 1697/8 Court: To the Commissioners of Prince Georges County these are humbly to Satisfie you that William Sessell, by the request of my wife as she lay on her death bed I have disposed of my children to Marreen Duval, and his heirs, till they are of age. John Sesell, aged seven years the 24th of December last past, Phillip Sesell, aged five years the 28th day of this instant and Susan Sessell, aged two years of January last /S/WILLIAM SESSELL."

This is the first time I have ever seen a record of children being given away, as they were usually bound out where there were no relatives to take care of them. In 1707 William Cecil appeared as a witness in a trial of Her Majesty vs Doctor Richard Pile. The Queen Ann's Parish Register shows he gave 50 pounds of tobacco to the church in 1709 and his son, John, was married there in 1718. The births of two of Phillip Cecil's daughters were recorded there in 1712 and 1716. In the November 1732 court, he made a petition for tax relief stating he was 67 years of age and had "spent most of his time in this Province." The Testamentary Proceedings show that Samuel Cecil, of Frederick County, was made administrator for the estate of William Cecil in July, 1749, and John Cecil was the bondsman. John was his son and Samuel was his grandson. In December, 1723, Phillip Cecil, the other son of William, bought 100 acres of land in Prince Georges County but in 1732-33 Phillip died and his wife, Elizabeth, was made Admnx of his estate, which was very small. In March, 1733, Elizabeth filed an inventory of the estate and in 1735 she rendered an account which was a rare find as it mentioned the heirs as "Phillip, John, William, Joshua, Elizabeth, and Mary, children of ye deceased."

Joshua Cecil and his brother, William, moved to Frederick County, Maryland, about 1753 as there is a record of a land patent to William that year. This land later fell into Montgomery County and the county court order books show Joshua Cecil was sued by Conrad Bladensburg for debt in 1775. Joshua Cecil was a soldier in the Revolutionary War and when he was an old man in 1805 he moved to Harrison County, Ohio. He died in 1814 and left a will naming his children including Joshua, Jr. Joshua Cecil, Jr., was married to Mary Reedon in Piscataway Parish, Prince George's County in 1787. Joshua Cecil was the name of my father's grandfather so I next went to Richmond, Va., to check the records of Tazewell County. Here again there were no land records so I had to fall back on the order books of the county court and here I found the following:

Order Book No. 1: Nov. 5, 1800. "The Commonwealth vs Joshua Cecil cont'd. Sept. 17, 1805. Joshua Cecil and Jane, his wife each prove two days attendance as witnesses."

Order Book No. 3: Feb. 27, 1821. "John Wynn is appointed administrator of the estate of Joshua Cecil, deceased." Jan. 28, 1823. "On the motion of John Wynn it is ordered that the overseers of the poor bind George Cecil and Joshua Cecil as the law directs."

By 1850 I could pick up the 3rd Joshua Cecil, and his family, from the census records but I had established proof of four ancestors in one line from the court order books. In the September 1967 issue of the NGS *Quarterly* an item I had written was published in which I cited another case where an ancestor was bound out in 1805 in Campbell County, Virginia. Copies of these records have been accepted by the Society of Colonial Wars, the Sons of the Revolution, and The Secretary of the War of 1812 as proof of descent. So I suggest that anyone having trouble tracing a family line try to search the county court order books or court judgment records as they are sometimes called.[8]

Memorials. The court may also order a memorial resolution as an expression of the community's respect for the deceased. Here is an 1849 example:

The death of Chapman Johnson occurred at the residence of John B. Baldwin in Richmond on the 12th of June 1849. The Court expressed respect and admiration for him. A motion to obtain a memorial to such a truly great and good man was made. He had many social and mental virtues and legal abilities, an ardent and unselfish patriotism, and monumental purity as a statesman.

Ordered that the court present to the presses of Staunton and Richmond for publication and a special copy to the family: 14 June 1849.

Having learned that Chapman Johnson, who was for many years a citizen of their town and acknowledged head of the legal profession, not only here but in the Commonwealth of Virginia, and who departed this life in the city of Richmond on the 12th of June it is due alike to their feelings and the public sentiment of the community that the Augusta County Bar Association gives publically their deep sense of loss, their affectionate regard for his memory, and their sympathy to his estimable family. Mr. Johnson became a resident of the town of Staunton more than 40 years ago. His profound learning as a lawyer and his distinguished eloquence as an orator endeared all to him. More than 20 years ago he removed himself to Richmond, but his removal did not sever the ties which bound him to Augusta County. A portion of each year was spent by him within our borders. In 1829, though of Richmond, he represented Augusta County at the convention to revise the State Convention. Our loss, with yours, is great.

It was further decided that the court would wear the badge of mourning for 30 days.[9]

This entry would be invaluable to the researcher unable to locate Chapman's whereabouts or unable to determine when or where he died.

Naturalizations. Often, the only reference to early naturalizations will be the court order granting citizenship. An 1851 example from the Augusta County, Virginia Court Order Book, announces:

> It is ordered by this court that Samuel Johnston formerly of Ireland who declared his intention to become a citizen of this state some 2 years ago having resided in the United States at least 4 years and in Virginia at least 1 year, be granted United States Citizenship.[10]

Furthermore, swearing-in formalities for a witness or a jury member often require a statement of citizenship status such as, "I, William Patrict, of Trenton, New Jersey, late of Dublin, Ireland, age 42, do declare. . ." This valuable information will usually only be found in the court minutes.

Appointment of Guardians. The following entry found in the Order Book of the Augusta County Court, Virginia, in 1750, is the only indication of the fact that James Berry is the guardian and not the father of these orphans: "Ordered that James Berry be appointed Guardian of John Berry, James Berry, and William Berry orphans of James Berry, dec'd." This item distinguishes between the three James Berrys.

Re-recording of Deeds. Order books are usually the places where deeds are re-recorded if the originals are not available. When the Rockingham County, Virginia, deed books were destroyed by fire, the county clerk reconstructed them from court orders and fragments that did not burn. This list of items appears in the February term in the order book:

> Deed Bryant to Moyus [Mavis] the wife of Thomas having acknowledged the same & their privy [private] examination taken as the law directs is OR [ordered recorded]
>
> A Deed Harrison to Read ackledged & OR
>
> A.D[eed]. of Lease Hudlow to Jackson proved by Witnefs thereto & OR
>
> A Deed Kyle to Stright proved by the Witnefs thereto & OR
>
> A Deed Fuzle to George Clemente ackledg wives acklgd taken and OR. . . .

A notation by the clerk establishes that these "entries are taken from the list of Deeds returned for record. . .and record thereof being wholly lost and neither the Original Deed nor certified copy being found for record."[11]

Judgments

In some jurisdictions, when judgment is given by the court and the case is closed, the court clerk is required to make an extensive minute entry with abridgement of the case and its resolution in a special book of judgments. These volumes are popular legal sources for lawyers and members of the bench because of their brevity; and before the days of printed court opinions, these judgments formed the precedents for future legal decisions. Here are some examples taken from the Eastowne (Westchester), New York, Mayor's Court for 1657:

> Eastowne May ye 1: 1657. where as it doth appeare in court that Roger miles Jarmia Akenes and hendrick corneloson waare the caus of kiling swine to the number of seven yet being a actidentall thing therefore the sentance of the coreut is yt they shall pay thirty shilings to anne quinbe proposinably and cost of coreut which is eighttene shilings and to be performed in ten days
>
> Eastowne may ye 1: 1657. whereas it appears in curuet that Larans Turner is in deted to hendrick Corneloson five pounds Sterling thirteen shilings yet becaus ten of the catel were not keept at winter ther fore the sentense of the couert is that Larans Turner shall pay to hendrick Corneluson five pounds Sterling acording to the complaint and [?] cost of coreut which is seven shiling
>
> mary Corneluson plantiv against gorg wright in an action of slander
>
> Eastowne may ye 1: 1657. it being proved in coreut that gorg wright hath ruyestly [illegible word] betwen mary Corneluson and good wife * * * that was formerly ended therefore the sentens of the cureut is that gorg wright is fined and shall pay to mary Corneluson three gilders and cost of court which is fourtene shilings to be performed in ten days
>
> Jun ye 12 1657. Richard Ponten plantive in the case of mary corneluson is plantive in atction of batrey against ales martin
>
> whereas Ales martine hath proseeded to the threattening of blodsheed with mary Corneluson and hat allso slandred her in a hey maner and hat charged the couert with in justice and hath charged one of the magstrates with speaking on truth therfor the sentanc of the couert is that Ales martine shall be punished by whipping her naked body as a magstrate or tow shall see caus to omit it and to pay all cost of couert
>
> September ye 1: 1657. Thomas martine plantive against Josiah Gilbord in a aktion of slander
>
> wher as it cannot be proved that Josiah Gilbord hath slanderd Thomas martin therfor for the sentanc of The cureut is that Thomas martin is to pay all cost of cureut which amounts to six shilings and three pense to be pad in 10 days.[12]

Case Files

These are among the most valuable of all court records because they contain original copies of evidence, writs, testimony, subpoenae, publications, etc., and thus are usually the most complete. It is in these files that details will be found which are never recorded in the minutes, orders, or judgments. In some jurisdictions, court clerks group all closed case files into one large bundle for each term of court and label it with that term. However, other court clerks assign case numbers to their files and access them through plaintiff-defendant cross indexes.

The contents of case files may vary from one document to hundreds. Even before shorthand, most significant testimony was taken down in writing and, if not signed by witnesses, at least attested by the court.

Witnesses Lists

Most courts reimbursed witnesses, an arrangement which encouraged participation from those who had to travel long distances or leave employment to appear. Witness books or lists show the names of witnesses and the amounts they received in payment. Some lists even include the addresses and ages of the witnesses named. (See Figure 6-5.)

These lists may not have been complete. Nevertheless, they still provide another means of identifying ancestral families in the cases where they exist.

Jury Records

You will likely find three types of juries: the grand jury, the petit jury, and the coroner's jury. The grand jury or indictment jury consists of one to twenty-three members and holds a preliminary hearing court to consider the evidence against a person accused of a crime and to determine if the evidence justifies holding the defendant for trial. They can also present those suspected guilty of law violations for punishment based upon their own personal knowledge.[13]

The petit jury, or trial jury, consists of six to twelve persons and acts as an impartial body to hear the evidence of the case and to reach a just decision based upon that evidence.

The coroner's jury consists of three to twenty-four members and is charged with hearing evidence about deaths under questionable circumstances. It is also called a jury of inquiry.

Most courts maintain separate records of jury duty. For each court term, a specific number of names is drawn from a list of all those eligible to serve, prepared from the tax records or voters' lists on file in the county. Figure 6-6 shows the jurors' names, addresses, occupations, and sometimes ages. Jurors excused or ex-

Spring Term 1842

Case	Witnesses' Names	No Days	No Miles	Amt	Whole Amt of Bill	Remarks
James B Trimble	John P. Harriman	3			1.59	Del[d]
vs	John Thompson	3	60	.25	4.24	"
Turner Wilson & Co	same	4	70	.25	5.17	"
John Brown	John Supple	3		1.50	3.09	Del[d]
vs	Gowen Hayes	4		.31	2.43	"
P.M. Hall						
Nelson & Gillihand	James Dodson	9		.25	5.02	At Fall Term
abt	same	2		.12	1.18	1841 Del[d]
C.B. Thompson						At this Term Del[d]
George Nevill	Henry Robinson	4			5.12	Del[d]
vs	George Nibert	5		.62	3.27	Del[d]
Noyes & Donnelly	Joseph C Harvey	6			3.18	"
	Thomas Scott	5			2.65	"
Donnelly & Noys	Ben F Scott	6		.12	3.30	Del[d]
abt						
George Nevill						

Figure 6-5. Brooke County, West Virginia Witness Book, Spring Term 1842; transcript from original in Brooke County Courthouse, Wellsburg, West Virginia.

empt are indicated with the reason for the dismissal. Each person selected is summoned to appear by the court. The coroner's jury is also called by drawing and summons—but it serves only for a specific case.

In most jurisdictions, jury call was mandatory unless the person had an acceptable excuse for refusing. The only records kept were the summons and minute entries made by the court clerk. Before long, however, many jurisdictions began to reimburse jurors for travel costs and loss of employment income while on duty and to keep careful records of jury service as a basis for payment.

When the court meets in session each day, a roll call of jurors determines who is present.

Many courts require grand juries to keep careful record of their investigations in separate volumes. These records contain the roll-call, description of the case under consideration including testimony of witnesses, reports, and findings of the jury. The actual trial record of a case after indictment contains a summary of the findings of the grand jury, but its own minutes are usually more complete.

In a jury book, you will find each case listed with the names of jurors who served on the case, the court term, the case number, and the number of the juror. Some courts prefer to record petit, grand, and coroner juries separately, while others use the same volume for all three types.

The attendance record gives the names and addresses of the jurors, the days served, the days defaulted, date excused from service, and the kind of jury—petit, grand, coroner—on which each juror served. From this attendance record, payment is made for the number of days served.

Not all jurisdictions use and/or preserve discharge certificates. Each certificate shows the name and address of the juror, the date of discharge from jury duty, and sometimes the reason for discharge—death, disability, end of term, etc.

The genealogical value of jury records lies in such information as names, occupations, and addresses. Jury records can also prove that the person named is still alive at that date, that he/she is a citizen of the jurisdiction, that he/she owns property—real estate or its equivalent—in the jurisdiction, and that he/she is of legal age. If a juror dies or moves from the jurisdiction during service, normally the record will note it.

Attorney Records

The attorneys who appear in court in behalf of the plaintiff or defendant are not always lawyers. In fact, several colonies in early years actually banned the practice of law by an attorney-at-law, a professional lawyer educated in techniques and procedures of law. Instead, their role was taken by an attorney-in-fact, a proxy for the plaintiff or defendant who pleads the case for someone else before the court.[14] In most colonies, they were literate and experienced individuals, though not technically trained.

As universities were founded and travel and communication with England improved, the number of attorneys-at-law increased, while attorneys-in-fact decreased in proportion. By the time of the Revolution, the colonies had trained lawyers and learned judges, but lay attorneys still acted for many decades.

You can expect to find two main types of records concerning attorneys. The first is letters of attorney, or permission for an attorney-in-fact to appear before the court in behalf of a plaintiff or defendant. Such a letter is very similar to the letters testamentary or administrative in a probate case and contains the name of attorney, the party granting proxy, the case involved, and the date when permission is granted.

The second is rolls of attorneys. Most courts maintain separate volumes of attorneys and members of the local bar who are licensed and approved to appear before that particular court. Each roll contains the name of the attorney, the sponsor, and the date of the admission to the bar. Some rolls also contain dates of death, disbarment, removal from the jurisdiction, etc. Some jurisdictions require law students to register as prospective bar members. These registrations contain the name and address of the student, the lawyer under whom the intern will serve, school, sponsors, and the report of the board of law examiners concerning qualifications. Sometimes the birthdate, birthplace, age, and even parents are included.

Coroners' Records

The coroner's foremost responsibility is to conduct inquests when a death occurs within his/her jurisdiction which involves a question of foul play, violence, or suicide. The inquest determines if a criminal act has been committed and, if so, the potential guilty party. No inquest is necessary in deaths from natural causes, illness, and accident with no indication of negligence. In some jurisdictions, the inquest is ordered by the court, in some by justices of the peace, and in some by the county attorney. In fact, in jurisdictions where an official coroner is not appointed, the justice of the peace or the county (district) attorney serves in this capacity. In

Figure 6-6. Payroll, Petit Jurors, April Term 1879, Probate Minutes, Utah County, Utah, 21 Oct. 1879; State Archives, State Capitol Bldg., Salt Lake City, Utah.

Names of Petit Jurors	Residence	Days	Amount	Miles	Amount	Total
John Bastian	Salem City Juab County	1	3 00	45	4 50	7 50
A. M. White	Diamond " "	1	3 00	45	4 50	7 50
H. Sanborn	Diamond " "	1	3 00	45	4 50	7 50
Richard Tyner	Salem City " "	1	3 00	45	4 50	7 50
J. W. Green	Diamond " "	1	3 00	45	4 50	7 50
M. A. Spafford	Anna Bella Springs [illegible]	1	3 00	140	14 00	17 00
James W. Rundy	Salem City Juab County	1	3 00	45	4 50	7 50
J. B. Honeyman	Diamond " "	1	3 00	45	4 50	7 50
Patrick Harrington	Diamond " "	1	3 00	45	4 50	7 50
E. K. Williams	Nephi " "	1	3 00	45	4 50	7 50
Roger Farrer Jr.	Provo City Utah Co	1	3 00	1	10	3 10
Amos W. Haws	" " "	1	3 00	1	10	3 10
David Cluff Jr.	" " "	1	3 00	1	10	3 10
Joseph W. Jones	" " "	1	3 00	1	10	3 10
John Whittbeck	Nephi Juab Co	1	3 00	45	4 50	7 50
Helen M. Huntley	Nephi Juab Co	1	3 00	45	4 50	7 50
Peter Madsen	Ephraim San Pete Co	1	3 00	80	8 00	11 00
Luke Cook	Provo City Utah Co	1	3 00	1	10	3 10
David Holdaway	" " "	1	3 00	1	10	3 10
Wm Fairbanks	Payson Utah Co	1	3 00	18	1 80	4 80
Jno W. Holliday	Santaquin " "	1	3 00	24	2 40	5 40
John M. Allred	Spring City San Pete Co	1	3 00	75	7 50	10 50
Joseph P. Allred	Chester " "	1	3 00	75	7 50	10 50
M. K. Kelsey	Springville Utah "	1	3 00	6	60	3 60
Calvin Van Leuven	" " "	1	3 00	6	60	3 60
Wm J. Bringhurst	" " "	1	3 00	6	60	3 60

more modern times, coroners have been replaced by medical examiners—especially in urban areas.

Here are the documents produced in one coroner's inquest in 1844: the warrant, which convenes the inquest and calls jurors; the inquisition, which determines the facts of the case; and the deposition, which records the witnesses' testimony. The case is titled as The State v. the dead body of a Negro woman Violet, the property of John Dinkins, Edgefield District, South Carolina. The warrant is issued by the coroner in the name of South Carolina.

> To the Sheriff or any lawful constable
> of Edgefield District
>
> Greating:
>
> These are to require you to immediately upon receipt and sight hereof, to summon and warn, verbally or otherwise, 4 men of the said district to be and appear before me the Coroner of said District at John Dinkins as within the said District between the hours of 8 and 9 o'clock on tomorrow am. there and then to inquire upon the view of a body of a certain person there lying dead how she came to her death. Fail not herein as you will answer to the contrary at your peril. Given under my hand and seal at Edgefield Courthouse
>
> 24 Mar AD 1844
> by me Dan Holland, Coroner

The coroner's inquisition produced a document summarizing the facts of the case as the jury determined them:

> An inquisition indented and taken at John Dinkins in Edgefield District on 25 Mar AD 1844 before me Daniel Holland, Coroner for the said district upon view of the body of a negro woman (slave) named Violet the property of said John Dinkins then and there being dead by the oaths of J.R. Tillman, John Doby, M.L. Gantry, James Dinkins, William Lundy, James Johnson, William Walker, Reuben Cooper, William I. Walker, John Cooper, William Doby, and Joseph Morris being a lawful jury of inquest who being charged and sworn to inquire for the State of South Carolina where and by what means said negro woman Violet came to her death upon their oaths do say, that the said Violet did on yesterday morning about 9 oclock near the said John Dinkins spring in said District violently, willfully and feloniously destroy her own life, by hanging herself by the neck with a rope to the limb of a tree and so the jurors aforesaid upon their oaths do say that the aforesaid Violet in manner and form aforesaid then and there voluntarily and feloniously herself did kill, against the peace and the dignity of the county aforesaid. In witness whereof, I Dan Holland Coroner aforesaid and the jurors aforesaid to this inquisition have interchangeably put our hands and seals this day and year aforesaid.
>
> J. R. Tillman — Wm Walker
> John Doby — Reuben Cooper
> M. L. Gantry — William I. Walker
> James Dinkins — Jno Cooper
> William Lundy — Wm Doby
> James Johnson — Joseph Morris
>
> Danl Holland Coroner

Two depositions follow:

> John Dinkins the owner of Violet and first person that found the dead body was sworn and says: that on yesterday the 24 Mar 1844 about 11 oclock in the morning he found the dead body of Violet near his spring

hanging by the neck with a rope to the limb of a tree, that she had been missing from his house about 2 or 3 hours before he found her dead, that himself and several of his neighbors took her from the tree (where hung) last evening and laid her in the house where she now lies, with the rope around her neck, just as she is now and he verily believes that she hung herself without the agency or assistance of any other person that from what he has learned, the hussy had it in contemplation to destroy herself for sometime past Sworn to this 25 Mar Ad 1844

John Dinkins

Before me
Dan Holland Coroner

Simeon Dinkins was sworn and says: that about 3 o clock yesterday (having previously heard that Violet had hung herself) he came to the spring of John Dinkins and there he saw the dead body of Violet hanging by the neck with a rope to the limb of a tree, that it appeared from all circumstances that she hung herself, that he saw her body taken from the tree and brought to the house just as it is now, with the rope around her neck that he has owned Violet and she was a negro of a very unhappy and ungovernable disposition that he has no doubt (from all circumstances) that she had had it in contemplation for sometime past to destroy herself and he has no doubt but that she hung herself without the agency or assistance of any other person Sworn to this 25 Mar AD 1844

his
Simeon X Dinkins
mark

before me
Dan Holland Coroner

The coroner is also responsible to carry out the regular duties of the sheriff should he become personally involved in a particular case. However, as the records produced are almost always filed with the sheriff's records, no problem arises from this occurrence.

Sheriff (Marshall, Constable, Chief of Police) Records

In every action filed in the courts of record, a sheriff is called upon to perform some service. He serves the official writs, summons, and subpoenae; and he must execute all final judgments of the court. The sheriff is responsible for the preservation of the peace; enforcement of laws; arresting felons and committing them to jail; and executing the mandates, orders, and directions of the court. He has the power to command every person above fifteen years of age to respond for the protection of the jurisdiction and preservation of the peace in times of emergency or be subject to fine or imprisonment. In so acting, he represents the sovereignty of the state, and no one in the county is superior to him.

The counterpart of the sheriff in a large municipality would be the chief of police, in the federal court system, the marshall. The constable serves in a like manner within the area served by a magistrate or justice of the peace – he serves as the sheriff in any matter within the jurisdiction of the local magistrate. He has the same powers and responsibilities within his more limited sphere of authority.

We can conveniently divide the records preserved by the sheriff into those produced as executive officer of the court and those produced as an instrument of law enforcement.

Records Produced as Court Executive. The sheriff is responsible to serve all writs issued by the court. Original writs are unserved writs. They may be current ones about to be served or old ones for persons whose whereabouts are unknown or whose fees for service have not been paid. Some jurisdictions require that the sheriff preserve a copy of all writs which he served. Some sheriffs maintain a running list of the writs they have received for service. This list contains the type of writ, the date issued, the names and addresses of the parties, the court term, case number, and the date filed.

In some jurisdictions, record of all writs is kept in the same volume. In others, various kinds of writs are recorded in separate volumes, i.e., capias, summons, warrants, executions, sales of condemned property, etc.

Most sheriffs also preserve a docket recording all writs served and any resultant sales of property. This docket will give the names of the parties, court, term and case number, title of the action, date filed, attorney named, costs and fees, disposition (judgment and execution) of the case, and the sheriff's signature.

Some sheriffs keep a special volume recording all deeds transferred by sheriff's sale. These show the description of the property, the date and amount of sale, the name and address of the grantee, and the date of the deed.

A lien book is similar, recording all liens on property within their jurisdiction which have resulted from court order. They will show the date of the lien, the parties involved, date of sale notice, location, and description of property.

Because the sheriff is frequently responsible to select as well as summon the jurors for each court term, he will often have a copy of the court's jury records.

Records Produced in Law Enforcement. Many sheriffs maintain a fingerprint and "mug" file; however, they are of such recent origin it is rare for the genealogical researcher to encounter them.

In most jurisdictions, the sheriff is responsible for the care and supervision of the local jail and its occupants. Unknown to most researchers, jail records are available as early as 1695 and perhaps earlier. Not only that, but the majority of incarcerations in the past were for debt, not crime.[15]

Before the American Revolution, jails were used to detain offenders awaiting trial, debtors, and witnesses. Violators of laws sometimes had to wait as long as a year before being brought to trial, and debtors were held until their property could be condemned and sold to pay the debts. Debtors with no property were released.

Some jurisdictions, Georgia, for example, "farmed out" convicts and debtors for labor and board[16] beginning during the last quarter of the eighteenth century or the first quarter of the nineteenth century. (For a more complete treatment of jail records, see Chapter 9, "Institutional Records.") Jail records include a journal, kept by the sheriff, jail warden, or deputy. It is similar to a daybook and shows the name and sex of every prisoner, the type of sentence and its length, dates of commitment and discharge, and reason for discharge: death, pardon, termination of sentence, etc.

The register of prisoners contains a physical description of the prisoner (hair, eyes, weight, height – later records contain fingerprints and photo), name and address, age, occupation, date and place of birth, habits and distinguishing characteristics, crime committed, sentence, education, previous prison record, dates of commitment and discharge, name of committing official, etc. This record can also be called the admission record, commitment register, prisoner's docket, or discharge book, and is required by law in most jurisdictions. Some even include the destinations of discharged offenders.

Some jurisdictions have required medical records since the early days of the jail. This register contains the name, physical description, age, sex, mental condition, and a brief medical history of each prisoner requiring medical attention. As part of this history, names and ages of parents, brothers and sisters, spouses, and children are often included.

The prisoners' daily record shows the daily roll of prisoners, their names, the date, the number of meals served, the total cost per day for each prisoner, etc.

Because the United States had no penitentiaries for several decades for those convicted in federal courts under federal laws, a separate record was kept on these prisoners in regular jails so that claims for costs could be submitted to the federal government.

Since 1814, jail keepers have been required to keep a separate record of all prisoners of war either awaiting trial or imprisoned after conviction – again for reimbursement by the government. The contents of these registers are similar to the regular registers, but also contain information concerning capture and military unit.

Most jurisdictions require that the jail keeper prepare an inventory of prisoners' property taken into custody during their term of imprisonment. The prisoner's name and signature is usually found in these records, along with the list of property.

Some jails preserve a record of all prisoners who are transferred to another jail showing the name, date of commitment, date and place of transfer, reason for transfer, etc.

In one family research project, Bridget Nixon proved decidedly elusive. A family tradition said her alcoholism alienated her family. Her children were housed with relatives, the husband finally divorced her, then remarried, and reunited the children. Finding documents to support the tradition, however, was difficult until a search of the jail records revealed her activities in St. Paul, Minnesota, 1856-60.

Aug 1856 p. 77	Criminal Court City of St. Paul vs Bridget Nixon Disorderly conduct, no return of process
20 Nov 1856 p. 84	Cited Bridget Nixon for drunkenness arrested by officer White W.R. Miller, City Marshall
Nov 1856 p. 90	Police Court of St. Paul United States vs Bridget Nixon Threats of violence Defendant committed in default of recognizance to keep the peace Orlando Simons, City Justice. . . .
May 26 1857	Report of the Chief of Police W.R. Miller submits claims for boarding of prisoners Mrs. Bridget Nixon, intoxication arrested by Officer Powers 25 May
11 June 1957 (*sic*)	Mrs. Nixon arrested for intoxication by Officer Wollers, 26 May
21 July 1857	Bridget Nixon arrested for assault and battery by Officer Morton, 16 July. . . .
7 Dec. 1858 p. 156	Arrests – Mrs. Nixon, intoxication by Officer Morton, 1 Dec. . . .
17 June 1859 p. 39	Report, Chief of Police, W. Crosby Mrs. B. Nixon, disorderly conduct arrested by Officer Miller
20 May 1859	City of St. Paul vs Bridget Nixon Disorderly conduct Defendant fined $10.00 and committed in default of payment
27 June 1859 p. 46	Identical entry [duplicate or repeat of offense not clear][17]

How to Search Court Records

Before 1800

Search page by page, unless your jurisdiction is lucky enough to have an every-name index. Begin on the first page for the period of time your ancestor lived in the area and work through each page. Where printed volumes or abstracts are available, use them as indexes to take you to the pages where your ancestor is recorded. Where there are no printed copies, search page by page, entry by entry, and extract entries with pertinent data.

To make positive and direct connections between each pedigree generation, especially if you have one of the 2,000 most common names in America, you will have to be very thorough. The professional genealogist, searching records for a fee for a client, will have to take some calculated risks since the costs of page-by-page searching are high in both time and money. Even so, such methodology is often necessary before 1800, for identifying information is otherwise too sketchy to make the right connection.

Since 1800

Colin James recommended in 1972 a search procedure that has proved consistently successful in his "United States Court Records, Part II: Genealogical Data to be Found in Court Records," a paper presented to the Utah Genealogical Association, Salt Lake City, Utah, 1972.

Figure 6-7. Index to Equity Cases, Cass Co., Ill., photocopy of original in Cass County Courthouse, Sigourney, Ill.

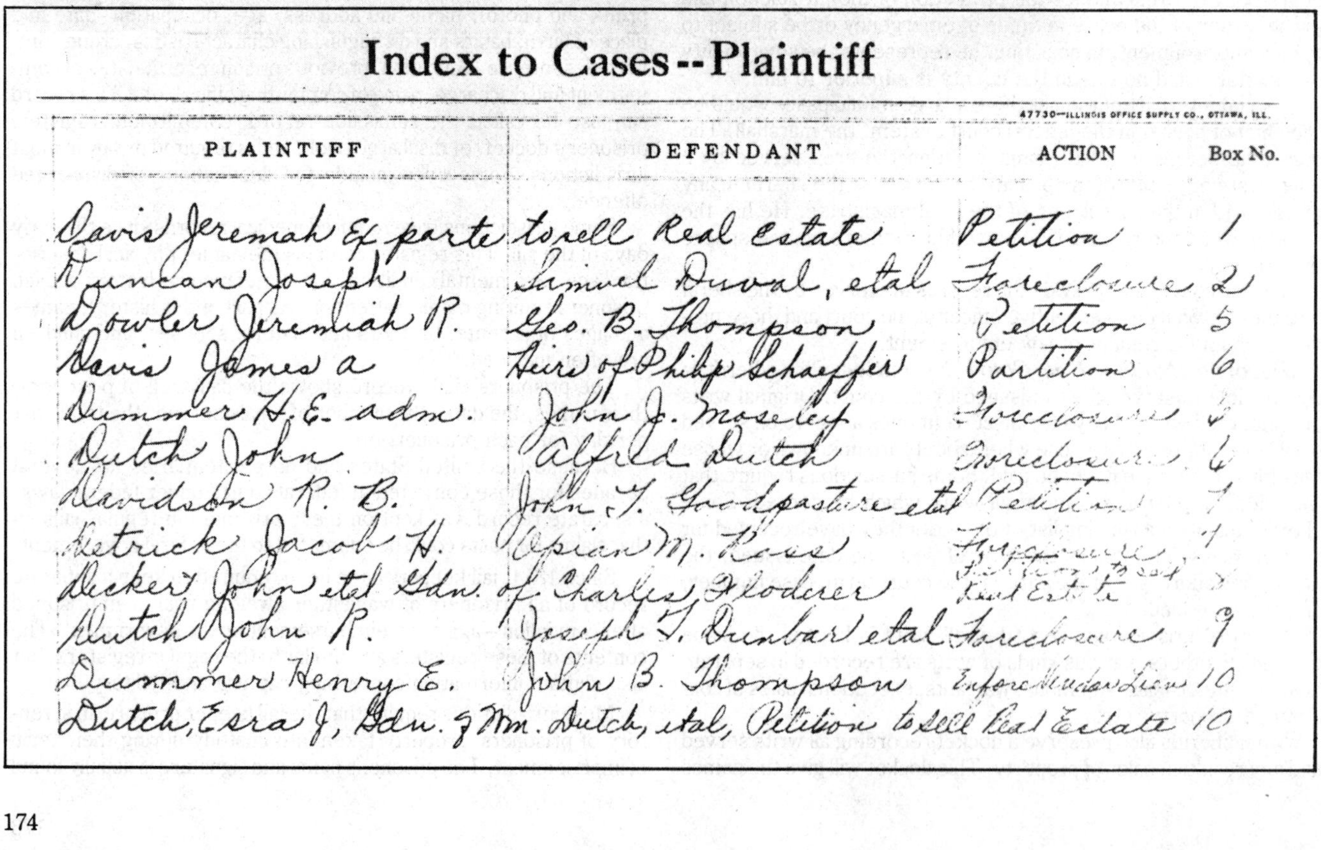

Index to Cases -- Plaintiff

47730—ILLINOIS OFFICE SUPPLY CO., OTTAWA, ILL.

PLAINTIFF	DEFENDANT	ACTION	Box No.
Davis Jeremah Ex parte	to sell Real Estate	Petition	1
Duncan Joseph	Samuel Duval, etal	Foreclosure	2
Dowler Jeremiah R.	Geo. B. Thompson	Petition	5
Davis James a	Heirs of Philip Schaeffer	Partition	6
Dummer H.E. adm.	John J. Moseley	Foreclosure	3
Dutch John	Alfred Dutch	Foreclosure	6
Davidson R. B.	John T. Goodpasture etal	Petition	7
Detrick Jacob H.	Apian M. Ross	Foreclosure	7
Decker John etal Gdn.	of Charles Flodecer	Petition to sell Real Estate	
Dutch John R.	Joseph T. Dunbar etal	Foreclosure	9
Dummer Henry E.	John B. Thompson	Enforce Mechanic Lien	10
Dutch, Esra J, Gdn. of Wm. Dutch, etal,		Petition to sell Real Estate	10

First, ask for the index to court cases – civil, criminal, or equity – whichever you wish to begin with. (See Figure 6-7.) Since about 1840, most courts have both a plaintiff and a defendant (or reverse) index. This index will give you the case number, or the box in which the case file or packet (also called a case jacket) is stored.

Next, ask the clerk for the case jacket or file by case or box number. You will receive a small packet of documents folded or rolled into a bundle and secured with a string or a rubber band. This file has the loose documents and copies of the important papers of the case.

Then examine the docket book entries, using the dates for the beginning of the case and the date it was closed by judgment, which you will find on the outside of the case file. Entries are either made numerically by case number or chronologically by date of case. A quick glance will tell you which applies. Examine all the entries for that case to see if there are other references you need to check. For example, the docket book may note: "Exhibits 1-14 in storage vault" or "Companion case, No. 4321."

From the case packet, decide whether you will begin with the orders, judgments, or other documents. Wherever you find a reference to another document which does not appear in your file, seek it out. Watch carefully for evidence that the case was appealed to a higher court or that the parties settled by arbitration.

Most search strategies suggest that you begin with the index and docket entries and then search the bound volumes for each court case. This procedure works if you don't know the case number or if there is no index to cases. It also takes longer since bound volumes provide fewer details.

Many court records are on microfilm through the Genealogical Society of Utah, including some case files. Especially noteworthy are the collections for York County, Maine, the eastern counties of Tennessee, much of Georgia, the Northern Neck of Virginia, and the adjoining counties of West Virginia. Some states and counties have microfilmed their early records to provide better access for users without handling fragile volumes. They are kept in state archives and county offices.

The vast majority of court records are still in local courthouse vaults and storage areas. To search these, request a photocopy of the indexes or dockets for the period of time and the surnames you are searching. This is a short, easy request, for which you can expect to pay between $5 and $15 depending upon the county. When you get your index copies, then order the files you wish, giving specific case numbers. It is wise to ask for a cost estimate before the files are copied, although some courts will bill you. Then you can send the right amount when you order the files. Some courts will supply estimates over the phone.

If you have a whole list of cases to check, hire a local genealogist to search them for you and provide extracts or photocopies of both the recorded copies in bound volumes and the case files, omitting duplicate documents.

Do not ask court personnel to make extensive searches for you. They have neither the time nor the interest to do a careful job; and a missed entry can be misleading.

Printed Court Records

Court records are being printed in extract form and as verbatim transcriptions so rapidly it is difficult to keep current. While it is usually best to rely upon original documents for research accuracy, the condition of original court records varies considerably: some are still firmly bound and easy to read, some are faded and crumbling, some are torn or have missing pages, some have been restored through lamination, and many have been destroyed or lost. As a result of these circumstances, printed transcripts can prove invaluable to the researcher who knows their limitations and uses them wisely.

Most printed volumes with verbatim transcripts are also indexed, including the names of all witnesses, jurors, court personnel, attorneys and litigants. In addition, they usually give the volume and page number of the original record and sometimes the case number. Thus, the printed volumes can serve as an effective and accurate index to the originals.

Original court records are difficult to read due to the unfamiliar handwriting of the court clerk, the prevalence of legal terms, Latin and French words, unknown abbreviations, and fading ink. A well-trained, experienced editor can often make a better transcript than an untrained researcher. Such a copy can be used as a guide to understand the words in each document and can thus save hours of poring over hard-to-read documents.

Many transcripts of early records were made during the 1800s. Since that time, the originals have been destroyed or lost. Although they vary widely in quality, these transcripts may represent the only existing copies of many records.

Extracts/abstracts are abbreviated versions of the original documents; no attempt is made to copy them entirely. Here is an example. The number in parentheses refers to the original page number.

March 16, 1779

(400) Garrat Wheeler exempted from levy.

(400) Commission for examination of Jane, wife of Robert Buchanan. Deed to Philip Sciler.

(402) Elizabeth, wife of James Thorpe, soldier in the Continental Army, with small children, allowed £25.

(402) Joseph Crouch recommended as Captain, Alexr. Maxwell as Lieutenant, and Patrick Hamilton as Ensign.

(403) John Lewis, Wm. Lowther and Andrew Davidson qualified Justices.

(404) William Robertson, Captain, and Nicholas Sybert, as First Lieutenant – qualified.

(406) Commission for priv. examination of Mille, wife of Charles Cummins, as to deed to Robert Cummins.

(406) Joseph Crouch as Captain, Jacob Warwick and Alexr. Maxwell as First Lieutenants – qualified.

(407) Elizabeth Wilson, soldier's wife, with small children, allowed £20.

(407) Admn. of estate of William Wallace granted widow Jane.

(408) Court appoints John Graham guardian of Joseph Graham, orphan of David Graham.[18]

Verbatim transcripts record every word with original punctuation and spelling. The editor will indicate in brackets any additions he/she makes. The following are examples:

Records of the Court of Sessions of Westchester County (New York): (Westchester Historical Society Publications, Vol. 1)

At a Court of Sessions held at Westchester for Ye County of Westchester by their Maj[es]ties Authority p[r]esent John Pell Justice & Quorum presed[en]t of the Court: John Palmer Justice of ye peace & Quorum & Daniel Strang & William Barnes Esqrs Justices of ye peace Decem[ber] ye 1st: 1691 – absent Joseph Theale Esqr Justice of ye Peace [1692 crossed out: 1691 inserted]

The Court opened

The Grand Jury Called & Appeared (Viz.)

Robert Hustead	John fforgeson
John fferis Senjor	Robt Hustead Junjor
John Mullenax	John Hadden Senjor
Joseph Hunt	Edwd Hadden
John Hunt	John Winter
John Quinby Junjor	Tho. Bedient
John Baly	Samll Palmer
	William Chadderton

The Court Adjurnes till Thursday morning

Constables Called

Westchester	
Eastchester	x
Rochell	Same
Momoroneck	x
Rye	x
& per younkers	x
Bedford	x all absent but westchester Rochell Same

[Page 2]
Mary Bayly Enters a Compl[ain]t against her husband Nathan baly by Mr. Antill her Atturney by petition

[next is crossed out] the Court hears the Complt and orders that Nathan Baly shall be sent for by a special warr[an]tt & that he appear on ye 17th Instant to Answer ye above said Complt directed to ye Sherrif or his Deputy And if he doth not appeare at the time appointed at westchester Court the matter is deferred for further Examination unto Justice pell & Justice Theale.[19]

Annotated transcripts are verbatim transcriptions with records from other courts, case files, and/or court opinions to reconstruct the whole case. (Rarely, however, are all papers in the case file used.)

Evaluating Printed Records

As with any copied record, errors are frequently made. Here is a checklist to help you determine the accuracy and completeness of the printed copy:

1. Compare a few pages of the transcribed copy selected at random with the original document, where it exists, to spot errors or omissions.
2. What is the editor's reputation? Is the editor known for correct work or does he/she sacrifice accuracy to save time or money? Does the editor have the proper training, education, and experience to insure a good job?
3. Based on your experience or that of a genealogist specializing in court records, do the number of cases covered appear sufficient for the approximate number of people living in the jurisdiction?
4. Is it listed in an annotated bibliography? Here is the notation for one work from a bibliography of published New England court records:

> 21. *Records of the Suffolk County Court, 1672-1680.* Edited by Samuel Elliot Morison with an Introduction by Zachariah Chafee, Jr. In publications of the Colonial Society of Massachusetts, *Collections*, Vols. 29-30. Boston: Published by the Society, 1933. These volumes represent a high-water mark in the editing of American colonial legal records. The editor has supplemented the records with copious extracts from the relevant file papers, and Professor Chafee has contributed a valuable essay. There is a most ample general index of names and subjects, and a separate table of reference to the General Laws and Liberties. Absolutely definitive for the court and period covered.[20]

What do reviewers say? Reliable publications are *Journal of American Legal History, The American Genealogist, The Genealogical Journal,* and other specialized historical and genealogical journals.

In the preface or introduction, the editor will explain his/her editorial policies, changes made in the original, and describe the original itself. For example:

> In reproducing these old records the manuscript has been faithfully followed, even when this means repeating obvious slips made by the old scribes, such as omissions of words, repetitions of words, or the use of words clearly wrong. The only liberty taken with the original text has been. . .to supply in brackets the missing word or words, where the old paper. . .has left enough letters of the defective word to justify this.[21]

Finding Printed Court Records

Many volumes of printed court records are available, but there is no complete bibliography of titles or locations. Here are some suggestions about places to look:

1. Published state archives. Most of the original colonies/states authorized publication of original court records in series called archives. Such compiled volumes as *Pennsylvania Archives, Maryland Archives*, and *Connecticut Archives* are examples. Complete sets are available in most research libraries.

AMS Press, 56 East 13th Street, New York, NY 10003, has reprinted the volumes for all thirteen original colonies except New Jersey and Louisiana, Maine, and Mississippi.

2. Local histories, particularly those published around the turn of the nineteenth century, frequently contain extracts or transcribed court records. Some are accurately reproduced with careful indexes; some have many errors. Be sure to check for appendixes, special sections of documents, and quotations in the middle of town and family sections.
3. Extracts, indexes, and complete transcripts of court records can be found in journals, occasional publications, annual volumes, and special series. See Chapter 13, "Genealogical Tools and Indexes."
4. Jeffrey, William, Jr. "Early New England Court Records: A Bibliography of Published Materials."*American Journal of Legal History* 1 (1957): 119-47. Reprinted from the *Boston Public Library Bulletin*. Contains a listing of the records published, the dates covered, name of court; title, author, and bibliographic data of printed volume; description and index; brief analysis of editing done and omissions.
5. Greene, Evarts B., and Richard B. Morris. *A Guide to the Principal Sources for Early American History (1600-1800) in the City of New York.* 2nd ed. New York: Columbia University Press, 1953. This reference volume contains a separate section of printed sources, including court records, found in various record depositories in New York City. They are arranged by subject and thereunder by state and locality.
6. Chapin, Bradley. *Criminal Justice in Colonial America, 1606-1660.* Athens, Ga.: The University of Georgia Press, 1983. This is a valuable description of courts and their jurisdiction, and specific crimes for which punishment was meted out before 1660 in America. The author includes a list of selected cases and a full bibliography of early sources. Since there are no printed reports, few indexes, and missing volumes for this period, the list is especially valuable. The genealogist who is searching for an American ancestor in this early period will benefit from a careful study of this book.
7. Volumes of court records have been published through the American Legal Records Series of the American Historical Association:

Bond, C. T. and Richard B. Morris, eds. *Proceedings of the Maryland Court of Appeals.* Washington, D.C.: American Historical Association, 1933.

Morris, Richard B., ed. *Select Cases of the Mayor's Court of New York City.* Washington, D.C.: American Historical Association, 1935.

Towle, Dorothy S., ed. *Records of the Court of Vice Admiralty of Rhode Island.* Washington, D.C.: American Historical Association, 1939.

Ferrell, J. T., ed. *The Superior Court Diary of William Samuel Johnson, 1773-93.* Washington, D.C.: American Historical Association, 1942.

Reed, H. Clay, and G. J. Miller, eds. *The Burlington Court Book.* Washington, D.C.: American Historical Association, 1944.

Gregoria, Anne K., ed. *Records of the Court of Chancery of South Carolina, 1671-1679.* Washington, D.C.: American Historical Association, 1950.

Ames, Susie, ed. *County Court Records of Accomack-Northampton, Virginia, 1632-40.* Washington, D.C.: American Historical Association, 1954.

Smith, Joseph H., ed. *Colonial Justice in Western Massachusetts (1639-1702): The Pynchon Court Record.* Cambridge: Harvard University Press, 1961.

Crowl, Philip A., and Joseph H. Smith, eds. *Records of the Court of Prince Georges' County.* Annapolis, Md.: American Historical Association with Maryland Hall of Records, 1964.

Since the initial series was completed, other volumes have been published by university or trade press publishers which come within the same scope. For example, the University Press of Virginia published in 1973, Susie M. Ames, ed., *County Court Records of Accomack-Northampton, Virginia 1640-1645. The Plymouth Court Records, 1686-1859,* are edited by David T. Konig in sixteen indexed and annotated volumes, available from Michael Glazier, Inc., 1210 King St., Wilmington, DE 19801.

Probate

Probate cases are distinctive enough to be discussed separately from civil, criminal, and equity proceedings. The records they generate are among the most valuable genealogical materials we have in America. They are also among the most complicated, filled with pitfalls for the unwary.

The probate process transfers the legal responsibility for payment of taxes, care, and custody of dependent family members, liquidation of debts, and transfer of property title to heirs from the deceased to an executor/executrix (where there is a will), to an administrator/administratrix (if the person dies intestate—without a will), or to a guardian/conservator if there are heirs under the age of twenty-one years or in cases where a person has become incompetent through disease or disability.

Testate Estates

When a person makes a last will and testament, he/she leaves a testate estate. Originally, a will devised real estate (or land) and property attached to it—buildings, mills, timber, water rights, etc. A testament bequeathed personalty (personal property) made up of movables (lump sums of money, books, jewelry, furniture, clothing, horses, cattle, pigs, sheep, grain, tools, slaves, services of indentured servants) and receivables (book debts, mortgages, bills of exchange, and loans). American laws generally leave a person free to distribute his/her estate at will as long as it does not leave the heirs dependent for their upkeep on the state.

Wills are of three different kinds: (1) Attested wills are prepared in writing, signed by responsible witnesses who certify to the court that the will was written at the instance of the deceased of his/her own free will and choice and that he/she was of sound mind at the time he/she did it. (2) Holographic wills are written completely in the handwriting of the person making the will, signed, dated, and not witnessed. If any other person writes on the will, it is invalid. In addition, the will must be found among the individual's important papers. It cannot be filed with an attorney or other third party unless all valuable papers are so filed. In some jurisdictions, this kind of will is not valid. (3) Nuncupative wills are oral, death-bed wills dictated to witnesses who convert them to writing at the earliest possible moment and present them to the court within a specified period of time after the person dies. In some jurisdictions, this kind of will is also invalid.

Intestate Estates

When a person dies without making a will, his/her property becomes an intestate estate. It is divided according to settlement shares determined by law. In most states, if the deceased is a married man, the widow receives one-third (known also as her dower rights) and the rest is divided equally among the children. If a child is dead, his share is divided among his own legal heirs. An illegitimate child is entitled to inherit from his/her mother; unless the father has acknowledged his parenthood in writing, duly witnessed and accepted by the court, or unless he later marries the mother, a child cannot inherit by law from the father. Some states allow the father to petition for a legislative act to legitimize his children so they can inherit, and some allow naturalization of deceased persons by special act so their heirs can inherit.

If a person dies without issue, his/her estate passes to his/her spouse and if he/she has no spouse, then to his/her parents and brothers and sisters. In some states, descent of property goes no further than this. In some, lines of descent become quite complicated with provision even for nephews, second cousins, and others.

In community property jurisdictions (Louisiana, California, Washington, Idaho, etc.) the property that a husband and wife own at the time of marriage and the property that each individually inherits afterwards remain separate property; the property which they acquire together during their married life becomes community property in which each has an undivided one-half interest. Upon the death of one, the common estate automatically reverts to the surviving spouse in fee simple.

In noncommunity property states, a woman has a dower right or life-estate in one-third of her husband's property. This right must be legally recognized in all transactions including transfers of land. A man has the right of curtesy or a life-estate in any property his wife owned when they married or in any she inherits in her own right during the marriage, providing they have at least one living child who can inherit from them. Otherwise, he has a right to one-third of her property only.[22] Marriage settlements contracted at the time of marriage can change these provisions. Under recent legislation, however, a woman has the right to renounce her dower claim to her husband's estate. She must acknowledge that full disclosure of the total worth of the estate was made and she understands what she is renouncing. This protects the estate against undue litigation. A man cannot legally disinherit his wife and leave her destitute, on the public's mercy. In most jurisdictions, welfare help is denied, even in cases of divorce, if the husband is in a position to pay for the wife's upkeep.

Guardianship

A guardian is a responsible individual of legal age appointed or acknowledged by the court to manage the property ownership of those incompetent by reason of youth or mental or physical handicap to handle their own affairs. A guardian may also be called a conservator, a curator, a tutor, or a receiver.

An orphan is a minor whose father is dead or whose deceased mother left separately owned property to her child but excluded the father. In both cases, a guardian is appointed to assume the legal responsibilities of property ownership. In other words, the "orphan" may have a living parent in either case. Such a child may also be called a ward or infant. It is also common for a mother or father to be appointed guardian of his/her own children without implying adoption, formal or otherwise.

The appointment of a guardian for a minor may be a separate court process from probate, handled by a different court. The appointment of a guardian for an adult who is incompetent to handle his/her own affairs may require two additional court processes—depending on the jurisdiction, the first to declare him/her incompetent and the second to appoint someone to act in his/her behalf.

Probate Proceedings

Since the procedures followed in both testate and intestate cases are almost identical, we can consider both together. Most states require that probate begin the first term of court following the death of a property owner, between thirty and ninety days after death.

1. Usually the principal heir petitions the court for authority to begin the probate process. Until recent years these petitions were made verbally and recorded only in the probate minute books; however, some jurisdictions require written petitions bearing the name of all heirs, their residences, and their ages, and these are filed with the original estate papers. Such petitions are especially valuable because this may be the only place all the heirs are listed. (See Figure 6-8 for an example of a petition to commence probate.)

In a testate estate, the executor petitions for letters testamentary or authority to probate the will. In an intestate case, the surviving spouse or oldest son normally petitions for letters of administration or authority to administer the estate according to the laws of the jurisdiction.

It is the responsibility of the executor or the administrator to look out for the best interest of the estate, the needs of the heirs,

Petition for Probate of Will and Letters Testamentary In the County Court of Johnson County, Nebraska In re Estate of George Hindenach Deceased.

PETITION

Your petitioner, Hannah Hindenach who is of legal age, shows: That George Hindenach late a resident of Spring Creek Precinct, in Johnson County Nebraska, died at his residence, in Johnson County Nebraska, on or about the 9 day of September A.D. 1895 leaving a last will and testament, executed in due form of law, as your petitioner believes which is now on file in this Court: that the subscribing witnesses to said instrument are T. Appelget of Tecumseh, Nebraska, and T. E. Fairall of Tecumseh, Nebraska; that said Will nominated Hannah Hindenach as executrix thereof, and that Hannah Hindenach is willing to accept the trust as Executrix that said decedent died seized of real estate in said Johnson County of the estimated value of $5000.00; that the said decedent was possessed of personal property in the said State of Nebraska of the estimated value of $600.00.

Your petitioner further shows that the devisees, legatees, heirs at law in the absence of a will, and other persons interested in said matter are as follows:

Name	*Age*	*Residence*	*Relationship To Deceased*
Hannah Hindenach	45	P.O. Tecumseh	Widow
George Hindenach Jr.	25	" "	Son
Lillie Hindenach	22	" "	Daughter
Bessie Hindenach	17	" "	"
Ella Hindenach	15	" "	"
Anna Hindenach	13	" "	"
Josie Hindenach	11	" "	"
Charles Hindenach	8	" "	Son
Mary Hindenach	6	" "	Daughter
Stella Hindenach	4	" "	"

Your petitioner therefore prays that a day may be fixed for hearing the proof of the execution of said instrument; that all the persons listed herein may be notified by Publication three weeks prior to said hearing, to show cause if any there be, why said instrument shall not be recorded as the last will and testament of said decedent.

Figure 6-8. Petition to Commence Probate by Hannah Hindenach, 9 Sept. 1895, Johnson County Court; typescript of holograph in Johnson County Courthouse, Tecumseh, Neb.

and the claims of the creditors.

2. Proving the will is a step that applies only to testate cases. The document is presented to the court. The witnesses to the will appear and attest that they saw the individual sign the will, that he/she was in sound mental condition and that he/she expressed his/her own free will. The court, after hearing this sworn testimony, will order that the will be recorded. Wills judged invalid are not proved and, hence, not recorded in the will book but can often be found among the loose or miscellaneous papers of the courthouse or town hall. They will not appear in the index to probate records, and they are rarely microfilmed. You have to ask for these records to be searched at the courthouse.

Some jurisdictions require that all heirs of the estate be notified and present at the reading and recording of the will. If any one has argument against the admission of the will to probate, he/she may make claim then or generally forfeit any future right to contest the will.

3. The executor designated in the decedent's will must be formally approved by the court; and, in intestate cases, the court appoints the administrator. Each state prescribes the order in which persons are entitled to be appointed, but in general this order is maintained: spouse, one of the children, parents, grandparents, brothers or sisters, uncles, aunts, nephews, nieces, great-uncles, great-aunts, first cousins, creditors, anyone legally competent, public administrators, etc.

4. An administrator must post a bond equal to the worth of the assets of the estate to insure his/her faithful performance of duty and protect the heirs in cases of misconduct. In most states, an executor is not required to file a large bond if the decedent's will exempts him/her from that trust.

Bondsmen were usually relatives or family friends until recently, when bonding companies replaced personal sureties. If the wife is executrix, the bondsmen will usually be her relatives. If a brother or son is executor, they will be chosen from the family of the deceased. Bondsmen can also be heirs to the estate.

5. In most testate and all intestate estates, three disinterested men (often relatives who are not potential heirs) are appointed by the court to inventory and appraise all the property of the estate. They are usually ordered to submit the inventory at the next term of court or within ninety days. (See Figure 6-9.) This inventory protected the executor or administrator from excessive claims against the estate and protected heirs against fraud or pilfering of their inheritance. The court used it to set probate fees as in modern practice. As a result, the values given to each item were close to current market value although there seems to have been a tendency to keep them low. Thus, the fees levied against the estate were lower and the sale of items at auction were ensured.

6. As soon as the inventory is made, publication of the pending probate is published. In early times, notices were tacked on the doors of courthouses, townhalls, churches, etc. Later, the court required public posting at the town hall and publication three successive weeks in the major county, town, or district newspaper before probate to give interested parties opportunity to be present to voice disagreement or to present claims against the estate. The law required preservation of those publication notices. Some jurisdictions keep copies of the newspapers at the county courthouse or town hall in which notices appeared, while others clip the notices and preserve them with the case packet. It is thus possible to find missing issues of newspapers at the probate authority.

7. Another step taken before probate begins is assigning an allowance for the dependents from a portion of the estate (usually the amount is determined annually) until the estate is settled and distributed. It may take the form of cash, income-producing property, like a herd of cattle, or money from the court-authorized sale of certain property. Usually the property so designated is exempt from creditor's claims. At this time, also, the widow's dower right will often be set off to provide for her support.

8. In estates involving minors or incompetent individuals, a guardian is appointed to receive and assume stewardship over their respective shares. Figure 6-10 is a petition of minor children for their mother to be appointed guardian. As with administrators and executors, guardians must post a bond equal to the worth of the orphan's estate. Figure 6-11 is an example of the required bond.

9. To raise funds for the support of the widow and children or to convert perishables to cash, it is frequently necessary to conduct periodic sales of property under the surveillance of the court. First, the administrator/executor or guardian petitions the court for authority to sell, stipulating the items, why the income is needed, and how much he expects to realize. If the court authorizes the sale, a public auctioneer is appointed and a careful account is kept of what was sold, how much each item brought, and to whom the item went.

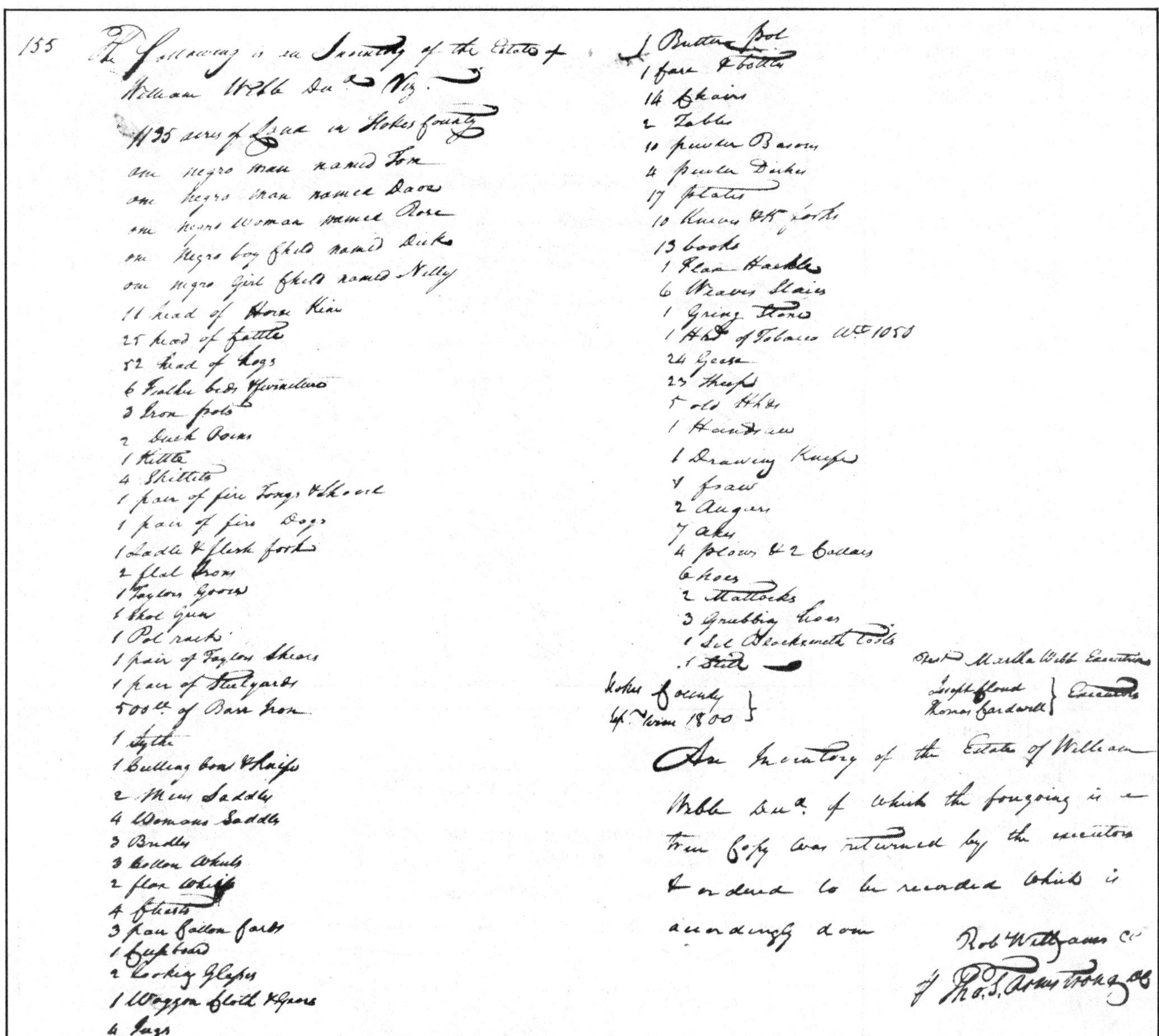

155 The following is an Inventory of the Estate of William Webb Dec^d Viz.
435 acres of Land in Stokes County
one negro man named Tom
one negro man named Dave
one negro Woman named Rose
one negro boy child named Duke
one negro Girl child named Nelly
11 head of Horse Kind
25 head of Cattle
52 head of hogs
6 Feather beds & furniture
3 Iron pots
2 Dutch Ovens
1 Kittle
4 Skillets
1 pair of fire Tongs & Shovel
1 pair of fire Dogs
1 Ladle & flesh fork
2 flat Irons
1 Taylors Goose
1 Shot Gun
1 Pot rack
1 pair of Taylors Shears
1 pair of Stilyards
500 lb of Barr Iron
1 Sythe
1 Cutting box & Knife
2 Mens Saddles
4 Womans Saddles
3 Bridles
3 Cotton Wheels
2 flax Wheels
4 Chests
3 Pair Cotton Cards
1 Cupboard
2 Looking Glasses
1 Waggon Cloth & Gears
4 Jugs
1 Butter Pot
1 Jar & bottle
14 Chairs
2 Tables
10 pewter Basons
4 pewter Dishes
17 plates
10 Knives & forks
13 books
1 Flax Hackle
6 Weavers Slays
1 Grind Stone
1 Hhd of Tobacco W^t 1050
24 Geese
23 Sheep
5 old Hhds
1 Handsaw
1 Drawing Knife
4 Fraws
2 Augers
7 Axes
4 plows & 2 Collars
6 hoes
2 Mattocks
3 Grubbing hoes
1 Set Blacksmith Tools
1 Still

Test Martha Webb Executrix
Joseph Cloud } Executors
Thomas Cardwell

Stokes County } Sept. Term 1800

An Inventory of the Estate of William Webb Dec^d of which the foregoing is a true Copy was returned by the executors & ordered to be recorded which is accordingly done

Rob Williams C.C.
by Thos. Armstrong D.C.

Figure 6-9. Inventory of the Estate of William Webb, by Rob Williams and Thos Armstrong, Will Book 1-4, 1790-1864, Book 1, Sept. Term 1800, Stokes Co., N.C.; GS 546,241.

10. In some jurisdictions, executors/administrators or guardians must account annually to the court for income received and expenses paid out of the estate, and for what purposes. In others, executors may only be required to account upon request from heirs or creditors. Because these records show heirs who die and women who marry before final settlement, they are extremely valuable for the genealogist.

11. Prior to the final settlement and distribution of the estate among the heirs, additional publication notices are issued to give claimants one last chance to voice their desires.

12. The executor/administrator must make a final accounting of receipts and disbursements of the estate before the remaining property can be divided and the responsibility ended. Figure 6-12 shows a final accounting.

13. When all parties concerned come to an agreement or when all heirs are twenty-one years of age, the property is divided and distributed to those heirs entitled to receive it; the case is closed; and the executor or administrator is released. In many probate jurisdictions, lengthy division documents will be found listing all heirs and their addresses, husbands of female heirs, and second marriages of widows. In some states, these settlement documents are found in the office of the land recorder – Division of Real Estate – as Figure 6-13 shows.

14. As each heir receives his/her portion of the estate, he/she signs a receipt or release to the executor/administrator. These receipts give the name of the heir, the amount and description of property received, the name of the executor/administrator, the names of guardians of minor children, and the name of the deceased. These releases are filed among the original estate papers. (See Figure 6-14.)

In this case, the cancelled checks act as the release of heirs in this probate case and provide the cities of residence of the heirs. Among those in this probate are Davenport, Council Bluffs, Somers, and Deep River, Iowa; Cleveland, Ohio; and Brainerd, Minnesota.

Probate records can provide an intimate glimpse into the life style of your ancestor and specific facts about the family. From wills you can discover how often the men on your pedigree entrusted their assets to a wife, whether all sons inherited equally, how the daughters fared in comparison, whether a man distributed

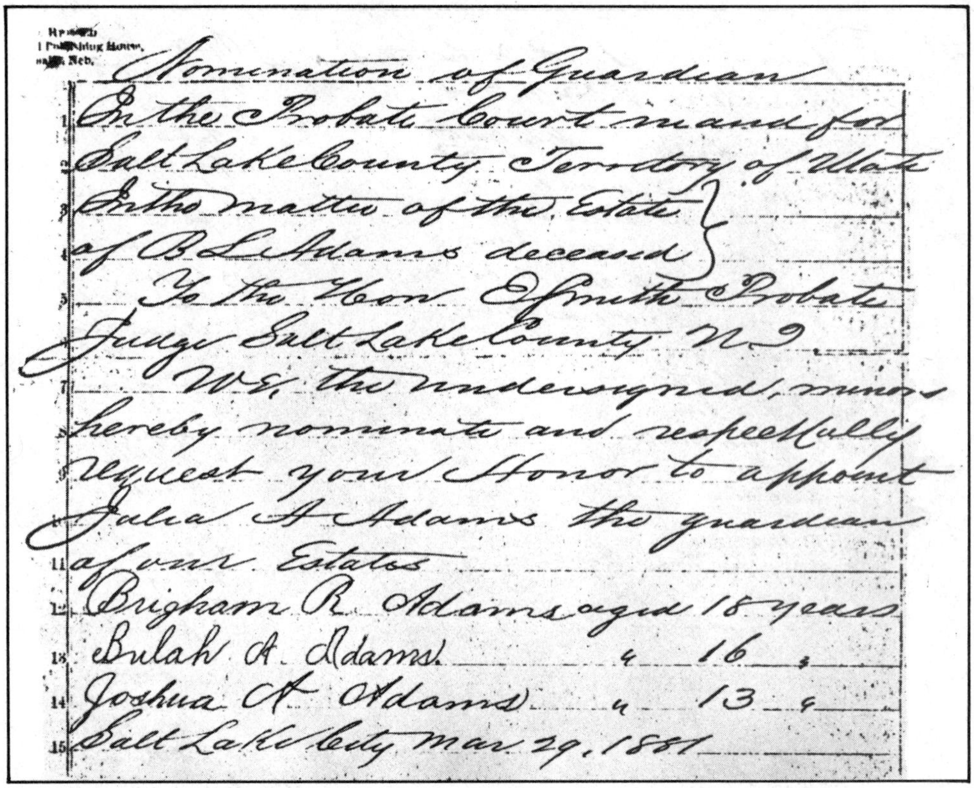

Figure 6-10. Nomination of Guardian Petition of Julia A. Adams by Brigham R., Bulah A., and Joshua A. Adams, Salt Lake Co., Utah Territory.

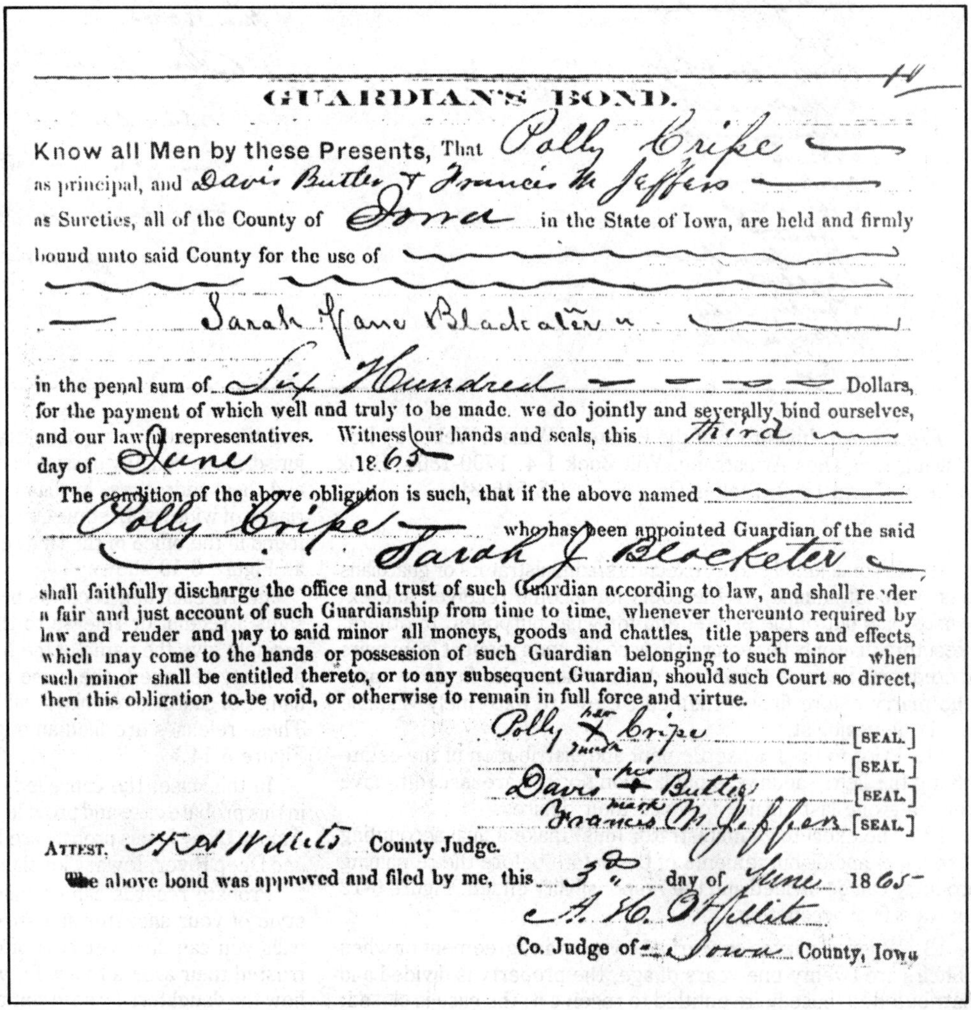

Nomination of Guardian
In the Probate Court in and for
Salt Lake County Territory of Utah
In the matter of the Estate
of B L Adams deceased
To the Hon E Smith Probate
Judge Salt Lake County U T
We, the undersigned, minors
hereby nominate and respectfully
request your Honor to appoint
Julia A Adams the guardian
of our Estates
Brigham R Adams aged 18 years
Bulah A. Adams " 16 "
Joshua A Adams " 13 "
Salt Lake City Mar 29, 1881

Figure 6-11. Guardian's Bond of Polly Cripe for Sarah Jane Blackater, 3 June 1865, Iowa Co., Iowa; originals in Iowa County Courthouse, Marengo, Iowa.

GUARDIAN'S BOND.

Know all Men by these Presents, That Polly Cripe as principal, and Davis Butler & Francis M Jeffers as Sureties, all of the County of Iowa in the State of Iowa, are held and firmly bound unto said County for the use of Sarah Jane Blackater in the penal sum of Six Hundred Dollars, for the payment of which well and truly to be made, we do jointly and severally bind ourselves, and our lawful representatives. Witness our hands and seals, this third day of June 1865

The condition of the above obligation is such, that if the above named Polly Cripe who has been appointed Guardian of the said Sarah J Blacketer shall faithfully discharge the office and trust of such Guardian according to law, and shall render a fair and just account of such Guardianship from time to time, whenever thereunto required by law and render and pay to said minor all moneys, goods and chattles, title papers and effects, which may come to the hands or possession of such Guardian belonging to such minor when such minor shall be entitled thereto, or to any subsequent Guardian, should such Court so direct, then this obligation to be void, or otherwise to remain in full force and virtue.

Polly her X mark Cripe [SEAL.]
[SEAL.]
Davis his X mark Butler [SEAL.]
Francis M Jeffers [SEAL.]

ATTEST, H. H. Willits County Judge.

The above bond was approved and filed by me, this 3d day of June 1865
A. H. Willits
Co. Judge of Iowa County, Iowa

Receved Marengo January 2d 1869
of Polly Cripe Guardian of
Sarah Jane Blackater Minor
heir of Henry Blacktar deceased
three hundred thirty Eight dollars
& twenty six cents in full
of all demands against said
Guardian for pension Back
pay & Baunty together, with
all orther claims against
said Guardian
Sarah ~~Jane Moore~~ formerly
Attest Sarah Jane Blackiter
Isaac Goodin John his x mark Moore

Figure 6-12. Final Account of Polly Cripe, guardian of Sarah Jane Blacketer; 3 June 1865, original in Iowa County Courthouse, Marengo, Iowa.

Figure 6-13. Partition of Lands From the estate of John Q. Shaver, Knox County, Tenn., Land Entry Book, pp. 238-39; GS 589,484. This illustration of the division is about one-fourth of the full map.

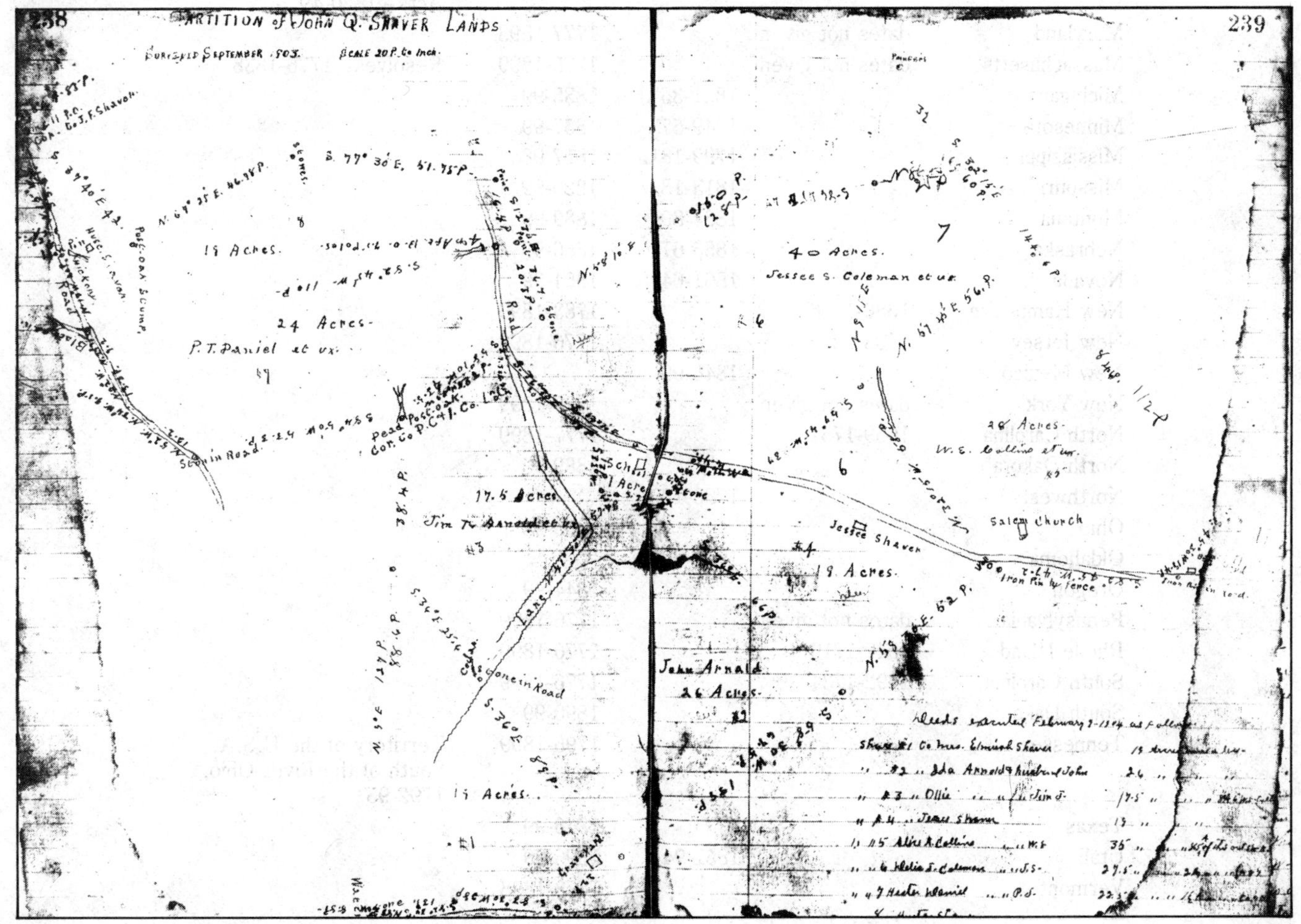

Table 6-2

Printed Laws of the United States

State	*Colony*	*Territory*	*State*	*Special Laws*
Alabama		1818	1819-99	
Arizona		1864-99		
Arkansas		1818-35	1836-99	
California			1849-99	
Colorado		1861-76	1876-99	Jefferson Territory, 1859-61
Connecticut	1639-73		1776-1899	Special Acts 1837-99
Dakota		1862-89		
Delaware	1704-41		1776-1899	
Florida		1822-45	1845-99	
Georgia	dates not given		1787-1899	
Idaho		1863-88	1890-99	
Illinois		1809-17	1818-99	
Indiana		1801-51	1816-99	
Iowa		1838-45	1846-98	
Kansas		1855-61	1861-99	
Kentucky			1792-1898	
Louisiana			1812-99	District (Under Jurisdiction of Indiana Territory) 1804; Territory of Orleans, 1804-11
Maine			1820-99	Resolves – 1820-39 Private and Special Acts – 1820-49
Maryland	dates not given		1777-1898	
Massachusetts	dates not given		1775-1899	Resolves – 1776-1838
Michigan		1821-35	1835-99	
Minnesota		1849-57	1857-99	
Mississippi		1799-1816	1817-98	
Missouri		1813-18	1820-99	
Montana		1864-89	1889-99	
Nebraska		1855-67	1866-99	
Nevada		1861-64	1864-99	
New Hampshire	1680-1726		1783-1899	
New Jersey	1703-22		1776-1899	
New Mexico		1846-99		
New York	dates not given		1777-1899	
North Carolina	1669-1751		1777-1899	
North Dakota			1889-99	
Northwest		1788-1801		
Ohio			1803-98	
Oklahoma		1890-99		
Oregon			1844-99	
Pennsylvania	dates not given		1776-1899	
Rhode Island	1647-1719		1776-1899	
South Carolina	1692-1734		1776-1899	
South Dakota			1890-99	
Tennessee			1796-1899	Territory of the U.S.A. South of the River Ohio, 1792-95
Texas			1846-99	
Utah		1851-94	1896-99	
Vermont			1778-1898	

State	Colony	Territory	State	Special Laws
Virginia			1776-1899	
Washington		1854-87	1889-99	
West Virginia			1861-99	
Wisconsin		1836-48	1848-99	
Wyoming		1869-90	1890-99	

his property to his children before his death, and who was instructed to care for the widow and younger children or for incapacitated or handicapped family members. Servants were sometimes released by will and slaves freed.

What provision is made for the widow? Firewood delivered to her door? Living quarters and a cash allowance for needed purchases? Does the allowance end on remarriage? What happens to her portion of the estate if she remarries?

What are the demographics of your family? Who lived in the household? What was the ratio of adults to children, males to females? Did the men live to see their grandchildren? Did women outlive their men? How many children reached adulthood before their parents died? What were the sizes of your family units?

What standard of living did your family have? Did they read and write? Did bequests include paintings, family Bible, fine furniture, a carriage, or musical instruments?

Also revealed in a will is biographical information: title, occupation, religious affiliation, age, place of residence, place of property ownership, associates of the family, and relationship to prominent families in the area.

Did your ancestor bequeath assets to charities like schools, hospitals, churches? Did he make a contribution for the upkeep of roads and bridges? Did he support a political party?

How did your ancestor speak? Indications of local dialect and pronunciation can be found in spelling variants, especially when a will is a holograph. It can also reveal personality, character, and level of formal education.

The probate inventory gives other insights into your family's life and how your family compared to others in the community.[23] (See Figure 6-15.) Where items are listed room by room and the rooms labeled, you get who slept where. A man was often judged by the kind of bed he slept in, so inventories usually listed bed and bedding in considerable detail: bed curtains imply a canopied bed to keep out cold drafts. Featherbeds, sheets, coverlets, blankets, and spreads may also be listed separately.

Table linens may be listed (damask, diaper, flaxen, canvas); cooking utensils and dishes (pewter, wood, china, porcelain, silverplate, brass); lighting (candles, lamps, wicks, lantern glass, and lighter fluids). In poor households, a clock may represent almost a quarter of the estate's total value. Pots and pans may be valued by weight, since that is the way they were bought and sold. Unknown objects like kimblins, piggins, and eshons (cheese vats and presses) may appear.

The processes of cooking, brewing, baking, dairying, and washing are described in the kinds of utility tubs and bowls used. The presence of smoothing tables or boards and flat irons indicate that clothes were ironed before wearing, and bedding may also have been "smoothed." Sanitary facilities inside the house could consist of chamber pots and close stools, often both. The larder hints at diet—butter, cheese, ham, bacon, hanging beef, salt pork, and potatoes. Particular trades or occupations emerge from tools, mercantile inventory, record books, contents of barns, granaries, and crops standing in the field.

A comparison of inventories from one generation of the family to another will show improvements in living conditions from fireplace cooking to stoves, from enclosed bedsteads to heated bedrooms, from wooden platters to china. Glass in windows, unless bequeathed as heirlooms to a family member, could be sold separately from the house, so panes may be listed in the inventory too.

Sometimes an item will be missing from an inventory because the owner gave it away before his/her death, it was sold to cover debts prior to death, or because it is specified in the will and falls in the executor's charge. Some inventories will end with "things unseen or forgotten," a category with an arbitrary dollar value assigned.

An inventory is also useful for distinguishing between persons of the same name by matching inventory contents like horses, cattle, and pigs with tax rolls and agricultural census entries. You can also prove the relationship between a man and his children with property, real or personal, listed in inventories and wills from one generation to the next.

American Probate Law

Despite their usefulness, probate records are filled with traps for the unwary genealogist. The first pitfall is contemporary law.

Probate is a function of state authority, with only one federal prohibition. Primogeniture, or passing a landed estate automatically to the eldest son, is forbidden; and by 1811 all former colonies had revoked it by statute. As a result, probate procedures vary from state to state and also change over time.

A useful background is knowing what laws were in effect in the state at the time your ancestor lived there. The printed laws for several American colonies have been published in eighteen volumes by Michael Glazier, Inc., 1210 King Street, Wilmington, DE 19801. Copies can be found at most law libraries. The *Sessions Laws of American States and Territories Prior to 1900* are available on microfiche from Redgrave Information Resources Corporation, 53 Wilton Road, Westport, CT 06880. For laws not cited in full, references to the revisions in each state law code are given, and you have a handy reference to follow the changes backward in time. The years for which printed laws are available are summarized in Table 6-2.

Tracing the history of a law is not difficult. Most law libraries are open for public use. A call before you go can verify public access, hours open, availability of copy machines, and fees if any.

In addition to the pitfalls presented by ignorance of legal language and past laws, another problem may arise if a researcher concentrates only on the case files or probate packet. You should not overlook other records leading to probate which appear among the records of other courts. For example, the Court of Common Pleas in Pennsylvania was responsible for hearing evidence of incompetency and determining the status of such individuals.

Appearance Docket, Vol. A, p. 536, Perry County, Pennsylvania, contains the petition of John River, brother-in-law of Peter Arnold of Buffalo Township, to issue a writ of incompetency since Peter Arnold was an habitual drunkard. His heirs are listed as George, Peter, William, and daughter Barbara, wife of George Varns. The court confirmed the petition on 16 March 1824. By 10 Nov. 1827, Peter had reformed and petitioned the court to have his rights restored. The court granted his request and released the guardian.[24]

Figure 6-14. Photocopy of cancelled check, to H.F.[?] Spracklin, distribution from D. D. Spracklin Estate, 14 March 1917; original in case file, Iowa County Courthouse, Marengo, Iowa.

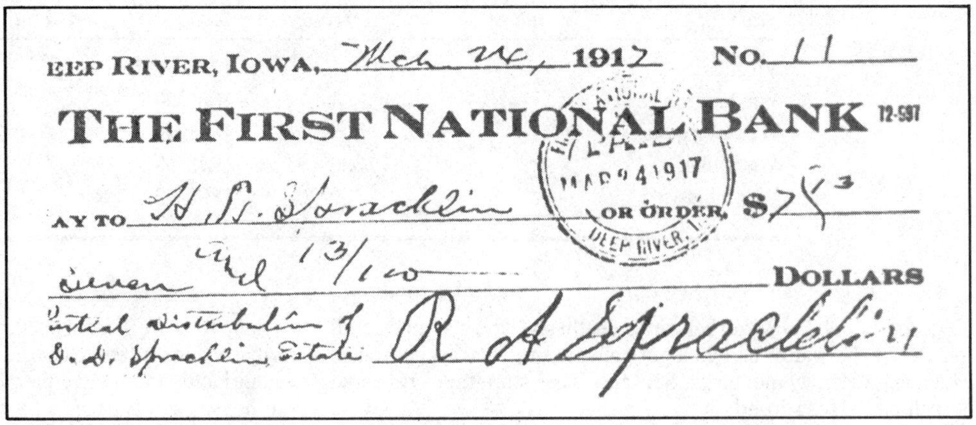

EEP RIVER, IOWA, Mch 14, 1917 No. 11

THE FIRST NATIONAL BANK 72-597

PAID MAR 14 1917 DEEP RIVER, I.

AY TO H. F. Spracklin OR ORDER, $7 13/100

Seven and 13/100 DOLLARS

Partial distribution of D. D. Spracklin Estate — R A Spracklin

Figure 6-15. Inventory of the Estate of Jacob Frank, 10 Sept. 1755, Lancaster County (Pennsylvania) Will Book B, vol. 1, p. 23. Original in Lancaster County Courthouse, Lancaster, Penn.

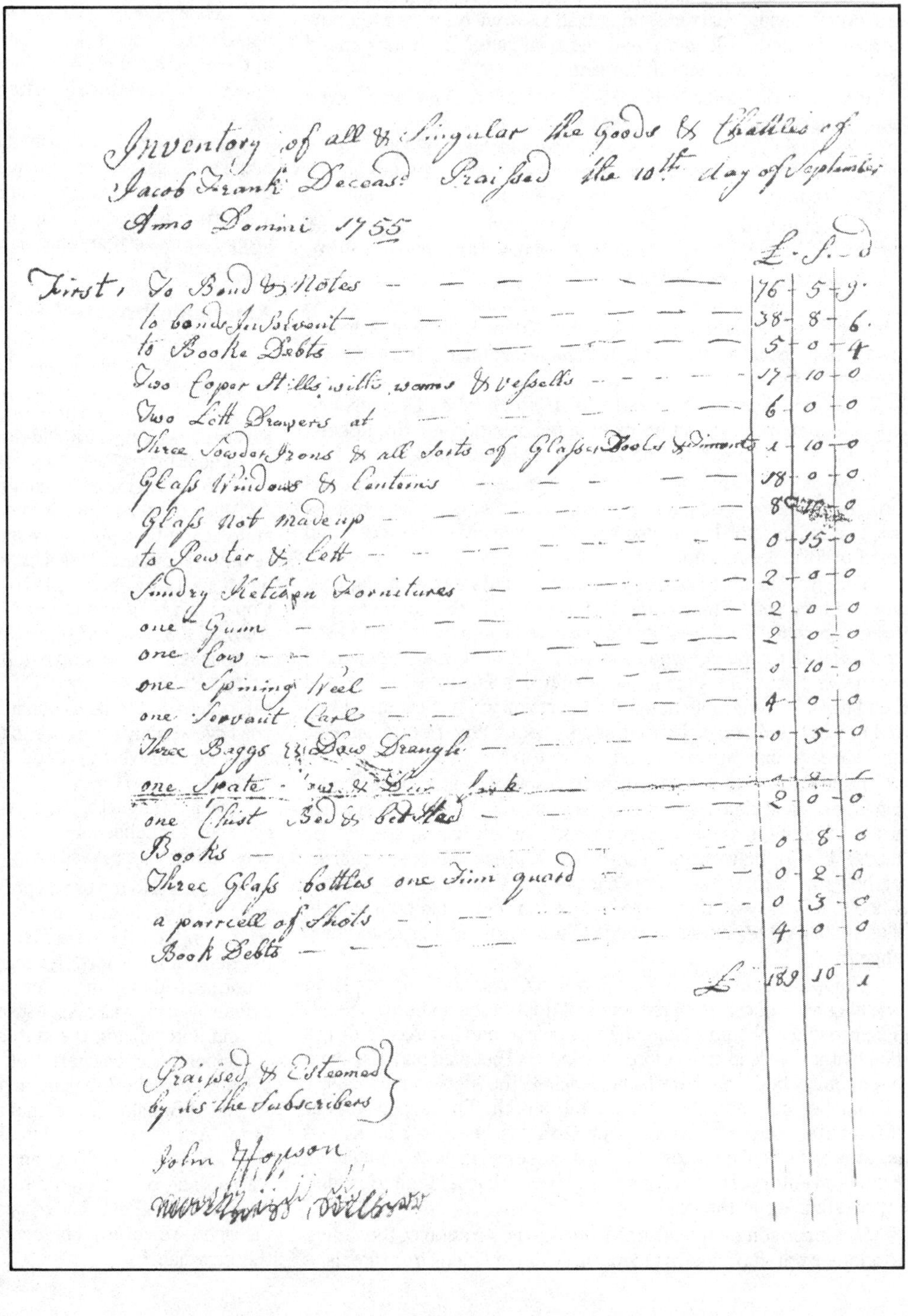

Inventory of all & Singular the Goods & Chattles of Jacob Frank Deceas^d Praissed the 10th day of September Anno Domini 1755

	£	S	d
First, To Bond & Notes	76	5	9
to bonds Insolvent	38	8	6
to Booke Debts	5	0	4
Two Coper Stills with worms & vessells	17	10	0
Two Lott Drawers at	6	0	0
Three Sowder Irons & all sorts of Glasier Tools & diments	1	10	0
Glass Windows & Lanterns	18	0	0
Glass Not made up	8	[illegible]	0
to Pewter & Lett	0	15	0
Sundry Kitchen Fornitures	2	0	0
one Gum	2	0	0
one Cow	2	0	0
one Spining Weel	0	10	0
one Servant Carl	4	0	0
Three Baggs & Dow Drangle	0	5	0
~~one Spate ... & ... ...~~			
one Chist Bed & bedstead	2	0	0
Books	0	8	0
Three Glass bottles one Tiin guard	0	2	0
a parcell of Shots	0	3	0
Book Debts	4	0	0
£	189	10	1

Praissed & Esteemed by us the Subscribers

John Hopson

[illegible]

Here is a checklist of documents produced by probate courts:[25]

COURT RECORDS

- ____ Estate docket
- ____ Guardianship docket
- ____ Claims docket
- ____ Minutes
- ____ Orders
- ____ Decrees
- ____ Judgments
- ____ Executions
- ____ Appeals
- ____ Indexes

PETITIONS

- ____ Letters testamentary
- ____ Administration
- ____ Guardianship
- ____ Appointment or change of guardian
- ____ Redress for misuse or waste of property
- ____ List of heirs
- ____ Renunciation

WILLS

- ____ Written
- ____ Nuncupative
- ____ Holographic
- ____ Codicils

BONDS

- ____ Administrator
- ____ Executor
- ____ Guardian
- ____ Appraiser
- ____ Trustee

INVENTORIES

- ____ Real estate
- ____ Personal property
- ____ Guardians
- ____ Conservators
- ____ Partnership
- ____ Minors' estates
- ____ Appraisals
- ____ Appraisers' warrants
- ____ Reports

PUBLICATIONS

- ____ Advertisements
- ____ Announcements
- ____ Notice to heirs
- ____ Notice of sales
- ____ Notice to creditors

ACCOUNTS

- ____ Administrator
- ____ Executor
- ____ Guardian
- ____ Trustee
- ____ Conservator

DIVISIONS

- ____ Commission reports
- ____ Settlements
- ____ Decrees of distribution
- ____ Dower rights
- ____ Courtesy rights
- ____ Awards
- ____ Private disbursement
- ____ Ledgers
- ____ Guardians' final report
- ____ Probate decrees
- ____ Certificates of devize
- ____ Assignments of real estate
- ____ Order of distribution
- ____ Decree of heirship

RELEASES

- ____ Executor
- ____ Administrator
- ____ Trustee
- ____ Guardian
- ____ Heirs
- ____ Conservator

CLAIMS

- ____ Petitions
- ____ Registers
- ____ Accounts
- ____ Appeals

MISCELLANEOUS

- ____ Unrecorded wills
- ____ Widows' allowances
- ____ Orders to find heirs
- ____ Sales documents
- ____ Marriage settlements
- ____ Waivers
- ____ Changes of name
- ____ Legitimation
- ____ Memoranda
- ____ Appeals
- ____ Judgments
- ____ Estate taxes

Important supporting legal documents can also be found in these nonprobate categories of records:[26]

Bastardy papers	Dower releases
Legitimation of children	Marriage contracts
Child custody papers	Marriage settlements
Name changes	Lis Pendens
Aliases	Foreclosures
Loose papers	Deeds
Unfiled documents	Leins
Inquisitions of lunacy	Tax leins
Manumissions	Land sold for back taxes
Petitions for freedom	Legislative papers
Certificates of freedom	Congressional petitions
Apprenticeships	Divorces
Annulments	Appeals
Adoptions	Claims
Orphans court records	Attachments of property

Also available at the law library are the state law codes. To locate a law effective when your ancestor was alive, check the current law code (dower rights, for instance, or age when a minor could make a will). Get the reference to the next earliest code when the law was changed or modified and work backward in time until you find the law as it was.

Although this process seems tedious, it is sometimes necessary and nearly always illuminating. The law determines the specifics in much of the probate process. Court officials do not explain what they are doing or their reasons for acting in a certain way in the record. They expect you to know that already.

The law also determines the ages at which your ancestors could transact legal business. Table 6-3 summarizes the most common ages (and exceptions) in the United States.

When courthouse fires occur, these other court documents may survive if they have been filed in other buildings or kept among the personal papers of justices or court officials.

Some of these records are used legally in lieu of probate processes. For example, Jacob Hoofman (Hoffman), Sr., died intestate in Fairfield County, Ohio, leaving sixteen children. The probate clerk, when a search was requested, found no will, but a careful search of the deeds brought this extremely detailed document in Figure 6-16 to light.

Jacob had distributed his lands to his children before his death, but died before the deed he executed for his son Simon could be recorded. The property went into his estate. Jacob had recorded the transaction in his own account book and the court accepted the transaction, requiring only that a quitclaim deed be signed by all sixteen children and their spouses. The document is invaluable, but it is found in the deeds, not the probate records.

In the past ten years, many printed probate records have appeared by societies and individuals. As is true with any extract, some transcripts are complete and others are incomplete or misread.

For example, the *South Carolina Genealogical Register,* June 1967, pp. 216-17, which extracts Will Books A-D, 1787-1810, shows this will among Newberry District Wills on p. 123:

> Mathew SIMS, Sr.
> Wife - Jeminah
> Sons - Charles, Matthew, Nathan and Reuben
> Daus. - Hannah Henderson, Drucilla Backley (deceased), Mary Sanders and Ann Henderson
> Executors - Reuben Simms and Bernard Glenn
> Witnesses - John Stequart, George Wilson and Fanny Stewart
> Will dated - 14 April 1795
> proved - 18 May 1795

In contrast, George Leland Summers, *Historical and Genealogical Newberry* (N.p.: for the author, 1950), p. 463, shows the same will as being on a different page, and provides much more detailed information.

> Matthew Sims, Sr., decd. Will 4-14-1795; proved 5-18-1795. Wife: Jemima (to have all lands remaining in her hands during her life or widowhood, under care of the Exrs.). Sons: Charles; Matthew (to his wife, Mary); James (dead) – to his heirs; Nathan (dead) – to his heirs; Reuben; David. After death of my wife, 200 acres whereon I live, on Tyger and Broad Rivers, to be sold and money equally divided among my four daughters, or their children. The daughters: Hannah Henderson, Drucilla Backley, Mary Sanders, and Ann Henderson. If Matthew's wife, Mary, should take her third part or right of dower of a certain tract of land in Hanover County, Va., which land I did purchase from my son, Matthew, and did give to my son, Nathan, I direct my Exrs. to stop and detain out of my son's, Mathew parts, as much as will fully satisfy my son's, Nathan, estate; and to pay to Admrs. of estate of said Nathan, dec. In case my widow does not claim dower, my Exrs. are not to detain any part of my son's, Matthew, decd., share. Gr-children:

Table 6-3

Ages of Legal Action*

Legal Action	Legal Age	Exceptions/ Comments
Inherit	From birth	An unborn child can also inherit
Be enumerated in census	From birth	Usually heads of household only until 1850
Attend school	5	Some schools accepted 3 year-olds
Witness documents	14 (male) 12 (female)	The age of discretion under the common law was 14(males) and 12 (females). Some exceptions are listed below.
Testify in court	14 (male) 12 (female)	
Choose guardian	14 (male) 12 (female)	Must be 21 in New York. No choice until age of discretion; then, if guardian appointed by court is unacceptable, can select another subject to court approval.
Serve as apprentice	14 (male) 12 (female)	Standard term was 21 (male), 18 (female) or time of marriage. If apprenticed before age of discretion, bound only to ages 14/12. Must have written deed which allowed for apprentice's consent, except for orphans on the public charge.
Show land to processioners	14 (male) 12 (female)	Males only; Southern states. Procession means to walk around the boundary lines of local property owners.
Be punished for crime	14 (male) 12 (female)	Some general exceptions before 1860. Complicated changes in the 20th century.
Sign contracts	14 (male) 12 (female)	May be required to confirm contract after arriving at majority.
Act as executor	14 (male) 12 (female)	Usually administrator with will annexed so the court had some controls. Age 17 in Massachusetts, Rhode Island, Missouri; age 18 in Mississippi. Bondsman who could act as co-executor required in Vermont.
Bequeath personal property by will	14 (male) 12 (female)	Age 18 in Connecticut, Massachusetts. Virginia; age 18 (male) and 16 (female) in New York; age 21 in Vermont. Property may be held in custody of court pending review.
Marry	14 (male) 12 (female)	Parental consent required in most states until age 21 (male) and 18 (female). Married child not subject to control of parents, could remarry on death of spouse without consent if underage. Age 18 (male) and 14 (female) in Mississippi, Ohio, Indiana; age 18 (male) and 15 (female) in Minnesota; age 17 (male) and fourteen (female) in Illinois; age sixteen (male) and fourteen (female) in Iowa. Marriage is valid without parental consent, but officiator could be fined. Annulment or divorce only way to void the marriage.
Be taxed	16	Males only were counted, females appear as "heirs of. . ."
Muster into militia	16	Males only.
Procession land	16	Procession means to walk around the boundary lines of local property owners.
Take possession of land holdings	16	"In possession of" on tax rolls signifies that the person named is at least 16.
Practice trade	18	Some cities licensed tradesmen to practice their profession/occupation at age 18.
Release of guardian	21 (male) 18 (female)	
Own land	21	Some states allowed females these rights at age 18.
Devise land by will	21	
Be taxed	21	Full poll responsibility unless exempt.
Plead or sue in court	21	
Be naturalized	21	After meeting residence requirements.
Fill public office	21	Age 25 or older required for some offices.
Serve on jury	21	Grand jury, petit jury, coroner jury.
Vote	21	Linked to 21 as age of land ownership, a prerequisite to voting in colonies.

*Based in part on Judge Tapping Reeve, *The Law of Baron and Femme, of Parent and Child, Guardian and Ward, Master and Servant, and of the Powers of the Courts of Chancery; with an Essay on the Terms Heir, Heirs, Heirs of the Body*, 3rd ed. (1862; reprint ed., New York: Source Book Press, 1970). This is an important legal treatise on family law describing the common law in America and exceptions created by statute law or specific traditions inherited from Spanish or French law codes. The author assumes legal knowledge on the part of the reader, so use Black's *Law Dictionary*. The original text predates the abolition of slavery and includes a discussion of law relating to slaves and their rights. It also predates much of the legal reform of the late nineteenth century which substantially changed the laws in several states. For the modern period, consult Chester G. Vernier, *American Family Laws: Comparative Study of the Forty-Eight American States, Alaska, District of Columbia, and Hawaii to 1 Jan. 1931*, 5 vols. (Stanford, Calif.: Stanford University Press, 1931), a state-by-state study of marriage, parent-child relationships and responsibilities, divorce, and probate in all aspects. These volumes have extensive indexes, making it easy to check specifics. Both works can be found in most law libraries.

William Sims and Sarah Shelton (the children of my son, Charles Sims). Exrs: Reuben Sims (son), Bernard Glenn (kinsman). Witnesses: John Stewart, George Wilson, Fanny Stewart.

Even more striking than the differences in content are the errors: the first lists four sons and four daughters, one deceased; the second lists six sons, two deceased, and four daughters, all living. The second also lists two grandchildren unmentioned in the first. Use the printed version as an index to the originals, but check the originals.

Two important printed projects are Carol Willsey Bell, *Ohio Wills and Estates to 1850: An Index,* available from the author at 4801 Mockingbird Court South, Columbia, OH 43229, and Brent Holcomb's abstracts of South Carolina wills for several counties available through Southern Historical Press, Box 738, Easley, SC 29740. These two projects are models for needed work in other areas.

Another problem is that New England demographic research comparing wills and probate inventories with tax rolls and other inhabitants' lists show that less than 50 percent of the male population was included among inventories and less than 40 percent left wills. In some areas, the percentage slips below 25 percent. Less than 10 percent of the women had either wills or inventories. While some people had little or no property to inventory, a substantial number seem to have deliberately made provision for their estates to pass to their heirs without probate.[27]

Probate records have uneven value when it comes to establishing specific death dates. Some probate records include the date of death. Some indexes record the death date, while the probate record does not. Where the death date is not given, the date of the acknowledgment of witnesses is usually the first record made in the probate process followed by the admission of the will to probate. In some jurisdictions, however, the witnesses acknowledged their signatures and certified the mental soundness of the testator at the time the will was drafted – not after the person's death. In others, probate of the will occurred before death and the testator was given some freedom as executor to insure that his wishes were carried out. To avoid these problems, the safest date to use is the date the will was recorded – between thirty and ninety days after the death of the testator.

Relationships between legatees and testator were seldom defined. As a consequence, brothers and nephews are mistaken for sons, sisters-in-law and daughters-in-law appear as unmarried daughters, and daughters with unknown married names may be unidentifiable. The legatees sometimes are mentioned by first names only.[28] "In-law" was often a synonym for "step" and adopted kin. Because of these problems, it is wise to corroborate all relationships with other sources.

However, probate records can provide valuable leads to those relationships. Here are some clues:[29]

1. In states that allowed the eldest son a double portion of his father's estate, an estate with seven shares has six heirs, not seven.

2. Daughters unmarried at the time a will is drafted may be married by the time it is probated. The will and subsequent documents will contain differing names. Watch given names carefully and always check all males listed in the final settlement, especially if they are not listed in the will as potential sons-in-law.

3. Statements like "my daughters Mary and Martha shall have five shillings each with what I have already given them" and "my daughter Grace shall have £30 to make her equal with her sisters" imply that some daughters are married and have already received their portions.

4. Special terminology may reveal relationships: "a femme sole" means an unmarried woman while "coverture" refers to a married woman.

5. Where two executors are named in a will, one is usually the relative of the testator and the other a relative of the spouse. Both sides of the family are represented to safeguard the interests of all parties and to keep peace.

6. Bondsmen are usually relatives who are willing to stand the risks and who have some leverage over the persons they guarantee. If the wife is executrix, the bondsmen will usually be her relatives. Where her maiden surname is unknown, look carefully at these names.

7. Guardians are usually relatives who have no potential interest in the estate. With some careful calculations, you can decide who these would be and perhaps identify missing surnames.

8. When the court has to determine who inherits, unless extenuating circumstances dictate otherwise, the estate is usually awarded to heirs of the whole blood (related by blood to both sides of the family) rather than an heir of the half blood (related to one side only). In this way, the property is more likely to stay in the family.

9. Second marriages of widows are most frequently documented among probate and guardianship records, as their new husbands assume responsibilities of the estate. This makes probate records especially valuable.

Some family members are omitted from a will because they are otherwise provided for. A man can settle a jointure on his wife at the beginning of the marriage in lieu of dower rights or subsequent claims against the estate. During colonial times when the law of primogeniture was in effect, the eldest son was frequently not mentioned in the will, for the real property descended automatically to him if the estate was entailed. Most American men also owned other lands in fee simple which could be described and left to younger sons.

As daughters married, they were customarily given their portion in cash, land, household furnishings, food, horses, slaves, etc. Sons were given their property when they reached majority or planned to marry. A family account book recorded the property conveyed to each child. If, when the father's estate was later settled, a child contested the settlement, this account showed what each marriage portion was. Thus, children who had received their share are frequently omitted from the will.

Special Court Proceedings

A number of special court proceedings are invaluable to the genealogist. Some, like name changes, are straightforward sources with easy-to-use indexes. Others, like the records of extra-legal courts, must be hunted down without an index. Yet these special processes can provide the key which opens a locked pedigree:

- Naturalizations
- Oaths of allegiance
- Name changes
- Adoptions
- Appeals and court reports
- Admiralty
- Claims
- Courts-martial
- Extra-legal courts
- Special courts: Indians, blacks, and foreign powers

Naturalization and administering oaths of allegiance are court functions discussed in detail in Chapter 15. Divorces, closely related to name changes and often indexed together, are discussed in Chapter 3.

Name Changes

Every state provides for legal name changes. The circumstances, however, vary from state to state and so do the courts having jurisdiction to authorize name changes. Here is a list of finding aids for the states where they exist.

California. "Record of Name Changes, 1866-1883." typescript, in California State Archives; GS 978,907, item 2.

Figure 6-16. Deed of Jacob Hoofman, 13 April 1839, Deed Book, Fairfield County, Ohio, Vol. 5, pp. 554-56; GS 295,286.

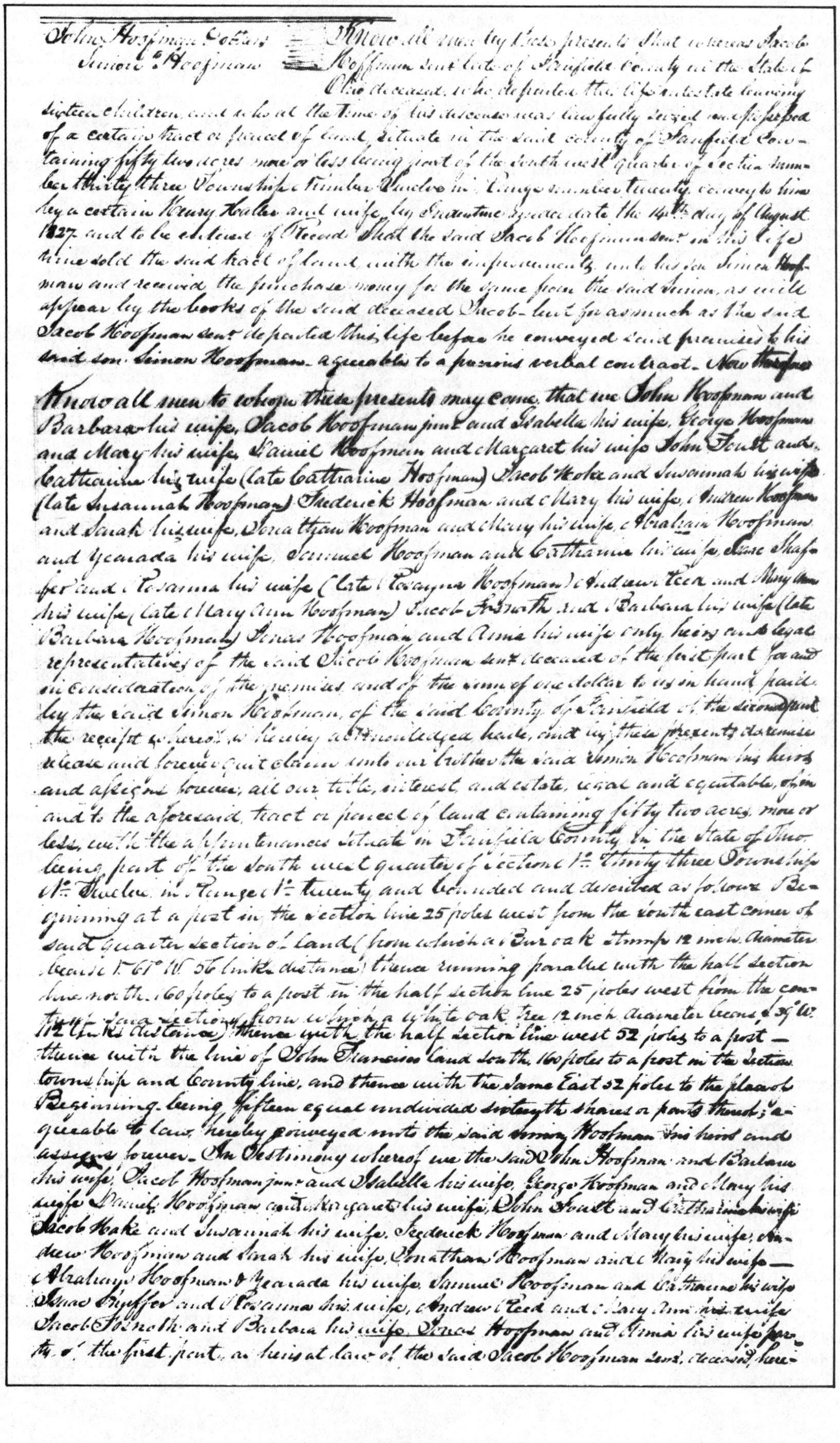

John Hoofman & others
Simon Hoofman

Know all men by these presents that whereas Jacob
Hoofman sen^r late of Fairfield County in the State of
Ohio deceased, who departed this life intestate leaving
sixteen children, and who at the time of his decease was lawfully seized and possessed
of a certain tract or parcel of land, situate in the said county of Fairfield con-
taining fifty two acres more or less being part of the south west quarter of section num-
ber thirty three Township number twelve in Range number twenty, convey to him
by a certain Henry Hoaler and wife, by Indenture bearing date the 14th day of August
1827 and to be entered of Record. That the said Jacob Hoofman sen^r in his life
time sold the said tract of land with the improvements unto his son Simon Hoof-
man and received the purchase money for the same from the said Simon, as will
appear by the books of the said deceased Jacob — but forasmuch as the said
Jacob Hoofman sen^r departed this life before he conveyed said premises to his
said son Simon Hoofman agreeable to a previous verbal contract — Now therefore

Know all men to whom these presents may come, that we John Hoofman and
Barbara his wife, Jacob Hoofman jun^r and Isabella his wife, George Hoofman
and Mary his wife, Daniel Hoofman and Margaret his wife, John Foust and
Catharine his wife (late Catharine Hoofman) Jacob Hoke and Susannah his wife
(late Susannah Hoofman) Frederick Hoofman and Mary his wife, Andrew Hoofman
and Sarah his wife, Jonathan Hoofman and Mary his wife, Abraham Hoofman
and Yearada his wife, Samuel Hoofman and Catharine his wife, Isaac Shaf-
fer and Rosanna his wife (late Rosanna Hoofman) Andrew Reed and Mary Ann
his wife (late Mary Ann Hoofman) Jacob Forsnoth and Barbara his wife (late
Barbara Hoofman) Jonas Hoofman and Anna his wife only heirs and legal
representatives of the said Jacob Hoofman sen^r deceased of the first part for and
in consideration of the premises and of the sum of one dollar to us in hand paid
by the said Simon Hoofman, of the said County of Fairfield of the second part
the receipt whereof is hereby acknowledged have, and by these presents do remise
release and forever quit claim unto our brother the said Simon Hoofman his heirs
and assigns forever, all our title, interest, and estate, legal and equitable, of in
and to the aforesaid tract or parcel of land containing fifty two acres more or
less, with the appurtenances situate in Fairfield County in the State of Ohio
being part of the south west quarter of Section N^o thirty three Township
N^o twelve in Range N^o twenty and bounded and described as follows Be-
ginning at a post in the section line 25 poles west from the south east corner of
said quarter section of land (from which a Bur oak stump 12 inch diameter
bears S. 61° W. 56 links distance) thence running parallel with the half section
line north 160 poles to a post in the half section line 25 poles west from the cen-
tre of said section (from which a white oak tree 12 inch diameter bears S. 39° W.
112 links distance) thence with the half section line west 52 poles to a post —
thence with the line of John Francisco land south 160 poles to a post in the section
township and County line, and thence with the same East 52 poles to the place of
Beginning. being fifteen equal undivided sixteenth shares or parts thereof; a-
greeable to law, hereby conveyed unto the said Simon Hoofman his heirs and
assigns forever. In Testimony whereof we the said John Hoofman and Barbara
his wife, Jacob Hoofman jun^r and Isabella his wife, George Hoofman and Mary his
wife Daniel Hoofman and Margaret his wife, John Foust and Catharine his wife
Jacob Hoke and Susannah his wife, Frederick Hoofman and Mary his wife, An-
drew Hoofman and Sarah his wife, Jonathan Hoofman and Mary his wife —
Abraham Hoofman & Yearada his wife, Samuel Hoofman and Catharine his wife
Isaac Shaffer and Rosanna his wife, Andrew Reed and Mary Ann his wife
Jacob Forsnoth and Barbara his wife, Jonas Hoofman and Anna his wife par-
ties of the first part as heirs at law of the said Jacob Hoofman sen^r deceased, here-

unto set their hands and seals this thirteenth day of April in the year of our Lord one thousand eight hundred and thirty nine

Executed in the presence			
of Henry King	John Hoffman (Seal)	Jonas Hoffman (Seal)	Isaac Schaefer (Seal)
William Hartranft	Barbery her x mark Hoffman (Seal)	Margaret her x mark Hoffman (Seal)	Rosanna her x mark Shafer (Seal)
Julius Hoffman	Jacob Hoffman (Seal)	Abraham his x mark Hoofman (Seal)	Frederick his x mark Hoofman (Seal)
Ambrose Hoffman	Isabella her x mark Hoofman (Seal)	Yerada her x mark Hoofman (Seal)	Mary her x mark Hoofman (Seal)
John Henderson	George Hoffman (Seal)	Samuel his x mark Hoofman (Seal)	Andrew Reed (Seal)
Daniel Pickel	Mary her x mark Hoofman (Seal)	Catharine her x mark Hoofman (Seal)	Anna Maria her x mark Reed (Seal)
Andrew Foust	Andrew Hoffman (Seal)	Jonas his x mark Hoofman (Seal)	Jonathan his x mark Hoofman (Seal)
Jeremiah Moore	Sarah her x mark Hoofman (Seal)	Anna her x mark Hoofman (Seal)	Mary her x mark Hoofman (Seal)
George Ponting	Jacob his x mark Hoke (Seal)	Jacob his x mark Kashnaht (Seal)	John Faust (Seal)
William his x mark Hickman	Susannah her x mark Hoke (Seal)	Barbara her x mark Kashnaht (Seal)	Catharine her x mark Foust (Seal)

The State of Ohio Fairfield County ss. Personally appeared before me the subscriber a Justice of the Peace in and for the said County of Fairfield the above named Jacob Hoofman and Isabella his wife, George Hoofman and Mary his wife, Andrew Hoofman and Sarah his wife, Jacob Hoke and Susannah his wife, Daniel Hoofman and Margaret his wife, Abraham Hoofman and Yerada his wife, Samuel Hoofman and Catharine his wife, Jonas Hoofman and Anna his wife, Jacob Kosnath and Barbara his wife, Isaac Shaffer and Rosanna his wife, Frederick Hoofman and Mary his wife, Andrew Reed and Mary Ann his wife, Jonathan Hoofman and Mary his wife, signers and sealers of the above instrument, and severally acknowledged the signing and sealing of the same to be their act and deed for the purposes therein expressed. And the said Isabella Hoofman and Mary Hoofman, Sarah Hoofman and Susannah Hoke, Margaret Hoofman, Yerada Hoofman, Catharine Hoofman, Anna Hoofman and Barbara Kosnath, Rosannah Shaffer and Mary Hoofman and Mary Ann Reed and Mary Hoofman being severally of lawful age, separate & apart from their said respective husbands by me examined and the contents of the above Deed by me made known to them, declared that they did voluntarily sign seal and acknowledge the same, and that they are still fully satisfied therewith. Given under my hand this thirteenth day of April Anno Domini 1839 —

Andrew Foust Justice of the Peace

State of Indiana Vigo County to wit Be it remembered that the within named John Hoffman and Barbery his wife came this day personally before me the undersigned one of the Justices of Vigo county [illegible] township and acknowledged that they signed sealed and and delivered the within indentures as their act and deed for the the purposes therein specified and the said Barbery being of full age and being by me duly examined separate and apart from her said husband and the contents of the said indenture being made known to her declared that she relinquished all her right and titel of dower in and to the lands and tenements in the within indentures set forth and described and that she voluntarily and of her own free will and accord and without any coercion or compulsion of her husband signed sealed and delivered the said indentures as her husband signed sealed and delivered the said indenture as her act and deed for the purposes aforesaid Given under my hand and seal [illegible] in Vigo county [illegible] Township aforesaid this six day of May in the year of our Lord eighteen hundred thirty nine — — — — — — — Thomas Davis J. P. [illegible]

State of Ohio Sandusky County ss Personally appeared the signers & sealers of the within Deed of Conveyance John Foust & Catharine Foust the said Catharine formerly Catharine Hoffman & did acknowledge the signing sealing & to be their free act & deed for the purposes therein expressed & the said Catharine Foust wife of John Foust being by me seperate and and apart from her said husband examined says she signed the same of her own free will without any fear of her said husband

October 23 1839 — William Fields Mayor of [illegible]

Attest of John & Catharine Foust signing of the the within Deed William Fields George Dickson — Rec. Nov 18th 1839 & Recorded [illegible] next month attest W. C. King R. F. C.

(12)

Georgia. Rowland, Arthur R., "Names Changed Legally in Georgia, 1800-1856." *National Genealogical Society Quarterly* 55 (1967): 177-210.

Indiana. Newhard, Malinda E., comp. *Name Changes Granted by Indiana General Assembly to 1852.* Available from Mrs. Newhard, Box 86, Harlan, IN 46743.

Maryland. Meyer, Mary K., comp. *Divorces and Names Changed in Maryland by Act of the Legislature, 1634-1854.* Pasadena, Md.: For the author, 1970; updated in "Names Changed in Maryland, 1855-1867: A Supplement to Divorces and Names Changed. . ." *Maryland Historical Magazine* 68 (1973): 335-39.

Massachusetts. Matokov, Albert. *List of Persons Whose Names Have Been Changed in Massachusetts, 1780-1892.* 2nd ed. 1893; reprint ed., Baltimore: Genealogical Publishing Comnpany, 1972.

North Carolina. McBride, Ransom, comp. "Legal Name Changes by Act of North Carolina Assembly, 1790-1799." *North Carolina Genealogical Society Journal* 1 (1975): 68-74; expanded "1800-1804," ibid. 2 (1976): 18-23; "1805-1808," ibid., 162-67.

An early source which includes the American colonies to 1782, is W. P. W. Phillimore and Edward A. Fry, comps., *An Index to Changes of Name Under Authority of Act of Parliament 1760-1901* (1905; reprint ed., Baltimore: Genealogical Publishing Company, 1968). The original introduction includes an essay on the "Law and Practice of Change of Name" by Phillimore, one of the foremost genealogists of his day.

Legislative control of name changes continued until roughly 1850-65 in America. Some state legislatures still have power to legalize names, although it is rare for them to do so. Regular courts with divorce jurisdiction usually have the power to legalize name changes today. Some have separately indexed volumes where these are recorded. Some list them in the regular court orders or judgments.

Name changes are especially important where divorce or adoption has occurred. For this reason it is a good idea to run the indexes name-by-name for all pedigree surnames and for those names which married into your lines. List any entries which appear promising. Then check the case files referred to for essential information.

Adoption Records

Adoption proceedings are usually court processes, although there are three methods through which adoption can take place: agreement without judicial proceedings, agreement filed in a court of law and accompanied by court order, and petition filed in a court of law and accompanied by court order. The first method is not considered legally binding in most states today.

Under Roman civil law, which forms the basis of the legal systems in Louisiana and Texas, adoption was an integral part of family law and was often used to increase prestige and family wealth. American Indians also practice adoption to varying extents. English common law, upon which the legal systems of most of the states are based, had no provision for adoption until 1926. Even though adoption statutes in America precede this date by nearly a century in some states, the majority did not provide for legal adoption until the latter half of the nineteenth century. Hence, legal adoption of a child by two people not the biological parents is a farily recent action. Table 6-4 indicates when the first statutes granting adoption were passed in the original thirteen states and selected others and the court which was given jurisdiction by the state codes.

Adoptions, even those later recognized by court action, often began within the family. For this reason, family traditions are important. Collect what the family members know from as many as are living. Include favorite nieces and grandsons who have been confidants of family members most likely to know the facts.

Next check the facts in actual documents. The documents and traditions in the case of Harry Chester Lee which follows is an example. According to a granddaughter:

> Great-Grandma Bandina Hinkle Lee, as you know, was Grandpa's [Harry Chester Lee's] adopted mother. However. . .his. . .real mother was Aunt Mary [Bell Hinkle] Garwood, Bandena's [*sic*] sister. I know she died [1927] after I was born & indications show Grandpa knew it. It must have been very hard for the poor woman, because she was living in Chicago by that time & she couldn't acknowledge her granddaughter & her first great grandchild. Anyhow the narrative is very interesting.

Table 6-4

Statutes Granting Adoption Jurisdiction

State	*Date*	*Court*
Connecticut	1864	Probate
Delaware	1890	Orphans'
Georgia	1855	Superior
Hawaii	1903	Circuit
Kentucky	1860	Circuit, equity, criminal
Maine	1867	Probate
Maryland	1892	Circuit
Massachusetts	1851	Probate
New Hampshire	1862	Probate
New Jersey	1877	Orphans'
New York	1873	Surrogate
North Carolina	1872	Superior
Ohio	1859	Probate
Pennsylvania	1855	Common pleas
Rhode Island	1872	Probate, Municipal
South Carolina	1882	Common pleas
Tennessee	1852	County, Circuit
Texas	c.1848	
Vermont	1853	Probate
Virginia	1891	Chancery
West Virginia	1882	Circuit

This Harry Chester Lee was born 21 June 1883, in a Chicago foundling home under the name of Chester Perry. Bandina Hinkle Lee picked him up from the foundling home at the age of three days, and he lived with her and her husband, Benjamin P. Lee, until they adopted him, at age thirteen. Bandina was Mary Bell's half-sister from Peoria County, Illinois.

A 1974 letter requesting the adoption papers brought the information from the presiding judge of Cook County Circuit Court that "all adoption files in Cook County are impounded."

However, an in-person request yielded a copy of the adoption petition dated 13 August 1897 and the decree of adoption entered a few days later. (See Figure 6-17.) Note that the petition also included a request that the boy's name be changed from Chester Perry to Harry Chester Lee.

Attempts to find a documented connection between Harry Chester Lee (Chester Perry) and Mary Bell failed. Cook County birth records yield no data for Chester Perry. An inquiry to Cook County Court regarding maternity was not answered, and there were no other records on file in Cook County. It is interesting, however, that Harry cared for Mary Bell Garwood in her later years. He was present at her death and provided the information on her death certificate. He also selected and paid for her burial place and funeral marker. Family members concluded that she was Harry's mother.

The Adoption Process

The petition sets out information concerning the child (or sometimes adult requiring custodial care) to be adopted, the biological parents, and the adopting parents. State statutes vary in the amount and type of data required, but generally they contain the name, residence, age or date of birth of the child; a description of any property the child might possess; the agency or person having present custody of the child; sometimes the sex, race, religion, place of birth, brothers and sisters if any, names and residences of the parents or guardian; the adoptive parents' names, residences,

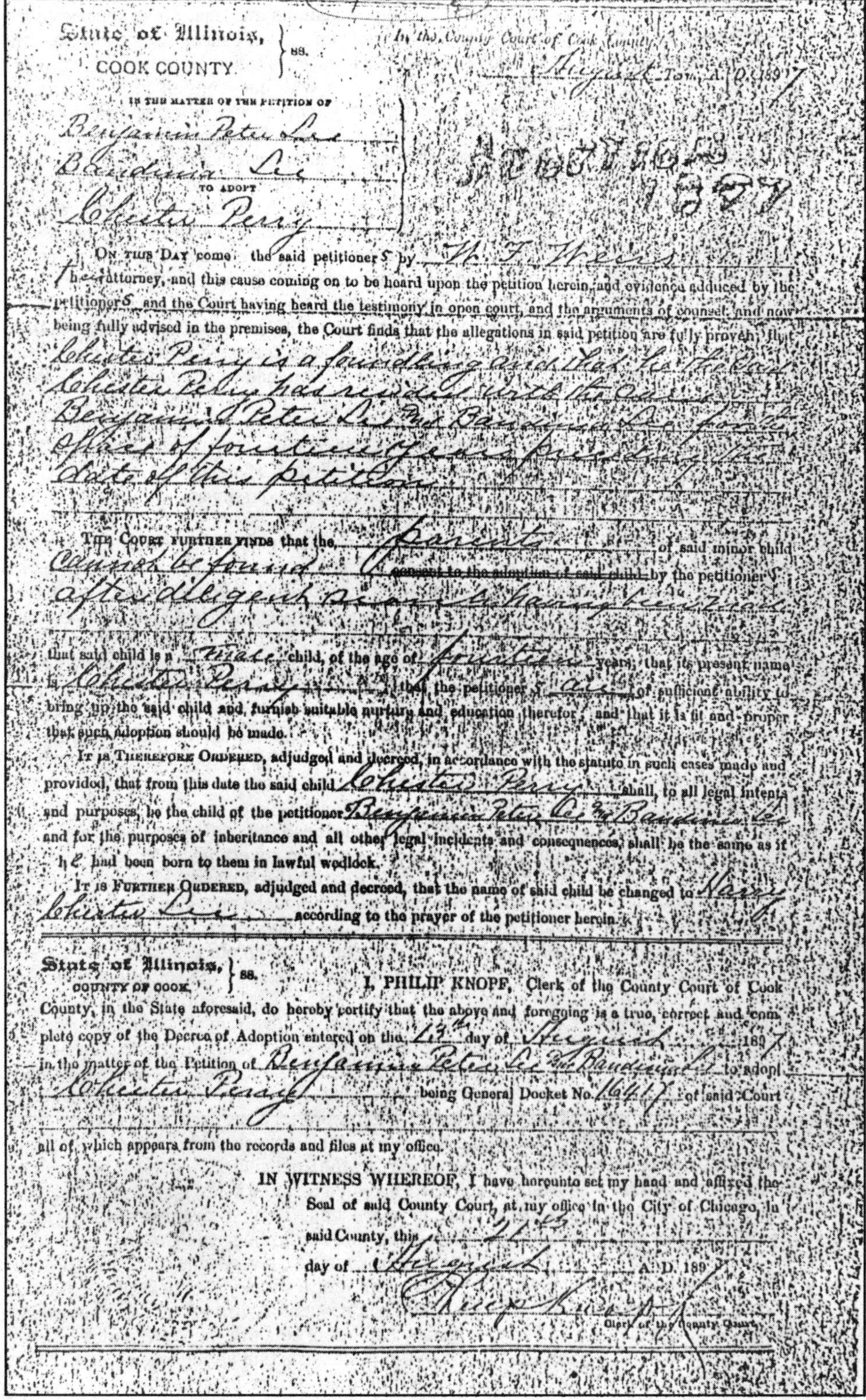

State of Illinois, } ss.
COOK COUNTY.

In the County Court of Cook County,
August Term, A.D. 1897

IN THE MATTER OF THE PETITION OF
Benjamin Peter Lee
Bandinia Lee
TO ADOPT
Chester Perry

RECORDED 1897

ON THIS DAY come the said petitioners by W. F. Weeks their attorney, and this cause coming on to be heard upon the petition herein, and evidence adduced by the petitioners and the Court having heard the testimony in open court, and the arguments of counsel, and now being fully advised in the premises, the Court finds that the allegations in said petition are fully proven; that Chester Perry is a foundling and that the said Chester Perry has resided with the said Benjamin Peter Lee and Bandinia Lee for the space of fourteen years preceding the date of this petition.

THE COURT FURTHER FINDS that the parents of said minor child cannot be found consent to the adoption of said child by the petitioners after diligent search having been made that said child is a male child, of the age of fourteen years; that its present name is Chester Perry that the petitioners are of sufficient ability to bring up the said child and furnish suitable nurture and education therefor, and that it is fit and proper that such adoption should be made.

IT IS THEREFORE ORDERED, adjudged and decreed, in accordance with the statute in such cases made and provided, that from this date the said child Chester Perry shall, to all legal intents and purposes, be the child of the petitioners Benjamin Peter Lee and Bandinia Lee and for the purposes of inheritance and all other legal incidents and consequences, shall be the same as if he had been born to them in lawful wedlock.

IT IS FURTHER ORDERED, adjudged and decreed, that the name of said child be changed to Harry Chester Lee according to the prayer of the petitioner herein.

State of Illinois, } ss.
COUNTY OF COOK.

I, PHILIP KNOPF, Clerk of the County Court of Cook County, in the State aforesaid, do hereby certify that the above and foregoing is a true, correct and complete copy of the Decree of Adoption entered on the 13th day of August 1897 in the matter of the Petition of Benjamin Peter Lee and Bandinia Lee to adopt Chester Perry being General Docket No. 16417 of said Court all of which appears from the records and files at my office.

IN WITNESS WHEREOF, I have hereunto set my hand and affixed the Seal of said County Court, at my office in the City of Chicago, in said County, this 21st day of August A.D. 1897

Philip Knopf
Clerk of the County Court.

Figure 6-17. Petition of Benjamin Peter Lee and Bandinia [sic] Lee to adopt Chester Perry, 13 Aug. 1897, Cook County Court, Ill., and decree of adoption, 21 Aug. 1897. Case file ffl16417, Cook County, Ill. Documents in possession of Harry L. Carle, 8035-186th S.W., Edmonds, WA 98020. Used with permission.

ages, religious affiliations, marital status, place and date of marriage, and fitness to adopt. In many states, if the child is illegitimate, the father is not recorded. Massachusetts, Illinois, New York, and Pennsylvania require that no indication of illegitimacy be given.

All parties who have an interest in the proceedings are notified of the date and time of the proceedings. Copies of these notifications are found in the case file. In Vermont, publication of adoption proceedings and proposed name changes had to appear for three successive weeks in the local newspapers before the hearing was held. Then the clerk of the probate court was required to submit annual returns of all such proceedings and name changes to the Secretary of State. See *General Statutes of Vermont* (1863), pp. 416-17. In this case, duplicate records are available in newspapers and in state archives.

Consent of the biological parents and their sworn and written statement relinquishing their rights to the child must be part of the case file. If the child is in the care of a guardian or institution, it provides consent. Children over a certain age – varying from eight to fourteen – are also required to give formal consent to the adoption.

Only five states – Alaska, Mississippi, Oklahoma, Oregon, and South Carolina – do not require a formal investigation of the adopting parents and the child. The proposed home, financial status, health, mental condition, occupation, and social standing in the community of the adopting parents are investigated along with the physical and mental condition and heritage of the child. Reports of these investigations become a part of the case file.

The hearing may be closed or open according to the judgment of the court. Evidence, testimony, and the above documents presented at the hearing provide the basis for a judgment and court decree. The decree may be interlocutory (requiring a waiting period of six months to one year before the adoption is final) or final (no waiting period). Usually as part of the decree, the child's name is changed to that of the adopting parents and the birth certificate is also changed accordingly.

If any party involved disagrees with the adoption, the case file will contain petitions for pending appeals to reconsider, annul, or revoke the decree. The grounds and procedures for such appeals vary considerably from state to state.

The records produced in adoption proceedings are still open in most states prior to 1930. Since that time, however, in an attempt to care for and protect both children and adoptive parents, some states have passed laws restricting the records. Wisconsin, Arkansas, California, Alabama, Minnesota, North Dakota, and Delaware limit adoption records only to the parties involved with court permission. In Pennsylvania, New Jersey, Louisiana, and Texas, the decree is open to the public, but the case files can be examined only with court permission. Most other states leave the choice of access up to the court.[30]

Records of adoptions which predate these laws are usually found among the regular records of the courts having adoption or family law jurisdiction. There is little problem in searching the early ones, if you follow this simple procedure. Ask to see the court docket or indexes covering the period of time of the search. Check carefully all surnames relating to your pedigree, for a relative may have adopted the child. Write out the number and name of the case. Ask the clerk for the case files you wish by number and name only, not by subject. If you wish copies and cannot make them yourself, request them by page or document date, not by name of document.

In some courthouses, there is little problem since the records are in files accessible to the public and coin-operated copy machines are nearby.

For sealed records, you will have to follow the rules of access set down by the court or the legislature. In most cases, the individual concerned must request the records *in person*.

The original birth certificate is released to the adoptee on demand in Alabama, Alaska, Kansas, Montana, and Pennsylvania. Court records are opened to adoptees on demand in South Dakota. Records are opened at court discretion in Connecticut, Minnesota, North Dakota, Tennessee, and Nebraska.

Rights of Inheritance. The primary purpose behind early adoption laws was to provide a legal heir for the adoptive parent. Hence, in most states adopted children inherit just as though they were "heirs of the body." In some jurisdictions, rights of inheritance are severely restricted. Property which is designated for "heirs of the body" by the testator cannot be inherited by adopted children in Maine, New Jersey, Ohio, Oklahoma, Rhode Island, Vermont, Utah, and West Virginia. Parents cannot inherit from adoptive children in Georgia, Oklahoma, and Tennessee.[31]

Citizenship. Alien children adopted by American parents do not automatically become citizens of the United States; however, the residence requirement is lowered to two years. The proceedings for children are less complicated than for adults.

Appeals Courts

Appeals courts review cases begun initially in other courts upon request of one or more litigants in the case. Some appeals courts may also transfer a case from a lower court for review upon some crucial point of law. This power is called certiorari. Few appeals courts concern themselves with questions of fact. That is, no witnesses appear to testify, and no jury determines the facts of the case. The court accepts the evidence of the previous trial and reviews questions of law – points on which an alleged error has been committed by the lower court. An exception is the Maryland Provincial Council, which will hold a full retrial, but usually, appeals made on new evidence are sent back to the lower court for retrial.

During the colonial period, however, most appeals courts also had original jurisdiction in cases involving land title, admiralty, probate, equity, divorce, criminal cases involving life or limb (capital cases), and all civil suits over £20 (increased eventually to £100).

Usually these appeals courts consisted of the royal governor and his council in judicial session following the model of the Privy Council of the King. Naturally, they were reluctant to surrender such judicial powers. These courts were called by various titles: Court of Assistants (Connecticut), Court of Magistrates (New Haven), Supreme Court (New Hampshire), General Court (Virginia), Court of Appeals (New Jersey and Georgia), and Provincial Court (Maryland).

In some of the colonies, the legislative assembly also handled appeals: Connecticut, Maryland, and Virginia assemblies heard divorce and land title cases until 1683, then these were transferred to the governor and council. Rhode Island, New York, and Delaware assemblies heard equity cases. In contrast, Pennsylvania, Rhode Island, and Massachusetts established supreme courts very early with jurisdiction equivalent to that of the English Court of King's Bench.

After the American Revolution, most state constitutions established supreme courts as the highest appellate courts in most states, although in theory, appeal can be made to the United States Supreme Court.

Appeals courts also issue these standard administrative enforcement writs: mandamus, ordering government officials to perform their duties; certiorari, ordering the review of a case from a lower trial court; habeas corpus, ordering the presentation of the accused before a magistrate for trial; and quo warrantis, ordering an office-holder to prove by what authority an office is held.

The courts of ultimate appeal during the colonial period were the King in Privy Council and/or Parliament. Such appeals were expensive and time consuming, involving amounts over £100 to £500 in value and taking almost two years to reach a verdict. As a result, only 265 cases were appealed. Some legislative assemblies restricted appeals to the King, and the Palatines (the Carolinas and Maryland) required the proprietor's permission to appeal.[32]

During the Revolution itself, appeals were limited to admiralty and military cases heard by the Continental Congress. The unsettled conditions and costs involved resulted in few appeals until the new government began to function. Then claims and cases were appealed to Congress as well as the Supreme Court.

Some state supreme courts did not assume conventional shape until after the Revolution. For example, Kentucky at one point in the early eighteenth century century had two courts of appeal to handle an enormous number of land title disputes, and the Texas Supreme Court in the Reconstruction period was so erratic that its rulings are never cited as serious precedents.[33]

Special courts of appeal were created from time to time to meet specific needs: In Virginia, the General Court (governor and council) heard criminal appeals well into the nineteenth century, before they were transferred to the Virginia Supreme Court. In Tennessee, it was impossible to survey land prior to settlement, resulting in overlapping and duplicate claims. The Tennessee Supreme Court of Errors and Appeals tried these land cases until 1834. In North Carolina the circuit court judges met regularly in a Court of Conference to discuss important cases and points of law. Gradually, it became a full-blown supreme court. New Jersey's Prerogative

Court and Maryland's Court of Delegates handled probate of wills and administration of estates.

Intermediate appeals courts relieved the workload of the state supreme courts and are courts of last resort for most cases. County and superior courts like Common Pleas and Quarter Sessions for appeals from justice and municipal courts are some examples.

Records of appeals courts are similar to those discussed above under civil, criminal, and equity cases, with two important exceptions: trial briefs and court opinions.

Trial Briefs. Since appeals courts did not usually hear trials, summaries of evidence and testimony – trial briefs – transmitted the facts of the case. These summaries have survived in most courts, and they are extremely valuable where the original case files no longer exist. Each judge in the court has a copy, with copies for the case file and trial attorneys. The earliest are in manuscript, but surprisingly soon they were printed. Supreme Court briefs were printed and bound from 1832 on.

Court Opinions. Court opinions are decisions of the judges in each case along with reasoning, and references to precedents. The first opinions were given orally and noted briefly in the court minutes or orders. Written opinions were required of all Supreme Court judges by a Congressional Act of 1834, and they became popular in other appeals courts, for they could be printed, circulated, and cited in similar cases, thus saving a great deal of research and correspondence.

Many appeals court records have been summarized, indexed by plaintiff (some defendant cross-indexes are available), and printed. (See Figure 6-18 for courts with printed reports.) More than 6,000 volumes representing some 500,000 different cases were in print in legal libraries across the United States by 1896. Many more have appeared since then.

The multi-volume *American Digest System*, published by West Publishing Company, 50 West Kellogg Blvd., St. Paul, MN 55102 is a partial index to printed reports of all fifty states from 1658 to the present, and its many volumes are available in almost any law library. The Century Edition or Digest covers cases from 1658 to 1896. The Decennial Edition or Digest covers cases from 1897 to date by decades: the First Decennial Digest covers 1897-1900, the Second Decennial Digest covers 1907-1916, and so forth to 1966 when the General Digest, 4th edition, begins.

An important feature of the Decennial Digest (volumes 21-25) is the Table of Cases, an alphabetical listing of printed cases 1658-1906, with subsequent tables for each ten-year increment in later volumes. For each case it gives the correct title, parallel citations to the National Reporter System and the State Reports (citation to State Reports are not included in the American Digest Table of Cases since 1966), the history of the case (i.e., whether it has been affirmed, reversed, or modified on appeal or rehearing), and the topics and key numbers under which the various points

Figure 6-18. Courts with Printed Reports, from *Guide to Legal Materials in the University of California, Santa Barbara Library: Case Law,* 4th rev. ed. (Santa Barbara, University of California, 1978).

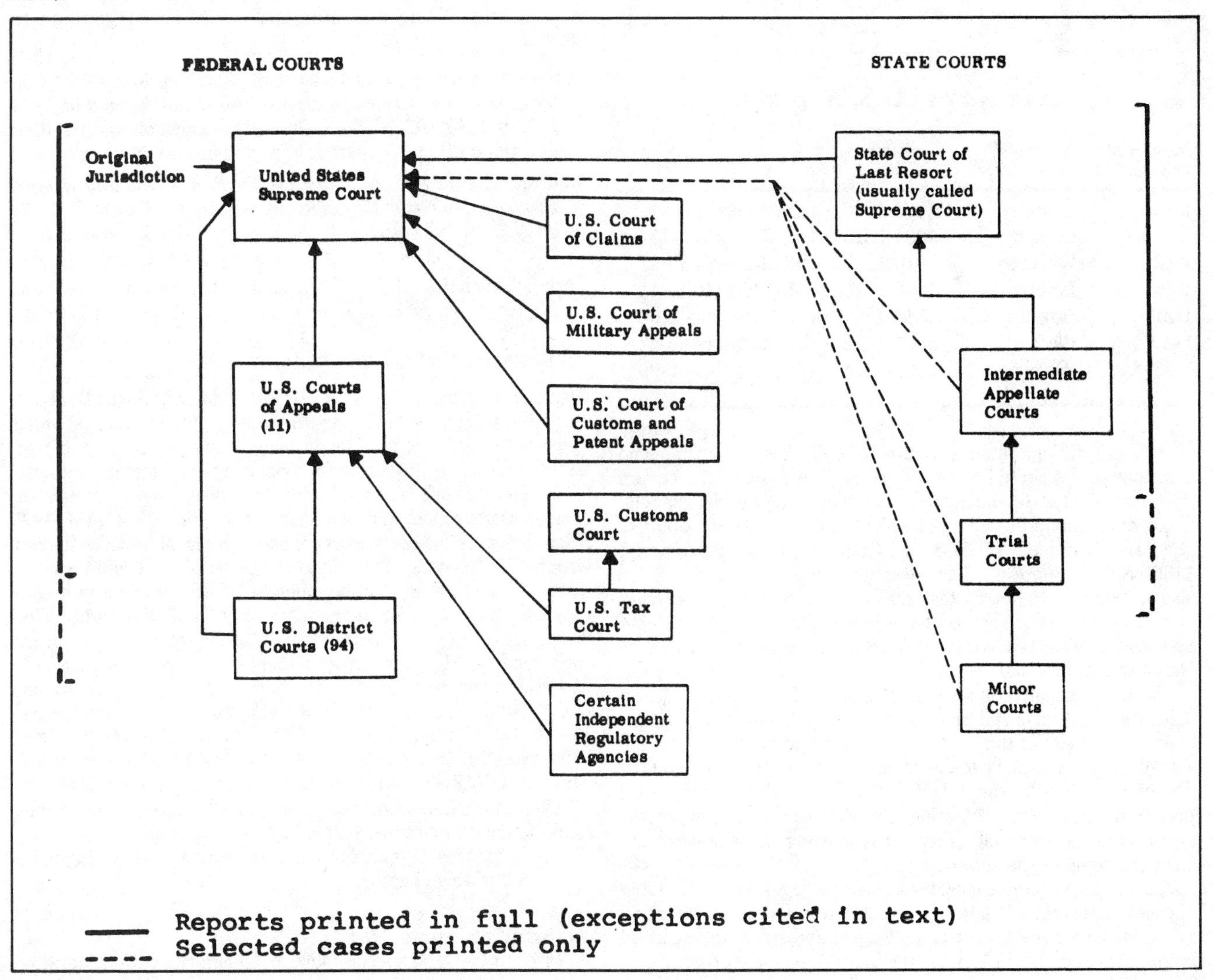

of laws in the case have been classified.

The Table of Cases has several limitations: (1) Cases are listed by plaintiff only. Defendants are cross-referenced in later digests and may be indexed in state and specialized reports. (2) Reports for county courts are often omitted. If your ancestor was A. P. Beard of Pennsylvania, you would not find his case listed, for it was tried before the county court. Yet the printed reports for Pennsylvania included his case. (3) Cases are described in abbreviated terms, so you must use the glossary carefully to find the case you want. (4) Cases 1897 to the present require checking several ten-year volumes.

Even with its limitations, every genealogist should be familiar with this reference tool. Including 500,000 cases, it is too valuable to be overlooked.

In addition to the Digest, you can check the printed reports for the states in which your ancestors lived. Each state has a series of printed reports, and some special courts have reports devoted to their cases. For example, *United States Reports* includes cases tried before the Supreme Court of the United States. (See Table 6-5.) The first ninety volumes were originally designated by the name of the court reporter and are cited, for example, 1 Dallas 295. 1 is the volume, Dallas is the name of the court reporter, and 295 is the page number. Articles in legal periodicals and law reviews are cited in the same volumes with an established abbreviation for the publication in the place of the reporter's name. Volume 91 was the first to carry the title *United States Reports,* but reprints of the first ninety volumes are labeled *U.S. Reports,* with a consecutive volume number, along with the original designation of the reporter's name for ease in identification.

Table 6-5

Summary of U.S. Reports

Number of Volumes	*Name of Court Reporter*	*Years Covered*	*Report Volume*
1-4	Dallas	1790-1800	U.S. Reports 1-4
1-9	Cranch	1801-1815	U.S. Reports 5-13
1-12	Wheaton	1816-1827	U.S. Reports 14-25
1-16	Peters	1828-1845	U.S. Reports 26-41
1-24	Howard	1843-1860	U.S. Reports 42-65
1-2	Black	1861-1862	U.S. Reports 66-67
1-23	Wallace	1863-1874	U.S. Reports 68-90

1 Dallas, though the first volume of *U.S. Reports,* contains no decisions of the United States Supreme Court. Instead it covers Pennsylvania reports: the Supreme Court of Pennsylvania, 1754-89; Court of Common Pleas, Philadelphia County, 1785-89; Court of Oyer and Terminer, 1785-88; and Court of Errors and Appeals, 1786-88. The Supreme Court decisions begin in 2 Dallas, which also includes the United States Court of Appeals, 1781-87. 4 Dallas includes the decisions of the United States Circuit Court for Pennsylvania, 1799-1806, and the Court of Errors and Appeals of Delaware, September Term, 1788.

Each case reported includes names of the plaintiff and the defendant, the court term and case number, the court involved, a summary of the facts of the case, a statement and clarification of the legal issues, a summary of the law pertaining to the case, and the decision reached by the judge(s). Obviously, these reports are prepared for the legal profession, but when they deal with property, probate, divorce, and other family matters, genealogical data form the basis of the report.

Each printed volume includes an index of legal subjects, a table of cases reported, and a table of cases cited. Later cases include a defendant cross-reference table. Plaintiff and defendant are listed in the table of cases only, not in the index. The table of cases also lists cases used as precedents.

Reports of state appellate and trial courts are also printed, usually by order of the state judiciary and are available in law libraries.

West Publishing of St. Paul, Minnesota, divided the United States into seven districts in 1879 and published the cases of the highest appellate courts for each state in that area. The Pacific area includes Alaska, Hawaii, Washington, Oregon, California, Idaho, Montana, Wyoming, Colorado, Utah, Nevada, Arizona, New Mexico, Kansas, and Oklahoma. The northwestern area includes the Dakotas, Nebraska, Minnesota, Iowa, Wisconsin, and Michigan. The southwestern area includes Texas, Arkansas, Missouri, Kentucky, and Tennessee. The Atlantic area includes Pennsylvania, Maryland, New Jersey, Delaware, Connecticut, Rhode Island, Vermont, New Hampshire, and Maine. The northeastern area includes New York, Massachusetts, Ohio, Indiana, and Illinois. The southeastern area includes West Virginia, Virginia, the Carolinas, and Georgia. The southern area includes Florida, Alabama, Mississippi, and Louisiana. Some published cases begin as early as 1658, but the majority date from the Civil War. These reports are included in the *Decennial Digest* Table of Cases.

As nearly as can be determined, all Supreme Court cases with written opinions from 1790 to 1815 have been printed. From 1816 to 1883, some 351 cases were unreported, with 310 written opinions not included. These cases are listed and described by J. C. Bancroft Davis, the court reporter, in the Appendix to 131 *United States Reports* (1889), lxiv-ccxxxi. Cases with no written opinions are not included.

See Table 6-6 for a summary of other published reports from federal courts. Here are three useful sources for getting into Supreme Court records:

Browning, James R., and Bess Glenn. "The Supreme Court Collections at the National Archives." *American Journal of Legal History* 4 (1960): 241-56. Includes a checklist of records, their description, years covered, and the number of feet per film.

Johnson, Marion M., et al. *Index to the Manuscript and Revised Printed Opinions of the Supreme Court of the United States in the National Archives, 1808-1873.* Special Lists, 21. Washington, D.C.: National Archives and Records Service, 1965.

Cocke, William Ronald, Jr. "Genealogical Notes from Supreme Court Reports." *William and Mary Quarterly,* 2nd series, 12 (1932): 167-72; 13 (1933): 49-54; 14 (1934): 24-35. Genealogical applications of data in appellate courts.

Opinions are listed alphabetically by justice, then by case title. Each entry gives the title of the case, the citation of the report in *United States Reports* by volume number, name of court reporter, and page number, whether the decision is concurring or dissenting, the case file number for appellate cases or the term docket number for cases of original jurisdiction. Almost all opinions are printed in *United States Reports.* Supporting documents are part of National Archives Record Group 267, Records of the Supreme Court of the United States. A detailed description can be found in NARS Preliminary Inventory 139, *Records of the Supreme Court of the United States.* This finding aid also shows the relationship of the reports to the other court records. Microfilm copies of these court records are available for purchase on microfilm from the National Archives, Washington, D.C. 20408. They are from: Revolutionary War Prize Cases, 1776-87 (M215); Appellate Case Files, 1792-1831 (M214); Minutes, 1790-1950 (M215); Dockets, 1791-1950 (M216); Attorney Rolls, 1790-1951 (M217); and Index to Appellate Case Files (M408).

The United States Court of Claims did not handle claims for pensions, although many were submitted to Congress.

For further readings on the Court of Claims, see the bibliography at the end of this chapter.

Admiralty Courts

Prior to 1697, no special courts of admiralty existed. Maritime matters were handled by existing common law courts, sitting with a jury. The English government asked these courts to enforce the Trade and Navigation Acts, but juries, who had themselves been guilty of violating those same laws, were reluctant to convict their fellow citizens. These breaches included failure to enter, clear, and register vessels, neglecting to carry the proper certificate, trading in ships not English built, navigating without the proper number of seamen, smuggling, and illicit trade. The Boston Tea Party was a revolt against the harshness of these acts.[34]

In 1697, American Courts of Vice-Admiralty were established by the English government in the chief seaports or districts (groups of colonies), completely separate from the courts of the colony in which the seaports happened to be. The governor served as vice-admiral of the colony but usually appointed someone else to be the judge of the court. Prosecutors attempted to bypass sympathetic juries by bringing their cases before the vice-admiralty where jury trial was prohibited and they could hope for convictions. Colonial judges, however, were also hesitant about convicting Americans of violating the admiralty laws, particularly smuggling and illegal trade.

In 1763, a vice-admiralty court for all America was established in Halifax, Nova Scotia, with British officials and judges. It heard its first cases in 1764, but protests from the colonies forced its removal to Boston with branch courts at Philadelphia and Charleston. This court gradually fell into disuse although it was not formally abolished.

With the outbreak of the American Revolution and the collapse of the British courts, the Continental Congress suggested that each

Table 6-6

Published Reports from Federal Courts*

U.S. Appeals Court/Cases	*Dates*	*Title and Contents of Reports*
Supreme Court	1790 to present	*U.S. Reports*. First 90 volumes identified by court reporter; reprint of volumes 1-90 labeled *U.S. Reports* with reporter's name; volumes 91 on titled *U.S. Reports*.
U.S. Court of Appeals	1781 to present	*U.S. Reports* 1781-1787 printed in 2 Dallas (vol. 2, *U.S. Reports*).
U.S. District Courts	1789 to present	*The Federal Reporter*, selected cases only.
U.S. Court of Claims	1855-63	*Reports of the Court of Claims Submitted to the House of Representatives*
	1863 to present	*Cases Decided in the Court of Claims in the U.S.*, vol. 30 indexes vols. 1-29, vol. 54 indexes vols. 30-54, vol. 62 indexes vols. 55-61.
U.S. Court of Military Appeals		*Decisions of the Court of Appeal*.
U.S. Court of Customs and Patent Appeals	1930 to date	*Reports of the Court of Customs and Patent Appeals of the U.S.* Each volume has plaintiff-defendant index.
U.S. Court of Customs Appeals	1909-29	Reports published by the Treasury Department under various titles. Indexes in each volume.
Prize Cases appealed to Continental Congress	1776-80	Includes Committee on Appeals cases referred to Court of Appeals. 109 cases listed 131 *U.S. Reports* (1889), xix-xlix. Each listing gives the title of the case, a brief description, court from which the appeal was made, dates of appeal and consideration, whether referred to Committee or Court.
Prize Cases of Revolutionary War, Committee on Appeals	1776-80	38 cases.
Prize Cases of Revolutionary War, Court of Appeals	1776-80	56 cases from all states except New York, which had no prize court.

*Lawrence F. Schmeckebier, *Government Publications and Their Use*, 3rd rev. ed. (Washington D.C.: Brookings Institution, 1961), pp. 266-78.

state provide a court of admiralty or give admiralty jurisdiction back to the regular courts. Jury trial was a prominent feature in these courts. The Constitution later vested admiralty jurisdiction in the federal district courts. See Table 6-7 for a state-by-state summary.

Admiralty Jurisdiction. Originally, admiralty courts limited their coverage to the mouths of rivers and the seacoasts of America. Gradually the jurisdiction was expanded to cover a wide variety of cases. This breadth of action yields some valuable data for genealogists.

Jurisdiction of matters includes wages of seamen – the most common cause the courts treated – bottomry (mortgaging a ship as security for payment of a loan), charter parties (contracts between merchants and mariners for merchandise to be carried), partnership (where two or more agree to share and share alike in some venture and one or more refuses to keep his part of the bargain), salvage (rescuing goods from wrecked vessels), claims for injuries to property or persons, contracts for building and furnishing ships, claims for money loaned or advanced, collisions, brutality, neglect of duty, insufficient food, and impressment (being kidnapped and forced to serve against one's will). These courts also had jurisdiction over prizes – seizure of enemy vessels and their cargo during wartime. Such cases were common in New York and South Carolina. Violations of pine masts were also handled by the admiralty courts – the King reserved to himself all white pines of more than twenty-four inches in diameter and three feet high for ships' masts for the Royal Navy. Anyone caught cutting them was tried before an admiralty court.

Admiralty courts had civil and criminal jurisdiction over merchants dealing with mariners, owners of ships, all persons having any relation to maritime transactions: those who build ships; those who equip, man, and supply them; those who land, load, and unload them; those who freight them; those employed in their service; those who violate, damage, injure, or violate their duty to or on the ship; all matters of business done in, or upon, or by the sea, public streams, fresh water, ports, rivers, and creeks with the ebbing and flowing of the tide as far as the high-water mark on shores or banks. If your ancestors lived along the water lines, most of their legal business would have been transacted in admiralty courts, not the local county courts.

Admiralty records have been preserved on both sides of the Atlantic. English records are in the Public Record Office among the records of the Lords of Trade, Board of Trade, and High Courts of Admiralty. Many of them have been calendared or abstracted and printed by order of Parliament. English records sometimes fell

Table 6-7
State Admiralty Courts 1776-89

State	*Title of Court*	*Date Formed*	*Appeals to Congress Allowed*	**Jury Trial*
Connecticut	County Maritime Courts (Long Island Sound Counties)	1776	No	
Delaware	Court of Admiralty	Before 1778	No	
Georgia	Court of Admiralty	1777	No	
Massachusetts	District Admiralty Courts (3), Boston	1775 1776	No No	After 1778
Maryland	Court of Admiralty	1763, renewed 1776	Yes	1776
North Carolina	Court of Admiralty	1777	No	1777
New Hampshire	Court of Admiralty	1776	Yes	
New Jersey	Court of Admiralty	1776 (abolished 1799)	No	
New York	No court established. British-occupied after 1776			
Pennsylvania	Court of Admiralty for Port of Pennsylvania	1778 (abolished 1780)	After 1780	Before 1780
Rhode Island	Maritime Court Court of Admiralty	1776 1780	Before 1780	
South Carolina	Court of Admiralty	1776	After 1777	1776
Virginia	Court of Commissioners in Admiralty, Court of Admiralty	1775 1776	After 1779, cases between two persons of the state excluded	

Based upon 131 *U.S. Reports*, Appendix, xx-xxii. Jurisdiction of state admiralty courts transferred to United States District Courts in 1789, under the Federal Judiciary Act 1st Congress, Sess. I, Ch. 20. (Statute 1, 24 Sept. 1789).

*Almost all states permitted trial by jury for prize cases.

into the hands of the American courts at the time of the Revolution. For example, the records of the Vice-Admiralty Court of New York are among the federal archives of New York City.[35] American records are found among the files of the court which exercised the jurisdiction. Records for the state admiralty courts are in the state archives, and some extracts are published.

In addition to the regular court records like dockets, minutes, and case files, admiralty courts include such evidence as ships' records and records kept by seamen: ship registers, enrollments, licenses, crew lists, manifests, passenger lists, seamen's contracts, clearance papers, log books, private letters, and other correspondence carried by the ship seized as part of its cargo.

For additional reading on admiralty courts, see the bibliography at the end of this chapter.

Claims Courts

The right – first guaranteed by the English government and incorporated into federal and state constitutions – to petition the government for redress of grievances is an excellent source of genealogical data because our ancestors used it so freely.

Common "grievances" were damages for supplies and provisions supplied in war, for unfair dealings of the government and its personnel; for unpaid wages, pensions, or other compensation promised; for lack of protection against local enemies and foreign powers; and for jurisdiction and boundary changes.

Although this discussion is limited to claims against the United States government and its courts, equivalent actions and records can be found in state court files and among the records of counties, towns, and cities.

Table 6-8 summarizes the types of claims made from 1774 through World War II with the agency responsible to deal with them, the record group number, and a brief description of the contents and/or location.

Most claims against the United States government before 1855 were presented to Congress and referred to committees on claims of the Senate and the House of Representatives. The inability of these committees to examine in detail all the claims submitted, together with the difficulty of getting Congress to appropriate the necessary funds to pay favorable claims, amounted to a denial of justice to many citizens. In addition, the number of claims became too great. A separate Court of Claims, established in 1855, did not solve the problem as it had no authority to render judgment. Its job was to investigate the claim and forward all evidence, testimony of witnesses, law briefs of solicitors and claimants, opinions and recommendations of the court to the Committee on Claims, House of Representatives, for final consideration of those cases recommended favorably. Those reported unfavorably were placed upon the calendar for Congressional consideration. This amounted to having each case tried twice and solved nothing. In 1863, the court was given power to render final judgment in all cases with the right of appeal to the Supreme Court for cases over $3,000. From 1855 to the end of 1881, it heard over 13,000 cases. By an amendment passed in 1868 to the Act of 1863, the clerk of the court was required to submit an annual return to Congress containing a list of all judgments rendered by the court, the amount of redress granted, the parties involved and a brief synopsis of the nature of the claim. See William A. Richardson, "History, Jurisdiction and Practice of the Court of Claims of the United States," *Southern Law Review*, new series., 7 (1882): 790. Such reports would be valuable, but I have been unable to locate any reference to them among the records of Congress.

The procedures and practices of the Court of Claims are very similar to those followed in regular courts of law except that all testimony and evidence is in writing. Twenty-five printed copies of all briefs must be filed (if the case is under $3,000, the briefs are printed at public expense) with the clerk of the court at least one day prior to the hearing of the case. No court costs are required except those of the claimant's personal attorney. Cases must be presented by legal counsel. There is no jury. Prior to 1868, all claimants had to prove that they had been loyal citizens of the Union during the Civil War. Since that time, the amnesty oath pardoning Confederates voided this provision. See Table 6-9 for a summary of its growing jurisdiction.

The records of the Court of Claims are similar to the records found in any court – dockets, minutes, judgments, and case files. The National Archives has published listings of the case files and related records with descriptions of what they contain, how they are filed, and indexes which can be used in Preliminary Inventories 47 and 58. Therefore, it will not be necessary to go into detail concerning these records here. Table 6-10, prepared for the convenience of the researcher from these inventories, gives the kind of records produced, the dates covered, and the locations of the original records themselves. Congressional records – both original and printed – contain pertinent information concerning the Court of Claims and its cases through the annual reports submitted by the court. The procedures outlined above for use with claims presented to Congress can be followed to use Court of Claims information.

Even though the court and parts of its jurisdiction were not established until the latter half of the nineteenth century, documents and evidence sometimes date from the Revolutionary period. In addition, many claims are submitted by and awarded to heirs of the original claimant.

For example, the French Spoliation cases include ledgers, account books, insurance policy registers, notarial records, letter books, day books, executors' accounts of liquidation of estates, ships' registers and logs, lists of crew members who served aboard vessels, etc. (See Appendix 1 in Preliminary Inventory 58.) Case files also include certificates of appointments of administrators, executors, legal representatives, powers of attorney, and proof of death. The Court of Claims, in an effort to substantiate the claims submitted, ordered evidence collected from customs and marine records in French ports and archives. Authenticated copies of these French materials, together with English translations, were sent to the State Department, and certified copies were introduced as evidence in the claims cases. Even though these records are copies of copies and thus subject to error, most originals have since been destroyed or lost. Maritime records kept by United States Customs officials at ports of entry – registrations, registers, oaths, proofs of ownership, licenses, enrollments – were also included.

Among the case files of the Congressional-jurisdiction records are muster rolls, certificates of death and burial, oaths of allegiance, inventories of property, statements and records of military service, records of courts martial, and tax lists. The naval-bounty claims contain lists of seamen who served on vessels during the Spanish-American War.

The United States Court of Claims did not handle claims for pensions, although many were submitted to Congress.

For further readings on the Court of Claims, see the bibliography at the end of this chapter.

Courts-Martial Records

The purpose of military courts is to insure orderly operations and exact obedience. The United States is and has been a non-military nation, maintaining a small standing army during times of peace and depending upon local militia or civilian armies to supplement these troops in times of war.

Local militias and state-authorized troops made up the bulk of the armed forces used in any war effort in the United States from colonial times until the Civil War. Even the troops mustered during the Revolutionary War, which were classified as the Continental Army, were drawn from these local units. As a result, records exist both at the federal level for the Continental troops and at the colonial/state level.

Prior to 1689, all military offenses were tried before regular law courts. With the passage of the English Mutiny Act in 1689,

Table 6-8
Claims Made Against the U.S. Government

Table of Claim	*Date*	*Name Index*	*NARS Record Group*	*Comments/Description*
Claims Barred by Statute of Limitations, Adjusted and Allowed.	1810	See Comments		Printed in *American State Papers* (036-216) available in most Government Documents sections of public and university libraries. Some claims indexed in Phillip W. McMullin, *Grassroots of America* (Provo, Utah: Gendata Corporation, 1972). Volume indexes are unreliable.
Claims of Persons, Circumstances Barred by Limitations	1792	Yes		1,500 Revolutionary Soldiers pensioned under an act of 27 March 1792. See Mary G. Ainsworth, "Recently Discovered Records Relating to Revolutionary War Veterans Who Applied for Pensions Under the Act of 1792," *National Genealogical Society Quarterly* 46 (1958): 8-13, 73-78
Private Claims Submitted to Congress	1774-89	Yes	360	Papers of the Continental (and Confederation) Congresses, 204 rolls (microfilm number 247); *Journals of the Continental Congress* (includes Confederation), 34 vols, printed by the Library of Congress, 1904-37. Every name indexes: *Index: Journals of the Continental Congress, 1774-1789* (NARS, 1976); *Index: Papers of the Continental Congress, 1774-1789.* 5 vols. (NARS, 1978). Film and indexes available in Federal Archives branches and other research libraries.
	1789 to present		46 (Senate) 233 (House)	Published as *Congressional Documents* arranged alphabetically to form an easily accessible index 1789-1891 (House), 1815-1909 (Senate).

Congress	Date	Congressional document containing list*
Senate		
14th-16th	1815-81	46th Cong., 3d sess., S. Misc. Doc 14, serials 1945-46.
47th-51st	1881-91	53rd Cong., 2d sess., S. Misc. Doc. 266, serial 3175.
52d-55th	1891-99	56th Cong., 1st sess., S. Doc. 449, serial 3881
56th and 57th	1899-1903	57th Cong., 2d sess., S. Doc. 221, serial 4433
58th	1903-05	59th Cong., 1st sess., S. Doc. 3, serial 4917
59th and 60th	1905-09	60th Cong., 2d sess., S. Doc. 646, serial 6165
House of Representatives		
1st-31st	1789-1851	32d Cong., 1st sess., H. Misc. Doc. (unnumbered), serials 653-655
32d-41st	1851-71	42d Cong., 3d sess., H. Misc. Doc. 109, serial 1574
42d-46th	1871-81	47th Cong., 1st sess., H. Misc. Doc. 53, serial 2036
47th-51st	1881-91	53d Cong., 2d sess., H. Misc. Doc. 213, serial 3268

*These claims have been reprinted in three volumes by Genealogical Publishing Company, Baltimore, Maryland.

Senate documents more than fifty years old are open for research. House documents may be used only by permission of the clerk of the House. Contact your congressman for authorization.

Table of Claim	Date	Name Index	NARS Record Group	Comments/Description
				For details see Arlene H. Eakle, *American Congressional Records* (Salt Lake City: The Genealogical Institute, 1974); *Preliminary Inventory 113: Records of the U.S. House of Representatives*, 2 vols.; *Preliminary Inventory 46: Records of the United States Senate;* and *Special List 32: Hearings in the Records of the U.S. Senate and Joint Committees of Congress; Special List 35: Printed Hearings of the House of Representatives Found Among Its Committee Records, 1824-1958.* For pension claims, see also Leroy P. Graf, et al., "The Pension Office to Congressman Andrew Johnson: A List, 1843-1853," *East Tennessee Historical Society Publications* 38 (1966): 97-108 for a list of pension claims Johnson introduced; originals are in possession of the U.S. Pension Office.
Quartermaster Claims	1839 1860	Volume indexes	92	4 manuscript vols., claims relating to services, supplies, or transportation furnished to or requisitioned for the Army. Supporting documents may have been destroyed. Includes Mexican War claims, 1847-58; civilian claims (mostly Mexican War teamsters), 1848-60.
4th of July Claims	1861-70 1871-90	Volume indexes Partial indexes only	92	68 vols. (manuscripts with supporting case files). Includes rejected claims. Volumes arranged by auditor's numbers, related papers filed by register numbers. 29 vols. (manuscripts and supporting case files). Arranged by year. Rejected claims arranged by box numbers. Incomplete 2-vol. register to rejected claims. Must prove loyal citizen of loyal state. Valuable, covers country. 36 vols. (manuscripts with supporting correspondence and case files).
Civil War Claims	1861-94	Some volume indexes	92	Transportation, personal services for persons later deceased, horses and mules, extra-duty, bounty arrears, property damage, rents, and other matters. Indexes, where they exist, are incomplete. See *Genealogical Research in the National Archives (1982)*, p. 230; and *Preliminary Inventory 135, Records Relating to Civil War Claims, U. S. and Great Britain.*
Transportation Claims	1871-87	Some volume indexes	92	131 registers including ocean and lake vessels, railroads accounts connected with military operations, ferries.
Confederate Horse Claims	1901-14	No	92	Claims for paroled Confederate soldiers whose arms and horses were seized by Union troops in violation of the terms of surrender. Files arranged by members from general correspondence of quartermaster general, 1890-1914.
Alabama Claims	1872	Yes		List of documents and correspondence in the cases of U. S. and Great Britain indexing the claims for losses to Confederate ships: *Alabama, Shenandoah, Florida, Tallahassee.* Description of cases in *Revised List of Claims. . .Known as the Alabama Claims.*
Southern Claims Commission	1871-80	Yes	217 233	Approved claims. Disallowed claims filed with records of House of Representatives. Gary B. Mills, comp., *Civil War Claims in the South: An Index of Civil War Damage Claims Commission, 1871-1880* (Laguna Hills, CA: Aegean Park Press, 1980). 22,298 claims were submitted by Southerners who swore they were loyal to the Union; 7,092 were allowed. Includes interrogatories (detailed questionnaries) filled out by all applicants. See Frank W. Klingberg, *The Southern Claims Commission* (Berkeley: University of California Press, 1955) and Sarah Larson, "Records of the Southern Claims Commission," *Prologue*, 1980, pp. 207-18.

Table of Claim	Date	Name Index	NARS Record Group	Comments/Description
Claims of Citizens of Kansas	1858-61	Volume indexes		35th Cong., 2d sess., H. Misc. Doc. 43, serial 1017 (1858-59); 36th Cong., 2d sess., H. Reports 104, serial 1106. Indexes are incomplete. Claims awarded for property damage by marauding raiders, i.e., Quantrell.
Hearings, Committee on War Claims	1910-14	Volume indexes		63d Cong., 2d sess., H. Reports 124. Many claims available on microfiche.
Claims Commissions, United States and Mexico	1839-1938	Yes	76	Include cases of seizure of property, quartering of troops, illegal arrest and maltreatment of prisoners, boundary claims, prize cases submitted by local residents. Several thousand claims were accepted. See *Preliminary Inventory 136: Records of United States and Mexican Claims Commission.*
War Relocation Authority (Japanese-Americans)	1941-46	Master Index of Evacuees (Microfilm of cards)	210	9,000 Japanese-Americans moved out of military zones in California, Oregon, Washington, Arizona, Arkansas, and Hawaii voluntarily. More than 100,000 were forced to evacuate by War Relocation Authority. See *Preliminary Inventory 77: Records of the War Relocation Authority.* Legislation before Congress (1983) to compensate each family up to $10,000.
World War II Exclusion Files	1941-48		153	Relocation of German and Italian aliens, U.S. citizens of German and Italian heritage in military zones. Alphabetically arranged by surname.

Table 6-10

Court of Claims Record Locations

Original Records	Dates Covered	Located
Original indexes, dockets, minutes, judgments books, register of attorneys	1855 to present	Court of Claims
Case Files: General Jurisdiction	1855-1939	Court of Claims, Record Group 123, National Archives.
	1939-46	Federal Records Center, Suitland, MD
	1946 to present	Court of Claims
Other	1855-1943	Court of Claims, Record Group 123, National Archives.
	1943 to present	Court of Claims
Attorney General Records	1855-1945	Court of Claims Section, Department of Justice, Record Group 205, National Archives.
	1945 to present	Attorney General Office, Department of Justice.
Reports to Congress	1855-63	Committee on Claims, records of House of Representatives, Record Group 233, National Archives.
Printed Record		
Reports to Congress	1855-63	Congressional Documents and Reports, Government Documents libraries.
Court Reports	1863	*Cases Decided in the Court of Claims of the United States,* Vols. 1 to present available in most large law libraries. Each volume indexed separately, general indexes Vol. 30 (Vols. 1- 29); Vol. 54 (31-54); Vol. 62 (55-62).

Table 6-9

United States Court of Claims

Jurisdiction	*Date Established*	*Date Abolished*	*Indexes Located*
Investigate, report findings to Congress. General jurisdiction, violations of contracts entered into by government agencies, violations of Indian treaties, patent infringements, unlawful imprisonment, overassessment or overpayments of taxes, payment of Army, Navy, civilian personnel, and unlawful seizure of property.	1855	1863	Court of Claims
Try claims, render final judgment	1863		Court of Claims
Admiralty claims		1930[1]	Court of Claims
Equity claims	1870		Court of Claims
Appeals to Supreme Court, plaintiff over $3,000, defendant all cases	1866[2]	1925[3]	Supreme Court records in the National Archives
District of Columbia—jurisdiction cases. Cases originally handled by Congressional committees. The majority were claims for seizure of stores, supplies, and damages resulting from the occupation of Union troops during the Civil War.	1880 1883, 1887	 1915[4]	Court of Claims Court of Claims
Claims under interdepartmental agencies. Also includes naval-bounty claims arising from the Spanish-American War.	1883, 1887		Court of Claims
Claims arising from depredations by French warships and privateers on American commerce, 1793-1801 (French spoilations). Court to investigate and report to Congress. The U.S. abandoned all claims for reparations against France in 1801, but the claimants continued to press for payment. 5,574 claims were filed with the court; all claims were settled with heirs.	1885	1908	Court of Claims Section, Dept. Of Justice, National Archives Record Group 205. Lists of claimants; 16th Cong., 2d sess. Sen. Doc. 118, serial 45; 19th Cong., 2d sess. H. Doc. 68, serial 157; 22d Cong., 2d sess. H. Doc. 147, serial 235; 38th Cong., 1st sess., Sen. Reports 41, serial 1178; 48th Cong., 1st sess. Sen. Exec. Doc. 205, serial 2168; 49th Cong. 1st sess. Sen. Exec. Doc. 102, serial 2340; 50th Cong. 1st Sess. H. Exec. Doc. 309, serial 2561. See Donald L. Jacobus, "Genealogy, the Law, and French Spoliation Claims," *American Genealogist* 46 (1970): 81-84.
Concurrent Jurisdiction given to federal district courts under $1,000, to circuit courts $1,000-$10,000.	1887		Pertinent district or circuit courts
Claims for property taken or destroyed by Indians under treaty with the U.S. government, 1814-91 (Indian Depredations). Cases usually involve isolated miners, ranchers, towns, stage coaches, wagon trains, and railroad lines.	1891[5] 1915	1920 1920	Same as French cases above. List of claims 49th Cong., 1st sess. H. Exec. Doc. 125, serial 2399
Indian Claims In 1946, Indians were given the right to present claims against the U.S. government like other U.S. citizens.	1946		Court of Claims 400 cases to 1960.

1. Since 1930, only foreigners can sue for admiralty claims in this court. Citizens must petition federal Admiralty Courts.

2. The law of 1863 gave right of appeal to the Supreme Court, but the court refused to hear appeals which were reviewable by the Department of the Treasury. Treasury jurisdiction abolished in 1866.

3. Since 1925, Supreme Court has right to choose cases it hears.

4. A large number of cases arising from long-standing Civil War claims were canceled. Number of cases handled after 1915 was small.

5. From 1796 to 1891, cases heard by Department of Interior and its predecessors, report made to Congress. Few awards made till 1891.

courts-martial heard military violations at both county/town and colonial levels.

Every able-bodied man from sixteen to sixty, fully armed at his own expense (except those specifically exempted by law), was required to serve in the county or town militia. These militia units were required to hold at least four private (local) musters and one or two general (county) musters per year at which they were to drill and to become proficient in the use of arms. At all musters, the captains of the companies were to keep an attendance record on each man and a record of the offenses and delinquencies of attendance and equipment of all men of their respective companies and report the same to the court-martial. The court-martial convened once a year in each county after the general muster of the county. In this militia court sat a majority or all of the captains of the county. They reviewed the ages and capabilities of all those on the muster lists, dropped those too old or disabled, inquired into the absences and delinquencies reported, and imposed fines. Militia watches were outlined, assigned, and reported on also. In some jurisdictions, the militia captain was also responsible for tax assessment, and tax districts coincided with militia districts. Figure 6-19 reports such an agenda, while Figure 6-20 specifies boundaries.

The professional, standing army of the United States dates from

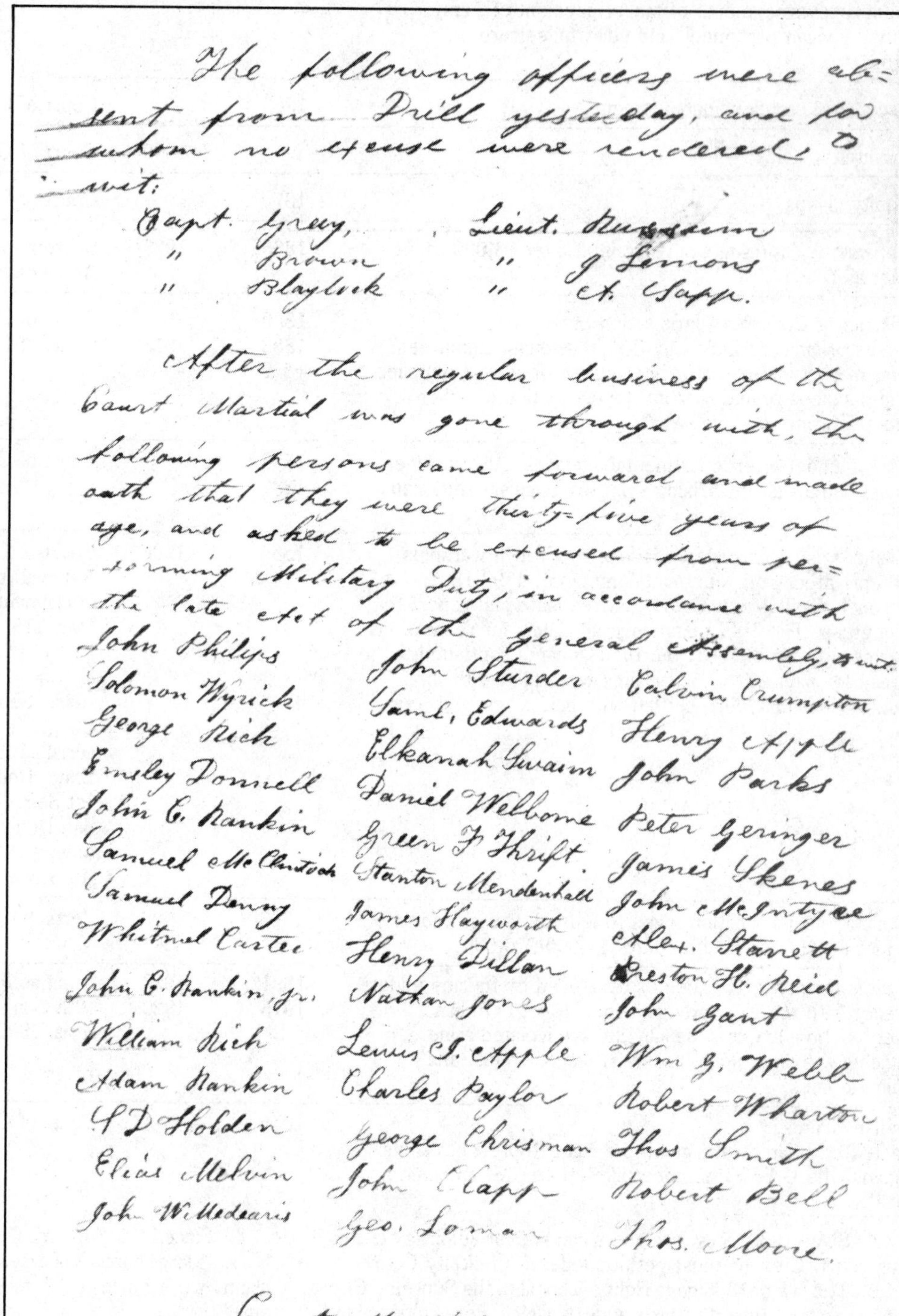

Figure 6-19. Court-Martial Minutes, 1841 Guilford County (North Carolina) Militia Book, Southern Historical Collection, manuscript 2307, Wilson Library, University of North Carolina, Chapel Hill, N.C. Used with Permission.

The following officers were absent from Drill yesterday, and for whom no excuse were rendered, to wit:

Capt. Grey, Lieut. Russum
" Brown " J. Lemons
" Blaylock " A. Sapp.

After the regular business of the Court Martial was gone through with, the following persons came forward and made oath that they were thirty-five years of age, and asked to be excused from performing Military Duty, in accordance with the late act of the General Assembly, to wit:

John Philips	John Sturder	Calvin Crumpton
Solomon Wyrick	Saml. Edwards	Henry Apple
George Rich	Elkanah Swaim	John Parks
Emsley Donnell	Daniel Welborne	Peter Geringer
John C. Rankin	Green F. Thrift	James Skenes
Samuel McClintock	Stanton Mendenhall	John McIntyre
Samuel Denny	James Hayworth	Alex. Starrett
Whitmel Carter	Henry Dillan	Preston H. Reid
John C. Rankin, jr.	Nathan Jones	John Gant
William Rich	Lewis I. Apple	Wm G. Webb
Adam Rankin	Charles Paylor	Robert Wharton
S D Holden	George Chrisman	Thos Smith
Elias Melvin	John Clapp	Robert Bell
John Willedearis	Geo. Loman	Thos. Moore

Court Martial adjourned

M. C. Sherwood
Judge Advocate

1789. In times of war, it is supplemented by National Guard and reserve units, state militias, and conscripted civilians. There are three types of military jurisdiction: military law, or the Code of Military Justice; martial law, or temporary rules enforced by soldiers governing both military and civilian populations; and military governments, or administrative functions exercised by military personnel and organizations over civil populations.

The Code of Military Justice outlined by Thomas Jefferson and John Adams in 1776 to govern Washington's volunteers has evolved into the Uniform Code of Military Justice adopted 31 May 1951 so all branches of the armed forces are subject to the same courts, trial procedures, and appellate review.

The National Guard is subject to this system when nationalized, in training, and under police actions. Reserve units are subject to military law while on active duty and during annual training camps. All members of the U.S. Armed Forces are subject to the code at all times. This code is enforced in military courts-martial. Although provided for by the Constitution, these tribunals derive their authority from the executive branch rather than the judicial and thus are completely separate from the regular system. Cases are not reviewable by civil courts nor can appeal be made to civil courts. Table 6-11 summarizes the types of courts-martial.

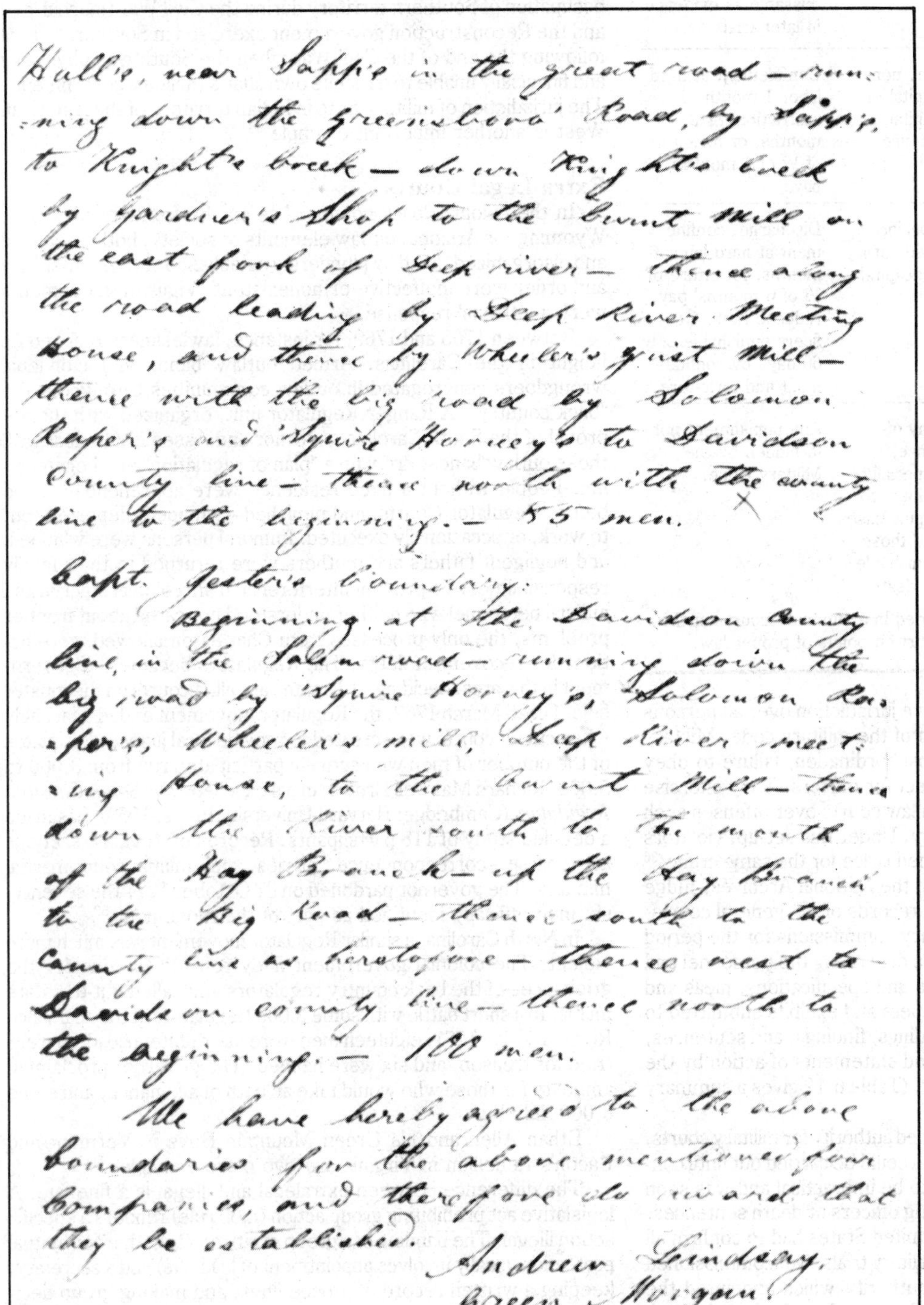

Hull's, near Sapp's in the great road—run-
-ning down the Greensboro' Road, by Sapp's,
to Knight's Creek—down Knights Creek
by Gardner's Shop to the burnt mill on
the east fork of Deep river—thence along
the road leading by Deep River Meeting
House, and thence by Wheeler's grist Mill—
thence with the big road by Solomon
Raper's and Squire Horney's to Davidson
County line—thence north with the county
line to the beginning.—85 men.

Capt. Jester's Boundary:
Beginning at the Davidson County
line, in the Salem road—running down the
big road by Squire Horney's, Solomon Ra-
-per's, Wheeler's mill, Deep River meet-
-ing House, to the burnt Mill—thence
down the River south to the mouth
of the Hay Branch—up the Hay Branch
to the Big Road—thence south to the
County line as heretofore—thence west to
Davidson County line—thence north to
the beginning—100 men.

We have hereby agreed to the above
boundaries for the above mentioned four
Companies, and therefore do award that
they be established.

Andrew Lindsay.
Green Morgan.

Figure 6-20. Court-Martial Minutes, 1841, Guilford County (North Carolina) Militia Book, p. 95; Southern Historical Collection, manuscript 2307, Wilson Library, University of North Carolina, Chapel Hill, N.C. Used with permission.

Table 6-11

Types of United States Courts-Martial

Court	*Membership*	*Offenses*	*Punishment*
Court of Inquiry	Appointed upon request of the accused	Any non-capital or capital offense	Determined by nature of offense. If there is sufficient evidence for court-martial, records are admissable as evidence in later trial.
Summary court-martial[1]	1 commissioned officer	Any non-capital or capital offense	Confinement at hard labor 1 month, restriction for 2 months, or forfeiture of 1/2 of 1 month's pay.
Special court-martial	3 or more commissioned officers	Specific cases of a noncapital nature	Discharge, confinement at hard labor 6 months, forfeiture of 2/3 of 6 months' pay, reduced rank. Officers punishable only 60 days by confinement and forfeiture.
General court-martial	5 or more commissioned officers and 1 law officer[2]	Any offense, especially subject to capital cases and those punishable by death	Any punishment not forbidden by the Military Code.

1. Cadets and officers cannot be tried in a summary court-martial.
2. The law officer instructs the court on points of proper law.

Courts-martial exercise exclusive jurisdiction over all persons subject to military law for violation of the military code. Military offenses under the code include insubordination, failure to obey orders, being AWOL, and disrespect for officers. They exercise concurrent jurisdiction with civilian law courts over offenses such as murder, theft, rape, and burglary. Under this set-up, violators may be tried, convicted, and punished twice for the same crime.[36]

Courts-martial files deposited in the National Archives, Judge Advocate General's Office, contain records of the general courts-martial, courts of inquiry and military commissions for the period 1809-1938. Included are documents describing the personnel and organization of the courts, changes and specifications, pleas and arraignments of the defendants, papers and exhibits submitted to the court for consideration, proceedings, findings, and sentences, reports of reviewing authorities, and statements of action by the Secretary of War and the President. (Table 6-12 gives a summary of these records.)

In 1776, when Congress established authority for military courts, no sentence of a general courtmartial could be carried out until confirmed by Congress. This proved to be impractical and was soon modified to apply only to high-ranking officers or death sentences. A little later, the President of the United States had to confirm all convictions of the death penalty in military trials. Noncommissioned soldiers could appeal only to the authority which appointed the military court. Under the National Defense Act of 4 June 1920, a Board of Review was established for review of all general courts-martial cases before punishment could be carried out. In 1952, Congress provided for a Court of Military Appeals through which civilian judges could review all military convictions and appeals from lower tribunals. In its first year, it heard 108 suits on appeal and in 50 percent of the cases reversed the decision rendered by the Board of Review.[37]

Martial Law and Military Governments. Martial law consists of rules temporarily applied to civilians under the direction of military officers. Authority for martial law must originate from Congressional grant or Presidential power and is enforced by military tribunals. If local units of government are unable to cope with war, insurrection, invasion, or other disruptive forces, Congress or the President can order a military government to replace these local units and supply administrative controls. Examples include federal occupation of Southern territory during the Civil War (martial law) and the Reconstruction government exercised in Southern States following the end of the Civil War when the South was physically and financially unable to direct its own affairs (military government). The jurisdiction of military forts in Indian territory of the American West is another important example.[38]

Extra-Legal Courts

In the colonial "back country," as on the frontiers of Texas, Wyoming, or Arizona, outlaw elements of society, both organized and disorganized, lived by plundering established settlements. Law and order were ineffective or nonexistent. Vigilante movements were a citizens' response.

Between 1765 and 1769, for instance, lawlessness reached its height in the Carolinas. Armed outlaw bands and individual wrongdoers congregated in outlaw communities throughout the "back country." A Ranger-Regulator unit, organized with the approval of the South Carolina governor and Assembly to deal with these outlaw bands, drew up a "plan of regulation" and began acting. People without a fixed residence were apprehended, tried before Regulator Courts, and punished—whipped, deported, put to work, or occasionally executed. Immoral persons were whipped, and negligent fathers and mothers were returned to their family responsibilities. To prevent interference from colonial officials and judicial personnel who neither understood nor cared about frontier problems, the only processes from Charleston allowed were actions for recovery of debts. The Regulators became the government in this area, deciding all disputes at militia courts on the muster field. On 25 March 1769, the Regulator movement ended peaceably when circuit courts were created to provide local justice. Estimates of the number of men who actually participated run from 3,000 to 5,000. Richard Maxwell Brown, in his excellent *The South Carolina Regulators* (Cambridge: Harvard University Press, 1963), has made a detailed study of 118 participants. Records of Regulator actions are sparse—correspondence, diaries, and militia court-martial minutes. The governor pardoned on 31 October 1771 the seventy-six men officially identified as part of the movement.[39]

In North Carolina, a similar Regulator movement was much more violent. The colonial government flatly refused to consider the grievances of the back country regulators and called out the state militia. In a short battle with some 2,000 Regulators at the Alamance River, 16 May 1771, eighteen men were killed, fifteen leaders were tried for treason, and six were hanged. The governor proclaimed amnesty for those who would take an oath of allegiance, and some 6,000 did.[40]

Ethan Allen and his Green Mountain Boys in Vermont and Bacon's Rebellion in Virginia are two more examples.

The difference between extralegal and illegal is a fine line. A legislative act prohibiting group action (mob rule) renders a specific action illegal. The banding of a group of citizens together for mutual protection usually involves appointment of leader(s) and a secretary, keeping a written record of proceedings, and making group decisions (rules) binding upon all regardless of approval. This kind of action is extralegal—outside of the law.

Extralegal courts do produce records—a wide variety of "official" or approved documents as well as reports of investigations, newspaper accounts, and correspondence between participants, witnesses, and government officials. For a provocative and fact-filled description of archives relating to extralegal bodies, see Richard Maxwell Brown, "The Archives of Violence," *American Archivist* 41 (1978): 431-44.

To provide legislative, executive, and judicial functions when regular government institutions had ceased to function effectively during the Revolutionary War, the colonials used the same system adopted by the Puritans a century earlier when they overthrew and executed Charles I.

By 1774, two separate governments functioned in most of the colonies: assemblies and governors under British control, and those created by the revolutionary colonial leadership. These two governments met in immediately successive sessions, frequently with the same membership. When Parliament abolished the regular assemblies, the revolutionary governments assumed complete control. Each colony sent representatives to the Continental Congress; each appointed a provincial assembly, a provincial council, and various district, county, and town governing committees. By the time the war started, each of the colonies had created a functioning system of local and provincial self-government. They operated under a mixture of martial and civil law until state constitutions could be ratified and regular government reestablished.

1. Some meetings of freeholders (freemen) had been organized as early as 1766. In Westmoreland County, Virginia, 114 freemen joined for common defense and safety, formed the basis for subsequent citizen action as the Revolution approached, and selected patriot representation for their extralegal provincial congress in the 1770s.[41]

2. Committees of Correspondence (Observation) corresponded with members in the colony and with committees in other colonies. They provided political information, creating and consolidating pre-Revolutionary sentiment with frequent meetings. By 1774, every colony but Pennsylvania and North Carolina had Committees of Correspondence.

3. Committees of Safety were the executive power to carry out the orders of the Continental Congress and to enforce the Articles of Association which all colonies had signed. County-level committees frequently usurped the powers of the regular county courts, some even requiring that every suit brought before a regular court of law had to be authorized by the committee. They also appointed military officials and judicial personnel for certain courts, appointed patrols to control Negroes, exchanged prisoners, fined militia men for refusal to serve, relocated, paroled, or jailed Loyalists (Tories), punished counterfeiters, administered loyalty and test oaths, supervised elections to provincial and Continental Congresses, ordered lists of taxable property and census rolls, censored publications and speech, frequently jailing offenders, passed moratoria on collection of debts or confiscations to be paid to creditors, corresponded and cooperated with other committees, offered bounties and premiums for manufacture of needed items – cotton, wool, limes, steel, etc. – regulated travel, controlled horse-racing, billiard playing, and dances, seized vessels and prizes, made lists of inhabitants to submit to Provincial Councils, and inventoried estates of suspected Loyalists.

The local militia was under their direct control. They tried all cases of disobedience and reported to the Provincial Congress.

Once state constitutions were ratified, the extralegal units were replaced by regular government.

The original minutes, correspondence, and loose papers of these committees are located, almost without exception, in state archives. Unfortunately, they are almost never used in genealogical research although they are often the earliest indication of Revolutionary War activity possible. Their minutes also provide judicial records for the years 1774-82 between the discontinuance of crown courts and the establishment of state courts. See Figure 6-21 for an example of judicial proceedings.

Table 6-12

Records of United States Courts-Martial

Records	*Dates*	*Record Group Number*	*Comments*
Records of General Courts-Martial and Courts of Inquiry, Navy	1799-1867	125, microfilmed in 198 reels, no. M237	Originals cover 1799-1943. Partially name-indexed. Must know approximate date; for some records must know offense as well. Records include name, rank, ship or station, alleged offense, place and date of trial, sentence. May include medical fitness for duty, prison reports, requests to change discharge from dishonorable to honorable. Dossiers include transcript of testimony.
Proceedings of General Courts-Martial, Marine Corps.	1798-1866	27	Arranged chronologically, must know date of court-martial.
Court-Martial Records, Office of Judge Advocate General (Army)	1805-1939	153	Case files for general courts-martial, courts of inquiry, military commissions. Arranged by case number. Name index 1891-1917. NARS is compiling name index for pre-1891 files. Some files include dates of birth, places of residence, dependents, as well as transcripts of trial. Separate series of files exist for 1805-15 (incomplete) and for 1861-65. Registers showing name, rank, unit, place, and date of court provide a partial index to all series. Files dated before 1812 are incomplete.

Mar. 11, 1777

The Committee met according to adjournment, Mr. Thomas Jordan in the Chair.

Upon complaints being made by a certain Allis Read, of Wyoming Township, that he the said Read, had a horse strayed or stolen from him some time ago, and was found in the custody of a certain John Drake, when said Read replevied the horse and got him and kept him in his possession for about six months, and then the widow of said Drake came and took him forcibly out of said Read's stable, he not being at home himself, and now keeps the horse and absolutely refuses to give him up again to the said Read.

Resolved, That Messrs. James McClure, Peter Milleck and John Clingman, with the assistance of the Committee of Wyoming Township, be a joint committee to meet at the house of James McClure in said township, on Saturday the 22nd day of this instant, March, to hear the complaint and defence of both parties concerning the said horse, and that the Chairman of this Committee issue summons for the evidences of the complainer to attend at said meeting, which summons are to be served by the complainer himself, as also a summons for the said Widow Drake to attend with the horse and her evidences or reasons, if any she have, why the complainer should not have his horse upon proper proofs being made of his being his property, and the aforesaid persons are hereby authorised to judge and determine betwixt both parties, and upon proper proofs being made, give their final judgment in the matter.

A certain Captain Jacob Links, of Buffalo Township, appealed to this Committee in consequence of a resolve of the Committee of said township, a copy of which is as follows, viz:

Resolved, That Jacob Links does return several sums of money which a number of the inhabitants of this township did deliver to him for the use of purchasing salt, he, said Links, acknowledging he could have had salt, but it being troublesome times he was afraid he should suffer loss if he would purchase the salt, and a certain evidence did declare that he said he was going on his own business to Philadelphia, and he, said Links, did not bring salt.

Dec. 21, 1776. By the Committee of Buffalo Township.

WILL IRWIN, Chairman.

In consequence of said appeal, Mr. Links was called in before this Committee and asked if he had evidence to produce. He said he had, but that he had them not then ready. *Resolved,* That Mr. Links's appeal be referred till the next meeting of Committee, and that his evidence be summoned to attend.

Figure 6-21. Minutes of the Northumberland County, Pennsylvania Committee of Safety, 11 March 1777, *Pennsylvania Archives,* 2nd series., vol. 14, pp. 375-77.

Some of these Committee of Safety records have been published:

Connecticut

Public Records of the State of Connecticut: Journals of the Council of Safety. Hartford: Case, Lockwood, and Brainerd Co., 1894-1942. Vols. 1-4 include Committees of Safety, 1776-84.

Maryland

"Committees of Observation." *Maryland Historical Magazine* 3 (1908): 387.

"Committee of Observation for Elizabethtown District." *Maryland Historical Magazine* 13 (1918): 28-53; 227-48.

"Journal of the Committee of Observation of the Middle District of Frederick County, Maryland." *Maryland Historical Magazine* 10 (1915): 301-31; 11 (1916): 50-66; 157-75; 237-60; 304-21; 12 (1917): 10-21.

Hoyt, William D., Jr. "Civilian Defense in Baltimore, 1814-15: Minutes of the Committee of Vigilance and Safety." *Maryland Historical Magazine* 39 (1944): 199-224; 293-309; cont. in Vol. 40.

"Journal and Correspondence of the Maryland Council of Safety, 1775-1793." *Archives of Maryland* 11 (1892): 12 (1893); 16 (1897); 21 (1901); 43 (1924); 45 (1927); 47 (1930); 48 (1931); 71 (1970); 72 (1972).

"Proceedings of the Eastern Shore Branch of the Council of Safety of Maryland." *Maryland Historical Magazine* 5 (1910): 153-66.

Vivian, Jean H. "Thomas Stone and the Reorganization of the Maryland Council of Safety, 1776." *Maryland Historical Magazine* 69 (1974): 271-78.

Massachusetts

Brown, Richard D. *Revolutionary Politics in Massachusetts: The Boston Committee of Correspondence and the Towns, 1772-1774.* Cambridge: Harvard University Press, 1965.

Fisch, Theodore. "The Revolutionary Committee System in Massachusetts, Virginia, and New York, 1772-1775." Master's thesis, University of Illinois, 1945. Comparative study, describes records used and their locations.

North Carolina

Waddell, Alfred M. "Proceedings of the Safety Committee of the Town of Wilmington, with Occasional Minutes of Joint Meetings of a Committee of New Hanover County and the Committees of the District of Wilmington, 1774-1776," in *A History of New Hanover and the Lower Cape Fear.* Wilmington: n.p., 1909, pp. 85-165.

Whitaker, Bessie Lewis. *The Provincial Council and Committee of Safety in North Carolina.* Chapel Hill: University of North Carolina Press, 1908. Includes list of meetings in sixteen counties and descriptions of records.

Pennsylvania

Minutes of the Pennsylvania Provincial Council. 10 vols. Philadelphia: J. Stevens, 1851-52. Includes "Council of Safety Minutes."

"Minutes of the Committee of Safety." *Pennsylvania Archives,* 1st series, 4-6; 2nd series, 1, 3, 15; 3rd series, 10; 4th series, 3.

South Carolina

"Miscellaneous Papers of the General Committee, Secret Committee, and Provincial Congress, 1775." *South Carolina Historical Magazine* 8 (1907); 9 (1908).

"Papers of the First Council of Safety of the Revolutionary Party in South Carolina, June-November, 1775." *South Carolina Historical Magazine* 1 (1900); 2 (1901); 5 (1904); 6 (1905); 7 (1906).

"Papers of the Second Council of Safety of the Revolutionary Party in South Carolina, November, 1775-March, 1776." *South Carolina Historical Magazine* 3 (1902); 4 (1903).

"Revolutionary Association in Public Defense of South Carolina, 1775." *National Genealogical Society Quarterly* 18 (1930): 1-2.

Virginia

Bowman, Larry. "The Virginia County Committees of Safety, 1774-1776." *Virginia Magazine of History and Biography* 79 (1971): 321-27.

Coleman, Charles W. "The County Committees of 1774-75 in Virginia." *William and Mary Quarterly,* 1st series, 5 (1896-97): 9-106; 245-55.

Harwell, Richard B. *The Committees of Safety of Westmoreland and Fincastle: Proceedings of the County Committees, 1774-1776.* Richmond: Virginia State Library, 1956.

Leake, James M. *The Virginia Committee System and the American Revolution.* Baltimore: Johns Hopkins University Press, 1917.

McIlwaine, H. R. "Proceedings of the Committee of Safety: Caroline and Southampton Counties, 1774-76." *Bulletin of the Virginia State Library* 17 (1920).

____________. "Proceedings of the Committee of Safety for Cumberland and Isle of Wight Counties, Virginia, 1775-76." *Fifteenth Annual Report, Virginia State Library Board.* Richmond: Virginia State Library, 1919.

Miller, E. I. "The Virginia Committee of Correspondence, 1759-70." *William and Mary Quarterly,* 1st series, 22 (1913-14): 1-19; 99-113.

"Proceedings of the Virginia Committee of Correspondence, 1759-1767." *Virginia Magazine of History and Biography* 10 (1902-03): 11 (1903-04); 12 (1904-05).

Westerberg, Frank B. "Vehicles of Discontent: The Committees of Correspondence in the Southern Colonies, 1773-1776." Ph.D. diss., University of North Carolina, 1967.

The Sons of Liberty, artisans and professional men organized in urban areas, were another extra legal Revolutionary group. Samuel Adams and his Boston Tea Party "Indians" were Sons of Liberty.[42]

Other important extralegal groups were the "Associators" who drafted the first instruments of government in new communities. These extralegal articles of association, signed by all males over age twenty-one, enabled settlers to handle basic legal needs. Examples are the Mayflower Compact of the early Pilgrims, the Watauga Association of Tennessee, and the Kentucky Resolves.[43]

Mining Districts and Their Records

In areas richly endowed with mineral resources – Pennsylvania, West Virginia, Alabama/Georgia, and the entire Western United States – are many jurisdictions called mining districts. Like the New England towns, they kept order until county local government functioned smoothly. In 1866, there were 500 districts in California, 200 in Nevada, 100 in Arizona, 100 in Idaho, 100 in Oregon, 50 in Montana, 50 in New Mexico, and 50 in Colorado. Twelve California counties were called mining counties for their principal industry.[44]

Here, as on a county level, we find the recording of deeds, transfers of title, claims, abstracts, surveys, mortgages, probates, and other court processes. For example, the Mining Records of Buckskin Joe District, Park County, Colorado, record the election of officers, mining claims, and transfers of title:

> July 12, 1860.
> Meeting in house of J. T. Berger.
> Discussion to who was to be regular recorder some claiming the office for D. J. Grist others for J. B. Stansell.
> Grist and Stansell retired.
> Charles Hitchcock moved meeting vote on recorder and Stansell was elected by a vote of 26 to 18.
> Moved by Stansell that meeting be held regularly the first Saturday in each month at 4 of the clock P.M. at the house of J. T. Berger. . . .
> Buckskin Joe Diggins May 23d 1860. . . .
> Know all men that I Buck Skin Joe Claim 100 feet of min^{g} ground for min^{g} purposes it being situated in Buck Skin Diggins Bounded on the Lower End by D. Griest and on upper end by Moore and Company.
>
> Buck Skin Joe.
>
> May 22, 1860
>
> Know all men by these presents that I, Frank Obena of Buckskin Diggins, J. T. (Jefferson Territory) for and in consideration of the sum of $50 to me in hand paid, the receipt of which is hereby acknowledged and receipted. Do sell Transfer and assign unto A. Fall my right title and interest in and to certain mining claims situated in Buckskin Diggins between Mr. Belden and Buckskin Joes claim, said claim being 50 feet up to the creek and 300 feet across. In testimony of which I have hereunto set my hand and seal this 28th day of April A. D. 1860.
>
> F. Obena
>
> W. G. Swimez (Witness
> B. S. Peabody (Witness[45]

Almost every mining district kept written records of some sort from the beginning, as claims had to be registered, although many did not survive fire, migration, or a thin vein. In other areas, major mining camps became county seats and their records were the first public records.

Mining district records, though rare, are valuable precisely because of that rarity. Almost invariably they are the only written evidence available for their period. In California, where the 1848 population was 14,000, and, by the close of 1849, over 100,000, no government records could hope to be comprehensive.

Miners Courts. In the absence of legally appointed law enforcement personnel, citizens of mining communities had to provide their own system of justice. Although the criminal cases confronting these "popular tribunals" have caught the public imagination, the miners' courts or *alcades*[46] dealt much more frequently with civil problems. They fixed the size of claims (which varied greatly from one camp to another), determined the boundaries of districts, and made simple rules governing the working and abandoning of claims and trespassing on the claims of others.

These courts were called into activity only when occasion arose. In smaller camps, guilt and punishment were often determined by the whole assembly of miners; in the larger mining communities, this responsibility was delegated to a jury, and sometimes legal counsel was available for the litigating parties. Justice was usually summary.

Compared with the "lynch-law" of cattle ranges, vigilante committees in mining towns represented a more formal administration of justice, more closely paralleling indictment and trial in statutory courts. Justice in Montana and other territorial mining camps was based in part on the examples set in the preceding decade by California, from which state many of the Montana miners had come.

For further study, see the bibliography at the end of this chapter.

Vigilante Societies

Some whites in northern cities became alarmed about 1830-40 with the flow of blacks fleeing slavery. Other whites openly encouraged the blacks to come, operating the "underground" networks, and providing new identities, work, and schooling once they arrived. Both types of groups kept records. The Vigilance Committee of Philadelphia is one example.[47] See also Chapter 19, "Black Ancestral Records."

New Jersey's numerous vigilante groups have been documented in Anthony S. Nicolosi's comprehensive study by location, county, name, place of meeting, date established, earliest meeting, latest meeting, and date dissolved. He also includes mutual protection associations for merchants. His notes include locations of records.[48]

Many frontier vigilance committees disbanded as soon as a specific emergency was over. Others had a long tenure.[49] An example of a formal vigilance society is the one organized in 1851 in San Francisco with a constitution, bylaws and newspaper publication. The organization grew from 200 initial signatories keeping painstaking records, until it was superceded by state-organized court systems in August 1856. It continued to meet as an organization until late in 1859. Between 6,000 and 8,000 men were formal members.[50]

Figure 6-22. Index, *House Reports,* 42nd Cong. 2nd sess. from 4 Dec., vol. 2, pt. 8, no. 22; Testimony, Alabama, vol. 6, p. 28.

Henderson, William, attempt to drown 540, 557, 558, 577–581, 583, 584, 636–638
character of 636
HENDERSON, WILLIAM, (colored,) testimony of.......... 576–590
lives in Huntsville; lived last August at Mr. Calvin Goodloe's, Colbert County; is married.......... 576
details of outrage upon him by disguised men, and their attempt to drown him.......... 577–581, 583, 584
character of the disguises worn 579
recognizes three of the party.......... 579, 580
previous difficulty with some of them.......... 581, 582
the parties arrested, tried before the United States commissioner, and acquitted.......... 582, 583, 584
alibis proven.......... 588
accounts between witness and Mr. Malone.......... 589, 590

Figure 6-23. *House Reports, Testimony, Alabama,* 42nd Cong. 2nd sess., vol 6, pp. 628, 631.

The following is the record of the evidence in the trial of Holscapple, Lindsay, and Malone, before United States Commissioner Day, at Huntsville, Alabama, September 1, 1871, referred to in the testimony of Lionel W. Day, page 590.

UNITED STATES
vs.
HOLSCAPPLE, LINDSAY, MALONE. } Trial September 1, 1871.

WM. HENDERSON:

Question. What is your name?
Answer. William Henderson.
Question. Where do you live?
Answer. With C. Goodloe.
Question. In what county?
Answer. Colbert County.
Question. How long have you been living there?
Answer. Moved there two weeks after Christmas.
Question. Men came to your house disguised; how many?
Answer. On Tuesday night, the 15th day of August, I had been talking to Mr. Goodloe until 11 o'clock at night, and then went to bed. Four men came to my room and woke me up and told me to strike a light. I shook Mack, my boy; woke him up instead of getting up myself. He got up and made a light, and they then told me to get up and put on my clothes; that they wanted me to go and show them where Cater Thompson was. I told them I did not know where he was and did not know him when I saw him. At that time I had a gun in the south corner of the house. One man was standing between me and the gun. I aimed to get at it and he shoved me back. Two of the men had pistols and two of them shot-guns, which they presented at me and told me to go out of the door; and as I turned around to go out of the door I saw Mr. Duce Lindsay, who put his hand on my shoulder; did not hurt me. I knew him by a veil on his hat being turned back over his hat from over his face. The veil came down over the face and the shoulders behind. Am well acquainted with him and knew it was him.

MARK HENDERSON: Uncle Henderson is my father; he is my mother's husband. I live with him. Some men came one night; been three weeks to-day, five men came. I was asleep when they came; they told Uncle Henderson to make up a light; Uncle Henderson woke me up, and I made up a light. Three of them came into the house and two stood in the door. Knew Holscapple; saw his face; had on a straw hat; am well acquainted with him; he did nothing. I started out of the door, and he told me to go back. They took William Henderson out of the house. I staid in Lewis's house the balance of the night; the houses adjoined. I saw William Henderson 8 o'clock the next day; went after Dr. Cross. William Henderson came after me; do not know what he wanted; I got back home before he saw me. I don't know where William Henderson was the day before the night they took him out.

Cross-examined:

Never told anybody what I would swear before I came here. Uncle Jim Carter asked me a while ago, but I did not tell him. Henderson told me this morning to tell nothing, only what I had seen and heard. Three men came in; Holscapple stood at the door; I saw his face; had a small piece of a veil over his face; I looked through the veil and saw his face; am certain only three men came in; did not look in the faces of the rest. Mr. Holscapple had on a straw hat; wore a little straw hat about there; he spoke to me, and I knew his voice; could see his features through the veil. No one in Lewis's house but himself and wife; I staid all night. Don't know where Henderson was the day before. I wasn't there.

his
MARK × HENDERSON.
mark.

Ku Klux Klans. At the close of the Civil War, the South not only faced the momentous task of reconstruction, but also the punitive acts of Congress and frequently corrupt "carpet-bag" administration. Federal armies were quartered on Southern soil, and martial law was exercised in the five newly established military districts. All those loyal to the Confederacy in some areas were stripped of their civil rights, while blacks were permitted to vote, hold public office, and bear arms.

Ex-Confederate soldiers, ignored by government and judiciary, organized the first Ku Klux Klan in Pulaski, Giles County, Tennessee, on 24 December 1865.[51] Initially social, within a month, it had taken a political slant, initiating several hundred members. From here it spread to every Southern state. In May 1867, at a conference in Nashville, Tennessee, of individual Klans, the Invisible Empire of the South was established under the leadership of General Nathan B. Forrest, a trusted and experienced Confederate officer. Each member took an oath in which he swore to "defend the Constitution and laws of the United States in their original purity[,] care for widows, females, and their households[,] aid brothers in distress[,] abstain totally from intoxicating liquors[,] oppose the radical [Reconstruction] party[,and] never divulge membership or activities."

In September 1878, five years after a federal investigation of terrorist activities, the Klan formally disbanded. During its existence, Forrest estimated 550,000 men had participated.[52]

In 1915, Georgia granted a charter to a new group of Ku Klux Klansmen who had organized themselves into a patriotic society of white, Protestant, native-born Americans. Shortly after World War I, legal Klans appeared throughout the South and in many other states of the Union. By 1926, there were over fifteen million members. Several of these Klans are still in existence today.

Since Klan activities are secret, few written records survive. However, the 1871-72 Congressional investigations generated testimony including pages and pages of first-hand biographical accounts, oral descriptions of neighbors, relatives, business associates, and deaths, violent and otherwise. It is also loaded with family history details. These transcripts are extremely valuable for tracing black (indexed as "colored") ancestry.

Poore, *A Descriptive Catalog of the Government Publications of the United States, 1744-1881,* compiled by order of Congress, 1885, identifies the volumes containing KKK investigations. Each volume is indexed, though only important and frequently named persons are indexed. Lesser parties and witnesses are not included. A review of the index for Alabama, in the *House Reports, Testimony, Alabama,* vol. 6, shows several index entries for William Henderson, a witness, whose stepson, Mark, is not indexed, though he was also a witness. Figure 6-22 is the Henderson index entry, while Figure 6-23 shows the kinds of information included in these reports.

Other extra legal jurisdictions include claims clubs, land and cattle companies (both described in some detail in Chapter 7, "Land and Tax Records"), and labor union activity (described in Chapter 10, "Business and Employment Records").

Special Courts

The American court system includes separate courts for such specific population groups as Indians, who were treated as a foreign power; slaves, who had few civil rights (in some areas free persons of color were legally treated as slaves); Confederates, whose governments abolished federal power in local courts; and foreign powers, who exercised jurisdiction over American soil at varying times. Only the Indian courts still function.[53]

Indian Courts. Records of Indian-white cases, settled according to treaty provisions, are scattered among state records for New York, North Carolina, and many of the western states. Sometimes they are clearly identified in archival finding aids, but usually they are filed with treaty papers, or among court or commission case files, and the genealogist must read archive inventories carefully. See the bibliography at the end of this chapter and Chapter 17.

Indians not living on reservations and not enrolled on tribal rolls have assumed American citizenship. Their records will be found in the local courts. Since Indians could expect juries to rule in favor of whites, they thus avoided court processes as much as possible. Jail records and cases brought before justices of the peace may be more common but are also more difficult to locate.

Black Courts. Slaves were usually tried in a separate set of courts presided over by one or two justices of the peace with assistance from local land holders. Free persons of color, although not slaves, were rarely treated like whites and could be required to appear before slave courts.

Manumission – setting a slave free – was a court process. A certificate of freedom was issued to each member of the family manumitted and also recorded by the court. Look for a formal marriage ceremony following manumission, since freedom brought with it other rights as well.

Some jurisdictions made a distinction between freedmen and free persons of color who had never been slaves or where freedom was won very early in their ancestry. Both are usually identified by color in the records and thus are distinguishable from whites of the same name.

The Inferior Court minutes for Jones County, Georgia, record the petition of a free black for recognition of his freedom. He had been seized as property of a debtor, sold at a sheriff's sale in 1811, and finally, eight years later, had come to court seeking his freedom again. The same court granted the petition for a guardian for three free black minors to protect their property.[54]

North Carolina records show cases where a man would free his blacks by will at the time of his death. Some even provided them with land or other property. Because emancipation was against the law in North Carolina, the county records rarely disclose details. Usually, the land is left by will in the hands of an executor who will have been instructed privately about the wishes of the testator. Among the appeals cases, however, will be details from relatives who feel slighted or neighbors who resent living next to blacks.

In South Carolina, the Magistrates and Freeholders Court handled all matters under the laws for "the better ordering of slaves" under authority originally granted in 1690, revised in 1740, 1743, and 1783. This court could inflict any punishment allowed by law. Death sentences were carried out immediately. Before 1783, the proceedings were written and sent to the clerk of the crown in Charleston. Later they were recorded in the district courts. This duplication is important when fires in South Carolina courthouses destroyed their early records, as occurred in Abbeville County.

Slave courts and proceedings have not been studied in any depth, but the bibliography at the end of the chapter contains a few references.

Other Courts

Other powers have exercised jurisdiction on American soil at varying times. Examples are the Confederate courts, 1861-65, the Spanish systems in Florida, the Mississippi River delta area, Texas, and the American Southwest; the French control of the Mississippi River Valley and its tributaries; the Mexican claims and jurisdiction in the Southwest; and the Dutch occupation of New Netherlands. See the bibliography at the end of this chapter for an introduction to these systems and their records.

Notes

1. The word *people* is misleading. At first, it meant all white men, then all men regardless of color eligible to vote, and finally, in 1918, all adults eligible to vote. It did not then, and does not now, mean all persons.

2. Bradley Chapin, *Criminal Justice in Colonial America, 1606-1660* (Athens, Ga.: University of Georgia Press, 1983), pp. 99-142.

3. See Bruce C. Daniels, *Town and Country: Essays on the Structure of Local Government in the American Colonies* (Middletown, Conn.: Wesleyan

University Press, 1978).

4. Based on Clarence N. Callender, *American Courts: Their Organization and Procedures* (New York: McGraw-Hill Book Co., 1927).

5. See H. J. Connant, "Imprisonment for Debt in Vermont: A History," *Vermont History* 19 (1951): 67-80.

6. Chester County Court, Penn., 1685, *Records of the Court at Upland in Pennsylvania*, 1681-92, Vol. 8. (Philadelphia: Pennsylvania Historical Society, 1860).

7. Joseph H. Smith, ed. *Colonial Justice in Western Massachusetts, 1639-1702: The Pynchon Court Record* (Cambridge: Harvard University Press, 1961), introduction.

8. In *National Genealogical Society Quarterly* 58 (1970): 171-72; reprinted with permission.

9. Memorial Upon the Death of Chapman Johnson, Order Book, Spring Term 1849, Augusta Co., Va. Transcribed from original in Augusta County Courthouse, Staunton, Va.

10. Order of Naturalization for Samuel Johnston, July Term, 1851, Order Book, Augusta Co., Va. Transcript from original in Augusta County Courthouse, Staunton, Va.

11. Re-recorded Deeds, Feb. Term 1800, Court Orders, vols. 0-0000, 1778-1810, Rockingham County, Va., originals in Rockingham County Courthouse, Winchester, Va. Microfilm copy, Genealogical Society of Utah (hereafter GS) microfilm 033,452.

12. Minutes of the Mayor's Court, Borough Town of Westchester, New York, printed in "Minutes of Court of Sessions, 1657-78," *Westchester County Historical Publications* 2 (1926): 1-39.

13. An excellent description of how a grand jury functions is Richard D. Younger, "The Grand Jury on the Frontier," *Wisconsin Magazine of History* (Autumn 1956): 3-8 ff. Not consecutive.

14. See Anton H. Chroust, *The Rise of the Legal Profession in America*, 2 vols. (Norman Okla.: University of Oklahoma Press, 1965.)

15. A very interesting, well-documented study of the use of jails and punishment in New York State is Philip Klein, *Prison Methods in New York State* (New York: Columbia University Press, 1920). It traces the development and history of most of the penal institutions in the state. See also Douglas Greenberg, "The Effectiveness of Law Enforcement in Eighteenth Century New York," *American Journal of Legal History* 20 (1976): 173-207.

16. See Derrell Roberts, "Joseph E. Brown and the Convict Lease System," *Georgia Historical Quarterly* 44 (1960): 399-410.

17. Police Court Minutes, St. Paul, Minn. Printed as appendix in Annual Report of City Council, St. Paul, Minn., 1856-60. Copies available in rare book vault, St. Paul Public Library, St. Paul, Minn.

18. Lyman Chalkley, *Chronicles of the Scotch-Irish Settlement in Virginia, Extracted From the Original Court Records of Augusta County, 1745-1800*, 3 vols. (1962; reprint ed., Baltimore: Genealogical Publishing Co., 1965.)

19. "Records of the Court of Sessions of Westchester County (New York)," *Westchester Historical Society Publications*, 1 (1924): 33, 44 ff.

20. William Jeffrey, Jr., "Early New England Court Records: A Bibliography of Published Materials," *American Journal of Legal History* 1 (1957): 119-47.

21. "Introduction," *Archives of Maryland: Proceedings of the Court of Chancery of Maryland, 1669-1679* (Baltimore: Maryland Historical Society, 1934), vol. 51.

22. For a more complete discussion, see "Dower Rights in the United States," *Harvard Law Review* 61 (1948): 42 ff. and George L. Hoskins, "Curtesy in the United States," *University of Pennsylvania Law Review* 100 (1951): 196-223.

23. "Inventories as a Source of Local History: Houses, Farmers, Industries, and Professions," *Amateur Historian* 4 (1958-59): 157-61; 186-95; 227-31; 320-24; and B. C. Jones, "Inventories of Goods and Chattels," *Amateur Historian* 2 (1955-56): 76-79.

24. As cited in Harry A. Focht, "Hidden Genealogical Data in Court Records," *The Perry Historians* 8 (1983): 2-3. The record also documents Peter Arnold's second marriage.

25. From Vincent L. Jones, et al., *Family History for Fun and Profit* (Salt Lake City: The Genealogical Institute, 1972), used with permission.

26. See Juliette Tomlinson, "Local History in Legal Records," *Old Time New England*, vol. 58, pp. 1-7, for other examples.

27. Kenneth Lockridge, "A Communication," *William and Mary Quarterly*, 3rd ser., 25 (1968): 516-17, and Daniel Scott Smith, "Underregistration and Bias in Probate Records: An Analysis of Data from Eighteenth Century Hingham, Massachusetts," *William and Mary Quarterly*, 3rd ser., 32 (1975): 100-110.

28. Gilbert S. Walker, "Old Land Deeds," *Pennsylvania Magazine of History and Biography* 41 (1917): 365-67.

29. Donald L. Jacobus, "Probate Law and Custom," *American Genealogist* 9 (1932): 4-9.

30. See Walter Lee Sheppard's interesting article "Confidential and Sealed Records: Their Effect on Genealogical Research," *American Genealogist* 50 (1974): 203-9.

31. Jean J. McVeetney, "Comparative Study of Laws of Adoption of Minors," *Women Lawyers Journal* 47 (1961): 13-21.

32. See A. M. Schlesinger, "Colonial Appeals to the Privy Council," *Political Science Quarterly* 28 (1913): 279-97, and Joseph Henry Smith, *Appeals to the Privy Council from the American Plantations* (New York: Columbia University Press, 1950). For Palatinate jurisdiction, see Gaillard Lapsley, *The County Palatinate of Durham* (Cambridge, Mass.: Harvard University Press, 1900). There was little difference in the powers granted the Palatinate in England and America; the problems arose in enforcing them so far away from the support of the royal government.

33. Edward H. Hilliard, "When Kentucky Had Two Courts of Appeal," *Filson Club Historical Quarterly* 34 (1960): 228-36; and George Shelley, "The Semicolon Court in Texas," *Southwestern Historical Review* 48 (1944-45): 449-68.

34. See O. M. Dickerson, *The Navigation Acts and the American Revolution* (Philadelphia: Lippincott, 1951).

35. Some of these records have been edited by Judge Charles M. Hough, *Reports of the Cases in the Vice-Admiralty of the Province of New York* (New Haven: Yale University Press, 1925), but these represent only about 40 percent of the total number. See Richard B. Morris, "The Federal Archives of New York City," *American Historical Review* 42 (1936-37): 272.

36. See Hubert D. Hoover, "Army Courts-Martial," *Legal Essays in Honor of O. K. McMurray* (Berkeley: University of California Press, 1935), pp. 165-86.

37. See Daniel Walker and C. George Niebank, "The Court of Military Appeals: Its History, Organization and Operation," *Vanderbilt Law Review* 6 (1952-53): 228-40.

38. John R. Kirkland, "Military Occupation in the South Atlantic States During Reconstruction, 1865-1876," Ph.D. diss., University of North Carolina, 1967; "The Reconstruction Courts of Texas, 1867-1873," *Southwestern Historical Quarterly* 62 (1958): 141; and James E. Sefton, *The U. S. Army and Reconstruction, 1865-1877* (Baton Rouge: Louisiana State University Press, 1967).

39. Regulator Pardon of 31 Oct. 1771, in *Miscellaneous Records, South Carolina Department of Archives and History*, vol. PP, pp. 45-47. (Charleston: N.p., n.d.), published by government order.

40. See John S. Bassett, "The Regulators of North Carolina, 1765-1771," *American Historical Association, Annual Report*, 1894 (Washington, D.C.: AHA, 1895), pp. 143-212; Arthur P. Hudson, "Songs of the North Carolina Regulators," *William and Mary Quarterly*, 3rd ser., 4 (1947): 470-85; Elmer Douglas Johnson, "The War of the Regulators: Its Place in History," Master's thesis, University of North Carolina, 1942; William S. Powell, ed., *The Regulators of North Carolina: A Documentary History, 1759-79* (Raleigh: State Department of Archives and History, 1971); and James P. Whittenburg, "Planters, Merchants, and Lawyers: Social Change and the Origins of the North Carolina Regulation," *William and Mary Quarterly*, 3rd ser., 34 (1977): 215-38; 693-95.

41. "Westmoreland Resolutions," *Virginia Historical Register* 2 (1849): 15-18. Originals in Virginia Historical Society, Richmond, Va.

42. "The Baltimore Artificers Company," *Maryland Historical Magazine* 2 (1907): 367-68; Richard Walsh, *Charleston's Sons of Liberty: A Study of the Artisans, 1763-1789* (Columbia: University of South Carolina Press, 1959); "Charleston's Sons of Liberty: A Study of the Mechanics, 1760-1785 (Ph.D. diss., University of South Carolina, 1958); and Henry B. Dawson, *The Sons of Liberty in New York"* (1959; reprint ed., New York: Arno Press, 1969). Read footnotes carefully for locations of records.

43. See "Associations and Associators in the American Revolution," *Maryland Historical Magazine* 6 (1911): 241-54; and "Records of the Cumberland Association," *American History Magazine* 7 (1902): 114-35, 254-66.

44. *Reports on U.S. Mineral Resources* (Washington, D.C.: Government Printers, 1866), p. 236.

45. As cited in Roy A. Davidson, "Some Early Manuscript Records of Park County, 1859-1863," *Colorado Magazine* 18 (1941): 168-79.

46. An alcade was a Mexican court after which many miners' courts were patterned and named. See Charles H. Shinn, *Land Laws of Mining Districts* (Baltimore: Johns Hopkins University Studies in History and Political Science, 2nd ser., 1884).

47. Joseph A. Borome, "The Vigilant Committee of Philadelphia," *Pennsylvania Magazine of History and Biography* 92 (1968): 320-51.

48. Anthony S. Nicolosi, "The Rise and Fall of the New Jersey Vigilant Societies," *New Jersey History* 86 (1968): 29-53. See also "The Vigilance Committee: Richmond During the War of 1812," *Virginia Magazine of History and Biography* 7 (1900): 225-41; 406-18.

49. J. W. Caughey, "Their Majesties the Mob: Vigilantes Past and Present," *Pacific Historical Review* 26 (1957): 217-34.

50. Richard Maxwell Brown, "San Francisco Vigilantes of 1856," in John Alexander Carroll, ed., *Reflections of Western Historians* (Tucson: University of Arizona Press, 1969); and Porter Garnett, "Papers of the San Francisco Committee of Vigilance, 1851," *Academy of Pacific Coast History* 1 (1910); 2 (1911); 4 (1913) edited by Mary Floyd Williams. See also her *History of the San Francisco Committee of Vigilance of 1851* (1921; reprint ed., New York: De Capo Press, 1970). The original papers are deposited in the Huntington Library, San Marino, California. For a careful analysis of 2,500 applications for membership, see Richard Maxwell Brown, *Strain of Violence: Historical Studies of American Violence and Vigilantism* (New York: Oxford University Press, 1975).

51. See Allen W. Trelease, *White Terror: The Ku Klux Klan Conspiracy and Southern Reconstruction* (New York: Harper & Row, 1971). Based in part on personal testimony of ex-Klansmen is Margaret S. Bearnson, "The Ku Klux Klan," M.A. thesis, University of Utah, 1931, containing a copy of the prescript (constitution and by-laws) and a cipher code used by the Klan in Pulaski, Tennessee, for all messages. See also William D. Bell, "The Congressional Investigations of the Ku Klux Klan, 1871-1972," Ph.D. diss., Louisiana State University, 1967.

52. The reports of this investigation, which contain reports of trials, testimony of witnesses, names of Klansmen, and descriptions of their activities, can be found in *Reports of Committees of the House of Representatives and of the Senate,* 2nd sess., 42nd Cong., 1871-72, *Affairs in the Late Insurrectionary States: The Ku Klux Conspiracy.*

53. Jack Kleiner, "United States Law on American Indians," *Case and Comment,* July-Aug. 1972, pp. 3-7, summarizes the legal rights of Indians on reservations, the impact of the Civil Rights Act of 1968, which included the Indian Bill of Rights, tribal judicial systems, and the impact of recent legislation.

54. See Inferior Court Minutes, 13 April 1819, Jones County, Georgia, pp. 61-63, and January Term, 1817, p. 97 for examples. Originals in County Courthouse, Georgia.

Bibliography

This bibliography begins with guides, bibliographies, and sources of general interest on law in the colonies and early states, then continues with specific subject bibliographies. Some attempt is made not to duplicate sources cited in the notes unless they apply to more than one subject area.

Guides

Important guides to National Archives records include numerous references to court documents. These guides are available in most research libraries – sometimes in goverment document sections.

Guide to Genealogical Research in the National Archives. 1982. 304 pp.

Guide to the National Archives of the United States. 1974. 884 pp.

Guide to Federal Archives Relating to the Civil War. 1962. 721 pp.

Guide to the Archives of the Government of the Confederate States of America. 1968. 536 pp.

Handbook of Federal World War Agencies and Their Records, 1917-21. 1943. 666 pp.

Federal Records of World War II. Vol. 1: *Civilian Agencies.* 1950. 1,075 pp. Vol. 2: *Military Agencies.* 1951. 1,061 pp.

List of Record Groups in the National Archives and the Federal Records Centers. 1981. 70 pp.

National Archives Microfilm Publications. 1974. 137 pp. Updated with titles 1974-82.

In addition to these guides, the National Archives has issued preliminary inventories describing in detail the holdings of specific record groups. These inventories are so detailed that you can often order documents directly from them. Special lists provide finding aids for selected record series. And the microfilm publications of NARS have accompanying pamphlets which list the specific contents of film rolls and give the historical background to help you use the records more effectively. These publications are free upon request. Institutions and local genealogical societies can be placed on the regular mailing list to receive inventories and lists as they are produced. A catalog is available on request from National Archives and Records Service, General Services Administration, Washington, DC 20408.

Bibliographies

Blume, William and Elizabeth Gaspar Brown. *Digests and Lists Pertaining to the Development of Law and Legal Institutions in the Territories of the United States: 1787-1954.* 6 vols. Ann Arbor: University Microfilm, 1965-79.

Flaherty, David H. "A Select Guide to Manuscripts Court Records of Colonial New England." *American Journal of Legal History* 9 (1967): 107-26.

Gersack, Dorothy Hill. "Colonial, State, and Federal Court Records: A Survey." *American Archivist* 36 (1973): 33-42.

Greene, Jack P. "The Publication of the Official Records of the Southern Colonies." *William and Mary Quarterly,* 3rd ser., 14 (1957): 268-80.

Hasse, Adelaide R. *Materials for a Bibliography of the Public Archives of the Thirteen Original States Covering Colonial Period and State Period to 1789.* 1908; reprint ed., New York: Argonaut Press, 1966.

Jeffrey, William, Jr. "Early New England Court Records: A Bibliography of Published Material." *Boston Public Library Quarterly,* 1954 as reprinted in *American Journal of Legal History* 1 (1957): 119-47.

Kammen, Michael G. "Colonial Court Records and the Study of Early American History: A Bibliographical Review." *American Historical Review* 70 (1965): 732-39.

Keitt, Lawrence. *An Annotated Bibliography of Bibliographies of Statutory Materials of the United States.* Cambridge: Harvard University Press, 1934.

Low, Erick Baker. *A Bibliography on the History of the Organization and Jurisdiction of State Courts.* Williamsburg: National Center for State Courts, 1980.

McReynolds, Michael. *List of Pre-1840 Federal District Court Records Located in Federal Record Centers.* Washington, D.C.: Government Printing Office, 1972. Special List, 31.

National Association of State Libraries. *A Checklist of Legislative Journals of the States of the U.S.A.* New York: Oxford Press, 1938.

____________. *Preliminary Checklists of Sessions Laws, to 1933.* New York: Oxford Press, 1934.

Nunis, Doyce B., Jr. "Historical Studies in United States Legal History, 1950-59: A Bibliography of Articles Published in Scholarly Non-Law Journals." *American Journal of Legal History* 7 (1963): 1-27.

Prager, Herta, and William W. Price. "A Bibliography on the History of the Courts of the Thirteen Original States, Maine, Ohio, and Vermont." *American Journal of Legal History* 1 (1957): 336-62; 2 (1958): 35-52, 148-54.

Sell, Gary L. *Legal Materials on Microform: A Bibliography.* 3rd ed. Provo, Utah: Brigham Young University, 1976.

Tompkins, Dorothy Campbell. *Court Organization and Administration: A Bibliography.* Berkeley: University of California Press, 1973.

Using Legal Records

Ball, Walter V. "Family Records from County Court Order Books." *National Genealogical Society Quarterly* 58 (1970): 3.

Bramwell, B. S. "Frequency of Cousin Marriages." *Genealogists' Magazine* 8 (1939): 305-16.

Connor, Seymour V. "Legal Materials as Sources of History." *American Archivist* 23 (1960): 157-65.

Dorman, John Frederick. "Colonial Laws of Primogeniture." World Conference on Records, 1969 (Salt Lake City, Utah: Genealogical Society of Utah, 1969).

Dumbauld, Edward. "Legal Records in English and American Courts." *American Archivist* 36 (1973): 15-32.

Farnham, Charles W. "Lower Court Cases: A Genealogist's Tool." *National Genealogical Society Quarterly* 49 (1961): 200.

Gilliam, C. E. "Mr. in Virginia Records Before 1776." *William and Mary Quarterly,* 3rd ser., 19 (1939).

Greenwood, Val D. "Court Records in the United States." *Genealogical Journal* 6 (1977): 159-68.

________. *The Researcher's Guide to American Genealogy.* Baltimore: Genealogical Publishing Co., 1973.

Haskins, George L. "Court Records and History." *William and Mary Quarterly,* 3rd ser., 5 (1948): 547-52.

________. "Curtesy in the United States." *University of Pennsylvania Law Review* 100 (1951): 196-223.

Jacobus, Donald Lines. "Probate Law and Custom." *American Genealogist* 9 (1932): 4-9.

Johnson, Guion G. "Courtship and Marriage Customs in Antebellum North Carolina." *North Carolina Historical Review* 8 (1931): 384-402.

Johnston, G. D. "Legal Terms and Phrases." *Amateur Historian* 3 (1956-57): 249-52.

Jordan, Philip D. "In Search of Local Legal Records." *American Archivist* 33 (1970): 379-82.

Keim, C. Ray. "Primogeniture and Entail in Colonial Virginia." *William and Mary Quarterly,* 3rd ser., 25 (1968): 545-86.

King, George H. S. "Maiden Names Used After Marriage." *American Genealogist* 47 (1971): 44.

Klein, Fannie J. *Federal and State Court Systems: A Guide.* Cambridge: Ballinger Publishers, 1977.

MacLeod, D. "Natural Child." *Genealogists' Magazine* 5 (1930): 250. In America, "natural birth" means the legitimate "heirs of the body," as opposed to step- or adopted children.

Maduell, Charles R. "Genealogy from Law Books." *New Orleans Genesis* 9 (1972): 42-43. Specific examples from state court reports.

Merritt, H. A., Jr. "Preservation of Court Records." *Wisconsin Bar Bulletin* 33 (1960): 43.

Morris, Richard B. "Early American Court Records: A Publication Program." *Anglo American Legal Series.* New York: New York University School of Law, 1941.

________. "Primogeniture and Entailed Estates in America." *Columbia Law Review,* vol. 27, p. 47.

________. *Studies in the History of American Law with Special Reference to the Seventeenth and Eighteenth Centuries.* New York: Columbia University Press, 1930, pp. 82-125.

"Mrs. for Unmarried Women." *Genealogists' Magazine* 10 (1950): 493, 538, 579-80.

Myrick, Shelby, Jr. "Legal Terminology in Genealogical Research in the U.S.A." Salt Lake City: World Conference on Records, 1969. Area 1-10. Includes a useful glossary with terms often omitted from modern dictionaries.

Padgett, Patricia Ann. "Legal Status of Women in Colonial Virginia, 1700-1785." Master's thesis, College of William and Mary, 1967.

Pound, Roscoe. *Organization of Courts.* Boston: Little, Brown, 1940.

Russell, George Ely. "Court Depositions and Affidavits as Evidence of Age in Maryland, 1637-1657." *Maryland Magazine of Genealogy* 2 (1979): 68-75.

Rutman, Darrett B., and Anita H. Rutman. "Now-wives and Sons-in-law: Parental Death in a Seventeenth Century Virginia County." In their *Chesapeake in the Seventeenth Century.* Chapel Hill: University of North Carolina Press, 1979, pp. 153-82.

Semonche, John E. "Common-Law Marriage in North Carolina: A Study in Legal History." *American Journal of Legal History* 9 (1965): 320-49.

Stevenson, Noel. "Genealogical Research in the Law Library." *American Genealogist* 18 (1941): 100-03. Genealogical applications of printed court reports.

Surrency, Edwin C. "The Courts in the American Colonies." *American Journal of Legal History* 11 (1969): 253-76, 347-76.

"Terms of Relationship in Colonial Times." *American Genealogist* 55 (1979): 52-54.

Southwick, Neal S. "The Coordinate Use of Wills and Deeds." *Journal of Genealogy* 2 (1973): 154-56.

Walker, Gilbert S. "Old Land Deeds." *Pennsylvania Magazine of History and Bibliography* 41 (1917): 365-67.

Weinberg, Allen. "Court Records: Orphans Among Archives." *American Archivist* 23 (1960): 167-74.

Weiner, Carol Z. "Is a Spinster an Unmarried Woman?" *American Journal of Legal History* 21 (1977): 27-31.

Wyatt-Brown, Bertram. *Southern Honor: Ethics and Behaviour in the Old South.* New York: Oxford University Press, 1982.

Admiralty Court Records

Andrews, Charles M. *The Colonial Period of American History: England's Commercial and Colonial Policy.* New Haven: Yale University Press, 1938. Vol. 4. An excellent historical treatment of the Courts of Admiralty in the colonies.

Towle, Dorothy S. *Records of the Vice-Admiralty Court of Rhode Island: 1716-1752.* Washington, D.C.: American Historical Association Committee on Legal History, 1939. Contains incomplete extracts of cases, and a history of admiralty jurisdiction in Rhode Island.

Ubbelhide, Carl. *The Vice-Admiralty Courts and the American Revolution.* Chapel Hill: University of North Carolina Press, 1960. A good description of the courts before 1763 and their influence on the American Revolution.

Whitney, Edson L. *Government of the Colony of South Carolina.* Baltimore: Johns Hopkins Press, 1895. Ch. 2 describes South Carolina's pre-Revolutionary Admiralty Courts.

Adoption Records

Much information has become available in the past ten years for adoptees seeking access to information. Resources, support groups, and texts are listed here.

The many studies on current adoption laws seldom cover the historical changes which affect tracing family lines. The impact of current law on pre-1930 adoption has been primarily to make access to early records more difficult. See the Introduction for a discussion of Freedom of Information laws that may be used to get access.

"Adoption in South Carolina." *South Carolina Law Quarterly* 9 (1957): 210.

Askin, Jayne. *Search: A Handbook for Adoptees and Birthparents.* New York: Harper & Row Publishers, 1982. The best how-to book available for adoptive research.

Barran, Annette, et al. "The Dilemma of Our Adoptees: Secret Adoption Records." *Psychology Today,* Dec. 1975, p. 38.

Brosnan, J. F. "The Law of Adoption (New York)" *Columbia Law Review* 22 (1922): 332.

Cavanaugh, Karen B. "Adoption and Genealogy." *Indiana Genealogical Informer* 2 (July 1981): 88-89; 3 (Aug. 1981): 1-2

Cutter, Simon. "Parent and Child, The Law of Adoption in Massachusetts." *Boston University Law Review* 15 (1935): 171.

Howard, Mary. "I Take After Somebody; I Have Real Relatives; I Possess a Real Name." *Psychology Today,* Dec. 1975, pp. 33-37.

Huard, Leo Albert. "The Law of Adoption: Ancient and Modern." *Vanderbilt Law Review* 9 (1955-56): 743.

Kupersmith, Nancy. "The Fight to Open Up Adoption Records." *Reader's Digest,* June 1978.

Leary, Morton L. *The Law of Adoption Simplified.* New York: Oceana Publications, 1948.

McLeod, R. M. "Adoption in Virginia." *Virginia Law Review* 38 (1952): 627.

Murphy, Harry J. *Where's What: Sources of Information for Federal Investigators.* New York: Warner Books, 1976. Important reference on how to access current records.

Merlin, William. "The Tennessee Law of Adoption." *Vanderbilt Law Review* 3 (1950): 627.

Neier, Aryeh. *Dossier: The Secret Files They Keep on You.* New York: Stein and Day, 1965. Provides insights into consulting records protected by privacy laws.

Rillera, Mary Jo. *The Adoption Searchbook: Techniques for Tracing People*. Huntington Beach, Calif.: Triadoption Publications, 1981. Available from publisher, Box 5218, Huntington Beach, CA 92646, or Everton Publishers, Box 368, Logan, UT 84321.

Robie, Diane C. *Searching in Florida: A Reference Guide to Public and Private Records*. ISC Publications, Box 10857, Costa Mesa, CA 92627.

Sanders, Patricia. Searching in California: A Reference Guide to Public and Private Records. Costa Mesa, Calif.: Independent Search Consultants, Inc., 1982. Available through ISC Publications, Box 10857, Costa Mesa, CA 92627, or Everton Publishers, Box 368, Logan, UT 84321.

Silberman, Curt C. "Adoption in New Jersey: An Analysis of Its Legal Effects and Consequences." *Rutgers University Law Review* 1 (1947): 250.

Strahorn, John S., Jr. "Adoption in Maryland." *Maryland Law Review* 7 (1943): 275.

Zainaldin, Jamil. "The Emergence of a Modern American Family Law, Child Custody, Adoption, and the Courts, 1796-1851." *Northwestern University Law Review* 73 (1979).

___________. "The Legal Origins of Modern Adoption." Ph.D. diss., University of Chicago, 1976.

Search and Support Organizations

Adoption Assistance Agency
18645 Sunburst Street
Northridge, CA 91324

Orphan Train Children
Elizabeth A. Ward
Route 2
Oak Crest Estates
Rogersville, MO 65742, or

Mrs. Eloise Thomsen
5843 Grant Street
Omaha, NE 68104

Tracers
39 Broadway
New York, NY 10006
(212) 558-6550

Tracers has some 300,000 computer entries of children seeking their parents; 40 percent of names are biological parents seeking their children.

Triadoption Library
7571 Westminster Avenue
Westminster, CA 92683
(714) 892-4098

Ask for their free reading list, international list of search and support groups, reunion registries (including state registries), and list of laws for states where records are available.

Courts of Claim Records

Field, Kate. "Notable and Curious Cases in the Court of Claims." *Green Bag* 7 (1895): 12.

National Archives. *Genealogical Research in the National Archives*. Washington, D.C.: General Services Admistration, 1982.

___________. Preliminary Inventory 47 (1953). "Records of the Court of Claims Section of the Department of Justice."

___________. Preliminary Inventory 58 (1954). "Records of the United States Court of Claims."

Indian Court Records

Brown. "The Choctaw-Chickasaw Court Citizens." *Chronicles of Oklahoma* 16 (1938): 425.

Davis. "Court of Reform in the Navajo Nation." *Journal of American Judicature Society* 43 (1959): 52. Describes the establishment of the tribal court.

Fullerton. "Courts in the Quapaw Country." *Indian Territory Bar Association Proceedings* 4 (1903): 63.

Givens. "The Creek Courts." *Indian Territory Bar Association Proceedings* 4 (1903): 43. Describes the establishment of Creek Courts in 1850 following resettlement.

Hastings. "The Cherokee Courts." *Indian Territory Bar Association Proceedings* 4 (1903): 39.

Hill, Edward E. *Guide to Records in the National Archives of the United States Relating to American Indians*. Washington, D.C.: NARS, 1981. This guide is well indexed and gives specifics on the courts maintained by Indian agencies. The records themselves are not described in detail.

Kawashima, Yasu. "Legal Origins of the Indian Reservation in Colonial Massachusetts." *American Journal of Legal History* 13 (1969): 42-56.

Knight. "Fifty Years of Choctaw Law, 1834-1884." *Chronicles of Oklahoma* 31 (1953): 76.

"Notes and Documents: The Brush Court of Indian Territory." *Chronicles of Oklahoma* 46 (1968): 201.

Reid, John. *A Law of Blood: The Primitive Law of the Cherokee Nation*. New York: New York University Press, 1970.

Sharp. "The Chickasaw Court." *Indian Territory Bar Association Proceedings* 4 (1903): 54. Describes the creation of Chickasaw courts in 1867.

Thompson. "Courts of the Cherokee Nation." *Chronicles of Oklahoma* 2 (1924): 63.

Mining District Records

Directory of Nevada Mines. rev. ed. Reno: Mining Press, 1940.

Greever, William S. *The Bonanza West: The Story of the Western Rushes, 1848-1900*. Norman: University of Oklahoma Press, 1963.

Griffen, Helen S. *California Mining Town Newspapers, 1850-80*. Glendale: J. E. Reynolds, 1954.

Griswold, Don L., and Jean H. Griswold. *The Carbonate Camp Called Leadville*. Denver: For the authors, 1951.

Hult, Ruby. *Lost Mines and Treasures of the Pacific Northwest*. 3rd ed. Portland: Binfords and Mort, 1968. Includes descriptions by oldtimers for mines open only a short time.

Marshal, Thomas Maitland. "Miners Laws of Colorado." *American Historical Review* 25 (1919-20): 426.

Mumrey, Nolee. *Early Mining Laws of Buckskin Joe, 1859*. Boulder, Colo.: For the author, 1961.

___________. *History and Proceedings of Buckskin Joe*. Boulder, Colo.: For the author, 1961.

Records of R. C. Barry, Justice of the Peace, Sonoma, California, 1850-51. Printed in *Miners and Business Directory*. Columbia, Calif.: Heckendorf and Wilson, 1856.

Shinn, Charles H. *Institutional Beginnings of a Western State*. Baltimore: Johns Hopkins University Studies in History and Political Science, 2nd series (1880), vol. 7. Discusses the lead mines of Iowa.

___________. *Mining Camps: A Study in American Frontier Government*. 1884; reprint ed., New York: Harper Torchbooks, 1965.

___________. *Land Laws of Mining Districts*. Baltimore: Johns Hopkins University Studies in History and Political Science, 2nd ser., (1884), vol. 12.

Smith, Duane A. *Rocky Mountain Mining Camps*. Indianapolis: Indiana University Press, 1975.

Other Court Records

Aiken, John. "New Netherlands Arbitration in the 17th Century." *Arbitration Journal* 29 (1974): 145.

Brown. "Legal Systems in Conflict: Orleans Territory, 1804-1812." *American Journal of Legal History* 1 (1957): 35.

Dart. "Influence of the Ancient Laws of Spain on the Jurisprudence of Louisiana." *InterAmerican Law Review* 1 (1959): 303.

Dupuy. "The Earliest Courts of the Illinois Country." *Illinois Law Review* 1 (1906): 81.

Fielder, George. *The Illinois Law Courts in Three Centuries 1673-1973: A Documentary History*. Chicago: Physician's Record Company, 1973.

Ford, Jeanette W. "Federal Law Comes to Indian Territory." *Chronicles of Oklahoma* 58 (1980-81): 432-39.

Gilbert. "Mexican Alcades of San Francisco, 1835-1846." *Journal of the West* 2 (1963): 245.

Grivas, Theodore. *Military Government in California, 1846-1850, With a Chapter on their Prior Use in Louisiana, Florida and New Mexico*. Glendale, Calif.: Arthur H. Clarke Co., 1963.

Hershkowitz, Leo. "The Troublesome Turk: An Illustration of Judicial Process in New Amsterdam." *New York History*, vol. 46, p. 299.

Lang, Margaret. *Early Justice in Sonora*. N.p.: Mother Lode Press, 1963.

McKnight. "The Spanish Legacy to Texas Law." *American Journal of Legal History* 3 (1959): 222, 229.

Robinson, William M., Jr. *Justice in Grey: A History of the Judicial System of the Confederate States of America*. Cambridge: Harvard University Press, 1941.

Shinn, Charles H. *Mining Camps: A Study in American Frontier Government*. 1884; reprint ed., New York: Harper Torchbooks, 1965. Includes an excellent description of the Spanish/Mexican legal system.

Twitchell. "Spanish Colonization and the Founding of the Cuidades and Villas in the Time of Don Juan Onate." *New Mexico Bar Association Minutes* (1919): 27.

Wiener, Frederick B. *Civilians Under Military Justice: British Practice since 1689, Especially in North America*. Chicago: University of Chicago Press, 1967.

Slave Court Records

Crawford, Paul. "A Footnote on Courts for Trial for Negroes in Pennsylvania," *Journal of Black Studies* 5 (Dec. 1974): 167-74.

Klebaner, Benjamin J. "American Manumission Laws and the Responsibility for Supporting Slaves." *Virginia Magazine of History and Biography* 63 (1955): 443-53.

McCain. "Magistrates' Courts in Early North Carolina." *North Carolina Historical Review* 48 (1971): 23.

McPherson, Robert G. "Georgia Slave Trials, 1837-1849." *American Journal of Legal History* 4 (1960): 257-84; 364-77. Includes cases.

Senesé, Donald J. "The Free Negro and the South Carolina Courts, 1790-1860." *South Carolina Historical Magazine* 68 (1967): 140-53; 265.

Sisk. "Crime and Justice in the Alabama Black Belt, 1875-1917." *Mid-America* 40 (1958): 106.

Steel, Edward M., Jr. "Black Monongalians: A Judicial View of Slavery and the Negro in Monongalia County, 1776-1865." *West Virginia* 34 (1972-73): 331-59.

INFORMATION GUIDE

Genealogical Information in the Record Group	*Patent*	*Deed*	*Military Bounty*	*Tax*	*Marriage Contracts*
Surname/name	●	●	●	●	●
Date of Birth					
Place of Birth					
Sex				●	
Race/color					
Physical Description					
Occupation	●				
Education					
Military Service			●		
Slave Status					
Property Owned	●	●		●	●
Religion					
Citizenship	●	●	●	●	●
Marital Status		●		●	●
Spouse's Name		●		●	●
Children's Names		●		●	
Father's Name		●		●	
Mother's Name		●		●	
Father's Birthplace					
Mother's Birthplace					
Date of Death		●			
Cause of Death					
Name of Cemetery		●			
Residence	●	●	●	●	●
Age				●	
Literacy/signature		●			●
Map	●		●		
Neighbors	●	●		●	

COULD YOU USE THIS CHAPTER?

Type of Record	*Kept from*	*Clues That You Should Consult These Records*
Deeds	All periods	A majority of free adult males owned land before the Civil War. Land was the symbol of power, wealth, and social status in the Old World and immigrants flocked to the U.S. to acquire the one commodity the New World had to offer in rich abundance—land. Deeds often state relationships; for those that don't, relationships can be inferred from the transactions themselves. Records of ownership will tell where the land came from—often the estate of a parent or grandparent; dower rights include the name of the wife who must assent to the sale before witnesses or land title is not clear; quit-claim deeds list married names of daughters and signatures of heirs to undivided land; deeds of gift include slaves given to grandchildren or aging parents; settlements describe property divided among heirs. Deeds are thus indispensible for all pedigrees even for ancestors who resided in cities.
Grants, patents	Colonial period to early 20th century	Over 5 million federal grants have transferred land to individuals in various parts of the U.S. The original thirteen colonies, Texas, and Hawaii issued several million more. These grants are essential for searching a colonial ancestor, especially frontier families. The application files give more genealogical details than actual patents. Post-Civil War homestead files are rich in personal data, often including naturalization papers.
Claims	Colonial period to early 20th century.	Private land claims document titles for land originally owned by France or Spain. If your ancestor lived in an area that changed flags, you may find up to six generations of genealogy in the case file.
Bounty land	About 1770 to 20th century	Veterans in many military engagements not just formal wars, were eligible for land grants in lieu of pay for services. And many soldiers claimed but promptly sold their land, so don't conclude there was a move unless other records support such a hypothesis.
Tax records	All periods	Taxes paid by "adult" (ages varied from state to state) males or female heads of household can help you locate your ancestor in a given place and distinguish him/her from others with the same name. By comparing lists for several consecutive years, you can see when young men come of age or marry, move into or out of the area, and die leaving minor heirs. Sometimes the heirs are named.

Chapter 7

LAND AND TAX RECORDS

William Thorndale

Land records provide two types of important evidence for the genealogist. First, they often state kinship ties, especially when a group of heirs jointly sell some inherited land. Second, they place individuals in a specific time and place, allowing the researcher to sort people and families into neighborhoods and closely related groups. By locating persons with reference to creeks and other natural features, the deeds, land grants, and land tax lists help distinguish one John Anderson, son of Mark, from another John Anderson in the same county. Prior to the Civil War, most free adult males owned land; so if the land records of an area survive and do not mention your ancestor, you should reevaluate the assumption that he lived in the area.

Most beginning genealogists underestimate the importance of using land records to pin persons to specific locales. Donald Lines Jacobus, considered the founder of scientific New England genealogy, wrote of Connecticut: "The most important town records, genealogically, are the land records."[1] In the South, which has far fewer vital records than New England, the land records are even more crucial to genealogical success.

This chapter on land is divided into two major parts. The first half describes deeds, survey systems, military bounty land, taxes, and something of real property law. The second half is a synopsis of each state's land grant records, along with historical notes and bibliographic references. Observe especially the distinction between "state-land states" (where the state made the land grants) and "public-domain states" (where the federal government made the grants). The first part of the chapter explains these two systems; the state-by-state synopsis tells the system used in each state.

Many of the land records mentioned in this chapter have been microfilmed. The Genealogical Society of Utah includes state land grants and county and some city deeds among its routinely filmed records. Consult its catalog at the branches listed in Appendix D. The society formerly filmed deed books only up to 1850, later up to the Civil War, and still later – in some cases but not all – the subsequent volumes. Sometimes cumulative deed indexes exist but were not filmed. Thus, despite the society's vast number of land records on microfilm, you should not treat its catalog as a complete inventory to what survives.

Other microfilmed records belong to libraries and archives that have made their manuscript collections of private land company papers and other records available. The millions of federal land patents have also been filmed and are available through the Bureau of Land Management as described in the state-by-state synopsis of public-domain states.

Deeds

Deeds are the bulk and backbone of American land records. They are fairly uniform in format and content, can normally be located in routinely predictable jurisdictions – usually the county – and should present few difficulties for the average researcher. Being one of the most important parts of the workaday civil law (as opposed to criminal law), they do have their share of legal terms. Val Greenwood, with the advantage of a law degree, has discussed some basic legal concepts about land in his *Researcher's Guide to American Genealogy* (Baltimore: Genealogical Publishing Co., 1973), pp. 286-96. *Black's Law Dictionary* also provides definitions. An authoritative encyclopedia such as the *Encyclopedia Britannica* in an older edition will contain a good review of "real property and conveyancing." Also check indexes in encyclopedias under *deeds*. This section contains an overview of deeds and other records found in deed books. Some remarks on more technical aspects are given below in the section on the "Use of Land Records."

The term *deed* can be used broadly to mean a legal document of transfer, bargain, or contract, or narrowly for a warranty deed where the seller warrants (guarantees) the title to the land being sold. Deed books contain many types of title conveyances and contracts: deeds in fee simple granting absolute ownership, mortgages transferring property rights as security for a debt, dower releases waiving a wife's rights, quitclaim deeds releasing whatever title or right is held whether valid or not, deeds of gift transferring land without a reciprocal consideration except perhaps "love and affection," powers of attorney appointing legal agents, marriage property settlements between spouses either before or after the marriage, bills of sale transferring property that is usually not land, and various forms of contracts such as leases, partnerships, indenture papers, and other performance bonds. These last four were not ordinarily recorded, though probate bonds were common in probate volumes. Deed books from before the Civil War and especially in colonial years were more miscellaneous in their contents, even including animal brands, occasional wills, slave manumissions, apprentice papers, petitions, depositions, tax lists, and whatever else the clerk decided to preserve on a convenient page.

European settlers and their governments brought to the colonies the principle that before land could be privately owned the government had to pass title into private hands. Thus, for any tract of land there should be a first-title deed, which is normally called a grant or patent. Usually the authorities sought from the local Indian tribes a cession of Indian title, though this concept of owning land was foreign to the Indian view of communal occupancy. Once the Indian title was terminated to the satisfaction of the whites, the government could grant title for a tract to an individual, corporation, or in the case of federal grants, even to a state. All subsequent transfers of that tract are by deed or analogous conveyance, or by inheritance.

In the United States, responsibility for guaranteeing legal title rests with the buyer and seller, who nowadays usually employ professional title searchers and lawyers to trace the chain of title back to the first-title grant if possible, attempting to verify a valid, unencumbered title transfer at each step. The government limits itself to the role of a referee supplying the rules, recording the results, and adjudicating disputes brought to court. To simplify such title searches, title abstract and insurance companies have arisen to make professional searches and sell insurance against defective titles.

Such companies have compiled indexes to title transfers in their local area. If a genealogist can afford the high expense, such a title company could compile an ancestor's local land records. Also, there are cases where the local deed office has been destroyed recently but abstracts survive in the private title company records.

An important fact follows from the American system of deed registrations: The records are usually sought by the names of the buyer or seller rather than the tract name or number. This means that a break in the chain of recorded owners can complicate a genealogist's understanding of why, in the absence of a deed, John Smith now owns land that Mary Smith owned ten years ago. The land could have passed from mother to son by will with proof only in the probate records, or it could have passed by intestate probate and not be recorded at all. It could also be that the two persons are unrelated and Mary sold the land to Paul Williams, who then sold it to John Smith, neither of the deeds being recorded, perhaps to save the cost of the clerk's fees. Or perhaps the deed from Mary Smith to John Smith was by sheriff's sale and indexed under the sheriff's name as seller. Such a sheriff's sale for delinquent taxes raises the point that tax foreclosures affecting the land would be in court records, while a bankruptcy suit might be processed in another county entirely.

A registry system called Torrens attempts to meet some of these problems. Named for Robert Richard Torrens, the South Australian legislator who developed it in the late 1850s, Torrens ideally records in one place under the title of the tract all former owners and all rights, interests, and liens to which the property is subject. Having established the registry as mandatory and complete, the government can then issue guaranteed certificates of title to a new owner. While available in about twenty states, Torrens in the United States has not operated as intended for several reasons, including constitutional questions of right of appeal to the courts, the great expense of the first registration, inadequate insurance funds to insure title guarantees, the statutory exclusion of certain encumbrances from the Torrens records, and–it is said–sabotage by private title companies and lawyers fearing loss of business.

For the genealogist, the advantage of a Torrens chain of title may be offset by the deed indexes being by tract rather than buyer and seller, a situation said to operate in parts of Iowa. Usually, there are two sets of indexes, one by tract and one by buyer and seller. If there are no buyer and seller indexes, the genealogist would need to search each tract record to insure comprehensive coverage of an ancestor's land transactions in the county. However, Torrens has never flourished in the United States, so the chances are small that the researcher will encounter this particular problem.

The variety of records in deed books requires the user to develop certain hunting and abstracting skills. Since few researchers have the time to read, page by page, the forty, fifty, or a hundred volumes of deeds in an average county or independent city, the user usually turns to the index. Seller indexes are also called direct and grantor indexes; buyer indexes are indirect and grantee indexes. Some counties have alphabetical indexes only for sellers, which requires reading all index entries A to Z to check the buyers (e.g., the buyers would be listed next to the sellers, but only the sellers are alphabetized). Before relying on a deed index, it is wise to make an informal sampling of the contents of the deed volumes to see if they contain records significantly different from deeds and if these different sorts of records are indexed along with the deeds. There actually exist deed volumes containing wills omitted from the deed index and not found in the probate indexes either.

While cumulative deed indexes are usually in alphabetical order (alpha order), running indexes cannot be, since more names are continually being added. Some running indexes merely group surnames under their first letter (initial order), so all *A* surnames are together unalphabetized, all *B* surnames together, etc., with special pages for *Mc* and *O'*. Occasionally, a clerk ignored the patronymic prefix and indexed MacDonald with *D* surnames and O'Carroll under *C*. More elaborate running indexes were sold commercially by companies vying for sales by inventing unique, eye-catching systems. Such complicated indexing systems must be mastered when encountered, though usually there are instructions in the front of the volume. Some allocate separate pages for vowels (surnames *Ba, Be, Bi,*. . .), some for consonants (the l-m-n-r-t system brings Chalkley, Cullison, and Czeskleba to the same page, since each has an *l* as the first internal "key" letter). Some running indexes use an initial surname order subdivided by initial letters of the given name (so Gregory Buck, Gary Ball, and Gertrude Brown are all on the same page). There are several more approaches, too many to explain. Some are illustrated in Morris L. Radoff, et al., *The County Courthouses and Records of Maryland. Part Two: The Records* (Annapolis: Hall of Records Commission, 1963), pp. 20-36.

Other problems with indexes are sins of omission–creating only a grantor index, mistakenly omitting a name, or ignoring nondeed items. This last problem is fairly common, especially in alphabetized master-deed indexes compiling all the deed volumes of the last hundred or two hundred years. Whether the indexer will consider the barrel brand of Thomas Forehall, cooper, worth indexing is doubtful, especially since it was recorded 150 years ago and can serve no purpose now. The researcher must always choose between trusting the index or checking the book or needed years page by page. Deeds with more than one buyer or seller may be indexed under the first person's name only, another reason to take the time to read page by page if the problem warrants it. There is also the occasional deed that provides information on a surname different from either the seller or buyer. On 7 May 1763, William and Betty Eskridge of Northumberland County, Virginia, sold land to Thomas Williams and, in passing, the deed gave a beautiful account of the Neale family, former owners of the land.[2]

Having found an actual entry in the deed volume, either by using the index or by page-by-page scanning, you should have a fairly standard format for abstracting entries. It is wise to train yourself to *first* write down the source (or if you have photocopied the entry, to immediately write the source on the photocopy). *Source* includes the archive or library where you found the record, as well as the record type, volume, and page. Here are three examples:

Maryland Hall of Records–Charles Co., Md., deeds 10:231 (microfilm)
King Co., Wa., courthouse, county auditor's office, deeds 27:13
Draper Papers (State Historical Society of Wisconsin, Madison), 6BB35 (microfilm 889,101, Genealogical Society, Salt Lake).

Printed notekeeping forms help some people remember to copy such sources.

As for abstracting a deed, the style is up to the researcher. Find a format that you like and try to standardize it within adaptable limits. Records tend to follow standard formats, which makes abstracting easier. Here is one example of an abstracted deed:

Barnwell Dist, SC, deeds vol. H 1814-15. p. 318 27 Oct 1813: Samuel Sprawls, Barnwell Dist, to John Ashley, residence not given, $20 46 acres on branch of Tinkers Creek, adj. Mary Collins and said John Ashley

Signed: Samuel Sprawls

wit: Edmond Brown, J. C. Starpkin (also Starkin)

Recorded 21 Nov 1814.

Some users forget that the deed book is a copy of an original paper and therefore the deed book signatures are usually in the clerk's handwriting, not holographs. Some jurisdictions, however, did require a signature on the copy they retained, so watch for them. Likewise, the seal–in wax and later in paper–beside the seller's signature was real on the original; but, in the deed book, the clerk drew a stylized circle surrounding the word "seal." The use of personal wax seals has long been out of fashion; but in the colonies, men were expected to have or borrow some sort of sealing device, which usually supplemented the illiterate's mark. Even English peasants as early as the thirteenth century were required by law to seal their signatures; in fact, there was a time when the seal was the official attestation, and the person's mark was auxiliary.

By the late seventeenth century, the seal was merely a traditional ornament.[3] Consequently, heraldic devices on colonial seals probably do not prove a signator had a coat of arms. In fact, George Washington had a seal with a device different from the family coat of arms, a fairly typical situation.

Seals and signatures are, however, minor problems compared to late recording. Since running indexes show names in chronological order, a 1735 deed recorded in 1802 is so out of place that the researcher may not carry the search far enough to spot it. I discovered a deed dated 31 March 1800 and recorded 21 March 1896 in Montgomery County, Georgia, with another in the same place dated 30 Dec. 1791 and recorded 30 July 1901 – 110 years later.[4] In the same general category is the deed re-recorded after the courthouse or town hall burned. Also be alert to indexes that show only the recording date, since behind the 1827 date could be an 1818 deed. If the ancestor died in 1823, the researcher might mistakenly conclude from the index that this 1827 deed could not be his.

State-Land States

Deeds normally locate the land tract by some legal description within a survey. The thirty states where the federal government granted land use the federal township and range system and include a special subcategory called private land claims. I will first, however, describe the remaining twenty states, called state-land states, which granted their own lands and have various surveying systems.

The twenty state-land states are the thirteen original states from New Hampshire to Georgia, plus Maine, Vermont, West Virginia, Kentucky, Tennessee, Texas, and Hawaii. For the latter two, consult the "Summary of State Land Records" at the end of the chapter. The remaining eighteen can be divided between the six New England states which used the New England town system, the transitional state of New York, and the remaining states from Pennsylvania and New Jersey south which used the Southern system of metes and bounds.

Southern Land Grants

The tomahawk grant is part of American folklore. The buckskin-clad squatter cuts blazes on a perimeter of trees that surround his newly picked tract of wilderness, and then off he goes to a land office to get a deed. He enters his claim (the petition) and gets official authorization (a warrant) to have the tract surveyed to produce a legal description (the plat) so the government can grant title for this specific piece of land (the first-title deed, usually called a grant or patent).

In the absence of a surveyed grid of meridians, baselines, townships, and ranges by which the land can be legally described, the description must use local features, usually called metes and bounds, which means "measuring" and "naming" boundary features. The distances in patents and deeds were usually in poles, rods, or perches (all synonyms) of sixteen and a half feet.

Here is part of a simple description: "Starting at the ash tree in the split rock, then 139 poles to where the spring branch enters Crooked Creek, then up said creek its meanders to a three-notch oak, then. . . ." A surveyed compass course reads: "Starting at the ash tree in the split rock, then North 41° East 139 poles to where the spring branch enters Crooked Creek, then up said creek its meanders South 14 poles, South 3° West 25 poles, South 9° East 13 poles to a three-notch oak. . . ."

Strictly speaking, because they used compass bearings, nearly all Southern tracts were not in metes and bounds. A more correct term is the indiscriminate survey, meaning that the survey was not tied to any larger survey grid. This chapter, however, will employ the common composite term of indiscriminate metes and bounds. Since the natural or manmade features of the description tended to disappear over the years, the property owner, in the company of local officials, neighbors, and sometimes a surveyor, might retrace the property bounds and mark again from memory or from a new survey those points that were disappearing or lost. This walking and remarking of the bounds was called "processioning."[5]

Unlike New England, lands in the Southern system were usually allotted directly to individuals. In New York, a transistion zone, large grants were often made to wealthy individuals who subdivided and sold the grants in small parcels. In Pennsylvania, New Jersey, and the colonies to the south, the allotted lands were usually farm-size tracts that went directly to individuals. There were some very large grants in the Southern colonies, especially Virginia. Two of the largest were 92,000 acres to Benjamin Borden and 118,000 acres to William Beverley, both in 1739 in the upper Shenandoah Valley, both part of the total 539,000 acres granted by 1740 to eight individuals or partnerships.[6] (Incidentally, Beverley's papers, including account books for his valley tract, are in the New York Public Library, which illustrates how far the genealogist might have to look for pertinent records.)

Land offices handled the paperwork of petitioning and obtaining the individual grants. It is extraordinary that in the colonies from Pennsylvania to Georgia plus their offspring of West Virginia, Kentucky, and Tennessee, none of their land offices were destroyed in a major fire. In the Civil War, the state capitals of Virginia, South Carolina, and Georgia were burned, yet the land office records survived. Nearly every one of the early states from Pennsylvania south still has a land office either as a distinct section of the state archives or as a division of an active state office.

The authority granting colonial lands was not always the government. There were three variations: (1) The English monarch controlled the government and granted the land through the governor. Examples are New York after 1689, South Carolina after 1729, and Georgia after 1754; (2) the monarch controlled the government but gave a private citizen or citizens (proprietors) the right to grant the land. Examples are the Northern Neck Proprietary of Lord Fairfax in Virginia, and the Granville District of Earl Granville in North Carolina; or (3) the English monarch allowed a private citizen or citizens to control the government and grant the land, as in Pennsylvania under the Penns and in Georgia under the trustees, 1733-54. Where the proprietors were distinct from the government, there will be land office records distinct from government records, as in New Jersey, Virginia, and North Carolina, though these records may later have been added to the government archives, as in Virginia and North Carolina, but not New Jersey. (See the state-by-state summary at the end of this chapter.)

There were several ways to acquire first title to lands, but usually they followed the four steps of petition, warrant, survey/plat, and grant/patent. (*Patent* and *grant* sometimes have different meanings, such as, the colony made patents but the state gave grants. In this chapter, however, they are used interchangeably to mean the first-title deed.)

The petition is a request to take up land. The petitioner may go before the appropriate officials – the colony's council or the land office clerk – and present a satisfactory reason for getting land, such as paying the purchase price, being promised land for military service, bringing an immigrant into the colony and thus becoming eligible for the headright land bounty (especially used in the South), or being able to produce a government order for a specified amount of land.

The warrant certifies the right to a specific acreage and authorizes an official surveyor to survey it, assuming no prior and conflicting claims. The plat, sometimes called a survey, is the surveyor's drawing of the legal description so the land is identifiable, his certification that everything is in order so far as the warrant, approved acreage, and legal description are concerned.

The patent/grant is the government's or proprietor's passing of title to the patentee/grantee. This is the first-title deed and the true beginning of private ownership of the land.

The government or proprietor usually entered a copy of the patent in a bound volume as a permanent, official record. The plats were sometimes recorded in volumes, and the surveyor's loose copy was also sometimes kept. The North Carolina Land Office, for example, has many loose surveys. Some land offices kept permanent warrant records; some did not. The petition was rarely recorded because the warrant was the formal statement of an authorized petition, though petitioner information is occasionally found in council minutes—especially for colonial headrights.

Bringing oneself or another to the colonies entitled the importer to a "headright" of land at specific historical periods. Virginia granted fifty acres per importation, but sailors abused it by claiming fifty acres every time they sailed to Virginia, then sold their claims. In the case of indentured servants, the fifty acres went to the one who paid the servant's passage. These headrights could be bought and sold, so the person claiming 200 acres for importing four persons was not necessarily the person who actually paid the passage costs. Thus, if Mark Randle claimed 450 acres for transporting nine persons including Mary Randle, it is possible Mark merely bought headrights to nine persons and never saw or knew Mary. It is also possible that Mary paid her own passage and sold her headright rather than claim the land. Furthermore, the nine persons need not have come on the same ship nor arrived in the same year.

New England did not have this system of headrights as a rule, though granting free land to town settlers was a form of reward for immigration. The Southern proprietors rarely gave headrights—the Calverts did for a while—because they sold land for a profit. The crown tried at times to make the colonies grant lands to indentured servants at the end of their service, but this was uncommon. Despite these caveats, the headright lists are valuable as the major or only immigration record for most colonial immigrants from the British Isles to the South.

The patent and related documents rarely give kinship information, so their great value is in locating the grantee in a specific time and place. On 11 August 1774, the following grant was made by the royal colony of South Carolina:

> George the Third by the Grace of God, of Great Britain, France and Ireland, King, Defender of the Faith, and so forth, To all to whom these presents shall come, Greeting: Know ye, that we of our special grace, certain knowledge and mere motion, have given and granted, and by these presents, for us, our heirs and successors, do give and grant unto Ezekiel Backler his heirs and assigns, a plantation or tract of land containing four hundred & fifty acres on Four Hole Swamp St. Mathews Parish Berkley County bounding northeast on Samuel Young & Ezekiel Backler Senr's land and all other sides on vacant land. . . .[7]

This grant names the owners of two adjoining tracts: Samuel Young and Ezekiel Backler, Sr. Is this Ezekiel, Sr., the same person as the grantee? Or is the grantee a younger Ezekiel living next to his father or uncle? Are there any other Backlers in the area? What are the names of other neighbors? Could any be in-laws? Did these neighbors come from the same former home as our grantee? A beginning toward answering these questions would be to draw the surveyed tracts in the area. Drawing a plat map is laborious and time-consuming, but such a map can identify neighbors with a precision it is hard to overestimate.

The surveys of the 1600s were quite crude. Early Virginia surveys often merely give a distance along a river and say the rectangle into the woods is a certain number of acres. Descriptive bounds giving only "up the meanders of the creek" must be approximated based on the remaining precise bounds, sometimes with the help of neighboring tracts. Copy errors by clerks—N 56° E 76 poles instead of the correct N 56° W 176 poles—could make it impossible to close the tract's perimeters, though the contiguous tracts may supply the corrections. Figure 7-1 explains how to draw plat maps.

Occasionally early colonial descriptions have strange directions such as SE ½ E or ES ½ S or even WNW ¼ N. These refer to the thirty-two-point compass card, which is described in Sarah S. Hughes, *Surveyors and Statesmen: Land Measuring in Colonial Virginia* (Richmond: Virginia Surveyors Foundation and The Virginia Association of Surveyors, 1979), a book worth reading by anyone interested in Southern indiscriminate surveys. In the thirty-two-point card the directions beginning at north toward east are:

north	N	N
north by east	N by E	N 11° 15′ E
north northeast	NNE	N 22° 30′ E
northeast by north	NE by N	N 33° 45′ E
northeast	NE	N 45° E
northeast by east	NE by E	N 56° 15′ E
east northeast	ENE	N 67° 30′ E
east by north	E by N	N 78° 45′ E
east	E	E

Fortunately, these compass card directions were rarely used. Dividing 90° into eight parts gives eight 11° 15′ sections which, given the imprecision of a modern small protractor and the surveyor's very rough angles in the 1600s, means the angles can be treated as N = 0°, N by E = 11°, NNE = 22°, N = 34°, . . ., E by N = 11°, E = 0°. Sometimes the angle will be NE by N½ N, meaning halfway between NE by N and NNE.

When researching deeds and surveys, you must decide whether to copy the detailed bounds. Much depends on whether the records will be easily available for future checking. Photocopies can help but are expensive when they start accumulating. A wise approach may be to not copy the precise bounds unless time is no problem or platting is planned but instead to abstract the usual information noting carefully all neighbors. Thus copies can later be ordered of those descriptions that seem to adjoin. If the bounds are to be copied, a simple notekeeping system is:

John Lemon, Northern Neck patent K171 1 Jly 1760, Frederick Co, Va, survey by Thomas Rutherford, Jr., Begin locust and black oak,

w/ Lemon	S 10 W 38	locust
w/ Francis Lilburn	N 80 W 40	white oak
"	S 20 W 190	black oak
	N 70 W 200	locust on hill
	N 20 E 240	2 black oaks
	S 70 E 235	to begin

311 acres[8]

Sometimes a course says "with Francis Lilburn's line" and gives the bearings and distance; sometimes it gives a bearing and direction and then tells what feature is met. By centering the bearing and distance information on the page, the researcher leaves space right and left for such descriptions. These natural features and adjoining landowners are important because they help match contiguous tracts. The difficulty of drawing tract maps is well worth the trouble for difficult lineage problems.[9]

New England Towns

While the Southern and New England land systems shared most of the same terminology, they differed fundamentally in that New England grants usually went to a group of men called town proprietors. Upon receipt of a block of land, these town proprietors surveyed parts of their large tract, apportioned out village homesites and field strips for themselves and others, and oversaw the subsequent disbursements of "divisions" of land until all the grant had passed into private ownership except for the town commons and local government lots. Thus, whereas the Southern grants to individuals created a rural landscape of scattered farms with very few towns, the New England grants created a society of villages.

The origin of the New England town runs back to the first settlers of Plymouth and Massachusetts Bay, where the Pilgrims and Puritans strove to establish a congregation-community uniting church and civil government into God's commonwealth. As new lands were needed to feed the growing population, groups of prospective settlers would petition a colony's government for land to

Figure 7-1. How to Draw a Plat Map in Indiscriminate Metes and Bounds.

Drawing Plat Maps

To plat a tract using metes and bounds bearings, you need only an ordinary protractor, pencil, scissors, and lined paper to provide constant east-west lines to orient the protractor.

The degrees begin at the first direction – cardinal point: north, south, east, west – and move toward the second given direction. Thus N 53° E is 53° east of north. If, as is occasionally done, the bounds read E 53° N, this is 53° north of east. N 53° E and E 53° N are not the same; N 53° E and E 37° N are.

For distance, which is measured in 16½ – foot lengths called poles/rods/perches (synonymous terms), a homemade scale can be made of 320 parts to the mile (320 poles × 16½ feet = 5280 feet). To make such a scale, cut a narrow strip of paper perhaps a quarter-inch wide to the length you want one mile to equal. Double, redouble, and redouble again.

Folding three times creates a strip divided into eight parts each 40 poles long. Then visually divide each 40 poles into four parts, thus creating a scale of ten poles to each mark. The U.S. Geological Survey's 1:24,000 topographic maps are a very good scale for drawing plats because small tracts such as thirty and forty acres come out at a good working size, not so tiny that they easily get lost. To fix exactly on the topographic map where a tract lay, it is usually necessary to bring together enough adjoining tracts to create sufficient known points on a creek so the whole series can be adjusted to match the bends of the creeks and rivers.

To order topographic maps, request the appropriate state index to maps from Branch of Distribution, USGS, 1200 South Eads Street, Arlington, VA 22202.

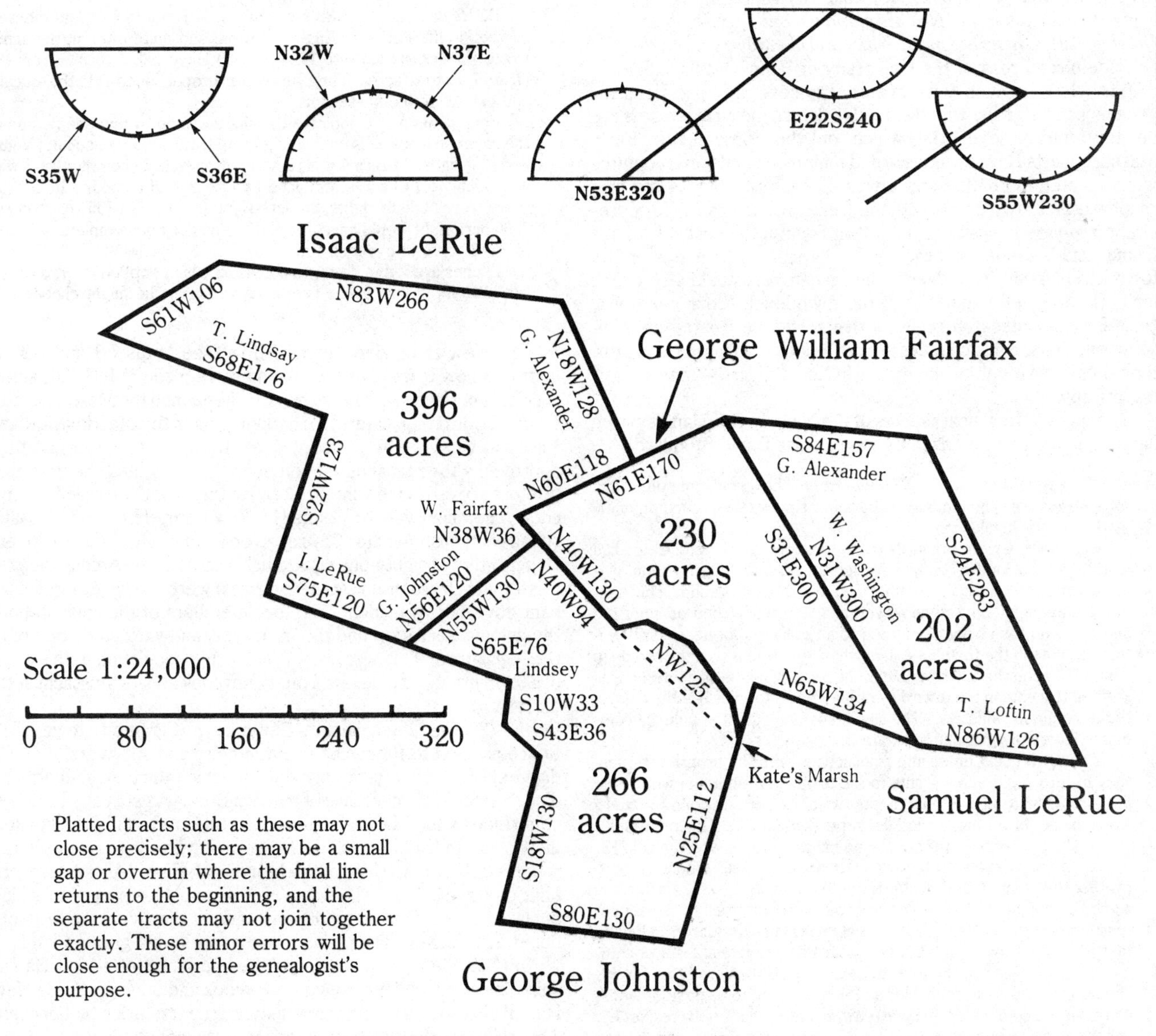

establish a new town, praying to be constituted the official proprietors to distribute the land within the town. The town was a geographical unit extending beyond the village to some agreed boundaries with the neighboring towns. The early towns were irregularly shaped; the later ones tended to run six miles by six miles in size. Thus, the town bounds had to be established so that a formal grant could be issued to the proprietors. The religious fervor of Puritanism later declined, but the town form of the congregation- community survived and was carried throughout most of New England and even a little ways into eastern New York and northeastern New Jersey. There was, however, a pressing tendency for people to move out of the village to be nearer their fields, which led to the buying and exchanging of land parcels to consolidate property into farms.

The classic analysis of the origins of the New England town is Sumner Chilton Powell, *Puritan Village: The Formation of a New England Town* (Middletown: Wesleyan University Press, 1963), a book with valuable English local sources on the origins of English immigrants. The literature is accessible through David Grayson Allen, *In English Ways: The Movement of Societies and the Transferral of English Local Law and Custom to Massachusetts Bay in the Seventeenth Century* (Chapel Hill: University of North Carolina Press, 1981). For colonial land history in New England, see Marshall Harris, *Origin of the Land Tenure System in the United States* (Ames: Iowa State College Press, 1953); and Roy Hidemichi Akagi, *The Town Proprietors of the New England Colonies; a Study of Their Development, Organization, Activities and Controversies, 1620-1770* (Philadelphia: Press of the University of Pennsylvania, 1924).

The New England town system has several implications for genealogists, starting with the need to determine what records are on the county level and which on the town level. Early Massachusetts Bay towns recorded their own deeds until counties were created in 1643. Early towns on eastern Long Island also recorded their own deeds until the Duke of York's New York proprietary required registration in Suffolk County. Connecticut, Rhode Island, and Vermont recorded and still record their deeds on the town level. Aside from deeds, the researcher should also check for early proprietor minutes on the town level. More generally, New England research requires that towns be treated as mini-counties. Thus, while counties are not as important as in the South, there are three levels of jurisdiction in New England– state, county, and town.

Some of the technical aspects of the New England land system have been well summarized by genealogist David Stoddard:

> A. *Commoners and Non-Commoners*. . .The term "commoner" and "proprietor" are synonomous. "Proprietor" simply replaces "commoner" as the proper legal term.
>
> Commoners were originally those to whom the General Court had made a grant of land in common for settlement, very often without giving them entire control. They formed a quasi-corporation. The right of a commoner might be conveyed in a land transaction or inherited and one who thus became entitled to a right was not necessarily entitled to vote in the town meetings when township privileges had been conferred upon the inhabitants. On the other hand, because a man was entitled to a vote in the town did not entitle him to a voice in the control of the common lands. . . . The land community and the political community were distinct and separate bodies.
>
> The town could enter into transactions with the proprietors; and they in turn could make grants to the town. In plantations where the inhabitants were all commoners, the two bodies acted as one and there would be no "proprietors' records" kept. For instance, Groton, Mass., was settled in 1655, yet there are no proprietors' records until 1713.
>
> As the population of the towns increased, it became necessary to protect the commoners' rights. Hampton, now in New Hampshire, is a good example: (1) 1641–Persons who were not freemen present at town meetings; (2) 1662–Voted "that no man be considered an inhabitant, or act in town affairs but he that hath one share at least of commonage, according to the first division"; (3) 1700–Voted that no one should vote unless a freeholder and none to vote to dispose of lands, unless he is a commoner. In towns such as these, the serious researcher will generally find separate proprietors' records either in a separate book or as the initial part of the first town book. . . .
>
> Two ways existed for the satisfying of claims by non-commoners: (1) Increase the number of commoners; (2) Grant lands to newcomers without accompanying the rights to commonage, either to an individual by name or to all of a given class; such as Barnstable granting 4 acres to every widow.
>
> B. *Division of Common Lands*. . .The valuation of a man's estate, made from the tax-list, was the principal basis of division (Haverhill, Ipswich, Dedham, Hartford, many Connecticut River towns, settlements along Long Island Sound).
>
> C. *Restrictions Upon Alienation*. . .Great care was taken to preserve the original character of the community and to control its membership. A Connecticut law of 1659 declared no inhabitant shall make sale of house and lands until put forth to the town for approval; an item in Guilford, Connecticut, Town Book refers to no one being able to sell OR purchase unless by consent of the community; Watertown, Massachusetts, in 1638 had a provision "against selling town lots to forrainers".
>
> D. *Common Field*. . .The proportions of land cultivated in common varied greatly throughout New England; largely based on necessity. Connecticut and Massachusetts laws gave authority to townsmen or selectmen, or, when there were none, to the major part of the freemen.
>
> Common fields were found in most towns. They were formed: (1) Due to lack of means to fence separately; (2) Due to difficulty of fencing (land along the Connecticut River); (3) Due to convenience. Fences were maintained by each owner according to his share of land enclosed.
>
> E. *Home Lots, Acre Rights, Pitches*. . .Home/house lots differed in size in different New England towns, and quite often in the same town; (1) Barnstable; 6 to 12 acres; (2) Haverhill, 5 to 22 acres; (3) Groton, 10 to 20 acres. They were often proportioned as to the "quality and estate" of the possessor. . . .
>
> Acre rights or lots indicate the share owned by any one person in the common lands. It is entirely different from home/house lots. Value varied greatly. In Billerica a 10 acre lot or right in common land was equivalent to 113 acres of upland or 12 acres of meadow. In Groton there were 60 acre rights; 20 acre rights;, etc. with 755 rights in all. A 60 acre right would have entitled the owner one complete partition to 3242 acres of common land.
>
> Pitches are rights drawn in a division which entitled the drawer to lay out a lot of land in the commons wherever he might choose.[10]

The New Hampshire town of Bow (see Maps 7-1 and 7-2) illustrates how town divisions of land were made.[11] In 1725, some residents of Haverhill, Massachusetts, petitioned the Massachusetts General Court (legislature) for a town grant in the Merrimack River Valley at what is now Concord, New Hampshire. The legislature approved a town of about seven by eight miles, and the first proprietors arrived in the winter of 1726 at this new town called Pennycook. The valley was also claimed by New Hampshire, whose coastal ruling esatablishment in 1727 received from its legislature an overlapping grant of eighty-one square miles called Bow. Among the proprietors (each promised 500-acre shares) were the governor, lieutenant governor, president, and four members of the council, both the colonial secretary and the treasurer, and various members of the legislature. This was, in short, a land speculation in the guise of a town grant, far different from Pennycook and its Massachusetts farmers.

In 1728, the Massachusetts General Court granted a town called Suncook, next to Pennycook, to the heirs and survivors of an Indian expedition two years previous in which thirteen soldiers had died. Suncook, predecessor of modern Bow, was surveyed in 1729, confirmed by the Massachusetts General Court, and made its first division of land in 1730. Field lots averaging fifteen to twenty acres were laid along both sides of the Merrimack River. All houses were built on the east side. The rival New Hampshire proprietors also declared a land division on the east side of the river, the first lots being forty acres. Thus, rival town proprietors granted lands.

In 1740, George II established the Massachusetts-New Hampshire line as it is today, placing Pennycook and Suncook inside New Hampshire and directing that existing property titles be honored. This ruling made the Bow proprietors the sole legal proprietors,

Map 7-1. Pennycook and Suncook in Relation to Bow, New Hampshire. Adapted from David A. Bundy, *100 Acres More or Less: The History of the Land and People of Bow, New Hampshire* (Canaan, N.H.: Bow Town History Committee and Phoenix Publishing, 1975); pp. 28, 32, 44.

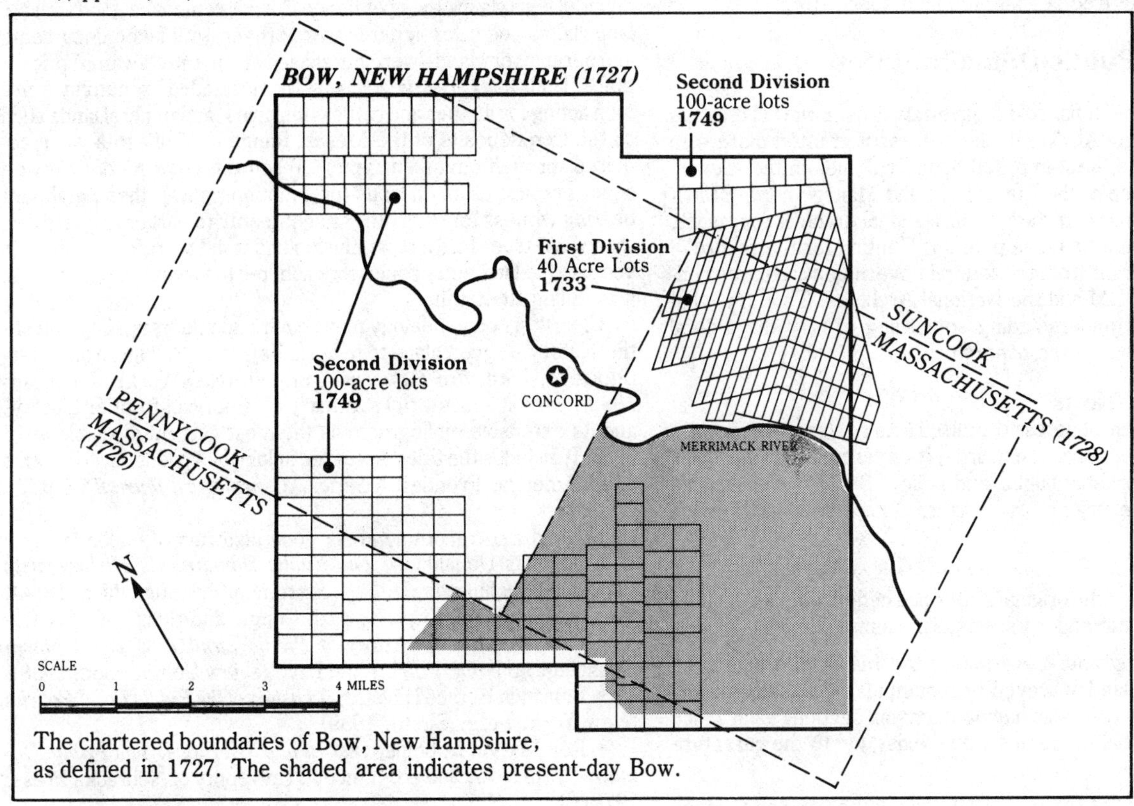

The chartered boundaries of Bow, New Hampshire, as defined in 1727. The shaded area indicates present-day Bow.

Map 7-2. Modern Bow, New Hampshire, Showing Its Surveyed Lots, Ibid., p. 106.

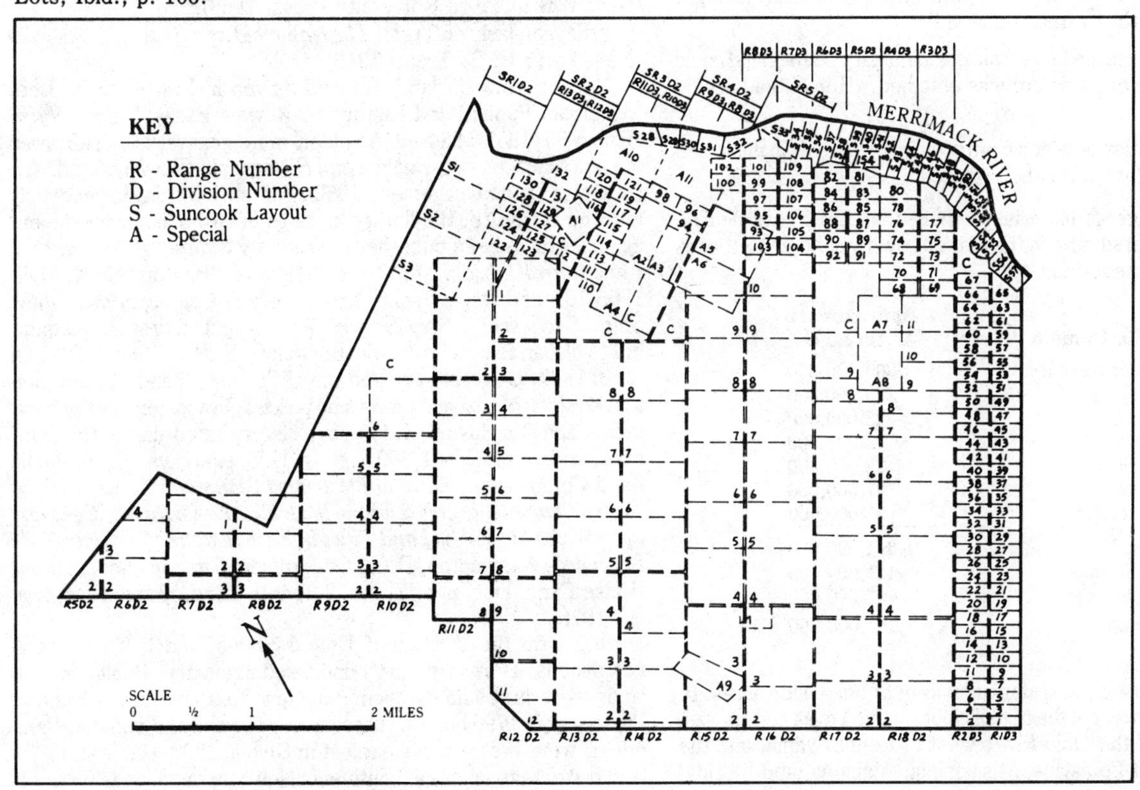

but the ex-proprietors of Suncook had the advantage of possession. The resulting legal battles were long and expensive, going all the way to England more than once. The present modern town gained a grant of town government from New Hampshire in 1767. When the Bow proprietors ceased functioning in 1786, the town of Bow was finally free of absentee land speculators.

Public-Domain States

The U.S. Government has sold or given away over one billion acres of land not including Alaska. In the process it granted more than five million patents, kept in 8,978 bound volumes in the Alexandria, Virginia, office of the Bureau of Land Management (BLM). An even greater mass of records in the National Archives represents the paperwork granting those patents. Hunting for the record of a particular land grant from the federal government requires contacting both the BLM and the National Archives. To know what to request means understanding something of how the federal government processed the paperwork.

Federal Land Grants

From 1776 when Congress promised land to Hessian deserters and for a quarter century afterwards, it experimented, mostly in Ohio, to find a workable public land policy. By 1803, when Ohio became a state, the major characteristics of the federal land system had been set:

1. The federal government, not the state, would dispose of the western lands which the original states had ceded, Georgia in 1802 being the last to surrender its western claims.

2. Before any grants were made, the Indian title had to be removed and the land surveyed in rectangular townships of six-mile squares, each township having thirty-six sections each a mile square. Some partial townships would exist due to the curvature of the earth.

3. The disposal of the vacant land would be handled through land offices located near settlers.

4. War service (at least prior to the Civil War) usually brought the veterans a right to free land.

5. Legally registered entry claims and military bounty land could usually be sold before a patent was obtained. (Homesteads could not.)

6. Valid land titles obtained from previous French, Spanish, and British governments would be honored.

By 1880, Congress had passed more than 3500 laws dealing with public lands. In summary, the federal government granted lands in seven broad categories:

Disposed Public Domain	Approximate Acreage
1. Sales and miscellaneous	300,000,000
2. Homesteads	285,000,000
3. Grants to states	225,000,000
4. Military bounty	73,000,000
5. Private land claims	22,000,000
6. Railroad grants	91,000,000
7. Timber culture, etc.	35,000,000
Total disposed	1,031,000,000
Remaining federal lands	411,000,000
State-owned lands	462,000,000
Total U. S. acreage	1,904,000,000[12]

Thus, the disposed public domain was over one billion acres. It included all states west of the Mississippi except Texas and Hawaii, all states north of the Ohio River west of Pennsylvania, and the four Gulf states of Louisiana, Mississippi, Alabama, and Florida. Much of the public domain was transferred to private or state title, though not so smoothly as a description of the system might pretend. Engineering Indian cessions was often both slow and deceitful; white settlers lived for years on Indian land without any legal claims to the land they cleared and farmed; land speculators amassed doubtful legal claims they petitioned Congress to make good; private land claims under foreign title were proven with faked documents and perjury; dry lands were purchased at cut-rate "swamp" prices; timber lands and cattle ranges were "homesteaded" by dummy frontmen acting for lumber and cattle companies, and mineral lands such as the iron deposits of the Mesabi Range in Minnesota were acquired through bogus entrymen. When the government allowed squatters first claim on lands (preemption rights), then neighbors bearing witness for each other might testify to earlier arrival dates than were true. In short, confusion and fraud were common. Just because the land-entry paperwork adheres to formula does not mean it is telling the truth.

Clearly, good genealogy may require an understanding of frontier history. A good place to begin is Ray Allen Billington and Martin Ridge, *Westward Expansion*, 5th ed. (New York: Macmillan, 1982). This is a masterful summary of American frontier history, and its extensive bibliography is the most current available as of 1983. It includes the titles discussed in John F. Vallentine, "Histories of the American Frontier: A Series," *Genealogical Journal* 6 (1977): 200-205.

I would also recommend six good histories of public lands:

- Thomas Donaldson, *The Public Domain: Its History, with Statistics* (Washington, D.C.: Government Printing Office, 1884), House Misc. Doc. 45 pt. 4, 47th Cong., 2nd Sess.
- Paul W. Gates, *History of Public Land Law Development* (Washington, D.C.: Public Land Law Review Commission, 1968).
- Benjamin Horace Hibbard, *A History of the Public Land Policies* (New York: Peter Smith, 1939).
- Roy Marvin Robbins, *Our Landed Heritage: The Public Domain, 1776-1970*, 2nd ed. (Lincoln: University of Nebraska Press, 1976).
- Malcolm J. Rohrbough, *The Land Office Business: The Settlement and Administration of American Public Lands, 1789-1837* (New York: Oxford University Press, 1968).
- Payson Jackson Treat, *The National Land System, 1785-1820* (New York: E. B. Treat, 1910).

Recent work on land history is given in Lawrence B. Lee, "American Public Land History: A Review Essay," *Agricultural History* 55 (1981): 284-99. An older, more general work is Bureau of Land Management, *Public Land Bibliography* (Washington, D.C.: Bureau of Land Management, 1962). For those wishing to get deeply into the literature, the library catalogs of two major government agencies have been published: *Dictionary Catalog of the National Agricultural Library, 1862-1965*, 73 vols. (Boston: G. K. Hall, 1965-70); and Department of the Interior, *Catalog of the United States Geological Survey Library*, 24 vols. plus a first supplement of 11 vols. and a second of four (Boston: G. K. Hall, 1964, 1972-74).

In 1879, Congress created the U.S. Public Land Commission to take stock of past and future land policies. In addition to its general report and Donaldson's 1,500-page history listed above, the commission also compiled 1,300 pages of U. S. land laws in U.S. Public Land Commission, *Laws of the United States of a Local or Temporary Character and Exhibiting the Entire Legislation of Congress upon Which the Public Land Titles in Each State and Territory Have Depended* (Washington, D.C.: Government Printing Office, 1881), House Exec. Doc. no. 47, pts. 2-3, 46th Cong., 3rd sess., serial no. 1976.

In short, the subject of United States land law history is voluminous. Here is a very condensed summary. Public domain lands were first sold by auction in New York City in 1787 and in Pittsburgh in 1796 but not successfully. Then on-the-spot local land offices were created, the earliest in Ohio in 1800, the first of 362 land districts to span the continent. Newly opened lands were offered at auction, then at a set minimum price—$2 an acre from 1796 to 1820. Credit was allowed on ever-easier terms, and the minimum tract size was reduced from 640 to 320 acres. Over-extension of credit and the resulting panic of 1819 caused the elimination of long-term credit in favor of eighty-acre minimums at $1.25 an acre. Congress passed many relief acts for those still owing money under the abolished credit system, and it also gave general preemption rights in 1841.

From the 1820s Congress became increasingly generous in giving away lands to finance military wagon roads (from 1823), canals (1827), river improvement (1828), swamp reclamation (1849), railroads (1850), colleges (1862), and desert reclamation (1894). In 1832, minimum purchases dropped to forty acres, and from 1842 to 1853, land was donated to early settlers in Florida, Oregon/Washington, and New Mexico/ Arizona. The famous 1862 Homestead Act gave a settler 160 acres (80 within railroad grant areas) for living on the land for five years and improving it. The donation and homestead acts required the claimant to show United States citizenship or an already-filed declaration of intent to become a citizen, valuable information for a genealogist. Later laws increased homestead acreage in arid areas, including the Desert Land Act of 1877 for 640 acres in a dozen Western states; the Kincaid Act of 1904 for 640 acres in western Nebraska; the Enlarged Homestead Act of 1909 for 320 acres in seven Mountain West states; and the Stock-Raising Homestead Act of 1916 for 640 acres. Homesteading essentially ended in the 1930s, although Western "sagebrush rebellions" have offered some state lands as late as 1983. General cash sales and preemption rights had been stopped in 1891, though some sales and much leasing of federal mineral and grazing lands continue to the present.

As always, the researcher should understand the paperwork flow. After the Indian title was extinguished and private land claims, if any, were adjudicated and surveyed, the surveyor-general's office established a principal meridian and base line surveyed at six-mile intervals to create townships of thirty-six sections, each a mile square. The manner of describing these resulting squares is the legal description, illustrated in Figure 7-2. Since many states have more than one principal meridian, they are part of the legal description, e.g., NW¼ of SE¼, sec. 9, T13S, R11E, 6th P.M. The standard descriptive text on surveying systems used is Bureau of Land Management, *Manual of Instructions for the Survey of the Public Lands of the United States* (Washington, D.C.: Department of the Interior, 1973), Technical Bulletin 6.

Figure 7-2. Legal Descriptions in the Federal Township and Range System.

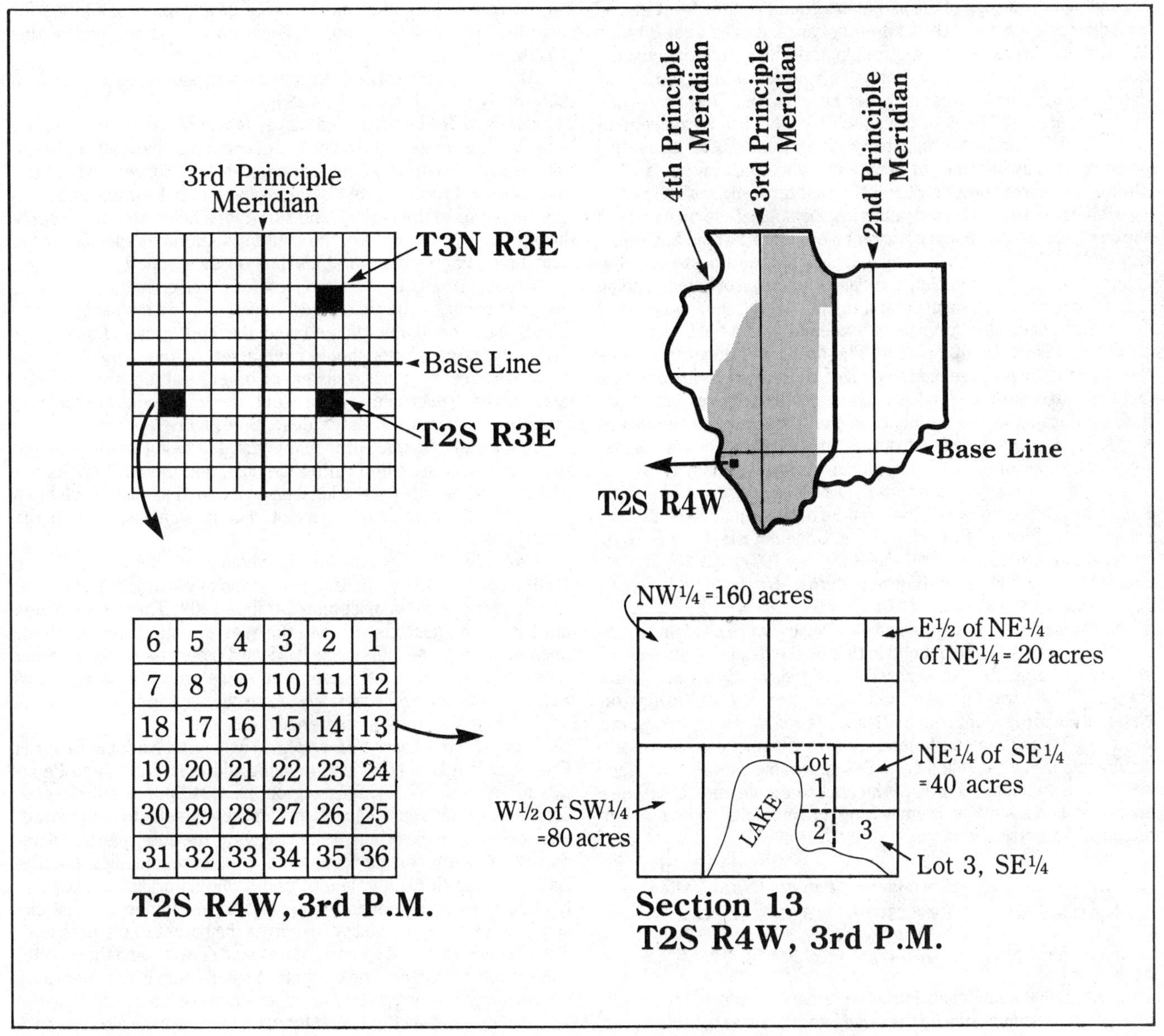

Once the land was surveyed and could be legally described, a local land office was opened, the auction was held, then land was available at the minimum price to claimants/entrymen who paid a credit installment (if prior to 1820) or a down payment on a cash purchase. Homesteads required a very small fee. Each land office was run jointly by two officials; a registrar who recorded entries and kept track of which tracts were claimed or still open and a receiver who handled the money. These officials kept daily journals and account ledgers and sent periodic summaries to the national headquarters, first the Treasury Department, and, from 1812, the newly created General Land Office (GLO). The local land office kept a separate file for each entry and two indexes by area: (1) the tract book, which was a written description of each entry on sheets arranged by township and range (Figure 7-3), and (2) a township plat, illustrated in Figure 7-4, which was a map of entries for each township showing patented tracts.

Once the entryman had fulfilled the requirements of purchase or homesteading, the local officials sent the case file (his paperwork and their final certificate of entitlement to a patent) to GLO headquarters in Washington, which confirmed that all paperwork was in order and issued a patent (first-title deed) transferring the land from the government to the private individual (or to the states, railroads, canal companies, etc.). The GLO headquarters recorded chronologically a copy of the patent in a bound volume by state and land district and stored the land-entry case file. The post-30 June 1908 patents were recorded chronologically in one continuous, national series regardless of state. This series is indexed for all patentees. The new owner may then have had the patent recorded in the county deed book or the state may have had an agreement with the GLO that the appropriate county and state authorities would be automatically informed of all patents, since the new lands were often exempt from property taxes for a set term such as five years.

Homestead case files are richer in genealogical information than the cash, credit, and bounty-warrant files. A homestead final certificate file includes the homestead application, certificate of publication of intention to complete the claim, final proof of homesteading (testimony from the claimant and his/her witnesses), a certified copy of the naturalization papers if needed, and a final certificate authorizing issuance of a patent. The final-proof documents give the claimant's name, age, and post office address, describe the tract and the house, date the establishment of residence, give the number and relationship of the members of the family, and note citizenship, crops, acres under cultivation, and testimony of witnesses. For illustrations of some of these documents, see E. Kay Kirkham, *The Land Records of America and Their Genealogical Value* (Salt Lake City: Deseret Book, 1964). A brief background of federal land records is in Richard F. Lackey, "The Genealogists' First Look at Federal Land Records," *Prologue* 9 (Spring 1977): 43-45; and W. Frank Meek, "Federal Land Office Records," *University of Colorado Law Review* 43 (1971-72): 177-97.

Not all claims – homestead and otherwise – were brought to patent. If the entryman did not obtain title by the deadline for the final charges or complete the homestead residency of five years, then the entry claim was cancelled and stored, now in the Washington National Records Center in Suitland, Maryland. However, some went to state and regional federal archives. From the genealogist's viewpoint, these cancelled case files, traceable through the tract books, are valuable records of the ancestor's life and sometimes give clues about why the claim was never completed. The number of cancelled entries is large:

	Entries	Patents	Percent Cancelled
Homestead Act	1,968,264	783,053	60.2
Timber Act	290,300	67,382	76.8
Desert Land Act	87,247	23,984	72.5

Over 1,185,000 homestead entries were never patented but should have files containing some of the same information as patented case files, plus a date and reason for the cancellation.

In 1946 the GLO and the Grazing Service were consolidated into the Bureau of Land Management (BLM), which today holds many GLO records or is the agency title under which the National Archives and its regional branches store GLO records – Record Group 49. Soon afterwards, the BLM initiated a "records improvement program" to repair the old GLO records, microfilm the tract, plat, and patent books, some used since 1800, and create clean copies of Western tract books. In 1983, it began a computerized master-index to patentee names. At present there is no such patent index prior to 1 July 1908, except for Alabama, Alaska, Arizona, Florida, Louisiana, Nevada, and Utah, none of whose pre-1 July 1908 indexes include private land claims.

The BLM (as of 1983) is divided into Eastern and Western states. Its working records – the tract books, plats, and patents – for all the Eastern states are at the Eastern States Office, 350 South Pickett Street, Alexandria, VA 22304. The Eastern states are all public-domain states east of the Mississippi River, plus all states on the river's west bank (Louisiana to Minnesota). Each Western state usually has its own office with the exceptions that Washington is with the Portland, Oregon, office and the Great Plains states are placed under adjoining states farther west. The local land office and the GLO headquarters made duplicate tract and plat books, so the researcher often has a choice of several repositories for microfilm or original records. (See summary at the end of this chapter.)

Each step of the process from survey to patent has left a record potentially helpful to the genealogist:

Survey Field Notes. The surveyor general's records for a state may be in that state's land office (most common), the state archives, or the appropriate regional federal archives. Surveys have little information directly usable by genealogists; but for ancestors on the land prior to the survey, the surveyor's field notes may supply background descriptions of the area and sometimes specific, crude drawings of homes and outbuildings on the property.

Tract Books. In the absence of a precise legal description, the tract books can be consulted for entrymen in a township. These books have been microfilmed and the appropriate Eastern or Western states offices should have a set for their region. Some state archives, regional archives, or other local research libraries may also have microfilms. At present, the tract books are the best index to claimants and patentees. (See Figure 7-3.)

Township Plats. After many years of being written on and over, the plats are often rather illegible, and the tract books are a better finding tool for the legal description. The plats have been microfilmed and are usually deposited in the same locations as the tract books. (See Figure 7-4.)

Patents. The originals for the whole public domain are in the Eastern States Office, recorded in chronological order by state and thereunder by land district up to 30 June 1908. They lack indexes but have been microfilmed, and the Western states patents have been mounted, one patent per IBM card (aperture card), allowing them to be sorted into township and range order for ease of location. Patents should be obtained from the appropriate BLM local office. (See summary at the end of chapter.)

Land-Entry Case Files. The Washington National Records Center in Suitland, Maryland (mailing address: Eighth and Pennsylvania Avenue, N.W., Washington, DC 20408), holds all the case files except for some cancelled files never sent to GLO headquarters. These files contain such things as the entryman's declaration of intent, supporting documents, witness testimonies, bounty-land warrants (if used in lieu of cash), and naturalization papers. No copy of the patent is in the file except under unusual circumstances such as inability to deliver the patent to the patentee. The files are arranged by acts, state, land district, and thereunder numerically. The tract book or patent should supply the necessary information, but the Suitland archives does not have either, so the information must accompany the request for the case file. The case

Figure 7-3. Typical Page from a General Land Office Tract Book. Courtesy of the Bureau of Land Management.

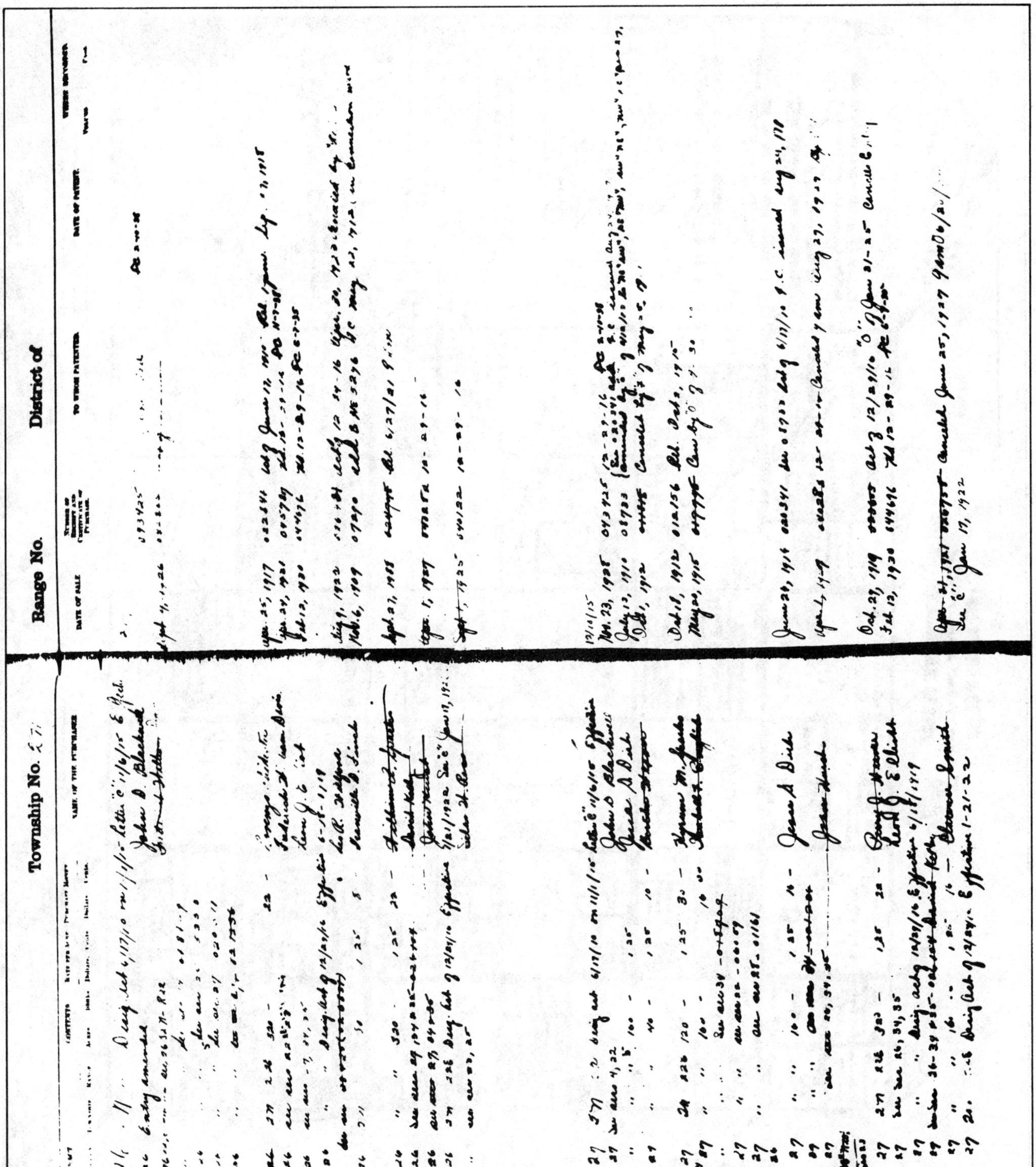

Township No. Range No. District of

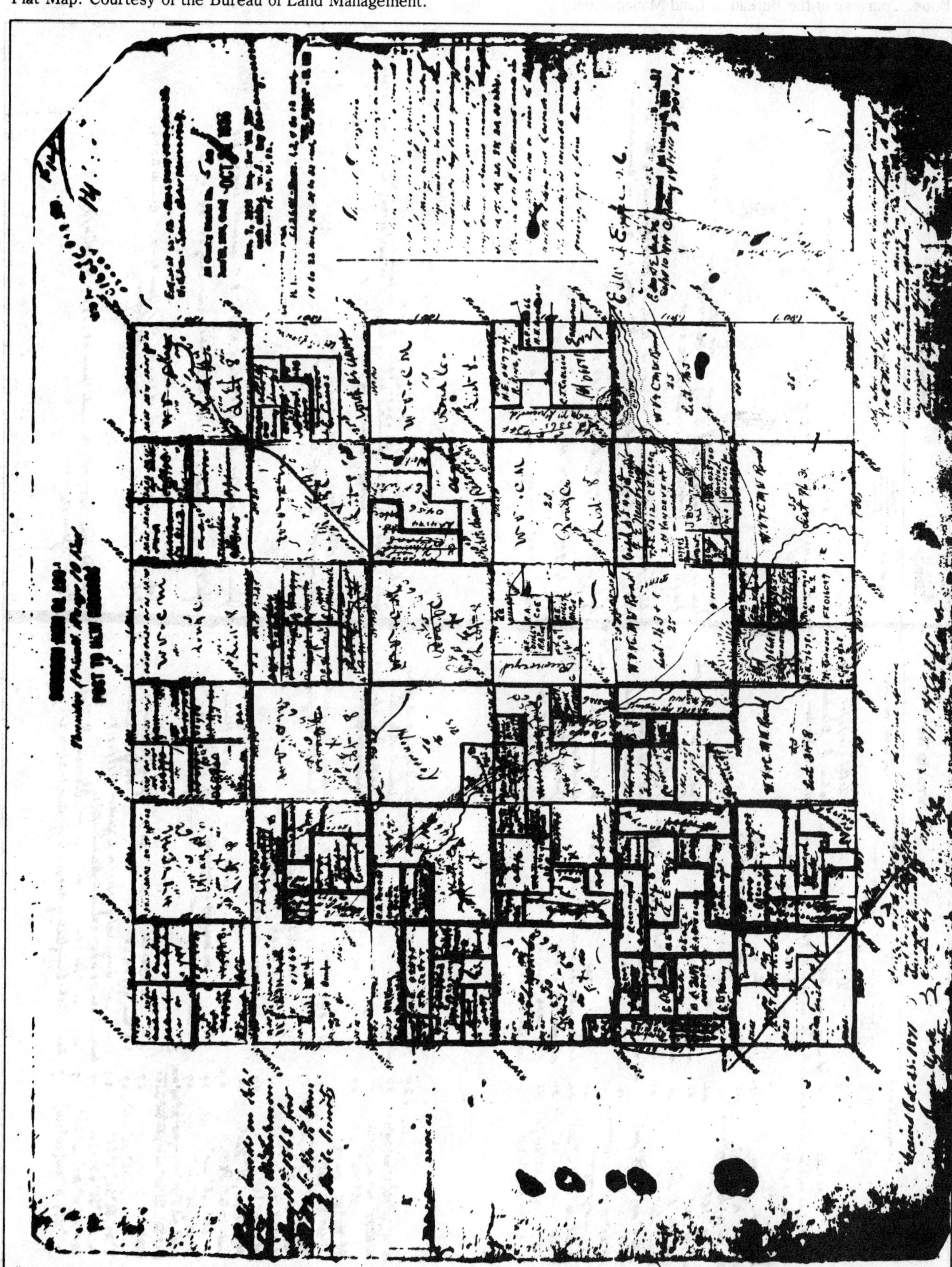

Figure 7-4. Typical Page from a General Land Office Township Plat Map. Courtesy of the Bureau of Land Management.

files are briefly described in Harry P. Yoshpe and Philip P. Brower, *Preliminary Inventory of the Land-Entry Papers of the General Land Office* (Washington, D.C.: National Archives, 1949).

The legal description is the key to finding a patent and case file except for post-30 June 1908 records and for the seven states listed above as indexed for pre-1 July 1908. The BLM state offices will do research by the quarter hour pre-paid, but genealogists may find this does not work well for fishing expeditions. The cost is too high, and genealogists usually want the names of the kin and in-laws living in the ancestor's neighborhood and cannot usually afford to send all the possible names. Therefore, try to search the tract books yourself at a convenient repository or use a private agent, first confirming where the tract books are in original and/or microfilm. Microfilm copies of the tract books are increasingly available at nearby research libraries.

Two other ways to obtain the legal description may be even easier: (1) a reference in the county deeds either recording the original patent or making reference to the tract in a deed, and (2) the legal description calculated from a historical atlas. These historical atlases are often called plat books, since they featured land ownership plat maps. Some good discussions concerning these atlases are: Richard W. Stephenson, *Land Ownership Maps* (Washington, D.C.: Library of Congress, 1967); Library of Congress, *List of Geographical Atlases in the Library of Congress*, 8 vols. (Washington, D.C.: Library of Congress, 1909-74); Michael J. Fox, "The Map Collection," in James P. Danky, ed., *Genealogical Research: An Introduction to the Resources of the State Historical Society of Wisconsin*, (Madison: State Historical Society of Wisconsin, 1979). Historical atlases—and subscription county histories, for that matter—were a Midwestern phenomenon which makes especially valuable the Newberry Library, *Checklist of Printed Maps of the Middle West to 1900*, 11 vols. (Boston: G. K. Hall, 1980), which lists all known pre-1900 plat maps and plat books for the eleven states of Indiana, Illinois, Iowa, Kansas, Michigan, Missouri, Nebraska, North Dakota, Ohio, South Dakota, and Wisconsin.

For the early years, the patent references may be in Clifford Neal Smith, *Federal Land Series*, 4 vols. to date (Chicago: American Library Association, 1972-in progress). Among the records he lists are the outgoing correspondence of the GLO and its predecessor office, which include the cover letters to transmitted patents as found on National Archives microfilm M25. Volumes 1 and 3 bring this correspondence down to August 1814.

From 1830 to 1934, the government dissolved many Indian reservations by first allotting each Indian a tract of land, then selling the remainder. The records of such allotments are voluminous, and many have been filmed as Bureau of Indian Affairs agency records. For instance, the records of the Winnebago Agency, Nebraska, are in the Kansas City federal archives and include land sales 1902-10, Santee acknowledgments of allotments 1885, lists of Ponca and Santee tribe members never receiving allotments 1936-41, etc.

The problem of settlers claiming land before the surveyors arrived was a very pressing one which Congress attempted to solve by preemption rights. That this was not a complete solution is shown by the existence of claims clubs, which were private associations sworn to enforce their members' claims when local land was offered for sale or homesteading. Often armed and intimidating, members would attend land office auctions as a group to convince nonmembers not to enter lands the members claimed. Such clubs were often quite formal in organization and kept records, some of which have survived. Claims clubs may be more interesting for historians than for genealogists but are definitely worth searching where they exist. Claims clubs were especially numerous and active in Iowa and Minnesota and the adjoining states to the west.

Such extralegal policing of land claims existed wherever the federal government's land title system came later than the settlers. The mining camp law of the California Gold Rush is an obvious instance of trying to avoid the violence of claim-jumping. In Utah, the settlers arrived twenty-two years before the land office and were openly worried about their legal position. Brigham Young once threatened, "If they jump my claim here, I shall be very apt to give them a preemption right that will last them to the last resurrection."[13]

State land offices of the public domain states will not be described here. These states received title to large acreage from the federal government and in turn sold or leased it to individuals. These records are in state land offices and archives. If you suspect that your ancestor had land dealings with a state, you can write either the state archives or the state secretary of state's office and ask where the records are. For many states, they are still held by the equivalent of a state land commissioner.

Private Land Claims

There was a special type of federal land grant called the private land claim, wherein the American government recognized as valid certain land grants made by the earlier French, Spanish, and British governments in areas acquired by the United States after the Revolution. These areas were the Old Northwest north of the Ohio River, the Gulf States from Florida to Louisiana, the tier of states on the west bank of the Mississippi, and the Spanish Southwest from New Mexico to California but not including Texas.

Sometimes the foreign legal titles were quite old and meticulously documented; often they were vague claims without clear bounds. Near villages it was common to find communal fields divided into long, individually owned arable strips surrounded by a communally maintained fence. Also characteristic, though not universal, were the "long lots," narrow adjoining tracts each a few hundred feet wide along a road or river, and each running far back into the woods or prairie—sometimes a mile or more. The French and Spanish authorities also made larger grants, such as the square leagues common in Texas and the rancheros in California. Barring the usual losses, the Spanish and French administrations usually kept adequate records, and land titles were recorded and preserved. The Texas General Land Office today has a series of sixty-nine volumes of Spanish and Mexican records. (See Chapter 18 for Hispanic records.) The Spanish land system is discussed in detail for Texas, New Mexico (with Colorado), Arizona, and California in Henry Putney Beers, *Spanish & Mexican Records of the American Southwest: A Bibliographical Guide to Archive and Manuscript Sources* (Tucson: University of Arizona Press and the Tucson Corral of the Westerners, 1979), pp. 44-60, 141-56, 247-68, 328-39.

When the United States government assumed control of areas containing Spanish and French grants, it had to create private land claims commissions to separate the authentic and legal titles from the fraudulent and dubious. (It is said that 900 Kaskaskia, Illinois, claims were perjured.[14]) By international law, the new government was obliged to recognize the valid property titles of the previous regime.

The private land claims ruled valid by the claims commissions of the United States state and federal courts are first-title deeds surveyed outside the regular federal system of townships and ranges. For example, on Map 7-3, a survey of Vincennes, Indiana, the federal survey lines stop at the irregular lots and tracts of the private land claims of the old French outpost called Vincennes Common. Even today, the legal titles run back to the confirmed first-title patents of the Vincennes private claims validated by the governor of the Northwest Territory, as directed by a Congressional Resolution of 1788. The legal description of this land is not in terms of sections, townships, and ranges, but in terms of the lot numbers the governor assigned to the validated and surveyed private land claims at Vincennes. The general system of private land claims, however, did not always run smoothly. Some perfectly good pre-American titles were not presented to claims commissions, engendering litigation much later.

"Private land claims" can also refer to the claims directly presented to Congress for private relief. These papers could be

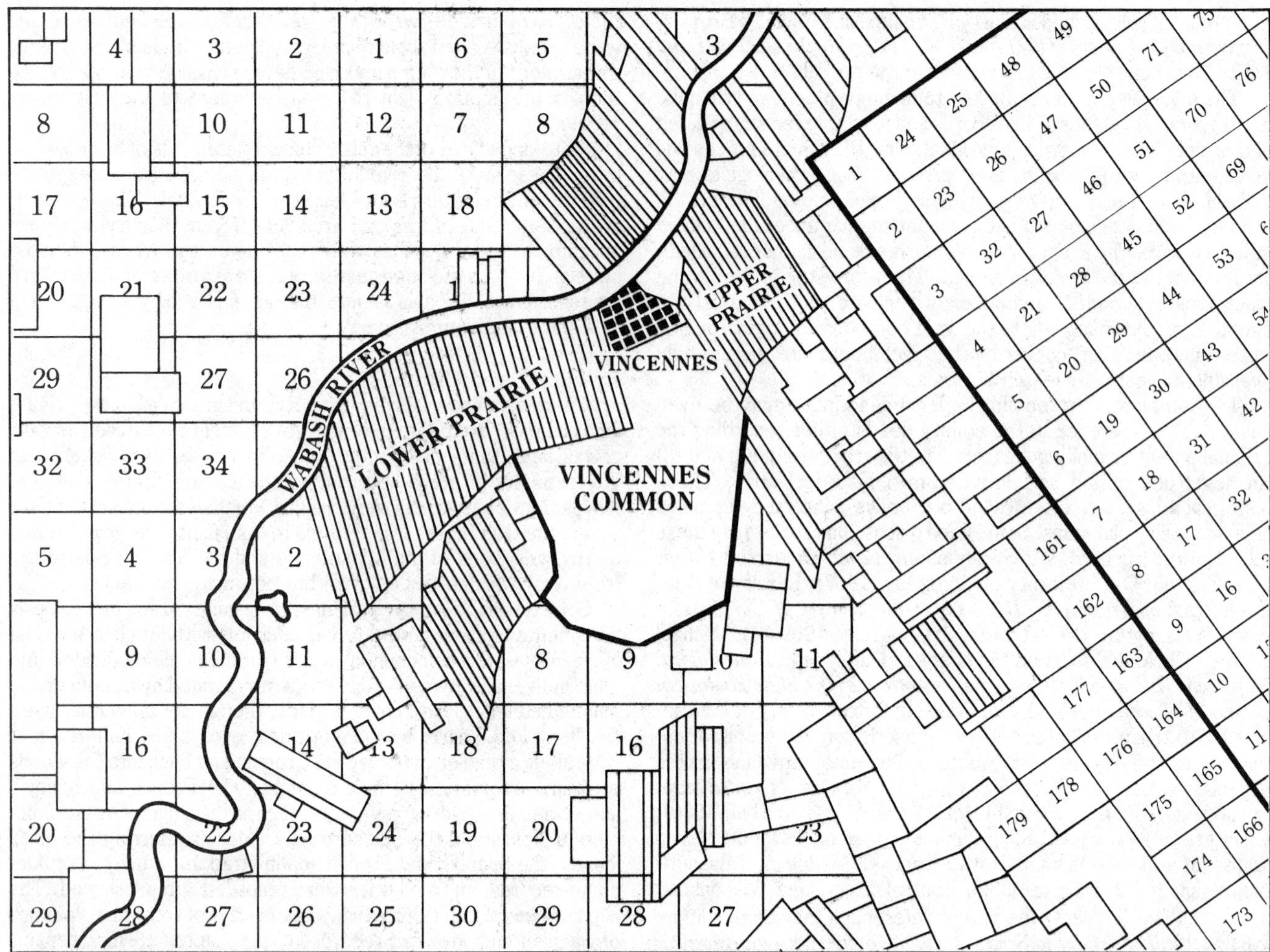

Map 7-3. Vincennes, Indiana. Private land claims surveyed within the federal township and range system. Adapted from Leonard Lux, *The Vincennes Donation Lands* (Indianapolis: Indiana Historical Society, 1949), map in pocket.

in different archives, depending on the administrative route taken. Claims to 1837 are recorded in U.S. Congress, *The American State Papers, Public Lands* (Washington, D.C.: Gales and Seaton, 1832-61) and are indexed in Phillip W. McMullin, *Grassroots in America* (Salt Lake City: Gendex, 1972). The National Archives has Congressional records, case files, and plat maps of private claims. Its *Guide to Genealogical Research in the National Archives* (1982), says on page 222:

> Originals of the committee reports to Congress on private land claims are among Records of the U. S. Senate, Record Group 46, and Records of the U. S. House of Representatives, Record Group 233. They are filed by Congress, thereunder by name of committee, and thereunder chronologically.
>
> Committee reports on individual land claims considered from 1826 to 1876 by the two congressional committees on private land claims are collected and published in *Reports of the Committees on Private Land Claims of the Senate and House of Representatives*, 2 volumes (45th Cong., 3d sess. Misc. Doc. 81, serial 1836). Each volume is indexed by name of claimant or subject, but many names were omitted. There is also an "Index to Reports of Committee on Private Land Claims, House of Representatives" on pages 5-20 of *House Index to Committee Reports* by T. H. McKee (Y1.3:C73/2). The Congressional Serial Set provides digested summaries and alphabetical lists of private claims presented to the U. S. Congress from the 1st to 51st Congress (1789-1891).

The *Guide*'s Table 25 shows which Congressional documents list private claims brought before Congress. Major university libraries and other large research libraries are usually repositories for such government documents, since the early publications have been filmed.

Private land claims are also found in various court records, since disapproved claims could be taken to court. In fact, Congress, in abolishing particular claims commissions, routinely authorized the holders of unsettled claims to prosecute their cases through the courts.

For further reading, see Paul W. Gates, *History of Public Land Law Development* (Washington, D.C.: Public Land Law Review Commission, 1968), pp. 87-119; his "Private Land Claims in the South," *Journal of Southern History* 22 (1956): 183-204; Louis Pelzer, "The Private Land Claims of the Old Northwest Territory," *Iowa Journal of History and Politics* 12 (1914): 363-93; T. P. Martin, "The Confirmation of French and Spanish Land Titles in the Louisana Purchase" (M.A. thesis, University of California, Berkeley, 1914); Lemont K. Richardson, "Private Land Claims in Missouri," *Missouri Historical Review* 50 (1955-56): 132-44, 271-86, 387-99; Clark S. Knowlton, ed., "Spanish and Mexican Land Grants in the Southwest: A Symposium," *Social Science Journal* 13 (Oct. 1976): 1-63.

Military Bounty Land

Granting military bounty land in the United States to encourage enlistments or reward previous service began in colonial times, but its legislative heyday was 1788-1855, though claims were still dribbling into the federal government in the 1960s. Genealogists find bounty-land records especially attractive because they serve the dual role of locating persons in time and place and of proving military service. Applications sometimes contain a wealth of information, especially when heirs claimed lands.

Colonial legislatures gave land for military service, such as in the Narragansett campaign of King Philip's War, 1675-76, but these were mostly private acts passed to reward meritorious service to the colony. In 1701, Virginia passed an act promising 200 acres free of quitrents for twenty years to those who would make armed settlements on the Indian frontier. The Crown's Proclamation of 1763 ordered the colonies to give bounty land for service in the French and Indian War to "reduced" (indigent) officers and to British Army privates mustered out in the colonies who intended to remain there. This did not include militia units. In 1776, Congress promised Hessian deserters fifty acres but had few takers. Also in 1776, the Congress promised bounty land to soldiers of the continental line, with privates and noncommissioned officers to get 100 acres, captains 300 acres, and other ranks various amounts. States that likewise promised, or afterwards gave, bounty lands were Massachusetts (with Maine), New York, Pennsylvania, Maryland, Virginia, the Carolinas, and Georgia. The states not giving Revolutionary bounty lands were New Hampshire, Rhode Island, Connecticut, New Jersey, and Delaware.

North Carolina was the most generous with its 640 acres (a square mile) to a private in the continental line. Maryland gave the smallest amount with fifty acres to a private, but Maryland also had very little western land to give. Map 7-4 and Table 7-1 show the locations of the military reserves and the acreage for each rank for each state and the federal government. Massachusetts grants were in Maine, but in no specific reserve; privates who got a 100-acre warrant from the federal government were not eligible for the state's. Soldiers of the continental line in other states could take both the federal and their state land bounties. (See the state summaries at the end of this chapter for brief references to bounty-land records. For Massachusetts, see Maine.) Paul Gates's 1968 *History of Public Land Law Development* discusses aspects of various state grants. He says, without elaborating, that Connecticut gave bounty land; but this seems to refer to the Fire Lands in Ohio granted to individuals burned out in the Revolution rather than to grants to soldiers.[15] Virginia is discussed below because its bounty-land records are widely scattered, some in the National Archives.

Congress was slow to redeem its promise of land for its soldiers. In 1788, it directed that bounty-land warrants should start being issued to those applying. But the U.S. Military District in Ohio, the only federal lands where federal Revolutionary warrants could be used until 1830, did not open until 1796—a full fifteen years after Yorktown. A planned second federal reserve at the south end of Illinois was not created; instead, the district in Ohio was enlarged. The Ohio Company and John Cleves Symmes in 1787 and 1788 had purchased millions of Ohio acres on credit from Congress and were permitted to pay one-seventh of the price in federal bounty-land warrants. Therefore, land offices of the two speculations accepted some federal warrants, the earliest locales where they could be used. Congress also created three military reserves for veterans of the War of 1812, but there were no federal reserves after these three in Illinois, Arkansas, and Missouri. Warrants usable in the Virginia and United States military districts in Ohio were made redeemable by scrip acts in 1830 and 1832 respectively, in any GLO land offices in Ohio, Indiana, and Illinois. In 1842, all federal bounty-land warrants were made good for purchases at any GLO land office.

The 1788 act stipulated that warrants were assignable, meaning the soldier could sell his warrant and not wait to take the land. This created an instant market in bounty warrants and allowed land speculators to accumulate large quantities of warrants and land. Paul Gates shows that fewer than one soldier (or his heirs) in ten got land by using his warrant under any federal bounty-land act. Since few soldiers actually used their warrants to patent land, patents and land-entry case files are much less valuable than the warrants and the warrant applications in locating a soldier's military service. Most soldiers sold their rights, using the back of the warrant to assign it to the buyer, who might in turn assign the warrant to another buyer. Sometimes the assignment left the buyer's name blank, to be filled in by the last purchaser. The warrant certificates issued to Mexican War veterans were folios, with the insides and back unprinted so they could be used for assignments.

The warrant market was big business, especially when warrants were no longer restricted to military reserve lands. Major brokerage firms dealt extensively in warrants, buying in the Eastern states and selling to Western land brokers and settlers. Financial newspapers in the boom years of the 1850s frequently carried price quotations. The government set a price ceiling from 1820 by charging a flat $1.25 per acre for most of its lands. The average market price peaked at about $1.20 an acre in 1854-55 for 160-acre warrants, just before the market was flooded by the act of 1855.[16] More warrants were used in Iowa than any other state, and it is estimated that half of Iowa was purchased with bounty-land warrants.

The federal government gave no bounty land for service after 1855, but Union veterans received special homestead rights: in 1870, the right to claim 160 acres within railroad grant areas (other homesteaders got only 80) and in 1872, the right to deduct their length of war service from the five-year residency needed to prove a homestead.

To get a federal bounty-land warrant it was necessary, under any act from 1788 to 1855, for the soldier or heirs to apply. The warrant applications are in Record Group 15 in the Military Service Records section in the downtown Washington building of the National Archives. The surrendered warrants (those used to obtain land) are in land-entry case files of the patentees in Record Group 49 in the Washington National Records Center, Suitland, Maryland. The case file categories are briefly described in Harry P. Yoshpe and Philip P. Brower, *Preliminary Inventory of the Land-Entry Papers of the General Land Office* (Washington, D.C.: National Archives, 1949), pp. 7-9, called Inventory No. 22 for short. The patents, obtained by using land warrants, were like any other GLO patents. The official copies are in the Eastern States Office of the Bureau of Land Management in Alexandria, Virginia. In seeking the various records related to a federal bounty-land warrant, the researcher should try to learn the warrant number, the acreage claimed, and the act used, e.g., warrant #8256, forty acres, act of 1852. This could be unnecessary information since the National Archives may handle the searching, but having this information in full or part allows for more precise requests, thereby increasing the chances of success. The best source is the bounty-land application files.

The following summary of the various warrant acts comes from Inventory No. 22, to which explanatory remarks are added. The number of warrants issued gives the researcher an idea of how many soldiers or their heirs applied under each act. Reference citations are to the respective acts of Congress. Citation 2 *Stat.* 236 means volume 2 of *U.S. Statutes at Large*, p. 236. M804 means National Archives microfilm publication M804.

1. ***Revolutionary War Warrants in the U. S. Military District in Ohio.***

9 July 1788	Continental Congress *Journals* 34:307	#1-14220
16 March 1803	2 *Stat.* 236	1-272
15 April 1806	2 *Stat.* 378	273-2500

Initially these assignable warrants were redeemable only for land in the U.S. Military District in Ohio. Soldiers of the continental line from any state received 100 acres (privates and NCOs), 150 (ensigns), 200 (lieutenants), 300 (captains), 400 (majors), 450 (lieutenant colonels), 500 (colonels), 850 (brigadier generals), and 1,100 (major generals). The initial minimum grants in the district were for quarter townships of the five-mile dimensions, that is,

Map 7-4. Federal and State Military Bounty Land Reserves for Veterans of the Revolutionary War and the War of 1812.

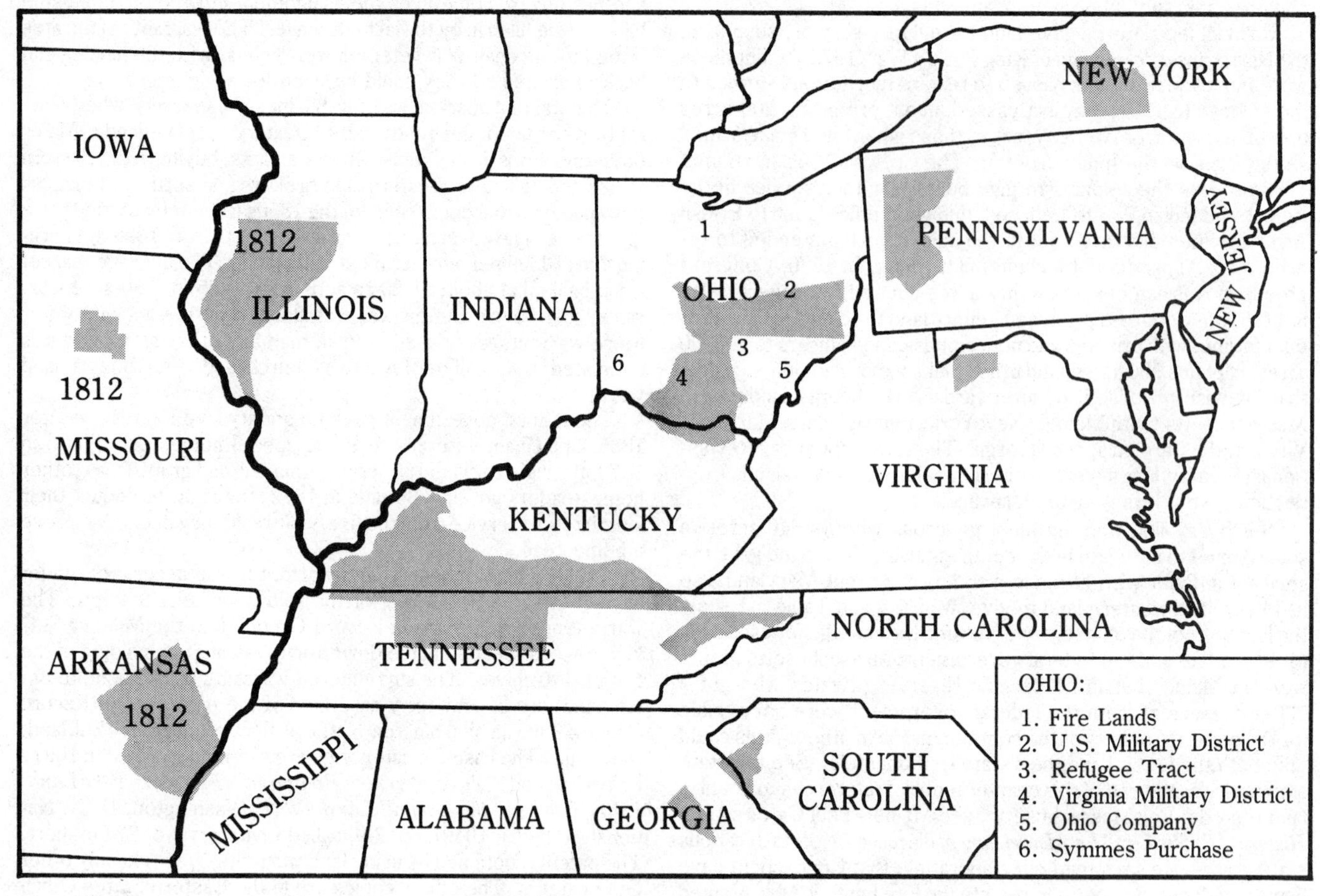

Table 7-1

Federal and State Bounty—Land Acreage, Revolutionary War

Rank	*U.S.*	*Georgia*[1]	*Maryland*	*Massachusetts*[2]	*New York*[3]		*North Carolina*	*Pennsylvania*	*South Carolina*	*Virginia*[5]
Major General	1,100	–	50	100	5,500	–	25,000[4]	2,000	100	15,000
Brigadier General	850	1,955	50	100	4,250	–	12,000	1,500	100	10,000
Colonel	500	1,150	50	100	2,500	2,000	7,200	1,000	100	6,667
Lieutenant Colonel	450	1,035	50	100	2,250	2,000	5,760	800	100	6,000
Major	400	920	50	100	2,000	2,000	4,800	600	100	5,333
Captain	300	575-690	50	100	1,500	1,500	3,840	500	100	4,000
Lieutenant	200	460	50	100	1,000	1,000	2,560	400	100	2,666
Ensign	150	460	50	100	1,000	1,000	2,560	300	100	2,666
Non-commissioned Officer	100	345	50	100	500	500	1,000	250	100	200-400
Private	100	230-287½	50	100	500	500	640	200	100	100-300

1. Georgia sometimes distinguished between the same rank in the state militia and the continental (federal) line. The private in the continental line received less than in the militia, but a captain in the continental line got the larger share. Refugees from Georgia who were forced to flee their homes and then joined the North or South Carolina militia received far greater proportional grants: privates 575, sergeants 632½, lieutenants 747½, and captains 977½ acres. The Georgia militia disintegrated under the British occupation, so Georgia rewarded those citizens who fought in neighboring states.

2. Massachusetts gave 100 acres only to those not receiving the 100-acre federal grant.

3. The first column shows the grant to all under the Resolution of 1783. The second column contains the grants to the two regiments under the Act of 1781.

4. Specific grant to General Nathanael Greene.

5. Privates and non-commissioned officers enlisting for three years were given twice as much as those enlisting for shorter periods. This was later increased to 300 acres for all privates remaining till the end of the war. An additional increase of fifty acres was given for each year's service over six. These last grants were made retroactive.

Paul V. Lutz, "Land Grants for Service in the Revolution," *New-York Historical Society Quarterly* 48 (1964): 230. Used with permission.

five miles to a side or 16,000 acres, thereby requiring warrantees to band together through an agent to reach 4,000 acres or sell out to get some value from their warrants. By 1800, lots down to 100 acres were available. In 1832, all entries in the district were ended, and those still holding warrants were allowed to trade them for scrip negotiable at GLO land offices in Ohio, Indiana, and Illinois. From 1842, such scrip was accepted at any GLO land office.

Many warrant application files for the 1788 act are destroyed. Where the warrantee's name is known, a substitute card was made with the note "no papers." These cards and the surviving application files are interfiled with the surviving Revolutionary pension files, all filmed on M804, "Revolutionary War Pension and Bounty-Land Warrant Application Files," in 2,670 rolls. This series is indexed for pensions and warrantees in National Genealogical Society, *Index of Revolutionary War Pension Applications in the National Archives* (Washington, D.C.: National Genealogical Society, 1976).

Congress, to aid soldiers who had not met the deadline of the 1788 act, passed a time extension in 1803 amended 1806. The warrants of these acts are numbered in one sequence. Nearly all surrendered warrants from numbers 1-6912 of the 1788 act were destroyed. Surviving surrendered warrants of the 1788, 1803, and 1806 acts are filed in land-entry case files and are filmed on M829, "U.S. Revolutionary War Bounty Land Warrants Used in the U.S. Military District of Ohio and Related Papers (Acts of 1788, 1803, 1806)" in sixteen rolls. Since patents were rarely placed in the case files, the U.S. Military District land-entry case files usually contain just the surrendered warrant. The files are filmed sequentially and missing warrants were either lost, misplaced, or never surrendered for land. The few surrendered for scrip under the 1832 and later acts are in that series, but cross-referenced on M829. On Roll 1 of M829 are two ledgers indexed in Smith's *Federal Land Series*, vol. 2, once used to record the issuance of warrants. Roll 1 of M829 also has indexes to the ledgers done and/or filmed by the National Archives. The pamphlet accompanying M829 describes these records and is available upon request from the National Archives.

2. War of 1812 Warrants in U.S. Military Districts in Illinois, Arkansas, and Missouri.

24 Dec. 1811	2 *Stat.* 669	#1-28085 for 160 acres
11 Jan. 1812	2 *Stat.* 672	
6 May 1812	2 *Stat.* 729	
27 July 1842	5 *Stat.* 497	
10 Dec. 1814	3 *Stat.* 147	1-1101 for 320 acres

The acts of 1811-12 promised 160 acres to privates and NCOs who enlisted in regiments raised by Congress and who served for five years, unless discharged sooner or killed. The 1814 act doubled the acreage for those who enlisted after 10 December 1814. Officers were given no bounty lands until the acts of 1850-55. The warrants were not legally assignable except by inheritance, and the GLO retained the warrant certificates, issuing the veteran a certificate of notification. These warrants were redeemable only in military reserves in Illinois, Arkansas, and Missouri until the act of 1842 made them redeemable at any GLO land office. The warrants became legally assignable in 1852.

These War of 1812 warrants, preserved mostly in bound volumes, are filmed on M848, "War of 1812 Military Bounty Land Warrants 1815-1858," in fourteen rolls. Patentees in the Arkansas and Missouri reserves are indexed on Roll 1, plus Illinois patentees with C and D surnames. The Illinois State Library's computer index to all federal patents in Illinois should include the military reserve. Since War of 1812 warrants were not legally assignable until 1852, the patent indexes should serve as indexes to prior warrantees, though Gates shows (pp. 263-70) that the land speculators got large parts of the reserves, presumably by having the patents processed in the names of the warrantees. This means many veterans patented land they probably never saw. The pamphlet accompanying M848 describes these records and is available upon request from the National Archives. Aside from these filmed warrants, there should also be unfilmed warrant application files and land-entry case files in Record Groups 15 and 49 respectively.

3. Applications for Bounty-land Scrip.

30 May 1830	4 *Stat.* 422	#1-1994
13 July 1832	4 *Stat.* 578	
2 March 1833	4 *Stat.* 665	1-225
3 March 1835	4 *Stat.* 770	1-970
31 Aug. 1852	10 *Stat.* 143	1-1689

The land available for patenting in the Virginia and U.S. military districts ran out long before all the outstanding warrants were redeemed, so Congress issued scrip for the remaining warrants. At first good only in GLO land offices in Ohio, Indiana, and Illinois, the scrip, printed in acreage denominations, was good at any GLO land office from 1842.

4. Mexican War Bounty-Land Warrants.

11 Feb. 1847	9 *Stat.* 125	1-7585 for 40 acres
		1-80689 for 160 acres

Congress, in the Mexican War, authorized ten regiments and offered privates and NCOs (but not officers) 160 acres for serving one year or more and 40 acres for serving less than a year. Alternately, the veteran could apply for $100 or $25 in scrip at 6 percent interest, acceptable for any payment due to the U.S. government. (This dollar scrip was different from the acreage scrip listed in entry 3 above.) There were no military districts created for Mexican War bounty land, the warrants being redeemable at any GLO land office. They were assignable. As usual, few warrantees or their heirs actually patented land using their warrants. The surrendered warrants are in the land-entry case files of the patentees. The best finding aid to Mexican War warrantees is their warrant application files.

5. The Acts of 1850-1855.

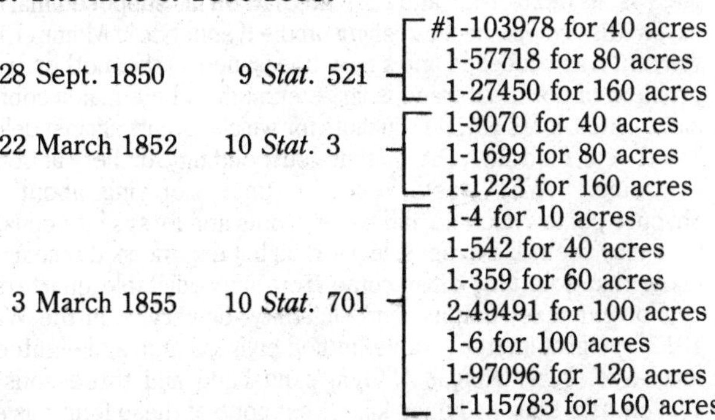

28 Sept. 1850	9 *Stat.* 521	#1-103978 for 40 acres
		1-57718 for 80 acres
		1-27450 for 160 acres
22 March 1852	10 *Stat.* 3	1-9070 for 40 acres
		1-1699 for 80 acres
		1-1223 for 160 acres
3 March 1855	10 *Stat.* 701	1-4 for 10 acres
		1-542 for 40 acres
		1-359 for 60 acres
		2-49491 for 100 acres
		1-6 for 100 acres
		1-97096 for 120 acres
		1-115783 for 160 acres

The acts of 1850-55 were not to encourage enlistments but to reward former service. The act of 1850 extended bounty land to officers and enlisted men who had not previously received land and who had served in any war since 1790, including the Indian wars. Nine months' service brought 160 acres, four months' service 80 acres, and one month's service 40 acres. Since there was initial confusion over whether the act made warrants assignable, the GLO commissioner later ruled that it did not. The act of 1852 explicitly made them assignable and extended the 1850 act to militiamen who served after 1812.

The 1855 act extended bounty-land privileges even further by making 160 acres the minimum entitlement and reducing service to fourteen days or even less. Those who traveled 1,200 miles in service were eligible even if they served less time. A veteran or his heirs who had previously received fewer than 160 acres could apply for the balance. Eligibility was extended to chaplains, wagon masters, militia rangers, and volunteers of certain campaigns such as Kings Mountain, the Nickojack Campaign in Tennessee, and the Cook County volunteers in the Black Hawk War. An act of 14 May 1856 extended the 1855 benefits to naval veterans and any Revolutionary service.

Using these figures as given by Inventory No. 22 and omitting scrip because it redeemed already issued warrants, the warrant totals issued by these categories of acts are:

Revolutionary War	16,720
War of 1812	29,186
Mexican War	88,274
Acts of 1850-55	464,419
Total	598,599

Considering that 77.6 percent of these bounty-land warrants are in the miscellaneous categories of the 1850-55 acts and that each warrant should have an application file with the veteran's documentation of service or kin documenting their relationship to him, how do genealogists locate what they need?

National Archives Trust Fund (NATF) Form 80 should be used to request pre-World War I pension and military service records and pre-1856 bounty-land warrant application files. It costs $5 prepaid (in 1983) for each category ($15 for all three) and is a bargain. If the requester has: (1) such definite information as service in a specific war or unit, (2) a soldier of uncommon name, or (3) extensive background information on the person sought, there should be few unanticipated problems. But many requests are fishing expeditions with little background identification on men with ordinary names, or the genealogist attempts to compile branches of a large family by plowing page-by-page through collections. It is difficult to see how these problems can be solved comprehensively by mail with much confidence. In such cases, a personal search or the services of an agent already in Washington, D.C., should be considered.

A special problem is fraudulent warrant applications, especially where heirs claim a soldier's rights. Mrs. Ellen Reed and her two children received bounty-land warrant #61,656 in 1849 for the Mexican War service of Richard Reed, private, Company D, First U.S. Artillery Regiment. Two months later, Richard's mother applied as his next-of-kin and showed that, on his supposed marriage day in Mississippi, he was fishing on the Kennebec in Maine. Ellen's warrant was cancelled and a new one issued to the mother.[17] This problem of potential fraud is large enough to be a major contaminant. Gates notes 59,190 warrants for which caveats against delivery had been filed by 1856, thus suspending further action on patenting.[18] Why waste research time worrying about such obscure points? Double and triple proofs and forays into collateral lines may seem like expensive overkill; but experienced researchers know that solutions often come from unpredictable quarters.

For example, bounty-land eligibility for service in the War of 1812 was first limited to able-bodied enlisted men age eighteen to forty-five. Mrs. Abigail O'Flyng's husband and three sons had served, two sons had been killed, yet none of these four was eligible for bounty land. Her husband had been over forty-five, one son was under eighteen, and the two dead sons had been promoted to officers just before they died. The Abigail O'Flyng Act of 1816 ended the age restrictions and allowed enlisted men promoted to officers to receive land. Also, by private act of Congress, her husband received 480 acres, the youngest son 160 acres, and the heirs of the dead sons their half pay for five years.[19]

This case tests a genealogist's expertise. Does he/she understand the scope and intent of the record group searched? Nearly all government records – federal, state, and local – are created as a result of statutes which should be read. Would a check of bounty-land applications filed have "proved" that none of the four O'Flyng men served in the war? Have offbeat records such as private acts of Congress been searched? Has the researcher screened other records many years later in which some legal actions resurface?

This last question is not rhetorical. Colonel Robert Porterfield was killed in the Revolution. His son Robert received from Congress a warrant for "about 6,000 acres." But the land was in Kentucky and from superior conflicting claims was lost. In 1860, Congress authorized scrip for Robert's heirs, to whom 153 warrants for forty acres each were issued. In 1900, twenty-one of these warrants were still outstanding and unlocated for land given on Revolutionary War service.[20]

For background on bounty lands, see National Archives, *Guide to Genealogical Research in the National Archives* (Washington, D.C.: National Archives and Records Service, 1982), pp. 133-39; Rudolf Freund, "Military Bounty Land and the Origins of the Public Domain," *Agricultural History* 20 (1946): 8-18; Gates's "Military Bounty Land Policies," in his *History of Public Land Law Development* (New York: Public Land Law Review Commission, 1968), pp. 249-84; C. Lichtenberg, "Beginnings of the United States Military Land Bounty Policy, 1637-1812" (M.A. thesis, University of Wisconsin, 1945); Paul V. Lutz, "Land Grants for Service in the Revolution," *New-York Historical Society Quarterly* 48 (1964): 221-35; Jean H. Vivian, "Military Land Bounties During the Revolutionary and Confederation Periods," *Maryland Historical Magazine* 61 (1966): 231-56; A. M. Lingegren, "The History of the Land Bonus of the War of 1812" (M.A. thesis, University of Wisconsin, 1922); James W. Oberly, "Military Bounty Land Warrants of the Mexican War," *Prologue* 14 (1982): 25-34.

Virginia Military District

An extraordinary flood of Revolutionary bounty-land warrants poured from Richmond, partly because Virginia had the largest state population and partly because it granted warrants not only to its continental line but to its state line as well. The distinction rests on who paid the troops, Congress or Virginia.

The first military reserve was created south of Green River in Kentucky and subsequently expanded west of the Tennessee. There were no bounty lands within present-day Virginia or West Virginia. In 1784, Virginia ceded its claim to the area north of the Ohio River, reserving the four million acres between the Scioto and Little Miami rivers for redemption of its bounty-land warrants. This Virginia Military District in Ohio was federal land whose first-title land grants were reserved solely for the Virginia warrants of veterans of the continental line. A series of ever more liberal acts broadened where warrants could be used and by whom until in 1852 Congress agreed that all Virginia Revolutionary warrants could be exchanged for scrip accepted at any GLO land office. Large numbers of these assignable warrants were sold; an estimated one-quarter of the Virginia Military District was acquired by twenty-five men.[21]

The paperwork flow was: (1) warrant application to Richmond, (2) warrant issued to warrantee, (3) selection of desired land in Kentucky or Ohio reserves and survey by official surveyor, (4) paperwork for Kentucky lands to the Virginia Land Office or from 1792, the Kentucky Land Office, or the federal capital for Ohio lands, and (5) patent for Kentucky land sent to patentee or federal patent sent to Richmond for relay to Ohio patentee.[22]

Thus, there should be four major repositories today for Virginia bounty-land records. There are, however, actually six. The land offices of Virginia, Kentucky, and Ohio are described in the state summaries at the end of this chapter. The microfilmed federal patents are in the BLM Eastern States Office in Alexandria, Virginia. The surrendered warrants are in Record Group 49 at the Washington National Records Center in Suitland, Maryland. The sixth major collection is the Illinois Historical Survey Collection in the University of Illinois Library, Urbana-Champaign, which has the papers of Richard Clough Anderson, surveyor of the Virginia Military District in Ohio. Clifford Neal Smith has brought this collection to the attention of a wide audience by his indexes in the *Federal Land Series*, especially volume 4, which is devoted to the district. He estimates that "about 64 percent of Virginia's obligations to its veterans were satisfied by the land grants in the Virginia Military District of Ohio."[23]

See also Clifford Neal Smith, "Virginia Land Grants in Kentucky and Ohio, 1784-1799," *National Genealogical Society Quarterly* 61 (1973): 16-27; John Salmon, "Revolutionary War Records in the Archives & Records Division of the Virginia State Library," *Genealogy*, no. 70 (July 1982): 2-10; Gaius Marcus Brumbaugh, *Revolutionary War Records. . . Virginia Army and Navy Forces with Bounty Land Warrants for Virginia Military Scrip; from Federal and State Archives* (Washington, D.C.: n.p., 1936); Willard Rouse Jillson, *Old Kentucky Entries and Deeds: A Complete Index to All of the Earliest Land Entries, Military Warrants, Deeds and Wills of the Commonwealth of Kentucky,* Filson Club Publication No. 34 (Louisville: Filson Club, 1926).

Loyalist Lands

The confiscation of Loyalist lands in the Revolution – what might be called "negative bounty land" – is a subject that deserves both extended research and a bibliographical source essay. What it receives here are brief comments.

Since the British government made a commendable effort to compensate Loyalist losses, the Loyalists had to list their lost property to claim that compensation. One of the best sources is Alexander Fraser, ed., *United Empire Loyalists Inquiry into the Losses and Services in Consequence of Their Loyalty. Evidence in the Canadian Claims*, 2 vols. (Toronto: The King's Printer, 1905), Second Report of the Bureau of Archives for the province of Ontario. From this excellent sourcebook comes the following example:

The claim (p. 293) of John Fowler, formerly of Stockbridge, Massachusetts, says he was a native of Guilford, Connecticut, lived in Stockbridge, fled to New York during the war and hired a farm on Long Island, was carried a prisoner to Stamford, Connecticut, and ultimately settled in Kingston, Ontario. "Produces deed dated 19th July, 1770, whereby Mark Hopkins in considn. of £30 lawful Conveys to Claimt. forty acres in Stockbridge. Says he purchased 35 acres adjoining, from his Br., in 1770 for about £25." And so on. "Produces a letter from his Father in Law saying that his Personal Property had been sold to the amount of £100 Lawful." Aside from separating the various John Fowlers, this record helps fill a page in the Fowler family genealogy.

Such claims name only a small percentage of Loyalists. Two New Jersey studies revealed that of 275 known Loyalists of Bergen County, only 29 claims could be found, while for the approximately 1,200 estates confiscated in New Jersey, there exist only 239 Loyalist claims.[24]

The official files of Loyalist claims are in the Public Record Office in London, partly summarized in Peter Wilson Coldham, *American Loyalist Claims: Abstracted from the Public Record Office, Audit Series 13, Bundles 1-35 & 37* (Washington, D.C.: National Genealogical Society, 1980). The manuscript sources are identified in Gregory Palmer, ed., *A Bibliography of Loyalist Source Material in the United States, Canada, and Great Britain* (Westport and London: Meckler Publishing and the American Antiquarian Society, 1982), a helpful book but one intended for experts. Another bibliography which is useful but which may be hard to find is Robert S. Allen, *Loyalist Literature: An Annotated Bibliographic Guide to the Writings on the Loyalists of the American Revolution* (Toronto and Charlettetown: Dundurn Press, 1982). There is no comprehensive bibliography to literature on confiscations of Loyalist estates. (See also Chapter 8, "Military Records."

One land record of potential help in identifying children is the land given in Canada and Nova Scotia to Loyalists under royal instructions of 1783, which promised 100 acres to heads of Loyalist families and fifty acres each to their children and to single men.

Taxes

Things taxed have included carriages and watches, windows and whiskey, land and slaves. Taxes on documents and tea helped start a war. Arkansas Territory's sudden tax on bounty lands in the 1820s was enacted and due before the news had time to reach the out-of-state owners, permitting the quick seizure and sale of "delinquent" lands. As this variety suggests, name lists of such taxes must be used with a cautious understanding of who should be on the list and who should not.

Colonial and antebellum counties and towns usually taxed free adult males a set, uniform amount called the poll (head, capitation) tax, which became due when a young man reached twenty-one (sixteen or eighteen years in some areas) and ceased to be due when a man reached some age such as fifty or sixty. Searching a series of such annual tax lists can catch sons coming of age. Sometimes the law made a father liable for a head tax for sons sixteen to twenty so that sons first move through the yearly tax lists as unnamed tallies under their father's name. The great failing of the system is that it does not work for women, who were not subject to such a poll tax but who might own and be taxed for land. North Carolina illustrates the variability of the poll tax ages. In colonial years, it set the white male poll at ages sixteen and upward, changed it to twenty-one and upward from the Revolution, exempted men over fifty from 1801, made it twenty-one to forty-four beginning in 1835, and from 1868 laid the poll tax on males between twenty-one and fifty.[25] The wary researcher must be aware of these shifting limits.

However, for all their limitations, poll tax lists can be combined with property tax lists as a substitute census. To identify clearly who owed what, clerks sometimes added useful descriptors. For example, the 1799 list for Warren County, Kentucky, has John Taylor Slick, John Taylor Cooksland, John Taylor gambler, John Taylor one eye, and John Taylor hatter.[26] The first two mean "on Salt Lick Creek" and "on land owned by Cook." A long series of such county tax lists can be crucial to identifying men with common names and showing when men entered and left the county, though lists often omit a man for a year or two when he is obviously still living on the same land. This means researchers should read at least eight years before and after a man first appears and disappears.

Names are often listed in initial order, meaning all surnames beginning with A are together but not alphabetically. Apparently clerks received tax lists from various justices of the peace, constables, or militia captains, and copied from each list first all the A surnames, then all the B surnames, etc. While some of the neighborhood proximities are lost, initial-order lists are easy to search for one surname. Researchers should always check the end of the county list where the clerk would add late, delinquent, and insolvent names.

Other typical omissions are children, slaves and indentured servants (except as unnamed but taxed property), landless men over the poll tax age, paupers, ministers, justices of the peace, militia officers, tax assessors, and men granted exemption for whatever reason. An Indiana statute of 1826 exempted "all persons who had served in the land or naval service of the United States, during the Revolutionary War, from the payment of a poll tax, and a tax upon personal property" if the veteran gave an affidavit to a justice of the peace.[27] There are also, inevitably, those who were overlooked.

Original lists as received by the clerk survive for 1771 Bute County, North Carolina, and have been compared to the final county-wide copy.[28] On the left are nine adjoining entries of a local list compared with the poll entries on the right of the final county list (in initial order on the original):

Local List	County List with Polls	
Joshua Taylor	not listed	
John Linch Jr.	John Lynch Jr.	1
John Faulcon, Henry Brown	John Falcon	2
John Baxter, John Weedon, Sharp Balthrop (& 1 sl.)	John Baxter	4
Rossen Allen, Drury Allen	Rossen Allan	2
Geo. Elliott Sr., Wm Steverson (& 7 sl.)	George Elliott	9
James Elliott, Thos. Rosser	James Elliott	2
Richd. Towns	Richard Town	1
David Towns, sons David & John	David Towns	3

Obviously, the final county list has significantly fewer names. It is surprising that so many of the hidden surnames differ from the head of the household.

Several reconstituted state "censuses" have been compiled from county tax lists such as for 1790 Kentucky and 1840 Texas "censuses." They can be a great time-saver in localizing a man's state residence, but calling these reconstitutions "censuses" runs counter to the need of researchers to understand the nature of their sources. The 1790 federal census attempted to record everyone under some head of household. The 1790 Kentucky tax lists did not. Thus, the 1790 reconstituted Kentucky census cannot completely replace the lost 1790 Kentucky census schedules.

One great advantage of the county tax lists is that many states also received and stored copies. Thus, when Buckingham County, Virginia, lost its records by fire, its main surviving record became the yearly tax lists in Richmond.

The quitrent was a land tax typical of colonies from New York south; New Englanders took pride in being free of this remnant of feudal dues. In English manorial society the land obligations due the manor, such as plowing and haying the lord's land, were commuted to an annual money payment. Upon payment, the obligations were "quit" for the year. Land patents in New York and colonies to the south stipulated a yearly quitrent that went either to the crown as in Virginia south of the Rappahannock River or to the proprietor as in Virginia in the Northern Neck. The Revolution generally abolished quitrents.

Broken runs of annual quitrent books survive, along with their relations the rent rolls, though no colony has complete yearly series. Locating surviving quitrents is not simple, especially since many were the private property of proprietors and thus lost during and after the Revolution. Significant numbers of landowners successfully avoided the lists, and there was great resistance to paying quitrents in general, especially for lands held for speculation and not farmed. Producing even approximately complete lists was often administratively impossible. One massive effort was made in Virginia in 1704 and provides a good but incomplete survey of surnames south of the Rappahannock River, the area north of the river being in the Northern Neck and its quitrents due not to Virginia but to the proprietary. The standard, though dated, general study is Beverley W. Bond, Jr., *The Quit-Rent System in the American Colonies* (New Haven: Yale University Press, 1919).

There have been three federal direct tax series that produced name lists, all to raise money for armies. In 1798, the French war scare led to a direct tax on real property and slaves (1 *Stat.* 580 and 597), which produced extensive name lists, though how complete and far down the economic scale is not clear. One local historian praises the comprehensiveness of this tax on dwelling houses: "In common with other towns, the Federal Direct Tax on Rehoboth [Massachusetts] lists the names of the owners and tenants of every dwelling house in the town, data which are found in no other record. . . . This 1798 dwelling house list, together with the census for 1800 . . . enables us to reconstruct a far more complete record for Rehoboth at the end of the eighteenth century than is possible in any other period of that century."[29]

Unfortunately, the 1798 direct tax has survived only in pieces. A janitor of the Boston Customs House used sections of the Massachusetts/Maine lists to fire his stoves.[30] Most surviving lists have been microfilmed but not in a single series. The known manuscripts, many very incomplete, follow. Addresses of state historical societies are in Appendix C:

Maine, New Hampshire, Massachusetts: New England Historic Genealogical Society
Vermont: none found
Rhode Island: Rhode Island Historical Society
Connecticut: Connecticut Historical Society
New York (vicinity of Clinton and Franklin counties): Vermont Historical Society
New Jersey: none found
Pennsylvania: National Archives (717 volumes filmed as M372)
Delaware: Historical Society of Delaware
Maryland and District of Columbia: Maryland Historical Society; Hall of Records Virginia/West Virginia: none found
Kentucky: none found
Tennessee: Tennessee State Library
North Carolina: none found
South Carolina: none found
Georgia (part of Burke County): Georgia State Archives

To raise money for the War of 1812, the federal government again resorted to a direct tax in 1814-16. Even fewer lists survive. The Connecticut Historical Society holds lists for 1814-16 "for many towns," and Hancock County, Maine, survives for 1815. The 1813 law directed that $3 million be collected and apportioned among the states by population. The state governments were allowed to pay the federal treasury the amount levied on their citizens (less 15 percent for saving the cost of collection) and in 1814 seven states did so, with four states doing the same in 1815 and 1816.[31] Perhaps this explains why few lists seem to be around. Few were made.

The greatest number of federal direct tax lists are those from the Civil War to as late as 1917, when the government levied income taxes, property taxes, and license fees. These taxes were directed more to wealth rather than the broader earlier taxes and therefore capture a smaller proportion of the adult male population; however, they do provide specific information on propertied individuals. The records surviving are massive. The National Archives is filming them, focusing primarily on 1862-66 lists and, as of 1982, had completed thirty-three states and the District of Columbia in 681 rolls. These microfilms are listed in the National Archives, *Guide to Genealogical Research in the National Archives* (1982), p. 247, which also lists some later schedules in its regional archives. As the Confederate states were conquered, the direct taxes were extended to them. Since many Southerners were unable to pay, the government sold much Southern land for taxes. In using the National Archives films of Civil War direct taxes, you should note that each state has a different microfilm publication number—M754 Alabama, M756 California, etc.—and therefore a separate pamphlet explaining each state's lists. These pamphlets are available from the National Archives upon request. (New York and New Jersey are filmed together as M603.)

For a detailed description of tax records and their direct application to genealogy see Arlene H. Eakle, *Tax Records: A Common Source With an Uncommon Value* (Salt Lake City: Family History World, 1978).

Use of Land Records

With some exceptions, American land law still reflects its English origins. The important exceptions are the French civil law in Louisiana, Spanish law in the Southwest, and Polynesian communal-use concepts in Hawaii. English property law, which means both land conveyance and inheritance law, was extremely complex and plagued by a nearly crushing mass of technicalities. This was especially true in the seventeenth and eighteenth centuries, when the United States was founded. The colonies lacked the judges, lawyers, law schools, and elaborate court system to implement English property law in all its complexity, but most of the basic concepts crossed the Atlantic and exist in the land records genealogists use.

One major distinction is between "real" and "personal" property, which arose in Norman England between property the courts could restore to a dispossessed owner and property for which the courts would grant compensation for losses. The distinction is conveniently—if only roughly—between land (and its "fixtures") and moveables. Since leases were deemed personal property and since deed registries record mostly real property, leases were normally not recorded. Hence, for reasons of early English law, tracing Americans who rented rather than bought farms can be very frustrating because their leases probably do not appear in the land records.

Another English concept is between freehold and copyhold, the first being for lands held in England by free men and the latter by villeins (i.e., peasants bound legally to the manor). The villein succeeded to the lands of his father upon payment of customary dues (fines), whereupon the record of such holdings was copied into the manor court roll, hence the name copyhold. In the American colonies such copyhold was never successfully established, since feudal and manorial structures did not exist in the colonies. The few instances where provincial proprietors tried to establish them, such as in Maryland and the Carolinas, were short-lived experiments in the face of so much unoccupied land surrounding these artificial manors. Thus, the American genealogist encounters freehold law that developed in contrast to a concept – copyhold – not normally met in American records. The one important remnant of feudalism that did gain a partial foothold in the colonies from New York to Georgia was the quitrent, which is explained in the section on taxes.

A third aspect of property law in England was the doctrine of estates, which assumed that all land in England was owned only by the crown and thus any subject held merely an "estate" in that land. Such holdings (tenures) could be with right to will or deed the land to another (fee simple), with right to a life interest that ended at the tenant's death (life estate), or with right for the land to pass inalienably to one's direct descendants so long as any existed (fee tail). This latter – "to X and the heirs of his body" – might be land entailed without a sex restriction or it might be entailed only to male heirs (tail male) or, rarely, only to female heirs (tail female).

Out of these various historical concepts from the feudal-manorial world as they survived in English common law came legal records the genealogist will encounter and need to understand. Not only did copyhold fail to flourish in the colonies, the idea also failed that the crown "really" owned all the land. So American law was centuries ahead of England in developing the legal sense of fee simple as an absolute (allodial) ownership. *Absolute* in this sense is restricted by eminent domain, taxation, zoning, and the public interest. Public interest, as an example, might restrict a private citizen from damming a fishing stream that ran through his land.

Two remnants of English law encountered in colonial records mostly south of New England are livery of seizen and the lease and release. Livery of seizen was a very old method of transferring land tenure by actually handing pieces of the property to the new owner. It means to take delivery of possession. Here is how lawyer William Blackstone described it:

> Livery in *deed* is thus performed. The feoffor [seller], lessor, or his attorney, together with the feofee [buyer], lessee, or his attorney, . . . come to the land, or to the house; and there, in the presence of witnesses, declare the contents of the feoffment or lease, on which livery is to be made. And then the feoffor, if it be of hand, doth deliver to the feofee, all other persons being out of the ground, a clod or turf, or a twig or bough there growing, with words to this effect. 'I deliver these to you in the name of seizen of all the lands and tenements contained in this deed.'[32]

Whether Americans performed all these steps is conjectural. Certainly such deeds were occasionally used in the colonial period in both New England and the South. In 1744, in Westmoreland County, Virginia, Arthur Harris "made Livery and Seizen of the Lands and Appurtinances within mentioned by delivering Turff and Twigg and the Ring of the Door of the Chief Mansion House on the Lands."[33] These odd phrases were formula and nothing individual should be read into them.

Though livery of seizen was uncommon, the system of lease and release – two parts – flourished in Southern colonies in the 1700s. The intent of this document in seventeenth-century England was to avoid the legal fee of having deeds recorded publicly. Under Henry VIII, the Statutes of Uses dictated that the person having the use of any land had the obligations of that land as well, such as taxes, feudal dues, etc. If land were leased, then by the Statute of Uses the only interest remaining to the leasor was the reversion of the land at the end of the lease's term. If that reversion were then released to the leasee, the land was sold without a bargain and sale, thus circumventing the law requiring public registration and fee. Here again, the form is formula and not a lease at all. The genealogist should read both documents since the lease often omits the wife's name because her husband could lease property without her consent. Also, the two serve as duplicate copies for such easily miscopied information as intricate metes and bounds descriptions and difficult-to-read proper names.

English property law (land law and inheritance) prior to the Victorian reforms was extraordinarily complex, dependent on technicalities, and steeped in a vocabulary now long obsolete. How property was inherited contains many subtle clues which nearly all researchers will pass by in ignorance. It is unfortunate that legal history studies in America are both rare and usually inadequate and that genealogists have no convenient compilation of American property law that is aimed toward the nonlawyer.

Property was divided into the real (mostly land) and the personal (usually moveables). In seventeenth- and eighteenth-century England, in intestate cases where no legal will existed, the personal property but not land was probated through the eccelesiastical courts with equal distribution to all children, while land was given under the common law to the heir-at-law. These differing courts for personal and real property account for why, at least in the colonial South, land is rarely mentioned in estate inventories: in England, such inventories were generally made by the ecclesiastical probate courts only, which did not usually probate land.

Primogeniture developed elaborate rules for identifying the heir-at-law in the absence of children; but if there were children, the heir-at-law was the eldest son (or, if dead, his heir-at-law) and, in the absence of a son, the daughters jointly inheriting as heirs-at-law. After 1540, the testator (maker of the will) could bequeath land, but lands not mentioned in the will were treated as intestate and went to the heir-at-law. The major exception was entailed lands, meaning lands bequeathed by an ancestor to a person and that person's lineal descendants. The legal entailing phrase was "to X and the heirs of his [or her] body lawfully begotten." (The phrase "to his heirs and assigns forever" is not an entail.) Such land entailed to X could not be bequeathed by will so long as it remained entailed, since entailed lands went to the heir-at-law. Widows had a right to a life interest in one-third of their husband's lands, to be surrendered if they remarried.

The genealogist interested in colonial lineages should watch how the land is inherited and how the personal property is disposed, if the inheritance exists in a time and colony governed by primogeniture and entail. If something strange seems to be happening, try to determine the local inheritance laws governing that time and place. Entailed lands and dower rights were protected from the debts owed by the estate, which may also give clues.

Unfortunately, there is no simple summary for each colony of which laws were in effect for which years for real/personal property and for testate/intestate probates. John Frederick Dorman's "Colonial Laws of Primogeniture," I-12, World Conference on Records (Salt Lake City: Genealogical Society of Utah, 1969) does the best job. A disappointingly disjointed discussion is Richard B. Morris's chapter on "Colonial Law Governing the Distribution and Alienation of Land" in his *Studies in the History of American Law with Special Reference to the Seventeenth and Eighteenth Centuries* (New York: Columbia University Press, 1930), pp. 69-125. Morris says that colonial practice was varied, uncertain, and debatable even to the colonial judges.

Two English laws worth knowing are the 1670 Statute of Distribution (22 & 23 Charles II c. 10 as amended 1 James II c. 17) and the 1677 Statute of Frauds (29 Charles II c. 3). (An English statute is cited by chapter number of the acts passed by the Parliament sitting in a regnal year of the sovereign. Thus, the 1677 act is chapter 3, 29th regnal year of Charles II.) The 1670 statute dictated that personal property (not real property) was distributed like this:

1. To children where no widow survived: Whole property divided equally among the children; a lone child received all.

2. To children and widow: Two-thirds to the children or their heirs and one-third to the widow.

3. To widow where no children survived: One-half to widow and one-half to the father of the deceased if alive or, failing him, to mother or the brothers and sisters.

4. When no widow and children survived, property went to father if alive or, failing him, to mother or the brothers and sisters.

The Statute of Frauds provided that personal property could no longer be disposed by oral testament and that executors/administrators must distribute such property as stipulated by will. Personal property not disposed by will was treated as intestate.

Although there are many local exceptions, English law was in force in the colonies to some degree where more specific colonial statutes did not exist, but the colonies could and did enact differing laws if "not repugnant" to English law and custom. The New England colonies, Pennsylvania, and Delaware granted equal divisions of land and moveables in intestates with a double share to the eldest son. (The eldest daughter in the absence of brothers had no like double portion.) If the land could not be conveniently divided, it could go to the inheriting son provided he justly compensated the other heirs. Rhode Island seems to have used primogeniture until 1770 (except 1718-28). Maryland abolished primogeniture in 1715, substituting equal division. The remaining colonies, all royal, retained primogeniture until the Revolution: New York, New Jersey, Virginia, the Carolinas, and Georgia. Georgia in its earliest years experimented with entailing lands by patent to male heirs, but it was an unpopular system.

If the heir-at-law automatically inherited entailed and intestate lands, then the eldest son need not be mentioned in his father's will. For example, in 1713, a John Taylor of Julian Creek, Norfolk County, Virginia, made a deed stating that the will of his brother Richard (Richard was alive) did not leave seventy-five acres to Richard's eldest son and in fact did not name this eldest son at all. Since the land had come to Richard from their father, John feared that if the land were not specifically transferred to the eldest son, he himself or his heirs would inherit this tract because John was the eldest son and primogeniture was the law in Virginia. Therefore John in his deed gives this seventy-five acres belonging to Richard to Richard's eldest son, Richard, Jr. Richard, Sr.'s, will survives and indeed does not mention the seventy-five acres or his eldest son.[34]

No English law required a testator in disinheriting a child to name him/her or leave such disinherited child the proverbial one shilling. As an unfortunate result, many wills ignore some children, leaving the genealogist in doubt whether the omission means that person was disinherited, dead, or not a child of the testator. Other records must be used to establish such points.

However, good genealogy is a conjunction of many types of records that together reinforce a pedigree and simultaneously test it. Land records are an essential strand in that web of proof but only one part. For example, the problem was to identify which of several Isaac Lindseys in Maury County, Tennessee, married in 1808 and died in Navarro County, Texas, in 1852.[35] An 1810 will by John Lindsey named a son Isaac who was a good chronological fit for the Texan, but this John had no deeds in Maury. Since Maury was opened to white settlement by an 1805 Indian cession and since the Lindsey family was certainly there by 1807, this absence of deeds or patents from the state of Tennessee was puzzling until the local history provided an explanation.

In 1783 North Carolina had allowed the purchase of Tennessee lands still held by Indians. The Maury County area had been claimed in 5,000-acre tracts by wealthy North Carolinians, but only in 1805-06 could whites actually settle there. So the Lindseys had arrived to legally "new" lands that had already been long owned.

The deeds, court minutes, tax lists, marriages, and other usual records sorted out four groups of Lindseys – a justice of the peace who lived in the eastern part of the county, a late-coming family who settled in the southwestern corner, two brothers who owned land but never settled in the county, and the group to whom the Texan apparently belonged.

In the absence of deeds, the Texan's family was localized by three steps: (1) the 1809 court minutes contained an oath about a lease from Long heirs to John Lindsey; (2) various road overseer appointments placed the targeted Lindseys on Little Bigby Creek in the center of the county; and (3) the 5,000-acre tract of the Long family, purchased in 1783, was plotted, locating it on Duck River, which runs through the center of Maury County, and overlying Little Bigby Creek. Thus, the Long acres included Little Bigby Creek. Clearly, John Lindsey had leased his Little Bigby land from the Longs, not purchased it.

The rest of the proof included tracing the family back through Georgia into South Carolina. John had a brother who died leaving three small sons who had come to Maury with their uncle John. One of these sons was named Isaac, while a second son had a son of his own named Isaac, neither being the Isaac who had married in 1808 and gone to Texas. Thus, the Texan was the one named in the 1810 will. By reading many volumes page-by-page, by plotting land grants, by following clues through several states, and by lucky survivals of records, it was possible to see these Lindseys in Maury in the years 1805-30, to sort out the different families, and to single out individuals. Land records underlay the whole proof though alone they could never have untangled the lineage.

Summary of State Land Records

The following summary locates the first-title grants for each state, although it is painfully brief. Since all states except Connecticut, Rhode Island, and Vermont record deeds and mortgages in the county and independent city, the deeds are assumed to be there unless otherwise stated. In short, the deeds should be easy to find, assuming they have not been destroyed. By contrast, the location of the land grants is complicated, varying widely from state to state.

The addresses of state land offices (where relevant) and the appropriate Bureau of Land Management (BLM) office are given. For addresses of state historical societies and state archives, see Appendix C. The BLM's Eastern States Office is at 350 South Pickett Street, Alexandria, VA 22304. The Federal Archives and Records Centers (FARC) are given in Appendix A. Questions involving private land titles are usually referred first to *American State Papers, Public Lands* (Washington, D.C.: Gales and Seaton, 1832-61) as indexed in Philip W. McMullin, *Grassroots in America* (Salt Lake City: Gendex, 1972). Inventory No. 22 refers to Harry P. Yoshpe and Philip P. Brower, *Preliminary Inventory of the Land-Entry Papers of the General Land Office* (Washington, D.C.: National Archives, 1949). Titles cited are obviously only a small part of what is available. I have doubtless overlooked still other titles.

Finally, you should remember that generalizations have exceptions and records are sometimes transferred. Joseph Martin Glynn, Jr., summarizes:

> Suppose I say, "The 1880 Soundex cards are at the National Archives in Washington, D. C., and on microfilm." This statement was true in 1945 but false by 1975. After some New England states cards were destroyed the remainder were sent to the Waltham Branch [of the National Archives]. If I say that[,] it's true in 1975 but false by 1979 because the cards were given to NEHGS [New England Historic and Genealogical Society] where they now [1982] are. Suppose I say the Waltham Branch has no ship passenger records. It's true in 1973 but

later surplus copies of some of the films were given to them. What a repository doesn't have [it] can acquire and what [it has] can be lost, stolen, destroyed, transferred, abstracted, microfilmed, and indexed, etc.[36]

This summary gives record locations for the early months of 1983. A note or phone call to verify locations should be standard operating procedure before beginning research.

Alabama

Public-domain state with two principal meridians (established 1805 and 1807) and fifteen GLO land districts. The first opened at St. Stephens in 1806. The last closed at Montgomery in 1927. These GLO local records were sent to the National Archives in Washington. Obtain patents from the BLM Eastern States Office, which also has copies of the tract books and township plats. The National Archives has the land-entry case files as described in Inventory No. 22, and a card index to Alabama federal patentees to 30 June 1908 (excluding private land claims). State and some county copies of ledgers, tract books, and plats are in the state archives and the Lands and Trademark Division, 528 State Office Building, Montgomery, AL 36130. See "Old Land Records of Madison County, Alabama," *Family Puzzlers*, no. 622 (20 Sept. 1979), pp. 2-3. Marilyn Davis Hahn is abstracting GLO district records, using mostly state duplicates rather than GLO originals. Her first three volumes are *Old Cahaba Land Office Records & Military Warrants, 1817-1853* (Birmingham: Banner Press, 1982); *Old St. Stephen's Land Office Records & American State Papers, Public Lands, Vol. 1, 1768-1888* (Easley, S.C.: Southern Historical Press, 1983), and *Old Sparta & Elba Land Office Records & Military Warrants, 1822-1860* (Easley, S.C.: Southern Historical Press, 1983). Many private land claims were processed through the St. Stephens office; also see the *American State Papers, Public Lands* as indexed by McMullin's *Grassroots*. Pre-1813 records for Alabama south of 31° should be in Tallahassee in the West Florida archives. Also see James F. Doster, "Land Titles and Public Land Sales in Early Alabama," *Alabama Review* 16 (1963): 108-24; David Lightner, "Private Land Claims in Alabama," ibid., 20 (1967): 187-204.

Alaska

Public-domain state with five principal meridians (three established 1905-11, and two 1956). Alaska was under the jurisdiction of the Russian-American Company until 1867, whose papers (1802-67) are microfilmed, NARS M11, 77 rolls. Trade, not settlement, was the company's goal, and the NARS pamphlet accompanying the microfilm collection does not mention any land title collection. An act of 1884 first authorizing a civilian governor expressly excluded general U.S. land law from Alaska except for mines and mining claims. The earliest of three GLO land districts opened at Sitka in 1885. Inventory No. 22 lists exactly 56 cash entries and 133 homestead patents for all of Alaska. The National Archives in Washington has the land-entry case files as described in Inventory No. 22, and a card index to Alaska patentees to 30 June 1908 (excluding private land claims). Obtain patents from the BLM Alaska State Office, Anchorage Federal Office Building, 701 "C" Street, Box 13, Anchorage, AK 99513, which also has copies of the tract books and township plats. Researchers with access to the Seattle FARC should inquire there concerning Alaska tract books, township plats, and the records of the GLO local Alaska land districts. Seek deeds in the judicial districts, Alaska's equivalent to counties.

Arizona

Public-domain state with two principal meridians (established 1865 and 1869). The earliest of Arizona's three GLO land districts opened in Prescott in 1870. Obtain patents from the BLM Arizona State Office, 201 North Central, Phoenix, AZ 85004, which also has copies of the tract books and township plats. The National Archives in Washington has the land-entry case files as described in Inventory No. 22, the GLO headquarters tract books and township plats, and a card index to Arizona patentees to 30 June 1908 (excluding private land claims). The *Guide to Genealogical Research in the National Archives* (1982), p. 222, reports some GLO local office records in the Denver FARC, but most are in the Los Angeles (Laguna Niguel) FARC. For private land claims, write the BLM New Mexico State Office, Federal Building, Box 1449, Santa Fe, NM 87501.

Arkansas

Public-domain state with one principal meridian (established 1815). There were eight GLO land districts, beginning and ending with Little Rock 1821-1933. The GLO local office records are in the Arkansas State Land Office, State Capitol, Little Rock, AR 72201. Obtain patents from the BLM Eastern States Office, which also has copies of the tract books and township plats. The National Archives in Washington has the land-entry case files as described in Inventory No. 22. Arkansas had one of the War of 1812's three military reserves. The warrants and an index are available on NARS microfilm M848, "War of 1812 Military Bounty Warrants, 1815-1858," fourteen rolls. A circa-1860 listing of patentees in the reserve is Katheren Christensen, *Arkansas Military Bounty Grants (War of 1812)* (Hot Springs, Ark.: Arkansas Ancestors, 1971). For private land claims, see the *American State Papers, Public Lands* as indexed in McMullin's *Grassroots*. Also see Joseph O. Van Hook, "Mexican Land Grants in the Arkansas Valley," *Southwestern Historical Quarterly* 40 (1936-37): 58-75.

California

Public-domain state with three principal meridians (established 1851-53). The first of ten GLO land districts opened at Los Angeles and Benicia in 1853. The records of these offices are at the San Francisco (San Bruno) FARC, except for the Los Angeles local district records, which are at the Los Angeles (Laguna Niguel) FARC. Obtain patents from the BLM California State Office, Federal Office Building, 2800 Cottage Way, Sacramento, CA 95825, which also has copies of the tract books and township plats. The National Archives has the land-entry case files as described in Inventory No. 22, and the GLO headquarters has originals of the tract books and township plats. For private land claims, see the state archives (indexed) and the Bancroft Library at the University of California, Berkeley. A Board of Land Commissioners to adjudicate Spanish and Mexican grants met 1852-56. Its files and other private claims papers, mostly collected at the surveyor-general's office in San Francisco, were destroyed in the earthquake and fire of 1906, but some parts or duplicates survive. See J. N. Bowman, "Index to the Spanish-Mexican Private Land Grant Records and Cases of California," (typescript at Bancroft Library, Berkeley, 1958, microfilmed). The Mexican Archives (1833-45) of the surveyor-general's office are microfilmed (fourteen rolls) at the state archives. The National Archives has microfilmed federal California court records regarding private land claims (NARS microfilms T910, T1207, T1214, T1215, and T1216).

Since the government could not control the hordes of 1849 miners, it pretended they did not exist, and there are no GLO records of '49 gold rush claims. See Joseph Ellison, "The Mineral Land Question in California, 1848-1866," *Southwestern Historical Quarterly* 30 (1926): 34-55; William Wilcox Robinson, *Land in California, the Story of Mission Lands, Ranchos, Squatters, Mining Claims, Railroad Grants, Land Scrip [and] Homesteads* (Berkeley: University of California Press, 1948); Rose H. Avina, *Spanish and Mexican Land Grants in California* (New York: Arno Press, 1976); and Paul W. Gates, "Public Land Disposal in California," *Agricultural History* 49 (1975): 158-78.

Colorado

Public-domain state with three principal meridians (established 1855 and 1880). The earliest of thirteen GLO land districts opened at Golden City in 1863. The Denver FARC holds GLO local office records for the more than seventy land districts formerly covering Colorado, New Mexico, Montana, the Dakotas, and Utah. Obtain patents from the BLM Colorado State Office, 1600 Broadway, Denver, CO 80203, which also has copies of the tract books and township plats. The National Archives in Washington has the land-entry case files as described in Inventory No. 22, and the GLO headquarters originals of the tract books and township plats. See LeRoy R. Hafen, "Mexican Land Grants in Colorado," *Colorado Magazine* 4 (1927): 82-93; George L. Anderson, "The Canon City or Arkansas Valley Claim Club, 1860-1862," ibid., 16 (1939): 201-10; "The Middle Park Claim Club, 1861," ibid., 10 (1933): 189-93; and a series of articles collectively titled "Spanish Land Grants in New Mexico and Colorado," *Journal of the West* 19 (July 1980): 1-99.

Connecticut

State-land state surveyed in variations of the New England town. First settled in 1634-35 in the Connecticut River Valley, its river towns formed a united government in 1639 without a charter from England. The New Haven colony was founded in 1638 and absorbed into Connecticut under the royal charter of 1662, which authorized a corporate colony (one that chooses its own governor). Connecticut was thus always free to grant its own lands, which it did through the General Court (legislature), usually to town proprietors but sometimes to individuals by grant or sale. The records are at the state archives in the Connecticut State Library; the colonial land records are being microfilmed. The Connecticut State Library also has such pertinent papers as the Robert C. Winthrop Collection, 1631-1794, and the William F. J. Boardman Collection, 1661-1835, both of which include land papers. Conveyances are recorded in the towns, not the counties. Proprietor records are rich in land records. See Nelson P. Mead, "Land System of the Connecticut Towns," *Political Science Quarterly* 21 (1906): 59-76; and Dorothy Deming, *The Settlement of the Connecticut Towns* (New Haven: Tercentenary Commission, 1953).

Delaware

State-land state surveyed in indiscriminate metes and bounds. Delaware is unique among the thirteen colonies in not having some colonial jurisdiction within its bounds that granted first titles to its lands. See Edward F. Heite, ed., *Delaware's Fugitive Records: An Inventory of the Official Land Grant Records Relating to the Present State of Delaware* (Dover: Delaware Division of Historical and Cultural Affairs, 1980), Hall of Records Inventory No. 2. The successive absorption of New Sweden into the Dutch colony of New Netherland and then into the English proprietary of James, Duke of York, means the early Delaware grants were made in New York. In 1682, the Duke of York conveyed his claims in present-day Delaware to William Penn, whose Pennsylvania proprietary granted Delaware's lands until the Revolution. In 1770, the Delaware legislature ordered the New York grants transcribed, since published as *Original Titles in Delaware Commonly Known as the Duke of York Record* (Wilmington: Delaware General Assembly, 1903), abstracted in the *Maryland and Delaware Genealogist*, vols. 5-15, 18 (1964-74, 1977). See also B. Fernow, *Documents Relating to the History of the Dutch and Swedish Settlements on the Delaware River* (Albany: Argus, 1877). Warrants and surveys from the Penn proprietary 1682-1776 are in the Delaware Hall of Records in Dover, as are tax records of the levy courts. The proprietary quitrents are at the Historical Society of Pennsylvania in Philadelphia. Forty-five Maryland grants are listed in Percy G. Skirven, "Durham County: Lord Baltimore's Attempt at Settlement of His Lands on the Delaware Bay, 1670-1685," *Maryland Historical Magazine* 25 (1930): 157-67. See also A. R. Dunlop, "Dutch and Swedish Land Records Relating to Delaware. . .," *Delaware History* 6 (1954-55): 25-51.

District of Columbia

Federal district of the United States, originally a ten-mile square taken from Maryland and Virginia by an act of 1790. The federal government arrived in 1800 and two counties, divided by the Potomac River, were created in 1801: Washington County to use Maryland law and Alexandria County (renamed Arlington in 1920) to use Virginia law. Within these counties were the chartered cities of Georgetown, Washington, and Alexandria. The land records (1792-1886) of the district's Recorder of Deeds are filmed in 694 rolls. For various land-related records of the District, see the *Guide to Genealogical Research in the National Archives* (1982), p. 242. In 1846, Alexandria County was retroceded to Virginia. During its years within the District of Columbia, it recorded its own deeds, as did the city of Alexandria. See John Frederick Dorman, "A Guide to the Counties of Virginia: Alexandria County (Arlington County)," *Virginia Genealogist* 3 (1959): 126-27.

Florida

Public-domain state with one principal meridian (established 1824). Of the five GLO land districts, the earliest opened at Tallahassee in 1825; the last closed at Gainesville in 1933. Obtain patents from the BLM Eastern States Office, which also has copies of the tract books and township plats. The National Archives in Washington has the land-entry case files and a card index to Florida patentees to 30 June 1908 (excluding private land claims). It also has Florida donation entry files (c 1842) under the Florida Armed Occupation Act of 1842 granting 160 acres to settlers able to bear arms. In 1821, Spain surrendered to the United States present-day Florida, including British/Spanish East Florida and, west of the Apalachicola River, the portion of British/Spanish West Florida that remained after the United States had seized western West Florida in 1810. Parts of the surviving British/Spanish provincial archives formerly at Saint Augustine and Pensacola are now in the Florida state archives in Tallahassee.

Several Congressional land commissions and many courts grappled with private land claims. The East Florida private land claims (1824-28) are filmed (seventeen reels), as are East Florida Spanish land grant archives (1764-1844) (eight reels). The Historical Records Survey published five volumes on *Spanish Land Grants in Florida* (Tallahassee, 1940-41). The county tax rolls of 1839-91 in the Florida Tax Commission have been filmed. See also George C. Whatley and Sylvia Cook, "The East Florida Land Commission: A Study in Frustration," *Florida Historical Quarterly* 50 (1971): 39-52; Charles L. Mowat, "The Land Policy in British East Florida," *Agricultural History* 14 (1940): 75-77; and S. W. Martin, "The Public Domain in Territorial Florida," *Journal of Southern History* 10 (1944): 174-87.

Georgia

State-land state surveyed partly in indiscriminate metes and bounds and partly in lottery lots. The Georgia Surveyor-General Department in the Georgia State Archives and Records Building, Atlanta, holds the grants, surveys, and related papers for Georgia from the colony's founding. Its major records and indexes are microfilmed. The department is one of the most active in the United States in indexing land records and publishing guides, including an admirable work, Marion R. Hemperley, *Georgia Surveyor General Department: A History and Inventory of Georgia's Land Office* (Atlanta: State Printing Office, 1982). A sampling of other titles issued by the department include Marion R. Hemperley and Pat Bryant, *English Crown Grants, 1755-1775*, 9 vols. (1972-74); Pat Bryant, *Entry Claims for Georgia Landholders, 1733-1775* (1975); Alex M. Hitz, *Authentic List of All Land Lottery Grants Made to Veterans of the Revolutionary War by the State of Georgia (1820, 1827, 1832)* (1955), and his *Georgia Bounty Land Grants* reprinted from the *Georgia Historical Quarterly* 38 (1954): 337-48. For a price-list, write the Georgia Surveyor-General Department, Archives and Records Building, Atlanta, GA 30334.

The three major means of granting land in Georgia were headrights (usually 200 acres for heads of households plus 50 acres for each family member and slave), Revolutionary bounty warrants (for citizens purportedly loyal to the Revolutionary government), and lotteries. The headrights are listed in *Index to the Headright and Bounty Grants of Georgia, 1756-1909* (Vidalia, Ga.: Georgia Genealogical Reprints, 1970). The Revolutionary bounty warrant files are very incomplete. The lotteries began with an act of 1803 and disposed of public lands in ceded Indian territories in 1805, 1807, 1820, 1821, 1827, and 1832. Eligibility required Georgia residency with extra draws for special categories such as Revolutionary service. The state-wide lists for all lotteries have been published but give only winning draws except for the 1805 list which shows all persons eligible under the enabling act of 1803. Its year's residency requirement from May 1802 makes it a good substitute for the missing 1800 Georgia federal census. There are some county eligibility lists in manuscript for later lotteries, and these might identify additional Revolutionary veterans. See also Robert S. Davis, Jr. and Silas Emmett Lucas, Jr., *The Georgia Land Lottery Papers, 1805-1914: Genealogical Data from the Loose Papers Filed in the Georgia Surveyor General Office Concerning the Lots Won in the State Land Lotteries and the People Who Won Them* (Easley, S.C.: Southern Historical Press, 1979). Prior to 1777, Georgia conveyances were recorded only in Savannah and survive mostly in the state archives. See *A Preliminary Guide to Eighteenth-Century Records Held by the Georgia Department of Archives and History* (Atlanta: Georgia Department of Archives and History, 1976). The R. J. Taylor, Jr., Foundation of Atlanta has published indexes to several of these colonial records and promises more. The State Tax Commission lists for 1787-1899 are microfilmed. See also Robert Scott Davis, Jr., *Research in Georgia* (Easley, S.C.: Southern Historical Press, 1981); Robert G. Lipscomb, "Land Granting in Colonial Georgia" (Master's thesis, University of Georgia, 1970); and Samuel Guyton McLendon, *History of the Public Domain of Georgia* (Atlanta: Foot and Davies, 1924).

Hawaii

State-land state unique in the Union for the Polynesian origins of its land titles. Hawaiian lands have never been part of the federal public domain. Prior to European settlement, the idea of absolute fee-simple land titles did not exist. Instead there was a hierarchy of right of use descending from the king through chiefs and subchiefs to commoners. The royal family or high chiefs gave Europeans and Americans similar rights of use which the foreigners interpreted as absolute ownership. In 1848, a Royal Land Commission sought to resolve the confusion and allocate permanent ownership by confirming royal patents or allocating land to the government, which then awarded grants. Records of original titles by the Land Commission are in the state archives, while the grants by purchase are at the Land Management Section of the Department of Land and Natural Resources, 1151 Punchbowl Street, Honolulu, HI 96813. The major parts of both collections are microfilmed. Deeds for all of the islands (1844-1900) with an index (1845-1917) are microfilmed in 108 reels. See also Jon J. Chinen, *Original Land Titles in Hawaii* (n.p.: By the author, 1961), and his *The Great Mahele: Hawaii's Land Division of 1848* (Honolulu: University of Hawaii Press, 1958); Thomas Marshall Spaulding, *Crown Lands of Hawaii* (Honolulu: University of Hawaii, 1923); Robert H. Horwitz, *Public Land Policy in Hawaii: An Historical Analysis* (Honolulu: University of Hawaii, 1969).

Idaho

Public-domain state with one principal meridian (established 1867). Of the five GLO land districts, the earliest offices opened in Boise City and Lewiston in 1867. The township plats are in the Seattle FARC. Obtain patents from the BLM Idaho State Office, 3380 Americana Terrace, Boise, ID 83706, which also has copies of the tract books and township plats. The National Archives in Washington has the land-entry case files as described in Inventory No. 22 and also the GLO headquarters originals of the tract books and township plats.

Illinois

Public-domain state with three principal meridians (established 1805 and 1815). Of the ten GLO land districts, the earliest opened at Kaskaskia in 1809 and the last closed at Springfield in 1876. The records of these offices are in the state archives. The Illinois State Archives also has a computer index to all federal patents in Illinois. For an excellent account of its land records, see Victoria Irons and Patricia C. Brennan, *Descriptive Inventory of the Archives of the State of Illinois* (Springfield: Illinois State Archives, 1978), pp. 549-60. The Shawneetown GLO records are indexed in Lowell M. Volkel, *Shawneetown Land District Records* (n.p., c 1978). Obtain patents from the BLM Eastern States Office, which also has copies of the tract books and township plats. The National Archives has the land-entry case files as described in Inventory No. 22. For private land claims, see the *American State Papers, Public Lands* as indexed in McMullin's *Grassroots*. One of the War of 1812 military reserves for bounty-land warrants was in Illinois. Its records are in the state archives and also on NARS microfilm M848, "War of 1812 Military Bounty Land Warrants, 1815-1858," in fourteen rolls. House Doc. 262, 26th Congress, 1st sess., 1840, has been reprinted with an index as Lowell M. Volkel, *War of 1812 Bounty Lands in Illinois* (Thomson, Ill.: Heritage House, 1977); it identifies patentees in the military tract. See Theodore L. Carlson, *Illinois Military Tract: A Study of Land Occupation, Utilization and Tenure* (Urbana: University of Illinois Press, 1951), Illinois Studies in the Social Sciences, vol 32, item 2. See also Paul W. Gates, "The Disposal of the Public Domain in Illinois, 1848-1856," *Journal of Economics and Business History* 3 (1931): 216-40; James E. Wright, *The Galena Lead District: Federal Policy and Practice, 1824-1847* (Madison: State Historical Society of Wisconsin, 1966).

Indiana

Public-domain state with two principal meridians (established 1799 and 1805). Of the six GLO land districts, the earliest opened at Vincennes in 1807; the last closed at Indianapolis in 1876. The records of these local offices were transferred to the Auditor of State but are now in the state archives. Obtain patents from the BLM Eastern States Office, which also has copies of the tract books and township plats. The National Archives in Washington has the land-entry case files as described in Inventory No. 22. The land entries for the Cincinnati land district (1801-40) and Vincennes land district (1807-77) are indexed in Margaret R. Water, *Indiana Land Entries*, 2 vols. (1948; reprint ed., Knightstown, Ind.: Bookmark, 1977). Vincennes had been settled since 1733 and experienced a large influx of Americans after the Revolution, a white enclave within Indian lands. For records on the resulting private land claims, see Leonard Lux, *The Vincennes Donation Lands* (Indianapolis: Indiana Historical Society, 1949), Indiana Historical Society Publications, vol. 25, item 4, and also the *American State Papers, Public Lands* as indexed in McMullin's *Grassroots*. See also Malcolm J. Rohrbough, "The Land Office Business in Indiana, 1800-1840," in *This Land of Ours: The Acquisition and Disposition of the Public Domain* (Indianapolis: Indiana Historical Society, 1978), pp. 39-59; Stephen Frederick Strausberg, "The Administration and Sale of Public Land in Indiana 1800-1860" (Ph.D. diss., Cornell University, 1970).

Iowa

Public-domain state with one principal meridian (established 1815 in Arkansas). Iowa had nine land districts, the earliest opening in 1838 in Burlington and Dubuque, the last closing at Des Moines in 1910. Their records are in the Kansas City FARC. Obtain patents from the BLM Eastern States Office, which also has copies of the tract books and township plats. The National Archives has the land-entry case files as described in Inventory No. 22. Over 20,000 settlers were in Iowa prior to the first land sales and thus had no legal title to their claims. To prevent speculators and latecomers from buying such improved lands at land office auctions, the settlers and speculators formed claims clubs to rig the auctions on grounds of first settlement. See Allan G. Bogue, "The Iowa Claims Clubs: Symbols and Substance," *Mississippi Valley Historical Review* 45 (1958): 231-35; Benjamin F. Shambaugh, ed., *Constitution and Records of the Claim Association of Johnson County, Iowa* (Iowa City: University of Iowa Press, 1894); Roscoe L. Lokken, *Iowa Public Land Disposal* (Iowa City: State Historical Society of Iowa, 1942); and Robert P. Swierenga, *Pioneers and Profits: Land Speculation on the Iowa Frontier* (Ames: Iowa University Press, 1968).

Kansas

Public-domain state with one principal meridian (established 1855). Of the eleven GLO land districts, the first opened at Lecompton in 1856, and the last closed at Topeka in 1925. The Kansas GLO records are in the Kansas City FARC but are reportedly incomplete. Obtain patents from the BLM Wyoming State Office, 2515 Warren Avenue, Box 1828, Cheyenne, WY 82003, which also has copies of the tract books and township plats for Kansas. The National Archives in Washington has the land-entry case files as described in Inventory No. 22 and the GLO headquarters original tract books and township plats. Significant portions of Kansas fell within railroad land grants, the land offices of the Santa Fe and the Rock Island railroads being especially important. The Kansas State Historical Society holds some of these papers. See Paul W. Gates, *Fifty Million Acres: Conflicts over Kansas Land Policy, 1854-1890* (Ithaca: Cornell University Press, 1954), and G. L. Anderson, "The Administration of Federal Land Laws in Western Kansas, 1880-1890: A Factor in Adjustment to a New Environment," *Kansas Historical Quarterly* 20 (1952): 233-51.

Kentucky

State-land state surveyed in indiscriminate metes and bounds east of the Tennessee River and in townships and ranges west of it. The Kentucky Land Office, Capitol Building, Frankfort, KY 40602, is an active department of the Office of Secretary of State and still issues an occasional new grant, since the land-grant process, though rare, is still in effect in Kentucky for vacant, ungranted lands. Warrants, surveys, patents, and other records are in the land office, indexed and microfilmed, open to public research. In 1792, Virginia sent to Kentucky its loose land papers relevant to Kentucky along with copies of its Virginia grants to Kentucky lands.

The separate categories of Kentucky grants are:

1. Virginia Grants, 1782-1792, sixteen volumes of 10,000 warrants issued by Virginia, including service in the French and Indian War, and transcribed in Richmond in the 1790s by order of the Kentucky legislature. See Joan E. Brookes-Smith, *Master Index: Virginia Surveys and Grants, 1774-1791* (Frankfort: Kentucky Historical Society, 1976).

2. Old Kentucky Grants, 1793-1856, twenty volumes of military, seminary, academic, treasury warrant, and preemption grants made by Kentucky. See Kentucky Historical Society, *Index for Old Kentucky Surveys and Grants [and Tellico Surveys & Grants] Microfilmed by Kentucky Historical Society* (Frankfort: Kentucky Historical Society, 1975).

3. Grants South of Green River, 1797-1866, eighteen volumes of nonmilitary headrights of 200 acres in the military reserve. These grants were first given as a relief for squatters.

4. Kentucky Land Warrants, 1816-73, forty-three volumes covering lands east of the Tennessee River purchased from the state.

5. Tellico Grants, 1803-53, two volumes describing 572 grants in the small Cherokee cession of 1805 in eastern Kentucky. See *Index* listed in #2 above.

6. County Court Orders, 1836-1924, 126 volumes on warrants sold by each county court east of the Tennessee River for any vacant lands within its bounds.

7. Grants west of the Tennessee River, 1822-58, eleven volumes surveyed in townships and ranges.

8. Grants South of Walker's Line, 1825-1923, loose papers from Kentucky's right to grant lands in Tennessee north of 36° 30', the intended state line. Walker ran the (present) line too far north. Researchers should also check the Tennessee land records for these grants. See James W. Sames III, *Four Steps West: A Documentary Concerning the First Dividing Line in America. . .Virginia, North Carolina, Kentucky, Tennessee* (Versailles, Ky.: By the author, 1971).

9. Warrants for Headrights, 1827-49, one volume containing fifty-five grants that probably belong in one of the other collections but became separated.

These and some other early land records are indexed in Willard Rouse Jillson, *The Kentucky Land Grants: A Systematic Index to All of the Land Grants Recorded in the State Land Office at Frankfort, Kentucky, 1782-1924*, Filson Club Publication No. 33 (Louisville: Filson Club, 1925), and his *Old Kentucky Entries and Deeds: A Complete Index to All of the Earliest Land Entries, Military Warrants, Deeds and Wills of the Commonwealth of Kentucky*, Filson Club Publication No. 34 (Louisville: Filson Club, 1926). These categories of land records have been summarized here because Kentucky probably suffered more than any other state from land-title litigation, because of the convergence of three unfortunate circumstances: Liberal land-granting by Virginia in an area distant from its supervision; Kentucky's settlement during the turmoil of the Revolution and its Indian wars, which meant that claims were frequently abandoned; and a tendency toward do-it-yourself rather than professional surveying. The resulting litigation produced a bonanza of depositions about first settlers, though such records are scattered in various courthouses and manuscript collections. An important collection is the microfilmed Kentucky Court of Appeals deed books, 1780-1909, in thirteen reels, and Hattie M. Scott, "Heirs in Court of Appeals Deeds," *Register of the Kentucky State Historical Society* 42 (1944): 6-18, 158-73, 256-62, 348-53. A Virginia Land Court sat at several Kentucky forts in 1780 to hear claims involving land north of Green River. Its transcripts appear in "Certificate Book of the Virginia Land Commission, 1779-80," *Register of the Kentucky State Historical Society* 21 (1923): 3-323. There were never any private land claims in Kentucky. The county tax lists 1782-c1875 are filmed.

See Beverley West Hathaway, *Kentucky Genealogical Research Sources* (West Jordan, Utah: Allstates Research, 1974), pp. 25-42, 119-22; Jack F. Royce, *The Preservation of Land Office Records*, Information Bulletin 89 (Frankfort: Legislative Report Commission, 1971); Philip Fall Taylor, *A Calendar of the Warrants for Land in Kentucky, Granted for Service in the French and Indian War* (Baltimore: Genealogical Publishing Co., 1967); Samuel M. Wilson, *Catalogue of Revolutionary Soldiers and Sailors of the Commonwealth of Virginia to Whom Land Bounty Warrants Were Granted* (Baltimore: Genealogical Publishing Co., 1967), reprinted from the *Yearbook of the Society, Sons of the American Revolution in the Commonwealth of Kentucky, 1894-1913*; and George Mark Harding, "The Uncertainty of Early Kentucky Land Titles," *Genealogy*, no. 64 (Oct. 1981): 1-4.

Louisiana

Public-domain state with two principal meridians (established 1807 and 1819). Of the five GLO land districts, the first opened at Opelouses in 1805, and the last closed at Baton Rouge in 1927. The papers of these offices are now in the Louisiana State Land Office, Box 44124, Baton Rouge, LA 70804. Obtain patents from the BLM Eastern States Office, which also has copies of the tract books and township plats. The National Archives has the land-entry case files as described in Inventory No. 22 and a card index to Louisiana patentees to 30 June 1908 (excluding private land claims). The French and Spanish governments of Louisiana left many pre-1804 papers, but the land grant papers seem to have suffered more losses than other categories of records. The Spanish Louisiana Cabildo judicial records (1769-1804) at the Louisiana Historical Center in New Orleans are microfilmed and rich in land transactions. Since a researcher needs a fairly fluent knowledge of French and Spanish to read longhand records, these pre-American records are beyond the average genealogist's reach, except that the Historical Records Survey (HRS) transcribed in nineteen volumes the records from the District of Baton Rouge in Spanish West Florida, and these are indexed in Stanley Clisby Arthur, *Index to the Archives of Spanish West Florida, 1782-1810* (New Orleans: Polyanthos, 1975). See also NARS microfilm T1116 in seven rolls of the HRS typescripts of the Archives of the Spanish Government of West Florida, 1789-1816. The Historical Records Survey issued a *Survey of Federal Archives in Louisiana: Land Claims and Other Documents* (Baton Rouge: HRS, 1940). The private land claims to 1837 are in the *American State Papers, Public Lands* as indexed in McMullin's *Grassroots*. Some of these materials in *American States Papers, Public Lands* are reorganized along geographical lines in Charles R. Maduell, *Federal Land Grants in the Territory of Orleans; the Delta Parishes* (New Orleans: Polyanthos, 1975). Seek deeds in the parishes, Louisiana's equivalent of counties. See also Harry L. Coles, Jr., "Applicability of the Public Land System to Louisiana," *Mississippi Valley Historical Review* 43 (1936-37): 39-58; Frances P. Burns, "The Spanish Land Laws of Louisiana," *Louisiana Historical Quarterly* 11 (1928): 557-81; Elizabeth Gaspar Brown, "Legal Systems in Conflict: Orleans Territory 1804-1812," *American Journal of Legal History* 1 (1957): 35-75; and Harry L. Coles, Jr., "The Confirmation of Foreign Land Titles in Louisiana," *Louisiana Historical Quarterly* 38 (1955): 1-22.

Maine

State-land state surveyed in coastal areas in the usual New England towns and into townships in the backwoods areas. In the 1620s and 1630s a number of vaguely defined large tracts were granted that overlapped each other and snarled later land titles. Then Massachusetts exploited the English Civil War to assert claims in 1652-74 to Maine, which further confused titles, as did the abandonment of nearly all Maine settlements during the Indian wars beginning in the 1670s.

Here is a drastic simplification of history: The Kennebec River was a dividing line, the area west (i.e., south) being in the Ferdinando Gorges proprietary (granted 1622 and 1639) that was purchased by Massachusetts in 1677, while the area east (i.e. north) of the Kennebec to the Saint Croix River was granted to James, Duke of York, in 1664. Reverting to the crown upon his overthrow, this eastern area was granted to Massachusetts in 1691 with reservation to the crown of rights to grant first titles. Thus, until the Revolution, Massachusetts granted Maine lands west of the Kennebec as proprietor, while it granted lands east of the river only with crown confirmation. Also scattered along the coast were those large and small overlapping early grants, which land developers/speculators purchased and resurrected by many lawsuits. A fifteen-mile strip on each side of the Kennebec itself was an outstanding example as described in Gordon E. Kershaw, *The Kennebec Proprietors, 1749-1775* (Portland: Maine Historical Society, 1975). In 1783 Massachusetts created the Committee for the Sale of Eastern [i.e. Maine] lands. The Maine State Archives considers these records to be the beginning of the Maine Land Office that is now a division of the archives in Augusta. The enabling act for Maine's 1820 statehood reserved half its public lands for disposal by Massachusetts, these lands being surveyed into blocks intermixed with Maine's half. In 1853, Maine bought Massachusett's remaining Maine lands. The Maine Land Office, State Capitol—Station 84, Augusta, ME 04333, has essentially the records since the Revolution, including microfilms of Massachusetts land sales. Both Massachusetts and Maine issued military bounty warrants, but no specific reservation was established. Revolutionary War veteran land grants are microfilmed in thirteen reels. See also Charles J. House, *Names of Soldiers of the American Revolution Who Applied for the State Bounty under Resolves of March 17, 1835, March 24, 1836 and March 20, 1836 as Appears of Record in Land Office* (Augusta: By order of the Governor and Executive Council, 1893). The various Maine and Massachusetts genealogical journals have useful lists as well. York County was created in 1640 and was Maine's only functioning county until 1760. Its deeds (1642-1737) were published as *York Deeds*, 18 vols. (Portland: John T. Hull, et al., 1887-1910). The counties of Aroostook and Oxford each have two deed-registration districts. See also James Sullivan, *History of Land Titles in Massachusetts* (Boston: I. Thomas and E. T. Andrews, 1801); *Note by the Commissioner on the Sources of Land Titles in Maine* in *Revised Statutes of Maine, 1883;* Frederick S. Allis, ed., *William Bingham's Maine Lands, 1790-1820* (Boston: Colonial Society of Massachusetts, 1954), vols. 36-37 in *Collections, Colonial Society of Massachusetts*; and the microfilm publication of papers of Bingham's estate agent, John Black, in Lawrence Donald Bridgham, "Maine Public Lands 1781-1795: Claims, Trespassers, and Sales" (Ph.D. diss.: Boston University, 1959).

Maryland

State-land state surveyed in indiscriminate metes and bounds except for lots in the military tract in the extreme western end of the state. The Calverts, Lords Baltimore, were proprietors of the colony from its founding in 1634 until the Revolution. Their political control passed into other hands in 1654-60 and 1692-1715 but not their land-granting rights. In 1641, a surveyor-general was appointed, in 1680 a specific land office was established, and in 1684 a land council was created to oversee disposals of land. At about the same time, the previous headright system was replaced by cash sales of proprietary lands. Those persons transported and claimed for headright grants are listed in Gust Skordas, *The Early Settlers of Maryland, an Index to Names of Immigrants Compiled from Records of Land Patents, 1633-1680* (Baltimore: Genealogical Publishing Co., 1968). The Maryland Hall of Records, Box 828, Annapolis, MD 21404, holds the land office papers, all microfilmed, including the warrants and patents from 1634. See Elizabeth Hartsook and Gust Skordas, *Land Office and Prerogative Court Records of Colonial Maryland* (Annapolis: Hall of Records Commission, 1946).

The Hall of Records has extensive card indexes to its land records, including the tract names of Maryland properties, but as of early 1983, these indexes were not microfilmed. See *A Guide to the Holdings at the Hall of Records*, Bulletin No. 17 (Annapolis: Hall of Records, October 1972). Colonial deeds were recorded at the county courts but have been collected at the Hall of Records and microfilmed. The deed books are inventoried in Morris L. Radoff et al., *The County Courthouses and Records of Maryland, Part Two: The Records* (Annapolis: Hall of Records Commission, 1963). There were also conveyances in the Provincial and the General Court of the Western Shore, all likewise at the Hall of Records.

Maryland surveyed fifty-acre lots in its western panhandle and granted them as military bounty lands to Revolutionary veterans. For details, see John M. Brewer and Lewis Mayer, *The Laws and Rules of the Land Office of Maryland* (Baltimore: Kelly, Piet, 1871) and a list of recipients in J. Thomas Scharf, *History of Western Maryland* (Philadelphia: Louis H. Everts, 1882), pp. 145-61. The proprietary patents stipulated a quitrent, which was payable to the proprietor, not the government. See Beverley W. Bond, "The Quitrent System in Maryland," *Maryland Historical Magazine* 5 (1910): 350-65. The manuscript rent rolls listing the tracts within each county and the debt books listing individuals and their lands are scattered and many lost, but there are significant collections in the Hall of Records in Annapolis and in the Calvert Papers of the Maryland Historical Society in Baltimore. See also Clarence P. Gould, *The Land System in Maryland, 1720-1765*, (Baltimore: Johns Hopkins Press, 1913); Paul H. Giddens, "Land Policies and Administration in Colonial Maryland, 1753-1769," *Maryland Historical Magazine* 28 (1933): 142-71; and Canville D. Benson, "Notes on the Preparation of Conveyances by Laymen in the Colony of Maryland," ibid., 60 (1965): 428-38.

Massachusetts

State-land state surveyed in irregular New England town bounds in the east and in more regular town rectangles in the west. Massachusetts pioneered the New England system of towns with its grants by the legislature (General Court) to groups of settlers (town proprietors), who in turn oversaw land distributions within their town area. Often the General Court had likely frontier areas surveyed into convenient town-size tracts – six-mile squares were common – and offered publicly to potential proprietors for settlement.

The Massachusetts Bay colonial records of such grants are in Nathaniel B. Shurtleff, ed., *Records of the Governor and Company of the Massachusetts Bay in New England* (Boston: Order of the Legislature, 1853-54), 5 vols. published in six vols. Plymouth colonial records are in Shurtleff, *Records of the Colony of New Plymouth in the New England* (Boston: Order of the Legislature, 1855-61), 12 vols., of which volume 12 is deeds (1620-51). The deeds for Massachusetts Bay were recorded in town records until the creation of counties, roughly 1643. Plymouth colony was joined by charter with Massachusetts Bay in late 1691. In 1685, it had been divided into three counties that recorded conveyances. Several Massachusetts counties were later divided into deed-registration districts: Berkshire into three districts in 1788, Bristol into two in 1837, Middlesex into two districts in 1854, Essex into two in 1869, and Worcester into two in 1884, each with its own courthouse. The Salem registry of Essex County, aside from its own deeds, also has those of old Norfolk County (1637-1714) and Ipswich (Newbury and later Rowley) town deeds 1640-94. The important county of Suffolk (Boston) has its deeds (1629-97) published as *Suffolk Deeds*, 14 vols. (Boston: Rockwell and Churchill Press, 1880-1906). It should be obvious from these brief facts that you must allow for variations in where, when, and what local land records survive. Town proprietor records also often survive and some are published. Property valuations and taxes for 1760-71 and 1780-1811 have been microfilmed in four and nineteen rolls respectively. See also James Sullivan, *The History of Land Titles in Massachusetts* (Boston: I. Thomas and E. T. Andrews, 1801); Mark D. Howe, "Recording of Deeds in the Colony of Massachusetts Bay," *Boston University Law Review* 28 (1948): 1-6; William I. Davisson and Dennis J. Dugan, "Land Precedents in Essex County, Massachusetts," *Essex Institute Historical Collections* 106 (1970): 252-76.

Michigan

Public-domain state with one principal meridian (established 1819). Michigan was under British jurisdictions until 1796, when the American government assumed control of Detroit. The five-to-eight mile Toledo Strip on the Michigan-Ohio border, now in Ohio, was under Michigan jurisdiction until 1835. The earliest GLO land office opened in 1804 in Detroit, and the last closed in Marquette in 1925. The location of Michigan's eight GLO district records could not be learned, except that the BLM turned over to the Bentley Historical Library of the University of Michigan, 1150 Beal Avenue, Ann Arbor, MI 48109, a set of the tract books and township plats. There are microfilms at some other Michigan libraries. Obtain patents from the BLM Eastern States Office, which also has copies of the tract books and township plats. The National Archives in Washington has the land-entry case files as described in Inventory No. 22. For private land claims, see the *American State Papers, Public Lands* as indexed in McMullin's *Grassroots*. See also D. Jones, "The Survey and Sale of the Public Land in Michigan, 1815-1862" (M.A. thesis, Cornell University, 1952); LeRoy Barnett, "Milestones in Michigan Mapping," *Michigan History* 63 (Sept./Oct. 1979): 34-43, and 63 (Nov./Dec. 1979): 29-38. Detroit property owners in 1805 are discussed in detail in Clarence M. Burton, with A. Agnes Burton, ed., *Governor and Judges Journal. Proceedings of the Land Board of Detroit* (Detroit: n. pub., 1915).

Minnesota

Public-domain state with two principal meridians (established 1831 and, far south in Arkansas, 1815). Of the dozen GLO land districts, the earliest opened in 1848 at Falls Saint Croix River, Wisconsin, and moved to Stillwater, Minnesota, in 1849; the last closed at Cass Lake in 1933. The tract books and township plats from these offices are in the Land Bureau, Department of National Resources, 658 Cedar Street, St. Paul, MN 55101. The bulk of their other records are in the state archives. Obtain patents from the BLM Eastern States Office, which also has copies of the tract books and township plats. The National Archives in Washington has the land-entry case files as described in Inventory No. 22. See Matthias N. Orfield, *Federal Land Grants to the States with Special Reference to Minnesota*, University of Minnesota Studies in the Social Sciences (Minneapolis: By the author, 1915); C. J. Ritchey, "Claim Associations and Frontier Democracy in Early Minnesota," *Minnesota History* 9 (1928): 85-95; and C. E. Worth, "The Operation of the Land Laws in the Minnesota Iron District," *Mississippi Valley Historical Review* 13 (1927): 483-98.

Mississippi

Public-domain state with five principal meridians (established 1803-1833). Of the six GLO land districts, the earliest opened in Washington in 1807, and the last closed in Jackson in 1925. The records of these offices are in the National Archives in Washington, not in Mississippi. The Mississippi Land Office, a state agency, existed from 1892 to 1980, and its records are now in the state archives, including some early records for the southern part of the state. Territorial land and court records (1798-1817) at the state archives have been microfilmed in five rolls. Obtain patents from the BLM Eastern States Office, which also has copies of the tract books and township plats. The National Archives in Washington has the land-entry case files as described in Inventory No. 22. For private land claims, numerous along the Gulf and the Mississippi River, see the *American State Papers, Public Lands* as indexed in McMullin's *Grassroots*. Early land claims are also given in May Wilson McBee, *The Natchez Court Records, 1767-1805: Abstracts of Early Records* (Greenwood, Miss.: By the author, 1954). It should be remembered that the area south of 31° was part of Spanish West Florida until 1810-11; thus, West Florida archives are partly in the state archives at Tallahassee and partly in Seville, Spain. See Richard S. Lackey, "Credit Land Sales, 1811-1815: Mississippi Entries East of the Pearl" (Master's thesis, University of Southern Mississippi, 1975); and Robert V. Haynes, "The Disposal of Lands in Mississippi Territory," *Journal of Mississippi History* 24 (1962): 226-52.

Missouri

Public-domain state with one principal meridian (established 1815). The earliest of the eight GLO land districts opened at Saint Louis in 1818, and the last closed in Springfield in 1922. Their records are in the state archives. See Missouri Records Management and Archives Service, "Missouri Public Domain: United States Land Sales, 1818-1922," *Archives Information Bulletin* 2, July 1980, which summarizes Missouri's land history, gives maps of the GLO land district boundaries, and lists the land records in the state archives. Obtain patents from the BLM Eastern States Office, which also has copies of the tract books and township plats. The National Archives has the land-entry case files as described in Inventory No. 22.

The opening of the first land office was delayed by extensive private-land claims requiring adjudication, then delayed again by the New Madrid earthquakes of 1811-12. Congress in 1815 granted scrip for up to 640 acres to sufferers in such "injured lands" with claims to be processed prior to opening the federal lands to public sales. For private land claims, see the *American State Papers, Public*

Lands as indexed by McMullin's *Grassroots*. See also *Missouri Land Claims* (New Orleans: Polyanthos, 1976), reprint of Congressional Document, 24th Congress, 1st Session, no. 16, 1835. It is noteworthy that, by 1793, Spanish Upper Louisiana had five administrative districts, from north to south: Saint Charles, Saint Louis (the provincial capital), Sainte Genevieve, Cape Girardeau, and New Madrid (which included Arkansas). These districts became the new American counties.

In 1795, a Spanish surveyor-general was appointed for Upper Louisiana. The archives of the Spanish districts are at several localities. Those at the Missouri Historical Society have been microfilmed and include major land records. There are also several hundred rolls of microfilmed land records at the state archives. One of the War of 1812 bounty-land reserves was in Missouri, for which an index and other records are available on NARS microfilm M848, "War of 1812 Military Bounty Land Warrants, 1815-1858," in fourteen rolls. See also Lemont K. Richardson, "Private Land Claims in Missouri," *Missouri Historical Review* 50 (1955-56): 132-44, 271-86, 387-99; and Paul W. Gates, *History of Public Land Law Development* (Washington, D.C.: Public Land Law Review Commission, 1968), pp. 96-108.

Montana

Public-domain state with one principal meridian (established 1867). The earliest of the nine GLO land districts opened at Helena in 1867. The records of these offices are in the Denver FARC. Obtain patents from the BLM Montana State Office, 222 North 32nd Street, Box 30157, Billings, MT 59107, which also has copies of the tract books and township plats. The National Archives in Washington has the land-entry case files as described in Inventory No. 22, and also the GLO headquarters original tract books and township plats. See William S. Peters and Maxine C. Johnson, *Public Lands in Montana; Their History and Current Significance*, Regional Study no. 10 (Missoula: Bureau of Business and Economic Research, 1959).

Nebraska

Public-domain state with one principal meridian (established 1855). Of the thirteen GLO land districts, the earliest opened in 1855 in Omaha, the last closed at Alliance in 1933. The records of these offices are in the state archives in the Nebraska State Historical Society, which has microfilmed all the tract books in fifty-three rolls and indexed some. Obtain patents from the BLM Wyoming State Office, 2515 Warren Avenue, Box 1828, Cheyenne, WY 82003, which also has copies of the tract books and township plats for Nebraska. The National Archives in Washington has the land-entry case files as described in Inventory No. 22 and the GLO headquarters original tract books and township plats. The land grant to the Union Pacific Railroad totaled a tenth of Nebraska, but its land office records were mostly destroyed in a fire. See Barry B. Combs, "The Union Pacific Railroad and the Early Settlement of Nebraska, 1868-1880," *Nebraska History* 50 (1969): 1-26; Addison Erwin Sheldon, "Land Systems and Land Policies in Nebraska," *Publications of the Nebraska State Historical Society* 22 (1936): 302-15; and Homer Socolofsky, "Land Disposal in Nebraska, 1854-1906: The Homestead Story," *Nebraska History* 48 (1967): 225-48.

Nevada

Public-domain state with one principal meridian (established 1851 in California). Nevada had four GLO land districts, the first opening in 1864 at Carson City. Obtain patents from the BLM Nevada State Office, 300 Booth Street, Box 12000, Reno, NV 89520, which also has copies of the tract books and perhaps some township plats. The National Archives in Washington has the land-entry case files as described in Inventory No. 22 and the GLO headquarters original tract books and township plats. It also has a card index to Nevada patentees to 30 June 1908. The San Francisco (San Bruno) FARC has the records of the Nevada GLO district offices, including the originals of the local office tract books and township plats. See John M. Townley, "Management of Nevada's State Lands, 1864-1900," *Journal of the West* 17 (1978): 62-73.

New Hampshire

State-land state surveyed in irregular New England town bounds along the coast and in fairly rectangular towns farther west and north. In the 1620s, John Mason was granted the land between the Merrimack and Piscataqua rivers, but he and his heirs failed to establish a successful proprietary colony. Beginning about 1641-42, Massachusetts claimed jurisdiction over the area, which fell within old Norfolk County, Massachusetts. The land records for old Norfolk are now at Salem in Essex County, Massachusetts. In 1679, New Hampshire escaped from Massachusetts control and became a royal province, while the Masonian assignees received qualified right to grant lands subject to local court decisions.

Massachusetts prior to 1741 also claimed the Merrimack Valley and established several towns there until New Hampshire's authority was confirmed by royal decree in 1741. New Hampshire then began granting land west of the Connecticut River in what is now Vermont – the Hampshire Grants – but never prevailed against the competing New York claims. The state archives has the major early land records and has published *Documents and Records Relating to the Province*, also called the *New Hampshire Provincial Papers* or the *New Hampshire State Papers*. Records on the town charters are in volumes 24-25 (1894-95), the town grants in volumes 27-28 (1895), the Masonian patent papers in volume 29 (1896), and the Hampshire Grants in Vermont in volume 26 (1895). Deeds from 1679 were recorded at the provincial capital until about 1771. They are all microfilmed and located in the state archives. The first counties were created in 1769 and took over the recording of conveyances. See Jonathan Smith, "Town Patents under Belcher," *Massachusetts Historical Society Proceedings* 45 (1911-12): 197-210; John F. Looney, "Benning Wentworth's Land Grant Policy: A Reappraisal," *Historical New Hampshire* 23 (1968): 3-13; and Maurice H. Robinson, *A History of Taxation in New Hampshire* (New York: n. pub., 1903).

New Jersey

State-land state (though the state never owned the land) surveyed in indiscriminate metes and bounds, plus some New England towns south of Staten Island. Compared to the other colonies, New Jersey had complex political and land-granting jurisdictions. After the fall of New Sweden and then New Netherland, the area was granted to James, Duke of York, who regranted it to two proprietors. After several more transfers and agreements, a 1686 West Jersey existed with its capital at Burlington while a corresponding East Jersey was governed from Perth Amboy. The dividing line between the two was poorly surveyed and caused conflicting land grants. In 1702, the proprietors surrendered governance to the crown but retained the right to grant vacant lands. From 1702 to 1738, New York and the reunified New Jersey had the same royal governor. In the late 1740s, land riots in East Jersey opposed the titles of the proprietors.

New Jersey is unique among the thirteen colonies in that its proprietors retained their rights after the Revolution to grant lands and receive back escheated land. They still retain these rights. Proprietary shares pass down the generations by inheritance and purchase like any other property. Consequently, proprietary land records (warrants, surveys, and patents) remain at the proprietary offices in Burlington and Perth Amboy. The major series have been microfilmed. Since colonial deeds had also been recorded at the two Jersey capitals, the New Jersey legislature in 1795 ordered them all transferred to Trenton. They are now in the state archives and have been microfilmed in separate series. Deeds after 1785 should be in the counties. The early Jersey deeds are published in William Nelson, *Calendar of Records in the Office of the Secretary of State, 1664-1703* (Paterson, N.J.: State of New Jersey, 1899), as volume 26 in *Documents Relating to the Colonial History of the State of New Jersey* (commonly called the *New Jersey Archives*). This book has been reprinted under the title *Patents and Deeds and Other Early Records of New Jersey, 1664-1703* (Baltimore: Genealogical Publishing Co., 1976). Kenn Stryker-Rodda has noted three special problems concerning early New Jersey property conveyances: (1) only an estimated 25 percent of the colonial deeds were recorded; (2) Jerseymen tended to record deeds when they needed to mortgage property, hence monied people are less likely to appear in the land records than the impecunious; and (3) "No one can pretend to do research on East Jersey families without careful examination of the contents of most of the 32 boxes of Alexander papers at the New-York Historical Society, where are preserved surveys, deeds, letters concerning property, litigation, etc.; nor on West Jersey families without similar examination of the Penn and Logan papers in Philadelphia."[37] See John E. Pomfret, *The New Jersey Proprietors and Their Lands, 1664-1776* (Princeton: D. Van Nostrand, 1964); Edgar J. Fisher, "Colonial Land Conflicts in New Jersey," *Historical Society of Hudson County Papers* no. 6; Crestview Lawyers Service, *Colonial Conveyances: Provinces of East & West New Jersey*, 2 vols. (Summit, N.J.: Crestview Lawyers Service, 1974); Charles H. Winfield, *History of the Land Titles in Hudson County, N.J., 1609-1871* (New York: Wynkoop & Hallenbeck, 1872), pp. 1-25; and James C. Connolly, "Quit Rents in Colonial New Jersey," *Union County Historical Society Proceedings* 1 (1923): 3-12.

New Mexico

Public-domain state with one principal meridian (established 1855). The first of New Mexico's four GLO land districts opened at Santa Fe in 1858. Their records are in the Denver FARC. Obtain patents from the BLM New Mexico State Office, Federal Building, Box 1449, Santa Fe, NM 87501, which also has copies of the tract books and township plats. The National Archives in Washington has the land-entry case files as described in Inventory No. 22 and the GLO headquarters original tract books and township plats. The 1854 Donation Act for New Mexico seems to have been little used, for the *Guide to Genealogical Research in the National Archives* (1982), p. 216, does not even mention this act in its section on donation lands, and the National Archives' Inventory No. 22, pp. 55-56, lists only 344 New Mexico donation patents. New Mexican private land grants are still being adjudicated and occasionally provoke violence. The large secondary literature is conveniently listed in Annabelle M. Oczon, "Land Grants in New Mexico: A Selective Bibliography," *New Mexico Historical Review* 57 (1982): 81-87. For information on the microfilm series of Spanish and Mexican archives, including land papers and private land claims, write the New Mexico State Records Center and Archives, 404 Montezuma, Santa Fe, NM 87503. See also Victor Westphall, *The Public Domain in New Mexico, 1854-1891* (Albuquerque: University of New Mexico Press, 1965); W. A. Keleher, "Law of the New Mexico Land Grant," *New Mexico Historical Review* 4 (1929): 350-71; and a series of articles collectively titled "Spanish Land Grants in New Mexico and Colorado," *Journal of the West* 19 (July 1980): 1-99.

New York

State-land state surveyed in several systems: indiscriminate metes and bounds, large manors with tenant farms, New England towns on eastern Long Island and along the Connecticut border, and large tracts in central and western New York often subdivided into townships and sections. Very large grants were always a common feature of New York land policy, the government officials finding it convenient (and lucrative both for fees and sharing the spoils) to have entrepreneurs do the subdividing and selling or leasing in farm-size parcels. Maps locating these major tracts have been printed often. One source is J. R. Bien, *Atlas of the State of New York* (New York: J. Bien & Co., 1895).

Several mammoth tracts in the western part of the state came into the hands of the Phelps-Gorham and Holland Land companies. Holland Land Company papers are located in the Buffalo and Erie County Historical Society, 25 Nottingham Court, Buffalo, NY 14216; the state archives in Albany; and the Cornell University Library, Ithaca, NY 14853. The Phelps-Gorham papers, more than 200 file boxes and some 235 volumes of original material, are located at the state archives, Albany. These records contain many credit sales. Likewise, the private papers of the large Hudson River manors may be necessary to complete a genealogy, since tenants who leased but did not buy land may never appear in the county conveyance records. See B. Fernow, *Documents Relating to the History and Settlement of the Towns Along the Hudson and Mohawk Rivers (with the Exception of Albany) from 1630 to 1682* (Albany: Weed, Parsons, 1881). The background history is excellently summarized in Sung Bok Kim, *Landlord and Tenant in Colonial New York: Manorial Society, 1664-1775* (Chapel Hill: University of North Carolina Press, 1978). In 1650, the Dutch government of New Netherland recognized Connecticut's title to Long Island east of Oyster Bay, though Long Island was soon reunited with New York under the Duke of York's proprietary (1664-89). See B. Fernow, *Documents Relating to the History of the Early Colonial Settlements Principally on Long Island* (Albany: Weed, Parsons, 1883). Deeds in these early New England towns were recorded in the town, not the county, prior to the successful extension of Suffolk County jurisdiction. This is also sometimes true of the debatable land east of the Hudson adjoining Connecticut and Massachusetts, where New Englanders settled on lands claimed by New York. (See Vermont entry for lands granted in what is now that state by New York.)

The major land records—patents, deeds, and land grant applications—of the colonial and state government are in the state archives, listed in New York State Archives, *Public Records Relating to Land in New York State* (Albany: New York State Archives, 1979). They are microfilmed. Land grant applications are partly available in New York Secretary of State, *Calendar of N. Y. Colonial Manuscripts, Indorsed Land Papers, in the Office of the Secretary of State of New York, 1643-1803* (Albany: Weed, Parsons, 1864). In 1784, the Board of Commissioners of the Land Office was established to dispose of the state's remaining public lands. In 1979, the Division of Land Utilization (Office of General Services) still held the land grant applicant files from 1799.

New York allotted its Revolutionary soldiers bounty land, giving privates 500 acres. The military reserve in the Finger Lakes region was surveyed into 600-acre lots so the veterans could take their 100-acre federal bounty alongside their state bounty in lieu of taking 100 acres in Ohio. Most veterans sold their claims and never settled in the military tract. The surveyed land in this reserve was distributed by lottery drawings, hence the title of the state's published list of recipients: New York Legislature, *The Balloting Book, and Other Documents Relating to Military Bounty Lands in the State of New York, New York Legislature* (Albany: Packard & Van Benthuysen, 1825). See Robert S. Rose, "The Military Tract of Central N. Y." (M.A. thesis, Syracuse Universiy, 1935). An earlier military tract was established northeast of the Adirondacks, but very few accepted this poor land. For background on New York's varied land tenure and law, see Robert L. Fowler, *History of the Law of Real Property in New York* (New York: Baker, Voorhis, 1895); S. G. Nissinson, "The Development of a Land Registration System in New York," *New York History* 20 (1939): 16-21; Armand LaPotin, "The Minisink Grant: Partnerships, Patents, and Processing Fees in Eighteenth Century New York," ibid., 56 (1976): 28-50; Charles W. Spencer, "The Land System of Colonial New York," *New York State Historical Association Proceedings* 16 (1917): 150-64; Arthur E. Sutherland, "The Tenancy on the New York Manor," *Cornell Law Quarterly* 41 (1956): 620-39; and H. Gresham Toole, "The Dutch Land System of New Netherland," *Marshall Review* 2 (1938): 31-39.

North Carolina

State-land state surveyed in indiscriminate metes and bounds. By charter 1663 (amended 1665), eight proprietors received a grant of all lands between 29° and 36° 30', the latter being the present North Carolina-Virginia line. In 1729, George II bought seven of the eight shares and made the Carolina proprietary a royal colony (actually three colonies – the two Carolinas and, in 1732, Georgia). The eighth share belonged to Lord Carteret, later Earl Granville, whose one-eighth part was laid off using the already surveyed Virginia line. Thus the northern half of present-day North Carolina composed the Granville District, where Earl Granville had the right to grant lands and collect quitrents, though not to govern. The boundary of the Granville District was the present southern line of the counties of Rowan-Davidson-Randolph projected east to the ocean. This Granville line was not even partially surveyed until the 1740s, when a land office was opened, only to close permanently about 1763. See E. Merton Coulter, *The Granville District*, James Sprunt Historical Publications, vol. 13, no. 12 (Chapel Hill: University of North Carolina, 1913), pp. 33-56.

The Granville grants, with an index, are in the state archives. The remaining grants from the early proprietary, the royal colony, and the state government, are in the land office, Secretary of State, Administration Building, Raleigh, NC 27603. These records also contain many Granville grants, since the legislature once ordered them recorded. The land office has a card index to the grants, but users should be alert to its peculiar arrangement, described in Margaret M. Hofmann, "Land Grants," *North Carolina Research: Genealogy and Local History*, eds., Helen F. M. Leary and Maurice R. Stirewalt (Raleigh: North Carolina Genealogical Society, 1980), pp. 299-315. Hofmann has also abstracted the early grants in *Province of North Carolina, 1663-1729, Abstracts of Land Patents* (Weldon, N.C.: Roanoke News, 1979). Headrights were offered throughout the colonial period, though the requirements and acreage varied. For such stipulations, see "Land Grants in Colonial North Carolina," *Family Puzzlers*, no. 653 (24 April 1980), pp. 1-4.

Deeds were recorded in the counties, though irregularly in the earliest years. North Carolina's military bounty-land act was the most generous of the states in granting 640 acres (in Tennessee) to a private in the continental line. Researchers should read George Stevenson's description of the state's bounty land records as given in Leary and Stirewalt's *North Carolina Genealogy*, cited above, pp. 371-79, one of the best chapters in an admirable book. See also Kenneth B. Pomeroy and James G. Yoho, *North Carolina Lands: Ownership, Use, and Management of Forest and Related Lands* (Washington: American Forestry Association, 1964); George Henry Swathers, *The History of Land Titles in Western North Carolina* (Ashville: Miller Printing, 1938); Lawrence N. Morgan, *Land Tenure in Proprietary North Carolina*, James Sprunt Historical Publications, vol. 12, No. 2 (Chapel Hill: University of North Carolina, 1912), pp. 41-63; Dan Lacy, "Records in the Offices of Registers of Deeds in N. C.," *North Carolina Historical Review* 14 (1937): 213-29; Jacquelyn H. Wolf, "Patents and Tithables in Proprietary North Carolina, 1663-1729," ibid., 56 (1979): 263-77; and Marvin L. Michael Kay, "The Payment of Provincial and Local Taxes in North Carolina, 1748-1771," *William and Mary Quarterly*, 3rd series, 26 (1969): 218-40.

North Dakota

Public-domain state with one principal meridian (established 1815 in Arkansas, North Dakota being surveyed much later). The earliest of North Dakota's seven GLO land districts opened at Pembina in 1870. The bulk of their records are in the State Historical Society of North Dakota. The original township plats are at the North Dakota Water Commission, State Office Building, 900 East Boulevard, Bismark, ND 58505. Obtain patents from the BLM Montana State Office, 222 North 32nd Street, Box 30157, Billings, MT 59107, which also has copies of the tract books and township plats for North Dakota. The National Archives in Washington has the land-entry case files as described in Inventory No. 22 and the GLO headquarters original tract books and township plats. See N. Thomas, "Distribution of the Public Domain in Dakota Territory" (M.A. thesis: University of South Dakota, 1944).

Ohio

Public-domain state with a complicated surveying history. Aside from the Virginia Military District's indiscriminate metes and bounds, Ohio has a dozen different township-and-range surveys, the major principal meridians being established 1785-1819. Some of these surveys do not use the usual federal numbering system but have five-mile-square townships. Researchers should be alert to four different boundary jurisdictions in early Ohio:

1. The actual surveys with their meridians and baselines (or lack of same in the Virginia Military District). See C. E. Sherman, *Original Ohio Land Subdivisions*, 4 vols. (Columbus: Ohio State Reformatory, 1925). Volume 3 recounts the history of the various surveys and gives detailed maps showing the numbering of townships. This book is a must for early Ohio research.

2. The various tracts as they opened for settlement, such as the Seven Ranges, the U.S. Military District, the Congress Lands east of Scioto River, and the Congress Lands west of Miami River. A map of these tracts is frequently reproduced in Ohio how-to books and articles. See, for instance, Carol Willsey Flavell and Florence Clint, *Ohio Area Key* (Denver: Area Keys, 1977), p. 45.

3. The land office districts, such as Symmes's private land office at Cincinnati, the GLO's Chillicothe land office (1801-76), and the Virginia Military District's land office also at Chillicothe. For GLO districts, see National Archives Inventory No. 22, pp. 57-59. The National Archives and the Ohio State Land Office, 88 E. Broad Street, Columbus, OH 43215, have guides to the changing GLO district boundaries.

4. The counties with their registries of deeds. See Randolph Chandler Downes, "Evolution of Ohio County Boundaries," *Ohio Archaeological and Historical Publications* 26 (1927): 340-477.

The state auditor of Ohio is in charge of the State Land Office, which welcomes letters but not visits, lacking (in 1983) sufficient visitor facilities. It has issued a pamphlet entitled "Ohio Land Grants" that helps orient the beginning researcher. The office also has an index to all Ohio patentees except the Symmes Purchase and the Connecticut Western Reserve, both of which were issued as single patents. Most Symmes land papers apparently burned. The Connecticut Land Company papers are in the Litchfield Historical Society, Box 385, Litchfield, CT 06759. There are land papers for the Western Reserve both in the Western Reserve Historical Society and in the Connecticut State Library, Hartford.

Settlers in the Western Reserve sometimes dealt through the Susquehannah Land Company and the Phelps-Gorham Land Company. See Julian P. Boyd and Robert J. Taylor, *The Susquehannah Company Papers*, 11 vols. (Wilkes-Barre: Wyoming Historical & Geological Society, and Ithaca: Cornell University Press, 1930-71). The original papers in the Connecticut State Archives, entitled "Susquehannah Settlers, 1755-1796" and "Western Lands, 1783-1789," include many references to the Fire Lands and the Connecticut Land Company. The papers and an every-name index are microfilmed. The Phelps-Gorham papers in the New York State Archives in Albany also include numerous references to Ohio lands, such as "Vol. 145. Book of Conveyances of Lands in Ohio, 1795-1808, and Vol. 156. Book of Conveyances of Lands in Ohio, 1801-1822."

A major listing of early Ohio entrymen and patentees is Clifford Neal Smith, *Federal Land Series*, 4 vols. to date (Chicago: American Library Association, 1972-in progress). Smith is plowing through various manuscript collections meticulously listing their contents and indexing their name lists. While not limited to Ohio, these first volumes are heavy on Ohio entrymen because the earliest federal land sales were mostly there. Smith's introductions should be read by any genealogist working in early Ohio records.

The earliest of Ohio's nine GLO land districts opened in 1800 in Marietta and Steubenville; the last closed at Chillicothe in 1876. The records of these land offices are split between the State Land Office, which has survey field notes, tract books, township plats, and related material, and the state archives in the Ohio Historical Society, 1982 Velma Avenue, Columbus, OH 43211, which has the remaining records, such as the ledger volumes concerning purchases and payments. Obtain patents from the BLM Eastern States Office, which also has copies of the tract books, township plats, and a five-volume index to Ohio patents c1800-1820. The National Archives in Washington has the land-entry case files as described in Inventory No. 22. The two major military reserves in Ohio for Revolutionary veterans – the Virginia Military District and the U.S. Military District – were discussed earlier in this chapter under Bounty Lands. Also see William Thomas Hutchinson, "Military Bounty Lands of the American Revolution in Ohio" (Ph.D. diss., University of Chicago, 1927).

The Connecticut Western Reserve was not a military reserve nor did Connecticut grant its soldiers bounty land. Several categories of sufferers in the Revolution were granted lands in Ohio. The inhabitants of Connecticut towns burned by British/Loyalist raiders received compensation in the Fire Lands of the Western Reserve, also called the Sufferers' Lands. Pro-Independence refugees from Canada and Nova Scotia received land in the Refugee Tract. See Smith's *Federal Land Series,* volume 1, sources F and G, for sufferers and refugees. Tax records for 1800-38 at the Ohio Historical Society are microfilmed.

See William E. Peters, "Ohio Lands and Their History," *Bulletin of the History and Philosophy Society of Ohio* 15 (1957): 340-48, and his *Ohio Lands and Their Subdivision,* 2nd ed. (Athens, Ohio.: William E. Peters, 1918); his seventeen-volume typescript, "Code of Land Titles in Ohio. A Compilation from Official Records of All Charters, Indian Treaties, Grants,. . ." (1935), is microfilmed and available at several major Ohio research libraries. See also Carol Willsey Flavell, *Ohio Genealogical Guide* (Youngstown, Ohio.: Carol Willsey Flavell, 1978), pp. 25-33 (but note the BLM Silver Springs office, p. 31, has since moved to Alexandria); Kenneth Duckett, "Ohio Land Patents," *Ohio History* 72 (1963): 51-60; Mayburt Stephenson Riegel, *Early Ohioans' Residences from the Land Grant Records* (Mansfield, Ohio.: Ohio Genealogical Society, 1976).

Oklahoma

Public-domain state with two principal meridians (established 1870 and 1881). Of the eleven GLO land districts, the earliest opened at Guthrie and Kingfisher in 1889, and the last closed at Guthrie in 1927. The records of these local offices are in the state archives. While it never had a unified territorial government, eastern Oklahoma was called the Indian Territory after an 1830 act of Congress. It continued until 1907, the major tribes each having their organized governments complete with tribal capitals. Only in 1889 was present-day Oklahoma opened to the federal land disposal process operated by the GLO. What made Oklahoma settlements spectacularly different were the formal land rushes with their opening-day stampedes to stake claims to already surveyed quarter sections. Those who illegally jumped the gun were called "sooners." The last major land tract was distributed by lottery rather than land rush. Obtain patents from the BLM New Mexico State Office, Federal Building, Box 1449, Santa Fe, NM 87501, which also has copies of the tract books and township plats for Oklahoma. The National Archives in Washington has the entry-land case files as described in Inventory No. 22 and the GLO headquarters original tract books and township plats.

Before Indian lands were opened for white settlement, each tribal member received an individual land allotment. While there is no one repository for the Indian allotment records, the researcher should check the Kansas City and Fort Worth FARCs and also the National Archives microfilm publications. The Indian Archives Division of the Oklahoma Historical Society, Oklahoma City, holds the records of many tribes. See Jean C. Brown, *Oklahoma Research: The Twin Territories* (Sapulpa, Okla.: Jean C. Brown, 1975); *Guide to Genealogical Research in the National Archives* (Washington, D.C.: National Archives and Records Service, 1982), pp. 159-70; Berlin Basil Chapman, "Federal Management and Disposition of the Lands of Oklahoma Territory, 1866-1907" (Ph.D. diss., University of Wisconsin, 1932).

Oregon

Public-domain state with one principal meridian (established 1851). Of the six GLO land districts, the earliest opened in Oregon City in 1855. Obtain patents from the BLM Oregon State Office, 825 NE Multnomah Street, Box 2965, Portland, OR 97208, which also has copies of the tract books and township plats. The GLO office records are in the Seattle FARC. The National Archives in Washington has the land-entry case files as described in Inventory No. 22 and the GLO headquarters original tract books and township plats.

Oregon's earliest white and mixed-blood settlers were entitled to free federal land under the Donation Act of 1850. An index and abstracts are on NARS microfilm M145, "Abstracts of Oregon Donation Land Claims, 1852-1903," in six rolls, which serves as an index to the case files reproduced in NARS microfilm M815, "Oregon and Washington Donation Land Files, 1851-1903," in 108 rolls. Because of a law forbidding their reproduction, the naturalization certificates in M815 case files were not filmed. The law was changed in the 1970s, so naturalization records referred to in these files can now be obtained from the National Archives. Donation case files are valuable because they should contain a statement of the date and place of birth of the entryman. See Genealogical Forum of Portland, Ore., *Genealogical Material in Oregon Donation Land Claims,* 5 vols. (Portland: Genealogical Forum of Portland, 1957-75). See also Jerry A. O'Callaghan, "The Disposition of the Public Domain in Oregon" (Ph.D. diss., Stanford University, 1952); James M. Bergquist, "Oregon Donation Act and National Land Policy," *Oregon Historical Quarterly* 58 (1957): 17-35.

Pennsylvania

State-land state surveyed mostly in indiscriminate metes and bounds, though the donation and depreciation lands north of Pittsburgh were surveyed in rectangular, numbered lots. William Penn as proprietor established a land office in 1682 that continues to the present as the Division of Land Records, Bureau of Archives and History, William Penn Memorial Museum Building, Box 1026, Harrisburg, PA 17120. The Division of Land Records holds such major land series as applications for warrants, original warrants, original surveys, patents, military grants – these are all microfilmed in many hundreds of reels. There are also smaller but no less valuable collections, such as depositions 1683-1881, caveats 1699-1890, title papers 1784-1852, etc., which are also microfilmed.

The Penn proprietary was very business-like in disposing of its lands at a fixed price (no headrights) as supervised by an appointed surveyor and a commission/board of property, which helps explain its wealth of records. The Division of Land Records is constructing tract maps for each county and, by 1982, had completed these "Warrantee Township Maps" for about one-third of the counties. They are available for purchase. One valuable feature of many Pennsylvania grants is their tract names – at least for earlier tracts – such as "Lithuania" or Levi Andrew Levi's "Uncircumcision." Such names may give ethnic and religious clues. To the records mentioned above should be added the first nine volumes of Pennsylvania grant records, discovered in the Philadelphia City Hall of 1952 and now indexed in Allen Weinberg and Thomas E. Slattery, *Warrants and Surveys of the Province of Pennsylvania Including the Three Lower Counties, 1759* (Philadelphia: Philadelphia Department of Records, 1965). See John E. Pomfret, "The First Purchasers of Pennsylvania, 1681-1700," *Pennsylvania Magazine of History and*

Biography 80 (1956): 137-63. The *Pennsylvania Archives,* 3rd series, contains William Henry Egle, *Warrantees of Land in the Several Counties of the State of Pennsylvania, 1730-1898* (Harrisburg: State Printer, 1898-1899), vols. 24-26. The *Pennsylvania Archives,* 2nd series, volume 19 (1893) contains minutes of the Board of Property, 1687-1732, and has been reprinted as William Henry Egle, *Early Pennsylvania Land Records* (Baltimore: Genealogical Publishing Co., 1976).

The lands north of Pittsburgh reserved for the Pennsylvania continental line were called the Donation Lands. Certificates were also issued to Pennsylvania troops entitling them to cheap lands in compensation for the ravages of inflation on their pay; these were called Depreciation Lands. The records are in the Division of Land Records, though most soldiers sold their rights rather than settle on the lands. See John E. Winner, "The Depreciation and Donation Lands," *Western Pennsylvania Historical Magazine* 8 (1925): 1-11. The Pennsylvania State Archives itself has some land records, such as land warrant and patent receipts 1781-1809, mortgages and valuations 1773-93, and colonial quitrent books and rent rolls.

Pennsylvania had several major boundary controversies with its neighbors, and various colonies gave grants of their neighbors' lands. Connecticut, about 1753-82, claimed and settled the upper Delaware River Valley (the Delaware Company papers are mostly lost) and the Wyoming Valley along the Susquehanna River. Its records are published as Julian P. Boyd and Robert J. Taylor, *The Susquehannah Company Papers,* 11 vols. (Wilkes-Barre: Wyoming Historical & Geological Society, and Ithaca: Cornell University Press, 1930-71). The Pennsylvania Surveyor General's Office papers on Connecticut patents in seventeen townships in Luzerne County, 1785-1810, are microfilmed in twenty-five reels. Also on microfilm are the "Susquehannah Settlers, 1755-96" and "Western Lands, 1783-89." An every-name index makes these papers valuable for genealogical research, especially since many men died before their claims were satisfied, necessitating mention of heirs as well as other property details.

In southwestern Pennsylvania around the time of the Revolution were three active Virginia counties. See Raymond M. Bell, "Virginia Land Grants in Pennsylvania," *Virginia Genealogist* 7 (1963): 78-83, 103-7, 152-62, and 11 (1967): 126-27, and John F. Vallentine, "Research in Virginia's District of West Augusta," *Genealogical Journal* 4 (1975): 141-47. See also W. R. Shepherd, *The Land System of Provincial Pennsylvania,* American Historical Association *Annual Report* (1895), pp. 117-25; Joseph C. Ruddy, "The Policy of Land Distribution in Pennsylvania since 1779" (M.A. thesis, Pennsylvania State College, 1933). For early settlers living along Pennsylvania's southeastern border, be alert to possible Maryland land records.

The Holland Land Company also had lands in Pennsylvania and operated a land office in Philadelphia. Original materials are scattered, with many at the Buffalo and Erie County Historical Society, Buffalo, New York. See Walter J. McClintock, "Title Difficulties of the Holland Land Company in Northwestern Pennsylvania," *Western Pennsylvania Historical Magazine* 21 (1938): 119-38.

Rhode Island and Providence Plantations

State-land state surveyed in New England towns. These towns in the colonial period were particularly strong relative to the colony's central government. Deeds were recorded by the towns, not the counties, although the colonial government for a while also recorded some conveyances. The earliest volume is abstracted in Dorothy Worthington, *Rhode Island Land Evidences, Vol. 1, 1648-1696, Abstracts* (Providence: Rhode Island Historical Society, 1921); no more published. These land evidence volumes are the major land record held by the state archives, though it has a few other records with land information. Information on town grants can be found in John R. Bartlett, *Records of the Colony of Rhode Island and Providence Plantations in New England,* 10 vols. (Providence: Rhode Island General Assembly, 1857-1865).

South Carolina

State-land state surveyed in indiscriminate metes and bounds. A proprietary colony 1670-1719 and a royal colony 1719-75, South Carolina's gradual separation from North Carolina was recognized by Parliament in 1729 and confirmed by the partial running of their dividing line in 1735. Subsequent segments were later run ever farther west, and many settlers unexpectedly found themselves inhabitants of the neighboring colony. Each colony made some grants in the other's territory. South Carolina had headright grants, which are sometimes in council journals about 1749-73. See also A. S. Salley, Jr., *Warrants for Land in South Carolina, 1672-1711,* rev. ed. (Columbia: University of South Carolina Press, 1973). No other recorded land warrants survive.

The colonial and state surveys/plats and grants are in the state archives and microfilmed. There are separate series with indexes for the proprietary, royal, and state periods. Land office business was suspended all through the 1720s, South Carolina having expelled the proprietary government in 1719. The situation was resolved when George II bought out the proprietors in 1729. In 1731, a more regularized processing of land titles was implemented, with the proprietary titles and claims to be registered as "memorials." In 1744, this memorializing of land titles was required of all titles granted from 1731, a system that helped the government identify quitrent obligations. Five manuscript volumes of quitrents exist for 1733-1774. See Alan D. Watson, "The Quit Rent System in Royal South Carolina," *William and Mary Quarterly,* 3rd series, 33 (1976): 183-211.

Prior to the Revolution, South Carolina land records may refer to the counties of Colleton, Craven, Berkeley, and Granville; these were nonfunctioning but useful as geographical locators. Deeds and mortgages were recorded only at Charleston until 1769-72; and until 1785, such records from local courthouses continued to be sent to and stored in Charleston. Pre-1719 are at the state arhives in Columbia. See Silas Emmett Lucas, Jr., *An Index to Deeds of the Province and State of South Carolina 1719-1785 and Charleston District 1785-1800* (Easley, S.C.: Southern Historical Press, 1977). In 1785-99, there were first seven and then nine "old" districts, where conveyances were stored. About 1799 these large districts were abolished and conveyances were recorded and stored at twenty-four small "new" districts. (These districts have been called counties since 1868.) See James M. Black, "The Counties and Districts of South Carolina," *Genealogical Journal* 5 (1976): 100-13. The need, until about 1769-72, to go to Charleston to record conveyances, the turmoil of the Revolution 1775-1783, and the loss of many "old" district records means South Carolina deeds prior to 1800 are very incomplete. The original tracts in the upcountry vicinity of the Broad, Tyger, and Enoree rivers have been platted and published as Union County Historical Foundation, *Land Grant Maps* (Union, S.C.: A Press, 1976). South Carolina passed a bounty-land act and established a small military reserve. See "Bounty Grants to Revolutionary Soldiers," *South Carolina Historical Magazine* 7 (1906): 173-78, 217-24. A unique land source is the state's Reconstruction attempt to buy land for black freedmen. Some records exist showing whites selling to the project and blacks buying. See Carol K. Rothrock, *The Promised Land; The History of the South Carolina Land Commission, 1869-1890* (Columbia: University of South Carolina Press, 1969). See also "Granting of Land in Colonial South Carolina," *South Carolina Historical Magazine* 77 (1976): 208-12; Robert Kilgo Ackerman, "South Carolina Colonial Land Policies" (Ph.D. diss., University of South Carolina, 1965); David A. Means, "The Recording of Land Titles in South Carolina. . .," *South Carolina Law Quarterly* 10 (1957-58): 346-419; Marion C. Chandler and Earl W. Wade, *The South Carolina Archives: A Temporary Summary Guide,* 2nd ed. (Columbia: South Carolina Department of Archives and History, 1976), pp. 5, 8-9, 41; Robert L. Meriwether, *The Expansion of South Carolina 1729-1765* (Kingsport, Tenn.: Southern Publishers, 1940).

South Dakota

Public-domain state with three principal meridians (established 1855 and 1878, and in Arkansas in 1815). Of South Dakota's eight GLO land districts, the earliest opened in Vermillion in 1861. The records of these offices are in the Denver FARC. Obtain patents from the BLM Montana State Office, 222 North 32nd Street, Box 30157, Billings, MT 59107, which also has copies of tract books and township plats for South Dakota. The National Archives in Washington has the land-entry case files as described in Inventory No. 22 and the GLO headquarters original tract books and township plats. See Charles L. Green, *The Administration of the Public Domain in South Dakota* (Pierre, S.D.: Hipple Printing, 1939); and N. Thomas, "Distribution of the Public Domain in Dakota Territory" (M.A. thesis, University of South Dakota, 1944).

Tennessee

State-land state surveyed in indiscriminate metes and bounds, except the lands west of the Tennessee River which were surveyed in roughly rectangular tracts within townships. In 1790, North Carolina ceded political control over Tennessee to the U.S. government but continued into the 1820s to issue military bounty warrants it expected to be redeemed with Tennessee lands. In 1806, the state of Tennessee was given title to the eastern two-thirds of the public lands, while the western third–called the Congressional Reservation–was to be incorporated into the GLO land system, with the proviso that North Carolina warrants would be satisfied in the Congressional Reservation if Tennessee's two-thirds proved insufficient. In 1818, Tennessee received the right to perfect titles in the federal portion and in 1841 to grant lands there. In 1846, the United States ceded all the undisposed lands in the Congressional Reservation to Tennessee. The plan to survey the Reservation in federal townships and ranges was never implemented nor did the United States open a land office. Tennessee was technically the first public-domain state, but the total acreage granted by the United States government in the state was the 640-acre townsite of Pulaski.

This history is recounted for two reasons. First, title grants in the Congressional Reservation were delayed many years while the government waited to see if its land would be needed to redeem North Carolina warrants. This caused population pressures along the boundaries of the reservation and enticed many squatters onto these empty lands. Thus they disappeared into areas without county records. Second, Tennessee grew so impatient waiting for the opening of the Reservation that in 1819 it created an interim title called "Middle Tennessee occupant grants." These preemption grants survive in the state archives and have been microfilmed along with other grants. The surveys, patents, and many North Carolina bounty-land warrants are in the state archives, also microfilmed.

The grants are in several series–North Carolina grants 1783-1800, Tennessee grants 1806-1927, the Hiwassee District, etc.–but are all indexed in a composite, microfilmed card index. By Congressional resolution, a survey was taken in the early 1790s to see how much land had already been granted in its newly acquired territory. This survey is available on NARS microfilm M68 in one roll and published as Betty G. C. Cartwright and Lillian Johnson Gardiner, *North Carolina Land Grants in Tennessee, 1778-1791* (Memphis: Cartwright and Gardiner, 1958). Early land records for northeastern Tennessee are sparse since settlers reached the Watauga and Holston rivers ahead of county government. The North-of-Holston settlements were treated as part of Washington County, Virginia, until about 1779. See also Thomas B. Jones, "The Public Lands of Tennessee," *Tennessee Historical Quarterly* 27 (1968): 13-36. Land laws and county boundary changes are collected in Henry D. Whitney, *The Land Laws of Tennessee* (Chattanooga: J. M. Deardorff & Sons, Printers, 1891).

Texas

State-land state surveyed in often rectangular metes and bounds with some large tracts subdivided into numbered blocks often a mile square. Many rivers have parallel long lots running back from the water. The first Spanish settlements in Texas were at Nacogdoches in 1716 and San Antonio in 1718; over the next 120 years about 26 million acres were granted by the Spanish and Mexican governments. Empresarios such as Stephen Austin, Sterling Robertson, Martín de León, and Benjamin Milam contracted with the Mexican government to bring settlers into Texas. In return, they received large grants and established their own land offices. The Texas Constitution of 1836 validated all Spanish and Mexican land grants provided they conformed to the laws in effect at their issuance, though title disputes were heard by the state courts. Also in 1836, the Texas legislature created the Texas General Land Office, which still manages 22 million acres, including lucrative gas and oil lands. When Texas entered the Union in 1845, it retained its right to sole disposal of its public domain.

The Texas General Land Office has, since 1836, overseen the transfer of most of the public land into private ownership. Its archives, along with the county deeds, are the major Texas land source for researchers. The Texas General Land Office, Stephen F. Austin State Office Building, Room 811, 1700 N. Congress Avenue, Austin, TX 78701, encourages both written queries and research in person. Here is the land office's summary of its major collections, excluding its important Spanish Archives of the pre-Republic period:[38]

Bounty grants for service in the Army of the Republic of Texas were awarded at the rate of 320 acres per three months of service.

Donation grants of 640 acres were given for special service during the Texas Revolution. Men who fought at any battle, such as the Siege of Bexar, Goliad, the Alamo, San Jacinto, etc., were eligible, and later donations were given to widows and surviving veterans.

Headrights were given to the heads of families and single men who settled in the Republic of Texas. First-class grants were given to any man who arrived in the Republic prior to 2 March 1836. Married men received one league (4,423.4 acres) and one labor (177.1 acres), and single men received one-third of a league (1,476.1 acres). Second-class grants were given to any man who arrived in the Republic after 2 March 1836 but prior to 1 October 1837. Married men received 1,280 acres, and single men received 640 acres. Third-class grants were given to any man who arrived in the Republic after 1 October 1837 but prior to 1 January 1840. Married men received 640 acres, and single men received 320 acres. Fourth-class grants were given to men who arrived in the Republic after 1 January 1840 but prior to 1 January 1842. Married men received 640 acres, and single men received 320 acres.

Preemption grants (homestead or settler's claims) went to individuals who actually resided on a tract of no more than 320 acres for at least three consecutive years from 22 January 1845. Under an act of 1854, preemptors could locate no more than 160 acres. Under an act of 1870, married men could locate no more than 160 acres and single men no more than 80 acres. The last preemption was approved in 1899.

School lands were sold to individuals under an act of 1874, and the proceeds went into the common school fund.

The land office has county maps showing the original surveys for each county and indexes by county to all grant records. A major guide is Texas General Land office, *Abstracts of All Original Texas Land Titles*, 8 vols. plus supplements (Austin: General Land Office, 1941-42), which can be purchased from the land office on microfiche. In 1855, the Texas Adjutant-General's office was destroyed along with its bounty warrants, donation records, and muster rolls, which necessitated creating a Court of Claims (1856-60) whose records are in the land office. Two major indexes to early grants are Virginia H. Taylor, *Index to Spanish and Mexican Land Grants in Texas* (Austin: Lone Star Press, 1974); and Thomas Lloyd Miller, *Bounty and Donation Land Grants of Texas, 1835-1888* (Austin: University of Texas Press, 1967). Miller's introduction (pp. 3-56) describes these grants in detail. There are also published indexes to some of the other grant series. The land office has issued a pamphlet summarizing the history of Texas land, but the standard treatment is Thomas Lloyd Miller, *The Public Lands of Texas 1519-1970* (Norman: University of Oklahoma Press, 1972). The Fort Worth FARC reports no GLO or private land claims records. See also Reuben McKitrick, *The Public Land System of Texas, 1823-1910* (Madison: University of Wisconsin, 1918), Bulletin no. 905; J. J. Bowden, *Spanish and Mexican Land Grants in the Chihuahuan Acquisition* (El Paso: Texas Western Press, 1971); and Florence Johnson Scott, *Royal Land Grants North of the Rio Grande, 1777-1821* (Rio Grande City: Texian Press, 1969).

Utah

Public-domain state with two principal meridians (established 1855 and 1875). Of Utah's three GLO land districts, the earliest opened in 1869 at Salt Lake City. Obtain patents from the BLM Utah State Office, 136 East South Temple, Salt Lake City, UT 84101, which also has copies of tract books and township plats. The National Archives has the land-entry case files as described in Inventory No. 22 and the GLO headquarters original tract books and township plats. It also has a card index to all Utah patentees to 30 June 1908. The records of the local GLO land offices are in the Denver FARC, summarized in Joel Barker, *Preliminary Inventory of the Records of the Bureau of Land Management–Utah* (Denver: Denver Archives and Records Center, 1979).

When the first Mormons settled in Utah in 1847, their church allotted lands and encouraged communal irrigation systems and living in villages rather than on farms. While these practices adapted well to semi-arid Utah, they did not conform to the federal policy of having people live on 160-acre homesteads. Thus it was often necessary when the first GLO land office opened in 1869 to have entrymen–often LDS Church officials–take out homestead patents and then redeed them piecemeal to actual owners. These transactions are recorded in county deed books. See Lawrence L. Linford, "Establishing and Maintaining Land Ownership in Utah Prior to 1869," *Utah Historical Quarterly* 42 (1974): 126-43; and Lawrence B. Lee, "Homesteading in Zion," ibid., 28 (1960): 28-38.

Vermont

State-land state surveyed in fairly rectangular New England towns. Although New Hampshire, New York, and Massachusetts all made grants in present-day Vermont, many of the settlers were from Connecticut, having migrated up the Connecticut River Valley. Any standard history of colonial Vermont will explain the New Hampshire-New York dispute of 1749 over control of Vermont, and the latter's simple solution of declaring itself independent of any jurisdiction during the period 1776-91. A brief account is in William H. Dumont, "The New York-Vermont Land Dispute, 1749-1791," *New York Genealogical and Biographical Record* 100 (1969): 91-95. The standard discussion is Matt Bushnell Jones, *Vermont in the Making* (Cambridge: Harvard University Press, 1939). Check also the Phelps-Gorham Collection at the New York State Archives, Albany, for documents relating to the Gore, a narrow strip of land along the New York-Connecticut-Vermont border.

The state's official land records are mostly in the Division of State Papers, Office of the Secretary of State, 109 State Street, Montpelier, VT 05602. The Vermont Secretary of State's *State Papers of Vermont* has published several volumes on land records: volume 2 by Franklin H. Dewart, *Charters Granted by the State of Vermont* (1922); and vols. 5-7, Mary Greene Nye, *Petitions for Grants of Land 1778-1811* (1939); *Sequestration, Confiscation and Sale of [Loyalist] Estates* (1941); and *New York Land Patents 1688-1786 Covering Land Now Included in the State of Vermont (Not Including Military Patents)* (1947). Volume 2 listed above has been indexed in Jay Mack Holbrook, *Vermont's First Settlers* (Oxford, Mass.: Holbrook Research Institute, 1976). Also see Hiram A. Huse, *The New Hampshire Grants, Being Transcripts of the Charters of Townships and Other Minor Grants of Land Made by the Provincial Government of New Hampshire Within the Present Boundaries of the State of Vermont, from 1749 to 1754*, New Hampshire State Papers, vol. 26 (Concord: Edward N. Pearson, Printer, 1895); and Herbert W. Denio, "Massachusetts Land Grants in Vermont," *Publications of the Colonial Society of Massachusetts* 24 (1920-22): 35-59. Vermont deeds are recorded in the towns, surviving records being microfilmed at least to 1850. See also Florence May Woodward, *The Town Proprietors in Vermont: New England Town Proprietorship in Decline* (New York: Columbia University Press, 1936).

Virginia

State-land state surveyed in indiscriminate metes and bounds. Virginia settlement began under a private stock company called the Virginia Company of London, whose charter was revoked in 1624. Only near the end of this period did the company begin granting land for private ownership, there being a few references in surviving records to grants in 1619-24. The fifty-acre headright existed 1618 to 1725; long headright lists of transported persons survive in the early patents and provide by far the most significant list of early Virginia settlers. Since these are often the earliest reference by several years to an immigrant in Virginia, the researcher must be alert to clerical and transcription errors, for which see Noel Currer-Briggs, "Headrights and Pitfalls," *Virginia Genealogist* 23 (1979): 45-56.

Virginia's land office records in the royal period (1624-1776) and in statehood are in the Virginia State Library at Richmond and have been microfilmed with indexes. The first fourteen patent books (1623-1732) are abstracted in Nell Marion Nugent, *Cavaliers and Pioneers*, 3 vols. (Richmond: Virginia State Library, 1934-79). Researchers should read her introduction in volume 1. The Fairfax Northern Neck Proprietary north of the Rappahannock River was selling lands before 1700. Its patent books are in the Virginia State Library and are microfilmed with an index. The Northern Neck's southern boundary first ran in 1746 in a straight line from the southern tip of Maryland's western boundary to the head of the North Rappahannock River at the north end of Rappahannock County and then down the river to Chesapeake Bay. It was moved south in 1753 by order of the crown, the line to run from the Maryland tip southeast along the southern boundary of now-Shenandoah County extended to the head of the South Rappahannock River, now called the Rapidan, and down to the bay.

Virginia had entail until 1776 and primogeniture to 1786. A special complication with Virginia entail was the absence for estates worth more than £200 of a way to terminate (dock) the entail except by an act of the legislature. Some eighteenth-century Virginia quitrent rolls survive. The 1704 record is in the Public Records Office in England, but it has been published several times. The most reliable readings of this 1704 list are in Louis des Cognets, Jr., *English Duplicates of Lost Virginia Records* (Princeton, N.J.: By the author, 1958), pp. 123-232, and Thomas J. Wertenbaker, *The Planters of Colonial Virginia* (New York: Russell & Russell, 1959), pp. 183-247. It covers only south of the Rappahannock, since the Northern Neck quitrents belonged to the Fairfax proprietary. There are Northern Neck quitrents for fourteen counties at the Huntington Library in San Marino (Los Angeles), California, which the genealogist must obtain on microfilm since the Huntington restricts access to its collections. Extensive personal and property tax lists are in the Virginia State Library 1782-1863 and have been microfilmed. See D. Forrest, "A History of Taxation in Colonial Virginia, 1607-1775" (M.A. thesis, William and Mary College, 1931); Frederick T. Neeley, "The Development of Virginia Taxation, 1775-1860" (Ph.D. diss., University of Virginia, 1956); and Mrs. G. Dice, "Lord Fairfax Rent Rolls," *National Genealogical Society Quarterly* 39 (1951): 113-18.

There are other Virginia records with some relation to land that deserve mention. The microfiche publication Ransome B. True, *Biographical Dictionary of Early Virginia, 1607-1660* (Jamestown:

The Association for the Preservation of Virginia Antiquities, 1982), lists in its 1982 edition about 120,000 entries for over 33,000 persons and includes deeds (though few of Nugent's patents). The bounty-land warrants by Virginia for the French and Indian War, Dunmore's War, and especially the Revolution are numerous. (See earlier discussion of bounty lands.)

Virginia in the 1770s and 1780s had several active counties in what is now southwestern Pennsylvania. See John F. Vallentine, "Research in Virginia's District of West Augusta," *Genealogical Journal* 4 (1975): pp. 141-47; Raymond M. Bell, "Virginia Land Grants in Pennsylvania," *Virginia Genealogist* 7 (1963): 78-83, 103-7, 152-62; and 11 (1967): 126-27. Virginia has a significant number of independent cities, and they keep their own conveyances; some have records from colonial times. George B. Everton, Sr., *The Handy Book for Genealogists*, 7th ed. (Logan, Utah.: Everton Publishers, 1981), lists Virginia's independent cities.

The secondary literature on Virginia land is large. For instance, see Fairfax Harrison, *Virginia Land Grants, a Study of Conveyancing in Relation to Colonial Politics* (Richmond: Old Dominion Press, 1925); W. Stitt Robinson, *Mother Earth: Land Grants in Virginia, 1607-1699* (Williamsburg: 350th Anniversary Celebration Corporation, 1957); Manning C. Voorhis, "The Land Grant Policy of Colonial Virginia, 1607-1774" (Ph.D. diss., University of Virginia, 1940), and his "Crown versus Council in the Virginia Land Policy," *William and Mary Quarterly*, 3rd series, 3 (1946): 499-514; Faye B. Reeder, "The Evolution of the Virginia Land Grant System in the Eighteenth Century" (Ph.D. diss., Ohio State University, 1937); Daphne S. Gentry, "Colonial and Commonwealth Land Records of Virginia," *Genealogical Journal* 4 (1975): 127-40; Sarah S. Hughes, *Surveyors and Statesmen: Land Measuring in Colonial Virginia* (Richmond: The Virginia Surveyors Foundation and the Virginia Association of Surveyors, 1979); William H. Seiler, "Land Processioning in Colonial Virginia," *William and Mary Quarterly*, 3rd series 6 (1949): 416-36; and Robert Young Clay, *Virginia Genealogical Resources* (Detroit: Detroit Society for Genealogical Research, 1980), pp. 11-12, 19-26.

Washington

Public-domain state with one principal meridian (established 1851). Of Washington's seven GLO land districts, the earliest opened in 1855 in Olympia, and the last closed in Seattle in 1927. The records of these offices are in the Seattle FARC. Obtain patents from the BLM Oregon State Office, 825 NE Multnomah Street, Box 2965, Portland, OR 97208, which also has copies of the tract books and township plats. The National Archives in Washington, D.C., has the land-entry case files as described in Inventory No. 22 and the GLO headquarters original tract books and township plats. Washington's earliest white and mixed-blood settlers were entitled to free federal land under the Donation Act of 1850. An index and abstracts are on NARS microfilm M203, "Abstracts of Washington Donation Land Claims, 1855-1902," in one roll, which serves as an index to the case files reproduced on NARS microfilm M815, "Oregon and Washington Donation Land Files, 1851-1903," in 108 rolls. Donation case files are valuable because they should contain a statement of the date and place of birth of the entryman. Because of a law forbidding their reproduction, the naturalization certificates in the M815 case files were not filmed. They can now be obtained from the National Archives. See Frederick Jay Yonce, "Public Land Disposal in Washington" (Ph.D. diss., University of Washington, 1966); and Roy Otto Hoover, "The Public Land Policy of Washington State: The Initial Period, 1889-1912" (Ph.D. diss., Washington State University, 1967).

West Virginia

State-land state surveyed in indiscriminate metes and bounds. Since West Virginia was part of Virginia until 1863, its first-title grants prior to the Civil War were made by Virginia. The colonial grants are in separate series for the Virginia royal government and for the Northern Neck Proprietary. They include significant portions of present West Virginia. (For the Northern Neck boundary, see the Virginia entry.) West Virginia land records are at the State Auditor, Capitol Building, West Wing 231, Charleston, WV 25305. The Virginia royal/commonwealth and Northern Neck grants are in the Virginia State Library, microfilmed with indexes. The West Virginia State Auditor has extensive grant records 1754-1864 and 1748-1912, also microfilmed. Pursuant to a 1951 act of the legislature, the state auditor attempted to collect and index all identifiable grantees: Edgar B. Sims, *Sim's Index to Land Grants in West Virginia* (Charleston: Auditor's Office, 1952), 866 pp. with 16 pp. supplement. See also Edgar B. Sims, *Making a State; Formation of West Virginia, Including Maps, Illustrations, Plats, Grants*,. . . (Charleston: State Auditor, 1956).

Researchers doing colonial and antebellum genealogy in West Virginia must remember that they are really working with Virginia records. Thus the bounty-land laws for the French and Indian War, Dunmore's War, and the Revolution apply to West Virginia. Likewise, the extension of Virginia counties into southwestern Pennsylvania in the 1770s and 1780s has ramifications for early West Virginia migrations – parts of those counties included West Virginia. The *Virginia Genealogist* and other Virginia genealogical and historical journals have much on early West Virginia lands.

Wisconsin

Public-domain state with one principal meridian (established 1831). Of the nine GLO land districts, the earliest opened in 1834 at Mineral Point, the last closed in 1925 at Wausau. The local records of these districts are at the Commissioner of Public Lands, 127 West Washington Avenue, Madison, WI 53703. Obtain patents from the BLM Eastern States Office in Alexandria, Virginia, which also has copies of the tract books and township plats. The National Archives has the land-entry case files as described in Inventory No. 22 and also the GLO headquarters original tract books and township plats. For private land claims, see the *American State Papers, Public Lands* as indexed in McMullin's *Grassroots*.

See also Paul W. Gates, "Frontier Land Business in Wisconsin," *Wisconsin Magazine of History* 52 (1962): 306-27; Frederick N. Trowbridge, "Confirming Land Titles in Early Wisconsin," ibid., 26 (1942): 314-22; and Michael Fox, *Maps and Atlases Showing Land Ownership in Wisconsin* (Madison: State Historical Society of Wisconsin, 1978).

Wyoming

Public-domain state with two principal meridians (established 1855 and 1875). Of Wyoming's six GLO land districts, the earliest opened in Cheyenne in 1870. The records of these offices are mostly in the Denver FARC, though the Wyoming state archives has records for entries not brought to patent. Obtain patents from the BLM Wyoming State Office, 2515 Warren Avenue, Box 1828, Cheyenne, WY 82003, which also has copies of the tract books and township plats. The National Archives has the land-entry case files as described in Inventory No. 22 and the GLO headquarters original tract books and township plats.

Notes

1. Donald Lines Jacobus, "Connecticut," in Milton Rubincam and Kenn Stryker-Rodda, eds., *Genealogical Research Methods and Sources*, 2 vols. (Washington, D.C.: American Society of Genealogists, 1960-71),1:129.

2. Indenture from William Eskridge and wife Betty to Thomas Williams, 7 May 1763, Northumberland County, Va., Deed Book 6, pp. 220-22, Genealogical Society (GS) of Utah microfilm 032,675 (7761 pt. 4).

3. J. Harvey Bloom, "Seals," *Genealogists' Magazine* 13 (1959): 111.

4. Indenture from Dempsey Wood, Sr., to Hardy Wood, 31 March 1800 (recorded 21 March 1896), Montgomery County, Ga., Deed Book 2W, pp. 404-05, GS 218,775 (29180 pt. 30); Indenture from Glasingham Haney, Sr., to Dempsy [sic] Wood, 30 Dec. 1791 (recorded 30 July 1901), ibid., Deed Book 2U, pp. 5-6, GS 218,779 (29180 pt. 34).

5. Kip Sperry, "Processioning in the Southern States," *Genealogical Journal* 4 (1975): 150-54.

6. Robert D. Mitchell, *Commercialism and Frontier: Perspectives on the Early Shenandoah Valley* (Charlottesville, Va.: University Press of Virginia, 1977), pp. 31-33.

7. Royal Grant to Ezekiel Backler, 11 Aug. 1774 (recorded 15 March 1773), South Carolina Royal Grants, Book 32, p. 49; GS 022,596 (5342 pt. 16).

8. Grant to John Lemon, 1 July 1760 (no recording date), Northern Neck Grants, Book K, p. 11; GS 029,515 (7117 pt. 8).

9. For an absorbing narrative of how such a reconstruction can provide an intimate understanding of the evidence, see James Franklin Sutherland, *Some Original Land Grant Surveys along Green River in Lincoln and Casey Counties, Kentucky (1781-1836)* (n.p.: Casey County Bicentennial Committee, 1975), pp. 1-27.

10. David F. Stoddard, "Land System of the New England Colonial Colonies," *Connecticut Nutmegger* 11 (1979): 556-64; capitalization standardized.

11. The historical summary which follows is drawn from David A. Bundy, *100 Acres More or Less: The History of the Land and People of Bow, New Hampshire* (Canaan, Conn.: Bow Town History Committee, by Phoenix Press, 1975).

12. "Brief Notes on the Public Domain," (n.p.: Bureau of Land Management, 1957), p. 21.

13. As quoted in Lawrence L. Linford, "Establishing and Maintaining Land Ownership in Utah Prior to 1869," *Utah Historical Quarterly* 42 (1974): 139.

14. Payson Jackson Treat, *The National Land System, 1785-1820* (New York: E. B. Treat, 1910), p. 215.

15. Paul Gates, *History of Public Law Land Development* (Washington, D.C.: Public Land Law Review Commission, 1968), pp. 251-57.

16. Ibid., p. 278.

17. James W. Oberly, "Military Bounty Land Warrants of the Mexican War," *Prologue* 14 (1982): 28.

18. Gates, *History of Public Land Law Development*, p. 279.

19. Treat, *The National Land System*, pp. 252-253.

20. Ibid., p. 340.

21. Gates, *History of Public Law Land Development*, p. 256.

22. Ibid., p. 255.

23. Smith, *Federal Land Series*, vol. 4, pt. 1, (1982), p. x.

24. Kenn Stryker-Rodda, "Limit of 18th Century Sources in New York and New Jersey," *Families* 11 (1972): 121.

25. Raymond A. Winslow, Jr., "Tax and Fiscal Records," in Helen F. M. Leary and Maurice K. Stirewalt, *North Carolina Research: Genealogy and Local History* (Raleigh: North Carolina Genealogical Society, 1980), pp. 214-15.

26. Poll Tax List, 1799, Warren County, Ky., Tax Lists 1799, pp. 5-6, 14, 17; GS 008,255 (2638 pt. 405).

27. *Laws of the State of Indiana. . .Tenth Session* (Indianapolis, Ind.: Douglas and Maguire, printers, 1826), p. 68, chap. 57.

28. "Bute Co., N. C.: 1771 Tax List," *The North Carolinian* 7 (1961): 899-907; "Franklin-Warren-Vance Cos. Area: Father-Son Relationships in 1771," ibid., 11 (1965): 1,499-1,515.

29. Richard LeBaron Bowen, *Early Rehoboth: Documented Historical Studies of Families and Events in this Plymouth Colony Township* (Rehoboth, Mass.: By the author, 1950), vol. 4, pp. 143-45.

30. Edward W. Hanson and Homer Vincent Rutherford, "Genealogical Research in Massachusetts: A Survey and Bibliographical Guide," *New England Historical and Genealogical Register* 13 (1981): 177.

31. Dall W. Forsythe, *Taxation and Political Change in the Young Nation, 1781-1833* (New York City: Columbia University Press, 1977), p. 59.

32. William Blackstone, *Commentaries on the Laws of England* (Oxford: Clarendon Press, 1766), book 2, ch. 20, p. 315.

33. Deed of Feofment from Arthur Harris to James Heaburn, 26 March 1744 (recorded 5 April 1744), Westmoreland County, Va. Deeds and Wills, Book 9, pp. 347-48; GS 034,272 (8166, pt. 6).

34. Deed of Release from John Taylor the Aged to Richard Taylor, 17 July 1713 (date of recording unknown), Chesapeake City, successor to Norfolk Co., Va., Deed Book 9, pp. 261-62; GS 032,829 (7799, pt. 9); and Will of Richard Taylor, 26 Sept. 1729, proved 19 Feb. 1730/1 (never officially recorded), Chesapeake City, successor to Norfolk County, Va., Unrecorded Wills Book 1722-36, p. 22.

35. William Thorndale, "The Lindseys of Maury County, Tennessee," typescript, in Genealogical Society of Utah, Salt Lake City, Utah, n. d.

36. *Guide to New England Genealogy* (Newton, Mass.: New England Family History Society, 1982), p. NE25.1.

37. Kenn Stryker-Rodda, "That Genealogical Quagmire: New Jersey," *National Genealogical Society Quarterly* 48 (1960): 62-64.

38. General Land Office, "Guide to Genealogy," (Austin, Tex.: General Land Office, 1982), pamphlet.

INFORMATION GUIDE

Genealogical Information in the Record Group	*Service*	*Pensions*	*Draft*	*Discharge*	*Burials*	*Veterans Homes*
Surname/name	●	●	●	●	●	●
Date of Birth	●					●
Place of Birth	●	●	●	●		●
Sex	●	●			●	●
Race/color	●	●				
Physical Description	●	●	●	●		●
Occupation	●	●	●	●		●
Education		●				
Military Service	●	●	●	●	●	●
Slave Status		●				
Property Owned		●				●
Religion						
Citizenship	●	●	●		●	●
Marital Status		●	●			●
Spouse's Name		●				●
Children's Names		●				●
Father's Name		●				
Mother's Name		●				
Father's Birthplace						
Mother's Birthplace						
Date of Death	●	●			●	●
Cause of Death	●	●			●	●
Name of Cemetery	●	●			●	●
Residence	●	●	●	●	●	●
Age	●	●	●	●	●	●
Literacy/signature		●				●
Photograph/sketch		●			●	●
Relatives					●	●

COULD YOU USE THIS CHAPTER?

Type of Record	*Kept from*	*Clues That You Should Consult These Records*
Service records and pension files	1775-on	If a family record, a notation in a county history, or other document hints that your ancestor may have applied for a pension—whether it was granted or not—you may be close to a genealogical goldmine. Such records, along with bounty-land applications, and military service records go back to the Indian wars that predated the Revolution, enabling you to locate your ancestor, distinguish him from others by the same name, and trace his movements between military service and the time he applied for the pension — — even determine the color of his eyes. If his widow applied for the pension allowed her by law, you can also establish both their deathdates and sometimes even those of their heirs. If your ancestor did not serve in the military, a brother or uncle who did will sometimes supply equally valuable information about the previous generation. Don't overlook the possibility that your ancestor may have been a Loyalist in the Revolution who received compensation for losses from the British government.
Draft records	1863 on	All white male citizens and aliens who had declared their intent to naturalize had to register for the draft if they were between the ages of eighteen and forty-five. Thus, these records for states under Union control during the Civil War supply a state-by-state list of men eligible for the draft with specific information about age, residence, occupation, and marital status. Draft records are often more complete than city directions for urban ancestors.
Confederate records	1861-on	If your ancestor was in the South during the Civil War, there is a good chance that his military records were turned over to the War Department in Washington, D.C., unless he belonged to a state unit that never became part of the Confederate military arm. Among these records are lists of Confederate prisoners of war who died in Northern prison.
Burial records	Since 1861	If you know that your ancestor made the military his career or died in active service or in a soldier's "home" after retirement, then records of his burial in one of the national or other military cemeteries probably exist. These records will give his name, date and place of burial, place of residence before enlistment, survivors, cause of death, and date and place of death in addition to military information.
Regiment or unit histories	Since Revolutionary War	If you can identify your ancestor's military unit, look at the many printed regimental or unit histories to see if something has been written about his company. Many of these try to identify every individual in a given military unit and their contributions.

Chapter 8

MILITARY RECORDS

Johni Cerny

The uses and value of military records in genealogical research for ancestors who were veterans are obvious, but military records can also be important to researchers whose direct ancestors were not soldiers in any war. The fathers, grandfathers, brothers, or other close relatives of the ancestor may have served in a war and their service or pension records may contain information that will assist in further identifying the family of primary interest. Due to the amount of genealogical information contained in some military pension files, they should never be overlooked during the research process. Those records not containing specific genealogical information are of historic value and should be included in any overall research design. The United States has been involved in at least eleven major wars, numerous Indian wars, and two "conflicts" since the first colonial settlements were established. For our purposes, the wars are grouped into these six periods:

Colonial Wars	
King Philip's War	1675-76
King William's War	1689-97
Queen Anne's War	1702-13
King George's War	1744-48
French & Indian War	1754-63
Revolutionary War	1775-83
Post-Revolutionary Wars	
War of 1812	1812-14
Indian Wars	1817-58
Mexican War	1846-48
Civil War	1861-65
Spanish-American War	1898
Modern Wars	
World War I	1917-18
World War II	1942-45
Korean Action	1950-53
Vietnam Action	1961-73

At least remnants of records exist for every war that the colonies and states were involved in; but as with other records maintained in the United States during the first centuries of its existence, there is little uniformity of content or style in those records.

This chapter will discuss the two principal categories of military records in detail: service records and records of veteran's benefits. Other record categories are referenced where they supply genealogical information.

Service Records

Colonial Wars (1675-1763)

Service records of soldiers in the colonial wars have more historical than genealogical information and usually provide only the name of the soldier and the colonial unit in which he served. They consist primarily of rosters, rolls, and lists that survived the wars and several fires. Most of these rosters and rolls have been published and can be found in genealogical and historical libraries throughout the nation. (See bibliography at the end of this chapter.)

Despite the scanty genealogical information these records provide, you should not ignore them. They may be sparse but few records in general exist for that period to help locate an ancestor. The presence of a soldier in a particular unit may be a valuable clue to his place of residence as well as useful in identifying his family in other records of the same location, even though there may be problems in distinguishing between two or more soldiers with the same name.

Revolutionary War (1774-1811)

Some of the original service records for the Revolutionary War were destroyed by fire, but those remaining are on file at the National Archives, compiled primarily from rosters and rolls of soldiers serving in the Continental Army and the colonial/state militia units, with additions from correspondence and field reports of military officers. These service records contain much more genealogical information than colonial records: name, rank, and military organization of the soldier. Included in some records are "the name of the state from which he served; the date that his name appears on one or more of the rolls; sometimes the date or dates of his enlistment, or the date of his appointment; and, rarely, the date of his separation from the service."[1] His physical description, date and place of birth, residence at the time of enlistment, and other personal details are also included in some categories. For example, in the size roll for Captain Aaron Ogden's Company, 1st Regiment of New Jersey, we find these men:

> WILLIAM JONES, private, 22, 5'4"; brown [eyes], fair [hair]; taylor, [tailor]; b. & res. Woodbridge, Essex Co., enl. 15 June '77.
>
> JONAS KENT, private, 32, 5'3"; black, dark; laborer; b. & res. Horse Neck, Essex Co.; enl. 7 Mar. '77.
>
> JOSEPH KING, private, 30, 5' 5 1/2", bloomer; b. & res. Morris, Morris Co.; enl. 24 Dec. '76; on detail at Wyoming all of '82.
>
> WILLIAM LEGEER, private, 19, 5'9"; light, fair; laborer; b. & res. Amwell, Hunterdon Co.; enl. 15 Apr. '79.
>
> WILLIAM McMULLIN, private, 36, 5' 8 1/2"; black, fair; laborer; b. Glenarm, Embrim, Ireland; res. Mendham, Morris Co.; enl. 16 Feb. '78; deserted at Morris Hutts, 18 Apr. '82, retaken 28 June '82, 100 lashes.
>
> (Book 75, 1782. Old Loan Records, NARS M1015, Roll 4)

Revolutionary War service records are indexed, most of the indexes have been microfilmed, and many libraries have copies. The service records themselves can be searched at the National Archives and its branches, or at the Genealogical Society of Utah and its branches. (See Appendix A and Appendix D for addresses.)

Genealogists who have access to the microfilmed records can search them more efficiently by following the guide in Table 8-1.

Table 8-1

Index to Microfilmed Revolutionary War Records

Record	NARS Microfilm Publication	Reels	Index	NARS Microfilm Publication	Reels	Comments/Access
Compiled Service Records of Soldiers who served in the American Army during the Revolutionary War	M881	1097	General Index to Compiled Military Service Records of Soldiers, Sailors, Army Staff Departments	M860	58	Available at National Archives and branches, Genealogical Society of Utah and branches, other selected libraries.
			Index to Compiled Service Records of Volunteer Soldiers who served. . .from North Carolina	M257	2	
			Index to Compiled Service Records of Volunteer Soldiers who served . . . from Connecticut	M290	1	
			Index to Compiled Service Records of Volunteer Soldiers who served. . .from Georgia	M1051	1	
			Other card indexes for Delaware, Maryland, Massachusetts, New Hampshire, New Jersey, New York, Pennsylvania, Rhode Island, South Carolina, Vermont, and Virginia			Available only at NARS: not on microfilm.
Compiled Service Records of American Naval Personnel and Members of Dept. of Quartermaster General and Commissary General of Military Stores who served during the Revolutionary War	M880	4				
Revolutionary War Rolls, List of Jackets, 1775-83	M246	138	Index to Revolutionary War Rolls (Soldiers, Regiments)	T515	58	Original records from which compiled service records were made. *Search in this order:* **1. T-515;** (a) Index of Soldiers (Army). 58 rolls. Cards on each person. Notations in lower left corner of index cards frequently give *volume number to original record.* Example: Joseph Smith, 136, William Douglas Regiment of Connecticut. (b) Index of Regiments. Arranged in continental then state units. Gives jacket number under which all documents for that regiment are found. Example: William Douglas Regiment #203. **2. M-246 Roll List of Jackets, 1775-83.** 138 rolls. Militia rolls, payrolls, supply lists for each regiment. These are the volumes in which the men will be listed. Most of the men will appear in more than one list, so be sure to check them all. Example: Jacket #203, William Douglas Regiment is on Roll 27 of the 138 rolls.
Numbered Record Books Concerning Military Operations and Service Pay, Settlements of Accounts, Supplies, War Department Collection of Revolutionary War Records	M853	41				Available only at NARS.
Miscellaneous Numbered Records (The Manuscript File) War Department Collection of Revolutionary War Records	M859	125	Special Index to Numbered Records in the War Department Collection of Revolutionary War Records, 1775-83	M847		Original records, ca. 35,000 items. Includes civilians in war service: paymasters, wagoneers, judges, chaplains, medical officers, teamsters, and others. Available at NARS and Genealogical society of Utah.
Compiled Service Records of Volunteer Soldiers who served from 1784-1811	M905	32	Index to Compiled Service Records. 1784-1811	M694	9	

Record	NARS Microfilm Publication	Reels	Index	Comments/Access
War Department Collection of Post Revolutionary War Manuscripts. 1784-1811	M904	4	Every-name card index.	Includes muster rolls. Index not on microfilm; search only at NARS.
Central Treasury Records of the Continental and Confederation Government Relating to Military Affairs, 1775-89	M1015	7		Includes military pay and muster rolls which can be used as evidence of service. Also included are company and accounts books of officers. For example, Capt. Aaron Ogden's company book, 1st New Jersey Regiment, 12782-83, is found on Roll 4. Available only at NARS.
Papers of the Continental Congress 1774-89	M247	204	John P. Butler, comp., *Index to Papers of the Continental Congress*,5 vols. (Washington: NARS, 1978).	Every-name index. Includes muster rolls, payrolls, wagoneer lists, claims for pay by Revolutionary soldiers and officers, many of whom did not live long enough to file for pension. film and printed index available at NARS. Index only available at Genealogical Society of Utah.
Miscellaneous Papers of the Continental Congress	M332	10		

Those using the collection of the Genealogical Society of Utah in Salt Lake City or one of its branches should check the *Military Records Register* for the appropriate call numbers for the above films. The collection of the Genealogical Society of Utah is almost as large as that of the National Archives, making these records more widely available throughout the United States, especially since the NARS interlibrary loan program for military records has been discontinued. Copies can, however, be obtained from the National Archives and Records Service in Washington, D.C. Patrons must use NATF Form 26 (revised May 82) to request a particular record. See Figure 8-1 for a blank form.

Three types of records are available from NARS: (1) pensions (2) bounty-land warrant applications, and (3) military service records. All three types of records can be requested for any soldier on the same form. Simply check all three types of records and enclose a $5 fee for each type requested. A search of these records cannot be completed without the full name of the veteran, his branch of service, the state from which he served, and the war in which he served. You may also use this form to request records pertaining to soldiers of wars other than the Revolutionary War. Expect a six-to-eight week processing time before you receive the records. If you want them quicker, use a record agent in Washington.

There may be instances in which information about a veteran of a particular war will not be found in federal military records. In this case, contact the archives of the state from which he served to obtain a copy of his service record, pension record, or bounty-land application.

Military records for the Revolutionary War can also be found in printed state and colonial archives and such other record sources as newspapers, broadsides which have survived in scattered collections, and in private record collections held by descendants from officers and other personnel. (See Figure 8-2 and Figure 8-3.)

Loyalists

Many researchers become frustrated when there is no evidence in any of the records of ancestors who would have been of prime age to have served in the Revolutionary War. Consider that an estimated 30 percent minimum of the population in 1776 in some areas was Loyalist. Many Loyalists went to Canada, Florida, to the West Indies, or even to England to avoid the conflict. Although research in British sources is outside the scope of this chapter, these published sources on the movements of the Loyalists during and after the Revolution should provide a place to begin:

Brown, Wallace. *The Good Americans: The Loyalists in the American Revolution*. New York: William Morrow and Co., 1969.

Bruce, R. M. *Loyalist Trail*. Kingston, Ontario: no pub., n.d.

Coldham, Peter Wilson. *American Loyalist Claims. Vol. I: Abstracted from the Public Record Office*. Washington, D.C.: National Genealogical Society, 1980.

DeMond, Robert O. *Loyalists in North Carolina During the Revolution*. Hampden, Conn.: Archer Books, 1964.

Dubeau, Sharon. *New Brunswick Loyalists: A Bicentennial Tribute*. Lambertville, N.J.: Hunterdon House, 1983.

Gilroy, Marion, comp. *Loyalists and Land Settlement in Nova Scotia*. Halifax: Public Archives of Nova Scotia, 1937.

Harrell, Isaac Samuel. *Loyalism in Virginia*. Durham, N.C.: Duke University Press, 1926.

Kelby, William. *Orderly Book of the Three Battalions of Loyalists Commanded by Brigadier-General Oliver de Lancey, 1776-1778*. Baltimore: Genealogical Publishing Co., 1972.

Palmer, Gregory. *A Bibliography of Loyalist Source Material in the United States, Canada, and Great Britain*. Westport, Conn.: Meckler Publishing Co., 1982. Compiled under the auspices of the American Antiquarian Society and a special university consortium.

Reid, William D. *The Loyalists of Ontario: Sons and Daughters of the American Loyalists of Upper Canada*. Lambertville, N.J.: Hunterdon House, 1983.

Ryerson, Adolphus E. *The Loyalists of America and Their Times; 1620-1816*. 2 vols. Toronto: n. pub., 1880.

Sabine, Lorenzo. *Biographical Sketches of Loyalists of the American Revolution*. 2 vols. Port Washington, N.Y.: Kennekat Press, 1966.

Siebert, Wilbur Henry. *The Colony of Massachusetts Loyalists at Bristol, England*. Boston: Massachusetts Historical Society, 1912.

__________. *Loyalists of East Florida 1774-1785*. 2 vols. DeLand, Florida: Florida State Historical Society, 1929.

Starke, James H. *The Loyalists of Massachusetts and the Other Side of the American Revolution*. Boston: By the author, 1910.

Van Tyne, Claude Halstead. *Loyalists in the American Revolution*. New York: Peter Smith, 1929.

Figure 8-1. NATF Form 26 (Revised May 82), Order for Copies of Veterans Records.

Date Received (NNMS)

NIC 155

ORDER FOR COPIES OF VETERANS RECORDS

INSTRUCTIONS FOR COMPLETING THIS FORM

Submit a separate set of forms for each veteran. Do NOT remove any of the pages of this 3 part set. A payment of $5.00 is required for EACH file checked in Block 1. **PREPAYMENT IS REQUIRED.** Make check payable to **National Archives Trust Fund (NNMS).**

Mail completed form with payment to

Cashier (NJC)
National Archives Trust Fund
8th & Pennsylvania Avenue, N.W.
Washington, DC 20408

AMOUNT ENCLOSED

ORDER FILLED Partial Complete

1. CHECK RECORD DESIRED
   - [ ] PENSION
   - [ ] BOUNTY-LAND WARRANT APPLICATION *(Service before 1856 only)*
   - [ ] MILITARY

REQUIRED MINIMUM IDENTIFICATION OF VETERAN

Items 2, 3, 4, 5 (and 6, when applicable) MUST be completed or your order cannot be serviced.

2. VETERAN *(Give last, first, and middle names)*
3. BRANCH OF SERVICE IN WHICH HE SERVED [ ] Army [ ] Navy [ ] Marine Corps
4. STATE FROM WHICH SERVED
5. WAR IN WHICH, OR DATES BETWEEN WHICH HE SERVED
6. IF SERVICE WAS CIVIL WAR [ ] Union [ ] Confederate

PLEASE PROVIDE THE FOLLOWING INFORMATION, IF KNOWN

7. UNIT IN WHICH HE SERVED *(Name of regiment or number, company, etc., name of ship)*
8. IF SERVICE WAS ARMY, ARM IN WHICH HE SERVED [ ] Infantry [ ] Cavalry [ ] Artillary *If other, specify:*
9. KIND OF SERVICE [ ] Volunteers [ ] Regulars
10. Pension or Bounty Land File No.
11. DATE OF BIRTH
12. PLACE OF BIRTH *(City, County, State, etc.)*
13. NAME OF WIDOW OR OTHER CLAIMANT
14. DATE OF DEATH
15. PLACE OF DEATH *(City, County, State, etc.)*
16. IF VETERAN LIVED IN A HOME FOR SOLDIERS, GIVE LOCATION *(City & State)*
17. PLACE(S) VETERAN LIVED AFTER SERVICE
18. YOUR NAME & ADDRESS

Print or type your name and address within the block below.

(Zip Code)

Do NOT write below — Space is for our reply to you.

[ ] RECORD FILE ENCLOSED — [ ] Pension $5 [ ] Bounty Land $5 [ ] Military $5

NUMBER OF FILES FROM WHICH COPIES WERE REPRODUCED

[ ] WE WERE UNABLE TO COMPLETE YOUR ORDER

[ ] REQUIRED MINIMUM IDENTIFICATION OF VETERAN WAS NOT PROVIDED. Please complete items 2 (give full name), 3, 4, and 5, and resubmit. Your order and remittance are returned to you.

[ ] A SEARCH WAS MADE BUT THE RECORDS YOU REQUESTED WERE NOT FOUND.
- [ ] Pension
- [ ] Bounty Land
- [ ] Military

[ ] When we do not find a record for a veteran, this does not mean that he did not serve. You may be able to obtain information about him from the State archives.

[ ] Your order and your remittance are returned to you.

[ ] Because extended search time was involved, a formal refund must be issued by the US Treasury, which will take 6 8 weeks for processing.

REFUND AUTHORIZING SIGNATURE *(Complete Name)*

REFUND AMOUNT

[ ] We found _____ pension or bounty land files and _____ military service files of the same name (or similar variations). You may order copies by returning the enclosed, marked forms.

[ ] See attached forms/leaflets/information sheet.

[ ] Other

19. NUMBER OF THESE BLANK FORMS YOU WOULD LIKE SENT TO YOU

SEARCHER

DATE

FILE DESIGNATION

NATIONAL ARCHIVES TRUST FUND BOARD

NATF Form 26 (Rev. 5-82)

CUSTOMER

A LIST of the Soldiers who have deserted from the three New Hampshire Battalions, in the Continental Service.

Thomas Low,	of Pennsylvania.	Daniel Bain,	Newbury-Port.	Samuel Ase,	Newtown.
Matthew Winfield.	Ditto.	Hix Small,	Cape-Cod.	Ebenezer Judkins,	Brintwood.
Peter Hanes,	Providence.	John Kelly,	Nottingham.	Jonathan Jennes,	Mitchel.
John Finley,	Marblehead.	James Wall,		John Sanborn,	Kensington.
William Shaw.		Thomas M'Loy,	Portsmouth.	John Foss.	Newbury-Port.
John Kaine,	New-Britain.	John Tecman,	New Ipswich.	Thomas Holmes,	Otter-Creek.
Johnson Smith,	New-Boston.	Asa Holt,	Hartford	Daniel Chandler,	Concord.
Thomas Hammon.		Samuel Harper,	Akworth.	Charles Hacket,	Tamworth.
Michael Laney.		Thomas Harper.	Ditto.	James Gorden,	Epping.
Matthew Holcomb,	Boscawin.	John Harper,	Ditto.	Charles Briant.	
John Lawrey,	Litchfield.	Elkiah Frost,	New Jersey.	John Ayers,	Londonderry.
Simon Nowles,	Brintwood.	John Baldwin,	Hanover.	Peat Chase,	Concord.
Phillip Judkins,	Unity.	William Page.		Thomas Adams,	
Thomas Johnson,	Walpole.	Christopher Billings,	Hartford.	Thomas Berry,	
Joseph Gaffe,	Waterbury.	Seth Rice.	Chester.	Richard Emerson,	Haverhill.
Thomas Wheeler,	Malden.	George Hogg,	Dunbarton:	Paul Wells,	Rumney.
Reuben Thorn.		John Reams,	Chester.	John Burton,	
James Chesley,	Durham.	Joseph Frost,	Ditto.	John Martin,	Goffstown.
Edward Thomas,	New York.	James Randlet,	Exeter.	Isaac Gay.	
James Hooper,	Ditto.	Jeremiah Robinson,	Epping.	John Willson.	
John Gardner.	Canterhook.	George Yeaton,	Portsmouth.	John Bradshaw.	
David Thompson,	Chesterfield.	Thomas Pace,	Mitchel.	Francis Carr,	
Thomas Smith,	Worcester.	Oliver Beacon,	Rindge.	John M'Derman.	
James Parker,	Taunton.	Daniel Russel,	Ditto.	Nathaniel Chase,	Salem.
William Allds,	Merrimack.	Samuel Witten,	Ditto.	John Wooley,	Winchester.
Edward Robinson	New York.	Daniel M'Carte.		Samuel Britain,	Westmoreland.
John Robinson,	Hallstown.	John Edwards.		Levi Fuller,	Chesterfield:
John Willey,	Charlestown, No. four.	James Patten.		Caleb Aldridge,	Westmoreland.
John Smith,	Ditto.	Abraham Clifford,	Rye.	William Goody,	New-Castle.
James Thomas,	Piermont.	Asa Knowlton,	Epsom.	Samuel Colk,	Casco-Bay.
William Wheeler.		Aaron Fiale,	Dunbarton.	Epneus Reed,	New-Salem.
William Sharper.		Caleb Hunt	Dublin.	William Young,	Dover.
John Taylor,	Amherst.	John Swan,	Ditto.	Daniel Clarke,	New-Castle.
Ebenezer Barker,	Dover.	Thomas Parks.		Robert Bragg,	Isle of Shoals.
David Hill,	Candia.	John Colkin,	Brattleborough.	Nathan Finn	Mason.
Duncan Campbell:		James Sloyn,	New York.	Joseph Costo	
Nehemiah Eastman.		Duncan Cambell,	Boston.	Joseph Gilbartelmey	
James Goodwin.		Robert M'Knight,	Deerfield.	Gaspral Tripp	
Joseph Smith,	Boston.	John Rawlins,	Greenland.	Jack Hannaway	
Benjamin Elker.		Gideon Gilson,	Lee.	Matthew Witherinton	
Edward Smith,	Portsmouth.	Matthias Welch,	Nottingham.	John Talvor	
James Aikin,	Chester.	William Griffin.	Portsmouth.	Charles Vorron	
Robert Holland,	Newmarket.	Matthew Mallom,	Great-Island.	Matthew Gotey	
William Frazer,	Pembroke.	John Ellefon,	Ditto.	Antoney Barber	
Moses Perry.	Portsmouth.	Benj'a Hicks,	Nottingham.	Bartelmey Cobey	
Daniel Daily.		John Stapels,	Dover.	John Row	
Andrew M'Donald.		David Batchelder,	Raymond.	Luas Devinow	
James Eastman.		Samuel Smith,	Gilmantown.	Venson Anailas	
John Powell,	Exeter.	Enos Jewell,	Unity.	Joseph Chartard	

STATE OF NEW-HAMPSHIRE

In COMMITTEE of SAFETY, Exeter, July 23, 1779.

ALL Officers, Civil and Military, in this State, are required; and all others Persons, who have the Good of their Country at Heart, are earnestly requested (without Delay) to apprehend, and properly secure in some Goal in this State, any, and all the above Deserters; and to give Notice to the Committee of Safety; for which Service a reasonable Allowance will be made.

M. WEARE, *President.*

Figure 8-2. List of Deserters from New Hampshire, printed as a public notice in the *New Hampshire Gazette* by the Committee of Safety, 23 July 1779; reproduced on microfiche in Evans' Early American Imprints.

Wallace, W. Stewart. *The United Empire Loyalists. A Chronicle of the Great Migration*. Toronto: Glasgow, Brook and Co., 1914.

Yoshpe, Harry Beller. *Disposition of Loyalist Estates in the Southern District of the State of New York*. New York: Columbia University Press, 1939.

Post-Revolutionary Wars (1812-48)

There are service records for the War of 1812, Indian Wars, and the Mexican War. The information included, similar to that in the service records of soldiers in the colonial wars and the Revolutionary War, has been indexed and microfilmed. See Table 8-2.

If a personal search of the microfilmed indexes at the National Archives or the Genealogical Society of Utah is not possible, you may request a search of the indexes of the National Archives using NATF Form 26 (revised May 82).

During the Mexican War, special units came from the Indian nations, the Mormons (Mormon Battalion) and New Mexico (Santa Fe Battalion of the Missouri Mounted Volunteers). Each of these units compiled its own records.

Civil War (1861-65)

Union Army Records. Union Army records contain enlistment papers, muster rolls, prisoner-of-war papers, death reports, and others. The records are indexed by state and by military units for those units organized within a specific state. You must know that state in which a soldier served or the unit with which he served to obtain his service records. Table 8-3 summarizes Union Army indexes and service records.

Enlistment papers often contain a description of the soldier and the place where he enlisted. Typically, a soldier enlisted near his home. This information can be valuable in helping you pinpoint the movements of an ancestor between 1850 and 1880 when pioneers were on the move in great numbers. Since the federal censuses for 1860 and 1870 are not indexed, knowing where a soldier enlisted provides a clue about where to search for his family in those enumerations and in other county records.

The National Archives will search its index to service records if you know the branch of service and the state from which a soldier served in the Civil War. Use NATF Form 26 to request Civil War service records for the Union Army. There are microfilmed copies of the indexes at the National Archives and its branches, the Genealogical Society of Utah and its branches, and at various other libraries throughout the country. The actual service records are available, however, only at the National Archives.

Figure 8-3. Revolutionary Muster Roll of Captain Daniel Detwiler's Company, Alsace Township, Berks Co., Penn., 21 May 1777; originals in Pennsylvania Historical Society, printed in *Historical Review of Berks County*, July 1936, p. 123.

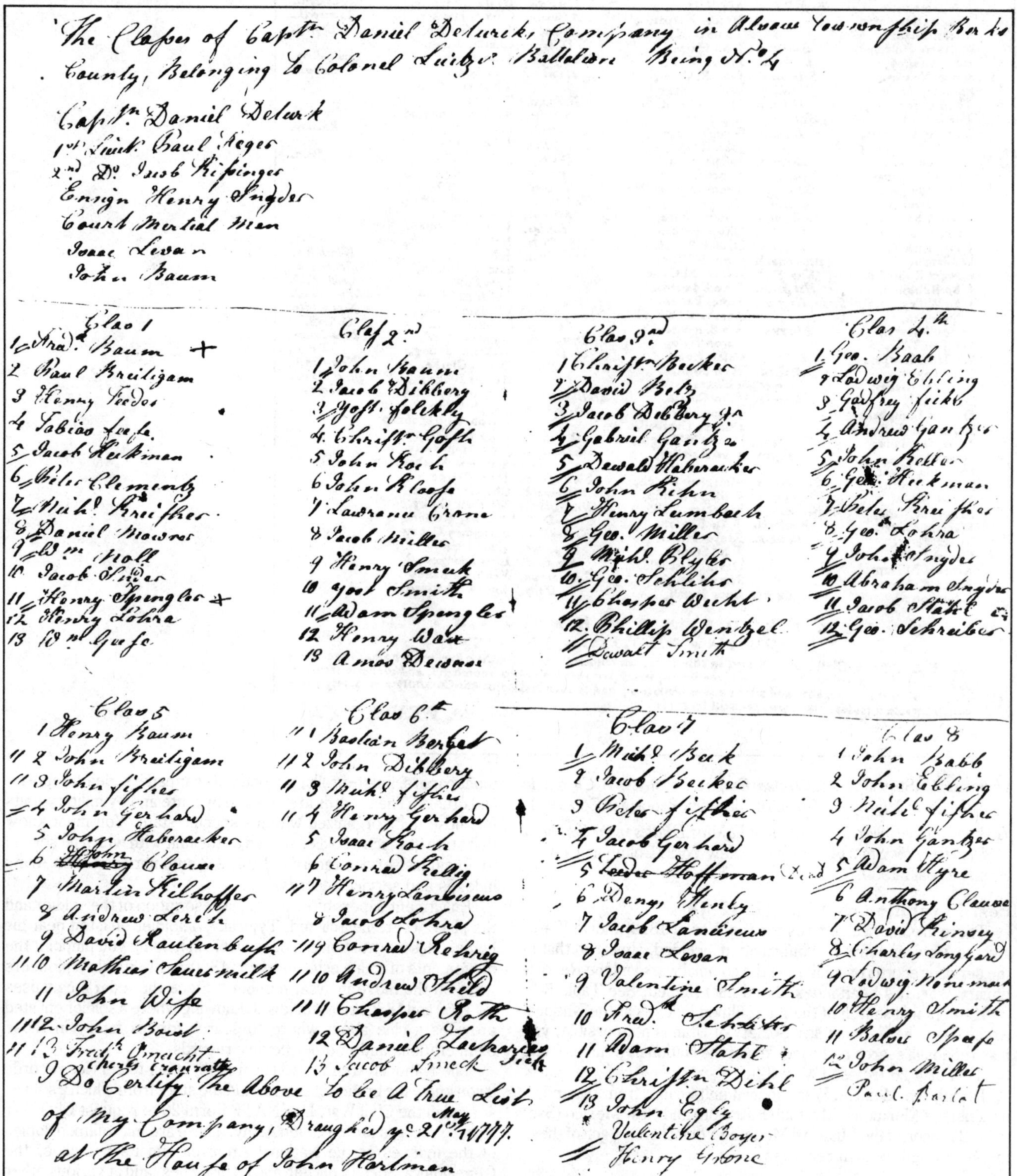

The Classes of Captn. Daniel Detwrek's Company in Alsace Township Berks County, Belonging to Colonel Lutz's Battalion Being No. 4

Captn. Daniel Detwrk
1st Lieut. Paul Reger
2nd Do. Jacob Kissinger
Ensign Henry Snyder
Court Martial Men
Isaac Levan
John Baum

Class 1
1 Fredk. Baum +
2 Paul Breitigam
3 Henry Feeder
4 Tobias Feese
5 Jacob Heckman
6 Peter Clementz
7 Michl. Kreisher
8 Daniel Maurer
9 Wm. Noll
10 Jacob Snider
11 Henry Spengler +
12 Henry Lohra
13 Wm. Geese

Class 2nd
1 John Baum
2 Jacob Dibbery
3 Yost Folckly
4 Christn. Gosh
5 John Koch
6 John Kloss
7 Lawrance Crane
8 Jacob Miller
9 Henry Smeck
10 Yost Smith
11 Adam Spengler
12 Henry Wax
13 Amos Deisner

Class 3rd
1 Christn. Becker
2 David Betz
3 Jacob Dibbery Jr.
4 Gabriel Gantzer
5 Dewald Haberacker
6 John Kuhn
7 Henry Lumbach
8 Geo. Miller
9 Michl. Blyler
10 Geo. Schleiher
11 Chasper Wicht
12 Phillip Wentzel
Dewalt Smith

Class 4th
1 Geo. Baab
2 Ludwig Ebling
3 Godfrey Ficke
4 Andrew Gantzer
5 John Keller
6 Geo. Heckman
7 Peter Kreisher
8 Geo. Lohra
9 John Snyder
10 Abraham Snyder
11 Jacob Stahl
12 Geo. Schreiber

Class 5
1 Henry Baum
2 John Breitigam
3 John Fisher
4 John Gerhard
5 John Haberacker
6 ~~Henry~~ John Clouse
7 Martin Kilhoffer
8 Andrew Lerch
9 David Rautenbush
10 Mathias Sauermilk
11 John Wise
12 John Boist
13 Fredk. Omacht

Class 6th
1 Bastian Berket
2 John Dibbery
3 Michl. Fisher
4 Henry Gerhard
5 Isaac Koch
6 Conrad Kellig
7 Henry Lanciscus
8 Jacob Lohra
9 Conrad Rehrig
10 Andrew Shield
11 Chasper Roth
12 Daniel Zacharias Sick
13 Jacob Smeck Sick

Class 7
1 Michl. Beck
2 Jacob Becker
3 Peter Fisher
4 Jacob Gerhard
5 Leeder Hoffman Dead
6 Deny Wenly
7 Jacob Lanciscus
8 Isaac Levan
9 Valentine Smith
10 Fredk. Schlitter
11 Adam Stahl
12 Christn. Diehl
13 John Egly
Valentine Boyer
Henry Grone

Class 8
1 John Babb
2 John Ebling
3 Michl. Fisher
4 John Gantzer
5 Adam Wyre
6 Anthony Clause
7 David Kinsey
8 Charles Longyard
9 Ludwig Nonemaker
10 Henry Smith
11 Balser Speese
12 John Miller
Paul Parlet

I Do Certify The Above to be A True List of My Company, Draughted ye 21st May 1777 at the House of John Hartman
By Me Daniel de Turck

Table 8-2

Service Records Indexes, 1812-48

Title	*NARS Microfilm Publication*	*Reels*	*Comments*
Index to Compiled Records of Volunteer Soldiers Who Served During the War of 1812	M602	234	There are also separate microfilm indexes for Mississippi (M678, 22 rolls), Louisiana (M229, 3 rolls), North Carolina (M250, 5 rolls), and South Carolina (M6652, 7 rolls). Numerous records for the War of 1812 are unindexed, unarranged, and thus inaccessible to genealogists. A volunteer project, sponsored by the National Genealogical Society, is currently indexing them.

Title	*State*	*Disturbance and Date*	*Microfilm Publications*	*No. of Rolls*
Indexes to Compiled Military Service Records of Volunteers During the Indian Wars, 1836-39	Alabama	Creek War, 1836-37	M244	2
	Alabama	Cherokee Removal, 1838	M243	1
	Alabama	Florida War, 1836-38	M254	1
	Florida	Florida War, 1835-38	M1086	63
	Georgia	Cherokee Disturbances and Removal, 1836-38	M907	1
	Louisiana	Florida War, 1836	M239	1
	Louisiana	War of 1836-38	M241	1
	Michigan	Patriot War, 1838-39	M630	
	New York	Patriot War, 1838	M631	1
	North Carolina	Cherokee Disturbances and Removal, 1837-38	M256	1
	Tennessee	Cherokee Disturbances and Removal, and Field and Staff of the Army of the Cherokee Nation	M908	2

Title	*NARS Microfilm Publication*	*Reels*	*Comments*
Index to Compiled Records of Volunteer Soldiers Who Served During the Mexican War, 1836-48	M616	41	Separate indexes are available for Mississippi (M863, 9 rolls), Pennsylvania (M1028, 13 rolls), Tennessee (M638, 15 rolls), Texas (M278, 19 rolls), Mormon Battalion (M351, 3 rolls)

Indian Wars information reprinted from *Genealogical Records in the National Archives* (Washington, D.C.: National Archives Records Service, 1983), p. 95.

Civil War Soldier Draft Records, 1863-65. By act of Congress, March 1863, the federal draft system was created. Men between ages twenty-five and forty, both white male citizens and aliens who had declared their intent to naturalize, were eligible for the draft. Males twenty to thirty-five and unmarried males thirty-five to forty-five had to serve unless physically disabled. Males seventeen to twenty could serve with the permission of a parent or guardian. The draft applied only to men residing in the United States under Union control.

The draft created three types of records:

1. Consolidated Lists. These are the most important individual records. An entry for a man gives his name, place of residence, age as of 1 July 1863, occupation, marital status, state, territory, or country of birth, and the military organization (if a volunteer) of which he was a member. The records are arranged by state and thereunder by congressional or enrollment district.

2. Descriptive Rolls. These rolls give additional information on men eligible for service. Although many of the entries are not completely filled out, they may give a personal description, exact place of birth, and whether accepted or rejected for service. The records are also filed by state and thereunder by congressional district.

Neither the consolidated lists nor the descriptive rolls have been microfilmed. They are part of National Archives Record Group 110 and are available only at the National Archives in Washington, D.C. To use the records you must know the number of the congressional district for the county in which a man lived. This can be determined by using *Congressional Directory for the Second Session of the 38th Congress of the United States* (Washington, D.C.: For the Joint Houses of Congress, 1865.)

3. Case Files on Drafted Aliens. These case files concern only aliens who were drafted and released 1861-64. The files may include name, district from which drafted, country of citizenship, age, length of time in United States, and a physical description. The files are in alphabetical order by surname in record group 59 available only at the National Archives.

The draft records, available for a historical period in which tracing families is sometimes very difficult, are invaluable for men living in cities. They are more complete and give important details not in corresponding censuses. Furthermore, their alphabetical arrangement makes searching them easier.

Confederate Service Records. When Richmond was evacuated by the Confederate Government in April 1865, the centralized military personnel records of the Confederate Army were taken to Charlotte, North Carolina, by the Confederate Adjutant and Inspector General, Samuel Cooper. When the Confederate civil authorities left Charlotte after agreeing to an armistice between the armies in North Carolina, President Jefferson Davis instructed Cooper to turn the records over, if necessary, to "the enemy, as

Table 8-3

Microfilmed Indexes and Compiled Service Records for Union Army Volunteers

State	Index: Microfilm publication	Index: Number of rolls	Compiled Military Service Records: Microfilm publication	Compiled Military Service Records: Number of rolls
Alabama	M263	1	M276	10
Arizona Territory	M532	1		
Arkansas	M383	4	M399	60
California	M533	7		
Colorado Territory	M534	3		
Connecticut	M535	17		
Dakota Territory	M536	1		
Delaware	M537	4		
District of Columbia	M538	3		
Florida	M264	1	M400	11
Georgia	M385	1	M403	1
Idaho Territory (see Washington Territory)				
Illinois	M539	101		
Indiana	M540	86		
Iowa	M541	29		
Kansas	M542	10		
Kentucky	M386	30	M397	515
Louisiana	M387	4	M396	50
Maine	M543	23		
Maryland	M388	13	M384	238
Massachusetts	M544	44		
Michigan	M545	48		
Minnesota	M546	10		
Mississippi	M389	1	M404	4
Missouri	M390	51	M405	854
Montana (see Washington Territory)				
Nebraska Territory	M547	2		
Nevada	M548	1		
New Hampshire	M549	13		
New Jersey	M550	26		
New Mexico Territory	M242	4	M427	46
New York	M551	159		
North Carolina	M391	2	M401	25
Ohio	M552	122		
Oklahoma (see Dakota Territory)				
Oregon	M553	1		
Pennsylvania	M554	136		
Rhode Island	M555	7		
South Carolina	None			
Tennessee	M392	16	M395	220
Texas	M393	2	M402	13
Utah Territory	M556	1	M692	1
Vermont	M557	14		
Virginia	M394	1	M398	7
Washington Territory	M558	1		
West Virginia	M507	13	M508	261
Wisconsin	M559	33		
Wyoming (see Washington Territory)				
U.S. Colored Troops	M589	98		
U.S. Volunteers (1st & 6th Regiments only)			M1017	65
Veteran Reserve Corps	M636	44		
Former Confederates Who Served in Union Army		65		

Reprinted from National Archives Trust Fund Board, *Guide to Genealogical Research in the National Archives* (Washington, D.C.: National Archives Record Service, 1982), p. 97.

Table 8-4

Microfilmed Indexes and Compiled Military Service Records for Confederate Army Volunteers

State	Index: Microfilm Publication	Index: Number of Rolls	Compiled Military Service Records: Microfilm Publication	Compiled Military Service Records: Number of Rolls
Alabama	M374	49	M311	508
Arizona Territory	M375	1	M318	1
Arkansas	M376	26	M317	256
Florida	M225	9	M251	104
Georgia	M226	67	M266	607
Kentucky	M377	14	M319	136
Louisiana	M378	31	M320	414
Maryland	M379	2	M321	22
Mississippi	M232	45	M269	427
Missouri	M380	16	M322	193
North Carolina	M230	43	M270	580
South Carolina	M381	35	M267	392
Tennessee	M231	48	M268	359
Texas	M227	41	M323	445
Virginia	M382	62	M324	1,075
Organizations Raised Directly by the Confederate Government			M258	123
General and Staff Officers			M331	275
Consolidated Index	M818	26		

Reprinted from *Genealogical Research in the National Archives* (Washington, D.C.: NARS, 1982), p. 102.

essential to the history of the struggle." When General Joseph E. Johnston learned, after the armistice, that the records were at Charlotte, he turned them over to the Union Commander in North Carolina, saying, "As they will furnish valuable materials for history, I am anxious for their preservation, and doubt not that you are too."

These military personnel records were taken to Washington along with other Confederate records captured by the Union Army and preserved in the War Department. Between 1878 and 1901, a former Confederate general, Marcus J. Wright, was employed by the War Department to locate missing Confederate records and borrow them for copying if the possessors did not wish to donate them to the War Department. In 1903, Secretary of War Elihu Root persuaded the governors of most of the Southern states to lend all Confederate military personnel records still in their possession to the War Department for copying.

The Confederate records surrendered or captured at the end of the war augmented by other records collected or copied since, resulted in a unique body of official information about the service of Confederate soldiers. The Confederate Army, unlike the Union Army, did not provide the states with copies of muster rolls for military units under its command, and the states also kept no muster rolls for units they had furnished. In the years after the war, copies of muster rolls kept by unit commanders were, in many cases, turned over to the states where the units originated. Those interested in the military service of Confederate soldiers had to rely on information contained in the War Department Collection of Confederate Records, now in the National Archives. The need for access to this information first became acute when Southern states began providing benefits for Confederate veterans. It has continued to be important to patriotic organizations composed of proven descendants of Confederate veterans.

To make information about the service of the Confederate soldiers more readily and completely available, the War Department began in 1903 to compile a service record for each soldier by copying off the entries pertaining to him in the muster rolls and other original records. This project was interrupted by World War I but was completed in 1927 with the aid of special appropriations. The result is an immense file of "compiled military service records" from which inquiries about Confederate soldiers are answered. Because of the efforts made over many years to incorporate all available information into this file, it is by far the most complete and accurate source of information about Confederate soldiers. A special study has shown that the chances of finding the record of a Confederate soldier from North Carolina in this file are about 50 percent greater than the chances of finding the soldier's record in John W. Moore, *Roster of North Carolina Troops in the War Between the States*, 4 vols. (Raleigh: For the author, 1882), long the standard reference, and compiled from the Confederate muster rolls in the custody of the federal War Department.

The compiled military service record of a Confederate soldier is kept in a jacket envelope filed with envelopes for other soldiers in the same regiment or similar unit. The record consists of one or more card abstracts and usually one or more original documents. Each card abstract is a copy made in the twentieth century by the federal War Department of an entry in such original records as Confederate muster rolls, returns, descriptive rolls, and Union prison and parole records. If the original record of a soldier's service was complete, the card abstracts may serve to trace his service from beginning to end, but they normally do little more than account for where he was at a given time. The compiled military service record may provide the following information of genealogical interest: age, place of enlistment, places served, place of discharge or death, and often, physical description.

The original Confederate records from which the cards were made are among the holdings of the National Archives. Microfilm copies of all indexes and some records are available at the National Archives and at the Genealogical Society of Utah. The Genealogical Society has the single largest collection of microfilmed state Confederate records. See Table 8-4. The index will provide the rank, unit, and name of the soldier and the pertinent file can be ordered from the National Archives.

The National Archives also compiled histories of Confederate military units and vessels (M861). They are arranged alphabetically by state and then by unit.

Because prisoner exchanges late in the Civil War were not working, approximately 28,000 Confederate soldiers, sailors, and citizens died in the North. While federal legislation from 1867 to 1873 provided for the reburial of Union soldiers in national cemeteries and for durable headstones, this early legislation made no specific provision for Confederate dead. Their graves were sometimes given thin headstones with a grave number and the soldier's name. Many of the non-Union graves, however, were marked with wooden headboards that disintegrated, although the names were often preserved in cemetery burial registers.

Finally in 1912, a typescript register of Confederate soldiers and sailors buried in federal cemeteries was compiled in accordance with a 1906 statute, to provide for marking the graves of Confederate soldiers and sailors who died in Union prisons. This register (M918) was generally arranged alphabetically by name of prison camp, other location where the death occurred, or occasionally by cemetery name. The individual burial lists are also arranged alphabetically by name of deceased and generally include rank, company, regiment, date of death, and number and location of grave. Some cemeteries did not bury the dead in numbered graves. Some regimental and company designations or death dates are not entered in the register. The registers also include few entries for private Confederate citizens. Some are unknown. Other entries are for bodies "removed," "sent home," and "taken home by friends." Entries for the Green Lawn Cemetery in Indianapolis, Indiana, have been lined through and a notation added, "Remains of above removed to lot 285, sec. 32, Crown Hill Cemetery, Indianapolis, Indiana, and reinterred as unknowns on October 27, 1931." (Check other explanatory notes at the begining or end of the burial list.) This register is now part of Record Group 92: Records of the Quartermaster General.

Record Group 92 also includes some records of the Office of the Commissioner for Marking the Graves of Confederate Dead not reproduced on M918: a two-volume 1914 register of Confederate soldiers and sailors who died in the North, the commissioner's incoming and outgoing correspondence, (two of his files are in the Office of the Quartermaster General, files 128991 and 342020), Confederate burial registers, lists, and correspondence pertaining to particular cemeteries.

The War Department Collection of Confederate Records, Record Group 109, includes registers of Confederates who died in Union prisons, National Archives M598, "Selected Records of the War Department Relating to Confederate Prisoners of War 1861-1865." Particularly useful is a two-volume series of registers of prisoner deaths compiled by the Office of the Commissary General of Prisoners (rolls 5 and 6). The volumes are alphabetically arranged by name of deceased and show the name; rank; regiment; company; place and date of capture; place, date, and cause of death; and number and locality of grave for each individual. The information in these registers may be used to supplement the information on M918, but burial information is frequently unavailable or obsolete. Rolls 10-12 are a five-volume series of registers of prisoner deaths, compiled by the Surgeon General's Office and arranged by the states in which the deceased served. They contain most of the information described above.

State Confederate Records. The War Department Collection of Confederate Records is not complete, even though great efforts were made to assemble all official information. A soldier may have served in a state militia unit never mustered into the service of the Confederate States government. Records of service in such units, if extant, may be in the state archives or in the custody of the state adjutant-general. Since the federal government of the

Table 8-5

Northern Cemeteries Where Confederate Soldiers/Sailors are Buried

Allegheny Cemetery 524
Alton, Illinois 1
Annapolis, Maryland 42
Baltimore, Maryland 43
Barryville, New York 51
Boston, Massachusetts (See Fort Warren)
Bowling Green, Kentucky 51
Brooklyn, New York 53
Cairo, Illinois (See Mound City)
Camp Butler, Illinois 67
Camp Chase, Ohio 90
Camp Dennison, Ohio (See Camp Chase)
Camp Douglas, Chicago, Illinois 145
Camp Morton, Indianapolis, Indiana 253 Reinterred 1931 at Crown Hill, Indianapolis
Camp Nelson, Kentucky (See Nicholasville)
Camp Randall, Madison, Wisconsin (See Madison)
Cave Hill, Kentucky, National Cemetery 502
Chambersburg, Pennsylvania 294
Chester, Pennsylvania (See Philadelphia)
Chicago, Illinois (See Camp Douglas)
Cincinnati, Ohio (Camp Dennison) (See Camp Chase)
Clarksburg, West Virginia 295
Clarysville, Maryland (See Cumberland)
Columbus, Ohio (See Camp Chase)
Covinton, Kentucky 296
Cumberland, Maryland 297
Cypress Hills National Cemetery 53
Danville, Kentucky 298
David's Island, NYC (See Brooklyn)
Deer Island, Boston Harbor 434
Elmira, New York 301
Evansville, Indiana 375
Finn's Point, New Jersey 376
Forest Hill Cemetery, Madison, Wisconsin 510
Fort Columbus, NYC (See Brooklyn)
Fort Delaware, Delaware (See Finn's)
Fort Layfayette, NYC (See Brooklyn)
Fort Leavenworth, Kansas 437
Fort McHenry, Maryland (See Baltimore)
Fort Scott, Kansas 436
Fort Warren, Boston Harbor, Massachusetts 439; removed to Deer Island
Fort Wood, NYC (See Brooklyn)
Frederick, Maryland 440
Gallipolis, Ohio 449
Gettysburg, Pennsylvania, removed South
Grafton, West Virginia (See New Creek)
Harpers Ferry, West Virginia 450
Harrisburg, Pennsylvania 451
Harrodsburg, Kentucky 452
Hart's Island, NYC (See Brooklyn)
Indianapolis, Indiana (See Camp Horton)
Jefferson Barracks, Missouri 456
Johnson's Island, Ohio 488
Kansas City, Missouri 495
Keokuk, Iowa 496
Lafayette, Indiana 497
Lexington, Kentucky 498
Loudon Park National Cemetery 43
Louisville, Kentucky 502
Madison, Wisconsin 510
Martinsburg, West Virginia 514
Mound City, Illinois 515
New Albany, New York (See Brooklyn)
New Creek (Keyser), West Virginia 518
New York, New York (See Brooklyn)
Nicolasville, Kentucky 519
Oak Woods Cemetery, Chicago, Illinois 145
Paducah, Kentucky (See Mound City, Illinois)
Perryville, Kentucky (See Mound City)
Philadelphia, Pennsylvania 522
Pittsburg, Pennsylvania 529
Point Lookout, Maryland 530
Portsmouth Grove, Rhode Island (See Brooklyn)
Rock Island, Illinois 613
St. Louis, Missouri (See Jefferson Bar)
Salem, New Jersey (See Finn's Point)
Sandusky, Ohio (See Johnson's Island)
Santa Fe, New Mexico 661
Shohola, Pennsylvania (See Elmira & Barryville)
Springfield, Illinois (See Camp Butler)
Terra Haute, Indiana 662
Thorntown, Indiana 663
Washington, DC 654
Wheeling, West Virginia 665
Willett's Point, NYC (See Brooklyn)
Woodlawn National Cemetery, Elmira, New York 57 & 201
York, Pennsylvania removed South

List of Cemeteries Containing Confederate Soldiers' Remains, from "Introduction," by Robert W. Gruber to the *Register of Confederate Soldiers, Sailors, and Citizens Who Died in Federal Prisons and Military Hospitals in the North, 1861-1865.*, NARS microfilm publication M918, also available at Genealogical Society of Utah. Numbers following cemetery name refer to pages in the register.

Table 8-6

Microfilm in the Genealogical Society of Utah Collection

If a state name is missing, no microfilm records are available.

State	*Rolls of Film or Volumes*	*Comments*
Alabama	3 vols cataloged by county	Muster lists; 1907 Census of Confederate veterans and widows
Florida	5 rolls	Officers' service records
	5 rolls	CSA service records
	113 rolls	State service records
	169 rolls	Pensions
Georgia	1 roll	Minutes, veterans at camp Quitman
	1 roll	Military commissions
	3 rolls	Abstracts of service records
	251 rolls	Pensions
	255 rolls	Pension applications
Kentucky	6 rolls	Index of soldiers
Louisiana	1 roll	1911 census of veterans and widows
Mississippi	94 rolls	Pension applications
Missouri	9 vols.	Muster lists
North Carolina	2 rolls	Pensions index
	19 rolls	Roster of soldiers
Tennessee	181 rolls	Pension applications
	3 rolls	Confederate soldiers' home records
	9 rolls	Veterans' biographical and genealogical questionnaire with printed index
Texas	15 rolls	Soldiers and officers index
	700 rolls	Pension files
	8 vols.	Muster lists
Virginia	42 rolls	Service records; includes West Virginia

Most series are being added to the collection yearly as budgets allow. Call numbers for each roll of film are recorded in the *Military Records Register* at the Genealogical Society of Utah and its branches.

United States did not pay benefits to Confederates, pensions and other state benefits are recorded only in state records.

The Genealogical Society has the single largest collection of microfilmed *state* Confederate records. Table 8-6 summarizes these materials. The call numbers for ordering the microfilms through branch libraries are most easily located in the *Military Records Register, Vol. II: Civil War.* If the branch library does not have a copy, have the librarian request a copy from the main library in Salt Lake City.

Two additional categories of records require special mention: military academy records and Reconstruction court records. Many officers in the Confederate troops received their early training in Southern military academies. Others had attended West Point and had to choose which side to support. Consult Bvt. Major-General George W. Cullum, *Biographical Register, Officers and Graduates of the U.S. Military Academy, West Point, New York*, 3rd ed., 9 vols. (Boston: Houghton-Mifflin, 1891); Stanley P. Tozeski, *Preliminary Inventory of the Records of the U.S. Military Academy* (Washington, D.C.: National Archives and Records Service, 1976); and Jon L. Wakelyn, *Biographical Dictionary of the Confederacy* (Westport, Conn.: Greenwood Press, 1977). Second, the confiscation of land by the Reconstruction government led to lengthy and bitter court battles. Genealogists seldom check these records, which can yield numerous details about Southern soldiers even though they are not technically military records. See also Chapter 6, "Court Records."

The checklist in Figure 8-4 represents most of the types of records created by state and local government units which apply to Confederate soldiers. Many have been microfilmed.

Spanish-American War Through Modern Wars, 1898 to the Present

Service records for soldiers serving in the armed forces after the Civil War are not as readily available, even though the records of these later wars are more detailed. See records index list in Table 8-7.

Using records for soldiers who served within the last seventy-five years is restricted to immediate family members under the provisions of the Right-to-Privacy Acts. Most of the federal records in this category are housed at the National Personnel Records Center, 9700 Page Boulevard, St. Louis, MO 63132. Living veterans can request their records or give written consent for others. Records protected by the privacy laws cannot be copied or viewed by the public, but some information contained in the records can be provided upon request. Use Form 180 (revised Sept. 81). (See Figure 8-5 for a blank.)

Documents issued to the veteran at time of discharge (or to his/her next of kin, in case of death) usually contain important genealogical information. The National Personnel Records Center candidly acknowledges that its priority is providing information for benefits, not genealogical data, and encourages contacting the veteran or next of kin. However, under the Freedom of Information Act (FOIA), (amended 1974), it will release an individual's age or date of birth, salary, photographs, source of commission, duty status, office telephone number, military and civilian educational level, decorations and awards (including a copy of the citation, if available), present and past duty assignments (including geographical location), future assignments which have been finalized, records of court martial trials (unless classified), marital status, education/schooling, rank/grade, serial/service number, date of rank/grade, promotion sequence number, and dependants, including name, sex, and age.

If the identity needs to be verified, the center will also add such items as name of father and/or mother, home address, etc. This service takes several weeks; you will be billed for researching, processing, and photocopying.

On 12 July 1973, fire broke out on the top floor of the National Personnel Records Center in St. Louis, destroying millions of military records and damaging millions more. According to James E. Cole, Jr., acting assistant archivist for federal records centers, 80 percent of the army records for 1912-59, 60 percent of the air force records for 1947-63, and 1 percent or less of Army records for personnel discharged since 1 January 1973 were destroyed.[2]

The center has since reconstructed the records of living military personnel who need the data to apply for pensions and other benefits. There are no plans at this time to reconstruct the records of deceased personnel where no benefits are owing.

Draft records housed at the Federal Archives and Records Center in Atlanta and veterans' medical treatment records were not in the fire. To obtain medical records information from the Veterans Administration Computer database, you will need a soldier identification number. A military unit and a name are not sufficient.

Draft records for World War I, 1917-18, are filed by the Selective Service Board of Registration. You will need your ancestor's exact address at the time of registration to locate the right entry. These records are scattered among several federal records centers. At this writing, the records for Oregon, Rhode Island, Utah, Vermont, Virginia, Washington, and Wyoming are at the Federal Archives and Record Center, 2306 E. Bannister Road, Kansas City, MO 64131; for Illinois check with the Federal Archives and Records Center, 7358 South Pulaski Road, Chicago, IL 60629. For all other states, contact the Federal Archives and Records Center, 221 St. Joseph Avenue, East Point, GA 30044. The records are being microfilmed for safekeeping. When this is done, they may be shifted again.

Discharge Records. Each county in the United States was required to record the honorable discharge of soldiers and sailors who served in World War I. Some discharges for the Civil War and Philippine Insurrection are also on record, as well as some dishonorable and medicial discharges. The records are kept in the local

Table 8-7

Service Records Indexes, 1898-1902

Title	*Number*	*Rolls*	*Comments*
General Index to Compiled Service Records of Volunteer Soldiers Who Served During the War with Spain, 1898-1901	M871	126	Separate indexes for each state and for special units of U.S. volunteers
Index to Compiled Records of Volunteer Soldiers Who Served During the Philippine Insurrection, 1899-1902	M871	24	Numerous miscellaneous records. The personnel file for one veteran injured at Kutubic Bay, Philippines, exceeds 200 pages. Files include newclippings and printed reports as well as original documents. Other records available at the Historical Reference Section, U.S. Army Military Research, Carlisle Barracks, Pennsylvania 17013

Figure 8-3. Research Outline and Checklist for Confederate Records, adapted with permission from *Family History for Fun and Profit,* © 1982, Family History World, Salt Lake City, Utah.

Research Outline and Checklist for Confederate Records Relating to the Civil War

Local Jurisdiction: County, Town, Independent City, City-County, Parish

Militia Records

____ Pay rolls
____ Muster rolls
____ Size rolls
____ Appointment of officers
____ Delinquents
____ Court martial minutes
____ Court martial files
____ List of males over 16
____ Enrollments
____ Slave patrol reports
____ Watch reports
____ Discharges
____ Pensions
____ Resolutions
____ Subscriptions
____ Exemptions
____ Train bands
____ Levy register
____ Widows' support
____ Widows' burials
____ Veterans' burials
____ Application for burial
____ Survivors' burials
____ Logbooks
____ Commissions
____ Deportations
____ Oaths
____ List of arms
____ Letters
____ Orders

Miscellaneous Records

____ Confiscated lands
____ Fines and forfeitures
____ Prisoners petitions
____ Vigilance committees

Bounties

____ Prisoners of war

Slavery Records

____ Manumissions
____ Freedom certificates
____ Petitions
____ Register of slaves
____ Register of free Negroes
____ Bills of sale

Claims

____ Registers
____ Accounts
____ Appeals

State Jurisdiction

Special Indexes

____ Cemeteries
____ Land claims
____ Military pensions
____ Military grave sites
____ Censuses

Property Records

____ Condemned land
____ Confiscated land
____ Abandoned land
____ Land memorials
____ Caveats
____ Alienations
____ Fines
____ Distraints
____ Abstracts
____ Insolvencies
____ Accounts
____ Arrears
____ Disclaimers
____ Petitions
____ Complaints
____ Inquests
____ Escheats
____ Transfer of rights
____ Devises lists
____ Heir lists
____ Quit claims
____ Tax sales
____ Tax exemptions
____ Tax liens
____ Tax lists
____ Tax farms
____ Chattel bills of sale

Military Academies

____ Register of cadets
____ Register of graduates
____ Admissions
____ Dismissals
____ Daybooks
____ Medical registers
____ Clothing accounts
____ Appointments
____ Nominations

Soldiers' Homes

____ Minutes of trustees
____ Donations
____ Reports
____ Accounts
____ Daybooks
____ Death register
____ Medical register
____ Visitors' register
____ List of personal effects

Military Records

____ Census of pensioners
____ Militia returns
____ Troop returns
____ Muster rolls
____ Muster-in rolls
____ Muster-out rolls
____ Enlistments
____ Enrollments
____ Substitutes
____ Journals
____ Logbooks
____ Letter books
____ Morning reports
____ Pay rolls
____ Paymaster rolls
____ Bounties paid
____ Expenses
____ Vouchers
____ Orders
____ Accounts
____ Orderly books
____ Training rolls
____ Inventory of effects
____ Final settlements
____ Gallantry reports
____ Rolls of honor
____ Drill rolls
____ Induction orders
____ Desertions
____ Prisoners
____ Service affadavits
____ Quartermaster rolls
____ Ordnance records
____ Equipment inventories
____ Clothing rolls
____ Discharges
____ Missing roster
____ Dead rolls
____ Deceased soldiers
____ Resignations
____ List of recruits
____ Casualty lists
____ Claims
____ Battle reports
____ Transfer rolls
____ List of rejected men

Courts Martial

____ Minutes
____ Depositions
____ Trials of regulations
____ Courts of inquiry
____ Articles of war
____ Orders

Hospitals

____ Daybooks
____ Sick reports
____ Wounded reports
____ Morning reports
____ Medical inspections
____ Substitutes
____ Death registers
____ Surgeon's register
____ Admissions
____ Transfers
____ Burials

Military Prisons

____ Register of prisoners
____ Medical register
____ List of personal property
____ Work register
____ Daybooks
____ Admissions
____ Transfers
____ Releases
____ Death register

Officers' Records

____ Commissions
____ Lists
____ Promotions
____ Rosters
____ Service records
____ Examinations
____ Correspondence
____ Retired officers
____ Personal papers
____ Oaths of office

Pension Board

____ Minutes
____ Correspondence
____ Examiners' reports
____ Applications
____ Survivors' applications
____ Proof of service
____ Military claims
____ Depositions
____ Disabled veterans

This list is a guide to the documents which could be found. Compare it with a current bibliography or guide to the record holdings of the state archives, state library, or state historical society where your ancestors lived.

____ Death claims
____ Claims settlements
____ Tax exemptions
____ War claims
____ Commissary claims
____ Confiscated property
____ Abandoned property
____ Exchange of prisoners
____ Slave patrols
____ Oaths of allegiance
____ Passports
____ Certificates of citizenship
____ Prisoner lists
____ Invasion records
____ Grave site indexes
____ Petitions for pardon
____ Debt certificates
____ Bill of credit
____ Substitutions
____ Adjutant general's report
____ Recruiting agents' reports
____ Recruiting books
____ Recruiting accounts
____ Recruiting rolls
____ Draft records
____ Enlistment contracts

State Employees—Officers

____ Oaths of office
____ Oaths of allegiance
____ Appointments
____ Removals
____ Resignations
____ Bonds

Court Records

____ Indexes
____ Dockets
____ Minutes
____ Orders
____ Writs
____ Precepts
____ Petitions
____ Judgments
____ Decrees
____ Verdicts

Appeals

____ Transcripts
____ Briefs
____ Exhibits
____ Files
____ Opinions

Attorney General Files

____ Dockets
____ Daybooks
____ Writs
____ Petitions
____ Correspondence
____ Case files
____ Accounts
____ Briefs

courthouse and usually consist of typed or handwritten transcripts of the original documents given to the soldier. Some of these discharge records from county collections have been microfilmed by the Genealogical Society of Utah, but most have not.

The records contain the individual's name, race, rank, serial number, reason for discharge, birthplace, age at time of enlistment, occupation, and a personal description. His/her service record, sometimes included with the discharge record, gives the length of service, prior service, marital status, arms and horsemanship qualifications, advancement, battles, decorations, honors, leaves of absence, physical condition, and character evaluation.

The same requirement for recording discharges was in effect for World War II veterans. The information contained in these records is the same as that on file for veterans of World War I.

United States Merchant Marines. Records pertaining to the service of merchant marines are on file with the United States Coast Guard. Records of discharged, deceased, and retired merchant marines are in the custody of the National Personnel Records Center, Military Personnel Records, 9700 Page Boulevard, St. Louis, MO 63132. Records of officers and active or reserve personnel prior to 1929 are in the custody of the Commandant of the U.S. Coast Guard, Washington, DC 20590.

Records of Veterans' Benefits

The provision of benefits to veterans was not widely adopted until after the Revolutionary War, although the separate colonies sometimes provided pensions for veterans disabled with injuries incurred in their service. Fighters in Indian skirmishes and local riots submitted claims for supplies, equipment, and time spent to both legislative assemblies and county courts. These records are discussed at greater length in Chapter 6, "Court Records." Bounties were also paid in both land and money for some military actions.

Pension Records (1774-1811)

The first congressional legislation authorizing the payment of pensions for Revolutionary War service was dated 26 August 1776, but the government did not begin paying pension allowances until 28 July 1789; applications for pensions were made to the federal government from that date. Many of the early applications were destroyed by fire in 1800 and 1814. A partial record of the earlier pensioners is included among reports to Congress in 1792, 1794, and 1795.

Revolutionary War Pension Dates

Date	*Action*
26 Aug. 1776	Invalid pensions for officers and soldiers, half-pay during disability, continental line.
24 May 1780	Widows and orphans of officers of Continental Army, half-pay for seven years, rescinded 29 July 1789.
21 Oct. 1780	Service pension for life for officers of Continental Army only, rescinded 4 Aug. 1790.
28 July 1789	Federal government assumes state invalid pensions, continental line.
3 March 1804	Federal government assumes all of South Carolina invalid pensions, continental line.
3 March 1805	Invalid pensions to those disabled since the war for wounds incurred during the war, continental line.
10 April 1806	Invalid pensions extended to volunteers, militia and state troops.
1813	Military records burned in War of 1812, including pension applications prior to 1813.
18 March 1818	Service pension for "cont. Establish 'T'." Act of 1820 removed many.
15 May 1828	Service pension for officers and soldiers eligible for pension under resolution of 21 Oct. 1780, full pay for life.
7 June 1832	First service pension for all Revolutionary soldiers and sailors, continental and state. Widows and orphans entitled to balance of money due a pensioner.
4 July 1836	Widow's pension for widow of Revolutionary soldier, on pension rolls of 1828, married during last term of service or before 3 Nov. 1783.
7 July 1836	Pension for widow if married before 1 Jan. 1794.
3 March 1837	Revolutionary widow entitled to pension even if remarried.
3 Feb. 1853	Revolutionary widow entitled to pension, regardless of date of marriage.
5 April 1869	Daniel F. Bakeman, last Revolutionary pensioner, dies.
11 Nov. 1906	Esther S. Damon, last pensioned Revolutionary widow, dies.

Figure 8-6. Important Revolutionary War Pension Acts and Resolutions, prepared in 1958 by Dr. Harold I. Meyer, President, Illinois Society, Sons of the American Revolution.

Figure 8-5. Request portion (back) of Form R6-7231 (Rev. 9/81), Genealogical Statement.

THIS PORTION OF THIS FORM WILL SERVE AS A REQUEST IF COMPLETED AND RETURNED TO THIS CENTER

PRIVACY ACT OF 1974 COMPLIANCE INFORMATION. The following information is provided in accordance with 5 U.S.C. 552a(e)(3) and applies to this form. Authority for collection of the information is 44 U.S.C. 2907, 3101, and 3103, and E.O. 9397 of November 22, 1943. Disclosure of the information is voluntary. The principal purpose of the information is to assist the facility servicing the records in locating and verifying the correctness of the requested records or information to answer your inquiry. Routine uses of the information as established and published in accordance with 5 U.S.C. 552a(e)(4)(D) include the transfer of relevant information to appropriate Federal, State, local, or foreign agencies for use in civil, criminal, or regulatory investigations or prosecution. In addition, this form will be filed with the appropriate military records and may be transferred along with the record to another agency in accordance with the routine uses established by the agency which maintains the record. If the requested information is not provided, it may not be possible to service your inquiry.

SECTION I - INFORMATION NEEDED TO LOCATE RECORDS

NAME USED DURING SERVICE *(Last, first, and middle)*	SOCIAL SECURITY NO.	DATE OF BIRTH	PLACE OF BIRTH

ACTIVE SERVICE, PAST AND PRESENT

BRANCH OF SERVICE	DATES OF ACTIVE SERVICE		*Check one*		SERVICE NUMBER DURING THIS PERIOD
	DATE ENTERED	DATE RELEASED	OFFICER	ENLISTED	

SECTION II - REQUEST

☐ I request the informational data available under FOIA. I realize that a fee may be applicable.

☐ Please verify the following additional data to ensure that NPRC has identified the correct veteran's record:

IDENTIFICATION OF REQUESTER *(Check appropriate box)*

☐ NEXT OF KIN *(relationship)*:

☐ OTHER *(specify)*:

SIGNATURE OF REQUESTER

RELEASE AUTHORIZATION, IF REQUIRED
(Read second-to-last paragraph on front side)

I hereby authorize release of the requested information/documents to the person indicated at left.

SIGNATURE OF VETERAN OR NEXT OF KIN

(If signed by other than veteran, show relationship to veteran):

REQUESTS SHOULD BE SUBMITTED TO:

Director
National Personnel Records Center
9700 Page Boulevard
St. Louis, Missouri 63132

COMPLETE RETURN ADDRESS OF REQUESTER *(Please type or print clearly)*

NAME

NUMBER AND STREET

CITY, STATE AND ZIP CODE

TELEPHONE NO. *(Include area code)*

R6-7231 (REV. 9/81) BACK

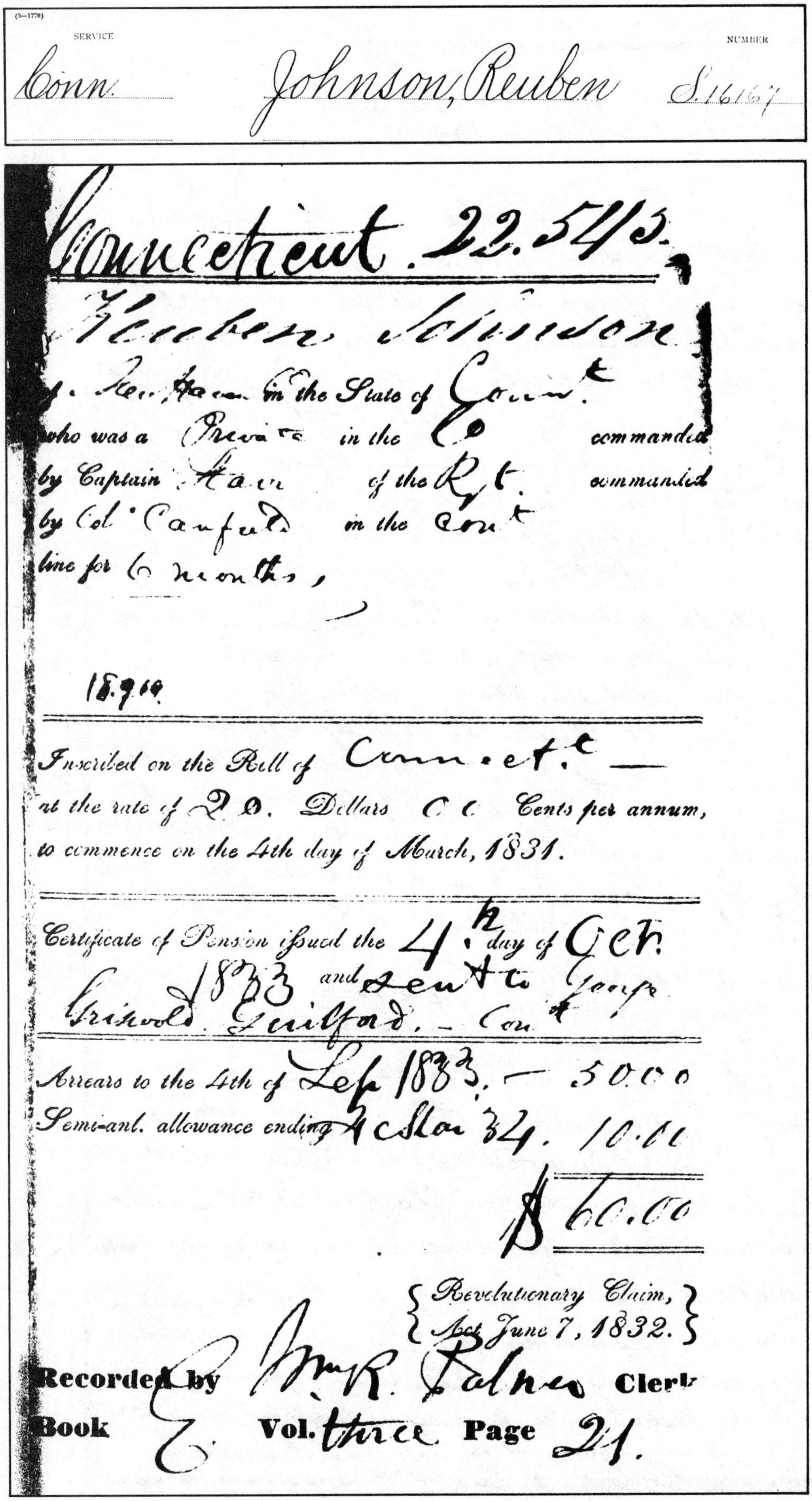

(3—1778)

SERVICE NUMBER

Conn. Johnson, Reuben S.16167

Connecticut 22.545.

Reuben Johnson

of New Haven in the State of Conn^t.

who was a Private in the Co commanded by Captain Ham of the Reg^t commanded by Col. Canfield in the Cont^t line for 6 months,

18.9.14.

Inscribed on the Roll of Connect^c — at the rate of 20. Dollars 00 Cents per annum, to commence on the 4th day of March, 1831.

Certificate of Pension issued the 4^h day of Oct. 1833 and sent to Geo. Griswold. Guilford. — Con^t

Arrears to the 4th of Sep 1833. — 50.00

Semi-anl. allowance ending 4 Mar 34. 10.00

$60.00

{Revolutionary Claim, Act June 7, 1832.}

Recorded by Wm R. Palmer Clerk

Book E Vol. three Page 21.

Figure 8-7. "Revolutionary War Pension File of Reuben Johnson," 19 Nov. 1832, National Archives no. W10156; Genealogical Society of Utah (hereafter GS) microfilm 971,428.

***Figure* 8-7.** Continued.

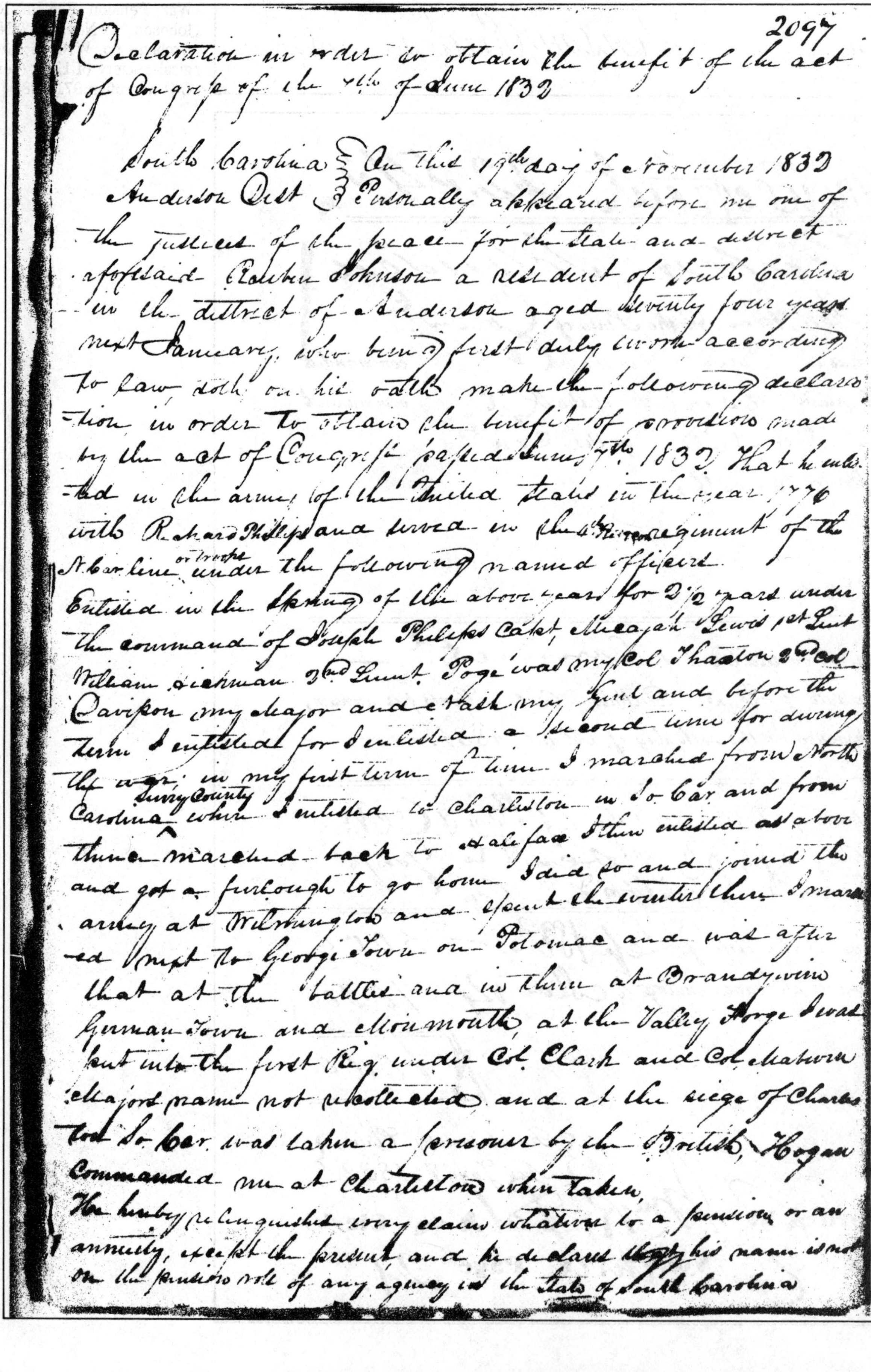

2097

Declaration in order to obtain the benefit of the act of Congress of the 7th of June 1832

South Carolina } On this 19th day of November 1832
Anderson Dist } Personally appeared before me one of
the justices of the peace for the State and district
aforesaid Reuben Johnson a resident of South Carolina
in the district of Anderson aged Seventy four years
next January who being first duly sworn according
to law doth on his oath make the following declara-
tion in order to obtain the benefit of provisions made
by the act of Congress passed June 7th 1832 That he enlis-
ted in the army of the United States in the year 1776
with Richard Phillips and served in the 4th Regiment of the
N. Car. line or troops under the following named officers
Enlisted in the Spring of the above year for 2½ years under
the command of Joseph Philips Capt, Micajah Lewis 1st Lieut
William Dickman 2nd Lieut. Pope was my Col Thaston 2nd Col
Davison my Major and Nash my Genl and before the
term I enlisted for I enlisted a second time for during
the war. in my first term of time I marched from North
Carolina Surry County where I enlisted to Charleston in So. Car. and from
thence marched back to Halifax I then enlisted as above
and got a furlough to go home I did so and joined the
army at Wilmington and spent the winter there I march-
ed next to George Town on Potomac and was after
that at the battles and in them at Brandywine
German Town and Monmouth, at the Valley Forge I was
put into the first Reg under Col. Clark and Col. Mabane
Majors name not recollected and at the siege of Charles
ton So. Car. was taken a prisoner by the British, Hogan
Commanded me at Charleston when taken,
He hereby relinquishes every claim whatever to a pension or an
annuity except the present, and he declares that his name is not
on the pension roll of any agency in the State of South Carolina

Sworn to, and subscribed, the day and year aforesaid

Reuben Johnson

We Robert King a clergyman residing in the State and district aforesaid, and Elisha Kelley residing in (the same) hereby certify we are well acquainted with Reuben Johnson who has sworn and subscribed to the above declaration; that we believe him to be as old as he had above stated, that he is reputed and believed in the neighbourhood where he resides, to have been a soldier of the revolution and we concur in that opinion

Sworn and subscribed the day and year aforesaid

Robert King
Elisha Kelley

And I the subscribing justice of the peace do declare after the investigation of the matter, and after putting the interrogatories prescribed by the War Department, that the above mentioned applicant, ~~as~~ I do believe was a revolutionary soldier and served as he states. And I do further ... that Robt King who has signed the preceeding, is a clergyman, resident as above stated, and that Elisha Kelley who has also signed the same is a resident of the same, and is a credible person, and that their statement is entitled to credit. Given under my hand and seal ~~the day and year~~ year aforesaid

Joseph Cox J.P. (seal)

And the above named applicant Reuben Johnson and on the same day did before me declare on oath that from the bodily infirmities that he was labouring under (say, the gravel) it render him so ~~unhappy~~ that he could not attend a court of the kind required by the War Department unless to his very great inconvenience

Sworn to and subscribed before me Joseph Cox J.P.

Reuben Johnson

Figure 8-7. Continued.

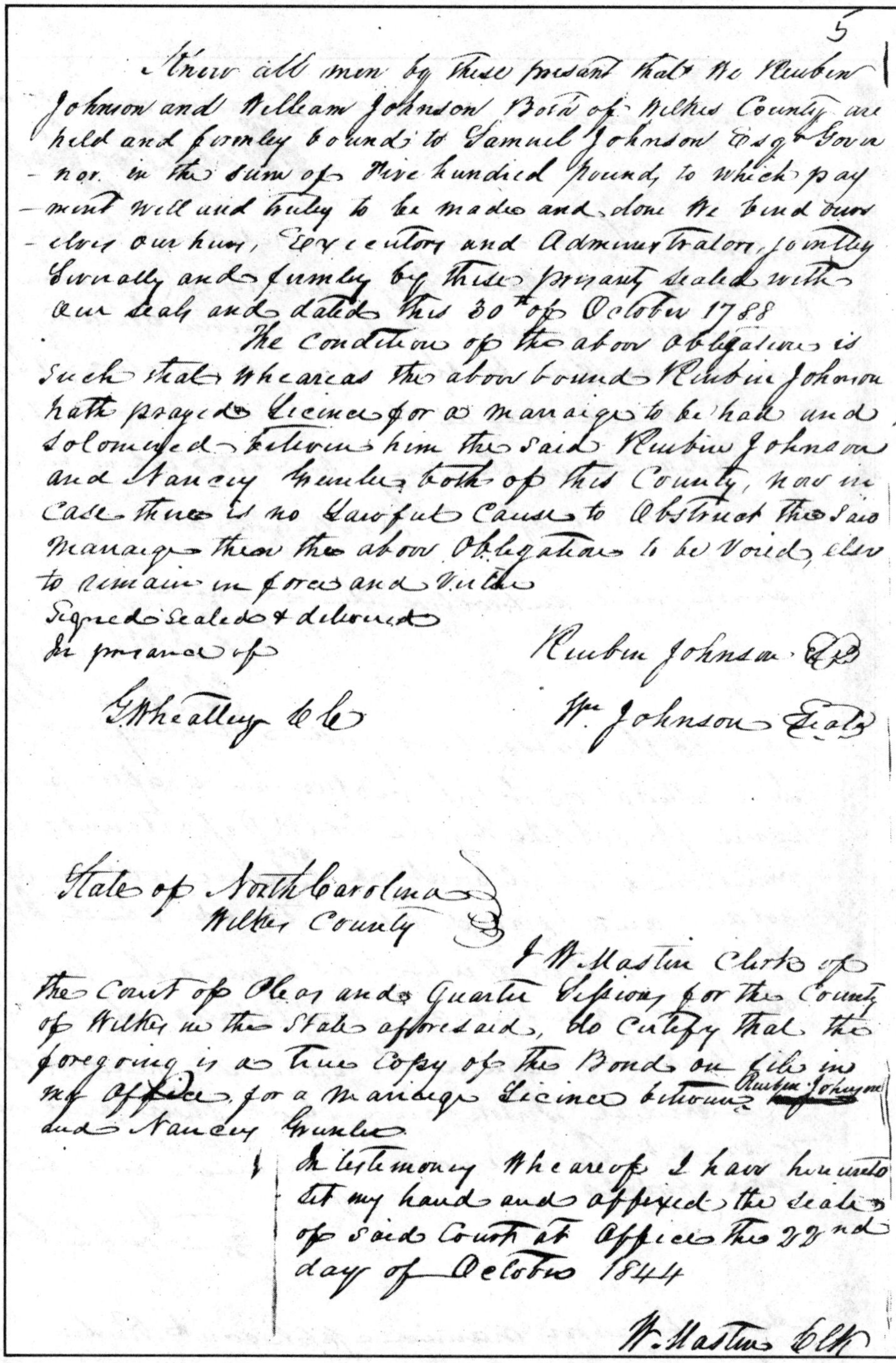

5

Know all men by these present that We Reuben Johnson and William Johnson Both of Wilkes County are held and firmly bound to Samuel Johnson Esqr Governor in the sum of Five hundred pound, to which payment well and truly to be made and done We bind our selves our heirs, Executors and Administrators, jointly Severally and firmly by these presents sealed with our seals and dated this 30th of October 1788

The Condition of the above Obligation is such that Whereas the above bound Reubin Johnson hath prayed Licince for a marriage to be had and solomnized between him the said Reubin Johnson and Nancy Grunler both of this County, now in case there is no Lawful Cause to Obstruct the said marriage then the above Obligation to be Voided, else to remain in force and Virtue

Signed Sealed & delivered
In presance of

G Wheatley C C

Reuben Johnson (Seal)

Wm Johnson (Seal)

State of North Carolina
Wilkes County

I W. Mastin Clerk of the Court of Pleas and Quarter Sessions for the County of Wilkes in the State afforesaid, do Certify that the foregoing is a true Copy of the Bond on file in my office for a marriage Licince between Reubin Johnson and Nancy Grunler

In testimony Whereof I have hereunto set my hand and affixed the seal of said Court at Office the 22nd day of October 1844

W. Mastin Clk

Although applications for pensions were made to the United States government, they were initiated in the courts of the counties and towns in which the veteran lived. The genealogist should also remember that a Pension Board refusal often led the claimant to seek relief from Congress directly. See Chapter 6, "Court Records," for more details.

The pension records for the Revolutionary War and later wars are more complete than earlier pension records and contain more information of genealogical value: affidavits made by the veteran and his neighbors or associates to support his claim, summaries of his service, the military organization in which he served, the dates of his service, his date and place of birth, names of heirs, relationship to others who served with him, his movements after the war, and information from family Bible records. Sometimes the Bible pages, torn out of the book, are enclosed as evidence.

For example, the Revolutionary War pension file of Reuben Johnson was filed in Anderson District, South Carolina, on 19 November 1832. The file is too long to reproduce in its entirety but is illustrative even in summary (Figure 8-7). Reuben Johnson filed a sworn statement with the justice of the peace of Anderson District to apply for a pension for his Revolutionary War services as a member of the Fourth Regiment of the North Carolina Line (troops). He enlisted with Richard Phillips in 1776 at Surry County, North Carolina, and served for two and one-half years in the command of Captain Joseph Philips. In his statement he also named the marches in which he took part. After re-enlisting he was present at the siege of Charleston, where he was taken prisoner by the British.

While his affidavit does not tell his birthdate or place, many applications do contain that information, as well as the veteran's

Figure 8-8. Certificate of Pension for Revolutionary War services awarded to Nancy (Greenlee) Johnson, widow of Reuben Johnson, 8 May 1846; GS 971,428.

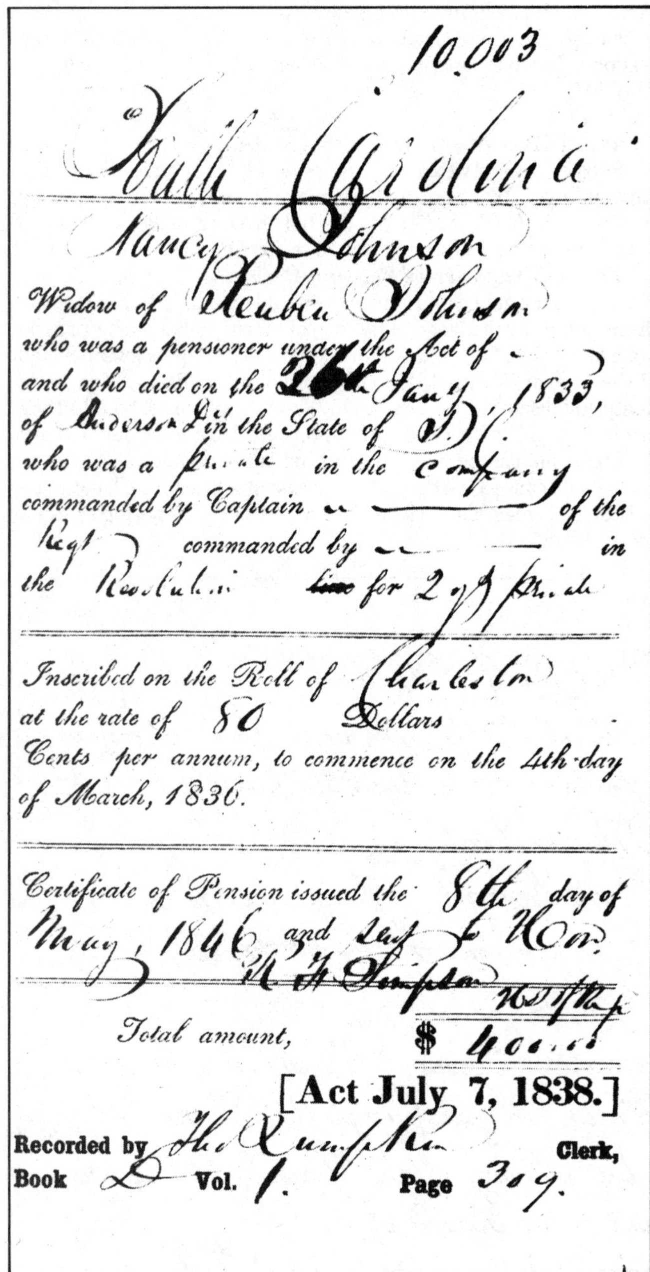

10,003

North Carolina

Nancy Johnson

Widow of Reuben Johnson

who was a pensioner under the Act of —

and who died on the 26th Jany 1833,

of Anderson Dis in the State of S.C.

who was a private in the company

commanded by Captain — of the

Regt commanded by — in

the Revolution ~~line~~ for 2 yr Private

Inscribed on the Roll of Charleston

at the rate of 80 Dollars

Cents per annum, to commence on the 4th day

of March, 1836.

Certificate of Pension issued the 8th day of

May, 1846 and sent to Hon. [illegible]

Total amount, $ 400.00

[Act July 7, 1838.]

Recorded by [illegible] Clerk,

Book D Vol. 1. Page 309.

residences after the war.

Reuben's wife applied for a widow's pension after her husband's death. This document contains information of greater importance. Nancy Johnson's affidavit of 29 March 1843 states that she was the widow of Reuben Johnson, that they were married 20 November 1788, and that her husband died 26 January 1833. Her sister Margaret Burroughs made a sworn statement that her sister was Nancy Johnson, née Greenlee, who had married Reuben Johnson in North Carolina many years before. Margaret was six years old when Nancy and Reuben were married and did not know the exact date of their marriage, but she knew Reuben and Nancy had moved to South Carolina with her father, Peter Greenlee, and that the two families lived on the same plantation. Peter died about forty years before her testimony. Her mother died 1 December 1842.

Reuben Johnson's file also contained a copy of his marriage record from Wilkes County, North Carolina. Figure 8-8 is the pension certificate issued to Nancy Johnson.

The documents in Reuben Johnson's file permit the researcher to outline his movements from the time of his enlistment to his death and documents two generations of ancestry.

A useful finding aid is the National Genealogical Society's Special Publication no. 40, *Index of Revolutionary War Pension Applications in the National Archives*, which indexes the applicant's name, the state from which he served, and the names of other applicants filing by reason of his service. (See Figure 8-9.) This information in followed by a coded suffix: The letter indicates the type of application on file: S (survivor was issued a pension); R (application rejected); W (widow's pension); BLWt (Bounty Land Warrant claim). The number after the letter is the claim number assigned by the government.

FULLERTON (continued)
James, N.H., S13099
John, Cont., Mass. Sea Service Sarah, W24263
John, Pa., S10714
Richard, Pa., BLWt. 747-200-Lt. Iss. 8/19/1789. No papers
Samuel, Mass., Persis, R3842
Thomas, Pa., Hannah, W3408
FULLILOVE, Anthony, Va., S31045
FULLINGTON, Arunah, Mass. See FULLERTON
Ezekiel, Cont., N.H., Jane, W24260
Mary, former wid. of Jonathan Bean, N.H., which see
FULLOM, Oliver. See FULLAM
FULLONTON, Ezekiel, See FULLINGTON
FULLTON, James B. See FULTON
FULLUM, Oliver, See FULLAM
FULLWOOD, William, S.C., S18829
FULMER, Casper, Armand's Corp., LLWt 13060-100. Iss. 3/10/1791. No papers.
Casper, Cont., Pa., Mary, W4676
George, N.Y., BLWt. 7133-100-Pvt. Iss. 4/21/1791 to Hendrick Kyser, ass. No papers
Jacob, N.Y., Margaret, R3844
Jacob, S.C., Elizabeth, W7343; BLWt. 34818-160-55
John, Cont., Pa., War of 1812, Mary, R3845
FULMORE, Joseph, Pa., S10667
FULNER, Jacob, S.C. See FULMER
FULP, Michael, N.C., Phebe, W1004
Peter, N.C., Elizabeth, W5278
FULPER, William, N.J., S34361
FULTON, Andrew, Va., (?), Elizabeth, R3848
David, N.C., S8539
James, Pa., S22779
James, Va., R3849
James B., Md., Anastasia, W8835
Jesse, Pa., S23645
John, N.Y., BLWt. 7120-100-Pvt. Iss. 9/15/1790 to Wm. Bell, ass. no papers
Robert, Crane's Cont. Art., Mass., BLWt. 4197-100-Sgt. Iss.1/26/1790 to John May. No papers.
Robert, Va., S8532
Samuel, Pa., Catherine, W2783
Samuel, Pa., R3850
Thomas, Va., R3851 & R14317

Figure 8-9. From National Genealogical Society, *Index of Revolutionary War Pension Applications in the National Archives*, National Genealogical Society Special Publication no. 40 (Washington, D.C.: National Genealogical Society, 1976), p. 202. Note that John Fulmer was also a veteran of the War of 1812. The index also includes notes to indicate that no papers are available.

Rejection of Revolutionary War pension applications did not necessarily mean that the applicant made a dishonest claim. Hundreds of applicants simply could not provide the necessary proof of service to be awarded a pension. The majority of applications were filed when Congress granted pensions to all veterans in 1832. Discharges had often been lost or, in many cases, never issued. Comrades-in-arms who could have attested to service were often deceased or had moved away.

The Revolutionary War pension application files have been microfilmed by the National Archives, and copies are on file at libraries throughout the country, including the Genealogical Society of Utah and its branches. This library has facilities for inexpensive photocopying or you may request copies from the National Archives, using form NATF 26 (revised May 82).

The Act of 1832 mentioned earlier required pension applications to include the birthplace, age, and residence of the applicant, and more. Applications may also include mention of a soldier substituting for another relative who was drafted into service. Once all of the applications pertaining to a veteran were received, including those of widows and other claimants, they were combined into one file.

Bounty Land Records

Bounty-land warrants were authorized by Congress in 1776 as a substitute for the wages it was unable to pay its soldiers. See section on bounty lands in Chapter 7, "Land and Tax Records." If the soldier was deceased, his heirs took claim to the land after the war. The number of acres granted was based upon the soldier's rank, and ranged from 100 to 1,100 acres. This method of decreasing military costs worked so well that bounty-land warrants were granted until 1855 and were also awarded to veterans of the post-Revolutionary Wars.

The number of applicants for bounty lands far exceeded the number of persons applying for pensions, but the bounty-land warrant application file is basically the same as that of the pension application file. The application provides the veteran's name, age, residence, the military organization in which he served, and the term of his service. If his widow or other heirs made a claim, their names, ages, and places of residence are given. Not all veterans actually farmed the land granted to them. Many assigned their warrants to others for a fee. Figure 8-10 shows Bounty Land Warrant 8057 designating Philip van Cortlandt the assignee of Eleazar Yeomans, a soldier in the New York line. Yeomans's 100 acres was authorized by an act of Congress on 9 July 1788, and assigned to van Cortlandt on 16 July 1790.

Not all bounty land applications were approved. The veteran had to prove his service in the war in exactly the same manner that a pensioner had to prove his service. Again, a rejected claim did not necessarily indicate that service was not rendered, only that the claimant was not able to provide sufficient proof.

An estimated 450,000 bounty land claims are on file in the National Archives. Some early claims were destroyed by the fires previously mentioned, but those remaining are available from the National Archives upon request, using NATF Form 26 (revised May 82).

Pension Records from 1789 to 1861

Pension records exist for the period between the end of the Revolutionary War and the beginning of the Civil War, primarily dealing with the War of 1812, the Indian Wars, and the Mexican War. These records are classified in four groups:

The Old Wars Series Pension Records. These records pertain to pension applicants who were disabled or killed while serving in any war after the close of the Revolutionary War and before the start of the Civil War, except for the War of 1812 pensions included in the regular War of 1812 pension application files. A few early death and disability claims of Civil War veterans prior to July 1861 are included. The original applications are located at the National Archives and can be requested in the same manner as all of the records discussed earlier. These pension applications have been indexed; the microfilmed index is available at the Genealogical Society of Utah.

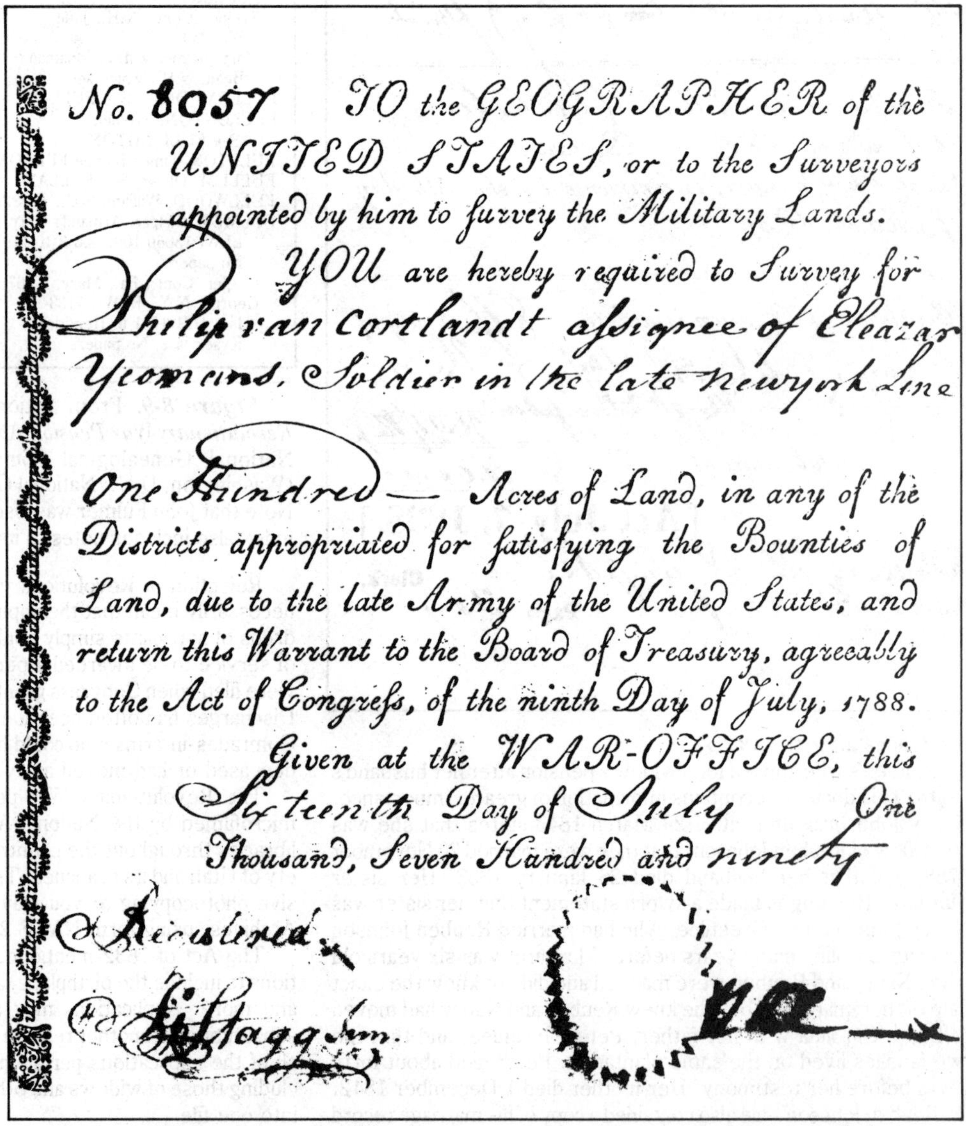

Figure 8-10. Bounty Land Warrant 8057, 15 July 1790, Philip van Cortlandt, assignee of Eleazar Yeomans, National Archives; GS 1,025,145.

No. 8057 TO the GEOGRAPHER of the UNITED STATES, or to the Surveyors appointed by him to survey the Military Lands.

YOU are hereby required to Survey for Philip van Cortlandt assignee of Eleazar Yeomans, Soldier in the late New York Line

One Hundred — Acres of Land, in any of the Districts appropriated for satisfying the Bounties of Land, due to the late Army of the United States, and return this Warrant to the Board of Treasury, agreeably to the Act of Congress, of the ninth Day of July, 1788.

Given at the WAR-OFFICE, this Sixteenth Day of July One Thousand, Seven Hundred and ninety

Registered

J. Stagg Jun.

Pension application files for veterans of the War of 1812 include applications of veterans still living after 1871 when Congress authorized their pensions. Applications for death, disability, regular service, widows, and other claimants are included in the same collection. A second act of Congress in 1878 authorized pensions for veterans who saw as few as fourteen days active duty.

These pension files will give you the veteran's name, age, and place of residence. If he was married, the marriage date and the maiden name of his wife are stated. The unit in which he served, the date and place of enlistment, and the date and place of discharge are also given. The widow's pension file will provide her name, age, and place of residence, their pertinent marriage information, the date and place of the veteran's death, his enlistment date and place, and the date and place of his final discharge. The pension files are available from the National Archives, but the microfilmed indexes are available in various libraries throughout the country.

Indian Wars. There were innumerable Indian Wars between 1817 and 1858. Veterans of these wars received pensions for and claims dating from 1892 to 1926. The files are classified as Indian survivors' originals, Indian survivors' certificates, Indian widows' originals, and Indian widows' certificates. These files are indexed and the microfilmed indexes are available at various libraries throughout the country. The pension files are located at the National Archives.

The Mexican War. Pension application files from the Mexican War were authorized by Congress in 1887 permitting veterans and their widows to file claims with the government. New restrictions specified a minimum of sixty days service, a minimum age at application of sixty-two, or being disabled or dependent.

These files contain basically the same information required in other pension applications but also required the maiden name of the wife, the names of former wives, death or divorce information about previous wives, and the names and dates of birth of living children. Pension applications were accepted between 1887 and 1926. They are indexed by name, and the index has been microfilmed. Copies of the files can be obtained from the National Archives.

Civil War and Later. Pension applications filed for the Civil War and later include records of Union Army soldiers. The files are arranged in nine categories: navy survivors' originals, navy survivors' certificates, navy widows' originals, navy widows' certificates, survivors' originals, survivors' certificates, widows' originals, widows' certificates, "C" and "XC" files.

Civil War Pensions

Pensions of Civil War veterans and their widows or minor children have been indexed by the name of the veteran. The indexes have been microfilmed and are available at local libraries. Figure 8-11 shows the index card of John W. Fulton, who served in three different companies of the Twelfth Illinois Cavalry, applied for a pension 20 Nov. 1901 in Pennsylvania, and was granted a certificate of pension based on his application. The same information would be included for a widow's or minor's pension.

Civil War pension application files are the best of the early military documents compiled and contain valuable genealogical information. These files do not all contain the same amount of information, but one can expect to find the name of the veteran, the military or naval unit in which he served, the date and place of his enlistment, his birthdate and place (in some files only), the date and place of his marriage, the names and birthdates of his children, the maiden name of his wife, information about subsequent marriages, the date and place of his discharge, the physical disabilities connected with service-related injuries, and his residences since his discharge. There will also be general affidavits of individuals who could attest to his disabilities and copies of the findings of examining physicians at the time of his injury and during subsequent periodic physicals.

Each pension applicant was required to complete a Declaration for an Original Invalid Pension. Figure 8-12 shows the declaration filed by James W. Reddish on 2 February 1891. In addition to most of the information noted above, his declaration also provides his physical description.

Figure 8-13 is the Declaration for a Widow's Pension filed by James's widow, Matilda Sweat, who stated that he died on 19 February 1894, that she was married on 5 January 1886 at Owensboro, Kentucky, and that both she and James were widowed at the time of their marriage. She had one minor child, Alonzo Reddish, who had been born in March 1884.

The Declaration for Dependent Pension of a Mother or Father (Figure 8-14) was submitted by Polly Ann Right, the mother of Markus L. Reddish and James. She stated that Markus had died of measles while in the service at Corinth, Mississippi, on 6 July 1862. She had married his father 2 October 1836 at Daviess County, Kentucky. After her husband died 1 March 1863 at Ohio County, Kentucky, she married Amos Right who had in turn died 5 July 1880.

Polly Ann Right had four sons in the Union Army at one time, and her husband was killed by Confederate troops as he worked

(3-8-3)

NAME OF SOLDIER: Fulton, John W.

NAME OF DEPENDENT: Widow, Minor,

SERVICE: D, 45 U.S. Vol. Inf. F 20 U.S. Inf.

DATE OF FILING.	CLASS.	APPLICATION NO.	CERTIFICATE NO.	STATE FROM WHICH FILED.
1901 Nov. 20	Invalid,	1277512	1,286,889	Pa.
	Widow,			
	Minor,			

ATTORNEY: Byington & Wilson.

REMARKS: C2 871,293

Figure 8-11. Civil War Pension Index Card of John W. Fulton, #1349885, 20 Nov. 1901, National Archives; GS 540,921.

Figure 8-12. Civil War Pension Application File of James W. Reddish, 2 Feb. 1891, Hancock County, Kentucky, National Archives; photocopy in author's possession.

[No. 1.]

DECLARATION FOR AN ORIGINAL INVALID PENSION.

This must be Executed before a Court of Record or some Officer thereof having custody of the Seal.

State of Kentucky County of Hancock, ss:

ON THIS Second day of February A. D. one thousand eight hundred and ninety one, personally appeared before me W. J. Morrison Notary Public of the County of Hancock ~~a COURT OF RECORD~~ within and for the county and State aforesaid James W. Reddish aged 52 years, who, being duly sworn according to law, declares that he is the identical James W. Reddish who was ENROLLED as a private on the 25th day of October 1861, in Company "K" of the 17th Regiment of Kentucky Infy Volr commanded by Col. McHenry and was honorably DISCHARGED at Calhoun Ky on the 31st day of December, 1861; that his personal description is a follows: age 52 years; height 5 feet 5 inches; complexion light; hair brown; eyes gray. That while a member of the organization aforesaid, in the service and in the line of duty, at Hartford, in the State of Kentucky, on or about the latter part day of November, 1861, he whilst on the march, was injured in the right foot by a wagon running over and crushing the same, and being thereby rendered unable to walk, he was placed on a commissary wagon to ride, from which said wagon he was thrown, with his left elbow dislocated, was thereupon taken to regimental hospital at Calhoun Ky for treatment. Whilst in said hospital contracted measles, from the effects of which he lost the sight of his left eye entirely.

(Here state the name or nature of disease, or the location of the wound or injury. If disabled by disease state fully its cause, if by wound or injury, the precise manner in which received.)

That he was treated in hospitals, as follows: Regimental Hospital at Calhoun Ky - November and December 1861
(Here state the names or numbers, and the localities of all hospitals in which treated, and the dates of treatment.)

That he has not been employed in the military or naval service otherwise than as stated above save and except as a Home Guard from 1862 to 186[illegible]
(Here state what the service was, whether prior or subsequent to that stated above, and the dates at which it began and ended.)

That he has not been in the military or naval service of the United States since the 31st day of December 1861. That since leaving the service this applicant has resided in the Ohio Co Ky, Rockport Ind and Daviess ~~in the State of~~ & Hancock Counties Ky, and that his occupation has been that of a Farmer since Jany 1862. That prior to his entry into the service above named he was a man of good, sound physical health, being when enrolled a Farmer. That he is now disabled from obtaining his subsistence by manual labor by reason of his injuries above described, received in the service of the United States; and he therefore makes this declaration for the purpose of being placed on the invalid pension roll of the United States. He hereby appoints, with full power of substitution and revocation [illegible] of Washington, D. C. his true and lawful attorney to prosecute his claim. That he has never received or applied for a pension; that his residence is ~~No.~~ Hawesville Hancock Co ~~street~~ Ky and that his post-office address is Hawesville Hancock Co Ky

Robert E. Duncan
Joe B. Vickers
(Two witnesses who can write sign here.)

James his X mark W Reddish
(Signature of Claimant.)

Figure 8-13. Declaration for Widow's Pension filed by Matilda (Sweat) Raddish [sic], wife of James W. Reddish.

DECLARATION FOR WIDOW'S PENSION.

Under act approved June 27, 1890.

STATE OF Kentucky COUNTY OF Daviess ss:

ON THIS 4th day of December A. D. one thousand eight hundred and ninety Eight personally appeared before me E. G. Adams a Notary Public within and for the County and State aforesaid Matilda Raddish aged 56 years, a resident of the city of Owensboro County of Daviess, State of Ky, who, being duly sworn according to law, makes the following declaration in order to obtain the Pension provided by Acts of Congress granting Pensions to widows: That she is the widow of James W. Raddish who enlisted under the name of James W. Raddish at Calhoun, Ky on the 25 day of Oct A. D., 1861, in Co F, 17 Reg't Ky. Inf Vols., and served at least ninety days in the late war of the rebellion, who was *honorably discharged* on the ✓ day of ✓ A. D. 186✓, and who died on the 19 day of February A. D. 1894.

That she was married under the name of Matilda Sweat to said James W. Raddish on the 5 day of Jan. 1886, by E. G. Adams, J. P. at Owensboro, Ky., there being no legal barrier to such marriage Former husband died Dec. 74 Former wife died Jan. 1. 85, that she has to the present date remained his widow.
Give date of death or divorce of former husband or wife, if any.

That she is without other means of support than her daily labor; that names and dates of birth of all the children now living under sixteen years of age of the soldier are as follows:

Alonzo Raddish, born March – 1884. , born 18 .
, born 18 . , born 18 .
, born 18 . , born 18 .
, born 18 . , born 18

That she has not heretofore received nor applied for Pension a claim was filed by soldier 987.165 That she makes this declaration for the purpose of being placed on the Pension roll of the United States under the provisions of the act of June 27, 1890.
If you previously applied, so state, giving number of claim.

She hereby appoints, with full power of substitution and revocation,

Jas. H. Vermilya & Co., of Washington, D. C.,

her true and lawful attorneys to prosecute her claim. That her Post Office Address is % E. G. Adams Owensboro County of Daviess State of Ky

Matilda her X mark Raddish
Signature of Claimant.

Nora Adams
Anna Duguid
Two witnesses who can write sign here.

PENSION B DEC 17 1898 U. S. OFFICE.

ATT'Y FILED

Figure 8-14. Declaration for Dependent Pension of a Mother or Father filed by Polley [sic] Ann Right, ibid.

Declaration for Dependent Pension of a Mother or Father

UNDER ACT OF CONGRESS APPROVED JUNE 27, 1890.

This must be Executed before a Court of Record or some Officer thereof having Custody of the Seal.

State of Kentucky County of Ohio, ss:

ON THIS 23rd day of July, A. D. one thousand eight hundred and ninety ......, personally appeared before me a Deputy Clerk of the Ohio Co. Court, a Court of Record within and for the County and State aforesaid Polley Ann Right, aged 70 years, who, being duly sworn according to law, makes the following declaration in order to obtain the Pension provided by Act of Congress approved June 27 1890. That She is the mother (Mother or Father) of Markus D Reddish (Name of Soldier), who enlisted under the name of Markus D. Reddish, at Hartford Ky on the 10" day of Oct—, A. D. 1861 in Co "F" 17" Ky Infft (Here state Company and Regiment, if in the Army; or vessel and Rank, if in the Navy.) in the war of the rebellion 1861, who was honorably discharged at ...... on the ...... day of ...... 18..., and who died at Corinth Miss. on the 6" day of July, 1862 of Measles while in the united states service & without fault on his part & said measles killed the said son & said son contracted & [illegible] while in U.S. service & in line of duty

that said soldier left neither widow nor child under sixteen years of age surviving; that the said declarant was married to the father (Mother or Father.) of said son at Davies Co Ky, on the 2d day of Oct—, A. D. 1836, by Rubin Cotter; that She is now wholly dependent upon others not legally bound for her support; that the father (Mother or Father.) of said son died at Ohio Co Ky. on the 1st day of March, A. D. 1863

That She has heretofore received applied for pension (If the Mother or Father of the Soldier had previously applied, so state, giving number of claim.) No 252,831

and that She has remarried & married Amos Right & he died 5 Jan (If mother's claim, here add "she has not again married.") Declarant hereby appoints, with full power of substitution and revocation, R R Wedding of Rosine Ohio Co Ky her (His or her) true and lawful attorney, to prosecute this claim; that her residence is No. ...... street ...... and her Post Office address is Horton Ohio Co Ky.

J. Raleigh
J. B. Wallace [illegible] (Two witnesses who can write, sign here.)

Polley Ann Right her mark (Signature of Claimant.)

on their farm. This unusual family situation is fully explained in the collected Civil War Pension files of the entire family. This family's files are representative of the majority of the records on file.

In addition to sworn statements attesting to marriages, the files also contain certified documents pertaining to marriages. Figure 8-15 shows a marriage record included in the pension file of Calvin R. Johnson, Indiana veteran.

Pensioners also completed periodic requests for additional information. For example, Figure 8-16 shows documentation of the maiden name of Solomon Winne's wife, the date of their marriage, and the names and dates of birth of their living children. Because she predeceased her husband by a few months, his pension file included a copy of her death certificate (Figure 8-17). The document provides the exact date of her death, her age at the time of her death, the names and birthplaces of her parents, and where she was buried.

Winne's file also included an unusual document. His daughter Mary H. Swarthout of Kingston, New York, filed an application to be reimbursed for expenses related to his last illness. He died 20 July 1909 at the Old Soldier's Home in Bath, New York, owing $75 for his board at the time of his death. He owned no real estate, personal property, or money. Figure 8-18 is a photocopy of the application.

Another document in the pension file is the termination of the pension. If the cause is death – the most common reason – the death date is usually listed.

One of the most valuable contributions that a pension file can make in genealogical research is listing the veteran's residences after discharge. Westward expansion sent many families leapfrogging states between censuses in the post-Civil War years. Tracing the exact movements of individuals and families during that period is difficult at best and sometimes impossible without the assistance of the "road maps" provided in these pension files.

Since the Confederacy dissolved after the war, no central governmental agency provided pensions for service or disability to the Confederate soldier; but some former Confederate states, including Alabama, Arkansas, Florida, Georgia, Louisiana, Mississippi, North Carolina, South Carolina, Tennessee, Texas, and Virginia, author-

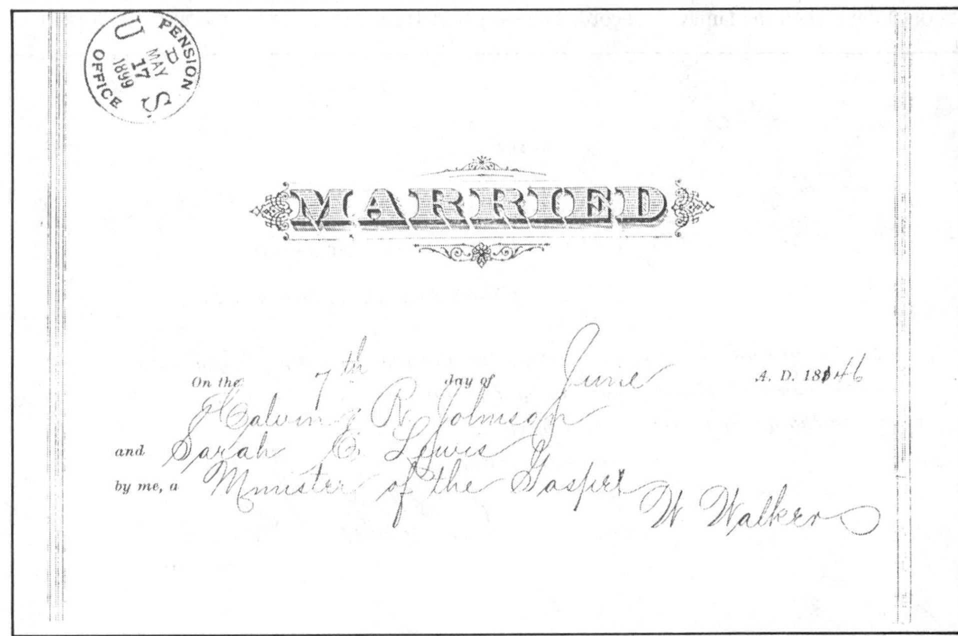
U.S. PENSION OFFICE MAY 17 1899

MARRIED

On the 7th day of June A. D. 1846

Calvin R. Johnson

and Sarah E. Lewis

by me, a Minister of the Gospel W. Walker

Figure 8-15. Marriage Return of Calvin R. Johnson and Sarah E. Lewis, 7 June 1846, Hamilton County, Ohio, and Certification, 14 April 1899, in Civil War Pension Application File, 11898, Richmond, Indiana: National Archives; photocopy of file in author's possession.

THE STATE OF OHIO, HAMILTON COUNTY, O. } SS. PROBATE COURT.

I, HOWARD FERRIS, *Sole Judge and Ex-Officio Clerk of the PROBATE COURT, within and for the County aforesaid, do hereby certify that the foregoing entry of the marriage of* Calvin R. Johnson *and* Sarah E. Lewis *is correctly copied from the record of marriages in said County, which record is now in said Probate Court in pursuance of law.*

In Testimony Whereof, *I have hereunto set my hand and affixed the Seal of the said Court at Cincinnati, this* 14th *day of* April *A. D. 189*9

Howard Ferris *Probate Judge and Ex-Officio Clerk.*

By F. J. Beble *Deputy Clerk.*

Form 800—1000—6-97.

ized pensions to veterans and their widows. Some of these pension files have been microfilmed by the Genealogical Society of Utah. Others are in the possession of various state archives or government custodians.

Figure 8-19 illustrates the Soldier's Application for Pension for the State of Tennessee. The record lists the veteran's name, date and place of enlistment, residence, date and place of birth, injuries resulting from military service, marital status, the number and ages of his children, the age of his wife, the number of years he resided in Tennessee, and his occupation. There is no standard format for pension applications for the Confederacy, but the Tennessee application is representative of most of the others.

Tennessee also compiled a valuable and little used record consisting of the biographical sketches of veterans of the Civil War who were still living in 1922. (See Figure 8-20.) These records are filled with valuable genealogical information, including the veteran's name, residence, age, place of birth, occupation, the unit he served in during the war, his parents' names and birthplaces, the names of his paternal grandparents, and their residence. The residence of the veteran's father, all facts known about parents, grandparents, and great-grandparents (including when the family came to America, property owned by the veteran and his parents, education and the general quality of the veteran's life) are included in these sketches.

Soldier Burial Records

Soldiers and veterans of the military services have had the benefit of being buried in one of the many national and other federally administered cemeteries since 1861, the most famous of which is Arlington National Cemetery just outside Washington, D.C. Records pertaining to almost all soldiers and veterans buried in cemeteries under federal jurisdiction are in the custody of the Cemetery Service, National Cemetery System, Veterans Administration, 810 Vermont Avenue, Washington, DC 20420. The names of the deceased are indexed and information will be furnished on request.

Some soldiers were buried on U.S. military installations between 1807 and 1939. Records of those buried in the U.S. Soldiers Home Cemetery in Washington, D.C., national cemeteries, military installations in the United States, and post cemeteries in Cuba, the Phillipines, Puerto Rico, and China are also included in this collection. You must know where the soldier is buried to find the burial record. The early burial registers record primarily burials of active-

Figure 8-16. Civil War Pension Application File of Solomon Winne, Kingston, New York, 13 April 1898; National Archives; photo copy in author's possession.

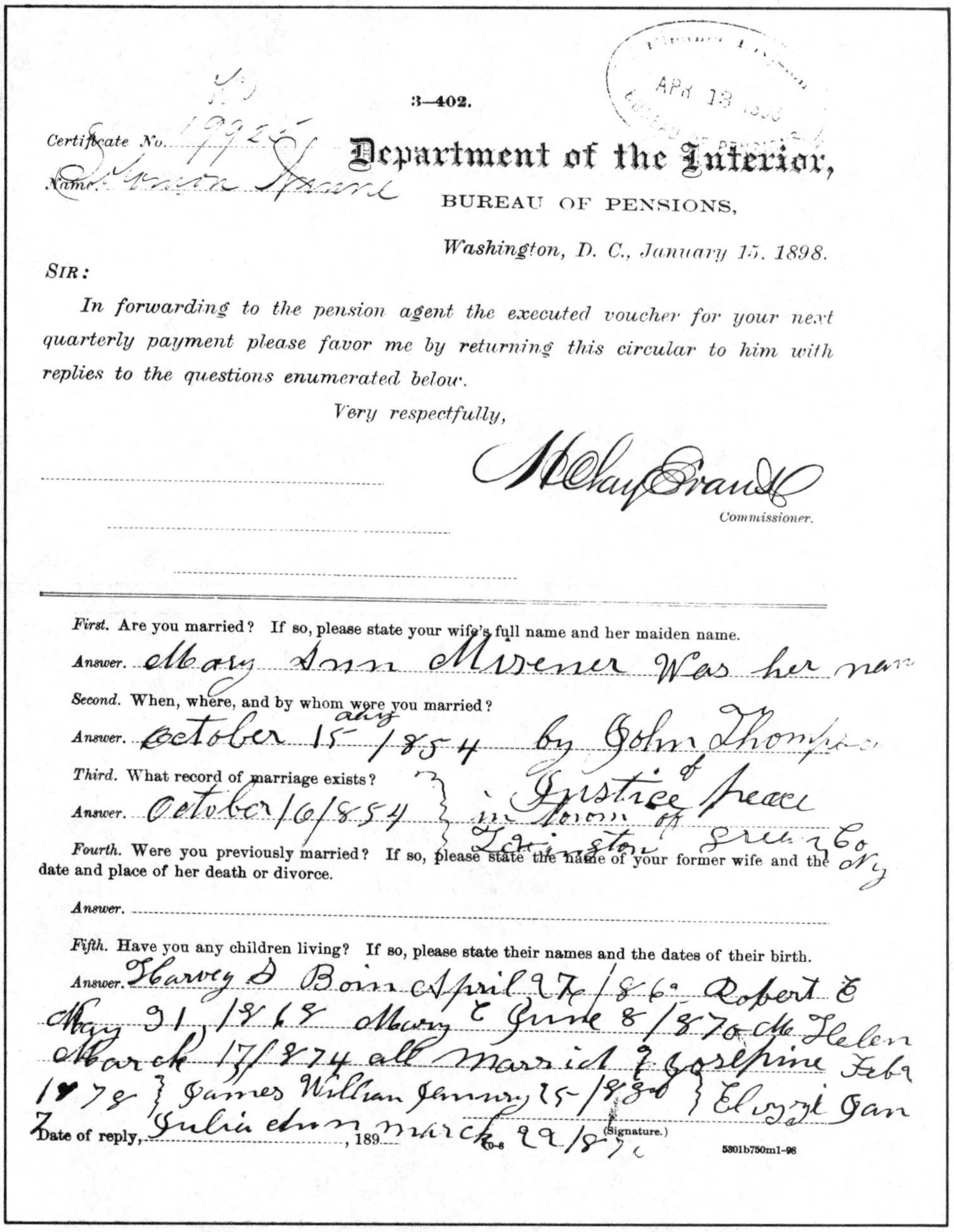

3—402.

Certificate No. 19925

Name. Soloman Winne

Department of the Interior,

BUREAU OF PENSIONS,

Washington, D. C., January 15, 1898.

SIR:

In forwarding to the pension agent the executed voucher for your next quarterly payment please favor me by returning this circular to him with replies to the questions enumerated below.

Very respectfully,

H. Clay Evans

Commissioner.

First. Are you married? If so, please state your wife's full name and her maiden name.

Answer. Mary Ann Mirener Was her name

Second. When, where, and by whom were you married?

Answer. October 15 day 1854 by John Thompson

Third. What record of marriage exists?

Answer. October 16/1854 } in Town of Lexington Greene Co NY Justice of Peace

Fourth. Were you previously married? If so, please state the name of your former wife and the date and place of her death or divorce.

Answer.

Fifth. Have you any children living? If so, please state their names and the dates of their birth.

Answer. Harvey S Born April 27/1860 Robert E May 31, 1868 Mary E June 8/1870 M Helen March 17/1874 all Married } Josephine Feb 1878 } James William January 25-1880 } Elizzi Jan 7 Julia Ann

Date of reply, March 29/1897, 189

(Signature.)

5301b750m1-98

duty soldiers except in the case of frontier army posts, where family members and civilian dependents were also buried in the post cemetery.

Four volumes of records dated 1861-68 pertain to burials of soldiers at the U.S. Soldiers Home Cemetery. The registers will provide the soldier's name, military organization, date and place of burial, rank, place of residence before enlistment, name and residences of the soldier's widow or other relative, age, cause of death, and place and date of death. Each volume is indexed by the initial letter of the soldier's surname.

Three correspondence files also contain information pertaining to soldiers' burials: letters relating to buried soldiers (1864-90), quartermaster's notifications (1863-66), and reports of Arlington National Cemetery Sexton (1864-67).

Applications for headstones to be placed at the graves of soldiers and veterans cover from 1879 to 1924. The information in the applications includes the name and address of headstone applicant, name of the veteran, rank, years of service, place and date of burial, and sometimes the date and cause of death. Most of these applications are filed by state, then by county, then by cemetery. Applications for headstones for soldiers, sailors, and marines buried outside the United States between 1911 and 1924 are arranged by country of burial. Soldiers buried in the cemeteries of the National Home for Disabled Volunteer Soldiers for whom headstone applications were made are arranged by the name of the home.

A card file indexing applications for headstones for 1870-1903 has been compiled and includes the serviceman's name, military organization, date and place of death, name and location of the cemetery, and date of the application. These cards are alphabetical by the surname of the soldier and they include Confederate, and post-Civil War veterans' applications.

There are also card file records of World War I-era soldiers who died overseas between 1917 and 1922. These files consist mainly of grave registrations, records of American names in European chapels, and records of American soldiers who were buried in Russia. They are arranged alphabetically by surname of the soldier or name of the cemetery. The collection of grave registrations includes the name of the soldier, military organization, date of death, a statement that he was killed in action, name and address of the nearest relative or guardian, and name of the chapel. The record of American names in European chapels includes the name of the soldier, military organization, date of death, statement that the soldier was killed in action, name and address of the nearest relative or guardian, and name of the chapel. These records are all on file in Record Group 92, Records of the Quartermaster General, in the National Archives.

A list of soldiers missing in action is in the custody of the National Archives under the Records of American Battle Commission, Record Group 117. The information includes the name of the missing soldier, the unit in which he served, and the date of disappearance.

Veterans' Homes

Records pertaining to the federal veterans' homes are housed in the National Archives in Record Group 15, Records of the Veterans' Administration, and in Record Group 231, Records of the U.S. Soldiers' Home. Here is a list of the National Homes for Disabled Volunteer Soldiers (now known as Veterans Administration Centers) and the dates of their creation:

Eastern Branch, Togus, Maine 1866
Central Branch, Dayton, Ohio 1867
Northwestern Branch, Wood, Wisconsin 1867
Southern Branch, Kecoughtan, Virginia 1870
Western Branch, Leavenworth, Kansas 1885
Pacific Branch, Sawtelle, California 1888

N. B.—WRITE PLAINLY, WITH UNFADING INK—THIS IS A PERMANENT RECORD. Every item of information should be carefully supplied. AGE should be stated EXACTLY. PHYSICIANS should state CAUSE OF DEATH in plain terms, so that it may be properly classified. Exact statement of OCCUPATION is very important. See instructions on back of certificate.

New York State Department of Health
BUREAU OF VITAL STATISTICS
STANDARD CERTIFICATE OF DEATH
STATE OF NEW YORK
Registered No. 11520

1 PLACE OF DEATH
County Ulster
Town
Village
City Kingston (No. ..., St.; ... Ward) [If death occurred in a hospital or institution, give its NAME instead of street and number]

2 FULL NAME Mary Ann Winne

PERSONAL AND STATISTICAL PARTICULARS
3 SEX Female
4 COLOR OR RACE White
5 SINGLE, MARRIED, WIDOWED, OR DIVORCED (Write the word) Married
6 DATE OF BIRTH March 10th 1909 (Month) (Day) (Year)
7 AGE 71 yrs. 1 mos. 6 ds. If LESS than 1 day, how many hrs. or min.?
8 OCCUPATION (a) Trade, profession, or particular kind of work Not given
(b) General nature of industry, business, or establishment in which employed (or employer)
9 BIRTHPLACE (State or country) Town of Shandaken, N.Y.
PARENTS
10 NAME OF FATHER John Misener
11 BIRTHPLACE OF FATHER (State or country) Scotland
12 MAIDEN NAME OF MOTHER Lamy Misener
13 BIRTHPLACE OF MOTHER (State or country) Holland
14 THE ABOVE IS TRUE TO THE BEST OF MY KNOWLEDGE
(Informant)
(Address)
15 Filed ..., 191... REGISTRAR

MEDICAL CERTIFICATE OF DEATH
16 DATE OF DEATH March 10, 1909 (Month) (Day) (Year)
17 I HEREBY CERTIFY, That I attended deceased from ..., 191..., to ..., 191..., that I last saw h... alive on ..., 191..., and that death occurred, on the date stated above, at ... m. The CAUSE OF DEATH* was as follows:
Organic heart disease
(Duration) ... yrs. ... mos. ... ds.
Contributory (SECONDARY) Arteriosclerosis
(Duration) ... yrs. ... mos. ... ds.
(Signed) E. E. Norwood, M.D.
..., 191... (Address) Kingston, N.Y.
*State the DISEASE CAUSING DEATH, or, in deaths from VIOLENT CAUSES, state (1) MEANS OF INJURY; and (2) whether ACCIDENTAL, SUICIDAL, or HOMICIDAL.
18 LENGTH OF RESIDENCE (FOR HOSPITALS, INSTITUTIONS, TRANSIENTS, OR RECENT RESIDENTS). At place of death ... yrs. ... mos. ... ds. In the State ... yrs. ... mos. ... ds.
Where was disease contracted, if not at place of death?
Former or usual residence
19 PLACE OF BURIAL OR REMOVAL Wiltwyck Cemetery
21 DATE OF BURIAL ..., 191...
20 UNDERTAKER
ADDRESS

PENSION OFFICE AUG 8 1910 U.S.

Burial or Transit Permit issued by ... Date of Issue ...

Form 68 V. S.

Figure 8-17. Death certificate of Mary Ann (Misener) Winne in Civil War pension file of Solomon Winne, ibid.

Figure 8-18. Application for Reimbursement to Mary H. Swarthout for expenses connected with the final illness of her father, Solomon Winne, in his pension file.

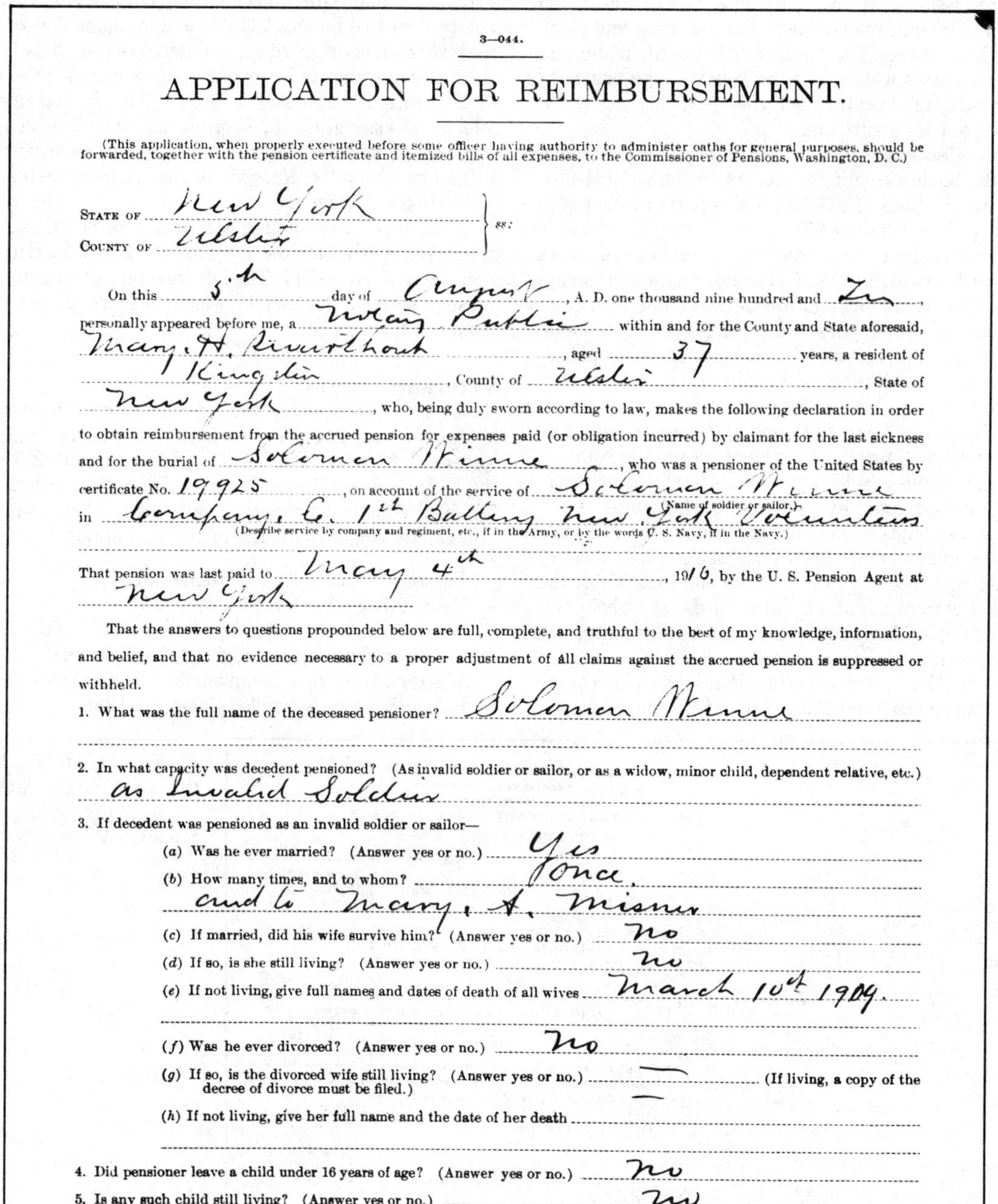

3—044.

APPLICATION FOR REIMBURSEMENT.

(This application, when properly executed before some officer having authority to administer oaths for general purposes, should be forwarded, together with the pension certificate and itemized bills of all expenses, to the Commissioner of Pensions, Washington, D. C.)

STATE OF New York } ss:
COUNTY OF Ulster

On this 5th day of August, A. D. one thousand nine hundred and Ten, personally appeared before me, a Notary Public within and for the County and State aforesaid, Mary H. Swarthout, aged 37 years, a resident of Kingston, County of Ulster, State of New York, who, being duly sworn according to law, makes the following declaration in order to obtain reimbursement from the accrued pension for expenses paid (or obligation incurred) by claimant for the last sickness and for the burial of Solomon Winne, who was a pensioner of the United States by certificate No. 19925, on account of the service of Solomon Winne (Name of soldier or sailor.) in Company, C. 1st Battery New York Volunteers (Describe service by company and regiment, etc., if in the Army, or by the words U. S. Navy, if in the Navy.)

That pension was last paid to May 4th, 1910, by the U. S. Pension Agent at New York

That the answers to questions propounded below are full, complete, and truthful to the best of my knowledge, information, and belief, and that no evidence necessary to a proper adjustment of all claims against the accrued pension is suppressed or withheld.

1. What was the full name of the deceased pensioner? Solomon Winne
2. In what capacity was decedent pensioned? (As invalid soldier or sailor, or as a widow, minor child, dependent relative, etc.) as Invalid Soldier
3. If decedent was pensioned as an invalid soldier or sailor—
   (a) Was he ever married? (Answer yes or no.) Yes
   (b) How many times, and to whom? Once, and to Mary. A. Misner
   (c) If married, did his wife survive him? (Answer yes or no.) no
   (d) If so, is she still living? (Answer yes or no.) no
   (e) If not living, give full names and dates of death of all wives March 10th 1909.
   (f) Was he ever divorced? (Answer yes or no.) No
   (g) If so, is the divorced wife still living? (Answer yes or no.) — (If living, a copy of the decree of divorce must be filed.) —
   (h) If not living, give her full name and the date of her death
4. Did pensioner leave a child under 16 years of age? (Answer yes or no.) no
5. Is any such child still living? (Answer yes or no.) no
6. Was there insurance (life, accident, or health) in force on life of pensioner at time of death? (Answer yes or no.) no
7. If so, give the name of each company in which a policy was carried and the amount in which each policy was written —
8. Who was the beneficiary named in each policy? —
9. What was the relation of each beneficiary to the pensioner? —
10. Were the premiums paid by the deceased pensioner? —
11. If not paid by the deceased pensioner, state the amount of premiums paid by each person who made payment on that account —

PENSION N AUG 8 1910 U. S. OFFICE

6—1572

12. Was pensioner a member of any society paying sick or death benefits? (Answer yes or no.) no
13. Is there an executor or administrator, or will application be made for appointment of any person as administrator? no
14. Did the deceased pensioner leave any money, real estate, or personal property? No Money, Real Estate or Personal Property
15. If so, state the character and value of all such property —
16. What was the assessed value (last assessment) of the real estate? —
17. How was the pensioner's property disposed of? None to dispose of.
18. Did pensioner leave an unindorsed pension check? (Answer yes or no.) no
19. What was your relation to the deceased pensioner? Daughter
20. Are you married? (Answer yes or no.) Yes
21. What was the cause of pensioner's death? Senile Dementia at Home
22. When did the pensioner's last sickness begin? Cannot say, admitted to Hospital in [illegible]
23. From what date did the pensioner become so ill as to require the regular and daily attendance of another person constantly until death? Was at Soldiers Home, Bath, N.Y. cannot give date
24. Give the name and post-office address of each physician who attended the pensioner during last sickness Attended by the Physicians at the Soldiers Home Bath, N.Y.
25. State the names of the persons by whom the pensioner was nursed during the period or any portion of the period of last sickness and the period covered by such service in each instance Nursed at the Home
26. Where did the pensioner live during last sickness? Soldiers Home, Bath N.Y.
27. Where did the pensioner die? Soldiers Home, Bath N.Y.
28. When did the pensioner die? July 20th 1909.
29. Where was the pensioner buried? Bath, N.Y.
30. Has there been paid, or will application be made for payment to you or any other person, any part of the expenses of the pensioner's last sickness and burial by any State, County, or municipal corporation? (Answer yes or no.) No
31. State below the expenses of the pensioner's last sickness and burial. Write the word *none* where no charge is made in case of any item of expense noted.

(Each charge entered below should be supported by an itemized bill of the person who rendered the service or furnished any supplies for which reimbursement is demanded, and should show, over his signature, by whom paid, or who is held responsible for payment, and contain the name of the pensioner for whom the expense was incurred or service rendered.)

Names.	Nature of Expenses.	State Whether Paid or Unpaid.	Amount.
	Physician		
	Medicine		
	Nursing and care		
	Undertaker		
	Livery		
	Cemetery		
	Other expenses and their nature:		
	Board &c	unpaid	75 00
	Total		

32. **Is the above a complete list of *all* the expenses of the last sickness and burial of the deceased pensioner?** (Answer yes or no.) Yes

That my post-office address is No. 28, on Taylor street, town or city of Kingston, County of Ulster, State of New York

(When the claimant for reimbursement is a married woman, she is required to sign the application with her own full name, not using the Christian name or the initials of her husband, and all bills should be receipted to her in her own name.)

Mary H. Swarthout
(Claimant's signature in full.)

6—1572

Figure 8-18. Continued.

3

Also personally appeared *Emma Fr[illegible]*

and *Dorothy P. Booth*, persons whom I certify to be respectable and entitled to credit, and who, being by me duly sworn, say that they were present and saw *Mary H. Swarthout*, the claimant, sign *her* name (or make *—* mark) to the foregoing application, and that they know the claimant therein; that they have read all the questions, answers, and declarations in said application and believe the facts therein set forth to be true; and that they have no interest, direct or indirect, in this claim.

[illegible]
171 [illegible]
[illegible]
[illegible]
(Signatures and post-office addresses of witnesses.)

Subscribed and sworn to before me this *5th* day of *August*, A. D. 19*10*; and I certify that the contents of the foregoing application, etc., were fully made known and explained to the claimant and witnesses before swearing, including the words *—* erased and the words *—* added; and that I have no interest, direct or indirect, in the prosecution of this claim.

F. W. Fr[illegible]
(Signature.)
Notary Public
(Official character.)
177 [illegible]

STATEMENT OF ATTENDING PHYSICIANS.

Give date of the pensioner's death

Give date of commencement of pensioner's last sickness

From what date did the pensioner require the regular and daily attendance of another person constantly until death?

During what period did you attend the pensioner?

State nature of disease from which pensioner died

Give name of each person who rendered service as nurse, and who has made or will make a charge for such service

Give name of any other physician who attended the pensioner in last sickness

Does your bill include a charge for all medicine furnished the pensioner during last sickness?

State whether you have read the questions in the foregoing application, and the claimant's answers thereto, and whether such answers are correct according to your best knowledge, information, and belief?

Mention any other facts within your knowledge which in your opinion would be helpful in adjusting this claim for reimbursement:

I certify that the foregoing statement is correct.

_______________, 191 _______________ *Attending Physician.*

_______________, 191 _______________ *Attending Physician.*

6—1572

PENSION N AUG 8 1910 U. S. OFFICE.

Marion Branch, Marion, Indiana 1888
Roseburg Branch, Roseburg, Oregon 1894
Danville Branch, Danville, Illinois 1898
Mountain Branch, Johnson City, Tennessee 1903
Battle Mountain Sanitarium, Hot Springs, South Dakota 1907
Bath Branch, Bath, New York 1894
Saint Petersburg Home, Saint Petersburg, Florida 1930
Biloxi Home, Biloxi, Mississippi 1930
Tuskegee Home, Tuskegee, Alabama 1933

Military Census Records

For a thorough discussion of military censuses, see Chapter 4. Briefly, military census enumerations were taken in 1840 and 1890. The 1840 information is available, but most of the 1890 census was destroyed by fire in 1921. The surviving enumerations have been microfilmed and are available in research libraries throughout the country.

The 1840 census simply provides the veteran's name, age, and residence. The 1890 census lists his name, rank, company, regiment or vessel, dates of enlistment and discharge, length of service in years, months, and days, aliases, post office address or the name of the institution in which he was living at the time of the enumeration, and disabilities incurred in the service.

Printed Volumes

Hundreds of volumes pertain to the military history of the United States and to the service and pension/bounty land applications that have been granted prior to the modern wars. There is no known comprehensive bibliography of those printed sources, but a partial list of sources is provided at the end of this chapter. A few examples of the information contained in randomly selected printed volumes are included for your study. On this page from the *Roster of Revolutionary Soldiers in Georgia,* note that the information included is extensive for one veteran while it is scant for others.

JESSE POPE, b. in Chowan Co., N. C.; d. Hancock Co., Ga., 1820. Received bounty grant of land in Ga. for his services, in N. C. Troops. Married Mary Fort.

JOHN POPE, b. 1755, Halifax Co., N. C.; d. 1819, Wilkes Co., Ga. Served as Capt., Ga. Troops. Received bounty grant of land in Ga. for his services. Married Elizabeth Smith, d. 1829.
Children:
1. Huldah, mar. Henry Jossey, Jr.
2. Keturah, mar. James Mathews, Jr.
3. Mary L., mar. — Henderson.
4. Wylie.
5. Rowena.
6. Louisa.
7. Martha, mar. Rev. Wm. A. Callaway.
8. Augustine Burwell.

JOHN HENRY POPE, b. 1756; d. 1821, Wilkes Co., Ga. Received bounty land in Ga. for his services with N. C. Troops. Married Mary Burwell.

OLIVER PORTER (son of JOHN PORTER, REV. SOLDIER of Va. and Mary Anthony), b. Prince Edward Co., Va., 1763; d. Greene Co., Ga., 1838. Enlisted in the Reg. of his brother WILLIAM PORTER, and was at the Siege of Yorktown. Received land in Greene Co., Ga. for his services. Married Margaret Watson, b. 171- (dau. of DOUGLASS WATSON, b. 1750 in Va.; d. 1797, Wilkes Co., Ga. Served in Va. and received bounty grant of land in Wilkes Co., Ga. for his services, and his wife Margaret Parker).
Children: (known)
1. Ann (1793-1875); mar. 1815, Adam Goudylock Saffold (son of WILLIAM SAFFOLD, REV. SOLDIER who received land in Ga. for his services; d. in Ga.; mar. Ann Goudelock).
2. Douglass Watson, mar. Annabelle Burwell (dau. of JOHN BURWELL, REV. SOLDIER, and his wife Ann Powell).
3. James, b. Greene Co., Ga.; mar. Athline (or Abijah) Cox, b. Morgan Co., Ga. (dau. of John Cox and his wife Elizabeth Hyde, dau. of JAMES HYDE, REV. SOLDIER who d. from effects of wounds received in service).

Mrs. Howard H. McCall, comp., *Roster of Revolutionary Soldiers in Georgia,* vol. 3 (Baltimore: Genealogical Publishing Co., 1969), p. 189

Figure 8-19. Tennessee Civil War Pension Application File of L. H. Hathcock, Rutherford County, Tennessee, 3 Aug. 1891, Tennessee Historical Library; GS 969,942.

ACCEPTED

No. 415

Soldier's Application for Pension.

(The Board Reserve the Right to Call for Additional Testimony if they Deem it Necessary.)

L. H. Hathcock

Filed Aug 3. 1891

Allow[illegible] Aug 3. 1891

Quarte[illegible] *llowance,* $ 25 00

Pension allowed from filing

Rejected —

[illegible] *President.*

Jno. P. Hickman *Secretary.*

Board Pension Examiners.

A. B. TAVEL, Printer to the State.

Figure 8-19. Continued.

SOLDIER'S APPLICATOIN FOR PENSION.

I L. H. Nathcock a native of the State of Tennessee and now a citizen of Tennessee, resident at Carlockville in the County of Rutherford in said State of Tennessee, and who was a soldier from the State of Tennessee in the war between the United States and the Confederate States, do hereby apply for aid under the Act of General Assembly of Tennessee, entitled "An Act for the benefit of the indigent and disabled soldiers of the late war between the States, and to fix the fees of attorneys or agents for procuring such pensions, and fixing a penalty for the violation of the same." And I do solemnly swear that, while in the discharge of my duty in the service of the Confederate ~~United~~ States, as a member of Company "F" 44th Tennessee Regiment of Infantry

I was wounded in the battle or battles of Stones River or Murfreesboro

and that from the effects of such wound or wounds I was disabled as follows: I was through the left hip, causing the bone to work out and made my left leg shorter, smaller & weaker than the other, amounting to the loss of the use of that leg.

and that by reason of such wound and disability, I am now entitled to receive the benefits of this Act. I further swear that I do not hold any national, State or county office, nor do I receive aid or a pension from any other State, or from the United States, and that I am not an inmate of any soldiers' home, and that I am unable to earn a reasonable support for myself and family. I do further solemnly swear that the answers given to the following questions are true:

In what county, State and year were you born?

Ans. In Coffee Co, Tenn, about the year 1844

When did you enlist, and in what command? Give the names of regimental and company officers under whom you were serving at date of wound or wounds.

Ans. I enlisted in Fall of 1861 in Co F. 44th Rg. When I was wounded Col. McDaniel was commanding the Rg. Jas. Hill was Capt. Jno Ashley was 1st Lieut. the second Lieut was not then with the Co.

In what battle or battles were you wounded, and if not in battle state under what circumstances you received the injury or injuries?

Ans. I was wounded in the battle of Stones River during the fight I was shot through the thigh with a minnie ball which worked out 13 months afterwards.

What was the precise nature of your wound or wounds?

Ans. I was shot through the left thigh.

What limb, if any, did you lose by reason of said wound or wounds, and if no limb, state fully the disability caused by said wound or wounds, and is said disability permanent?

Ans. I lost no limb, I have lost the use of my left leg by said wound. The disablity is permanent.

Were you incapacitated for service by reason of said wound, wounds or service?

Ans. Yes

Were you discharged from the army by reason of said wound, wounds or service?

Ans. I never was discharged but was carried home.

If discharged from the army, where were you and what did you do until the close of the war?

Ans. I remained at home and after I got able I tried to work on the farm.

What was the name of the surgeon that attended you?

Ans. Dr. Mankin

Are you married, or have you been married?

Ans. I am married

READ THIS ACT BEFORE FILLING OUT APPLICATION.

CHAPTER 64, LAWS OF TENNESSEE, 1891.

AN ACT for the benefit of the indigent and disabled soldiers of the late war between the States, and to fix the fees of attorneys or agents for procuring such pensions, and fixing a penalty for the violation of the same.

SECTION 1. *Be it enacted by the General Assembly of the State of Tennessee,* That the Comptroller, Attorney-general of the State, and three ex-Confederate soldiers, to be suggested by the Tennessee Division of Confederate Veterans, appointed by the Governor, and hold their office for two years, without pay, shall constitute the "Board of Pension Examiners," who are invested with full power and authority to hear and determine all applications for pensions under the provisions of this Act, and to prescribe such rules and regulations touching such applications at such times as they may deem necessary for the proper conduct of their business as such board; and to hear evidence touching such applications, at such times and places, and in such manner, as they may desire; and to allow or refuse pensions according as justice and law may require. They are invested with full power over the entire pension roll at all times, and it is their duty to strike from the roll such names as may be improperly there, after proper notice and hearing. Their decision shall be final.

SEC. 2. *Be it further enacted,* That only disabled soldiers, Federal and Confederate, that enlisted from the State of Tennessee in Tennessee regiments, or citizens of this State at the time of their enlistment in regiments of other States, who are now residents of this State; or citizens of other States who enlisted in Tennessee or other States, but who are now and have been citizens of this State for one year, shall be entitled to the benefits of this Act; and they must be *bona fide* residents of the State at least one year before making their application for pension; and their characters as soldiers must have been free from dishonor; and it must appear that they are not pensioners entitled to pension under the laws of the Federal Government or of any other State, and that they are not already in possession of a competency—the object of this statute being to provide for the indigent and disabled.

SEC. 3. *Be it further enacted,* That the rates of pensions to be paid under this Act shall be as follows:

1. For total disability, such as the loss of both arms, both legs or both eyes, or the use of the same either in battle, skirmish or on picket, or from sickness, exposure or other injuries received during the war, in prison, or on the way home, $25 per month.

2. For partial disability, such as the loss of *one leg and one arm,* either in battle, skirmish or on picket, or one of the aforesaid limbs lost in battle, or skirmish, or on picket, and the other so disabled as to since render it useless or made amputation necessary, $10 per month.

3. For smaller disability, such as the loss of one leg or one arm, or the use of the same, either in battle, skirmish or on picket, or in prison, $8.33⅓ per month.

The Board of Pension Examiners shall pass on all applications, give their approval before a pension shall be granted; when granted, the Comptroller shall issue his warrant quarterly to the pensioner for the amount of the pension, on the Treasurer, who shall pay the same out of any moneys not otherwise appropriated.

SEC. 4. *Be it further enacted,* That no pension shall be allowed to any one unless it shall clearly appear that his disabilities resulted from some injury received while engaged in the military service, and while in the line of duty, or in prison.

SEC. 5. *Be it further enacted,* That the pensions allowed under this Act shall be paid quarterly; and that no arrears shall be allowed beyond the date of making application, and in no case for more than one year. If, from inheritance or otherwise, any pensioner shall acquire a competency sufficient for his support, cease to be a resident of the State, or die, it shall be the duty of the board to strike such pensioner from the pension roll.

SEC. 6. *Be it further enacted,* That the Board of Pension Examiners shall keep a book in which shall be recorded the names of each pensioner, company and regiment, date, place, and nature of wound received, date and place where paroled or discharged, date of granting and amount of pension.

SEC. 7. *Be it further enacted,* That it shall be the duty of the board to fix the fees of attorneys prosecuting applications for pensions, which shall in no case exceed $10, which shall be paid directly to the attorney.

SEC. 8. *Be it further enacted,* That it shall be a misdemeanor punishable by a fine of not less than $500 and imprisonment not less than ten days, for any person to contract for or receive, directly or indirectly, more than the legal fees for prosecuting pension claims under this Act. The grand jury are given inquisitorial power over this offense, and the "Board of Pension Examiners" are required to investigate such matters, and have them brought before the courts.

SEC. 9. *Be it further enacted,* That the Board shall have power, with the consent of the Trustees, in case of applicants having no families, to allow them a support in the Confederate Soldier's Home in lieu of a pension.

SEC. 10. *Be it further enacted,* That it shall be the duty of the Board to withhold pension from any pensioner who may habitually waste the State's bounty in dissipation or other dishonorable manner.

SEC. 11. *Be it further enacted,* That this Act take effect from and after its passage, the public welfare requiring it; and that all former laws on the subject of pensions be and the same are hereby repealed.

Passed March 10, 1891.

THOMAS R. MYERS,
Speaker of the House of Representatives.

W. C. DISMUKES,
Speaker of the Senate.

Approved March 12, 1891.

JOHN P. BUCHANAN,
Governor.

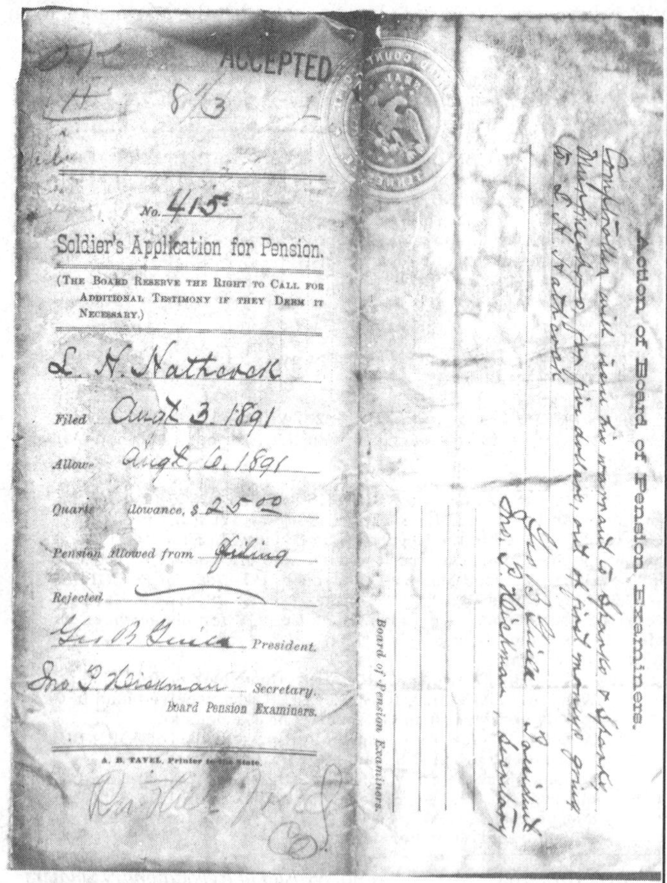

ACCEPTED

No. 415

Soldier's Application for Pension.

(THE BOARD RESERVE THE RIGHT TO CALL FOR ADDITIONAL TESTIMONY IF THEY DEEM IT NECESSARY.)

L. H. Nathcock

Filed Augt 3. 1891

Allowed Augt 6. 1891

Quarterly Allowance, $25.00

Pension Allowed from Filing

Rejected

Geo B. Guild President.

Jno. P. Hickman Secretary.

Board Pension Examiners.

A. B. TAVEL, Printer to the State.

Action of Board of Pension Examiners.

Board of Pension Examiners.

If so, what is the size of your family?

Ans. A wife and three children

What are the respective ages of your wife and children?

Ans. Wife is 47 yrs old. Children are 20, 13, & 11 respectively

To what sex do your children belong?

Ans. Oldest girl, next one is a boy & youngest is a girl

In what business are you now engaged, if any; and what do you earn?

Ans. I am trying to farm. With the help of my wife & children I can hardly make a living. My neighbors are good to me and help me some.

What estate have you in your own right, real and personal, and what is its value?

Ans. Nothing

What estate has your wife in her own right, real and personal, and what is its value?

Ans. Nothing

How have you derived support for yourself and family for the last five years?

Ans. By my labor, what I could do — my family helped me

Do you use intoxicants to any extent?

Ans. No I do not

How long have you been an actual resident of the State of Tennessee?

Ans. All my life 47 years

Have you an attorney to look after this application?

Ans. Yes

If so, give his name and address.

Ans. Sparks & Sparks
Murfreesboro Tenn

Witness my hand, this 10th day of July 1891.

L H his X mark Hathcock

WITNESSES:

J B Murfree Physician.

W M Green Witness.

Edmond his X mark Hassell Witness.

Witness J W Sparks Jr.

State of Tennessee, Rutherford County. } Personally appeared before me Frank White Clerk of the County Court of said county, the above named L H Hathcock the applicant, with whom I am personally acquainted, and having the application read and fully explained to him, as well as the statements and answers therein made, made oath that the said statements and answers are true.

Witness my hand at office this 10th day of July 1891.

Frank White Clerk.

State of Tennessee, Rutherford County. } Personally appeared before me Frank White Clerk of the County Court of said county, the above named J B Murfree one of the subscribing witnesses to the foregoing application, and who is a physician of good standing, and being duly sworn, says that he has carefully and thoroughly examined L H Hathcock the applicant, and finds him laboring under the following disabilities:

Loss of the use of the left leg caused by a Gunshot wound in the left hip joint causing fracture of the head of the thigh bone (femur). The bone was so much fractured that a good deal of it came away. There is now a stiffness of the hip joint with shortening of the limb. The left limb is (3) three inches shorter than the right. The injury is such as to disable him from any active manual labor as he has but imperfect use of it, and in my opinion the disability is permanent.

Witness my hand at office, this 1st day of August 1891.

Frank White Clerk.

(If possible the two witnesses as to Character should have served with the Applicant in the Army, and if so let them, or either, state it in their oath.)

State of Tennessee, Rutherford County. } Personally appeared before me Frank White Clerk of the County Court of said county, the above named W M Green and Edmond Hassell two of the subscribing witnesses to the foregoing application, with whom I am personally acquainted, and known to me to be citizens of veracity and standing in this community, and who make oath that they are personally acquainted with the foregoing applicant, and that the facts set forth and statements made in his application are correct and true, to the best of their knowledge and belief, and that they have no interest in this claim, and that said applicant's habits are good and free from dishonor. And they both further make oath to the following facts touching the applicant's service in the Confederate army.

Mr Green says he served in the same Co & Regiment with the applicant and knows that he made a good soldier. He was wounded as stated and that he is now badly crippled. Mr Hassell says he served in the army with applicant in the same Co & Reg. He made a good soldier and was badly wounded and is now badly crippled.

Witness my hand, at office, this 10th day of July 1891.

Frank White Clerk.

Figure 8-19. Continued.

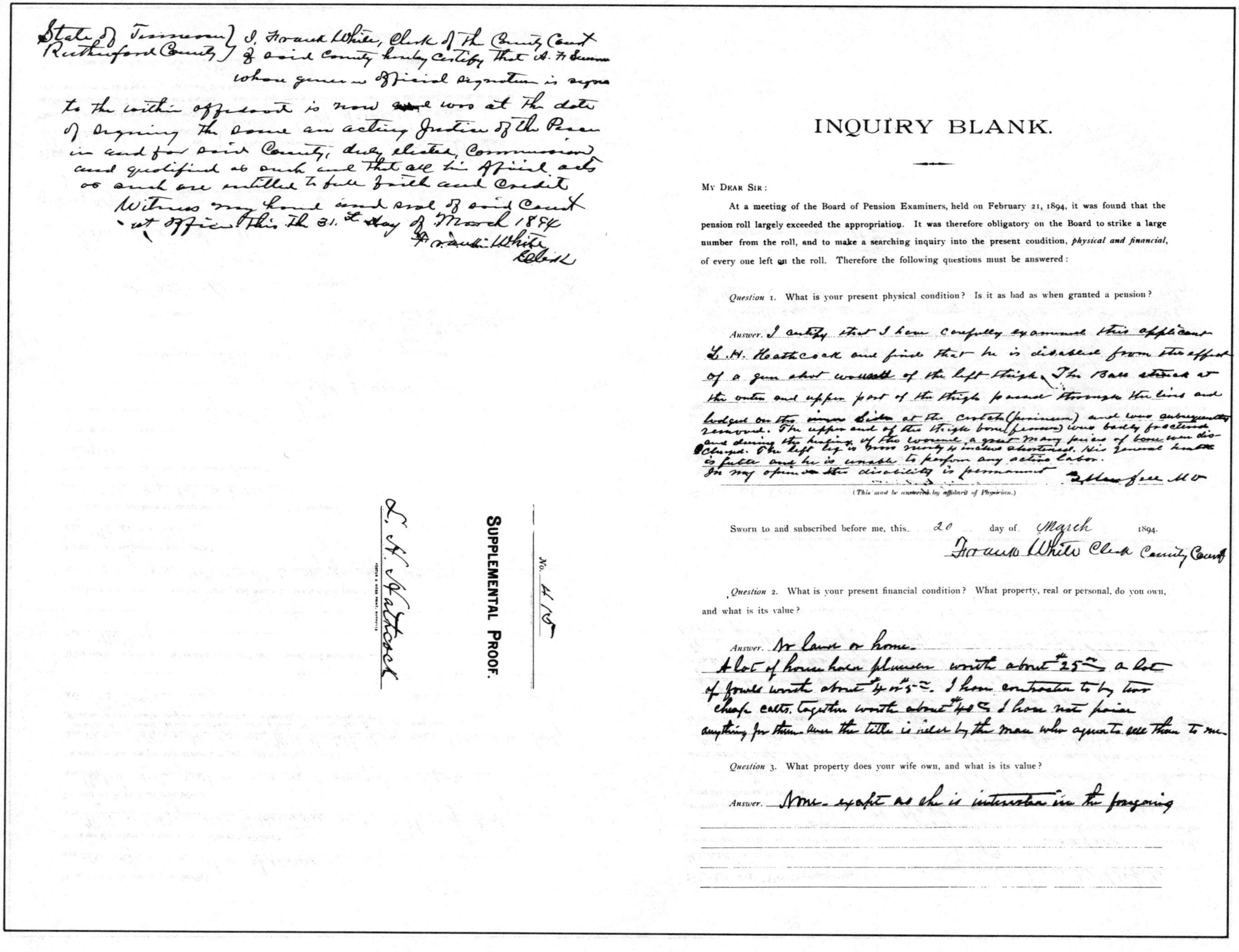

State of Tennessee }
Rutherford County } I, [illegible] White, Clerk of the County Court of said County hereby certify that A. H. [illegible] whose genuine official signature is signed to the within affidavit is now and was at the date of signing the same an acting Justice of the Peace in and for said County, duly elected, Commissioned and qualified as such and that all his official acts as such are entitled to full faith and credit.

Witness my hand and seal of said Court at office this the 31st day of March 1894

[illegible] White
Clerk

No. 415

SUPPLEMENTAL PROOF.

L. H. Hathcock

FOSTER & WEBB PRINT, NASHVILLE

INQUIRY BLANK.

MY DEAR SIR:

At a meeting of the Board of Pension Examiners, held on February 21, 1894, it was found that the pension roll largely exceeded the appropriation. It was therefore obligatory on the Board to strike a large number from the roll, and to make a searching inquiry into the present condition, *physical and financial*, of every one left on the roll. Therefore the following questions must be answered:

Question 1. What is your present physical condition? Is it as bad as when granted a pension?

Answer. I certify that I have carefully examined this applicant L. H. Hathcock and find that he is disabled from the effect of a gun shot wound of the left thigh. The Ball struck at the outer and upper part of the thigh passed through the limb and lodged on the inner side at the crotch (perineum) and was subsequently removed. The upper end of the thigh bone (femur) was badly fractured and during the healing of the wound a great many pieces of bone were discharged. The left leg is now nearly 4 inches shortened. His general health is feeble and he is unable to perform any active labor. In my opinion the disability is permanent. [illegible] M.D.

(This must be answered by affidavit of Physician.)

Sworn to and subscribed before me, this 20 day of March 1894.

[illegible] White Clerk County Court

Question 2. What is your present financial condition? What property, real or personal, do you own, and what is its value?

Answer. No land or home. A lot of household furniture worth about $25.00 a lot of fowls worth about $4 or $5.00. I have contracted to buy two cheap calves together worth about $40.00 I have not paid anything for them since the title is held by the man who agrees to sell them to me.

Question 3. What property does your wife own, and what is its value?

Answer. None except as she is interested in the foregoing

Question 4. What is the present size of your family?

Answer. We have [illegible] family

Question 5. How many children have you, and what are their ages and sex?

Answer. 2 daughters 18 & 19 years of age. the latter has been married, her husband is dead. she has two children both boys. one is 1½ years old, and the other is 3 years old and one son 15 years of age.

Question 6. Are not some of your children able to support you?

Answer. No

Question 7. What is your present occupation, and how much do you earn thereby?

Answer. Trying to make a living by working the land of other persons

Witness to mark W. R. Singleton

L. H. his X mark Hathcock

Sworn to and subscribed before me, this 20 day of March 1894.

Frank White Clerk County Court

We, D. R. Summers and Jonathan Oneal know the above answers to be literally true.

x D. R. Summers

x Jonathan Oneal

Sworn to and subscribed before me, this 27th day of March 1894.

A. T. Summers
Justice of the Peace

THESE questions must be answered and returned to me by the next meeting of the Board (May 21, 1894), or it will be taken for granted that you are not now in condition to draw a pension.

This action is taken by the Board on account of the meager appropriation allowed for pensions by the Legislature. The Board, at the last meeting of the Legislature, asked for an increased appropriation, but the Legislature refused to grant its request.

It is also obligatory on the Board that these questions should be answered, from time to time, by all men remaining on the pension roll. This is a positive requirement of the law. (See Section 5.)

Very respectfully,

JNO. P. HICKMAN, *Secretary.*

Figure 8-19. Continued.

Question 1. What is the present physical condition of the pensioner?

Answer Disabled for active manual labor on account of fracture of the neck of the left thigh bone produced by a gun shot wound received at the Battle of Stones River which shortens the left leg about four inches. His disability is permanent and is equal to the loss of the ~~[illegible]~~ of a limb

Signature J. B. Murfree

(This must be answered by affidavit of a physician, taken by an officer using a seal.)

Sworn to and subscribed before me, this 27th day of June 1903.

G H Wilkinson Clerk

For Rutherford County, Tenn.

Question 2. What is your present financial condition? What property, real and personal, do you own and what is its value?

Answer: It is light – have no Real Estate – 1 mare, but not paid for, 4 hogs household furniture value about $125.00

Question 3. What property does your wife own and what is its value?

Answer: nothing but poultry about $6.00 worth

(Questions 2 and 3 must be answered by affidavit of the pensioner before an officer using a seal.)

(In addition to the above the following certificate of the County Trustee must be filled out.)

I, J W Dejarnatt Trustee of Rutherford County, Tennessee, hereby certify that the property assessed on the tax books of this County to L H Hathcock a pensioner, and his wife Elvera Hathcock amount to $ 60 real estate and $ Nothing assessed to them on 70's Book personal.

J W Dejarnatt Trustee.

For Rutherford County, Tenn

Question 4. What is the present size of your family? How many children have you living with you? Give their sex and ages.

Answer: Five – 1 and 2 Grandchildren My Daughter is 25 My Grandchildren both boys 10 and 12 years old

Question 5. What is your present occupation and how much do you earn thereby?

Answer: I do a little farming, very little

Question 6. How did you get out of the army? When and where?

Answer: I was wounded in Battle of Murfreesboro, shot in the thigh near the hip joint, permanently disabled, not able to do any more service, was carried to my fathers house and remained there

Question 7. Did you take the oath of allegiance to the U. S. Government? If so, when, where and under what circumstances?

Answer: I never did - I remained at my fathers house in a permanently crippled condition during the remainder of the war

(If the pensioner was discharged or paroled let him file the papers if he has them. If they have been lost or destroyed let him make proof by affidavit of some officer or comrade who knows the fact.)

STATE OF TENNESSEE, } ss.
______ County.

Personally appeared before me, L. H. Hathcock a pensioner of the State of Tennessee, to me well known, who makes oath that the answers given to the questions asked him in the foregoing paper are true.

Witness W. W. McLemore

(Signature of Pensioner) L. H. his x mark Hatchcock

Sworn to and subscribed before me this 24" day of June 1903.

[Seal]

G. H. Wilkinson Clerk
For Rutherford County, Tenn.

TO TENNESSEE PENSIONERS.

Nashville, Tenn., May ______ 1903.

The Pension Laws of the State as amended by the Legislature of 1903 require the Special Examiner to "fully investigate the pensioners now on the roll; and in case a doubt exists as to the worthiness of a pensioner, or where charges are preferred by reputable persons, to visit the said pensioner, and fully investigate his condition, both physical and financial, and make a written report of his investigation to said board."

In order that the requirements of the law may be carried out, you will at once answer the following questions under oath before an officer using a seal, and mail to the Special Examiner in the enclosed envelope.

TENNESSEE BOARD OF PENSION EXAMINERS.

By FRANK A. MOSES,
Special Examiner.

Figure 8-20. Biographical Questionnaire of Civil War Veteran Samuel S. M. Blankenship, Lafayette Co., Tenn., 1821, Tennessee Historical Commission GS 975,591.

FEDERAL MAR 2 4 1922 Received

MANUSCRIPT DIVISION AC. NO. 449

STATE OF TENNESSEE
TENNESSEE HISTORICAL COMMITTEE
DEPARTMENT OF LIBRARIES, ARCHIVES AND HISTORY
JOHN TROTWOOD MOORE, DIRECTOR

NOTE.—Should this Questionnaire fall into the hands of one who is not a Veteran of the Civil War, or who did not live during those days, you will confer a favor on this Department by giving it to some Soldier who has not received a copy, or return to us.

The chief purpose of the following questions is to bring out facts that will be of service in writing a true history of the Old South. Such a history has not yet been written. By answering these questions you will make a valuable contribution to the history of your State.

In case the space following any question is not sufficient for your answer, you may write your answer on a separate piece of paper. But when this is done, *be sure* to put the number of the question on the paper on which the answer is written, and number the pages of the paper on which you write your answer.

Read all the questions before you answer any of them. After answering the questions here given, if you desire to make additiona statements, I would be glad for you to add just as much as you desire.

1. State your full name and present postoffice address Samuel S. M. Blankenship LaFayette Tennessee
2. State your age now age 80 3rd march 1921
3. In what State and county were you born? Tennessee, County Macon
4. Were you a Confederate or Federal soldier? Federal
5. Name of your Company? D. 9th Kentucky (B) Number of Regiment 9th Kentucky Infantry
6. What was the occupation of your father? Farmer
7. Give full name of your father. David Blankenship Born at Franklin Virginia in the County of Franklin State of Virginia He lived at Moved to Smith County Tennessee 1820.
Give also any particulars concerning him, as official position, war services, etc., books written by, etc. No war service. Books none.
8. Maiden name in full your mother. Judie Holland She was the daughter of John Holland (Full Name) and his wife Polly Holland (Full Name) Who lived at LaFayette Tenn.
9. Remarks on Ancestry. Give here any and all facts possible in reference to your parents, grandparents, great-grandparents, etc., not included in the foregoing, as were they lived, offices held, Revolutionary or other war service; what country the family came from to America; first settled, county and State; *always* giving *full* names (if possible), and *never* referring to an ancester simply as such without giving the name. It is desirable to include every fact possible, and to that end the full and exact record from old Bibles should be appended on seperate sheets of this size, thus preserving the facts from loss virginia. No office held. great uncle served in Revolutionary War. Came from Holland. Virginia. Bedford County.
10. If you owned land or other property at the opening of the war, state what kind of property you owned, and state the value of your property as near as you can No land or other property.
11. Did you or your parents own slaves? If so, how many? No slaves.
12. If your parents owned land, state about how many acres about 300 acres.
13. State as near as you can the value of all the property owned by your parents, including land, when the war opened Value of land about $300 other property about $750.
14. What kind of a house did your parents occupy? State whether it was a log house or frame house or built of other material, and state the number of rooms it had Log house. only three rooms
15. As a boy and young man, state what kind of work you did. If you worked on a farm, state to what extent you plowed, worked with a hoe and did other kinds of similar work. (Certain historians claim that white men would not do work of this sort before the war.) Worked on farm practically every day plowed and used hoe to great extent

45. Give the names of all the members of your Company you can remember. (If you know where the Roster is to had, please make special note of this.)

L. Pate Cox	Lafayette	Tennessee
Tom Dixon	Trousdale Co.	"
Albert Meador	Lafayette	"
(all of these	are living)	
9 same Regiment		
Capt. Reid	Scottsville	Kentucky
M. Reed		"
Gov. Whitney	Red Boiling Springs	Tennessee

46. Give here the NAME and POST OFFICE ADDRESS of living Veteerans of the Civil War, whether members of your Company or not; whether Tennesseans or from other States:

Name	Post Office	State
Pate Pinkerton	Scottsville	Kentucky
W. E. Durham	"	"
Pate Cox	Lafayette	Tennessee
Robert Deckerd	"	"
Wilson Bray	"	"
Wesley Snyder	"	"
Jesse Bertram	"	"
Will Dillard	"	"
Jim Meador	Westmorland	"
Logan White	Lafayette	"
Gilbert Wakefield	"	"
Will West	"	"
Jim Bill	"	"
Jim Pidigon	"	"
Mike Brandon	"	"
Mont Marsh	Red Boiling Springs	"

16. State clearly what kind of work your father did, and what the duties of your mother were. State all the kinds of work done in the house as well as you can remember—that is, cooking, spinning, weaving, etc. Father worked on farm all of life. Mother did work house chores, wove and spun all the cloth to make clothing for the children, husband, and herself.

17. Did your parents keep any servants? If so, how many? None

18. How was honest toil—as plowing, hauling and other sorts of honest work of this class—regarded in your community? Was such work considered respectable and honorable? Among most classes it was considered respectable and honorable for anyone to do.

19. Did the white men in your community generally engage in such work? yes

20. To what extent were there white men in your community leading lives of idleness and having others do their work for them? practically all did their own work. Very few had slaves

21. Did the men who owned slaves mingle freely with those who did not own slaves, or did slaveholders in any way show by their actions that they felt themselves better than respectable, honorable men who did not own slaves? Cant remember

22. At the churches, at the schools, at public gatherings in general, did slave-holders and non-slave-holders mingle on a footing of equality? Cant remember

23. Was there a friendly feeling between slave-holders and non-slave-holders in your community, or were they antagonistic to each other? So far as can remember they were alright to each [illegible]

24. In a political contest in which one candidate owned slaves and the other did not, did the fact that one candidate owned slaves help him any in winning the contest? Cant Remember

25. Were the opportunities good in your community for a poor young man, honest and industrious, to save up enough to buy a small farm or go in business for himself? opportunities were poor unless one had a good capital of which he had helped

26. Were poor, honest, industrious young men, who were ambitious to make something of themselves, encouraged or discouraged by slaveholders? Those that depended on daily labor for their support were discouraged because of less work to do and also for smaller [illegible]

27. What kind of school or schools did you attend? Country school

28. About how long did you go to school altogether? Lasted about three months each year, in all about 30 months

29. How far was it to the nearest school? about one mile. Roads leading to the school was rough.

30. What school or schools were in operation in your neighborhood? only one school could have handily been reached while boarding at home.

31. Was the school in your community private or public? Most public

32. About how many months in the year did it run? About three months

33. Did the boys and girls in your community attend school pretty regularly? yes

[T]eacher of the school you attended a man or a woman? All men teacher

5. In what year and month and at what place did you enlist in the service of the Confederacy or of the Federal Government? December 1, 1861 at Columbia Kentucky

36. After enlistment, where was your Company sent first? Glasgow Kentucky and and shortly to Nashville

37. How long after enlistment before your Company engaged in battle? 4 months

38. What was the first battle you engaged in? Battle of Shiloh engaged in this battle only one day.

39. State in your own way your experience in the War from this time on to its close. State where you went after the first battle—what you did, what other battles you engaged in, how long they lasted, what the results were; state how you lived in camp, how you were clothed, how you slept, what you had to eat, how you were exposed to cold, hunger and disease. If you were in hospital or in prison, state your experience here. Had experience which proved to be beneficial after leaving army. After battle went to Corinth Mississippi. Made preparation for battle but enemy left. Before any battle Murfreesboro [illegible] about two days, result good. Well taken care of in hospital

40. When and where were you discharged? Huntsville Alabama January 8 1865

41. Tell something of your trip home. From Huntsville we came to Nashville to Bowling Green Kentucky thence to Scottsville Kentucky and then home

42. What kind of work did you take up when you came back home? Working on farm with father.

43. Give a sketch of your life since the close of Civil War, stating what kind of business you have engaged in, where you have lived, your church relations, etc. If you have held any office or offices, state what it was. You may state here any other facts connected with your life and experience which has not been brought out by the questions. Working on farm as long as physical ability allowed me. Lived in Macon county Tennessee since I came from army. Was married to Katherine Jane White March 8 1865. 7 children were born six boys and one girl all of whom are living except one. Four of them have taught school in Macon County one after made a Medical Doctor and also he served in the Spanish American War 1898 and in the Worlds war as first Lieutenant but did not go overseas. Another Jr M. Blankenship studied law and afterwards went to Los Angeles California. Other four are farmers. Belong to Missionary Baptist Church

44. On a separate sheet give the names of some of the great men you have known or met in your time, and tell some of the circumstances of the meeting or incidents in their lives. Also add any further personal reminiscences. (Use all the space you want).

Virginia Soldiers of 1776 is rich in genealogical information:

William Brown, Midshipman.

Exec. Dept. July 23rd, 1835. The heirs of William Brown are allowed L. B. for his services as a Midshipman in the Va. State Navy, for three years, Littleton Tazewell, Gov.

Matthews Co. court. Aug. 13, 1835. On motion of John Borun, and by the oath of Matthias Gayle it was proved that Thomas Brown, William, Francis, Ralph, Ann, Mary and Judith Brown are the children of William Brown a Midshipman in the Rev. war. That all the children died intestate except Judith Brown and Mary (who married Robert Weston); that the said Mary and Robert Weston are both dead and that they left one child only, named, Judith Weston; that Judith Brown and Judith Weston are the only surviving heirs of Midshipman William Brown. Copy teste, Shepard G. Miller Clerk of court.

Note. Written at the bottom of this paper is a memorandum of names:—1. Th. Brown, 2, Wm. B., 3, Ralph B. 4, Frs Brown. Whether or not these are relatives I know not.

Abstract of the will of William Brown of Gloucester Co., Parish of Kingston. "To my loving wife, Judith Brown; all my children:—Thomas, William, Francis, Ralph, Ann, Mary and Judith". Signed, 20th Oct., 1791. Witnesses, Simon Laughlin, Ann Laughlin, Dorothy Buckner.

Matthews Co., 10th Dec., 1792 the will was proven. Teste, John Cary, Clerk. Copy teste, Shepard G. Miller.

Warrant 8228 for 2666-2/3 acres issued 19 Aug., 1835 to Judith Brown and Judith Weston, heirs of William Brown. Recorded, Book 3, page 95, Va. L. Off.

Louis A. Burgess, comp., *Virginia Soldiers of 1776* (Richmond: Richmond Press, Inc., 1927), p. 202.

The Roster and Record of Iowa Soldiers in the War of the Rebellion shows still another approach:

COMPANY "A"

Babcock, Charles W. (Veteran.) Age 22. Residence Clayton County, nativity New York. Re-enlisted Jan. 4, 1864. Re-mustered Feb. 2, 1864 Mustered out July 6, 1865, Louisville, Ky. Transferred from company A, Third Battalion.

Baker, James H. (Veteran.) Age 28. Residence Cedar Falls, nativity Pennsylvania. Re-enlisted Dec. 17, 1863. Re-mustered Dec. 23, 1863 Discharged July 1, 1865, Louisville, Ky. Transferred from company A Third Battalion.

Barrett, George W. (Veteran.) Age 19. Residence Boone County, nativity New York. Re-enlisted Jan. 4, 1864. Re-mustered Feb. 2, 1864 Mustered out July 12, 1865, Louisville, Ky. Transferred from company A, Third Battalion.

Billick, Joseph. (Veteran.) Age 22. Residence Columbus City, nativity Pennsylvania. Re-enlisted Jan. 4, 1864. Re-mustered Feb. 2, 1864 Mustered out July 12, 1865. Transferred from company A, Third Battalion.

State of Iowa, *Roster and Record of Iowa Soldiers in the War of the Rebellion*, vol. 1 (Des Moines: Emory H. English, State Printer, 1908), p. 441

State Military Records

Military records were also created and preserved by state and local jurisdictions. Their contents are much like those described above. They will be found scattered through state archives, historical societies and museums, military forts (both those still active and museums for those discontinued), and among the papers in the county clerk's office. The militia records, however, are often the first to be disposed of, since local militias no longer exist. These records can be located using state and local record inventories.

Private collections of military records are also scattered through record repositories. Check the National Union Catalog of Manuscripts Collections of the Library of Congress (NUCMC) and the National Historic Trust for Records Preservation, available in most research libraries of any size, to discover their locations.

Special projects and collections are more difficult to locate. Brigham Young University Library has a card Index to Graves of American Revolutionary Soldiers with some 60,000 entries based on the reports of the Daughters of the American Revolution. This index gives entrée to the DAR Patriot Index, Revolutionary War pension files, bounty-land warrants, census records, and numerous other sources.[3] Watch the pages of the *Genealogical Helper*, *Illinois State Genealogical Society Newsletter*, *History News*, and other periodicals which announce these special projects.

For example, Morristown National Historical Park, Morristown, New York, has an extensive collection of Revolutionary War materials including account books, letter books, and 17,500 original manuscripts. To learn more of their holdings, check the *Directory of Museums* listing for Morristown Park.

Notes

1. National Archives Trust Fund Board, *Guide to Genealogical Research in the National Archives* (Washington, D.C.: National Archives and Records Service, 1982), p. 85.

2. *The Office*, Dec. 1973, p. 30, as quoted in *Utah Genealogical Association Newsletter*, Oct. 1974, p. 6.

3. Preston J. Owens, "Index to Graves of American Revolutionary Soldiers," *Genealogical Journal* 5 (1976): 47-50.

Selected Bibliography of American Military Records

Hamersly, Thomas H. S. *Complete Regular Army Register of the United States for One Hundred Years, 1799-1879.* Washington, D.C.: T. H. S. Hamersly, 1880.

Kirkham, E. Kay. *Some of the Military Records of America Before 1900.* Salt Lake City, Utah : Deseret Book Co., 1964.

deKraft, E. *A List of All the Pensioners of the United States; The Sum Paid to Each.* Baltimore: Southern Book Co., 1959.

National Archives Trust Fund Board. *Genealogical Research in the National Archives.* Washington, D.C.: General Services Administration, 1982.

Pappas, George S. *U.S. Army Unit Histories: A Bibliography.* Carlisle Barracks, Penn.: U.S. Army Military History Research Collection, 1971.

Smith, Paul Tincher. "Militia of the United States from 1846-1860." *Indiana Magazine of History* 15 (1919): 20-47.

U.S. Bureau of Census. *Eleventh Census of the United States, 1890.* Washington, D.C.: The National Archives, 1945.

U.S. Bureau of Pensions. *Annual Report of the Commissioner of Pensions for the Year Ending June 30, 1881.* Washington, D.C.: Government Printing Office, 1881.

____________. *List of Pensioners on the Roll January 1, 1883.* 5 vols. Baltimore: Genealogical Publishing Co., 1970.

____________. *Report of the Commissioner of Pensions for the Year Ending June 30, 1892.* Washington, D.C.: Government Printing Office, 1892.

U.S. Congress, House Committee on Military Affairs. *Mustering-Out Pay.* Washington, D.C.: Government Printing Office, 1943.

U.S. Department of the Interior. *Report of the Secretary of the Interior, With a Statement of Rejected and Suspended Applications for Pension.* 1852; reprint ed., Baltimore: Genealogical Publishing Co., 1969.

U.S. National Archives. *Registers of Enlistments in the United States Army, 1789-1877.* Washington, D.C.: National Archives Microfilm Publications, 1963.

U.S. Veterans Administration. *Pension File, Service Records, Land Warrants, 1775-1913.* Washington, D.C.: National Archives, 1970.

U.S. War Department. *Letter from the Secretary of War Transmitting a Report of the Names, Rank, and Line of Every Person Placed on the Pension List, in Pursuance of the Act of January 20, 1820.* Baltimore: Southern Book Co., 1959.

____________. *The Pension Roll of 1835.* 4 vols. Baltimore: Genealogical Publishing Co., 1968.

____________. *A Transcript of the Pension List of the United States for 1813.* Baltimore: Southern Book Co., 1959.

Colonial Wars

Andrews, Frank DeWitte, comp. *Connecticut Soldiers in the French and Indian War*. Vineland, N.J.: By the compiler, 1923.

Bodge, George M. *Soldiers in King Philip's War, Being a Critical Account of That War, with a Concise History of the Indian Wars of New England from 1620-1677, Official Lists of the Soldiers of Massachusetts Colony Serving in Philip's War...* 3rd ed. 1906; reprint ed., Baltimore: Genealogical Publishing Co., 1967.

Buckingham, Thomas. *Roll and Journal of Connecticut Service in Queen Anne's War, 1710-1711*. New Haven: Acorn Club of Connecticut, 1916.

Chapin, Howard Miller. *Rhode Island in the Colonial Wars. A List of Rhode Island Soldiers and Sailors in King George's War, 1740-1748*. Providence: Rhode Island Historical Society, 1920.

____________. *Rhode Island in the Colonial Wars. A List of Rhode Island Soldiers and Sailors in the Old French and Indian Wars, 1755-1762*. Providence: Rhode Island Historical Society, 1918.

____________. *Rhode Island Privateers in King George's War, 1739-1748*. Providence: Rhode Island Historical Society, 1926.

Connecticut Historical Society. *Rolls of Connecticut Men in the French and Indian War, 1755-1762*. 2 vols. Hartford: By the society, 1903-05.

Crozier, William Armstrong. *Virginia Colonial Militia, 1651-1776*. Baltimore: Southern Book Co., 1954.

Kentucky Land Office. *A Calendar of the Warrants for Land in Kentucky, Granted for Service in the French and Indian War*. Baltimore: Genealogical Publishing Co., 1967.

Lewis, Virgil A. *Soldiery of West Virginia in the French and Indian War; Lord Dunmore's War; The Revolution; The Later Indian Wars; The Whiskey Insurrection; The Second War with England; The War with Mexico, and Addenda Relating to West Virginians in the Civil War*. Baltimore: Genealogical Publishing Co., 1967.

MacLean, John P. *A Historical Account of the Settlements of Scotch Highlanders in America Prior to the Peace of 1783*. Baltimore: Genealogical Publishing Co., 1968.

New York Historical Society. *Muster Rolls of New York Provincial Troops, 1755-1764*. New York: By the society, 1892.

Nolan, James Bennett. *Officers and Soldiers in the Service of the Province of Pennsylvania, 1744-1764*. Philadelphia: The University of Pennsylvania Press, 1936.

Rhode Island. Society of Colonial Wars: *Nine Muster Rolls of Rhode Island Troops Enlisted During the Old French War*. Providence: By the society, 1915.

Robinson, George Frederick, and Albert Harrison Hall. *Watertown Soldiers in the Colonial Wars and The American Revolution*. Watertown, Mass.: Historical Society of Watertown, 1939.

Shepard, James. *Connecticut Soldiers in the Pequot War of 1837*. Meriden, Conn.: Journal Publishing Co., 1913.

Society of Colonial Wars, Illinois. *List of Officers and Members Together with a Record of the Service Performed by Their Ancestors in the Wars of the Colonies*. Chicago: Society of Colonial Wars, 1900.

Taylor, Philip F. *A Calendar of the Warrants for Land in Kentucky, Granted for Service in the French and Indian War, Excerpted from the Year Book of the Society of Colonial Wars of Kentucky*. 1917; reprint ed., Baltimore: Genealogical Publishing Co., 1967.

Revolutionary War

Ainsworth, Mary Bouvier. "Recently Discovered Records Relating to Revolutionary War Veterans who Applied for Pensions Under the Act of 1792." *National Genealogical Society Quarterly* 46 (March/June 1958).

Allen, Penelope Johnson. *Tennessee Soldiers in the Revolution*. Bristol, Tenn.: King Printing Company, 1935.

Armstrong, Zella. *Some Tennessee Heroes of the Revolution*. 5 vols. Chattanooga: Lookout Publishing Company, 1935.

Bailey, J. D. *Some Negroes of the American Revolution*.

Bell, Annie W. B. *Revolutionary War Soldiers who Settled and Lived in Kentucky Counties*. (Salt Lake City: Genealogical Society of Utah, 1935.

Blair, Anna. "A List of Revolutionary Soldiers Buried in North Carolina." *Historical Collections of the Georgia Chapters, Daughters of the American Revolution*, 1926, pp. 353-64.

Bowman, J. E. *Obituary Notices of Revolutionary Soldiers from Connecticut, Maine, Pennsylvania, Rhode Island and some Central, Western and Southern States*.

Burgess, Louis Alexander. *Virginia Soldiers of 1776*. 3 vols. Richmond: Richmond Press, 1927-29.

Chamberlain, George Walter. *Soldiers of the American Revolution of Levanon, Maine*. Weymouth, Mass.: Weymouth and Braintree Publishing Co., 1897.

Chandler, Ora. *Copies of Pension Papers of Revolutionary, 1812, and Indian War Soldiers Who Settled in Henderson County, Kentucky*. Corydan, Ky.: n. pub., n.d.

Clark, H. A. "A Connecticut Revolutionary Roll," *New England Historical and Genealogical Register* 60 (Oct. 1906): 331.

Clark, H. C. "Report on Publication of Revolutionary Military Records." *Annual Report, American Historical Association, 1915-16*. pp. 193-99.

Coggins, Jack. *Ships and Seamen of the American Revolution; Crews, Weapons, Gear, Naval Tactics and Actions of the War for Independence*. Harrisburg: Stackpole Books, 1969.

Connecticut Historical Society. *Lists and Returns of Connecticut Men in the Revolution 1775-1783*. Connecticut Historical Society Collections, vol. 12. Hartford: By the society, 1909.

____________. *Rolls and Lists of Connecticut Men in the Revolution, 1775-1782*. Connecticut Historical Society Collections, vol. 8. Hartford: By the society, 1901.

Crockett, Walter Hill. *Revolutionary Soldiers Buried in Vermont. 1903-07*; reprint ed., Baltimore: Genealogical Publishing Company, 1959.

Dandridge, Danske. *American Prisoners of the Revolution*. Baltimore: Genealogical Publishing Company, 1967.

Daughters of the American Revolution. "Graves of Revolutionary Soldiers." *National Historical Magazine*, June 1940, pp. 36-37.

Daughters of the American Revolution, North Carolina. *Roster of Soldiers from North Carolina in the American Revolution*. 1932; reprint ed., Baltimore: Genealogical Publishing Co., 1967.

DeMarce, Virginia Easley. *Canadian Participants in the American Revolution—An Index*. Sparta, Wis.: Lost in Canada, 1980. Includes a forty-five page descriptive bibliography of little-known sources documenting Revolutionary War service.

Deutrich, Mabel E. *Preliminary Inventory of the War Department Collection of Revolutionary War Records*. Record Group 93. Washington, D.C.: National Archives and Records Service, 1970.

Draper, Belle (Merrill). *Honor Roll of Massachusetts Patriots Heretofore Unknown, Being a List of Men and Women who Loaned Money to the Federal Government During the Years 1777-1779*. Boston: n. pub., 1899.

Eckenrode, Hamilton J. *List of Revolutionary Soldiers of Virginia*. Special Report of Department of Archives and History, 1911. Richmond: Virginia State Library, 1912.

Eckling, Max von. *The German Allied Troops in the North American War of Independence, 1776-1783*. Transcribed and abridged from German by J.G. Rosengarten. 1893; reprint ed., Baltimore: Genealogical Publishing Co., 1969.

Egle, William Henry. *Old Rights, Property Rights, Virginia Entries and Soldiers Entitled to Donation Lands*. Harrisburg, Va.: C. M. Busch, State Printer, 1896.

Ervin, Sara Sullivan. *South Carolinians in the Revolution*. 1949; reprint ed., Baltimore: Genealogical Publishing Company, 1965.

Flagg, Charles Alcott. *An Alphabetical Index of Revolutionary Pensioners Living in Maine*. 1920; reprint ed., Baltimore: Genealogical Publishing Company, 1967.

The Genealogical Society of the Church of Jesus Christ of Latter-day Saints. *A General Index to a Census of Pensioners for Revolutionary or Military Service, 1840*. Baltimore: Genealogical Publishing Company, 1965.

Georgia Department of Archives and History. *Georgia Roster of the Revolution*. Atlanta: Index Printing Company, 1920.

Giller, Sadye. *Corrections to the Index of Revolutionary War Pension Applications*. Washington, D.C.: By the author, 1965.

Gilmer, Georgia, and Elmer Parker. *American Revolution Roster of Fort Sullivan, 1776-1780*. Moultrie, S.C.: Fort Sullivan Chapter, D.A.R., 1980. Available from Georgia M. Gilmer, 409 Church St., Mt. Pleasant, SC 29464.

Gleason, William, and David Kinley. "Federal Military Pensions in the United States," *Journal of Genealogy* 4 (1979): issues 6-12.

Godfrey, Carlos E. *The Commander-In-Chiefs Guard: Revolutionary War.* Baltimore: Genealogical Publishing Company, 1972.

Goodrich, John E. *Rolls of the Soldiers in the Revolutionary War, 1775-1783.* Rutland, Vt., 1904.

Gould, Edward Kalloch. *Revolutionary Pensioners of Knox County, Maine.* Rockland, Maine: The Courier-Gazette, 1935.

Gwathmey, John H. *Historical Register of Virginians in the Revolution; Soldiers, Sailors, Marines, 1775-1783.* Richmond: Dietz Press, 1938.

Hammond, Isaac Weare. *Rolls of the Soldiers of the Revolutionary War.* 4 vols. Concord: Parsons B. Cogswell, State Printer, 1885-89.

Heddon, J. S. *Connecticut Soldiers of 1775-1783 Buried in New Haven, Connecticut.* New Haven, Conn.: n. pub., 1934.

Historical Records Survey. *Index of Official Register of the Men of New Jersey in the Revolutionary War.* Newark, N.J.: Works Progress Administration, 1941.

House, Charles J. *Names of Soldiers of the American Revolution Who Applied for State Bounty Under Resolves of March 17, 1835; March 24, 1836; and March 20, 1836, as Appears of Record in the Land Office.* Baltimore: Genealogical Publishing Company, 1967.

Houston, Martha L. *Six Hundred Revolutionary Soldiers and Widows of Revolutionary Soldiers Living in Georgia, 1827-1828.* (Athens, Ga.: 1965. Available from Heritage Press, Danielsville, Georgia.

Houts, Alice K. *Revolutionary Soldiers Buried in Missouri.* Kansas City: By the author, 1966.

Hoyt, Max Ellsworth, et al. *Index of Revolutionary War Pension Applications.* Washington, D.C.: National Genealogical Society, 1966.

Jones, Chester. *New Jersey Revolutionary War Veterans.* New Brunswick, N.J. Filmed by the Genealogical Society of Utah, 1971.

Jordan, John W. "Military Hospital at Bethlehem and Lititz During the Revolution." *Pennsylvania Magazine of History and Biography* 20 (1896): 137-57.

Kaminkow, Marion J., and Jack Kaminkow. *Mariners of the American Revolution.* Baltimore: Magna Carta Book Co., 1967.

Knight, Lucian L. *Georgia's Roster of the Revolution.* Baltimore: Genealogical Publishing Company, 1967.

____________. *List of American Seamen with Name and Vital Information About Each of Providence District, Pursuant to the Act for and Protection of American Seamen, Found at the U.S. Customs House Providence, Rhode Island, 1829 Through 1857.*

____________. *List of Hessian Prisoners, War of the Revolution.*

Maryland Historical Society. *Muster Rolls and Other Records of Service of Troops in the American Revolution, 1775-1783.* Baltimore: Genealogical Publishing Co., 1972.

Massachusetts Secretary of the Commonwealth. *Massachusetts Soldiers and Sailors of the American Revolutionary War.* 17 vols. Boston: Wright and Potter Printing Company, State Publishing Co., 1972.

Mather, Frederic Gregory. *The Refugees of 1776 from Long Island to Connecticut.* Baltimore: Genealogical Publishing Co., 1972.

McAllister, Joseph T. *Virginia Militia in the Revolutionary War.* Hot Springs, Va.: McCallister Publishing Co., c1913.

McCall, Ettie S. *Roster of Revolutionary Soldiers in Georgia and Other States.* 3 vols. Vol. 1, 1941; reprint ed., Baltimore: Genealogical Publishing Co., 1968-69.

McGhee, Lucy K. *Pension Abstracts of Maryland Soldiers of the Revolution, War of 1812, and Indian Wars Who Settled in Kentucky.* Washington, D.C., n.d.

Mell, Annie R. W. *Revolutionary Soldiers Buried in Alabama.* Montgomery, 1904.

____________. *New York Pension Roll (Revolutionary War), 1815-1840.*

Muster and Pay Rolls of the War of the Revolution, 1775-1783. Collections of the New York Historical Society. 2 vols. New York: By the society, 1914-15.

New York Secretary of State. *The Balloting Book, and Other Documents Relating to the Military Bounty Lands in the State of New York.* Albany, N.Y.: Packard and Benthuysen, 1825.

North Carolina State Archives. *Register of Continental Line from North Carolina.* Atlanta: Georgia Society, Daughters of the American Revolution, John T. Hancock, 1941.

O'Byrne, Mrs. Estella. *Roster of Soldiers and Patriots of the American Revolution Buried in Indiana.* 2 vols. Brockville, Ind.: Indiana DAR, 1938, 1966.

Ohio Adjutant-General's Office. *Grave Registration of Soldiers Buried in Ohio.* Columbus, Ohio: Filmed by Genealogical Society of Utah, 1958.

Owen, Thomas M. *Revolutionary Soldiers in Alabama.* Alabama State Archives Bulletin 5. 1911; Reprint ed., Baltimore: Genealogical Publishing Co., 1967.

Peterson, Clarence S. *Known Military Dead During the American Revolutionary War, 1775-1782.* 1959; reprint ed., Baltimore: Genealogical Publishing Company, 1967.

Quisenberry, Anderson C. *Revolutionary Soldiers in Kentucky.* Excerpted from the *Year Book, Kentucky Society, Sons of the American Revolution.* 1896; reprint ed., Baltimore: Genealogical Publishing Co., 1959.

Ready, Anne W. *West Virginia Revolutionary Ancestors Whose Services Were Non-Military and Whose Names, Therefore, Do Not Appear in Revolutionary Indexes of Soldiers and Sailors.* 1930; reprint ed., Baltimore: Genealogical Publishing Co., 1963.

Rosegarten, Joseph George. *American History from German Archives with Reference to the German Soldiers in the Revolution and Franklin's Visit to Germany.* Lancaster, Pa.: The Pennsylvania-German Society, 1904.

Schweitzer, George K. *Revolutionary War Genealogy.* Available from the author, 7914 Glenson, Knoxville, TN 37919.

South Carolina Treasury. *Stub Entries of Indents Issued in Payment of Claims Against South Carolina Growing Out of the Revolution.* 12 vols. Columbia, S.C.: Department of Archives and History, 1910-57.

Stryker, William S. *Official Register of the Officers and Men of New Jersey in the Revolutionary War.* 1872; reprint ed., Baltimore: Genealogical Publishing Co., 1967.

Tate, Mrs. Percy L. *Roster and Ancestral Roll: Maine Daughters of the American Revolution and the List of Maine Soldiers at Valley Forge, 1777-1778.* N.p.: Daughters of the American Revolution, 1948.

U.S. Bureau of Census. *A Census of Pensioners for Revolutionary or Military Services: With Their Names, Ages, and Places of Residence Taken in 1840.* 1841; reprint ed., Baltimore: Genealogical Publishing Co., 1967.

U.S. Bureau of Pensions. Pension Records of the Revolutionary Soldiers from Connecticut. Washington, D.C.: Government Printing Office, 1919.

U.S. House of Representatives. *Digested Summary and Alphabetical List of Private Claims Which have been Presented to the House of Representatives from the First to the 31st Congress, Exhibiting the Action of Congress on Each Claim.* 3 vols. Reprint ed., Baltimore: Genealogical Publishing Co., 1970.

U. S. Congress, Senate. *List of the Names of Such Officers and Soldiers of the Revolutionary Army as Have Acquired a Right to Lands from the United States and Who Have Not Yet Applied Therefor.* Washington, D.C.: Duff Publishers, 1828.

U.S. General Land Office. *Registers of Revolutionary War Land Warrants, Act of 1788; Military District of Ohio. 1789-1805.*

U.S. Veterans Administration. *Selected Records from Revolutionary War Pension and Bounty Land Warrant Application Files.* Washington, D.C.: National Archives Microfilm Publications, 1969.

U.S. War Department. *Claims Against the U.S. Government for Services of the Militia of Georgia, in the Years 1793 and 1794.*

Virginia Department of Archives and History. *List of the Revolutionary Soldiers of Virginia.* Richmond: Virginia State Library, 1913.

Waters, Margaret R. *Revolutionary Soldiers Buried in Indiana. Three Hundred Names Not Listed in the Roster by Mrs. O'Byrne.* 2 vols. 1949, 1954; reprinted in 1 vol. Baltimore: Genealogical Publishing Co., 1970.

Welch, Alice T. *Family Records, Mississippi Revolutionary Soldiers, Mississippi Daughters of the American Revolution.* 1956; reprint ed., Baltimore: Genealogical Publishing Co., 1969.

Whiteley, William Gustavus. *The Revolutionary Soldiers of Delaware.* Wilmington, 1896.

Wilson, Samuel M. *Catalogue of Revolutionary Soldiers and Sailors of the Commonwealth of Virginia for Military Service in the War for Independence.* 1913; reprint ed., Baltimore: Genealogical Publishing Co., 1953.

War of 1812, Indian Wars, and Mexican War

Barton, Henry W. *Texas Volunteers in the Mexican War.* Wichita Falls, Tex.: Texian Press, 1970.

Carr, Deborah Edith Walldridge. *Index to Certified Copy List of American Prisoners of War, 1812-15.* N.p.: United States Daughters of 1812, 1924.

Clark, Byron N. *A List of Pensioners of the War of 1812, Vermont Claimants*. Baltimore: Genealogical Publishing Co., 1969.

Connecticut General Assembly. *Record of Service of Connecticut Men in the Revolution, The War of 1812, and The Mexican War 1889.*

Graf, LeRoy P., et al. "The Pension Office to Congressman Andrew Johnson: A List, 1843-1853," *East Tennessee Historical Society Publications* 38 (1966): 97-108.

Indiana Adjutant-General's Office. *Indiana in the Mexican War*. Indianapolis: W. B. Burford, 1908.

Kentucky Adjutant-General's Office. *Report of the Adjutant General of Kentucky Soldiers of the War of 1812*. Frankfort, 1891.

Larson, Sarah. "The War of 1812 Papers: State Department Records for Genealogy and Local History," *Prologue*, Summer 1981, pp. 115-26.

Linn, John B., and William H. Egle. *Muster Rolls of the Pennsylvania Volunteers in the War of 1812-1814*. Baltimore: Genealogical Publishing Co., 1967.

Massachusetts Adjutant-General's Office. *Records of Massachusetts Volunteers Militia Called out by the Governor of Massachusetts to Suppress a Threatened Invasion During the War of 1812-1814*. Boston: By Brigadier General Gardner W. Pearson, the Adjutant General of Massachusetts, 1913.

Miller, Alice Turner. *Soldiers of the War of 1812 Who Died in Michigan*. Ithaca, Mich.: By the author, 1962.

Nebraska Secretary of State. *Roster of Soldiers, Sailors and Marines of the War of 1812, The Mexican War, and The War of the Rebellion Residing in Nebraska, June 1, 1891*. Lincoln: State Journal Co., 1892.

New Jersey Adjutant General's Office. *New Jersey in the War of 1812, Books 1-52* Trenton: Filmed by the Genealogical Society of Utah, 1969.

North Carolina Adjutant General's Office. *Muster Rolls of the Soldiers of the War of 1812 Detached from the Militia of North Carolina in 1812 and 1814*. Winston-Salem, N.C.: Barber Publishing Co., 1969.

Oberly, James W. "Military Bounty Land Warrants of the Mexican War." *Prologue*, Spring 1982, pp. 25-34.

Ohio Adjutant General's Office. *Roster of Ohio Soldiers in the War of 1812*. Baltimore: Genealogical Publishing Co., 1968.

Rowland, Mrs. Dunbar. *Mississippi Territory in the War of 1812*. Baltimore: Genealogical Publishing Co., 1968.

Sapio, Victor A. *Pennsylvania and The War of 1812*. Lexington: University of Kentucky Press, 1970.

U.S. Adjutant General's Office. *Muster Pay and Receipt Rolls of Indiana Territory Volunteers or Militia of the Period of The War of 1812*. 4 vols. Washington, D.C.: Adjutant General, n.d.

U.S. National Archives. *Compiled Service Records of Volunteer Soldiers Who Served During the Mexican War in Mormon Organizations*. Washington, D.C.: National Archives Microfilm Publications, 1961.

___________. *Index to War of 1812 Pension Application Files*. Washington, D.C.: National Archives Microfilm Publications, 1961.

___________. *Mexican War Service Records, 1845-1877*. Washington, D.C.: National Archives Microfilm Publications, 1960.

U.S. Veterans Administration. *Mexican War Index to Pension Files 1887-1926*. Washington, D.C.: National Archives, 1967.

Vermont Adjutant General's Office. *Roster of Soldiers in the War of 1812-1814*. Montpelier: Herbert T. Johnson, the Adjutant General, 1933.

Wilder, Minnie S. *Kentucky Soldiers of The War of 1812*. Baltimore: Genealogical Publishing Co., 1969.

Civil War

Army Department of Northern Virginia. *The Appomattox Roster*. New York: Antiquarian Press, 1962.

Britzell, Edwin W. *Point Lookout Prison Camp for Confederates*. Available from Edwin W. Britzell, Box 107, Abell, MD 20606.

California Adjutant General's Office. *Records of California Men in The War of the Rebellion, 1861 to 1867*. Sacramento: State Office, 1890.

Candler, Allen D. *The Confederate Records of the State of Georgia*. Atlanta: C. P. Byrd, State Printer, 1909-11.

Cooling, B. Franklin. *Bibliography of the Era of the Civil War, 1820-1876*. Carlisle Barracks, Penn.: U.S. Army Military History Research Collection, 1974.

Georgia Department of Archives and History. *Confederate Pension Rolls*. Atlanta: Filmed by the State of Georgia, 1963.

Groene, Bertram Hawthorne. *Tracing Your Civil War Ancestors*. Rev. ed., Winston-Salem, N.C.: John F. Blair Publisher, 1980.

Guide to the Archives of the Government of the Confederate States of America. Washington, D.C.: National Archives and Records Service, 1968.

Guide to Federal Archives Relating to the Civil War. Washington, D.C.: National Archives and Records Service, 1962.

Henderson, Lillian. *Roster of the Confederate Soldiers of Georgia, 1861-1865*. Haperville, Ga.: Longings and Porter, 1960-64.

Illinois Adjutant General's Office. *Report of the Adjutant General of the State of Illinois, 1861-1866*. 9 vols. Springfield, Ill.: Phillips Brothers, 1900-02.

Iowa Adjutant General's Office. *Roster and Record of Iowa Soldiers in the War of the Rebellion*. 6 vols. Des Moines: E. H. English, State Printer, 1908-11.

Kansas Adjutant General's Office. *Report of the Adjutant General, C. K. Holliday, December 31, 1864*. Leavenworth: By the Adjutant General, 1865.

___________. *Report of the Adjutant General, T. J. Anderson, of the State of Kansas in 1861-1865*. 2 vols. Topeka: By the Adjutant General, 1867-70.

Katz, Irving I. *The Jewish Soldier from Michigan in the Civil War*. Columbus: Ohio State University Press, 1961.

Langley, Elizabeth B. *Taney County, Missouri Soldiers Who Fought in the Civil War Including Soldiers of Southwest Missouri and Northwest Arkansas; also the Cherokees under Stand Watie*. Billings, Mo.: By the author, 1963.

Libby Prison General Hospital. *Morning Report of Sick and Wounded in the Libby Prison General Hospital at Richmond, Virginia, Monday, May 15, 1865*. Filmed by the Genealogical Society of Utah, 1968.

Manarin, Louis H. *North Carolina Troops, 1861-1865, A Roster*. Raleigh: North Carolina Department of Archives and History, 1966.

Maryland General Assembly. *History and Roster of Maryland Volunteers, War of 1861-1865*. 2 vols. Baltimore: N.p., 1898-99.

Maryland Hall of Records Commission. *Index to the Maryland Line in the Confederate Army, 1861-1865*. Publication no. 3. Annapolis: By the Adjutant General.

Massachusetts Adjutant General's Office. *Record of Massachusetts Volunteers, 1861-1865*. 2 vols. Boston: The Adjutant General's Office, 1868-70.

Massachusetts Bureau of Labor Statistics. *A List of Soldiers, Sailors, and Marines of the War of the Rebellion in the Commonwealth of Massachusetts on May 1, 1905*. Boston.

Mills, Gary B. *Civil War Claims in the South: An Index of Civil War Damage Claims Filed Before the Southern Claims Commission, 1871-1880.*

Missouri Adjutant General's Office (Union). *Alphabetical Register of Officers of Missouri Volunteer and Missouri State Militia Accompanying Adjutant General's Report for 1865*. Jefferson City, Mo., 1865.

Munden, Kenneth White. *Guide to Federal Archives Relating to the Civil War*. Washington: National Archives and Record Service, 1962.

National Society of Andersonville. *Atwater Report: List of Prisoners Who Died in 1864-65 at Andersonville Prison*. Andersonville, Ga.: For the society, 1981.

Nebraska Adjutant General's Office. *Roster of Nebraska Volunteers from 1861-1869*, Hastings: Wigton and Evans, 1888.

New Hampshire Adjutant General's Office. *Revised Register of the Soldiers and Sailors of New Hampshire in the Rebellion, 1861-1866*. Concord: I.C. Evans, Public Printer, 1895.

Nix, Bennie Edgar. *Compiled List of Confederate Soldiers of Shelby County, Texas*. Center, Tex.: J. B. Sanders, c1965.

North Carolina General Assembly. *Roster of North Carolina Troops in the War Between the States*. 4 vols. Raleigh: J. W. Moore, 1882.

Ohio Roster Commission. *Official Roster of the Soldiers of the State of Ohio in the War of the Rebellion, 1861-1866*. 12 vols. Akron, 1886-95.

Pompey, Sherman Lee. *Civil War Veteran Burials*. 2 vols. Independence, Calif.: Historical and Genealogical Publishing Co., 1965.

___________. *Civil War Veteran's Burials from California, Nevada, Oregon, and Washington Regiments Buried in Colorado*. Independence, Calif.: Historical and Genealogical Publishing Co., 1965.

___________. *Confederate Soldiers Buried in Colorado*. Independence, Calif.: Historical and Genealogical Publishing Co., 1965.

____________. *Interment of Union Soldiers in United States Territories During the Civil War.* Independence, Calif.: Historical and Genealogical Publishing Co., c. 1965.

____________. *Military Records; Alabama, Arizona, Arkansas, Indians of North America, Maryland, Missouri, Texas, Georgia, Mississippi, Tennessee.* Independence, Calif.: Historical and Genealogical Publishing Co., 1965.

____________. *Muster Lists of the American Rifles of Maryland, Baltimore Artillery, Dias Maryland Artillery, Maryland Guerilla Zouaves, and Captain Walter's Company.* Bakersfield, Calif.: Historical and Genealogical Publishing Co., c1965.

____________. *Muster Lists of the Arkansas Confederate Troops.* 2 vols. Independence, Calif.: Historical and Genealogical Publishing Co., c1965.

____________. *Muster Lists of the Cherokee Confederate Indians.* Independence, Calif.: Historical and Genealogical Publishing Co., 1965.

____________. *Muster Lists of the Creek and Other Confederate Indians.* Independence, Calif.: Historical and Genealogical Publishing Co., 1966.

____________. *Muster Lists of the Missouri Confederates.* 9 vols. Independence, Calif.: Historical and Genealogical Publishing Co., c1965.

____________. *Muster Lists of the Texas Confederate Troops.* 8 vols. Independence, Calif.: Historical and Genealogical Publishing Co., c1966.

Rhode Island General Assembly. *Official Register of Rhode Island Officers and Soldiers Who Served in the United States Army and Navy from 1861 to 1866.*

Robertson, James I., Jr. *The Civil War.* Washington, D.C.: U.S. Civil War Centennial Commission, 1963.

Schweitzer, George K. *Civil War Genealogy.* Available at 7914 Gleason, C-1136, Knoxville, TN 37919.

Sluby, Paul E., Sr. *Civil War Cemeteries of the District of Columbia Metropolitan Area.* Washington, D.C.: Columbia Harmony Society, n.d. Includes listings of interments.

Stillwell, Leander. *The Story of a Common Soldier of Army Life in the Civil War, 1861-1865.* Erie, Kan.: Franklin Hudson Publishing Co., 1920.

U.S. Adjutant General's Office. *Compiled Service Records of Volunteer Union Soldiers who Served in Organizations from the Territory of Utah, 1862.* Lot Smith's Company, Utah Cavalry.

____________. *Official Army Register of the Volunteer Force of the United States Army for the Years 1861, 1864, 1865.* 8 vols. Washington, D.C.: U.S. Adjutant General's Office 1865-1867.

U.S. National Archives. *Consolidated Index to Compiled Service Records of Confederate Soldiers.* Washington, D.C.: National Archives Microfilm Publications, 1957.

U.S. Record and Pension Office. *Compiled Service Records of Confederate General and Staff Officers and Nonregimental Enlisted Men.* Washington, D.C.: National Archives Microfilm Publications, 1962.

____________. *Compiled Service Records of Confederate Soldiers Who Served in Organizations from the State of Arkansas.* Washington, D.C.: National Archives Microfilm Publications, 1962.

____________. *Index to Compiled Service Records of Confederate Soldiers Who Served in Organizations from the State of Florida.* Washington, D.C.: National Archives Microfilm Publications, 1962.

____________. *Index to Compiled Service Records of Confederate Soldiers Who Served in Organizations from the State of Florida.* Washington, D.C.: National Archives Microfilm Publications, 1959.

U. S. Veterans Administration. *General Pension Index File, 1861-1934.* Washington, D.C.: Veterans Administration Publications Service, 1953.

Vermont Adjutant General's Office. *Revised Roster of Vermont Volunteers and Lists of Volunteers Who Served in the Army of the United States During the War of the Rebellion, 1861-1866.* Montpelier: Press of the Watchman Publishing Co., 1892.

Volkel, Lowell M. *Illinois Soldiers and Sailors Homes.* N.p.: McDonnell Publications, n.d.

Wright, Edward Needles. *Conscientious Objectors in the Civil War.* New York: A. S. Barnes, 1961.

INFORMATION GUIDE

Genealogical Information in the Record Group	*Prison Registers*	*Mortician's Registers*	*Coroner*	*Schools*	*Orphanages*	*Hospitals*
Surname/name	●	●	●	●	●	●
Date of Birth						●
Place of Birth	●	●			●	●
Sex	●		●	●	●	●
Race/color	●		●		●	●
Physical Description	●				●	●
Occupation	●	●	●			●
Education	●			●		
Military Service		●				●
Slave Status						
Property Owned					●	●
Religion	●	●			●	●
Citizenship						
Marital Status	●	●				●
Spouse's Name		●				●
Children's Names		●		●		●
Father's Name		●		●		●
Mother's Name		●				●
Father's Birthplace						
Mother's Birthplace						
Date of Death	●	●	●		●	●
Cause of Death	●	●	●			●
Name of Cemetery		●	●		●	●
Residence	●	●	●	●	●	●
Age	●	●	●	●	●	●
Literacy/signature	●			●		●
Photograph/sketch	●		●	●	●	●
Hereditary Diseases			●			●

COULD YOU USE THIS CHAPTER?

Type of Record	*Kept from*	*Clues That You Should Consult These Records*
Prison Records	Ca. 1800 to present	Are there family traditions that an ancestor "did time", was executed for a crime, imprisoned but pardoned, etc.? Newspaper clippings, journal accounts, county and local histories may also provide clues.
Mortuary records	Ca. 1800 to present	Did your family live in a city of any size during this early time period? Even rural areas had access to such services.
Coroners' records	All periods	Any family traditions or clues around the time of death of foul play or suspicious circumstances? In more recent times, did death take place without a physician present?
School records	About twenty years	Does the Census say "attended school during the year" or is "Cannot read and write" column unmarked? Do report cards survive? Did your ancestor's inventory list books other than the family Bible? Do local or county histories tell of an ancestor with a continuing concern in education? Does the county atlas show a schoolhouse on or near your ancestor's property? If schools are in operation in ancestral areas, ask for their records and search them.
Orphanage records	After 1850 for most government agencies; church and poorhouse facilities available since eighteenth century.	Are there family traditions that an ancestor was placed in an orphanage after the death/desertion of one/both parents? Was an ancestor formally adopted rather than just being taken in by kin or friends? After searching traditional sources like census, marriage, land, probate, and military records, are you still without names of parents for your ancestor? Was your family ancestor exempt from paying taxes?

Chapter 9

INSTITUTIONAL RECORDS

Johni Cerny

Institutional records are some of the least used and most valuable sources of genealogical information available to the researcher. School, hospital, mortuary, coroner's, orphanage, and prison records require more sophisticated research methods, apply to a restricted population, and are not always available to the public, since some are modern, protected by the laws of privacy which are discussed in the Introduction. Still, because these and less modern records contain valuable genealogical information, it is important for the researcher to understand the record types, content, availability, and special problems in use.

Few of the records in this category have received the attention given to the major record sources, but they have developed into valuable genealogical sources during this century. Each record has existed in one form or another for nearly 150 to 200 years. Such an accumulation of information is obviously important, yet almost everything remains to be done before the records of, say, orphanages and prison systems in the United States become familiar tools in the working genealogist's hands. The magnitude of the task of compiling the information available and putting it in a usable format for the researcher is beyond the scope of this work, but it should be done in the future.

Much of the information in this chapter is available here for the first time. The section on prison records provides more detailed information than that offered in any other source publication and includes a list of the correctional agencies in the federal and state jurisdictions.

Prison Records

Prisons as they currently exist began as innovations about 200 years ago. Prior to that time the offender was confined in dungeons or jails awaiting trial. The principal trial court for crimes was called Gaol Delivery, because it emptied the jail. The first modern prison is believed to have been the Walnut Street Jail in Philadelphia, which opened its doors in 1790. It was fashioned after the workhouses of London and other European cities.

Penologists saw a need for more sophisticated correctional institutions and designed what was considered a model prison at Auburn, New York, in 1825. It was followed by Eastern State Penitentiary at Cherry Hill in Philadelphia in 1829. Thousands of prisons, reformatories, correctional institutions, and related penal groups have been established since.

The early criminal judicial system was more likely to convict an offender for violations less serious than those of the modern offender. Probation was instituted in the United States at about the same time the model prison was established at Auburn, New York. The purpose of probation was the same then as it is now – to provide supervision to the first-time offender who committed a lesser crime and to avoid imprisoning juveniles.

Jurisdictions

Early prisons were operated, as they are today, by federal, state, local, and military authorities. The correctional institutions of all four jurisdictions are listed in *Juvenile and Adult Correctional Departments, Institutions, Agencies and Paroling Authorities* (1981). This directory includes organizational descriptions of each institution. Most of the institutions listed were founded within the last fifty years and are not within the time period of primary interest to most genealogists, but Table 9-1 gives the names of those functioning by 1900, plus some federal institutions that began operations after 1900. The list also includes some institutions which were once operational but are no longer functioning. You should contact the correctional agency of the same state to determine the exact scope of the prison's existence and the disposition of its records.

Types of Records

Unfortunately, there is no complete inventory of the records maintained by each of the early correctional institutions in the United States. The types of records compiled by early Pennsylvania correctional institutions are representative of those found in other states for the same time period and include admission and discharge books, biographical registers, hospital record books, descriptive registers, convict dockets, reception descriptive books, registers of prisoners, death warrants, clemency files, pardon books, and lists of executions.

Admission and Discharge Books. These books contain the name of the inmate, date of admission, race, sex, health, habits (temperance), marital status, immunizations, family diseases, number of convictions, length of sentence, time in county jail, birthplace, occupation, physical and mental health at release, time in prison, and pardon information. Figure 9-1 is a page from the 1844 admissions register of the Eastern Pennsylvania State Penitentiary.

Registers of Prisoners. Registers of prisoners are similar to admission books and list the name of the prisoner, age, race, birthplace , number of convictions, county of residence, court of sentencing, date of sentencing, crime, maximum sentence, and remarks (usually about release). Figure 9-2 is a page from the Register of Prisoners, 1889-1901, of the Pennsylvania Industrial Reformatory.

Biographical Registers. The Biographical Register of the Pennsylvania Industrial Reformatory is a good example of the valuable information found in these registers. The information is divided into data about the inmate and data about his family. (See Figure 9-3.)

INMATE		FAMILY
Name	Physical stature	Insanity
Date of record	Mental capabilities	Epilepsy
Crime	Moral susceptibility	Dissipation
Maximum sentence	Health	Education
Family	Culture	Pecuniary condition
Schools	Addresses of correspondents	Occupations
Labor		Pauper or criminal
Religion		Religion
Associations		

Table 9-1

Correctional Institutions Before 1900 And Contemporary Federal/State Agencies

FEDERAL AGENCIES AND INSTITUTIONS

	Bureau of Prisons 320 First Street N.W. Washington, DC 20534
North Central Region:	K.C.I. Bank Building 10920 Ambassador Drive Kansas City, MO 64153
South Central Region:	1607 Main, Suite 700 Dallas, TX 75201
Western Region:	330 Primrose Road, 5th Floor Burlingame, CA 94010
Southern Region:	523 McDonough Boulevard, S.E. Atlanta, GA 30315
Northeast Region:	Scott Plaza II, Industrial Highway Philadelphia, PA 19113

PENITENTIARIES

	Date Established
United States Penitentiary, Atlanta, GA 30315	1902
United States Penitentiary, Leavenworth, KS 66048	1895
United States Penitentiary, Lewisburg, PA 17837	1932
United States Penitentiary, Marion, IL 62959	1963
United States Penitentiary, Terre Haute, IN 47808	1940

MILITARY

Commandant
U. S. Army Disciplinary Barracks
Fort Leavenworth, KS 66027 (1874)

Commandant
Fort Riley Confinement Facility
1st Infantry Division
Fort Riley, KS 66442 (1880)

Correctional Facility
Marine Corps Recruit Depot
Parris Island, SC 29905

STATE AND LOCAL AGENCIES AND INSTITUTIONS

Alabama

State Department of Corrections
101 South Union Street
Montgomery, AL 36130

No correctional institutions listed prior to 1900.

Alaska

Department of Health & Social Services
Division of Adult Corrections
Pouch H03
Health & Social Services Building
Juneau, AK 99811

No correctional institutions listed prior to 1900.

Arizona

Department of Corrections
1601 West Jefferson
Phoenix, AZ 85007

No correctional institutions listed prior to 1900.

Arkansas

Department of Correction
Box 8707
Pine Bluff, AR 71611

No correctional institutions listed prior to 1900.

California

Department of Corrections
630 K Street
Sacramento, CA 95814

California State Prison at San Quentin
San Quentin, CA 94964 (1852)

California State Prison at Folsom
Box W
Represa, CA 95671 (1880)

Colorado

State Department of Corrections
6385 North Academy Boulevard
Colorado Springs, CO 80907

Canon Correctional Facility
Box 1010
Canon City, CO 81212 (1871)

Buena Vista Correctional Facility
Box R
Buena Vista, CO 81211 (1889)

Connecticut

Department of Correction
340 Capitol Avenue
Hartford, CT 06106

Connecticut Correctional Institution–Somers
Box 100
Somers, CT 06071 (1827)

Delaware

Department of Correction
80 Monrovia Avenue
Smyrna, DE 19977

No correctional institutions listed prior to 1900.

Washington, D.C.

Department of Corrections
614 H Street N.W.
Washington, DC 20001

No correctional institutions listed prior to 1900.

Florida

Department of Corrections
1311 Winewood Boulevard
Tallahassee, FL 32301

Florida State Prison
Box 747
Starke, FL 32091 (1871)

Georgia

Department of Offender Rehabilitation
800 Peachtree Street, N.E.
Atlanta, GA 30308

No correctional institutions listed prior to 1900.

Hawaii

Department of Social Services and Housing
Corrections Division
Box 339
Honolulu, HI 96809

No correctional institutions listed prior to 1900.

Idaho

Department of Corrections
Box 7309
Boise, ID 83707

Idaho State Correctional Institution
Box 7309
Boise, ID 83707 (1870)

Illinois

Department of Corrections
1301 Concordia Court
Springfield, IL 62702

Joliet Correctional Center
Box 515
Joliet, IL 60434 (1860)

Menard Correctional Center
Box 711
Menard, IL 62259 (1878)

Pontiac Correctional Center
Box 99
Pontiac, IL 61764 (1871)

Indiana

Department of Correction
804 State Office Building
Indianapolis, IN 46204

Indiana State Prison
Box 41
Michigan City, IN 46360 (1859)

Indiana Boys' School
Box 211
Plainfield, IN 46168 (1867)

Iowa

Bureau of Correctional Institutions
5th Floor, Hoover Building
Des Moines, IA 50319

Men's Reformatory
Box 8
Anamosa, IA 52205 (1872)

Iowa State Penitentiary
Box 316
Fort Madison, IA 52627 (1839)

Kansas

Kansas State Department of Corrections
535 Kansas Avenue, Suite 200
Topeka, KS 66603

Kansas State Industrial Reformatory
Box 1568
Hutchinson, KS 67501 (1895)

Kansas State Penitentiary
Box 2
Lansing, KS 66043 (1864)

Kentucky

Bureau of Corrections
State Office Building
Frankfort, KY 40601

Kentucky State Penitentiary
Box 128
Eddyville, KY 42038 (1888)

Louisiana

Department of Corrections
Box 44304
State Capitol Station
Baton Rouge, LA 70804

Louisiana State Penitentiary
Angola, LA 70712 (1866)

Maine

Department of Mental Health and Corrections
State Office Building
Augusta, ME 04333

Maine State Prison
Box A
Thomaston, ME 04861 (1824)

Maine Youth Center
675 Westbrook Street
South Portland, ME 04106 (1853)

Maryland

Department of Public Safety and Correctional Services
Division of Correction
6314 Windsor Mill Road
Baltimore, MD 21207

Maryland Penitentiary
954 Forrest Street
Baltimore, MD 21202 (1811)

Maryland House of Correction
Box 534
Jessup, MD 20794 (1879)

Boys' Village of Maryland
Cheltenham, MD 20623 (1870)

Massachusetts

Executive Office of Human Services
Department of Correction
Saltonstall Office Building
100 Cambridge Street
Boston, MA 02202

Massachusetts Correctional Institution
Box 366
Bridgewater, MA 02324 (1855)

Massachusetts Correctional Institution
Box 99
Framingham, MA 01701 (1877)

Massachusetts Correctional Institution
Box 00
West Concord, MA 01742

Michigan

Department of Corrections
Stevens T. Mason Building
Lansing, MI 48909

Michigan Reformatory
Ionia, MI 48846 (1877)

State House of Correction
and Branch Prison
Marquette, MI 49855 (1899)

State Prison of Southern Michigan
4000 Cooper Street
Jackson, MI 49201

Adrian Training School
Box 218
Adrian, MI 49221 (1881 for juveniles)

Minnesota

Department of Corrections
30 Metro Square Building
7th & Robert Streets
St. Paul, MN 55101

Minnesota Correctional Facility-
St. Cloud
Box B
St. Cloud, MN 56301 (1889)

Minnesota Correctional Facility–
Red Wing
Box 45
Red Wing, MN 55066 (1889)

Mississippi

Department of Corrections
23 North President Street
Jackson, MS 39202

Mississippi State Penitentiary
Parchman, MS 38738 (1900)

Missouri

Department of Social Services
Division of Corrections
East Capitol Avenue
Jefferson City, MO 65101

Missouri State Penitentiary for Men
Box 236
Jefferson City, MO 65101 (1835)

Training School for Boys
Boonville, MO 65233 (1889)

Training School for Girls
Chillicothe, MO 64601 (1889)

Montana

Department of Institutions
Corrections Division
1539 11th Avenue
Helena, MT 59601

Montana State Prison
Box 7
Deer Lodge, MT 59722 (1869)

Pine Hills School
Miles City, MT 59301
(1894 for juveniles)

Nebraska

Department of Correctional Services
Box 94661
Lincoln, NE 68509

Nebraska State Penitentiary
Box 2500
Lincoln, NE 68501 (1869)

Nevada

Department of Prisons
Box 607
Carson City, NV 89701

Nevada State Prison
Box 607
Carson City, NV 89701 (1861)

Nevada Youth Training Center
Box 469
Elko, NV 89801

New Hampshire

New Hampshire State Prison
Box 14
Concord, NH 03301 (1880)

New Hampshire Youth Development
Center
Box 303
Manchester, NH 03105 (1858)

New Hampshire has no central
Department of
Corrections.

New Jersey

Department of Corrections
Box 7387
Whittlesley Road
Trenton, NJ 08628

New Jersey State Prison
Third Street
Trenton, NJ 08611 (1798)

New Mexico

Corrections and Criminal
Rehabilitation
Department
113 Washington Avenue
Santa Fe, NM 87501

Penitentiary of New Mexico
Box 1059
Santa Fe, NM 87501

New York

New York State Commission
of Correction
Tower Building
Empire State Plaza
Albany, NY 12223

Albion Correctional Facility
Albion, NY 14411 (1893)

Auburn Correctional Facility
Box 618
Auburn, NY 13011 (1817)

Clinton Correctional Facility
Dannemora, NY 12929 (1845)

Elmira Correctional Facility
Elmira, NY 14902 (1876)

Fishkill Correctional Facility
Beacon, NY 12508 (1892)

Ossining Correctional Facility
154 Hunter Street
Ossining, NY 10562 (1825)

New York City

New York City Department
of Corrections
100 Centre Street
New York, NY 10013

North Carolina

Department of Correction
840 West Morgan Street
Raleigh, NC 27603

Division of Prisons
831 West Morgan Street
Raleigh, NC 27603

Central Prison
835 West Morgan Street
Raleigh, NC 27602 (1871)

North Dakota

Director of Institutions
State Capitol
Bismarck, ND 58505

North Dakota Penitentiary
Box 1497
Bismarck, ND 58501 (1885)

Ohio

Department of Rehabilitation
and Correction
1050 Freeway Drive North
Columbus, OH 43229

Ohio State Reformatory
Box 788
Mansfield, OH 44901 (1896)

Oklahoma

Department of Corrections
400 North Eastern
Box 11443
Oklahoma City, OK 73111

No correctional institutions
listed prior to 1900.

Oregon

Department of Human Resources
Corrections Division
2575 Center Street N.E.
Salem, OR 97310

Oregon State Penitentiary
2605 State Street
Salem, OR 97310 (1853)

Pennsylvania

Department of Justice
Bureau of Correction
Box 598
Camp Hill, PA 17011

State Correctional
Institution – Huntingdon
Huntingdon, PA 16652 (1889)

State Correctional Institution
and Correctional Diagnostic
and Classification Center
Box 9901
Pittsburgh, PA 15233 (1826)

Philadelphia

Philadelphia Prisons
8201 State Road
Philadelphia, PA 19136

House of Correction
8001 State Road
Philadelphia, PA 19136 (1874)

Holmsburg Prison
8215 Torresdale Avenue
Philadelphia, PA 19136 (1896)

Rhode Island

Department of Corrections
75 Howard Avenue
Cranston, RI 02920

Rhode Island Training School
for Youth
300 New London Avenue
Cranston, RI 02920 (1850)

South Carolina

Department of Corrections
4444 Broad River Road
Box 21787
Columbia, SC 29221

Central Correctional Institution
Capitol Station A
Box 11159
Columbia, SC 29211 (1868)

Wateree River Correctional Institution
Route 1, Box 144
Rembert, SC 29129 (1892)

South Dakota

Office of Correctional Services
Suite 402-403, Foss Building
Pierre, SD 57501

South Dakota Penitentiary
Box 911
Sioux Falls, SD 57101 (1882)

South Dakota Training School
Box 7
Plankinton, SD 57368
(1887 for juveniles)

Tennessee

Department of Correction
State Office Building
5th & Charlotte
Nashville, TN 37219

Tennessee State Penitentiary
Centennial Boulevard
Nashville, TN 37209 (1898)

Tennessee Prison for Women
Stewart's Lane
Nashville, TN 37218 (1898)

Brushy Mountain Prison
Petros, TN 37218 (1898)

Texas

Department of Corrections
Box 99
Huntsville, TX 77340

Huntsville Unit
Box 32
Huntsville, TX 77340 (1849)

Jester Unit
Route 2
Richmond, TX 77469 (1885)

Wayne Unit
Route 1, Box 1
Huntsville, TX 77340 (1899)

Utah

Department of Social Services
Division of Corrections
150 West North Temple
Salt Lake City, UT 84103

Utah State Prison
Box 250
Draper, UT 84020 (1868)

Vermont

Agency of Human Services
Department of Corrections
103 South Main Street
Waterbury, VT 05676

No correctional institutions listed prior to 1900.

Virginia

State Department of Corrections
Box 26963
4615 West Broad Street
Richmond, VA 23261

Powhatan Correctional Center
State Farm, VA 23160 (1895)

Virginia State Penitentiary
500 Spring Street
Richmond, VA 23219 (1800)

Beaumont Learning Center
Beaumont, VA 23014 (1898)

Hanover Learning Center
Hanover, VA 23069 (1898)

Washington

Department of Social and Health Services
Adult Corrections Division
Mail Stop FN-61
Olympia, WA 98504

Washington State Penitentiary
Box 520
Walla Walla, WA 99362 (1887)

West Virginia

Department of Corrections
116 Quarrier Street
Charleston, WV 25301

West Virginia Penitentiary
Moundsville, WV 26041 (1866)

West Virginia Industrial School for Boys
Grafton, WV 26354 (1891)

West Virginia Industrial Home for Girls
Salem, WV 26426 (1899)

Wisconsin

Department of Health and Social Services
Division of Corrections
Box 7925
Madison, WI 53701

Waupun Correctional Institution
Box C
Waupun, WI 53963 (1851)

Green Bay Correctional Institution
Box WR
Green Bay, WI 54305 (1898)

Wyoming

Adult and Juvenile Institutions
State Board of Charities and Reform
Capitol Building 002
Cheyenne, WY 82002

Wyoming State Penitentiary
Box 400
Rawlins, WY 82301 (1892)

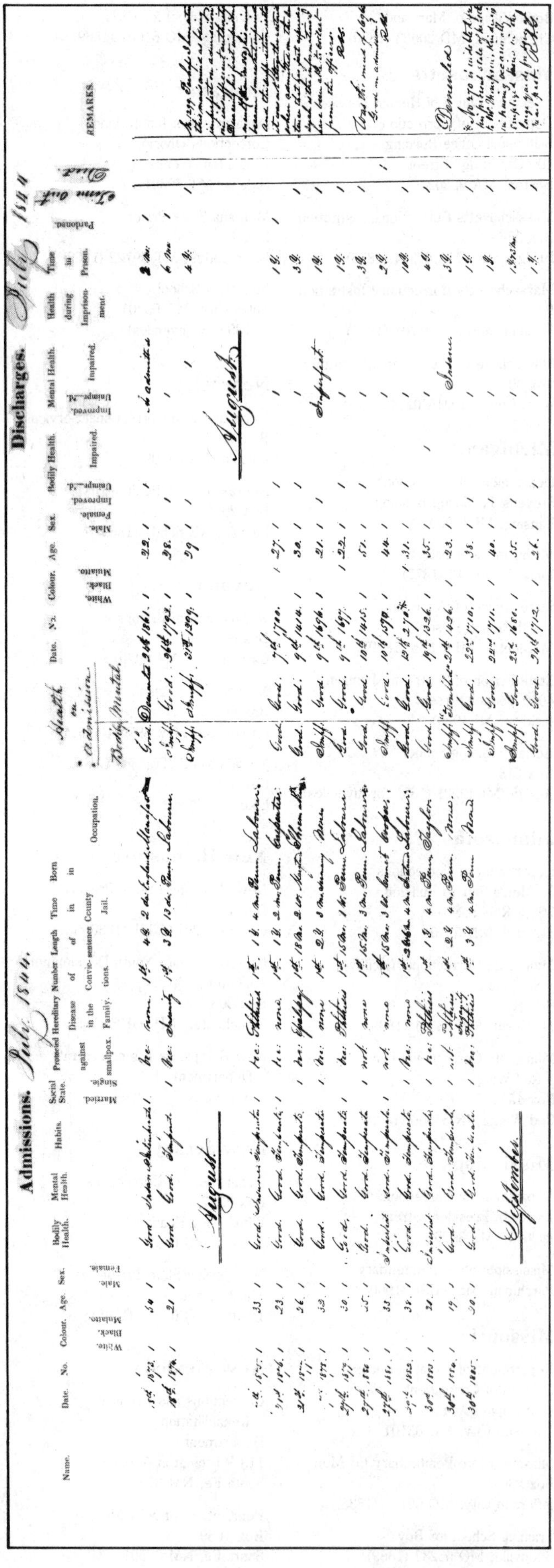

Figure 9-1. July 1844 Admissions, Admissions and Discharge Book, Eastern Pennsylvania State Penitentiary, vol. 1, p. 1; Genealogical Society of Utah microfilm (hereafter cited as GS) 1,032,652, item 2.

Received.	Number	NAME.	AGE	COLOR.	NATIVITY.	No. of Conv.	COUNTY.	COURT.	DATE OF SENTENCE. 1889	CRIME.	MAXIMUM SENTENCE.	REMARKS.
[illegible] 16	1	Moore John G	21	White	Penn^a	1	Huntingdon	Quar. Sessions	Feby 13	Larceny	3 Years	[illegible] Dis. [illegible]
21	2	Schaeffer Frank	19	"	"	1	Dauphin	do	" 18	Same	3 "	Paroled Mch. 8. 189[illegible]
21	3	Moran James	17	"	"	1	do	do	" 18	Same	3 "	Paroled June [illegible] Dis. Nov. 17. 9[illegible]
21	4	Crawford Marion	17	"	"	1	do	do	" 18	Same	4 "	Paroled May Dis. Oct 21-9[illegible]
23	5	Rafferty Thomas	16	"	"	1	Clearfield	do	" 20	Break'g & Ent'g & Larceny	4 "	Paroled May Dis. Dec. 13.
March 1	6	Keller Chas E	19	"	"	1	Snyder	do	" 26	Larceny	3 "	Paroled Mch. 7. 1890 Dis. Mch. 2. [illegible]
5	7	Gassenmeyer William	16	"	"	1	Philadelphia	do	March 2	Same	3 "	Paroled Mch. 24. 189[illegible] Dis. Nov. 25. [illegible]
5	8	Neibauer Charles	18	"	"	1	do	do	" 2	Same	3 "	Paroled May [illegible] Dis. May [illegible]
5	9	Carr James	22	"	"	1	do	do	" 2	Burglary	10 +	Dis. [illegible]
5	10	Humphries George	20	Black	No. Carolina	1	do	do	" 2	Larceny	3 "	Paroled May Dis. Nov. 2[illegible]
5	11	Flood James	20	White	Penn^a	1	do	do	" 2	Same	3 "	Paroled May 1[illegible]
5	12	Evard Thomas	20	"	"	1	do	do	" 2	Same	3 "	[illegible] Paroled [illegible]
5	13	Pasquella John		"	Italy	1	do	do	" 2	Assault & Battery to Kill	3 "	[illegible] Dis. Dec. [illegible]
5	14	Burns Michael	18	"	Penn^a	1	do	do	" 2	Larceny	3 "	Paroled [illegible] Disch. Mar. [illegible]
7	15	Jackson Montgomery	15	Black	"	1	Indiana	do	" 6	Entering dwelling with intent to commit Felony	4 "	Dis. Nov. 17 [illegible]
12	16	De Ford Chas (alias)	17	White	"	1	Franklin	do	Feby 26	Horse Stealing	10 "	Paroled [illegible] Dis. Nov. 20 [illegible]
14	17	Mitchell John	18	"	"	1	Beaver	do	March 8	Casting Missiles upon a RR car & Assault	3 "	Paroled May Dis. Oct 2[illegible]
14	18	Donovan John	19	"	"	1	do	do	" 8		3 "	Paroled A[illegible]
15	19	Reed Hiram E	18	"	"	1	Lycoming	do	" 14	Robbery	10 "	
17	20	O'Herron William	17	"	"		Allegheny	do	" 7	Larceny	3 "	Dis. Oct [illegible] Paroled [illegible]
17	21	McKinney James	21	"	Ohio		do	do	" 7	Same	3 "	Died July [illegible] Paroled [illegible]
17	22	Brooks James	19	"	Penn^a		do	do	" 14	Receiv'g Stolen Goods	3 "	Dis. [illegible] Paroled [illegible]
17	23	Geiger Samuel	18					Oyer & Ter		[illegible]	10	Brought [illegible] Paroled [illegible]

Figure 9-2. Register of Prisoners, 1889-1901, Pennsylvania Industrial Reformatory, p. 1; GS 1,032,656, item 3.

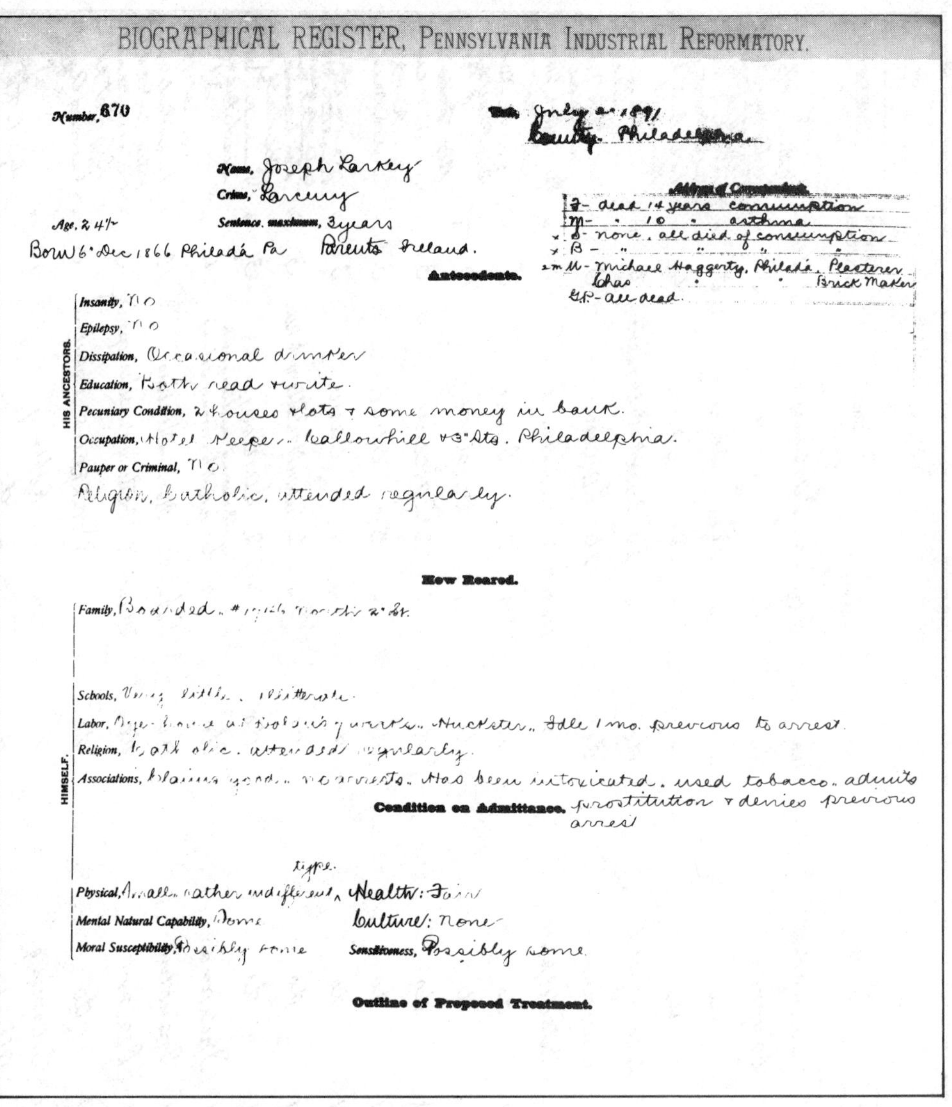

BIOGRAPHICAL REGISTER, PENNSYLVANIA INDUSTRIAL REFORMATORY.

Number, 670

Date, July 2nd 1891

County, Philadelphia

Name, Joseph Larkey

Crime, Larceny

Age, 24 7/12

Sentence, maximum, 3 years

Born 6 Dec 1866 Phila. Pa. Parents Ireland.

Address of Correspondents.

F – dead 14 years consumption
M – " 10 " asthma
S – none. all died of consumption
B – " " " "
2 m U – Michael Haggerty, Phila. Plasterer
Chas " " Brick Maker
G.P. – all dead.

Antecedents.

HIS ANCESTORS.

Insanity, No

Epilepsy, No

Dissipation, Occasional drinker

Education, Both read & write.

Pecuniary Condition, 2 houses & lots & some money in bank.

Occupation, Hotel keeper – Callowhill & 3rd Sts. Philadelphia.

Pauper or Criminal, No

Religion, Catholic, attended regularly.

How Reared.

Family, Boarded – [illegible]

HIMSELF.

Schools, Very little – illiterate.

Labor, [illegible] Huckster. Idle 1 mo. previous to arrest.

Religion, Catholic. attended regularly.

Associations, [illegible] no arrests. Has been intoxicated. used tobacco. admits prostitution & denies previous arrest

Condition on Admittance.

Physical, Small, rather indifferent type. Health: Fair

Mental Natural Capability, None Culture: None

Moral Susceptibility, Possibly some Sensitiveness, Possibly some

Outline of Proposed Treatment.

Figure 9-3. Biographical Register. Pennsylvania Industrial Reformatory, No. 670; GS 1,032,655, item 1.

The information in Figure 9-3 gives more details than is called for by the form. Joseph Larkey's parents are not named, but the dates and causes of their deaths are noted. His living relatives were two uncles, Michael and Charles Haggerty of Philadelphia. His grandparents were not identified by name but were listed as deceased. Other records list the names of parents, grandparents, and other relatives in the space for addresses of correspondents. All of this information is, of course, helpful to a genealogical effort.

Hospital Record Books. Sometimes detailed in their information about the inmate's medical treatment while imprisoned, these books may include specifics on the date and cause of death, or they may be statistical accounts of the types of illnesses treated and the frequency of treatment.

Descriptive Registers. Descriptive registers are similar to registers of prisoners, giving the date of entry, name, age, birthplace, occupation, complexion, color of eyes, color of hair, stature, physical marks, sentence, when sentenced, number of convictions, when and how discharged, expiration of sentence, and remarks. Figure 9-4 is the 1826 Descriptive Register of the Pennsylvania State Penitentiary.

Convict Dockets. Some of the information found in convict dockets is provided in other records, including name of inmate, crime, sentence, when sentenced, court of sentencing, name of prosecutor, date admitted, physical description, when discharged and how. This list is part of the A page from the index to the 1826 Convict Docket of Western Pennsylvania State Penitentiary.

	Folio
Atherton, Peter	1
Allman, Jesse	8
Anderson, Margaret J.	9
Atkinson, George	13
Armstrong, Robert	15
Anderson, Abraham	17
Anderson, Abraham	31
Austin Alpheus	37
Adkins Martin	45

Convict Docket, 1826, Western Pennsylvania State Penitentiary, p. 1; G S 1,032,653, item 1.

Reception Descriptive Lists of Convicts. An expanded form of early prison registers, the reception descriptive lists contain detailed information about the prison inmate. The information listed in these records includes the convict's name, age, race, crime, date

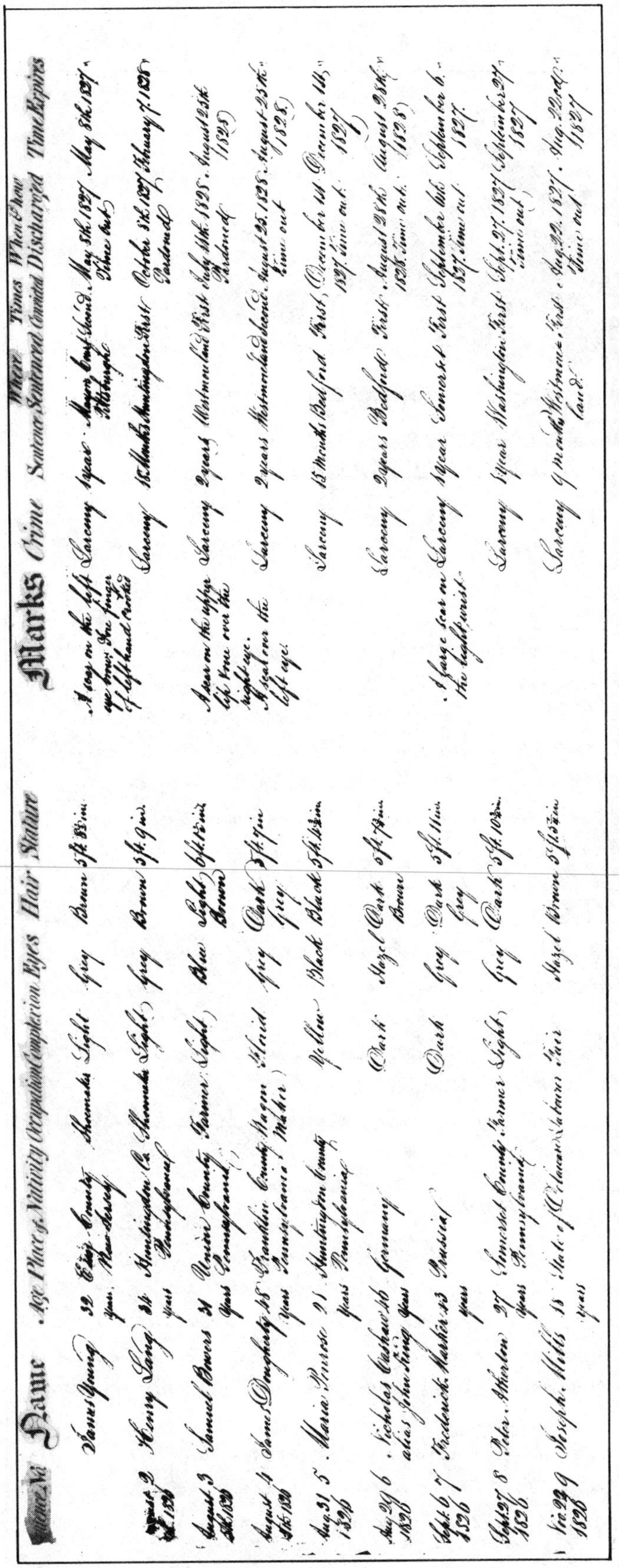

Figure 9-4. Descriptive Register, May 1826-Feb. 1827, Pennsylvania Western State Penitentiary, p. 1; GS 1,032,653, item 2.

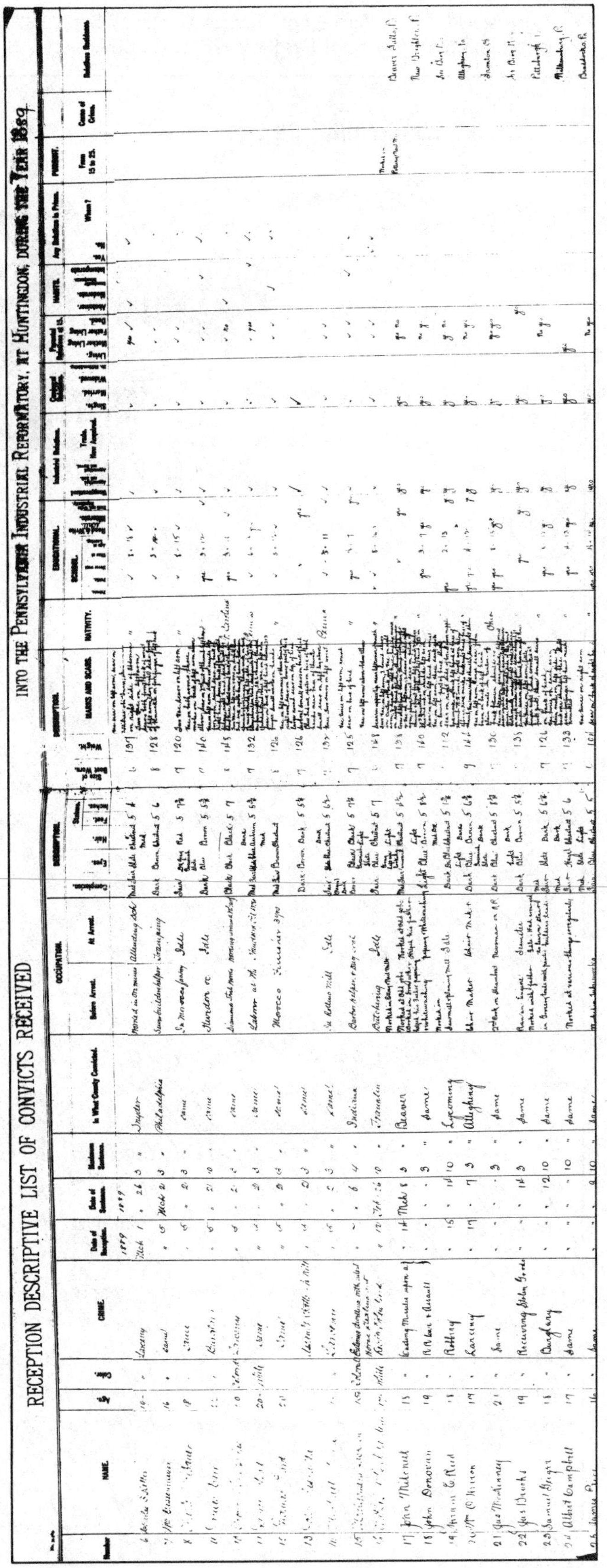

Figure 9-5. Reception Descriptive List of Convicts Received, 16 Feb. - 17 March 1889, Pennsylvania Industrial Reformatory, p. 1; GS 1,032,655, item 2.

Figure 9-6. Death Warrant of Thomas Munley, 7 Sept. 1876, Pennsylvania State Board of Pardons; GS 1,032,659.

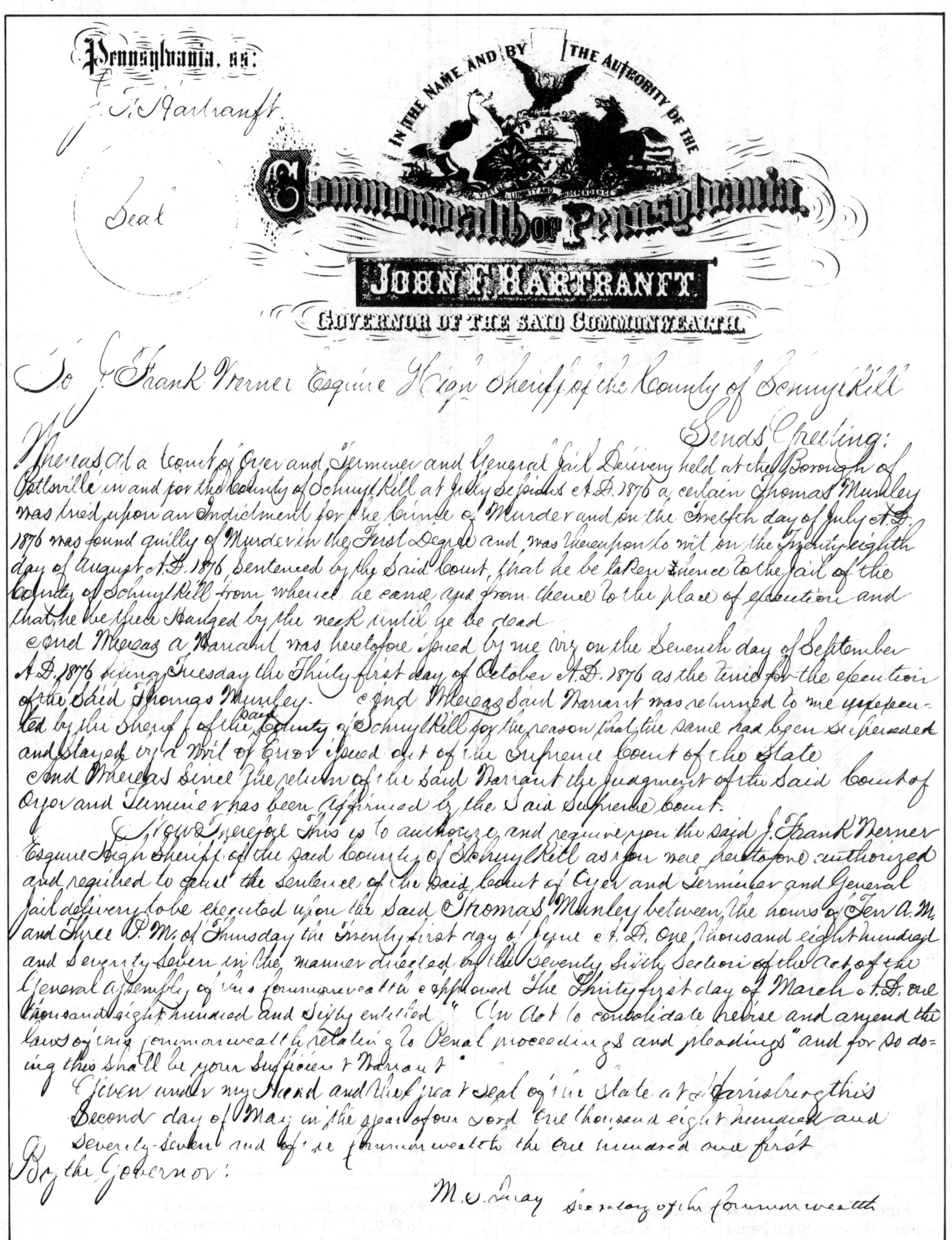

Pennsylvania, ss:

J. F. Hartranft

Seal

IN THE NAME AND BY THE AUTHORITY OF THE

Commonwealth of Pennsylvania

JOHN F. HARTRANFT

GOVERNOR OF THE SAID COMMONWEALTH.

To J. Frank Werner Esquire High Sheriff of the County of Schuylkill

Sends Greeting:

Whereas at a Court of Oyer and Terminer and General Jail Delivery held at the Borough of Pottsville in and for the County of Schuylkill at July Sessions A.D. 1876 a certain Thomas Munley was tried upon an Indictment for the Crime of Murder and on the Twelfth day of July A.D. 1876 was found guilty of Murder in the First Degree and was thereupon to wit on the Twenty eighth day of August A.D. 1876 Sentenced by the Said Court, that he be taken thence to the Jail of the County of Schuylkill from whence he came and from thence to the place of execution and that he be there Hanged by the neck until he be dead.

And Whereas a Warrant was heretofore issued by me viz on the Seventh day of September A.D. 1876 fixing Tuesday the Thirty first day of October A.D. 1876 as the time for the execution of the Said Thomas Munley. And Whereas Said Warrant was returned to me unexecuted by the Sheriff of the said County of Schuylkill for the reason that the same had been superseded and stayed by a Writ of Error issued out of the Supreme Court of the State

And Whereas since the return of the said Warrant the Judgment of the Said Court of Oyer and Terminer has been affirmed by the Said Supreme Court.

Now Therefore This is to authorize and require you the said J. Frank Werner Esquire High Sheriff of the said County of Schuylkill as you were heretofore authorized and required to cause the sentence of the said Court of Oyer and Terminer and General Jail delivery to be executed upon the said Thomas Munley between the hours of Ten A.M. and Three P.M. of Thursday the Twenty first day of June A.D. One thousand eight hundred and Seventy Seven in the manner directed by the Seventy Sixth Section of the Act of the General Assembly of this Commonwealth approved The Thirty first day of March A.D. One thousand eight hundred and Sixty entitled "An Act to consolidate revise and amend the laws of this Commonwealth relating to Penal proceedings and pleadings" and for so doing this shall be your sufficient Warrant.

Given under my Hand and the Great Seal of the State at Harrisburg this Second day of May in the year of our Lord One thousand eight hundred and Seventy-seven and of the Commonwealth the One hundred and first

By the Governor:

M. S. Quay Secretary of the Commonwealth

of reception, date of sentence, county of conviction, occupation before and at the time of arrest, physical description, shoe size, weight, birthplace, education, occupational training, marital status, parental relations at fifteen, drinking habits, relatives in prison, cause of crime, relatives' residence. Figure 9-5 is from the 1889 Reception Descriptive List of the Pennsylvania Industrial Reformatory.

Death Warrants. These files, which consist of the actual warrant and all the supporting documentation of the conviction, contain information of greater historical than genealogical value. The disposition of appeals for clemency and commutation are often included in the file. Figure 9-6 is the death warrant of Thomas Munley, inmate of the Pennsylvania prison system, from the records of the Pennsylvania State Board of Pardons.

Clemency Files. Clemency files contain requests to the governor for clemency in the sentence of a convict. A narrative in these files explains the circumstances involved in the commission of the crime, the reasons for clemency, and attestations to the character of the convict. The petition is signed by individuals who support the granting of clemency. Figure 9-7 is the 1833 clemency file of Isaac F. Clarke, inmate of the Western Pennsylvania Penitentiary.

Pardon Books. These brief records attest to pardons granted to convicts by the state governor and contain little genealogical information. They do, however, include references to the place of conviction and the court of sentencing. Figure 9-8 is a page from the pardon book of the State of Pennsylvania.

Lists of Executions. Some descriptive information about the convict is provided in these lists including date and time of execution, name, age, weight, and color, name of the person murdered, and the sheriff's name. Figure 9-9 shows three entries from the Execution Book of the Commonwealth of Pennsylvania.

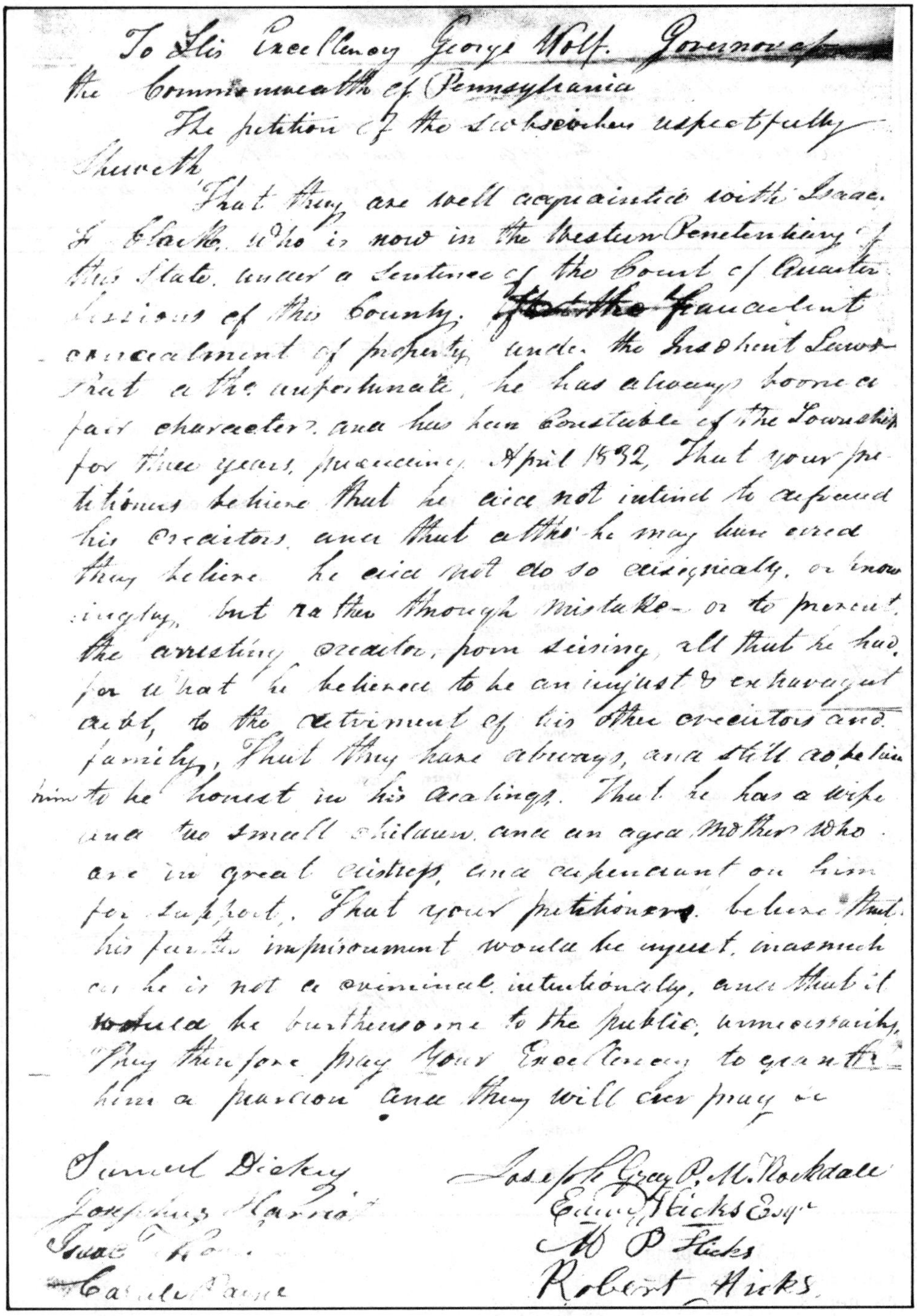

To His Excellency George Wolf Governor of the Commonwealth of Pennsylvania

The petition of the subscribers respectfully Showeth

That they are well acquainted with Isaac F. Clarke who is now in the Western Penitentiary of this State under a Sentence of the Court of Quarter Sessions of this County for the fraudulent concealment of property under the Insolvent Laws that he the unfortunate, he has always borne a fair character and has been Constable of the Township for three years preceeding April 1832, That your petitioners believe that he did not intend to defraud his creditors and that altho he may have erred they believe he did not do so designedly or knowingly but rather through mistake or to prevent the arresting creditor from seizing all that he had for what he believed to be an unjust & extravagant debt, to the detriment of his other creditors and family, That they have always, and still do believe him to be honest in his dealings. That he has a wife and two small children and an aged Mother who are in great distress and dependent on him for support. That your petitioners believe that his further imprisonment would be unjust, inasmuch as he is not a criminal intentionally, and that it would be burthensome to the public unnecessarily. They therefore pray Your Excellency to grant him a pardon and they will ever pray &c

Samuel Dickey
Josephus Harris
Isaac [illegible]
Caleb Paine

Joseph Gray P.M. Rockdale
Edward Hicks Esqr
W P Hicks
Robert Hicks

Figure 9-7. Clemency Files of Isaac F. Clarke, 1833, Department of State, Secretary of the Commonwealth of Pennsylvania; GS 1,018,404.

Figure 9-8. Record of pardon, Joseph Burwell, 11 July 1818, and Abraham Brown, 11 July 1818, Pardon Books, Department of State, Secretary of the Commonwealth of Pennsylvania, p. 398; GS 1,032,591.

Commonwealth vs Joseph Burwell	Was convicted of Manslaughter at a Court of Oyer and Terminer for Allegheny County on the 13th January 1818, and sentenced to four years imprisonment at hard labour, 6 months whereof in the cells - & pay costs.	Pardon granted July 11th 1818.
Commonwealth vs Abraham Brown	Was convicted of a Misdemeanor at a Mayors Court of the City of Philadelphia on the 31st March 1818, and sentenced to one years imprisonment & pay costs.	Pardon granted July 11th 1818.
Commonwealth vs William McKim	Was convicted of Assault and Battery upon three indictments at a Court of Quarter Sessions for Chester County, on the 5 May 1818,	Pardoned August 10 1818. so far as respects the

Note.
Blaise Skupinski
was also Indited for the Murder of the Battles family, May 3. 1851 But was Never Tried. He being Executed in Connection with the Murder of Lehman

Arthur Spring. for Killing Ellen Lynch and Hannah Shaw, at their home Federal St above Seventh. The Motive was robbery. Spring was also supposed to have killed a Stationer named Rink, on Chestnut St below 9th.

LIST OF EXECUTIONS.

No. 7. Date, December 3 [illegible]
Name, Blaise Skupinski
Age, Years. Weight, Lbs. Color, White
Time,
Murder of Jacob Lehman.
Sheriff, H. Lelar

No. 8. Date, June 10. 1853.
Name, Arthur Spring
Age, Years. Weight, Lbs. Color, White
Time,
Murder of Ellen Lynch and Hannah Shaw
Sheriff, Allen

No. 9. Date, May 23. 1856
Name, Peter Mattex
Age, Years. Weight, Lbs. Color, Black
Time,
Murder of
Sheriff, Magee

Figure 9-9. Execution List for Blaise Skupinski, Arthur Spring, and Peter Mattex, County Prison, Philadelphia County, Pennsylvania, 1839-1916, p. 3, GS 975,748, item 3.

Availability of Records

Locating early prison records can be challenging. The records of Pennsylvania prisons have been microfilmed by the Genealogical Society of Utah, but the actual records are still on file at the prison or at the state archives. When you know the place or state of imprisonment, you should write to the prison itself or to the state department of corrections at the address given in Table 9-1 asking for photocopies of the records available and the location of the records, if they are no longer maintained by the prison authorities. Requests should list the specific record desired—"the entries from the biographical register, the reception descriptive list, and the clemency file," for instance, to insure receiving records of maximum genealogical value.

Use of Prison Records

Most family genealogists will not need prison records regularly, but professional genealogists should know how to use them. The incarceration of an ancestor may go unnoticed unless the court records index a criminal conviction, the newspapers describe and report the trial, or family members remember the story. One of my clients told me that his great-grandfather was convicted of arson and negligent homicide in the death of his first wife. Research revealed that the ancestor was actually married five times. The alleged murder involved his second wife, whom he had divorced before 1880. She sued for fraudulent divorce after his third marriage. The suit was filed in Missouri, although she was a resident of Tennessee. The ancestor was reportedly so enraged by the suit that he returned to Tennessee to burn down her house, unknowingly causing her death in the fire. The court records of Greene County, Missouri, supported the information about the fraudulent divorce suit. There was, however, no record of a criminal trial, arrest, or incarceration in Missouri or Tennessee.

Since he was a veteran of the Civil War and had received a disability pension, I requested his pension files to determine his movements after being discharged and to gain additional information about his marriages. The pension file shows that the ancestor received a periodic physical at Lansing, Kansas, in 1884, where the Kansas State Prison is located. He had been a resident of Montgomery County, Kansas, just prior to living in Lansing. A document in his file states that he misplaced his pension certificate when he was arrested at Cherryvale, Kansas, just prior to his being taken to the prison at Lansing.

The Montgomery County records produced nothing about his arrest and trial. I requested his prison record, but officials at Lansing responded disappointingly that they had no record of him in their files. In a second letter I included the document from the pension file to assist in identifying the records. The prison officials indicated that the records had been transferred to the Kansas State Historical Society. The historical society would not provide photocopies but affirmed that the ancestor had served a three-year sentence in the Kansas State Prison at Lansing for larceny.

Researchers must often use a variety of records to lead them to the prison in which an ancestor was incarcerated. Once that has been determined, finding the actual prison records should be no more complicated than my own process. Obtaining the records is worth the effort, however, since they will help identify other family members. For instance, the biographical register shown in Figure 9-3 contains at least five leads to follow:

1. Joseph Larkey was born in Philadelpha 6 December 1866. The 1866 city directory should list all of the Larkey families in that city during the year of his birth, possibly giving clues to parents, grandparents, and other relatives with the same surname.

2. Joseph's father was a hotelkeeper who died fourteen years prior to his son's incarceration (1877). The city directory of Philadelphia should be searched specifically for a hotelkeeper named Larkey also. Later directories should list his widow.

3. Joseph Larkey named Michael and Charles Haggerty as uncles. They are probably maternal uncles, so his mother's family should be sought among the Haggerty families of Philadelphia.

4. Information gained from city directories should lead to a search of the 1870 census for a Larkey family living in Philadelphia, with both parents having been born in Ireland and the head of the household employed as a hotelkeeper.

5. Records of the Catholic Church closest to Callowhill and 3rd Street in Philadelphia where Joseph's father worked should be examined to see if the family was involved in the nearest parish.

The records of the court in which a convict was sentenced should also be searched for additional historical information.

Problems in Using Prison Records

The problems encountered in using prison records are similar to those encountered in using any other early records. Early records of the correctional institutions are sometimes difficult to locate. Modern prison records within the last seventy-two years fall under the jurisdiction of privacy laws and cannot be released. Family members may obtain the records of deceased convicts and ex-convicts under some circumstances, but you should inquire about those conditions at the prison or correctional agency by letter or telephone.

Legibility is also a problem. Early records are handwritten and can be difficult to read. Others are faded and damaged. Microfilmed copies may be fuzzy and unclear. When filmed copies are poor, it may be necessary to obtain a copy of the original.

Although prison records will only occasionally be included in the research process, they are valuable sources of genealogical and historical information. Researchers should take the time and effort to track them down. Sometimes prison records cannot be used alone and require the information included in court records, newspaper articles, coroners' records, and other sources to complete the picture of the individuals and circumstances involved in the events that led to imprisonmnent.

Mortuary Records

Mortuaries and funeral homes in the United States are privately owned business establishments many of whose proprietors have maintained records for over 125 years. The amount of genealogical information recorded in the early years of record keeping was limited compared to the amount of information compiled later; but at a minimum, the early records list the name of the deceased, death date, place of death, cause of death, and name of the informant. Occasionally, the age, residence, occupation, birthplace , and next of kin of the deceased are included. Most early mortician records are available to the public. Figure 9-10 illustrates printed mortuary records that date from 1914.

Modern morticians' records are more complete. The mortician gathers information needed to compile both the death certificate and obituary notice. Figure 9-11 is a sample of the form completed by Larkin Mortuary in Salt Lake City, Utah, and kept in its files. These records are not available to the public, but can be obtained by close relatives of the deceased. Figure 9-12 is a sample of the form morticians complete to compile the death certificate required by the State of Utah Department of Health. It is also protected by the privacy laws and is not available to the public.

Morticians' records are extremely valuable sources of information for the period before vital records were kept. The records are maintained at the mortuary and contain facts not available in other sources. Locating morticians' records is not difficult if the place of death is known. The *National Directory of Morticians* (Youngstown, Ohio: National Directory of Morticians, annual), which lists the names and addresses of most morticians and funeral directors in the United States, can be found in the collections of numerous genealogical libraries and in the offices of local mortuaries. Records of mortuaries and funeral homes that are no longer in operation or that have changed proprietorship can often be found in the custody of the town or county clerk, the local public

Figure 9-10. Typescript of Chalfant-Perry Funeral Home Mortuary Records, 1914-54 (Fort Wayne, Indiana: Fort Wayne Public Library, 1965), p. 1.

Adair, Clifford Angeline	wid-Harvey	b. 9-25-18[illegible]
p. Cloyd Ellenwood		d. 5-26-19[illegible]
Nancy Closterman	int; Lindenwood	b. Ft. Wayne
Adair, Harvey F.	m-Clifford A.	b. 6-13-1890
p. Sloan Adair		d. 5-16-1953
Julia Ann Neirelter	int; Lindenwood	b. Hoagland
Adair, Julia A.	wid-Sloan	b. 10-18-1859
p. Henry Neirleiter-Germany		d. 5-25-1940
Elizabeth Young-Unknown	int; Antioch, Hoagland	b. Indiana

Figure 9-11. Biographical Data Form, Larkin Mortuary, Salt Lake City, Utah.

NO.

NAME OF DECEDENT — First, Middle, Last | SEX | RACE (White, Black, Am. Indian, etc.) Specify | DATE OF DEATH (Month, Day, Year)

WAS DECEDENT OF SPANISH ORIGIN? YES ☐ NO ☐ If yes, indicate type - Mexican ☐ Puerto Rican ☐ Cuban ☐ Other ☐ (If other, specify) | DATE OF BIRTH (Month, Day, Year) | AGE (Last Birthday) YEARS | IF UNDER 1 YEAR: MONTHS, DAYS | IF UNDER 24 HOURS: HOURS, MINUTES

BIRTHPLACE (State or Foreign Country) | CITIZEN OF WHAT COUNTRY? | Married ☐ Never Married ☐ Divorced ☐ Widowed ☐ Other ☐ | EDUCATION (Specify only highest grade comp.) Elem or Second. (0-12) College (13-16 or 17+) | SOCIAL SECURITY NUMBER

USUAL OCCUPATION (Give kind of work done during most of working life, even if retired) | KIND OF BUSINESS OR INDUSTRY | NAME OF SURVIVING SPOUSE (If Wife, Enter Maiden Name)

NAME OF FATHER | MAIDEN NAME OF MOTHER | WAS DECEDENT EVER IN U.S. ARMED FORCES? YES ☐ NO ☐

USUAL RESIDENCE (Street and number or location and zip code) | INSIDE CITY LIMITS? YES ☐ NO ☐ | NAME & MAILING ADDRESS OF INFORMANT

CITY OR TOWN | COUNTY | STATE

NAME of hospital, nursing home or other institution where death occurred. (If outside an institution, give street address or location.) | ☐ In patient ☐ E.D. patient ☐ DOA | CITY OR TOWN | COUNTY

MEDICAL CERTIFIER (Doctor) Name | ADDRESS

Burial ☐ Removal ☐ Entombment ☐ Cremation ☐ Other ☐ | DATE (Month, Day, Year) | MISCELLANEOUS | TIME OF DEATH (24 Hour Clock)

CEMETERY OR CREMATORY - Name | LOCATION | CITY OR TOWN | STATE

FUNERAL DATE | TIME | PLACE

VIEWING

CLERGYMAN OFFICIATING | SERVED BY (Staff Member)

HONORARIUM | LARKIN MORTUARY - Salt Lake City, Utah

DATE OF MARRIAGE | PLACE OF MARRIAGE

IS SPOUSE LIVING? IF NOT, DATE OF DEATH

CHURCH AFFILIATION

ACTIVITIES - CIVIC, FRATERNAL, POLITICAL, RELIGIOUS, SOCIAL OR OTHER ACCOMPLISHMENTS

SURVIVORS

MISC.

OBITUARY HANDLED BY FAMILY ( ) MORT. ( ) PICTURE - YES ( ) NO ( )

DATE AND TIME GIVEN IN .... TRIBUNE ( ) DESERET ( )

GIVEN IN BY .... FAMILY PHONE NUMBER ....

ORGANIST - FAMILY ( ) MORT. ( ) SOLOIST - FAMILY ( ) MORT ( ) NAME ....

FUNERAL SERVICES DISCUSSED ( ) CLOSE CASKET BEFORE ( ) AFTER ( ) FAMILY PRAYER YES ( ) NO ( )

REMOVE FLOWER CARDS - FAMILY ( ) MORT. ( ) PALLBEARERS ( ) CARS EXPLAINED HEARSE ( ) FLORAL TRUCK ( ) FAMILY CAR ( ) PALLBEARERS CAR ( )

ESCORT - YES ( ) NO ( ) TIME FUNERAL NOTICES DISCUSSED ( )

CLOTHING - FAMILY ( ) MORT ( ) BOTH ( ) CEMETERY DISCUSSED ( ) BURIAL CONTAINER ( ) ....

FAMILY CAR TO RESIDENCE - NO ( ) YES ( ) IF YES - ADDRESS AND TIME ....

FAMILY MEET AT CHURCH ( ) REGISTER BOOK AND THANK YOU CARDS ( ) CERTIFIED COPIES DISCUSSED ( ) HAIR ( )

SOCIAL SECURITY DISCUSSED ( ) VETERAN BENEFIT DISCUSSED ( ) MILITARY HONORS ( ) ....

CASKET SELECTED ( ) DEVICE AND GREENS TO BE USED YES ( ) NO ( ) JEWELRY (RING) ....

PROGRAMS - YES ( ) NO ( ) NUMBER

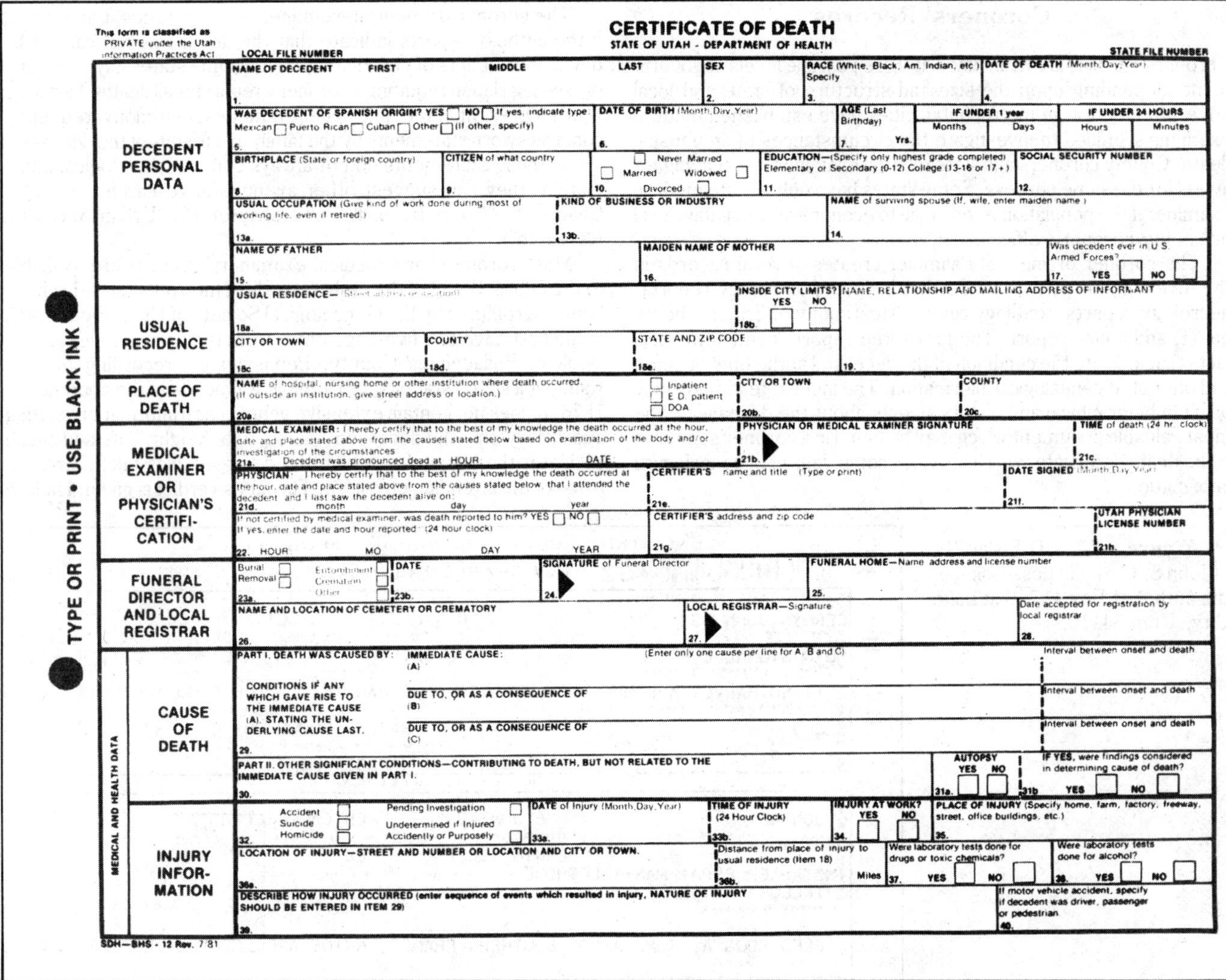

This form is classified as PRIVATE under the Utah Information Practices Act

CERTIFICATE OF DEATH
STATE OF UTAH - DEPARTMENT OF HEALTH

LOCAL FILE NUMBER
STATE FILE NUMBER

TYPE OR PRINT • USE BLACK INK

DECEDENT PERSONAL DATA
1. NAME OF DECEDENT FIRST MIDDLE LAST
2. SEX
3. RACE (White, Black, Am. Indian, etc.) Specify
4. DATE OF DEATH (Month, Day, Year)
5. WAS DECEDENT OF SPANISH ORIGIN? YES NO If yes, indicate type: Mexican Puerto Rican Cuban Other (If other, specify)
6. DATE OF BIRTH (Month, Day, Year)
7. AGE (Last Birthday) Yrs. IF UNDER 1 year Months Days IF UNDER 24 HOURS Hours Minutes
8. BIRTHPLACE (State or foreign country)
9. CITIZEN of what country
10. Never Married Married Widowed Divorced
11. EDUCATION—(Specify only highest grade completed) Elementary or Secondary (0-12) College (13-16 or 17+)
12. SOCIAL SECURITY NUMBER
13a. USUAL OCCUPATION (Give kind of work done during most of working life, even if retired.)
13b. KIND OF BUSINESS OR INDUSTRY
14. NAME of surviving spouse (If, wife, enter maiden name.)
15. NAME OF FATHER
16. MAIDEN NAME OF MOTHER
17. Was decedent ever in U.S. Armed Forces? YES NO

USUAL RESIDENCE
18a. USUAL RESIDENCE—
18b. INSIDE CITY LIMITS? YES NO
18c. CITY OR TOWN
18d. COUNTY
18e. STATE AND ZIP CODE
19. NAME, RELATIONSHIP AND MAILING ADDRESS OF INFORMANT

PLACE OF DEATH
20a. NAME of hospital, nursing home or other institution where death occurred. (If outside an institution, give street address or location.) Inpatient E.D. patient DOA
20b. CITY OR TOWN
20c. COUNTY

MEDICAL EXAMINER OR PHYSICIAN'S CERTIFICATION
21a. MEDICAL EXAMINER: I hereby certify that to the best of my knowledge the death occurred at the hour, date and place stated above from the causes stated below based on examination of the body and/or investigation of the circumstances. Decedent was pronounced dead at HOUR DATE
21b. PHYSICIAN OR MEDICAL EXAMINER SIGNATURE
21c. TIME of death (24 hr. clock)
21d. PHYSICIAN: I hereby certify that to the best of my knowledge the death occurred at the hour, date and place stated above from the causes stated below, that I attended the decedent and I last saw the decedent alive on: month day year
21e. CERTIFIER'S name and title (Type or print)
21f. DATE SIGNED (Month Day Year)
22. If not certified by medical examiner, was death reported to him? YES NO If yes, enter the date and hour reported (24 hour clock) HOUR MO DAY YEAR
21g. CERTIFIER'S address and zip code
21h. UTAH PHYSICIAN LICENSE NUMBER

FUNERAL DIRECTOR AND LOCAL REGISTRAR
23a. Burial Removal Entombment Cremation Other
23b. DATE
24. SIGNATURE of Funeral Director
25. FUNERAL HOME—Name address and license number
26. NAME AND LOCATION OF CEMETERY OR CREMATORY
27. LOCAL REGISTRAR—Signature
28. Date accepted for registration by local registrar

MEDICAL AND HEALTH DATA

CAUSE OF DEATH
29. PART I. DEATH WAS CAUSED BY: IMMEDIATE CAUSE: (A) (Enter only one cause per line for A, B and C) Interval between onset and death
CONDITIONS IF ANY WHICH GAVE RISE TO THE IMMEDIATE CAUSE (A), STATING THE UNDERLYING CAUSE LAST.
DUE TO, OR AS A CONSEQUENCE OF (B) Interval between onset and death
DUE TO, OR AS A CONSEQUENCE OF (C) Interval between onset and death
30. PART II. OTHER SIGNIFICANT CONDITIONS—CONTRIBUTING TO DEATH, BUT NOT RELATED TO THE IMMEDIATE CAUSE GIVEN IN PART I.
31a. AUTOPSY YES NO
31b. IF YES, were findings considered in determining cause of death? YES NO

INJURY INFORMATION
32. Accident Suicide Homicide Pending Investigation Undetermined if Injured Accidently or Purposely
33a. DATE of Injury (Month, Day, Year)
33b. TIME OF INJURY (24 Hour Clock)
34. INJURY AT WORK? YES NO
35. PLACE OF INJURY (Specify home, farm, factory, freeway, street, office buildings, etc.)
36a. LOCATION OF INJURY—STREET AND NUMBER OR LOCATION AND CITY OR TOWN.
36b. Distance from place of injury to usual residence (Item 18) Miles
37. Were laboratory tests done for drugs or toxic chemicals? YES NO
38. Were laboratory tests done for alcohol? YES NO
39. DESCRIBE HOW INJURY OCCURRED (enter sequence of events which resulted in injury, NATURE OF INJURY SHOULD BE ENTERED IN ITEM 29)
40. If motor vehicle accident, specify if decedent was driver, passenger or pedestrian.

SDH—BHS - 12 Rev. 7/81

Figure 9-12. Certificate of Death Form, Larkin Mortuary, Salt Lake City, Utah.

library or historical society, and even university collections with local focus. Check NUCMC (*National Union Catalog of Manuscript Collections*) for morticians records deposited locally.

Once the mortician's record has been obtained, you should evaluate it carefully for both the information it contains and the research it suggests, such as:

1. Occupation. If the occupation of the deceased was unusual or governed by a labor union, you should investigate employment or union records.

2. Service in the armed forces. You should request military service records if the ancestor was a veteran. The branch of service may not be listed in the mortician's records, but it may be found in the obituary notice or in the documents created by the mortician to apply for veteran's burial benefits. Department of Defense Form 214, Record of Discharge, must accompany the application for burial benefits, and a photocopy may be in the mortician's files. Figure 9-13 is a copy of my father's DD Form 214, placed in the mortuary files at the time of his burial.

3. Name and address of the informant. You may be able to contact the informant. If he/she is deceased, an heir of either the informant or the deceased may own or reside in the residence listed.

4. Hospital, nursing home, or institution where the death occurred. These establishments maintain excellent records which are discussed in detail later in this chapter.

5. Cemetery or crematory. If the deceased is buried in a family cemetery plot, cemetery records and tombstone inscriptions will provide information about other family members buried in that plot. Figure 9-14 is a form from the cemetery file, obtained after reviewing the mortician's records of George F. Myers.

6. Marriage. You should follow up on the marriage record to obtain details about the spouse of the deceased.

7. Church affiliation. The name and location of the church attended by the deceased may be recorded. The religion of the deceased will also be stated, if known. Church records may offer extensive information about the parents, grandparents, brothers, sisters, and children of the deceased.

8. Fraternal organizations. If the deceased was a member of the Masons, Order of the Elks, Knights of Columbus, or similar organization, their records may provide extensive biographical information.

9. Survivors. The list of survivors usually includes the residences of family members and the married names of daughters, excellent clues to other avenues of research in previously unknown locations.

Morticians' records are not totally without problems for the researcher. The information contained in the records is only as accurate as the knowledge and memory of the informant. Therefore, inaccuracies can occur if the informant was not closely related to the deceased, lacked detailed knowledge, or became confused while grief-stricken. When the information is fragmented or disagrees with previously known facts, you will need to conduct additional searches to clarify the discrepancies.

Coroners' Records

Coroners' records are maintained at three possible levels of government, depending upon the size and structure of state and local governments. Large metropolitan cities have established medical examiners' offices to investigate the circumstances of an unusual death. County coroners and state medical examiners exist at higher levels for the same purpose. Some states have only a state medical examiner if the population is too small to economically maintain local or county coroners' offices.

The coroner or medical examiner creates several records in the investigation of unusual deaths, including pathology reports, necrology reports, toxology reports, testimony offered at the inquest, and a jury report. The first three reports contain medical facts that indicate the condition of the deceased at the time of death and offer little genealogical information. The inquest testimony may provide biographical and historical facts about the deceased. The most valuable document which may be found in a coroner's records is the death certificate, which provides some degree of genealogical information.

The coroner or medical examiner may not request an inquest if the autopsy reports indicate that the death was not caused by negligence or acts of violence, although some states have recently passed legislation requiring a coroner's report for all deaths if a doctor was not present at the time of death. Inquest testimony frequently contains sworn statements by the family and friends of the deceased. While these statements do not always contain genealogical information, they can suggest other avenues of research. (See also Chapter 6, "Court Records," and Chapter 16, "Urban Ancestral Research").

Most coroners' and medical examiners' records are available to the public. Some of the early records of metropolitan cities have been microfilmed by the Genealogical Society of Utah. Figure 9-15 is the first page of a five-page entry from the Coroner's Evidence Book of Philadelphia County, Pennsylvania, recording Isadore Raimonda's fatal stabbing of Dominic Raimonda in the abdomen in 1876. It does not contain extensive genealogical information, stating specifically only the deceased's name, age, height, date and cause of death, the hospital to which the deceased was taken, and the name of the attending physician. The jury's verdict is given; Isadore

Figure 9-13. DD Form 214 of John S. Cerny in possession of the author at Box 417, Salt Lake City, Utah 84110.

ENLISTED RECORD AND REPORT OF SEPARATION
BOOK 40253 PAGE 22 — HONORABLE DISCHARGE

1. Last name – First name – Middle initial: CERNY JOHN S
2. Army serial no.: 36 346 273 — 3. Grade: S SGT — 4. Arm or service: SC — 5. Component: AUS
6. Organization: 563D SIGNAL CORPS
7. Date of separation: 6 OCT 45 — 8. Place of separation: SEPARATION CENTER CAMP MC COY, WIS
9. Permanent address for mailing purposes: 2511 SO HARVEY AVE BERWYN ILLINOIS
10. Date of birth: 2 JAN 16 — 11. Place of birth: CHICAGO ILLINOIS
12. Address from which employment will be sought: SEE 9
13. Color eyes: HAZEL — 14. Color hair: BROWN — 15. Height: 5-5½ — 16. Weight: 133 — 17. No. dependents: 2
18. Race: White X — 19. Marital status: Married X — 20. U.S. citizen: Yes X
21. Civilian occupation and no.: GRADER MEAT

MILITARY HISTORY

22. Date of induction: 6 JUN 42 — 23. Date of enlistment: — 24. Date of entry into active service: 6 JUN 42 — 25. Place of entry into service: CHICAGO ILLINOIS
Selective service data: 26. Registered: X — 27. Local S.S. board no.: #2 — 28. County and state: BERWYN ILL — 29. Home address at time of entry into service: SEE 9
30. Military occupational specialty and no.: INSTALLER REPAIRMAN TELEPHONE & TELEGRAPH 097
31. Military qualification and date: RIFLE MKM
32. Battles and campaigns: NAPLES-FOGGIA, ROME-ARNO, SOUTHERN FRANCE, RHINELAND, CENTRAL EUROPE
33. Decorations and citations: GOOD CONDUCT MEDAL SO #156 JUL 43; MERITORIOUS SERVICE UNIT AWARD GO #452 HQ 7TH ARMY AUG 45
34. Wounds received in action: NONE
35. Latest immunization dates: Smallpox JUL 44 — Typhoid JAN 45 — Tetanus MAY 45 — Other (specify) TYPHUS MAY 45

36. Service outside continental U.S. and return:

Date of departure	Destination	Date of arrival
19 AUG 43	NATO	2 SEP 43
16 NOV 43	MTO	23 NOV 43
7 SEP 44	ETO	9 SEP 44
20 SEP 45	US	28 SEP 45

37. Total length of service: Continental service: Years 1, Months 2, Days 21 — Foreign service: Years 2, Months 1, Days 10
38. Highest grade held: S SGT
39. Prior service: NONE
40. Reason and authority for separation: CONVENIENCE OF THE GOVT, RR1-1 (DEMOBILIZATION) AR 615-365, 15 DEC 44
41. Service schools attended: ILLINOIS BELL TELEPHONE SCHOOL CHICAGO
42. Education (years): 8 3 0

PAY DATA

43. Longevity for pay purposes: Years 3, Months 4, Days 1 — 44. Mustering out pay: Total 300, This payment 100 — 45. Soldiers deposits — 46. Travel pay: 1320.00, 15.25 — 47. Total amount, name of disbursing officer: 1657.58 H L OLDENBURG MAJ FD

INSURANCE NOTICE

IMPORTANT: If premium is not paid when due or within thirty-one days thereafter, insurance will lapse. Make checks or money orders payable to the Treasurer of the U. S. and forward to Collections Subdivision, Veterans Administration, Washington 25, D. C.

48. Kind of insurance: Nat. Serv. X — 49. How paid: Allotment X — 50. Effective date of allotment discontinuance: 31 OCT 45 — 51. Date of next premium due: 30 NOV 45 — 52. Premium due each month: 6.80 — 53. Intention of veteran to: Continue X

54. Right thumb print
55. Remarks: EUROPEAN-AFRICAN-MIDDLE EASTERN THEATER SERVICE MEDAL; FOUR (4) OVERSEAS SERVICE BARS; NO TIME LOST UNDER AW 107; LAPEL BUTTON ISSUED; ASR SCORE (2 SEP 45) 101
56. Signature of person being separated: John S. Cerny
57. Personnel officer: CARL C BUTLER 2D LT AC ASSISTANT ADJUTANT

WD AGO Form 53-55, 1 November 1944. This form supersedes all previous editions of WD AGO Forms 53 and 55 for enlisted persons entitled to an Honorable Discharge, which will not be used after receipt of this revision.

Figure 9-14. Catholic Cemeteries Associations of the Diocese of Pittsburgh to Lineages, March 1983 re Myers Family Cemetery Records, original in possession of the author, Box 417, Salt Lake City, Utah 84110.

CEMETERY COPY

THE [C]ATHOLIC CEMETERIES A[S]SOCIATIONS
OF THE DIOCESE OF PITT[SBU]RGH
718 HAZELWOOD AVE., PITTSBU[RG]H 17, PA.

03177

DIVISION 2

ACCOUNT NAME Myers George DATE 6-26- 19

ADDRESS 1437 Page St. CITY Pitts Pa

☑ INTERMENT DATE OF DEATH 6-25- 19

☐ REMOVAL AGE 43

☐ RECEIVING VAULT PLACE OF DEATH 1437 Page St.

NAME OF DECEASED Myers George ADDRESS same

BURIAL DATE 6-29- 19[5]3 TIME 9 a.m. CHURCH St. Gabriel PRIEST PERMIT ☑ UNDERTAKER [illegible]

DEED IN NAME OF Meyers Mrs Bridget RELATIONSHIP TO DECEASED grandmother ☐ NON-CATHOLIC ☑ CATHOLIC BURIAL

1. ☐ SINGLE GRAVE SEC. ROW NO. ☐ POOR GROUND ☐ D. P. A.

2. ☐ LOT SEC. E LOT 153 GRAVES

3. ☑ OPEN GRAVE # 4 ☑ O. D. ☐ E. D. O. T. ☐ ☑ ADULT ☐ CHILD 30

4. ☑ LOWERING DEVICE AND GREENS 30

5. ☐ TENT

6. TYPE VAULT ☐ OURS ☐ OTHERS — COMPANY P. V. cave proof SIZE 6

7. ☐ DISINTERMENT OF ORIGINAL INT. MADE 19 TYPE VAULT

FROM SEC. LOT GR. TO SEC. LOT GR. ☐ O. D. ☐ E. D.

8. REASON TO RECEIVING VAULT TIME ALLOWED

9. OTHER SERVICES

SECTION	LOT NO	MONTH	YEAR	DAY	PRICE	FOLIO NUMBER
E	153					

NAME

Bridget Meyers

STREET TOWN STATE

GRAVE	BURIED	DATE	GRAVE	BURIED	DATE
1	Martin Meyers 3-20-1900 Bridget Myers 1-7-10				
2	Anna M. Meyers 1-27-36 George Meyers 5-4-51				
3	John & Ella Kane 3-20-1900				
4	Andrew Cain 12-14-03 Patrick Cain 2-17-13 removed to 602 M #2, 10-29-13				
5	George Myers [6]-29-53				
6					

Raimonda was convicted of manslaughter, suggesting a search of prison records.

Modern coroners' records may contain more detailed information, have greater historical value, and thus should be used in addition to vital records.

The value of coroners' records is similar to that of morticians' records. The information found in the records should be carefully analyzed for genealogical facts and clues to other record sources that may prove helpful. The information found in Figure 9-15 suggests several possibilities for additional research:

1. Names of the deceased and the defendant. Although not specifically stated, the record implies that Isadore and Dominic were cousins. Any further research should be approached with this possibility in mind.

2. Translator. Because the police officer interviewed the wounded Dominic with a translator, the dying man may have been a recent immigrant. Naturalization records may show if either Dominic or Isadore had petitioned for or received citizenship.

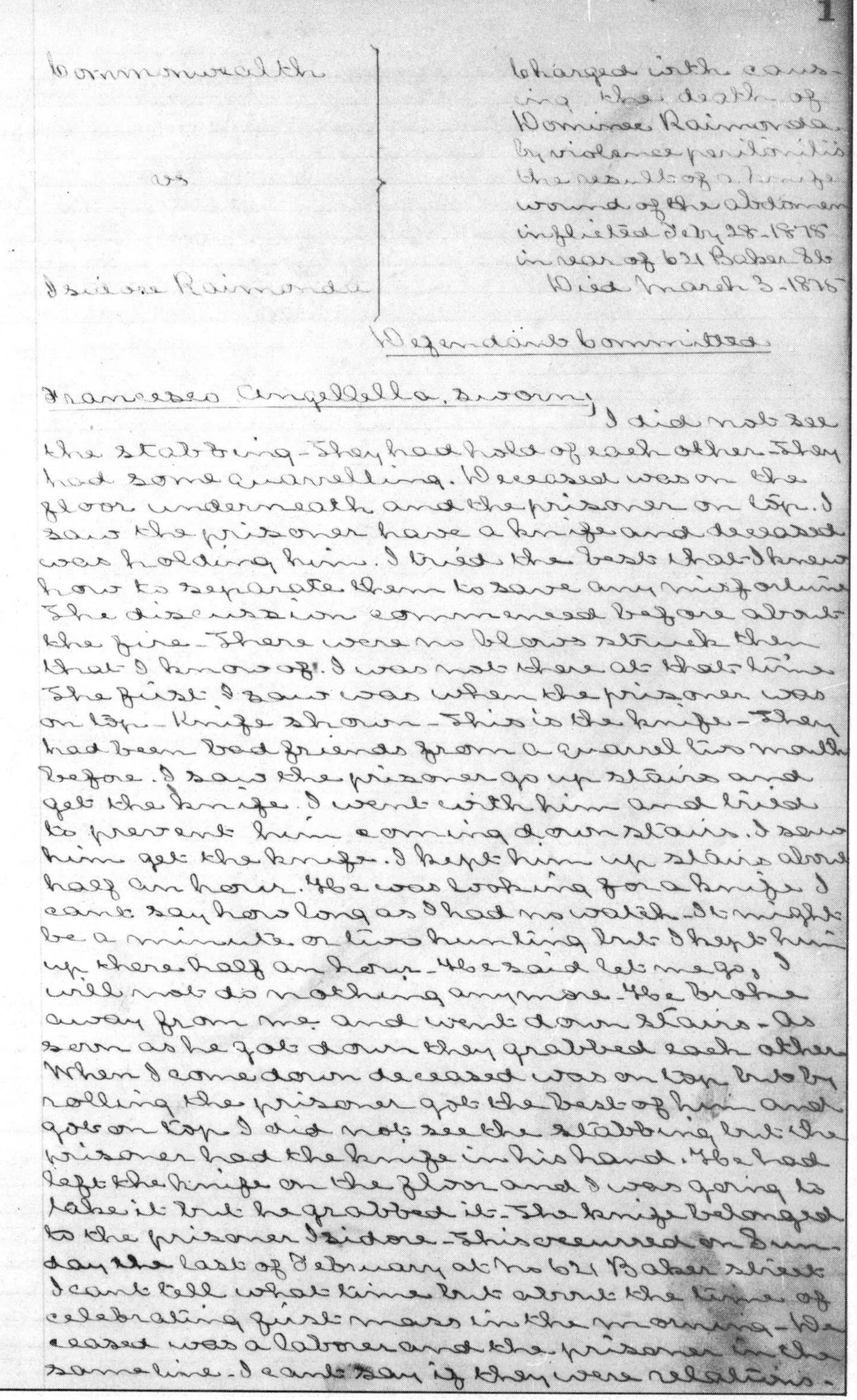

1

Commonwealth vs Isidore Raimonda

Charged with causing the death of Dominic Raimonda by violence peritonitis the result of a knife wound of the abdomen inflicted Feby 28-1875 in rear of 621 Baker St. Died March 3-1875

Defendant Committed

Francesco Angelella, sworn

I did not see the stabbing - They had hold of each other - They had some quarrelling. Deceased was on the floor underneath and the prisoner on top. I saw the prisoner have a knife and deceased was holding him. I tried the best that I knew how to separate them to save any misfortune. The discussion commenced before about the fire - There were no blows struck then that I know of. I was not there at that time. The first I saw was when the prisoner was on top - Knife shown - This is the knife - They had been bad friends from a quarrel two months before. I saw the prisoner go up stairs and get the knife. I went with him and tried to prevent him coming down stairs. I saw him get the knife. I kept him up stairs about half an hour. He was looking for a knife. I can't say how long as I had no watch - It might be a minute or two hunting but I kept him up there half an hour - He said let me go, I will not do nothing anymore - He broke away from me and went down stairs - As soon as he got down they grabbed each other. When I came down deceased was on top but by rolling the prisoner got the best of him and got on top. I did not see the stabbing but the prisoner had the knife in his hand. He had left the knife on the floor and I was going to take it but he grabbed it - The knife belonged to the prisoner Isidore - This occurred on Sunday the last of February at No 621 Baker street. I can't tell what time but about the time of celebrating first mass in the morning - Deceased was a laborer and the prisoner in the same line. I can't say if they were relations.

Figure 9-15. Commonwealth vs. Isadore Raimonda, Coroner's Evidence Book, Philadelphia County, Pennsylvania, p. 1, GS 965,369, item 1.

3. Hospital. The hospital records may still exist and should be checked for more information.

4. Verdict. The record concludes with the report that Isadore was convicted of manslaughter and sentenced, a notation made later after the appropriate court has dealt with the case. Prison records may contain additional biographical facts about Isadore Raimondo.

The coroner also issues death certificates. This document generally provides the deceased's name, age, sex, place of birth, race, occupation, marital status, place of death, date of death, and cause of death.

In contrast to the very full record on the fatal Raimonda quarrel is a seven-line entry in the Coroner's Evidence Book of the New York City coroner in 1862. (Figure 9-16).

Most family researchers will not need coroners' and medical examiners' records to establish genealogical facts, but professional genealogists should find them most valuable. Usually the records are on file at the office of the coroner or medical examiner. Early records may have been transferred to the city or county clerk's office, the local historical society, or a state archives. The coroner's office will know where the old records are located. Some offices will not release the records without proof of relationship to the deceased and a statement indicating how the information in the record will be used. Usually family history is considered a valid reason.

Once you have located the records, there should be few problems in using them. However, they may have suffered deterioration over the years, making all or part of the records difficult to read. Unless the witnesses at an inquest perjured themselves, the testimony should be factual, eliminating erroneous information about the deceased. The major problem in using coroner's records is locating the old records, a process that may involve writing several letters of inquiry to various levels of government, local clerks, and historical societies.

Still, despite the specialization and inconvenience involved in using coroner's records, they should not be ignored, especially when you need historical information.

School Records

The records of schools, colleges, and universities in the United States have gradually developed into valuable sources of genealogical information. Early school records lack uniformity, especially in rural primary school systems; and many no longer exist. What you will usually find is school board minutes. (See Figure 9-17.) While board

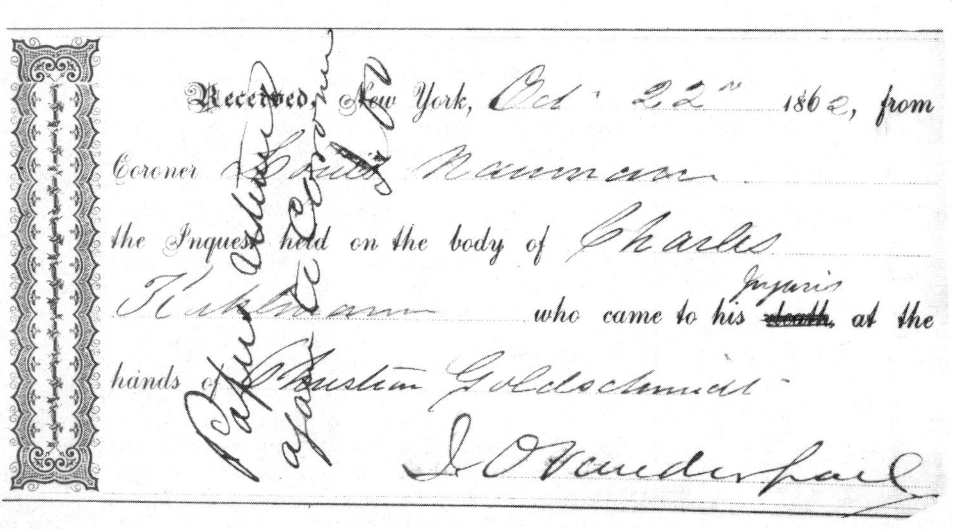

Recived Oct 2, 1862 from Coroner Rainey the inquisition on view of the body of Joseph P. Thompson
Dist. Attys Office
J. O. Vanderpool

Received, New York, Oct 22nd 1862, from Coroner [illegible] Naumann the Inquest held on the body of Charles Kiklman who came to his ~~death~~ injuries at the hands of Gustav Goldschmidt
J. O. Vanderpool

Figure 9-16. Inquest reports on Joseph P. Thompson, 2 Oct. 1862, and Charles Kikleman [?], 22 Oct. 1862, Coroner's Office Inquests to Deaths, New York City, 1862-64; GS 514,332.

minutes deal primarily with administrative and financial matters involved in operating the school, they may include such potentially valuable information as the names of administrators and teachers, and reference to other records that might be available. For instance, these 1873 minutes from McDuffey County, Georgia, refer to a school census. Does that census still exist in the files of the county school district or the county clerk?

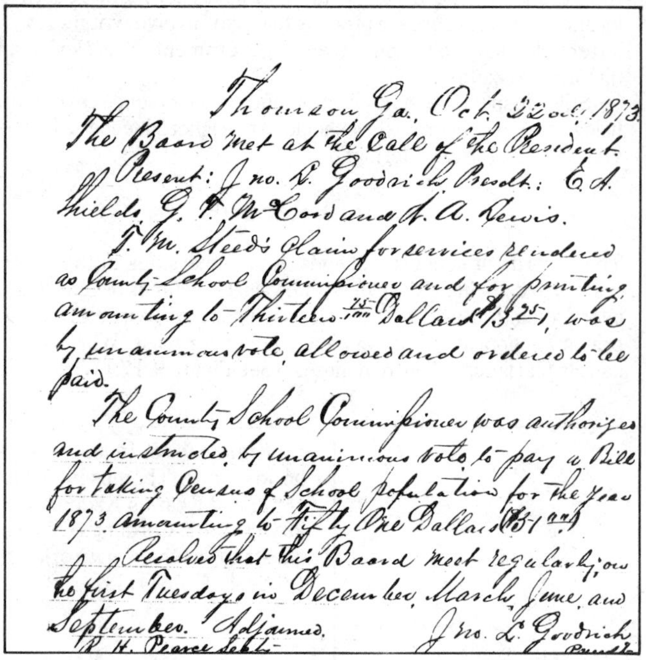
Thomson Ga. Oct. 22nd 1873
The Board met at the Call of the President.
Present: Jno. L. Goodrich Presdt.: E. A. Shields, G. F. McCord and A. A. Lewis.
T. M. Steed's Claim for services rendered as County School Commissioner and for printing amounting to Thirteen 25/100 Dollars $13.25, was by unanimous vote, allowed and ordered to be paid.
The County School Commissioner was authorized and instructed by unanimous vote to pay a Bill for taking Census of School population for the year 1873 amounting to Fifty One Dollars $51.00.
Resolved that this Board meet regularly on the first Tuesdays in December, March, June and September. Adjourned.
R. H. Pearce Secty. Jno. L. Goodrich Presdt.

Figure 9-17. School Board Minutes, 22 Oct. 1873, McDuffey County, Georgia, 1872-1960, p. 25; GS 220,521, part 1.

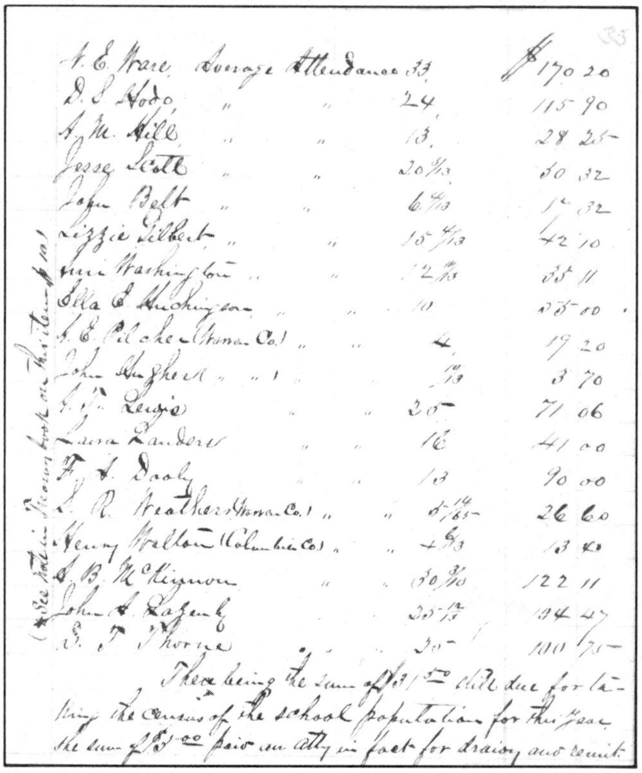

A. E. Ware	Average Attendance	33	$170 20
D. S. Hodo	" "	24	115 90
A. M. Hill	" "	13	28 25
Jesse Scott	" "	20 2/3	60 32
John Belt	" "	6 2/3	17 32
Lizzie Gilbert	" "	15 2/3	42 10
Annie Washington	" "	12 2/3	35 11
Ella S. Hutchinson	" "	10	25 00
A. E. Pilcher (Thomas Co.)	" "	4	19 20
John Hughes	" "	1/3	3 70
A. J. Lewis		30	71 06
Laura Landers		16	41 00
F. A. Dooly		13	90 00
L. R. Weathers (Warren Co.)	" "	5 14/65	26 60
Henry Walton (Columbia Co.)	" "	4 2/3	13 40
A. B. McKinnon	"	30 2/3	122 11
John A. Lazenby		35 1/3	104 47
S. F. Thorne		35	100 75

There being the sum of $31.00 still due for taking the census of the school population for this year the sum of $51.00 paid an atty in fact for drawing and remit.

Figure 9-18. School Board Minutes, 22 Oct. 1873, McDuffey County, Georgia, 1872-1960, p. 33.

Figure 9-18 lists the amount McDuffey County paid each teacher for services during 1874. Salaries were set by the number of students in attendance rather than by the number of school days taught. McDuffey County required licensing earlier than most rural school systems, and Figure 9-19 shows the applicants who were granted licenses to teach in 1876 and the number of years for which the license was granted.

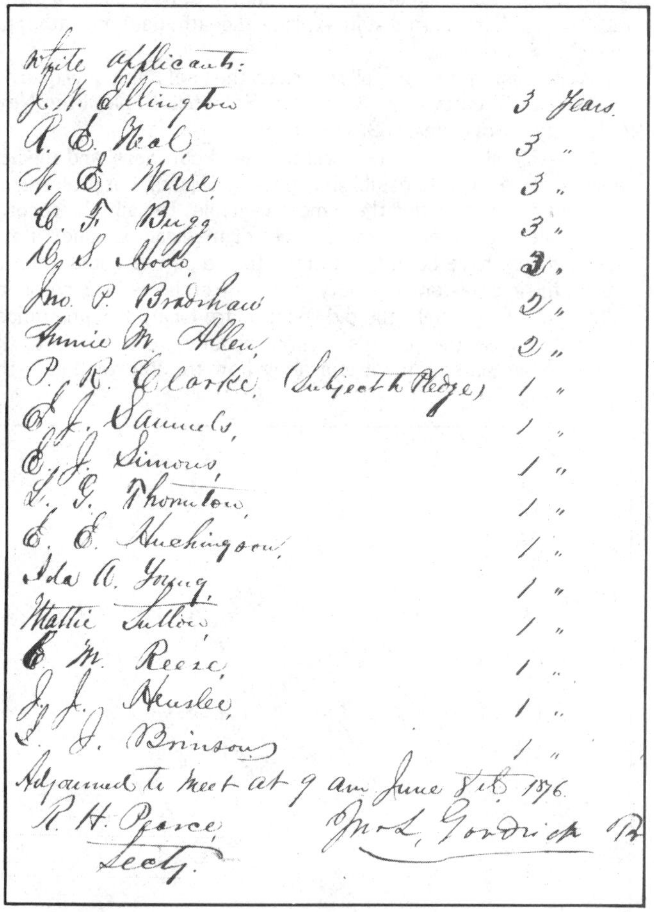
White Applicants:

J. W. Ellington	3 Years
R. E. Neal	3 "
A. E. Ware	3 "
C. F. Bugg	3 "
D. S. Hodo	3 "
Jno. P. Bradshaw	2 "
Annie M. Allen	2 "
P. R. Clarke (Subject to Pledge)	1 "
E. J. Samuels	1 "
E. J. Simons	1 "
L. G. Thornton	1 "
E. E. Hutchinson	1 "
Ida A. Young	1 "
Mattie Fullon	1 "
C. M. Reese	1 "
J. J. Henslee	1 "
L. J. Brinson	1 "

Adjourned to meet at 9 am June 8th 1876.
R. H. Pearce Secty. Jno. L. Goodrich Pr.

Figure 9-19. School Board Minutes, 22 Oct. 1873, McDuffey County, Georgia, p. 40.

Many metropolitan and rural schools received funds from the local government to cover the cost of educating poor children. Records of children receiving an education at government expense can be found in court records, school board minutes, or town meeting records. Figure 9-20 lists the 1829 page containing the names of these children of Oglethorpe County, Georgia. The information—name, age, and sex of the child—is typical of all early school records.

Some of the best early primary school records were kept by private preparatory and boarding schools whose students were from the region's wealthy families. References to the child's parents, residence, curriculum, and activities, as well as individual and class photographs can more often be found in these school records.

As with most other records in the United States, school records became more comprehensive after the turn of the twentieth century. Schools maintained by the Bureau of Indian Affairs are excellent sources of information and reflect the type of information found in modern school records. These records, maintained by the federal government, have been microfilmed. Records of the Juneau Indian Agency in Alaska are housed at the Federal Records Center at Seattle, Washington, and were microfilmed by the Genealogical Society of Utah in 1969. Figure 9-21 shows thirteen-year-old Oswald Willard Booth's application for admission to boarding school in 1946

Childrens Names

Age Sex

7 Alfred Stewart 14 Male
8 Silas Bowers 12 Male.
9 James Hartley 11 "
120. Sarah Tweedle female.
121 James Brackman x.
122 Sarah Kimball 8 F x

Figure 9-20. Names of Poor Children and Expenditures for Poor School – 1829, Oglethorpe County, Georgia; GS 21,526.

5-192
Revised (March, 1942)
Incorporates
Form 5-262

UNITED STATES
DEPARTMENT OF THE INTERIOR
Office of Indian Affairs
Field Service

Leave blank
Accepted ________ (Lenght of term)
Date ________

APPLICATION FOR ADMISSION TO BOARDING SCHOOLS*

(This application should be forwarded through the Reservation and Area Superintendents to the Superintendent of the school to which admission is being sought and his approval received before the student is permitted to depart)

Agency and reservation Metlakatla , Alaska Date 9/3/46

Application for admission to Wrangell Institute School, to enter grade 7th grade

Oswald Willard Booth (Name of applicant) M x F (Sex) Home Address Metlakatla

Tribe Tshimpsean Degree of Indian blood Full How verified

Born Jan. 17, 1933 (Month Day Year) at Metlakatla, Alaska (Town, County and State) Present age 13

I am a member x I attend ___ I prefer the Presbyterian church.
(Draw a line under the one applicable)

Intelligence test given? ___ Name test and by whom administered ________ Date ________ Score ________

PUBLIC OR DAY SCHOOL NEAREST HOME TO WHICH APPLICANT IS ELIGIBLE

Name of School Metlakatla Gov. Location: Metlakatla, Alaska (Post Office District County State)

Grades taught to 9th Annual term (Months) ___ Miles from home Local Is transportation furnished? ___

Why does applicant not attend this school? Training at a Boarding School

SCHOOLS FORMERLY ATTENDED

	Name	Place	Years	Grades	Reason for leaving
1.	Metlakatla Government		7	6	to attend bigger school
2.					
3.					
4.					
5.					

Can applicant pay tuition (particularly if high-school graduate, or if applicant for commercial or advanced trade course)? ________

Can applicant pay own transportation? Yes.

If applicant has individual funds state amount and source None

Is applicant eligible for any local, county, or State assistance? (Indicate specific type and estimate amount)? no

What effort has been made to obtain this assistance? ________

*This form also should be used for care of children with special needs -- Deaf☐, Blind☐, Mentally deficient☐, Delinquent☐, In need of boarding home care☐, Mission School☐, Or other (Specify) ________.
In these special cases file 2 copies of each application with Indian Office.

Figure 9-21. Application for Admission to Boarding School of Oswald Willard Booth, 3 Sept. 1946, Metlakatla Alaska Indian Agency, United States Department of the Interior, Office of Indian Affairs; GS 1,030,798.

Figure 9-22. School Census of Indian Children. Afognak, Alaska, 1939-49, United States Department of the Interior, Office of Indian Affairs; GS 1,030,793.

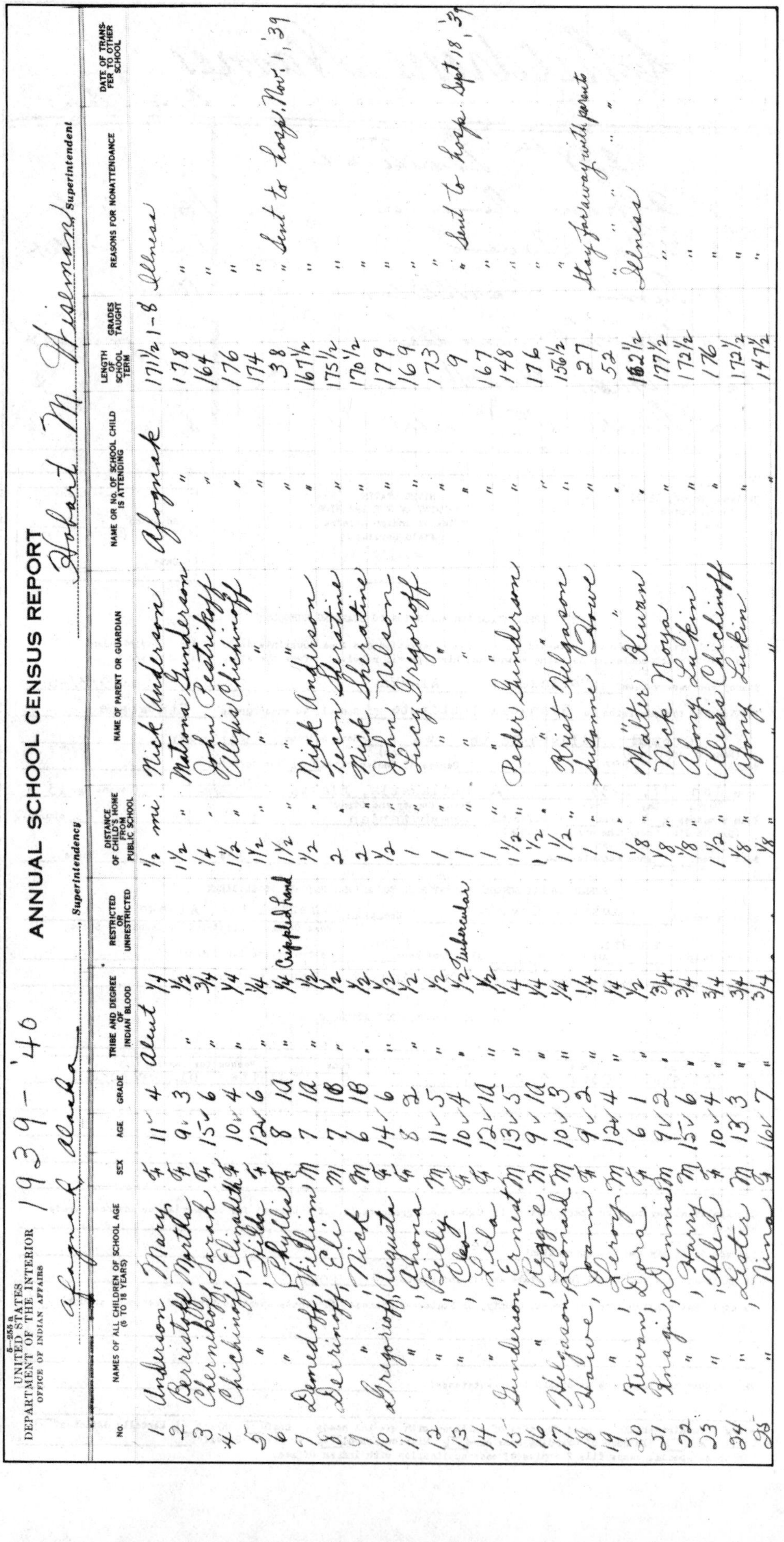

5—255 a
UNITED STATES
DEPARTMENT OF THE INTERIOR
OFFICE OF INDIAN AFFAIRS

1939 - '40

ANNUAL SCHOOL CENSUS REPORT

Afognak, Alaska, Superintendency

Hobart M. Wiseman, Superintendent

No.	Names of all children of school age (6 to 18 years)	Sex	Age	Grade	Tribe and degree of Indian blood		Restricted or unrestricted	Distance of child's home from public school	Name of parent or guardian	Name or No. of school child is attending	Length of school term	Grades taught	Reasons for nonattendance	Date of transfer to other school
1	Anderson, Mary	F	11	4	Aleut	1/4		1/2 mi.	Nick Anderson	Afognak	171½	1-8	Illness	
2	Berristoff, Martha	F	9	3	"	1/2		1½ "	Matrona Gunderson	"	178		"	
3	Chernikoff, Sarah	F	15	6	"	3/4		1/4 "	John Pestrikoff	"	164		"	
4	Chichinoff, Elizabeth	F	10	4	"	1/4		1½ "	Alexis Chichinoff	"	176		"	
5	" , Hilda	F	12	6	"	1/4		1½ "	" "	"	174		"	
6	" , Phyllis	F	8	1A	"	1/4	Crippled hand	1½ "	" "	"	38		" Sent to hosp. Nov. 1, '39	
7	Demedoff, William	M	7	1A	"	1/2		1/2 "	Nick Anderson	"	167½		"	
8	Derrinoff, Eli	M	7	1B	"	1/2		2 "	Lecon Sheratine	"	175½		"	
9	" , Nick	M	6	1B	"	1/2		2 "	Nick Sheratine	"	170½		"	
10	Gregorioff, Augusta	F	14	6	"	1/2		1/2 "	John Nelson	"	179		"	
11	" , Anona	F	8	2	"	1/2		1 "	Lucy Gregorioff	"	169		"	
12	" , Billy	M	11	5	"	1/2		1 "	" "	"	173		"	
13	" , Cleo	F	10	4	"	1/2	Tubercular	1 "	" "	"	9		" Sent to hosp. Sept. 18, '39	
14	" , Lila	F	12	1A	"	1/2		1 "	" "	"	167		"	
15	Gunderson, Ernest	M	13	5	"	1/4		1½ "	Peder Gunderson	"	148		"	
16	" , Reggie	M	9	1A	"	1/4		1½ "	" "	"	176		"	
17	Helgason, Leonard	M	10	3	"	1/4		1½ "	Krist Helgason	"	156½		"	
18	Howe, Joann	F	9	2	"	1/4		1 "	Susanne Howe	"	27		Stay far away with parents	
19	" , Leroy	M	12	4	"	1/4		1 "	" "	"	52		" " " "	
20	Kewan, Dora	F	6	1	"	1/2		1/8 "	Walter Kewan	"	162½		Illness	
21	Knagin, Dennis	M	9	2	"	3/4		1/8 "	Nick Noya	"	177½		"	
22	" , Harry	M	15	6	"	3/4		1/8 "	Afony Lukin	"	172½		"	
23	" , Helen	F	10	4	"	3/4		1½ "	Alexis Chichinoff	"	176		"	
24	" , Lester	M	13	3	"	3/4		1/8 "	Afony Lukin	"	172½		"	
25	" , Nina	F	16	7	"	3/4		1/8 "	" "	"	147½		"	

submitted to the Department of Interior Office of Indian Affairs.

The Office of Indian Affairs also compiled school censuses of Indian children taken at the town and county levels throughout the United States at one time or another but without any predictable format or consistency. The 1939-49 census of the Indian children on the Afognak, Alaska, reservation is shown in Figure 9-22. See Chapter 4, "Census Records," for further information about school censuses.

University and college records are excellent sources of genealogical information compared to early primary school records. Records document admission, registration, course of study, and graduation. Additionally, many alumni associations and school archivists have compiled biographies and histories of former students. Many schools have preserved applications for admission containing valuable family information. Yearbooks and annuals are on file with alumni associations and in college and university libraries.

Many colleges, universities, prep schools, and boarding schools have directories, while listings of local primary schools are difficult to locate and usually pertain only to a specific area. County histories often mention the early county schools and sometimes list students of a particular graduating year. Local or state historical societies may also have information about the area's early schools.

Modern school records are protected by privacy laws, but family members are sometimes able to obtain the information or photocopies of the documents in the files. Because state, local, and school policies govern the availability of school records, you should write to the local school of interest to determine what procedure to follow.

Early school records may be located in the archives of the present school district, in the office of the city, town, or county clerk, in local or state libraries and/or in local or state archives or historical societies. Ask the local school board where records are presently deposited.

Orphanage Records

Orphanages, dating from the seventeenth century in England, were originally workhouses, poorhouses, and asylums. The orphanages of today hardly resemble those depicted by Charles Dickens, but their purpose is the same – to provide refuge for the orphaned or abandoned child. Such institutions in the United States have existed for at least two centuries, operated by civil authorities, religious groups, and private benefactors. The types of records kept vary and are often difficult to locate.

During the early history of the United States, town and county officials appointed or elected overseers of the poor to deal with paupers and orphaned children. Local courts usually appointed guardians to care for orphans who might be heirs to property. When relatives or local residents were unwilling or unable to care for the child, he/she, if old enough, was bound out to learn a trade. If the child was too young, he/she was sent to an institution, usually maintained on a local level. County court records or probate records give the date the child was apprenticed, to whom, and the trade to be learned. These are often indexed under "orphans," "apprentices," or "paupers" in court indexes and dockets. For example, the Overseer of the Poor of Ohio County, Indiana made this report and financial accounting in May, 1827:

> May Term 1827
>
> And now at this time comes Alexander Dale Overseer of the Poor in and for Harrison Township in Ohio County and exhibits an account of Monies by him Received of Wilkerson McCarty Administrator of the Estate of Samuel McCarty Deceased, which the said Administrator States is the Sum which was coming to Nancy Smith (Now a pauper of said Harrison Township) as one of the Heirs at Law of the said Decedent amounting to Twenty-two Dollars and Ninety Cents $22.90. Out of which Sum of $22.90 it appears he (Dale) has paid to Eleazur Carver the Sum of Sixteen Dollars and Ninety Three ¾ cents for keeping said pauper the Last half of the Year ending on the first Monday of May 1827 it being the full of the balance due said Carver for keeping the said pauper the year aforesaid. Leaving in the hands of the said Alexander Dale Overseer as aforesaid the Sum of Five Dollars and Ninety Seven Cents.
>
> Aside he (Dale) also exhibits an account against the County for Services by him rendered as Overseer afsd as follows towit:
>
> | | |
> |---|---|
> | To Tending court one day with Carver | $1.00 |
> | To Binding out a poor boy to the Cabinet making business | 1.00 |
> | To Advertising and letting out Nancy Smith pauper aforesd for 1827 | 2.00 |
> | For making report of Sale to Clerk | 1.00 |
> | For going to Carver's to see pauper and settling with him for keeping pauper one year, the half of his pay | 1.00 |
> | Amounting in the whole to the sum of | $6.00 |
>
> Which account of Six Dollars is allowed by the Board for the Services aforesaid. And the said Overseer agrees to retain and keep in his hands the aforesaid Five Dollars & Ninety Seven Cents in full satisfaction of the aforesaid Charge against the County to Six Dollars which is approved by the Board.[1]

Orphanages maintained by state and local governments were funded agencies that maintained better records than private and church agencies. Their files usually include the child's name, age or date of birth, birthplace, date of admission, names of parents, birthplace of parents, name and residence of nearest kin, date of discharge, to whom indentured and when, whether the child was orphaned or abandoned, and any remarks. These records are available at the orphanage if it is still in operation. Otherwise, the records of a state-operated establishment may be with the state archivist or state's Department of Social and Welfare Services. Write to both offices to insure that you have identified and obtained all existing records. Records of closed orphanages operated below the state level may be deposited with the town, city, or county clerk, the local agency responsible for currently operating orphanages, or a local historical society or research library. Some records may still be in possession of the families of institution officials.

Orphanages operated by religious groups and private benefactors kept records similar to those of government-operated orphanages. The Vine Street Orphan's [*sic*] Home of Chattanooga, Tennessee, operated by the Women's Christian Association of Chattanooga, maintained excellent records, including a diary of the home, lists of subscribers, names and ages of children there, matron's reports, secretary's reports, minutes of the Women's Christian Association meetings, and manager's books and journal between 1879 and 1903.

Figure 9-23 is a page from the matron's report dated 30 May 1887. It notes which children were placed with families ("Laura Henry taken from the Home by Mrs. DeGrummond May 10th.") and also their retrieval ("Martha Bennett taken from Dr. Hall May 16th on account of ill useage by them.").

The Applications for Children record book provides more information on placement. Sometime between her admission in May 1887 and an entry dated December 1888, Laura Henry's grandmother asked for custody but "investigation showed her to be unworthy." Another child, Frankie Tipton, was adopted by an F. McCullum family of Wilmington, Ohio, in December 1888.

The minutes of board meetings also contain valuable information. The August 1887 minutes report that Jennie Davis, who had left two children with the home two or three years, had remarried a man named Holmes, and they had a child of their own. She "intends applying for them," and her husband "prefers a request for the two children. He represents himself as their father. Decided to let them have the one in the Home," but the second, in "a good home with Mrs. Frank George. . .would be left there at least for the present."

---

[1]County Commissioners' Minutes, Book B, Fayette County, Indiana, May Term 1827; typescript courtesy of Arlene H. Eakle, The Genealogical Institute, Salt Lake City, Utah.

The manager's books contain administrative information about employee salaries, statistics, health and financial reports, and other information unrelated to a specific orphan.

A much briefer and more formal record, the 1876 Register of the Jewish Foster Home and Orphan Asylum in Philadelphia (Figure 9-24), gives the child's name, age, admission date, birthplace, names and birthplaces of parents, closest kin and address, date of discharge, indenturing, and trade. This register does not explain the circumstances surrounding the child's placement in the home, but most records do.

The early records of nongovernment-operated orphanages no longer in existence may be difficult to locate. If the orphanage is or was operated by a religious group, the records may be at its headquarters. The Catholic Church, which operated the largest number of nongovernmental orphanages in metropolitan cities, usually maintains a diocesan archives. State and local historical societies may have some early orphanage records, university libraries are anxious to get them, and many are in possession of families of institution officials. Check NUCMC under name of institution, names of officials, and localities where orphanages existed.

Problems with using orphanage records include legibility, availability, damage, and determining location. Court records sometimes can be substituted for incomplete or nonexistent orphanage records.

The information found in orphanage records can be critically important. The Vine Street matron's report of 30 May 1887 notes that Alice Moore was "taken by Mrs. Day, Ringold, Georgia." Unless family records reflect her transfer to the Day household in Georgia, the researcher might spend endless hours searching Chattanooga records for her. If her name was changed to Day, it might be impossible to trace her parents without the orphanage link to Moore.

Hospital and Medical Records

Hospital and physicians' medical records are also excellent sources of genealogical information. However, as confidential documents, they are difficult to obtain and are often not made available even to immediate family members. Some hospital records from the nineteenth century have been released and microfilmed by the Genealogical Society of Utah, including the early records of the St. Louis City Hospital, which are fairly representative of the content in most records of this period. Figure 9-25 shows a page from the St. Louis City Hospital register in 1860.

Normally, early hospital registers will tell you the patient's name, age, birthplace, date of admission, illness or disease, and date of discharge or death. Some records, are, however, less informative.

In addition to registers, hospitals maintained early death records such as those compiled by the Almshouse Hospital in Philadelphia in 1893. (Figure 9-26) The information on death records varies from hospital to hospital, but almost always you can expect to find the

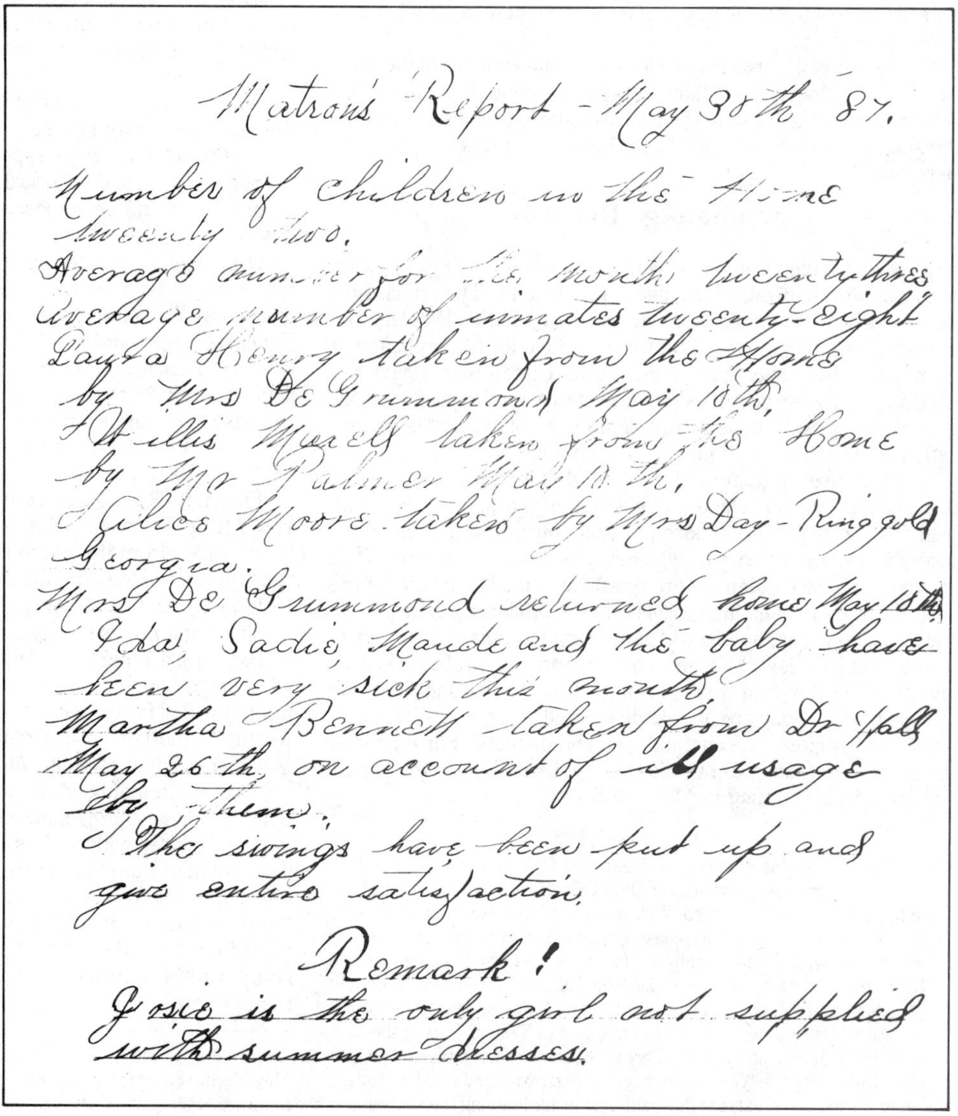

Figure 9-23. Matron's Report – Vine Street Orphan's Home, Chattanooga, Tennessee, 30 May 1887; GS 987,757.

Matron's Report - May 30th 87.

Number of children in the Home twenty two.
Average number for the month twenty three
Average number of inmates twenty-eight
Laura Henry taken from the Home by Mrs De Grummond May 10th,
Willis Merell taken from the Home by Mr Palmer May 11th,
Alice Moore taken by Mrs Day-Ringgold Georgia.
Mrs De Grummond returned home May 18th,
Ida, Sadie, Maude and the baby have been very sick this month
Martha Bennett taken from Dr Hall May 26th, on account of ill usage by them.
The swings have been put up and give entire satisfaction.

Remark!

Josie is the only girl not supplied with summer dresses.

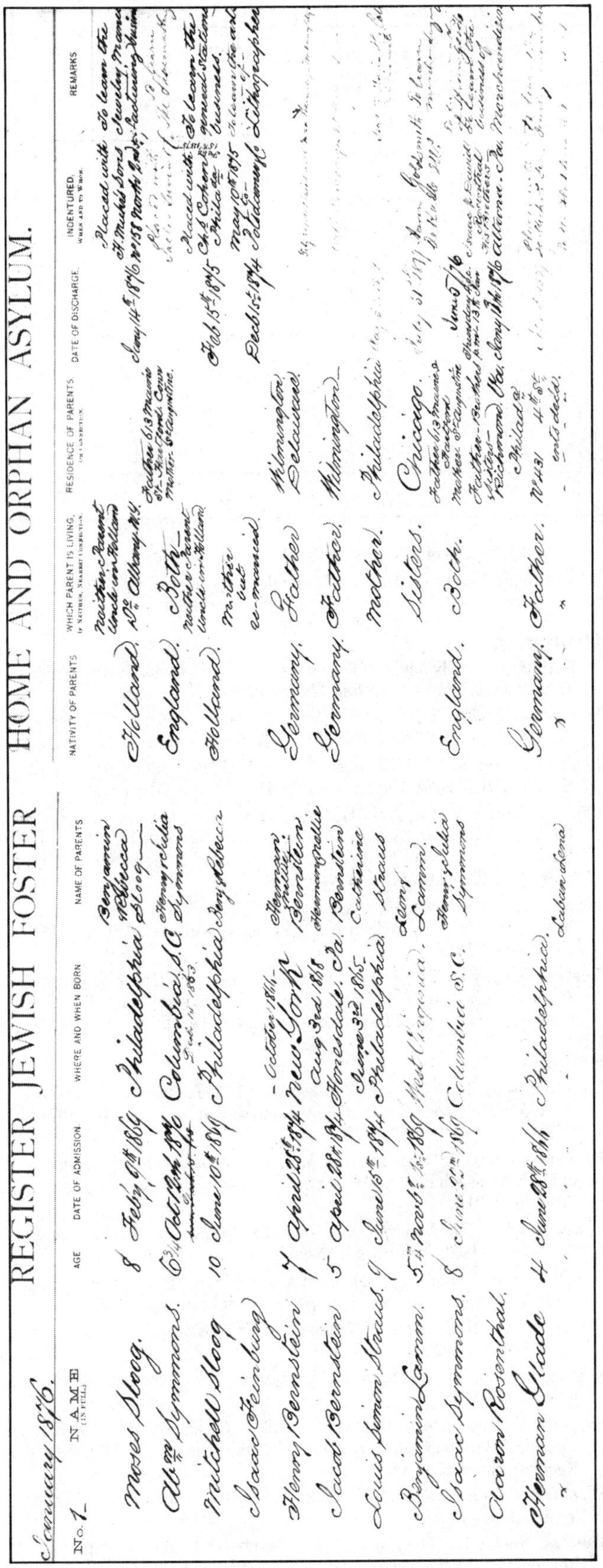

Figure 9-24. Register Jewish Foster Home and Orphan Asylum, 1876-1911, Philadelphia, Pennsylvania, Jan. 1876, pp. 1-2; GS 1,013,425, item 3.

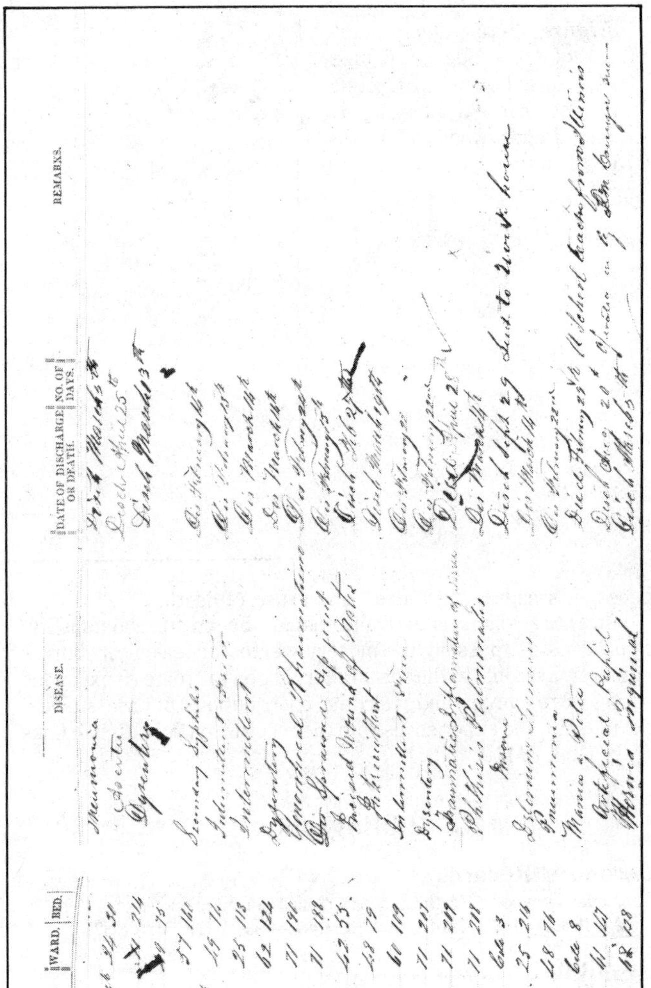

Figure 9-25. Register, St. Louis City Hospital, 1860; GS 980,610.

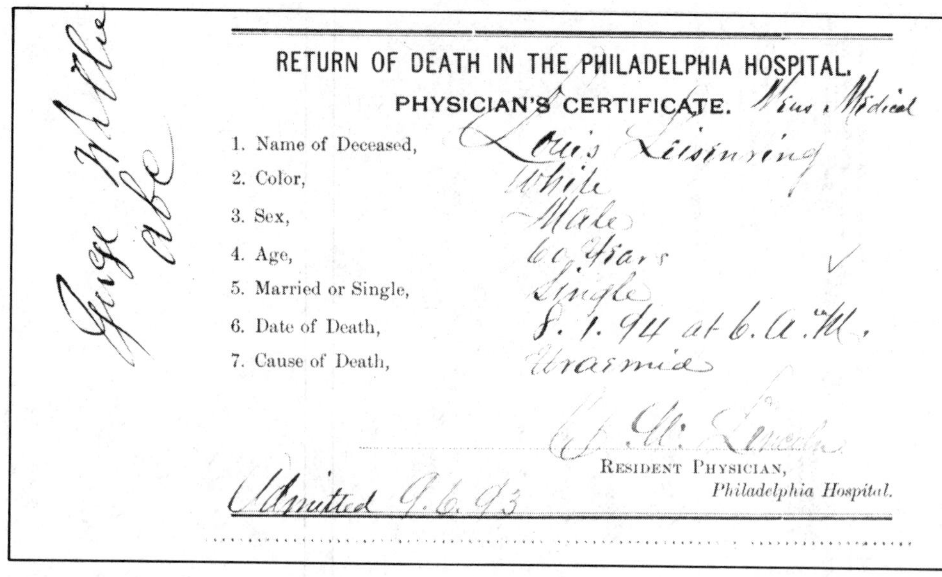

RETURN OF DEATH IN THE PHILADELPHIA HOSPITAL.

PHYSICIAN'S CERTIFICATE.

1. Name of Deceased,
2. Color, White
3. Sex, Male
4. Age, 66 Years
5. Married or Single, Single
6. Date of Death, 8. 1. 94 at 6. A. M.
7. Cause of Death, Uraemia

Resident Physician,
Philadelphia Hospital.

Admitted 9. 6. 93

Figure 9-26. Death Certificate of Annie Spence, 6 June 1894, Almshouse Hospital, Bureau of Charities, Philadelphia County, Pennsylvania, p. 1; GS 975,748, item 1.

deceased's name, death date, and cause of death.

An entire volume could – and should – be written about institutional records, possibly the most neglected genealogical sources currently available to the researcher. I hope to create an expanded listing of resources and welcome contributions of case studies, documents, and experiences with the records to Box 417, Salt Lake City, Utah 84110.

Bibliography

Coroners' Records

Roebuck, Haywood. "North Carolina Colonial Coroners' Inquests, 1738-75." *North Carolina Genealogical Society Journal* 1 (1975): 11-37.

Hospitals

Clay, Robert Y. "Patients in the Hospital at Williamsburg, 1800-37." *Virginia Genealogist* 24 (1980): 23-28, 90-94.

"Continental Hospital Returns." *Pennsylvania Magazine of History and Biography* 23 (1899): 35-50.

Gilliam, Charles Edgar. "Mount Malado." *Tyler's Quarterly* 20 (1938-39): 138-42, 250. Virginia's earliest hospital.

Hunter, Robert J. "The Origins of the Philadelphia General Hospital." *Pennsylvania Magazine of History and Biography* 57 (1933): 32-57.

New York Down-State Medical Center. *History of Long Island College Hospital: Alumni Association Highlights, 1880-1955 and Biographies of Graduates, 1900-1955.* New York: New York Alumni Association, 1961.

Johns, Frank S. and Anne Page. "Chimborazo Hospital and J. B. McCaw, Surgeon in Chief." *Virginia Magazine of History and Biography* 62 (1954): 190-200. Excellent description of Revolutionary War hospital records with examples and locations.

Jordan, John W. "Military Hospital at Bethlehem and Lititz during the Revolution." *Pennsylvania Magazine of History and Biography* 20 (1896): 137-57. Undocumented account with patient lists.

Kelner, Joseph. "Examination of Hospital Records." *Case and Comment* 84 (1979): 51-54. Describes access to modern records.

Larrabee, Eric. *The Benevolent and Necessary Institution: New York Hospital, 1771-1971.* Garden City, N.Y.: Doubleday, 1971.

Uppedegraff, Marie. *The Story of Stamford Hospital, 1896-1971.* Stamford, Conn.: Stamford Hospital, 1971.

Williams, William H. "The Industrious Poor and the Founding of the Pennsylvania Hospital." *Pennsylvania Magazine of History and Biography* 97 (1973): 431-43. Established 1751.

Morticians

Elder, Charlotte DeVolt. "New Englanders in the Mortuary Records of Savannah, Georgia." *New England Historic and Genealogical Register* 125 (1971): 28-44. Covers 1803-22.

"Undertakers Records," *Maryland Genealogical Bulletin*, vols. 20 (1979), 21 (1980).

Orphanages

Fink, Arthur E. "Changing Philosophies and Practices in North Carolina Orphanages." *North Carolina Historical Review* 48 (1971).

Harland, Thomas. "Of Franklin, Whitfield, and the Orphans." *Georgia Historical Quarterly* 29 (1945): 201-16. Bethesda Orphanage in Georgia.

Jones, Newton B. "The Charleston Orphan House, 1860-1876." *South Carolina Historical Magazine* 62 (1961): 203-14. Organized 1790.

Langson, Miriam Z. *Children West: A History of the Placing-out System of the New York Children's Aid Society, 1853-1896.* Madison: State Historical Society of Wisconsin, 1964. Describes records for one of the most important social institutions in New York City.

Pickett, Robert S. *House of Refuge: Origins of Juvenile Reform in New York State, 1815-1857.* Syracuse, N.Y.: Syracuse University Press, 1969. Established 1825.

Teeters, Negley K. "The Early Days of the Philadelphia House of Refuge." *Pennsylvania History* 27 (1960): 165-87. Established 1828. Based on minutes of the Board of Inspectors, journals, and daybooks of the house.

Prisons

Carleton, Mark T. *Politics and Punishment: The History of the Louisiana State Penal System.* Baton Rouge: Louisiana State University Press, 1971.

Haskins, George L. "Ecclesiastical Antecedents of Criminal Punishment in Early Massachusetts." *Massachusetts Historical Society Proceedings* 72 (1963): 21ff.

Lewis, Orland F. *The Development of American Prisons and Prison Customs, 1776-1845.* 1922; reprint ed., New York: Arno Press, 1962.

New York State Temporary State Committee of Investigation. *County Jails and Penitentiaries in New York State.* Albany: n. pub., 1966.

Phelps, Richard H. *A History of Newgate [Prison] of Connecticut.* New York: Arno Press, 1969.

Reynolds, John. *Recollections of Windsor Prison [Vermont].* Boston: n. pub., 1839.

Shepard, William. "Records from Old Jail at Cumberland Courthouse, Virginia." *William and Mary Quarterly*, 2nd series, 12 (1932): 39-40. Records dated 1782-86.

Sing Sing: The View Within. New York: Winter House, 1972. Photos taken by inmates.

Teeters, Negley K. "The Early Days of the Eastern State Penitentiary at Philadelphia." *Pennsylvania History* 16 (1949): 261-302.

Schools

Ambler, Charles H. "Poor Relief Education, 1818-1847." *West Virginia History* 3 (1941-42): 285-304. Based on school records transferred from the courthouse in Kanawha County to West Virginia University, Morgantown.

Andrews, Edward D. "The County Grammar Schools and Academies of Vermont." *Vermont Historical Society Proceedings*, Sept. 1936, pp. 174ff.

Finkelstein, Barbara J. "Schooling and Schoolteachers: Selected Bibliography of Autobiographies in the Nineteenth Century." *History of Education Quarterly* 14 (1974): 293-300. Important bibliography.

Fuller, Wayne E. *The Old Country School: The Story of Rural Education in the Middle West* (Chicago: University of Chicago Press, 1982. Includes description of the records.

Gersman, Elinor M. "A Bibliography for Historians of Education: Historical Perspectives on the Educational Experience in the United States." *History of Education Quarterly* 14 (1974): 279-92.

Hogue, Arthur R. "The Record of an Indiana School District, 1837-1844." *Indiana Magazine of History* 48 (1952): 185-92.

Index to Georgia Poor-School and Academy Records, 1826-1850. Atlanta: R. J. Taylor, Jr., Foundation, 1980. Records include lists of children with names, ages, school attendance, records of parents, and tuition payments.

McMahon, Clara R. P. "A Note on the Free School Idea in Colonial Maryland." *Maryland Historical Magazine* 54 (1959): 149-52.

Morison, Samuel Eliot. *The Founding of Harvard College*. Cambridge: Harvard University Press, 1935. Excellent description of the records kept by a university. Alumni registers for many original universities in the United States have been published and will be found in major research libraries.

"Records of Pennsylvania School Children, 1802-1809," *National Genealogical Society Quarterly* 50 (1962): 78. Tax lists included school-age children with their ages.

Sloane, Eric. *The Little Red Schoolhouse: A Sketchbook of Early American Education*. Garden City, N.Y.: Doubleday, 1972.

Staubo, Merete. *History of the Council of School Superintendents, Cities and Villages of the State of New York, 1883-1967*. Ithaca, New York: Cornell University Press, 1971.

INFORMATION GUIDE

Genealogical Information in the Record Group	*Apprenticeship*	*Account Books*	*Insurance*	*Credit Reports*	*Poor Law*	*Personnel*
Surname/name	●	●	●	●	●	●
Date of Birth			●			
Place of Birth	●		●			●
Sex	●	●	●		●	●
Race/color			●			●
Physical Description	●		●		●	●
Occupation	●		●	●		●
Education						●
Military Service						●
Slave Status	●					
Property Owned				●	●	
Religion					●	
Citizenship						
Marital Status		●	●		●	●
Spouse's Name		●	●		●	●
Children's Names			●		●	●
Father's Name	●				●	
Mother's Name	●				●	
Father's Birthplace						
Mother's Birthplace						
Date of Death		●	●		●	●
Cause of Death			●			
Name of Cemetery						
Residence	●	●	●	●	●	●
Age	●		●	●	●	●
Literacy/signature	●		●			●
Photograph/sketch			●			●
Relatives			●			●
Social Security No.			●			●

COULD YOU USE THIS CHAPTER?

Type of Record	*Kept from*	*Clues That You Should Consult These Records*
Indenture/ apprentice	All periods	Has your family preserved any tradition that a given ancestor learned his/her trade as an apprentice? Children as young as seven or eight were apprenticed, even those who had two living parents. It was also common for orphans to be "bound" by magistrates to insure that they would be taken care of, not become public charges, and learn a useful trade. Indentures, a somewhat similar system, resembled apprenticeships and would be most interesting if an immigrant ancestor thus arranged to pay for his/her passage to the New World.
Account books	All periods	If you can locate your ancestor in a given community, whether large or small, for a period of time, it is worthwhile to check for surviving business records, particularly during the colonial period when other records are sparse. Businesses kept track of customers and services in account ledgers that have been preserved, thus enabling you to locate your family in time and place, reconstructing some of the family background. Some include deathdates, relationships, places of origin, and other essential information.
Insurance records	Mainly after 1840	If family traditions mention a life insurance policy or if records of payment or old certificates hint at the existence of one, it is worthwhile to check insurance companies. Generally these records are detailed and companies have preserved them for a long time. If your ancestor lived in Chicago (1871), San Francisco (1906), or other city during a major fire or disaster, always check. These events almost bankrupted even large insurance companies in the East.
Credit reports	1840 to present	If your ancestor had a business of his/her own, even though it was small, records of its activities might be printed in likely places like county or local histories and referenced in unlikely places like credit reporting agency files (R.G. Dun's ledgers – 2,580 volumes arranged by county – date from the 1840s).
Employee records	About 1750 to present	If your ancestor did not own his/her own business, employee records can help round out a life story. City and county directories frequently identify those listed by occupation or profession; labor union records, and Social Security records provide otherwise unavailable birth data for persons born as early as the 1850s. Business records of modern small businesses and large corporations are also available. Many large businesses go back well over fifty years and many small businesses, established before 1800, as you trace their history, later merged with larger ones and their records have been preserved along with those of company "descendants." This chapter explains how to find such records and access them whether they are in private hands or public repositories.

Chapter 10

BUSINESS AND EMPLOYMENT RECORDS

Kory L. Meyerink

This chapter discusses a class of records usually overlooked by genealogists even though they often reveal as much or more than such standard sources as censuses and death certificates. These sources are business and employment records. Businesses have had customers since at least the first mill was built to grind grain or saw wood, and a surprising number of employer-employee or buyer-seller records were kept and have survived. When we remember that many vital events were not always recorded by the family and official records were not required by some states until after 1900, the value of business and employment records which predate many standard genealogical records becomes evident.

The most common objection to using business records is our image of rural America, composed largely of farmers until the last generation or so. The six American great-grandfathers of my own children included three farmers living in the western states, a painter in Chicago and western Montana, a physician in Manhattan, and a coal and grain merchant in western Massachusetts. All of them lived from about the 1850s to the 1930s, and Andrew Sticht (born 1860), the painter, was a classic research "dead end." Using the family tradition from a carved box that his father—whose name wasn't even known—was a cabinetmaker in New York City was enough clue to lead back two more generations to the immigrant ancestor.

Another great-grandfather, Francis Cromwell, was reportedly born in a town called Woodstock, but not even the state was specified. We found a pension application for Civil War service, but the information on it turned out to be false. A photograph of his mother, however, had the photographer's name and town of Woodstock on the back of the photograph. This business record, the photograph, led us to the Canadian province of Ontario, where the only Woodstock large enough to have a photographer in the 1860s was located. Francis was a farmer, not a businessman or a business employee. Thus, even for our farmer ancestors, business records are relevant.

As evidence of the first point, it is not well known that by 1880 more than half of the population had nonfarming occupations.[1] A breakdown by profession shows that agriculture was outnumbered by the combination of manufacturing and trades by 1910.[2]

The value of employment records is especially apparent for immigrant ancestors, many of whom settled in large cities where the nation's largest businesses were also typically located. See Chapter 16 for information on city research.

However, using these records can pose challenges. You must know your ancestor's location and profession. Many records no longer exist. Of those that do, some are much more complete than others, including birthplace, residence (previous and concurrent to the employment), relatives and family members, education level, and employment history. Some businesses are no longer extant, and tracking down their records becomes a challenge. Almost none of the records are indexed. Many are stored in locations that make consulting them very difficult, and many have been destroyed or lost through the years. Still, the kind of information and breakthrough possibilities mean that business records simply cannot be overlooked.

Determining an ancestor's profession begins with home and family sources, obituaries and census, probate or perhaps property records. (See the chapters on those topics in this volume.) City directories, even in small towns, often include the employer's name in the listings. If all else fails, you should search local histories to learn who major employers were in that area for the relevant time period.

Probably your ancestor did not work for the same employer his/her entire lifetime. Give priority to the records of the company where he/she worked longest or to the most recent employer, since recent records are typically more complete. Other suggestions for locating pertinent records occur throughout the chapter.

Most of this chapter will deal with the specific types of records in each historical period and how to locate them, followed by a bibliography. Generally, the records fall into three time frames: colonial (to about 1780), early American (about 1780 to 1870), and modern American (about 1870 to the present). Records which fall into one or more time periods are fully described in the era where they are most helpful.

Colonial Business and Employment Records

The predominance of farming as employment naturally curtails the number of original business and employment records in this time period. Also, the hazards of the intervening 200 years limit surviving documents. But the 10 to 20 percent of the colonial population involved in nonfarming activites often recorded their transactions with the rest of the population. Virtually all tradesmen had apprentices with whom they had formal written agreements. Most farmers bought some supplies or had their grain milled and lumber sawn. Often this was a credit arrangement, recorded by the tradesman in an account book. Schoolteachers charged for their services, and some kept records. Careful searching of these kinds of documents in the years before 1780 can yield important facts.

Apprentice Records

The Old World system of indenturing apprentices to learn a trade was one of the first imports to America. In colonial days most apprentices were boys in their teens, often younger than fourteen. The agreement (often called an indenture) was signed by the master as well as the parent or guardian of the boy.[3] The trades were often family businesses, and many fathers formally took their sons as apprentices. (Paul Revere learned the silversmith trade from his father, and Benjamin Franklin was indentured as a printer to his brother James.)

Since apprentices were usually bound until they were twenty-one, the length of the indenture specified in the document gives an excellent indication of a boy's age. If a boy was bound to his master for twelve years and five months, the boy was probably about eight and a half years old when the indenture was signed.

In New England it was not uncommon, especially among poorer families, for children under ten to be bound out. This 1676 indenture illustrates the kinds of genealogical and historical information available in such records:

> This Indenture witnesseth that I, Nathan Knight, sometime of Black Point, with the consent of my father-in-law, Harry Brooken and Elend, his wife, have put myself apprentice to Samuel Whidden, of Portsmouth, in the county of Portsmouth, mason, and bound after the manner of an apprentice with him, to serve and abide the full space and term of twelve years and five months, thence next following, to be full, complete and ended; during which time the said apprentice his said master faithfully shall serve, his lawful secrets shall keep, and commands shall gladly do, damage unto his said master he shall not do, nor see to be done of others, but to the best of his power shall give timely notice thereof to his said master. Fornication he shall not commit, nor contract matrimony within the said time. The goods of his said master, he shall not spend or lend. He shall not play cards, or dice, or any other unlawful game, whereby his said master may have damage in his own goods, or others, taverns, he shall not haunt, nor from his master's business absent himself by day or by night, but in all things shall behave himself as a faithful apprentice ought to do. And the said master his said apprentice shall teach and instruct, or cause to be taught and instructed in the art and mystery as mason; finding unto his said apprentice during the said time meat, drink, washing, lodging, and apparel, fitting an apprentice, teaching him to read, and allowing him three months towards the latter end of his time to go to school to write, and also double apparel at end of said time. As witness our hands and seals, interchangeably put to two instruments of the same purpose, November the twenty-fifth, one thousand six hundred and seventy-six.[4]

An indenture from 1807 is shown in Figure 10-1 as it appears in the Pilot Indentures book for the Port of Philadelphia. The text includes the full name of the boy and both parents, as well as his exact age and residence (which was not in Pennsylvania). The conditions of the apprenticeship are also interesting.

If your ancestor was a tradesman, seeking out his apprenticeship could provide a wealth of information.

Other Indenture Records

The word *indenture* means to bind one person to another for a given period of time in payment for some service. The most common type of indenture was probably that used to pay for passage to America. Many former prisoners from England, indentured as servants for a number of years to pay for their passage, settled in the Southern states. In other cases, children were bound out to help earn money for a family or so daughters could learn "housewifry."

Figure 10-2 from the Philadelphia Mayor's Office, Records of Indentures, shows several different types of indentures and the kinds of information included in each.

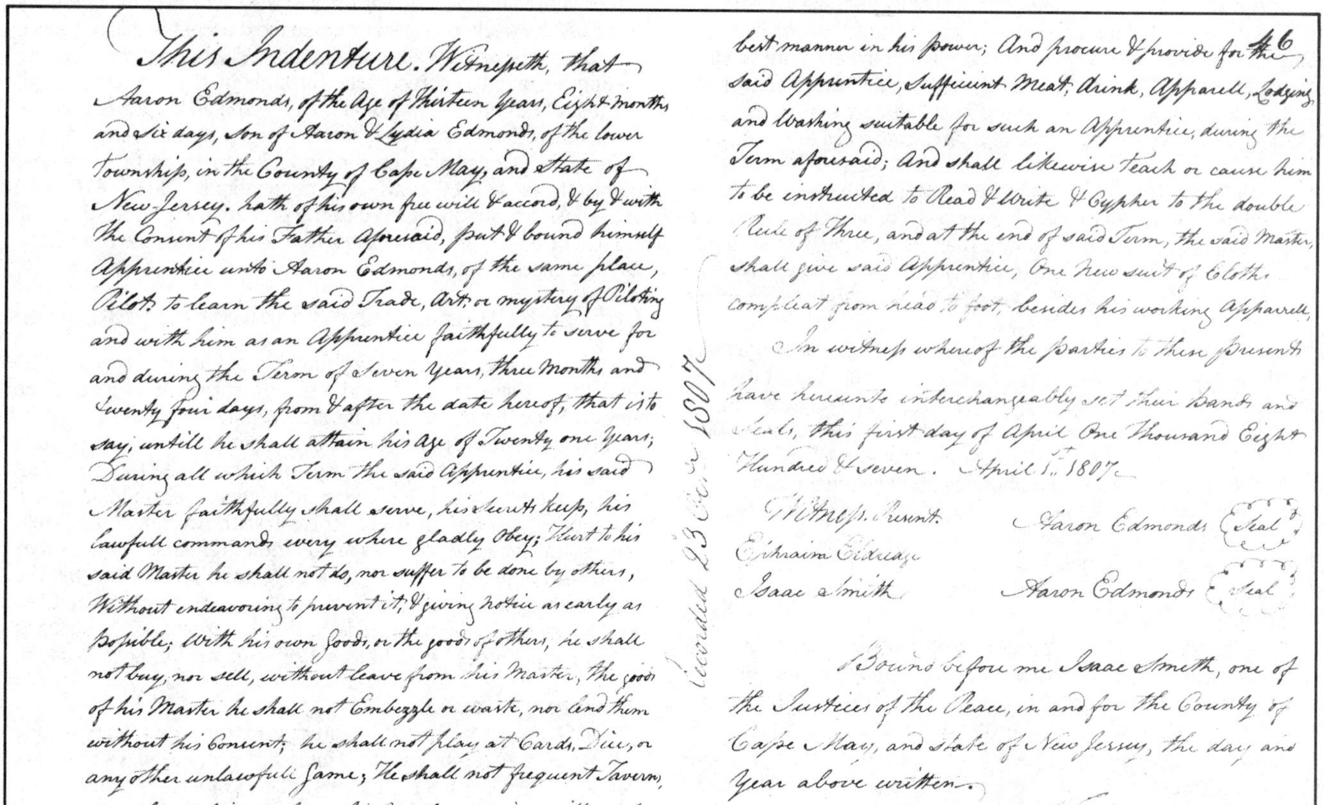

Figure 10-1. Indenture of Aaron Edmonds to Aaron Edmonds, 23 Oct. 1807, Port of Philadelphia, Pa.; Pilot Indenture 1806-15, p. 45; Genealogical Society of Utah (hereafter GS) microfilm 1,018,398, item 2.

This Indenture. Witnesseth, that Aaron Edmonds, of the Age of Thirteen Years, Eight Months, and Six days, Son of Aaron & Lydia Edmonds, of the lower Township, in the County of Cape May, and State of New-Jersey. hath of his own free will & accord, & by & with the Consent of his Father aforesaid, put & bound himself Apprentice unto Aaron Edmonds, of the same place, Pilot. to learn the said Trade, Art, or mystery of Piloting and with him as an Apprentice faithfully to serve for and during the Term of Seven Years, three Months and twenty four days, from & after the date hereof, that is to say, untill he shall attain his Age of Twenty one Years; During all which Term the said Apprentice, his said Master faithfully shall serve, his Secrets keep, his lawfull commands every where gladly Obey; Hurt to his said Master he shall not do, nor suffer to be done by others, Without endeavouring to prevent it, & giving notice as early as possible; With his own Goods, or the goods of others, he shall not buy, nor sell, without leave from his Master, The goods of his Master he shall not Embezzle or waste, nor lend them without his Consent; he shall not play at Cards, Dice, or any other unlawfull Game; He shall not frequent Taverns, nor absent himself from his Masters service, without his Leave; He shall not commit Fornication, nor contract Matrimony, within said Term; But in all things behave himself as a good & faithfull Apprentice toward his said Master, & all that are his, during the said Term; And the said Aaron Edmonds shall & will teach & cause the said Apprentice to be taught & Instructed in the Art & Mystery of Piloting, in the Bay & River Delaware, after the best

46

best manner in his power; And procure & provide for the said Apprentice, Sufficient Meat, drink, Apparell, Lodging, and Washing suitable for such an Apprentice, during the Term aforesaid; And shall likewise teach or cause him to be instructed to Read & Write & Cypher to the double Rule of Three, and at the end of said Term, the said Master shall give said Apprentice, One new suit of Cloths compleat from head to foot, besides his working Apparrell.

In witness whereof the parties to these Presents have hereunto interchangeably set their hands and Seals, this first day of April One Thousand Eight Hundred & seven. April 1st 1807.

Witness Present. Aaron Edmonds (Seal)
Ephraim Eldredge
Isaac Smith Aaron Edmonds (Seal)

Recorded 23 Octr 1807

Bound before me Isaac Smith, one of the Justices of the Peace, in and for the County of Cape May, and state of New Jersey, the day and Year above written.

Isaac Smith

This record shows that Mary Stamper was to learn "Housewifry" and also gives her mother's full name. Since the term of service is seven years, she was probably almost fourteen years old. Mary Barrett was apparently indentured to pay for passage to America as her service lasted only one year, beginning with her arrival in America. The reference to the Mayor of Cork in her indenture is a strong clue about her specific town of residence in Ireland, a necessary fact to know before seeking her Irish records. Jacob Grubb was apparently transferred from the apprenticeship of one cordwainer (shoemaker) to another. (For a list of definitions of older occupations, see Appendix 1 at the end of the chapter.) Mary Barbara Leichtin was bound five years to pay a debt of twenty-one pounds, nine shillings, the cost of her passage from Rotterdam. Such records can provide clues to age, vocation, country of origin, and lines for future research on the homes or businesses where they were to serve. Sometimes the original certificates of indenture still exist as well.

Less formal records of indentures are also valuable. My own research on William Plaskett of Trenton, New Jersey, led me to the New Jersey Archives, which include extracts of newspaper articles published between 1704 and 1780 relative to New Jersey citizens regardless of where the paper was printed. An item extracted from the 17 September 1747 *Pennsylvania Gazette* (printed in Philadelphia) indicated that Plaskett had a bound servant named "Sarah Davis, about 27 years of age, middle stature, somewhat freckled, [who] has a small scar in her forehead, and is slow of speech." A Welshwoman, she had run away on September 11 wearing "a callicoe gown, a black fur hat, shagged on the under side, with a patch on the crown, and an ozenbrigs apron."[5] The clue turned my research to indenture records where I found that Plaskett also had another indentured servant, "Abigail Edwards (a servant from Ireland in the ship Pomona). . .for four years from Sept. 18th 1746, consideration 13 £.: customary dues."[6]

The fact that William Plaskett had at least two servants during the same year (1746-47) indicates his social standing. Even though no new genealogical information was located, these business records contribute important biographical information.

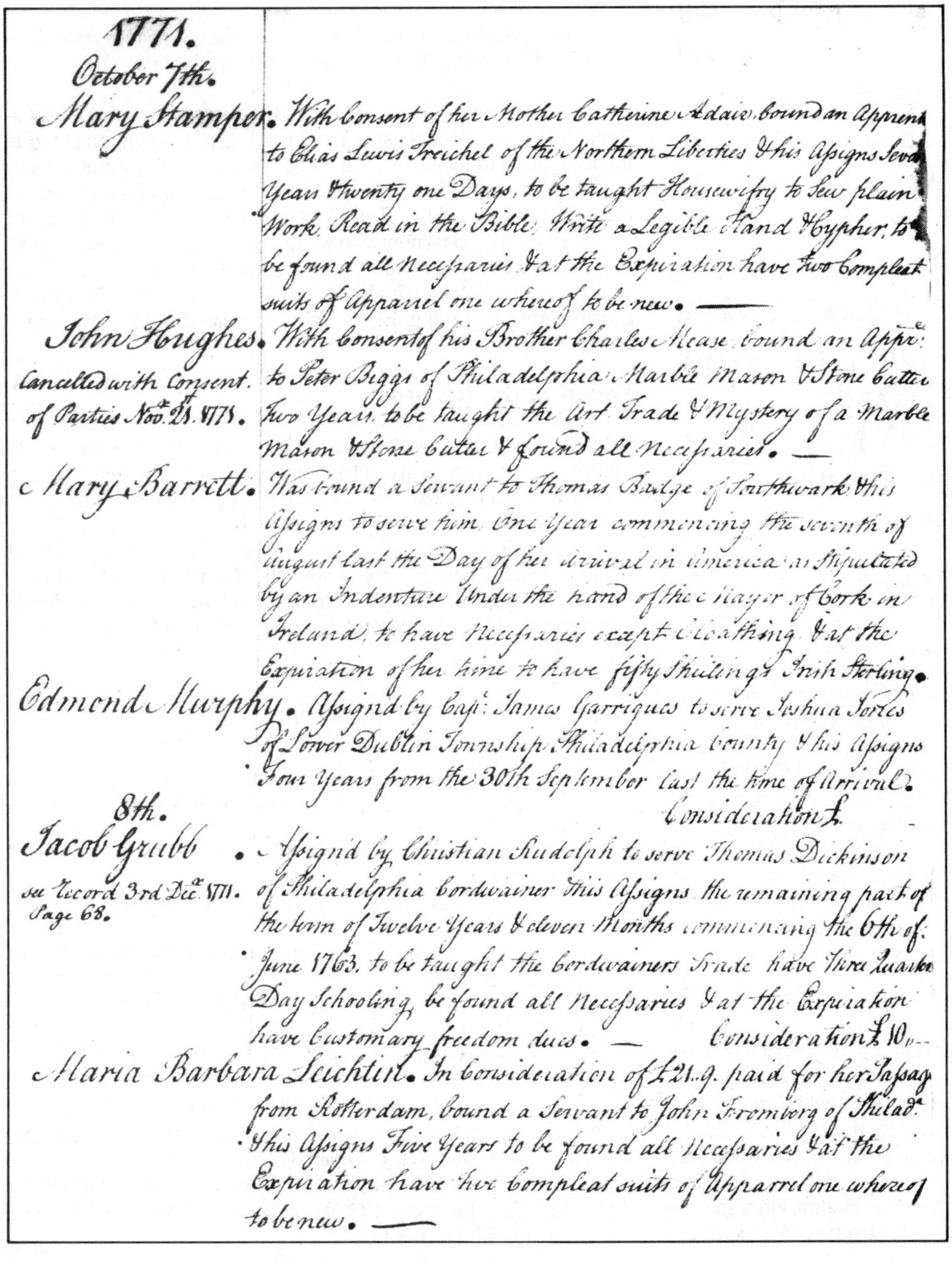

1771.
October 7th.

Mary Stamper. With Consent of her Mother Catherine Adair bound an Appren[tice] to Elias Lewis Treichel of the Northern Liberties & his Assigns Seven Years & twenty one Days, to be taught Housewifry to Sew plain Work, Read in the Bible, Write a Legible Hand & Cypher, to be found all Necessaries & at the Expiration have two Compleat suits of Apparel one whereof to be new. —

John Hughes. With Consent of his Brother Charles Mease bound an Appre: to Peter Biggs of Philadelphia Marble Mason & Stone Cutter Two Years to be taught the Art Trade & Mystery of a Marble Mason & Stone Cutter & found all Necessaries. —
Cancelled with Consent of Parties Nov. 28. 1771.

Mary Barrett. Was bound a Servant to Thomas Badge of Southwark & his Assigns to serve him One Year commencing the seventh of August last the Day of her arrival in America as Stipulated by an Indenture Under the hand of the Mayor of Cork in Ireland, to have Necessaries except Cloathing & at the Expiration of her time to have fifty Shillings Irish Sterling.

Edmond Murphy. Assignd by Capt. James Garrigues to serve Joshua Jones of Lower Dublin Township Philadelphia County & his Assigns Four Years from the 30th September last the time of Arrival. Consideration £ -

8th.

Jacob Grubb. Assignd by Christian Rudolph to serve Thomas Dickinson of Philadelphia Cordwainer & his Assigns the remaining part of the term of Twelve Years & eleven Months commencing the 6th of June 1763, to be taught the Cordwainers Trade have Three Quarters Day Schooling, be found all Necessaries & at the Expiration have Customary freedom dues. — Consideration £10..
see Record 3rd Dec. 1771. Page 68.

Maria Barbara Leichtin. In Consideration of £21..9. paid for her Passage from Rotterdam, bound a Servant to John Fromberg of Philad. & his Assigns Five Years to be found all Necessaries & at the Expiration have two Compleat suits of Apparrel one whereof to be new. —

Figure 10-2. Philadelphia Mayor's Office, Record of Indentures of Redemptioners 1771-73, p. 5, (GS 976,801, item 1).

Account Books

Even if our ancestors did not employ others or run a business, they were dependent on other businesses for some of their daily goods. The most common and genealogically useful records of such early businesses are storekeepers' account books. They seldom record those who paid at the time of purchase. Transactions with friends and relatives may not be recorded in the business ledger, although they show up in personal daybooks and memoranda as well as in probate inventories of assets and debts. These records are often overlooked. This example is from a printed account book where the storekeeper noted family relationships to identify the individuals involved. The *d* means that the goods were delivered to that person and *nr* means "near" or possibly "neighbor."

Addedle (Adedle, Addle), William, June 38-Dec 42, nr Peter Demun of Peapck; d John Brady, Andrew Jones; d to Peter Demun, Samuel Alexander, Jerry Rolandt; paid James Alexander note

Adkinson, *see* Atkinson

Ake, Jacob, Jly 35-Apr 39, son to Jerry; d to Jacob Bodine

Jerry, Jly 36-Sep 39, at the Society, Peter Jarvis nr; d to Jacob Bodine

Akeman (Akerman), John, Jly 42-Jly 43, nr Samuel Alexander

Akerly, Arther, Apr. 35-May 37; & joint account with Obediah Seward

Kenn Stryker-Rodda. "The Janeway Account Books 1735-1746,"*Genealogical Magazine of New Jersey* 33 (Jan.- April 1958): 4.

Another example of the ways these records can be valuable is the account books of John Avery, a schoolmaster in Huntingdon, Long Island, 1763-79, who kept a record for each year the children were taught. (See Figure 10-3.) The Conkling family was a fairly large family in the Huntingdon area, and it is often difficult now to sort out who belongs to whom.[7] Imagine how illuminating the following notations about the various Conkling families would be, especially since children are linked to their parents and they can be definitely located in Huntingdon for the specified years. Although abstracts like these are very useful, other historical (if not genealogical) information may be found in the originals, the locations of which are mentioned in the periodical in which the abstracts appear.

Other Records

Periodically during the colonial period, small companies were formed for various purposes, most frequently to buy land outside the township or to construct a road or a major new building within the town. These companies would formulate policy, elect officers, collect money, and delegate and supervise the work. They also kept records (usually called minutes), some of which survived and have been published. Histories of various occupations in a specific area are another valuable source. Compiled from several sources, they are usually secondary rather than primary sources carefully prepared by professional historians. This example of a silversmith in Staunton, Virginia, is one selection from an excellent book-length study of local professions.

C. E. EVARD & BROTHER opened a "New Jewellery and Watch Establishment" in Staunton in June 1849. There were two persons in the silversmith and jewelry business in this vicinity who might have been the principal in this firm, Charles Eugene Evard of Winchester and Charles Edward Evard of Leesburg. This was undoubtedly the Leesburg jeweler, for the same illustration was used in the advertising in Staunton and Leesburg. The name of the brother is unknown. This firm advertised clocks, watches, and jewelry repaired and warranted at its shop, one door above M. Cushing's Confectionery Store.[1] On July 9, following, the firm had just received from their manufactory a large supply of "silver Table and Tea Spoons, also Dessert and Salt Spoons, Sugar Tongs, Butter Knives, all superior articles and manufactured especially to order. . . . The public generally are informed that the subscribers will sell all kinds of jewellery and spoons much lower than the Baltimore prices."[2] How long this firm continued in business here is not definitely known, but on March 1, 1850 C. E. Evard announced to the public of Leesburg that he had returned to and permanently located himself in Leesburg; so that the firm did business in Staunton not longer than nine months.

George Barton Cutten, *The Silversmiths of Virginia from 1694 to 1850* (Richmond: Diete Press, 1952), p. 172.

See the bibliography at the end of the chapter for other occupational histories. An ancestor need not be exclusively engaged in an occupation to be included in these records. For example, Mary Q. Elliott, *Biographical Sketches of Knox County [Ohio] Writers* (Mount Vernon, Ohio: N.p., 1937), included a brief sketch of James Blair, a local farmer who wrote poems that were occasionally published in local newspapers. The sketch indicated that Blair originally came from Blairs Valley, Washington County, Maryland. Subsequent research in Blairs Valley extended the line two more generations.

Locating the Records

In general, locating business records of the colonial time period is less difficult than working with later records. Most available records are preserved in local or state historical societies. The first place to look is in town records. The local town clerk or historian can help you determine where these records are now. Many historical societies have published detailed guides to their published or unpublished records. For example, the Historical Society of Pennsylvania has approximately 500 volumes of business, professional, and personal account books dated as early as 1676 and covering an impressive range:

COUNT BOOKS, 1676-1904. Approx. 500 vols. Presented by various persons.

Records of miscellaneous business enterprises:

Nehemiah Allen, Philadelphia merchant and cooper, account book, 1698-1736, 1 vol.

Andrews and Meredith, merchants and shippers, invoice book, 1794-95, 1 vol.

Isaac Archer, business and personal receipt book, 1795-1841, 1 vol.

Joséph Archer, engaged in Canton silk, rice, tea trade, letter books, 1833-34, 2 vols.

William Armstrong, merchant and army contractor, receipt book, 1778, 1 vol.

William H. Ashurst, Philadelphia merchant, receipt book, 1839-44, 1 vol.

Aurora, office account book, 1822-24, 2 vols.

Backhouse, Jones and Backhouse, Philadelphia merchants, raccoon and beaver skins, ledger, 1773-75, 1 vol.

Robert and Francis Bailey, Philadelphia printers, day book, 1791-97, waste book, 1794-1829, memorandum book, 1795-1841, journal, 1799-1856, 4 vols.

Robert Baily, Philadelphia liver oil merchant, fish and general merchandise, letter book, 1796-1807, 1 vol.

Abel Baker and William Sill, general merchants, whiskey, shoes, tobacco, muslin, ledger, 1813-15, 1 vol.

Charles H. Baker, account book, 1812, letter book, 1812-13, 2 vols.

John and Samuel Baker, receipt book, 1786-95, 1 vol.

John R. Baker, receipt book, 1824-29, 1 vol.

Guide to the Manuscript Collections of the Historical Society of Pennsylvania, 2nd ed., Phildelphia: Historical Society of Pennsylvania, 1949, item 108.

This Historical Society also has a volume of Philadelphia Insurance Company records (Item 1019 in the *Guide*), Philadelphia Dancing Assembly Records from 1749 (Item 1015) and other business records. "The Descriptive Inventory of the Archives of the City and County of Philadelphia," a looseleaf finding aid updated regularly by the staff, is replete with references to apprenticeship and indenture records, including an indexed volume as early as 1751-87.

Almost every manuscript collection has some kind of guide to indicate its contents. If the collection has been filmed by the Genealogical Society of Utah, it can be found in its catalog under the locality the record deals with and is available on interlibrary loan through its branch offices. Thus, indentures for Spottsylvania County, Virginia, would be found under that county in the catalog. Often records of areas neighboring an ancestor's residence are also helpful.

In New York City, the minutes of the Civil Court Quarter Sessions contain petitions of release from apprentices whose masters had moved from the town. Indenture records of passengers to America are usually in the city where the ship landed, such port cities as Philadelphia, Baltimore, or New York.

Many colonial business records are now in printed form, as some of these examples show. These may include books (usually filed by locality), or articles in genealogical magazines. A diligent genealogist will search carefully through the back issues of the county, state, and regional publications for the area he/she is searching. In this regard the *Genealogical Periodical Annual Index* (GPAI) may be helpful. See Chapter 13, "Genealogical Tools and Indexes" for more details.

Early American Business Records, 1780-1870

All of the business records discussed in the previous section carry forward into the early American time period, from 1790 to 1870. Forms of apprenticeship continued into the twentieth century and, in some forms, up to the present. Account books are still kept today, although they are usually less helpful to the genealogist because of the abundance of other sources. Indentures for indebtedness became less common during the first half of the nineteenth century and rarely appear in later years.

America remained very agrarian in the nineteenth century, but more businesses developed, nurtured by the laissez-faire policy of the government and more ancestors will appear in contemporary business records. Insurance companies began keeping voluminous records, simple account books evolved into credit reporting agencies, and an increasing professional class began generating more records. The records associated with these businesses are the major new sources in this time period.

Insurance Records

As more Americans left the relative security of the farm, life insurance became popular. Prior to 1843 a few attempts were made to develop life insurance programs, but only one, the Presbyterian Ministers Fund, 1759-present, survived. Other kinds of insurance societies thrived, notably fire and marine insurance. The growth of cities led directly to the establishment of life insurance companies.[8] Surviving till at least 1942, according to one historian, were sixteen major life insurance companies begun between 1843 and 1852 with nineteen more founded by 1875. (See Appendix 2 at the end of this chapter.)

The nature of life insurance makes such records very interesting for a genealogist. Early insurance contracts were brief and loosely worded, but they did contain certain kinds of information about their clients. Even then, policy holders had to provide information about their lifestyle, health, age, residence, and relatives (notably the beneficiaries). By 1865 medical information on diseases or health conditions was included, and in 1889 Mutual Life began attaching a medical examination to the policy.[9]

Since life insurance is usually paid after the death of the insured, the companies need to keep their records for many years. To protect themselves legally, most companies kept their records long past the death of the insured. For many years most companies had

Chaden, Henry: Jonathan (1770-1)
Chichester, James: Jemmy (1766-7); Ephraim (1767); Sally (1767); Sarah (1767)
Chichester, Joseph: schooling (betw. 1763-67)
Chichester, Widow: portion of wood for schoolhouse (betw. 1763-7)
Clocke, Mr.: Phebe (1778)
Conkline, Col Platt: Nathaniel (1775-6)
Conkline, Widow: Jacob (betw. 1763-7)
Conkling, Ananias: daughter (1777)
Conkling, Capt. Cornelius: Ebenezer Morgan (1767)
Conkling, David: 2 children (1777); Phebe (1778); David (1778-9)
Conkling, Ezekiel: Elizabeth Betsy (1776-8); Philetus (1776-8); Silas (1778)
Conkling, Hubbard: Charlotte (1777); Isaac Wood (1768)
Conkling, Isaac: Timothy (1767); Henry Titus (1766-7)
Conkling, Jeremiah: son (1765); Jacob (1767)
Conkling, John: Phebe (1770-1); Mary (1777); Sarah (1777)
Conkling, Joseph: John (1768)
Conkling, Philip: Patty (1770); Bennet (1776-9); Richard Titus (1765-6)
Conkling, Richard: Titus (1765, 67)
Conkling, Richard, Jr.: 2 children (1778)
Conkling, Stephen: daughter (betw. 1763-7)
Conkling, Thomas: Hannah (1778); Lucy (1778); Richard Hults (1777)
Conkling, Thomas, Jr.: son (betw. 1763-7); Selah (1767-8); Esther (1767); Zophar (1767)
Conkling, Timothy: Abel (1766, 68); Ezra (1767); Jonathan (1766-8); Timothy (1767)
Conkling, Widow, of West Neck: 2 children (1778)
Could, Ruth: 2 children (1776); Christian (1777); William (1777)

Figure 10-3. Kenneth Scott, "Some Huntington, Long Island Residents, 1763-1779," *National Genealogical Society Quarterly* 62 (Sept. 1974): 177.

no policy on discarding records. When one company, apparently Connecticut Mutual Life, prepared to move into a new home office about 1925, it decided to design a records retention policy. Its policy, as of 1941, is a model of what materials other life insurance companies retain.

For historical reasons, all correspondence from the company's first twenty years was kept. Applications which were the basis for the insurance contract are kept while the policy is in force. Applications not approved are destroyed after ten years, and the application of a deceased policy holder is destroyed after twenty. The abstract or history cards are retained permanently. These cards contain a complete history of each account. Other records kept permanently include account or renewal cards (records of premium payments), accumulated dividend cards, cancelled checks and bank statements, cash books, directors' minutes and committee records, ledgers, payrolls, and real estate records.[10] Since older records are the most likely to be discarded, it is wise to search relevant records as soon as possible.

As a genealogist, you would be most interested in the application since it would contain most of the personal information. Some companies may keep original applications permanently or microfilm them. Even if the application is discarded, other records may be helpful in providing relevant information about residence, health, age, etc.

In 1910, one company in the Northeast realized it had lost contact with a considerable number of policy holders or their beneficiaries to whom large sums of money were due. It undertook a systematic, often lengthy, search to find those heirs. Their files are very valuable to the family historian who finds an ancestor or relative in them.[11]

Although most insurance companies still exist under some name or another, many are unwilling to search their large files for a family historian. Therefore it may be better to offer to search yourself and be prepared to show proof of descent from the relevant ancestor. Most of these records are in corporation archives, and a pleasant letter to the home office will usually help locate the desired materials. A current agent of the company may help you gain access to old records.

The most common method of learning which company insured your ancestor is presently living family members. Old insurance certificates, cancelled checks, or personal account books among family papers may also provide this information. Although these may be among the most difficult records to pursue, they are also among the most helpful.

Credit Reporting Agencies

During the nineteenth century, most businessmen and women purchased goods from suppliers who did not know them personally. Credit was common, but suppliers needed to determine the credit worthiness of businesses. In 1841, the Mercantile Agency, the first commercial credit-reporting company, was launched. Later known as R. G. Dun and Company, it dominates the credit reporting field even today. By the early 1850s, it employed 2,000 correspondents in the United States and Canada, who sent at least semi-annual credit reports to the New York office about business people in their area.

Dun's 1841-90 ledger books are deposited in Baker Library at Harvard University – 2,580 volumes arranged by counties. The reports almost always indicated the subject's occupation, net worth, value of real and personal estate, and business prospects. Many reports also included age, marital status, former residence, personal character, and family background. The best information is in the 1850-80 period. Only those likely to apply for credit are usually represented. Since accuracy was vital to Dun's subscribers, the reports provide reliable data.[12]

These records are available to any interested researcher at Baker Library. Some indexes may be difficult to use; but if your ancestor was a merchant or businessman in this time period, a wealth of information may well be easily available. It should be noted that permission from Dun and Bradstreet is necessary before publishing material from this source, but such permission is not difficult to obtain.[13]

The Professions

Between 1780 and 1870, more and more of our ancestors became ministers, lawyers, doctors, architects, or entered professions, as distinct from trades. Such professions generated valuable records. (See Chapter 14, "Compiled Biographies," and Chapter 11, "City Directories and Their Cousins.") Most ministerial records are kept by the archives of each denomination. A great deal of information may be included in these records, especially if they are relatively recent or if the minister drew a pension. Some denominations have published directories of their ministers. Either old editions of a directory or a historical directory like this example, can give important geographical information on an ancestor who was an ordained clergyman or a notable church layman.

Brinkman, Benjamin F., b Graafschap, Mich, May 3, 1863. WTS, 1906. Ord UnitedPresby. Pas Second, Englewood, Chicago, Ill 1906-10; Second, Pella, Ia 1911-17; fin agt Central 1917-20; pas Calvary, Cleveland, O 1920-21. d Cleveland, O Mar 5, 1921.

Brock, John Randlett, b Newbury, Vt, Jun, 1831, s of Jacob R. AB, RutgersC, 1859; NBTS, 1862. Lic Cl Passaic, 1862; ord Cl Paramus, 1862. Pas West New Hempstead, N.Y 1862-65; Spring Valley, N.Y 1865-69; tchr 1869-71. d Marysville, Tenn Aug 7, 1872.

Brockles, Albert. Received Presby 1911; pas Ave B, NYC 1911-13; dismissed MethCh 1914.

Brodhead, Jacob, b Marbletown, N.Y, May 14, 1782, s of Charles W. AB, UnionC, 1801; NBTS, 1804; DD, QueensC, 1815. Lic Cl Albany, 1804; ord Cl Poughkeepsie, 1804. Pas Rhinebeck Flats, N.Y 1804-09; Collegiate, NYC 1809-13; Crown St, Philadelphia, Pa 1813-26; Broome St, NYC 1826-37; Flatbush, Ulster Co, N.Y 1837-41; Central, Brooklyn, N.Y 1841-46. Pres GenSyn, 1816-17 and 1825-26. d Springfield, Mass Jun 6, 1855.

Peter N. Vandenberge, *Historical Directory of the Reformed Church in America, 1625-1965* (New Brunswick, N.J.: Reformed Church in America, 1966), p. 22.

The current edition of *The Yearbook of American and Canadian Churches* is the most helpful source for locating the central headquarters of most denominations. (See Chapter 5, "Church Records.") It may help determine the present name of a church which has merged with others. It also includes lists of "Main Depositories of Church History Material and Sources," arranged by denomination, and "Standard Guides to Church Archives."

Lawyers and judges have occupied a prominent position in our society for the last 200 years. Since they dealt with the public trust, they were registered in many cities and very early established "the bar" as a means of determining qualifications. The most easily accessed records of this profession are again secondary, printed sources. In many large cities and counties, books have been written on "The Bench and Bar of. . ." These books contain biographical information on those practicing law in a locality at the time of and prior to publication. *Martin's Bench and Bar of Philadelphia*, for example, includes reference to most attorneys who ever practiced in Philadelphia and many colonial lawyers who worked any place in Pennsylvania. It also includes an alphabetical list of all those ad-

The Philadelphia Bar.

Being a List of the names of gentlemen who have been admitted to practice, as Attorneys-at-law in the County Courts of the City and County of Philadelphia, from 1682 to 1883, with the dates of their admission.

Abbreviations—A-age at death. ADM.-for admitted to practice. ATTY-GEN.-Attorney General. B-for born. B. G. or BRIG. GEN.-for Brigadier General. C. J.-Chief Justice. Co-for county. COL. OF VOLS.-Colonel of volunteers, 1861-65. COL.-before christian name, colonel of militia. C. P.-for Common Pleas. C. R.-Colonial Records. D-for died. D. C.-for District Court. DIRECT'RY-for Philadelphia Directory. IN. PRAC.-for in practice. J.-Judge. J. C. P.-Judge of the Common Pleas. J. O. C.-Associate Judge of the Orphans Court. M. C.-for Member of Congress. M. G.-Major General. PA.-for Pennsylvania. P. V.-Pennsylvania Volunteers, 1861-65. PA. MAG.-Pennsylvania Magazine. P. J.-President Judge. Q. M. G.-for Quarter-Master-General. S. C.-for Supreme Court of Pennsylvania. U. S.-for United States. U. S. C. C.-for United States Circuit Court. U. S. S. C.-for United States Supreme Court. * Name from Sheriff's Deed Book B, which is the date of admission in the Supreme Court, which I have used where an earlier date could not be found.

Abbett, Benjamin Franklin,		Jan. 25, 1868
Edwin L.,		Dec. 5, 1864
Leonidas,		Feb. 5, 1857
Abbey, William Burling,		Nov. 4, 1876
Abbott, Montelius,	*d. May 18, 1877, a. 38*	June 21, 1862
William Holloway,		July 13, 1844
Abrams (Rev.) Joseph,	*d. Mch 30, 1881, a. 69*	Nov. 2, 1839
Joseph Addison,		Nov. 30, 1878
Ackley, John Edward,		Dec. 13, 1879
Ackworth, Edmund,[1]	*Chester Co. Records*	Feb. 23, 1741
John,	*d. Dec. 14, 1744*	Before 1744
Adams, Frederick Mayhew,		Jan. 22, 1847
George Bethune,		Mch 2, 1878
John Bell,	*d. Jan. 4, 1874*	Mch 13, 1855
John,		Nov. 1, 1879
John Quincy,		May 3, 1856
Josiah Robert,		Dec. 5, 1874
Robert, Jr.,		Apl 27, 1872
Thomas Boylston,[2]	*Judge, d. 1832, a. 60*	Dec. 7, 1793

Figure 10-4. John Hill Martin, *Martin's Bench and Bar of Philadelphia* (Philadelphia: Rees Welsh and Co., 1883), p. 243.

mitted to practice in the courts of Philadelphia, both city and county, including death dates and ages at death for those no longer living at the time of publication. (See Figure 10-4.)

Another valuable source on lawyers is *Martindale-Hubbell Law Directory*, an annual publication, which lists every practicing lawyer in the country. This directory began in the 1860s; and while most public libraries have only recent editions, many law libraries retain the earliest copies. This source gives some biographical information, as well as residence and affiliation with a law firm.

Similar books exist in some areas for doctors or surgeons. They too were often registered by the city; and such certificates or licenses should be sought in city, county, and state archives. The Pennsylvania State Archives, for example, records medical licenses since 1894 and dental licenses since 1897. Earlier licenses are found in county archives.

Other Records

An ancestor need not be prominent to be included in a business record. In some cases, many people were recorded by cities because of their occupation. Figure 10-5 shows an 1863 register of prostitutes compiled by the Guardians of the Poor in Philadelphia. Remarkable for its completeness, it includes information about these women's ages, length of time in the city, literacy, marital status, number of children, how long and why they were involved in the profession, other trades they held, parents' occupations, and when, why, and from where they emigrated. Often parents' or siblings' names were also recorded.

A wide range of information is available on other occupations we may not expect to find documented. For example, the Pennsylvania State Archives houses applications for teaching certificates from 1866, a Register of Pilots' Homes and Securities from 1783 to 1876, Philadelphia licenses for peddlers and hawkers from 1820 to 1838, and tavern licenses applied for and granted from 1750 to 1855.[14]

Locating the Records

Much of what was said about locating colonial records applies to the 1780-1870 period. Original manuscript records are usually found in local or state archives and historical societies. Unlike colonial records, however, very few have been published, although guides to the archives are often available. For example, *The Guide to Genealogical Sources at the Pennsylvania State Archives* spends some twelve pages describing various collections which they have designated as "occupational records." Only a few were mentioned above.

Modern American Business and Employment Records, 1870-Present

With the conclusion of the Civil War and the reunification of the country, American business began to grow by leaps and bounds. As businesses grew, so did their records. Only two or four ancestors may have been in the labor force around the year 1900, but odds are that half of them were either working for someone else (hence

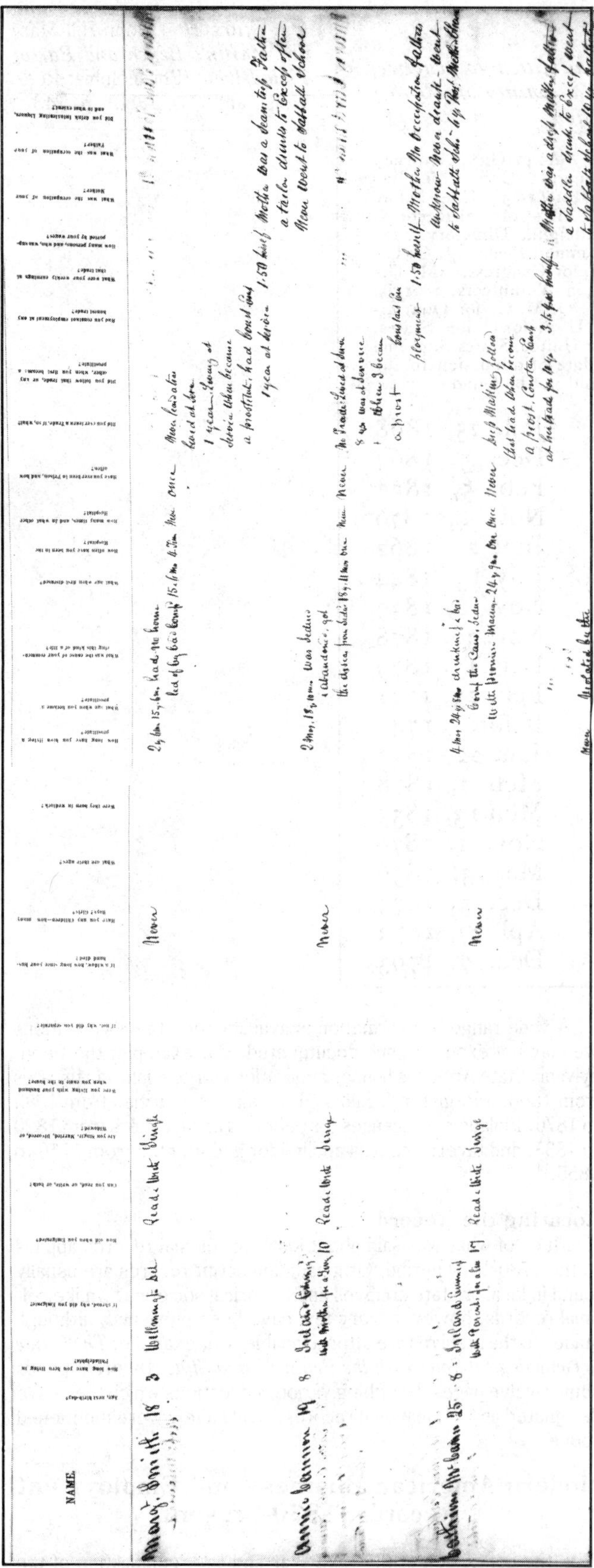

Figure 10-5. Philadelphia Guardians of the Poor, Prostitute Record, 1863, p. 63.

employed) or in business for themselves (thus creating their own business records). By 1880, farming involved only 50 percent of the work force and even they were more regularly documented. In difficult research problems, the records of collateral "ancestors" or siblings of your ancestor should not be overlooked.

Several topics are relevant to researching modern business records, most notably procedures for locating such records. Corporations began keeping more complete employee or personnel records, and several valuable new types of documentation began, including records of labor unions, mortuaries, and the Social Security system.

Obviously, knowledge of an ancestor's employer is crucial to this research. Again, family members and home records are the best source for this information. Most city directories include the employer's name on each listing. It does not matter if the ancestor lived in a small town or large city, as directories exist for most areas. This sample from the 1922 directory of Missoula, Montana, then considered a small town, shows the kind of information you can expect.

MISSOULA CITY DIRECTORY (1922) 271

Sterriet George H, lab Missoula White P S Co, h rear 601 Phillips
Stetson Harry E, mail carrier R F D 2
Stevens Clare, appr G A Meisinger, r 1529 De Foe
Stevens Harry H, driver, h 208 S 3d W
Stevens John M, carmn N P Ry, h 1619 De Foe
Stevens Lyman W, brkmn N P Ry, r 117 N 2d W
Stevens Myrta M (wid Albert M), h 117 N 2d W
Stevens Russell, student, r 405 S 1st W
Stevens Wm W, moved to Portland, Ore
Stevenson Derrick, moved to Bozeman, Mont
Stevenson Mrs F J, r Florence Hotel
Stewart C Donald, clk C M & St P Ry, h 246 Edith
Stewart Dee, chauf H L Haines, r 314 W Railroad
Stewart Fleming K, surveyor Forest Service, r Grand Hotel
Stewart Floyd E, r 405 S 3d W
Stewart Jas A, firemn N P Ry, h 402 W Cedar
Stewart L L, r 401 S 1st W
Stewart Leighton, formn N P Ry, h 1520 S 7th W
Stewart R D, clk, h Orchard Homes R F D 1
Stewart Thomas, car opr, h Orchard Homes R F D 4
Stewart Wm M, mgr Traffic Service Bureau, h Rattlesnake
Stewart Willie H, swtchmn N P Ry, h 929 Sherwood
Sticht Bert, lab Anton Vogt & Sons, h East Missoula
Sticht Glenn, lab Anton Vogt & Sons, h East Missoula
Stickney Earl W, rancher, h Orchard Homes R F D 1
Stickney Fred J, carmn N P Ry, h 530 N 2d W

Missoula City Directory (Missoula: R. L. Polk and Co., 1922), p. 271; *h* means *house*, *r* means *resides at*.

Note that both the occupation and employer are given. The Northern-Pacific Railroad (NPRR) appears to be a major employer. Bert and Glenn Sticht are laborers for Anton Vogt and Sons. This valuable information had never been mentioned to the Sticht family historian by the older members of the family.

Labor Unions

As American business grew, so did the desire of the employees for better working conditions. Labor unions were born. Since their purpose is improvement of employment conditions, accurate membership records are vital. Many unions have preserved volumes of records which may contain information relevant to your research. One description of the potential treasures vividly suggests the possibilities: "The ITU (International Typographical Union) Headquarters Basement is comprised of a labyrinth of corridors. Each corridor is replete with shelves, filing cabinets, boxes, etc. I would imagine an archivist would be delirious with joy to be loosened in this musty atmosphere."[15]

This description was part of an excellent 1960 survey conducted by the Society of American Archivists Committee on Labor Records. The table reproduced in Appendix 3 summarizes results of a survey sent to 265 organizations, to which 118–45 percent–responded. Thus their information represents about half the labor organizations in the country. It is unfortunate that several major unions such as the United Automobile Workers, International Ladies Garment Workers, United Mine Workers, the Teamsters, and most railroad and building trade unions did not reply.

The table in Appendix 3 will answer several questions about the unions covered and suggest what records the nonrespondent unions may have. Although the survey did not ask about membership records, some of the notes mention such information. The date of the earliest records and the quality of records also provide clues to the scope of their holdings.

Obviously, you need to know the union and the local to which an ancestor belonged before researching this source, but often the union can be deduced by occupation if family sources lack this information. An ancestor's residence or employer's name may be sufficient for a helpful union secretary to determine the relevant local. If the business is still in operation, you can identify present local members working there, and they may know the history of their union at that company. Most records will be at union or local headquarters, but some have been deposited in local archives. The Library of Congress's *National Union Catalogue of Manuscript Collections* includes labor union records, including some membership lists of union locals. (See section on Repositories.)

Small Businesses

If your ancestor owned a small business, there is probably a record of the business license in the city or state where he did business. The application for a license should include a variety of information such as age, birthplace, marital status, and residence, depending on when the license was applied for.

The number of employees of a small business varies greatly, but is often less than twenty and sometimes only two or three. Typically, they were friends or relatives of the owner, and few, if any, personnel records were kept. Payroll records, however, may still be preserved. If the business still exists, try contacting the present owner for information and records. In some cases, he may be a relative of the previous owner and may have been a small child when "Uncle Jake" worked there. Records of defunct businesses are discussed at the end of this chapter.

Corporations

Big business employs a large portion of the labor force and typically has kept better employee records for a longer period. Also, they are more likely to be in business still, making it easier to locate their records. Information recorded will vary greatly, and it is more important to discuss how to locate those records (see below) than to describe what one may find. Before beginning research into a corporation's records, you should do some basic background research: read its company history if it has one, check periodicals for articles, or request reading suggestions from its public relations office. Showing an interest in and knowledge of the company will make it easier for the company to want to help you.

One interesting group of corporations is the Fortune 500, *Fortune* magazine's annually compiled list of the 500 largest United States companies. These "premiere" United States companies have records commensurate with their size. When *Fortune* started rating the companies in 1954, its 500 employed about eight million people, or about 12 percent of the labor force.[16] Some changes occur in the list each year (about twenty different companies appear with each new ranking), but most companies remain on the list. Currently *Fortune* also rates a second 500 as well as listing separate lists of fifty top businesses in seven different service categories, leaving the first and second 500 as industrial and not service companies. This creates a total of 1,350 businesses ranked by *Fortune*. In 1981, they employed over thirty-three million people, almost one-third of the work force.

The complete *Fortune* listing is available in most public libraries, and the "First 500" with corporate address and telephone are included in Appendix 5 at the end of this chapter. The numbers assigned to these companies' manuscript collections in archives as cataloged by the Library of Congress's *National Union Catalogue of Manuscript Collections* are also given. The seven separate service categories of "50 largest" are life insurance, (Appendix 6), transportation, (Appendix 7), retailing (Appendix 8), utilities (Appendix 9), commercial banks (Appendix 10), diversified service (Appendix 11), and diversified financial companies (Appendix 12). They are listed with addresses and phone numbers where available; and the insurance and transportation companies include the year of incorporation when available.

Social Security

The largest group of employment records in the world are those of the United States Social Security system. These records are fairly recent, since the Social Security Administration began in 1934, and they are also restricted. However, people have had success in obtaining records from the file of a deceased direct ancestor.

The greatest benefit of these records may be that applicants for Social Security needed documentation of their birth to prove their age. The early Social Security files include many people born in the 1850s, 1860s, 1870s, and later. Among this group would be naturalized citizens from foreign countries. The information on specific birthplace may not be recorded anyplace else but is vital for further research. This is especially true for people naturalized before 1906, when detailed birth information was not required.

If an ancestor lived past about 1935 he/she may have a Social Security file. If you provide proof of his/her death (a death certificate) and his/her Social Security number (often on the death certificate), then you should be able to obtain a copy of his/her original application for a number or his/her claim for benefits. Write to the Social Security Administration, 6401 Security Blvd., Baltimore, MD 21235. Briefly explain what information you need and that it is unavailable anywhere else. If they refuse to process your request (remember it may take several weeks), then ask your congressman or senator for assistance. See Jayne Askin, *Search* (New York: Harper & Row, 1982) for other search approaches.

Don't give up. If your ancestor is dead and if you are a bona fide descendant, the Freedom of Information Act gives you the right to this information. Even the Social Security number gives you a clue to the ancestor's residence. The first three digits of the number indicate the state where the number was applied for. (See Table 10-1.)

Mortuary Records

During the contemporary period, almost all of our ancestors were recorded in one final business record, that of the local mortician. These records can be very complete and include information not found elsewhere. In the case of an Irish mining family in upstate New York, the mortuary records of two sons of the immigrants named the specific towns in Ireland both parents came from. Although the parents came about 1850, their sons' burials in 1939 and 1942 provided the most important clues to their origins.

In most cases the mortician is named either on the death certificate, the sexton's burial records, or in the obituary, if not on all three. To locate a particular mortuary or any mortuary in a particular town, consult the *National Directory of Morticians*. See Figure 10-6.

If this directory is not available at the local public library, consult one of your local morticians. Often if a mortuary went out of business, it was purchased by another mortuary and its records were transferred to the new company.

Figure 10-6. *National Directory of Morticians,* Vol. KK (Youngstown, Oh.: National Directory of Morticians, 1970), p. 553; published irregularly.

OHIO—Continued 553

THE McGOWAN-REID FUNERAL HOME

CUYAHOGA FALLS LEADING FUNERAL HOME

Area Code 216

Phone 928-1313

Newly Redecorated Private-Ample Parking

Shrine NFDA Kiwanis

STOW AND THIRD STREETS CUYAHOGA FALLS, OHIO

Shipping Point Akron, Ohio

CORNING—Perry Co.
Population, 1065

POST Funeral Home
24 Hour Ambulance Service
Oxygen Equipped
Area Code 614 Phone 347-4723
CORNING, OHIO 43730

Hermey, Carl W.
Post Funeral Home

CORTLAND—Trumbull Co.
Population, 1957
Love, J. H. & Son

COSHOCTON—Coshocton Co.
Population, 113,106
Dawson, Arthur & Son
Gibson and **Bontrager**
Glass Funeral Home

COVINGTON—Miami Co.
Population, 2473
Reutzahn Funeral Home

CRESTLINE—Crawford Co.
Population, 6500
Beck Funeral Home
Garverick Funeral Home
(See Ad Next Column)

CRESTON—Wayne Co.
Population, 1522
Murray, John C., Fune. Home

GARVERICK FUNERAL HOME
Area Code 419 Ph. 683-2020
NFDA
Complete Rolling Stock and Equipment
336 North Thoman St.
CRESTLINE, OHIO 44827

CRIDERSVILLE—Auglaize Co.
Population, 1053
Bayliff Funeral Home

CROOKSVILLE—Perry Co.
Population, 2960
Cannon & Cannon
Driggs, C. S.

CUMBERLAND—Guernsey Co.
Population, 493
Tom, E. R.

CUYAHOGA FALLS—
Summit Co. Pop., 47,922
Billow, The Co.
Carr Memorial Home
(See Ad Next Column)
Clifford Funeral Home
McGowan-Reid
(See Ad Top of Page)

CARR Memorial Homes
Phone
216—434-1997
810 Portage Trail
CUYAHOGA FALLS, OHIO

DALTON—Wayne Co.
Population, 1067
Monbarren Funeral Home

DANVILLE—Knox Co.
Population, 926
Dusthimer Funeral Home

DAYTON—Montgomery Co.
Population, 262,232
Baker, Eugene Funeral Home
5555 Philadelphia Drive
Banta Funeral Home
3419 West 3rd St.
Boyer's, O. P. Sons Co.
60 W. Riverview Ave.
Bradford & Connelly
42 Linden Ave.
Far Hills & Schantz Ave.
1849 Salem Ave.
Carrigan Funeral Home
2201 N. Main St.
Graham Funeral Home
1850 Wayne Ave.
Harris Funeral Home
49 Linden Ave.
CONTINUED NEXT PAGE

Locating Modern Records

The most difficult problem facing the user of business and employment records is locating those records. They may not be easily accessible or they may not include your ancestor; but if they cannot be located, your other problems are irrelevant. (See also "How to Find Business and Employment Records," following this chapter.)

Obviously, if a company (large or small) still exists, the problem of locating its records should not be great. Someone in the home office should know where they are, what information is in them, and how to get that information. Some companies have deposited their records in various archives, a matter covered in Repositories, the next section of this chapter.

The best method of finding records of existing businesses is to contact the business directly. Addresses for the largest companies (and hence the largest employers) are found in Appendixes 5 through 12, but there are thousands of smaller companies. Several useful books can help locate these other companies. (See bibliography at the end of this chapter.)

An excellent layman's guide to 317 of the largest United States companies is *Everybody's Business, An Almanac.* This book profiles each company in everyday terms rather than business jargon or technical language. Among information of interest to a genealogist would be the year of founding, some history of the company, the number of employees, and, most importantly, whom to contact at the home office for general information, including phone numbers. A list of companies in this guide is in Appendix 4.

The complicated world of modern business often makes it difficult to determine whether a company is independent or a subsidiary of a larger corporation. Dun and Bradstreet's annual *Directory of Corporate Affiliations* (Skokie, Ill.: National Register Publishing Company) helps clarify the confusion. It includes the "family tree" of every major corporation and tells who owns whom. It lists the mergers, acquisitions, name changes (1976-81), divisions, subsidiaries, affiliates, and parent companies of most major American corporations.

Once you know the company you're looking for, you still need to know where its office is. *Ward's Directory of 55,000 Largest Corporations* is often considered the best directory in its field. Each company is listed alphabetically, geographically, and by size of sales. The current business address is given, including phone numbers. The same company also publishes a directory of 45,000 private United States companies, which should help in locating somewhat smaller companies.

Another helpful tool is Dun's annual *Million Dollar Directory,* which lists about 115,000 United States businesses with a net worth over $500,000. It also lists companies alphabetically and geographically. Figure 10-7 illustrates the kind of information included in each entry.

Table 10-1

Social Security Area Designations

Social Security Number	*Area Allocations*	*Social Security Number*	*Area Allocations*
001-003	New Hampshire	449-467	Texas
004-007	Maine	468-477	Minnesota
008-009	Vermont	478-485	Iowa
010-034	Massachusetts	486-500	Missouri
035-039	Rhode Island	501-502	North Dakota
040-049	Connecticut	503-504	South Dakota
050-134	New York	505-508	Nebraska
135-158	New Jersey	509-515	Kansas
159-211	Pennsylvania	516-517	Montana
212-220	Maryland	518-519	Idaho
221-222	Delaware	520	Wyoming
223-231	Virginia	521-524	Colorado
232	West Virginia and North Carolina	525	New Mexico
		526-527	Arizona
233-236	West Virginia	528-529	Utah
237-246	North Carolina	530	Nevada
247-251	South Carolina	531-539	Washington
252-260	Georgia	540-544	Oregon
261-267	Florida	545-573	California
268-302	Ohio	574	Alaska
303-317	Indiana	575-576	Hawaii
318-361	Illinois	577-579	District of Columbia
362-386	Michigan	580	Virgin Islands and Puerto Rico
387-399	Wisconsin		
400-407	Kentucky	581-584	Puerto Rico
408-415	Tennessee	585	New Mexico
416-424	Alabama	586	Guam, Philippine Islands, and American Samoa
425-428	Mississippi		
429-432	Arkansas		
433-439	Louisiana	587	Mississippi
440-448	Oklahoma	700-728	Railroad Retirement Board (all states)

Smaller companies are not as difficult to locate since they are less tangled in the web of corporate ownerships. Usually, if an ancestor worked for a smaller company, the headquarters were probably in the same town or state where he/she lived. If the business still exists, then you can probably locate it in the local phone book or current city directory. Never underestimate the ability of your local public or university librarian to help you locate the address of a small or large company.

The success or failure of your search may depend on your correspondence with the company, whether it is big or small. Remember when contacting companies that, while they may be consumer-conscious, genealogy is not their business. In the initial letter, it may help to explain that you have an interest in the company's history because of a family connection and would like to know where information like personnel and employment records has been stored. Ask if there are company or corporate archives and who the archivist or librarian is. Don't expect to achieve your goal in a single letter. The first task is to locate somebody who knows what you're looking for. Then you can begin to acquire the records.

It may be more efficient to make an initial contact by telephone so that you can learn whom you need to speak with. Be patient, for you will probably be shuttled from department to department and put on hold several times. Many companies will have a WATS line or an 800 number which you can call at no charge to you. You can determine if the company you're seeking has a toll-free number by calling 1 (800) 555-1212.

If you are still not successful, ask for the customer relations department and briefly explain your problem. Once you find the right person, be clear, courteous, and brief in your letters or conversations. Ask if the records are open to public research by someone like yourself or an agent representing you. If possible, offer to search the records personally, as they will probably be voluminous and unindexed. Most records custodians do not want to search such records but will allow you to. Always offer to pay necessary charges. Again, a little background on the company can be very helpful in opening the proper doors to the records you are seeking.

Defunct Businesses

Unfortunately, many of our ancestors worked for companies no longer in existence. Fortunately, many seemingly defunct companies have not actually disappeared but continue under a different name and/or ownership. If an ancestor worked for Victor Talking Machine, for example, you would have to learn that the name is now RCA before pursuing further research. Whenever a business folds, there are usually customers who are attractive to the competition. Therefore, the records of the old company may be transferred to another firm, often the one which bought them out. In a small city, try contacting present businesses in the same line of work for information about an ancestral company.

Perhaps the defunct business belonged to a trade association or some other group of businesses in the same trade or locality. These types of organizations may have information on the company in question and may know where their records are. Anthony T. Kruzas and Robert C. Thomas, eds., *Business Organizations and Agencies Directory* (Detroit: Gale Research Co., 1980) lists and provides addresses of trade, business, and commercial organizations, stock exchanges, labor unions, and chambers of commerce, and many other groups. Better Business Bureaus, as well as federal and state government agencies, are also included. It incorporates sixty pages of addresses of business libraries and information centers with a geographic index. Another good source book is David M. Brownstone and Gordon Carruth, *Where to Find Business Information* (New York: John Wiley and Sons, 1979), a source which can help locate agencies particular to the business you are seeking. (See Figure 10-8). If you are looking for employee information about a railroad company, the source-finder section will refer you to several sources of information. Note that the entry on "Railroads, Employee Benefits" refers you to two periodicals by the Railroad Retirement Board.

Information on old companies may appear in articles in various business magazines. One of the best ways to search this source is the *Business Periodicals Index,* which began in 1958 and is readily available in public libraries. Articles are listed under the industry or company name. The format is like that of *Reader's Guide to Periodical Literature.*

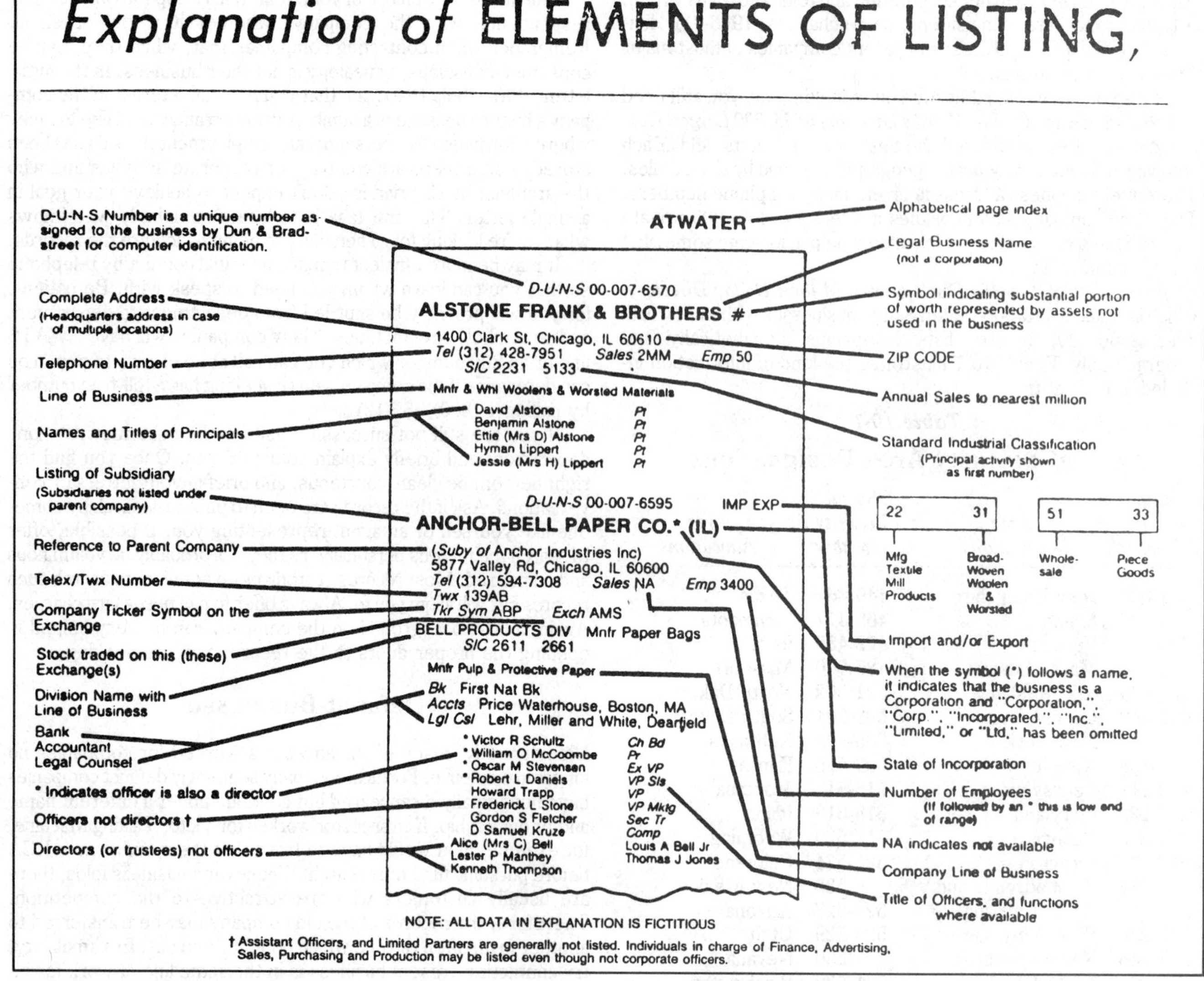

Figure 10-7. Dun's Marketing Services, *Million Dollar Directory* (New York City: Dun and Bradstreet Corporation, 1983).

If you know where a business was located you can then write to the local Chamber of Commerce or the state archives for information on what became of it and its records. The secretary of state in each state should have incorporation records specifying the years a company was in business or if the name was changed. A local town or county historical society may also have knowledge of a business's demise. As mentioned earlier, local cities or counties may have business licenses for unincorporated businesses within their boundaries. Their records may indicate when a business folded and if the owner started a new and similar business.

To locate local historical societies which may have information on defunct businesses and record repositories, consult Tracy Linton Craig, ed., *Directory of Historical Societies and Agencies in the United States and Canada,* (Nashville: American Association for State and Local History, published annually). It lists almost every historical society in both countries, including a brief description of their collections and major programs. These societies are usually quite knowledgeable about history in their areas and can help determine what happened to a local business.

Railroad Employees

The special status of railroading in America has been recognized several ways. Railroad workers received special Social Security numbers and their own pension plan. As many as two and a quarter million people worked for the railroad companies at their peak around 1920. Furthermore, many railroad company records are very easily located.

A *Biographical Directory of Railroad Officials of America* was issued periodically during the last century. The California State Railroad Museum Library at 111 I Street in Sacramento has copies from 1885, 1906, 1913, and 1922. The same library also has some fifty drawers of employment cards for the Southern Pacific Railroad, dating back to 1903. A location list of major railroad archives is in Table 10-2. See appendixes of this volume for addresses of the repositories.

To determine which railroad lines merged with any given major service, consult *Moody's Transportation Manual,* issued annually by Moody's Investors Service, Inc., 99 Church Street, New York, NY 10007, (212) 267-8800. Current and back issues are available at most public and research libraries.

If an ancestor received a pension from a railroad, then he should be on record at the Railroad Retirement Board, 844 Rush Street, Chicago, IL 60611. The board is very helpful in answering requests for information if you can provide the employee's name, position, the railroad he worked for, and where and when he was employed.

Repositories

In 1959 the Library of Congress began a catalog of manuscripts

SOURCE FINDER

RAILROAD ADJUSTMENT BOARD, NATIONAL (US)

National Mediation Board Annual Report 3393
National Mediation Board Reports of Emergency Boards 3394

RAILROAD RETIREMENT BOARD (US)

Railroad Retirement Board Annual Report 3991
Railroad Retirement Board Quarterly Review 3992

RAILROADS

International Railway Journal 2724

Railroad Revenues, Expenses and Income 3993
Railway Age 3995
Reference Book of Transportation 4041
Yearbook of Railroad Facts 5097

Canada

Railway Operating Statistics 3998
Railway Transport Service Bulletin 3999
Uniform Classification of Accounts for Class 1 Common Carriers by Railways 4747

New England

Boston Marine Guide 577

United States

Government and Private Expenditures for Transport Facilities 2237
Information Letter 2573
Interstate Commerce Commission Annual Report 2745
Modern Railroads 3265
National Mediation Board Annual Report 3393
Railroad Mileage by States 3990
Transportation Service 4694

Washington (DC)

Railroad Mileage by States 3990

RAILROADS, ACCIDENTS AND SAFETY

Railway Accidents 3994
Regulations for Transportation of Dangerous Commodities by Rail 4057

RAILROADS, ASSOCIATION OF AMERICA

Indexes of Railroad Material Prices and Wage Rates 2498
Yearbook of Railroad Facts 5097

RAILROADS, EMPLOYEE BENEFITS

Railroad Retirement Board Annual Report 3991
Railroad Retirement Board Quarterly Review 3992

RAILROADS, EQUIPMENT

Indexes of Railroad Material Prices and Wage Rates 2498

Figure 10-8 David M. Brownstone and Gordon Carruth, *Where to Find Business Information* (New York: John Wiley and Sons, 1979), p. 150.

housed throughout the country. Known as the *National Union Catalog of Manuscript Collections* (NUCMC), it is issued yearly with information on over 2,000 newly cataloged manuscript collections each year. By 1980, about 46,640 collections located in 1,122 repositories had been cataloged. The catalogs are indexed each year with cumulative indexes covering 1959-62, 1963-66, 1967-69, 1970-74, and every five years subsequently. A wealth of information can be found on defunct and current business and employment records in these indexes.

For example, Joseph Stulb of Philadelphia worked for Schrack and Company, a nineteenth-century paint firm. The NUCMC index lists:

> STULB, Joseph Jr. 71-121
> SCHRACK (C.) and Company, Philadelphia, Pa 72-121

This citation means that they both appear in the collection cataloged 72-121, which was the 121st collection cataloged in 1972. The Schrack entry in the 1972 catalog reads:

MS 72-121

Schrack (C.) and Company, Philadelphia, Pa.
Records, 1808-1938. ca. 200,000 items.

In Eleutherian Mills Historical Library (Greenville, Del.) (various accessions)

Correspondence, accounts, bills and receipts, stock books, formulae books (1844-1912), orders, shipping records, banking records, and other business records of a paint, varnish, and color manufacturing firm. Persons represented include Christian Schrack (ca. 1790-1854), founder of the firm, who began business as a carriage builder; his partner, Joseph Stulb (d. 1898); Stulb's sons, Edwin H. Stulb (1850-1920) and Joseph Stulb, Jr.; his grandsons, Joseph Reichert Stulb (b. 1883) and Edwin H. Stulb, Jr.; and Townsend Willits.

In part, described in A Guide to the Manuscripts in the Eleutherian Mills Historical Library, by John B. Riggs (1970) p. 970-971.

Gift, 1966, and purchases, 1965-68.

National Union Catalog of Manuscript Collections (Washington, D.C.: Library of Congress, 1972), p. 20.

Table 10-2
Location of Railroad Archives

Railroad	Location	Description of Collection
Burlington Northern	Minnesota State Historical Society	Historical archives, deposited 1975. Cataloging to take an estimated eight to ten years.
Northern Pacific and Great Northern	Minnesota State Historical Society	Historical archives.
Illinois Central, 1851-1906	Newberry Library, Chicago	Includes personnel applications and pension files, large map collection of all routes including subsidiary lines, many of which run into the deep South. Printed guide by Carolyn Curtis Mohr, 1951, available.
Chicago Burlington and Quincy Railroads	Newberry Library, Chicago	Includes numerous trunk and subsidiary lines, most acquired during the late 1870s and 1880s, throughout the Midwest and the eastern Rockies area. Printed guide by Elisabeth C. Jackson and Carolyn Curtis, 1949, available.
Chicago and Northwestern	Northern Illinois University	Includes Minneapolis & St. Paul and Chicago Great Western lines. Almost 300 boxes of documents, including an employee card file in possession of Chicago and Northwestern Historical Society as of 11 July 1982. Organizing it for deposit in DeKalb will take an estimated year. Collection 51 includes employee military service, personnel data, employee pass lists, and lists of officers and agents already on deposit. Contact Craig Pfannkuche, 8612 Memory Trail, Wonder Lake, IL 60097.

This collection is a wonderful find—about 200,000 items pertaining to Schrack and Company, Joseph Stulb, his sons, and his grandsons. It indicates that the collection is not in Philadelphia or even in Pennsylvania, but rather in a historical library in Delaware. NUCMC also includes the manuscript collections of several labor unions.

Obviously not all manuscript collections have been cataloged in NUCMC. Thousands of specific archives also exist which may be affiliated with the company you are researching. National Historical Publications and Records Commission, *The Directory of Archives and Manuscript Repositories in the United States* (Washington, D.C.: National Archives and Records Service, 1978) lists 3,250 repositories and briefly describes the holdings of 2,675 of them. Arranged geographically, the directory also includes a list of repositories by type, including corporate archives, local historical societies, organizational archives, state and university archives, and thirteen other types of repositories. Here is an example:

AKRON

OH11-240
The Firestone Tire & Rubber Company
Archives Department
2930 West Market Street
Akron OH

MAILING ADDRESS:
1200 Firestone Parkway
Akron OH 44317

(216) 867-8220

OPEN: M-F 7:45-4:45; closed weekends and holidays
ACCESS: generally restricted to Firestone executives and certain other employees; others by appointment
COPYING FACILITIES: no
MATERIALS SOLICITED: Company mailings to the field, Public Relations Department press releases on personnel changes, new plants, new products, and price increases, and proofs of magazine advertisements.

HOLDINGS:
Total volume: 750,000 items
Inclusive dates: 19th century -
Description: Personal papers and records of Harvey S. Firestone and his family, and his business papers from the founding of the Company to his death in 1938; business correspondence, speeches, photographs, and other materials of Harvey S. Firestone, Jr. (1920-73); and non-current Company records of archival value.

SEE: Hamer.

National Historical Publications and Records Commission, *The Directory of Archives and Manuscript Repositories in The United States* (Washington, D.C.: National Archives and Records Service, 1978), p. 497.

Even this list is not complete, as it has been estimated that between six and eleven thousand such repositories exist in this country, any number of which may contain business records.[17]

Finally, the use of published guides to manuscript collections in larger archives cannot be overlooked. The *Guide to Genealogical Records in the Pennsylvania State Archives* was mentioned earlier as a good example. Another example is the section from the *Guide to Manuscripts Collections and Institutional Records in Ohio*. (See bibliography.)

Notes

1. *1982 Information Please Almanac, Atlas, and Yearbook*, 35th ed. (New York: Simon and Schuster), p. 48; table, "Persons in the Labor Force."

2. U.S. Bureau of Census, "Labor Force and Employment by Industry: 1800 to 1960," *Historical Statistics of the United States, Colonial Times to 1970*, part 1, series D, (Washington D.C.: U.S. Government Printing Office, 1975), pp. 165-81.

3. U.S. Department of Labor, *Apprenticeship Past and Present*, rev. ed. (Washington, D.C.: U.S. Department of Labor, 1964), p. 4.

4. Ibid., p. 11.

5. William Nelson, ed., *Documents Relating to Colonial History of New Jersey*, 1st series (Patterson, N.J.: Press Printing and Publishing Co., 1895), Vol. 12, pp. 401-2.

6. George W. Neible, "Account of Servants Bound and Assigned before James Hamilton, Mayor of Philadelphia," *Pennsylvania Magazine of History and Biography* 32 (Oct. 1908): 369.

7. Conklin Mann, "The Family of Conchelyne, etc., in America," *American Genealogist*, vol. 21, pp. 48-58, 133-47, 210, 215, 246-53, and vol. 22, pp. 111-21, 226-36, documents the difficulty of distinguishing Conklins.

8. Shepard B. Clough, *A Century of American Life Insurance: A History of the Mutual Life Company of New York, 1843-1943* (New York: Columbia University Press, 1946), p.5.

9. Ibid, p. 8.

10. Harold F. Larkin, "Retention of Life Insurance Records," *The American Archivist* 5 (April 1942): 95-98.

11. Ibid., p. 98.

12. James H. Madison, "The Credit Reports of R. G. Dun and Co. as Historical Sources," *Historical Methods Newsletter* 8 (Sept. 1975): 128-30.

13. For a more detailed history of early credit reporting, see James H. Madison, "The Evolution of Commercial Credit Reporting Agencies in Nineteenth Century America," *Business History Review* 48 (1974): 164-86.

14. Robert H. Dructor, *A Guide to Genealogical Sources at the Pennsylvania State Archives* (Harrisburg: Pennsylvanical Historical and Museum Commission, 1980), pp. 54-64.

15. Paul Lewinson and Morris Rieger, "Labor Union Records in the United States," *American Archivist* 25 (Jan. 1962): 39.

16. Ibid., pp. 41-42.

17. National Historical Publications and Records Commission, *Directory of Archives and Manuscript Repositories in the United States* (Washington, D.C.: National Archives and Records Service, 1978), p. 8.

Bibliography

Research and Finding Aids

Brownstone, David M., and Gordon Carruth, *Where to Find Business Information*. New York: John Wiley and Sons, 1979.

Cochran, Thomas Childs. *200 Years of American Business*. New York: Basic Books, 1977.

Craumer, Lucille V., ed. *Business Periodicals Index*. New York: H. W. Wilson Company, annual since 1958.

Daniels, Lorna M. *Business Information Sources*. Berkeley: University of California Press, 1976.

Milner, Anita Cheek. *Newspaper Indexes: A Location and Subject Guide For Researchers*. Metuchen, N.J.: Scarecrow Press, 1977.

Vallentine, John F., ed. *Handbook for Genealogical Correspondence*. Salt Lake City: Bookcraft, 1963.

Directories

Craig, Tracy Linton, ed. *Directory [of] Historical Societies and Agencies in the United States and Canada*. 12 ed. Nashville: American Association for State and Local History, 1982.

Directory of Corporate Affiliations. Skokie, Ill.: National Register Publishing Co., annually since 1967.

Dun's Marketing Services. *(Dun's) Million Dollar Directory*. New York: Dun and Bradstreet Corp., annually since 1963.

Fortune Magazine. *Fortune Double 500 Directory*. Trenton: Fortune Magazine, annually since 1970.

Jacques, Constant H., ed. *Yearbook of American and Canadian Churches*. Nashville: Abington Press, annually since 1935.

Kruzas, Anthony T. and Robert C. Thomas, eds. *Business Organizations and Agencies Directory*. Detroit: Gale Research Co., 1980.

The National Directory of Morticians. Vol. KK Youngstown, Ohio.: National Directory of Morticians, 1970.

National Historical Publications and Records Commission. *Directory of Archives and Manuscript Repositories in the United States*. Washington, D.C.: National Archives and Records Services, 1978.

Standard and Poor's Register of Corporations, Directors and Executives. New York: Standard and Poors Corp., annually since 1928.

Ward, Baldwin H., ed. *Ward's Directory of 55,000 Largest Corporations*. Petaluma, Calif.: Baldwin H. Ward Publications, 1981.

Typical Guides to Manuscript Collections

Dructor, Robert M. *A Guide to Genealogical Sources at the Pennsylvania State Archives*. Harrisburg: Pennsylvania Historical and Museum Commission, 1980.

Guide to the Manuscript Collections of the Historical Society of Pennsylvania. 2nd ed. Philadelphia: Historical Society of Pennsylvania, 1949.

Larson, David R., ed. *Guide to Manuscripts Collections and Institutional Records in Ohio*. N.p.: Society of Ohio Archivists, 1974.

The National Union Catalog of Manuscript Collections. Washington, D.C.: Library of Congress, annually since 1962.

Some Printed Primary Business Records

Kingsbury, Susan Myra, ed. *The Records of the Virginia Company of London*. 4 vols. Washington, D.C.: U.S. Government Printing Office, 1938.

Neible, George W. "Account of Servants Bound and Assigned Before James Hamilton, Mayor of Philadelphia." *Pennsylvania Magazine of History and Biography* 32 (1908): 88-103, 237-49, 351-70.

Nelson, William, ed. *Documents Relating to the Colonial History of the State of New Jersey*. 1st series, vol. 12. Patterson, N.J.: Press Printing and Publishing Co., 1895.

Pennsylvania German Society. *Record of Indentures of Individuals Bound Out as Apprentices, etc.,. . .Philadelphia. . .1771 to 1773. . . .* Baltimore: Genealogical Publishing Co., 1973.

Scott, Kenneth. "Some Huntington, Long Island Residents, 1763-1779." *National Genealogical Society Quarterly* 61 (Sept. 1974): 173-77.

The Stoystown and Greensburgh Turnpike Road Company: Minutes 1815-1826. N.p.: Southwest Pennsylvania Genealogical Services, 1976.

Stryker-Rodda, Kenn. "The Janeway Account Books 1735-1746." *Genealogical Magazine of New Jersey* 33 (Jan./April 1958): 1-4.

Some Compiled Business Records

Cutten, George Barton. *The Silversmiths of Virginia from 1694 to 1850*. Richmond: Dietz Press, 1952.

Elliott, Mary Quigley. *Biographical Sketches of Knox County Writers*. Mount Vernon, Ohio.: n. pub., 1937.

Hutslar, Donald A. *Gunsmiths of Ohio 18th and 19th Centuries. Longrifle Series*. York, Pa.: George Shumway, 1973.

Martin, John Hill. *Martins Bench and Bar of Philadelphia*. Philadelphia: Rees Welsh and Co., 1883.

R. L. Polk and Co. *Missoula City Directory*. Missoula, Mont.: R. L. Polk and Co., 1922.

Vandenberge, Peter N., ed. *Historical Directory of the Reformed Church in America 1628-1965*. New Brunswick, N.J.: Reformed Church in America, 1966.

Historical Information on Businesses and Records

Apprenticeship Past and Present. Rev. ed. Washington, D.C.: U.S. Department of Labor, 1964.

Clough, Shepard B. *A Century of American Life Insurance: A History of the Mutual Life Insurance Company of New York 1843-1943*. New York: Columbia University Press, 1946.

Herrick, Cheesman A. *White Servitude in Pennsylvania*. 1926; reprint ed., New York: Negro University Press, 1969.

Historical Statistics of the United States Colonial Times to 1970. Washington, D.C.: U.S. Department of Commerce, 1975.

Information Please Almanac, Atlas and Yearbook. 35th ed. New York: Simon and Schuster, 1982.

Larkin, Harold F. "Retention of Life Insurance Records." *American Archivist* 5 (April 1942): 93-99.

Lewinson, Paul, and Morris Rieger. "Labor Union Records in the United States." *American Archivist* 25 (Jan. 1962): 39-57.

Madison, James H. "The Credit Reports of R. G. Dun and Co. as Historical Sources." *Historical Methods Newsletter* 8 (Sept. 1975): 128-31.

Moskowitz, Milton, Michael Katz, and Robert Levering, eds. *Everybody's Business: An Almanac*. San Francisco: Harper and Row, 1980.

Continued
on page 342

Appendix 1

Old Trades and Occupations

The following Appendix was adapted from *Journal of the Hampshire Family History Society* 7 (May 1980): pp. 16-18.

Ale-draper: innkeeper.

Backster/baxter: originally a female baker, later used for either sex.

Badger: one who buys corn and other commodities and carries them elsewhere to sell, i.e., an itinerant dealer between producer (farmer, fisherman, etc.) and consumer. Also known in various dialects as *cadger, hawker, huckster.*

Barker: a tanner of leather.

Bowyer: a maker of and dealer in bows, or an archer.

Brewster: a female brewer.

Bunter: a rag and bone woman.

Cadger: *see* badger.

Caper: a cap maker.

Carter: a wagoner or stable headman.

Cashmarie: one who takes fish from the coast to inland markets. *See* rippier.

Chamber master: in the boot and shoe trade, a shoemaker who works in his own home, either executing contracts for shops or selling his own products to them.

Chapman: a man whose business is buying and selling, either from a market stall or booth, or itinerantly.

Cobbler: a repairer of shoes.

Collier: one occupied in the production or sale of coal; a coal miner.

Cooper: one who makes and repairs wooden vessels formed of staves and hoops, e.g., casks, buckets, tubs.

Copeman: a dealer or chapman; in the seventeenth century, a receiver of stolen goods.

Cordwainer: a maker of good-quality shoes.

Costermonger: originally a seller of apples; a fruiterer, especially in the open street.

Couper: one who barters, deals, or buys and sells.

Cursitor: a chancery court clerk who draws up wills.

Dexter: a dyer.

Eggler: an egg dealer or poulterer.

Farandman: a stranger or traveller, especially a travelling merchant.

Fellmonger: a dealer in animal skins and hides, especially sheepskin.

Flesher: a butcher.

Fletcher: a maker of and dealer in arrows, and occasionally in both bows and arrows.

Fogger: a petty chapman carrying small wares from village to village; a low-class lawyer, usually as pettifogger; a middleman in the nail and chain trade; an agricultural laborer who feeds cattle.

Furbisher: an armor polisher.

Furner: a baker, i.e., one in charge of the ovens.

Garthman: one who owned, or worked in a fish-garth (a dam in a river for catching fish); a yardman or herdsman.

Greave/grieve: a bailiff, foreman, or sheriff.

Hacker: a user or maker of hoes, mattocks, etc.

Hawker: an itinerant dealer who carries his wares on his back.

Hellier/hillier: a slater or tiler of roofs.

Higgler: an itinerant dealer like a cadger; one who haggles or bargains.

Hind: farm laborer; household or domestic servant.

Huckster: a retailer of small wares in shop or booth.

Jagger: a carrier, carter, peddler or hawker. In mining, a man who carries ore on a pack-horse from a mine to the place where it is smelted; a boy who has charge of the 'jags' or train or trucks in a coal mine.

Lattener: a maker of or worker in latten, a mixed metal of yellow color, either identical with or closely resembling brass.

Lavender: a washerwoman.

Leightonward: a gardener.

Litster: a dyer.

Lorimer: a maker of bits and metal mountings for horse bridles, also a spurrier and generally a maker of small ironware and a worker in wrought iron.

Navigator: a laborer digging canals and later railways.

Neatherd: a cowherd.

Owler: a smuggler of sheep and/or wool out of England.

Pigman: a seller of crockery, also called a muggler.

Pikeman: a miller's assistant.

Rippier: *see* cashmarie. There might be a distinction in that the rippier took his/her fish from the riverbank and the cashmarie took his/her fish from the sea coast.

Roper: a rope and net maker.

Salter: a maker of and dealer in salt, a drysalter.

Say weaver: a weaver of say, a cloth of fine texture resembling serge.

Scrivener: a clerk specializing in drawing up bonds.

Slop-seller: a seller of ready-made clothes.

Smith: a metal worker. The blacksmith worked in iron, the whitesmith in tin, *also* goldsmith, silversmith, etc.

Spurrier: a spur maker. *See* lorimer.

Swailer/swealer: a miller, or dealer in corn.

Tasker: a reaper or thresher.

Tinker: one who repairs utensils made of tin.

Tucker: a fuller (one who cleanses and thickens cloth).

Webster: a weaver.

Whig: a Scottish horse drover.

Whitear: a cleanser of hides.

Whitesmith: a maker of utensils in tin, especially dairy utensils.

Whittawer: a saddler.

Wright: a constructor, e.g., wheelwright, shipwright, etc.

Appendix 2

Life Insurance Companies Commencing Business Prior to 1876 and in Active Operation in 1942*

Name of Company	Home Office	Year and Date of Commencing Business
Presbyterian Ministers' Fund	Philadelphia	1759
Mutual Life Insurance Company of New York	New York City	1 Feb 1843
New England Mutual Insurance Company	Boston, Mass.	1 Dec. 1843
Mutual Benefit Life Insurance Company	Newark, N.J.	1 April 1845
New York Life Insurance Company	New York City	12 April 1845
State Mutual Life Assurance Company	Worcester, Mass.	1 June 1845
Connecticut Mutual Life Insurance Company	Hartford, Conn.	15 Dec. 1846
Penn Mutual Life Insurance Company	Philadelphia, Pa.	25 May 1847
Union Mutual Life Insurance Company	Portland, Maine	1 Oct. 1849
National Life Insurance Company	Montpelier, Vt.	1 Feb. 1850
U.S. Life Insurance Company	New York City	4 March 1850
Aetna Life Insurance Company	Hartford, Conn.	July 1850
Manhattan Life Insurance Company	New York City	1 Aug. 1850
Phoenix Mutual Life Insurance Company	Hartford, Conn.	May 1851
Massachusetts Mutual Life Insurance Company	Springfield, Mass.	1 Aug. 1851
Berkshire Life Insurance Company	Pittsfield, Mass.	4 Sept. 1851
German Mutual Life Insurance Company (Name changed to St. Louis Mutual Life Insurance Co., 1919)	St. Louis, Mo.	12 April 1858
Northwestern Mutual Life Insurance Company	Milwaukee, Wis.	25 Nov. 1858
Equitable Life Assurance Society of the United States	New York City	28 July 1859
Home Life Insurance Company	New York City	1 May 1860
Germania Life Insurance Company (Name changed to Guardian Life Insurance Company of America, 1918)	New York City	16 July 1860
John Hancock Mutual Life Insurance Company	Boston, Mass.	27 Dec. 1862
Maryland Life Insurance Company	Baltimore, Md.	12 July 1865
Provident Life & Trust Company of Philadelphia (Name changed to Provident Mutual Life Insurance Company of Philadelphia, 1908)	Philadelphia, Pa.	31 July 1865
Connecticut General Life Insurance Company	Hartford, Conn.	Oct. 1865
Travelers Insurance Company	Hartford, Conn.	July 1866
Metropolitan Life Insurance Company	New York City	Jan. 1867
Equitable Life Insurance Company of Iowa	Des Moines, Iowa	March 1867
Union Central Life Insurance Company	Cincinnati, Ohio	1867
Pacific Mutual Life Insurance Company	Louisiana, Calif.	April 1868
Masonic Mutual Relief Association (Name changed to Monumental Life Insurance Company, 1935)	Washington, D.C.	3 March 1869
Mutual Life Insurance Company of Baltimore	Baltimore, Md.	1870
Pennsylvania Mutual Insurance Company	Philadelphia, Pa.	1870
Life Insurance Company of Virginia	Richmond, Va.	April 1871
Prudential Insurance Company of America	Newark, N.J.	13 Oct. 1875

*Shepard B. Clough, *A Century of American Life Insurance: A History of the Mutual Life Company of New York*, 1843-1943 (New York: Columbia University Press, 1946), pp. 30, 46.

Appendix 3

U.S. Labor Union Records

1	2	3	4	5	6	7	8	9	10	11	12	13	14	15	16	17
	Types of Records—Earliest Years															
Organization Name	Earliest Records	Contracts	Correspondence	Educational Material	Financial	Minutes	Negotiations	Press Releases etc.	Research	Scrapbooks	Newsletters etc.	Quantity	Weeded	Losses	Complete Since	See Notes
Federations																
American Federation of Labor and Congress of Industrial Organizations	1883		1888		1901	1893		1898			1906	435 c., 1,110 b., 75 ft.	Yes	Yes	1888	(1)
AFL-CIO Industrial Union Dept.	1955		1955	1955	1955	1955		1955	1955		1955		No	No	1955	
AFL-CIO Railway Employes' Dept.	1908	1914	1908	1920	1920	1908	1908	1919	1914		1919	147 c., 393 ft.	Yes	Yes	1908	(2)
AFL-CIO Railway Labor Executives' Assn.	1926					1926										(3)
National Independent Union Council	1951	1951	1951	1951	1951	1951		1951			1951	5 c.	No	No	1951	
National and International Unions																
Actors' Equity Assn.	1913		1945		1913	1913					1920	45 c.	Yes	No	1913	(4)
American Federation of Television and Radio Artists	1937	1939	1937	1937	1937	1937	1937	1937		1937		70 c.	Yes	No	1937	(5)
American Guild of Musical Artists, Inc.	1936	1936	1936	1936	1936	1936	1936	1936	1936	1936	1936	135 c.	No	No	1936	(6)
Screen Actors Guild, Inc.		1937	1933	1934	1933	1933	1937	1934			1944		Yes	No		(7)
Agricultural Workers Union, National	1934		1934									30 c.	No	No	1934	(8)
Air Line Communication Employees Assn.																(9)
Air Line Dispatchers Assn.	1939	1939	1939		1940	1939	1942	1956			1934	36 c.	Yes	No	1950	(10)
Air Line Pilots Assn., International	1930	1938	1930	1930	1930	1938	1930	1930	1930	1930	1930	100 c., 400 b., 2,700 ft.	Yes	Yes	1930	(11)
Aluminum Workers International Union	1933	1933	1933		1933	1933					1933	18 c., 10 b., 125 ft.	No	Yes	1953	(12)
Associated Unions of America	1939	1941	1939		1939	1939	1941				1939	5 c., 7 b.	Yes	No		(13)
Bakery and Confectionery Workers' International Union, American																(14)
Brewery, Flour, Cereal, Soft Drink, and Distillery Workers of America, International Union of United	1886	1886		1910	1886	1886	1886		1937		1886		Yes	Yes	1886	(15)
Bricklayers, Masons, and Plasterers' International Union of America	1865											150 c.	Yes			(16)
Broadcast Employees and Technicians, National Assn. of	1933	1933	1933	1950	1945	1933	1933			1936	1936	16 c., 20 b.	Yes	Yes		(17)
Building Service Employees' International Union	1940	1946	1956	1945		1940		1945	1945		1945		Yes	Yes	1955	(18)
Cement, Lime, and Gypsum Workers International Union, United	1936	1936	1936	1952	1936	1937	1937		1935		1946	54 c.	No	No	1936	(19)
Chemical Workers Union, International	1940	1944	1940	1949	1940	1940	1940	1944	1949	1944	1940		No	No	1944 and 1949	
Christian Labor Assn. of the U. S. A.																(20)
Cigar Makers' International Union of America		1856	1928		1879					1880		8 c., 100 b., 110 ft.	Yes	Yes	1879	(21)
Clothing Workers of America, Amalgamated	1911	1911	1914	1920	1915	1911	1913	1914	1917	1910	1921	20 c., 15 ft.	Yes	Yes		(22)
Communications Workers of America	1937	1939	1939	1945	1939	1939	1945	1945	1945		1939		Yes	No	1939	(23)
Coopers' International Union of North America		1951	1953		1929							6 c., 6 b., 36 ft.	Yes	No		(24)
Electrical, Radio, and Machine Workers, International Union of	1950	1950	1950		1950	1950	1950	1950	1951	1950	1950	200 c.	No	No		(25)
Engineers, American Federation of Technical	1918	1945	1950		1950	1930	1950	1950			1950	12 c., 8 b., 100 ft.	Yes	Yes	1950	(26)
Federal Employees, National Federation of																(27)
Fire Fighters, International Assn. of	1918	1948	1953		1918	1918			1918		1953	50 c.	Yes	No		(28)
Firemen and Oilers, International Brotherhood of												60 c., 30 b., 110 ft.	No	No		(29)
Flight Engineers, International Assn.		1948	1948	1952	1948	1950	1950	1955	1955	1958	1950	14 c., 6 b., 30 ft.	No	No		
Glass Bottle Blowers Assn. of the U. S. and Canada	1842		1952	1954					1950			6 c., 4 b., 3 ft.	Yes	No		(30)
Glass and Ceramic Workers of North America, United	1933	1934	1934	1942	1934	1934	1934		1942	1936		50 c.		No		(31)
Glass Cutters League of America, Window	1917	1917	1917		1917	1917	1917				1917	26 c., 81 b.	No	Yes	1917	(32)
Government Employees, American Federation of	1932		1932	1950	1950	1932		1941	1945		1956	56 c.	Yes	Yes	1950	
Grain Millers, American Federation of	1935	1936	1936		1936	1936	1936					1 c.	Yes	No	1945	(33)
Granite Cutters' International Assn. of America	1877				1877	1877							No	No	1877	(34)
Hatters, Cap and Millinery Workers International Union, United	After 1850	1919	1927		1934	1934		1948	1937				Yes	No	1934	(35)
Hosiery Workers, American Federation of	1913	1929	1920		1920	1913						328 b.	Yes	No	1913	(36)
Industrial Workers of America; International Union, Allied		1955	1941	1946	1942	1938	1939	1946	1946		1946		Yes	Yes	1954	(37)

(Continued on Next Page)

Paul Lewinson and Morris Rieger, "Labor Union Records in the United States," *American Archivist* 25 (Jan. 1962): 46-57; reprinted with permission.

1 Organization Name	2 Earliest Records	3 Contracts	4 Correspondence	5 Educational Material	6 Financial	7 Minutes	8 Negotiations	9 Press Releases etc.	10 Research	11 Scrapbooks	12 Newsletters etc.	13 Quantity	14 Weeded	15 Losses	16 Complete Since	17 See Notes
		Types of Records—Earliest Years														
Industrial Workers Union, National	1955	1956	1955	1955	1955	1955	1956	1955			1956	1 c.	No	No	1955	(38)
Iron Workers, International Assn. of Bridge, Structural and Ornamental	1901	1919	1919	1919	1919	1919	1919	1919			1919	300 c., 200 b.	No	Yes	1919	(39)
Lace Operatives of America, Amalgamated	1906				1906	1906	1906					5 c., 12 b.	No	No		(40)
Lathers International Union, The Wood, Wire, and Metal	1899	Current year	1902		1899					1899	1953	16 ft.	Yes	No		(41)
Laundry and Dry Cleaning International Union																(42)
Leather Workers International Union of America	1955	1955	1955	1955	1955	1955	1955	1955	1955	1955	1955	5 c., 6 b.	No	No	1955	
Letter Carriers of the U.S.A., National Assn. of				1946	1892	1892		1952	1900	1946	1946		Yes	No		(43)
Letter Carriers' Assn., National Rural	1903		1957		1900s	1952					1952					(44)
Lithographers of America, Amalgamated		1949	1943			1904	1949		1953			12 c.	Yes		1952	(45)
Locomotive Engineers, Brotherhood of																(46)
Locomotive Firemen and Enginemen, Brotherhood of		1887	1930	1956			1907		1900			200 c.	Yes	No	1930	(47)
Longshoremen's and Warehousmen's Union, International	1934	1934	1934	1934	1934	1934	1934	1934	1934	1934	1934	49 c., 111 b., 81 ft.	No	No	1946	(48)
Marine Engineers' Beneficial Assn., National		1910	1925		1900	1875						4 c.	Yes	Yes		(49)
Marine and Shipbuilding Workers of America, Industrial Union of	1933												Yes	No		(50)
Mine, Mill, and Smelter Workers, International Union of		1944	1945			1936			1946			150 b., 100 ft.			1945	(51)
Musicians, American Federation of	1896	1920	1912	1931	1896	1896	1920					43 c.	No			(52)
Newspaper Guild, American	1933															(53)
Packinghouse Workers, National Brotherhood of	1939	1942	1939	1941		1939					1939	4 c., 6 b.	Yes	No	1949	(54)
Photo-Engravers' Union of North America, International	1900	1906	1905		1906	1900	1905					224 c.	Yes	No	1925	
Plate Printers', Die Stampers' and Engravers' Union of North America, International	1906		1906			1906					1906	1 b.	Yes	No	1906	
Post Office Motor Vehicle Employees, National Federation of	1925		1956		1956	1929					1956	4	Yes	No		(55)
Postal Clerks Union, National	1959		1959		1959			1959			1959	5 c.	Yes	No		(56)
Postal Employees, National Alliance of	1913		1920	1920	1920	1920	1920	1920	1920	1920	1920	15 c.	No	No	1955	(57)
Postal Transport Assn., National												40 c., 70 ft.	Yes	No		(58)
Printing Pressmen and Assistants' Union of North America, International	1889	1918	1890		1890		1890		1937			100 c.	No	No		(59)
Protection Employees in the Electrical and Machine Industry, Independent Union of Plant	1950	1950										10 c.	Yes	No		(60)
Radio Assn., American		1937					1949						Yes	Yes		(61)
Railroad Operating Crafts, United																(62)
Railroad Signalmen, Brotherhood of																(63)
Railroad Telegraphers, The Order of	1886	1895			1886	1886			1920		1922	60 c., 50 b., 3,000 ft.	Yes	Yes	1920	(64)
Railroad Trainmen, Brotherhood of	1883												Yes	No		(65)
Railroad Yardmasters of North America, Inc.	1925	1925	1925	1930	1925	1925	1925	1930				10 c.	No	No		(66)
Retail Clerks International Assn.	1888	1945	1900	1950	1888	1888							Yes	Yes	1945	(67)
Roofers, Damp and Waterproof Workers Assn.; United Slate, Tile, and Composition	1942		1942									17 c.	Yes	No	1942	(68)
Seafarers' International Union of North America (Great Lakes District)	1916															(69)
Inlandboatmen's Union of the Pacific (Puget Sound Division)	1931	1931	1931		1931	1931						20 ft.	Yes	No	1940	
Marine Cooks' and Stewards' Union	1951	1952	1951		1951	1952	1952	1952		1957	1952	19 c.	No	Yes	1955	
Pacific Coast Marine Firemen, Oilers, Watertenders, and Wipers Assn.	1903	1934	1933	1949	1933	1933	1934				1944	25 c., 40 b., 269 ft.	Yes	Yes	1933	(70)
Sailors' Union of the Pacific	1885	1936	1936	1936	1936	1936	1936	1936	1936	1950	1936	100 b.	Yes	Yes		(71)
State, County, and Municipal Employees, American Federation of	1935	1944	1935	1944	1935	1935	1935	1944	1944		1935	74 c., 20 b., 504 ft.	Yes	No	1944	(72)
Steelworkers of America, United	1936	1937	1936	1936	1936	1936	1937	1936	1936	1936	1936	600 c.	Yes	No		(73)
Stereotypers' and Electrotypers' Union of North America, International	1888	1900	1902		1902	1902						30 c.	Yes	No		(74)
Stove Mounters' International Union of North America	1882	1950		1950	1950	1950						18 c.	Yes	No	195[illegible]	
Street, Electric Railway, and Motor Coach Employes' of America; Amalgamated Assn. of	1892		1935		1923							175 c.	Yes	Yes	1923	

(Continued on Next Page)

(continued)

		Types of Records—Earliest Years														
1	2	3	4	5	6	7	8	9	10	11	12	13	14	15	16	17
Organization Name	Earliest Records	Contracts	Correspondence	Educational Material	Financial	Minutes	Negotiations	Press Releases etc.	Research	Scrapbooks	Newsletters etc.	Quantity	Weeded	Losses	Complete Since	See Notes
Teachers, American Federation of	1916	1919	1916	1916	1916	1916	1916	1916	1916	1916	1916	30 c., 100 b., 300 ft.	Yes	Yes		(75)
Telephone Unions, Alliance of Independent	1949		1949		1953	1949		1954			1954	1 c.	Yes	No	1954	(76)
Textile Workers Union of America	1937	1937	1937	1937	1937	1937	1937	1937	1937	1937	1937		No	No		(77)
Tobacco Workers International Union	1900	1900	1896		1895	1897			1900		1900	15 c., 10 b.	Yes	No		(78)
Tool Craftsmen, International Assn. of	1953	1955	1952		1953	1953	1955				1952	3 c., 6 b.	No	No		(79)
Toy Workers of the U.S. and Canada, International Union of Doll and	1952		1952	1952	1952	1952		1952	1952	1952		4 b.	Yes	No	1955	
Train Dispatchers Assn., American	1918	1918	1918		1918	1918	1918		1918			30 c.	Yes	No	1918	(80)
Transport Service Employees, United													No		1945	(81)
Typographical Union, International	1851	1800s	1950		1852	1852	1800s						Yes	No	1850	(82)
Upholsterers' International Union of North America	1879	1937	1916	1923	1846	1879		1940		1940	1917		Yes	Yes	1937	(83)
Watchmen's Assn., Independent		1937	1937	1937	1937	1937	1937	1937	1937	1937	1937	15 c., 24 b., 60 ft.	No	No		(84)
Welders of America, National Union, United	1936	1938	1937			1944						5 c., 4 b.	Yes	Yes		(85)
Writers Guild of America, East, Inc.	1954	1954	1954		1954	1954	1954	1954		1956	1954	10 c.	Yes	No	1954	(86)
Writers Guild of America, West, Inc.	1926	1942	1937		1947	1926	1941				1945	30 c., 70 b.	No	No		(87)
State Federations																
Alabama Labor Council	1926	1960	1930	1960	1926	1906		1960	1960		1956	11 c.	Yes	Yes	1933	(88)
Colorado Labor Council					1896	1896						32 c., 100 ft.	Yes		1928	(89)
Idaho State AFL–CIO	1916		1916		1916	1916		1958		1958		3 c.	Yes	No	1916	
Illinois State AFL–CIO	1884												No	No	1884	(90)
Indiana State AFL–CIO																(91)
Iowa Federation of Labor			1955	1956	1931	1937					1959	8 c.	Yes	No	1945	(92)
Kentucky State AFL–CIO	1917	1917		1939				1947				1 c.	No	Yes		(93)
Maryland State and District of Columbia AFL–CIO	1957		1957		1957	1957					1957	5 c.	Yes	No		(94)
Minnesota AFL–CIO Federation of Labor	**1896**			**1956**	**1896**	**1896**		**1950**			**1947**	**8 c., 2 b.**	**Yes**	**Yes**	**1956**	**(95)**
Missouri State Labor Council	**1891**		**1953**	**1953**	**1891**	**1891**		**1953**			**1953**	**4 c.**	**No**	**Yes**	**1953**	**(96)**
Montana State AFL–CIO	**1908**		**1908**		**1908**			**1908**				**9 c., 15 b.**	**No**	**No**	**1908**	**(97)**
New Jersey State Industrial Union Council	**1953**		**1953**	**1953**	**1953**	**1948**		**1955**	**1955**	**1956**	**1956**	**7 c., 16 ft.**	**Yes**	**Yes**	**1955**	
Ohio AFL–CIO																**(98)**
Oklahoma State AFL–CIO	**1903**		**1903**									**10 c.**	**Yes**	**Yes**		**(99)**
South Dakota State Federation of Labor	**1920**	**1925**	**1920**		**1920**	**1920**						**1 c.**	**Yes**	**Yes**		**(100)**
Tennessee State Labor Council													**Yes**	**Yes**	**1956**	**(101)**
Texas State AFL–CIO			**1952**		**1942**	**1937**				**1940**		**21 c., 33 b.**	**No**	**Yes**	**1939**	**(102)**
Utah State AFL–CIO																**(103)**
Vermont State Labor Council												**3 c., 3 b.**	**No**	**No**	**1958**	**(104)**
West Virginia Federation of Labor			**1940**		**1950**	**1940**		**1957**		**1957**	**1957**	**6 c.**	**Yes**	**No**	**1957**	**(105)**

Notes to the preceding tabulation of the results of the survey of labor union records begin on the next page. These notes are especially important to persons seeking to make interpretive judgments on the basis of the data presented in the tabulation.

Notes to Tabulation

1. (Cols. 5, 10) The records include educational material and research records, but earliest dates are not given. (Col. 7) Minutes are restricted. Legislative records also exist since 1924. AFL records since 1888 are transferred to the State Historical Society of Wisconsin after microfilming. CIO records, similarly, will go to the Catholic University of America, Washington, D. C. Scrapbooks and other personal papers of Samuel Gompers were sent to the New York Public Library after 1924. The AFL–CIO retains 16 cabinets of "early labor history and biographical material on Labor leaders." It films "documents of importance" continuously, and has at this time "over two million documents on film."

2. Correspondence before 1945 is on microfilm.

3. (Cols. 3, 4, 9, 12) The presence of these types is indicated, without beginning date; "1926" (Col. 7) may refer to them, too. "Not open to public use."

4. (Col. 3) Contracts are included, but without beginning date. News clippings have been given to the Theatre Collection, New York Public Library.

5. The Federation of Radio Artists, chartered 1937, and the Television Authority, 1949, merged in 1952.

6. Has compiled a history.

7. (Col. 10) "Spasmodic" research records are included. (Col. 16) Complete since earliest days. Materials, not clearly archives, have been given to a number of industrial relations institutes and the like, to university and other libraries, etc.; a list of institutions is available from the Society of American Archivists.

8. Started as Southern Tenant Farmers Union, 1934; name changed to National Farm Labor Union, 1944, and to present form, 1952; merged with Amalgamated Meat Cutters and Butcher Workmen of North America, Aug. 1960. (Cols. 5–12) All these types of records are present, but from an unspecified date; perhaps 1934? The union also has a file of its newspapers, films, and tape recordings. Records, 1934–57, have been deposited in the Southern Historical Collection, Library of the University of North Carolina; and a four-year accretion is to be sent later. Columbia University's Oral History Project has a transcription of a recording by H. L. Mitchell.

9. Reply states that this union is now a part of Communications Workers of America; see below.

10. Has given convention minutes, constitution and bylaws, and financial reports to a restricted list of public and university libraries and research organizations.

11. (Col. 3) Year of the association's first contract.

12. Predecessor or earlier title: International Council of Aluminum Workers Unions—AFL. Has given convention proceedings, contracts, and constitution to libraries, etc.

13. Formerly Wisconsin Association of Independent Unions. (Cols. 9 and 11) Press releases, speeches, etc., and scrapbooks are present from an unspecified date.

14. The union intends "to place historical material and relevant records with one of the universities particularly interested in labor matters."

15. (Col. 4) Correspondence and memoranda are included, but without beginning date. A history was published in 1910; a new one was in view for 1961 publication. The union has an unbroken file of its publications.

16. Membership records and printed officers' reports and convention proceedings retained since 1865. By convention instructions of 1948 a ten-year retention period was established for "correspondence, contracts, circular letters, etc." Records prior to the ten-year period have been destroyed.

17. (Cols. 4, 6, 8, 12) are returned as "partial." Present organization name dates from 1943; 1940–43, National Association of Broadcast Engineers and Technicians; 1933–40, Association of Technical Employees.

18. Quantity is returned as "very large."

19. Records include file of monthly publication (since 1937), roster of salaried representatives (since 1941), and a brief history (1945). Also included are records of the predecessor National Council of Cement Workers.

(continued)

8–10, 12) These types of records are present, but from unspecified dates. Return calls attention to a "history to 1937."

37. Return states "Our union was chartered in August 1935 as the United Automobile Workers of America. When the AFL–CIO merged our name was changed as above."

38. Constitution has been sent to various colleges and universities.

39. (Col. 14) "Routine records are microfilmed after they are several years old." (Col. 15) Return notes a "large" loss of records in 1919, when headquarters were moved from Indianapolis to St. Louis.

40. (Col. 16) Return states records substantially complete since a more recent date than "earliest days."

41. (Col. 16) Return states records substantially complete since earliest days.

42. (Col. 16) Letter reply: chartered 1958, records "consist of correspondence, minutes, and financial records from that time."

43. (Col. 13) Return indicates "several shelves," and (Col. 16) substantially complete since "earliest days." Some records (publications?) have been given to libraries, etc. Reference is made to complete files, from 1892, of *Proceedings*, *Postal Record*, and *Bulletins*, and to William C. Doherty, *Mailman, U.S.A.*, a "reasonably comprehensive study" by the president of the organization.

44. (Col. 16) Records substantially complete since "earliest days." Attention is called to bound-volume file of weekly magazine and to its 1953 golden anniversary issue.

45. (Cols. 5, 6, 9) Return indicates the presence of these types, but from unspecified years.

46. Letter return: it is the "policy of this Organization . . . to release records . . . only to accredited Governmental agencies."

47. (Col. 6) Return indicates the presence of financial records, but from an unspecified year.

48. Return calls attention to a completely indexed bound file of the biweekly *Dispatcher* from 1942, and a bound file of the *ILWU Reporter*, monthly Hawaiian paper, from 1949. Copies of publications are sent to university libraries, etc., on request. The union has made a special collection of "Bridges [Harry] case materials, beginning with the first one in 1935."

49. (Col. 16) Records substantially complete since "earliest days."

50. (Cols. 3–10) Earliest records are variously given as "from signature" (Cols. 1–3) or "from inception" (Cols. 4–12); there is also a file of the union newspaper. "Printed proceedings" have been given to libraries, universities, etc. Attention is called to Joseph A. Raffaele, "The Rise of Industrial Unionism in the American Shipbuilding Industry" (thesis).

51. (Col. 6) The presence of financial records is indicated, but earliest date is queried.

52. (Col. 15) "Do not know" of any losses. (Col. 16) Records substantially complete "from earliest days." Magazine *International Musician* is on "several public libraries' mailing list." On file are recorded speeches by James C. Petrillo and a book outlining AFM history to about 1950.

53. Letter return states that "detailed financial records" exist from 1947; earlier ones are scattering; contract file is "virtually intact"; early negotiation records "nonexistent or sketchy, although . . . nearly complete" since 1955; membership records "fairly complete" since founding (1933).

54. Formerly International Brotherhood of Swift Employees. (Col. 6) Financial records "kept by Natl. Treasurer—not known by dates." (Cols. 8–10) These records are present, but earliest dates are not provided. Has given proceedings, constitutions, etc., to "school libraries" on request.

55. (Col. 16) Records substantially complete since a date more recent than earliest days. Include a file of "Rotor" (publication?) since 1936. Has given "Rotor," constitution and bylaws, and convention minutes copies to libraries, etc.

56. (Col. 16) Records substantially complete since earliest days, including a file of

20. "Everything we have dates from 1931."

21. (Col. 3) This date is marked "Toronto." (Col. 6) This date is marked "Local Unions." (Col. 15) A notation indicates that many early records were destroyed in the Chicago fire of 1871. (Col. 16) An ambiguity in the return suggests that 1928 may be the date from which records are substantially complete. The present name of the organization dates from 1867; from June 1864 to that year it was Cigar Makers National Union of the United States. Material has been given to the Library of Congress, the New York Public Library, and "various universities, colleges, and city public libraries," but it is not clear whether anything but publications are included.

22. The ACW was formed from former locals of the United Garment Workers of America in 1914. (Col. 8) Includes arbitration cases. (Col. 11) Scrapbooks include newspaper clippings, periodical articles, and some unpublished speeches, memoranda, correspondence, pamphlets, and photographs. (Col. 16) The union does not feel that its records are complete. The records also include organizing and strike leaflets since 1910. The union has used its records for its own publications on union history and has made them available for biographies, studies, and dissertations. Copies or duplicates, chiefly of published material, 1910 to date, have been given to the New School for Social Research, New York.

23. Name until 1948: National Federation of Telephone Workers; now includes Air Line Communication Employees Association. (Col. 3) In some cases, from 1945. (Col. 13) Many records are kept in district offices; all records up to 1955 have been microfilmed, except research department files (which include contracts); these unmicrofilmed files occupy about 10 filing cabinets at Washington, D. C., headquarters.

24. Records also include "Board Letters—copy of all important letters sent to General Executive Board members," since 1948. (Col. 16) The union believes its records are complete in all important kinds from its earliest days.

25. (Col. 5) Educational material is present from an unspecified date. (Col. 16) The union believes its records are complete in all important kinds since its earliest days.

26. Has given convention proceedings to "colleges, etc."

27. "We have not completed this questionnaire as the NFFE is not a 'labor union' within the meaning and intent of the Labor and Management Improper Practices Act."

28. Return calls attention to history: *The International Association of Fire Fighters*, by James Joseph Gibbons (M. A. thesis, University of Notre Dame).

29. (Cols. 3–9) These types of records are returned as present, as are also "journals." (Col. 16) "From earliest days."

30. Former title, Green Glass Bottle Blowers. (Col. 16) "Complete . . . from earliest years" according to return. Material (publications) sent to libraries on request.

31. (Col. 12) May also be present. (Col. 13) May be additional boxes and shelved material. (Col. 14) Return checks both "yes" and "no." (Col. 15) "Complete . . . since earliest days."

32. (Col. 9) May also be present. An "Incorporated Assn." (of window glass workers?) joined the league in 1930; the Window Glass Cutters and Flatteners Protective Association in 1934; and the Window Glass Cutters and Flatteners Association of America at an unspecified date.

33. Originally National Council of Grain Processors, later American Federation of Grain Processors.

34. Return indicates as also present "Monthly Journal and Circular" since 1877, and "general registers of members' dues payments" since 1906.

35. (Col. 7) A few late nineteenth- and early twentieth-century items in addition. "Legal records" are also present since "early 1900's." The union has given some material to the Rand School of Social Science and the "Bund Archives of the Jewish Labor Movement." Return also calls attention to Donald B. Robinson, *Spotlight on a Union*, 1948; Charles H. Green, *The Headgear Workers*, 1944; and *Max Zaritsky at Fifty*, 1935.

36. Formerly American Federation of Full-Fashioned Hosiery Workers. (Cols. 5,

(continued)

U. S. LABOR UNION RECORDS

union newspaper since 1959. Has had requests for records from libraries, etc., "which we intend to comply with as soon as feasible."

57. Has made up special historical collections.

58. (Cols. 4–9, 12) Return indicates the presence of these types of records, without beginning date. (Col. 16) Believes records complete since "earliest days." Calls attention to a brochure *The Editor Speaks*, based on "writings of a former Editor of our official publication, Mr. J. L. Reilly."

59. (Col. 16) Records substantially complete since earliest days, but "dates vary in some kinds of materials"; "membership records, financial records rather complete, contracts fairly well since about 1920." Has union periodicals "back to beginning."

60. (Cols. 3–12) The 1950 beginning year for contracts may also be intended to cover the other specified types. The union also has a file of photographs. (Col. 16) Records substantially complete since earliest days.

61. (Cols. 4–7, 9–12) Return gives "various" for beginning dates. (Col. 16) Records not substantially complete since earliest days, but no beginning date is given.

62. Across the questionnaire has been written: "How much is this all to cost now or in the future? What are you selling and to whom?"—and more in the same vein.

63. Only letter return received. "The majority of our old records have been destroyed, and copies of old contracts, memorandums, correspondence, etc. have been filed in our basement for years."

64. (Cols. 4, 8) These types of records are checked as present, but without beginning dates.

65. (Cols. 3–12) "We have something on practically everything listed, dating back to the date of our organization." (Col. 13) "Many, many file cabinets at our headquarters . . . Cleveland." (Col. 14) On weeding: "very few, no valuable historical records." Also: "We have a fine library in Cleveland headquarters, and even a small museum of early mementos. . . . Our publication, first a monthly and later (1947) a weekly, TRAINMAN NEWS, would be a valuable source for historical research."

66. (Col. 16) Records substantially complete since earliest days.

67. Formerly Retail Clerks National Protective Association. Return calls attention to *A Brief History of the RCIA*.

68. (Cols. 1, 8) Returned "Not Applicable." (Cols. 6–7) Returned "Published."

69. (Cols. 3–12) Only Col. 7 is checked. A note states "Minutes of Conventions, etc., are in New York . . . these go back to 1916."

70. "The Marine Firemen, our news publication, is sent every month to approximately 150 libraries, labor schools, and universities."

71. (Col. 16) Return indicates records not substantially complete since earliest days but gives no other date. Calls attention to "An Anniversary Edition of 'West Coast Sailors,' official organ . . . commemorating 100th Anniversary of the birth of Andrew Furuseth . . . March 5, 1954," and other pamphlets and briefs; also to Hyman G. Weintraub, *Andrew Furuseth* (University of California Press, 1959).

72. (Col. 11) Scrapbooks are present, but no beginning date is given.

73. Includes records of the Steelworkers Organizing Committee—CIO, 1936–42. (Col. 13) In addition to the stated quantity of paper records, there are "5½ million microfilmed documents." "Philip Murray historical material was donated to the Catholic University (25 cases of documents)." The union's public relations department publishes a "historical resume each 10 years." Since May 1953 the union has had a considerable records management program in operation, which includes the preservation of "historical data."

74. "Part of the Internatl. Typographical Union" from 1888 to 1902, "known as the Stereotypers and Electrotypers Trade District Union." (Col. 16) Records substantially complete since earliest days. "We hope to write a history of our union if we ever have time."

75. (Col. 16) Substantially complete since earliest days. Has file of *American Teacher Magazine* since 1916. Has given material (publications?) to libraries, etc., but is "not certain of amount."

76. The Alliance "is a Federation . . . Each member union is autonomous and main-

tain their own records . . . Practically all the activities of the Alliance are incorporated in the minutes of the Quarterly Conferences . . . not published for distribution outside of the Alliance."

77. (Col. 16) Records substantially complete since earliest days. Has file of "magazines, newspaper, convention reports, convention proceedings."

78. (Col. 16) Records substantially complete since a more recent, unspecified, date than earliest days. Has file of publication *The Tobacco Worker* since 1900. Furnishes copies of "material" (publications?) to "any library, labor school, etc., upon request."

79. (Col. 16) Records substantially complete since a more recent (unspecified) date than earliest days. Sends constitution and "Question and Answer booklets" upon request. Has a special collection, "Our history."

80. (Col. 12) Has newsletters, etc., from "various" beginning dates. Has bound volumes of magazine *The Train Dispatcher* from 1919, and has sent it to "a few libraries and universities."

81. (Cols. 3, 4, 6, 7, 9, 11, 12) The presence of these types is indicated, without beginning dates. Has made up special historical collections, unspecified.

82. This union returned two questionnaires with comments, which include the sentences set in italic type at the head of this article. The respondents speak of a "considerable" quantity of "invaluable documents," dating from the union's founding in 1850. As the union officers in the first 30 years could not devote full time to their administrative work, some early correspondence may not be in the archives; but some of the officers did leave their correspondence in the union's hands. Other records from the earliest date include applications for membership, for pensions, and for admission to the Union Printers Home; receipts for union expenditures; issues of publications; and contracts negotiated by local unions. In recent years the ITU has begun a program of microfilming its records. "The wealth of material on the ITU is fantastic but to date no comprehensive history of our organization has even been written. There were three attempts [including] a 1200-page Tome by George A. Tracey (1st Vice-President, 1909–12) . . . published in 1913."

83. (Col. 5) "Journals since 1923." (Col. 6) "of locals." (Col. 13) "Two attic store rooms full." The union also has financial records from 1846, of the Sailmakers Union of the Port of New York, founded in 1835. It has "tentatively assigned" the minutes of Local 21, St. Louis, 1879–1900, to the U. S. Department of Labor. A history of the union (1,700 ms. pages) was begun in 1952, for the period 1881–1931, and completed in 1955, by John Newton Thurber; and a shorter version based thereon, but with additional material to 1955, was completed by Peter A. Stone in 1956. A revised and reedited version is scheduled for 1961 publication.

84. (Col. 16) Records substantially complete since earliest days.

85. Since 1960 convention, the International Union United Welders. Formed in 1936 as the Aircraft Welders Association of America; later the United Aircraft Welders of America and then the National Union, United Welders of America. (Cols. 6 & 8) "Partial." Also has file of "paper" (periodical?) from 1959. (Col. 16) Records substantially complete since unspecified date more recent than earliest days. Has given copies of contracts to libraries and universities.

86. (Col. 2) "With some scattering of records prior to reorganization of Authors League of America, Inc., in August, 1954 at which the . . . Guild . . . was formed."

87. (Col. 16) Records complete since earliest days, date unspecified. "The organization came into being in 1954 as a result of an amalgamation of Screen Writers Guild, Inc. and Radio Writers Guild, Inc., both of which were affiliated at that time with the Authors League of America."

88. Formerly Alabama State Federation of Labor. Sends printed *Proceedings* to libraries, etc., on request.

89. (Cols. 4, 5, 9–12) These types present, but no beginning dates given. Calls attention to Barron B. Beshoar, *Out of the Depths* (1942; reissued 1957), a "study of John Lawson."

90. (Cols. 4–7, 9, 10, 12) These types present, but no beginning dates given.

91. No return, but a letter to the committee from Prof. Marshall Smelser, History

(continued)

Department, University of Notre Dame, states that the "Indiana CIO Council" has files from the 1930's, consisting of council minutes, convention reports, and correspondence (Feb. 28, 1956).

92. (Col. 5) Return indicates five-year retention period. (Col. 12) Return indicates one-year retention period. Return indicates presence, also, of convention proceedings from 1939, constitutions from 1927, audits from 1951, and year books from 1945.

93. (Col. 16) Records not substantially complete since earliest days; no beginning date given.

94. (Col. 16) Records substantially complete since earliest days.

95. Has given "several scrapbooks dating quite far back" to the Minnesota Historical Society. Calls attention to George Lawson, *History of Labor in Minnesota* (published by the Federation, 1955; still available).

96. Previous names: Missouri State Federation of Labor AFL, 1891–1956; Missouri State Industrial Union Council CIO, 1941–1956. Has given convention *Proceedings* to libraries, etc., since 1953.

97. Formerly Montana State Federation of Labor.

98. Return indicates the presence of: "Convention Proceedings and Officers Reports Ohio CIO Council 1938–1957 (complete)," "Ohio State Federation of Labor Convention Proceedings and Officers Reports 1892– (not complete)," and "Ohio AFL–CIO Convention Proceedings and Officers Reports (complete)."

99. Organized as Twin Territories Federation of Labor, 1903; name changed to Oklahoma State Federation of Labor, 1907; "merged with Oklahoma AFL–CIO," 1957. (Cols. 5–7, 9–10, 12) The presence of these types indicated without beginning dates. Has a file of monthly *Oklahoma Federationist*. "Practically all record[s] 1903 through 1953" have been given to the "University of Oklahoma—Labor Archives."

100. Records not substantially complete since earliest days, but no beginning date given.

101. (Cols. 5–7, 9, 12) Return indicates the presence of these types without beginning dates. (Col. 13) "small amount." (Col. 15) "Fire destroyed CIO records." Calls attention to a "history . . . compiled by university student."

102. Merger of Texas State Federation of Labor and Texas State CIO Council, 1957. (Col. 6) 1942 CIO, 1952 AFL. (Col. 7) CIO only. (Col. 16) CIO records "complete since 1939"; "unable to find Texas St. Fed. of Labor records prior to 1952"; "records of Fed. are very incomplete prior to 1957"; "records since . . . merger date are complete." Publications "are being placed in U. of Texas Main Library"; "Ar. [*sic*—archives?] in the Barker Texas History Library as we find them." Has a photograph collection from 1950, a clipping file from 1953, a "personality" file from 1953, and "a small collection of historical items" for display. Calls attention to two dissertations, histories of the State Federation of Labor and the State AFL–CIO, available also through the University of Texas Library.

103. (Cols. 4, 6, 7, 12) The presence of these types is indicated, without beginning dates. "Such records as have been maintained have been turned over to the Institute of Industrial Relations of the University of Utah."

104. *Proceedings* of annual conventions given to libraries, etc.

105. Has convention *Proceedings* since 1903. "Have published book recently."

Appendix 4

Index of Companies Profiled in Everybody's Business: An Almanac, 1981.

A&P
ABC
Abbott Labs
Aetna
Albertson's
Alcan
Alcoa
AMAX
American Airlines
American Brands
American Cyanamid
American Express
American Home Products
American Hospital Supply
American Motors
American Standard
American Stores
Amfac
Amtrak
Anaconda
Anderson Clayton
Anheuser-Busch
ARA Services
Archer-Daniels-Midland
Armstrong
Asarco
Associated Dry Goods
AT&T
Atlantic Richfield
Avon
Bally
Bank of America
Bantam
B-A-T Industries
Beatrice Foods
Bechtel
Bekins
Bendix
Black & Decker
Blue Bell
Boeing
Boise Cascade
Borden
Borg-Warner
Braniff International
Bristol-Myers
Brown Group
Burlington Industries
Burlington Northern
Campbell Soup
Cargill
Carnation
Carter Hawley Hale
Castle & Cooke
Caterpillar Tractor
CBS
Central Soya
Champion International
Charter Oil
Chase Manhattan
Chesebrough-Pond's
Chrysler
Citicorp
City Investing
Cluett-Peabody
Coca Cola
Colgate-Palmolive
Columbia Pictures
Conoco
Consolidated Foods
Continental Airlines
Continental Baking
Continental Grain
Continental Illinois
Control Data
Adolph Coors
CPC International
Crane
Crown Zellerbach
Cummins Engine
Dart Industries
Dayton Hudson
John Deere
Dekalb Agresearch
Del Monte
Delta Air Lines
Diamond International
Dillon
Walt Disney
Doubleday
Dow Chemical
Dow Jones
Du Pont
Eastern Airlines
Eastman Kodak
Jack Eckerd
Engelhard
Esmark
Exxon
Federal Company
Federated Department Stores
Firestone
Fisher Foods
Fleming
Fluor
Ford Motor
Foremost McKesson
Fruehauf
Gallo
Gannett
General Dynamics
General Electric
General Foods
General Mills
General Motors
General Telephone
General Tire
Genesco
Georgia Pacific
Gerber
Giant Food
Gillette
B.F. Goodrich
Goodyear
W.R. Grace
Green Giant
Greyhound
Grumman
Gulf Oil
Gulf + Western
Hallmark
Harcourt Brace Jovanovich
Harper & Row
Hart Schaffner & Marx
H.J. Heinz
Hershey
Heublein
Hewlett-Packard
Hilton Hotels
Hoffmann-La Roche
Holiday Inns
Honeywell
Geo. A. Hormel
IC Industries
IBM
Inco
Interco
International Flavors & Fragrances
International Harvester
International Paper
Interpublic Group
Iowa Beef Processors
ITT
Jewel
Johns-Manville
Johnson Wax
Johnson & Johnson
Johnson Products
K Mart
Kaiser Aluminum
Kaufman & Broud
Kellogg
Kennecott
Kentucky Fried Chicken
Kerr-McGee
Kimberly-Clark
Knight-Ridder
Kohler
Kraft
Kroger
Land O'Lakes
Levi Strauss
Libby's
Liggett Group
Eli Lilly
Litton Industries
Lockheed
Loews
Longs Drug Stores
Lowe's Companies
Lucky Stores
Macy's
Malone & Hyde
Marriott
Mars
Mattel
Oscar Mayer
MCA
McDonald's
McDonnell Douglas
McGraw-Hill
Mead
Melville
Merck
Merrill Lynch
MGM
Metropolitan Life
Miles Laboratories
3M
Missouri Pacific
Mobil
Monsanto
J.P. Morgan
Morton-Norwich
Nabisco
National Airlines
NCR
Nestlé
Newhouse
New York Times
A.C. Nielsen
Norfolk and Western
Northrop
Northwest Orient
Northwest Industries
Norton Simon
Occidental Petroleum
Off-Track Betting
Pan American
Park Newspapers
Peabody Coal
J.C. Penney
Pepsico
Pet
Pfizer
Philip Morris
Phillips Petroleum
Pillsbury
Playboy
Polaroid
Proctor & Gamble
Prudential
PSA
Quaker Oats
Ralston Purina
Random House
RCA
Reader's Digest
Resorts International
Revco
Revlon
R.J. Reynolds
Reynolds Metals
Richardson-Merrell
Roadway Express
Rockwell International
Safeway Stores
Santa Fe Industries
Schering-Plough
Jos. Schlitz Brewing
Schlumberger
Scott Paper
Scovill
Seagram
Sears, Roebuck
Shaklee
Shell Oil
Singer
SmithKline
Sohio
Southern Pacific
Southern Railway
Southland
Springs Mills
Squibb
A.C. Staley
Standard Brands
Standard Oil of California
Standard Oil of Indiana
Sterling Drug
J.P. Stevens
Stop & Shop
Sunbeam
Supermarkets General
Super Valu Stores
Tampax
Tandy
Tenneco
Texaco
Texas Instruments
J. Walter Thompson
Time Inc.
Times Mirror
Transamerica
Triangle Publications
TWA
Twentieth Century-Fox
Union Camp
Union Carbide
Union Pacific
Uniroyal
United Airlines
United Brands
U.S. Air
U.S. Gypsum
U.S. Home
U.S. Steel
United Parcel Service
United Technologies
Upjohn
Walgreen
Jim Walter
Warner Communications
Warner Lambert
Washington Post
West Point Pepperell
Westinghouse
Weyerhaeuser
Whirlpool
White Consolidated
Wickes
Wilson Foods
Winn-Dixie
F.W. Woolworth
Wm. Wrigley, Jr.
Xerox
Zenith

UNITED STATES COMPANIES RANKED BY *FORTUNE*: AN ADDRESS LIST*

Elaine Barton, Compiler

Appendix 5

500 Top United States Companies

ACF Industries (321)
750 3rd Avenue
New York, NY 10017
(212) 986-8600

AM International (342)
130 E. Randolph Street
Chicago, IL 60601
(312) 565-2800

AMAX (152)
Amax Center
Greenwich, CT 06830
(203) 622-2000

AMF (245)
777 Westchester
White Plain, NY 10604
(914) 694-9000

AMP (274)
Eisenhower Blvd.
Harrisburg, PA 17105
(717) 564-0100

Abbott Laboratories (172)
Abbott Park
North Chicago, IL 60064
(312) 937-6100
NUCMC 71-157, -1514

Agway (100)
Box 4933
Syracuse, NY 13221
(315) 477-7061

Air Products & Chemicals (228)
Box 538
Allentown, PA 18105
(215) 398-4911

AIRCO (282)
85 Chestnut Road
Montvale, NJ 07645
(201) 573-0800

AKZONA (279)
1 W. Pack Square
Asheville, NC 28802
(704) 253-6851

Allegheny International (204)
Washington National
Pittsburgh, PA 15222
(412) 562-4000

Allied (55)
Box 2245R
Morristown, NJ 07960
(201) 455-2000

Allis-Chalmers (188)
Box 512
Milwaukee, WI 53201
(414) 475-2000
NUCMC 60-798; 72-124

ALUMAX (284)
400 S. El Camino
San Mateo, CA 94402
(415) 348-3400

Aluminum Company of America (78)
1501 Alcoa Bldg.
Pittsburgh, PA 15219
(412) 553-4707
NUCMC 62-1902, -2567; 68-906; 78-960

Amerada Hess (33)
Box 3208
New York, NY 10043
(212) 997-8500

American Bakeries (451)
10 S. Riverside
Chicago, IL 60606
(312) 454-7400

American Brands (96)
245 Park Avenue
New York NY 10017
(212) 880-4200

American Can (81)
American Lane
Greenwich, CT 06830
(203) 552-2000
NUCMC 64-1262; 73-333

American Cyanamid (106)
Berdan Avenue
Wayne, NJ 07470
(201) 831-2000

American Greetings (478)
10500 American
Cleveland, OH 44144
(216) 252-7300

American Hoechst (225)
1041 Rt. 202-206
Somerville, NJ 08876
(201) 685-2000

American Hoist & Derrick (437)
63 S. Robert Street
St. Paul, MN 55107
(612) 228-4321

American Home Products (93)
685 3rd Avenue
New York, NY 10017
(212) 986-1000

American Motors (162)
27777 Franklin
Southfield MI 48034
(313) 827-1000
NUCMC 76-1443; 80-1553

American Petrofina (164)
Fina Plaza
Dallas, TX 75206
(214) 750-2400

*NUCMC numbers are added after the address where available. 72-157, -1514 means 157th collection cataloged in 1972, with another related collection in collection 1514, by the Library of Congress, *National Union Catalogue of Manuscript Collections.*

American Standard (165)
40 W. 40th
New York, NY 10018
(212) 840-5100

AMPCO-Pittsburgh (493)
700 Porter Bldg.
Pittsburgh, PA 15219
(412) 471-6950

AMSTAR (197)
1251 Avenue of the Americas
New York, NY 10020
(212) 489-9000

Amsted Industries (345)
3700 Prudential
Chicago, IL 60601
(312) 645-1700

Anchor Hocking (319)
109 N. Broad
Lancaster, OH 43130
(614) 687-2111

Anderson Clayton (202)
Box 2538
Houston, TX 77001
(712) 651-0641
NUCMC 77-1746

Anheuser-Busch (99)
721 Pestalozzi
St. Louis, MO 63118
(314) 577-2000
NUCMC 66-1151, -1155; 78-957; 79-787

ARCATA (373)
2750 Sand Hill
Menlo Park, CA 94025
(415) 854-5222

Archer-Daniels-Midland (107)
Box 1470
Decatur, IL 62525
(217) 424-5200

ARMCO (51)
703 Curtis St.
Middletown, OH 45043
(513) 425-6451

Armstrong Rubber (448)
500 S. Sargent Drive
New Haven, CT 06507
(203) 562-1161

Armstrong World Industries (256)
Box 30001
Lancaster, PA 17604
(717) 397-0611
NUCMC 80-102

Arvin Industries (476)
1531 13th Street
Columbus, IN 47201
(812) 372-7271

ASARCO (234)
120 Broadway
New York, NY 10005
(212) 669-1000

Ashland Oil (35)
Box 391
Ashland, KY 41101
(606) 329-3333
NUCMC 66-723

Atlantic Richfield (10)
515 S. Flower Street
Los Angeles, CA 90071
(213) 486-3511
NUCMC 72-1192

Avery International (416)
415 Huntington
San Marino, CA 91108
(213) 682-2812

AVNET (266)
767 5th Avenue
New York, NY 10022
(212) 644-1050

Avon Products (160)
9 W. 57th Street
New York, NY 10019
(212) 593-4017

BASF Wyandotte (307)
100 Cherry Hill Road
Parsippany, NJ
(201) 263-0200

Batus (90)
Citizen's Plaza
Louisville, KY
(502) 581-8000

Baker International (185)
Box 5500
Orange, CA 92667
(714) 634-2333

Ball (358)
345 S. High Street
Muncie, IN 47302
(317) 747-6100
NUCMC 79-1905

Bally Manufacturing (339)
2640 W. Belmont
Chicago, IL 60618
(312) 267-6060

Bangor Punta (361)
1 Greenwich Place
Greenwich, CT 06830
(203) 622-8100

Barnes Group (494)
123 Main Street
Bristol, CT 06010
(203) 583-7070

Baush & Lomb (433)
1 Lincoln 1st Street
Rochester, NY 10004
(212) 344-6900

Baxter Travenol Laboratories (239)
1 Baxter Park
Deerfield, IL 60015
(312) 948-7000

Beatrice Foods (41)
2 N. LaSalle
Chicago, IL 60602
(312) 482-3820

Beckman Instruments (423)
2500 Harbor Blvd.
Fullerton, CA 92634
(714) 871-4848

Becton Dickinson (300)
Mack Centre Dr.
Paramus, NJ 07652
(201) 967-3700

BELCO Petroleum (484)
1 Dag Hammarskjold Plaza
New York, NY 10017
(212) 644-2200

Bell & Howell (393)
7100 McCormick
Chicago, IL 60645
(312) 673-3300

Bemis (386)
800 Northstar Circle
Minneapolis, MN 55402
(612) 340-6000

Bendix (86)
Bendix Center
Southfield, MI 48037
(313) 827-5000
NUCMC 68-2134; 70-413

Bethlehem Steel (47)
701 E. 3rd Street
Bethlehem, PA 18016
(215) 694-2424
NUCMC 61-2311; 72-70

Big Three Industries (351)
3535 W. 12th Street
Houston, TX 77008
(712) 868-0333

Black & Decker Manufacturing (248)
701 E. Joppa Road
Towson, MD 21204
(301) 828-3900

Blue Bell (249)
Box 21488
Greensboro, NC 27420
(919) 373-3400

Boeing (31)
7755 E. Marginal
Seattle, WA 98108
(206) 655-2121

Boise Cascade (143)
1 Jefferson
Boise, ID 83728
(208) 384-6161

Borden (85)
277 Park Avenue
New York, NY 10017
(212) 573-4000
NUCMC 62-4508; 70-1071; 73-370

Borg-Warner (155)
200 S. Michigan
Chicago, IL 60604
(312) 322-8500
NUCMC 71-622

Briggs & Stratton (442)
Box 702
Milwaukee, WI 53201
(414) 259-5333

Briston-Myers (113)
345 Park Ave.
New York, NY 10022
(212) 644-2100

Brockway Glass (368)
McCullough Avenue
Brockway, PA 15824
(814) 268-3015

Brown-Forman Distillers (472)
Box 1080
Louisville, KY 40201
(502) 778-5531

Brown Group (263)
8400 Maryland Avenue
St. Louis, MO 63105
(314) 997-7500

Brunswick (260)
1 Brunswick Place
Skokie, IL 60077
(312) 470-4700

Buckrus-Erie (475)
Box 56
S. Milwaukee, WI 53172
(414) 768-4000

Burlington Industries (132)
Box 21207
Greensboro, NC 27420
(919) 279-2000

Burroughs (128)
Burroughs Place
Detroit, MI 42232
(313) 972-8026

CBI Industries (326)
800 Jorie Blvd.
Oak Brook, IL 60521
(312) 654-7000

CF Industries (303)
Salem Lake Drive
Lake Zurich, IL 60047
(312) 438-9500

CPC International (89)
International Place
Englewood, NJ 07632
(201) 894-4000

Cabot (223)
125 High Street
Boston, MA 02110
(617) 853-1000

Cameron Iron Works (324)
Box 1212
Houston, TX 77001
(713) 939-2211

Campbell Soup (153)
Campbell Place
Camden, NJ 08101
(609) 964-4000

Campbell Taggart (270)
Box 222640
Dallas, TX 75222
(214) 358-9211

Capital Cities Communications (438)
485 Madison Avenue
New York, NY 10022
(212) 421-9595

Carnation (121)
5045 Wilshire Blvd.
Los Angeles, CA 90036
(213) 931-1911

Carpenter Technology (440)
Box 662
Reading, PA 19603
(125) 372-4511

Caterpillar Tractor (37)
100 N.E. Adams St.
Peoria, IL 61629
(309) 675-1000
NUCMC 78-310

CECO (497)
1400 Kensington
Chicago, IL 60650
(312) 579-1400

Celanese (104)
1211 Avenue of the Americas
New York, NY 10036
(212) 764-7640
NUCMC 76-862

Central Soya (199)
1300 Fort Wayne N.
Fort Wayne, IN 46802
(219) 425-5100

Certain Teed (334)
Box 860
Valley Forge, PA 19482
(215) 687-5000

Cessna Aircraft (302)
5800 E. Pawnee
Wichita, KA 67201
(316) 685-9111

Champion International (97)
1 Landmark Square
Stamford, CT 06921
(203) 358-7000

Champion Sparkplug (354)
900 Upton Ave.
Toledo, OH 43661
(419) 535-2567

Charter (75)
Box 2017
Jacksonville, FL 32231
(904) 358-4111

Chesebrough-Ponds (236)
33 Benedict Place
Greenwich, CT 06830
(203) 661-2000

Chicago Pneumatic Tool (482)
6-8 E. 44th Street
New York, NY 10017
(212) 692-4000
NUCMC 80-1180

Chromalloy American (253)
120 S. Central
St. Louis, MO 63105
(314) 726-9200

Chrysler (26)
12000 L. Townsen
Highland Park, MI 48288
(313) 956-5252
NUCMC 67-8, -15; 71-653

Cincinnati Milacron (322)
4701 Marburg Avenue
Cincinnati, OH 45209
(513) 841-8100

Cities Service (39)
Box 300
Tulsa, OK 74102
(918) 561-2211
NUCMC 75-151, -2069

Clark Equipment (259)
Circle Drive
Buchanan, MI 49107
(616) 697-8000

Clorox (389)
7901 Oakport Street
Oakland, CA 94621
(415) 635-9666

Cluett Peabody (348)
510 5th Avenue
New York, NY 10036
(212) 930-3021

Coastal (59)
9 Greenway Place
Houston, TX 77046
(713) 877-1400

Coca-Cola (58)
Box 1734
Atlanta, GA 30301
(404) 897-2121
NUCMC 72-157

Colgate-Palmolive
300 Park Avenue
New York, NY 10022
(212) 751-1200

Collins & Aikman (431)
210 Madison Avenue
New York, NY 10171
(212) 486-6400

Colt Industries (179)
430 Park Avenue
New York, NY 10016
(212) 949-5000
NUCMC 78-1052

Combustion Engineering (102)
900 Long Ridge
Stamford, CT 06902
(203) 329-8771

Commonwealth Oil Refining (314)
3626 Tesoro Drive
San Antonio, TX 78217
(512) 828-8444

Cone Mills (406)
1201 Maple St.
Greensboro, NC 27405
(919) 379-6220

Consolidated Foods (63)
135 S. LaSalle Street
Chicago, IL 60603
(312) 726-6414

Consolidated Papers (455)
231 1st Avenue North
Wis. Rapids, WI 55494
(715) 422-3111

Continental Group (74)
633 3rd Avenue
New York, NY 10017
(212) 551-7000

Control Data (144)
Box O
Minneapolis, MN 55440
(612) 853-8100

Cooper Industries (142)
2 Houston Cen.
Houston, TX 77002
(713) 654-4451

Coors (323)
Golden, CO 80401
(303) 279-6565

Copperweld (424)
2 Oliver Plaza
Pittsburgh, PA 15222
(412) 263-3200

Corning Glass Works (226)
Houghton Park
Corning, NY 14830
(607) 974-9000
NUCMC 78-1001

Crane (224)
300 Park Avenue
New York, NY 10022
(212) 980-3600

Crown Central Petroleum (242)
1 N. Charles Street
Baltimore, MD 21203
(301) 539-7400

Crown Cork & Seal (257)
9300 Ashton Road
Philadelphia, PA 19136
(215) 698-5100

Crown Zellerbach (140)
1 Bush Street
San Francisco, CA 94104
(415) 915-5000
NUCMC 67-2209, -2240; 71-617; 76-1229

Cummins Engine (200)
1000 5th Street
Columbus, IN 47201
(812) 372-7211

Cyclops (309)
650 Washington
Pittsburgh, PA 15228
(412) 343-4000

DPF (399)
141 Central Park
Hartsdale, NY 10530
(914) 428-5000

Dan River (417)
Box 6126
Greenville, SC 29606
(803) 298-9000

Dana (158)
Box 1000
Toledo, OH 43697
(419) 535-4500

Dart & Kraft (29)
Glenview, IL 60025
(312) 998-4550

Data General (379)
4400 Computer Drive
Westborough, PA 01581
(617) 366-8911

DAYCO (364)
333 W. 1st Street
Dayton, OH 45402
(513) 226-7000

Dean Foods (382)
3600 N. River Rd.
Franklin Park, IL 60131
(312) 625-6200

Deere (65)
John Deere Road
Moline, IL 61265
(309) 792-8000

Deluxe Check Printers (470)
Box 43399
St. Paul, MN 55165
(612) 483-7111

Dennison Manufacturing (441)
275 Wyman Street
Waltham, MA 02154
(617) 890-6350

Dexter (463)
1 Elm Street
Windsor Locks, CT 06096
(203) 627-9051
NUCMC 66-422

Diamond International (261)
733 3rd Avenue
New York, NY 10017
(212) 697-1700

Diamond Shamrock (112)
2300 Southland
Dallas, TX 75201
(214) 745-2000

Digital Equipment (137)
146 Main Street
Maynard, MA 01754
(617) 896-5111

Donnelley (R.R.) & Sons (271)
2223 Martin Luther King
Chicago, IL 60616
(312) 326-8000

Dorchester Gas (390)
Box 31049
Dallas, TX 75231
(214) 750-3500

Dorsey (456)
400 W. 45th Street
Chattanooga, TN 37410
(615) 821-6551

Dover (311)
277 Park Avenue
New York, NY 10172
(212) 826-7160
NUCMC 60-1151

Dow Chemical (24)
2030 Dow Center Avenue
Midland, MI 48640
(517) 636-1000
NUCMC 80-945

Dow Corning (384)
2200 West Salzburg
Midland, MI 48640
(517) 496-4000

Dow Jones (414)
22 Cortland St.
New York, NY 10007
(212) 285-5000

Dresser Industries (83)
Box 718
Dallas, TX 75221
(214) 746-6000

Du Pont (E.I.) De Nemours (12)
1007 Market Street
Wilmington, DE 19898
(302) 774-1000
NUCMC 60-1315, -1361, -1370, -3013; 62-4644; 71-1721, -1724; 72-157; 73-531

EG & G (391)
45 William Street
Wellesley, MA 02181
(617) 237-5100

E-Systems (439)
Box 22603L
Dallas, TX 75266
(214) 661-1000

Eagle-Picher Industries (422)
Box 779
Cincinnati, OH 45201
(513) 521-7010

Eastman Kodak (28)
343 State Street
Rochester, NY 14650
(716) 724-4000
NUCMC 61-1220

Eaton (139)
100 Erieview Place
Cleveland, OH 44114
(216) 523-5000

Economics Laboratory (421)
370 Wabasha Street
St. Paul, MN 55102
(612) 224-4678

Emerson Electric (118)
8100 Florissant
St. Louis, MO 63136
(314) 553-2000

Emhart (215)
Box 2730
Hartford, CT 06101
(203) 677-4631

Engelhard (180)
1221 Avenue of the Americas
New York, NY 10020
(212) 764-3700

Envirotech (485)
3000 Sand Hill
Menlo Park, CA 94025
(415) 854-2000

Esmark (127)
55 E. Monroe Street
Chicago, IL 60603
(312) 431-3600

Ethyl (214)
Box 2189
Richmond, VA 23217
(804) 644-6081

Evans Products (243)
Box 3295
Portland, OR 97208
(503) 222-5592

Ex-Cell-O (292)
2855 Coolidge
Troy, MI 48084
(313) 649-1000

EXXON (1)
1251 Avenue of the Americas
New York, NY 10020
(212) 398-3000

FMC (109)
200 East Randolph
Chicago, IL 60601
(312) 861-6000

Fairchild Industries (262)
Fairchild Drive
Germantown, MD 20767
(301) 428-6000

Farmers' Union Central Exchange (265)
1185 N. Concord
South St. Paul, MN 55075
(612) 451-5151
NUCMC 60-546

Farmland Industries (64)
3315 N. Oak Traf.
Kansas City, MO 64116

Federal Co. (296)
Box 17236
Memphis, TN 38117
(901) 761-3610

Federal-Mogul (347)
Box 1966
Detroit, MI 48235
(313) 354-7700

Federal Paper Board (465)
75 Chestnut Ridge
Montvale, NJ 07645
(201) 391-1776

FERRO (392)
1 Erieview Plaza
Cleveland, OH 44114
(216) 641-8580
NUCMC 69-229

Fiat-Allis (473)
106 Wilmot Road
Deerfield, IL 60015
(312) 948-5500

Fieldcrest Mills (460)
Box 307
Eden, NC 27288
(919) 623-2123

Figgie International (371)
4420 Sherwin Rd.
Willoughby, OH 44904
(216) 946-9000

Firestone Tire & Rubber (88)
1200 Firestone
Akron, OH 44317
(216) 379-7000

Ford Motor (6)
American Road
Dearborn, MI 48121
(313) 322-3000
NUCMC 67-11; 77-230, -1335; 78-1435; 80-932, -1206, -1478

Fort Howard Paper (486)
Box 130
Green Bay, WI 54305
(414) 435-8821

Foster (L.B.) (458)
415 Holiday Drive
Pittsburgh, PA 15220
(412) 928-3400

Foster Wheeler (220)
666 5th Avenue
New York, NY 10019
(212) 581-7770

Foxboro (430)
38 Neponset Avenue
Foxboro, MA 02035
(617) 543-8750

Frederick & Herrud (490)
1487 Farnsworth
Detroit, MI 48211
(313) 832-6080

Freeport Minerals (346)
200 Park Avenue
New York, NY 10017
(212) 578-9297

Fruehauf (183)
Box 238
Detroit, MI 48213
(313) 267-1000

GAF (403)
140 W. 51st Street
New York, NY 10020
(212) 621-5000

GATX (278)
120 S. Riverside
Chicago, IL 60606
(312) 621-6200

Gannett (258)
Lincoln Tower
Rocheser, NY 14604
(716) 546-8600
NUCMC 70-1082

Gates Learjet (444)
Box 7707
Wichita, KS 67277
(316) 946-2000

General Cinema (350)
27 Boylston Street
Chestnut Hill, MA 02167
(617) 232-8200

General Dynamics (76)
Pierre Laclede
ST. Louis, MO 63105
(314) 862-2440
NUCMC 78-1768

General Electric (11)
3135 Easton Turnpike
Fairfield, CT 06431
(203) 383-2431
NUCMC 61-249, -930; 65-496; 66-1230; 70-502, -1059; 71-1172; 73-225; 76-1639, -1640, -1642; 77-1955, -1956

General Foods (52)
250 North Street
White Plain, NY 10625
(914) 683-2500
NUCMC 68-2190

General Instrument (349)
1775 Broadway
New York, NY 10019
(212) 541-8200

General Mills (80)
Box 1113
Minneapolis, MN 55440
(612) 540-2311
NUCMC 66-860; 67-863, -2241; 79-1919

General Motors (3)
767 5th Avenue
New York, NY 10022
(212) 486-5000
NUSMC 64-1469; 66-1526; 71-118, -590; 72-1420; 73-279; 78-1768; 80-932, -1206, -1478

General Signal (219)
High Ridge Park
Stamford, CT 06904
(203) 357-8800

General Tire & Rubber (163)
1 General Street
Akron, OH 44329
(216) 798-3000
NUCMC 77-2047

GENESCO (387)
111 7th Avenue N.
Nashville, TN 37202
(615) 367-7000

Georgia Kraft (489)
1700 Redmond Circle
Rome, GA 30161
(404) 291-6920

Georgia-Pacific (67)
900 S.W. 5th Avenue
Portland, OR 97204
(503) 222-5561

Geosource (381)
2700 S. Post Oak
Houston, TX 77056
(712) 961-1111

Gerber Products (419)
445 State Street
Fremont, MI 49412
(616) 928-2000

Getty Oil (23)
3810 Wilshire Blvd.
Los Angeles, CA 90010
(213) 381-7151

Gifford-Hill (446)
Box 42127
Dallas, TX 75247
(214) 627-3860

Gillette (173)
Prudential Tower
Boston, MA 02199
(617) 421-7000

Gold Kist (212)
244 Perimeter Circle
Atlanta, GA 30301

Goodrich (B.F.) (138)
500 S. Main
Akron, OH 44318
(216) 379-2000

Goodyear Tire & Rubber (38)
1144 E. Market Street
Akron, OH 44316
(216) 794-2121
NUCMC 75-1173, -1576

Gould (178)
10 Gould Center
Rolling Meadow, IL 60008
(312) 640-4000

Grace (W. R.) (53)
1114 Avenue of the Americas
New York, NY 10036
(212) 764-5555

Great Northern Nekoosa (240)
75 Prospect Street
Stamford, CT 06901
(302) 359-4000

Greyhound (82)
Greyhound Tower
Phoenix, AZ 85077
(602) 248-4000
NUCMC 62-765

Grumman (203)
1111 Stewart Avenue
Bethpage, NY 11714
(516) 575-2659

Gulf Oil (9)
Box 1166
Pittsburgh, PA 15230
(412) 263-5000
NUCMC 75-2069; 77-2047; 79-1896

Gulf Resources & Chemical (459)
1100 Milam Building
Houston, TX 77002
(713) 658-0471

Gulf & Western Industries (61)
1 Gulf & Western
New York, NY 10023
(212) 333-7000

Hammermill Paper (254)
Box 1440
Erie, PA 16533
(814) 456-8811

Handy & Harman (425)
850 3rd Avenue
New York, NY 10022
(212) 752-3400

Harcourt Brace Jovanovich (453)
757 3rd Avenue
New York, NY 10017
(212) 888-4444
NUCMC 59-199; 69-583

Harnischfeger (412)
Box 554
Milwaukee, WI 53201
(414) 671-4400

Harris (229)
1025 W. NASA Blvd.
Melbourne, FL 37202
(305) 727-9100

HARSCO (286)
350 Poplar Church Road
Camp Hill, PA 17011
(717) 763-7064

Hart Schaffner & Marx (357)
36 S. Franklin Street
Chicago, IL 60606
(312) 372-6300
NUCMC 80-187

Heileman (G.) Brewing (360)
Box 459
La Crosse, WI 54601
(608) 785-1000

Heinz (H.J.) (111)
Box 57
Pittsburgh, PA 15230
(412) 237-5757

Hercules (157)
910 Market Street
Wilmington, DE 19899
(302) 575-5000

Hershey Foods (244)
100 Mansion East
Hershey, PA 17033
(717) 534-4000

Heublein (227)
Munson Road
Farmington, CT 06032
(203) 677-4061

Hewlett-Packard (110)
1501 Page Mill
Palo Alto, CA 94304
(415) 857-1501

Honeywell (69)
Honeywell Plaza
Minneapolis, MN 55408
(612) 870-5200

Hoover (376)
101 E. Maple Street
North Canton, OH 44720
(216) 499-9200

Hoover Universal (445)
Box 1003
Ann Arbor, MI 48106
(313) 429-2552

Hormel (Geo. A.) (247)
501 16th Avenue N.E.
Austin, MN 55912
(507) 437-5611

Hughes Tool (213)
Box 2539
Houston, TX 77001
(713) 926-3101
NUCMC 66-1402

Hyster (420)
Box 2902
Portland, OR 97208
(503) 280-7000

IC Industries (92)
111 E. Wacker Drive
Chicago, IL 60601
(312) 565-3000

Interco (170)
Box 8777
St. Louis, MO 63102
(314) 231-1100

Ideal Basic Industries (483)
Box 8789
Denver, CO 80201
(303) 623-5661

Idle Wild Foods (436)
Box 118
Worcester, MA 01613
(617) 242-0600

Illinois Tool Works (498)
8501 W. Higgins
Chicago, IL 60631
(312) 693-3040

Ingersoll-Rand (120)
200 Chestnut Ridge
Woodcliff Lane, NJ 07675
(201) 573-0123

Inland Steel (103)
30 W. Monroe Street
Chicago, IL 60603
(312) 346-0300

INSILCO (398)
1000 Research Park
Meriden, CT 06450
(203) 634-2000

Intel (363)
3065 Bowers Avenue
Santa Clara, CA 95051
(408) 987-8080

Interlake (313)
2015 Spring Road
Oak Brook, IL 60521
(312) 986-6600

International Harvester (46)
401 N. Michigan
Chicago, IL 60611
(312) 670-2427
NUCMC 62-797, -3513; 64-798; 71-1146; 75-692; 77-1374

International Minerals & Chemicals (196)
2315 Sanders Road
Northbrook, IL 60062
(312) 564-8600

International Multifoods (298)
8th and Marquette
Minneapolis, MN 55402
(612) 340-3300

International Paper (77)
220 E. 42nd Street
New York, NY 10017
(212) 490-6000
NUCMC 62-1183; 71-1648

International Telephone & Telegraph (14)
320 Park Avenue
New York, NY 10022
(212) 752-6000
NUCMC 62-2708

James River Corp. of Virginia (447)
Box 2218
Richmond, CA 23217
(804) 644-5411

Johnson Controls (291)
Box 423
Milwaukee, WI 53201
(414) 276-9200

Johnson & Johnson (68)
501 George Street
New Brunswick, NJ 08903
(201) 524-0400

Joy Manufacturing (297)
537 Smithfield Street
Pittsburgh, PA 15222
(412) 562-4500

Kaiser Aluminum & Chemical (136)
300 Lakeside Drive
Oakland, CA 94643
(415) 271-3300

Kaiser Steel (310)
Box 58
Oakland, CA 94666
(415) 271-2211

Kane-Miller (401)
Box 7
Tarrytown, NY 10591
(914) 631-6900

Kellog (175)
235 Porter Street
Battle Creek, MI 49016
(616) 966-2000

Kellwood (435)
Box 14374
St. Louis, MO 63178
(314) 576-3100

Kerr Glass Manufacturing (479)
501 S. Shatto Place
Los Angeles, CA 90020
(213) 487-3250

Kerr-McGee (101)
Box 25861
Oklahoma City, OK 73125
(405) 270-1313

Kidde (149)
9 Brighton Road
Clifton, NJ 07012
(201) 777-6500

Kimberly-Clark (147)
4 Lake Street
Neenah, WI 54956
(414) 729-1212
NUCMC 68-2245; 78-1040

Knight-Ridder Newspapers (272)
1 Herald Plaza
Miami, FL 33101
(305) 350-2413

Knudsen (496)
Box 2335
Los Angeles, CA 90051
(213) 747-6712

Koppers (190)
Koppers Building
Pittsburgh, PA 15219
(412) 227-2000
NUCMC 78-767; 79-1086; 80-214, -707

LTV (40)
Box 225003
Dallas, TX 75265
(214) 746-7711

Land O'Lakes (115)
Box 116
Minneapolis, MN 55440
(612) 331-6330
NUCMC 72-980

Lear Siegler (235)
3171 S. Bundy Drive
Santa Monica, CA 90406
(213) 391-7211

Lever Brothers (281)
390 Park Avenue
New York, NY 10022
(212) 688-6000
NUCMC 61-3050

Levi Strauss (148)
2 Embarcadero
San Francisco, CA 94106
(415) 544-6000
NUCMC 77-1964

Libbey-Owens-Ford (275)
811 Madison Avenue
Toledo, OH 43695
(419) 242-5781

Lilly (Eli) (340)
307 E. McCarty Street
Indianapolis, IN 46285
(317) 261-2000

Lipton (Thomas J.) (340)
800 Sylvan Avenue
Englewood, NJ 07632
(201) 567-8000

Litton Industries (79)
360 N. Crescent
Beverly Hills, CA 90210
(213) 273-7860

Lockheed (57)
Box 551
Burbank, CA 91520
(213) 847-6121
NUCMC 67-608; 71-1162; 76-707; 78-1768; 80-490

Lone Star Industries (328)
1 Greenwich Place
Greenwich, CT 06830
(203) 661-3100

Louisiana Land & Exploration (273)
Box 60350
New Orleans, LA 70160
(504) 566-6500

Louisiana Pacific (312)
1300 S.W. 5th Avenue
Portland, OR 97201
(503) 221-0800

Lowenstein (M.) (432)
1430 Broadway
New York, NY 10018
(212) 930-5000

Lubrizol (337)
29400 Lakeland
Wickliffe, OH 44092
(216) 943-4200

M/A-COM (464)
South Avenue
Burlington, MA 01803
(617) 272-9600

MAPCO (182)
1800 S. Balitimore
Tulsa, OK 74119
(918) 584-4471

Macmillan (487)
866 3rd Avenue
New York, NY 10022
(212) 935-2000
NUCMC 60-1713; 64-903, -913; 66-1567; 67-112; 69-943, -967; 76-1288, -1340, -1869

Magic Chef (402)
740 King Edward
Cleveland, TN 37311
(615) 472-3371

Mallinckrodt (477)
Box 5840
St. Louis, MO 63134
(314) 895-0123

Manville (181)
342 Rockwell
Pontiac, MI 48053
(313) 334-4583

Marathon Oil (36)
539 S. Main Street
Findlay, OH 45840
NUCMC 71-1140

Marion (495)
Box 3027
Mobile, AL 36652
(205) 626-3300

Marmon Group (208)
39 S. LaSalle
Chicago, IL 60603
(312) 372-9500

Martin Marietta (130)
6801 Rockledge
Bethesda, MD 20034
(301) 897-6000

Maryland Cup (411)
10100 Reisterst
Owings Mills, MD 21117
(301) 363-1111

MASCO (338)
21001 Van Born
Taylor, MI 48180
(313) 274-7400

Masonite (454)
19 N. Wacker Drive
Chicago, IL 60606
(312) 372-5642

Mattel (330)
5150 Rosecrans
Hawthorne, CA 90250
(213) 978-5150

McCormick (408)
11350 McCormick
Hunt Valley, MD 21031
(301) 667-7301

McDermott (108)
1010 Common Street
New Orleans, LA 70112
(504) 587-4411

McDonnell Douglas (45)
Box 516
St. Louis, MO 63166
(314) 232-0232

McGraw-Edison (168)
1701 Golf Road
Rolling Meadow, IL 60008
(312) 981-3800

McGraw-Hill (294)
1211 Avenue of the Americas
New York, NY 10020
(212) 997-1221
NUCMC 78-1467

McLouth Steel (385)
300 S. Livernois
Detroit, MI 48209
(313) 843-3000

Mead (146)
Courthouse Plaza
Dayton, OH 45463
(513) 222-6323

Merck (145)
Lincoln Avenue
Rahway, NJ 07065
(201) 564-4000
NUCMC 67-2160

Mid-America Dairymen (283)
800 W. Tampa
Springfield, MO
(417) 865-9641

Midland Cooperatives (467)
45 Progress Parkway
Hazelwood, MO 63043
(314) 434-0327

Midland-Ross (332)
20600 Chagrin
Cleveland, OH 44122
(216) 491-8400

Miles Laboratories (372)
1127 Myrtle Street
Elkhart, IN 46515
(219) 264-8111

Minnesota Mining & Manufacturing (54)
3M Center
St. Paul, MN 55144
(612) 733-1110

Mitchell Energy & Development (395)
1 Shell Plaza-3
Houston, TX 77002
(713) 224-4522

Mobil (2)
150 E. 42nd Street
New York, NY 10017
(212) 883-4242
NUCMC 75-2069

MOHASCO (415)
57 Lyon Street
Amsterdam, NY 12010
(518) 841-2211

Monfort of Colorado (355)
Box G
Greeley, CO 80632
(303) 353-2311

Monsanto (50)
800 N. Lindbergh
St. Louis, MO 63166
(324) 694-1000

Morton-Norwich Products (318)
110 N. Wacker Drive
Chicago, IL 60606
(312) 621-5200
NUCMC 75-415, -416

Motorola (126)
1303 E. Algonquin
Schaumburg, IL 90067
(213) 277-3311
NUCMC 80-2017

Murphy Oil (167)
200 Jefferson
El Dorado, AR 71730
(501) 862-6411

NCR (116)
1700 S. Patterson
Dayton, OH 45479
(513) 449-2000
NUCMC 60-168; 75-1139

NL Industries (156)
1230 Avenue of the Americas
New York, NY 10020
(212) 399-9400

NVF (308)
Yorklyn Road
Yorklyn, DE 19736
(302) 239-5281

Nabisco Brands (60)
425 Park Avenue
E. Hanover, NJ 07936
(201) 884-0500
NUCMC 64-870

NALCO Chemical (407)
2901 Butterfield
Oak Brook, IL 60521
(312) 887-7500

Nashua (410)
44 Franklin Street
Nashua, NH 03061
(603) 880-2323
NUCMC 60-1232; 64-240; 73-230; 80-1879

National Can (233)
8101 Higgins Road
Chicago, IL 60631
(312) 399-3000

National Cooperative Refinery Association (374)
1 Mile S. McPherson
McPherson, KS 67460
(316) 241-2340

National Distillers & Chemical (218)
99 Park Avenue
New York, NY 10016
(212) 949-5000

National Gypsum (317)
4100 1st International Bank
Dallas, TX 75270
(214) 653-8511
NUCMC 71-1801

National Semiconductor (287)
2900 Semiconductor
Santa Clara, CA 95051
(408) 737-5000

National Service Industries (343)
1180 Peachtree
Atlanta, GA 30309
(404) 892-2400

National Starch & Chemical (405)
Fiderne Avenue
Bridgewater, NJ 08807
(201) 685-5000

National Steel (94)
2800 Grant Building
Pittsburgh, PA 15219
(412) 263-4100

NATOMAS (232)
601 California
San Francisco, CA 94108
(415) 981-5700
NUCMC 80-1812, -1851

New York Times (344)
229 W. 43rd Street
New York, NY 10036
(212) 556-1234
NUCMC 62-2226, -2428, -4554; 65-1733; 66-995, -1397; 68-1055, -2262; 72-1004, -1873; 76-147, -1520, -1524; 77-621; 78-37, -717, -945, -1000, -1017, -2352; 30-831, -1886, -2045

Newmont Mining (333)
300 Park Avenue
New York, NY 10022
(212) 753-4800

North American Philips (131)
100 E. 42nd Street
New York, NY 10017
(212) 697-3600

Northrop (194)
1800 Century Park
Los Angeles, CA 90067
(213) 553-6262

Northwest Industries (105)
6300 Sears Tower
Chicago, IL 60606
(312) 876-7000

Northwestern Steel & Wire (488)
121 Wallace Street
Sterling, IL 61081
(815) 625-2500

Norton (264)
1 New Bond Street
Worcester, MA 01606
(617) 853-1000
NUCMC 64-240

Norton Simon (141)
277 Park Avenue
New York, NY 10017
(212) 832-1000

NUCOR (450)
4425 Randolph Road
Charlotte, NC 28211
(704) 366-7000

Oak Industries (468)
Box 28759
Rancho Bern, CA 92128
(714) 743-7533

Occidental Petroleum (18)
10689 Wilshire Blvd.
Los Angeles, CA 90024
(213) 879-1700

Ogden (174)
277 Park Avenue
New York, NY 10017
(212) 754-4000

Olin (193)
120 Long Ridge
Stamford, CT 06904
(203) 356-2000

Outboard Marine (362)
100 Sea Horse Drive
Waukegan, IL 60085
(312) 689-6200

Owens-Corning Fiberglas (169)
Fiberglas Tower
Toledo, OH 43659
(419) 249-8000
NUCMC 77-283

Owens-Illinois (98)
Box 1035
Toledo, OH 43666
(419) 247-5000
NUCMC 77-267; 80-1950

PACCAR (216)
777 106th Avenue S.E.
Bellevue, WA 98004
(206) 455-7464

PPG Industries (122)
1 Gateway Center
Pittsburgh, PA 15222
(412) 434-3131

Pabst Brewing (397)
917 W. Juneau Avenue
Milwaukee, WI 53201
(414) 347-7300

Pacific Resources (299)
Box 3379
Honolulu, HI 96842
(808) 547-3111

Palm Beach (474)
400 Pike Street
Cincinnati, OH 45202
(513) 241-4260

Parker-Hannifin (295)
17325 Euclid Avenue
Cleveland, OH 44112
(216) 531-3000

Peabody International (449)
4 Landmark Square
Stamford, CT 06901
(203) 348-0000

Peavey (352)
Peavey Building
Minneapolis, MN 55402
(612) 370-7500

Penn Central (123)
245 Park Avenue
New York, NY 10167
(212) 599-8000
NUCMC 77-1593

Pennwalt (280)
3 Parkway
Philadelphia, PA 19102
(215) 587-7000

Pennzoil (159)
Box 2967
Houston, TX 77001
(713) 236-7878

Pepsi Co. (49)
Anderson Hill
Purchase, NY 10577
(914) 253-2000

Perkin-Elmer (293)
Main Avenue
Norwalk, CT 06856
(203) 762-1000

Pfizer (133)
235 E. 42nd Street
New York, NY 10017
(212) 573-2323

Phelps Dodge (246)
300 Park Avenue
New York, NY 10022
(212) 940-6400

Philip Morris (43)
100 Park Avenue
New York, NY 10017
(212) 679-1800

Phillips Petroleum (15)
Keeler Avenue 333 S.W.
Bartlesville, OK 74003
(918) 661-6600
NUCMC 75-2069

Pillsbury (129)
608 2nd Avenue S.
Minneapolis, MN 55402
(612) 330-4966

Pitney Bowes (252)
Walter H. Wheeler
Stamford, CT 06926
(203) 356-5000

Polaroid (251)
549 Technology
Cambridge, MA 02139
(617) 577-2000

Porter (H.K.) (418)
Porter Building
Pittsburgh, PA 15219
(412) 391-1800

Potlatch Forests, Inc. (336)
1 Maritime Plaza
San Francisco, CA 94111
(415) 981-5980

Procter & Gamble (25)
301 E. 6th Avenue
Cincinnati, OH 45202
(513) 562-1100
NUCMC 67-588; 76-1868

Purex Industries (396)
5101 Clark Avenue
Lakewood, CA 90712
(213) 634-3300

Quaker Oats (161)
Merchandise Market
Chicago, IL 60654
(312) 222-7111

Quaker State Oil Refining (327)
255 Elm Street
Oil City, PA 16301
(814) 676-0661

RCA (44)
30 Rockefeller Plaza
New York, NY 10020
(212) 621-6000
NUCMC 68-2043; 70-502; 71-1814; 77-1269

Ralston Purina (73)
Checkerboard Square
St. Louis, MO 63188
(314) 982-1000

Rath Packing (491)
Sycamore at Elm
Waterloo, IA 50703
(319) 235-8900
NUCMC 73-333

Raychem (461)
300 Constitution Drive
Menlo Park, CA 94025
(415) 329-3333

Raytheon (62)
141 Spring Street
Lexington, MA 02173
(617) 862-6600

Reichhold Chemicals (320)
525 N. Broadway
White Plain, NY 10603
(914) 682-5700

Republic Steel (87)
25 W. Prospect Avenue
Cleveland, OH 44101
(216) 574-7100
NUCMC 61-3050; 71-897; 75-1576

Research Cottrell (492)
Box 1500
Somerville, NJ 08876
(201) 685-4570

Revere Copper & Brass (353)
605 3rd Avenue
New York, NY 10016
(212) 578-1500

Revlon (171)
767 5th Avenue
New York, NY 10022
(212) 758-5000

Rexnord (290)
3500 1st Wisconsin
Milwaukee, WI 53202
(414) 643-3000

Reynolds (R.J.) Industries (32)
401 N. Main Street
Winston-Salem, NC 27102
(919) 748-4000

Reynolds Metals (114)
6603 West Broad
Richmond, VA 23261
(804) 281-2000

Richardson-Vicks (268)
10 Westport Road
Wilton, CT 06897
(203) 762-2222

Riegel Textile (499)
25 Woods Lake Road
Greenville, SC 29607
(803) 242-6050

Robertson (H.H.) (413)
2 Gateway Center
Pittsburgh, PA 15222
(412) 281-3200

Rockwell International (48)
600 Grant Street
Pittsburgh, PA 15219
(412) 575-2000

Rohm & Haas (206)
Independence Mall West
Philadelphia, PA 19105
(215) 592-3000

Rohr Industries (452)
Box 878
Chula Vista, CA 92012
(714) 575-4111

SCM (201)
299 Park Avenue
New York, NY 10017
(212) 752-2700

St. Regis Paper (151)
150 E. 42nd Street
New York, NY 10017
(212) 573-6000
NUCMC 62-4085; 66-792

Savannah Foods & Industries (462)
Box 339
Savannah, GA 31402
(912) 234-1261

Saxon Industries (388)
1230 Avenue of the Americas
New York, NY 10020
(212) 246-9500

Schering-Plough (210)
2000 Galloping
Kenilworth, NJ 07033
(201) 931-2000

Schlitz (Jos.) Brewing (335)
Box 614
Milwaukee, WI 53201
(414) 224-5020
NUCMC 71-1140

Scott & Fetzer (409)
14600 Detroit Avenue
Lakewood, OH 44107
(216) 228-6200

Scott Paper (176)
Scott Plaza
Philadelphi, PA 19113
(215) 521-5000

Scovill (331)
99 Mill Street
Waterbury, CT 06720
(203) 757-6061
NUCMC 70-1217; 78-257

Seagram (Joseph E.) & Sons (238)
375 Park Avenue
New York, NY 10022
(212) 572-7000

Searle (G.D.) (304)
Box 1045
Skokie, IL 60076
(312) 982-7000
NUCMC 71-1398

Shaklee (500)
1900 Powell Street
Oakland, CA 94608
(415) 428-8000

Shell Oil (13)
Box 2463
Houston, TX 77001
(713) 241-4083
NUCMC 75-2069; 76-1030, -1582; 77-2047

Sheller-Globe (466)
Box 962
Toledo, OH 43697
(419) 255-8840

Sherwin-Williams (231)
101 Prospect Avenue
Cleveland, OH 44115
(216) 566-2573
NUCMC 71-778

Signal Companies (70)
11255 Torrey Place
LaJolla, CA 92037
(714) 455-7392

Signode (394)
3600 W. Lake Avenue
Glenview, IL 60025
(312) 724-6100

Singer (150)
8 Stamford Forum
Stamford, CT 06904
(203) 356-4200
NUCMC 62-4242; 68-2329

Smith (A.O.) (366)
Box 584
Milwaukee, WI 53201
(414) 447-4000

Smith International (277)
4667 MacArthur Blvd.
Newport Beach, CA 92660
(714) 752-9000

Smithkline (195)
Box 7808
Boise, ID 83729
(208) 345-5000

SONOCO Procucts (457)
N. 2nd Street
Hartsville, SC 29550
(803) 383-7000

Southwest Forest Industries (369)
Box 7548
Phoenix, AZ 85011
(602) 279-5381

Sperry (66)
1290 Avenue of the Americas
New York, NY 10104
(212) 956-2121
NUCMC 62-720; 79-1592, -1984

Springs Mills (329)
Box 70
Fort Mill, SC 29715
(803) 547-2901

Square D (289)
1415 S. Roselle
Palatine, IL 60067
(312) 397-2600

Squibb (207)
40 W. 57th Street
New York, NY 10019
(212) 489-2000

Staley (A. E.) Manufacturing (192)
2200 E. El Dorado
Decatur, IL 62525
(217) 423-4411
NUCMC 77-1171

Standard Oil of California (5)
225 Bush Street
San Francisco, CA 94104
(415) 894-7700
NUCMC 64-1174; 65-78, -941; 67-489, -1290; 69-1807; 77-208; 70-560

Standard Oil (Indiana) (7)
200 E. Randolph
Chicago, IL 60601
(312) 857-6111
NUCMC 64-1174; 65-78, -941; 67-489, -1290; 69-1807; 77-208

Standard Oil (Ohio) (21)
101 Prospect Avenue
Cleveland, OH 44115
(216) 575-4141
NUCMC 64-1174; 65-78, -941; 67-489, -1290; 69-1807; 77-208

Stanley Works (315)
195 Lake Street
New Britain, CT 06050
(203) 225-5111

Stauffer Chemical (217)
Nyala Farms Road
Westport, CT 06880
(203) 222-3000

Sterling Drug (211)
90 Park Avenue
New York, NY 10016
(212) 972-4141

Stevens (J.P.)
1185 Avenue of the Americas
New York, NY 10036
(212) 575-2000
NUCMC 79-258

Stokely-Van Camp (443)
Box 1113
Indianapolis, IN 46206
(317) 631-2551

Storage Technology (325)
2270 S. 88th Street
Louisville, CO 80027
(303) 673-5151

Sun (17)
100 Matsonford
Radnor, PA 19087
(215) 293-6000

Sun Chemical (434)
200 Park Avenue
New York, NY 10166
(212) 986-5500

Sunbeam (237)
5400 W. Roosevelt
Chicago, IL 60650
(312) 854-3500

Sundstrand (305)
4751 Harrison
Rockford, IL 61101
(815) 226-6000

Superior Oil (187)
First National City Bank Bldg.
Houston, TX 77001
(713) 751-4111

Sybron (365)
174 Passaic Street
Garfield, NJ 07026
(201) 773-4000

TRW (71)
23555 Euclid Avenue
Cleveland, OH 44117
(216) 383-2121
NUCMC 75-1745

Tecumseh Products (356)
100 E. Patterson
Tecumseh, MI 49286
(517) 423-4811

Tektronix (301)
Box 500
Beaverton, OR 97005
(503) 644-0161

Teledyne (134)
1901 Avenue of the Stars
Los Angleas, CA 90067
(213) 277-3311

TENNECO (16)
Box 2511 Tenneco
Houston, TX 77002
(713) 757-2131

Texaco (4)
200 Westchester
White Plains, NY 10650
(914) 253-4000
NUCMC 70-816, -1972; 72-700; 77-1745

Texas Instrument (91)
Box 225474
Dallas, TX 75222
(214) 238-2011

TEXTRON (124)
40 Westminster
Providence, RI 02903
(401) 421-2800
NUCMC 64-240; 73-230; 80-1879

Thiokol (383)
Box 1000
Newton, PA 18040
(215) 968-5911

Time Inc. (125)
Rockefeller Center
New York, NY 10020
(212) 586-1212
NUCMC 62-3439; 66-1158; 69-983, -1832; 71-976; 78-1031

Times Mirror (186)
Times Mirror Square
Los Angeles, CA 90053
(213) 972-3838

Timken (250)
1835 Dueber Avenue
Canton, OH 44706
(216) 453-4511

Titanium Metals Corp. of America (469)
400 Rouser Road
Corapolis, PA 15108
(412) 262-4200

Todd Shipyards (426)
1 State Street Place
New York, NY 10004
(212) 344-6900
NUCMC 66-493

TOSCO (117)
10100 Santa Monica
Los Angeles, CA 90067
(213) 552-7000

Trane (359)
3600 Pammel Creek
La Crosse, WI 54601
(608) 782-8000

Trinity Industries (380)
Box 10587
Dallas, TX 75207
(214) 631-4420

Tyler (370)
3100 Southland
Dallas, TX 75201
(214) 747-8251

Tyson Foods (471)
2210 W. Oakland
Springdale, AR 72764
(501) 756-4000

Union Camp (222)
1600 Valley Road
Wayne, NJ 07470
(201) 628-2000
NUCMC 69-478; 80-893

Union Carbide (30)
270 Park Avenue
New York, NY 10017
(212) 551-2345
NUCMC 69-1346

Union Oil of California (27)
461 S. Boylston
Los Angeles, CA 75265
(213) 746-7711
NUCMC 61-1815

Union Pacific (56)
345 Park Avenue
New York, NY 10154
(212) 826-8200
NUCMC 60-48, -1211; 61-3650; 62-1167, -1401, -2436, -4047, -4717, -4959; 64-904; 65-920, -1190, -1843; 66-1568; 67-2071; 68-341, -381; 69-382, -687; 76-442; 77-1503; 80-678

Uniroyal (177)
World Headquarters
Middlesbury, CT 06749
(203) 573-2000

United Brands (95)
1271 Avenue of the Americas
New York, NY 10020
(212) 397-4000

United Merchants & Manufacturers (404)
1407 Broadway
New York, NY 10018
(212) 564-6000

U.S. Gypsum (241)
101 S. Wacker Drive
Chicago, IL 60606
(312) 321-4000

U.S. Industries (285)
250 Park Avenue
New York, NY 10017
(212) 697-4141

U.S. Steel (19)
600 Grant Street
Pittsburgh, PA 15230
(412) 433-1121
NUCMC 60-781, -1215; 62-766; 64-798; 66-216; 69-448

United Technologies (20)
United Technology Building
Hartford, CT 06101
(203) 728-7000

Universal Leaf Tobacco (306)
Box 25099
Richmond, VA 23260
(804) 359-9311

Upjohn (205)
7000 Portage Road
Kalamazoo, MI 49001
(616) 323-4000
NUCMC 65-407; 77-1593; 80-1676

VF (378)
1047 North Park Road
Reading, PA 19610
(215) 378-1151

Vulcan Materials (367)
Box 7497
Birmingham, AL 35253
(205) 877-3000

Wallace Murray (428)
299 Park Avenue
New York, NY 10171
(212) 486-6400

Walter (Jim) (191)
Box 22601
Tampa, FL 33622
(813) 871-4811

Wang Laboratories (341)
1 Industrial Avenue
Lowell, Ma 01851
(617) 851-4111

Warnaco (481)
350 Lafayette Street
Bridgeport, CT 06602
(203) 579-8094

Warner Communications (135)
75 Rockefeller
New York, NY 10019
(212) 484-8000

Warner-Lambert (119)
201 Mount Tabor
Morris Plains, NJ 07950
(201) 540-9000

Washington Post (375)
1150 15th Street NW
Washington, D.C. 20071
(202) 223-6000
NUCMC 60-1824; 65-914; 80-825, -1748

West Point-Pepperell (276)
120 E. Morris Street
Dalton, GA 30720
(404) 278-1100

Western Electric (22)
222 Broadway
New York, NY 10038
(212) 571-2345
NUCMC 64-1561; 77-730

Westinghouse Electric (34)
Gateway Center
Pittsburgh, PA 15222
(412) 255-3800
NUCMC 61-2643; 66-981; 69-1750; 70-502; 71-1696; 73-225; 77-2044; 80-262, -713

Westmoreland Coal (480)
2500 Fidelity Place
Philadelphia, PA 19109
(215) 545-2500

WESTVACO (230)
299 Park Avenue
New York, NY 10171
(212) 688-5000

Weyerhauser (84)
1021 A Street
Tacoma, WA 98477
(206) 924-2345
NUCMC 70-273, -505, -1386; 71-617; 72-996

Wheelabrator-Frye (209)
Liberty Lane
Hampton, NH 03842
(602) 926-5911

Wheeling-Pittsburgh Steel Co. (288)
Box 118
Pittsburgh, PA 15230
(412) 288-3600

Whirlpool (166)
2000 US 33 North
Benton Harbor, MI 49022
(616) 926-5000

White Consolidated Industries (184)
11770 Berea Road
Cleveland, OH 44111
(216) 252-3700

Whittaker (221)
10880 Wilshire
Los Angeles, CA 90024
(213) 475-9411

Willamette Industries (316)
3800 1st National Bank
Portland, OR 97201
(503) 277-5581

Williams Companies (198)
1 Williams Center
Tulsa, OK 74172
(918) 588-2000

WITCO Chemical (267)
277 Park Avenue
New York, NY 10017
(212) 644-6300

Wrigley (Wm. Jr.) (429)
410 N. Michigan
Chicago, IL 60611
(312) 644-2121

Wyman-Gordon (427)
105 Madison Street
Worcester, PA 01612
(617) 765-5111

Xerox (42)
Xerox Square
Stamford, CT 06904
(203) 329-8700

Zenith Radio (269)
1000 Milwaukee
Glenview, Il 60025
(312) 391-7000
NUCMC 80-1888

Zurn Industries
1 Zurn Place
Erie, PA 16512
(704) 824-4605

Appendix 6

Fifty Largest Life Insurance Companies*

Aetna Life (4)
151 Farmington
Hartford, CT 06156
(203) 273-0123
(1853)

Aetna Life and Annuity (34)
151 Farmington
Hartford, CT 06156
(203) 273-0123

Allstate Life (50)
Allstate Plaza
Northbrook, IL 60062
(312) 291-5000
(1931)

American National (30)
1 Moody Plaza
Galveston, TX 77550
(713) 763-4661
(1905)

American United Life (48)
Box 368
Indianapolis, IN 46206
(317) 923-7201
(1877)

Bankers Life (12)
711 High Street
Des Moines, IA 50307
(515) 247-5627
(1879)

Capitol Life (46)
Box 1200
Denver, CO 80201
(303) 861-4065
(1905)

Connecticut General Life (7)
900 Cottage Grove
Bloomfield, CT 06002
(203) 726-6000
(1865)

Connecticut Mutual (16)
140 Garden Street
Hartford, CT 06115
(203) 727-6500
(1846)

Continental Assurance (21)
CNA Plaza
Chicago, IL 60685
(312) 822-5000

Equitable Life Assurance (3)
1285 Avenue of the Americas
New York, NY 10019
(212) 554-1234
(1859)

Franklin Life (28)
Franklin Square
Springfield, IL 62713
(217) 528-2011

General American Life (41)
700 Market
St. Louis, MO 63101
(314) 231-1700
(1933)

Guardian of America (33)
201 Park Avenue South
New York, NY 10003
(212) 473-3000
(1860)

Home Life (37)
253 Broadway
New York, NY 10007
(212) 233-6400
(1860)

IDS Life (32)
IDS Tower
Minneapolis, MN 55402
(612) 372-3131
(1957)

Jefferson Standard (47)
Box 21008
Greensboro, NC 27420
(919) 378-2011

John Hancock Mutual (6)
Box 111
Boston, MA 02117
(617) 421-4506
(1862)

Liberty National (44)
Box 2612
Birmingham, IL 35202
(205) 325-2722

Life Insurance of Virginia (49)
Box 27601
Richmond, VA 23261
(804) 281-6000
(1871)

Lincoln National Life (17)
1300 S. Clinton
Fort Wayne, IN 46801
(219) 424-5421

Massachusetts Mutual (11)
1295 State Street
Springfield, MA 01111
(413) 788-8411
(1851)

Metropolitan (2)
1 Madison Ave.
New York, NY 10010
(212) 578-2211
(1868)

Minnesota Mutual Life (39)
345 Cedar Street
St. Paul, MN 55101
(612) 298-3500
(1880)

Mutual Benefit (15)
520 Broad Street
Newark, NJ 07101
(201) 481-8000
(1845)

Mutual of New York (13)
1740 Broadway
New York, NY 10019
(212) 708-2000
(1842)

National Life (27)
National Life Drive
Montpelier, VT 05602
(802) 229-3333
(1848)

National Life and Accident (23)
National Life Center
Nashville, TN 37250
(615) 749-1000

Nationwide Life (25)
1 Nationwide
Columbus, OH 43216
(614) 227-7111
(1929)

New England Mutual (14)
501 Boylston Street
Boston, MA 02117
(617) 266-3700
(1835)

New York Life (5)
51 Madison Avenue
New York, NY 10010
(212) 576-7000
(1841)

Northwestern Mutual (9)
720 E. Wisconsin
Milwaukee, WI 53202
(414) 271-1444
(1857)

Northwestern National (43)

Pacific Mutual (24)
Box 9000
Newport Beach, CA 92660
(714) 640-3011
(1936)

Penn Mutual (18)
530 Walnut Street
Philadelphia, PA 19172
(215) 629-0600
(1847)

Phoenix Mutual (20)
1 American Road
Hartford, CT 06115
(203) 278-1212
(1851)

Provident Life & Accident (38)
Fountain Square
Chattanooga, TN 37402
(615) 755-1011
(1887)

Provident Mutual (36)
Box 7878
Philadelphia, PA 19101
(215) 472-5000
(1865)

Prudential (1)
Prudential Plaza
Newark, NJ 07101
(201) 877-6000
(1873)

Southwestern Life (42)
1807 Ross Avenue
Dallas, TX 75201
(214) 655-5111
(1903)

State Mutual of America (29)
440 Lincoln Street
Worcester, MA 01605
(617) 852-1000
(1844)

Teachers Insurance & Annuity (10)
730 3rd Avenue
New York, NY 10017
(212) 490-9000
(1918)

Transamerica Occidental Life (26)
Hill and Olive at Twelfth Street
Los Angeles, CA 90015
(213) 742-4242

Travelers (8)
1 Towers Square
Hartford, CT 06115
(203) 277-0111

Union Mutual (31)
Box 9548
Portland, ME 04104
(207) 780-2211
(1848)

United of Omaha Life (40)
Mutual of Omaha Life
Omaha, NB 68175
(402) 342-7600
(1926)

Variable Annuity Life (35)
2777 Allen Parkway
Houston, TX 77019
(713) 526-5251

Western & Southern (22)
400 Broadway
Cincinnati, OH 45202
(513) 421-1800
(1888)

*The company's ranking by size follows its name in parenthesis while the date of incorporation, where known, is on the line under the telephone number.

Appendix 7

Fifty Largest Transportation Companies*

Alexander & Baldwin (44)
Box 3440
Honolulu, HI 96801
(808) 525-6611

Allied Van Lines (39)
Box 4403
Chicago, IL 60680
(312) 681-8000
(1928)

American Airlines (6)
Box 61616
DFW Airport, TX 75261
(214) 355-1234
(1934)

ARCO Pipeline (30)
Arco Bldg.
Independence, KS 67301
(316) 331-1300
(1950)

Arkansas Best (43)
Box 48
Fort Smith, AR 72902
(501) 785-6000
(1966)

BP Pipelines (33)
1 Dag Hammarskjold Plaza
New York, NY 10017
(212) 644-2200

Braniff International (19)
Drawer 61747
Dallas, TX 75261
(214) 358-6011
(1930)

Burlington Northern (4)
176 E. 5th Street
St. Paul, MN 55101
(612) 298-2121
(1961)

CSX (1)
701 East Byrd Street
Richmond, VA 23200
(804) 782-1400

Chicago Milwaukee St. Paul & Pacific Railroad (41)
666 N. Lake Shore
Chicago, IL 60611
(312) 337-0400

Chicago & North Western Transportation (26)
400 W. Madison Street
Chicago, IL 60606
(312) 454-6000

Consolidated Freightways (20)
601 California
San Francisco, CA 94108
(415) 397-4161
(1929)

Continental Air Lines (23)
LA International Airport
Los Angeles, CA 90009
(212) 646-2810
(1934)

Delta Air Lines (9)
Atlanta International Airport
Atlanta, GA 30320
(404) 765-2600
(1930)

Eastern Air Lines (8)
Miami International Airport
Miami, FL 33148
(305) 873-2211
(1938)

Emery Air Freight (35)
Box 322
Wilton, CT 06897
(203) 762-8601
(1946)

EXXON Pipeline (29)
800 Bell Avenue
Houston, TX 77002
(713) 656-4364
(1941)

Federal Express (36)
Box 727
Memphis, TN 38194
(901) 365-3600
(1971)

Frontier Airlines (37)
8250 Smith Road
Denver, CO 80207
(303) 398-5151
(1950)

Illinois Central Gulf Railroad (25)
233 N. Michigan
Chicago, IL 60601
(312) 565-1600

Kansas City Southern Industries (48)
114 W. 11th Street
Kansas City, MO 64015
(816) 556-0303

Leaseway Transportation (27)
3700 Park East
Beachwood, OH 44123
(216) 991-8800
(1960)

McLean Trucking (34)
Box 213
Winston-Salem, NC 27107
(919) 721-2000
(1934)

Missouri Pacific (12)
210 N. 13th Street
St. Louis, MO 63103
(314) 622-0123
(1894)

Norfolk & Western Railway (14)
8 N. Jefferson
Roanoke, VA 24042
(703) 981-4530
(1896)

Northwest Airlines (13)
100 South 7th Street
St. Paul, MN 55111
(612) 726-2111
(1934)

Overseas Shipholding Group (49)
1114 Avenue of the Americas
New York, NY 10036
(212) 869-1222

Ozark Airlines (45)
Lambert Airfield
St. Louis, MO 63145
(314) 895-6600
(1943)

PSA (40)
3225 N. Harbor
San Diego, CA 92101
(714) 297-4781
(1945)

Pan American World Airways (7)
Pan Am Building
New York, NY 10017
(212) 880-1234
(1927)

Piedmont Aviation (32)
Box 2720
Winston-Salem, NC 27102
(919) 767-5100
(1940)

RLC (50)
Box 1791
Wilmington, DE 19899
(302) 658-8541
(1954)

Republic Airlines (17)
7500 Airline Drive
Minneapolis, MN 55450
(612) 726-7406
(1943)

Rio Grande Industries (42)
Box 5482
Denver, CO 80217
(303) 892-1215

Roadway Express (21)
Box 471
Akron, OH 44309
(216) 434-1641
(1930)

Santa Fe Industries (10)
224 S. Michigan
Chicago, IL 60604
(312) 427-4900
(1967)

Sohio Pipe Line (17)
Midland Building
Cleveland, OH 44115
(216) 575-4141
(1937)

Southern Pacific (11)
1 Market Plaza
San Francisco, CA 94105
(415) 362-1212
(1917)

Southern Railway (15)
Box 1808
Washington, DC 20013
(202) 686-4460

Telecom (38)
1200 Travis
Houston, TX 77002
(713) 658-9961

Texas International Air (31)
8451 Lockheed Street
Houston, TX 77017
(214) 357-6522

Tiger International (16)
1888 Century Park
Los Angeles, CA 90067
(213) 552-6330
(1969)

Trans World (2)
605 3rd Avenue
New York, NY 10016
(212) 556-3000
(1934)

UAL (3)
Box 66919
Chicago, IL 60666
(312) 952-4000
(1968)

United Parcel Service (5)
643 W. 43rd Street
New York, NY 10036
(212) 736-5544
(1930)

US Air (22)
Washington National
Washington, DC 20001
(703) 892-7000

United Van Lines (47)
1 United Drive
Fenton, MO 63026
(314) 326-3100
(1942)

Western Air Lines (24)
6060 Avion Drive
Los Angeles, CA 90009
(213) 327-4400
(1925)

World Airways (46)
International Airport
Oakland, CA 94614
(415) 577-2000
(1948)

Yellow Freight System (28)
Box 7270
Shawnee Mission, KS 66207
(913) 383-3000
(1950)

*The company's ranking by size appears in parenthesis after the name with the date of incorporation, where known, following the telephone number.

Appendix 8

Fifty Largest Retailing Companies

ARA Service (21)
Independence Square
Philadelphia, PA 19106
(215) 923-7700

Albertson's (18)
Box 20
Boise, ID 83726
(208) 344-7411

Allied Stores (23)
1114 Avenue of the Americas
New York, NY 10036
(212) 764-2000

American Stores (8)
Box 27447
Salt Lake City, UT 84127
(801) 539-0112

Associated Dry Goods (25)
417 5th Avenue
New York, NY 10016
(212) 679-8700

Carter Hawley Hale Stores (22)
550 S. Flower Street
Los Angeles, CA 90071
(213) 620-0150

Dayton Hudson (16)
777 Nicollet Mall
Minneapolis, MN 55402
(612) 370-6948

Dillon Companies (27)
Box 1266
Hutchinson, KS 67501
(316) 663-6801

Jack Eckerd (35)
Box 4689
Clearwater, FL 33518
(813) 531-8911

Federated Department Stores (9)
7 W. 7th Street
Cincinnati, OH 45202
(513) 579-7000

First National Supermarkets (43)
17000 Rockside
Maple Heights, OH 44137
(216) 587-7100

Fisher Foods (38)
5300 Richmond
Bedford Heights, OH 44146
(216) 292-7000

Giant Food (39)
Box 249
Carlisle, PA 17013
(717) 249-1424

Grand Union (17)
100 Broadway
Elmwood Park, NJ 07407
(201) 796-4800

Great Atlantic & Pacific Tea (10)
Box 418
Montvale, NJ 07645
(201) 573-9700

Household Merchandising (15)
1700 S. Wolf Road
Des Plaines, IL 60016
(312) 298-8800

Jewel Companies (14)
5725 North River Road
Chicago, IL 60631
(312) 693-6000

K Mart (3)
3100 West Big Beaver
Troy, MI 48084
(313) 643-1000

Kroger (5)
1014 Vine Street
Cincinnati, OH 45201
(513) 762-4000

Lucky Stores (7)
6300 Clark Avenue
Dublin, CA 94566
(415) 828-1000

R.H. Macy (26)
151 W. 34th Street
New York, NY 10001
(212) 560-3600

Marriott (32)
Marriott Drive
Washington, DC 20058
(301) 897-9000

Marshall Field (45)
25 E. Washington
Chicago, IL 60690
(312) 236-7272

May Department Stores (19)
611 Olive
St. Louis, MO 63101
(314) 247-0300

McDonald's (28)
McDonald's Plaza
Oak Brook, IL 60521
(312) 887-3200

Melville (24)
3000 Westchester
Harrison, NY 10528
(914) 253-8000

Merchantile Stores (42)
128 W. 31st St.
New York, NY 10001
(212) 560-0500

Montgomery Ward (12)
1 Montgomery Ward
Chicago, IL 60671
(312) 467-2000

Pantry Pride (44)
500 E. Las Olas
Ft. Lauderdale, FL 33300
(305) 467-7436

J.C. Penney (4)
1301 Avenue of the Americas
New York, NY 10019
(212) 957-4321

Pneumo (48)
4800 Prudential
Boston, MA 02199
(617) 272-9300

Rapid-American (29)
888 7th Avenue
New York, NY 10019
(212) 399-4500

REVCO Drug Stores (41)
1925 Enterprise
Twinsburg, OH 94660
(216) 425-9811

Safeway Stores (29)
4th & Jackson
Oakland, CA 94660
(415) 891-3000

SCOA Industries (48)
155 E. Broad Street
Columbus, OH 43215
(614) 221-5421

Sears Roebuck (1)
Sears Tower
Chicago, IL 60684
(312) 875-2500

Service Merchandise (50)
Box 24600
Nashville, TN 37202
(615) 251-6666

SIGMOR (33)
Box 20267
San Antonio, TX 78220
(512) 223-2361

Southland (13)
Box 719
Dallas, TX 75221
(214) 463-7000

Stop & Shop Companies (31)
Box 369
Boston, MA 02101
(617) 463-7000

Supermarkets General (20)
301 Blair Road
Woodbridge, NJ 07095
(201) 499-3000

Tandy (37)
Box 17180
Fort Worth, TX 76102
(817) 390-3700

Thrifty (49)
5051 Rodeo Road
Los Angeles, CA 90016
(213) 293-5111

U.S. Shoe (47)
1658 Herald Avenue
Cincinnati, OH 45212
(513) 841-4111

Wal-Mart (30)
Box 116
Bentonville, AR 42712
(501) 273-7741

Waldbaum (40)
Hemlock Blvd.
Central Isle, NY 11722
(516) 582-9300

Walgreen (36)
200 Wilmot Road
Deerfield, IL 60015
(312) 948-5000

Winn-Dixie Stores (11)
Box B
Jacksonville, FL 32203
(904) 783-1800

F.W. Woolworth (6)
233 Broadway
New York, NY 10279
(212) 227-1000

Zayre (34)
770 Chochituate
Framingham, MA 01701
(617) 620-5000

---

*The company's ranking by size appears in parentheses after the name with the date of incorporation, where known, following the telephone number.

Appendix 9

Fifty Largest Utilities

Allegheny Power System (43)
320 Park Avenue
New York, NY 10022
(212) 752-2121

American Electric Power (5)
2 Broadway
New York, NY 10004
(212) 440-9000

American Natural Resources (28)
1 Woodward Avenue
Detroit, MI 48226
(313) 965-1200

American Telephone & Telegraph (1)
195 Broadway
New York, NY 10007
(212) 393-9800

Arizona Public Service (38)
Box 21666
Phoenix, AZ 85036
(602) 271-7900

Baltimore Gas & Electric (42)
Box 1475
Baltimore, MD 21203
(301) 234-5000

Carolina Power & Light (21)
Box 1551
Raleigh, NC 27602
(919) 836-6111

Central & South West (13)
2700 One Main Place
Dallas, TX 75250
(214) 745-3700

Cleveland Electric Illuminating (37)
Box 5000
Cleveland, OH 44101
(216) 623-1350

Columbia Gas System (24)
20 Montchanin
Wilmington, DE 19807
(302) 429-5000

Commonwealth Edison (6)
Box 767
Chicago, IL 60690
(312) 294-4321

Consolidated Edison (9)
4 Irving Place
New York, NY 10003
(212) 460-4600

Consolidated Natural Gas (46)
30 Rockefeller
New York, NY 10020
(212) 245-5100

Consumers Power (22)
212 W. Michigan
Jackson, MI 49201
(517) 788-0550

Continental Telephone (36)
56 Perimeter
Atlanta, GA 30346
(404) 391-8000

Detroit Edison (14)
2000 2nd Avenue
Detroit, MI 48226
(313) 237-8000

Duke Power (15)
Box 33189
Charlotte, NC 28242
(704) 373-4011

El Paso (35)
Box 2185
Houston, TX 77001
(713) 515-9400

Enserch (50)
301 Harwood
Dallas, TX 75201
(214) 651-8700

Florida Power & Light (17)
9250 W. Flagler
Miami, FL 33101
(305) 552-3552

General Public Utilities (19)
100 Interpace Place
Parsippany, NJ 07054
(201) 263-6500

General Telephone & Electronics (2)
1 Stamford Forum
Stamford, CT 06904
(203) 357-2000

Gulf States Utilities (40)
Box 2951
Beaumont, TX 77701
(713) 838-6631

Houston Industries (18)
611 Walker Avenue
Houston, TX 77002
(713) 228-2474

Illinois Power (48)
500 S. 27th Street
Decatur, IL 62525
(216) 424-6600

Internorth (34)
2223 Dodge Street
Omaha, NE 68102
(402) 348-4000

Long Island Lighting (25)
230 Old Country
Mineola, NY 11501
(516) 228-2890

Middle South Utilities (8)
Box 61005
New Orleans, LA 70161
(504) 529-5262

Niagara Mohawk Power (27)
300 Erie Blvd. W.
Syracuse, NY 13202
(315) 574-1511

Northeast Utilities (33)
174 Brush Hill
Springfield, MA 01089
(413) 785-5871

Northern Indiana Public Service (44)
5265 Hohman Avenue
Hammond, IN 46320
(219) 853-5200

Northern States Power (45)
414 Nicollet Mall
Minneapolis, MN 55401
(612) 330-5500

Ohio Edison (26)
76 S. Main
Akron, OH 44308
(216) 384-5100

Pacific Gas & Electric (4)
77 Beale Street
San Francisco, CA 94106
(415) 781-4211

Pacific Lighting (49)
810 S. Flower Street
Los Angeles, CA 90017
(213) 689-3481

Pacific Power & Light (32)
920 SW 6th Avenue
Portland, OR 97204
(503) 243-1122

Panhandle Eastern Pipe Line (30)
3000 Bissonet Avenue
Houston, TX 77005
(713) 664-3401

Pennsylvania Power & Light (20)
2 N. 9th Street
Allentown, PA 18101
(215) 821-5151

Philadelphia Electric (16)
2301 Market Street
Philadelphia, PA 19101
(215) 841-4000

Public Service Co. of Indiana (41)
1000 E. Main
Plainfield, IN 46168
(317) 839-9611

Public Service Electric & Gas (11)
80 Park Plaza
Newark, NJ 07101
(201) 430-7000

SONAT (47)
1900 Fifth Avenue North
Birmingham, AL 35200
(205) 325-3800

Southern California Edison (7)
Box 800
Rosemead, CA 91770
(213) 572-1086

Southern Company (3)
Box 720071
Atlanta, GA 30346
(404) 393-0650

Texas Eastern Corp. (29)
Box 2521
Houston, TX 77001
(713) 759-3131

Texas Utilities (10)
2001 Bryan Tower
Dallas, TX 75201
(214) 653-4600

TRANSCO Companies (39)
Box 1396
Houston, TX 77001
(713) 871-8000

Union Electric (31)
Box 149
St. Louis, MO 63166
(314) 621-3222

United Telecommunications (23)
Box 11315
Kansas City, MO 64112
(913) 676-6000

Virginia Electric & Power (12)
Box 26666
Richmond, VA 23261
(804) 771-3000

Appendix 10

Fifty Largest Commercial Banking Companies

Ameritrust Corp. (44)
900 Euclid Avenue
Cleveland, OH 44101
(216) 687-5000

Bancohio Corp. (45)
155 E. Broad
Columbus, OH 43265
(614) 463-8100

Bank of New York Co. (25)
48 Wall Street
New York, NY 10015
(212) 530-1784

Bankamerica Corp. (1)
555 California
San Francisco, CA 94104
(415) 622-3456

Bankers Trust New York Corp. (9)
Box 318
New York, NY 10017
(212) 775-2500

Barnett Banks of Florida (46)
Box 40789
Jacksonville, FL 33231
(904) 791-7720

Centerre Bancorp (48)
1 Centerre Plaza
St. Louis, MO
(314) 554-6500

Chase Manhattan Corp. (3)
1 Chase Manhattan Plaza
New York, NY 10081
(212) 552-2222

Chemical New York Corp. (7)
20 Pine Street
New York, NY 10087
(212) 770-1234

Citicorp (2)
399 Park Avenue
New York, NY 10043
(212) 559-1000

Continental Illinois Corp. (6)
231 S. LaSalle
Chicago, IL 60693
(312) 828-2345

Crocker National Corp. (13)
1 Montgomery Street
San Francisco, CA 94104
(415) 477-0456

Detroitbank Corp. (39)
211 W. Fort
Detroit, MI 48226
(313) 222-3300

European American Bancorp. (27)
10 Hanover Square
New York, NY 10015
(212) 437-4300

First Bank System (20)
Box 522
Minneapolis, MN 55480
(612) 370-5100

First Chicago Corp. (10)
1 First National Plaza
Chicago, IL 60670
(312) 732-4000

First City Bankcorp of Texas (23)
Box 2387
Houston, TX 77001
(713) 658-6109

First Interstate Bancorp (8)
Box 54068
Los Angeles, CA 90054
(213) 614-3019

First National Boston Corp. (18)
Box 2016
Boston, MA 02106
(617) 434-2200

First Pennsylvania Corp. (50)
16th & Market
Philadelphia, PA 19101
(215) 786-5000

First Union Corp. (49)
1st Union Plaza
Charlotte, NC 28288
(704) 374-4269

Harris Bancorp. (30)
111 W. Monroe
Chicago, IL 60603
(312) 461-2121

Interfirst Corp. (17)
1201 Elm Street
Dallas, TX
(214) 744-7100

Irving Bank Corp. (16)
1 Wall Street
New York, NY 10005
(212) 487-2121

Manufacturers Hanover Corp. (4)
New York, NY
(address unavailable at press time)

Marine Midland Corp. (14)
140 Broadway
New York, NY 10015
(212) 440-1000

Mellon National Corp. (15)
Box 15629
Pittsburgh, PA 15244
(412) 787-5534

Mercantile Texas Corp. (33)
Box 225415
Dallas, TX 75265
(214) 698-5000

Michigan National Corp. (38)
Box 589
Bloomfield, MI 48013
(312) 255-6400

J.P. Morgan & Co. (5)
23 Wall Street
New York, NY 10015
(212) 483-2323

National Bank of Detroit Corporation (24)
Woodward Avenue at Fort Street
Detroit, MI 48232
(313) 225-1000

NCNB Corp. (28)
1 NCNB Plaza
Charlotte, NC 28255
(704) 374-5000

National Bank of North America (41)
44 Wall Street
New York, NY 10005
(212) 623-4000

National City Corp. (47)
623 Euclid Avenue
Cleveland, OH 44115
(216) 575-2000

Northern Trust Corp. (37)
50 S. LaSalle
Chicago, IL 60675
(312) 630-6000

Northwest Bancorp. (19)
1200 Northwestern
Minneapolis, MN 55480
(612) 272-8123

Philadelphia National Corp. (35)
Broad & Chestnut
Philadelphia, PA 19101
(215) 629-3100

Pittsburgh National Corp. (31)
5th Avenue & Wood
Pittsburgh, PA 15222
(412) 355-2666

Rainier Bancorp. (42)
Box 3966
Seattle, WA 98124
(206) 621-4111

Republic New York Corp. (29)
425 5th Avenue
New York, NY 10018
(212) 930-6000

Republic of Texas Corp. (22)
Box 222105
Dallas, TX 75222
(214) 653-5031

Seafirst Corp. (26)
Box 3586
Seattle, WA 91824
(206) 583-3131

Security Pacific Corp. (11)
Box 2097
Los Angeles, CA 90051
(213) 613-6211

Southeast Banking Corp. (34)
100 S. Biscayne
Miami, FL 33131
(305) 577-4000

Texas Commerce Bancshares (21)
Box 2558
Houston, TX 77001
(713) 236-4865

Union Bank (32)
445 S. Figueroa
Los Angeles, CA 90071
(213) 687-6877

U.S. Bankcorp. (43)
210 Main Street
Portland, OR 97208
(503) 225-6111

Valley National Corp. (40)
Box 71
Phoenix, AZ 85001
(602) 261-2900

Wachovia Corp. (36)
Box 3099
Winston-Salem, NC 27102
(919) 748-5000

Wells Fargo & Co. (12)
420 Montgomery
San Francisco, CA 94104
(415) 396-0123

*The company's ranking by size appears in parentheses after the name with the date of incorporation, where known, following the telephone number.

Appendix 11

Forty-five Largest Diversified Service Companies

AGRI Industries (9)
2829 Westown Parkway
West Des Moines, IA
(515) 223-3700

ALCO Standard (12)
Box 834
Valley Forge, PA 19842
(215) 296-8000

American Broadcasting (14)
1330 Avenue of the Americas
New York, NY 10019
(212) 887-7777

American Hospital Supply (10)
1 American Plaza
Evanston, IL 60201
(312) 866-4000

American Medical International (50)
404 N. Camden Drive
Beverly Hills, CA 90210
(213) 278-6200

AMFAC (17)
Box 3230
Honolulu, HI 96801
(808) 945-8111

Associated Milk Producers (11)
6609 Blanco Road
San Antonio, TX 78284
(512) 341-8651

CBS (6)
51 W. 52nd Street
New York, NY 10019
(212) 975-4321

CFS Continental (48)
100 S. Wacker Drive
Chicago, IL 60606
(312) 368-7500

Centex (39)
4600 Republic National Bank
Dallas, TX 75201
(214) 748-7901

Commercial Metals (33)
Box 1046
Dallas, TX 75221
(214) 631-4120

Dairymen (41)
10140 Linn Station
Louisville, KY 40223
(502) 426-6455

Dillingham (26)
Box 3468
Honolulu, HI 96801
(808) 946-0771

Dravo (28)
1 Oliver Plaza
Pittsburgh, PA 15222
(412) 566-3000

Dun & Bradstreet (34)
299 Park Avenue
New York, NY 10171
(212) 593-6800

Fischbach (38)
485 Lexington Avenue
New York, NY 10017
(212) 986-4100

S.M. Flickinger (36)
Box 1086
Buffalo, NY 14240
(716) 674-7200

Fleming Companies (7)
Box 26647
Oklahoma City, OK 73126
(405) 848-7721

Fluor (3)
3333 Michelson
Irvine, CA 92730
(714) 975-2000

Foremost-McKesson (5)
1 Post Street
San Francisco, CA 94104
(415) 983-8300

Foster Wheeler (25)
110 S. Orange
Livingston, NJ 07039
(201) 533-1100

GDV (31)
767 Fifth Avenue
New York, NY 10000
(212) 759-4826

Genuine Parts (27)
2999 Piedmont Avenue N.E.
Atlanta, GA 30339
(404) 953-1700

Grain Terminal Association
Division of Harvest States Cooperative
1667 Snelling Avenue
St. Paul, MN 55100
(612) 646-9433

Halliburton (2)
2600 Southland
Dallas, TX 75201
(214) 748-7261

Holiday Inns (24)
3742 LaMar
Memphis, TN 38118
(901) 362-4001

Humana (32)
Box 1438
Louisville, KY 40201
(502) 561-2000

Hospital Corp. Of America (19)
1 Park Plaza
Nashville, TN 37203
(615) 327-9551

IU International (15)
1500 Walnut
Philadelphia, PA 19102
(215) 985-6600

Landmark (47)
35 E. Chestnut
Columbus, OH 43215
(614) 225-8711

MCA (35)
100 Universal Circle
Universal City, CA 91608
(213) 985-4321

Malone & Hyde (31)
1991 Corporate
Memphis, TN 38132
(901) 345-4200

Morrison-Knudsen (20)
Box 7808
Boise, ID 83729
(208) 345-5000

Parsons (37)
100 W. Walnut Street
Pasadena, CA 91124
(213) 440-2000

Petrolane (23)
1600 E. Hill Street
Long Beach, CA 90806
(213) 427-5471

Phibro (1)
212 Avenue of the Americas
New York NY 10000
(212) 575-5900

Pittston (18)
1 Pickwick Place
Greenwich, CT 06830
(203) 622-0900

Raymond International (40)
Box 27456
Houston, TX 77027
(713) 623-1500

Ryder System
Box 520816
Miami, FL 33152
(305) 593-3726

Super Food Services (43)
3185 Elbu Road
Dayton, OH 45429
(513) 294-1731

Super Value Stores (4)
Box 990
Minneapolis, MN 55440
(612) 935-8844

SYSCO (30)
1177 W. Loop Street
Houston, TX 77002
(713) 877-1122

TESORO Petroleum (8)
8700 Tesoro Drive
San Antonio, TX 78286
(512) 828-8484

Turner Construction (21)
150 E. 42nd Street
New York, NY 10017
(212) 573-0400

U.S. Home (45)
Box 2863
Houston, TX 77001
(713) 877-2311

*Companies no longer qualified were dropped from list at time of last printing.

Appendix 12

Fifty Largest Diversified Financial Companies

Aetna Life & Casualty (2)
51 Farmington
Hartford, CT 06156
(203) 273-0123

H.E. Ahmanson (6)
3731 Wilshire Blvd.
Los Angeles, CA 90010
(213) 949-0300

Alleghany (35)
350 Park Avenue
New York, NY 10004
(202) 752-2121

American Express (3)
American Express Building
New York, NY 10004
(212) 480-2000

American Financial (33)
1 E. 4th Street
Cincinnati, OH 45202
(513) 579-2121

American General (15)
Box 3247
Houston, TX 77001
(713) 522-1111

American International Group (17)
70 Pine
New York, NY 10005
(212) 770-7000

American Savings (43)
77 W. 200 S.
Salt Lake City, UT 84101
(801) 531-5600

American Savings & Loan Assn. of Florida (44)
17801 NW 2nd Avenue
Miami, FL
(305) 653-5353

AVCO (20)
1275 King
Greenwich, CT 06830
(203) 531-2800

Bache Group (29)
100 Gold Street
New York, NY 10038
(212) 791-1000

Baldwin-United (24)
1801 Gilbert Avenue
Cincinnati, OH 45202
(513) 852-7821

Beneficial (18)
1300 Market Street
Wilmington, DE 19899
(302) 658-5171

Broadview Financial (49)
6000 Rockside Way
Cleveland,OH 44131
(216) 584-8157

Capitol Holding Co. (36)
Box 32830
Louisville, KY 40232
(502) 584-8157

Chubb (39)
100 William Street
New York, NY 10038
(212) 285-2850

City Federal Savings & Loan Assn. (37)
1141 E. Jersey Street
Elizabeth, NJ 07201
(201) 355-3300

Continental Corp. (16)
80 Maiden Lane
New York, NY 10038
(212) 374-3518

Crum & Forster (31)
110 William Street
New York, NY 10038
(212) 791-8200

Donaldson Lufkin & Jenrette (25)
140 Broadway
New York, NY 10005
(212) 943-0300

Federal National Mortgage Assn. (1)
1133 15th Street N.W.
Washington, DC 20005
(202) 293-6000

Financial Corp. of America (32)
6420 Wilshire Blvd.
Los Angeles, CA 90048
(213) 653-9550

Financial Corp. of Santa Barbara (47)
Box 1109
Santa Barbara, CA 93102
(805) 963-2025

Financial Federation (42)
615 S. Flower Street
Los Angeles, CA 90017
(213) 624-1901

First Boston (9)
20 Exchange Place
Boston, MA 10005
(212) 825-2000

First Charter Financial (11)
9465 Wilshire
Beverly Hills, CA 90212
(213) 273-3300

General Reinsurance (30)
600 Steamboat Road
Greenwich CT 06830
(203) 622-4000

Gibraltar Financial Corp. of Calif. (26)
9111 Wilshire Blvd.
Beverly Hills, CA 90213
(213) 278-8720

Golden West Financial (23)
1970 Broadway
Oakland, CA 94612
(415) 645-9420

Great Western Financial (8)
8484 Wilshire Blvd.
Beverly Hills, CA 90211
(213) 658-6060

Guarantee Financial Corp. of California (50)
1177 Fulton Mall
Fresno, CA 93721
(209) 268-8111

Walter E. Heller International (19)
105 W. Adams Street
Chicago, IL 60603
(312) 346-2300

Household Finance (21)
2700 Sanders Road
Prospect Heights, IL 60070
(312) 564-5000

E.F. Hutton Group (22)
1 Battery Plaza
New York, NY 10004
(212) 742-5000

INA (7)
Box 7728
Philadelphia, PA 19101
(215) 241-4000

Imperial Corp. of America (14)
Box 631
San Diego, CA 92112
(714) 236-1222

Kemper (34)
Kemper Center
Lake Zurich, IL 60047
(312) 540-2000

Lincoln National (12)
1300 S. Clinton
Fort Wayne, IN 46801
(219) 424-5421

Loews (39)
666 5th Avenue
New York, NY 10019
(212) 841-1000

Merrill Lynch & Co. (5)
1 Liberty Plaza
New York, NY 10080
(212) 637-7455

Northern California Savings & Loan (48)
300 Hamilton Avenue
Palo Alto, CA 94301
(415) 326-7290

Paine Webber (38)
140 Broadway
New York, NY 10005
(212) 437-2121

Reliance Group (41)
919 3rd Avenue
New York, NY 10022
(212) 750-7500

Safeco (40)
Safeco Plaza
Seattle, Wa 98185
(206) 545-5000

St. Paul Companies (28)
385 Washington
St. Paul, MN 55102
(612) 221-7911

Transamerica (13)
600 Montgomery
San Francisco, CA 94111
(415) 983-4055

Transohio Financial (46)
1 Penton Plaza
Cleveland, OH 44114
(216) 696-2341

Travelers (4)
1 Tower Square
Hartford, CT 06115
(203) 277-0111

U.S. Fidelity & Guaranty (27)
100 Light Street
Baltimore, MD 21202
(301) 547-3000

Western Financial (45)
3443 N. Central
Phoenix, AZ 85012
(602) 248-4620

---

*The company's ranking by size appears in parentheses after the name with the date of incorporation, where known, following the telephone number.

HOW TO FIND BUSINESS AND EMPLOYMENT RECORDS

Arlene H. Eakle

Finding Aids

If you know your ancestor's business firm or place of employment, several finding aids are available in most public and research libraries to locate business records:

1. *Directory of Business Archives in the United States and Canada*. Chicago: Society of American Archivists, 1975. Some 2,000 corporations, private companies, and institutions, with employees were surveyed, including the *Fortune* 500. The directory describes the holdings of each of the 196 business firms who responded.

The major reason for this low response was that no archives had been established. Although a few companies established historical archives as early as 1925, most of them date from 1950 as a result of the massive awareness program launched after the Second World War by the Society of American Archivists.[1] See Table 10-3 at the end of this chapter for a summary of business archives.

Interestingly enough, the survival of historical business records may turn out to be more common before 1900 than since, for early records were kept in bound volumes. Some had subject or name indexes. Thus, customer orders were kept in order books and invoices in invoice books. Correspondence was copied into letter books and accounts were entered transaction-by-transaction in ledger books. The pre-1890 system was based on double-entry bookkeeping often unfamiliar to genealogists today. After 1890, index cards became popular because data could be more easily sorted and arranged. Carbon copies came into use around 1900, with looseleaf binders, folders, and envelope-like jackets available by the 1920s.[2]

While the modern system is easier to understand and use, it is also more vulnerable to destruction, since loose papers tend to accumulate faster and take up more storage space than bound ledgers.

2. *National Union Catalog of Manuscript Collections (NUCMC)*. Washington, D.C.: Library of Congress, 1959-____. Published annually, with cumulative indexes. These volumes are available in most public and research libraries, although they may be shelved in the cataloging department. Each volume is completely indexed in each descriptive entry by subject, locality, title, and persons mentioned.

Sample entries from the 1981 volume are:

MS 81-42

Consolidated Virginia Mining Company. Records, 1876-1955. ca.1300 items. In Henry E. Huntington Library (San Marino, Calif.)

Correspondence, business papers, reports, ledgers (1919-46), and 112 maps (1876-1947), chiefly relating to the mine's later period of operation, 1919-55. Maps cover other mines of the Comstock Lode in Nevada. Unpublished finding aid in the repository. Purchased from Neil Weinstein, 1975.

MS 81-376

Seward Forest records, 1860-1974. 21 ft. In University of Virginia Library (Charlottesville 10026). Workmen's timebooks and payrolls, applications, surveying notes, lumber delivery and sawmill records, farm account books, bills, receipts, income records, gradebooks for classes held there, and other records of Seward Forest, Brunswick County, Va., entrusted to the University of Virginia for instruction in forestry by Dr. Walter Merritt Seward in 1932. Includes correspondence of first manager Joseph S. Branscomb and Directors Alfred Akerman and Guy Estes, relating to lumber operations; Akerman's correspondence, diary (1921-23), lecture notes, and other files, from his career at Seward Forest and as Georgia State Forester, professor of forestry at University of Georgia, and district forester for Southside Virginia; correspondence, column entitled "Outdoors Here" for Richmond News-Leader, and lists and indexes of area flora and fauna, of field naturalist in residence John Barzillai Lewis; correspondence, class notes, patient records (1888-1914), and other papers, of Dr. Seward, relating to his medical practice in New York City, Virginia farm, and law suit over his land holdings in Brunswick County; and forestry clipping file, issues (1910-14) of Biltmore Doings (newsletter of Biltmore Forest School, N.C.), issues (1934-36) of Clatonia (publication of Virginia Academy of Science Committee on State Flora), and notes from a lecture (1901) by Gifford Pinchot.

Unpublished finding aid in the repository. Archival transfers from Seward Forest, 1974-76.

MS 81-744

Sparrows Point Shipyard records, 1892-1976. 99 sheets. In Maryland Historical Society Library (Baltimore) (2370) Photocopies of originals at Bethlehem Steel Corporation, Sparrow Point Shipyard, Baltimore, Md.

List of all 649 ships built at the yard, 1892-1976, arranged by hull number, with vessel's name, type, owner, and technical and construction data; and index by vessel types and owners. The shipyard was owned by Maryland Steel Corporation, 1888-1916, and by Bethlehem Steel Corporation afterwards.

3. *Historical Society Publications*. Numerous business archives have been deposited in historical societies across the country. Most societies publish an annual report, a quarterly journal, archive inventories, and/or guides to their principal collections where each set of records is described with dates, names of owners, types of records deposited, restrictions on use (if any), and size of collection. Sample entries from *Manuscripts of the Historical Society of Pennsylvania* follow. (Philadelphia: For the society, n.d.). The collection includes both company and personal business records.

1009. PHILADELPHIA CENTRE SQUARE WATER WORKS, 1801-6. 1 vol. Presented by the Jenkintown Trust Co., 1936. List of first subscribers.

1019. PHILADELPHIA INSURANCE COMPANY, 1814-45. 1 vol. Presented by Mrs. Howard W. Page, 1934. Minutes, accounts, names of officers, and records of general transactions.

1025. PHILADELPHIA SUGAR REFINING COMPANY RECORDS, 1812. 1 vol. Presented by A. C. Kline, 1863. Articles of association, list of stockholders, constitution, bylaws, and other data.

108: PERSONAL and PROFESSIONAL RECORDS, 1676-1904. Approximately 500 vols.

John Q. A. McConkey, canal boat owner and shipper (Delaware and Raritan Canal), invoice book, 1877-79, 1 vol.

Mary Ann, John Q. A., and James McConkey, canal boat transportation, boat book, 1847-80, 1 vol.

William McCorkle, advertising and periodical dealer, ledger 1804-87, 1 vol.

James McCurrach and Company, shipping agents, accounts current, 1790-96, 1 vol.; letter book, 1794-1800, 1 vol.

George Meade, shipper and general merchant, receipt book, 1784-88, 1 vol.

David Meredith, Philadelphia merchant, memorandum, and account book, 1813-17, 1 vol.

Jesse Meredith, Downington, merchant, shoemaker, school accounts, vital statistics, ledger, 1795-1850, daybook, 1805-50, 2 vols.

Jonathan Meredith, Philadelphia tanner, hide accounts, waste, leather, sales, bark, ledger, day, and blotter books, 1784-1800, 34 vols.

4. *Subject Collections*. This reference work, edited by Lee Ash (New York: R. R. Bowker Company, 1978), is especially valuable for special manuscript collections in public libraries which are not described in other publications.

Sample entries under *BUSINESS* are:

Atlanta Public Library, Ivan Allen, Jr. Dept. of Science.
Industry & Government. Richard L. Tubesing, Head.
10 Pryor Street Atlanta, GA 30303
Vols. (15,000) Cat. Microforms
Budget ($75,000)
Notes: This collection incl. on microform annual reports and Securities Exchange Commission 10-K reports for some 11,000 companies from 1976 to date; current and retrospective stock quotations, stock reports, corporate and industry records and directories and supporting looseleaf services; information file on Atlanta's largest 10,000 companies from 1976 to date, with annual updates; and current plat maps for the five county Metro-Atlanta area. Atlanta and Georgia business history sections are being developed. Most material in this collection is noncirculating. Telephone ready reference service is provided.

Harvard University Library, Graduate School of Business Administration, Baker Library.
Robert W. Lovett, Cur. of Manuscripts and Archives.
Soldiers Field, Boston, MA 02163 Vols.
(65,000) Cat. Mss. Pix.
Notes: Baker Library strong in historical aspects of business and economics incl. company histories, business biographies, histories of industries, etc. 6500 pictures. Ms. collection of more than 75,000 incl. original records of business firms from 1400 (Medici Collection) to present; especially strong in 19th century. New England enterprises, textile firms, China trade, railroads, papers of several Northeast merchant families. Also incl. pictures, trade cards, clipper ship cards, money, trade catalogs, business cartoons, prices current and exhibit items. See Robert W. Lovett and Eleanor C. Bishop, comps., *List of Business Manuscripts in Baker Library* (Boston: The Library, 1969), 334 pp. Mss. are described in the *National Union Catalog of Manuscript Collections* and in Hamer's *A Guide to Archives and Manuscripts in the United States*. Kress Library see Economics History. Restricted use: Manuscripts and Kress Library noncirculating. Downs: 1636, 2122, 2616, 2675, 2677, 2698, 2700, 2701, 2702, 2706, 2708, 2711, 2713-15, 2716, 2717-18, 2721-26, 2734, 2737, 2774, 2814, 4300, 5162: Supplement 964, 965, 968, 998.

Los Angeles Public Library, Business and Economics Dept.
Billie M. Connor, Principal Libn.
630 W. 5th St.
Los Angeles, CA 90071
Uncat. Microforms
Notes: Reports of 50,000 corporations traded on the New York, American and Pacific Exchanges, as well as many western over-the-counter corporations, are received on a current basis. Those for New York and American Stock Exchanges are retained for 5 years; western companies indefinitely. Annual reports and 10-Ks for New York and American Stock Exchange corporations are available in microfiche, 1970-1976. Beginning with 1977, 10-K reports for all U.S. publicly traded corporations are collected. Standard sources of information on corporations are available, current and retrospective.

Minneapolis Public Library and Information Center, Business and Science Dept.
Leonard J. Pignatello, Head.
300 Nicollet Mall
Minneapolis, MN 55401
Vols. (100,000) Cat. Phonorecords Audiotapes Videotapes Microforms
Budget ($100,000)
Notes: Separate card catalog, telephone reference service, and directory service. Over 1300 current periodical titles. Large file of corporation annual reports. 32-drawer file local company histories and annual reports. 925 domestic and foreign telephone directories. 900 trade and industrial directories. Historical U.S. stock quotations, 1891-date. Local OTC quotations, 1933-date. 85 indexes and abstracting services. Over 100 looseleaf reference services.

Pomona Public Library, Special Collections.
David Streeter, Libn.
625 S. Garey Avenue
Mailing add.: P. O. Box 2271,
Pomona, CA 91766
Uncat. Mss.
Notes: 165 linear feet of Pomona Valley business records incl. 16 water companies and 28 citrus companies; diaries; clubs and organizations; Laura Ingalls Wilder.

5. *Bibliographies*. Special bibliographies also carry references to business archives.[3] An example is Alan M. Meckler and Ruth McMullin, comps. and eds., *Oral History Collections* (New York: R. R. Bowker Company, 1975). Oral history programs are listed by company, project or person. Here are some sample entries:

WEYERHAEUSER, C. D. with C. S. Martin, Weyerhaeuser Timber Company (98 pages, permission required) *Columbia University NY*

WEYERHAEUSER, CHARLES A. Discussed in Columbia University interview with William L. Maxwell

WEYERHAUSER, FREDERICK KING (1895-__) Industrialist. Weyerhaeuser Timber Company (1956, 167 pages, permission required) *Columbia University* NY

WEYERHAEUSER, JOHN PHILIP, JR. (1899-1956)
Weyerhaeuser Timber Company (41 pages, permission required) *Columbia University* NY
Discussed in Columbia University interview with Albert B. Curtis

WEYERHAEUSER TIMBER COMPANY

Participants and pages: Volume I: A. E. Aitchison, 85: John Aram, 98; David H. Bartlett, 59; Jack Bishop, 32; Ralph Boyd, 26; Hugh B. Campbell, 32; Norton Clapp, 32; R. V. Clute, 65; T. S. Durment, 45; O. D. Fisher, 73; A. N. Frederickson, 71; John H. Hauberg, 126; E. F Heacox, C. S. Martin and C. D. Weyerhaeuser, 98; F. W. Hewitt, 66; Robert W. Hunt, 85; C. H. Ingram, 12; R. E. Irwin, 40; S. P. Johns, Jr., 46; Don Lawrence, 66; George S. Long, Jr., 46; R. R. Macartney, 44; Charles J. McGough, 66; William L. Maxwell, 112; Howard Morgan, 54; C. R. Musser, 27; Leonard H. Nygaard, 49; Harold H. Ogle, 47; Arthur Priaulx and James F. Stevens, 75; Al Raught, 54; Otto C. Schoenwerk, 40; A. O Sheldon, 41; H. C. Shellworth, 77; Frank Tarr, 17; G. Harris Thomas, 63; David S. Troy, 36; Roy Voshmik, 16; John A. Wahl, 18; Frederick K. Weyerhaeuser, 167; J. Philip Weyerhaeuser, 41; Maxwell W. Williamson, 38. Volume II: Earl R. Bullock, 32; Albert B. Curtis, 103; Wells Gilbert, 26; Roy Huffman, 68; W. K. McNair, 33; Leslie Mallory, 13; S.G. and C. D. Moon, 32; Jack Morgan, 43; J. J. O'Connell, 77; R. E. Saberson, 81; Hugo Schlenck, 113; Gaylord M. Upington and Lafayette Stephens, 75 (1956, 2981 pages, permission required) *Columbia University NY.*

6. *American Archivist*. Each issue of the *American Archivist* published quarterly by the Society of American Archivists since 1936, contains reviews of new archival guides and "News and Notes" describing the transfer of business records to local repositories. The Milwaukee-Downer College archives, 1852-1964, and the Plankton Bank records, 1866-1907, are deposited at the University of Wisconsin, Milwaukee (Wisconsin). The Del Monte Corporation (originally the Pacific Improvement Company) archives have been deposited in the Graduate School of Business History, Stanford University (California). The Brewster Company, a New Haven and New York carriage company, deposited 155 bound volumes of account books and business ledgers in the New York Public Library collection. Keeping track of new collections made available for research requires that genealogists review every issue of the *American Archivist*. Copies are readily available at public and research libraries.

Colleges and Universities

Although not usually considered business records as such, personnel and student files of colleges and universities and the records of civil and military personnel of the United States government are also of genealogical value.

There are 1,700 four-year colleges, and 1,000 junior colleges in the United States today, many of them dating before 1850. More than 1,300 have historical archives. Today these institutions of higher learning employ 730,000 faculty and enroll 10,217,000 students. Some faculty and student materials, like the matriculation records of Harvard College since 1636, have been published.[4] For addresses and phone numbers consult Rod Nordland, *Names and Numbers: A Journalist's Guide to the Most Needed Information Sources and Contacts* (New York: John Wiley and Sons, 1978), pp. 263-77, or the current *American Library Directory* published bi-annually by R. R. Bowker Company of New York.

U.S. Government Personnel

Personnel files retained by the federal government for employees and civil service personnel, 1860-1951, have topped 60 million. These are available for research, with some restrictions on files dealing with living persons. Some files require invoking the Freedom of Information Act for access.

Personnel files for military personnel and their dependents were seriously depleted by fire in 1973. The records center in St. Louis, which housed army and air force records for World War I through the Korean War caught fire and an inadequate water supply resulted in massive loss of personnel files. Reconstruction of these records from other documents and records held by individual soldiers is limited to living veterans and heirs currently drawing benefits. Even so, this body of source material is very large and includes 13 million army personnel files, 4 million air force files, 22 million navy files, 3 million marine corps files, and 600,000 coast guard files.

Access is limited to files of a dead veteran, or where the request comes from next of kin or a legal representative. The Freedom of Information Act may expedite access in some instances. Write National Personnel Records Center, 111 Winnebago, St. Louis, MO 63132.[5]

Service records for wars before 1914 are in the National Archives and thoroughly described in the *Guide to Genealogical Research in the National Archives* (Washington, D.C.: NARS, 1982).

Research Hints

In addition to the sources to identify business firms discussed in the chapter, centennial histories or local scrapbooks published in special sections of the newspaper and/or issued separately for distribution at local celebrations also carry lists of historical businesses pursued by local families. Photographs in family records, even unidentified ones, often show owners and employees of local shops and mercantile businesses standing in front of the company sign.

Incorporation Registers and Files.

Next check both the county and state incorporation registers where the business was located.[6] Some businesses are recorded at the county level while some are filed only with the state. Some are chartered or licensed by a federal government agency and may not be listed at the local level. This is especially true of federally chartered banks. The Secretary of State (or equivalent) in most states maintains two registers: one of current companies (now available by computer access) and one of defunct or dissolved companies. Each company in the register has a file number to locate loose documents. With this number ask for the corporate case files which include the original charter, amendments to articles of incorporation, correspondence dealing with name changes and appointments of new directors, statement of dissolution with cause, and court proceedings or claims (if any) against the corporation or its officers.

Your initial contact can be made by telephone to determine which government agency has the records, what information you must send, and how much a search costs. Telephone numbers for state and county officials can be found in *Names and Numbers* (New York: John Wiley and Sons, 1978 and subsequent editions) or *National Directory of Addresses and Telephone Numbers* (New York: Nicholas Publishing Company, published annually).

Many county registers have been transferred to state archives or historical societies. An example is Weber County, Utah, whose corporate records include incorporation index 1871-1959, incorporation records (including articles and by-laws) 1958-65, and affidavits of business firms and partnerships 1913-63, with indexes. These volumes have all been deposited in the Utah State Archives in Salt Lake City. Weber County articles of incorporation before 1958 are found in the Secretary of State's (lieutenant-governor's) office. The Utah lieutenant governor also maintains state incorporation records which are located in the new state offices several miles away from the archives.

"Dragnet" Sources

Several other sources list business firms from the past or supply the clues needed to determine what the name of a historical business was and when it was in operation. Using these records is complicated and the process is called a "dragnet" strategy by William G. Roy in his "Collecting Data on American Business Officials in the Late Nineteenth and Early Twentieth Century," *Historical Methods* 15 (Fall 1982): 143-51. Since these materials are easily found in public and research libraries, even beginners can locate both current and historical businesses.

Stock Market Directories. An important stock market directory is the *Manual of Statistics* published annually since 1886 with listings for industrial securities traded on the major stock exchanges. The *Manual* covers most of the railroads, larger firms with extensive capitalization, and later, some of the Fortune 500. Other directories include Poor's *Manual of Railroads* and Moody's *Manuals* with separate volumes for railroads, municipal governments, banks and finance, and public utilities. Published annually since 1900 by Moody's Investors Service Inc., a division of Dun and Bradstreet, these directories omit some of the most important companies like Carnegie Steel and Standard Oil. They are also less likely to cover decentralized industries such as books, shoes and boots, and the lumber industry.

The biggest difficulty in locating information on specific companies is identity. Firms go out of business. They merge to form new companies. They are acquired by another, usually larger, company. They change names, directors, and even locations. The directories which keep track of these identities are modern sources. Our ancestors recorded changes with county and state officials or announced them in newspapers and trade publications.

In addition to Dun and Bradstreet's *Directory of Corporate Affiliations* and Dun's *Million Dollar Directory* discussed in the chapter is Robert D. Fisher, *Manual of Valuable and Worthless Securities,* which lists businesses reorganized, liquidated, or dissolved. Each of these directories is published annually and is available in most public and university libraries in the business/economics section.

Biographical Dictionaries. These include the *Dictionary of American Biography* (first published in 1922), the *National Cyclopedia of American Biography,* and a wide variety of Who's Who publications. (See Chapter 14, "Compiled Biographical Sources.") The *Cyclopedia* was begun in 1898 by the James T. White Company of New York to give biographical coverage to business leaders, especially young men from the West, with information supplied by the subjects themselves. More specialized is the *Biographical Directory of Railway Officials of America* published since 1885.

Most of these dictionaries are indexed in the eight-volume *Biography and Genealogy Master Index: A Consolidated Index to More Than 3,200,000 Biographical Sketches in over 350 Current and Retrospective Biographical Dictionaries.* It is easy to check and available in most research libraries.[7]

A close kin to these dictionaries are the county atlases published following the Civil War and the "mug books" where local residents purchased immortality by placing their pictures and their biographical sketches in books circulated throughout the county and its environs.

Trade Association Directories. Farley's *Reference Directory of Booksellers, Stationers, and Printers in the U.S. and Canada* published since 1886 and the *Pocket Directory of Shoe Manufacturers* published by the *Boot and Shoe Reporter* since 1907 are examples of trade directories. The National Electric Light Association (1923), the National Retail Dry Goods Association (1934), and the National Fire Protection Association (1935) are examples of trade associations that publish directories of members with their specific affiliations.

The *Encyclopedia of Associations*, published biannually by Gale Research Company of Detroit, includes precise addresses, phone numbers, titles and frequency of bulletins and newsletters published, library information services offered, employment exchanges, and many other facts and figures for trade associations, many of which have a continuous history from the mid-nineteenth century to the present.

Corporate Histories. Many American businesses have written official corporate histories. The history of Standard Oil Company took some eighteen years to write, in part because its 35,000 boxes of records took so long to study and digest. Some years ago, the Harvard University Graduate School of Business History began to chronicle individual American business histories. Some of the titles in their series include: Ralph M. Hower, *History of Macy's of New York, 1858-1939: Chapters in the History of a Department Store* (Cambridge: Harvard, 1943), and *The History of an Advertising Agency: N. W. Ayer & Son at Work, 1869-1949* (Cambridge: Harvard, 1949); John S. Ewing and Nancy P. Norton, *Broadloom and Businessmen: A History of the Bigelow-Sanford Carpet Company, 1825-1953* (Cambridge: Harvard, 1955); Gerald T. White, *A History of the Massachusetts Hospital Life Insurance Company* (Cambridge: Harvard, 1955); and George S. Gibb, *The Whitesmiths of Taunton: A History of Reed and Barton, 1824-1943* (Cambridge: Harvard, 1943).

For other histories consult:

Business History, published quarterly by Harvard Graduate School of Business History. Includes reviews and announcements of historical studies of American businesses.

Cochran, Thomas. *Railroad Leaders, 1845-1890: The Business Mind in Action*. Cambridge: Harvard University Press, 1953. Based on 100,000 letters from sixty-one railroad officials.

Daniells, Lorna M. *Studies in Enterprise*. Boston: Little, Brown, 1957. Includes list of business histories.

Larson, Henrietta. *Guide to Business History*. Cambridge: Harvard University Press, 1948. Bibliography of histories and printed sources.

Trade Journals. Periodicals and newssheets have been published for the shipping and maritime industry, for agriculture,[8] and for many others since the mid-nineteenth century. These sources are traditional materials to consult in checking for historical businesses of any size, and they are as close as your nearest public or research library. However, if your local libraries do not have the volumes you want, check collections in libraries of those cities and towns where the industry was most common. Try Pittsburgh for the steel industry, San Francisco or Seattle for the pacific shipping trade, Atlanta and Savannah for the turpentine industry.[9]

Notes

1. A more recent survey in 1977 showed that some 310 business archives had been created. See Gary D. Saretsky, "North American Business Archives: Results of a Survey," *American Archivist* 40 (Oct. 1977), 413-20.
2. Oliver Wendell Holmes, "Evaluation and Preservation of Business Archives," *American Archivist* 1 (Oct. 1938): 171-85.
3. Karen M. Benedict, *A Select Bibliography on Business Archives and Records Management* (Chicago: Society of American Archivists, 1981), pp. 144. Annotated list of more than 400 articles and books on business archives.
4. Maynard Brickford, "Academic Archives," *American Archivist* 43 (1980): 449-60.
5. Dr. Marvin H. Kabakoff, "Have You Overlooked Military Records?" *Genealogy Digest*, Oct. 1982, pp. 28-31.
6. The process of incorporation and how it has changed over time is described in George H. Evans, Jr., *Business Incorporations in the United States, 1800-1943* (Princeton: Princeton University Press, 1948). He also has a useful appendix of business firms and their dates of incorporation.
7. 2nd ed. (Detroit: Gale Research Company, (1980), 8 vols.; supplement, 1981-82, 3 vols. Other updates are planned.
8. A list of agricultural journals can be found in Albert L. Demaree, *The American Agricultural Press, 1819-1860* (New York: Columbia University Press, 1941), pp. 393-400.
9. Lee Ash, *Subject Collections* (New York: R. R. Bowker and Company, 1978), p. 169

Table 10-3

Summary of Business Archives

Business Firm	*Address*	*Archive Created*	*Description*	*Date Covered*	*Access*
Aerospace Corp.	2350 El Segundo Drive Los Angeles, CA 90045	1961			Open to scholars
Air Reduction Co., AIRCO	85 Chestnut Road Montvale, NM 07645 (201) 455-2000	1915	Archives, 140 E. 42nd Street, New York, NY 10017. Includes financial records, newsclippings		Open to employees only.
Aluminum Company of America, ALCOA (78)	1501 Alcoa Bldg. Pittsburgh, PA 15219 (412) 553-4707	1949	Archives include photos	From 1888	Open to company personnel
American Brass Company			Originally Aaron Benedict, button-maker. Archives include his original ledgers	From 1826	

[1]Numbers in parentheses after the name refer to its Fortune ranking.
[2]NUCMC=Annual volume and collection number for materials deposited in outside libraries. Consult the National Union Catalog of Manuscript Collections described above.

American Machine and Foundary Company	261 Madison Avenue New York, NY 10016		Archives include family papers, photos	From 1909	Open to company personnel.
American Motors	27777 Franklin Southfield, MI 48034, (313) 827-1000	1946	NUCMC 76-1443, 80-1553	From 1900	
Ampex Corporation (Electronics)	401 Broadway Redwood City, CA 94000 (415) 367-0011	1960	Includes photos	From 1944	Open to study. Index available at Records Center.
Anheuser-Busch (99)	721 Pestalozzi St. Louis, MO 63118 (314) 577-2000		NUCMC 66-1151, -1155, 78-957, 79-787		
Armour and Company	401 North Wabash Avenue Chicago, IL 60611	1900		Some records from 1868	Open to company personnel. Guide available.
Armstrong Cork, now Armstrong World Industries	Box 30001 Lancaster, PA 17604	1946	Includes photos NUCMC 80-102	From 1860	Open with some restrictions. Guide available.
American Can Company (81)	American Lane Greenwich, CT 06830 (203) 552-2000		Maintains own business library of 2,500 volumes, microforms. NUCMC 64-1262, 73-333		Catalog available.
Atchison, Topeka and Santa Fe Railroad Company	80 East Jackson Chicago, IL 60604 (312) 427-4900	1895	Archives, Box 1738, Topeka, KS 66601	From 1858	Open to scholars, advance arrangements required.
Atlantic Richfield ARCO (10)[1]	515 S. Flower Street Los Angeles, CA 90071 (213) 486-3511	1979	Includes records for Anaconda Copper Mining Company. 58 boxes of documents. Computerized index to photograph collection. NUCMC 72-1192[2]	From 1920s	Microform copy deposited at Waterbury, CT museum for greater access.
Atlas Chemical Industries	Wilmington, DE 19899	1920	2,723 drawers of documents	From 1854	Open to company personnel. Guide available. Anniversary history available in manuscript.
Bank of America Corp. (1 in banking)	Box 37000 San Francisco, CA 94137 (415) 622-4997	1958	Includes photos, oral history recordings	1906-80	See O.G. Wilson, "Bank of America's Archival Program," *American Archivist* 29 (Jan. 1966): 43-48. Open to scholars.
Bank of Hawaii	Box 2900 Honolulu, HI 96846		Maintains own business research library with over 4,000 volumes. Building a history of banking in Hawaii collection.		Open to study, indexes available.
Bennett Office Inc.	1210 Baker Building Minneapolis, MN 55402	1952	Includes early mining records of Minnesota	From 1890	Open to scholars. Index available.
B.F. Goodrich Co. (138)	500 S. Main Akron, OH 44317 (216) 379-2000	1965	Includes photos, oral history	From 1869	Open to scholars.
Bigelow-Sanford Carpet Company				From 1825	History: John S. Ewing and Nancy P. Norton, *Broadloom and Businessmen: A History of the Bigelow-Sanford Carpet Company, 1825-1953*. Cambridge: Harvard University Press, 1955.
Black and Decker Manufacturing Co. (248)	701 E. Joppa Rd. Towson, MD 21204 (301) 828-3900	1966	Includes photos, products	From 1910	Open to study on approval.
Boeing Aircraft (31)	7755 E. Marginal Seattle, WA 98108 (206) 655-2121	1962	Pacific Museum of Air History, Seattle. 400 record boxes, 500 cubic feet of records.	From 1916	Open to scholars. Guide available. See Peter M. McLellan, "The Boeing Archival Program," *American Archivist* 29 (Jan. 1966): 37-42.

Business Firm	Address	Archive Created	Description	Date Covered	Access
Boeing Company Vertol Division	Boeing Center Box 16850 Philadelphia, PA 19142	1969		From 1943	
Borden, Inc. (85)	277 Park Avenue New York, NY 10017 (212) 573-4000	1900	NUCMC 62-4508, 70-1071 73-370	From 1805	Open to scholars. Guide available.
Boston Edison Company	800 Boylston Street Boston, MA 02199 (617) 424-2000	1866	Includes photos and oral history.		Open to scholars. Guides available.
Brewster & Company		1936	Originally New Haven and New York Carriage Company. 155 bound volumes of accounts, ledgers at New York Public Library.		
Burlington Industries (132 textiles)	Box 21207 Greensboro, NC 27420 (919) 279-2000		NUCMC 68-1544, -1583 Historical records deposited in educational institutions.		Open to company personnel, to scholars with limits. Historical records subject to rules of institutional depository.
Butterick Patterns	161 Sixth Avenue New York, NY 10013		A division of American Can Co.	From 1867	Open to scholars with some restrictions. Guide available.
Caterpiller Tractor (37)	100 N.E. Adams Street Peoria, IL 61629 (309) 675-1000	1982	NUCMC 78-310		
Central Security National Bank	20th and Broadway Lorain, OH 44052		Includes photos, oral history.		Open to study on arrangement.
Chase Manhattan Bank	1 Chase Manhattan Plaza New York, NY 10015 (212) 552-2222	1975	Includes oral history.		Records for last 75 years closed to research.
Chicago Board of Trade	141 West Jackson Chicago, IL 60600 (312) 435-3500	1968			
Chrysler Corp. (26)	12000 L. Townsen Highland Park, MI 48288 (313) 956-5252		NUCMC 67-8, -15; 71-653		
Citicorp (2, commercial banking)	399 Park Ave. New York, NY 10043 (212) 559-1000	1977			
Civil Service Employees Insurance Company	989 Market Street San Francisco, CA	1952	Includes oral history.	From 1951	Open to company personnel.
Cleveland Electric Illuminating Co. (37, utilities)	Box 5000 Cleveland, OH 44101 (216) 623-1350	1949	12,000 cubic feet of records, includes subscribers, records of easement and right of way.	From 1900	Open to scholars on approval.
Cluett, Peabody and Company, Inc. (348, men's apparel)	510 5th Avenue New York, NY 10036 (212) 930-3021	1954	4,000 boxes of records.	From 1900	Open to scholars, Kardex index.
Coca Cola USA (58)	Box 1734 Atlanta, GA 30301 (404) 897-2121		NUCMC 72-157 Archives in Coca Cola USA Building, some in University of Illinois, Urbana-Champaign. Includes oral history.		Open to scholars by appointment. See Linda M. Mathews, "The Archives of Coca-Cola Company," *Georgia Archive* (Spring 1973): 12-20. History: Charles Howard Candler, "Thirty-three Years with Coca-Cola, 1890-1923," typescript, 1945, Coca-Cola archives; Asa Griggs Chandler [founder]. N.p.: Emory University Press, 1950.

Colonial Williamsburg Foundation	Drawer C Williamsburg, VA 23185 (703) 229-1000				
Colorado Interstate Gas Company	Box 1087 Colorado Springs, CO 80901	1955	Includes photos.	From 1927	Open to company personnel. Guide available.
Columbia Broadcasting CBS (6, diversified service)	51 W. 52nd Street New York, NY 10019 (212) 975-4321				
Colwell Company	3223 West 6th Los Angeles, CA	1962	2,000 boxes. Includes oral history.	From 1958	Open to scholars. Guide available.
Container Corporation of America	38 S. Dearborn Street Chicago, IL 60603	1926			Open to company personnel. Guide available.
Continental Illinois National Bank and Trust of Chicago	231 S. LaSalle Street Chicago, IL 60693		14,000 volumes in own business library. Includes photos.		Open to study.
Corning Glass Works (226)	Houghton Park Corning, NY 14830 (607) 974-9000	1973	Includes oral history. NUCMC 78-1001		
Cummins Engine Co. (200)	1000 5th Street Columbus, IN 47201 (812) 372-7211		Maintains own business library.		
Deere & Company (65)	John Deere Road Moline, IL 61265 (309) 792-8000	1955		From 1840	Open for limited use by scholars. Deere Museum has unique, 3-dimensional history of John Deere's life and contribution to America. Guides available.
Del Monte	Box 567 Pebble Beach, CA 93953 (408) 649-8500		Originally Pacific Improvement Company. Early ledgers and account books deposited Stanford University, J. Hugh Jackson Library, Stanford, CA 94305.		Guide available.
Diamond Reo Truck Division, White Motor Corporation	320 S. Sangamon Street Chicago, IL 60607	1958	Includes photos.		Open to company personnel.
Dow Chemical (25)	2030 Dow Center Ave. Midland, MI 48640 (517) 636-1000		Includes family papers, executives' personal papers, oral history	From 1890	Open to scholars.
Dun and Bradstreet (34)	299 Park Avenue New York, NY 10171 (212) 593-6800		Originally Lewis Tappan Mercantile Agency, est. 1841. Historical records, including nineteenth century credit ledgers, deposited in Harvard University Baker Library. Maintains extensive business library.	From 1840	Open to scholars. Materials to be published must be submitted to Dun for screening and permission. Guide available. Separate guide for Harvard collection: Robert W. Lovett and Eleanor C. Bishop. *List of Business Manuscripts in the Baker Library, Harvard University.* 4th ed. Boston: Houghton-Mifflin, 1978. 400 pp.
ESB, Inc.	Box 8109 Philadelphia, PA 19101		Formerly Electric Storage Battery.	From 1871	Open to study. Locator-Index file.
E. I. DuPont DeNemours and Company (15)	1007 Market Street Wilmington, DE 19898 (302) 774-1000	1952	Eleutherian Mills Hagley Foundation, Greenville, Delaware, houses historical records. These include family and company records. Other records in institutional libraries. NUCMC 60-1315, -1361, -1370, -3013; 62-4644; 71-1721, -1724, -157; 73-531. Henry Francis DuPont Winterthur Museum houses Dominy and Wister family papers and others for mercantile families in the Delaware Valley.	Before 1805	Open to study. Guide: John B. Riggs, *A Guide to the Manuscripts in the Eleutherian Mills Historical Library* (Greenville, Del.: DuPont, 1970). 1205 pp.

Business Firm	Address	Archive Created	Description	Date Covered	Access
Eastern Gas and Fuel Associates	2900 Prudential Tower Boston, MA 02199	1950		From 1900	Open to study, card index available.
Eastman Kodak (28)	343 State Street Rochester, NY 14650	1949	NUCMC 61-1220		
Educational Testing Service (ETS)	Princeton, NJ 08540 (609) 921-9000	1969	Includes oral history collection.		
Eli Lilly and Company (340)	307 E. McCarty Street Indianapolis, IN 46285 (317) 261-2000	1956	Includes family and personal papers, photos, tape recordings, motion pictures.	From 1780 (family), From 1876 (company)	See Helen L. Davidson, "The Indispensability of Business Archives," *American Archivist* 30 (Oct. 1967): 593-97. Open to study, mail requests answered. Card catalog.
Employees Insurance of Wausau, Wisconsin				From 1911	Open to scholars upon request. There is a company history in manuscript.
Ethyl Corporation (214)	Box 2189 Richmond, VA 23217 (804) 644-6081		Maintains own business library of 15,000 volumes at Gulf States Road, Box 2246, Baton Rouge, LA 70821.		
Export-Import Bank of the United States (EXIM Bank)	811 Vermont Avenue N.W. Washington, DC 20571		Maintains extensive business library, including maps, tape recordings, oral history.		Open to study. Catalog available.
Farmers and Mechanics Savings Bank of Minneapolis	90 S. Sixth Street Minneapolis, MN 55402	1953	Some stored in the Salt Mines (These are indexed but not open to study.)	From 1874	Open to company personnel.
Federal Reserve Bank of Chicago	230 S. LaSalle Street Chicago, IL 60690				Restricted use. No photocopying.
Field Enterprises, Inc. (*World Book Encyclopedia*)	Merchandise Mart Plaza Chicago, IL 60654	1964	Includes oral history, photos, newspaper clippings file. Division of Marshall-Field.	From 1876	Open to scholars with permission.
Firestone Tire and Rubber Company (88)	1200 Firestone Akron, OH 44317 (216) 379-7000	1943			See William D. Overman, "The Firestone Archives and Library," *American Archivist* 16 (Oct. 1953): 305-09.
First Church Christ Scientist	107 Falmouth Street Boston, MA	1934	Includes Christian Science Publishing Society. Important historical manuscripts collection.	From 1892	Open to scholars with permission, preliminary inventories.
First National Bank of Atlanta	Box 4148 Atlanta, GA 30302				Some records confidential, rest open to study.
Ford Foundation	320 E. 43rd Street New York, NY 10017 (212) 573-5000				
Ford Motor Company (6)	Greenfield Village and Henry Ford Museum Dearborn, MI 48121 (313) 271-1620	1951	Business records at Greenfield Village and Henry Ford Museum. Personal and family records, historical collections deposited in Edison Institute in 1964. Includes oral history. NUCMC 67-11; 77-230, -1335; 78-1435; 80-932, -1206, -1478	From 1903	Archives open to company personnel. Edison Institute collection open to scholars. See Henry E. Edmonds, "The Ford Motor Company Archives," *American Archivist* 15 (April 1952): 99-104. Rumored that personnel files destroyed except for last twenty-five years.
General Electric (11)	3135 Easton Terrace Fairfield, CT 06431 (203) 383-2431		NUCMC 61-249, -930; 65-496; 66-1230; 70-502, -1059; 71-1172; 73-225; 76-1639, -1640, -1642; 77-1955-56		

Company	Address	Date	Description	Records	Access
General Mills (80)	Box 1113 Minneapolis, MN 55440 (612) 540-2311		NUCMC 66-860; 67-863, -2241; 79-1919		
General Public Utilities Corporation (19, utilities)	100 Interspace Plaza Parsippany, NJ 07054 (201) 263-6500	1946	Historical records stored in separate location.		Not open to scholars.
Georgia Pacific Co. (67)	900 S.W. Fifth Avenue Portland, OR 97204 (503) 222-5561	1977			
Gerber Products (419)	445 State Street Fremont, MI 49412 (616) 928-2000	1976			
Goodyear Atomic Corporation	Box 628 Piketon, OH 45661	1954		From 1952	Open to company personnel.
W.R. Grace Co.	1114 Avenue of the Americas New York, NY 10036 (212) 764-5555	1929	7,500 square feet of historical records.	From 1882	Open to company personnel.
Goodyear Tire and Rubber Co. (38)	1144 E. Market Street Akron, OH 44316 (216) 794-2121	1905	7,000 cubic feet of historical archives. Includes photos, oral history. NUCMC 75-1173, -1576		Open to company personnel.
Great Northern Railway Co.	175 E. Fourth Street St. Paul, MN 55101	1937	Historical records kept in Record Storage Building. Includes scrapbooks, printings, photos.	From 1862	Open to scholars upon approval, guide available.
Great Western Financial (8, diversified financial)	8484 Wilshire Blvd. Beverly Hills, CA 90211 (213) 658-6060	1963	Formerly Great Western Savings and Loan Association.	From 1938	Open to scholars.
Gulf Oil (9)	Box 1166 Pittsburgh, PA 15230 (412) 263-5000	1965	Historical Archives deposited University of Texas, Austin. NUCMC 75-2069, 77-2047, 79-1896. Participant in Oil Industry Oral History Program.		
Hercules, Inc. (157)	910 Market Street Wilmington, DE 19899 (302) 375-5000	1940		From 1912	
Houston Industries (18, utilities)	611 Walker Avenue Houston, TX 77002 (713) 228-2474	1959	Formerly Houston Natural Gas Corporation. 7,500 boxes of records.	From 1927	Open to company personnel.
Illinois Bell Telephone	225 W. Randolph Street Chicago, IL 60606		Maintains own business library with 11,000 volumes.		
Illinois Central Gulf Railroad Company (25, transportation)	233 N. Michigan Chicago, IL 60601 (312) 565-1600		Historical records are deposited in Newberry Library (1851-1906) and in company vault, Champaign (1851-1950).		Newberry records open to scholars with permission of railroad. Guide: Carolyn Curtis Mohr, *Guide to Records of the Illinois Central Railroad, 1851-1906*. Chicago: Newberry Library, 1951. Champaign records open to 1951. Company officials only.
Industrial Credit Co.	6th Floor Hamm Building St. Paul, MN	1967	1,732 square feet of historical records. Records are culled according to Federal Record Retention Schedule.		Open to company personnel, guide available.
Insurance Company of North America (INA) (7, diversified financial)	1600 Arch Street Box 7728 Philadelphia, PA 19101 (215) 241-3293	1944	Records include policies, personnel files, French spoliation claims (1790-1960), San Francisco (1906), and Chicago (1871) Fire Claims, tontines (life insurance lotteries, 1792-1941), records of merged companies.	1735-1974	Open to scholars. *Guide to INA Corporation Archives*. Philadelphia: INA, 1975.

Business Firm	*Address*	*Archive Created*	*Description*	*Date Covered*	*Access*
International Business Machines (IBM) (8)	Old Orchard Road Armonk, NY 10504 (914) 765-1900	1961	Includes photos, oral history.	From 1885	Open to scholars with restrictions.
International Harvester (46)	401 N. Michigan Chicago, IL 60611 (312) 670-2427	1971	NUCMC 62-797, -3513; 64-798; 71-1146; 75-692; 77-1374		
International Minerals & Chemicals Corporation (196)	2315 Sanders Road Northbrook, IL 60062 (312) 564-8600		Maintains own business library of 40,000 volumes and maps at 421 E. Hawley St., Mundelein, IL 60060.		
International Paper Company (77)	220 E. 42nd Street New York, NY 10017 (212) 490-6000	1898	NUCMC 62-1183, 72-1648		Open to company personnel, open to scholars with restrictions
Jet Propulsion Laboratory	4800 Oak Grove Drive Pasadena, CA	1940	10,000 cubic feet of records including technical flight data reports.		Open to approved scholars
John Hancock Mutual Life Insurance Co.	200 Berkely St. Box 1111 Boston, MA 02117 (617) 421-6000	1948	Commenced business 27 Dec. 1862, absorbed records of mutual benefit societies. Includes family papers.	From 18th century	Open to scholars with permission. Guide available.
Johnson and Johnson (68)	501 George Street New Brunswick, NJ 08903 (201) 524-0400	1929	Large collection of historical records, includes illustrations, patents, product development records.	From 1886	Open to scholars.
Jones and Laughlin Steel Corporation	3 Gateway Center Pittsburgh, PA 15230		Includes personal and family papers.	From 1853	Open to scholars. Guide available.
Kimberly-Clark Corporation (147)	4 Lake Street Neenah, WI 54956 (414) 729-1212	1941	NUCMC 68-2245, 78-1040. Includes oral history, photos.	From 1872	Open to scholars upon approval. Guide available.
LTV Aerospace	Box 909 Warren, MI 48090	1963	Missile and Space Division of LTV Electrosystems.		Open to scholars
LTV Electrosystems	Box 1056 Greenville, TX	1955	13,000 cubic feet, includes personnel data, photos, oral history materials.	From 1943	Open to scholars upon request.
Lederle Laboratories	Pearl River, NY 10965	1955	Division of American Cyanamid Company (106). Includes highly selected personal papers, family papers, oral history. Also a museum containing early products, photos.	From 1906	Open to company personnel. Index available.
Lehman Brothers	1 William Street New York, NY 10004	1900	Includes personal and family papers	From 1948	Open to company personnel. Guide available.
Lever Brothers (281)	390 Park Avenue New York, NY 10022	1895	NUCMC 61-3050. Includes photos, oral history.		Open to company personnel. Index available.
Lockheed Aircraft (57)	Box 551 Burbank, CA 91520 (213) 847-6121	1954	Includes photos. NUCMC 67-608, 71-1162, 76-707, 78-1768, 80-490	From 1932	Open to scholars upon approval.
Lockheed Electronics Company	U.S. Highway 22 Plainfield, NJ 07061	1962	Division of Lockheed Aircraft (57).	From 1948	Open under specific conditions (unstated).
Logetronics, Inc.	7001 Loisdale Road Springfield, VA 22150			From 1955	Open to company personnel.
Los Angeles Times	Times Mirror Square Los Angeles, CA 90053 (213) 625-2345	1978			
Macy's Department Store (R.H. Macy) (26, retailing)	151 W. 34th Street New York, NY 10001 (212) 560-3600		Includes personal and family papers		History: Ralph M. Hower, *History of Macy's of New York, 1858-1939: Chapters in the History of a Department Store*, Cambridge: Harvard University Press, 1943

Marathon Oil Company (36)	539 S. Main Street Findlay, OH 45840 (419) 422-2121	1938	NUCMC 71-1140. Includes photos, personal papers of company officials.	From 1887	Open to company personnel.
Marshall-Field (45)	25 E. Washington Chicago, IL 60690 (312) 236-7272				
Massachusetts Mutual Life Insurance Company	1295 State Street Springfield, MA 01111	1932-36	Est. 1 Aug. 1851. Includes personal papers of company executives, oral history materials. Maintains own business library.	From 1861	Open to company personnel.
Massachusetts Hospital Life Insurance Company			Records deposited Harvard University Baker Library.		History: Gerald T. White, *A History of the Massachusetts Hospital Life Insurance Company* (Cambridge: Harvard University Press, 1955).
Mattel Toys (330)	5150 Rosecrans Hawthorne, CA 90250 (213) 978-5150	1967	Includes personal papers of company personnel, oral history, photos, catalogs.	From 1947	Open to scholars. Guide available.
Maytag Company	Newton, OH 50208	1959	Includes personnel records, photos, other records.	From 1893	Open to company personnel. Guide available.
McGraw-Hill, Inc. (294)	1221 Avenue of the Americas New York, NY 10020 (212) 997-1221	1958	NUCMC 78-1467. Includes personal and family papers, photos, more than 100 oral interviews, complete files of magazines published by the firm.	From 1884	Open to scholars.
Mead Johnson and Company (146)	Courthouse Plaza Dayton, OH 45463 (513) 222-6323	1966	Includes personnel records, clippings, photos and slides, oral history tapes.	From 1905	Open to scholars upon approval.
Merrill, Lynch, Pierce, Fenner & Smith, Inc. (5)	1 Liberty Plaza New York, NY 10080 (212) 637-7455			From 1939	Open for study with written permission.
Miles Laboratories (372)	1127 Myrtle Street Elkhart, IN 46515 (219) 264-8111		Maintains own business library of 58,000 volumes, microforms, including advertising of products, international marketing files.		
Miller Chemical Co.	1441 California Street Omaha, NE 68100		Includes photos.	From 1932	Open for study upon approval.
Minnesota Mutual Life Insurance Company	345 Cedar Street St. Paul, MN 55101		Records preserved are those required to satisfy company policy and legal requirements.	From 1880	Open for study upon approval.
Mitre Corporation	Bedford, MA		86,000 documents and volumes.	1945-65	Open to company personnel. Printed guide subject to controlled distribution.
Montgomery Ward & Co., Inc. (12, retailing)	1 Montgomery Ward Plaza Chicago, IL 60671 (312) 467-2000		Est. 1872. Includes full set of Montgomery Ward catalogs. Maintains own business library, includes photos.		Selected portions open to scholars upon approval.
Mutual of New York	1740 Broadway New York, NY 10019	1962	Est. 1 Feb. 1843. Includes photos, scrapbooks, news clippings.	From 1843	Open to scholars. Card catalog available.
Mutual of Omaha	3316 Farnum Street Omaha, NE 68100	1942	Includes applications.	From 1909	Open to scholars. Kardex file available.
NEGEA Service Corp.	130 Austin Street Cambridge, MA 02139		Est. 1853. Archives in 2-story building, includes photos.		Open to scholars.
Nabisco Brands (60)	425 Park Avenue E. Hanover, NJ 07936 (201) 884-0500	1982	NUCMC 64-870		
National Bank of Detroit	611 Woodward Detroit, MI 48232	1960	Includes photos, scrapbooks.	From 1933	Open to company personnel.

Business Firm	Address	Archive Created	Description	Date Covered	Access
Nationwide Mutual Insurance Co.	246 North High Street Columbus, OH 43215	1948	Includes oral history materials.	From 1926	Open to study.
New England Merchants National Bank	28 State Street Boston, MA 02106		Maintains own business library with collection of theses and dissertations.		
New York Life Insurance Company	51 Madison Avenue New York, NY 10010	1955	Est. 12 April 1845. Extensive historical archives.	From 1845	Open to scholars.
New York Stock Exchange	11 Wall Street New York, NY 10005 (212) 623-3000	1979			
Northeast Airlines, Inc.	Logan Airport Boston, MA	1967	40 drawers of records, includes photos.	From 1903	Open to company personnel.
Northwestern National Life Insurance Co.	20 Washington Ave. S. Minneapolis, MN 55440	1950		From 1888	Open to scholars on limited basis.
N.W. Ayer & Son			Records deposited Harvard University, Baker Library	From 1869	History: Ralph M. Hower, *The History of an Advertising Agency: N.W. Ayer & Son at Work, 1869-1949.* Cambridge: Harvard University Press, 1949.
Otis Elevator Co.	260 Eleventh Avenue New York, NY 10001	1950	Includes personal and family papers.	From 1833	Selected material open to scholars.
PPG Industries, Inc.	1 Gateway Center Pittsburgh, PA 15222	1900	Includes licenses, long-term contracts, deeds and leases.		Open to scholars, card index.
Pan American World Airways (7, transportation)	Pan Am Building New York, NY 10017 (212) 880-1234	1948	Est. 1927. 80,000 cubic feet of records, includes personal and family papers, photos, oral history.	From 1927	Open to scholars on request. Guide available. History of company in manuscript.
Parke, Davis & Co.	Box 118 Detroit, MI 48232		Maintains own business library, includes maps, photos.		
Pennzoil United (159)	900 S.W. Tower Box 2967 Houston, TX 77001 (713) 236-7878	1967	Archives available on microfilm.		Open to company personnel.
Pet Incorporated	1401 Arcade Building St. Louis, MO 63101	1959		From 1903	Open to company personnel. Guide available.
Pittsburgh Steel	Box 118 Pittsburgh, PA 15230		Includes photos.	From 1901	Open to company personnel.
Plantation Pipe Line Company	Atlanta, GA	1964	Miscellaneous historical records.	1930-50	Open to public relations personnel.
Proctor & Gamble (25)	301 E. 6th Avenue Cincinnati, OH 45202 (513) 562-1100	1957	NUCMC 67-588, 76-1868. 260 document cases, including personal papers of the founders, photos, magazines.	From 1837	Specific requests answered. Guide available.
Pullman Sleeping Car Company			Ceased business in 1967. Employed nearly 1 million persons including many blacks, immigrants. Records in (1) Chicago Public Library, Special Collections: photographs, brochures, clippings, reports mostly dealing with Pullman neighborhood; (2) Newberry Library – Family & Community History Center. See "Reconstructing Work Histories by Computer: Pullman Shop Workers," *Historical Methods Newsletter* 15 (Summer 1982): 139-42. Unskilled laborers, porters,	1880-1949	Must have written permission of family to look at records.

			laundresses, maids; shopworkers, foremen, office personnel; (3) South Suburban Genealogical Society, 161st and Louis Avenue, South Holland, IL 60473, (312) 333-9474. Compiling an index 1880-1940, 900 boxes; 1 million documents from Hammond and Michigan City, Ind.; Roseland and Pullman, Ill.		
Radiation, Inc.	Box 37 Melbourne, FL 32900	1966	2,000 cubic feet of documents.		
Ralston Purina Co. (73)	Checkerboard Square St. Louis, MO 63188 (314) 982-1000		Est. 1894.		Open to scholars with approval.
Raytheon Company (62)	141 Spring Street Lexington, MA 02173 (617) 862-6600		87,000 cubic feet of records.	From 1939	Open to scholars with restrictions.
Reed and Barton	Taunton, MA 02780		Historical records deposited Baker Library, Harvard University		History: George S. Gibb, *The Whitesmiths of Taunton: A History of Reed and Barton 1824-1943.* Cambridge: Harvard University Press, 1943.
Revere Copper and Brass, Inc. (353)	605 3rd Avenue New York, NY 10016 (212) 578-1500	1928		From eighteenth century	Open to company personnel. Annual histories circulated to stockholders.
Rexall Chemical Co.	Box 37 Paramus, NJ 07652	1967	Includes personal papers and photos.	From 1960	
Rio Grande Industries (42, transportation)	Box 5482 Denver, CO 80217 (303) 892-1215		Records deposited in State Historical Society of Colorado. Originally Denver & Rio Grande Railroad.		
Rockefeller Family and Associates	30 Rockefeller Plaza New York, NY	1954	4,000 boxes of personal and business records, including 372 letterbooks, memorabilia.	1839-1961	Open to scholars upon approval. Guide available. See Joseph W. Ernst, "Omnes Unum Sint: The Rockefeller Archives," *American Archivist* 26 (Jan. 1966): 61-67.
Rockwell International (48)	600 Grant Street Pittsburgh, PA 15219 (412) 565-2000	1947		From 1888	Open to company personnel. Guide available.
Rohm and Haas Co. (206)	Independence Mall W. Philadelphia, PA 19105 (215) 592-3000	1966	Includes personal papers, photos.	From 1926	Open to scholars on authorized request.
S.S. Kresge Company	2727 Second Avenue Detroit, MI		Includes oral history, photos, copies of company newspapers.	From 1912	Open to company personnel. Company history available in manuscript.
Safeway Stores (2, retailing)	4th and Jackson Oakland, CA 94660 (415) 891-3000	1926	Includes personal papers, photos.		Authorized internal use only.
Schlage Lock Co.	Box 3324 San Francisco, CA 94119	1958	Includes personal papers, oral history, photos.	From 1909	Open to company personnel, "indirectly to scholars."
Sears, Roebuck and Co. (1, retailing)	Sears Tower Chicago, IL 60684 (312) 875-2500	1955	Includes 300 oral history interviews, photos, slides, company catalogs.	From 1888	Open to scholars. Guide available.
Security First National Bank	Sixth & Spring Streets Los Angeles, CA	1929	Includes photos, personal and family papers.	From 1850	Open to responsible research. Guide available.
Shell Oil Company (13)	Box 2463 Houston, TX 77001 (713) 241-4083	1945	NUCMC 75-2069; 76-1030, -1582; 77-2047	From 1930	Open to company personnel. Guide available.
Southern Pacific Railroad (11, transportation)	1 Market Plaza San Francisco, CA 94105 (415) 362-1212	1917	Historical records deposited in institutional libraries.		

Business Firm	Address	Archive Created	Description	Date Covered	Access
Southland Corporation (13, retailing)	2828 N. Haskell Avenue Dallas, TX 75221 (214) 463-7000			From 1920	Open for study. Guide available.
Standard Oil of California (5)	225 Bush Street San Francisco, CA 94104 (415) 894-7700		NUCMC 79-560. 35,000 boxes of records.	1914-53	Corporate history took eighteen years to write by Harvard School of Business because of wealth of data available.
Standard Oil of Indiana (7)	200 E. Randolph Chicago, IL 60601 (312) 856-6111	1950	NUCMC 64-1174; 65-78, -941; 67-489, -1290; 69-1807; 77-208	From 1889	Open to scholars.
Standard Oil of Kentucky	Box 1446 Louisville, KY 40201	1965	Includes payroll records.	1800-1950	Open to scholars. Guide available.
Standard Oil of New Jersey (EXXON Corp.)	1221 Avenue of the Americas New York, NY 10020 (212) 398-3000		Some records deposited in University of Wyoming.		
Standard Oil of Ohio (21)	101 Prospect Avenue Cleveland, OH 44115 (216) 575-4141				
Texaco, Inc. (4)	200 Westchester White Plains, NY 10650 (914) 253-4000	1950	NUCMC 70-816, -1972; 72-700; 77-1745 Includes biographical files, historical photos.	From 1901	Open to qualified researchers. Index available.
Time, Inc. (125)	Rockefeller Center New York, NY 10020 (212) 586-1212	1946	NUCMC 62-3439; 66-1158; 69-983, -1832; 71-976; 78-1031		
Transcontinental Gas Pipe Line Corp. TRANSCO Companies (39)	Box 1396 Houston, TX 77001 (713) 871-8000	1960		From 1948	Open to company personnel. Guide available.
Union Mutual Life Insurance Company	400 Congress Street Portland, ME 04112	1964	Includes personal papers, photos. Est. 1 Oct. 1849.	From 1848	Open to scholars. History of company published in 1964.
Union Oil Company of California (27)	461 S. Boylston Los Angeles, CA 75265 (213) 746-7711		NUCMC 61-1815. Includes personal papers, photos.	From 1880	Open to company personnel.
Union Pacific (56)	345 Park Avenue New York, NY 10154 (212) 826-8200		NUCMC 60-48, -1211; 61-3650; 62-1167, -1401, -2436, -4047, -4717, -4959; 64-904; 65-920, -1190, -1843; 66-1568; 67-2071; 68-341, -381; 69-382, -687; 76-442; 77-1503; 80-678.		
United Air Lines, Inc. (3, transportation)	Box 66919 Chicago, IL 60666 (312) 952-4000	1963	Includes personal and family papers, maps, scrapbooks, oral history tapes.	From 1918	Open for study. Mail requests answered.
United Texas Petroleum	Box 2120 Houston, TX 77000	1960	6,320 cubic feet of records, stored in a separate location.	From 1896	Open to company personnel. Guide available.
Wagner Electric Corporation	1 Summer Avenue Newark, NJ 07100	1900	1,200 boxes of records.		Open to company personnel.
Walt Disney Productions	500 S. Buena Vista Street Burbank, CA 91521 (213) 845-3141	1955	5,000 cubic feet. Includes sound recordings, musical scores, print formulas, oral history collection.	From 1929	Open to company personnel. See David R. Smith, "Comics and Cels," *California Historical Quarterly* 56 (Fall 1977): 270-74; "It All Started with a Mouse: The Walt Disney Archives," *California Librarian* 33 (Jan. 1972): 23-28; "A Mouse Is Born,"

					College and Research Libraries 39 (Nov. 1978): 492-94.
Washington Gas Light Company	1100 H Street N.W. Washington, DC 20005	1960	Includes scrapbooks, photos.	From 1830	Open to scholars. Guide available.
Wells Fargo & Co. (12, commercial banks)	420 Montgomery San Francisco, CA 94104 (415) 396-0123	1975			See Janis Mackenzie, "Wells Fargo & Co.: Banking on the Past," *San Francisco Business*, April 1979, pp. 6-11.
Western Electric (22)	222 Broadway New York, NY 10038 (212) 571-2345	1942	NUCMC 64-1561, 77-730. Est. 1869 as Grey and Barton of Cleveland and Chicago. Manufacturing and supply unit of Bell Telephone Systems.	1869-1981	See John Buchanan, "The Western Electric Historical Library," *American Archivist* 29 (Jan. 1966): 55-59.
Weyerhauser (84)	1021 A Street Tacoma, WA 98477 (206) 924-2345	1974	NUCMC 70-273, -505, -1386; 71-617; 72-996		
Women's Federal Savings & Loan Association of Cleveland		1965			Open to scholars.

[1]Numbers in parentheses after the name refer to its Fortune ranking.
[2]NUCMC=Annual volume and collection number for materials deposited in outside libraries. Consult the National Union Catalog of Manuscript Collections described above.

PART II
PUBLISHED GENEALOGICAL SOURCES

INFORMATION GUIDE

Genealogical Information in the Record Group	*City and Telephone*	*County & Regional*	*Professional*	*College*	*Religious*
Surname/name	●	●	●	●	●
Date of Birth	●	●	●		
Place of Birth		●	●	●	
Sex					
Race/color	●				
Physical Description					
Occupation	●	●	●		●
Education			●	●	
Military Service			●	●	
Slave Status					
Property Owned		●			
Religion					●
Citizenship					
Marital Status	●			●	●
Spouse's Name	●			●	●
Children's Names	●				●
Father's Name	●			●	
Mother's Name	●				
Father's Birthplace					
Mother's Birthplace					
Date of Death	●	●	●	●	●
Cause of Death					
Name of Cemetery					
Residence	●	●	●	●	●
Age	●	●	●	●	
Literacy/signature		●	●	●	●
Photograph/sketch		●	●	●	●

COULD YOU USE THIS CHAPTER?

Type of Record	*Kept from*	*Clues That You Should Consult These Records*
City and telephone directories	After 1800; early years are sporadic	If you have an ancestor in an urban area, directories can be invaluable in giving you an exact address, cutting hours off the time it will take to find the family in the censuses between 1860 and 1910. Directories also narrow down death dates, so you can make an educated guess whether to search probate, land, and naturalization records. You can also pinpoint religious records by identifying the clergyman who may have officiated at a wedding or funeral. A careful look at addresses will enable you to identify all family members over eighteen years of age living in the same home including those attending universities. Father, mother, and sibling relationship are implied.
County and regional directories	After 1800; early years are sporadic	Business directories are particulary helpful when you have rural ancestors. They are usually organized on a county basis. Because they are readily available and easy to use, they can sometimes help you locate an ancestor in an area very quickly, let you know what kinds of property he held, and whether other adult members of the family were nearby.
Professional directories	After 1820	If family tradition or a census indicates that your ancestor was a doctor, lawyer, military person, or in the civil service, you should be able to find him/her easily by using these directories. Military lists, by order of Congress, started as early as 1816, although most are considerably later. Even though the number of details differ from directory to directory, at the least they will locate your ancestor in time and place. At most, they will provide a biographical outline. Many specialized directories also exist: was your ancestor involved in transporting goods on the Great Lakes? Consult a shipping directory.
College directories	1649 to the present	If there is a possibility, either by tradition or because of your ancestor's profession, that he/she attended college, explore fraternity/sorority directories and those maintained by alumni associations. Not only can such directories provide information about the school years and studies of the ancestor, but many of them will identify his/her parents, location at the time the directory was made, or even, his/her dates of birth and death. The Ivy League schools have published alumni directories since their establishment.
Religious directories	After 1800	If your ancestor was a clergyman with an established church, there is an excellent chance that he appears in one of its directories, some of which date from the 'teens of the nineteeth century.
Post office and street directories	After 1900	Do you have letters with street addresses but no city? Do photographs bear the address of the photographer's shop? With post office and street directories you can see which city, in the year of publication, had a street by that name, eliminate unlikely candidates, and zero in with other sources on the right one.

Chapter 11

CITY DIRECTORIES AND THEIR COUSINS

Gordon Lewis Remington

D*IRECTORY: A Book containing one or more alphabetical lists of the inhabitants of any locality, with their addresses and occupations; also a similar compilation dealing with the members of a particular profession, trade, or association, as a Clerical or Medical Directory, etc.*[1]

While a directory can often in itself be a source of interesting genealogical and biographical information, its chief value lies in its use as an aid to locating a person in place and time. One type of directory groups people by a common residence. The second groups them by a common association or attribute. In addition, many directories cover organizations rather than individuals and are sometimes called registers, catalogs, annuals, yearbooks, or guides. Whatever its title, contents, or method, then, a directory will always list and locate members of a group. This chapter will give a history of directories, describe the limitations and resources of six kinds, and provide numerous examples of how to use them.

The most comprehensive guide to find whether a directory exists is James A. Ethridge, ed., *Directory of Directories* (Detroit: Gale Research Co., 1980). This source is available at most public and university libraries. It will, however, cover only those directories in publication in 1980. Its chief value for pre-1920 research is to provide current addresses and telephone numbers of publishing companies with directory libraries. The Library of Congress has two volumes of the same title published by R. L. Polk in 1912 and 1916.

The *Oxford English Dictionary* cites J. Brown's *The Directory or List of Principal Traders in London* (1732) as the earliest use of the word *directory* as defined above. Lists of inhabitants or associates are extant from at least two hundred years earlier. Dorothea N. Spear, in the introduction to her *Bibliography of American Directories Through 1860*, gives a concise account of the history of directories in the United States.

> Although as early as 1665, in New York a grouping of residents by streets was shown in the Records of the Dutch Magistrates, the first directory-type listing the inhabitants of an American city of which we have knowledge is a Baltimore broadside. It is entitled *The Following List of Families, And Other Persons Residing in the Town of Baltimore, Was Taken in the Year 1752, by a Lady of Respectability*, and is believed to have been printed between 1830 and 1840 by Joseph Townsend (1756-1841) from the original manuscript in the Maryland Historical Society. Next came the two Charleston directory lists of 1782 and 1785 printed in the *South Carolina and Georgia Almanack* for those years, owned by the Charleston Library Society and reprinted in 1951. Philadelphia has the honor of having produced the first separately printed directories in this country, two rivals issued in 1785, the earlier being *MacPherson's Directory for the City and Suburbs of Philadelphia*, first issued on November 16, 1785, and the second, *The Philadelphia Directory*, by Francis White, first issued on November 29, 1785. The John MacPherson edition is to be found in the Philadelphia Free Library and in the Historical Society of Pennsylvania, while the White volume is owned by the Phildelphia libraries and the American Antiquarian Society. . . . New York quickly followed Philadelphia with *The New-York Directory* of 1786, by David Franks, which was frequently reprinted in later years. The New-York Historical Society and the New York Public Library own original copies of this directory. Following the lead of the most progressive cities, many others throughout the country began to issue directories in rapid succession.
>
> The compilation of the early directories was usually a side issue rather than the principal line of the compiler's work. Therefore . . . some of the authors combined the listing with their duties as letter carriers, postmasters, county constables, school principals, teachers, and brokers. Often the modest compiler's own name and address were not even included in the alphabetical listing. The majority of these publications, however, were issued by newspaper offices. From the mid-nineteenth century we find separate directory publishers such as the well-known firms of George Adams and of Damrell & Moore of Boston, C.S. Wiliams of Cincinnati, and the John F. Trow and John Doggett Companies of New York, William H. Boyd who had offices in New York, Philadelphia, and Washington, and many others. Boyd advertised in 1859 that he owned the largest collection of directories in the world and was prepared to publish the directory of any city or state. We know that he did issue directories for many of the eastern and mid-western cities. Then came the R. L. Polk Company of New York and Detroit, with numerous branch offices, which presumably became the largest directory publisher and so continues today. The price of directories ranged from twenty-five cents to four dollars by the end of the 1850s, whereas our comprehensive Polk publications of today cost us fifty dollars a copy. It is true that the earliest attempts were quite crude, often with the names sorted only under each letter but not completely alphabetized. In the early volumes there were no house numbers so that the locations given were quite general, and some times the millers and merchants were located merely "next the bridge" or "opposite the town hall."[2]

Originally, the two basic types of directories (residence and attribute) were more or less combined. The early directories' business orientation influenced their development and content. Just as the census was designed primarily for congressional apportionment and not for genealogical purposes, so the directory is limited as a genealogical source by the intent of its compilers. The early English directories listed "principal traders" and "gentleman of accompte." It is doubtful that the "Lady of Respectabilty," who compiled the *List of Families, and Other Persons* in Baltimore, 1752, included in her list those families and "other persons" who weren't respectable. Although such economic and class distinctions are less apparent later, it was not until the second half of the nineteenth century that directories included common laborers with any regularity, and even then they usually left out transients.

As cities grew in the nineteenth century, the directories became more detailed. They included special sections devoted to businesses, organizations, churches, and even steamship lists along with the list of general inhabitants. These special sections eventually evolved into nongeographic directories by the late 1800s. Those considered in this chapter are:

1. City and telephone directories
2. County and regional business directories
3. Professional directories
4. Organizational directories
5. Religious directories
6. Post office and street directories

This chapter will consider those directories published within the jurisdiction of the United States before 1920. Although this leaves out one city directory for Sitka, Alaska, from the period of Russian ownership, the following excerpt from the foreword to the *Alaska Directory and Gazetteer for 1934-1935* will perhaps make up for this omission and explain the difficulties of listing people constantly on the move.

> This Second Biennial Edition of the *Alaska Directory and Gazetteer* represents a complete new compilation of the residents and business houses of the Territory of Alaska . . . .
>
> Extreme care has been taken to secure the most complete and accurate information possible but the publishers cannot assume responsibility for any accuracies [*sic*] or omissions.
>
> A frontier country, one-fifth the size of the United States, with its approximately 29,000 white population distributed among more than 400 widely scattered towns and settlements, present[s] difficulties which subscribers will appreciate. The shift of population from point to point in the Territory by seasonal occupation and winter vacationing in the States, offer further problems of reporting proper locations of many residents.
>
> In order to meet these situations, the issuing of supplements from time to time prior to publication of the next directory proper will be continued. Also, all purchasers are entitled to two years reference, inquiry and tracing service.[3]

General Problems with Directories

Finding a directory, the first step in use, is also the most difficult, particularly for researchers far from major record centers. This chapter provides source locations for the major types of directories. If major record centers and local libraries do not have a directory for the year desired, a copy may no longer exist. The law which requires copyrighted material to be deposited in the Library of Congress dates only from 1870. Also, some directories were originally published for short-term use and have been disposed of.

Another consequence of short-term use is low-quality paper. Individual pages may deteriorate badly. A binding can always be replaced; but when segments of the printed page tear off and are swept up at the end of the day by the library custodian, they are gone forever. Microfilming has helped; but in many cases, small reduction and poor lighting make the film copies hard to read.

When consulting any directory, keep in mind why it was compiled. No directory can substitute for the census. If an individual was not at home when the directory agent called, his name may not appear for that particular year. Business and professional directories may have required a fee for inclusion. If you can't find an ancestor in the alphabetical sequence, be sure to check the beginning section for listings "received too late to be included."

If the ancestor is not there but should be, check for misplaced letter spellings—Tohmson, instead of Thomson, for instance. Names may also be spelled wrong. Early New York City directories often contained lists of variant name spellings. Pittsburgh city directories listed the names Meyers, Meyer, Myers, and Myer together until the 1860s. Consider type style when using early directories, particularly those from the eighteenth century. Don't misread the old double ess character *ſſ* as "f."

The date on the title page of a directory is usually that of publication and does not necessarily indicate when the information was compiled. As a general rule, search one year on either side of the year being sought, especially when you are trying to determine an address. If a particular address is given in 1870, but the family is not there in the census, check the 1871 directory to see if they moved.

City and Telephone Directories

Directories are primarily useful in locating people in place and time. They can tell you generally where an ancestor lived and give an exact location for census years. They are also useful for linkage with sources other than censuses.

Telephone directories are marginally useful as genealogical sources. In 1876, when the telephone was invented, only three people had telephones. By 1900, this number had climbed to 1,356 or 17 people per 1000 of population. In 1920, 13,329 or 23 people per 1,000 population had telephones.[4] Early telephone directories may tell you nothing more than that a person had a telephone. Nevertheless, even this scanty data tells you a certain amount: telephone owners are more affluent than non-phone owners, and if there are two or more persons of the same name or characteristics, the telephone directory can help you distinguish between them.

City directories' usefulness for gaining access to census records cannot be overstated. While census indexes exist for the years 1790 through 1850, 1860 and 1870 have been indexed only for specific states, 1880 is indexed only for those families with children under ten, and 1910 is indexed only for certain states. Where these indexes fail, city directories can help. For those censuses as yet unavailable to the general public (from 1920 on), the census bureau will search if a precise address is known for the census year.

Later city directories will list grown children who live with their parents but who are working or going to school. Read the entries' surnames for persons residing at the same address. These yearly directories show which children belong to which households, when they marry and start families of their own, when they establish themselves in business, and, sometimes, whom the daughters marry. In cases where a specific occupation is given, you can search records pertinent to that occupation.

Some city directories also give special facts: separate listings for blacks, places of birth and death, removals, and which steamships are operating where. These notations are usually for one year only and are not the norm.

City directories were at least partly responsible for the specialized directories considered elsewhere in the chapter. Always check the city directory for separate business, organizational, and church listings, often on different-colored pages at the end of the volume.

How to Use City Directories

Once an ancestor has been found in a city directory, there are several ways this information can be used to gain access to, or link with, such sources as censuses, death and probate records, church records, naturalizations, and land records. Table 11-1 summarizes the compatibility between directories and censuses.

Table 11-1 lists 149 places in the United States with a population of over 10,000 that were divided into wards or other subdistricts in the 1870 census. It will help you locate families with a city directory. The list is based on information in the *Ninth Census of the United States*: *Statistics of Population*, Table 3 (Washington, D.C.: Government Printing Office, 1872).

The list shows the number of wards and the number of National Archives microfilm reels for each place in the 1860 and 1870 censuses. As we've mentioned, these two censuses present the most problems for locating a family in a large city. An 1860 census reel contains about 20,000 names, while the average in 1870 is 25,000. We chose the number 10,000 to represent slightly over one-third of a microfilm reel. Genealogists who don't have time to search many reels will find the infomation on these smaller places useful. Obviously, hunting down the right directory may be a waste of time, where less than a full reel of microfilm is in question. It is up to you to make that judgment each time.

In 1870, over 380 places in the United States were divided into wards. These ranged from Yankton, Dakota Territory (population: 737; wards: 3), to New York City (population: 942,292; wards: 22). Pennsylvania had the most places divided into wards with forty-three, while Colorado Territory, Florida, Montana, New Mexico Territory, Oregon, Vermont, and Washington Territory had none.

In 1870, many major cities were divided into election districts or precincts below the ward level. The twenty-two wards of New York City were subdivided into 387 election districts with varying numbers of districts per ward. Five of the twelve wards of San

Francisco were subdivided into fourteen election districts. These divisions are irrelevant and do not affect the use of city directories, as city directories rarely make note of election districts.

Here is an explanation of the categories on the list:

City/State. Self-explanatory. Note that some places were still territories in 1870.

Status. C=City, B=Burrough, V=Village, T=Township. The status reflects the political nature of the place in 1870. The date following the abbreviation is the date of incorporation or chartering. Note that many places had directories published before they were chartered as cities.

Population. The population in 1860 and 1870 should indicate the time you will need to search for a particular place. The data is from the *Ninth Census* mentioned above. (1860: 1 reel = 20,000; 1870: 1 reel = 25,000).

Wards. If the city was divided into wards for census purposes, the number of wards is given in 1860. Many of the cities were not divided into wards for census purposes but may have been in reality. The data on wards is also from the *Ninth Census*.

NARS mf. The number of National Archives microfilm reels. This information comes from the *Catalogue of Census 1790-1880*, published by the National Archives. Where a place is less than a full reel of microfilm or has not been specified as a full reel or more, the county in which the town can be found is listed.

Directories. *Earliest*: the earliest directory in the above-mentioned *Bibliography of American Directories Through 1860* by Dorothea N. Spear; *GS*: whether the Genealogical Society of Utah in Salt Lake City has a directory for the place in 1860 and 1870, *LC*: whether the Library of Congress has a directory for each census year, *RP:* whether Research Publications has produced a microfilm of the directories and which segments are available. Research Publications is in the process of microfilming city directories in the Spear bibliography.

Census Records and Directories. For a city directory to be useful in making a census search, you must know the wards for the census year desired, since the census was taken ward by ward. First, find the ancestor's address in the directory closest to the census year. For example, our ancestor lived at 1357 Clifford Avenue, Rochester, New York, in 1912. The closest directory to the 1910 census is the 1913 directory published by the Drew Allis Company of Rochester. (See Figure 11-1.)

The street directory gives all of the addresses on Clifford Avenue, but Clifford runs through five different wards. At this point, we check the cross streets. The nearest cross street to 1357 is Renwood. Turning to Renwood Street, we find it is entirely in the twenty-second ward of the city. We can now search this ward in the 1910 census with near certainty that we will find our ancestor there.

Some directories do not list all of the minor cross streets that fall in the same ward. Combine these directories with maps to find the address you want. Most directories include maps showing ward boundaries for this very purpose. In most copies, however, the maps are usually missing; and since you will be using microfilms more than originals, you will need other maps to do the job.

Some directories also give exact address and street coordinates, so places can be pinpointed quickly on a map. See Sarah Street in this Pittsburgh Street Directory.

SARAH, from 79 S Seventh to City line, 24th, 25th, 26th, 28th and 29th wards—S15-20.

SARDIS AY, from Leech to Thirty-seventh, 15th ward—H20.

SARONEY AY, from Manhattan to Leon ay, 18th ward—C29.

R. L. Polk and Co., *Pittsburgh, Allegheny City, and Allegheny County Business Directory for 1900* (Pittsburgh: R. L. Polk and Co., 1900), p. 46.

Figure 11-1. *Rochester, [New York] Directory Containing a General Directory of the Citizens, a Business Directory, and the City and County Register*, no. 64, 1913, (Rochester: Drew Allis Co., 1913), pp. 26, 41.

Clifford Avenue, from 1012 St. Paul, east, to Culver road; wards 5, 8, 17, 18, 22

Left.	*Rt.*	
2	1	St. Paul
	87	Durgin
96		Harris
164	163	Conkey avenue
—	—	R., W. & O. R.R.
232		Roth
276		Lill
390	389	Clinton av. N.
490		Remington
590	589	Joseph avenue
628		Loomis
	629	Theodore
652	651	Maria
676		Standinger alley
700	699	Thomas
764	775	Henry
816	815	Barons
	859	Dudley
902	901	Hudson avenue
944		Orphans' alley
1032	1031	North
	1083	Lincoln
	1123	Hollister
1170		Carter
1174	1167	Portland avenue
1268	1265	Miller
1310		Spiegel park
	1345	Rohr
1352		Renwood
	1377	First
	1393	Coleman terrace
1400		Manitou
1434	1435	Portage
	—	Seifert
1464		Clairmount
1498	1495	Sixth
1520		Nichols
	1555	Priscilla
1564		Jerold
	1579	Garnet
1606		Newcomb
1646		Rustic
1686		Arbutus
1706	1703	North Goodman
	1745	Winterroth
	1787	Pansy
	1827	Cummings
	1863	Ellison
1914	1911	Morton
2024		Lyceum
	—	Arden
	—	Longview avenue
	—	Sarona avenue
	—	Ventura avenue
	2281	Martinet avenue
2272		Waring road
	2373	Culver road

Clifton, from 47 Prospect, west, to 100 Genesee; ward 11

Left.	*Rt.*	
1	2	Prospect
31	32	Reynolds
39		Hall alley
49		Caffery place
65	64	Jefferson avenue
87		St. Clair
105		Morgan

Raymond, from 1147 Clinton avenue South, southwest, to Howard, at city line; ward 14

Redfield, from Freeman, south; ward 5

Reed Park, from 492 Hudson avenue, east, to 813 North; ward 8

Regent Place, from 181 Milburn, south; ward 12

Remington, fr. 490 Clifford avenue, north, to 459 Norton; ward 17

Left.	*Rt.*	
1	2	Clifford avenue
39		LaForce
	46	DeJonge
67		Mead
	78	Boston
105		Carl
	118	Langham
139		Avenue A
	156	Wilkins
171		Ketchum
201		Morrill
	218	Dale
233		Bloomingdale
263	264	Avenue D
—		Bismark terrace
	298	Pardee
	332	Farbridge
329		Kohlman
	364	Leo
373		Ereth
	390	Zimbrich
399		Oscar
	422	Weaver
441		Borchard
	450	Wolfert terrace

Renwood. fr. 1352 Clifford avenue. north. to 135 Fernwood avenue; ward 22

Reservoir Avenue. from 922 Mt. Hope avenue, east, to Highland Park; ward 14

Reynolds, from 281 West avenue. south. to 435 Seward: wards 11, 19

Left.	*Rt.*	
2	1	West avenue
6		Rice alley
	7	Lapey place
18	19	Troup
40	39	Clifton
60		Atkinson
88	87	Adams
102	101	Knowles alley
116	117	Tremont
	129	Penn
144	145	Bronson avenue
170	171	Cady
190		Faxon alley
198	199	Champlain
212	211	Ruff alley
226	225	Frost avenue
238	237	Whittlesey alley
250	255	Bartlett

Table 11-1
Directory/Census Compatibility

City	*State*		*Population*		*Wards*		*NARS F*		*Earliest Directory In Spears*	*Directories*				
										GS		*LC*		*RP*
			1860	*1870*	*1860*	*1870*	*1860*	*1870*		*1860*	*1870*	*1860*	*1870*	
Akron	OH	C/1865	3,477	10,006	-	3	Summit		1859	no	no	yes	yes	1859-1860
Albany	NY	C/1686	62,367	69,422	10	10	2	3	1813	no	no	yes	yes	1813-1901
Alexandria	VA	C/1852	12,652	13,570	-	4	Alexandria		see Washington D.C.					
Allegheny City	PA	C/1840	28,702	53,180	4	8	2	2	see Pittsburgh, PA					
Allentown	PA	C/1867	8,025	13,884	5	6	Lehigh		see Reading, PA					
Altoona	PA	C/1868	3,591	10,610	-	6	Blair		1873	no	no	no	no	none
Atlanta	GA	C/1847	9,554	21,789	5	6	1	Fulton	1859	yes	yes	yes	yes	1859-1901
Auburn	NY	C/1848	10,986	17,225	-	7	1	Cayuga	1857	no	no	yes	no	1857-1860
Augusta	GA	C/1817	12,493	15,389	4	4	Richmond		1841	no	no	yes	yes	1841-1860
Aurora	IL	C/1853	6,011	11,162	-	11	Kane		1859 co.	no	no	yes	no	none
Baltimore	MD	C/1797	212,418	267,354	20	20	10	10	1752/1796	no	no	yes	yes	1752-1901
Bangor	ME	C/1834	16,407	18,289	7	7	Penobscot		1834	no	no	yes	yes	1834-1860
Biddeford	ME	C/1855	9,349	10,282	-	7	York		1856	no	no	no	no	1856-1860
Binghamton	NY	C/1867	8,325	12,692	-	5	Broome		1857	no	no	yes	no	1857-1860
Boston	MA	C/1822	117,840	250,526	12	16	6	10	1789	yes	yes	yes	yes	1789-1901
Bridgeport	CT	C/1836	13,299	18,969	-	3	Fairfield		1855	no	no	no	no	1855-1860
Brooklyn	NY	C/1834	266,661	396,099	19	22	13	17	1822	yes	yes	yes	yes	1822-1901
Buffalo	NY	C/1832	81,129	117,714	13	13	5	4	1828	yes	yes	yes	yes	1828-1901
Burlington	IA	C/1838	6,706	14,930	-	7	Des Moines		1856	yes	yes	yes	no	1856-1860
Cambridge	MA	C/1846	26,060	39,634	5	5	1	2	1847	no	no	yes	yes	1847-1860
Charleston	SC	C/1783	40,522	48,956	9	8	1	2	1782	yes	yes	yes	yes	1782-1901
Charlestown	MA	C/1847	26,065	28,323	-	3	1	Middlesex	1831	no	no	yes	no	1831-1860
Chelsea	MA	C/1857	13,395	18,547	-	4	Middlesex		1847	no	no	yes	no	1847-1860
Chicago	IL	C/1837	109,260	298,977	10	20	7	14	1839	yes	yes	yes	yes	1839-1901
Cincinatti	OH	C/1819	161,044	216,239	17	24	9	9	1819	yes	yes	yes	yes	1819-1901
Cleveland	OH	C/1836	43,417	92,892	11	15	2	5	1837	yes	yes	yes	yes	1837-1901
Cohoes	NY	C/1870	8,800	15,357	-	4	Albany		see Albany, NY					
Columbus	OH	C/1834	18,554	31,274	5	9	1	1	1843	yes	no	yes	yes	1843-1901
Concord	NH	C/1849/53	10,896	12,241	7	7	1	Merrimack	1830	no	no	yes	no	1830-1860
Council Bluffs	IA	C/1853	2,011	10,020	5	6	Pottawattamie		n/a	no	yes	no	no	none
Covington	KY	C/1834	16,471	24,505	7	9	Kenton		see Cincinatti, OH					
Davenport	IA	C/1851	11,267	20,038	-	6	Scott		1853	yes	yes	yes	yes	1853-1881
Dayton	OH	C/1841	20,081	30,473	6	11	1	1	1850	no	no	yes	yes	1850-1901

Des Moines	IA	C/1857	3,965	12,035	-	7	Polk		n/a	no	no	no	yes	1861-1901
Detroit	MI	C/1806	45,619	79,577	10	10	2	4	1837	no	no	yes	yes	1837-1901
Dubuque	IA	C/1841	13,000	18,434	-	5	Dubuque		1856	yes	yes	yes	no	1856-1860
Easton	PA	B/1789	8,944	10,987	3	3	Northampton		see Reading, PA					
East Saginaw	MI	C/1859	3,001	11,350	-	6	Saginaw		n/a	no	no	no	no	none
Elizabeth	NJ	C/1855	11,567	20,832	3	8	Union		1859 (co.)	no	no	yes	no	none
Elmira	NY	C/1864	8,682	15,863	-	6	Chemung		1857	no	no	yes	no	1857-1860
Erie	PA	C/1851	19,419	19,646	2	6	Erie	1	1853	no	no	yes	yes	1853-1901
Evansville	IN	C/1847	11,484	21,830	-	9	Vanderburgh		1858	no	yes	yes	yes	1858-1901
Fall River	MA	C/1854	14,026	26,766	6	6	Bristol		1853	no	no	yes	yes	1853-1901
Flushing	NY	V/	10,188	14,650	-	3	Queens	1	1889	no	no	no	no	none
Fond Du Lac	WI	C/1852	5,450	12,764	5	5	Fond Du Lac		1857	no	no	no	yes	1857-1860
Fort Wayne	IN	C/1840	n/a	17,718	n/a	9	Allen		1858	no	no	yes	yes	1858-1881
Galveston	TX	C/1839	7,307	13,818	4	4	Galveston		1856	no	no	yes	yes	1856-1901
Georgetown	DC	C/1789	8,733	11,384	4	-	DC		see Washington DC					
Grand Rapids	MI	C/1850	8,085	16,507	5	5	Kent		1856	no	no	yes	yes	1856-1901
Hamilton	OH	C/1857	7,223	11,081	3	4	Butler		1858	no	no	yes	no	1858-1860
Hannibal	MO	C/1839	6,505	10,125	3	5	Marion		n/a	no	no	no	no	none
Harrisburg	PA	C/1860	13,405	23,104	6	9	Dauphin		1839	no	no	yes	no	1839-1901
Hartford	CT	C/1784	29,152	37,180	3	7	1	2	1799	no	no	yes	yes	1799-1901
Haverhill	MA	C/1869	9,995	13,092	-	6	Essex		1853	no	no	yes	no	1853-1860
Hoboken	NJ	C/1855	9,662	20,297	3	4	1	1	see Jersey City, NJ					
Indianapolis	IN	C/1847	18,611	48,244	7	9	1	2	1855	no	no	yes	yes	1855-1901
Jackson	MI	C/1857	4,799	11,447	4	4	Jackson		1869	no	no	no	no	
Jersey City	NJ	C/1838	29,226	82,546	4	16	1	3	1849	no	no	yes	yes	1849-1901
Kansas City	MO	C/1853	4,418	32,260	-	4	Jackson	1	1859	no	yes	yes	yes	1859-1901
Keokuk	IA	C/1848	8,136	12,766	4	6	Lee		1854	yes	yes	yes	no	1854-1860
Lafayette	IN	C/1854	9,387	13,506	-	6	Tippecanoe		1858	no	no	yes	no	1858-1860
Lancaster	PA	C/1818	17,603	20,233	-	6	1	Lancaster	1843	no	no	yes	no	1843-1860
Lawrence	MA	C/1853	17,639	28,921	6	6	Essex	1	1847	no	no	yes	no	1847-1860
Leavenworth	KS	C/1855	7,429	17,873	4	4	Leavenworth		1859	no	no	yes	no	1859-1860
Lewiston	ME	C/1861	7,424	13,600	-	7	Androscoggin		1872	no	no	no	no	none
Lexington	KY	C/1832	9,321	14,801	-	4	Fayette		1806	no	no	yes	yes	1806-1860
Little Rock	AR	C/1836	3,727	12,380	-	4	Pulaski		1899	no	no	no	no	none
Lockport	NY	C/1865	13,523	12,426	-	4	Niagara		1866	no	no	no	no	none
Louisville	KY	C/1828	68,033	100,753	8	12	2	4	1832	yes	yes	yes	yes	1832-1901
Lowell	MA	C/1836	36,827	40,928	6	6	1	2	1832	no	no	yes	yes	1832-1901
Lynn	MA	C/1850	19,083	28,233	7	7	Essex	1	1832	no	no	yes	no	1832-1860
Madison	IN	C/1836	8,130	10,709	9	6	Jefferson		1859	no	no	yes	no	1859-1860

(contiuned)

City	*State*		*Population*		*Wards*		*NARS F*		*Earliest Directory In Spears*	*Directories*				
										GS		*LC*		*RP*
			1860	*1870*	*1860*	*1870*	*1860*	*1870*		*1860*	*1870*	*1860*	*1870*	
Manchester	NH	C/1846	20,107	23,536	8	8	1	1	1844	no	no	yes	yes	1844-1901
Memphis	TN	C/1849	22,623	40,226	8	10	Shelby		1849	no	no	yes	yes	1849-1901
Milwaukee	WI	C/1846	45,246	71,440	9	9	3	3	1847	no	yes	yes	yes	1847-1901
Minneapolis	MN	C/1867	2,564	13,066	4	4	Hennepin		1847	no	no	yes	yes	1861-1901
Mobile	AL	C/1819	29,258	32,034	7	8	Mobile	1	1836	no	no	yes	yes	1837-1901
Montgomery	AL	C/1837	8,843	10,588	-	6	Montgomery	1	1859	no	no	n/a	no	none
Nashua	NH	C/1853	10,065	10,543	8	8	Hillsborough		1841	no	no	no	no	1841-1860
Nashville	TN	C/1806	16,988	25,865	8	10	Davidson		1853	no	yes	yes	yes	1853-1901
New Albany	IN	C/1839	12,647	15,396	-	6	Floyd		1856	no	no	yes	no	1856-1860
Newark	NJ	C/1836	71,941	105,059	12	13	2	4	1835	no	no	yes	yes	1835-1901
New Bedford	MA	C/1847	22,300	21,320	6	6	1	Bristol	1836	no	no	yes	no	1836-1860
New Brunswick	NJ	C/1730	11,256	15,058	-	3	Middlesex		1855	no	no	no	no	1855-1860
Newburgh	NY	C/1865	15,196	17,014	-	4	Orange	1	1856	no	no	yes	no	1856-1860
Newburyport	MA	C/1851	13,401	12,595	-	6	Essex		1849	no	no	yes	no	1849-1860
New Haven	CT	C/1784	39,267	50,840	8	8	2	2	1840	no	yes	yes	yes	1840-1901
New Orleans	LA	C/1805	138,675	191,418	11	15	8	7	1805	yes	yes	yes	yes	1805-1901
Newport	RI	C/1853	10,508	12,521	-	5	Newport		1856	no	no	no	no	1856-1860
New York City	NY	C/1653	805,658	942,292	22	22#	34 39/40	1	1786	yes	yes	yes	yes	1786-1901
Norfolk	VA	C/1845	14,620	19,229	-	4	Norfolk	1	1801/1851	no	no	yes	yes	1801-1860
Norristown	PA	B/1812	8,848	10,753	-	3	Montgomery		1860	yes	no	yes	no	1860
North Providence	RI	T/	11,818	20,495	-	3	Providence		see Providence RI					
Norwich	CT	C/1784	14,048	16,653	-	4	New London		1846	no	no	yes	no	1846-1860
Ogdensburg	NY	C/1868	7,409	10,076	-	3	St. Lawrence		1857	no	no	no	no	1857-1860
Omaha	NE	C/1857	1,883	16,083	3	6	Douglas		1867	no	no	no	yes	1861-1901
Oshkosh	WI	C/	6,086	12,663	5	5			1857	no	no	no	no	1857-1860
Oswego	NY	C/1848	16,816	20,910	4	8	1	Oswego	1852	no	no	yes	no	1852-1860
Paterson	NJ	C/1851	19,586	33,579	5	9	Passaic	1	1855	no	no	yes	yes	1855-1901
Peoria	IL	C/1845	14,045	22,849	5	7	1	1	1844	no	no	yes	yes	1844-1901
Petersburg	VA	C/1850	18,266	18,950	4	6	Petersburg		1859	no	no	yes	no	1859-1860
Philadelphia	PA	C/1701	565,529	674,022	24	28	25	28/28	1785	yes	yes	yes	yes	1785-1901
Pittsburgh	PA	C/1816	49,217	86,076	9	23	3	4	1813	yes	yes	yes	yes	1813-1901
Portland	ME	C/1832	26,341	31,413	7	8	Cumberland	1	1823	no	no	yes	yes	1823-1901
Portsmouth	OH	C/1851	6,268	10,592	-	5	Scioto		1859	no	no	yes	no	1859-1860
Portsmouth	VA	C/1858	9,496	10,492	-	2	Norfolk		see Richmond, VA					
Pottsville	PA	B/1828	9,444	12,384	-	6	Schuylkill		see Reading, PA					
Poughkeepsie	NY	C/1854	14,726	20,080	4	6	Dutchess		1843	yes	yes	yes	no	1843-1860
Providence	RI	C/1832	50,666	68,904	7	9	3	3	1824	no	no	yes	yes	1824-1901

Quincy	IL	C/1839	13,718	24,052	6	6	1	Adams	1848	no	no	yes	no	1848-1860
Reading	PA	C/1847	23,162	33,390	5	9	1	1	1806/1856	no	no	yes	yes	1856-1901
Richmond	VA	C/1782	37,910	51,038	3	5	2	2	1818	no	no	yes	yes	1818-1901
Rochester	NY	C/1834	48,204	62,386	12	14	3	2	1827	no	no	yes	yes	1827-1901
Rockford	IL	C/1852	6,979	11,049	-	5	Winnebago		1857	no	no	yes	no	1857-1860
Rome	NY	C/1870	3,584	11,000	3	5	Oneida		1857	no	no	yes	no	1857-1860
Roxbury	MA	C/1846	25,137	(see Boston)	5	(see Boston)	1		1847	no	no	yes	n/a	1847-1860
Sacramento	CA	C/1850	13,785	16,283	4	4	Sacramento		1851	no	no	yes	yes	1851-1881
St. Joseph	MO	C/1851	8,932	19,565	3	5	Buchanan		1882	no	no	no	no	none
St. Louis	MO	C/1823	160,773	310,864	10	12	9	13	1821	yes	yes	yes	yes	1821-1901
St. Paul	MN	C/1854	10,401	20,030	4	5	Ramsey		1856	no	no	yes	yes	1856-1901
Salem	MA	C/1858	22,252	24,117	6	6	1	1	1837	yes	no	yes	no	1837-1860
Salt Lake City	UT	C/1851	8,236	12,854	20	20	Salt Lake		1867	no	yes	no	yes	1861-1901
San Antonio	TX	C/1837	8,235	12,256	-	4	Bexar		n/a	no	no	no	yes	1861-1901
Sandusky	OH	C/1845	8,408	13,000	-	5	Erie		1855	no	no	yes	no	1855-1860
San Francisco	CA	C/1850	56,802	149,473	12	12#	2	7	1850	yes	yes	yes	yes	1850-1901
Savannah	GA	C/	22,292	28,235	4	4	Chatham	1	1848	no	no	yes	yes	1848-1901
Schenectady	NY	C/1798	9,579	11,026	5	5	Schenectady		1841	no	no	yes	no	1841-1860
Scranton	PA	C/1866	9,223	35,092	-	12	Lackawanna	1	1867	no	no	no	yes	1861-1881
Springfield	IL	C/1840	9,320	17,364	-	4	Sangamon		1855	no	no	yes	no	1855-1860
Springfield	MA	C/1852	15,199	26,703	-	8	Hampden	1	1845	no	no	yes	no	1845-1860
Springfield	OH	C/1850	7,002	12,652	4	5	Clark		1852	no	no	yes	no	1852-1860
Stockton	CA	C/1850	3,679	10,066	-	3	San Joaquin		1852	see S.F.	no	see S.F.	no	1852-1860
Syracuse	NY	C/1847	28,119	43,051	8	8	1	2	1844	no	no	yes	yes	1844-1901
Taunton	MA	C/1864	15,376	18,679	-	8	Bristol		1850	no	no	yes	no	1850-1860
Terre Haute	IN	C/1853	8,594	16,103	5	5	Vigo		1858	no	no	yes	no	1858-1860
Toledo	OH	C/1837	13,768	31,584	4	8	Lucas	1	1858	no	no	yes	yes	1858-1901
Trenton	NJ	C/1792	17,228	22,874	6	7	1	Mercer	1844	no	no	yes	no	1844-1860
Troy	NY	C/1816	39,235	46,465	10	10	2	2	1829	no	no	yes	yes	1829-1901
Utica	NY	C/1832	22,529	28,804	7	9	1	1	1817	no	no	yes	yes	1817-1901
Vicksburg	MS	C/1836	4,591	12,443	-	8	-	Warren	1860	no	no	yes	no	1860
Washington	DC	C/1802	61,122	109,199	7	7	3	4	1822	no	no	yes	yes	1822-1901
Waterbury	CT	C/1853	10,004	10,826	-	4	New Haven		1869	no	no	no	yes	none
Wheeling	WV	C/1836	14,083	19,280	6	7	Ohio		1839	no	no	yes	no	1839-1860
Wilkes-Barre	PA	B/1806	4,253	10,174	-	3	Luzerne		1871	no	no	no	no	none
Williamsport	PA	C/1866	5,664	16,030	2	8	Lycoming		1866	no	no	no	no	none
Wilmington	DE	C/1832	21,258	30,841	5	9	1	1	1814	no	no	yes	yes	1814-1901
Worcester	MA	C/1848	24,960	41,105	8	8	2	2	1828	no	no	yes	yes	1829-1901
York	PA	B/1787	8,605	11,003	-	5	York		1877	no	no	no	no	none
Zanesville	OH	C/1850	9,229	10,011	4	6	Muskingum		1851	no	no	yes	no	1851-1860

Maps. If the street directories alone cannot provide the proper ward, maps can. There are basically three kinds of maps: those without ward boundaries, those with ward boundaries, and those with boundaries added after publication.

Maps without ward boundaries will help you if you can find a description of the ward boundaries. Sometimes you will find these in city directories which do not indicate the wards for each street. In this case, you can draw on the map of ward boundaries. This is, however, a time-consuming process.

Maps with ward boundaries are the most useful. First, identify a few main streets; then it will be fairly easy to find smaller streets. You can find such maps at the Library of Congress. The Genealogical Society of Utah, which has a good map collection, is in the process of acquiring maps for all major cities from 1840 to 1900 from the Library of Congress.

There are also maps with census enumeration district boundaries. You can find these maps at the Washington National Records Service, 4205 Suitland Road, Suitland, Maryland, for those censuses with designated enumeration districts: 1880, 1900, 1910.

Maps with ward boundaries added after publication are time-savers. Take care however, that such maps have been drawn correctly or you will have to search a long time to find the right entries. The Newberry Library in Chicago has constructed a 1900 atlas for the city of Chicago from the enumeration district maps. This atlas is especially valuable for finding alleys, courts, and other short streets. The Genealogical Society of Utah is adding ward boundaries to maps already in its collection. The Federation of Genealogical Societies will compile a 1910 city atlas through the National Archives Record Centers Gift Fund. Another general source of city maps is E. Kay Kirkham, *A Handy Guide to Record Searching in the Larger Cities of the United States* (Logan, Utah: Everton, 1974). The maps include street indexes, so this is a useful compilation. Take care here also, as this book does not cover all of the major cities for which such maps are available nor do the maps always cover every census year.

When maps and street indexes are available, locating the exact ward where an ancestor lived becomes a priority before you can make best use of city directories. For example, finding an ancestor in the Philadelphia census illustrates the process. The earliest known ancestor of the Patton family was John Quincy Adams Patton. These facts are known about him: he lived in Philadelphia; his wife's name was Agnes Boyd; he had a child named James Abram Garfield Patton. James's date of birth is unknown. It might have been during the 1880s because of his unusual name (James Abram Garfield was president in 1881). We could not locate this family in the 1900 census but there is a possible family in the 1880 census:[5]

1321 S. 8th St.	John Patton		Age 39	huckster	b. Pennsylvania
	Agnes	wife	36		b. Pennsylvania
	Joseph	son	16		"
	Emma	dau	13		"
	John	son	10		"
	Agnes	dau	8		"
	Robert	son	6		"
	Anna F.	dau	11/12 (June)		"[5]

No James Abram Garfield appeared in this family, but the mother was young enough that he might have been born after 1880. Fur-

---

Figure 11-2. 1870 U.S. Census, Pennsylvania, Philadelphia Co., Philadelphia City, 3rd Division, 1st Ward, 2nd Enumeration; p. 19;. Genealogical Society of Utah (hereafter cited as GS) microfilm 552,914.

Page No. 19 } ☞ Inquiries numbered 7, 16, and 17 are not to be asked in respect to infants. Inquiries numbered 11, 12, 15, 16, 17, 19, and 20 are to be answered (if at all) merely by an affirmative mark, as /.

Schedule 1.—Inhabitants in 3rd Dist 1st Ward, **in the County of** Philadelphia, **State of** Penna, **enumerated by me on the** 17th **day of** Nov, **1870.**

80

Post Office: Phila Pa

John H Frederick, *Ass't Marshal.*

	Dwelling-houses, numbered in the order of visitation.	Families, numbered in the order of visitation.	The name of every person whose place of abode on the first day of June, 1870, was in this family.	Description: Age at last birth-day. If under 1 year, give months in fractions, thus, 3/12.	Description: Sex.—Males (M.), Females (F.)	Description: Color.—White (W.), Black (B.), Mulatto (M.), Chinese (C.), Indian (I.)	Profession, Occupation, or Trade of each person, male or female.	Value of Real Estate Owned: Value of Real Estate.	Value of Real Estate Owned: Value of Personal Estate.	Place of Birth, naming State or Territory of U. S.; or the Country, if of foreign birth.	Parentage: Father of foreign birth.	Parentage: Mother of foreign birth.	If born within the year, state month (Jan., Feb., &c.)	If married within the year, state month (Jan., Feb., &c.)	Attended school within the year.	Education: Cannot read.	Education: Cannot write.	Whether deaf and dumb, blind, insane, or idiotic.	Constitutional Relations: Male Citizens of U. S. of 21 years of age and upwards.	Constitutional Relations: Male Citizens of U. S. of 21 years of age and upwards, whose right to vote is denied or abridged on other grounds than rebellion or other crime.	
	1	2	3	4	5	6	7	8	9	10	11	12	13	14	15	16	17	18	19	20	
1	727		Friedline Emily	43	F																1
2			Emma	20	F																2
3			Ella	18	F																3
4			Frank	12	M																4
5			Maggie	10	F																5
6	729		Schabacker John	47	M																6
7			Adelaide	43	F																7
8			John	15	M																8
9			Henry	12	M																9
10			Sophia	7	F																10
11			Anna	4	F																11
12			George	2	M																12
13	731		Patton John	35	M																13
14			Agness	22	F																14
15			Joseph	7	M																15
16			Emma	4	F																16
17			John	2	M																17

ther confirmation was needed before accepting this family as ancestral. The first step was to find John Patton in the Philadelphia directories after 1880. We checked the directories through 1888 that were available in Salt Lake City and found these entries:

> 1880 Patton, John Huckster 1321 South 8th St.
> 1881 Patton, John Q.A. Laborer 1321 South 8th St.[6]

This information told us that the family was almost certainly ancestral. The next step was to find this family in the 1870 census, to locate older children, and to estimate a marriage date. These are the entries in the 1869 and 1870 city directories:

> 1869 Patton, John Huckster 731 Medina St.
> 1870 Patton, John Peddlar 731 Medina St.[7]

Since the 1870 census is not indexed, we had to find the ward where Medina Street was located. The directory's street index was organized both by wards and by cross streets. Medina's street directory index was in the first ward. The next step was to search the census itself.

Philadelphia in 1870 had two enumerations, one taken in June and one taken in November. Unlike the first, the second enumeration listed only the population's names, ages, and sex. Also, the street names were written at the top of each page. By reading these street names and the exact house number, the John Patton family was located in the 1870 Philadelphia census without much trouble. (See Figures 11-2, 11-3.)

Once we had found the family in the second enumeration, we searched the first enumeration. Philadelphia's first ward covered an entire microfilm reel, but knowing from the second enumeration that the family lived in the third district of the first ward helped considerably.

Death and Probate Records. When you know that an ancestor died in a large city, you can use his or her presence in a directory to approximate the date of death. This makes voluminous city death and probate records much easier to search. It is often easier, however, to estimate a man's death, since, unlike a recently widowed woman, a widower will not be designated as such. Take care with this method: an individual's nonappearance in a directory does not always indicate death. Sometimes a person will disappear for a year or so and then mysteriously reappear at the same address. More likely than not, the ancestor was there all the time. Remember how the source was compiled. Even today, the general population must cooperate to put together a city directory. The agent or compiler usually leaves a notice on the door if the resident is not home, and not everyone will take the time or trouble to write the information which might be given verbally when the agent calls. The compiler may or may not follow up if it is too costly. Methods in the nineteenth century may have been considerably worse. Therefore, it is best to check directories for a reasonable time period after an individual's first disappearance to determine if that ancestor died or moved away.

Unless a man appears in one directory at a particular street address and his widow appears at the same address in the year following his disappearance, you should not assume that you will find a death or probate record in the year immediately following. This is especially true where older individuals (particularly widows) are involved. They may still be alive and living with children. Nevertheless, even a date with which to begin a death or probate search is valuable.

Figure 11-3. 1870 U.S. Census, Pennsylvania, Philadelphia Co., Philadelphia City, 3rd Division, 1st Ward, 1st Enumeration; p. 68; GS 552,886.

Page No. 68 ; ☞ Inquiries numbered 7, 16, and 17 are not to be asked in respect to infants. Inquiries numbered 11, 12, 15, 16, 17, 19, and 20 are to be answered (if at all) merely by an affirmative mark, as /.

SCHEDULE 1.—Inhabitants in 3rd Div. Philadelphia, in the County of Philada., State of Penna., enumerated by me on the 17th day of June, 1870.

Post Office: 1502 So. 5th St. Phila.

F. L. Taylor, *Ass't Marshal.*

	Dwelling-houses, numbered in the order of visitation.	Families, numbered in the order of visitation.	The name of every person whose place of abode on the first day of June, 1870, was in this family.	Description: Age at last birthday. If under 1 year, give months in fractions, thus, 3/12.	Description: Sex.—Males (M.), Females (F.)	Description: Color.—White (W.), Black (B.), Mulatto (M.), Chinese (C.), Indian (I.)	Profession, Occupation, or Trade of each person, male or female.	Value of Real Estate Owned: Value of Real Estate.	Value of Real Estate Owned: Value of Personal Estate.	Place of Birth, naming State or Territory of U. S.; or the Country, if of foreign birth.	Parentage: Father of foreign birth.	Parentage: Mother of foreign birth.	If born within the year, state month (Jan., Feb., &c.)	If married within the year, state month (Jan., Feb., &c.)	Attended school within the year.	Education: Cannot read.	Education: Cannot write.	Whether deaf and dumb, blind, insane, or idiotic.	Constitutional Relations: Male Citizens of U. S. of 21 years of age and upwards.	Constitutional Relations: Male Citizens of U. S. of 21 years of age and upwards, whose right to vote is denied or abridged on other grounds than rebellion or other crime.	
	1	2	3	4	5	6	7	8	9	10	11	12	13	14	15	16	17	18	19	20	
1			Fredline Maggie	10	F	W				Penna					/						1
2	485	523	Schabacker John	46	M	W	Tailor	1200	200	Hesse Cassel	/	/							/		2
3			—— Margaret	42	F	W	Keeping House			Hanover	/	/									3
4			—— John	14	M	W	App to Brick Making			Penna	/	/									4
5			—— Henry	11	M	W				Penna	/	/			/						5
6			—— Sophia	6	F	W				Penna	/	/									6
7			—— Anne	4	F	W				Penna	/	/									7
8			—— George	1	M	W				Penna	/	/									8
9	486	524	Patton John	28	M	W	Huckster		200	Penna	/	/				/	/		/		9
10			—— Agnes B.	22	F	W	Keeping House			Penna	/	/									10
11			—— Joseph	6	M	W				Penna							X				11
12			—— Emma	3	F	W				Penna											12
13			—— John	2	M	W				Penna											13
14			Gibson Sallie	25	F	W	Seamstress			Penna	/	/									14
15	487	525	Brown Margaret	37	F	W	Tailoress		200	Ireland	/	/									15
16			—— Mary E.	7	F	W				Penna	/	/			/						16
17			—— Simon	2	M	W				Penna	/	/									17
18			Smith Ann	60	F	W	Keeping House			Ireland	/	/				/	/	—			18

For example, James Renwick and Ellen/Helen Gibson were married in Scotland in 1814. They had three known children: Andrew, born 1815; Alexander, born 1818; and Marion, born 1820. Sometime between 1820 and 1840 they immigrated to New York City (Manhattan). We found James in the 1840 census. In the 1850 Manhattan census, Ellen was living alone, presumably as a widow. A search of *Doggett's New York City Directories 1845-46* and *1846-47* (New York: John Doggett, Jr.), pp. 302 and 326 respectively, revealed the following entries:

1845-46	*1846-47*
Renwick Alexander, stonecutter, 400 Washington	Renwick Ellen, widow James, boarding, 400 Washington
Renwick James, boarding, 400 Washington	

We can draw several conclusions from these entries. In 1845-46 there are two entries for a James Renwick. Additional research showed that Alexander, the son, was a mason. An Alexander Renwick, stonecutter, also appears at the 400 Washington Street address. Thus it is probable that the James Renwick at that address is the ancestor. We verified this conclusion with the 1846-47 directory. Although neither Alexander nor James appears, the entry for "Renwick Ellen, widow James, boarding 400 Washington" indicated that James had died sometime between 1845 and 1846. We knew from previous research that Alexander had moved to Pittsburgh by this time.

Manhattan death registers also exist for this time period. These records are arranged alphabetically by the first letter of each surname for each year. To search the entire 1840-50 decade would be tedious and time-consuming. A search in the 1845 death registers quickly yielded this entry:

5 June 1845
James Renwick, age 59
400 Washington St.
Disease of Heart
Place of burial: Scotch Presbyterian Cemetery
Sexton: C. A. Stewart[8]

As it turned out, this record quickly and efficiently provided the only mention of James Renwick's age at a given date.

Church Records. You can use city directories to gain access to church records. In most major cities, civil marriage records have existed longer than in rural areas. In Philadelphia, for example, civil marriages have been recorded since 1860, while in the rest of Pennsylvania the normal starting date is 1885. Similarly, Pittsburgh records begin in 1875. Since there was little governmental apparatus to record marriages effectively, it was up to the clergyman who performed the service to return the information to the city authorities. In states where marriages were recorded at the county level, large cities benefited from this registration by being included on the county level.

Whatever the circumstances under which marriages were recorded, the information given is very similar: the names of the bride and groom, the license date, the marriage date, sometimes names of witnesses, and almost always the name of the clergyman or magistrate who performed the marriage.

For example, according to Philadelphia's 1900 census, Christian and Sophia Hochwald had been married for thirty-eight years.[9] Christian had lived in Philadelphia before this date, so a check in the marriage registers might determine Sophia Hochwald's maiden name. The microfilm copy of the Board of Health Marriage Registers for 1862 was extremely faded but clear enough to identify Christian Hochwald's marriage date as 3 May 1862.[10] Unfortunately, the bride's name was illegible.

Reverend G. Wiehle performed the marriage, and his address was 531 St. John Street. The Philadelphia city directories showed that this man was the pastor of the Salem German Reformed Church on St. John Street.[11] Now a check in church records can be made for this couple's marriage, membership, and children's baptisms.

Naturalization and Land Records. It may seem odd to group naturalization and land records, but methodologically they are very similar. They both reflect the parameters of residence in an area. If a person owned a home in a city, there should be some record of its purchase when the family moved into the city and its sale when the family changed residences or moved out of the city. Finding the first and last years of residence narrows down the search for these land records, which in a city like New York or Boston, can be voluminous.

Similarly, finding an immigrant's first year of residence in a city narrows down the naturalization records you'll have to search. In cases where these records are indexed, knowing that one of two naturalized immigrants of the same name lived in the city before the other may differentiate the two.

Remember James Renwick? He appeared in the city directories of New York back to 1833.[12] According to New York City naturalization records, he made his declaration of intention 3 February 1835.[13] During that time period, declarations were usually filed after three years of residence; the information in James Renwick's case corresponds nicely with his residence in New York City. He may have arrived too late in 1832 for that year's directory.

Renwick is an uncommon name, but this method, for both land and naturalization records, also works well when the surname involved is more common and differentiation using auxilliary sources is necessary.

Problems Special to City Directories

Surprisingly, access is not a big problem with directories. An agent in Washington, D.C., can use those in the Library of Congress, and the same method applies where a particular state historical society or a local public library is concerned.

All of the general problems with directories apply to city directories; but in the area of completeness, the problem of jurisdiction seems peculiar to city directories.

Particularly in the second half of the nineteenth century, cities continually annexed territory from surrounding townships. You have to study the area history to know what parts of a city were previously under different jurisdictions. Pittsburgh provides a case in point. Before the 1850s the south side of the Monongahela River was all part of Lower Saint Clair Township. Beginning in that decade, as the population of Pittsburgh spilled over the river, independent boroughs were created. Eventually, boroughs with names like South Pittsburgh, Birmingham, East Birmingham, and Ormsby dwarfed Lower Saint Clair Township. Ormsby was created in 1869 and lasted only until 1872, when all of the south side was incorporated into the city of Pittsburgh. People continued to call it "Pittsburgh, South Side" – so individuals who were later married or died in Pittsburgh often wrote "South Side" as their birthplace. For pre-1872 censuses, you will need to determine which borough they resided in. The Pittsburgh city directories often abbreviate the names of the boroughs in the listings and shorten your search time.

To determine jurisdictional changes where boroughs are not listed, consult city and county histories. Also check the descriptive notes at the beginning of city directories themselves.

Source Locations. You can find city directories in almost every library in the nation. Go first to the public library nearest the place you are researching; if you can't travel there, phone its reference desk. Most libraries, historical societies, and archives on the state level will have a fairly extensive collection of in-state directories and may also have directories from major out-of-state cities. The reference librarian may be willing to photocopy the pages you need and send them to you. Reference staffs are quite busy, however, so a letter may be better if you're not in a hurry.

On the national level, the Library of Congress in Washington, D.C., and the American Antiquarian Society in Worcester, Massachusetts, contain major collections of directories. The Library of Congress also has microfilm copies of all of the directories available at the American Antiquarian Society through the efforts of Research Publications, Inc., which completed the first segment of its three-phase project early in 1967, by microfilming city directories through 1860 listed in Spear's bibliography, including the collection of the American Antiquarian Society, whose collection contains almost two-thirds of Spear's titles. Almost one hundred libraries contributed one or more additional directories. Of Spear's almost 1600 titles, all but forty-five were filmed, a completion record of better than 97 percent.

Positive response to the first segment encouraged microfilming city directories for 1861-81. To keep the project manageable, it was limited to the fifty largest cities of the period, with some others added for regional representation. Research Publications, Inc., used the collection of the American Antiquarian Society, created its own bibliography, and arranged for filming.

The third segment covers the same cities and uses the same format but extends coverage from 1881 to 1901. The editors note: "During the period included, and running through the years covered by Segment 3, the city directories were printed on very poor paper. Many of the directories are literally falling to pieces. The microfilm collection will insure continued availability and access to this important research source."[14]

For further information and orders, write:

Customer Order Dept.
Research Publications, Inc.
12 Lunar Drive
New Haven, CT 06525

The Genealogical Society of Utah also has microform copies of directories for most of these major cities up to 1901.

If you can't locate the directory you want through any of the above places, you may need to write to or visit a private directory library maintained by the publishing companies. You will find private directories libraries for the following companies. Check the yellow pages for specific locations.

Burch Directory Company
Akron, Ohio

Calkin-Kelly Directory Company
Binghamton, New York

Cleveland Directory Company
Cleveland, Ohio

Hill Directory Company
Richmond, Virginia

Hudspeth Directory Company
El Paso, Texas

H. A. Manning Company
Schenectady, New York

R. L. Polk and Company:
Boston, Massachusetts
Chicago, Illinois
Columbus, Ohio
Dallas, Texas
Denver, Colorado
Detroit, Michigan
Honolulu, Hawaii
Kansas City, Missouri
Monterey Park, California
New York City, New York
Philadelphia, Pennsylvania
St. Louis, Missouri
St. Paul, Minnesota
Salt Lake City, Utah
Seattle, Washington
Washington, D.C.

Tower Directory Company
Portland, Maine

Williams Directory Company
Cincinnatti, Ohio

Wright Directory Company
Milwaukee, Wisconsin

County and Regional Business Directories

Business directories as a distinct entity evolved partly from the special sections in city directories and partly from the needs of people in sparsely populated rural areas to communicate their services to one another. Because the rural economy often centered on the county seat, these early business directories were usually organized by county. In addition to the names of farmers and businessmen, they contained advertisements of goods and services; and although they were primarily business oriented, they also served as general directories in those rural areas. Much like a modern almanac, they often included other useful information.

A regional (multi-county, state, or market area) business directory combines a city directory's specialized business sections with a county directory's wide geographic market coverage. As communications developed, nineteenth century manufacturers, farmers, and service-oriented businesses found that directories covering more than their own county were quite useful and even necessary. These regional business directories vary in comprehensiveness. The earlier ones, often called "advertising directories," mention only those businesses which could afford to be included. By the late 1800s, however, statewide business directories listed nearly every place and a variety of businesses from farming to pharmacy.

The information obtained from a county or regional business directory helps locate people in place and time. County business directories which include farmers, like city directories, narrow down census searches to specific townships. This is especially useful when the ancestor married someone from another township in the same county. Some county business directories also contain dates and places of birth, dates of marriage, length of residence in the town, names of children, and other biographical details on their subjects as well as names.

You can use regional business directories in the same way. If you know which state the ancestor lived in but not the exact place, regional directories can help, although they are less likely to give such extensive biographical information, and their coverage may be limited.

How to Use County and Regional Business Directories

The 1869-70 gazetteer and business directory of Monroe County, New York, is a typical county business directory. On the left page are four advertisements, directed to a rural market. On the right page the residents of rural Henrietta Township are listed alphabetically. (See Figure 11-4.) The information following each name, when properly interpreted, is very enlightening.

For example, the entry on Alvy Remington tells us that his post office was West Henrietta and thus the closest settlement as well. His land was in lot 10, range 6, according to the township and range system of surveying. (See Chapter 7 on land records.) By occupation he was a farmer and owned ninety-five acres. If he had leased his land, it would have been indicated.

There are three other Remingtons in Henrietta in this directory: George T., Seth W., and William T. Without knowing anything about the family, one could conclude that there is some relationship between Alvy, Seth, and William on the basis of the lot and range information. In fact, William and Seth were Alvah (the correct spelling) Remington's sons. A bit of family history can also be gleaned: William had fifty-seven acres, the directory tells us, while Seth had only one. Thomas Remington, Alvah's father, originally purchased

Figure 11-4. Hamilton Child, *The Gazetteer and Business Directory of Monroe County, New York for 1869-1870* (Rochester: Erastus Darrow, 1870), p. 195.

Quirk, Mathew, (Brighton,) lot 11, R. 6, farmer 72.
Raas, Frederick, (West Henrietta,) lot 25, R. 5, farmer 23.
Raynor, Leonard, (West Henrietta,) lot 12, R. 6, farmer leases 90.
REEVE, JOHN, (Henrietta,)(*with Thomas,*) lot 22, R. 1, farmer 340.
Reeve, Thomas, (Henrietta,) (*with John,*) lot 22, R. 1, farmer 340.
Reeves, George, (West Brighton,) lot 1, R. 3, farmer 1¼.
Remington, Alvy, (West Henrietta,) lot 10, R. 6, farmer 95.
Remington, George T., (Henrietta,) lot 22, R. 2, farmer 11.
Remington, Seth W., (West Henrietta,) lot 10, R. 6, farmer 1.
Remington, William T., (West Henrietta,) lot 10, R. 6, farmer 57.
Renner, John, (West Brighton,) lot 3, R. 5, farmer 21.
Richardson, David H., (Henrietta,) lot 10, R. 3, farmer 180.
Roberts, George M. C., (Henrietta,) lot 11, R. 3, farmer leases 116.
Sherman, Oliver B., (West Henrietta,) lot 25, R. 4, farmer 100.
Shilling, Frederick, (West Henrietta,) lot 23, R. 6, farmer 35.
Sholts, Henry, (West Brighton,) lot 4, R. 5, farmer 63.
Short, Andrew, (Henrietta,) lot 15, R. 3, farmer 34.
Sibbey, Elisha, (Henrietta,) lot 16, R. 1, farmer 99.
SIBLEY, ELISHA, (North Rush,) lot 18, Scott Tract, farmer 106.
SIMMONS, EDWARD, (Henrietta,) lot 16, R. 3.
Sipperly, John, (Henrietta,) lot 19, R. 2, farmer 50.
Skilton, William, (Henrietta,) lot 17, R. 1, farmer 30.
Slade, Hannah Mrs., (Henrietta,) lot 15, farmer 50.
Slow, Jacob, (West Henrietta,) lot 22, R. 5, wagon maker.
Smith, Charles J., (West Henrietta,) lot 31, R. 4, farmer 80.
Smith, David, (Henrietta,) lot 2, R. 2, retired farmer 80.

lot ten, range six, in the 1820s. Alvah bought out his brothers and sisters and then distributed the land among his own children. The fact that Seth had only one acre in 1870 helps clarify the relationship between father and son: When Alvah died in 1888, he left nothing to Seth's children because Seth had been unable to pay back a debt to his father before he died in 1885.

One of the earliest regional directories is *The American Advertising Directory Manufacturers and Dealers in American Goods for the Year 1831*. Most of the listings are in the northeast manufacturing area, but places as far (that is, for 1831) from the East Coast as Nashville, Tennessee, had at least one listing. This contrasts starkly with the *New Mexico Business Directory* for 1907-08, which mentions every city, town, and village in New Mexico as well as El Paso, Texas, and Denver, Colorado. The town of Central had 450 inhabitants, but only fifteen entries were given:

CENTRAL.

Postoffice and important town in Grant county, 9 miles east of Silver City, the most convenient railroad point. Mining, stockraising, farming and fruitgrowing the principal industries. Population 450.

Bayard Smelting & Mining Co, W D Murray mgr.
Crowley J, postmaster, justice peace, drugs.
GOULD BROS, general merchandise.
Hamilton A, mines and mining.
Helde Mrs G W, millinery and dressmaker.
Link B T, fruitgrower and dairy.
McMillen Geo, mines and mining.
MURRAY BROS, general merchandise.
MONTGOMERY & DALRYMPLE, meat market.
Reed Mrs W, restaurant.
Rendall L G, notary public.
Rodgers Clark, fruitgrower.
Stephens Chas, fruitgrower.
SWEENEY W H, general merchandise.
Wiley J A, saloon.

New Mexico Business Directory . . . 1907-1908 (Denver: The Gazetteer Publishing Co., 1907), p. 217.

The postmaster was also the justice of the peace and pharmacist for the town. The directory does not list the men who worked on the fruit farms and in the mines.

Special Problems

Business directories are limited in that every editor selects which businesses to include. If your ancestor was a businessman, but not mentioned, this does not mean that he wasn't there.

Another problem with regional directories is availability. These directories seem to have been published much less regularly than the yearly city directories; consequently, they may be harder to find.

Source Locations. If you're looking for a particular business directory, the best place to start is the local public library in that area. State libraries also have excellent collections of local and regional business directories. Both the Library of Congress and the Genealogical Society of Utah have such directories, but the collection of the Library of Congress is more comprehensive. A list of the Library of Congress's directories as of 1931 was printed in *The American Genealogist*, vol. 13, pp. 51-53, and reprinted in Colleen Neal's *Lest We Forget: A Guide to Genealogical Research in the Nation's Capital* (Annandale, Va.: n. pub., 1982). Since these business directories were often published by the same companies that published city directories, private directory libraries should also be consulted.

Professional Directories

The late nineteenth-century business directory, as we might expect, coincided with a proliferation in specialized professions. As the *Directory of Directories* can attest, the number of professional directories at present is astounding. For pre-1920 research, however, we will consider only law, medicine, civil and military service, and a category called miscellaneous. We will consider each of these professions separately due to the different circumstances under which each directory was published. Since the use and problems of professional directories are generally similar, these will be considered together with exceptions noted where appropriate.

Law

The *Directory of Directories* describes law directories like this:

> Background: 'Law Lists' refers to a group of directories which provide varying amounts of information about lawyers, and which were formerly certified by a committee of the American Bar Association as being ethically appropriate sources in which lawyers could make known their availability for consultation. As a result of the United States Supreme Court decision in 1977 governing advertising by lawyers and subsequent actions by the ABA, the Standing Committee on Law Lists no longer certifies law lists, state or national, as being in compliance with any rules or standards. (In response to requests for guidance from some states, the committee prepared proposed guidelines for state regulation of law lists which were submitted to committees of the ABA and reported to the ABA House of Delegates in August 1979.) About sixty law lists were formerly certified by the committee and described in the 'Directory Information Service.' These listings, revised as needed, are

continued in this volume. The law list which has operated longest under a single title is 'Campbell's List,' established in 1879. 'Martindale-Hubbell Law Directory,' resulted from a merger of 'Martindale's American Law Directory,' founded in 1868, and 'Hubbell's Legal Directory,' founded 1870; it is currently the largest of the law lists and among the most highly regarded. Covers: Martindale-Hubbell, a national list, and the state and regional directories published by the Legal Directories Publishing Company, Inc., are the only comprehensive law lists which include every attorney nationally or in an area. There are no law lists which attempt to include every attorney in a special field. In fact, the essence of the appeal of law lists is exclusivity: all lists charge fees for inclusion (usually based on the population of the area where a given attorney practices, and ranging to $600 or more), except [that] comprehensive lists include a minimum listing without a fee; many lists operate on the basis of 'exclusive representation,' i.e., they list only one firm in a given locality. A few, such as the 'Rand McNally List of Bank-Recommended Attorneys,' operate on the basis of recommendations or sponsorships. Some lists use rating systems, and firms listed are coded for ability, diligence, etc., as evaluated by peers. Entries include: Even within a single law list, entries may run from a brief name-and-address notation to one or two pages or more, depending upon the size of the firm and how much it is willing to spend for its listing. In a typical full entry, a firm name, address, and phone will be given along with names and backgrounds of partners and names of typical clients; associates may also be listed. Many lists include uniformly less data. Arrangement: The most frequent use of a law list is in finding a lawyer in a location where the user has no contacts. Therefore, nearly all law lists are geographical in arrangement. Indexes: Alphabetical indexes by personal name may or may not be provided. Price: Part of the service provided by law list publishers is the free distribution of their lists to lawyers listed and to others who can be assumed to be users of the services of lawyers listed. There is no ethical restriction on the sale of law lists, but it was the experience of the DOD staff in compiling law list material that many publishers are not anxious to give laypersons information about their publications or to promote commerical sales; whether this lack of cooperation resulted from a desire to enhance the exclusive image of their lists or for other reasons is not clear.[15]

Law directories are generally arranged state by state and are frequently not indexed. In the past, law directories could generally be found on the local and state level. In areas where such regional directories are not available prior to the advent of the national directories in the 1870s, you can usually find lawyers in general business directories. Most law directories today are national-level directories, but there are still some on the state and local level, particularly in the large metropolitan areas.

Law directories locate an individual in place and time for purposes of gaining access to, or linking with, other sources, including other directories. Other significant data may include the law school graduated from, or, in cases where law was read, the state in which the lawyer was first admitted to the bar. You may also find other biographical information which will help you trace the individual lawyer's career and suggest other records to search.

Source Locations. All law libraries should have at least one current law directory. How many—if any—back issues are kept and for how far back depends on the individual library and its storage capabilities. Even if the library has kept old directories, access to them may be limited. Large public libraries often keep back issues for reference. You might also find law directories through local and state bar associations. Again, whether they have back issues may depend on their space limitations. The American Bar Association has not kept past directories since 1981.

The Library of Congress has a complete set of the Martindale-Hubbell Directory from 1931 on. The library has only sporadic copies of earlier issues with the earliest Hubbell directory being 1871, and the earliest Martindale-Hubbell directory being 1885.

The publishing companies themselves maintain libraries, but access is a problem. They may share the *Directory of Directories* (DOD) reluctance to sell their directories to lay people or to assist genealogists with research questions. Undoubtedly, the best approach is a specific written request; if they don't respond, follow with a telephone call. Don't be surprised if they refuse to help. The publisher's librarian is often quite busy. The addresses of the two oldest law list compilers are:

Martindale-Hubbell Inc. One Prospect Street Summit, NJ 07901	Campbell's List Inc. Campbell Building Maitland, FL 32751

Medicine

The American Medical Directory, published under the auspices of the American Medical Association, has only existed since 1906. Unlike law directories, it is published erratically, so that a complete collection may not cover every year since 1906. The directory is arranged by state, and the later editions also contain alphabetical listings. Before 1906 medical directories were published by private companies or by local and state medical associations. Some city directories contained separate lists for doctors, and doctors were listed in general business directories as well.

The *American Medical Directory* presently contains the following information: name, address, year licensed, medical school, type of practice, primary and secondary specialties, and board certifications. Some of the earlier editions also contain year of birth and year graduated from medical school.

Medical directories will help you locate a person in place and time and will provide links with other sources.

Source Locations. Medical school libraries should have the most current edition of the *American Medical Directory* readily available. Your access to back issues may depend on the individual library's policy. The Eccles Health Science Library at the University of Utah medical school keeps a complete collection of the directory available to the general public. Local and state medical associations may also maintain old directories, including those published on a regional level.

R. L. Polk published a *Medical and Surgical Register* of the United States and Canada which was in its fifth edition by 1898. You may have a hard time finding early issues of this register; the Library of Congress does not seem to have any. But, as a last resort, try sending a letter to one of the R. L. Polk libraries listed in the section on city directories.

The Library of Congress maintains a complete collection of the *American Medical Directory*. If you can't get to a large medical library, consider sending a letter to the current publisher of the *American Medical Directory*:

PSG Publishing Co., Inc.
545 Great Road
Littleton, MA 01460

Civil and Military Service Directories

In 1816, Congress passed a bill providing for the biennial publication of a register "containing correct lists of all the officers and agents, civil, military, and naval, in the service of the United States." This list contained the individual's name and office, pay, place of birth, and place of residence. In 1851, the state from which the person was appointed was added.[16]

Although the main register of government civil servants contained the names of military and naval officers, separate registers for these two services were also eventually published. These registers are considerably more detailed than the general register. They contain the date of enlistment or entry into the service and the date the most recent rank was achieved. These army and navy registers include officers only.

The general register is arranged alphabetically. The army register is arranged by regiment, with a name index and a list of where each regiment was stationed in the year of publication. The Navy register is arranged by ship rather than regiment and includes the location of each ship. The Marine Corps is listed in the navy register.

The resolution further provided that the registers should be current as of 30 September the year preceding the publication date. Thus, the civil register for 1864 reflects information collected in 1863.

Army and navy registers accounted for regular (career) service only. An ancestor known to be an officer in the Civil War may not be listed if he was part of the volunteer army. In addition, the state of birth and state from which he was appointed are invaluable as links to other sources when service records are not readily available.

The government of the United States has probably generated more paper than any single organization in the history of this country. If an ancestor worked for the government, there should be a record of it somewhere. These registers can connect you with those records when more specific information than "he worked for the government" or "he was an army officer" is available.

Source Locations. According to the 1816 bill, twenty-five copies of the register were to be deposited in the Library of Congress. In 1851, a provision was added which allowed for a copy to be sent to each Secretary of State. Presumably the Library of Congress and state libraries and archives contain copies today.

The Library of Congress has apparently transferred the older registers to the National Archives, but you should check both repositories. State libraries and archives may not have kept all of the registers from each year, so there may be gaps. States in the former Confederacy may not have copies of the registers for 1861-65.

Miscellaneous Professions

Directories dated earlier than 1920 exist for a number of professions. R. L. Polk published the following directories:

Dental Register of the United States
Architects and Builders' Directory of the United States
Marine Directory of the Great Lakes
Ohio Architects and Builders' Directory
Pennsylvania Architects and Builders' Directory
Western New York Architects and Builders' Directory

The Library of Congress has these early professional directories: *The Dentist Register* (1879); *Banker's Almanac and Year Book* (1844); *Rand McNally Banker's Blue Book* (1872); *Polk's World Bank Directory* (1895). Perhaps the best way to find out whether a professional directory exists prior to 1920 is to find that profession in the *Directory of Directories* and contact the publisher. One directory which has been published only since 1932 is nevertheless relevant to pre-1920 research: *The American Blue Book of Funeral Directors*, published every two years. Any professional directory will locate an ancestor in time and place, but the funeral directors' bluebook will let you trace a funeral home to the present day and, where it has gone out of business, perhaps determine the successor and thus where the records might be. A funeral home in business in 1932 may have existed for fifty years and, in a given community, its records could almost substitute for death registers.

Source Locations. The Library of Congress and local and state archives will probably have some directories relevant to their areas of interest. If you can find a publisher of pre-1920 professional directories who is still in business today, see if it maintains a directory library. The publisher of *The American Blue Book of Funeral Directors* is:

Kates-Boylston Publications
1501 Broadway
New York, NY 10036

How to Use Professional Directories

Here are two examples relevant to your use of various professional directories:

The ancestor in question was known to be a doctor in the New York City area about 1910. The *American Medical Directory* for 1909 had an alphabetical listing, and Lucy Criddle Jones was easily located in its New York City section.

JONES, CATESBY⊕—Md.1,'93; 7 E. 32d St.; 9-1, 4-5.
JONES, CHAS. NOALE DIXON⊕—N.Y.1,'83; 601 W. 179th St.; 8-10, 6-7; Or.
JONES, DAVID H. (b 1874)⊕-N.Y.5,'97; 215 W. 101st St.; 12-1, 4-7:30.
Jones, Henry Woodward (b 1847)—Mich.7,'74; 301 W. 107th St.
Jones, Horace Loomis—Pa.2,'81; 126 W. 127th St.; 7-9, 6-8.
JONES, ISRAEL C.⊕—O.9,'74; Home for Incurables, Fordham; until 10.
Jones, Leonard W.—Ont.5,'02; office, Manhattan Eye and Ear Hospital.
JONES, LUCY CRIDDLE (b 1872)⊕—N.Y.15,'98; 212 E. 53d St.; 12-1:30, 6-7.
Jones, Robt. Mortimer — H — N.Y.9,'06 136 Madison Ave.; 11-1, 5-6; ALR.
Jones, Roland D.—Pa.1,'81; 56 E. 59th St.; 9-1.
JONES, S. BEACH — N.Y.1,'72; Park Ave. and 62d St.; 12-1; N.
Jones, Walter Hastings—H—N.Y.9,'86; The Ansonia, 73d St. and Broadway; 9-10, 1-2, 5-6.
Jones, Wm. Fredk.—Vt.2,'83; 323 W. 19th St.; 8-9, 1-2, 6-8.
JONES, WM. J., Jr. — N.Y.20,'99; 238 W. 118th St.; 5-7.

American Medical Directory, 1909, 3rd ed. (Chicago: American Medical Association Press, 1909), p. 799.

This listing tells us that Lucy Criddle Jones was born in 1872, that she graduated from Syracuse University Medical School in 1898, and that in 1909 she lived at 212 East 53rd Street. (Offices separate from home addresses are indicated.) From this information, I could make positive identification in the census and also start looking up medical school records.

In the second example, Figure 11-5, Robert Nelson Eagle was known to have been a lieutenant in the U.S. Army before the Civil War, and there was a tradition that he had served with Robert E. Lee. Starting with the Army Register for 1860, I found Eagle serving with the Second Regiment of Cavalry, of which Robert E. Lee was lieutenant colonel. Eagle had entered the service as a first lieutenant on 3 March 1855. He was born in New York but appointed from Texas. Since the register also gave the location of the Second Regiment in 1860, I could consult the 1860 census as well as military records.

College-Related Directories

Like professional directories, organizational directories are highly specialized and suited to the needs of a particular organization. Two examples of such directories are university alumni directories and fraternity directories.

These sorts of directories may not be published yearly and may not appear in the *Directory of Directories*. You may even have to locate a directory of organizations to find a specific directory for the particular organization in which you are interested. In some cases, an organizational directory will not tell you the names of its members but may provide the addresses of various branches to which you can write. This would be helpful in cases where an ancestor belonged to an organization in the 1800s that is no longer active and for which you must locate records. The kind of information given in an organizational directory can range from a mere address to dates of membership, or birth and death.

16	SECOND REGIMENT OF CAVALRY.						
NAME.	Rank in the Reg't.	Rank in the Army.		Original entry into service.		Born in.	
Colonel.							
Albert S. Johnston,	3 Mar. 55	B. G. bvt.	18 Nov. 57	(d) Bvt. 2 lt. 2 inf.	1 July, 26	Ky.	T
Lieutenant Colonel.							
Robert E. Lee,	3 Mar. 55	Col. bvt.	13 Sept. 47	Bvt. 2 lt. eng.	1 July, 29	Va.	V
Majors.							
William J. Hardee,	3 Mar. 55	L. C. bvt.	20 Aug. 47	2 lt. 2 drag.	1 July, 38	Ga.	G
		Comm't cadets, M. A. with loc. rank of L. C.					
George H. Thomas,	12 May, 55	Bvt.	23 Feb. 47	2 lt. 3 art.	1 July, 40	Va.	V
Captains.							
Earl Van Dorn,	3 Mar. 55	M. bvt.	20 Aug. 47	Bvt. 2 lt. 7 inf.	1 July, 42	Miss.	M
Edmund K. Smith,	3 Mar.	Bvt.	20 Aug.	Bvt. 2 lt. 5 inf.	1 July, 45	Fla.	Fl
James Oakes,	3 Mar.	Bvt.	8 Sept.	Bvt. 2 lt. 2 drag.	1 July, 46	Pa.	Pa
Innis N. Palmer,	3 Mar.	Bvt.	13 Sept.	Bvt. 2 lt. m. rifles,	1 July,	N. Y.	N.
George Stoneman,	3 Mar.			Bvt. 2 lt. 1 drag.	1 July,	N. Y.	N.
William R. Bradfute,*	3 Mar.			Capt.	3 Mar. 55	Tenn.	Te
Albert G. Brackett,*	3 Mar.			Capt.	3 Mar.	N. Y.	In
Charles J. Whiting,	3 Mar.			(e) Bvt. 2 lt. 2 art.	1 July, 35	Mass.	Ca
Nathan G. Evans,	1 May, 56			Bvt. 2 lt. 1 drag.	1 July, 48	S. C.	S.
Richard W. Johnson,	1 Dec.			Bvt. 2 lt. 6 inf.	1 July, 49	Ky.	Ky
First Lieutenants.							
Joseph H. McArthur,	3 Mar. 55			Bvt. 2 lt. 2 inf.	1 July, 49	Mo.	M
Charles W. Field,	3 Mar.			Bvt. 2 lt. 2 drag.	1 July,	Ky.	Ky
Kenner Garrard,	3 Mar.			Bvt. 2 lt. 4 art.	1 July, 51	Ky.	Oh
Walter H. Jenifer,*	3 Mar.			(f) 1 lt. 3 drag.	9 Apr. 47	Md.	M
William B. Royall,*	3 Mar.			1 lt.	3 Mar. 55	Va.	M
William P. Chambliss,*	3 Mar.			1 lt.	3 Mar.	Va.	Te
Robert Nelson Eagle,*	3 Mar.			1 lt.	3 Mar.	N. Y.	Te
John T. Shaaff,	1 May, 56			Bvt. 2 lt. 6 inf.	1 July, 51	D. C.	D.
George B. Cosby,	1 May,			Bvt. 2 lt. m. rifles,	1 July, 52	Ky.	Ky
William W. Lowe,	1 Dec.	Adjt.	31 May, 58	Bvt. 2 lt. 2 drag.	1 July, 53	Ind.	Io
John B. Hood,	18 Aug. 58			Bvt. 2 lt. 4 inf.	1 July,	Ky.	Ky

Figure 11-5. Adjutant General's Office, *Official Army Register for 1860* (Washington, D.C.: Government Press, 1860), p. 16.

How to Use This Source

Here is an example of the joint use of two organizational directories. A modern descendant of the Weed family discovers an old fraternity pin in the attic, bearing the Greek letters *Alpha Delta Phi*. On the back of the pin, the initials H.A.W. have been inscribed. Some time ago, it so happened that this family moved to the West Coast from New York and lost all touch with the family in the East. In fact, Grandpa Weed had been reluctant to talk about his ancestors beyond the information that "they came from New York."

Seizing on this artifact as a potential key to the Weed family mysteries, the modern Weed tries to locate information on H.A.W. His best approach would be to find some list of past fraternity members, but there was none listed in the *Directory of Directories* at the local library. There was, however, a listing for *Baird's Manual of American College Fraternities*. Upon calling the publisher (the local library did not have this source), the modern Weed obtains—not without difficulty—the information needed. The publisher would rather have sold him the book than have given out free the address of the Alpha Delta Phi Fraternity Alumni Association. After Weed sends a request for information, the Alumni Association sent him this copy of the following page from the 1966 *Catalogue of the Alpha Delta Phi*:

1836

•Hillyer, Giles Mumford
•Hobart, John Henry
•Jay, John
•McVickar, Henry
•Ward, Henry, Jr.
•Waters, George Gilfert
•Weed, Harvey Augustus

1837

•Aldis, Charles
•Blatchford, Samuel
•Chittenden, Nathaniel William
•Fessenden, Henry Partridge
•Halsey, Anthony
•Leggett, William Henry
•MacMullen, John
•Tucker, John Ireland
•Vanderbilt, John, Jr.
•Whitlock, Samuel H.

Executive Council of the Alpha Delta Phi, *Catalogue of the Alpha Delta Phi, 1832-1866*, (New York: Alpha Delta Phi, 1966), p. 101.

A letter accompanying the page indicated that this was the only Weed with the initials H.A. in the general index to the catalog, which also listed him as deceased.

This information led Weed to examine the *Columbia University Alumni Register*, which revealed that although Harvey Augustus Weed did indeed graduate in 1836, he went on to receive a higher degree in 1839.

1910, 634 Lenox Av Westfield NJ, *bank*
Weed, Edgar Theodore MD 1881, 39 W 87 NYC
Weed, Edwin Dunning AB 1894, 2218 E 1 Duluth Minn, *clergy*
Weed, Eleanor Hill (see Sharp, Eleanor Weed)
Weed, Ethel Georgine AM 1906, Maplewood NJ
Weed, G B ent 1834 P&S, decd.
Weed, Harvey Augustus AB 1836, AM 1839 C, d. 1872
Weed, John W ent 1819 P&S, decd.
Weed, John Waring LLB 1868, d. Nov 7, 1915
Weed, Lowry Albert AB 1916 (cl 1914). Internat'l Composition Co 25 Broadway NYC

The Committee on [the] General Catalogue, *Columbia University Alumni Register, 1754-1931* (New York: Columbia University Press, 1932), p. 931.

The register also indicated that H. A. Weed died in 1872. Without knowing his exact date of birth, the modern Weed estimated, based on the date of Harvey's first degree, that Harvey was in his late forties when he died. Grandpa Weed had been born in 1870; perhaps this was the reason he knew little of his past. With the information from the *Alumni Register*, the modern Weed checked Columbia University's records, and these allowed him to extend the line by linking it with other sources.

Special Problems

Locating directories is the major problem. Since many of them are published after the fact, that is, they are really books which contain membership lists since the organization's inception, more recent copies may be just as valuable as earlier copies. Check the organization itself and the Library of Congress first, then go to major university and public libraries in the same area where the school is located.

Religious Directories

The original religious directories were books containing directions for the order of public or private worship. As time passed, some denominational directories began to include lists of clergy and/or churches. Eventually the listings outweighed the directions, and these books became directories in the modern sense. Some denominational directories have dropped all statements of creed, such as *The Official Catholic Directory*, first published in 1817. Religious directories may also be called registers, annuals, and yearbooks. The information they include differs from denomination to denomination, the minimum amount being the name of the church and its pastor.

The information contained in religious directories is significant in two ways. If the ancestor was a clergyman, they can guide you to the places of service. This is especially true in the case of itinerant ministers; religious directories narrow down these ministers' assigned working areas. Also, like funeral directories, religious directories may suggest where the ancestor worshipped and where to find the contemporary records.

How to Use Religious Directories

Suppose the ancestor was a Baptist in Rochester, New York, in the first half of the nineteenth century. *The American Baptist Register* for 1852 shows four Baptist churches in Rochester, the two earliest having been established in 1818 and 1834. Since we know the ancestor lived in Rochester before 1834, he probably belonged to the First Baptist Church. A check of Baptist churches in modern Rochester shows that the First Baptist Church still exists, and we write to its pastor requesting a check in early records for mention of our ancestor.

In another example, it is known that the ancestor was a Baptist minister named Henry Smith and that before he moved to Michigan in 1863, he lived somewhere in New York. A check of all of the Baptist Associations in New York revealed only one Henry Smith, who preached at Hastings, Westchester County. (See Figure 11-6.) With this information, we don't need to check all of the Henry Smiths in the 1850 census index of New York; we can zero in on the relevant one.

Problems Special to Religious Directories

Access continues to be the major problem with these directories. Common designations such as "Baptist" and "Methodist" may comprise several distinct denominations. So you will need to research the ancestor's exact religion to find the appropriate directory. Also, the denomination as it existed in the nineteenth century may now be defunct or merged with another group. In this case, lack of a modern directory showing church locations may limit your access to the original records.

Source Locations. Taking into consideration these problems, the best way to determine the existence and location of a directory for the denomination of interest is to look for a church archives for that particular denomination. Such archives may have back issues of these directories, as well as information on where to find the records in modern churches. Also check the seminary or training college libraries. (See Chapter 5, "Church Records in the United States.")

Among public repositories, check the Library of Congress, state and local libraries, and general university libraries (particularly those which were once denominational); but don't stop there. The Library of Congress, for example, has *The Official Catholic Directory* only as early as 1886 although it has been published since 1817. In such a case contact the publisher:

P. J. Kenedy and Sons
866 Third Avenue
New York, NY 10022

Post Office and Street Directories

Post office and street directories were originally published by the government to help deliver the mail correctly before ZIP codes. Post office directories list all active post offices in the year of publication. For instance, *The Street Directory of the Principal Cities of the United States . . . to April 1908*, 5th ed. (1908; reprint ed., Detroit Gale Research Company, 1973) contains the names of streets and the cities with streets by those names. This was necessary in cases where the sender listed only a street address, no city of addressee, and no return address. The directory was published mainly for the use of the Division of Dead Letters and should not be confused with the street directories discussed with city directories.

How to Use Post Office and Street Directories

You can use both of these directories with old family letters. If you have a letter that bears only the name of a "town" and state and this "town" cannot be found in any modern gazetteer, it may no longer exist or perhaps the name was changed. A post office directory from the right period will give you the location.

New York Association.

CHURCHES.	CONST.	COUNTIES.	PASTORS.	BAPT.	MEMBERS.
First Church, N. Y.,	1762	New York,	S. H. Cone, D. D.,	15	557
First Church, Staten Island,	1785	Richmond,	Samuel White,	2	177
Middletown,	1792	Rockland,	J. W. Griffiths,		56
Abyssinian, N. Y.,	1808	New York,	J. T. Raymond,	8	373
North Beriah, N. Y.,	1809	New York,	J. S. Backus,	26	235
Ebenezer, N. Y.,	1825	New York,	G. L. Marsh,	2	98
Greenport, L. I.,	1832	Suffolk,	C. J. Hopkins,		151
Zion, N. Y.,	1832	New York,	Thomas Henson,		378
Newburgh,	1833	Orange,	James Scott,	5	103
Sixteenth St., N. Y.,	1833	New York,	J. W. Taggart,	54	714
Berean, N. Y.,	1838	New York,	J. R. Stone,	20	420
Sag Harbor, L. I.,	1844	Suffolk,	E. W. Bliss,	9	137
Welsh, N. Y.,	1833	New York,	Thomas H. Davies,		167
Monticello,	1836	Sullivan,	———		49
Piermont, First,	1839	Rockland,	———	1	48
Bethesda, N. Y.,	1841	New York,	N. B. Baldwin,	16	130
Middletown, First,	1842	Orange,	S. S. Barrett,	4	62
Hempstead,	1842	Rockland,	E. J. Williams,		21
Cold Spring, L. I.,	1842	Suffolk,	W. B. Harris,		40
Bloomingdale, N. Y.,	1843	New York,	S. Wilkins,	3	130
Parksville,		Sullivan,	Wm. W. Murphy,		67
First Mariner's,	1843	New York,	J. R. Steward,	11	122
Providence, N. Y.,	1845	New York,	———	1	66
Newtown, L. I.,		Queens,	———		15
Central, Brooklyn,	1847	Kings,	J. W. Sarles,	11	172
West, Staten Island,	1848	Richmond,	William Pike,	5	31
Olive Branch, N. Y.,	1849	New York,	———	19	183
Oyster Bay, L. I.,	1724	Suffolk	Marmaduke Earle,		39
East Marion, L. I.,	1847	Kings,	Erastus Denison,	4	35
Hastings, First,	1850	West Chester,	Henry F. Smith,	9	28
Shiloh, Newburg,	1848	Orange,	Elisha Hawkins,	14	27
			Total,	239	4582

Figure 11-6. J. Lansing Burrows, ed., *American Baptist Register for 1852* (Philadelphia: American Baptist Publication Society, 1853), p. 237.

If the letter bears only the address on Religious Street and the date of 13 January 1908, the original envelope having been lost, the street directory can help. The 1908 directory already cited shows:

Reliance Place
Flushing, N.Y.
(Elmhurst)
Relic Alley
Pittsburg, Pa.
Relief
Oil City, Pa., 1-20
Relief Alley
Allegheny, Pa.
Pittsburg, Pa.
Relief Ave.
Poplar Bluff, Mo., 200-600
Religious
New Orleans, La., 1400-1999
Reilis
Saginaw, Mich., 200
Relyea Place
New Rochelle, N.Y., 1-20
Rembert
Memphis, Tenn., N.
61-662 S.

Street Directory of the Principal Cities of the United States Embracing Letter-Carrier Offices Established to April 30, 1908 (Washington, D.C.: Postmaster General, 1908) p. 637.

Thus, in 1908, Religious Street existed only in New Orleans. If, however, the name is Relief, you would have more cities to consider. This method can be used with any stray street address, including photographers' addresses on the backs of old photographs.

Source Locations

Most research libraries of any size have one or both directories available in their reference sections. The Library of Congress and the Genealogical Society of Utah both have copies.

Notes

1. *The Oxford English Dictionary* (Oxford: Clarendon Press, 1961), p. 393.

2. Dorothea N. Spear, *Bibliography of American Directories Through 1860* (Worcester, Massachusetts: American Antiquarian Society, 1961), pp. 5-10.

3. *Alaska Directory and Gazetteer 1934-1935* (Seattle: Alaska Directory Co., 1935), foreword.

4. U. S. Bureau of the Census, *Historical Statistics of the United States, Colonial Times to 1957* (Washington, D.C.: Government Printing Office, 1960), pp. 480-81.

5. 1880 U.S. Census, Philadelphia Co., Philadelphia City, Penn., vol. 66, enumeration district (E.D.) 3, p. 23, line 14; Genealogical Society of Utah (hereafter GS) 1,255,166.

6. *Gopsill's Philadelphia Directory 1880* (Philadelphia: James Gopsill, 1880) p. 1327; 1881, p. 1289.

7. Ibid., 1869, p. 1167; 1870, p. 1202; both on GS 1,000,897.

8. Death Certificate for James Renwick, 5 June 1845, Manhattan Death Register; GS 447,550.

9. 1900 U.S. Census, Philadelphia Co., Philadelphia, Penn., vol. 167, enumeration district (E.D.) 412, sheet 7, line 24; GS 1,241,461.

10. Marriage Record of Christian Hochwald and Sophia [illegible], 3 May 1862, Philadelphia Marriage Registers 1862, p. 193; GS 978,997.

11. *McElroy's Philadelphia City Directory 1862* (Philadelphia: E.C. and J. Biddle, 1862), p. 862; GS 1,000,895.

12. *Doggett's New York Directory* (New York: John Doggett, Jr., 1833-40) 1833, 1834, 1835, 1836, 1837, 1838, 1839, 1840.

13. Declaration of Intention of James Renwick to Become a Naturalized Citizen of the United States, New York Co., N.Y., Naturalization Records (loose papers) Court of Common Pleas, 1845; GS 953,637.

14. 1982 Information Brochure Supplied by Research Publications, Inc., 12 Lunar Drive, New Haven, CT 06525. Copies available on request.

15. James M. Ethridge, ed. *The Directory of Directories* (Detroit: Information Enterprises, 1980), p. 245; reprinted by permission.

16. Adjutant General's Office, *Register of Officers and Agents, Civil, Military and Naval in the Service of the United States 30 Sept. 1863* (Washington, D.C.: Government Printing Office, 1864), notes.

Bibliography

Burton, Robert E. "City Directories in the United States, 1784-1820: A Bibliography with Historical Notes." M.S. thesis, University of Michigan, 1956. Gives locations of directories.

Catalog of City, County, and State Directories Published in North America. New York: North American Directory Publishers, 1967.

Davis, Marjorie V. *Guide to American Business Directories*. Washington, D.C.: Public Affairs Press, 1948.

"Directories in the Library of Congress." *American Genealogist* 13 (1937): 46-53; 27 (1951): 142.

Hofstetter, Eleanore O. and Harold C. Livesay. "Pre-Civil War Directories: Sources in American History." *RQ* 8 (1968): 174-76.

Klein, Bernard. *Guide to American Directories*. 5th ed. Englewood Cliffs, N.J.: Prentice-Hall, 1962.

Knights, Peter R. "The Plain People of Boston." *Scientific American*, Nov. 1981. Includes a perceptive appendix on directories.

Moriarity, John H. "Directory Information Materials for New York City Residents, 1626-1786: A Bibliographic Study." *Bulletin New York Public Library*, Oct. 1942.

Murphy, Harry J. *Where's What; Sources of Information for Federal Investigators*. New York: Warner Books, 1976.

Spear, Dorothea N. *Bibliography of American Directories Through 1860*. Worcester, Mass.: American Antiquarian Society, 1961.

INFORMATION GUIDE

Genealogical Information in the Record Group	
Surname/name	●
Date of Birth	●
Place of Birth	●
Sex	●
Race/color	●
Physical Description	
Occupation	●
Education	●
Military Service	●
Slave Status	●
Property Owned	●
Religion	●
Citizenship	●
Marital Status	●
Spouse's Name	●
Children's Names	●
Father's Name	●
Mother's Name	●
Father's Birthplace	●
Mother's Birthplace	●
Date of Death	●
Cause of Death	●
Name of Cemetery	●
Residence	●
Age	●
Literacy/signature	
Photograph/sketch	●
Relatives Residing Elsewhere	●

COULD YOU USE THIS CHAPTER?

Type of Record	*Kept from*	*Clues That You Should Consult These Records*
Vital Statistics	About 1750 to present	Newspapers were published first in major population centers, but it was a rare community that was not served by at least a county paper in the nineteenth century. Notices of births, marriages, and deaths could and did appear almost anywhere in the paper, ranging from the briefest of mentions to extensive coverage. Births were mentioned less frequently than either deaths or marriages in the earliest papers, but are still worth searching for.
Social events	About mid-nineteenth century	Such events as school plays with complete casts, and graduations, minutes of meetings in which participants are named, parades and celebrations describing who did what, and biographical sketches are also featured. If you can identify your ancestor as the resident of a community for at least a ten-year period, it is worth searching local papers page-by-page. Not only will you find information about your ancestors, you will also gain insights into their milieu and society.
Legal notices	From eighteenth century	Because of legal requirements that public notices be published, even if courthouse records no longer exist, local newspapers may help you reconstruct land sales, tax rolls, probate of wills, settlement of estates, divorce proceedings, and reports of civil and criminal cases.
Advertisements	From eighteenth century	If your ancestors lived in a city, the newspaper can identify their professions and show how they advertised for business. Many new residents in an area announced their services and availability with an advertisement. Advertisements also become important in identifying runaway slaves and members of the family who moved away.
Migrations information	From eighteenth century	Did your ancestor seem to disappear? Local newspapers included news reports of trips, letters to the editor from wanderers, advertisements from newly arrived or departing merchants, names of ships leaving or departing, and lists of people whose mail was accumulating in the post office. All of these sources can be helpful in pinpointing the time ancestors left a particular area and where they went.

Chapter 12

NEWSPAPERS

Loretto Dennis Szucs

The genealogist who ignores newspapers misses a great mass of valuable material. Newspapers are, for those who become proficient in their use, the day-to-day diaries of local community events, clearly mirroring the lifestyle and environment of ancestors long dead. They are thus an excellent source for family history, giving accounts of events from a contemporary point of view.

The newspaper is intended for general readers, usually addresses a geographic region, and may also specialize in an ethnic, cultural, social, or national group. Because newspapers preserve the collected thoughts of many minds, they reflect moral, cultural, educational, and political development more broadly than do the isolated thoughts of an individual's correspondence or diary. Nowhere can a clearer idea be gained of public sentiment than in the American newspaper.

While records of birth, marriage, and death are the most commonly used and the most consistently helpful, only the genealogist's imagination and resourcefulness limit the paper's usefulness in supplying clues about historical events, local news items, probate court and legal notices, real estate transactions, political biographies, announcements, notices of new and terminated partnerships, business advertisements, and notices for settling debts.

The newspaper takes on an added importance for genealogical research when official public records have been destroyed. Cook County, Illinois, for example, lost all official county records in the Great Chicago Fire of 1871. Newspapers consequently became important in reconstructing the history of the city and tracing the roots of its settlers. Whatever the status of the public records, however, the researcher cannot come away from newspapers without new insight into the social and cultural context of times past.

How to Find Newspapers

Locating local newspapers of the past can be difficult. The first step in the search is to identify papers which served the area of interest and which have survived.

County histories are a good starting point to learn the names of newspapers. Lengthy treatment is often given to the newspapers from the beginning until the date of the history. If a newspaper is still being published, *Ayers Directory* will provide location and correct title. The predecessor of this directory began publishing in 1869, so newspapers that have ceased publication since that time can be identified in earlier issues. Newspapers are listed by town of publication.

Union lists are also helpful in locating newspaper files; Clarence Brigham, *History and Bibliography of American Newspapers, 1690-1820;* Gregory's *American Newspapers, 1821-1926;* and the Library of Congress, *Newspapers on Microfilm* (various editions) are essential (See bibliography at the end of the chapter for citations.) For most states, other union lists exist. Arranged by state, county, and town, these union lists give information on specific libraries, historical societies, newspaper offices, and private collections where these newspapers have been located. They also tell the time period covered by each newspaper and its frequency of publication. Most reference departments in public and university libraries also have these union lists. For specific titles, see the bibliography at the end of this chapter.

If there were no newspapers published in a particular town or county of interest, a nearby town may have been the news center serving the area. The area served might include another county, or even a county across state lines. Make a careful study of maps for clues of area coverage.

Before going to the librarian, you should be armed with as much information about the newspaper for the area of search as possible including the source from which you obtained that information. Do not expect librarians to identify newspapers. That is your job. Once you know the location of the newspaper, however, the librarian can usually request copies on interlibrary loan.

United States Newspaper Project

Since the publication of Gregory's *American Newspapers,* covering from 1821 to 1936, historians and librarians have been interested in bringing it up to date. State historical societies, state libraries, university libraries, archives, and many state consortia of libraries have become involved.[1] The result is that every state in the nation at present has some kind of newspaper program, and many have published lists of their specific holdings. (See bibliography.)

Far and away the most comprehensive program directed at updating Gregory's list began in 1973. The Organization of American Historians, with the help of funds from the National Endowment for the Humanities, began planning for what is now known as the United States Newspaper Project.[2] Within a few years, as a result of this effort, American genealogists will have easy access in one form or another, to almost every extant newspaper file in the United States.

The pilot project, known as the Iowa Pilot Project, was completed in 1979 and is cited in the bibliography. The outcome of the project was the listing of Iowa newspapers in both an automated index and a published list, thus demonstrating that a national project was possible. The Indiana Project, to be completed by summer 1985, is also cited in the bibliography.

In 1981, the Online Computer Library Center (OCLC) in Dublin, Ohio, agreed to accept newspaper records into its database, thereby acting as the computer network for the U.S. Newspaper Project. This makes 5,000 terminals available in 3,000 libraries, archives, and historical societies in North America. In 1982 and 1983 respectively, the Library of Congress and six national newspaper repositories began to enter their holdings into the OCLC database.[3] This database extends to national networks that cover every state and will provide the bibliographies and the holdings records of an estimated 35,000 newspaper titles from all fifty states. This pioneer effort will test the guides and procedures developed for the national plan and is the first phase of a multi-year project. Ultimately it will make available all surviving copies of the 300,000 newspapers published in the United States since 1690 to every interested person and subscribing institution.

In the fall of 1982 the National Endowment for the Humanities (NEH) invited universities, libraries, archives, and historical societies to submit applications for grants covering their own states.[4] In July 1983, the first awards were made, and the United States Newspaper Project was no longer in pilot or testing stages. All newspapers published since 13 September 1690 will eventually be produced in microform, identified in the computer network, and made available through local interlibrary loan services. Until this is a reality, the National Endowment for the Humanities will continue to fund, state by state, projects to identify, locate, and preserve newspapers.

It is an immense project–impossible to complete without the remarkable degree of cooperation shown. The project was conceived by the Council for Learned Societies, planned by the National Endowment for the Humanities, assisted by the Library of Congress, and accepted by the Online Computer Library Center for network service. They merit the thanks of historians and genealogists.

Newspapers on Microfilm

The high acid content of newsprint, the bulky size of newspapers, and myriad storage difficulties have led to mass microfilming. This, in turn, makes newspapers one of the most accessible sources genealogists have. Libraries and historical societies will loan film at a nominal cost. It is usually unnecessary to contact the original publisher or successor, since most historical papers are now in public repositories.

To determine what papers are currently available on microfilm consult the published catalogs of these companies:

Bell and Howell
Micro-Photo Division
Old Mansfield Road
Wooster, OH 41691

Microfilming Corporation of America
1620 Hawkins Ave.
Box 10
Sanford, NC 27330

University Microfilms
300 North Zeeb Road
Ann Arbor, MI 48106

University Microfilms has runs of small local papers as well as local historical society proceedings long out of print.

Evans Early American Imprints

Charles Evans compiled *American Bibliography: A Chronological Dictionary of all Books, Pamphlets, and Periodical Publications Printed in the United States, 1639-1820* in twelve volumes. Most of the titles in this series have been reproduced from the best copies onto microfiche, including all of the state news gazettes and some of the smaller papers published before 1820, and newsletters published during the American Revolution. The fiche collection is called Evans Early American Imprints, and copies can be found in most university and some public library collections, making pre-1820 newspapers readily available to most genealogists.

Photocopies from pages of the fiche are usually impractical in most cases, because the fiche is covered with protective plastic.

How to Search Newspapers

Once a copy of the newspaper from the ancestor's time and location has been procured, what information can you find? Just look and see. There really is no better way to learn about old newspapers than to spend some time reading them.

Format and content varied greatly from place to place and from year to year. Metropolitan dailies were primarily concerned with international, national, and state affairs. Municipal events were often general. Little, if any, attention was given to personals, except for advertisements. Metropolitan papers would also occasionally pick up items from distant or rural areas which had news appeal outside their own community.

In contrast, small country or community newspapers were always concerned with local people and their immediate surroundings. Genealogically, these small papers are especially valuable. To fully tap their potential, begin at the front page of the first issue available in the time period of your search and proceed–issue by issue, page by page–through the entire publication. Obviously, the size of large metropolitan papers makes this approach impossible. In these larger papers, narrow your search to specific dates determined by other sources.

Vital Statistics

In older newspapers, statistical notices of births, deaths, and marriages appear almost anywhere in the publication; and unless you read every page thoroughly, you may miss a notice. Column headings can be misleading too. An unsuspecting researcher looking for the death notice or obituary of an ancestor who had died in a construction accident might miss the article headed "Blown to Eternity," if he/she concentrates his/her search around a personal name. A twentieth-century attitude toward newspapers will not be much help in reading an eighteenth-century publication.

Deaths. One of the most useful genealogical applications of newspapers is for vital statistics, particularly the obituary or death notice. There is a difference in death lists, lists of burial permits, notices, and obituaries.

Official lists of the dead are commonly found in newspapers. This kind of list gives the meager information supplied to the newspaper from city or county records and was included as a free service to the readers. Military casualty lists are included in this kind of death record.

Deaths Reported 2 and 3 Jan. 1900, *New York Times*.

PHILIPPINE CASUALTIES.

WASHINGTON, Jan. 2.—Gen. Otis's latest casualty report is as follows:

Deaths since last report: Wounded by natives, Dec. 16, George A. Wagner, F, Fourteenth Infantry. Drowned accidentally at Bacoor, Nov. 19, Patrick Hart, F, Fourteenth Infantry; Manila, Dec. 27, William Ott, Corporal, D, Twenty-first Infantry. Acute dysentery, Dec. 23, John H. Buckner, musician, E, Thirteenth Infantry; Dec. 18, George W. Magann, K, Twenty-second Infantry; Dec. 8, Troy Hamilton, I, —— Cavalry. Chronic dysentery, Dec. 23, Andrews McKielland, H, Thirty-first Infantry; Dec. 21, Joseph H. Bolter, K, Twenty-second Infantry; Dec. 26, James Shanahan, A, Twenty-eighth Infantry; John A. Renan, M, Thirteenth Infantry. Chronic diarrhoea, Dec. 24, William Crabb, E, Fourteenth Infantry, Dec. 25, John C. Cain, I, Twenty-first Infantry; Dec. 23, Michael Kane, civilian, late I, Twenty-second Infantry. Typhoid, Dec. 28, Andrew L. Gilken, M, Eleventh Cavalry; Dec. 20, James Croffey, D, Sixth Infantry; Dec. 30, George P. Leets, hospital steward. Variola, Dec. 26, Hume Dulin, L, Twenty-fourth Infantry; William W. Adams, M, Thirty-fourth Infantry. Pneumonia, Oct. 19, John I. Williams, K, Twenty-second Infantry. Malaria, Dec. 20, Robert Culhane, H, Sixth Infantry. Cachexia, Dec. 27, Edward J. Kelly.

DIED.

GARDNER.—At Flatlands, on Jan. 2, of pneumonia, Elizabeth Marion Crane, wife of the Rev. John S. Gardner, and daughter of the late Rev. Oliver Crane.

Funeral at parsonage of Flatlands Reformed Church on Friday, at 2 P. M.

McGILL.—At midnight, Dec. 31, 1899, John Walter McGill, for thirty years associated with his brother, George W. McGill, in business in New York City.

His funeral will be from his late residence, 18 Halstead Street, Brick Church, East Orange, N. J., Wednesday, Jan. 3, 1900, at 2:30 o'clock P. M.

McMILLAN.—On Jan. 2, at Bath Beach, of pneumonia, Eleanor Bowen, wife of Charles L. McMillan, and daughter of the late Alfred S. Bowen.

Notice of funeral hereafter.

MITCHEL.—On Dec. 31, at her residence, Bedford Park, New York City, Jane Verner Mitchel, widow of John Mitchel.

Friends are invited to attend her funeral from St. James's Church, Jerome Avenue and St. James's Place, Fordham, at a quarter past 2 P. M., on Thursday, Jan. 4.

Interment private. Please omit flowers.

NICHOLS.—Tuesday morning, Jan. 2, William N. Nichols, 3d, infant son of William H. Nichols, Jr., and [illegible] Nichols.

Funeral private.

RIGNEY.—At his late residence, 118 West One Hundred and Twenty-third Street, on the morning of Jan. 2, Thomas Rigney, in the eighty-eighth year of his age.

Funeral private.

DEATH LIST OF A DAY.

Charles MacRae.

Charles MacRae, who died on Saturday at Seabreeze, Fla., and whose funeral took place yesterday morning at the Church of the Intercession, Broadway and One Hundred and Fifty-eighth Street, was one of the oldest and best known real estate brokers in the city.

Mr. MacRae had been in the real estate business all his life with the exception of a brief period following the panic of 1873, and numbered among his clients some of the wealthiest men who have dealt in Manhattan realty. His specialty was property in Fifth Avenue and those adjacent streets which make up the Fifth Avenue section. He purchased the site for the residence of the late Cornelius Vanderbilt, Fifth Avenue, Fifty-seventh to Fifty-eighth Street, and represented John D. Rockefeller when the latter bought the ground for his house in Fifty-fourth Street near Fifth Avenue. At one time and another Mr. MacRae also acted as broker for Collis P. Huntington, the late Robert Bonner, and the Havemeyers. Through him William C. Whitney bought his country seat, Wheatley Hills, at Roslyn, L. I.

Mr. MacRae was born in this city sixty-six years ago. He leaves a widow and four sons—Elmer, Charles, Cecil, and Jesse

Figure 12-1. The *New York Times,* Wednesday, 3 Jan. 1900.

The *New York Times* has a master index, including vital statistics, from 1851 to the current year. A separate Obituary Index with 390,000 entries is also available. Official death lists and casualty lists are not indexed. References may appear for casualty lists under the subject heading of "Philippines Insurrection, casualty lists. . . ."

Death or funeral notices were paid announcements. Unlike the obituary, the notice states only the name of the decedent, when and where the death occurred, and occasionally the name of a survivor. An example might be: "Dyer, Harry, 26th inst., funeral from St. James at 1 pm, thence by carriage to Greenwood Cemetery." Even this simple statement can provide needed clues to continue research. Many ancestors will not be found in paid announcements because survivors either did not deem them necessary or couldn't afford them. In hard economic times such as the Great Depression, there were noticeably fewer paid announcements.

In Figure 12-1 are three death announcements – all on the same page, all in the same issue – of the *New York Times,* Wednesday, 3 January 1900. Each carried its own price; all three are included in the *Times* Obituary Index.

Death information found in newspapers will not be consistent over the years. Different customs also predominated in different parts of the country. Very early obituaries tended to limit the announcement to one or two lines. A typical early nineteenth-century entry states the name of the deceased, perhaps an age or estimated age, the date of death, and the late residence; funeral information may follow in some cases. More details of the death may have been included, but rarely were survivors named. The fact that a husband or wife "is left with ten children to mourn the loss" may be the extent of the help provided in such an article. Parents' names were rarely given except in the case of a child, and even these may merely say: "Baby Mary departed this life to live with the angels."

As the century progressed, an increasing amount of information was furnished. It was not uncommon to find biographical accounts including birthdates, marriage dates and places, and children's and grandchildren's names. While the small-town newspaper could afford space to print details on the deaths of even the common man, this policy was not practical for the metropolitan press. Large dailies printed lengthy obituaries only on the prominent, the powerful, the wealthy – those for whom the fee was paid to laud their lives.

In short, there are no set rules on the amount of information which can be expected. I'll describe what you can generally expect but there will be exceptions.

When using the newspaper as a source for death information, do not restrict the search to one publication. You should examine all the papers covering the ancestor's community because accounts in one paper may differ from those in another publication. Consider also the possibility that an obituary might appear several days, a week, or a month after the death. Sometimes all the area deaths are noted simultaneously at the end of the year.

The circumstances of the death will determine where information will appear within the newspaper itself. Accidental deaths, murders, and suicides were news items and were therefore placed in an attention-getting spot but might not be mentioned in other notices. These news items often mention that an inquest was held and you might find more information from a coroner's records. The word *suddenly* is a clue that the death was unnatural and that an inquest may have been held, even if it is not reported.

In some situations, the only information identifying a person's birthplace may be in an obituary. Notice of death in a city the ancestor formerly inhabited may tell where to search for death and burial records in the new location. This is especially true when an aged parent, known to reside with a child, dies while visiting another town or state. The notice may be printed in locations where other children reside and in the place of residence of the deceased.

Also providing needed death dates or places are lists of war dead, disaster victims, and deceased members of a fraternal organization. Names of policemen and firemen who have died within the year are often published periodically.

Marriages. Marriage license notices appear frequently in both city and rural newspapers. Often, these are posted weekly and in many instances will note the age of the bride and groom as well as their places of residence.

The *Central Illinois Gazette* for 12 May 1858 ran this fairly typical notice:

> The following marriage licenses have been issued since our last report:
>
> P. Haynes to Temps Green,
> J. R. Thomas to M. J. Stacy,
> W. I. Traywick to Willella Gray,
> J. Y. Pearce to Cora Pearce.
>
> COLORED
> Charley Weathers to Van King

A Great Golden Wedding.

On October 23rd 1851. Joseph V. Parkison and Miss Fannie Kenton were married at the home of the bride's parents, Mr. and Mrs J. C. Kenton, on the old Kenton homestead, a few miles north of Rensselaer. We can't say at their "palatial residence," but it was a good log house, like nearly all the early settlers occupied in those days. And they were early settlers indeed; the bride's father, universally called "Coon" Kenton in those days, from his proclivities for killing coons and other wild denizens of the forest, and the groom's father John G. Parkison, both being pioneers of pioneers and among our very earliest settlers.

Both were directly descended from the most distinguished pioneer ancestry. Mr. Parkison being a grand-son of no less a person than Gen. Simon Kenton, the great scout and Indian fighter, and partner of Daniel Boone. His wife was his 2nd or 3rd cousin and a grand daughter of Mark Kenton, a brother of Simon's.

The marriage ceremony was performed by Rev. Samuel Benjamin, a "hard-shell" Baptist minister and a brother of Jared Benjamin and Mrs. David Nowels, still residents of Rensselaer.

Mr. and Mrs. Parkison lived for a year or two with his father, in Barkley Tp., and then in their own home, in the same township, for nearly 25 years, and since then in their present home 4 miles east of Rensselaer, near the small station of Pleasant Ridge. They very lately sold that home, and next year will build them a new house, just outside the corporation line of Rensselaer, where their declining years will be passed in the peace and quietude their busy but honorable, gentle and kindly lives have so well merited. They are abundantly rich in the love of children, grand-children and great grand-children. They also are excellently well to do in this world's goods of the more obvious, but not more desirable kind, and can well afford to take life easy henceforth.

Of those present at the original wedding 50 years ago, the only survivors, besides the couple themselves, are Addison Parkison, Uncle Joe's older brother, Mr. and Mrs. David Nowels, Simon and Jasper Kenton, the bride's brothers, the latter, no doubt, being the "irrepressible kid" of the affair and Mrs. Cynthia Weathers, of Howard, Kans. Of these only "Uncle Ad," Simon Kenton and Mrs. Weathers were present at the golden wedding, Mrs. Nowels being too feeble to attend, and Jasper Kenton being out of town.

It is a most notable fact, which may be mentioned in this connection, that there are not less than ten grand-children of old Gen. Simon Kenton still living: Namely, Addison Parkison, Mrs Margaret Robinson, Mrs. Mary J. McCoy, of Rensselaer, Joseph V. Parkison, of Pleasant Ridge, Wm. W. Murray, of Barkley Tp., Jasper Co., Henry L. Murray, of Monon, Mrs. Isabel Parker, of Frankfort, Lewellyn Kenton, of Monticello, Mrs. Mary Tyler, of Delphi, and and Joseph Kenton, of Kansas.

The celebration Wednesday was no doubt, the greatest affair of the kind ever held in Jasper county, and participated in by not less than 225 persons. All of their six children were present, as follows: Mrs. Matilda Collins, Wallace Parkison, Mrs. H. B. Porter, Mrs W. V. Porter, Mrs Josie Milligan of Garnett, Kans. and Mrs. Maggie Yeoman of Chickasaw, I. T. There were also present sixteen grand children and four great grand children. Five brothers and sisters of either Mr. or Mrs Parkison also came to do them honor. Among the guests from outside the county, not mentioned above, were Henry Murray and wife of White Co., Erastus Smith and wife of Tippecanoe Co., Mrs. Elizabeth Kauffman and Mrs. Jennie Dugan of Iowa, Mrs. Mattie Rinehart, of Buffalo, Mrs. Sarah Wood, Miss Mary Wood, of Lee, Miss Ada Mayhew, of California.

About one hundred and twenty relatives of all degrees were in the company. Besides these there are one hundred or more of friends, many of whom were old settlers and life-long acquaintances. In all there were 207 person partook of the elegant dinner besides such children as were held in the arms of others. The dinner was served in a large tent that was erected for the occasion and a wonderful dinner it was, as all present will testify. Full justice was done to it and we are sure that more than the traditional twelve basketfuls were taken up after all had "eaten and were filled."

As a preliminary, however, to the meal came the formal presentation of the presents. This was done by Rev. C. D. Royse in behalf of the assembled guests and then Matilda Collins on behalf of the children to each of their parents a handsome gold watch, chains also were presented by their grand-children. Both watches and chains were as nearly alike except in size as could be secured, and the watches were each engraved with the initials of the recipients. The presents from others were both numerous and handsome. Space will not admit of special mention of any individual gifts. These included various articles of artistically decorated chinaware, pictures, gold and pearl handled umbrellas, gold spectacles, a gold thimble, knives and forks. But no attempt has been made to even enumerate the different articles. The family of Wm. Parkison, a deceased brother, presented a handsome set of china dishes.

In connection with the dinner festivities a touching incident was the reading of the following verses prepared for the occasion by Miss Josephine Kenton, and read by her:

Their Golden Wedding Day.

Just fifty years ago dear wife
Since you and I were wed,
Today's our golden wedding day
Where can the years have fled?

Am I that shy and awkward youth?
Are you that maiden fair
With silver threads among the curls,
That once was jet black hair?

Our children number six just even
Among the living here,
While three we trust are safe in heaven,
Away from care and fear.

Our children, brothers, sisters, friends,
Have met to cheer us on
While our grand-children, too attend
To make our joys all one.

Dear friends all pray that you and I
May walk life's golden sands
Until we reach that better place
The house not made with hands.

We are able to make you farm loans at a very low rate of interest.
BRUNER & RANDLE.

Feed of all kinds at the Feed Store, Such as hominy meal, bran, chop feed, corn, hay and straw. COX & BRANCH, Prop.

For sale, heating stoves, piano, and various other articles of slightly used furniture. Residence Division street, opposite Catholic church. MRS MABEL HAAS.

Wagons for Sale.

For sale, cheap, two good second-hand farm wagons. For name of party enquire at this office.

Figure 12-2. "A Great Golden Wedding," *Rensselaer Semi-Weekly Republican*, 25 Oct. 1901, p. 1.

Again, the best sources for engagement and marriage information are local papers. Generally only the socially and politically elite were newsworthy enough to get coverage in metropolitan dailies.

Marriage anniversaries celebrating twenty-five, fifty, or more years of marriage were of special interest in local papers. For example, the golden wedding of Mr. and Mrs. Joseph V. Parkinson merited two full columns on the front page, including a complete review of their fifty years together, in The *Rensselaer Semi-Weekly Republican*, Jaspar County, Indiana, in 1901. See Figure 12-2.

Or, consider this interesting account from the *Nashville Banner*, 6 October 1897.

> DISAPPOINTED IN LOVE
>
> Clarksville, October 11, Disappointment in love is the reason assigned for J. C. Northington, a well-known planter of Fort Royal, becoming demented. He was brought here yesterday but was refused admission into the county jail without proper papers. Miss Olive Sockett married Walter Nayler, of this place, several days ago. A license had been issued for her and Northington, but she changed her mind at the last moment.

Few eyes would miss this bit of sensational gossip. For the genealogist, however, perplexed by a Sockett-Northington wedding license, this little item provides a much-needed explanation.

Births. Even prior to the time that birth registration was required by law, birth announcements, though uncommon, could be found in certain papers. Notices of births may appear in the society column several days, weeks, or even months after the event.

Local News

The weekly editions of community newspapers give a personal glimpse of people found nowhere else. Country papers would allow plenty of space for a column prepared by a local resident to tell of recent births, upcoming or recent marriages, illnesses, visitors to the community, out-of-town visitors or former residents vacationing with relatives in their old home, and news of a more personal nature. A common example of the kind of clues to be found is one which reads, "Miss Marjorie Dyer of our town is visiting her cousin Miss Margaret Howley in Fort Wayne." This example gives another location of family members and possibly a surname previously unknown. These columns also note anniversaries, parties, reunions, and achievements such as a promotion or a Boy Scout award. Newcomers to a community often received the attention of the columnist and former residents were natural for inclusion.

LITTLE LOCALS.

The Week's Occurrences Put in Cold Type.

A Record of Events, Prospective and Retrospective.

John Barr's baby is quite sick.

These are lovely nights when, it is not raining.

Mrs. R. H. Caldwell is reported sick this week.

Nath Peoples killed two white cranes this week.

Hogs are dying in this section of the county with what is called red mange.

The negros had a big day here last Saturday. Everything passed off quietly.

Mrs. Will Collins presented her husband with a fine girl last Monday evening.

Parties owing the DEMOCRAT will confer a favor by calling around and settling.

George Woodard, who lives near Bennert's mill, has a chicken without wings.

Little Locals in Carroll County Democrat, Huntingdon, Tenn., 12 July 1889.

School news might include awards won and detailed coverage of a graduation, complete with a class picture or even individual photographs of the graduates. School board minutes, lists of teachers and pupils, and other school events are also frequently recorded. A social event that prints the guest list, like this 12 May 1858 report in the *Central Illinois Gazette* of a masquerade party, is a genuine find:

> The young people did themselves proud last Friday night in the masquerade party at Mr. R. H. Carter's. It was the first of the kind they had gotten up for some time and the occasion was looked too [sic] with considerable interest. A large number of both ladies and gentlemen were en-masque, while there were many who attended that did not conform to the rules of the entertainment, but appeared in their customary dress. The following are the parties who were en-masque and the characters represented:

Miss Cora Townes........Flower Girl
" Lena Hawkins........Dinah
" Jessie Hawkins........Cinderella
" Corinia Hilliard........Minnehaha
" Jessie Priest........Night
" Lottie Wade........Day
" Ernest Hilliard........Western Girl [sic]
" Florence Carter........Chinese Woman
" Mabel Young........Sailor Girl
" Linnie McCracken........Highland Lass
" Sallie Leach........Becky Stubbs
" Ivy Williams........Tambourine Girl
" Lulu Hawkins........Red Riding Hood
" Eva Prince........Witch
" Dora Elliot........Nun
" Ethel McClain........Spanish Girl
Miss [?] Luther Carter........Innocence
John Neely........Sambo
Frank Johnson........Prince
Prof. Westbrooks........Priest
Jeb Anderson........Uncle Sam
Walter Carnes........Chinaman
Will Townes........Old Gentleman
Lewis Parker........Page
Fred Walters........Judge Bluebottle
Rufe McClain........Owl
Priest Clark........Sailor Boy
Dr. Cox........Spanish Cavalier
Ed Leach........Old Father Hubbard
Will Carter........Pair of Dudes
Jim McCall........Pair of Dudes
Warren Parsons........Cowboy
Elwood Watson........Farmer

Local news columns are one of the most important sources for data on women and children—two groups of people who rarely appear in other records in their own right. Local columns also provide clues leading to other records. If great-grandmother belonged to a Methodist charitable organization or a sewing circle sponsored by a church, it is a clear indication of church membership. If the religious affiliation was previously unknown, the researcher has a valuable lead.

Biographical Sketches

Newspapers carry biographical sketches in a variety of guises—birthday announcements, testimonials, feature articles, and other items. Sometimes these are indexed. Sometimes they can only be found when searching page by page. An example with a touch of humor is this obviously muckraking letter to the editor of the *Central Illinois Gazette* in West Urbana, Illinois, 12 February 1858, passed on by the addressee, John G. Oiler:

> Dear Sir:—I am requested by many good citizens (Hodges, McLaurie & Co., we suppose) of our Town to enquire of you concerning one Dr. Scroggs who is said to have lived for some time in your town. Scroggs came here about a year ago and he is making himself a great nuisance. He proposes to be a great temperance man and officiously seeks to enlighten the Barbarians out here as he calls them. I am told you can give some light on his true character. We wish to know whether Scroggs ever carried on a Drug Store in your place or rather a dram shop. Did he sell whiskey to back door customers? Did he keep a station on the underground R.R.? Was your neighborhood glad when he left? Was he a man of integrity, of good moral character, was he a notorious s—t-as" or a gentleman?
>
> If you will please answer the above inquiries and give his true character to us you will much oblige many good citizens of our Town who think him a great bore. Answer soon.
>
> Very truly, J. S. Jones
>
> N.H. Tell us especially whether he traded in liquor.

Loyally, Scroggs's friends replied on 1 April 1858 from Harveysburg, Ohio:

> We whose names are hereunto annexed do certify that we have known J. W. Scroggs for some years past—known him as a physician, and as one who kept a drug store—do not think he would or ever did sell whiskey to any persons who were in the habit of drinking to excess; and our understanding was, that he did not sell whisky or any other kind of spirituous liquors, except for medical purposes, and always looked upon him as one of our best Temperance men. He always took part in favor of Temperance when any occasion offered in our place.

Ausahem Antram,
A. L. Antram,
Samuel G. Welch,
John Howe,
B. D. Gaddis,
C. Sikes,
Jos. T. Mistletoe,
Ephraim Mills,
John D. Abbott,
Joseph Williamson,
Christian Ilirey,
E. L. Macy,
James Astram,
Joseph Nedery,
Joseph Lippincott,
G. W. Ham,
M. T. Macy,
A. T. Sabia,
Joshua Garwood
S. O. Garwood,
David Mason, M.D.,
F. D. Harian,
Jabes H. Crew
Nathan Macy
Thomas Wilson
Wm. Macy
Mark Haynes
Jesse Randall
Wm. Randall
Thos. Wilson, Jr.
Finley Ham,

Membership lists, printed minutes, and summaries of events for fraternal organizations, benevolent associations, lists of retirees, political groups, musicians, firemen, and policemen are common. You will even be able to find group photographs.

Judgments.

The following judgments were filed yesterday, the first name being that of the debtor:

ANDREWS, Herbert F., and Theodore S. Miller—L. Gross $331
BLOOM, Edward L.—B. E. Guntert 71
BOHNET, Philip, and William Emrich—H. Harrison 560
CROOKS, John J., and Catharine Goulstil—H. Augusta Davidson 1,650
COHN, Samuel and Gottschalk—G. W. Walmuth 6,990
COVENTRY, Eva—Louise Veitis 201
CONKLIN, George W., individually and as executor—James J. Stettheimer and others 49
CONKLIN, George W., individually and as executor—James J. Stettheimer and others 42
CONKLIN, George W., individually and as executor—James J. Stettheimer and others 42
CARO, Esek, Edward N. Dickerson, De Lancey Nicoll, and Edwin H. Brown—E. Stephens, costs 120
CALLAHAN, Thomas—A. Halliday & Co. 149
DAVIS, David—J. H. Knoepfel 46
DEAN, Robert J.—J. H. Stoutenburgh 801
D'NICOLE, Giuseppe—G. W. Smith and another 82
EHRGOTT, George M., and Elizabeth J. Wilder—Louis Bauer 156
EGENBERGER, William, and Elizabeth Messmann—A. Egenberger, costs 96
FITZPATRICK, John—J. Meyer 88
FISK, George B.—M. Hershfield 61
GALLIGAN, Patrick H.—N. Zabriskie 147
GETZOFF, Sofie—J. J. Milbury 78
GOSS, Mary—H. G. Waters 10
GUNTHER, George—H. E. Artheimer 231
GUNTHER, George—A. H. Sprung 147
HILGERS, William—E. Bramble 73
HOOPER, William B.—L. Horton 40
KRAUTMAN, Elias—H. B. Claflin Company 41

Real Estate Transfers.

Hans Erickson to Arnette M. Erickson Dec. '99, pt nw sw 4-31 5 39 a Walker $175

Anna L. Kirk to William W. Watson Nov. 24, '99, bl 2-11 s½ 3-10 lts 3, South add. Rensselaer. 1,000

Wallace Robinson to John A. Zahn Dec. 27, '99, e½ ne 3-30-5, 80 a. Gillam 2,500

William Pierson to Peter T. Hordeman Dec. 28, '99, pt w½ nw 27-30-7, 78 a Union 2,184

William H. Ade to Joseph Hall Jr., Nov. 20, '99, w½ nw 8-28-7-80 Jordan pt sw sw 5-28-7, 8 a Newton 4,000

Ferdinand DeMuynck to Chas. Sigo, Aug. 5, '99, ne 18-27-6 Carpenter 8,000

Harvey J. Kannal to William S. Day Dec. 28, '99, pt se sw 30-29-6 Newton .... [illegible]

James M. Carr to Ray D. Thompson Dec. 21, '99, pt nw sw 25-29-7 pt e½ se 26-29-7 pt nw sw 25-29-7 pt e½ se 26-29-7 Newton 2,000

David M. Carson to James B. Albertson Feb 11, '99, nw se, sw ne 12-30-5, Gillam 1,000

Ira Gay et ex to Martha J Willcox Dec. 19, '99, lots 2 and 6 nw 19-29-6 Marion 650

David B. Nowels to Wm. B. Austin Dec. 21, '99, lts 22-23 bl 32 Rensselaer Weston add w½ nw se 34-30-5 20 a 1,800

Wm B. Austin to Henry Lee Dec. 27, '99, e½ ne 28-29-5 80 a Hanging Grove 3,000

Figure 12-3. Judgments, the *New York Times,* 3 Jan. 1900, Real Estate Transfers, *Rennselaer Semi-Weekly Republican,* Jasper Co., Indiana, 9 Jan. 1900; Notice, *Hocking Sentinel,* Logan, Ohio, 16 April 1845.

Notice.

The State of Ohio, } Court of Com Pleas
Hocking county SS } March Term 1845

NOTICE is hereby given that the following Executors and Administrators filed their accounts current and vouchers for inspection and settlement at the next term of said court, to wit:

Alexander White, Administrator of John Campbell, deceased.

Joseph Whipple, Executor of Samuel Moore, deceased.

Jeremiah Rose, Administrator of William Rose, deceased.

David Shultz, Administrator of Joseph Funk, deceased.

John S. Hawk, Administrator of Jesse Dowd, deceased.

David Young, Administrator of Henry Hendlebaugh, deceased.

Attest, C. W. JAMES, Clk.

Robert Smith, } Hocking Common Pleas,
vs
Mary Smith, } Petition for Divorce.

The defendent is hereby notified that the above named Robert Smith did, on the 18th day of March, A. D. 1845, file in the Clerks office in this Court his petition therein alledging that she has been wilfully absent from him more than three years, that she has been guilty of Adultery, and guilty of gross neglect of duty, and praying to be divorced for these causes, and that said petition will be for hearing before said court at its next May term.

C. W. JAMES, Clerk.

March 28, 1845. 6w38

Legal Notices

The requirement that some judicial actions (in cases including more persons than the principals) cannot be concluded without public notice carries side benefits for the genealogist. Legislatures either provided for and supported an official county or community publication or they designated existing newspapers for these purposes. Examples include land sales for payment of taxes, administration in probate, proving of wills, heirship determination and the settlement of estates, pending divorce proceedings, sales of properties of insolvent estates, and more. When court records are not available for any reason, these public notices can fill the gap. (See Figure 12-3.)

Other types of periodicals may pick up legal notices too. For example, the *Chicago Daily Law Bulletin*, a special kind of professional newspaper which began publication in 1854, has calendars, reports, and public notices from every court for Chicago and Cook County. For the genealogist, these entries can be the key to locating original case files.

Actually, any legal record could be printed in the newspaper, where local authorities were required to make public a specific set of facts or where they felt it to be in the public interest to do so. For example, review this 1764 tax roll.

The Proprietors of that Part of

Coxhall, so called, in the County of *York*, purchased by *Roger Haskins* and 36 others, of *Harrisseekeing Symonds*, are hereby notified that at their Meeting by Adjournment at *Ipswich*, *May* 13. 1763. they agreed upon and ordered a Tax of 12*s* to be laid on each 100 Acre Right in said Tract, and at a further Adjournment on the 6th Day of October last, they agreed upon and ordered a further Tax of 6*s* on each 100 Acre Lot in that Tract, making in the whole 18*s*. on each 100 Acre Right, and in that Proportion, for defreying the necessary Charges which have already arisen, or may hereafter arise in bringing forward a Settlement of said Lands, and to be paid to Capt. *Francis Goodhue*, of *Ipswich*, their Treasurer. The Purchasers subject to said Taxes are as follows, *viz*.

	Acres.		Acres.
Roger Haskins	200	Richard Walker	300
Edward Bishop	200	John Brownsfarmer	300
William Baker	200	Nathaniel Brown	300
George Herrick	100	Zechariah Herrick	100
Thomas Edwards	100	Thomas Higgiason	100
Samuel Ingalls, jun.	200	John Staniford	200
John Low, jun.	200	Thomas Low	200
William Dixee	200	Samuel Ingalls	100
Thomas Shepherd	200	Robert Lord, jun.	100
William Goodhue	500	Robert Bradford	100
Samuel Giddings	200	Nicholas Woodbury	100
Barnard Thorn	100	Mark Haskell	100
Michael Farlow	200	William Haskell	100
[illegible] Farlow	200	William Cleaves	100
[illegible]	200	John Harris	600
Matthew Perkins	200	John [illegible]	600
John Giddings	200	Nathaniel Rust	200
Paul Thorndike	200	Andrew Elliot	100
Isaac Fellows.	300		

And the said Proprietors are hereby notified, that if they fail to make such Payment within the Time limited by Law for Payment thereof, so much of their common Land belonging to such delinquent Rights will be sold, as will be necessary for Payment thereof according to an Act of this Province, made in the 26th Year of the Reign of King *George* the Second, intitled *An Act in Addition to an Act* intitled An Act directing how Meetings of Proprietors of Lands lying in common may be called.

Ipswich, March 26. 1764.

Boston Gazette and Country Journal, 21 May 1764, p. 3.

Public Announcements and Advertisements

Paid ads, common from the beginning of news publication, chronicle the products, housing, transportation, dress, and reading habits of our ancestors. Particularly relevant for the genealogist are advertisements about insolvent debtors, forced land sales, educational opportunities, and professional services.

Missing People. Early newspapers frequently carried touching advertisements from worried relatives who had lost contact with loved ones. These ads often provided the missing individual's personal description, clothing description, last known whereabouts, and the destination, if known, of a lost traveler. For example, *Sower's Newspaper* of Philadelphia, on 22 June 1759, ran this notice:

> Nicholas Emrich, Allemangel, Albany Township, Berks County, inquires for his two sons, and one daughter. The older son, Valentin, is married; the other son, Friedrich, is single.[5]

Common, too, were notices that horses and other property had been lost or stolen, claims against estates, and even announcements by irate husbands like this one in 1776:

> Whereas the Wife of Joseph Cartwright having eloped from him sundry times, he requests all persons not to trust her, as he will not pay any debts she may contract.
>
> Joseph Cartwright[6]

One wife defended herself vigorously in the *Boston Evening Post* in 1762:

> I find in your last Monday's Papers that my husband has informed the Publick That I have eloped—and that I run him into Debt, and has given a Caution not to Trust me on his Account. Although I am very sensible that neither he or I are of much Importance to the Publick, for he has no Estate to entitle me to any Credit on his account; yet I desire you to be so kind to me, as to let the Publick know That I never run him in Debt in my Life, nor ever eloped, unless it was to Day Labour, to support me and the Children, which I am of necessity Obliged to do; and shall be ever glad to do my Duty to him, and wish he would for the future behave to me in such a Manner that I may do it with more Ease than heretofore.
>
> Her
> Mary X Wellington[7]
> Mark

A fascinating background to an eighteenth-century marriage comes from this protest advertisement paid for by the groom:

ADVERTISEMENT.

O Yes! O Yes!

BENJAMIN HALL of Cornish! BENJAMIN HALL of Cornish! mind what your relations say, and carry your wifes, sisters child home, or you will have a bill of COST to pay.—Hark'ee! Brother, Benjamin, " Hear me, for I will speak," your abuse to your sister, turning her into the highway for crossing your will in marrying me, after introducing me into her company—violating the agreement made with your brother at Sutton—still detaining her child—by slighting the addresses made to you from your relation at Whitingham—together with my inviolable promise of publishing your uncivil usage (in a small pamphlet,) agreeable to law and evidence, unless you give me satisfaction. know ye, that if you don't settle with your wifes mother, brother and sister within one month from this date, I will lay open your whole proceedings in this affair, with an address to the Judges of Law and good breeding in this county, wishing you to save me the trouble, and yourself the disgrace, I subscribe myself your affectionate brother in law..

AMOS TAYLOR.

Keene, Jan. 26, 1796.

Advertisement, *New Hampshire Gazette,* 26 Jan. 1796.

Immigration, Migrations, and Shipping Data

Newspapers are especially helpful in tracing migrations from one place to another. In the personal and local news columns, we can trace visits to relatives, trips to other places, and general movements. Announcements, letters to the editor, and "Marine Intelligence" include such useful entries as lists, names of ships docking or cleared for departure, letters of gratitude for a safe journey, or descriptions of the ocean voyage. Ads for goods and services frequently announce newly established merchants and others new to the community who are setting up business for the first time. A helpful source is Rita S. Gottesman, *The Arts and Crafts in New York, 1777-1799: Advertisements and News Items from New York City Newspapers* (New York: New York Historical Society, 1954).

When mail and packages sent general delivery were not called for or when the addressee had moved without leaving a forwarding address, local papers frequently printed letter lists. Here is one first printed in the *Western Bugle* of Council Bluffs, Iowa, 16 June 1852, then picked up by the *Deseret News* in Salt Lake City, Utah. Many Mormons living in Winter Quarters completed their migration to Utah in 1852.

> Anderson, James M.
> Anthony, John
> Atherton, Joseph
> Anderson, Hiram
> Alcock, Robert
> Armstrong, A.
> Ashley, Thomas
> Alexander, N. B.
> Adams, A. J.
> Armstrong, John A.[8]
>
> and on through several hundred names.

The *South Carolina Gazette* is filled with notices of men and women setting up business. Robert Catherwood, "surgeon to the hospitals and garrisons in East Florida" (16 February 1767), opens a practice with an announcement, and a Mrs. Grant "proposes to practice midwifery "having studied that art regularly and practised it afterwards at Edinburgh: Certificates of which she can produce from the Gentlemen whose lectures she attended, and likewise from the professors of Anatomy and Practice of Physick in that city. . . ." (29 Dec. 1768)[9]

BY

HEWLETT & BRIGHT.

SALE OF

VALUABLE

SLAVES,

(On account of departure)

The Owner of the following named and valuable Slaves, being on the eve of departure for Europe, will cause the same to be offered for sale, at the NEW EXCHANGE, corner of St. Louis and Chartres streets, on *Saturday,* May 16, at Twelve o'Clock, *viz.*

1. **SARAH, a mulatress, aged 45 years, a good cook and accustomed to house work in general, is an excellent and faithful nurse for sick persons, and in every respect a first rate character.**

2. **DENNIS, her son, a mulatto, aged 24 years, a first rate cook and steward for a vessel, having been in that capacity for many years on board one of the Mobile packets; is strictly honest, temperate, and a first rate subject.**

3. **CHOLE, a mulatress, aged 36 years, she is, without exception, one of the most competent servants in the country, a first rate washer and ironer, does up lace, a good cook, and for a bachelor who wishes a house-keeper she would be invaluable; she is also a good ladies' maid, having travelled to the North in that capacity.**

4. **FANNY, her daughter, a mulatress, aged 16 years, speaks French and English, is a superior hair-dresser, (pupil of Guilliac,) a good seamstress and ladies' maid, is smart, intelligent, and a first rate character.**

5. **DANDRIDGE, a mulatoo, aged 26 years, a first rate dining-room servant, a good painter and rough carpenter, and has but few equals for honesty and sobriety.**

6. **NANCY, his wife, aged about 24 years, a confidential house servant, good seamstress, mantuamaker and tailoress, a good cook, washer and ironer, etc.**

7. **MARY ANN, her child, a creole, aged 7 years, speaks French and English, is smart, active and intelligent.**

8. **FANNY or FRANCES, a mulatress, aged 22 years, is a first rate washer and ironer, good cook and house servant, and has an excellent character.**

9. **EMMA, an orphan, aged 10 or 11 years, speaks French and English, has been in the country 7 years, has been accustomed to waiting on table, sewing etc.; is intelligent and active.**

10. **FRANK, a mulatto, aged about 32 years speaks French and English, is a first rate hostler and coachman, understands perfectly well the management of horses, and is, in every respect, a first rate character, with the exception that he will occasionally drink, though not an habitual drunkard.**

☞ All the above named Slaves are acclimated and excellent subjects; they were purchased by their present vendor many years ago, and will, therefore, be severally warranted against all vices and maladies prescribed by law, save and except FRANK, who is fully guaranteed in every other respect but the one above mentioned.

TERMS:—One-half Cash, and the other half in notes at Six months, drawn and endorsed to the satisfaction of the Vendor, with special mortgage on the Slaves until final payment. The Acts of Sale to be passed before WILLIAM BOSWELL, *Notary Public,* at the expense of the Purchaser.

New-Orleans, May 13, 1835.

Figure 12-4. Slave Auction Announcement, Broadside, New Orleans, 13 May 1835.

Runaway Slaves or Indentured Servants. Early American newspapers are full of announcements from masters about their slaves or servants. Notices offered slaves for sale or hire, listed runaways, reported captures, and sought the return of runaways, indentured servants, and apprentices. Physical descriptions and descriptions of clothing are usually very detailed.

Newspapers are important sources for tracing blacks before the Civil War. Announcements of sales, with complete physical descriptions can be combined with probate files, slave census schedules, cemetery inscriptions, and sometimes ships' manifests to trace blacks to the ocean's edge. (See Figure 12-4.) For blacks involved in rebellions or accused of local crimes, the news accounts can be combined with court and coroner's records to round out information.

Religious Newspapers

Many denominations sponsored newspapers.[10] If you know an ancestor's religious affiliation, the effort to find copies of the religious newspaper is usually worthwhile because it offers details not found in another source. A respected member of a religious group will often command more attention within that community than elsewhere. In one case, I searched all existing daily papers printed in Chicago at the time of my subject's death. Each paper noted his death, age, and last known address. Only a few of the papers provided funeral information. However, the weekly Catholic diocesan newspaper included his town of origin in Europe, the year he emigrated to the United States, the year he arrived in Chicago, the year he became a member of the parish, the date of his marriage, the maiden name of his wife, the names of their children, and those of their children's spouses. The flowery eulogy that one expects to find in a turn-of-the-century publication was also provided, along with the names of the clergy in attendance at the funeral service.

Foreign Language Newspapers

Immigrants arrived in the United States with their own culture, customs and language. They were all hungry for news from their homelands, where most had left relatives and friends. The foreign language press opened a natural channel of communication to bridge the Old World and the new environment.

As in religious communities, a person had a better opportunity to be recognized. Where the local English language newspaper glosses over or carries one-line death notices of persons of foreign birth and tongue, he/she will get detailed notice in his/her ethnic newspaper.

Ethnic organizations are still numerous throughout the United States and most of them publish their own foreign language papers. Large collections can be found in the Immigrant Archives, University of Minnesota, Minneapolis, and the Balch Institute, 18 S. 7th Street, Philadelphia, PA 19106. Both of these centers seek and preserve immigrant materials for all groups. More specialized collections include the Swenson Swedish Immigration Research Center, Augustana College, Rock Island, Illlinois, and the Balzekas Museum of Lithuanian Culture, 4012 Archer Avenue, Chicago, IL 60632. (For more details, see Chapter 15, "Tracking the Immigrant Ancestor.")

The holdings of the Balzekas Museum are available on microfilm at the Genealogical Society of Utah and contain death notices from Lithuanian newspapers:

Deaths 1900-1979, including those in Chicago, Boston, New York, Los Angeles, Toronto, Argentina, Australia, London, and several states in the United States:

Abar–Biej ---------- 1206173
Biek–GiLa ---------- 1206174
GiLa–Knys ---------- 1206175
Kobe–Mork ---------- 1206176
Mork–Rzoz ---------- 1206177
Saba–Urba ---------- 1206178
Urba–Zymo ---------- 1206179

Other ethnic archives and libraries are listed in Donna McDonald, ed., *Directory of Historical Societies and Agencies in the U. S. and Canada,* 11th ed. (Nashville: American Association for State and Local History, 1978). See also Chapter 13, "Genealogical Indexes and Catalogs."

College and university libraries frequently have large collections of foreign newspapers. Some of these are extracted and indexed. (See bibliography at the end of this chapter.) If you have a problem locating your specific immigrant group, a foreign consulate can often provide help. Check the immigrant maps in Chapter 15 for local areas where immigrant groups settled. Then consult public libraries and museums for newspaper collections and special, local indexes.

Current Newspapers

Current newspapers are especially useful in locating unknown relatives. Distant relatives may still be living in old hometowns though the direct ancestor moved away. A well-prepared advertisement, placed in a local paper with sufficient identifying information, will sometimes open the door to assistance from descendants of a common ancestor. Consult Vincent L. Jones et al., *Family History for Fun and Profit* (Salt Lake City: The Genealogical Institute, 1972) for sample ads and how to place them.

Most current newspapers at least occasionally feature historical articles about the community and its people. These articles may also provide useful leads. Several have genealogical columns which accept inquiries from outside the circulation area. Anita Cheek Milner, *Newspaper Genealogy Columns* (Bowie, Md.: Heritage Books, 1981) lists most of these.

Indexes

The same basic reference tools that help us in using periodicals guide the intelligent use of newspapers. The three most needed tools are bibliographies, inventories of library and depository holdings, and indexes. (See bibliography at the end of the chapter for citations.) Anita Milner's three-volume *Newspaper Indexes* locates unpublished indexes and card files, and Betty Jarboe, *Obituaries: A Guide to Sources*, is a good state-by-state directory for obituary indexes. About half of all current newspaper indexes were begun in the 1970s.

The most commonly used newspaper index in American libraries is the *New York Times Index,* because of the tremendous volume of material it prints and because both the microfilm edition of the paper and the index are available in so many public, college, and university libraries. The *New York Times Index* now reaches back to 1851 (with some gaps) and is most useful. This index covers published articles by subject matter and provides name indexing too. Since most metropolitan newspapers report important events at approximately the same time, the *Times* index becomes an index to other newspapers for the same subjects. For example, The *New York Times Index* will identify major battles of the Civil War and print some casualty lists. Using that specific date, you can check other newspapers for similar lists of local men killed or wounded in the same engagement. The index is especially valuable when the casualty lists are issued weeks or even months after the battle was fought.

The American Antiquarian Society of Worcester, Massachusetts, pioneered the indexing of many early newspapers. Among other newspapers, the society indexed marriages and deaths appearing in the *Columbian Sentinel* of Boston 1784-1840, a major achievement because this newspaper printed marriage and death notices from all over the country and includes 80,000 names. Other indexing projects of the society have been a death index to the *Christian Intelligencer* of the Reformed Dutch Church, 1830-71, an index to marriages and deaths in the *New York Weekly Museum*, 1788-1817, and an index of obituary notices of the *Boston Transcript*, 1875-1930. Copies of these newspaper indexes have been deposited in the Library of Congress, the New York Public Library, and the New England Historic Genealogical Society.

Index of Obituaries of Boston Newspapers 1704-1800, 3 vols. (Boston: G. K. Hall, 1968) in Boston covers abstracts of deaths within Boston (1794-1800) and deaths outside of Boston (1704-95). The late Gertrude Barber abstracted and indexed the marriages and deaths that were reported in the *New York Evening Post* (1801-90) and in the *Brooklyn Eagle* (1841-81). Kenneth Scott has compiled vital records and other genealogical information printed in the *New York Post-Boy* and other eighteenth-century New York and Philadelphia papers.

Most of these indexes are covered by Betty Jarboe in her book on obituaries. Of the hundreds of partial indexes to be found in this country in obscure genealogical society newsletters and publications, it is unfortunate that more are not published and generally available. Jarboe correctly suggests that each researcher is probably aware of specialized newspaper indexes. For example, I have found valuable John Corrigan, "Index to Names of Irish Americans in Chicago Newspapers" ($1/surname, John Corrigan, 6458 S. Campbell, Chicago, IL 60629) and Charles Banet, *Index to Allen County (Indiana) French Immigrants* compiled from Fort Wayne newspapers located at Saint Joseph College, Rennselaer, IN 47978. The Polish Genealogical Society of Chicago has published indexes of the obituaries in *Jednosc-Polonic*, the Polish newpaper in Baltimore, as well as other aids to finding Polish newspaper information. (See bibliography for citations.)

Indexing newspapers is a favorite ongoing project for hundreds of genealogical societies across the nation. The Chicago Genealogical Society has published *Index to Vital Records from Chicago Newspapers* which covers 1833 to 1848 in seven volumes. Many of these indexes are known only to the compilers and those who may be familiar with local library collections. The ambitious and imaginative researcher should make inquiries about the existence of such tools.

For many years before it ceased publication, the *Boston Transcript* published genealogical queries and answers. The Boston Public Library has indexed the names in the *Boston Transcript* genealogical section. They are available on microcards in many of the important genealogical libraries such as the Newberry Library in Chicago, the Fort Wayne-Allen County Public Library in Fort Wayne, Indiana, and the Genealogical Society of Utah and its branches.

Finally, the Works Progress Administration compiled, among other things, a *General Index to Contents of Savannah Georgia Newspapers*, which covers 1763 to 1830 in twenty-seven volumes. The *Virginia Gazette* has also been indexed from 1736 to 1780. Both indexes are in the Library of Congress.

Since most newspaper indexes compiled by newspaper personnel are subject-oriented, individuals are indexed only if a major article is devoted to them. Few indexes cover gossip columns, ads, announcements, passenger lists, and other equally important items. For these, search page by page. A shortcut of sorts is to check the vital records indexes first to narrow down time periods when the family lived in each area, and then search these periods page by page in the local papers, covering all columns. Quality of information found in newspapers varies greatly. Genealogists, like historians, should be cautious. Historians exercise scholarly judgment about the reliability of stories and records as eyewitness accounts of events and facts. The hurried nature of news-gathering—then as now—often leads to error. Not everything found in print is to be taken without question. Two accounts will always be better than one. However, newspaper accounts may often be the only available record of a particular event. In general, since the newspaper account was drawn from contemporary sources, we can hope for accuracy and appreciate anew the flavor of the times.

Notes

1. Icko Iten, "The Place of the Newspaper," *Library Trends* 4 (Oct. 1955): 140-55, describes principal newspaper collections state by state.

2. National Endowment for the Humanities, *United States Newspaper Project: A National Project*, Feb. 1983, pp. 1-27.

3. "Newspaper Data Bank to be Developed," *Editor and Publisher* 116 (15 Jan. 1983): 11.

4. "The Newspaper Project and NELINET: The American Antiquarian Society," *The Nelinet Liaison* 5 (March 1983): 4.

5. Hocker, Edward W. *Genealogical Data. . .from Advertisements in German Newspapers. . .1743-1800* (Baltimore: Genealogical Publishing Co., 1980), p. 82. See also David H. Koss, "Advertisements for Missing Relatives in Der Christliche Botschafter, 1839-1865," *National Genealogical Society Quarterly* 66 (1978): 33-41; and James L. Morgan, *Marriages, Deaths, and Other Notices in the "Arkansas Gazette," 1819-1822* (Newport, Ark.: Northeast Arkansas Genealogical Association, 1971), p. 7.

6. *The Pennsylvania Evening Post*, 6 July 1776.

7. *The Boston Evening Post*, 1 July 1762.

8. A similar list, containing sixty-one names is in possession of Marie Dickoré, 3411 Clifton Ave., Cincinnati, Ohio, for the *Rising Sun Times* of Rising Sun, Indiana near Cincinnati, Ohio. The original volumes of the *Rising Sun Times* are now missing.

9. In Hennig Cohen, the *South Carolina Gazette, 1732-1775* (Columbia: University of South Carolina Press, 1953), p. 47.

10. See Henry Smith Stroupe, *The Religious Press in the South Atlantic States, 1802-1865* (Durham, N.C.: Duke University Press, 1956.

Bibliography

The following list of works related to newspapers is extensive but by no means exhaustive. Some of the works cited are only a few pages in a periodical, while other works are comprehensive or multivolumed. The list has been compiled largely from Arlene H. Eakle, *Were Your Ancestors Front-Page News?* (Salt Lake City: Genealogical Institute, 1974), pp. 33-41. All of the titles have been verified in the OCLC database on-line in some 5,000 libraries across the country. This bibliography is designed as a guide to primary sources. It includes research aids, identifying and locating specific newspapers with content descriptions and suggestions on use where appropriate as well as abstracts of newspaper data.

The OCLC database includes universities and other institutions as authors, frequently referencing compilers or editors only in the annotation. If you are unable to locate any item by author/compiler/ editor, try title first, then the university press or department responsible for its printing.

Your local library is a starting point for searching for ancestors in published works. Files kept by historical societies, archives, and publishers' offices have been identified by states; thus, some standard checklists for most of the states are provided, suggesting the kinds of guides and lists available in libraries. Most of the titles in this bibliography can be found under one of several subject headings in card catalogs: Newspapers, Microfilm, Obituaries, Birth Records, Marriage Records, and Death Records, each with these subject subdivisions: Bibliographies, Union Lists, or Indexes. Card catalogues will quickly identify the library's holdings.

As this chapter is concerned with American newpapers, no reference is made to British or non-U.S. foreign newspapers, American newspapers in England and elsewhere, or English language newspapers elsewhere in the world.

How-Tos, Analytical Studies

(* = especially valuable)

Bond, Donovan H., and W. Reynolds McLeod. *Newsletters to Newspapers: Eighteenth-Century Journalism, A Bi-Centennial Symposium*. Morgantown: West Virginia University, 1977. Includes accounts of women journalists and women's papers.

Clark, Thomas D. "The Country Newspaper as a Source of Social History." *Indiana Magazine of History* 48 (1952): 217-32.

*"A File of Old Newspapers." *Wisconsin Magazine of History* 8 (1924-25): 454-58.

*Eakle, Arlene H. *Were Your Ancestors Front-Page News?* Salt Lake City: The Genealogical Institute, 1974. 61 pp. Includes how to advertise for genealogical information.

*Kobre, Sidney. *Development of the Colonial Newspaper*. 1944; reprint ed., New York: Peter Smith, 1960.

Karolevitz, Robert F. *Newspapering in the Old West: A Pictorial History of Journalism and Printing on the Frontier*. Seattle: Superior Publishing Company, 1965. 191 pp. Includes samples of underground, hand written newspapers.

Lantz, Herman R. "Use of the Local Press in Historical Research." *Mid-America* 38 (1956): 172-79.

Merrit, Richard L. *Symbols of American Community*. New Haven: Yale University Press, 1966.

Nelson, William. "American Newspapers of the Eighteenth Century as Sources of History." *Report, American Historical Association* 1 (1908).

Pease, Janet K. "Your Ancestors and How to Find Them: Newspapers." *Tri-State Trader*, 28 Aug. 1982. Discusses indexing, abstracting, copying newspapers.

Piercy, J. W. "The Newspaper as a Source of Historical Information." *Indiana History Bulletin* 10 (1933): 387.

Scorza, Joseph C. "The Care and Feeding of a Newspaper Index." *The U*N*A*B*A*S*H*E*D Librarian* 24 (1978): 11-12.

*Tanselle, G. Thomas. *Guide to the Study of U. S. Imprints*. 2 vols. Cambridge: Belknap Press, 1971. 403 pp. Discusses early newspapers in depth.

Thomas, Isaiah. "History of Printing in America." *Transactions of the American Antiquarian Society* (1874), Volume 5 (bound in two parts).

*Wallace, Wesley H. "Property and Trade: Main Themes of Early North Carolina Newspaper Advertisements." *The North Carolina Historical Review* 32 (1955): 451-82.

Directories

Ayers Directory of Publications. 115th ed. Fort Washington, Penn.: IMS Press, 1983. "The professional's directory of print media published in the United States. . .economic descriptions of the states, provinces, cities and towns in which all listees are published; 15 separate, classified lists; 69 custom-made maps on which all publication cities and towns are indicated." 360 pp. Includes newspapers (dailies and weeklies), magazines, newssheets.

American Newspaper Directory. First published in 1869 by George P. Rowell & Co.; merged with N. W. Ayer & Sons, *American Newspapers* to become the *Ayers & Sons Directory of Newspapers and Periodicals*. Now called *Ayers Directory of Publications*.

Editor and Publisher. *International Year Book*. New York: Editor and Publisher, 1959. Comprehensive directory of U.S. and foreign newspaper business, giving circulation, advertising rates, personnel for most papers listed, and statistics for newspaper industry as a whole. "Every daily newspaper in every country of the world."

National Directory of Weekly Newspapers. New York: Weekly Representatives, Inc., 1958-76. Includes semi-weekly and tri-weekly newspapers; previously *Annual Directory of Country and Suburban Home Town Newspapers*.

Parch, Grace D., ed. *Directory of Newspaper Libraries in the U.S. and Canada*. New York: Special Libraries Association, 1976. 319 pp. Includes availability of indexes, published and unpublished, of microfilm files, and services to public.

Working Press of the Nation, 1945-present. Burlington, Iowa: National Research Bureau, 1945-present. Annual. Includes daily newspapers, with names of key personnel; weekly, special interest newspapers, principal U.S. foreign language newspapers, Sunday magazine supplements, news services, photo services, and newsreel companies. Absorbed by *Gebbie House Magazine Directory* in 1976. Continued by *Internal Publication Directory*, vol. 29, 1978.

Bibliographical Studies

Brigham, Clarence S. "Additions and Corrections to History and Bibliography of American Newspapers." *Proceedings of the American Antiquarian Society* 72 (1971): 15-62. This set, along with *American Newspapers 1821-1936* (see Graham below) provides a comprehensive record of newspaper files from 1690 to 1936.

Amon Carter Museum of Western Art. *Newspapers on Microfilm*. Fort Worth, Tex.: By the museum, 1968. 80 leaves. A listing of newspapers acquired by the museum 1964-68.

Barnes, Timothy M. "Loyalist Newspapers of the American Revolution, 1763-1783; A Bibliography." *American Antiquarian Society Publications 83 (1973;): 217-83.*

Brigham, Clarence S. *History and Bibliography of American Newspapers, 1690-1820*. 2 vols. Worcester, Mass.: American Antiquarian Society, 1947.

Center for Research Libraries. *The Center for Research Libraries Catalogue: Newspapers*. 2nd ed. Chicago: By the center, 1978. 233 pp.

Chicago Historical Society. *A Checklist of the Kellogg Collection of "Patent Inside" Newspapers of 1876*. Chicago: WPA Historical Records Survey Project, 1939. 99 leaves.

Consortium of Western Universities and Colleges. *Union List of Newspapers Currently Received by the Member Libraries*. Stanford, Calif.: Hoover Institution, 1969. 41 pp.

Cook, Elizabeth C. "Newspapers in the American Colonies." *Literary Influences in Colonial Newspapers, 1704-1750*. New York: n.p., 1912. pp. 268-72.

Cooper, Gayle. *A Checklist of American Imprints for 1830*. Metuchen, N.J.: Scarecrow Press, 1972.

Delmatier, Royce D. *American Newspaper Files in Eight California Libraries, 1900-1954: A Listing of Metropolitan Newspapers Having a Circulation of Over 50,000*. Berkeley: Regional Resources Coordinating Committee of the California Library Association, 1954. 47 leaves.

Denver Public Library, Western History Department. *Western Newspapers on Microfilm*. 2nd ed. Denver: Public Library, 1972. 14 pp.

Fessler, Aaron L., and Saro J. Ricardi. *Current Newspapers: United States and Foreign; A Union List of Newspapers Available in the Libraries of the New York Metropolitan Area*. New York: New York Public Library, 1957. 66 pp.

Graham, Mrs. Walter. *Census of American Newspapers and Periodicals 1690-1800 in American Libraries*. Urbana, Ill.: n.p., 1934.

Gregory, Winifred. *American Newspapers, 1821-1936: A Union List of Files Available in the United States and Canada*. 1937; reprint ed., New York: Kraus, 1967. Includes references to 3,663 repositories.

Griswold, Ada Tyng, comp. *Annotated Catalogue of Newspaper Files in the Library of the State Historical Society of Wisconsin*. 2nd ed. Madison: State Historical Society of Wisconsin, 1911. 591 pp.

Guide to Microforms in Print: Author/Title. Incorporating International Microforms in Print. Westport, Conn.: Microform Review, Inc., 1982. "Cumulative annual listing of microform titles, comprising. . . newspapers,. . . which are currently available from micropublishing organizations throughout the world. Purpose of the Guide is to serve as a means of bibliographic control of international micropublications."

Hale, Richard W., Jr. *Guide to Photocopied Historical Materials in the United States and Canada*. Ithaca, N.Y.: Cornell University Press for the American Historical Association, 1961. 241 pp.

Haskell, Daniel C., comp. *Checklist of Newspapers and Official Gazettes in the New York Public Library*. New York: New York Public Library, 1915. 579 pp. (Reprinted from *NYPL Bulletin*, July-Dec. 1914.)

Jones, Edgar A., comp. *Catalog of Newspapers on Microfilm in the William F. Maag, Jr., Library*. Youngstown, Ohio: Youngstown State University, 1982. Revised by Jeffrey Luttrell.

Lathem, Edward Connery, comp. *Chronological Tables of American Newspapers, 1690-1820; Being a Tabular Guide to Holdings of Newspapers Published in America Through the Year 1820*. Barre, Mass.: American Antiquarian Society, 1972. 131 pp. Companion to Brigham, above.

Lutz, Earle. "Soldier Newspapers of the Civil War." *Papers of the Bibliographical Society of America* 46 (1952): 373-86.

Maloney, Hazel, ed. *Union List of Newspapers*. Milwaukee: Library Council of Metropolitan Milwaukee, 1979. 55 pp.

Milner, Anita Cheek. *Newspaper Genealogical Column Directory*. Rev. ed. Escondido, Calif.: For the author, 1982. 26 pp.

Mott, Frank Luther. *American Journalism, A History: 1690-1960*. 3rd ed. New York: Macmillan, 1971. 901 pp. Histories of significant newspapers are found under the name of the newspaper.

New York Metropolitan Reference and Research Library Agency. *Union List of Selected Microforms in Libraries in the New York Metropolitan Area*. 3rd ed. New York: By the agency, 1980. 181 pp.

Newspapers and Periodicals for Research on Microfilm. Glen Rock, N.J.: Microfilming Corporation of America, 1971. 78 pp. Updated by individual catalogs published annually for U.S. regions.

Newspapers on Microfilm. Wooster, Ohio: Bell & Howell, Micro-Photo Division, 1979-present. Annual catalog and price list. Special collections include black newspapers, underground newspapers, foreign newspapers published in America.

North, Simon Newton Dexter. *History and Present Condition of the Newspaper and Periodical Press of the United States, with a Catalogue of the Publications of the Census Year*. Washington, D.C.: Government Printing Office, 1884. 446 pp. In U.S. Census Office. 10th Census, vol. 8. Appendix D; Bound Files of American Newspapers in the Possession of the American Antiquarian Society, Worcester, Mass. Index.

Park, Robert Ezra. *Immigrant Press and Its Control*. Westport, Conn.: Greenwood, 1970. 487 pp.

Parsons, Henry S., comp., U. S. Library of Congress, Periodical Division. *Check List of American 18th Century Newspapers in the Library of Congress*. Rev. ed. Washington, D.C.: Government Printing Office, 1936. 401 pp. Originally compiled by John Van Ness Ingram. Bibliography of those publications still in existence in 1870 and 1880 arranged by state and county, with name, date established, owner, and migration of newspaper files. Found in research libraries or U.S. Government Documents Section of university and public libraries.

Philadelphia Bibliographical Center and Union Library Catalogue. Committee on Microphotography. *Union List of Microfilms*. Cumulation 1949-59, 2 vols. Ann Arbor, Mich.: J. W. Edwards, 1961. This does not include newspapers which are listed in Library of Congress Newspapers in Microform.

Saxon, Mary Esther. *Newspapers on Microform in the Bizzell Library*. Norman, Okla.: University of Oklahoma Press, 1975. 209 pp.

Stewart, R. C. and Margaret Byrnes. *Special Microform Collections*. Ann Arbor, Mich.: University of Michigan Libraries, 1977. Lists only those collections for which there are indexes; includes *Early American Newspapers* but excludes library's holdings of American newspapers.

Thomas, Isaiah. "History of Printing in America." *Transactions of the American Antiquarian Society* 2 (1871); bound in two parts. Volume 2 includes a list of newspapers published 1775-1810 by state and ante-Revolution publications year by year.

U. S. Library of Congress, Catalog Publication Division. *Newspapers in Microform: United States 1948-1972*. Washington, D.C.: Library of Congress, 1973. 1057 pp. Preface: "a continuing cumulative series designed to bring under bibliographic control U.S. newspapers that have been reduced to microfilm (microform) and are housed permanently in U.S., Canadian, and foreign libraries, as well as in vaults of domestic and foreign libraries, as well as in vaults of domestic and foreign commerical publishers." *The Union List of Microfilms* began in 1941 as "Union List of Microfilms, 1942," and supplements 1-5, 1943-47, cumulated into *Union Lists of Microfilms*, rev. and enl. and cumulated ed. 1951. Supplements 1949-52, and 1952-55. The final cumulation 1955-59 is replaced by *Newspapers on Microfilm* (microform) published by the Library of Congress.

___________. *Newpapers in Microform, United States: 1973-1977*. Washington, D.C.: Library of Congress, 1978. 642 pp.

___________. *Newspapers in Microfilm, 1978-*. Washington, D.C.: Library of Congress, 1st annual issue, 1978. (144 pp.); 1979 (211 pp.); 1980 (107 pp.).

University Microfilms, Ann Arbor, Michigan. *Catalogue of Newspapers on Microfilm*. Annual edition.

University of Chicago. *Newspapers in Libraries of Chicago, A Joint Check List*. Chicago: University of Chicago Libraries, Document Section, 1936. 258 pp.

Wallace, William S. *A Check List of Western Newspapers in the Mills Collection*. Albuquerque: n.p., 1955. Reprinted from *New Mexico Historical Review* 30 (April 1955). "Byron T. Mills gave his collection to Rodgers Library, New Mexico Highlands University, Las Vegas."

Yale University Library. *List of Newspapers in the Yale University Library*. New Haven: Yale University Press, 1916.

State-by-State Bibliography

Alabama

Alabama State Department of History and Archives. *Checklist of Newspapers and Periodical Files in the Department of Archives and History*. Montgomery: Brown Printing Co., 1904. 65 pp.

Ellison, Rhoda C. *History and Bibliography of Alabama Newspapers in the 19th Century*. Birmingham: University of Alabama Press, 1954. 209 pp.

Samford University Library. *Newspapers on Microfilm*. Birmingham, Ala.: By the library, 1970. 13 leaves.

Arizona

Lutrell, Estelle. "Newspapers and Periodicals of Arizona, 1859-1911." *General Bulletin of the University of Arizona* 20 (July 1949), no. 3.

Arkansas

Historical Records Survey. *Union List of Arkansas Newspapers, 1942. A Partial Inventory of Arkansas Newspaper Files Available in the Offices of Publishers, Libraries, and Private Collections in Arkansas*. Little Rock, Ark.: Historical Records Survey, Division of Community Service Programs, Work Projects Administration, 1942. 240 pp.

Hudson, John A., and Robert L. Peterson. "Arkansas Newspapers in the University of Texas Newspaper Collection." *Arkansas Historical Quarterly* 14 (1955): 207-24.

California

Budenz, Justine, Paul Jordan Smith, and J. H. Young, comps. *Early Newspapers and Periodicals of California and the West, Including the Only Known Complete Copy of the First Volume of the Californian*. San Francisco: W. R. Howell, 1970. 115 pp.

California Library Association, Southern District. *A Union List of Newspapers in Offices of Publishers and in Libraries of Southern California*. Los Angeles: Sixth District, California Library Association, 1936. 200 pp.

California State University, Fullerton. *Union List of Newspapers on Microforms in the California State University and Colleges Libraries*. Edited, compiled, and programmed by the California State University, Fullerton, Library. 2nd ed. Fullerton: California State University, 1975. 416 pp.

Chandler, Katherine. *List of California Periodicals Issued Previously to the Completion of the Transcontinental Telegraph (August 15, 1846-October 24, 1861)*. Library Association of California. Publication No. 7. San Francisco: Hicks-Judd Press, 1905.

Cooperative Information Network (CIN). *Union List of Newspapers*. Stanford, Calif.: Cooperative Information Network, 1978.

Dawson, M. *History and Bibliography of Southern California Newspapers, 1851-1876*. Los Angeles: Dawson's Bookshop, 1950. 86 pp.

Delmatier, Royce D. *American Newspaper Files in Eight California Libraries, 1900-1954*. Berkeley: Regional Resource Coordinating Committee, 1954. 47 leaves.

Flint, Marion D., ed. *Union List of Newspapers in the Libraries of San Diego and Imperial Counties*. 2nd ed. San Diego: San Diego State University Library, 1981. 85 pp.

Giffen, Helen S. *California Mining Town Newspapers, 1850-1880; A Bibliography*. Van Nuys, Calif.: J. E. Reynolds, 1954. 102 pp.

Kemble, Edward C. *A History of California Newspapers, 1846-1858*. Los Gatos, Calif.: Talisman Press, 1962. 398 pp.

Newspaper Holdings of the San Francisco Public Library as of 31 Jan. 1970.

Union List of Newspapers in Offices of Publishers and Libraries of Southern California. Los Angeles: n.p., 1936.

Wheeler, J. F. "Santa Clara County (CA) Newspapers, 1850-1971, An Inventory of Selected Resources, and a Checklist of Newspaper Titles." M.A. thesis, California State University, San Jose, 1972. 193 pp.

Colorado

McMurtrie, Douglas C., and Albert H. Allen. "Early Colorado Newspapers." *Early Printing in Colorado*. Denver: n.p., 1935. 223-86 pp.

Oehlerts, Donald E. *Guide to Colorado Newspapers, 1859-1963.* Denver: Rocky Mountain Bibliographic Center, 1964. 184 pp.

Rex, Wallace H. *Colorado Newspapers Bibliography, 1859-1933.* Denver: Bibliographical Center for Research, Rocky Mountain Region, 1939. 69 pp.

Connecticut

Cutler, C. L. *Connecticut's Revolutionary Press.* Chester: Pequot Press, 1975. 61 pp.

Morse, Jarvis M. *Connecticut Newspapers in the Eighteenth Century.* New Haven: Published for the Tercentenary Commission by the Yale University Press, 1935. 31 pp.

Smith, James E. *One Hundred Years of Hartford's "Courant" from Colonial Times Through the Civil War.* New Haven: Yale University Press, 1949. 343 pp.

Delaware

Delaware University, Newark Library. *Union List of Newspapers in Microform.* Newark: Delaware University Press, 1964. 11 leaves.

District of Columbia

Millington, Yale O. "A List of Newspapers Published in the District of Columbia, 1820-1850." *Papers of the Bibliographic Society* 18 (1924): 60; 19 (1925): 43-65.

Florida

Emig, Elmer J. "A Check-List of Extant Florida Newpapers, 1845- 1846." *Florida Historical Society Quarterly* 11 (1932): 77-87.

Knauss, James O. "List of Florida Newspapers Published Before July 1845." *Territorial Florida Journalism.* Deland, Fla.: n.p. 1926. pp. 86-128.

Georgia

Brantley, Rabun L. *Georgia Journalism During the Civil War Period.* George Peabody College for Teachers, Contributions to Education, No. 58. Nashville, Tenn.: George Peabody College for Teachers, 1929.

Flanders, Ralph B. "Newspapers and Periodicals in the Washington Memorial Library, Macon, Georgia." *North Carolina Historical Review* 7 (1930).

Griffith, Louis T., and John E. Talmadge. *Georgia Journalism, 1763-1950.* Athens, Ga.: University of Georgia Press, 1951. 413 pp.

Illinois

James, Edmund J. *A Bibliography of Newspapers Published in Illinois Prior to 1860.* Illinois State Historical Library Publications, No. 1. Springfield, Ill.: Phillips Bros., 1899. 94 pp. Appendix A: Chronological List of Missouri and Illinois Newspapers 1808-1897, in the Saint Louis Mercantile Library. Appendix B: List of County Histories of Illinois.

Mabbott, Thomas O., and Philip D. Jordan. *A Catalogue of Illinois Newspapers in the New York Historical Society.* Springfield: Journal Printing Co., 1931. 58 pp. Reprint from *Illinois State Historical Society Journal* 24 (1931): 187-242.

Scott, Franklin W. *Newspapers and Periodicals of Illinois, 1814-1879.* Collections of ISHS Library, vol. 6. Rev. and enl. ed. Springfield, Ill.: Trustees of the Illinois State Historical Society, 1910. 610 pp.

Stark, Sandra M. "Newspapers in the Illinois State Historical Library." *Illinois Libraries* 64 (March 1982): 203-334. Updated publication in *Illinois Libraries* every three years. 1982 lists over 60,000 reels of newspaper microfilm acquired since 1959.

University of Chicago. *Newspapers in the Libraries of Chicago.* Chicago: University of Chicago Library, 1936. 258 pp.

Wrone, D. R. "Newspapers of DeWitt County, Illinois, 1854-1960; a Bibliography and Checklist." *Illinois Libraries* 46 (May 1964): 367-92.

Indiana

Etchason, Jerri. *A History of Family-Owned Newspapers in Hartford City, Indiana: 1852-1977.* Muncie, Ind.: Ball State University, 1980. 29 pp.

Miller, John W. *Indiana Newspaper Bibliography: Historical Account of All Indiana Newspapers Published from 1804-1980 and Locational Information for all Available Copies, Both Original and Microfilm.* Indianapolis: Indiana Historical Society, 1982. 538 pp. In process April 1983 is a National Endowment for the Humanities proposal to update this bibliography. Nearly one million pages of Indiana newspapers have been microfilmed since the inception of a microfilming project in spring of 1980. Between ten and twenty thousand pages are filmed per week.

Iowa

Cheever, L. D., comp. *Newspaper Collection of the State Historical Society of Iowa.* Iowa City: State Historical Society of Iowa, 1969. 118 pp.

Iowa Pilot Project of the Organization of American Historians. The Library of Congress, United States Newspaper Project. *A Bibliography of Iowa Newspapers, 1836-1976.* Iowa City: Iowa State Historical Department, 1979. 371 pp.

Petersen, W. J. *The Pageant of the Press, A Survey of 125 Years of Iowa Journalism.* Iowa City: Iowa State Historical Society, 1962. 118 pp.

Pittman, Edward F. *Index to Bound Newspapers in Iowa State Department of History and Archives.* Des Moines: State of Iowa, 1947. 35 pp.

Kansas

Kansas State Historical Society. *History of Kansas Newspapers, 1854-1916.* Topeka: W. R. Smith, 1916. 373 pp.

Kentucky

Evans, Herndon. *The Newspaper Press in Kentucky.* Lexington: University of Kentucky, 1975.

Henry, Edward A. "The Durrett Collection of Kentucky Newspapers Now in the University of Chicago." *Papers of the Bibliographic Society* 8 (1914): 57-94.

Jillson, Willard R. *Newspapers and Periodicals of Frankfort, Kentucky, 1795-1945.* Lexington: Kentucky State Historical Society, 1945. 82 pp.

"Kentucky Newspaper Collections Available in Lexington." *Tri-State Trader* 2 (April 1983): 39. The University of Kentucky has 8,000 reels of Kentucky newspapers 1788 to present, important because of disastrous losses of public records: 66 of 120 Kentucky courthouses suffered floods, fires, and/or tornadoes.

Kinkead, Ludie, and T. D. Clark. *Checklist of Kentucky Newspapers Contained in Kentucky Libraries.* Lexington, 1935. 44 pp.

Perrin, William H. *The Pioneer Press of Kentucky, 1787-1830.* Louisville: Filson Club, 1888. 93 pp.

Rawlings, Kenneth W. "Trial List of Titles of Kentucky Newspapers and Periodicals Before 1860." *Kentucky Historical Society Register* 36 (1938): 263-87.

Louisiana

Historical Records Survey. *Louisiana Newpapers, 1794-1940. List of Louisiana Newspaper Files in Offices of Publishers, Libraries, and Private Collections in Louisiana.* Baton Rouge: Louisiana State Library, 1941. 295 pp.

Louisiana State University and Agricultural and Mechanical College Library. *Newspaper Files in Louisiana State University Library.* Baton Rouge: State University Library, 1961. 211 leaves.

McMullen, T. N., ed. *Louisiana Newspapers, 1794-1969; a Union List of Louisiana Newspaper Files Available in Public, College, and University Libraries in Louisiana.* Baton Rouge: Louisiana State University and Agricultural and Mechanical Library, 1965. 281 pp.

McMurtrie, Douglas C. *Early Printing in New Orleans, 1764-1810, With a Bibliography of the Issues of the Louisiana Press.* New Orleans: Searcy & Pfaff, 1929. 151 pp.

__________. "The French Press of Louisiana. Notes in Supplement to Edward Larocque Tinker's Bibliography of French Newspapers and Periodicals of Louisiana." *Louisiana Historical Quarterly* 18 (1935): 947-65.

Tinker, Edward L. "Bibliography of French Newspapers and Periodicals of Louisiana." *Proceedings of the American Antiquarian Society* 26 (Oct. 1932): 247-370.

Maine

Fassett, Frederick G., Jr. *A History of Newspapers in the District of Maine, 1785-1820.* Orono, Maine: University Press, 1932. 242 pp.

Maryland

Hofstette, E. O., and M. S. Eustis, comps. *Newspapers in Maryland Libraries: A Union List.* Baltimore: State Department of Education, Div. of Library Services, 1977. 139 pp.

Keidel, George C. *Earliest German Newspapers of Baltimore.* Baltimore: privately printed, 1927. Library of Congress has a copy.

___________. "Early Maryland Newspapers: A List of Titles." *Maryland Historical Magazine* 28 (1933); 29 (1934); 30 (1935).

Maryland Gazette. *Two Hundred Years with the Maryland Gazette, with Notes and Illustrations of Historical Maryland.* Annapolis: Capital-Gazette Press, 1927. 180 pp.

Wroth, Lawrence C. *A History of Printing in Colonial Maryland, 1686-1776.* Baltimore: The Typothetae of Baltimore, 1922. 275 pp.

Massachusetts

Ayer, Mary Farwell. *Check-List of Boston Newspapers, 1704-1780.* Boston: Colonial Society of Massachusetts, 1907. 527 pp.

Boston Public Library. *A List of Periodicals, Newspapers in Principal Libraries of Boston and Vicinity.* Boston: Trustees of the Library, 1897. 143 pp.

Michigan

Brown, Elizabeth Read. *A Union List of Newspapers Published in Michigan Based on the Principal Newspaper Collections in the State with Notes Concerning Papers Not Located.* Ann Arbor: University of Michigan, Department of Library Science, 1954. 263 pp.

Doll, Louis W. *A History of the Newspapers of Ann Arbor, 1829-1920.* Wayne State University Studies, No. 5, History. Detroit: Wayne State University Press, 1959. 174 pp.

McMurtrie, Douglas C. "Newspaper Record of Michigan Newspapers, 1796-1850." *Early Printing in Michigan, With a Bibliography of the Michigan Press.* Chicago: John Calhoun Club, 1931. pp. 227-320.

Michigan Newspapers on Microfilm, With a Description of the Michigan Newspapers on Microfilm Project. 4th ed. Lansing: Michigan Bureau of Library Services, 1973. 53 pp.

Sullivan, H. A., and T. Friedes. *Newspaper Resources of Metropolitan Detroit Libraries.* Detroit: Wayne State University Press, 1965. 46 pp.

Minnesota

Hage, George S. *Newspapers on the Minnesota Frontier, 1849-1860.* St. Paul: Minnesota Historical Society, 1967. 176 pp.

Minnesota University Library, Newspaper and Microform Division. *Newspapers in the University of Minnesota Library: A Complete List of Holdings.* Minneapolis: University of Minnesota Press, 1964. 52 pp.

South-Central Minnesota Inter-Library Exchange (SMILE). *Newspapers in the Region Nine Area: A Listing of All Newspapers Published in Blue Earth, Brown, Faribault, LeSueur, Martin, Nicollet, Sibley, Waseca, and Watonwan Counties.* Mankato, Minn.: SMILE, 1976. 11 pp.

University of Minnesota, Immigration History Research Center. *Newspapers on Microfilm.* St. Paul: By the center, 1978.

Mississippi

Historical Records Survey. *Mississippi Newspapers, 1805-1904.* Jackson, Miss.: Works Progress Administration, 1942. 323 pp.

Mitchell Memorial Library, Mississippi State University, comp. *Union List of Newspapers.* Mississippiana, vol. 2. Jackson: Mississippi Library Commission, 1971. 86 pp.

Missouri

Dunbar, Laverne J. "A Missouri State Newspaper Morgue." *Missouri Historical Review* 19 (1924-25): 304-7.

Lyon, William H. *The Pioneer Editor in Missouri, 1808-1860.* Columbia: University of Missouri Press, 1965. 202 pp.

Organ, Minnie. "History of the County Press of Missouri." *Missouri Historical Review* 4 (1909-10): 111-33; 149-66; 252-308.

___________. "Old Newspaper Files in the State Historical Society at Columbia." *Missouri Historical Review* 5 (1910-11): 34-42.

St. Louis Mercantile Library Association. *Missouri and Illinois Newspapers, 1808-1897.* St. Louis:. For the association, 1897.

Taft, William H. *Missouri Newspapers, When and Where, 1803-1963.* Columbia: State Historical Society of Missouri, 1964. 428 pp.

Nebraska

Nebraska State Historical Society. *A Guide to the Newspaper Collection of the State Archives.* Lincoln: By the society, 1969. 89 pp.

Nevada

Lingenfelter, Richard E. The Newspapers of Nevada, 1858-1958; A History and Bibliography. Introduction by David F. Myrick. San Francisco: J. Howell Books, 1964. 228 pp.

McMurtrie, Douglas C. "A Bibliography of Nevada Newspapers, 1858 to 1875." Inclusive in *Gutenberg-Jahrbuch* Mainz (1935): 292-312.

New Jersey

Johnston, Elma L. *Trenton's Newspapers, 1778-1932.* Trenton: Trenton Times Newspapers, 1932. 66 pp.

Nelson, William. "Some Account of American Newspapers, Particularly of the 18th Century." *Documents Relating to the Colonial Revolutionary and Post-Revolutionary History of the State of New Jersey.* Series 1, vols. 11, 12, 19 (1917).

Union List of Newspaper Holdings in Libraries in Somerset County and the Somerset County Area. n.p., 1980. 13 pp.

New Mexico

Groves, P. S., et al., ed. *New Mexico Newspapers; A Comprehensive Guide to Bibliographical Entries and Locations.* Albuquerque: University of New Mexico Press, 1975. 641 pp.

Stratton, Porter A. *The Territorial Press of New Mexico, 1834-1912.* Albuquerque: University of New Mexico Press, 1969. 306 pp.

New York

Chautauqua County Historical Society. *A Guide to Newspapers in Microform in Chautauqua County, New York.* Westfield, N.Y.: By the society, 1982. 100 leaves. Part 1, Guide; Part 2, Microfilm Index.

"Checklist of New York City Newspapers Arranged by Year, 1725-1811," *Stokes' Iconography,* vol. 2, pp. 431-52.

Faibisoff, Sylvia G., and Abigail S. Kelly. "A Bibliography of Newspapers in Fourteen New York State Counties." *New York History* 53 (1972). Continues to present.

Fox, Louis H. "New York City Newspapers, 1820-1850; A Bibliography." *Papers of the Bibliographic Society* 21 (1927): 1-131.

Hamilton, Milton W. *The Country Printer of New York State.* New York: Columbia University Press, 1936. 360 pp.

Mercer, Paul, comp. *Bibliographies and Lists of New York State Newspapers: An Annotated Guide.* Albany: State Library, 1981. 79 pp.

New York State Library. *A Checklist of Newspapers in Microform in the New York State Library, the University of the State of New York, State Education Department.* Albany: The New York State Library, 1979. 35 pp.

Newspapers on Microfilm: A Listing of Newspapers on Microfilm in Allegheny, Chemung, Schuyler, Steuben, and Yates Counties. Corning, N.Y.: Southern Tier Library System, 1981. 47 pp.

Rochester Public Library. *Union List of Serials in the Libraries of Rochester, Including Periodicals, Newspapers, Annuals, Publications of Societies, and Other Books Published at Intervals.* Rochester: Rochester Public Library, 1917. 147 pp.

Shultes, Dorothea, for Syracuse University Libraries. *Newspapers on Microfilm in Syracuse University Libraries.* Syracuse, N.Y.: Syracuse University Press, 1971. 30 leaves.

North Carolina

Crittenden, Charles C. *North Carolina Newspapers Before 1790.* The James Sprunt Historical Studies, vol. 10, no. 1. Chapel Hill: The University of North Carolina Press, 1928. 83 pp.

Jones, H. G., and Julius H. Avant. *Union List of North Carolina Newspapers, 1751-1900.* Edited in cooperation with the Committee on Conservation of Newspaper Resources of the North Carolina Library Association. Raleigh: State Department of Archives and History, 1963. 152 pp.

Jones, Roger C. *Guide to North Carolina Newspapers on Microfilm: North Carolina Newspapers Available on Microfilm from the Division of Archives and History.* 5th rev. ed. Raleigh, N.C.: North Carolina Division of Archives and History, 1982. 92 pp.

Wallace, Wesley H. "Property and Trade: Main Themes of Early North Carolina Newspaper Ads." *North Carolina Historical Review* 32 (1955): 451 ff.

North Dakota

Kolar, Carol K. *Union List of North Dakota Newspapers, 1864-1976.* Fargo: North Dakota Institute for Regional Studies, 1981. 448 pp.

Ohio

Gutgesell, Stephen, ed. *Guide to Ohio Newspapers, 1793-1973: Union Bibliography of Ohio Newspapers Available in Ohio Libraries.* Columbus: Ohio Historical Society, 1976. 412 pp.

Galbreath, C. B., for Ohio State Library. *Newspapers and Periodicals in Ohio State Library, Other Libraries of the State, and Lists of Ohio Newspapers in the Library of Congress, and the Library of the Historical Society of Wisconsin.* Columbus, Ohio: Fred J. Heer, 1902. 268 pp.

Oklahoma

Foreman, Carolyn T. *Oklahoma Imprints, 1835-1907; A History of Printing in Oklahoma Before Statehood.* Norman, Okla.: University of Oklahoma Press, 1936. 499 pp.

Ray, Grace E. *Early Oklahoma Newspapers: History and Description of Publications from Earliest Beginnings to 1889.* University of Oklahoma Bulletin, n.s. No. 407, Studies No. 28. Norman, Okla.: University of Oklahoma Press, 1928. 119 pp.

Oregon

Oregon University Library. *Newspapers on Microfilm.* Occasional Paper, No. 2, Eugene, Ore.: Oregon University Library, 1963. 17 leaves.

Turnball, G. S. *History of Oregon Newspapers.* Portland; Binsfords, 1939. 560 pp.

Pennsylvania

Hocker, Edward W. *Genealogical Data Relating to the German Settlers of Pennsylvania and Adjacent Territory: From Advertisements in German Newspapers Published in Philadelphia and Germantown, 1743- 1800.* Indexed by Thomas L. Hollowak. Baltimore: Genealogical Publishing Co., 1980. 242 pp.

Knauss, James O. "Tables of German-American Newspapers of the Eighteenth Century." *Social Conditions Among the Pennsylvania Germans in the Eighteenth Century.* Lancaster, Penn.: Proceedings of the Pennsylvania-German Society, 1922. pp. 160-202.

Nolan, James B. *Newspapers of Berks County, Pennsylvania, 1789-1900.* Reading: Historical Society of Berks County, 1951. 69 pp.

Pennsylvania Historical Survey. *A Checklist of Pennsylvania Newspapers prepared by the Pennsylvania Historical Survey, Division of Community Service Programs, Work Projects Administration.* Harrisburg: Pennsylvania Historical Commission, 1944-present. Vol. 1, Philadelphia County.

Pennsylvania State University Library. *Newspapers on Microform, Pattee Library, Pennsylvania State University.* New ed. University Park: By the library, 1978. 90 leaves.

Pennsylvania State Library. *Holdings of Pennsylvania Newspapers.* Harrisburg: General Library Division, 1965. 67 leaves.

Salisbury, Ruth. *Pennsylvania Newspapers: A Bibliography and Union List.* Pittsburgh: Pennsylvania Library Association, 1969. 179 pp.

Steirer, William F., Jr. "Mirror of Revolution: A Study of Pennsylvania in Newspapers, 1764-1794." Ph.D. diss., University of Pennsylvania, 1967.

South Carolina

Cohen, Hennig. *The South Carolina Gazette: 1732-1775.* Columbia: University of South Carolina Press, 1953. 273 pp.

South Carolina Newspapers Issued on Microfilm. Charleston: South Carolina Library Society, 1956.

Woody, Robert H. *Republican Newspapers of South Carolina.* Charlottesville, Va.: The Historical Publishing Co., Inc., 1936.

Tennessee

John Willard Brister Library. *Newspapers on Microforms.* Memphis: Memphis State University, 1975. 25 pp.

Tennessee State Library and Archives. *Collection of Newspapers on Microfilm.* Nashville: Tennessee State Library, 1958-59.

__________. *Tennessee Newspapers: A Cumulative List of Microfilmed Tennessee Newspapers in the Tennessee State Library.* Nashville: State Library, 1969. 126 pp. Progress report.

Texas

McCausland, Walter. "Some Early Texas Newspapers." *Southwestern Historical Review* 49 (1945-46): 384-89.

Historical Records Survey. *A Union List of Texas Newspapers, 1831-1939.* San Jacinto: Museum of History Association, 1941. 293 pp.

Murphy, Virginia B. *Newspaper Resources of District V, Texas Library Association: A Union List.* Houston: University of Houston Library, 1968. 46 pp.

__________. *Newspaper Resources of Southeast Texas.* Houston: University of Houston Libraries, 1971. 63 pp.

Texas State Library, Austin, Information Services Division. *Newspapers on Microfilm.* Austin: Public Services Department, 1978. 13 leaves.

Wittenmyer, M. O., ed. *Union List of Newspapers in the Libraries of Fort Worth-Dallas Major Resource Centers.* Fort Worth: Texas Christian University Library, 1969. 144 pp.

Utah

Alter, J. Cecil. *Early Utah Journalism: A Half Century of Warfare Waged by the West's Most Militant Press.* Salt Lake City: Utah State Historical Society, 1938. 405 pp.

McMurtrie, Douglas C. *Notes on Early Printing in Utah Outside of Salt Lake City.* Los Angeles: Press of Frank Wiggins Trade School, 1938. 9 pp. Reprinted from *Utah Historical Quarterly* 5 (July 1932): 83-87.

Utah Daily Newspapers on Microfilm. List available from University Microfilming Corporation, 3322 South 3rd East, Salt Lake City, UT 84106.

Vermont

Forbes, Charles S. "History of Vermont Newspapers." *The Vermonter,* Aug. 1905.

Virginia

Cappon, Lester J. *Virginia Newspapers, 1821-1935: A Bibliography with Historical Introduction and Notes.* New York: Appleton-Century, 1936. 299 pp.

Minor, Kate P., and Susie B. Harrison. *A List of Newspapers in the Virginia State Library, Confederate Museum, and Valentine Museum.* Richmond: Virginia State Library, 1912. *Virginia State Library Bulletin* 5 (1912): 285-425.

Richmond Area Reference Group. *Union List of Newspapers.* Ashland, Va.: for reference only, 1971. 14 leaves.

Smith, Glenn C. *Checklist of Newspapers to 1821 in the Alderman Library, University of Virginia.* Ninth Annual Report of Historical Collections of the University of Virginia, n.d.

"Virginia Newspapers in Public Libraries: Annotated List of Virginia Newspapers in the Library of Congress." *Virginia Magazine of History and Biography* 8 (1900-01); 9 (1901-02); 10 (1902-03).

Washington

"Newspapers of Washington Territory to 1890." *Washington Historical Quarterly* 13 (1922): 181-95, 251-68; 14 (1923): 21-29, 100-7, 186-200, 269-90; 26 (1935): 34-64, 129-43.

Smith, Charles W. "The Bagley Collection of Pacific Northwest History." *Washington Historical Quarterly* 10 (1919): 83-87.

Washington Newspapers and Historical Materials on Microfilm in the Washington State Library. Olympia: Washington State Library, 1966. 27 pp.

Hamilton, Katryn S., comp. *Newspapers on Microfilm in the Washington State Library.* Olympia: Washington State Library, 1980. 86 pp.

West Virginia

Kiplinger, John L. "The Press in the Making of West Virginia." *West Virginia History* 6 (1944-45): 127-76.

Nonona, Delf, and Charles Shetler. *West Virginia Imprints, 1790-1863. A Checklist of Books, Newspapers, Periodicals.* Moundsville, W.V.: n.p., 1958.

West Virginia University Library. *Newspapers in the West Virginia University Library.* Morgantown, W.V.: West Virginia University Library, 1964.

Wisconsin

"File of Old Newspapers." *Wisconsin Magazine of History* 6 (1924-25): 454-58.

Hansen, James L. *Wisconsin Newspapers, 1833-1850: An Analytical Bibliography*. Madison: State Historical Society of Wisconsin, 1979. 100 pp.

Oehlerts, Donald E., comp. *Guide to Wisconsin Newspapers 1833-1957*. Madison: State Historical Society of Wisconsin, 1958. 338 pp.

Blair, Emma Helen. *Annotated Catalogue of Newspapers in the Library of the State Historical Society of Wisconsin*. Corrected to 1 January 1896. Madison: State Historical Society of Wisconsin, 1896. (Cover date 1898) 208 pp. 2nd ed., 1911. 591 pp.

Wyoming

Keen, Elizabeth. "Guide to Wyoming Frontier Newspapers." *Annals of Wyoming* 33 (1961): 135-68; 34 (1962): 218-33; 35 (1963): 88-101.

Homsher, Lola. *Guide to Wyoming Newspapers, 1867-1967*. Cheyenne: Wyoming State Library, 1971. 130 pp.

McMurtrie, Douglas C. "Early Printing in Wyoming." *Papers of the Bibliographic Society* 36 (1942): 267-304.

Ethnic, Religious, Foreign-Language, Occupational, and Specialty Newspapers

American Council for Nationalities Service. *Ethnic Press in the U.S., Lists of Ethnic Newspapers and Periodicals in the U. S.* New York: Nationalities Press, 1974.

Arndt, Karl J. R., and May E. Olson. *German-American Newspapers and Periodicals 1732-1955, History and Bibliography*. 2nd rev. ed. New York: Johnson Reprint Corp., 1965. 810 pp. Vol. 2: 1732-1968. Pullach/München: Verlag Documentation. Addenda to 1732-1955 volume. 708 pp.

Black Press Periodical Directory, 1975. Newark, N.J.: Black Press Clipping Bureau, 1974. 61 pp.

Boonstra, Harry. *Dutch-American Newspapers and Periodicals in Michigan, 1850-1925*. Chicago: University of Chicago, 1967. 108 pp.

Culkin, Harry M. *Guide to Current Catholic Diocesan Newspapers in Microfilm*. New York: Catholic Committee, American Theological Association, 1979.

Demaree, Albert L. *The American Agricultural Press*. New York: Columbia University Press, 1941. 430 pp.

Fraenkel, Joseph. *The Jewish Press of the World*. 7th ed. London: Cultural Department of the World Jewish Congress, 1972. 128 pp. 1st ed. 1953.

Golembiewski, Thomas E. *The Study of Obituaries as a Source for Polish Genealogical Research*. Chicago: Polish Genealogical Society, 1983. 70 pp. Chicago reference tool.

Hebrew Union College, American Jewish Periodical Center. *Jewish Newspapers and Periodicals on Microfilm, Available at the American Jewish Periodical Center*. Cincinnati: Jewish Institute of Religion 1957. 56 pp. Supplement 1, by H. C. Zafren. Cincinnati, 1960. 28 pp. Reprint from *Studies in Bibliography and Booklore* 4 (Dec. 1959).

Hollowak, Thomas L. *Indices of the Obituaries in the Jednosc-Polonia*. Chicago: Polish Genealogical Society, 1983. 150 pp. *Jednosc-Polonia* was the most important Polish newspaper in Baltimore.

Joseph Jacobs Organization. *Joseph Jacobs Directory of the Jewish Press in America*. New York: By the author, 1974. 144 pp.

Keidel, J. C. *Earliest German Newspapers of Baltimore*. Baltimore: For the author, 1927. Copy at Library of Congress.

Kolehmainen, John I. "Finnish Newspapers and Periodicals in Michigan." *Michigan History* 24 (1940): 119-27.

"Lithuanian American Publications." In Algirdas M. Budreckis, comp. and ed. *The Lithuanians in America, 1651-1975*. Dobbs Ferry, N.Y.: Oceana Publications, 1976. Appendix, pp. 157-59.

Norlie, O. M. *Norwegian-American Papers, 1847-1946*. Northfield, Minn.: Eilron Press, 1946.

Norton, Wesley. *Religious Newspapers in the Old Northwest to 1861: A History, Bibliography, and Record of Opinion*. Athens: Ohio University Press, 1977. 196 pp. Study of religious publications in the Midwest.

Radical Periodicals in the United States 1890-1960. Westport, Conn.: Greenwood Press, 1976. Includes color chart showing when each was published.

Setterdahl, Lilly. *Swedish-American Newspapers: A Guide to the Microfilms Held by the Swenson Swedish Immigration Research Center, Augustana College, Rock Island, Illinois*. Augustana Library Publications, No. 35. Rock Island, Ill.: Augustana College Library, 1981. 36 pp.

Stroupe, Henry S. *The Religious Press in the South Atlantic States, 1802-1865*. Durham, N.C.: Duke University Press, 1956.

Wynar, Lubomyr Roman, and Anna T. Wynar. *Encyclopedic Directory of Ethnic Newspapers and Periodicals in the United States*. 2nd ed. Littleton, Colo.: Libraries Unlimited, 1976. 248 pp. 1st ed. 1972. 2nd ed. eliminates defunct publications, lists 977.

General Indexes and Abstracts

Brayer, Herbert O. "Preliminary Guide to Indexed Newspapers in the United States, 1850-1900." *Mississippi Valley Historical Review 33 (1946): 237-58.*

Chicago Public Library. *Guide to Indexes and Abstracts*. Chicago: Chicago Public Library, 1977. Newspaper index pp. 10-11.

Evans, Helen F. *Index of References to American Women in Colonial Newspapers through 1800*. Bedford, N.H.: The Bibliographer, 1979. Volume 1, New Hampshire.

Holloway, Lisabeth M., et al. *Medical Obituaries: American Physicians' Biographical Notices in Selected Medical Journals Before 1907*. New York: Garland Publishing Co., 1981.

Jarboe, Betty M. *Obituaries: A Guide to Sources*. Boston: G. K. Hall, 1982. 340 pp.

Martin, George A. *Marriage and Death Notices from the National Intelligencer, Washington, D.C., 1800-1850*. Washington, D.C.: National Genealogical Society, 1976.

Milner, Anita Cheek. *Newspaper Indexes; A Location and Subject Guide for Researchers*. 3 vols. Metuchen, N.J.: Scarecrow Press, 1977-82. Includes unpublished indexes and card indexes.

New England Library Association, Bibliography Committee. *A Guide to Newspaper Indexes in New England*. Holden, Mass.: New England Library Association, 1978. 91 pp.

Sell, Kenneth D. "Checklist of Published Indexes to Current American Daily Newspapers." *RQ* 17 (1977): 13-16. These are published indexes. Circulation over 100,000, 150 titles, 29 published indexes.

State-by-State Indexes and Abstracts

Alabama

Foley, Helen S. *Marriage and Death Notices of Alabama Newspapers, 1819-1890*. Easley, S.C.: Southern Historical Press, 1981. 200 pp.

__________. *Obituaries from Barbour County (Alabama) Newspapers, 1890-1905*. Easley, S.C.: Southern Historical Press, 1976. 146 pp.

Gandrud, Pauline Jones. *Marriage, Death, and Legal Notices from Early Alabama Newspapers, 1818-1880*. Easley, S.C.: Southern Historical Press, 1981. 618 pp.

California

Genealogical Society of Riverside California. *Newspaper Abstracts, Births, Marriages, Deaths, 1878*. Riverside: For the society, 1976. 16 pp.

Newspaper Index: Los Angeles Times. Jan. 1972. Wooster, Ohio: Bell and Howell Microphoto Division, 1972-present.

"Vital Statistics from the San Diego Union." *Leaves and Saplings* (San Diego Genealogical Society) 1 (1973): 149 ff.

Colorado

Gladden, Sanford C. *Index to Boulder County Newspapers, 1877-1905*. Manuscript index at Norlin Library, University of Colorado, Boulder.

Connecticut

Ireland, Norma Olin, and Winifred Irving. *Index to the Hartford Times; Genealogical Gleanings, 1912-1916*. Fallbrook, Calif.: Ireland Indexing Service, n.d.

Scott, Kenneth, and Roseanne Conway, comps. *Genealogical Data from Colonial New Haven Newspapers*. Baltimore: Genealogical Publishing Company, 1979. 547 pp.

District of Columbia

Newspaper Index: Washington Post. Jan. 1971. Wooster, Ohio: Bell and Howell Microphoto Division, 1971-present.

Georgia

Annals of Savannah, 1850-1937: Digest and Index to the "Savannah Morning News." Savannah: n.p., 1961. Copy in Library of Congress.

Colket, Meredith B., Jr. "Indexes to Savannah, Georgia, Newspapers." *National Genealogical Society Quarterly* 79 (Sept. 1981): 181-83.

"Indexing Newspapers." *National Genealogical Society Quarterly* 57 (1969): 92. Description of indexes to *Augusta Chronicle*, 1861-73.

LeMaster, Mrs. Vernon. *Abstracts of Georgia Death Notices from the Southern Recorder, 1830-1855.* Orange, Calif.: Orange County Calilfornia Genealogical Society, 1971. 115 pp.

__________. *Abstracts of Georgia Marriages from the Southern Recorder, 1830-1955.* Orange, Calif.: Orange County California Genealogical Society, 1971. 108 pp.

Newspaper Index: Atlanta Constitution. Jan. 1979. Sanford, N.C.: Microfilming Corporation of America, 1980.

Warren, Mary Bondurant. *Marriages and Deaths, Adstracted from Extant Georgia Newspapers.* 2 Vols. Danielsville, Ga.: Heritage Papers, n.d. vol. 1: 1763-1820. 155 pp. vol. 2: 1820-30, 191 pp.

Indiana

Beeson, Cecil. *Newspaper Items from the Hartford City Telegram, Hartford City, Indiana.* Fort Wayne: Public Library, 1972. 402 pp.

Capt. Jacob Warrick Chapter, NSDAR. *Warrick County, Indiana Newspapers, Standard and Enquirer of Boonville,* Owensboro, Ky.: McDowell Publications, n.d. 271 pp.

Cox, Carroll O. and Gloria M. Cox. *New Harmony, Indiana, Newspaper Gleanings, 1825-1844.* Owensboro, Ky.: McDowell Publications, n.d. 265 pp.

Fort Wayne and Allen County Public Library. *Index to Obituary Records as Found in the "Journal Gazette," Fort Wayne, Indiana.* Fort Wayne, Ind.: By the library, 1973-76. 1 (1900-18) 360; 2 (1938-49) 449; 3 (1971-75) 297.

Smith, W. W. *Newspapers Abstracts of Owensville and Gibson County, Indiana, 1872-1915, Being a Reprint of the Information Contained in the Several Editions of a True Record.* Michael L. Cook, ed. and indexer. Evansville, Ind.: Tri-State Genealogical Society, 1978. 160 pp.

Wilke, Katherine. *Newspaper Gleanings, Union City, Randolph County.* Union City, Ind.: for the author, 1969. Vol. I: 1873-83.

Illinois

Chicago Genealogical Society. *Vital Records from Chicago Newspapers, 1833-1848.* Vols. 1-7. Chicago: Genealogical Society, n.d. Recreates records destroyed by the Chicago Fire in 1871, includes other counties in northern Illinois and in New York State.

Hutchinson, Ruth A. *Abstracts of Marriage, Death, and Estate Notices from the "Oquawka Spectator", Henderson County, Illinois, 1848-1852.* Rowlett, Tex.: For the author, 1979.

Koss, David. "Chicago Obituaries in Der Christliche Botschafter, 1844-1871", *Chicago Genealogist*, Summer, 1979, pp. 5-11.

Newspaper Index: Chicago Sun Times. Jan. 1979-present. Wooster, Ohio: Bell and Howell Microphoto Division, 1979-present.

Newspaper Index: Chicago Tribune. Jan. 1972-present. Wooster, Ohio. Bell and Howell Microphoto Division, 1972-present.

Smith, Lilah, and Verda Gerwick. *Marriage Records of McLean County, Illinois.* Danville, Ill.: Heritage House, 1971. 25 pp. Extracts from newspapers.

Wrone, D. R. "Newspapers of DeWitt County, Illinois, 1854-1960; A Bibliography and Checklist." *Illinois Libraries* 46 (May 1964): 367-92.

Kentucky

Smith, Pearl O. *Genealogical Excerpts from Ohio County, Kentucky Newspapers, 1881-1899.* Owensboro, Ken.: McDowell Publications, n.d. 92 pp.

Louisiana

Newspaper Index: The New Orleans Times-Picayune. Jan. 1972-present. Wooster, Ohio: Bell and Howell Microphoto Division, 1972-present.

Maryland

Arps, Walter E., Jr. *Before the Fire, Genealogical Gleanings from the Cambridge (MD) Chronicle, 1830-1855.* Lutherville, Md.: Bettie Carothers, 1978. 54 pp.

Barnes, Robert. *Marriages and Deaths from Baltimore Newspapers, 1796-1816.* Baltimore: Genealogical Pubishing Co., 1978. 383 pp.

__________*Marriages and Deaths from the Maryland Gazette, 1727-1839.* Baltimore: Genealogical Publishing Co., 1973. 234 pp.

Hollowak, Thomas L. *Index of Marriages and Deaths in the (Baltimore) Sun, 1837-1850.* Baltimore: Genealogical Publishing Co., 1978. 787 pp.

__________*Index to Marriages and Deaths in the (Baltimore) Sun, 1851-1860.* Baltimore: Genealogical Publishing Co., 1978. 292 pp.

Massachusetts

Boston Evening Transcript. Index 1879-1899. Worcester, Mass.: American Antiquarian Society, n.d.

The Christian Intelligencer. Index 1830-1871. Worcester, Mass.: American Antiquarian Society, n.d.

The Columbia Sentinel. Index 1784-1840. Worcester, Mass.: American Antiquarian Society, 1961.

Index of Obituaries of Boston Newspapers, 1704-1800: Boston Athenaeum. 3 vols. Boston: G. K. Hall, 1968.

Works Progress Administration. *Index to Local News in the Hampshire Gazette, 1786-1937.* 3 vols. Boston: Historical Records Survey, 1939.

Michigan

Cowles, Jane A., et al. *Condensed Transcripts of Obituaries in the Region of Southeast Isabella County, Michigan and Surrounding Area.* Owensboro, Ky.: McDowell Publications, n.d. 109 pp.

Newspaper Index: The Detroit News. Jan. 1976. Wooster, Ohio: Bell and Howell Microphoto Division, 1976-present.

Mississippi

Mississippi Genealogical Society. *Newspaper Notices of Mississippiana 1820-1860.* Jackson, Miss., 1960. 152 pp. Reprinted from *Journal of Mississippi History*, vols. 18-21.

Missouri

"Death and Estate Notices, Missouri Gazette, 1808-1822," *National Genealogical Society Quarterly* 65 (1977); 67 (1979). 17 pp.

McManus, Thelma S. *Ripley County (Missouri) Records: Obituary, 1874-1910.* Doliphan, Mo.: By the author, 1979. 259 pp.

Kentucky

Clift, G. Glenn. "Kentucky Marriages and Obituaries, 1787-1860." *Kentucky Historical Society Register* 36 (1938); 37 (1939); 38 (1940); 39 (1941); 40 (1942); 41 (1943).

Sisson, Sarah, and Janice Mercer. *Newspaper Articles.* Lawson, Mo.: By the authors, 1978. 87 pp.

Stanley, Lois, George F. Wilson, and Maryhelen Wilson. *Death Records from Missouri Newspapers: The Civil War Years, Jan. 1861-Dec. 1865.* St. Louis, Mo.: By the authors, 1983. 193 pp.

Nebraska

Dale, R. E. *Index to the Plattsmouth Weekly Herald, 1865-1872.* 4 vols. Lincoln: Nebraska State Historical Society, 1957.

New Hampshire

Hammond, Otis G. *Death and Marriage Notices from the New Hampshire Gazette, 1765-1800.* Bowie, Md.: Heritage Books, n.d. 246 pp.

New York

Gottesman, Rita S. *The Arts and Crafts in New York: Advertisements and News Items from New York City Newspapers.* 3 vols. New York: Printed for the New York Historical Society, 1938-1949. (Reprinted from *Collections of the New York Historical Society* for the years 1936, 1948, 1949, The John Wats De Peyster Publication Fund Series, 69, 81-82.) Vol. 1: 1726-76, vol. 2: 1777-99, vol. 3: 1800-04.

New York Daily Tribune. Index. 1875-1906. 10 vols.

New York Morning Herald. After the *New York Post,* the best source for marriage and death notices. No index available to the public. A manuscript subject index 1873-1924, owned by the *New York Telegram,* superficially extended back to 1840, including incomplete obituaries from 1848 and marriages from 1858.

New York Times. Index. 1851-1982. Published annually since 1913. Provides coverage from September 1851 through 1912 with indexes originally printed for use by the *New York Times* staff, as well as newly prepared indexes.

New York Times. Obituaries Index, 1858-1968. New York: New York Times, 1970. 1136 pp. More than 390,000 listings compiled from the *New York Times Index.* Alphabetically arranged list of names giving year of death and reference to the obituary in the *New York Times.*

Falk, Byron A., and Valerie R. Falk. *Personal Name Index to "The New York Times Index" 1851-1974.* 21 vols. Succasunna, N.J.: Roxbury Data Interface, 1976-81. Single Alphabetical listing of millions of names buried in the *New York Times Indexes.* Death listings included with citations preceded by "d". There are no *Times* indexes for 1907, 1908, 1910. Very few references for years 1909, 1911, 1912, and especially 1905 due to contents of the *Times* indexes for those years.

Scott, Kenneth. *Genealogical Data from Colonial New York Newspapers.* 1964-76. Reprint. Baltimore: Genealogical Publishing Co., 1977. 278 pp.

__________. *Genealogical Abstracts from the American Weekly, 1719-1746.* Baltimore: Genealogical Publishing Co., 1974. 180 pp.

__________. *Genealogical Data from the New York Post-Boy, 1743-1773.* Washington, D.C.: National Genealogical Society, 1973. 188 pp.

__________. *Rivington's New York Newspaper: Excerpts from a Loyalist Press, 1773-1783.* New York: New York Historical Society, 1973. 470 pp.

North Carolina

Broughton, Carrie L. *Marriage and Death Notices from "Raleigh Register" and "North Carolina State Gazette," 1799-1825.* 1945; reprint ed., Genealogical Publishing Co., 1975. 178 pp.

__________. *Marriage and Death Notices in "Raleigh Register" and "North Carolina State Gazette," 1826-1845.* 1947; reprint ed. Baltimore: Genealogical Publishing Co., 1968. 402 pp.

__________. *Marriage and Death Notices in the "Raleigh Register" and "North Carolina State Gazette," 1846-1867.* 1949-50; reprint ed., Baltimore Genealogical Publishing Co., 1975. 205 pp.

__________. *Marriage and Death Notices in the "Raleigh Register" and "North Carolina State Gazette," 1846-1893.* (Microform). Sanford, N.C.: Microfilming corp. of America, 1979. 6 microfiches. Originally published in the *Bulletin of North Carolina State Library* (1947).

Cotten, Elizabeth H. *Marriage and Death Notices from Raleigh, N. C., Newspapers, 1796-1826.* Easley, S.C.: Southern Historical Press, 1977. 164 pp.

Grantham, Rose L., and Carol Haywood, comps. *Death Notices from the "Mecklenberg Jeffersonian," Charlotte, N.C., 1841-1849: An Index Microform.* Sanford, N.C.: Microfilming Corp. of America, 1979. 2 microfiches. (Microreproduction of original published Charlotte, N.C.: Public Library of Charlotte and Mecklenburg County, 1966).

Lucas, Silas Emmett, Jr., and Brent Holcomb. *Marriages and Death Notices from Raleigh, North Carolina Newspapers, 1796-1826.* Easley, S.C.: Southern Historical Press, 1978. 168 pp.

Neal, Lois Smathers. *Abstracts of Vital Records from Raleigh, North Carolina Newspapers.* 2 vols. Spartanburg, S.C.: Reprint Company, 1979-1980. Vol. 1: 1799-1819; Vol. 2: 1820-29.

Topkins, Robert M. *Marriage and Death Notices from Extant Asheville Newspapers, 1830-1870: An Index.* Raleigh, N.C.: North Carolina Genealogical Society, 1877. 139 pp.

__________. *Marriage and Death Notices from the "Western Carolinian" (Salisbury, N.C.) 1820-1842: An Indexed Abstract.* 1975; reprint ed., Spartanburg, S.C.: Reprint Co., 1982.

Wright, F. Edward. *Marriages and Deaths from Caroline County Newspapers, 1830-1874.* Silver Springs, Md.: Family Line, 1972. 60 pp.

Ohio

Cleveland Newspapers, Index. January 1976- . Cleveland: Public Library, 1976-present.

Cleveland Press and Cleveland Plain Dealer Index. Copy at Henry E. Huntington Library, San Marino, Calif.

Gilbert, Audrey. *Obituary Abstracts . . . from . . . Preble County, Ohio Newspapers: Eaton Register, Eaton Democrat.* 2 vols. Owensboro, Ken.: McDowell Publications, 1981-present. (Vol. 1: 1850-90; Vol. 2: 1877-95.

Index to Obituaries in the Toledo Blade, 1837 to Present. Manuscript card index, Toledo Public Library, Toledo, Ohio.

Timman, Henry R. *Newspaper Abstracts, Huron County, Ohio, 1822-1835.* Norwalk, Ohio: By the author, 1974. 70 pp.

Wilke, Katherine. *Newspaper Death Records, Darke County, Ohio.* 4 vols. Union City, Ind., 1968. Vol. 1: 1850-80; Vol 2: 1880-85; Vol. 3: 1886-91; Vol. 4: 1892-98.

Oregon

Oregon Spectator. "Oregon Spectator" Index, 1846-1854. Prepared by WPA Newspaper Index Project. Sponsored by the City of Portland and the Oregon Historical Society. 2 vols. Portland: Historical Records Commission, 1901. Vol. 1: A-J; Vol. 2: K-Z.

Pennsylvania

"Marriage and Death Notices from the Philadelphia Saturday Evening Post." *Pennsylvania Magazine of History and Biography (1971-1973).*

"Marriage Notices in the Pennsylvania Gazette, 1766-1787." *National Genealogical Society Quarterly* 64 (1976), no. 3.

McRae, Joan M. *Marriage and Death Notices Extracted from Warren County, Pa. Newspapers, 1848-1865.* N.p.: For the author, 1982.

Rentmeister, Jean R. *Marriage and Death Notices Extracted from the Genius of Liberty and Fayette Advertiser of Uniontown, Pa., 1805-1854.* Apollo, Pa.: Closson Press, 1981. 52 leaves.

Scott, Kenneth. *Abstracts from Ben Franklin's Pennsylvania Gazette, 1728-1748.* Baltimore: Genealogical Publishing Co., 1975. 720 pp.

__________, and Janet R. Clarke. *Abstracts from the "Pennsylvania Gazette," 1748-1755.* Baltimore: Genealogical Publishing Co., 1977. 376 pp.

__________. *Abstracts (Mainly Deaths) from the "Pennsylvania Gazette," 1725-1748.* Baltimore: Genealogical Publishing Co., 1976. 58 pp.

__________. *Genealogical Abstracts from the "American Weekly Mercury," 1719-1746.* Baltimore: Genealogical Publishing Co., 1974. 180 pp.

__________. *Genealogical Data from the Pennsylvania Chronicle, 1767-1774.* Washington, D.C.: National Genealogical Society, 1976. 170 pp.

South Carolina

Cohen, Hennig. *"The South Carolina Gazette," 1732-1775.* Columbia: University of South Carolina Press, 1953.

Elliott, Colleen M., ed. *Marriage and Death Notices from the Keowee Courier, 1849-1883.* Easley, S.C.: Southern Historical Press, 1979. 186 pp.

Hart, Joseph E. *Marriage and Death Notices from Yorkville, S.C., Newspapers.* 2 vols. York, S.C.: For the author, 1971.

Herd, Elmer Don. *Marriage and Death Notices from the Abbeville Banner, 1846-1860.* N.p., 1980. 74 pp.

Holcomb, Brent H. *Marriage and Death Notices from Baptist Newspapers of South Carolina, 1835-1865.* Spartanburg, S.C.: Reprint Co., 1981. 143 pp.

__________. *Marriage and Death Notices from Camden, South Carolina*

Newspapers, 1816-1865. Easley, S.C.: Southern Historical Press, 1978. 166 pp.

__________. *Marriage and Death Notices from the Up-country of South Carolina: as taken from Greenville Newspapers, 1826-1863.* Columbia, S.C.: South Carolina Magazine of Ancestral Research, 1983. 269 pp.

__________. *Marriage and Death Notices from Columbia, South Carolina Newspapers, 1792-1839.* Easley, S.C.: Southern Historical Press, 1982. 114 pp.

__________. *Marriage and Death Notices from the Charleston Observer, 1827-1845.* Spartanburg, S.C.: Reprint Publishers, 1980. 283 pp.

__________. *Marriage and Death Notices from the "Charleston Times," 1800-1821.* Baltimore: Genealogical Publishing Co., 1979. 374 pp.

__________. *Marriage, Death, and Estate Notices from Georgetown, S. C. Newspapers, 1791-1861.* Easley, S.C.: Southern Historical Press, 1978. 250 pp.

__________. *Marriage and Death Notices from the "Pendleton (South Carolina) Messenger," 1807-1851.* 1977. Reprint ed., Easley, S.C.: Southern Historical Press, 1979. 123 pp.

__________. *Marriage and Death Notices from the "Lutheran Observer," 1831-1861; Southern Lutheran, 1861-1865.* Easley, S.C.: Southern Historical Press, 1979. 233 pp.

__________. *Marriage and Death Notices from the "Southern Christian Advocate."* Easley, S.C.: Southern Historical Press, 1979.

__________. *Marriage and Death Notices from Upper South Carolina Newspapers, 1843-1865.* Easley, S.C.: Southern Historical Press, 1977. 176 pp.

Revill, Janie, comp. *Marriage and Death Notices Abstracted from Newspapers Published in Camden, South Carolina, 1822-1842.* Columbia, S.C., 1936. 66 pp.

__________. "Marriage and Death Notices Abstracted from Various Old Newspapers on File in the Library of the University of South Carolina. 1804-1865." n.p., c1936. 49 leaves. Typewritten.

Salley, Alexander S. *Marriage Notices in "Charleston Courier," 1803-1808.* 1919. Reprint ed., Baltimore, Md.: Genealogical Publishing Co., 1976.

__________. *Marriage Notices in the "South Carolina" and "American General Gazette," 1766-1781; "The Royal Gazette," 1781-1782.* 1914. Reprint ed., Baltimore: Genealogical Publishing Co., 1976. 52 pp.

__________. *Marriage Notices in the "South Carolina Gazette" and Its Successors (1732-1801).* 1902; reprint ed., Baltimore: Genealogical Publishing Co., 1976. 174 pp.

Wilkinson, Tom C. *Early Anderson County, South Carolina Newspapers Marriages and Obituaries, 1841-1882.* Easley, S.C.: Southern Historical Press, 1978. 272 pp.

Wilson, Teresa E., and Janice L. Grimes. *Marriage and Death Notices from the Southern Patriot.* Easley, S.C.: Southern Historical Press, 1982. Vol. 1, 1815-30.

Webber, Mabel L. "Marriage and Death Notices from the City Gazette." *South Carolina Historical and Genealogical Magazine* 21 (1980): 77-87; 31 (1930): 264.

Woody, R. H. *Republican Newspapers of South Carolina.* Charlottesville: Virginia Historical Publications, 1936. In *Southern Sketches,* no. 10, 1st series.

Tennessee

Baker, Russell P. *Marriages and Obituaries from the "Tennessee Baptist," 1844-1862.* Easley, S.C.: Southern Historical Press, 1879. 137 pp.

Garrett, Jill K. *Obituaries from Tennessee Newspapers, 1851-1899.* Easley, S.C.: Southern Historical Press, 1980. 434 pp.

Lucas, Silas Emmett, Jr. *Marriages from Early Tennessee Newspapers, 1794-1851.* Easley, S.C.: Southern Historical Press, 1978. 544 pp.

__________. *Obituaries from Early Tennessee Newspapers, 1794-1851.* Easley, S.C.: Southern Historical Press, 1978. 432 pp.

Tennessee State Library and Archives. *Marriages from Early Tennessee Newspapers, 1794-1851.* 1978; reprint ed., Nashville: By the Library, 1980. 544 pp.

Texas

Cawthon, Juanita Davis. *Marriage and Death Notices, Marion County, Texas and Environs, 1853-1927.* Shreveport, La.: For the author, 1980. 160 pp.

El Paso Genealogical Society. *Births, Deaths, and Marriages in El Paso Newspapers.* Easley, S.C.: Southern Historical Press, 1980. 350 pp.

Newspaper Index: "The Houston Post". January 1977- . Wooster, Ohio: Bell and Howell Microphoto Division, 1977-present.

Vermont

McCorison, M. A. *Vermont Imprints, 1778-1820: A Checklist.* Worchester, Mass.: American Antiquarian Society, 1963. 597 pp.

Works Progress Administration. *Index to Burlington Free Press.* Burlington: University of Vermont, 1940.

Virginia

McIlwaine, H. R. *Index to Obituary Notices, "Richmond Enquirer," May 9, 1804-1829; "Richmond Whit", 1824-1838.* 1923; reprint ed., Baltimore: Genealogical Publishing Co., 1979. 89 pp.

Cappon, Lester J., and Stella F. Duff. *Virginia Gazette Index.* 2 vols. Williamsburg: Institute of Early American Culture, 1950.

Wisconsin

Obituary Index, 1939-1971, the New North, Rhinelander Daily News; 1972-1975. Rhinelander Daily News. Microform. 3 reels. n.p., 1983.

Gee, Patricia, and Wilma Foley. *Marriages and Deaths in the "Depere News", 1871-1883.* Dearborn, Mich.: For the authors, 1976. 91 pp.

__________. *Deaths in the "Green Bay Advocate," 1870-1880.* Dearborn, Mich.: For the author, 1976. 67 pp.

__________. *Marriages in the "Green Bay Advocate," 1870-1880.* Dearborn, Mich.: For the author, 1976. 115 pp.

Special Indexes

American Banker, Index. 1971- . Wooster, Ohio: Bell and Howell, Microphoto Division, 1971-present.

Bogle, Dixie. *Cherokee Nation Births and Deaths 1884-1901.* Abstracted from *Indian Chieftain Newspapers.* Venita, Okla.: Northeast Oklahoma Genealogical Society, 1980. 135 pp.

__________, and Dorthy Nix. *Cherokee Nation Marriages 1884-1901.* Abstracted from *Indian Chieftan Newspapers.* Venita, Okla.: Abraham Coryell Chapter, DAR, 1980. 140 pp.

Index to Black Newspapers. January 1977- . Wooster, Ohio: Bell and Howell Microphoto Division, 1977-present. Ten black newspapers indexed for personal names and subject. Annual.

Christian Science Monitor. Index. Wooster, Ohio: Bell and Howell Microphoto Division, 1950-present.

Christian Science Monitor. Cumulative Index, 1960-1964. 5 vols. Corvallis, Ore.: H. M. Cropsey, 1960-64.

The Wall Street Journal. Vol. 1-present. New York: Dow-Jones and Co., 1955.

INFORMATION GUIDE

Genealogical Information in the Record Group	*IGI*	*FGRA*	*Printed Histories*	*DAR Sources*
Surname/name	●	●	●	●
Date of Birth	●	●	●	●
Place of Birth	●	●	●	●
Sex	●	●	●	
Race/color			●	
Physical Description				
Occupation		●	●	●
Education		●	●	●
Military Service		●	●	●
Slave Status				
Property Owned			●	
Religion	●		●	●
Citizenship				
Marital Status	●	●	●	●
Spouse's Name	●	●	●	●
Children's Names		●	●	●
Father's Name	●	●	●	●
Mother's Name	●	●	●	●
Father's Birthplace			●	●
Mother's Birthplace			●	●
Date of Death		●	●	●
Cause of Death				●
Name of Cemetery		●	●	●
Residence	●	●	●	●
Age	●	●	●	●
Literacy/signature			●	
Photograph/sketch			●	

COULD YOU USE THIS CHAPTER?

Type of Record	*Kept from*	*Clues That You Should Consult These Records*
International Genealogical Index (IGI)	Like other records in this chapter, it was created in modern times to access records that go back to 1650 and earlier.	Indexes are like doing research with a partner. They save time and lead you to sources you might not otherwise consider. The IGI indexes over 68 million personal names in a birth/marriage database where seven to ten million new names are added annually. It is particularly strong for New England ancestors. If you know the state but not the county of origin, the IGI is especially useful. It also accesses specific record sources like church registers allowing you to determine if an ancestor appears in that source *before* searching it. Several other important research aids have been prepared by the Genealogical Society of Utah. This chapter tells how to use them
American Genealogical Biographical Index	From 1952 for much older records	Although unfinished (through "Orchard" in 1983), it will reference over twelve million persons in articles, books, and brief biographies published in newspapers, county and local histories, collections of biographies, magazines, and other sources from the eigthteenth century on. Other indexes also exist for published collections and printed histories.
Biography and Genealogy Master Index	1980, to access biographies of all periods.	Consolidated index to 3,200,000 biographical sketches in more than 350 dictionaries. An invaluable modern tool especially for twentieth century biographies.
National Union Catalog of Manuscript Collections (NUCMC)	Modern but not limited in time for what it indexes	This catalog is in the process of indexing all manuscript (unpublished) sources in American libraries and archives many of which are biographical or have genealogical interest. Begun in 1959, NUCMC has indexed about 7,500 entries under "genealogy" alone (to 1980) and adds at least one new volume every year. Most libraries also house catalogs, registers, or guides to their manuscript holdings. This chapter explains how to find and use them.
DAR Collections	Modern to access earlier records	A potpourri of abstracted family and local sources like Bibles, letters, diaries, cemetery tombstones, marriage records, These often have every name indexes. Finding aids for these are also described in this chapter.

Chapter 13

GENEALOGICAL TOOLS AND INDEXES

Kory L. Meyerink

A genealogist reconstructing a family history or pedigree faces mountains of records which may contain some reference to that family or ancestor. This chapter focuses on the major tools and indexes needed for each genealogist to sift through these records and locate appropriate information. This chapter also mentions several minor tools as examples of others available for use. Indexes, especially in the last decade, have become the most important tool in genealogical research. In fact, with the present information explosion and the increased availability of earlier records, indexes are the only way a genealogist can search these records successfully.

Some genealogical indexes have broad application while others have very limited use. Generally, they cover two different types of records: compiled or secondary sources (family or local histories, genealogies written by others, articles in journals, and family group sheets based on analysis of a series of records) and primary or original sources (military rolls, immigration lists, and census records).

Indexes may include given names of each subject (personal name indexes) or just the last name with page references for each occurrence of that name (surname indexes). They can also be comprehensive (meaning that every name in the source is included) or selective (meaning that only the major occurrences of the name are indexed). There may be locality, topical, or major-entry indexes as well. In this case only the head of the family will be indexed although the whole family is described by name in the entry itself.

Indexes compiled by government clerks for wills, deeds, and court cases are personal-name indexes; they reference only the principals in each transaction. Witnesses, jurors, clerks, and others mentioned in the documents are rarely indexed. Indexes to compiled histories include topical or surname entries only. Comprehensive, every-name indexes are usually compiled by genealogists or for genealogical use. These may be bound into the original record, written or typed into a separate volume, or added to the pages of the original index. As you search a record, whether it is compiled or original, check carefully for multiple indexes. You may find them at the end, in the middle, or conveniently at the front of the record. They may not be indicated in the table of contents.

Genealogical tools are any item which enables the genealogist to get at data faster, less expensively, and more effectively. Sometimes the tool was originally compiled for an entirely different purpose like census maps showing enumeration districts. These maps were compiled as an aid for enumerators in contacting family households in their districts. Today we use them to find our ancestors in specific dwellings so we can search the census without looking at every entry. City directories serve the same general purpose, although they were originally compiled to help consumers locate persons offering goods and services.

Genealogical indexes and tools have limitations. The most obvious is that no index is 100 percent accurate. Indexing is tedious and time-consuming work. People make mistakes in copying entries, classifying them, and preparing them for publication. The use of computers may limit the errors, but every genealogist will experience computer errors too at some time or another.

The index is only as accurate as the source. If a family history has errors, these errors will be indexed. Misspelled words, garbled names, and incorrect page references will be indexed as well. It is not the place of the indexer to correct errors even where they are obvious, although he/she will sometimes add a preface or footnote to warn the user. If the record is in a foreign language or badly damaged, names may be indecipherable or illegible. A skilled indexer, dealing with unfamiliar names may misinterpret spellings, placing the name in an entirely different part of the index than it belongs. Cross references for spelling variants and for multiple entries may be omitted due to space or financial considerations.

Many indexes are not strictly alphabetical. All the A entries are together but Abbott may come after Arnold. Some indexes file names by the first letter of the given name, the first three letters of the surname, or the first and third letters of either name. Some are alphabetized by the *given* name irrespective of first letter of surname. Others, like Soundexes, are arranged so that names pronounced alike are indexed together.

Indexers are biased, selecting entries to be indexed according to their own criteria. Some will list their selection process to alert the reader, some say nothing at all. For example, Schneider and Snyder may be indexed together or separately in a surname index. If the index is topical, who chooses the topics? Are public officials indexed all together, individually by name, or by separate government agency? Entries may be divided into descendants, spouses who marry into the family, ancestors of the central couple, and places where the family members lived—each in a separate index. Check them all.

Women may be omitted from the index. If you are looking for Mary Loomis and the index lists only John, Joseph, Michael, and Stephen, check these entries. The indexer may have included only her brothers and father. Children and grandparents may be handled in the same way.

Every name can be spelled some other way. The *Cole* family in New York sometimes appears as *Kool* due to Dutch influence or *Kohl* due to German influence, yet most of the family stem from the New England Coles. In strictly alphabetical indexes, such spelling variants must be checked to get all the data. Be especially careful for variations with a vowel as the initial letter. Even simple names like *Ott* can appear as *Ot, Otte, Utt,* or *Autt.*

Both personal and family names may be translated from another form. Jacob is the Latin and German form of James. The Slavic Vojtech becomes Adelbert or Albert in English. Polly equals Mary and Sally is Sarah. The Huguenot *Le Counte* becomes the Dutch *de Graff* and *de la Maistre* becomes *Delamater*. The Germans liked to translate their names into English: *Zimmerman* becomes *Carpenter* and *Schwartz* becomes *Black*. Be wary when you are dealing with the first and second American generations.

If you are looking for a Mary Loomis-John Smith marriage, the usual suggestion for searching is to check Loomis first because it is less common. If you are searching a Loomis family history, however, reverse the process. Check for John Smith married to Mary Loomis. This is faster and usually more effective.

An excellent article on using indexes is Donald Lines Jacobus, "Tricks in Using Indexed Genealogical Books," *The American Genealogist* 30 (April 1954): 85. Jacobus covers some of these rules in greater detail. Keep in mind that indexes are just tools. Both compiled genealogies and primary sources must be carefully analyzed for accuracy and completeness before building any pedigree upon them. In fact, pedigree construction should be done in primary sources whenever possible.

Some tools and indexes have several genealogical applications even though they are discussed here under one topic only. The vast number of indexes available permit limited discussion on each one, but references will provide additional details and applications.

Indexes Generated by the Church of Jesus Christ of Latter-day Saints

During the last century the Church of Jesus Christ of Latter-day Saints has been actively engaged in genealogical research as a corporate entity. Its individual members have also researched their own ancestry. Throughout this period of time, several indexes with universal application have been created. These indexes, not limited to members of the Church, constitute the largest compiled genealogical indexes in the world.

International Genealogical Index (IGI)

Formerly called the Computer File Index (CFI), this index contains over 68 million entries (1981 edition). It is a personal-name index, in strict alphabetical sequence, to the computer database of births and marriages. Few death entries are included.

Seven to ten million names are added to the index each year; updates are issued every three to four years. The current edition was published on microfiche in 1981. The U.S./Canadian section has over nine million entries with Massachusetts having the greatest number – 1.7 million names. Ohio, New York, Connecticut, and Pennsylvania follow with about half-million each. A new edition is projected for mid-1984 with some twelve million new entries worldwide.

The entries in the IGI come from two main sources: names supplied by genealogists from family records and the results of their own research, and names extracted by trained volunteers from selected sources – church registers, birth and marriage records, probate and census documents – from many areas of the world. Each entry includes the name of the person, names of parents or spouse, sex, date and place of event, LDS ordinance dates, and input sources reference number. The names are arranged alphabetically with cross-references for marriages only. Parents of children christened or born are not individually indexed. The input source reference number is coded to indicate the type of record used and whether it is submitted by a genealogist or as part of the name-extraction project. See Figure 13-1 for an annotated example.

The source number (batch number as it is called) can be used to refer to the original input source where additional data is usually recorded for each person. The index is available on microfiche at the Genealogical Society of Utah, its 460 branches, and selected genealogical and public libraries throughout the United States. (See Appendix D for the branch nearest you.) Most of the input sources are available on microfilm through the same libraries.

Several guides explain the IGI and its genealogical applications:[1]

1. *Genealogical Research Paper Series F, No. 6, 1983* (stock no. PRGS2020) available for $2.50 from the Genealogical Society of Utah in Salt Lake City, or from the General Church Distribution Center, 1999 West 1700 South, Salt Lake City, Utah 84104. This newly published research paper is a forty-nine page pamphlet with some excellent illustrations and the following sections: What Is the IGI (sources of information, uses, limitations); How to Use the IGI; IGI Format (name, father/mother or spouse, sex, type [of event], event date, event place, LDS ordinance dates, source); How to Find the Source of an IGI Entry; Why You May Not Find a Name in the IGI; Guidelines for Using the IGI (places, names, dates); Requesting Searches by Mail (relationship requirement, minimum information); Index to Old Parochial Registers of Scotland; the Computer Printout; Appendixes – Sources of IGI Entries by Batch Number, IGI Localities and Their Regions, How to Find an IGI Entry for German Empire Areas; and Index.

The format of the paper (8½ x 11 inches, in double columns except where the illustrations take nearly whole pages) and its illustrations and explanations make this research paper a very friendly research aid to use.

2. "IGI Instructions and Regions" (on microfiche, available wherever copies of the IGI are found) dated September 1983 or later.

This instruction consists of two separate documents on the same microfiche. The first is "IGI Instructions and Regions," and "Introduction to the IGI Batch Number Index." The instructions included in this microfiche are kept up to date and should always be available with the IGI. The instruction provided here was later adapted to *Research Paper F-6* described above. The microfiche instructions do not include illustrations. The twenty-two page "IGI Instructions and Regions" include the following headings: Instruction, Sources of Information, Uses, Limitations, How to Use the IGI, IGI Format (name, father/mother or spouse, sex, type [of event], event date, event place, LDS ordinance dates, sources); Guidelines for Using and Interpreting the IGI; (places, names, dates); IGI Countries and Their Regions; and How the IGI Lists Localities for the German Empire Areas.

The second document on the microfiche (which also appears as the introductory pages on each microfiche of the IGI Batch Number Index in editions published September 1983 and later) includes Introduction, Before Using This Index, To Use This Index, Explanation of Symbols, and Explanation of Each Batch Number – (what type of record each batch number will lead the user to). Use this instruction to help you while at the library using the IGI.

3. Elizabeth L. Nichols, "The International Genealogical Index," *New England Historical Genealogical Register* 87 (July 1983): 193-217. This article includes background information in a general question-and-answer format, including: What is the IGI? What is the IGI not? Who publishes the IGI? Why was the IGI created? For what purposes can the IGI be effectively used? Where is the IGI available? What information is included in the IGI? How is the IGI arranged? What records may be found in the IGI? Can a person make corrections to entries in the IGI? How does one locate the source used for entering a name in the IGI? What is a computer printout? What is the Parish and Vital Records Listing? Do IGI entries ever lead to sources other than the input source? What are some general problems one may find in using the IGI? What are the chances of my finding a record for my New England ancestor in the IGI? It also includes a glossary of terms, special symbols and their meanings, and two case studies.

The first case study begins with looking for the entry in the IGI and takes the reader through ten steps to locate and evaluate the information as it is found in the IGI entry, the computer printout, and the original input sources, using the IGI batch number index. The example includes illustrations and written explanation for each step.

The second case study explains how to use the "Parish and Vital

Figure 13-1. The International Genealogical Index (IGI).

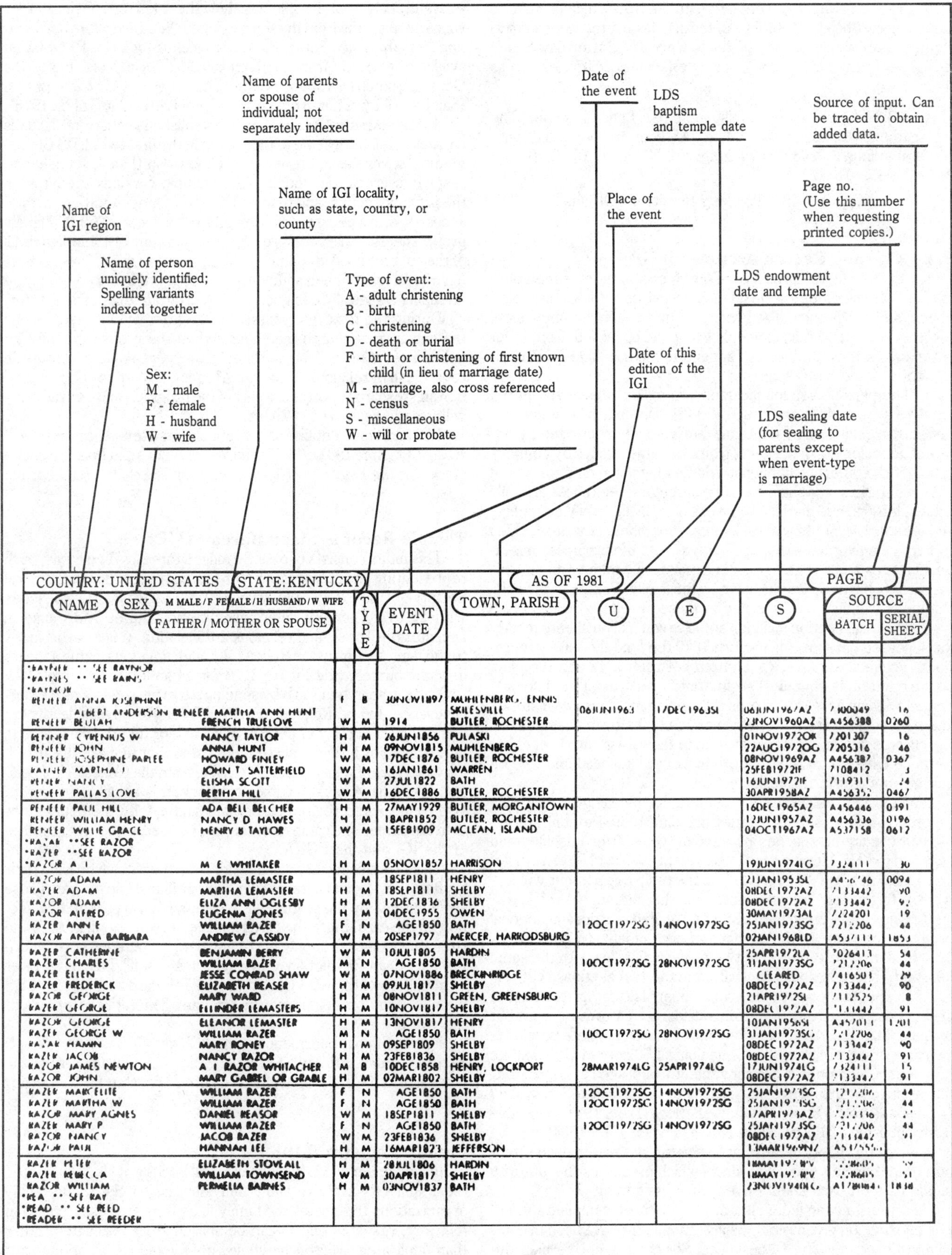

COUNTRY: UNITED STATES — STATE: KENTUCKY — AS OF 1981 — PAGE

M MALE / F FEMALE / H HUSBAND / W WIFE

NAME	SEX	FATHER / MOTHER OR SPOUSE	TYPE	EVENT DATE	TOWN, PARISH	U	E	S	SOURCE BATCH	SOURCE SERIAL SHEET
*RAYNER ** SEE RAYNOR										
*RAYNES ** SEE RAINS										
*RAYNOR										
RENEER ANNA JOSEPHINE	F	ALBERT ANDERSON RENEER MARTHA ANN HUNT	B	30NOV1897	MUHLENBERG, ENNIS SKILESVILLE	06JUN1963	17DEC1963SL	06JUN1967AZ	7100049	16
RENEER BEULAH	W	FRENCH TRUELOVE	M	1914	BUTLER, ROCHESTER			23NOV1960AZ	A456388	0260
RENNER CYRENIUS W	H	NANCY TAYLOR	M	26JUN1856	PULASKI			01NOV1972OK	7201307	16
RENEER JOHN	H	ANNA HUNT	M	09NOV1815	MUHLENBERG			22AUG1972OG	7205316	46
RENEER JOSEPHINE PARLEE	W	HOWARD FINLEY	M	17DEC1876	BUTLER, ROCHESTER			08NOV1969AZ	A456387	0367
RAYNER MARTHA J	W	JOHN T SATTERFIELD	M	16JAN1861	WARREN			25FEB1972IF	7108412	3
RENER NANCY	W	ELISHA SCOTT	M	27JUL1822	BATH			16JUN1972IF	7119311	24
RENEER PALLAS LOVE	W	BERTHA HILL	M	16DEC1886	BUTLER, ROCHESTER			30APR1958AZ	A456352	0467
RENEER PAUL HILL	H	ADA BELL BELCHER	M	27MAY1929	BUTLER, MORGANTOWN			16DEC1965AZ	A456446	0391
RENEER WILLIAM HENRY	H	NANCY D HAWES	M	18APR1852	BUTLER, ROCHESTER			12JUN1957AZ	A456336	0196
RENEER WILLIE GRACE	W	HENRY B TAYLOR	M	15FEB1909	MCLEAN, ISLAND			04OCT1967AZ	A537158	0612
*RAZAR **SEE RAZOR										
*RAZER **SEE RAZOR										
*RAZOR A I	H	M E WHITAKER	M	05NOV1857	HARRISON			19JUN1974LG	7324111	30
RAZOR ADAM	H	MARTHA LEMASTER	M	18SEP1811	HENRY			21JAN1953SL	A456746	0094
RAZER ADAM	H	MARTHA LEMASTER	M	18SEP1811	SHELBY			08DEC1972AZ	7133442	90
RAZOR ADAM	H	ELIZA ANN OGLESBY	M	12DEC1836	SHELBY			08DEC1972AZ	7133442	92
RAZOR ALFRED	H	EUGENIA JONES	M	04DEC1955	OWEN			30MAY1973AL	7224201	19
RAZER ANN E	F	WILLIAM RAZER	N	AGE1850	BATH	12OCT1972SG	14NOV1972SG	25JAN1973SG	7212206	44
RAZOR ANNA BARBARA	W	ANDREW CASSIDY	M	20SEP1797	MERCER, HARRODSBURG			02JAN1968LD	A537113	1853
RAZER CATHERINE	W	BENJAMIN BERRY	M	10JUL1805	HARDIN			25APR1972LA	7026413	54
RAZER CHARLES	M	WILLIAM RAZER	N	AGE1850	BATH	10OCT1972SG	28NOV1972SG	31JAN1973SG	7212206	44
RAZER ELLEN	W	JESSE CONRAD SHAW	M	07NOV1886	BRECKINRIDGE			CLEARED	7416503	29
RAZER FREDERICK	H	ELIZABETH REASER	M	09JUL1817	SHELBY			08DEC1972AZ	7133442	90
RAZOR GEORGE	H	MARY WARD	M	08NOV1811	GREEN, GREENSBURG			21APR1972SL	7112525	8
RAZER GEORGE	H	ELLINDER LEMASTERS	M	10NOV1817	SHELBY			08DEC1972AZ	7133442	91
RAZOR GEORGE	H	ELEANOR LEMASTER	M	13NOV1817	HENRY			10JAN1956SL	A457011	1201
RAZER GEORGE W	M	WILLIAM RAZER	N	AGE1850	BATH	10OCT1972SG	28NOV1972SG	31JAN1973SG	7212206	44
RAZAR HAMIN	H	MARY RONEY	M	09SEP1809	SHELBY			08DEC1972AZ	7133442	90
RAZER JACOB	H	NANCY RAZOR	M	23FEB1836	SHELBY			08DEC1972AZ	7133442	91
RAZOR JAMES NEWTON	M	A I RAZOR WHITACHER	B	10DEC1858	HENRY, LOCKPORT	28MAR1974LG	25APR1974LG	17JUN1974LG	7324111	15
RAZOR JOHN	H	MARY GABREL OR GRABLE	M	02MAR1802	SHELBY			08DEC1972AZ	7133442	91
RAZER MARCELLITE	F	WILLIAM RAZER	N	AGE1850	BATH	12OCT1972SG	14NOV1972SG	25JAN1973SG	7212206	44
RAZER MARTHA W	F	WILLIAM RAZER	N	AGE1850	BATH	12OCT1972SG	14NOV1972SG	25JAN1973SG	7212206	44
RAZOR MARY AGNES	W	DANIEL REASOR	M	18SEP1811	SHELBY			17APR1973AZ	7223316	27
RAZER MARY P	F	WILLIAM RAZER	N	AGE1850	BATH	12OCT1972SG	14NOV1972SG	25JAN1973SG	7212206	44
RAZOR NANCY	W	JACOB RAZER	M	23FEB1836	SHELBY			08DEC1972AZ	7133442	91
RAZOR PAUL	H	HANNAH LEE	M	16MAR1823	JEFFERSON			13MAR1969NZ	A517555	
RAZER PETER	H	ELIZABETH STOVEALL	M	28JUL1806	HARDIN			18MAY1972PV	7228605	59
RAZER REBECCA	W	WILLIAM TOWNSEND	M	30APR1817	SHELBY			18MAY1972PV	7228605	51
RAZOR WILLIAM	H	PERMELIA BARNES	M	03NOV1837	BATH			23NOV1940LG	A178084	1838
*REA ** SEE RAY										
*READ ** SEE REED										
*READER ** SEE REEDER										

Records Listings," its purpose and value, what is found, and what it means.

This article can be found at all LDS branch genealogical libraries, through a special arrangement between the New England Historic Genealogical Society (publisher of the article) and the Genealogical Department of the Church of Jesus Christ of Latter-day Saints (publisher of the index), and at many other major libraries across the country.

4. A British perspective on using the IGI. Lance J. Jacob, "The International Genealogical Index: A Tool to be Used with Understanding," *Genealogical Magazine* 21 (June 1983): 60-63; (Sept. 1983): 165-70.

See also Chapter 15, "Tracking Immigrant Origins."

Family Group Record Archives (FGRA)

From 1924 to 1978 the LDS Church encouraged its members to submit family group sheets on their ancestors to the Genealogical Society of Utah library. The almost 10 million family group sheets represent about 40 million people living and deceased. Some, but not many, of these names also appear on the IGI. The FGRA collection is divided into sections:

1. The patrons section includes two million sheets submitted 1962-78 for people born about 1850 (the last four or five generations). It includes many duplicate family sheets submitted by different genealogists descending from the same family. By comparing all of the different versions, you find names and addresses of potential cousins who share the same ancestors; references to family Bibles, letters, and diaries in possession of living family members, and personal accounts written by family members now dead; clues to family naming patterns, spelling variants of surnames, migrational routes and places of residence for family members; and exact dates of birth and death known by the family. Variations of family traditions can also be discerned in these sheets.

2. The main section includes some seven million sheets mostly for deceased persons born before 1870 (beyond the third generation). These sheets were submitted between 1942 and 1969 and documentation is limited—usually "family records" if the information is based on personal records or knowledge, or printed histories and parish registers if the information comes from research.[2]

There is a cross-reference system to show if a group sheet exists (or once existed) for a parent or child of the husband and wife on any given sheet in the main section.

Names and addresses for submitting genealogists are also recorded on these sheets but they pre-date 1969. Persons still living can usually be reached by sending your letter unsealed and stamped to LDS Membership Department, 50 East North Temple, Salt Lake City, UT 84150. The membership department will forward it to the last known address for the person.

The group sheets in both sections are filed in strict alphabetical order by the name of the husband of each family and chronologically by date where there are two or more families with the same husband. There is some duplication in the two sections, but it is limited. The hard copy of the group sheets is incomplete as some sheets have been removed by inconsiderate patrons or worn out from constant use and photocopying. A more complete version is available on microfilm at the Genealogical Society of Utah and its branches. Call numbers are conveniently published in Laureen R. Jaussi and Gloria D. Chaston, *Register of Genealogical Society Call Numbers*, 2 vols., Provo, Utah: Genealogy Tree, 1981; (available from publisher, 31 East 2050 North, Provo, UT 84604).

The group sheets in these two sections will eventually be computer input using a special program which preserves the integrity of the data on each sheet—even those with errors.

This tool is not an index. It is an alphabetized, compiled source. The information given is only as accurate as the care used in compiling the record. The Genealogical Society has not verified the research and the family sheets are known to have errors, especially those for colonial American lines going into England and Europe. Sources are usually given at the bottom of the group sheet; however, a careful analysis of the data will show that there are obvious items which do not come from the sources listed. See *LDS Church Records and Research Aids*, Series F. No. 1, 1978. (Stock No. PRGS0659) available for $2.50 from the Genealogical Society of Utah or the General Church Distribution Center and *From You to Your Ancestors* (Salt Lake City: Church of Jesus Christ of Latter-day Saints, 1978).

3. The Ancestral File is a newly established section and includes correct versions of some of the sheets in the first two. LDS Church members were asked to verify each item on their family sheets, resolve discrepancies found in the multiple versions submitted in the patrons' section, and resubmit the first four generations of their ancestry with a pedigree chart in July 1981. Nearly 200,000 family group sheets were received, over 19 percent of them listing all of the sources used in compiling the new sets of data. These sheets have been microfilmed and, at this writing, are being computer input using a specially designed, linked program to eliminate error.

During the next few years, the program will be tested using the ancestry of church members. When the project is ready for public use, data will be solicited from genealogists worldwide regardless of religious affiliation. Meticulous care for documentation and research updates are part of the program, and its availability will greatly assist researchers.

For additional details, see "Genealogy's New Ancestral File," *Ensign* 11 (April 1981): 76-77; and Wilma Adkins and Lois V. Knight, *Documenting Your Four Generations* (Salt Lake City: KIN Forms, 1980).

Temple Records Index Bureau (TIB)

This index consists of over 30 million three-by-five cards, each representing one individual's record submitted to the Genealogical Society of Utah, 1842-1969 (pre-IGI). It is also a worldwide index with 25 to 30 percent referencing United States and Canadian ancestors. All areas and religions are included. It is a partial index to the main section of the FGRA, although not every name appears in both sources. See Figure 13-2 for an annotated example.

You can search the TIB by sending a written request on Temple Ordinance Index Request Form PFGS0073, available at the Genealogical Society of Utah in Salt Lake or its branches, and $1 per name or by hiring an accredited researcher to make the search for you. A list of researchers is available from the Genealogical Society. If you have several names to check, it is usually less expensive to get an accredited researcher and pay by the hour rather than the name. The same form can also be used to request searches of the IGI and the FGRA.

The TIB is especially valuable for those persons who gave their birthdate, place, and parents from their personal knowledge. These are identified by the word "self" in the family representative section on the card. Since the cards include persons living in 1842 and later, the index can supply first-hand data for persons born before the American Revolution. Although these "self" TIB cards refer to members of the LDS Church, most TIB cards are not for LDS members but for their ancestors for many generations throughout the world.

For additional information, see *A Brief Guide to the Temple Records Index Bureau*, Series F, No. 2, available from the Genealogical Society or General Church Distribution Center for $1.25.

Family Registry (FR)

In November 1983, the Genealogical Society of Utah announced the Family Registry to allow individual researchers and family organizations to register the family lines they are researching. In this way, research efforts can be shared and coordinated rather than duplicated. Microfiche copies of indexed registration forms

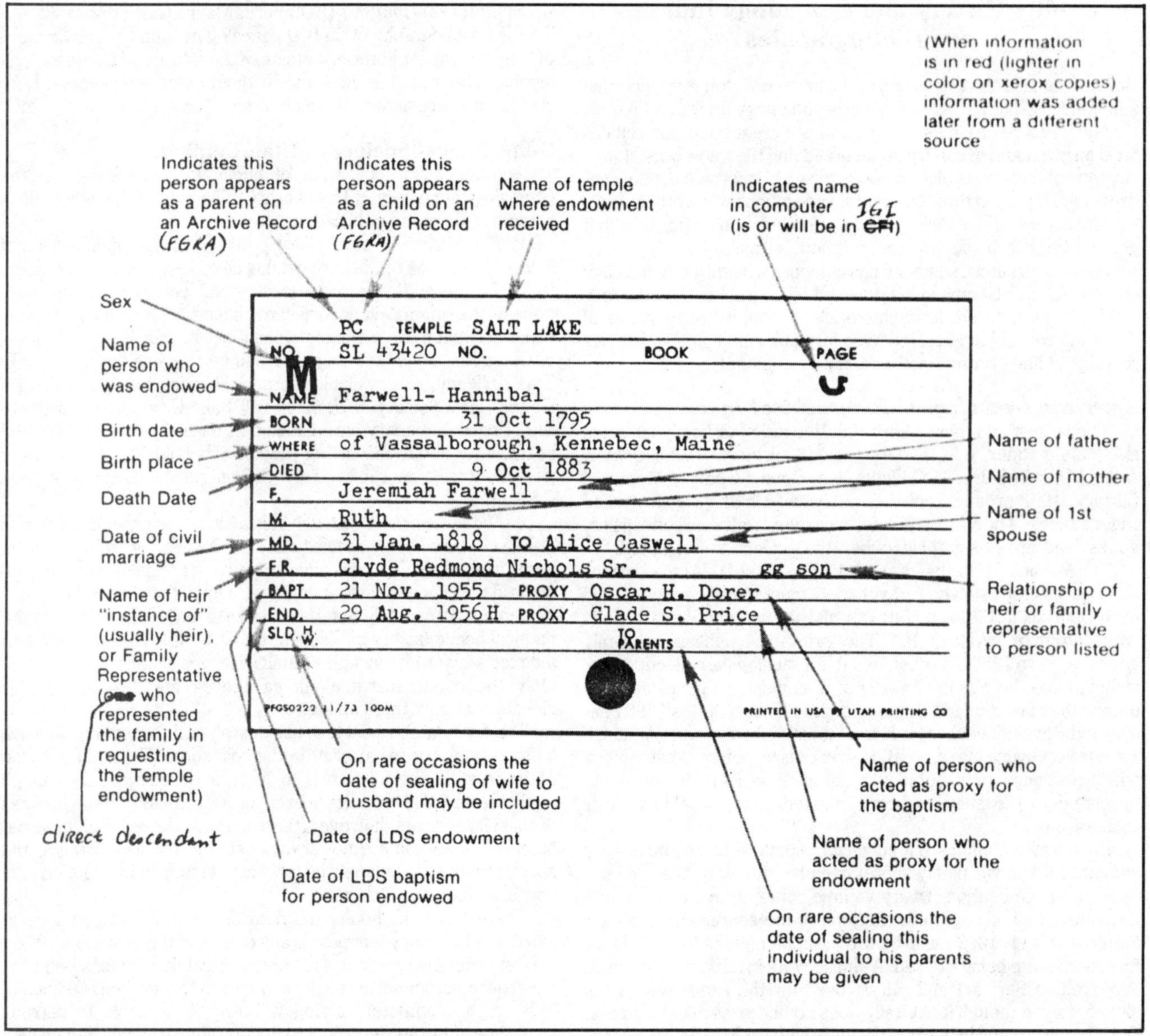

Figure 13-2. An Index Card from the Temple Records Index Bureau (TIB).

are available for search and inquiry at the Genealogical Society of Utah and its branches. Request form PFGS2512 (organizations) or PFGS2501 (individuals) to register. Registration and inquiry are free.

Other specialized indexes and research tools are also available through the Genealogical Society of Utah. These include both records pertaining to members of the LDS Church and to records in the society 's microfilm holdings of genealogical records. These tools are described and cataloged in:

LDS Church Records and Research Aids. Series F, No. 1 (Stock No. PRGS0659). Available for $2.50 from Genealogical Society of Utah or the General Church Distribution Center.

Jaussi, Laureen R., and Gloria D. Chaston. *Fundamentals of Genealogical Research*. 3rd ed. Salt Lake City, Utah: Deseret Book Co., 1977.

___________. *Register of Genealogical Society Call Numbers*. 2 vols. Provo, Utah: Genealogy Tree, 1981.

Finding Aids to the Microfilmed Manuscript Collections of the Genealogical Society of Utah, Salt Lake City: University of Utah Press, 1978-80. Each volume includes descriptive entries for special tools, indexes, and finding aids created by the Genealogical Society to make access to its microfilmed holdings quicker and more effective. They can be ordered from Family History World, 57 West S. Temple, Suite 255, Salt Lake City, UT 84101. Price list available on request.

• Cottler, Susan M., Roger M. Haigh, and Shirley A. Weathers. *Preliminary Survey of the Mexican Collection* 1978, 216 pp.

• Haigh, Roger M., and Shirley A. Weathers. *Supplement to the Preliminary Survey of the Mexican Collection* 1979, 28 pp.

• Eakle, Arlene H., Arvilla Outsen, and Richard S. Tompson. *Descriptive Inventory of the English Collection* 1979, 184 pp.

• ___________, and L. Ray Gunn. *Descriptive Inventory of the New York Collection* 1980, 292 pp.

• Jensen, C. Russell. *Preliminary Survey of the French Collection* 1980, 475 pp.

• Smelser, Ronald. *Preliminary Survey of the German Collection* 1979, 638 pp.

Family History and Genealogy Indexes and Bibliographies

Before you search very far into your ancestry, you often find that someone else has already published a genealogy (or family history) for one of your surnames. Such a find is a great boon, for you can build on previous research instead of redoing the same work. Literally tens of thousands of such books exist. Many trace the descendants of one person through several generations while others trace the ancestors of a couple. Various combinations also exist but generally these books are based on one surname.

How do you find if someone has compiled a history or genealogy on your family? Compiled indexes and bibliographies are the only efficient way to locate family histories. Through a combination of these indexes, I have located over fifty published family histories relating to lines on my mother's ancestry alone!

American Genealogical-Biographical Index

The largest and most comprehensive index to family histories is Fremont Rider, ed., *The American Genealogical-Biographical Index (AGBI)*, Series 2, (Middletown, Conn.: Godfrey Memorial Library, 1952-present, vol. 127 published 1983). It is also called Rider's Index. The editor will reference over twelve million articles, books, and brief biographies when the project is completed.

Therein lies its biggest drawback. The size of this index means that it progresses slowly. An average of four volumes are published each year (six in 1983). It is strictly alphabetical and Vol. 127 ends with "Orchard, William H." The primary emphasis is family genealogies to 1950 but other valuable genealogical collections are included like the *Boston Transcript* (a newspaper genealogy column with wide circulation), the complete United States 1790 census, and Revolutionary records from most of the colonies. Although not an every-name index, AGBI is an extensive personal-name index which excludes only persons mentioned incidentally or those unrelated to the subjects being indexed such as witnesses or authors.

Each entry contains the subject's complete name, birth year and state if known, highly abbreviated biographical data, and the book and page citation. Every volume contains an explanation of the index. Full bibliographic citations to the sources indexed are found in Vols. 1, 10, 34, and 54 with a supplement in Vol. 70. Over 850 sources are being indexed. A similar work in forty-eight volumes appeared as Series 1 and can be used for the remainder of the alphabet even though it naturally does not index as many sources. Both series are available at major genealogical libraries as well as public and university libraries with large genealogy collections.

Genealogy Library Catalogs

Several genealogical libraries have published their catalogs in some form. A recent example is Mary L. Strong, comp., *Library Shelf List of the Genealogical Forum of Portland* (Portland, Ore.: Genealogical Forum of Portland, 1983). Over 6,000 histories, genealogies, and source books are listed. These catalogs serve as indexes to genealogies since they are cataloged by family surname. Remember that libraries acquire books after the catalog is published, often issuing supplements to previous publications to inform readers of their new holdings.

One major catalog is Marion J. Kaminkow, *Genealogies in the Library of Congress: A Bibliography*, 2 vols. (Baltimore: Magna Carta Books, 1972); Supplement, 1972-76. These books can be found in most genealogical or research libraries. Altogether, they list over 23,000 entries with 30,000 cross references.

Arranged alphabetically by surname, the entries contain complete bibliographic citations. *See* and *see also* entries lead the user to genealogies which would usually be overlooked. The books indexed are of course available in the Library of Congress but many can also be found at other major genealogical libraries.

The same editor has also prepared *A Complement to Genealogies in the Library of Congress* (Baltimore: Magna Carta Books, 1981). This is a bibliography of 20,000 genealogies found in one or more of forty-five major libraries outside of the Library of Congress collection. The format is the same (without cross references). It includes an abbreviation of which library has the book.

Genealogical Society of Utah Catalog

Another major collection of family histories exists in the Genealogical Society of Utah library. The bulk of the collection is listed in two micro-publications.

1. *The Microfilm Card Catalog* (MCC), a microfilm edition of selected portions of the card catalog as of 1972 with supplements to 1977. This edition includes locality, subject, and surname sections of the original dictionary card catalog. The cards in the surname collection are arranged alphabetically and, like the Library of Congress, cover the major surnames contained in each book. This 1972 edition is available in branch libraries but *not* at the main Genealogical Society of Utah. In Salt Lake City, direct access to the original dictionary card catalog on three-by-five cards is still possible for about one-half of the library's holdings. These cards will eventually be replaced by the microfiche Computer Card Catalog.

2. *The Microfiche Computer Genealogical Library Card Catalog* (GLC) contains library acquisitions since November 1978 and those items from the MCC cards which have been recataloged. The society is in the process of recataloging all acquisitions received before November 1978, including the vast DAR collection filmed at the national headquarters in Washington, D.C. The surname section, indexed separately, includes family histories acquired since 1978. Only the major surnames in each book are included in this alphabetical surname catalog.

The fiche entries include detailed, analytical descriptions for each source, book, or manuscript in the collection. The main purpose of the recataloging program is to describe the entries fully enough so that practical choices for searching can be made. In the process of changing formats, however, there are some losses. For instance, facts of publication are not always listed in the fiche catalog and specific identity for a family history may be subject to question until you examine the work itself.

There are many books and records which have been accessioned which do not yet appear in any portion of these catalogs. They are retrieved by checking the computer catalog database on line. Reference personnel at the society can do this for you. Online access to the computer catalog will also be available to patrons sometime after the Genealogical Society library moves into its new building (projected for late fall 1985). The society also plans to make the catalog a union catalog to family histories and other sources located in libraries throughout the United States. These are developments for the future, however.

Other sources not in the catalogs can be found by consulting special registers of call numbers compiled by library staff. Citations to these registers are in the catalogs.

Hard copies of both catalog cards and microfiche entries can be ordered at 15 cents a frame through Patron Services, Genealogical Society of Utah, 50 East North Temple, Salt Lake City, UT 84150. Cost estimates will be supplied on request.

From its early years, the Genealogical Society, like many genealogical libraries, indexed articles, genealogies, and family histories in periodicals as well as books. Most of these apply to Mormons and residents of Utah. The original cards are arranged alphabetically in the Utah/LDS Church collection of the library. They are not available on microfilm and new entries are being added to this file each week. For those genealogists who visit the library in person, this index may be of interest.

Computer Index to Microfilmed Holdings, Harold B. Lee Library

Brigham Young University in Provo, Utah, has a genealogical

collection that includes some 500,000 rolls of records rich in family Bible notations, cemetery inscriptions, family histories, and other sources compiled or transcribed by DAR chapters throughout the Southern United States. An every-name index to these rolls of film is being compiled by volunteers at the Harold B. Lee Library under the direction of Roger Flick at the rate of about 50,000 per month. Eventually, the index will be available online at computer terminals throughout the BYU library.

New York Public Library Card Catalog

The genealogy and local history section of the New York Public Library has been published as *Dictionary Catalog of the Local History and Genealogy Division*, 18 vols. (Boston: G. K. Hall, 1974). Entries for families and individuals are found as well as subject and locality cards. This source indexes only the major surnames in each book, but it remains very useful. It is available in most genealogy libraries as well as large public and university libraries.

Other library catalogs published by G. K. Hall include the Peabody Library (Baltimore), Boston Atheneaum (Boston), Los Angeles Public Library, American Antiquarian Society (Worcester, Mass.), and others. These can be found in most university and some public libraries.

Books on Demand

University Microfilms, 300 North Zeeb Road, Ann Arbor, MI 48106 can supply microfilm or xerox copies of out-of-print family histories for 25 cents per page. Its "Genealogy and Heraldry" catalog lists some 1,100 books currently on microfilm. The catalog is free upon request.

If you know the title of the book you want and where a copy is located, University Microfilms will obtain permission to copy it (including copyright clearance if needed) and supply you with a microfilm or xerox copy for 25 cents per page. This is a valuable service. While the cost seems great, it is less expensive than reprint services or hiring a genealogist to search the book for you. (See Introduction, "Photocopied Books," for additional information.)

Publishers and Booksellers Catalogs

Another source for family histories are the catalogs of various publishers who are selling new, old (used or rare), and reprinted family histories. These are surname catalogs or have surname sections and are arranged similarly to library catalog indexes. The major source in this field is Netti Schreiner-Yantis, *Genealogical and Local History Books in Print* (Springfield, Va.: Genealogical Books in Print, 1976-Present; 3 vols. to 1983). Thousands of genealogical books are listed for sale in this source from over a thousand vendors. One of the larger sections of the book is the "Family Histories for Sale" section. A separate index to this section in the third volume (1981) references 5,400 different surnames. Brief descriptions are given for each family history as well as the location of the vendor. One great advantage is that many of these are new books not included in other indexes or catalogs. The volumes are not cumulative so all three should be checked. A fourth volume is scheduled for 1984. Most genealogical libraries have this catalog. Personal copies can be ordered from Genealogical and Local History Books in Print, 6818 Lois Drive, Springfield, VA 22150.

The following publishers' catalogs may also be helpful: *Genealogy and Local History Guide*, parts 1-4, Microfilming Corporation of America (formerly of Sanford, North Carolina, now part of University Microfilms, Ann Arbor, Michigan). See address above. These catalogs contain 814 genealogies, 15 genealogical periodicals, 1,567 local histories and 267 printed primary sources on microfiche well indexed. MCA's stated goal is to microfiche all printed genealogy and local history works. Catalogs are available upon request. Microfiche publications are available for research in the Library of Congress; Allen County Public Library, Fort Wayne, Indiana; Fort Bragg, North Carolina; Fort Campbell, Kentucky; Onondaga County Library, Syracuse, New York; Morristown Public Library, New Jersey; Boston Public Library, Massachusetts; Pennsylvania State Library, Harrisburg; Atlanta Public Library; Ricks College Library, Rexburg, Idaho; Knoxville Public Library, Tennessee; Hawaii State Library, Honolulu; Genealogical Society of Utah, Salt Lake City; Brigham Young University, Provo, Utah; American Antiquarian Society Library, Worcester, Massachusetts; Balch Institute, Philadelphia; Mechanics Library, Charleston, South Carolina; Henry E. Huntington Library, San Marino, California; Newberry Library, Chicago; Folger Shakespeare Library, Washington, D.C.; and DAR Library, Washington, D.C. (See Appendix G for addresses.)

Genealogical Catalog. Goodspeeds Book Shop, 18 Beacon Street, Boston, MA 02108. Family histories and genealogies in out-of-print books have been reprinted separately for each surname. Reprints are on sale at Goodspeeds; copies can also be found in many genealogical libraries.

Genealogy and Local History Catalog. Charles E. Tuttle Co., Inc. Rutland, VT 05701.

Genealogy, Heraldry, Local History Catalogs. Genealogical Publishing Company, 111 Water Street, Baltimore, MD 21202. Publishers listed in Appendix H also issue catalogs of value.

Manuscript Catalogs

Thousands of libraries across America have manuscript collections which include genealogies, family histories, and the research notes of professional and amateur genealogists on the many families they researched during their lives. A manuscript is any unpublished document: journals, diaries, letters, business records, and church registers, among others. A manuscript may also be a genealogy, pedigree chart, family history nicely typed or written in almost illegible, abbreviated notes. A manuscript can also be a printed volume which has handwritten annotations. In a genealogy or family history, these notes can be corrections to previously printed errors or new information, like missing maiden surnames.

Since 1959, the Library of Congress has solicited detailed descriptions of such manuscript collections in public, private, and university libraries. These indexed and cross-referenced descriptions are published in the *National Union Catalog of Manuscript Collections* (Washington, D.C.: Library of Congress, 1962-present). This multi-volume catalog (NUCMC) includes 46,000 collections in 1,122 repositories (to 1980) many of which are personal and family papers. The indexes include headings for personal names as well as surnames under the topic "Genealogy." Under that topic alone about 7,500 entries have been listed since the catalog was begun in 1959.

Each volume is indexed and every three or four years the indexes are cumulative. The Library of Congress has announced a master index for all volumes published to date which will merge these volumes and cumulative indexes together in one alphabet.

To search NUCMC, look for your surname of interest—let's say it's Johnson—and the reference to "genealogy," as below.

JOHNSON, Josephine Winslow, 1910-   70-2061

JOHNSON, Katharine (McMahon) d. 1924.
70-126

JOHNSON, Laura Grace (Mosher) b. 1876.
70-409

JOHNSON, Lionel.   70-1903

JOHNSON, Louis Arthur, 1891-   70-151

JOHNSON, Lyndon Baines, Pres. U S.. 1908-
70-708, 70-711, 70-844

As correspondent. 70-185, 70-1416, 70-1446, 70-1681

Speeches. 70-1384

JOHNSON, Magnus, 1871-1936. 70-255

JOHNSON, Mary Louise (Hays) d. 1903. 70-409

JOHNSON, Merle De Vore, 1874-1935 70-1745

JOHNSON, Moses, ca. 1808-1853. 70-834

National Union Catalog of Manuscript Collections (Washington, D.C.: The Library of Congress, 1970), p. 417.

Take the reference number and check the volume. For example, 70-2050 means the 2050th collection cataloged in 1970. That particular collection number was assigned to the manuscript entry for Martha Frances (Woodroof) Hiden, a professional genealogist in Virginia whose files include Johnsons.

MS 70-2050

Hiden, Martha Frances (Woodroof) 1883–1959.
Papers, ca. 1900–58. ca. 1750 items.
In Virginia Historical Society collections (Richmond)
Correspondence, genealogical notes, and notebooks, concerning the Allen, Almond, Banks, Bell, Bibb, Bohannan, Bradford, Burton, Campbell, Claiborne, Clark, Cole, Cowherd, Crafton, Crittenden, Croshaw, Daniel, Early, Elkins, Fowler, Goodloe, Graves, Groom, Hawkins, Hazelrigg, Helm, Hiden, Holladay, Hudson, Johnson, Jones, Kirtley, Mallicote, Marr, Martiau, Martin, Mills, Morgan, Naff, Nalle, Peacock, Petty, Pittman, Powell, Quarles, Roane, Roberts, Robinson, Rowland, Runkle, Shipp, Smith, Spiller, Tandy, Taylor, Terrell, Thompson, Towles, Tucker, Tunstall, Vivion, Webb, Woodroof, and Wyatt families.
Gift of Mrs. Hiden's family, Newport News, Va., through the courtesy of Mrs. Annie Lash Jester, Tabb, Va., 1969.

National Union Catalog of Manuscript Collections (Washington, D.C.: The Library of Congress, 1970) p. 260.

Many genealogists stop here for they are looking for a compiled genealogy. Check also for the specific locality your ancestors lived in, the churches and schools they attended, other families they were associated with, and so on. These entries could disclose current locations for your family's Bible, diaries kept by your great-grandmother as she crossed the ocean to America, or Civil War letters written by your great-grandfather to his sweetheart.

These volumes are especially valuable for records carried to places not associated with your family by relatives or family friends who moved away. For example, the personal papers of Zachariah Johnston, a resident of Rockbridge County, Virginia, ended up in Durham, North Carolina. Searches in Rockbridge County disclosed the location of some of his papers in the Virginia Historical Society in Richmond but failed to mention that a much larger collection had been deposited in Duke University, Durham, North Carolina, where one of the family members later settled. This collection was cataloged in *National Union Catalog of Manuscript Collections*.

A more concise reference is the *Directory of Archives and Manuscript Repositories* (Washington, D.C.: National Historical Records Publications and Records Commission, 1978). This volume is less useful because the descriptions are too concise to include most families and individuals mentioned in the manuscripts themselves. However, it does contain references to collections for ethnic and immigrant groups.

Both of these tools are available in most research libraries.

DAR Library Catalog

A recent addition to published manuscript catalogs is National Society Daughters of the American Revolution, *Library Catalog, Volume One: Family Histories and Genealogies* (Washington, D.C.: DAR, 1982). Arranged alphabetically by the primary family treated, the entries include full bibliographic citations and the DAR library call number. Many of the more than 14,000 entries refer to typescript genealogies found in few other libraries. There is also an author and surname index to locate other major families treated in books cataloged under a different surname such as Cromwells in the Bullock genealogy. Copies of this valuable index are in most genealogy libraries or it can be purchased from the DAR. This may well have been the most important index to appear recently.

Bibliographic Search Networks

Many major public, private, and university libraries have entered the computer age in full. These libraries are connected to one of several computer networks that allows them to locate and catalog books much faster by sharing information with others in the network. One of the major networks is OCLC (Online Computer Library Center). This network is an online card catalog for some 5,000 university, public, and private libraries who subscribe to the service. They supply a copy of their card catalog for input into the master database.

At the present time, there is no subject entry for OCLC. If you have a specific title or an author's name, you can retrieve the full citation and locate the copy nearest you which can be borrowed on interlibrary loan.

Almost every university library and many public and private libraries have a special computer reference services department. Library personnel are trained to obtain information from over 100 databases, including *Comprehensive Dissertation Abstracts, Encyclopedia of Associations, National Newspaper Index, Ulrich's International Periodicals Directory, Historical Abstracts,* Standard's and Poor's News Services, ERIC (Educational Resources Information Center), and many others.

These databases can be searched in a few short minutes, providing reference bibliographies, including locations of specific reference materials which can be borrowed on interlibrary loan. You pay by the minute for computer time and by the entry for the bibliographies generated. In a recent search, twenty-two minutes of time to search ten years of 9,000 periodicals yielded thirty-two entries of specific interest for a cost of $28.45. It would have taken at least four months to physically search those periodicals even with the best of indexes. See Chapter 22 for more information on computer databases.

Genealogists often avoid using university libraries because they are large and organized for academic studies. They are, however, financed with tax money which genealogists help to pay. They have the funds to purchase some of the most important research tools available – many of them discussed throughout the chapters of this book. Sign up as a Friend of the Library (usually a $10-$15 fee per quarter) so you have borrowing privileges and your own library card. Then drop into the computer services department and investigate what they have to offer.

Local Histories Indexes and Tools

Many printed genealogies and biographies are buried in the thousands of local histories published throughout the country in the last century and a half. The genealogist needs a shovel to dig them out. Once found they can produce added insight on a particular ancestor, mention a father's name or place of origin, or add several generations to a lineage. Proper usage of available indexes will greatly help the digging in these sources. Several indexes with narrower scopes will be briefly mentioned in the section on Regional Indexes, but here are several which are generally nationwide in scope.

Index to American Genealogies (Munsell's Index)

One of the first attempts to index every printed genealogical work was done by Joel Munsell's Sons, an Albany publishing house in the late nineteenth century. This *Index to American Genealogies*, could fit well in the previous section on family histories or the next section on periodical indexes, but its greatest value lies in the inclusion of genealogical material from town, county, and local histories. First printed in 1900, it went through five editions and a supplement (1900-08). It was reprinted by Gale Research Company of Detroit in 1966 and is currently available in another reprint edition from Genealogical Publishing Company of Baltimore, 1979. Although somewhat outdated, it is very useful. Many local histories, which included lengthy genealogies, were published before 1908.

This work indexes surnames with brief titles and page numbers given to identify where a family history may be found. The approximately 63,000 references are not comprehensive but do include the major occurrences of family information in the books cited. The brief citations can be located in the companion volume, *The American Genealogist,* 5th ed. (Albany, N.Y.: Joel Munsell's Sons; 1900; reprint ed., Detroit: Gale Research Co., 1975) which is a bibliography of family histories published in America to 1900. Every genealogical library collection should have this book. A helpful description of this tool and how to use it can be found in Roger Scanland, "The Munsell Genealogical Indexes," *Genealogical Journal* 2 (Sept. 1973): 103-8.

Newberry Index

One of the largest genealogical libraries in the country is the Newberry Library in Chicago. Between 1896 and 1917 the staff there compiled a detailed surname index to genealogical periodicals and local history books. Although not an every-name index it is fairly comprehensive. The references include brief mentions of the surname as well as biographies and family genealogies. The *Genealogical Index of the Newberry Library,* 4 vols. (Boston, Mass.: G. K. Hall, 1960) contains 512,000 entries arranged alphabetically by surname. Very brief citations are included to the books indexed—usually a short title, author, year of publication. They are arranged by region or state. Since the index was discontinued in 1917 no books published after that date are included.

Greenlaw Index

A similar index is William Prescott Greenlaw, comp., *The Greenlaw Index of the New England Historic Genealogical Society,* 2 vols. (Boston, Mass.: G. K. Hall, 1979). Greenlaw was librarian of the New England Historic Genealogical Society 1894 to 1929. It is similar in size and scope to the Munsell and Newberry indexes; however, the citations reference works carrying a family through three or more generations in books published 1900-40. The over 35,000 entries are arranged alphabetically by surname and given names on three-by-five cards which are reduced and printed in two large volumes. The citations also include the ancestor, residence, and time period. Oriented towards New England, as is Munsell's Index, Greenlaw's complements the Midwest orientation of the Newberry Index nicely. All three indexes have coverage outside those areas as well.

Library of Congress Index to Local History Biographies

Another card file to biographical material was made by the Library of Congress and recently published on microfilm: *The Library of Congress Index to Biographies in State and Local Histories,* 40 reels (Baltimore: Magna Carta Book Co., 1979). This index includes about 170,000 names of persons whose biographical sketches appear in 340 state, county, regional, and city histories. The names are arranged alphabetically but the index is not comprehensive. Of the 340 histories indexed, twenty-six states are represented only once. The remaining twenty-four states show this distribution:

Alabama	8	Louisiana	21
Alaska	3	Maryland	2
Arkansas	10	Mississippi	13
Arizona	6	Nevada	11
California	34	North Carolina	10
Connecticut	3	North Dakota	3
Delaware	3	New York	2
District of Columbia	3	Oklahoma	3
		Ohio	2
Georgia	36	South Carolina	13
Hawaii	3	Tennessee	32
Idaho	12	Texas	27
Kentucky	50		

Comparatively intensive coverage for the South makes this tool especially helpful. An excellent review pointing out some limitations is J. Carlyle Parker, "Book Reviews," *Genealogical Journal* 9 (March 1980): 39.

Genealogical Indexing Associates (GIA)

A relatively new development is statewide indexes to local histories. Many every-name indexes have been published for individual local histories. Now works are beginning to appear which include many histories in one alphabetical index. These are personal-name indexes for those for whom a sketch or important information is available. In using these indexes it is good to check every sketch in an area of interest (county, city) for all people of the surname of interest. This way the ancestor may be found even if he isn't the subject of a sketch. GIA (Box 102, Bountiful, UT 84087) has already published a microfiche index to Indiana biographies containing almost a quarter of a million names from 537 sources. An Illinois index should appear in 1984, and volumes for other Midwestern and Eastern states are planned.

Periodical Indexes

For over a hundred years genealogists and genealogical societies have been printing periodicals (serials or magazines) which include a large variety of original sources, "how-to" articles, and compiled family histories. Over the years several incomplete periodical indexes have appeared for genealogists. While they are not every-name indexes, they are very helpful. Some of the indexes mentioned above include some genealogical periodicals, but the following are the most helpful.

Index to Genealogical Periodicals (Jacobus's Index)

One of the foremost modern genealogists, Donald Lines Jacobus, saw the need to access the information hidden in periodicals. He published three volumes (1932-53) as a partial index to major genealogical periodicals. His *Index to Genealogical Periodicals* (reprint ed., 3 vols. in 1, Baltimore: Genealogical Publishing Co., 1978) is available in all genealogical libraries and collections. It includes about 20,000 references to people, places, and records appearing in periodicals from 1870 to 1952 by surname, personal name, and locality. Unfortunately, he did not index periodicals with their own comprehensive index, and he indexed articles by their main subject rather than including every name. Thus, the family record of the Wilsons of Newport is indexed as: Wilson; Family Record, Newport. No individuals are specified. His introduction to each volume is invaluable. Table 13-1 lists some of the major periodicals he indexed and specifies the volumes covered. An invaluable new edition of *Donald Lines Jacobus' Index to Genealogical Periodicals* has been completed by Carl Boyer, III, (Newhall, Calif.: Boyer Publications, 1983), available from Box 333, Newhall, CA 91322.

Table 13-1

Some Major Genealogical Periodicals Included in Jacobus' Index to Genealogical Periodicals

Title Codes	Journal	Volumes or Years Indexed Vol. 1 (1936)	Vol. 2, (1949)	Vol. 3 (1953)
A1	*New England Historical and Genealogical Register*	51-85, 1897-1931	86-100, 1932-1946	101-106, 1947-52
A2	*New York Genealogical and Biographical Record*	1-62, 1870-1931	63-77, 1932-46	78-83, 1947-52
B1	*Genealogical Magazine of New Jersey*	1-6, 1925-31	7-20, 1931-45	21-25, 1946-50
B2	*Nebraska and Midwest Genealogical Records*	1-9. 1923-31	10-18, 1932-43	---
B3	*Connecticut Magazine*	1-12, 1895-1908	---	---
B4	*The American Genealogist*	1-8, 1923-32	9-23, 1932-47	24-28,1948-52
Dt	*Detroit Society for Genealogical Research Magazine*	---	2-10,1938-47	10-16, 1947-52
E	*"Old Northwest" Genealogical Quarterly*	1-15, 1885-95	---	---
J	*South Carolina Historical and Genealogical Magazine*	1-30, 1900-1929	31-47, 1930-46	48-53, 1947-52
M	*National Genealogical Society Quarterly*	1-19, 1912-31	20-34, 1932-46	35-40, 1947-52
P	*Genealogical Society of Pennsylvania Publications* (later *Pennsylvania Genealogical Magazine)*	1-11, 1895-1931	11-1, 1932-45	15-19, 1947-52
Q1	*Pennsylvania Magazine of History and Biography*	1-54, 1877-1930	55-63, 1931-39	---
U	*Utah Genealogical and Historical Magazine*	1-22, 1910-31	23-30, 1932-39	---
V1	*Tyler's Quarterly*	1-12, 1919-31	13-28, 1931-47	29-32, 1947-51
V3	*Virginia Magazine of History and Biography*	under Regional Indexes, Southern States.	40-53, 1932-46	55-60, 1947-52
X	*Maryland Genealogical Bulletin*	1-2, 1930-31	3-17, 1932-46	18-21, 1947-51
Y1	*Collections of the Essex Institute*	51-67, 1915-31	68-82, 1932-46	83-88, 1947-52
Z	*DAR Magazine*	1-64, 1892-1930 (in part)	68-82, 1932-46	---

Annual Index to Genealogical Periodicals and Family Histories (Waldenmaier)

Jacobus's Index ends with 1952 periodicals. The next decade is only partially covered in an eight-volume index by Inez B. Waldenmaier, *Annual Index to Genealogical Periodicals and Family Histories,* Washington, D.C.: By the author, 1956-63. It was primarily a list of new family histories and records printed each year either in book form or in periodicals. It is incomplete but slightly more comprehensive in its later volumes. However, it is the only such source available for those years. Major genealogical libraries will have a copy; all eight volumes are currently out of print.

Genealogical Periodical Annual Index (GPAI)

Since 1962 a *Genealogical Periodical Annual Index* has been published which is a great boon to genealogists except for a gap 1970-73. Several editors have tackled this task over the years. Table 13-2 shows the chronological status of periodical indexes and provides a good overview.

Currently Catherine M. Mayhew, comp., and Laird C. Towle, ed., produce the *Genealogical Periodical Annual Index* (Bowie, Md.: Heritage Books, 1974-present). This index is in virtually every genealogy library collection. It is not cumulative from year to year. Thus, each year must be searched separately. It is not an every-name index and includes a personal name only when the individual is the subject of an article. Book reviews and other articles are also indexed. Only about half of the genealogical periodicals currently available are indexed – those periodicals which provide free copies of their issues to the compiler. Fortunately, most major periodicals participate. Many small local periodicals (based on one or two counties for example) are not included. Still, GPAI is a very helpful tool and can save hours of research if used carefully.

Specific Periodical Indexes

Many long-lived genealogical periodicals have published comprehensive, cumulative indexes of their own magazine. While most publish annual indexes, those with cumulative indexes are more helpful to the genealogist. A partial list of such periodicals and the volumes covered in each cumulative index follows. Most of them are every-name indexes.

New England Historic and Genealogical Register, vols. 1-50, 51-112 ("abridged").

New York Genealogical and Biographical Record, vols. 1-20, 20-40, 39-76, and 77-94. (Subject only).

National Genealogical Society Quarterly, vols. 1-50 (topical index).

Daughters of the American Revolution Magazine, vols. 1-84, then every five years to 104. ("Genealogy Index").

New Jersey Genealogical Magazine, vols. 1-30, 31-40.

Virginia Genealogist, vols. 1-20.

Detroit Society for Genealogical Research Magazine, vols. 1-10, then every five years to vol. 30.

Mayflower Descendant, vol. 1-34, "Index of Persons."

South Carolina Historical and Genealogical Magazine, vol. 1-40, 41-71.

Table 13-2

Overview of Genealogical Periodical Indexes

Volume Number	*Indexes Periodicals Published in:*	*Number of Genealogical Periodicals Indexed*	*Number of Entries*	*Number of Surname Periodicals*	*Year Published*	*Compiler and/or Editor*
			Index to Genealogical Periodicals			
1	1870-1931	51	About 8,850	0	1932	Donald L. Jacobus
2	1931-46	50	About 9,750	0	1948	Donald L. Jacobus
3	1947-52	24	About 2,500	0	1953	Donald L. Jacobus
			Annual Index to Genealogical Periodicals and Family Histories			
1-8	1956-62	111		Very few	1956-62	Inez B. Waldenmaier
			Genealogical Periodical Annual Index (GPAI)			
1	1962	78	unknown	0	1963	Ellen S. Rogers
2	1963	118	unknown	0	1964	Ellen S. Rogers
3	1964	115	unknown	37	1965	Ellen S. Rogers
4	1965	115	unknown	0	1967	Ellen S. Rogers
5	1966	97	About 3,050	0	1967	George E. Russell
6	1967	124	3,700	0	1969	George E. Russell
7	1968	133	3,983	60	1970	George E. Russell
8	1969	151	4,624	72	1973	George E. Russell
9-12	1970-73		(not yet published)			
13	1974	95	3,500	45	1976	Laird C. Towle
14	1975	117	4,400	39	1977	Laird C. Towle
15	1976	120	4,500	0	1978	Laird C. Towle
16	1977	132	7,600	0	1979	and Catherine Mayhew
17	1978	140	7,600	0	1980	and Catherine Mayhew
18	1979	147	7,700	0	1983	and Catherine Mayhew

Although publication is presently lagging four years behind, there are plans to become current shortly.

Notes and Queries Relating to Pennsylvania, 7 vols. First-Fourth Series. Eva D. Schory, *Every Name Index to Egle's Notes and Queries* (Decatur, Ill.: Decatur Genealogical Society, 1981.

Subject Index to Genealogical Periodicals (Sperry)

The GPAI and related indexes are strong on names but not on other genealogical topics like research techniques or content articles. Kip Sperry compiled an index to fill this void: *Index to Genealogical Periodical Literature 1960-1977,* Gale Genealogy and Local History Series, Vol. 9 (Detroit, Mich.: Gale Research Co., 1979). It indexes articles on research procedure, descriptions of genealogical collections, sources, histories of localities, and other topical material of interest. It does not include compiled genealogies or printed source records. Nevertheless it is a helpful index for genealogists needing information about a source or area.

Indexes to Records

Military Indexes

Almost every United States genealogist has one or more ancestors who were involved in the military. Many lineage societies are formed around service in a particular war, thus creating great interest in military records. A few select military indexes are mentioned here.

Revolutionary War. Most colonial states have now published books listing people who served from that state in the Revolutionary War. There are, however, three nationwide indexes of note: *Index of Revolutionary War Pension Applications in the National Archives,* National Genealogical Society Special Publication No. 40 (Washington, D.C.: By the society, 1976) is an alphabetical index of all those who applied for a pension or who received bounty land based on Revolutionary service. Some *see* references are included. The index thus includes only those soldiers/sailors who lived until pension laws went into effect or widows who could prove the Revolutionary War Service for their husbands: about 80,000 names. The index is available in most genealogical libraries. The actual pension files are in the National Archives with microfilm copies at the Genealogical Society of Utah library, and other repositories. See Chapter 8, "Military Records."

The *DAR Patriot Index* 2 vols. (Washington, D.C.: National Society DAR, 1966) is a list of over 105,000 people who aided the cause of the Revolution with one descendant or more who joined the DAR. In most cases, lineage papers are available showing some documentation on the patriot and his family. Volume 2, a supplement (1979), added about 10,500 new names and made corrections to Volume 1. The DAR lineage books have been published through National Number 164,000 (Vol. 164). The *Index of the Rolls of Honor in the Lineage Books* (Washington, D.C.: DAR 1939-present) may also help identify a patriot ancestor. See Chapter 23, for more information on lineage society records.

Civil War. State-wide indexes exist for those who served from specific states in the Civil War (both Union and Confederate) but the major indexes are in the National Archives or genealogical libraries that have purchased microfilm copies. The three-by-five card index to Civil War pension applications is the largest single index for this war: *General Index to Pension Files 1861-1934* (Washington, D.C.: National Archives T288, 544 rolls) is available at many major genealogical libraries. It covers only those serving the Union cause or Confederate soldiers who later switched.

Compiled service records have also been indexed and microfilmed for each state that sent soldiers to war. These are indexes to every known soldier, not just those who applied for a pension. However, they are state by state. No consolidated, nation-wide index of service in the Civil War exists.

Many books have been compiled on those who served in other United States wars as described in Chapter 8 and Chapter 23.

Immigration Indexes

The topic of immigration to the United States is also discussed in Chapter 15. Immigration records are generally available in two forms: printed lists taken from manuscripts or compilations and unpublished manuscript lists. A mammoth work seeking to index all printed immigration records is P. William Filby and Mary K. Meyer, eds. *Passenger and Immigration Lists Index,* 3 vols. and 1982 supplement (Detroit, Mich.: Gale Research Co., 1981, 1982). It contains 700,000 personal names filed alphabetically including age (if given), destination, and source citations for over 1,300 printed immigration lists. Another supplement is planned for 1983-84 with 200,000 names. Over 2,000 printed sources have been identified, in all, 600 more to be included in future supplements. Two excellent articles by P. William Filby in the *Genealogical Journal* explain this project: "Published Passenger Lists" 8 (Dec. 1979): 177 and "Published Passenger Lists" 12 (Fall 1983): 112. Several other projects and indexes are mentioned in the latter article.

There are, however, over 20 million people who came to the United States in the nineteenth century who are not included on printed immigration lists. Arrival lists compiled by ports of entry survive and they have been microfilmed by the National Archives. Indexes exist for arrivals at the following ports for the years indicated:

Baltimore	1820-74, 1852-97, 1853-66
Boston	1848-91
Mobile, Alabama	1820-62
New Bedford, Mass.	1823-74
New Orleans	1820-50 and 1853-99
New York City	1820-46 and 1897-1902
Philadelphia	1800-1906, 1820-74

These indexes are available at the National Archives and the Genealogical Society of Utah as well as at larger genealogical libraries. See also *Guide to Genealogical Research in the National Archives* (Washington, D.C.: National Archives and Records Services, 1982).

Census Indexes

See Chapter 4, "Census Records," for a thorough discussion. Statewide census indexes exist for every federal census through 1850 and some later years. Caution should be observed in using census indexes. Blacks are usually omitted. Often the indexers were not well trained in early American handwriting. Also most indexes were made from microfilm copies and the writing may have been faded or difficult to read. In some cases, two or more indexes exist for the same census. If possible use both.

However, do not depend on the index alone. If an ancestor was known to have lived in a county when a census was taken but does not appear in the index, search the entire township or county. In larger cities for the post-1850 period, city directories may be helpful as a type of index. See Chapter 16, "Sources for Urban Research," and Chapter 11, "City Directories and Their Cousins."

Accelerated Indexing Systems (AIS) produced indexes for censuses 1850 and earlier, but very few for later years. Index Publishing (Box 11476, Salt Lake City, UT 84147) in 1983 published its first post-1850 census index, *1856 Utah Census Index.* Currently it plans to publish seven indexes for 1860, two for 1870, two for 1910, and three for the 1890 veteran census in 1984.

Currently no nationwide census index is available except for the 1790 census, which is included in the Rider Index (AGBI). Also *Century of Population Growth 1790-1900* (1909; reprint ed., Baltimore: Genealogical Publishing Co., 1967) includes (pp. 227-70) a table of names grouped by similar spellings, showing in which states each map appears. It thus creates a quasi-index.

Regional Indexes

Here are some indexes of great value in certain regions. This list is by no means exhaustive.

New England

Austin, John Osbourne. *Genealogical Dictionary of Rhode Island with Additions and Corrections.* Baltimore: Genealogical Publishing Co., 1969.

Barbour, Lucius A. *Index to Connecticut Vital Records.* Microfilm Hartford, Conn.: Connecticut State Library, n.d.

Holmes, Frank R. *Directory of Ancestral Heads of New England Families 1620-1700.* Baltimore: Genealogical Publishing Co., 1964.

Ireland, Norma Olin, and Winifred Irving. *Cutter Index, A Consolidated Index of Cutters 9 Genealogy Series.* Fallbrook, Calif: Ireland Indexing Service, n.d.

New England Historic and Genealogical Register, Index of Persons and Index of Subjects and Places Vol. 1-50. Baltimore: Genealogical Publishing Co., 1972.

Noyes, Sibyl, et al. *Genealogical Dictionary of Maine and New Hampshire.* Baltimore: Genealogical Publishing Co., 1979.

Parsons, Margaret Wellington. *Index (Abridged) to the New England Historic and Genealogical Register Vol. 51-112.* Marlborough, Mass.: n. pub., 1959.

Savage, James. *A Genealogical Dictionary of the First Settlers of New England.* 4 vols. Baltimore: Genealogical Publishing Co., 1981.

Mid-Atlantic States

Hoenstine, Floyd. *Guide to Genealogical and Historical Research in Pennsylvania.* Hollidaysburg, Penn.: n. pub., 1978. Contains thousands of references to surnames in over 2,500 printed family and local histories.

Magruder, James M., Jr. *Index of Maryland Colonial Wills 1634-1777* . N.p., n.d., Indispensable due to loss of early Maryland records.

Montgomery, Thomas Lynch, ed. *Pennsylvania Archives, Seventh Series*. 5 vols. Harrisburg, Penn.: n. pub., 1914. An index to the valuable and lengthy sixth series.

Smeal, Lee, and Ron Jackson, eds. *Index to New Jersey Wills (1689-1789; The Testators*. Salt Lake City, Utah: Accelerated Indexing Systems, Inc., 1979.

Strassburger, Ralph Beaver with William Hinke. *Pennsylvania German Pioneers*. vol. 3 Norristown, Penn.: Pennsylvania German Society, 1934. Indexes about 30,000 arrivals in Philadelphia.

Stryker-Rodda, Kenn. *Index to the Genealogical Magazine of New Jersey*. 3 vols. Cottonport, La.: Polyanthos, 1973, 1977. Every-name index to a significant genealogical publication.

Midwestern States

Bell, Carol Willsey. *Ohio Wills and Estates to 1850: An Index*. Columbus, Ohio: For the author, 1981; 4801 Mockingbird Court S., Columbus, Ohio 43229. Includes excellent introduction, cites entries for records no longer in existence as well as referencing documents in county courthouses.

First Families of Ohio Official Roster, Vol. 1 Columbus: Ohio Genealogical Society, 1981. Lists 2,273 settlers of Ohio before 1820 with at least one descendant doing genealogical research.

Heiss, Willard, comp. *Index to Indiana Source Books*. Indianapolis: Family History Section of Indiana Historical Society, 1983. Includes 115,000 names from the sources reprinted from the *Hoosier Genealogist*, 1961-79.

Indiana Biographical Index. Bountiful, Utah: Genealogical Indexing Associates, 1983. Contains over 247,000 personal names from Indiana biographical sources on sixteen microfiche.

McMullin, Phillip W. *Grassroots of America*. Salt Lake City, Utah: Gendex Corp. 1972. An index to the *American State Papers: Land Grants and Claims*. Covers early landowners in Southern and Midwestern states.

Morford, Charles. *Biographical Index to the County Histories of Iowa*. Vol. 1, Baltimore: Gateway Press, 1979.

Smith, Clifford Neal. *Federal Land Series. Vol. 1: 1788-1810; Vol. 2: 1799-1835; Vol. 3: 1810-1814; Vol. 4: Grants in the Virginia Military District of Ohio*. Chicago: American Library Association, 1972-82.

Sopp, Elsie L. *Personal Name Index to the 1856 City Directories of Iowa*. Gale Genealogy and Local History Series, Vol. 13. Detroit, Mich.: Gale Research Co., 1980.

Surname Index by the Iowa Genealogical Society. 3 vols. Iowa: By the society, 1972-77. A total of 96,000 names of ancestors members in the Iowa Genealogical Society are researching.

Southern States

Dorman, John Frederick, and Netti Schreiner-Yantis. *Index to the Virginia Genealogist Vol. 1-20*. Washington, D.C.: n. pub., 1981. Contains over 175,000 citations to records published in the *Virginia Genealogist*.

Georgia Secretary of State Office. *Indexes to the Various Georgia Land Lotteries*. Augusta, Ga.: n. pub., n.d. Personal-name indexes to those who received land in land lotteries, 1805-32.

Hollingsworth Genealogical Card File. Atlanta, Ga.: R. J. Taylor, Jr., Foundation, 1979 microfilm. A prominent genealogist's card file alphabetically by surname; given names out of order.

Kirkham, E. Kay. *An Index to Some of the Family Records of the Southern States*. Logan, Utah: Everton, 1979. "35,000 microfilm references from the National Society DAR files and elsewhere."

Munn, Robert F. *Index to West Virginia*. Charleston, W.V.: Education Foundation, 1960.

Stewart, Robert Armistead. *Index to Printed Virginia Genealogies*. Baltimore: Genealogical Publishing Co., 1970.

Swem, Earl Gregg. *Virginia Historical Index*. Roanoke, Va.: Stone Publishing Co., 1934-36. The primary Virginia and Southern states index. Comprehensive index to six major southern historical and genealogical periodicals.

Western States

Genealogical Material in Oregon Donation Land Claims. Portland Ore. Genealogical Forum of Portland, 1957-63. Indexes 5,289 pre-1853 land claims in Oregon Territory.

Jenson, Andrew. *LDS Biographical Encyclopedia*. 4 vols. Salt Lake City, Utah: A. Jenson History Co., 1901-36.

Office of the County Clerk (Various Counties). *Great Registers, California Voter Registration Lists*. Microfilmed (various dates).

Parker, J. Carlyle. *An Index to the Biographies in Nineteenth Century California County Histories*. Gale Genealogy and Local History Series, Vol. 7. Detroit, Mich.: Gale Research Co., 1979.

Parker, Nathan C. *Personal Name Index to the 1856 City Directories of California*. Gale Genealogical and Local History Series, Vol. 10. Detroit, Mich.: Gale Research Co., 1980.

Other Name Indexes

Several other indexes exist which can be a boon to the genealogist. They do not fit well into any category so a sampling is included here.

Miranda C. Herbert and Barbara McNeil, *Biography and Genealogy Master Index*, 2nd ed., 8 vols. (Detroit, Mich.: Gale Research Co., 1980; 3 vol. supplement, 1982), is a personal-name index citing biographical sketches or reports from 350 "Who's Who" types of publications. As one strictly alphabetical sequence (plus supplements), it is an invaluable tool to locating over three million references to notable people. It concentrates heavily in the twentieth and late nineteenth centuries, including living people. See also Chapter 14, "Compiled Biographical Sources."

Anita Cheek Milner, *Newspaper Indexes*, 2 vols. (Metuchen, N.J.: Scarecrow Press 1977, 1979), is an excellent guide to newspapers with indexes. It tells where those indexes are located and their scope. It is arranged by state, subdivided by city or county. See also her "Newspaper Indexes," *Genealogical Journal* 8 (Dec. 1979): 185 and Chapter 12, "Newspapers."

Computerized "Roots" Cellar is a computerized query service of Everton Publishers in Logan, Utah. Most genealogical periodicals have "Query" sections where subscribers can advertise for information on a surname or a research "dead end," but this is by far the largest. By mid-1983 some 20,000 participants had submitted over 175,000 names for computer input. Updates are printed in each issue of the *Genealogical Helper* and the entire database will be searched for a surname or individual for a fee. Details are in each issue of the *Helper*.

Computerized Genealogy Library, a division of American Computing Centers (ACC), has about 330,000 names in its database that are lineage-linked. In other words, if a child is located in this collection the computer automatically locates his/her parents, grandparents, etc. This information can be printed on pedigree charts, family group sheets, and descendancy tables for a relatively small per-name charge. For information, write CGL, 1864 S. State, Salt Lake City, Utah 84115.

Ronald V. Jackson, Jr., *Early American Series* (Salt Lake City, Accelerated Indexing Systems 1981-present) is a set of personal-name indexes in book form much like his census indexes. These indexes are statewide and typically cover the colonial and early periods. Tax lists, state censuses, and passenger lists are included in the indexes. Many of these books are at large genealogy libraries.

John P. Butler, comp. *The Papers of the Continental Congress,* 5 vols. (Washington, D.C.: Government Printing Office, 1980) is an every-name index to the original papers of the Continental and Confederation Congresses, 1774-89. Petitions from residents of Kentucky and Illinois in 1785, requests for pay and reimbursement for expenses incurred during the Revolutionary War, letters of recommendation, obituaries, and newspaper clippings are just a few of the documents included in this index. Copies of these volumes can be found in federal record centers and selected research libraries. The 204 rolls of microfilm they reference are available in the same libraries.

Frank Willing Leach, comp., "Genealogy of the Signers of the Declaration of Independence," is a collection of manuscripts with extensive indexes for each signer at the end of each section. The materials have been microfilmed and copies can be found in the Filson Club, Louisville, Kentucky; National Society of the Sons of the American Revolution, Washington, D.C.; and the Genealogical Society of Utah, Salt Lake City. These include documented materials on the descendants of the signers. The work he did on their ancestors is unlocated at this writing. Table 13-3 includes the list of signers and the call numbers for the films at the Genealogical Society of Utah and its branches.

Table 13-3

Signers of the Declaration of Independence*

State	*Name of Signer*	*Film Call Number at the Genealogical Society*
New Hampshire	Josiah Bartlett	F 001,751
	Matthew Thornton	F 001,751
	William Whipple	F 001,751
Massachusetts	John Adams	F 001,751
	Samuel Adams	F 001,751
	Elbridge Gerry	F 001,751
	John Hancock	F 001,751
	Robert Treat Paine	F 001,751
Rhode Island	William Ellery	F 001,751
	Stephen Hopkins	F 001,751
Connecticut	Samuel Huntington	F 001,751
	Roger Sherman	F 001,751
	William Williams	F 001,751
	Oliver Wolcott	F 001,751
New York	William Floyd	F 001,752
	Francis Lewis	F 001,752
	Philip Livingston	F 001,752
	Lewis Morris	F 001,752
New Jersey	Abraham Clark	F 001,752
	John Hart	F 001,752
	Francis Hopkinson	F 001,753
	Richard Stockton	F 001,753
	John Witherspoon	F 001,753
Pennsylvania	George Clymer	F 001,753
	Benjamin Franklin	F 001,753
	John Morton	F 001,753
	Robert Morris	F 001,753
	George Ross	F 001,754
	Benjamin Rush	F 001,754
	James Smith	F 001,754
	George Taylor	F 001,754
	James Wilson	F 001,754
Delaware	Thomas McKean	F 001,754
	George Read	F 001,754
	Caesar Rodney	F 001,754
Maryland	Charles Carroll	F 001,754
	Samuel Chase	F 001,754
	William Paea	F 001,754
	Thomas Stone	F 001,754
Virginia	Carter Braxton	F 001,754
	Benjamin Harrison	F 001,755
	Thomas Jefferson	F 001,755
	Francis Lightfoot Lee	F 001,755
	Richard Henry Lee	F 001,755
	Thomas Nelson, Jr.	F 001,755
	George Wythe	F 001,755
North Carolina	Joseph Hewes	F 001,756
	William Hooper	F 001,756
	John Penn	F 001,756
South Carolina	Thomas Heyward, Jr.	F 001,756
	Thomas Lynch, Jr.	F 001,756
	Arthur Middleton	F 001,756
	Edward Rutledge	F 001,756
Georgia	Button Gwinnett	F 001,756
	Lyman Hall	F 001,756
	George Walton	F 001,756

*Reprinted from David W. Putnam, Jr., "Genealogy of the Signers of the Declaration of Independence," *Genealogical Journal* 5 (Winter 1976): 125. Used with permission.

Directories of Genealogists

Occasionally a genealogist will want to contact another genealogist who is known to be working on the same line or in the same area. Generally the name is known from previous publications by that genealogist or recommendations of others. Several directories or indexes to genealogists are available.[3]

William D. Anderson and Associates, *Genealogists in the U.S. and Canada,* Memphis, Tenn.: Anderson and Associates, 1983, is the largest such directory and lists some 1,428 genealogists alphabetically by state of residence. Usually only the name and address appear. A 1984 edition will be available in April: 2935 Cordell, Memphis, TN 38118.

P. William Filby and Mary K. Meyer, eds., *Who's Who in Genealogy and Heraldry* (Detroit: Gale Research Co., 1981) gives much more information about a select number of genealogists chosen for their contributions to the field. Most of them are professional genealogists. A second volume is in process.

The Association of Professional Genealogists (APG) publishes an annual directory of its several hundred members. Many members have expanded listings giving background information. It is in most genealogy libraries or is available from APG, Box 11601, Salt Lake City, UT 84147.

The Board for Certification of Genealogists publishes an annual list of genealogists and record searchers it has certified for competency in specific areas. This list is alphabetical by state and includes areas of specialization. The list is available for $2 at Box 19165, Washington, DC 20036.

The Genealogical Department of the LDS Church maintains a list of Accredited Genealogists, tested for ability in specific regions and countries. Updated quarterly and listed by rotation in each area of accreditation this list is free from 50 East North Temple, Salt Lake City, UT 84150.

If one is seeking information on a genealogist from an earlier generation who is now presumed dead there are fewer indexes. The best is Frederick A. Virkus, ed., *The Handbook of American Genealogy,* Vols. 1-4 (Chicago: Institute of American Genealogy 1932-43).

This source includes a list of 2,341 genealogists both amateur and professional with some background. Volume 4 (1943) is the most complete but omits some names from earlier volumes. It also includes a list of almost 11,000 genealogies then in progress with the names of genealogists then working on them, as well as a state and county breakdown of genealogists.

Other directories include: Family Data Exchange
314 West Center #134
Bountiful, UT 84010
(801) 295-6880

Computerized data bank to bring genealogists together on a periodical basis. Costs not given.

International Genealogical Directory
Box 20425
Cleveland, OH 44120
First directory published in 1981, $7.50 plus 50 cents postage in U.S., additional $1 overseas. Registration of twenty surnames, with additional listings at 25 cents per name. Copy of directory included in fee.

National Missing Persons Register
Box 182
Madison, TN 37115
Registration fee: $50. Register of missing persons with location data: $5.

Nationwide Surname Index
L. Pero
Box 488
Bend, OH 97709
Reports per surname: $1 each. No charge if no information found. Thousands of surnames on file.

Ray's Surname Index File
Box 482
McCook, NE 69001
List of others searching your names, $1 per surname and SASE. Clearing house for surnames of Ray, Rey, Rae, etc.

Surname interests are published each issue in most genealogical periodicals, but at present there is no master index to these. Some publications are largely surname-interest publications and others include extensive listings. Among these are:

Genealogy Today
2815 Clearview Place, #400
Atlanta, GA 30340
(404) 457-7801
Listings five names, five issues: $24. Includes simultaneous listings in "Surnames in Genealogy Today." No limit on the number of names accepted.

Directory of Genealogical Societies, Libraries, Periodicals, and Professionals
July-August issue of *Genealogical Helper*
Everton Publishers
Box 368
Logan, UT 84321
(801) 752-6022
Annual. Registration fees published in the *Helper*. Subscription, $15 per year for six issues. Queries published in every issue, 25 cents per word. Display ads accepted, $13/inch.

National Directory of Local Researchers
The Family Tree
450 Potter Street
Wauseon, OH 43567
Annual. Directory, mostly professional genealogists with their credentials and interests. Published April, September. Some advertising. Listing $3/$6 includes directory. Directory only, $5.

Conclusion

Genealogical indexes are perhaps the most important tools a genealogist has. They enable him/her to access information previously difficult, if not impossible, to search. The computer makes indexing simultaneously more feasible and more necessary.

How can the genealogist learn about new indexes? Involvement with colleagues in a local professional society or local genealogy societies is important. So are regular surveys of major genealogical periodicals and those in your area of interest. Book reviews alert the reader to new indexes. Some recommended periodicals for this purpose are the *Genealogical Helper, Genealogical Journal, National Genealogical Society Quarterly,* and the *New England Historic and Genealogical Register*. More research aids are cited in the bibliography which follows.

Notes

1. Edited from Elizabeth L. Nichols, "Descriptions of Guides," Genealogical Society of Utah, December 1983. Used with permission.
2. Another section referred to as the Old Patron Section contains sheets submitted 1924-62. The hard copy sheets are no longer available, but they were microfilmed separately in 1952 and 1965. The 1965 filming is the most complete copy of these early sheets.
3. Expanded from Arlene H. Eakle, ed. *Research News* 2 (Sept. 1983): 2.

Bibliography of Additional Research Aids

American Library Association. *American Library Directory*. 32nd ed. New York: R. R. Bowker, 1982-83.

Crouch, Milton, and Hans Raum, comps. *Directory of State and Local History Periodicals*. Chicago: American Library Association, 1977.

Crowther, George Rodney, III. *Surname Index to Sixty-Five Volumes of Colonial and Revolutionary Pedigrees*. Washington, D.C.: National Genealogical Society, 1964.

Filby, P. William. *American and British Genealogy and Heraldry*. 3rd ed. Boston: New England Historic Genealogical Society, 1983.

Glenn, Thomas Allen. *A List of Some American Genealogies Which Have Been Printed in Book Form*. 1897; reprint ed., Baltimore: Genealogical Publishing Company, 1969.

Guide to Genealogical Research in the National Archives. Washington, D.C.: National Archives and Records Service, 1982.

Ireland, Norma Olin. *Local Indexes in American Libraries: A Union List of Unpublished Indexes*. 1947; rev. ed., Boston: Gregg Press, 1972.

____________, and B. P. Hayes. *An Index to Indexes: A Subject Bibliography of Published Indexes*. Rev. ed., Westwood, Mass.: Faxon, 1974.

Konrad, J. *Directory of Genealogical Periodicals*. Munroe Falls, Ohio: Summit Publications, 1979.

Kruzas, Anthony et al. *Directory of Special Libraries and Information Centers*. 4th ed. Detroit, Mich.: Gale Research Co., 1977.

Meyer, Mary K. *Directory of Genealogical Societies in the U. S. and Canada*. $15, Libra Publications, Box 29, Linthicum Heights, MD 21099.

Parker, J. Carlyle. *Library Service For Genealogists*. Gale Genealogy and Local History Series, Vol. 15. Detroit, Mich.: Gale Research Co., 1981.

Schwartz, Mary, et al. *A Guide to Reference Aids for Genealogists*. 3rd ed. rev. Los Angeles: GPS Publishing, 1983.

Sperry, Kip. *A Survey of American Genealogical Periodicals and Periodical Indexes*. Gale Research and Local History Series, Vol. 3. Detroit, Mich.: Gale Research Co., 1978.

Vallentine, John F. *Locality Finding Aids for U.S. Surnames*. Logan, Utah: Everton Publishers, 1977.

INFORMATION GUIDE

Genealogical Information in the Record Group	*Biographies*	*Dictionaries*	*Local Histories*
Surname/name	●	●	●
Date of Birth	●	●	●
Place of Birth	●	●	●
Sex	●	●	●
Race/color			
Physical Description			●
Occupation	●	●	●
Education	●	●	●
Military Service	●	●	●
Slave Status			
Property Owned	●		●
Religion	●	●	●
Citizenship	●		●
Marital Status	●	●	●
Spouse's Name	●	●	●
Children's Names	●	●	●
Father's Name	●	●	●
Mother's Name	●	●	●
Father's Birthplace	●		●
Mother's Birthplace	●		●
Date of Death	●	●	●
Cause of Death			
Name of Cemetery	●		●
Residence	●	●	●
Age	●	●	●
Literacy/signature			●
Photograph/sketch	●	●	●

COULD YOU USE THIS CHAPTER?

Type of Record	*Kept from*	*Clues That You Should Consult These Records*
Compiled biographies	About 1800 to present	One of the most valuable of the sources we have and one which requires careful analysis of its contents since biographies are often compiled from inadequate research or from secondary sources. Even so, they provide specific data not found in other sources. This chapter tells what biographies contain, how to evalute them, and describes indexes and tools created for their effective use
Local histories	About 1850 to present	Local histories usually include biographical sketches of prominent residents and early settlers. These biographies are especially valuable as they often draw on data nearer the actual life span of the ancestors they chronicle, even including oral interviews with family members or close neighbors.

Chapter 14

COMPILED BIOGRAPHIES

Jimmy B. Parker

Compiled biographies can provide genealogical researchers with valuable information and clues about an individual or a family. Often printed in local histories and encyclopedias or compendia, these biographies are available in many libraries and are therefore more widely accessible to most researchers than such documents as probate, land, vital, census, military, and church records which must usually be consulted on microfilm at a few research centers.

Biographies, often based on information supplied by the subject himself, can include data which would be difficult, if not impossible, to obtain from other sources. For example, biographies can sketch the outlines of a family tree for a researcher to verify from other sources. Or biographies which might suggest former residences, church affiliation, political party, length of time in a county, or unit of military service can point to other documents the researcher should check. The disadvantage, of course, is that these works are selective, rather than comprehensive. Your ancestor had to fall within the book's area of interest to be considered for inclusion. Only a few women are included in most.

Types of Biographies

General Biographical Encyclopedias

Many biographies are general compilations such as *Who's Who in America, Who's Who in the Midwest, Who's Who in Science*, and *Dictionary of American Biography*. (See bibliography for a partial listing of such sources.) The main advantage of the *Who's Who* type of biography is that it is generally available in public and university libraries. The main disadvantage is that it includes only fairly prominent men.

A typical *Who's Who* entry will provide information about a person's birthdate and birthplace, parents, education, marriage date, spouse, children, and then general information about occupation and special honors attained—whatever made the person famous enough to be included in the first place. An entry may also list the person's home or business address and, in a more detailed biography such as the *Dictionary of American Biography*, the references from which the life history was compiled and also the author of the specific entry. The following fairly brief example is from *Who's Who in the West*. The other more detailed and less compressed example is from *Dictionary of American Biography*. From them, you can see the kind of information which might be listed and the varying scope of such compilations.

FULLER, RICHARD EUGENE, museum ofcl,; b. N.Y.C., June 1, 1897; s. Eugene and Margaret Elizabeth (Mactavish) F.; Ph.B. [Bachelor of Philosophy], Yale, 1918; B.S., U. Wash., 1924, M.S., 1925, Ph.D., 1930, Alumnus Summa Laude Dignatas, 1961; LL.D., Wash. State Coll., 1944; m. Elizabeth Morrison Emory, October 9, 1951; 1 dau., Elizabeth Ann Hansen (Mrs. E. H. Friday). Asst. prof. U. Wash., 1930-34, research appointment, asso. prof., 1934-40; research prof., 1940-55; dir. Barkon Tube Lighting Corp., 1933-35, chmn., 1935-37, pres., 1937-39; dir. Cornucopia Gold Mines, Seattle, 1935-36, v.p., treas., 1936-38, pres., 1938-41; dir. Northwestern Glass Co., 1940-48, chmn. 1948-68; treas. Pacific Sci. Found., 1962-66; co-chmn. Pacific N.W. Met. Opera auditions, 1956-61; chmn. N.W. Met. Opera Guild, 1962; pres. Art Inst. Seattle, 1930-33, Western Assn. Mus. Dirs., 1935-37; pres. dir. Seattle Art Mus. (donor with his mother), 1933, emeritus, 1973; mem. Pres.'s Adv. Com. Nat. Cultural Center and redecoration of White House; founder Seattle Found., also pres., 1946-50. Trustee Seattle C. of C. (chmn. arts and edn. com., 1946-48). Served A.F.S., France, 1917; lt. 42d CAC AEF, 1918-19; maj. Army Specialist Corps, 1942-43. Recipient Ann. award Seattle Real Estate Bd. for outstanding civic service, 1939: King's medal (Great Britain) for service in cause of freedom, 1946; Raymond J. Huff award World Affairs Council of Seattle, 1960; also various citations. Dir. Seattle War Chest, 1942-44, Brit. Am. War Relief, 1941-44, Russian War Relief, 1941-45, chmn. Seattle Com., 1943-45; dir., exec. com. mem. Community Chest; chmn. Pacific N.W. div. Inst. Pacific Relations, 1950-51; chmn. U.S. Com. for Study Paricutin (Mexican volcano), div. geology NRC, 1944-50. Fellow Geol. Soc. Am., Mineral. Soc. Am., A.A.A.S.; mem. Am. Geophys. Union (pres. volcanology sect. 1944-47), A.I.A. (hon.), A.I.D. (hon.), Am. Assn. Museums (council 1954-63), Brit. Order St. John Jerusalem (asso. officer 1964, asso. comdr. 1970), Internat. Council Museums (U.S. nat. com., v.p. 1958-62), Assn. Art Museums Dirs. (v.p. 1956-57, 61-62, pres. 1963-64), Japan Soc. Seattle (pres. 1957-58), Newcomen Soc., Phi Beta Kappa, Phi Beta Kappa Assoc., Sigma Xi. Clubs: Rainier, University (Seattle); Yale, Century Assn. (N.Y.C.) Contrb. articles on geology to sci. jours. Home: 1227 Lexington Way E., Seattle WA 98112. Office: Seattle Art Museum Seattle WA 98112.[1]

DEWING, THOMAS WILMER (May 4, 1851-Nov. 5, 1938), painter, was born in Boston, the third son and the youngest of five children of Paul and Sophronia (Durant) Dewing and seventh in descent from Andrew Dewing, who emigrated from England to Dedham, Mass., in the 1640's. Paul Dewing was an expert millwright and was at one time engaged in paper manufacturing. Young Dewing received his education at home from an older sister. At an early age he developed a lifelong interest in natural history. He worked for a time in Boston as a lithographer, but his art work attracted the interest of a wealthy patron, who reportedly encouraged him to go to Albany and draw portraits. After a year or two there he had saved enough money to go abroad, and from 1876 to 1879 he studied in Paris under Jules J. Lefebvre. On his return he settled in New York City, where he remained for the rest of his life. His wife, Maria Richards Oakey Dewing [*q.v.*], whom he married in 1881, was a painter of flower subjects. They had one daughter, Elizabeth Bartol, who became a novelist.

Dewing specialized in small figure paintings of women—misty portrayals of what the art critic Royal Cortissoz characterized as "fair women in idle meditation" in "a world where it is always afternoon and never wind blows loudly." Cortissoz found the "exquisitely dehumanized beauty" of Dewing's work altogether admirable in its lyrical appeal and its subtle and original color. In his refinement, as Charles H. Caffin [*q.v.*] noted in 1907, Dewing became less and less concerned with form, to the point where he was occupied with the mere suggestion of abstract expressionism, as in "Le Jaseur" and "La Peche." Samuel Isham [*q.v.*], writing in 1905, compared the figures of Dewing with the landscapes of Dwight W. Tryon [*q.v.*] and found both artists moving into the realm of dreams. Dewing's idealized figures have also been compared with those of Abbott H. Thayer [*q.v.*], and numerous examples of the works of both painters were acquired by the collector John Gellatly [*q.v.*]. In its flowerlike delicacy an oriental note is seen in Dewing's work, a quality which undoubtedly attracted the attention of another collector, Charles Lang Freer [*q.v.*].

Besides figure painting, Dewing also did portraits of men, women, and children. He was a close friend of architect Stanford White [*q.v.*], who designed frames for a number of his pictures. For White's Imperial Hotel in New York City Dewing painted a notable composition, "Dawn," on a circular ceiling fifteen feet in diameter (later in the Gellatly Collection), which won praise from the critic Sadakichi Hartmann in 1902.

Dewing painted very little after 1920. His work found a place in museums throughout the country, with the major concentrations in two collections under the Smithsonian Institution in Washington: the Freer Gallery, with thirty-one paintings and drawings, and the John Gellatly Collection in the National Collection of Fine Arts, with seventeen. The two jointly honored the centennial of the artist's birth by an exhibition of his work in 1951.

In 1880 Dewing was elected a member of the Society of American Artists. He taught at the Art Students' League in New York City from 1881 to 1888 and became an honorary member of that organization. In 1887 he was elected an Associate of the National Academy of Design and in the next year an Academician. He resigned from the Society of American Artists in 1897 and in the following year joined a new, progressive group called the Ten American Painters, along with J. Alden Weir, John H. Twachtman, and Willard L. Metcalf [*q.v.*]. He was elected to the National Institute of Arts and Letters in 1908. Dewing died at his home in New York City of hardening of the arteries at the age of eighty-seven and was buried in Mt. Auburn Cemetery, Cambridge, Mass.

B. F. Dewing, *Descendants of Andrew Dewing of Dedham, Mass.* (1904); Nelson C. White in *Art and Archaeology*, June 1929; C. H. Caffin, *The Story of Am. Painting* (1907); Royal Cortissoz, *Am. Artists* (1923); Sadakichi Hartmann, *A Hist. of Am. Art* (1902); Samuel Isham, *The Hist. of Am. Painting* (1905); Holger Cahill and Alfred H. Barr, Jr., eds., *Art in America in Modern Times* (1934); Nat. Collection of Fine Arts, *Catalog of Am. and European Paintings in the Gellatly Collection* (3rd ed., 1945); Freer Gallery of Art, *Paintings, Pastels, Drawings, Prints, and Copper Plates by and Attributed to Am. and European Artists* (1948); *Am. Art Annual* and *Who's Who in Am. Art*, 1921-38; *Who's Who in America*, 1920-21 to 1938-39; *N.Y. Herald Tribune*, Nov. 5, 1938; *N.Y. Times*, Nov. 5 and 6, 1938; *N.Y. Herald Tribune*, Nov. 5, 1938; *N.Y. Times*, Nov. 5 and 6, 1938; N.Y. Pub. Lib. Art Division reference file; interview with Mrs. Elizabeth Dewing Kaup, daughter of the artist. A portr. of Dewing by William Merritt Chase [*q.v.*] is owned by the Nat. Acad. of Design.

Mary Bartlett Cowdrey[2]

Occupational Biographies

Some biographical encyclopedias are based on occupation, for instance, all of the scientists or doctors or artists in a specific locale. Such biographies include general information: name, residence, birthplace and birthdate, education, perhaps the spouse or children, but the main emphasis of course is the occupation: the person's professional reputation, honors received, and publications. Depending on the scope of a compilation, a person need not have been unusually prominent in order to be included. However, a researcher must know or at least suspect the occupation before such volumes are useful.

For example, *A Medical History of the State of Indiana* (1911) tells us that Dr. Joseph H. D. Rogers was born in Lexington, Kentucky, in 1805, graduated from Transylvania University, served in the Texan rebellion, settled in Madison, Indiana, in 1840, practiced there until his retirement in 1875, and died there in 1885. "He was a man of large physique and strong personality" and had a "widespread reputation as a surgeon," according to a grandson. He was present at the organization of the State Medical Society in 1849 and was the father of a doctor, Dr. Joseph G. Rogers.[3]

Mary Q. Burnet compiled a similar volume of *Art and Artists of Indiana* (New York: The Century Co., 1921). The book provides the following kind of information about artists like Ellen M. Ingraham: birthdate and place, death date and place, art teacher, art experience, art awards, art exhibitions, and address. Neither the doctor nor the artist had a national reputation, so the editors had made an effort to be comprehensive.

Similar books can be found for other occupations and other locales. Some national occupational biographies have been compiled such as Clark A. Elliott, *Biographical Dictionary of American Science* (Westport, Conn.: Greenwood Press, 1979).

Political Biographies

The common denominator of some biographical compilations is political party or political offices held. This kind of volume may include very wide-ranging material about the background of a legislator. For example, in Rebecca A. Shepherd and others, comps., *A Biographical Directory of the Indiana General Assembly, Vol. 1, 1816-1899* (Indianapolis: Select Committee on the Centennial History, 1980), the following information is listed about a legislator in addition to the time served and offices held: birthdate and birthplace, education, wife, marriage date, death date of wife, number of children, military service, residence, occupations, political affiliation and offices held, membership in other organizations, death date and place, and cross-references to other biographical references on this person.

The Biographical Directory of the American Congress, 1774-1971 (Washington, D.C.: Government Printing Office, 1971), in contrast, limits itself to the politician's name, office, residence, birthplace, birthdate, education, military service, work experience, and political offices.

Although you must already know a very specific kind of information about the person – his or her political activity – these entries may be included in state-wide indexes. Encouragingly too, a politically active person who was not "famous" may still be included.

Religious Affiliation Biographies

Some biographies were compiled into a single reference work based on religious preference. Again, this kind of volume requires knowing an ancestor's religious affiliation; and the material included is usually heavily weighted in favor of ecclesiastical offices and honors. Such records may also include general background information, however. For example, *The Mennonites in Indiana and Michigan* gives compressed information about preacher and bishop John P. Speicher (1833-94):

> Born in Somerset County, Pennsylvania, July 9, 1833. United with the Mennonite Church in 1853. Married Magdalena Hershberger (1840-1909) on May 23, 1858. One son and one daughter survived him. Ordained preacher at the Bowne Mennonite Church, May 25, 1867. Ordained bishop the fall of 1869. Served until within three months of his death, when ill health forced him to become inactive. Died in Kent County, Michigan, June 26, 1894, at the age of 60. Burial at Bowne.[4]

Depending on the scope of a volume and the makeup of a specific religious community, a broader cross-section of people may be included in such a work. A reference such as Andrew Jenson's *LDS Biographical Encyclopedia* gives this type of detailed information. Because the Mormon Church has a lay clergy, a broad cross-section of the community is included. It thus becomes important to know something about the history and practices of a particular religion to know what kind of information might be found in a religious affiliation reference.

> HALES, Jacob Lehman, Bishop of the Cedar Valley Ward, (Lehi Stake) Utah Co., Utah, was born March 11, 1864, at Enterprise, Morgan Co., Utah, the son of Henry William Hales and Sarah Jane McKinney. He moved with his parents to Cedar Fort when eight years old, and after reaching the age of thirteen he moved to Millard County, settling near Deseret. He was educated in Cedar Fort and Deseret.
>
> He was baptized Aug. 15, 1880, by David K. Crafts; was ordained an Elder, May 15, 1899, by Frank Hinckley; ordained a Seventy, May 17, 1899, by Joseph W. McMurrin, and filled a mission to the Eastern States in 1899-1901, laboring in West Virginia. In 1901 (Oct. 16) he married Mary Matilda Crafts in the Salt Lake Temple; two children have blessed this marriage, viz: Myron Lehman and Katherina Rebecca. Brother Hales was ordained a High Priest, March 12, 1911, by George

Cunningham. He served as assistant superintendent of the Cedar Fort Sunday School, and as second counselor to Bishop James E. Garn (being set apart to the latter position Feb. 25, 1912). After serving as first counselor to Bishop Hacking about one year, he was sustained as Bishop of the Cedar Valley Ward, Jan. 22, 1922, being ordained to that office Jan. 29, 1922, by Apostle Richard R. Lyman, and still acts as Bishop in Cedar Valley. Brother Hales is a farmer by avocation.[5]

Military Service Biographies

Military service also forms a basis for the compilation of biographies, on a national, local, or military unit basis. Of course the emphasis in such volumes is on military service; other information is brief and sketchy. The scope of a volume points to the relative prominence of those included: the smaller the military unit, the more complete the listing. This entry on Daniel R. Merritt, for instance, is relatively detailed because the history deals only with four Kentucky regiments.

Daniel R. Merritt

Surgeon Daniel R. Merritt, M.D., of Mayfield, was born and reared in Kentucky, and educated at Lebanon. In 1859 he was graduated professionally at the Jetterson Medical College, Philadelphia, and he then began the practice, which was interrupted in 1861, by the Civil War. When the issue came he promptly devoted himself to the cause of the Southern independence, and enlisted in the Seventh Kentucky Infantry (Colonel Crossland's regiment). He was made regimental surgeon. He was on duty with this regiment in the hospital service for two years during its service at Shiloh, Vicksburg, Baton Rouge, and in Mississippi during [the] Vicksburg campaign. Subsequently he served with the Thirty-fifth Alabama Infantry, in charge of field hospital, in Mississippi until the Third Kentucky, Colonel A. P. Thompson's regiment, with which the Seventh was consolidated, was mounted. He was then assigned to that command, with which he served with General Forrest, participating in the battle of Guntown, the raid to Paducah, Ky., the North Alabama campaign, and the operations of Forrest's cavalry during Hood's winter campaign in Tennessee. Finally, at the battle of Selma, Ala., in the spring of 1865, he was taken prisoner by the Federal troops of General J. H. Wilson, ending his Confederate service. After the close of the war Dr. Merritt engaged in the practice of medicine in Graves County, and continued it with success, achieving a high standing in his profession, until his retirement in 1897. In 1867 he was married to Sophia, daughter of James Briggs, and by this union has five children living—Beauregard Merritt, M.D., a graduate of Marion Simms College, St. Louis, now practicing in Graves County; Orlando M., William, Ernest, Ella (wife of G. W. Thorpe), and Ivan. Dr. Merritt is a great favorite socially, and in business affairs is active and enterprising. In 1899 he was elected president of the Exchange Bank, of Mayfield.[6]

Local Histories

Residents of a geographical area often compile a reference work for that locality. The focus of such local histories may be a state, county, local village, or township. Usually, the smaller the locality the more detailed the information included. Many of these local histories were prepared on the county level around the turn of the century.

Biographies are usually included in local histories. Some biographies are very abbreviated, especially those on a state level. A listing in James C. Mercer and Edward K. Rife's *Representative Men of Ohio* (Columbus: James K. Mercer, 1903), for example, only lists name, occupation, birthplace and birthdate, education, work experience, residences, political affiliation, and membership in certain organizations.

County and township histories as a rule include more detailed data and chronicle a broader cross-section of a community. The following example, from a history of Fond du Lac County in Wisconsin, includes the name, occupation, residence, birthplace and birthdate, parents' names and background information about them education, marriage date and place, background information about spouse, detailed work experience, and personal characteristics. The grandly eloquent tone of the entry is characteristic of local histories from this period. This biography also includes a portrait and an example of the subject's signature. (See Figure 14-1.)

Sanford Hazen, manufacturer of windmills, harrows and rollers, is one of the leading and enterprising citizens of Ripon, Wis. He was born in Copenhagen, Lewis Co., N. Y., on the 6th of April, 1821, and is a son of John and Polly (Blodgett) Hazen, who passed their entire married lives in Lewis County, where a family of nine children was born unto them. For genealogy see sketch of Chester Hazen, in this volume. John Hazen died at his home in Lewis County, N. Y., in 1839. Five years later, in 1844, his wife emigrated to this county, settling in Oakfield Township, but subsequently removed to Springvale township, where her death occurred.

The subject of this sketch passed the days of his boyhood and youth in his native county, receiving his education in a common school such as were in existence in that early day. In the month of February, 1844, having attained to man's estate, he formed a matrimonial alliance with Miss Susan B. Wright, who was also born in Lewis County. The same year the young couple settled in the town of Oakfield, Fond du Lac County. The country was then in a wild and uncultivated state, and gave little promise of future brightness. They continued to reside in the community until the following spring, when they returned to Copenhagen, and remained in the East until 1858. By that time the country had become more thickly settled, civilization had made great progress, and the growth and development of the community was very marked. Purchasing land in Green Lake County, not far from the present city of Ripon, Mr. Hazen embarked in farming, which he followed successfully until 1874, when he removed to Ripon, where in company with his brother, he opened an establishment for the manufacture of windmills. They began business in a small way, but since that time their trade has increased to gigantic proportions, and they are now owners of one of the leading enterprises of the county. The Laning planing mill was their first business location, but while there situated, within two years their stock was destroyed by fire. In the meantime their windmills were gaining a reputation, and in order to have sufficient room in which to carry on the work, and thereby supply the increasing demand, they removed to the old carriage shop of Dodge & Manville on East Scott street.

Figure 14-1. Portrait and signature of Sanford Hazen.

In 1876, the firm became S. Hazen & Son, W. F. Hazen becoming a partner in the business. Since that time its growth has been marked and rapid, the manufactured implements being windmills, drags and harrows. In the fall of 1881, it became necessary to seek still more commodious quarters, and the firm purchased the old Lyman elevator and warehouse property, and a lot, situated north of the Chicago, Milwaukee & St. Paul Railroad depot. Not long after this, work was discontinued at Shaffer's foundry, which was torn down, and they were thus deprived of all facilities for casting and repairing. It became apparent that they must at once supply the needed machinery, or their orders would far exceed the supply on hand; so, late that season they erected a building on the lot which they had purchased, and fitted it up for foundry purposes. The Hazen windmill is now well-known in Wisconsin and adjoining States. They have received orders from almost every township between Fond du Lac County and Northern Michigan, while their market also extends far to the East, West and South. The mills are in all sizes, from ten to twenty-five feet, and are equal, if not superior to any others on the market.

As a citizen, Mr. Hazen is ever ready to aid in the support of those enterprises which are calculated to benefit the public, and is recognized as one of the leading men of the community. He possesses strong temperance views, and aided in the organization of the first Washingtonian Temperance Society at Oakfield. He is a man of strong convictions, and when once he has determined that he is pursuing a right course, neither fear, ridicule or persuasion can cause him to adopt opposite views. None question his honesty of purpose, but all regard him as a man of sterling worth, and tender him the respect which is his just due. See portrait.[7]

Local histories, in addition to information about individual citizens, also include county atlases and plat (land ownership) maps, and sometimes portraits of residents and drawings of businesses in the area. (See Figure 14-2.)

Many also included directories of residents and/or lists of patrons who financially supported the publication of the book. Such directories might include such information as name of owner, description of business, place of business, residence, birthplace, date of settlement in county. (See Figure 14-3.)

Unpublished Biographies

Other biographies have never been published. They may be included in journals or diaries or in family correspondence, or they may be stored in the personnel files of businesses, in church historical files, and records of mortuaries. Such manuscript biographies may be more difficult to find but, as a last resort, may be useful.

Evaluation of Biographies

All biographical materials should be used with a great deal of caution. Usually only the most glowing parts of a person's life are included, but it is just as often the problems and difficulties which shape a person's personality and character. Remember that there is much more to a person's life than a biography would tell.

To evaluate the relative value of a particular biography, ask yourself a series of questions:

1. How was the biography compiled? Was the subject asked to submit a life history or did the author of the volume prepare

Figure 14-2. Residence of Patrick McCormick, Bethlehem Township, Stark County, Ohio in *Combination Atlas Map of Stark County, Ohio* (Philadelphia: L. H. Everts & Co., 1875), p. 101.

Figure 14-3. Township Personals and Directories in *Combination Atlas Map of Stark County, Ohio* (Philadelphia: L. H. Everts & Co., 1875), p. 118.

TOWNSHIP PERSONALS AND DIRECTORIES

STARK COUNTY,

GIVING NAMES AND LOCATIONS OF PRINCIPAL PRODUCERS, ETC., IN THE YEAR 1875, WHO PATRONIZE THIS WORK.

CANTON TOWNSHIP.

NAME.	LOCATION.	Date of Settlement.	NATIVITY.	Post-Office Address.	DESCRIPTION OF BUSINESS.
Barnett, J. F.	District 2	1869	Pennsylvania	Canton	Farmer.
Bachtel, Maggie	" 1	1848	Ohio	"	Tailoress.
Bechtel, Abraham	" 1	1853	"	"	Tailor.
Browning, O. F.		1842	"	"	Miller.
Bowman, J. R.	" 4	1864	"	N. Industry	Teacher.
Bair, William	" 4	1833	"	Canton	Farmer.
Caley, Joseph					
Criswell, B. F.	" 4	1872	"	"	"
Deckard, Henry	" 2	1873	"	"	"
Ford, Henry	" 4	1874	Pennsylvania	N. Industry	"
Gitneier, John	" 7	1871	"	Canton	Butcher.
Giessen, Otto	" 4	1872	Germany	"	Brewer.
Henry, Jacob	" 4	1852	Ohio	N. Industry	Farmer.
Hale, Charles	" 9	1871	England	Osnaburg	" and mining.
Hoffman, J. F.	" 1	1872	Pennsylvania	Canton	"
Kreibwill, Peter	" 1	1865	France	"	"
Klopfenstein, Jos.		1874	"	"	Brewer.
Lichtenwalter, Jno.	" 2	1859	Ohio	"	Farmer.
Longabaugh, Jacob	" 4	1818	Germany	N. Industry	"
Lind, D. & Co.	" 5	1874	Pennsylvania	Canton	Millers.
Lind, L. M.	" 5	1874	Ohio	"	Miller.
Lind, Luther	" 5	1874	"	"	"
Leonard, Henry		1870	"	"	Brick maker.

NAME.	LOCATION.	Date of Settlement.	NATIVITY.	Post-Office Address.	DESCRIPTION OF BUSINESS.
Niesz, Joseph					
Niesz, J. F.	District 1	1873	Ohio	Canton	Market gardening.
Packer, H. R.		1874	"	"	Teacher.
Pearson, J. M.	" 4	1874	"	"	Farmer.
Pratzmann, D.	" 2	1854	Germany	"	Small fruits and wine.
Rank, John	" 5	1853	Ohio	"	Farmer.
Roth, J. F.		1853	"	"	"
Rowland, Henry	" 2	1852	"	"	"
Richards, E. B.		1844	"	"	"
Richards, Daniel	" 4	1873	Pennsylvania	N. Industry	" and mining.
Rohrer, E. W.	" 2	1848	Ohio	Canton	"
Rohrer, D. H.	" 1	1874	"	"	"
Stauffer, J. E.	" 1	1872	"	"	"
Stauffer, D. E.		1872	Pennsylvania	"	"
Shock, Jacob		1848	Ohio	"	"
Sponseller, David	" 2	1837	"	"	"
Sponseller, J. H.	" 5	1872	"	"	Teacher.
Staub, John	" 2	1874	Pennsylvania	"	Miller.
Schwalm, I.	" 1	1848	France	"	Building and contracting.
Smith, Geo. E.		1859	Pennsylvania	"	Tanner and farmer.
Sprankle, Jacob		1825	"	"	Farmer.
Stover, Joel	" 5	1868	Ohio	"	"
Shrover, G. A.	Section 29	1874	"	"	"

the biography from information furnished by the family? Or did a researcher look at original records and write the biography himself? Most "mug books" (compilations during the late 1800s and early 1900s) were prepared from information supplied by the subject's family. Information based on personal knowledge is valuable, but the family's sense of what is important may be very different from what a genealogist would consider important. And all information still needs to be checked.

2. What is the quality of the workmanship of the volume? Often a book quite literally can be "told by its cover." If the book is poorly printed and badly bound, the information within may have been sloppily gathered as well.

3. How well documented is the biography? Does the compiler list the sources used and the information extracted from the sources so the reader can evaluate the information and arrive at his/her own conclusions? Or does the compiler simply list facts as he/she sees them without volunteering a source? If sources are listed, do they come from original documents or have they been lifted from other compilations, perhaps of doubtful authenticity? Does the compiler evaluate his/her sources? How well are the facts extracted from the sources listed?

4. How well is the volume itself indexed? The care of indexing is often an indication of the care of the compiler about other aspects of the project.

Biographical materials, then, are wonderful tools for the genealogical researcher. But they must be used with caution as well as gratitude.

Finding Aids

Indexes to many types of biographical compilations have been prepared although the editors' approaches to such indexes have been many and varied.

See United States Department of the Interior, *Biographical and Historical Index of American Indians and Persons Involved in Indian Affairs* (Boston: G. K. Hall and Co., 1966), for an example of a subject approach to indexing biographical materials. Another approach concentrates on a region. An example is the *Indiana Biographical Index*, available on microfiche from Genealogical Indexing Associates, Box 102, West Bountiful, UT 84087. The statewide approach indexes all sources, regardless of type or scope for that particular state, allowing a researcher to locate a biography very quickly, even when the ancestor's county of residence, religious affiliation, political persuasion, etc., are not known.

This list gives examples of the types of finding aids which should be consulted:

Filby, P. William, comp. *American and British Genealogy and Heraldry.* 3rd ed. Boston: New England Historic Genealogical Society, 1983.

Herbert Miranda C. and Barbara McNeil. *Biography and Genealogy Master Index.* 8 vols. 2nd ed. Detroit: Gale Research Co., 1980. Supplement. 3 vols. 1982. Cites more than 3.5 million biographies or biographical references in 350 different "Who's Who Publications," including most of those cited in the bibliography below. It is an invaluable tool for the genealogist and copies can be found in most research librairies.

Kaminkow, Marion, J., ed. *United States Local Histories in the Library of Congress.* Baltimore: Magna Carta Book Co., 1975.

New York Public Library. *Dictionary Catalog of the Local History and Genealogy Division, the Research Libraries of the New York Public Library,* 18 vols. Boston: G. K. Hall, 1974.

New York Public Library. *United States Local History Catalog.* 2 vols. Boston: G. K. Hall, 1974.

Peterson, Clarence Stewart. *Consolidated Bibliography of County Histories in Fifty States in 1961.* 1961; reprint ed., Baltimore: Genealogical Publishing Co., 1973.

Schreiner-Yantis, Netti, comp. *Genealogical and Local History Books in Print.* 3rd ed. Springfield, Va.: Genealogical Books in Print, 1981.

Wolf, Joseph C. *A Reference Guide for Genealogical and Historical Research in Illinois.* Detroit: The Detroit Society for Genealogical Research, Inc., 1967. (This last reference is only an example of the type of listing that may be found for most states.)

Notes

1. *Who's Who in the West,* 15th ed. (Chicago: Marquis's Who's Who, Inc., 1978), p. 245.

2. Robert Livingston Schuyler, ed., *Dictionary of American Biography,* supplement 2 (New York: Charles Scribner's Sons, 1958), p. 149.

3. William Harrison Kemper, *A Medical History of the State of Indiana* (Chicago: American Medical Association Press, 1911), p. 335.

4. John Christian Wenger, *The Mennonites in Indiana and Michigan,* No. 10 in Studies in Anabaptist and Mennonite History (Scottsdale, Pa.: Herald Press, 1961), p. 330.

5. Andrew Jenson, *LDS Biographical Encyclopedia,* 4 vols. (Salt Lake City: Deseret News Press, 1936), 4: 144.

6. Henry George, *History of the 3rd, 7th, 8th and 12th Kentucky C.S.A.* (Lyndon, Ky.: Mull-Wathen Historic Press, 1911), p. 151.

7. *Portrait and Biographical Album of Fond du Lac County, Wisconsin* (Chicago: Acme Publishing Co., 1889), pp. 603-4.

Bibliography of General Biographical Compilations

Canadian Who's Who. London, England: The Musson Book Co., Ltd., 1910. Concise biographies of distinguished Canadians living at the time.

Encyclopedia of American Biography. New York: The American Historical Society, Inc., 1934-70. Formerly *American Biography: A New Cyclopedia, 1916-33.* Old series—fifty-four volumes with main index and detailed information. Most entries both nineteenth and twentieth centuries. Some born eighteenth century. Includes many military personnel. New series—forty volumes, each with own index. Covers nineteenth and twentieth centuries.

Johnson, Allen, ed. *Dictionary of American Biography.* New York: Charles Scribner's Sons, 1928-36 plus supplements, 1944 and 1958. Twenty volumes with two supplements. General index to all names. Most entries born eighteenth or nineteenth centuries. Some date back to seventeenth century. Very detailed information.

National Cyclopedia of American Biography. New Jersey: James T. White and Co., 1975-. Sixty-one volumes to date, A-M. Each volume indexed with a general index to all volumes. Dates, places, occupations, and achievements are listed. Biographies from early 1700s to present.

Rider, Fremont, ed. *American Genealogical Biographical Index.* Middletown, Conn.: The Godrey Memorial Library, 1952-; vols. 1-127 cover through *Orchard, William H.* Over 127 volumes. Indexes alphabetically by surname; people treated in many family histories and various state and county records. Volume 1 has the main key to references in the series. Covers 1620 to 1900s.

Roberts, Sir Charles G. D. and Arthur L. Tunnell, eds. *Dictionary of Canadian Biography.* Toronto: Trans-Canada Press, 1966-72. Ten volumes cover A.D. 1000-1880.

Rose, George Maclean. *Cyclopedia of Canadian Biography.* Toronto: Rose Publishing Co., 1888. Collection of people distinguished in professional and political life, leaders in Canadian commerce and industry, and successful pioneers.

Virkus, Frederick A., ed. *Compendium of American Genealogy.* Chicago: A. N. Marquis and Co., 1925. Seven volumes, each indexed separately. Usually lists a person from nineteenth century and his direct lineage back to the immigrant. Scanty information—often just a name or approximate dates. Many errors.

Who's Who in America. Chicago: Marquis's Who's Who Inc. Since 1899, a new edition has been published about every two years. This same publisher also publishes several other titles in the same format, including *Who Was Who in America, Who's Who in the World, Who's Who in the East, Who's Who in the South and Southwest, Who's Who in the West, Who's Who in the Midwest, Who's Who of American Women, Who's Who in Finance and Industry, World Who's Who in Science, Who's Who in Government, Directory of Medical Specialists, Directory of Osteopathic Specialists.*

Wilson, James Grant and John Fiske, eds. *Appleton's Cyclopedia of American Biography.* New York: D. Appleton and Co., 1887. Six-volume set with additional six-volume supplement and main index. Names arranged alphabetically. Contains mainly Americans but also some royal or famous families from Europe, England, Mexico, etc. Covers 1400s to 1900s. Small paragraph on each individual.

PART III
SPECIAL RESOURCES

INFORMATION GUIDE

Genealogical Information in the Record Group	*Letters of Recommendation*	*Permits to Emigrate*	*Hospital Records*	*Passenger Lists*	*Oaths of Allegiance*	*Naturalization*
Surname/name	●	●	●	●	●	●
Date of Birth						●
Place of Birth		●			●	●
Sex		●	●	●		●
Race/color			●	●		
Physical Description		●	●	●		
Occupation		●	●	●		●
Education						
Military Service		●				●
Slave Status			●			
Property Owned						
Religion	●					
Citizenship		●		●	●	●
Marital Status	●	●	●	●		●
Spouse's Name	●	●		●		●
Children's Names	●	●		●		
Father's Name						
Mother's Name						
Father's Birthplace						
Mother's Birthplace						
Date of Death			●			
Cause of Death			●			
Name of Cemetery						
Residence	●	●	●	●	●	●
Age	●	●	●	●	●	●
Literacy/signature		●		●	●	●
Photograph/sketch		●				●

COULD YOU USE THIS CHAPTER?

Type of Record	*Kept from*	*Clues That You Should Consult These Records*
Emigration/ immigration records	1607 to present	If you have traced your pedigree to the immigrant ancestor, or are within a generation of the immigrants, this chapter is for you. The examples have been drawn from German and English immigration records, which will make it more helpful if your family's root go into those area. However, the Nationality Reference Directory at the end of the chapter deals nation-by-nation with immigration from almost every country in Europe and adds Australia, Canada, the Philippines, and Russia. No examples are cited for South or Central American, African, or Asian nations. Even for these areas, although the emigration records generated in the country of departure may differ somewhat from English/German examples, the immigration records generated upon their arrival in this country are the same in each time period: agreements signed with merchants, "pest" hospital records, health certificates, entry permits, letters to the editor, passenger lists, oaths of allegiance, and other documents.
Newspapers	1709 to present	If your ancestors settled initially or permanently in an ethnic community, you will find valuable the records generated by that community: newspapers, churchs, and immigrant aid societies.
Naturalization records	1740 to present	Alien registration cards; certificates of registry, of lawful entry, of arrival; declarations of intent to seek citizenship; petitions and certificates of naturalization are all important documents. This chapter will also give you hints on how to trace the ancestor who came to the United States via another country where the stay may have lasted for several years or even, in the case of some groups, two or three generations.

Chapter 15

TRACKING IMMIGRANT ORIGINS

Arlene H. Eakle

Since 1607, some fifty million immigrants have come from other lands to America. Some nine million passed through on their way to some other place or returned to their original homeland, leaving a net gain of over forty million persons:

400,000	1607-1790
5,000,000	1820-60
25,900,000	1880-1920
14,000,000	1925-80

The year 1907 was the peak: 1,285,349.[1]

Between 1607 and 1790 early immigration was basically British (England, Scotland, Ulster Ireland, Southern Ireland, Wales) and German. A classification of the white population of the United States in 1790 by national or linguistic stock shows: English and Welsh 60.1 percent, Scots 8.1 percent, Ulster Irish 5.9 percent, Southern Irish 3.6 percent, German 8.6 percent, Dutch 3.1 percent, French 2.3 percent, Swedish .7 percent, Spanish .8 percent, and unassigned 6.8 percent.[2]

Distribution of these national groups, however, differed from state to state in ways that impact on genealogical research during the colonial period. Immigration and naturalization policies, settlement and occupational patterns, and even cultural traditions are affected by the concentration of national groups as Table 15-1 shows.

Table 15-1

State-by-State Distribution of National Groups in the United States, 1790

National Group	*Percentage of Distribution by State*			
English and Welsh	Pennsylvania	35.3	North Carolina	82
Scots	Connecticut	2.2	Georgia	15.5
Irish	Rhode Island	2.8	Georgia	15.3
Germans	Vermont	.2	Pennsylvania	33.3
Dutch	New Hampshire	.1	New York	17.5
French	South Carolina	3.9	Northwest Territory	57.1
Spanish			Southwest Territory	96.5

John F. Vallentine, "Tracing the Immigrant Ancestor," *Genealogical Journal* 3 (1974): 4.

Even with the close contact between French Canada and Vermont, during the colonial period, less than 1 percent of the Vermont population was French in 1790. This ratio would change in the nineteenth century as Canadians entered the United States to work. The area which became Ohio in 1803 was over 50 percent French; only one-third of Pennsylvania was actually "Dutch" (German).

Map 15-1. Settlement to 1790.

Before 1790, the population was confined to the area east of the Appalachian Mountains with only a scattering of Americans over the line along the frontiers. Between 1820 and 1860, Ireland supplied the largest single group of immigrants – Germany, especially Prussia, sent 20 percent of the immigrants during those years. A smattering from other parts of Europe and an introduction of people from China and Mexico rounded out the population.[3]

Map 15-2. Settlement, 1820-60.

Settlement flowed into New York and Boston as the Irish came in droves to build canals and railroads, and the Europeans answered the call for settlement on vacant lands in the Midwest. The discovery of gold in California brought an overnight American population to the West Coast. See Map 15-2.

Before 1885, immigrants originated north of the Alps and west of the Elbe River. After 1885, the so-called New Immigration came from Southern and Eastern Europe, with the largest number of immigrants from Italy and Russia, mostly Jews.

These immigrants concentrated in urban centers where jobs were available and where churches, neighbors, and immigrant aid societies cushioned the immigrant experience. See Map 15-3. Most of these families were too poor to buy land when they arrived in America, and many heads of families had skilled and semi-skilled occupations.[4]

Map 15-3. Settlement, 1880-1920.

Russian immigrants comprised 20 percent of the foreign population of New York State and 25 percent of New York City; Austrian-Hungarian comprised 12 percent and 14 percent respectively; and Italy supplied 17 percent of the foreign population in New York, 18 percent in the city. By 1910, one-fourth of the foreign born population of New York City had arrived within the last five years, speaking a variety of languages, practicing a variety of religious customs, and demanding a wide range of food.[5] See Figure 15-1.

American immigrant records remain constant for all national groups while personal records may vary. Place of settlement, time of arrival, language and custom, points of contact between generations and families, religion and school policies – these also vary.

Emigration/Immigration Records

The emigration/immigration process generated a wealth of records, both personal and administrative, to keep track of who left, where they were going, the status of their personal affairs at the time they left, and their ability to care for their own needs on arrival. Most of these records are ancient in origin; and while their contents usually expand with the amount of information requested from each person, the types remain quite constant from 1700 to the present.

Some of these records have lain hidden in archives and personal papers for generations. Some are indexed and abstracted by government order or by genealogists who need quicker access. Many more are available on microfilm through the National Archives and its federal records centers and through the Genealogical Society of Utah and its branches. (See Appendixes A and D for those nearest you.)

Emigration (Departure) Records

When a family or an individual decided to emigrate, there were several steps they followed, some to comply with the law, some to prepare for their journey, and some from local custom or tradition. Each generated records.

Letters of Manumission. If the head of the house was tied to the soil on which he lived by medieval serf-lord commitments, the first step was to obtain a letter of manumission. This document freed him – usually with payment of a fee – from these obligations. See Figure 15-2 for a 1730 German example.

Sale of Property. If the head of the house owned property, he would advertise it for sale or dispose of it among family members who stayed behind. Some emigrants left their property in the care of relatives or friends and returned to sell it after they were sure they could make a success of their move to a new world. These documents are duly recorded with the proper authorities, often with direct statements of intent to emigrate or precise locations in the New World.

Letters of Recommendation. Letters of recommendation from local church authorities stating that the emigrant was a member of the congregation in good standing were next obtained. With these documents in hand, the emigrant then approached the local police authority for permission to leave.

Permit to Emigrate. The permit to emigrate certified that the man had paid his bills, settled his affairs in the community, and was free to leave. The passport allowed him to cross jurisdictional boundaries. In some countries, the permit to emigrate and the passport were combined in a single exit visa issued by district or provincial authorities. These identification papers were carried on the person of the emigrant, and local clerks recorded information from them first in court or council minute books and, by the nineteenth century, in emigration registers. Sometimes duplicate copies of the documents were made, labeled and folded, and filed alpha-

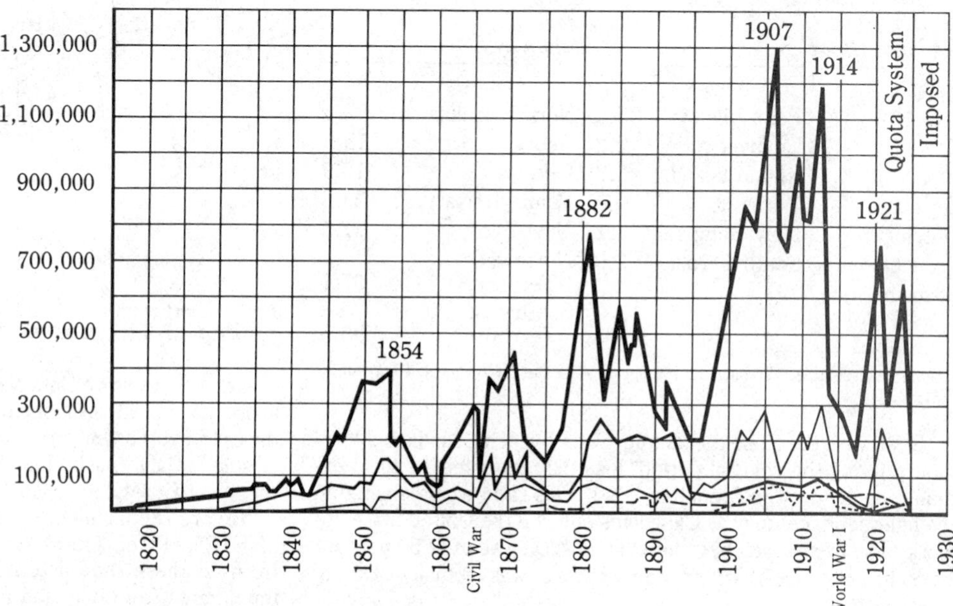

Figure 15-1. From Philip Taylor, *The Distant Magnet: European Immigration to the U.S.A.* (London: Eyre & Spottiswoode, 1971) and Antonia Stella, *Some Aspects of Italian Immigration to the United States* (New York: Arno Press, 1975).

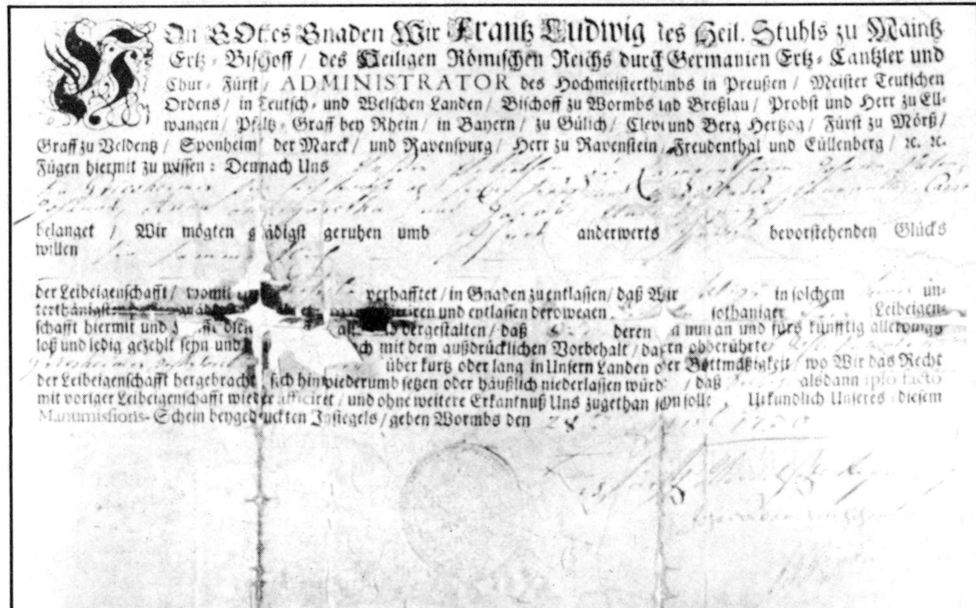

Von GOttes Gnaden Wir Frantz Ludwig des Heil. Stuhls zu Maintz Ertz-Bischoff / des Heiligen Römischen Reichs durch Germanien Ertz-Cantzler und Chur-Fürst / ADMINISTRATOR des Hochmeisterthumbs in Preußen / Meister Teutschen Ordens / in Teutsch- und Welschen Landen / Bischoff zu Wormbs und Breßlau / Probst und Herr zu Ellwangen / Pfaltz-Graff bey Rhein / in Bayern / zu Gülich / Clev und Berg Hertzog / Fürst zu Mörß / Graff zu Veldentz / Sponheim / der Marck / und Ravenspurg / Herr zu Ravenstein / Freudenthal und Cüllenberg / rc. rc. Fügen hiermit zu wissen: Demnach Uns [illegible] belanget / Wir mögten gnädigst geruhen umb [illegible] anderwerts [illegible] bevorstehenden Glücks willen [illegible] der Leibeigenschafft / [illegible] verhafftet / in Gnaden zu entlassen / daß Wir [illegible] in solchem unterthänigst [illegible] und entlassen derowegen [illegible] sothaniger Leibeigenschafft hiermit und [illegible] dergestalten / daß [illegible] deren [illegible] nun an und fürs künfftig allerdings loß und ledig gezehlt seyn und [illegible] mit dem außdrücklichen Vorbehalt / daß [illegible] obberührte [illegible] über kurtz oder lang in Unsern Landen oder Bottmäßigkeit / wo Wir das Recht der Leibeigenschafft hergebracht / sich hinwiederumb setzen oder häußlich niederlassen würd[illegible] / daß [illegible] alsdann ipso facto mit voriger Leibeigenschafft wieder afficiret / und ohne weitere Erkantnuß Uns zugethan seyn solle. Urkundlich Unseres diesem Manumissions-Schein beygedruckten Insiegels / geben Wormbs den 28 [illegible] 1730.

Figure 15-2. Letter of Manumission, granted by the Archbishop of Mayence to John Valentine Griesheimer, 28 April 1730. Printed in Ralph B. Strassburger with William J. Hinke, *Pennsylvania German Pioneers*, 3 vols. (Lancaster, Pa.: Pennsylvania German Society, 1934), 3: 67. Reprinted in 2 vols. without illustrations; Baltimore: Genealogical Publishing Company, 1966.

betically or by number in the local archives. When emigrants left illegally, without paying the fees and getting the proper papers, they were also recorded in the emigrant registers. In some cases, interviews about their whereabouts are recorded too, with notations that potential inheritance rights would be paid to the government in lieu of emigration fees.

Emigration Agent. The purchase of tickets and travel accommodations was usually done through an emigration agent. Early agents were appointed by church or emigrant groups to secure the best price and to insure that fellow travelers were not cheated. These agents traveled with the group to their destination. Some of them were pastors or church clerks.[6] Later agents worked for shipping lines to fill steerages so the trip was profitable for the company. They were licensed by local authorities and paid on commission or percentage, some by the length of the journey, and some by the total cost of the ticket and provisions. For a more detailed description of how these agents operated see R. J. Dickson, *Ulster Emigration to Colonial America, 1718-1775* (London: Routledge and Kegan Paul, 1966), Chapter 7; Norman McDonald, *Canada: Immigration and Colonization, 1841-1903* (Toronto: Macmillan of Canada, 1976); and Clifford Neal Smith and Anna P. Smith, *American Genealogical Resources in German Archives* (New York: R. R. Bowker, 1977).

Indentures. Emigrants too poor to pay their own way could agree to sell themselves into service for the cost of their passage. Those who contracted through an emigrant agent before they left their country of origin were referred to as *indentured servants*. They carried a copy of the contract with them, knowing in advance how much time they owed. These contracts would be sold to employers in the New World. Those who did not negotiate contracts before they left redeemed the cost of their passage and provisions by selling themselves to the highest bidder once they arrived in America. These were called *redemptioners*. English emigrants were most often indentured with articles signed before a magistrate;[7] Germans usually redeemed their passages at auction. Richard B. Morris, *Government and Labor in Early America* (New York: Harper and Row, 1965) is the classic work on the subject. Other studies examine servitude in individual colonies, for example, Warren B. Smith, *White Servitude in Colonial South Carolina* (Danielsville, Ga.: Heritage Papers, 1972). A list of these local studies is included in Barbara Bigham, "Colonists in Bondage: Indentured Servants in America," *Early American Life* 10 (1979): 30-33, 83-84.

Emigrants traveling from German principalities to Pennsylvania faced a long, three-part journey. See Map 15-4. The first stage was the trip down the Rhine to Rotterdam or Amsterdam. Wrote one 1750 voyager:

> This journey lasts from the beginning of May to the end of October, fully half a year, amid such hardships as no one is able to describe adequately with their misery. The cause is because the Rhine boats from Heilbronn to Holland have to pass by 26 custom houses, at all of which the ships are examined, which is done when it suits the convenience of the custom-house officials. In the meantime the ships with the people are detained long, so that the passengers have to spend much money. The trip down the Rhine lasts therefore four, five, and even six weeks. When the ships come to Holland, they are detained there likewise five to six weeks. Because things are very dear there, the poor people have to spend nearly all they have during that time.[8]

The second stage was from Rotterdam to the English port of Cowes on the Isle of Wight, then the principal port for immigrant traffic, although ships also stopped at Dover, Plymouth, London, and other ports. Here was another delay while ships awaited customs clearance, provisioning, and favorable winds. This phase took fourteen to twenty-one days.

The final stage of the journey was the seven-to-twelve week ocean crossing, later shortened by steam to fewer than fourteen days. The passengers were densely packed into the steerage decks below the water line of the ship. Shipping companies, to increase profits and cut expenses, often filled the cargo spaces with people too, rather than carry adequate food and water. By the mid-nineteenth century, government authorities required minimum rations of food and water from the ships' provisions; but earlier travelers risked disease, storm, and a high mortality rate. For a detailed description of the ocean voyage, see Philip Taylor, *The Distant Magnet: European Emigration to the U.S.A.* (London: Eyre & Spottiswoode, 1971) and Strassburger with Hinke, *Pennsylvania German Pioneers*.

Travel Documents. Documents which chronicle this part of the emigration process include personal records kept by the emigrant: personal accounts of provisions and fees advanced or receipts for payment of fees and purchases made, agreements with ships' masters, haulage receipts or claim checks for baggage loaded in cargo holds or shipped on other vessels (*quittung* in German); and travel journals which described weather, travel conditions, scenery, and enroute deaths, births, or marriages. Sometimes they recorded complete passenger lists. All of these, except the travel diaries, have been vulnerable to destruction and few survive today. There are examples among personal papers in the collec-

Map 15-4. Map of Rhineland, Germany, showing the sources of the Palatine Emigration. Adapted from Walter A. Knittle, *Early 18th Century Palatine Emigration* (Philadelphia: Dorrence and Co., 1937).

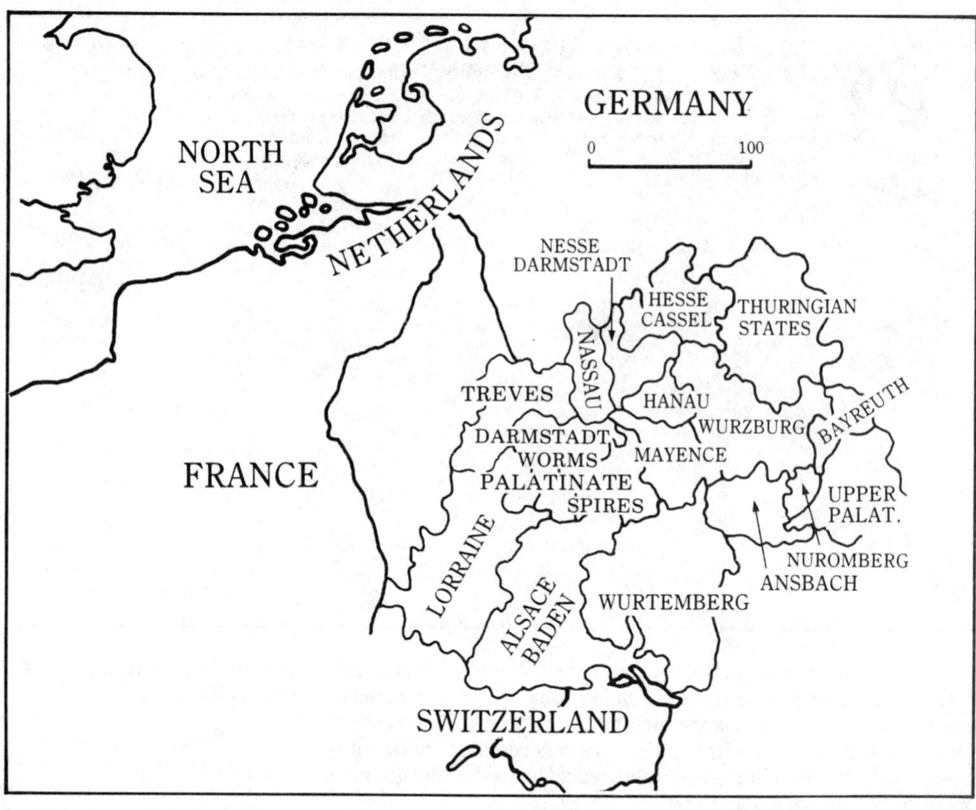

tions of the Pennsylvania Historical Society in Philadelphia. Travel diaries are being published in genealogical periodicals. Examples include Dr. Hale T. Shenefield, "From Herrnhut to Hagerstown: Johann Christoph Poet's Journal of His Trip from Herrnhut Down the Elbe and Thence to Haarlem," *Maryland Magazine of Genealogy* 3 (Spring 1980): 1-10; Willard Heiss, "A German Immigration Diary: 1848, Michael Friedrich Radke," *Genealogy* 66 (Jan. 1982): 1-6; and Hannah B. Roach, "Brief Report on How Certain Germans Have Fared, Who Have Come to Pennsylvania in this Year, 1749," *Pennsylvania Genealogical Magazine* 22 (1961): 236-37. See also Davis Bitton, *Mormon Diaries and Autobiographies* (Provo, Utah: Brigham Young University Press, 1977), a bibliography of 2,894 first-person accounts. Many are emigrant diaries or include travel accounts, especially significant for Scandinavian emigrants.

Customs Records. Customs officials were reponsible to see that each ship docking and clearing port was licensed and registered. Officials also recorded ships' manifests listing crew, passengers, and cargo; ships' logs which record weather and directional notations with statements on the conditions of the passengers, and births, marriages, and deaths; payroll accounts with signatures for seamen; ships' accounts for provisions advanced to emigrants; and miscellaneous documents which relate to the ship itself. These documents, sometimes called shipping records, sometimes referred to as customs records, will be found either in possession of the shipping company, the customshouse, or in local and government archives.

By the time the emigrants arrived in the new land, they often had acquired additional personal documents like certificates for marriages contracted in Rotterdam, in Cowes, or on board river or ocean vessels.

Another source awaiting genealogists is church records in emigrant ports of call. Here travellers attended services, took communion, christened newly born children, or buried those who died along the emigrant route. Although most of these are written in non-English languages, there are a substantial number on microfilm among the holdings of the Genealogical Society of Utah and its branch libraries.

For example, a Welsh family enroute to New York in the 1840s ran short of funds in Liverpool. They interrupted their journey for four years while the father earned enough money to continue the trip. While there, two children were born to the family and recorded in the Welsh Methodist (Calvinist) congregation. Clues of these births, later recorded in U.S. census records, were documented from this congregation's birth register.

Ahnenpass. During the Nazi regime, each citizen of Germany was required to carry an *Ahnenpass* (ancestor passport) with six generations of ancestry for government and military personnel and three generations for all others. This requirement was also imposed on some of the countries which capitulated to the Reich during World War II including Holland and Belgium. Copies were filed with the Reich. The German pedigrees were published as *Stamm-und-Ahnentafelwerke* (Pedigree and Ancestor Tables) (Leipzig: Zentralstelle für deutsche Personen-und-Familiengeschichte, various dates). Volumes for Italians of Aryan descent were also published.

The Genealogical Society of Utah has microfilmed the *Ahnenpass* for the area of Mittelfranken in the Brenner Collection (671 reels) with supporting documents. The following description from Ronald Smelser, ed., *Preliminary Inventory of the German Collection at the Genealogical Society of Utah* (Salt Lake City: University of Utah Press, 1980), pp. xviii-xvix, may help American genealogists unfamiliar with these documents.

> The collection is in nine parts:
>
> 1. An alphabetical listing (A-We) by surname of families along with vital record information.
>
> 2. Records from the Reichsbauernschaft and other agencies indicating where background research was done.
>
> 3. Miscellaneous family information not integrated into the bulk of the collection (part 1).
>
> 4. Marriage records from the eighteenth and nineteenth century of soldiers stationed in the area.
>
> 5. Directory of locations in Mittelfranken where research was done.
>
> 6. *Erbhofliste*—a pedigree of families living in the area for 200 years or more. An interesting example of the Nazi combination of "blood and soil."

7. Verification material including vital and parish records dating to the sixteenth century as well as pertinent correspondence.

8. Pedigree of Heinrich Himmler's family.

9. A file of genealogists who were appointed to do research. Correspondence between various genealogists and the Reichsbauernschaft dealing with their employment and the results of their work.

A rough sampling of thirty-five rolls revealed that the family information provides names, dates of birth and death, place of residence, occupation as well as names and occupations of parents, and a confirmation of whether the person in question was considered *Arier* or *Jude*. The sampling also revealed a sprinkling of other materials including genealogical journals, local newspapers, essays, and pedigrees of a number of famous Germans, including Schiller, Moerike, Uhland, and Schelling.

For further details, see Milton Rubincam, "Researching European Origins of Pennsylvania German Families." *Pennsylvania Genealogical Magazine* 25 (1967-68): 242; Milton Rubincam and John I. Coddington, "The *Ahnenpass* of Nazi Germany," *National Genealogical Society Quarterly,* vol. 45, pp. 208-10.

Emigrant Lists. These emigration sources deal with persons who are leaving the country. Thus, they were created for and are preserved in foreign archives. Emigration registers may include passenger lists (discussed under Immigrant Records below), passport applications, emigrant lists returned to the central government from district offices or courts, agreements to serve in America, accounts of servants bound, and intentions to leave the country which appeared as advertisements in local newspapers and periodicals. Since 1815 in Baden, German emigrants were required to announce their intention to leave the country in local newspapers, alerting creditors and local authorities. A government project sponsored by the Third Reich extracted selected ads for 1815-17. Friedrich Wollmershauser, a professional genealogist in Stuttgart, has announced a computer project to extract and index these ads for 1818-50 and perhaps as late as 1866.[9] See Table 15-2 for a port or jurisdiction summary of European emigration.

Additional documents are listed country by country and state by state in Olga K. Miller, *Migration, Emigration, Immigration: Principally to the United States and in the United States,* 2 vols. (Logan, Utah: Everton Publishers, Inc., 1974-78); includes Genealogical Society of Utah call numbers; Clifford Neal Smith and Anna P. Smith, *American Genealogical Resources in German Archives (AGRIGA): A Handbook* (New York: R. R. Bowker, 1977); P. William Filby with Mary K. Meyer, *Passenger and Immigration Lists Index,* 6 vols. (Detroit: Gale Research Company, 1981-84); Arlene H. Eakle, "Emigrant Sources for Tracing Pennsylvania German Ancestors," *APG Newsletter* 5 (May 1981): 8-11; and David H. Pratt, "British Immigration to North America," *Families* 20 (1981): 233-39. See also Research Approaches in this chapter.

Shipping Company Records. An invaluable tool for English research is P. Mathias and A. W. H. Pearsall, *Shipping: A Survey of Historical Records* (Newton Abbot, England: David and Charles, 1980). The survey is in two parts: (1) shipping companies and their record holdings and (2) shipping records in county and other record offices. There is an index of named ships, an index of persons and firms, and an index of places and principal trades. These are the firms with separate entries:

Shipping Companies

Anchor Line
Belfast Steamship Company Ltd.
The Ben Line Steamers Ltd.
Bolton Steam Shipping Company Ltd.
Booker Bros. (Liverpool) Ltd.
The Bowater Steamship Company Ltd.
The Bristol City Line of Steamships Ltd.
The Bristol Steam Navigation Company Ltd.
The British & Commonwealth Shipping Company Ltd.
Burns & Laird Lines Ltd.
Coast Lines Ltd.
William Cory & Son Ltd.
Cunard Steamship Company Ltd.
Elder Dempster Lines Ltd.
Furness, Withy & Company Ltd.
Glen Line Ltd.
Henderson Line Ltd.
Hogarth Shipping Company Ltd.
Houlder Bros & Company Ltd.
Inman Steamship Co. Ltd.
London and Edinburgh Shipping Co. Ltd.
Manchester Liners Ltd.
Moor Line Ltd. and Walter Runciman & Co. Ltd.
North of Scotland, Orkney & Shetland Shipping Co. Ltd.
Ocean Steam Ship Co. Ltd.
Palm Line Ltd.
Peninsular & Oriental Steam Navigation Co. Ltd.
Sir Walter Reardon Smith & Sons Ltd.
Royal Mail Steam Packet Company
Walter Runciman & Co. Ltd. *See* Moor Line Ltd.
Chr. Salvesen & Co. (shipowners)
Silver Line Ltd.
William Sloan & Company, Ltd.
Tyne-Tees Steam Shipping Company, Ltd.
Other known shipping company papers:
Blue Funnel Line
C. T. Bowring & Co. Ltd.
British-Indian Steam Navigation Co.
Canadian Pacific Line
Commercial Steam Packet Co.
Inman Steamship Co. Ltd.
Okil and Co. Ltd.
George Robinson and Co. Ltd.

You can substitute passenger lists retained by shipping companies for official lists missing for English ports. Where lists exist in United States or European ports they can be compared for details. Included among the collections are pictures of ships sailing for each line.

If you know the name of the ship your ancestor came on, but not the date or port of arrival, you can check the *Morton Allan Directory of European Passenger Steamship Arrivals* (New York: Immigration Information Bureau, Inc., 1931) for New York (1890-1930) and the ports of Philadelphia, Boston, and Baltimore (1904-26). Also valuable are the *Calendar of Archives of the Pacific Coast Steamship Companies of Alaska and America* (Claremont, Calif.: Claremont College, 1941) and William Armstrong Fairburn, *Merchant Sail,* 6 vols. (Center Lovell, Maine: Fairburn Marine Educational Foundation, Inc., 1945-55). Volume 6 indexes 13,278 vessels named in the six volumes. These volumes also have photographs and drawings of most of the ships with short historical sketches of each one.

You should be aware that many ships changed names, moved to another home port, or wore out or went down only to have another ship built with its specifications and name. In several instances, more than one ship carried the same name at the same time. Be sure to check all ships with the same name for the time period your ancestor migrated.

The Immigration Process

The process of arrival in the new country generated another series of records. The Reverend Henry M. Muehlenberg, described the arrival process in a report to his superiors in Halle, 1769:

> After much delay one ship after another arrives in the harbor of Philadelphia, when the rough and severe winter is before the door. One or more merchants receive the lists of the freights and the agreement which the emigrants have signed with their own hand in Holland, together with the bills for their travel down the Rhine and the advances of the "newlanders" for provisions, which they received on the ships on account. Formerly the freight for a single person was six to ten louis d'ors, but now it amounts to fourteen to seventeen louis d'ors [one louis d'ors equalled about $4.50]. Before the ship is allowed to cast anchor at the harbor front, the passengers are all examined, according to the law in

Table 15-2

Availability of European Emigrant Lists

Port or Jurisdiction	*Document*	*Date*	*Index*	*Originals*	*Copies*	*Comments*
Australia Victoria	Passenger lists (outwards)	1852-1924	No	Australian Archives, Outer Cresent, Middle Brighton, Melbourne, Victoria 3186	Genealogical Society of Utah (GS), 121 reels microflim 35983 pts 1-121	
Belgium Antwerp	Passport applications	1854-55	No	Stadsarchief Venustraat II Antwerp, Belgium	"Passenger Lists," GS, 3 reels microfilm 392,910-12	Many immigrants from Austria-Hungary, Italy, Switzerland, through Antwerp
Denmark Copenhagen		1868-1911	Alphabetical by year	Landsarkivet Sjaelland, Copenhagen, Denmark	GS 35 reels of microfilm, 898,564-622; 1868-1911	Separate register for Mormons only, 1872-94
England London	Lists	1709		Public Record Office, Chancery Lane, London WC2A 1LR England #C.O. 388/76 No. 56, 56i, 56ii, 64, 68-70	Microfilm copies available from Public Record Office, London	
All shires	Licenses to pass beyond the seas	Elizabeth I to 1677		Public Record Office E.157 (Exchequer), 2 boxes	Printed in John C. Hotten, *Original Lists of Persons of Quality* (Reprint, Baltimore: Genealogical Publishing Company, 1974)	Indexed in Filby, *Passenger and Immigration Lists Index*
Liverpool	"Settlers"	1817-76	No	Public Record Office, Original correspondence. Settlers (C.O. 384/14-18)		Applications from intending emigrants
British Mission (LDS)	Emigration records	1849-1923	Alphabetical	LDS Church Historical Department, Salt Lake City, Utah	GS, 15 reels microfilm	Church leaders acted as licensed emigration agents
France Le Havre		c1750-1850		Archives de la Chambre de Commerce et d'Industrie du Havre, Place Leon-Meyer (B.P. 1410) 76600 Le Havre, France		Many Italians came through Le Havre
LaRochelle	Lists of passengers embarking in Louisiana for France	1732-33 1737, 1748-49, 1752, 1754, 1758, 1765	No	Archives Nationales de la France, 60 rue des Francs-Bourgeois, Paris Cedex, France	Library of Congress (LC), microfilm copy. French Archives Nationales; Colonie Serie F5B, Selected Transcripts. Vol 34	Includes lists from other French ports as well as LaRochelle
	Lists of soldiers and passengers embarking for Louisiana	1717-20	No		Same, vol. 39	

Port of Jurisdiction	*Document*	*Date*	*Index*	*Originals*	*Copies*	*Comments*
Germany Braunschweig	German emigration index				GS 1,125,001	Names from periodicals, compiled 1976
Baden	Emigration index	1866-1911	Cards, alphabetical	Badisches Generallands-Archiv Nordl. Hiedapromenade 2, 7500 Karlsruhe, Germany	GS, 38 reels microfilm	Copies of emigrant lists sent from district offices to central government. Fee charged to search originals. Index called Baden-Wurttemberg, but Wurttemberg not included
Bremen	Emigration lists			Destroyed during World War II	LC, 3 reels microfilm: Bremen, Germany. Archive der Handel-Skammer, A.I.I. Auswanderer, 1841-75	Many Austria-Hungary emigrants through Bremen
Hamburg	Emigration lists	1850-1934	Alphabetical in sections		LC, Microfilm, 1850-72; GS, 361 reels microfilm 1850-1934; includes index	30 percent of all European emigrants passed through Hamburg including Russians and Austrians. See "Hamburg Passenger Lists." Research Paper C-30 (Salt Lake City: Genealogical Society of Utah, 1976)
Hessen	Emigration index	1800-1900	Alphabetical in sections		GS, 5 reels microfilm	
Westfalen	List of emigrants				Printed in *Beitrage zur Westfalischen Familien forschung,* vols. 22-24 (Munster: Verlag Aschendorff, 1966)	
Alsace	Passport applications	1817-66	Alphabetical		GS, 6 reels microfilm	Includes Bas-Rhin, Haut-Rhin
Trier	Emigration lists	19th Century	Alphabetical		Josef Jergen, "Emigration to America from District of Trier," typescript, 5 vols. GS 928, 106	
Ireland Antrim				Public Record Office, Northern Ireland		
Netherlands	Emigration register	1847-77	Alphabetical		Computer Listing, GS 1,181,553	
	Dutch nationals on U.S. passenger lists	1820-80	Alphabetical		Computer Listing, 4 vols.	Copy at GS 973/W25W. See also Robert P. Swierenga. *Dutch Immigrants in United States Ship Passenger Manifests, 1820-1880,* 2 vols. (Wilmington, Del.: Scholarly Resources, 1983)
	Emigration naar America en andere landen	1831-77		Algemeen Provincial Archive, Loosduinseweg 17, The Hague 2028 Netherlands	GS, 12 reels microfilm 487, 360-371	

Port or Jurisdiction	*Document*	*Date*	*Index*	*Originals*	*Copies*	*Comments*
Rotterdam	Embarkation lists	1709		Public Record Office, T1/119: 6-10, 19-26, 58-65, 68-72, 79-82		German Palatines to New York only. Rotterdam lists reported destroyed
Netherland Mission (LDS)	List of emigrants	1904-14		LDS Church Historical Department	GS 6,186	
Norway Bergen		1874-1924	Yes		GS, 78 fiche; microfilm 357,704	
Kristiansand		1873-1901			GS 365,931	
Nedenes Amt		1873-1901			GS 1 reel microfilm	
Oslo		1867-1902	Yes		GS, 18 reels microfilm 353,081-98	
Trondheim		1867-1900	No		GS, 3 reels microfilm 362,609-11	
Tromsö		1850-1900		Statsarkivkontoret I Tromsö Petersborggata 21-24 9000 Tromsö		Not filmed as of winter 1983-84
Portugal Lisbon				Reparticão Do Arquivo E Bibliotéca Do Ministerio Dos Negócios Estrangeiros, Palácio das Necessiodades, Lisboa 3		
Scotland	Treasury papers	1715-1820		Public Record Office, Chancery Lane, London WC2A 1LR England Treasury Papers. T.47. Emigration Registers, 23 vols.	Portion published *New England Historical and Genealogical Register* (1911)	
				Misc. 12. 1773-1776 Lists from Scottish Ports: Greenock, Kirkaldy, Wigtown, Kirkwall, Stornaway, Stranraer, Lerwick, Glasgow. Misc. 1: 500, 231-35. Scots Highlanders to America, 1774. Misc. 1: 338. Scots Highlanders to America, 1776		Formerly "misc. Refugees, Carolina, 6(1)."
Spain	Asientos de pasajeros	1509-1701		Archivo General de Indias, Seccion de Contración, Sevilla, Spain	GS, 11 reels of microfilm 1,223,690-700	Passengers to the New World
Sweden Goteborg	Emigration lists	1869-1951	1869-93	Göteborg Provincial Archives, Göteborgs Arkivkontar Box 2258 403 14 Göteborg, Sweden. 143 vols.	GS, 67 reels microfilm, 1869-1920	Provincial archives one of centers indexing emigrants. Many indexes underway. Göteborg principal port for Sweden
Helsingborg		1907-64		Göteborg Provincial Archives		

Port or Jurisdiction	*Document*	*Date*	*Index*	*Originals*	*Copies*	*Comments*
Kalmar City	Emigrant contracts	1880-92		Göteborg Provincial Archives		
Karlstad	Emigrant index			Emigrantregistret i Karlstad Box 331, S-651 05 Karlstad, Sweden		100,000 emigrants from Varmland
Malmö		1874-1939	1874-1891	Malmö City Archives Stadsarkivet 1 Malmo S:t Petrigatan 7 A 211 22 Malmö, Sweden	GS, 3 reels microflm. 1,043,345-347	
Swedish Mission (LDS)	Emigrants lists	1904-32		LDS Church Historical Department	GS, 025,700	
Norrkoping		1859-1919	Indexes	Göteborg Provincial Archives 1 vol.		
Stockholm	Emigration lists	1869-1944	1869-86 1883-86 (incomplete)	Stockholm City Archives Stockholms Stadsarkiv Kungsklippan 6, Box 22063 104 22 Stockholm 22	GS, 402,933; 1869-1904 only	Includes some emigrants from Finland
	Passport journals	1737-1879		Göteborg Provincial Archives	On microfilm at GS	
	Passport journals (Navy Pension Fund Departure Lists)	1798-1851	1817-50	Royal Swedish Military Record Office, Fack, 100 26 Stockholm 34	GS 275 reels microfilm	Cataloged by city
Värmland				Emigrantregistret for Värmland Drottninggatan 1 A 652 24 Karlstad, Sweden Index only at Goteborg Provincial Archives		Collections on emigration from Varmland
Broderne Larrson & Co.	Emigration Agency records	1873-1913	No	Göteborg Provincial Archives	GS, 9 reels microfilm. 479,331; 479,587-479, 605	Central and Southern Sweden. Includes letters, ticket stubs. Gives destinations
	Emigration extracts	1851 to present	1851-60	[National Central Bureau of Statistics] Statistiska Centralbyråns Arkiv Karlavägen 100, 115 26 Stockholm, Sweden	GS, 567 reels microfilm. 1851-1940	From Swedish parish registers. Some by county, some by parish. From 1865 uniform schedules of emigrants extracted
West Indies Santo Domingo	Passports	1799-1801			Printed, Nellis H. Fowler, *National Genealogical Society Quarterly* 56 (1968): 263-75	

force, by a physician, as to whether any contagious disease exists among them. Then the arrivals are led in procession to the City Hall and there they must render the oath of allegiance to the king of Great Britain. After that they are brought back to the ship. Then announcements are printed in the newspapers, stating how many of the new arrivals are to be sold. Those who have money are released. Whoever has well-to-do friends seeks a loan from them to pay the passage, but there are only a few who succeed. The ship becomes the market-place. The buyers make their choice among the arrivals and bargain with them for a certain number of years and days. They then take them to the merchant, pay their passage and their other debts and receive from the government authorities a written document, which makes the newcomers their property for a definite period."[10]

Bills for Provisions and Passenger Agreements. The original agreements, bills, and receipts for passage and provisions are surrendered by the passengers to merchants so the ship's master can be reimbursed for commodities advanced on the journey. These documents, where they have survived, will be found among the merchants' records. The Historical Society of Pennsylvania, like many historical societies, has many collections of merchants' records. The Genealogical Society of Utah has microfilmed several for New York.

"Pest" Hospital Records. Ellis Island is an intriguing if grim reminder of the screening newly arrived immigrants received. What most genealogists don't realize is that the screening process began very early. Passengers traveling for six months with short rations, cramped sleeping and living quarters, and close proximity to disease and death often arrived in unfit condition. As early as 1718, health officers boarded immigrant ships to determine how many of the passengers carried infectious diseases. None of the passengers were allowed ashore until the doctor had licensed the ship's master to disembark them. In 1743, the city of Philadelphia bought Province Island where the Delaware and Schuylkill rivers joined, as a "pest" island for diseased passengers. In 1750, a hospital was erected on the island.[11] The records of this hospital are in the Historical Society of Pennsylvania.

Undertakers' and Merchants' Accounts. Local undertakers, usually joiners or carpenters by trade, contracted to collect bodies and bury them at public expense. These costs were then passed on to the merchants to whom the passengers were originally consigned. Undertakers kept accounts so they could be paid from the public treasury. For example, Jacob Shoemaker's 1754 "Account of the Palatines Buried this Year," lists:

for Alexander Stedman	[£] 62
for Henry Cepley	39
for Benjamin Shoemaker	57
for Daniel Benesett	87
for Michael Hilligass	8
	253

Jacob Shoemaker upon his affirmation saith the above acct of Burials since 14 Sept. last is exact & read from his Book & the Acct of Coffins except those from Michael Hilligass which he thinks may be 6 or 8 more.

Jacob Shoemaker

Affirmed before me,
Chas. Willing Nov. 14, 1754

This report and request for payment was presented to the city council of Philadelphia. Shoemaker was an undertaker/joiner and the men listed are local merchants.[12] The city kept accounts so they could collect from the merchants. The merchants kept track of their business investment in taking, on consignment, a whole shipload of human cargo. Many of these account books are also located in the Historical Society of Pennsylvania. See *Guide to the Manuscript Collections of the Historical Society of Pennsylvania*, 2nd ed. (Philadelphia: For the society, 1949), #108.

Every port city soon had some provision to receive immigrants to protect their inhabitants from epidemics and their treasuries from being drained by the needs of newly arrived immigrants, most of whom were unable to bear their own expenses.

Newspapers and Hospital Reports. Local newspapers often printed the monthly hospital reports. For example, in the *Quebec Mercury*, published from July 1829 through November 1830, the monthly reports from the Quebec Emigrants Hospital included patients' names and places of origin, and whether they had died in the hospital:[13]

Ade, John (d), Kilkenny
Allet, James, Longford
Anderson, James, Glasgow
Anderson, John, London
Anderson, John (d), Glasgow
Anderson, Sarah, Cork
Arley, John (d), Tyrone
Armond, Mary, Louth

Health Certificates. Health certificates, some of which have survived among the immigrant records in the Pennsylvania State Archives, were issued to those who recovered. This same practice of certifying patient recovery was followed until well into the twentieth century for immigrants entering the United States.

Passenger Lists. Passenger lists, often called manifests, emigrant/immigrant lists, and arrival lists, are among the most important sources of information we have access to. Even those which do not yield specific places of residence or destination are valuable.

Passenger lists were never intended to be genealogical documents. They were created for administrative control over the millions of people who swarmed into the United States from 1620 to the present. But the United States is not the only country to keep track of people on the move. Countries of origin also felt a need to monitor the out-flow.

There were, as a result, at least seven different passenger lists created and many more for some groups of passengers. These include lists made and filed with (1) the port of embarkation, (2) ports of call along the route, (3) the port of arrival, (4) newspapers at the port of departure, (5) newspapers at cities of arrival, (6) a copy kept with or as part of the ship's manifest, (see Figure 15-3) and (7) notations of passengers in the ship's log. In addition, travelers recorded their fellow passengers in diaries, journals, and letters home. If the group was chartered by a government agency, a specific church, or an emigrant aid society, (see Figure 15-4), a list was kept with the official archives of the project. If the ship was quarantined for disease, a copy of the list was attached to medical reports. Pennsylvania Germans were required to take an oath of allegiance and an oath of abjuration when they landed in Philadelphia. All able-bodied heads of families were taken immediately before a magistrate when they arrived.

Some ot these are official lists required by law; others are private recordings. For the genealogist, the fact that so many copies were made insures that at least one will have survived for almost each immigrant. The main problem is finding the lists.

Official passenger lists are available from 1820 through 1945 for most of the ports in the United States with customshouses. Those available in the National Archives on microfilm are tabulated in "Passenger Arrival Lists," *Genealogical Research in the National Archives* (Washington, D.C.: National Archives Trust Fund, 1982), Chapter 2. They are divided into Customs Passenger Lists, (original lists, copies, or abstracts) and Immigration Passenger Lists (State Department Transcripts, Lists) with pertinent indexes. Microfilm publications call numbers are given where appropriate. Copies are also available for searching at the Genealogical Society of Utah and its branches.

No official records exist during the nineteenth century for persons entering the United States through Canada or Mexico. Lists for the Pacific Coast ports are in the possession of the customs service in those ports or have been transferred to federal archives branches on the West Coast. The National Archives does not have records for these ports. There are a few passenger lists for San Francisco (1920) at the Federal Archives, San Bruno, California.

Figure 15-3. Report and Manifest of the *Langdon Cheves*. Philadelphia to New York via St. Thomas, 1824; Port of Philadelphia Passenger Lists, 1820-54; microfilm copy at the Genealogical Society of Utah (hereafter GS) 419,614.

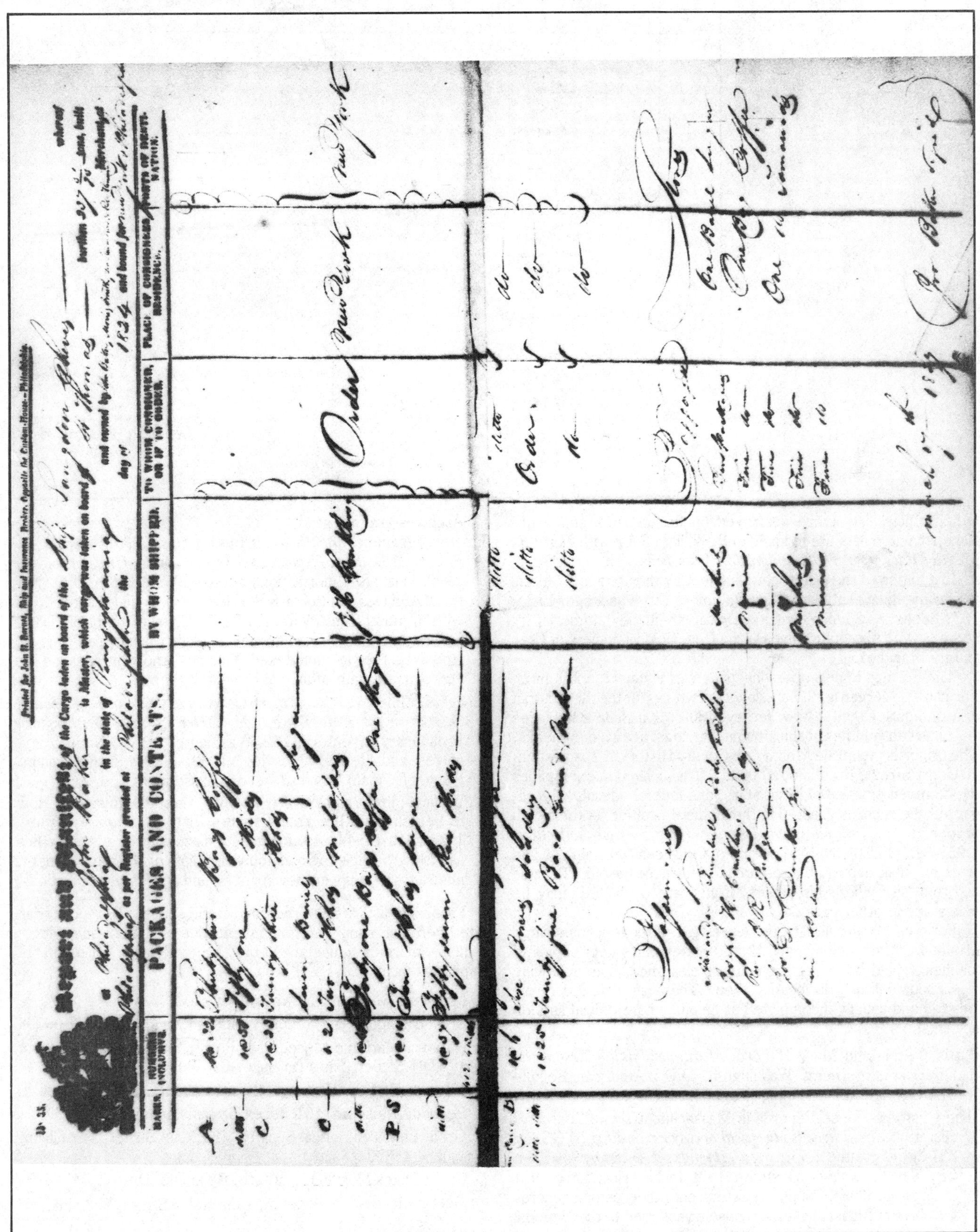

Figure 15-4. List of Emigrants, 1852-57, assisted by the Highland and Emigration Society; GS 404,437.

List of Emigrants assisted by the Highland and Island Emigration Society, and embarked on board the Ship Georgiana which sailed from Glasgow for Port Phillip on the 13th July 1852.

Number of Family	Name	Age	Residence	Estate	Remarks
36	Macquien Peter	40	Glen	Skeabost	[illegible]
	(wife) Jane	36	"	"	
	John	13	"	"	Healthy family
	Alexander	6	"	"	
	Donald	6	"	"	
	Kenneth	3	"	"	
37	Nicolson, Alexdr	36	Aird	Ditto	[illegible]
	Mary	29	"	"	Eligible couple - fine healthy children
	Alexander	8	"	"	
	John	6	"	"	
	Donald	3	"	"	
	Infant (not named)	—	"	"	
38	McLeod, Dougald	36	Ditto	Ditto	[illegible]
	Mary	33	"	"	Man appears to have suffered much for want of food.
	Peggy	11	"	"	Lived in a gravel pit covered
	Norman	9	"	"	in with heather for 10 months.
	Donald	7	"	"	
	Malcom	1	"	"	

Other official lists were destroyed by fire in 1851 and 1940. Reconstructed lists are indexed in P. William Filby with Mary K. Meyer, *Passenger and Immigration Lists Index,* cited earlier.

In addition to the passenger lists kept by the state and federal governments are city lists. The Baltimore City Passenger Lists, 1833-66, have a Soundex index. Originals are in the Baltimore City archives with microfilm copies at the Genealogical Society of Utah and its branches.

The Forman Papers, personal papers of Samuel I. and John S. Forman who served as commissioners of wrecks for the third district of Monmouth County, New Jersey, 1800-51, include 238 pieces and nineteen volumes of ships' manifests, logs, and account books. The originals are at the Monmouth County Historical Association, 70 Court Street, Freehold, NJ 07728. This collection exemplifies the common practice of local, state, and federal officials who regarded the records created in their official position as their own property. The *National Union Catalog of Manuscripts Collections* (1958-82), published by the Library of Congress, will help you find those on public deposit; but research to determine the official's name and then see where his papers, if any, are deposited, may be necessary in other cases.

For pre-1820 official lists, the genealogist can consult ships' cargo manifests. Many colonial and United States ports kept copies of manifests filed as a requirement of clearance. The following references will help in locating them. These records are rarely indexed and usually incomplete but helpful where official lists do not exist.

Bartis, Peter, and Mary Hufford. *Maritime Folklife Resources: Directory and Index.* Washington, D.C.: American Folklife Center, 1980. Lists finding aids, collections, and publications.

"The Customs-House Records in Massachusetts as a Source of History." *Massachusetts Historical Society Proceedings* 54 (1921): 324-30. Reprinted in *Tracing an Immigrant Ancestor.* Salt Lake City: The Genealogical Institute, 1974. Includes location in 1921 of cargo manifests, shipping registers, and other customs records for ports of Massachusetts. Those transferred to the National Archives are indicated.

Finster, Jerome. *Major Sources in Customs Bureau Records in Statistical Data on Exports and Imports of the United States to 1900.* Reference Information Paper, 49. Washington, D.C.: National Archives and Records Service, 1973. Includes appendixes with twentieth-century foreign cargo manifests for major United States ports. These foreign manifests also include passengers. However, they are unindexed. You must know the port and the approximate date of arrival to search them.

Lindgard, Elmer W. *Records of the Collector of Customs Puget Sound District in the Federal Records Center, Seattle, Washington.* Preliminary Inventory, 122. Washington, D.C.: National Archives and Records Service, 1960. These include ships' manifests, many of which record passengers.

McWilliams, Jerry, and Waverly Lowell. "Maritime Museums: How to Search Them for Your Family's History." *Family Heritage* 1 (Oct. 1978): 141-45. Includes a discussion of research aids like Lloyd's Registers and equivalent lists of ships and owners, photographs, shipping newspapers, and oral history collections.

Passenger lists are also recorded in ships' logs. The repositories listed here can supply archive inventories or lists of ships' logs. Principal maritime museums in the U.S. with large collections of ships logs include:

Mariner's Museum, Newport News, VA 23606

Mystic Seaport, G.W. Blunt White Library, Mystic, CT 06355

National Maritime Museum, J. Porter Shaw Library, Foot of Polk Street, San Francisco, CA 94109

Newport Historical Society, 82 Touro Street, Newport, RI 02840

Peabody Museum, 161 Essex Street, Salem, MA 01970

Great Lakes Historical Society, 480 Main Street, Vermillion, OH 44089

Great Lakes Maritime Institute, Belle Isle, Detroit, MI 48207

Bernice P. Bishop Museum, 1355 Kalihi Street, Honolulu, HI 96819

The amount of literature included for each passenger varies from list to list. Some lists give names of ship and passengers, country of origin, and port of arrival only. Others will add sex, age, occupation, and place of residence when ticket was purchased. Some group the passengers into family units, some list them by tickets, some arrange them in alphabetical order, and others arrange them in the order in which the passengers boarded the ship. Name of the ship's master and dates of departure and arrival will be found on some. Later lists, like those for Hamburg, give birthdate and place, date and parish of confirmation, marital status, and state or city of destination.

Passenger lists are usually separate documents after 1820 if the ship was a passenger liner. If the ship was a cargo vessel which also carried passengers, they will be listed on the ship's manifest with the master, crew, and cargo. Some ancestors were actually shipped by the pound as if they were trunks of books or bales of wool. Before 1820, most of them were not declared as passengers, and many were landed in harbors where customshouses had not been established.

Masters who landed passengers without permission, however, could be forced to return them or give security to customs officials by bond to cover costs of removal for illegal entry. Some ports required the payment of a head tax and issued certificates or permits to land. When the federal government began to regulate immigration in 1820, each ship was required by law to submit an official list of passengers carried. Masters failing to comply could be severely fined and denied port clearance.

Federal control created three types of passenger arrival records: customs passenger lists, immigration passenger lists, and customs lists of aliens. All of them are available for searching, with some restrictions.

Customs Passenger Lists (1820-1905). These lists were filed by the masters of the ships with the collector of customs in each port. The original lists were prepared in duplicate on board ship and signed by the master of the vessel (under oath) and the customs authority. One copy was filed with the collector of customs. The other copy was returned to the master to be kept with the ships papers.[14] On the list, the master was also required to record births and deaths during the voyage. Under a British/American law of 1855, a copy of the passenger lists for British ships was also given to the British consul in the American port. Some may have been filed with the consul as early as 1820 when federal regulation began.[15]

Original lists are extant for seven U.S. ports only. Copies or abstracts of the original lists were made by the collectors of customs and sent once each quarter to the Secretary of State. The information is usually abbreviated and there are undoubtedly copy errors. Transcriptions were also made for 1819-32 from the copies sent to the Department of State. These are arranged by name of district or port, name of vessel, and name of passenger. The transcripts are third-generation copies and contain many errors.

Immigration Passenger Lists (1883-1945). These lists date from 1891 for most ports and from 1883 for the Port of Philadelphia. The indexes are arranged chronologically, first by shipping line, then by initial letter of surname. Six have been indexed. Thirty-six ports are included in these lists.

Customs Lists of Aliens (1798-1800). From time to time, aliens have been recorded by customs collectors. Most of these are indexed in Filby's *Passenger and Immigration Lists*.

An additional passenger list rarely consulted by genealogists is the registration rolls recorded in port clearing centers like Castle Garden and Ellis Island (New York), Angel Island (San Francisco), and Province Island (Philadelphia). These rolls are difficult to use. They are unindexed and nationalities are intermixed. Still they can fill gaps in other materials. Each registration clerk by 1890 had some four or five thousand immigrants to register each day. Dates, names, and nationalities are imperfectly recorded as a result. Registration of emigrants in foreign clearing centers was much more precise and carefully done.[16]

Fitting the documents together can lead to some difficulty if the emigrant did not arrive in the port of destination. If the ship sank, newspapers often printed the list of survivors and sometimes printed the original list of passengers and crew. If the persons on board were turned away, petitions to mayors or governors for admission can disclose which colony finally accepted the ship. Pirates might capture the ship on the open sea and carry the passengers as hostages to be ransomed or set them ashore somewhere along the coast. Petitions for acceptance, news accounts of the raid, correspondence between pirates and government, court trial testimony – these also yield clues.

These documents are time-consuming to hunt for; but thanks to the generous time of genealogists throughout the country, reports and documents are being published in periodicals and small publications. And since we work on a pedigree in reverse, we have the information on the port the ancestor arrived in before we know the circumstances of the voyage. If your ancestor settled in the Carolinas, one of the sources you will already have searched will be the *North Carolina Genealogical Journal* which carries lists of immigrants and arrivals regularly. An article such as Ransom McBride, "A Change of Destination for Some 100 Emigrants from Virginia and Maryland to South Carolina, 1718," August 1983, pp. 165-67, links your ancestor to a place of origin.[17]

Oaths of Allegiance. There were three passenger lists compiled for Pennsylvania German immigrants: (1) the captain's lists made on board the ship by the ship's mate from the manifest; (2) lists of oaths of allegiance to the king of Great Britain signed by all male immigrants over sixteen who were well enough to march in procession to a magistrate (these two lists were submitted to the Pennsylvania government on large, loose sheets of paper and not all of them have survived); and (3) lists of signers of the oath of fidelity and abjuration. (See Figure 15-5.) The oath was a renunciation of claims to the throne of England by "pretenders" and a denial of the right of the Pope to outlaw a Protestant monarch. Those males over sixteen well enough to walk to the courthouse also signed these renunciations in a series of bound ledger volumes. They have survived intact. Strassburger and Hinke estimate that only two out of five passengers are recorded on the signed lists.

The original order of the names on the lists is important. The first signatures are often the leaders, for the Palatines (immigrants from the Rhine River Valley of Germany – the Palatinate) came in groups. The names themselves are significant, for they may represent a whole church group or a group of related families. For these reasons, I suggest that you copy the whole passenger list where your ancestor appears and study the names carefully. The list can be a check for identifying the correct ancestor in church registers, census lists, news announcements, and other records.

The spelling of names on the captains' lists is often inaccurate and different from the way the names appear on the other two. The mate wrote what he heard. The signatures represent the way your ancestor spelled his own name. When you compare the two, you can often determine how the name was originally pronounced. For example, Johann Herman Ekell (his signature) is listed on the captain's list as Johann Harmon Akel. In Pennsylvania and Maryland, where Harmon Eakle settled, the surname is still pronounced *Aykle* rather than *Ee-kle* as in the West.

The signatures are significant too. The original printed volumes of *Pennsylvania German Pioneers* in which these lists appear contain the printed versions of all three lists, with the second volume reproducing in facsimile the original signatures as they appear on the third list. When the Genealogical Publishing Company reprinted the set, it did not reproduce the volume of signatures.

The majority – a surprising number – of the German immigrants were literate and signed their own names. These signatures are evidence for identity. When you compare Harmon Eakle's signature on deeds in Washington County, Maryland, with Johann Herman Ekell's signature on the passenger list, they are the same.

Andrew Hoffman of Dauphin County, Pennsylvania, signed his will with a mark, his deeds with marks, and his Revolutionary War oath of allegiance with a mark. The passenger lists include Andreas Hofman, age twenty-two in 1730, who signs his own name; Johann Andreas Hoffman in 1754, who signs his name; and Andrew Hoffman in 1772, who signs with a mark. While identity is not proven with this evidence, the first two are less likely to be the same man as the Andrew in Dauphin County.

Newspaper Announcements. After the oaths were taken, the passengers returned to the ship to negotiate terms of service. The newspaper becomes the principal public document at this point since announcements of new arrivals to be sold were printed in each issue, with dates of auction. After the negotiations were over, the results were also printed in the newspapers:

> Account of Servants bound and Assigned Before James Hamilton, Mayor of Philadelphia, Oct. 9, 1745. George Okill assigned Roger McDonnell (a servant from Ireland, in Brigt Cliveland, Wm Robinson, master) to William Miller, Chester Co. to serve three years from October 5, 1745. Consideration £11.5 with customary dues. John Inglis assigned Agnes Mein (a servant from Scotland on ship Anne Galley, Capt Houston) to William Miller, Chester Co. to serve five years from Sept. 20, 1745. Consideration £15, to have customary dues.[18]

This announcement records the arrival of two immigrants who do not appear in *Pennsylvania German Pioneers* because Roger McDonnell was Irish, not German. Already a British subject, he did not need to take the oaths on arrival. Agnes Mein was a woman and therefore not required to sign. A few captains interpreted the law to mean they recorded all passengers including women and children in this early period, but most included only males sixteen and older.

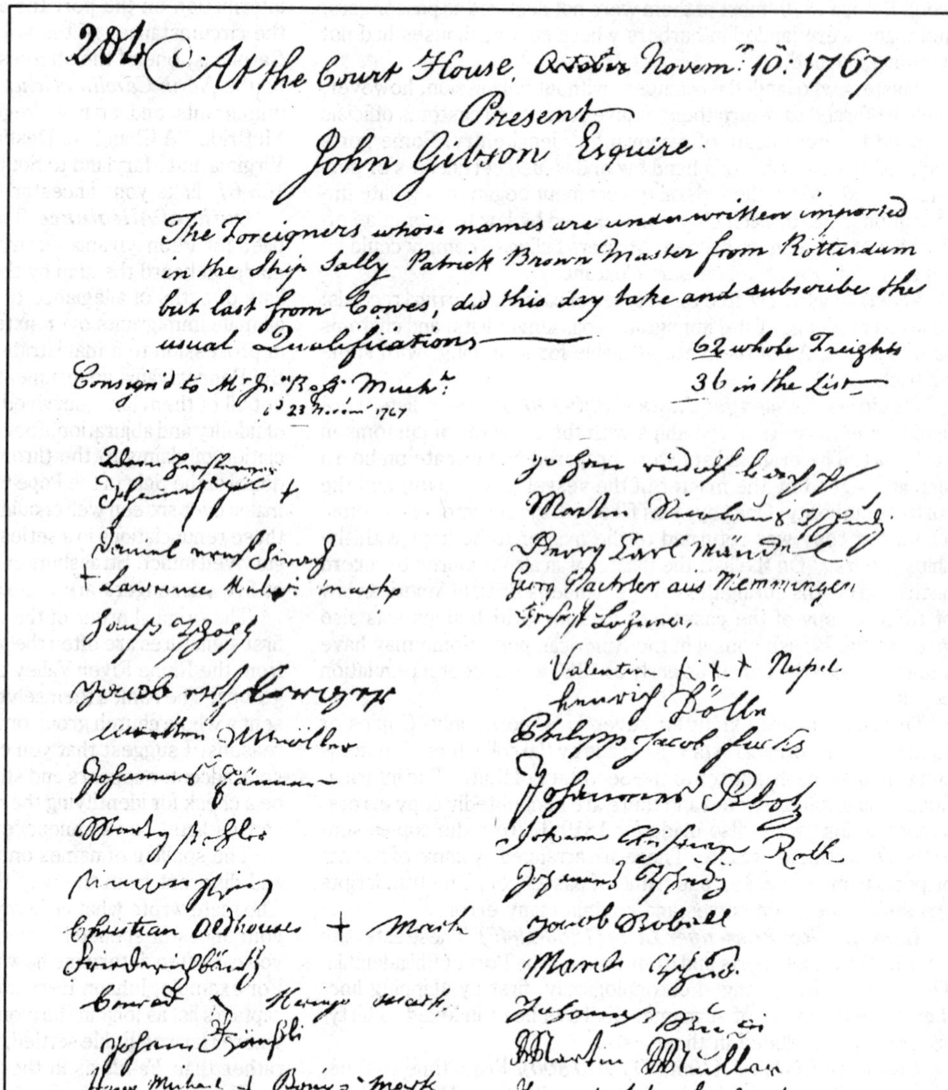

Figure 15-5. Printed in Ralph B. Strassburger with William J. Hinke, *Pennsylvania German Pioneers*, 3 vols. (Norristown, Pa.: Pennsylvania German Society, 1934), 2: 829.

204 C At the Court House, October Novemr 10: 1767
Present
John Gibson Esquire

The Foreigners whose names are underwritten imported in the Ship Sally Patrick Brown Master from Rotterdam but last from Cowes, did this day take and subscribe the usual Qualifications —

62 whole Freights
36 in the List

Consign'd to Mr. Jn. Ross Merchant

Indentures. The actual indentures or agreements for service were signed and certified by the mayor's court. Some were recorded by the court clerk but most were simply noted in the minutes. Immigrants' names and the persons to whom they were bound were listed in some.

Letters of Thanks. It was also customary for the immigrants to thank the captain and his crew in writing for a safe and speedy voyage. The letter of thanks may be published in the newspapers.

Letters announcing safe arrival were also submitted to news sheets in the country of origin. This saved each passenger from writing a separate letter to family and friends at home. Several of these letters are reproduced in Jean Stephenson, *Scotch-Irish Migration to South Carolina* (Strasburg, Va.: Shenandoah Publishing House, Inc., 1971). Such letters described the voyage, reported births, deaths, and marriages on board, and included names of passengers—usually the heads of house only.

Immigration/emigration sources, even if they are carefully indexed, may not include your ancestor. Illegal departures and arrivals may not be recorded except in court minutes or annotations by police clerks on emigrant registers. Children who emigrate with their parents will not be listed by name. Compiled sources and translations often contain errors or missed entries. The original and the extract may include different information. Filby, who used many correspondents in compiling his *Passenger and Immigration Lists Index,* found it was not unusual for each passenger list from each genealogist to contain a different number of entries and differences in spelling.

Annotations are extremely valuable. (See Figure 15-6.) Some compilers have worked with their data so long that their direct knowledge of the source is quite helpful. However, even a skilled genealogist can combine data incorrectly and give immigrants an identity which they do not have in the original records. Wherever possible, *check the original.*

The Process of Settlement

Newspapers. Many of the immigrants had relatives and friends who had already come to America and frequently tried to locate them with newspaper advertisements. Some ten German-language newspapers served German immigrants in or near Philadelphia by 1776. In addition there were the English-language papers. Extracts of inquiries and ads have been made by two genealogists: Anita L. Eyster, "Notices by German and Swiss Settlers Seeking Information of Members of their Families, Kindred, and Friends Inserted between 1742-1761" in *Pennsylvania Berichte* and 1762-1779 in *Pennsylvania Staatsbote," Pennsylvania German Folklore Society* 3 (1938): 32-41; and Edward Hocker, *Genealogical Data Relating to the German Settlers of Pennsylvania from Advertisements in German Newspapers Published in Philadelphia and Germantown, 1743-1800* (Baltimore: Genealogical Publishing Company, 1981).

Newspapers carry more than letters and announcements seeking relatives. They also publish probate processes originating in Europe and obituaries of family members who died in Europe. I recommend that you research both the original papers, often available on microfilm through interlibrary loan, and the abstracts cited here. (See also Chapter 12, Newspapers.)

Arndt, Karl J. R., and May E. Olson. *German-American Newspapers and Periodicals, 1732-1955: History and Bibliography.* Heidelberg: Quelle and Meyer, 1961. Distributed in U.S. through Clark University, Worcester, Mass.

Miller, Daniel. *Early German-American Newspapers.* Lancaster: Pennsylvania German Society, 1911.

__________. "The German Newspapers of Berks County." *Transactions of the Berks County Historical Society.* 3 (1910-11): 4-23.

Scott, Kenneth, and Janet R. Clarke. *Abstracts from the Pennsylvania Gazette, 1748-1755.* Baltimore: Genealogical Publishing Company, 1977.

Wittke, Carl F. *German-Language Press in America.* Louisville: University of Kentucky Press, 1957.

Wynar, Lubomyr. *Encyclopedic Directory of Ethnic Newspapers and Periodicals in the U.S.* Littleton, Colo.: Libraries Unlimited Inc., 1972.

Common-Language Sources. Some aspects of the immigrant experience were traumatic—selling all they owned, traveling for weeks to reach a new land, watching loved ones sicken and die away from the rest of the family. These took their toll. Many immigrants cushioned the shock by living, at least temporarily, with family and friends who had already immigrated. As you search in census records, write down all boarders listed in a multiple-family dwelling, for they are often related to the head of house even if the surname is different. As the family head of house acquired work and earned some income, the family moved into its own residence, often rented, sometimes owned.

Immigrants of the same background tended to cluster in areas so language would be less of a problem. These immigrant clusters have been plotted on maps by historians. If your ancestor does not appear in a city directory right away, check these immigrant maps. Examples include Leo F. Schnore, *The New Urban History*

Figure 15-6. Friedrich Krebs, "Palatine Emigration Materials from the Neckar Valley, 1726-66, ed. and trans., Don Yoder, *Pennsylvania Folklife* (Summer 1975): 23.

23. ERNST RUDI, citizen of Weiler, emigrant of 1727, paid 18 florins 47 kreuzer emigration tax. His name appears as *Hans Ernst Rudi* in the passenger lists of the *William and Sarah,* 1727.

[According to records of the Heimatstelle Pfalz, Kaiserslautern, *Hans Ernst Rudi,* son of *Hans Conrad Rudi,* cooper, of Weiler, and his wife *Anna Maria,* nee *Schopf,* was baptized in Weiler February 5, 1682. He married, January 25, 1707, in Hilsbach (Reformed Church Register of Hilsbach-Weiler), *Anna Catharina Doll,* of Hilsbach, daughter of the Attorney Doll.

In the same ship lists appears the name of *Johann Dietrich Rudi,* born January 1, 1702, at Reihen, Kreis Sinsheim, son of *Sebastian* and *Anna Margaretha Rudi. Dietrich Rudi* settled first in Germantown, Pennsylvania, in 1737 was in Upper Salford, Philadelphia (now Montgomery) County, then to Rockhill, Bucks County, and finally settled at Indian Creek. See Price, *History of Christ Reformed Church at Indian Creek,* p. 67.

Other early Rudi emigrants included (1) *Bastian Rudi,* born at Reihen, Kreis Sinsheim, December 21, 1708, baptized the 23rd, son of *Dietrich* and *Anna (Schuch) Rudi,* arrived at Philadelphia on the Ship *Plaisance,* September 21, 1732; and (2) *Hans Conrad Rudi,* born August 5, 1683, at Dühren, son of *Hans Rudi* from Frenkendorf, Canton Basel, Switzerland, and his wife *Anna Dorothea Bender,* nee *Lang* (Heimatstelle Pfalz). According to the church registers of Dühren *Hans Conrad Rudi* went to the New Land before 1747 (Heimatstelle Pfalz).]

(Princeton, N.J.: Princeton University Press, 1973) with his map showing the locations of German, Irish, native-born, and mixed populations in the city of Milwaukee; and Donald B. Cole, *Immigration City: Lawrence, Massachusetts, 1845-1921* (Chapel Hill, N.C.: University of North Carolina Press, 1963). Within one mile of the local textile mills, immigrants representing fifty-one different countries settled.

The Philadelphia Project, described in "A Special Issue: The Philadelphia Social History Project," *Historical Methods Newsletter* 9 (March-June 1976), is mapping the city of Philadelphia house by house to show its Irish, German, and black populations. Sources are population censuses, black censuses compiled by the Abolition Society and the Society of Friends, city directories, and manufacturing census schedules. Similar maps for Chicago have been constructed at Hull House, now a museum administered by the University of Illinois, Chicago Circle. Each neighborhood with its ethnic make-up is indicated with colored pins. Churches and immigrant aid societies nearby are also indicated.

Immigrant Aid Societies. Immigrant aid societies sprang up to supply information on lodgings, work opportunities, and local resources; to provide credit references and sometimes cash or food where needed; to advise and caution immigrants against the unscrupulous; to collect and forward mail; to coordinate group insurance and benefits for living family members; and to aid in burial of loved ones and with legal transactions unfamiliar to new immigrants. It also helped some immigrants return to their homelands. See Wilbur S. Shepperson, *Emigration and Disenchantment: Portraits of Englishmen Repatriated from the United States* (Norman, Okla.: University of Oklahoma Press, 1965). In 1931, 43,000 aliens came to America and 89,000 departed. By the 1950s, about 3 million persons in Europe had lived part of their lives in America. See also William L. Sachse, "The Migration of New Englanders to England, 1640-1660," *American Historical Review* 53 (Jan. 1948).

These societies kept some invaluable records. See G. A. Dobbert, "An On-Line System for Processing Loosely Structured Records," *Historical Methods* 15 (Winter 1982): 16-22, for the use of 1,700 obituaries clipped by the German Immigrant Society of Cincinnati, Ohio; and John Guertler and Adele Newburger, *Records of Baltimore's Private Organizations: A Guide to Archival Resources* (New York: Garland Press, Inc., 1981) for ethnic and immigrant societies in the city of Baltimore. The YWCA operated institutes for women to help them adjust, learn English, and care adequately for their families. See Nicholas V. Montalto, *The International Institute Movement: A Guide to Records of Immigrant Society Agencies in the United States* (St. Paul: Immigration History Research Center, 1978) for a state-by-state listing of aid societies for women immigrants. An excellent article is Erna Risch, "Immigrant Aid Societies Before 1820," *Pennsylvania History* 3 (Jan. 1936): 15-32, reprinted in *Tracing Immigrant Ancestors* (Salt Lake City: Genealogical Institute, 1974), which discusses societies for Germans, Scots, Irish, and others throughout the American colonies. Also excellent is Bradford Luckingham, "Benevolence in Emergent San Francisco: A Note on Immigrant Life in the Urban Far West," *Southern California Quarterly* 55 (1973): 431-44, which describes societies for French, Germans, Catholics, Protestants, seamen, ladies, Hebrews, and others.

Societies in the area your ancestors settled can be located through corporation records in county and city offices, directories of associations published biannually by Gale Research Company of Detroit and R. R. Bowker of New York, WPA inventories of social welfare agencies in each state, and current yellow pages in local telephone directories under Welfare Agencies or Social Welfare Agencies. Some cities also published annual almanacs with names and addresses of those agencies reporting to city government.

Church Records. A local church congregation could also cushion culture shock for the immigrant. The church was a familiar friend with services in a familiar tongue. Its officials and members were often known to the immigrant. The formality of christening a child born enroute or solemnizing a marriage begun as a shipboard romance provided a ritual sanction for the move. Letters of recommendation for church membership were surrendered within four to twelve weeks of arrival. These loose documents have seldom survived. In the early eighteenth century, church services may have been held in private homes for several years before the church was built. Itinerant ministers could not carry certificates or letters with them and they were frequently left behind or lost. So were minute books in many instances. Evidence of membership comes from communicant lists, and entries of christening in the register or burial in the churchyard. By the mid-nineteenth century, well-established churches will have collections of letters of recommendation, with notations in registers of "received by letter." See Chapter 5.

The Process of Americanization

Becoming an American took more than a trip to the United States. The process took several years to complete and some immigrants made the transition more easily than others. Men, with the need to speak English and appear American in order to move up the employment ladder, seem to have made the adjustment with less stress than women.

Photographs

Family photographs can provide evidence of how rapidly the process occurred in your family. When did family members first begin to wear American-style clothing? Look at hats and shoes. Scan the wearing apparel of males especially. If your people came from Eastern Europe, watch for the disappearance of women's head scarves and aprons worn even at festive gatherings and celebrations. When did the children begin to attend public school?

Alien Registration

Registration of aliens with a local court of record was required from 1802 to 1828. Customs officers in Salem and Beverly, Massachusetts, recorded passenger lists with aliens clearly marked, 1798-1800. These records are in the National Archives.

Enforcing this law during the War of 1812 has given us some valuable data for persons immigrating after 1800. Many of these are indexed by P. William Filby with Mary K. Meyer, *Passenger and Immigration Lists Index.*

Under the 1929 Alien Registration Act, aliens were again required to register their current residences and place of employment annually with the federal government. Immigrant identification cards, certificates of registry, certificates of lawful entry, certificates of arrival (see Figure 15-7), and alien registration cards (see Figure 15-8) are forms of identification. All aliens must carry one of these identification cards on their person to be considered legal aliens. Any alien without one of the above can be deported without a hearing. These cards or certificates will usually be preserved in home sources. You must have the registration number to order other documents.

Alien registration cards are valuable because they give a precise address. They can also be valuable to trace the foreign-born children of American citizens, foreign-born children adopted by American parents, and children transported out of the United States by their parents. Their birth certificates will be on file with the Passport Agency, U.S. Department of State or the Immigration and Naturalization Service of the Department of Justice. These records can be obtained through the Freedom of Information Act when adoption agencies refuse to give out similar information. See L.G. Sherick, *How to Use the Freedom of Information Act: FOIA* (New York: Arco Publishing Company, 1978), and Jayne Askin with Bob Oskam, *Search: A Handbook for Adoptees and Birthparents* (New York: Harper & Row Publishers, 1982).

Also valuable are records of the U. S. Attorney General's Office which include letters of identity, affidavits of birth and identity, passenger lists, and correspondence regarding visas and travel per-

U. S. DEPARTMENT OF JUSTICE
IMMIGRATION AND NATURALIZATION SERVICE No. 23-104495

CERTIFICATE OF ARRIVAL

[C]ERTIFY that the immigration records show that the alien named below arrived at the port, [a]nd in the manner shown, and was lawfully admitted to the United States of America for [resi]dence.

[N]ame: Pinzin, Secondo
[P]ort of entry: New York, N. Y.
[D]ate: July 2, 1920 VFP 265453
[M]anner of arrival: SS Dante Alighieri

[I] CERTIFY that this certificate of arrival is issued under authority of, and in conformity with, [...] of the Act of June 29, 1906, as amended, solely for the use of the alien herein named and only [...]tion purposes.

IN WITNESS WHEREOF, this Certificate of Arrival is issued

September 11, 1941
(Date)

Figure 15-7. Certificate of Arrival of Secondo Pinzin, 2 July 1920; U. S. Dept. of Justice #23-104495. Copy courtesy of Vivienne J. Pencin, Box 3203, Quail Valley, CA 92380.

Form AR-3 *Registration Number* 5321724

ALIEN REGISTRATION RECEIPT CARD

John Menkalski
8819 Bellevue Ave.,
Cleveland, Ohio

KEEP THIS CARD. Keep a record of the number.

Figure 15-8. Alien Registration Card of John Menkalski, no. 5321724. Copy courtesy of Viviene J. Pencin, Box 3203, Quail Valley, CA 92380.

mits for 1937-65. These materials can also be accessed through the Freedom of Information Act from the National Archives.

Naturalization Records

Owning land or an equivalent estate in merchandise for city dwellers required citizenship during the colonial period. In practice, the filing of declaration of intent to become a citizen was considered sufficient to buy land or apply for a land grant. At all times, citizenship was required to serve in public office or to vote. Most aliens became citizens within ten years of the time they were eligible. See Table 15-3.

Immigrants can obtain citizenship in a variety of ways. See Table 15-4. When the federal government acquires territory by treaty or purchase, it also acquires jurisdiction over people living on that land at the time. It acquired Louisiana in 1803, Florida – including Mississippi and Alabama – in 1819, and Alaska in 1867. The United States has always agreed to validate property titles of these persons who become citizens by purchase. To validate the title, however, a private land claim must be be filed and these claims can be very valuable. The current land owner must document claim to title; and if the grant was originally given to a father or grandfather, the claimant must also prove descent. Some files contain four to seven generations of genealogical proof through family Bible pages, original land transactions, genealogy charts, and affidavits and testimony of neighbors and relatives. These records are in the National Archives. See Chapter 7, "Land and Tax Records," and Chapter 6, "Court Records," for examples and indexes. See also *Guide to Genealogical Research in the National Archives* (Washington, D.C.: National Archives Trust Fund, 1982), Chapters 15-16.

Table 15-3

Percentages of Eligible Aliens Naturalized, 1901

Nationality	*Percent Naturalized*	*Percent Declarations*
Armenian	58.2	20.9
Bohemian/Moravian	62.1	23.2
Croatian	19.4	19.1
Dutch	77.8	14.8
English	65.0	15.7
Finnish	56.3	23.9
German	65.4	14.1
Greek	3.7	6.4
Hebrew	24.1	29.5
Irish	79.1	7.1
Italian, North	32.9	22.0
Italian, South	18.1	9.9
Lithuanian	21.9	11.8
Magyar	15.0	19.3
Polish	21.6	13.9
Portuguese	5.3	.9
Russian	8.3	8.3
Ruthenian	14.7	8.3
Scotch	68.5	9.6
Serbian	0	5.7
Slovak	17.1	14.7
Swedish	84.9	11.1
Syrian	20.0	15.0
Turkish	84.0	10.0

U.S. Immigration Commission, *Report of Immigration Commission: Abstracts of Reports of the Immigration Commission, with Conclusions and Recommendations and Views of the Minority* (Washington, D.C.: Government Printing Office, 1911), vol. 1, pp. 486-87.

A second form of naturalization was a sort of amnesty act passed by the legislative bodies of American colonies or by the United States Congress granting citizenship to all residents. For example, in 1776, the newly established Continental Congress declared that all non-English residents of the American Colonies were citizens of the new government. Some states ratified this declaration for their own citizens. By joint resolution of Congress, Texas residents were granted citizenship in 1845. By acts of Congress, citizenship was conferred upon residents of Hawaii in 1900, of Puerto Rico in 1917, of the Virgin Islands in 1927, on American Indians in 1924, and on blacks by Constitutional amendment in 1868. Women and children

Table 15-4
Historical Summary of U.S. Naturalization Provisions

Title, Date of Act	Treaty or agreement	Legislative Act	Court of records	Residence requirement in years	Years resident in state	Years resident to declare intent	Eligibility	Comments
1740*		●	●	7			Free, white males, 21 years old.	Declaration of intention required to own land; sacrament certificate required within 3 months before application. Could be naturalized in groups.
1776	●						All white residents of European descent born in the colonies or loyal to Revolutionary cause.	Several states passed their own naturalization laws; exceptions: Connecticut, Georgia, New Hampshire, North Carolina, Pennsylvania. Abolished 1790. States retained right to set local residence requirements. Statehood automatically conferred citizenship in most states on all residents.
1778		●		None			All free, white residents in all states have common U.S. citizenship.	
1790			●	2	1		Free, white males, 21 years old	Loyal indentured servants residing in the colonies at time of Revolution automatically citizens.
1795			●	5	1	3	Free, white males, 21 years old.	Wives and children automatically became citizens. Single women over twenty-one years could apply for citizenship.
1798				14		5		Revoked in 1802.
1802*			●	5	1	3	Free, white males, 21 years old.	Aliens to register with court on arrival. Repealed 1828. If alien dies after declaring intent, widow and children became citizens automatically. Those in military could become citizens after honorable discharge. Typical records created: unbound declarations of intention, sometimes called applications; proofs of residence; bound volumes of recorded declarations of intention; bound volumes of admissions to citizenship; certificates of naturalization; minute entry in court journal docket entries; indexes.
1808		●						Importation of blacks prohibited.
1868 Fourteenth Amendment to Constitution.		●					Blacks	Became citizens automatically when amendment passed.

*Definitive immigration–naturalization acts.

Compiled from Darrell H. Smith, *Bureau of Naturalization* (New York: AMS Reprints, 1926) before 1918; Gilmar G. Udell, *Naturalization Laws* (Washington, D.C.: Government Printing Office, 1968) since 1918; and James C. Neagles and Lila Lee Neagles, *Locating Your Ancestor: A Guide to Naturalization Records* (Logan, Utah: Everton Publishers, 1975).

Title, Date of Act	Treaty or agreement	Legislative Act	Court of records	Residence requirement in years	Years resident in state	Years resident to declare intent	Eligibility	Comments
1882		●						Chinese excluded. Prior to 1868, among Chinese admitted to work on railroads, opium traffic became a problem.
1906*			●	5	1	2	Aliens must register at port of entry on arrival.	Application must record name, age, occupation, personal description, place of birth, last foreign residence, date of arrival, name of vessel, U.S. residence, marital status. Children under 18 years and wives become citizens automatically when man is naturalized.
1918		●		3		Waived	Resident aliens, Filipinos, Puerto Ricans with honorable discharge from military service; seamen aliens must file intent.	Automatic citizenship. Must appear in court with two written affidavits attesting character.
1922				3		Waived	Women, age 21 years, regardless of marital status.	Women do not gain or lose citizenship by marriage.
1924 Immigration Quota Act			●	5	1		Same as 1906, 1918, 1922	Specific numbers of immigrants admitted from each national group based on percent of 1920 population already resident. Aliens unable to support themselves to be deported.
1927		●					Residents of Virgin Islands born after 17 Jan. 1917.	
1929 Alien Registration Act		●		5		Waived	Legal entry before 3 June 1921.	Certificates of entry issued on application with two character affidavits.
1931		●						Aliens who traffic in drugs could be deported.
1940 Alien Registration Act of 1940		●					Aliens over 14 years of age.	Registration at local post office required within 30 days of arrival, with fingerprints in duplicate. One copy of print attached to alien card.
Nationality Act of 1940*		●					American Indians given citizenship.	Extended definiton of eligibility, procedures, punishments for non-compliance, entry documents, adjustments of quotas
1941			●	Waived		Waived	Honorable discharge from military service in World War I or II	Two character affidavits, copy of discharge filed with court of record.
1943		●					Chinese given low quota.	

Title, Date of Act	Legislative Act	Residence requirement in years	Years resident in state	Eligibility	Comments
1946	●			Filipinos, natives of India given quotas	
1948 Displaced Persons Act	●			Persons and dependents fleeing persecution, must reside in occupied territory.	Granted legal entry and asylum at public expense. Must qualify with quotas. Some quotas waived.
1949 Agricultural Act	●			Mexican aliens admitted on work agreements with employers.	
1952* Immigration and Nationality Act		5	1	Africans given quota.	Quotas, entry documents, and photographs required; exclusion, registration, eligibility defined.
1953 Refugee Relief Act	●				Special nonquota visas granted to refugees, escapees, German expellees. Specific number for each national group.
1963	●				Noncertified copies can be made of all naturalization records.

prior to 1928 automatically became U.S. citizens when the husband/father did. Individual names of persons given citizenship by legislative act are often omitted and the group may be referred to as a whole.

Aliens could go before any court of record and declare their intent to become a citizen after they had resided in the United States for at least three years. Many made the initial declaration to buy land but have no formal citizenship right recorded by the local courts during the nineteenth century. Paying taxes over an established length of time seemed sufficient to grant also the right to vote, hold office, and serve on juries. See Kenneth Scott, "Resident Aliens Enabled to Hold Land in New York State, 1790-1825," *National Genealogical Society Quarterly* 67 (March 1979): 42-57 and Kenneth Scott and Roseanne Conway, *New York Alien Residents, 1825-1848* (Baltimore: Genealogical Publishing Company, 1975).

Soldiers, after honorable discharge, were granted citizenship without formal petition.

Even with these exceptions, there are many naturalization records on file before state and federal courts of record. These are summarized for each state in James C. Neagles and Lila Lee Neagles, *Locating Your Immigrant Ancestors: A Guide to Naturalization Records* (Logan, Utah: Everton Publishers, Inc., 1975; new edition in preparation).

Before 1906, the records were kept by federal, state, and local courts. After 1906, copies were forwarded to the Immigration and Naturalization Service as well. Since 1968, uncertified copies of these papers can be requested for research purposes.

There are five-by-eight-inch photocopies of naturalization records 1780-1906 for New York City and the New England states (Record Group 85) – Maine, Massachusetts, New Hampshire, and Rhode Island – reproduced for a WPA project. They usually consist of two pages for each person; and many include petition for citizenship, oath of allegiance, record of previous citizenship, place and date of birth, occupation, place and date of arrival in the United States, name of the ship, and names and addresses of witnesses and applicants. These records are indexed on three-by-five-inch cards. The National Archives announced plans at Hartford, 15 July, 1983, to microfilm these cards so they will be more accessible.

For a state-by-state description of the records in each federal district court, see *Guide to Genealogical Research in the National Archives*, Chapter 3.

Record contents vary with period of time – later records contain more information than earlier ones. Figure 15-9, dated 10 April 1765 contains the minimum data you can expect to find. Figure 15-10, dated 9 September 1911, is an example of information available for a later period. Each record you get will have different information, but you can expect some or all of the following:[19]

Sacrament Certificate: Name, date, and place of sacrament.

Oath of Allegiance: Date, name, renunciation of allegiance to any foreign government, name of monarch or government, and place of residence.

Declaration of Intention (First Papers): Name, address, occupation, birthplace, nationality, country from which emigrated, birthdate or age, personal description, date of intention, marital status, last foreign residence, port of entry, name of ship, date of entry, and date of document.

Petition (Second or Final Papers): Name, address, occupation, date emigrated, birthplace, country from which emigrated, birthdate or age, time in the United States, date of intention, name and age of spouse, names of children, ages of children, last foreign

Pennſylvania, ſſ.

I *Edward Shippen Junr* Prothonotary of the Supream Court of the Province of *Pennſylvania*, DO hereby certify, That at a Supream Court held at *Philadelphia*, for the Province of *Pennſylvania*, before *William Allen, William Coleman and Alexander Stedman* Eſquires, Judges of the ſaid Court, the *Tenth* Day of *April* in the Year of our Lord, *One Thouſand Seven Hundred* and *Sixty five* between the Hours of Nine and Twelve of the Clock in the Forenoon of the ſame Day, *Wyrick Seltzer* of *Tulpehocken* in the County of *Berks* being a Foreigner, and having inhabited and reſided for the Space of Seven Years in his Majeſty's Colonies in *America*, and not having been abſent out of ſome of the ſaid Colonies for a longer Space than Two Months at any one Time during the ſaid Seven Years. And being one of the People who conſcientiouſly ſcruple and refuſe the taking an Oath, did take and ſubſcribe the Affirmations and Declarations, according to the Directions of an Act of Parliament, made in the thirteenth Year of the Reign of his late Majeſty King GEORGE, the Second, intituled, *An Act for naturalizing ſuch foreign Proteſtants, and others, therein mentioned, as are ſettled, or ſhall ſettle, in any of his Majeſty's Colonies in* America, and according to an Act of General Aſſembly of this Province of *Pennſylvania*, made in the ſixteenth Year of his ſaid late Majeſty, intituled, *An Act for naturalizing ſuch foreign Proteſtants, as are ſettled, or ſhall ſettle within this Province, who not being of the People called* Quakers, *do conſcientiouſly refuſe the taking of any Oath*, and thereupon was admitted to be his Majeſty's natural born Subject of the Kingdom of *Great Britain*, and of this Province, purſuant to the Direction and Intention of the ſaid Act of Parliament, and Act of Aſſembly *In Teſtimony* whereof I have hereunto ſet my Hand, and affixed the Seal of the Supream Court, the *Tenth* Day of *April* in the Year firſt above-mentioned.

Edw. Shippen Jr

Figure 15-9. Certificate of Naturalization of Wyrick Seltzer, 10 April 1765, Pennsylvania Supreme Court, printed in Earl W. Ibach, *Hub of the Tulpehocken* (Womelsdorf, Pa.: For the author, 1975), p. 52. Used with permission.

residence, port and mode of entry, name of ship, date of entry, names of witnesses, date of document, address of spouse, and photograph (after 1940).

Certificate of Naturalization: Name, address, birthplace or nationality, country from which emigrated, birthdate or age, personal description, marital status, name of spouse, age or birthdate of spouse, address of spouse, names, ages, and addresses of children, and date of document.

Other Records

Other records will also give evidence of citizenship with indications of date naturalized and country of origin. Census records, 1870-1910, give varying details from foreign-born parents to the year of immigration and how many years naturalized. Applications for donation lands, for homesteads, and other federal grants include naturalization records, since only citizens can apply for a federal grant. Church records, especially letters of transfer or recommendation, give places of birth or residence. Passports and oaths of allegiance already referred to yield valuable clues. Employment files and voters' registration records may give the date and court of naturalization, port and date of arrival, ship, and country of birth. These records are created as a result of residence in the United States. As ancestors reappear in these materials, the process of Americanization becomes more complete.

Immigrants may come directly to the United States from their place of birth. Many, however, have come via some other country where they stay sometimes five years or so. For others, they may already be removed two or three generations from their homelands. French Huguenots stayed in Germany, Switzerland, Holland, and England before coming to America. The Palatines who immigrated in 1709 to New York came via England and Ireland. Englishmen may stop in Canada or Australia, Scots in Barbados and Canada, Germans in Russia or Lithuania and Brazil, and Italians in Brazil and Canada before coming here. The process of emigration, immigration, settlement, and acculturation occurs in each of these countries. If you go directly to the country of birth in such cases, you will miss deaths of parents, marriages, births of children, deaths of spouses, and much more.

Research Approaches

Some approaches for tracking an immigrant ancestor to a place of origin have a high degree of success. Some are a waste. The majority of Americans are foreign-born or descended from foreign-born people. This obvious fact conceals a snare for the unwary—the assumption that a pedigree can be extended best by going directly to the country of origin. In reality, the solution to the problem most frequently lies in American records and archives.

Certain well-known genealogical sources provide enough information to tantalize us but not enough to meet our research needs. For example, federal census schedules have been indexed and are easily accessible in research libraries. Using these indexes, we quickly arrive at the port of entry only to discover that we lack the date of entry and the name of the ship on which our ancestor sailed. What's more, we have no idea if the ancestor traveled alone

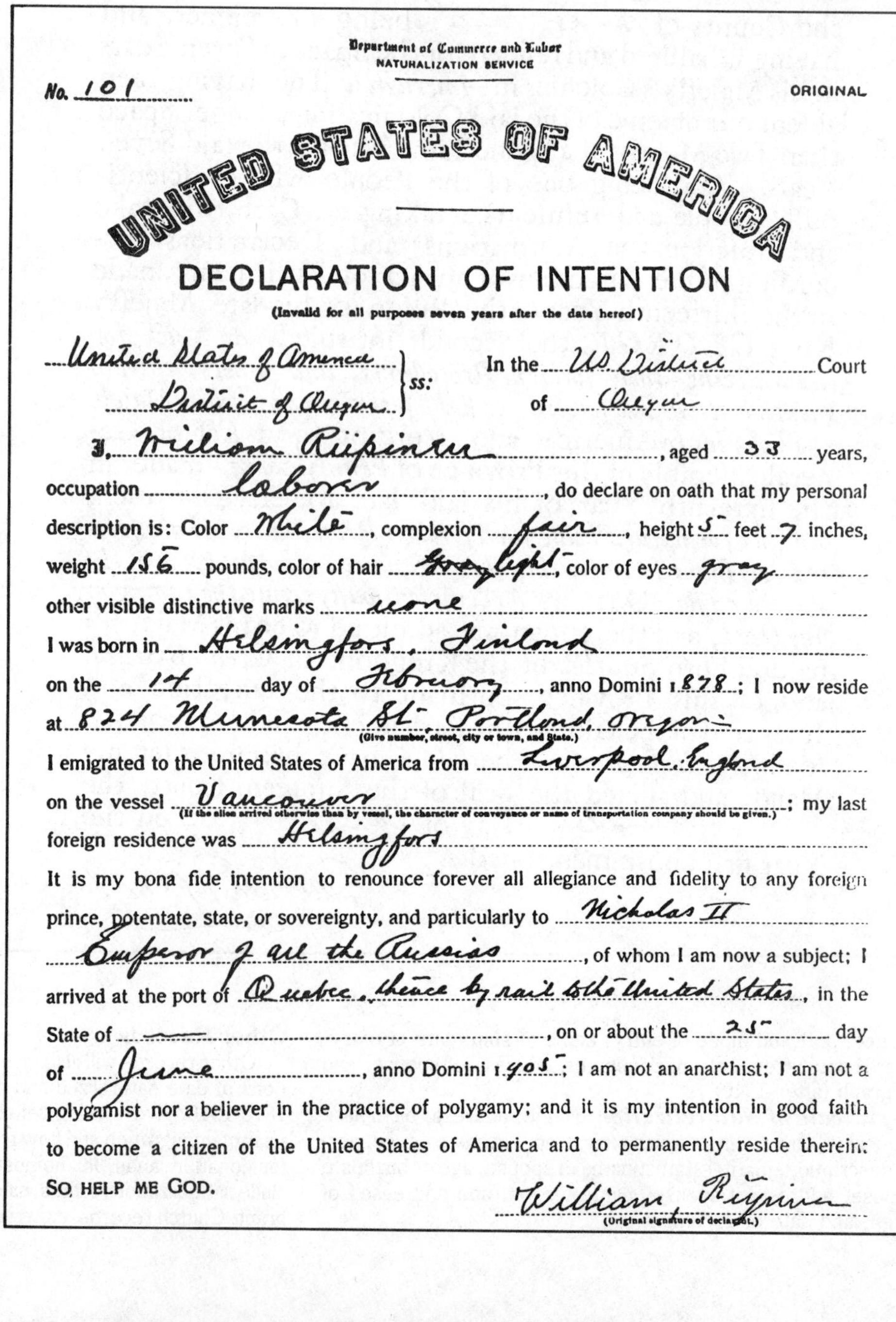

Department of Commerce and Labor
NATURALIZATION SERVICE

No. 101 ORIGINAL

UNITED STATES OF AMERICA

DECLARATION OF INTENTION

(Invalid for all purposes seven years after the date hereof)

United States of America } ss: In the US District Court
District of Oregon } of Oregon

I, William Rüpinen, aged 33 years, occupation laborer, do declare on oath that my personal description is: Color White, complexion fair, height 5 feet 7 inches, weight 156 pounds, color of hair gray light, color of eyes gray other visible distinctive marks none

I was born in Helsingfors, Finland on the 14 day of February, anno Domini 1878; I now reside at 824 Minnesota St. Portland, Oregon (Give number, street, city or town, and State.)

I emigrated to the United States of America from Liverpool, England on the vessel Vancouver (If the alien arrived otherwise than by vessel, the character of conveyance or name of transportation company should be given.); my last foreign residence was Helsingfors

It is my bona fide intention to renounce forever all allegiance and fidelity to any foreign prince, potentate, state, or sovereignty, and particularly to Nicholas II Emperor of all the Russias, of whom I am now a subject; I arrived at the port of Quebec, thence by rail to the United States, in the State of —, on or about the 25 day of June, anno Domini 1905; I am not an anarchist; I am not a polygamist nor a believer in the practice of polygamy; and it is my intention in good faith to become a citizen of the United States of America and to permanently reside therein: SO HELP ME GOD.

William Riipinen
(Original signature of declarant.)

Figure 15-10. Declaration of Intention of William Rüpinen, 29 Sept. 1911, U.S. District Court of Oregon; photocopy in possession of the author.

or with other family members, as an adult or a child, or under a different (or differently spelled) name. In short, the very information we need to identify that foreign ancestor from the multitude of immigrants and to locate a place of origin is missing from our notes.

In almost every case, the genealogist has to pull back a generation to solve the problem. It can be avoided to begin with by collecting every piece of information available in America: from relatives (home sources); from compiled genealogies and pedigrees; from census, land, and probate records in the ancestor's county or township of residence; from employers, fraternal organizations, insurance companies, and churches in the ancestor's hometown; from state military and customs files; and federal court and immigration records.

If these sources do not tell specifically where to look, migrational patterns can come to the rescue. Painstaking research is necessary, however, if history is the only guide.

A second research mistake is to look in foreign archives for documents available in United States libraries and record repositories either in original or photocopy form. For example, the Huntington Library in San Marino, California, has the original manuscripts of the Hastings family of Great Britain. These 50,000 manuscript items of one of the most important noble families cover c1101 to 1892. They cannot be searched in Great Britain, for they exist only in America. The Genealogical Society of Utah has several thousand reels of microfilmed emigration registers directly available to all genealogists who have access to a branch library.

The Genealogical Society also has microfilm copies of original records pertaining to the Jews in Poland and at Hebrew University in Jerusalem. (See Chapter 21, "Jewish-American Records.") It takes two full catalog drawers to hold the cards on which they are described. Although these records are written in Polish, their accessibility in Poland today is extremely limited. In America they are available to anyone within driving distance of a branch library.

Here is a case study. For almost fifty years, the Robinson family organization had been searching for its immigrant ancestor, John Rowlandson Robinson, in England. Professional researchers, hired to extend the pedigree, had performed extensive searches in Yorkshire parishes. Family members had made additional searches

(Invalid for all purposes seven years after the date hereof)

United States of America } ss: In the U.S. District Court
District of Oregon } of Oregon

I, William Riepinen, aged 33 years,
occupation laborer, do declare on oath that my personal description is: Color White, complexion fair, height 5 feet 7 inches,
weight 156 pounds, color of hair gray light, color of eyes gray
other visible distinctive marks none
I was born in Helsingfors, Finland
on the 14 day of February, anno Domini 1878; I now reside
at 824 Minnesota St. Portland, Oregon
(Give number, street, city or town, and State.)
I emigrated to the United States of America from Liverpool, England
on the vessel Vancouver (If the alien arrived otherwise than by vessel, the character of conveyance or name of transportation company should be given.); my last foreign residence was Helsingfors
It is my bona fide intention to renounce forever all allegiance and fidelity to any foreign prince, potentate, state, or sovereignty, and particularly to Nicholas II Emperor of all the Russias, of whom I am now a subject; I arrived at the port of Quebec, thence by rail to the United States, in the State of ——, on or about the 25 day of June, anno Domini 1905; I am not an anarchist; I am not a polygamist nor a believer in the practice of polygamy; and it is my intention in good faith to become a citizen of the United States of America and to permanently reside therein: SO HELP ME GOD.

William Riepinen
(Original signature of declarant.)

Subscribed and sworn to before me this 29th
[SEAL] day of Sept, anno Domini 1911
Amburn
Clerk of the U.S. District Court.
By G Clark, Deputy Clerk.

11—2526

in several other records. Yet fifty years and hundreds of dollars later, the pedigree still ended with John himself. Why?

The first problem was confused organization of family materials. Each genealogist kept a record of the searches he/she made but did not compare or correlate these searches in a centralized set of records. As a result, some records have been searched several times while many records have not been searched at all.

The second problem was going too quickly into English sources with the result that the family could not recognize John and his parents when they began searching. Searches were made in forty-four jurisdictions to determine church affiliation and every parish within a twenty-mile radius of Clapham, Yorkshire. There are too many Robinsons in this section of England to know who is who.

A more effective way would have been to begin where John Robinson died and to follow him, record by record, back to his place of birth. The information gathered in each jurisdiction enables the search to be carried to the next with greater success.

Such a procedure can also identify other family members or close associates who emigrated to America to build a "totality" of data about them. This data can identify them in their precise place of origin in England as well.

The third problem was overlooking living relatives, some of whom had corresponded with or visited relatives in England. Living relatives can provide street addresses and towns of residence for family members in their places of origin. They may also possess family Bibles, letters, pictures, journals, and diaries. A cousin living in Southern California had John's original journals. John had corresponded with relatives in England shortly after the family emigrated; and his journals contain lists of family members, death notices, tombstone inscriptions, names and addresses of family members, the ship the family emigrated on, its port and date of arrival, and several family ancestors.

Survey work among family members, their home source collections, and interviews with living grandchildren of John Rowlandson Robinson was badly needed. The importance of working thoroughly from the last localities to the first, picking up associated families and other family members who emigrated, cannot be overemphasized.

Tracing immigrants seems very difficult but the problems are usually procedural. The immigrant has left a trail, but the genealogist has overlooked the footprints.

A useful way to organize information and clues is to keep a summary of the people your ancestor comes in contact with—potential relatives (father-in-law, spouses for children, brothers-in-law) and traveling companions. After you have tracked the ancestor through life, make a summary of contact points: sponsors and godparents for children, witnesses for deeds and wills, fellow soldiers or officers in military units, neighbors who settled near each other, business partners, traveling companions, surnames marrying into your ancestor's family, and coreligionists who worshipped in the same church and were buried in the same cemetery. Such a summary list appears in Table 15-5.

When you can't locate your own ancestor, track these neighbors and associates. Watch for these names on passenger and immigration lists. When you find their places of origin, see if your own ancestor is nearby.

In Duke University Library, Durham, North Carolina, is an account book among the personal papers of Zachariah Johnston. It includes money loaned to family members and close associates from the time the Johnston family left Ireland, to their initial settlement near Bethlehem, Pennsylvania, to their stop in Augusta County, Virginia, to their residence in Lexington, Virginia, just south of the Augusta County line. The same names appear and reappear. The whole group left Ireland in 1709 and stayed together at least until Zachariah died in 1800. They are recorded, along with their specific townland in Ireland, in that little account book. These families intermarried more than ten times during that century.

For other examples of this approach, read Henry Z. (Hank) Jones, Jr., "Finding the Ancestral Home of a Palatine Forefather: The Case of Martin Zerbe," *Pennsylvania Genealogical Magazine* 29 (1975): 129-32, and "The Braun and Loesch Families: Neighbors in Germany and America;" *Quarterly of the Pennsylvania German Society* 10 (April 1976); Sumner Chilton Powell, *Puritan Village: The Formation of a New England Town* (Garden City, N.Y.: Doubleday & Company, 1965); and Jean Stephenson, *Scotch-Irish Migration to South Carolina, 1772: Reverend William Martin and His Five Shiploads of Settlers* (Strasburg, Va.: Shenandoah Publishing House, Inc., 1971).

European/British Sources

The production of country-wide indexes and finding aids makes it possible today to research both sides of the Atlantic at the same time in ways that were not possible ten years ago. The two nationality groups selected to demonstrate this approach are English and Pennsylvania German.

International Genealogical Index (IGI)

First check the International Genealogical Index at the Genealogical Society of Utah, one of its branches, or selected libraries across the country. It is the largest genealogical database: 68 million entries in the 1981 edition. It indexes sources: births and marriages in civil and church records with some probate and census entries for the United States. It also indexes family data and results of research by Mormon genealogists since 1969. The index is easy to check because it is on microfiche and combines spelling variants in one alphabetized sequence, state by state and province by province. Some sections are country-wide, like the entries for Scotland, Belgium, Switzerland, Italy, and the Netherlands.

Searches are inexpensive: if you are unable to check the index yourself, the personnel of the Genealogical Society of Utah will check it for you at $1 per name. Write Genealogical Society of Utah, 50 East North Temple, Salt Lake City, UT 84150 for order forms or pick up some at your nearest branch library. (Addresses in Appendix D.)

If you have an ancestor, Hezekiah Mitchell, who emigrated to Illinois in 1851 from Yorkshire, England, but you are unable to locate his parish of birth, check the International Genealogical Index (Figure 15-11):

There is no entry for Hezekiah. Perhaps the records for his parish are not yet in the database. About 85 percent of all parish registers or Bishops' Transcripts (official copies of register entries sent to the bishop of the diocese) for Yorkshire have been input, but not all of them appear in the 1981 edition of the database.

How do you determine which records are in the database? The *Parish and Vital Records Listings*, available in hard copy and microfiche with the IGI, is updated monthly and lists country-by-country every source input into the database.

Figure 15-12 is a sample section for the parish of Almondbury, Yorkshire, England. Note the double ** which means that these records have been input but do not appear in the current edition of the database.

Perhaps Hezekiah was a Nonconformist. The Colne River Basin, in which Almondbury is located, was heavily Nonconformist in the early nineteenth century when Hezekiah was born.

How do you determine if all church registers extant are in the database? *Parish and Vital Records Listings* for Almondbury show that several Nonconformist records are in the Index. By comparing this list with the *List of Non-Parochial Registers, Main Series and the Society of Friends Series preserved at the Public Records Office in London* (London: List and Index Society, 1969), GS 924,808, Figure 15-13, and "List of Nonconformist Chapels, Excluding Jews and Society of Friends," typescript, n.d., GS 962,176, Figure 15-14, it is possible to determine if all of the church records, both Anglican and Nonconformist, have been input. There are some chapels for

Table 15-5

Summary of Contact People for Andrew Hoffman

Name	*Connection*	*Place*	*Date*
Thomas Willy, wife Elizabeth	Sponsors at christening of daughter, Elizabeth	St. John's Reformed Church (Hain's) Lower Heidelberg, Berks Co., Penn., close to Reading, Penn.	1773
Matheyss Jaeger	Wife, Anna Margaretha, is sponsor for christening of child	St. David's Reformed Church (Killinger's Church)	1775
Catherine Richards (Ritscheric)	Sponsor at christening of daughter, Catherine	St. John's Reformed Church (Hain's Church)	1776
Margaret Linnewelt	Sponsor at christening of daughter, Margareth	Same place	1781
Christopher Schaeffer, wife Anna Maria	Sponsor at christening of daughter, Anna Maria	Same place	1784
Casper Stone	Buys Andrew's land	Heidelberg, Berks Co., Penn.	1784
John Deell	Buys Andrew's land	Same place	1785
M. Magd. Umholz	Sponsor at christening of daughter	Klinger's Lutheran Church, Upper Paxton, Dauphin Co., near Gratz Penn.	1789
George Klinger	Executor of Andrew's will	Dauphin County, Penn.	written, 1795 proved, 1802
Jacob Laudenslager	100 acres, one-story cabin adjoins in Wisconisco Valley	Dauphin County, near Gratz, Penn.	1798
Peter Wiljer, Sr.	Wife, Anna Margaretha, is sponsor for christening of children	Hoffman's Reformed Church, Dauphin Co., near Gratz, Penn.	1800
George Mayer	Wife, Anna Margaretha, is sponsor for christening of children	Klinger's Lutheran Church, Dauphin Co.	1803
Frederick Stein (Stone)	Tenant in common for land patent	Upper Paxton, Dauphin	1804

which there are no extant records. All chapels are accounted for except Linthwaite Schools Methodist Chapel for which there is no record on file.

The christenings in the Church of England parish of Almondbury are complete from 1557 to 1805, and in the Bishops' Transcripts from 1806 to 1835. The marriages are complete from 1557 through 1835 as well. All records are accounted for; and even though four segments are not yet in the database, all have been input.

Since Hezekiah does not appear in the Index, searching the birth entries in the original records will probably not locate him either. The new edition of the IGI, expected spring of 1984, can be checked for the four segments not yet on the fiche. If he does not appear there, the chances are 92 percent that he is not recorded – for the database has less than an 8 percent error factor. Another source is needed to locate our immigrant.

The Robinson family above had to check the original records to determine if John Rowlandson Robinson was recorded in them. In Hezekiah Mitchell's case, we can bypass that lengthy effort with its almost certainly negative results and proceed to other sources.

The German section of the IGI is a little different and presents some problems in its use, especially for American genealogists. (See Figure 15-15.)

Finding the right place to look is the first challenge. The boundaries of the German principalities have changed over time and the name given by an ancestor to a county clerk may no longer be used. For example, the city of Baden did not receive that name until the mid-twentieth century. If an ancestor said Baden-Baden, he/she probably meant the province (granddukedom) rather than the city.[20]

Maps 15-5 show sixteenth-century boundaries in comparison with the modern countries of Europe.

The Genealogical Society of Utah has prepared an instruction sheet (Figure 15-16) for the German IGI showing which territories are indexed in which sections. Since census enumerators are known

COUNTRY: ENGLAND — COUNTY: YORK — AS OF JUN 1981 — PAGE 67,111

NAME	FATHER MOTHER OR SPOUSE (SEX: M MALE F FEMALE H HUSBAND W WIFE)	S	E	EVENT DATE	TOWN, PARISH	B	E	S	SOURCE BATCH	SERIAL SHEET
MITCHELL, HENRY WILLIAM										
MITCHELL, HENRY WILLIAM		M	C	11JUN1866	HALIFAX	CLEARED	CLEARED	CLEARED	C007692	21653
	GEORGE MITCHELL/ELLEN AMELIA									
MITCHELL, HENRY WILLIAM	HENRY MITCHELL/MARY	M	C	25MAR1868	KIRKBY FLEETHAM	16JUN1973LG	30OCT1973LG	08NOV1973LG	C015072	0666
MICHELL, HENRYE	WILLM. MICHELL/	M	C	08SEP1611	HEPTONSTALL	26JUN1965LA	27OCT1965LA	21JUN1972HE	P007681	2899
MYCHELL OR BAWDWAYN, HENRYE		M	C	30DEC1611	HEPTONSTALL	26JUN1965LA	28OCT1965LA	UNCLEARED	P007681	2955
	ROBERT MYCHELL/SUSAN BAWDWAYN									
MITCHELL, HEPHZIBAH	WILLIAM THOMAS	W	M	06APR1826	HALIFAX			22AUG1980SL	M007692	6666
MITCHELL, HEPHZIBAH	JOHN MITCHELL/SALLY	F	C	11MAR1829	SOWERBY NEAR HALIFAX	CLEARED	CLEARED	CLEARED	C107861	3675
MITCHELL, HEPHZIBAH	CORNELIUS FLANERY	W	M	02MAY1831	HALIFAX			20AUG1980SL	M007692	11106
MITCHELL, HEPHZIBAH		F	C	09MAR1845	HALIFAX	CLEARED	CLEARED	CLEARED	C007692	22240
	WILLIAM MITCHELL/ELIZABETH									
MITCHELL, HERBERT	JOHN MITCHELL/ALICE	M	C	29OCT1833	HALIFAX	CLEARED	CLEARED	CLEARED	C007692	16055
MITCHELL, HERBERT	JOHN MITCHELL/ELIZABETH	M	C	05FEB1866	WENTWORTH	CLEARED	CLEARED	CLEARED	C108021	3696
MITCHELL, HERBERT	THOMAS MITCHELL/JANE	M	C	22MAR1867	MARKET WEIGHTON	CLEARED	CLEARED	CLEARED	C109071	3228
MITCHELL, HERBERT	JOSEPH MITCHELL/EMMA OGDEN	M	B	31JUL1878	LEEDS	08AUG1973LD	09OCT1973LD	22JAN1974LD	7308729	66
MITCHELL, HERBERT SYDNEY		M	C	27 [illegible]1847	OSSETT	CLEARED	CLEARED	CLEARED	C107721	3351
	JOSEPH MITCHELL/MARY ANN									
MICHELL, HESTER	HENRICI MICHELL/	F	C	20JAN1571	ELLAND	03DEC1936	16JAN1935SL	12AUG1976SW	C009302	1069
MITCHELL, HESTER	WILLIAM MITCHELL/	F	C	27NOV1662	EMLEY	28AUG1965OK	05FEB1966OK	26JUN1969SL	P007601	0479
MAICHELL, HEW	LANCLOTT MAICHELL/	M	C	28FEB1684	SKIPTON	01MAY1967SL	20MAY1967SL	27FEB1969SG	P009361	5313
MITCHELL, HIRAM	WILLIAM MITCHELL/MARY LAWTON	M	C	03SEP1835	PENISTONE	15NOV1975LA	09DEC1975LA	20JAN1976LA	C042681	12627
MITCHELL, HIRAM	/CH[illegible]OTTE MITCHELL	M	C	24OCT1844	PENISTONE	15NOV1975LA	10DEC1975LA	UNCLEARED	C042681	13875
MITCHELL, HIRAM	E[illegible] SHACKLETON	H	M	23APR1820	BRADFORD			23APR1980AL	M107651	3291
MITCHELL, HIRAM	[illegible]HELL/MARY	M	C	16AUG1829	BRADFORD	CLEARED	CLEARED	CLEARED	C107652	5268
MITCHELL, HIRAM	THOMAS M[illegible]HELL/MARY	M	C	03JUL1831	BINGLEY	21MAY1980IF	16MAY1980IF	29MAY1980IF	C007372	4471
MITCHELL, HOLLIS PEEL	JAMES MITCHELL/MARTHA	M	C	07AUG1831	SOWERBY NEAR HALIFAX	CLEARED	CLEARED	CLEARED	C107841	3833
MITCHELL, HONOUR	JOHN MITCHELL/AGNES	F	B	11DEC1813	BRADFORD,WESTGATE BAPTIST	CLEARED	CLEARED	CLEARED	C093291	0365
MITCHELL, HORATIO	THOMAS MITCHELL/ELLEN	M	C	31OCT1841	OSSETT	CLEARED	CLEARED	CLEARED	C107721	2872
MITCHELL, HOUGH	WILLIAM MITCHELL/AGNES	M	B	04JAN1736	SETTLE	26JUN1965	30OCT1965HZ	30JAN1979OG	7816336	16
MITCHEL, HUGH	THOS. MITCHEL/	M	C	13OCT1768	SANDAL MAGNA	12APR1976SL	27MAY1976SL	17AUG1976SL	7525513	17
MITCHELL, HUGH	ALICE WILSON	H	M	28APR1756	BRADFORD			27NOV1966AL	A170754	0686
MITCHEL, HUGH	ELIZABETH KNAPTON	H	M	11OCT1830	CAWTHORNE BY BARNSLEY			20NOV1979MT	M107861	0197
MITCHELL, HUMFRAY	ELLEN ELLIS	H	M	07FEB1609	SKIPTON IN CRAVEN			03MAY1974LG	7327614	30
MITCHELL, HUMFRUS	HENRICI MITCHELL/	M	C	16JUN1639	SHEFFIELD,SAINT PETER	31MAR1965SL	08JUL1965SL	11JUN1969SL	P007751	12529
MITCHELL, HUMPHREY	ELLEN ELLIS	H	M	07FEB1608	SKIPTON			03MAR1960AL	A455806	0156
MITCHELL, HUMPHREY	THOMAS MITCHELL/ANN	M	C	07MAY1803	HUDDERSFIELD,QUEENS STREET WESLEYAN	19SEP1978PV	02DEC1978PV	24JAN1979PV	C088611	0356
MITCHELL, IDAW [illegible]	WILLM. MITCHELL/	F	C	07FEB1593	LEEDS,SAINT PETER	15JAN1929	22FEB1929SG	29OCT1971LG	P009621	4196
MITCHELL, IMMANUEL	ELI MITCHELL/ANN	M	C	24DEC1820	HALIFAX	CLEARED	CLEARED	CLEARED	C007692	4520
MICHELL, IS	H[illegible]NAH GILLET	H	M	08APR1667	HALIFAX			17JAN1978SL	7721709	8
MYCHELL, ISAAC	JAMES MYCHELL/	M	C	28NOV1575	HALIFAX	20MAY1944	31OCT1944SG	16OCT1969LA	P007691	11039
MYCHELL, ISAAC	HENRY MYCHELL/	M	C	28MAR1585	HALIFAX	20MAY1944	28SEP1944SG	22OCT1969LA	P007691	14599
MITCHELL, ISAAC	PARSEBELL MITCHELL/	M	C	01NOV1597	LEEDS,SAINT PETER	INFANT	INFANT	27OCT1969SL	P009621	5501
MITCHELL, ISAAC	JOHN MITCHELL/	M	C	15SEP1667	SKIPTON	INFANT	INFANT	26FEB1969SG	P009341	4293
MITCHEL, ISAAC	ISAAC MITCHEL/HANNAH	M	C	1677	SOWERBY NEAR HALIFAX	12MAY1978LA	29JUN1978LA	02SEP1978LA	7808131	25
MITCHELL, ISAAC	SUSAN BARRIT	H	M	29JUN1696	HALIFAX			20APR1978LA	7725506	39
MITCHELL, ISAAC	SUSAN BARRIT	H	M	29JUN1697	HALIFAX			16FEB1973SG	7225526	13
MITCHELL, ISAAC	ISAAC MITCHELL/	M	C	JUN1725	HAWORTH	09NOV1968MT	24APR1969MT	07OCT1970MT	P018511	2280
MITCHEL, ISAAC	MARY CROWTHER	H	M	13JAN1728	HALIFAX			17JAN1973MT	7127116	69
MITCHEL, ISAAC	JAMES MITCHEL/SARAH	M	C	1735	SOWERBY NEAR HALIFAX	20MAR1979HA	20MAR1979HA	08FEB1980HA	7834834	54
MITCHEL, ISAAC	SUSAN SUTCLIFFE	H	M	25MAR1745	HALIFAX			28OCT1978PV	7808630	56
MITCHEL, ISAAC	MARTHA WILKINSON	H	M	13JUN1749	BINGLEY			23APR1974SL	7317328	43
MITCHEL, ISAAC	ISAAC MITCHEL/	M	C	22APR1753	BINGLEY	06DEC1974OG	14JAN1975OG	14FEB1975OG	7406733	91
MITCHEL, ISAAC	SARAH ECELS	H	M	19APR1762	HALIFAX			28OCT1978PV	7808630	48
MITCHEL, ISAAC	WILLIAM MITCHEL/	M	C	17JUL1763	BINGLEY	INFANT	INFANT	17NOV1977SL	7708133	15
MITCHEL, ISAAC	MARY ECCLES	H	M	12AUG1764	HALIFAX			22SEP1978SL	7808131	28
MITCHEL, ISAAC	ISABEL WARDEL	H	M	13JUN1774	HALIFAX			26MAY1978SL	7809033	9
MITCHEL, ISAAC	GRACE BINNS	H	M	15JAN1775	HALIFAX			26MAY1978SL	7809033	7
MITCHELL, ISAAC	BETTY MIDGLEY	H	M	02SEP1779	HALIFAX			26MAY1978SL	7809033	19

Σ = EVALUATED ENTRY

A = ADULT CHRISTENING B = BIRTH C = CHRISTENING D = DEATH OR BURIAL F = BIRTH OR CHRISTENING OF FIRST KNOWN CHILD M = MARRIAGE N = CEN: US W = WILL ALL OTHERS - MISCELLANEOUS

Figure 15-11. International Genealogical Index, Mitchell surname, Yorkshire, England; Genealogical Society of Utah.

to have written Baden or Bavaria because they were easier to spell even though the ancestor said Wuerttemburg or Hessen, you might search all German sections for your ancestor. The alphabetical and chronological arrangement of the entries makes the search easier.

A second difficulty can be finding the right entries. You may know your ancestor by an Americanized name, Jacob Hoffmann, unaware that the first given name for both Catholic and Lutheran children in Germany is usually a christening name – Georg Jakob Hoffmann. Since many of the entries in the IGI come from christening registers, you must search the whole list of entries for your surname so you won't miss the right one. Looking for Jacob Hoffman alone may be unsuccessful.

Another problem arises if either the given name or the surname has been changed in spelling, from Rudisille to Rutschly, Schneider to Snyder, or translated from Schwartz to Black or Zimmerman to Carpenter. In an alphabetized index with many pages per letter you must check for specifics.

Other genealogists have encountered these problems and developed ways to deal with them. Some selected study in their writings will ease the job ahead for you:

Bason, William H. "German/Dutch Names." *North Carolina Genealogy*, Winter 1968, p. 2244. List of suffixes.

Foreign Versions of English Names. Publication M-131, prepared under the direction of the U.S. Immigration and Naturalization Service. See Figure 15-17.

Gerberich, Albert H. "Geographical Aspects of Pennsylvania German Genealogical Study." *National Genealogical Society Quarterly* 34 (1946): 113-17. Discusses examples of German names from cities, towns, rivers, topographical landmarks – some 25 percent of the names.

Johnson, Arta F. *A Guide to the Spelling and Pronunciation of German Names*. Columbus, Ohio: For the author, 1981.

Schelbert, Leo, and Sandra Luebking. "Swiss Mennonite Family Names: An Annotated Checklist." *Pennsylvania Folklife*, Summer 1977, pp. 2-24. Includes spelling variants.

Smith, Clifford Neal. *Encyclopedia of German-American Genealogical Research*. New York: R. R. Bowker Company, 1976; pp. 91-103. Indepth study of dialectical clues in German names.

———— and Anna P. Smith. "German Surnames in America." *National Genealogical Society Quarterly* 62 (1974): 13-16.

Strassburger, Ralph B. *Pennsylvania German Pioneers, 1727-1808*. William J. Hinke, ed. 3 vols. Norristown, Penn.: Pennsylvania German Society, 1934. 1: 229-55. Includes Christian name directory with variants and Americanized versions.

Yoder, Don. "Is Your Name Dutchified?" *Pennsylvania Dutchman*, Dec. 1949, pp. 70-71. Discusses vowel changes.

ENGLAND — PARISH AND VITAL RECORDS LISTINGS — NOV 1983 — PAGE 8

1. COUNTY	2. TOWN AND/OR PARISH	3. PERIOD FROM - TO	4. RECD TYPE	5. PRINT OUT CALL NO.	6. PROJECT	7. SOURCE CALL NO.
YORKS	ALMONDBURY	1557-1667	CHR	0820527	C 1712-2	230649
YORKS	ALMONDBURY	1668-1726	CHR	0820577	C 1712-3	230649
YORKS	ALMONDBURY	1727-1761	CHR	1235386	P 1712-1	230649
YORKS	ALMONDBURY	1761-1769	CHR		C 1712-3	
YORKS	ALMONDBURY	1770-1782	CHR	0820592	C 1712-4	230649
YORKS	ALMONDBURY	1771-1774	CHR		P 1712-1	
YORKS	ALMONDBURY	1783-1789	CHR		C 1712-4	230650
YORKS	ALMONDBURY	1790-1793	CHR	0820566	C 1712-5	230650
		1793-1805	CHR			230651
YORKS	ALMONDBURY	1557-1766	MAR	NONE	M 1712-1 **	230649
YORKS	ALMONDBURY, BERRY BROW SALEM CHAPEL METHODIST NEW	SEE: BERRY BROW SALEM CHAPEL, METHODIST NEW CONNEXION				
YORKS	ALMONDBURY, BROADLANDS BAPTIST	1809-1838	BIR	NONE	C 9324-1	816604 (RG4 3377)
YORKS	ALMONDBURY, BTS	1806-1812	CHR	NONE	C 1712-8 **	990854
YORKS	ALMONDBURY, BTS	1813-1835	CHR	NONE	C 1712-6	990854,990855,9908
YORKS	ALMONDBURY, BTS	1766-1773	MAR	NONE	M 1712-7 **	990853
YORKS	ALMONDBURY, BTS	1774-1812	MAR	NONE	M 1712-8 **	990854
YORKS	ALMONDBURY, BTS	1813-1835	MAR	NONE	M 1712-6	
YORKS	ALMONDBURY, DEADMANSTONE WESLEYAN	1835-1837	CHR	* 0883999	C 7998-1	816617 (RG4 3028)
YORKS	ALMONDBURY, HOLMFIRTH LANE INDEPENDENT	SEE: HOLMFIRTH, LANE INDEPENDENT				
YORKS	ALMONDBURY, HOLMFIRTH WESLEYAN	SEE: HOLMFIRTH, WESLEYAN				
YORKS	ALMONDBURY, HOLY TRINITY BTS	1829-1846	CHR	NONE	C 7157-1	990857
YORKS	ALMONDBURY, HONLEY MOOR COTTOM INDEPENDENT	SEE: HONLEY, HONLEY MOOR COTTOM INDEPENDENT				
YORKS	ALMONDBURY, HONLEY WESLEYAN METHODIST	SEE: HONLEY, WESLEYAN METHODIST				
YORKS	ALMONDBURY, LINTHWAITE WESLEYAN METHODIST	SEE: LINTHWAITE, WESLEYAN METHODIST				
YORKS	ALMONDBURY, MELTHAM WESLEYAN	SEE: MELTHAM, WESLEYAN				
YORKS	ALMONDBURY, NETHERTHONG WESLEYAN	SEE: NETHERTHONG, WESLEYAN				
YORKS	ALMONDBURY, WESTGATE WESLEYAN	1812-1832	CHR	* 0883976	C 7576-1	816604 (RG4 3666)

* THE PRINTOUT IS ON MICROFILM ONLY ** RECORDS IN THIS BATCH AND PERIOD ARE NOT IN THE CURRENT IGI

Figure 15-12. International Genealogical Index, Parish and Vital Records Listing, Almondbury, Yorkshire, England, Nov. 1983; Genealogical Society of Utah.

No.	Place.	Denomination and Date of Foundation.	Number of Register Books Deposited, and Description of Entries therein.	What Period extending over.
	YORKSHIRE.			
1	Aberford - - - -	Catholic - - 1786	1. Births and Baptisms	1806—1838
2	Addingham - - - -	Independent - 1829	1. Births - -	1829—1836
	Aiskew (*see* 25).			
	Aldborough (*see* 102).			
3	Allerton, near Bradford - -	Independent - 1814	1. Births and Baptisms	1815—1837
3A*	——— - - - -	Wesleyan - -	1. Baptisms - -	1835—1857
4	——— Park, St. Mary's - -	Catholic - 1807	1. Births and Baptisms	1816—1840
5	*Almondbury, Broadlands Chapel* -	*Baptist* - - *1816*	1. *Births* - -	*1809—1837*
6	———, Westgate Chapel - -	Wesleyan - - 1817	1. Births and Baptisms	1812- 1837
7	———, Berry Brow, near Huddersfield, Salem Chapel.	Methodist New Connexion - - 1826	1. Births and Baptisms	1826—1837
	——— (*see* 77, 242, 259, 274).			

Figure 15-13. *List of Non-Parochial Registers. . .* (London: List and Index Society, 1969), p.79.

– 4 –

	PLACE	COUNTY	DENOMINATION	PERIOD	PLACE OF DEPOSIT
ALLESTREE		Derby	W. Meth.		
ALMONDBURY	Broadlands	Yorks.	Bapt	1809-1837	PRO
	Berry Brow	Yorks.	Meth. N. Conn.	1826 - 1837	PRO
	Westgate	Yorks.	W. Meth.	1812 - 1837	PRO
	Linthwaite Schools	Yorks.	Meth.	1822	
	Linthwaite	Yorks.	W. Meth.	1807 - 1837	PRO
	Deadmanstone	Yorks.	W. Meth.	1835 - 1837	PRO
	Honley	Yorks.	Ind.	1795 - 1837	PRO
	Honley	Yorks.	W. Meth.	1819 - 1837	PRO
	Netherthong	Yorks.	W. Meth.	1807 - 1837	PRO
ALMONDSBURY		Gloucs.	W. Meth.		

Figure 15-14. Genealogical Society of Utah Research Department, "List of Non-Conformist Chapels. . ." typescript, n.d., p.4; GS 962,176.

P 138 | P 138

REGION: CENTRAL EUROPEAN   COUNTRY: GERMANY   AS OF AUG 1981   PAGE [illegible]

NAME (SEX M MALE F FEMALE H HUSBAND W WIFE)	FATHER MOTHER OR SPOUSE	SEX	TYPE	EVENT DATE	COUNTY, TOWN, PARISH	B	E	S	SOURCE BATCH	SERIAL SHEET
HOFFMANN, HEINRICH JOHANN FRIEDRICH	JOHANN JOACHIM LUDWIG HOFFMANN/CHARLOTTE SOPHIA LANGE	M	C	17DEC1843	MECKLENBURG-SCHWERIN,RECKNITZ	28APR1971OK	21JUL1971OK	23JUL1971OK	7027819	62
HOFEMANN, HEINRICH JOHANN FRIEDRICH CRISTIAN	LUDWIG JOHANN HEINRICH HOFEMANN/CATHARINA MARIA SOPHIA FISCHER	M	C	18AUG1850	MECKLENBURG-SCHWERIN,SCHWERIN	INFANT	INFANT	19SEP1972LA	7022402	15
HOFFMANN, HEINRICH JOHANNES ALBERT	AUG. FRIEDRICH WILHELM HOFFMANN/MAGDALENA DOROTHEA ELISABETH WESTPHAL	M	C	10FEB1859	MECKLENBURG-SCHWERIN,WISMAR	31JAN1980SL	06MAY1980SL	19JUN1980SL	7928522	13
HOFMANN, HEINRICH WILHELM ELWIN	JOHANN FRIEDRICH WILHELM HOFMANN/ERNESTINE LOUISE PHILIPPINE HENRIETTE STIEL	M	B	14JUL1864	WALDECK,KORBACH	INFANT	INFANT	20JUN1973SL	7220803	76
HOFEMANN, HELENE SOPHIE WILHELMINE	CHRISTIAN JOHANN HEINRICH HOFEMANN/LOUISE SOPHIA JOHANNA KOEHLER	F	C	02MAY1851	MECKLENBURG-SCHWERIN,SCHWERIN	19MAR1971LA	23JUL1971LA	21SEP1972LA	7022402	27
HOFFMANN, HELLMUTH JOHANN LUDWIG	MARIA JOHANNE FRIEDERIKE CHRISTOFFERS	H	M	23APR1852	MECKLENBURG-SCHWERIN,GUESTROW			19JUL1972OK	7134658	96
HOFFMANN, HELMUTH JOHANN LUDWIG	DIETRICH HOFFMANN/CHARLOTTA WULFF	M	C	06AUG1816	MECKLENBURG-SCHWERIN,KRITZKOW	13APR1972OK	28APR1972OK	18JUL1972OK	7134658	84
HOFFMANN, HENRICH	DIETRICH HOFFMANN/DORTHE SCHREY	M	C	01OCT1679	LUBECK,RENSEFELD	19MAY1970	12JUN1970LG	22JUN1970LG	7929525	17
HOFFMANN, HENRICUS	CAROLI HOFFMANN/THERESIAE KAS	M	C	27APR1828	OLDENBURG,BUNDENBACH,KATHOLISCH	CLEARED	CLEARED	CLEARED	C980274	0516
HOFFMANN, HENRIETTE	JOHANN CARL CHRISTOPH SCHROEDER	W	M	14DEC1838	MECKLENBURG-SCHWERIN,GASEDOW			05DEC1975SF	7507709	46
HOFFMANN, HENRIETTE		F	B	21AUG1904	OLDENBURG,WESTERSTEDE	26JUN1975WA	29OCT1975WA	UNCLEARED	7460011	0
HOFFMAN, HENRY	THEODOR HOFFMAN/CAROLINE MARIA KRAMER	M	B	10AUG1905	BREMEN,BREMEN	07DEC1973OG	18JAN1974OG	PARENTS LVG	7308719	6
HOFFMANN, HERMANN EMIL	ANNA CATHARINA NIEBLING	H	M	06AUG1889	HAMBURG,HAMBURG			25MAR1976[illegible]	7500033	19
HOFFMANN, HERTHA		F	B	11JUN1898	OLDENBURG,JEVER	29JUL1975WA	15NOV1975WA	UNCLEARED	7460007	0
HOFFMANN, HEINRICH FRIEDRICH	CATHARINA MAGDALENE DREWS	H	M	28JUN1816	LUBECK,RENSEFELD			11APR1972OG	7117428	8
HOFFMANN, HINRICH FRIEDRICH HERMANN	HINRICH FRIEDRICH HOFFMANN/CATHARINA MAGDALENE DREWS	M	C	19MAR1824	OLDENBURG,RENSEFELD	24FEB1972AZ	07MAR1972AZ	15JUN1972AZ	7118022	6
HOFFMANN, HINRICH MATHIES	DIETRICH HOFFMANN/ELSABE FRANKE	M	C	25FEB1713	LUBECK,RENSEFELD	11JUL1972LG	18JAN1973LG	13MAR1973LG	7204810	3
HOFEMANN, ILSABE DOROTHEA	JOCHIM HINRICH HOFEMANN/	F	C	12MAY1745	MECKLENBURG-SCHWERIN,SCHWERIN	13MAR1971LA	22JUL1971LA	14SEP1972LA	7022401	19
HOFEMANN, ILSABE MAGDALENA	JOCHIM HINRICH HOFEMANN/	F	C	04JAN1752	MECKLENBURG-SCHWERIN,SCHWERIN	13MAR1971LA	22JUL1971LA	14SEP1972LA	7022401	19
HOFFMANN, JACOB	DIETRICH HOFFMANN/ELSABE FRANKE	M	C	21OCT1708	LUBECK,RENSEFELD	11JUL1972LG	18JAN1973LG	13MAR1973LG	7204810	2
HOFFMANN, JACOB CHRISTIAN	MARIA SOPHIA KOEPKE	H	M	19JUL1796	MECKLENBURG-SCHWERIN,KRAKOW			23SEP1976LG	7602211	74
HOFMANN, JACOB MATHIAS	MARIA CHRISTIANA TIMMEN	H	M	26OCT1797	MECKLENBURG-SCHWERIN,KARGOW			26APR1977OK	7620116	83
HOFFMANN, JAKOB	JOHANN CARL HOFFMANN/CHARLOTTE BURBES	M	C	26AUG1849	OLDENBURG,BIRKENFELD,EVANGELISCH	CLEARED	CLEARED	CLEARED	C994758	0089
HOFEMANN, JETTE WILHELMINE	AUGUST HEINRICH CHRISTOPH HOFEMANN/SOPHIA WILHELMINA MARIA MEIER	F	C	18SEP1859	MECKLENBURG-SCHWERIN,SCHWERIN	INFANT	INFANT	14SEP1972LA	7022401	1
HOFEMANN, JOACHIM FRIEDRICH	ULRICH CHRISTOPH HOFEMANN/	M	C	27AUG1749	MECKLENBURG-SCHWERIN,SCHWERIN	30APR1971LA	22SEP1971LA	19SEP1972LA	7022402	24
HOFEMANN, JOACHIM FRIEDRICH	VIECK DOROTHIE HOFEMANN	H	M	25NOV1774	MECKLENBURG-SCHWERIN,SCHWERIN			23NOV1971OK	7022426	72
HOFEMANN, JOACHIM FRIEDRICH	MAGDALENA MARIA DOROTHEA ADEL	H	M	18NOV1791	MECKLENBURG-SCHWERIN,SCHWERIN			23NOV1971OK	7022426	72
HOFFMANN, JOACHIM FRIEDRICH CHRISTOPH	JACOB MATHIAS HOFFMANN/MARIA CHRISTIANA TIMMEN	M	C	14MAR1800	MECKLENBURG-SCHWERIN,KARGOW	13FEB1976LA	26FEB1976LA	09MAR1976LA	7520308	23
HOFEMANN, JOACHIM JOHANN FRANZ	HANS JOACHIM DIEDRICH HOFEMANN/WILHELMINE HEDWIG FISCHER	M	C	13JUL1823	MECKLENBURG-SCHWERIN,SCHWERIN	26APR1971LA	17SEP1971LA	15SEP1972LA	7022401	33
HOFEMANN, JOACHIM JOHANN FRANZ	CATHARINA SOPHIA ELISABETH BRUHN	H	M	05APR1850	MECKLENBURG-SCHWERIN,SCHWERIN			24OCT1972HA	7023924	88
HOFFMANN, JOANNA FRIEDERICA	HENRICH HOFFMANN/ELISABETH VAHLING	F	C	07OCT1829	OLDENBURG,BAKUM,ROEMISCH-KATHOLISCHE	CLEARED	CLEARED	CLEARED	C990022	1310

Σ = EVALUATED ENTRY

A = ADULT CHRISTENING B = BIRTH C = CHRISTENING D = DEATH OR BURIAL F = BIRTH OR CHRISTENING OF FIRST KNOWN CHILD M = MARRIAGE N = CENSUS W = WILL ALL OTHERS = MISCELLANEOUS

Figure 15-15. International Genealogical Index. Hoffman surname, Central European, Germany; microfiche copy, Genealogical Society of Utah.

Yoder, Eleanor. "Nicknaming in an Amish-Mennonite Community." *Pennsylvania Folklife*, Spring 1974, pp. 30-37. Includes a list of personal and family names.

Immigration Lists Indexes

One of the most significant developments in genealogy in the past ten years is the publication of indexes to immigration lists. The largest project is P. William Filby with Mary K. Meyer *Passenger and Immigration Lists Index*, 6 vols. (Detroit: Gale Research Company, 1981-84), containing one million of the almost two million entries for the British Isles and Europe. (See Figure 15-18.) Another 750,000 are ready for print and Filby processes some 2,000 entries per week which come in from correspondents throughout the country.

This index is easy to scan. The surname and reference key are printed in bold type and overrun lines are indented enough that the eye moves easily down the page. Where maiden names are found in the source, the women are indexed under both married and maiden names. All names in each list are indexed. If a man has two or more given names then he is listed under each of his given names in the source. For example, Strassburger and Hinke in *Pennsylvania German Pioneers*, record Johannes Andreas Hoffman on three different lists. All three lists however, are indexed under *Johannes Andreas* only. Thus, if you are looking for Andrew Hoffman, you will find only two in the index, when there are actually three. Filby indexes him under both *Johannes* and *Andreas*, thus making him retrievable from the Strassburger and Hinke compilation as well.

Each immigrant is identified by name (spelled as it appeared in the source), age (if given), place of arrival, year of arrival, source code, and page number. All persons traveling together are listed with the head of household as a group and cross-referenced to all family members who immigrated together.

Passenger and Immigration Lists Index covers only lists in print. It does not include entries from the original passenger arrival records. As these materials are published however, they will be indexed in future volumes. The list of sources appears in two forms: short title with key and full bibliographic entry. It is easy to photocopy the short title list on four pages and keep it with your research notes.

Included in the series is P. William Filby, comp., *Passenger and Immigration Lists Bibliography, 1538-1900* (Detroit: Gale Research Company, 1981). This bibliography updates Harold Lancour's original *Bibliography of Passenger Lists* (New York: New York Public Library, 1937); revised and enlarged by Richard Wolfe (New York:

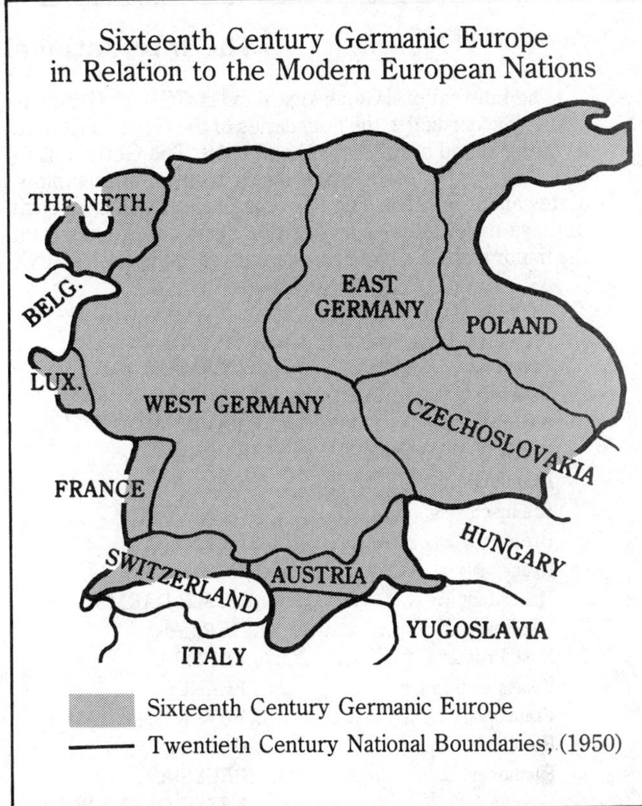

Map 15-5. Sixteenth-and Twentieth-Century Germany. Lee C. Hopple, "European Religious and Spatial Origins of the Pennsylvania Dutch," *Pennsylvania Folklife,* Autumn 1979, pp. 2-11.

New York Public Library, 1963), and expands it from 262 titles to more than 1,300. Each source indexed is cited in full with a descriptive annotation of contents, coverage, and related immigration lists. See Figure 15-19. If the sources have been reprinted, facts of publication for the reprint are given. This bibliography will continue to expand as Filby adds new sources to the index.

Of the original 262 lists described in Lancour's bibliography drawn from printed sources, 30 percent are emigrant lists recorded at the port of embarkation, 8 percent are passenger lists recorded at the port of arrival, 4 percent are ships, lists, and about 15 per cent are compiled works on settlers in specific localities drawn from church records, convict and pauper lists, naturalizations, customs lists, legal papers and petitions, county histories, oaths of allegiance, and other records. Filby's series of volumes continues this broad coverage.

Printed Immigration Sources

Several genealogists and publishing houses are at work to provide us with access to the sources indexed by P. William Filby. Table 15-6 summarizes this publishing effort.

Emigrant/Immigrant Computer Databases

A number of computer projects dealing with immigrants, mostly supported by public grants to universities, will enter the public domain when the project is completed. Inquiries can be addressed to the project directly in care of the sponsoring university or institution.

1. Don Yoder, retired folklife professor, University of Pennsylvania, and former editor of *Pennsylvania Folklife*, began a project to link Pennsylvania German emigrant lists with American church records and other local sources in Pennsylvania thus bridging the Atlantic. Under his editorship, *Pennsylvania Folklife* published several lists which he translated from the German. See Arlene H. Eakle, "Emigrant Sources for Tracing Pennsylvania German Ancestors," *APG Newsletter* 3 (May 1981): 8-13 for titles.

2. Dr. Richard Vann, Professor of History and Letters, Wesleyan University, has created a database of 35,000 English Quakers. Taken from alphabetized registers in the Public Record Office, his project includes data on Quakers who immigrated to the colonies before the American Revolution.

3. Ulf Beijbom, Director of the House of Emigrants, Vaxjo, Sweden, is linking over one million emigrants who left Sweden with those who settled in America, using church registers, passenger lists, and other sources on both sides of the Atlantic. Some of the materials are being published in ***Emigrantinstitutet, Svensk-Amerikansha Kyrkoarkiv Med Canada*** (Upsala: i foljande ordning, n.d.)

4. Temple University, National Immigration Archives, is using the Customs Passenger Lists of the United States, 1820-50, to study immigration in a variety of aspects. As it inputs data from the lists, it codes and makes the entries available for publication by Genealogical Publishing Company. See Table 15-6 above for titles currently available.

Reference sources for English ancestors which can be checked inexpensively and quickly are also available.

English Marriage Indexes

Even though most English marriage indexes are arranged by county rather than country-wide, a check in all can be made at the same time. (See Table 15-7.)

Women Friends Petition, 1659

An unusual source with great value is the Women Friends Petitioners against Tithes, 1659. This petition was submitted to "the Parliament of England, who are set in place to do justice, to take off oppression, and to stop the oppressors. We whose hands are hereunder writen do testifie and declare against the oppression of

The International Index for Germany

The International Genealogical Index (IGI) for Germany is set up according to the boundaries of the German Empire as they existed between 1871 and 1918. The German Empire consisted of seven major states plus numerous minor states and free cities. The IGI separates entries from each of these major states into separate sections. Entries from the minor states and free cities are listed in the GERMANY section. The eight sections of the IGI for Germany are: BADEN, BAVARIA, GERMANY, HESSEDARMSTADT, PRUSSIA, SAXONY, THURINGIA, and WUERTTEMBERG. In addition, entries from the former German area of Alsace-Lorraine are listed under FRANCE. FRANCE is found in series L: *Southern European*; all others in Series K: *Central European*.

German Territory	*IGI Section*
Alsace-Lorraine	FRANCE
Anhalt	GERMANY
Baden	BADEN
Bayern	BAVARIA
Berlin	PRUSSIA
Brandenburg	PRUSSIA
Braunschweig	GERMANY
Bremen	GERMANY
Brunswick	GERMANY
Darmstadt	HESSE-DARMSTADT
Detmold	GERMANY
East Prussia	PRUSSIA
Elsass-Lothringen	FRANCE
Franconia	BAVARIA
Hamburg	GERMANY
Hannover	PRUSSIA
Hessen	HESSE-DARMSTADT or PRUSSIA
Hessen-Kassel	PRUSSIA
Hessen Nassau	PRUSSIA
Hohenzollern	PRUSSIA
Holstein	PRUSSIA
Lippe	GERMANY
Luebeck	GERMANY
Mecklenburg-Schwerin	GERMANY
Mecklenburg-Strelitz	GERMANY
Nassau	PRUSSIA
Niedersachsen	PRUSSIA or GERMANY
Oldenburg	GERMANY
Ostfriesland	PRUSSIA
Ostpreussen	PRUSSIA
Palatinate	BAVARIA or PRUSSIA
Pfalz	BAVARIA or PRUSSIA
Poland	POLAND or PRUSSIA or USSR
Pomerania	PRUSSIA
Pommern	PRUSSIA
Posen	PRUSSIA
Preussen	PRUSSIA
Rheinland	PRUSSIA
Saarland	PRUSSIA
Sachsen	SAXONY or PRUSSIA
Saxony	SAXONY or PRUSSIA
Schaumburg-Lippe	GERMANY
Schlesien	PRUSSIA
Schlëswig-Holstein	PRUSSIA or DENMARK
Schwarzburg	THURINGIA
Silesia	PRUSSIA
Swabia	BAVARIA or WUERTTEMBERG
Thueringen	THURINGIA
Waldeck	GERMANY
Westfalen	PRUSSIA
Westphalia	PRUSSIA
Westpreussen	PRUSSIA
Wuerttemberg	WUERTTEMBERG

Figure 15-16. Genealogical Society of Utah Library, Sept. 1981. Copyright 1981 by Corporation of the President of the Church of Jesus Christ of Latter-day Saints. Used with permission.

Tithes, and against the injustice of them, which hath set up by the commands and laws of men were they set up since the Apostles where by many have been prisoned till death for not paying of them &c &c . . . ."

The petition was signed by almost 7,000 women throughout England who were members of the Society of Friends in 1659. Gilbert Cope, an American Quaker genealogist, prepared an alphabetical digest of these women with page references. (See Figure 15-20.) The original list is arranged by county of residence.

1851 Census, England

A glance at a migrational map for England shows that the bulk of movement about 1851 was to London and its environs. Migration into other cities was also taking place at the same time. This makes the 1851 census especially critical, for it lists the parish of birth. Unlike American census indexes compiled for rural areas long before cities were indexed, British indexes for 1851 begin with major cities like London, Norwich, Liverpool, and Sheffield. The first volumes are now available from local family history societies and interested genealogists. Unlike costly American indexes, the English volumes are inexpensive typescripts.

Projects are listed as they are completed in *Family History News and Digest,* the bulletin of the Federation of Family History Societies, available in many American libraries or by subscription from Mrs. Ann Chiswell, Secretary, 96 Beaumont Street, Milehouse, Plymouth, Devon PL2 3AQ, $4 by surface mail. A list of member societies is available on request. For Liverpool, contact Lyman DePlatt, RR2 Box 216, American Fork, UT 84003.

German Records

A large body of the essential source material you need to identify your ancestor in Germany is available in the United States in print and microfilm. You do not need to hire a research agent in Germany or correspond with record officials until you have exhausted these sources here. You can search most of them yourself by buying your own copies, using copies from public and university

ENGLISH	BULGARIAN	FRENCH	GERMAN	GREEK	HUNGARIAN	ITALIAN	LITHUANIAN	NORWEGIAN	POLISH	RUMANIAN	RUSSIAN	SERB and CROATIAN	SWEDISH	UKRANIAN	YIDDISH	SPANISH
JOACHIM			JOACHIM	IOAKEM, IOAKIEM,		GIOACCHINO	JOAKIMAS	JOAKIM		IOAKIM	IOAKIM		JOAKIM			
JOB				JOB		GIOBBE					JOV					
JOCUNDAS						GIOCONDO										
JOHN	JOAN	JEAN	JOHANNES	JOANNES JOANNIS	JANOS	GIOVANNI JIOVANNI	JONAS	JOHAN, JENS	JAN, IWAN IGNAC	IOAN	IVAN	IVAN	JONAM, JENS	IVAN	YOCHANAN	JUAN · JOAO
JACK JOHAN JOHNNIE JOHNNY ZANE		JEANNOT JEHAN	HANS JOHANN	GIANNES		GIAN			JANEK		VANIA JOVAN					JOAO JUANITO
JONAH JONAS			JONAS			GIUSEPPE									JONAH	JONAS
JOSEPH	JOSIF	JOSEPHE	JOSEF	JOSIF	JOZSEF, JOSZEF	GIUSEPPE, GUISEPPE	JUOZAPAS	JOSEF	JUZEF, JOZEF	IOSIF, YOUSEF	IOSIF	JOSEP	JOSEF	OSIP, OSYP	JOSEF, YOUSEF	JOSE
JOSEPHINE JOSEPHA JOSEPHINA		JOSEPHE FINETTE	JOSEPHA	JOSEPHINI JOSEFINA	JOZEFA	GIUSEPPINA GUISEPPINA GIUSSEPPINA	JUOZAPINA	JOSEFIN	JOZEFA	IOSEFINA		JOSEFINA	JOSEFINA			JOSEFA
JOSHUA JOSH		JOSUE	JOSUA			GIOSUE									YEHOSHA	
JOSIAH JOSIAS		JOSIAS			JOZSUE	GIOSIA										
JUDAH JUDA JUDE			JUDAH	IOUDAS		GIUDA	JUDAS	JUDAS		IUDAN			JUDAS		YEHUDI	
JUDITH		JUDITHE	JUDITH	IOUDITH	JUDIT	GIUDITTA	JUDITA	JUDIT				JUDITA	JUDIT		HUDES	
JULIA		JULIANE JULIETTE JULIE	JULIE	IOULIA	JULISKA	GIULIA	JULIJA	JULIA	JULIA	IULIA	IULIA	JULIANA	JULIA	YULIA		JULIETTA
JULIAN JULE		JULIEN JULIE	JULIANUS JULIAN			GIULIANO										JULIAN
JULIET		JULIETTE			JULCSA	GIULIETTA										
JULIUS		JULES JULOT	JULIUS	IOULIOS	GYULA	GIULIO	JULIJUS	JULIUS	JULIUSZ	JULIU		JULIO	JULIUS			
JUST JUSTIN		JUSTIN	JUSTIN			GIUSTINO			JUSTYN							JUSTINO
KATE KATHERINE KATINKA		CATANT CATHERINE	KAETHE KATHERINE KATINKA	KATINA EKATERINE KATINKA	KATALIN KATARINA	CATERINA	KOTRYNA KOTRYNA	KATLA KATHERINE	KASIA KATARZYNA	ECATERINA ECATERINA	KATIA EKATERINA	KATA KATICA KATICA	KAISA KATRINA	KATERYNA		CATALINA
KELLIOPI				CALIPSO KALIPSO CALIOPE KALIOPE												
KENNETH								KNUT			INNOKENTY		KNUT			
LACHLAN																

Figure 15-17. Foreign Versions of English Names (Washington, D.C.: U.S. Government Printing Office, 1962).

Figure 15-18. Sample sheet from P. William Filby, *Passenger and Immigration Lists.* Reproduced from promotional brochure issued by Gale Research Company, 1982.

Name of passenger

Specific source containing arrival record (and possible additional information). No need for endless and perhaps fruitless search through many different books, magazines, and manuscripts.

Date of arrival

Port of arrival

Accompanying dependents or relatives

Ages

Special Feature: "See" references guides users to family entries.

PASSENGER AND IMMIGRATION LISTS INDEX

Blume, Johanne Schramm n.a. *SEE* Blume, Hein
Blumenhart, Martin 24; Charles Town, S.C., 1764 ***3751*** *p37*
Blumenthal, Dr. n.a.; Texas, 1845 ***1481*** *p82*
Blumentskin, Maria 16; Charles Town, S.C., 1764 ***3751*** *p38*
Blumerstock, Andrew 8; Charles Town, S.C., 1764 ***3751*** *p40*
Blundell, Catherine 18; Charles Town, S.C., 1766 ***3751*** *p58*
Blundell, Charles 21; Maryland, 1774 ***1271*** *p69*
Blundell, Charles 29; Maryland, 1775 ***1271*** *p148*
Wife: Mary 29
Blundell, George n.a.; America, 1753 ***691*** *p27*
Blundell, Mary 29 *SEE* Blundell, Charles
Blunderfield, Thomas n.a.; America, 1697 ***691*** *p27*
Blundy, Charles n.a.; America, 1771 ***691*** *p27*
Blunt, Charles n.a.; Barbados, 1668 ***691*** *p27*
Blunt, Hannah 10; New York, N.Y., 1820 ***4761*** *p12*
Blunt, Isaac n.a.; Barbados, 1694 ***691*** *p27*
Blunt, James n.a.; America, 1756 ***691*** *p27*
Blunt, Jane n.a ; America, 1772 ***691*** *p27*
Blunt, John n.a.; Maryland and/or Virginia, 1718 ***691*** *p27*
Blunt, Joseph 40; New York, N.Y., 1820 ***4761*** *p12*
Blunt, Mary 10; New York, N.Y., 1820 ***4761*** *p12*
Blunt, Melliant 11; New York, N.Y., 1820 ***4761*** *p12*
Blunt, Phoebe 13; New York, N.Y., 1820 ***4761*** *p12*
Blunt, Richard n.a.; Maryland, 1737 ***691*** *p27*
Blunt, Samuel 12; New York, N.Y., 1820 ***4761*** *p12*
Blunt, Sarah 40; New York, N.Y., 1820 ***4761*** *p12*
Blunt, Sarah, Jr. 19; New York, N.Y., 1820 ***4761*** *p12*
Blunt, William 15; New York, N.Y., 1820 ***4761*** *p12*
Bluthard, Gottfried n.a.; Texas, 1846 ***1481*** *p82*
With family
Bluyman, Hannah n.a.; Maryland, 1739 ***691*** *p27*
Bly, Elizabeth 21; Virginia, 1774–1775 ***1271*** *p117*
Bly, Manuel Giano 21; Charleston, S.C., 1820 ***4761*** *p29*
Bly, Mr. n.a.; Boston, Mass., 1765 ***5001*** *p40*
Blynn, Nath n.a.; Boston, Mass., 1769 ***5001*** *p88*
Blyth, John 32; Carolina, 1774 ***1271*** *p110*
Blyth, Sarah 30; Jamaica, 1774 ***1271*** *p21*
Blyth, Thomas n.a.; America, 1699 ***691*** *p27*
Blythe, Ann 12; Boston and/or Charlestown, Mass., 1820 ***4761*** *p149*
Blythe, George 14; Boston and/or Charlestown, Mass., 1820 ***4761*** *p149*
Blythe, Jno 6 wks; Boston and/or Charl[estown, Mass.,] 1820 ***4761*** *p149*
Blythe, Margaret 2; Boston and/or Cha[rlestown,] Mass., 1820 ***4761*** *p149*
Blythe, Margaret 38; Boston and/or Cha[rlestown,] Mass., 1820 ***4761*** *p149*
Blythe, Samuel 9; Boston and/or Charle[stown, Mass.,] 1820 ***4761*** *p149*
Blythe, Samuel 37; Boston and/or Charlestown, Mass., 1820 ***4761*** *p149*
Blythe, Sarah n.a.; America, 1772 ***691*** *p27*
Boado, J Sanchez 25; New York, N.Y., 1820 ***4761*** *p101*
Boami, Thos n.a.; Boston, Mass., 1716 ***5001*** *p17*
Boandner, Wm 40; New York, N.Y., 1820 ***4761*** *p108*
Board, John 36; Virginia, 1774 ***1271*** *p92*
Boardman, J 23; Baltimore, Md., 1820 ***4761*** *p85*
Boardman, Jerry 8; Boston, Mass., 1848 ***2881*** *p8*
Boardman, Jerry 60; Boston, Mass., 1848 ***2881*** *p8*
Boardnave, Wm 40; New York, N.Y., 1820 ***4761*** *p13*
Boardrey, Paul n.a.; Maryland and/or Virginia, 1728 ***691*** *p27*
Boardsey, Paul n.a.; Maryland and/or Virginia, 1728 ***691*** *p27*
Boarey, John 22; Texas, 1902 ***306*** *p3*

Bodame, Salvatore 21; Texas, 1898 ***306*** *p3*
Bodazean, Colas n.a.; Charles Town, S.C., 1763–1764 ***3751*** *p21*
Bodden, Samuel n.a.; America, 1774 ***691*** *p28*
Boddin, Ann Mary n.a.; Pennsylvania, 1773 ***3701*** *p320*
Boddington, Martha n.a.; Barbados, 1669 ***691*** *p28*
Boddon, James n.a.; Richmond, Va., 1820 ***4761*** *p83*
Boddon, Z n.a.; Richmond, Va., 1820 ***4761*** *p83*
Bode, Christina n.a. *SEE* Bode, Hein
Bode, Conrad n.a. *SEE* Bode, Hein
Bode, Conrad 18; Texas, 1845 ***1481*** *p82*
Bode, Elisa Armgard n.a. *SEE* Bode, Hein
Bode, Ferdinand n.a. *SEE* Bode, Hein
Bode, Friedr 25; Texas, 1845 ***1481*** *p82*
Bode, Hein n.a.; Texas, 1845 ***1481*** *p82*
Wife: Elisa Armgard n.a.
Child: Conrad n.a.
Child: Christina n.a.
Child: Ferdinand n.a.
Bode, Joh Hein Christoph n.a ; Texas, 1846 ***1481*** *p82*
Bodemann, Gustav 27; Texas, 1846 ***1481*** *p82*
Bodemann, Robert 27; Texas, 1846 ***1481*** *p82*
Bodemeyer, Dorothea n.a.; Texas, 1846 ***1481*** *p82*
Boden, James n.a.; Charles Town, S.C., 1767–1768 ***3751*** *p103*
Boden, James 50; Charles Town, S.C., 1767–1768 ***3751*** *p105*
Boden, Jane 36; Charles Town, S.C., 1767–1768 ***3751*** *p105*
Boden, John, Jr. n.a.; Pennsylvania, 1772 ***3701*** *p98*
Boden, Margaret n.a.; Charles Town, S.C., 1767–1768 ***3751*** *p103*
Boden, Margaret 18; Charles Town, S.C., 1767–1768 ***3751*** *p105*
Boden, Sarah 2; Charles Town, S.C., 1767–1768 ***3751*** *p105*
Bodenstedt, Fritz n.a.; Texas, 1845 ***1481*** *p82*
Bodeymyer, Daniel n.a.; America, 1747 ***691*** *p28*
Bodger, Thomas n.a.; America, 1764 ***691*** *p28*
Bodie, Johann n.a.; Texas, 1846 ***1481*** *p82*
Bodie, Mr. n.a.; Boston, Mass., 1768 ***5001*** *p84*
Bodieu, Francis Rudolph n.a.; Maryland, 1666–1750 ***4026*** *p11*
Bodle, John 18; Charles Town, S.C., 1766 ***3751*** *p57*
Bodle, Samuel 15; Charles Town, S.C., 1766 ***3751*** *p57*
Bodmer, F n.a.; Texas, 1845 ***1481*** *p82*
Boe, Ellen 16; Boston, Mass., 1849 ***2881*** *p7*

Boehringer, Christian 37; Texas, 1845 ***1481*** *p82*
Wife: Christine R 33
With boy
Child: Elis 9
Child: Jane 5
Child: Justina 3

Boeckel, E Asmus 22; Texas, 1844 ***1481*** *p82*
Boeckel, Erasmus 22; Texas, 1844 ***1481*** *p82*
Boecker, Christine Dannsmann 45 *SEE* Boecker, Fried
Boecker, Fried 28; Texas, 1845 ***1481*** *p79*
Wife: Christine Dannsmann 45
Child: Johanna 2
Boecker, Johanna 2 *SEE* Boecker, Fried
Boeddeker, Angela Roth n.a. *SEE* Boeddeker, Anton
Boeddeker, Anton n.a.; Texas, 1846 ***1481*** *p82*
Wife: Angela Roth n.a.
Boedecker, Carl n.a.; Texas, 1846 ***1481*** *p82*
Son: Louis n.a.
Son: Theo n.a.
Boedecker, Louis n.a. *SEE* Boedecker, Carl
Boedecker, Theo n.a. *SEE* Boedecker, Carl
Boehl, Christoph 24; Texas, 1846 ***1481*** *p82*
Boehl, Georg 21; Texas, 1846 ***1481*** *p82*

Boettcher, Aug n.a.; Texa
Boettcher, August 27; Te
Boettcher, Johannes n.a.;
Wife: Anna Rose n.a.
Bogaert, Theunis Gysberts 1687 ***3306*** *p659*
Bogan, Ann 20; Boston, M
Boger, Henry Conrad n.a. *p220*
Boger, Henry Conrad n.a. *p236*
Bogg, Daniel n.a.; Americ
Bogg, Daniel n.a.; Americ
Boggin, J 18; New York,
Boggs, Elizabeth 10; Char ***3751*** *p69*
Boggs, Elizabeth 33; Char ***3751*** *p69*
Boggs, Robert n.a.; Charl ***3751*** *p67*
Boggs, Samuel n.a.; Charl ***3751*** *p68*
Boggs, Thomas n.a.; Char *p122*
Boggust, John n.a.; Massa
Bogle, Robt 50; Grenada,
Bogue, Bernard 50; Bosto
Bogue, Eliza 5; Boston, M
Bogue, Jane 9; Boston, M
Bogue, John 7; Boston, M
Bogue, Rose 45; Boston, M
Bogue, William 27; Philad
Bohannan, James n.a.; Am
Bohannan, John 30; Philad
Boheme, A 32; Baltimore,
Bohilly, John n.a.; Pennsy
Bohls, Heinrich n.a.; Texa
With wife & 3 children
Bohme, Fried 25; Texas, 1
Bohmer, G 32; Baltimore,
Bohmerth, Bernard 34; Te
With wife & sister & mo
With 2 children
Bohn, Elizabeth n.a.; Penn
Bohn, Philip n.a.; Pennsyl
Bohrmann, Fr n.a.; Texas,
Boice, Sarah n.a.; Virginia
Boies, William n.a.; Penns
Boill, John 22; Barbados,
Bois, Thomas 26; Boston,
Boisbilland, John n.a.; Ne *p661*
Bokermann, Hein n.a.; Te
With wife
Bokus, Carl n.a.; Texas, 1
Bolaender, Andreas n.a.; T
Boland, L 25; Baltimore, M
Boland, M 30; Boston and 1820 ***4761*** *p221*
Boland, Sally 24; Philadel
Bolde, F W n.a.; Texas, 1
Boldrick, S J 38; Texas, 1
Boldt, Wilh n.a.; Texas, 1
Boles, Jane 21; Boston, M
Bolgiano, Wm G 20; Balti
Bolgians, Wm 21; Norfolk
Boliarga, J B M 32; New
Bolingbroke, Mary n.a.; M
Bollard, George 21; Virgin
Bollard, Wilhelmina n.a.; *p134*
Bollis, Henry n.a.; Americ
Bollon, Hugh 24; Philadel

Figure 15-19. Sample sheets from P. William Filby, *Passenger and Immigration Lists Bibliography, 1538-1900* (Detroit: Gale Research Company, 1981). A second volume to be published in April, 1984, will add 600 more lists to the total.

Page 149 **Passenger and Immigration Lists Bibliography** **In**

Australia, Germans to
1800s 1858
1825-1846 5085
1835-1854 3474
1847-1886 4460
1850-1903 ..3914
Hamburg ships
1850 ....
Poles (Old Luth
1835-1854 ...
Wends to, 19th
Austria, Salzburg
1734-1739 .....
Austrians
arrivals, 1850-1
from Guessing,
from Imperial C
1843-1877 ...
to Georgia, 173
to Texas, 1858-

B

Bacon, Anthony,
1740 ....
Baden, Duchy of,
Germans from,
Germans from,
Germans from
Baden-Durlach, G
1710-1815 ....
1738 ....
1749 ....
1749-1751 ....
1749-1755 ....
1751 ....
1752 ....
1753 ....
Baden-Wuerttemb
1727-1775 ....
18th, 19th c ...
Baltimore
arrivals
from Bremen
from the Neth
Central and Eas
Dutch to, 1847
Germans to, fro
Germans to, fro
1873-1876 ..

Baltimore County, Md., servants to,
1772-1774 1
Baptismal records, French in "New France," 1621-1700 6
Baptist Herald, obituaries of Germans from Russia, 1800s to 1950s 6

2765-2768 **Passenger and Immigration Lists Bibliography**

2765-2768
GREAT REGISTER, TULARE CO. [CALIFORNIA], 1888, NATURALIZATION DATA. In *Sequoia Genealogical Society Newsletter.*
2765
---Vol. 1:1 (Jan. 1975), p. 4; vol. 1:2 (Feb. 1975), p. 3; vol. 1:3 (Mar. 1975), p. 4; vol. 1:4 (Apr. 1975), p. 4; vol. 1:5 (May 1975), p. 4.
2766
---Vol. 2:1 (Sept. 1975), p. 3; vol. 2:2 (Oct. 1975), p. 4; vol. 2:3 (Nov. 1975), p. 4 vol. 2:4 (Jan. 1976), p. 4; vol. 2:5 (Feb. 1976), p. 4; vol. 2:6 (Mar. 1976), p. 4; vol. 2:7 (Apr. 1976), p. 4; v
2767
---Vol. 3:1 (S
3:3 (Nov. 197
(Feb. 1977),
1977), p. 4; v
2768
---Vol. 4:1 (S
vol. 4:4 (Jan.
vol. 4:6 (Mar
vol. 4:8 (May

From vol.
of Tulare C
of arrival
tries. Cove
the years
1890. Thi
1978 issue

2772
GREER, G
grants, 1623-
Co., 1912, 37
Co., Baltimo

Includes 2
Office. Ex
published

2802
GRUCHALLA, ROBER
der Personen, welche mit
nach Quebec zur Auswan
engagirt sind." In *Bism*
Genealogical Society [*Ne*
pp. 8-24.

A list of persons emigrat
Hamburg to Quebec, 186
in Minnesota, and their d
area of North Dakota. F

Page 57 **Passenger and Immigration**

2960
HAYNES, EMMA SCHWABENLAND. "Arrival Dates in New York of Steamships Given in *Work Papers* 9 Through 14." In *Journal of the American Historical Society of Germans from Russia*, vol. 3:1 (Spring 1980), pp. 60-61.

Gives date of departure from Hamburg and date of arrival in New York between 1873 and 1878 of the ships mentioned in *Work Papers* 9 through 14, all by Gwen Pritzkau, nos. 6920-6925. Included in this article are a few names omitted from the lists in *Work Papers* 9 through 14.

• • •

2966
HAYNES, EMMA S. "Passenger Lists." In *Journal of the American Historical Society of Germans from Russia*, vol. 1:1 (Spring 1978), pp. 76-78.

Names 400 German passengers, most from Bremen to New York, 1875-1876, and one to Baltimore, 1875.

• • •

2969

Figure 15-20. Gilbert Cope, "Alphabetical Digest of the Names of over Seven Thousand Women Who Petitioned Against Tithes, 1659," typescript; Cope Collection, Pennsylvania Historical Society; GS 441,488, item 3.

A L P H A B E T I C A L   D I G E S T

Of the Names of over Seven Thousand Women
Who Petitioned against Tithes

1 6 5 9.

ABBAT,
Elizabeth, 50 p
ABBOT,
Elizabeth 31 h
Sarah 53 q
ABERE,
Anne 61 t
ABERY,
Alice 62 t
ABEY,
Jone 48 o
ABLY,
Anne 28 f
ABRA,
Jane 61 t

ADDAMS
Elizabeth 44 m
Frances 44 m
Mary 67 v
ADDANS
Mary 44 m
ADDISON
Rebeccha 26 f
ADISON
Elizabeth 9 b
ADKINS
Susan 57 r
ADKINSON
Jenet 9 b
ADLAM

ALBRIGHT
Eliz. 60 s
Jane 60 s
ALCOCK
Anne 31 i
Comfort 13 c
Dorothy 60 s
Elenor 49 o
Ellen 24 e
Mary 31 i
Patience 13 c
ALCOCKE
Eliz. 48 o
Hannah 48 o
ALCOP

ALESOP
Hester 53 q
ALEXANDER
Dorothy 23 e
Sarah 56 r
ALFIELD
Sarah 40 l
ALFORD
Elizabeth 47 o
Rachel 56 r
ALICE
Anne 55 r
ALLASON
Agness 16 d
Elizabeth 18 d

Table 15-6

Printed Immigration Sources

Author	*Dates*	*Titles, Publishers*	*Comments*	*Indexed by Filby/ Meyer*
Carl Boyer, III	1538-1825	*Ship Passenger Lists*, 4 vols. 1977-80: *National and New England, 1600-1825, New York and New Jersey, 1600-1825; Pennsylvania and Delaware, 1641-1825; The South 1538-1825*. Available from Carl Boyer, Box 333, Newhall, CA 91322.	Includes annotated entry for lists in print; reproduction of lists for those out of print or published in foreign periodicals. Foreign articles are untranslated and less useful than the translated versions in *Pennsylvania Folklife*.	Yes
Peter W. Coldham	1615-1775	*Bonded Passengers to America*, 9 vols. in 3 (1981-83); Available from Genealogical Publishing Company, 1001 N. Calvert, Baltimore, MD 21202.	Comprehensive list of 50,000 indentured servants from England including an excellent introduction describing the indenture system. Comprehensive list from Middlesex sessions rolls and gaol delivery reports; Newgate prison pardons, transportation bonds, landing certificates; and sentence books for Corporation of London.	No*
David Dobson	1650-1775	*Directory of Scots Banished to the American Plantations, 1650-1775* (1983): available from Genealogical Publishing Company, 1001 N. Calvert, Baltimore, MD 21202.	Compiled from court cases, prison records, local and family sources. 3,000 Scots.	No*
Genealogical Publishing Company	1846-51	*The Famine Immigrants Series: Lists of Irish Immigrants Arriving at the Port of New York* (1982-84): vol. 1 (Jan. 1846-June 1847); vol. 2 (July 1847-Dec. 1848); vol. 3 (July 1848-March 1849).	Series will include 5-6 vols. Compiled under supervision of Temple University's National Immigration Archives from U.S. passenger arrival records.	No*
Werner Hacker		**Auswander Series**, 8 vols.: *Auswanderunger aus dem fruheren Hochstift Speyer nach Sudosteuropa und Ubersee im XVIII. Jahrhundert. Schriften zur Wanderungsgeschichte der Pfalzer.* Catholic emigrants from Speyer territory, most to Hungary, 400 to Cayenne in the 1760s. *Auswanderungen aus Baden und dem Breisgau.* Stuttgart und Aalen: Konrad Theiss Verlag, 1980. 743 pp. 11,544 emigration cases, many of them to America. *Auswanderungen aus dem Sudostlichen Schwarzwald zwischen Hochrhein, Baar und Kinzig.* Munchen: Buchreihe der sudostdeutschen historischen Kommission 29, 1975. Covers Catholic areas of southeast Black Forest. *Auswanderer vom Oberen Neckar nach Sudosteuropa.* Munchen: Buchreihe der sudostdeutschen historischen Komission 23, 1970. Mostly Catholic territories along upper Neckar River. *Auswanderungen aus dem nordlichen Bodensee im 17. und 18. Jhdt.* Hegau-Bibliothek bd. 29. Singen: Hegau-Geschichtsverein, 1975. 400 pp. Catholic territories north and west of Lake Constance.	120,000 emigrants, mostly Catholics, from Southwestern Germany. Compiled from manumissions, debt clearances, protocols, emigration registers.	No*

*Printed lists not yet indexed by Filby/Meyer will be indexed in future volumes.

(continued)

Author	Dates	Titles, Publishers	Comments	Indexed by Filby/ Meyer
		"Auswanderungen aus dem Raum der spateren Hohenzollerischen Lande nach Sudosteuropa im 17. und 18. Jahrhundert." *Zeitschrift fur Hohenzollerische Geschichte* 5 (1969): 45-230. Catholic territories which later became Hohenzollern. *Auswanderungen aus Oberschwaben.* Stuttgart und Aalen: Konrad Theiss Verlag, 1977. 799 pp. Area between Lake Constance and Danube River, mostly Catholic emigrants. "Auswanderer aus dem Territorium der Reichsstadt Ulm, vot allem im ausgehenden 17. und 18. Jahrhundert." *Ulm und Oberschwaben* 42/43 (1978): 161-257. Contains 813 emigration cases from the territory of Ulm City, about a third of them to America. Many of these joined the Salzburgers and went with them to Georgia. Available from Naturwiss und Histor. Verein, Willi-Hofmann-Strasse Z, 4930 Detmold, West Germany.		
Henry Z. (Hank) Jones, Jr.	1709-76	"Palatine Families of New York," unpublished. Contact Jones, Box 8341, Universal City, CA 91608	Three-generation, genealogical study of the 1709-era immigrants and their descendants to 1776, some 14,000 family groups, an ancestral study of the 800 original families who emigrated from the Palatine. Project described in "The Palatine Families of New York: A Comprehensive Study," *Genealogical Journal* 5 (1976): 126-28 with selected family names under study.	No*
Olga K. Miller		*Emigration, Immigration, Migration: Principally of the United States, and in the United States.* 2 vols. Available from Everton Publishers, Inc., Box 368, Logan, UT 84321.	Bibliography of immigration materials country by country. Includes Genealogical Society of Utah call numbers.	Part*
Sylvia Lee Nimmo	1849-68	*Passenger Lists: Transcriptions from National Archives Copies Made by Michael Cassady* (Omaha, Neb.: For the author, 1983). Available from Nimmo, 6201 Kentucky Road, Route 21, Papillion, NE 68133.	Contains 15,000 names for port of New York.	No*
Clifford Neal Smith	1700-1900	**German-American Genealogical Research Series:** *Brunswick Deserter-Immigrants of the American Revolution* (1973); *Mercenaries from Ansbach and Bayreuth, Germany, Who Remained in America after the Revolution,* rev. ed. (1979); *Muster Rolls and Prisoner-of-War Lists in American Archival Collections Pertaining to the German Mercenary Troops Who Served with the British Forces during the American Revolution,* three parts separately bound (1974, 1976); *Emigrants from Saxony (Grandduchy of Sachsen-Weimar-Eisenach) to America, 1854, 1859.* (1974; reprint ed, 1980); *Mercenaries from Hessen-Hanau Who*	Monographs are based upon original manuscripts in the Hamburg and Marburg state archives, the Public Records Office in London, and local communal files in eastern and western Germany and Poland. The manuscripts have been abstracted, translated into English, annotated, and fully indexed.	Part*

Author	*Dates*	*Titles, Publishers*	*Comments*	
		Remained in Canada and the United States after the American Revolution (1976); *Emigrants from the Principality of Hessen-Hanau, Germany, 1741-1767* (1979); *Nineteenth-Century Emigration of "Old Lutherans" from Easten Germany (mainly Pmerania and Lowe Silesia) to Australia, Canada, and the United States (1979); Nineteenth-Century Emigration from Kreis Simmern (Hunsruecck), Rheinland-Pfalz, Germany, to Brazil, England, Russian Poland, and the United States of America* (1980); *Nineteenth-Century Emigration from the Siegkreis, Nordrhein-Westfalen, Germany, Mainly to the United States* (1980); and *Immigrants to America and Central Europe from Beihingen am Neckar, Baden-Wuerttemberg, Germany, 1727-1934 (1980).* **German and Central European Emigration Series:** *Reconstructed Passenger Lists for 1850; Hamburg to Australia, Brazil, Canada, Chile, and the United States,* in three parts bound separately; part 3 contains supplementary notes on the emigrants' places of origin or birth covering all three parts (1980). **British-American Genealogical Research Series:** *British Deportees to America, Part 1: 1760-1763* (1974, reprint ed. 1980); *British Deportees to America, Part 2: 1764-1765* (1979); *Part 3: British Deportees to America, 1765-75* (1982). Available from Westland Publications, Box 117, McNeal, AZ 85617.		
Clifford Neal Smith and Anna P. Smith		*American Genealogical Resources in German Archives (AGRIGA): A Handbook* (1977). *Encyclopedia of German-American Genealogical Research* (1976). Available from R.R. Bowker and Co., 1180 Avenue of the Americas, New York, NY.	Emigration lists, court records, and other documents arranged alphabetically by village and individuals. Includes a bibliography of published emigration lists printed in German (English titles in brackets). It also has an excellent section on German surnames and how Americanization has changed them. These two volumes are indispensible for anyone tracing a German ancestor.	Part*
Robert P. Swierenga	1820-1880	*Dutch Immigrants in United States Ship Passenger Manifests, 1820-1880: An Alphabetical Listing by Household Heads and Independent Persons,* 2 vols. (Wilmington, Del.: Scholarly Resources, 1983). *Dutch Emigrants to the U.S., South Africa, South America, and Southeast Asia, 1835-1800: An Alphabetical Listing by Household Heads and Independent Persons* (Wilmington, Del.: Scholarly Resources, 1983).	55,000 names. Also available in typescript at the Genealogical Society of Utah, GS 973/w25w. 21,800 names	No*

(continued)

Author	Dates	Titles, Publishers	Comments	Indexed by Filby/ Meyer
Michael H. Tepper	1820-50	*Customs Passenger Lists Series; Passenger Arrivals at the Port of Baltimore, 1820-1834* (1983). Available from Genealogical Publishing Company, 1001, N. Calvert, Baltimore, MD 21202.	Compiled from the copies, abstracts and originals at Temple University. Future volumes will cover New York, Philadelphia, Boston, and New Orleans. Each volume will list about 50,000 immigrants with every-name indexes.	No*
		Immigration Lists, 5 vols. 1975-79: Emigrants to Pennsylvania *(Pennsylvania Magazine of History and Biography);* Passenger Lists (*New York Genealogical and Biographical Record);* Passengers to America *(New England Historical and Genealogical Register);* New World Immigrants (various periodicals), 2 vols. Available from Genealogical Publishing Company, 1001 N. Calvert, Baltimore, MD 21202.	Facsimile reprints of articles in major historical and genealogical journals. Some overlap with Boyer; includes many not in Boyer.	Yes

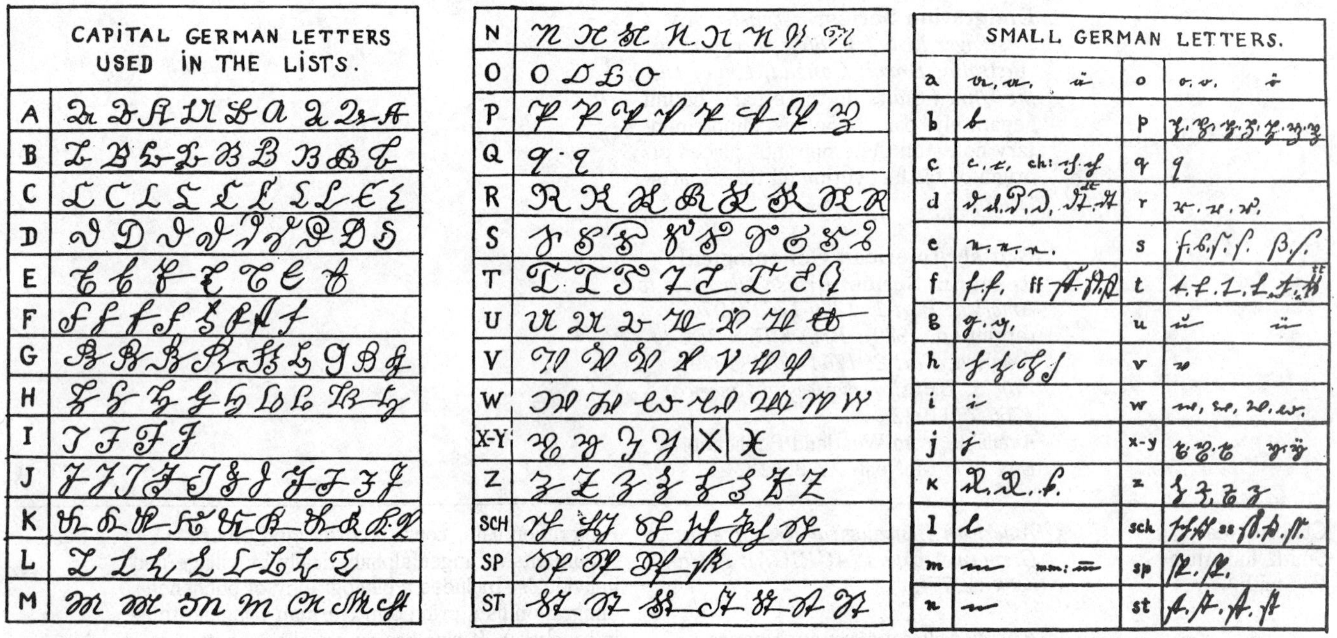

CAPITAL GERMAN LETTERS USED IN THE LISTS.

SMALL GERMAN LETTERS.

Figure 15-21. Reprinted from Ralph B. Strassburger, *Pennsylvania German Pioneers, 1727-1808,* William J. Hinke, ed., 3 vols. (Norristown, Pa.: Pennsylvania German Society, 1934), vol. 1, pp. 891-93. These letters are based on the actual handwriting of the immigrants themselves.

libraries on interlibrary loan, or requesting them through a branch library of the Genealogical Society of Utah. With the guide sheets in Figures 15-21 and 15-22 you can negotiate your way through indexes and at least the printed volumes, even when you do not read German. A more detailed research aid is Arta F. Johnson, *How to Read German Church Records Without Knowing Much German,* available from Johnson, 153 Aldrich Road, Columbus, OH 43214).

Reference sources for tracing Pennsylvania German pedigrees are also available inexpensively and easily.

Pennsylvania County Historical Societies "Family Reports." Several of the county historical societies have "family reports" with information previously collected and filed by family name. To get a report, simply send your surname or ancestor's full name and $10 to the county where the family lived. The society will send photocopies of the materials they have on hand. This service is available from York, Chester, Lancaster, Dauphin, and others. Some of these files are also available on microfilm at the Genealogical Society of Utah and its branches. Check card catalog for specifics.

Julius Billeter Swiss Collection. Julius Billeter was a Swiss genealogist who traced many Swiss families between 1896 and 1950. His files are available on microfilm at the Genealogical Society of Utah. A list of family names and abbreviations included in his files is available on request with SASE from Genealogical Society of Utah, 50 East North Temple, Salt Lake City, UT 84150.

Familiengeschichtliche Quellen. Some 2,000 family histories published in Germany are available in a thirteen-volume, family-name index compiled between 1926 and 1950 by Oswald Spohr. The index has been reprinted by Franz Heinzmann Verlag,

Table 15-7

English Marriage Indexes

Index	*Access*
Index to Civil Registration of Births, Marriages, and Deaths for England and Wales 1837-1906. 1,077 reels.	Call numbers are printed in a separate register. Genealogical Society of Utah and its branches have the index to Civil Registration only. If you use it at a branch library, have a librarian request a copy of the register. Certificates can be ordered from General Register office, St. Catherine's House, 10 Kingsway, London WCZB 6JP England.
Malcolm Pinhorn, comp., Pinhorn's Marriage Index 1538-1837, three-fourths million cards.	Pinhorn's Manor Farmhouse, Hulverstone, Isle of Wight P030 4EH England. Send SASE (2 International Reply Coupons, Addressed Envelope).
Index to Births, Marriages, Deaths in the *London Times*, 1785-1933. 99 reels. Includes a five-page "How to Use..." section.	Genealogical Society of Utah and branches; *London Times* available on microfilm in most university libraries.
David E. Gardner and Judith Ison, "English Marriage Indexes," *Genealogical Journal*, June 1975, pp. 73-76.	Describes these indexes and where to find them.
Pallott's Marriage Index, London Middlesex, 1780-1837. 4.5 million cards.	Achievements, Ltd., Northgate, Canterbury, Kent CT2 9NN England.
Boyd's Marriage Index* (Percival Boyd) 3 series, 4,836 parishes, 174 reels of film.	Original copy at Society of Genealogists (37 Harrington Gardens, London SW7 4JX); typed carbon copy, microfilm copy, compiled county-by-county. Genealogical Society of Utah and branches.

*Total number of parishes completed in Boyd's Marriage Index:

County	*Parishes Completed*	*Total Parishes*	*County*	*Parishes Completed*	*Total Parishes*
Bedfordshire	8	127	Lincolnshire	99	627
Berkshire	13	162	London and Middlesex	202	–
Buckinghamshire	64	206	Norfolk	278	691
Cambridgeshire	170	171	Northamptonshire	127	292
Cheshire	18	130	Northumberland	–	96
Cornwall	200	204	Nottinghamshire	161	220
Cumberland	35	143	Oxford	36	217
Derbyshire	86	184	Rutland	23	50
Devonshire	170	472	Shropshire	125	229
Dorset	79	260	Somerset	123	486
Durham	73	93	Staffordshire	4	183
Essex	381	405	Suffolk	492	504
Gloucestershire	182	347	Surrey	69	146
Hampshire	107	307	Sussex	56	305
Herefordshire	6	223	Warwickshire	30	208
Hertfordshire	48	132	Westmoreland	13	68
Huntingtonshire	16	93	Wight (Isle)	28	–
Kent	129	400	Wiltshire	73	318
Lancashire	101	211	Worcestershire	40	209
Leicestershire	140	256	Yorkshire	212	751

Figure 15-22. German Genealogical Words and Abbreviations, prepared by the European Reference Section, Genealogical Society of Utah, for patrons. Reproduced exactly (with accent marks omitted). Used with permission.

abend	evening
abends, des abends	in the evening
adel	nobility
ahnentafel	pedigree
allgemeine	general
allhier	in this place
alt	old
absterben	to die
adoptiert	adopted
alter	age
am Altar getraut	married at altar
am folgenden Tag	on the following day
am gleichen Tag	on the same day
amt	office; usually some type of local office
am erlimgen	remarks
aufbieten	public banns
aufenthaltsort	residence
ausser Dienst	formerly employed, retired
auswanderer	emigrant
auswanderung	emigration
Baiern	Bavaria
band	volume
bauer	farmer, peasant
Bayern	Bavaria
Bd.	see "band"
bedingt getauft	conditionally baptized
beerdigt	buried
beerdigung	interment
begraben	buried
begraebnis	burial
beichtvater	father confessor
bemerkungen	remarks
berg	hilltop, mountain
besitz	occupation
bez.	see "bezirk"
bezirk	district
Bibliothek	library
BRD	see "Bundersrepublik Deutschland"
braut	bride
brautigam	bridgegroom
bruder	brother
bube	boy
buerger	citizen
burg	castle, fortress
burger	citizen (male)
burgerin	citizen (female)
burgerregister	citizen register
Bundesrepublik Deutschland	German Federal Republic (West Germany)
Canton	lower level governmental subdivision used during Napoleonic occupation (1807-1812)
d.a.	see "der Altere"
DDR	see "Deutsche Demokratische Republik"
d.J.	see "der Juengere"
dirndel	girl, maid
Departement	an upper-level political subdivision (1807-1812)
de Altere	the elder; senior
der Juengere	the younger; junior
Deutsche Demokratische Republik	German Democratic Republic (East Germany)
Dioezese	diocese
dorf	village
ehe	marriage
ehelich	married
eheliches	legitimate
ehebrecher	adulterer
ehefrau ehelich	legitimate
eheleute	married couple
ehemann	husband
einwanderung	immigration
einwilligung	permission
Elsass	Alsace
eltern	parents
enkel	grandson
erbschaft	inheritance
Ev.	see "Evangelisch"
Evangelisch	Evangelical
familie	family
familiename	surname
familienregister	family register
familienforschung	genealogical research
familiengeschichte	genealogy
findling	orphan
firmung	confirmation
forscher	research
fraeulein	Miss
Frankreich	French
Frau	wife, woman, Mrs.
Freiherr	baron
Fuerstentum	principality
gatte	spouse (husband)
gattin	spouse (wife)
geb.	see "geboren"
geboren	born
geburst(en)	birth(s)
geburtsbrief	birth certificate
geburtstag	birthday
gedenktag	anniversary
geheiratet	married
geistliche	clergyman
gemeinde	community, village
Gericht	a court of law
genannt	alias, called
geschieden	divorced
geschlecht	sex
Geschichte	history
geschlect	family
geschlechtsname	surname
geschwister	siblings
gestern	yesterday
gestorben	died
get.	see "getauft"
getauft	christened, baptized
getraut	married
getrauten	married couple
gevatter	godfather
gevatterin	godmother
gewerbe	trade
Graf	count; earl
Grafschaft	the area under control of a Graf
grenze	boundary
grossherzogthum	grand dukedom
grosselthern	grandparents
grossmutter	grandmother
grossvater	grandfather
grundbuch	land register
(zu) hause	(at) home
hebamme	midwife
haben	to have
heirat	marriage
heiraten	to marry
heimat	home
Herkunft	origin
Herrschaft	a large landholding
Herzogthum	duchy (Herzog-duke)
hiesiger Ort	of this place
hinterbliebenen	survivors
hinterlassen	left behind
hochstift	bishopric
Hochzeit	wedding
Hoheit	highness, nobility
hurenkind	illegitimate child
im gleichen Monat	in the same month
Jahr	year
Jahrhundert	century
Jh.	see "Jahrhundert"
Jahrestag	anniversary
Jahreszeit	season
jungfrau, jungfer	virgin
junge	boy
junggeselle, jungling	bachelor
Kanton	see "Canton"
Kath.	see "Katholisch"
Katholisch	Catholic
kaufmann	merchant
KB	see "Kirchenbuch"
kind	child
kinder	children
Kirche	church
Kirchenbuch	church/parish book
Kirchgemeinde	parish
Kirchenspiel, Kirchspiel	parish
Kirchensprengel	parish
Kirchenvorsteher	church warden
kaufen	to buy
knabe	boy
Konfirmation	confirmation
Kopulation	marriage
Kr.	see "Kreis"
krankheit	disease
Kreis	district or county
Kt.	see "Canton"
Kurhessen	Electorate of Hesse
Kurpfalz	Electorate of the Pfalz
Kusine	cousin (female)

Kuster	sexton	Rodel	register	Urgrossmutter	great-grandmother
Land	a state	(im) Ruhestand	retirement	Urgrossvater	great-grandfather
Landarchiv	state archive	s.	see "siehe"	Unrwe	under, below, lower
Landkreis	a rural administrative area	S.	see "Seite"	Urkunde(n)	document(s)
lebending	living	S.v.	see "Sohn von"	v.	see "von"
ledig	single	Sachsen	Saxony	Vater	father
legitimiert	legitimate	Schein	certificate	Vereinigten Staaten	United States
letzer Wille	last will	schenkungen	donations	Verh.	see "verheiratet"
leichen	funeral	Schlesien	Silesia	verehelichung	marriage
Lexikon	dictionary	Schloss	castle	verehelicht	married
Lothringen	Lorraine	schmied	smith	verheiratet	married
madchen	girl	schuster	shoemaker	sich verlogen	to become engaged
magd	maid, maiden, girl	schwanger	pregnant	verlobung	betrothal
maennlich	male	Schweiz	Switzerland	Verlobte	bride (fiancee)
mann	husband, man	Schwester	sister	Verlobte	bridegroom (fiance)
Matrikel	register	Schwiegersohn	son-in-law	verrichtet	performed
mittel	middle	Seite	page	Verstorbene	the deceased
Monat	month	siehe	see: refer to	verwitwete	widowed
morgen	tomorrow	Sippe	clan, tribe	verstorben	deceased, defunct
Morgen	morning	Sohn	son	verwandt	relatives
Mutter	mother	Sohnlein, Sohnchen	little son	Verz.	see "Verzeichnis"
nachgelassene(r)	surviving	Sohn von	son of	Verzeichnis	list, register
Nachmittag	afternoon	Staat	state	Vetter	male cousin
Nacht	night	sollen	should	Volkszahlung	census
Name	name	Stadt	city	von	of, from
Nebenfrau	concubine	Staatarchiv	state archive	vormund	guardian
Neffe	nephew	Stadtkreis	an urban (city or town) administrative area	vorname	given name
nichte	cousin(female)	Stammbaum	family tree	vollzogen	performed
neue	new	stand	occupation	Vorfahr	ancestor
nieder	lower	Standesamt	registrar's office	waise	orphan
N.N. (nomen nescio)	unknown name	sterben	to die	Wappen	coat-of-arms
Nord	north	Stiefkind	stepchild	Waeppenkunde	heraldry
Nottaufe	emergency baptism	Stiefmutter	stepmother	wehmutter	midwife
ober	over, above	Stiefvater	stepfather	weib	wife, woman
Oesterreich	Austria	Strasse	street	weiblich	female, feminine
Onkel	uncle	stunde	hour	weiland	deceased
ort	place	Sud	south	an welchem (Tag)	on which (day)
Ost	east	T.v.	see "Tochter von"	Westfalen	Westphalia
pate	witness (male)	Tag	day	werden	to become
patin	witness (female)	Tag der Taufe	day of baptism	witwe	widow (abbre.—Wwe.)
paten	witnesses	tal	valley	witwer	widower (abbre.—Wwer.)
Pfarramt	parish	Tante	aunt	wohnen	to live
Pfarrbuch	parish book	taufe	baptism	wohnung	residence
Pfarrer	minister, pastor	taufen	to baptize	Wohnort, Wohnplatz	place of residence
platz	place	taufpaten	godparents	wollen	to want
Pommern	Pomerania	Testament	will	wurde geboren	was born
Praefektur	office of a prefect, the administrator of French dept.	Tochter	daughter	wurde getauft	was baptized
Preussen	Prussia	Tochterchen, tochterlein	little daughter	Zehnten	tithing
Priester	priest	Tochter von	daughter of	Zehntbuch, Zehntenbuch	tithing book
quellen	source	Tod	death	Zeit	time
Rathaus	townhall	tot	dead	Zeit der Geburt	time of birth
reformiert	reformed	totgeborenes Kind	stillborn child	Zeuge	witness
Regierung	central government; the highest level of government	Trauung	marriage	Zivilstandsamt	civil register office
rentner	retired person	u.	and	Zuname	surname
		und des, und der	and of	zwilling	twins
		unehelich	illegitimate		
		unehelichkeit	illegitimate		
		ungefahr	about, circa		

Am Gengelstraesschen 19, 4000 Düsseldorf 30, West Germany. Volume 14 was issued in 1983. A microfilm copy of the complete set is available at the Genealogical Society of Utah and its branches.

Notes

1. Allan L. Damon, "A Look at the Record: The Facts Behind the Current Controversy Over Immigration," *American Heritage* 33 (Dec. 1981): 51.

2. John F. Vallentine, "Tracing the Immigrant Ancestor," *Genealogical Journal* 3 (1974): 4.

3. Ibid., p. 5.

4. Peter Roberts, *The New Immigration: A Study of the Industrial and Social Life of East Europeans in America* (New York: Arno Press, 1970), reprint of 1912 ed., p. 157.

5. Philip Taylor, *The Distant Magnet: European Emigration to the U.S.A.* (London: Eyre & Spottiswoode, 1971), pp. 192-95.

6. The Mormon Church used only in-house emigrant agents, licensed and registered in the localities where they worked, to procure tickets and provisions. See Arlene H. Eakle, *The Pingree Legacy* (Salt Lake City, Utah: Job Pingree Family Organization, 1983), Chapter 2.

7. Most emigration lists which have survived for England are lists of

servants who bound themselves by contract or persons sentenced to transportation by English courts. Some writers claim that the majority of English immigrants to America before 1776 were indentured servants or redemptioners—between 60 and 70 percent. See Damon, "A Look at the Record," p. 54. Voluntary immigration does not seem to have generated official lists except the Pennsylvania German lists published in *Pennsylvania German Pioneers* and a few English lists. Supporting documents, i.e., indentures, announcements of auctions of servants in the newspapers, court records, and local histories, do not support equally high percentages for these Germans. I believe that the figures are inflated because of lack of evidence. Once the index to published lists undertaken by P. William Filby and Mary K. Meyer is completed, we may be able to challenge this theory that a majority of early Americans were forced immigrants.

8. Gottlieb Mittelberger, "Journey to Pennsylvania in the Year 1750," Carl T. Eben, trans., in Strassburger with Hinke, *Pennsylvania German Pioneers* 1: xxxiii.

9. See *APG Newsletter* 4 (April 1982): 3.

10. Quoted in Strassburger with Hinke, *Pennsylvania German Pioneers*, p. xxxvii.

11. Ibid., p. xxxvi.

12. Ibid.

13. Joan McKay, "Emigrants' Hospital Reports from the *Quebec Mercury*," *Ottawa Branch News* 15 (July-Aug. 1982): 42-45.

14. Lavona L. Ness, "Passenger Arrival Lists." Lecture before the Washoe County Genealogical Society, Reno, Nevada, Oct. 1981, typescript in author's possession.

15. P. A. M. Taylor, "Passenger Lists as an Historical Source," *Genealogists' Magazine* 12 (1954): 197-200.

16. Kristian Hvidt, "Along the Scandinavian Emigrant Trail: Part 1, Denmark," World Conference on Records and Genealogical Seminar, 5-8 Aug. 1969, Salt Lake City, Utah, p. 2.

17. See also "Petition to King George II from Persons Identifying Themselves as Palatines or Descendants of Palatines," *North Carolina Genealogical Journal* 1 (1975): 61, and Luther R. Kelner, "Memorial to Governor Shute of Massachusetts from Residents of North Ireland," *History of Dauphin County, Pennsylvania*, 2 vols. (New York: Lem's Publishing Company, 1907), 2: 23-26.

18. In *Pennsylvania Magazine of History and Biography* 30 (1906): 427.

19. Adapted from information sheet prepared by Marilyn Deputy, Genealogical Society of Utah, 1982.

20. Friedrich Wollmershauser, Otelsheim, West Germany, to Editor, *APG Newsletter* 4 (April 1982): 2-3.

NATIONALITY REFERENCE DIRECTORY

This Nationality Reference Directory which follows has been compiled to help the genealogist deal with variables in the immigrant mosaic. It includes search tips for each national group, a map showing settlements within the United States, subject collections located in selected American libraries and archives with finding aids where they are available, research projects underway, and a bibliography of immigrant studies, especially those telling where a group originated, how it migrated to America, and where it settled. A list of how-to books for each national group is also included.

While the location of national settlements for the group your ancestor belonged to may be a matter of interest to historians, it is a matter of necessity for genealogists. A typical immigrant ancestor arriving in America will travel with others of the same national group or be headed for their settlement. This ancestor will move from place to place along a migration route already established by others. Once a pattern of movement is established, others follow as if it were a habit hard to break.

Czech community papers in one area will often carry articles, vital statistics, and obituaries about Czechs living in another. Family Bibles, letters from one family to another, or marriage records within the national group may be deposited in a library many miles distant from where your family currently lives. A small public library in a Czech community in Texas may have compiled a biographical file or indexed the vital records in foreign-language newspapers which record your ancestor and his family. This directory will help you locate these records.

Map symbols:

- • Individual settlements
- ■ Areas of settlement clusters
- ▤ Scattered settlement, often occupation-oriented

*This reference in a bibliography is specially recommended because it shows immigrant origins and destinations, usually with specific maps.

General Bibliographies

Brye, David L. *European Immigration and Ethnicity in the United States and Canada*. Santa Barbara, Calif: ABC-CLIO, 1983. Includes statistical studies, histories, series, etc.

Buenker, John D., and Nicholas C. Burckel. *Immigration and Ethnicity: A Guide to Information Sources*. Detroit: Gale Research Company, 1977. Annotated citations for published sources including books, articles, dissertations with addresses of societies, repositories, publishers. Omits Afro-American, native Americans, foreign language works, genealogical publications.

*Filby, P. William. *American-British Genealogy and Heraldry. A Selected List of Books*. 3rd ed. Boston: New England Historic Genealogical Society, 1983. Includes section on ethnic groups.

Janeway, W. Ralph. *Bibliography of Immigration in the U.S., 1900-1930*. Columbus, Ohio: H. L. Hedrick, 1934. Includes many references for books not picked up by later bibliographies.

*Mannion, John J. "Selected Bibliography on European Ethnic Group Settlement in Rural North America." *Irish Settlements in Eastern Canada*. Toronto: University of Toronto Press, 1973. Excellent; includes articles on settlement patterns.

*Miller, Olga K. *Migration, Emigration, Immigration*. 2 vols. Logan, Utah: Everton Publishers, 1974-81. The most complete bibliography of emigration sources compiled for genealogists. Includes call numbers at the Genealogical Society of Utah, articles, pamphlets, books, and foreign language titles.

Miller, Wayne C., et al. *A Comprehensive Bibliography for the Study of Ethnic Minorities*. 2 vols. New York: New York University Press, 1976. Includes books and articles for each ethnic group.

Wasserman, Paul, and Jean Morgan. *Ethnic Information Sources of the U.S.* Detroit: Gale Research Company, 1976. Includes eighty-six ethnic groups omitting blacks, American Indians, and Eskimos covered in other publications. Lists ethnic organizations and their publications.

Immigration and Reprint Series

Request catalogs and ordering instructions from each publisher below.

American Immigration Collection. Arno Press, 330 Madison Avenue, New York, NY 10017. Series 1, 41 titles; Series 2, 33 titles. Includes separate set of volumes for each ethnic group, i.e., *The Italian American Experience Series*.

American Immigration Library. Jerome S. Ozer, Publisher Inc., 475 Fifth Avenue, New York, NY 10017. Thirty titles issued to 1972.

Ethnic Americans Series. R and E Research Associates, Inc., 4843 Mission Street, San Francisco, CA 94112. Short, descriptive bibliographies for major ethnic groups.

How and Where to Research Your Ethnic-American Cultural Heritage. Robert D. Reed, 18581 McFarland Avenue, Saratoga, CA 95070. Separate volumes for German, Polish, Jewish, Italian, Scandinavian, Russian, black, Irish, Chinese, native American, Japanese, Mexican groups. Includes addresses for general information sources, embassies, historical societies, bookstores, and directories with basic bibliographies. Suitable for beginners. Some addresses may not be current.

Of Immigrant Ways Series. Barnes and Noble Books, Dillon Press, Inc. 500 South Third Street, Minneapolis, MN 55415. Series includes Swedish, Irish, Scottish, and German. Discusses traditions, customs, immigration, and language.

World Conference on Records Papers. Genealogical Society of Utah, 50 East North Temple, Salt Lake City, UT 84150. List for 1969 includes many emigrant/immigrant subjects. Papers for 1980 available individually for $1 each or the whole conference in thirteen volumes including index for $48. Lists free upon request.

Immigrant Registers

American Immigrant Ancestry Register. Lineages, Box 417, Salt Lake City, UT 84111. Membership group, $10/year. Computer file of immigrant ancestors.

Chicago Irish. John E. Corrigan, 6458 S. Campbell, Chicago, IL 60629 $1/surname. SASE for entries in Chicago Irish newspapers, 1870-1930. Other material available.

Colonial Immigrants. *The Second Boat*, Downeast Ancestry, Box 398, Machias, ME 04654. Focus on pre-1650 immigrants and their descendants to the American Revolution period.

Irish Immigrants. Irish Studies Program, Northeastern University, 101 Newbury Street, Boston, MA 02116. Cosponsored by New England Historic Genealogical Society. "Missing Friends" listed in the Catholic newspaper, *Boston Pilot*, 1836-1920s.

Lost Ancestors from Wurttemberg? Freidrich R. Wollmershauser, Stuttgarter Strasse 133, 7261 Ostersheim, West Germany. $1 per name. Alphabetized population lists.

New Jersey Emigrant Register. Dr. John Anderson, 1 Myrtle Road, East Brunswick, NJ 08816. New Jersey residents who moved to other states. Register will be filed in Special Collections, Rutgers University Library, New Brunswick, NJ 08901.

Scots-Irish Immigrants. David Rencher, 12523 S. 1450 W., Riverton, UT 84065. Compiling lists of groups and individuals.

Scottish Immigrants. Norman Moyes, 84 E. 760 S., Orem, UT 84057. Compiling register of groups and their members.

National Source Papers

The Genealogical Society of Utah Research Papers Series has compiled major source papers available country by country. These papers are available from LDS Church Distribution Center, 1999 West 1700 South, Salt Lake City, UT 84104 or Genealogical Society of Utah, 50 East North Temple, Salt Lake City, UT 84150. Titles and prices available on request.

Argentina	Germany	Nicaragua*
Australia	Guatamala	Norway
Austria	Honduras*	Panama*
Belgium	Hong Kong	Poland
Canada	Hungary	Samoa
Chile*	Iceland	Scotland
Columbia*	Ireland	South Africa
Costa Rica*	Isle of Man	Sweden
Denmark	Italy	Switzerland
Ecuador	Japan	Taiwan
El Salvador*	Mexico	United States
England/Wales	Netherlands	Uruguay*
France	New Zealand	Venezuela*

*Available in Spanish also.

Specialty Genealogical Periodicals

Overseas Ancestors. The Hartwell Company, 1617 West 261 Street, Harbor City, CA 90710. Periodicals include: *French Genealogist; Italian Genealogist, East European Genealogist* (Poland, Russia, Czechoslovakia, Hungary, Roumania, Yugoslavia, Bulgaria, Albania); *Be-Ne-Lux Genealogist* (Belgium, Netherlands, Luxembourg); *East Asian Genealogist* (Japan, Korea, China, Indo-China, Burma, Thailand, Malaya); *Germanic Genealogist* (Germany, Austria, Switzerland, Mennonites); *English Genealogist, Scottish Genealogical Helper, Irish Genealogical Helper*, and *Spanish Genealogical Helper*. Each issue has articles, queries, and ads for products and services.

For others consult Mary K. Meyer, *Directory of Genealogical Societies in the U.S. and Canada* (Libra Publications, Box 29, Linthicum Heights, MD 21090. 1982 edition included as Appendix G. See also Tracy L. Craig, *Directory of Historical Societies and Agencies in the U.S. and Canada*, AASLH, 708 Berry Road, Nashville, TN 37204.

Special Research Aids

Between 1906 and 1932, the Carnegie Institute of Washington, D.C., in collaboration with the American Historical Association, financed the compilation and publication of guides to manuscript materials relating to American history located outside the continental United States. The bulk of this material, however, remains in foreign depositories.*

Andrews, C. M. *Guide to the Materials for American History, to 1783, in the Public Record Office of Great Britain.* 2 vols. Washington, D.C., 1912-14. Reprint ed., New York: Kraus Reprints, 1965.

Andrews C. M., and F. G. Davenport. *Guide to the Manuscript Materials for the History of the United States to 1783, in the British Museum, in Minor London Archives, and in the Libraries of Oxford and Cambridge.* Washington, D.C., 1908.

Bell, H. C., et al. *Guide to British West Indian Archive Materials in London and in the Islands, for the History of the United States.* Washington, D.C., 1926.

Bolton, H. E. *Guide to Materials for the History of the United States in the Principal Archives of Mexico.* Washington, D.C., 1913.

Chapman, C. E. *Catalogue of Materials in the Archivo General de Indias for the History of the Pacific Coast and the American Southwest.* Berkeley, 1919.

Faust, A. B. *Guide to the Materials for American History in Swiss and Austrian Archives.* Washington, D.C., 1916. (See Figure 15-23.)

Fish, C. R. *Guide to the Materials for American History in Roman and Other Italian Archives.* Washington, D.C., 1911.

Golder, F. A. *Guide to Materials for American History in Russian Archives.* 2 vols. Washington, D.C., 1917-37.

Hill, R. R. *Descriptive Catalogue of the Documents Relating to the United States in the Papeles procedentes de Cuba. Deposited in . . .Seville.* Washington, D.C., 1916.

Jameson, J. F., ed. "Guide to the Items Relating to American History in the Reports of the English Historical Manuscripts Commission," American Historical Association *Reports*, 1898, p. 611. Addenda to 1927 are in the *Cambridge History of the Empire*, vol. 1, p. 837.

Learned, M. D. *Guide to the Manuscript Materials Relating to American History in the German State Archives.* Washington, D.C., 1912.

Leland, W. G., and J. J. Meng. *Guide to Materials for American History in the Libraries and Archives of Paris.* 2 vols. Washington, D.C., 1932-43. Two volumes remain to be published.

Matteson, D. M. *List of Manuscripts Concerning American History Preserved in European Libraries.* Washington, D.C., 1925.

Parker, D. W. *Guide to the Materials for United States History in Canadian Archives.* Washington, D.C., 1913.

Paullin, C. O., and F. L. Paxson. *Guide to the Materials in London Archives for the History of the United States since 1783.* Washington, D.C., 1914.

Paz, Inlian. *Catalogo de manuscritos de America existentes en la Biblioteca Nacional.* Madrid, 1933.

Perez, L. M. *Guide to the Materials for American History in Cuban Archives.* Washington, D.C., 1907.

Report on American Manuscripts in the Royal Institution of Great Britain. 4 vols. London, 1904-09. Many of these have since been transferred to American repositories.

Rubincam, Milton, ed. "Materials in Foreign Archives for Writing Pennsylvania History." *Pennsylvanian* 2 (1944-45): 17.

Shepherd, W. R. *Guide to the Materials for the History of the United States in Spanish Archives.* Washington, D.C., 1907.

*Revised from Vincent L. Jones, et al., *Family History for Fun and Profit* (Salt Lake City: The Genealogical Institute, 1972), pp. 279-80.

Figure 15-23. Sample entry from A. B. Faust, *Guide to the Materials for American History in Swiss and Austrian Archives* (Washington, D.C.: 1916).

PROTOKOLLE DES KLEINEN RATHS.

No references to Carolina, Pennsylvania, or other American colonies until 1734.

Vol. 106, 1734-1735.

p. 144. "Hans Heinrich Breitenstein um Reisegelt in Carolinam." Oct. 23, 1734. (4 Gulden were voted to be given him when aboard ship.)
Jacob Müller (informator, Lehrer) begs to go to Carolina with wife and 3 children, and asks for help (Reisegelt). Nov. 17, 1734. Kl. R. Beschluss: "Ist abgewiesen, und solle weder er, noch andere, die in Carolinam reisen wollen, oder reisen zu wollen vorgeben, nicht weiter angehört werden."

p. 146. "In Carolinam reisende arme leut aus d. Zürich Gebiet" (ungefähr 100 Personen). Oct. 27, 1734.

Figure 15-24. Sample entry from Public Records Office of Northern Ireland, County Antrim, B. R. Crick and Miriam Alman, *A Guide to the Manuscripts Relating to America in Great Britain and Ireland* (London: Oxford University Press, 1961).

EMIGRANT PASSENGER LISTS: 1792–1870 (incomplete).

The Office contains various transcripts and photostats of lists of emigrants sailing to America, culled from newspapers and other sources: of 1792 (T. 711), of 1802–4 and 1833–5 (T. 1011), of 1804–5 (T. 521), of 1836 (T. 671), and of 1860–70 (T. 1428).

Additions to these guides include:

Beers, Henry P. *The French and British in the Old Northwest: A Bibliographic Guide to Archives and Manuscript Sources*. Detroit: Wayne State University Press, 1964.

Crick, B. R. and Miriam Alman. *A Guide to the Manuscripts Relating to America in Great Britain and Ireland*. London: Oxford University Press, 1961. Revised by John W. Raimo. Westport, Conn.: Meckler Books, 1979. (See Figure 15-24.)

Gipson, L. H. *Guide to Manuscripts Relating to the History of the British Empire, 1748-1776*. New York: Alfred J. Knopf, 1970.

Stevens, B. G. *Facsimiles of Manuscripts in European Archives Relating to America, 1773-1783*. 25 vols. New York: AMS Press, 1972. Includes descriptions, notes, references, translations.

Genealogical Society of Utah Microfilm Collections

The library of the Genealogical Society of Utah contains the largest collection of filmed manuscripts in the world – over a million 100-foot rolls. The scope of the collection is truly international, with the society's declared intention "to gather records on everyone who has ever lived." This astonishing statement is backed by significant collections of microfilmed manuscripts for the United States, Europe, Latin America, and the Far East.

The bulk of the collection contains civil and parish registers of births, marriages, deaths, and other register information. The remaining rolls of film alone, however, constitute the largest collection of non-parish or non-civil registers in the world – letters, maps, factory records, guild records, and immigration documents. While the parish and civil registers are usually adequately cataloged, these other kinds of records are not. Roger M. Haigh, ed., *Finding Aids to Microfilm Manuscript Collections, Genealogical Society of Utah* (Salt Lake City: University of Utah Press, 1978), is designed to acquaint users with the nature and location of these historical manuscripts.

The *Finding Aids* survey, document, and explain the minutely detailed information available in the Genealogical Society's archives. The Introduction to the *Preliminary Survey of the Mexican Collection* offers an example of the guidance available in the publications:

Often overlooked by scholars evaluating the use of the collection are the thousands of rolls of filmed manuscripts which are not vital statistics of one type or another. The purpose of this section is to familiarize the academic community more fully with the "other material" held in this repository. In the Mexican areas this category includes between 10,000 and 20,000 rolls of film. Most of the manuscripts filmed are in the Archivo de la Curia and the Archivo del Metropolitano Cabildo Eclesiástico in Mexico City and the Archivo del Antiguo Arzobispado de Michocán in Morelia.

The documents in these collections reveal intimate glimpses of the internal infrastructure of the Roman Catholic Church – its financial situation, its parishes, its procedure for selection of clerics and its operation of the commercial enterprises which it controlled. Because of the enormity of church influence, particularly in the colonial period, these manuscripts contain the type of data desired by anyone interested in the socioeconomic situation of Mexico from 1560 to 1860.

The largest body of film [in the Morelian Collection] (2,325 rolls) is catalogued as "Marriage Information and Miscellaneous Transactions" – each entry includes a date or time span as well. . . . The largest number [of rolls] reflects the role played by the Archbishop of Michoacán in whom was vested the highest authority within the Archdiocese. Included in the filmed material are records of investigations of problematic marriage applications, i.e., one partner or the other being suspected of being married already, being a non-Catholic, or, in the case of mulattoes, being bound, etc. Divorce cases are also included where the circumstances involved similar problems. Murder cases, land title disputes, estate controversies, claims against landowners (often the Catholic Church) brought by *mayordomos*, and claims against priests and other clerics for misbehavior ranging from laxity to various forms of scandalous dealings appear in the records as well. Of a more routine nature, the Archbishop of Michoacán was apparently also called upon to investigate applicants for clerical vacancies and to arrive at final decisions on their appointments; in addition, he perused the credentials of aspirants to religious orders and reviewed the accounts of parroquias, hospitals, convents, confradías, and foundling homes.

Finding Aids

*Preliminary Survey of the Mexican Collection,** Susan M. Cotler, Roger M. Haigh, and Shirley A. Weathers, 1978, 216 pages.

Descriptive Inventory of the English Collection, Arlene H. Eakle, Arvilla Outsen, and Richard S. Tompson, 1979, 184 pages.

*Supplement to the Preliminary Survey of the Mexican Collection,**
Roger M. Haigh and Shirley A. Weathers,
1979, 28 pages.

*Preliminary Survey of the German Collection,**
Ronald Smelser,
1979, 638 pages.

*Descriptive Inventory of the New York Collection,**
Arlene H. Eakle and L. Ray Gunn,
1980, 292 pages.

*Preliminary Survey of the French Collection,**
C. Russell Jensen,
1980, 475 pages.

*Includes microfilm call numbers.

COUNTRY-BY-COUNTRY SUMMARY OF AIDS

Australia

Special Collections

Library	*Address*	*Description of Material*
International Marine Archives, Inc.	21 Orange Street Nantucket, MA 02554	Whaling, merchant marine surveying materials.
Genealogical Society of Utah	50 East North Temple Salt Lake City, UT 84150	Large collection on microfilm. Also available at branch libraries. Especially rich in emigration/immigration records.

How-to Books: Australian Ancestry

Geeves, Philip. *Local History in Australia: A Guide for Beginners*. Sydney: Library of Australian History, n.d. 58 pp.

Gray, Nancy. *Compiling Your Family History: A Guide to Procedure*. 14th ed. Sydney: Society of Australian Genealogists, 1984. 40 pp.

Hansen, Niel T. *Guide to Genealogical Sources – Australia and New Zealand*. Melbourne: Stake Genealogical Committee, LDS Church, 1962.

MacDonald, Lillyan. "Genealogical Research in Australia," *Descent* 13 (Sept. 1983): 118-32.

Peake, Andrew Guy. *Sources for South Australian Biography*. Adelaide: South Australian Genealogy and Heraldry Society, 1982. 151 pp.

__________. *Sources for South Australian Family History*. Adelaide: South Australian Genealogy and Heraldry Society. 1982. 75 pp.

Canada

The open border between Canada and the United States has a revolving-door effect on migration. Canadians move into and out of the states along the border seeking work and opportunity. Americans move back and forth seeking refuge from war, cheaper land, or better markets for their goods. Intermarriage across boundary lines is also common. These are more widely known, however, than the immigrant patterns which flow across one country into another. Agents, paid commissions on the length of the immigrants' journey, routed Canadian immigrants across the United States from as far away as New Orleans. And Europeans, seeking the least costly routes of travel, came by way of the St. Lawrence, entering the United States at Ogdensburg, New York (Irish); Chicago, Illinois (Poles and Scandinavians); and Sheboygan, Michigan (Swedes). If you have ancestors along the border, check both sides for records. (See Map 15-6.)

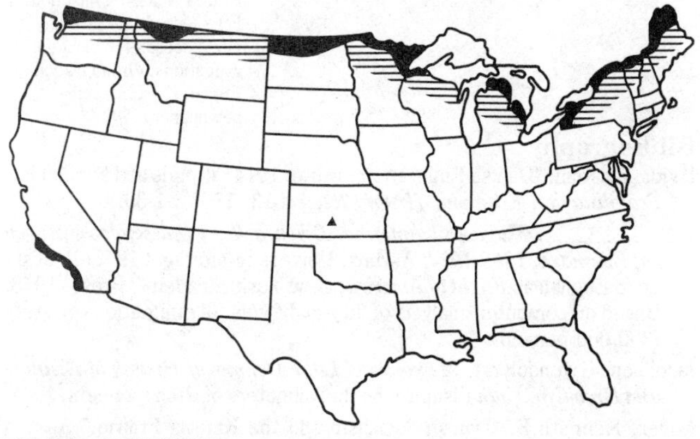

Map 15-6. Canadian Settlement Patterns.

Special Collections

Library	*Address*	*Description of Material*
University of Minnesota, James Ford Bell Library	309 19 Avenue S. Minneapolis, MN 55455	Library of European expansion, 1400-1800.
Yale University, Beinecke Manuscripts	121 Wall Street New Haven, CT 06520	Local histories, periodicals, family and estate papers, land company records. Largest collection of Canadiana in the U.S.
University of Maine at Orono, Northeast Archives of Folklore, Oral History	South Stevens Hall Orono, ME 04473	Local history of the Maritime provinces, settlers back and forth across the border. Guide: Florence Ireland, "The Northeast Archives of Folklore and Oral History: A Brief Description and Catalog of its Holdings, 1958-72," *Northeast Folklore* 13 (1972).
California State University, Department of Geography	Sierra Hall Northridge, CA 91324	Computer project of migration of French Canadians to New England based on censuses, directories, naturalization records.
University of Vermont Bailey Memorial Library	Burlington, VT 05401	2,000 volumes, large collection of manuscripts on Canada.
Cleveland Public Library	325 Superior Avenue Cleveland, OH 44114	55,000 volumes, maps, pictures.
Minnesota State Historical Society	Cedar Street and Central Avenue St. Paul, MN 55101	240,000 volumes, maps, including early settlers histories, directories, native peoples.
University of Minnesota Library	Minneapolis, MN 55455	Especially rich for the Prairie Provinces.
Cox Library	1701 North 11th Street Box 5167 Tucson, AZ 85703	10,000 volumes, many pertaining to Canada; many local histories. Collection also on microfilm through Genealogical Society of Utah.
University of Arizona	Tucson, AZ 85721	8,000 volumes, local and printed histories on the West; manuscripts including Canada.
Buffalo and Erie Historical Society	25 Nottingham Court Buffalo, NY 14216	Over 25,000 volumes, slides, one million manuscripts, photographs dealing with Niagara Frontier. Strong War of 1812 Collection.
New York Historical Society	170 Central Park West New York, NY 10024	Small collection relating to Canada.
University of Rochester, Rush Rhees Library	Rochester, NY 14627	French Canadian history.
Brown University, John Carter Brown Library	Providence, RI 02912	Some French Canadian materials, early prints and drawings.
Indiana University, Lilly Library	Bloomington, IN 47401	2,500 volumes, numerous outlines. History of French conquest of Canada.
Maine Historical Society	485 Congress Street Portland, ME 04111	Collection on Maritime Provinces.

American Antiquarian Society	185 Salisbury Street Worcester, MA 01609	United Empire Loyalists Collection, Union List of Manuscripts in forty-one Canadian libraries.
Acadia University Acadia Institute	Wolfville, Nova Scotia BOP 1XO	Biographical index to Nova Scotia heads of families, 1749-76 includes planters from Connecticut and Rhode Island, fishermen from Massachusetts and Maine, Germans from Pennsylvania. Similar projects at College of St. Anne and Université de Moncton on Acadians.
Maritime History Group Archival Association of Atlantic Canada		Atlantic Canada Shipping Project, 1846-1920, based on crew lists, shipping registers, admiralty records, newspapers, etc. Records for all maritime ports in computer database. See Report on Project in *Archival Association of Atlantic Canada Newsletter*, 6 (June 1978), 1827.

Bibliography

Allen, James P. "Migration Fields of French Canadian Immigrants to Southern Maine." *Geographical Review* 62 (1972): 366-83.

*Bagnell, Kenneth. *The Little Immigrants: The Orphans who Came to Canada*. Toronto: Macmillan of Canada, 1980. Includes description of records and how to access them.

Canadian Manuscripts in the Boston Public Library: A Descriptive Catalog. Boston: G. K. Hall, 1970.

*DeMarce, Virginia E. *Canadian Participants in the American Revolution: An Index*. Sparta, Wis.: For Lost in Canada, 1980. Includes a forty-page bibliography of original and printed sources.

Directory of Canadian Archival Depositories. Ottawa: Archives Section, Canadian Historical Association, 1971.

Dunn, Charles. *Highland Settler: A Portrait of the Scottish Gael in Nova Scotia*. Toronto: University of Toronto Press, 1953.

Hansen, Marcus L., and John R. Brebner. *The Mingling of the Canadian and American Peoples*. New Haven: Yale University Press, 1940.

Hill, Douglas. *The Opening of the Canadian West*. London: Heinemann, 1967.

____________. *Scots to Canada*. London: Gentry Books, 1972.

Hope, Louise. "A Canadian Colony in Kansas." *Families* 13 (Winter, 1974): 22-24.

*Macdonald, Norman. *Canada: Immigration and Colonization, 1841-1903*. Toronto: Macmillan of Canada, 1976. Excellent study. Includes list of emigrant/immigrant aid societies and their records.

*Mannion, John J. *Irish Settlements in Eastern Canada: A Study of Cultural Transfer and Adaptation*. Toronto: University of Toronto Department of Geography, 1974. Significant study for transfer of cultural elements to new environment and how this evidence aids identity.

Palmer, Greg. *Bibliography of Loyalist Source Materials in Archives in the United States, Canada, and Great Britain*. Westport, Conn.: Meckler Books, 1982.

Parker, Jimmy B. "Canadian Immigration and Emigration." *Genealogical Journal* 3 (1974): 103-8.

How-to-Books: Canadian Ancestry

Auger, Roland J. "Genealogy in the Province of Quebec." *National Genealogical Society Quarterly* 67 (1979): 34-41.

Baker, Eunice R. *Searching For Your Ancestors in Canada*. Ottawa: For the author, 1974.

Baxter, Angus. *In Search of Your Roots: A Guide for Canadians Seeking Their Ancestors*. Toronto: Macmillan of Canada, 1978. 292 pp.

Blakeley, Phyllis R. "Some Sources for Nova Scotia Genealogy." *National Genealogical Society Quarterly* 57 (1969): 83-87.

Fellows, Robert F. *Researching Your Ancestors in New Brunswick*. Fredericton: n. pub., 1979. 303 pp.

Gilchrist, Brian J. "The Ontario Archives: Records and Research Methods." *Families* 15 (1976): 168-76.

Jonasson, Eric. *The Canadian Genealogical Handbook*. 2nd ed., Winnipeg, Wheatfield Press, 1978. 352 pp.

____________. "Genealogical Sources in the Province of Manitoba." *Genealogical Journal* 8 (1979): 91-114.

____________. "Family History Resources in Western Canada." *British Columbia Genealogist* 12 (March 1983); 2-10.

Keffer, Marion C. "Ontario Genealogical Resources." *National Genealogical Society Quarterly* 67 (1979): 14-24.

Punch, Terrence M. *Genealogical Research in Nova Scotia*. Halifax: n. pub., 1978. 132 pp.

Denmark

Three hundred thousand Danish emigrants came to the United States between 1845 and 1915. About 250,000 settled in Iowa, Kansas, Minnesota, Illinois, and New York. Some 18,000 became Mormons and went to Utah. From here they spread into other areas. (See Map 15-7.) These Danes tended to merge into the American population. They did not retain their own culture or identity as a group.

In Denmark, the research of Kristian Hvidt (see bibliography) shows that the Danes came mostly from the southeastern part of Denmark along the Baltic Sea. They moved from country to town or city to try their luck. When they failed to make a living, they migrated to America to try again. As a result, places of residence given on immigrant records and places of birth are usually different.

Special Collections

Library	*Address*	*Description of Material*
Danebod High School	Tyler, MN 56178	Folklife collection of an old Danish settlement.
Dana College	Blair, NE 68008	890 volumes; Rev. P. S. Vig Collection, copies at Dane Worldwide Archives. Include Danish-American newspapers, emigrant/immigrant letters.
Grandview College	1351 Grandview Avenue, Des Moines, IA 50316	About 3,000 volumes, rich in church records. Most records are in Danish.
Danish-American Association	30 North Dearborn Street, Chicago, IL 60611	Archives, records of immigrant assistance. Copies at Dane Worldwide Archives
Dane Worldwide Archives	Konvalvej No. 2, Aalborg, Denmark	Personal records of many individuals; private collection of Rasmus Anderson, 1874-1922 (Anderson organized congregations for Danish State Church in the Midwest), 50 vols. of correspondence with Danish immigrants across the United States. Collection of F.L. Grandtvig includes vital records for local congregations, "Immigration Register" from Danish newspapers.

Bibliography

Hvidt, Kristian. "Danish Emigration Prior to 1914: Trends and Problems." *Scandinavian Economic History Review* 13 (1965): 1-30.

*____________. *Flugten til Amerika: Drivkraefter i Massendvandringen fra Denmark, 1868-1914*. Aarhns: Universitetsforlaget 1971. Published in English as *Flight to America*. New York: Academic Press, 1975. Based on computer-analysis of fifty-eight vols. of emigration registers (300,000 names).

Jacobsen, Gwendolyn J. *Memories of Little Denmark: History of Elsinore and Brooklyn, Utah* Elsinore, Utah: Daughters of Utah Pioneers, 1964.

Miller, Kenneth E. "Danish Socialism and the Kansas Prairie." *Kansas Historical Quarterly* (Summer 1972).

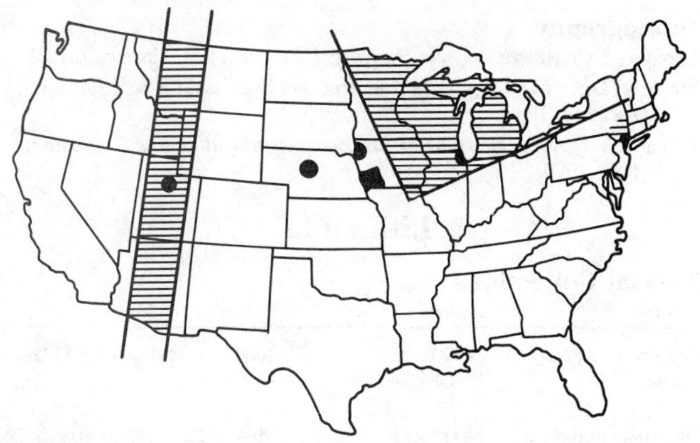

Map 15-7. Danish Settlement Patterns.

Schmidt, Jorgen W., ed. *Oh du Zion i Vest.* Kovenhagen: Rosenkilde og Bagger, 1965. Collection of original sources of Mormon emigrants, bibliography of original narratives in Danish.

How-to Books; Danish Ancestry

Smith, Frank, and Finn A. Thomsen. *Genealogical Guidebook and Atlas of Denmark.* Salt Lake City: Bookcraft, 1969.

Eastern Europe

The peoples of Bulgaria, Greece, Hungary, Lithuania, and Roumania each have a separate identity with different customs, different languages, different surnames, and different migration patterns. In too many American books (this book is no different), these are all blended together as "Eastern Europe." They do tend to live in the same general areas, as shown on Map 15-8, with the greatest numbers congregated in Eastern United States cities. Especially valuable for these ancestors are the museums being created at Ellis Island and the Statue of Liberty, for these collections cover the years when Eastern European peoples were flocking to these shores.

Among the collections which will soon be available are large numbers of photographs of entering immigrant families lined up by size and age. Sometimes places of origin, ship, port, date, and destination are written on the photo. Not all are identified by family name.

Special Collections

Library	*Address*	*Description of Material*
University of Minnesota Immigrant Archives	Minneapolis, MN 55455	International collection for records of immigrants from Eastern and Southern Europe – includes twenty nationality groups, large collection of foreign language newspapers published in America, and records of fraternal organizations. See *Guide to the Manuscript Holdings of the Immigrant Archives* (St. Paul: Center for Immigration Studies 1974). The center also publishes *Immigrant History Newsletter* with notices of published works, acquisitions, and new research projects. The archives had 23,000 volumes, 2,000 reels of microfilm, and 2,100,000 manuscripts in 1974.
Balch Institute for Ethnic Studies	18 S. 7th Street Phildelphia, PA 19106	Outstanding collection of photographs. Original records for immigrants from Europe including family Bibles, passports, letters, diaries.
Immigrant Library	5043 Lankershim Blvd., North Hollywood, CA 91601	Private library with a large collection of European telephone directories, reference books, some microfilm. Strongest in German materials.
Public Archives of Canada, Immigration Ethnic Archives	Ottawa, Canada	Includes original passports, family documents, official emigrant/immigrant archives from foreign embassies, photographs for European settlers – many of whom later migrated into the United States. Exchange program with or through Institute for Migration Studies (Turku, Finland), Australian Ethnic Affairs Council, Czechoslovak National Association (Canada), Center for American Studies (Japan) is bringing copies from foreign archives to Canada.
New York Public Library	5th Ave. and 42nd Street, New York, NY 10018	Large collection of histories, printed volumes for European nationalities. Card catalog for Slavonic collection published in 26 vols by G. K. Hall.
Indiana University	Bloomington, In 47401	Slavic and East European collection, especially periodicals.
Stanford University Hoover Institution	Stanford, CA 94305	East European collection of 14,000 vols., mss., maps, emigration groups, periodicals, newspapers, etc.
Center for Migration Studies	209 Flagg Place, Staten Island, NY 10304	Immigrant experience in America, Catholic Church as a cultural cushion for immigrants. Includes records of social welfare organizations, church records and agencies, private papers of immigrants. See Otlha della Cava, *A Guide to the Archives of the Center for Migration Studies* (New York: For the Center, 1974).
American Museum of Immigration, Statue of Liberty National Monument	Liberty Island, New York 10004	Includes oral history, photographs, immigrants' personal papers.
Ellis Island Museum	New York, NY	Research center to be established on Ellis Island with a repository for immigrant materials for those researching family roots. Prof. August C. Bolino, Catholic University of America, Cardinal Station, Box 1314, Washington, DC 20064, is seeking donations of family records, photographs, personal papers, and immigrant records for persons who came through Ellis Island to be housed at the university until the research center is completed. See *Illinois State Genealogical Society Newsletter* 3 (Oct. 1982): 4.

How-to Books: European Ancestry

Handy Guide to Austrian Genealogical Records. Logan, Utah: Everton Publishers, 1979. 97 pp.

Handy Guide to Hungarian Genealogical Records. Logan, Utah: Everton Publishers, 1980. 100 pp.

Kowallis, Otto K., and Vera Kowallis. *Genealogical Guide and Atlas of Silesia*. Logan, Utah: Everton Publishers, n.d. 442 pp.

St. Angelo, Mabel. "Some Microfilm Sources for the Ukranian Genealogist." *Generations* 5 (1980): 11-17.

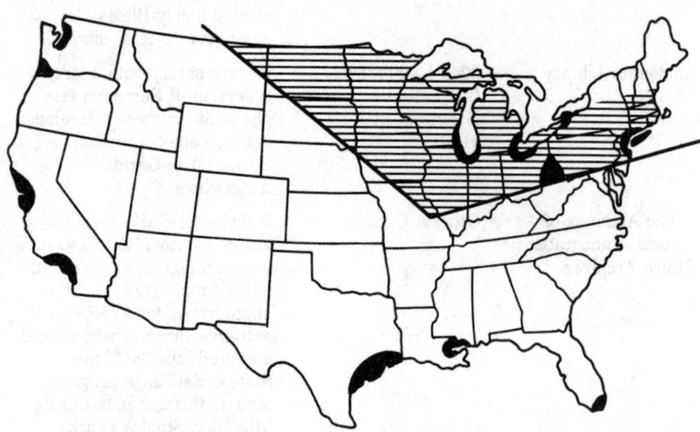

Map 15-8. Eastern European Settlement Patterns.

Bulgaria

Special Collections

Library	*Address*	*Description of Material*
University of Illinois	Urbana, IL 61801	6,200 volumes, emphasis on history.

Bibliography

Punderf, Marion V. *Bulgaria: A Bibliographic Guide.* 1965; reprint ed. New York: Arno Press, 1968.

Greece

Special Collections

Library	*Address*	*Description of Material*
Holy Cross Greek Orthodox Theological School	50 Goddard Avenue Brookline, MA 02146	Over 30,000 vols. on history of modern Greece, Greek Orthodox Church.
Greek Archives Western Americana Div., Marriott Library	University of Utah Salt Lake City, UT 84112	Six percent of Utah population in 1910 was Greek. Includes family papers, histories, newspapers, church records, oral history, and photographs.

Bibliography

Fairchild, Henry P. *Greek Immigration to the United States.* New Haven: Yale University Press, 1911.

Saloutos, Theodore. *The Greeks in the United States.* Cambridge: Harvard University Press, 1964.

Panagopaulos, E. P. *New Smyrna: An Eighteenth Century Greek Odyssey.* Gainesville, Fla.: University of Florida Press, 1966. A group of 1,200 Greeks in East Florida in 1768

Papanikolas, Helen Z. "Toil and Rage . a New Land: The Greek Immigrants in Utah." *Utah Historical Quarterly* 38 (1970): 155-77.

Hungary

Special Collections

Library	*Address*	*Description of Material*
American Hungarian Library and Historical Society	215 East 82nd Street, New York, NY 10028	Collection of about 3,000 vols. of archival materials, manuscripts, maps, and photographs. Includes rare diplomatic correspondence and other original documents relating to Hungarian immigrants.

Bibliography

Lengyel, Emil. *Americans from Hungary.* New York: J. B. Lippincott, 1948.

Sonders, D.A. *The Magyars in America.* San Francisco: R & E Research Associates, 1969.

Weinstock, S.A. *Hungarians in America: Acculturation and Occupation.* Nijhoff, 1970.

Lithuania

Special Collections

Library	*Address*	*Description of Material*
University of Pennsylvania	3420 Walnut, Philadelphia, PA 19104	4000 vols. on history of Lithuania.
University of Kansas Spencer Library	Lawrence, KS 66045	Medieval history of Lithuania.
Balzekas Museum of Lithuanian Culture	4012 Archer Avenue, Chicago, IL 60632	Unpublished memoirs, personal papers, records of Lithuanian organizations. Alphabetical card file of death notices from Lithuania newspapers, 1900-1979. Microfilm copy at the Genealogical Society of Utah and its branches.

Bibliography

*Kucas, Antanas. *Lithuanians in America.* Boston: Catholic University of America, 1981. Discusses why they left, where they came from, organizations established to cushion the immigrant experience.

Roumania

Bibliography

Galitzi, Christine A. *A Study of Assimilation Among the Roumanians in the United States.* New York: AMS Press, 1968.

Wertsman, Vladimir. *The Roumanians in America and Canada: A Guide to Information Sources.* Detroit: Gale Research Company, 1981. Excellent work.

England

A map for English settlement is ineffective, for the majority of the population in America has British ancestry, and the 1980 census showed that 40 million living Americans descend from English stock. English immigrants who came to America can present a difficult research problem for their places of residence and places of birth usually differ. The English population is a mobile one with major shifts of people from rural to urban centers and city to city in search of work.

Major movements occurred 1795-1830 with a shift toward the industrial areas of Manchester and Liverpool and from 1841-91 toward London. The next step was migration to America, Canada, and Australia. There was also some triangular traffic from England to Canada to America and from England to Australia to America. Marriages, births of children, and deaths of spouses will be found along the way. Other English families arrived after stopovers in the West Indies or Latin America.

Military service brought 125,000 British troops to America before and during the American Revolution. Many soldiers mustered out and stayed or returned with families later. British troops also served in Europe, migrating to America after discharge.

Special Collections

Library	*Address*	*Description of Material*
Allen County Public Library	230 Jefferson Street, Fort Wayne, IN 46802	Excellent collection of local history materials, publications of parish register societies, English, Scots, Irish, and Welsh periodicals.

The Francis Bacon Library	655 No. Dartmouth Avenue, Claremont, CA 91711	2,500 volumes of contemporary histories of England, sixteenth and seventeenth century; material on Francis Bacon.
Sutro Library	480 Winston Drive, San Francisco, CA 94102	Special collection of material in British history.
Henry E. Huntington Library	1151 Oxford Road, San Marino, CA 91108	Collections of printed materials, manuscripts 11th century to 1837, estate papers, military correspondence, manorial documents. A valuable collection.
Newberry Library	60 West Walton, Chicago, IL 60610	British history to World War I, oral history collections, special genealogical section rich in family and local history.
Harvard University Library	Cambridge, MA 02138	Special collections of local histories to 1715.
Washington University	6600 Millbrook Way, St. Louis, MO 63130	Collection of British Parliamentary publications.
New York University Law School	Vanderbilt Hall, Washington Square South, New York, NY 10003	Collection of ancient legal documents, many uncataloged.
Cleveland Public Library	325 Superior Avenue, Cleveland, OH 44114	Excellent British history collection.
Yale University Sterling Memorial Library	120 High Street, New Haven, CT 06520	One of the largest collections especially of Parliamentary papers, English maps, and printed local histories.
Virginia State Library	11th and Capitol Street, Richmond VA 23219	Over 10,000 volumes of county histories, parish registers, photographs.
Newark Public Library	5 Washington Street, Newark, NJ 07101	Charles Cummings, private collection of New Jersey Loyalist papers.
William L. Clements Library, University of Michigan	South University Avenue, Ann Arbor, MI 48109	Eighteenth-century documents relating to royal forests, sheriffs, smuggling, included among the Shelburne Mss. Large collections of printed histories, newspapers. Arlene P. Shy, *Guide to Manuscript Collections* (Boston: G. K. Hall, 1978).
Library of Congress Annex	2nd Street and Independence Avenue, S.E., Washington, DC 20540	Microfilmed collection of documents prepared for the American Council of Learned Societies, 2,000,000 manuscripts. See Grace G. Griffin, *A Guide to Manuscripts Relating to American History in British Depositories Reproduced for the Library of Congress*. Washington, D.C.: Library of Congress, 1946.
Folger Shakespeare Library	201 East Capitol Street, Washington, DC 20003	40,000 English manuscripts: diaries, letters, account books, Parliamentary reports. See *Catalog of Manuscripts of the Folger Shakespeare Library*. Boston: G. K. Hall, 1970. 3 vols.
Union Theological Seminary	Broadway at 120th Street, New York, NY 10006	400,000 volumes, manuscripts, maps dealing with church history of Great Britain. Includes the McAlpin collection of history and theology, 1500-1700. Multi-volume printed list of holdings available in many research libraries.
Georgetown University Special Collection	37th and O Street, S.W. Washington, DC 20057	Louis C. Hagerty collection of British regimental histories and personal narratives.
British Information Services	45 Rockefeller Plaza, New York, NY 10020	Maps, government publications, guides to archives.
University of Georgia Special collections	Athens, GA 30602	Earl of Egmont papers relating to early Georgia colonists.
Enoch Pratt Free Library, George Peabody Collection.	17 East Mt. Vernon Place, Baltimore, MD 21202	Extensive collection of British materials; including genealogies, parish registers. and maps.

Bibliography

Berkley, Francis Lewis. *British Manuscript Sources for Virginia History*. Charlottesville: Alderman Library, University of Virginia, 1952.

Berthoff, Rowland T. *British Immigrants in Industrial America, 1790-1950*. Cambridge: Harvard University Press, 1953.

Bridenbaugh, Carl. *Vexed and Troubled Englishmen, 1590-1642*. New York: Oxford University Press, 1967.

Campbell, Mildred. "English Emigration on the Eve of the American Revolution." *American Historical Review* 61 (1955): 1-20.

Carrothers, W. A. *Emigration from the British Isles*. 1929; reprint ed., New York: A. M. Kelley: 1969.

"The Cavalier Emigration." *William and Mary Quarterly*, lst series, 6 (1897-98): 89-90.

Cell, Gilliam T. *English Enterprise in New Foundland, 1577-1660*. Toronto: University of Toronto Press, 1969.

Cowan, Helen I. *British Emigration to British North America: The First Hundred Years*. Toronto: University Press, 1961.

Crouse, N. M. "The Causes of the Great Migration, 1630-1640." *New England Quarterly* 5 (1932): 3-36.

Currer-Briggs, Noel. *English Adventurers and Virginia Settlers. The Coordinated Use of Seventeenth Century British and American Records by Genealogists*. 3 vols., London: Phillimore, 1969.

Hepbnan, A. C., ed. *Minorities in History*. London: n.p., 1979. Includes English settlers in Ireland and Virginia, 1550-1650.

Hill, Douglas. *Great Emigrations: The English to New England*. London: Gentry Books, 1975.

James, Alfred, P. "The First English-Speaking Trans-Appalachian Frontier." *Mississippi Valley Historical Review* 17 (1930-31): 55-71.

Johnson, Stanley C. *A History of Emigration from the United Kingdom to North America, 1763-1912*. 1913; reprint ed., New York: A. M. Kelley, 1966.

Mowat, Charles L. "East Florida as a British Province, 1763-84." *University of California Publications* 32 (1943). Maps, excellent bibliography.

Myers, Albert C. *Quaker Arrivals at Philadelphia, 1682-1750*. Baltimore: Southern Book Co., 1957.

Newsome, A. R. *Records of Emigrants from England and Scotland in North Carolina, 1774-75*. Raleigh, N.C.: n. pub., 1962.

Newton, A. P. *Colonizing Activities of the English Puritans*. New Haven: Yale University Press, 1914.

Pennington, Loren E. *The Origins of the English Promotional Literature for America, 1553-1625*. Ann Arbor: University of Michigan 1962.

Population Movements in England, 1821-1851. Salt Lake City: Genealogical Society of Utah, 1971. Parish-by-parish account of reasons for movement in and out.

Pratt, David H. "English and Welsh Immigrants." *Genealogical Journal* 3 (1974): 8-12.

Rabb, T. K. *Enterprise and Empire: Merchant and Gentry Investment in the Expansion of England, 1575-1630*. Cambridge: Harvard University Press, 1967.

Rouse, A. L. *The Cousin Jacks: Cornish in America*. New York: Charles Scribner's Sons, 1969.

Salley, A. S. *Early English Settlers of South Carolina*. Columbia, S.C.: Colonial Dames, 1946.

Shammas, Carole. "English-born and Creole Elites in Turn-of-the-Century Virginia." *Chesapeake in the Seventeenth Century.* Chapel Hill, N.C.: University of North Carolina Press, 1979, pp. 274-96.

Shepperson, Wilbur S. *British Emigration to North America: Projects and Opinions in the Early Victorian Period.* Minneapolis: University of Minnesota Press, 1957.

__________. *The Promotion of British Emigration by Agents for American Lands, 1840-1860.* Reno: University of Nevada Press, 1954. Important study.

"Staffordshire Pedigrees, Visitations, 1664-1700." *Tyler's Quarterly* 11 (1929-30): 141. Staffordshiremen to Virginia.

Tyack, N. C. P. "Migration from East Anglia to New England before 1660." Ph.D. diss., London University, 1951.

Weslager, C. A. *The English on the Delaware, 1610-82.* New Brunswick: Rutgers University Press, 1967.

How-to-Books: English Ancestry

Bethell, David. *English Ancestry.* Salt Lake City: Accelerated Indexing Systems, 1981. 387 pp.

Boreham, John M. *The Census [English] and How to Use It.* Brentwood, Essex: Essex Society for Family History, 1982. 20 pp.

Burness, Lawrence R. "Genealogical Research in Gibraltar." *Genealogists' Magazine* 24 (March 1983): 41-44.

__________. "Genealogical Research in the Channel Islands." Ibid., 19 (1978): 169-72; 257-58.

Colwell, Stella. *The Family History Book.* Oxford, England: Phaidon Press, Limited, 1980. 176 pp. Over 150 illustrations.

Currer-Briggs, Noel and Royston Gambier. *Debrett's Family Historian.* London: Debrett, Webb, & Bower, 1981. 208 pp.

Eakle, Arlene, et. al. *Descriptive Inventory of the English Collection at the Genealogical Society of Utah.* Salt Lake City: University of Utah Press, 1979. 184 pp.

__________. *Finding English Ancestors.* Salt Lake City: Family History World, 1983. 34 pp.

Elton, G. R. *England 1200-1600.* London: Hodder and Stoughton, 1969.

Emmison, F. G. *Archives and Local History.* Chichester: Phillimore & Co., 1978. 128 pp.

Field, D. M. *Step-by-Step Guide to Tracing Your Ancestors.* London: Hamlyn, 1982.

Hamilton-Edwards, Gerald. *In Search of British Ancestry.* 4th ed. Baltimore: Genealogical Publishing Co., 1983. 224 pp.

MacFarlane, Alan. *Reconstructing Historical Communities.* Cambridge: Cambridge University Press, 1977. 222 pp.

Peskett, Hugh. *Discover Your Ancestors: A Quest for Your Roots.* Tisbury, Wiltshire: For Debrett's Peerage, 1978.

Phipps, Alan J. "An Overview of English Genealogical Research for Those Not Residing in the United Kingdom." *Relatively Speaking* 9 (Winter 1981): 5-8.

Pine, Leslie G. *American Origins.* 1960; reprint ed., Baltimore: Genealogical Publishing Co., 1967.

__________. *Your Family Tree: A Guide to Genealogical Sources.* Rev. ed. London: H. Jenkins, 1962.

__________. *Genealogists Encyclopedia.* Newton-Abbott, England: David & Charles, 1969.

Pratt, David H. "British Immigration to North America." *Families* 20 (1981): 233-39.

Round, John Horace. *Family Origins and Other Studies.* 1930; reprint ed., Baltimore: Genealogical Publishing Co., 1970. 303 pp.

__________. *Pedigree and Peerage: Studies in Peerage Law and Family History.* 2 vols. Baltimore: Genealogical Publishing Co., Inc., 1970.

__________. *Studies in Peerage and Family History.* Baltimore: Genealogical Publishing Co., Inc., 1970. 496 pp.

Smith, Frank, and David E. Gardner. *Genealogical Research in England and Wales.* 3 vols. Salt Lake City: Bookcraft, 1956-64.

Steen, Doris. "A Study of Some of the Records of the British East India Company." *Genealogical Communications Journal*: Vol. 1, pp. 21-33.

Steel, Don J. *Discovering Your Family History.* London: British Broadcasting Corporation, 1980. 172 pp.

__________. *National Index of Parish Registers: Sources for Births, Marriages, and Deaths Before 1837.* London: Society of Genealogists, 1968, 439 pp.

__________. *National Index of Parish Registers: Sources for Nonconformist Genealogy and Family History.* Chichester: Phillimore & Co., 1973.

__________. *National Index of Parish Registers: Sources for Roman Catholic Genealogy and Family History.* Chichester: Phillimore & Co., 1974. 264 pp. Includes section on Jewish records.

Storey, Richard, and L. Madden. *Primary Sources for Victorian Studies.* Chichester: Phillimore & Co., 1977.

Summers, Peter G. *How to Read a Coat of Arms.* London: Standing Conference on Local History, 1979. 23 pp.

Tate, George F. "Migration Sources--Britain to America." Paper for Genealogy 310 class, Brigham Young University, 1969. Includes several unused emigrant sources in the Public Record Office. Copy in author's possession.

Thoyts, E. E. *How to Read Old Documents.* 1893; reprint ed., Chichester: Phillimore and Co., 1980. 153 pp.

Finland

Several Finns settled among the Swedes in colonial New York and along the Delaware River. They are hard to recognize because their names were spelled in Swedish with resulting loss of identity. (See Map 15-9).

Map 15-9. Finnish Settlement Patterns.

Special Collections

Library	*Address*	*Description of Material*
Lutheran Church in American Archives	1100 East 55th Street, Chicago, IL 60615	Records for Illinois and Iowa synods, Lutheran church in America. Official depository for United Lutheran Church (German), Augustana Lutheran Church (Swedish), Evangelical Lutheran Church (Danish), Suomi Evangelical Lutheran Church (Finnish) Congregations, 1887-1960.
Suomi College, Finnish Library	Houghton, MI 49931	Excellent collection of Finnish printed vols., many histories.
University of Michigan, Bentley Library	Ann Arbor, MI 48103	Collecting archival material on film and xerox copies from Institute for General History, University of Turku, includes emigration records, 1860-1914; records of temperance societies, churches, oral history, and American letters written home to Finland. Collection now contains 91 reels of Finnish-language newspapers printed in Michigan.

Bibliography

Haglund, A. William. *Finnish Immigrants to America, 1820-1920*. Madison: University of Wisconsin Press, 1960.

*Karni, Michael G., et al. *The Finnish Experience in the Western Great Lakes Region: New Perspectives*. Vammala, Finland: n. pub. 1975.

Kaups, Matti E. "Finnish Place-names in Michigan." *Michigan History* 51 (1967).

Keijo, Virtanen. "Letters to Finland." *Michigan Historical Collections* 26 (1976), whole issue.

Kolehmainen, John I. "Founding of the Finnish Settlements in Ohio." *Ohio Archaeological and Historial Society Publications*, 49 (1940): 150-59.

Wuorinen, John H. *The Finns on the Delaware, 1638-1655*. New York: Columbia University Press, 1938.

How-to Books: Finnish Ancestry

Johnson, Amandus, "Scandinavian and Finnish Genealogy: A Bibliography." *National Genealogical Society Quarterly*, 48 (1960): 1-11.

France

One problem with tracing French ancestry is the ease with which they merge into the national group they live with, the original name being anglicized. A second obstacle is that French-sounding surnames may actually be Belgian. Genealogists tracing a pedigree into Dutch New York or the Wisconsin-Canadian border area can watch for subtle ties in language and settlement patterns. Sometimes a useful check is the International Genealogical Index (IGI) for Belgium and France to see in which country pockets of the surname appear. See Map 15-10.

Map 15-10. French settlement patterns.

Special Collections

Library	*Address*	*Description of Materials*
Southwestern Louisiana Institute, Stephens Memorial Library	Lafayette, LA 70501	French in Louisiana, Acadians-4,000 vols., French in North America.
Louisiana State University Library	Baton Rouge, LA 70803	3,000,000 manuscripts, rich on French in Louisiana.
Tulane University Howard-Tilton Memorial Library	Audubon Place New Orleans, LA 70118	500,000 manuscripts, newspapers, family papers–and documents, lower Mississippi Valley.
d'Entremont Collection	Rev. Clarence d'Entremont, 71 Center Street, Fairhaven, MA 02719	Fine private library of Acadian materials. 4 x 6 card index. Will answer requests by mail.
Donald J. Hebert	Cecilia, LA 70521	Private library. Acadian materials. Open house for researchers held once a year.
Northwestern University Library	Evanston, IL 60201	Over 10,000 manuscripts and documents for 1784-1800.
University of Michigan	Ann Arbor, MI 48104	10,000 vols., most of which deal with French societies and associations.
Smith College Library	Northampton, MA 01060	French Canadian collection of about 7,000 vols.
Paris Library	1330 13th Terrace Miami Beach, FL 33139	Union collection of books about Paris; in English.
Harvard University	Cambridge, MA 02138	French local history collection.
Mt. Allison University Ralph Pickard Bell Library	Sackville, New Brunswick, Canada EOA 3CO	Winthrop P. Bell Collection of Acadian History
Eleutherian Mills Historical Library	Greenville, DE 19807	French manuscripts, periodicals, family documents, DuPont family records. See John B. Riggs, *Guide to the Manuscripts in the Eleutherian Mills Historical Library* (Greenville, Del.: DuPont, 1970).
Detroit Public Library	5201 Woodward Avenue, Detroit, MI 48202	Manuscripts, maps, photographs, local history on French Canadian history.
Library of the French Institute in the U.S.	22 East 60th Street, New York, NY 10022	French civilization collection, emphasis on cultural development.
American Antiquarian Society	185 Salisbury Street Worcester, MA 01609	French Louisiana collection, history, newspapers, etc. About 25,000 vols. on French
Association Canado Americaine	52 Concord Street Manchester, NH 03101	About 25,000 vols. on French in North America.
Center of Acadian Studies, University of Moncton	Moncton, New Brunswick	History and genealogy of Acadians.
Illinois History Survey University of Illinois	Urbana, IL 61801	French colonial archives, 1671-1808 on boundaries, military affairs, missions, naval records (1684-1741).
Basque Studies Program University of Nevada Library	Reno, NV 89557	Documents on Basques who settled in Nevada and California. Materials in French-Spanish, English, Italian. Newsletter, language studies also offered.

Acadians

Bibliography

Doughty, Arthur G. "The Acadian Exile," *Chronicles of Canada* 9 (1922).

d'Entremont, Clarence J. "The Acadians and Their Genealogical Records." *Genealogical Journal* 5 (Dec. 1979): 136-45.

Griffiths, Naomi. *The Acadians: Creation of a People*. Toronto: McGraw-Hill, 1973.

*Hebert, Donald J. *Acadians in Exile*. Cecilia, La: Hebert Publications, 1982. Introduction is especially valuable.

Hoyt, William D., Jr. "A Contemporary View of the Acadian Arrival in Maryland, 1755." *William and Mary Quarterly*, 3rd series, 5 (1948): 571-75.

Ledet, Wilton Paul. "Acadian Exiles in Pennsylvania." *Pennsylvania History* 9 (1942): 118-28.

Millard, Clifford. "The Acadians in Virginia," *Virginia Magazine of History and Biography* 40 (1932): 241-58.

Sollers, Basil. "The Acadians (French Neutrals) Transported to Maryland." *Maryland Historical Magazine* 3 (1980): 1-21.

Winzerling, Oscar W. *Acadian Odyssey*. Baton Rouge: Lousiana State University, 1955.

French

Bibliography

Baillargeon, Le P. Noë. "The Missions of the Quebec Seminary in the Mississippi Valley, 1698-1699." *French Canadian and Acadian Genealogical Research* (1969).

Bennett, Charles E. *Settlement of Florida*. Gainesville: Florida University Press, 1968.

Bugg, James L., Jr. "The French Huguenot Frontier Settlement of Manakin Town." *Virginia Magazine of History and Biography* 61 (1953): 359-94.

Childs, St. Julien R. "The Petit-Guerard Colony." *South Carolina Historical Magazine* 43 (1942): 1-17, 88-97.

Cooke, James J. *New French Imperialism, 1880-1910: The Third Republic and Colonial Expansion*. Newton Abbott, England: David & Charles, 1973.

Delafosse, Marcel. *Des Rivedoux à la Caroline du Sud*. B. Assoc. Amis Ile de Ré, 1969.

DeVille, Winston. *Gulf Coast Colonials: A Compendium of French Families in Early Eighteenth Century Louisiana*. Baltimore: Genealogical Publishing Company, 1968.

Douglas, Donald. *The Huguenots: Story of Huguenot Emigration, Particularly to New England*. New York: n.p., 1954.

Dupre, Huntley. "The French in Early Kentucky." *Filson Quarterly*, 15 (1941): 78-104.

Franco-American Overview. 6 vols. Cambridge: National Assessment and Dissemination Center for Bilingual Education, 1979-83.

Fregault, Guy. "18th Century French America." *French Canadian and Acadian Genealogical Review* (1968).

Gilbert, Chinard. *Les Refugiés Huguenots in Amérique*. Paris: Société d'Edition, 1925.

Hamer, P. M. "Anglo-French Rivalry in the Cherokee Country, 1754-57." *North Carolina Historical Review* 2 (1925): 303-22.

Harvey, D. C. *The French Regime in Prince Edward Island*. New York: AMS Press, 1970.

Holmes, Abiel. "Essay on History of the French Protestants." Massachusetts Historical Collection vol. 22, 1832.

Hondaille, Jacques A. "French Refugees in the United States, 1790-1810." *National Genealogical Society Quarterly* 51 (1963): 209-13.

Jordan, Terry G. "Antecedents of the Long-lot in Texas," *Annals, Association of American Geographers* 64 (1974): 70-86.

Kellog, Louise Phelps. *The French Regime in Wisconsin and the Northwest*. New York: Cooper Square Publication, 1968.

Kent, Donald H. *French Invasion of Western Pennsylvania 1753*. Harrisburg, Pa.: n. pub., 1954.

Kingdon, Robert M. "Pourquoi les refugiés huguenots aux colonies américaines sont-ils devenus épiscopaliens?" *Le Refuge Huguenot*, Colloque Montpellier (1969).

Land, Mary Wilson. *The Establishment of the Huguenots in Virginia*. Master's thesis, William and Mary, 1942.

McDermott, John F. *The French in the Mississippi Valley*. Urbana: University of Illinois Press, 1965.

__________. *French Men and French Ways in the Mississippi Valley*. Urbana: University of Illinois Press, 1969.

McCall, Grant Edwin. *Basque-Americans and a Sequential Theory of Migration and Adaptation*. San Francisco: San Francisco State College, 1968.

Menk, Patricia H. "Notes on Some Early Huguenot Settlements in Virginia." *Virginia Magazine of History and Biography* 52 (1944): 194-96.

Nasatir, Abraham P. *French Activities in California: An Archival Calendar-Guide*. Stanford: University Press, 1945.

Potter, Elisha R. *Memoir Concerning the French Settlement in the Colony of Rhode Island*. Providence: Sidney S. Rider, 1879.

Reaman, George E. *The Trail of the Huguenots in Europe, the United States, South Africa, and Canada*. Baltimore: Genealogical Publishing Company., 1983.

Rieder, Milton P., Jr., and Norma Rieder. *The Acadians in France*. Metairie, La.: n. pub., 1972.

Thwaites, Rueben Gold. *France in America, 1497-1763*. Westport, Conn.: Greenwood Press, 1970.

Trudel, Jean-Paul. *Quelque noms français dans l'histoire de Chicago et du Middlewest*. Astican, 1969.

Vance, John L. *French Settlement and Settlers of Gallipolis*. Ohio Archeological and Historical Society Publication 3 (1890) 45-81.

Weilbrenner, Bernard. *Archival Resources in Quebec for the History of the Mississippi Valley*. French Canadian and Acadian Genealogical Research (1969).

Weiner, Margary. *The French Exile, 1789-1815*. London: Murray, 1960.

Wessel, B. B. *An Ethnic Survey of Woonsocket, Rhode Island*. New York: Arno Press, 1970.

Winthrop, Pickard B. *The "Foreign Protestants" and the Settlement of Nova Scotia*. Toronto: University of Toronto Press, 1961.

Wyllys, Rufus Kay. *The French in Sonora 1850-1854: The Story of French Adventurers from California into Mexico*. Berkeley: University of California Press, 1932.

How-to Books: French Ancestry

Bird, Jack. "Some Sources for French Genealogy and Heraldry." *Genealogists' Magazine* 13 (1960): 237.

de Borgomale, H. L. Rabino. "Genealogical Research in France." *Genealogists' Magazine* 10 (1946): 1-7.

Douglas, William A., and Richard W. Etulain. *Basque Americans: A Guide to Information Sources*. Detroit: Gale Research Co., 1982.

Durye, Pierre. *Genealogy: An Introduction to Continental Concepts*. New Orleans: Polyanthos, 1977. 143 pp.

Jensen, C. Russell. *Preliminary Survey of the French Collection at the Genealogical Society of Utah*. Salt Lake City: University of Utah Press, 1980. 475 pp.

Germany

The Germans who came to America before the American Revolution were mostly Protestants–Lutheran and Reformed–with relatively few Catholics. The migrations between 1820 and 1920 brought many Catholics. In towns where German Protestants and Catholics settled, they tended to establish themselves in separate sections of town with their own churches and their own cemeteries. (See Maps 15-11.) With the exception of the large number of Germans from Russia who came with the New Immigration, the flow of Germans was from the same areas along the Rhine River as the early migrations. German immigrants surpassed all the others from 1850 to 1885, peaking in 1882 with 250,630 persons.

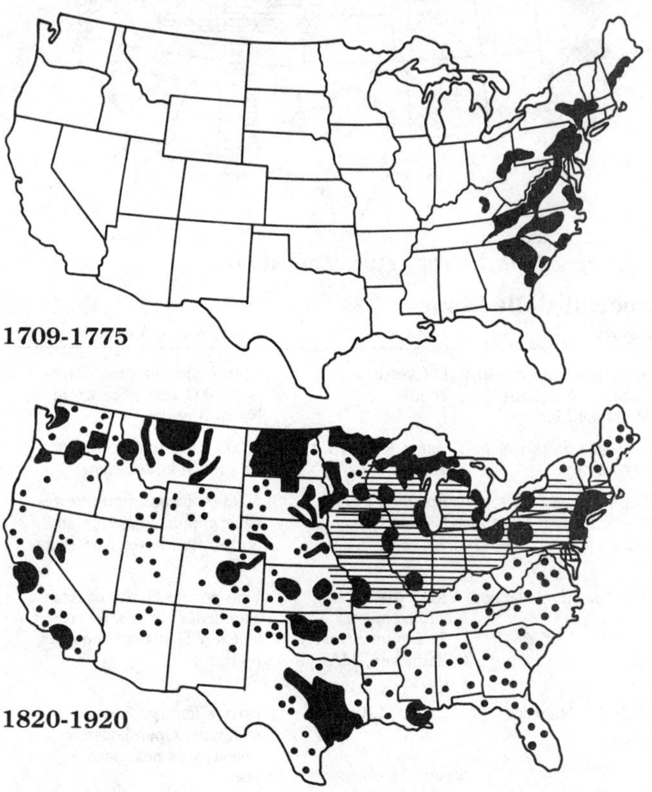

Maps 15-11. German Settlement Patterns.

Special Collections

Library	Address	Description of Material
Free Library of Philadelphia Rare Book Dept.	Logan Square Philadelphia, PA 19103	2,400 vols., 1,000 mss. of Pennsylvania German *fraktur*. Largest collection in United States.
Bucks County Historical Society	Pine and Ashland Streets, Doylestown, PA 18901	Large collection of Pennsyvania German *fraktur*.
Lebanon Valley College Library	Annville, PA 17003	1750 vols. of Pennsylvania German *fraktur*.
Society for the History of Germans in Maryland	231 St. Paul Place Baltimore, MD 21202	Immigrants from Germany and their descendants.
Franklin & Marshall College	Lancaster, PA 17604	Manuscripts for Pennsylvania German studies. Special card-index (160,000 entries) to periodicals and learned society publications. Large collection of church records. Microfilm copies of much of this material available through Genealogical Society of Utah.
Immigrant Library	5043 Lankershim Boulevard, Hollywood, CA 91601	Printed volumes and microforms. Complete set telephone directories, East Germany and West Germany. List of surnames already researched available on request.
German Society of Pennsylvania	Spring Garden & Marshall Streets Philadelphia, PA 19123	Over 45,000 vols., mostly in German, includes history and biography.
Carl Schurz Memorial Foundation	420 Chestnut Street, Phildelphia, PA 19106	Photographs, mss., printed volumes. Union Catalog of of German-Americana.
Goethe House	120 E. 56th Street, New York, NY 10020	Currently published books in German about Germany. Over 175 current German newspapers received regularly.
National Archives and Records Services	NARS General Services Administration Washington, DC 20408	Records of the German Third Reich, Nuremberg War Crime Trials, German Foreign Ministry, and others. Requires good working knowledge of German. Most are available on microfilm. See Robert Wolfe, ed., *Captured German and Related Records: A National Archives Conference* (Athens, Ohio: University of Ohio Press, 1974.), 279 pp. Describes finding aids, collections.
University of Texas Barker Texas History Center	Austin, TX 78712	Maps, manuscripts, private volumes. Includes records for the German-Wendish settlement in Texas.
American Historical Society, Germans from Russia	631 D Street, Lincoln, NE 68502	Genealogies, family Bibles and records, German language, newspapers, articles on immigrants, histories, etc. See Emma S. Haynes, *Bibliography of the AHSGR Archives and Historical Library, Greeley, Co.* Lincoln, Neb.: AHSGR, 1981.
York County Historical Society	250 E. Market Street, York, PA 17403	Ten-volume collection of emigrant/immigrant articles with three-volume index, giving European origins of settlers in Pennsylvania. Genealogies, histories, oral history tapes.
Colorado State University Germans from Russia Study Project	Fort Collins, CO 80523	Family documents, oral history tapes, theses and dissertations, articles, histories.
Pennsylvania German Society	Box 97, Breinigsville, PA 18031	Active publishing progam of original sources relating to Pennsylvania Dutch.
Lehigh County Historical Society	Old Courthouse Hamilton and Fifth, Allentown, PA 18101	German language newspapers collection, genealogies, family histories, original records for Lehigh county.
Mennonite Historical Library, Goshen College	Goshen, IN 46526	Special Amish projects, underwritten by Johns Hopkins University School of Medicine, including a composite index of names listed in Amish genealogies and a composite genealogy of all living married Amish persons.

Bibliography

Albrecht, Abraham. *Mennonite Settlement in Kansas*. Master's thesis, University of Kansas, 1925.

Bernheim, Gotthardt. *History of the German Settlements and the Lutheran Church in North and South Carolina*. 1872; reprint ed.,Baltimore: Genealogical Publishing Company, 1975.

Bisele, Rudolph L. *History of the German Settlements in Texas, 1831-61*. Austin: Von Boeckmann Jones Co., 1930.

Bittinger, Lucy F. *The Germans in Colonial Times*. 1901; reprint ed. New York: Russell and Russell, 1968.

Boam, Thomas L. "German Migration to America." *Genealogical Journal* 3 (1974): 13-17.

Brink, Benjamin M. "Palatine Settlements in New York." *New York State Historical Association Proceedings* 11 (1912): 136-43.

Brown, J. H. "Early German Settlers Along the Hudson and Schoharie." *Americana* 8 (1913): 794-803.

Caldwell, Lillie M. *Texas Wends, Their First Half Century*. Salado, Tex.: For the author, 1959.

Cunz, Dieter. *The Maryland Germans: A History*. Princeton: University Press, 1948.

Dahl, John A. "The German-Wendish Settlement of Serbin, Texas." *Genealogical Journal* 7 (March 1978): 17-20.

Diffenderffer, Frank R. *The German Immigration into Pennsylvania, 1700-1775*. 1900; reprint ed., Baltimore: Genealogical Publishing Co., 1979.

Dolan, Jay P. *The Immigrant Church: New York's Irish and German Catholics, 1815-1865*. Baltimore: Johns Hopkins Press, 1975.

Earl, Samuel. "The Palatines and their Settlement in the Valley of the Upper Mohawk." *Oneida Historical Society Transactions*, 1881, pp. 31-51.

Ellsworth, Wolcott W. "The Palatines in the Mohawk Valley." *New York State Historical Association Proceedings* 14 (1915): 295- 311.

Faust, Albert B. *The German Element in the United States*. 2 vols. Boston, 1909. Includes maps showing settlement locations.

Fecher, Vincent J. *A Study of the Movement for German National Parishes in Philadelphia and Baltimore, 1787-1802*. Rome, Italy: n. pub., 1955.

"A Forgotten Moravian Settlement in New Jersey." *Pennsylvania Magazine of History and Biography* 37 (1913): 248-52.

Fries, Adelaide L. *The Moravians in Georgia, 1735-40*. Raleigh: Edwards & Broughton, 1905.

Furer, Howard B., ed. *The Germans in America, 1607-1970: A Chronology and a Fact Book*. Dobbs Ferry, N.Y.: Oceana Publications, 1973.

*Guenther, Karen. "Germans in America: German Settlement of Colonial Pennsylvania Compared to that of Antebellum Texas." *Historical Review of Berks County* 48 (Winter 1982): 10-29. Includes excellent maps.

Heavener, Ulysses S. A. *German New River Settlement: Virginia*. 1929; reprint ed., Baltimore: Genealogical Publishing Co., 1981.

Hostetler, John A., and Gertrude E. Huntington. *The Hutterites in North America*. New York: Holt, Rinehart, and Winston, 1967.

Johnson, Hildegard, "Location of German Immigrants in the Middle West." *Annals, Association American Geographers* 41 (1951): 1-41. Includes map.

Huebener, Theodore. *The Germans in America*. Philadelphia: Chilton Book Company, 1962.

Kieffer, Henry M. *Some of the First Settlers on the Forks of the Delaware and Their Descendants*. Easton, Penn.: For the author, 1902.

Knittle, Walter A. *Early Eighteenth Palatine Emigration: A British Government Redemptioners Project to Manufacture Naval Stores*. Philadelphia: Dorrence & Company, 1937.

Kriebel, H. W. "The Schwenkfelders in Pennsylvania: A Historical Sketch." *Pennsylvania German Society Proceedings*, vol. 13 (1904).

Kuhns, Oscar. *The German and Swiss Settlements of Colonial Pennsylvania*. New York, 1900.

Luebke, Frederick C. *Immigrants and Politics: Germans of Nebraska, 1800-1900*. Lincoln: University of Nebraska Press, 1969.

Mellick, Andrew D., Jr. "German Emigration to the American Colonies: Its Cause and the Distribution of the Emigrants." *Pennsylvania Magazine of History and Biography* 10 (1886): 241-50, 375-91.

Meynen, Emil. *Bibliography on German Settlements in Colonial North America*. 1937; reprint ed., Detroit: Gale Research Co., 1966.

Myers, Raymond E. "The Story of Germanna." *Filson Quarterly* 48 (1974): 27-42.

Nead, Daniel W. *The Pennsylvania German in the Settlement of Maryland*. 1914; reprint ed., Baltimore: Genealogical Publishing Company, 1980.

Rosenberger, Homer T. "Migrations of the Pennsylvania Germans to Western Pennsylvania." *Western Pennsylvania Historical Magazine* 53 (1970): 319-35; 54 (1971), 58-76.

Rubincam, Milton. "Materials in Foreign Archives for Writing Pennsylvania History." Pennsylvanian 2 (1944-45):17

Ruth, Jacob E. "A Journey in the Mid-Nineteenth Century." *Mennonite Quarterly Review* 42 (1968). Mennonite immigration to America.

Sachse, J. F. *The German Pietists of Provincial Pennsylvania, 1694- 1708*. Philadelphia: For the author, 1895.

Sallet, Richard. *Russian-German Settlements in the U. S.* Fargo, N.D.: n. pub., 1974.

*__________. *Russian-German Settlements in the United States*. Fargo: North Dakota Institute for Regional Studies, 1974. Includes place names of German settlements in Russia. Excellent maps.

Schelbert, Leo, and Henvig Rappolt. *Alles ist ganz anders hier*. Breisgau: Walter-Verlag Olten and Freiburg, 1977. Immigrant letters written home to Germany. In German.

Scheuerman, Richard D. *Pilgrims on the Earth: A German-Russian Chronicle*. Fairfield, Wash.: Ye Galleon Press, 1974. Includes several immigrant lists.

Schultz, Arthur R., et al. *Bibliography of German Culture in America to 1940*. Madison: University of Wisconsin Press, 1953.

Schuricht, Herrmann. *The German Element in Virginia*. 2 vols. 1898-1900; reprint ed. Baltimore: Genealogical Publishing Company, 1977.

Smith, C. Henry. "The Mennonite Immigration to Pennsylvania, 18th Century." *Pennsylvania German Society Proceedings* 25 (1929): 1-142.

Smith, Guy H. "Notes on the Distribution of the German-Born in Wisconsin in 1905." *Wisconsin Magazine of History* 13 (1929-30): 107-20.

Spalek, John M. *Guide to Archival Materials of German-Speaking Emigration to the United States after 1933*. Charlottesville, Va.: University Press of Virginia, 1981. Valuable.

Strobel, P. A. *The Salzburgers and their Descendants*. Baltimore: Newton Kurtze, 1855.

Swehla, H. "Bohemians in Central Kansas." *Kansas State Historical Society Collections* 13 (1913-14): 469-512.

__________. "German Element in Central Kansas." Ibid., pp. 513-34.

Tolzmann, Don H. *Americana Germania: A Bibliography*. Metuchen, N.J.: Scarecrow Press, 1975.

Walker, Mack. *Germany and the Emigration, 1816-1885*. Cambridge: Harvard University Press, 1964.

Wayland, John W. *The German Element in the Shenandoah Valley in Virginia*. Charlottesville: University of Virginia Press, 1907.

Wust, Klaus. *Virginia Germans*. Charlottesville: University of Virginia Press, 1969.

__________. "German Mystics and Sabbatarians in Virginia, 1700- 1764." *Virginia Magazine of History and Biography* 72 (1964): 330-47.

How-to Books: German Ancestry

Arndt, Karl J. R. "How to Find Your Hessian Ancestor." *Genealogical Journal* 6 (March 1977): 15-18.

Epp, Frank H. "The Mennonites: Genealogical Opportunity and Genealogical Problems." *Families* 15 (1976): 150-59.

Genealogical Research in German-Speaking Lands: A Symposium. Washington, D.C.: National Genealogical Society, 1958.

Genealogical Society of Utah. *The Hamburg Passenger Lists*. Research Paper, C-30. Salt Lake City: Genealogical Society of Utah, 1976. 25 pp. Includes glossary of column titles.

Gerberich, Albert H. "Geographical Aspects of Pennsylvania German Genealogical Study," *National Genealogical Society Quarterly* 34 (1936): 113-17.

Hostetler, John A., and Beulah S. Hostetler. "Amish Genealogy: A Progress Report." *Pennsylvania Folklife* 19 (Autumn 1969): 23-27.

Jensen, Larry O. *A Genealogical Handbook of German Research*. 2 vols. Rev. ed. Pleasant Grove, Utah: For the author, 1980-84.

Johnson, Arta F. *How to Read German Church Records Without Knowing Much German*. Columbus, Ohio: For the author, 1982.

__________. *Bibliography and Source Materials for Researching German-Speaking Ancestry*. Columbus, Ohio: For the author, 1982.

Jones, Henry Z., Jr. "Finding the Ancestral Home of a Palatine Forefather: The Case of Martin Zerbe." *Pennsylvania Genealogical Magazine* 29 (1975): 129-32. Includes how to trace neighbors and associates to document your own ancestor.

__________. "The Palatine Families of New York: A Comprehensive Study." *Genealogical Journal* 5 (1976): 126-28.

Konrad, J. *German Family Research Made Simple*. Rev. ed. Munroe Falls, Ohio: Summit Publications, 1982. 103 pp.

Nelson, Vernon H. "Moravian Genealogical Research." *Pennsylvania Genealogical Magazine* 29 (1975): 41-50.

Reschke, Horst A. *German Genealogical Research*. Salt Lake City: Privately printed, 1966.

Roberts, Charles R. *Genealogical Research Among Pennsylvania German and Huguenot Families*. Washington, D.C.: National Genealogical Society, 1933. 15 pp.

Sala, Karl. "East Germany: Field Research." *APG Newsletter* 5 (May 1983): 5-6.

Smelzer, Ronald. *Preliminary Survey to the German Collection at the Genealogical Society of Utah*. Salt Lake City: University of Utah Press, 1979. 638 pp.

Smith, Clifford Neal, and Anna P. Smith. *Encyclopedia of German-American Genealogical Research*. 2 vols. New York: R. R. Bowker, 1976-77.

__________. *American Genealogical Resources in German Archives (AGRIGA): A Handbook*. New York: R. R. Bowker Company, 1977.

Ward, Robert E. "German and German-American Genealogical Guides and Sources since 1850." *Genealogical Journal* 6 (March 1977): 3- 14.

Wellauer, Maralyn A. *Tracing Your German Roots*. Milwaukee: For the author, n.d., 88 pp.

Iceland

Iceland sent about 30 percent of its total population, which was small to begin with, to the United States, Brazil, and Manitoba, Canada. Mormon missionaries converted some as early as 1854 who went to Utah, but the majority of immigrants came between 1873 and 1890. (See Map 15-12.)

Special Collections

Library	*Address*	*Description of Collections*
Johns Hopkins University, Milton S. Eisenhower Library	North Charles and 34th Street, Baltimore, MD 21218	18th-19th century manuscripts for Icelandic history, some printed volumes.
University of Wisconsin Madison	728 State Street Madison, WI 53706	Collection of printed vols. for Icelandic history.
Genealogical Society of Utah	50 East N. Temple Salt Lake City, Utah 84150	Microfilm copies (800 reels) of parish registers, emigrant materials; printed volumes of Icelandic history.
Cornell University Olin Library	Ithaca, NY 14853	Willard Fishe Collection

Map 15-12. Icelandic Settlement Patterns.

Bibliography

Jackson, Thorstina. *History of Icelanders in North Dakota.* Reykjavik: n. pub., 1936.

Thorsteinsson, T. T., and Tryggvi Olesen. *History of the Icelanders in the Western World.* 5 vols. Reykjavik: n. pub., 1940-55.

How-to Books: Icelandic Ancestry

Jonasson, Eric. *Tracing Your Icelandic Family Tree.* Winnipeg: Wheatfield Press, 1975. 51 pp.

Ireland

Ireland responded eagerly to immigration promotions from the United States. Emigrant agents operated out of Londonderry, Portrush, Newry, Belfast, and Larne (1718-75), selling tickets as far away as Dublin. Some thirty American states, seeking Irish settlers, promoted their benefits within Ireland, and so did the canal and railroad companies, who often gave bonuses to those who signed up.

In the early 1840s, Canada increased the immigrant tax, so Irish who would have gone first to Canada came directly to the United States. Irish immigration peaked 1846-53 and again in 1863 (although there seems to be no tie between the newly arrived Irish and the need for soldiers in the Civil War). The Irish avoided steam vessels until after 1850 because they were more expensive.

Many thousands of Irish settled first in northern England for a few years to a generation or two before migrating to the United States, clustering in Liverpool, Manchester, and other northern cities. And many Irish served as foreign mercenaries on the Continent before migrating to America. If you have been looking for your Irish ancestor in Ireland without success, check these possibilities.

One migration pattern rarely noted is the route from Liverpool to Cork to Galway by ship. Irish could and did travel to Liverpool for work and return to their families by this route. Important "ports" of entry in America for Irishmen were Ogdensburg and Buffalo, New York; Chicago; and Boston. See Map 15-13.

Special Collections

Library	*Address*	*Description of Material*
American Irish Historical Society	991 Fifth Avenue New York, NY 10028	12,000 volumes including local histories of provinces, counties, cities, towns, parishes. About 1,250 manuscripts, family records.
St. John's University	75 Lewis Avenue Brooklyn, NY 10206	1,000 volumes on Irish history. 16th- and 17th-century patent rolls, ancient laws of Ireland.
Henry E. Huntington Library	1151 Oxford Road San Marino, CA 91108	Irish printed collections, manuscripts, bibliographies.
New England Historic Genealogical Society	101 Newsbury Street, Boston, MA 02116	Periodicals, manuscripts, maps, genealogical collection.
Friends Historical Library, Swarthmore College	Swarthmore, PA 19081	Microfilm copies of Quaker Irish records.
Samford University Harwell G. Davis Library	800 Lakeshore Drive Birmingham, AL 35209	Irish collection includes genealogies, heraldry, histories, periodicals.
University of Chicago Library, Dept. of Special Collections	1100 East 57th Street Chicago, IL 60637	Irish collection covers 17th-19th centuries. Includes large collection of newspapers. See *A Preliminary Guide to the Manuscripts and Archives in the University of Chicago Library* (Chicago: University Press, 1973).
Diocese of Ogdensburg Archives	622 Washington Street Ogdensburg, NY 13669	Includes births, marriages, deaths of Irish immigrants coming into United States via Ogdensburg.
Irish-American Cultural Institute	683 Osceola Avenue St. Paul, MN 55105	Publishes *Eire: A Journal of Irish Studies.* Maintains Irish publications and media, library of printed Irish materials.
Boston College Bapst Library	Chestnut Hill MA 02167	Irish collection of 3,700 vols. which include transcriptions of mss., legal documents, printed materials.
Providence Public Library	150 Empire Street Providence, RI 02903	Small Irish collection.
Villanova University Falvey Memorial Library	Villanova, PA 19085	Joseph McGarrity collection of Irish-American materials

Map 15-13. Irish Settlement Patterns.

Bibliography

Adams, William F. *Ireland and Irish Immigration to the New World, 1815 to the Famine.* New Haven: Yale University Press, 1932.

Byrne, Stephen. *Irish Emigration to the United States.* 1873; reprint ed., New York: Arno Press, 1969.

Fitzpatrick. "Early Irish Settlers in Kentucky." *Journal of the American Irish Historical Society* 2 (1899): 139-44.

Gibson, Florence E. *The Attitudes of the New York Irish Toward State and National Affairs, 1848-1892.* New York: Columbia University Press, 1951.

Hackett, J. Dominick. "Philadelphia Irish." *Journal of the American Irish Historical Society* 30 (1932): 103-17.

"Irish Builders in North Carolina." *Journal of the American Irish Historical Society* 10 (1911): 258-61.

"Irish Settlers on the Opequan." *Journal of the American Irish Historical Society* 6 (1906): 71-74.

Lawless, Joseph T. "Some Irish Settlers in Virginia." *Journal of the American Irish Historical Society* 2 (1899): 161-66.

Linehan, John C. "Irish Pioneers and Builders of Kentucky." *Journal of the American Irish Historical Society* 3 (1900): 78-88.

__________. "The Irish Pioneers of Texas." *Journal of the American Irish Historical Society* 2 (1899): 120-38.

__________. "Early Irish Settlements in Virginia." *Journal of the American Irish Historical Society* 4 (1904): 30-42.

Mann, A. P. "The Irish in New York in the Early 1860s." *Irish Historical Studies* 7 (1950): 87-108.

McDonald, M. J. *History of the Irish in Wisconsin in the Nineteenth Century: A Dissertation.* Washington: Catholic University of America Press, 1954.

Morehouse, Frances. "The Irish Migration of the Forties." *American Historical Review* 33 (1927-18): 579-92.

O'Brien, Michael J. "An Interesting Example of the Extent of Irish Emigrations to the American Colonies." *Journal of the American Irish Historical Society* 27 (1928): 179-83.

__________. "Irish Pioneers in Berks County, Pennsylvania." *Journal of the American Irish Historical Society* 27 (1928): 39-45.

__________. "Irish Pioneers in Maryland." *Journal of the American Irish Historical Society* 14 (1915): 207-19.

__________. "The Irish in Montgomery and Washington Counties, Maryland in 1778." *Journal of the American Irish Historical Society* 24 (1925): 157-61.

__________. "Irish Settlers in Pennsylvania." *Journal of the American Irish Historical Society* 6 (1906): 37.

__________. "North Carolina. Some Early MacCarthys, McGuires, Ryans, Fitzpatricks, O'Quinns, Sullivans, Burkes, and Learys." *Journal of the American Irish Historical Society* 12 (1913): 161-67.

O'Grady, Joseph P. *How the Irish Became Americans.* New York: Twayne Publishers, 1973.

O'Leary, Cornelius F. "The Irish in the Early Days of St. Louis." *Journal of the American Irish Historical Society* 9 (1910): 206-13.

Purcell, R. J. "Irish Settlers in Early Delaware." *Pennsylvania History* 14 (1947): 94-107.

Rice, Bernadine. "The Irish in Texas." *Journal of the American Irish Historical Society* 30 (1932): 60-70.

Roth, Cecil. "A Description of America, 1785." *American Jewish Archives* 17 (1965): 27-33.

Rowly, William E. "The Irish Aristocracy of Albany, 1798-1878." *New York History* 52 (1971): 275-304.

Schrier, Arnold. *Ireland and the American Emigration, 1850-1900.* St. Paul: University of Minnesota Press, 1958.

Walsh, Francis R. "Who Spoke for Bostons' Irish? The Boston Pilot in the Nineteenth Century." *Journal of Ethnic Studies* 10 (1982).

*Wittke, Carl. *The Irish in America.* 1956; reprint ed., Russell and Russell, 1970.

How-to Books: Irish Ancestry

Begley, Donal F. *Irish Genealogy: A Record Finder.* Dublin: Heraldic Artists, Ltd., 1981. 252 pp.

Clare, Wallace. *A Simple Guide to Irish Genealogy.* London: G. E. J. Coldwell, 1938. 34 pp.

DeRoo, Virginia M. "The Process I Used in the Search for Information about My Clifford Reilly Ancestors in Ireland." *Genealogical Helper,* March/April 1978: pp. 9-14.

Flolliot, Rosemary. "Genealogy in Ireland." *American Genealogist* 52 (1976): 210-15.

Hackett, James Dominick. "How to Trace Your Irish Relatives and Ancestors." *Journal of the American Irish Historical Society* 28 (1929-30): 124-39.

Handbook on Irish Genealogy. 5th ed. Dublin: Heraldic Artists, 1980. 145 pp.

O'Laughlin, Michael C. *The Complete Book for Tracing Your Irish Ancestors.* North Kansas City, Mo.: For the author, 1980. 179 pp.

Trainor, Brian. "Sources for Genealogical Research in Ireland." *Canadian Genealogist* 1 (1979): 132-54.

Ward, William R. *A Primer for Irish Genealogical Research.* Salt Lake City: William R. Ward, 1976. 35 pp.

Italy

Heavy concentrations of Italians occur in the major Northern and Western cities although small pockets can be found in other areas. See Map 15-14. Most of the Italians who emigrated in the colonial period were Waldenses (Protestants), largely from the Piedmont area with close kinship to the Huguenots. Those who came after 1820 were Catholic. By 1907 Italians made up the third largest immigrant group coming into the United States. Principal ports of entry were New York City, Baltimore, and Boston.

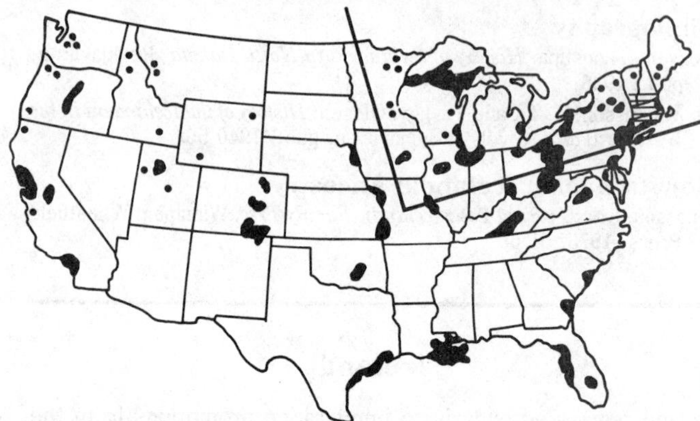

Map 15-14. Italian Settlement Patterns.

Special Collections

Library	*Address*	*Description of Materials*
University of Wisconsin Memorial Library	728 State Street Madison, WI 53706	Microfilm copies of Archivio Stato Genoa materials, registers, and cartularies of Genoa Notaries beginning 1154.
Providence Public Library	150 Empire Street Providence, RI 02903	Sherman Italian collection of about 4,000 volumes on Italian history and culture.
Italian Cultural Institute	686 Park Avenue N.W., New York, NY 10021	13,000 vols of Italian materials.
Dominican House of Studies, Order of Preachers, Province of St. Joseph	487 Michigan Avenue, N.E. Washington, DC 20017	Growth of Roman Catholic church in Ohio and Mississippi valleys, especially Ohio and Kentucky. Large archives for Dominican order in the United States.
Center for Migration Studies	209 Flagg Place Staten Island, NY 10304	Immigrant experience of Italians to America, role of Catholic church in immigration and assimilation. Records of social welfare agencies, labor unions, Catholic organizations, family papers, unpublished memoirs. See Otha della Cava, *A Guide to the Archives of the Center for Migration Studies* (New York: For the Center for Migration Studies, 1974).

Bibliography

Bjork, Robert M. *The Italian Immigration into France, 1870-1954*. Ann Arbor: University Microfilms, 1955.

Caroli, Betty B. *Italian Repatriation from the United States, 1900-1914*. New York: Center for Migration Studies, 1974.

Cordasco, Francesco, and Salvatore LaGumina. *Italians in the United States: A Bibliography of Reports, Texts, Critical Studies, and Related Materials*. New York: Oriole Editions, 1972.

__________. *Italian Americans: An Annotated Bibliography*. Detroit: Gale Research Company, 1978.

Falconer, Margaret. *Italian Reference Aids in the University of Toronto Library*. Toronto: University Library, 1967.

Lord, E., et al. *The Italian in America*. New York: Books for Libraries, 1970.

Nelli, Humbert S. *The Italians in Chicago, 1880-1930: A Study in Ethnic Mobility*. New York: Oxford University Press, 1970.

Schiaro, Giovanni. *The Italians in America before the Civil War*. New York: Vigo Press, 1934.

Stella, A. *Some Aspects of Italian Immigration to the United States*. San Francisco: R & E Research Associates, 1970.

How-to Books: Italian Ancestry

Camajani, Guelfo G. *Genealogy in Italy*. Florence: Instituto Genealogico Italiano, 1979. 30 pp.

Handy Guide to Italian Genealogical Records. Logan, Utah: Everton Publishers, 1978. 30 pp.

Konrad, J. *Italian Family Research*. Munroe Falls, Ohio: Summit Publications, 1980. 49 pp.

"Some Sources for Italian Genealogy." *Genealogists' Magazine* 14 (1962): 66-69.

The Netherlands

The greatest incidence of Dutch immigration occurred in the seventeenth century when the Dutch East India Company established trading cooperatives in New York and New Jersey, and at selected sites along the eastern coastline of the United States; in 1847 with the Great Migration into Michigan and Iowa; and in the inter-war migration which brought pockets of Dutch settlers into the Midwest and along the West Coast. Farms established in Washington state by Dutch settlers via New York and Michigan and those laid out by twentieth-century immigrants direct from Holland differ subtly in the layout of the farm buildings and the angles of the main barn to the mountains. Many of the surnames on mail boxes are the same, however. (See Map 15-15.)

Special Collections

Library	Address	Description of Material
Syracuse University Library, George Arents Research Library	Syracuse, NY 13210	Dutch Reformed Church manuscripts. Manuscript catalog available.
Holland Society of New York	122 East 58th Street New York, NY 10022	More than 4,000 vols., manuscript collections of Dutch Reformed Church, genealogies of early Dutch settlers and their descendants in New York, Pennsylvania, Delaware and New Jersey.
Los Angeles Public Library	603 W. 5th Street Los Angeles, CA 90071	100,635 vols of Dutch language, literature, history.
University of Michigan Bentley Historical Library	1150 Beal Avenue Ann Arbor, MI 48109	Dutch in the United States. See Thomas Powers and William McNitt, *Guide to Manuscripts in the Bentley Historical Library* (Ann Arbor: University of Michigan, 1976).
Herrick Public Library	300 River Avenue Holland, MI *49423*	"Dutch Family Histories and Genealogies." *Michigan Heritage* 14 (1972): 56. Church records, genealogies, oral history collection.
Hope College Archives	Holland, MI 49423	History of Dutch in Western Michigan, photographs, diaries, personal papers. See Andrew Vander Zee, *Guide to the Archives of Hope College* . (Holland, Mich.: Hope College, 1972).
Netherlands Museum	City Hall Holland, MI 49423	Dutch settlements in Michigan. Dutch migration to the Midwest. See Elton J. Bruins, *A Guide to the Archives of the Netherlands Museum* (Holland, Mich: n. pub., 1971).
Calvin College and Seminary Library Colonial Origins Collection	3207 Barton Street S.E., Grand Rapids, MI 49506	Minutes of 688 Christian Reformed Churches, Midwest, New York, New Jersey, Colorado, California, Washington, and Canada. Original letters of Dutch immigrants. See Herbert Brinks, ed., *Guide to the Dutch-American Historical Collections of Western Michigan* (n.p.: Dutch-American Historical Commission, 1967).
Dordt College Dutch Memorial Collection	498 4th Avenue, N.E., Sioux Center, IA 51250	Dutch settlers in the Midwest: Iowa, Minnesota, North Dakota, South Dakota, and parts of Canada. School and church records, letters, diaries, oral history tapes.
Netherlands Information Service Library	711 Third Avenue New York, NY 11232	Collection of over eighty current Dutch periodicals.
Northwestern University	Evanston, IL 60201	Netherlands under Nazi occupation, underground periodicals from Denmark, and several hundred Dutch periodicals.

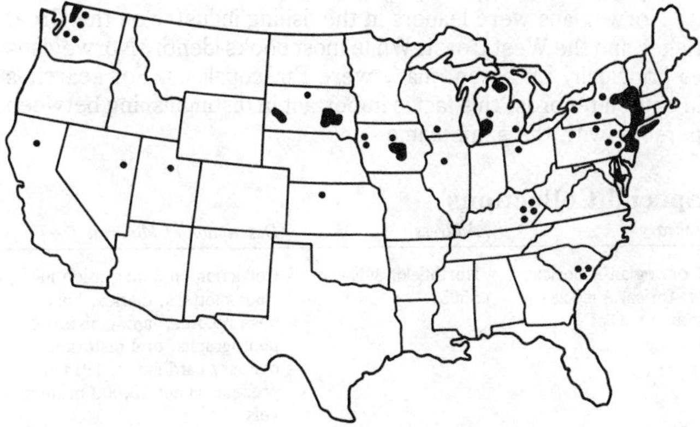

Map 15-15. Dutch Settlement Patterns.

Bibliography

Coolhaas, W. *A Critical Survey of Studies on Dutch Colonial History*. Nijhoff: n. pub., 1960. Includes New Netherland.

Doezema, Linda P. *Dutch Americans*. Detroit: Gale Research Co. 1979. Bibliography of Dutch immigrants, culture, communities in the United States.

The Dutch in New Netherlands and the United States, 1609-1909. 1909; reprint ed., San Francisco: R & E Research Associates, 1970.

Flippin, Percy Scott. "The Dutch Element in Kentucky." *Mississippi Valley Historical Review* 9 (1915-17): 135-50.

*Hinte, J. Van. *Nederlanders in Amerika*. Groningen: P. Noordhoff, 1928. Contains description and maps for settlements in the Midwest. In Dutch.

Leiby, Adrian C. *Early Dutch and Swedish Settlers of New Jersey*. New York: Van Nostrand, 1964. Includes maps.

*Lucas, Henry S. *Netherlanders in America: Dutch Immigration to the United States and Canada, 1789-1950*. Ann Arbor: University of Michigan Press, 1955.

Mulder, Arnold. *Americans from Holland*. New York: J. B. Lippincott, 1947. Good discussion of the patroon system.

Putnam, Ruth. "The Dutch Element in the United States." *Annual Report of the American Historical Association* 1909, pp. 205-18.

Stille, Charles J. "Archivium Americanum in the Consistory Court of the Archbishop of Upsal." *Pennsylvania Magazine of History and Biography* 15 (1891): 481-85.

Wabeke, Bertus H. *Dutch Emigration to North America, 1624-1860*. 1944; reprint ed., Books for Libraries, 1970.

How-to Books: Dutch Ancestry

Fahy, T. G. "Genealogical Research in the Netherlands." *Genealogists' Magazine* 13 (1961): 366-71.

Franklin, Charles M. *Dutch Genealogical Research*. Indianapolis: Ye Olde Genealogie Shoppe, 1981. 96 pp.

Nederhand, Erica H. *Ancestral Research in the Netherlands: Advanced Study in Dutch Records and Methods of Genealogical Research*. 2 vols. Salt Lake City: privately printed, 1967.

Wijnaendts von Resandt, W. *Searching for Your Ancestors in the Netherlands*. Hague: Centraal Bureau voor Genealogie, n.d.

van Weezep, John. "American-Dutch and Belgium Research." *Genealogical Journal* 3 (1974): 19-22.

Norway

In 1850, only 1,800 persons in the United States were of Norwegian birth. These were concentrated in the Fox River area of Illinois, in southeast Minnesota, and in Wisconsin where over one-fifth of the population of Dane County (Madison) was Norwegian. By 1890, there were over one million. The majority of those who came after 1850 settled in Minnesota and North Dakota (15 percent of the total population). See Map 15-16.

Norwegians were leaders in the fishing industry on the Great Lakes and the West Coast. While most books identify Norwegians as principally Lutheran, many were Episcopalians. For searches in church records, this fact is important in distinguishing between persons with the same name.

Special Collections

Library	*Address*	*Description of Material*
Norwegian-American Historical Association, St. Olaf College	Northfield, MN 55057	Collection on immigration includes letters, diaries, business records, family histories, photographs, oral histories; obituary card index, 1914 to present; about 15,000 printed vols.
Luther College, Koren Library	Decorah, IA 52101	Some 20,000 Norwegian manuscripts, 1,000 vols. of Norwegian American newspapers. Also Synod for Norwegian Lutheran Church of America, 1853-1917 records, and records of lumber industry for Iowa.
University of Wisconsin, Madison, Library	728 State Street Madison, WI 53706	Includes 2,000 Norwegian local histories; periodicals and historical publications for Norway
Minnesota Historical Society	690 Cedar Street St. Paul, MN 55101	Large collection of Norwegian immigration materials including guidebooks written for prospective immigrants. About 10,000 manuscripts.
State Historical Society of Wisconsin	816 State Street Madison, WI 53706	Family and local histories, oral history for Norway. Includes Rasmas B. Anderson papers, 1841-1931, fifty-five boxes of family and personal papers.
Carnegie Institution of Washington	1530 P Street N.W. Washington, DC 20005	Archive materials relating to Norwegian migration collected in Norway.
Gerhard Naeseth	4909 Sherwood Road Madison, WI 53711	Biographies of first 18,000 Norwegians to America, 1825-50.
Amundsen Book Co.	108 Washington Street Decorah, IA 52100	Specializes in Norwegian maps and books.

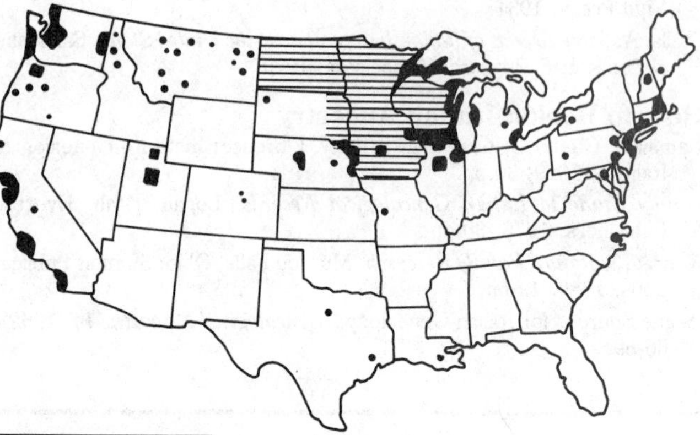

Map 15-16. Norwegian Settlement Patterns.

Bibliography

Blegan, Theodore C. *Norwegian Migration to America*. 2 vols. Northfield, Minn.: Norwegian-American Historical Association, 1931- 40.

Bjork, Kenneth. *West of the Great Divide: Norwegian Migration to the Pacific Coast, 1847-1893*. Northfield, Minn.: Norwegian- American Historical Association, 1958.

Flom, George T. *A History of Norwegian Immigration to the United States to 1848*. Iowa City: University of Iowa Press, 1909.

Gjerset, Knut. *Norwegian Sailors in American Waters*. Northfield, Minn.: Norwegian-American Historical Association, 1958.

Haugen, Einar. *The Norwegians in America. A Student's Guide to Lcoalized History*. New York: Teachers College Press, 1967.

Hodnefield, Jacob. "Norwegian-American Bygdelags and their Publications." *Norwegian-American Studies and Records*, vol. 18, pp. 163-222.

Horde, Bryjolf J. "Norwegian Migrations to the U. S. before the Civil War." *Norwegian-American Historical Association Studies* 6 (1931). 162-67.

Naeseth, Gerhard B. "Norwegian Settlements in the United States: A Review of Printed and Manuscript Sources for the Study of Norwegian Sources in America." E-10. World Conference on Records, Salt Lake City, Utah, 1969.

Naess, Harald S. *Norwegian Influence on the Upper Midwest*. Duluth: University of Minnesota Press, 1976.

Norlie, Olaf M. *History of the Norwegian People in America*. Minneapolis: Augsburg Publishing House, 1925. Norwegian-American Studies and Records. Multi-volume series of printed letters, journals, documents, and historial studies of specific Norwegian groups and where they settled. Over forty volumes published since 1926.

*Qualey, Charlton C. *Norwegian Settlement in the United States*. Northfield, Minn.: Norwegian-American Historical Association, 1938.

*Rosdail, J. Hart. *The Sloopers, Their Ancestry and Posterity*. Broadview, Ill.: For the author, 1961. Includes genealogy.

Semmingsen, Ingrid. "Norwegian Emigration in the Nineteenth Century." *Scandinavian Economic History Review* 8 (1960): 150-60.

*____________. *Norway to America: A History of the Migration*. Minneapolis: University of Minnesota Press, 1980.

How-to Books: Norwegian Ancestry

Brown, Forrest. "Norwegian-American Family History." *Genealogy* 45 (1979): 1-13.

Did Your Ancestors Come From Norway? Oslo: Royal Ministry of Foreign Affairs, 1971. 8 pp.

Smith, Frank, and Finn A. Thomsen. *Genealogical Guidebook and Atlas of Norway*. Logan, Utah: Everton Publishers, n.d.

Wellauer, Maralyn A. *Tracing Your Norwegian Roots*. Milwaukee: For the author, 1979. 70 pp.

The Philippines

Special Collections

Library	Address	Description of Material
Philippine Foundation of America	Library of Congress Washington, DC 20540	Correspondence, photos, records of post-World War II activities
Rutherford B. Hayes Library	1337 Hayes Avenue Fremont, OH 43420	Manuscripts relating to the Insurrection in the Philippines 1899-1901. Includes maps.
Newberry Library	60 West Walton Chicago, IL 60610	Ayer Collection which includes over 6,000 photographs and volumes on Philippine history to 1900.
University of Michigan Bentley Historical Library	1150 Beal Avenue Ann Arbor, MI 48109	Philippine collection.
Indiana University Lilly Library	7th and Jordan Bloomington, IN 47401	Philippine collection. See C.R. Boxer. "Preliminary Report on a Collection of Documents Looted at Manila in 1762-64 and now in the Lilly Library," *Southeast Asian Archives* 2 (July 1969) and *Catalogue of Philippine Manuscripts in the Lilly Library* (Bloomington, Ind.: Asian Studies Research Institute, 1968).
U.S. Military History Institute	Carlisle Barracks, PA 17013	War records, reports of Philippine Insurrection.

Bibliography

Norell, Irene P. *Literature of the Filipino-American in the United States: A Selective and Annotated Bibliography*. San Francisco: R & E Associates, 1976.

Saito, Shiro. *Philippine Ethnography: A Critically Annotated and Selected Bibliography*. Honolulu: University of Hawaii, n.d.

Selected Bibliography of the Philippines. Chicago: University Philippine Studies Program, 1956.

How-to Books: Filipino Ancestry

Vance, Lee W. *Tracing Your Philippine Ancestors*. 3 vols. Denver: Philippine Ancestors, 1980. 771 pp. Definitive.

Poland

For immigrants from Poland, the family, the church and parochial school, and the neighborhood societies provided cushions against the trauma of immigration. Some 92 percent of all American Poles attended parochial school at least one year as children. Here they were taught English, the three R's, and Catholicism in Polish. See Map 15-17.

As new immigrants arrived, it was common for them to live in boarding houses operated by family members or associates who had immigrated first. As you search census records, be sure to copy all persons living under the same roof as your ancestor—many of them will be relatives.

Watch for tombstones. The surname is often given there as it was spelled in Europe. This name will be essential to identify your ancestor in Old World records while the name by which the ancestor goes in America will be more useful in searching immigration sources.

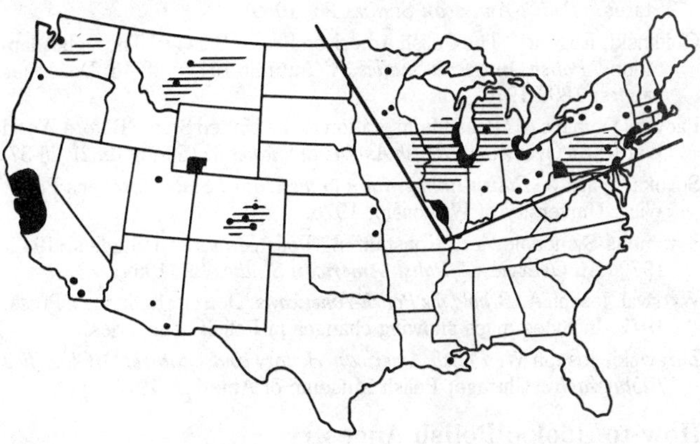

Map 15-17. Polish Settlement Patterns.

Special Collections

Library	Address	Description of Material
The Hoover Institution Stanford University	Stanford, CA 94305	History, underground movement, government in exile, emigré groups, 450 periodicals, newspapers, government documents and archives. See *Archival and Manuscript Materials: A Checklist of Major Collections* (Stanford: Hoover Institution, 1975).
University of Kansas Spencer Library	Lawrence, KS 66045	Polish history through the 18th century, maps, photos.
Holy Family College	Grant and Frankford Avenues, Philadelphia, PA 19114	About 1200 vols. of Polish history, Torresdale area of Philadelphia, histories of Polish parishes, documents for war relief.
Polish-American Historical Association	984 N. Milwaukee Avenue Chicago, IL 60622	Polish language newspapers, personal papers, church records.
Polish Genealogical Society	984 N. Milwaukee Avenue Chicago, IL 60622	Ancestor index file, family charts, original family records.
Joseph Pilsudski Institute of Americans for Research in Modern History of Poland	381 Park Avenue S. New York, NY 10016	19th and 20th century Polish history. Includes embassy records, photographs, personal papers, Polish-American newspapers. Mimeographed guide to holdings available on request.
Central Council of Polish Organizations Polish Historical Commission	4291 Stanton Avenue Pittsburgh, PA 15201	Polish immigrants in Pittsburgh, small collection of manuscripts.
University of Pittsburgh Archives of Industrial Society	Pittsburgh, PA 15260	Local business and public records for Pittsburgh and Allegheny County, including labor unions, fraternal organizations, churches, schools.

Bibliography

Duker, Abraham G. *The Polish "Great Emigration" and the Jews*. Ann Arbor: University Microfilms, 1956.

Dworaczyk, E.J. *The First Polish Colonies of America in Texas*. San Francisco: R & E Research Associates, 1969.

Fox, P. *The Poles in America*. New York: Arno Press, 1970.

Haiman, M. *Polish Pioneers of California*. San Francisco: R & E Research Associates, 1969.

Lerski, Jerzy Jan. *A Polish Chapter in Jacksonian America: The United States and the Polish Exiles of 1831*. Madison: University of Wisconsin, 1958. Includes list of exiles.

Mostwin, Danuta. "Post-World War II Polish Immigrants in the United States." *Polish-American Studies* 26 (1969).

Obidinski, Eugene. "The Polish American Press: Survival Through Adaptation." *Polish American Studies* 34 (Autumn 1977): 38-46. Describes papers, 1890-1976.

Pacyga, Dominic A. "Polish Immigration to the United States Before World War II: An Overview." *Polish American Studies* 39 (Spring 1982): 28-37.

Soroka, Waclaw. *Polish Immigration to the United States*. Stevens Point, Wis.: University of Wisconsin, 1976.

Symmons-Symonolewicz, Konstantin. "Polish-American Studies, 1942-1970: An Overview." *Polish-American Studies* 22 (1969).

Wytrwal, Joseph A. *Behold the Polish-Americans*. Detroit: Endurance Press, 1977. Includes maps showing changes in Polish boundaries.

Zurawski, Joseph W. *Polish American History and Culture: A Classified Bibliography*. Chicago: Polish Museum of America, 1975.

How-to Books: Polish Ancestry

Gnacinski, Jan, and Len Gnacinski. *Polish and Proud: Tracing Your Polish Ancestry*. West Allis, Wis.: Janlen Enterprises, 1979. 78 pp.

Konrad, J. *Polish Family Research*. Rev. ed. Munroe Falls, Ohio: Summit Publications, 1982. 49 pp.

Wellauer, Maralyn A. *Tracing Your Polish Roots*. Milwaukee: For the author, 1979. 87 pp.

Russia

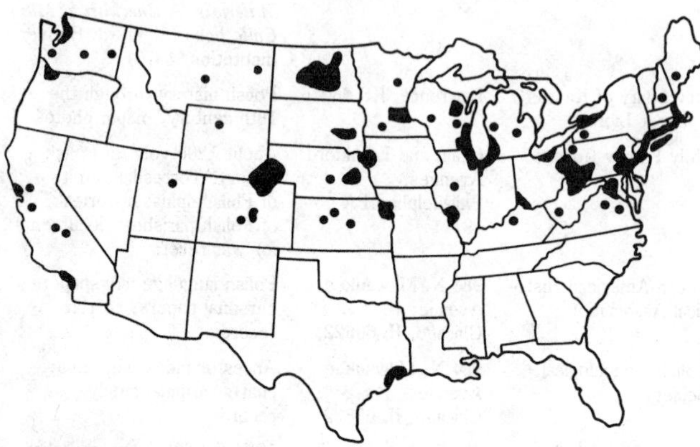

Map 15-18. Russian Settlement Patterns.

Special Collections

Library	*Address*	*Description of Collections*
Public Archives of Canada, Likhachev-Ragozin-Mathers Archives	Ottawa, Canada	Vast collection of original records and copies for immigration (1900-22), settlement, military affairs and service, religious activities of Russian and other East Europeans. Also includes Russian embassy and consular records at the time of the Russian Civil War. See John H. Brown, "The Disappearing Russian Embassy Archives, 1922-49," *Prologue*, Spring 1982, pp. 5-13. Very significant collection for genealogy as the documents give birth information, places of origin, family relationships.
Library of the Ukranian Museum of Chicago	2453 West Chicago Chicago, IL 60622	Over 150 Ukranian periodicals, printed volumes of history, geography, photographs.
Hoover Institution, Stanford University	Stanford, CA 94305	Extensive collection dealing with the 1917 Revolution, including private archives, correspondence, books, pamphlets, leaflets, and personal papers of the principal revolutionaries. Okhrana Archives with Russian secret police dossiers and correspondence, 1895-1917. See Charles G. Palm and Dale Reed, *Guide to the Hoover Institution Archives* (Stanford: Stanford University Press, 1980), 418 pp.
American Russian Institute	90 McAllister Street San Francisco, CA 94102	Manuscripts, printed volumes, maps, photographs, and slides in Russian and English.
Library of Congress	Washington, DC 20540	Largest collection outside Russia; includes Russian-American newspapers.
New York University	70 Washington Square New York, NY 10012	100,000 vols. for the study of Russian history, maps, manuscripts. Winter Palace collection of military documents.
Columbia University Archive of Russian and East European History	210 International Affairs Building, 420 West 118th Street New York, NY 10027	Broad collection of Russian materials for Russian Empire, Soviet Union, Eastern Europe since 1700. See Philip E. Moseley, "Columbia's New Treasure-House of Russian History," *Columbia Library Columns* 2 (1953): 17-24; 7 (1958): 32-36.
Byelorussian Charitable Educational Fund, Inc.	1716 NE 7th Terrace Gainesville, FL 32601	Original documents and printed volumes. Immigrant aid records.

Bibliography

Anuta, Michael J. *East Prussians from Russia*. Menomine, Mich.: For the author, 1980. Includes immigrant lists.

Davis, Jerome. *The Russian Immigrant*. 1922; reprint ed., New York: Arno Press, 1969.

*Hiebert, Clarence. *Brothers in Deed to Brothers in Need: A Scrapbook about Mennonite Immigrants from Russia, 1870-1885*. Newton, Kan.: Faith and Life Press, n.d. Includes numerous examples of immigrant records, shipping companies, passenger lists.

*Kulychy, M. *Resettlement of Displaced Persons in the U.S.A. by the United Ukranian American Relief Committee*. 1950, map.

Kuznets, Simon. *Immigration of Russian Jews to the U. S.: Background and Structure*. Cambridge: Harvard University Press, 1975.

*Maichel, Karol. *Guide to Russian Reference Books*. 2 vols. Stanford, Calif.: Hoover Institution on War, Revolution, and Peace, 1964. Vol. 2 includes history, genealogy, ethnography, geography.

Sallet, Richard. *Russian-German Settlements in the U.S.* Fargo, N.D.: n. pub., 1974.

Simicenko, Alex. *Pilgrims, Colonists, and Frontiersmen: Generation to Generation Changes in a Russian Ethnic Community*. New York: MacMillan, 1964.

Smith, C. Henry. *The Coming of the Russian Mennonites, 1874-1884*. Berne, Ind.: Mennonite Book Concern, 1937.

Scotland

For several generations, the Scots Highlanders, from the mountainous area of Scotland, did not intermarry with the Scots-Irish, Scots from the lowlands who settled in Ireland for several generations before migrating to America. They were, however, frequently found in the same areas and sometimes shared the same names. There were periodic migrations of Scots from Nova Scotia through New England and New York into the South during the colonial period. There was also some contact between Scots in the West Indies and in the Carolinas. (See Map 15-19).

Map 15-19. Scottish Settlement Patterns.

Special Collections

Library	*Address*	*Description of Material*
New York Public Library	5th Avenue & 42nd Street, New York, NY 10018	Printed histories, periodicals, finding aids for Scotland.
Duke University Perkins Library	Durham, NC 27706	Southern history collection includes family papers, letters, diaries, immigrant documents.
South Caroliniana Library, University of South Carolina	Columbia, SC 29208	Printed volumes, manuscripts, and maps dealing with Scots settlers in the South.
New York State Archives	Cultural Education Center, Empire State Plaza Albany, NY 12230	Records of Phelps-Gorham Purchase include documents on Scots settlers in central New York.

Bibliography

Adams, Margaret I. "Causes of Highland Emigration of 1783-1803." *Scottish Historical Review* 17 (1919-20): 73-89.

__________. "Eighteenth Century Highland Landlords and the Poverty Problem." *Scottish Historical Review* 19 (1921-22): 1-20, 161-79.

__________. "Highland Emigration of 1770." *Scottish Historical Review* 16 (1918-19): 280-93.

"Arrival of the Cardross Settlers," *South Carolina Historical Magazine* 30 (1929): 69-80.

Banks, Charles E. "Scotch Prisoners Deported to New England by Cromwell, 1651-52." *Massachusetts Historical Society Proceedings* 61 (1928): 4-29.

Chamberlain, George W. "The New York Scots Colony." *Magazine of History* 4 (1906): 43-46.

Coldham, Peter Wilson. "Scottish Rebels Transported to Maryland." *National Genealogical Society Quarterly* 63 (1975); 137-38.

Cummings, Hubertis M. *Scots Breed & Susquehanna.* Pittsburgh: University of Pittsburgh Press, 1964.

"Emigration Lists of Scots, to America in the 1770s." Public Records Office, London, SP 54/45 f164 c, d, e, f.

Gordon, G. A. "The Arrival of Scotch Highlanders at Darien." *Georgia Historical Quarterly* 20 (1936): 199-209.

Graham, Ian C. *Colonists from Scotland: Emigration to North America, 1707-1783.* Ithaca: Cornell University Press, 1956.

Hancock, P. D. *A Bibliography of Works Relating to Scotland, 1916- 1950.* 2 vols. Edinburgh: The University Press, 1960.

Insh, George P. *Scottish Colonial Schemes, 1620-1686.* Glasgow: Maclehose, Jackson & Co., 1922.

*Maclean, John P. *An Historical Account of the Settlements of Scotch Highlanders in America.* Baltimore: Genealogical Publishing Co., 1968. Discusses the Darien Scheme and its investors, early settlements.

*Meyer, Duane G. *The Highland Scot of North Carolina, 1732-1776.* Chapel Hill: University of North Carolina Press, 1961.

Pryde, George S. "The Scots in East New Jersey." *Proceedings of the New Jersey Historical Society*, vol. 15.

__________. "Scottish Colonization in the Province of New York." *New York History*, vol. 16.

Ross, Peter. *The Scot in America.* New York, 1896.

Steven, William. *The History of the Scottish Church, Rotterdam.* Edinburgh: Wangh and Innes, 1833. Important study.

How-to Books: Scottish Ancestry

Hamilton-Edwards, Gerald. *In Search of Scottish Ancestry.* Chichester: Phillimore & Co., 1972. 252 pp.

James, Alwyn. *Scottish Roots: A Step-by-Step Guide for Ancestor-Hunters.* Gretna, La.: Pelican Publishing Co., 1982. 181 pp.

McLeod, Dean L., and Norman L. Moyes. *Aids to Scottish Research.* Salt Lake City, Utah: Professional Genealogists, 1978. 50 pp.

Steel, Don J. *National Index of Parish Registers: Sources for Scottish Genealogy and Family History.* Chichester: Phillimore & Co., 1970. 320 pp.

Whyte, Donald. *Introducing Scottish Genealogical Research.* 3rd ed. Edinburgh: Scottish Genealogy Society, 1980.

Scots-Irish

Little distinction was made between the Scots-Irish and the Irish in the colonial period. About the time of the Revolution, distinctions began to appear. The majority of the Irish who came to the United States before 1820 were Protestants from Ulster – the Scots-Irish. They tended to farm on the frontier and in the hill country. They spread into the Midwest and West, into the Deep South and Texas, and gave Appalachia its rich folk heritage. The Irish who came after 1820 were Catholics from southern Ireland, often laborers working on railroads or canals, and they tended to cluster in urban areas. There are, of course, exceptions to both patterns. (See Map 15-20.)

Special Collections

Library	*Address*	*Description of Material*
Historical Society of Pennsylvania	1300 Locust Street Philadelphia, PA 19107	Personal papers, church records. See *Guide to the Manuscript Collections of the Historical Society of Pennsylvania*, 2nd ed. (Phildelphia: For the society, 1949).
Waveland State Shrine	Higbee Mill Road Lexington, KY 40503	Business records, family history charts, diaries, photographs.
Western Kentucky University Folklore Archives	Bowling Green, KY 42101	Folklore and oral history collections preserving the traditions of Scotch-Irish folk. See "Research Guide to Western Kentucky University Folklore and Folklife Archives," *Academic Services Library Bulletin* 8 (1974).
Tennessee Valley Authority Technical Library	400 Commerce Avenue Knoxville, TN 37902	Cemetery relocation files, tombstone inscriptions, more than 500,000 maps. Only record for some small East Tennessee communities.
Historical Foundation of Presbyterian and Reformed Churches	Georgia Terrace Montreat, NC 28757	Extensive collection of church records, histories, personal papers.
South Caroliniana Library, University of South Carolina	Columbia, SC 29208	Over one million manuscripts, 45,000 volumes of printed material, 4,500 rolls of microfilm for the history and development of South Carolina.

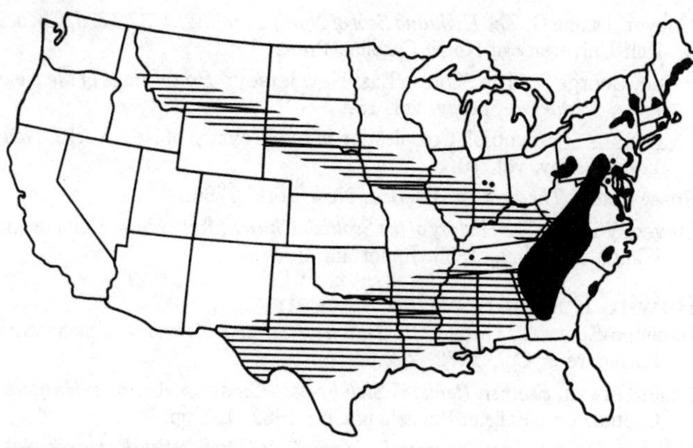

Map 15-20. Scots-Irish Settlement Patterns.

Bibliography

Armor, William C. *Scotch-Irish Bibliography of Pennsylvania.* Nashville: Barbee & Smith, 1896.

Bolton, Charles K. *Scotch-Irish Pioneers in Ulster and America.* Boston: Bacon & Brown, 1910.

Clyde, John C. *Genealogies, Necrology, and Reminiscences of the "Irish Settlement."* Frazer, Penn., 1879.

*Dickson, R. J. *Ulster Emigration to Colonial America, 1718-75.* London: Routledge and Kegan Paul, 1966.

Dinsmore, John W. *The Scotch-Irish in America.* Chicago: Winona Publishing Company, 1906.

Dunaway, Wayland F. *The Scotch-Irish of Pennsylvania.* Chapel Hill: University of North Carolina, 1944.

Ford, Henry J. *The Scotch-Irish in America.* Princeton: University Press, 1915.

Franz, Genge W. "The Pennsylvania Frontier and the Scotch-Irish, 1717-65." Ph.D. diss., Rutgers, 1967.

Glasgow, Maude. *The Scotch-Irish in Northern Ireland and in the American Colonies.* New York: G. P. Putnam's Sons, 1936.

Green, E. R. R., ed. *Essays in Scotch-Irish History.* London: Routledge and Kegan Paul, 1969.

__________. "Queensborough Township: Scotch-Irish Emigration and the Expansion of Georgia, 1763-1776." *William and Mary Quarterly,* 3rd series, 17 (1960): 183-99.

Hanna, Charles A. *The Scotch-Irish.* New York: G. P. Putnam's Sons, 1902. Includes map showing precise locations of 123 communities.

Hartin, Mellie Scot. "A History of the Scotch-Irish and their Influence in Kentucky." *Filson Club Quarterly* 34 (1960): 248-55.

Howe, George. "The Scotch-Irish and their First Settlements on the Tyger River." 1861 Centennial Discourse delivered at Nazareth Presbyterian Church. Copy in possession of author.

Klett, Guy S. *Presbyterians in Colonial Pennsylvania.* Philadelphia: University of Pennsylvania Press, 1937.

Leyburn, James G. *The Scotch-Irish: A Social History.* Chapel Hill: University of North Carolina Press, 1962.

Linehan, John C. *The Irish Scots and the "Scotch-Irish."* Concord, The American Irish Historical Society, 1902.

Puckett, James M., Jr. "The Scotch-Irish Emigration." *Georgia Genealogical Society Quarterly* 3 (1966-67): 402-4. Includes map.

Stephenson, Jean. *Scotch-Irish Migration to South Carolina, 1772: Rev. William Martin and His Five Shiploads of Settlers.* Strasburg, Va.: Shenandoah Publishing House, Inc., 1971. Includes methodology for tracking places of origin using newspapers and land records.

Woodburn, James A. *The Scotch-Irish Presbyterians in Monroe County, Indiana.* Indianapolis: E. J. Hecker, 1910.

How-to Books: Scotch-Irish Ancestry

Bell, Raymond M. "Sources for Genealogy and Local History of the Scotch-Irish of Central Pennsylvania." *National Genealogical Society Quarterly* 33 (1945): 114-17.

Falley, Margaret Dickson. *Irish and Scotch-Irish Ancestral Research.* 2 vols. Strasburg, Va.: Shenandoah Publishing House, 1961-62. Significant work.

Parker, Donald D. *Scottish and Scotch-Irish Ancestry Research.* Santa Fe, N.M.: For the author, n.d. 32 pp.

Stephenson, Jean. *Scotch-Irish Migration to South Carolina.* Strasburg, Va: For the author, 1971. Includes methodology on connecting families in South Carolina and Ireland using newspapers, records, and other sources.

South Africa

Special Collections

Library	*Address*	*Description of Material*
New York Public Library	5th Avenue & 42nd Street, New York, NY 10018	South African collection described in *New York Public Library Bulletin* 4 (1899): 429-61, 502-5. Includes Boer War, government documents, histories, news reports.
Northwestern University Library, Africana Division	1935 Sheridan Road, Evanston, IL 60201	Archives for Church Missionary Society activities in Africa, materials on race relations.
Billy Graham Archives Wheaton College	Box 607, Wheaton, IL 60187	Pledge cards for twentieth-century crusades.

How-to Books: South African Ancestry

Lombard, R. T. J. "Genealogical Research in South Africa." *Genealogists' Magazine* 19 (Dec. 1978): 274-76.

__________. *Handbook for Genealogical Research in South Africa.* Pretoria: Human Sciences Research Council, 1977. 129 pp.

Spain

Spanish, Mexican, Cuban, Puerto Rican, and West Indian ancestors are often included together as Spanish-American or Hispanic. This creates some blurring of origins, especially for nineteenth- and twentieth century pedigrees. Naming patterns can be unreliable too. The Bureau of the Census, in preparation for taking the 1980 census, put together a master Spanish surname list, using a team of genealogists and linguists. You can consult this list for a questionable surname by writing the U.S. Department of Commerce, Bureau of the Census, Washington, DC 20233 or Arlene H. Eakle, Genealogical Institute, 57 W. South Temple, Salt Lake City, UT 84101.

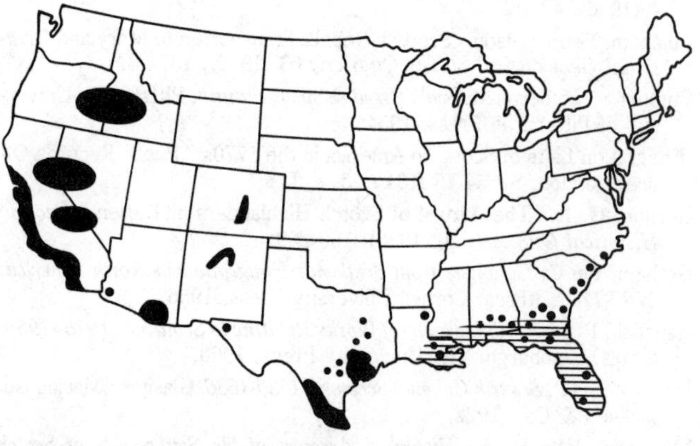

Map 15-21. Spanish Settlement Patterns.

Special Collections

Library	Address	Description of Material
Louisiana State University	Baton Rouge, LA 70803	Louisiana Collection, books and documents on Spanish Louisiana 1762-1806.
University of Texas	El Paso, TX 79968	Spanish land grant documents; Mexican acquisitions, Latin-American collection (1770-1843), 160,000 vols. Card catalog printed, 39 vols. Boston: G. K. Hall, 1969. Available in many research libraries.
Arizona State University, Hayden Library	Tempe, AZ 85281	Brazilian collection, folklore, periodicals.
Northwestern University	1935 Sheridan Road Evanston, Il 60201	Nicolas Acosta Collection of Bolivian mss. (1500-1890). 40,000 items.
University of California	Berkeley, CA 94720	Spanish-American collection.
University of Illinois (Illinois History Survey)	Urbana, IL 61801	American documents in Spanish archives, microfilm copies of 101,000 pp.
Loyola University Spanish Documents Project	6363 St. Charles Avenue New Orleans, LA 70118	Santo Domingo papers relating to Spanish colony of Louisiana. Important collection.
Fort Lewis College Center of Southwest Studies	College Heights Durango, CO 81301	Microfilm and original documents relating to Spanish in Colorado. See *Center of Southwest Studies: Opportunities for Research* (Durango, Colo.: n.p., n.d.)
University of Texas Bexar Archives	Austin, TX 78712	Nettie Lee Benson Latin American collection, 500 feet of manuscripts, 2,250 reels of film. Maps, personal papers, church archives. See University of Texas Library, *Catalog of the Latin American Collection* (Boston: G. K. Hall, 1969.) Biannual supplements. Bexar Archives, 1717-1836. Spanish and Mexican records of Texas, 250,000 mss., 4,000 printed pages.
Sutro Library San Francisco State University Campus	480 Winston Drive San Francisco, CA 94132	Large collection of Spanish American, Mexican documents.

Bibliography

Bannon, J. A. *The Spanish Borderlands Frontier, 1513-1821.* New York: Holt-Rhinehart, 1970.

Chandler, Michael John. *A Guide to Records in Barbados.* Oxford: B. Blackwell, 1965.

Fisher, L. E. *The Intendant System in Spanish America.* New York: Gordian Press, 1969.

Gallardo, Jose Miguel. "The Spaniards and the English Settlement in Charlestown." *South Carolina Historical Magazine* 37 (1936): 49-64, 91-99, 131-41.

Holmes, Jack D. L. *A Guide to Spanish Louisiana, 1762-1806.* New Orleans: n. pub., 1970.

Moses, B. *Spain Overseas.* New York: Kraus Reprint, 1970.

New Mexico Records Center. *Calendar of Microfilm Edition of Spanish Archives of New Mexico, 1621-1821.* Santa Fe, 1968. *Calendar of Microfilm Edition of Mexican Archives of New Mexico, 1821-1846.* Santa Fe, 1970. *Guide to Microfilm Edition.* Myra Ellen Jenkin ed., Santa Fe, 1967.

Northrup, Marie E. *Spanish-Mexican Families of Early California, 1769-1850.* New Orleans: Polyanthos, 1976.

Platt, Lyman De. "Spanish and Mexican Immigration to the United States." *Genealogical Journal* 3 (1974): 23-24.

Taylor, Virginia H. *The Spanish Archives of the General Land Office of Texas.* Austin: Lone Star Press, 1955.

Tudela, José. *Los Manuscriptos de Ameŕica en las bibliotecas de Espana.* Madrid: Ediciones Cultura Hispanica, 1954.

Twitchell, Ralph E. *The Spanish Archives of New Mexico.* 2 vols., Cedar Rapids, Iowa: Torch Press, 1914.

University of Texas Library. *Calendar of the Manual E. Sondra Manuscript Collection in the University of Texas Library.* Mexico: Editorial Jus., 1952.

Waring, Joseph L. "An Account of the Invasion of South Carolina by the French and Spaniards in August 1706." *South Carolina Historical Magazine* 66 (1965): 98-101.

How-to Books: Spanish Ancestry

Barton, Noel R. "Genealogical Research in the Records of the California Spanish Missions." *Genealogical Journal* 4 (March 1975): 13-33.

Hoffman, Paul E. "A Guide to Field Research in Spain for the Family Historian with Special References to Louisiana." *New Orleans Genesis* (1980).

Platt, Lyman De, ed. *Genealogical-Historical Guide to Latin America.* Detroit: Gale Research Co., 1978. 273 pp. Available in English and Spanish.

Sweden

The Emigrantinstitutet in Vaxjo, Sweden, has been computer-linking Swedes in church records on both sides of the Atlantic. American church records include christening and confirmation information usually giving the parish of birth in Sweden at the time of marriage. The Genealogical Society of Utah has the largest collection of microfilmed Swedish records (over 60,000 reels of film) in America. The Vaxjo collection includes many churches not yet microfilmed, so both collections must be searched. U.S. access to Vaxjo collection can be made by correspondence at the address below.

Swedes were heavily involved in the logging industry and employed in the building of the Northern Pacific Railroad. These occupations carried them across the northern part of the United States. See Map 15-22.

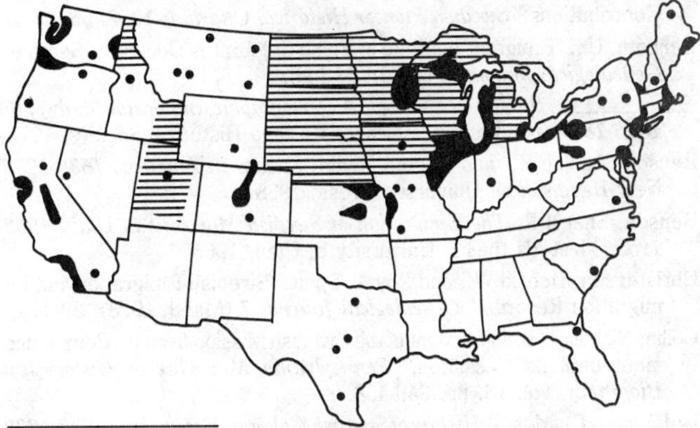

Map 15-22. Swedish Settlement Patterns.

Special Collections

Library	Address	Source of Collections
Kennebunk Free Library	Kennebunk, ME 04043	Oral history collection for Swedish settlers, Swedes in logging industry.
Augustana College Swenson Swedish Immigration Research	Rock Island, IL 61201	Immigrant letters, records, papers of church clergy including journals and correspondence. Small printed collection. Large collection of Swedish-American newspapers. See Lilly Setterdahl, *Swedish-American Newspapers: A Guide to Microfilms* (Rock Island: Augustana College, 1981).

University of Michigan Bentley Library	Ann Arbor, MI 48109	Letters, records sent by immigrants to entice others to come and to describe their lives in the New World. Collecting Swedish-language newspapers published in Michigan.
Emigrantinstitutet (House of Emigrants)	Box 201 351 04 Vaxjo 1 Sweden	Swedish-American church records on microfilm, Swedish American newspapers, 7,000 American letters cataloged by name of town where mailed in Minnesota, Iowa, Michigan. Large collection of photos.
Pennsylvania Historical Society	1300 Locust Street, Philadelphia, PA 19107	Correspondence and documents of Swedish Church missionary activities in Delaware, 17th century. See Charles J. Stille, "Archivium Americanum in the Consistory Court of Archibishop of Upsal," *Pennsylvania Magazine of History and Biography* 15 (1891): 481-85.
Minnesota Historical Society	690 Cedar Street St. Paul, MN 55101	Excellent printed and periodical collection.
American Swedish Institute	2601 Oakland Avenue Minneapolis, MN 55407	Settlement of Swedes in America, family and personal papers, oral history, correspondence and record books of Swedish immigrant organizations, Bibles, genealogies photographs, microfilm copies of Swedish churches in Minnesota.

Bibliography

Acrelius, Israel. *A History of New Sweden or Settlements on the River Delaware*. Translated from Swedish edition of 1758. Philadelphia: Historical Society of Pennsylvania, 1876.

Ander, Oscar F. "A Bibliography on Swedish Immigration and Emigrant Contributions." *Swedish Pioneer Historical Quarterly* 1952, pp. 35-44.

Beijbom, Ulf. "Emigrant Institute in Vaxjo Celebrates Decade of Service." *Genealogical Journal* 8 (1979): 192-96.

________. *Swedes in Chicago: A Demographic and Social Study of the 1846-1880 Immigration*. Chicago: Chicago Historical Society, 1972.

Benson, Adolph B., and Naboth Hedin. *Swedes in America, 1638-1938*. New Haven: Yale University Press, 1938.

Benson, Sheryl R. *The Emigration of Swedish Mormons to Utah, 1905-1955*. Master's thesis, University of Utah, 1965.

Christensen, Donald W., and Roy A. Spjut. "Swedish Emigration and Immigration Records." *Genealogical Journal* 7 (March 1978): 38-47.

Collin, Nicholas. "Brief Account of the Swedish Mission from Its Commencement until its Cessation." *Pennsylvania Magazine of History and Biography*, vol. 16, pp. 349-458.

DeLannoy, Charles. *A History of Swedish Colonial Expansion, 1638-1938*. Newark: University of Delaware, 1938.

Flom, George T. "The Early Swedish Immigration to Iowa." *Iowa Journal of History and Politics*, 1905, pp. 583-615.

Janson, Florence E. *The Background of Swedish Immigration, 1840- 1930* Chicago: University of Chicago, 1931.

Johnson, Amandus. *Swedish Settlers on the Delaware, 1638-65*. 2 vols. Reprint ed., Baltimore: Genealogical Publishing Company, 1969.

*Larson, Esther G. *Swedish Commentators on America, 1638-1865: An Annotated List of Selected Manuscript and Printed Materials*. Chicago: Swedish Pioneer Historical Society, 1963.

Lindberg, John S. *The Background of Swedish Emigration to the U. S.* Minneapolis: University of Minnesota Press, 1930.

Mawe, Carl-Erik. *Varmlanningar I Nordamerika* Saffle, Saffletidns. Translated in 1971 as *Swedish Emigration*.

Mulder, William. *Homeward to Zion: Mormon Migration from Scandinavia, 1850-1905*. Minneapolis: University of Minnesota Press, 1957.

*Nelson, Helge. *The Swedes and the Swedish Settlements in North America*. New York: Arno Press, 1970. Includes map showing where each settlement is located.

Nilsson, Fred. *Emigrationen fran Stockholm till Nordamerika, 1880 -1893*. Stockholm: Svenska Bokforlaget, 1970.

*Nordstom, Byron, ed. *The Swedes in Minnesota*. Minneapolis: T. S. Denison & Co., 1976. Includes maps showing settlements in comparison with other ethnic groups.

Olson, E. W. *History of the Swedes in Illinois*. 3 vols. Chicago: University of Chicago Press, 1908.

Olsson, Nils William. "Swedes in America." *National Genealogical Society Quarterly* 49 (1961): 193-99.

*________. *Swedish Passenger Arrivals in New York, 1820-1850*. Chicago: Swedish Pioneer Historical Society, 1967. Entries are annotated. A valuable work.

Russell, George Ely. "The Swedish Settlement in Maryland, 1654." *American Genealogist* 54 (1978): 203-10.

Schersten, Albert F. *The Relation of the Swedish-American Newspaper to the Assimilation of Swedish Immigrants*. Rock Island, Ill.: Augustana Library, 1935.

Stephenson, George M. "The Background of the Beginnings of Swedish Immigration, 1850-1875." *American Historical Review* 31 (1926): 708-23.

________. *Religious Aspects of Swedish Immigration: A Study of Immigrant Churches*. Minneapolis: University of Minnesota Press, 1932.

Stomberg, Andrew A., ed. "Letters of an Early Emigrant Agent in the Scandinavian Countries who Visited Scandinavia in 1854-1861 to Stimulate Emigration." *Swedish-American Historical Bulletin* 3 (1930): 7-52.

Thomas, W. W., Jr. "Swedish Colonization in Maine and New England." *The New England States* (New York, 1897), vol. 3, pp. 1244-58.

Westman, Erik G., ed., et al. *The Swedish Element in America*. 4 vols. Chicago: Swedish American Biographical Society, 1931-34.

How-to Books: Swedish Ancestry

Heckscher, Ella. "Genealogical Sources in Sweden." *Utah Genealogical and Historical Magazine* 29 (1938): 99-111. Excellent description of sources.

________. *Sex Kapitel am slaktforskning: kort handledning for amatores*. Stockholm: Monnier, 1954. Six editions published by 1966.

Johansson, Carl-Erik. *Cradled in Sweden: A Practical Help for Genealogical Research in Swedish Records*. Rev. ed. Logan, Utah: Everton Publishers, 1977. 205 pp.

Routledge, Carin. "Tracing Your Swedish Ancestry." *Relatively Speaking* 10 (1982): 19-23.

Nils, William Olsson. "Tracing Your Swedish Ancestry." *Swedish Pioneer Historical Quarterly* 13 (1962). Reprint ed. Stockholm: Royal Swedish Ministry of Foreign Affairs, 1965.

Swedish Foreign Office Press. *Finding Your Forefathers*. Stockholm: Swedish Foreign Office Press and Information Service, 1957.

Switzerland

Map 15-23. Swiss Settlement Patterns.

Special Collections

Library	Address	Description of Material
New York Public Library	Fifth Avenue and 42nd Street New York, NY 10018	Printed archives, inventories of archives, periodicals, public documents, 1,500 volumes of Swiss history, genealogies.
Mennonite Historical Library	Bluffton College Bluffton, OH 45817	Church records, Swiss settlers in Ohio.
Historical Society of Pennsylvania	1300 Locust Street Philadelphia, PA 19107	Genealogies, family and business papers, histories newspapers, and periodicals for Swiss settlers into Pennsylvania and Delaware in the 18th century.
Swiss American Historical Society	216 E. 39th Street Norfolk, VA 23504	Important collection for Swiss settlers in the southern U.S.

Bibliography

Billigmeier, Robert H., and Fred A. Picard. *The Old Land and the New: The Journals of Two Swiss Families in America in the 1820s*. Minneapolis: University of Minnesota, 1965.

"Documents Relating to Early Projected Swiss Colonies in the Valley of Virginia, 1706-09." *Virginia Magazine of History and Biography* 29 (1921): 1-17, 180-90, 287-91.

Faust, Albert B. "Swiss Emigration to the American Colonies in the Eighteenth Century." *American Historical Review* 22 (1916-17): 21-44, 98-132.

__________. *Guide to the Materials for American History in Swiss and Austrian Archives*. Washington, D.C.: Carnegie Institution, 1916. Important inventory of records.

*von Grueningen, John Paul. *The Swiss in the United States*. Madison: Swiss-American Historical Society, 1940. Includes maps showing precise settlements in each state.

Kelsey, R. W. "Swiss Settlers in South Carolina." *South Carolina Historical Magazine* 23 (1922): 85-91.

Kuhns, Oscar. *The German and Swiss Settlements of Colonial Pennsylvania*. N.p.: Gryphon Books, 1970.

Macco, Herman Freidrich. *Swiss Emigrants to the Palatine in Germany and to America 1650-1800*. n.p.: Aachen, 1954.

*Schelbert, Leo. "Eighteenth Century Migration of Swiss Mennonites to America." *Mennonite Quarterly Review* 42 (1968).

Voight, Gilbert P. "Swiss Notes on South Carolina, 1736-37." *South Carolina Historical Magazine* 21 (1920): 93-104.

See also section on Germans.

How-to Books: Swiss Ancestry

Handy Guide to Swiss Genealogical Records. Logan, Utah: Everton Publishers, 1978. 92 pp.

Nielson, Paul A. *Swiss Genealogical Research: An Introductory Guide* Norfolk, Va.: Doning, 1979. 83 pp.

Wellauer, Maralyn A. *Tracing Your Swiss Roots*. Milwaukee: For the author, n.d. 115 pp.

Wales

Until about 1830, the majority of the Welsh who came to America were farmers and pursued agriculture when they arrived here. By 1840, the Welsh who came were skilled miners from South Wales attracted by the opening of mining districts through the Midwest (iron) and the Appalachian Mountains (bituminous coal) or engaged in mining-support occupations. Later these miners would trek to the gold fields and coal mines in the West. Some would return as mining gained momentum in West Virginia and Kentucky. See Map 15-24.

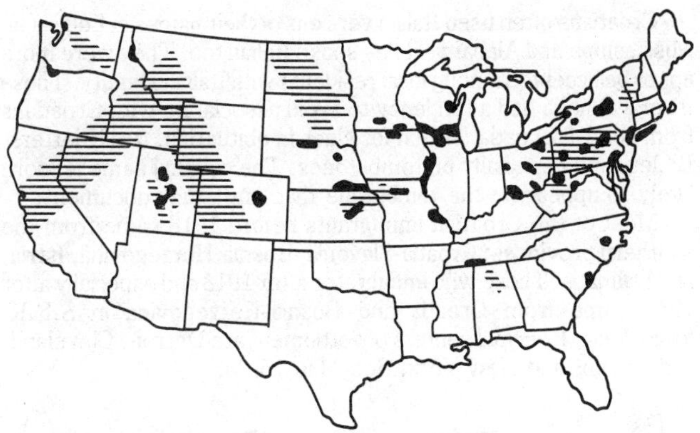

Map 15-24. Welsh Settlement Patterns.

Special Collections

Library	Address	Description of Material
University of Wisconsin Library	728 State Street Madison, WI 53706	850 volumes on Welsh literature.
Carnegie Library of Pittsburgh	4400 Forbes Street Pittsburgh, PA 15213	Welsh Library, 550 vols.
University of Pittsburgh, Urban Archives, Archives of Industrial Society.	Pittsburgh, PA 15260	Local records documenting urban growth and industrial development. Includes schools, churches, fraternal, and ethnic organizations.
Welsh Society	450 Broadway Camden, NJ 08103	Founded 1729, membership records 1800 to present.

Bibliography

Bibliography of the History of Wales. 2nd ed. 1962. Printed from *Bulletin of the Board of Celtic Studies* 20 (May 1963); Supp. II, 22 (Nov. 1966).

Browning, Charles H. *Welsh Settlement of Pennsylvania*. Philadelphia: W. J. Campbell, 1912.

Conway, Alan. *The Welsh in America, Letters from Immigrants*. Minneapolis: University of Minnesota Press, 1961. Originals are in Welsh.

Dodd, A. H. *Character of Early Welsh Immigration to the United States*. 1953; reprint ed., Cardiff: University of Wales Press, 1953.

Ellis, David M. "The Assimilation of the Welsh in Central New York." *New York History* 53 (1972): 299-333.

Glenn, Thomas A. *The Welsh Settlements in Pennsylvania*. Philadelphia: n.p., 1910.

__________. *The Welsh Founders in Pennsylvania*. 2 vols. Baltimore: Genealogical Publishing Co., 1970.

Hartman, Edward G. *Americans from Wales*. Boston: Christopher Publishing House, 1967. Includes lengthy description of settlements, migrations, and a list of counties where the Welsh settled.

Hughes, D. *Welsh People of California, 1849-1909*. San Francisco: R & E Research Associates, 1969.

Jones, William H. "The Welsh Settlements in Ohio." *Ohio Archaeological and Historical Society* 16 (1907): 194-227.

How-to Books: Welsh Ancestry

Jones, Frances T. D. "An Approach to Welsh Genealogy." *Transactions Honorable Society of Cymmrodorion* 1948 (1949): 303-466.

Wood, H. G. L. "The Value of Welsh Pedigrees." *The Ancestor*, 1903.

Yeatman, Pym. "Welsh Manuscript Pedigrees." *Notes and Queries Series*, 1901.

Yugoslavia, Czechoslovakia

Californians of Croatian origin may be listed as Russian on the census. Names are similar and census takers did not seem to pay careful attention to what the people said.

Croatians often used Italian versions of their names in Louisiana, Mississippi, and Alabama. They spoke Italian too. They were more apt to be accepted among local residents with Italian identity. Those from Dalmatia had a tendency to avoid association with Croatians from central Croatia. Watch for clues in obituaries, family letters, Bibles, and especially on tombstones. The original name is more likely to appear on the tombstone than any other document.

Most of the Croatian immigrants before 1918 came from the southern provinces: Croatia-Slavonia, Bosnia-Herzegovina, Istria, and Dalmatia. Those who immigrated after 1918 and especially after 1945 came from Croatia and Bosnia-Herzegovina in S.F.R. Yugoslavia. Principal centers of settlement are Detroit, Cleveland, Pittsburgh, and New York. See Map 15-25.

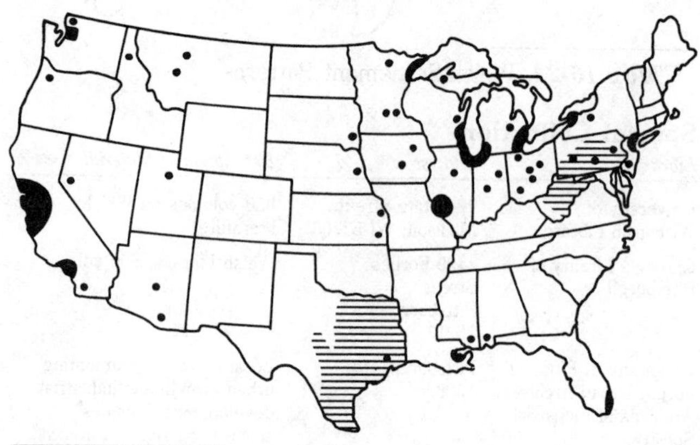

Map 15-25. Yugoslavian/Czechoslovakian Settlement Patterns.

Yugoslavia

Special Collections

Library	*Address*	*Description of Material*
Croatian Ethnic Institute, Inc.	4851 S. Drexel Blvd., Chicago, IL 60615	Excellent collection of histories, newspapers, oral history.

Bibliography

*Colakovic, Branko Mita. *Yugoslav Migrations to America*. San Francisco: R & E Research Associates, 1973. Includes maps, questionnaire for interviews of living Slavs and descendants of immigrants, internal migration in United States. Maps colonies in principal cities. Excellent for census research.

Gazi, Stjephan. *Croatian Immigration to Allegheny County, 1882-1913*. Pittsburgh: Croatian Fraternal Union, 1956.

Govorchin, Gerald Gilbert. *Americans from Yugoslavia*. Gainesville, Fla.: University of Florida Press, 1961. Includes maps.

Kraljic, Frances. *Croatian Migration to and from the United States, 1900-1914*. Palo Alto, Calif.: Ragusan Press, 1978. Excellent bibliography.

Prpic, George J. *The Croatian Immigrants in America*. New York: Philosophical Library, 1971. Excellent bibliography, includes genealogical records.

Stipanovich, Joseph, and Maria K. Woroby. *Slavic Americans: A Study Guide and Source Book*. San Francisco: R & E Associates, 1977.

Vujrovich, Milos M. *Yugoslavs in Louisiana*. Gretna, La.: Pelican Publishing Company, 1974. Includes a list of Slav businesses by name, address, year established and a list of fishermen from Dalmatia in Placquemines Parish.

Czechoslovakia

Special Collections

Library	*Address*	*Description of Material*
Los Angeles Public Library	630 West 5th Street Los Angeles, CA	300 vols. Czech history, periodicals, newspapers.
Syracuse University	Syracuse, NY 13210	2,000 vols., manuscripts, economic history of Czechoslovakia, other European peoples.
University of Illinois	Urbana, IL 61801	31,800 vols. history and periodicals; large collection of royal letters patent; original documents, Czech-American newspapers.
Illinois Benedictine College Library	5700 College Road Lisle, IL 60532	10,000 vols. history, collection of Czech family Bibles.

Bibliography

Czechoslovakia National Council of America. *Panorama: A Historical Review of Czechs and Slovaks in the United States of America*. Cicero, Ill.: Czechoslovakia National Council, n.d.

Dwyer, Joseph D. *Slovenes in the U.S. and Canada: A Bibliography*. St. Paul: Minnesota Immigration History Research Center, 1981.

Jerabeh, Esther. *Czechs and Slovaks in North America: A Bibliography*. Chicago: Czechoslovak National Council of America, 1976. Includes extensive section on organizations, newspapers.

Maresh, Henry R. "Czech Settlements in Texas." 1946. Map in Texas State Archives, Austin.

Miller, Olga K. "Czech and Slovak Immigration to the United States." *Genealogical Journal* 5 (1976): 146-54. Excellent, select bibliography.

*__________. *Genealogical Research for Czech and Slovak Americans*. Detroit: Gale Research Co., 1978.

Sturm, Rudolf. *Czechoslovakia: A Bibliographical Guide*. Washington, D.C.: Library of Congress, 1967.

Wellauer, Maralyn A. *Tracing Your Czech and Slovak Roots*. Milwaukee: For the author, 1977.

INFORMATION GUIDE

Genealogical Information in the Record Group	*Utility*	*Undertaker*	*Printed Histories*	*Selective Service*	*Neighborhood Books*	*Settlements*
Surname/name	●	●	●	●	●	●
Date of Birth		●	●	●	●	
Place of Birth		●	●	●	●	
Sex		●	●			●
Race/color						
Physical Description						
Occupation		●	●	●	●	●
Education			●			●
Military Service			●	●		
Slave Status						
Property Owned	●		●			
Religion			●		●	
Citizenship			●	●		●
Marital Status		●	●	●	●	
Spouse's Name		●	●		●	●
Children's Names			●		●	●
Father's Name			●		●	
Mother's Name			●		●	
Father's Birthplace			●			
Mother's Birthplace			●			
Date of Death		●	●		●	●
Cause of Death						
Name of Cemetery		●				
Residence	●	●	●	●	●	●
Age		●	●	●	●	●
Literacy/signature			●	●		●
Photograph/sketch		●	●		●	
Relatives		●	●	●	●	

COULD YOU USE THIS CHAPTER?

Type of Record	*Kept from*	*Clues That You Should Consult These Records*
"Standard" city records	Seventeenth century to present	If your ancestors lived in an urban center—New York City, Boston, Philadelphia, St. Louis, Chicago, New Orleans—you will be delighted at the number of records that are available in cities. Directories will locate an ancestor with an exact address so that the task of searching the census becomes simpler. Land records, maps, census records, vital records, coroners' records, undertakers' records, cemetery records, and church records—the standard sources for any genealogical research projects—are sometimes easier to search in a city because more finding aids have been prepared and because the records are easier to find. Naturalization records, voting records, draft records, and court records are others that accumulated naturally in cities.
Neighborhood sources	About 1880 to the present	If your ancestors seem to be associated with a particular neighborhood, church or occupation for a long period of time, the chances are good that local histories and newspapers included them. If your ancestor lived in an ethnic neighborhood or one that took its identity from a particular profession (the Garment District), the neighborhood library may have business records, indexes to local histories; and oral histories with people who remember things the way they were a generation or two ago. Also valuable are records of institutions and settlement houses.
Utility records	About 1880 to present	If your ancestor lived in an urban area after 1800, check utility records: sprinkling systems, sidewalk widening, sewer, water, power, gas, garbage pick-up records. These are especially valuable for identifying addresses for immigrants who move from one part of the city to another as their economic conditions improve. Second-, third-, and fourth-class cities also keep these records.

Chapter 16

SOURCES FOR URBAN ANCESTORS

Loretto Dennis Szucs
David S. Weber

Very early in the process of developing a family history, you will probably discover yourself face to face with the problem of locating data about ancestors who lived in a large American city. The United States today is very much an urban nation—73.5 percent of the population lives in cities—but the trends began well over a century ago. Most people, with the image of a rural America, do not know that over 50 percent of the population lived in urban areas as early as 1920. Moreover, many specific ethnic groups had higher percentages of urbanization than the general population. About 72 percent of the foreign-born by 1910, lived in cities.[1] The economics of migration, as well as the personal goals of the migrants, many of whom hoped to make a fortune and return home, necessitated settlement in urban centers like New York, Cleveland, or Chicago. There, burgeoning industries welcomed unskilled laborers, ethnic clusters offered a familiar setting for the homesick, and cheap housing and food let them accumulate some savings.

City research reflects the confusing variety, color, bustle, and adjustments of the urban surroundings new to the immigrant in its maze of metropolitan records. Much of the training in these resources must be self-taught. No two cities were born of a common history nor were their political natures, commercial interests, ethnic makeup, or geographical locations ever identical. Research sources readily found in one city may be closed or destroyed in the next. The experience of the Afro-American, the German Jew, the Irish Catholic, and the white Anglo-Saxon Protestant frequently differed, and those differences dictate the types of records to be used.

Despite their differences, cities have one thing in common: a reputation of being more difficult to research by reason of their multi-layered bureaucracy and the lack of printed indexes and access to sources. The advantage, of course, is the fact that urban areas often include the resources, human and financial, to preserve and to disseminate information about the past. City governments ask more questions of their residents than do their rural counterparts. Employers like Inland Steel or Pullman-Standard retain more complete employment records than a small rural business like Lippincott Dairy Company. Historical societies, libraries, and universities collect manuscripts, newspapers, rare books, and similar materials from which a sociologist, demographer, urbanologist, or social historian can draw. It is no accident that some of the most dynamic contemporary research is occurring in urban-related topics. The resources are vast.

This chapter will survey the many record types that you can expect to find in a city, some of them brief views of the chapter-length studies available elsewhere in this book.

City Records

The basic approach to urban genealogy is similar to that followed for any other research problem. Every genealogist begins with certain facts and progresses to the unknown. If tradition says that great-grandfather emigrated from Germany and settled first in Chicago, then you should educate yourself on the background and existing materials for research in that city. Guides have been published for many major cities which outline in broad terms the location and accessibility of sources, eliminating some blind alleys.

For example, one of the best introductory volumes is Rosalie Fellows Bailey, *Guide to Genealogical and Biographical Sources for New York City, 1783-1898* (New York: By the author, 1954). Even if New York City is not your area of interest, Bailey's forty separate categories of records with select bibliographies will give you an analogue for the city in which you are interested. Not all of these will apply to every research problem, but knowing of them can stimulate innovative approaches when other paths seem closed.

A second valuable aid for laying the groundwork in city searching is John D. Buenker, Gerald Michael Greenfield, and William J. Murin, *Urban History: A Guide to Information Sources* (Detroit: Gale Research Co., 1981) an annotation of 1,921 scholarly works covering eleven broad topical areas. Anyone with an interest in any major city can find pertinent literature listed here. Many of the sources cited are standard metropolitan histories; others are contemporary works with bibliographies which are potential goldmines in themselves, pointing to the *original sources* on which the author based his study. Such references can lead directly to manuscripts, special collections, and other hidden tools.[2]

City Directories

A city directory is often the place to begin a particular search. (See Chapter 11, "City Directories and Their Cousins.") If family tradition says James Miller was a teamster who settled on the north side of Chicago around 1850, you should search the directories for that period. Multiple listings for the common name complicate the issue, but you will be able to eliminate all of the James Millers who were not teamsters, drivers, cartmen, or expressmen living on the north side, thus narrowing the search.

Cities often had several directory publishers—Chicago had three in 1871—and you should look at all of them, for each contains unique details. *Edward's Chicago Census Directory* (Chicago: Richard Edwards, 1871) lists not only the name, occupation, and address of the individual but also provides the ward number, the number of males, females, and total in residence as well as the birthplace of the head of the household. *Gager's 1857 Chicago Directory* (Chicago: John Gager & Co.) adds the birthplace and years of residency in Chicago to the usual information. One publication lists "Miller, Emma, widow" and a second notes "Emma, widow James." By limiting a search to one directory, you may miss precious clues.

Street Directories. One of the frustrations in research is finding incomplete information in any given source, for example, the beautiful old portrait which bears the name and street address of the photographer but gives no city, a candid shot of a group of people on the porch of a charming old house at 4124 Trowbridge Street, or the letter which states, "Your brother remains close to the shop in the city but has taken up new quarters on Madison Street." Nearly

Figure 16-1. *Sanborn Insurance Maps of Salt Lake City, Utah* (New York: Sanborn Map Co., 1911), p. 103.

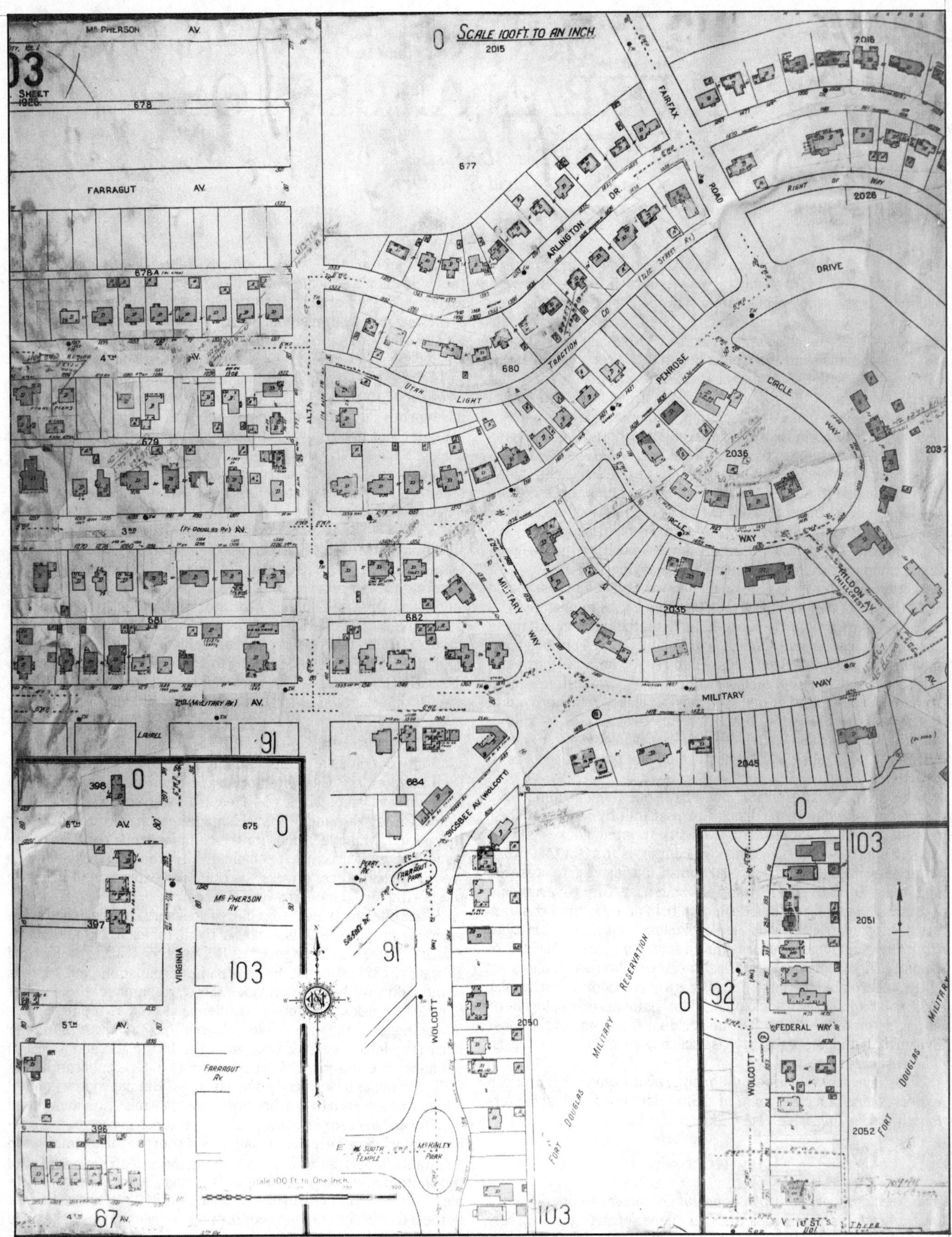

a century later, these notes are useless if the town name is unknown. *The Street Directory of the Principal Cities of the United States*, originally published by order of the Postmaster-General in 1908 and republished by Gale Research Company (Detroit, 1973) contains the names of the streets, avenues, courts, places, lanes, roads, and wharves to which mail was delivered.

Land Records

Even though the city dweller is not always dependent upon real estate for a livelihood, that quarter acre is usually as valuable as the agriculturalist's quarter section. Not only the deed books but many court cases bear record of this.

Most American cities are under the jurisdiction of county governments, and city land records are almost always found with the county recorder. City lots, however, may be recorded in volumes separate from county land with their own indexes or finding aids. They are easy to miss.

The municipal library, designed to collect data useful to the governance of the city, is a good place to learn the procedures of land searching. One may find plat maps or tract books centralized there. Otherwise, detailed plat maps of city blocks are usually available from municipal agencies or from the recorder of deeds.

If the ancestor you are interested in is consistently listed at a certain address for a number of years in city directories, he/she may have owned that piece of property. When you find frequent address changes, you may assume that he/she was renting. Both of these hypotheses need further proof; however, the ancestor who rented property in one location may have also owned land in another, especially a vacant lot. To find his/her land records, check land indexes or abstracts, tax rolls, and less commonly consulted sources like building permits or building improvement files; street, sidewalk, and sewer assessment records; or utility cards for water, lighting, and refuse collection, which also identify an owner with a specific lot or address. These records are normally not subject to privacy laws. Land abstracts compiled from deeds and other property documents by title and abstract companies provide an alternate source when the original land records have been destroyed. They were especially valuable in Chicago after the fire of 1871 when they were used to reestablish property title in burned areas.

Maps

A solid knowledge of the city's layout as it existed in an ancestor's time is also important. While current maps may provide an introduction, and a point of reference for library card catalogs,[3] ward boundaries, street names, and street numbers change over the years. A good source of nineteenth-century maps is E. K. Kirkham's *A Handy Guide to Record Searching in the Larger Cities of the United States* (Logan, Utah: Everton Publishers, 1974) which includes thirty-nine maps for twenty-three major cities along with their respective street indexes.

Jonathan Sheppard Books, Box 2020, Plaza Station, Albany, NY 12220 offers a packet of maps reproduced from Fannin's *Atlas of 1853* which includes maps for the cities of Baltimore, Boston, Buffalo, Charleston, Chicago, Cincinnati, Milwaukee, New Orleans, New York, Philadelphia, Pittsburgh, St. Louis, San Francisco, and Washington, D.C. Write for prices. Francis J. Reynolds, *The New World Atlas* (New York: P.F. Collier & Son Company, 1925) includes maps for Boston, New York, and other large United States cities which are helpful for census research after 1900.

Many American city maps are available for purchase from the Photoduplication Section of the Library of Congress. Catalogs and finding aids to this vast collection can be found in most research libraries and in government documents sections of public and university libraries. For urban ancestors, one special category deserves a more detailed description: Fire Insurance Maps.

The Sanborn Map Company produced some 700,000 sheets of detailed maps for 12,000 cities and towns in North America from 1867 to the present. (Other companies began producing maps as early as 1846.) These maps were used by insurance agents to determine hazards and risk in underwriting specific buildings. Each map is produced on a large over-size sheet in gentle pastel colors: olive drab for adobe, pink for stone, blue for brick, yellow for wood, gray for iron. Size, shape, and construction of homes, businesses, farm buildings; locations of windows, doors, firewalls, roof types; widths and names of streets; property boundaries; ditches, water mains, sprinkling systems; and other details are clearly indicated. (See Figure 16-1.)

Individual residents do not appear on the maps by name, although specific addresses are shown. Businesses appear by name. Once you find your ancestor in census, directory, or utility files, you can determine precisely what house or business the family lived and worked in. It is possible to combine city directories and census entries with fire insurance maps and place each resident on the map.

Fire Insurance Maps in the Library of Congress, prepared by the Geography and Map Section of the Library of Congress (Washington, D.C., 1981, 773 pp.) lists the maps available for each town and city. Copies will be supplied upon request from the Library of Congress, Photoduplication Services, Washington, DC 20540. Because the size varies, it is a good idea to write ahead and ask for a cost estimate for each copy. The pastel colors will not reproduce distinctly in black and white.

Duplicate copies of the maps are also available at selected libraries across the country and in state historical societies and local public libraries. For example, the maps for Tacoma, Washington, are in the Taoma Public Library in their original, multicolored form. Those for Utah cities are found at the Utah State Historical Society.

The Chicago Historical Society maintains a separate guide to its map collection, which is catalogued by date, enabling the searcher to pinpoint a particular time period to coordinate the city directory-census study. Maps are also listed by subject. School district and cemetery maps may help to locate records from those agencies. Fire insurance maps offer details of the metropolitan area seldom found elsewhere. The New York Public Library also has one of the largest city map collections in the country.

Most libraries will not have special equipment for the reproduction of large maps nor will they allow photocopying because of potential damage to the maps. You may improvise a makeshift map by superimposing wards or old street locations on a current map.

Census Records

Federal, state, and special censuses are productive genealogical tools (see Chapter 4), for probably no other records in existence contain more data about individuals or families. Searching through the lists for a metropolitan area, however, presents special problems.

The Soundex and other census indexes are helpful but somewhat limited. Often names were misspelled or completely omitted in transcription from the original schedules. For the 1880 census, only households with children ten years of age or under were listed in the Soundex.[4] Very few indexes exist for 1860 and 1870, especially for cities. If you know the family's configuration, you can go over a census line by line in hopes that names, ages, birthplaces, and other known facts will catch your eye, even though the name is misspelled or the page barely legible. However, the ward is the smallest division of the city that you can identify to limit the search for the 1850-70 censuses; they do not provide street names or numbers.

The geographical arrangement of the census schedules makes finding aids vital when searching for urban residents. Recently, historian Keith Schlesinger devised a system to locate individuals overlooked by the Soundex. Schlesinger gleaned addresses from city directories, which he found both accurate and accessible, then plotted them on maps of census enumeration districts, which normally followed the boundaries of voting precincts in most cities. By narrowing the search for the nonindexed individual to one or two enumeration districts, this scheme permits the historian to escape the confinement of the Soundex. Research institutions are beginning to acquire enumerator district maps and finding aids which trace the route taken during the count, and enumeration district boundary descriptions are available on microfilm through the National Archives and Records Service (NARS). The Newberry Library and Schlesinger have refined several methods for searching the 1850-1900 censuses for Chicago. See Keith Schlesinger and Peggy Tuck Sinko, "Urban Finding Aid for Manuscript Census Searches," *National Genealogical Society Quarterly* 69 (Sept. 1981): 171-80. The techniques, of course, are applicable to other cities as well.

Establishing the whereabouts of your own urban ancestor does not exhaust the possibilities of census schedules. The microfilm contains the raw data necessary to understand the life of a neighborhood. What, for example, was the ethnic and occupational configuration of the street? Did the family settle with or near relatives? When combined with historical or sociological studies, a census can provide a better insight on what it meant to live in a nineteenth-century city.

Nor should you overlook state censuses, mortality schedules, and other special censuses. The New York State Census for 1855, for example, is far more important than the federal census since it includes information on the value and construction of the dwelling; the number of families occupying it; household members by name, age, sex, and relation to the head of the family; state or country of birth for each; marital status; profession, trade, or occupation; number of years resident in the city; voting status; and literacy of adults. The 1855 census takers took the local election districts in each city ward for their districts, enabling the searcher to focus on a desired household faster than in a corresponding federal census, which was organized by ward. Local genealogists have compiled indexes for several areas. While this census does not specify bounds of the election districts, for New York City, the *New York Times* published the polling place of each of the 128 election districts in the twenty-two wards for the previous election on 7 November 1854.

Vital Records

Vital records (births, marriages, deaths) contain varying information according to the locality and the year. (See Chapter 2, "Vital Records and Cemetery Research," and Chapter 3, "Marriage and Divorce Records.") Many cities began collecting vital records information before their states did. Their interest was partly a response to the overcrowding and greater health problems of cities, and some states with large urban populations were the first to require registration for precisely the same reasons, particularly when the so-called Progressive Movement was strong. Neither Illinois nor New York had statewide registration by 1910. As a rule of thumb, when double sets are available, you can usually get an answer more quickly from the municipal agency than from the state. For instructions for access to vital records kept since the instigation of municipal or statewide registration, see "Where to Write for Vital Records," Appendix F. Periodic revisions keep information about prices, geographic location, and controlling agencies current.

Births. Birth certificates will usually list the date, time, and place of a birth; sex of the baby; the names of the infant and parents; and the attending midwife or physician. One collection (over 100,000 entries) of midwives' records for Chicago is at the Northwestern Memorial Hospital Archives, recently made accessible by the microfilming project of the Genealogical Society of Utah, available at its main or branch libraries. Similar manuscripts exist for other places although you have to search to locate them.

Marriages. Marriage certificates will often list the man's name and age, the woman's maiden name and age, and the name of the presiding minister or official. If necessary, one can connect the minister to the religious institution through contemporary city directories. The marriage license application is more desirable because it usually has more information, but in many areas (like Chicago) the application is either no longer extant or not publicly available. Marriage indexes, often compiled from newspapers, are also very useful for pinpointing a date.

In Cincinnati, the marriage records were destroyed when the Hamilton County courthouse burned – not once but three different times (1814, 1849, 1884). The Works Progress Administration (WPA) reconstructed the marriages from surviving pages and compiled a new set of indexes. The Daughters of the American Revolution also reconstructed the marriage records using ministers' diaries, church registers, justice dockets, original certificates, and newspapers. The combination of both reconstructed sets is more complete for some surnames than they were before the fires.

Deaths. A death certificate usually contains at least the name and age of the decedent, the date, place, and cause of death, the name of the attending physician, and the place of burial. Later records contain more information. In metropolitan areas, you will need at least an approximate death date to request a death records search. With the exact date of death from the certificate and the individual's address, you can also access the obituary, undertaker's record, cemetery record, and probate. With the social security number, recorded on the death certificate since 1937, you can often access other sources.

The Genealogical Society of Utah has microfilmed vital records for many municipalities, and the society's branch libraries may provide the only opportunity to do a competent search. The original city records are rarely open to the public. The sheer volume of documents in the care of the metropolitan agency makes the search difficult; vital statistics agencies are usually overworked, understaffed, and ill-prepared to do a lengthy or thorough search; and when the exact date of an event is unknown, the name common or misspelled, the handwriting questionable or illegible, the complications can become insurmountable.

New York City printed vital records by order of the borough governments. Each annual volume was individually indexed. Today these records are available ***on microfilm*** only at the Municipal Archives, Department of Records and Information Services, 52 Chambers Street, New York, NY 10007 and the Genealogical Society of Utah and its branches. Here is a borough-by-borough list of the existing birth, death, and marriage records.

Manhattan	Births:	July 1847-48; July 1853-97
	Deaths:	1795-1804; 1812-1919
	Marriages:	June 1847-1948; July 1853-65
Brooklyn	Births:	1866-97
	Deaths:	1847-53; 1857-1919
	Marriages: (Flatbush only)	1847-52
Bronx*	Deaths:	1898-1919
Queens	Deaths:	1898-1919
	Scattered birth, death, and marriage records:	1880s-1890s.
Richmond	Deaths:	1898-1919
Staten Island	Scattered birth, death, and marriage records:	1880s-1890s

Special indexes can be of great assistance where they exist. The Works Projects Administration (WPA) compiled an index to Chicago deaths 1871-1933 during 1933. Unaccessible except to agency officials until recently, it is now available on microfilm through Genealogical Society branch libraries.

*Before the creation of the Bronx as a separate borough in 1898, it was part of Westchester County, except for certain western areas which were annexed by New York (Manhattan) in 1874, and eastern areas annexed in 1895. Vital records for these areas are with Manhattan records.

ILLINOIS, COOK, CHICAGO - VITAL RECORDS

Chicago (Illinois). Board of Health.
Chicago deaths, 1871-1933.

U.S. & CAN
FILM AREA

Microfilm of original records at the Cook County courthouse, Chicago, Illinois.

Alphabetical listing of Chicago city and county deaths returned to the City Board of Health and later forwarded for filing with the county clerk. Includes name, address, date of death, and register number.

Deaths, A-Bou	1871-1933	1295943
Deaths, Bou-Cul	1871-1933	1295944
Deaths, Cul-Fol	1871-1933	1295945
Deaths, Fol-Haw	1871-1933	1295946
Deaths, Haw-J	1871-1933	1295947
Deaths, K-Lap	1871-1933	1295948
Deaths, Lap-McB	1871-1933	1295949
Deaths, McC-Obr	1871-1933	1295971
Deaths, Obr-Res	1871-1933	1295972
Deaths, Rep-Sik	1871-1933	1295973
Deaths, Sik-Ste	1871-1933	1295974
Deaths, Ste-Wal	1871-1933	1295975
Deaths, Wal-Z	1871-1933	1295976

Figure 16-2. Works Project Administration, Chicago Deaths 1871-1933.

Obituaries provide valuable biographical data and are often the only printed source with such information. Betty M. Jarboe, *Obituaries: A Guide to Sources* (Boston: G. K. Hall and Co., 1982) is an invaluable finding aid for obituaries in newspapers or periodicals, particularly when the population of the city makes searching for a death date unusually difficult. A typical citation from this source shows that the Colorado Historical Society Library has files of newspaper birth, marriage, and death notices from the 1860s to the 1940s. Another entry tells us that the New Orleans Public Library has a card file of approximately 523,000 obituary cards which it is expanding by 25,000 new cards per year. The New Orleans project, still in progress, will eventually cover the period from 1804 to 1972.

An unusual example of combining records to find a death date is the case of Solomon Schwartz. His descendants moved away from Chicago, and his death date and burial place had been lost in that time although they remembered it was in a Jewish cemetery. His great-grandchildren could not find his name in the city death index. They could not use cemetery records since they are arranged chronologically and by lot numbers. However, in the county recorder's records, a deed book marked "Cemeteries" contained original title records arranged by cemetery. Solomon Schwartz's record was in the second Jewish cemetery consulted. Only the number of the conveyance, the date, name of the grantor (cemetery) and the grantee (Solomon), and the legal description of the cemetery lot were given; but further investigation in the cemetery's records proved that this was the correct man.

Coroners' Inquests

An infrequently used record is the coroner's inquest. (See Chapter 2.) If there is any reason to believe that your ancestor may have died of any violent, unnatural, or unknown cause, the resulting inquest may contain a wealth of information rarely found in other sources and date to the mid-seventeenth century in Maryland and Virginia. Many of the deaths reported annually in a city end up in the coroner's files, now commonly under the jurisdiction of the city or county medical examiner. As a rule, the earlier records may contain more details than later files do. In addition to the death information, one early coroner's record for a Chicagoan listed his personal effects. The rosary in his pocket was a clue which led to a successful search in Catholic sources not previously considered because the family was Protestant. An added bonus was the wife's name; she had been called as a witness.

Coroner's files may also provide personal histories of the victim through exact birthplaces, dates, names of parents and other relatives, educational and occupational background, military service, Social Security number, and much more. A doctor's statement may incorporate a medical history and physical traits. Eyewitness accounts often contain insights into the character of a victim and record the drama of the death itself. A coroner's verdict concluded early case histories but more recent reports do not determine guilt. They also provide leads to subsequent court cases.

Usually you need an exact death date since this record type is usually arranged chronologically, and some are not indexed. Inquests stemming from catastrophes will sometimes be grouped under the name of the disaster such as the Iroquois Theatre Fire, Our Lady of the Angels School Fire, etc. Coroners' inquests combine effectively with news accounts of disasters, which provide casualty lists and background details on each event.

Undertakers' Records

Undertakers' records will often add more detailed information about a decedent than the official county death certificate. However, mortuaries may be difficult to locate in the city because of shifting neighborhoods. Use the city directories to trace a family-owned establishment to a new location in the city. (See section on morticians' directories in Chapter 11 and section on coroners' records in Chapter 2.) A successor might know the whereabouts of records from extinct establishments.

Cemetery Records

There is no direct route to cemetery records in metropolitan areas. (See Chapter 2.) Nonsectarian cemeteries generally maintain their own files. Policies vary somewhat, but many cemetery officials will give minimal information over the telephone: names of individuals interred in a single plot, exact grave locations, and current owners of the plot. Additional data usually requires a fee. Since records are, in most instances, cross-indexed by location and chronology, seldom does a comprehensive index exist. The key to cemetery record use is an exact death date for at least one of the individuals buried in a given plot. This, in turn, can generate names of others in the same place.

Religious Sources

The location of urban religious records presents a unique challenge. (See Chapter 5.) Population, geography, and ethnicity are confusing enough; but to complicate matters further, different denominations kept different types of records. For example, presbyteries transferred membership records with the departure of the member. Immigrants commonly chose to worship in their own tongues and often went far out of their neighborhoods to find the congenial atmosphere of the national parish. Churches as well as people responded to the dynamics of the city, some closing, consolidating, or moving as neighborhoods changed, while others shifted from their ethnic orientation to accommodate new circumstances. Thus, any researcher having difficulty tracing the church or synagogue of his/her ancestor might save time by backtracking to study the history of that particular religion in the locale of interest. Though finding religious records may be difficult, it usually repays the time and effort spent. Church records usually predate civil records and supply information not found elsewhere – sometimes telling even the European church or parish where people being married were christened or confirmed.

An invaluable guide for research in this area is the Historical Records Survey of the Works Progress Administration (WPA). WPA workers inventoried church and public records extant in the 1930s for any areas in the United States. Their lists for urban churches are especially valuable. A typical entry for church vital records would contain the name and address of the institution at the time of publication, ethnic orientation (if any), and comprehensive dates for each type of vital record. If the organization housed documents from other congregations, the survey noted that fact and gave a range of dates. Map 16-1 shows Chicago parishes as they were constituted in 1873. For example, *A Guide to Church Vital Statistics Records in California – San Francisco and Alameda Counties* (San Franscisco: Northern California Historical Records Survey, 1940), breaks the individual churches down by geographical area and denomination. A summary of baptisms, marriages, and death records follows for each. Additionally, it notes that Holy Family was a Chinese mission while Saint Anthony of Padua was German. In most cases the founding dates are listed.

The obvious limitation to the survey is that many of the records may have since been moved. But it is still a place to start.

For those inventories which were printed, consult Sargent B. Child and Dorothy P. Holmes, *Bibliography of Research Project Reports*, WPA Technical Series No. 7 (1943; reprint ed.,), Bountiful, Utah: Printing by Faisal (365 North Main, Bountiful, UT 84010), 1979 as *W.P.A. Bibliography 9*. Many inventories were never printed and they can be located by consulting Loretta L. Hefner, *The WPA Historical Records Survey: A Guide to the Unpublished Inventories, Indexes, and Transcripts* (Chicago: Society of American Archivists, 1980).

Early city or county histories, biographical sketches, and jubilee books provide other background on religious institutions in the local

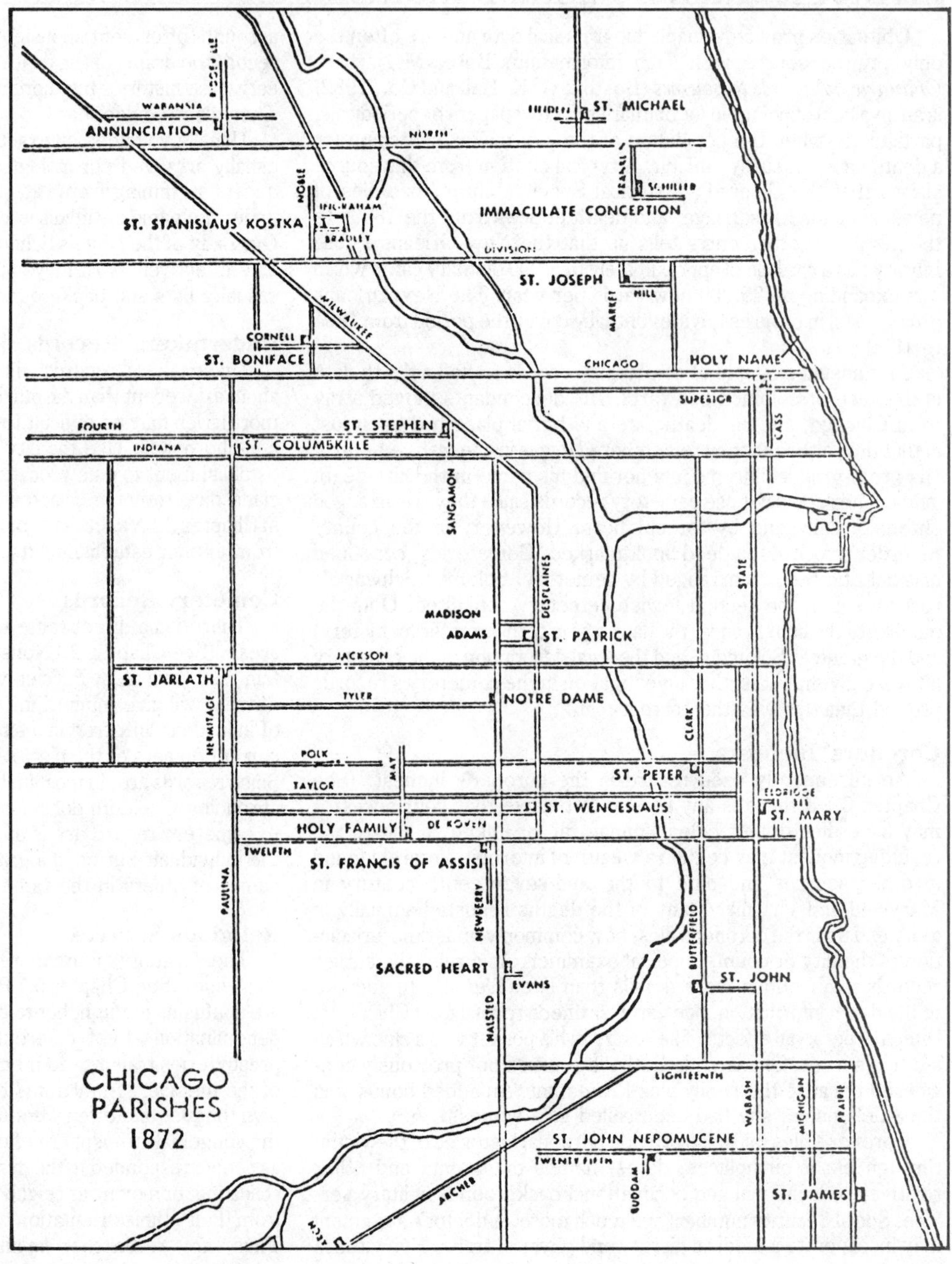

Map 16-1. Rev. Francis J. Epstein, *A Necrology of Diocesan Priests of the Chicago Archdiocese 1837-1959* (Chicago: Catholic Archdiocese of Chicago [c1906]. An updated though still undated version by Rt. Rev. Msgr. Malachy P. Foley, P.A., is also extant.

area. Through these descriptions one may trace the church, its development, and ethnic makeup. Modern studies also are a tremendous help, and their bibliographies enhance their utility. George Lane and Alginantes Kezys, comps., *Chicago Churches and Synagogues* (Chicago: Loyola University Press, 1981) single out 125 houses of worship with architectural, historical, or social significance. Further, they provide a detailed description and history of each building and its congregation, ethnic classification, architectural attributes, and location by exact address, and area of city. The acknowledgements and notes give the researcher numerous sources for locating denominational repositories.

Even though there is no comprehensive guide to American church records, one should mention two major works: August B. Suelflow, *A Preliminary Guide to Church Records and Repositories*, a standard reference of denominational archives; and, for those with a Roman Catholic interest, the *Official Catholic Directory*, published annually since 1817 by P.J. Kenedy and Sons, which lists American dioceses, parishes, and institutions with their respective addresses. In some instances, successor repositories for closed churches are given. Major libraries and Catholic churches are likely to maintain copies of these volumes. For churches which have changed names and denominational affiliation, consult Julia Pettee, *List of Churches: Official Forms of the Names for Denominational Bodies with Brief Description and Historical Notes* (Chicago: American Library Association, 1948).

A few church records are available in book or microform. The Newberry Library in Chicago has a large collection of sources from the eastern United States as well as from local institutions. The Detroit Society of Genealogical Research is one of many metropolitan groups engaged in publication of local church records. The Genealogical Society of Utah has filmed church registers from numerous localities, and its branch library system allows access in every state to these records. Also available through the Genealogical Society of Utah is the International Genealogical Index rich in church registers for New York City, Boston, Hartford, Philadelphia, and other northern cities.

Used in combination with other sources, church vital records may help illuminate even the most perplexing problems. For example, Karl Johnson was known to have lived at a certain address in Chicago for several years near the beginning of the twentieth century, but his death date was unknown. The Works Progress Administration Index to Chicago Deaths indicated that he died at that address in 1911. This death year led to a certificate which in turn pointed to the cemetery records. The cemetery gave the officiating minister's name, and a directory search identified him as belonging to the Swedish Covenant Church. It had since moved, but inquiries at another congregation of the same denomination pinpointed the new location of the records. Not only did the church have many records on the family, it had a jubilee book with biographical sketches which included Karl Johnson as a founding member. The biography gave his exact birthplace, his date of arrival in this country, and his prior residence before settling in Chicago in 1884.

Printed Sources

One of the distinct advantages of city research is the profusion of printed materials. The numerous local histories published in the last quarter of the nineteenth century were a greater service to posterity than publishers of that time realized. Compiled and printed for a localized citizenry, they form a body of research material fascinating to genealogists. Though not of uniform quality or content, they exist in abundance for cities and counties in the United States. Topics include the establishment and development of social, political, and economic institutions, military information, municipal histories, chronologies, portraits of individuals, and photographs or engravings of the urban scene. Many early printed town and city plats (maps) are also extremely useful.

Of greatest importance, perhaps, to the genealogist is the wealth of biographical material in these volumes. At the city level, most of the biographies deal with persons who have achieved prominence in one field or another. Prominence is a very relative term. If you assume that your ancestors were common people, then you may assume you will find no help in such sources. This is not invariably true. Futhermore, though direct ancestors may not be included, sometimes descendants of these ancestors on other lines may be. Since these persons descend from a common ancestor, the value is much the same. Important clues on migrational patterns, ethnic communities, political involvement, religious affiliation, and occupations can be gleaned from the biographical sketch of a member of a group to which an ancestor belonged. With these clues, you may then start looking for records of less prominent members of that group.

Naturalizations

Yet another type of record which urban researchers commonly mine for information are the naturalizations, because so many urbanites were immigrants.

Until 1906 naturalization was strictly a function of the courts. In that year Congress created the Bureau of Immigration and Naturalization to standardize the system. One byproduct was a greatly expanded set of questions for the immigrant to answer; another was retention of duplicate copies of all final petitions in the Washington office of the Bureau.

Passage of an Alien Registration Law in 1940 caused the Immigration and Naturalization Service (INS) to touch the lives of resident noncitizens as well. Alien registration files are closed to all but direct descendants who invoke the Freedom of Information Act process. Very limited repatriation records also survive in the central files of the agency.

Naturalization records require a petition for naturalization number for reference purposes. This number is usually available through indexes maintained by the court of record where the petition was filed. Boston, New York City, and Chicago are blessed with comprehensive Soundex indexes which cover local and federal naturalizations. The New York records are further indexed by national group (Germans, Italians, etc.) for several years. When the Soundex fails, as it occasionally does, ancillary records like order books (which show all naturalizations approved on a given day) and registers (which list petitioners by first initial of surname) may also exist.

Because naturalization conferred voting rights on aliens, voting records are another possible source of information for the urban genealogist. Voter registration lists included the native-born as well as the naturalized, of course, but have the built-in limitation that they cover only those who made the effort to register. Still, voting records are sometimes indexed or registered by ward, and they may provide an avenue for identification when censuses or directories are unavailable. Precinct block books might substitute for assessment books in areas where few people owned property. Voting lists can provide a test for community involvement. They reflect local mores in other ways, for the linkage between citizenship and voting was not always visible. Voting did not always guarantee full-fledged citizenship, just as citizenship did not always result in the exercise of the ballot. For those writing a detailed family history, a study of official election returns, especially those predating the secret ballot, might prove intriguing as a means of identifying political participation.

Selective Service

Not everyone voted, even when eligible; but every male born between 1873 and 1900 was supposed to register with the Selective Service System during World War I. The draft cards identified the date and place of birth, occupation, residence at the time of registration, and physical description of the registrant. Aliens were expected to register, although they could request an exemption from service on the grounds of conflicting allegiance. The alien registration and the bulk of the actual draft cards are in the NARS

Regional Archives Branch, 1559 Saint Joseph Avenue, East Point, GA 30344.

The cards are arranged by local board and thereunder alphabetically; cities like Chicago and New York had many local boards. It is thus necessary to have an exact address, which the National Archives staff at East Point can convert into a draft board number in order to pick the correct card.

Court Records

Court records are potentially the most valuable yet the most underutilized sources in the city. (See Chapter 6.) Again, the case volume created by the vast population and the bureaucracy involved may intimidate even an enthusiastic searcher. Court jurisdictions and procedures have puzzled many a searcher, but books on local government can guide one through the maze. For example, a particularly handy source for Illinois is the Louis L. Emerson, ed. (Secretary of State), *Blue Book of the State of Illinois 1925-1926* (Springfield: Illinois State Journal Co., 1925) with its descriptions of the various levels in the political structure.

By far the most commonly used court records are the probates because of their helpfulness in identifying heirs. Some counties will have master indexes for court proceedings; but more often than not, you must examine registers by year. When names are distinguished only by case number, a search of the docket books may be in order. The shortcut approach is especially good in cities where old cases are warehoused and must be requested a few at a time. Dockets provide a synopsis of the case, the decedent's name and date of death, name of the administrator, and names of widowed spouse and heirs. This information enables the searcher to order the correct case from the warehouse or to retrieve it from its court location without going through all the other cases of the same name.

In divorce cases, testimony provides personal accounts from the principals of the lawsuit as well as the testimony of witnesses. It is not uncommon to find exact marriage dates and places, former residences, children's names as well as those of other relatives and acquaintances, a list of assets explicitly defining real estate, and the cause for the action. Guardianship documents are also full of genealogical information.

Suits concerning property, real or otherwise, demanded proof of ownership in court, which may enlighten us about family relationships. Consider the case of James Miller who died intestate. Some years later, after the death of his wife, the children became engaged in a dispute over the property. The testimony provided birthdates and places of all children born in the house on the property in question and their married names, while a sister who had raised the children and had since repatriated to Ireland entered the controversy. As she had returned to her home village, the land controversy also supplied, after much searching elsewhere, the origin of the immigrant family.

Name-change petitions are often helpful also, for they applied to the entire family, who are named in the official document.

One unlikely place to find many a lost court case will be under the letter "I" in the Plaintiff indexes. Thousands of cases, regardless of the subject, are mysteriously filed under the heading *In re*,"in regard to" or "in the matter of."

City courts can also yield information of value. If the city is subject to the county jurisdiction (see "Urban Jurisdictions Not Subject to County Authority" at the end of the chapter) police courts and local justice courts take care of trivial matters where the fines and fees are limited. More important cases go automatically to county and state tribunals. If the city is independent, however, mayors' courts, hustings (so-called in Virginia, Maryland, and the Carolinas), had substantial jurisdiction.

These city courts issued business licenses for taverns, mercantile establishments, hotels, and other shops; and received petitions from local citizens regarding many of the functions which are today handled by commissioners or separate agencies of government such as road repair, runoff water drainage, watch and ward (police patrol and security of business and personal property), volunteer fire department personnel, and numerous other activities necessary to provide services and protection for city dwellers. Another important function was providing for the poor. Among the references to the poor in city court minutes are notices of removals of persons and families who are not residents of the city and who might become public charges on the poor rolls. Minutes record that these people are transported to the city line at public expense.

Records for these courts were often printed annually by public order and these volumes are found in the local public library. For example, the printed minutes and reports of city officials for St. Paul, Minnesota, are in the St. Paul Public Library with a second copy available at the Minnesota Historical Society. The city minutes for Nashua, New Hampshire, are found only at the Nashua Public Library, where there is a complete run of volumes until well into the twentieth century. The Genealogical Society of Utah has microfilmed the city court volumes for Savannah, Georgia, and several other southern cities and towns. The minutes of the Mayor's Court of New York City are published in the New York Historical Society Collections. There is a great interest in city court minutes and many of them are easy to locate.

Somewhat less well-known than probate or other local court records, are federal court files. The federal courts have traditionally heard cases involving interstate disputes and often served as a court of appeal for litigation which originated at the local level. In addition, the federal courts were usually indexed by plaintiff and/or defendant, making the search a time-consuming project.

The material in a file varies with the significance of the case and the state that it reached during the trial process. But depositions describing the acquisition and retention of property were not unusual in land disputes, which often appeared as equity suits. These were accompanied many times by maps of the place in question or copies of deeds submitted as exhibits. Such cases can produce literally thousands of pages of testimony and may detail facts about the family and its environment which are unattainable elsewhere. One extraordinary example recorded specifics about the Hyde Park area of Chicago during its settlement years, which had survived in no other form.

Bankruptcy filings included schedules of assets and liabilities, outlining the business and financial dealings of the bankruptcy claimant. Small partnerships and proprietorships, along with personal bankruptcies, comprised the preponderance of cases heard in bankruptcy court. When federal bankruptcy laws were not in effect, "involuntary" bankruptcies were entered as equity proceedings. Federal criminal prosecutions were a minor portion of the case load until the 1920s, when prohibition violations swelled the numbers. Other types of federal cases of genealogical interest might include confiscation cases from the Civil War, when the Union government seized the available property of Confederate sympathizers, and personal injury suits against interstate carriers (usually railroads).

The federal government touched urban residents in other ways than through its courts. The Internal Revenue Service (IRS) was less visible before World War I than it is now, but an assortment of IRS assessment lists sheds light on the wealth of many individuals during the Civil War and again after 1913. The Civil War vintage assessments (arranged by collection district and thereunder alphabetically) have been microfilmed; those for the early twentieth century have not. Original monthly assessment lists survive for San Francisco, Denver, Chicago, and Detroit, and are deposited in the Federal Archives and Records Centers (FARC) serving those cities. Taxable income was defined at a level which limited the assessment to the middle and upper classes; nevertheless, thousands of entries appear in the volumes pertaining to urban districts.

A source with particular interest to those whose roots lie in the South comes from the records of the Southern Claims Commission, organized to settle with Union sympathizers who had supplied Northern forces without compensation. Case files included depositions, affidavits, reports, and receipts. A geographical index, arranged by state and county, allows the researcher to pinpoint people in a specific territory, while the consolidated index serves as a name entry. See *Records of the Commissioners of Claims (Southern Claims Commission), 1871-1880*, Micropublication M87 (Washington, D.C.: National Archives and Record Service), consolidated index edited by Gary B. Mills. These records are not limited to cities, but the major locales of Atlanta and New Orleans are included.

Business/Occupational Records

Bankruptcy and tax records lead naturally to another source: professional, business, and employment records. (See Chapter 10, "Business and Employment Records.") Occupational specialization and the related drive to license specific trades or skills both resulted from urbanization and mass society. Many of these collections belong to institutions which lack the resources to undertake extensive searches; indexes and finding aids may prove spotty; and privacy restrictions sometimes limit access. Still, these records are definitely worth searching.

National professional associations, with membership lists often dating back into the 1800s, are one place to look. (See section on occupations in Chapter 11.) The American Medical Association, for example, has files on its members, and a doctor residing in New York after about 1880 had to register his license with the county clerk and submit an affidavit of his admission to practice. Private associations printed directories, almanacs, and collective biographies with information on their compatriots. This filled a dual need, providing exposure for the budding professional and assuring clients that it was possible to find an upright and competent practitioner of a given skill in a mobile society. Whatever the purpose, the result for the genealogist is additional information about the newly emergent managerial and professional classes.

Increased interest in business regulation during the same time period[5] stemmed from the same concerns and generated another body of records. The demand for honest retailing inspired Boston to inspect the weights and measures of merchants in that city as early as 1881. Inspection reports, an early type of consumer protection, gave the owner's name and address and described any action taken as a result of the visit. Similar departments eventually appeared elsewhere in the country. A parallel to this idea in the private sector was the credit report, developed in 1842 by Dunn and Bradstreet. National in scope and detailed in coverage, the reports in the company archives, now at Harvard University Library, can increase your understanding of nineteenth-century business life as well as knowledge of some particular firm. For example, credit investigators recorded many aspects in their reports. One noted that his subject had married well; her name and a comment on her father buttressed the opinion that this party was a good risk. If you can identify an ancestor with a specific company or business, you may be able to search the records of that business, assuming that it is still extant or that the records have been deposited in a historical society or corporate archives. Business archives must usually be examined in person; the libraries simply do not have the personnel to respond to mail requests.

Most major metropolitan areas began as transportation centers, and many records of transportation companies have survived. Maritime records in the National Maritime Museum of San Francisco, the Great Lakes Maritime Institute of Detroit, and the Great Lakes Historical Society in Vermillion, Ohio, near Cleveland, may contain documentation in the form of crew lists or log books. The National Archives in Washington contains applications for seamen's protection certificates and files on merchant seamen; regional archives branches are currently accessioning inspection and licensing documents from maritime and riparian ports. Boston, Cleveland, Detroit, and Chicago records have already been transferred; others will follow as they are found. Rail transportation workers may be traced through corporate archives, union records, or government agencies. The Newberry Library in Chicago has manuscripts from the Chicago, Burlington, and Quincy Railroad and some from the Pullman Standard Car Company. Figure 16-3 is an example of an employee's service card with Pullman. The Chicago Historical Society recently acquired some files of the Brotherhood of Sleeping Car Porters. The Railroad Retirement Board, also located in Chicago, is the national pensioning agency for rail workers; its records should be interesting for anyone with an ancestor eligible for a railroad pension. The Railroad Retirement Board, however, did not begin operations until the mid-1930s. Records are limited to individuals associated with the rail industry at or since that time or who were receiving a private rail pension which was assumed by the Board

Form 1729. 11-06. 5M.
NAME Avigni Aurelio E. D. O.
ADDRESS AUG 20 1907
Dep't Frt CB Occup'n Lab long gang
Age 30 yrs. Born Month Year Date last Birthday
Old Check No. Total Service with Co. yrs. months
Boards ☑ Rents ☐ Owns ☐ Single ☐ Married ☑ Widower ☐
Dependents Wife ☑ No. of Children 2 and in Italy
Country of birth Italy How long in U. S. 2 mos Citizen ☐
When last empl'd by Co. Month Year When at Pullman shops
Where How long
Occup'n Reason for leaving
Foreman Old Check No.
Other record with Co.
OTHER EMPLOYMENT DURING PAST 12 MONTHS.
Employer R R Labor
Address
Occup'n Foreman Check No.
P'rd of empl. Reason for leaving Date quit, mo. year
Wrote Answered File No.
Employer
Address
Occup'n Foreman Check No.
P'rd of empl. Reason for leaving Date quit, mo. year
Wrote Answered File No.
RELATIVES IN COMPANY'S EMPLOY.

NAME	RELATIONSHIP	DEP'T	CHECK NO.

6203

Name Avigni Aurelio
Address 205 - 115th St Age 30

	Check No.	Dep't and Occup'n	Rate	Change of Rate	Hired	Dropped	
1	6203	Frt CB Lab	16 2/3		8 20 7	9 19 7	Q
2							
3							
4							
5							
6							
7							
8							
9							
10							
11							
12							
13							
14							
15							
16							

SIGN FULL NAME
Avigni Aurelio

Figure 16-3. Employment card of Aurelio Avigni, Pullman Standard Car Manufacturing Company, 20 Aug. 1907. Original records at South Suburban Genealogical and Historical Society, 161st Place and Louis Avenue, Box 96, South Holland, IL 60473. Genealogists seeking family members or ancestors may use this collection.

in 1937.

Many municipalities have records of city employees dating back to founding days. Police and firemen pension records are often the greater part of these municipal collections. Municipal archives or reference libraries are good sources for these records. Sometimes the individual department still holds the documents.

The union movement has many of its roots in the major industrial centers of the country, and some records have survived. Wayne State University in Detroit is the site of the Archives of Labor History, which has collected manuscripts from unions all over the country. Its major holdings have come from the United Auto Workers, as one might expect, but some records have come from the American Federation of Teachers, the Newspaper Guild, and the Industrial Workers of the World. The Ohio Historical Society has gathered labor union documents as well, placing many of them in regional repositories like the Western Reserve Historical Society in Cleveland.

Union records at the local level often include membership lists, minutes of meetings, clippings files, scrapbooks, and similar materials. In San Francisco, scene of intense labor strife during the 1930s, the police monitored radical organizations quite closely. The WPA Historical Records Survey of Northern California, cited earlier, cataloged several series of police files, some indexed, which surveyed the activities of Communists, IWWs and even some antiwar aliens.[6] Like business archives, many labor archives lack the resources to respond to mail requests, and you may need to search these records in person. As in most cases, it is wise to find out what the policy is before making any long-distance trips.

Neighborhood Sources

Anyone who looks at a city history will immediately realize that only a small fraction of the population gains municipal recognition. A citizen prominent enough to be found in a major printed historical source is inevitably the same individual who will be easily found in every other source. He will have remained at the same address for years, his land records are easily traced, his church recorded every event, the census enumerator never missed him, and he left a probate that proved almost everything.

For most city ancestors, a more manageable and productive search area is the neighborhood or community. Usually, the neighborhood will have its own library where a researcher can expect to find more information on that immediate area including local histories, sometimes still in manuscript, and even neighborhood newspapers. Community newspapers allowed a great deal of space for local events and personalities ignored by the big city papers. Local libraries may also be the place to begin a search for school records which are sometimes scattered rather than in compact collections. The school records themselves are usually kept at the municipal level, but the library can provide area school addresses and district jurisdictions.

City neighborhoods and districts may have their own historical societies and museums, often affiliated with the public library. Even if they are not, the local librarian will know about them. Neighborhood historical societies, usually manned by volunteers and open at irregular hours, are rarely listed in phone books; but when they exist, they can be gold mines of information about local residents and may have community photographs, scrapbooks, and personal mementos. One of these neighborhood treasures is a personal note from a proud young businessman.

The Bicentennial in 1976 prompted many communities and neighborhoods to investigate their heritage. Old-timers were interviewed, relics came out of attics, and basements disgorged documents. Indexes of newspaper obituaries and cemeteries were compiled. When local studies were published, neighborhood libraries usually received copies. Libraries of universities or community colleges in the area may also have copies.

The main branch of the city public library, the municipal library, and the city or county historical library should also be checked for neighborhood sources. If the ethnic makeup of a neighborhood has changed or if the old neighborhood no longer exists, then the central repository for the city is the logical place to search for needed information. When searching major libraries for neighborhood information, you should check not only listings of the neighborhood itself, but also its surrounding neighbors, especially if they shared a district or area name. Or the dominant nationality of a neighborhood may be the key to locating information. Chicago examples include Germans in Old Town Area; South Side Irish; and Poles of the Milwaukee Avenue District. Still other neighborhoods were settled by mixed ethnic groups who shared a common occupation in a particular part of the city. The Garment District, the stockyard area, the steelmill area – all might be classifications in a library card catalog. Modern urban studies frequently focus on specific neighborhoods, which serve as a microcosm of city life. Their bibliographies of masters' theses, dissertations, or books can help further searches.

Photographic archives or graphics departments maintained by some libraries may provide photographs of cities, neighborhoods, streets, business establishments, and ancestral homes. The Graphics Department of the Chicago Historical Society catalogs

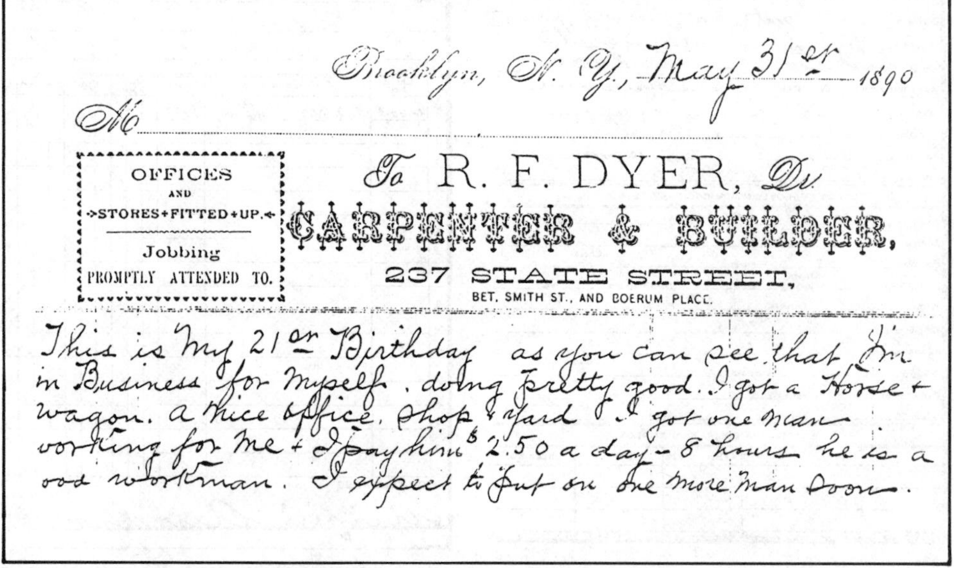

Brooklyn, N. Y., May 31st 1890

M

OFFICES AND
->STORES+FITTED+UP.<-
Jobbing
PROMPTLY ATTENDED TO.

To R. F. DYER, Dr.
CARPENTER & BUILDER,
237 STATE STREET,
BET. SMITH ST., AND BOERUM PLACE.

This is My 21st Birthday as you can see that I'm in Business for myself. doing pretty good. I got a Horse + wagon. a nice office. Shop + yard. I got one man working for me + I pay him $2.50 a day – 8 hours he is a ood workman. I expect to put on one more man soon.

Figure 16-4. R. F. Dyer to unidentified correspondent, 31 May 1980, holograph example of a neighborhood scrapbook in possession of the author, 3629 W. 147th Ave., Midlothian, IL 60445.

its photos by street address as well as subject (landmark, neighborhood, event). To draw from this collection you need to know the changes in the names of streets and in the city's numbering system but such efforts usually add a valuable graphics dimension to the family history. Ask reference personnel for street directories and other such finding aids.

Ethnic Sources

Nowhere is the dramatic increase in recent genealogical interest more evident than in ethnic research with a parallel increase in guides and tools. Genealogical societies nationwide are bringing sophistication to the collection, preservation, and use of ethnic materials. The microfilming projects of the Genealogical Society of Utah have brought the records of the world to our doorsteps. Lubomyr R. Wynar, *Encylopedic Directory of Ethnic Organizations in the United States* (Littleton, Colo.: Libraries Unlimited, 1976), the first comprehensive guide to major organizations created by various communities, demonstrates the pluralism of the American city. Ethnic press and organizations are primary indicators of the group's social structure, but interdisciplinary efforts by colleges and universities are also important. The "Italians in Chicago Project," operated by the University of Illinois at Chicago, has not only collected materials and interviewed neighborhood veterans, but has also begun to disseminate its information through bibliographies which circulate to libraries. Similar projects and collections exist for other major cities, and they are certainly worth investigating.

Settlements

An institution which served a grass-roots clientele in urban areas was the settlement house. Numerous settlements sprang up in the working-class neighborhoods where they sought to reach a maximum number of residents with programs ranging from citizenship classes to ethnic musical societies. Like the unions, papers of settlement houses contain membership lists and minutes of meetings. They also have a wealth of information about happenings in the neighborhood in which they were situated: the daily pulse of life on the surrounding streets, ethnic conflicts, the struggle between good and evil (as seen by the middle-class employees of the house), and the drive to attain success. Settlements reached only a small proportion of those who resided in the overcrowded tenements beyond their doors, but the larger ones often had 2,000 members or more on their rolls at any given time.

Chicago has annual listings of social service agencies which date back to the 1920s. These include settlements, orphanages, placing-out societies, family shelter, and others. Similar directories can be found for most large cities in the collections of the local public libraries. City directories also list social welfare groups in a special section of the directory beginning about the same time. Using a modern telephone directory and moderate telephone time, you can determine which of the current agencies are the same as those listed earlier and under what circumstances their records are available. See also Chapter 6, "Court Records," for procedures in locating records of adoption agencies.

Other Urban Records

The New York Historical Society has a large collection of indentures and apprenticeships. Almshouse admissions and discharges, sheriffs' sales, records of burials at city expense and even case files from asylums and hospitals can be found there for varying dates of New York City's history.

Records of the poor have been little used by American genealogists to trace their ancestors. When you realize that from 10 percent to 25 percent of the population of Philadelphia, New York City, Baltimore, and Boston appeared on the poor rolls at some time in their lives, these records assume a new importance.[7]

Municipal Archives and Libraries

It is impossible to generalize about municipal archives and municipal libraries because they vary so much. An overview of what can be found in three major cities, however, may suggest their potential.

The Baltimore City Archives offers perhaps one of the best resources for municipal research in the country. Of special interest to the genealogist is the WPA alphabetical name index covering the years 1756-1938 to over 300,000 individual items, including all personal names appearing in petitions, licenses, correspondence, applications, bonds, muster rolls, inquests, and certain police and health reports. The Baltimore Archives also has passenger list indexes for ships arriving in that city from 1833 to 1866, some taxation records, voter registrations, a police census for 1868, and extensive fire department files.

The Municipal Archives of New York City has a tremendous amount of material, some dating back to the Dutch settlements in 1670. Many of the old treasures are not currently catalogued or accessible; however, federal grants made in the last few years will finance this work. The most important collection for the genealogist is the vital records of the city prior to 1898. Florence Clint, in the *New York Area Key* (Elizabeth, Colo.: Keyline Publishers, Inc., 1979), gives a summary of what is there, a policy statement for using the archives, and application forms which may be reproduced for ordering birth, marriage, and death records.

Chicago does not have an official archives, but maintains the Chicago Municipal Reference Library. Established in 1900 as the Bureau of Statistics, the library's primary purpose is to serve city agencies while also acting as a public reference library. The collections cover the many interests of municipal government, including public administration, city planning, human relations, urban renewal, environment, and public safety. Special collections include a newspaper clipping file of eighty-one legal-sized filing drawers of classified clippings since 1956 from Chicago daily papers and from some of the neighborhood papers. Community area information is available in census data (statistical), newspaper clippings, and some published material on Chicago's seventy-six officially recognized neighborhoods. Chicago campaign literature is arranged by date of election from 1902 to the present. A Chicago street name file of WPA research information gives the origin of the street names and the dates when street names were changed. There are copies of Chicago departmental reports from 1871 to date and proceedings of the City Council from 1865 to date. Except for the most prominent Chicago citizens, they contain very little genealogical information, but these resource materials may serve as finding tools. Contrary to a popular belief, it is not possible to find records of individual policemen or firemen here, although lists of names may show up in precinct files and the like. John J. Flinn, *The History of Chicago Police* (1887; reprint ed., Montclair, N.J.: Patterson Smith Publishing Corp., 1973) is among the printed sources in the library and though limited in time coverage it could solve some genealogical puzzles. A typical entry is: "John Fleming, patrolman; born Ireland 1855; came to Chicago 1878; entered the force 15 December 1884."

Notes

1. U.S. Bureau of the Census, *Historical Statistics of the United States: Colonial Times to 1970* (Washington, D.C.: Government Printing Office, 1975), pp. 11-12; Charles N. Glaab and A. Theodore Brown, *A History of Urban America* (New York: The Macmillan Co., 1967), pp. 133-67.

2. See also Loretto Dennis Szucs, *Cook County Research (Chicago, Illinois Area): Not an Impossible Dream* (Chicago: By the author, 1981); and Robert Scott Davis, Jr., *Research in Georgia* (Easley, S.C.: Southern Historical Press, 1981).

3. Library card catalogs are frequently organized by modern (post-1970) civil boundaries even though the records cataloged carry colonial dates; e.g., a suburban cemetery will be cataloged under the metropolitan name *as if it had always been a part of the metropolis*.

4. The Genealogical Society of Utah is currently extracting the 1880 census as part of its International Genealogical Index. When the data has been input into this database, an every-name index will be available for the whole United States.

5. See Robert Wiebe, *The Search for Order, 1887-1920* (New York:

Hill and Wang, 1967).

6. To learn the extent of such records, see Richard Maxwell Brown, "The Archives of Violence," *American Archivist* 41 (1978), and Roger W. Lotchin, *San Francisco, 1840-1856: From Hamlet to City* (New York: Oxford University Press, 1974).

7. Gary B. Nash, "Poverty and Poor Relief in Pre-Revolutionary Philadelphia," *William and Mary Quarterly*, 3rd series, 33 (Jan. 1976): 3-30.

Selected Bibliography of Urban Sources

Akey, Denise S., ed. Encyclopedia of Associations: Detroit: Gale Research Co., 1983.

Ash, Lee, ed. *Subject Collections: A Guide to Special Book Collections and Subject Emphases as Reported by University, College, Public and Special Libraries and Museums in the United States and Canada*. 4th ed., New York: R. R. Bowker, 1974.

Buenker, John D., Gerald Michael Greenfield, and William J. Murin. *Urban History—A Guide to Information Sources*. Detroit: Gale Research Co., 1981.

Child, Sargent B., and Dorothy Holmes. *Check List of Historical Records Survey Publications: Bibliography of Research Project Reports*. Baltimore: Genealogical Publishing Co., 1969.

The Directory of Directories: An Annotated Guide to Business and Industrial Directories, Professional and Scientific Rosters, and Other Lists and Guides of All Kinds. Detroit: Gale Research Co., 1980.

Directory of Special Libraries and Information Centers. Detroit: Gale Research Co., 1976.

Encyclopedia of American Associations. Detroit: Gale Research Co., 1970.

Greenwood, Val D. *The Researcher's Guide to American Genealogy*. Baltimore: Genealogical Publishing Co., 1973.

Historical Societies and Agencies in the United States and Canada. 10th ed. Nashville, Tenn.: American Association for State and Local History, 1975.

Kenedy, P. J. *The Official Catholic Directory*. New York: P. J. Kenedy and Sons, annual editions from 1819 to date.

Kirkham, E. Kay. *A Handy Guide to Record Searching in the Larger Cities of the United States*. Logan, Utah: Everton Publishers, 1974.

Lane, George A., and Alginantes Kezys. *Chicago Churches and Synagogues*. Chicago: Loyola University Press, 1981.

Library of Congress, Geography and Map Division. *Fire Insurance Maps in the Library of Congress*. Washington, D.C.: Library of Congress, 1981.

McWilliams, Jerry, and Lowell Waverly. "Maritime Museums: How to Search Them for Your Family's History." *Family Heritage* 1 (Oct. 1978): 140-46.

Meyer, Mary Keysor, ed. *Meyer's Directory of Genealogical Societies in the U.S.A. and Canada* (with appended list of Independent Genealogical Periodicals). 4th ed. Pasadena, Md.: Mary Keysor Meyer, Pub., 1982.

National Historical Publications and Records Commission. *Directory of Archives and Manuscript Repositories in the United States*. Washington, D.C.: National Archives and Records Service, 1978.

Neagles, James C., and Lila Neagles. *Locating Your Immigrant Ancestor*. Logan, Utah: Everton Publishers, 1975.

Preuss, Arthur. *A Dictionary of Secret and Other Societies: Comprising Masonic Rites, Lodges, and Clubs; Concordant, Clandestine, and Spurious Masonic Bodies; Non-Masonic Organizations to Which Only Freemasons Are Admitted; Mystical and Occult Societies; Fraternal, Benevolent and Beneficiary Societies; Political, Patriotic, and Civic Brotherhoods; Greek Letter Fraternities and Sororities; Military and Ancestral Orders; Revolutionary Brotherhoods, and Many Other Organizations*. Detroit: Gale Research Co., 1966.

Rodda, Dorothy, and John Harvey. *Directory of Church Libraries*. Philadelphia: Drexel Press, 1967.

Suelflow, August R. *A Preliminary Guide to Church Records Repositories*. Chicago: Society of American Archivists, 1969.

Wynar, Lubomyr R. *Encyclopedic Directory of Ethnic Organizations in the United States*. Littleton, Colo.: Libraries Unlimited, 1976.

Urban Research Archives, Sources, and Guides

Atlanta

Atlanta Public Library
126 Carnegie Way, N.W.
Atlanta, GA 30303

Atlanta Historical Society Archives
3099 Andrews Drive, N.W.
Atlanta, GA 30355

Georgia Department of Archives and History
330 Capital Avenue, S.E.
Atlanta, GA 30308

See its nine-page pamphlet, *Genealogical Research in Georgia Papers*.

Genealogical Society
Georgia Genealogical Society
Box 38066
Atlanta, GA 30334

Adams, Marilyn. *Georgia Local and Family History Sources in Print*. 1982. 72 pp. Available from Heritage Research, Box 742, Clarkston, GA 30021.

Davis, Robert Scott, Jr. *Research in Georgia*. Easley, S.C.: Southern Historical Press, 1981. Focuses on the collections of the Georgia Department of Archives and History. Describes the microfilm and manuscript collections, the law room, the periodical room, and the available guides to collections. Microfilm collection includes pre-1900 state and county records and book lists. Also has a bibliography of county histories and genealogies.

Russell, James M. *Atlanta, Gate City of the South, 1847 to 1885*. Princeton: Princeton University Press, 1972. 401 pp. From his dissertation.

Starbuck, James C. *Historic Atlanta to 1930: An Indexed Chronological Bibliography*. Monticello, Ill.: Council of Planning Librarians, 1974. Many good academic citations.

Boston

Boston Public Library
Copley Square
Boston, MA 02117

Massachusetts Secretary of State
Archives Division
State House
Boston, MA 02133

Genealogical Society
New England Historic Genealogical Society
101 Newberry Street
Boston, MA 02116

Massachusetts Society of Genealogists
Box 215
Ashland, MA 01721

Bowen, Richard Le Baron. *Massachusetts Records: A Handbook for Genealogists, Historians, Lawyers and Other Researchers*. Rehoboth, Mass.: By the author, 1957. 66 pp.; index.

Handlin, Oscar. *Boston's Immigrants: A Study of Acculturation*. 1959. reprint ed., New York: Atheneum, 1970.

Haskell, John D., Jr. *Bibliographies of New England History: Massachusetts: A Bibliography of Its History*. 1976. 584 pp. Prepared by the Committee for a New England Bibliography.

Historical Records Survey. *Inventory of Town and City Archives of Massachusetts*. No. 13. Suffolk County, Vol. I. Boston, Part 5. Boston, Mass.: Works Progress Administration, 1940.

New England Library Association. *A Genealogist's Handbook for New England Research*. Boston: By the author, 1980.

Chicago

Chicago Public Library
Department of Social Science & History
425 North Michigan Avenue
Chicago, IL 60610

Chicago Historical Society
Clark Street at North Avenue
Chicago, IL 60614

Chicago Municipal Reference Library
Room 1004, City Hall
121 North LaSalle Street
Chicago, IL 60602

Illinois Office of the Secretary of State
Archives Division
Archives Building
Springfield, IL 62756

Genealogical Society
Chicago Genealogical Society
Box 1160
Chicago, IL 60690

Jewell, Frank. *Annotated Bibliography of Chicago*. Chicago: Chicago Historical Society, 1979.

Mayer, Harold M., and Richard C. Wade. *Chicago: Growth of a Metropolis*. Chicago: 1969.

Szucs, Loretto Dennis. *Cook County Research (Chicago, Illinois Area): Not an Impossible Dream*. (Springfield Ill.: Illinois State Genealogical Society, 1981. 13 pp.

Cleveland

Cleveland Public Library
325 Superior Avenue
Cleveland, OH 44114

Western Reserve Historical Society
History Library
10825 East Blvd.
Cleveland, OH 44106

Ohio State Library
65 South Front Street
Columbus, OH 43215

Genealogical Societies
Great Cleveland Genealogical Society
Box 40254
Cleveland, OH 44140

Ohio Genealogical Society
Box 2625
Mansfield, OH 44906

Flavell, Carol Willsey, and Florence Clint. *Ohio Area Key*. Denver: Area Keys, 1977. Available from Genealogical Research Foundation, Inc., Box 333, Kiowa, CO 80117.

Guide to the Manuscripts and Archives of the Western Reserve Historical Society. Cleveland: 1972, 425 pp.

Rose, William G. *Cleveland, The Making of a City*. Cleveland: World Publishing Company, 1950. 1272 pp.

A Selective Guide to Genealogical Aids in the Cleveland Public Library History Department. Cleveland: 1976. 29 p.

Denver

Denver Public Library
Genealogy Division
1357 Broadway
Denver, CO 80203

State Historical Society of Colorado
Documentary Resources Department
1300 Broadway
Denver, CO 80203

Colorado Department of Administration
Division of State Archives and Public Records
1313 Sherman Street
Denver, CO 80203

Genealogical Society
The Colorado Genealogical Society
Box 9671
Denver, CO 80209

Denver: A Pictorial History from Camp to Queen City of the Plains. Boulder: Pruett Publishing Company, 1973. 336 pp.

Dorsett, Lyle. *The Queen City: A History of Denver*. Boulder: Pruett Publishing Co., 1977. 320 pp.

Frech, Mary L. *Chronology and Documentary Handbook of the State of Colorado. Chronologies and Documentary Handbooks of the States*, vol. 6, Dobbs Ferry, N.Y.: Ocean Pub., 1973.

Detroit

Detroit Public Library
5201 Woodward Avenue
Detroit, MI 48202

Burton Historical Collection
Detroit Public Library
5201 Woodward Avenue
Detroit, MI 48202

Michigan State Library (Archives)
735 East Michagan Avenue
Lansing, MI 48933

Genealogical Society

The Detroit Society for Genealogical Research
c/o Burton Historical Collection
Detroit Public Library
5201 Woodward Avenue
Detroit, MI 48202

Anderson, Alloa, and Polly Bender. *Genealogy in Michigan, What, When, Where*. 2nd ed. Ann Arbor: Genealogical Society of Washtenaw County, Michigan, 1978, 44 pp.

Family Trails. Lansing, Michigan: Michigan Department of Education, 1967-1982. 5 vols. Reprinted by Michigan Genealogical Council, 215 West Peterson Drive, Brighton, MI 48116.

Fine, Sidney. *Frank Murphy: The Detroit Years*. Ann Arbor: University of Michigan Press. 1975. 608 pp.

Parkins, Almon. *The Historical Geography of Detroit*. 356 pp. 1918; reprint ed. 1970.

New Orleans

New Orleans Public Library
Louisiana Division
219 Loyola Avenue
New Orleans, LA 70140

The Historic New Orleans Collection
Archives-Manuscripts Division
533 Royal Street
New Orleans, LA 70130

Louisiana State Library
State Capitol Ground
Baton Rouge, LA 70804

Genealogical Society

Genealogical Research Society of New Orleans
Box 51751
New Orleans, Louisiana 70151

Bolding, Gary. "Change, Continuity, and Commercial Identity of a Southern City: New Orleans, 1850-1950." *Louisiana Studies* 14 (1975): 161-78.

Reed, Merl E. *New Orleans and the Railroads: The Struggle for Commercial Empire 1830-1860*. Baton Rouge: Louisiana State University Press, 1966.

New York

The New York Public Library
The Research Libraries
5th Avenue & 42nd Street
New York, NY 10018

Long Island Historical Society
128 Pierrepont Street
Brooklyn, NY 11201

State Archives
The New York Office of State History
The State Education Department
Empire State Plaza
Albany, NY 12234

Municipal Archives and Records Center
23 Park Row, N.
New York, NY 10038

Genealogical Society

New York Genealogical and Biographical Society
122 East 58th Street
New York, NY 10022

Baily, Rosalie Fellows. *Guide to Genealogical and Biographical Sources for New York City (Manhattan). 1783-1898*. New York: By the author, 1954. 96 pp.

Clint, Florence. *New York Area Key*, Elizabeth, Colo.: Keyline Publishers, Inc., 1979.

Eichholz, Alice, and James M. Rose. *Free Black Heads of Households in the New York State Federal Census, 1790-1830*. Detroit: Gale Research Company, 1981. 301 pp.

Greene, Evarts B., and Richard B. Morris. *A Guide to the Principal Sources for Early American History (1600-1800) in the City of New York*. 2nd ed. New York: Columbia University Press, 1953. 400 pp.

Guide to Dutch Manuscripts Relating to New Netherland. Albany, N.Y.: University of State of New York, 1978. 138 pp.

Kouevenhoven, John A. *The Columbia Historical Portrait of New York*. New York: Octagon Press, 1978. 550 pp.

New York Historical Society. *Old New York in Early Photographs, 1853-1901*. Introduction and Commentary by Mary Black. New York: Dover, 1973. 228 pp.

Photographic Views of New York City, 1870s-1970s. Microfiche edition of 54,000 photos from the New York Public Library Collections. University microfilms, 300 North Zeeb Road, Ann Arbor, MI 48106. Catalog available on request.

Philadelphia

Free Library of Philadelphia
Logan Square
Philadelphia, PA 19103

Philadelphia Historical Commission
1313 City Hall Annex
Juniper and Filbert Streets
Philadelphia, PA 19107

State Archives
Pennsylvania Historical and Museum Commission
William Penn Memorial Museum and
Archives Building, Room 1026
3rd and North Streets
Harrisburg, PA 17120

Genealogical Society

Genealogical Society of Pennsylvania
1300 Locust Street
Philadelphia, PA 19107

Clint, Florence. *Pennsylvania Area Key*. 2nd ed. Denver: Area Keys, 1976.

Filby, P. William, ed. *Philadelphia Naturalization Records*. Detroit: Gale Research Co., 1982. 716 pp.

Lafore, Lawrence, and Sarah Lee Lippencott. *Philadelphia: The Unexpected City*. Garden City, N.Y.; Doubleday, 1965. 178 pp.

Pennsylvania Line: A Research Guide to Pennsylvania Genealogy and Local History, 3rd ed., Laughlintown, Pa.: Southwest Pennsylvania Genealogical Services, 1983.

Scharf, Thomas J., and Westcott Thompson. *History of Philadelphia 1609-1884*. Philadelphia: L.H. Everts and Company, 1884. 3 vols.

Wolf, Stephanie Gruuman. *Urban Village: Population, Community and Family Structure in Germantown, Pennsylvania, 1683-1800*. Princeton, University Press, 1976. 361 pp.

The Philadelphia Social History Project describing Philadelphia County at 1850, 1860, 1870, and 1880 has the following resources:

1. The federal census schedules show for the study of individual mobility, blacks: all persons (94,000), Irish: all males 18 + (142,000), Germans: all males 18+ (84,000); For the study of stratification: native white Americans: (50,000) sample males 18+; for the study of family structure: 2,000 households with ca. 6 persons per household for each ethnic group (Irish, German, native American) in each census year. Total sample: 144,000; variables for each of 500,000 individuals: name, grid location, age, sex, race, color, occupation, real and personal property, place of birth, literacy; and for the study of neighborhood: total population: 1850-408,000; 1860-565,000; 1870-674,000; 1880-840,000. A grid pattern, one X one-and-one quarter blocks, was imposed on the map of the entire county. For each inhabitant of the 7,100 grid squares which emerged, the age in eight categories, sex, and ethnicity are recorded.

Pennsylvania Abolition Society and Society of Friends Manuscript Census Schedules for 1838, 1837, and 1856 give data for 11,500 households – all black households in Philadelphia County; variables for each household head and his household including occupation, wages, real and personal property, literacy, education, religion, membership in beneficial societies, temperance societies, taxes, rents, dwelling size, address, and grid location, sex and slave or free birth.

U.S. Manufacturing Manuscript Census Schedules give data for ca. 29,000 individual firms, a 100 percent sample: firms-4,700 (1850)-8,500 (1880), including name of firm, type of product, amount of capital investment, type of power, type and number of machines, number of employees by sex, average wages paid by sex, number of months in operation each year, raw materials (kinds, quantities, and values), and address and grid location.

4. City business directories include 127,000 individual firms – a 100 percent sample: 10,000 (1850) and 47,000 (1880), including name of suscriber, type of product or service, and address.

5. Transportation network data describes a total of 140 routes including all horse-drawn street cars and railroads, the date of incorporation, company name, and date of merger. Block-by-block routes have been reconstructed and precise "X"-"Y" coordinates have been converted to machine-readable form.

For details see "The Philadelphia Social History Project," *Historical Methods Newsletter* 9 (March-June 1976): Special Issue.

San Francisco

San Francisco Public Library
San Francisco Room
Civic Center
San Francisco, CA 94102

California Historical Society Library
2099 Pacific Avenue
San Francisco, CA 94109

San Francisco Maritime Museum
J. Porter Shaw Library
Foot of Polk
San Francisco, CA 94109

University of California at San Francisco
Archives Division
513 Parnassus Avenue
San Francisco, CA 94143

Genealogical Society

California Genealogical Society
2099 Pacific Avenue
San Francisco, CA 94109

Hansen, Gladys, ed. *San Francisco: The Bay and Its Cities*. New York: Hastings House, 1973. 496 pp. Uses material from the 1970 census to update what was originally the result of Federal Writer's Project in the 1930s.

Lotchin, Roger W. *San Francisco 1846-1856: From Hamlet to City*. New York: Oxford University Press, 1974. 406 pp.

Williams, Mary Floyd. *History of the San Francisco Committee of Vigilance, 1851-1921*; reprint ed., New York: De Capo Press, 1970.

Urban Jurisdictions Not Subject to County Authority

Based on Bureau of the Census, *1967 Census of Governments*, vol. 1, *Government Organization*. Washington, D.C.: United States Government Printing Office, 1968.

Areas with governments legally designated as city-county: San Francisco, Denver, and Honolulu.

Areas designated as metropolitan: Nashville and Davidson County, Tennessee.

Areas subject to some county jurisdiction, but operating as cities. Jacksonville, Duval County, Florida; Indianapolis, Marion County, Indiana; New Orleans, Orleans Parish, Louisiana; Baton Rouge, East Baton Rouge Parish, Louisiana; Nantucket, Nantucket County, Massachusetts; Boston, Suffolk County, Massachusetts; New York City, borough/county: Bronx, Kings (Brooklyn), New York (Manhattan), Queens, and Richmond; and Philadelphia, Philadelphia County, Pennsylvania.

Areas designated as independent cities, not subject to the county: Washington D.C.; Baltimore City, Maryland; St. Louis, Missouri; Carson City, Nevada; and the following burgs of Virginia: Alexandria, Bedford, Bristol, Buena Vista, Charlottesville, Chesapeake, Clifton Forge, Colonial Heights, Covington, Danville, Emporia, Fairfax, Falls Church, Franklin, Fredericksburg, Galax, Hampton, Harrisonburg, Hopewell, Lexington, Lynchburg, Martinsville, Newport News, Norfolk, Norton, Petersburg, Portsmouth, Radford, Richmond, Roanoke, Salem, South Boston, Staunton, Suffolk, Virginia Beach, Waynesboro, Williamsburg, and Winchester.

Unorganized areas functioning as counties: Fairfield, Hartford, Litchfield, Middlesex, New Haven, New London, Tolland, and Windham, Connecticut; and Bristol, Kent, Newport, Providence, and Washington, Rhode Island.

Unorganized areas attached to other counties for government purposes: Shannon, Todd, and Washington, South Dakota.

Other unorganized areas: twenty-nine census divisons in Alaska including its ten boroughs which function as counties, and Yellowstone National Park in Montana, park areas located in Idaho and Wyoming are included in the counties of those states. In addition to these cities, many other cities, some so small you would never think of them as having separate jurisdiction, have the right to keep vital statistics. When you can't locate your ancestor in county records, remember that you may be dealing with a city and check for separate records.

INFORMATION GUIDE

Genealogical Information in the Record Group	*Census Rolls*	*Payrolls*	*Land Allotments*	*Applications*	*Tribal Enrollments*	*Annuity Rolls*
Surname/name	●	●	●	●	●	●
Date of Birth	●			●	●	
Place of Birth				●		
Sex	●	●	●	●	●	●
Race/color	●	●	●	●	●	●
Physical Description						
Occupation	●	●		●	●	
Education						
Military Service						
Slave Status	●				●	
Property Owned	●		●		●	
Religion						
Citizenship/Tribe	●	●	●	●	●	●
Marital Status	●	●		●	●	
Spouse's Name	●	●		●		
Children's Names	●	●	●	●	●	
Father's Name	●	●		●	●	
Mother's Name	●	●		●	●	
Father's Birthplace				●		
Mother's Birthplace				●		
Date of Death	●	●		●	●	
Cause of Death						
Name of Cemetery						
Residence	●	●	●	●	●	●
Age	●	●	●	●	●	●
Literacy/signature	●			●	●	
Photograph/sketch						
Indian Name/Number	●	●		●	●	●

COULD YOU USE THIS CHAPTER?

Type of Record	*Kept from*	*Clues That You Should Consult These Records*
Indian censuses, allotment rolls, tax rolls, etc. for the Five Civilized Tribes.	From the 1820s on for some tribes	If you have a tradition of Indian ancestry or if your ancestors came from the areas shown on the maps, it would be worth your while to check the ciizenship applications for the Five Civilized Tribes described in this chapter. Membership in these tribes was established firmly on the basis of kinship; and the applications, involving the payment of federal funds as they did, are thorough. Even if a family was refused citizenship, the applications could still be there, documenting the exact generation when the Indian-white marriage occurred and who the contracting parties were. Records also exist for schools, Indians who served in the military in many wars including both sides in the Civil War, and for Christian missions to the Indians. The bibliography lists books and articles devoted to other tribes as well.

Chapter 17

RECORDS RELATING TO NATIVE AMERICAN RESEARCH: THE FIVE CIVILIZED TRIBES

George J. Nixon

This chapter focuses on selected records that make up the foundation of American Indian research in an area of great interest to genealogists researching today. When asked "What is your most difficult research problem?" some 15 percent of active genealogists polled in a 1983 survey by the Genealogical Institute of Salt Lake City, said, "Tracing Cherokee ancestry."

The Fort Worth Federal Record Center, the National Archives, and the Oklahoma Historical Society in Oklahoma City house the record examples cited in this chapter which, due to limited space here, concentrate on the records of the Five Civilized Tribes (Cherokee, Choctaw, Chickasaw, Creek, and Seminole), with special attention to Cherokee sources. These records are representative of those existing for other tribes which came under the jurisdiction of the Bureau of Indian Affairs (BIA), although the exact content and time period may differ.

The bibliography at the end of the chapter references a wider range of records and tribes for those genealogists who require help in other areas. Appendix 1 lists the agencies within the jurisdiction of the Bureau of Indian Affairs with the location (1982) of records for all existing tribes.

Records Relating to the Five Civilized Tribes, Federal Archives and Records Center, Fort Worth, Texas

Tribal citizenship is rooted securely in kinship, and the federal records described in this section document and preserve these kinship ties. In fact, the genealogical data which these federal records include are more precise and detailed than equivalent sources for non-Indian ancestors.

Cherokee Records East of the Mississippi

In 1838, while the majority of the Cherokee were being gathered in the East for the removal to the West, several hundred Cherokees escaped into the mountains of North Carolina to avoid the removal, thus forming the Eastern Band of Cherokees.

At the same time, many heads of Cherokee families elected to take advantage of Article 12 of the 1835 treaty which stated that those individuals and families of the Cherokee Nation averse to a removal west of the Mississippi and desirous of becoming citizens of the states where they resided could remain upon the certification of a special commission that they were qualified to take care of themselves and their property.

From this time until the final rolls were made in 1902, these two groups were encouraged to move west and become citizens of the Cherokee Nation there. Several hundred actually did and were enrolled on the final rolls. However, until the time of their removal, these Cherokees will be found upon the rolls of the Eastern Band.

Their records include a register of Cherokees who wished to remain in the East 1817-19 (2 vols.), emigration registers of Indians who wished to migrate 1817-38 (18 vols.), applications for reservations 1819, and the Henderson roll index of 1835.

Cherokee Census of 1835 (Henderson Roll)

This census was actually the product of five census takers: Nathaniel Smith, George W. Underwood, C. H. Nelson, Regin Rawlins, and Daniel Henderson.

Major Benjamin F. Currey was placed in charge of the taking of the census. The purpose of the census, as stated by Major Currey was that "to be fully possessed of a knowledge of their number, the number of each man's houses, the number of his farms, with the quantity of land under cultivation, the proportions of tillable land, the mineral resources and water privileges of the country, etc., the commissioners would be able to fix a true estimate upon the value of the country in case the whole title does not approve of the gross sum fixed upon already."

The census lists 1,959 persons of the Cherokee Nation in North Carolina, Tennessee, Alabama, and Georgia, and was submitted by Major Currey on 27 February 1836 to the Commissioner of Indian Affairs.

The original of this census is found in the National Archives, Washington, D.C., filling sixty-six pages. It requests information in these categories: heads of families (Indians, half-breeds, quadroons, and whites), residence (state, county, and watercourse), males (under eighteen and over eighteen), females (under sixteen and over sixteen), slaves (male, female, and total slaves), total Cherokees, whites connected by marriage, farms, acres in cultivation, houses, bushels of wheat raised, bushels of corn raised, bushels of wheat sold, for how much, bushels of corn sold, for how much, bushels of corn bought, for how much, mills, ferryboats, farmers over eighteen, merchants over eighteen, readers of English, readers of Cherokee, half-breeds, quadroons, full-blooded, mixed Catawbas, mixed Spaniards, mixed Negroes, weavers, spinsters (operators of spinning wheels), reservees, descendants of reservees, and remarks.

This census is the only known census listing the whole Cherokee Nation east of the Mississippi (with the exception of the already migrated Old Settler Cherokees).

Next came the Mullay roll of 1848. It was the first census of the Eastern Band of Cherokee after the general removal. It was made by John C. Mullay, a clerk in the Commissioner of Indian Affairs office. Mullay was instructed to enroll those individuals and families who were in North Carolina at the time of the ratification of the Treaty of New Echota on 23 May 1836 and who had not removed to the West or had not received the commutation for removal and subsistence. Children born after that date (1836) were therefore excluded, as were whites who had married a Cherokee after that date. Cherokees outside North Carolina in 1836 were not included although individuals who had died since then were included and their date of death was given.

This roll includes 1,557 Cherokees and records information by the headings of number, name, age, and "remarks," which generally include family relationships and date of death (where applicable). Occasionally other information is given such as "orphaned," "crippled," or "blind." The Mullay census was followed by an annuity roll taken by John Drennen in 1851, and the Emigrant Roll, an enumeration of Eastern Cherokee who moved west after 1835 and were residing in Indian Territory by 1851.

On 25 April 1851, the Secretary of the Interior appointed David W. Silar to take a census of the Cherokees east of the Mississippi to determine who could be eligible to participate in a per capita payment based on the 1835 treaty. Silar submitted his completed report in October 1851. This census lists 1,959 individuals by state and county in North Carolina, Tennessee, Alabama, and Georgia. The last few pages contain 170 disputed cases.

The columns for this roll are number, name, age, relationship to head of household, sex, blood ("I" for Indian, "W" for white), and "remarks."

Alfred Chapman was appointed in 1851 to make a per capita payment to the Eastern Cherokee based upon the census taken by Silar. These payments were made in December of 1851 and January of 1852 to 2,134 individuals. This payroll census designates recipients by number, name, the amount received, and the signature of the recipient. The arrangement is similar to that of the Silar Roll, in that individuals are listed by family groups and by state and county.

This roll played an important part in Guion Miller's preparation of his roll completed in 1910. Anyone who could trace his ancestry to an individual listed on the Chapman Roll was included on the Guion Miller Roll.

By an Act of Congress approved 27 July 1868, S. H. Swetland was appointed to take a census of the North Carolina Cherokees. He was instructed to use the Mullay Roll of 1848 as his basis and to enroll all individuals enrolled by Mullay who were still living and the heirs or legal representatives of those deceased. Additionally, he was instructed to take a separate census of all Eastern Cherokees whether they were living in North Carolina or the adjoining states and to appraise the value of their property, farm products, horses, cattle, etc.

The census was completed 24 May 1869 and gives families, number, name, age, sex, blood, estate, horses, mules, cows, oxen, cattle, hogs, sheep, wheat, corn, oats, rye, literacy, parents living or dead, and other remarks.

Joseph G. Hester was appointed 26 September 1882 to take a fifth census of the Eastern Band of Cherokees. Copies of the Mullay Roll, Silar Roll, Chapman Roll, and Swetland Roll were made available for his use. Hester was required to account for all persons on the previous rolls by either including them on the new roll, noting their deaths on the old rolls, or describing their whereabouts as unknown either to Hester or to any of the Indians.

The completed roll was submitted to the Secretary of the Interior on 24 January 1884. It contained 2,956 persons residing in North Carolina, Georgia, Tennessee, Alabama, South Carolina, Kentucky, New Jersey, Virginia, Illinois, Kansas, Colorado, and California. Those living west of the Mississippi and listed by Hester were descendants of members of the Eastern Band who had not severed their connection with the Eastern Band and had no affiliation with the Cherokee Nation in the West.

The Hester Roll contains the following information: number on Hester Roll, number on Chapman Roll, number on Swetland Roll, Indian name, relationship to head of family, age, ancestor on previous rolls, relationship to ancestor, present place of residence, and remarks. Guion Miller also used this roll in the preparation of his roll in 1910.

Other enumerations include the Powell Roll (1867), a census roll of Cherokees residing in The Cherokee Nation (1867) taken by H. Tompkins, an index to freedmen on Tompkins's roll (1867), and a list of rejected claimants taken 1878-80 by the Cherokee Commission on Citizenship. A separate 1869-71 Swetland enumeration covers only the Sequoyah District of the Cherokee Nation within Indian Territory.

Among other records available are a census roll 1875-76, Lipe receipt roll 1879-80, Cherokee census and index 1880, pay or receipt roll 1880, census roll 1883, Cherokee receipt roll 1883, Cherokee roll 1883, Cherokee freedmen roll 1883 (Wallace Roll), Cherokee census roll 1886, Cherokee census 1890, Cherokee receipt roll 1890, Cherokee census roll 1893, Starr Roll 1894, Cherokee payroll index 1894, Cherokee census roll 1894, lists of Cherokee children 1895-97 (children born between 1894-97 with date of birth and parents' names), Shawnees admitted to Cherokee citizenship 1895, Cherokee census roll 1896, Cherokee freedmen roll 1896 (Clifton Roll), list of applicants for Cherokee citizenship 1896 and those admitted, roll of Cherokee Shawnee 1896, Cherokee colored persons roll (after 1897), Cherokee equalization payroll about 1900, Delaware-Cherokee (no date) index to Delaware payroll, the Delaware payroll 1886, 1890, 1894, and the per capita payroll for Delawares 1904. From these rolls, the births of children, deaths of grandparents, and marriages of young couples can be documented.

Rolls of Cherokee Residing West of the Mississippi (Indian Territory)

In 1782, a group of Cherokee who had fought on the British side during the Revolution petitioned the Spanish governor at New Orleans for permission to settle on the west side of the Mississippi within the Spanish territory. Permission was granted in 1794 and a group of Cherokee settled in the St. Francis River valley in what is now southeastern Missouri. From time to time, more tribesmen joined them.

During the winter of 1811-12 the Cherokees moved en masse to the Arkansas region. Other Cherokees who decided to emigrate from the old nation periodically joined them in small groups.

With the treaty signed 8 July 1817 at Turkey Town, these emigrants received title to their lands. Under this treaty, the Cherokees ceded two large tracts of land and two smaller tracts of land east of the Mississippi River for an area of equal value in the West between the Arkansas and White rivers. As encouragement for others to remove, the treaty promised "to give all poor warriors who remove a rifle, ammunition, blanket, and brass kettle or beaver trap each, as full compensation for improvements left by them." The treaty further promised to compensate them for improvements, provide transportation, and provide subsistance for those who would agree to remove. Consequently, over 1,100 Cherokees emigrated from the East to the West between 1818 and 1819.

By a treaty signed 6 May 1828, the Cherokees ceded their lands in present Arkansas for lands in the present state of Oklahoma. Unfortunately, no record exists of an estimated 2,000 Cherokees who emigrated before 1817, but the rolls for those who moved because of the treaties of 1817 and 1828 are in the National Archives in Washington, D.C.

The Treaty of New Echota, 29 December 1835, represented the final cession of all Cherokee lands east of the Mississippi and the forced migration of these remaining tribal members west on the "Trail of Tears." Cherokees who had emigrated prior to 1835 became known as Old Settler Cherokees.

The 1851 Old Settler Roll. The 1851 Old Settler Roll lists each individual by district and his/her children unless the mother was an emigrant Cherokee. In this case, the children were listed with their mother on the Drennen Roll. Forty-four family groups are listed as non-residents. No other information is given. Guion Miller used this roll in compiling his 1910 record.

1896 Payment Roll. This payroll is based on the 1851 Old Settler Roll and is of major genealogical importance. The names of those still living in 1896 are listed first, followed by those who had died and their heirs, and each heir's relationship. The payroll lists each payee's 1851 roll number, name, agency pay number, age, sex, amount received, and post office address.

Cherokee Census of 1880. On 3 December 1879, the Cherokee National Council authorized a census and a per capita payment for purchase of "bread stuffs." This census later became very important to the Dawes Commission in preparing the final rolls of 1902. Any Indian or intermarried white listed on this census was accepted without challenge by the Dawes Commission. A notation on the 1902 census card showed his location and the name by which he was enrolled on the 1880 census.

The 1880 census was arranged by District and within the Cherokee Nation and thereunder by the six schedules: (1) Cherokee citizens including native, adopted white, Shawnee, Delaware, and freedmen; (2) orphans under sixteen; (3) those rejected; (4) those whose citizenship claims were pending; (5) "intruders" (unauthorized white "squatters" on Cherokee land); and (6) those living in the Cherokee Nation by permit granted by the Cherokee Council. Each schedule gives the individual's name by family group, age, race, occupation, sex, and roll number.

Cherokee Census of 1883 and 1886. On 19 May 1883, the Cherokee National Council authorized another census upon which to base a per capita payment of monies received ("Gross Money") from leased land. This census is arranged by districts like the first and includes an orphans' roll, those in national prisons, and a supplemental roll, showing the name and age of each individual.

A receipt roll shows the individual's name and roll number, the total number in the household, the total amount paid each household, the name of person receiving payment, and the name of a witness to the payment.

More money was available from the same source in 1886 and was disbursed after another census. In addition to the information given in the 1883 payment roll, it identifies individuals by their relationship to the head of household, thus becoming a valuable genealogical aid.

The 1890 Cherokee Census. This census contains the most complete information of any census for the Cherokee Nation. It is arranged by district and includes six schedules: (1) native Cherokees and adopted whites, Shawnees, and Delawares; (2) orphans under sixteen; (3) those denied citizenship by the Cherokee authorities; (4) those whose claims to citizenship were pending; (5) "intruders"; and (6) whites living in the Cherokee Nation by permit. The 1890 census's 105 columns include such detailed information as farm improvements, products, livestock, etc.

1893 Cherokee Census. This census distinguishes Cherokee citizens by blood, adopted whites, freedmen, Shawnees, Delawares, intermarried persons, and Creeks. Arranged by district, this census provides the individual's name, age, sex, admission reference, name of guardian, place of residence, and name of person providing identification.

The Starr Roll (1894). On 3 March 1893, the United States Congress passed an act that resulted in the sale of the Cherokee Outlet (or "Cherokee Strip") to the United States. Its 5,574,487 acres were sold for $8,595,736.12. In 1894, a per capita payment of $365.70 was made.

E. E. Starr, treasurer of the Cherokee Nation, prepared the receipt roll, arranged by district and thereunder by enrollment number. It contains the name of the head of household, the name of the person receiving payment, and the name of a witness to the transaction. An orphans' roll is also included.

1897 Roll. On 28 July 1897, the Cherokee National Council authorized a census from the 1894 "Strip Payment" roll. This census specifies the individual's enrollment number, name, age, and sex with occasional mention of the names of deceased parents or names used on previous rolls.

Chickasaw Records

These records include a census and muster roll 1837-39, annuity rolls 1867 and 1878, census roll (Pickens & Pontotoc County) 1890, payroll 1893, census 1896, and a roll for the "leased district" 1905.

Choctaw Records

Choctaw records include a census of Choctaws before removal 1831, the emigration roll 1831-57, a register of claims for reservations 1834-57, the Cooper census roll 1856, freedmen roll 1885, 1896, a census 1896 with an index, Choctaw national warrants (no date), indexes and records of testimony by Mississippi Choctaw 1899 with additional "evidence" in 1901, an undated index to Mississippi Choctaw children, per capita payrolls in 1906 and 1913, the annuity payroll, 1917-29, miscellaneous court cases and marriage licenses 1888-97, an index to enrollment cases c1900, some 1902 "proceedings of identity" for Mississippi Choctaws with an alphabetical index, an index to applications, and rejected appeals for citizenship, both Choctaw and Chickasaw; 1900 rolls and lists of parties admitted to Choctaw citizenship in South McAlester and Ardmore 1900 with a 1903 roll and index to citizens, and a 1902 roll of Choctaw freedmen; Choctaw and Chickasaw indexes 1902-07; and a land lottery, an annuity roll for Choctaws and Chickasaws at Murrow Indian Orphan Home 1907-08, and application for per capita payments 1910-28, for Choctaws and Chickasaws.

Creek Records

Creek records include a Creek census 1833; an emigration list 1836-38; a census of freedmen 1867-69; a census of orphans and their heirs entitled to benefits from the treaties of 1832 and 1870; a register of entries under the Settlers Relief Act of 1875, an index to old Creek freedmen 1868-79; an annuity roll 1890; noncitizens in Muscogee Nation 1893; citizenship cases 1895-96; a census by towns 1895; a census for the districts of Coweta, Deep Fork, Eufala, Muscogee, Okmulgee, and Wewoka 1895; a list of persons admitted to Creek citizenship 1899, a roll (original emigrants and heirs) 1904; an annuity roll 1918, annuity payments to Creek and freedmen on the Union side 1869-70 with payroll continuing to loyal Creeks in 1904 and 1906.

Seminole Records

Seminole records include, most importantly, the 1900 census, a certified and indexed copy of Seminole Indians alive on 31 December 1899. It is organized by the blood (clan) bands of Thomas Palmer, Echo Emarthoge, Simon Brown, Yaha Harjo, Tusekia Harjo, Kinkehe, Thomas Little, Obtiarche, Echoille, William Cooper, Nuthcup Harjo, and Osaske Harjo. Freedmen are listed in two separate bands, those of Dosar Barkus and Caesar Bruner. There is also an annuity payroll 1901 and a miscellaneous roll 1908.

Records Relating to the Five Civilized Tribes, National Archives, Washington, D.C.

Of the numerous record groups described in Edward E. Hill, *Preliminary Inventory of the Records of the Bureau of Indian Affairs*, 2 vols. (Washington, D.C.: National Archives and Records Service, 1965) and his *Guide to Records in the National Archives of the United States Relating to American Indians* (Washington, D.C.: National Archvies and Records Service, 1981) this chapter selects seven available to the researcher at the National Archives.

1. Records of the Bureau of Indian Affairs (Record Group 75).
2. Records of the United States Regular Army Mobile Units (Record Group 391).
3. Records of the Supreme Court of the United States (Record Group 267).
4. Records of the District Courts of the United States (Record Group 21).
5. Records of the United States Court of Appeals (Record Group 276).
6. Records of the United States Court of Claims (Record Group 123).
7. Records of the Veterans Administration (Record Group 15).

Records of the Bureau of Indian Affairs (Record Group 75)

Indian Removal Records. During the administration of Andrew Jackson, removing Indians in the East to an Indian territory west of the Mississippi River became an explicit policy. As early as 1803 with the Louisiana Purchase, such removals were officially encouraged and some Indians did migrate west.

However, under Jackson, treaties were negotiated trading tribal lands in the East for land in the unorganized territory west of the Mississippi. An act of 28 May 1830 (4 *Stat.* 411), specifically authorized the President to exchange these lands. The actual removals were conducted between 1830 and 1836 by the Office of the Commissary General of Subsistance and supervised by military officers. Some Indians, however, were allowed to move by themselves and individual Indians who wished to stay in the East could accept a "reservation" of land (usually farm-sized) in fee simple and remain as citizens, giving up all rights of tribal membership. The removals were mainly completed by the late 1840s.

The removal was not without problems, most of which concerned reservations granted to Indians in the East and the compensation of Indians for losses. The three most troublesome treaties were the Treaty of 29 December 1835 with the Cherokee Nation, the Treaty of 29 September 1830 with the Choctaws, and the Treaty of 24 March 1832 with the Creeks.

Four commissions were appointed successively in an attempt to settle different kinds of claims arising from the Cherokee Treaty. Most of the difficulties concerning the Choctaw Treaty arose from the article which entitled Choctaw families to secure title to a reservation and remain in the East. The Creek Treaty provided for the allotment of land to all heads of families with the intention that they would then sell the land. Fraud cases multiplied, and most of the Creek removal records relate to the attempted settlement of these cases.

The best treatment of the removal policy is Annie H. Abel, *The History of Events Resulting in Indian Consolidation West of the Mississippi*, Annual Report of the American Historical Association, 1906 (Washington, D.C.: Government Printing Office, 1908). For an excellent discussion of the actual removal process, see Grant Forman, *Indian Removal* (Norman: University of Oklahoma Press, 1932).

Here is a brief list of some of the Bureau of Indian Affairs records relating to removals that you will find useful:

Cherokee removal records include a register of Cherokees who wished to remain in the East 1817-19 (2 vols. and unbound papers); applications for reservations 1819; East Cherokee census rolls 1835-84 (19 vols. and unbound papers) including the Henderson Roll 1835, Mullay Roll 1848, Silar Roll 1851, Chapman Roll 1852, Powell Roll 1867, Swetland Roll 1869, and Hester Roll 1884 (Henderson, Mullay, etc., were the individuals or officials responsible for compiling the rolls); emigration rolls 1817-38 (18 vols. and unbound papers); ledger recording debts of Indians 1831-36 (1 vol.); and miscellaneous Cherokee removal records 1820-54.

Records of First Board of Cherokee Commissioners, 1836-39 include letters sent 1835-39 (1 vol.), property valuations 1835-39 (24 vols. and unbound papers), changes in assignment of property valuations 1837-38 (1 vol.), abstracts of returns of property 1838, returns of property 1838 (4 vols.), pocket book for reservation claims 1837-39 (1 vol.), reservation claim papers 1837-39, decisions on reservations claims 1837-39, (2 vols.) spoliation claim papers 1838-39, decisions on spoliation claims 1838 (2 vols.), papers relating to claims for debts against Cherokee Indians 1837-39, record of judgments against Cherokee Indians 1837 (1 vol.), decisions on claims of attorneys against the Cherokee Nation 1837-38, miscellaneous claim papers 1836-39, certificate stubs 1838 (1 vol. and unbound papers), and general abstract of valuations and spoliations allowed and of balances due 1839 (3 vols.).

Records of the Second and Third Board of Cherokee Commissioners, 1842-45 include letters sent 1842-45 (1 vol.), proceedings of Second Board 1843 (1 vol.), schedule of claims adjudicated by the Second Board 1843 (1 vol.), pocketbooks of the Second and Third Boards 1842-44 (2 vols.), claim papers of the Second and Third Boards 1843-45, decisions of the Second and Third Boards 1842-45, pocketbook of the Second and Third Boards 1842-45, pocketbooks of claims presented in the West 1845 (2 vols. and unbound papers), and register of payments 1837-45 (5 vols.).

Records of the Fourth Board of Cherokee Commissioners, 1846-47 include letters sent 1846-47, minutes 1846-47, claim papers 1846-47, and register of payments 1847.

Chickasaw removal records include letters sent 1832-61 (3 vols.), census and muster rolls 1837-39 (1 vol.), abstracts of locations of land 1836-44 (2 vols.), reports of land sales and deeds 1836-39, journal of expenditures 1833-36 (1 vol.), and statements concerning proceeds of sales of land 1849 (1 vol.).

Choctaw removal records include a census roll 1831 (1 vol.), alphabetical list of Choctaw reserves (1 vol.), census roll 1856, emigration lists 1831-57 (5 vols.), register of claims for reservations 1834-36 (1 vol.), reports concerning claims for reservations 1836-41 (1 vol.), statements concerning sales of Choctaw orphan lands 1838-83 (2 vols.), statements and schedules 1831-1906, and miscellaneous Choctaw removals 1825-58.

Creek removal records include census roll 1833 (1 vol.), index to Creek reserves, not dated (1 vol.), land location registers 1834-86 (5 vols.), location registers and certificates of contracts 1834-36 (2 vols.), abstracts of Creek contracts 1836 (1 vol.), abstracts of approved contracts for sales of reservations 1839-42 (1 vol.), reports concerning land of deceased reservees 1844 (1 vol.), miscellaneous records concerning contracts 1833-57, emigration lists 1836-38 (8 vols.), and miscellaneous Creek removal records 1827-59.

Other removal records include five volumes of miscellaneous muster rolls for 1832-36 that record removals for Apalachicola and Seminole, Kickapoo, Ottawa, Potawatomi, Quapaw, and Wyandot.

Records of the Land Division. Since colonial times, a major goal of Indian policy was to induce Indians to give up their lands. The Land Division was established in 1846 as the Land Statistics, Reservations, and Grants Division (sometimes the Land and Law Division). Most removals had taken place by then. It administered the sale of parts – sometimes all – of reservations ceded by Indians who had agreed to move to Indian Territory.

In 1887, the General Allotment Act (24 *Stat.* 388) allowed the division of tribal lands into individual allotments. During an initial twenty-five-year trust period, the United States acted as guardian for the allotments, and Indians could not sell their land without government approval. After the expiration of the trust period, the Indians received a fee patent and full control of the land. A Certificate of Competency testified to the ability of individual Indians to conduct their own affairs and authorized them to sell their land.

Records relating to Cherokee citizenship include letters received relating to Cherokee citizenship 1875-89, affidavits 1889-90, affidavits of questioned Cherokee freedmen 1889-91, affidavits 1891-92, affidavits 1893, drafts of census rolls 1889-90, welfare rolls 1890, supplementary census rolls 1891-92, indexes to revised copies of Wallace Roll of Cherokee freedmen 1890-93 (2 vols.), revised copies of Wallace Rolls 1890-96 (6 vols.), rolls of Shawnee Cherokee 1889, 1896 (2 vols.), and roll of Cherokee freedmen 1896-97 (1 vol.).

Records Relating to the Enrollment of Eastern Cherokee. These records deserve special attention. They are frequently referred to as the Guion Miller Rolls after Guion Miller who, after 1906, was appointed by the United States Court of Claims to determine who was eligible to participate in a fund awarded to persons who were Eastern Cherokees at the time of the treaties of 1835-36 and 1845 or to their descendants. Miller submitted his report and roll on 28 May 1909 with a supplementary report in 1910.

In the meantime, Frank C. Churchill, acting under instructions from the Secretary of the Interior, had been compiling a roll of the Eastern Band of Cherokee. He submitted his report and roll on 20 May 1908. It contained far fewer names than Miller's because it was intended to include only persons then recognized as members of the Eastern Band of Cherokees of North Carolina.

People omitted from Churchill's roll voiced strong objections, and members of the tribe claimed that unentitled persons had been enrolled. Further investigations were made by Special Bureau of Indian Affairs Agent Charles L. Davis in 1910-11 and by an enrollment committee headed by Special Agent Orlando M. McPherson in 1913-14.

An act of Congress of 4 June 1924 (43 *Stat.* 376) providing for the final disposition of the affairs of the Eastern Band, required still another roll. The Eastern Cherokee Enrolling Commission submitted its final report and roll on 1 December 1928. It was approved by the Secretary of the Interior in 1931.

The Guion Miller Report and Exhibits 1908-10 in twenty-nine volumes consist of ten volumes of transcripts of testimony, arranged chronologically; a report dated 5 January 1910 concerning exceptions to findings; a printed copy of the completed roll with two 1910 supplements; and copies of the Drennen, Chapman, and "Old Settler" rolls of 1851-52 with a consolidated index for the Chapman and Drennen rolls and a separate index for the Old Settler Roll. The volumes are arranged numerically as parts of classified file "33931-11-053 Cherokee Nation," which also contains other pertinent records. The applications submitted for enrollment are described under the Records of the United States Court of Claims. Other records in the Miller report include a roll of Eastern Cherokee 1909 (1 vol.), correspondence, reports, and related records concerning Eastern Cherokee Enrollment 1907-16, index to council roll of Eastern Band of Cherokee 1907 (1 vol.), council roll of Eastern Band of Cherokee 1907 (2 vols.), and rolls of Eastern Band of Cherokee 1908 (2 vols.).

The records produced by the 1924-28 Eastern Cherokee Enrolling Commission include a numerical index to enrollment records 1929, applications and related records 1925-28, alphabetical index to names appearing in testimony 1929, transcripts of testimony 1927-28 (5 vols.), decisions 1926-28 (5 vols.), rolls of Eastern Band of Cherokee 1928 (1 vol.), and the report of the Commissioners of Indian Affairs 1930.

Other records relating to the enrollment of the Five Civilized Tribes include letters received relating to Choctaw freedmen 1878-84, rolls of Choctaw freedmen 1885 (1 vol.), records relating to applications for identification as Mississippi Choctaw 1901-07, and records relating to applications for enrollment from the Five Civilized Tribes 1910-15.

Records of the Law and Probate Divisions. An Act of 25 June 1910 (36 *Stat.* 855), authorized the Secretary of the Interior to determine the heirs of deceased Indian allottees. In 1913, the Heirship Section was transferred to the Law Division. The records of the Law and Probate Divisions that are now in the National Archives stop at 1923 and include Indian wills 1911-21 (8 vols.), reports of examiners of inheritance 1919-23, decisions of the Attorney General 1848-66 (1 vol.), and court decisions 1904-12.

Records of the Civilization Division. This division, first known as the Civilization and Statistics Division, was established in 1846. The records are fragmentary, mainly because its functions were inherited by other divisions who received the pertinent records. Those remaining include census rolls 1835-69 (for the main series of census rolls see records of the Statistics Division); and schedules of Indians, soldiers, and citizens killed or captured 1873-1875.

Records Relating to Indian Civil War Claims. During the Civil War, many Indians loyal to the United States were driven from their homes or suffered property damages from Confederate forces. Treaties negotiated later provided for investigation and compensation. These records include records relating to claims of loyal Choctaw and Chickasaw 1866, receipt book for loyal Choctaw and Chickasaw claims 1868 (1 vol.), records relating to loyal Creek claims 1869-70, and abstracts of loyal Creek claims 1869-70 (1 vol.).

Records of the Finance Division. The Finance Division, established in 1846, was responsible for administrative examination of accounts, appropriations, remittance stock investments, settlement of claims, and other expenditures for or on account of Indians. Its records concerning payments to tribes or individuals include annuity payment rolls 1841-1949 (959 vols. and miscellaneous unbound papers), an index to Cherokee Freedmen Payment Rolls 1897 (1 vol.), a Cherokee Freedmen Payment Roll 1897 (1 vol.), an Index to Supplemental Payment Roll for Cherokee Freedmen (2 vols.), the Supplemental Roll for Cherokee Freedmen 1897 (1 vol.), exhibits for Cherokee Freedmen Payment Rolls 1897 (9 vols.), an Old Settler Cherokee census roll 1895 (1 vol.), an Index to Payment Roll for Old Settler Cherokee 1896 (1 vol.), and a roll of Creek orphans and list of payments to be made 1870 (1 vol.).

Records of the Miscellaneous Divisions. Established in 1889 and discontinued in 1908, this division was responsible for matters concerning trade with the Indians. Its only records now in the National Archives relate to traders' licenses: letters received concerning traders' licenses 1878-80, 1889-1905, applications for traders' licenses 1892-99, register of traders' licenses 1847-73 (1 vol.), 1876-82 (1 vol.), traders' licenses 1865-98 (15 vols.), roster of licensed traders 1885-98 (15 vols.), and roster of licensed traders 1885-1909 (2 vols.).

Records of the Statistics Division. Organized in 1909, this division processed census rolls, reports of births and deaths, health reports, and numerous other kinds of reports and statistical data. Its census rolls and supplements go back to 1885 and up to 1940. The information concerning individuals varies but usually includes the English and/or Indian name, roll number, age, date of birth, sex, and relationship to head of family. Beginning in 1930, the censuses also give the degree of Indian blood, marital status, ward status, residence, and sometimes other information. There are a few post-1940 rolls. The rolls are arranged alphabetically by name of agency or school and thereunder by year.

Records of the United States Regular Army Mobile Units, 1821-1942 (Records Group 391)

In August 1866, the War Department's General Order 56 authorized the President to enlist and employ a force of Indians within the territories and Indian country. This force, not to exceed 1,000, was to act as scouts. These units are referred to by their designation at the time they were created. Their records include descriptive books for Companies A, B, C, and F (1872-86), descriptive books for a battalion consisting of companies A, B, C, and D (1882-84), letters sent by Company A (January 1891-October 1899), a register of letters received by Company A (January 1891-August 1899), letters and telegrams sent by Company C (August 1878-December 1881), descriptive rolls of Warm Springs and Chiricahua Apache Indian bands (1884-85), and a descriptive book for a detachment of Seminole Indian scouts (1889-93). Although the scouts were active in the regular army well into the twentieth century, the records do not extend beyond 1899.

The descriptive books contain rolls and lists of noncommissioned officers, men discharged, and deaths. These and the muster rolls show the name of each scout, his age, physical description, place of birth, date and place of enlistment, the officer who enrolled him, payroll information, and remarks.

On 9 March 1891, War Department General Order 28 authorized the enlistment of one company of Indians for each twenty-six regiments of white cavalry and infantry. The order specified that Troop L of each cavalry regiment except for the Ninth and Tenth, and Company I of each of the infantry regiments, except the Sixth, Eleventh, Fifteenth, Nineteenth, Twenty-fourth, and Twenty-fifth, would be recruited by the enlistment of up to fifty-five Indians for each troop or company.

By 1894 it was decided to discontinue the enlistment of Indians except as scouts. The last Indian unit, Troop L of the Seventh Cavalry, was disbanded in 1895.

Record books for these Indian units consist of letters sent by Troop L, Third Cavalry (1891-94); letters sent by Company I, Twelfth Infantry (1891-94); descriptive book, Troop L, Third Cavalry (1891- 94); orders issued (1891-94) and special orders received by Company I, Twelfth Infantry 1891-93); register and letters received by Company I, Twelfth Infantry (1891-94); and register of letters received by Company I, Twenty-first Infantry, (September 1891-November 1892).

Records of The Supreme Court of the United States (Record Group 267)

The original and appellate case files of this court are in the National Archives. The Indian lawsuits touch upon almost every aspect of Indian life including such cases as the determination of an individual membership in a tribe, the political status of a tribe, tribal property rights, the scope of federal power over Indian affairs, and jurisdiction over criminal acts on reservations.

Records of District Courts of the United States (Records Group 21)

Indians have been involved in almost every conceivable kind of legal dispute, both civil and criminal. The majority of cases which involved Indians were tried in the areas where they lived but could be held in any court—federal, district, or circuit. Since the records of cases involving Indians are rarely separated and the names of the plaintiffs do not necessarily indicate whether Indians are involved, you should have a particular case to research rather than hoping for results from a fishing expedition.

The kinds of records in case files will vary according to the nature of the case, but typical examples would be petitions, indictments, briefs, affidavits, depositions of witnesses, documents submitted as evidence, subpoenas, judgments, and other documents created by the courts. (See Chapter 6 for more information on these court records and how to use them.)

Records of the United States Courts of Appeals (Record Group 276)

The records of this court consist primarily of appellate case files but only records of the Sixth and Eleventh Districts have been placed in the National Archives. The courts that appear to have the most records concerning Indians are the Eighth Circuit Court and the Tenth Circuit Court. The records of the Eighth Circuit Court (St. Louis) are at the Federal Archives Records Center in Kansas City. The Tenth Circuit Court records are at the Federal Archives Records Center in Denver, Colorado. (See Appendix A for addresses.)

Records of the United States Court of Claims (Record Group 123)

This court's general jurisdiction includes any claim against the United States based upon the Constitution, any act of Congress, any regulation of an executive department, and any expressed or implied contract with the United States. The National Archives has case files for general jurisdiction cases (1855-1939), congressional jurisdiction cases (1884-1933), and departmental jurisdiction cases (1883-1943). There are files for approximately two hundred tribal cases within these three categories.

Case files include transcripts of testimony, petitions, briefs, affidavits, depositions, finding of facts, and other documents customarily found in records of court cases.

A special record group involves three general jurisdiction cases filed as a result of Cherokee grievances over the treaties providing for their removal to the West. In 1905, the court awarded more than $1 million to the Eastern Cherokees (those still living in the East at the time of the Treaty of 1835 and their descendants). Between 1906 and 1909, more than 45,000 claimants submitted applications providing detailed information on their families. Descriptions of other records in this case appear under Records of the Land Division of the Bureau of Indian Affairs.

Records of the Veterans Administration (Record Group 15)

Until 1833, the President, Congress, and the Departments of War, Navy, and the Treasury shared responsibility for administering pensions. In 1833, Congress authorized the appointment of a Commissioner of [Military] Pensions to act under the direction of the Secretary of War. In 1849, this commissioner was transferred to the Department of the Interior.

Among the 54,000 pension application files and several thousand bounty land warrant applications are those for individual Indians based on service as scouts and soldiers. Other soldiers claimed pensions and bounty lands for service in Indian wars throughout the nineteenth century. Reading the complete file is the only way to verify that a given applicant is an Indian, although service in a particular company of infantry, for example, is an excellent clue. (See Chapter 7 for more information on land records and Chapter 8 for more information on military records.)

A pension or bounty land warrant on file may contain several applications of a veteran or his dependents and heirs; documents supporting the identity, service, or character of the claimant; and evidence of the action taken on the claim. The application was a sworn statement that might include the date, name, address, age, birthplace, and date of birth of the veteran; date and place of enlistment and discharge; rank, company, and commanding officer; physical description; occupation; date and circumstances of any disability resulting from service; medical treatment received; other enlistments or military service; date, number and amount of any other pension and bounty land warrants received; names of the veteran's parents, the date and place of their marriage; the date and place of his own marriage and (if applicable) divorce; names and dates of birth of his children; his addresses since his discharge; his signature or mark; and his date and place of death.

Unfortunately, the applications of Indians generally are brief and usually lack the extensive narrative accounts of battles and campaigns that are frequently included in the accounts of other soldiers.

Claimants also often submitted such documentary evidence to support their applications as marriage certificates, wills, commissions, discharges, and affidavits of other veterans or knowledgeable persons.

The records of the Veterans Administration also include many series of pension payments and control registers that could be used to locate records pertaining to qualifying Indians. Among the records of the Special Examination Division of the Bureau of Pensions are correspondence and memoranda 1917-30 concerning verification of Indian scouts' military service and alleged violations of pension laws.

Non-Federal Records

Confederate War Department Records (Record Group 109)

In 1938, the Adjutant General's Office transferred its collection of Confederate records to the National Archives. It is unfortunate that many of these records had been destroyed before they were seized by the Union Army during its occupation of Richmond. The Confederate War Department had received jurisdiction over Indian Affairs by an act passed 21 February 1861, establishing a Bureau of Indian Affairs. Apparently none of its central office records have survived.

A large part of the surviving Confederate records relating to Indians have been published in the multi-volume War Department publication, *The War of the Rebellion: A Compilation of the Official Records of the Union and Confederate Armies,* 70 vols. (Washington, D.C.: Government Printing Office, 1880-1901). The chapter and volume citations in the following section are to this publication.

A Trans-Mississippi District was established on 9 January 1862, embracing parts of Louisiana, Indian Territory (now Oklahoma), Arkansas, Missouri, and a few months later, Texas. Four volumes of letters and telegrams sent (1863-65) contain copies of correspondence with successive commanders of the Indian Territory district and commanders of Indian troops in the field (Chapter 2, covering vols. 70-72 and half of vol. 73). These letters relate primarily to military operations and troops in Indian Territory and help locate an ancestor in time and space.

The majority of Indian operations under the Confederacy centered in western Arkansas and the Indian Territory. The Indian Territory Department had been created in 1861, merged into the Trans-Mississippi Department in 1862, and became a separate district in 1864. Four volumes of letters sent (1863-65) are found in Chapter 2, Volumes 258, 267, 268, and 270. These letters were written to military officers in the field, including commanders of Indian troops, Indian leaders, and officials in the Confederate War Department.

Muster rolls have also survived for various Indian organizations that operated in the Indian Territory. Much of the relevant information contained in these muster rolls was later abstracted onto cards by the Adjutant General's Office, which has custody of the records. The information is currently available in compiled military service records, which include a file for each individual who served in an organization. There are also cards (called caption and record of events cards), which contain activities of the unit as a whole. The caption cards are available on microfilm as *Compiled Records Showing Service of Military Units in Confederate Organizations*. Roll 74 contains information about the Indian Organizations.

Pertinent compiled military service records that have been reproduced on microfilm by the National Archives include *Compiled Service Records of Confederate Soldiers Who Served in Organizations Raised Directly by the Confederate Government* and *Compiled Service Records of Confederate General and Staff Officers and Nonregimental Enlisted Men*. The former include records of the Cherokee, Chickasaw, Choctaw, Creek, Osage, and Seminole organizations, while the latter contains files for staff officers—Brigadier General Stand Watie, Douglas H. Cooper, and Albert Pike. These men were all deeply involved in Confederate relations with Indian tribes west of the Mississippi (principally the Indian Territory).

Casualty lists and battle reports have also survived and have been reproduced on microfilm by the National Archives as *Confederate States Army Casualties: Lists and Narrative Reports, 1861-1865*. The documents pertaining to battles in Indian Territory appear on Roll 17.

Records Relating to the Five Civilized Tribes, Oklahoma Historical Society

No discussion of Indian records would be complete without reference to the Indian Archives in the Oklahoma Historical Society, Oklahoma City. This collection of Indian documents contains approximately 3 million pages of manuscripts and 6,000 bound volumes—the largest collection of Indian documents in the United States outside of the National Archives. These records were placed in custody of the Oklahoma Historical Society by a Congressional act 27 March 1934. See Table 17-1 for an inventory.

Oklahoma is the pivotal state in Indian study because the state itself was created from Indian Territory. Citizens of the Five Civilized Tribes were relocated there when their lands were exchanged but other Indian tribes were also moved onto allotments and reservations within the original territory. Today the actual location of the land is now Missouri, Kansas, Arkansas, Oklahoma, or Texas. Maps 17-1 and 17-2 show the locations of these tribes in relationship to the Five Civilized Tribes. Intermarriage among the various Indian groups in The Nations (as the territory was called) comingled these tribes, and descendants today may have lost memory of these marriage ties, designating themselves as "Cherokee" when in reality they are something else.

The Oklahoma Historical Society collections include numerous references to all of the tribes inhabiting the territory. Other collections can be located by using NUCMC and the *Directory of Archives and Manuscripts Depositories* discussed in other chapters of this volume.

Maps can be significant research tools often overlooked by genealogists. On these maps, the location of Indian settlements provides important genealogical facts: if your ancestors settled originally in the shaded area of Map 17-1 or the Indian Territory portion of Oklahoma (Map 17-2), your chances of having Indian blood on one or more of your ancestral lines is better than 75 percent, even if the assimilation of that Indian tie into your American family has become blurred or the generation when the Indian-white marriage took place is lost. See the case study of Earl Davis later in this chapter. County and state records alone may give no indication of such origins. Only a check in the Indian sources, identifying the precise generation of the tie can resolve the problem.

Private collections, also housed at the Oklahoma Historical Society, are the work of several noted Indian Studies historians. The collections are the result of years of research and will be of immense value to the more advanced genealogist. These collections are:

- Grant Foreman: Transcripts of records in Office of Commission of Indian Affairs and Superintendent Five Civilized Tribes.
- Grant Foreman: Collection of letters, notes, newspaper clippings, etc.
- Grant Foreman: Collection of John R. Thomas Papers.
- Frederick B. Severs: Collection of Accounts Books as trader, Creek Nation.
- Indian Pioneer History: The John Meserve Collection concerning Chiefs of the Five Civilized Tribes, the John H. Adair Collection of Early Cherokee Papers, the G. A. Rost Collection of Newspaper Clippings on Oklahoma land openings, the Edwin Ludlow Collection, Eva Lewers Collection, Peter Hanranty Collection, Katie Edward Bemo Mitchell Collection, and the papers of Anna Eliza Worcester Robertson, Alice Robertson, and Grace Merriam.

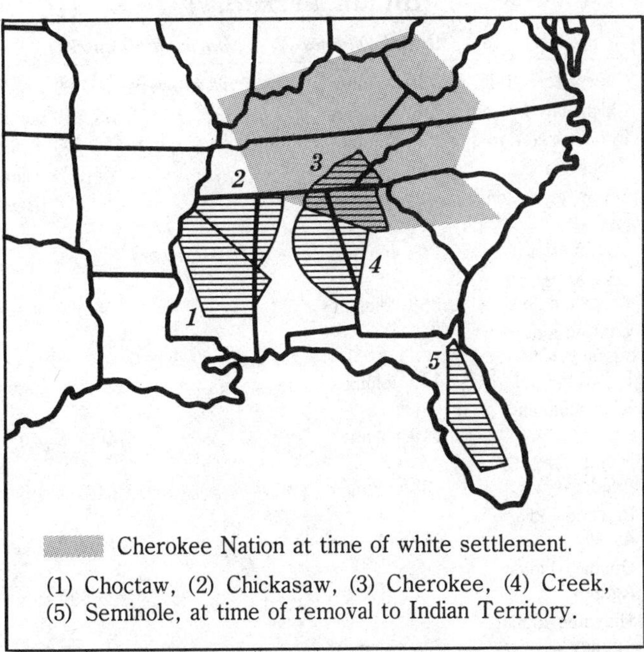

Map 17-1. Locations of Five Civilized Tribes in the South.

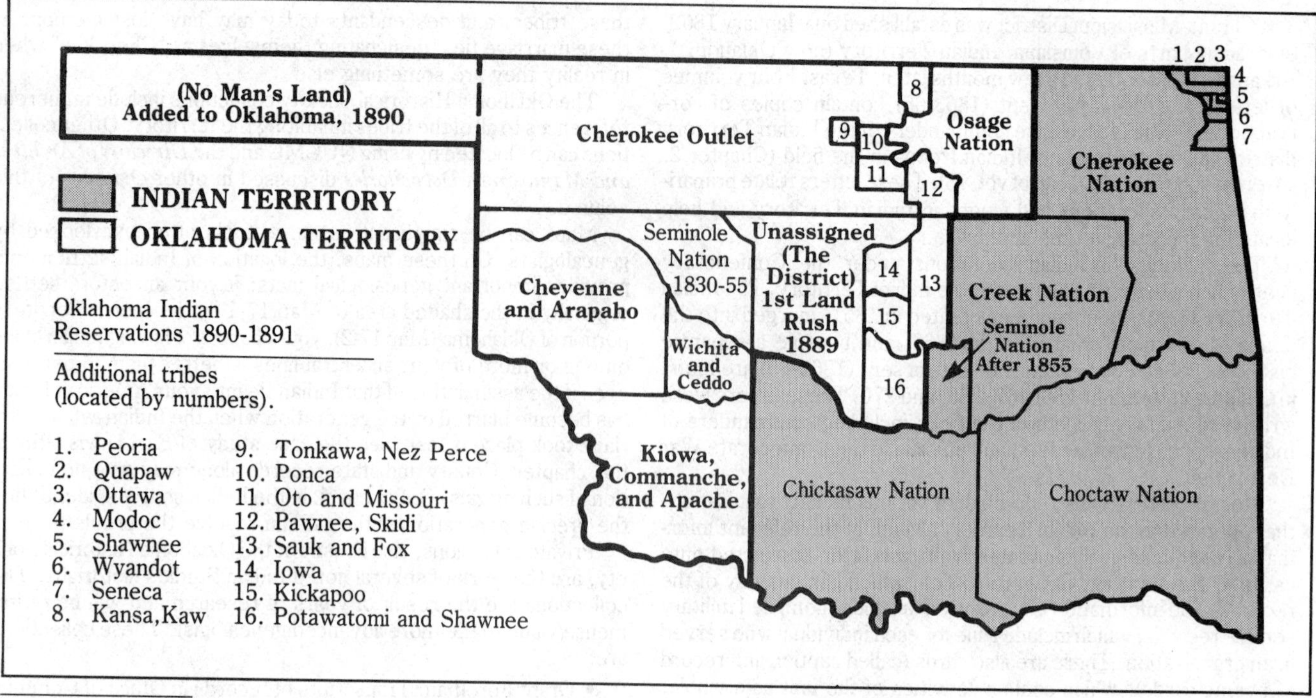

Map 17-2. Based on Muriel Wright, *A Guide to the Indians of Oklahoma* (Norman: University of Oklahoma Press, 1971), and John Morris, et al., *Historical Atlas of Oklahoma* (Norman: University of Oklahoma Press, 1976). The Choctaws arrived west of the Mississippi in 1820; the other four Civilized Tribes soon followed. After the Civil War other Indian tribes migrated into the Nations, settling primarily in the Western sections and along the Arkansas, Missouri, Kansas borders. In 1889, the area was divided into Indian Territory (eastern part) and Oklahoma Territory (western part) as a prelude to non-Indian settlement. Specific reservations and allotments were assigned 1890-91. By 1907, counties were formed throughout Oklahoma and the reservation boundaries disappeared.

Table 17-1

Records of the Five Civilized Tribes Including Records of the Cheyenne, Arapahoe, Kiowa, Pawnee, Quapaw, Shawnee, and Other Tribes Assigned Lands in The Nations (Indian Territory)

Tribes	*Bound Volumes*	*Unbound Manuscripts*
Cherokee Nation	740 volumes	25 file drawers 430,000 pages
Chickasaw Nation	106 volumes	17,510 pages
Choctaw Nation	499 volumes	54,083 pages
Creek Nation	88 volumes	55,973 pages
Seminole Nation	12 volumes	228 pages
Dawes Commission	242 volumes	29 file drawers
Cheyenne and Arapahoe Agency	886 volumes	556,686 pages
Cantonment Agency, Chilocco Indian School	140 volumes	127,356 pages
Kiowa Indian Agency	519 volumes	749,335 pages
Mekusukey Academy	30 volumes	64,314 pages
Pawnee Indian Agency	902 volumes	211,200 pages
Quapaw Indian Agency		26,089 pages
Shawnee Indian Agency	623 volumes	

Additionally, the Oklahoma Historical Society maintains an excellent collection of Oklahoma newspapers. By 1897, ten daily newspapers, eighty weekly newspapers, and twelve monthly newspapers served the Oklahoma Territory with several more in the Indian Territory. Many of these newspapers are at least partially indexed.

Case Studies

Samuel Sixkiller

Assume for the moment that your ancestor is one Samuel Sixkiller, born about 1850 in the Indian Territory. Family memories and traditions, when assembled, give you a little information. His wife's name was Nancy. There were five or six children but you only know names for three: Arch, supposedly the oldest son, born before 1880, and two daughters, Emma and Delia.

Prior to statehood, Oklahoma was divided into two territories – Indian Territory and Oklahoma Territory, organized in 1889 out of Indian Territory. The 1900 Soundex of Oklahoma Territory does not reveal your ancestor, so you turn to the 1900 Soundex of Indian Territory. Just as you had hoped, Samuel Sixkiller was indeed living in Indian Territory. A copy of the Soundex card is shown in Figure 17-1. You will notice that, in this case, there are two cards for the family.

This family fits the description you have so far. Samuel was born in 1850. His wife is Nancy, and the oldest son, Arch, was born in 1876. The two daughters, Emma and Delia, are also listed among the other children: Lynch, George, and Ned.

The information just below Samuel's name tells you that the family was living in Township 15 North, Range 25 East, Cherokee Nation, Indian Territory. In the upper right hand corner are references to the volume, sheet, district, and line of the census from which the Soundex information was extracted.

S246

INDIAN TERRITORY VOL. 4 E. D. 36 SHEET 26 LINE 35

SixKiller, Samuel (HEAD OF FAMILY)

In (COLOR) nov (MONTH) 1850 (YEAR) 49 (AGE) Indian Territory (BIRTHPLACE) (CITIZENSHIP)

Cherokee nation (COUNTY) Twp 15 N.R. 25 E (M. C. D.)

(CITY) (STREET) (HOUSE NO.)

OTHER MEMBERS OF FAMILY

NAME	RELATION-SHIP	BIRTH MONTH	BIRTH YEAR	AGE	BIRTHPLACE	CITIZEN-SHIP
SixKiller, Nancy	W	Jan	1848	52	Indian Territory	
Arch	S	sept	1876	23	Indian Territory	
Lanch	S	Oct	1879	20	Indian Territory	
George	S.	Dec	1881	18	Indian Territory	
Emma	D	nov	1886	13	Indian Territory	

1900 CENSUS—INDEX DEPARTMENT OF COMMERCE BUREAU OF THE CENSUS 1 are 2

A-1a

U. S. GOVERNMENT PRINTING OFFICE

STATE Indian Territory

SixKiller, Samuel (HEAD OF FAMILY—Continued)

OTHER MEMBERS OF FAMILY—Continued

NAME	RELATION-SHIP	BIRTH MONTH	BIRTH YEAR	AGE	BIRTHPLACE	CITIZEN-SHIP
Ned	S	may	1889	11	Indian Territory	
Delia	D	Dec	1892	8	Indian Territory	
Hanson, Julie	"	Jan	1878	22	Territory	

1900 CENSUS—INDEX 2 are 1

A-1b

Figure 17-1. 1900 Soundex Indian Territory, Samuel Sixkiller, (Code S-246); Genealogical Society of Utah (hereafter GS) 1,249,686.

The 1900 census schedule is basically the same for Indians as for whites, but Figure 17-2 shows the full schedule, while Figure 17-3 shows the additional section which applies to Indians.

The "special inquiries" tell us that Samuel and Nancy are both Cherokees as were Samuel's parents, even though he is listed as only one-half Cherokee. He was not living in polygamy, was not taxed, and his dwelling was permanent.

This census tells us that Samuel was born in Indian Territory in November 1850, is forty-nine years old, has been married for twenty-six years (about 1874), and farms his own land which he holds without a mortgage. His parents were both born in North Carolina. He does not read or write but speaks English. Nancy was born in January of 1848 and is fifty-two. Four of her twelve children died before 1900. If Samuel had used an Indian name, there would also be a Soundex entry for that name.

More information and more questions emerge from the 1910 census, taken when Oklahoma had been a state for three years. Samuel and Nancy Sixkiller are living in Lees Creek Township, Adair County. (Are they in the same place, or have they moved?) Much of the information is the same, but Nancy states that seven of her children are living. One child has died in the last decade. (Are all twelve children Samuel's? Nancy, who is three years older, has been married twice.) Samuel now states that he is three-quarters Cherokee and one-quarter white. Both he and Nancy had received an allotment of land in 1900. (Was it the farm Samuel said he owned or another piece of property?) Our research has answered some questions and raised still more.

Prior to 1900, there are no federal census records available for Indian Territory. Here's where we use the Indian records described previously.

In 1893 the Commission to the Five Civilized Tribes (Dawes Commission) was established to negotiate agreements to exchange tribal lands for individual allotments. The Curtis Act of 1898 (30 *Stat.* 495) provided for the preparation of tribal rolls and the allotments themselves. One of the most important group of records this Commission produced was the "Final Rolls of Citizens and Freedmen of the Five Civilized Tribes."

Several categories of tribal membership are distinguished in

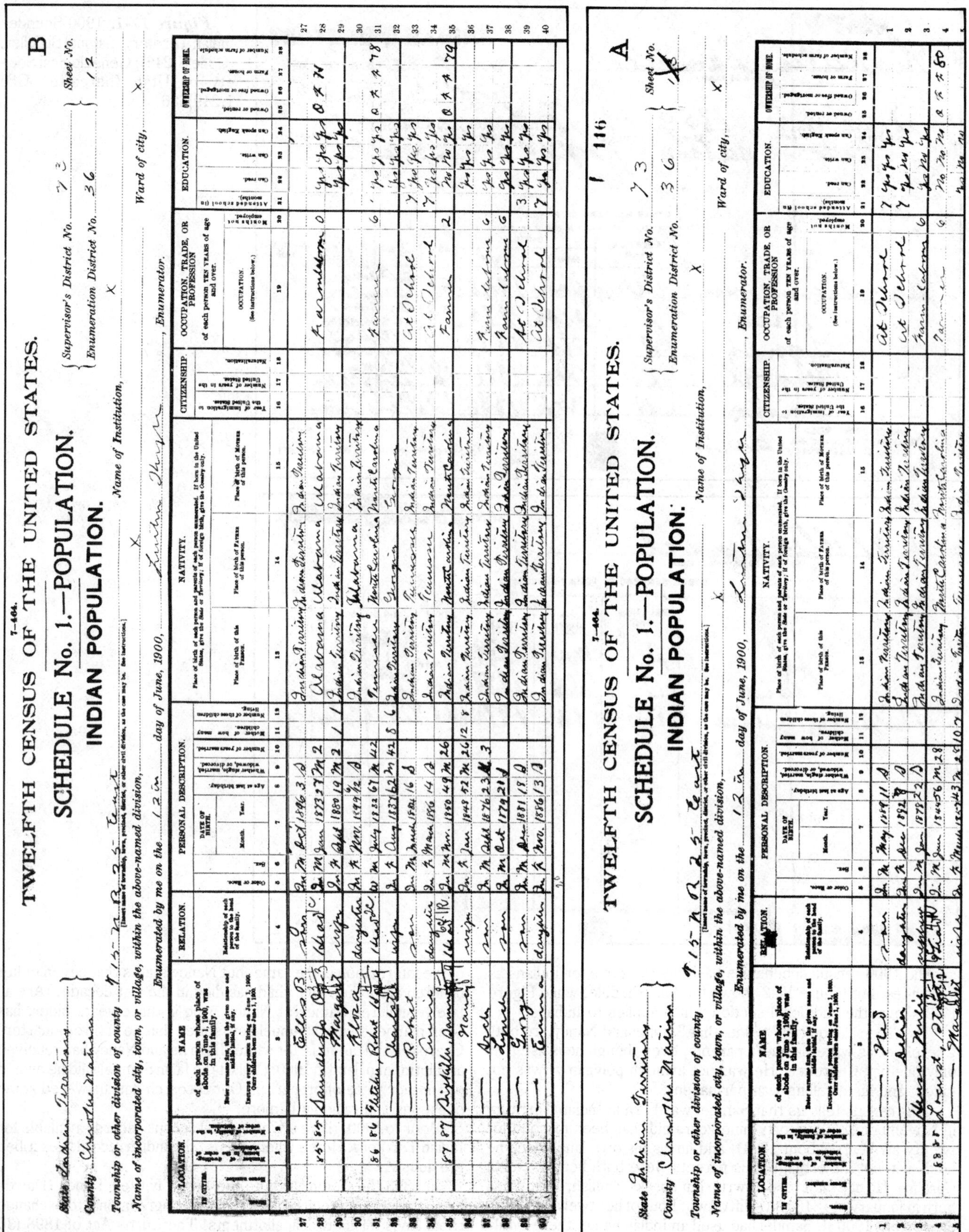

Figure 17-2. 1900 Census Cherokee Nation, District 36, Township 15 North, Range 25 East, vol. 4, enumeration district (ED) 36, sheet 26, line 35; sheet 27, lines 1-3. GS 1,241,845.

SCHEDULE No. 1.—POPULATION—Continued.

SPECIAL INQUIRIES RELATING TO INDIANS.

OTHER NAME, IF ANY.	NATIVITY. Tribe of this Indian.	Tribe of Father of this Indian.	Tribe of Mother of this Indian.	MIXED BLOOD. Has this Indian any white blood; if so, how much? (0, ½, ¼, or ⅛.)	CONJUGAL CONDITION. Is this Indian, if married, living in polygamy?	CITIZENSHIP. Is this Indian taxed? (See instructions.)	Year of acquiring citizenship.	Was citizenship acquired by allotment?	DWELLINGS. Is this Indian living in a fixed or in a movable dwelling?
29	30	31	32	33	34	35	36	37	38
— Ellis B	Cherokee	Cherokee	Cherokee	1/2		No			Fixed
Saunders, Jo B	Cherokee	Cherokee	Cherokee	1/2	No	No			Fixed
— Margaret	Cherokee	White	Cherokee	1/2	No	No			Fixed
— Flora	Cherokee	Cherokee	Cherokee	1/2		No			Fixed
Fletcher, Robert H.	White	White	White		No	No			Fixed
— Charlotte	Cherokee	Cherokee	Cherokee	1/2	No	No			Fixed
— Robert	Cherokee	White	Cherokee	1/2		No			Fixed
— Annie	Cherokee	White	Cherokee	1/2		No			Fixed
Sixkiller, Samuel	Cherokee	Cherokee	Cherokee	1/2	No	No			Fixed
— Nancy	Cherokee	Cherokee	Cherokee	1/2	No	No			Fixed
— Arch	Cherokee	Cherokee	Cherokee	1/2	No	No			Fixed
— Lynch	Cherokee	Cherokee	Cherokee	1/2		No			Fixed
— George	Cherokee	Cherokee	Cherokee	1/2		No			Fixed
— Emma	Cherokee	Cherokee	Cherokee	1/2		No			Fixed
— [illegible]	Cherokee	Cherokee	Cherokee	1/4		No			Fixed
— A-ge	Cherokee	Cherokee	Cherokee	1/4		No			Fixed
— A-nee	Cherokee	Cherokee	Cherokee	1/4		No			Fixed
— [illegible]	Cherokee	Cherokee	Cherokee	1/4		No			Fixed
— Ah-he-ah-dah-ge	Cherokee	Cherokee	Cherokee	1/2		No			Fixed
— Le-wee	Cherokee	Cherokee	Cherokee	1/4		No			Fixed
— [illegible]	Cherokee	Cherokee	Cherokee	1/4		No			Fixed
— [illegible]	Cherokee	Cherokee	Cherokee	1/4		No			Fixed
— Lit-tee	Cherokee	Cherokee	Cherokee	1/4		No			Fixed
[illegible]	Cherokee	Cherokee	Cherokee	0	No	No			Fixed
[illegible]	Cherokee	Cherokee	Cherokee	1/4	No	No			Fixed
— [illegible]	Cherokee	Cherokee	Cherokee	1/4		No			Fixed
— Es-tah	Cherokee	Cherokee	Cherokee	1/4		No			Fixed
Glass, Je-nee	Cherokee	Cherokee	Cherokee	0		No			Fixed
[illegible]	Cherokee	Cherokee	Cherokee	0	No	No			Fixed

INSTRUCTI
(co

The following instru
Column 29.—Write
to the English name giv
Indian or English, repea
Columns 30, 31, a
answers should be obtai
be obtained. If the In
made both in columns 1
ance with the facts.
Column 35.—An I
detached from his or h
vidual, and as such su
taxes or not; also if he
an allotment of land, an
two cases the answer to
An Indian on a res
settled territory, is cons
to this inquiry is "No."
Column 36.—If the
American citizenship, w
has not acquired citizen
Column 37.—If the
of land from the Gover
by other means, write "
ship, leave the column b
Column 38.—If th
structure, write "mova
of any kind, write "fixe

B side). Each Indian
end of the line on whi
from column 1 to colu
answered.
Columns 1 to 28.-
population schedule.
accordance with the in
general population sch
relation to filling colu
Columns 1 and 2
the general populatio
population, make two
series in each kind of
when added together
of families visited an
Column 19.—If
on the Government fo
supporting and partly
and then the letter "
age and receives ratio

INSTRUCT

Figure 17-3. Ibid., "Special Inquiries Relating to Indians."

these rolls. For the Cherokee, the categories are: Cherokee by blood, Cherokee by intermarriage, Cherokee freedmen, and minor Cherokee freedmen. There is some variance in the categories for Choctaws, Creeks, Seminoles, and Chickasaws; but basically they are the same.

In the index to these rolls (Figure 17-4), Samuel, Nancy, Lynch, George, Emma, Ned, and Delia are all listed with the appropriate roll number. We notice that the Sixkiller family, despite its distinctive name, is part of a large clan. We also notice that Arch is not in the index.

Using this index, we easily find Samuel and Nancy's family in the second volume. Sam Sixkiller and his family appear on page 253, second column. The first number is the individual's roll number. The columns following the roll number are the name, age, sex, degree of Indian blood, and card number.

2314	Starr, Hooley	11	M	5-16	846
2315	Starr, Nancy	9	F	5-16	846
2316	Sixkiller, Sam	51	M	3-4	847
2317	Sixkiller, Nancy	54	F	3-4	847
2318	Sixkiller, Lynch	22	M	3-4	847
2319	Sixkiller, George	21	M	3-4	847
2320	Sixkiller, Emma	16	F	3-4	847
2321	Sixkiller, Ned	13	M	3-4	847
2322	Sixkiller, Delia	11	F	3-4	847
2323	Sixkiller, Walter	47	M	5-8	848
2324	Sixkiller, Julia	45	F	1-8	848
2325	Sixkiller, Martha	17	F	3-8	848
2326	Sixkiller, Henry	15	M	3-8	848
2327	Sixkiller, Narcissa	12	F	3-8	848
2328	Sixkiller, Frank	9	M	3-8	848
2329	Sixkiller, Stella	6	F	3-8	848
2330	Sixkiller, Walter R.	4	M	318	848
2331	Brackett. Benjamin	53	M	1-16	849

The Final Rolls of Citizens and Freedmen of the Five Civilized Tribes in Indian Territory (Washington, D.C.: Government Printing Office, 1907), vol. 2, p. 253; GS 908,371, item 2.

The full roll card, Figure 17-5, gives us some very specific information.

Samuel Sixkiller, at the time of his enrollment (1903) was residing in the Flint District of the Cherokee Nation, Indian Territory. The lefthand column is the Dawes Roll Number. In addition to the other information, the column on tribal enrollment gives us the number he was assigned in the 1896 Cherokee Tribe census, the names of his and Nancy's parents, and their own enrollment. His parents are Arch and Charlotte Sixkiller. Nancy's parents were Sam Leslie (or Laslie) and Susie Scott.

It's a genealogical boon that the 1900 federal census and the Final Rolls are two different records of about the same date. Thus one supports the other. Similarly, the Guion Miller Rolls were closed

Figure 17-4. The Commission and Commissioner to the Five Civilized Tribes, "Index to the Final Roll of Citizens and Freedmen of the Five Civilized Tribes in Indian Territory," (Washington, D.C.: Government Printing Office, 1907), p. 386; GS 962,366.

386 CHEROKEES BY BLOOD

Name.	Roll No.
Sittingdown, Nancy	2136
Sittingdown, William	25634
Sittingdown, Stephen	26362
Sittingdown, James	26363
Sittingdown, Thadius	26364
Sittingdown, Minnie	26365
Sittingdown, Agnes	26366
Sittingdown, Edgar	26367
Sittingdown, Ella	29820
Sitsler, George W.	30135
Sitsler, James Lewis	30136
Sitten, Naomi A.	31698
Sitten, Theodore L.	31699
Sixkiller, Glover	768
Sixkiller, Nancy	1357
Sixkiller, Sam	2316
Sixkiller, Nancy	2317
Sixkiller, Lynch	2318
Sixkiller, George	2319
Sixkiller, Emma	2320
Sixkiller, Ned	2321
Sixkiller, Delia	2322
Sixkiller, Walter	2323
Sixkiller, Julia	2324
Sixkiller, Martha	2325
Sixkiller, Henry	2326
Sixkiller, Narcissa	2327
Sixkiller, Frank	2328
Sixkiller, Stella	2329
Sixkiller, Arch	2418
Sixkiller, Walter R.	2330
Sixkiller, Joshua	2547
Sixkiller, Johnie	2548
Sixkiller, Luke	7397
Sixkiller, Emma	7398
Sixkiller, James	10732
Sixkiller, Nancy	10733
Sixkiller, Carrie	10734
Sixkiller, Pearl	10735
Sixkiller, Joseph	10736
Sixkiller, Henry	11223
Sixkiller, Linnie M.	11224
Sixkiller, William F.	11225
Sixkiller, Artemecie M.	11226
Sixkiller, Charles	12339
Sixkiller, Martin	12340
Sixkiller, Hooley	12885
Sixkiller, Jesse M.	12886
Sixkiller, James T.	13397
Sixkiller, Claude L.	13398
Sixkiller, Robert M.	13399
Sixkiller, Ida M.	13400
Sixkiller, Pleasant T.	13401
Sixkiller, Jesse	14348
Sixkiller, Sarah	14349
Sixkiller, Katie	14350
Sixkiller, Ethel	14351
Sixkiller, Josie	14967
Sixkiller, Fannie	16040
Sixkiller, Samuel R.	16877
Sixkiller, Sallie	18313
Sixkiller, Charlie	18605
Sixkiller, Eliza	18606
Sixkiller, Rufus	18607
Sixkiller, Sampson	18608
Sixkiller, Charlotte	18913
Sixkiller, George	18914
Sixkiller, Sam	18915
Sixkiller, Annie	19002
Sixkiller, John	19067
Sixkiller, Winnie	19068
Sixkiller, Ora	19069
Sixkiller, Nannie	19070
Sixkiller, Gafford	19245
Sixkiller, Susie	19246
Sixkiller, Nellie	19248
Sixkiller, Laura	19249
Sixkiller, Abraham	19666
Sixkiller, Margaret	19667
Sixkiller, Dennis	19668
Sixkiller, Sarah	19669
Sixkiller, Kate	19670
Sixkiller, Lincoln	19671
Sixkiller, Retta	19672
Sixkiller, Johnson	20059
Sixkiller, Lula	20060

Name.	Roll No.
Sixkilller, Samuel	20061
Sixkiller, Bluford	20267
Sixkiller, Annie	20268
Sixkiller, Maud	23599
Sixkiller, Lola	23600
Sixkiller, Blanche	23601
Sixkiller, Mabel	23602
Sixkiller, Henry	23603
Sixkiller, Mary A.	23604
Sixkiller, Linnie	25562
Sixkiller, Young Wolfe	25563
Sixkiller, Mintie	25763
Sixkiller, Hattie	26937
Sixkiller, John B.	27220
Sixkiller, Cicero	27221
Sixkiller, Dora	27222
Sixkiller, Joseph	27470
Sixkiller, Lucy	27471
Sixkiller, Gracie	27472
Sixkiller, Bertha	28556
Sixkiller, Carrie B.	28730
Sixkiller, Jennie	29721
Sixkiller, Peggie	29722
Sixkiller, Henry	32313
Six, John W.	6368
Six, Ida	17773
Six, Enoch	17772
Six, John	17807
Six, Groundhog	30551
Six, Humphrey	30552
Six, Tincup	30553
Skaggs, Myrtle A.	11457
Skaggs, Roy	11458
Skaloll, James	21290
Skelley, Cora	32247
Skelley, Charles	32248
Skelley, Joseph	32249
Skinner, Thomas F.	7545
Skinner, Morgan D.	7546
Skinner, Galuga T.	7547
Skinner, Bettie A.	7548
Skinneer, Mary A.	7549
Skinner, Laura C.	26558
Skinner, John	28810
Skinner, Ray N.	28811
Skillman, Sarah E.	9210
Skillman, Bessie D.	9211
Skillman, John O.	9212
Skitt, Patsey	19663
Skitt, Martha	20137
Skitt, Sam	20138
Skitt, Nancy	20139
Skitt, Ben	20140
Skitt, Ella	20141
Skitt, Alice	20142
Skitt, Mattie	20143
Skitt, Calvin	20144
Skitt, Margaret	22788
Skitt, Lucy	25821
Skidmore, Annie F.	21764
Skidmore, Eugene O.	21765
Skidmore, Otis T.	21766
Skidmore, Elizabeth A.	21767
Skidmore, Henry C.	21768
Skidmore, Letitia F.	21769
Skidmore, Benjamin F.	21770
Sleeper, Cricket N.	15249
Sleeper, Nannie I.	15250
Sleeper, Minnie	17352
Sleeper, Julia	17353
Sleeper, Gideon D., Jr.	17354
Sleeper, Walter J.	17355
Sleeper, Mattie	17356
Slack, Olive A.	31499
Slack, Edith	31500
Slagle, Minnie H.	24377
Slagle, Gordon	24378
Slagle, Dennis	24379
Slagle, Hattie F.	24380
Slagle, Ellsworth	24381
Sloan, Mary E.	887
Sloan, Alexander G.	5116
Sloan, Nora C.	5117
Sloan, Lizzie H.	5118
Sloan, Cora E.	5119
Sloan, Robert D.	7210

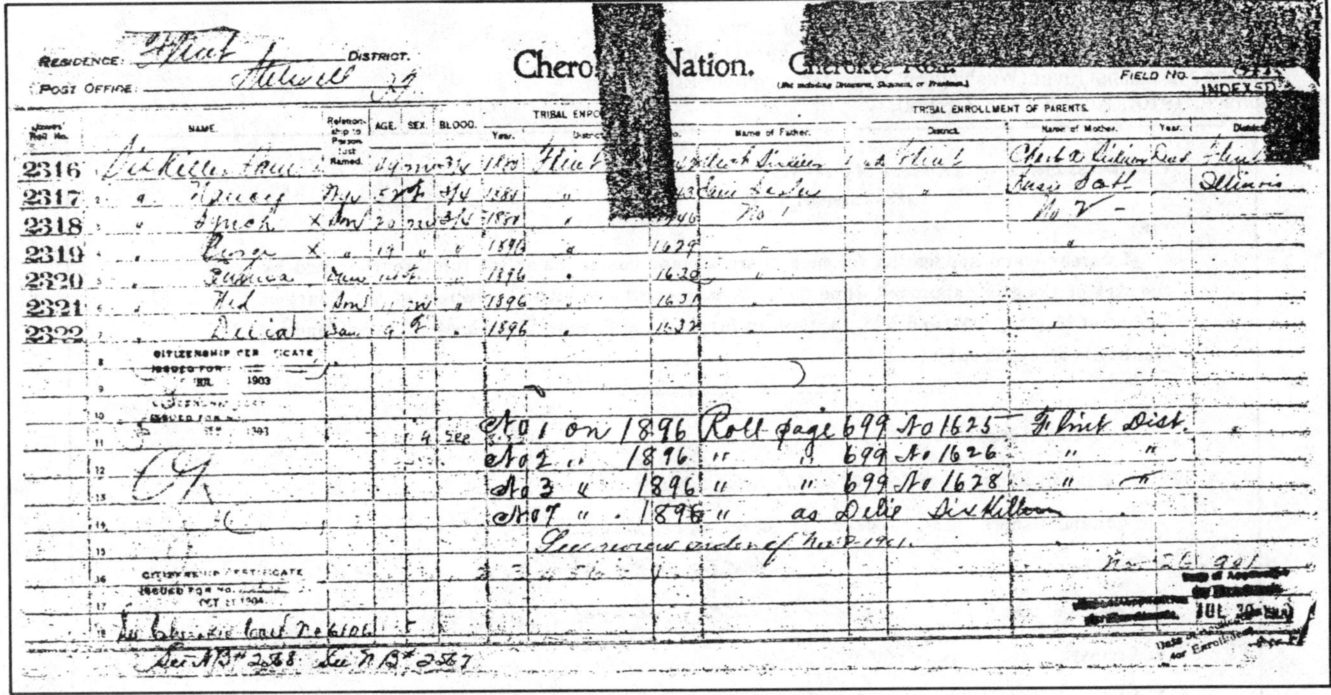

Residence: Flint District.
Post Office: Stilwell I.T.

Cherokee Nation. Cherokee Roll.

Field No.

INDEXED

Dawes' Roll No.	Name	Relationship to Person first Named	Age	Sex	Blood	Tribal Enrollment Year	District	No.	Name of Father	Year	District	Name of Mother	Year	District
2316						1880	Flint				Flint			Flint
2317						1880						Lucy Salt		Illinois
2318						1880			No 1			No 2		
2319						1896		1627						
2320						1896		1630						
2321						1896		1631						
2322						1896		1632						

Citizenship Certificate Issued for ... 1903

No 1 on 1896 Roll page 699 No 1625 Flint Dist.
No 2 " 1896 " " 699 No 1626 " "
No 3 " 1896 " " 699 No 1628 " "
No 7 " 1896 " as Delie Sixkiller

Citizenship Certificate Issued for No ... Oct 21 1904

Date of Application for Enrollment. Jul 30 1900

See NB 2588 See NB 2587

Figure 17-5. Samuel Sixkiller, Card No. 847, Cherokee Nation; GS 022,530.

shortly before the 1910 federal census, thus making another convenient research pair. The most interesting item in the 1910 federal census, however, is that only one daughter is living with Samuel and Nancy; but this is hardly surprising. The other children were certainly of an age to marry and leave home.

Even if Samuel had not been accepted on the Guion Miller Rolls as eligible to share the money awarded to the Cherokees, the information in his application would have made the search worthwhile. In researching a family that lived in Oklahoma or Indian Territory, I routinely check the indexes. If I find my target person in the index to the applications, I know I have a genealogical goldmine.

Guion Miller's rolls are divided into Cherokees east of the Mississippi and those residing west of it. A check of the index locates him in the eastern portion, on page 127.

24592	23516	2318	Sixkiller, Lynch	Stilwell, Okla.		27
24593	2873	14560	Maggie		W	27
24594		3148m	Felix		S	3
24595	5590	23602	Sixkiller, Mable	Choteau, Okla.		15
24596		23603	Henry		B	9
24597		23604	Mary A.		S	7
			By Belle Sixkiller, Gdn.			
24598	23927	2325	Sixkiller, Martha	Stilwell, Okla.		21
24599	27967	2937	Sixkiller Mattie B.	Afton, Okla.		32
24600	16583	1357	Sixkiller, Nancy	Baptist, Okla.		89
24601	761	2316	Sixkiller, Samuel	Stilwell, Okla.		47
24602	786	2317	Nancy		W	58
24603	761	2321	Ned		S	17
24604		2322	Delia		D	13
24605	16721	20061	Sixkiller, Samuel	Baptist, Okla.		13
24606		32313	Henry		B	10
			By Johnson Sixkiller, Gdn.			
24607	16328	16877	Sixkiller, Samuel R.	Muskogee, Okla.		29
24608	770	2323	Sixkiller, Walter	Stilwell, Okla.		51

Guion Miller, comp., *Eastern Cherokees Residing West of the Mississippi River,* p. 126 (Washington, D.C.: Government Printing Office, 1910); GS 378,594.

The first column contains his number assigned by Guion Miller. In the second column is his Eastern Cherokee application number (761), the key to the rest of the important records in this roll. The third refers to Samuel's Dawes number. Nancy's number is 786.

For our purposes, we will follow only Samuel and Nancy, but in a genuine research situation, I would routinely examine the applications of all of Samuel's children and their spouses.

The usual length of an Eastern Cherokee application is about four pages. However, other documents and correspondence may be included. Samuel's application, Figure 17-6, bears the label on the exterior that "Applicant is the son of Arch Fields, enrolled by Drennen in 1851 as Arch Six Killer in Flint District Group 46 – and Annie Bigfeather his grandmother enrolled at same time and place under Group #36. Misc. List 4019." (The reference to Drennen is to the Old Settler Roll of 1851.)

The application cover also bears the notation, "Grouped herewith are nos 764, 770, 769, 4227, 5690, 5591, 5592, 10688, 27103, 27104, . . .claims through Anny [sic] Bigfeather, Flint 36," These are the application numbers of persons who are in some way related to Samuel Sixkiller, most likely other descendants of his grandmother. Of course, as a matter of standard procedure, I would review these applications especially since Samuel names three uncles through whom he makes his claim. The value of these applications is apparent immediately. Samuel's gives us an exact birthdate (25 November 1851) and birthplace (Flint District, Cherokee Nation). Samuel identifies his parents as Arch Fields, (Indian name: Ar-chi Sixkiller) and Charlotte Adair (Cr-haw-hah). Both parents were born in Georgia and died in Flint District, Arch in 1863 and Charlotte in 1886. The other children in the family were Jennie Henson, born 1852, Walter Sixkiller, born 10 Oct. 1855, and John M. Sixkiller, born June 1857, died 1886. The application goes back another complete generation. Samuel's father's parents were Sixkiller Fields and Annie Bigfeather while Samuel's maternal grandparents were Samuel and Polly Adair. The Adair children are also named. Samuel adds the interesting note that "my fathers name was changed from Arch Fields to Six Killer, taking fathers given name instead of his Sir Name."

Following Samuel's application is the Supplemental Application for Minor Children, in this case, Ned, Delia, and a twelve-year-old nephew of Nancy's they had taken into their home. Nancy's maiden name is given as Lasley. After the affadavit of witnesses is attached a deposition from Samuel's brother, Walter, which adds the further information that Charlotte Adair was three-quarters white and an "old settler."

A following page of field investigation notes identifies Arch Field and his half-brother, George Bigfeather, as "the only persons through whom this group of cases can be O.K.'d." The trail now leads us to their mother, Annie Bigfeather, and the Drennen (Old Settler) Roll of 1851.

Figure 17-6. Eastern Cherokee Application of Samuel Sixkiller, Guion Miller, comp., Final Roll for Those [Cherokees] Living East of the Mississippi River (Washington, D.C.: Government Printing Office, 1910), No. 761; GS 378,600.

Commissioner of Indian Affairs,
Washington, D. C.

Sir:

I hereby make application for such share as may be due me of the fund appropriated by the Act of Congress approved June 30, 1906, in accordance with the decrees of the Court of Claims of May 18, 1905, and May 28, 1906, in favor of the Eastern Cherokees. The evidence of identity is herewith subjoined.

1. State full name—

English name: Samuel Sixkiller

Indian name: Samie Su-tul-le-te-hi

2. Residence: Flint District Cherokee Nation

3. Town and post office: Stilwell Ind Ter

4. County: Flint

5. State: Ind Ter

6. Date and place of birth: Nov 25 1851 Flint District Cher, Nat,

7. By what right do you claim to share? If you claim through more than one relative living in 1851, set forth each claim separately: Arch. Fields (my father) Annie Bigfeather (My Grandmother) my uncle (Hitcher Bigfeather) Uncle Hawk Bigfeather Uncle Tom Sixkiller,

8. Are you married? Yes

9. Name and age of wife or husband: Nancy Sixkiller 58 yrs of age

10. Give names of your father and mother, and your mother's name before marriage.

Father—English name: Arch Fields Sixkiller 46 Mlt

Indian name: Ar-chi Sululleleke

Mother—English name: Charlotte Fields O.S. 11. 16.

Indian name: Oo haw-hah

Maiden name: Charlotte Adair

11. Where were they born?

Father: In Georgia

Mother: In Georgia

12. Where did they reside in 1851, if living at that time?

Father: Flint District Cherokee Nation

Mother: Flint District Cherokee Nation

13. Date of death of your father and mother—

Father: In August 1863 **Mother:** 1886

6—524

14. Were they ever enrolled for annuities, land, or other benefits? If so, state when and where: Unknown.

15. Name all your brothers and sisters, giving ages, and if not living, the date of death:

	NAME.	BORN.	DIED.
(1)	Samuel Sixkiller	25th of Nov 1857	
(2)	Jennie Anson	1853	
(3)	Walter Sixkiller	10th of Oct. 1855	
(4)	John M. Sixkiller	June 1857	1886
(5)			
(6)			

16. State English and Indian names of your grandparents on both father's and mother's side, if possible:

FATHER'S SIDE.	MOTHER'S SIDE.
Sixkiller Fields	Samuel Adair
Annie Bigfeather	Polly Adair

36 Flt

17. Where were they born? In Georgia

18. Where did they reside in 1851, if living at that time? In Flint District Cherokee Nation

19. Give names of all their children, and residence, if living; if not living, give dates of deaths:

(1) English name: George Adair 1876
Indian name: Charlotte ~~Adair~~ Ar-tal-uck Tayou ~~1886~~
Residence: Flint District C.N. 1886

(2) English name: Ca Kaw Kah
Indian name:
Residence:

(3) English name: Malinda Adair
Indian name: A-lee 1881
Residence: Flint District Cher Nation

(4) English name: John B Adair
Indian name: Oo-u-tee
Residence: Sallisaw Cherokee Nation

(5) English name:
Indian name:
Residence:

20. Have you ever been enrolled for annuities, land, or other benefits? If so, state when and where. Nothing only Enrolled by the Dawes Commission for Allotments of Lands

6—624

Figure 17-6. Continued.

21. To expedite identification, claimants should give the full English and Indian names, if possible, of their paternal and maternal ancestors back to 1835: Unknown

REMARKS.

(Under this head the applicant may give any additional information that he believes will assist in proving his claims.)

My fathers name was changed from Arch Fields to Sixkiller, ~~father~~ taking fathers given name instead of his Sir Name

NOTE.—Answers should be brief but explicit; the words "Yes," "No," "Unknown," etc., may be used in cases where applicable. Read the questions carefully.

I solemnly swear that the foregoing statements made by me are true to the best of my knowledge and belief.

(*Signature.*) Samuel his x mark Sixkiller

Subscribed and sworn to before me this 8 day of Oct, 1906.

My commission expires

Nov. 21, 1908 Hugh M. Adair *Notary Public.*

AFFIDAVIT.

(The following affidavit must be sworn to by two or more witnesses who are well acquainted with the applicant.)

Personally appeared before me John B. Adair and John Houseberg, who, being duly sworn, on oath depose and say that they are well acquainted with Samuel Sixkiller, who makes the foregoing application and statements, and have known him for 55 years and 25 years, respectively, and know him to be the identical person he represents himself to be, and that the statements made by him are true, to the best of their knowledge and belief, and they have no interest whatever in his claim.

Witnesses to mark. Signatures of witnesses.

John B Adair

John Houseberg

Subscribed and sworn to before me this 8 day of Oct, 1906.

My commission expires

Nov. 21, 1908 Hugh M. Adair *Notary Public.*

NOTE.—Affidavits should be made, whenever practicable, before a notary public, clerk of the court, or before a person having a seal. If sworn to before an Indian agent or disbursing agent of the Indian service, it need not be executed before a notary, etc.

6—621

	Anny Big Feather	(761)
36	Ioe-hue-ka	
	Hawk	
	Cloud	
37	George Hughs, Sr.	
	Tah-lee-skie	
	Tow-wae-hee	
	Te-saw-we-skee	
38	Tune-wa-le-see	
	Isaac	
	Polly	
	Ach-enne	
	Ally	
39	Ah-ke-lo-hee	
	Sul-la-kee	
40	Jane Glenn	(1601-1683)
	George	(1601)
	Christopher	(1601)
	Edward	(1601)
	Nancy	(1601)
	Thompson	
	Amy	
41	Rachel	
	Ti-a-neh	
	Water-falling	
42	Charles Overtaker	
	Nelly	
43	Samuel	
	Johnson Lec	(16590)
	Toky	(16590)
	Alick	
44	Chu-wa-loo-kee	
	Jerry	
	Cun-la-we-skie	
	Se-cowie	
	Oo-cha-lun-na-hi	
45	Ben-about	
46	Arch Six Killer	

The 1851 Drennen Roll of the Cherokee Indians, p. 34; GS 970.1, A1 #31.

Earl Davis

A research case involving the Eastern Cherokees is equally interesting, taking place almost completely in Georgia. An act of Congress of 4 June 1924 (43 *Stat.* 376) providing for the final disposition of affairs of the Eastern Band of Cherokee, required a new census. Initially assigned to an Eastern Cherokee Enrolling Commission, it became, in 1928, the sole responsibility of Fred A. Baker, examiner of inheritance. His final report and roll were submitted on 1 December 1928 and approved in 1931 by the Secretary of the Interior. Between 1925 and 1928, the Eastern Cherokee Enrolling Commission received and considered applications for enrollment. The decisions concerning applicants claiming descent from the same ancestor are arranged alphabetically by surname of the ancestor.

The decision of the Enrolling Commission in the case of Earl Davis is twenty-six pages long and lists ninety-five applicants who claimed a common ancestor, in this case, Rachel Martin Davis and Coleman J. Davis. Earl Davis, Sr., was number 873.

According to the testimony of his application, Earl Davis, Sr., one of the oldest, was born in 1861 at Dahlonega, Lumpkin County, Georgia, where he had spent his life. His mother was white and his father was one-eighth Cherokee through his paternal grandmother, Rachel, who was one-fourth Cherokee.

Earl had received money in 1910 as had several other relatives who were on the Guion Miller Roll. They had also been enrolled by Hester (1884), Swetland (1868-9), Chapman (1852), and Henderson (1835).

Rachel is not identified on the Henderson roll of 1835 since only the head of the family was named. According to the family, Rachel was married to Daniel Davis, also of Lumpkin County, who was listed as an "intermarried" white man. Since "one member of his family is enrolled as a reservee," his ten children are enrolled as "descendants of reservees." Daniel Davis and his family had taken the option of acquiring a farm and staying in the county where they had all been born. The commission took a dim view of this multigenerational separation from the ancestral band and rejected the application. The important thing for the researcher is the amazingly detailed genealogical information that can be gleaned from this document and the various rolls upon which members of the family appeared.

The information on Earl's application, for instance, provides the exact date and place of his birth, as well as those of his parents, brothers and sisters, and the approximate date of death for his aunts and uncles. Earl must have visited Indian Territory (Oklahoma) at least once as he was enrolled at Vinita, Indian Territory, in 1893. The Supplemental Application for Minor Children lists the names and dates of birth of his children. On the last page, Earl adds, "my Grandfather Daniel Davis was married to Rachel Martin Nov. 1st 1808. She was the youngest daughter of John Martin of Virginia."

Interestingly, in keeping with the commission's ultimate decision, Earl Davis does not describe himself as an Indian on the 1910 census. He lived in a white community and was married to a white woman. Because he was not on a reservation, he appears in the same federal censuses as other non-Indians.

Just as interesting is the fact that Earl's family and his ancestors are found in *both* the records of the Cherokee nation and the records of local jurisdiction in Lumpkin County, Georgia. The 1850 federal census of Davis District shows the family of Daniel Davis (Earl's grandfather), but without Rachel his mother, and the family of Earl's father. Daniel left a will in which he mentions Earl among "the rest of my heirs" and Earl's death record is preserved in the county. He died 26 March 1937 at the age of seventy-six. Incidentally, his race is given as white.

Although Indian genealogy could hardly be described as trouble-free, these examples from a very narrow segment of the total records described in this chapter, will show that one of the pleasant surprises may be, precisely, how many records are available.

Bibliography

General Reference Guides

Bledsoe, Samuel T. *Indian Land Laws, Being a Treatise on Indian Land Titles in Oklahoma*. Kansas City, Mo.: Venn Law Books, 1913.

Curtis, Mary B. "Five Civilized Tribes: The Cherokee, Chickasaw, Choctaw, Creek, and Seminole Indians." *Magazine of Bibliographies* 1 (1972): whole issue. Also available separately as *Bibliography of the Five Civilized Tribes*. Fort Worth: Magazine of Bibliographies, 1973. Available from 1209 Clover Lane, Fort Worth, TX 76107.

Dockstadter, Frederick J. *The American Indian in Graduate Studies: A Bibliography of Theses and Dissertations*. New York: Museum of the American Indians, 1967.

Ethnogeographic Guide to the Indian Claims Commission Papers. New York: Clearwater Publishing Company, 1975.

Hargrett, Lester. *Bibliography of the Constitution and Laws of the American Indians*. New York: Oklahoma Imprints, 1951.

Heard, J. Norman, *An Annotated Bibliography of the Indians North of Mexico and South of Canada*. Ph.D. diss., Lousiana State University, 1967.

Henry, Jeanette, ed. *The Indian Historian Press: Index to Literature on the American Indian.* San Francisco: For the press, 1970-____. Annual. Includes tribal publications.

Hill, Edward E., comp. *Guide to Records in the National Archives of the United States Relating to American Indians.* Washington, D.C.: NARS, 1981.

___________. *The Office of Indian Affairs, 1824-1880: Historical Sketches.* New York: Clearwater Publishing Company, 1974.

___________, *Preliminary Inventory of the Records of the Bureau of Indian Affairs.* 2 vols. Washington, D.C.: NARS, 1965.

Hodge, Frederick W., ed. *Handbook of American Indians North of Mexico.* 2 vols. 1907-10; reprint ed., New York: Pageant Books, 1959. Includes alphabetical listing of all North American Tribes.

Housman, Reginald. *Expansion and American Indian Policy, 1783-1812.* East Lansing, Mich.: Michigan State University Press, 1967.

"Indian Cessions Within the Northwest Territory." *Illinois Libraries* 61 (June 1979): whole issue. Includes maps, index to treaties, other valuable materials for Illinois.

Indians of the Americas: A Bibliography. Regina, Saskatchewan: Provincial Library, 1973.

Jackson, Curtis E., and Marcia J. Galli. *A History of the Bureau of Indian Affairs and Its Activities Among Indians.* San Francisco: R & E Research Associates, 1977.

Johnson, Steven L. *Guide to American Indian Documents in the Congressional Serial Set: 1817-1899.* New York: Clearwater Publishing Co., 1977.

Kappler, Charles Joseph. *Indian Treaties, 1778-1883.* New York: Interland Publishing Company, 1973.

Kawashima, Yash. "Legal Origins of the Indian Reservation in Colonial Massachusetts." *American Journal of Legal History* 13 (1969): 42-56. Helpful for New England Indian background.

Morris, John W., et al. *Historical Atlas of Oklahoma.* 2nd ed. Norman: University of Oklahoma Press, 1976.

Prucha, Francis Paul. *American Indian Policy in the Formative Years: The Indian Trade and Intercourse Acts, 1790-1834.* Lincoln: University of Nebraska Press, 1962.

___________. *American Indian Policy in Crisis: Christian Reformers and the Indian, 1865-1900.* Norman: University of Oklahoma Press, 1976.

Ruth, Kent. *Great Day in the West: Forts, Posts, and Rendezvous Beyond the Mississippi.* Norman: University of Oklahoma Press, 1975.

Schmeckebier, Laurence Frederick. *The Office of Indian Affairs.* Baltimore: The Johns Hopkins Press, 1927.

Schoolcraft, Henry R. *Historical and Statistical Information Respecting the History, Condition and Prospects of the Indian Tribes of the United States.* Philadelphia, 1851. 7 vols. This collection performed a very important service for Indian history in collecting and preserving an immense amount of history: vocabularies of Indian languages, legends of various tribes, biographies of chiefs and warriors, emigrations and theories of origin.

Shirk, George. *Oklahoma Place Names.* Norman: University of Oklahoma Press, 1976.

Shorey Publications on the Pacific Northwest, the West, Alaska, and the Indians. Reprints of scarce and rare materials at reasonable prices. Write for current catalog to Shorey Book Store, 110 Union Street, Box 21616, Seattle, WA 98111.

Smith, Dwight L. *Indians of the United States and Canada: A Bibliography.* 2 vols. Santa Barbara: ABC-CLIO. 1974, 1983. Invaluable index to some 5,000 periodical articles from the *America: History and Life* database. Each entry is annotated.

Smith, Jane F., and Robert M. Kvasnicka. *Indian-White Relations, A Persistent Paradox.* Washington, D.C.: Howard University Press, 1976.

Swanton, John R. *The Indian Tribes of North America.* Washington, D.C.: Smithsonian Institute Press, 1952, reprint ed. 1974.

U.S. Department of Commerce. *Federal and State Indian Reservations and Indian Trust Areas.* Washington, D.C.: U.S. Government Printing Office, nd.

U. S. Department of the Interior. *Biographical and Historical Index of American Indians and Persons Involved in Indian Affairs.* 8 vols. Boston: G. K. Hall, 1966.

Vestal, Stanley. *New Sources of Indian History, 1850-1891: A Miscellany.* Norman: University of Oklahoma Press, 1934.

White, Joy Vincent. *Taxing Those They Found Here: An Examination of the Tax Exempt Status of the American Indian.* Albuquerque, N.M.: Institute for the Development of Indian Law, 1972.

Wissler, Clark. *Indians of the United States; Four Centuries of Their History and Culture.* 1940; reprint ed., Garden City, N.Y.: Doubleday, 1966. 319 pp. Illustrated, bibliography.

Wright, Muriel H. *A Guide to the Indian Tribes of Oklahoma.* Norman: University of Oklahoma Press, 1971. Includes a list of early articles relating to Indians in *Chronicles of Oklahoma* (quarterly published by Oklahoma Historical Society, 1921-____.); excellent maps of Indian and Oklahoma Territories showing lands occupied by Commanche, Kiowa, Apache, Quapaw, Peoria, Ottawa, Shawnee, Modoc, Wyandot, Seneca, Cheyenne, Arapahoe, Sac and Fox, Iowa, Ponca, Otto, Missouri, Kaw, Pawnee.

Printed Sources

American State Paper. Washington, D.C.: Gales and Seaton, 1832-1861. Of particular interest are Class II – Indian Affairs, and Class V – Military Affairs.

Baker, Jack D., trans. *Cherokee Emigration Rolls, 1817-1835.* Oklahoma City: Baker Publishing Co., 1977.

Campbell, John B. *Campbell's Abstract of Creek Indian Census Cards and Index.* Muskogee, 1915. 430 pp.

Carter, Clarence E., comp. and ed. *Territorial Papers of the U.S.* Washington, D.C.: U.S. Government Printing Office, 1934-62. 26 vols.

Fries, Adelaide L., ed. *Records of the Moravians in North Carolina, 1752-1820.* Raleigh: North Carolina Historical Commission, 1922-43. 7 vols.

Hastain, E. *Index to Choctaw-Chickasaw Deeds and Allotments.* Muskogee: n.p., 1908.

___________. *Hastain's Township Plats of the Seminole Nation.* Muskogee: n.p., 1913.

___________. *Hastain's Township Plats of the Creek Nation.* Muskogee: n.p., n.d. Available Oklahoma Historical Society.

McGhee, Lucy Kate. *Historical Records of the Cherokee Indians Compiled to Honor the Famous Indian Woman, Nancy Ward, of Tennessee and Her Noted Uncle, Atta Cullaculla and Son-in-Law, General Joseph Martin and Daughter, Mrs. General Joseph (Betsy Ward) Martin.* Washington: n.d. Records were taken from Volume 1, Cherokee Minute Docket of the 4th Commission in Washington, D.C., which met in Washington 1846-47 under the Treaty of 1835-36. Contains references to marriages and other Indian family data.

___________. *Cherokee Walkers: Claims of People by the Name of Walker Intermarried with the Cherokee Indians.* Washington, D.C.: For the author, 1958-59. 3 vols. Vol. 1 has title, *Eastern Cherokee Walkers.* 62 pp. This was coedited by Annie Walker Burns.

North American Indians. Microform publications on more than seventy tribes including oral history, out-of-print books, periodicals, pamphlets; Indian Rights Association Papers, 1864-1973; bulletins and reports of the Smithsonian Institute Bureau of American Ethnology. Write for catalogs, University Microfilms, 300 Zeeb Road, Ann Arbor, MI 48106.

Thwaites, Reuben G., ed. *The Jesuit Relations and Allied Documents: Travels and Explorations of the Jesuit Missionaries in New France, 1610-1791.* 73 vols. Cleveland: 1896-1901. Original text in French, Latin, or Italian with parallel English translations, bibliography, notes, and some facsimiles. Includes Lousiana, Illinois, New York, and New England areas. See analysis in Lawrence C. Wroth, "The Jesuit Relations from New France," Papers of the Bibliographical Society of America 30 (1936): 110-49.

Tyner, James W., and Alice Tyner Timmons, comp. *Our People and Where They Rest.* Norman: American Indian Institute, University of Oklahoma, c1969-82. 11 vols. Tombstone inscriptions and death documents.

Wallace, Paul A. W. "The Moravian Records." *Indiana Magazine of History* 48 (1952): 141-60.

Washburn, Wilcomb E., ed. *The American Indian and the United States: A Documentary History.* 4 vols. Westport, Conn.: Random House, Inc., 1973. Comprehensive research collection of 216 reports, treaties, laws, judicial decisions affecting the American Indian.

Winfrey, Dorman H., ed. *The Indian Papers of Texas and the Southwest, 1825-1916.* Austin: Texas State Library, 1959-66. 5 vols.

Impact of American Indian Policy on Individual Tribes

Berthong, Donald J. *The Southern Cheyenne*. Norman: University of Oklahoma Press, 1963.

Corkran, David H. *Carolina Indian Frontier*. Columbia: University of South Carolina, 1970. 70 pp.

___________. *The Cherokee Frontier; A Conflict and Survival 1740-1762*. 1961; reprint ed. Norman: University of Oklahoma Press, 1966. 302 pp. Illustrated, bibliography.

___________. *Creek Frontier, 1540-1783*. Norman: University of Oklahoma Press, 1967.

Corn, James F. *Red Clay of Rattlesnake Springs: A History of the Cherokee Indians of Bradley County, Tennessee*. Cleveland, 1959. 108 pp. Bibliography.

Cotterill, Robert S. *The Southern Indians: The Story of the Civilized Tribes Before Removal*. 2nd ed. Norman: University of Oklahoma Press, 1971.

Dale, Edward E. *The Indians of the Southwest: A Century of Development Under the United States*. Norman: University of Oklahoma Press, 1976.

___________. *Cherokee Cavaliers: Forty Years of Cherokee History as Told in the Correspondence of the Ridge-Watie-Boudinot Family*. Norman: University of Oklahoma Press, 1969.

Debo, Angie. *A History of the Indians of the United States*. Norman: University of Oklahoma Press, 1977.

___________. *The Rise and Fall of the Choctaw Republic*. 2nd ed. Norman: University of Oklahoma Press, 1972.

___________. *And Still the Waters Run*. Princeton: Princeton University Press, 1940. 417 pp. Map, bibliography. An account of the liquidation of the Five Civilized Tribes of the Indian Territory.

___________. *The Five Civilized Tribes*. Philadelphia: J. B. Lippincott, 1951. 35 pp. Sequel to *And Still the Waters Run*.

de Charlevoix, P. F. X. *History and General Description of New France*. Chicago, 1962. 6 vols. Translated with notes by John G. Shea.

De Rosier, Arthur H., Jr. *The Removal of the Choctaw Indians*. Knoxville: University of Tennessee Press, 1970.

Devorsey, Louis. *The Indian Boundary in the Southern Colonies, 1763-1775*. Chapel Hill: University of North Carolina, 1966. 280 pp.

Dorn, Edward. *The Shoshoneans: The People of Basin-Plateau*. New York: Morrow, 1966.

Foreman, Carolyn T. *Indians Abroad*. Norman: University of Oklahoma Press, 1963.

___________. *Indian Women Chiefs*. Muskogee: For the author, 1954.

Foreman, Grant. *Advancing the Frontier 1830-1860*. 2nd ed. Norman: University of Oklahoma Press, 1968.

___________. *A History of Oklahoma*. Norman: University of Oklahoma Press, 1942.

___________. *Fort Gibson*. Norman: University of Oklahoma Press, 1936.

___________. *The Five Civilized Tribes*. Norman: University of Oklahoma Press, 1974.

___________. *Indian Removal: The Emigration of the Five Civilized Tribes*. Norman: University of Oklahoma Press, 1975.

___________. *Indians and Pioneers*. Norman: University of Oklahoma Press, 1937.

Fritz, Henry E. *The Movement for Indian Assimilation, 1860-90*. Philadelphia: University of Pennsylvania Press, 1963. 244 pp.

Gibson, Arrell M. *The Chickasaws*. Norman: University of Oklahoma Press, 1979.

___________, and Edwin C. Bears. *The Kickapoos: Lords of the Middle Border*. Norman: University of Oklahoma Press, 1969.

Graebner, Norman A. "Public Land Policy of the Five Civilized Tribes," *Chronicles of Oklahoma* 23 (1945-46): 107-18. Excellent study.

Gray, Elma E. *Wilderness Christians: The Moravian Mission to the Delaware Indians*. 1956; Reprint ed., New York: Russell and Russell, 1973. 354 pp.

Gunnerson, Dolores A. *The Jicarilla Apaches*. Dekalb, Ill.: Northern Illinois University Press, 1972.

Guttmann, Allen. *States' Rights and Indian Removal: The Cherokee Nation v. The State of Georgia*. Lexington, 1965. 94 pp. Bibliography. A brief but excellent work on the origins of American Indian policy from the removal controversy to the historical debate of the present time. Quotations from the documents of the period are the major part of the book.

Haines, Frances. *The Nez Percés: Tribesmen of the Columbia Plateau*. Norman: University of Oklahoma, 1955.

Hewes, Leslie. "The Oklahoma Ozarks as the Land of the Cherokees." *Genealogical Review* 32 (1942): 269-81.

Hoebel, Edward A. *The Cheyennes; Indians of the Great Plains*. New York: Holt, 1960. 103 pp.

Hyde, George. *Red Cloud's Folk: A History of the Ogallala Sioux Indians*. Norman: University of Oklahoma Press, 1937.

Jacobs, Wilbur R. *Dispossessing the American Indian*. New York: Scribner's, 1972.

___________. *Indians and Whites on America's Early Frontier*. New York: Scribner's, n.d.

___________. *Indians of the Southern Frontier*. Columbia: University of South Carolina Press, 1945.

___________. *Wilderness Politics and Indian Gifts, the Northern Colonial Frontier, 1748-1761*. Stanford, Calif.: Stanford University Press, 1950.

Johnson, Neil R. *The Chickasaw Rancher*. Stillwater: Redlands Press, 1961.

Johnson, Row M. *Oklahoma History South of the Canadian [River]*. Chicago: University of Chicago Press, 1925. 3 vols.

Kelly, Lawrence C. *The Navajo Indians and Federal Indian Policy, 1900-1935*. Tucson: University of Arizona Press, 1968.

Lumpkin, Wilson. *The Removal of the Cherokee Indians from Georgia*. 2 vols. New York: For the author, 1907. Includes some first-hand accounts.

McReynolds, Edwin. *Oklahoma, A History of the Sooner State*. Norman: University of Oklahoma Press, 1976.

___________. *The Seminoles*. Norman: University of Oklahoma Press, 1957. 397 pp. Maps, bibliography.

Malone, Henry T. *Cherokees of the Old South*. Athens: University of Georgia, 1956. 238 pp. Bibliography.

Malone, James H. *The Chickasaw Nation*. Louisville, 1922. 537 pp. Maps, bibliography. The first six chapters were printed for private distribution in 1919.

Mathews, John Joseph. *The Osages: Children of the Middle Waters*. Norman: University of Oklahoma Press, 1961.

Mayhall, Mildred P. *The Kiowas*. 2nd ed. Norman: University of Oklahoma Press, 1971.

Newe. *A Western Shoshone History*. Reno: Intertribal Council of Nevada, 1976.

O'Beirne, Harry F., comp. *Leaders and Leading Men of the Indian Territory*. Chicago: n.p., 1891. 328 pp. With interesting biographical sketches and brief history of Choctaws and Chickasaws. 200 portraits.

O'Beirne, Harry F., and E. S. O'Beirne. *The Indian Territory: Its Chiefs, Legislators, and Leading Men*. St. Louis: n.p., 1892. 485 pp. Page 82 notes that the first halfbreed Cherokee was born in North Virginia as far back as 1620 and was the son of an Irish adventurer named Dogherty.

O'Donnell, James H. "The Virginia Expedition Against the Overhill Cherokee, 1776." *East Tennessee Historical Society Publications* 39 (1967): 13-25.

O'Neil, Floyd A. "An Anguished Odyssey: The Flight of the Utes, 1906-08." *Utah Historical Quarterly* 36 (Fall 1968): 315-27.

Otis, D. S. *The Dawes Act and the Allotment of Indian Land*. Norman: University of Oklahoma Press, 1973.

Peake, Ora Brooks. *A History of the United States Indian Factory System: 1795-1822*. Denver: For the author, 1954.

Rister, Carl C. *Baptist Missions Among the American Indians*. Atlanta: For the author, 1944.

Schell, Herbert S. *History of South Dakota*. Lincoln: University of Nebraska, 1961. Includes a detailed discussion of Plains Indians.

Semple, W. F. *Oklahoma Indian Land Titles Annotated*. St. Louis: Thomas Law Books, 1952.

Seymour, Flora W. *Indian Agents of the Old Frontier*. New York, 1941. 402 pp.

Sherer, Lorraine, M. *The Clan System of the Fort Mojave Indians*. Los Angeles: Ward Ritchie Press, 1965. 85 pp.

Thompson, Gregory C. *Southern Ute Lands, 1848-1899: The Creation of a Reservation*. Durango, Colo.: Fort Lewis, 1977.

Williams, Samuel C. *Beginnings of West Tennessee in the Land of the Chickasaws, 1541-1841*. Johnson City: For the author, 1930.

Woodward, Grace S. *The Cherokees*. Norman: University of Oklahoma, 1963. 359 pp.

Genealogical Applications

Allen, John R. "18th Century Cherokee Archives." *American Archivist* 5 (1942): 2-44.

Bell, George M. *Genealogy of the "Old" and the New Cherokee Indian Families*. Bartlesville, Okla.: For the author, 1972.

Clark, Dick. *Cherokee Ancestor Research*. Modesto, Calif.: Rich-Nor-Lin Publications, 1979.

Faux, David. "Documenting Six Nations Indian Ancestry." *Families* 20 (1981): 31-42.

"Indians of Southern Virginia, 1650-1711: Depositions in the Virginia and North Carolina Boundary Case." *Virginia Magazine of History and Biography* 7 (1899-1900): 337-58; 8 (1900-01): 1-11.

Jordan, Julia A. "Oklahoma's Oral History Collection: New Sources for Indian History." *Chronicles of Oklahoma* 69 (1971).

Kirkham, E. Kay, comp. "The American Indian Census Rolls, 1885-1940 (NARS M595)." 1978. Typescript register to Record Group 75 with Genealogical Society of Utah call numbers and alphabetical tribe/ band index. Copies available at Genealogical Society of Utah and at branch libraries on request.

___________. "The American Indian and His Records of Genealogical Value." *Genealogical Helper*, May-June 1979, pp. 5-7.

___________. *Our Native Americans and Their Records of Genealogical Value*. 2 vols. Logan, Utah, Everton Publishers, 1980-83. Covers federal records, Oklahoma Historical Society, and the Genealogical Society of Utah.

"The Lost Archives of the Cherokee Nation, 1763-1772," *East Tennessee Historical Society Publications*. 43 (1971): 112-22. This is Part 1. The study continues for several issues.

McEvers, Julie. *Indian Genealogy: A Guidebook to Native American Ancestry*. New Orleans, La.: Polyanthos, 1978. 300 pp.

Parker, Jimmy B. "American Indian Genealogical Records." *National Genealogical Society Quarterly* 63 (March 1975): 15-21.

___________. "American Indian Records and Research." In Jessie Carney Smith, ed. *Ethnic Genealogy: A Research Guide*. Westport, Conn.: Greenwood Press, 1983, pp. 210-38.

___________. "The Cherokee Phoenix," *American Genealogist* 51 (1975): 136-41. Newspaper that printed vital records.

___________. "Sources of American Indian Genealogy." *Genealogical Journal* 6 (Sept. 1977): 120-25.

Spindel, Donna. *Introductory Guide to Indian-Related Records (to 1876) in the North Carolina State Archives*. Raleigh: North Carolina State Division of Archives and History, 1977.

Younkin, C. George. *Historical and Genealogical Records of the Five Civilized Tribes and Other Indian Records*. Salt Lake City: World Conference on Records, 1969.

___________. "Searching for American Indian Genealogy." *Stirpes* 17 (1977): 167-82.

Appendix 1

Bureau of Indian Affairs Field Office Records

School or Agency	*Location*
Aberdeen Area Office	FARC Kansas City
Abiquiu and Cimarron Agencies	FARC Denver
Albuquerque Indian School	FARC Denver
Anadarko Area Office	FARC Fort Worth
Arapaho, Cheyenne (and agency)	FARC Fort Worth
Bannock, Shoshone (and agency)	
(Wind River Agency)	FARC Denver
(Fort Hall Agency)	FARC Seattle
Billings Area Office	FARC Seattle
Birch Cooley School (Pipestone Indian School)	FARC Kansas City
Bismarck Indian School	FARC Kansas City
Blackfeet Agency	FARC Seattle and FARC Denver
California Agency (Sacramento Area Office)	FARC San Francisco
California Agency (Riverside Area Field Office)	FARC Los Angeles
Camp Apache Agency (Fort Apache Agency)	FARC Los Angeles
Camp McDowell Agency (Pima Agency)	FARC Los Angeles
Canton Asylum for Insane Indians (Pipestone Indian School)	FARC Kansas City
Cantonment Agency (Conho Agency)	FARC Fort Worth
Carlisle Indian Industrial School	National Archives
Carson School and Agency	FARC San Francisco
Carter and Laona Agencies	FARC Chicago
Charles G. Burke Indian School	FARC Denver
Chamberlain Indian School	National Archives
Chemawa Indian School	FARC Seattle
Cherokee Agency, East	National Archives
Cherokee Agency, North Carolina	FARC Atlanta
Cherokee Agency, West	National Archives
Cheyenne and Arapaho Agency (Concho Agency)	FARC Fort Worth
Cheyenne River Agency	FARC Kansas City
Chickasaw Agency, East	National Archives
Chilocco Indian School	FARC Fort Worth
Chocktaw Agency, East	National Archives
Cimarron Agency (Abiquiu Agency)	FARC Denver
Coeur d'Alene Agency (Colville Agency)	FARC Seattle
Colorado River Agency	FARC Los Angeles
Colville Agency	FARC Seattle
Concho Agency	FARC Fort Worth
Consolidated Chippewa Agency	FARC Kansas City and National Archives
Choctaw and Chickasaw Agency (Muskogee Area Office)	National Archives
Creek Agency, East	National Archives
Crow Creek Agency	FARC Kansas City
Cushman School (Puyallup Agency)	FARC Seattle

Reprinted from *Guide to Genealogical Research* in the National Archives (Washington, D.C.: NARS, 1982), pp. 163-67. Names in parentheses are how the agency is mentioned in Edward E. Hill, *Guide to Records in the National Archives Relating to American Indians* (Washington, D.C., NARS, 1981).

School or Agency	*Location*
Devil's Lake Agency (Fort Totten Agency)	FARC Kansas City
Digger Agency	FARC San Francisco
Fallon School and Agency	FARC San Francisco
Five Civilized Tribes Agency (Muskogee Area Office)	FARC Fort Worth
Flandreau School and Agency	FARC Kansas City
Flathead Agency	FARC Seattle
Fond du Lac Agency (Red Lake Agency)	FARC Kansas City and FARC Chicago
Fort Apache Agency	FARC Los Angeles
Fort Belknap Agency	FARC Seattle
Fort Berthold Agency	FARC Kansas City
Fort Bidwell School and Agency	FARC San Francisco
Fort Bridger Agency (Wind River Agency)	FARC Denver
Fort Defiance Subagency (Navajo Agencies)	FARC Denver
Fort Hall Agency	FARC Seattle
Fort Lapwai Agency (Northern Idaho Agency)	FARC Seattle
Fort Lewis Indian School	FARC Denver
Fort Peck Agency	FARC Seattle
Fort McDermitt Agency (Reno Agency)	FARC San Francisco
Fort Mohave School (Colorado River Agency)	FARC Los Angeles
Fort Shaw Indian School	National Archives
Fort Totten Agency	FARC Kansas City
Fort Yuma Agency	FARC Los Angeles
Fox Day School (Sac and Fox Agency)	FARC Chicago
Gila River Agency (Pima Agency)	FARC Los Angeles
Grand Portage School (Consolidated Chippewa Agency)	National Archives
Grand Rapids Agency	FARC Chicago
Grand River Agency (Standing Rock Agency)	FARC Kansas City
Grand Ronde-Siletz Agency	FARC Seattle
Great Lakes Consolidated Agency	FARC Chicago
Great Nemaha Agency (Potawatomi Agency)	FARC Kansas City
Green Bay Agency (Menominee Agencies)	FARC Chicago
Greenville School and Agency	FARC San Francisco
Haskell Institute	FARC Kansas City
Hayward Indian School	FARC Chicago
Hoopa Valley Agency	FARC San Francisco
Hope School (Springfield School)	National Archives
Hopi Agency	FARC Los Angeles
Horton Agency (Potawatomi Agency)	FARC Kansas City
Jicarilla Agency	FARC Denver
Juneau Area Office	FARC Seattle
Kansas Agency (Potawatomi Agency)	FARC Kansas City
Kaw Agency (Pawnee Agency)	FARC Fort Worth
Keshena Agency (Menominee Agency)	FARC Chicago
Kickapoo Agency (Potawatomi Agency)	FARC Kansas City
Kiowa Agency (Anadarko Area Office)	FARC Fort Worth
Klamath Agency	FARC Seattle
Lac du Flambeau Agency and School	FARC Chicago
Laguna Sanatorium	FARC Denver
Laona Agency (Great Lakes Consolidated Agency)	FARC Chicago
LaPointe Agency (Hayward Indian School and Lac du Flambeau Agency)	FARC Chicago
Leech Lake Agency	National Archives and FARC Kansas City
Lemhi Agency (Fort Hall Agency)	FARC Seattle
Leupp Training School (Navajo Agencies)	FARC Denver
Lovelocks School (Fallon School)	FARC San Francisco
Lower Brulé Agency	FARC Kansas City
Mackinac Agency	FARC Chicago
Malheur Agency	National Archives
Menominee Agencies, Minneapolis Area Office	FARC Kansas City
Menominee Agencies in Wisconsin	FARC Chicago
Mescalero Agency	FARC Denver
Mesquakie Day School (Sac and Fox Agency)	FARC Chicago
Miami Agency	FARC Fort Worth
Milk River Agency (Fort Peck Agency)	FARC Seattle
Minneapolis Area Office	FARC Kansas City
Minnesota Agency	FARC Kansas City
Mission Tule River Agency (Pala Subagency)	FARC Los Angeles
Moqui Pueblo Agency	National Archives
Mount Pleasant Indian School	FARC Chicago
Muskogee Area Office	FARC Fort Worth and National Archives
Navajo Agencies	FARC Denver and Los Angeles
Neah Bay Agency (Taholah Agency)	FARC Seattle
Neosha Agency (Miami Agency)	FARC Fort Worth
Nett Lake Agency	National Archives and FARC Kansas City
Nevada Agency	FARC San Francisco
New York Agency	National Archives
Nez Perce Agency (Northern Idaho Agency)	FARC Seattle
Nisqually and Skokomish Agency (Puyallup Agency)	FARC Seattle
Northern Cheyenne Agency	FARC Seattle
Northern Idaho Agency	FARC Seattle
Northern Pueblos Agency	FARC Denver
Oakland Agency (Pawnee Agency)	FARC Fort Worth
Omaha Agency (Winnebago Agency)	FARC Kansas City
Oneida School and Agency	FARC Chicago

School or Agency	*Location*
Osage Agency	FARC Fort Worth
Otoe Agency (Pawnee Agency)	FARC Fort Worth
Ouray Agency (Uintah and Ouray Agency)	FARC Denver
Pala Subagency	FARC Los Angeles
Palm Springs Agency	FARC Los Angeles
Papago Agency	FARC Los Angeles
Paiute Agency (Uintah and Ouray Agency)	FARC Denver
Pawnee Agency	FARC Fort Worth
Pechanga Agency (Pala Subagency)	FARC Los Angeles
Phoenix Area Office	FARC Los Angeles
Pierre Agency	FARC Kansas City
Pierre Indian School	FARC Kansas City
Pima Agency	FARC Los Angeles
Pine Ridge Agency	FARC Kansas City
Pipestone Indian School	FARC Kansas City
Ponca Agency (Pawnee Agency)	FARC Fort Worth
(Winnebago Agency)	FARC Kansas City
Portland Area Office	FARC Seattle
Potawatomi Agency	FARC Kansas City
Prairie du Chien Agency (Winnebago Agency)	FARC Kansas City
Pueblo and Pueblo and Jicarilla Agencies	FARC Denver
Pueblo Day Schools at Albuquerque and Santa Fe	FARC Denver
Pueblo Indian Agency and Pueblo Day Schools	FARC Denver
Puget Sound District Agency	FARC Seattle
Puyallup Agency and Cushman School	FARC Seattle
Quapaw Agency (Miami Agency)	FARC Fort Worth
Quinaielt Agency (Puyallup Agency)	FARC Seattle
Rapid City Indian School	FARC Kansas City
Red Cliff School and Agency	FARC Chicago
Red Cloud Agency (Pine Ridge Agency)	FARC Kansas City
Red Lake Agency	FARC Kansas City
Red Moon Agency (Concho Agency)	FARC Fort Worth
Reno Agency	FARC San Francisco
Rice Boarding School (San Carlos Agency)	FARC Los Angeles
Riggs Institute (Flandreau School)	FARC Kansas City
Riverside Area Field Office	FARC Los Angeles
Rosebud Agency	FARC Kansas City
Roseburg Agency	FARC San Francisco
Round Valley Agency	FARC San Francisco
Sac and Fox Agency and Sanatorium	FARC Chicago
Sacramento Agency and Area Office	FARC San Francisco
Salem (Chemawa) School (Grand Ronde-Siletz Agency)	FARC Seattle
San Carlos Agency	FARC Los Angeles
San Jacinto Agency (Tule River Agency)	FARC San Francisco
Santa Fe Indian School	FARC Denver
Santee Agency (Flandreau Agency)	FARC Kansas City
Seger Agency (Concho Agency)	FARC Fort Worth
Seminole Agency, Florida	FARC Atlanta
Seneca School (Miami Agency)	FARC Fort Worth
Shawnee Agency in Oklahoma	FARC Fort Worth
Sherman Institute	FARC Los Angeles
Shiprock Boarding School (Navajo Agencies)	FARC Denver
Shiprock Subagency (Navajo Agencies)	FARC Los Angeles
Shoshone and Bannock Agency (Wind River Agency)	FARC Denver
Siletz Agency (Grand Ronde-Siletz Agency)	FARC Seattle
(Roseburg Agency)	FARC San Francisco
Sioux Sanatorium	FARC Kansas City
Sisseton Agency	FARC Kansas City
Six Nations Agency (New York Agency)	National Archives
Skokomish Agency (Tulalip Agency)	FARC Seattle
Southern Apache Agency	National Archives
Southern Mission Agency (Pala Subagency)	FARC Los Angeles
Southern Pueblos Agency	FARC Denver
Southern Ute and Consolidated Ute Agencies	FARC Denver
Spokane Agency	FARC Seattle
Spotted Tail Agency (Rosebud Agency)	FARC Kansas City
Springfield (Hope) Indian School	National Archives
Standing Rock Agency	FARC Kansas City
Taholah Agency	FARC Seattle
Toadlena Day School	FARC Denver
Tomah Indian School and Agency	FARC Chicago
Tongue River Agency (Northern Cheyenne Agency)	FARC Seattle
Truxton Canyon Agency	FARC Los Angeles
Tuba City Subagency	FARC Los Angeles
Tulalip Agency	FARC Seattle
Tule River Agency	FARC San Francisco
Turtle Mountain Agency	FARC Kansas City
Uintah and Ouray Agency	FARC Denver
Umatilla Agency	FARC Seattle
United Pueblos Agency	FARC Denver
Union Agency (Muskogee Area Office)	National Archives
Utah Agency (Abiquiu Agency)	FARC Denver
Upper Arkansas Agency (Concho Agency)	FARC Fort Worth
Upper Missouri Agency (Crow Creek Agency)	FARC Kansas City
Upper Platte Agency (Rosebud Agency)	FARC Kansas City
Vermillion Lake Agency	FARC Chicago
Vermillion Lake School (Nett Lake Agency)	National Archives
Wahpeton Indian School	FARC Kansas City
Walker River Agency	FARC San Francisco
Warm Springs Agency	FARC Seattle
Western Shoshone Agency	FARC San Francisco
Western Washington Agency (Taholah and Tulalip Agencies)	FARC Seattle
Whetstone Agency (Rosebud Agency)	FARC Kansas City
White Earth Agency	National Archives and FARC Kansas City

School or Agency	Location
White River Agency (Lower Brulé Agency)	FARC Kansas City
Wichita Agency (Anadarko Area Office)	FARC Fort Worth
Window Rock Area Office (Navajo Agencies)	FARC Denver and FARC Los Angeles
Wind River Agency	FARC Denver
Winnebago Agency	FARC Kansas City
Wittenberg Agency	National Archives
Yakima Agency	FARC Seattle
Yankton Agency	FARC Kansas City
Zuni Agency	FARC Denver

INFORMATION GUIDE

Genealogical Information in the Record Group	*Census*	*Citizenship*	*Land Grants*	*Mission Register*	*Land Claims*	*Government Correspondence*
Surname/name	●	●	●	●	●	●
Date of Birth				●		
Place of Birth	●	●	●	●	●	●
Sex	●	●		●	●	
Race/color	●	●		●	●	●
Physical Description						
Occupation	●	●	●	●	●	●
Education						
Military Service	●		●		●	●
Slave Status	●	●		●	●	●
Property Owned			●		●	●
Religion				●	●	
Citizenship	●	●	●		●	●
Marital Status	●	●	●	●	●	●
Spouse's Name	●		●	●	●	
Children's Names	●		●	●	●	
Father's Name			●	●	●	
Mother's Name				●	●	
Father's Birthplace					●	
Mother's Birthplace					●	
Date of Death				●	●	●
Cause of Death				●	●	
Name of Cemetery				●		
Residence	●	●	●	●	●	●
Age	●	●	●	●	●	●
Literacy/signature				●		●
Photograph/sketch						
Relatives				●	●	

COULD YOU USE THIS CHAPTER?

Type of Record	*Kept from*	*Clues That You Should Consult These Records*
Spanish archives and local records	Sixteenth to eighteenth certuries	If you can trace an ancestor into the present states of Texas, New Mexico, Arizona, and California to the time period before these areas became part of the United States, a wealth of information has been preserved. Families can be reconstructed from wills and land records, while provincial histories and court records of many kinds will document movements, purchases, and dates of birth, marriage, and death. A reading knowledge of Spanish is helpful but not essential in all cases since many of the documents have been translated or indexed or the essential information can thus be extracted with the aid of a Spanish-English dictionary.
Catholic mission records	About 1540 to 1910	Church registers of births, marriages, and deaths; correspondence including immigrant lists and records or orphans settled in California with local families, also help to reconstruct families and trace places of origin. Spanish and Indian names are also to be found in these records as the missionaries often assigned new or Christianized names to converts. Evidence of genetic diseases may also be traced in these records.

Chapter 18

GENEALOGICAL AND HISTORICAL SOURCES IN THE SPANISH AND MEXICAN SOUTHWEST

George J. Nixon

This chapter presents a general and brief overview of some of the records available to those of Spanish and Mexican descent. Geographically, it centers on the present states of Texas, New Mexico, Arizona, and California. See Map 18-1 for more complete territorial acquisitions.

This survey should not be considered complete by any means. A complete compilation would require several volumes. One source in particular, Henry Putnam Beers, *Spanish and Mexican Records of the American Southwest* (Tucson: University of Arizona Press, 1979) will be extremely helpful to the genealogist and historian on the location, content, and history of records of the Spanish and Mexican Southwest.

This chapter emphasizes provincial history, land records, records of local jurisdiction, and Catholic Church records. Many of these records have been transcribed and/or translated by the staff of the various depositories or independent scholars and historians. Many, however, are untranslated documents. At the end of the chapter is a list of depositories with addresses, and a bibliography of guides, inventories, and catalogues.

Records under Spanish Sovereignty and Mexican National Government

Provincial Archives

The provincial records of Texas can be divided into two groups: the Bexar Archives and the Nacogdoches Archives.

The Bexar Archives consist of over 250,000 pages of manuscripts and some 4,000 pages of printed material covering 1717 to 1836. Among the numerous items in this collection are correspondence of presidio commanders; correspondence of other army officers; correspondence of local officers; correspondence of clergymen; correspondence of enlisted men and citizens; diaries; passports; cattlebrand licenses; censuses of Texas settlements, usually showing heads of families, numbers of men, women, and children, and occupation; and judicial proceedings, containing trials of smugglers, highwaymen, traitors, murderers, foreigners, deserters, and others who violated Spanish and Mexican laws.

These records reflect the administration of civil affairs, ecclesiastical matters, exploration, local history, immigration, colonization, and genealogy. They have been arranged into five subgroups, each of which is in chronological order without regard to province:

1. Coahuila and Texas official publications 1826-35.
2. General government publications 1730-1836.
3. Nongovernmental publications 1778, 1811-36.
4. Undated and dated fragments.
5. General manuscript series 1717-1836.

Calendar cards for individual documents have been prepared. They total some 81,000 entries and provide the date, number of pages, writer's name, place of writing, addressee's name, summary of the contents in English, and type of document. This collection is indexed and has a separate calendar of printed laws and decrees of Coahuila and Texas, 1821-35, in addition to bound and indexed volumes of translated documents, 1717-79 and 1804-8.

The 172 microfilm rolls of the Bexar Archives are prefaced by a general description of the material and contain calendar entries.

The Bexar Archives are presently in the custody of the University of Texas Archives, Austin, Texas. The transcribed portions are deposited in the Bexar County Courthouse, San Antonio, Texas, and the Stephen F. Austin State College Archive Collection. The microfilm edition of the Bexar Archives is available at the University of Texas Archives.

The Nacogdoches Archives, covering 1731 to 1836, are arranged in chronological order and classified according to the administrative organization of the Mexican government from 1824 to 1836. The six subgroups are further divided into series or files as follows:

- *Mexico:* Spanish and Mexican decrees 1812-35 and miscellaneous materials 1756-1835.
- *Chihuahua:* Monterrey 1791-1835.
- *San Antonio de Bexar Saltillo Monclova:* Residencias of governors; Manuel de Sandoval 1736, Francisco Garcia Larios 1748, and Pedro del Bario Junco y Espriella 1751; correspondence from the governor of Texas and Coahuila 1749-1835; decrees of Coahuila and Texas 1834-35; and miscellaneous material 1823-35.
- *Bexar:* Correspondence of the Bexar political chief 1823-35, miscellaneous material relating to the municipality of Bexar 1823-35, and correspondence of the principal commandant 1825-35.
- *Nacogdoches:* Alcaldes' correspondence 1832-36, primary judges' correspondence 1834-35, political chief's correspondence 1834-36, and proceedings of the *ayuntamiento* of Nacogdoches 1826-36, lawsuits 1824-35, citizenship papers 1826-36, miscellaneous material 1826-36, commandant of the frontier's correspondence 1827-35, and places subordinate to Nacogdoches—Attoyac, Ayish Boyou, San Augustine 1824-35, Sabine 1824-35, and Anahuac 1832-35.
- *General—Coahuila and Texas:* Census reports for various missions and towns 1783-1835, civil elections 1824-35, including tally sheets, returns of elections, minutes of electoral assemblies and lists of officers elected in Nacogdoches and other areas; reports of military companies stationed at Bexar, La Bahia, Aguaverde, Rio Grande, Monclova, Lampozos and Trinity 1773-1813, 1835; and miscellaneous material 1785-1835.

The Nacogdoches Archives have been transcribed in eighty-nine volumes, with a card index to the transcriptions.

The Nacogdoches Archives are presently located at the Texas State Library, Archives Division, Austin, Texas. Transcribed copies and other records have been deposited with the University of Texas Archives, the Stephen F. Austin State College Library in Nacogdoches, the North Texas State College Library in Denton, and the Newberry Library in Chicago. Transcriptions of other Nacogdoches records are in custody of the Nacogdoches County

Map 18-1. Territorial Acquisitions by the United States, 1790-1867, U.S. Government Printing Office, 1959.

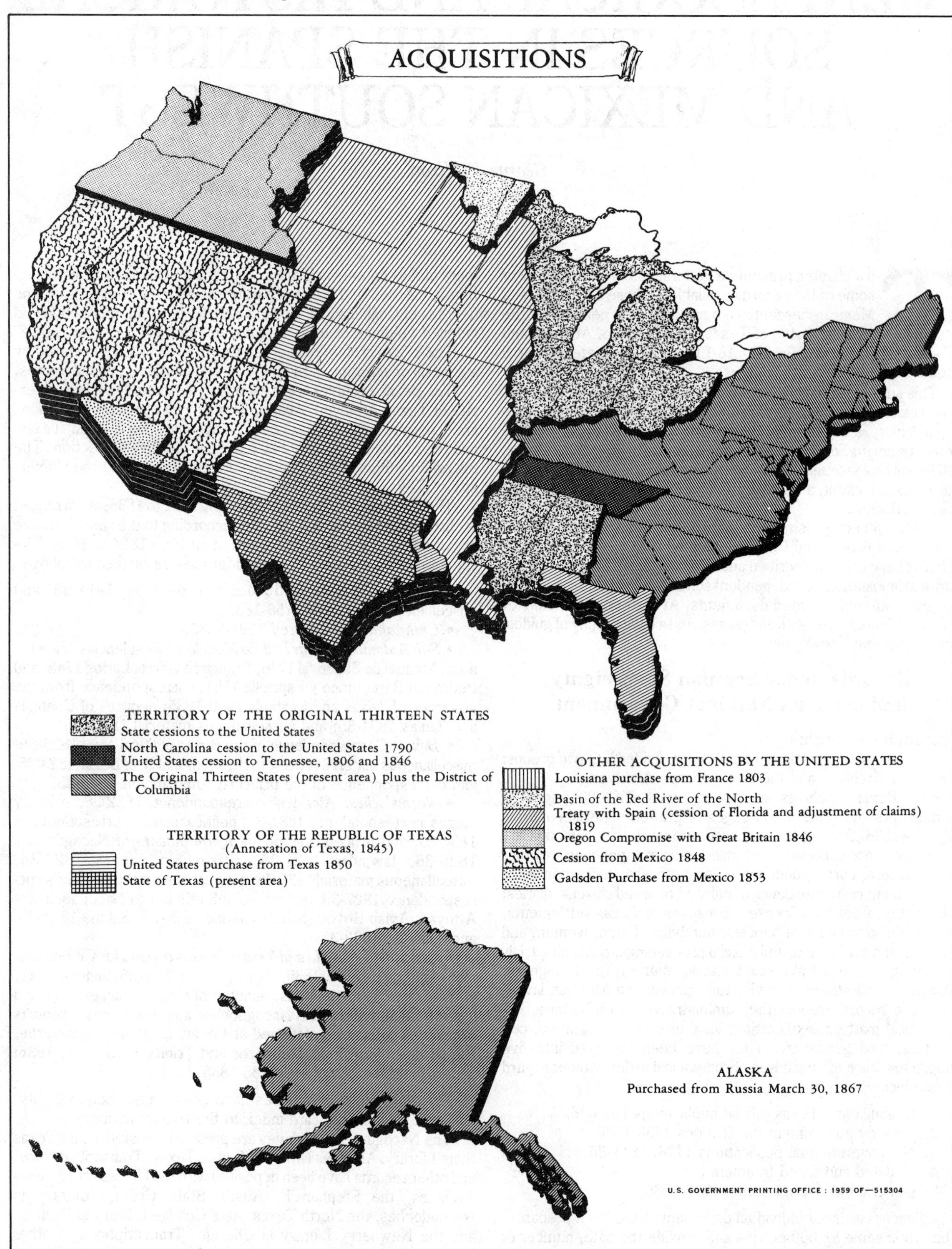

Clerk. Twenty transcribed volumes are in the Texas State Archives with other sets of these transcribed records in the University of Texas Archives, the Stephen F. Austin State College Library, the North Texas State College, and the Newberry Library.

Seventy-five bound volumes, 1744-1837, prepared by Robert Blake, are kept in the Blake Collection in the Houston Public Library. The collection includes correspondence, diaries, election returns, bills of sale, a record of foreigners who settled in Nacogdoches, 1827-34, lists of foreigners residing in Nacogdoches, judicial proceedings, marriage contracts, accounting and financial papers, orders, commissions, and other documents. Censuses for Nacogdoches and surrounding settlements, 1792-1835, list the name of head of household, race, marital status, birthplace, age, occupation; wife's name, her age, birthplace, and race; and the number and ages of children. Some censuses supply information on real estate, but few give the numbers of inhabitants at various settlements and missions. A calendar of the Blake Collection is available in the University of Texas Archives.

Finding Aids and Guides

Helpful published aids are:

Censuses of Nacogdoches, Tenehaw, and Sabine, Bevil's Settlement. *Microfilm of Censuses, 1828-36, of Nacogdoches, Tenehaw, and Sabine, Bevil's Settlement (Jasper, Texas), William's Settlement, and San Augustine*. These and other materials in the National Archives are in the Library of Congress. See William S. Jenkins, ed., *Guide to the Microfilm Collection of Early State Records, Supplement*, pp. 5-6, 101.

Kielman, Chester V. *Guide to Microfilm of Bexar Archives 1717-1803*. Austin: University of Texas Archives, 1967.

__________ *Guide to Microfilm Edition of Bexar Archives 1804-21*. Austin: University of Texas Archives, 1969.

__________ *Guide to Microfilm Edition of Bexar Archives 1822-36*. Austin: University of Texas Archives, 1971.

Mullins, Marion D., ed. *First Census of Texas, 1829-36, to Which Are Added Texas Citizenship Lists 1821-35, and Other Early Records of the Republic of Texas*. Washington, D.C., 1959.

Texas, Department of Agriculture, Insurance, Statistics, and History. "Report of the Classifier and Translator of Manuscripts in the Texas State Library." In *The Twenty-Ninth Annual Report of the Commissioner of Agriculture, Statistics, and History for the Year 1903*. Austin: Von Boeck Mann-Jones Co., 1904, pp. xiii-xxvi. See also "Classification Scheme of the Nacogdoches Archives, pp. xx-xxii.

Land Records

To promote settlement, the Spanish Government dispensed land grants quite liberally. The procedure for obtaining a grant was to apply to the governor, who then sent an order of approval to the local officer to make an examination, survey, and appraisal of the tract, before placing it in the applicant's possession. The notary recorded the receipt of the order and with the commissioned officer and petitioner, certified the act. A visual inspection, survey, and demarcation of the tract was then made by the local officer, the applicant, appraisers, witnesses, and adjacent land owners. A written report of the proceedings, during which the applicant was put into possession, was prepared. All of these documents constituted the owner's title, which had to be approved by the viceroy of New Spain at Mexico City. The files of *expedientes*, or land records, were archived in San Antonio, Nacogdoches, Laredo, and the other towns on the Rio Grande; and the grants were registered in the provincial capital, the seat of intendancy (San Luis Potosi) after 1786, and Mexico City. During Spanish rule, local officials permitted settlers to occupy land long before the legal requirements had been fulfilled, but eventually the documents were filed in the appropriate town archives.

Numerous large grants of premium land were made to contractors or *empressarios* for bringing in settlers. This alphabetical listing of *empressario* contracts also indicates dates land was granted:

Arispe, Manuel R.	1828
Austin, Moses	1821
Austin, Stephen Fuller	1825
Austin, Stephen Fuller	1827
Austin, Stephen Fuller	1828
Austin, Stephen Fuller and Samuel Williams	1831
Beales, John Charles and Jose Manuel Royuela	1832
Beales, John Charles and Mexicans	1832
Beales, John Charles and James Grant	1832
Beales, John Charles (see Mexican Company)	
Cameron, John	1827
Cameron, John	1828
Chambers, Thomas J., (see Padilla, Juan A.)	
Cherokee Indians	1831
De Leon, Martin	1825
De Leon, Martin	1829
DeWitt, Green	1825
Dominguez, Juan	1829
Dominguez, Marciano (see Mexican Company)	
Edwards, Haden	1825
Exeter, Richard and Stephen J. Wilson	1828
Filsola, Vicente	1831
Galveston Bay and Texas Land Co.	1830
Grant, James (see Beales, John C.)	
Heweston, James and James Power	1828
Johnson, Frank W. (see Williams, Samuel)	
Leftwich, Robert	1825
Lovell, Benjamin D. (see Purnell, John G.)	
McMullen, John and James McGoin	1828
Mason, John Thompson	1834
Mexican Company (Marciano Dominguez, Fortunato Soto, Juan Ramon Milda de la Rosa, and John Charles Beales)	1830
Milam, Benjamin R.	1826
Milan de la Rosa and Juan Ramon (see Mexican Land Company)	
Padilla, Juan Antonio and Thomas Jefferson Chambers	1830
Peebles, Robert (see Williams, Samuel)	
Power, James	1825
Power, James (see Heweston, James)	
Purnell, John G. and Benjamin D. Lovell	1825
Robertson, Sterling C.	1834
Shawnee Indians	1825
Soto, Fortunato (see Mexican Land Company)	
Soto, Fortunato and Henry Egerton	1834
Thorn, Frost	1825
Vehlein, Joseph (see Woodbury, John L.)	
Vehlein, Joseph and Company	1826
Vehlein, Joseph and Company	1828
Wavell, Arthur Goodall	1826
Williams, Samuel (see Austin, Stephen F.)	
Williams, Samuel, Robert Peebles, and Frank W. Johnson	1835
Wilson, Stephen J. (see Exeter, Richard)	
Wilson, Stephen J.	1826
Woodbury, John L. and Joseph Vehlein and Company	1826
Zavala, Lorenzo de	1829

The land records acquired by the General Land Office have been classified, indexed, and bound with the title papers of the various colonies in separate volumes. Translations of *empresario* contracts and other materials fill twelve of the 175 volumes, which cover 1720 to 1836. This collection contains: laws, decrees, resolutions, regulations, treaties, *empresario* contracts and correspondence, census reports, lists of colonists, petitions and remonstrances, land grants, titles, surveys and field notes, messages of the governors of Coahuila and Texas, appointments of officers, reports of municipal officers, records relating to mission lands, registers of families, and oaths of allegiance.

The General Land Office has microfilmed these records, the Spanish titles requiring forty-two rolls, and the surveys and field notes requiring twelve rolls. The original Spanish archives consisting of 28,786 pages in sixty-nine volumes have been laminated for preservation. Also, data on the land records has been indexed on IBM cards, permitting easier access.

The records in the General Land Office have been classified and arranged into a number of series. The title papers for the various colonies have been bound into sixty-nine volumes, the first twenty-three pertaining to the various colonies. (See Table 18-1.)

Table 18-1

General Land Office Records, 1720-1836 (Colonies)

Series	Volume Numbers	Index Numbers
Austin's first colony	1-2	A
Austin's second colony	3-6	A
Austin's third colony	7-8	A
Austin's fourth colony	9	A
Austin and William's colony	10-11	A
DeWitt's colony	12-13	A
Robertson's colony	14-15	A-B
Milam's colony	16	A
Power and Heweston's colony	17	A-B
Burnet's colony	18-19	A-B
Vehlein's colony	20-21	A-B
Zavala's colony	22-23	A-B

The remaining forty-six volumes of this series (vol. 24-69) are composed of documents relating to special grants, grants to volunteers, and miscellaneous documents. Volumes 24-43 are indexed, but 44-69 are not.

Additionally, there are several unnumbered volumes, which contain registers of grants in Austin's colony, 11 July 1825-2 December 1831; in Wavell's colony, 1830-31; in Milam's colony, 1830-31; and in Robertson's colony, 1835-36.

These land records are currently located in the Texas General Land Office, Austin, Texas. In addition, several counties have transcribed copies of some of these records, deposited with the respective county clerks.

Records of Local Jurisdiction

The early settlements in Texas were classified as missions, presidios, or pueblos. The Franciscan Order supervised the missions, but the military commander governed the presidio, while the pueblo, a civil settlement developed at or near a mission or presidio, was partially self-governing. Each local government had a *cabildo* or *ayuntamiento* (municipal council) composed of *regiodores* (councilmen) who were presided over by the *alcalde* (mayor). Generally, there were two *alcalde ordinarios* (municipal judges), the *alguacil mayor* (sheriff), and the *mayordomo de propios* (administrator of public lands). The *mayordomo de propios* also functioned as the *procurado* (attorney). The *escribanos* kept the *cabildo* minutes, served as notary, prepared legal documents, took depositions, and maintained the local archives.

One of the largest collections of local records is at San Antonio, partially described in the section on provincial records. The local record groups at San Antonio are:

1. Land grants and sales 1736-1836, arranged alphabetically by surname of grantee and chronologically thereunder.
2. Mission records, consisting of inventories of the San Antonio missions: San Antonio de Valero, San Juan de Capistrano, Purisima Conception de Acuna, San Francisco de la Espada, San Jose y San Miguel de Aguayo, and Mission Nuestra Senora del Refugio.
3. Lands outside Bexar County 1778-1835.
4. Wills and estates 1742-1836, arranged alphabetically by surnames and chronologically thereunder.
5. Rebel property 1813-36, arranged chronologically.
6. Powers of attorney 1770-1836, arranged alphabetically by surname and chronologically thereunder.
7. Contracts, agreements, and receipts, instruments of varied nature, including adoptions, business partnerships, and marriage doweries, arranged chronologically.
8. Various legal papers including land grants, wills, military discharges, and municipal accounts arranged chronologically.
9. Litigations 1757-1830, arranged chronologically.
10. Decrees, edicts, laws, and proclamations 1761-1835, arranged by government and chronologically thereunder.
11. Military reports 1781-1832, arranged chronologically.
12. Postal administration 1816-35, arranged chronologically.
13. Customs house reports 1824-34, arranged chronologically.
14. *Oficios* 1770-1833, arranged chronologically.
15. Fragments, unidentified manuscripts.
16. Post-1836 records.
17. Broadsides 1761-1822, arranged chronologically.

After the Velasco Treaty of 1836 which removed all Mexican troops from the region south of the Rio Grande River, the region between the Rio Grande and the Nueces River became a no-man's land. When American soldiers occupied Texas and the Mexican War broke out in 1846, Laredo and all its records became property of the United States. The collection consists of some 8,000 documents (1768-1868, a few as early as 1749), including census reports, vital statistics, allotments of land tax renditions, wills, settlements of estates, and civil and criminal litigations. Transcription of these records was completed in 1941. A partial set of transcriptions, covering only 1755 to 1830 with many gaps, is in the Texas State Archives. The Laredo Archives have also been microfilmed for the Southwest Collection at Texas Technological University, Lubbock, Texas. The Colorado State Archives has a positive copy of this microfilm edition, extending to 1847. The original collection of the Laredo Archives is now in the custody of St. Mary's University Library, San Antonio, and is available on sixteen rolls of microfilm covering 1749-1872. Access to the original manuscripts is also possible with special permission. Texas State Archives, Laredo Junior College, and Bexar County Archives also have microfilm copies. There is no index or calendar available for these records.

The original records of the villa of San Jose de Palafox, 1810-27, are presently at St. Mary's University Library, San Antonio, Texas. It was founded in 1810 by Captain Juan J. Diaz and some families from Coahuila on the east side of the Rio Grande in what is now Webb County. The town was abandoned 1818-26 because of Indian depredations, resettled, and destroyed finally in 1829 by Indians. These records, published in facsimile with translations, include lists of persons living in the town, and censuses of 1815 and 1816, which give the names of heads of families; the number of children, men, and women; and lists of mulattoes, mixed breeds, and Indians.

Some of the records of Nacogdoches have previously been described, but several other collections relating to Nacogdoches are also important. Records of the Nacogdoches district court 1834-62 are in the Stephen F. Austin State College Archive Collection, and copies of the court proceedings are in the University of Texas Archives. The Texas History Collection of Baylor University has Nacogdoches records 1770 to about 1900.

Records of the municipality of San Felipe de Austin are found at the Belleville county clerk's office and contain:

1. Colonial archives 1824-37, including deeds, grants, powers of attorney, title bonds, agreements, and bills of sale, arranged alphabetically by surname and numerically thereunder.
2. Colonial papers 1810-37, powers of attorney, wills, agreements, alphabetically by surname and chronologically thereunder.
3. Marriage bonds and contracts 1824-36.
4. Miscellaneous documents.
5. Judicial records of San Felipe: dockets of Alcalde Court

1829-33 and Superior Court 1827-28, civil case papers 1834-37, and probate case papers 1824-37.

City records of Brazoria are in the custody of the county clerk at Angelton, and are similar in content to those previously described.

Catholic Church Records

The Catholic missions in Texas had a two-fold purpose: Christianizing the Indians and promoting settlement. Missionary efforts by the Franciscans had begun as early as 1659 with the establishment of the Mission Nuestra Senora de Guadalupe del Paso at El Paso del Norte (Ciudad Juarez, Mexico). By the close of the eighteenth century, the missions had nearly achieved their goals of frontier settlement; and about 1793, records of the numerous missions were placed in the hands of parish churches. Figure 18-1 shows the first page of burial records from Mision de la Purisima Conception de Acuna dated 5 March 1731.

The records of the San Antonio missions were transferred to the parish church of San Fernando in 1793. Surviving records are located at the San Fernando Cathedral, seat of the Archdiocese of San Antonio:

1. Burial register of San Antonio de Valero 1703-82, San Francisco Solano 1703-13, San Xavier de Noxera 1722, and San Antonio de Valero 1718-82.
2. Register of marriages and baptisms of San Antonio de Valero 1703-83, baptismal records of San Francisco Solano 1703-08, and San Xavier de Noxera 1721-26, including a register of baptisms of Hyerbipiamo Indians who were settled at the mission in 1722.
3. Register of marriages and marriage applications of San Antonio de Valero 1709-1825, including marriages recorded at San Francisco Solano 1709-16.
4. Register of baptisms, marriages, and burials of San Francisco Solano 1703-08 (in the Archives of the College of Santa Cruz of Queretaro).
5. Marriage register of Purisima Conception de Acuna 1777-90.

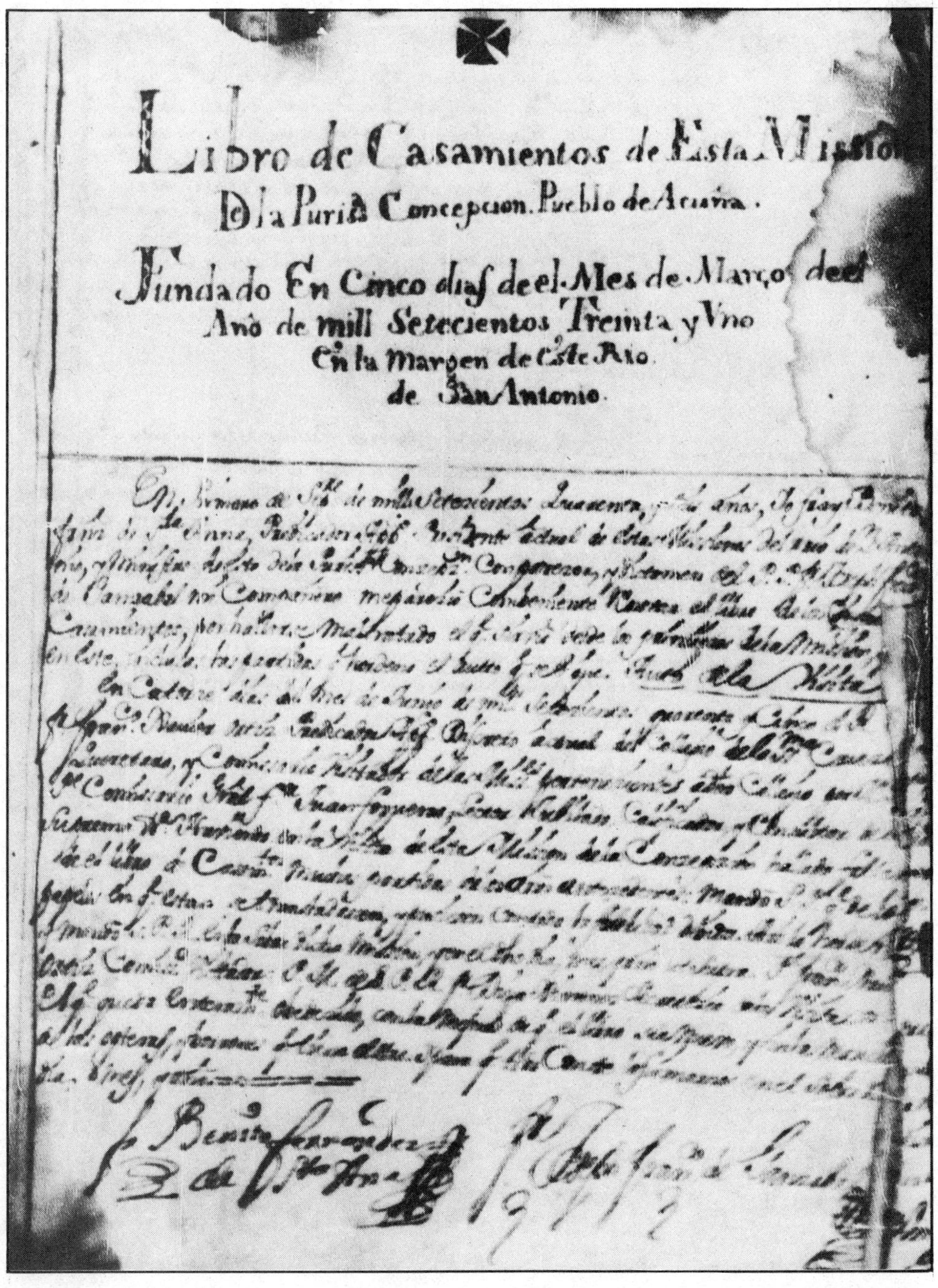

Libro de Casamientos de Esta Mission
De la Purisa Concepcion. Pueblo de Acuña.
Fundado En Cinco dias de el Mes de Março de el
Año de mill Setecientos Treinta y Vno
En la Margen de Este Rio
de San Antonio.

Figure 18-1. Burial Record of Mision de la Purisima Conception de Acuna, 5 March 1731, p. 1; San Fernando Cathedral, San Antonio, Texas; Genealogical Society of Utah (hereafter GS) microfilm 025,433.

6. Baptism register of San Jose y San Miguel de Acuna 1777-1823.
7. Marriage register of San Jose y San Miguel de Acuna 1778-1822.
8. Register of burials for San Juan Capistrano 1781-1824.
9. Scattered entries for San Francisco de la Espada 1818-24.

Most of the baptismal and burial registers of Purisima Conception de Acuna and most of the records of San Francisco de la Espada are missing. Figure 18-2 shows one of the few surviving baptismal records from Purisima Conception.

The Bancroft Library of the University of California has a few records from San Antonio de Valero including its baptismal and burial register 1720-21, marriage register 1748-54, and burial register 1754.

Records held by San Fernando Cathedral have been microfilmed and are available in the Genealogical Society of Utah. These records have also been photocopied and are available in the San Fernando Archives and the Catholic Archives of Texas in the Chancery Archives in Austin, Texas.

Records of the parish church of San Fernando dating from 1721 also are in the Archdiocese of San Antonio in the San Fernando Cathedral:

1. Register of baptisms 1731-1858.
2. Register of marriages 1731-1856.
3. Register of burials 1731-1860.
4. Register of confirmations 1731-1860.
5. Miscellaneous unbound records 1775-78.

The records of Nuestra Senora del Refugio presently in the parish church at Matamoros, Tamaulipas, include its baptism register 1807-27 and burial register 1807-25.

Photostatic copies of these registers are available in the Catholic Archives of Texas in the chancery office in Austin, Texas. Addi-

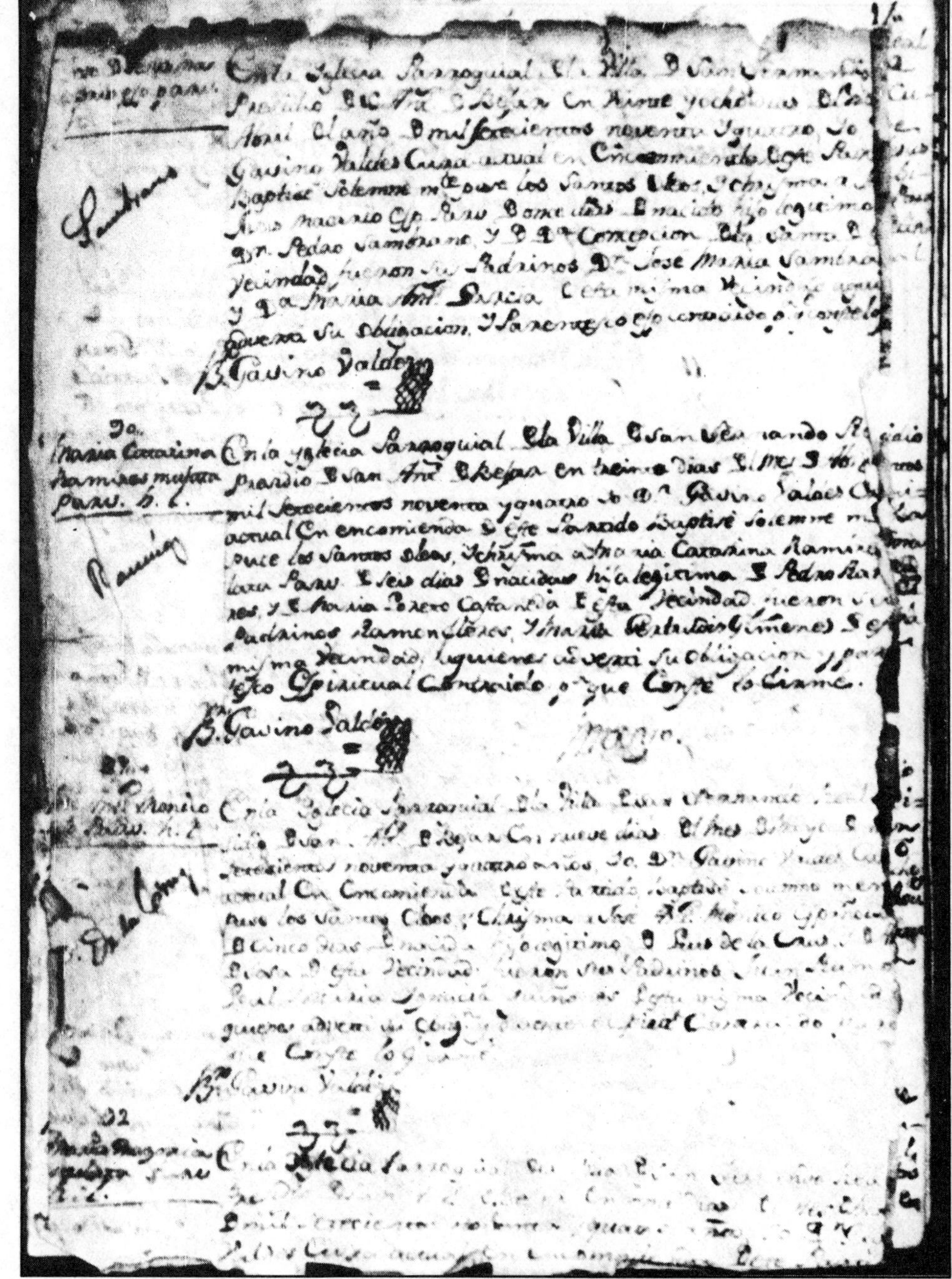

Figure 18-2. Baptism record of Mision de la Purisima Conception de Acuna, p. 34; San Fernando Cathedral, San Antonio, Texas; GS 025,433, item 2.

tional copies are available in the Church of Our Lady of Refuge at Refugio. Also available in the chancery office are the records of Saint Augustin Church of Laredo, which include:

1. Register of baptisms 1788-1860.
2. Register of marriages 1790-1881.
3. Register of burials 1836-48.
4. Book of confirmations 1834-54.

Records of New Mexico under Spanish Sovereignty and Mexican National Government

Provincial Archives

The Spanish archives of New Mexico 1621-1821, presently held at the Archives Division of New Mexico State Records Center, concern the administration of the region from the period of Spanish colonial sovereignty to the establishment of the Mexican government in 1821. Excluded from these archives are official land grant documents and land conveyances in special collections.

The Spanish archives, microfilmed in twenty-two rolls, are calendared chronologically, identified briefly, and located by frame number.

1. Communications and decrees received from the viceroy and commandant-general.
2. Copies of communications to the viceroy and commandant-general.
3. Reports from local officials and instructions sent to them.
4. Censuses.
5. Appointments, governors' edicts, minutes, and petitions of the *cabildo* of Santa Fe.
6. Military records, including lists of troops, muster rolls, orders, journals of operations, reports of inspections, and service records.
7. Judicial records containing litigation proceedings in civil and criminal cases, judgments of the governor and captain general, auxiliary documents (affidavits, petitions, depositions, testimonies, writs, declarations, etc.), and probate records.

The New Mexico State Records Center has forty-two rolls of New Mexican archives microfilm consisting of documents relating to the Mexican government, 1821-46. Included are items from the following private collections:

1. State Records Center Special Collections: Ralph Emerson Twitchell Papers, Donaciano Vigal Papers, Benjamin M. Read Papers, L. Bradford Prince Papers, Maria G. Duran Papers, Mrs. James Seligman Papers, Tyler Dingee Collection-Delgado Family Papers, Ortez Family Papers, Ina Ortero Collection, Ted Ortero Collection, and Valencia County Papers.
2. Zimmerman Library, University of New Mexico: L. Bradford Prince Papers, D'Armond Papers, Miguel Antonio Lovato Papers, and Julius Seligman Papers.
3. Bureau of Land Management, Santa Fe Office: Governor's letterbook of communications sent to authorities within New Mexico 1840-42, Journal of Diputacion Provincia (provincial deputations) 1822-24, Journal of Deputacion Territorial 1824-37, and Journal of Asemble Departmental (departmental assembly) 1845-46.

The Mexican archives have been organized into several record groups, according to agency of function, and then subdivided by subject matter within each record group with documents in each section arranged chronologically: instructions, investigations, journals, judicial proceedings, orders, petitions, reports, and *residencias* (residences of various officials).

There are also similar records at the Huntington Library relating to New Mexico. The Bancroft and Huntington documents have been microfilmed and are available at the New Mexico State Record Center.

Land Records

The Spanish and Mexican governments adopted liberal land grant policies for New Mexican territory similar to those for their Texan lands. The procedure for obtaining a land grant in New Mexico was also the same as it was in Texas. The individual desiring the land grant first submitted a petition of application for a grant to an alcalde, which was then forwarded by him to the governor. The governor, in turn, directed the alcalde to make an investigation. The alcalde then would submit his report and a sketch map to the governor. The governor would then order the alcalde to place the grantee in possession. In order to prevent conflicts over boundaries, the alcalde executed an act of possession before witnesses. The original title paper was given to the grantee, and a copy was filed in an *expediente* in the secretary's office at Santa Fe. Final title papers were not issued, however, until the alcalde certified that the land had been occupied for four years. Much controversy arose, as the boundaries of the grants were natural landmarks and very vague. Surveys were generally not made and title papers not completed, so the *expedientes* remained incomplete. Transfers, exchanges, donations, and partitions of land were made before the governor or alcalde and recorded in the archives. Disputes over titles to lands, boundaries, and water rights were heard by the same officials.

In 1846, General Steven W. Kearny created the office of register of lands for the Territory of New Mexico. The secretary of the territory held this office and was responsible for recording documents concerning lands in the Territory of New Mexico previously issued by the Spanish or Mexican governments. Persons having written land claims could have them recorded after payment of a fee, and those without written claims were required to record statements within five years. The register of lands was authorized to furnish certified copies of documents and directed to safeguard the records.

As a result of this authorization, the first register of lands in 1847, Donaciano Vigal, Secretary of New Mexico appointed in 1846 by Governor Stephen W. Kearny when civil government was established, created three land registers. Book A, 1847-49, and Book C, 1849, are in the State Records Center. Book B has been lost. Books A and C have been microfilmed and are in the Microfilm Collection of Early State Records in the Library of Congress and the University of New Mexico Library.

Spanish and Mexican land grant records that came into possession of the surveyor general are still owned by the federal government. These records have been microfilmed in sixty-six rolls and contain:

1. Spanish land grant records taken over by the surveyor general in 1855.
2. Pueblo land grants including Spanish documents.
3. The Vigal list of Spanish archives received by the Americans.
4. Vigal's register of land titles 1847-53.
5. The case files of private land claims adjudicated by the surveyor general 1855-90.
6. Transcription of the documents filed with the surveyor general.
7. Case files and other records of the Court of Private Land Claims.
8. Correspondence of the surveyor general.
9. Muniments of title of the claim of the Baron of Arizona (James Addison Reavis). This complicated court case involved land fraud and the removal of the baron's title to an enormous land claim.

The Spanish land grant records contain a variety of documents, including acts of possession, boundary proceedings, circular letters, correspondence, decrees, decisions and reports of the departmental assembly, claims for lands, compromises, controversies of land, confirmations of grants, conveyances, copartnerships, deeds, distributions of estates, donations of lands, dowers, exchanges, gifts and grants, grants of lead mines, inventories and partitions of estates, lawsuits, laws and regulations relating to lands, letters, mining regulations, mining suits, mortgages, orders for possession, orders for the settlement of towns, partitions of lands, petitions for land, petitions for permission to remove, powers of attorney, proceedings for locations, proceedings regarding contested wills, proceedings regarding the establishment of towns, proceedings regarding the settlement of estates, protests against the sale of lands, registrations of mines, reports, revocations of grants, titles, trespasses, and wills.

Figure 18-3, the first page of an 1812 will probate that runs forty pages in Spanish typescript with accompanying English translation, is a remarkable document that begins with the widow's petition, attestation of witnesses, authorization to read the will, the will itself (its first provision is offering the captain's soul to God, the second, a specification that his body shall be buried directly within the cemetery gate so that the living may "stomp *[sic]* and trample" upon it), the codicil, which reemphasizes certain provisions of the will (primarily his desire that the mother of his dead first wife not be considered an heir), and the record of litigation which followed. His fears about his former mother-in-law had not been in vain.

The records of the surveyor general, accumulated or prepared while adjudicating land claims, are now in the custody of the State Records Center at Santa Fe. The case files of private land claims adjudicated by the surveyor general 1855-90 are the most extensive and are filed in numerical order by report number. They contain a variety of documents including petitions of claimants, sketch maps, original Spanish documents on the grants, translations, testimonies of witnesses, affidavits, survey documents, copies of decrees of the Court of Private Land Claims, copies of patents, correspondence, and memoranda.

A private land claims docket lists cases in the above file and records documents submitted during the proceedings. This docket is indexed by report number and alphabetically by names of grantees. Land claims records contain copies of many of the documents recorded in the docket described, and an old grant docket contains ninety-three entries for claims adjudicated by the surveyor general. A record of private land claims supplies extensive information on reports 1-139 of the total 162 recorded in the docket.

Records of grants made to Pueblo Indians contain Spanish documents relating to the Pueblo grants and to the Acoma Pueblo

Figure 18-3. Will and Probate Proceedings of Captain Francisco Amangual, 1812 Bexar County Spanish Archives 1736-1836, Wills and Estates Book 1-9, 1736-1838; typescript; GS 1,019,360.

TESTAMENTO DEL CAPITAN RETIRADO FRANCISCO AMANGUAL

AÑO DE 1812

1

Prova. de Texas, año de 1812, Sn. Ferndo. de Bexar.

Diligencias practicadas para la apertura del textamto. serrado del Capn. retirado, Don Franco. Amangual, a peticion de su viuda.

Govno. E.

Sor. Govr:

Doña Maria Trenidad Garzia, biuda del Capitan retirado, Don Franco. Amangual, que fallesio a las nueve y media de la noche del dia de aller, con el devido respecto y como mas alla lugar a drcho. ante V. S. se presenta y dise qe. entre los papeles de dho. su esposo encontro su testamto. o ultima disposicion serrado y un documto. abierto los qe. devidamte. aconpaña a V. Sa. a fin de qe. sirviendose abrir el primero tenga a bien mandar se cunpla lo en el dispuesto, ynterpondo. su autoridad judicl. en forma legal pa. su mallor firmeza y balidazn. como el de qe. se le de una copia testimonda. pa. su Governo. Por tanto, a V. Sa. pide y suplica se sirva hazer como pide de qe. recibira merzed y justicia. Juro no ser de malicia y en la necesario, &a.

Maria Trinidad Garcia

[Rúbrica]

survey investigation of 1884 followed by English translations.

The Federal Records Center in Denver, Colorado, has records of the surveyor general of New Mexico which include:

1. Letters sent to the registers and receivers at La Mesilla and Las Cruces 1875-91.

2. Letters sent relating to land grants 1893-96, concerning surveys, plats, conflicts of claims, and the status of cases before the Court of Private Land Claims.

3. Documents showing cost of grant surveys under confirmation by the Court of Private Land Claims.

4. Letters sent 1884-1910, containing letters to General Land Office, private individuals, and surveyors.

5. Letters received at Las Cruces from General Land Office 1875-91.

6. Surveyor general's letters sent 1887-97.

The Bureau of Land Management in Washington, D.C., has accumulated files of land grants in New Mexico, Colorado, and Arizona. The surveyor's field notes provide identifying information on private land claims and areas of public domain. The survey plats contain general descriptions of the land and are filed by state, township, and range, in looseleaf form. Tract books contain a record of the disposition of every tract of land and serve as an index to the patents and case files of public land transactions. Patents and titles issued by the bureau are maintained in a series of volumes (about 7,000,000 patents in over 12,000 volumes). The bureau also has an index to private land claims. See Chapter 7, "Land Records," for greater detail.

Records of the Court of Private Land Claims are in the New Mexico State Records Center and Archives in Santa Fe. Records of private land claims adjudicated by the court contain original grants or copies of grants, sketch maps, applications for survey, testimonies of witnesses on boundaries, reports of the surveyor general on surveys, notices of surveys, decrees and opinions of the court, and an appearance docket or register of actions showing case numbers, title, nature, name of attorney, memoranda of papers filed, proceedings on the case, and index by name of grant.

Records of Local Jurisdiction

The majority of local jurisdiction records of the Territory of New

WILL OF CAPTAIN FRANCISCO AMANGUAL

1812

1

Province of Texas, 1812. San Fernando de Bexar.

Proceedings on opening the sealed will of the retired Captain Francisco Amangual on the petition of his widow.

To the Governor:

I, Maria Trinidad Garcia, widow of the retired Captain, Francisco Amangual, who died at half past nine last night, appear before you with all due respect and declare:

That among the papers of my said husband I found his last will and testament which was sealed and another document which was not sealed which I produce herewith in order that you may break the seal of the first document and that you will also order compliance with its provisions and I pray that you will employ your judicial authority for its greatest force and validity; I also pray you to have a certified copy issued to me by your office.

Wherefore I pray you to decree as I request that I may be awarded right and justice. I swear that this petition is not filed with malice but of necessity, etc.

Maria Trinidad Garcia,

[Rubric]

Mexico for the pre-American period have disappeared. Portions of the journal of proceedings of the *Ayuntamiento* of Santa Fe 1829-36 are in the Zimmerman Library of the University of New Mexico with a typescript in the Bancroft Library of the University of California. These records are also available on microfilm at the New Mexico State Records Center.

Catholic Church Records of New Mexico

In 1598 Juan de Onate, accompanied by ten Franciscan missionaries, established missions at a number of Indian pueblos, then constructed churches and schools. In the second half of the eighteenth century, the Franciscan missions in New Mexico began to decline. However, the amount of historical material generated during this period is significant.

Only a portion of the ecclesiastical records of the Spanish and Mexican periods have survived and are now in the Archives of the Archdiocese of Santa Fe. Since there is only limited access to these original records by accredited scholars, the State Records Center, the Henry E. Huntington Library, the Genealogical Society of Utah, and the Archdiocesan Archives have microfilm editions. Following is a list of available records, arranged according to mission and church:

Abiquiu: Register of baptisms 1754-1850, register of marriages 1756-1826, book of official letters 1822-41, and inventory book 1777-1813.

Acoma: Register of baptisms 1725-77, register of marriages 1726-70, register of burials 1726-77, register of burials (fragmentary) 1810, and register of confirmations 1736, 1760.

Albuquerque: Register of baptisms 1706-36, register of baptisms 1743-1802, register of baptisms 1822-50, register of baptisms 1736 (fragmentary), register of marriages 1726-1841, register of marriages 1845-66, register of burials 1726-1823, register of burials 1838-53, book of official letters 1745-1810, book of official letters 1818-51, account book of church fabric, *majordomos,* and inventories 1818-61, and accounts of church and *majordomos* 1816-18.

Belen: Register of baptisms 1810-34, register of baptisms 1843-81, register of marriages 1826-56, index to register of baptisms and marriages, register of baptisms 1793-1850, register of marriages 1826-84, register of burials 1838-85, register of baptisms, marriages, and burials 1793-1826, and official letters 1819-51.

Bernalillo: Register of baptisms, marriages, and burials 1700-12.

Cochiti: Register of baptisms 1736-1831, register of marriages 1776-1873, register of burials 1776-1873, book of official letters 1775-1817, index to Spanish and Indian baptisms 1845-73, and inventory book 1753-1829.

Galisteo: Register of burials 1711-29, register of marriages 1725-1826 (fragmentary), register of marriages and burials 1727-74 (unbound), register of burials 1778-1829, book of official letters 1783-1815, and inventories (fragmentary).

Isleta: Register of baptisms 1720-76, 1829-42; register of marriages 1726-1846; register of burials 1726-76; and book of official letters 1746-1818, 1789-1823.

Jemez: Register of baptisms 1701-1829, register of marriages 1720-76, register of burials (fragmentary), register of baptisms, marriages, burials 1701-26.

Laguna: Register of baptisms 1720-76, register of marriages 1700-77, register of burials 1715-19 (fragmentary), register of burials 1726-76, and inventory book 1736-77.

Mansos: Register of marriages 1691 (fragmentary).

Nambe: Register of baptisms 1707-27, 1771-1837; register of marriages 1707-28, 1772-1862; and register of burials 1707-1869.

Pecos: Register of baptisms 1726-63, 1776-1829; register of marriages 1699-1765; register of burials 1726-72; and book of official letters 1716-49.

Picuris: Register of baptisms 1750-71, 1776-1830, 1835-50; register of marriages 1726-1837; register of burials 1712-1858 (early portion is fragmentary); and inventory book 1743-67 (fragmentary).

Pojoaque: Register of baptisms 1779-1839, register of marriages 1744-1853, and register of burials 1779-1852.

Sandia: Register of baptisms 1771-1846 and register of marriages 1771-1858.

San Felipe: Register of baptisms 1769-1829, register of marriages 1726-1814, register of burials 1696-1796 (fragmentary), register of burials 1841-70, book of official letters 1755-1823.

San Ildefonso: Register of baptisms 1725-1834; register of marriages 1700-1853; register of burials 1840-55; and book of official letters 1824-52, 1817-34.

San Juan: Register of baptisms 1726-1837; register of marriages 1726-76, 1850-55; register of burials 1726-1826, 1836-57; book of official letters 1779-1816, 1817-34; and inventory of books and papers 1818-46.

San Miguel del Vado: Register of baptisms 1829-47, register of marriages 1829-46, register of burials 1829-47, account book 1842-55, prenuptial investigations 1829-34, and inventory 1828 (fragmentary).

Santa Ana: Register of baptisms 1771-1844; register of marriages 1694-1711, 1722-1828; register of burials 1739-52, 1765-71; book of official letters 1746-60; and inventory book 1712-53.

Santa Clara: Register of baptisms 1728-1805, 1841-45; register of marriages 1726-1830, 1844, 1846 (fragmentary); register of burials 1712-13, 1714-19, 1723, 1724, 1800-01, 1726-1843; book of official letters 1815-32; inventory book 1712-42; and census book 1818.

Santa Cruz de la Canada: Register of baptisms 1710-21, 1731-67, 1769-1850 (several incomplete years 1759-81); register of marriages 1726-1869; register of burials 1726-89, 1795-1859; book of official letters 1721-95, 1803-33, 1834-53; and miscellaneous incomplete registers, inventories, etc.

Santa Fe: Register of baptisms 1747-91, 1796-1848, 1848-51; register of marriages 1728-1843, 1846-57; register of burials 1726-1834, 1845-52; book of official letters 1697-1725, and miscellaneous account books.

Santa Fe Castrense: Register of baptisms 1798-1833, register of marriages of soldiers 1779-1833, and register of burials 1779-1833.

Santo Domingo: Register of baptisms 1771-73, 1829-46; register of marriages 1771-77, 1846-62; register of burials 1771-1846, and some baptisms and marriages from Santa Ana included.

Socorro: Register of baptisms 1821-50, register of marriages 1821-53, register of burials 1821-63, and book of official letters 1831-50.

Tesuque: Register of baptisms 1694-1724 (includes some marriages and burials).

Tome: Register of baptisms 1793-1826, 1809-47; register of baptisms, marriages, burials 1793-1826; register of marriages 1776-1846; and register of burials 1809-55.

Truches: Register of confirmations 1845 (fragmentary).

Zia: Register of baptisms 1694-1772, register of burials 1709, 1727-72; and register of marriages 1697-17.

Zuni: Register of baptisms 1709, 1727-72; register of marriages 1705-76; and register of burials 1706-19.

Records of Arizona under Spanish Sovereignty and Mexican National Government

During the Spanish period, the present area of southern Arizona was known as Pimeria Alta. This area also included a portion of northern Sonora, Mexico. This was the northwestern frontier of New Spain, inhabited by the Pima and Papago tribes. The region of Arizona remained under Spanish and Mexican government until the United States purchased it in 1853 for $10 million under the Gadsden Treaty. The Territory of Arizona was created by an Act of Congress on 24 February 1863.

The researcher interested in documentary sources on the activities of the Spanish and Mexicans in Arizona should consult the archives of Mexico, Spain, Sonora, Nueva Vizcaya, and Chihuahua. Information regarding missionaries and military personnel serving in Arizona from Mexico can be found in the records of Spanish towns and churches south of the border, particularly in Sonora.

Although space does not allow a detailed listing of the numerous Arizona sources now in Mexican archives, here is a brief list:

Archivo General de la Nacion: Correspondence, reports, diaries concerning political and financial administration, military affairs, ecclesiastical affairs, relations with the Indians, explorations, expeditions, and mining.

Archivo Historico de Hacienda, Seccion de Temporalidades: Documents concerning the exploration of the Colorado River 1729-63, and papers regarding hostilities of the Apache, Seris, and Pima Indians 1755-60.

Archivo Historico del Estado Sonora in Hermosillo: Official correspondence, reports, memoranda, executive decrees, minutes, debates of the state legislature, judicial reports, documents concerning general administration, elections of officials, establishment of missions, administration of community property, documents on the California expedition 1772-83, and American fur traders on the Gila and Colorado rivers in the 1820s.

Archivo General de Notarias: Documents beginning in the eighteenth century containing material relating to business and legal transactions.

Archives at Durango: Documents of the colonial period covering Nueva Vizcaya.

Archivo de Estado: Unclassified collection including correspondence of governors, intendents, military commandants, reports of inspections of presidios, decrees, proclamations, criminal and civil trials, and probate records.

The Parral Archives (Chihuahua) 1631-1821: Neuva Vizcaya records arranged chronologically by year within classifications of administrative business and war measures, land and mining claims, protocols, civil actions, criminal actions, and unclassified material.

Microfilm editions of these records are available in the United States at the University of Alabama; University of Arizona; University of California at Berkeley; Fort Lewis College, Durango, Colorado; Northern Illinois University, DeKalb; University of Minnesota; State University of New York, Stony Brook; State University of New York, Buffalo; Temple University, Philadelphia; University of Texas, Austin; University of Texas, El Paso; Texas Agricultural and Mechanical College, College Station; Texas Christian University, Fort Worth; Tulane University, New Orleans; University of Utah, Salt Lake City; and Library of Congress.

The University of Texas Library also has an extensive collection of photo-reproductions from several areas in Mexico and microfilms of the presidial archives of Janos Archives 1721-1900, and Chihuahua Archives. The Janos Archives are available on microfilm at the El Paso Centennial Museum and the University of Arizona Library as well. Microfilm from the Durango Archives is available in the Library of the University of Texas, El Paso.

Reproductions from Mexican repositories are also available in the Bancroft Library of the University of California, Berkeley.

Land Records

Very few land grants were made in southern Arizona. The Gadsden Treaty of 1853 provided that land titles in the ceded territory be recognized, but settlement of private land claims was not initiated by the United States for many years.

The original Spanish land grant records are now in the custody of the National Archives and have been microfilmed by the Arizona State Library and Archives.

Catholic Church Records

The existing records of the Catholic missions of Arizona are very incomplete. The archives of the Diocese of Tucson has some baptismal, marriage, and burial registers of Guevavi 1739-67, and some baptismal, marriage and burial registers of Tumacacori 1768-1825. Microfilms of these records are available at the University of Arizona Library, St. Louis University Library, and the Arizona Historical Society.

Records of California under Spanish Sovereignty and Mexican National Government

Provincial Records

California was ceded to the United States under the treaty of Guadalupe Hidalgo in 1848. Until September of 1850, when California was admitted as a state, the territory continued under military government.

Provincial records of California until 1846 were divided between Los Angeles and Monterey. After much shuffling between various repositories, these records were finally placed in the custody of the surveyor general in San Francisco, but were nearly all destroyed by the fire of 1906. The land records escaped, and some other documents had fortunately been issued as broadsides or pamphlets and were thus preserved in libraries. The various types of documents include laws, decrees, proclamations, instructions, regulations, tables, orders, notices, manifestoes, reports, and expositions.

The Bancroft Library has a nearly complete collection of such materials, and a large collection of Mexican documents is also available at the Sutro Library, San Francisco State College.

Land Records

Free grants of land were made under Spanish rule to encourage settlement in upper California. Each pueblo was allowed four square leagues of land; and under instructions of the viceroy in 1773, San Diego and Monterey were authorized to make grants within the limits of the town or mission. In 1781, the pueblos were authorized to grant house lots and agricultural tracts to new settlers, supplying them with livestock, agricultural implements, and pastureland. In 1791, the capitans of presidios were ordered to grant house lots and fields to soldiers and settlers, who in turn were obliged to do militia duty and sell surplus produce to the presidios. Indians worked the land occupied by the Franciscan missions, but the government retained ownership of the land.

The Mexican government, however, used a more liberal land grant system. The governor in 1828 authorized grants to heads of families, private persons, and *empresarios* who were to contract for the introduction of colonists. The *empresario* contracts were to be approved by the supreme government in Mexico and the other grants by the territorial deputation. The governors also made numerous grants in payment for approval of the departmental assembly.

Surveys of the land grants were not made with any degree of regularity by either Spanish or Mexican governments; descriptions based on landmarks were often indefinite, causing difficulties for later United States land commissioners.

Laws and regulations enacted in California in the 1780s required documentation of land grants, resulting in the accumulation of a number of records for each grant. These were filed in separate *expedientes* and kept by the secretary. A complete *expediente* included the original petition of the applicant to the governor, the sketch of the land solicited, the report of the local official, the decree of concession, the approval of the departmental assembly, the governor's certificate, and a copy of the title.

This documentation is, more often than not, incomplete. The procedures and conditions of occupation were seldom complied with, and the certificate of approval by the departmental assembly is frequently missing.

The treaty of Guadalupe Hidalgo mandated that the United States respect a legitimate title. Congress passed legislation for the settlement of private land claims in California while Spanish records were transferred to the United States Surveyor General for California. In 1851, Congress appointed a board of land commissioners to determine the validity of private land claims.

The private land grant records that came into the custody of the surveyor general's office were arranged into several series. The private land grant files 1784-1846 contained petitions for land, the governor's references to local authorities for reports, the reports, the governor's concessions, the reports of actions of the legislative assembly, the title or patent, the reports of measurement, depositions of witnesses, judicial proceedings, notice of sales, boundary disputes, land suits, wills, and correspondence.

Files that survived the San Francisco fire of 1906 are in the Bureau of Land Management Records (Record Group 49) in the National Archives. Transcripts of private land grants made before the fire are in the California State Archives.

Originally, eight registers of land grants were issued, but only the register for 1839-43 has survived. Photostats of this register are in the California State Archives and the Bancroft Library of the University of California at Berkeley. A transcript of the entries for 1784-1831 is in the Bancroft Library. Transcripts of the second (1833-36), fourth, and the sixth (1844-45) registers are in the California State Library. The sixth register has been published.

The Spanish and Mexican land grant records that survived the San Francisco fire were transferred to the National Archives in 1937 and included records relating to private land claims of California. These records comprise an index to complete *expedientes*, an index to incomplete *expedientes*, an alphabetical list of 580 complete *expedientes*, an alphabetical list of 315 incomplete *expedientes*, a list of documents relative to land claims deposited in the Spanish Archives since the annexation of California, correspondence, lists, affidavits, petitions concerning certified copies of land documents furnished by the surveyor general to the Board of Land Commissioners 1852-53, docket of district land cases, receipts for patents 1857-98, and transcripts of incomplete *expedientes* numbers 75-315.

The Bureau of Land Management Land Office in Sacramento has files of field notes of surveys, survey plats, and tract books.

The Federal Records Center in San Francisco has a file of American documents relating to Spanish and American land grants 1856-90 containing survey notes, court orders, surveyor's depositions, and miscellaneous items.

A board of land commissioners decided the validity of private land claims in California. Part of these records were given to the surveyor general's office in San Francisco and, consequently, burned in the fire of 1906. In 1939, the remainder of the board's records were taken to the National Archives and assigned to Record Group 49, Records of the Bureau of Land Management. These files contain title papers, copies of *expedientes* from Spanish and Mexican archives, originals or transcripts of deeds, wills, assignments, transfer of titles, decrees, orders of the Spanish government, and certificates of legislative approval.

An index to these case files has been prepared by the National Archives. Other records include a general Index of Spanish and Mexican archives in the surveyor general's office, an index to land titles received from the surveyor general, an index to land grants and persons to whom they were conceded, an index to land holdings, and an index to land cases with docket numbers.

A more extensive collection of records of the Board of Land Commissioners, also in the National Archives and a part of the Bureau of Land Management Records, contains record of evidence, record of petitions, record of decisions, docket, journal of proceedings, letters sent 1852-56, and index to private land claims with localities, names of original grantees, names of present claimants, names of counties, and docket numbers.

The bibliography at the conclusion of this chapter gives additional information on land records of California.

Records of Local Jurisdiction

The settlement of California followed the usual pattern of Spanish colonization – the mission, the presido, and the pueblo.

The Franciscan order had extensive civil authority and established missions throughout lower and upper California. The presidos were garrisoned by soldiers, the commandants having civil and judicial authority within their respective districts located at San Diego, Monterey, Santa Barbara, and San Francisco.

Local records were transferred in 1850 to the nine existing counties: San Diego, Los Angeles, Santa Barbara, San Luis Obispo, Monterey, Branciforte, San Francisco, Santa Clara, and Sonoma. These records were later transferred to the surveyor general's office in San Francisco and consequently burned in the 1906 fire.

An extensive collection of Monterey records now held by that county includes criminal proceedings of the Monterey Court 1807-43; military affairs 1781-1843; papers from the prefect's office 1837-49; papers regarding tithes, missions, and religious affairs 1782-1844; papers connected with Indians 1833-48; land grants, sales, transfers, suits, and location claims 1803-49; power of attorney 1834-49; register of cattle brand 1835-49; papers on the probate of estates and wills 1830-48; papers relating claims against the Mexican government 1841-42, 1846-47; naturalization papers 1829-42; political affairs, censuses, elections 1828-49; acalde and *ayuntamiento* records 1828-50; official acts of judges 1842-46; papers regarding ships at sea 1833-49; index to the Spanish archives; and deeds of grants 1822-50.

The Bancroft Library has transcripts and abstracts of some of these records while the Huntington Library has sixteen volumes on microfilm.

Los Angeles records available from the Huntington Library on microfilm include alcalde correspondence 1823; *ayuntamiento* minutes from 1832; judicial records of civil and criminal cases; records of the Los Angeles prefecture from 1834; register of cattle brands and marks 1833-52; notarial records; petitions for land; claims for mines; deeds, mortgages, contracts, bankruptcy papers, wills; inventories of personal and household goods; court-martial papers; censuses; and decrees and proclamations.

The Historical Society of Southern California also has photostats of this collection, and the Los Angeles County Recorder's Office has indexed transcriptions and translations.

The Los Angeles County Law Library has court records from 1839-82 including criminal cases 1839-50, civil cases 1839-44, and miscellaneous Spanish records 1840-50.

The Los Angeles Archives has translations of archives 1826-45 including a voters' register of 1830 and censuses of 1836 and 1844. Transcripts of these records are in the Bancroft Library with official documents of San Francisco 1835-57.

Records of San Diego are now in the Records of the Bureau of Land Management (Record Group 49) in the National Archives. Other early records of San Diego are in the Junipero Serra Museum in San Diego, the Bancroft Library, and the San Diego Historical Society Archives.

Records of San Jose are presently in the Santa Clara county recorder's office. Transcripts of this collection are in the Bancroft Library along with collections of Spanish and Mexican records relating to Santa Cruz, San Luis Obispo, and numerous early settlements.

Catholic Church Records

Surviving mission records are at the chancery office of the Archdiocese of San Francisco and include the following:

San Francisco de Asis (Delores): Register of baptisms 1776 -1870, register of marriages 1777-1859, register of burials 1776-1856, and account book 1805-28.

San Jose: Register of baptisms 1797-1859, register of marriages 1796-1859, and register of burials 1797-1837.

San Rafael: Register of baptisms 1817-39, register of marriages 1818-39, and register of burials 1818-39.

Mission records at the chancery of the Archdiocese of Los Angeles include:

San Buenaventura: Book of official letters 1806-42.

San Diego de Alcala: Book of official letters 1806-42.

San Fernando Rey: Register of baptisms 1797-1855, register of marriages 1798-1954, register of burials 1798-1852, and book of letters and inventories 1806-47.

The chancery office of the Diocese of Monterey has records that include:

San Antonio de Padua: Register of baptisms 1771-1882, register of marriages 1773-1872, register of burials 1819-72, and register of confirmations 1778-1872.

San Carlos de Borromes (Carmel): Register of baptisms 1770-1896, register of marriages 1772-1908, register of burials 1770-1915; and register of confirmations 1778-1896.

San Juan Bautista: Register of baptisms 1797-1843.

San Luis Obispo: Register of baptisms 1772-1821, register of marriages 1772-1824, register of burials 1772-1838, register of confirmations 1778-1906, book of official letters 1806-16, and census records 1775-1836.

San Miguel: Register of deaths 1798-1858.

Santa Cruz: Register of baptisms 1791-1857, register of marriages 1791-1902, and register of burials 1791-1894.

Nuestra Sonora de la Soledad: Register of baptisms 1791-1854 and register of marriages 1791-1854.

The Santa Barbara Mission archives includes:

San Jose: Register of burials 1837-59 and register of confirmations 1835-55.

San Luis Obispo: Book of official letters and inventories 1806-9 .

San Luis Rey: Register of baptisms 1827, 1828; book of official letters, inventories 1806-33; and census rolls 1798-1834, 1811-20.

Santa Barbara: Register of baptisms 1786-1858; register of marriages 1787-1857; register of burials 1787-1841; book of official letters 1791-1843; annual reports 1787-1836; book of orders 1798-1848; account books 1805-18, 1813-15, 1816-22; account book and record of masses 1787-1807; account book of merchandise 1842; and census rolls 1815, 1840.

The Bancroft Library has microfilms of Santa Barbara records for Santa Ynez (account book 1830-38) and Nuestra Senora de Soledad (register of confirmations 1792-95).

Records in the custody of parishes include:

La Purisima Conception: Register of baptisms 1788-1850, register of marriages 1788-1850, register of burials 1789-1850, and account book 1806-34.

San Antonio de Padua: Register of burials 1771-1819.

San Buenaventura: Register of baptisms 1782-1873, register of marriages 1782-1893, and register of burials 1782-1912.

San Diego de Alcala: Register of baptisms 1775-1846, register of marriages 1775-1938, register of burials 1775-1880, and register of confirmations 1789-1904.

San Francisco de Asis: Register of baptisms 1776-1856, register of marriages 1777-1860, register of burials 1776-1856, and book of confirmations 1838-40.

San Francisco Solano: Register of baptisms 1840-68, register of marriages 1840-1908, and register of burials 1840-78.

San Gabriel: Register of baptisms 1771-1855, register of marriages 1774-1855, and register of burials 1774-1855.

San Juan Bautista: Register of baptisms 1797-1931, register of marriages 1797-1934, and register of burials 1797-1934.

San Juan Capistrano: Register of baptisms 1776-1853, register of marriages 1777-1915, register of burials 1777-1850.

San Luis Obispo: Register of baptisms 1821-69.

San Miguel: Register of baptisms 1797-1861 and register of marriages 1797-1860.

Santa Ynez: Register of baptisms 1804-50, register of marriages 1804-50, and register of burials 1805-60.

Mission records now in the custody of the Bancroft Library include the following:

San Antonio de Padua: Census rolls 1803-34, inventories 1836, 1845, and loose documents 1774-1836, including matrimonial investigations, marriage dispensations, and miscellaneous papers.

San Diego de Alcala: Inventory book 1777-84.

San Fernando Rey: List of neophytes.

San Francisco Solano: Register of baptisms 1824-39, register of marriages 1824-39, and register of burials 1823-39.

San Jose: Book of official letters and inventories 1807-44.

Santa Ynez: Inventory 1845.

Soledad: Census rolls 1818-34.

Records of the Santa Clara Mission now held by the Orradre Library, University of Santa Clara, include register of baptisms 1777-1862, register of marriages 1778-1863, register of burials 1777-1866, register of confirmations 1779-1896, and book of official letters 1806-46.

Repositories

See Appendix A for addresses of Federal Archives and Records Centers, Appendix B for addresses of state archives, and Appendix C for addresses of state historical societies.

Arizona

Phoenix

Arizona Department of Library and Archives
1700 West Washington
Phoenix, AZ 85007

U. S. Bureau of Land Management
Arizona State Office

Tucson

Arizona Historical Society

Roman Catholic Diocese of Tucson
Chancery Archives
192 S. Stone Avenue, Box 31
Tucson, AZ 85702

San Xavier del Bac Mission, Oblasser Library
(Papago Indian Affairs)
Box 645, R.R. 11
Tucson, AZ 85706

University of Arizona Library
Tucson, AZ 85721

California

Berkeley

Pacific School of Religion Library
Graduate Theological Union Library
2400 Ridge Road
Berkeley, CA 93010

University of California
Bancroft Library
Berkeley, CA 94720

Camarillo

St. John's Seminary Library
5012 East Seminary Road
Camarillo, CA 93010

Claremont

Libraries of the Claremont Colleges
Pomona College Library
6th and College Avenue
Claremont, CA 91711

Fresno

Roman Catholic Diocese of Fresno
1550 N. Fresno Street
Fresno, CA 93717

Chancery Archives
Chancery Office
Box 1668
Fresno, CA 93717

Jolon

San Antonio Mission
Jolan, CA 93928

Laguna Niguel

Federal Archives and Records Center
(formerly at Bell, California)

Los Angeles

Los Angeles County Law Library
301 W. First Street
Los Angeles, CA 90012

Los Angeles County Museum Library

Office of the City Clerk

Office of the County Recorder

Roman Catholic Archdiocese of Los Angeles
Chancery Archives
Chancery Office
1531 West 9th Street
Los Angeles, CA 90015

Roman Catholic Church, Our Lady Queen of the Angels Church
100 Sunset Boulevard
Los Angeles, CA 90012

Southwest Museum
Braun Research Library
234 Museum Drive
Box 128, Highland Park Station
Los Angeles, CA 90042

University of California at Los Angeles Library
405 Hilgard Avenue
Los Angeles, CA 90024

Palos Verdes

Palos Verdes Public Library
650 Deep Valley Drive
Palos Verdes, CA 90274

Pasadena

Pasadena Public Library
285 E. Walnut Street
Pasadena, CA 91101

Sacramento

California State Archives
1020 "O" Street
Sacramento, CA 95814

California State Library
914 Capital Mall
Library and Courts Building
Box 2037
Sacramento, CA 95809

U. S. Bureau of Land Management
California Land Office

San Bruno

Federal Archives and Records Center
(formerly at San Francisco)

San Diego

San Diego Historical Society
Library and Manuscripts Collection
Serra Museum, Presidio Park
Box 81825
San Diego, CA 92138

San Diego de Alcala Mission

San Diego Public Library
820 E Street
San Diego, CA 92101

San Francisco

California Historical Society

California State Library, Sutro Branch
2495 Golden Gate Avenue
San Francisco, CA 94118

City Archives

Dolores Mission
Mission Dolores Basilica
16th and Delores Streets
San Francisco, CA

Roman Catholic Archdiocese of San Francisco
Chancery Archives
445 Church Street
San Francisco, CA 94114

Society of California Pioneers
456 McAllister Street
San Francisco, CA 94102

U.S. District Court, Northern District of California

San Gabriel

San Gabriel Archangel Mission

San Jose

San Jose Historical Museum

San Juan Bautista

San Juan Bautista Mission
Box 410
San Juan Bautista, CA 95045

San Juan Capistrano

San Juan Capistrano Mission

San Luis Obispo

San Luis Obispo Mission
San Luis Obispo, CA 93401

San Marino

Henry E. Huntington Library and Art Gallery
1151 Oxford Road
San Marino, CA 91108

San Miguel

San Miguel Mission
Box 69
San Miguel, CA 93451

Santa Ana

Charles W. Bowers Memorial Museum
2002 N. Main Street
Santa Ana, CA 92706

Santa Barbara

Our Lady of Sorrows Church
Santa Barbara Mission Archives
21 E. Sola Street
Santa Barbara, CA 93101

Santa Clara

University of Santa Clara
Orradre Library

Solvang

Santa Ynez Mission
1760 Mission Drive
Box 408
Solvang, CA 93463

Stanford

Stanford University Library
Dept. of Special Collections, Manuscripts Division
Stanford, CA 94305

Ventura

San Buenaventura Mission
211 E. Main Street
Ventura, CA 93001

Colorado

Denver

Colorado Dept. of Administration

Division of State Archives and Public Records

Federal Archives and Records Center

State Historical Society of Colorado

U.S. Bureau of Land Management
Colorado State Office Library
1037 20th Street
Denver, CO 80202

New Mexico

Albuquerque

Roman Catholic Archdiocese of Santa Fe
Chancery Archives
202 Morningside Drive, S.E.
Albuquerque, NM 87108

University of New Mexico Library
Albuquerque, NM 87131

Las Vegas

New Mexico Highlands University Library
Donnelly Library
National Avenue
Las Vegas, NM 87701

Santa Fe

Historical Society of New Mexico

New Mexico State Records Center and Archives

U.S. Bureau of Land Management
New Mexico State Office Library
Box 1449
Santa Fe, NM 87501

Texas

Angleton

Brazoria, County Clerk's Office

Austin

Austin Public Library
401 Guadalupe
Box 2287
Austin, TX 78767

Catholic Archives of Texas (Texas Catholic Historical Society)
16th and Congress
Box 13327 Capital Station
Austin, TX 78711

Roman Catholic Diocese of Austin
Chancery Archives

Texas General Land Office

Texas State Library, Archives Division
1200 Brazos
Box 12927, Capital Station
Austin, TX 78711

University of Texas
Eugene C. Barker Texas History Center
Texas Archives
10100 Burnet Road
Box "P"
Austin, TX 78712

University of Texas Library
Latin American Collection
(same as above)

Bay City

Matagorda, County Clerk's Office

Belleville

Austin, County Clerk's Office

Dallas

Dallas Historical Society
Research Center
Hall of State
Fair Park
Box 26038
Dallas, TX 75226

Southern Methodist University
De Golyer Foundation Library
Dallas, TX 75275

Southern Methodist University
Hendren Library
(same as above)

Denton

North Texas State College Library
Box 5188, NT Station
Denton, TX 76203

El Paso

University of Texas at El Paso Library
El Paso, TX 79968

Galveston

Rosenberg Library
2310 Sealy Avenue
Galveston, TX 77550

Gonzales

Gonzales Memorial Museum

Houston

Houston Public Library
500 McKinney Avenue
Houston, TX 77002

Laredo

Laredo Junior College
West End Washington Street
Laredo, TX 78040

St. Augustin Church

Webb, County Clerk's Office

Lubbock

Texas Technological University Library
Lubbock, TX 79409

Nacogdoches

Nacogdoches, County Clerk's Office

Refugio

Our Lady of Refuge Church
1008 S. Alamo Street
Refugio, TX 78377

Dawgood Library
601 E. Ymbacion Street
Box 267
Refugio, TX 78377

District Court Clerk's Office

San Antonio

Alamo Museum

Bexar, County Clerk's Office

Lady of the Lake College
411 S.W. 24th Street
San Antonio, TX 78285

Old Spanish Mission Historical Research Library
San Jose Mission

Roman Catholic Archdiocese of San Antonio
9123 Lorene Lane
Box 32648
San Antonio, TX 78284

San Fernando Cathedral Archives
114 Military Plaza
San Antonio, TX 78205

St. Mary's University Library
1 Camino Santa Maria
San Antonio, TX 78284

Trinity University Library
715 Stadium Drive
San Antonio, TX 78284

San Augustin

San Augustin, County Clerk's Office

San Jacinto

San Jacinto Museum

Waco

Baylor University
Texas History Collection
Box 6307
Waco, TX 76706

Bibliography of Guides, Inventories, and Catalogs

Abajian, James DeT. "Preliminary Listing of Manuscript Collections in Library of California Historical Society." *California Historical Society Quarterly* 33 (Dec. 1954): 372-76.

Arno Press Collection. *The Chicano Heritage*. 55 titles, description and order form available upon request. Arno Press, 3 Park Avenue, New York, NY 10017. Includes reprints, bibliographies, original studies, archive guides.

"Bandelier Collection of Copies of Documents Relative to the History of New Mexico and Arizona." *In Report of the United States Commission to the Columbian Historical Commission at Madrid, 1892-93, with Special Papers*, pp. 305-26. House Executive Document No. 100, 53rd Cong., 3rd sess., Serial 3322. Washington, D.C.: Government Printing Office, 1895.

Barker, Eugene C. "Report on the Public Archives of Texas." *American Historical Association, Annual Report* 2 (1901): 353-58.

Barton, Noel R. "Genealogical Research in the Records of the California Spanish Missions." *Genealogical Journal* 4 (March 1975): 13-33. Includes a table of record locations.

Beers, Henry Putnam. *Spanish and Mexican Records of the American Southwest*. Tucson: University of Arizona Press: 1979.

Boulton, Herbert E. *Guide to Materials for the History of the United States in the Principal Archives of Mexico*. Carnegie Institution of Washington, Publication No. 163. Washington, D.C.: Carnegie Institution, 1913.

___________. "Spanish Mission Records at San Antonio." *Texas State Historical Association Quarterly* 10 (April 1907): 297-307.

Borges, Pedro. "Documentacion americana en el Archivo General O.F.M. de Roma." *Archivo iber-americano* 19 (enero-junio 1959): 5-119.

Bowman, Jacob N. "California Private Land Grant Records in the National Archives." 24 Jan. 1956. Photostat of typescript, National Archives Library.

___________. "Index of Private Land Grants and Land Grant Papers." 1942. Manuscript in the Bancroft Library, University of California.

___________. "Index of the Spanish-Mexican Private Land Grant Records and Cases of California." Berkeley, 1958. Photocopy of typescript in the National Archives; original in the Bancroft Library, University of California.

___________. "The Parochial Books of the California Missions." *Historical Society of Southern California Quarterly* 43 (Sept. 1961): 303-15.

Burrus, Ernest J. *A History of the Southwest: A Study of the Civilization and Conversion of the Indians in Southwestern United States and Northwestern Mexico from the Earliest Times*. Vol. 1 of Catalogue of the Bandelier Collection in the Vatican Library. Rome: Jesuit Historical Institute, 1969.

Butler, Ruth L. *A Check List of Manuscripts in the Edward E. Ayer Collection*. Chicago: Newberry Library, 1937.

California, State Library. "Index to Spanish Archives on File in the State Library, XIV – Spanish Archives Collected in Monterey in 1851, by Order of the Legislature." In United States, Appellant. *U.S. District Court, Northern District of California, No. 424: The United States v. Jose Y. Limantour; Transcript of the Record from the Board of United States Land Commissioners, in Case. No. 548, Filed February 19, 1856*, pp. 267-72. San Francisco: Whitton, Towne & Co. Excelsior Steam Presses, 1857.

___________, Surveyor General. "Corrected Report of Spanish and Mexican Grants in California, Complete to February 25, 1886." In *Report of the Surveyor-General of the State of California from August 1, 1884, to August 1, 1886, Appendix to the Journals of the Senate and Assembly of the Twenty-Seventh Session...*, 1:11-29. Sacramento: 1887. Also published separately in Sacramento, 1886.

___________, ___________. "Report of Spanish or Mexican Grants in California, prepared by James S. Stratton." In *Report of the Surveyor-General of the State of California, from August 1st, 1879, to August 1st, 1880*. California, Legislature, *Appendix to the Journals of the Senate and Assembly of the Twenty-Fourth Session*, 1:15-54. Sacramento, 1881.

___________, University, Los Angeles, Library. *Guide to Special Collections in the Library of the University of California at Los Angeles*. UCLA Library, Occasional Papers No. 7. Los Angeles, 1958.

Carrera Stampa, Manuel. *Archivalia Mexicana*. Universidad Nacional Autonoma de Mexico, Publicaciones del Instituto de Historia, 1st Series, Num 27. Mexico: Editorial Jus, 1952.

Casteneda, Carlos E. *A Report on the Spanish Archives in San Antonio, Texas*. San Antonio: Yanaguana Society, 1937.

__________, and Jack A. Dabbs. *Guide to the Latin American Manuscripts in the University of Texas Library*. Committee on Latin American Studies, American Council of Learned Societies, Miscellaneous Publication, No. 1. Cambridge: Harvard University Press, 1939.

__________. *Independent Mexico in Documents: Independence, Empire and Republic; A Calendar of the Juan B. Hernandez y Davalos Manuscript Collection*. Mexico: Editorial Jus, 1954.

Cavazos Garza, Israel. *Catalogo y sintesis de los protocolos del Archivo Municipal de Monterrey, 1599-1700, 1700-1725*. Indices de los archivos del noreste de Mexico, 2; Instituto Tecnologico y de Estudias Superiores de Monterrey, Publicaciones, Series: Historia 4. Monterrey: Instituto Tecnologico y de Estudias Superiores de Monterrey, 1966, 1973.

Chapman, Charles E. *Catalogue of Materials in the Archivo General de Indias for the History of the Pacific Coast and the American Southwest*. University of California, Publications in History, vol. 8. Glendale: Arthur H. Clark Co., 1919.

Chavez, Angelicco. *Archives of the Archdiocese of Santa Fe, 1678-1900*. Publications of the Academy of American Franciscan History, Bibliographical Series, vol. 3. Washington, D.C.: Academy of American Franciscan History, 1957.

__________. "Some Original New Mexico Documents in California Libraries." *New Mexico Historical Review* 25 (July 1950): 244-53.

Colley, Charles C. *Documents of Southwestern History: A Guide to the Manuscript Collections of the Arizona Historical Society*. Tucson: Arizona Historical Society, 1972.

Connor, Seymour V. *A Preliminary Guide to the Archives of Texas*. Austin: Texas State Library, 1956.

Cottler, Susan M., et al. *Preliminary Survey of the Mexican Collection at the Genealogical Society of Utah*. Salt Lake City: University of Utah Press, 1978. Supplement, 1979.

Cowan, Robert G. *Ranchos of California: A List of Spanish Concessions, 1775-1822, and Mexican Grants, 1822-46*. Fresno: Academy Library Guild, 1956.

Cox, Isaac J. "The Early Settlers of San Fernando." *Quarterly, Texas State Historical Association* 5 (Oct. 1901): 142-60. Includes biographies, census entries.

Coy, Owen C. *Guide to the County Archives of California*. California Historical Survey Commission Publication. Sacramento: California State Printing Office, 1919.

Daly, Lowrie J. "Microfilmed Materials from the Archives of the Sacred Congregation 'De Propaganda Fide.'" *Manuscripta*, Nov. 1966, pp. 139-44.

Day, James M., Ann B. Dunlap, Mike Smyers, and Kenneth Parker. *Maps of Texas, 1527-1900: The Map Collection of the Texas State Archives*. Austin: Pemberton Press, 1964.

Day, James M., and Donna Yarbrough. *Handbook of Texas Archival and Manuscript Depositories*. Texas State Library, Monograph Series, No. 5. Austin: Texas Library and Historical Commission, 1966.

Diaz, Albert J. *A Guide to the Microfilm of Papers Relating to New Mexico Land Grants*. University of New Mexico Publications, Library Series, No. 1. Albuquerque: University of New Mexico Press, 1960.

__________. *Manuscripts and Records in the University of New Mexico Library*. Albuquerque: University of New Mexico Library, 1957.

__________. "University of New Mexico Special Collections." *New Mexico Historical Review* 33 (July, Oct. 1958): 235-51, 316-21.

Dixon, Ford. "Texas History in Maps: An Archival and Historical Examination of the James Perry Bryan Map Collection." *Texana* 5 (Summer 1967): 99-116; (Fall 1967): 238-67.

Dobyns, Henry F. *Spanish Colonial Tucson: A Demographic History*. Tucson: University of Arizona Press, 1976. Meticulous analysis of population enumerations.

Edwards, Mrs. Ben C. *Chronological List of Framed Documents from Dr. Wm. E. Howard Collection* [in the Daughters of the Republic of Texas Library]. San Antonio, 1950.

Ericson, Carolyn R. *Nacogdoches – Gateway to Texas: A Biographical Directory, 1773-1849*. Fort Worth: Arrow-Curtis Printing Co., 1974.

Evans, G. Edward. "A Guide to Pre-1850 Manuscripts in the United States Relating to Mexico and the Southwestern United States, with Emphasis on Their Value to Anthropologists." *Ethnohistory* 17 (Winter-Spring 1970): 63-90.

Ewing, William S. *Guide to the Manuscript Collections in the William L. Clements Library*. Ann Arbor: Clements Library, 1953.

Ezell, Paul, and Greta Ezell. *The Aguir Collection in the Arizona Pioneers' Historical Society*. San Diego: San Diego State College Press, 1964.

Fish, Carl R. *Guide to the Materials for American History in Roman and Other Italian Archives*. Carnegie Institution of Washington, Publication, no. 128. Washington: Carnegie Institution, 1911.

Fisher, Mary Ann. *Preliminary Guide to the Microfilm Collection in the Bancroft Library*. Berkeley: University of California, 1955.

Geiger, Maynard J. *Calendar of Documents in the Santa Barbara Mission Archives*. Publications of the Academy of American Franciscan History, Bibliographical Series, vol 1. Washington: Academy of American Franciscan History, 1947.

Genealogical Society of the Church of Jesus Christ of Latter-day Saints. *Major Genealogical Records Sources in Mexico*. Research Paper, Series H, No. 2. Salt Lake City: Genealogical Society, 1970.

Goddart, Jeanne, Charles A. Kritzler, and Archibald Hanna. *A Catalogue of the Frederick W. & Carrie S. Beinecke Collection of Western Americana*, vol. 1, *Manuscripts* [in the Yale University Library]. New Haven and London: Yale University Press, 1965.

Gomez Canedo, Lino. *Los archivos de la historia de America, periodo colonial espanola*. 2 vols. Instituto Panamericano de Geografia e Historia, Comision de Historia. Publicacion Num. 225. Mexico City: Comision de Historia. 1961.

Greenleaf, Richard E., and Michael C. Meyer. *Research in Mexican History: Topics, Methodology, Sources, and a Practical Guide to Field Research*. Lincoln: University of Nebraska Press, 1973. One of the best guides for Mexican and borderlands research.

Hale, Richard W., Jr. *Guide to Photocopied Historical Materials in the United States and Canada*. Ithaca, N.Y.: Cornell University Press, 1961.

Hamer, Philip M. *A Guide to Archives and Manuscripts in the United States*. New Haven: Yale University Press, 1961.

Hammond, George P. *A Guide to the Manuscript Collections of the Bancroft Library*, vol. 2. Bancroft Library, Bibliographical Series, Vol. 2: *Manuscripts Relating Chiefly to Mexico and Central America*. Berkeley and Los Angeles: University of California Press, 1972.

Hilton, Ronald. *Handbook of Hispanic Source Materials and Research Organizations in the United States*. Stanford: Stanford University Press, 1956.

Historical Records Survey, Arizona. *Inventory of the County Archives of Arizona, No. 10, Pima County (Tucson)*. Phoenix: The Historical Survey, 1938.

__________, Colorado. *Inventory of the County Archives of Colorado No. 2, Alamosa County (Alamosa)*. Denver: Historical Records Survey, 1942.

__________, __________. *Inventory of the County Archives of Colorado, No. 12, Costilla County (San Luis)*. Denver: Historical Records Survey, 1938.

__________, New Mexico. *Inventory of the County Archives of New Mexico, No. 1, Bernalillo County (Albuquerque)*. Albuquerque: Historical Records Survey, 1938.

__________, __________. *Inventory of the County Archives of New Mexico, No. 4, Colfax County (Raton)*. Albuquerque: Historical Records Survey, 1937.

__________, __________. *Inventory of the County Archives of New Mexico, No. 7, Dona Ana County (Las Cruces)*. Albuquerque: Historical Records Survey, 1940.

__________, __________. *Inventory of the County Archives of New Mexico, No. 17, Mora County (Mora)*. Albuquerque: Historical Records Survey, 1940.

__________, __________. *Inventory of the County Archives of New Mexico, No. 23, Sandoval County (Bernalillo)*. Albuquerque: Historical Records Survey, 1939.

__________, __________. *Inventory of the County Archives of New Mexico, No. 31, Valencia County (Los Lunas)*. Albuquerque: Historical Records Survey, 1940.

__________, Northern California. *Inventory of the County Archives of California, No. 20, Napa County (Napa)*. San Francisco: Northern California Historical Records Survey Project, 1941.

__________, __________. *Inventory of the County Archives of California, No. 36, San Benito County (Hollister)*. San Francisco: Northern

California Historical Records Survey Project, 1940.

__________, __________. *Inventory of the County Archives of California, No. 39. The City and County of San Francisco (San Francisco)*, Vol. 2. San Francisco: Northern California Historical Records Survey Project, 1939.

__________, __________. *Inventory of the County Archives of California, No. 41, San Luis Obispo (San Luis Obispo)*. San Francisco: Northern California Historical Records Survey Project, 1939.

__________, __________. *Inventory of the County Archives of California, No. 44, Santa Clara County (San Jose)*. San Francisco: Northern California Historical Records Survey Project, 1939.

__________, Southern California. *Guide to Depositories of Manuscripts in the United States: California*. Los Angeles: Southern Historical Records Survey Project, 1941.

__________, __________. *Inventory of the Bixby Records Collection in the Palos Verdes Library and Art Gallery*. Los Angeles: Southern California Historical Records Survey Project, 1940.

__________, __________. *Inventory of the County Archives of California, No. 20, Los Angeles County (Los Angeles) County Clerk's Office*. Los Angeles: Southern California Historical Records Survey Project, 1943.

__________, Texas. *Inventory of the Colonial Archives of Texas, No. 3, Municipality of Brazoria, 1832-1837 (Brazoria County Courthouse, Angleton, Texas)*. San Antonio: Texas Historical Records Survey, 1937.

__________, __________. *Inventory of the Colonial Archives of Texas, 1821-1837, Municipality of San Felipe de Austin (Austin County Courthouse, Belleville, Texas)*. San Antonio: 1938. Photocopy of manuscript in the University of Texas Library.

__________, __________. *Inventory of the County Archives of Texas, No. 28, Caldwell County (Lockhart)*. San Antonio: Texas Historical Records Survey, 1941.

__________, __________. *Inventory of the County Archives of Texas, No. 75, Fayette County (Langrange)*. San Antonio: Texas Historical Records Survey, 1940.

Hoffman, Ogden. "Table of Land Claims, Presented to the Commission Pursuant to the Provisions of the Act of Congress of March 3d, 1851, Entitled 'An Act to Ascertain and Settle the Private Land Claims in the State of California.' " In Hoffman, *Reports of Land Cases Determined in the United States District Court for the Northern District of California*, appendix 1. San Francisco, 1862. Also in *The Federal Cases* 30:1217-57, listed under "Printed Sources."

Howard, William E. *Calendar of the Howard Collection of Texana: A Collector's Item*. Dallas, 1944.

Hoyo, Eugenio del. *Indice del Ramo de Causas Criminales del Archivo Municipal de Monterrey*. Instituto Tecnologico y de Estudios Superiores de Monterrey, Serie de Historia. Monterrey: Instituto Tecnologico y de Estudios de Monterrey, 1963.

Hughes, Ann E. *The Beginnings of Spanish Settlement in the El Paso District*. Berkeley: University of California Press, 1914. Includes biographies.

Hutchinson, Cecil A. *Frontier Settlement in Mexican California: Hijar-Padres Colony and Its Origins, 1769-1835*. New Haven: Yale University Press, 1969. Includes complete list of settlers.

Jenkins, Myra E. *Calendar of the Mexican Archives of New Mexico, 1821-46*. Santa Fe: State of New Mexico Records Center, 1970.

__________. *Guide to the Microfilm of the Spanish Archives of New Mexico, 1621-1821, in the Archives Division of the State of New Mexico Records Center*. Santa Fe: State of New Mexico Records Center, 1967.

__________. *Guide to the Microfilm Edition of the Mexican Archives of New Mexico, 1821-1846, in the Archives Division of the State of New Mexico Records Center*. Santa Fe: State of New Mexico Records Center, 1969.

Jenkins, William S., comp., and Lillian A. Hamrick, ed. *A Guide to the Microfilm Collection of Early State Records*. Prepared by the Library of Congress in association with the University of North Carolina. Washington: Photoduplication Service, Library of Congress, 1950. *Supplement*. Comp. and ed. by W. S. Jenkins. Washington, D.C., 1951.

Jones, Oakah L., Jr. *Los Paisanos: Spanish Settlers on the Northern Frontier of New Spain*. Norman: University of Oklahoma Press, 1979.

Kenneally, Finbar, ed. *United States Documents in the Propaganda Archives: A Calendar*. 5 vols. Publications of the Academy of American Franciscan History. Washington, D.C.: Academy of American Franciscan History, 1966-74.

Kielman, Chester V. *Guide to the Microfilm Edition of the Bexar Archives, 1717-1803*. Austin: University of Texas Archives, 1967.

__________. *Guide to the Microfilm Edition of the Bexar Archives, 1804-1821*. Austin: University of Texas Archives, 1969.

__________. *Guide to the Microfilm Edition of the Bexar Archives 1822-1836*. Austin: University of Texas Archives, 1971.

__________. *The University of Texas Archives: A Guide to the Historical Manuscripts in the University of Texas Library*. Austin: University of Texas Press, 1967.

Lane, (Sister) M. Claude. *Catholic Archives of Texas: History and Preliminary Inventory*. Houston: Sacred Heart Dominican College, 1961.

Leonard, Olen E. *The Role of the Land Grant in the Social Organization and Social Process of a Spanish American Village in New Mexico*. Albuquerque: Calvin Horn Publishers, Inc., 1970. Study of El Cerrito. Includes excellent photographs of the Spanish social heritage.

Martinez, Pablo L. *Guia Familiar de Baja California, 1700-1900*. Mexico City: Imprenta "Laura," 1965. Includes biographies, vital records.

Mexico, Direccion de Archivo Historico Militar. *Guia del Archivo Historico Militar de Mexico, formado de Orden de la Direccion del Archivo Militar*. Prologo de Vito Alsessio Robles. Mexico City: Taller Autografico, 1948.

__________, Ministerio de Hacienda y Credito Publico Archivo. *Guia del Archivo Historico del Archivo Historico de Hacienda Siglos XVI a XIX*. Mexico City: Los talleres de impresiones de estamphillas y valores de la Sria. de hda., 1940-45.

Miller, David J. "Private Land Claims [Adjudicated]; Private Land Claims Not Yet Adjudicated." In New Mexico (Territory), Secretary's Office. *The Legislative Blue-Book of the Territory of New Mexico*. Santa Fe: Charles W. Greene, Public Printer, 1882, pp. 129-34.

Morgan, Dale L., and George P. Hammond, eds. *A Guide to the Manuscript Collections of the Bancroft Library*. Bancroft Library Publications, Bibliographical Series, vol. 1: *Pacific and Western Manuscripts, except California*. Berkeley and Los Angeles: University of California Press, 1963.

Mundo Lo, Sara de. *Bibliography of Hispanic-American Collection Biography*. Boston: G. K. Hall and Co., 1980.

Murrieta, Cynthia R. de, and Maria L. Torres Chavez. *Catalogo del Archivo Historico del Estado Sonora*. 2 vols. Hermosillo: Centro Regionalde Norests, Instituto Nacional de Antropologia e Historia, Secretaria de Educacion Publica, 1974-75.

National Archives Trust Fund. *Genealogical Research in the National Archives*. Washington, D.C.: National Archives, 1982.

New Mexico, State Records Center and Archives. *Calendar of the Mexican Archives of New Mexico, 1821-1846*. Prep. by Myra Ellen Jenkins. Santa Fe: State of New Mexico Records Center and Archives, 1970.

__________. *Calendar of the Spanish Archives of New Mexico, 1621-1821*. Santa Fe: State of New Mexico Records Center and Archives, 1968.

New York Historical Society. *Survey of the Manuscript Collections in the New York Historical Society*. New York: New York Historical Society, 1941.

Nogales, Luis G. *The Mexican-American: A Selected and Annotated Bibliography*. Stanford, Calif.: Stanford University Press, 1971.

Northrop, Marie E. *Spanish-Mexican Families of Early California: 1769-1850*. New Orleans: Polyanthos, 1976. Volume 1 of a projected series on California family origins.

__________. *Spanish-American Families of Early California, 1769-1850*. Burbank, Calif.: Southern California Genealogical Society, Inc., 1984. Volume 2 on early California families, including 265 family genealogies.

Olmstead, Virginia L. "Spanish Enlistment Papers of New Mexico, 1732-1820." *National Genealogical Society Quarterly*, vol. 67 (1979).

O'Rourke, Thomas P. *The Franciscan Missions in Texas, 1690-1793*. Washington, D.C.: Catholic University of America, 1927.

Parish, John C. "California Books and Manuscripts in the Huntington Library." *Huntington Library Bulletin*, no. 7 (April 1935) 1-58.

Parral, Mexico, Archivo. *English Translation of the Index to El Archivo de Hidalgo del Parral, 1631-1821*. Trans., Consuelo P. Boyd. Tucson: Arizona Silhouettes, 1971.

__________. "Index to El Archivo de Hidalgo del Parral, 1631-1821." Tucson: Arizona Silhouettes, 1961. Photocopy in the Library of Congress.

Peckham, Howard H. *Guide to the Manuscript Collections in the William*

L. Clements Library. Ann Arbor: University of Michigan Press; London: H. Milford, Oxford University Press, 1942.

Platt, Lyman De. *Genealogical-Historical Guide to Latin America*. Detroit: Gale Publishing Company, 1978. Also available in Spanish: *Una Guia Genealogico-Historica de Latin America*. Ramona, Calif.: Acoma Books, 1978.

__________. "Hispanic-American Records and Research." In Jessie Carney Smith, ed., *Ethnic Genealogy: A Research Guide*. Westport, Conn.: Greenwood Press, 1983, pp. 365-401. Includes case studies.

__________. "Spanish and Mexican Immigration to the United States." *Genealogical Journal* 3 (1974): 23-24.

Pompey, Sherman L. *Genealogical Records of California*. Fresno, Calif.: For the author, 1968. Typescript. Microfilm copy at Genealogical Society of Utah.

Read, Benjamin M. *Chronological Digest of the "Documentos Ineditos del Archivo de las Indias."* Albuquerque: Albright & Anderson, 1914.

Rio, Ignacio del. *Guia del archivo franciscano de la Biblioteca Nacional de Mexico. vol. 1. Guias, no. 3.* Mexico: Instituto de Investigaciones Bibliograficas, Universidad Nacional Autonoma de Mexico, 1975.

Rubio Mane, Jorge Ignacio. *El Archivo General de la Nacion, Mexico, D.F.*. pp. 63-169. Mexico City: Editorial Cultura, 1940. Also published in *Revista de la Historia de America 9* (1940): 63-169.

Saint John's Seminary, Camarillo, California, Library, Estelle Doheny Collection. One Hundred Manuscripts and Books from the Estelle Doheny Collection in the Edward L. Doheny Memorial Library, St. John's Seminary, Camarillo, California. Los Angeles: Anderson & Ritchie, 1950.

Sanchez, Jose de la Cruz. "The Inventory of All the Archives [of Yerba Buena] from the Foundation of the Ayuntamiento in 1835, to the End of the Present Year [1845]." *The Pioneer: or, California Monthly Magazine* 1 (March 1843): 142-44.

San Diego Historical Society. *A Guide to the Research Collections of the San Diego Historical Society Located in the Serra Museum, Presidio Hill, Birthplace of California*. San Diego: The Society, 1964.

San Jacinto Museum of History, San Jacinto Monument, Texas. *A Check List of Manuscripts Including a Transcript of a Letter from the Battleground, an Eyewitness Account of the Battle of San Jacinto*. San Jacinto: San Jacinto Museum of History Association, 1949.

Santos, Richard G. "An Annotated Survey of the Spanish Archives of Laredo at Saint Mary's University of Texas." *Texana* 4 (Spring 1966): 41-46.

__________. "Documentos para la historia de Mexico en los archivos de San Antonio, Texas." *Revista de Historia de America* 63-64 (enero-diciembre, 1967): 343-49.

Scholes, France V. "Manuscripts for the History of New Mexico in the National Library in Mexico City." *New Mexico Historical Review* 3 (July 1928): 301-23.

Shepherd, William R. *Guide to the Materials for the History of the United States in Spanish Archives*. Carnegie Institution of Washington, Publication No. 91. Washington, D.C.: Carnegie Institution, 1907.

Sherburne, George, et al. "Huntington Library Collections." *Huntington Library Bulletin*, No. 1 (May 1931): 33-106.

Smithsonian Institution. *Catalogue of the Berlandier Manuscripts Deposited in the Smithsonian Institution, Washington, D.C.* New York: Folger & Turner, Printer, 1853.

Spain, Archivo General de Simancas. *Guia del Archivo General de Simancas*. [Madrid]: Direccion General de Archivos y Bibliotecas; [Valencia, Tipografia Moderna], 1958.

__________, Archivo Historico Nacional. *Guia del Archivo Historico. Por Luis Sanchez Belda*. [Madrid], 1958.

__________, Direccion General de Archivos y Bibliotecas. *Guia de los archivos de Madrid*. Madrid: Nuevas Graficas, 1952.

__________, __________. *Guia de las bibliotecas de Madrid*. Madrid: Talleres Graficos Escelices, 1953.

Spell, Lota M. *Research Materials for the Study of Latin America at the University of Texas*. Austin: University of Texas Press, 1954.

Strout, Clevy L. *A Catalog of Hispanic Documents in the Thomas Gilcrease Institute*. Tulsa: The Thomas Gilcrease Institute of American History and Art, 1962.

Taylor, Virginia H., trans. and ed. "Calendar of the Letters of Antonio Martinez, Last Spanish Governor of Texas, 1817-1822." *Southwestern Historical Quarterly* 59 (Jan.-April 1956): 372-81, 473-86; 60 (July 1956-April 1957): 80-99, 292-305, 387-400, 533-47; 61 (July-Oct. 1957): 125-46, 288-304.

__________. *The Spanish Archives of the General Land Office of Texas*. Austin: Lone Star Press, 1955.

Texas, General Land Office. "Key to the Spanish Archives of the General Land Office of Texas." Photocopy in possession of the author supplied by the Texas General Land Office.

Timmons, W. H. "The El Paso Area in the Mexican Period, 1821-1848." *Southwestern Historical Quarterly* 84 (July 1980): 1-28. Includes family history.

__________. "The Population of the El Paso Area – A Census of 1784." *New Mexico Historical Review* 52 (Oct. 1977): 311-16. Annotated with biographical and family data.

Torok, Mildred. *Guide to Collections: The University of Texas at El Paso Archives*. El Paso, 1972.

Tudela, Jose. *Los manuscritos de America en las bibliotecas de Espana*. Madrid: Ediciones Cultura Hispanica, 1954.

Twitchell, Ralph E. *The Spanish Archives of New Mexico*. 2 vols. Glendale, Calif.: Arthur H. Clark Co., 1914.

U.S. Federal Records Center, Bell, California. *Preliminary Inventory of the Records of the Bureau of Land Management (Record Group 49)*. Comp., Gilbert Dorane. Los Angeles: 1966.

__________, San Francisco, California. *Preliminary Inventory of the Records of the Bureau of Land Management (Record Group 49)*. Comp., John P. Heard. San Francisco, 1969.

U.S. Library of Congress. *Archives of Government Offices Outside of Washington*. House Document No. 1443, 62nd Cong., 3rd Sess. (Serial 6501). Washington: Government Printing Office, 1913.

__________, Division of Maps. *The Lowery Collection: A Descriptive List of Maps of the Spanish Possessions within the Present Limits of the United States, 1502-1820*. Prep. by Woodbury Lowery; ed. by Philip Lee Phillips. Washington, D.C.: Government Printing Office, 1912.

__________, Manuscript Division. *Handbook of Manuscripts in the Library of Congress*. Washington, D.C.: Government Printing Office, 1918.

__________, __________. *Manuscripts on Microfilm: A Checklist of the Holdings in the Manuscript Division*. Comp., Richard B. Bickel. Washington, D.C.: Government Printing Office, 1975.

__________, __________. *The National Union Catalog of Manuscript Collections*, 1959/61-74. 12 vols. 1959-61, Ann Arbor, Mich.: J. W. Edwards, Inc., 1962; 1962, Hamden, Conn.: Shoe String Press, Inc., 1964; 1963/64-74, Washington, D.C.: Library of Congress, 1965-75.

U. S. National Archives. "Alphabetical Index to the California Board of Land Commissioners Expedientes for Private Land Claims Dockets." Records of the General Land Office. Record Group 49. Washington, D.C., 1969. Typescript.

__________. "Alphabetical Index to the California Private Land Claims Dockets," Records of the General Land Office. Record Group 49. Washington, D.C.: 1969. Typescript.

__________. *Guide to the National Archives of the United States*. Washington, D.C.: Government Printing Office, 1974.

__________. "Land Grant Records That Survived a Great Fire." *Historical Society of Southern California Quarterly* 26 (March 1944): 38-44.

__________. *List of Cartographic Records of the General Land Office (Record Group 49)*. Comp., Laura E. Kelsay. Special Lists No. 19. Washington, D.C.: National Archives, 1964.

__________. "Preliminary Inventory of the Cartographic Records of the Bureau of Land Management (Record Group 49)." Comp., Laura E. Kelsay. Washington, D.C., 1965. Typescript.

__________. *Preliminary Inventory of the Records of the Supreme Court of the United States (Record Group 267)*. Comp., Marion M. Johnson. Preliminary Inventories No. 139. Washington, D.C.: National Archives, 1962.

__________. "Records of Mexican Land Claims in California." Prep. by Ralph G. Lounsbury. Washington, D.C.: n.d. Typescript.

U.S. Survey of Federal Archives, Arizona. *Inventory of Federal Archives in the States, Series VIII, The Department of the Interior, No. 3, Arizona*. Tucson: Survey of Federal Archives, 1939.

__________, California. *Inventory of Federal Archives in the States, Series II, Federal Courts, No. 5, California*. San Francisco: Survey of Federal Archives, 1939.

__________, __________. *Inventory of Federal Archives in the States, Series V, Department of Justice, No. 5, California*. San Francisco: Survey of Federal Archives, 1939.

__________, __________. *Inventory of Federal Archives in the States, Series VIII, The Department of the Interior, No. 8, California*. San Francisco: Survey of Federal Archives, 1941.

__________, __________. "Lists of Maps in the Spanish and Mexican Land Claims Cases in the United States District Court for the Northern District of California." San Francisco, 1940. Typescript in the National Archives.

U.S. Surveyor General of California. "Alphabetical List of Approvals of Grants of Land, by the Departmental Assembly of California, Recorded in the Book of Sessions." In U.S. Department of the Interior, *Annual Report*, 1880, pp. 912-16. Washington, D.C.: Government Printing Office, 1880.

__________. "Alphabetical List of Names of Ranchos, the Claims of Which Have Been Acted upon by the Former Governments." In U.S. Department of the Interior, *Annual Report*, 1880, pp. 899-912. Washington, D.C.: Government Printing Office, 1880.

__________. "Catalogue of the Original Expedientes or Records in Relation to Land Claims in Upper California under the Spanish and Mexican Governments, with References to Registries of the Same, Arranged in Alphabetical Order, Now on File in the Spanish Archives of the Office of the United States Surveyor-General for California." In U.S. Department of the Interior, *Annual Report*, 1880, pp. 859- 99. Washington, D.C.: Government Printing Office, 1880.

__________. "List of Original Documents in Cases Presented to the United States Land Commission, Now on File in the Office of the United States Surveyor-General for California." In United States Department of the Interior, *Annual Report*, 1880, pp. 799-858. Washington, D.C.: Government Printing Office, 1880.

__________. "List of Original Land Grants on File in the Land Commission Papers of the United States Surveyor General's Office for California." In U.S. District Court, California (Northern District), *The United States, Appellants v. Jose Y. Limantour, Appellee, Nos. 424 and 428, Land Commission Exhibits.... [San Francisco, 1958]*. Exhibit K.

U.S. Surveyor General of New Mexico. "List of Documents Relating to Grants of Land by the Spanish and Mexican Governments in the Archives of the Office of the Surveyor-General of New Mexico, June 30, 1885." In U.S. Department of the Interior, *Annual Report*, 1855, 1:535-52. Washington, D.C.: Government Printing Office , 1885. Also in House Executive Document No. 2, 49th Cong., 1st sess. (Serial 2378).

__________. "Private Land Claims Against the Public Domain in New Mexico on File in the Office [of the] United States Surveyor-General for New Mexico, June 30, 1855." In U.S. Department of the Interior, *Annual Report*, 1855, 1:554-61. Washington, D.C.: Government Printing Office, 1885. Also in House Executive Document No. 1, pt. 5, 49th Cong., 1st Sess., Serial 2378.

__________. "Schedule of Documents Relating to Grants of Land by the Spanish and Mexican Governments, Forming the Archives of the Surveyor General of New Mexico—Abstract of the Grants of Lands Selected from the Public Records of the Territory, Found in the Archives of Santa Fe, New Mexico." In U.S. Department of the Interior, *Annual Report*, 1856, pp. 413-32, 433-39. Senate Executive Document No. 5, 34th Cong., 3rd Sess., Serial 875. Washington, D.C.: A.O.P. Nicholson, Printer, 1856. Also in House Executive Document No. 1, 34th Cong., 3rd Sess. (Serial 893).

Van den Eynde, Damian. "Calendar of Spanish Manuscripts in John Carter Brown Library." *Hispanic American Historical Review* 16 (Nov. 1936): 564-607.

Vasquez, Nadine M. *Sinaloa Roots: An Account of the 1781 Expedition to Alta California and Ancestral Records of Early California Settlers, 1723-1808*. Carmichael, Calif.: For the author, 1974. Includes family history of the settlers.

Vaughan, John H. "A Preliminary Report on the Archives of New Mexico." *American Historical Association, Annual Report* 1909, pp. 465-90.

Villasenor, Espinosa, Roberto, et al. *Indice del Ramo de Californias*. 2 vols. Mexico City: Archivo General de la Nacion, 1977. Index to sources, family history, and biographical data for upper and lower California.

Weber, Francis J. "The Los Angeles Chancery Archives." *The Americas* 21 (April 1965): 410-20.

__________. "The San Francisco Chancery Archives." *The Americas* 20 (Jan. 1964): 313-21.

Withington, Mary C. *A Catalogue of Manuscripts in the Collection of Western Americana Founded by William Robertson Coe, Yale University Library*. New Haven: Yale University Press, 1952.

Woods, Richard D. *Reference Materials on Mexican Americans: An Annotated Bibliography*. Metuchen, N.J.: Scarecrow Press, 1976. Includes guides to genealogical material.

Wright, Doris M. *A Guide to the Mariano Guadalupe Vallejo Documentos para la Historia de California, 1780-1875*. Berkeley: University of California Press, 1963.

INFORMATION GUIDE

Genealogical Information in the Record Group	*Freedmen's Bureau*	*Plantation*	*Manumissions*	*Underground Railroad*	*Slave Declarations*	*Registers of Negroes*	*Abolition Societies*
Surname/name	●	●	●	●	●	●	●
Date of Birth		●					
Place of Birth	●	●					
Sex	●	●	●	●	●	●	●
Race/color	●	●	●	●	●	●	●
Physical Description	●	●	●	●		●	
Occupation	●	●	●		●	●	
Education	●						
Military Service	●		●				
Slave Status	●	●	●			●	●
Property Owned	●						●
Religion						●	●
Citizenship	●		●			●	
Marital Status	●	●	●			●	●
Spouse's Name	●	●		●			●
Children's Names	●	●		●		●	●
Father's Name	●	●				●	●
Mother's Name	●	●				●	●
Father's Birthplace	●						●
Mother's Birthplace	●						●
Date of Death		●					●
Cause of Death							
Name of Cemetery		●					●
Residence	●			●	●	●	●
Age	●	●	●	●	●	●	●
Literacy/signature	●		●			●	●
Photograph/sketch	●						

COULD YOU USE THIS CHAPTER?

Type of Record	*Kept from*	*Clues That You Should Consult These Records*
Oral tradition	All periods	Oral traditions and formal oral histories are essential for black genealogy since they glean family "knowns" available nowhere else.
Basic American sources	Post-1865	Census records, wills, deeds, marriage and vital records, military files, and other record types which apply to the non-black population also apply to blacks after the Civil War. For these records see other chapters in this book.
Plantation records	Seventeenth century to about 1870	Accounts and registers list births and deaths for slaves, as well as some marriages (marriage among slaves was basically illegal in most jurisdictions). Purchase and sale of slaves, breeding records, and deeds of gifts include value, sex, age, and sometimes relationships. Other slave records discussed include slave trade and shipping records, estate proceedings, bills of sale, manumission registers and certificates of freedom, slave declarations made by owners transporting slaves across state lines. This chapter discusses two myths commonly believed in black research: births of children born to white fathers and black mothers are impossible to document and that all American blacks descend from slaves. It also describes the omission of blacks from compiled sources and indexes even when the original records document them, and the research strategy of tracing slave owners simultaneously with their slaves to prove relationships and origins of slave ancestors.
Freedmen's Bureaus	1865-74	These Bureaus supplied food rations, clothing, loans for land and tools; administered hospitals and relocation camps; provided employment and schooling; legalized marriages and reunited families. Records discussed in this chapter, are invaluable in tying modern black families to their slave ancestors.
Register of free blacks	About 1800 to 1865	Registers of free blacks were kept in most states bordering the slave states to record the status of blacks living in the community. They are especially valuable for tracing places of origin.
Anti-slavery societies	About 1807 to 1863	Numerous schemes to free blacks, transport them back to Africa or the West Indies, aid their flight to freedom to Canada or northern United States cities, generated records used by genealogists until recently. Although these records take some effort to find, they are especially valuable for places of residence and origin. The Underground Railroad, with map of stations, is also discussed.

Chapter 19

BLACK ANCESTRAL RESEARCH

Johni Cerny

Interest in black American ancestral research was shared by only a small segment of America's black population prior to the advent of Alex Haley's *Roots*. The surge of interest during the post-*Roots* era overwhelmed libraries, professional genealogists, and genealogical societies. At this writing, some seven years later, interest still remains high, as does the need for guidance. A number of instruction manuals have been written to guide the amateur, including the best, *Black Genesis,* by James Rose and Alice Eichholz, which was published in 1977. Professional genealogists specializing in Southern states research have become skilled in tracing slave ancestry and are available for hire by those seeking professionally compiled lineages and family histories. Additionally, libraries, archives, and genealogical societies have begun to requisition sources to add to their previously sparse black research collections.

Black ancestral research can be difficult. It should be approached initially just as any American genealogical research project is begun. You begin with yourself and work backward, employing the basics of genealogical research methods and sources in the United States. There are a number of excellent general instruction manuals available for consultation. See the bibliography at the end of this chapter for a list of those I recommend. *Black Genesis* provides a brief outline of the major record sources to use during the initial stages of research and a state-by-state description of resources available.

Along with basic research skills, you'll need a broad understanding of black American history and the country's slave system. The references at the end of the chapter will provide you with this background. Particularly significant is the work of Gary B. Mills and Elizabeth Shown Mills on some black families of Louisiana which specifically refutes two research myths, largely constructed by genealogists experienced in tracing white ancestries who are unaware that American printed indexes and sources omit black entries even though the original records include them.[1]

The first myth is that births of children born to white fathers and black mothers are impossible to document except from oral tradition. In reality, some 75 percent of American blacks have at least one white ancestor and 15 percent have a predominately white ancestry.[2] The second myth is that American blacks descend from slaves. By 1860, one out of every eight blacks was already free. As early as 1830, some 3,765 free blacks owned slaves themselves. Men often purchased their wives and children born in slavery and then set them free.

Blacks, regardless of whether their ancestors were free or slave, are usually able to trace their ancestry back to the end of the Civil War without too much difficulty using the same sources white Americans use. These sources are referred to in this chapter and described in detail in other chapters of this book. Descendants of free blacks will find their ancestors prior to the Civil War documented in vital, church, land, estate, military, and other public records. Some specific records oriented to color, like residence licenses, manumission papers, and other proofs of freedom, will also be found. These ancestors are color-coded as B[lack] or M[ulatto] or designated as "free men of color" to distinguish them from white Americans of the same name.

Pre-Emancipation slave families were considered the personal property of their owners and as such were without legal rights. They were prohibited from owning real or personal property themselves and do not appear in these records as owners although they may appear as slaves, named or unnamed.

One of the most effective approaches to identify slave ancestors is to identify the plantation at which the ancestor worked and the owner of the slave family. Research then focuses upon the owner's family and the records it produced as slave owners, as well as on the slave family itself.

When slaves were sold to a plantation, their African identity and names were disregarded. They were given only first names, such as Tom, Eliza, Mattie, or Sarah. Most slave names were not duplicated on the same plantation, although occasionally you will find slaves named "Old Jim," "Big Jim," and "Young Jim" on one plantation, the adjectives helping to distinguish between three slaves.

When the Civil War ended, slaves legally adopted surnames. Some slaves took surnames prior to being freed, but they generally kept their choice a secret from the white community. Many researchers approach slave family research with the misconception that freed slaves took the surnames of their last owner. Slaves were often known by several surnames and made a final choice at the time they were emancipated. They often took the surname of their father, who may have been a white slave master or overseer, a deceased slave, or a slave sold to another owner years prior to the emancipation. Their name may have been the name of a current owner, a former owner, a prominent American (Washington and Lincoln were the most popular), a locally prominent citizen, or the given name of the father of the family. Immediately after the emancipation, it was not uncommon to find some black families using more than one surname. Missouri Gordy, for example, born a slave in 1856, was the granddaughter of Sibby Morgan who was owned by the Brown and Morgan families of Hancock County, Georgia. Missouri Gordy used the name Missouri Brown when, after the Civil War, she applied for a marriage license.

Once you have established the owners of a slave ancestor, it is a good practice to go back to previously searched records and look for emancipated ancestors under the surname of the owner(s). Searching for slave ancestors always requires a thorough investigation of the white slave-owning family in all public and historical records.

Another area of critical importance is oral history. Since slave ancestors are rarely found in such public records as vital, land, and estate records, there are few clues to follow in your search. The tradition of maintaining an oral history began in Africa with the *griot*, the tribal historian whose role is described in detail in *Roots*. African tribes relied upon *griots* to preserve their tribal and family histories. The *griot* would commit names, relationships, and events to memory and repeat them generations at a time when called upon. American slaves also maintained a tradition of oral history. From memory, slaves, and later, freedmen,* passed family histories on for generations. Sometimes known as "storytellers," they were the centers of attention on many a hot summer night. Researchers should contact as many older family members as possible to gather fragments of a family's oral history. While surviving story fragments may not contain specific details about the family's slave residence or owner, the narratives may include clues that will lead to some valuable sources of information.

Oral histories are best taken by tape recorder. There are several excellent books on the market which outline the type of questions to ask during an interview. Willa K. Baum, *Oral History for the Local Historical Society* is recommended by James Rose and Alice Eichholz in *Black Genesis*. Her work is published by the Conference of California Historical Societies in Stockton, California (1969). You should also read the oral history chapter in *Black Genesis*.

Compilers and collectors of genealogical sources ignored black Americans in private and public documents for decades. It will take years to bring black research sources up to the current level of white sources. The authors of *Black Genesis* list twenty-one projects which would improve the availability of black research sources and lessen the time and energy presently required to extend black lineages and compile black family histories. Many of the projects have not been funded and are incomplete, if begun at all. Local groups around the country are working to compile source material in their specific areas, but a national organization dedicated to the retrieval of black historical and genealogical source material is badly needed. The wide dispersion of compiled information does not preclude success in identifying your black ancestry, but success will come more slowly. You will have to pursue research sources more doggedly and do some skillful analysis of the information you are able to locate.

Federal Census Schedules

While federal census schedules include information about the country's entire population, they are especially valuable in black ancestral research. The 1982 *Guide to Genealogical Research in the National Archives*, published by the National Archives and Records Service, discusses information on blacks in the census schedules, as well as in other federal records:

> The first listing of all blacks by name in a federal census was made in 1870, in the first federal census taken after the Civil War. In 1850 and 1860, slave statistics were gathered, but the census schedules did not list slaves by name; they were tallied unnamed in age and sex categories. These slave schedules are useful, however, as circumstantial evidence that a slave of a certain age and sex was the property of a particular owner in 1850 and 1860.
>
> Free blacks who were heads of households were enumerated by name in the censuses from 1790-1840, and the names of all free household members were included in the censuses of 1850 and 1860. Slaves, however, were listed in total numbers or recorded in age and sex categories, 1790-1840. *List of Free Black Heads of Families in the First Census of the United States, 1790*, Special List 34, compiled by Debra L. Newman (Washington[, D.C.]: National Archives and Records Service, rev. 1974), lists roughly 4,000 free blacks recorded as heads of families.[3]

Census records up to and including 1910, are available on microfilm at various libraries and Federal Records Centers throughout the nation. The Genealogical Society of Utah has a complete collection of federal census schedules, as well as an extensive collection of census indexes. However, you should be aware that indexing firms did not always include black families. Long, tedious searches of entire counties may be necessary to find your ancestors in the 1870 census enumerations. While many recently freed blacks remained near their pre-emancipation residences, many were already on the move. If you do not find your ancestors in the county in which they lived prior to the emancipation, be certain to search surrounding counties. Before beginning a census search for your ancestry, read Chapter 4, "Census Records," to understand the best use, special problems, and special applications of census records including black censuses taken in specific areas.

The *Guide to Genealogical Research in the National Archives* devotes Chapter 12 to records of black Americans, including, in addition to census records, military service and related records. It covers the Revolutionary War-Civil War period, Freedmen's Bureau and related records, records of slaves in the District of Columbia, and records relating to slave trade and African colonization. Cherokee freedmen records are also included.

Military Records

Black Americans began serving in military units during the Revolutionary War. Their service records and pension applications are included in the record groups discussed in the Military Records chapter. Debra L. Newman compiled a list of black servicemen from the *War Department Collection of Revolutionary War Records*, Special List 36 (Washington, D.C.: National Archives and Records Service, 1974). Blacks are also listed in records of the Continental and Confederation congresses and the Constitutional Convention, Record Group 360.

The *Guide* also describes infrequently used collections:

> When the British evacuated New York in 1783, they took with them many former slaves. Lists of those who left with the British, called "inspection rolls," were created so that reparation could be made to former owners under the terms of the Treaty of Paris of 1783. Consequently, carefully accurate information was recorded for each evacuee. Given are name, sex, sometimes age, and brief physical description of each individual; name and residence of former owner; and additional information in a "remarks" column. The lists are available on roll 7 of Miscellaneous Papers of the Continental Congress, 1774-1789, M332, and roll 66 of Papers of the Continental Congress, 1774-1779, M247.[4]

Black soldiers were also members of the Union and Confederate armies during the Civil War. Black Union soldiers served in regiments of U.S. colored troops and in other branches of the armed forces. You can search the microfilm *Index to Compiled Service Records of Volunteer Union Soldiers Who Served with the United States Colored Troops*, M589, (98 rolls) to determine if your ancestor served in the Union Army during the Civil War. Soldiers are listed alphabetically by name. The index is available for search through the National Archives and the Genealogical Society of Utah. Other record sources pertaining to the black Union soldier include:

- *Compiled Records Showing Service in Volunteer Union Organizations*, (M594), rolls 204-17; historical information about volunteer organizations.
- *Tabular Analysis of the Records of the U.S. Colored Troops and Their Predecessor Units in the National Archives of the United States*, Special List 33, compiled by Joseph B. Ross (Washington, D.C.: National Archives and Records Service, 1973); regimental records, correspondence, orders, descriptive books, and morning reports.
- Colored troops division records included in Record Group 94; fifty-four indexed volumes of descriptive lists of black soldiers who enlisted in Missouri in 1864. They list name, age, eye and hair color, complexion, height, place of birth, occupation, and date of enlistment. Those who were freed slaves will list former owners' names in some instances.

Black Civil War veterans were afforded disability pensions. They are included in the microfilm *General Index to Pension Files, 1861-1864*, T288, discussed at length in Chapter 8, "Military Records." The index is available on microfilm at various libraries

* "Freedman": slave who is emancipated. "Free man of color": black who is free from birth or freed many years earlier. Both are different from a freeman who is *always* white in a legal sense. In Pennsylvania, a freeman is a single, white male over twenty-one years of age. In New York, a freeman is a citizen or man free to ply a trade within city limits. In Massachusetts, a freeman is white, age twenty-one, and owns enough land to vote.

and Federal Records Centers throughout the nation. Application forms must be requested from the National Archives and Records Service following the procedure outlined in Chapter 8, "Military Records." Pension application files of black soldiers are very valuable.

Blacks served extensively in Confederate Army units composed primarily of white soldiers, but little genealogical information is found in Confederate service records. Rarely are indications of race included in service records, except when a physical description is given. The most important information included is the soldier's place of enlistment, which was near his residence in most instances. Of course, that's where you would begin your search for the slave owner.

Finding an ancestor in Union Army records does not imply that he was a free black citizen prior to the Civil War. Many escaped slaves joined the Union Army during the war. Some researchers become confused when there is no trace of their black ancestors in the northern area in which the ancestor enlisted. Whenever a black citizen disappears from the records of an area in which he previously appeared, the possibility that he was a slave prior to that time should be considered.

A substantial bibliography of black Americans serving in the armed forces exists although information varies from names and service dates to simple histories of the unit. Some of the more helpful are listed in the bibliography at the end of this chapter.

Freedmen's Bureau and Related Records

The Bureau of Refugees, Freedmen, and Abandoned Lands, more commonly called the Freedmen's Bureau, was created by Congress in 1865 as a division of the War Department. The organization was given the task of administering to refugees and freedmen after the war's end and was directly responsible for helping former slaves adjust to freedom. The bureau issued rations and clothing to needy freedmen, operated hospitals and relocation camps, found jobs for freed slaves, established schools, and leased or supervised the working of abandoned lands. It also legalized marriages entered into during slavery and reunited families split through sales and

Table 19-1

Freedmen's Bureau Field Office Records

		Assistant Commissioner		*Superintendant of Education*		
District Field Office	*Headquarters*	*Microfilm Publication*	*Rolls*	*Microfilm Publication*	*Rolls*	*Historical Study*
Alabama	Montgomery	M 809	23	M 810	8	
Arkansas, including Missouri, parts of Kansas	St. Louis	M 979	52	M 980	5	
	Washington, D.C.	M1055	21	M1056	24	
Disctrict of Columbia, including parts of Maryland, Virginia, West Virginia, and Delaware						
Florida	Tallahassee					
Georgia (originally part of South Carolina)	Beaufort, S.C.	M 798	36	M 799	28	
	Nashville					
Kentucky (originally part of Tennessee)						
Louisiana	New Orleans	M1027	36	M1026	12	
Maryland, including parts of West Virginia and Delaware						James H. Whyte, "Activities of the Freedmen's Bureau in Southern Maryland 1865-70," *Chronicles of St. Mary's* 7 (1959): 11-18 and "The Freedmen's Bureau in West Virginia," *West Virginia History* 39 (Jan.-April 1978): 99-142.
Mississippi	Vicksburg	M 826	50			
North Carolina	Raleigh	M 843	38	M 844	16	
South Carolina	Beaufort	M 869	44			Martin Abbott, *The Freedman's Bureau in South Carolina, 1865-72.* (Chapel Hill: University of North Carolina Press, 1967).
Tennessee	Nashville	M 999	34	M1000	9	Weymouth T. Jordan, "Freedmen's Bureau in Tennessee," *East Tennessee Historical Society Publications* 11 (1939): 49-61.
Texas	Galveston	M 821	32	M 822	18	Barry A. Crouch, "Hidden Sources of Black History: The Texas Freedmen's Bureau Records as a Case Study." *Southwestern Historical Quarterly* 83 (1980): 211-26.
Virginia	Richmond	M1048	67	M1053	20	William T. Alderson, *The Freemen's Bureau in Virginia.* M.A. thesis, Vanderbilt University, 1949.

estate transfers of slaves.

Most of the bureau's records are nongenealogical, but many records are useful. Record Group 105 is divided into two groups:

1. Bureau Headquarter's Records, 1865-72 (described in *Preliminary Inventory of the Records of the Bureau of Refugees Freedmen, and Abandoned Lands, Washington Headquarters,* compiled by Elaine Everly (Washington, D.C.: National Archives, 1973) This collection includes freedmen's marriage certificates between 1861 and 1869. In addition to actual marriage licenses, the collection also includes proofs of marriage. You must know where the marriage of interest took place to locate the record since documents are arranged alphabetically by the groom's surname within each state's file.

There are no statistics available on the number of marriages documented for each state. Some states have several hundred and others have none. Records sometimes include, in addition to the names of the marrying parties, their residences, date and place of marriage, their complexions, their parents' complexions, periods of time living with previous spouses, causes for separation in previous marriages, and numbers of children by previous and present marriages.

2. Records of District or Field Offices also contain marriage records. These registers were maintained by local superintendents and agents of the bureau. Registers include the same basic information as the bureau headquarters records. Researchers must know the place and date of the marriage to find it in the records. Arkansas, Kentucky, Louisiana, and Mississippi are heavily represented in the collection. Marriage records recorded by the bureau were also simultaneously recorded in local county records. (See Table 19-1.)

3. The Freedmen's Savings and Trust Company was founded by Congress as a banking institution with thirty-three branches established between 1865 and 1870. Its records are part of Record Group 101 of the Office of the Comptroller of the Currency and are reproduced as National Archives Microfilm Publication M816 in Table 19-2.

Each person applying for an account with the Freedmen's Savings and Trust Company was required to provide specific information. Recorded in "Registers of Signatures of Depositors," the applications generally include account number, name of depositor, date of entry, birthplace, place of residence as a child, residence at date, age, complexion, occupation, employer, name of wife or husband, names of children, names of parents, brothers, and sisters, and remarks. The names of former slave owners and the name of the plantation of residence are sometimes included. Some applications do not contain all this information.

These registers are not indexed, but there are indexes to deposit ledgers (1865-74) which are microfilmed as National Archives Microfilm Publication M817 (5 rolls). These indexes list depositors' names, account numbers, and page number in the deposit ledgers. Indexes are arranged alphabetically by state and then by branch within the state. Names are arranged alphabetically by first letter of the surname of the depositor.

Many other Freedmen's Bureau records contain information of genealogical value, but the way the records are arranged and the lack of usable indexes makes research in the records an arduous task. For a full discussion of Freedmen's Bureau and related records, consult the *Guide to Genealogical Records in the National Archives* from which I have quoted earlier.

All of the records discussed above are in the custody of the National Archives and Records Center. You can use microfilmed records at the Federal Records Centers or you may employ an agent located in Washington, D.C., to search those records of interest to you. The Board for Certification of Genealogists, Box 19165, Washington, DC 20036, has a list of certified record searchers which will be supplied upon request. The Association of Professional Genealogists, Box 11601, Salt Lake City, Utah 84147 also has a list of qualified searchers.

Table 19-2

Microfilmed Records of the Freedmen's Savings and Trust Company

Roll No.	*State*	*Branch*	*Dates Covered*
1	Alabama	Huntsville	28 Nov. 1865-21 Aug. 1874
2	Alabama	Mobile	18 June 1867-29 June 1874
3	Arkansas	Little Rock	27 Feb. 1871-15 July 1874
4	Washington, D.C.	Washington	11 July 1865-30 Dec. 1871
5	Washington, D.C.	Washington	24 May 1872-22 July 1874
5	Florida	Tallahassee	25 Aug. 1866-15 Jan. 1872
6	Georgia	Atlanta	15 Jan. 1870-15 July 1872
7	Georgia	Augusta	23 Nov. 1870-29 June 1874
8	Georgia	Savannah	10 Jan. 1866-17 Dec. 1870
9	Georgia	Savannah	17 Dec. 1870-22 Oct. 1872
10	Georgia	Savannah	22 Oct. 1872-1 Sept. 1874
11	Kentucky	Lexington	21 March 1870-3 July 1874
11	Kentucky	Louisville	15 Sept. 1865-8 July 1874
12	Louisiana	New Orleans	20 June 1866-29 June 1874
12	Louisiana	Shreveport	11 Feb. 1871-29 June 1874
13	Maryland	Baltimore	3 May 1866-23 June 1874
14	Mississippi	Columbus	1 Aug. 1870-16 June 1874
14	Mississippi	Natchez	29 March 1870-18 June 1874
15	Mississippi	Vicksburg	28 July 1868-29 June 1874
16	Missouri	St. Louis	6 April 1869-8 Oct. 1869
17	New York	New York City	20 Feb. 1871-6 July 1874
18	North Carolina	New Bern	2 Nov. 1869-25 July 1874
18	North Carolina	Raleigh	9 April 1868-20 April 1868
18	North Carolina	Wilmington	3 Sept. 1869-30 Oct. 1869
19	Pennsylvania	Philadelphia	7 Jan. 1870-26 June 1874
20	South Carolina	Beaufort	20 June 1868-3 July 1874
21	South Carolina	Charleston	19 Dec. 1865-2 Dec. 1869
22	South Carolina	Charleston	4 Dec. 1869-25 Feb. 1871
23	South Carolina	Charleston	25 Feb. 1871-2 July 1872
24	Tennessee	Memphis	28 Dec. 1865-1 July 1874
25	Tennessee	Nashville	23 Dec. 1871-23 June 1874
26	Virginia	Lynchburg	8 July 1871-22 Aug. 1871
26	Virginia	Norfolk	4 Dec. 1871-29 June 1874
26	Virginia	Richmond	18 July 1867-20 June 1870
27	Virginia	Richmond	21 June 1870-29 June 1874

Records of Slaves and Slavery

There is no central repository of records pertaining to slaves and slavery, although one is certainly needed. Records which have been located and preserved are usually found in local and state libraries or archives. A major contribution to slave research would be extracting and indexing all slave holders in the 1860 federal census slave schedules for each county, then determining from the available county records the name of the slave owner's plantation and its geographic location. In the absence of compiled research sources, the researcher must contact each local and state repository for a description of its black history and genealogy collections. The types of records included in their collections will vary.

Plantation Records

If a slave owner's identity cannot be established by family members, the next place to look is plantation records. Usually they include birth, marriage, and death information. They also mention the sale of slaves and list the new owner's name. The number of surviving plantation records is unknown. No concerted effort to locate those records has been made. While many records are certainly lost or destroyed, a large number may still exist. Since plantation records are one of the most valuable sources of black genealogical information, every possible effort should be made to determine if the records of the plantation where your ancestors lived and worked still exist.

Birth, Marriage, and Death Records

While vital records—records of birth, marriage, and death—were not required nation-wide by statute until early in this century, some Southern states and a number of New England states required such records. Although most states insisted that marriage records be compiled by each county, very few Southern states registered slave marriages. Most of those marriages were by agreement of the slave couple and were not recognized as legal.

Birth records were another matter. Virginia began registering births and deaths in 1853. Interestingly, the early registrations reflect, on a per capita basis, the tendency to register slave births more often than those of the slave owner's own children. One reasonable explanation is the slave owner's need to protect his personal property by officially recording it. West Virginia was formed from Virginia in 1863 and its counties continued to maintain birth and death records after achieving statehood. The Genealogical Society of Utah has microfilmed Virginia's county records, including the early birth and death records important to black research. If you know the birthdate of a slave ancestor, you can search the birth records for a male or female slave born on that date. The baby's gender will be recorded but not his/her name or the parents' names. The owner's name, however, will be given. Sometimes the name of the plantation or, at a minimum, the area in which the birth took place will be recorded.

Bills of Slave Sales

Slaves were considered personal property. While most personal property was not recorded in civil records, slave sales frequently appear in property records. If a slave owner died indebted, his/her real and personal property was often sold by court order to satisfy the debts. Court records, especially probate court records, will contain bills of sale which list the name and value of the slave sold along with the name of the buyer. Sometimes members of the original slave owner's family will purchase the slaves. Bills of sale will be found among land records, estate records, or miscellaneous county records.

Most of these records are on file in the county in which the transaction took place. Other miscellaneous records can be found in local and state libraries or archives.

Slave Trade Records

Identifying a specific slave in the shipping lists of slave importations is not easy. Most of the ships' manifests list only the number of slaves transported, the African port of embarkation, the port of entry into this country, the shipper's name, and the name and address of the person to whom the cargo was delivered. Manifests for ships transporting slaves between domestic ports are sometimes more descriptive, including in this listing the slave's first name, age, and sex, the name of the shipper, and the name and address of the person to whom the slaves were delivered.

Manifests have been preserved for ships arriving in New Orleans, Savannah, and Mobile; but they are not indexed, so you would need to know when, where, and by whom a slave was sold to use the records. Microfilm copies of the early slave-trade manifests are available at the National Archives and at the Genealogical Society of Utah.

Estate Records

Few researchers will be able to trace slave ancestry without consulting wills, administration records, and inventories. Slaves did not have legal rights and hence did not own property, but they are usually included in the estate records of their owners.

At the time of a slave owner's death, the courts required that his /her estate be settled according to the law. The slave owner may have made a will specifying the distribution of his/her real and personal property, including slaves, among his/her heirs. If the owner died without a will (intestate), the court appointed an administrator to settle the estate. The administrator was responsible to see that the real estate and personal property were inventoried to arrange for the sale of property if there were debts to be satisfied. The information included in these estate records is invaluable to the black genealogist.

A case history may help illustrate the research process. This example involves not only estate records but other records consulted in the search for the ancestry of Burton F. Fuller. When the search began, his father was not known but his mother was believed to be Jane Fuller, a woman born into slavery in Georgia.

Burton F. Fuller was living in the Meriweather District of Baldwin County, Georgia, when the 1900 federal census was taken. (See Figure 19-1.)

His mother, Jane, was living in the household listed as a widow who had given birth to twelve children, five of whom were still living when the census was taken. She had been born in Georgia and so had her parents. Burton had been born in March 1874, and we assumed he died some time between 1874 and 1900.

Then we worked backward. Twenty years earlier, when the 1880 census had been taken, Jane Fuller, a widow, was the head of her household in the Pittsburg District of Baldwin County, Georgia. (See Figure 19-2). Three of her twelve children were living with her including six-year-old Burton. Thus we narrowed the time of this father's death to between 1874 and 1880.

Moving back another ten years to the 1870 census, we found Jane Fuller enumerated with her husband, Washington, still in Baldwin County, with Milledgeville as the closest post office. (See Figure 19-3.)

There were no probate records or estate inventory in the county court minutes, but the June 1879 term included a petition for support of Jane Fuller and her seven minor children. (See Figure 19-4.)

A study of Baldwin County's deeds showed that Jane Fuller sold two and a half acres to Jeff Walker of the county, on 4 December 1897. The land bordered that owned by Burton Walker's heirs. The plot was so small it may have been a portion of a divided estate. Since her youngest son was named Burton, she may have been related to the Walker family.

Pursuing that clue, we examined the estate records of Baldwin County, Georgia, and found a very interesting document, a long will by an Alex Walker with a codicil. They had been proved in court 26 May 1888. See Figure 19-5.

From this will we could reconstruct Alex Walker's family. His wife was named Clarissa.

TWELFTH CENSUS OF THE UNITED STATES.

SCHEDULE No. 1.—POPULATION.

State Georgia — County Baldwin — Township or other division of county Meriwether district 318 — Supervisor's District No. 6 — Enumeration District No. 3 — Sheet No. 6 — 233 A

Enumerated by me on the 6th day of June, 1900, J. D. McGriff, Enumerator.

Figure 19-1. 1900 U.S. Census, Meriweather District, Baldwin County, Georgia, p. 233, lines 26-30; Genealogical Society of Utah (hereafter GS) microfilm 1,240,178.

Children:	*Grandchildren*:
Lucious Walker (deceased)	Ebbie Walker
	June Walker
	Alice Walker
	Laman Walker
	Becky Walker
	Mat (*sic*) Walker
	Mary Walker
	Zander Walker
Seaborn Walker	Holt Walker
	Day Walker
	Mitchell Walker
	Lizzie Walker
	Patsy Walker
Alex Walker, Jr.	Gabriel Walker
	Joseph Walker
	Charly Walker
	Ann Walker
	Lula Walker
Jeff Walker	Ardel Walker
Clarissa Quacom	Hall Quacom
	Young Quacom
	Gertrude Quacom
Susan Reynolds	Ella Reynolds
	Emma Reynolds
	Simon Reynolds
	Roy Reynolds
	Lucious Reynolds
	Howard Reynolds
	Flagg Reynolds
Burton Walker	Seaborn Walker
	Augustus Walker
	________ Walker
	(child due in December)
Isabella Humphries	Jeff Humphries
	Sammie Humphries
	Juky Humphries
Sabina Banks	Sampson Banks
	Virginia Banks
	(infant) Banks
Zack Walker	
Matilda Walker	
(Adopted Daughter)	
Jane Fuller	

Alex Walker died 9 May 1888 at age seventy-seven in Baldwin County, Georgia. The land records of that county did not disclose the source of the property he left to his heirs.

Alex Walker could not be linked to any white Walker families mentioned in Baldwin County, Georgia, records. There was no oral history to provide the name(s) of his owner(s) as a slave. We systematically searched the Baldwin County inventories included in the Baldwin County Ordinary Court records and found Alex in the inventory of Zachariah Lamar's estate, dated 10 January 1835 (pp. 187, 189):

Ellick [Alex]	$650
Clarissa his wife	$450
Jenny their child	$150
Burton child of Ellick	$125
Eliza child of Ellick	$100

Zachariah Lamar's will, proven in Baldwin County, Georgia, 1 November 1834, mentions Alex and his family:

> Item and clause Second I give and bequeath and devise unto Lucius Q. C. Lamar & Jesse Robinson and survivors of them as trustees for my beloved daughter Mary Ann Lamar and such child or children as she may have living at the time of her death the real and personal estate

Dwelling	Family	Name	Color	Sex	Age	Relationship	Single	Married	Widowed	Occupation	Unemployed	Cannot read	Cannot write	Place of Birth	Father's Birth	Mother's Birth
		— Lucius	B	M	5	Son	/			at school				Georgia	Georgia	Georgia
		— Emma	B	F	4	daughter	/							Georgia	Georgia	Georgia
		— Josephine	B	F	1	daughter	/							Georgia	Georgia	Georgia
250	257	Deacon Young	B	M	30			/		Farmer	/	/	/	Georgia	Georgia	Georgia
		— Clarissa	B	F	28	wife		/		work on farm	/	/	/	Georgia	Georgia	Georgia
		— Wall	B	M	5	Son								Georgia	Georgia	Georgia
		— Young	B	M	3	Son								Georgia	Georgia	Georgia
		— Lucenia	B	F	1	daughter	/							Georgia	Georgia	Georgia
251	260	Humphris Peter	B	M	24			/		Farmer	/	/	/	Georgia	Georgia	Georgia
		— Isabella	B	F	22	wife		/		work on farm	/		/	Georgia	Georgia	Georgia
		— Samuel	B	M	2	Son	/							Georgia	Georgia	Georgia
		— Infant not named	B	M	6/80	Son	/							Georgia	Georgia	Georgia
252	261	Underwood Margaret	B	F	22				/	Farm laborer	/	/	/	Georgia	Georgia	Georgia
		— Green	B	M	4	Son	/							Georgia	Georgia	Georgia
		— Burton	B	M	2	Son	/							Georgia	Georgia	Georgia
		— Infant not named	B	F	7/12	daughter	/							Georgia	Georgia	Georgia
253	262	Fuller Jane	B	F	49				/	Farmer	/	/	/	Georgia	Georgia	Georgia
		— Clarissa	B	F	18	daughter	/			Farm laborer	/		/	Georgia	Georgia	Georgia
		— Henry	B	M	12	Son	/			work on farm	/		/	Georgia	Georgia	Georgia
		— Burton	B	M	6	Son	/			at school				Georgia	Georgia	Georgia

Figure 19-2. 1880 U.S. Census, Pittsburg District, Baldwin County, Georgia, p. 257, lines 32-36, GS 1,254,133.

Page No. 118 ; Inquiries numbered 7, 16, and 17 are not to be asked in respect to infants. Inquiries numbered 11, 12, 15, 16, 17, 18, and 20 are to be answered (if at all) merely by an affirmative mark, as /.

SCHEDULE 1.—Inhabitants in ______, **in the County of** Baldwin, **State of** Georgia, **enumerated by me on the** 5th **day of** July, **1870.**

Post Office: Milledgeville [illegible], **Ass't Marshal.**

Line	Dwelling	Family	Name	Age	Sex	Color	Occupation	Place of Birth	Cannot read	Cannot write	Male citizens 21+
28	1012	1017	Reynolds Simon	27	M	B	Farm laborer	"		/	/
29			[illegible]	22	F	B	Keeping house	"	/	/	
30			[illegible]	3	F	B		"			
31			Isabella	1	F	B		"			
32	1013	1018	Fuller Washington	85	M	B	Farm laborer	"		/	/
33			Jane	45	F	B	Keeping house	"	/	/	
34			Curtis Scott	21	M	B	Farm laborer	"	/	/	
35			Fuller Moriah	12	F	B	at home	"	/	/	
36			Mary	13	F	B	"	"	/	/	
37			Clarissa	7	F	B		"			
38			James	5	M	B		"			
39			Henry	3	M	B		"			
40			[illegible]	1	F	B		"			

Figure 19-3. 1870 U.S. Census, Baldwin County, Georgia, p. 118, lines 32-40; GS 545,633.

Figure 19-4. Petition of Jane Fuller for support, 28 May 1879, Baldwin County, Georgia, Minutes of Ordinary Court, (Book), p. 108; GS 423,185.

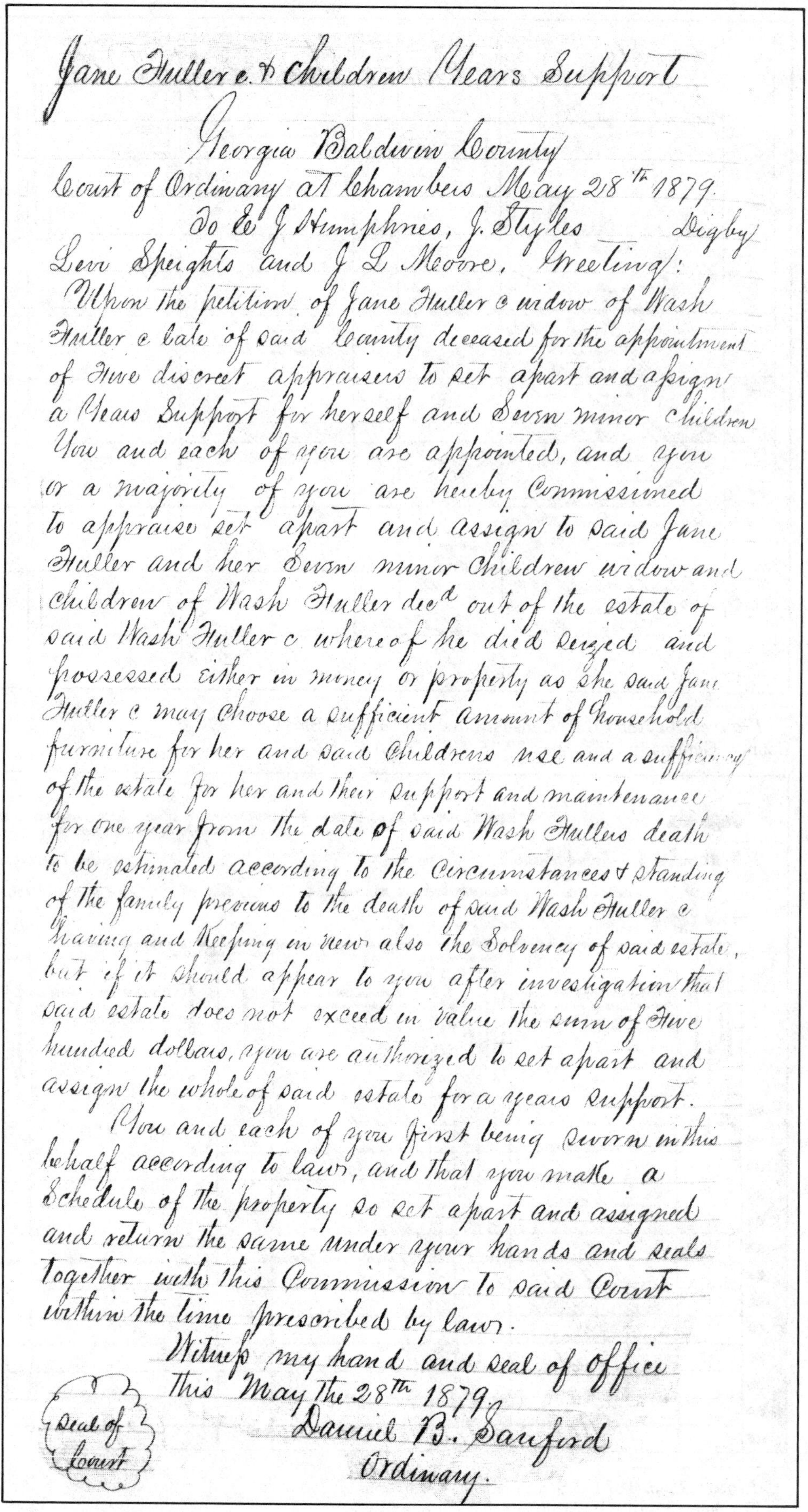

Jane Fuller c. & Children Years Support

Georgia Baldwin County
Court of Ordinary at Chambers May 28th 1879
To E J Humphries, J. Styles Digby
Levi Speights and J L Moore, Greeting:
Upon the petition of Jane Fuller c widow of Wash Fuller c late of said County deceased for the appointment of Five discreet appraisers to set apart and assign a Years Support for herself and Seven minor Children You and each of you are appointed, and you or a majority of you are hereby Commissioned to appraise set apart and assign to said Jane Fuller and her Seven minor Children widow and Children of Wash Fuller decd out of the estate of said Wash Fuller c whereof he died seized and possessed either in money or property as she said Jane Fuller c may Choose a sufficient amount of household furniture for her and said Childrens use and a sufficiency of the estate for her and their support and maintenance for one year from the date of said Wash Fullers death to be estimated according to the Circumstances & standing of the family previous to the death of said Wash Fuller c having and Keeping in view also the Solvency of said estate, but if it should appear to you after investigation that said estate does not exceed in value the sum of Five hundred dollars, you are authorized to set apart and assign the whole of said estate for a years support.

You and each of you first being sworn in this behalf according to law, and that you make a Schedule of the property so set apart and assigned and return the same under your hands and seals together with this Commission to said Court within the time prescribed by law.

Witness my hand and seal of Office
this May the 28th 1879

(Seal of Court)

Daniel B. Sanford
Ordinary.

Figure 19-5. Will of Alex Walker, proved 26 May 1888, Will Book 1, Baldwin County, Georgia, pp. 182-85; GS 415,161.

Will and Codicil of Alex Walker deceased

Georgia
Baldwin County } In the name of God Amen
I Alex Walker Sr. of said State & County being in health & of sound
& disposing Mind & Memory & wishing to arrange my worldly
affaires. so that there will be no wrangling or disputing among
my heirs when I am dead hereby make & declair this as my last
Will and Testament, revoking all others will heretofore made
by me. Item First. I desire that my body be decently buried
in the place known as Walkers cemmetary. near my present
home.
Item Second. I desire that all my debts just, be paid.
Item Third — I give & bequeath to my grand Children. Children of
my son Lucius Walker now dead) to wit. Ebbie Walker, Jim
Walker. Alice Walker. Laura Walker. Becky Walker, & Mat Walker
Mary Walker & James Walker — Twenty Nine Acres of land it being
portion of my plantation whereon they now live with their
Annie Andrews formerly Annie Walker, & which has been surveyed
& measured off for them — I appoint my son Seaborn Walker
Guardian for said Children.
Item Fourth — I give & bequeath to my son Seabor Walker this
Children now living to wit. Holt. Day. Mitchell. Lizzie and
Patsy Walker. & such as may be borned to him hereafter
Thirty (30) Acres of land on my plantation, it beinging the
portion whereon seaborn now lives & which has been surveyed & measured
off to him.
Item Fifth — I give & bequeath to my son Alex Walker for his children now
living. to wit Gabriel. Joseph. Charly. Ann. & Lula Walker & such
as may be hereafter borned to him. Twenty five (25) Acres of the
the same being that portion of my plantation. whereon said Alex
Walker now lives and which has been surveyed & measured
off for him.
Item Sixth, I give & bequeath to my son Jeff Walker and his
Children Arch & such others Children, as may be borned to him
Twenty Seven (27) Acres of land, same being that portion of
my plantation on which said Jeff Walker now lives & which
has been surveyed & measured off to him.
Item Seventh — I give & bequeath to my daughter Clarissa Duggan &
her Children now living. to wit. Paul. Young. Seny. & Gertrude
~~Gio~~ and such children as may hereafter be borned to her
Twenty five (25) Acres of land same being that portion of my
plantation whereon said Clarissa ~~Walker~~ Duggan now lives & which
has been surveyed & measured off to her.
Item Eight — I give & bequeath to my daughter Susan Reynolds and
their Children now living. to wit — Ellen. Emma, Simon,
Lucius. Howard. & Flagg Reynolds & such other Children

Figure 19-5. Continued.

Will and Codicil of Alex Walker deceased Continued

as my hereafter be borned to her. Twenty Five (25) Acres of land, same being that portion of my plantation whereon the said Susan Reynolds now lives & which has been surveyed & measured off to her.

Item–Ninth I give & bequeath to my son Burton Walker & his children now living. to wit: Seaborn. Augustus & — Walker (three in number) & such other children as my hereafter be borned to him. Twenty Five (25) Acres of land. to be measured off from that portion of my plantation not already measured off.

Item. Ten. I give & bequeath to my daughter. Isabella Humphries & her three children. now living. to wit: Jeff. Sammie & Lucky Humphries & such other children as my be borned to her. Twenty five (25) Acres of land to be measured off from that portion of my plantation, not already measured off

Item, Eleven. I give & bequeath to my daughter Sabena Banks & her three children. now living to wit. Sampson, Virginia. — Banks (infant) & such others children as my hereafter be borned to her. Twenty five (25) of land. to be measured off from that portion of my plantation, not already measured off.

Item twelve I give & bequeath to Zack Walker. a boy that I have taken to nurse & who is now living with me. Twenty five (25) Acres of land to be measured off from that portion of my plantation no already measured off.

Item, thirteen I give & bequeath to Matilda Walker. a girl that I have taken to nurse & who is now living with me Twenty five (25) Acres of land. to be measured off from that portion of my plantation. not already measured off

Item, fourteen. To my beloved wife Clarissa Walker. I give & bequeath the following. Twenty Five (25) Acres of land to be measured off immediately around my dwelling house, also my dwelling house & all out houses. where I now live — all my household & kitchen furniture of every sort. including bedding &c. all wearing apparel — also all my horses, mules. cows. hogs. & stock of every kind.

Item. fifteen. I desire that the land given in this will. to Burton Walker, Isabella Humphries. Sabena Banks. Zack Walker & Matilda Walker. be not divided. until after the death of my wife Clarissa Walker. as it is my intention that all of my land except. that mentioned in Items: 3. 4. 5. 6. 7. & 8. remain undivided until after the death of my wife.

Item Sixteen. The piece of wood land. lying just across the road from my dwelling house I. desire to be equally divided amongst all mentioned in this will (each having a childs part) except my daughters Clarissa [illegible] & Susan Reynolds. they having already. all that I. desire them to have.

Item – Seventeen, — I nominate & appoint my two sons. Jeff Walker & Seaborn Walker. as Executors of this my last Will & Testament.

Alex his X Walker
mark

Will and Codicil of Alex Walker deceased Continued

Signed declared & published by Alex Walker Sr. as his last Will and Testament in presence of us the subscribers who subscribed our names hereto in the presence of said Testator at his instance & request & and of each other he signing in our presence & we signing in his presence
This 9th day of May 1888.

R. W. Ivey
Dennis Walker
Walter Paine

State of Georgia }
Baldwin County } Whereas I Alex Walker Sen. did on the 9th day of May 1888 — Sign Seal declare & Publish my last Will & Testament in presence of R. W. Ivey, Dennis Walker & Walter Paine. Who Signed the said Will & Testament as Witnesses & Whereas I am desirous of adding a bequest to said Will. I therefore Make & publish this Codicil to said Will & Testament. I give & bequeath to my Daughter Jane Fuller. The Five Acres of land and houses & improvements thereon on which She now lives
This May 26th 1888.

Alex his Walker Sr (X)
mark

Signed Sealed declared & published by Alex Walker Sen as a Codicil to his last Will & Testament of the 9th day of May 1888 in the presence of the undersigned who subscribed our names hereto in the presence of said Testator & at his special instance request & in presence of each other.
This May 26th 1888.

P. L. Fair
W. E. Hernandez
Walter Paine

Georgia
Baldwin County }
I Walter Paine do Swear that I as Witness R. W. Ivey and Dennis Walker saw the within named Alex Walker Sign and publish the within paper as his last Will and Testament, that I subscribed the same as a Witness thereto at the Special instance and request of the said Alex Walker and in his presence as did also R. W. Ivey & Dennis Walker, that the said Alex Walker Signed the same freely and voluntarily and was at the time of such signing of Sound and disposing mind and memory.
Sworn to and subscribed before me
this August 3rd 1891 } Walter Paine
W. W. Bell
Ordinary B. C.

Figure 19-5. Continued.

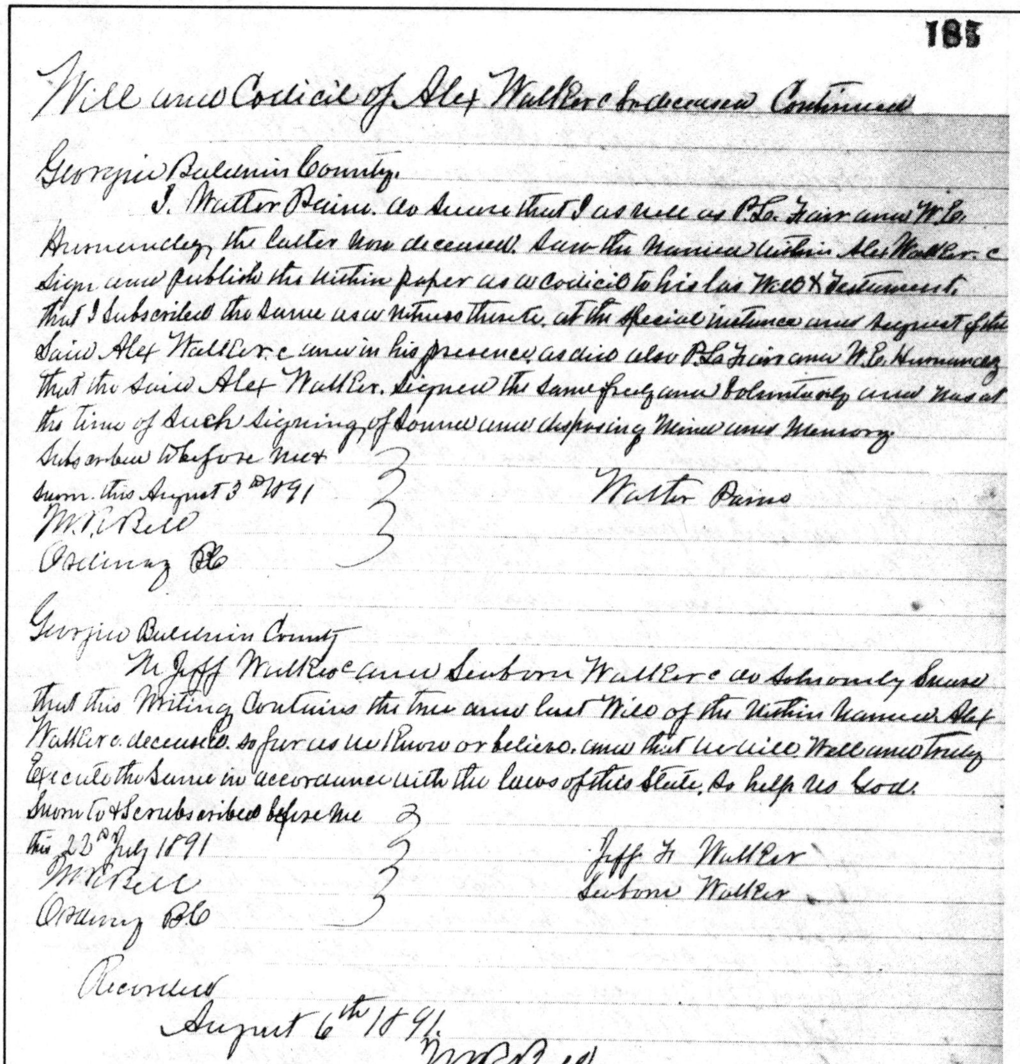

185

Will and Codicil of Alex Walker Sr deceased Continued

Georgia Baldwin County.

I, Walter Paine, do swear that I as well as P. L. Fair and W. E. Hemandez, the latter now deceased, saw the named within Alex Walker Sr sign and publish the within paper as a codicil to his last Will & Testament, that I subscribed the same as a witness thereto, at the special instance and request of the said Alex Walker Sr and in his presence, as did also P. L. Fair and W. E. Hemandez, that the said Alex Walker signed the same freely and voluntarily and was at the time of such signing of sound and disposing mind and memory.

Subscribed before me &
Sworn this August 3rd 1891 } Walter Paine
M. R. Bell
Ordinary B.C.

Georgia Baldwin County

We Jeff Walker Sr and Seaborn Walker Sr do solemnly swear that this writing contains the true and last Will of the within named Alex Walker Sr deceased, so far as we know or believe, and that we will well and truly execute the same in accordance with the laws of this State. So help us God.

Sworn to & subscribed before me
this 23rd July 1891 } Jeff F. Walker
M. R. Bell } Seaborn Walker
Ordinary B.C.

Recorded
August 6th 1891.
M. R. Bell
Ordinary B.C.

herein after mentioned to wit my Hurricane plantation and adjoining lands in the county of Baldwin containing twenty-four hundred and thirty six acres and the following negroes to wit Levin Nancy (his wife) Nelly Elizabeth and Delia (children of Levin) Ellick & Clarissa his wife and Jenny their child. . . .

No mention is made of Burton and Eliza, the other children listed in the inventory. They may have been born after Zachariah's will was written in 1832 and before the inventory was taken in 1835.

Mary Ann Lamar married General Howell Cobb, Georgia Solicitor-General, member of Congress, Speaker of the U.S. House of Representatives, governor of Georgia, Secretary of the U.S. Treasury, President of the Provisional Congress of the Confederate States, and Major General in the Confederate Army.

This example is typical of the research process and types of records used to extend slave ancestry. The Genealogical Society in Salt Lake City has microfilmed most of the county records in the slave states or you can write to the appropriate court for specific documents. Research by correspondence will, however, be difficult due to the extensive searches required. You may consider using the services of a professional genealogist to solve the more complex research problems.

Manumission Records

Prior to the Emancipation Proclamation, slaves were frequently given their freedom. Some were able to purchase their freedom, especially if they lived in urban areas where they could "moonlight" for extra money. Some slave owners freed favored slaves, a slave mistress and her children, or slaves who provided valiant services. Freed slaves received documents attesting to their manumission, and the action was recorded in county court or land records. Some manumission records are also housed in local and state historical libraries or archives.

Blacks born as freemen also held certificates attesting to their free status although such documents were not always protection against being kidnapped and sold.

Slave Advertisements

Newspaper ads (see figure 19-6) appeared in hundreds of newspapers throughout the slave states advertising sales or runaways. With no indexes or catalogued collections, you will have to learn the names of newspapers for the areas in which your slave ancestors lived and then search them page by page to determine if the slave owner advertised.

The Underground Railroad 1786-1860

From 1786 onward, fugitive slaves could escape northwards on the Underground Railroad which covered fourteen Northern states by 1830. From 1840 to 1860 some 50,000 slaves travelled it to settle in the North or Canada. The Federal Fugitive Slave Law of 1793 was countered by the "personal liberty laws" of many northern states.

If any portion of your family settled in a northern city, in Canada, or in a black community in the Midwest established before the Civil War, the chances are excellent that they travelled on the Underground Railroad at least some of the way. See Wilbur H. Seibert, *The Underground Railroad from Slavery to Freedom* (1898; reprint ed., New York: Russell and Russell, 1967) and William Still, *The Underground Railroad* (1872; reprint ed., New York: Arno Press, 1968). These two works list stationkeepers and agents of the Underground network. Once you have their names and where they were in operation, you can check the National Union Catalog of Manuscript Collections (NUCMC) to see if they kept journals, diaries, or account books and, if so, where these records are located.

$100 REWARD

Ranaway from the subscriber living in Cass County, Georgia, a negro man named Jess. He is a dark mulatto, 45 years old, a scar on one side of his forehead and his right shoulder bone has been broken. The said slave was raised in Lexington, Ky., where he will doubtless endeavor to go.

Lexington Observer and Reporter, 1 Jan 1840.

I wish to sell a negro woman and four children. The woman is 22 years old, of good character, a good cook and washer. The children are very likely, from 6 years down to 1 1/2. I will sell them together or separately to suit purchaser. J. T. Underwood.

Louisville Weekly Journal, 2 May 1849.

Negroes for sale! A yellow negro woman of fine constitution, and two children, from the country and sold for no fault but to raise money. Will not be sold to go down the river. Her husband, a fine man, can be had also. Apply at the store of Jarvis & Trabue 3rd & Main.

Louisville Weekly Journal, 3 Sept. 1845.

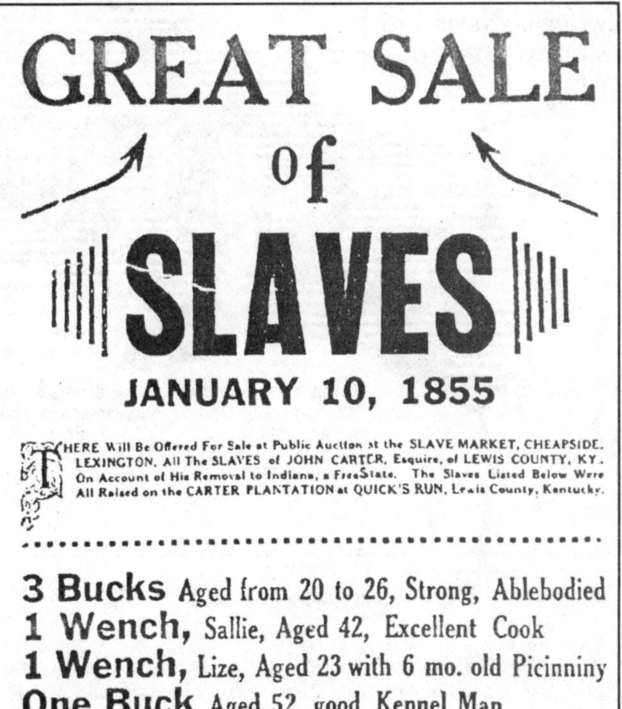

GREAT SALE

of

SLAVES

JANUARY 10, 1855

THERE Will Be Offered For Sale at Public Auction at the SLAVE MARKET, CHEAPSIDE, LEXINGTON, All The SLAVES of JOHN CARTER, Esquire, of LEWIS COUNTY, KY., On Account of His Removal to Indiana, a Free State. The Slaves Listed Below Were All Raised on the CARTER PLANTATION at QUICK'S RUN, Lewis County, Kentucky.

3 Bucks Aged from 20 to 26, Strong, Ablebodied
1 Wench, Sallie, Aged 42, Excellent Cook
1 Wench, Lize, Aged 23 with 6 mo. old Picinniny
One Buck Aged 52, good Kennel Man
17 Bucks Aged from twelve to twenty, Excellent

TERMS: Strictly CASH at Sale, as owner must realize cash, owing to his removal to West Offers for the entire lot will be entertained previous to sale by addressing the undersigned.

JOHN CARTER, Esq.

Po. Clarksburg Lewis County, Kentucky

Figure 19-6. Broadside of slave sale, 10 Jan. 1855, printed by the *Lexington Observer* as a public announcement.

In addition to the individual keepers and agents, vigilance committees in urban centers like Philadelphia, Boston, Cleveland, and Cincinnati also kept journals and accounts of the monies they expended from donations to transport blacks over the system. These are sometimes called Fugitive Journals. They give names, sex, ages, and destinations. Sometimes comments include information on groups traveling together, origins, children accompanying parents, and other details.

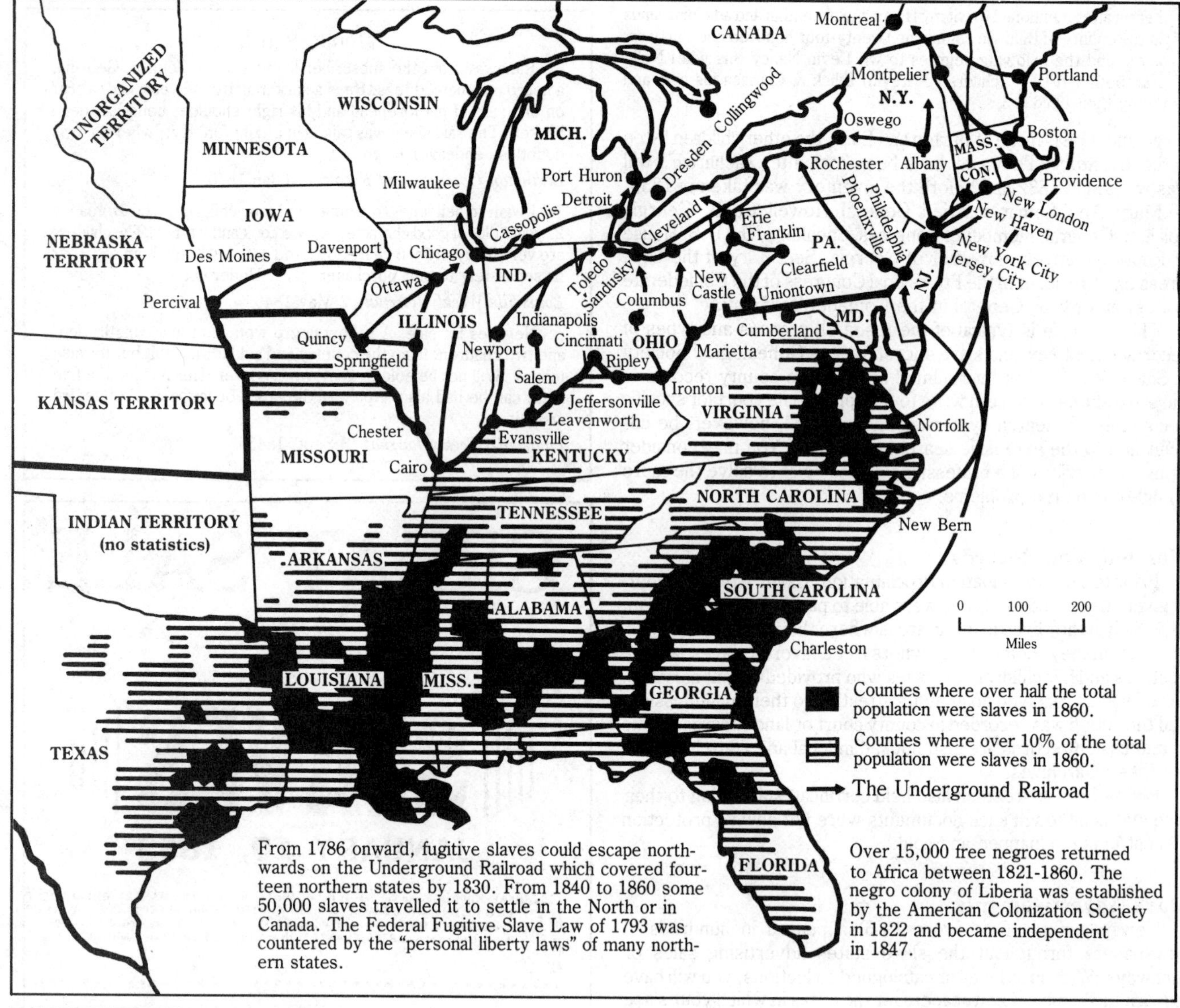

Map 19-1. The Underground Railroad, 1786-1860.

Entries for these committees can also be found in NUCMC and in the *Directory of Archives and Manuscripts Repositories* (Washington, D.C.: National Historical Publications and Records Commission, 1978) under the headings of *Afro-American* or *Anti-Slavery*.

A must is Robin W. Winks, *The Blacks in Canada: A History* (New Haven: Yale University Press, 1971). Don't let the title of the book mislead you. His "Note on Sources" (pp. 497-520) includes a description of United States historical collections pertaining to blacks in general and the Underground Railroad in particular. These twenty-four pages are among the most valuable you will encounter for an introduction to the private papers available. Winks acknowledges that his survey of collections is just a beginning, however.

If you suspect or have proof that your ancestor was assisted by the Underground Railroad, you might search along the usual routes followed by the escaping slaves. Map 19-1 shows these routes, many of which ended across the border in Canada.

Slave Declarations

After the abolition of the slave trade in 1808, several states forbade the importation of slaves into the state for resale and required that emigrants to the state, regardless of their places of origin, must appear before a local justice within a specified time after their arrival and declare their intent to keep the law. This meant that a man moving from Virginia to Kentucky appeared before the local justices and declared who he was and where he came from. If he brought slaves, he recorded who they were by name, sex, and age, and certified that he moved with the intent of becoming a resident of the area, not with the intent to sell his slaves. These slave declarations are valuable records of migration, settlement, and place of origin.

Registers of Negroes

Most jurisdictions where free blacks resided required that they register with local authorities and carry certificates of their free status as a guard against runaway-slave charges. These registers are especially common in the border states of Maryland, Delaware, Tennessee, Kentucky, Missouri, and Arkansas.

Illinois counties preserve a variety of registers dealing with blacks: Record of Indentured Slaves/Servants (many were actually slaves, although slavery was outlawed in Illinois at an early date), Record of Children of Color, Record of Freedom Certificates Issued to Men of Color, and Register of Negroes and Mulattoes. Register of Slaves, Emancipation Register, and Affidavits of Color also served to provide citizenship status, although limited by numerous laws restricting activities of blacks. If your black ancestors migrated to Illinois as slaves and applied for free status in Illinois, these records frequently give places of origin in the slave state they came from.[5]

Anti-Slavery Groups and Their Records

An important source of information referred to by writers on black genealogy but rarely treated in a how-to publication is the mass of information created by anti-slavery organizations and their activities. These sprang up in the early nineteenth century and continued until the Emancipation Act in 1863.

An abortive although interesting project was conceived by the Manumission Society of Guilford County, North Carolina, in the mid-1830s.[6] The society chartered a ship to transport blacks to the West Indies, collected several thousand dollars through donations, compensated owners for the loss of their property, transported the blacks to the port, and then discovered two major obstacles to their plans. Finding a place to land them in the West Indies was the first obstacle, for the local economy was unable and unwilling to absorb them. Then the blacks refused to leave America. So the society had no recourse but to find another place to send them. The final decision was to transport them in wagon trains to Indiana and Illinois where clusters of blacks formed their own small communities on the fringes of settlements. Black communities were also established in parts of Ohio, Pennsylvania, and later in Canada.

Records for these groups have been deposited in historical collections across the United States and in Canada. Table 19-3 lists a few of these. The bibliography at the end of the chapter will enable you to locate others. These records are rarely indexed, they are scattered, and their access is subject to some restriction. Badly needed is a complete finding aid that lists their locations and indexes.

What do abolition society records include that has genealogical value? Journals, registers, correspondence, and accounts include money expended to move blacks from one place to another. These often name the blacks in family units, give places of origin, ages, and even record births, deaths, and marriages taking place along the way. Reports of arrival and settlement may also be included.

Blacks were enumerated in the city of Philadelphia by abolition society personnel and these censuses are invaluable for the genealogical details they contain. See Chapter 4, "Census Records," for a description of their contents.

Registry of Black Ancestry

Genealogical societies, private groups, and religious organizations have been collecting and preserving genealogies of white Americans for decades, but until recently there was no effort to collect black genealogical information already compiled by family and professional genealogists. The recently established Registry of Black American Ancestry is currently accepting for preservation and future computerization family group records, lineage charts, and biographical sketches from those interested in preserving and sharing their private research materials. Records can be submitted to the Registry of American Black Ancestry, Box 417, Salt Lake City, UT 84110.

Table 19-3

Abolition Society Records

Source	*Location*	*Specific Projects or Collections*	*Description*
American Missionary Association	Chicago Public Library 425 N. Michigan Avenue Chicago, IL 60611		Vivian G. Harsh Collecton, microfilms of 450,000 documents; 200 titles of Afro-American newspapers, 1827 to present.
American Colonization Society	Chicago Historical Society Clark Street at North Avenue Chicago, IL 60614		American Colonization Society, 1820-1858. Accounts, letters, African settlements. See Tom W. Schick, "Afro-American Immigration to Liberia: An International Perspective on Black Genealogy," *National Genealogical Society Quarterly* 66 (1978): 285-90.
American Anti-Slavery Society	Sutliff Museum Warren Public Library 444 Mahoning Avenue, NW Warren, OH 44483		Accounts, journals, correspondence, 1834-40.
Maryland State Colonization Society	Maryland Historical Society 201 W. Monument Street Baltimore, MD 21201		Includes minutes, manumissions, censuses, deeds, return of Negroes to Liberia, 1823-63. See William D. Hoyt, Jr., "The Papers of the Maryland State Colonization Society," *Maryland Historical Magazine* 32 (1937): 247-71, and Penelope Campbell, "Maryland State Colonization Society, 1831-1857." Ph.D. diss., Ohio State 1967.
Baltimore Association for Moral and Educational Improvement of Colored People	Maryland Historical Society 201 W. Monument Street Baltimore, MD 21201		See Richard P. Fuke, "The Baltimore Association for the Moral and Educational Improvement of the Colored People, 1864-70," *Maryland Historical Magazine* 66 (1971).
Quaker Anti-Slavery Movement (various activities.)	Swarthmore College Friends Historical Library Swarthmore, PA 19081		Abolition manuscripts, Underground Railroad, valuable collection.

(continued)

Source	*Location*	*Specific Projects or Collections*	*Description*
Manumission Society of Guilford County, North Carolina	Southern Historical Collection University of North Carolina Chapel Hill, NC 27514	Papers of Richard Mendenhall, #2055	Manumission Society Papers, 1794-1845, Guilford County, N.C. Includes emigration of freed Negroes to Haiti, passenger lists, legal papers liberating slaves, and Quaker records and correspondence. The Southern Historical Collection also has many plantation records.
New York Manumission Society	New York Public Library 5th Avenue and 42nd Streets New York, NY 10018		See Charles C. Andrews, *The History of the New York African Free Schools from Establihsment in 1787 to Present [1830]...and Brief Account of Successful Labors of New York Manumission Society.* 1830; reprint ed., New York: Negro University Press, 1969.
Black Families in Southern Maryland	Hall of Records Box 828 Annapolis, MD 21404	Dictionary of Maryland Legislators, 1634-1900	Includes documents on black families drawn from collections in the Maryland State Archives.
Slavery: The Definitive collection of Primary Sources	University Microfilms 300 Zeeb Road Ann Arbor, MI 48106	Slavery Micropublishing Program	27,000 microfiche from historical collections in the New York Historical Society, New York Public Library, State Historical Society of Wisconsin, John Olin Library at Cornell University, Historical Society of Pennsylvania, the Library Company of Philadelphia, and other repositories. Catalog available upon request.
Plantation records	Henry E. Huntington Library 1151 Oxford Road San Marino, CA 91108	Robert A. Brock Collections	Plantation records, personal papers, letters, estate collections for "King" Carter and other Virginia slaveowners.
Negro source materials on microfiche and microfilm	NCR Microcard Editions 901 Twenty-Sixth Street N.W. Washington, D.C. 20037	Includes WPA Slave Interviews conducted in the 1930s.	Includes slave narratives, oral histories, periodicals, 1825-1960; printed laws, pamphlets, books on emancipation.

Notes

1. See Gary B. Mills, *The Forgotten People: Cane River's Creoles of Color* (Baton Rouge: Louisiana State University Press, 1977) and Elizabeth Shown Mills and Gary B. Mills, "Slaves and Masters: The Louisiana Metoyers," *National Genealogical Society Quarterly* 70 (Sept. 1982): 163-89.

2. Roger Brown, *Social Psychology* (New York: The Free Press, 1965), p. 165, and Gunnar Myrdal, *An American Dilemma* (New York: Harper and Row, 1962), p. 133.

3. National Archives and Records Service, *Guide to Genealogical Research in the National Archives* (Washington, D.C.: National Archives Trust Fund Board, 1982), p. 173.

4. Ibid., p.173.

5. W. Wesley Johnston, "Illinois Free Black Records," *Illinois State Genealogical Society Quarterly* 14 (Summer 1982): 72-73.

6. Manumission Society of Guilford, North Carolina, 1794-1855, Southern Historical Collection, 2055, University of North Carolina, Chapel Hill, NC 27514.

Bibliography

Abajian, James. *Blacks in Selected Newspapers, Censuses, and Other Sources: An Index to Names and Subjects*. Boston: G. K. Hall, 1977.

Bailey, Rosalie Fellows. *Guide to Genealogical and Biographical Sources for New York City, 1783-1898*. New York: By the author, 1954.

Ballagh, James Curtis. *A History of Slavery in Virginia*. Baltimore: Johns Hopkins Press, 1902.

Baum, Willa K. *Oral History for the Local History Society*. Stockton, Calif.: Conference of California Historical Societies, 1969.

Bell, Barbara. *Black Biographical Sources*. New Haven, Conn.: Yale University Press, 1970.

Bentley, George R. *A History of the Freedmen's Bureau*. 1955; reprint ed., Philadelphia: Octagon Books, 1970.

Berlin, Ira. *Slaves Without Masters*. New York: Pantheon Books, 1974.

Black Studies: Select Catalog of National Archives and Records Service Microfilm Publications. Washington, D.C.: General Services Administration, 1973.

Blassingame, John W. *The Slave Community: Plantation Life in the Antebellum South*. New York: Oxford University Press, 1979.

Blockson, Charles L. "Black American Records and Research." ed. Jessie Carney Smith. *Ethnic Genealogy: A Research Guide*. Westport, Conn.: Greenwood Press, 1983, pp. 309-64. Good bibliography.

________, with Ron Fry. *Black Genealogy*. Englewood Cliffs, N.J.: Prentice-Hall, 1977.

Brewer, James H. *The Confederate Negro*. Durham, N.C.: Duke University Press, 1969.

Brown, Barbara W., and James M. Rose, eds. *Black Roots in Southeastern Connecticut, 1650-1900*. Detroit: Gale Research Co., 1980. Includes "every piece of information that could be found on blacks" in that region.

Brown, Letitia Woods. *Free Negroes in the District of Columbia, 1790-1846*. New York: Oxford University Press, 1972.

Brown, Warren Henry. *Checklist of Negro Newspapers in the United States, 1827-1946.* Jefferson City, Mo.: Lincoln University, 1946.

Brumbaugh, Gaius Marcus. *Maryland Records.* 2 vols. 1924; reprint ed., Baltimore: Genealogical Publishing Company, 1975.

Cappon, Lester J., and Stella F. Duff. *Virginia Gazette Index, 1736-1780.* Williamsburg, Va.: Institute of Early American History and Culture, 1950.

Cashin, Hershel V. *Under Fire with the Tenth U.S. Cavalry.* New York: Arno Press, 1969.

Catterall, Helen Honor Turncliff, ed. *Judicial Cases Concerning American Slavery and the Negro.* Carnegie Institution of Washington, Publication No. 374. 5 vols. 1926-37; reprint ed., New York: Negro University Press, 1981.

Cockrum, William M. *History of the Underground Railroad.* New York: Negro University Press, 1969.

Conneau, Theophilus. *A Slaver's Log Book.* Englewood Cliffs, N.J.: Prentice-Hall, 1976.

Crawford, Paul. "Footnote on Courts for Trial of Negroes in Colonial Pennsylvania." *Journal of Black Studies* 5 (Dec. 1974): 167-74.

Douglas, William. *The Douglas Register.* Richmond: J. Fergusson, 1928.

Dunn, Lynn P. *Black Americans: A Study Guide and Source Book.* San Francisco: By the author, 1970.

Everly, Elaine. *Preliminary Inventory of the Records of the Bureau of Refugees, Freedmen, and Abandoned Lands.* Washington, D.C.: National Archives and Records Service, 1973.

Fletcher, Marvin. *The Black Soldier and Officer in the United States Army, 1891-1917.* Columbia: University of Missouri Press, 1974.

Foner, Philip Sheldon. *Blacks in the American Revolution.* Contributions in American History, No. 55. Westport, Conn.: Greenwood Press, 1976.

Fowler, Arlen L. *The Black Infantry in the West, 1869-1891.* Westport, Conn.: Greenwood Press, 1971.

Franklin, John Hope. *From Slavery to Freedom: A History of Negro Americans.* 4th ed. New York: Alfred A. Knopf, 1974.

Gara, Larry. *The Liberty Line: The Legend of the Underground Railroad.* Lexington: University of Kentucky Press, 1967. Provocative account, carefully documented, valuable footnotes.

Guild, June Purcell. *Black Laws of Virginia.* 1936; reprint ed., New York: Negro University Press, 1969.

Gutman, Herbert. *The Black Family in Slavery and Freedom, 1750-1925.* New York: Vintage Books, 1976.

Harris, Norman Dwight. *The History of Negro Servitude in Illinois and of Slavery Agitation in that State, 1719-1864.* 1904; reprint ed., New York: Haskell House, 1969.

Henri, Florette. *Black Migration, 1900-1920.* New York: Doubleday Anchor Press, 1975. In-depth study of migration to northern cities.

Herbert, Donald J. *Southwest Louisiana Records: Church and Civil Records of Settlers.* Vol. 2: 1811-30. Eunice, La.: By the author, 1974.

Hess, James W., comp. *Guide to Manuscripts and Archives in the West Virginia Collection.* Morgantown: West Virginia University Library, 1974.

Huggins, Nathan Irvin. *Black Odyssey: The Afro-American Ordeal in Slavery.* New York: Pantheon Books, 1977.

Jones, Ruby Mae. *The Negro in Colonial Georgia, 1735-1805.* Bell and Howell Culture Collection, no. 564-2. Wooster, Ohio: Bell and Howell, 1938.

LaBrie, Henry G. *A Survey of Black Newspapers.* New York: Ferdinand Teubner, 1979.

Lamon, Lester C. *Black Tennesseans, 1900-1930.* Knoxville: University of Tennessee Press, 1977.

Leckie, William H. *The Buffalo Soldiers: A Narrative of the Negro Cavalry in the West.* Norman: University of Oklahoma Press, 1967.

Mannix, Daniel P., with Malcolm Cowley. *Black Cargoes: A History of the Atlantic Slave Trade, 1518-1865.* New York: Viking Press, 1962. Ninth printing, 1969.

Menn, Joseph Karl. "The Large Slaveholders of the Deep South, 1860." Ph.D. diss., University of Texas, 1964. University Microfilms, Ann Arbor, Mich. 65-4333.

Mills, Elizabeth Shown and Gary B. Mills. "Slaves and Masters: The Louisiana Metoyers," *National Genealogical Society Quarterly* 70 (Sept. 1982).

Mooney, Chase Curran. *Slavery in Tennessee.* 1957; reprint ed., Westport, Conn.: Negro University Press, 1971.

Nash, Gary B. "Slaves and Slaveowners in Colonial Philadelphia." *William and Mary Quarterly*, 3rd series, 30 (April 1973): 223-56.

Nell, William Cooper. *The Colored Patriots of the American Revolution.* 1862; reprint ed., New York: Arno Press, 1968.

Nichols, Charles Harold. *Many Thousands Gone: The Ex-Slaves' Accounts of Their Bondage and Freedom.* Bloomington, Ind.: Indiana University Press, 1969.

Newman, Debra L. *List of Free Black Heads of Families in the First Census of the United States.* Washington, D.C.: National Archives, 1973.

Phillips, Ulrich Bonnell. *American Negro Slavery.* New York: D. Appleton & Co., 1918.

Puckett, Newbell. *Black Names in America: Origins and Usage.* Boston: G. K. Hall, 1975.

Quarles, Benjamin. *The Negro in the American Revolution.* Chapel Hill: University of North Carolina Press, 1961.

Rawick, George P. *The American Slave: A Composite Autobiography.* 16 vols. Westport, Conn.: Greenwood Press, 1972.

Reed, Robert D. *How and Where to Research Your Ethnic-American Cultural Heritage: Black Americans.* Saratoga, Calif.: By the author, 1979.

Rose, James, and Alice Eicholz. *Black Genesis.* Detroit: Gale Research, 1978.

Rose, Willie Lee, ed. *A Documentary History of Slavery in North America.* New York: Oxford University Press, 1976.

Ross, Alexander Milton. *Recollections of an Abolitionist from 1855-1865.* Northbrook, Ill.: Metro Books, Inc. 1972.

Schatz, Walter. *Directory of Afro-American Resources.* New York: R. R. Bowker. 1970. Includes special research collections, libraries.

Sloan, Irving J. *Blacks in America: 1492-1976: A Chronology and Fact Book.* 4th ed., rev. Dobbs Ferry, N.Y.: Oceana, 1977.

Smedley, Robert C. *History of the Underground Railroad.* New York: Arno, 1969.

Spears, John R. *The American Slave Trade.* 1907; reprint ed., New York: Charles Scribner's & Sons, 1970.

Steward, T. G. *The Colored Regulars in the United States Army.* Philadelphia: M. E. Book Concern, 1904.

Sterkx, H. E. *The Free Negro in Ante-Bellum Louisiana.* Rutherford, N.J.: Fairleigh Dickinson University Press, 1972.

Still, William. *The Underground Railroad.* Philadelphia: Porter and Coates, 1872.

Strick, Lisa W. *The Black Presence in the Era of the American Revolution, 1770-1800.* Washington, D.C.: Smithsonian Institution, 1973.

Welsh, Erwin K. *The Negro in the U.S.: A Research Guide.* Bloomington: Indiana University Press, 1965.

Westmoreland, Guy T., Jr. *An Annotated Guide to Basic Reference Works on the Black American Experience.* Wilmington, Del.: Scholarly Resources, Inc., 1974.

Wharton, Vernon Lane. *The Negro in Mississippi, 1865-1890.* 1947; reprint ed., New York: Harper & Row, 1965.

Winks, Robin W. *The Blacks in Canada: A History.* New Haven: Yale University Press, 1971.

Work, Monroe N. *A Bibliography of the Negro in Africa and America.* New York: Octagon Books, 1970.

Woodson, Carter G. *A Century of Negro Migration.* 1918; reprint ed., New York: AMS Press, 1970.

____________. *Free Negro Heads of Families in the United States Census of 1830.* Association for the Study of Negro Life and History, 1925.

INFORMATION GUIDE

Genealogical Information in the Record Group	*Kenkai (Assoc.)*	*Newspapers*	*Household Registers*	*Temple Death Registers*	*Mortuary Tablets*	*Clan Genealogies*
Surname/name	●	●	●	●	●	●
Date of Birth	●	●				●
Place of Birth	●	●	●			●
Sex						●
Race/color						
Physical Description						
Occupation		●	●			
Education		●				●
Military Service	●	●	●			●
Slave Status						
Property Owned			●			
Religion						
Citizenship	●		●			
Marital Status	●	●	●	●		●
Spouse's Name	●	●	●	●		●
Children's Names	●	●	●			●
Father's Name		●	●	●	●	●
Mother's Name		●	●	●	●	●
Father's Birthplace		●				●
Mother's Birthplace		●				●
Date of Death	●	●	●	●	●	●
Cause of Death						●
Name of Cemetery		●	●	●	●	
Residence	●	●	●			
Age		●	●	●	●	
Literacy/signature			●			
Photograph/sketch		●			●	
Buddhist Name			●	●	●	

COULD YOU USE THIS CHAPTER?

Type of Record	*Kept from*	*Clues That You Should Consult These Records*
Family sources	All periods	If your ancestors are part of the post World War II migrations, begin your family genealogy with home sources described in this chapter as well as Chapter 1.
Basic American sources	All periods	If your ancestors were part of the major migrations of Asian peoples to the United States at the end of the nineteenth century, next consult the basic American documents described in other chapters of this book: census records, vital statistics, naturalizations, business and employment records, etc.
Asian sources	Varies with record type	When you reach the point of research in the country of origin, language facility is a prerequisite. If you do not know the language, you will need to consult an expert. This chapter describes the major documentary resources availabe in China, Korea, and Japan, with some comments on other Asian countries, and suggests the most profitable lines of inquiry. Substantial bodies of Asian materials located in this country are also described in this chapter.

Chapter 20

ASIAN AMERICANS: SOURCES FOR ANCESTRAL RESEARCH

Spencer J. Palmer

According to the 1980 U.S. census, over 3.5 million Asians live in America. They have been emigrating to the United States for over 150 years. This migration, though slow at first, brought approximately 300,000 Orientals to this country by the end of the nineteenth century. It continues to bring over 200,000 annually. Although the religious and cultural backgrounds of these immigrants are vastly different than those of emigrants from Europe, they have come for many of the same reasons; chief among these is the opportunity for economic betterment.

Ethnic Groups in the United States

Chinese

The first East Asian ethnic group to arrive in America, according to the U.S. Immigration Commission, was the Chinese in 1820. During the next thirty years the number of Chinese climbed gradually to a few hundred. After the 1848 discovery of gold near San Francisco, the demand for cheap labor in the mines brought thousands of Chinese to California, largely from the southern Chinese province of Guangdong (Kwangtung), especially its port cities of Canton, Macau (a Portuguese possession), and Hong Kong (British). By the end of 1851, the number of Chinese in California had reached 25,000.

More than the incentive of gold, though, was spurring the Chinese to leave their homeland and seek a new life in America. In the mid-nineteenth century, China was suffering social decay. A corrupt government, high taxes, and unfair treaties forced upon her by Western powers, especially Britain, weakened China's economy severely. With their society on the brink of upheaval, many Chinese received the news of economic opportunity in America as a means of deliverance from their problems.

Census figures reveal that, of the roughly 65,000 Chinese who arrived in the United States during the 1850s, almost half did not stay but apparently returned to China. Since the political and economic unrest in the homeland had not decreased, such returning indicates the strength of their attachment to their homeland.

Although the Chinese were initially welcomed in California as laborers in the mines and on the railroads, prejudice soon appeared in the form of legislation. Chinese immigration to the United States can, in fact, be grouped into four general time periods according to the liberality of the laws: free immigration (1820-82); discriminatory restrictions (1882-1904); absolute exclusion (1904-43); and liberalization (1943-to present).

Since the liberalization period began, the profile of Chinese immigrants has become more balanced. Where early arrivals were mostly laborers and merchants, modern immigrants have included professional people, educators, and businessmen.

The 1980 U.S. census numbered over 800,000 Chinese in this country, the largest single Asian ethnic group. Ninety-five percent live in urban areas, with the largest concentration in San Francisco's Chinatown and the Bay area in general, although smaller "Chinatowns" also exist in New York, Chicago, and other major cities. The Chinese migration to the United States has increased in recent years and with it, the desire of Chinese Americans to know their roots.

Japanese

Although the history of the Japanese in America is shorter than that of the Chinese, it is also fraught with similar difficulties. However, the Japanese government, unlike that of the Chinese, to some degree controlled the affairs of its emigrants to America.

The first Japanese arrived in 1843, but significant immigration did not occur until twenty-five years later when a group of 148 contract laborers arrived in Hawaii. The first group of Japanese immigrated to the mainland in 1869. But it wasn't until the 1890s that the bulk of Japanese immigration began, the result of Japan's 1886 rescission of a ban on emigration to Hawaii due to the mistreatment of Japanese workers there eighteen years earlier. By 1898, when Hawaii was annexed as a United States territory, 60,000 Japanese were living there. Permission to continue to the United States without passports was granted, beginning an influx of thousands of Japanese to the mainland within the next few years. In 1900, for example, 12,635 Japanese arrived on the West Coast from Hawaii.

Although San Francisco and Los Angeles were the principal ports of entry for Japanese immigrants, Seattle and Portland also received many immigrants. Mining and railroad work drew Japanese workers to Utah, Wyoming, and Colorado in the 1890s and early 1900s. By 1910 small groups of farmers began settling in Utah and Idaho, raising vegetables on marginal lands. In larger towns, like Denver and Salt Lake City, a Japanese store, restaurant, tailor shop, or laundry clustered on a central city street. Most of the early immigrants were male laborers who continued to come until 1924, when the Immigration Exclusion Act prohibited immigration by persons "ineligible for citizenship."

This act was essentially an Asian exclusion law, directed against the Japanese and other Orientals. Several organizations were formed on the West Coast to fight this legislation and to petition for Japanese rights. The Japanese American Citizens League (JACL) organized in 1930, and the first such group formed on a national level, became the chief vehicle for Japanese in the United States to solve their problems.

During World War II, from 1942-45, over 100,000 West Coast Japanese were evacuated to relocation centers around the United States. The cooperation of these Japanese Americans in submitting to the evacuation was evidence of their loyalty to the United States.

Ethnic colonies on the West Coast after World War II were greatly diminished as Japanese moved into white-collar and technical jobs in large numbers. Restrictions on intermarriage almost totally disappeared, and Japanese Americans were finally able to own land and to become citizens of the United States.

The American occupation of Japan at the end of World War II

(1945-53), the Korean conflict (1950-53), with the subsequent stationing of American troops in Japan, resulted in about 25,000 "war brides" entering the United States by 1960. A special amendment to the Soldier Brides Bill allowed the pre-1952 Japanese spouses and children of American servicemen to immigrate despite exclusion.

Today the Japanese population in the U.S. is over 700,000, the majority (80 percent) of which is found in the western states.

Koreans

The Koreans, like the Japanese and the Chinese, came first to Hawaii before migrating to the United States mainland. Although some Koreans had come to America as early as 1882, the first Korean immigrant of record to Hawaii came in 1901. From 1903 to 1905, over 7,000 Koreans, with the blessing of their government, were recruited to work on sugar plantations. In 1905, with the establishment of Japan's protectorate in Korea, the Korean government was forced to halt all emigration.

The Korean independence movement – the desire to free the Korean peninsula from Japanese rule – was a strong bonding influence among Korean Americans. The Korean National Association, founded in 1909, led the independence movement in the United States by publishing its own newspapers and urging the U.S. government to press Japan to withdraw.

The Korean Christian churches there fervently supported the independence movement. The church was and still is one of the most important organizations of the United States Korean community for several reasons. Besides assisting Koreans in adjusting to their new life in America, most local congregations sponsored classes to teach Korean children the language, culture, and history of their homeland. The Christian churches (mainly Presbyterian, Methodist, and Catholic), thus helped preserve and transmit Korean culture.

The majority of Koreans now in America have arrived within the last fifteen years. The Korean-American population, just 70,000 in 1970, was 350,000 in 1980 – an increase of 400 percent. Hence, most Koreans in the United States have to search records in Korea to trace their ancestry.

Filipinos

The United States, through the Treaty of Paris, acquired the Philippine Islands from Spain in 1898. The first Filipinos to arrive in the United States were a group of 100 students in 1903. Studying at United States government expense, the "Pensionados" completed their educations and returned to their homeland. This program was in effect until World War II. The second group of immigrants, farm laborers, were enlisted to work on the sugar plantations of Hawaii until the 1930s. The third influx was by far the largest. Beginning with the Immigration Act of 1965, Filipino immigration rose 950 percent in ten years, bringing over 200,000 Filipinos to the United States.

Immigration has continued to spiral upward; in 1980 the Filipino population had reached 775,000, an increase of almost 440,000 over the total ten years previously. According to the 1980 U.S. Census, Filipinos ranked second only to Chinese in population among Asian ethnic groups. Should the present trend continue, Filipinos may soon be the dominant nationality among Asian Americans.

East Indians

The first East Indians to come to the United States, students and businessmen, arrived in the early 1900s. Restrictive policies limited their number to just a few thousand until 1946, when a new immigration law raised the annual quota to 100 individuals.

Between the passage of the 1946 law and the 1965 Immigration Act, about 6,500 East Indian immigrants, most of whom were nonquota, entered the United States. The high proportion of nonquota immigrants is evidence that many East Indians brought their families. From 1965 to 1975 immigration from India increased 2,000 percent, escalating the number of Indians to over 85,000. The Census Bureau reported that in November of 1979, 182,000 people in the United States claimed Asian Indian ancestry.

Several patterns have developed in East Indian immigration from 1946 to the present: 1) the youth of the immigrants – 60 percent have been under thirty years old; 2) job status – many are professionals; 3) geographic background – most emigrated from India's large cities rather than, like most of the early immigrants, its rural areas; 4) even population distribution throughout the United States – East Indians are more evenly spread across the country than any Asian ethnic group.

Southeast Asians

The most recent group of Asians to immigrate are the Southeast Asian refugees whose countries (Cambodia, Laos, and South Vietnam) were torn by strife in the 1960s and 1970s. In 1975, when the Communists gained control, many Cambodians, including ethnic Chinese and Vietnamese, as well as Khmer (Cambodian) and Laotians, fled to Thailand. When the South Vietnamese capital of Saigon fell, a chaotic evacuation of 100,000 people including ethnic Chinese and Khmer took place within a few days.

These Southeast Asian refugees immigrated rapidly; by September 1979, the Immigration and Naturalization Service recorded the arrival of 116,350 Vietnamese and Laotian refugees. By 1980, California alone had a Vietnamese population of 90,000, while the U. S. Census Bureau reported almost 200,000 people of Vietnamese ancestry.

Though still comparatively small minorities, Asian ethnic groups are becoming more visible and are having an increasing social, economic, and political impact on America. Not only have Americans in general become more keenly interested in Asian groups in America, but Asian Americans have become increasingly interested in their own ethnicity and cultural heritage and in understanding their own roots.

Tracing Asian Ancestry in the United States*

In tracing your ancestry, you should begin with yourself or what you can find out about yourself from members of your family. (See Chapter 1 on home sources.) Start with a pedigree chart and a family group record and list the names and vital statistics of your parents, your brothers and sisters, and if you are married, your spouse and children.

From memory fill in as much as you can; then go to the home sources. Traditional Japanese and Western home sources include journals, diaries, notes, old newspapers, letters, clippings, obituaries, paper or wooden mortuary tables, family records, household registers, family death registers, church certificates and records, employment records and correspondence, materials relating to memberships in ethnic associations, diplomas, school records, yearbooks, records of cremation and burial, records of residence, travel or transfer, records of military service, immigrant ancestor's passport or papers, receipts, financial records, deeds and wills, photograph albums, family crests, and relics.

Ask family members and friends of the family living in this country, as well as overseas, if they have any of these sources in their possession. If you cannot visit your relatives in person, you may want to write or telephone them. Indicate a genuine family interest but calls and letters, particularly at first, should be brief, polite, and to the point.

Consult vital records – records of births, deaths, marriages, and divorces that are available within any given jurisdiction – the state,

---

*What follows in this section is drawn from the findings, writings, and suggestions of Greg Gubler in unpublished materials he has made available to me. Professor Gubler, who now teaches at BYU-Hawaii, is a recognized expert in Japanese genealogical research and was for years associated with the Genealogical Society of Utah.

province, city, town, or country. Since many Asians are recent immigrants to the United States, vital records, which are kept in city, state, and national archives, will be useful. For example, a copy of your own birth certificate will confirm details of your father's and mother's data. (See Chapter 2, "Vital Records and Cemetery Research.")

Birth records usually list complete names of individuals, birthplace and date, sex, name of father, maiden name of mother, legitimacy, and the age of each parent at the time of birth. Death records include the complete name of the deceased, sex, age of the individual at death, date and place of death, burial, cause of death, marital status, and sometimes valuable details about parents. Divorce decrees are granted by courts at the county or local level and vary in how much useful information they contain. (See Chapter 3, "Marriage and Divorce Records.")

In the United States, birth records are generally kept at the state level by a bureau of vital statistics and/or health department. Marriage and divorce records are found either at the county or state level and sometimes both. See Appendix F, "Where to Write for Vital Records," for the addresses of the respective offices.

Records before Hawaii's annexation are kept in the Hawaii State Archives and are on microfilm at the Genealogical Society of Utah. The large Asian-American community in Hawaii makes up a significant portion of vital records during the Hawaiian Kingdom and Republic periods.

The 1890 and 1896 census reports for Hawaii include some Japanese immigrants, but later census reports are sometimes incomplete. (See Chapter 4, "Census Records.") Items included are name, address, age, country of origin or race, number of years in Hawaii, occupation, religious category (Catholic, Protestant, or Mormon. Buddhists were apparently filed as Protestants in early census records.), languages familiar with, and ownership of land or house. Federal census reports since 1900 are located in the National Archives in Washington, D.C. Records within the last seventy-five years are restricted to direct-line ancestors or children of the deceased. (See "Privacy Laws" in Introduction.)

Translation and spelling problems will arise if you are tracing Asian ancestry in the United States. Because many immigrants never learned much English, they often made errors in filling out forms or in providing information orally. Many had trouble with dates and in adjusting to the Western calendar.

Locating your ancestor in time and space will help you do more effective research. First, find a good map in order to locate cities, towns, and villages. In looking for relatives or friends of the family in the United States, you may wish to consult telephone books or directories. (See Chapter 11, "City Directories and Their Cousins.") University libraries often collect local histories and materials of ethnic groups in their respective areas. For example, the University of Hawaii, UCLA, the University of California at Berkeley, and the University of Washington have books, manuscripts, and microfilms relating to Japanese-Americans in their respective communities. The Bishop Museum in Honolulu is also building an excellent collection.

Ethnic Associations in America

Since many of these sources are in Oriental languages, you may need help in reading them. *The examples that follow are Japanese, but counterpart sources are available for other Asian-American groups.*

Prefectural Associations. People originating from the same prefecture (similar to but smaller than a state) in Japan shared common dialects, experiences, and affinities, providing a natural basis for identity. The associations they formed in America, called *kenkai* or *kenjinkai,* sought to help immigrants adjust to their new life in America.

In Hawaii, which had the largest number of immigrants, there were strong prefectural associations for those from Hiroshima, Yamaguchi, Jumamonto, Okinawa, Niigata, Fukushima, and Fukuoka. More than a score of *kenjinkai* were listed in the 1964 Los Angeles phone book, though many of these have subsequently disappeared. Seattle *kenkai* include prefectures of Hiroshima, Okayama, Yamaguchi, Fukuoka, Kuymamoto, Wakayama, Shiga, and Ehime.

Most prefectural associations produced membership directories, mimeographed or published newsletters, and corresponded regularly with individual members. If the *kenkai* no longer has an office, search out children of former leaders and/or inquire at the local branch of the Japanese American Citizens League (or Japanese Canadian Citizens Association) about the existence of such records.

Japanese American Citizens League. Formed in Seattle in 1930 to represent the interests of American-born Japanese, JACL has advocated minority rights in the United States since the post-World War II era. Many branches publish newspapers and newsletters on the affairs of the community, while a number of branches collect Japanese ancestry materials. The local JACL branch may help in locating an ancestor. Addresses of JACL branches may be obtained from the national office: JACL, Japan Center, Suite 203, San Francisco, CA 94115.

Japanese Newspapers. Japanese language newspapers were printed in Hawaii and the urban centers of California almost immediately after the arrival of the first immigrants. To attract Nisei (second-generation Japanese Americans) and Sansei (third-generation) readers, most of the papers added English sections as the communities expanded. In both the Japanese and English sections, items of genealogical and historical value such as obituaries, births, marriages, and anniversaries were included. Many ethnic newspapers are still printed in Hawaii and in the major West and East Coast cities of the United States.

Employment records, school records, church records, Japanese mortuary records, Buddhist sects and temples, cemeteries, Chinese, Korean, Japanese, and other Asian consulates in the United States, travel agencies, and the records of the Genealogical Society of Utah, are valuable resources.

At the outset, you should ask yourself some basic questions. Tracing your family can be a difficult task best begun by determining your ancestors' place of origin. Greg Gubler has suggested the following questions in beginning your search:

1. Do you, your parents, or relatives know an ancestor in the country, region, and, if possible, home town–that may be able to help you find appropriate records on your immigrant ancestor?
2. Can these contacts help you obtain family and household registers, Buddhist death records, etc., that will extend your pedigree?
3. Do you know the name of your immigrant ancestor?
4. Do you know when and where your immigrant ancestor died?
5. Do you know the descendants of your immigrant ancestor?
6. Did your immigrant ancestor marry before or after emigrating?
7. Do you know the port at which your ancestor arrived?
8. Do you know when your ancestor arrived?
9. Do you know where your ancestor established his or her first residence after arrival?
10. What family traditions exist concerning the reasons your immigrant ancestors emigrated?

The records of the Immigration and Naturalization Service of the United States provide arrival information for the West Coast ports and post-1900 Hawaii. They also contain alien registration forms submitted after 1940, as well as naturalization records and certificates created on or after 27 September 1906. Information from these records may be obtained by filling out Form G-641, available at the fifty local INS offices in major United States cities.

Genealogical Sources in Asia

Because of the recentness of Asian immigration, the American historical data is quite limited. Once you have exhausted all records and sources available in the United States for tracing your ancestors, you will need to search primary sources in Asia. Becoming aware of genealogical records in the country of your ancestry is necessary, as the principal sources differ from country to country in Asia.*

Chinese Sources

Historical Records. Written histories and clan genealogical records are the two most important Chinese ancestral sources. The *fang-chi*, or local histories of traditional China, contain rich ancestral information. To consult the appropriate local history, you must know the region from which your progenitors came.

The *fang-chih*, in addition to geographical, religious, and educational records, include categories helpful in researching family and clan lineages. Professor Tsun Leng, then chairman of the Sociology Department, New Asia, University of Hong Kong, describes the two most important as:

1. "Elites and personalities" which list leaders from all walks of life: scholars, farmers, artisans, merchants, retired generals, and high-ranking officials. It also includes biographies of Chinese who have achieved the traditional standards of loyalty, filial piety, chastity, and righteousness.

2. "Clan and family" which mention the influential and famous families and clans with their family stories, lines, traditions, standings, achievements, and their contributions to the community or nation.

Genealogical Records. Genealogical records in China, often extensive, have been kept by clans and families for many hundreds of years. Most genealogical records include: 1) lineage and branches of the family – essentially pedigree charts and family trees; 2) ancestral halls and graveyards – one or two chapters detailing the construction of halls for worshipping ancestors and the ceremonies performed; 3) academic degrees and official ranks; and 4) outstanding persons of a given clan. The last two categories focus on individuals within a clan who rose to high positions in government or in society.

Such genealogical records are scattered throughout the world, with many housed in libraries in the United States and Japan but particularly in China (the People's Republic of China) and in the Republic of China on Taiwan. According to the survey research of Hisang-lin Lo, pp. 49-50 in *Studies in Asian Genealogy*, the largest library collections of Chinese genealogies extant today are in the Peking University Library, the Chinese Provincial Library of Guangdong, the Fun P'ing-shan Library of the University of Hong Kong, the Tokyo Bunko (Library) of Japan, the Japan Congress Library, and the East Asian Library of Columbia University in New York. Almost all genealogical records contained in these libraries are from the Ch'ing period (1644-1911), China's last traditional dynasty, or from the first thirty-eight years of the Republic (1911-49).

Since 1949 many valuable privately kept genealogies have been lost or destroyed. Of those surviving, most are records of clans and families from southern China. Since the bulk of Chinese immigrants to the United States came from the south China province of Guangdong, the library collections at Hong Kong and Guangdong province may be especially fruitful sources of information.

---

*What follows here is drawn primarily from Spencer J. Palmer, *Studies in Asian Genealogy* (Provo, Utah: Brigham Young University Press, 1972), which contains papers presented at the 1969 World Conference on Records in Salt Lake City, Utah. For those who can read the local languages and scripts of Asia, the book is a useful source of names, terms, and words. The Tsun Leng quotation which follows is from pp. 13-16.

Japanese Sources

As in China, the earliest known Japanese writings, dating from the sixth century A.D. contain stories about ancient heroes and genealogical records of the imperial family. Later in the seventh century, under imperial commission, the *Kojiki* and the *Nihon Shoki*, the two earliest Japanese books dealing with Shinto legends and myths, were produced and are the two oldest surviving chronicles.

Clans throughout Japanese history have established private academies and libraries to preserve genealogical records, as have Buddhist monasteries and the various governments. Genealogy has also been an integral part of Japan's samurai or military tradition, with records of the Tokugawa period (1600-1868) still extant in Japan. Written genealogies were required by many of the traditional military houses.

Household Registers (Koseki). These extensive and rich sources on Japanese society originated in 1871 and grew out of earlier systems of public registration. Virtually all cities, towns, and villages of Japan kept registration offices where family record books were deposited. Prior to World War II, most entries were handwritten on a folded printed form. Post-war entries are usually typed on thin rice paper and inserted into binders. These records are available only to close descendants of the head of the house.

Buddhist Death Registers (Kakocho). Death registers are kept in Buddhist temples for ancestor veneration and ritual. The dead are given a posthumous Buddhist name. This parish temple record also serves as an obituary providing names and other essential information. If you have Buddhist ancestry, ask a relative in Japan to search for you or write directly (in Japanese) to the appropriate regional or local temple.

Buddhist Mortuary Tablets (Ihai). These tablets, prepared for ancestor veneration and the remembrance of the dead, are made of wood, lacquered in black, and inscribed in gold leaf, although some in the United States and Hawaii are merely paper strips. These tablets are most often found in the family *butsudan* (Buddhist household shrine) in homes where Japanese Buddhist customs are still strong and contain at least the posthumous names and dates of death of individuals.

Tombstone Inscriptions. Inscriptions on tombstones are often productive sources of information for you in tracing your ancestry in Asia or in any other place in the world. The importance of cemetery visits cannot be overemphasized.

Family Crests (Kamon). Like coats of arms in European genealogical research, family crests can be significant sources of information in Japan. Often found on tombstones, mortuary tablets, ceremonial dress, and family documents, these crests also appear on feudal records. Crests usually do not represent surnames but are linked with family branches in particular areas of Japan. These hereditary insignia, tied in with the history of a family, may help you identify a surname or a pedigree.

Korean Sources

The basic sources listed for research in China and Japan are also available in Korea with the addition of two other areas of information.

Korean clan genealogies, the ***chokpo***, are of immense importance to Korean research as Edward Wagner, associate professor of Korean Studies at Harvard, has shown in *The Literati Purges: Political Conflict in Early Yi Korea* (Cambridge: Harvard University Press, 1974). The *chokpo* are a mirror of Korean society during the 500 years of Yi Dynasty (1392 to 1910), Korea's last historic dynasty. They describe the elite ruling class. These clan records are held in repositories throughout Korea along with extensive collections in the Seoul National University Library and the Korean National Library. Many Korean *chokpo* records have been microfilmed and are available through the Genealogical Society of Utah.

For the Yi period, the government examination rosters (***pangmok***) reveal the names of all successful candidates who took government examinations for public office. They are recorded in classical Chinese, and you will likely need some help in examining them.

Bibliography of Asian-American Materials in United States Libraries

Asians in America

Conroy, Hilary, and T. Scott Miyaka, eds. *Historical and Sociological Studies of Japanese Immigration and Assimilation*. Santa Barbara, Calif.: American Bibliographical Center, Clio Press, 1972.

Gubler, Greg. "Asian-American Records and Research," Jessie Carney Smith, ed. *Ethnic Genealogy*, Westport, Conn.: Greenwood Press, 1983, pp. 239-308.

Kort, Blanche L., and Mitsuo Yamato. *A Bibliographic Record of Americans of Japanese Ancestry*. Honolulu: Stowe and Associates, 1963.

Melendy, Howard B. *The Oriental Americans*. New York: Hippocrene Books, 1972.

________________. *Asians in America*. New York: Hippocrene Books, 1981.

Palmer, Spencer J., ed. *Studies in Asian Genealogy*. Provo, Utah: Brigham Young University Press, 1972.

Chinese Americans

Chinese American Christian Identity and Calling. Berkeley, Calif.: Pacific and Asian American Center for Theology and Strategies (PACTS), 1979.

Chinese Local Histories as a Source for the Genealogist. Genealogical Research Papers, Series J, No. 3, Salt Lake City: Genealogical Department of the Church of Jesus Christ of Latter-day Saints, 1974.

Chinn, Thomas W. *The Chinese Six Companies*. Chinese Historical Society of America, n.d.

________________. *Genealogical Methods and Sources for the Chinese Immigrants to the U. S.* Paper presented at the World Conference on Records of the Genealogical Society of Utah, Salt Lake City, 1969.

Culin, Stewart. *The I Hing or "Patriotic Rising."* San Francisco: R and E Research Associates, 1970.

Gibson, Otis. *The Chinese in America*. Cincinnati: Hitchcock and Walden, 1877.

Huang, Joe. *Chinese Americans*. San Francisco: Association of Chinese Teachers, 1977.

Kung, Shien-woo. *Chinese in American Life*. Seattle: University of Washington Press, 1962.

Lai, H. Mark. "The Chinese Language Sources Bibliography Project: Preliminary Findings." *AMERASIA* 5 (1978): 95-107.

Lee, Calvin B. T. *Chinatown, U. S. A.* Garden City, N.Y.: Doubleday, 1965.

Lee, Rose Hum. *The Chinese in the United States of America*. Hong Kong: Hong Kong University Press, 1960.

Major Genealogical Record Sources in Hong Kong. Genealogical Research Papers, Series J, No. 4. Salt Lake City: Genealogical Department of The Church of Jesus Christ of Latter-day Saints, 1974.

Major Genealogical Record Sources in Taiwan. Genealogical Research Papers, Series J, No. 2, rev. ed. Salt Lake City: Genealogical Department of The Church of Jesus Christ of Latter-day Saints, 1976.

Miller, Stuart C. *The Unwelcome Immigrant*. Berkeley, Calif.: University of California Press, 1969.

Japanese Americans

Aubert, Louis. *Americains et Japonais*. Paris: A. Colin, 1908.

Boddy, E. Manchester. *Japanese in America*. San Francisco: R and E Research Associates, 1970.

Conroy, Hilary, and T. Scott Miyakawa, eds. *East Across the Pacific: Historical and Sociological Studies of Japanese Immigration and Assimilation*. Santa Barbara, Calif.: American Bibliographical Center, Clio Press, 1972.

Fukei, Budd. *The Japanese American Story*. Minneapolis: Dillon, c1976.

Japanese Immigration: An Exposition of its Real Status. 1907; reprint ed. San Francisco: R and E Research Associates, 1972.

Kitano, Harry H. L. *Japanese Americans*, 2nd ed. Englewood Cliffs, N.J.: Prentice-Hall, c1976.

Leathers, Noel L. *The Japanese in America*. Minneapolis: Lerner Publications Company, c1974.

Levine, Gene N. *The Japanese American Community*. New York: Praeger, 1981.

Major Genealogical Record Sources in Japan. Genealogical Research Papers, Series J, No. 2, rev. ed. Salt Lake City: Genealogical Department of the Church of Jesus Christ of Latter-day Saints, 1974.

Millis, Harry A. *The Japanese Problem in the United States*. New York: Macmillan, 1915.

Personal Justice Denied. Washington, D.C.: U. S. Government Printing Office, 1982.

Petersen, William. *Japanese Americans*. Washington, D.C.: University Press of America, c1971.

Stein, R. Conrad. *Go For Broke: The Nisei Regiment*. Chicago: Children's Press, 1983.

They Work for Victory. Salt Lake City, Utah: The Japanese American Citizens League, 1945.

Stanley, Sue, and Nathaniel N. Wagner, eds. *Asian-Americans: Psychological Perspectives*. Palo Alto: Science and Behavior Books, Inc., 1973.

Weglyn, Michi. *Years of Infamy, The Untold Story of America's Concentration Camps*. New York: Morrow Quill Paperbacks, 1976.

Korean Americans

Hurh, Won Moo. *Comparative Study of Korean Immigrants in the United States*. San Francisco: R and E Research Associates, 1977.

Kim, Won-Yong. *Koreans in America*. Seoul: Po Chin Chai Printing Company, 1971.

Melendy, Howard B. *Asians in America*. Boston: Twayne Publishers, c1977.

Patterson, Wayne. *The Koreans in America*. Minneapolis: Lerner Publication Co., c1977.

Sociological Studies of Korean Immigration and Assimilation in North America. Santa Barbara, Calif.: American Bibliographical Center, Clio Press, 1972.

INFORMATION GUIDE

Genealogical Information in the Record Group	*Synagogue*	*Circumcision*	*Bar/Bar Mitzvah*	*Mortuary*	*Communal Histories*	*Hebrew Immigrant Aid Society*
Surname/name	●	●	●	●	●	●
Date of Birth		●				
Place of Birth		●		●	●	●
Sex			●			
Race/color						
Physical Description						
Occupation				●	●	●
Education			●		●	
Military Service					●	
Slave Status						
Property Owned					●	●
Religion	●	●	●	●	●	
Citizenship						
Marital Status	●				●	●
Spouse's Name					●	●
Children's Names					●	●
Father's Name	●	●	●	●	●	
Mother's Name	●			●	●	
Father's Birthplace					●	
Mother's Birthplace					●	
Date of Death	●			●	●	
Cause of Death						
Name of Cemetery	●			●	●	
Residence	●	●	●	●	●	●
Age	●	●	●	●	●	●
Literacy/signature						●
Photograph/sketch					●	●
Hebrew Name		●	●	●		

COULD YOU USE THIS CHAPTER?

Type of Record	*Kept from*	*Clues That You Should Consult These Records*
American synagogue records	After 1800	If there is a family tradition that your ancestor was Jewish, chances are that he/she came to the United States in the great migrations between 1880 and 1920 and settled in an urban area. Synagogue records include account books, religious school registers, birth and circumcision records, bar/bat mitzvah and confirmation records, marriage records, and death and cemetery records that could confirm his/her presence and add genealogical information.
Congregational and community histories	After 1895	Even if your ancestor did not live in a Jewish population center in the United States, he/she could still be included if he/she had family ties to a Jewish center. Jews in urban centers are, of course, prime candidates for inclusion. All of the records above could help in the vital step of locating the ancestral hometowm in Europe but other records are also useful: the 1900/1910 censuses, naturalization records, Hamburg passenger lists, and Hebrew Immigrant and Aid Society (HS) records.
East European and German records	Primarily nineteenth century	This chapter also describes the records available in the United States from Jewish communities in Germany, Poland, Hungary, Lithuania, and France that survived until the 1960s.

Chapter 21

JEWISH-AMERICAN RESEARCH

Johni Cerny

It is no secret that Jews have been persecuted and expelled from country after country for centuries. As they departed they took little more than honored traditions, an enduring religious heritage, and the will to survive in new surroundings. Today there are over 14 million Jews residing in eighty-four countries. Slightly more than 42 percent of the total Jewish population lives in the United States, primarily in the country's urban centers.

The first group of Jews arrived in colonial America from Brazil in 1654, settling in the Dutch colony of New Amsterdam. They were mostly Sephardic Jews, descendants of a segment of the Jewish people who lived along the Iberian Peninsula during the Middle Ages until the Spanish Inquisition of 1492 required all religious groups to convert to Catholicism. The Jewish population dispersed to other Mediterranean countries, Latin America, and northern Europe.

The Dutch did not welcome this first group of Jews, but they allowed them to remain, and New York became the first focal point of Jewish settlement. Today the city boasts a population of nearly 2 million Jews, slightly less than the total Jewish population of the Soviet Union. New York's Jewish population grew slowly. Early Newport, Rhode Island, was more tolerant and permitted Jews to settle without the restrictions New York imposed. The Newport community, however, was never large and died out about 1823. In the 1880s, Rhode Island Jewry was reestablished with the arrival of Jews from Eastern Europe. During the eighteenth century, small numbers of Jews began to move out of New York to settle first in Philadelphia and then at other locations in Pennsylvania, augmented by Spanish-Portuguese Jews by way of Holland and England. They were skilled artisans and merchants who preferred city life styles and were only rarely found among the westward-moving pioneers. A few German Jews also arrived in the colonial period. Southern colonial Jews settled in Savannah, Georgia (refugees from Portugal by way of London in 1733), and in Charleston, South Carolina (from the West Indies and Brazil). By 1820, Charleston had the largest Jewish population in the United States, a colony of some seven hundred. Other communities were established in Philadelphia (1745), Montreal (1760s), and Richmond (1789) before the turn of the nineteenth century. See Rabbi Malcolm H. Stern, "Jewish Migrations," in Kenn Stryker-Rodda, ed., *Genealogical Research: Methods and Sources,* Vol. 2 (Washington, D.C.: American Society of Genealogists, 1983), pp. 341-59 for locations of other communities in America.

Today only a small portion of Jewish Americans are descended from these colonial Americans. The majority of America's Jews trace their origins to ancestors who arrived in this country after 1881. They are Ashkenazic Jews, descendants of German and Eastern European peoples. Although many Jews from Germany immigrated to the United States between 1850 and 1870, the enormous waves of refugees from Czarist Russia did not begin until 1881. The change in Russian leadership after Alexander II was assassinated precipitated the influx of Jews beginning in that year. Jews living in the Pale, an area in Russia that permitted Jews, were subjected to the first of a series of harsh pogroms. Nearly one-third of the eastern European Jewish population left its homes to resettle in America; nearly two million arrived between 1881 and 1914. According to Irving Howe in *World of Our Fathers,* their

> . . .departure from Russia, Poland, Romania, and Austro-Hungary can be traced along four main routes:
>
> 1. Jews coming from the Ukraine and southern Russia would usually cross the Austro-Hungarian border illegally, travel by train to Vienna or Berlin, and regroup themselves for the journey to one of the major ports of embarkation: Hamburg and Bremen in Germany, Rotterdam and Amsterdam in Holland, and Antwerp in Belgium.
>
> 2. Jews emigrating from western or northwestern Russia would surreptitiously cross the German border and proceed to Berlin and then the northern ports.
>
> 3. Jews from the Austro-Hungarian empire would legally cross the German border, journey to Berlin, and there join the mass of Jews from Russia to proceed to the ports.
>
> 4. Jews from Romania whose mass migration first began in 1899, traveled mostly through Vienna, Frankfurt-am-Main, and then the Holland ports, though a few took the sea voyage from Trieste or Fiume.[1]

Before the Jews' expulsion from eastern Europe, many Jewish communities were plundered and burned. Their records and cemeteries were destroyed wholesale, especially in Russia. Occasionally synagogue records were hidden and preserved, and later brought to America or carried to Israel.

Jewish Americans seeking to trace their ancestry initially feel that their history makes the task impossible. That is far from true. Arthur Kurzweil's excellent guide to Jewish genealogy in America and Europe, *From Generation to Generation* (New York: Schocken Books, 1982) is available today at most better bookstores and Jewish bookstores throughout the country. I recommend it highly to both the professional and the family genealogist.

American Jews whose ancestors arrived in this country before 1881 should begin tracing their family like other Americans. Begin with family and home sources and interviews with living relatives. Then expand your search to include vital records (birth, marriage, and death), census records, naturalization records, passenger lists, and local histories, to name a few. The early chapters of this book will provide you with a thorough understanding of these records' content, use, availability, and location.

Since most American Jews are of Ashkenazic descent who will reach their immigrant ancestor within a generation or two, this chapter will focus on European records and their availability as well as American records peculiar to Jewish-American ancestral research. Records exist in England and in Mediterranean countries for Sephardic Jews. Some of these are available in the United States. See bibliography at the end of the chapter for guides.

---

1. Irving Howe, *World of Our Fathers* (New York: Harcourt, Brace Jovanovich, 1976), p. 28. Rabbi Stern's researches have shown that many Jews sailed from Trieste and Fiume.

Figure 21-1. Congregation of B'nai Jeshurun, New York City, 1884, General Minutes Book, 1883-1927, p. 5; Genealogical Society of Utah (hereafter GS) microfilm 978,417.

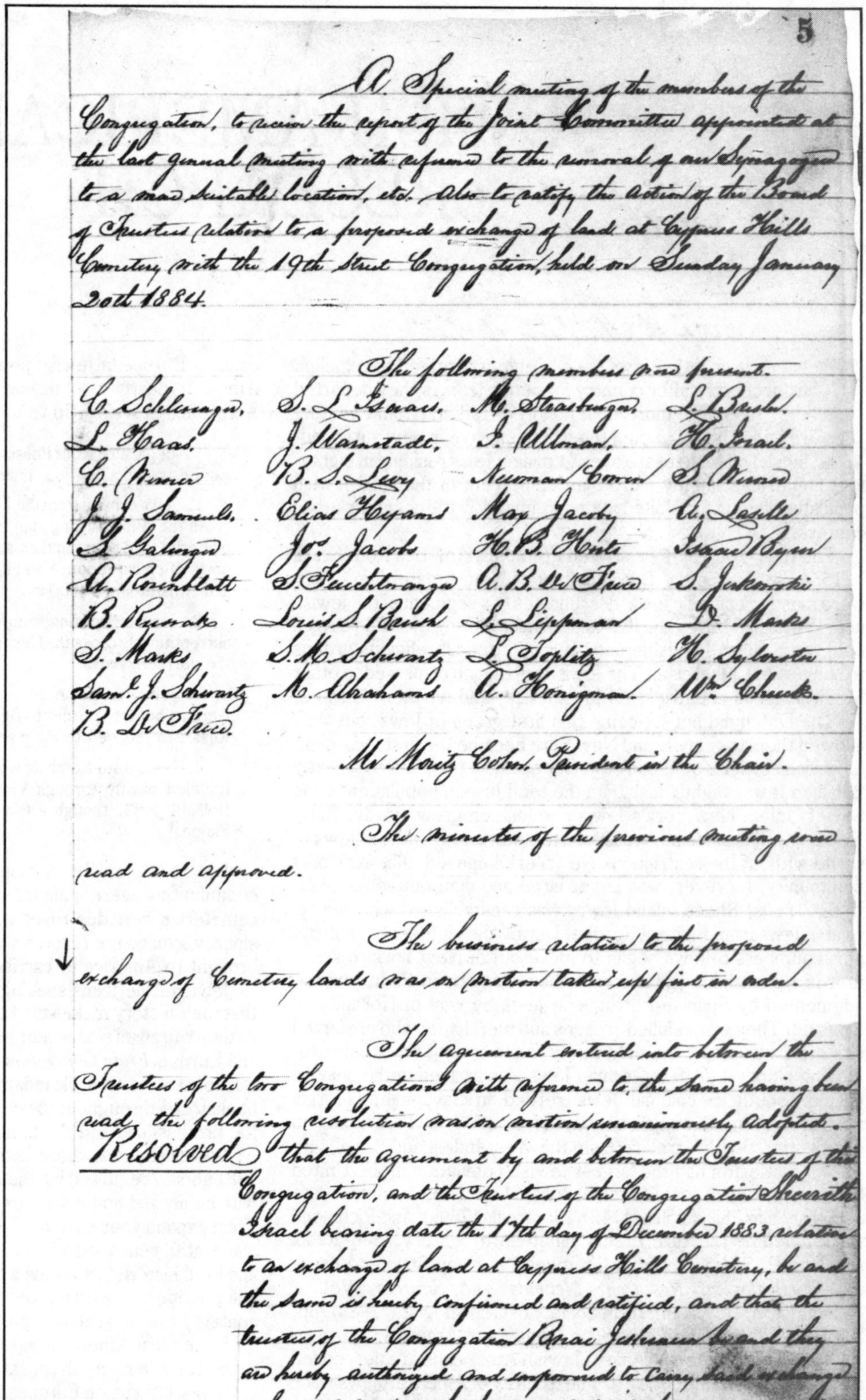

5

A Special meeting of the members of the Congregation, to receive the report of the Joint Committee appointed at the last general meeting with reference to the removal of our Synagogue to a more suitable location, etc. Also to ratify the action of the Board of Trustees relative to a proposed exchange of land at Cypress Hills Cemetery with the 19th Street Congregation, held on Sunday January 20th 1884.

The following members were present.

C. Schlesinger.	S. L. Isaacs.	M. Strasburger.	L. Bissler.
L. Haas.	J. Wamstadt.	I. Ullman.	H. Israel.
C. Werner	B. S. Levy	Newman Cowen	S. Werner
J. J. Samuels.	Elias Hyams	Max Jacoby	A. Lasalle
L. Galinger	Jos. Jacobs	H. B. Hertz	Isaac Byer
A. Rosenblatt	S. Feuchtwanger	A. B. De Frece	S. Jeskowski
B. Rusack	Louis S. Baush	L. Lippman	D. Marks
S. Marks	S. M. Schwartz	L. Soplitz	H. Sylvester
Saml. J. Schwartz	M. Abrahams	A. Honigman	Wm. Chuck.
B. De Frece			

Mr Moritz Cohen, President in the Chair.

The minutes of the previous meeting were read and approved.

The business relative to the proposed exchange of Cemetery lands was on motion taken up first in order.

The agreement entered into between the Trustees of the two Congregations with reference to the same having been read, the following resolution was on motion unanimously adopted.

Resolved that the agreement by and between the Trustees of this Congregation, and the Trustees of the Congregation Shearith Israel bearing date the 17th day of December 1883 relative to an exchange of land at Cypress Hills Cemetery, be and the same is hereby confirmed and ratified, and that the trustees of the Congregation B'nai Jeshurun be and they are hereby authorized and empowered to carry said exchange of lands into effect by the execution of such instruments as

Jewish Synagogue Records in America

Synagogue records differ somewhat from records of other American religious groups. The records will vary from synagogue to synagogue both in the United States and other countries. Thus, you will not be able to find all of the records discussed here for every synagogue.

Minute Books

Most American and a few European synagogues compiled several types of minute books, but few early examples survive, especially if the synagogue relocated, as most did, in urban areas with the change of population. The Congregation of B'nai Jeshurun in New York City kept extensive minute books, including general minute books, minutes of the trustees, electors' minutes, and minutes of the joint committee on the cemetery. I have featured its records extensively, but it has a remarkable archives matched by few others in America. It is up to the researcher to determine what records still exist for the congregations attended by the ancestor of interest. Minute books ordinarily contain little genealogical information, but lists of members present at congrega-

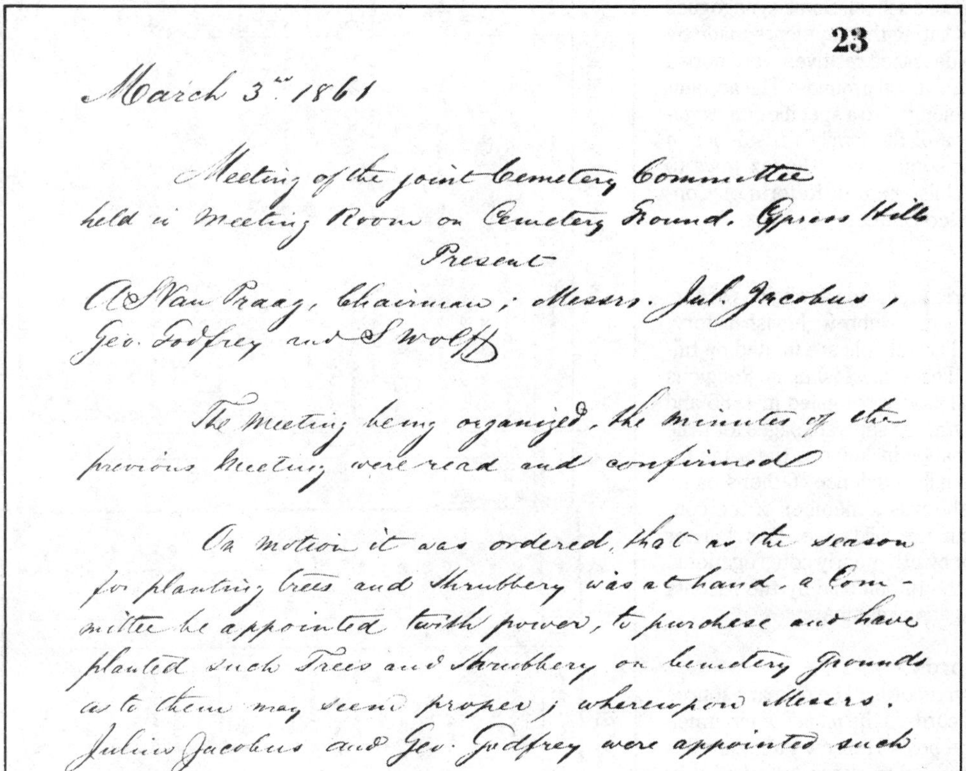

23

March 3rd 1861

Meeting of the joint Cemetery Committee held in Meeting Room on Cemetery Ground. Cypress Hills

Present

A S Van Praag, Chairman; Messrs. Jul. Jacobus, Geo. Godfrey and S Wolff

The Meeting being organized, the minutes of the previous Meeting were read and confirmed

On motion it was ordered, that as the season for planting trees and shrubbery was at hand, a Committee be appointed with power, to purchase and have planted such Trees and Shrubbery on Cemetery Grounds as to them may seem proper; whereupon Messrs. Julius Jacobus and Geo. Godfrey were appointed such Committee.

On Motion it was agreed to appropriate a piece of ground by each of the respective congregations for raising and cultivating shrubbery for future use of the Ground.

On motion it was ordered, that the Keeper, Mr. de Youngh, be authorized to have reception-room of House papered, as also to purchase a Grinding-Stone Shovel and Saw Buck, and present bill for same to the Committee at next Meeting.

On motion adjourned

J. Blumenthal
Secty pro tem

Figure 21-2. Congregation of B'nai Jeshurun, New York City, Minutes of the Joint Cemetery Committee, p. 23; GS 978,420.

tional meetings and changes of the synagogue's location will help you. Figure 21-1 is a page from the 1884 General Minute Book of Congregation B'nai Jeshurun. Figure 21-2, a page from the Minutes of the Joint Committee on Cemetery, names the cemetery operated by the same congregation. The greatest value of minute books lies in the history of the congregation that they include.

Account Books

Some synagogues maintained separate account books, and others included the information in the general or trustees' minutes. Account books are valuable to genealogists because they include lists of members of the synagogue who contributed financially to its operation or to maintaining its religious school. Some synagogues also kept cemetery account ledgers listing the payments made by members of the congregation whose deceased relatives were buried in the synagogue-owned and -operated burial grounds. The account lists indicate how long an ancestor belonged to a specific congregation but not necessarily the duration of the family's residence in the area. It was not uncommon for some less orthodox Jews to change congregations with the establishment of Reform or Conservative congregations in the United States.

Religious School Registers

Nearly every synagogue in America operates a religious school to educate its children in religious subjects, Hebrew, Jewish history, and Jewish traditions and lifestyle. The schools are funded by tuition and members' contributions. The B'nai Jeshurun Religious School Register shown in Figure 21-3 was compiled in 1885 and offers some valuable information. There are separate pages for male and female students, but the information included is the same for both: date of admission, name of pupil, residence, father's name (occasionally the mother's), if he/she was a member of the congregation, and, in the remarks column, the child's age. This register is fairly representative of those kept by other early congregations. The school account books will list the tuition paid by the parents and contributions by other congregation members.

Birth and Circumcision Records

Only a few synagogues kept birth records. The primary source of birth information in synagogue records is the *mohel* or circumcision register. The registers list the boy's Hebrew name and his father's Hebrew name. In some instances they also include the family name, as in Figure 21-4, a page from the 1848-49 Circumcision Record of Temple Rodelph Shalom in Philadelphia. The *mohel* also gives the date of circumcision (usually the eighth day after the boy's birth), the names as indicated above, and the residence of the child's father. This source is, of course, silent about the births of daughters. Since *mohel* records were kept by individual circumcisers, it is unusual to find circumcision registers among synagogue records.

Bar/Bat Mitzvah and Confirmation Records

When a Jewish boy reaches the age of thirteen, he is considered mature enough to assume responsibilities in the synagogue. About 150 years ago, Reform Judaism borrowed confirmation from Protestantism and applied it equally to boys and girls. Further equality was achieved with the recent introduction by many American congregations of bat mitzvah for girls.

There are few records of bar/bat mitzvah ceremonies. Generally, only an announcement in the synagogue bulletin or a printed program will survive the event. You will more likely find records of these events in family and home sources.

Confirmations take place in group ceremonies, indicating completion of a specific program or period of religious study. Confirmation classes are usually listed in synagogue bulletins in late spring, and parents' names are included.

Marriage Records

A few congregations maintain marriage records like those shown in Figure 21-5 from the records of the Congregation of B'nai Jeshurun

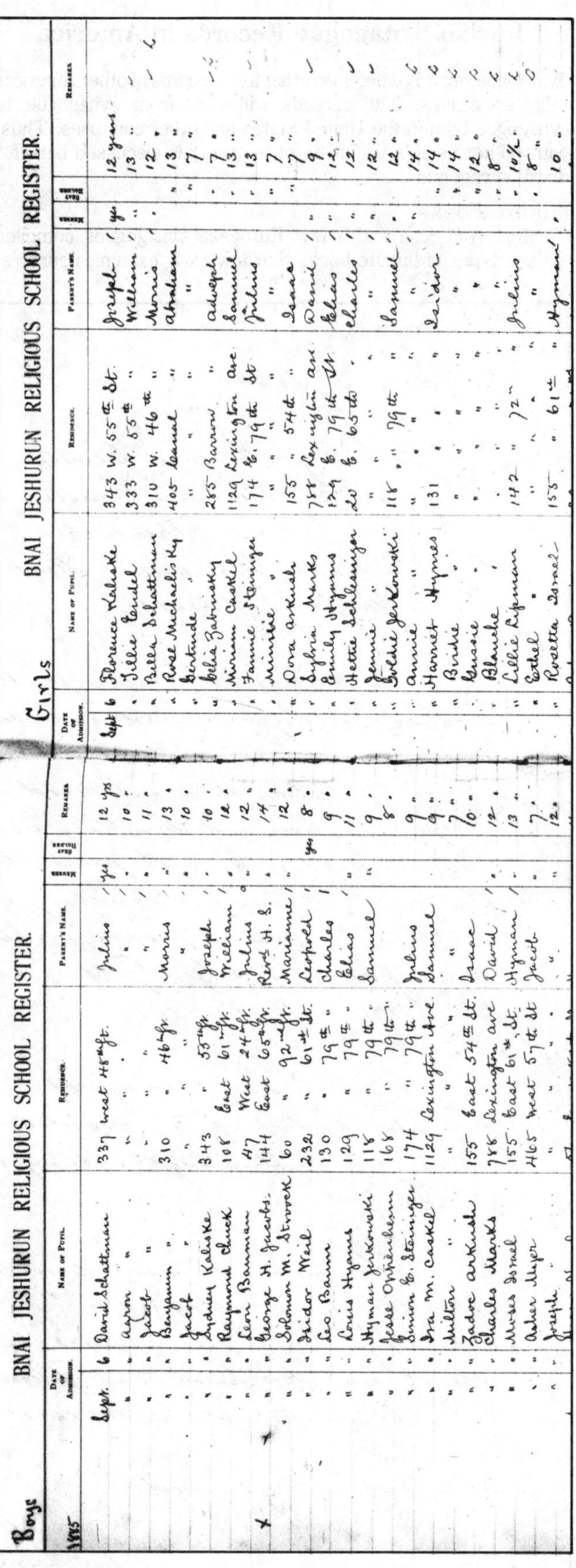

Boys 1885 — BNAI JESHURUN RELIGIOUS SCHOOL REGISTER.

Date of Admission	Name of Pupil	Residence	Parent's Name	Member	Seat Holder	Remarks
Sept. 6	David Schattman	337 West 48th St.	Julius	yes		12 yrs
" "	Aaron "	" " "	"			10 "
" "	Jacob "	" " "	"			11 "
" "	Benjamin "	310 " 46th St.	Morris			13 "
" "	Jacob "	" " "	"			10 "
" "	Sydney Kaliske	343 " 55th St.	Joseph			10 "
" "	Raymond Chuck	108 East 61st St.	William			12 "
" "	Leon Bauman	47 West 24th St.	Julius			12 "
" "	George H. Jacobs	144 East 65th St.	Revd. H. S.			14 "
" "	Solomon M. Strook	60 " 92nd St.	Marianne			12 "
" "	Isidor Weil	232 " 61st St.	Leopold		yes	8 "
" "	Leo Baum	130 " 79th "	Charles			9 "
" "	Louis Hyams	129 " 79th "	Elias			11 "
" "	Hyman Jerkowski	118 " 79th "	Samuel			9 "
" "	Jesse Oppenheim	168 " 79th "				8 "
" "	Simon E. Steiniger	174 " 79th "	Julius			9 "
" "	Ira M. Caskel	1129 Lexington Ave.	Samuel			9 "
" "	Milton "	" "	"			7 "
" "	Zadoc Arkush	155 East 54th St.	Isaac			10 "
" "	Charles Marks	788 Lexington ave	David			12 "
" "	Moses Israel	155 East 61st St.	Hyman			13 "
" "	Asher Myer	465 West 57th St	Jacob			7 "
" "	Joseph "	" " "	"			12 "

Girls — BNAI JESHURUN RELIGIOUS SCHOOL REGISTER.

Date of Admission	Name of Pupil	Residence	Parent's Name	Member	Seat Holder	Remarks
Sept 6	Florence Kaliske	343 W. 55th St.	Joseph	yes		12 years
"	Tillie Eudel	333 W. 55th "	William	"		13 "
"	Bella Schattman	310 W. 46th "	Morris			12 "
"	Rose Michaelisky	405 Canal "	Abraham			13 "
"	Gertrude "	" "	"			7 "
"	Celia Zabinsky	285 Barrow "	Adolph			7 "
"	Miriam Caskel	1129 Lexington ave	Samuel			13 "
"	Fannie Steiniger	174 E. 79th St	Julius			13 "
"	Minnie "	" " "	"			7 "
"	Dora Arkush	155 " 54th "	Isaac			7 "
"	Sylvia Marks	788 Lexington ave	David			9 "
"	Emily Hyams	129 E. 79th St	Elias			12 "
"	Hettie Schlesinger	20 E. 65th "	Charles			12 "
"	Jennie "		"			12 "
"	Goldie Jerkowski	118 " 79th "	Samuel			12 "
"	Annie "	" " "	"			14 "
"	Harriet Hymes	131 " " "	Isidor			14 "
"	Birdie "	" " "	"			14 "
"	Gussie "	" " "	"			12 "
"	Blanche "	" " "	"			8 "
"	Lillie Lipman	142 " 72nd "	Julius			10½ "
"	Ethel "	" " "	"			8 "
"	Rosetta Israel	155 " 61st "	Hyman			10 "

Figure 21-3. Congregation B'nai Jeshurun, New York City, 6 Sept. 1885, Religious School Register, 1885-1919, pp. 1-2; GS 978,422.

Figure 21-4. Temple Rodelph Shalom, Philadelphia, Circumcision Record, 1845-64, p. 12; GS 1,013,426, item 1.

1848 Born	שנת תר"ט מלתי ביום	שם אביו ואמו	שם הילד	No.
10th December Philada	מקץ	יונה	ברוך	ז 7
		Silvester		
16th December Philad.	שבת חנוכה מקץ	יוסף צבי הכהן Cohn	משה	ח 8
5th November	ויגש	מנחם Emanuel Strauss	יוסף	ט 9
1849 5th Januar Philada	שמות	שמואל הלוי Sturm	יהודה Löb	י 10
9th Januar Philada	וארא	ישי Isaac Löffel	בנימין Wolf	יא 11
11th Januar Philada	וארא	משה Rosenthal	אליהו	יב 12

in New York City. These are older marriage records, dated 1833. The certificate of marriage includes the names of the bride, the groom, and the bride's father, the place of the marriage, and the date of the marriage. These records are written in Hebrew and English but may also be in German, Hebrew, Yiddish, or one of several eastern European languages, depending on the congregation. More recent records may not include the name of the bride's father.

Death, Burial, Cemetery, and Mortuary Records

Jewish law concerning death, burial, and cemetery maintenance is voluminous. The interpretation and implementation of the law differ, depending upon whether the congregation is Orthodox, Conservative, or Reform. One universal law is that the body must be buried on the day of death whenever possible. Also, Jews must be buried in a consecrated cemetery. Law dictates that the *matseva*, or gravestone, not be placed on the grave until the first anniversary of the death, although Sephardic Jews place the gravestone on the burial plot after thirty days.

Some congregations maintain death records, such as the 1853-1928 death register of Congregation B'nai Jeshurun. (See Figure 21-6).

Most synagogue death records will list the name of the deceased, his/her Hebrew name, age, birthplace, parents' names, Jewish death date, date of interment, where interred, and miscellaneous remarks.

Figure 21-6. Congregation B'nai Jeshurun, New York City, 1853-1928, unpaginated; GS 978,420.

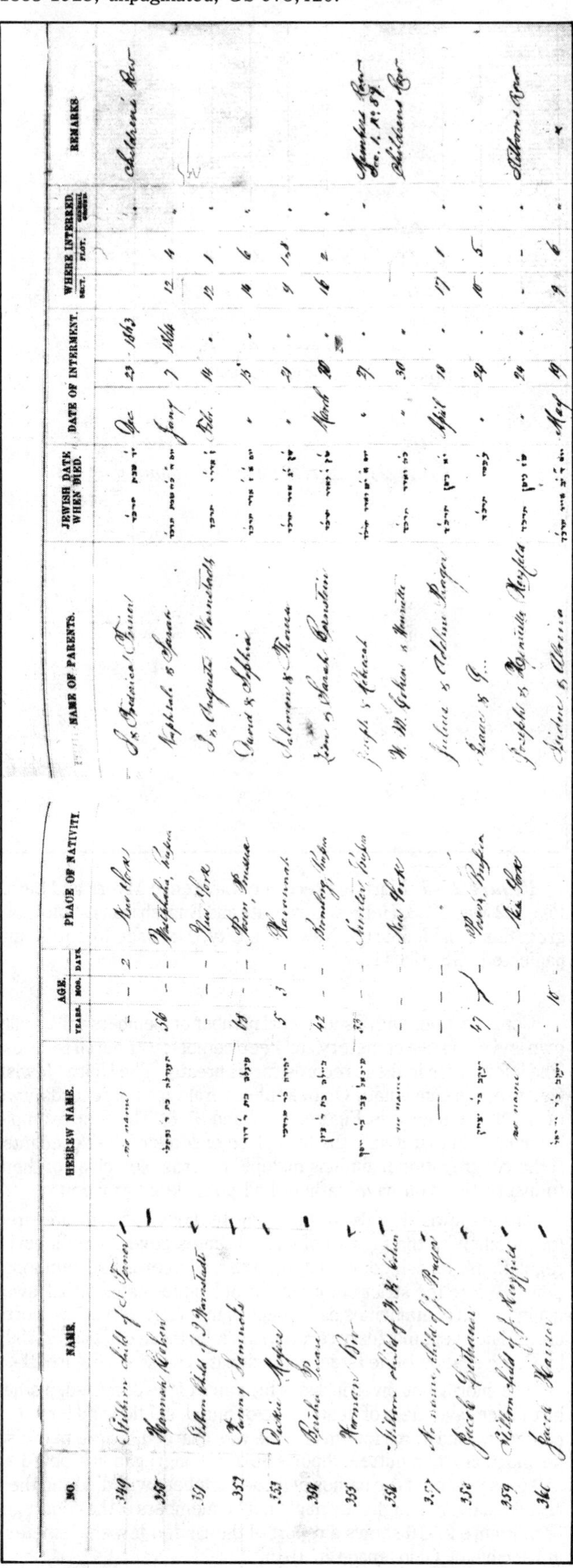

No.	Name	Hebrew Name	Age Years	Age Mos.	Age Days	Place of Nativity	Name of Parents	Jewish Date When Died	Date of Interment	Where Interred Sect.	Where Interred Plot	Where Interred General Ground	Remarks
349													
350													
351													
352													
353													
354													
355													
356													
357													
358													
359													
360													

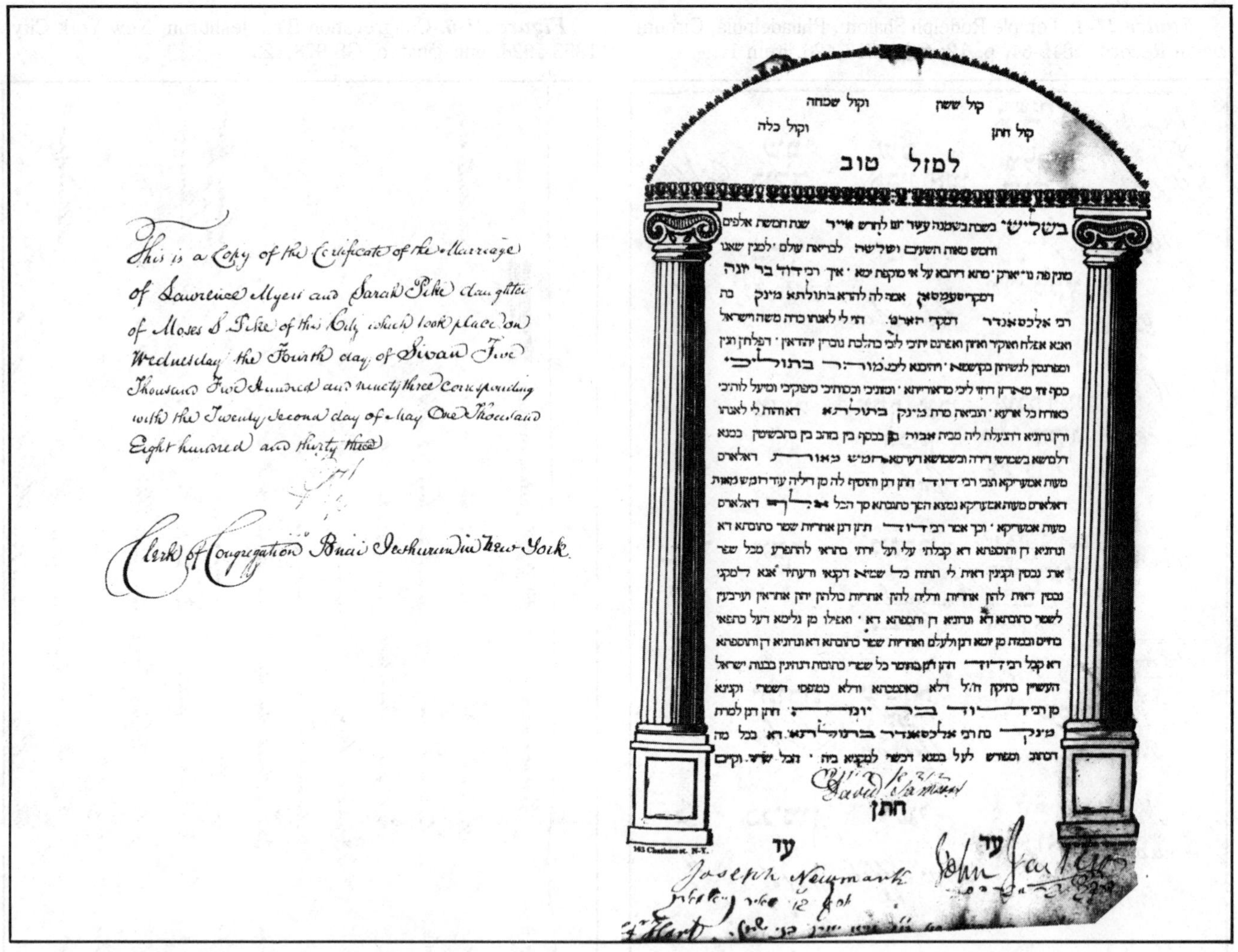

This is a Copy of the Certificate of the Marriage of Lawrence Myers and Sarah Pike daughter of Moses S. Pike of this City which took place on Wednesday the Fourth day of Sivan Five Thousand Five hundred and ninety three corresponding with the Twenty second day of May One Thousand Eight hundred and thirty three

Clerk of Congregation Bnai Jeshurun in New York.

קול ששון וקול שמחה
קול חתן וקול כלה
למזל טוב

חתן

עד
עד

Joseph Newmark

Figure 21-5. Marriage record of Lawrence Myers and Sarah Pike, 22 May 1833, Hebrew certificate and English translation, Congregation B'nai Jeshurun, New York City, Marriage Records, unpaginated; GS 978,412.

Congregations with a substantial number of members will usually own and operate a cemetery and keep cemetery or burial records. The information in these records varies greatly. The United Jewish Cemetery in Cincinnati, Ohio, kept several types of records, two of which are shown in Figures 21-7 and 21-8. The first example is valuable in that it lists the birthplace of some of the decedants. If the congregation maintains multiple records, search all of them to insure that you have gathered all possible information.

Ancient Jewish law also dictated how the body was to be prepared for burial. With the growth of United States governmental burial regulations, Jewish communities have made certain accommodations. Before the strict enforcement of United States burial laws, many Jewish communities had groups of members serving as morticians. They kept mortuary records similar to those compiled in 1895 by Congregation Bene Israel in Cincinnati, Ohio. See Figure 21-9.

The information given includes the name of the deceased, his/her birthplace, age, date of death, date of burial, section and lot in the cemetery, and items for which a fee was charged. There may also be mortuary committee reports to the congregation's board of trustees which list the names of those members who died and their relatives, even though they might not be members of the congregation. Figure 21-10 shows a report of the United Jewish Cemetery in Cincinnati, Ohio, made in 1915.

It is also customary for those who so desire to place memorial tablets or plaques on the walls of the synagogue upon which the deceased relative's name and death date is inscribed.

Congregations with smaller memberships rarely own their own cemeteries. They may operate a cemetery jointly with other congregations or they may purchase an area within a city or public cemetery for their members' exclusive use. This portion of the public cemetery is consecrated according to Jewish law.

With few exceptions, all practicing Jews are buried in Jewish cemeteries. Those exceptions are suicides or apostates. Establishing suicide is subject to rigorous proof, almost depending upon an eyewitness to the death. Apostates are those who are known to have ritually become members of another faith, such as by Christian baptism.

Jewish tombstones provide much more genealogical and biographical information than those of other religious groups. See the section on tombstones in Kurzweil's *From Generation to Generation* for detailed instructions on how to read a Jewish tombstone.

Congregational and Jewish Community Histories

The practice of publishing congregational or community histories to commemorate an anniversary or special event developed and increased during the twentieth century. Some of these publications are excellent sources of information about the lives of one's ancestors in their religious and community settings.

Locating records maintained by Jewish synagogues and congregations in the United States can be challenging. Many synagogues

22

Location	Name =1866=	age	Death	Burial
O. G.	Mrs Guiterman	✓	Sept 2	
"	Max Meyer	✓	" 12	
"	Henry Oppenheimer	✓	" 16	
"	Mr. Cohn	✓	" 18	
"	Mrs. Jacob Oppenheimer	✓	" 28	
6-2	Yette Cohen	✓ 75	Oct 10	Oct 12
23-2	Jacob Childs	✓ 53	" 13	" 14
O. G.	Daughter of Sam Weiler	✓	" 15	
"	Mrs. Friedman	✓	" 17	
"	Francis Simmons	✓	" 18	
"	Emile Berg	✓	" 18	
76-2	Helen Bohm	9 Mo	" 18	Oct 19
137-2	Tillie Stadler	✓ 35	" 18	" 20
73-2	Rosette Lowenthal	✓ 1	" 19	" 21
O. G.	Child of Levi	✓	" 20	
"	Francis Meyer	✓	" 24	
"	Jacob Reitler	✓	" 19	
52-2	Eliza Davis	✓	" 25	Oct 27
20-2	Carrie May	✓ 6	Nov 1	Nov 3
O. G.	Mrs. Baum	✓	" 2	
"	Child of David Bing	✓	" 3	

Figure 21-7. United Jewish Cemetery Association, Cincinnati, Ohio, Record Book, 1850-1951, p. 22; GS 899,904.

No 78 — A premature birth of Herz Mayerfelt on Friday 31 May 1850

N 91 — A premature birth of Isaac & Elizabeth Hyams on Monday 3d June 1850

Row 9 GR-13 Tomb — Jacob Wertheimer a native of Bavaria who died on Tuesday June ... aged 70 years

N 103 — (Columbus) Infant Son of Joseph Alexander who died June 2d 1850 age 2 years

Row 9 GR. 10 Tomb — Hartwick Berlinsky Mann a native of Posen who died Thursday 11 April 1850 aged 21 years

Figure 21-8. Burial Records of the United Jewish Cemetery, 1850-1930, Cincinnati, Ohio, p.5; GS 899,905.

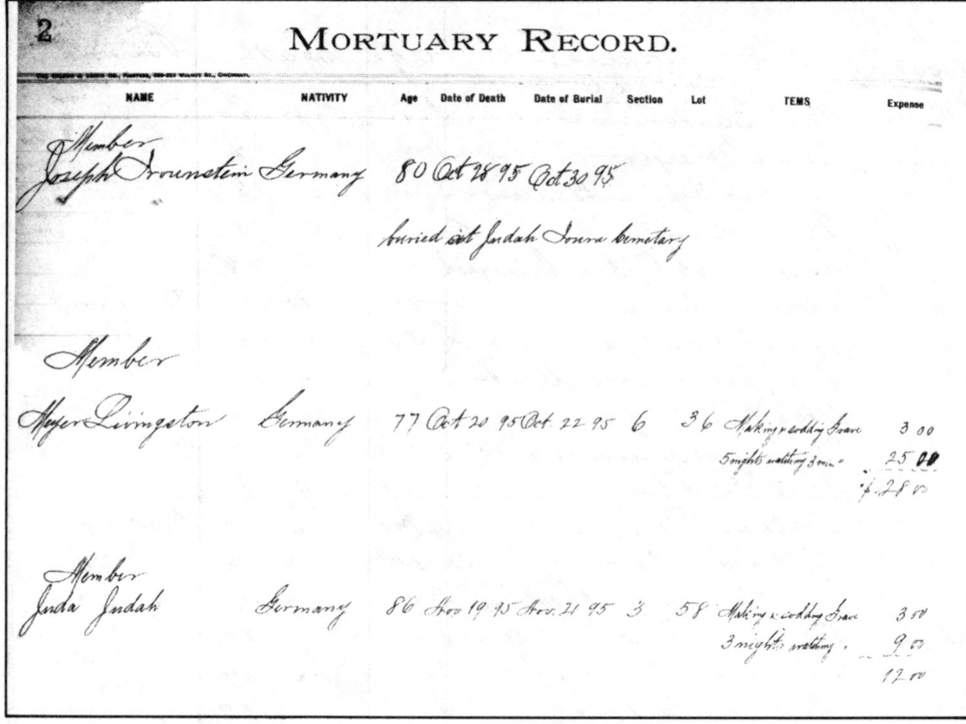

2

MORTUARY RECORD.

NAME	NATIVITY	Age	Date of Death	Date of Burial	Section	Lot	ITEMS	Expense
Member Joseph Trounstein	Germany	80	Oct 28 95	Oct 30 95				
buried at Judah Touro Cemetery								
Member Meyer Livingston	Germany	77	Oct 20 95	Oct 22 95	6	36	Making & walling grave	3 00
							5 nights watching	25 00
								28 00
Member Juda Judah	Germany	86	Nov 19 95	Nov 21 95	3	58	Making & walling grave	3 00
							3 nights watching	9 00
								12 00

Figure 21-9. Congregation Bene Israel, Cincinnati, Ohio, Mortuary Records, 1895-1942, p. 2; GS 1,012,750, item 10.

have continued to house their old records, but the American Jewish Archives, 3101 Clifton Avenue, Cincinnati, OH 45220, has acquired many old records. Most of its collection has been microfilmed by the Genealogical Society of Utah and can be used in Salt Lake City or at one of the society's many branch libraries. The American Jewish Historical Society, 2 Thornton Road, Waltham, MA 02514, also has an excellent collection of synagogue records. See Table 21-1 for archives and holdings.

Searching records in person may be difficult. The synagogue or library may not be set up to allow research or may not have the staff to perform the searches you request. If the synagogue is close enough to your home, you may be able to search the records personally, providing the rabbi or other synagogue official will grant permission. The American Jewish Archives and the American Jewish Historical Society can provide a list of competent persons you can hire to perform the searches for you or you can hire a professional genealogist to assist with the searches. However, only a few competent professionals specialize in Jewish ancestral research. Be sure to examine his/her credentials before concluding an agreement. Few synagogues have archives, and the older records are often locked away in inaccessible areas, making it difficult for anyone to use them. It is better to ascertian whether the synagogue records in which you are interested have been microfilmed by the American Jewish Archives.

Locating the Immigrant Ancestral Home

As I mentioned earlier, most American Jews will reach their immigrant ancestors in one or two generations. Now begins one of the most difficult research processes you will face: determining the immigrant's exact European residence or birthplace. Like the United States, European countries rarely have national programs for the registration of births, marriages, and deaths. Records are almost always maintained town by town. Ordinarily, if you find the European residence or birthplace of your Jewish ancestors, you will find it in this country's records.

Begin the search for this information in family records, papers, and memorabilia in family possession or deposited in a research library or archives. You should interview older family members to determine if they remember hearing stories about the homeland, town, or village of the immigrant ancestors. If this approach fails to produce the needed information, some painstaking searches must follow.

Census Records

Most of our Jewish immigrant ancestors were already in the United States when the 1910 federal census was taken. This census enumeration and the 1900 enumeration list the year the individual arrived in the United States if he/she was foreign-born. The enumerations also state the immigrant's citizenship status. If no action had been taken to acquire American citizenship, *al* for "alien" will be entered. If the immigrant has petitioned the court for citizenship, *Pa* will be entered. *Na* indicates that the immigrant is a naturalized citizen. These enumerations will also list the immigrant's birthplace. The 1910 census will also specify the native language spoken by the immigrant. (See Chapter 4, "Census Records.")

Naturalization Records

Citizenship was not required in the United States, but most immigrants eventually applied for it. Naturalization records consist of declarations of intent, petitions to become a citizen, and naturalization records. Not all naturalization records contain the same information, and sometimes the information is too general to help identify the immigrant's residence or birthplace. However, if you're fortunate, the record can include the place and date of birth, emigration date, port of entry, arrival date, and place of origin. These records were maintained by the United States county or district court where your ancestor resided if the naturalization action took place before September 1906. After that date, naturalization records were compiled and maintained by the Bureau of Immigration and Naturalization and are available from the Office of Immigration and Naturalization, 425 I Street, N.W., Washington, DC 20530.

You can obtain a request form there or at the nearest United States Federal Building. The Genealogical Society of Utah has microfilmed some early naturalization records, including those for metropolitan Chicago and Cook County, Illinois. For more information on naturalization records, see Chapter 15, "Tracking Immigrant Origins."

Cincinnati, Ohio, October 28th, 1915.

To the Officers & Members of the

K. K. BENE ISRAEL:

I respectfully submit the following report for the year 1915:

We have lost by death the following sixteen members:

Ferdinand Jacobs	Judah H. Hart
Joseph Freiberg	Lewis Seasongood
Max Schottenfels	Harry M. Selig
Henry W. Mack	Benjamin L. Bing
Carl S. Weihl	Sallie Mihalovitch
Wallace Holzman	Adeline Liebenstein
Seymour Samuels	Louis F. Bowman
Louis Loeb	Sol. Fox

In addition to the above, there have been seven deaths in the families of members.

Miriam Holzman	Hannah Levy
Bella Bowman Gottlieb	Carrie Hess Powers
Fannie S. Johnson	Johanna Kronacher

Tillie Mayer

There have been /√ of non-members of the Congregation.

Emma Bloom Kramer	Chas. Schiff
Amelia Patlis	David Cahn
Samuel Hollander	Jacob Pulasky
Solomon Levy	Sade R. Miller
Edgar J. Bernheim	Gus. Frank
Walter E. Bernheim	Henrietta Traub
Samuel B. Marks	Gertrude Newman

Bella Berman

The United Jewish Cemetery, as well as the old cemetery at Chestnut and Central Avenue, are in good condition.

Respectfully submitted,

Warden.

Figure 21-10. Warden's Report of Deaths, 1915, with Mortuary Records, 1895-1942, Congregation Bene Israel.

Table 21-1

Jewish Archives and Their Holdings

Archives	Holdings	Guides and Comments
1. American Jewish Archives 3101 Clifton Avenue Cincinnati, OH 45220	Rich collection of genealogies vital and church records, newspaper indexes, family and personal papers. Large collection of Jewish periodicals and newspapers on microfilm.	*Manuscripts Catalog of the American Jewish Archives*. 4 vols. Boston: G. K. Hall, 1971. Many available on microfilm at the Genealogical Society of Utah.
2. American Jewish Historical Society 2 Thornton Road Waltham, MA 02154	Synagogue and educational records, personal and family papers.	See NUCMC for detailed descriptions.
3. Jewish Theological Seminary Library 3080 Broadway New York, NY 10027	*Pinkasim* (record books) of European Jewish communities, including tax lists, local community meetings; Hebrew subscription lists for 8,767 communities in Europe and North Africa with more than 350,000 names of Jews who paid toward the publication of Hebrew books.	
4. Leo Baeck Institute 129 East 73rd Street New York, NY 10021	One of the most important repositories for records of German-speaking Jews, includes congregational histories, vital records, family papers. Hundreds of genealogies and family histories reaching into the seventeenth century are on file there. Its Rudolf Simonis Collection includes the genealogies, correspondence, and histories of hundreds of Jewish families in Berlin, northern Germany, and Sweden. The institute also includes the collection of Berthold Rosenthal which specializes in the Jews of Baden and the Palatinate.	Close relationship with agencies in London and Jerusalem. *Bibliothek und Archiv, Katalog*. Band 1: Register s.v. *Genealogie* (New York: Leo Baeck Institute, 1970). In German.
5. Philadelphia Jewish Archives Center 625 Walnut Street Philadelphia, PA 19106	Hebrew Immigrant Aid Society records for Jews arriving in Philadelphia, neighborhood center day nursery records, orphans' records, records of local synagogues.	Free newsletter describes holdings, programs, accessions.
6. Western Jewish History Center Judah L. Magres Memorial Museum 2911 Russell Street Berkeley, CA 94705	Family histories and memoirs of Western families	Moses Rischin, *Family History Guide* (Berkeley Calif: For the center, n.d.)
7. Yivo Institute for Jewish Research 1048 Fifth Avenue New York, NY 10028	Depository for East-European Jewry including congregational histories and records. Majority in Yiddish. Hebrew Immigrant Aid Society files for immigrants assisted from 1920 on, autobiographies of East European immigrants 1882-1955, testimonies of Holocaust survivors Yizkor books (Holocaust survivors) for many towns of East Europe.	See Library of Congress, *National Union Catalog of Manuscript Collections* (NUCMC) for descriptions. Institute maintains a card catalog listing *Landmannschaften* (immigrant societies with current names and addresses of officers.

Ship's Passenger Lists

United States ships' passenger lists may provide the name of the town in which your immigrant ancestor lived. These records generally list the passenger's name, age, and country of origin. Only occasionally will the exact place of residence or birth be listed if the immigrant arrived before 1890. Lists compiled after that date will more likely give you the information you need. The National Archives in Washington, D.C., has the most complete set of passenger lists and indexes to those lists and will provide a copy of the passenger list entry if you can tell them the date of arrival and port of entry. You must obtain Form GSA 7111 from Passenger Lists (NNCC), National Archives (GSA), Washington, DC 20408, before requesting the information. The Genealogical Society of Utah has microfilmed copies of United States ships' passenger lists before 1900. Unfortunately, there are few indexes for those years of heaviest immigration. (See Chapter 15 for more information.)

Hamburg Passenger Lists

A large number of central and eastern European Jews embarked from Hamburg, Germany, en route to the United States. The passenger lists of ships leaving Hamburg between 1850 and 1934 have been indexed and are on microfilm at the Genealogical Society of Utah. (See Figure 21-11.) One index lists the ships sailing directly to the United States, while a second indexes ships that

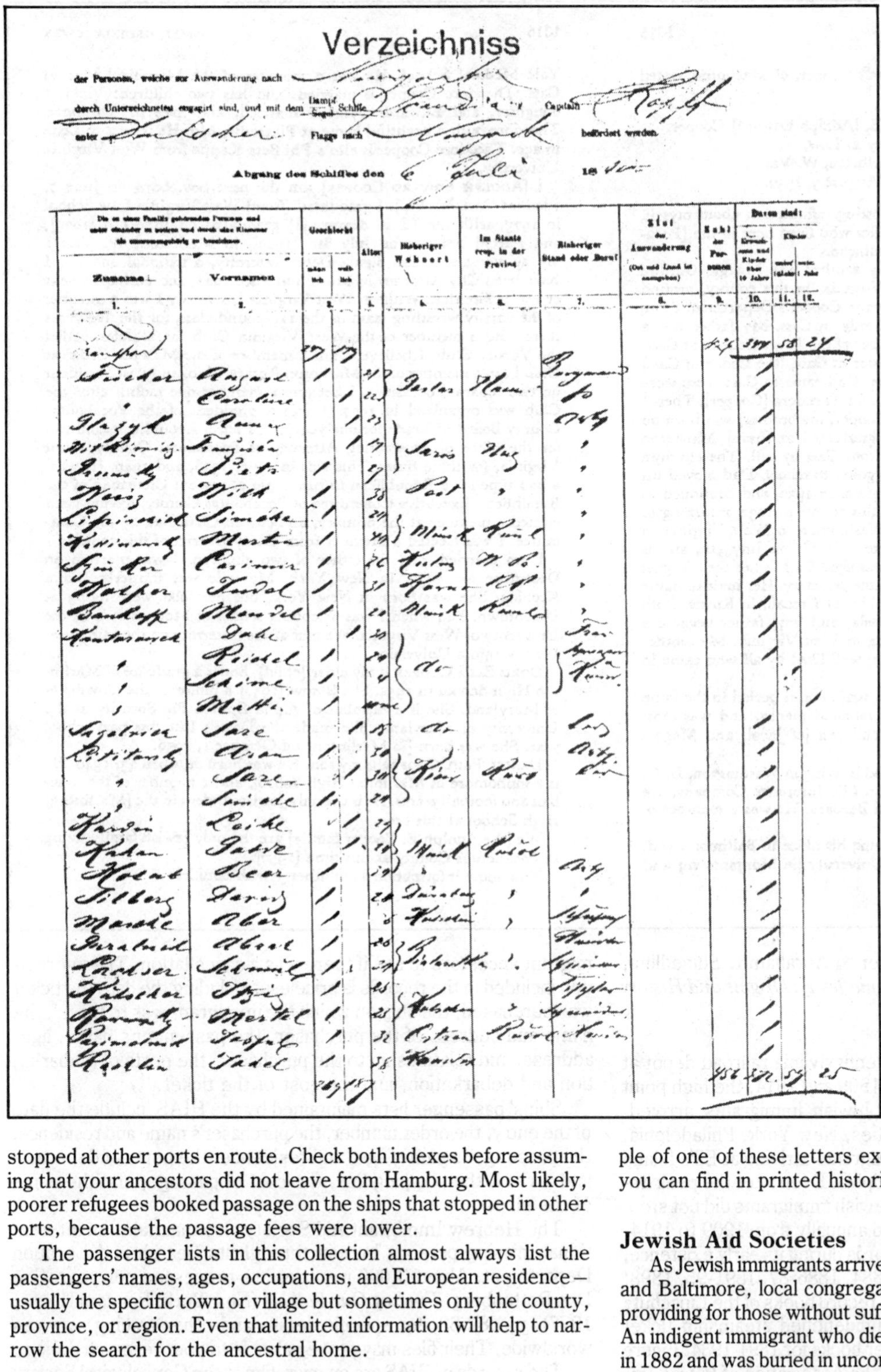

Figure 21-11. Hamburg Passenger Lists.

stopped at other ports en route. Check both indexes before assuming that your ancestors did not leave from Hamburg. Most likely, poorer refugees booked passage on the ships that stopped in other ports, because the passage fees were lower.

The passenger lists in this collection almost always list the passengers' names, ages, occupations, and European residence – usually the specific town or village but sometimes only the county, province, or region. Even that limited information will help to narrow the search for the ancestral home.

Printed Histories

If your immigrant ancestor arrived before 1880 and settled in a rural area, the family, including its place of origin, may be mentioned in the biographical section of a local or county history. Some states and large cities also have volumes chronicling the history of Jews in their area. One of the finest publications of this type is Abraham I. Shinedling, *West Virginia Jewry: Origins and History 1850-1958*, 3 vols. (Philadelphia: Maurice Jacobs, Inc., 1963). The biographical material included in this publication was obtained in writing from living family members. See Figure 21-12 for an example of one of these letters exemplifying the valuable information you can find in printed histories.

Jewish Aid Societies

As Jewish immigrants arrived in New York, Philadelphia, Boston, and Baltimore, local congregations assumed the responsibility of providing for those without sufficient funds to establish themselves. An indigent immigrant who died shortly after arriving in New York in 1882 and was buried in unconsecrated ground inspired the founding of the Hebrew Sheltering Society. A Philadelphia branch followed in 1883. The society met new immigrants on the city's docks and provided them with shelter, settled them in new jobs all over the country, and assisted them in their adjustment to a new culture and environment. The Hebrew Immigrant Aid Society (HIAS) groups in New York and Philadelphia were the most aggressive in organizing immigrant aid during the 1880s.

The Association for the Protection of Jewish Immigrants (APJI) was founded in 1884, and, with HIAS, took care of 1,076 immigrants that same year. A total of 2,310 were aided in 1885, and the number continued to increase into the 1890s. The APJI's reception station

MARLINTON 1015

[Letter from A. E. (Adolph Edward) Cooper, of Marlinton, dated August 3, 1956]

"A. E. [Adolph Edward] Cooper,
"Attorney at Law,
"Marlinton, W. Va.
"August 3, 1956.

This is in reply to your letter requesting information about myself, family, and other former Jewish families who lived here in the [Pocahontas] county, and especially at Marlinton.

My father was Jacob Cooper. My mother was Maggie Gordon Cooper. They came to Cass, West Virginia, in this county, around 1905. Dad was a merchant, operating the Cooper's Department Store at Cass. We were the only Jewish family in Cass. My father was a most respected citizen. He was a member of the Town Council at Cass. He was a member of the Masonic Order at Cass, [the Lodge in Cass] being Riverside Lodge No. 124. When Dad came to Cass there were three children, namely, Veeda, Leon, and Theodore [Cooper]. Then I was born on June 7th, 1906. Lewis [Cooper, my brother] was born on July 20th, 1907. All [the] children graduated at [from] Marlinton High School. Marlinton is 25 miles from Cass by rail. The children had to board away from home while going to school. Dad moved his store from Cass to Durbin, West Virginia, in 1930, and continued in business for a couple of years and left this county in 1932, returning to Washington, D. C. He came from Washington to West Virginia in 1905. Dad died in 1943 in Washington, D. C., on July 4th, and is buried in Adas Israel Cemetery. He was aged 69. Mother died August 25th, 1947, and is also buried in the same cemetery. Her maiden name was Gordon, and her father was a rabbi, as I recall, in Russia. Both my parents originally came from Russia, and [my] father became a naturalized citizen prior to his coming to West Virginia. My mother was a very well-read person, and [was] well liked by all who came in contact with her.

My sister, Veeda [Cooper], died in 1928, and is buried in the same cemetery in Washington. She was a talented pianist, and was most popular. She was the oldest of the children [of Jacob and Maggie Gordon Cooper].

Leon [Cooper] is the oldest boy, and is living in Washington, D. C. He is connected with the Metropolitan Life Insurance Company, He is married, and has one child, named Barbara. He was a member of the Masonic Lodge at Cass.

Theodore Cooper is a doctor, having his office in Baltimore, Md. He graduated [from] West Virginia University [in Morgantown] and

1016 WEST VIRGINIA JEWRY

Yale Medical School. He was a member of the Masonic Lodge at Cass. Theodore Cooper is married, and has two children: Vicki, a daughter, and Edward. Vicki is married, and lives in Baltimore. Theodore built a beautiful home at Pikesville, Md. He is next to Leon in age. Theodore Cooper is also a Phi Beta Kappa from West Virginia University.

I [Adolph Edward Cooper] am the next boy, born on June 7, 1906 [at Cass, W. Va.]. I graduated [from] West Virginia Law School in 1929, with the LL.B. degree. [I] graduated on June 8th [1929], and started practice on July 8th [1929], in Marlinton, W. Va. [I am a] member of Phi Sigma Delta fraternity, a national one. . . . I have been City Attorney in Marlinton since 1941, and perhaps a year or two before that. While at West Virginia University I was a member of the varsity wrestling team in the 118-pound class, for the five years there, and a member of the West Virginia Club for athletes, called the Varsity Club, I believe. I am a member of the Masonic Order at Cass. I am a member of the Marlinton Rotary Club, and Past President on two separate occasions. I became a member one month after the Club was organized in 1937. I was a president of the Pocahontas County Board of Trade for one year. . . . I am a Republican, and ran for the office of Prosecuting Attorney of Pocahontas County, West Virginia, for three times. This was in 1932, 1936, and 1940. [It was] a bad time for a Republican to run. I am at present Chairman of the Republican Executive Committee of Pocahontas County, having been elected a member at the primary, and chosen Chairman by the Committee. I was elected a Member from Edray District of this county.

I am married, and the father of two children. I was married on December 24, 1933, in New York. My wife was formerly Diana Kronick. She was born in New York, but her folks were living at Uniontown, Pa., when I was attending school at Morgantown at the University of West Virginia. We met at the fraternity on the campus at West Virginia University.

Doris Ella Cooper is my elder [child]. She is a graduate of Marlinton High School in 1954. She is now [1956] a junior at the University of Maryland. She is a member of Alpha Epsilon Phi Sorority at the University of Maryland. She made the Dean's List this past school year. She was born [in Marlinton] on October 1, 1936.

Daniel Paul Cooper is my son. He was born on April 23, 1940. He is a sophomore in Marlinton High School, and a member of the baseball and football teams. He is the only Jewish student in the [Marlinton] High School at this time.

We [the Adolph E. Cooper family] are the only Jewish family living in Pocahontas County at this time [1956].

Now some information as to other Jewish families:

Figure 21-12. Adolph E. Cooper to Abraham I. Shinedling, 3 Aug. 1856, in Shinedling, *West Virginia Jewry: Origins and History 1850-1958*, vol. 3, p. 1015.

was established in 1886 at the old Pennsylvania railroad depot at 32nd and Market streets. Between 1909 and 1914, the high point of unlimited immigration, 138,051 Jewish immigrants arrived. Representatives from four major cities, New York, Philadelphia, Baltimore, and Boston, met the immigrants arriving at Ellis Island and brought many of them to Philadelphia. Even after the peak immigration period ended, the flow of Jewish immigrants did not stop. Approximately 100,000 Jews arrived annually from 1909 to 1914. HIAS maintained some excellent records during its early existence, including ships' passenger lists for 1884, 1886-87, 1891-95, 1898, 1901, 1903, 1905, 1909, 1912, 1913; record books of the Lipschutz Steamship Company for 1923-48; unidentified steamship ticket records for 1907-10; and passage order books for 1894-1934. Figure 21-13 is a page from the Register of the Association of Jewish Immigrants, providing the date, name of immigrant, his/her age, marital status, place emigrated from, number of nights' lodging provided, number of meals provided, whether paid for or free, departure date, and remarks (usually where the individual went to work or to live).

The Lipshutz Steamship Company record books (Figure 21-14) are interesting and valuable. They include ticket requests made by persons in this country for the passage of relatives and friends in Europe. Some of the entries are marked "cancelled," indicating that the individual either arranged other transportation or did not emigrate. Thus, it may be worthwhile to search here for your immigrant ancestors to see if there was a cancellation. The information included in the records is priceless, including the date the ticket was purchased, the ship on which the immigrant was to travel, the name and address of the purchaser, the passenger's name, age, address, and relationship to the purchaser, the ports of embarkation and debarkation, and the cost of the ticket.

Ships' passenger lists maintained by the HIAS include the date of the entry, the order number, the purchaser's name and residence, the passenger's name, age, and residence, the ports of departure and arrival, the shipping line, the cost of passage, and the name of the ship.

The Hebrew Immigrant Aid Society also maintains an international missing persons bureau through its Search and Location Department. About 3,000 inquiries are processed per year. See Dan Rottenberg, *Finding Our Fathers* (New York: Random House, 1977), pp. 82-83, for specific details and other tracing services worldwide. Their files may prove valuable to your research project.

The records of HIAS are on microfilm at the Genealogical Society of Utah and available through its branch libraries. The originals are at the Yivo Institute (see Archive Table 21-1) and other repositories.

Jewish Ancestral Research Outside the United States

Once you know the immigrant ancestor's residence or birthplace, there are more challenges ahead. You must turn to European records for most Jewish-American families. Since the scope of this volume does not permit me to examine the record sources of all

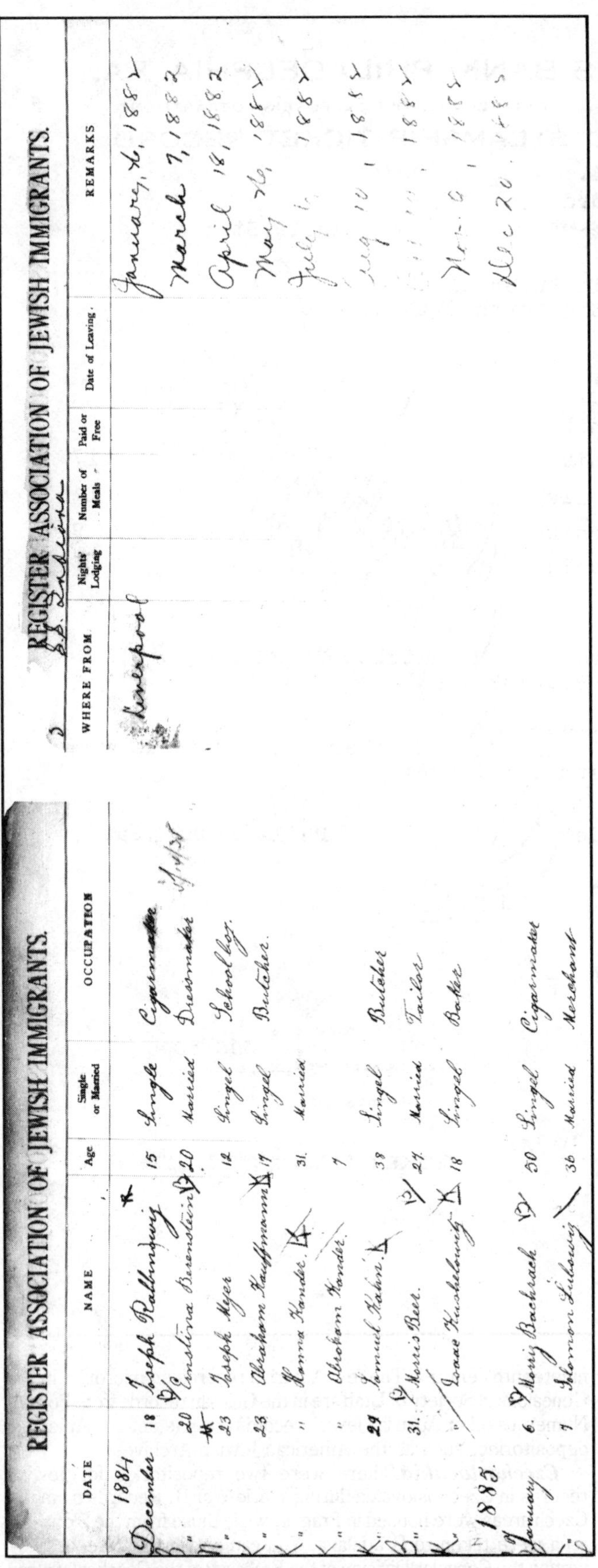

REGISTER ASSOCIATION OF JEWISH IMMIGRANTS.

S.S. Indiana

DATE	NAME	Age	Single or Married	OCCUPATION	WHERE FROM	Nights' Lodging	Number of Meals	Paid or Free	Date of Leaving	REMARKS
1884 December 18	Joseph Rabinowitz	15	Single	Cigarmaker	Liverpool					January 6, 1885
20	Ernestina Berenstein	20	Married	Dressmaker						March 7, 1885
23	Joseph Myer	12	Singel	Schoolboy						April 18, 1885
23	Abraham Kauffmann	17	Singel	Butcher						May 26, 1885
"	Hanna Kander	31	Married							July 6, 1885
"	Abraham Kander	1								Aug 10, 1885
29	Samuel Kahn	38	Singel	Butcher						[illegible] 1885
31	Morris Beer	27	Married	Tailor						Nov 6, 1885
"	Isaac Kushelowitz	18	Singel	Baker						Dec 20, 1885
1885 January 6	Morris Bachrach	50	Singel	Cigarmaker						
7	Solomon Lubowitz	36	Married	Merchant						

Figure 21-13. Register of the Association of Jewish Immigrants 1884-1921, Hebrew Immigrant Aid Society, 1885, among pp. 5-8, Philadelphia Jewish Archives; GS 1,026,150.

the nations in which Jews have lived or currently live, I will emphasize German and East European records, the homeland of a majority of the Jews who immigrated from the 1850s on.

It is not uncommon to hear discouraged researchers claim that it is impossible to trace Jewish roots into Germany, Poland, or other East European countries. It is true that pogroms and Nazi persecution made a determined effort to destroy all Jewish life, communities, and Jewish records—to wipe out all signs of Jewish existence in Europe. Despite their determination, however, records still survived.

The Genealogical Society of Utah successfully negotiated the microfilming of records in Germany, Poland, Hungary, Lithuania, and France in the late 1960s. These records are primarily civil and church records which chronicle births, marriages, and deaths; but other types of records exist and are obtainable with some effort.

Toledot: The Journal of Jewish Genealogy published a partial list of the Genealogical Society's holdings for Germany, Poland, and Hungary in its 1977-78 issues. Since then, many additional records have been added to the society's collection. (See the bibliography of German, Hungarian, Polish, Lithuanian, and French Jewish records available at the time of this printing at the end of this chapter.) The microfilms are available at the Genealogical Society of Utah library in Salt Lake City and in its branch libraries across the nation.

Germany

The records microfilmed by the Genealogical Society are those of West German towns and villages. East Germany has not permitted microfilming. Germany did not uniformly implement civil registration of Jewish births, marriages, and deaths until 1875 although some locations maintained civil registrations earlier. The records of some eastern German towns and provinces, then part of the territory now claimed by East Germany, can be found in Polish records, due to boundary changes after World War II.

Some agencies in Israel and the United States have gathered the Jewish documents and synagogue records surviving the widespread destruction of World War II. The Central Archive for the History of the Jewish People in the Sprinzak Building, Hebrew University Campus, Jerusalem, is one of the major repositories of Jewish records from Europe. Its guide to the archives in Israel is available from Box 1149, Jerusalem, Israel. The Genealogical Society of Utah is presently microfilming Jewish materials in the Central Archive at Hebrew University.

Hungary

The old kingdom of Hungary once included parts of what is now Czechoslovakia, the Soviet Union, Yugoslavia, Romania, and Austria. The Genealogical Society of Utah has filmed all of the available records pertaining to Hungarian Jews up to 1895 including the 1848 Jewish census for several Hungarian counties that are now part of the Soviet Union and Czechoslovakia.

Poland

The Polish collection of the Genealogical Society of Utah is extensive, including birth, marriage, and death records dating from 1808. You can also find some Jewish records in Catholic Church registers through 1826 when separate civil registers were established for Jews. It is important to realize that a large portion of the collection includes Jewish vital records from areas that were formerly part of Germany or the Soviet Union.

Only a few records from the Austrian area of Poland are on microfilm. There are also many unmicrofilmed Jewish records in the Polish State Archives including those dated after 1870. If the records you need are not in the Genealogical Society's collection, you can request them from Naczelna Dyrekcja, Archiwow Panstwowych, ul. Dyuga 6 s.p. 1005, 00-950-Warszawa, Poland.

France

Civil registration in France began in 1792 and included vital

Figure 21-14. Cancelled ticket purchased by Louis Sukonick, 9 Feb. 1924, among first few entries in Lipschutz Steamship Record Book, Hebrew Immigrant Aid Society, Philadelphia Jewish Archives; GS 1,026,296.

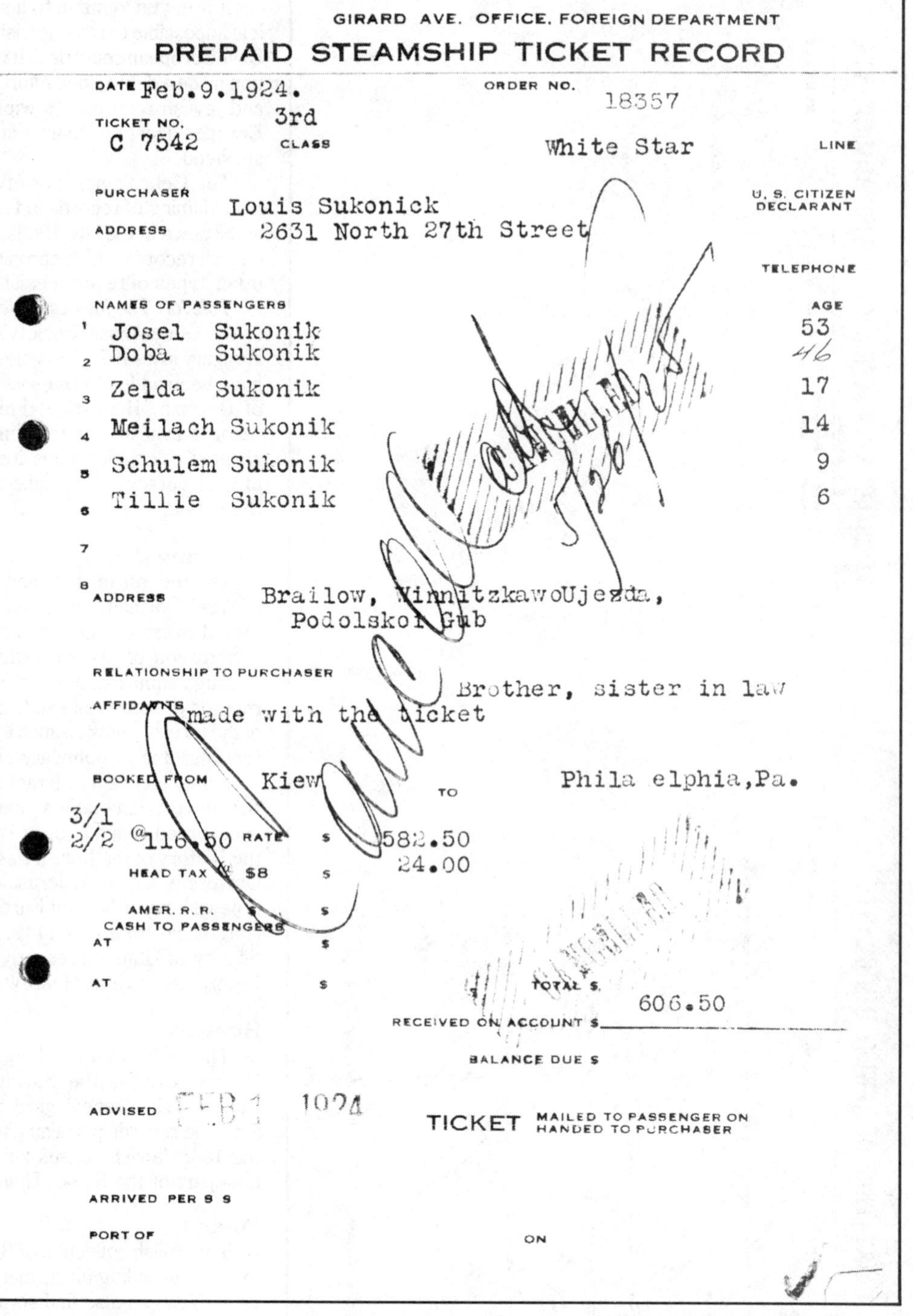
PEOPLES BANK, PHILADELPHIA, PA.
GIRARD AVE. OFFICE. FOREIGN DEPARTMENT
PREPAID STEAMSHIP TICKET RECORD

DATE Feb.9.1924. ORDER NO. 18357
TICKET NO. C 7542 3rd CLASS White Star LINE
PURCHASER Louis Sukonick U. S. CITIZEN DECLARANT
ADDRESS 2631 North 27th Street
TELEPHONE

NAMES OF PASSENGERS	AGE
1 Josel Sukonik	53
2 Doba Sukonik	46
3 Zelda Sukonik	17
4 Meilach Sukonik	14
5 Schulem Sukonik	9
6 Tillie Sukonik	6
7	
8	

ADDRESS Brailow, Winnitzkawo Ujezda, Podolskoi Gub
RELATIONSHIP TO PURCHASER Brother, sister in law
AFFIDAVITS made with the ticket
BOOKED FROM Kiew TO Phila elphia,Pa.
3/1 2/2 @116.50 RATE $ 582.50
HEAD TAX @ $8 $ 24.00
AMER. R. R. $
CASH TO PASSENGERS AT $
AT $
TOTAL $ 606.50
RECEIVED ON ACCOUNT $
BALANCE DUE $
ADVISED FEB 1 1924 TICKET MAILED TO PASSENGER ON / HANDED TO PURCHASER
ARRIVED PER S S
PORT OF ON
CANCELLED

records for the French Jews as well. The Genealogical Society of Utah has filmed records from some, but not all, departments or counties.

Other Countries

Of course Jews emigrated from other European countries and from Russia. Negotiations to microfilm these records are underway by the Genealogical Society of Utah, but there is no assurance that arrangements can be made with each country. Meanwhile, here is a status report on records from these countries:

Austria. The Austrian government required civil registration as early as 1788, but compliance was not complete until late in the nineteenth century. The few Austrian records on microfilm in the Genealogical Society of Utah are in the Galician records from Poland. Numerous other Austrian Jewish records are in Israeli and American depositories, such as the American Jewish Archives.

Czechoslovakia. There were two repositories for Jewish records in Czechoslovakia during World War II. Records from the Czech areas were housed in Prague, while those from the Slovakian area were taken to Bratislava. You can obtain these records by writing the Consular Division of the Embassy of the Czechoslovakian Socialist Republic, 3900 Linnean Avenue N.W., Washington, DC 20008.

Netherlands. Holland became the home of hundreds of Sephardic Jews whose ancestors settled in Holland in the seventeenth century both from Spain and Portugal, Germany and Poland. Many then embarked for other countries including the United States, but a substantial number remained for over four centuries, until the Nazi holocaust when they fled to America and Israel. Many genealogies have been compiled and printed for Jewish families in Holland. Netherland Joods Familienarchief, Amsteldijk 67, Amsterdam, The Netherlands, will receive inquiries about these genealogies.

The Soviet Union. Today nearly three million Jews live in the Soviet Union; only the United States and Israel have larger Jewish populations. Many of those presently living in the Soviet Union originally resided in areas politically assigned to the USSR after World War II. Little is known about the records maintained for Jews in Russia before the 1917 Revolution. Most of them had been kept by individual congregations and hence were vulnerable to destruction. When persecution began, many rabbis refused to keep records which could later be used against their congregations. A few survive in Israeli, western European, Warsaw, and United States archives. Correspondence to each archive listed at the end of this chapter may provide information about your town of interest.

Tracing Victims and Survivors of the Holocaust

Few Jewish families in Europe were unaffected by the Holocaust. The Central Tracing Bureau was established in 1943 in Frankfort-am-Main, West Germany, to help locate displaced persons and to reunite separated families. This organization is now the International Tracing Service, Arolsen D-3548, Federal Republic of West Germany. It gathered available concentration camp records and any other documents that recorded the fate of Jews who disappeared during the war. The index to their records includes 39,700,000 names. The International Tracing Service will provide the name of the camp in which an individual was confined, his/her place of birth, personal information, and the individual's fate. The organization will trace your relatives if you provide the names and other identifying information. The name alone is not sufficient. The more details you provide about an individual, the greater the prospects for success.

Another agency dedicated to the identification of victims of the Holocaust is Yad Vashem, Box 3477, Jerusalem, Israel. Unlike the International Tracing Service, Yad Vashem will not trace your relatives, but they will inform you if the individual in question has been identified in their records as deceased. They have compiled testimonies from survivors of the Holocaust which include information about those who were killed.

Memorial Books

Memorial or *yizkor* books tell the story of a European Jewish town or area. There are over 500 memorial books in print today, published by *landsmannschaften*, people who cherish the memory of their homelands. The size of the town or village is unimportant. Even the smallest village may have a memorial book. Most of the publications were compiled after the Holocaust, but many predate that time period, and all of them contain valuable information.

Most of the memorial books available are listed in David Bass, "Bibliographic List of Memorial Books Published in the Years 1943-1972," *Yad Vashem Studies on the European Jewish Catastrophe and Resistance*, vol. 10, (Jerusalem: Yad Vashem, 1973). Copies of the books are at the YIVO Institute for Jewish Research, 86th Street and 5th Avenue, New York City, NY 10028; at the New York Public Library, Jewish Division, 5th Avenue & 42nd Street, New York City, NY 10018; and at the Jewish Theological Seminary Library, 3080 Broadway, New York City, NY 10027.

Printed Genealogies and Family Histories

While there are not as many printed genealogies and family histories for Jewish ancestors as for others, the number of excellent publications increases daily. Most of the libraries and archives I have mentioned have collections of printed genealogies. Malcolm H. Stern, genealogist of the American Jewish Archives, has compiled *First American Jewish Families: 600 Genealogies, 1654-1977* (New York: KTAV Publishing House, 1978), an enlarged revision of *American of Jewish Descent: A Compendium of Genealogy* (Cincinnati: American Jewish Archives, 1960). One or both editions are available in research libraries. Figure 21-15 shows a page from the genealogy of the Etting family. Figure 21-16 is a page outlining the Levy, Baruch, and Fannie families from "Jewish Family Genealogies and Histories," a collection of materials arranged alphabetically by surname in the Hebrew Union College Collection. The material is available on microfilm at the Genealogical Society of Utah.

Research into Jewish ancestry is challenging and sometimes difficult, but interest in Jewish ancestry is only now beginning to blossom and the decades ahead promise substantial development. The recently formed Registry of Jewish Ancestry, Box 417, Salt Lake City, UT 84110, is currently accepting material to be exchanged and published to preserve the research that has been finished and will be done in the future.

Bibliography

Cooper, Wyatt. *Families: A Memoir and Celebration.* New York: Harper and Row, 1975.

Joseph, Anthony P. "On Tracing Australian Jewish Genealogy." *Genealogists' Magazine* 14 (Dec. 1964): 425.

Kranzler, David. *My Jewish Roots: A Practical Guide to Tracing Your Genealogy and Family History.* New York: Sepher-Harmon Press, 1979.

*Kurzweil, Arthur. *From Generation to Generation: How to Trace Your Jewish Genealogy and Personal History.* New York: Schocken Books, 1981. Paperback edition of the best how-to-book. Emphasizes East European Jewish genealogy.

Munitz, Benzion. "Identifying Jewish Names in Russia." *Soviet Jewish Affairs* 3 (May 1972): 66-76.

*Rottenberg, Dan. *Finding Our Fathers: A Guide to Jewish Genealogy.* New York: Random House, 1977. Includes a 234-page "Guide to Jewish Family Genealogies," and a country-by-country description of archives and finding aids.

Samuel, Wilfred. "Sources of Anglo-Jewish Genealogy." *Genealogists' Magazine,"* Dec. 1932, p. 146; updated in "Jewish Ancestors and Where to Find Them," by Edgar Samuel, ibid., Dec. 1953, p. 412.

Shiloah-Discovering Jewish Identity Through Oral/Folk History: A Source Book. New York: Institute for Jewish Life, 1976.

Shilstone, E. M. *Jewish Memorial Inscriptions in Barbados.* Waltham, Mass.: American Jewish Historical Society, 1957. Includes description of records in Barbados.

Smith, Clifford Neal, and Anna P. Smith. *Encyclopedia of German-American Genealogical Research.* New York: R. R. Bowker, 1976. German villages where Jews lived in eighteenth and nineteenth centuries, ship passenger lists, and other local records.

*Steel, D. J., and Edgar R. Samuels. *Sources for Roman Catholic and Jewish Genealogy and Family History.* London: Phillimore, 1974. Nineteen-page section of British sources on Jews.

Stern, Malcolm H. "Jewish Migrations." In Kenn Stryker-Rodda, ed., *Genealogical Research: Methods and Sources*, vol. 2 (Washington, D.C., American Society of Genealogists, 1983), 341-59. Revised and updated bibliographic essay of the printed sources available on Jewish ancestry. Includes description of principal Jewish archives and manuscript collections. Lists locations of primary congregations of Jews.

____________. *Jewish Genealogy: An Annotated Bibliography.* Nashville, Tenn.: American Association of State and Local History, 1981. Technical leaflet, no. 138.

____________. "American Reform Judaism: A Bibliography." *American Jewish Historical Quarterly,* Dec. 1973, pp. 120 ff. Includes a list of congregational histories.

Wolf, Lucien, "Anglo-Jewish Coats of Arms." *Transactions of the Jewish Historical Society of England, 1894-95.* pp. 153-69.

*These items also include excellent bibliographies.

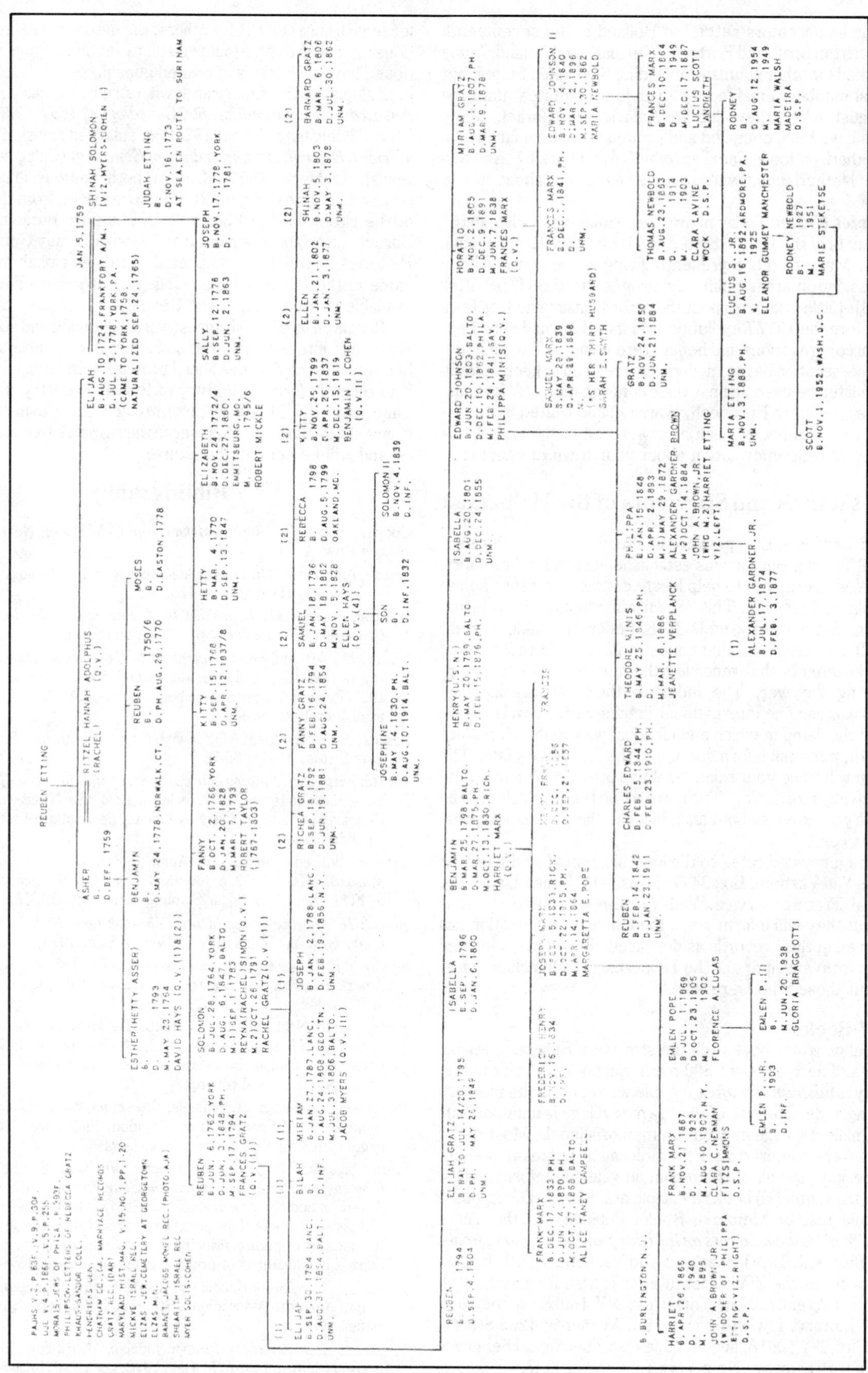

Figure 21-15. "Etting Family Genealogy" in Malcolm H. Stern, comp., *Americans of Jewish Descent: A Compendium of Genealogy*, (New York: KTAV Publishing, Inc., 1971).

Copy of Original Copy of Record in Recorder's Office,
Landau, Bavaria.

- - - - - - - - - - - - - -

Great-grandparents,-

Were named Baruch and Fannie Levy, and came to
Landau from Odratzheim, Elsas.

Grand-parents,-

Levy, Simon, married on June 17, 1794,
Jeannette Mayer formerly named Rachel.

Children,-

Raphael born July 20, 1800.
Joseph " Dec. 17, 1802.
Jacob (formerly Meier) born Apl. 19, 1805.
Julia born March 22, 1808.

Ludwig (formerly Leon - Leob. - born July 17, 1798;
Died March 12, 1861.
Feis born Oct. 26, 1796. Died Feb. 28, 1799.

Father,-

Levy, Joseph married first time 27th May, 1828,
to Malche Lang aus Horstein Grenichte Algemon in
Unterfranken. First wife died July 24, 1830.

Child Alphonse. Born Mch. 7, 1829. Died Dec. 23, 1829.

Second Marriage to -

Regina Chau on Feb. 1, 1831.

Regina Chau born Feb. 24, 1803. Daughter of
Zacharies Chau, merchant in Mannheim, and
Blumle Aberle.

Children -

Sigismund-	Born Dec.	10,	1831.	Died June 21, 1832.
Beda -	" "	15,	1832.	" Jan. 3, 1833.
Bertha -	" "	2,	1833	To America in 1851.
Michael -	" "	2,	1834.	Died May 2, 1838
Johannette	" Nov.	2,	1835.	" Jan. 8, 1836.
Fannie -	" Apl.	12,	1837.	" Sep. 26, 1867.
Augustina -	" Mch.	23,	1839.	" Feb. 26, 1840.
Julia -	" Sep.	12,	1840.	
Emelie -	" Feb.	9,	1842.	
Oskar -	" June	26,	1843.	
David -	" Dec.	27,	1844.	
Wilhelm -	" Sep.	4,	1849.	Died Sep. 13, 1849.

Family Levy emigrated lawfully to America in the year 1853.

Figure 21-16. "Genealogy of the Levy, Baruch, and Fannie Families," in "Jewish Family Genealogies," Hebrew Union College Collection, Cincinnati, Ohio; GS 1,013,430.

German-Jewish Records on Microfilm

The following list of German-Jewish records available at the library of the Genealogical Society of Utah appeared in *Toledot: The Journal of Jewish Genealogy* 2 (Summer 1978): 16-26 (Vol. 2, No. 1). Additional records have been added to this collection since 1978, and the collection continually expands. If you do not find records you need in this list, check the library's current catalogs. See also Ronald Smelzer et al., *Finding Aids to the Microfilmed Records of the Genealogical Society of Utah: Preliminary Survey of the German Collection* (Salt Lake City: University of Utah Press, 1979).

The collection is primarily composed of birth, marriage, and death records of Jews in German communities in the 1800s. Other types of genealogical records pertaining to Jews and some material for this century are included. This collection of records was microfilmed in various archives in Germany and in Poland.

The list does *not* include the name of every town in Germany where Jews once lived. Some Jewish records may still be in the local communities; some have been transferred to the Central Archives for the History of the Jewish People in Jerusalem. Other Jewish communities may have kept no records, or the records that were kept may have been lost or destroyed over the years.

Many small villages and towns in Germany did not keep their own vital records but instead were under the jurisdiction of a nearby larger community. Consequently, the vital records of their Jewish inhabitants, like those of the German residents, may be found in the registers of the larger communities.

Civil registration has been compulsory throughout Germany since 1876 and, in some areas, since much earlier. In some cases, Jews were not recorded in a separate register but included in a general register of the community. General registers should be looked up in the library's catalogs.

Some of the communities in this list became part of Polish territory following World War I. The remaining communities became part of West Germany, East Germany, Poland, or the Soviet Union after World War II. The original German place names are used in this list, with the corresponding Polish or Russian place name and province shown with an asterisk following the entry, (* now ..., ..., Poland).

This list is arranged alphabetically by the name of the German community (column 1). Place names in parentheses which occasionally follow an entry indicate a larger neighboring community or district. "Kr."[*Kreis*] and "Bez." [*Bezirk*] are German terms for "district."

The second column is a code for the name of the present-day or former German province in which the community is or was located. For towns now in West Germany (BRD) or East Germany (DDR), the current province is noted. For towns now in Poland or the USSR, the former German province is usually listed. The following codes are used:

Ba	Baden	Ne	Neubrandenburg (DDR)
Bd	Baden-Wéurttemberg (BRD)	Ni	Niedersachsen (BRD)
Be	Berlin (BRD/DDR)	No	Nordrhein-Westfalen (BRD)
Bn	Bayern (BRD)	Ns	Niederschlesien (pre-war)
Br	Brandenburg (pre-war)	Ob	Oberschlesien (pre-war)
Ch	Karl-Marx-Stadt [Chemnitz] (DDR)	Os	Ostpreussen (pre-war)
		Pm	Pommern (pre-war)
Dr	Dresden (DDR)	Pt	Potsdam (DDR)
Er	Erfurt (DDR)	Rh	Rheinland-Pfalz (BRD)
Fr	Frankfurt a.d. Oder (DDR)	Ro	Rostock (DDR)
Ha	Hanover	Sc	Schwerin (DDR)
He	Hessen (BRD)	Sl	Schlesien (pre-war)
Hl	Halle (DDR)	Su	Suhl (DDR)
Hm	Hamburg (BRD)	We	Westpreussen (pre-war)
Ma	Magdeburg (DDR)	Wf	Westfalen

The third column refers to the type of records available on microfilm for that place. "B", "M", and "D" indicate, respectively, birth, marriage, and death records. "-Ind" following "B", "M", or "D" refers to an index for that particular group of records. The following additional abbreviations are used in column 3:

Recs-1	Records about Jews.
Recs-2	Representatives and administrative employees of the Jewish community.
Recs-3	Jewish records for this locality are included on a series of microfilm reels of the civil registers. If reel numbers are omitted, consult the library of the Genealogical Society of Utah in Salt Lake City.
Recs-4	Naturalization of foreigners including Jews.
Recs-5	Jewish records for this locality are included on a series of microfilm reels of Roman Catholic records.
Recs-6	Family Book of the Jewish community, including names and birthdates.
Recs-7	Cemetery records 1830-1930 and Chronicle 1889-1901.
Recs-8	Family burial plots.
Recs-9	Naturalized Jews 1814, unidentified index, and deaths nineteenth century.
Recs-10	Jewish school records.
Recs-11	Military duty.
Recs-12	Cemetery records.
Recs-13	Voting Lists.
Recs-14	Lists of incoming/outgoing Jews.
Recs-15	Register of naturalized Jews and of heads of families.
Recs-16	List of Jews.
Recs-17	Circumcisions.
Recs-18	Conversions.
Recs-19	List of Jews paying duties.
Recs-20	Family records of Jews.
Recs-21	Alphabetical card index of Jews baptized into the Roman Catholic Church.
Recs-22	Baptisms of Jews in the Evangelical Lutheran Church.
Recs-23	Divorces.
Recs-24	Name changes of Jewish families.
Recs-25	Probate records, including Jews.
Recs-26	Guardianship records.
Recs-27	Women's snyagogue seats.
Recs-28	Persons leaving the Jewish communities.

Column 4 indicates the span of years for which records in column 3 are available. It must be noted, however, that the records may not be complete for the entire span indicated, as there are often gaps in the records.

The last column refers to the microfilm reel number used by the library of the Genealogical Society of Utah to identify that particular set of records. This number is used in ordering film from Salt Lake City. A particular reel sometimes contains records for more than one community, although quite frequently the records for a particular town occupy more than one reel.

Community	Province	Record Type	Record Span	Genealogical Society Record Number
Abterode	He	Recs-3	1808-09	800,125
Abterode	He	Recs-3	1810-11	800,126
Abterode	He	Recs-3	1808-12	800,127
Adelsheim	Bd	B	1812-46	1,192,020
Adelsheim	Bd	MD	1817-54	1,192,020
Adelsheim	Bd	B	1847-69	1,192,021
Adelsheim	Bd	MD	1855-69	1,192,021
Adelsheim	Bd	BMD	1812-1912	1,192,021
Ahaus	No	Recs-5	1827	1,044,959
Allendorf*	He	BMD	1822-75	870,522
*a.d. Lumda (Giessen).				
Altenstadt	He	BMD	1824-70	870,523
Altlandsberg	Fr	B	1847-74	1,184,462
Altmark *		Recs-12	unknown	1,184,377
*Kreis Stuhm, now Stary Targ, Gdańsk, Poland.				
Amelunsen	Wf	BMD	1808-13	1,050,592
Angelturn	Bd	BMD	1826-70	1,192,020
Annaberg-Bocholz	Ch	D	1900-36	1,184,462
Apolda	Er	See Eisenach		
Argenau*		BMD	1815-47	719,220
*now Gniewkowo (Inowrocaw), Bydgoszcz, Poland.				
Arheilgen*	He	BMD	1823-72	870,524
*now part of Darmstadt				
Arnswalde*	Br	BD	1779-1812	1,184,377
*now Choszczno, Szczecin, Poland.				
Arnswalde		BMD	1847-53	544,649
Aschenhausen	Su	BMD	1739-1919	1,184,462
Aschenhausen		Recs-12	1713-1880	1,184,463
Aschenhausen		M	1904-27	1,184,463
Aschenhausen	See also Eisenach.			
Aschersleben	Hl	BM	1809-15	1,184,463
Assenheim	He	BMD	1856-73	870,527
Augsburg	Bn	Recs-1	1298-1802	580,429
Augsburg		Recs-1	1550-1756	580,430
Augsburg		Recs-1	1556-1802	580,431
Augsburg		Recs-1	1555-1731	580,432
Augsburg		Recs-1	1732-43	580,433
Augsburg		Recs-1	1743-45	580,434
Augsburg		Recs-1	1745-1802	580,435
Augsburg		Recs-1	1570-1701	580,436
Augsburg		Recs-1	1702-22	580,437
Augsburg		Recs-1	1733-50	580,438
Augsburg		Recs-1	1751-60	580,439
Augsburg		Recs-1	1761-72	580,440
Augsburg		Recs-1	1773-1804	580,441
Augsburg		Recs-1	1805-17	580,442
Augsburg		Recs-1	1534-1813	580,443
Aurich	Hz	BMD	1782-1935	1,257,051
Bad Dürkheim	Rh	BMD	1808-10	587,607
Bad Dürkheim		B	1869-71	587,616
Bad Gundersheim	Ni	Recs-20	1775-1852	949,296
Bad Sülze	Ro	BD	1815-1904	068,936

Bad Sülze		BD	1815-1904	1,185,018
Baiertal	Bd	BMD	1811-70	1,192,021
Ballenstedt	Hl	BMD	1828-71	1,184,463
Bamberg	Bn	Recs-21	Unknown	536,187
Baranowitz *		BMD	1812-70	879,596
Baranowitz *		BMD	1810-74	879,597
Baranowitz *		BMD	1810-70	879,598
*now Baranowice (Rybnik), Katowice, Poland.				
Barchfeld	Su	BD	1849-74	809,959
Bartenstein*	Os	D	1852-1938	1,184,377
*now Bartoszyce, Olsztyn, Poland.				
Battenberg	He	BMD	1823-46	809,965
Battenberg			1847-54	809,966
Battenberg			1862-74	809,967
Bauerbach	Su	BMD	1738-1939	1,184,463
Beerfelden	He	BMD	1810-75	068,870
Beienheim	He	BMD	1826-73	870,524
Belgard Persante *		BMD	1870-72	1,184,377
Belgard Persante *		BMD	1853-1929	1,184,378
*now Białogard, Koszalin, Poland.				
Bellmuth	He	See Ortenberg.		
Berent*	We	BM	1847-65	742,795
Berent *		Recs-1	1847-73	474,721
Berent *		Recs-1	1873-1919	474,715
*now Koscierzyna, Gdańsk, Poland.				
Bergen*	He	M	1829-81	070,819
*(Kr. Hanau), now part of Bergen-Enkheim.				
Bergstadt	Sl	See Leschnitz.		
Berkach	Su	BMD	1831-75	1,184,463
Berkach		BMD	1831-1931	1,184,464
Berlin	Be	Recs-22	1830-1920	070,321
Berlin	Be	B	1812-40	477,280
Berlin	Be	B	1812-40	477,281
Berlin	Be	B	1815-41	477,282
Berlin	Be	B	1813-47	477,283
Berlin	Be	B	1812	477,284
Berlin	Be	B	1812	477,285
Berlin	Be	B	1820-40	477,286
Berlin	Be	B	1812-27	477,287
Berlin	Be	M	1844-48	477,287
Berlin	Be	M	1812-47	477,288
Berlin	Be	MD	1841-47	477,289
Berlin	Be	Recs-23	1812-47	477,290
Berlin	Be	MD	1813-46	477,290
Berlin	Be	D	1812-47	477,291
Berlin	Be	D	1812-47	477,292
Berlin	Be	B	1847-53	477,293
Berlin	Be	B	1851-59	477,294
Berlin	Be	B-Ind	1847-53	477,294
Berlin	Be	B	1857-63	477,295
Berlin	Be	B-Ind	1853-59	477,295
Berlin	Be	B	1861-66	477,296
Berlin	Be	B-Ind	1859-63	477,296
Berlin	Be	B, B-Ind	1866-69	477,297
Berlin	Be	B	1869-73	477,298
Berlin	Be	B	1873-74	477,299
Berlin	Be	B-Ind	1869-73	477,299
Berlin	Be	B-Ind	1873-74	477,300
Berlin	Be	M, M-Ind	1847-56	477,300
Berlin	Be	M	1856-67	477,301
Berlin	Be	M-Ind	1856-62	477,301
Berlin	Be	M	1865-71	477,302
Berlin	Be	M-Ind	1847-56	477,302
Berlin	Be	M	1871-74	477,303
Berlin	Be	M	1867-74	477,304
Berlin	Be	M-Ind	1862-67	477,304
Berlin	Be	D, D-Ind	1847-55	477,304
Berlin	Be	D	1855-67	477,305
Berlin	Be	D, D-Ind	1855-62	477,305
Berlin	Be	D	1865-71	477,306
Berlin	Be	D-Ind	1862-67	477,306
Berlin	Be	D	1871-74	477,307
Berlin	Be	D-Ind	1867-74	477,307
Berlin	Be	B, B-Ind	1848-74	477,308
Berlin	Be	M	1847-62	477,308
Berlin	Be	M	1862-72	477,309

Berlin	Be	M-Ind	1847-66	477,309
Berlin	Be	M	1872-74	477,310
Berlin	Be	M-Ind	1866-74	477,310
Berlin	Be	D	1850-74	477,310
Berlinchen*	Br	BMD	1847-53	544,649
*now Barlinek, Szczecin, Poland.				
Berlinchen*	Neumark	Recs-16	1736-1816	1,184,378
*now Berlinek, Bydgoszcz, Poland.				
Bernburg	Hl	Recs-1	1809-63	1,184,464
Bernberg	Hl	BMD	1827-75	1,184,465
Bernstadt*	Ns	BMD	1847-87	1,184,378
Bernstadt*	Ns	Ind	1847-87	1,184,379
*now Bierutów, Wroclaw, Poland.				
Bernstein*	Br	BMD	1825-74	1,184,379
*Neumark, now Peczyce, Szczecin, Poland.				
Berstadt	He	BMD	1824-75	870,524
Berwangen	Bd	BMD	1804-50	1,192,020
Berwangen	Bd	D	1851-69	1,189,140
Bessungen*	He	BMD	1823-74	870,525
*now part of Darmstadt.				
Betsche*		Recs-1	1877-1918	474,925
*now Pszczew (Miedzyrzecz), Zielona Góra, Poland.				
Beuern	He	BMD	1823-75	870,525
	(Giessen)	See also Gensungen.		
Beuthen*	Ob	B	1880-86	1,184,404
Beuthen*	Ob	MD	1840-1940	1,184,405
*now Bytom, Katowice, Poland.				
Bibra	Su	BMD	1838-1937	1,184,466
Binau	Bd	BMD	1811-37	1,192,022
Birklar	He	BMD	1835-75	870,525
Bischofsheim*	He	B	1850-67	814,341
*Hanau				
Bleichenbach	He	See Ortenberg.		
Bleicherode	Er	BMD	1809-76	1,184,466
Bleicherode	Er	BD	1795-?	1,184,467
Blesen *		Recs-1	1839-88	474,923
*Bledzew (Miedzyrzecz), Zielona Góra, Poland.				
Bodigheim	Bd	BMD	1813-69	1,192,024
Boizenburg	Sc	BMD	1813-1920	068,935
Bomst*	Sl	Recs-1	1847-99	474,924
Bomst*	Sl	Recs-2	1848-1916	474,931
*now Babimost (Sulechow), Zielona Góra, Poland.				
Bönstadt*	He	BMD	1857, 1861	870,525
*now part of Niddatal.				
Borgentreich	Wf	BMD	1815-18	1,050,768
Bornberg*	He	BMD	1809-22	870,534
*now part of Gross-Gerau.				
Boxberg	Bd	BMD	1826-70	1,192,020
Brandenburg*	Pt	BMD	1789-1870	1,184,467
*Havel				
Brätz*	Br	BM	1847	807,873
*now Brόje (Miedzyrzecz), Zielona Góra, Poland.				
Braunschweig	Ni	BMD	1808-14	958,059
Breitenbach*	He	B	1849-67	815,011
*Kassel				
Breitenbach*	He	BD	1838-63	815,013
*Ziegenhain				
Breslau*	Ns	B	1760-1804	1,184,379
Breslau*	Ns	B	1804-46	1,184,380
Breslau*	Ns	B	1827-38	1,184,381
Breslau*	Ns	B	1838-46	1,184,382
Breslau*	Ns	B	1846-72	1,184,383
Breslau*	Ns	B	1847, 1933-39	1,184,384
Breslau*	Ns	B-Ind	1766-1812	1,184,384
Breslau*	Ns	M	1772-73	1,184,384
Breslau*	Ns	M	1784-96	1,184,385
Breslau*	Ns	M	1797-1811	1,184,386
Breslau*	Ns	M	1804-12, 1846-47	1,184,387
Breslau*	Ns	M	1832-47	1,184,388
Breslau*	Ns	M	1846-47, 1887-98	1,184,389
Breslau*	Ns	M-Ind	1772-1812	1,184,389
Breslau*	Ns	M-Ind	1873-1930	1,184,389
Breslau*	Ns	M	1903-19	1,184,389
Breslau*	Ns	M	1903-38	1,184,390

Community	Province	Record Type	Record Span	Genealogical Society Record Number
Breslau*	Ns	D	1791-1812	1,184,390
Breslau*	Ns	D	1813-59	1,184,391
Breslau*	Ns	D	1815-27	1,184,392
Breslau*	Ns	D	1860-74	1,184,393
Breslau*	Ns	D	1910-21	1,184,394
Breslau*	Ns	D	1914-27	1,184,395
Breslau*	Ns	D	1914-27	1,184,396
Breslau*	Ns	D	1918-26	1,184,397
Breslau*	Ns	D	1928-40	1,184,398
Breslau*	Ns	D	1928-40	1,184,399
Breslau*	Ns	Recs-12	18th-19th century	1,184,400
Breslau*	Ns	Recs-12	18th-19th century	1,184,401
Breslau*	Ns	Recs-12	1761-1856	1,184,402
Breslau*	Ns	D-Ind	1780-1874	1,184,402
Breslau*	Ns	Recs-12	unknown	1,184,403
Breslau*	Ns	Recs-17	1743-1813	1,184,403
Breslau*	Ns	Recs-18	1932-39	1,184,403
Breslau	*	Recs-6	1791	1,184,403
Breslau	*	Recs-6	1791	1,184,404
*now Wrocaw, Wrocaw, Poland.				
Breunigweiler	Rh	Recs-24	1808	488,217
Brieg (Bez, Besiau)*	NS	M	1809-74	1,184,405
Brieg (Bez, Besiau)*	Ns	D	1810-74	1,184,406
Brieg (Bez, Besiau)*	Ns	B	1794-1874	1,184,407
*now Brzeg, Opole, Poland.				
Bröckeln	Ni	BMD	1809-10	949,343
Bromberg*	We	BMD	1823-65	813,087
Bromberg*	We	Recs-4	1852-53	475,863
Bromberg*	We	Recs-4	1854-55	475,864
Bromberg*	We	Recs-4	1870-71	475,865
Bromberg*	We	Recs-4	1871-72	475,866
*now Bydgoszcz, Bydgoszcz, Poland.				
Bromskirchen	He	BMD	1823-46	815,014
Brüel	Sc	BMD	1787-1903	068,935
Bublitz *		BMD	1816-18	1,184,406
*now Bobolice, Koszalin, Poland.				
Bunde	Hz	BMD	1855-58	1,187,668
Bunzlau*	Ns	Recs-12	1840-1933	1,184,406
*now Bolesawiec, Wrocaw, Poland.				
Burg*	Ma	BD	1825-63	1,184,467
*Magdeburg				
Burg-Gräfenrode	He	BMD	1851-75	870,526
Bürgeln	He	BMD	1808-12, 1864-67	815,170
Burgholzhausen	He	BMD	1823-75	870,526
Burgsteinfurt	Wf	BMD	1814-74	1,046,926
Burgsteinfurt	Wf	BMD	1840-74	1,046,927
Burkhardsfelden	He	BMD	1823-74	870,526
Busecker-Tal*	He	BMD	1809-22	870,527
Busecker-Tal*	He	BMD	1828-75	870,540
Busecker-Tal*	He	BMD	1823-75	870,522
*now Grossen-Buseck and Alten-Buseck.				
Butzback	He	BMD	1810-50	870,528
Butzback	He	BMD	1851-60	870,529
Butzback	He	BMD	1861-65	870,530
Butzback	He	BMD	1866-75	870,531
Bützow	Sc	BMD	1813-98	068,935
Caldern	He	BM	1810-12, 1849-67	815,196
Calvörde	Ma	BD	1738-1889	949,296
Castrop	Wf	BMD	1818-26	936,716
Castrop	No	Recs-5	1818, 1826-34	936,716
(Bez. Dortmund), now part of Castrop-Rauxel.				
Cosel*	Ob	Recs-1	1810-1917	1,184,406
*now Koźle, Opole, Poland.				
Coswig (Anhalt)	Hl	BMD	1800-78	1,184,468
Crivitz	Sc	BMD	1813-77	068,935
Crivitz	Sc	BMD	1813-77	1,184,468
Crossen Ober*	Br	Recs-12	1825-1955	1,184,406
*now Krosno Odrzański, Zielona Góra, Poland.				
Czempin*		Recs-12	unknown	1,184,406
*now Czempín, Poznań, Poland.				
Danzig*	We	B	1847-54	742,680
Danzig*	We	B	1854-57	742,681
Danzig*	We	B	1850-62	742,682
Danzig*	We	B	1861-64	742,683
Danzig*	We	B	1864-65	742,684
Danzig*	We	M	1848-51	742,684
Danzig*	We	M	1851-55	742,685
Danzig*	We	M	1853-57	742,686
Danzig*	We	M	1857-59	742,687
Danzig*	We	M	1860-63	742,688
Danzig*	We	M	1860-63	742,777
Danzig*	We	M	1862-63	742,778
Danzig*	We	M	1864-65	742,779
Danzig*	We	D	1852-55	742,780
Danzig*	We	D	1855-59	742,781
Danzig*	We	D	1859-64	742,782
Danzig*	We	D	1864-65	742,783
Danzig-Weinberg*	We	B	1905-39	1,184,407
Danzig*	We	BMD	1837-83	1,184,407
Danzig*	We	D	1889-1940	1,184,408
Danzig*	We	Recs-8	1848-1906	1,184,409
Danzig*	We	Recs-9	unknown	1,184,410
*now Gdańsk, Gdańsk, Poland.				
Dargun	Ne	BMD	1813-74	1,184,468
Darmstadt	He	BM	1823-75	870,532
Darmstadt	He	D	1823-75	870,533
Darmstadt	He	BMD	1788-1808	1,190,506
Daubringen	He	BMD	1826-75	870,534
Deisel*	He	BMD	1810, 1811	816,450
*now part of Trendelburg.				
Dessau	Hl	BMD	1811-71	1,184,468
Dessau	Hl	BMD	1847-1936	1,184,469
Dessau	Hl	Recs-12	1869-1910	1,184,470
Deutsch	We		See Rosenberg.	
Eylau, now Lawa, Olsztyn, Poland.				
Dielmissen	Ni	BMD	1810-13	949,317
Diersburg	Bd	B	1860-69	1,192,006
Diersburg	Bd	M	1813-69	1,192,006
Diersburg	Bd	B	1813-59	1,192,007
Diersburg	Bd	D	1813-69	1,192,007
Dirschau	*	BMD	1828-48	743,206
Dirschau	*	Recs-1	1882-1919	475,221
*now Tczew, Gdańsk, Poland.				
Dömitz	Sc	BMD	1812-1933	1,184,481
Domitz	Sc	BD	1847-48	1,185,013
Dörningheim	He	BMD	1811	832,395
Dornum	Ha	BMD	1815-1911	1,257,052
Dossenheim	Bd	BMD	1810-70	1,192,007
Dramburg*		BMD	1779-1874	1,184,481
*now Drawsko Pomorskie, Koszalin, Poland.				
Dreissigacker	Su	BD	1811-70	1,184,481
Dresden	Dr	BMD	1786-1864	1,184,471
Dresden	Dr	BMD	1790-1834	1,184,472
Dresden	Dr	BMD	1786-1835	1,184,473
Dresden	Dr	BMD	1786-1890	1,184,474
Dresden	Dr	B	1865-90	1,184,475
Dresden	Dr	BM	1865-1910	1,184,476
Dresden	Dr	D	1865-94	1,184,477
Dresden	Dr	D	1894-1910	1,184,478
Dresden	Dr	Recs-1	unknown	1,184,479
Dresden	Dr	Recs-1	1899-?	1,184,480
Dresden	Dr	Recs-1	1899-?	1,184,481
Drossen*	Br	BMD	1813-99	1,184,410
*now Ośno (Lubuskie), Zielona Góra, Poland.				
Eberbach	Bd	BMD	1816-70	1,192,007
Eberstadt	He	B	1781	1,190,527
Eberstadt	He	History	1724	1,190,527
Eberstadt	He	History	1717-56	1,190,527
Eberstadt	He	BMD	1788-1807	1,190,527
Eberstadt	He	B	1808-39	1,190,527

Eberstadt	He	B	1808-67	1,190,527
Eberstadt	He	D	1808-70	1,190,537
Eberstadt	He	D	1871-83	1,190,538
Eberstadt	He	B-Ind	1650-1790	1,190,538
Eberstadt	He	M	1839-40	1,190,544
Eberstadt*	He	BMD	1823-73	871,592
*now part of Darmstadt.				
Ebsdorf	He	BMD	1849-72	816,480
Eckardroth	He	BD	1826-75	816,480
Egeln	Ma	BM	1867-74	1,184,482
Egelsbach	He	BMD	1844-69	870,534
Ehrstadt	Bd	BMD	1811-70	1,192,024
Ehrsten	He	BMD	1808-10	806,721
Eichstetten	Bd	B	1843-70	1,192,009
Eichstetten	Bd	6	1851-70	1,192,009
Eimeldingen	Bd	B	1821-56	1,192,016
Eimeldingen	Bd	M	1839	1,192,016
Eimeldingen	Bd	D	1823-62	1,192,016
Eisenach	Er	B	1838-58	1,184,482
Eisenach	Er	B	1859-1904	1,184,483
Eisenach	Er	M	1838-93	1,184,484
Eisenach	Er	M	1857-1906	1,184,485
Eisenach	Er	BMD	1817-38	1,184,485
Eisenach	Er	BMD	1872-1939	1,184,486
Eisenach	Er	D	1838-58	1,184,487
Eisenach	Er	D	1858-1906	1,184,488
Elben	He		See Naumburg.	
Elbing*	Os	BMD	1812-71	742,026
*now Elblag, Gdańsk, Poland.				
Eigerhausen*	He	BMD	1808-12	806,722
*Kassel				
Emden	Hz	BMD	1816-44	1,257,052
Emden	Hz	BM	1844-74	1,257,052
Emden	Hz	B	1924-26	1,257,052
Emden	Hz	M	1874	1,257,052
Emden	Hz	D	1844-76	1,257,052
Emden	Hz	D	1924-25	1,257,052
Emden	Hz	BMD	1844-56	1,258,184
Emden	Hz	BMD	1865	1,258,184
Emden	Hz	BMD	1844-66	1,258,191
Emden	Hz	M	1844-68	1,258,192
Emmendingen	Bd	BMD	1800-19	1,185,203
Emmendingen	Bd	BMD	1820-32	1,185,204
Emmendingen	Bd	BMD	1833-38	1,185,205
Emmendingen	Bd	BMD	1839-45	1,185,206
Emmendingen	Bd	BMD	1846-53	1,185,541
Emmendingen	Bd	BMD	1854-60	1,185,542
Emmendingen	Bd	BMD	1861-69	1,185,543
Emmendingen	Bd	B	1811-70	1,192,010
Emmendingen	Bd	M	1814-70	1,192,010
Emmendingen	Bd	D	1811-69	1,192,011
Engelthal*	He	BMD	1826-70	870,535
*now part of Altenstadt.				
Epfenbach	Bz	D	1842-70	1,192,036
Epfenbach	Bz	M	1842-69	1,192,036
Eppingen	Bz	D	1844-69	1,192,025
Eppingen	Bz	M	1811-69	1,192,025
Eppingen	Bz	D	1811-43	1,192,025
Eppingen	Bz	B	1811-35	1,192,025
Eppingen	Bz	B	1836-70	1,192,025
Erbstadt	He	B	1852	817,258
Erksdorf	He	BMD	1808-12, 1856-74	817,259
Erksdorf	He	BMD	1808-61	860,106
Ernsthausen (Frankenberg)	He	BMD	1808-13, 1856-73	817,260
Erzhausen	He	BMD	1822-72	870,535
Eshelbach	Bd	BMD	1811-70	1,192,024
Eschershausen (Holzminden)	Ni	Recs-20	1763-76	949,296
Eschershausen (Holzminden)	Ni	B	1810	949,329
Eschollbrücken	He	BMD	1809-75	871,592
Esens	Hz	BMD	1845-1938	1,257,052
Eschwege	He	BMD	1808-12	806,724
Eschwege	He	BMD	1825-1930	071,178

Ettlingen	Bd	B	1810-22	1,237,687
Ettlingen	Bd	B	1823-45	1,237,813
Ettlingen	Bd	B	1846-60	1,237,814
Ettlingen	Bd	B	1861-69	1,237,815
Ettlingen	Bd	M	1810-49	1,237,815
Ettlingen	Bd	M	1850-69	1,237,816
Ettlingen	Bd	D	1810-35	1,237,816
Ettlingen	Bd	D	1836-58	1,237,817
Ettlingen	Bd	D	1859-69	1,237,818
Fechenheim*	He	Recs-25	1849-66	817,483
*now part of Frankfurt/Main.				
Felsberg	He	BMD	1824-52	817,495
Festenberg	Ns	BMD	1812-74	1,184,411
Kr. Gross Wartenberg, now Twardogóra, Wrocaw, Poland.				
Flatow*	We	BMD	1813-46	1,184,410
Flatow*	We	Recs-6	unknown	1,184,411
*now Zótow, Koszalin, Poland.				
Flehingen	Bd	6	1857-	1,192,026
Flehingen	Bd	D	1811-69	1,192,026
Flehingen	Bd	M	1810-69	1,192,026
Flehingen	Bd	D	1810-69	1,192,026
Fordon	*	BMD	1820-51	814,573
Fordon	*	BMD	1823-51	814,574
Fordon	*	BMD	1849-88	814,575
*now Fordon (Bydgoszcz), Bydgoszcz, Poland.				
Frankenau*	He	BMD	1808-13	817,498
*Canton				
Frankenberg	He	BMD	1808-12	817,501
*Canton. See also Frankenau (Canton).				
Frankenstein*	Ns	Recs-12	19th, 20th century	1,184,411
*now Zabkowice Slaskie, Wrocaw, Poland.				
Frankfurt/Oder	Fr	BMD	1847-63	584,092
Frankfurt/Oder	Fr	BMD	1864-78	584,093
Fraustadt*		D	1802-33	1,184,411
Fraustadt*		BMD	1763-1936	1,184,412
Fraustadt*		BMD	1800-99	1,184,413
Fraustadt*		BMD	1838	896,082
Fraustadt*		Recs-19	1890-1919	474,930
*now Wschowa, Zielona Góra, Poland.				
Freiamt	Bd	BMD	1800-17	1,185,544
Freiamt	Bd	BMD	1818-49	1,185,545
Freiamt	Bd	BMD	1850-69	1,185,546
Freystadt*	We	D	1893-1930	1,184,413
*now Kisielice, Olsztyn, Poland.				
Freystadt*	Ns	M	1849-73	896,080
*now Kozuchów (Nowa Sól), Zielona Góra, Poland.				
Freiburg	Bd	BMD	1845-70	1,192,011
Freidburg	He	BMD	1828-38	870,536
Friedberg	He	BMD	1839-73	870,537
Friedeberg*	He	BMD	1847-53	544,649
*Neumark, now Strzelce Krajenskie, Zielona Góra.				
Frielendorf	He	BM	1790-1871	828,533
Friesenheim	Bd	6	1843-70	1,192,012
Friesenheim	Bd	BMD	1813-70	1,192,012
Freisenheim	Bd	BMD	1800-21	1,257,284
Freisenheim	Bd	BMD	1821-35	1,257,285
Freisenheim	Bd	BD	1846-51	1,257,286
Freisenheim	Bd	M	1846-50	1,257,286
Freisenheim	Bd	BD	1852-55	1,257,286
Freisenheim	Bd	M	1851-55	1,257,287
Freisenheim	Bd	BMD	1856-68	1,257,287
Freisenheim	Bd	BMD	1868-69	1,257,288
Fritzlar	He	BMD	1810-12, 1824-71	828,534
Frohnhausen (Frankenberg)	He	BMD	1814-50 See also Oberasphe.	828,535
Gadebusch	Sc	BMD	1793-1922	068,935
Garbenteich	He	BMD	1825-75	870,537
Gedern	He	BMD	1824-75	870,538
Gehaus	Su		See Eisenach.	
Geisa	Su		See Eisenach.	
Geismar (Frankenberg)	He	BMD	1851-74	828,698
Gelnhausen	He	BMD	1811-13, 1823-33	828,721

Community	Province	Record Type	Record Span	Genealogical Society Record Number
Gemmingen	Bd	B	1846-70	1,192,027
Gemmingen	Bd	D	1811-66	1,192,027
Gemmingen	Bd	B	1812-45	1,192,027
Gemmingen	Bd	M	1811-69	1,192,027
Gemmingen	Bd	D	1866-69	1,192,027
Gemünden (Canton)	He		See Frankenau (Canton).	
Gensungen	He	BMD	1808-12	806,645
Georgehausen	He	BMD	1828-75	801,155
Gernsbach	Bd	BMD	1815-69	1,188,124
Giessen	He	BMD	1809-75	801,155
Giessen	He	B	1809-22	870,538
Gissingheim	Bd	Recs-5	1848-69	1,044,161
Glatz*	Ns	D	1832-1940	1,184,414
*now Kodzko, Wrocaw, Poland.				
Glauberg	He	BMD	1841-70	870,539
Gleiwitz*	Ob	BMD	1812-61	875,339
Gleiwitz*	Ob	D	1800-1940	1,184,414
*now Gliwice, Katowice, Poland.				
Glogau*	Ns	Recs-16	1812	1,184,415
Glogau*	Ns	BMD	1812-70	1,184,416
Glogau*	Ns	D	1818-1938	1,184,417
*now Gogów, Zielona Góra, Poland.				
Gnesen*		BMD	1840-47	719,426
*now Gniezno, Poznań, Poland.				
Gochsheim	Bd	BMD	1812-65	1,192,030
Goldberg	Sc	BMD	1814-1916	068,935
Goldberg	Sc	BM	1847-48	1,185,013
Gollnow*	Pm	Recs-6	1860-1934	1,184,417
*now Zgorzelec, Wrocaw, Poland and Görlitz.				
Gombeth	He		See Grossenenglis.	
Gondelsheim	Bd	B	1811-49	1,192,030
Görlitz*	Ns	Recs-12	1850-1940	1,184,417
Görlitz*	Ns	BMD	1864-1932	1,184,418
*now Zgorzelec, Wroclaw, Poland and Görlitz.				
Gossfelden	He	BMD	1810-12, 1824-83	831,642
Gräfenhausen	He	BMD	1823-72	870,539
Grebenstein	He	BMD	1827-87	831,658
Greene	Ni	BMD	1809, 1812	949,334
Greetsiel	Ha	BD	1815-17	1,257,052
Griesheim	He	BMD	1823-72	870,541
Gross-Bieberau	He	BMD	1827-75	870,540
Grosseicholtzheim	Bd	BMD	1811-69	1,192,029
Gross-Mühlingen	Ma	BMD	1778-1871	1,184,497
Gross Wartenberg*	Ns	Recs-12	1820-67	1,184,417
*Bez. Breslau, now Syców, Wroclaw, Poland.				
Grossalsleben	Ma	BMD	1801-03, 1832-48	1,184,497
Grossen-Linden	He	BMD	1823-75	870,541
Grossenenglis	He	BD	1808-12	806,664
Grossropperhausen	He	BD	1849-74	853,749
Grotzingen	Bd	BD	1811-69	1,192,027
Grotzingen	Bd	BMD	1811-69	1,192,028
Grotzingen	Bd	6	1811-69	1,192,028
Grotzingen	Bd	B	1811-unknown	1,192,028
Grüningen	He	BMD	1823-75	870,542
Gudensberg	He	BMD	1808-12	806,662
Gudensberg	He	Recs-3 (M)	1849-74	
Gustrow	Sc	BMD	1813-1935	068,935
Guttentag*	Ob	D	1846-80	1,184,419
*now Dobrodzién, Katowice, Poland.				
Guttstadt*	Os	D	1846-1937	1,184,419
*now Dobre Miasto, Olsztyn, Poland.				
Guxhagen	He	BM	1848-49	832,395
Habitzheim	He	BMD	1823-75	870,542
Hagenow	Sc	BMD	1813-1937	1,184,498
Hahn (Darmstadt)	He	BMD	1823-72	870,543
Hainchen	He	BMD	1830-70	870,544
Halle (Holtzminden)	Ni	BMD	1808-12	949,340
Hamburg	Hm	Recs-26	1783-1849	574,799
Hanau	He	B	1866-69	832,416
Harmuthsachen	He	BMD	1808-09	806,668
Harmuthsachen	He	BMD	1810-12	806,652
Hartum	Wf	6	1828-34	470,435
Hatzbach	He	BMD	1808-12, 1856-74	832,419
Haynau*	Ns	Recs-12	1888-1936	1,184,419
*now Chojnow, Wrocaw, Poland.				
Heegheim	He	BMD	1860-66	870,544
Heidelberg	Bd	BMD	1810-70	1,188,142
Heidelsheim	Bd	B	1814-70	1,192,028
Heidelsheim	Bd	D	1814-69	1,192,028
Heidelsheim	Bd	M	1816-69	1,192,028
Heinsheim	Bd	BMD	1812-69	1,192,029
Hehlen	Ni	Recs-20	1773-1893	949,296
Hehlen	Ni	BMD	1809-10	949,343
Heldenbergen*	He	BMD	1823-75	870,544
*now part of Nidderau.				
Helmarshausen	He	BMD	1803-89	832,422
Helmstedt	Ni	Recs-20	1847-74	949,296
Herbstein	He	BMD	1857-72	870,544
Herleshausen	He	BMD	1809-13	806,659
Heubach (Schluchtern)	He	BMD	1812-75	832,452
Heuchelheim (Giessen)	He	BMD	1824-75	870,545
Hildburghausen	Su	BMD	1826-1922	1,185,003
Hilsbach	Bd	BMD	1801-69	1,192,029
Hindenburg	Ob		See Zabrze.	
Hintersteinau	He	BMD	1859-74	833,862
Hirschberg*	Ns	Recs-12	1886-1938	1,184,419
*now Jelenia Góra, Wrocaw, Poland.				
Hochhausen	Bd	BMD	1812-69	1,192,030
Hochhausen (Tauberbischofsheim)	Bd	Recs-5	1830-69	1,044,167
Höchst (Büdingen)	He	BMD	1826-70	870,545
Hochstadt	He	BMD	1825-73	833,863
Hoffenheim	Bd	BMD	1858-69	1,189,199
Hoffenheim	Bd	D	1843-70	1,189,199
Hoffenheim	Bd	D	1870-1921	1,189,200
Hoffenhardt	Bd	BMD	1847-69	1,192,030
Hoffenhardt	Bd	BMD (Ind)	1811-46	1,192,046
Hoffenhardt	Bd	6	1820-69	1,192,046
Hoffenhardt	Bd	BD	1847-69	1,192,046
Hoffenhardt	Bd	BMD	1811-46	1,192,046
Hofgeismar	He	BMD	1809-1903	833,824
Hofgeismar	He	M	1869-74	833,825
Hofgeismar	He	Recs-3	1798-1808	833,824
Hofgeismar	He	Recs-3 (M)	1795-1865	833,864
Hohe	Ni	BMD	1809	957,306
Hohensalza	*		See Argenau.	
*now Inowrocaw, Bydgoszcz, Poland.				
Holzheim (Giessen)	He	BMD	1823-75	870,545
Holzminden	Ni	Recs-20	1839-76	949,296
Holzminden	Ni	B	1809	949,708
Hoof	He	BD	1849-60	834,010
Hornburg	Ni	BMD	1808-14	949,708
Hoym	Hl	BMD	1828-80	1,185,003
Hundsfeld*	Sl	BMD	1812-1923	1,184,419
*Bez. Breslau, now part of Wrocaw, Wrocaw, Poland.				
Horden	Bd	M	1811-70	1,192,012
Horden	Bd	D	1811-69	1,192,013
Hüttenberg AMT	He	BMD	1809-22	870,546
Hüttengesäss	He	BMD	1840-77	834,021
Iba	He	BMD	1808-12	806,638
Ihringen	Bd	M	1847-69	1,191,014
Ihringen	Bd	D	1846-69	1,191,014
Ihringen	Bd	B	1847-70	1,191,014
Ihringen	Bd	BMD	1811-45	1,191,014
Ilvesheim	Bd	BMD	1810-70	1,238,454
Immenhausen	He	BMD	1808-12	806,638

Ittlingen	Bd	BMD	1814-69	1,192,032
Jastrow*	We	BMD	1816-39	1,184,420
Jastrow*	We	BMD	1830-47	1,184,421
*now Jastrowie, Koszalin, Poland.				
Jauer*	Ns	BMD	1806-1939	1,184,422
Jauer*	Ns	Recs-6	1819-?	1,184,423
*now Jawor, Wrocaw, Poland			unknown	
Jengum	Hz	B	1816-83	1,257,052
Jengum	Hz	B	1935	1,257,052
Jengum	Hz	M	1821-82	1,257,052
Jengum	Hz	M	1819-40	1,257,052
Jengum	Hz	D	1822-83	1,257,052
Jengum	Hz	D	1933	1,257,052
Josbach	He	BMD	1808-11,	
			1856-74	834,165
Kaiserslautern	Rh	Recs-12	various	536,484
Kalisch*		BMD	1809-20	743,141
Kalisch*	Recs-3	1821-65		
*now Kalisz, Poznań, Poland.				
Kalme	Ni	BMD	1809-12	949,710
Kanth*	Ns	BMD	1812-1937	1,184,423
*Kr. Neumarkt, now Katy Wrocawskie, Wrocaw, Poland.				
Karlsruhe	Bd	BMD	1810-?	
			unknown	1,256,447
Karthaus	*	Recs-1	1848-73	475,222
*now Kartuzy, Gdańsk, Poland.				
Kassel	He	BMD	1808-10,	
			1848-67	839,331
Kattowitz*	Ob	B	1860-1936	1,184,423
Kattowitz*	Ob	D	1869-1934	1,184,424
Kattowitz*	Ob	D	1850-1939	1,184,425
Kattowitz*	Ob	D	1825-1939	1,184,426
Kattowitz*	Ob	Recs-27	1868-97	1,184,428
*now Katowice, Katowice, Poland.				
Kemnade	Ni	BMD	1809-12	949,710
Kempen*		BMD	1825-35	742,975
Kempen*		BMD	1836-41	742,976
Kempen*		BMD	1842-47	742,977
*now Kepno, Poznań, Poland.				
Kieferstädetel*	Sl	Recs-17	1806-65	1,184,428
Kieferstädetel*	Sl	Recs-12	1831-93	1,184,428
*now Sośnicowice, Katowice, Poland.				
Kirchardt	Bd	B	1816-69	1,192,032
Kirchardt	Bd	M	1818-64	1,192,032
Kirchardt	Bd	D	1818-37	1,192,032
Kirchardt	Bd	B	1821-41	1,192,033
Kirchardt	Bd	B	1840-70	1,192,048
Kirchardt	Bd	M	1858	1,192,048
Kirchardt	Bd	D	1833-37	1,192,048
Kirchen	Bd	BMD	1799-1819	1,257,017
Kirchen	Bd	BM	1820-69	1,257,018
Kirchen	Bd	D	1820-69	1,257,019
Kirchen	Bd	6	1811-38	1,192,015
Kirchen	Bd	BMD	1811-38	1,192,015
Kirchen	Bd	B	1839-70	1,192,015
Kirchen	Bd	D	1839-70	1,192,015
Kirchen	Bd	M	1839-69	1,192,015
Kirchhain	He	BMD	1810-12,	
			1856-74	841,263
Kirtorf	He	BMD	1809-23	870,546
Konigsbach	Bd	BD	1848-69	1,192,031
Konigsbach	Bd	BD	1811-47	1,192,031
Konigsbach	Bd	M	1812-68	1,192,031
Konigsberg*	Os	B-Ind:	1826-74	
Konigsberg*	Os	Males:	A-B	071,607
Konigsberg*	Os	Males:	B-C	071,608
Konigsberg*	Os	Males:	C-F	071,609
Konigsberg*	Os	Males:	F-G	071,610
Konigsberg*	Os	Males:	G-H	071,611
Konigsberg*	Os	Males:	H-Ka	071,612
Konigsberg*	Os	Males:	Ka-Kr	071,613
Konigsberg*	Os	Males:	Kr-L	071,614
Konigsberg*	Os	Males:	L-M	071,615
Konigsberg*	Os	Males:	M-P	071,616
Konigsberg*	Os	Males:	P-R	071,617
Konigsberg*	Os	Males:	R-Sch	071,618

Konigsberg*	Os	Males:	Sch-St	071,619
Konigsberg*	Os	Males:	St-V	071,620
Konigsberg*	Os	Males:	V-Z	071,621
Konigsberg*	Os	Females:	A-B	071,622
Konigsberg*	Os	Females:	B-D	071,623
Konigsberg*	Os	Females:	D-F	071,624
Konigsberg*	Os	Females:	F-H	071,625
Konigsberg*	Os	Females:	H-Ka	071,626
Konigsberg*	Os	Females:	Ka-Kr	071,627
Konigsberg*	Os	Females:	Kr-M	071,628
Konigsberg*	Os	Females:	M-N	071,629
Konigsberg*	Os	Females:	N-R	071,630
Konigsberg*	Os	Females:	R-Sch	071,631
Konigsberg*	Os	Females:	Sch-St	071,632
Konigsberg*	Os	Females:	St-W	071,633
Konigsberg*	Os	Females:	W-Z, A-S	071,634
Konigsberg*	Os	M-Ind	1790-1874	071,635
Konigsberg*	Os	B	1847-52, 1859	475,875
Konigsberg*	Os	B	1860-65	475,876
Konigsberg*	Os	M	1873-77	475,877
Konigsberg*	Os	B	1852-57	585,589
Konigsberg*	Os	B	1858-71	585,590
Konigsberg*	Os	M	1852-74	585,590
Konigsberg*	Os	M	1847-52	476,220
Konigsberg*	Os	BMD-Ind	1847-52	071,107
Konigsberg*	Os	Recs-16	unknown	071,112
*now Kaliningrad, Kaliningrad, Russia.				
Konigshütte*	Ob	D	1867-1940	1,184,430
*Królewska Huta, now part of Chorzów, Katowice, Poland.				
Königslutter	Ni	Recs-20	1872-74	949,296
Konstadt*	Ob	BD	1835-90	1,184,431
*now Woczyn, Opole, Poland.				
Konstanz	Bd	BMD	1863-69	870,274
Korb	Bd	B	1808-46	1,192,031
Korb	Bd	D	1831-46	1,192,031
Korb	Bd	B	1846-70	1,192,031
Korb	Bd	M	1832-44	1,192,031
Korb	Bd	6	1831-70	1,192,031
Korb	Bd	M	1846-70	1,192,031
Korb	Bd	D	1846-70	1,192,035
Korbach	He	BMD	1859-75	841,277
Koschmin*		BMD	1811-12	742,946
*now Koszalin, Koszalin, Poland.				
Koslin*	Pm	BMD	1812-46	896,086
*now Koszalin, Koszalin, Poland.				
Krakow	Sc	BMD	1813-74	068,935
Krappitz*	Ob	BMD	1819-48	1,184,431
(Kr. Oppeln)	See also Oppeln.			
*Krapkowice, Opole, Poland.				
Krautheim	Bd	Recs-5	1812-70	1,047,435
Kreuzburg*	Ob	BMD	1830-55	1,184,431
*now Kluczbork, Opole, Poland.				
Kriewen	*	BMD	1835-47	743,099
*now Krzywiń, Poznań, Poland.				
Krojanke*	We	Recs-1	1812-33	495,964
Krojanke*	We	Recs-1	1833-41	495,965
Krojanke*	We	Recs-1	1834-54	495,966
Krojanke*	We	Recs-1	1846	495,967
Krojanke*	We	BMD	1800-63	1,184,432
*now Krajenka, Koszalin, Poland.				
Krojanke Kulm	*	Recs-1	1829-32	495,967
*now Krajenka Chemo, Bydgoszcz, Poland.				
Krone	*	B	1847-74	813,169
*now Kronowo (Bydgszcz), Bydgoszcz, Poland.				
Kröpelin	Ro	BMD	1817-98	068,935
Krotoschin	*	BMD	1825-41	743,091
Krotoschin	*	BMD	1842-47	743,092
*now Krotoszyn, Poznań, Poland.				
Kurnik	*	BMD	1817-47	742,003
*now Kornik, Poznań, Poland.				
Laage	Sc	BMD	1813-1907	068,935
Lahr	Bd	B	1856-70	1,257 304
Lahr	Bd	MD	1856-70	1,257,304
Lahr	Bd	B	1858-69	1,192,016
Landau	Rh	BMD	1784-90	488,361
Landeck*	Ns	Recs-12	1922-34	1,184,432
*now Ladek-Zorój, Wrocaw, Poland.				

Community	Province	Record Type	Record Span	Genealogical Society Record Number
Landenburg	Bd	BMD	1812-70	1,192,034
Landenburg	Bd	BMD	1810-70	1,238,445
Landeshut*	Ns	BMD	1800-1938	1,184,432
*now Kamienna Góra, Wrocaw, Poland.				
Landsberg in Oberschlesien	Ob	D	1843-44	1,184,432
(Kreis Rosenberg) now Gorzów Slaski, Opole, Poland.				
Lang-Göns	He	BMD	1809-22	870,546
Lang-Göns	He	BMD	1822-75	870,546
Langen-Bergheim	He	BMD	1853-70	870,546
Langendiebach	He	BMD	1826-74	841,285
Langendiebach	He	BD	1849-67	841,285
Langendorf*	Sl	B	1810-57	1,184,432
Langendorf*	Sl	Recs-1	1762-1820	1,184,433
Langendorf* (Kr. Gleiwitz)	Sl	Recs-1	1828-89	1,184,434
*now Wielowieś, Katowice, Poland.				
Langenselbold	He	BD	1826-77	841,286
Langsdorf	He	BMD	1823-75	870,546
Lavenburg*	Pm	BMD	1829-46	1,184,433
Lavenburg*	Pm	Recs-12	1844-1936	1,184,433
Lavenburg*	Pm	Recs-12	1844-1936	1,184,434
*now Lebork, Gdańsk, Poland.				
Laurahutte*	Sl	Recs-1	1856-62, 1880	1,184,434
*now part of Siemianowice Slaskie, Katowice, Poland.				
Leer	Ha	BMD	1842-1939	1,257,052
Leidenhofen	He	BD	1850-73	841,290
Leidolsheim	Bd	BMD	1783, 1790	1,236,237
Leidolsheim	Bd	BMD	1800-24	1,236,257
Leidolsheim	Bd	BMD	1824-53	1,256,232
Leidolsheim	Bd	BMD	1854-69	1,236,233
Leihgestern	He	BMD	1823-75	870,547
Leiman	Bd	BMD	1812-40	1,192,035
Leiman	Bd	BMD	1840-69	1,192,035
Leiman	Bd	BMD	1810-70	1,188,237
Leobschutz*	Ob	D	1818-1937	1,184,434
*now Gubczyce, Opole, Poland.				
Leschnitz*	Ob	Recs-12	1855-1933	1,184,378
*Leśnica (Strzelce Opolskie), Opole, Poland.				
Lessen*	We	BMD	1824-85	1,184,434
*now Lasin, Bydgoszcz, Poland.				
Leuterhausen	Bd	BMD	1811-69	1,192,035
Leverkusen	No	BMD	1808	176,106
Lich	He	BMD	1822-75	870,547
Lichtenau	Bd	BMD	1812-70	1,192,016
Lichtenberg	He	BMD	1849-64	870,848
Liebenau	He	BMD	1828-88	841,299
Liedolsheim	Bd	BMD	1823-61	1,192,036
Liegnitz*	Ns	BM	1855-1940	1,184,435
Liegnitz*	Ns	D	1814-1940	1,184,436
Liegnitz*	Ns	Recs-16	1812-50	1,184,436
*now Legnica, Wrocaw, Poland.				
Lindheim	He	BMD	1823-69	870,548
Lohra	He	BD	1849-67	841,302
Lollar	He	BMD	1815-74	870,549
Lorrach	Bd	6	1728-1869	1,238,141
Lorrach	Bd	6	1827-67	1,192,015
Lorrach	Bd	B	1827-65	1,192,018
Lorrach	Bd	M	1829-67	1,192,018
Lorrach	Bd	B	1866-67	1,192,018
Lorrach	Bd	D	1827-67	1,192,018
Lorrach	Bd	D	1868-70	1,192,018
Lorrach	Bd	B	1868-70	1,192,018
Lowen*	Ns	BMD	1815-36	1,184,436
Lowen*	Ns	Recs-1	1836-1934	1,184,437
*now Lewin Brzeski, Opole, Poland.				
Lowenberg*	Ns	Recs-12	1815-1932	1,184,437
*now Lubliniec, Katowice, Poland.				
Lübz	Sc	BMD	1813-95	068,935
Ludinghausen	Wf	BM	1832-58	1,048,751
Ludinghausen	Wf	D	1832-47	1,048,751
Ludinghausen	Wf	D	1848-58	1,048,752
Ludinghausen	Wf	BMD	1859-74	1,048,752
Ludwigslust	Sc	BMD	1827-1920	068,935
Madgeburg	Ma	B	1829-30	1,185,004
Madgeburg	Ma	MD	1929-32	1,185,004
Madgeburg	Ma	BM	1832-47	1,185,005
Madgeburg	Ma	D	1815-1939	1,185,005
Mainzlar	He	BMD	1827-75	870,549
Malchen	Hn	B	1823-24	1,190,528
Malchen	Hn	D	1823-24	119,058
Malchen	Hn	M	1823-25	119,058
Malchen	Hn	D	1823	119,058
Malchin	Ne	BMD	1813-84	068,936
Malchin	Ne	BMD	1813-84	1,185,006
Malchow	Ne	BMD	1812-95	1,185,006
Malchow	Ne	BMD	1860	1,185,013
Mannheim	Bd	BMD	1810-60	1,238,466
Mannheim	Bd	BMD	1861-70	1,238,467
Mannheim	Bd	BMD	1810-60	1,238,463
Mannheim	Bd	BMD	1860-70	1,238,464
Mannheim	Bd	BMD	1805-14	1,238,457
Mannheim	Bd	BMD	1815-59	1,238,458
Mannheim	Bd	BMD	1860-70	1,238,459
Marburg	He	BMD	1808-13	801,069
Marburg	He	BD	1845-69	801,069
Marburg	He	BD	1849-64	850,224
Mardorf (Marburg)	He	BD	1856-73	846,196
Marienburg*	We	B	1847-65	742,802
Marienburg*	We	MD	1847-65	742,803
*now Malbork, Gdańsk, Poland.				
Marienwerder*	We	Recs-1	1818-24	496,013
Marienwerder*	We	Recs-10	1812-27	496,157
Marienwerder*	We	Recs-10	1827-28	496,158
Marienwerder*	We	Recs-10	1829-32	496,159
Marienwerder*	We	Recs-10	1832-35	496,160
Marienwerder*	We	Recs-10	1835-37	496,161
Marienwerder*	We	Recs-10	1837-40	496,162
Marienwerder*	We	Recs-10	1837-43	496,163
Marienwerder*	We	Recs-10	1843-48	496,164
Marienwerder*	We	Recs-10	1848-54	496,165
Marienwerder*	We	Recs-10	1814-60	496,166
Marienwerder*	We	Recs-11	1852	495,963
Marienwerder*	We	Recs-12	1833-1932	1,184,441
*now Kwidsyn, Gdańsk, Poland.				
Marisfeld	Su	BMD	1768-1888	1,185,006
Marisfeld	Su	BMD	1837-1936	1,185,007
Markt	Ba	B	1821-56	1,192,016
Markt	Ba	M	1839	1,192,016
Markt	Ba	D	1823-62	1,192,016
Märkish	We	BMD	1815-47	1,184,439
Friedland*	We	Recs-16	1799-1810	1,184,440
Friedland*	We	Recs-16	1799-1810	1,184,441
*now Mirosawiec, Koszalin, Poland.				
Marköbel	He	BD	1849-66	846,198
Marlow	Ro	BMD	1814-66	068,936
Marlow	Ro	BMD	1814-73	1,185,007
Mechtal	Ob		See Miechowitz.	
Meckesheim	Ba	BMD	1811-69	1,192,036
Meckesheim	Ba	B	1812-69	1,188,241
Meckesheim	Ba	M	1814-69	1,188,241
Meckesheim	Ba	D	1811-66	1,188,241
Mecklenburg-Schwerin		Recs-28	1912-33	1,185,007
Meerholz	He	B	1841-47	848,665
Meimbressen	He	B	1827-89	848,666
Meimbressen	He	BMD	1808-10	806,721
Meiningen	Su	BMD	1850-1937	1,185,008
Melbach	He	BMD	1826-72	870,550
Melsungen	He	BMD	1824-52	801,304
Melsungen	He	M	1849-74	801,304
Menzingen	Ba	B	1800-69	1,192,034
Menzingen	Ba	MD	1811-69	1,192,034
Merzhausen	He	BMD	1808-12	801,306
Merzhausen (Ziegenhain)	He	BMD	1824-72, 1883	801,306

Meseritz*	Br	BMD	1817-41	1,184,442
Meseritz*	Br	Recs-1	1846-75	474,926
Mesertiz*	Br	Recs-13	1848-1903	474,929
(Bez. Posen)				
*now Miedzyrzecz, Zielona Góra, Poland.				
Messel	He	BMD	1823-72	870,550
Messelhausen	Bd	Recs-5	1811-69	1,047,446
Michelfeld	Ba	BMD	1811-70	1,192,032
Miechowitz*	Ob	M	1880, 1885	1,184,442
*now Miechowice, Katowice, Poland.				
Mittelsinn	Bnn	BMD	1826-55	801,307
Mixstadt	*	BMD	1836-46	746,949
*now Mikstat, Poznań, Poland.				
Momberg	He	B	1856-73	801,308
Momberg	He	D	1856-73	801,309
Monzesheim	Ba	BMD	1811-70	1,192,033
Moschin	*	B	1835-36	746,967
*now Mosina, Poznań, Poland.				
Muhlbach	Ba	BMD	1812-70	1,192,033
Müllheim	Ba	BMD	1810-70	1.192,017
Münsterberg*	Ns	BD	1824-77	1,184,442
*now Ziebice, Wrocaw, Poland.				
Muschenheim	He	BMD	1835-75	870,551
Myslowitz*	Sl	B	1847-49, 1863-66	864,943
Myslowitz*	Sl	M	1849-60	864,944
Myslowitz*	Sl	M	1859-63	864,945
Myslowitz*	Sl	BMD	1847-70	864,946
*now Mysowice, Katowice, Poland.				
Nakel Netze	*	BMD	1848-74	715,114
Nakel Netze	*	BMD	1823-67	715,115
Nakel Netze	*	Recs-16	1833-35	1,184,443
*Nako Nad Notecia, Bydgoszcz, Poland.				
Namslau*	Ns	BMD	1812-47	1,184,443
Namslau*	Ns	Recs-12	1914-18	1,184,443
*now Namysów, Opole, Poland.				
Nauburg	He	BMD	1808-12	810,506
Neidenstein	Bd	D	1842-70	1,192,036
Neidenstein	Bd	M	1842-69	1,192,036
Neisse*	Ob	B	1809-1928	1,184,443
Neisse*	Ob	MD	1813-1930	1,184,444
Neisse*	Ob	Recs-28	1914-38	1,184,444
*now Nysa, Opole, Poland.				
Netra	He	BMD	1808-12	810,509
Neu-Berun	*	BMD	1847-70	864,953
*now Bieruń Nowy, Katowice, Poland.				
Neubukow	Ro	BM	1813-76	1,185,010
Neukalen	Ne	BMD	1813-75	068,936
Neukalen	Ne	BMD	1813-75	1,185,010
Neumarkt*	Ns	BM	1818-48	1,184,444
*now Sroda Slaska, Wrocaw, Poland.				
Neumittelwalde*	Ns	B	1810-83	1,184,441
Neumittelwalde*	Ns	Recs-12	1870-1906	1,184,444
(Meozibor)				
*now Miedzybŕz, Wrocaw, Poland.				
Neusalz*	Ns		See Freystadt.	
*now Wejherowo, Gdańsk, Poland.				
Neustadt*	Ob	Recs-1	1812-1939	1,184,444
*Now Prudnik, Opole, Poland.				
Neustadt-Giewe	Sc	BMD	1811-76	1,185,010
Neunstetten	Ba	BMD	1813-70	1,192,037
Neustettin*	Pm	Recs-12	1788-1870	1,184,444
*now Szczecinek, Koszalin, Poland.				
Nieder-Eschbach	He	BMD	1827-75	870,551
Nieder-Mockstadt	He	BMD	1823-66	870,552
Nieder-Ramstadt	He	BMD	1823-72	870,551
Nieder-Seemen	He		See Ortenberg.	
Niederklein	He	BMD	1856-71	849,122
Niederrodenbach	He	BMD	1811-12, 1849-67	850,173
Niederrodenbach	He	BD	1849-68	855,680
Nonnenweier	Ba	BMD	1808-32	1,257,310
Nonnenweier	Ba	BMD	1833-69	1,257,311
Nordeck	He	BMD	1849-64	850,175
Nordeck	He	BMD	1849-69	850,176
Nordhaussen	Er	BMD	1829-82	1,185,010

Nussloch	Ba	B	1810-70	1,188,251
Nussloch	Ba	MD	1812-69	1,188,251
Ober-Erlenbach	He	Recs-1	1875	870,553
Ober-Ramstadt	He	BMD	1823-72	870,552
Ober-Seemen	He	BMD	1826-75	870,553
Ober-Wöllstadt	He	Recs-1	1841-57	870,553
Oberasphe	He	BMD	1826-47	850,177
Oberasphe	He	B	1750-1810	828,635
Oberaula	He	B	1824-66	850,198
Oberaula	He	BD	1849-74	850,199
Obervorschütz	He	BM	1808-12	810,517
Oberzell	He	D	1826-75	850,223
Ohlau*	Ns	BMD	1817-1933	1,184,445
*now Oawa, Wrocaw, Poland.				
Öls*	Ns	Recs-1	1812-1930	1,184,444
Öls*	Ns	Recs-1	1812-1930	1,184,445
*now Oleśnica, Wrocaw, Poland.				
Oppeln*	Ob	BMD	1812-1938	1,184,445
*now Opole, Opole, Poland.				
Oranienburg	Pt	D	1815-39	1,185,010
Ortenberg	He	BMD	1831-75	.870,554
Ortenberg	He	BMD	1834-75	870,555
Ossenholz*	We	B	1826-1934	530,225
Ossenholz*	We	M	1826-1931	530,226
Ossenholz*	We	BMD	1826-92	530,227
Ossenholz*	We	D	1917-38	530,227
(Hermannsbad)				
*now Osieciny, Bydgoszcz, Poland.				
Osterode*	Os	BMD	1865-1936	071,081
*now Ostróda, Olsztyn, Poland.				
Osteriesland	Ha	BMD	1723-1939	1,257,051
Ottenstein	Ni	Recs-20	1768-1876	949,296
Ottenstein	Ni	BMD	1809-13	958,004
Ottrau	He	BD	1824-74	850,229
Pakosch	*	BMD	1823-47	719,232
*now Pakość, Bydgoszcz, Poland.				
Parchim	Sc	BMD	1813-1936	1,185,010
Pasewalk	Ne	D	1865-1906	1,185,010
Penzlin	Ne	BMD	1814-1915	068,936
Perleberg	Sc	BMD	1812-99	1,185,010
Pfaffenbeerfurth	He	BMD	1868-74	870,555
Pforzheim	Ba	BMD	1810-70	1,192,038
Pfungstadt	He	BMD	1823-72	870,555
Plau	Sc	BMD	1813-1917	068,936
Plau	Sc	BMD	1813-1913	1,185,011
Plaue	Er	BMD	1825-1920	1,185,011
Pless*	Sl	BMD	1847-74	1,184,446
*now Pszczyna, Katowice, Poland.				
Pleschen	*	BMD	1835-47	752,629
*now Pleszew, Poznań, Poland.				
Polzin*	Pm	D	1858-1936	1,184,446
(Bez. Koslin)				
*now Poczyn Zdrój, Koszalin, Poland.				
Potsdam	Pt	BMD	1810-63	1,185,011
Potsdam	Pt	D	1906-36	1,185,011
Potsdam	Pt	Recs-12	1745-1933	1,185,011
Potsdam	Pt	Recs-12	1838-1939	1,185,012
Preussisch*	Os	Recs-12	1825-1907	1,184,446
*Holland, now Pasek, Olsztyn, Poland.				
Preussisch-Stargard*	We	Recs-1	1847-62	474,723
Preussisch-Stargard*	We	Recs-1	1862-70	474,724
Preussisch-Stargard*	We	Recs-1	1882-1903	474,717
Preussisch-Stargard*	We	Recs-1	1904-20	474,718
Preussisch-Stargard*	We	BMD	1812-1939	185,355
Preussisch-Stargard*		B	1812-74	414,467
Preussisch-Stargard*	We	MD	1812-74	414,468
Preussisch-Stargard*	We	Recs-12	1848-1904	1,184,446
*now Starogard Gdański, Gdańsk, Poland.				

Community	Province	Record Type	Record Span	Genealogical Society Record Number
Putzig *		Recs-1	1812-55	474,720
Putzig *		Recs-1	1857-1920	474,714
*now Puck, Gdańsk, Poland.				
Pyritz*	Pm	Recs-16	1853-unknown	1,184,446
*now Pyrzyce, Szczecin, Poland.				
Rappenau	Ba	BMD	1813-69	1,192,037
Rastenburg*	Os	BMD	1813-74	1,184,447
*now Ketrzyn, Szczecin, Poland.				
Ratibor*	Ob	Recs-12	1888, 1940	1,184,447
Ratibor*	Ob	D	1865-1930	1,184,448
Ratibor*	Ob	BM	1814-74	1,184,449
*now Raciborz, Opole, Poland.				
Rauischholzhausen	He	BMD	1809-71	851,356
Rauschenberg	He	BMD	1849-74	851,403
Rehna	Sc	BMD	1814-82	068,936
Rehna	Sc	BMD	1813-82	1,185,012
Reichenbach*	Ns	Recs-7		
*now Dzierzoniow, Wrocaw, Poland.				
Reilingen	Ba	BMD	1811-69	1,192,038
Reinheim	He	BMD	1823-75	870,556
Reiskirchen*	He	BMD	1832-75	870,556
*Giessen				
Rennertehausen	He	BMD	1835-46	851,405
Rheinbishofsheim	Ba	BMD	1810-69	1,256,663
Rheinbishofsheim	Ba	6	1853-70	1,192,018
Rheinbishofsheim	Ba	BMD	1844-70	1,192,019
Reinbishofsheim	Ba	BMD	1810-43	1,192,019
Rhina	He	BMD	1811-12	851,409
Ribnitz-Damgarten	Ro	B	1812-75	1,185,012
Richelsdorf	He	MD	1851-1912	850,568
Riesenburg*	We	BMD	1823-74	1,184,449
Riesenburg*	We	B	1920	1,184,449
*now Prabuty, Olsztyn, Poland.				
Rimbach (Bergstrasse)	He	BMD	1823-58	870,556
Röbel*	He	BMD	1813, 1915	1,185,012
*Müritz				
Röddenau	He	BMD	1851-73	851,409
Rödgen*	He	BMD	1827-55	870,557
Rogasen	*	BMD	1817-39	752,799
Rogasen	*	BMD	1840-47	752,800
*now Rogoźno (Oborniki), Posnań, Poland.				
Rohrbach	Ba	BMD	1812-69	1,192,039
Rohrbach	Ba	BMD	1812-70	1,192,039
Rohrbruch *		BMD	1823-44	719,149
*now Rynarzewo, Bydgoszcz, Poland.				
Röhrenfurt*	He	BMD	1838-52	851,410
Röllshausen	He	BD	1849-70	853,745
Rommelhausen	He	BMD	1853-70	870,557
Ropperhausen	He	BD	1828-66	853,749
Rosenberg*	Ob	BMD	1812-47	1,184,449
Rosenberg*	Ob	D	1891-1938	1,184,449
Rosenberg*	Ob	Recs-14	1815-47	1,184,449
Rosenberg*	Ob	Recs-14	1815-47	1,184,450
*now Olesno, Opole, Poland.				
Rosenberg*	We	B	1847-74	904,700
*now Susz, Olsztyn, Poland.				
Rosenthal*	He	M	1849-67	853,760
Rosenthal*	He	M	1851	853,763
Rosenthal (Frankenberg)	He	BMD	1808-11	853,769
Rossdorf (Darmstadt)	He	BMD	1823-72	870,543
Rossdorf (Marburg)	He	BD	1856-73	853,771
Rossow	Ne	BMD	1814-45	068,936
Rostock	Ro	BMD	1839-74	068,936
Rotenburg	He	M	1849-74	853,780
Rotenburg	He	M	1827-32	853,783
Roth (Biedenkopf)	He	BMD	1824-74	855,679
Rothenkirchen	He	M	1811-12	855,680
Rückingen	He	BD	1849-68	855,680
Rudigershagen	Er	BD	1818-20	1,185,019
Rügenwalde*	Pm	B	1846-61	1,184,450
*now Darowo, Koszalin, Poland.				
Ruttershausen	He	BMD	1823-75	870,557
Rybnik			See Baranowitz.	
Sagan*	Ns	Recs-12	1841-1937	1,184,450
*now Zagań, Zielona Góra, Poland.				
Sandhausen	Ba	BMD	1810-70	1,188,254
Sandersleben	Hl	BMD	1750-1926	1,185,012
Santomischel	*	BMD	1817-39	1,184,450
*now Zaniemysl, Poznań, Poland.				
Schildberg *		BMD	1835-46	747,832
*now Ostrzeszow, Poznań, Poland.				
Schlichtingsheim*	Ns	BMD	1835-47	896,081
Schlichtingsheim* (Kr. Fraustadt)	Ns	BMD	1835-59	1,184,450
*now Szlichtyngowa, Zielona Góra, Poland.				
Schloppe*	We	Recs-6	1750-unknown	1,184,450
*now Czopa, Koszalin, Poland.				
Schluchtern	Ba	D	1816-69	1,192,040
Schluchtern	Ba	M	1823-69	1,192,040
Schluchtern	Ba	B	1810-69	1,192,040
Schmalkalden	Su	BMD	1798-1921	1,185,013
Schmalkalden	Su	BD	1849-74	860,506
Schmalkalden	Su	BMD	1811-12	811,120
Schöneck	*	Recs-1	1871-1919	475,222
*now Skarszewy, Gdańsk, Poland.				
Schöningen	Ni	BMD	1809-12	958,254
Schonholthausen	Wf	B	1804-08	1,238,094
Schonholthausen	Wf	B	1820	1,238,094
Schonholthausen	Wf	D	1818	1,238,094
Schönlanke (Bez. Schneidemuhl)	*	BMD	1817-47	1,184,451
*now Trzcianka, Poznań, Poland.				
Schönstadt	He	BMD	1849-66	860,511
Schrecksbach	He	BD	1849-75	860,512
Schrecksbach	He	BMD	1824-72, 1883	801,306
Schriesheim	Ba	BMD	1811-69	1,192,040
Schriesheim	Ba	BMD	1810-70	1,257,316
Schrimm *		BMD	1817-47	758,361
*now Srem, Poznań, Poland.				
Schulitz	*	BMD	1823-47	719,152
*now Solec Kujawski, Bydgoszcz, Poland.				
Schwaan	Sc	BMD	1813-83	068,936
Schwaan	Sc	BMD	1813-83	1,185,013
Schwarza	Su	BMD	1825-75	1,185,013
Schwarzenborn (Ziegenhain)	He	BD	1824-74	860,517
Schwedt Oder	Fr	BD	1750-1860	1,185,013
Schweidnitz*	Ns	BMD	1854-75	1,184,451
*now Swidnica, Wrocaw, Poland.				
Schweinsberg	He	BMD	1808-09	860,532
Schweinsberg	He	M	1809-12	860,535
Schweinsberg	He	BD	1856-74	860,535
Schwerin	Sc	BMD	1849-75	1,185,014
Schwerin*	Br	BMD	1808-38	1,184,452
Schwerin*	Br	B	1839-46	1,184,453
Schwerin*	Br	BMD	1808-47	1,184,454
Schwerin*	Br	D	1845-47	1,184,455
Schwerin*	Br	D	1875-1918	1,184,455
Schwerin* (Warthe)	Br	Recs-15	Unknown	1,184,455
*now Skwierzyna, Zielona Góra, Poland.				
Seelow	Fr	D	1800-76	1,185,014
Sennfeld	Ba	6	1855-66	1,192,041
Sennfeld	Ba	BMD	1811-70	1,192,042
Sindolsheim	Ba	BMD	1812-70	1,192,041
Sindolsheim	Ba	*Bescheinigungen* (certificates)	1831-62	1,192,041
Sinsheim	Ba	B	1812-69	1,192,041
Sinsheim	Ba	M	1829-69	1,192,041
Sinsheim	Ba	D	1813-70	1,192,041

Södel	He	BMD	1823-61	870,557
Sohrau*	Sl	D	1837-79	1,184,456
*now Zory, Katowice, Poland.				
Soldin*	Br	BMD	1833-47	1,184,456
*now Myslibórz, Szczecin, Poland.				
Sontra	He	BMD	1808-09, 1812	811,128
Sontra	He	BMD	1810-11	811,129
Sontra	He	BMD	1820-34	860,568
Spachbrücken	He	BMD	1823-75	870,559
Speckswinkel	He	BMD	1808-61	860,106
Sprottau*	Ns	BMD	1811-1933	1,184,456
Sprottau*	Ns	Recs-14	1813-45	1,184,456
*now Szprotawa, Zielona Góra, Poland.				
Staden	He	BMD	1823-70	870,557
Städtel*	Sl	BMD	1810-73	1,184,456
*now Miejsce, Opole, Poland.				
Stadtengsfeld*	Su	BMD	1720-1813	1,185,014
Stadtengsfeld*	Su	BMD	1817-38	1,185,015
Stadtengsfeld*	Su	BMD	1838-75	1,185,016
Stadtengsfeld	Su	D	1840-1936	1,185,017
See also Eisenach.				
Stadtoldendorf	Ni	Recs-20	1774-1876	949,296
Stammheim	He	BMD	1826-70	870,558
Stargard*	Pm	Recs-16	ca. 1761	1,184,456
*now Stargard Szczeciński, Szczecin, Poland.				
Staussfurt	Ma	Recs-12	1874-1902	1,185,017
Staufenberg	He	BMD	1829-46	870,558
Stebbach	Ba	BM	1811-70	1,192,042
Stebbach	Ba	D	1811-69	1,192,046
Steinbach (Giessen)	He	BMD	1825-75	870,558
Steinberg	He		See Ortenberg, Watzenborn.	
Stiensfurt	Ba	BMD	1813-69	1,192,043
Steinfurth	He	BMD	1863-72	870,558
Stendal	Ma	Recs-16	1852-80	1,185,017
Sterbfritz	He	BMD	1826-74	860,133
Sternberg	Sc	BMD	1806-1937	1,185,017
Sterzhausen	He	BD	1849-65	860,134
Stettin*	Pm	Recs-16	1841-47	1,184,457
Stettin*	Pm	D	1845-49	1,184,457
Stettin*	Pm	BD	1854-74	1,184,458
Stettin*	Pm	M	1901-39	1,184,458
*now Szczecin, Szczecin, Poland.				
Stockheim (Büdingen)	He	BMD	1837-75	870,559
Strasburg*	We	Recs-5 (B)	1823-97	544,875
Strasburg*	We	BMD	1840-47	808,142
*now Brodnica, Bydgoszcz, Poland.				
Strelitz*	Ne	D	1760-1923	1,185,018
*now Neustrelitz.				
Striegau*	Ns	Recs-12	1850-1939	1,184,458
*now Strzegom, Wrocaw, Poland.				
Strümpfelbrunn	Bd	BMD	1867-70	1,185,183
Strümpfelbrunn	Bd	BMD	1810-66	1,185,184
Stuhm*	We	Recs-12	unknown	1,184,458
*now Sztum, Gdańsk, Poland.				
Tangermünde	Ma	Recs-20	1820-60	1,185,018
Tarnowitz*	Sl	BMD	1847-70	877,402
Tarnowitz*	Sl	BMD	1813-71	1,184,458
Tarnowitz*	Sl	D	1871-85	1,184,459
Tarnowitz*	Sl	D	1895-1901	1,184,460
*now Tarnowskie Góry, Katowice, Poland.				
Tempelburg*	Pm	BD	1829-52	1,184,460
*now Czaplinek, Koszalin, Poland.				
Tessin	Ro	BMD	1813-85	1,185,018
Teterow	Ne	BM	1813-80	1,185,018
Themar	Su	B	1876-1938	1,185,018
Themar	Su	Recs-20	1820-1920	1,185,018
Tirschtiegel*	Br	Recs-15	1834-48	1,184,460
*now Trzciel, Zielona Góra, Poland.				
Thorn	*	Recs-1	1818	496,009
*now Toruń, Bydgoszcz, Poland.				
Tost*	Ob	M	1886	1,184,461
Tost*	Ob	D	1841-72	1,184,461
*now Toszek, Katowice, Poland.				

Trachenberg*	Ns	Recs-12	unknown	1,184,461
*now Zmigrod, Wrocaw, Poland.				
Trebbin	Pt	Recs-16	1801	1,185,019
Trebbin	Pt	Recs-1	1692-1812	1,185,020
Tremessen	*	BMD	1832-47	719,242
*now Trzemeszno, Bydgoszcz, Poland.				
Treysa	He	B	1824-1902	858,243
Tumringen	Ba	6	1827-67	1,192,015
Tumringen		*Eheverkundingen* (publishing bans)		
Tumringen	Ba	B	1827-67	1,192,018
Tumringen	Ba	M	1829-67	1,192,018
Tumringen	Ba	D	1827-67	1,192,018
Tumringen	Ba	BD	1868-70	1,192,018
Unruhstadt*	Br	BMD	1817-74	1,184,461
*now Kargowa, Zielona Góra, Poland.				
Unterschüpf	Ba	BMD	1811-69	1,192,043
Usenborn	He	BMD	1829-75	870,559
Uttrichshausen	He	BMD	1837-73	858,246
Vacha*	Su	BMD	1815-76	1,185,019
Vacha	Su	BMD	1838-1920	1,185,021
see also Eisenach.				
Vandsburg	*	BMD	1825-47	719,323
*now Wiecbork, Bydgoszcz, Poland.				
Völkershausen*	Su		See Eisenbach.	
*Kr. Bad Salzungen				
Vollmerz	He	BMD	1780-1887	858,305
Wachenbuchen	He	BD	1849-69	858,305
Waldenburg*	Ns	BMD	1934-38	1,184,461
*now Wabrzych, Wrocaw, Poland.				
Walldorf (Werra)	Su	BMD	1839-1938	1,185,022
Waldurn	Ba	BMD	1810-29	1,057,177
Waldurn	Ba	BMD	1830-41	1,057,178
Waldurn	Ba	BMD	1842-55	1,057,179
Waldurn	Ba	BMD	1856-66	1,057,180
Waldurn	Ba	BMD	1867-70	1,057,181
Wanfried	He	BMD	1808-12	859,944
Watzenborn*	He	BMD	1824-75	870,560
*now Watzenborn-Steinberg.				
Weckesheim	He	BMD	1836-72	870,560
Weener	Ha	BMD	1859-60	1,187,668
Weener	Ha	BMD	1861-62	1,187,669
Wehrda (Marburg)	He	B	1849-66	859,948
Weiler	Ba	BMD	1811-69	1,192,043
Weimar	Er		See Eisenach.	
Weingarten	Ba	B	1857-60	1,192,043
Weingarten	Ba	B	1857-59	1,192,043
Weingarten	Ba	BMD	1812-70	1,192,044
Weingarten	Ba	B	1832-59	1,192,044
Weinheim	Ba	BMD	1811-69	1,192,044
Weiterstadt	He	BMD	1823-72	870,561
Wenings	He	BMD	1834-75	871,590
Westpreussen Province		Recs-16	1812, 1845	1,184,441
Wieschowa* (Kr. Tarnowitz)	Sl	BD	1847-48	877,421
*now Wieszowa, Katowice, Poland.				
Wieseck*	He	BMD	1825-75	871,590
*now part of Giessen.				
Wiesloch	Ba	BM	1811-24	1,192,043
Wiesloch	Ba	MD	1811-24	1,192,043
Wiesloch	Ba	BMD	1811-24	1,192,043
Willingshausen	He	BD	1849-73	864,610
Willingshausen	He	BMD	1824-72, 1883	801,306
Windecken	He	BMD	1825-74	864,611
Wittelsberg	He	BMD	1849-65	868,036
Wittenberg	Sc	BMD	1813-77	068,936
Wittmund	Ha	B	1804-32	1,257,054
Wittmund	Ha	M	1844-72	1,257,054
Wittmund	Ha	D	1723-1886	1,237,054
Wohnbach	He	BMD	1823-75	871,591
Wohra	He	BD	1856-73	864,623
Woldenberg* (Neumarkt)	Pm	BMD	1770-1854	1,184,461
*now Dobiegniew, Zielona Góra, Poland.				

Wolfenbüttel	Ni	BMD	1808-14	958,025
Wolferode	He	BD	1856-73	864,624
Wollenberg	Ba	Index	1811-46	1,192,046
Wollenberg	Ba	6	1820-69	1,192,046
Wollenberg	Ba	M	1811-69	1,192,046
Wollenberg	Ba	BD	1811-69	1,192,046
Wommen	He	BMD	1809-13	806,659
Wronke (Warthe)	*	Recs-1	1832-unknown	1,184,461
*now Wronki, Poznań, Poland.				
Zabrze*	Ob	M	1882-83	1,184,461
Zabrze* (Hindenburg)	Ob	Recs-12	1873-1940	1,184,419
*now Zabrze, Katowice, Poland.				
Zielhard	He	BMD	1828-75	870,538
Ziegenhain	He	B	1849-73	868,694
Zimmersrode	He	BMD	1809-12	868,618
Züntersbach	He	BMD	1827-75	868,618

Polish Jewish Records On Microfilm

The following list of Polish Jewish records available at the library of the Genealogical Society of Utah in Salt Lake City is a compilation from a list prepared by *Toledot: The Journal of Jewish Genealogy* and those records added to the collection since 1978. The editors would like to express their gratitude to Steven W. Siegel of Toledot Press, 155 East 93rd Street, Suite C, New York, NY 10028 for kind permission to use the previously published portions of this list.

The collection consists mainly of birth, marriage, and death records of Jews in Polish communities during the 1800s. Some German communities which later became a part of Poland are also included. The records were filmed at the Polish State Archives. It is important to understand that:

1. Not all Polish towns with Jewish citizens are listed.
2. Not all Jewish records in the archives were filmed.
3. Not every community maintained records.
4. Some records have been lost or destroyed.
5. Small towns did not maintain their own records. Their records can be found in the collection of a larger neighboring community.
6. Jewish communities in Poland did not keep vital records until required by civil authorities in the various countries having jurisdiction: Austrian Poland, 1784 (most compiled by 1850), Russian Poland, 1808 (most begin in 1826), and German Poland, 1876.

The list is arranged alphabetically by the name of the Polish community (column 1). "See" and "see also" references indicate that records pertaining to a particular community may (also) be found with the records of the cross-referenced places.

The second column is a code for the name of the traditional province in which the community is situated. The following codes are used:

Bi	Bialystock	Kr	Krakow	Rz	Rzeszów
By	Bydgoszcz	Ló	Lódź	Sz	Szczecin
Gd	Gdańsk	Lu	Lublin	Wa	Warszawa
Ka	Katowice	Ol	Olsztyn	Wr	Wroclaw
Ki	Kielce	Op	Opole	Zi	Zielona Góra
Ko	Koszalin	Po	Poznań		

The third column refers to the type of records available on microfilm for that place. "B", "M", and "D" indicate, respectively, birth, marriage, and death records. "-Ind" following "B", "M", or "D" refers to an index for that particular group of records. (However, many of the records are indexed without such an indication in the list.) The following additional abbreviations are used in column 3:

Recs-1	Records about Jews.
Recs-2	Representatives and administrative employees of the Jewish community.
Recs-3	Jewish records for this locality are included on a series of microfilm reels of the civil registers. Consult the library of the Genealogical Society of Utah in Salt Lake City for the reel numbers of the Jewish materials.
Recs-4	Naturalization of foreigners including Jews.
Recs-5	Jewish records for this locality are included on a series of microfilm reels of Roman Catholic records. Consult the library of the Genealogical Society of Utah in Salt Lake City for reel numbers of the Jewish records.
Recs-6	Family book of the Jewish community, including names and birthdates.
Recs-7	Cemetery records 1830-1930 and Chronicle 1889-1901.
Recs-8	Family burial plots.
Recs-9	Naturalized Jews 1814, unidentified index, and deaths nineteenth century.
Recs-10	Jewish school records.
Recs-11	Military duty.
Recs-12	Cemetery records.
Recs-13	Voting lists.
Recs-14	Lists of incoming/outgoing Jews.
Recs-15	Register of naturalized Jews and heads of families.
Recs-16	List of Jews.
Recs-17	Circumcisions.
Recs-18	Conversions.
Recs-19	List of Jews paying duties.
Recs-20	Divorces.

Column 4 is the span of years for which records in column 3 are available. It must be noted, however, that the records may *not* be complete for the entire span indicated, as there are often gaps in the records.

The fifth column occasionally contains the letter "G", which means that the records are in German rather than in Polish. The "G" designation refers to those communities which were German territory at the time the records were created. However, not every former German town in this list is so indicated.

The last column refers to the microfilm reel number used by the library of the Genealogical Society of Utah to identify that particular set of records. Use this number to order film from Salt Lake City. A particular reel sometimes contains records for more than one community, although quite frequently the records for a particular town occupy more than one reel.

Community	Province	Record Type	Record Span	Genealogical Society Record Number
Aleksandrów*	Lo	BMD	1826-44	678,740
Aleksandrów*	Lo	BMD	1845-57	678,741
Aleksandrów*	Lo	BMD	1858-65	678,742
Aleksandrów (Lodzki)	Lo	BMD	1866-70	678,743
Aleksawdrow	Lo	BMD	1826-44	678,740
Aleksawdrow	Lo	BMD	1845-57	678,741
Aleksawdrow	Lo	BMD	1858-65	678,742
Aleksawdrow	Lo	BMD	1866-70	766,346
Aleksawdrow	Lo	BMD	1871-75	1,189,025
Aleksawdrow	Lo	BMD	1876	1,189,026
Andrzejewo	Wa	BMD	1808-19	808,606
Andrzejewo	Wa	BMD	1814-20	808,607
Andrzejewo	Wa	BMD	1819-25	808,608
Andrzejewo	Wa	BMD	1826-36	808,589
Andrzejewo	Wa	BMD	1838-59	808,590

Andrzejewo	Wa	BMD	1826-38	808,614
Andrzejewo	Wa	BMD	1839-50	808,615
Andrzejewo	Wa	BMD	1851-59	808,616
Annopol	Lu	BMD	1826-55	681,139
Babiak	Po	BMD	1826-59	810,118
Babimost	Zi	Recs-1	1847-99 G	474,924
Babimost	Zi	Recs-2	1848-1916 G	474,931
Bakalarzewo	Bi	BMD	1826-41	746,481
Bakalarzewo	Bi	BMD	1842-62	746,482
Bakalarzewo	Bi	BMD	1866-67	1,191,894
Bakalarzewo	Bi	BMD	1870-75	1,191,894
Bakalarzewo	Bi	BMD	1877	1,191,894
Baranów	Lu	BMD	1827-55	681,154
Baronów	Lu	BMD	1856-75	681,155
Baronów	Lu	BMD	1879-1905	681,156
Baranowice	Ka	BMD	1812-70 G	879,596
Baranowice	Ka	BMD	1810-74 G	879,597
Baranowice	Ka	BMD	1810-70 G	879,598
Barlinek	Sz	BMD	1847-53 G	544,649
Bartoszyce	Ol	D	1852-1938	1,184,377
Bedków	Lo	BMD	1826-46	681,063
Bedzin	Ka	BMD	1826-30	766,055
Bedzin	Ka	BMD	1831-44	766,056
Bedzin	Ka	BMD	1845-56	766,057
Bedzin	Ka	BMD	1857-59	766,058
Belchatów*	Lo	BMD	1824-43	681,038
Belchatów*	Lo	BMD	1844-51	681,039
Belchatów*	Lo	BMD	1852-60	681,040
Belchatów*	Lo	BMD	1861-65	681,041
*See also Szczerców.				
Belchow	Lo	BMD	1824	681,038
Belchow	Lo	BMD	1828-43	681,038
Belchow	Lo	BMD	1844-51	681,039
Belchow	Lo	BMD	1852-60	681,040
Belchow	Lo	BMD	1861-65	681,041
Belchow	Lo	BMD	1873-74	1,189,029
Belźyce	Lu	BMD	1826-42	681,163
Belźyce	Lu	BMD	1843-49	681,164
Belźyce	Lu	BMD	1830-54	681,165
Belźyce	Lu	MD	1826-59	681,166
Belźyce	Lu	BMD	1855-64	681,167
Belźyce	Lu	BMD	1866-68	767,802
Berlinek	Zi	BMD	1763-1936	1,184,378
Biala Podlaska	Lu		See Kodeń, Terespol.	
Biala Podlaska	Lu	BMD	1845	1,199,950
Biala Podlaska	Lu	BMD	1853-64	1,199,951
Biala Podlaska	Lu	BMD	1865-73	1,199,952
Biala Rawska	Lo	BMD	1826-68	681,070
Bialobrzegi	Ki		See Przybyszew.	
Bialogard	Ko	BMD	1870-72	1,184,377
Bialogard	Ko	BMD	1853-69	1,184,378
Bialystoki	Bi	BMD	1835-60 G	747,735
Bialystoki	Bi	BMD	1861-63 G	747,736
Bialystoki	Bi	BMD	1864-65 G	747,737
Bialystoki	Bi	B	1866, 1869	1,191,933
Bialystoki	Bi	M	1866-75	1,191,934
Bialystoki	Bi	D	1866-69	1,191,934
Bialystok	Bi	M	1878	1,191,934
Bialystok	Bi	B	1871-72	1,191,935
Bialystok	Bi	M	1871-72	1,191,935
Bialystok	Bi	D	1870-72	1,191,935
Bialystok	Bi	MD	1873	1,191,936
Bialystok	Bi	BMD	1874-77	1,191,936
Bialystok	Bi	B	1878	1,191,936
Bialystok	Bi	BM	1878	1,191,937
Biecz	Rz	BD	1850-68	753,059
Bielawy	Lo	BMD	1826-41	681,078
Bielawy	Lo	BMD	1842-55	681,079
Bielsk	Wa	BMD	1826-50	729,200
Bielsk	Wa	BMD	1851-65	729,201
Bielsk Podlanski	Bi	BMD	1835	1,191,937
Bieruń Nowy	Ka	BMD	1847-70 G	864,953
Bierutow	Wr	BMD	1847-77	1,184,378, 1,184,379
Biezuń	Wa	BMD	1857-58	702,625
Bilgoraj	Lu		See Józefów.	
Biskupice	Lu	BMD	1826-55	689,827
Biskupice	Lu	BD	1826-62	689,828
Blaszki	Po	BMD	1826-67	588,121
Blaszki	Po	B	1871-93	127,713
Blaszki	Po	B	1899-1921	127,714
Blaszki	Pd	BMD	1899-1939	127,715
Blaszki	Pd	BMD	1892-1939	127,716
Bledzew	Zi	Recs-1	1839-88 G	474,923
Bobolice	Ko	BMD	1816-18	1,184,406
Bobrownski	Wa	BMD	1826-28	689,496
Bobrownski	Wa	BMD	1829-33	702,431
Bobrownski	Wa	BMD	1834-50	702,432
Bobrownski	Wa	BMD	1851-58	702,433
Bochnia	Kr		See Wisnicz.	
Bodzanow	Wa	BMD	1826-50	729,202
Bodzanow	Wa	BMD	1851-65	729,203
Bodzentyn-Kielce		BMD	1869-70	1,192,415
Bodzentyn-Kielce		BMD	1869-74	1,192,416
Bogoria	Ki	BMD	1826-47	813,072
Bogoria	Ki	BMD	1848-65	588,927
Bogoria	Ki	BMD	1866-77	1,199,823
Boleslawiec	Lo	BMD	1826-38	681,099
Boleslawiec	Wr	Recs-12	1840-1933	1,184,406
Brzeg	Op	M	1809-74	1,184,405
Brzeg	Op	D	1810-74	1,184,406
Brzeg	Op	Recs-12	Unknown	1,184,406
Brzeg	Op	B	1794-98	1,184,407
Brzeg	Op	B	1809-74	1,184,407
Bolimów	Lo	BMD	1826-58	681,111
Bolimów	Lo	Recs-3	1737-1870	
Boźenica	Bi		See Rosochate, Rutki.	
Brodnica	By	B	1823-97 G	544,875
Brodnica	By	BMD	1840-47	808,142
Brójce	Zi	BM	1847	807,873
Brok	Wa	BMD	1826-56	808,604
Brok	Wa	BMD	1857-65	808,605
Brzesko	Kr	BM	1849-86 G	948,419
Brzeziny*	Lo	BMD	1826-44	689,703
Brzeziny*	Lo	BMD	1845-56	689,704
Brzeziny*	Lo	BMD	1857-65	689,705
Brzeziny*	Lo	BMD	1866-70	766,370
*See also Bedków, Jezów, Stryków, Ujazd.				
Brzeznica	Lo	BMD	1826-48	689,720
Brzeznica (Nowa Osada)	Lo	BMD	1849-64	689,721
Burzenin	Lo	BMD	1826-64	689,741
Bychawa	Lu	BMD	1826-55	689,851
Bychawa	Lu	D	1836-44	689,852
Bychawa	Lu	BMD	1845-54	689,853
Bydgoszcz*	By	BMD	1823-65 G	813,087
Bydgoszcz*	By	Recs-4	1852-53 G	475,863
Bydgoszcz*	By	Recs-4	1854-55 G	475,864
Bydgoszcz*	By	Recs-4	1870-71 G	475,865
Bydgoszcz*	By	Recs-4	1871-72 G	475,866
*See also Fordon, Koronowo.				
Bytom	Ka	BMD	1840-1940	1,184,404
Bytom	Ka	B	1880-86	1,184,405
Bytom	Ka	M	1880-85	1,184,405
Bytom	Ka	M	1921-25	1,184,405
Bytom	Ka	M	1935-38	1,184,405
Bytom	Ka	D	1889-1940	1,184,405
Bytom	Ka	D	1867-88	1,184,405
Ceglow	Wa	BMD	1826-36	702,434
Checiny	Ki	BMD	1866-68	1,192,416
Checiny	Ki	BMD	1869-73	1,192,417
Checiny	Ki	BMD	1874-77	1,192,418
Chelm*	Lu	D	1823, 1853-66	702,696
Chelm*	Lu	B	1826-28, 1857-64	702,674
Chelm*	Lu	M	1851-61	702,674
Chelm*	Lu	BMD	1828, 1855-60	702,680
Chelm*	Lu	BMD	1843-47	702,672
Chelm*	Lu	BMD	1848-54	702,673
Chelm*	Lu	BMD	1861-69	702,681
Chelm*	Lu	BMD	1870-84	702,682
Chelm*	Lu	BMD	1885-88	702,683

Community	Province	Record Type	Record Span	Genealogical Society Record Number
Chelm*	Lu	BMD	1889-94	702,684
Chelm*	Lu	BMD	1895-98	702,685
Chelm*	Lu	BMD	1899-1901	702,686
Chelm*	Lu	BMD	1902-04	702,687
Chelm*	Lu	BMD	1905-09	702,688
Chelm*	Lu	BMD	1910-13	702,689
Chelm*	Lu	M	1914	702,675
Chelm*	Lu	B	1923-25	702,675
Chelm*	Lu	M	1924-28, 1936	702,679
Chelm*	Lu	D	1924-27	702,679
Chelm*	Lu	BM	1915	702,679
Chelm*	Lu	B	1926-29	702,676
Chelm*	Lu	BMD	1930-31	702,690
Chelm*	Lu	B	1931, 1936	702,677
Chelm*	Lu	BMD	1932-33	702,691
Chelm*	Lu	BMD	1934	702,692
Chelm*	Lu	BMD	1935	702,693
Chelm*	Lu	BMD	1937	702,694
Chelm*	Lu	BMD	1938	702,695
Chelm*	Lu	B	1937, 1939	702,678
*See also Siedliszcze, Swierze, Wojslawice.				
Chelm	Lu	BMD	1843-47	702,672
Chelm	Lu	BMD	1848-54	702,673
Chelm	Lu	B	1826-28	702,674
Chelm	Lu	M	1851-61	702,674
Chelm	Lu	D	1857-64	702,674
Chelm	Lu	M	1914	702,675
Chelm	Lu	B	1923-25	702,675
Chelm	Lu	B	1926-29	702,676
Chelm	Lu	B	1931, 1936	702,677
Chelm	Lu	B	1937, 1939	702,678
Chelm	Lu	M	1924-36	702,679
Chelm	Lu	D	1924-27	702,679
Chelm	Lu	BD	1915	702,679
Chelm	Lu	MD	1828	702,680
Chelm	Lu	BMD	1855-60	702,680
Chelm	Lu	BMD	1861-69	702,681
Chelm	Lu	BMD	1870-84	702,682
Chelm	Lu	BMD	1885, 1887	702,683
Chelm	Lu	BMD	1888	702,683
Chelm	Lu	BMD	1889, 1890	702,684
Chelm	Lu	BMD	1894	702,684
Chelm	Lu	BMD	1895-98	702,685
Chelm	Lu	BMD	1899-1901	702,686
Chelm	Lu	BMD	1902-04	702,687
Chelm	Lu	BMD	1905, 1907	702,688
Chelm	Lu	BMD	1909	702,688
Chelm	Lu	BMD	1910-13	702,689
Chelm	Lu	BMD	1930-31	702,689
Chelm	Lu	BMD	1932-33	702,691
Chelm	Lu	BMD	1934	702,692
Chelm	Lu	BMD	1935	702,693
Chelm	Lu	BMD	1937	702,694
Chelm	Lu	BMD	1938	702,695
Chelm	Lu	BD	1823	702,695
Chelm	Lu	BMD	1853-59	702,692
Chelm	Lu	D	1859-66	702,696
Chmielnik	Ki	BMD	1876-77	1,192,418
Chojnów	Wr	BD	1888-1936	1,184,419
Chorzele	Wa	BMD	1826-41	723,213
Chorzele	Wa	BMD	1842-54	723,214
Chorzele	Wa	BMD	1855-63	723,215
Chorzow	Ka	D	1867-1940	1,184,430
Choszczno	Sz	BMD	1847-53 G	544,649
Choszczno	Sz	BD	1778-1812	1,184,377
Ciechanów	Wa	BMD	1826-41	702,466
Ciechanów	Wa	BMD	1842-54	702,467
Ciechanów	Wa	BMD	1855-63	702,468
Ciechanowiec	Bi	BMD	1847-51	1,186,427
Ciechanowiec	Bi	BMD	1853, 1856	1,186,427
Ciechanowiec	Bi	BMD	1868, 1869	1,186,427
Ciechanowiec	Bi	BMD	1888, 1890	1,186,427
Ciechanowiec	Bi	BMD	1899, 1901	1,186,427
Ciechanowiec	Bi	B	1935	1,186,427
Ciechanowiec	Bi	M	1843-44	1,186,427
Ciechanowiec	Bi	M	1846, 1859	1,186,427
Ciechanowiec	Bi	M	1860, 1867	1,186,427
Ciechanowiec	Bi	BMD	1839	1,191,937
Ciechanowiec	Bi	BMD	1843-47	1,191,937
Ciechanowiec	Bi	BMD	1849-51	1,191,937
Ciechanowiec	Bi	BMD	1853	1,191,937
Ciechanowiec	Bi	BD	1854, 1856	1,191,937
Ciechanowiec	Bi	BD	1857	1,191,937
Ciechanowiec	Bi	D	1858	1,191,937
Ciechanowiec	Bi	B	1859	1,191,937
Ciechanowiec	Bi	BM	1865	1,191,937
Ciechanowiec	Bi	BMD	1867-70	1,191,937
Ciepielów	Ki	BMD	1826-56	813,909
Ciepielów	Ki	BMD	1857-65	813,910
Ciepielów	Ki	BMD	1866-70	1,192,418
Ciepielów	Ki	BMD	1871-73	1,192,419
Czaplinek	Ko	BD	1829-52 G	1,184,460
Czemierniki	Lu	BMD	1810-59	723,592
Czempin	Po	Recs-12	unknown	1,184,406
Czersk	Wa	BMD	1828-36	723,683
Czerwińsk	Wa	BMD	1826-65	689,633
Czestochowa*	Ka	BMD	1826-40	875,326
Czestochowa*	Ka	BMD	1841-51	875,327
Czestochowa*	Ka	BMD	1852-59	875,328
Czestochowa*	Ka	BMD	1860-65	875,329
*See also Mstów, Przyrow.				
Czlopa	Ko	Recs-6	1750-unknown G	1,184,450
Czyzewo	Bi	BMD	1808-19	808,606
Czyzewo	Bi	BMD	1814-20	808,607
Czyzewo	Bi	BMD	1819-25	808,608
Czyzewo	Bi	BMD	1826-38	808,614
Czyzewo	Bi	BMD	1839-50	808,615
Czyzewo	Bi	BMD	1851-59	808,616
Czyzewo	Bi	BMD	1860-65	747,701
Czyew-Osada	Bi	BMD	1866-74	1,199,529
Czyew-Osada	Bi	B	1875	1,199,529
Dabie	Po	BMD	1826-49	810,675
Dabie	Po	BMD	1850-65	810,676
Daleszyce	Ki	BMD	1826-46	729,025
Daleszyce	Ki	BMD	1847-65	729,026
Daleszyce	Ki	BMD	1866-70	1,192,419
Darlowo	Ko	BMD	1846-61	1,184,450
Debica	Kr		See Tarnów.	
Dobiegniew	Zi	BMD	1770-1854	1,184,461
Dobre Miasto	Ol	D	1846-unknown	1,184,419
Dobrodzien	Ka	D	1846-80	1,184,419
Dobrzyn Nad Drweca			See Golub-Dobrzyń.	
Dobrzyn Nad Wisla	By	Recs-3	1808-65	
Drawskd Pomorskie	Ko	BMD	1779-1874	1,184,410
Drobin	Wa	BMD	1826-46	729,204
Drobin	Wa	BMD	1847-64	729,205
Dubienka	Lu	BMD	1826-39	729,418
Dubienka	Lu	BMD	1840-52	729,419
Dubienka	Lu	BMD	1853-63	729,420
Dzerzoniów	Wr	Recs-12	1830-1930	1,184,449
Dzialoszyce	Ki	BMD	1810-20	588,908
Dzialoszyce	Ki	BMD	1821-27	588,909
Dzialoszyce	Ki	B	1826-56	588,913
Dzialoszyce	Ki	BM	1826-64	814,603
Dzialoszyce	Ki	MD	1826-64	814,604
Dzialoszyce	Ki	BMD	1849-65	814,605
Dzialoszyn	Lo	BMD	1828, 1837	702,383
Dzierzgowo	Wa	Recs-3	1808-65	
Dzierżoniów	Wr	Recs-7		
Elblag	Gd	BMD	1812-71	742,026
Filipów	Bi	BMD	1829-55	746,504
Filipów	Bi	BMD	1856-65	746,505
Filipów	Bi	BMD	1866-67	1,191,984

Filipów	Bi	BMD	1870-77	1,191,985
Firlej	Lu	BMD	1826-31	729,183
Fordon	By	BMD	1820-51 G	814,573
Fordon	By	BMD	1823-51 G	814,574
Fordon	By	BMD	1849-88 G	814,575
Frombork	Ol	Recs-12	unknown	1,184,411
Gdańsk	Gd	B	1847-54 G	742,680
Gdańsk	Gd	B	1854-57 G	742,681
Gdańsk	Gd	B	1850-62 G	742,682
Gdańsk	Gd	B	1861-64 G	742,683
Gdańsk	Gd	B	1864-65 G	742,684
Gdańsk	Gd	M	1848-51 G	742,684
Gdańsk	Gd	M	1851-55 G	742,685
Gdańsk	Gd	M	1853-57 G	742,686
Gdańsk	Gd	M	1857-59 G	742,687
Gdańsk	Gd	M	1860-63 G	742,688
Gdańsk	Gd	M	1860-63 G	742,777
Gdańsk	Gd	M	1862-63 G	742,778
Gdańsk	Gd	M	1864-65 G	742,779
Gdańsk	Gd	D	1852-55 G	742,780
Gdańsk	Gd	D	1855-59 G	742,781
Gdańsk	Gd	D	1859-64 G	742,782
Gdańsk	Gd	D	1864-65 G	742,783
Gdańsk	Gd	B	1905-39 G	1,184,407
Gdańsk	Gd	BMD	1837-83 G	1,184,407
Gdańsk	Gd	D	1889-1940 G	1,184,408
Gdańsk	Gd	Recs-8	1848-1909 G	1,184,409
Gdańsk	Gd	Recs-9	G	1,184,410
Gebice	By	BMD	1832-47	719,219
Gliwice	Ka	BMD	1812-61 G	875,339
Gliwice	Ka	Recs-12	1903-40	1,184,450
Gliwice	Ka	D	ca. 1800	1,184,458
Glogow	Zi	BMD	1812-40	1,184,415
Glogow	Zi	BMD	1812-40	1,184,416
Glogow	Zi	Recs-12	1812-40	1,184,418
Glowno	Lo	BMD	1812-33	702,417
Glowno	Lo	BMD	1834-43	702,418
Glowno	Lo	BMD	1844-53	702,419
Glowno	Lo	BMD	1854-65	702,420
Glowno	Lo	BMD	1866-70	767,085
Glowno	Lo	BMD	1812-33	702,417
Glowno	Lo	BMD	1834-43	702,418
Glowno	Lo	BMD	1844-53	702,419
Glowno	Lo	BMD	1854-65	702,420
Glowno	Lo	BMD	1866-70	767,085
Glowno	Lo	BMD	1871-76	1,192,278
Glubczyce	Op	D	1818-1937	1,184,434
Gniewkowo	By	BMD	1815-47 G	719,220
Gniezno	Po	BMD	1840-47	719,426
Gdleniow	Sz	Recs-6	1860-1934	1,184,417
Golina	Po	BMD	1826-38	719,441
Golina	Po	BMD	1840-62	719,442
Golub-Dobrzýn	By	BMD	1808-19,	812,350,
			1819-25	812,349
Golub-Dobrzýn	By	BMD	1826-40	812,351
Golub-Dobrzýn	By	BMD	1826-50	812,352
Golub-Dobrzýn	By	BMD	1851-59	812,353
Golub-Dobrzýn	By	BMD	1858-65	812,354
Gora Kalwaria	Wa	BMD	1826-47	723,681
Gora Kalwaria	Wa	BMD	1848-59	723,682
Góra Pulawska	Lu	Recs-3	1810-65	
Gorlice	Rz		See Biecz.	
Gorzków	Lu	BMD	1826-46	808,092
Gorzków	Lu	BMD	1847-55	808,093
Gorzków	Lu	BMD	1856-70	767,825
Gorzow Slaski	Op	D	1843-44	1,184,432
Gowarczów	Ki	BMD	1826-40	716,402
Gowarczów	Ki	BMD	1841-59	716,403
Grabowiec	Lu	BMD	1826-36	808,189
Grabowiec	Lu	BMD	1837-54	808,190
Grabowiec	Lu	BMD	1855-65	808,191
Grabowiec	Lu	BMD	1866-67	767,826
Grajewo	Bi	BMD	1834-57	747,019
Grajewo	Bi	BMD	1871-73	1,199,529
Grajewo	Bi	BMD	1874-75	1,199,530
Grocholice	Lo	BMD	1826-45	723,499

Grocholice	Lo	D	1827-30	767,091
Grocholice	Lo	BMD	1831-69	767,091
Grodzisk				
Mazowiecki	Wa		See Wishitki.	
Grójec*	Wa	BMD	1826-36	723,673
Grójec*	Wa	BMD	1826-42	723,674
Grójec*	Wa	BMD	1843-57	723,675
Grójec*	Wa	BMD	1858-64	723,676
*See also Czersk, Mogielnica, Tarczyn, Warka.				
Gromadno	By	B	1874-76	1,257,375
Gromadno	By	B	1877	1,257,376
Gromadno	By	D	1874-77	1,257,376
Grupa	By	B	1874-75	1,257,371
Grupa	By	M	1874	1,257,371
Grupa	By	D	1874	1,257,372
Grupa	By	M	1875-76	1,257,372
Grupa	By	B	1875-76	1,257,372
Grupa	By	D	1876-77	1,257,372
Horodlo	Lu	BMD	1826-54	807,824
Hrubieszów	Lu	BMD	1826-38	807,844
Hrubieszów	Lu	BMD	1839-40	807,845
Hrubieszów	Lu	BMD	1841-46	807,739
Hrubieszów	Lu	BMD	1847-52	807,740
Hrubieszów	Lu	BMD	1853-59	807,741
Hrubieszów	Lu	BMD	1860-65	807,742
Hrubieszów	Lu	BMD	1866-67	767,828
Hrubieszów*	Lu	BMD		
*See also Grabowiec, Uchanie.				
Ilawa	Ol		See Susz.	
Ilza	Ki	BMD	1866-70	1,192,419
Ilza	Ki	BMD	1871-75	1,192,420
Ilza	Ki	BMD	1850-61	714,995
Ilza	Ki	BMD	1862-65	714,996
Inowroclaw	By		See Gniewkowo.	
Izbica	Lu	BMD	1826-46	807,755
Izbica	Lu	BMD	1847-58	807,756
Izbica-Kwawska	Po	BMD	1810-35	741,831
Izbica-Kwawska	Po	BMD	1836-52	741,832
Izbica-Kwawska	Po	BMD	1853-65	741,833
Jablonka Koscielna	Bi	BMD	1827-65	747,702
Jablonka Koscielna	Bi	BMD	1838, 1849	1,186,444
Jablonka Koscielna	Bi	BMD	1857, 1864	1,186,444
Jablonka Koscielna	Bi	BMD	1865, 1869	1,186,444
Jablonka Koscielna	Bi	M	1851, 1888	1,186,444
Jablonka Koscielna	Bi	M	1851, 1888	1,186,444
Jablonka				
Swierczewo	Bi	BMD	1838-88	1,046,484
Jablonka	Bi	BMD	1866, 1871	1,199,530
Janów Podlaski	Lu	BMD	1826-39,	807,766,
			1840-43	807,767
Janów Podlaski	Lu	BMD	1844-65	807,768
Janów Podlaski	Lu	BMD	1866-69	937,498
Janowiec	Lu	BMD	1817-41	813,880
Janowiec	Lu	BMD	1842-57	813,881
Janowiec	By	B	1874-75	1,257,377
Janowiec	By	M	1874-75	1,257,377
Janowiec	By	D	1874-75	1,257,377
Janowiec	By	BMD	1876-77	1,257,378
Jarczów	Lu	BMD	1827-50	813,882
Jarczów	Lu	BMD	1851-65	813,883
Jarczów	Lu	BMD	1866-70	937,498
Jaroszyn	Lu		See Góra Pulawska.	
Jastrowie	Ko	BMD	1816-39	1,184,420
Jastrowie	Ko	BMD	1840-47	1,184,421
Jastrowie	Ko	B	1830	1,184,421
Jawor	Wr	BMD	1806-39	1,184,422
Jedrzejów	Ki		See Sobków.	
Jezow	Lo	BMD	1826-60	723,535
Jezow	Lo	BMD	1861-65	723,536
Jezow	Lo	BMD	1866-70	767,101
Jezow	Lo	BMD	1871-76	1,257,770
Józefow*	Lu	B	1810-18	813,884
Józefow*	Lu	M	1810-18	813,885
(Bilgoraj)				
Józefow*	Lu	BMD	1810-25	813,886
Józefow*	Lu	BMD	1823-26	813,887

Community	Province	Record Type	Record Span	Genealogical Society Record Number
Józefow*	Lu	BMD	1826-43	813,893
Józefow (Bilgoraj)	Lu	BMD	1844-63	813,894
Józefów (Bilgoraj)	Lu	BMD	1826-45	813,895
Józefów (Opole Lubeiskie)	Lu	BMD	1846-62	813,896
Józefów Nad Wisla	Lu	B	1863	905,146
Józefów Nad Wisla	Lu	BMD	1866-68	905,146
Kalisz*	Po	BMD	1809-20	743,141
Kalisz*	Po	BMD	1821-28	743,142
Kalisz*	Po	BMD	1829-37	743,143
Kalisz*	Po	BMD	1838-45	743,144
Kalisz*	Po	BMD	1846-51	743,145
Kalisz*	Po	BMD	1852-57	743,146
Kalisz*	Po	BMD	1858-61	743,147
Kalisz*	Po	BMD	1862-65	743,148
*See also Blaszki, Stawiszyn.				
Kaluszyn	Wa	BMD	1826-32	702,435
Kaluszyn	Wa	BMD	1833-40	702,436
Kaluszyn	Wa	BMD	1841-46	702,437
Kaluszyn	Wa	BMD	1847-52	702,438
Kaluszyn	Wa	BMD	1853-59	702,439
Kaluszyn	Wa	BMD	1860-63	702,440
Kaluszyn	Wa	BMD	1864-65	702,441
Kamienna Góra	Wr	BMD	1800-1938	1,184,432
Kamiensk	Lo	BMD	1826-51	723,552
Kamiensk	Lo	BMD	1852-57	723,553
Kamionka-Lubartow	Lu	BMD	1826-65	813,843
Karczew	Wa	BMD	1826-41	702,442
Karczew	Wa	BMD	1842-64	702,443
Karczew	Wa	BMD	1842-72	702,444
Kargowa	Zi	BMD	1817-74	1,184,461
Kartuzy	Gd	Recs-1	1848-73 G	475,222
Katowice	Ka	B	1860-1936	1,184,423
Katowice	Ka	D	1869-1934	1,184,424
Katowice	Ka	D	1850-1939	1,184,425
Katowice	Ka	D	1825-1939	1,184,426
Katowice	Ka	Recs-12	1868-97	1,184,428
Katy Wroclawskie	Wr	BMD	1812-37	1,184,423
Kazanow	Ki	BMD	1828-57	730,310
Kazimierz	Lu	BMD	1826-41	813,859
Kazimierz	Lu	BMD	1842-63	813,860
Kepno	Po	BMD	1825-35 G	742,975
Kepno	Po	BMD	1836-41 G	742,976
Kepno	Po	BMD	1842-47 G	742,977
Ketrzyn	Ol	BMD	1813-74	1,184,447
Kielce	Ki		See Checiny.	
Kielce	Ki	BMD	1868-72	1,192,420
Kielce	Ki	BMD	1873-77	1,192,421
Kisielice	Ol	BMD	1893-1930	1,184,413
Klimontów	Ki	BMD	1826-39	809,129
Klimontów	Ki	BMD	1840-53	809,130
Klimontów	Ki	BMD	1854-61	809,131
Klimontów	Ki	BMD	1862-65	809,132
Klimontów	Ki	D	1861-70	1,199,823
Klimontów	Ki	BMD	1862-66	1,199,823
Klimontów	Ki	BMD	1862-66	1,199,824
Klimontów	Ki	BMD	1867-70	1,199,824
Klimontów	Ki	BMD	1866-74	1,199,825
Klimontów	Ki	BMD	1875-77	1,199,826
Klimontów	Ki	B	1874-78	1,199,826
Klobuck	Ka	BMD	1826-60	879,546
Klobuck	Ka	BMD	1856-64	879,547
Klobuck	Ka	BMD	1859-77	1,199,680
Klobuck			See also Krzepice.	
Klodawa	Po	BMD	1826-31	743,000
Klodawa	Po	BMD	1832-58	743,001
Klodawa	Po	BMD	1859-65	743,002
Klodzko	Wr	BMD	1832-1940	1,184,414
Klucbork	Op	BD	1813-15	890,725
Klucbork	Op	BMD	1830-55	1,184,431
Klukowo	Bi	M	1934, 1936	1,186,445
Klwow	Ki	BMD	1851-60	718,961
Klwow	Ki	BMD	1866-74	1,192,421
Kock	Lu	BMD	1826-42	813,989
Kock	Lu	BMD	1843-58	813,990
Kock	Lu	BMD	1859-65	813,991
Kodeń	Lu	BMD	1826-41	813,999
Kodeń	Lu	BMD	1843-54	814,000
Kolaki	Bi	Recs-5	1808-69	814,000
Kolbiel	Wa	BMD	1826-38, 1854	702,445
Kolo*	Po	BMD	1825-40	741,979
Kolo*	Po	BMD	1841-54	741,980
Kolo*	Po	BMD	1855-65	741,981
*See also Babiak, Dabie, Sompolno.				
Kamarow	Lu	BMD	1826-42	813,874
Kamarow	Lu	BMD	1843-60	813,875
Kamarow	Lu	BMD	1861-65	813,876
Kamarow	Lu	BMD	1866-70	905,158
Koniecpol	Ki	BMD	1826-42	730,078
Koniecpol	Ki	BMD	1844-55	730,079
Konin*	Po	M	1815	741,998
Konin*	Po	BMD	1826-45	741,998
Konin*	Po	BMD	1846-53	741,999
Konin*	Po	BMD	1855-65	742,000
*See also Golina, Skulsk, Slesin, Wilczyn.				
Końskie*	Ki	BMD	1826-36	716,412
Końskie*	Ki	BMD	1837-45	716,415
Końskie*	Ki	BMD	1846-59	716,416
Końskie*	Ki	BMD	1857-63	716,413
Końskie*	Ki	BMD	1864-65	716,414
Końskie*	Ki	BMD	1860-65	716,607
Końskie*	Ki	BMD	1866-68	1,192,421
Końskie*	Ki	BMD	1869-77	1,192,422
*See also Gowarczów, Przedbórz.				
Konskowola	Lu	BMD	1826-33	715,368
Konskowola	Lu	BMD	1836-40	715,368
Konskowola	Lu	BMD	1844	715,369
Konskowola	Lu	BMD	1845, 1850	715,369
Konskowola	Lu	BMD	1852, 1859	715,369
Konskowola	Lu	BMD	1860, 1862	715,369
Konskowola	Lu	BMD	1863	715,369
Konskowola	Lu	BMD	1866, 1870	905,160
Konskowola	Lu	Recs-5	1826-63	
Konskowola	Lu	BMD	1866-70	905,160
Konstantynów Nad Bugiem	Lu	BMD	1826-54	715,358
Konstantynów Nad Bugiem	Lu	BMD	1826-54	715,738
Koprzywnica	Ki	BMD	1857-58	809,133
Kórnik	Po	BMD	1817-47 G	742,003
Koronowo	By	B	1847-74 G	813,169
Koscierzyna	Gd	BM	1847-65 G	742,795
Koscierzyna	Gd	Recs-1	1847-73 G	474,721
Koscierzyna	Gd	Recs-1	1873-1919 G	474,715
Koscierzyna	Gd	B	1813-92 G	185,334
Kosów	Wa	BMD	1827-44	808,908
Kosów	Wa	BMD	1845-62	808,909
Koszalin	Ki	BMD	1812-46	896,086
Kozienice	Ki		See Magnuszów.	
Kozienice	Ki	MD	1810-11	729,351
Kozienice	Ki	BMD	1826-30	729,351
Kozienice	Ki	BMD	1831-38	729,352
Kozienice	Ki	BMD	1839-52	729,353
Kozienice	Ki	B	1826-30	729,354
Kozienice	Ki	M	1826-41	729,355
Kozienice	Ki	D	1826-30	729,355
Kozienice	Ki	B	1826-35	729,355
Kozienice	Ki	D	1831-41	729,356
Kozienice	Ki	B	1836-45	729,356
Kozienice	Ki	M	1842-59	729,357
Kozienice	Ki	D	1842-46	729,358
Kozienice	Ki	BMD	1846-61	729,358
Kozienice	Ki	BMD	1848	729,358
Kozienice	Ki	BMD	1849-58	729,359
Kozienice	Ki	BMD	1859-63	729,360

Kozlé	Op	BMD	1810-17	1,184,406
Kozmin	Po	BMD	1811-12	742,946
Kozuchów	Zi	M	1849-73 G	896,080
Krajenka	Ko	Recs-1	1812-33 G	495,964
Krajenka	Ko	Recs-1	1833-41 G	495,965
Krajenka	Ko	Recs-1	1834-54 G	495,966
Krajenka	Ko	Recs-1	1846 G	495,967
Krajenka	Ko	BMD	1800-63	1,184,432
Krajenka Chelmo	By	Recs-1	1829-32 G	495,967
Kraków	Kr	BD	1798-1819	718,912
Kraków	Kr	B	1820-29	718,913
Kraków	Kr	B	1830-36	718,914
Kraków	Kr	B	1837-43	718,915
Kraków	Kr	B	1844-50	718,916
Kraków	Kr	B	1851-55	718,917
Kraków	Kr	M	1798-1816	718,918
Kraków	Kr	M	1817-38	718,919
Kraków	Kr	M	1830-39	718,920
Kraków	Kr	M	1840-52	718,921
Kraków	Kr	D	1811-28	718,922
Kraków	Kr	D	1829-38	718,923
Kraków	Kr	D	1839-47	718,924
Kraków	Kr	D	1848-54	718,914
Krapkowice	Op	BD	1820-43 G	890,725
Krapkowice	Op	BMD	1819-48	1,184,431
Kraśniczyn	Lu	BMD	1826-36	715,450
Krasnik*	Lu	B	1826-49	715,440
Krasnik*	Lu	B	1850-65	715,441
Krasnik*	Lu	M	1826-70	715,442
Krasnik*	Lu	D	1826-47	715,443
Krasnik*	Lu	D	1847-67	715,444
*see also Annopol, Zaklików.				
Krasnik	Lu	B	1869-70	995,812
Krasnik	Lu	BD	1735-47	995,812
Krasnik	Lu	B	1735-1810	995,812
Krasnik	Lu	M	1735-47	995,813
Krasnik	Lu	M	1747-81	995,813
Krasnik	Lu	M	1767-90	995,813
Krasnik	Lu	D	1781-1818	995,813
Krasnik	Lu	B	1826-49	715,440
Krasnik	Lu	B	1850-65	715,441
Krasnik	Lu	M	1826-70	715,442
Krasnik	Lu	D	1826-47	715,443
Krasnik	Lu	D	1847-67	715,444
Krosnobrod	Lu	BMD	1827-46	715,421
Krosnobrod	Lu	BMD	1847-57	715,422
Krosno-Odrzańskie	Zi	Recs-12	1825-1955	1,184,406
Krasnopol	Bi	BMD	1836-62	746,651
Krasnopol	Bi	BMD	1866-68	1,191,985
Krasnopol	Bi	BMD	1870-75	1,191,985
Kranystaw*	Lu	BMD	1826-51	715,438
Kranystaw*	Lu	BMD	1852-60	715,439
Kranystaw*	Lu	BMD	1868-70	905,162
*See also Gorzków, Izbica, Turobin, Wysokie, Zolkiewka.				
Krepa Koscielna	Ki	BMD	1810-12	813,911
Krepa Koscielna	Ki	BMD	1816-24	813,911
Krepa Koscielna	Ki	BMD	1825-40	813,912
Krepa Koscielna	Ki	BMD	1841-55	813,913
Krepa Koscielna	Ki	BMD	1856-65	813,914
Krepa Koscielna	Ki	BMD	1866-70	1,257,420
Krepa Koscielna	Ki	BMD	1871-74	1,257,421
Krepa Koscielna	Ki	BMD	1875-77	1,257,422
Kromolów	Ka	BMD	1826-35	879,569
Kromolów	Ka	BMD	1836-54	879,570
Krotoszyn*	Po	BMD	1825-41 G	743,091
Krotoszyn*	Po	BMD	1842-47 G	743,092
*See also Koźmin, Zduny.				
Krylow	Lu	BMD	1826-40	715,463
Krylow	Lu	BMD	1841-59	715,464
Krzepice	Ka	BMD	1830-47	879,559
Krzepice	Ka	BMD	1848-65	879,560
Krzeszow Górny	Lu	BM	1826-34	718,678
Krzywiń	Po	BMD	1835-47	743,099
Kuczbork	Wa	BMD	1826-65	702,639
Kurów	Lu	BMD	1828-47	718,699
Kurozweki	Ki	BMD	1875-78	1,199,827
Kutno*	Lo	BMD	1808-12	730,039
Kutno*	Lo	BMD	1813-16	730,040
Kutno*	Lo	BMD	1817-21	730,041
Kutno*	Lo	BMD	1822-28	730,042
Kutno*	Lo	BMD	1829-33	730,043
*See also Lowicz.				
Kwidzyń	Gd	Recs-1	1818-24 G	496,013
Kwidzyń	Gd	Recs-10	1812-27 G	496,156
Kwidzyń	Gd	Recs-10	1827-28 G	496,158
Kwidzyń	Gd	Recs-10	1829-32 G	496,159
Kwidzyń	Gd	Recs-10	1832-35 G	496,160
Kwidzyń	Gd	Recs-10	1835-37 G	496,161
Kwidzyń	Gd	Recs-10	1837-40 G	496,162
Kwidzyń	Gd	Recs-10	1836-43 G	496,163
Kwidzyń	Gd	Recs-10	1843-48 G	496,164
Kwidzyń	Gd	Recs-10	1848-59 G	496,165
Kwidzyń	Gd	Recs-10	1814-60 G	496,166
Kwidzyń	Gd	Recs-11	1852 G	495,963
Kwieciszewo	By	BMD	1832-47	719,231
Labiszyn	By	B	1875	1,192,323
Labiszyn	By	BMD	1874-76	1,192,324
Labiszyn	By	BMD	1876-77	1,192,325
Labiszyn	By	BMD	1874-75	1,192,325
Labiszyn	By	BMD	1876-77	1,192,326
Ladek-Zorój	Wr	Recs-12	1922-34	1,184,432
Lask	Lo	BMD	1827-31	808,471
Lask	Lo	BMD	1832-41	808,472
Lask	Lo	BMD	1842-50	808,473
Lask	Lo	BMD	1851-59	808,474
Lask	Lo	BMD	1859-65	808,475
Laskowice	By	BMD	1874-75 G	1,192,318
Laskowice	By	B	1876	1,192,318
Laskowice	By	B	1877	1,192,319
Laskowice	By	MD	1876-77	1,192,319
Laszczow	Lu	BMD	1826-44	718,748
Laszczow	Lu	BMD	1845-54	718,749
Laszczow	Lu	BMD	1855-65	718,750
Laszczow	Lu	BMD	1866-69	905,178
Latowicz	Wa	BMD	1827-36	702,446
Lebork	Gd	BMD	1829-46	1,184,344
Lebork	Gd	Recs-12	1844-1936 G+H	1,184,344
Lebork	Gd	Recs-12	1844-1936	1,184,434
Leczyca*	Lo	BMD	1817-24	767,130
Leczyca*	Lo	BMD	1826-35	718,760
Leczyca*	Lo	BMD	1836-45	718,761
Leczyca*	Lo	BMD	1846-55	718,762
*See also Ozorkow.				
Legnica	Wr	B	1855-1938	1,184,435
Legnica	Wr	M	1855-1940	1,184,435
Legnica	Wr	D	1855-1940	1,184,436
Legnica	Wr	Recs-15	1812-50	1,184,436
Legnica	Wr	Recs-12	1814-1939	1,184,436
Lelow	Ki	BMD	1873-76	1,199,693
Lelow	Ki	BMD	1877	1,199,694
Lemberg			See Lwów.	
Lesnica	Op	Recs-12	1855-1933 G	1,184,378
Lewin Brzecki	Op	BM	1815-35	1,184,436
Lewin Brzecki	Op	D	1825-35	1,184,436
Lewin Brzecki	Op	Recs-12	1836-50	1,184,437
Lezajsk	Rz	D	1826-66	766,021
Lipno	By		See Dobrzyn Nad Wisla.	
Lipsko*	Ki	BMD	1826-50	813,919
Lipsko*	Ki	BMD	1851-58	813,920
Lipsko*	Ki	BMD	1837	723,731
*See also Ciepielow, Tarlow.				
Lipsko	Ki	BMD	1866-67	1,192,421
Lipsko	Ki	BMD	1868-74	1,192,422
Lisow	Ki	BMD	1810-36	723,731
Lisow	Ki	BMD	1837-59	723,732
Lniano	By	BMD	1874-77	119,321
Lodz*	Lo	BMD	1826-47	809,427
Lodz*	Lo	BMD	1848-58	809,428
Lodz*	Lo	BMD	1859-62	809,429
Lodz*	Lo	BMD	1863-65	809,430
Lodz*	Lo	BMD	1866-68	767,143

Community	Province	Record Type	Record Span	Genealogical Society Record Number
Lodz*	Lo	BMD	1869-70	767,144
Lodz	Lo	BMD	1871-72	1,191,746
*See also Lutomiersk, Tuszyn.				
Lodz	Lo	BMD	1873-74	1,191,747
Lodz	Lo	BMD	1875-77	1,191,748
Lodz	Lo	BMD	1877	1,191,749
Lodzki	Lo	BMD	1832-51	730,171
Lodzki	Lo	BMD	1852-65	730,172
Lodzki	Lo	BMD	1868-70	767,113
Lomazy	Lu	BMD	1826-37	718,770
Lomazy	Lu	BMD	1838-54	718,771
Lomza*	Bi	BMD	1827-38	747,709
Lomza*	Bi	BMD	1839-53	747,710
Lomza*	Bi	BD	1846-58	747,711
Lomza*	Bi	MD	1852-64	747,712
Lomza*	Bi	B	1859-64	747,713
Lomza*	Bi	BMD	1863-72	747,714
*See also Rosochate, Rutki, Sniadowd, Wizna.				
Lomza	Bi	B	1865-66	1,199,530
Lomza	Bi	D	1866	1,199,530
Lomza	Bi	BMD	1867-68	1,199,530
Lomza	Bi	B	1867-75	1,199,530
Lomza	Bi	MD	1868	1,199,531
Lomza	Bi	BMD	1869-72	1,199,531
Lomza	Bi	BMD	1872	1,199,532
Lomza	Bi	D	1869-73	1,199,532
Lomza	Bi	BMD	1873	1,199,532
Lomza	Bi	B	1873-79	1,199,533
Lomza	Bi	B	1875-79	1,199,533
Lomza	Bi	M	1857-71	1,199,533
Lomza	Bi	D	1875	1,199,533
Lomza	Bi	BMD	various	1,199,533
Losice*	Wa	BMD	1829-41	811,236
Losice*	Wa	BMD	1844-60	811,237
*See also Sarnaki.				
Lowicz*	Lo	BMD	1808-11	811,066
Lowicz*	Lo	BMD	1811-17	811,067
Lowicz*	Lo	BMD	1818-23	811,068
Lowicz*	Lo	BMD	1824-25	811,069
Lowicz*	Lo	BMD	1826-43	811,070
Lowicz*	Lo	BMD	1844-59	811,071
Lowicz*	Lo	BMD	1860-65	811,072
Lowicz*	Lo	BMD	1861-68	767,136
Lowicz*	Lo	BMD	1867-70	767,137
*See also Bielawy, Bolimow, Glowno.				
Lolazieje*	Bi	BMD	1827-54	746,680
*now Lazdijai, Kaunas, Lithuania.				
Lubartów*	Lu	BMD	1826-42	718,719
Lubartów*	Lu	BMD	1843-54	718,720
Lubartów*	Lu	BMD	1855-65	718,721
Lubartów*	Lu	BMD	1866-68	905,168
*See also Kamionka.				
Lublin*	Lu	B	1830-42	702,735
Lublin*	Lu	B		702,736
Lublin*	Lu	M		702,737
Lublin*	Lu	D		702,738
Lublin*	Lu	D	1841-50	702,739
Lublin*	Lu	BMD	1826-30	702,740
Lublin*	Lu	BMD	1831-37	702,741
Lublin*	Lu	BMD	1838-41	701,742
Lublin*	Lu	BMD	1842-43	702,743
Lublin*	Lu	BMD	1844-45	702,744
Lublin*	Lu	BMD	1846-47	702,745
Lublin*	Lu	BMD	1848-49	702,746
Lublin*	Lu	BMD	1849-51	702,747
Lublin*	Lu	BMD	1852-53	702,748
Lublin*	Lu	BMD	1854-55	702,749
Lublin*	Lu	BMD	1856	702,750
Lublin*	Lu	BMD	1857	702,751
Lublin*	Lu	BMD	1858-59	723,560
Lublin*	Lu	BMD	1860-61	723,561
Lublin*	Lu	BMD	1862-63	723,562
Lublin*	Lu	BMD	1864	723,563
Lublin*	Lu	BMD	1826-40	723,564
Lublin*	Lu	BMD	1841-53	723,565
Lublin*	Lu	BMD	1854-64	723,566
Lublin*	Lu	BMD	1865	905,172
Lublin*	Lu	BMD	1866	905,173
Lublin*	Lu	BMD	1867	905,174
Lublin*	Lu	BMD	1868-69	905,175
Lublin-Wieniawa*	Lu	BMD	1865-69	905,176
*See also Biskupice, Piaski.				
Lubliniec	Ka	D	1820-1900	1,184,437
Luków	Lu	BMD	1826-35	743,174
Luków	Lu	BMD	1836-47	743,175
Luków	Lu	BMD	1848-60	743,176
Luków	Lu	BMD	1861-65	743,177
Luków	Lu	BMD	1866-68	905,182
Lutomiersk	Lo	BMD	1826-33	810,239
Lutomiersk	Lo	BMD	1834-44	810,240
Lutomiersk	Lo	BMD	1845-59	810,241
Lutomiersk	Lo	BMD	1860-65	810,242
Lutomiersk	Lo	BMD	1866-68	767,124
Lwów	*	B	1814-37	905,274
*Lvov, Ukraine; formerly Lemberg, Galioa.				
Lwówek Slaski	Wr	Recs-12	1815-32	1,184,437
Magnuszów	Ki	BMD	1826-39	729,040
Malbork	Gd	B	1847-65 G	742,802
Malbork	Gd	MD	1847-65 G	742,803
Malogoszcz	Ki	BMD	1826-43	814,645
Malogoszcz	Ki	BMD	1844-64	814,646
Malogoszcz	Ki	BMD	1865-67	1,192,423
Markuszow	Lu	BMD	1826-46	743,200
Michow	Lu	BMD	1826-55	742,876
Miechowice	Ka	M	1880-85	1,184,442
Miedzyborz	Wr	B	1810-83	1,184,441
Miedzyborz	Wr	Recs-12	1870-1906	1,184,444
Miedzyrzec-Podlaski	Lu	BMD	1826-35	742,870
Miedzyrzec-Podlaski	Lu	BMD	1836-40	742,871
Miedzyrzec-Podlaski	Lu	BMD	1841-47	742,872
Miedzyrzec-Podlaski	Lu	BMD	1848-54	742,873
Miedzyrzec-Podlaski	Lu	BMD	1855-60	742,874
Miedzyrzec-Podlaski	Lu	BMD	1861-65	742,875
Miedzyrzec-Podlaski	Lu	BMD	1866-68	905,191
Miedzyrzecz*	Zi	Recs-1	1846-75 G	474,926
Miedztrzecz*	Zi	Recs-13	1848-1903 G	474,929
*See also Bledzew, Brójce, Pszczew.				
Miejsce	Op	BMD	1810-73 G	1,184,456
Mikstat	Po	BMD	1836-46 G	746,949
Mińsk-Mazowiecki*	Wa	BMD	1826-45	702,447
Mińsk-Mazowiecki*	Wa	BMD	1846-55	702,448
*See also Ceglów, Kaluszyn, Latowicz, Siennica, Stanislawow.				
Mlawa*	Wa	BMD	1823-47	702,504
Mlawa*	Wa	BMD	1848-59	702,505
Mlawa*	Wa	BMD	1860-65	702,506
*See also Radzanowo, Szreńsk.				
Mokobody	Wa	BMD	1837-60	808,846
Mordy	Wa	BMD	1826-45	808,853
Mordy	Wa	BMD	1846-58	808,854
Mosielnica		BMD	1826-42	723,668
Mosielnica		BMD	1843-58	723,669
Mosielnica		BMD	1859-65	723,670
Mosielnica		BMD	1836-64	723,673
Mosina	Po	B	1835-36 G	746,967
Mstow	Ka	BMD	1826-58	864,928
Mszczonów	Wa	BMD	1826-44	723,427
Mszczonów	Wa	BMD	1845-54	723,428
Myślibórz	Sz	BMD	1833-47 G	1,184,456

Myslowice	Ka	B	1847-66 G	864,943
Myslowice	Ka	M	1849-60 G	864,944
Myslowice	Ka	M	1859-63 G	864,945
Myslowice	Ka	BMD	1847-70 G	864,946
Naklo Nad Notecia	By	BMD	1848-74	715,114
Naklo Nad Notecia	By	BMD	1823-67	715,115
Naklo Nad Notecia	By	B D-Ind	1848-74	715,114
Naklo Nad Notecia	By	M	1854-67	715,114
Naklo Nad Notecia	By	BMD	1823-32	715,115
Naklo Nad Notecia	By	BMD	1835-40	715,115
Naklo Nad Notecia	By	BMD	1838-67	715,115
Namyslow	Op	BMD	1812-1918	1,184,453
Naruszewo	Wa	BMD	1808-25	689,612
Nowa Sól	Zi		See Kozuchow.	
Nowe Miasto				
Nad Pilica	Lo	BMD	1826-36	588,562
Nowe Miasto				
Nad Pilica	Lo	BMD	1837-54	588,563
Nowe Miasto				
Nad Pilica	Lo	BMD	1856-65	768,005
Nowogrod	Bi	BMD	1826-46	747,715
Nowogrod	Bi	BMD	1847-64	747,716
Nowogrod	Bi	M	1857-71	1,199,533
Nowogrod	Bi	B	1866	1,199,534
Nowogrod	Bi	BMD	1867-71	1,199,534
Nowogrod	Bi	D	1871-86	1,199,534
Nowogrod	Bi	BMD	1873	1,199,534
Nowogrod	Bi	B	1873-82	1,199,534
Nowogrod	Bi	B	1874	1,199,534
Nowogrod	Bi	BMD	1875	1,199,534
Nowy Dwór Maz.	Wa		See Wieliszew, Zakroczym.	
Nowy Korczyn	Ki	BMD	1826-39	1,192,423
Nowy Korczyn	Ki	BMD	1849-62	1,192,424
Nowy Korczyn	Ki	BMD	1875-76	1,192,424
Nur	Wa	BMD	1826-45	811,051
Nur	Wa	BMD	1846-59	811,052
Nysa	Op	B	1809-83	1,184,443
Nysa	Op	B	1810-1928	1,184,443
Nysa	Op	M	1816-83	1,184,444
Nysa	Op	M	1814-1928	1,184,444
Nysa	Op	D	1813-1930	1,184,444
Nysa	Op	D	1815-86	1,184,444
Oborniki	Po		See Rogoźno.	
Okuniew	Wa	BMD	1826-37	689,634
Olawa	Wr	BMD	1817-1933	1,184,445
Olesnica	Wr	Recs-12	1812-1930	1,184,444
Olesnica	Wr	Recs-12	1812-1930	1,184,445
Olesno	Op	BMD	1812-47 G	1,184,449
Olesno	Op	D	1891-1938 G	1,184,449
Olesno	Op	Recs-14	1815-47 G	1,184,449
Olesno	Op	Recs-14	1815-47 G	1,184,450
Oleszyce	Rz	BD	1814-64	766,035
Olita*	Bi	M	1835-65	747,740
*now Alytna, Kaunas, Lithuania.				
Olkusz*	Kr	BMD	1827-40	875,262
Olkusz*	Kr	BMD	1841-57	875,263
Olkusz*	Kr	BMD	1854-70	923,473
*See also Pilica, Wolbrom, Zarnowiec.				
Opatów*	Ki	BMD	1835-45	809,163
Opatów*	Ki	BMD	1843-55	809,164
Opatów*	Ki	BMD	1854-65	809,165
*See also Ożarów.				
Opoczno	Ki	Recs-5	1826-60	
Opoczno	Ki	BMD	1866-68	1,192,424
Opoczno	Ki	BMD	1869-74	1,192,425
Opole	Op	BMD	1812-1938	1,184,445
Opole Lubelskie*	Lu	B	1826-54	747,887
Opole Lubelskie*	Lu	M	1826-51	747,888
Opole Lubelskie*	Lu	D	1826-50	747,889
*See also Józefów, Józefów, Nad Wisla.				
Orla	Bi	BMD	1836-66	1,191,940
Osieciny	By	B	1826-1934 G	530,225
Osieciny	By	M	1826-1931 G	530,226
Osieciny	By	D	1826-92 G	530,227
Osieciny	By	D	1917-38 G	530,227
Osieciny	By	BM	1826-52 G	530,227

Osno	Zi	BMD	1813-99	1,184,410
(Lubuskie)				
Ostrów				
Mazowiecka*	Wa	BMD	1826-37	808,429
Ostrów				
Mazowiecka*	Wa	BMD	1837-43	808,430
Ostrów				
Mazowiecka*	Wa	BMD	1841-45	808,431
Ostrów				
Mazowiecka*	Wa	BMD	1843-48	808,432
Ostrów				
Mazowiecka*	Wa	BMD	1849-54	808,433
Ostrów				
Mazowiecka*	Wa	BMD	1847-59	808,434
Ostrów				
Mazowiecka*	Wa	BMD	1856-65	808,435
*See also Andrzejewo, Brok, Nur, Zareby, Kościelne.				
Ostrzeszów	Po	BMD	1835-46	747,832
Otwock	Wa		See Karczew, Kolbiel.	
Ożarów	Ki	BMD	1826-49	809,166
Ożarów	Ki	BMD	1844-57	809,167
Ozorkow	Lo	M	1923	1,046,468
Ozorkow	Lo	M	1872, 1883	1,186,428
Pabianice	Lo	BMD	1831-62	714,498
Pabianice	Lo	BMD	1853-65	714,499
Pabianice	Lo	BMD	1866-70	768,013
Pabianice	Lo	B	1831-62	714,498
Pabianice	Lo	M	1831-53	714,498
Pabianice	Lo	D	1831-50	714,499
Pabianice	Lo	D	1850-65	714,499
Pabianice	Lo	M	1853-65	714,499
Pabianice	Lo	D	1863-65	714,499
Pabianice	Lo	BMD	1866-70	768,013
Pabianice	Lo	BMD	1871-74	1,191,880
Pacanow*	Ki	BMD	1875-77	1,192,425
Pajeczno*	Lo	BMD	1826-37	716,008
Pajeczno*	Lo	BMD	1838-65	716,009
Pajeczno*	Lo	BMD	1866-70	768,015
*See also Brzeznica-Nowa Osada, Sulmierzyce.				
Pakość	By	BMD	1823-47	719,232
Parczew	Lu	BMD	1826-53	747,900
Paslek	Ol	BMD	1825-1907	1,184,446
Pelczyce	Sz	BMD	1825-74	1,184,379
Piaseczno*	Wa	BMD	1829-36	723,683
*See also Góra Kalwaria.				
Piaski	Lu	Recs-5	1810-64	
Piaski	Lu	BMD	1826-37	748,070
Piaski	Lu	BMD	1838-55	748,071
Pilica	Kr	BMD	1826-35	875,273
Pilica	Kr	BMD	1836-46	875,274
Pilica	Kr	BMD	1847-57	875,275
Pilica	Kr	B	1826-50	875,276
Pilica	Kr	BM	1826-65	875,277
Pilica	Kr	D	1836-65	875,278
Pilica	Kr	BMD	1858-70	923,477
Pilica	Kr	Recs-5	1808-70	
Pilzno	Rz		See Tarnów.	
Pińczów	Ki	BMD	1608-1810	716,155
Pińczów	Ki	BMD	1811-14	716,156
Pińczów	Ki	BMD	1815-20	716,157
Pińczów	Ki	BMD	1821-25	716,158
Pińczów	Ki	BMD	1826-28	716,159
Pińczów	Ki	BMD	1830-41	716,160
Pińczów	Ki	BMD	1842-51	716,161
Pińczów	Ki	BMD	1852-65	716,162
Pińczów	Ki	BMD	1810-27	716,163
Pińczów	Ki	BMD	1828-38	716,164
Pińczów	Ki	BMD	1839-47	716,165
Pińczów	Ki	BMD	1848-50	716,166
Pińczów	Ki	BMD	1851-64	716,167
Pińczów	Ki	BMD	1862-63	1,192,425
Pińczów	Ki	BMD	1865-71	1,192,426
Pińczów	Ki	BMD	1871-75	1,192,427
Pińczów	Ki	BMD	1866-67	1,192,358
Pińczów	Ki	BMD	1870	1,192,358
Pińczów	Ki	BMD	1870-75	1,192,359

Community	Province	Record Type	Record Span	Genealogical Society Record Number
Piotrkow Trybunalski*	Lo	BMD	1808-10	715,786
Piotrkow Trybunalski*	Lo	BMD	1810-16	715,787
Piotrkow Trybunalski*	Lo	BMD	1816-21	715,788
Piotrkow Trybunalski*	Lo	BMD	1821-24	715,789
Piotrkow Trybunalski*	Lo	BMD	1824-30	715,790
Piotrkow Trybunalski*	Lo	BMD	1831-38	715,804
Piotrkow Trybunalski*	Lo	BMD	1839-46	715,805
Piotrkow Trybunalski*	Lo	BMD	1847-53	715,806
Piotrkow Trybunalski*	Lo	BMD	1854-58	715,807
Piotrkow Trybunalski*	Lo	BMD	1858-64	715,808
Piotrkow Trybunalski*	Lo	BMD	1864-69	768,023
*See also Rozprza, Sulejów, Wólborz.				
Plawno	Lo	BMD	1826-42	715,816
Plawno	Lo	BMD	1843-63	715,817
Plawno	Lo	BMD	1864-65	715,818
Plawno	Lo	BMD	1866-70	768,052
Pleszew	Po	BMD	1835-47 G	752,629
Plock	Wa	BMD	1808-25	729,206
Plock	Wa	BMD	1815-25	729,207
Plońsk*	Wa	BMD	1826-40	689,635
Plońsk*	Wa	BMD	1841-47	689,636
Plońsk*	Wa	BMD	1848-52	689,637
Plońsk*	Wa	BMD	1853-63	689,624
Plońsk*	Wa	BMD	1864-65	689,625
*See also Czerwińsk, Smoszewo, Sochocin.				
Polńsk	Wa	B	1852-59	1,191,932
Polńsk	Wa	D	1854-70	1,191,932
Polńsk	Wa	B	1860-65	1,191,932
Polńsk	Wa	B	1865	1,191,987
Polńsk	Wa	M	1855-65	1,191,987
Polńsk	Wa	B	1866-70	1,191,987
Polńsk	Wa	BMD	1866, 1867	1,191,987
Polńsk	Wa	BMD	1868, 1869	1,191,988
Polńsk	Wa	B	1866-73	1,191,988
Polńsk	Wa	BMD	1870-71	1,191,988
Polńsk	Wa	BMD	1872	1,191,989
Polńsk	Wa	D	1872	1,191,989
Polaniec	Ki	BMD	1826-36	588,928
Polaniec	Ki	BMD	1837-60	588,929
Polaniec	Ki	BMD	1861-65	588,930
Polaniec	Ki	BMD	1866-73	1,199,827
Polaniec	Ki	BMD	1874-77	1,199,828
Prabuty	Ol	BMD	1823-74 G	1,184,449
Prabuty	Ol	B	1920 G	1,184,499
Praszka	Lo	BMD	1826-51	715,837
Praszka	Lo	BMD	1852-65	715,838
Praszka	Lo	BMD	1866-67	768,026
Pruchnik	Rz	B	1834-70	766,039
Prudnik	Op	BD	1812-1939	1,184,444
Przasnysz*	Wa	BMD	1826-37	702,526
Przasnysz*	Wa	BMD	1838-48	702,527
Przasnycz*	Wa	BMD	1849-57	702,528
Przasnycz*	Wa	BMD	1858-65	702,529
*See also Chorzele, Dzierzgowo.				
Przedbórz	Ki	BMD	1826-34	719,103
Przedbórz	Ki	BMD	1835-46	719,104
Przedbórz	Ki	BMD	1847-56	719,105
Przedbórz	Ki	BMD	1857-65	719,106
Przedbórz	Ki	BMD	1866	1,192,427
Przedbórz	Ki	BMD	1867-71	1,192,428
Przerosl	Bi	BMD	1866-77	1,191,985
Przerosl	Bi	BMD	1827-52	747,007
Przerosl	Bi	BMD	1853-65	747,008
Przybyszew	Ki	BMD	1826-34	723,683
Przyrow	Ka	BMD	1826-46	875,468
Przyrow	Ka	BMD	1847-58	875,469
Przyrow	Ka	BMD	1859-72	1,199,718
Przyrow	Ka	BMD	1873	1,199,718
Przyrow	Ka	BMD	1874-77	1,199,719
Przysucha*	Ki	BMD	1826-39	718,969
Przysucha*	Ki	BMD	1840-54	718,970
Przysucha*	Ki	BMD	1854-63	718,971
*See also Klwów.				
Przytyk	Ki	BMD	1826-64	729,066
Przytyk	Ki	D	1840-62	729,067
Przytyk	Ki	BMD	1826-42	729,068
Przytyk	Ki	BMD	1843-50	729,069
Przytyk	Ki	BMD	1851-59	729,070
Przytyk	Ki	Recs-5	1810-65	
Pszczew	Zi	Recs-1	1877-1918 G	474,925
Puck	Gd	Recs-1	1812-55 G	474,720
Puck	Gd	Recs-1	1857-1920 G	474,714
Pulawy*	Lu	BM	1838-66	753,304
*See also Baranów, Góra Pulawska, Janowiec, Kazimierz, Końskowola, Kurów, Wawolnica.				
Puńsk	Bi	BMD	1833-65	747,764
Pyrzyce	Sz	Recs-1	1853	1,184,446
Pyzdry	Po	BMD	1826-45	752,757
Pyzdry	Po	BMD	1846-65	752,758
Racibórz	Op	BM	1814-74	1,184,449
Radom*	Ki	BMD	1827-44	716,127
Radom*	Ki	BMD	1845-48	716,128
Radom*	Ki	BMD	1848-52	716,129
Radom*	Ki	BMD	1852-58	716,130
Radom*	Ki	BMD	1859-62	716,131
Radom*	Ki	BMD	1862-65	716,132
*See also Lisów, Przytyk, Wolanów.				
Radomsko*	Lo	BMD	1826-40	718,597
Radomsko*	Lo	BMD	1841-56	718,598
Radomsko*	Lo	BMD	1857-65	718,599
Radomsko*	Lo	BMD	1866-70	768,054
*See also Plawno.				
Radoszyce	Ki	BMD	1826-41	719,332
Radoszyce	Ki	BMD	1842-50	719,333
Radoszyce	Ki	BMD	1851-59	719,334
Radoszyce	Ki	BMD	1866-69	1,192,428
Radoszyce	Ki	BMD	1870-76	1,192,429
Radzanowo	Wa	BMD	1824-25	702,836
Radzanowo	Wa	BMD	1826-47	702,837
Radzanowo	Wa	BMD	1848-65	702,838
Radziejow	By		See Osieciny.	
Radzilow	Bi	BMD	1826-47	747,020
Radzyn Podlaski*	Lu	BMD	1826-36	753,330
Radzyn Podlaski*	Lu	BMD	1837-47	753,331
Radzyn Podlaski*	Lu	BMD	1829-62	753,332
*See also Biala, Czemierniki, Kock, Miedzyrzec, Podlaski, Wohyń.				
Rajgród	Bi	BMD	1826-50	747,021
Rawa Mazowiecka*	Lo	BMD	1809-23	718,609
Rawa Mazowiecka*	Lo	BMD	1824-39	718,610
Rawa Mazowiecka*	Lo	BMD	1841-52	718,611
Rawa Mazowiecka*	Lo	BMD	1853-62	718,612
Rawa Mazowiecka*	Lo	BMD	1865-66	768,029
*See also Nowe Miasto Nad Pilica.				
Rejowiec	Lu	BM	1826-59	753,346
Rejowiec	Lu	BMD	1826-53	753,347
Rogoźno	Po	BMD	1817-39 G	752,799
Rogoźno	Po	BMD	1840-47 G	752,800
Rosochate	Bi	Recs-5	1808-63	
Rozprza	Lo	BMD	1826-50	718,796
Rozprza	Lo	BMD	1851-65	718,797
Rozprza	Lo	BMD	1866-70	768,031
Rutki	Bi	BMD	1850-60	747,724
Rybnik	Ka		See Baranowice.	
Rychwal	Po	BMD	1826-55	752,823
Ryki	Wa		See Bobrowniki.	
Rynarzewo	By	BMD	1823-44 G	719,149
Rypin*	By	BMD	1808-20	715,061

Rypin*	By	BMD	1820-26	715,062
Rypin*	By	BMD	1827-41	715,063
Rypin*	By	BMD	1842-50	715,064
Rypin*	By	BMD	1851-58	715,065
Rypin*	By	BMD	1859-65	715,066
*See also Golub-Dobrzyn.				
Sandomierz*	Ki	BMD	1826-37	809,134
Sandomierz*	Ki	BMD	1838-44	809,141
Sandomierz*	Ki	BMD	1845-51	809,142
Sandomierz*	Ki	BMD	1852-65	809,136
*See also Klimontów.				
Sandomierz	Ki	BMD	1832	1,199,828
Sandomierz	Ki	M	1855	1,199,828
Sandomierz	Ki	D	1857	1,199,828
Sandomierz	Ki	B	1868	1,199,828
Sandomierz	Ki	B	1860-65	1,199,828
Sandomierz	Ki	M	1860-70	1,199,828
Sandomierz	Ki	D	1863	1,199,828
Sandomierz	Ki	BMD	1866-73	1,199,829
Sandomierz	Ki	BMD	1874-75	1,199,830
Sarbiewo	Wa	BMD	1808, 1813	689,643
Sarbiewo	Wa	BMD	1816-25	689,643
Sarbiewo	Wa	BMD	1826-39	689,644
Sarbiewo	Wa	BMD	1840-55	689,645
Sarbiewo	Wa	BMD	1856-65	689,646
Sarbiewo	Wa	BMD	1866-76	1,191,926
Sarbiewo	Wa	BMD	1877	1,191,927
Sarnaki	Wa	BMD	1836-47	810,575
Sarnaki	Wa	BMD	1848-58	810,576
Secemin	Ki	BMD	1826-45	716,107
Secemin	Ki	BMD	1846-65	716,108
Secemin	Ki	BMD	1866-69	1,192,429
Sejny	Bi	BMD	1826-65	747,778
Sejny	Bi	BMD	1866-75	1,191,986
Sereje*	Bi	BMD	1826-56	752,589
*Now Seirijar, Kaunas, Lithuania.				
Seroczyn	Wa	BMD	1841-59	808,635
Siedlce*	Wa	BMD	1828-40	808,645
Siedlce*	Wa	BMD	1841-44	808,646
Siedlce*	Wa	BMD	1845-57	808,647
*See also Mokobody, Moroy, Seroczyn, Wodynie.				
Siedliszcze	Lu	BMD	1827-29	753,411
Siemianowice		M	1856-80 G+H	1,184,434
Siennica	Wa	BMD	1826-36	702,449
Sienno	Ki	BMD	1866-73	1,192,429
Sienno	Ki	BMD	1826-44	813,931
Sienno	Ki	BMD	1845-55	813,932
Sienno	Ki	BMD	1856-65	813,933
Sienno	Ki	BMD	1866-73	1,192,429
Sieradz	Lo		See Burzenin, Zloczew.	
Sierpc*	Wa		1826-37	
*See Raciaz.				
Sierpc	Wa	BMD	1838-52	730,160
Sierpc	Wa	BMD	1852-53	730,161
Sierpc	Wa	BMD	1864-65	730,162
Sierpc	Wa	BMD	1826-37	730,159
Skarszewy	Gd	Recs-1	1871-1919 G	475,222
Skierniewice	Lo	BMD	1826-45	743,266
Skierniewice	Lo	BMD	1846-65	743,267
Skierniewice	Lo	BMD	1866	768,040
Skierniewice	Lo	BMD	1867	1,191,774
Skierniewice	Lo	BMD	1868-75	1,191,775
Skrzeszew	Wa	BMD	1821-46	810,577
Skrzeszew	Wa	BMD	1849-64	810,578
Skulsk	Po	BMD	1826-65	752,879
Skwierzyna	Zi	BMD	1808-38 G	1,184,452
Skwierzyna	Zi	B	1839-46 G	1,184,453
Skwierzyna	Zi	BMD	1808-47 G	1,184,454
Skwierzyna	Zi	D	1845-47 G	1,184,455
Skwierzyna	Zi	D	1875-1918 G	1,184,455
Skwierzyna	Zi	Recs-15	unknown	1,184,455
Slawatycze	Lu	BM	1847-76	753,441
Slesin	Po	BMD	1826-55	752,880
Slupca	Po		See Zagórów.	
Smoszewo	Wa	BMD	1809-12	689,628
Sniadow	Bi	BMD	1867-68	1,199,534
Sniadow	Bi	BMD	1869-73	1,199,535
Sniadowo	Bi	BMD	1808, 1832	996,527
Sniadowo	Bi	BMD	1826-38	747,725
Sniadowo	Bi	BMD	1839-48	747,726
Sniadowo	Bi	BMD	1849-64	747,727
Sniadowo	Bi	Recs-5	1810-65	
Sobkow	Ki	BMD	1810-53	715,872
Sobkow	Ki	BMD	1854-65	715,873
Sobkow	Ki	BMD	1866-76	1,192,430
Sobota	Lo	BMD	1826-65	743,026
Sochocin	Wa	BMD	1826-49	689,626
Sochocin	Wa	BMD	1850-59	689,627
Sochocin	Wa	BMD	1860-79	1,191,989
Sochocin	Wa	BMD	1808-20	689,638
Sochocin	Wa	BMD	1820-25	689,639
Sochocin	Wa	BMD	1820-25	689,640
Sochocin	Wa	BMD	1840-53	689,641
Sochocin	Wa	BMD	1854-60	689,642
Sochocin	Wa	BMD	1866-73	1,191,927
Sochocin	Wa	BMD	1874-75	1,191,928
Sokolow Pod-Laski*	Wa	BMD	1812-23	808,912
Sokolow Pod-Laski*	Wa	BMD	1823-25	808,913
Sokolow Pod-Laski*	Wa	BMD	1827-38	809,156
Sokolow Pod-Laski*	Wa	BMD	1839-46	809,157
Sokolow Pod-Laski*	Wa	BMD	1847-55	809,158
Sokolow Pod-Laski*	Wa	BMD	1856-64	809,159
*See also Kosów, Skrzeszew.				
Sokoly	Bi	BMD	1867	1,191,940
Sokoly	Bi	BMD	1869-72	1,191,940
Sokoly	Bi	BM	1875	1,191,940
Sokoly	Bi	BMD	1878	1,191,940
Sokoly	Bi	BMD	1826-65 G	747,741
Sokoly	Bi	BMD	1847-1930 G	1,046,485
Sokoly Nowosiolki	Bi	M	1840	1,186,448
Sokoly Nowosiolki	Bi	BMD	1881, 1886	1,186,448
Sokoly Nowosiolki	Bi	BMD	1887	1,186,448
Sokoly Nowosiolki	Bi	BMD	1872, 1910	1,186,448
Solec Kwawski	By	BMD	1823-47 G	719,152
Sompolno	Po	BMD	1826-47	758,352
Sompolno	Po	BMD	1848-65	758,353
Sosnicowice	Ka	Recs-7, 17	1806-96 G+H	1,184,428
Srem	Po	BMD	1817-47 G	758,361
Stanislawow	Wa	BMD	1826-36	702,450
Stargard-Szczecinski	Sz	Recs-16	c1761 G	1,184,456
Starogard-Gdański	Gd	Recs-1	1847-62 G	474,723
Starogard-Gdański	Gd	Recs-1	1862-70 G	474,724
Stargard-Gdański	Gd	Recs-1	1882-1903 G	474,717
Stargard-Gdański	Gd	Recs-1	1904-20 G	474,718
Stargard-Gdański	Gd	BMD	1812-1939 G	185,355
Starogard-Gdański	Gd	B	1812-74 G	414,467
Starogard-Gdański	Gd	MD	1812-1939 G	414,468
Stary Targ	Gd	Recs-12	unknown	1,184,377
Staszow*	Ki	BMD	1866-72	1,199,830
Staszow*	Ki	BMD	1873-77	1,199,831
*See Bogoria.				
Staszów	Wa	Recs-3	1810-25	
Staszów	Wa	BMD	1826-36	588,931
Staszów	Wa	BMD	1837-50	588,932
Staszów	Wa	BMD	1851-56	588,933
Staszów	Wa	BMD	1857-65	588,934

Community	Province	Record Type	Record Span	Genealogical Society Record Number
Stawiszyn	Po	BMD	1826-65	764,034
Stopnica	Ki	BMD	1875-77	1,192,430
Strykow	Lo	BMD	1826-35	747,973
Strykow	Lo	BMD	1836-53	747,974
Strykow	Lo	BMD	1854-65	747,975
Strykow	Lo	BMD	1866-70	768,049
Strzegom	Wr	BMD	1850-1939	1,184,458
Strzegom	Wr	Recs-12	1850-1939	1,184,458
Strzelce Krajeńskie	Zi	BMD	1847-53 G	544,649
Strzelce Opolskie	Op		See Leśnica.	
Strzelce Opolskie	Op	BMD	1828-1919	1,184,417
Sulechów	Zi		See Babimost.	
Sulejow	Lo	BMD	1826-42	747,995
Sulejow	Lo	BMD	1843-65	747,996
Sulejow	Lo	BMD	1866-70	760,106
Sulmierzyce	Lo	BMD	1826-55	748,109
Sulmierzyce	Lo	BMD	1856-65	748,110
Sulmierzyce	Lo	BMD	1866-70	760,108
Suraz	Bi	BMD	1870-74	1,186,429
Suraz	Bi	BMD	1880	1,186,429
Suraz	Bi	B	1881-1914	1,186,429
Suraz	Bi	M	1881-1913	1,186,429
Susz	Ol	B	1847-74 G	904,700
Suwalki*	Bi	BMD	1826-34	752,618
Suwalki*	Bi	BMD	1835-40	752,619
Suwalki*	Bi	BMD	1842-47	752,620
Suwalki*	Bi	BMD	1848-54	752,621
Suwalki*	Bi	BMD	1856-61	752,622
Suwalki*	Bi	BMD	1862-65	752,623
Suwalki*	Bi		1866-75	
*See also Wizajny.				
Suwalki	Bi	BMD	1866	1,191,986
Suwalki	Bi	BMD	1867-77	1,199,520
Suwalki	Bi	BMD	1869	1,199,520
Suwalki	Bi	BMD	1872-73	1,199,520
Suwalki	Bi	BMD	1875	1,199,520
Swidnica	Wr	BMD	1854-75 G	1,194,451
Swierze	Lu	BMD	1826-65	766,278
Sycow	Wr	Recs-12	1820-67	1,184,417
Szadek	Lo	BMD	1826-54	747,923
Szczebrzeszyn	Lu	BMD	1825-39	755,509
Szczebrzeszyn	Lu	BMD	1840-50	755,510
Szczebrzeszyn	Lu	BMD	1851-60	755,511
Szczebrzeszyn	Lu	BMD	1861-65	755,512
Szczebrzeszyn	Lu	BMD	1866-70	904,319
Szczecin	Sz	Recs-16	1841-47 G	1,184,457
Szczecin	Sz	D	1845-49 G	1,184,457
Szczecin	Sz	BD	1854-74 G	1,184,458
Szczecin	Sz	M	1901-39 G	1,184,458
Szczekociny	Ki	BMD	1826-43	716,115
Szczepankowo	Bi	M	1820-21	747,727
Szczerców	Lo	BMD	1826-47	747,932
Szczerców	Lo	BMD	1848-65	747,933
Szczerców	Lo	BMD	1866-70	760,113
Szczucyn	Bi	BMD	1826-30	767,022
Szczucyn	Bi	MD	1831	767,022
Szczucyn	Bi	B	1840-53	767,022
Szczucyn	Bi	BMD	1850-60	747,023
Szczucyn	Bi	BMD	1861-65	747,024
Szczuczyn	Bi	BMD	1866-70	1,199,535
Szczuczyn	Bi	B	1870-79	1,199,535
Szczuczyn	Bi	B	1870-79	1,199,536
Szczuczyn	Bi	BMD	1871-72	1,199,536
Szczuczyna	Bi	Recs-5	1727-1870	
Szczekociny	Ki	BMD	1826-46	1,199,732
Szczekociny	Ki	BMD	1847-52	1,199,733
Szczekociny	Ki	BMD	1858-66	1,199,733
Szczekociny	Ki	BMD	1867-77	1,199,734
Szlichtyngowa	Zi	BMD	1835-47 G	896,081
Szlichtyngowa	Zi	BMD	1835-59	1,184,450
Szlichtyngowa	Zi	BMD	1834-47	896,081
Szprotawa	Zi	BMD	1811-1933 G	1,184,456
Szprotawa	Zi	Recs-14	1813-45 G	1,184,456
Szreńsk	Wa	BMD	1809-16	702,854
Szrenńsk	Wa	BMD	1817-23	702,855
Szrenńsk	Wa	BMD	1826-43	702,856
Szrenńsk	Wa	BMD	1845-60	702,857
Szrenńsk	Wa	BMD	1861-68	702,858
Sztum	Gd	Recs-12		1,184,458
Szydlowiec	Ki	BMD	1826-43	716,419
Szydlowiec	Ki	BMD	1844-52	716,420
Szydlowiec	Ki	BMD	1853-61	716,421
Szydlowiec	Ki	BMD	1862-65	716,422
Tarczyn	Wa	BMD	1808-51	723,671
Tarczyn	Wa	BMD	1852-59	723,672
Tarlow	Ki	BMD	1826-51	813,946
Tarlow	Ki	BMD	1852-65	813,947
Tarlow	Ki	BMD	1866-68	1,192,430
Tarlow	Ki	BMD	1869-73	1,192,431
Tarnogóra	Lu		See Izbica.	
Tarnow*	Ki	BD	1808-55	742,702
Tarnow*	Ki	BD	1849-70	948,420
Tarnow*	Ki	B	1863-70	948,421
Tarnow*	Ki	MD	1849-70	948,422
*See also Brzesko.				
Tarnowskie Góry	Ka	B	1813-55	1,184,458
Tarnowskie Góry	Ka	M	1824-54	1,184,458
Tarnowskie Góry	Ka	D	1813-71	1,184,458
Tarnowskie Góry	Ka	D	1871-85	1,184,459
Tarnowskie Góry	Ka	D	1895-1909	1,184,460
Tarnowskie Góry	Ka	BMD	1847-70 G	877,402
Tarnowskie Góry	Ka	BMD	1813-71 G	1,184,458
Tarnowskie Góry	Ka	D	1871-85 G	1,184,459
Tarnowskie Góry	Ka	D	1895-1901 G	1,184,460
Tczew	Gd	BMD	1828-48 G	743,206
Tczew	Gd	Recs-1	1882-1919 G	475,221
Terespol	Lu	BMD	1826-34	756,981
Terespol	Lu	BMD	1835-43	756,982
Terespol	Lu	BMD	1844-54	756,983
Tobiasze	Lo		See Tomaszów Mazowiecki.	
Tomaszow	Lu	BMD	1826-36	757,366
Tomaszow	Lu	BMD	1837-45	757,367
Tomaszow	Lu	BMD	1847-50	757,368
Tomaszow	Lu	BMD	1851-55	757,369
Tomaszow	Lu	BMD	1856-61	757,370
Tomaszow	Lu	BMD	1862-69	757,371
Tomaszow	Lu	BMD	1870	904,324
Tomaszow Lubelski*	Lu	BMD	1870	
*See also Jarczów, Komorów, Tyszowce.				
Tomaszow Mazowiecki	Lo	BMD	1830-45	747,938
Tomaszow Mazowiecki	Lo	BMD	1846-57	747,939
Tomaszoe Mazowiecki	Lo	BMD	1858-65	747,940
Tomaszow Mazowiecki	Lo	BMD	1866-70	760,115
Toruń	By	Recs-1	1818 G	496,009
Toszek	Ka	M	1886	1,184,461
Toszek	Ka	D	1841-72	1,184,461
Trzcianka	Po	BMD	1817-47 G	1,184,451
Trzcianne	Bi	B	1871-72	1,186,454
Trzcianne	Bi	B	1857, 1880	1,186,454
Trzcianne	Bi	B	1883, 1885	1,186,454
Trzcianne	Bi	B	1888, 1914	1,186,454
Trzcianne	Bi	Divorce	1898, 1900	1,186,454
Trzcianne	Bi	Divorce	1902	1,186,454
Trzcianne	Bi	Divorce	1906-19	1,186,454
Trzciel	Zi	Recs-15	1834-48 G	1,184,460
Trzemeszno	Zi	BMD	1832-47	719,242
Turobin	Lu	BMD	1826-42	757,404
Turobin	Lu	BMD	1843-50	757,405
Turobin	Lu	BMD	1851-60	757,406
Turobin	Lu	BMD	1861-69	904,327
Tuszyn	Lo	BMD	1826-48	747,955
Tuszyn	Lo	BMD	1849-65	747,956
Tuszyn	Lo	BMD	1866-70	760,119

Twardogora	Wr	BMD	1812-74	1,184,411	Warta	Lo	BMD	1851-58	753,088
Tychy	Ka		See Bieruń Nowy.		Wasosz	Bi	BMD	1840-65	747,025
Tykocin	Bi	BMD	1866	1,191,940	Wasosz	Bi	BMD	1866-75	1,199,536
Tykocin	Bi	B	1867-73	1,191,940	Wawolnica	Lu	BMD	1826-90	761,160
Tykocin	Bi	BMD	1868-74	1,191,941	Wegrów	Wa	B	1826-48	811,273
Tykocin	Bi	B	1826-44	747,742	Wegrów	Wa	BMD	1826-48	810,101
Tykocin	Bi	BMD	1827-38	747,742	Wegrów	Wa	BMD	1838-53	810,102
Tykocin	Bi	BMD	1839-65	747,743	Wejherowo	Gd	Recs-1	1848-73 G	474,722
Tykocin	Bi	BMD	1857-62, 1864	747,744	Wejherowo	Gd	Recs-1	1882-1912 G	474,716
Tyszowce	Lu	BMD	1826-28	766,304	Wejherowo	Gd	Recs-1	1913-19 G	474,719
Tyszowce	Lu	BMD	1829-43	766,305	Widawa	Lo	BMD	1826-50	753,103
Tyszowce	Lu	BMD	1844-60	766,306	Widawa	Lo	BMD	1852-65	753,104
Tyszowce	Lu	BMD	1861-69	766,307	Widawa	Lo	BMD	1866-69	760,130
Tyszowce	Lu	BMD	1870	904,328	Wiecbork	By	BMD	1825-47	719,323
Uchanie	Lu	BMD	1826-44	766,425	Wiejsieje*	Bi	BMD	1840-53	752,634
Uchanie	Lu	BMD	1845-64	766,426	*now Vejseja, Kaunas, Lithuania.				
Ujazd	Lo	B	1826-65	747,077	Wieliszew	Wa	BMD	1808-17	689,647
Ujazd	Lo	BMD	1826-65	747,078	Wieliszew	Wa	BMD	1818-25	689,648
Ujazd	Lo	BMD	1866-70	760,121	Wieliszew	Wa	BMD	1826-41	689,649
Ujazd	Lo	Recs-5	1808-70		Wieliszew	Wa	BMD	1842-58	689,650
Walbrzych	Wr	BMD	1934-38	1,184,461	Wieliszew	Wa	BMD	1859-65	689,651
Warka	Wa	BMD	1826-41	723,677	Wielowies	Ka	B	1810-57	1,184,432
Warka	Wa	BMD	1842-54	723,678	Wielowies	Ka	Recs-1	1762-1820	1,184,433
Warka	Wa	BMD	1855-59	723,679	Wielowies	Ka	Recs-1	1817	
Warszawa	Wa	BMD	1826-30	689,510	Wielowies	Ka	M	1828-51	1,184,434
Warszawa	Wa	BMD	1828-29	689,511	Wielowies	Ka	Recs-1	1877-89	1,184,434
Warszawa	Wa	BMD	1830-31	689,512	Wieluń*	Lo	BMD	1826-53	753,121
Warszawa	Wa	BMD	1832-33	689,513	Wieluń*	Lo	BMD	1854-65	753,122
Warszawa	Wa	BMD	1834-36	689,514	Wieluń*	Lo	BMD	1866-70	760,136
Warszawa	Wa	BMD	1835-37	689,515	*See also Praszka.				
Warszawa	Wa	BMD	1837	689,516	Wieniawa	Lu	BMD	1865-69	905,176
Warszawa	Wa	BMD	1834-38	689,517	Wieniawa	Lu	BMD	1826-40	723,564
Warszawa	Wa	BMD	1839	689,518	Wieniawa	Lu	BMD	1841-53	723,565
Warszawa	Wa	BMD	1840	689,519	Wieniawa	Lu	BMD	1854-64	723,566
Warszawa	Wa	BMD	1841	689,520	Wieniawa	Lu	BMD	1865-69	905,176
Warszawa	Wa	B	1838-41	689,521	Wierzbowiec	Wa	BMD	1808-22	689,441
Warszawa	Wa	BMD	1842	689,522	Wierzbowiec	Wa	BMD	1824-25	689,441
Warszawa	Wa	BMD	1843	689,523	Wierzbowiec	Wa	BMD	1826-50	689,442
Warszawa	Wa	BMD	1826-44	689,524	Wieszowa	Ka	BD	1847-48 G	877,421
Warszawa	Wa	BMD	1837-44	689,525	Wilczyn	Po	BMD	1827-58	764,452
Warszawa	Wa	BMD	1843-45	689,526	Wiskitki	Wa	BMD	1826-45	723,429
Warszawa	Wa	BMD	1843-46	689,527	Wiskitki	Wa	BMD	1846-54	723,430
Warszawa	Wa	BMD	1846-47	689,557	Wislica	Ki	BMD	1826-46	588,922
Warszawa	Wa	BMD	1847	689,528	Wislica	Ki	BMD	1847-65	588,923
Warszawa	Wa	BMD	1847	689,529	Wislica	Ki	BMD	1866-75	1,192,431
Warszawa	Wa	BMD	1848-49	689,530	Wiśnicz	Kr	BM	1814-70	936,648
Warszawa	Wa	BMD	1851	689,531	Wisznice	Lu	B	1826-49	761,187
Warszawa	Wa	BMD	1851	689,532	Wizajny	Bi	BMD	1829-32	752,653
Warszawa	Wa	BMD	1852	689,533	Wizajny	Bi	BMD	1833-48	752,654
Warszawa	Wa	BMD	1852-53	689,534	Wizajny	Bi	BMD	1851-65	752,655
Warszawa	Wa	B	1847-54	689,535	Wizajny	Bi	BMD	1866-69	1,199,521
Warszawa	Wa	D	1851-53	689,536	Wizajny	Bi	BMD	1873-74	1,199,521
Warszawa	Wa	BMD	1854-55	689,537	Wizna	Bi	BMD	1828-36	747,728
Warszawa	Wa	BMD	1855	689,538	Wizna	Bi	BMD	1837-65	747,729
Warszawa	Wa	BMD	1853-56	689,539	Wizna	Bi	BMD	1868-73	1,199,536
Warszawa	Wa	BMD	1857	689,540	Wlodawa*	Ki	BMD	1844-59	761,192
Warszawa	Wa	BMD	1857	689,541	Wlodawa*	Ki	BD	1826-65	761,193
Warszawa	Wa	B	1857-60	689,542	*See also Slawatycze, Wisznice.				
Warszawa	Wa	BMD	1858-59	689,543	Wloszczowa*	Ki	BMD	1823-57	716,122
Warszawa	Wa	BMD	1860	689,544	Wloszczowa*	Ki	BMD	1858-65	716,149
Warszawa	Wa	BMD	1860	689,545	*See also Koniecpol.				
Warszawa	Wa	BMD	1860	689,546	Wloszczowa	Ki	BMD	1866-75	1,192,432
Warszawa	Wa	BMD	1861	689,547	Wloszczowa	Ki	BMD	1876	1,192,433
Warszawa	Wa	B	1862-63	689,548	Wodynie	Wa	BMD	1826-39	808,665
Warszawa	Wa	BMD	1862-64	689,549	Wodzislaw	Ki	BMD	1826-34	715,885
Warszawa	Wa	BMD	1862-63	689,550	Wodzislaw	Ki	BMD	1835-44	715,886
Warszawa	Wa	BMD	1863-66	689,551	Wodzislaw	Ki	BMD	1845-58	715,887
Warszawa	Wa	BMD	1863-64	689,552	Wodzislaw	Ki	BMD	1859-65	715,888
Warszawa	Wa	BMD	1864-66	689,553	Wodzislaw	Ki	BMD	1867-75	1,192,433
Warszawa	Wa	BMD	1864-65	689,554	Wodzislaw	Ki	BMD	1876-77	1,192,434
Warszawa	Wa	BMD	1865-66	689,555	Wohyn	Lu	BMD	1826-42	761,208
Warszawa	Wa	BMD	1865	689,556	Wohyn	Lu	BMD	1844-64	761,001
Warta	Lo	BMD	1809-15	753,084	Wojslawice	Lu	BMD	1826-50	767,024
Warta	Lo	BMD	1815-24	753,085	Wojslawice	Lu	BMD	1851-70	767,025
Warta	Lo	BMD	1823-32	753,086	Wolanów	Ki	BMD	1826-58	716,441
Warta	Lo	BMD	1833-50	753,087	Wolanów	Ki	Recs-5	1810-65	

Community	Province	Record Type	Record Span	Genealogical Society Record Number
Wolbórz	Lo	BMD	1826-46	753,174
Wolbórz	Lo	BMD	1847-56	753,175
Wolbórz	Lo	BMD	1857-67	760,149
Wolbrom	Kr	BM	1845-63	876,799
Wolbrom	Kr	BMD	1826-41	923,368
Wolbrom	Kr	BMD	1842-47	923,369
Wolbrom	Kr	BMD	1831-55	923,370
Wolbrom	Kr	BMD	1856-66	923,371
Wolbrom	Kr	BMD	1867-70	923,372
Wolczyn	Op	BD	1835-90	1,184,431
Wolomin	Wa		See Okuniew.	
Wroclaw	Wr	B	1760-1804 G	1,184,379
Wroclaw	Wr	B	1804-46 G	1,184,380
Wroclaw	Wr	B	1827-38 G	1,184,381
Wroclaw	Wr	B	1838-46 G	1,184,382
Wroclaw	Wr	B	1846-72 G	1,184,383
Wroclaw	Wr	B	1847, 1933-39 G	1,184,384
Wroclaw	Wr	B-Ind	1766-1812 G	1,184,384
Wroclaw	Wr	M	1772-73 G	1,184,384
Wroclaw	Wr	M	1784-96 G	1,184,385
Wroclaw	Wr	M	1797-1811 G	1,184,386
Wroclaw	Wr	M	1804-12, 1846-47 G	1,184,387
Wroclaw	Wr	M	1832-47 G	1,184,388
Wroclaw	Wr	M	1846-47, 1887-98 G	1,184,389
Wroclaw	Wr	M-Ind	1772-1812 G	1,184,389
Wroclaw	Wr	M-Ind	1873-1930 G	1,184,389
Wroclaw	Wr	M	1903-19 G	1,184,389
Wroclaw	Wr	M	1903-38 G	1,184,390
Wroclaw	Wr	D	1791-1812 G	1,184,390
Wroclaw	Wr	D	1813-59 G	1,184,391
Wroclaw	Wr	D	1815-27 G	1,184,392
Wroclaw	Wr	D	1860-74 G	1,184,393
Wroclaw	Wr	D	1910-21 G	1,184,394
Wroclaw	Wr	D	1914-27 G	1,184,395
Wroclaw	Wr	D	1914-27 G	1,184,396
Wroclaw	Wr	D	1918-26 G	1,184,397
Wroclaw	Wr	D	1928-40 G	1,184,398
Wroclaw	Wr	D	1928-40 G	1,184,399
Wroclaw	Wr	Recs-12	18th, 19th century G	1,184,400
Wroclaw	Wr	Recs-12	18th, 19th century G	1,184,401
Wroclaw	Wr	Recs-12	1761-1856 G	1,184,402
Wroclaw	Wr	D-Ind	1780-1874 G	1,184,402
Wroclaw	Wr	Recs-12	unknown G	1,184,403
Wroclaw	Wr	Recs-17	1743-1813 G	1,184,403
Wroclaw	Wr	Recs-18	1932-39 G	1,184,403
Wroclaw	Wr	Recs-6	1791 G	1,184,403
Wroclaw	Wr	Recs-6	1791 G	1,184,404
Wroclaw	Wr	BMD	1760-1940	1,184,379 1,184,404
Wroclaw	Wr	BMD	1812-1923	1,184,419
Wronki	Po	Recs-16	unknown	1,184,461
Wrzesnia	Po		See Pyzdry.	
Wrzesnia	Po	D	1867-69	1,186,460
Wrzesnia	Po	M	1859-60	1,186,460
Wschowa*	Zi	BMD	1838 G	896,082
Wschowa*	Zi	Recs-19	1890-1919 G	474,930
*See also Szlichtyngowa.				
Wschowa	Zi	BMD	1802-33	1,184,411
Wschowa	Zi	BMD	1763-1936	1,184,412
Wylatowo	By	BMD	1832-47	719,244
Wyrzysk	By		See Naklo Nad Notecia.	
Wysokie	Lu	BMD	1820-36	771,631
Wysokie Mazowieckie*	Bi	BMD	1826-48	747,730
Wysokie Mazowieckie*	Bi	BMD	1849-65	747,731
Wysokie Mazowieckie*	Bi	M	1859-1911	1,046,462
Wysokie Mazowieckie*	Bi	Recs-5	1665-1870	
*See also Czyzewo, Jablonka Koscielna, Jablonka Swierczewo.				
Wysokie Mazowieckie	Bi	D	1848-80	1,186,438
Wysokie Mazowieckie	Bi	BMD	1911	1,186,439
Wysokie Mazowieckie	Bi	M	1872	1,186,439
Wysokie Mazowieckie	Bi	M	1887-1911	1,186,439
Wysokie Mazowieckie	Bi	M	1908-09	1,186,439
Wysokie Mazowieckie	Bi	M	1936	1,186,439
Wysokie Mazowieckie	Bi	BM	1898-1927	1,186,440
Wysokie Mazowieckie	Bi	BMD	1834, 1861	1,186,440
Wysokie Mazowieckie	Bi	BMD	1863, 1867	1,186,440
Wysokie Mazowieckie	Bi	BMD	1869	1,186,440
Wysokie Mazowieckie	Bi	BMD	1898, 1905	1,186,441
Wysokie Mazowieckie	Bi	BMD	1909, 1910	1,186,441
Wysokie Mazowieckie	Bi	BD	1866	1,199,537
Wysokie Mazowieckie	Bi	MD	1868	1,199,537
Wysokie Mazowieckie	Bi	BMD	1869	1,199,537
Wysokie Mazowieckie	Bi	BMD	1862,1875	1,199,537
Wysokie Mazowieckie	Bi	BMD	1872	1,199,537
Wyszgrod	Wa	BMD	1826-35	730,206
Wyszgrod	Wa	BMD	1836-44	730,207
Wyszgrod	Wa	BMD	1845-51	730,208
Wyszgrod	Wa	BMD	1852-58	730,209
Wyszgrod	Wa	BMD	1859-65	730,210
Zabkowice Slaskie	Wr	Recs-12		1,184,411
Zabrize	Ka	M	1882-83	1,184,461
Zabrize	Ka	Recs-12+D	1873-1940	1,184,419
Zagan	Zi	Recs-12+D	1841-1937	1,184,450
Zagórów	Po	BMD	1826-43	765,779
Zagórów	Po	BMD	1844-65	765,780
Zaklików	Lu	BMD	1826-62	771,637
Zakroczym	Wa	BMD	1825-31	689,628
Zakroczym	Wa	BMD	1832-44	689,629
Zakroczym	Wa	BMD	1845-50	689,630
Zakroczym	Wa	BMD	1851-57	689,631
Zakroczym	Wa	BMD	1858-63	689,632
Zambrow*	Bi	BMD	1842-47	747,732
Zambrow*	Bi	BMD	1848-65	747,733
*See also Kolaki, Zawady.				
Zambrow	Bi	BMD	1867, 1869, 1870	1,199,537
Zambrow	Bi	BMD	1872-74	1,199,538
Zamość*	Lu	B	1832-43	771,650
Zamość*	Lu	BMD	1832-52	771,651
Zamość*	Lu	BMD	1826-65	755,697
Zamość*	Lu	Recs-5	1810-69	
*See also Krasnobród, Szczebrzeszyn.				
Zaniemyśl	Po	BMD	1817-39 G	1,184,450
Zareby Kościelne	Wa	BMD	1836-45	810,610
Zareby Kościelne	Wa	BMD	1846-59	810,611
Zarki	Ka	M	1826-29	1,199,847
Zarki	Ka	B	1826-29	1,199,847
Zarki	Ka	B	1833-40	1,199,848
Zarki	Ka	B	1841-48	1,199,848
Zarki	Ka	M	1830-36	1,199,848

Zarki	Ka	M	1838	1,199,848
Zarki	Ka	D	1826-48	1,199,848
Zarki	Ka	B	1849-60	1,199,849
Zarki	Ka	M	1855-57	1,199,849
Zarki	Ka	M	1859-60	1,199,849
Zarki	Ka	D	1848-52	1,199,849
Zarki	Ka	D	1850	1,199,849
Zarki	Ka	D	1853-56	1,199,849
Zarki	Ka	D	1859-68	1,199,850
Zarki	Ka	D	1870-74	1,199,850
Zarki	Ka	B	1861-62	1,199,850
Zarki	Ka	B	1867-74	1,199,850
Zarki	Ka	B	1875-76	1,199,851
Zarki	Ka	MD	1875-78	1,199,851
Zarki	Ka	B	1877-78	1,199,851
Zarnow	Ki	BMD	1826-53	718,949
Zarnow	Ki	BMD	1854-65	718,950
Zarnow	Ki	BMD	1866-73	1,192,434
Zarnowiec	Kr	BMD	1826-33	876,807
Zarnowiec	Kr	BMD	1834-52	876,808
Zarnowiec	Kr	BMD	1834-54	876,809
Zarnowiec	Kr	MD	1833-70	876,810
Zarnowiec	Kr	BMD	1858-68	923,375
Zarnowiec	Kr	BMD	1811-24	876,803
Zarnowiec	Kr	BMD	1825	876,804
Zarnowiec	Kr	BMD	1826-33	876,807
Zarnowiec	Kr	BMD	1834-52	876,808
Zarnowiec	Kr	BMD	1853-57	876,809
Zarnowiec	Kr	B	1826-54	876,809
Zarnowiec	Kr	M	1826-38	876,809
Zarnowiec	Kr	M	1839-70	876,810
Zarnowiec	Kr	D	1833-48	876,810
Zarnowiec	Kr	BMD	1858-68	923,375
Zawady	Bi	Recs-5	1808-70	
Zawichost	Ki	BMD	1826-38	809,137
Zawichost	Ki	BMD	1839-50	809,138
Zawichost	Ki	BMD	1851-58	809,139
Zawichost	Ki	BMD	1859-64	809,140
Zawichost	Ki	BMD	1865-66	1,199,831
Zawichost	Ki	BMD	1867-77	1,199,832
Zawichost	Ki	BMD	1877	1,199,833
Zawiercie	Ka		See Kromolów.	
Zouńska Wola	Lo	BMD	1826-54	753,220
Zouńska Wola	Lo	BMD	1850-65	753,221
Zouńska Wola	Lo	BMD	1866-67	760,161
Zouny	Po	MD	1818-47	765,799
Zgierz	Lo	BMD	1826-46	753,243
Zgierz	Lo	BMD	1847-59	753,244
Zgierz	Lo	BMD	1860-65	753,245
Zgierz	Lo	BMD	1866-70	760,165
Zgorzelec	Wr	Recs-12	1850-1940	1,184,417
Zgorzelec	Wr	BMD	1864-1932	1,184,418
Ziebice	Wr	MD	1824-77	1,184,442
Zloczew	Lo	BMD	1826-30	766,318
Zloczew	Lo	BMD	1831-58	766,319
Zloczew	Lo	BMD	1859-65	766,320
Zloczew	Lo	BMD	1866	760,168
Zloczew	Lo	Recs-5	1808-70	
Zlotów	Ko		See Krajenka.	
Zlotów	Ko	BMD	1813-46	1,184,410
Zlotów	Ko	BMD	1813-46	1,184,411
Zmigrod	Wr	Recs-12	unknown	1,184,461
Zólkiewka	Lu	BMD	1827-49	753,996
Zólkiewka	Lu	BMD	1850-60	753,997
Zólkiewka	Lu	BMD	1861-70	904,337
Zory	Ka	D	1837-79 G	1,184,456
Zuromin*	Wa	BMD		
Zuromin*	Wa	BMD		
*See also Biezuń, Kuczbork.				
Zwoleń	Ki	BMD	1826-33	716,373
Zwoleń	Ki	BMD	1834-51	716,374
Zwoleń	Ki	BMD	1852-58	716,375
Zwoleń	Ki	BMD	1859-65	716,376

Hungarian Jewish Records On Microfilm

The Genealogical Society of Utah's collection of Hungarian Jewish records was microfilmed at the Hungarian National Archives about twenty years ago. The records consist primarily of birth, marriage, and death entries compiled between 1800 and 1895, with most dating after 1845. Small communities did not maintain their own vital records and are included in the records of larger nearby communities. The name of the larger jurisdiction can be determined by using a gazetteer of old Hungary, *Magyarország Helységnévtára*, which is also on microfilm at the society (call numbers 599,564 and 973,041). Records not available on microfilm can be requested by correspondence.

The towns included in the following register are for the most part located in what is now Hungary, but there are some communities that are now a part of Austria, Czechoslavakia, Romania, or Yugoslavia. All of the communities listed were part of Hungary prior to 1918.

The society also has microfilmed copies of the 1848 Jewish census. The census lists the names of all members of the household, their ages, and their places of birth. The collection consists of six rolls of microfilm.

The following register was originally compiled by *Toledot: The Journal of Jewish Genealogy* (volume 1, no. 3) in 1977. It is reproduced here with permission. This list is arranged alphabetically by name of Hungarian community (column 1). The term *kerület* after a place name refers to the "district" surrounding that locality. "Neolog" and "Orthodox" refer, respectively, to the "reform" and "orthodox" components of the Jewish community.

The second column is a code for the name of the present-day county in which the community is situated. An asterisk (*) means that the locality is no longer in Hungary; the next line explains where it is. The following codes are used:

Ba	Baranya	Nó	Nógrád
BAZ	Borsod-Abaúj-Zemplén	Pe	Pest
Bé	Békés	So	Somogy
BK	Bács-Kiskun	SS	Szabolcs-Szatmár
Cs	Csongrád	Sz	Szolnok
Fe	Fejér	To	Tolna
GS	Gyór-Sopron	Va	Vas
HB	Hajdu-Bihar	Ve	Veszprém
He	Heves	Za	Zala
Ko	Komárom		

The third column refers to the type of records available on microfilm for that place. "B", "M", and "D" indicate, respectively, birth, marriage, and death records. "Circum" refers to circumcision records. "Census" means a census of Jews for that community. "-Ind" following "B", "M", or "D" refers to an index for that particular group of records.

Column 4 is the span of years for which records in column 3 are available. It must be noted, however, that the records may *not* be complete for the entire span indicated, as there are often gaps in the records.

The last column refers to the microfilm reel number used by the library of the Genealogical Society of Utah to identify that particular set of records. Use this number in ordering film from Salt Lake City. A particular reel frequently contains records for more than one community.

Community	Province	Record Type	Record Span	Genealogical Society Record Number
Aba	Fe	BMD	1800-95	642,794
Abaújszántó	BAZ	BMD	1842-88	642,726
Abaújszántó	BAZ	BMD	1888-95	642,727
Abony	Pe	BMD	1837-95	642,846
Ács	Ko	BMD	1868-95	642,837
Ádánd	So	BMD	1845-95	642,880

Community	Province	Record Type	Record Span	Genealogical Society Record Number
Adony	Fe	BMD	1850-85	642,794
Ajak	SS	BMD	1876-95	642,900
Akasztó	BK	BD	1883-90	642,848
Albertirsa	Pe	BMD	1847-95	642,848
Álmosd	HB	BMD	1852-85	642,750
Alpár	BK	BD	1883-85	642,849
Anarcs	SS	BMD	1876-95	642,900
Apagy	SS	BMD	1849-86	642,900
Apostag	BK	BMD	1825-95	642,849
Aszód	Pe	BMD	1837-95	642,849
Bácsbokod	BK	BMD	1858-85	642,728
Baja	BK	B	1853-85	642,728
Baja	BK	B	1886-95	642,729
Baja	BK	M	1853-95	642,729
Baja	BK	D	1853-77	642,729
Baja	BK	D	1877-95	642,730
Bajai kerület	BK	BMD	1886-95	642,730
Bakonszeg	HB	BMD	1876-85	642,750
Bakonyszentkirály	Ve	B	1840-84	642,940
Baksa és Szentlőrinc	Ba	BMD	1851-95	642,741
Baksa és Szentlőrinc	Ba	Census	Unknown	642,741
Balassagyarmat	Nó	BMD	1850-80	642,840
Balassagyarmat	Nó	D	1850-67	642,841
Balassagyarmat	Nó	D	1886-95	642,841
Balassagyarmat	Nó	B	1850-78	642,841
Balassagyarmat	Nó	M	1850-95	642,841
Balatonboglár	So	B	1768-1883	642,880
Balatonfőkajár	Ve	BMD	1815-95	642,940
Balatonfüred	Ve	BMD	1863-95	642,945
Balkány	SS	BMD	1845-62	642,900
Balkány	SS	BMD	1853-95	642,901
Balmazújváros	HB	BMD	1876-95	642,807
Bán	Ba		See Ivándárda és Bán.	
Baracska	Fe	BD	1842-72	642,794
Baracska és Csátalja	BK	BMD	1853-85	642,731
Báránd	HB	BM	1877-95	642,750
Bátaszék	To	BMD	1851-95	642,922
Bátmonostor	BK	BMD	1854-84	642,731
Bátorkeszi	*	BMD	1834-67	642,791
*now Vojnice, Západoslovenský kraj, Czechoslovakia.				
Battonya	Bé	BMD	1851-95	642,780
Becske	Nó	BMD	1856-82	642,841
Bedó	HB	BMD	1880-85	642,750
Békés	Bé	B	1851-95	642,742
Békés	Bé	MD	1855-95	642,742
Békéscsaba	Bé	B-Ind	1820-85	642,743
Békéscsaba	Bé	B-Ind	1886-95	642,744
Békéscsaba	Bé	M-Ind	1844-95	642,744
Békéscsaba	Bé	D-Ind	1844-95	642,744
Békéscsaba	Bé	MD	1850-90	642,745
Békéscsaba	Bé	B	1881-90	642,745
Békéscsaba-Orthodox		BMD	1883-95	642,745
Békésszentandrás	Bé	BMD	1850-85	642,745
Beled	GS	BMD	1836-95	642,897
Bercel	Nó	BMD	1884-88	642,841
Berekböszörmény	HB	BMD	1877-85	642,751
Berettyószentmárton	HB	BMD	1878-95	642,751
Berettyóújfalu	HB	BMD	1846-95	642,752
Besenyőd	SS	BMD	1849-85	642,902
Bezi	GS	BMD	1839-85	642,803
Bicske	Fe	BMD	1886-95	642,795
Biharkeresztes	HB	BMD	1877-92	642,753
Biharnagybajom	HB	BMD	1845-95	642,753
Bihartorda	HB	BMD	1877-86	642,753
Biharugra	HB	BMD	1877-85	642,753
Bócs	BAZ	B	1864-85	642,765
Bodrogkeresztúr	BAZ	BMD		642,952
Bojt	HB	BMD	1876-86	642,753
Bölcske	To	BMD	1846-85	642,924
Boldogasszony	*	BMD	1835-95	700,859
*now Frauenkirchen, Burgenland, Austria.				
Bonyhád	To	BMD	1851-95	642,923
Budai kerület	Pe		See Budapest.	
Budapest-Neolog, Pesti kerület	Pe	MD	1885	642,986
Budapest-Neolog, Pesti kerület	Pe	B-Ind	1836-74	642,986
Budapest-Neolog, Pesti kerület	Pe	B-Ind	1875-92	642,987
Budapest-Neolog, Pesti kerület	Pe	M-Ind	1836-79	642,987
Budapest-Neolog Pesti kerület	Pe	M-Ind	1880-95	642,988
Budapest-Neolog, Pesti kerület	Pe	D-Ind	1836-84	642,988
Budapest-Neolog, Pesti kerület	Pe	D-Ind	1885-95	642,989
Budapest-Neolog, Pesti kerület	Pe	B	1836-51	642,961
Budapest-Neolog, Pesti kerület	Pe	B	1851-62	642,962
Budapest-Neolog, Pesti kerület	Pe	B	1863-67	642,963
Budapest-Neolog, Pesti kerület	Pe	B	1868-71	642,964
Budapest-Neolog, Pesti kerület	Pe	B	1872-76	642,965
Budapest-Neolog, Pesti kerület	Pe	B	1876-79	642,966
Budapest-Neolog, Pesti kerület	Pe	B	1879-82	642,967
Budapest-Neolog, Pesti kerület	Pe	B	1882-86	642,968
Budapest-Neolog, Pesti kerület	Pe	B	1886-88	642,969
Budapest-Neolog, Pesti kerület	Pe	B	1889-90	642,970
Budapest-Neolog, Pesti kerület	Pe	B	1890-92	642,971
Budapest-Neolog, Pesti kerület	Pe	B	1892-94	642,972
Budapest-Neolog, Pesti kerület	Pe	B	1894-95	642,973
Budapest-Neolog, Pesti kerület	Pe	M	1836-59	642,973
Budapest-Neolog, Pesti kerület	Pe	M	1851-71	642,974
Budapest-Neolog, Pesti kerület	Pe	M	1871-88	642,975
Budapest-Neolog, Pesti kerület	Pe	M	1888-95	642,976
Budapest-Neolog, Pesti kerület	Pe	D	1836-46	642,976
Budapest-Neolog, Pesti kerület	Pe	D	1847-60	642,977
Budapest-Neolog, Pesti kerület	Pe	D	1847-60	642,977
Budapest-Neolog, Pesti kerület	Pe	D	1861-67	642,978
Budapest-Neolog, Pesti kerület	Pe	D	1868-75	642,979
Budapest-Neolog, Pesti kerület	Pe	D	1876-78	720,185
Budapest-Neolog, Pesti kerület	Pe	D	1879-83	642,980
Budapest-Neolog, Pesti kerület	Pe	D	1884-86	642,981
Budapest-Neolog, Pesti kerület	Pe	D	1886-88	642,982
Budapest-Neolog, Pesti kerület	Pe	D	1889-92	642,983
Budapest-Neolog, Pesti kerület	Pe	D	1892-94	642,984

Budapest-Neolog, Pesti kerület	Pe	D	1895	642,985
Budapest-Neolog, Pesti kerület	Pe	M	1848-66	642,985
Budapest-Orthodox, Pesti kerület	B		1872-95	642,990
Budapest-Orthodox, Pesti kerület	M		1871-85	642,990
Budapest-Orthodox, Pesti kerület	D		1890-95	642,990
Budapest-Neolog, Budai kerület	B		1820-95	642,991
Budapest-Neolog, Budai kerület	M		1823-85	642,991
Budapest-Neolog, Budai kerület	M		1886-95	642,992
Budapest-Neolog, Budai kerület	D		1831-95	642,992
Budapest-Orthodox, Budai kerület	B		1876-95	642,993
Budapest-Orthodox, Budai kerület	M		1876-95	642,993
Budapest-Orthodox, Kőbányi kerület	Circum		1876-95	642,993
Budapest-Orthodox, Kőbányi kerület	M		1877-95	642,993
Budapest-Orthodox, Kőbányi kerület	D		1885-95	642,993
Budapest-Obundai kerület	B		1802-85	642,994
Budapest-Obundai kerület	B		1886-95	642,995
Budapest-Obundai kerület	M		1851-95	642,995
Budapest-Obundai kerület	D		1851-73	642,995
Budapest-Obundai kerület	D		1874-95	642,996
Budapest-Obundai kerület	B-Ind		1803-95	642,997
Budapest-Obundai kerület	D-Ind		1851-95	642,997
Budapest-Obundai kerület	BMD		1889-95	642,997
Budapest-Cinkota			See Cinkota.	
Budapest-Kőbánya			See Budapest.	
Budapest-Nagytétény			See Nagytétény.	
Budapest-Soroksár			See Soroksár.	
Budapest-Újpest			See Újpest.	
Cece	Fe	B	1844	642,795
Cece	Fe	BMD	1851-95	642,795
Cegléd	Pe	BMD	1850-95	642,850
Celldömölk	Va	BMD	1877-95	642,933
Cinkota	Pe	BMD	1878-82	642,851
Csabrendek	Ve	B-Ind	1771-1895	642,945
Csabrendek	Ve	BMD	1828-95	642,946
Csátalja	Bk		See Baracska és Csátalja.	
Csécse	Nó	BMD	1850-95	642,841
Csenger	SS	BD	1851-95	642,919
Csepreg	Va	BMD	1886-95	642,898
Csökmö	HB	BMD	1854-95	642,754
Csongrád	Cs	BMD	1841-95	642,781
Csorna	GS	BMD	1850-95	642,898
Csurgó	So	B	1776-1895	642,881
Csurgó	So	M	1856-95	642,881
Csurgó	So	D	1856-95	642,882
Csurgó	So	BMD	1848-95	642,882

Dabas	Pe	BMD	1850-95	642,851
Darvas	HB	BMD	1877-95	642,754
Dávod	BK	BMD	1854-94	642,731
Debrecen	HB	B	1856-95	642,807
Debrecen	HB	M	1856-95	642,808
Debrecen	HB	D	1859-95	642,808
Debrecen-(Orthodox)	HB	BMD	1870-95	642,808
Debrecen	HB	Census	1848	719,823
Debrecen	HB	Census	1870	722,262
Derecske	HB	BMD	1871-95	642,755
Dévaványa	Bé	BMD	1846-95	642,827
Diósgyór	BAZ	BMD	1859-95	642,765
Döge	SS	BMD	1886-95	642,902
Dombóvár	To	BMD	Unknown	642,924
Dombrád	SS	BMD	1876-95	642,902
Domony	Pe	BMD	1840-84	642,851
Dömsöd	Pe	BMD	1876-82	642,851
Dunaföldvár	To	BMD	1851-95	642,925
Dunaföldvár	To	BMD	1852-95	642,926
Dunapataj	BK	BMD	1850-95	642,852
Dunspentele	Fe		See Dunaújváros.	
Dunaújváros	Fe	B	1843-95	642,795
Dunaújváros	Fe	MD	1851-95	642,795
Ecser	Pe	BD	1869-83	642,852
Eger	He	BM	1840-95	642,815
Eger	He	D	1850-95	642,816
Egyek	HB	BMD	1873-85	642,809
Encsencs	SS	BMD	1871-85	642,902
Enying	Fe	BMD	1845-95	642,941
Eperjes	*	Census	1848	719,823
*now Prešov, Východoslovenský kraj, Czechoslavakia.				
Ercsi	Fe	BMD	1882-95	642,796
Erdőbénye	BAZ	BMD	1840-95	642,952
Erdótelek	He	BMD	1876-85	642,816
Erk	He	BD	1876-85	642,816
Érpatak	SS	BMD	1870-85	642,902
Esztár	HB	BMD	1877-95	642,756
Esztergom	Ko	B	1828-95	642,791
Esztergom	Ko	M	1835-72	642,791
Esztergom	Ko	M	1872-95	642,792
Esztergom	Ko	D	1833-95	642,792
Esztergom-Orthodox	Ko	BMD	1872-75	642,792
Esztergom-Orthodox	Ko	BMD	1880-95	642,793
Fadd	To	BMD	1850-86	642,927
Farmos	Pe	BD	1878-95	642,852
Fehérgyarmat	SS	BMD	1851-95	642,919
Felsómindszent	Ba		See Mindszent.	
Fényeslitke	SS	BMD	1874-95	642,902
Földes	HB	BMD	1863-95	642,809
Fülek	*	BMD	1856-95	642,842
*now Filakovo, Středoslovenský kraj, Czechoslovakia.				
Furta	HB	BMD	1877-95	642,756
Füzesabony	He	BMD	1876-86	642,816
Füresgyarmat	Bé	BMD	1879-85	642,746
Gáborján	HB	BMD	1877-95	642,756
Galgagyörk	Pe	BMD	1848-95	642,852
Gara	BK	B	1857-82	642,731
Gara	BK	M	1860-79	642,731
Gara	BK	D	1861-85	642,731
Gáva	SS	BMD	1854-95	642,902
Gemzse	SS	BMD	1852-82	642,902
Geszt	Bé	BMD	1878-85	642,756
Gesztеréd	SS	BMD	1852-95	642,902
Gige	So	BMD	1862-85	642,883
Gödöllő	Pe	BMD	1851-95	642,853
Gödöllő kerület	Pe	BMD	1838-85	642,854
Gönc	BAZ	BMD	1850-82	642,728
Gyoma	Bé	BMD	1862-95	642,746
Gyömöre	GS	BMD	1841-95	642,803
Gyömrő	Pe	BD	1871-80	642,854
Gyón	Pe	BMD	1859-72	642,854
Gyöngyös	He	B	1846-76	642,816
Gyöngyös	He	B	1876-95	642,817

Community	Province	Record Type	Record Span	Genealogical Society Record Number
Gyöngyös	He	M	1846-95	642,817
Gyöngyös	He	D	1846-95	642,818
Gyöngyös-Orthodox	He	MD	1881-95	642,818
Gyöngyös-Orthodox	He	B	1846-63	642,818
Gyöngyös-Orthodox	He	D	1851-63	642,818
Gyöngyös-Orthodox	He	BMD	1864-78	642,819
Gyöngyös-Orthodox	He	BMD	1879-95	642,820
Gyöngyös-Orthodox	He	Census	1848	719,823
Gyöngyös-mellék	Ba	BMD	1848-95	642,883
Győnk	To	BMD	1831-95	642,927
Győr	GS	BMD	1846-95	642,804
Győr	GS	Census	1848	719,823
Győrasszonyfa	GS	BMD	1853-85	642,847
Győrszent-márton	GS	BMD	1850-95	642,847
Győrsziget	GS	BMD	1840-95	642,805
Gyula	Bé	BMD	1863-95	642,747
Gyulaháza	SS	BMD	1852-95	642,902
Hahót	Za.	BMD	1871-95	642,946
Hajdubagos	HB	BMD	1877-85	642,757
Hajdubös-zörmény	HB	BMD	1861-95	642,757
Hajdudorog	HB	BMD	1851-95	642,809
Hajduhadház	HB	BMD	1856-95	642,809
Hajdunánás	HB	BMD	1851-95	642,810
Hajdusámson	HB	BMD	1845-95	642,811
Hajduszoboszló	HB	BMD	1826-95	642,812
Hajduszovát	HB	BMD	1853-95	642,813
Hajduszovát	HB	BMD	1876-95	642,757
Hatvan	He	BMD	1850-95	642,821
Hédervár	Gs	BMD	1858-85	642,806
Hegyközszentimre	*	BMD	1869-77	642,757
*now in Crisana, Rumania.				
Hejőcsaba	BAZ		See Miskolc-Hejocsaba.	
Hencida	HB	BMD	1877-95	642,757
Hidas	Ba	BMD	1875-84	642,731
Hidas és Pécsváradi kerület	Ba	Census	1850	642,731
Hodász	SS	BMD	1876-85	642,919
Hódmezővas-árhely	Cs	BM	1844-95	642,782
Hódmezővas-árhely	Cs	D	1844-76	642,782
Hódmezővas-árhely	Cs	D	1877-95	642,783
Hódmezővas-árhely	Cs	B	1846-95	642,783
Hódmezővas-árhely	Cs	M	1849-95	642,783
Hódmezővas-árhely	Cs	D	1850-95	642,783
Hőgyész	To	BMD	1842-95	642,928
Hógyészkerület	To	BMD	1851-94	642,928
Hógyészkerület	To	BMD	1842-83	642,929
Hosszúpályi	HB	BMD	1877-85	642,757
Ivándárdaés Bán	Ba	BMD	1851-95	642,732
Izsák	BK	BMD	1843-95	642,854
Jánosháza	Va	BMD	1850-95	642,933
Jármi	SS	BMD	1806-85	642,919
Jász kerület	Sz	B	1877-85	642,830
Jász kerület	Sz	M	1862-85	642,831
Jász kerület	Sz	D	1854-85	642,831
Jászapáti	Sz	BMD	1878-89	642,827
Jászberény	Sz	B	1851-95	642,827
Jászberény	Sz	MD	1851-95	642,828
Jászberény kerület	Sz	B	1851-95	642,829
Jászberény kerület	Sz	BMD	1851-95	642,830
Jászszen-tandrás	Sz	B	1886-88	642,831
Jéke	SS	BMD	1886-91	642,902
Józsa	HB	BMD	1886	642,757
Kaba	HB	BMD	1835-95	642,757
Kaba	HB	BMD	1876-95	642,813
Kabold	*	Circum	1833-95	700,788
*now Kobersdorf, Burgenland, Austria.				
Kadarkút	So	BMD	1851-85	642,883
Kajászó	Fe	BMD	1813-95	642,796
Kállósemjén	SS	BMD	1870-95	642,902
Kalocsa	BK	BMD	1850-95	642,855
Kalocsa	BK	BMD	1850-95	642,856
Kántorjánosi	SS	M	1876-85	642,919
Kapolcs	Ve	BMD	1867-95	642,947
Kápolnás nyék	Fe	BMD	1777-95	642,797
Kaposmérő	So	BMD	1861-84	642,883
Kaposvár	So	B	1771-1895	642,884
Kaposvár	So	M	1851-95	642,884
Kaposvár	So	D	1851-85	642,884
Kaposvár	So	D	1886-95	642,885
Kaposvár	So	BMD	1844-77	642,885
Kaposvár	So	BMD	1878-95	642,886
Kapuvár	GS	BMD	1879-95	642,899
Karád	So	B	1881-85	642,887
Karcag kerület	Sz	BMD	1856-95	642,831
Kecskemét	BK	BMD	1832-95	642,857
Kékcse	SS	BMD	1886-95	642,902
Kemecse	SS	BMD	1875-95	642,903
Kerekegyháza	BK	B	1863-85	642,857
Keszthely	Ve	BMD	1852-95	642,947
Kisbér	Ko	BMD	1868-95	642,838
Kiskőrös	BK	B	1866-85	642,857
Kiskőrös	BK	M	1811-95	642,857
Kiskőrös	BK	D	1851-85	642,858
Kiskőrös - Orthodox	BK	B	1821-85	642,858
Kiskőrös - Orthodox	BK	BMD	1842-95	642,858
Kiskunfélegy-háza	BK	BMD	1851-95	642,860
Kiskunhalas	BK	BMD	1851-95	642,859
Kiskunmajsa	BK	BMD	1850-95	642,860
Kisléta	SS	BMD	1876-85	642,903
Kismarja	HB	BMD	1877-86	642,758
Kismarton	*	Circum	1833-95	700,794
Kismarton	*	MD	1833-95	700,794
*now Eisenstadt, Burgenland, Austria.				
Kistelek	Cs	BMD	1859-80	642,783
Kisújszállás kerület	Sz	BMD	1851-95	642,831
Kisvárda	SS	BMD	1851-85	642,904
Kisvárda	SS	BM	1886-95	642,904
Kisvárda	SS	D	1886-95	642,905
Kisvárda	SS	B	1851-95	642,905
Kisvárda	SS	M	1851-95	642,906
Kisvárda	SS	D	1852-95	642,906
Kisvarsány	SS		See Varsány.	
Kőbányai kerület	Pe		See Budapest.	
Kóka	Pe	BMD	1877-95	642,861
Kokad	HB	BMD	1877-85	642,758
Komádi	HB	BMD	1877-85	642,758
Komoró	SS	BMD	1881-95	642,907
Konyár	HB	BMD	1879-85	642,758
Köpscény	*	BMD	1835-95	700,871
*now Kittsee, Burgenland, Austria.				
Körmend	Va	B	1851-95	642,933
Körmend	Va	BMD	1841-95	642,934
Körösladány	Bé	BMD	1879-95	642,747
Körösnagy-haršany	Bé	BMD	1877-85	642,758
Körösszakál	HB	BMD	1877-85	642,758
Körösszegá-pati	HB	BMD	1877-95	642,758
Kőszeg	Va	BMD	1851-95	642,935
Kötegyán	Bé	BMD	1879-85	642,758
Kővágóörs	Ve	BMD	1847-95	642,948
Kunhegyes kerület	Sz	BMD	1851-95	642,832
Kunmadaras	Sz	BMD	1855-95	642,832
Kunszentmárton kerület	Sz	B	1850-79	642,832
Kunszentmiklós	BK	BMD	1855-95	642,861
Lajtakáta	*	BMD	1835-95	700,874
*now Gattendorf, Burgenland, Austria.				
Lakompak	*	Circum	1833-95	700,801

Lakompak	*	MD	1833-95	700,801
*Now Lackenbach, Burgenland, Austria.				
Laskod	SS	BMD	1886-95	642,907
Lengyeltóti	So	BMD	1846-95	642,887
Lepsény	Fe	B	1863-85	642,941
Lőrinci	He	BMD	1850-95	642,843
Losonc	*	B	1850-95	642,842
Losonc	*	B	1850-85	642,843
Losonc – Orthodox	*	B	1884-85	642,843
Losonc	*	BMD	1850-65	642,843
*now Lučenec, Středoslovenský kraj, Czechoslovakia.				
Lovasberény	Fe	BMD	1764-1895	642,797
Mád	BAZ	BMD	1827-95	642,952
Mágocs	Ba	BMD	1851-86	642,733
Mágocs	Ba	BD	1857-85	642,733
Mágocs	Ba	BMD	1833-95	642,734
Magy	SS	BMD	1852-84	642,907
Magyargencs	Ve	BMD	1893-95	642,935
Magyarhomorog	HB	BMD	1877-85	642,758
Makó	Cs	BMD	1833-95	672,780
Mándok	SS	BMD	1850-85	642,907
Mándok	SS	B	1886-95	642,907
Mándok	SS	MD	1886-95	642,908
Mándok	SS	BMD	1850-95	642,908
Marcali	So	B	1774-1895	642,887
Marcali	So	M	1807-95	642,887
Marcali	So	D	1851-95	642,888
Marcali	So	BMD	1845-95	642,888
Mátészalka	SS	BMD	1863-95	642,920
Mezőberény	Bé	BMD	1874-95	642,747
Mezőcsát	BAZ	BMD	1851-95	642,767
Mezőgyán	Bé	BMD	1878-85	642,758
Mezőkeresztes	BAZ	BMD	1851-95	642,767
Mezőkövesd	BAZ	BMD	1851-95	642,768
Mezőladány	SS	BMD	1858-85	642,908
Mezőpeterd	HB	BMD	1877-84	642,759
Mezőszilas	Fe		See Szilasbalhas.	
Mezőtúr	Sz	BMD	1850-95	642,832
Mihályfa	Ve	BMD	1866-95	642,948
Mikepércs	HB	BMD	1886	642,759
Mindszent	Ba	BMD	1851-80	642,733
Mindszent	Cs	BMD	1851-95	642,784
Miskolc	BAZ	B-Ind	1838-81	642,769
Miskolc	BAZ	BMD	1879-86	642,770
Miskolc	BAZ	B	1882-95	642,770
Miskolc	BAZ	M	1871-75	642,770
Miskolc	BAZ	M	1882-88	642,770
Miskolc	BAZ	M	1889-95	642,771
Miskolc	BAZ	D	1871-95	642,771
Miskolc	BAZ	B	1836-83	642,772
Miskolc	BAZ	B	1884-95	642,773
Miskolc	BAZ	M	1851-95	642,774
Miskolc	BAZ	D	1851-82	642,775
Miskolc	BAZ	D	1883-95	642,776
Miskolc	BAZ	Census	1848	719,823
Miskolc-Diósgyőr	BAZ		See Diósgyor.	
Miskolc-Hejőcsaba	BAZ	BMD	1851-95	642,766
Mohács	Ba	BMD	1851-95	642,735
Monor	Pe	BMD	1835-95	642,861
Monor	Pe	BMD	1837-95	642,862
Monostorpályi	HB	BMD	1889-95	642,759
Mór	Fe	BMD	1841-95	642,798
Mosonmagyaróvár	GS	BMD	1835-95	601,568
Muraszombat	*	BMD	1835-95	642,935
*now Murska Sobota, Slovenija, Yugoslavia.				
Nádudvar	HB	BMD	1850-95	642,813
Nagyatád	So	BM	1851-95	642,888
Nagyatád	So	D	1851-77	642,888
Nagyatád	So	D	1860-95	642,889
Nagyatád	So	BMD	1861-95	642,889
Nagybajom	So	BMD	1870-95	642,889
Nagybajom	So	BMD	1856-95	642,890
Nagybaracska	BK		See Baracska és Csátalja.	
Nagydobos	SS	BMD	1859-85	642,920
Nagyecsed	SS	BMD	1856-85	642,920
Nagykálló	SS	BMD	1844-95	642,909
Nagykanizsa	Za	BMD	1835-95	642,949
Nagykáta	Pe	BMD	1851-95	642,862
Nagykáta	Pe	BMD	1859-95	642,863
Nagykőrös	Pe	BMD	1834-95	642,864
Nagyléta	HB	BMD	1875-95	642,759
Nagymárton	*	Circum	1833-95	700,813
Nagymárton	*	MD	1833-95	700,813
*now Mattersburg, Burgenland, Austria.				
Nagyoroszi	Nó	BMD	1850-95	642,843
Nagyrábé	HB	BMD	1875-95	642,759
Nagysimonyi	Va	BMD	1851-95	642,936
Nagyszombat	*	Census	1848	719,823
*now Trnava, Západoslovenský kraj, Czechoslovakia.				
Nagytétény	Pe	B	1760-1895	642,865
Nagytétény	Pe	M	1820-95	642,865
Nagytétény	Pe	D	1851-95	642,865
Nagytétény	Pe	BMD	1850-95	642,866
Nagyvarsány	SS		See Varsány.	
Nagyvázsony	Ve	BMD	1842-95	642,941
Nemesszalók	Ve	BMD	1875-88	642,936
Németújvár	*	BMD	1841-95	700,702
*now Güssing, Burgenland, Austria.				
Nyírábrány	HB	B	1867-84	642,759
Nyíracsád	HB	BMD	1863-95	642,910
Nyíradony	HB	BMD	1871-85	642,759
Nyírbátor	SS	BMD	1845-90	642,911
Nyírbátor	SS	BMD	1851-95	642,912
Nyírbogát	SS	BMD	1851-85	642,913
Nyírderzs	SS	M	1876-85	642,920
Nyíregyháza	SS	BMD	1866-95	642,913
Nyírgelse	SS	BMD	1850-85	642,913
Nyíribrony	SS	BMD	1852-80	642,913
Nyírkarász	SS	BMD	1876-86	642,913
Nyírlugos	SS	BMD	1870-85	642,913
Nyírmada	SS	BMD	1851-95	642,914
Nyírmeggyes	SS	BMD	1853-95	642,921
Nyírmihálydi	SS	BMD	1850-85	642,915
Nyírtass	SS	BMD	1852-95	642,915
Obudai kerület	Pe		See Budapest.	
Okány	Bé	BMD	1877-85	642,759
Oláhapati	*	BMD	1877-82	642,759
*now in Crisana, Rumania.				
Olaszilszka	BAZ	BMD	1841-95	642,953
Onod	BAZ	BMD	1851-95	642,777
Opályi	SS	BMD	1874-85	642,921
Orosháza	Bé	BMD	1874-95	642,747
Oroszvár	*	BMD	1835-95	601,569
*now Rusovce, Západoslovenský kraj, Czechoslovakia.				
Ózd	BAZ	BMD	1867-95	642,777
Pacsa	Za	BMD	1838-95	642,950
Paks	To	BMD	1887-95	642,929
Paks - Orthodox	To	B	1830-93	642,931
Paks - Orthodox	To	BMD	1852-95	642,931
Pánd	Pe	BMD	1860-95	642,867
Pap	SS	BMD	1878-94	642,915
Pápa	Va	BMD	1848-95	642,942
Papos	SS	BMD	1874-85	642,921
Pásztó	Nó	BMD	1833-95	642,822
Patahaza	GS	BMD	1839-44	642,806
Pátroha	SS	BMD	1852-95	642,915
Pécel	Pe	BMD	1859-84	642,867
Pécs	Ba	BM	1851-95	642,736
Pécs	Ba	D	1851-95	642,737
Pécs	Ba	B	1860-95	642,737
Pécs	Ba	MD	1860-95	642,738
Pécs	Ba	Census	1848	719,823
Pécs kerület	Ba	BMD	1851-85	642,738
Pécs kerület	Ba	BMD	1864-88	642,739
Pécsvárad kerület	Ba	BMD	1851-95	642,739
Pécsvárad kerület	Ba	Census	1850	642,731
Penc	Pe	BMD	1862-80	642,843
Pesti kerület	Pe		See Budapest.	
Péteri	Pe	BMD	1877-80	642,867
Pétervására	He	BMD	1851-95	642,823
Petneháza	SS	BMD	1852-95	642,915
Pilis	Pe	BD	1877-80	642,867

Community	Province	Record Type	Record Span	Genealogical Society Record Number
Pilisvörös-vlar	Pe	BMD	1819-95	642,867
Pincehely	To	BMD	1851-95	642,930
Piricse	SS	BMD	1877-85	642,916
Pocsaj	HB	BMD	1852-95	642,759
Polgár	HB	BMD	1853-95	642,916
Polgár	HB	BMD	1854-95	642,814
Pomáz	Pe	BMD	1851-95	642,868
Poroszló	He	BMD	1850-95	642,823
Püspökladány	HB	BMD	1854-95	642,814
Pusztakovácsi	So	B	1867-77	642,890
Rácalmás	Fe	BMD	1877-85	642,799
Ráckeve	Pe	BMD	1862-95	642,869
Rajka	GS	BMD	1835-95	601,569
Regoce	*	BMD	1853-85	642,731
*now Ridica, Vojvodina, Yugoslavia.				
Rétközberencs	SS	BMD	1886-95	642,916
Rohonc	*	BMD	1834-95	700,726
*now Rechnitz, Burgenland, Austria.				
Sajókazinc	BAZ	BMD	1867-95	642,778
Sajószent-péter	BAZ	BMD	1851-95	642,778
Salgótarján	Nó	BMD	1874-95	642,844
Sáp	HB	BMD	1877-86	642,760
Sáránd	HB	BMD	1877-85	642,760
Sárbogárd	Fe	BMD	1843-95	642,799
Sarkad	Bé	BMD	1853-95	642,760
Sarkadkeresztúr	Bé	BMD	1877-95	642,760
Sárospatak	BAZ	BMD	1833-95	642,953
Sárrétudvari	HB	BMD	1877-95	642,760
Sárvár	Va	BMD	1882-95	642,936
Sárvár - Orthodox	Va	B	1851-85	642,936
Sárvár - Orthodox	Va	B	1886-95	642,937
Sárvár - Orthodox	Va	MD	1851-95	642,937
Sátoraljaúj-hely	BAZ	BMD	1851-95	642,954
Sátoraljaúj-hely	BAZ	BMD	1827-95	642,955
Sátoraljaúj-hely Orthodox	BAZ	BMD	1878-85	642,955
Sátoraljaúj-hely kület	BAZ	BMD	1886-95	642,957
Sellye	Ba	BMD	1881-85	642,739
Siklós	Ba	BMD	1851-95	642,740
Siófok	So	B	1865-77	642,943
Somogyszil	So	BMD	1850-95	642,891
Somogyszil	So	BMD	1846-95	642,892
Sopron	GS	BMD	1867-95	642,899
Sopron	GS	Census	1848	719,823
Sopronkeresztúr	*	Circum	1827-95	700,836
Sopronkeresztúr	*	MD	1827-95	700,836
*now Deutschkreutz, Burgenland, Austria.				
Soroksár	Pe	BMD	1850-95	642,869
Soroksár	Pe	Census	unknown	642,869
Sümeg	Ve	BMD	1876-95	642,950
Szabadszállás	BK	BMD	1858-95	642,870
Szabolcsbáka	SS	BD	1876-85	642,916
Szabolcsveresmart	SS	BMD	1886-95	642,916
Szakolca	*	Census	1848	719,823
*now Skalica, Západoslovenský kraj, Czechoslovakia.				
Szalárd	*	BMD	1852-95	642,761
*now Sälard, Crisana, Rumania.				
Szalonta	*	BMD	1854-95	642,761
*now Salonta, Crisana, Rumania.				
Szarvas	Bé	B	1850-70	642,748
Szarvas	Bé	BMD	1886-95	642,748
Szarvas	Bé	M	1852-82	642,748
Szarvas	Bé	D	1851-70	642,748
Szarvas - Orthodox	Bé	B	1872-85	642,748
Szarvas - Orthodox	Bé	M	1873-85	642,748
Szarvas	Bé	BMD	1871-95	642,749
Szécsény	Nó	BMD	1850-85	642,844
Szeged	Cs	B	1844-85	642,785
Szeged	Cs	MD	1852-85	642,786
Szeged	Cs	BM	1886-95	642,786
Szeged	Cs	B-Ind	1850-95	642,786
Szeged - Orthodox	Cs	B	1871-85	642,786
Szeged - Orthodox	Cs	D	1874-85	642,786
Szeged	Cs	B	1870-95	642,787
Szeged	Cs	M	1844-95	642,787
Szeged	Cs	D	1844-77	642,787
Szeged	Cs	D	1878-95	642,788
Szeged - Orthodox	Cs	B	1871-85	642,788
Szeged - Orthodox	Cs	M	1871-85	642,788
Szeged - Orthodox	Cs	D	1874-85	642,788
Szeghalom	Bé	BMD	1888, 1895	642,749
Székelyhid	*	BMD	1831-95	642,762
*now Säcueni, Crisana, Rumania.				
Székesfehérvár	Fe	BMD	1884-95	642,800
Székesfehérvár - Orthodox	Fe	BMD	1845-72	642,800
Székesfehérvár	Fe	B	1844-95	642,800
Székesfehérvár	Fe	M	1843-95	642,800
Székesfehérvár	Fe	D	1843-83	642,800
Székesfehérvár	Fe	D	1872-95	642,801
Székesfehérvár	Fe	BMD	1875-95	642,801
Székesfehérvár	Fe	BMD	1845-95	642,801
Székesfehérvár kerület	Fe	B	1776-1895	642,801
Székesfehérvár	Fe	M	1858-95	642,802
Székesfehérvár	Fe	D	1856-95	642,802
Székesfehérvár	Fe	BMD	1776-1895	642,802
Szendrő	BAZ	BMD	1851-95	642,779
Szentendre	Pe	BMD	1853-95	642,870
Szentes	Cs	BMD	1849-95	642,789
Szentes	Cs	MD	1850-95	642,790
Szentgotthárd	Va	BMD	1886-95	642,937
Szentgyörgy	*	Census	1848	719,823
*now Svätý Jur, Západoslovenský kraj, Czechoslovakia.				
Szentlőrinc	Ba		See Baksa és Szentlórinc.	
Szentlőrinckáta	Pe	BMD	1878-95	642,870
Szentmártonkáta	Pe	BMD	1875-95	642,870
Szentpéterszeg	HB	BMD	1878-95	642,763
Szerencs	BAZ	BMD	1827-95	642,958
Szerep	HB	BMD	1877-86	642,763
Szigetvár	Ba	B	1842-95	642,893
Szigetvár	Ba	M	1852-95	642,893
Szigetvár	Ba	D	1851-95	642,893
Szigetvár	Ba	BMD	1842-95	642,894
Szilasbalhás	Fe	BMD	1854-85	642,932
Szilasbalhás	Fe	BMD	1841-95	642,943
Szilsárkány	GS	BMD	1881-95	642,899
Szirák	Nó	BMD	1850-95	642,845
Szolnok	Sz	BMD	1833-95	642,833
Szolnok kerület	Sz	BMD	1850-95	642,834
Szombathely	Va	BMD	1850-95	642,938
Szombathely - Orthodox	Va	BMD	1850-95	642,939
Szügy	Nó	BMD	1850-95	642,845
Tab	So	B	1847-95	642,895
Tab	So	MD	1850-95	642,895
Tab	So	BMD	1845-95	642,896
Tab	So	Census	1819-52	642,896
Tab	So	BMD	1851-85	642,932
Tab kerület	So	BMD	1870-85	642,896
Tállya	BAZ	BMD	1827-95	642,959
Tápióbicske	Pe	BMD	1863-95	642,871
Tápióság	Pe	BMD	1860-95	642,871
Tápiósüly	Pe	BMD	1877-86	642,871
Tápiószecső	Pe	BMD	1855-95	642,871
Tápiószele	Pe	BMD	1837-95	642,871
Tápioószent-márton	Pe	BD	1881-95	642,872
Tapolca	Ve	BMD	1828-95	642,950
Tarcal	BAZ	BMD	1827-95	642,959
Tass	BK	BMD	1833-95	642,870
Tata	Ko	BMD	1868-95	642,839
Téglás	HB	BMD	1857-95	642,763
Temesvár	*	Census	1848	719,823
*now Timişoara, Timis, Rumania.				
Tépe	HB	BMD	1877-85	642,763
Tét	GS	BMD	1841-95	642,806

Tetétlen	HB	BMD	1886-95	642,763
Tinnye	Pe	BMD	1769-1885	642,872
Tiszabercel	SS	BMD	1854-95	642,916
Tiszabezdéd	SS	BMD	1876-95	642,916
Tiszabő kerület	Sz	BMD	1850-95	642,834
Tiszacsege	HB	BMD	1873-85	642,763
Tiszadada	SS	B	1886-95	642,916
Tiszaföldvár kerület	Sz	BMD	1856-95	642,834
Tiszafüred	Sz	BMD	1840-95	642,824
Tiszafüred kerület	Sz	BMD	1851-88	642,825
Tiszakanyár	SS	BMD	1888-95	642,916
Tiszakécske	BK	BMD	1851-95	642,872
Tiszalök	SS	BMD	1877-95	642,916
Tiszaszentimre kerület	Sz	BMD	1850-95	642,835
Tiszaszentmárton	SS	BD	1876-86	642,917
Tiszavasvári	SS	BD	1856-95	642,917
Tóalmás	Pe	BMD	1868-95	642,872
Tokaj	BAZ	BMD	unknown	642,959
Tolcsva	BAZ	B	1851-83	642,959
Tolcsva	BAZ	BMD	1821-95	642,960
Told	HB	BMD	1877-84	642,763
Tolna	To	BMD	1851-95	642,932
Törökszent-miklós	Sz	B	1886-95	642,835
Törökszent-miklós	Sz	M	1850-85	642,835
Törökszent-miklós	Sz	D	1851-85	642,835
Törökszent-miklós	Sz	BMD	1850-95	642,836
Törtel	Pe	BD	1881-85	642,872
Tótkomlós	Bé	BMD	1872-85	642,749
Trencsén	*	Census	1848	719,823
*now Trenčin, Západoslovenský kraj, Czechoslovakia.				
Tunyogmatolcs	SS	B	1871-85	642,921
Túrkeve	Sz	BMD	1851-95	642,836
Újfehértó	SS	BMD	1852-95	642,917
Újfehértó	SS	BMD	1844-95	642,918
Újpest	Pe	B	1851-92	642,873
Újpest	Pe	B	1892-95	642,874
Újpest	Pe	M	1851-85	642,874
Újpest	Pe	M	1886-95	642,875
Újpest	Pe	D	1850-95	642,875
Újvidéd	*	Census	1848	719,823
*now Novi Sad, Vojvodina, Yugoslavia.				
Üllő	Pe	BMD	1877-85	642,875
Üny	Ko	BMD	1822-71	642,793
Üri	Pe	BMD	1878-80	642,875
Vác	Pe	B	1853-85	642,876
Vác	Pe	B	1886-95	642,877
Vác	Pe	M	1853-95	642,877
Vác - Orthodox	Pe	M	1874-95	642,877
Vác	Pe	D	1853-95	642,877
Vác	Pe	BMD	1846-95	642,878
Vámospércs	HB	BMD	1876-86	642,763
Váncsod	HB	BMD	1877-95	642,763
Városszalónak	*	BMD	1841-95	700,744
*now Stadt Schlaining, Burgenland, Austria.				
Varsány	SS	BMD	1876-85	642,918
Vaskút	BK	B	1884-88	642,731
Vaskút	BK	M	1885	642,731
Vaskút	BK	D	1884-85	642,731
Vasvár	Va	BMD	1851-95	642,939
Vekerd	HB	BMD	1878-95	642,763
Verpelét	He	B	1851-74	642,825
Verpelét	He	Census	?	642,825
Verpelét	He	B	1875-95	642,826
Verpelét	He	M	1852-95	642,826
Verpelét	He	D	1851-95	642,826
Vértes	HB	BMD	1846-95	642,764
Veszprém	Ve	B	1851-95	642,943
Veszprém	Ve	BMD	1836-90	642,944
Veszprém kerület	Ve	BMD	1886-95	642,944
Vitka	SS	BMD	1862-85	642,921
Zalaegerszeg	Za	BMD	1835-95	642,951
Zalalövő	Za	BMD	1830-95	642,951
Zalaszentgrót	Za	BMD	1828-32	642,951
Zombor	*	Census	1848	719,823
*now Sombor, Vojvodina, Yugoslavia.				
Zsadány	Bé	BMD	1877-85	642,764
Zsáka	HB	BMD	1877-95	642,764
Zsámbék	Pe	BMD	1841-95	642,879

The 1848 Hungarian Census of the Jews

This census gives a wealth of information about Jewish households. It gives not only the age of all members of the household but also the specific birthplace, which can be extremely valuable in continuing research on a family which has moved in from another area. Many of those enumerated had moved in from other countries.

Jewish census returns are available on microfilm for the following old counties:

Baranya	719,824
Békés	719,823
Bihar	719,823
Csanád	719,824
Csongrád	719,824
Esztergom*	719,824*
Fejér	719,824
Győr	719,824
Hajdú	719,824
Komárom	719,824
Közép-Snolnok (later Szilágy)	719,824
Krassó	719,824
Kraszna (later Szilágy)	719,824
Máramaros	719,825
Moson	719,825
Szabolcs	719,825
Tolna	719,825
Trencsén	719,826
Turócz*	719,826*
Ung	719,826
Vas	719,827
Veszprém	719,827
Zala	719,828

*A better filming of Turócz and Esztergom County returns is available on film no. 754,368. These are the second items on the film, about halfway through the roll.

These county census returns are not necessarily complete because many larger cities were enumerated separately from the county they were in. Census returns for the following free cities are on film number 719,823.

Debreczen, Hajdú county
Eperjes, Saros county
Gyöngyös, Heves county
Győr, Győr county
Miskolcz, Borsod county
Modor, Pozsony county
Nagy-Szombat, Pozsony county
Pécs, Baranya county
Sopron, Sopron county
Szakolcza, Nyitra county
Ujvidék, Bács county
Temesvár, Temes (fragments)
Trencsén, Trencsén county
Zombor, Bács County

COULD YOU USE THIS CHAPTER?

Type of Record	*Kept from*	*Clues That You Should Consult These Records*
Computer database	Modern, with access to sources from all periods	If you already have, or are considering acquiring a personal computer, this chapter will explain some of its many genealogical applications. If you are a complete novice, the opening sections define database and describe how computers work. A glossary of computer terms is included along with extensive listings for software, hardware, existing genealogical programs, user groups, databases already entered on computers, services available such as library catalogs, newsletters, focused on computer use for genealogical world. The directory of online and genealogical databases is unique to this chapter.

Chapter 22

THE COMPUTER AND THE GENEALOGIST

Wade C. Starks

The modern genealogist, whether he/she knows it, is working with collections of information organized in a uniform fashion. These collections are known by the trendy term *databases*. A familiar example of a database is the telephone directory containing uniform "records" of individuals, including names, addresses, and telephone numbers. Other common databases include dictionaries, cookbooks, catalogs, accounting ledger books, and library card catalogs.

Not every collection of information is a database. Letters, novels, newspapers, and text books are not considered databases. Even though they also contain information, the formal organization distinguishes them from a database. In a database, each specific bit of information is organized in a uniform way that makes information retrieval easy for the user. In the telephone directory, the retrieval key is the individual's name, and the method of organization is alphabetical. The number or address can be found only by using the key of the name. Similarly, a dictionary contains two specific pieces of information, a word and a definition. The uniform arrangement is alphabetical by word.

Nearly every source a genealogist uses is a database. A birth record includes such specific information as the child's name, sex, birthdate, parents, and residence. A census may include the same data as well as occupation, status, and additional filial relationships. Other databases include probates, tax lists, passenger lists, voting registrations, marriage records, death records. . .the list can go on and on.

For hundreds of years, recording methods have been the same. Data has been recorded in manuscript or print in a manually organized format. Reorganization or modification was impossible without completely redoing the work by hand. Most chronologically organized documents would be easier for genealogists to use if they were organized differently – for instance, alphabetically. Because of this, millions of hours have been expended to produce indexes. With the technological revolution, all of this is changing.

The computer has altered our recordkeeping and access methods drastically. Though the future will doubtless bring marvelous advances in computer architecture and technology, we need wait no longer to acquaint ourselves with these new tools. Today, microcomputers are available in a wide variety of packages, capabilities, and prices. Many are affordable and suitable for the genealogist.

To understand why a computer is so important to serious research, we must first understand just what it can do for us. A computer can do very little more with a database than we ourselves could, but it can do those things infinitely faster and more accurately. Consider our telephone directory. If we had a phone number with no name on a scrap of paper, it would be extremely difficult to find who that number belonged to by searching in a printed alphabetical directory. If, however, the directory were in a computer database, the computer could provide the answer in moments. A computer can scan, move, change, or list data in a database faster than we can blink an eye. In the time it takes us to turn a page, a computer will already have scanned several equivalent pages of data. Yet, at its breakneck speed it can unerringly "read" each piece of target data it encounters. And it does it all without getting sleepy, blurry-eyed, or sidetracked by daydreaming.

The Computer Database

Before we can know how a computer can most effectively assist us in genealogical research and what type of computer is most suitable to this task, we must first understand how computer databases are organized, manipulated, and preserved. Computers, for all their abilities, are very stupid and require precise database organization and uniformity. The more complex the database, the more you must plan in developing it.

There are three general ways of handling data in a data base: relational, hierarchical, and network. The difference between the three systems is how the data are organized. The data used in genealogical research are relational by nature.

What do we mean by a relational database system? That data is handled and stored by how one item relates to another. For instance, in our telephone directory example, a computer printout would show:

Kunz Dale J	199 W 205 South	225-9699
Laird Robert S	611 N Belmont Ave.	364-4208
Larsen David M	121 W Penrose Dr.	375-6804
Muhlestein Steven S	1026 E Woodland Rd.	226-4330

This relational database looks just as it would if you were to make it with a pencil and paper. Each line of information has a fixed length; each piece of information is logically organized and is of uniform size. Each address and phone number relates directly to the person to whom they belong. There are actually two types of relational databases. The format of the one above is fixed length. A variable length format is essentially the same as above with one exception. The length of each piece of data in each line may be variable; for instance:

Kunz Dale J 199 W 205 South 225-9699
Laird Robert S 611 N Belmont Ave. 374-4208
Larsen David M 121 W Penrose Dr. 375-6804
Muhlestein Steven S 1026 E Woodland Rd. 226-4330

Notice that the data's logical relationship is still readily apparent. The latter method uses less storage space, while the former is easier and faster for the computer just as it is easier for us to visually separate its various components.

The computer organizes and maintains all this information with a system called a database manager. The database manager enables a user to create a database, add information to it, change it, reorganize it, and view it in various ways. A database manager is a program that tells the computer how to handle the information according to the user's instructions.

What does a computer database look like? Logically, a relational database resembles an ordinary file drawer. In fact, the largest logical aspect of a computer database is called a file. Just as a file drawer is subdivided by many file folders, a computer file is divided into smaller uniform subsets called records which are in turn divided into smaller subsets of dissimilar but related data called fields.

Each computer file is structured to accommodate a particular type of entry or record. One file might handle birth extracts, another marriage extracts, and still another census extracts. Each file can handle only one type of record. A file set up for births would not handle marriage entries, because each has a different structure. If we wanted to create a file in which to maintain a telephone directory, we might instruct the database manager program through the computer keyboard to organize the file so that each record in the file is in these fields:

FIELD	NAME	SIZE
Field 1:	surname	12
Field 2:	given name	24
Field 3:	address	16
Field 4:	phone nbr	8

As you can see, this particular record consists of four separate pieces of information fields. The first field, the surname, is arbitrarily limited to twelve characters. Field 2 is reserved for the individual's given name and is twenty-four characters long. The next field, which we named address, is sixteen characters long; and the last field, phone number, is eight characters long.

If we add up the length of all the fields, we get the total length of each record—sixty characters or bytes. One byte equals one character. A computer considers a blank space a character just like a letter, number, or other symbol, such as ?, &, -, etc. The larger the records, the fewer of them can be stored in a file. A file's length can vary depending upon the number of records in it and the physical limitations imposed by the particular computer system it is in.

A typical marriage file might look like this:

Field 1:	marriage date	11
Field 2:	marriage place	32
Field 3:	groom surname	12
Field 4:	groom given name(s)	24
Field 5:	bride surname	12
Field 6:	bride given name(s)	24
Field 7:	source	24
Total bytes		139

Obviously, a file structured for marriage entries would not accommodate a phone list. It would be wasteful to attempt to make it do so, since phone lists require only sixty bytes.

Using the Data

Once you have developed a database, what are you going to do with it? Here is a representative list of commands you will need to work with a database:

Append: add records to an existing file.
Edit: change or add data to an existing record
Copy: copy all or portions of a file into another file.
Create: create new files of a specified structure.
Delete: delete a record.
Find: find a record using an index file.
Insert: insert a record within a file.
List: list all records or a selected list of records in a file.
Locate: locate a record based on a particular characteristic.
Merge: merge all or portions of two files into another file.
Modify: modify the structure of an existing file.
Replace: make data replacements in a specified field of all or selected records.
Report: generate a printout on a screen or to the printer.
Rename: rename a file.
Sort: reorganize the database (alphabetically) on a certain field.
Sum: add the contents of numerical fields of selected records.
Update: change or add data in one file from data in another file.

These particular commands represent a portion of the vocabulary from a popular database manager called dBASE II. The syntax of other database managers may vary, but the functions will be similar.

After reading this list of functions, you can get an idea of some of the things a database manager can do for you. With a command like "list," you can have the computer call up all records that meet a certain criterion, such as all records in the telephone field which have the first three digits of 374. If your telephone list is organized by surname, but you want to know to whom a given phone number belongs, you may ask the computer to "locate" the record which has that number in the phone field. Upon receiving such a command, the computer will rapidly search the file until it finds the appropriate record.

A command like "sort" will permit you to input data randomly or in a convenient way, then rearrange it the way you wish to retrieve it. If you are producing an index of marriages in a certain county, it is convenient to input them by following the chronology of the original record but sort them alphabetically by surname.

Hardware

Now that you are beginning to see what a database manager can do for you, let's discuss the kind of equipment you need. The programs used to do database management, word-processing, accounting, or other special tasks are called software. They can be created or changed by a programmer. The machines they run on are called hardware. These are not so readily modified.

Each computer's architecture or internal design is unique. Some machines are dedicated to specific tasks while others can handle a variety of chores. Examples of "dedicated" computers are game machines, navigation computers, computers that manage automobile gasoline engines, and so on. They can do only those tasks for which they are designed. General purpose computers, on the other hand, are designed to run almost any program the operator wishes within the limitations of their design. At one moment one might be used as a word processor, at another time it might be used to run a mailing list, or for financial analysis, or some similar function.

General purpose computers are of most interest to the genealogist. They range from small units that are little more than glorified toys to very expensive and sophisticated machines well beyond the means of the average individual. A broad range of computer systems can be adapted to genealogy tasks. Some require individual programming, while others are designed to accommodate packaged programs. In most applications the latter are more suitable.

For the purpose of this study, let's investigate a typical practical computer system that might adequately meet the genealogist's needs. The system includes the following components:

CPU (central processing unit)
Operating system
RAM (random access memory)
Mass storage
Communication
Keyboard
Monitor
Packaging

Perhaps the most popular CPU's available are the 8080, the Z80, and the 8086. The first two are popular because they are compatible with a widely accepted disk-operating system called CP/M. Until recently, each computer had its own unique operating system, which was totally incompatible with other companys' computers. The CP/M operating system has been a big step toward compatibility between machines. CP/M has become so widely accepted by computer manufacturers that most of the software programs written in the past for the microcomputer market were written to run on CP/M machines. The 8086 is a different type of CPU which runs another disk-operating system called MSDOS. With the growing popularity of IBM's 16 byte systems, MSDOS also provides significant software.

Apple is the leading computer in use by genealogists today because of the software that has been available. The practical computer would be based upon either CP/M or MSDOS to keep up with the rapid expansion of good software for these systems. Apple plans to add an IBM compatible unit to its product line to draw on this software for its customers.

We need to consider two types of computer memory when evaluating a system: internal volatile memory called RAM, and mass storage memory, one of several types of magnetic media, like tape. RAM is electronic memory within the computer's circuitry. It is active and remembers only when the power is on. When the power is turned off, everything stored in RAM is lost. Unlike tape, which has to be searched sequentially, RAM consists of a series of memory cells or pigeonholes, each with its own access analogous to a long street with houses along one side. Each house has a street address. The first house is 1 and the numbers ascend to the end of the street. Just as you might go to any house in any order, the computer can go to any memory address to process data. Among other things, this capability allows the computer to index.

RAM comes in different sizes. The larger RAM can hold more data and can therefore process data more effectively than smaller RAMs. RAM size is measured by the number of bytes (remember, a byte equals a single character) it contains. Each byte is a memory cell or pigeonhole with its own unique address. In computer terminology, bytes are counted in units of K (kilobytes), where one K equals 1024 bytes rather than 1000 bytes. Computers use a special definition for kilo based on the powers of two. Two multiplied by itself eight times is 1024. Why eight times? Because on most microcomputers, each byte is made up of eight subparts called bits. For more about computer theory, check the topic in a public library.

The RAM size normally varies from 16k to 128k and beyond. A RAM must serve two functions: it must hold the operating system and application programs, and it must hold data to be processed. The operating system might reside in 10K bytes of RAM, while application programs (word processors, database managers, etc.) usually occupy many K bytes, ranging from a typical program of about 16K to perhaps as much as 50K or more in extreme cases. Obviously, a 1K RAM would not do the job. A system for genealogy should have at least 48K of RAM, and preferably 64K. More powerful micros have RAM of 128K, 256K, 512K, and so on. Generally, the computer system's cost is directly proportional to its capabilities.

The other aspect of computer memory is permanent mass storage. Since RAM has a limited amount of storage and because it is volatile, being electronic, there must be another way of saving all the information we use. This storage is on magnetic media similar to recording tapes. In fact, some systems use ordinary cassette recorders and tapes. More sophisticated storage devices use special magnetic records called disks. Some, made of thin plastic, are called floppy disks; others, called hard disks, are rigid, magnetically coated aluminum. Most micros incorporate floppy disk drives in their systems. They are less expensive than the more sophisticated hard-disk drives, yet are adequate for most micro applications.

The capacity of floppy-disk drives varies from one system to another. Some may hold 100K bytes of data, while others may have capacities of 200K, 400K, 800K, or even more in a few cases. A typical typewritten page may contain about 3500 characters or bytes of information. A simple calculation tells us, then, that 100K (102,400) bytes will accommodate up to about thirty pages of text, 200K about sixty pages, and so on. In database files, a file like our marriages mentioned above with 139 bytes per record could hold as many as 1400 records. Obviously, the larger the drive capacity the more information the system can handle at one time and the more convenient it is to use.

Let's say that our "practical" computer system will have 64K of RAM and at least two drives with a minimum of 200K disk capacity. Our "practical" computer should also be able to communicate conveniently with other computers to share information. It should have a standard-size typewriter-style keyboard and a monitor (a TV-like screen) on which to view what you type and the computer's responses. Another aspect of a computer system is the packaging. Most micros are relatively small and can fit nicely on a desk top. Some consist of several separate components: computer, keyboard, monitor, and disk drives. Others integrate them all into one unit. Still others are portable and can be carried around like a briefcase. Many genealogists will find portability desirable because it allows them to take the computer to their research. In addition to the computer, you will want a way to get "hard copies" (printouts on paper) of what is in the computer. For this, you will need a printer, ranging in price from several hundred to several thousand dollars. The less expensive dot-matrix printers are adequate for most applications. More expensive letter-quality daisy-wheel printers may be more suitable for some applications.

As I stated before, a great variety of computers is available on the market today. My "practical" computer model will enable you to narrow the choices down. Then you can further reduce the selection by other considerations. Which computer fits into your budget? Is it easy for you to use? Also consider company and dealer support and service. Follow-up support and service is extremely important to the beginning computerist.

Once you invest in a computer system, take the time to learn how to use it and the programs properly. You will be embarking upon a new and engrossing learning adventure. Using the computer may seem bewildering at first, but in time it will become second nature to you.

Computer Glossary

APL: A Programming Language. A high-level language developed by IBM but not widely used by others.

BASIC: Beginners All-purpose Symbolic Instruction Code. The most popular language in personal computers.

Bit: bytes are subdivided into eight bits. These bits determine what the computer displays on the screen.

Byte: the amount of memory space needed to store a simple character such as B or 5. Bytes are usually shown in thousands (K for kilobyte) or millions (M for megabyte).

COBOL: Common Business Oriented Language. Developed for business applications with large information databases. Many computers accept both BASIC and COBOL.

CP/M: a very popular operating system (*q.v.*).

CPS: characters per second.

CPU: Central Processing Unit. The "brains" controlling other parts of the computer.

Crash: system failure due to power loss, program bugs, or other problems.

CRT: Cathode Ray Tube, also called the video display terminal or VDT. The monitor or video screen where information is displayed.

Cursor: the flashing marker that shows where you are working on the video screen.

Databank: a central source of information stored in large computers and available to home computers and other computers over telephone lines.

Disk (disc) drive: a shoebox-size device which reads information off and on disks.

Documentation: a manual describing the software program or nardware equipment and how to use it.

DOS: Disk Operating System. The program that tells the disk drive to read from or write to a disk.

Floppy disk: a mass-storage device of flexible plastic that creates a memory similar to that of magnetic tape.

FORTRAN: Formula Translation. A language mostly used by scientists; business computers may not need it.

Hacker: an addict who cannot get enough of the computer screen and keyboard.

Hardware: the computer equipment.

K: kilobytes, approximately a thousand bytes.

LPM: lines per minute.

LPS: lines per second.

M: megabytes: approximately a million bytes.

Mainframe: the big computers such as those in banks, universities, and corporations.

Microcomputer: the low-line capacity personal computer, up to 64K. However, minicomputers are growing closer in size to microcomputers.

Minicomputer: the midrange size of computers, larger than the Radio Shack/Apple personal computers. A few years ago the distinction between micro- and mini- was clearer.

Modem: Modulator/demodulator. The device that allows you to connect your computer to the telephone line.

Online: the data the computer can access at one time.

Operating system: the set of programs that keep your "electronic file cabinet" organized. CP/M is probably the most widely used operating system, but some manufacturers such as Radio Shack/Tandy and Apple have developed their own. It is advisable to buy either a very popular personal computer (IBM, Radio Shack, Apple) or one with CP/M.

Pascal: an academic language named after the French mathematician.

RAM: Random Access Memory. The working memory space you use to store, retrieve, alter, or erase information.

ROM: Read Only Memory. The computer's "burned in" memory instructions that tell it how to behave and which you cannot erase or alter.

Software: the programs you buy for the computer.

Storage capacity: the capability to hold information for future retrieval; usually expressed in K or M.

Support: the service and/or warrantees that come with the computer or the service contract.

Turnkey: a complete, ready-to-go system that will work when you "turn the key."

VDT: Video Display Terminal. See CRT.

Word processing: Text-editing programs that facilitate composing and editing reports, etc.

BIBLIOGRAPHY OF COMPUTER DATABASE AND INFORMATION SOURCES

Wilma Adkins, Compiler

This source list is compiled from reviews or advertisements in the *APG Newsletter* (Box 11601, Salt Lake City, UT 84147) – especially its January 1982 special issue on computers; from *Genealogical Computing* (Data Transfer Associates, Inc., 5102 Pommeroy Drive, Fairfax, VA 22032); or from press releases or flyers distributed by vendors at genealogical conferences. Where possible the sources are quoted directly.

The application of computers to genealogy is just getting a good start; and in such a rapidly expanding field, prices are also subject to rapid fluctuations. We have included full addresses and telephone numbers since there is no single source which provides this data for genealogical users. Check the current issue of *Genealogical Computing* for prices or contact the vendors directly.

Buyer's Guides

Computers and People – Computer Directory and Buyers' Guide Issue

Berkeley Enterprises, Inc.
815 Washington Street
Newtonville, MA 02160
(617) 332-5453

The Directory of Directories (DOD), 2nd ed., p. 411.

Data Communications Buyers' Guide

McGraw-Hill, Inc.
1221 Avenue of the Americas
New York, NY 10020
(212) 997-3139

"Covers manufacturers of data communications, distributors of data processing, information network equipment and services, worldwide." *DOD*, 2nd ed., p. 411.

DATAGUIDE

Sentry Publishing Company, Subsidiary of Technical Publishing Company
Five Kane Industrial Drive
Hudson, MA 01749

"Covers 4,000 manufacturers and suppliers of data processing equipment and accessories, including software." *DOD*, 2nd ed., p. 411.

Datapro Directory of Microcomputer Software

Datapro Research Corporation
1805 Underwood Blvd.
Delran, NJ 08075
(609) 764-0100

"Covers about 1,220 vendors of software; 2,500 software descriptions. . . ." *DOD*, 2nd ed., p. 411.

Datapro Reports

Datapro Research Corporation
1805 Underwood Blvd.
Delran, NJ 08075
(609) 764-0100

"The *Datapro Reports* series include separate reports on minicomputers, data communications, electronic data processing, support systems and equipment, word processing, software . . ." *DOD*, 2nd ed., p. 411.

Directory of Small Computers

Datapro Research Corporation
1805 Underwood Blvd.
Delran, NJ 08075
(609) 764-0100

"Covers over 900 manufacturers and suppliers of small computers, software, peripheral equipment. . .personal computing clubs, user groups. . . ." *DOD*, 2nd ed., p. 139.

Directory of Computer Software and Related Technical Reports

National Technical Information Service
Commerce Department
5285 Port Royal Road
Springfield, VA 22161
(703) 487-4808

"Covers about 100 government agencies which offer over 350 software packages and technical reports. . . ." *DOD*, 2nd ed., p. 411.

INC.

Independent Computer Consultants Association
Box 27312
St. Louis, MO 63141.

INC., January 1982. If you want help determining what you need or if you need someone to write the software to your specifications, this group will tell you of freelance data systems specialists in your area.

Genealogy Programs (Software)

The following list includes references and citations to which the reader can refer for additional information concerning the software. Also, if a certain program runs on a particular computer, that computer model is listed.

"Ancestor File Programs"
J. P. Davis
10650 Hickory Ridge Road
Columbia, MD 21044
(301) 964-6063
IBM-PC

"=Ancestors="
Ancestors
Box 2434
Harbor, OR 97415
Atari 800

"Ancestors"
Christopher Meek
4132 Lay Street
Des Moines, IA 50317
TRS-80 Color

"Ancestry I/III"
Soft-Gene
11 John Swift Rd.
Acton, MA 01720
TRS-80 Model I and III
Genealogical Computing 2 (May 1983)

"Appleroots"
CDS Corporation
1285 Sumac Drive
Logan, UT 84321
(800) 453-2708 for toll free ordering
Apple II.

"Apple Tree Genealogy System"
J. Fiske Software Systems, Inc.
One University Place
New York, NY 10003

For Apple II, 48 K, 1 or 2 drives; includes a professional-level family recordkeeping system, 1,000 names of variable length, hierarchical data-structure. Easy to use. 100 user-definable fields, an automatic proofreader report, a self-teaching tutorial, and The Linkage Analyzer. See Tom L. Beckham, "John Fiske's Apple Tree Reviewed," *Genealogical Computing*, 2 (Jan. 1983).

"Apple Tree III"
Cyber Services, Inc.
Attn: Risdon W. Hankinson
701 Sooner Park Drive
Bartlesville, OK 74003

Sample program and booklet available. Apple II, Apple IIe. See *Genealogical Computing* 2 (May 1983).

"Cemetery Inscriptions Program"
P. A. Grasse
2805 Raven Avenue
Wausau, WI 54401
TRS-80 Model 1.

"Commodore 64"
Byteware
906 W. 6th Avenue
Monmouth, IL 61462

Menu-driven programs for genealogy, including family group sheet and pedigree chart. *Genealogical Helper* (Nov./Dec. 1983).

"Computer Genealogy Systems"
Patricia Cotter
1682 Roxanna Lane
New Brighton, MN 55112

Stores and updates complete genealogical records (vital statistics, parents, children, and notes). Prints complete set of family group sheets, ancestor and descendant charts, and indexes. Sample printouts and information available, IBM-PC, TRS-80 Model I, III, 48K and 2 disk drives. *Genealogical Computing* 2 (May 1983).

"FGS and PEDC"
Byteware
906 W. 6th Avenue
Mammouth, IL 61462
Commodore 64

"The Family Connection"
Discovery Software
Box 68821
Indianapolis, IN 46168
(317) 291-1433

Or

Box 9336
Cincinnati, OH 45209

For Apple II, IIe, and Apple compatibles. Includes up to 7,800 records. Fast and easy to use. Commas allowed. Complete support, excellent manual, includes pedigree charts, family group sheets, index. *Genealogical Computing* 2 (May 1983). See "Discovery," software announcement, *Genealogical Computing* 2 (July 1982).

"Familyfile"
Compugen Systems
Box 15604
Fort Wayne, IN 46885
IBM PC

"Family for CoCo"
TWM Box 232
Lititz, PA 17543

TRS-80 Color Computer *Genealogical Computing* 2 (May 1983).

"Family Group Sheet Program"
John A. Ashworth, Jr.
Box 809
Matthews, NC 28105
(704) 847-2058

Sample printout available. TRS-80 Color Computer *Genealogical Computing* 2 (May 1983).

"Family Records File System"
Hierarchal Systems Group
Box DB
College Station, TX 77841

TRS-80 Model II, 16, CP/M systems *Genealogical Computing* 2 (May 1983).

"Family Roots"
"Lineages"
Quinsept, Inc.
Box 216
Lexington, MA 02173
(617) 862-0404

For Apple II or IBM PC, Commodore 64, selected CP/M systems. Free brochure and printouts. Includes six types of charts and sheets; indexes; user fields; notes, footnotes, and sources. No limits. Adapts to your hardware. *Genealogical Computing* 2 (May 1983). See FAMILY ROOTS program by Steve Vorenberg, (User Review,) *Genealogical Computing* 2 (May 1983). Advertisement, ibid., 2 (Sept. 1982). Steve and Pat Vorenberg, Quinsept, Inc., "About the Author," *Genealogical Computing* 1 (March 1982). "Lineages" (User Review), *Genealogical Computing* 2 (Sept. 1982).

"Family Ties"
Wagstaff Computer Services
1050 E. 800 South
Provo, UT 84601

IBM-PC; CP/M versions for Osborne, Kaypro, Otroma, Televideo, Eagle, Morrow Micro decisions. NEC, ADDS Viewpoint, Socorc 120, Franklin; Apple II, II¢, IIe.

"Family Tree"
Genealogy Software
Box 1151
Port Huron, MI 48061
(519) 344-3990
Commodore 64, Vic

"Family Tree"
"Family Reunion"
Personal Software Company
Box 776
Salt Lake City, UT 84110
(801) 227-3174
IBM-PC

"Fretware Family Tree System"
Cecil Fretwell and Shela S. Fretwell
Fretware Family Tree System
2605 Highview Avenue
Waterloo, IA 50702

User friendly, 40-character display. Apple II Plus, Apple IIe. *Genealogical Computing* 2 (Sept. 1983).

"Genalog II" (Apple II)
"Genalog 80" (TRS 80 I)
Genalog Software
111 Woodgate Road
Middletown, NJ 07748
(201) 671-9211

Genealogical Data Systems
Box 6433
San Jose, CA 95150

For IBM/370 Series, and IBM 5110 and 5120 computers. These systems cost more than the average genealogist will pay but are very favorably reviewed in Jan M. Engle, "Preview: Genealogical Data Systems," *Genealogical Computing* 1 (July 1981). Jan M. Engle, "Kinology is Fun," *Genealogical Helper*, Nov.-Dec. 1981. Samples of his program; Engle: (software announcement), *Genealogical Computing* 2 (July 1982).

"Genealogical Record Programs"
Roderick H. Payne
100 Villa Avenue
Buffalo, NY 14216
IBM-PC and IBM-PC compatible

"Genealogy I and II"
RoNAN
5506 Camber Drive
San Diego, CA 92117
Atari 800

"The Genealogist's Right Hand"
User Friendly Systems, Inc.
6135 Ross Road
Fairfield, OH 45014
(513) 874-4550

Apple II, IIe, and Apple Compatibles; 48K, 1 disk. Includes relationships between millions of people; stores as much as you like about each person. Unlimited number of children and spouses; indexes; pedigree charts, mailing labels, and family sheets. *Genealogical Computing* 2 (May 1983). See George B. Wissing, "About the Authors," *Genealogical Computing* 2 (July 1982).

"Genealogy"
Bio
Box 423
Nannet, NY 10954
Northstar.

"Genealogy: Compiling Roots and Branches"
Armstrong Genealogical Systems
C/o John J. Armstrong
5009 Utah Street
Greenville, TX 75401
(214) 454-8209

TRS-80 Model II or 16 with 64K, 1 disk drive and 80 or more column printer. Prints and maintains a complete book of information; 1,000 persons per diskette. Descriptive booklet available. *Genealogical Computing* 2 (May 1983). See John J. Armstrong, "About The Authors," *Genealogical Computing* 1 (Sept. 1981). John R. Gilpin, "Genealogy – Compiling Roots and Branches" (User Review), *Genealogical Computing* 1 (Sept. 1981).

"Genealogy on Display"
Melvin O. Duke
Box 20836
San Jose, CA 95160
IBM-PC

"Genealogy Program"
John Ford
5561 Esplanada
Santa Maria, CA 93455
(805) 937-1732

Northstar, CP/M. *Genealogical Computing* 1 (May 1982).

"Genealogy Program"
Lanco Genealogical Research
Box 3011
Farmington, MI 48018-3011

Sample pedigree chart for SASE; IBM-PC; *Genealogical Computing* 2 (May 1983).

"Genealogy Program"
Frank Lerchen
2950 Espana Court
Fairfax, VA 22031

TRS-80 Model III, 48K, one disk drive. Generates family group records, search listings for parents' or childrens' names, pedigrees starting with any person in the file, and horizontal or vertical charts. See: "Lerchen:" (software announcement), *Genealogical Computing* 2 (July 1982).

"Genealogy Workshop"
Tenex
Box 6578
South Bend, IN 46660
(800) 348-2778
(219) 277-7726 (Indiana only)
TI 99/4a

"Geneas/Base"
Praxisoft Computer Enterprises
Box 1221
Muskegon, MI 49443
TRS-80 I, III and 4

"Genecom"
Ramon W. Martin
23 Rosemoor Grove
Chandler's Ford
East Leigh, Hants.
SOS ITB
England
Zenith/Heath

"Generations, The Genealogy Program"
Micro-80, Inc.
2665 No. Busby Grove
Oak Harbor, WA 98277
(800) 352-0458 Ext. 3005

Disk or cassette. TRS-80 Model I, III. *Genealogical Computing* 2 (May 1983).

"Gen-Pro"
D. Labue
DML Software
14 Wick Road
E. Brunswick, NJ 08816
Timex 1000, Sinclair 2X-81

"Genesis – 80"
Anthony J. Skvarek
1514 W. Mission #14
Pomona, CA 91766

Sample family history and pedigree available. TRS-80 Model III. *Genealogical Computing* 2 (May 1983).

"GenesisI"
GenesisI
Box 236
Lakeside, MT 59922

A short (5K) sample genealogy program for Northstar, TRS-80 Model I. Coming for Apple II, TRS-80 Model III. Based on the family group records you might otherwise put on three-by-five cards. Advertisement, *Genealogical Computing* 1 (July 1981).

"Genie"
Sinclair G. Cannon
Central Research of Utah
895 South 770 West
Bountiful, UT 84010
(801) 298-7713

Or:
Family History Center
Box 11394
Salt Lake City, UT 84147

IBM-PC, IBM-XT, and Tandy 2000. See Sinclair G. Cannon, "About the Authors," *Genealogical Computing* 4 (Jan. 1984).

"Genieology"
Warner Enterprises
Box 6276
Glendale, CA 91205-0276
CP/M systems, CP/M-86, MSDOS

"Gensystems"
John J. Armstrong
Armstrong Genealogical Systems
5009 Utah Street
Greenville, TX 75401
(214) 454-8209

"A complete system of nine computer programs which will record and publish a camera-ready family history." Automatically adds and prints narratives and family tables. Includes 335 to 705 persons per diskette. TRS-80 Model I or III with 48K, 2 disk drives and 80 or more column printer. Descriptive booklet available. See (advertisement), *Genealogical Computing* 2 (Sept. 1982). Ibid., 2 (May 1983).

"Heritage"
Creative Services
Box 580
Oak Harbor, WA 98277
TRS 80 I and III

"Irish Roots"
Eiron Computors
Eiron House, Park Road
Dun Ladire, Dublin
Ireland

Northstar, Horizon, Apple II, TRS-80, and PET, single or double density. *Genealogical Computing* 1 (Nov. 1981).

"Lineages"
Ervin A. Madern
Box 1746
Rohnert Park, CA 94928-1241

TRS 80 color. Cassette and program listing.

"Netplot"
Q Mu Nications Corp.
Box 2422
Ann Arbor, MI 48107
(313) 633-3161

General purpose family tree plotting system including multiple marriages. Capable of large plots. Available for any microcomputer with 64K RAM. *Genealogical Helper* (Nov./Dec. 1983).

"Patriarch I"
Cyclone Software
3305 Macomb Street NW
Washington, DC 20008
(202) 362-8740
Apple II, IIe

"Pedigree"
The Genea-rators!
5102 Pommeroy Drive
Fairfax, VA 22032
(703) 978-8490

TRS-80 I and III, one disk printer system, requires 32K or 48K memory. *Genealogical Computing* 1 (Nov. 1981).

"Port for Genealogists"
Team Approach Limited
4 Abingdon Drive
Ottawa, Ontario
K2H 7M3 Canada
(613) 829-7848

"Roots"
TSE-Hardside
6 South Street
Milford, NH 03055

TRS-80 Model I and III.

"ROOTS/M"
Commsoft, Inc.
665 Maybell Avenue
Palo Alto, CA 94306
(415) 493-2184

Free brochure available. Apple II, CP/M, TRS-80 Model II, Kaypro, Northstar, Zenith/Heath, Osborne I, Vector Graphic, Altos, Cromemco, Dynabyte, Imsai, Xerox 820. *Genealogical Computing* 2 (May 1983). See Howard L. Nurse, "About the Authors," *Genealogical Computing* 1 (Jan. 1982). William K. Johnson, "ROOTS89 and ROOTS/M User Group," *Genealogical Computing* 1 (Jan. 1982).

"RootsWriter"
Commsoft, Inc.
665 Maybell Avenue
Palo Alto, CA 94306
(415) 493-2184

Enhanced version of SPELLBINDER word processing program; special genealogical templates for LDS family group sheet and NGS MAC forms. CP/M systems. *Genealogical Computing* 2 (May 1983).

"ROOTS/34"
Gary Mokotoff
Northvale Systems
507 Crest Drive
Northvale, NJ 07647

Sample reports and screens available. IBM System/34. *Genealogical Computing* 2 (May 1983).

"ROOTS/89"
Commsoft, Inc.
665 Maybell Avenue
Palo Alto, CA 94306
(415) 493-2184

Zenith/Heath. *Genealogical Computing* 2 (May 1983).

"Text Indexing System"
Hierarchal Systems Group
Box DB
College Station, TX 77841

CP/M systems, Vector Graphic, TRS-80 Model II. *Genealogical Computing* 2 (May 1983).

"Treesearch" by Marie Irvine
Array Systems
Box 295
Brigham City, UT 84302

Portable unit compatible. IBM PC, Compaq, Columbia, Epson HX-20 collector. Marie Irvine, "Treesearch: A Research Program Plus a Record Keeping Program," *Genealogical Computing* 3 (July 1983).

"Your Ancestors"
Ken Barber Software
Box 140
Great Falls, MT 59403

Timex 1000, Sinclair 2X-81. Stores names and statistics of 7 generations, 128 people, and prints charts. Requires 16K RAM. Versions for Commodore VIC or 64 and Texas Instruments coming. *Genealogical Computing* 2 (Sept. 1983).

"Your Family Tree" by Chuck Acree
Acorn Software Products, Inc.
7655 Leesburg Pike
Falls Church, VA 22043
(703) 893-0868

TRS-80 Model III and IV, IBM PC. *Genealogical Computing* 2 (May 1983). See Chuck Acree, "About the Authors," *Genealogical Computing* 2 (May 1983).

Genealogical Computing has also printed some actual programs: "For every name a number" (July 1981), "Grpsheet" and "Findper" (Sept. 1981), and a mailing list program (January 1982). These are complete programs, written in BASIC for the Radio Shack TRS-80.

Genealogical Databases

ACC Computerized Genealogy Service
Box 27193
Salt Lake City, UT 84127
(801) 486-3111

Sample packet available. Lineage-linked computerized genealogy, Notable Cousins Project. Includes over 300,000 names in linked form; produces charts, indexes, family group sheets, etc., as print-outs of the data. Can supply descendants as well as ancestors; *Genealogical Computing* 2 (Sept. 1982). See David S. Barss, "Computerized Service Announcement," *Genealogical Computing* 2 (Sept. 1982).

"AFRA Computerized Database."
American Family Records Association,
311 E. 12th Street
Kansas City, MO 64106

Listing of names of persons with related genealogical data to bring genealogists searching for common lines together. Eventually telephone access will be available. AFRA Computerized Database. *Family Records Today* 3 (July 1982); *Genealogical Computing* 1 1982.

AIS Computer Searches
Accelerated Indexing Systems, Inc.
Box 2127
Salt Lake City, UT 84110

Name search by computer of 48,000,000 indexed names, mostly U.S. federal census records, 1790-1850. *Genealogical Computing* 2 (Sept. 1982).

America History and Life
ABC CLIO
Riviera Campus
2040 Alameda Padre Sierra
Box 4397
Santa Barbara, CA 93103

A comprehensive four-part bibliography of articles, books, and dissertations of U.S. and Canadian history and culture. The database is available for direct computer searching through Lockheed's DIALOG Information Retrieval Service. (See below). *America History and Life* is also available in book form in library reference sections.

Ancestral Charts
Dashes
Box 501
Sweeny, TX 77480

Prints up to twelve generations of family tree for $15, 20 cents per name.

"Ancestral File"
Genealogical Society of Utah
50 East North Temple
Salt Lake City, UT 84150

Many members of the LDS Church have turned in their first four generation pedigree charts and the accompanying family group sheets. Over 190,000 have been received, creating a paper file of an estimated million names. The church will computerize this massive collection, creating a family relationship file – a boon to genealogists as well as researchers in other fields. Computer input will be done by specially trained volunteers, and the file will be available within a few years. At that time public input into this file will be encouraged. Direct computer access is being considered. See "Mormon Computer Capability," *Genealogical Computing* 1 (Jan. 1982); "Genealogical Computing and the Mormons," *Genealogical Computing* 2 (Sept. 1982); "New Mormon Church Program," *Genealogical Computing* 4 (Jan. 1984).

BAM BAM
Boston Public Library
666 Boylston Street
Box 286
Boston, MA 02117

Worldwide book alert for rare books and manuscripts stolen or missing. Early Report, Channel 2, NBC-TV, 1 April 1982.

Bare Hunting Bevers
Box 3056
Wichita Falls, TX 76309
(817) 691-4015

South Carolina marriages, deaths.

Byron Sistler & Assoc.
1712 Natchez Trace
Nashville, TN 37212
(615) 297-3085

Tennessee census, marriage, church records.

Compu-Gen Surname Exchange
Compu-Gen
Box 684
Dover, OH 44622-0684

Data exchange; surnames registered at $3 per name. *Genealogical Computing* 2 (Sept. 1982).

Computer Center for Jewish Genealogy
Neil Rosenstein, M.D.
654 Westfield Ave.
Elizabeth, NJ 07208

$15 subscription ($21 overseas). Monthly printouts and periodic updates. *Genealogical Computing* 2 (Sept. 1982). See Neil Rosenstein, "Computing Center for Jewish Genealogy" *Genealogical Computing* 1 (March 1982).

Computer Genealogy Associates, Inc.
Ashville, N.C. 28800

Share IBM PC, letter-quality printer, office, modem. Stockholders only, no public service. *Genealogical Computing* 2 (Sept. 1982).

The Computerized Family File
Everton Publishers
Box 368
Logan, UT 84321
(801) 752-6022

Listing of family organizations, their publications, their research activities. *Genealogical Helper* (Jan.-Feb. 1983).

Computerized "Roots" Cellar
Everton Publishers, Inc.
Box 368
Logan, UT 84321

Exchange data on common ancestors with name and address of submitters published serially in *The Genealogical Helper*. Retrieval also by extraction service. *Genealogical Computing* 2 (Sept. 1982). *The Genealogical Helper* (Jan. -Feb. 1983). See "Evertons Announce New Service," *Genealogical Computing* 2 (March 1983). "Computerized 'Roots' Cellar," *Genealogical Computing* 1 (Sept. 1981).

Computerized Surname Magazine
Genealogical Center Library
Box 88534
Atlanta, GA 30356-8534

Queries in alphabetical order, over 3,400 per issue. Published quarterly. Names also published semi-monthly in *Genealogy Today* (see below). *Genealogical Computing* 2 (Sept. 1982).

"Consolidated Computer Output Index"
South Carolina Department of Archives and History
Box 11669
Capitol Station
Columbia, SC 29211
(803) 758-5816

The South Carolina Archives has created a major-name index to many of the state's colonial records. Will make a surname search for a nominal fee from the printout. List of sources available on request for SASE. "Computers," *APG Newsletter* 4 (Jan. 1982).

Data Base Services
New York State Library
Cultural Education Center
Empire State Plaza
Albany, NY 12230
(518) 474-3232

Computerized journal and report literature on New York State. Access through regional libraries.

Data-Search
3036 S. Alpine
Evergreen, CO 80439
(303) 674-8165

Genealogical data exchange.

The Family and Community History Program
The Newberry Library
60 W. Walton Street
Chicago, IL 60610

Illinois 1860 and 1870 computerized census project.

Family Name Exchange
Box 284
Detroit, MI 48234

Computer-indexed genealogical data. Surnames registered free. *Genealogical Computing* 2 (Sept. 1982).

Family Tree Data Center
Box 33927
San Diego,CA 92103
(714) 295-5693

Storage, expanding, retrieval, publishing of family data. Samples, $5.

Family Tree Services
Box 864
Palo Alto, CA 94301

Computer-organized data on standard forms.

Genealogical Branch Library
Brigham Young University
Harold B. Lee Library
Provo, UT 84603

A unique volunteer program will provide a computerized, every-name index to more than 500,000 rolls of microfilmed records including DAR records, Bible records, and family histories pertaining to the southern states. This index will be online through BYU to terminals in many parts of the U.S. when the project is completed. At last report entries were being extracted at the rate of 50,000 per week. See Roger Flick, "Getting the Most for Your Library Budget." *APG Newsletter* 4 (Nov. 1982): 1-5.

Genealogical Data-Computer Indexed
Box 6284
Detroit, MI 48234

Family name exchange database.

Genealogical Indexing Associates
Box 102
West Bountiful, UT 84087

Computer inquiry service. Includes 225,000-name Indiana biographical index. Will soon include Illinois, Iowa, Kentucky, Michigan, Ohio, Wisconsin, and other states. *Genealogical Computing* 2 (Sept. 1982).

Geneee's Exchange
Helen H. Pierrard
R. D. 4
West Chester, PA 19380

"GENEEE'S EXCHANGE" has the goal of answering these questions: Does a record exist? Where can this record be found? To whom and where do I write for a copy?"

Gary T. Hawbaker
Rt. 2 Box 409
Elizabethtown, PA 17022

Also prints Pennsylvania tax lists.

Historical Boundary Data File
Newberry Library
60 West Walton Street
Chicago, IL 60610
(312) 943-9090

See John H. Long, "Historical Boundary Data File," *Mapline* 3 (1979). Fourteen states were completed before the funds ran out. This source is disseminated both as a database and as printed atlases. University of Wisconsin Cartographic Laboratory (UWCL) offers a custom mapmaking service and will plot outline maps from the Historical Boundary Data File. Contact UWCL for order forms and current prices: Cartography Laboratory, M382 Science Hall, 550 N. Park Street, University of Wisconsin, Madison, WI 53706, (608) 262-1363. The data file itself will be available through the Inter-University Consortium for Political and Social Research at University of Michigan, Box 1248, Ann Arbor, MI 48106.

ICPSR Data Archive
Inter-University Consortium for Political and Social Research
Box 1248
Ann Arbor, MI 48106

Includes U.S. Censuses, 1790-1970; roll call votes for U.S. Congress; nineteenth and twentieth century French census data.

Illinois Computerized Census Project
Newberry Library
60 W. Walton Street
Chicago, IL 60610

Alphabetical index to 4,511,842 names in 1860 and 1870 federal census of Illinois.

Illinois Public Domain Computer
Conversion Project
Illinois State Archives
Archives Building
Springfield, IL 62756

Index of over 550,000 original sales of public lands in Illinois. Direct inquiries to Information Services/Reference. See *Illinois State Genealogical Society Quarterly*, (Summer 1982), p. 93.

"International Genealogical Index" (IGI)
(Formerly Computer File Index)
Genealogical Society of Utah
50 East North Temple
Salt Lake City, UT 84150

(See example in Chapter 13, "Genealogical Indexes.") IGI is a file indexed by surname with family relationships not shown except where given in the specific source used for each entry. It includes 68 million names from areas all over the world. It is available in microfiche printouts at the society and its branch libraries. Areas with greater activity in the file are updated more frequently. England and the United States are both high-activity areas, the United States being updated about every two years. The file prefers vital records (births, christenings, marriages) as sources, and accepts others only in the absence of these. This data is, however, of varying accuracy. Errors are quite low, due to the double checking of entries, specialized training of the volunteers, and the use of one "high integrity" source for each entry. Entries are grouped under one master spelling of a surname, so several spellings of the same name will be together. However, in some cases, the source record is hard to read, and some names could be interpreted two ways. The primary surname used for indexing of this file varies from area to area.

International Soundex Reunion Registry
Box 2312
Carson City, NV 89702
(702) 882-6270

Confidential, voluntary identification system and reunion agency for adoptees, birthparents, and those seeking genetic aid. 7,922 registrants. *Genealogical Computer Pioneer* 1 (March 1983).

Jacksoniana
Ernest H. Jackson
730 Parker Woods Drive
Rockford, IL 61102
(815) 962-0817

Computerized database of over 50,000 entries, primarily the Jackson surname. Portions published quarterly.

"Kentucky Guide Project"
Kentucky Department of Libraries and Archives
Frankfort, KY 40601

Sponsored by the federal government in four states, including Kentucky and Wisconsin. Database currently available in computer printout in Kentucky Department of Libraries and Archives. Computer file updated periodically. Online access expected in future. *Genealogical Computing* 2 (July 1982).

"Kentucky Cemetery Records Project"
Kentucky Historical Society
300 W. Broadway
Frankfort, KY 40601
(502) 564-3016

Brian D. Harney, "Letter to Editor," *Genealogical Computing* 2 (July 1982). Project sponsored by the Kentucky Historical Society. Input on IBM OS/6 computer.

Marriage Finding, Inc.
Box 233
Baton Rouge, LA

Database of 100,000 records for Louisiana, Mississippi, Georgia. Send SASE for details. *Genee's Exchange*, Feb. 1982.

Missing Persons
Box 195
Great Kills
Staten Island, NY 10308

Database of missing persons with name, address, birthdate. $50 per name per state to search.

Montrose Genealogical Services
Box 284
Tuart Hill, Western Australia 6060
Phone: (09) 349-4505

Constantly updated listing of others tracing branches of your family worldwide. Also central index of sources. Annual subscription: $9.50.

National Adoption Registry
(Div. of Yesterday's Children)
828 Davis Street
Evanston, IL 60201
(312) 475-1700

Includes 6,000 entries, mostly from the Midwest. Monthly meetings to reunite adoptees and natural children. "Computers," *APG Newsletter* 4 (Jan. 1982).

National Adoptive Search Registry
NASR, Inc.
Box 2051
Great Neck, NY 11022
(516) 466-4140

Includes entries for adoptees and their biological parents.

Ontario Computerized Land Records Index, 1780-1914
Ontario Provincial Archive
77 Grenville Street
Queen's Park
Toronto M7A 2K9
Canada

Includes Crown Lands Papers, Canada Company papers, Peter Robinson Papers. Available on microfiche at Genealogical Society of Utah and its branches. Ontario (Canada) land index is published on microfiche; see "Computers," *APG Newletter* 4 (Jan. 1982).

Ontario Genealogical Society
Box 66, Station Q
Toronto M4T 2L7
Ontario
Canada

"As the 25th anniversary project of the Ontario Genealogical Society, founded in 1961, it has been announced that all of the twenty-one branches of the society will undertake a joint project of indexing the 1871 provincial census. The details are at present still being worked out, but there will be a local township/district index and this will be merged into a master province-wide index."—J. Brian Gilchrist

Orphan Voyage of Florida
13906 Pepperrell Drive
Tampa, FL 33624

Computer surname listing from telephone books of all fifty states. Will supply a printout on request of all telephones and addresses for any surname. Fee varies; $150 minimum. *Family Records Today* 3 (July 1982).

Pedigree Information System
Computer Science Department
Brigham Young University
Provo, UT 84602

Computerized pedigree research.

Quebec Project
Department of Demography
Université de Montreal
Montreal, Quebec

Computerized reconstitution of Quebec's entire population from its origins to the year 1850. Estimated that the population descends from about 20,000 original people. The database includes parish registers and nominal censuses supplemented with confirmation lists, land records, military rolls, and ships' passenger lists. See Legore Jacques and Bertrans Desjardins, "Using Computers to Reconstitute Families: French Canadian Seventeenth-Century Families as an Example." World Conference on Records, 1980, 13 vols. (Salt Lake City: Genealogical Society of Utah, 1980), vol. 12, p. 333ff. Richard Hirst, in a letter to editor concerning computerized data banks in Canada notes that many groups (major repositories such as the Public Archives down to small public libraries, like Niagara-on-the -Lake) have been creating computerized databases. *Genealogical Computing* 2 (Sept. 1982).

Tracers
39 Broadway
New York, NY 10006
(212) 558-6550

Reunion registry for adoptees and their biological parents, missing persons, and other investigations. About 300,000 entries, of which about 40 percent are biological parents seeking their children. "Computers," *APG Newsletter* 4 (Jan. 1982).

"Virginia Settlers Research Project"
Association for the Preservation of Virginia Antiquities
2705 Park Avenue
Richmond, VA 23220
(804) 359-0239

The Association will search the microfiche edition at $10 per surname for up to five photocopy pages. "Computers," *APG Newsletter* 4 (Jan. 1982). Microfiche edition also available at Genealogical Society of Utah.

Judith Allison Walters
Box 129
Bothell, WA 98011

Computerized list of 1,800 photographers from 1840 to 1939 with cities and some operation dates.

Warling Computing Services
8530 Burnet Avenue Unit 201
Sepulveda, CA 91343

Data exchange for researchers.

Yochson Institute
Leonard Fink
Box FF
Brooklyn, NY 11219
(212) 435-0900

1980 press release announcing the "first computerized Jewish genealogical database system..." *Genealogical Computing* 4 (Jan. 1984).

How To Search Online Databases*

There are hundreds of major bibliographic databases that index subjects such as books in print, newspapers, stock market prices, and chemical periodicals. Genealogical professionals interested in North American history should already be familiar with the printed indexes called *Historical Abstracts, America: History and Life,* and the *Comprehensive Dissertation Abstracts,* both accessible by computer. Nowadays massive abstracting indexes such as *Psychological Abstracts, Population Bibliography,* or the *Canadian Business Periodicals Index* are not only on computer but compiled by computer and later printed on hard copy. "Online" means your computer terminal can access another computer across town or even across an ocean.

Many university libraries have or are creating special rooms with computer terminals attended by library specialists who will conduct online searches for set fees. For example, the University of Utah has access to about 250 such databases through three vendors, Bibliographic Retrieval Services, DIALOG Information Services, and System Development Corporation. They purchase databases which are periodically updated and sell access to users such as government agencies, corporations, universities, and in-

---

*Edited from William Thorndale, "Computer Search of Online Data," *APG Newsletter* 4 (Jan. 1982): 10-12.

dividuals. There are now no large online databases specifically for genealogists, though the Genealogical Society of Utah's upcoming computerized catalog will be online in a few years. Large online databases are more in the future than the present so far as genealogy is concerned, but serious researchers should keep alert to this new way of finding information.

As a genealogical experiment, I used the University of Utah terminal to search the single database called ERIC, the Educational Resources Information Center. Since 1966 the U.S. Department of Education has provided access to educational literature through ERIC, both by creating abstract indexes and by microfiching hard-to-find materials such as technical reports, speeches, conference proceedings, and professional papers. ERIC is available through DIALOG. A telecommunications link was made from Salt Lake City through San Francisco to the vendor's computer in nearby Palo Alto, California.

Using the search words *family history* and *genealogy*, the computer identified in ERIC sixty-eight items with *family history* in their titles or abstracts and fifty-four with *genealogy*, for a total (discounting overlap) of 117. Upon orders, the DIALOG computer relayed the titles and their bibliographic data to Salt Lake, where a matrix printer made a hard copy of all 117. This took nine minutes, and the library charged $4.69.

The titles without abstracts made judging contents very difficult. Clearly, "Black Roots; Using Genealogy in the Classroom," *Social Studies* 71:2 (March-April 1980): 68-70, was a valid title for our purposes—a "clean" reference. Just as obviously, "Knowledge and Human Values: A Genealogy of Nihilism," *Teachers College Records* 82 (Sept. 1981): 505-20, was a "dirty" item, not our kind of genealogy. But what was "A Badger Chemist Genealogy: The Faculty at the University of Wisconsin-Madison"? Getting the abstracts online along with the titles would resolve the confusion, so for purposes of cost comparison, all 117 titles were obtained online with their abstracts. This took seventy minutes and cost $38.37. In this case, it was about eight times more expensive to obtain the titles with abstracts as it was to obtain just the titles. However, before the more expensive title-abstract search was made, the terminal attendant said a cheaper way would be to tell the DIALOG computer to print the 117 titles-with-abstracts in California and then the printout would be mailed, arriving in three or four days. The estimated price of this offline retrieval was about $15. The cost is less because you are paying for computer time but not the hour or so of telecommunications.

Since ERIC is an index to educational literature, most of the "clean" family history and genealogy titles are on teaching children, many dealing with ethnic family history. Most of the "dirty" titles were on medical family histories. Possibly some terms could be defined that are common to medical family history but not to genealogical family history. If so, the computer could be told to reject any titles with these "dirty" identifiers and thus reduce considerably the number of family history titles not on genealogy. However, the terminal attendant doubted such screening would work in our case. The principle is valid in some situations, such as searching for astronomical stars while rejecting film, theater, and motion picture stars.

Among the 117 titles retrieved, seventy-three were valid items and forty-three were invalid. One was uncertain because it had no abstract: "The Algebra of Genealogy," *Mathematical Spectrum* 4:1 (1972): 7-9. The "Badger Chemist Genealogy" mentioned above proved to be a list of chemistry professors, a sort of genealogy of passing the torch.

As mentioned before, ERIC is also a microfiche collection of more ephemeral materials published and unpublished, items that would normally be hard to find. These are rich in ethnic entries, especially Indian and Hispanic individuals and families. Most major university libraries in North America subscribe to ERIC microfiche. My printout gave the ERIC document numbers, so it was very easy to find the microfiche copy of ERIC Document 192779 with Jessie Carney Smith, *Institute on Ethnic Genealogy for Librarians, Performance Report and Guide for Participants* (Nashville, Tenn.: Fisk University, 1979), 153 pp. It proved to be a project report on training librarians "to collect, preserve, interpret, and disseminate materials on ethnic genealogy. . . .", a useful source for those interested in such a subject.

It is illegal to offer photocopies of the printout, which is copyright. However, information such as the titles themselves cannot be copyrighted.

Interestingly, appendixes 4, 5, and 7 of the project report on ethnic librarianship could not be reproduced on microfiche because they were on colored paper. Materials will increasingly be preserved in microforms and should be designed by publishers with this in mind. Genealogical material—even APG's *Green $heet*—should not appear on colored paper.

An analogous problem is uninformative titles. "Win, Place, Show" appeared on our nine-minute titles printout, but we had to await the abstracts printout to get any idea how it dealt with family history and genealogy. (Answer: the genealogies of thoroughbred horses.) Cute titles are especially unhelpful. Since many indexes rely solely on key words in the title, the (fictitious) title *Links in the West* on the Rawley family's Alberta branch is not going to be found under *Rawley* in a key-word index, but the Link family may waste time hunting for the book. The conclusion is clear: as we move deeper into the information revolution and rely ever more on computerized data-retrieval systems, authors must remember their works should have self-explanatory titles and be reproducible on microforms for future economical storage.

On-Line Information Services

CompuServe Incorporated
5000 Arlington Centre Boulevard
Columbus, OH 43220
(800) 848-8990

Includes communication network. Subscription: $39.95; includes five introductory hours. Connect charge and monthly minimum required for prime time.

Dialog Information Services, Inc.
(Formerly Lockheed Information Services)
3460 Hillview Avenue
Palo Alto, CA 94304
(800) 227-1927; (800) 982-5838 in California

Time charge varies. Includes access to *Historical Abstracts, America: History and Life, Comprehensive Dissertation Abstracts,* and many more. Service available through most university computer centers.

Knowledge Index
3460 Hillview Avenue
Palo Alto, CA 94304
(800) 227-5510; (415) 858-3796

Subscription: $35. Connect charge includes network fees.

Source Telecomputing Corp.
1616 Anderson Road
McLean, VA 22102
(800) 336-3366

Subscription: $100, includes user's manual, lifetime subscription to newsletter, and other publications. Contact for connect, toll-call, and time charges.

On-Line Databases

Book Review Index
Gale Research Company
The Book Tower
Detroit, MI 48226
(313) 961-2242

Online through Dialog Information Services, Inc. . Periodical and book reviews.

Books in Print
R. R. Bowker Company
1180 Avenue of the Americas
New York, NY 10036
(212) 764-5100

Books currently available from publishers, complete citations.

COIN: Computerized Information in Canada
Information Systems
Alberta Research Council
Terrace Inn, 4th Floor
Edmonton, Alberta T6H 5R7,
Canada
(403) 438-0666

"Covers: Publicly available data bases in Canada and organizations which will search them." *The Directory of Directories (DOD)*, 2nd ed., p. 492.

CompuServe
Information Services
CompuServe Inc.
5000 Arlington Centre Boulevard
Columbus, OH 43220
(800) 848-8990

Online through CompuServe, Inc. Multifaceted information service providing many databases. May soon include genealogical databases.

Computer and Data Services
TYMNET, Inc.
20665 Valley Green Drive
Cupertino, CA 95014
(408) 446-6000

"Covers some seventy-five firms subscribing to TYMNET. . ., databases. . ., computer software. . . ." *DOD*, 2nd ed., p. 492.

Computer Readable Databases–A Directory and Data Source Book
American Society for Information Science
1010 16th Street, N.W.
Washington, DC 20036
(202) 659-3644

"Covers about 775 bibliographic databases which are machine readable, designed for information retrieval use, and publicly or commercially available." *DOD*, 2nd ed., p. 492.

Databases and Clearinghouses: Information Resources for Education
National Center for Research on Vocational Education
Ohio State University
1960 Kenny Road
Columbus, OH 43210
(614) 486-3655

"Covers fifty-five databases and thirty clearinghouses concerned with education." *DOD*, 2nd ed., p. 453.

Directory of Computer-Based Services [Telenet]
GTE Telenet Communications Corporation
8229 Boone Boulevard
Vienna, VA 22180
(703) 442-2300

"Covers about 300 databases." *DOD*, 2nd ed., p. 495.

Directory of ERIC Search Services
Educational Resources Information Center
National Institute of Education
Education Department
Washington, DC 20208

"Covers about 460 organizations which provide computerized ERIC database searches; other databases available to each organization are also mentioned. . . ." *DOD*, 2nd ed., p. 454.

Directory of Online Databases
Cuadra Associates, Inc.
1523 Sixth Street, Suite 12
Santa Monica, CA 90401
(21) 451-0644

"Covers over 860 online bibliographic and nonbibliographic databases." *DOD*, 2nd ed., p. 498.

Directory of Online Information Resources
Capital Systems Group, Inc.
11301 Rockville Pike
Kensington, MD 20895
(301) 881-9400

"Entries include database name, subject, description, coverage, file size. . . ." *DOD*, 2nd ed., p. 498.

Encyclopedia of Information Systems and Services
Gale Research Company
Book Tower
Detroit, MI 48226
(313) 961-2242

"Covers: More than 2,500 storage and retrieval services, database producers and publishers, online vendors. . ., networks. . ., databanks. . . ." *DOD*, 2nd ed., p. 149.

Espial Database Directory: Current Canadian Information Contained in Selected Databases and Databanks
Espial Productions Ltd.
Box 624
Station K
Toronto, Ontario M4P 2H1, Canada
(416) 485-8063

DOD, 2nd ed., p. 501.

GPO Monthly Catalog
Superintendant of Documents
U.S. Government Printing Office
Washington, DC 20402

Available by direct subscription or through Dialog Information Services, Inc.

Independent Computer Consultants Association
Box 27412
St. Louis, MO 63141

If you want help determining what you need or if you need someone to write software to your specifications, ask for freelance data systems in your area. *Inc.* (Jan. 1982).

Information Industry Market Place
R. R. Bowker Company
1180 Avenue of the Americas
New York, NY 10036
(212) 764-5100

"Covers about 2,500 firms and individuals who produce information products." *DOD*, 2nd ed., p. 508.

Information Sources: The IIA Membership Directory
[Information Services and Publishers]
Information Industry Association
316 Pennsylvania Ave., S.E., Suite 400
Washington, DC 20003
(301) 654-4150

"Covers over 130 companies producing information products, databases, microforms, online services. . . ." *DOD*, 2nd ed., p. 508.

International Software Data Base
Imprint Software Ltd.

Online through Dialog Information Services, Inc.; knowledge index, microcomputer software.

Library Networks
Knowledge Industry Publications
701 Westchester Avenue
White Plains, NY 10604
(914) 328-9157

"Publication includes list of twenty-five computer-based library networks and consortia." *DOD*, 2nd ed., p. 513.

Magazine Index
Information Access Corporation
404 Sixth Avenue
Menlo Park, CA 94025

Indexes to current periodicals. Available through Dialog Information Services, Inc.

Microcomputer Index

Online through Dialog Information Services, Inc.; knowledge index, microcomputer magazines.

National Online Circuit. New Directory of Self-Help Data Groups
Rebecca B. Gonzalez
IIT Research Institute
10 W. 35th Street
Chicago, IL 60616

INC., (Jan. 1982).

Online Bibliographic Databases
Aslib
Three Belgrave Square
London SWIX 8PL, England

"Covers about 190 online bibliographic databases worldwide." *DOD*, 2nd ed., p. 517.

Genealogical Networks

Computer-Assisted Genealogical Timesharing
Genealogical Time Sharing
1822 Harding Ave.
Abington, PA 19001

Share your research time with distant genealogists. $5 registration; $2 for each timesharing match made. *Genealogical Computing* 2 (Sept. 1982).

Family Historian's Network
Data Tranfer Associates, Inc.
5102 Pommeroy Drive
Fairfax, VA 22032
(703) 978-3532

A sheduled-use library of data and program files available to *Genealogical Computing* subscribers only. See *Genealogical Computing* 4 (Jan. 1984) for details.

LOCI' CORNER
Minneapolis, MN
(612) 571-5965

Genealogical Computing 1 (May 1982).

Spindex User's Network
Historical Records Project
Peterson Hall
Central Washington University
Ellensburg, WA 98926

Archives networking.

Genealogical User Interest Groups

Computer-Genealogy Associates
44 Haywood Street
Asheville, NC
(704) 252-7529

Computer Interest Group
Society of Genealogists
Coordinator, Don Francis
8 Fairborne Rise
Old Basing
Basingstoke, Hants.
RG24 DEH
England, UK

Dallas TRS-80 User's Group

See *Genealogical Computing* 1 (March 1982).

Kaypro Users Genealogy Interest Group
3010 Regency, Apt. 10
Ames, IA 50010

Minnesota Genealogical Society
Computer Group
Box 16006
St. Paul, MN 55105

National Genealogical Society
Computer Committee
1921 Sunderland Place N.W.
Washington, DC 20036
(202) 785-2123

Quinsept Users Group
5855 Santa Teresa Boulevard
San Jose, CA 95123

Publishes quarterly newsletter, $15 per year.

Roots Users Group (RUG)
7304 Mariposa Drive
Manassas, VA 22111

Publishes newsletter $9.50 per year.

Seattle Genealogical Society
Computer Interest Group
Box 549
Seattle, WA 98111

Library Catalogs

The LDS Church Genealogical Library Computer Catalog focuses on locality, "general-to-specific" or country, state, county, town arrangement for records of or about a certain area. For example, you will find deeds for Montgomery County, Ohio, under "US, Ohio, Montgomery–Land & Property." There are also listings by subject for records like prison camps (institutions) and by surname for family histories. For local records, the author is considered the office or jurisdiction which generated the records. Records are also listed by title. Helpful research information is given at the beginning of each state. It may include such data as burned records, county formation, or *see* references showing the county location of a given town or township. The source of entries is the library's own collection. It may eventually become a "union" catalog, showing sources located in other places. There is a monthly microfiche update for most states. The catalog is primarily on microfiche. Library personnel have limited access to terminals. Patrons will eventually be able to access through terminals also. Copies of catalog entries can be obtained by mail or by using a private researcher. At this writing, a little over 50 percent of the collection has been input. All branch libraries have printouts on microfiche.

The Online Computer Library Center, Inc. ("Ohio Network" or OCLC) has online terminals, available in most university libraries throughout the country, which provide access to holdings of all member libraries. The database is title/author oriented, subject entries are not included. Public/student use is encouraged; you must have an author or title to find the nearest copy. (See Chapter 12, "Newspapers," for other details.)

Spindex is a high-level system now in use by the Library of Congress, the National Archives, and the National Historical Publications and Records Commission to describe and index archival material and to prepare record inventories to manuscript collections.

For other libraries and archives see Judith P. Reid, "Library of Congress, SCORPIO! A Different Approach." *Genealogical Computing* 1 (Nov. 1981); Nancy Sahli, *Spindex: An Introduction for New and Prospective Users* (Ellensburg, Wash.: Spindex User's Network, 1980).

Computer catalogs are planned or underway in many institutions. We will see more union catalogs and have access to more catalogs on microfiche and microviewer. Others have already plugged into networks such as Knowledge Index, the Ohio Network, and Spindex. Access to this information is online within the library system to which the institution belongs.

Michael Cook, *Archives and the Computer* (Woburn, Mass.: Butterworth's, 1980), includes a valuable but select Directory of Archival Systems throughout the world.

Genealogical/Computer Serial Publications

Most periodicals honor a try before you buy policy. They will send a sample issue for a SASE (9 X 12 envelope and 3rd class postage) or current issue with invoice.

These periodicals include articles on computing for genealogists:

APG Newsletter
Association of Professional Genealogists
57 W. South Temple
Box 11601
Salt Lake City, UT 84147
(801) 532-3327

Bimonthly. Arlene H. Eakle, ed., $25/yr. in the U.S.; $35/yr. outside U.S.. Write for sample issue.

Computer-Ease for the Genealogist
Family History Center
Box 11394
Salt Lake City, UT 84147
(801) 277-6796

Quarterly. Wilma Adkins, ed. $3.95 a year. First two issues free with long SASE.

Computer in Genealogy: Society of Genealogists Newsletter
Society of Genealogists
37 Harrington Gardens
London SW7 4JX
England

Quarterly. David Hawgood, ed.

Computerized Surname Magazine
Genealogical Center Library
Box 88534
Atlanta, GA 30356
(404) 457-7801

Bimonthly. Diane Dieterle, ed. $26.50/yr.

Genealogical Computing
Data Transfer Associates, Inc.
5102 Pommeroy Drive
Fairfax, VA 22032
(703) 978-3532

Bimonthly newsletter from July 1981. Paul Andereck, ed. $20 per year in the U.S.; $25/yr. outside the U.S., plus $2 surcharge for checks not drawn on U.S. banks.

Genealogical Computer Pioneer
Posey Enterprises
Box 338
Orem, UT 84057

Quarterly journal. Joanna B. Posey, ed. $15/yr.

Genealogical Helper
Everton Publishers
Box 368
Logan, UT 84321

Bimonthly publication. George B. Everton, Jr., ed. $14.50/yr.

Genealogy Today
2815 Clearview Place #400
Atlanta, GA 30340
(404) 457-7801

Semi-monthly newspaper. Diane Dieterle, ed. $26/yr.

Indiana Genealogical Informer
Box 86
Harlan, IN 46743

Monthly newsletter. Melinda Newhard, ed. $9/yr.

NGS Computer Interest Group Digest
National Genealogical Society
1921 Sunderland Place N.W.
Washington, DC 20036
(202) 785-2123

Irregular. Wilma Adkins, ed.

NCS Newsletter
National Society of Computer Genealogists
2815 Clearview Place
Atlanta, GA 30340
(404) 457-7801

Organized 1 May 1983. Quarterly, *Computer/Genealogist* to begin 1 Jan. 1984. Diane Dieterle, ed. $25 charter membership.

Reading List

Genealogical Applications

Andereck, Paul A. *Genealogical Computing: The Beginning.* Fairfax, VA.: Data Transfer Associates, Inc., 1984. The best from *Genealogical Computing,* digested and up-dated. An effective way to access back issues if you have just discovered this valuable publication.

Andereck, Paul A. "The Computer: An Aid to the Historian." Annual All-day Seminar, 27 March 1982, Montgomery College, Rockville, Maryland. Paper available from author, 5102 Pommeroy Drive, Fairfax, VA 22032. (703) 978-8490. Computers and family history.

Appel, Eva, et al. "Computerized Family Reconsitution." Information Paper, The Demographic Database, University of Umea, S-90187, Umea, Sweden. Computer input of church registers in Sweden.

"Are Your Ancestors in a Computer?" *Genealogy Today* (1 March 1983).

Baldwin, Brad and Jackie Rae Baldwin. "Information Networks: A Sign of the Times." *Portable Companion,* Dec. 1983-Jan. 1983, p. 33.

Bechhoefer, Arthur S. "Electronic Publishing: The New Newsletter." *BYTE* 8 (May 1983): 124.

Brooke, N.M. "Some Problems Arising from the Computer Analysis of Armorial Records." *Family History* 11 (July 1976): 348-60.

"Claims, Committee Reports, and the Consolidated Computer Output Index: A Revolution in Access." *South Carolina Historical Magazine* 79 (1978): 313-18.

Collison, Robert L. *Indexes and Indexing: Guide to the Indexing of Books and Collections of Books,. . .and Other Material*. London: n.p., 1969.

Darwin, Kenneth. "The Use of the Computer in Indexing Records." *Archive* 9 (1970).

DeCoursey, Bill. "Telecommunications News." *Genealogical Computing* 1 (Sept. 1981).

Dieterle, Diane. *Basic Programming for Genealogists*. Atlanta, GA.: Genealogy Today, 1982. Written for the beginner.

Directory of Special Libraries and Information Centers, published annually and available from Gale Research Company, Book Tower, Detroit, MI 48226, (313) 961-2242. "Covers over 15,000 special libraries, information centers, 700 networks." *The Directory of Directories* (DOD), 2nd ed., p.499.

"Evertons Introduce the New Computerized Family File." *The Genealogical Helper* (Jan.-Feb. 1982).

Fishbein, Meyer H. "ADP and Archives: Selected Publications on Automatic Data Processing." *American Achivist* 38 (Jan. 1975): 31-42. Bibliography.

Garvin, Andrew P., and Hubert Bermont. *How to Win with Information or Lose Without It*. Bermont Books, 815 15th St. N.W., Washington, DC 20005. Includes the use of databanks, indexes, directories, reference sources, retrieval information networks, etc.

"Genealogical Telecommunications." *Genealogical Computing* 1 (Jan. 1982).

Grosswirth, Marvin. "Getting the Best from Databanks." *Personal Computing* (May 1983): 111. Includes a listing of thiry-two online databases and eighteen online services, information on how to find online databases, and more.

Harrison, I. R. "An Eye to the Future: Uses of the Computer in Genealogy." *Genealogists Magazine* 20 (Sept. 1980): 162-68.

Heiss, Willard. "The Use of the Personal Computer System in Genealogical Family Organizations." *Genealogy* (May 1982): 1-3.

Hogan, Thom. "From Afar: Playing with Electronic Bulletin Boards." *Portable Companion* (Dec.-Jan. 1983): 37.

INC. Independent Computer Consultants Association, Box 27312, St. Louis, MO 63141. *INC.*, January 1982. If you want help determining what you need or if you need someone to write the software to your specifications, this group will tell you of freelance data systems specialists in your area.

Interdisciplinary Studies in the Humanities. Available from Scarecrow Press, Inc., 52 Liberty Street, Metuchen, NJ 08840, (201) 548-8600. Covers about 800 colleges and universities which offer academic programs in humanities. *DOD*, 2nd ed., p. 508. May be useful in locating those which offer family studies, demography, etc. May also be creating databases.

James, David. "Databases Fulfill Needs on Demand." *Personal Computing* (July 1982): 32.

Long, John H. "The Case for Historical Cartographic Data Files." Paper presented at the Ninety-Second Annual Meeting of the American Historial Association, Dallas, 1977.

____________. "The Historical Boundary Data File: Resource for Frontier Studies." Paper presented at the Great Lakes History Conference, Grand Rapids, 1979.

"Letter to the Editor re: Special-Interest Users' Groups (SIGs) on CompuServe." *Genealogical Computing* 2 (1983).

Marsh, Warren L. *Search and Retrieval: The Application of Data Processing to Genealogical Research*. Available from Warren L. Marsh, 5 Windsor Court, Old Saybrook, CT 06475.

Montgomery, Austin H., Jr. "Speed Indexing of Genealogical Data by Computer." *National Genealogical Society Quarterly* 64 (1976): 35-43.

"New Search Tool Now Available." *SMAA Newsletter* (Jan. 1982): 9. *Southwest Missouri Adult Adoptees Newsletter* reports a computer surname listing from telephone books of all fifty states and Washington, D.C., acquired by Orphan Voyage of Florida, 13906 Pepperrell Drive, Tampa, FL 33624.

"Networking: Present Realities & Future Benefits." *Genealogical Computing* 2 (Jan. 1983).

"Network Queries Are Not Efficient." *Genealogical Computing* 2 (Nov. 1982).

Parker, Rita. "Computing Your Family Tree." *Personal Computing*, Jan. 1983, pp. 112-18.

Papenfuse, Edward. "The Public Records of the American Revolutionary Era: Some Suggestions for the Development of Bibliographic Guides." *Historical Methods Newsletter* 4 (Sept. 1971): 148-50.

Posey, Joanna W. "Tracing Your Roots by Computer." *Software Supermarket*. Jan. 1984, pp. 11-17.

"Reasons for Organizing A Computer Interest Group in Your Society." *Genealogical Computing* 1 (May 1982).

Saal, Harry. "Local Area Networks." *BYTE* 8 (May 1983): 60.

Skolnick, M. H. "A Computer Program for Linking Records." *Historical Methods Newsletter* 4 (Sept. 1971).

Stevens, Lawrence. "Doing Business from the Source." *Personal Computing*, April 1983 p. 72.

Stothers, Thomas, and A. K. Barsby. "Observations on Recording Pedigrees on Computers." 13th Internatonal Congress of Genealogical and Heraldic Sciences, 1 Sept. 1976, Imperial College, Kensington, England.

____________. "Identification of Ensigns Armorial by Computers." *Genealoigie et Heraldica*, 10th International Congress of Genealogical and Heraldic Sciences, Vienna, 1970. (Verlag der Wiener, Medizinischer Akademie, 1972) 1: 439-44.

Wagner, Richard L. "John Howland Goes Electronic." *Mayflower Quarterly* 47 (Nov. 1981): 208-11.

Witschey, Walter R. T. "Locating Land Described in Colonial Patents by Computer Analysis." *Virginia Magazine of History and Biography* 88 (1980): 155-69.

Wrege, Rachael. "The Human Roll Call: The Mormon Church Builds a Database—a List of Everyone Who Has Ever Lived." *Popular Computing*, Dec. 1982; pp. 48-55.

Readings on Equipment, Software, and Hardware

A CP/M Software Index Small Systems Group, Box 5429, Santa Monica, CA 90405. Lists almost 1,700 programs offered by 507 vendors.

Andereck, Paul. "The Genealogy of A Genealogical Computer." *Genealogical Computing* 1 (May 1982).

____________ and Sara Andereck. "The State of Genealogical Computing: A Report of Reader Survey Results." *Genealogical Computing* 22 (May 1983). Includes a discussion of computer ownership by *Genealogical Computing* readers and changing buying patterns. 1 (Nov. 1981); 1 (May 1982); 2 (July 1982); 2 (Sept. 1982); 2 (Nov. 1982); 2 (Jan. 1983); 2 (March 1983).

____________. "What Does A Genealogical Computer Cost?" *Genealogical Computing* 2 (March 1983).

____________. "How Would You Spend $4,500?" *Genealogical Computing* 2 (July 1982); 2 (Sept. 1982); 2 (Nov. 1982).

Brandon, Dick H., and Sidney Segelstein. *The Businessman's Guide to Minicomputers: How to Select Hardware, Software, and Services*. n.p., 1981.

Brown, Stuart, "An Inexpensive Letter-Quality Printer." *BYTE* 8 (May 1983): 242.

"Carry-About Computers?" *Genealogical Computing* 2 (Nov. 1982).

"Computer Shopping with the Editor." *Genealogical Computing* 2 (Jan. 1983).

Eakle, Arlene. "Thoughts About Business Computers." *APG Newsletter* 4 (Jan. 1982). Contains an annotated bibliography of published software and hardware consumer guides/directories. A thoughtful article on purchasing hardware, software, and services, and a section on "Genealogy Software Opportunities."

Eischen, Martha. *Compu-Guide: A Consumer's Guide to Small Business Computers*. Beaverton, Ore.: Dilithium Press, 1982.

Freiberger, Stephen, and Paul Chew, Jr. *A Consumer's Guide to Personal Computing and Microcomputers*. Rochelle Park, N.J.: Hayden Book Co., 1980.

Gabel, David. "How to Pick a Portable Computer." *Personal Computing*, May 1983, p. 96. Includes a buyer's guide to features and capabilities of portable and hand-held computers.

____________. "If It's Worth Its Weight in Paper. . . ." *Personal Computing* July 1982, p. 66. Includes a buyer's guide to printers.

"A Genealogy Computer: What's the Cost?" *Genealogical Computing* 1 (July 1981).

"A Great Little Computer But . . ." *Genealogical Computing* 2 (March 1983).

"How Long Should You Keep Computers?" *Genealogical Computing* 2 (Jan. 1983).

Kelly, Dr. Mahlon G. "Data Collection With a Microcomputer." *BYTE* 8 (March 1983).

"A Large Dose of Dots (Printers)." *Genealogical Computing* 1 (March 1982).

"Looking Ahead: OCR?" *Genealogical Computing* 1 (July 1981).

Mansfield, Richard, et al. *The Beginner's Guide to Buying A Personal Computer.* Greensboro, N.C.: Computer Books, 1982.

Osborne, Adam, and David Bunnell. *An Introduction to Microcomputers: Volume One – The Beginner's Book.* Berkeley, Calif.: Osborne/ McGraw-Hill, 1982.

"Portability, Not Transportability?" *Genealogical Computing* 2 (May 1983).

"Printers: An Editorial View." *Genealogical Computing* 1 (Jan. 1982).

"Putting Coin-Operated Computers in Libraries." *Venture,* July 1982.

Rinder, Robert M. *A Practical Guide to Small Computers.* New York: Monarch Press, 1981.

Rothfeder, Jeffrey. "The Well-Traveled Computer." *Personal Computing,* May 1983, p. 72.

Rubin, Charles. "Portable Power." *Personal Computing* May 1983, p. 87.

Sager, Ira. "You and Your Computer: Solving the Printer Puzzle." *Venture* June 1982, p. 26.

Sarisky, Larry. "Will Removable Hard Disks Replace the Floppy?" *BYTE* 8 (March 1983). Tells of another breakthrough in price and mass storage: a five-megabyte fixed and removable hard-disk system for under $2,000.

Sutherland, John. "Getting the System You Want." *Genealogical Computing* 2 (Jan. 1983).

"Too Great an Expectation?" *Genealogical Computing* 2 (March 1983). In response to readers' complaints about dealers.

Washington Post. "IBM Enters the Personal Computer Market." *Genealogical Computing* 1 (Sept. 1981).

"Yes, It Is What It Seems (Expansion in the Personal Computer Marketplace)." *Genealogical Computing* 2 (Sept. 1982).

Genealogical Programming, Database Management, Standards

"A Self-directed Approach (Users of Off-the-Shelf Database Management and Word-Processing Programs for Family Recordkeeping)." *Genealogical Computing* 1 (March 1982).

"About Indexing Programs." *Genealogical Computing* 2 (Jan. 1983).

Acree, Chuck. "What Are Your Genealogical Objectives?" *Genealogical Computing* 2 (Sept. 1982).

Clark, Clarence A. *Computerizing Your Genealogical Records.* College Station, Tex.: Computer Genealogical Services, 1976.

Elliott, Bob. "Genesis of A Genealogy Program, Part 2." *Genealogical Computing* 2 (March/May 1983). Discusses developing the program specifications and database record structure for each person.

Harrison, I. R. "Applied Genealogical Computing." *Genealogical Computing* 2 (Nov. 1982).

Howell, Barton J. "A File Management Code for Genealogical Records." *Genealogical Computing* 1 (Nov. 1981).

___________. "More on Genealogy Codes." *Genealogical Computing* 1 (Jan. 1982).

___________. "Howell on Numbering (continued)." *Genealogical Computing,* (March 1982).

___________. "Feedback: Numbering." *Genealogical Computing,* May 1982.

___________. "Howell's Numbering Windup." *Genealogical Computing* 2 (Sept. 1982).

Johnston, W. Wesley. "Data Processing for Genealogists." *APG Newsletter* 4 (Jan. 1982).

___________. "The Elements of A Data Processing System: An Introduction for Genealogists." *APG Newsletter* 4 (Jan. 1982).

Letter to editor concerning features needed in a genealogy program. *Genealogical Computing* 2 (May 1983).

Letter to editor concerning numbering. *Genealogical Computing* 2 (July 1982).

Letter to editor concerning standards in genealogical computing. *Genealogical Computing* 2 (May 1983).

Marsh, Warren L. *Search and Retrieval: The Application of Data Processing to Genealogical Research.* Old Saybrook, Conn.: n.p., 1970.

Mitchell, Edward. "An Intro to Data Structure." *Creative Computing* Oct./ Nov. 1982.

Pontius, James W. "Pontius on Dates." *Genealogical Computing* 2 (Sept. 1982).

"Pontius' Suggestion." *Genealogical Computing* 2 (March 1983).

Schreier, Jim. "Computing Your Genealogy." *Interface Age,* Jan, 1980, p. 124; 1 (July 1981).

"Standards in Genealogical Computing." *Genealogical Computing* 2 (March 1983).

Taylor, Nora M. "Design of A Unit Record for Genealogy." *Genealogical Computing* 1 (March 1982).

"The Genealogists Recommend Data Fields (Survey Response)." *Genealogical Computing* 2 (Sept. 1982).

Vorenberg, Steve. "Genealogy Program Requirements." *Genealogical Computing* 2 (Nov. 1982).

"What It Takes to Program." *Genealogical Computing* 1 (May 1982).

Genealogy and the Computer

Andereck, Paul A. "Personal Computing in Genealogy: An Evaluation." *Genealogical Computing* 1 (May 1982).

Anderson, Esther A. "On Getting Involved with Computers." *Genealogical Computing* 1 (March 1982).

Armstrong, John J. "Roots and Branches." *Personal Computing* Sept. 1979, p. 41. See also commentary: *Genealogical Computing* 1 (July 1981).

Cavanaugh, Karen B. "Computers – A Genealogist's Dream Come True." *The Indiana Genealogical Informer* 3 (April 1982).

"Computers." *APG Newsletter* 4 (Jan. 1982). Special issue on computers and genealogy.

Cook, Michael. *Archives and the Computer.* Woburn, Mass.: Butterworth's, 1980.

Dempsey, Jim. "Genealogical Systems Analysis." *Genealogical Computing* 2 (Nov. 1982).

Dieterle, Diane. "Computers and You." *Genealogical Computing* 1 (Jan. 1982).

Engle, Jan M. "Kinology is Fun." *Genealogical Helper.* (Nov./Dec. 1981). See also his author's comments, *Genealogical Computing* 1 (July 1981). Includes samples of his program.

"Genealogical Adequacy; Is it Relative?" *Genealogical Computing* 1 (Nov. 1981).

"Genealogical Uses of Computers." *Genealogical Computing* 1 (Sept. 1981).

Harney, Brian. "Could Computers Have a Place in Your Genealogical Work?" *The Circuit Rider,* Feb. 1982, pp. 3-5.

Harter, Stuart. "Genealogy and the Personal Computer." *The Indiana Genealogical Informer* 3 (April 1982).

Heaps, H. S. *Information Retrieval: Computational and Theoretical Aspects.* New York: n.p., 1978. Discusses search programs.

"History and the Computer: A Special Issue." *Historical Methods Newsletter* 7 (June 1974).

Legare, Jacques. "Using Computers to Reconstitute Families: French Canadian Seventeenth-century Families as an Example." World Conference on Records, 1980, Salt Lake City, Utah, Genealogical Society of Utah, vol. 12, pp. 333ff.

McCormick, Ida Skarson. "Feedback: What Is A Genealogically Adequate System?" *Genealogical Computing* 1 (March 1982).

McDowell, Scott, and Connie McDowell. "Living The Genealogical Computerist's Dream." *Genealogical Computing* 1 (Nov. 1981).

McKay, Jack. "Personal Computers for Genealogists." *National Genealogical Society Quarterly* 69 (March 1981).

Merril, Stan W. "Tracing Your Own Roots." *BYTE,* Oct. 1979, p. 22. See also commentary: *Genealogical Computing* 1 (July 1981).

"Micro Clinic: Abbreviate Your Entry Labor." *Genealogical Computing* 1 (May 1982).

"Micro Clinic: Computer Memory." *Genealogical Computing* 1 (Nov. 1981).

"Micro Clinic: Family Data Files." *Genealogical Computing* 1 (Jan. 1982).

Micro Clinic: Letter to the Editor, "The Family Data File." *Genealogical Computing* 1 (March 1982).

"Micro Clinic: Multiply Your Keystrokes." *Genealogical Computing* 2 (Nov. 1982).

"Micro Clinic: Sorting with Speed." *Genealogical Computing* 2 (Sept. 1982).

"Misconceptions of Genealogical Computing: Disadvantages of Computerized Genealogy – Another Viewpoint. Followed by Editorial Comment." *Genealogical Computing* 2 (Sept. 1982).

Montgomery, Austin H., Jr. "Speed Indexing of Genealogical Data by Computer." *National Genealogical Society Quarterly* 64 (1976): 35.

Parker, Rita. "Computing Your Family Tree." *Personal Computing* (Jan. 1983).

Posey, Joanna W. "The Use of Computers in Genealogical Family Organizations." *Genealogical Computing* 2 (July 1982).

Rogers, Herb. "Feedback: Genealogically Adequate." *Genealogical Computing* 1 (Jan. 1982).

Scofield, Norman E. "The Usefulness of Computers in Amateur Genealogy." *Genealogical Computing* 1 (Nov. 1981).

Skolnick, Mark H. "Computers in Genealogy." World Conference on Records, 1980, Salt Lake City, Genealogical Society of Utah, vol. 12, pp. 205ff.

Stothers, Thomas. "Identification of Ensigns Armorial by Computer." *Genealogicae et Heraldica* (1970).

Stothers, Thomas and A. K. Barsby. "Observations on Recording Pedigrees on Computers." *XIII International Congress of Genealogical and Heraldic Sciences*. Kensington, England: Imperial College, 1976.

"The Computers are Coming!" *Genealogical Computing* 2 (Nov. 1982).

Towne, William B. "Putting the 'Byte' on Genealogical Computerization." *A Lot of Bunkum* (Oct. 1981). See also comment in *Genealogical Computing* 1 (July 1981).

"UG Means Users' Group." *Genealogical Computing* 2 (May 1983). Roots Users' Group (RUG) and proposed directory of genealogy software users will be included in future *GC's*.

Word Processing

"Dictation: A Simple Idea." *Genealogical Computing* 2 (May 1983).

Drakeford, Richard. "Sorting Notes with MailMerge." *Portable Companion*, Feb./March 1983, p. 28.

Gabel, David. "Word Processing: Finding the Right Software." *Personal Computing* April 1983, p. 110. Includes "A Buyer's Guide to Word-Processing Software."

Green, John C. "Word-Processing for The Genealogist (Biblio)." *Genalogical Computing* 2 (Nov. 1982).

Leddy, Edward F. "The Academic and WordStar." *Portable Companion*, Feb./March 1983, p. 34. Preparing terms papers, dissertations, and theses.

Letter to the editor concerning word processing for family worksheets. *Genealogical Computing* 2 (Sept. 1982).

Napier, Edward D. "More on Typesetting and Publishing." *Genealogical Computing* 2 (Sept. 1982).

Pence, Dick. "Using Word Processing to Compile A Family History." *Genealogical Computing* 1 (March 1982).

Rainey, Scott. "Filling in Forms: WordStar Tackles Preprinted Forms." *Portable Companion*, Feb./March 1983, p. 37.

"Software Buyer's Guide." *Creative Computing*. Cited in *Genealogical Computing* 2 (July 1982).

"Typesetting: The Third Way to Print." *Genealogical Computing* 2 (July 1982).

"Word Processing for Genealogists." *Genealogical Computing* 2 (May 1983).

"Word-Processing Usage." *Genealogical Computing* 1 (Jan. 1982).

COULD YOU USE THIS CHAPTER?

Type of Record	*Kept from*	*Clues That You Should Consult These Records*
War societies Early settlers and ship societies Colonial societies Nationality (Ethnic) Societies Religious societies Royal and baronial societies	Most created after 1860 for societies pertaining to all periods	If you have evidence that an ancestor was an early settler or sailed on one of the original ships to America; or that he served in a public office before the Revolutionary War; or if he/she was Welsh, English, Irish, a Scot, a Swede, or a Huguenot who immigrated before 1800, your ancestry may already have been traced, documented, and printed with an everyname index just awaiting your discovery. If your ancestor served in any war from colonial Indian disturbances through World War II, your ancestry may have been traced and is waiting your discovery.
Family societies and organizatons		This chapter details each society, its qualifications for membership, provides names and addresses, lists the publications in which these lineages have been printed, and where to find them. Manuscript collections of applications and their public access are also described by the acknowledged American authority on the subject, who himself, belongs to more than 100 societies and serves as the official genealogist for several.

Chapter 23

RY AND LINEAGE TY RECORDS

omas Smallwood, Jr., C.A.L.S.

S... societies ...ghout the Unit... de range of registers, jou... mbership rosters. Many of the sources needed to establish membership in a hereditary society will be found in other chapters – vital, military, church, and pension records – and not repeated in this chapter. Hereditary societies can be classified under seven headings:

- "War" societies
- Early settler and ship societies
- Colonial societies
- Nationality (ethnic) societies
- Religious societies
- Royal and baronial societies
- Family organizations

Hereditary or lineage societies require a prospective member to complete an application form showing descent from the qualifying ancestor for that society. The application should be sufficiently documented to prove beyond any doubt the accuracy of the lineage set forth. A number of the hereditary societies do not wish to have their mailing addresses published. The majority of these are "by invitation only" societies. They require that new members be invited to join by a current member and provide letters of recommendation.

"War" Societies

The oldest, largest, and best-known of the hereditary societies are those with membership based on the military service of an ancestor. These societies are listed in chronological order of military service.

The Ancient and Honorable Artillery Company of Massachusetts

Founded in 1637 and chartered by Governor Winthrop in 1638, this is the oldest military body and chartered organization on the American continent. Membership is limited to 550 regular members, who do not have to descend from a former member. "Right of descent" membership is open to any male descendant of a former member of the company whose service dates prior to 1738. Unlike the regular members, "right of descent" applicants may reside outside of the New England area.

Address: The Armory, Faneuil Hall, Boston, MA 02109

Printed works: The Ancient and Honorable Artillery Company of Massachusetts, *Roll of Members of the Military Company of Massachusetts, Now Called the Ancient and Honorable Artillery Company of Massachusetts. With a Roster of the Commissioned Officers and Preachers, 1638-1894* (Boston: Alfred Mudge & Son, 1895).

National Society Women Descendants of the Ancient and Honorable Artillery Company

This society was founded in 1927 for women descendants of former member of the Ancient and Honorable Artillery Company of Massachusetts, 1637-1774.

Address: Mrs. Charles Ernest Loucks, 1408 20th Street, Arlington, VA 22202

Printed works: *History and Lineage Book*, 7 vols. (By the society, 1940, 1950, 1959, 1974; 3 vols. 1980).

The General Society of Colonial Wars

This society was founded in 1893 for descendants of an ancestor who served in the military from the settlement of Jamestowne, Virginia, in 1607, to the Battle of Lexington in 1775; or who held office as governor, lord proprietor, etc., or a member of the legislative body of a colony in that time period.

Address: The Secretary General Society of Colonial Wars, 840 Woodbine Avenue, Glendale, OH 45246

Printed works: Nearly all of the twenty-nine state societies have published, from time to time, their own registers. Two excellent examples are: The Society of Colonial Wars in the State of Connecticut, *Register of Pedigrees and Services of Ancestors* (Hartford: By the society, 1941), and The Society of Colonial Wars in the State of Maryland, *Genealogies of the Members and Record of Services of Ancestors* (Baltimore: The Friedenwald Company, 1905), which includes a pedigree chart for each member.

1. General Society of Colonial Wars, *An Index of Ancestors and Roll of Members*, 3 vols. (By the society, New York: 1922, Hartford 1941, Baltimore, 1977).
2. New York Historical Society, *Muster Rolls of the New York Provincial Troops, 1755-1764* (New York: By the society, 1892).
3. Frank DeWitte Andrews, *Connecticut Soldiers in the French and Indian War* (Vineland, N.J.: By the compiler, 1923).
4. Robert D. Benedict, "The Pequot War" in *New York Society of Colonial Wars Year Book 1906-1907* (By the society, 1907).
5. George Madison Bodge, *Soldiers in King Philip's War* (Baltimore: Genealogical Publishing Co., 1967).
6. Thomas Church, *The History of Philip's War, Also of the French and Indian Wars at the Eastward*, 1716 (See H. N. Dexter's revised edition of 1865).
7. Samuel A. Drake, *The Border Wars of New England Covering King William's War 1689-1697 and Queen Anne's War 1701-1714* (1897 edition).
8. Joseph K. Fornance, *The Pennymite Wars* (Philadelphia: The Society of Colonial Wars in the Commonwealth of Pennsylvania, 1941).
9. Francis Parkman, *A Half Century of Conflict: Queen Anne's War 1701-1714 and King George's War 1744-1748* (1892 edition).
10. Herbert Treadwell Wade, *A Brief History of the Colonial Wars in America, From 1607 to 1775* (Society of Colonial Wars in the State of New York, 1948).

National Society Daughters of Colonial Wars

This society was organized in 1932 for women descendants of participants in the colonial wars. The membership requirements are very similar to those cited above for the men's society.

Figure 23-1. Membership Support Affidavit of Grahame Thomas Smallwood, Jr., The Society of Colonial Wars in the Commonwealth of Pennsylvania.

THE SOCIETY OF COLONIAL WARS IN THE COMMONWEALTH OF PENNSYLVANIA

AFFIDAVIT

In support of application for membership of (give full name)

Grahame Thomas Smallwood, Jr.

Pennsylvania (State) ss.:
Philadelphia (City or County)

Grahame Thomas Smallwood, Jr. (Full name of deponent) being duly sworn, says:—

1. That the applicant was born on 26 February 1919 in Toledo, Ohio (Town, City or County) and is a resident of Philadelphia, Pennsylvania

2. That he is the son of Graeme Thomas Smallwood born in Revere, Mass. on 2 Aug. 1897, died in Washington, D.C. on 25 April 1947 and Dorothy Hubbell his wife, born in Toledo, Ohio on 17 December 1895 died in .... on .... married in Washington, D.C. on 12 March 1918

3. That the said Dorothy Hubbell was the daughter of Edward Parmelee Hubbell born in Buffalo, N.Y. on 7 February 1869, died in Washington, D.C. on 8 Aug. 1951, and Ermina Cadwell Pheatt his wife, born in Toledo, Ohio on 28 Dec. 1869 died in Washington, D.C. on 9 February 1956 married in Toledo, Ohio on 12 February 1895

4. That the said Ermina C. Pheatt was the daughter of Zebulon Converse Pheatt born in Cape Vincent, N.Y. on 21 December 1832, died in Toledo, Ohio on 7 July 1901, and Sarah Amanda Cadwell his wife, born in Turin, N.Y. on 17 Feb. 1832 died in Toledo, Ohio on 27 August 1903 married in Cape Vincent NY on 21 May 1867

5. That the said Sarah A. Cadwell was the daughter of Joseph Cadwell born in Lisle, N.Y. on 24 January 1796, died in Cape Vincent, New York on 2 Aug. 1865, and Julia Bush his wife, born in Turin, N.Y. on 29 July 1802 died in Turin, New York on 14 April 1843 married in Turin, N.Y. on 7 January 1827

6. That the said Julia Bush was the daughter of Oliver Bush born in Westfield, Mass. on 13 August 1770, died in Turin, New York on 9 Apr. 1844, and Electa Dewey his wife, born in Westfield, Mass on 16 Nov. 1772, died in Turin, New York on 8 February 1849 married in Westfield, Mass on 8 January 1795

7. That the said Electa Dewey was the daughter of Noble Dewey born in Westfield, Mass. on 15 June 1752, died in Westfield, Mass. on 23 Dec. 1830, and Eleanor Pomeroy his wife, born in Northampton, Mass on 20 Oct 1752, died in Turin, New York on 6 November 1823 married in Westfield, Mass on 20 August 1772

8. That the said Eleanor Pomeroy was the daughter of Daniel Pomeroy born in Northampton, Mass on 27 March 1709, died in Battle of Lake George on 8 Sept 1755, and Rachel Moseley his wife, born in ... on 1715, died in Northampton, Mass. on 1 February 1797 married in ... on 4 November 1736

9. That the said ... was the ... of ... born in ... on ..., died in ... on ..., and ... his wife, born in ... on ..., died in ... on ...

Both as to services of ancestor and descent give references to documentary or other authorities and submit same or certified copies. Allegations of fact based upon tradition cannot be considered. Mere titles of rank in town, church, probate, or registry records, and on gravestones cannot be accepted. Encyclopaedias, genealogies, and histories must have references in them to original authorities. Give volume and page for book references.

THAT TO THE BEST OF DEPONENT'S KNOWLEDGE AND BELIEF THE LINE OF DESCENT SET FORTH ABOVE IS LINEAL AND NOT IN ANY CASE BY ADOPTION.

THAT THE SERVICES OF DANIEL POMEROY in the American Colonial Wars upon which this claim of eligibility to membership is based, were as follows: Killed at the Battle of Lake George while serving as a Lieutenant in Colonel William's Regiment with his brother Lieut-Colonel Seth Pomeroy.

AUTHORITIES AS TO SERVICE

"The Journals & Papers of Seth Pomeroy" pgs.115,142 Published by the Soc. of Colonial Wars in the State of New York, 1926.; Soc.Col.Wars First Supplement to Index of Ancestor 1941, p.202. Mass. Soc. Col. Wars, 1906, p. 161.

AUTHORITIES AS TO DESCENT

Formal Proof Is Required For Each Statement In Every Generation

Generation	References	Generation	References
1	Birth certificate	8	Pomeroy Gen.A.A.Pomery, 1912, p.172 Journals & Papers of Gen.Seth Pomeroy 1926, pgs.115, 142. N.E.Hist.Gen.Reg. Vol 43, pgs. 41-43. Mass.Soc. Col.Wars 1906, p.161
2	Birth certificates, Marriage certif. Death certificate.	9	
3	Death certificates; Marriage certif. Family Bible records.	10	
4	Death certificates; D.A.R.Linage Book, Vol.135, p.178; Hist. Toledo & Lucas Co. Ohio, pgs 30, 422, 758.	11	
5	Kelloggs in the New World, p.230 ed of 1903; D.A.R.Lineage Book, vol.135, p.178; vol 27, p.40; vol.28, p.113. Cem.Church Recs, DAR 1932, vol 31, p181.	12	
6	Dewey Gen.1898, A.M.Dewey, p. 275; Westfield Marriages, 1781-1835, p.415; Westfield Births (1937), p.56; NYState D.A.R. Records, vol.31, p.180.	13	
7	Pomeroy Gen.A.A.Pomeroy, 1912, p.227; Noble Gen., Boltwood, 1878, p. 383; Dewey Gen., A.M.Dewey, 1898, p. 275. Cem.Church Recs.DAR vol.31, p 183. N.E.H.G.R., vol. 43, p.43.	14	

...ot encroach upon ...rgin, which is re... ...or binding.

Address: National Society Daughters of Colonial Wars, 1307 New Hampshire Avenue, N.W., Washington, DC 20009

Printed works: National Society Daughters of Colonial Wars, *Membership List and Index of Ancestors*, 2 vols. (Somerville, Mass.: 1941, 1950).

The Ancient and Honorable Order of the Jersey Blues

This society was organized in 1960 for male descendants of men who served in the Jersey Blues during any war from the colonial period through the Spanish-American War, provided he resided in New Jersey or served in the military or judicial service of that state.

Address: Not available.

Printed works: Malcolm B. Gilman, *The Story of the Jersey Blues* (Trenton: Trenton Publishing Co., 1962).

The Society of the Cincinnati

This society was founded in 1783 at the close of the Revolutionary War by a group of officers of the continental line. This mutual friendship society of officers was conceived to "endure as long as they shall endure, or any of their eldest male posterity; and in failure thereof, the collateral branches who may be judged worthy of becoming its members and supporters." Of the 2,269 original members, plus 1,257 eligibles who did not join or had been killed in battle, approximately 2,000 are presently represented by descendants.

Address: The Society of the Cincinnati, 2118 Massachusetts Avenue, N.W., Washington, DC 20008

Printed works: A number of state societies have published their own volumes on members and their ancestors. An excellent example is Francis S. Drake, *Memorials of the Society of the Cincinnati of Massachusetts* (Cambridge: John Wilson & Son, 1873).

1. Bryce Metcalf, *Original Members and Other Officers Eligible to the Society of the Cincinnati 1783-1838, With the Institutions, Rules of Admission, and Lists of the Officers of the General and State Societies* (Strasburg, Va.: Shenandoah Publishing House, Inc., 1938).
2. Edgar Erskine Hume, comp., *Society of the Cincinnati, Rules of the State Societies for Admission to Membership* (Washington, D.C.: By the society, 1934).
3. Francis B. Heitman, *Historical Register of Officers of the Continental Army during the War of the Revolution, 1914, With Addenda by Robert H. Kelby, 1932* (Baltimore: Genealogical Publishing Co., 1973).

The Daughters of the Cincinnati

Founded in 1894, the daughters have similar requirements for membership as the men's society, with one major exception: more than one member may represent an ancestor at a given time.

Address: Daughters of the Cincinnati, 122 East 58th Street, New York, NY 10022

Printed works: *A Salute to Courage* (New York: Columbia University Press 1979).

National Society Daughters of the American Revolution

Organized in 1890, this society is the largest and best known of the hereditary societies, with a membership exceeding 122,000. Since 1890 some 672,000 women have joined the DAR. Membership is based on descent from an ancestor who served the cause of American independence in the military, as a recognized patriot, or by rendering material aid.

Address: National Society DAR, 1776 D Street, N.W., Washington, DC 20006

Printed works: Over 200 volumes have been printed by various state societies, including membership rosters, lists of ancestors buried in a particular state, and biographies of the founders in various states.

1. *DAR Patriot Index*, 2 vols., (Washington, DC: By the society, vol. 1, 1966; vol. 2, 1979). These volumes list the Revolutionary soldier with known dates of birth and death, name of his wife or wives, military rank, and state from which he served.
2. *DAR Index of the Rolls of Honor,* 4 vols., 1916-40 (Washington, D.C.: By the society, 1980; reprint, 4 vols. in 2). These volumes index the ancestors of members as published in 160 volumes of lineage books.

General Society Sons of the Revolution

This society was founded in 1876 as a result of the stringent requirements of the Society of the Cincinnati, which made no provision for membership of younger sons of the original members. Membership is based on military service or descent from key civil officials.

Address: General Society Sons of the Revolution, Fraunces Tavern, 54 Pearl Street, New York, NY 10004

Printed works: Numerous state societies of the Sons of the Revolution have published annual volumes on membership and ancestry. Two excellent examples are the 1901-03 and 1907-09 *Register of the Sons of the Revolution in the State of Missouri* (St. Louis: Woodward & Tiernan Printing Co.). They contain ancestral lines from nearly all of the thirteen colonies.

1. Henry Hall, *Year Book of the Societies Composed of Descendants of the Men of the Revolution* (New York: The Republic Press, 1890). This rare and unusual volume unites the Sons of the Revolution, Sons of the American Revolution, Daughters of the American Revolution, and the Society of the Cincinnati.

National Society Sons of the American Revolution

Organized in 1889, the SAR is the largest hereditary society for men, with chapters in all fifty states, the District of Columbia, France, and England. Membership is based on descent from an ancestor who either served in the military, held high civil office, or was a patriot in the American cause.

Address: National Society SAR, 1000 South Fourth Street, Louisville, KY 40203.

Printed works: Numerous state societies of the SAR have printed yearbooks containing lineages, etc. The 1893-94 volume of the New York State Society presents a number of engravings of ancestors. The Register of the District of Columbia Society for 1896 is another splendid volume.

1. Louis A. Cornish and A. Howard Clark, *A National Register of the Society Sons of the American Revolution* (New York: Andrew H. Kellogg Press, 1902). This unusual volume contains the entire list of membership for the National Society to 31 December 1901, including all deceased members, with lines of descent from Revolutionary War ancestors.
2. John St. Paul, Jr., *The History of the National Society of the Sons of the American Revolution* (New Orleans: Pelican Publishing Company, 1962).

Microfilm: The Genealogical Society of Utah has microfilmed over 82,500 lineage papers of the National Society SAR and cross-indexed them by the name of the member and the name of ancestor.

National Society Children of the American Revolution

This society was organized under the auspices of the DAR. Membership is limited to boys and girls under the age of twenty-two. Membership requirements are the same as the DAR and SAR.

Address: National Society CAR, 1776 D Street, N.W., Washington, DC 20006

Hereditary Order of Descendants of the Loyalists and Patriots of the American Revolution

This society was organized in 1973 for those with descent from both a loyalist and a patriot of the American Revolution. The loyalist may be a collateral ancestor, but not more distant than the third degree. Application forms show the two lines of descent from the two ancestors.

Address: Roswell Levi Atwood, Governor General, 1701 Massachusetts Avenue, N.W., Washington, DC 20036

Printed works:

1. Wallace Brown, *The Good Americans. The Loyalists in the American Revolution* (New York: William Morrow & Co., 1969).

2. ________, *The King's Friends. The Composition and Motives of the American Loyalist Claimants* (Providence: Brown University Press, 1966).

3. Murtie June Clark, *The Loyalists in the Southern Campaign of the Revolutionary War*, 3 vols. (Baltimore: Genealogical Book Co., 1981).

4. Robert O. DeMond, *Loyalists in North Carolina during the Revolution* (1940; reprint ed., Hampden, Conn.: Archer Books, 1964).

5. Harold Bell Hancock, *Delaware Loyalists* (Wilmington: Historical Society of Delaware, 1940).

6. Isaac Samuel Harrell, *Loyalism in Viriginia* (Durham, N.C.: Duke University Press, 1926).

7. Edward Alfred Jones, *Loyalists in Massachusetts, Their Memorials, Petitions and Claims* (1930; reprint ed., Baltimore: Genealogical Publishing Co., 1969).

8. Lorenzo Sabine, *Biographical Sketches of Loyalists of the American Revolution*, 2 vols. (1864; reprint ed., Port Washington, N.Y.: Kennikat Press, 1966).

9. Paul H. Smith, *Loyalists and Redcoats* (Chapel Hill, N.C.: University of North Carolina Press, 1964).

10. James H. Starke, *The Loyalists of Massachusetts, and the Other Side of the American Revolution* (Boston: By the author, 1910).

11. The United Empire Loyalists, *The Old Empire Loyalist List* (1885; reprint ed., Baltimore: Genealogical Publishing Co., 1976).

12. Esther Clark Wright, *Loyalists of New Brunswick* (Fredericton, Neb.: By the author, 1955).

Society of the Descendants of Washington's Army at Valley Forge

This society was organized in 1976 at Valley Forge, Pennsylvania, for descendants of a soldier serving in the Continental Army at the Valley Forge encampment in 1777-78.

Address: Society of the Descendants of Washington's Army at Valley Forge, Box 915, Valley Forge, PA 19481

Printed works:

1. Calvin E. Chunn, *Not by Bread Alone* (By the society, 1981).
2. Ramona Worley, *In Search for the Winter Patriot* (By the society, 1979).

Society of the Whiskey Rebellion of 1794

This society was organized in 1959 for male lineal descendants of ancestors who served in the militia to put down the 1794 rebellion in western Pennsylvania against Alexander Hamilton's excise tax on whiskey.

Address: Society of the Whiskey Rebellion of 1794, 3311 Columbia Pike, Lancaster, PA 17603

Printed works: None located.

Military Order of Foreign Wars of the United States

This society was organized in 1894. Membership is conferred on officers with active military service in any of our foreign wars from the American Revolution to the Vietnam campaign. Descendants in the direct male line of such an officer may qualify for hereditary companionship.

Address: Military Order of Foreign Wars of the United States, Hill-Physick-Keith House, 321 South Fourth Street, Philadelphia, PA 19106

Printed works: *Register of Commanderies and Members, Military Order of Foreign Wars of the United States 1894-1900* (By the order, 1901).

General Society of the War of 1812

This society was organized 24 September 1814 at Fort McHenry, Baltimore, Maryland, at the close of the War of 1812. It was primarily a Maryland society known as "The Defenders of Baltimore." From 1814 to 1888 all of the presidents were 1812 War veterans. Membership is limited to male lineal descendants of participants in the military or privateer service of the United States. If the participant had no descendants, one collateral descendant may be admitted to the society.

Address: General Society of the War of 1812, Hearst Hall, Washington National Cathedral, Wisconsin Avenue & Woodley Road, N.W., Washington, DC 20016

Printed works: Biennial and triennial meetings of the general society have published their proceedings for the past ninety years.

1. Col. Frederick Ira Ordway, Jr., ed., *Register of the General Society of the War of 1812* (By the society, 1972).

2. ________, *Bicentennial Supplement to the 1972 Register* (Ann Arbor, Mich.: Edward Brothers, Inc., 1976).

3. General Society of the War of 1812, *The Constitution and Register of Membership of the General Society of the War of 1812*. (Washington, D.C.: The Law Reporter Printing Co., 1908).

National Society United States Daughters of 1812

Organized 8 January 1892 on the anniversary of the Battle of New Orleans, the society requires lineal descent from an ancestor who rendered military, naval, or civil service between the close of the American Revolutionary War in 1784 and the close of the War of 1812 in 1815. Military service may be in any one of sixteen recognized engagements between those dates.

Address: National Society United States Daughters of 1812, 1461 Rhode Island Avenue, N.W., Washington, DC 20005

Printed works: *1812 Ancestor Index* (Norcross, Ga.: Harper Printing Co., 1970). This volume lists some 20,000 established ancestors, names of spouses, and the name of the child (and spouse) through whom the member joined, also the state from which the ancestor served.

Aztec Club of 1847—The Military Society of the Mexican War 1846-1848

This society was organized in 1847 for lineal descendants of commissioned officers of the army, navy, or marine corps who served in Mexico or Mexican waters during the War with Mexico 1846-48.

Address: RADM Frank Paull Mitchell, USN, 8301 Thoreau Drive, Washington, DC 20034

Printed works:

1. K. Jack Bauer, *The Mexican War* (New York: By the author, 1974).
2. *The Aztec Club of 1847 Roster of Members* (By the society, 1972).

San Jacinto Descendants

This society was founded on Texas Independence Day, 2 March 1965, for lineal descendants of an ancestor who participated in the Battle of San Jacinto, 21 April 1836, or was assigned to the rear guard at Harrisburg.

Address: San Jacinto Descendants, 2911 University Boulevard, Houston, TX 77005

Printed works: None located.

The Military Order of the Loyal Legion of the United States

This society was founded in 1865, the year Lincoln died. Membership is limited to male lineal descendants of commissioned officers in the Union Forces, 1861-65, with hereditary membership open to male descendants of a brother or sister of such officer. Their war library contains some 11,000 volumes on the Civil War and numerous regimental histories.

Address: Military Order of the Loyal Legion of the United States, 1805 Pine Street, Philadelphia, PA 19103

Printed works: Numerous commanderies throughout the United States have printed rosters for nearly a century. An excellent example is the *Register of the Commandery of the State of Pennsylvania, 1865-1882*.

1. *Roster of the Military Order of the Loyal Legion of the United States* (Philadelphia: By the order, 1975). Contains membership rosters of sixteen state commanderies.

2. *Loyal Legion Historical Journal,* published periodically by the order for the past forty years.

Dames of the Loyal Legion of the United States

This society was founded in 1899 as a companion society to the Military Order of the Loyal Legion of the United States. Membership is limited to women descendants of Union Army commissioned officers and the wives of members of the MOLLUS.

Address: Dames of the Loyal Legion of the United States, 1805 Pine Street, Philadelphia, PA 19103

Printed works: *Roster of the Loyal Legion of the United States,* as cited above, contains a section devoted to the membership of the Dames of the Loyal Legion.

Sons of the Union Veterans of the Civil War

This society was founded in 1881 to perpetuate the memory of the Grand Army of the Republic. Membership is open to all male descendants of soldiers, sailors, or marines who served in the Union cause 1861-65.

Address: Sons of the Union Veterans of the Civil War, Box 24, Federal Building, Gettysburg, PA 17325

Printed works: *The Banner,* a quarterly published by the society with information on all posts.

Auxiliary to the Sons of the Union Veterans of the Civil War

This group was organized in 1883 as the "Ladies Aid Society." Membership today is in several categories: wives of sons of the Union veterans, widows of sons who were in good standing at death, mothers of sons, and all female lineal relatives.

Address: The national president's home, which changes each year. Write in care of the Sons of the Union Veterans of the Civil War.

Printed works: *The Banner,* although published by the Sons of the Union Veterans, also includes information on the auxiliary.

Daughters of Union Veterans of the Civil War 1861-65

Organized in 1885, this society is the oldest's women's hereditary society in the United States. Membership is limited to lineal descendants of military participants in the Civil War on the Union side.

Address: Daughters of Union Veterans of the Civil War, 503 South Walnut Street, Springfield, IL 62704.

Printed works: None located.

Ladies of the Grand Army of the Republic

This society was organized in 1885, combining the Loyal Ladies League and the Ladies of the Grand Army of the Republic. Membership is open to all mothers, wives, sisters, daughters, granddaughters, blood-kin nieces, and cousins of honorably discharged Union veterans.

Address: Changes each year with new national president. President for 1983: Lois Reffner, 419 Agatha Street, Pitcairn, PA 15140.

Printed works: None located.

United Daughters of the Confederacy

This group was organized in 1894 for women who are lineal or collateral descendants of men or women who served in the military or civil service of the Confederate States of America, or who gave material aid to the cause.

Address: United Daughters of the Confederacy, Memorial Building, 328 North Boulevard, Richmond, VA 23220

Printed works: Jefferson Davis, *Woman in the South in War Times,* and *The Rise and Fall of the Confederate Government.* (Both available through the society.)

Children of the Confederacy

Organized in 1896 by the United Daughters of the Confederacy, membership in this society is limited to boys and girls under twenty-one years of age who are lineal descendants or nieces or nephews of men or women who served honorably in the Confederate service or of members of UDC or SCV.

Address: Same as UDC

Printed works: None located.

Sons of Confederate Veterans

This group was organized in 1896 under the auspices of the United Confederate Veterans. Membership is limited to male descendants, lineal or collateral, of participants in the Confederate military, or participants who died in prison, were killed in battle, or were honorably discharged.

Address: Sons of Confederate Veterans, Box 5164, Hattiesburg, MS 39401

Printed works: None located.

The Order of Stars and Bars

This society was organized in 1938 for male descendants, lineal or collateral, of commissioned officers of the Confederate States of America.

Address: The Order of Stars and Bars, Southern Station, Box 1, Hattiesburg, MS 39401

Printed works: None located.

The Military Order of the World Wars

Organized in 1919 as "The American Officers of the Great War," this society's title changed in 1920, and in 1942 *War* became plural. Membership is open to male United States citizens who have served honorably on active duty as commissioned officers, between 6 April 1917 and 2 July 1921, or since 16 September 1940. Male descendants of members or of deceased officers are eligible for hereditary membership.

Address: Military Order of the World Wars, 1100 17th Street, N.W., Washington, DC 20036

Printed works: None located.

Early Settler and Ship Societies

This grouping of societies, listed by date of founding, is based on the earliest settlers of a town, state, or geographical area. Societies of early arrivals on specific ships are included, identified by the name of the ship as in *The Mayflower, The Welcome, The Ark,* and *The Dove.*

The Saint Nicholas Society of the City of New York

This group was founded in New York City in 1835 at the suggestion of Washington Irving, as a society for male descendants of residents of the city of New York or of New York State prior to 1785. Members must be proposed and seconded in writing. There is a limited membership.

Address: The Saint Nicholas Society of the City of New York, 122 East 58th Street, New York, NY 10022

Printed works:

1. *The Saint Nicholas Society of the City of New York Genealogical Record,* 9 vols. (New York: By the society, vol. 1, 1905; vol. 2, 1916; vol. 3, 1923; vol. 4, 1934; vol. 5, 1945; vol. 6, 1950; vol. 7, 1958; vol. 8, 1968; vol. 9, 1980). These volumes contain the complete lineages of all members, plus biographical sketches of the ancestors.

2. Sebastian Visscher Talcott, *Genealogical Notes of New York and New England Families,* (1883; reprint ed., Baltimore: Genealogical Publishing Co., 1973).

The Society of California Pioneers

This group was founded in 1850 for male lineal descendants of residents of California prior to 1 January 1850, the date of statehood.

Address: Society of California Pioneers, 456 McAllister Street, San Francisco, CA 94102

Printed works:

1. Hubert H. Bancroft, *California Pioneer Register and Index 1542-1858: Including Inhabitants of California 1769-1800 and List of Pioneers* (1884-90; reprint ed. Baltimore: Genealogical Publishing Co., 1964).

2. California State Society Daughters of American Revolution, *Records of the Families of California Pioneers,* vol. 2 only (By the society, n.d.).

3. Marie E. Northrup, *Spanish-Mexican Families of Early California, 1769-1850* (New Orleans: Polyanthos, 1976).

The Daughters of the Republic of Texas

This society was founded in 1891 for female lineal descendants of loyal citizens who established residence in Texas prior to the state's annexation on 19 February 1846.

Address: Daughters of the Republic of Texas, The Alamo, San Antonio, TX 78205

Printed works: See sources listed for the Sons of the Republic of Texas and:

1. Mrs. Harry Joseph Morris, comp., *Daughters of the Republic of Texas: Founders and Patriots of the Republic of Texas—Lineages of Members* (Austin: By the author, 1963).

2. Texas Society of the Daughters of the American Revolution, *The Roster of Texas Daughter's Revolutionary Ancestors* (Houston: By the society, 1976).

The Sons of the Republic of Texas

This group was organized in 1893 for male lineal descendants of a resident of Texas prior to annexation on 19 February 1846.

Address: Sons of the Republic of Texas, 2426 Watts Road, Houston, TX 77025

Printed works:

1. Chester W. and E. H. Geue, *A New Land Beckoned: German Immigrants to Texas 1844-1847* (Fort Worth: By the authors, 1966).

2. Alice Duggan Gracy, Jane Sumner, and Emma G. S. Gentry, *Early Texas Birth Records 1838-1870,* 2 vols. (Austin: Mrs. H. R. Gentry, 1970-71).

3. Norma Rutledge Grammer, *Marriage Records of Early Texas 1824-1846* (Fort Worth: Fort Worth Genealogical Society, 1972).

4. Thomas Lloyd Miller, *Bounty and Donation Land Grants of Texas 1835-1888* (Austin: By the author, 1967).

5. Florence Johnson Scott, *Royal Land Grants of the Rio Grande 1777-1821* (Rio Grande City: Rio Grande City Publishers, 1969).

National Society of New England Women

This group was organized in 1895 for women descendants of any ancestor born in New England prior to the signing of the Constitution of the United States 4 March 1789.

Address: Mrs. O. W. Shannon, President General, 3715 Warrensville Center Road, #340, Shaker Heights, OH 44122

The Order of the Founders and Patriots of America

This society was organized in 1896 for men descended in the male line of either parent from an ancestor who settled in one of the colonies prior to 13 May 1657 *and* whose intermediate ancestor, in the same line, served in the War of the American Revolution, adhering always as a patriot to the American cause. Since both founder and patriot must bear the surname of the applicant's father or mother, this has long been regarded as the most difficult lineage society to join.

Address: Order of the Founders and Patriots of America, 1701 Massachusetts Avenue, N.W., Washington, DC 20036

Printed works:

1. Meredith B. Colket, Jr., *Founders of Early American Families—Emigrants from Europe 1607-1657* (Oberlin, Ohio: Oberlin Printing Co., 1975). This most unusual volume documents some 3,500 male heads of families who appear to have descendants in the male line to the present day.

2. *The Order of the Founders & Patriots of America Registers,* vol. 1, (New York: J. J. Little & Ives Co., 1926); vol. 2, Arthur Adams, comp. (By the order, 1940); vol. 3 (New York: By the order, 1960); vol. 4 (New Hartford, Conn: By the order, 1981).

General Society of Mayflower Descendants

This group was founded in 1897 as a society for the lineal descendants of passengers on the *Mayflower,* which arrived in Plymouth harbor in December 1620.

Address: General Society of Mayflower Descendants, 4 Winslow Street, Box 297, Plymouth, MA 02361

Printed works: A number of state societies have published excellent volumes with complete lineages of members. An example is Frederick Ira Ordway, Jr., ed., *Register of the Society of Mayflower Descendants in the District of Columbia,* 2 vols. in 1 (Federalsburg, Md.: J.W. Stowell Printing Co., 1970, 1973).

1. Anne Borden Harding, ed., *Mayflower Families Through Five Generations: Family of George Soule,* vol. 1 (Plymouth, Mass: By the society, 1980).

2. Lucy Mary Kellogg, ed., *Mayflower Families Through Five Generations: Families of Francis Eaton, Samuel Fuller, and William White,* vol. 1 (Plymouth, Mass: By the society, 1975).

3. *The Mayflower Descendant,* 34 vols. and 2 vol. index (Plymouth, Mass: By the Massachusetts Society, 1899-1937).

4. Milton E. Terry and Anne Borden Harding, comps., *Mayflower Ancestral Index* (Plymouth, Mass.: By the society, 1981).

5. Robert M. Sherman, ed., *Mayflower Families Through Five Generations: Families of James Chilton, Richard More, and Thomas Rogers,* vol. 2 (Plymouth, Mass: By the society, 1978).

The National Society of the Daughters of Founders and Patriots of America

This group was founded in 1898 for women descended in the direct male line of either parent from an ancestor who settled in any of the colonies between 13 May 1607 and 13 May 1687. This last date is thirty years later than the men's organization.

Address: National Society of the Daughters of Founders and Patriots of America, Hearst Hall, Wisconsin Avenue & Woodley Road, N.W., Washington, DC 20016

Printed works: *Lineage Book of the National Society of Daughters of Founders and Patriots of America,* 45 vols. since 1909. Contains complete proven lineages.

National Society of the Daughters of Utah Pioneers

This group was founded in 1901 for female lineal descendants of those who came to Utah before the completion of the railroad 10 May 1869.

Address: National Society of the Daughters of Utah Pioneers, 300 North Main Street, Salt Lake City, UT 84103

Printed works:

1. *Daughters of Utah Pioneers,* 30 vols. (Salt Lake City: By the society, 1939-68).

2. James T. Jakeman, ed., *Daughters of Utah Pioneers and Their Mothers* (Salt Lake City: By the society, 1930). Contains a fabulous collection of over 500 photographs.

3. *Utah Pioneer Biographies,* 44 vols. (Salt Lake City: Utah Historical Society, 1935-64).

Society of the Founders of Norwich, Connecticut

Organized in 1901, this society is open to all interested in the history and preservation of Norwich. Applicants who prove lineal descent from an original proprietor or one of the earliest settlers receive a certificate of descent.

Address: Society of the Founders of Norwich, Connecticut, 348 Washington Street, Norwich, CT 06360

Printed works:

1. Frances M. Caulkins, *History of Norwich from Its Possession by the Indians to the Year 1866* (1886; reprint ed., Baltimore: Genealogical Publishing Co., 1976).

Sons and Daughters of Oregon Pioneers

This group was organized in 1901 for lineal descendants of settlers in the Oregon Country before statehood, 14 February 1859.

Address: Sons and Daughters of Oregon Pioneers, 1500 S.W. Spring Street, Portland, OR 97201

Printed works:

1. Oregon State Archives, *Pioneer Families of the Oregon Territory, 1850*, Bull. 3, pub. 17 (Salem: Oregon State Archives, 1961).
2. *Genealogical Material in Oregon Donation Land Claims Abstracted from Applications*, 4 vols. (Portland: Genealogical Forum, 1957-62).
3. *Genealogical Research in Oregon*, in *National Genealogical Society Quarterly* 47 (1959): 115-48.

Piscataqua Pioneers

This group was organized in 1905 for lineal descendants of early (prior to July 1776) settlers on both the New Hampshire and Maine sides of the Piscataqua River and its tributaries.

Address: Phyllis Tucker, Secretary, 7 Ann's Lane, Hampton, NH 03842

Printed works:

1. *Society of Piscataqua Pioneers, Register of Members and Ancestors, 1905-1981* (By the society, 1981).
2. Sybil Noyes, Charles Thornton Libby, and Walter Goodwin Davis, *Genealogical Dictionary of Maine and New Hampshire* (1928-39; reprint ed., Baltimore: Genealogical Publishing Co., 1972).
3. Charles Henry Pope, *The Pioneers of Maine and New Hampshire 1623-1660* (Baltimore: Genealogical Publishing Co., 1965).
4. Wilbur D. Spencer, *Pioneers on Maine Rivers with Lists to 1651.* (1930; reprint ed., Baltimore: Genealogical Publishing Co., 1973).

The Welcome Society of Pennsylvania

This group was founded in 1906 to honor the ship *Welcome* on which William Penn travelled to his colony. Applicants must prove lineal descent from a passenger arriving on the *Welcome* in October 1682 or on some other vessel arriving in Pennsylvania between 24 December 1681 and 31 December 1682.

Address: The Welcome Society of Pennsylvania, 316 South Juniper Street, Philadelphia, PA 19107

Printed works:

1. Walter Lee Sheppard, Jr., ed., *Penn's Colony, Passengers and Ships Prior to 1684*, vol. 1, (Baltimore: Genealogical Publishing Co., 1970).
2. George E. McCracken, ed., *Penn's Colony, The Welcome Claimants–Proved, Disproved and Doubtful, With an Account of Some of Their Descendants*, vol. 2 (Baltimore: Genealogical Publishing Co., 1970).

Sons of Utah Pioneers

This group was organized in 1907 for male lineage descendants of those who came to Utah prior to completion of the railroad 10 May 1869.

Address: Sons of Utah Pioneers, 3301 East 2920 South, Salt Lake City, UT 84109

Printed works:

1. *The Pioneer*, a monthly publication, 32 vols. to 1983.
2. *List of Pioneers of 1847 with Biographical Notes from the Journal of the History of the Church 1847 and The Historical Record*, vol. 9 (Salt Lake City: Genealogical Society of Utah).
3. *Biographies of the Members of the Salt Lake Chapter, Sons of Utah Pioneers* (Salt Lake City: Genealogical Society of Utah, 1980). A collection of sketches contributed by members.
4. Ronald Vern Jackson and David L. Grundvig, *Directory of Individuals Residing in Salt Lake City Wards 1854-1861.* Early Mormon Series, vol. 1 (Salt Lake City: By the authors, 1982).

National Society of the Sons and Daughters of the Pilgrims

This group was organized in 1908 for lineal descendants of a settler (Pilgrim) in any of the colonies prior to 1700.

Address: Arthur L. Finnell, Registrar General, 3917 Heritage Hills Drive, #104, Minneapolis, MN 55437

Printed works:

1. *Lineages of Members of the National Society of the Sons & Daughters of the Pilgrims to 1 January 1929* (Philadelphia: By the society, 1929).
2. *Lineages of Members of the National Society of the Sons & Daughters of the Pilgrims 1920-1952*, vol. 2 (By the society, 1953).
3. Mary E. Mayo, ed., *Sixteen Hundred Lines to Pilgrims, Lineage Book III* (Ann Arbor, Mich: Edwards Brothers, Inc., 1982).
4. *The Pilgrim News-Letter*, a semi-annual publication with news of various state branches and the annual General Court.

National Society of Old Plymouth Colony Descendants

This group was organized in 1910. Applicants must prove descent from a man or woman who came to Old Plymouth Colony prior to 1641.

Address: National Society of Old Plymouth Colony Descendants, R.D. 2, 24 Samoset Road, East Sandwich, MA 02537

Printed works:

1. *Records of Plymouth Colony–Births, Marriage, Deaths, Burials, etc. 1633-1689,* (1857; reprint ed. of *The Records of the Colony of New Plymouth in New England*, vol. 8 Baltimore: Genealogical Publishing Co., 1977]).
2. William T. Davis, *General Register of Plymouth Families*, from *Ancient Landmarks of Plymouth*, (1899; reprint ed. Baltimore: Genealogical Publishing Co., 1977).
3. Lucy Hall Greenlaw, *The Genealogical Advertiser*, 4 vols. (1898-1901; reprint ed. 4 vols. in 1, Baltimore: Genealogical Publishing Co., 1974. Contains Plymouth Colony marriages 1693-1733 and probate records 1686-88.
4. Bradford Kingman, *Epitaphs from Burial Hill, Plymouth, Massachusetts–1657-1892.* (1892; reprint ed., Baltimore: Genealogical Publishing Co., 1977).
5. Robert S. Wakefield, *Plymouth Colony Marriages to 1650* (By the author, 1978).
6. Alexander Young, *Chronicles of the Pilgrim Fathers of the Colony of Plymouth From 1602-1625,* (1844; reprint ed., Baltimore: Genealogical Publishing Co., 1974).

The Society of the Ark and the Dove

This group was founded in 1910 for lineal descendants of Sir George Calvert, the first Lord Baltimore, and settlers who came in either *The Ark* or *The Dove* in March 1634.

Address: Capt. Arthur C. Bushey, Jr., USN (Ret.), 4401 Roland Avenue, Baltimore, MD 21210

Printed works:

1. *Maryland Genealogies–A Consolidation of Articles from the Maryland Historical Magazine*, 2 vols. (Baltimore: Genealogical Publishing Co., 1980). Vol. 1 contains numerous descendants of the Calvert family.
2. Gus Skordas, *Early Settlers of Maryland*, (1968; reprint ed., Baltimore: Genealogical Publishing Co., 1979). An index of names of immigrants compiled from records of land patents 1633-80 in the Hall of Records at Annapolis, Maryland.
3. Albert L. Richardson, *The Maryland Original Research Society of Baltimore Bulletin*, 3 issues in 1 vol. Reprint ed., Baltimore: Genealogical Publishing Co., 1979).

Order of the First Families of Virginia

This society was founded in 1912 to honor Virginia, the first permanent English colony on this continent. Membership is by invitation only and is limited to lineal descendants of those who aided in the establishment of the Virginia Colony 1607-24.

Address: Not available.

Printed works: Annie Lash Jester and Martha Woodroof Hiden, *Adventurers of Purse and Person: Virginia 1607-1616,* 2nd ed. (By the society, 1964).

The Society of Indiana Pioneers

This group was founded in 1916 for lineal descendants of residents in the state during the pioneer period, which varies from 1825 to 1850 when the last two counties were added.

Address: Caroline Dunn, Secretary, 315 West Ohio Street, Indianapolis, IN 46202

Printed works: There are numerous early county histories for Indiana, plus a large collection in Colleen Ridlen, *Early Marriage Records*.

1. William M. Cockrum, *A Pioneer History of Indiana* (n. pub., 1907).
2. Willard Heiss, *Who's Your Hoosier Ancestor?*, 3-vol. reprint of columns in the *Indianapolis Times* (Indianapolis: By the author, 1963-65).
3. Leonard G. McCay, *Indiana Ancestors Index* (Indianapolis: By the author, 1975).

Louisiana Colonials

This society was founded in 1917 for all lineal descendants of colonists in the Lousiana Territory before it became a state, 30 April 1803.

Address: Louisiana Colonials, 1911 Octavia Street, New Orleans, LA 70115

Printed works:

1. Stanley C. Arthur and George C. H. de Kernion, *Old Families of Louisiana* (1931; reprint ed., Baltimore: Genealogical Publishing Co., 1971).
2. Winston DeVille, *Gulf Coast Colonials: A Compendium of French Families in Early 18th Century Louisiana* (Baltimore: Genealogical Publishing Co., 1968).
3. ________, *Lousiana Recruits* (Cottonport, La.: Polyanthos, 1973).
4. ________, *The New Orleans French 1720-1733* (Baltimore: Genealogical Publishing Co., 1973).
5. Herman deBachelle Seebold, *Old Louisiana Plantation Homes and Family Trees,* 2 vols. (1941; reprint ed., By the author, 1971).

Sons and Daughters of the First Settlers of Newbury, Massachusetts

This group was founded in 1927 for all lineal descendants of those who settled at Newbury prior to 1700.

Address: Sons and Daughters of the First Settlers of Newbury, MA, Box 444, Newburyport, MA 01950

Printed works:

1. John J. Currier, of Newbury Port, 1764-1905, 2 vols. (1906-09; reprint ed., Baltimore: Genealogical Publishing Co., 1977-78).
2. David W. Hoyt, *The Old Families of Salisbury and Amesbury. With Some Related Families of Newbury, Haverhill, Ipswich, and Hampton, and of York County, Maine* (1879-1919; reprint ed., Baltimore: Genealogical Publishing Co., 1982).
3. Charles H. Pope, *The Pioneers of Massachusetts* (1900; reprint ed., Baltimore: Genealogical Publishing Co., 1975).

Society of the Descendants of the Founders of Hartford

This group was organized in 1931 to honor the founder, the Reverend Thomas Hooker, and the early settlers, of Hartford, Connecticut. Membership requires lineal descent from an ancestor who settled in Hartford prior to February 1640.

Address: Society of the Descendants of the Founders of Hartford, 77 Welles Drive North, Newington, CT 06111

Printed works: Lucius Barnes Barbour, *Families of Early Hartford Connecticut,* 2nd rev. ed. (Baltimore: Genealogical Publishing Co., 1982).

The Jamestowne Society

This group was founded in 1936. Membership is open to descendants of stockholders in the Virginia Company of London or of settlers at Jamestowne or on Jamestowne Island prior to 1700.

Address: The Jamestowne Society, Box 7389, Richmond, VA 23221

Printed works:

1. Joseph Francis Inman, *Historical Highlights of the Jamestowne Society's First Quarter of a Century – Roster of Members 1936-1971* (Richmond: By the society, 1971).
2. *The Jamestowne Society – Roster of Members January 31, 1983* (Richmond: By the society, 1983). Includes articles of incorporation, bylaws of the society, and the qualifying ancestor of each member.

The First Families of Ohio

This society was founded in 1964, with membership restricted to members of the Ohio Genealogical Society with proven descent from an ancestor who settled in the territory, now the state of Ohio, before 1820.

Address: The First Families of Ohio, Box 2625, Mansfield, OH 44906

Printed works: The 1890 Howe Historical Collection of eighty-eight Ohio Counties has been reprinted in eighty-eight individual pamphlets containing biographies and history.

1. Albion M. Dyer, *First Ownership of Ohio Lands* (1911; reprint ed., Baltimore: Genealogical Publishing Co., 1982).
2. Marjorie Smith, ed., *Ohio Marriages 1790-1897. Extracted from the Old Northwest Genealogical Quarterly* (1977; reprint ed., Baltimore: Genealogical Publishing Co., 1980).

The Order of the First Families of Mississippi 1699-1817

This society was founded in 1967 for lineal descendants of a native or resident of the old territory now included in the state of Mississippi, between the French establishment of Old Biloxi in 1699 and statehood on 10 December 1817.

Address: Not available.

Printed works:

1. Norman E. Gillis, *Early Inhabitants of the Natchez District* (By the author, 1963).
2. Junie E. S. King, *Mississippi Court Records 1799-1835* (Beverly Hills: By the author, 1936).
3. May Wilson McBee, *The Natchez Court Records 1767-1805* (1953; reprint ed., Baltimore: Genealogical Publishing Co., 1979).
4. Mississippi State Daughters of the American Revolution, *Mississippi Daughters and Their Ancestry,* 2 vols. (Starkville, Miss.: Starkville Publishing Co., 1965).

Colonial Societies

All of these groups involve descent from an ancestor active during the colonial period. Generally the cutoff date is 4 July 1776 but there are exceptions which will be noted. The following societies are listed in order of founding.

The Colonial Dames of America

This society was founded in 1890 for women of lineal descent from a worthy ancestor who held public office or a commission in the armed forces, from the settlement of Jamestowne 13 May 1607 to 19 April 1775. There are chapters in fourteen major cities, the District of Columbia, London, Paris, and Rome.

Address: The Colonial Dames of America, 421 East 61st Street, New York, NY 10021

Printed works: *Ancestral Records and Portraits—A Compilation from the Archives of Chapter 1, Baltimore, Maryland, of The Colonial Dames of America,* 2 vols. (New York: Grafton Press, 1910).

The National Society of the Colonial Dames of America

This group was founded in 1891 for women of lineal descent from a resident of an American colony prior to 1750 who rendered efficient service to his/her country before 5 July 1776, including the signers of the Declaration of Independence. There are societies in some forty states and the District of Columbia.

Address: The National Society of the Colonial Dames of America, Dumbarton House, 2715 Q Street, N.W., Washington, DC 20007

Printed works:

1. *Register of Ancestors, The National Society of the Colonial Dames of America in the Commonwealth of Virginia,* (Richmond: By the society, 1979).
2. *Index of Pennsylvania Ancestors of the National Society of the Colonial Dames in the Commonwealth of Pennsylvania,* (Philadelphia: By the society, 1970).

The Colonial Order of the Acorn

This society was founded in 1894 for male lineal descendants of residents of an American colony prior to 4 July 1776. Membership is limited to 200 and applicants must be proposed in writing by a proposer and seconder. The society does not emphasize either military or civil service and can commemorate events not associated with wars. The New York chapter was the first organized; Maryland and Connecticut chapters were authorized, but it is believed that only the New York chapter is presently active.

Address: Colonial Order of the Acorn, 125 East 84th Street, New York, NY 10028

Printed works: *Views of Early New York with Illustrative Sketches* (New York: By the society, 1904).

The Colonial Society of Pennsylvania

This group was founded in 1895 for male lineal descendants of an ancestor who settled prior to 1700 in any of the American colonies.

Address: The Colonial Society of Pennsylvania, 1300 Locust Street, Philadelphia, PA 19107

Printed works: *The Colonial Society of Pennsylvania: Charter, Constitution, By-Laws, Officers, Members, etc.,* 4 vols. (Philadelphia: By the society, 1908, 1914, 1931, 1950). Contains a line of descent for each member.

The National Society of the Colonial Daughters of the Seventeenth Century

This group was founded in 1896 for women lineally descended from an ancestor who rendered service from 1607 through 1699, according to the society's eligibility list. Membership is by invitation only.

Address: Not available.

Printed works: *National Society of the Colonial Daughters of the Seventeenth Century Lineage Book,* 8 vols. (By the society, 1898, 1907, 1916, 1923, 1932, 1942, and 1968). The 1968 volume contains over 1,800 colonists and their qualifying service.

The Hereditary Order of the Descendants of Colonial Governors

This group was founded in 1896 for lineal descendants of those men who exercised supreme executive power in the American colonies prior to 1775. Membership is by invitation only.

Address: Not available.

Printed works:

1. John W. Raimo, ed., *The Biographical Directory of American Colonial Governors 1607-1789* (Westport, Conn.: Meckler Books, 1979).
2. *The Pennsylvania Society of Colonial Governors,* vol. 1 (Philadelphia: Allen, Lane & Scott, 1916).

The Vermont Society of Colonial Dames

This group was organized in 1897 as an independent society for women of lineal descent from ancestors whose service in the colonial period is of public record such as the founder of a colony, town, or church or those who served in any civil or military capacity.

Address: The Vermont Society of Colonial Dames, 102 Court Street, Middlebury, VT 05753

Printed works: None located.

Order of Americans of Armorial Ancestry

This society was founded in 1903 for lineal descendants of an immigrant in one of the original colonies who had a proven right to "bear coat armor" in the country of his/her origin.

Address: Nicholas D. Ward, 6654 Barnaby Street, N.W., Washington, DC 20015

Printed works:

1. Ruth Thayer Ravenscroft, comp., *Complete Register of Members with Coats of Arms, from 15 September 1903 to 15 December 1964* (Colorado Springs: Lithographic Press, 1965).
2. Louis Warner, comp., *Order of Americans of Armorial Ancestry, Officers and Members* (By the society, 1979).
3. *The Roll of Arms,* published in the *New England Historical and Genealogical Register,* in nine parts: 1928, 1932, 1936, 1940, 1946, 1954, 1958, 1971, and 1979.

Descendants of the Signers of the Declaration of Independence

This society was founded in 1907 for all lineal descendants of those who signed the Declaration of Independence.

Address: Mrs. Hans Bielenstein, Secretary General, 50 Riverside Drive, New York, NY 10024

Printed works: There have been numerous biographies printed on all the signers.

1. Frank Willing Leach, "Manuscript Collection Containing All the Known Lines of Descent of the Signers," Historical Society of Pennsylvania, Philadelphia.

The Order of Colonial Lords of Manors in America

This society was founded in 1911 for lineal descendants of the order's twenty-seven recognized patroons, lord of the manor, or seigniors. Membership is by invitation only.

Address: Not available.

Printed works: Family genealogies on the following names should be checked: Archer, Billop, Brooke, Claggett, de Lotbiniere, Heathcote, Herrman, Gardiner (2), Livingston, Lloyd, Mayhew, Melyn, Morris, Paine, Palmer, Pell, Philips, Sewell, Tangier Smith, Sylvester, Van Courtlandt (2), van der Donck, Van Rensselaer, Winthrop, and Wyllys.

The National Society of Colonial Dames of the XVII Century

This group was founded in 1915 for women of lineal descent from an ancestor who lived in one of the eleven British colonies of America prior to 1701, as an immigrant colonist or as a descendant of one.

Address: The National Society Colonial Dames XVII Century, 1300 New Hampshire Avenue, N.W., Washington, DC 20036

Printed works: *The Seventeenth Century Review,* 25 vols. to 1983.

National Society of the Daughters of the American Colonists

This group was founded in 1921 for female lineal descendants of those who rendered civil or military service in any of the colonies prior to 4 July 1776.

Address: National Society of the Daughters of the American Colonists, 2205 Massachusetts Avenue, N.W., Washington, DC 20008

Printed works: *The Colonial Courier,* 25 vols. to 1983.

The National Society of Dames of the Court of Honor

This group was founded in 1921 for female lineal descendants of a colonial governor or a commissioned officer during the American wars, 1607-1865; colonial wars and colonial governors, 1607-1775; the American Revolution, 1775-83; the War of 1812, 1784-1815; the Mexican War, 1836-38; and the War Between the States, 1861-65. Membership is by invitation only.

Address: Not available.

Printed works: Research sources for all of the war societies also apply to this society.

The Society of Descendants of the Colonial Clergy

This group was founded in 1933 for lineal descendants of any clergyman, regularly ordained, installed, or settled over any Christian church in the original colonies prior to 4 July 1776.

Address: Mrs. Donald J. Morton, Secretary General, 12 Westchester Drive, Auburn, MA 01501

Printed works:

1. Frederick Lewis Weis, *The Colonial Clergy and the Colonial Churches of New England* (Lancaster, Mass.: By the society, 1936).
2. ________, *The Colonial Clergy of Maryland, Delaware, and Georgia* (Lancaster, Mass.: By the society, 1950).
3. ________, *The Colonial Clergy of Virginia, North Carolina and South Carolina* (Boston: By the society, 1955).
4. ________, *The Colonial Clergy of the Middle Colonies, New York, New Jersey and Pennsylvania 1628-1776* (Worcester, Mass: By the society, 1957).

The National Society of Lords of the Maryland Manors

This group was founded in 1938 for lineal descendants of the first Baron Baltimore, or of one or more of the colonists who were "granted by the Lord Proprietor of Maryland, a manor in fee simple with manorial rights and privileges," prior to 1722. The society has placed markers at twenty-three manors. Membership is by invitation only.

Address: Not available.

Printed works: See sources listed for The Ark and The Dove Society.

National Society of the Children of the American Colonists

This group was founded in 1939 as a kindred society to the Daughters of the American Colonists. Any child from birth through twenty-one years of age is eligible through lineal descent from an ancestor who rendered civil or military service to any of the colonists prior to 4 July 1776.

Address: National Society of the Children of the American Colonists, 2205 Massachusetts Avenue, N.W., Washington, DC 20008

Printed works: Sources are the same as for the Daughters of the American Colonists.

National Society Southern Dames of America

This society was founded in 1962 for women of verified Southern ancestry. Membership is by invitation only.

Address: Mrs. James A. Koonce, 414 N. Walnut Street, Box 43, Florence, AL 35631

Published works: All lineage volumes on the South apply to this society.

Flagon and Trencher—Descendants of Colonial Tavernkeepers

This society was founded in 1962 for men and women who are lineal descendants of persons conducting a tavern, inn, ordinary, or other type of hostelry, on or prior to 4 July 1776.

Address: Flagon and Trencher—Descendants of Colonial Tavernkeepers, 421 Summit Avenue, South Orange, NJ 07079

Printed works: Harriet Stryker-Rodda, ed., *Colonial Tavernkeepers: Qualifying Ancestors of Flagon and Trencher Members*, 4 vols. (By the society, 1976, 1977, 1978, 1980).

Order of Descendants of Colonial Physicians and Chirurgieons

This group was organized in 1974 for men and women who are lineal descendants of a physician, chirurgieon, or licensed midwife, practicing on the North American continent during the colonial period through 1783. Membership is by invitation only.

Address: Not available.

Printed works: *Order of Descendants of Colonial Physicians and Chirurgieons Membership Roster*, 2 vols. (By the society, 1978, 1979 with supplements issued 1980, 1981, 1982).

Nationality (Ethnic) Societies

Among the oldest lineage societies established in this country, this category includes many charitable societies founded for English, Irish, Scottish, and Welsh immigrants in the major port cities of the Atlantic coast. These societies are listed by date of founding.

The Welsh Society of Philadelphia

This group was organized in 1729 for men of Welsh birth or descent. It is the oldest hereditary society in Philadelphia and was founded as a charitable society to aid distressed Welshmen.

Address: The Welsh Society of Philadelphia, 450 Broadway, Camden, NJ 08105

Printed works: Edward George Hartmann, *The Welsh Society of Philadelphia—History, Charter and By-Laws, and Membership List* (Philadelphia: By the society, 1980). Printed for the 250th anniversary of its founding.

The Saint Andrew's Society

This group was organized in Charleston, South Carolina, in 1729, Philadelphia, Pennsylvania, in 1747, Savannah, Georgia, in 1750, New York City in 1756, Alexandria, Virginia, in 1780, Albany, New York, in 1803, and Washington, D.C., in 1855. The society is for men of Scottish birth or descent, except in Charleston where there are no restrictions on lineage although membership is limited to thirty. Later societies have been organized throughout the United States.

Addresses: The Saint Andrew's Society, 1218 Chestnut Street, Philadelphia, PA 19107; 820 East 67th Street, Savannah, GA 31405; 281 Park Avenue South, New York City, NY 10010; 150 Washington Avenue, Albany, NY 12200.

Printed works:

1. *An Historical Sketch of the Catalogue of the Saint Andrew's Society of Philadelphia with Biographical Sketches of Deceased Members 1749-1913*, 2 vols. (Philadelphia: By the society, 1907-13).
2. *History of the Saint Andrew's Society of Charleston, South Carolina 1729-1929*, (Charleston: By the society, 1929).
3. David Baillie Morrison, ed., *Two Hundredth Anniversary 1756-1956 of the Saint Andrew's Society of the State of New York* (Philadelphia and New York: Clark Printing House, Inc., 1956).
4. Peter Kimmear, *Historical Sketch of the Saint Andrews Society of the City of Albany 1803-1903* (Albany: Weed-Parsons, 1903).

The Saint George's Society

This group was organized in Charleston, South Carolina, in 1733, New York in 1770, Philadelphia in 1772, and Baltimore in 1867. Membership is restricted to men of English birth or ancestry, except for the Charleston Society which has no ancestry restrictions but limits membership to thirty.

Addresses: The Saint George's Society, 110 Church Street, Charleston, SC 29401; 319 Fishers Road, Bryn Mawr, PA 19010; Box 383, Baltimore, MD 21203; 15 East 26th Street, New York, NY 10010

Printed works: Theodore C. Knauf, *A History of the Society of the Sons of St. George Established at Philadelphia, Etc.* (Philadelphia: By the society, 1923).

Figure 23-2. Applicant's Genealogical Chart of Grahame Thomas Smallwood, Jr., Dutch Colonial Society of Delaware.

APPLICANT'S GENEALOGICAL CHART

Dutch Colonial Society of Delaware

THIS WORKING SHEET SHOULD BE RETURNED WITH APPLICATION

Name Grahame Thomas Smallwood, Jr. Spouse ....

Descendant of Cornelis Maessen van Buren

1 I am the decendant of

Graeme Thomas Smallwood born on 2 August 1897 at Revere, Massachusetts
died at Washington, D.C. on 25 April 1947 and his (first or) spouse
Dorothy Hubbell born on 17 December 1895 at Toledo,Ohio
died at .... on .... married on 12 March 1918 Washington, D.C.

2 The said Dorothy Hubbell was the child of
Edward Parmelee Hubbell born on 7 February 1869 at Buffalo, New York
died at Washington, D.C. on 8 August 1951 and his (first or) spouse
Ermina Cadwell Pheatt born on 28 December 1869 at Toledo, Ohio
died at Washington, D.C. on 9 February 1956 married on 12 February 1895 Toledo, Ohio

3 The said Ermina Cadwell Pheatt was the child of
Zebulon Converse Pheatt born on 21 December 1832 at Cape Vincent, New York
died at Toledo, Ohio on 7 July 1901 and his (~~first~~ or second) spouse
Sarah Amanda Cadwell born on 17 February 1832 at Turin, New York
died at Toledo, Ohio on 27 August 1903 married on 21 May 1867 Cape Vincent, N.Y.

4 The said Zebulon Converse Pheatt was the child of
Isaac Tichenor Pheatt born on 15 April 1808 at Liverpool, New York
died at Toledo, Ohio on 11 May 1859 and his (first or) spouse
Ermina Frink born on 15 September 1809 at Herkimer, New York
died at Toledo, Ohio on 11 October 1881 married on 3 December 1829 Rochester, N.Y.

5 The said Isaac Tichenor Pheatt was the child of
David Pheatt born on 1778 at ....
died at Oswego, New York on 4 September 1834 and his (first or) spouse
Harriett Muller bapt ~~born~~ on 18 June 1785 at Kinderhook, New York
died at Oswego, New York on 24 August 1863 married on 1807 Fulton, New York

6 The said Harriett Muller was the child of
Cornelius H. Muller bapt ~~born~~ on 14 April 1759 at Claverack, New York
died at Fulton, New York on .... and his (first or) spouse
Maria Muller born on .... at ....
died at Hannibal, New York on .... married on 16 November 1781 Claverack, N.Y.

7 The said Cornelius H. Muller was the child of
Hendrick Muller bapt ~~born~~ on 5 May 1728 at Claverack, New York
died at .... on .... and his (first or) spouse
Harriet van Dusen bapt ~~born~~ on 9 February 1734 at Livingston, New York
died at .... on .... married on 3 January 1756

8 The said **Harriet (Ariaantje) van Dusen** was the child of
Tobias van Dusen bapt born on **16 August 1696** at **Claverack, New York**
died at .... on **17 October 1781** and his (first or) spouse
Ariaantje Muller bapt born on **19 July 1696** at **Claverack, New York**
died at .... on **Before 1772** married on **21 March 1723**

9 The said **Tobias van Dusen** was the child of
Robert Teuwis van Deusen born on .... at ....
died at .... on .... and his (first or) spouse
Cornelia M.van Buren born on **bapt. 1665** at ....
died at .... on **before 1717** married on **22 September 1689**

10 The said **Cornelia Martense van Buren** was the child of
MartenCornelius van Buren born on **1638/9** at ....
died at .... on **13 November 1703** and his (first or) spouse
Maritje Quackenbos born on .... at ....
died at **Albany, New York** on **7 May 1683** married on **1662**

11 The said **Marten Cornelius van Buren** was the child of
Cornelis Maessen van Buren born on .... at **Burmalsen,Gelderland**
died at **Papsknee, New York** on **1648** and his (first or) spouse
Catalyntje Martens born on .... at ....
died at **Papsknee, New York** on **1648** married on **1635/6**

12 The said .... was the child of
.... born on .... at ....
died at .... on .... and his (first or) spouse
.... born on .... at ....
died at .... on .... married on ....

RESIDENCE IN COUNTY AND STATE OF FAMILY IN EACH GENERATION DESIRED

DETAILS SHOWING THE FAMILY DESCENT: Give reference to verify the above statement of birth, marriage and death, by volume and page if reference is made to published work, and a duplicate certified or attested copy of facts where reference is made to Family Bible, tombstone, or other unpublished authority. Statements based upon TRADITION cannot be considered.

1st Gen. Birth certificates(Attached)Marriage and Death certificate (attached).
2nd Gen. Marriage certificate (attached); Death notices (attached)
3rd Gen. Death certificates (att.); Hough's Hist.Jefferson Co.N.Y.p.115; Hist.Toledo,Lucas Co. pgs.30;422;758.
4th Gen. Hist.Toledo,Lucas Co.Ohio,p.438,455,457,693,836;DAR Lineages vol.135,page 178.
5th Gen. Kinderhook,N.Y.,Vosburgh,vol 2,p.144; 1840 Census Oswego;1810 Census Oneida,N.Y.
6th Gen. DAR Patriot Index,1966 p.468;Columbia Co.N.Y.Wills,1935,vol.I,p.31;Dutch Ref.Church Claverack Records.
7th Gen. NY Gen & Biog.Rec. vol.74,p.16,56,127,147; VanDeusen Gen,Benson,1901,p.48, 133-4.
8th Gen. Van Deusen Gen,Benson,p.47; Van Deusen Gen.A.H.VanD.,1912,p.7,22,35.
9th Gen. Van Buren Fam.,H.van B.Peckham,1913,p.325-337;Van D.Gen.Benson,1901, p. 41.
10th Gen. St.Nicholas Soc.volVIII,1968 p.115;VanBuren Fam,Peckham,1913,p.17-28.
11th Gen. Van Buren Fam.Peckham,1913,pgs.17-28, 51,299; Holland Dames Register,p.102.
12th Gen. ....

The Society of the Friendly Sons of Saint Patrick

This group was organized in 1771 in Philadelphia for the relief of immigrants from Ireland, with membership restricted to men of Irish birth or descent.

Address: The Society of the Friendly Sons of Saint Patrick, 1218 Chestnut Street, Philadelphia, PA 19107

Printed works:

1. John M. Campbell, *The History of the Friendly Sons of St. Patrick and the Hibernian Society* (Philadelphia: By the societies, 1982).
2. Dennis J. Clark, *A History of the Society of the Friendly Sons of St. Patrick for Relief of Emigrants from Ireland in Philadelphia 1951-1981* (Philadelphia: By the society, 1982).
3. Daniel Dougherty, *History of the Friendly Sons of St. Patrick for the Relief of Emigrants from Ireland in Philadelphia*, (Philadelphia: By the society, 1892).
4. Samuel Hood, *A Brief Account of the Friendly Sons of St. Patrick* (Philadelphia: By the society, 1844).

Saint David's Society of the State of New York

This group was founded in 1835 for men of Welsh birth or descent of those connected by ties of consanguinity or marriage. Prior to this, Welshmen had participated in the Saint David's Benevolent Society, founded in 1801, and the Ancient Britons Benefit Society, founded in 1805.

Address: Saint David's Society of the State of New York, 71 West 23rd Street, New York, NY 10010

Printed works: *St. David's Society of the State of New York – Origin and Purpose of the Society* (New York City: By the society, n.d.).

The Holland Society of New York

This group was founded in 1885 for male descendants in the direct male line only of a Dutchman who was a native or resident of New York or the American colonies prior to 1675.

Address: The Holland Society of New York, 122 East 58th Street, New York, NY 10022

Printed works:

1. *Holland Society of New York Yearbook*, 38 vols. (New York: By the society, 1886-1937).
2. *Index to Publications of the Holland Society of New York* (New York: By the society, 1959).
3. *De Halve Maen*, Holland Society of New York quarterly magazine, from 1922-date.

The Netherlands Society of Phildelphia

This group was founded in 1892 for male lineal descendants of a Dutch ancestor who settled in the American colonies prior to 4 July 1776, or who, born in the Netherlands, emigrated to the United States after 1776.

Address: The Netherlands Society of Philadelphia, 1062 Lancaster Avenue, Rosemont, PA 19010

Printed works: *The Netherlands Society of Philadelphia – An Account of the Organization, Purposes and Traditions* (Philadelphia: By the society, 1966).

The Swedish Colonial Society

This group was founded in 1909 for men and women of lineal descent from Swedish colonists in the United States prior to 1783 (known as Forefather Members) as well as any person interested in the history of the early Swedes in America.

Address: The Swedish Colonial Society, 1300 Locust Street, Philadelphia, PA 19107

Printed works:

1. *The Swedish Colonial Society, Governor Johan Printz Memorial Edition, History, Charter, By-Laws, Officers, Members, Publications, Etc.* (Philadelphia: By the society, 1954).
2. Amandus Johnson, *The Swedish Settlements on the Delaware, 1638-1664*, 2 vols. (1911; reprint ed., Philadelphia: 1969).

The Dutch Settlers Society of Albany

This group was founded in 1924 for male and female descendants of residents of Fort Orange, the colony of Rensselaerswick, or the village of Beverwyck, before 1665.

Address: The Dutch Settlers Society of Albany, R. D. 2, Box 163, Troy, NY 12182

Printed works:

1. *The Dutch Settlers Society of Albany Yearbook*, 48 vols. (Albany: By the society, 1925-83).
2. Charlotte Wilcoxen, *Seventeeth Century Albany: A Dutch Profile* (Albany: Albany Institute, 1981).
3. *Records of the Dutch Reformed Church of Albany New York 1683-1809 as Excerpted from Year Books of the Holland Society of New York* (1904-27; reprint ed., Baltimore: Genealogical Publishing Co., 1978).

Religious Societies

All of these groups base membership on descent from French Huguenot ancestors who fled France because of religious persecution.

The Huguenot Society of America

This group was founded in 1883 in New York City for male and female lineal descendants of Huguenot families who immigrated to America prior to the Edict of Toleration 28 November 1787.

Address: The Huguenot Society of America, 122 East 58th Street, New York, NY 10022

Printed works: *Collections of the Huguenot Society of America – Registers of the Births, Marriages and Deaths of the Église François a la Nouvelle York, from 1688 to 1804*, vol. 1 (only one printed) (New York: By the society, 1886).

The Huguenot Society of South Carolina

This organization was founded in 1885 in Charleston, South Carolina, for male and female lineal descendants of Huguenot families who immigrated to American prior to the Edict of Toleration, 28 November 1787.

Address: The Huguenot Society of South Carolina, 25 Chalmers Street, Charleston, SC 29401

Printed works:

1. *Transactions of the Huguenot Society of South Carolina*, 87 vols. (Columbia: By the society, 1889-1983).
2. S. DuBose and F. Porcher, *History of the Huguenots of South Carolina* (n.p., 1887).

The Huguenot Society of the Founders of Manakin in the Colony of Virginia

This group was founded in 1922 for male and female lineal descendants of any Huguenot resident of Virginia prior to 1786. Associate membership is provided for descendants from Huguenots who resided outside of Virginia.

Address: The Huguenot Society of the Founders of Manakin in the Colony of Virginia, 4419 Washington Pike N.E., Knoxville, TN 37917

Printed works:

1. R. A. Brock, *Documents, History and Family Genealogy Relating to the Huguenot Emigration to Virginia and to the Settlement of Manakin Town, With an Appendix of Genealogy* (1886; reprint ed., Baltimore: Genealogical Publishing Co., 1979).
2. *The Huguenot*, 21 vols. (n. p.: By the society, 1924-66).

The National Huguenot Society

This group was organized in 1951 as a federation of state societies. In 1983 there were forty-two state society organizations, including the District of Columbia. Individual applicants join a local state society and automatically become a member of the national society.

Address: The National Huguenot Society, Hearst Hall,

Washington National Cathedral, Wisconsin Avenue and Woodley Road, N.W., Washington, DC 20016

Printed works:

1. Rev. Ammon Stapleton, *Memorials of the Huguenots in America* (Carlisle, Penn: Huguenot Publishing Co., 1901).

2. Charles W. Baird, *History of the Huguenot Emigration to America,* 2 vols. (1885; reprint ed., Baltimore: Regional Publishing Co., 1966).

3. Allan Forbes and Paul F. Cadman, *Boston and Some Noted Emigrés* (Boston: State Street Trust Company, 1938).

Royal and Baronial Societies

All of the societies in this grouping, listed by date of founding, require the applicant to trace the ancestry of an immigrant ancestor to his/her native country until noble or royal ancestry is reached. Establishing the proper "gateway" ancestor is the major problem for most applicants.

The first two volumes listed below are of great assistance in locating such ancestors.

1. Frederick Lewis Weis, *Ancestral Roots of Sixty Colonists Who Came to New England Between 1623 and 1650. The Lineage of Alfred the Great, Charlemagne, Malcolm of Scotland, Robert the Strong and Some of Their Descendants.* 5th ed., with additions and corrections by Walter Lee Sheppard, Jr. (Baltimore: Genealogical Publishing Co., 1976).

2. Frederick Lewis Weis and Arthur Adams, *The Magna Charta Sureties, 1215: The Barons Named in the Magna Charta 1215 and Some of Their Descendants Who Settled in America 1607-1650,* 3rd ed., with additions and corrections by Walter Lee Sheppard, Jr. (Baltimore: Genealogical Publishing Company, 1979).

3. George E. Cokayne, ed., *The Complete Peerage,* 13 vols., (London, 1910-59).

The first two volumes are the only editions with acceptable proof for the various royal and baronial lineage societies. While the majority of the *Ancestral Roots* ancestry is of the New England area, nearly half of *The Magna Charta* lines are Virginian. *The Complete Peerage* is the most acceptable proof for all peerage lines.

Order of the Crown in America

This society was founded in 1898 as an order for men and women of proven royal descent, with the stipulation that ladies be members in good standing of either the Colonial Dames of America or the National Society of Colonial Dames of America. Membership is limited and by invitation only.

Address: Not available.

Printed works:

1. *The History, Constitution and Officers of the Order of the Crown in America* (By the order, 1902, 1917, 1927).

2. *Order of the Crown in America Membership Roster* (By the order, 1962, 1968, 1971, 1975, 1981).

The Baronial Order of Magna Charta

This society was founded in 1898 for male lineal descendants of the earls and barons elected to be the sureties of the Magna Charta, shortly after 19 June 1215. Membership is by invitation only.

Address: Douglas Chandler Wright, Marshal, 462 Point Road, Little Silver, NJ 07739

Printed works:

1. Arthur Edwin Bye, *Magna Charta, King John and The Barons* (Bridgeport, Penn: Chancellor Press, 1967).

2. Frederick Lewis Weis and Arthur Adams, *The Magna Charta Sureties 1215,* 3rd ed., with additions and corrections by Walter Lee Sheppard, Jr. (Baltimore: Genealogical Publishing Co., 1979).

The National Society of Americans of Royal Descent

This group was founded in 1908 for men and women of proven royal descent. An applicant must be a member of a recognized lineage society of the colonial period, and female applicants must be a member of either the National Society of the Colonial Dames of America or of the Colonial Dames of America. Applicants also need to be known by at least one member of the group's executive council and be proposed and seconded in writing. Membership is by invitation only.

Address: Not available.

Printed works: *National Society of Americans of Royal Descent—History, Membership Roster, Constitution and By-Laws* (By the society, 1960, 1965, 1968, 1971, 1974, 1977, 1980).

The National Society of Magna Charta Dames

This group was founded in 1909 for female descendants of the Magna Charta Sureties of 1215. Membership is by invitation of the council, following proposal by a present member.

Address: The National Society of Magna Charta Dames, Box 4222, Philadelphia, PA 19144

Printed works: John S. Wurts, *Magna Charta,* 8 vols., (Philadelphia: By the author, 1942).

The National Society of Daughters of the Barons of Runnemede

This group was organized in 1921 for women of lineal descent from one or more of the barons who served as sureties of the Magna Charta in 1215. Membership is by invitation only, following proposal by a present member.

Address: Mrs. J. A. Grady, 1102 Westover Road, Wilmington, DE 19807

Printed works: *National Society Daughters of the Barons of Runnemede—Organization, History and Membership—With Full-color Arms of the Barons,* (Athens, Ga.: McGregor Co., 1937). Contains biographical sketches of the "gateway" ancestors of the members, and sketches of the founders of the society.

The Military Order of the Crusades

This group was founded in 1934 for men of lineal descent from one or more crusaders of the rank of knight or higher who participated in the Crusades 1096-1291. Membership is by invitation only.

Address: The Military Order of the Crusades, 104 Bladdyn Road, Ardmore, PA 19003

Manuscript documents in possession of the order:

1. William Hannis Perot, List of Crusaders Used as Qualifying Ancestors by the Order to 7 June 1977.

2. History, Constitution and By-Laws (By the order, 1960).

Order of Three Crusades 1096-1192

This group was founded in 1936 for men and women of lineal descent from a participant in one of the first three crusades, 1096-1192. A pilgrimage to Jerusalem as a religious gesture was not a crusade and is not acceptable. Membership is by invitation only. Applicants must be sponsored by two members and be known to at least one officer of the order.

Address: Not available.

Printed works: *Order of Three Crusades 1095-1192—History, Constitution and By-Laws, Membership Roster,* 4 vols. (By the Order, 1965, 1970, 1976, 1983).

Order of the Crown of Charlemagne in the United States of America

This society was founded in 1939 for men and women of lineal descent from the Emperor Charlemagne. Membership is by invitation only.

Address: Not available.

Printed works:

1. Marcellus Donald R. von Redlich, *Pedigrees of Some of the Emperor Charlemagne's Descendants,* vol. 1 (West Somerville, Mass: Somerville Printing Company, 1942).

2. Aileen Lewers Langston and J. Orton Buck, Jr., comps.,

Figure 23-3. Excerpts from the Life Membership Application of Grahame Thomas Smallwood, Jr., The Order of the Crown of Charlemagne in the United States of America.

National Number

The Order of the Crown of Charlemagne in the United States of America

SUPPLEMENTAL **Lineage Claim for Life Membership**

Name of Applicant Grahame Thomas Smallwood, Jr.

Maiden Name

Address The Union League

Philadelphia, Pa., 19102

The American Ancestor Alice Freeman wife of John Thompson

is the ancestor through whom my claim of eligibility is based.

S He settled in Roxbury in the colony of Massachusetts Bay

on or about 1627@1640 S He was born ca. 1595 S He died 11 Feb 1664/5

Endorsed by the undersigned members to whom the applicant is known.

1. Name

Address

2. Name

Address

The undersigned have investigated and ascertained that the Applicant meets the required qualifications. for membership and thus approve this application.

The Supplemental Membership fee of $ 40.00 was paid by

Date fee received by Treasurer — Treasurer General

Date this lineage was approved — Genealogist General

Date of election to membership — Registrar General

DO NOT WRITE ON THIS MARGIN

40. The said Arnold I, Count of Flanders & Artois was the child of
Baldwin II, Count of Flanders & Artois born at on ca. 865
died at on 2 Jan. 918; married on 884
to Alfthryth of England born at on
died at on 7 June 929; married at
Proof: Ibid

41. The said Baldwin II, Count of Flanders & Artois was the child of
Baldwin I of Flanders born at on
died at on 879; married on 862
to Princess Judith born at on ca. 846
died at on; married at
Proof: Ibid

42. The said Princess Judith was the child of
Charles II, the Bald, King of the Franks born at on 828
died at on 877; married on (1) 842
to Ermentrude of Orleans born at on
died at on; married at
Proof: Ibid

43. The said Charles II, King of the Franks was the child of
Louis I, King of the Franks born at on 778
died at on 840; married on
to Judith of Bavaria born at on
died at on 19 Apr. 843; married at
Proof: Ibid

44. The said Louis I, King of the Franks was the child of
The Emperor Charlemagne born at on 2 Apr. 747
died at Ais La Chapelle on 28 Jan. 813/4; married on ca. 771
to Hidegarde of Swabia born at on 758
died at on 30 Apr. 783; married at
Proof: Ibid

DO NOT WRITE ON THIS MARGIN

Pedigrees of Some of the Emperor Charlemagne's Descendants, vol.2, (Cottonport, La: Polyanthos, Inc., 1974).

3. J. Orton Buck and Timothy Field Beard, *Pedigrees of Some of the Emperor Charlemagne's Descendants,* vol. 3 (Nashville: Ambrose Printing Co., 1978).

Descendants of the Illegitimate Sons and Daughters of the Kings of Britain

This group was founded in 1950 by four fellows of the American Society of Genealogists, to improve scholarship and research on all "royal lineages." Membership is open to men and women who can prove by quality scholarship their descent in any line, from the illegitimate son, daughter, grandson, or granddaughter of a king or queen of England, Scotland, or Wales.

Address: Herman Nickerson, Jr., 107 Lake Lane Rock Creek, Jacksonville, NC 28540

Manuscript of "Royal Bastards from the Time of the Norman Conquest–The Constitution, Annual Reports, Lineages of Descents of Members, Etc." All of these are sent to members in loose-leaf form, to be added to three-ring binders as new members join. Approximately 200 lineages have been approved.

Printed works: Walter Lee Sheppard, Jr., "Descendants of the Illegitimate Sons and Daughters of the Kings of Britain," *National Genealogical Society Quarterly* 62 (Sept. 1974): 182-91.

Family Societies and Organizations

The proliferation of family societies in the past five years makes it impossible to list all of them in this relatively brief chapter. Many family groups publish extensive family genealogies, newsletters, and bulletins. They also hold family reunions throughout the country. Sources for information on these family associations include:

1. J. Konrad, ed., *Family Associations, Societies and Reunions* (1982). Contains 1800 entries. Available for $5 from The Augustan Society, Box P, Torrance, CA 90507.

2. Jane O. Berryman, comp. *National Index of Family Associations and Periodicals* (1982). For $2 and SASE, the index will be searched for a particular name. If there is no entry, the fee will be returned. The mailing address is 3638 Philadelphia Street, Chino, CA 91710.

3. *The Connecticut Nutmegger,* published quarterly by the Connecticut Society of Genealogists. The address is Box 435, 2906 Main Street, Glastonbury, CT 06033. Contains lists of family reunions, clan societies, and family histories, as well as Connecticut vital records. Annual dues and subscription are $20.

4. *The Hereditary Register of the United States of America.* Contains listing of some 550 family associations, societies, and publications. The 1982 edition is available for $40 from 444 W. Camelback Road, Suite 105, Phoenix, AZ 85013.

5. *Newsletter of the International Society for British Genealogy and Family History.* Contains listings of family reunions in this country and in England. Annual fee is $10. The address is Box 20425, Cleveland, OH 44120.

6. *The National Genealogical Society Newsletter.* Published six times a year, the newsletter has a column "About Families," which covers reunions and publications. The annual membership of $30 includes the excellent *National Genealogical Society Quarterly Magazine.* Mailing address is 1921 Sunderland Place, N.W., Washington, DC 20036.

Location of Lineage Society Source Material

The majority of volumes cited will be found in any major library with a substantial genealogical collection. Most of these, for instance, are available at the Genealogical Society of Utah in Salt Lake City, especially those printed since 1960 or reprints of earlier volumes.

The Hereditary Register of the United States of America, cited above, is the major single volume source for membership information on over 100 lineage societies.

Readers interested in obtaining copies of listed volumes for their personal libraries should contact Goodspeed's Genealogical Book Shop, 18 Beacon Street, Boston, MA 02108 and Genealogical Publishing Co., Inc., 1001 N. Calvert Street, Baltimore, MD 21202.

Comments for the Serious Lineage Society Researcher

Many professional genealogists specialize in preparing lineage papers for their clients. Those certified by the Board for Certification of Genealogists will list the intials C.A.L.S. (Certifed American Lineage Specialist) after their names.

A list of certified genealogists throughout the United States is available from the Board of Certification of Genealogists, Box 19165, Washington, DC 20036. Send $2 and a #10 SASE with postage for two ounces of first-class mail for a copy.

A Certified American Lineage Specialist should be familiar with the requirements for membership in all of the major hereditary societies and the format for documenting applications for each society. Individuals make application for membership in the society and receive the worksheets and application forms. The genealogist should never ask for application blanks for a client.

The sample lineage papers reproduced in this chapter show great variance in format and required documentation. The applicant or his/her genealogist should first make several photocopies of the worksheet and experiment on these before attempting to type the final applications.

Documentation is frequently misunderstood. The listing of a volume with pertinent page numbers is not sufficient for most societies. Photocopies of all proofs should accompany the application. This will speed up the approval by the society's verifying genealogist who often resides far from a major library and depends entirely on the material submitted. All original copies of vital records, family Bible records, and personal documents should be retained by the applicant. Photocopies from published volumes should include the title page. This is especially true when submitting family Bible records. The page showing the year the Bible was published is vital to establish the fact that the entries were made at that time period.

Never handletter applications, no matter how legibly. All applications should be typed with a good black ribbon. When two copies are required, both should always be original typings.

LIST OF CONTRIBUTORS
APPENDICIES
GLOSSARY
BIBLIOGRAPHY INDEX
SUBJECT INDEX

CONTRIBUTORS

Wilma Adkins, an accredited genealogist for the Southern and Midwestern States, is a graduate of Brigham Young University (B.S. in genealogy technology). She is a member of the Association of Professional Genealogists (co-founder and treasurer, 1979-80; executive secretary, 1980-81;) and the Utah Genealogical Association (board of trustees, 1979-81, first vice president, 1981-83). She has published, with others, an index to the 1840 Iowa census, an index to Irish sources, the *1979 Directory of Professional Genealogists,* and other works. Her areas of interest include professional procedures, ethics, and activities; computer services; and Southern and Midwestern research.

Elaine Barton, a professional genealogist, is a member of the St. Louis Genealogical Society, the York Family Association, the Wyckoff Family Organization, and Maeystown Preservation Society. President of Ances-Tree, Inc., she is a published author.

Johni Cerny, president and founder of Lineages, Inc., the nation's largest genealogical research firm, has been tracing people's ancestry for twenty years—first as a hobbyist and later as a professional genealogist after a career as a captain in the U.S. Army Ordinance Corps. A specialist in the Southern States, Colonial Virginia, and Black American research, she is treasurer and on the Board of Trustees of the Association of Professional Genealogists, has served as secretary (1980) and as president (1981) of the Utah Genealogical Association, and currently serves as president of the Genealogical Research Foundation and the Genealogical Development Foundation, two nonprofit organizations. She is the Director of First Families of America, the Registry of American Immigrant Ancestry, the Registry of Black American Ancestry, and America's Notable Cousins, divisions of Lineages, Inc. She is also a member of the National Genealogical Society.

The Source is her first major publication. Works in progress include *Ancestry's Guide to Research* with Arlene H. Eakle. Among her current clients are Berry Gordy, Jr., Quincy Jones, Ira A. Fulton, Michael Caine, Peggy Lipton, Mickey Rudin, and Mo Ostin. She is also directing the research for two major screen-plays scheduled for production in 1986.

Richard W. Doughtery, who holds a Ph.D. in History from the University of Wisconsin-Madison, has been a professional genealogist since 1979. A Fulbright Scholar at the University of Bonn, Germany, his research area of specialization is tracing German immigrant ancestors, as well as those from France, Poland, Czechoslovakia, and other East European countries. A member of Concordia Historical Institute, he is also serving (1984) as vice president of the Professional Chapter of the Utah Genealogical Association.

Arlene H. Eakle, president and managing director of the Genealogical Institute in Salt Lake City (1973-to-date), is a popular lecturer and has spoken at more than two hundred conferences in the United States and Canada between 1972 and 1983. She is a specialist with sixteen years experience in tracing immigrant and Pennsylvania German ancestors, searching U.S. colonial records, and solving southern research problems. She has served on the Utah State Historical Society Community History Workshop Team (1975-77), as a University of Utah Research Fellow, Center for Historical Population Studies (1977-79), as consultant to the U. S. Bureau of the Census for Spanish surnames (1978), and is a member of the Utah Genealogical Association, the Maryland Genealogical Society, the Council on British Studies, Utah Historical Society, and the Cambridge Group for the Study of Population and Social Structure. Founder in 1979 of the Association of Professional Genealogists, she served on its first Board of Trustees, represented Utah as trustee (1980-83), and was 1980-82 president. Currently, she is Registrar of the Federation of Genealogical Societies.

Her publications include: with Vincent L. Jones, the 1972 *Genealogical Research: A Jurisdictional Approach,* reprinted in 1974 as *Family History for Fun and Profit* now in its fifth printing; *Do Your Letters Beg for Attention?* (1973); *Teacher's Aid: Research Notekeeping* (1973); *How to Search a Cemetery* (1974); *Photograph Analysis: A Teaching Module for Family History in the Classroom;* Georgia L. Weber and Adelia Baird, *Woods Cross: Patterns and Profiles of a City* (1976); with Richard Tompson and Arvilla Outsen, *A Descriptive Inventory of English Records in the Genealogical Society of Utah* (1979); and with L. Ray Gunn, *Descriptive Guide to the Microfilmed Collection for New York at the Genealogical Society of Utah* (1980), among other works. Former (1979) editor of *World Heritage Magazine,* she edits the *APG Green $heet* and the *APG Newsletter.* Works in progress include an annotated bibliography of family and local histories in Great Britain, 1590-1800 (Ph.D. diss., University of Utah, 1984); a guide to genealogical research in Great Britian for Americans, a map resource book for American genealogists, and *Ancestry's Guide to Research* with Johni Cerny.

Kory L. Meyerink was born in Greenwich, Connecticut, in 1954 to a Dutch immigrant father and a mother whose roots go generations into New York/New England. His fifteen-year hobby of genealogy became his profession five years ago. A 1979 graduate of Brigham Young University, he also resided in Germany for two years and is conversant with German and Dutch records, specializes in northern and eastern United States research and in finding the hometowns of German immigrants. Accredited in both German and Midwestern United States research, he is currently the secretary-treasurer for the Utah State Society, Sons of the American Revolution.

George J. Nixon, a native of Grants Pass, Oregon, has been a professional genealogist since 1976. A former student at University of California, Los Angeles, he also served a tour of duty in the U.S. Navy (1957-60). His areas of specialization are research in the Southern, Midwestern, and Western states, and American Indian records. Current projects include lineages and family histories of Martha Jane Canary (Calamity Jane), Myra Shirley (Belle Starr), and the Dalton/ Young families.

Spencer J. Palmer, a native of Thatcher, Arizona, received his M.A. in East Asian Studies and Ph.D. in History from the University of California at Berkeley. He is professor of history and religion at Brigham Young University, where he served as Coordinator of Asian Studies, as Director of World Religions in the Religious Studies Center for several years, and is currently Director of the David M. Kennedy International Center. He is the author or editor of twelve books and numerous articles focusing primarily on Asian culture, history, and religion, as well as international affairs.

Jimmy B. Parker is an Accredited Genealogist in the Midwestern and eastern United States and New England. He has held various positions with the Genealogical Society of Utah, served on the Board of Trustees (1978-79) of the Utah Genealogical Association, as editor (1978) of *Genealogical Journal*, was named a fellow in the Utah Genealogical Association in 1979, and received an Award of Merit from the National Genealogical Society. He is (1984) president of the Association of Professional Genealogists and chairman of the Genealogical Coordinating Committee. Current research interests include a volume on American Indian genealogical research and a consolidated index to Indiana biographical sketches.

Richard W. Price, accredited by the Genealogical Society of Utah, has been engaged in genealogy for fifteen years, professionally for the last five. A Brigham Young University graduate, he specializes in English research, where he has made several on-site research trips; emigration to the American colonies from England, (particularly from Norfolk and Lincolnshire), and English military research problems. Founder and immediate past president of the Association of Professional Genealogists, he is the author of *John Lathrop, 1584-1653: Reformer, Sufferer, Pilgrim, Man of God,* and has presented papers for the Utah Genealogical Association and National Society meetings.

Gordon Lewis Remington is a native of upstate New York and an amateur genealogist since the age of ten. He worked for twelve years on his personal ancestry using sources in New England, the Midwest, Mid-Atlantic and Southern states, England, Scotland, and Germany. A professional genealogist since 1979, he is a member of New England Historic Genealogical Society. He has studied at Wesleyan University, the University of Rochester, and the University of Utah, from which he will receive a B.A. in History in 1983.

Grahame Thomas Smallwood, Jr. is a Certified American Lineage Specialist, educated in Europe and making his home in Salt Lake City. A specialist in preparing lineage papers for hereditary societies, he is himself a member of the Order of the Founders and Patriots of America (governor-general, 1968-72), Order of Descendants of Colonial Governors (governor-general 1963-67), National Society of Americans of Royal Descent (president-general 1971-73), Order of Americans of Armorial Ancestry (national president 1973-76); Baronial Order of Magna Charta (marshal 1974-76); American Friends of Lafayette (national president 1971); Military Order of the Crusades (commander-general 1977-78); Order of the Crown of Charlemagne; Order of the Crown in America (registrar general, life); Order of the Three Crusades, 1096-1192; Order of the Descendants of Colonial Physicians and Chirugieons; National Huguenot Society (genealogist-general 1980-84); National Society Sons and Daughters of the Pilgrims; National Gavel Society; National Society Sons of the American Revolution, General Society War of 1812; General Society of Colonial Wars (verifying general for the Pennsylvania Society 1975-date); General Society Sons of the Revolution (verifying General, Pennsylvania Society 1975-date); and others.

Among his honors are the Minuteman Award of the Sons of the American Revolution (1968); Patriot Award, Sons of the American Revolution (1964); Society of the Sons of St. George of Philadelphia Annual Cuthbert Pratt Memorial Award (1979); and first recipient of the Grahame Thomas Smallwood, Jr. Award of the Association of Professional Genealogists.

Wade C. Starks, an accredited genealogist with the Genealogical Society of Utah, is a Brigham Young University graduate in genealogy and family history where he has also served as an instructor at annual genealogy seminars. His special interests are Scandinavian research (Norway, Sweden, Denmark, Finland, the Faero Islands, and Iceland). He speaks Norwegian, Swedish, Danish, and some German and French, has published the first volume of *Norwegian Genealogical Research* (1981), and has further volumes in progress. He also has the reputation with his Utah colleagues of being the most knowledgeable person in the state in making genealogical computer applications among professional genealogists.

Loretto Dennis Szucs, a former teacher and legal secretary is presently a professional genealogist and lecturer. She is current chairman of the Council of Northeastern Illinois Genealogical Societies and its past vice-president and newsletter editor. She is also presently a director of the South Suburban Genealogical and Historical Society, of the Chicago Genealogical Society, and of the Illinois State Genealogical Society. Founding secretary and current delegate (publications) to the Federation of Genealogical Societies, she is also currently a volunteer at the Federal Archives and Records Center at Chicago. She has written *Cook County Research (Chicago, Illinois Area): Not An Impossible Dream* (Chicago: Illinois State Genealogical Society, 1981), published numerous articles and compiled "Eastern District of Michigan (Detroit) Circuit and District Court Naturalizations" (manuscript copies available at the Newberry Library, Chicago; Allen County Public Library, (Fort Wayne, Indiana); and Federal Archives and Records Center, Chicago).

William Thorndale is both an Accredited Genealogist and Certified Genealogist (southern states). He received his B.A. and M.A. in U.S. History from the University of Washington, was a U.S. Air Force civilian historian in Vietnam, is a specialist in Southern Revolutionary War Records, member and past newsletter editor for the Association of Professional Genealogists, and a member of the National Genealogical Society.

David S. Weber, who holds degrees from Mount Union College, Miami University, and Ohio State University (Ph.D.), was for five years an archivist with the National Archives and Records Service in Chicago. He is now chief of its Appraisal and Disposition Section. His publications include "Of Trials, Tribes, and Topographers: Holdings of the Chicago Regional Branch of the National Archives," *Illinois Libraries,* April 1981, pp. 283-87 (coauthored); "A Research Guide to Materials Relating to Native Americans Available in the Chicago Archives Branch," *Illinois Libraries,* Oct. 1981, pp. 621-25; "A Brief Guide to Naturalization Records at the Chicago Regional Archives Branch," *Polish Genealogical Society Newsletter,* Spring 1982, p. 3; and "The Papers of Rutherford B. Hayes," *National Historical Publications and Records Commission,* Microfilm edition, forthcoming.

Appendix A

REGIONAL FEDERAL ARCHIVES AND RECORDS CENTER

FARC branches receive the records of the field offices of U. S. Government agencies located in their area, except that agencies in the District of Columbia, Maryland, and West Virginia send their records to the Washington National Records Center, Washington, DC 20509. They will loan microfilm to libraries and research institutions in their service area given in parentheses after the address.

For each of the following, address inquiries to:

Chief, Archives Branch
Federal Archives and Records Center

Boston

380 Trapelo Road
Waltham, MA 02154
(Serves Connecticut, Maine, Massachusetts, New Hampshire, Rhode Island, and Vermont)

New York

Building 22-MOT Bayonne
Bayonne, NJ 07002
(Serves New Jersey, New York, Puerto Rico, and the Virgin Islands)

Philadelphia

5000 Wissahickon Avenue
Philadelphia, PA 19144
(Serves Delaware and Pennsylvania; for the loan of microfilm also serves the District of Columbia, Maryland, Virginia, and West Virginia)

Atlanta

1557 St. Joseph Avenue
East Point, GA 30344
(Serves Alabama, Georgia, Florida, Kentucky, Mississippi, North Carolina, South Carolina, and Tennessee)

Chicago

7358 South Pulaski Road
Chicago, IL 60629
(Serves Illinois, Indiana, Michigan, Minnesota, Ohio, and Wisconsin)

Kansas City

2306 East Bannister Road
Kansas City, MO 64131
(Serves Iowa, Kansas, Missouri, and Nebraska)

Fort Worth

4900 Hemphill Street (building address)
Box 6216 (mailing address)
Forth Worth, TX 76115
(Serves Arkansas, Louisiana, New Mexico, Oklahoma, and Texas)

Denver

Building 48, Denver Federal Center
Denver, CO 80225
(Serves Colorado, Montana, North Dakota, South Dakota, Utah, and Wyoming)

San Francisco

1000 Commodore Drive
San Bruno, CA 94066
(Serves California except southern California, Hawaii, Nevada except Clark County, and the Pacific Ocean area)

Los Angeles

24000 Avila Road
Laguna Niguel, CA 92677
(Serves Arizona; the southern California counties of Imperial, Inyo, Kern, Los Angeles, Orange, Riverside, San Bernardino, San Diego, San Luis Obispo, Santa Barbara, and Ventura; and Clark County, Nevada.)

Seattle

6125 Sand Point Way N.E.
Seattle, WA 98115
(Serves Alaska, Idaho, Oregon, and Washington)

Appendix B

STATE HISTORICAL ARCHIVES AND RECORD DEPOSITORIES

Alabama Department of Archives and History
624 Washington Avenue
Montgomery, AL 36104

Alaska Historical Library
Pouch G
Division of State Libraries
Juneau, AK 99801

Arizona State Department of Library, Archives, and Public Records
3rd Floor, State Capitol
Phoenix, AZ 85007

Arkansas Historical Commission
300 West Markham Street
Little Rock, AR 72201

California State Archives
1020 "O" Street
Sacramento, CA 95814

Colorado Division of State Archives and Public Records
1313 Sherman Street
Denver, CO 80203

Connecticut State Libary
231 Capitol Avenue
Hartford, CT 06115

Delaware Division of Historical and Cultural Affairs
Hall of Records
Dover, DE 19901

Florida Division of Archives, History, and Records Management
R.A. Gray Building/Pensacola and Bronough Streets
Tallahassee, FL 32304

Georgia Department of Archives and History
330 Capitol Avenue
Atlanta, GA 30334

Hawaii State Archives
Iolani Palace Grounds
Honolulu, HI 96813

Idaho State Historical Society
610 N. Julia Davis Drive
Boise, ID 83706

Illinois State Archives
Archives Building
Springfield, IL 62756

Indiana State Library
140 N. Senate
Indianapolis, IN 46204

Iowa Division of Historical Museum and Archives
E. 12th Street and Grand Avenue
Des Moines, IA 50319

Kansas State Historical Society
120 W. 10th Street
Topeka, KS 66612

Kentucky Department of Parks
10th Floor
Capitol Plaza Tower
Frankfort, KY 40601

Louisiana State Museum
751 Chartres Street
New Orleans, LA 70116

Maine State Archives
State Capitol
Augusta, ME 04333

Maryland Department of General Services
Hall of Records
Saint John's Street & College Avenue
Annapolis, MD 21401

State Library of Massachusetts
341 State House
Boston, MA 02133

Michigan History Division
Michigan Department of State
Lansing, MI 48910

Minnesota Historical Society Division of Archives and Manuscripts
1500 Mississippi Street
St. Paul, MN 55101

Mississippi Department of Archives and History
100 S. State Street
Jackson, MS 39201

Missouri Department of Natural Resources
100 East Capitol Avenue
Jeffeson City, MO 65101

Montana Historical Society and Archives Board of Education
225 N. Roberts Street
Helena, MT 59620

Nebraska Historical Society and Archives
1500 "R" Street
Lincoln, NE 68508

Nevada State, County, and Municipal Archives
1807 N. Carson Street
Carson City, NV 89710

New Hampshire State Historical Commission
71 S. Fruit Street
Concord, NH 03301

New Jersey Bureau of Archives
New Jersey State Library
185 W. State Street
Trenton, NJ 08625

New Mexico State Records Center and Archives
404 Montezuma 87503
Santa Fe, NM 87503

New York State Archives
Cultural Education Center
Empire State Plaza
Albany, NY 12230

North Carolina Division of Archives and History
109 E. Jones Street
Raleigh, NC 27611

State Historical Society of North Dakota
Liberty Memorial Building
Bismarck, ND 58505

Ohio Historical Society Division of Archives and Manuscripts
1982 Velma Avenue
Columbus, OH 43211

Oklahoma Department of Libraries
200 N.E. 18th Street
Oklahoma City, OK 73105

Oregon Divison of Archives
Office of Secretary of State
1005 Broadway, N.E.
Salem, OR 97301

Pennsylvania Historical and Museum Commission
William Penn Memorial Museum
3rd and North Street
Harrisburg, PA 17120

Rhode Island State Archives
314 State House
Providence, RI 02900

South Carolina Department of Archives and History
Box 11669
Columbia, SC 29211

South Dakota State Archives
E. Highway Bypass
Pierre, SD 57501

Tennessee State Library and Archives
403 7th Avenue North
Nashville, TN 37219

Texas Library and Historical Commission
1201 Brazos
Austin, TX 78701

Utah State Archives
Room 28
State Capitol
Salt Lake City, UT 84114

Vermont Divison of Public Records Agency of Administration
State Administration Building
Montpelier, VT 05602

Virginia State Library
11th and Capitol Streets
Richmond, VA 23219

Washington State Capitol Historical Association
211 W. 21st Avenue
Olympia, WA 98501

West Virginia Department of Archives and History
Science and Culture Center
Charleston, WV 25305

Wisconsin Historical Society Divison of Archives
816 State Street
Madison, WI 53706

Wyoming State Archives and Historical Department
Barrett Building
Cheyenne, WY 82002

Appendix C

HISTORICAL SOCIETIES AND AGENCIES IN THE UNITED STATES

Alabama Historical Association
3121 Carlisle Rd.
Birmingham, AL 35213
Telephone: (205) 324-0998
Publications: *The Alabama Review*

Alaska Historical Commission
3221 Providence Avenue
Anchorage, AK 99504
Telephone: (907) 274-6222
Publication: *Alaska History News*

Arkansas Historical Association
History Department
University of Arkansas
Fayetteville, AR 72701
Telephone: (501) 575-3001
Publication: *Arkansas Historical Quarterly*

Arizona Historical Society
949 E. 2nd Street
Tucson, AZ 85719
Telephone: (602) 882-5774
Publication: *The Journal of Arizona History*

California Historical Society
2090 Jackson Street
San Francisco, CA 94109
Telephone: (415) 567-1848
Publication: *California Historical Quarterly*

The State Historical Society of Colorado
1300 Broadway
Denver, CO 80203

The Connecticut Historical Society
1 Elizabeth Street
Hartford, CT 06105
Telephone: (203) 236-5621
Publication: *Bulletin*

The Historical Society of Delaware
505 Market Street Mall
Wilmington, DE 19801
Telephone: (302) 655-7161
Publication: *Delaware History*

Florida Historical Society
University of South Florida Library
Tampa, FL 33620
Telephone: (813) 974-2731
Publication: *Florida Historical Quarterly*

Georgia Historical Society
501 Whitaker Street
Savannah, GA 31401
Telephone: (912) 944-2128
Publication: *Georgia Historical Quarterly*

Hawaiian Historical Society
560 Kawaiahao Street
Honolulu, HI 96813
Publication: *The Hawaiian Journal of History*

Idaho State Historical Society
610 N. Julia Davis Drive
Boise, ID 83706
Telephone: (208) 384-2120
Publication: *Idaho Yesterdays*

Illinois State Historical Society
Old State Capitol
Springfield, IL 62706
Telephone: (217) 782-4836
Publication: *Journal of the Illinois State Historical Society*

Indiana Historical Society
315 W. Ohio Street
Indianapolis, IN 46202
Telephone: (317) 633-5277
Publication: *Indiana Magazine of History*

State Historical Society of Iowa
402 Iowa Avenue
Iowa City, IA 52240
Telephone: (319) 338-5471
Publication: *The Palimpsest*

Kansas State Historical Society
120 W. 10th St.
Topeka, KS 66612
Telephone: (913) 296-3251
Publication: *Kansas Historical Quarterly*

Kentucky Historical Society
300 W. Broadway
Frankfort, KY 40601
Telephone: (502) 564-3016
Publications: *Register; Kentucky Ancestors; Kentucky Heritage; Bulletin*

Louisiana Genealogical and Historical Society
Box 3454
Baton Rouge, LA 70821
Publication: *The Louisiana Genealogical Register*

Maine Historical Society
485 Congress Street
Portland, ME 04101
Telephone: (207) 774-1822
Publication: *Maine Historical Society Quarterly*

Maryland Historical Society
201 W. Monument Street
Baltimore, MD 21201
Telephone: (301) 685-3750
Publication: *Maryland Historical Magazine*

Massachusetts Historical Society
1154 Boylston Street
Boston, MA 02215
Telephone: (617) 536-1608
Publication: *Proceedings*

Historical Society of Michigan
2177 Washtenaw Avenue
Ann Arbor, MI 48104
Telephone: (313) 769-1828
Publication: *Chronicle*

Minnesota Historical Society
690 Cedar Street
St. Paul, MN 55101
Telephone: (612) 296-2747
Publication: *Minnesota History*

Mississippi Historical Society
100 S. State Street
Jackson, MS 39205
Telephone: (601) 354-6218
Publication: *Journal of Mississippi History*

State Historical Society of Missouri
Hitt and Lowry Streets
Columbia, MO 65201
Telephone: (314) 443-3165
Publication: *Missouri Historical Review*

Montana Historical Society
225 N. Roberts
Helena, MT 59601
Telephone: (406) 449-2694
Publication: *Montana, the Magazine of Western History*

Nebraska State Historical Society
1500 R Street
Lincoln, NE 68508
Telephone: (402) 432-2793
Publication: *Nebraska History*

Nevada Historical Society
1650 N. Virginia Street
Reno, NV 89503
Telephone: (702) 784-6397
Publication: *Nevada Historical Society Quarterly*

New Hampshire Historical Society
30 Park Street
Concord, NH 03301
Telephone: (603) 225-3381

The New Jersey Historical Society
230 Broadway
Newark, NJ 07104
Telephone: (201) 483-3939
Publication: *New Jersey History*

Historical Society of New Mexico
Box 4638
Santa Fe, NM 87501
Publication: *LaCronica*

New York State Historical Association
Lake Road, Route 80
Cooperstown, NY 13326
Telephone: (607) 547-2533
Publication: *New York History*

North Carolina Division of Archives and History
109 E. Jones Street
Raleigh, NC 27611
Telephone: (919) 733-7305
Publications: *North Carolina Historical Review; Carolina Comments*

State Historical Society of North Dakota
Liberty Memorial Building
Bismarck, ND 58505
Telephone: (701) 224-2666
Publication: *North Dakota History: Journal of the Northern Plains*

Ohio Historical Society
I-71 and 17th Avenue
Columbus, OH 43211
Telephone: (614) 466-4663
Publication: *Ohio History; Echoes*

Oklahoma Historical Society
2100 N. Lincoln Boulevard
Oklahoma City, OK 73105
Telephone: (405) 521-2491
Publication: *The Chronicles of Oklahoma*

Oregon Historical Society
1230 S.W. Park Avenue
Portland, OR 97205
Telephone: (503) 222-1741

Historical Society of Pennsylvania
1300 Locust Street
Philadelphia, PA 19107
Telephone: (215) 732-6200
Publication: *The Pennsylvania Magazine of History and Biography*

Rhode Island Historical Society
52 Power Street
Providence, RI 02906
Telephone: (401) 331-8575
Publication: *Rhode Island History*

South Carolina Historical Society
100 Meeting Street
Charleston, SC 29401
Telephone: (803) 723-3225
Publication: *South Carolina Historical Magazine*

South Dakota State Historical Society
Soldiers' & Sailors' Memorial Building
E. Capitol Avenue
Pierre, SD 57501
Telephone: (605) 224-3615
Publication: *South Dakota History*

Tennessee Historical Society
403 7th Avenue N.
Nashville, TN 37219
Telephone: (615) 741-2660
Publication: *Tennessee Historical Quarterly*

Texas State Historical Association
SRH 2-306, University Station
Austin, TX 78712
Telephone: (512) 471-1525
Publication: *Southwestern Historical Quarterly*

Utah State Historical Society
300 Rio Grande
Salt Lake City, Utah 84101
Telephone: (801) 533-5755
Publication: *Utah Historical Quarterly*

Vermont Historical Society
State Street
Montpelier, VT 05602
Telephone: (802) 828-2291
Publication: *Vermont History*

Virginia Historical Society
428 North Boulevard
Richmond, VA 23221
Telephone: (804) 358-4901
Publication: *Virginia Magazine of History and Biography*

Washington State Historical Society
315 N Stadium Way
Tacoma, WA 98403
Telephone: (206) 593-2830
Publication: *Pacific Northwest Quarterly*

West Virginia Historical Society
Science and Culture Center
Charleston, WV 25305
Telephone: (304) 348-2278

State Historical Society of Wisconsin
816 State Street
Madison, WI 53706
Telephone: (608) 262-3266
Publication: *Wisconsin Magazine of History*

Wyoming State Archives and Historical Department
Barrett Building
Cheyenne, WY 82002
Telephone: (307) 777-7518
Publication: *Annals of Wyoming*

THE GENEALOGICAL SOCIETY OF UTAH AND ITS BRANCHES

The main library of the Genealogical Society is currently housed in the west wing of 50 E. North Temple Street, Salt Lake City, UT 84150, (801) 531-2531, but a new building is under construction, to be completed in 1985 or 1986, one block west on West Temple Street opposite the west gate to Temple Square. The library is open extended hours on weekdays and weekends (except Sunday) to serve the public. However, since branch libraries, located in ecclesiastical units called stakes, are manned by volunteers and have irregular hours, it is usually best to inquire by mail about hours and instructions for ordering microfilms. Address all correspondence to Branch Genealogical Library.

Eastern States Branch Genealogical Libraries

Connecticut

Hartford Connecticut Stake
Box 500
Ellington, CT 06029

Delaware

Wilmington Delaware Stake
22 Minquil Drive
Newark, DE 19713

Maine

Augusta Maine Stake
2 Sylvan Road
Hallowell, ME 04347

Maryland

Silver Spring Maryland Stake
Box 4119
Silver Spring, MD 20904

Massachusetts

Boston Massachusetts Stake
14 Wedgewood Road
Natick, MA 01760

New Hampshire

Nashua New Hampshire Stake
Box 3477
Nashua, NH 03060

New Jersey

East Brunswick New Jersey Stake
PO Box 398
E. Brunswick, NJ 08816

Morristown New Jersey Stake
1 Club Road
Chatham, NJ 07928

New York

Albany New York Stake
Box 11251
Loudonville, NY 12211

Buffalo New York Stake
c/o Fred Stoner
5074 Clearview Drive
Williamsville, NY 14221

Ithaca New York Stake
c/o Richard F. Brecht
3805 Pembroke Lane
Vestal, NY 13850

Yorktown New York Stake
12 Green Meadow Lane
New Canaan, CT 06840

New York New York Stake
Two Lincoln Square (3rd Floor)
Broadway at 65th Street
New York, NY 10023

Plainview New York Stake
168 Ontario Avenue
Massapequa, NY 11758

Rochester New York Stake
635 Blue Spruce Road
Webster, NY 14580

Syracuse New York Stake
Box 5
Syracuse, NY 13205-0005

Pennsylvania

Philadelphia Pennsylvania Stake
Box 284
Broomall, PA 19008

Pittsburgh Pennsylvania Stake
Box 16217
Pittsburgh, PA 15242

Reading Pennsylvania Stake
Box 3556
Reading, PA 19605-0556

State College Pennsylvania Stake
Box 224
State College, PA 16801

York Pennsylvania Stake
Box 584
York, PA 17405

Rhode Island

Providence Rhode Island Stake
Box 285
Quaker Hill, CT 06375

Vermont

Montpelier Vermont Stake
Box 247
Montpelier, VT 05602

Wisconsin

Madison Wisconsin Stake
1711 University Avenue
Madison, WI 53706

Southern States Branch Libraries

Alabama

Birmingham Alabama Stake
Box 76074
Birmingham, AL 35253

Huntsville Alabama Stake
Box 12595
Huntsville, AL 35802

Arkansas

Little Rock Arkansas Stake
Box 275
Jacksonville, AR 72076

Florida

Cocoa Florida Stake
Mari L. Pope
Box 1807
Cocoa, FL 32922

Gainesville Florida Stake
Box 459
Alachua, FL 32615-1167

Hialeah/Ft. Lauderdale Florida Stake
213 East 61 Street
Hialeah, FL 33013

Jacksonville Florida Stake
Box 943
Orange Park, FL 32073

Jacksonville Florida West Stake
Box 7004
Jacksonville, FL 32238-0004

Lakeland Florida Stake
Box 3087
Lakeland, FL 33802

Marianna Florida Stake
Box 1601
Marianna, FL 32446

Miami Florida Stake
Box 570081
Miami, FL 33157

Orlando Florida Stake
100 Dundee Drive
Fern Park, FL 32730

Pensacola Florida Stake
Box 30011
Pensacola, FL 32504

St. Petersburg Florida Stake
Gateway Mall Station
Box 20962
St. Petersburg, FL 33742

Tallahassee Florida Stake
Box 6687
Tallahassee, FL 32301

Tampa Florida Stake
Box 16039, Temple Terrace
Tampa, FL 33617

West Palm Beach Florida Stake
Box 2350
Boca Raton, FL 33427-2350

Georgia

Macon Georgia Stake
2065 Regent Street
Macon, GA 31211

Marietta Georgia Stake
5245 Moon Road
Powder Spring, GA 30073

Sandy Springs Georgia Stake
5694 Throwbridge Drive
Dunwoody, GA 30338

Kentucky

Hopkinsville Kentucky Stake
Route 7, Box 244
Benton, KY 42025

Lexington Kentucky Stake
Box 12101
Lexington, KY 40580

Louisville Kentucky Stake
Shelbyville Road
Box 24241
Louisville, KY 40224

Louisiana

Baton Rouge Louisiana Stake
Istrouma Box 53247
Baton Rouge, LA 70805

Shreveport Louisiana Stake
Box 5514
Shreveport, LA 71105

Mississippi

Hattiesburg Mississippi Stake
Marie Wilson
Petal, MS 39465

Missouri

Columbia Missouri Stake
Box 1752
Columbia, MO 65205

Kansas City Missouri Stake
Box 8294
Shawnee Mission, KS 66208

Liberty Missouri Stake
Box 262
Liberty, MO 64068

Springfield Missouri Stake
Box 531
Springfield, MO 65801

St. Louis Missouri Stake
Box 5807
Berkeley, MO 63134

North Carolina

Asheville North Carolina Stake
Box 889
Arden, NC 28704

Charlotte North Carolina Stake
Box 241072
Charlotte, NC 28233

Fayetteville North Carolina Stake
c/o President Edward E. Brock
2325 Hope Mills Road
Fayetteville, NC 28304

Hickory North Carolina Stake
Box 344
Hickory, NC 28603

Kinston North Carolina Stake
Box 1518
Kinston, NC 28501

Raleigh North Carolina Stake
c/o Margaret Muster
10408 Noel
Bailey Road, NC 27614

Wilmington North Carolina Stake
Route 2, Box 5-H
Hampstead, NC 28443

Oklahoma

Norman Oklahoma Stake
Box 429
Norman, OK 73070

Oklahoma City Oklahoma Stake
Box 32306
Oklahoma City, OK 73132

Tulsa Oklahoma Stake
Box 4768
Tulsa, OK 74104-0768

South Carolina

Charleston South Carolina Stake
PO Box 9434
Hanahan, SC 29410

Columbia South Carolina Stake
115 Saddlemount Drive
Hopkins, SC 29061

Greenville South Carolina Stake
Box 129
Greenville, SC 29678

Tennessee

Chattanooga Tennessee Stake
3411 Roberts Road
Chattanooga, TN 37416

Kingsport Tennessee District
Box 1818
Kingsport, TN 37662

Knoxville Tennessee Stake
Box 11312
Bearden, TN 37919

Memphis Tennessee Stake
Box 381553
Memphis, TN 38138-0008

Nashville Tennessee Stake
Box 4373
Madison, TN 37115

Texas

Austin Texas Stake
702 River Bend Drive
Georgetown, TX 78626

Beaumont Texas Stake
1815 Peterson
Nederland, TX 77627

Corpus Christi Texas Stake
Box 6364
Corpus Christi, TX 78411

Dallas Texas Stake
Box 24906
Dallas, TX 75224

Dallas Texas East Stake
Box 18212
Dallas, TX 75218

Plano Texas Stake
Box 5751
Richardson, TX 75080

El Paso Texas Stake
3651 Douglas Avenue
El Paso, TX 79903

Hurst Texas Stake
Box 1201
Hurst, TX 76053

Friendswood Texas Stake
Box 360
Friendswood, TX 77546

Houston Texas Stake
Box 961
Bellaire, TX 77401

Houston Texas South Stake
Box 12295
Houston, TX 77121-2295

Houston Texas North Stake
Box 73173
Houston, TX 77273

Longview Texas Stake
Box 6218
Longview, TX 75608

Lubbock Texas Stake
Box 6454
Lubbock, TX 79413

Odessa Texas Stake
Box 662
Odessa, TX 79760

San Antonio Texas Stake
c/o Turley Chrio. Clinic
131 Babcock Road
San Antonio, TX 78201

Virginia

Annandale Virginia Stake
Box 89
Annandale, VA 22003

Charlottesville Virginia Stake
Box 647
Charlottesville, VA 22906

Fairfax Virginia Stake
Ravensworth Box 1447
Springfield, VA 22151

Norfolk Virginia Stake
Box 62526
Virginia Beach, VA 23462

Oakton Virginia Stake
Box 279
Oakton, VA 22124

Richmond Virginia Stake
Box 8264
Richmond, VA 23226

Roanoke Virginia Stake
Box 3189
Roanoke, VA 24015-1189

West Virginia

Huntington West Virginia Stake
Box 8247
Huntington, WV 25705

Midwestern States Branch Libraries

Illinois

Champaign Illinois Stake
8 McDonald Court
Champaign, IL 61821

Chicago Heights Illinois Stake
Box 304
Lossmoor, IL 60422

Naperville Illinois Stake
5301 Benton Avenue
Downers Grove, IL 60515

Rockford Illinois Stake
1856 Hutchins
Rockford, IL 61108

Wilmette Illinois Stake
2801 Lake Avenue
Wilmette, IL 60091

Indiana

Fort Wayne Indiana Stake
Box 5250
Hazelwood Station
Fort Wayne, IN 46895

Indianapolis Indiana Stake
720 Woodale Terrace #18
Greenwood, IN 46142

Iowa

Cedar Rapids Iowa Stake
Box 1705
Cedar Rapids, IA 52406

Davenport Iowa Stake
Box 2378
Davenport, IA 52809

Des Moines Iowa Stake
1100–63rd Street
Des Moines, IA 50311

Kansas

Topeka Kansas Stake
Box 5242
Topeka, KS 66605

Wichita Kansas Stake
Box 8232
Wichita, KS 67208

Michigan

Bloomfield Hills Michigan Stake
Box 584
Bloomfield Hills, MI 48013

Grand Blanc Michigan Stake
Box 805
Grand Blanc, MI 48439

Grand Rapids Michigan South Stake
2510 Lake Drive
Grand Rapids, MI 49506

Lansing Michigan Stake
Box 801
East Lansing, MI 48823

Midland Michigan Stake
1414 Timber Drive
Midland, MI 48640

Westland Michigan Stake
Box 70
Westland, MI 48185

Minnesota

Minneapolis Minnesota Stake
1001 E. 66th Street #B
Richfield, MN 55423

St. Paul Minnesota Stake
436 East Eldridge Avenue
St. Paul, MN 55117

Nebraska

Omaha Nebraska Stake
Box 83
Boys Town, NE 68010

North Dakota

Fargo North Dakota Stake
2426 9th Street South
Fargo, ND 58103

Ohio

Cincinnati Ohio Stake
5505 Bosworth Place
Cincinnati, OH 45212

Cleveland Ohio Stake
Sylvan K. Asbury
c/o Frederick Blackburn,
Technical Supervisor
4077 Dryden Drive
North Olmstead, OH 44070

Columbus Ohio East Stake
Box 208
Reynoldsburg, OH 43068

Dayton Ohio Stake
3089 Revlon
Jettering, OH 45420

Kirtland Ohio Branch Genealogical Library
c/o Mike Jennings
8800 Billings Road
Kirtland, OH 44094

Toledo Ohio Stake
Ward Collings
Box 430
Maumee, OH 43537

South Dakota

Rapid City South Dakota
PO Box 9001
Rapid City, SD 57701

Sioux Falls South Dakota Stake
Box 1356
Sioux City, SD 51101

Wisconsin

Appleton Wisconsin District
Box 321
Shawano, WI 54166

Beloit Wisconsin Stake
301 Garden Drive
Belvidere, IL 61008

Milwaukee Wisconsin Stake
3061 W. Green Avenue
Milwaukee, WI 53221

Mountain States Branch Libraries

Arizona

Camp Verde Arizona Stake
Box 1067
Cottonwood, AZ 86326

Flagstaff Arizona Stake
Box 446
Flagstaff, AZ 86002

Globe Arizona Stake
Box 2393
Globe, AZ 85501

Holbrook Arizona Stake
Box 455
Holbrook, AZ 86025

Mesa Arizona Stake
464 East First Avenue
Mesa, AZ 85204

Page Arizona Stake
Box 278
Page, AZ 86040

Phoenix Arizona Stake
2235 W. Verde Lane
Phoenix, AZ 85015

Phoenix Arizona North Stake
1144 West Myrtle Avenue
Phoenix, AZ 85063

Phoenix Arizona West Stake
Box 14304
Phoenix, AZ 85063

Prescott Arizona Stake
Box 2503
Prescott, AZ 86302

St. David Arizona Stake
Box 280
St. David, AZ 85630

Safford-Thatcher Arizona Stake
Box 1218
Safford, AZ 85546

St. Johns Arizona Stake
Box 59
St. Johns, AZ 85936

Show Low Arizona Stake
Box 443
Show Low, AZ 85901

Snowflake Arizona Stake
Box 800
Snowflake, AZ 85937

Tucson Arizona Stake
500 South Langley
Tucson, AZ 85710

Winslow Arizona Stake
Box 12
Winslow, AZ 86047

Yuma Arizona Stake
Box 1418
Yuma, AZ 85364

Colorado

Arvada Colorado Stake
Box 1247
Arvada, CO 80004

Boulder Colorado Stake
Box 3210
Boulder, CO 80307

Colorado Springs Colorado Stake
411 East Del Norte
Colorado Springs, CO 80907

Columbine Colorado Stake
Box 531
Littleton, CO 80160-0531

Cortez Colorado Stake
28103 Country Road H
Cortez, CO 81321

Denver Colorado Stake
Box 22403
Wellshire Station
Denver, CO 80222

Denver Colorado North Stake
Box 33008
Northglenn, CO 80233

Durango Colorado Stake
#5 Pine Tree Way
Durango, CO 81301

Fort Collins Colorado Stake
Box 9556
Fort Collins, CO 80525

Grand Junction Colorado Stake
Box 40003
Grand Junction, CO 81504

LaJara Colorado Stake
Box 146
LaJara, CO 81140

Littleton Colorado Stake
Box 2801
Southglenn Branch
Littleton, CO 80161

Meeker Colorado Stake
Box 126
Glenwood Springs, CO 81601

Montrose Colorado Stake
PO Box 1507
Montrose, CO 81401

Pueblo Colorado Stake
c/o Frieda Nielson
1820 Garwood Drive
Pueblo, CO 81005

Montana

Billings Montana Stake
3617 Poly Drive
Billings, MT 59102

Billings Montana East Stake
Box 50182
Billings, MT 59105

Bozeman Montana Stake
Box 697
Bozeman, MT 59715

Butte Montana Stake
220 Janney Road – Route 1
Butte, MT 59701

Great Falls Montana Stake
PO Box 803
Great Falls, MT 59403

Helena Montana Stake
PO Box 811
Helena, MT 59601

Kalispell Montana Stake
Box 3607
Kalispell, MT 59901

Missoula Montana Stake
Box 3026
Missoula, MT 59806

New Mexico

Albuquerque New Mexico Stake
Box 3568
Albuquerque, NM 87110

Albuquerque New Mexico East Stake
2281 35th Street
Los Alamos, NM 87554

Farmington New Mexico Stake
Box 23
Farmington, NM 87499

Gallup New Mexico Stake
Box 1728
Gallup, NM 87301

Grants New Mexico Stake
1305 Franciscan
Grants, NM 87020

Las Cruces New Mexico Stake
Box 471
Las Cruces, NM 88004

Roswell New Mexico Stake
Box 1417
Roswell, NM 88201

Santa Fe New Mexico Stake
Box 6012
Santa Fe, NM 87502

Wyoming

Afton Wyoming Stake
Box 293
Afton, WY 83110

Casper Wyoming Stake
Box 2171
Casper, WY 82609

Cody Wyoming Stake
1030 Red Butte
Cody, WY 82414

Evanston Wyoming Stake
250 County Road
Evanston, WY 82930

Gillette Wyoming Stake
Box 744
Sheridan, WY 82801

Green River Wyoming Stake
Box 486
Green River, WY 82935

Kemmerer Wyoming Stake
c/o Inez Morris
921 3rd West Avenue
Kemmerer, WY 83101

Lovell Wyoming Stake
Box 547
Lovell, WY 82431

Rock Springs Wyoming Stake
Box 1043
Rock Springs, WY 82901

Worland Wyoming Stake
Box 1296
Worland, WY 82401

Wyoming Stake
c/o Laramie County Library
2800 Central Avenue
Cheyenne, WY 82201

California Branch Libraries

Anaheim California Stake
Box 3786
Anaheim, CA 92803

Bakersfield California Stake
Box 9445
Stockdale Branch
Bakersfield, CA 93309

Barstow California Stake
Box 1258
Barstow, CA 92311

Blythe California Stake
1203 Broadway
Needles, Ca 92363

Camarillo California Stake
1487 Jilia Court
Camarillo, CA 93010

Carlsbad California Stake
3866 Althea Lane
Carlsbad, CA 92008

Cerritos California Stake
12310 Telegraph Road
Santa Fe Springs, CA 90670

Cerritos California West Stake
21122 So. Alburtis
Lakewood, CA 90715

Chico California Stake
Box 4274
Chico, CA 95927

Covina California Stake
Box 833
West Covina, CA 91793

Cypress California Stake
Box 5874
Buena Park, CA 90622

El Centro California Stake
Box 2537
El Centro, CA 92243

Escondido California Stake
609 N. Citrus
Escondido, CA 92027

Eureka California Stake
2734 Dolbeer Stake
Eureka, CA 95501

Fairfield California Stake
Box 373
Fairfield, CA 94533

Fresno California Stake
4974 No. Fresno Street
Suite 565
Fresno, CA 93726

Garden Grove California Stake
Box 1114
Garden Grove, CA 92641

Glendale California Stake
Box 9010
Verdugo Viejo Station
Glendale, CA 91206

Gridley California Stake
Box 902
Gridley, CA

Hacienda Heights Stake
Box 5038
Hacienda Heights, CA 91745

Hemet California Stake
Box 1346
Hemet, CA 92343

La Crescenta California Stake
Box 80333
La Canada, CA 91214

Lancaster California Stake
44143 Elm Street
Lancaster, CA 93534

Long Beach California East Stake
Box 4362
Long Beach, CA 90804

Los Angeles California East Stake
Box 141
Alhambra, CA 91802

Los Angeles California Santa Clarita Stake
Box 1683
Canyon Country, CA 91351

Menlo Park California Stake
Box 1084
Menlo Park, CA 94250

Mission Viejo California Stake
Box 3585
Mission Viejo, CA 92690

Modesto California Stake
2115 North Danair Avenue
Turlock, CA 95380

Monterey California Stake
Box 683
Seaside, CA 93962

Napa California Stake
Box 244
Napa, CA 94559-244

Newbury Park California Stake
613 Paeso LaPerla
Newbury Park, CA 91320

Oakland California Stake
4780 Lincoln Avenue
Oakland, CA 94602

Orange California Stake
596 So. Dumas Road
Orange, CA 92669

Palmdale California Stake
Box 879
Palmdale, CA 93550

Palm Springs California Stake
32-660 Whispering Palm
Cathedral City, CA 92234

Pasadena California Stake
Box 5182
East Pasadena, CA 91107

Redding California Stake
Box 3492
Redding, CA 96049-3492

Ridgecrest California Stake
Box 1090
Ridgecrest, CA 93555

Riverside California Stake
Box 4222
Riverside, CA 92514

Riverside California West Stake
Box 7665
Riverside, CA 91503

Sacramento California Stake
5343 Halsted Avenue
Carmichael, CA 95608

San Bernardino California Stake
Box 432
San Bernardino, CA 92403

San Diego California Stake
3705–10th Avenue
San Diego, CA 92103

San Jose California Stake
2175 Santiago Street
San Jose, CA 95150

San Luis Obispo California Stake
Box 695
San Luis Obispo, CA 93401

Santa Barbara California Stake
Box 26
Goleta, CA 93017

Santa Clara California Stake
c/o Naomi Gerns
1936 Bohannon Drive
Santa Clara, CA 95050

Santa Maria California Stake
c/o Janet Maughan
822 E. Laguna
Santa Maria, CA 93455

Santa Rosa California Stake
Box 6371
Santa Rosa, CA 95401

Simi Valley California Stake
Box 3276
Simi Valley, CA 93063

Southern California Area Branch Genealogical Library
10741 Santa Monica Boulevard
Los Angeles, CA 90025

Stockton California Stake
Box 7042
Stockton, CA 95207

Upland California Stake
Box 1290
Upland, CA 91786

Ventura California Stake
Box 3517
Ventura, CA 93004

Whittier California Stake
14043 Eastridge Drive
Whittier, CA 90606

Northwestern States and Hawaii Branch Libraries

Alaska

Anchorage Alaska Stake
Box 4-2560
Anchorage, AK 99509

Fairbanks Alaska Stake
Box 73263
Fairbanks, AK 99701

Hawaii

Hilo Hawaii Stake
17 Mikioi Street
Hilo, Hawaii 96720

Honolulu Hawaii Stake
1560 South Beretania Street
Honolulu, HI 96826

Honolulu Hawaii West Stake
Box 17761
Honolulu, HI 96819

Kaneohe Hawaii Stake
Box 1366
Kaneohe, HI 96744

Kona Hawaii Stake
Box C
Kailua, Kona, HI 96740

Laie Hawaii Stake
c/o BYU-Hawaii
Box 49
Laie, Oahu, HI 96762

Idaho

Bear Lake Idaho Stake
Bear Lake County Library
Montpelier, ID 83254

Blackfoot Idaho Stake
Box 759
Blackfoot, ID 83221

Blackfoot Idaho West Stake
Box C
Moreland, ID 83256

Boise Idaho Stake
Box 5775
Boise, ID 83705

Burley Idaho Stake
Box 1227
Burley, ID 83318

Caldwell Idaho Stake
Box 794
Caldwell, ID 83605

Driggs Idaho Stake
Box 95
Driggs, ID 83422

Firth Idaho Stake
Box #24
Firth, ID 83236

Idaho Falls Idaho Stake
720 North Wabash Avenue
Idaho Falls, ID 83401

Idaho Falls Ammon Stake
Box 1612
Idaho Falls, ID 83401

Idaho Falls Ammon West Stake
1975 Eagle Drive
Idaho Falls, ID 83401

Idaho Falls West Stake
854 Claire View Lane
Idaho Falls, ID 83401

Idaho Falls East Stake
1652 Johnson
Idaho Falls, ID 83401

Iona Idaho Stake
Box 514
Iona, ID 83427

Lewiston Idaho Stake
Box 267
Lewiston, ID 83501

Malad Idaho Stake
Box 214
Malad, ID 83252

Meridian Idaho East Stake
4167 Columbine Street
Boise, ID 83704

Moore Idaho Stake
Box 113
Arco, ID 83213

Nampa Idaho Stake
Box 592
Nampa, ID 83651

Pocatello Idaho Stake
156-1/2 South 6th Avenue
Pocatello, ID 83201

Post Falls Idaho Stake
Box 512
Post Falls, ID 83854

Salmon Idaho Stake
Box 768
Salmon, ID 83467

Shelley Idaho Stake
Box V
Shelley, ID 83274

Twin Falls Idaho Stake
401 Maurice St. No.
Twin Falls, ID 83301

Upper Snake River Stake
Ricks College Library
Rexburg, ID 83440

Nevada

Elko Nevada Stake
Box 651
Elko, NV 89801

Ely Nevada Stake
Box 599
Ely, NV 89301

Fallon Nevada Stake
Box 69
Fallon, NV 89406

Las Vegas Nevada Stake
509 S. Ninth Street
Las Vegas, NV 89101

Logandale Nevada Stake
Box 409
Logandale, NV 89021

Reno Nevada Stake
Washoe Public Library
301 South Center
Reno, NV 89501

Sparks Nevada
Box 1882
Sparks, NV 89431

Oregon

Beaverton Oregon Stake
Box 1562
Beaverton, OR 97075

Bend Oregon Stake
Box 6021
Bend, OR 97701

Coos Bay Oregon Stake
Box 1211
Coos Bay, OR 97420

Corvallis Oregon Stake
Box 986
Corvallis, OR 97339

Eugene Oregon West Stake
3550 West 18th Street
Eugene, OR 97402

Grants Pass Oregon
Box 121
Grants Pass, OR 97526

Gresham Oregon Stake
Box 339
Fairview, OR 97024

Klamath Falls Oregon Stake
Box 1477
Klamath Falls, OR 97601

LaGrande Oregon Stake
Box 31
LaGrande, OR 97850

Lake Oswego Oregon Stake
Box 25
West Linn, OR 97068

Medford Oregon Stake
Box 1801
Medford, OR 97501

Nyssa Oregon Stake
Route 1, Box 945
Ontario, OR 97914

Oregon City Oregon Stake
Box 684
Oregon City, OR 97045

Portland Oregon Stake
Box 14786
Portland, OR 97214

Portland Oregon East Stake
Box 20204
Portland, OR 97220

Prineville Oregon Stake
Box 709
Prineville, OR 97754

Roseburg Oregon Stake
Box 1143
Roseburg, OR 97470

Salem Oregon Stake
7305 Lardon Road NE
Salem, OR 97302

Salem Oregon North Stake
Box 7667
Salem, OR 97303

The Dalles Oregon Stake
Box 278
The Dalles, OR 97058

Utah

Beaver Utah Stake
Box 789
Beaver, UT 84713

Blanding Utah Stake
Box 772
Blanding, UT 84511

Bountiful Utah Heights Stake
c/o Bishop Edgar Drake
981 East 250 South
Bountiful, UT 84010

Brigham City Utah South Stake
10 South 4th East
Brigham City, UT 84302

Cache Stake
Box L
Logan, UT 84321

Castledale Stake
Box 415
Orangeville, UT 84537

Cedar City Utah Stake
Box G
Cedar City, UT 84720

Delta Utah Stake
Box 395
Delta, UT 84624

Duchesne Utah Stake
Drawer O
Duchesne, UT 84201

Fillmore Utah Stake
Box 1818
Fillmore, UT 84631

Heber City Regional Branch Genealogical Library
Box 146
Heber City, UT 84032

Hurricane Utah Stake
Box 1550
Hurricane, UT 84737

Kanab Utah Stake
Box 808
Kanab, UT 84741

Lehi Utah Stake
50 E. North Temple, Room 264W
Salt Lake City, UT 84150

Loa Utah Stake
Box 278
Loa, UT 84747

Moroni Utah Stake
Box 410
Moroni, UT 84646

Mount Pleasant Utah Stake
Box 797
Mount Pleasant, UT 84647

Nephi Utah Stake
Box 121
Nephi, UT 84648

Ogden Utah Stake
539 24th Street
Ogden, UT 84401

Parowan Utah Stake
Box 875
Parowan, UT 84761

Price Utah Stake
Box 14
Price, UT 84501

Richfield Utah Regional Branch Genealogical Library
Box 79
Richfield, UT 84701

Roosevelt Utah Stake
Box 1989
Roosevelt, UT 84066

Rose Park North Stake
c/o President Donald Phillips
1521 Goodwin Avenue
Salt Lake City, Utah 84116

Sandy Utah East Stake
10208 South 1280 East
Sandy, UT 84070

Santaquin Utah Stake
Box 657
Santaquin, UT 84655

South Jordan Utah Stake
1078 West 9840 South
Riverton, UT 84065

St. George Utah Stake
Box 417
St. George, UT 84770

Springville Utah Stake
686 E. Cutler Avenue
Springville, UT 84663

Tremonton-Garland Utah Stake
Box 126
Tremonton, UT 84337

Utah Valley Branch
Genealogical Library
4226 HBL Library
Brigham Young University
Provo, UT 84602

Uintah Basin Branch
Genealogical Library
Box 398
Vernal, UT 84078

Washington

Bellevue Washington Stake
Box 1502
Bellevue, WA 98009

Bellingham Washington Stake
Box 860
Ferndale, WA 98248

Bremerton Washington Stake
Box 26, Manette Stake
Bremerton, WA 98310

Everett Washington Stake
Box 1685
Everett, WA 98201

Kennewick Washington Stake
317 W. 10th Avenue
Kennewick, WA 99336

Longview Washington Stake
Box 247
Longview, WA 98632

Moses Lake Washington Stake
449 Fircrest
Moses Lake, WA 98837

Mount Vernon Washington
Stake
421 North Barker
Mount Vernon, WA 98273

Olympia Washington Stake
715 Hansen Street
Olympia, WA 98503

Pasco Washington Stake
Route 5, Box 5025
Pasco, WA 99302

Pullman Washington Stake
Box 5
College Station
Pullman, WA 99163

Puyallup Washington Stake
Box 612
Sumner, WA 98390

Ephrata Washington Stake
Box 516
Quincy, WA 98848

Richland Washington Stake
1406 Perkins
Richland, WA 99352

Seattle Washington North
Stake
5701 8th Avenue NE
Seattle, WA 98105

Spokane Washington Stake
N. 919 Pines Road
Spokane, WA 99206

Tacoma Washington Stake
5502–36th Street West
Tacoma, WA 98466

Vancouver Washington Stake
12009 SE 11th Street
Vancouver, WA 98664

Walla Walla Washington Stake
Box 1236
Walla Walla, WA 99362

Wenatchee Washington Stake
c/o Lois Carter
Box 7093
East Wenatchee, WA 98848

Yakima Washington Stake
Route 4, Box 280-A
Yakima, WA 98908

Appendix E

SELECTED RESEARCH LIBRARIES

This list of selected research libraries includes those mentioned as depositories in the text and others with substantial genealogy materials. Many specialized research archives and libraries are named with addresses in the various chapters that describe those problems. See Appendix A for addresses of National Archives and branches, Appendix B for state archives, Appendix C for state historical societies, Appendix D for addresses of branch libraries of the Genealogical Society of Utah, and Appendix G for other Genealogical Societies in the United States. Their holdings range from history to genealogy to heraldry. As research libraries, they collect books, periodicals, microforms, and newspapers of interest to genealogists. Public and university libraries also have substantial collections of interest to genealogists, some housed in special genealogy rooms, but most inter-filed with their other materials. Addresses and holdings of those nearest you and those in the areas where your ancestors come from are listed in the *American Library Directory*. published biannually by R. R. Bowker Company, the *Directory of Historical Societies in the U.S. and Canada* published biannually by the American Association for State and Local History; the *Directory of Genealogical Societies in the U.S. and Canada* published biannually by Libra Publications, Box 29, Linthicum Heights, MD 21090; and the *American Museums Directory*, published periodically by the American Museums Associtation. These directories are available at your local public library.

Alabama

Institute of Genealogical and Historical Research
Samford University Library
800 Lakeshore Drive
Birmingham, AL 35208

California

Los Angeles Public Library
630 West Fifth Street
Los Angeles, CA 90017

Genealogical Research Center
Dept. of Special Collections
San Francisco Public Library
Civic Center
San Francisco, CA 94102

Sutro Library
San Francisco State University
480 Westminster Drive
San Francisco, CA 94132

Huntington Library
1161 Oxford Road
San Marino, CA 91108

Colorado

Denver Public Library
1357 Broadway
Denver, CO 80203

District of Columbia

Folger Shakepeare Library
201 E. Capitol Street
Washington, DC 20003

Genealogical Dept.
Library of Congress
Washington, DC 20540

National Genealogical Society Library
1921 Sunderland Place N.W.
Washington, DC 20036

National Society of the Daughters of the American Revolution Library
1776 D Street N.W.
Washington, DC 20006

Georgia

Atlantic Public Library
126 Carnegie Way N.W.
Atlanta, GA 30303

Hawaii

DAR Memorial Library
1914 Makiki Heights Drive
Honolulu, HI 96822

Illinois

Newberry Library
60 W. Walton Street
Chicago, IL 60610

Indiana

Fort Wayne Public Library
900 Webster Street
Fort Wayne, IN 46802

Kentucky

Filson Club Library
118 W. Breckenridge Street
Louisville, KY 40202

Louisiana

New Orleans Public Library
Genealogy Section
219 Loyola Avenue
New Orleans, LA 70140

Massachusetts

Boston Athenean
10 ½ Beacon Street
Boston, MA 02108

Boston Public Library
Box 286
Boston, MA 02117

New England Historic and Genealogical Society Library
101 Newbury Street
Boston, MA 02116

Yenching Institute
Harvard University
Cambridge, MA 02138

American Antiquarian Society
185 Salisbury Street
Worcester, MA 01609

Maryland

George Peabody Collection
Enoch Pratt Free Library
400 Cathedral Street
Baltimore, MD

Michigan

Burton Historical Library
Detroit Public Library
5201 Woodward Avenue
Detroit, MI 48202

Nebraska

Nebraska DAR Library
202 West 4th Street
Alliance, NE 69301

New York

Columbia University East Asian Library
116th Street and Broadway
New York, NY 10027

New York City Public Library
Local History and Genealogy Division
Fifth Avenue & 42nd Street
New York, NY 10018

Roswell P. Flower Genealogy Library
229 Washington Street
Watertown, NY 13601

Ohio

Case Western Reserve University Libraries
11161 E. Boulevard
Cleveland, OH 44106

Cleveland Public Library
325 Superior Avenue
Cleveland, OH 44114

Oklahoma

State DAR Library
Historical Building
Oklahoma City, OK 73102

Oregon

Portland Genealogical Forum
Neighbors of Woodcraft Building
1410 SW Morrison
Portland, OR 97205

Pennsylvnia

Free Library of Philadelphia
Logan Square
Philadelphia, PA 19141

South Carolina

South Caroliniana Library
University of South Carolina
Columbia, SC 29201

Texas

Dallas Public Library
Texas Historic and Genealogical Department
1954 Commerce Street
Dallas, TX 75201

Genealogical Research Library
4524 Edmondson Avenue
Dallas, TX 75205

Utah

The Genealogical Helper Library
Everton Publishers, Inc.
3223 S. Main Street
Nibley, UT 84321

Genealogy and Microforms Library
Harold B. Lee Library
Brigham Young University
Provo, UT 84602

Genealogical Society of Utah
50 E. North Temple
Salt Lake City, UT 84150

Vermont

Genealogical Library
Bennington Museum
Bennington, VT 05201

Washington

Seattle Public Library
1000 Fourth Avenue
Seattle, WA 98104

Appendix F

WHERE TO WRITE FOR VITAL RECORDS

Taken from *Where To Write for Vital Records*, U.S. Department of Health and Human Services Publication No. (PHS) 82-1142.

Place of event	*Cost of copy*	*Address*	*Remarks*
ALABAMA			
Birth or Death	$5.00	Bureau of Vital Statistics State Department of Public Health Montgomery, AL 36130	State office has had records since January 1908. Additional copies at same time are $2.00 each. Fee for special searches is $5.00 per hour.
Marriage	$5.00	Same as Birth or Death	State office has had records since August 1936.
	Varies	See remarks	Probate Judge in county where license was issued.
Divorce	$5.00	Same as Birth or Death	State office has had records since January 1950.
	Varies	See remarks	Clerk or Register of Court of Equity in county where divorce was granted.
ALASKA			
Birth or Death	$3.00	Department of Health and Social Services Bureau of Vital Statistics Pouch H-02G Juneau, AK 99811	State office has had records since 1913.
Marriage	$3.00	Same as Birth or Death	Records since 1913.
Divorce	$3.00	Same as Birth or Death	Records since 1950.
	Varies	See remarks	Clerk of the Superior Court in judicial district where divorce was granted. Juneau and Ketchikan (First District), Nome (Second District), Anchorage (Third District), Fairbanks (Fourth District).
AMERICAN SAMOA			
Birth or Death	$1.00	Registrar of Vital Statistics Vital Statistics Section Government of American Samoa Pago Pago, AS 96799	Registrar has had records since 1900.
Marriage	$1.00	Same as Birth or Death	
Divorce	$1.00	Same as Birth or Death	
ARIZONA			
Birth or Death	$3.00	Vital Records Section Arizona Department of Health Services P.O. Box 3887 Phoenix, AZ 85030	State office has had records since July 1909 and abstracts of records filed in counties before then.
Marriage	Varies	See remarks	Clerk of Superior Court in county where license was issued.
Divorce	Varies	See remarks	Clerk of Superior Court in county where divorce was granted.
ARKANSAS			
Birth	$2.00	Division of Vital Records Arkansas Department of Health 4815 West Markham Street Little Rock, AR 72201	State office has had records since February 1914 and some original Little Rock and Fort Smith records from 1881.
Death	$3.00		
Marriage	$2.00	Same as Birth or Death	Records since 1917.
	$2.00	See remarks	Full certified copy may be obtained from County Clerk in county where license was issued.

Place of event	*Cost of copy*	*Address*	*Remarks*
Divorce	$2.00	Same as Birth or Death	Coupons since 1923.
	Varies	See remarks	Full certified copy may be obtained from Circuit or Chancery Clerk in county where divorce was granted.
CALIFORNIA			
Birth or Death	$3.00	Vital Statistics Branch Department of Health Services 410 N Street Sacramento, CA 95814	State office has had records since July 1905. For earlier records, write to County Recorder in county where event occurred.
Marriage	$3.00	Same as Birth or Death	State office has had records since July 1905. For earlier records, write to County Recorder in county where event occurred.
Divorce	$3.00	Same as Birth or Death	Fee is for search and identification of county where certified copy can be obtained. Certified copies are not available from State Health Department.
	Varies	See remarks	Clerk of Superior Court in county where divorce was granted.
CANAL ZONE			
Birth or Death	$2.00	Panama Canal Commission Vital Statistics Clerk APO Miami 34011	Records available from May 1904 to September 1979.
Marriage	$1.00	Same as Birth or Death	Records available from May 1904 to September 1979.
Divorce	$0.50	Same as Birth or Death	Records available from May 1904 to September 1979.
COLORADO			
Birth or Death	$2.00	Vital Records Section Colorado Department of Health 4210 East 11th Avenue Denver, CO 80220	State office has had death records since 1900 and birth records since 1910. State office also has birth records for some counties for years before 1910.
Marriage	See remarks	Same as Birth or Death	Statewide index of records for all years except 1940-75. Inquiries will be forwarded to appropriate office. Certified copies are not available from State Health Department.
	Varies	See remarks	County Clerk in county where license was issued.
Divorce	See remarks	Same as Birth or Death	Statewide index of records for all years except 1940-67. Inquiries will be forwarded to appropriate office. Certified copies are not available from State Health Department.
	Varies	See remarks	Clerk of District Court in county where divorce was granted.
CONNECTICUT			
Birth or Death Short form	$3.00 $2.00	Department of Health Services Vital Records Section Division of Health Statistics 79 Elm Street Hartford, CT 06115	State office has had records since July 1897. For earlier records, write to Registrar of Vital Statistics in town or city where event occurred.
Marriage	$3.00	Same as Birth or Death	Records since July 1897.
	$3.00	See remarks	Registrar of Vital Statistics in town where license was issued.
Divorce	See remarks	Same as Birth or Death	Index of records since 1947. Inquiries will be forwarded to appropriate office. Certified copies are not available from State office.
	$3.00	See remarks	Clerk of Superior Court in county where divorce was granted.
DELAWARE			
Birth or Death	$2.50	Bureau of Vital Statistics Division of Public Health Department of Health and Social Services State Health Building Dover, DE 19901	State office has records for 1861 to 1863 and since 1881 but no records for 1864 to 1880.
Marriage	$2.50	Same as Birth or Death	Records since 1847.
Divorce	See remarks	Same as Birth or Death	Records since 1935. Inquiries will be forwarded to appropriate office. Fee for search and verification of essential facts of divorce, $2.50. Certified copies are not available from State office.

Place of event	*Cost of copy*	*Address*	*Remarks*
	$2.00	See remarks	Prothonotary in county where divorce was granted up to 1975. For divorces granted after 1975 the parties concerned should contact Family Court in the county where the divorce was granted.
DISTRICT OF COLUMBIA			
Birth or Death	$3.00	Vital Records Branch 615 Pennsylvania Avenue, NW Washington, D.C. 20004	Office has had death records since 1855 and birth records since 1871, but no death records were filed during the Civil War.
Marriage	$3.00	Same as Birth or Death	Records since January 1, 1982.
	$5.00	Marriage Bureau 515 5th Street, NW Washington, D.C. 20001	Fee for proof of marriage, $2.50; proof of age, $2.50.
Divorce	$3.00	Same as Birth or Death	Records since January 1, 1982
	Varies	Clerk, Superior Court for the District of Columbia, Family Division 500 Indiana Avenue, NW Washington, D.C. 20001	Records since September 16, 1956.
	Varies	Clerk, U.S. District Court for the District of Columbia Washington, D.C. 20001	Records before September 16, 1956.
FLORIDA			
Birth or Death	$2.00	Department of Health and Rehabilitative Services Office of Vital Statistics P.O. Box 210 Jacksonville, FL 32231	State office has had some birth records since April 1865 and some death records since August 1877. The majority of records date from January 1917. (If the exact date is unknown, the fee is $2.00 for the first year searched and $1.00 for each additional year up to a maximum of $25.00. Fee includes one copy of record if found.)
Marriage	$2.00	Same as Birth or Death	Records since June 6, 1927. (If the exact date is unknown, the fee is $2.00 for the first year searched and $1.00 for each additional year up to a maximum of $25.00. Fee includes one copy of record if found.)
	$2.00	See remarks	Clerk of Circuit Court in county where divorce was granted.
Divorce	$2.00	Same as Birth or Death	Records since June 6, 1927. (If exact date is unknown, the fee is $2.00 for the first year searched and $1.00 for each additional year up to a maximum of $25.00. Fee includes one copy of record if found.)
	Varies	See remarks	Clerk of Circuit Court in county where divorce was granted.
GEORGIA			
Birth or Death	$3.00	Georgia Department of Human Resources Vital Records Unit Room 217-H 47 Trinity Avenue, SW Atlanta, GA 30334	State office has had records since January 1919. For earlier records in Atlanta or Savannah, write to County Health Department in county where event occurred. Additional copies of same record ordered at same time are $1.00 each.
Marriage	See remarks	Same as Birth or Death	Centralized State records since June 9, 1952. Certified copies are not issued at State office. Inquiries will be forwarded to appropriate office.
	$3.00	See remarks	Probate Judge in county where license was issued.
Divorce	See remarks	Same as Birth or Death	Centralized State records since June 9, 1952. Certified copies are not issued at State office. Inquiries will be forwarded to appropriate office.
	Varies	See remarks	Clerk of Superior Court in county where divorce was granted.
GUAM			
Birth or Death	$2.00	Office of Vital Statistics Department of Public Health and Social Services Government of Guam P.O. Box 2816 Agana, GU, M.I. 96910	Office has had records since October 26, 1901.

Place of event	*Cost of copy*	*Address*	*Remarks*
Marriage	$2.00	Same as Birth or Death	
Divorce	Varies	See remarks	Clerk, Superior Court of Guam, Agana, GU, M.I. 96910.
HAWAII			
Birth or Death	$2.00	Research and Statistics Office State Department of Health P.O. Box 3378 Honolulu, HI 96801	State office has had records since 1853.
Marriage	$2.00	Same as Birth or Death	
Divorce	$2.00	Same as Birth or Death	Records since July 1951.
	Varies	See remarks	Circuit Court in county where divorce was granted.
IDAHO			
Birth or Death	$4.00	Bureau of Vital Statistics, Standards, and Local Health Services State Department of Health and Welfare Statehouse Boise, ID 83720	State office has had records since 1911. For records from 1907 to 1911, write to County Recorder in county where event occurred.
Marriage	$4.00	Same as Birth or Death	Records since 1947.
	Varies	See remarks	County Recorder in county where license was issued.
Divorce	$4.00	Same as Birth or Death	Records since January 1947.
	Varies	See remarks	County Recorder in county where divorce was granted.
ILLINOIS			
Birth or Death	$3.00	Office of Vital Records State Department of Public Health 535 West Jefferson Street Springfield, IL 62761	State office has had records since January 1916. For earlier records and for copies of State records since January 1916, write to County Clerk in county where event occurred. ($3.00 fee is for search of files and one copy of record if found. Additional copies of same record ordered at same time are $2.00 each.)
Marriage	See remarks	Same as Birth or Death	Records since January 1962. All items may be verified (fee $3.00). Inquiries will be forwarded to appropriate office. Certified copies are not available from State office.
	$3.00	See remarks	County Clerk in county where license was issued.
Divorce	See remarks	Same as Birth or Death	Records since January 1962. Some items may be verified (fee $3.00). Certified copies are not available from State office.
	Varies	See remarks	Clerk of Circuit Court in county where divorce was granted.
INDIANA			
Birth or Death	$4.00	Division of Vital Records State Board of Health 1330 West Michigan Street P.O. Box 1964 Indianapolis, IN 46206	State office has had birth records since October 1907 and death records since 1900. Additional copies of same record ordered at same time are $1.00 each. For earlier records, write to Health Officer in city or county where event occurred.
Marriage	See remarks	Same as Birth or Death	Marriage Index since 1958. Inquiries will be forwarded to appropriate office. Certified copies are not available from State Health Department.
	Varies	See remarks	Clerk of Circuit Court or Clerk of Superior Court in county where license was issued.
Divorce	Varies	See remarks	County Clerk in county where divorce was granted.
IOWA			
Birth or Death	$4.00	Iowa State Department of Health Vital Records Section Lucas State Office Building Des Moines, IA 50319	State office has had records since July 1880.
Marriage	$4.00	Same as Birth or Death	State Office has had records since July 1880.

Place of event	Cost of copy	Address	Remarks
Divorce	See remarks	Same as Birth or Death	Brief statistical record only since 1906. Inquiries will be forwarded to appropriate office. Certified copies are not available from State Health Department.
	$4.00	See remarks	Clerk of District Court in county where divorce was granted.
KANSAS			
Birth or Death	$3.00	Bureau of Registration and Health Statistics Kansas State Department of Health and Environment 6700 South Topeka Avenue Topeka, KS 66620	State office has had records since July 1911. For earlier records, write to County Clerk in county where event occurred. Additional copies of same record ordered at same time are $2.00 each.
Marriage	$3.00	Same as Birth or Death	Records since May 1913.
	Varies	See remarks	Probate Judge in county where license was issued.
Divorce	$3.00	Same as Birth or Death	Records since July 1951.
	Varies	See remarks	Clerk of District Court in county where divorce was granted.
KENTUCKY			
Birth or Death	$4.00	Office of Vital Statistics Department for Human Resources 275 East Main Street Frankfort, KY 40621	State office has had records since January 1911 and some records for the cities of Louisville, Lexington, Covington, and Newport before then.
Marriage	$4.00	Same as Birth or Death	Records since June 1958.
	Varies	See remarks	Clerk of County Court in county where license was issued.
Divorce	$4.00	Same as Birth or Death	Records since June 1958.
	Varies	See remarks	Clerk of Circuit Court in county where decree was issued.
LOUISIANA			
Birth or Death	$3.00	Division of Vital Records Office of Health Services and Environmental Quality P.O. Box 60630 New Orleans, LA 70160	State office has had records since July 1914. Birth records for City of New Orleans are available from 1790, and death records from 1803.
Short Form	$2.00		
Marriage	See remarks	Same as Birth or Death	Certified copies are not available from State Health Department. Inquiries will be forwarded to appropriate office.
Orleans Parish	$3.00	Same as Birth or Death	
Other Parishes	Varies	See remarks	Certified copies are issued by Clerk of Court in parish where license was issued.
Divorce	Varies	See remarks	Clerk of Court in parish where divorce was granted. For Orleans Parish, copies may be obtained from State office for $2.00.
MAINE			
Birth or Death	$2.00	Office of Vital Records Human Services Building Station II State House Augusta, ME 04333	State office has had records since 1892. For earlier records, write to the municipality where event occurred.
Marriage	$2.00	Same as Birth or Death	
	$2.00	See remarks	Town Clerk in town where license was issued.
Divorce	$2.00	Same as Birth or Death	Records since January 1892.
	$5.00	See remarks	Clerk of District Court in judicial division where divorce was granted.
MARYLAND			
Birth or Death	$2.00	Division of Vital Records State Department of Health and Mental Hygiene State Office Building P.O. Box 13146 201 West Preston Street Baltimore, MD 21203	State office has had records since August 1898. Records for City of Baltimore are available from January 1875.

Place of event	*Cost of copy*	*Address*	*Remarks*
Marriage	$2.00	Same as Birth or Death	Records since June 1951.
	See remarks	See remarks	Clerk of Circuit Court in county where license was issued or Clerk of Court of Common Pleas of Baltimore City (for licenses issued in City of Baltimore).
Divorce	See remarks	Same as Birth or Death	Records since January 1961. Certified copies are not available from State office. Some items may be verified. Inquiries will be forwarded to appropriate office.
	Varies	See remarks	Clerk of Circuit Court in county where divorce was granted.
MASSACHUSETTS			
Birth or Death	$3.00	Registry of Vital Records and Statistics Room 105, McCormack Building 1 Ashburton Place Boston, MA 02108	State office has had records, except for Boston, since 1841. For earlier records, write to the City or Town Clerk in place where event occurred. Earliest records available in the Boston office are for 1848.
Marriage	$3.00	Same as Birth or Death	Records (except for Boston) since 1841. Earliest Boston records are for 1848.
Divorce	See remarks	Same as Birth or Death	Index only since 1952. Inquirer will be directed where to send request. Certified copies are not available from State office.
	$3.00	See remarks	Registrar of Probate Court in county where divorce was granted.
MICHIGAN			
Birth or Death	$10.00	Office of Vital and Health Statistics Michigan Department of Public Health 3500 North Logan Street Lansing, MI 48914	State office has had records since 1867. Copies of records since 1867 may also be obtained from County Clerk in county where event occurred. Detroit records may be obtained from the City Health Department for births occurring since 1893 and for deaths since 1897.
Marriage	$10.00	Same as Birth or Death	Records since April 1867.
	Varies	See remarks	County Clerk in county where license was issued.
Divorce	$10.00	Same as Birth or Death	Records since 1897.
	Varies	See remarks	County Clerk in county where divorce was granted.
MINNESOTA			
Birth or Death	$5.00	Minnesota Department of Health Section of Vital Statistics 717 Delaware Street SE Minneapolis, MN 55440	State office has had records since January 1908. Copies of earlier records may be obtained from Clerk of District Court in county where event occurred or from the Minneapolis or St. Paul City Health Department if the event occurred in either city.
Marriage	See remarks	Same as Birth or Death	Statewide index since January 1958. Inquiries will be forwarded to appropriate office. Certified copies are not available from State Health Department.
	$5.00	See remarks	Clerk of District Court in county where license was issued.
Divorce	See remarks	Same as Birth or Death	Index since January 1970. Certified copies are not available from State office.
	$5.00	See remarks	Clerk of District Court in county where divorce was granted.
MISSISSIPPI			
Birth	$10.00	Vital Records State Board of Health P.O. Box 1700 Jackson, MS 39205	State office has had records since 1912. Full copies of birth certificates obtained within 1 year after the event are $5.00. Additional copies of same record ordered at same time are $1.00 each.
Short Form	$5.00		
Death	$5.00		
Marriage	$5.00	Same as Birth or Death	Statistical records only from January 1926 to July 1, 1938, and since January 1942.
	$3.00	See remarks	Circuit Clerk in county where license was issued.
Divorce	See remarks	Same as Birth or Death	Records since January 1926. Certified copies are not available from State office. Inquiries will be forwarded to appropriate office.
	$2.00	See remarks	Chancery Clerk in county where divorce was granted.

Place of event	*Cost of copy*	*Address*	*Remarks*
MISSOURI			
Birth or Death	$1.00	Division of Health Bureau of Vital Records State Department of Health and Welfare Jefferson City, MO 65101	State office has had records since January 1910. If event occurred in St. Louis (city), St. Louis County, or Kansas City before 1910, write to the City or County Health Department. Copies of these records are $3.00 each in St. Louis City and County. In Kansas City, $6.00 for first copy and $3.00 for each additional copy ordered at the same time.
Marriage	No fee	Same as Birth or Death	Indexes since July 1948. Correspondent will be referred to appropriate Recorder of Deeds in county where license was issued.
	Varies	See remarks	Recorder of Deeds in county where license was issued.
Divorce	See remarks	Same as Birth or Death	Indexes since July 1948. Certified copies are not available from State Health Department. Inquiries will be forwarded to appropriate office.
	Varies	See remarks	Clerk of Circuit Court in county where divorce was granted.
MONTANA			
Birth or Death	$3.00	Bureau of Records and Statistics State Department of Health and Environmental Sciences Helena, MT 59601	State office has had records since late 1907.
Marriage	See remarks	Same as Birth or Death	Records since July 1943. Some items may be verified. Inquiries will be forwarded to appropriate office. Apply to county where license was issued if known. Certified copies are not available from State office.
	Varies	See remarks	Clerk of District Court in county where license was issued.
Divorce	See remarks	Same as Birth or Death	Records since July 1943. Some items may be verified. Inquiries will be forwarded to appropriate office. Apply to county where license was issued if known. Certified copies are not available from State office.
	Varies	See remarks	Clerk of District Court in county where divorce was granted.
NEBRASKA			
Birth or Death	$3.00	Bureau of Vital Statistics State Department of Health 301 Centennial Mall South P.O. Box 95007 Lincoln, NE 68509	State office has had records since late 1904. If birth occurred before then, write the State office for information.
Marriage	$3.00	Same as Birth or Death	Records since January 1909.
	Varies	See remarks	County Court in county where license was issued.
Divorce	$3.00	Same as Birth or Death	Records since January 1909.
	Varies	See remarks	Clerk of District Court in county where divorce was granted.
NEVADA			
Birth or Death	$4.00	Division of Health - Vital Statistics Capitol Complex Carson City, NV 89710	State office has had records since July 1911. For earlier records, write to County Recorder in county where event occurred. Additional copies of Death Records ordered at the same time are $4.00 each for second and third copies, $3.00 each for the next three copies, and $2.00 each for any additional copies.
Marriage	See remarks	Same as Birth or Death	Indexes since January 1968. Certified copies are not available from State Health Department. Inquiries will be forwarded to appropriate office.
	Varies	See remarks	County Recorder in county where license was issued.
Divorce	See remarks	Same as Birth or Death	Indexes since January 1968. Certified copies are not available from State Health Department. Inquires will be forwarded to appropriate office.
	Varies	See remarks	County Clerk in county where divorce was granted.
NEW HAMPSHIRE			
Birth or Death	$3.00	Bureau of Vital Records Health and Welfare Building Hazen Drive Concord, NH 03301	State office has had some records since 1640. Copies of records may be obtained from State office or from City or Town Clerk in place where event occurred.

Place of event	*Cost of copy*	*Address*	*Remarks*
Marriage	$3.00	Same as Birth or Death	Records since 1640.
	$3.00	See remarks	Town Clerk in town where license was issued.
Divorce	$3.00	Same as Birth or Death	Records since 1808. Fee includes search and one copy if found.
	$3.00	See remarks	Clerk of Superior Court where divorce was granted.
NEW JERSEY			
Birth or Death	$2.00	State Department of Health Bureau of Vital Statistics CN 360 Trenton, NJ 08625	State office has had records since June 1878. Additional copies of same record ordered at same time are $1.00 each. If the exact date is unknown, the fee is an additional $0.50 per year searched.
		Archives and History Bureau State Library Division State Department of Education Trenton, NJ 08625	For records from May 1848 to May 1878.
Marriage	$2.00	Same as Birth or Death	If the exact date is unknown, the fee is an additional $0.50 per year searched.
	No fee	Archives and History Bureau State Library Division State Department of Education Trenton, NJ 08625	Records from May 1848 to May 1878.
Divorce	$2.00	Superior Court, Chancery Division State House Annex, Room 320 CN 971 Trenton, NJ 08625	The fee is for the first four pages. Additional pages cost $0.50 each.
NEW MEXICO			
Birth or Death	$4.00	Vital Statistics Bureau New Mexico Health Services Division P.O. Box 968 Santa Fe, NM 87503	State office has had records since 1920 and delayed records since 1880.
Marriage	Varies	See remarks	County Clerk in county where license was issued.
Divorce	Varies	See remarks	Clerk of District Court in county where divorce was granted.
NEW YORK (Except New York City)			
Birth or Death	$5.00	Bureau of Vital Records State Department of Health Empire State Plaza Tower Building Albany, NY 12237	State office has had records since 1880. For records before 1914 in Albany, Buffalo, and Yonkers or before 1880 in any other city, write to Registrar of Vital Statistics in city where event occurred. For the rest of the State, except New York City, write to State office.
Marriage	$5.00	Same as Birth or Death	Records from January 1880 to December 1907 and since May 1915.
	Varies	See remarks	Records from January 1908 to April 1915. County Clerk in county where license was issued.
	$5.00	See remarks	Records from January 1880 to December 1907. Write to City Clerk in Albany or Buffalo or Registrar of Vital Statistics in Yonkers if marriage occurred in one of these cities.
Divorce	$5.00	Same as Birth or Death	Records since January 1963.
	Varies	See remarks	County Clerk in county where divorce was granted.
NEW YORK CITY			
Birth or Death	$3.50	Bureau of Vital Records Department of Health of New York City 125 Worth Street New York, NY 10013	Office has had birth records since 1898 and death records since 1920. For Old City of New York (Manhattan and part of the Bronx) birth records for 1865-1897 and death records for 1865-1919 write to Municipal Archives and Records Retention, 52 Chambers St., New York, NY 10038.
Marriage	$7.00	See remarks	Records from 1847 to 1865. Municipal Archives and Records Retention Center, New York Public Library, 23 Park Row, New York, NY 10038, except Brooklyn records for this period, which are filed with County Clerk's Office, Kings County, Supreme Court Building, Brooklyn, NY 11201. Additional copies of same record ordered at same time are $2.00 each.

Place of event	*Cost of copy*	*Address*	*Remarks*
	$7.00	See remarks	Records from 1866 to 1907. City Clerk's Office in borough where marriage was performed.
	$7.00	See remarks	Records from 1908 to May 12, 1943. New York City residents write to City Clerk's Office borough of bride's residence; nonresidents write to City Clerk's Office in borough where license was obtained.
	$7.00	See remarks	Records since May 13, 1943. City Clerk's Office in borough where license was issued.
Bronx Borough	$7.00	Marriage License Bureau 1780 Grand Concourse Bronx, NY 10457	
Brooklyn Borough	$7.00	Marriage License Bureau Municipal Building Brooklyn Borough Hall Brooklyn, NY 11201	
Manhattan Borough	$7.00	Marriage License Bureau No. 1 Center Street Municipal Building New York, NY 10007	
Queens Borough	$7.00	Marriage License Bureau Queens Borough Hall 120-55 Queens Boulevard Kew Gardens, NY 11424	
Staten Island Borough (no longer called Richmond)	$7.00	Marriage License Bureau Staten Island Borough Hall St. George Staten Island, NY 11201	
Divorce			See New York State
NORTH CAROLINA			
Birth or Death	$3.00	Department of Human Resources Division of Health Services Vital Records Branch P.O. Box 2091 Raleigh, NC 27602	State office has had birth records since October 1913 and death records since January 1, 1930. Death records from 1913 through 1929 are available from Archives and Records Section, State Records Center, 215 North Blount Street, Raleigh, NC 27602.
Marriage	$3.00	Same as Birth or Death	Records since January 1962.
	$3.00	See remarks	Registrar of Deeds in county where marriage was performed.
Divorce	$3.00	Same as Birth or Death	Records since January 1958.
	Varies	See remarks	Clerk of Superior Court where divorce was granted.
NORTH DAKOTA			
Birth or Death	$2.00	Division of Vital Records State Department of Health Office of Statistical Services Bismarck, ND 58505	State office has had some records since July 1893. Years from 1894 to 1920 are incomplete.
Marriage	$1.00	Same as Birth or Death	Records since July 1925. Requests for earlier records will be forwarded to appropriate office.
	Varies	See remarks	County Judge in county where license was issued.
Divorce	See remarks	Same as Birth or Death	Index of records since July 1949. Some items may be verified. Certified copies are not available from State Health Department. Inquiries will be forwarded to appropriate office.
	Varies	See remarks	Clerk of District Court in county where divorce was granted.
OHIO			
Birth or Death	$3.00	Division of Vital Statistics Ohio Department of Health G-20 Ohio Departments Building 65 South Front Street Columbus, OH 43215	State office has had records since December 20, 1908. For earlier records, write to Probate Court in county where event occurred.
Marriage	See remarks	Same as Birth or Death	Records since September 1949. All items may be verified. Certified copies are not available from State Health Department. Inquiries will be referred to appropriate office.
	Varies	See remarks	Probate Judge in county where license was issued.

Place of event	Cost of copy	Address	Remarks
Divorce	See remarks	Same as Birth or Death	Records since September 1949. All items may be verified. Certified copies are not available from State Health Department. Inquiries will be referred to appropriate office.
	Varies	See remarks	Clerk of Court of Common Pleas in county where divorce was granted.
OKLAHOMA			
Birth or Death	$2.00	Vital Records Section State Department of Health Northeast 10th Street & Stonewall P.O. Box 53551 Oklahoma City, OK 73152	State office has had records since October 1908.
Marriage	Varies	See remarks	Clerk of Court in county where license was issued.
Divorce	Varies	See remarks	Clerk of Court in county where divorce was granted.
OREGON			
Birth or Death	$5.00	Oregon State Health Division Vital Statistics Section P.O. Box 116 Portland, OR 97207	State office has had records since January 1903. Some earlier records for the City of Portland since approximately 1880 are available from the Oregon State Archives, 1005 Broadway, N.E., Salem, OR 97310.
Marriage	$5.00	Same as Birth or Death	Records since January 1906.
	Varies	See remarks	County Clerk in county where license was issued. County Clerks also have some records before 1906.
Divorce	$5.00	Same as Birth or Death	Records since 1925.
	Varies	See remarks	County Clerk in county where divorce was granted. County Clerks also have some records before 1925.
PENNSYLVANIA			
Birth Short Form **Death**	$4.00 $5.00 $3.00	Division of Vital Statistics State Department of Health Central Building 101 South Mercer Street P.O. Box 1528 New Castle, PA 16103	State office has had records since January 1906. For earlier records, write to Register of Wills, Orphans Court, in county seat where event occurred. Persons born in Pittsburgh from 1870 to 1905 or in Allegheny City, now part of Pittsburgh, from 1882 to 1905 should write to Office of Biostatistics, Pittsburgh Health Department, City-County Building, Pittsburgh, PA 15219. For events occurring in City of Philadelphia from 1860 to 1915, write to Vital Statistics, Philadelphia Department of Public Health, City Hall Annex, Philadelphia, PA 19107.
Marriage	See remarks	Same as Birth or Death	Records since January 1941. Certified copies are not available from State Health Department. Inquiries will be forwarded to appropriate office.
	Varies	See remarks	Marriage License Clerks, County Court House, in county seat where license was issued.
Divorce	Varies	Same as Birth or Death	Records since January 1946. Certified copies are not available from State Health Department. Inquiries will be forwarded to appropriate office.
	Varies	See remarks	Prothonotary, Court House, in county seat where divorce was granted.
PUERTO RICO			
Birth or Death	$0.50	Division of Demographic Registry and Vital Statistics Department of Health San Juan, PR 00908	Central office has had records since July 22, 1931. Copies of earlier records may be obtained by writing to local Registrar (Registrador Demografico) in municipality where event occurred or by writing to central office for information.
Marriage	$0.50	Same as Birth or Death	
Divorce	$0.60	See remarks	Superior Court where divorce was granted.
RHODE ISLAND			
Birth or Death	$4.00	Division of Vital Statistics State Department of Health Room 101, Cannon Building 75 Davis Street Providence, RI 02908	State office has had records since 1853. For earlier records, write to Town Clerk in town where event occurred. Additional copies of the same record ordered at the same time are $2.00 each.

Place of event	*Cost of copy*	*Address*	*Remarks*
Marriage	$4.00	Same as Birth or Death	Records since January 1853. Additional copies of the same record ordered at the same time are $2.00 each.
	$4.00	See remarks	City or Town Clerk in place where marriage was performed.
Divorce	$1.00	Clerk of Family Court 1 Dorrance Plaza Providence, RI 02903	
SOUTH CAROLINA			
Birth or Death	$3.00	Office of Vital Records and Public Health Statistics S.C. Department of Health and Environmental Control 2600 Bull Street Columbia, SC 29201	State office has had records since January 1915. City of Charleston births from 1877 and deaths from 1821 are on file at Charleston County Health Department. Ledger entries of Florence City births and deaths from 1895 to 1914 are on file at Florence County Health Department. Ledger entries of Newberry City births and deaths from late 1800's are on file at Newberry County Health Department. These are the only early records obtainable.
Marriage	$3.00	Same as Birth or Death	Records since July 1950.
	Varies	See remarks	Records since July 1911. Probate Judge in county where license was issued.
Divorce	$3.00	Same as Birth or Death	Records since July 1962.
	Varies	See remarks	Records since April 1949. Clerk of county where petition was filed.
SOUTH DAKOTA			
Birth or Death	$3.00	State Department of Health Health Statistics Program Joe Foss Office Building Pierre, SD 57501	State office has had records since July 1905 and access to other records for some events that occurred before then. Additional copies requested at the same time are $1.00 each.
Marriage	$3.00	Same as Birth or Death	Records since July 1905. Additional copies requested at the same time are $1.00 each.
	$2.00	See remarks	County Treasurer in county where license was issued.
Divorce	$3.00	Same as Birth or Death	Records since July 1905. Additional copies requested at the same time are $1.00 each.
	Varies	See remarks	Clerk of Court in county where divorce was granted.
TENNESSEE			
Birth or Death	$3.00	Division of Vital Records State Department of Public Health Cordell Hull Building Nashville, TN 37219	State office has had birth records for entire State since January 1914, for Nashville since June 1881, for Knoxville since July 1881, and for Chattanooga since January 1882. State office has had death records for entire State since January 1914, for Nashville since July 1874, for Knoxville since July 1887, and for Chattanooga since March 6, 1872. Birth and death enumeration records by school district are available for July 1908 through June 1912. For Memphis birth records from April 1874 through December 1887 and November 1898 to January 1, 1914, and for Memphis death records from May 1848 to January 1, 1914, write to Memphis-Shelby County Health Department, Division of Vital Records, Memphis, TN 38105.
Marriage	$3.00	Same as Birth or Death	Records since July 1945.
	Varies	See remarks	County Court Clerk in county where license was issued.
Divorce	$3.00	Same as Birth or Death	Records since July 1945.
	Varies	See remarks	Clerk of Court in divorce was granted.
TEXAS			
Birth or Death	$5.00	Bureau of Vital Statistics Texas Department of Health 1100 West 49th Street Austin, TX 78756	State office has had records since 1903. Additional copies of same *death* record ordered at same time are $2.00 each.
Marriage	See remarks	Same as Birth or Death	Records since January 1966. Certified copies are not available from State office. Fee for search and verification of essential facts of marriage is $1.00
	Varies	See remarks	County Clerk in county where license was issued.

Place of event	Cost of copy	Address	Remarks
Divorce	See remarks	Same as Birth or Death	Records since January 1968. Certified copies are not available from State office. Fee for search and verification of essential facts of divorce is $1.00.
	Varies	See remarks	Clerk of District Court in county where divorce was granted.
TRUST TERRITORY OF THE PACIFIC ISLANDS			
Birth or Death	$0.25 plus $0.10 per 100 words	Director of Medical Services Department of Medical Services Saipan, Mariana Islands 96950	Clerk of Court in district where event occurred. (If not sure of district in which event occurred, write to Director of Medical Services to have inquiry referred to the correct district.) Courts have had records since November 21, 1952. Beginning 1950, a few records have been filed with the Hawaii Bureau of Vital Statistics.
Marriage	Varies	See remarks	Clerk of Court in district where marriage was performed.
Divorce	Varies	See remarks	Clerk of Court in district where divorce was granted.
UTAH			
Birth or Death	$5.00	Bureau of Health Statistics Utah Department of Health 150 West North Temple P.O. Box 2500 Salt Lake City, UT 84110	State office has had records since 1905. If event occurred from 1890 to 1904 in Salt Lake City or Ogden, write to City Board of Health. For records elsewhere in the State from 1898 to 1904, write to County Clerk in county where event occurred.
Marriage	$5.00	Same as Birth or Death	State office has had records since 1978. Only short form certified copies are available.
	Varies	See remarks	County Clerk in county where license was issued.
Divorce	$5.00	Same as Birth or Death	State office has had records since 1978. Only short form certified copies are available.
	Varies	See remarks	County Clerk in county where divorce was granted.
VERMONT			
Birth or Death	$3.00	Vermont Department of Health Vital Records Section Box 70 115 Colchester Avenue Burlington, VT 05401	Town or City Clerk of town where birth or death occurred.
Marriage	$3.00	Same as Birth or Death	
	$3.00	See remarks	Town Clerk in town where license was issued.
Divorce	$3.00	Same as Birth or Death	
VIRGINIA			
Birth or Death	$3.00	Division of Vital Records and Health Statistics State Department of Health James Madison Building P.O. Box 1000 Richmond, VA 23208	State office has had records from January 1853 to December 1896 and since June 14, 1912. For records between those dates, write to the Health Department in the city where event occurred.
Marriage	$3.00	Same as Birth or Death	Records since January 1853.
	Varies	See remarks	Clerk of Court in county or city where license was issued.
Divorce	$3.00	Same as Birth or Death	Records since January 1918.
	Varies	See remarks	Clerk of Court in county or city where divorce was granted.
VIRGIN ISLANDS (U.S.)			
Birth or Death			
St. Croix	$2.00	Registrar of Vital Statistics Charles Harwood Memorial Hospital St. Croix, VI 00820	Registrar has had birth and death records on file since 1840.
St. Thomas and St. John	$2.00	Registrar of Vital Statistics Charlotte Amalie St. Thomas, VI 00802	Registrar has had birth records on file since July 1906 and death records since January 1906.
Marriage	See remarks	Bureau of Vital Records and Statistical Services Virgin Islands Department of Health Charlotte Amalie St. Thomas, VI 00801	Certified copies are not available. Inquiries will be forwarded to appropriate office.

Place of event	Cost of copy	Address	Remarks
St. Croix	$2.00	Chief Deputy Clerk Territorial Court of the Virgin Islands P.O. Box 929 Christiansted St. Croix, VI 00820	
St. Thomas and St. John	$2.00	Clerk of the Territorial Court of the Virgin Islands P.O. Box 70 Charlotte Amalie St. Thomas, VI 00801	
Divorce	See remarks	Same as Marriage	Certified copies are not available. Inquiries will be forwarded to appropriate office.
St. Croix	$2.00	Same as Marriage	
St. Thomas and St. John	$2.00	Same as Marriage	
WASHINGTON			
Birth or Death	$3.00	Vital Records P.O. Box 9709, LB11 Olympia, WA 98504	State office has had records since July 1907. For King, Pierce, and Spokane counties copies may also be obtained from county health departments. County Auditor of county of birth has registered births prior to July 1907.
Marriage	$3.00	Same as Birth or Death	State office has had records since January 1968.
	$2.00	See remarks	County Auditor in county where license was issued.
Divorce	$3.00	Same as Birth or Death	State office has had records since January 1968.
	Varies	See remarks	County Clerk in county where divorce was granted.
WEST VIRGINIA			
Birth or Death	$2.00	Division of Vital Statistics State Department of Health State Office Building No. 3 Charleston, WV 25305	State office has had records since January 1917. For earlier records, write to Clerk of County Court in county where event occurred.
Marriage	$2.00	Same as Birth or Death	Records since 1921. Certified copies have been available since 1964.
	Varies	See remarks	County Clerk in county where license was issued.
Divorce	See remarks	Same as Birth or Death	Index since 1968. Some items may be verified (fee $2.00). Certified copies are not available from State Office.
	Varies	See remarks	Clerk of Circuit Court, Chancery Side, in county where divorce was granted.
WISCONSIN			
Birth or Death	$4.00	Bureau of Health Statistics Wisconsin Division of Health P.O. Box 309 Madison, WI 53701	State office has scattered records earlier than 1857. Records before October 1, 1907, are very incomplete. Additional copies of the same record ordered at the same time are $2.00 each.
Marriage	$4.00	Same as Birth or Death	Records since April 1836. Records before October 1, 1907, are incomplete. Additional copies of the same record ordered at the same time are $2.00 each.
Divorce	$4.00	Same as Birth or Death	Records since October 1907. Additional copies of the same record ordered at the same time are $2.00 each.
WYOMING			
Birth or Death	$2.00	Vital Records Services Division of Health and Medical Services Hathaway Building Cheyenne, WY 82002	State office has had records since July 1909.
Marriage	$2.00	Same as Birth or Death	Records since May 1941.
	Varies	See remarks	County Clerk in county where license was issued.
Divorce	$2.00	Same as Birth or Death	Records since May 1941.
	Varies	See remarks	Clerk of District Court where divorce took place.

GENEALOGICAL SOCIETIES OF THE UNITED STATES*

Alabama

Anniston
AlaBenton Genealogical Society
c/o Anniston Public Library
Box 308, 36201

Birmingham
Birmingham Genealogical Society, Inc.
Box 2432, 35201

Alabama Genealogical Society, Inc.
Samford University Library–
Special Collections
800 Lakeshore Drive 35229

Centre
Southern Society of Genealogists
Box 295, 35960

Cullman
North Central Alabama Genealogical Society
200 Clark St.
N.E., 35055

Dadeville
The Genealogical Society of East Alabama, Inc.
Box 484, 36835

Decatur
North Alabama Genealogical Society, Inc.
c/o Mrs. T. M. Blaxton
Rt. 3
Box 510-A, 35603

Dothan
Southeast Alabama Genealogical Society
c/o Cecilia Minder
1115 Normandale Dr, 36301

Enterprise
Pea River Historical and Genealogical Society
Box 628, 36330

Florence
Natchez Trace Genealogical Society
Box 1645, 35631

Gadsden
Northeast Alabama Genealogical Society, Inc.
Box 674, 35902

Huntsville
Tennessee Valley Genealogical Society
Box 1568, 35807

Hurtsboro
Genealogical Society of East Alabama, Inc.
c/o Mrs. W. M. Hollingsworth, 36860

Mobile
Mobile Genealogical Society, Inc.
Box 6224, 36606

Montgomery
Montgomery Genealogy Club
c/o Nancy M. Weems
Correspondence Secretary
1919 Norden Lane, 36106

Selma
Central Alabama Genealogical Society
Box 477, 36701

Tuscaloosa
Tuscaloosa Genealogical Society
1439-49th Ave. East, 35404

Tuskegee
Genealogical Society of East Alabama
Box 569, 36083

University
The American College of Heraldry
Drawer CG, 35486

Winfield
Marion Pioneer Territorial Genealogical Society
c/o Northwest Regional Library
Drawer O, 35594

Alaska

Fairbanks
Fairbanks Genealogical Society
c/o Ruth Van Veldhuizen
Star Rt.
Box 40581
1 Mile Gilmore Trail, 99701

Ketchikan
Genealogical Society of Southeastern Alaska
518 Deermount, 99901

Arizona

Sierra Vista
Apache Genealogical Society
109 Kayetan Dr.
N.E., 85635

Sun City
Sun City Genealogical Society
Box 1448, 85351

Tucson
Arizona State Genealogical Society
Box 6027, 86733

Arkansas

Batesville
Batesville Chapter
Arkansas Genealogical Society
c/o Shirley Martin
460 Morrow, 72501

Camden
Ouachita-Calhoun Genealogical Society
c/o Mrs. Roberta Hollis
628 Banner St., 71701

Southern Arkansas Genealogical Society
976 Lyons Lane
S.W., 71701

Texarkana USA Genealogical Society
Rt. 7
Box 466
BA7, 75501

Clarksville
Johnson County Genealogical Society
c/o Mrs. Jewell Phillips
Rt. 1, 72830

El Dorado
Union County Genealogical Society
Box 1202, 71730

Fordyce
Dallas County Genealogical & Historical Society
Box 28, 71742

* This appendix is adapted from *Meyer's Directory of Genealogical Societies in the U.S.A. & Canada*, 4th ed., Mary K. Meyer, compiler and editor. The editors of the *THE SOURCE* would like to express their gratitude to Mrs. Meyer for her kind permission to reprint from her publication. The reader is advised that Mrs. Meyer updates her book every two years, and that a new edition is scheduled for publication in May 1984. Copies can be obtained by writing to the author at Libra Publications, Box 29, Linthicum Heights, MD 21090

Dallas County Genealogy Group
c/o Dallas County Library
501 E. Fourth St., 71742

Fordyce County Genealogical & Historical Society
Box 28, 71742

Fort Smith
Madison County Genealogical Society
701 N. 12th St., 72901

Harrison
Boone County Historical and Genealogical Society
Box 58, 72601

Hot Springs
The Melting Pot Genealogical Society
Box 2186, 71901

Little Rock
Arkansas Genealogical Society
c/o Mrs. M. B. Cia Sr.
4200 A St., 72205

Magnolia
So-We-Ar Genealogical Society
c/o T. O. Hamaker, Pres.
Box 9, 71753

Mountain Home
Baxter County Historical and Genealogical Society
Box 309, 72653

Nashville
Howard County Heritage Club
Hempstead & 2nd St., 71852

North Little Rock
Pulaski County Heritage Seekers
c/o Laman Library, 72114

Rogers
Northwest Arkansas Genealogical Society
Box K, 72756

Russellville
Pope County Genealogical Group
Rt. 5
Box 249-A, 72801

Yell County Historical & Genealogical Society
Mary V. Humphrey
Box 356, 72801

Searcy
White County Historical Society
Mrs. Leister Presley
1708 W. Center, 72143

State College
Crowley's Ridge Genealogical Society
Box 2091, 72467

Van Buren
Crawford County Genealogical Society
929 E. Main St., 72956

California

Anderson
Shasta County Genealogical Society
Box 793, 96007

Arroyo Grande
South County Branch
California Central Coast Genealogical Society
421 Cornwell, 93420

Bakersfield
Kern County Genealogical Society
Box 2214, 93301

Barstow
Mojave Desert Genealogical Society
Box 1320, 92311

Bellflower
Universal Genealogical Society
9512 Cedar St., 90706

Blythe
Colorado River-Blythe-Quartzite Genealogical Society
Box 404, 92226

Burbank
Southern California Genealogical Society
103 S. Golden Mall, 91502

Canoga Park
San Fernando County Genealogical Society
c/o Dwight Cushman
8009 Lena Ave., 91304

Carlsbad
North San Diego County Genealogical Society
Box 581, 92108

San Diego County Genealogical Association
Box 3, 92100

Columbia
Tuolumme County Genealogical Society
Box 1817, 95310

Concord
Contra Costa County Genealogical Society
Box 910, 94522

Davis
Davis (CA) Genealogy Club
630–2nd St., 95616

Desert Hot Springs
Coachella Valley Genealogical Society
27905 Hopper Rd., 92260

El Centro
Imperial County Genealogical Society
Box 2643, 92244

El Dorado
El Dorado Research
Box 56, 95623

Escondido
Escondido Genealogical Society
Box 2190, 92025

Fair Oaks
Sacramento Genealogical Society
5240 Tyosa St., 95628

Fairfield
Solano County Genealogical Society
Box 2494, 94533

Fort Bragg
Mendocino Coast Genealogical
c/o Mrs. K.M. Williams
19751 Myrtel St., 95437

Fresno
Fresno Genealogical Society
Box 1429, 93716

Goleta
Santa Barbara County Genealogical Society
Box 1174, 93116

Hawthorne
Jewish Genealogical Society of Los Angeles
Mel Hanberg, President
4444 W. El Segundo Blvd., 90250

Hayward
Hayward Area Genealogical Society
Box 754, 94543

Hemet
Genealogy Club of Hemet-San Jacinto
Box 2516, 92343

Jackson
Amador County Genealogical Society
829 Buena Vista Dr., 95642
Box 1323, 95453

Lakeport
Lake County Genealogical Society
Box 1323, 95453

La Mesa
Irish Family Names Society
Box 2095, 92041

Lancaster
Antelope Valley Genealogical Society
Box 1049, 93534

Lawndale
South Bay Cities Genealogical Society
Box 847, 90260

Long Beach
Questing Heirs Genealogical Society
Box 15102, 90815

Los Banos
Los Banos Genealogical Society
c/o Betty Bettencourt
Box 1106, 93635

Modesto
Genealogical Society of Stanislaus County
Mrs. Nadeen Marlett
1630 Victor Way., 95351

Morro Bay
California Central Coast Genealogical Society, Inc.
Box 832, 93442

Napa
The California Alliance of Genealogical Societies
Sandra K. Ogle, Chairman
45 Kreuse Canyon Dr. 94558

Napa Valley Genealogical & Biographical Society
Box 385, 94558

Novato
Marin County Genealogical Society
Box 1511, 94947

Oakland
East Bay Genealogical Society
3940 LaCresta Ave., 94602

Orange
Orange County California Genealogical Society
Box 1587, 92666

Oxnard
Ventura County Genealogical Society
Roberta Griffith
2221 Lavanda Dr., 93030

Palo Alto
Croatian-Slovenian-Serbian Genealogical Society
936 Industrial Ave., 94070

Paradise
Paradise Genealogical Society
Box 335, 95969

Pasadena
Genealogical Friends of the Pasadena Library
285 E. Walnut. 91101

San Gabriel Genealogical Society
Pasadena Public Library
285 E. Walnut, 91101

Pine Grove
Prospector Genealogical Society
Box 127, 95665

Pollock Pines
El Dorado County Genealogical Society
Box 723, 95726

Pomona
Pomona Valley Genealogical Society
Box 286, 91769

Redondo Beach
TRW Genealogical Society
One Space Parck [sic]
s/1435, 90278

Redwood City
Redwood City Genealogical Society
Box 645, 95540

Riverside
Genealogical Society of Riverside
Box 2557, 92516

Sacramento
Genealogical Association of Sacramento
Anne Broudes
7434 Center Pkwy., 95832

San Bernardino
San Bernardino Valley Genealogical Society
Box 2505, 92406

San Carlos
Croatian–Serbian-Slovene Genealogical Society
2527 San Carlos Ave., 94070

San Diego
German Research Association
Box 11293, 92111

San Diego Genealogical Society
Box 83448, 92138

Southern California Chapter
Ohio Genealogical Society
Ruth Parson, Treasurer
16863 Bellotta Dr., 92128

San Francisco
Balkan and Eastern European American Genealogical and Historical Society
c/o Adam S. Eterovich
4843 Mission St., 94112

San Francisco
California Genealogical Society
2099 Pacific Ave., 94109

Santa Clara
Santa Clara County Historical & Genealogical Society
2635 Homestead Rd., 95051

Santa Cruz
Genealogical Society of Santa Cruz County
Box 72, 95063

Santa Maria
Santa Maria Valley Genealogical Society
Box 1215, 93454

Santa Rosa
Sonoma County Genealogical Society
Box 2273, 95405

Seal Beach
Leisure World Genealogy Club
Mrs. Retha Hollenbeck
1440 Skokie Rd.-89L., 90740

Stockton
San Joaquin Genealogical Society
Box 4817, 95204

Sun City
Hadley Genealogical Society of Southern California
33210 Bailey Park Dr., 92381

Torrence
South Bay Cities Genealogical Society
Box 5341, 90510

Turlock
Turlock Genealogical & Historical Society
c/o J. Carlyle Parker, Asst. Dir.
California State College
Stanislaus Library
800 Monte Vista Ave., 95380

Ukiah
Ukiah Tree Tracers Genealogical Society
Box 72, 95482

Whittier
Whittier Area Genealogical Society
Box 4367, 90607

Victorville
Hi-Desert Genealogical Society
Box 616, 92392

Visalia
Sequoia Genealogical Society
Box 3473, 93277

Yorba Linda
Yorba Linda Genealogical Society
19684 Marino Plaza, 92686

Yreka
Genealogical Society of Siskiyou County, Inc.
Box 225, 96097

Yuba City
Sutter Yuba Genealogical Society
Box 1274, 95991

Yucca Valley
Genealogical Society of Morongo Basin
Box 234, 92284

Colorado

Arvada
Arvada Historical Society
Genealogy Committee
Robert Leishman, Chairman
6560 Upham St., 80003

Boulder
Boulder Genealogical Society
Box 3246, 80302

Colorado Springs
Pike's Peak Genealogical Society
Penrose Public Library
Box 1579, 80901

Denver
The Colorado Genealogical Society
Box 9671, 80209

Ft. Collins
Larimer County Genealogical Society
c/o American Baptist Church
600 S. Shields St., 80521

Georgetown
Georgetown Genealogical Society
Ronald J. Neely, Curator
3rd and Argentine Sts. 80444

Grand Junction
Mesa County Genealogical Society
Box 1506, 81502

Greeley
Weld County Genealogical Society
Box 278, 80631

Lakewood
Colorado Council of Genealogical Societies
David S. Vogels Jr., Pres.
1824 Robb St., 80215

Foothills Genealogical Society
Box 15382, 80215

Littleton
Columbine Genealogical Society
Box 2074, 80161

Pueblo
Southeastern Colorado Genealogical Society
Box 4086, 81003

Connecticut

Glastonbury

Connecticut Society of Genealogists
Box 435, 06033

Greenwich

The Jacobite Association
White Rose House
Box 66, 06830

Manchester

French-Canadian Genealogical Society of Connecticut
Henri E. Carrier, President
c/o 215 Adams St., 06040

Stamford

Stamford Genealogical Society
Box 294, 06904

Delaware

Dover

Downstate Chapter
Delaware Genealogical Society
Bob Lewis, Chairman
Dover Public Library
45 S. State St., 19901

Wilmington

Delaware Genealogical Society
505 Market St., 19801

District of Columbia

Washington

Afro-American Historical & Genealogical Society
Box 13006, 20009

Board For Certification of Genealogists
1307 New Hampshire Ave.
N.W., 20036

National Genealogical Society
1921 Sunderland Pl.
N.W., 20036,

Florida

Bradenton

Manasota Genealogical Society, Inc.
Box 9433, 33506

Cape Coral

Lee County Genealogical Society
Ernest England, President
411 S. E. 19th Pl., 33904

Cocoa

Brevard Genealogical Society
Box 1123, 32922

Daytona Beach

Volusia County Genealogical & Historical Society
Box 2039, 32014

Ft. Lauderdale

Genealogical Society of Broward County, Inc.
Box 485, 33302

Fort Walton Beach

Oskaloosa County Genealogical Society
Drawer 1175, 32548

Gainesville

Alachua County Genealogical Society
Box 12078, 32604

Jacksonville

Jacksonville Genealogical Society
4589 Amherst St., 32205

Southern Genealogists Exchange Society, Inc.
Box 2801, 32203

Key West

Monroe County Genealogical Society
c/o Rachel J. Lowe
21 Ventana Lane
Big Coppitt Key, 33040

Lake Wales

Ridge Genealogical Society
Billie Reading Lewis, Secretary
1104 Voncile St., 33853

Melbourne

Genealogical Society of South Brevard
Box 786, 32901

Miami

Genealogical Society of Greater Miami, Inc.
Box 015299, 33101

Miami Shores

Ukranian Genealogical and Heraldric Society
573 N.E. 102nd St., 33138

Orlando

Central Florida Genealogical and Historical Society
Box 177, 32805

Panama City

Genealogy Society of Bay County
Box 662, 32401

Pinellas Park

Florida Society for Genealogical Research, Inc.
8461–54th St.
North, 33565

Port Charlotte

Charlotte County Genealogical Society
Box 2682, 33592

Ruskin

South Hillsborough Genealogists
c/o Ruskin Branch Library
1 Dickman Dr.
S.E., 33570

Sarasota

Genealogical Society of Sarasota, Florida
c/o Betty Styer
8911 Midnight Pass Rd. Apt. 114, 33581

International Genealogy Fellowship of Rotarians
Charles D. Townsend, Editor
5721 Antietam Dr., 33581

Tallahassee

Florida State Genealogical Society
Box 10249, 32302

Tallahassee Genealogical Society, Inc.
Box 4371, 32303

Tampa

Florida Genealogical Society
Box 18624, 33609

Orphan Voyage
13906 Pepperrell Dr., 33624

Titusville

Genealogical Society of North Brevard
c/o Doris Yancey
3838 Champion Rd., 32780

West Palm Beach

Palm Beach County Genealogical Society
Box 1746, 33402

Georgia

Albany

Southwest Georgia Genealogical Society
c/o Frances Wynd
2009 Gail Ave., 31705

Atlanta

Genealogical Library for Blind & Physically Handicapped (Genealogical Center Library)
Box 88534, 30356

Georgia Genealogical Society
Box 38066, 30334

Augusta

Augusta Genealogical Society, Inc.
Box 3743, 30904

Carrollton

Carroll County Genealogical Society
Mrs. Rueben M. Word, President
805 Rome St., 30117

Columbus

The Genealogical Society of the Original Muscogee County
c/o Col. Sam Adams (USA Ret.)
4019 Calhoun Dr. 31903

Orangeburgh (South Carolina) German-Swiss Genealogical Society
Judge Alex. D. Williams, Secretary
Box 367, 31902

Cumming

Forsyth County Historical & Genealogical Society, Inc.
Box 762, 30130

Forsyth Heritage Foundation, Inc.
Box 762, 30130

Homerville

Huxford Genealogical Society
Box 595, 31634

La Grange

West Central Georgia Genealogical Society
Box 2291, 30241

Marietta

Northeast Cobb Genealogical Society
Box 1413, 30060

Newnan

Coweta County Genealogical Society, Inc.
Box 1014, 30264

Rome
Northwest Georgia Historical & Genealogical Society
Box 2484, 30161

Sylvania
Scriven County Historical & Genealogical Society
c/o Elizabeth Lee
239 Sylvan Circle., 30467

Summerville
Walker County Chapter
North Georgia Historical & Genealogical Society
D. P. Henley, President, 30747

Warner Robbins
Central Georgia Genealogical Society
Box 2024, 31099

Idaho

Boise
The Idaho Genealogical Society, Inc.
325 State St., 83702

German Research Group
c/o Ed Sarbach
Box 7683, 83707

Treasure Valley Chapter
Idaho Genealogical Society
325 State St., 83701

Burley
Burley Genealogical Society
Box 1227, 83318

Caldwell
Family Scanners Chapt.
Idaho Genealogical Society
Box 581, 83605

Grangeville
Idaho County Chapter
Idaho Genealogical Society
215 W. North, 83530

Hayden Lake
North Idaho Genealogical Society
Hayden Lake Free Library, 83835

Heyburn
Magic Valley Chapter
Idaho Genealogical Society
c/o Theo Henderson
Rt. 2
770 S. River Dr., 83336

Kellogg
Shoshone County Genealogical Society
Box 183, 83837

Lewiston
Twin Rivers Genealogical Society
c/o Lewiston Public Library
101-5th St., 83501

McCall
Intermountain Historical & Genealogical Society
c/o Frank L. Fry Jr.
Box 788, 83638

Moscow
Latah County Genealogical Society
c/o Latah County Historical Society
110 South Adams St., 83843

Nampa
Nampa Genealogical Society
c/o Nampa Public Library
101-11th Ave. S., 83651

Illinois

Albion
Edwards County Genealogical Society
c/o Miss Lois Goodson
318 N. Fifth St., 62806

Aledo
Mercer County Historical Society
Genealogy Division
Mrs. Ruth Giffen, Curator
604 N.E. 2nd St., 61231

Anna
Union County Genealogical/Historical Commission
101 E. Spring St., 62906

Augusta
Tri-County Genealogical Society
Box 355, 62311

Belleville
St. Clair County Genealogical Society
Box 431, 62221

Bolingbrook
Bolingbrook Genealogical Society
Clyde Ruble, Sec.
121 Cypress, 60439

Camargo
Douglas County Genealogical Society
Box 50, 61919

Canton
Fulton County Historical & Genealogical Society
c/o Mrs. Charles V. Petrovich
1040 North Main St., 61520

Carrollton
Green County Historical & Genealogical Society
Box 137, 62016

Carterville
Genealogical Society of Southern Illinois
c/o John A. Logan College
Rt. 2, 62918

Charleston
Coles County Genealogical Society
Box 225, 61920

Chicago
Afro-American Genealogical & Historical Society of Chicago
Helen Burnett, President
7933 S. Michigan Ave., 60619

Chicago Genealogical Society
Box 1160, 60690

Polish Genealogical Society, Inc.
984 N. Milwaukee Ave., 60622

Claremont
Richland County Illinois Genealogical Society
c/o Mrs. Jan Doan
Rt. 1, 62421

Clinton
DeWitt County Genealogical Society
Box 632, 61727

Danville
Illiana Genealogical Society
Box 207, 61832

Decatur
Decatur Genealogical Society
Box 2205, 62526

Illinois State Genealogical Society
Box A631, 62525

Des Plaines
Genealogical Questors
c/o Des Plaines Historical Society
789 Pearson, 60016

East Dubuque
Grant County Genealogical Society
c/o Bernita Jenkins
100 Elm St., 61025

Edwardsville
Madison County Genealogical Society
Box 631, 62025

Effingham
Effingham County Genealogical Society
Box 1166, 62401

Elgin
Elgin Genealogical Society
Box 1418
Elgin, Illinois 60121-0818

Fellowship of Brethren Genealogists
Gwendolyn Bobb, Sec./Treas.
518 Miller Dr, 60120

Elmhurst
Elmhurst Illinois Genealogical Group
Box 84, 60126

Evanston
Yesterday's Children
Box 1554, 60204

Freeport
Genealogical Committee
Stephenson County Historical Society
110 Coates Pl., 61032

Galesburg
Knox County Genealogical Society
Box 13, 61401

Geneva
Kane County Genealogical Society
Box 504, 60134

Greenup
Cumberland County Genealogical Society
Box 676, 62428

Greenville
Bond County Genealogical Society
Box 172, 62246

Harvey
Thornton Township Historical Society
154 East 154th St., 60426

Havana
Mason County Genealogical & Historical Society
Box 246, 62644

Henry
Henry Historical & Genealogical Society
610 North St., 61537

Jacksonville
Jacksonville Area Genealogical & Historical Society
Box 21, 62651

Kankakee
Kankakee Valley Genealogical Society
Kankakee Public Library
Box 1659, 60901

Lawrenceville
Lawrence County Genealogical Society
Mrs. George Maxfield
1703 - 15th St., 62439

Lexington
Lexington Genealogical & Historical Society
318 W. Main St., 61753

Libertyville
Lake County Illinois Genealogical Society
Cook County Memorial Library
413 N. Milwaukee Ave., 60048

Lincoln
Logan County Genealogical Society
Box 283, 62656

Litchfield
Montgomery County Genealogical Society
Box 212, 62056

Lombard
DuPage County Genealogical Society
Box 133, 60148

Macomb
McDonough County Genealogical Society
Box 202, 61455

Marion
Southern Ilinois Genealogical Society
c/o Alice L. Grant
607 N. Logan St., 62959

Marissa
Illinois Chapter
Pal-Am
Gloria F. Cox, Secretary
Rt. 2
Box 149C, 62257

Marissa Historical and Genealogical Society
Box 27, 62257

Marshall
Clark County Genealogical Society
Box 153, 62441

McHenry
McHenry County Genealogical Society
1011 N. Green St., 60050

Monmouth
Warren County Genealogical Society
Box 240, 61462

Monticello
Platt County Historical & Genealogical Society
Box 123, 61856

Mt. Prospect
Northwest Suburban Council of Genealogists
Box AC, 60056

Mt. Vernon
Mt. Vernon Genealogical Society
Elizabeth L. Kell, Secretary
Box 103, 62864

Nashville
Washington County Genealogical Society
c/o Wanda Groenhert
Rt. 1, 62263

Niles
Jewish Genealogical Society of Illinois
Box 48501, 60648

Normal
Bloomington-Normal Genealogical Society
Box 488, 61761

Odell
Odell Historical and Genealogical Society
Box 82, 60460

Olney
Richland County Genealogical Society
Box 202, 62450

Oregon
Ogle County Genealogical Society
Box 183, 61061

Ottawa
American College of Genealogists
c/o Richard E. Willson, Sec./Treas.
Starved Rock Library System
Box 354, 61350

Genealogy Guild
LaSalle County Historical Society
Box 577, 61350

Palestine
Fort LaMotte Genealogical & Historical Society
LaMotte Public Library, 62451

Pekin
Tazewell County Genealogical Society
Box 312, 61554

Peoria
Peoria County Genealogical Society
Box 1489, 61655

Quincy
Great River Genealogical Society
c/o Public Library
526 Jersey St., 62301

Robinson
Crawford County Genealogical Society
Box 110, 63454

Rock Island
Blackhawk Genealogical Society
Box 912, 61201

Rockford
Illinois Mennonite Historical & Genealogical Society
8015 Cameo Dr., 61111

North Central Illinois Genealogical Society
Box 1071, 61105

Rushville
Schuyler-Brown Historical and Genealogical Society
Jail Museum
Congress and Madison Sts., 62681

Salem
Marion County Genealogical & Historical Society
Box 342, 62881

Savanna
Carroll County Genealogical Society
c/o Savanna Public Library
Box 347, 61074

Shelbyville
Shelby County Historical and Genealogical Society
Box 287, 62565

South Holland
South Suburban Genealogical & Historical Society
Box 96, 60473

Springfield
Sangamon County Genealogical Society
Box 1829, 62705

Staunton
Staunton Area Genealogical Society
Box 95, 62088

Sterling
Whiteside County Genealogists
Box 145, 61081

Whiteside County Genealogical Society
c/o Y.W.C.A.
412-1st Ave., 61081

Stockton
Heritage League of Northwest Ilinois
Stockton Public Library
140 W. Benton St., 61085

Streamwood
Poplar Creek Genealogical Society
200 Kosan Circle, 60103

Sullivan
Moultrie County Historical & Genealogical Society
Box MM, 61957

Sycamore
The Genealogical Society of DeKalb County Illinois
Box 295, 60178

Toledo
Cumberland Coles County Genealogical Society
Rt. 1
Box 141, 62468

Troy
Madison County Genealogical Society
Box 89, 62294

Tuscola
Douglas County Genealogical Society
c/o Mrs. Philip White
303 South Indiana, 61953

Urbana
Champaign County Genealogical Society
Urbana Free Library
201 S. Race St., 61801

Utica
Genealogy Guild of LaSalle County
Box 278, 61373

Vandalia
Fayette County Genealogical Society
Box 177, 62471

Warsaw
Lee County Genealogical Society
c/o William M. King
Rt. 2, 62379

Waterloo
Monroe County Historical & Genealogical Society
Morrison-Talbot Public Library
219 Park St., 62298

Monroe County Genealogical Research Group
Mrs. William Schmitt
512 Mary Dr., 62298

Watseka
Iroquois County Genealogical Society
Old Courthouse Museum
103 W. Cherry, 60970

Waverly
Waverly Genealogical & Historical Society
c/o Mrs. Guy W. Martin
359 E. Tremont, 62692

Western Springs
Western Springs Historical Society
Genealogy Division
740 Hill Grove Ave., 60558

White Heath
Piatt County Historical & Genealogical Society
Rt. 1
Box 30, 61884

Winnetka
North Suburban Genealogical Society
768 Oak St., 60093

Zion
Zion Genealogical Society
Zion Public Memorial Library
2600 Emmaus Ave., 60099

Indiana

Albion
Noble County Genealogical Society
c/o Noble County Public Library
109 No. York St., 46701

Anderson
Madison County Historical Society, Inc.
Family History Section
Box 523, 46015

Bedford
Lawrence County Genealogical Society
Lawrence County Museum
Courthouse, 47421

Bloomfield
Greene County Historical & Genealogical Society
Gene Coombs, President
105 Mechanic St., 47424

Bloomington
Monroe County Genealogical Society
The Old Library
202 E. Washington, 47401

Brazil
Clay County Genealogical Society, Inc.
Box 211, 47834

Bourbon
Marshall County Genealogical Society
3383 E. Eighth Rd., 46504

Crawfordsville
Who's Your Ancestor Genealogical Society
Crawfordsville Library
222 S. Washington St., 47933

Danville
Hendricks County Genealogical Society
c/o Danville Public Library
101 S. Indiana St., 46122

Elkhart
Elkhart County Genealogical Society
1812 Jeanwood Dr., 46514

Evansville
Tri-State Genealogical Society
c/o Willard Library
21 First Ave., 47712

Fort Wayne
Allen County Genealogical Society of Indiana
Box 12003, 46862

Greencastle
Genealogy Club of Putnam County
Greencastle Public Library
102 E. Walnut St., 46135

Indianapolis
Indiana Chapter
Palatines to America
Mrs. Ruth Shelley, Secretary
4825 Straford Ave., 46201

Indianapolis
Indiana Historical Society
Family History Section
315 W. Ohio St., 46202

Kokomo
Howard County Genealogical Society
220 N. Union, Box 736, 46901

North Central Indiana Genealogical Society
c/o R. Tetrick
2300 Canterbury Dr., 46901

Lafayette
TIPCOA (Tippecanoe County Area Genealogical Society)
909 South St., 47901

Logansport
Cass County Genealogical Society
Box 373, 46947

Indiana Chapter I
Ohio Genealogical Society
Pauline Babb, Treasurer
Rt. 5, 46947

Monticello
White County Genealogical Society
Box 149, 47960

Marion
Grant County Genealogical Society
24 Herbal Dr., 46952

White County Genealogical Society
Box 149, 47960

Muncie
Delaware County Genealogical Society
c/o Mrs. Juanita Lewis
Y.W.C.A.
310 E. Charles St., 47305

New Albany
Southern Indiana Genealogical Society
Box 665, 47150

Peru
Miami County Genealogical Society
Box 542, 46970

Plymouth
Tri-County Genealogical Society
c/o Mrs. Robert Kirkley
Box 19, 46536

Rochester
Fulton County Historical Society, Inc.
7th & Pontiac, 46975

Warsaw
Kosciusko County Area Genealogy Researchers
Mrs. Willodean Metzger, President
Rt. 2
Box 97, 46580

Genealogy Section
Kosciusko County Historical Society
Box 1071, 46580

Washington
Daviess County Genealogical Society
c/o Eleanor Purdue
703 Front St., 47501

Westville
Northwest Indiana Genealogical Society
Box 403, 46391

Winchester
Randolph County Genealogical Society
c/o Monisa Wisner
Rt. 3, 47394

Winimac
Pulaski County Genealogical Society
Pulaski County Library
121 S. Riverside Dr., 46996

Iowa

Albia
Monroe County Chapter
Iowa Genealogical Society
Sarah Hindman
Rt. 3, 52531

Ames
Story County Chapter
Iowa Genealogical Society
c/o Chamber of Commerce
205 Clark Avenue, 50010

Ankeny
Ankeny Area Chapter
Iowa Genealogical Society
Carole Martin
422 N.E. 7th St., 50021

Atlantic
Southwest Iowa Genealogical Memory Writers Society
c/o Atlantic Public Library
507 Poplar. 50022

Cass County Genealogical Society
Box 392, 50022

Audubon
Audubon County Chapter
Iowa Genealogical Society
Mrs. Dorothy H. Hansen
104 Nasby Ave., 50025

Bellevue
Jackson County Chapter
Iowa Genealogical Society
Mrs. Evelyn Edleman
Rt. 3
Box 81A. 52031

Bloomfield
Davis County Chapter, Iowa Genealogcial Society
c/o Peggy Arnold
206 Grode St., 52537

Burlington
Des Moines County Genealogical Society
Box 493, 52601

Cedar Rapids
Linn County Chapter
Iowa Genealogical Society
Charlene Hansen, President
Box 175, 52406

Linn County Heritage Society
Box 175, 52406

Centerville
Appanoose County Chapter
Iowa Genealogical Society
Gladys M. DePuy
424 E. State St., 52544

Charles City
Cedar Valley Chapter
Iowa Genealogical Society
c/o Ethel Mae Krueger
804 N. Grand, 50616

Clarinda
Page County Genealogical Club
Mrs. Henry L. Ankenny, President
420 South 16th, 51632

Clarion
Wright County Genealogical Society
Box 225, 50525

Clinton
Gateway Chapter
Iowa Genealogical Society
Lyle Suthers
912 Pleasant Valley, 52732

Corydon
Wayne County Genealogical Society
Box 182, 50060

Creston
Union County Chapter
Iowa Genealogical Society
c/o Irma Miller
1002 N. Vine, 50801

Dallas Center
Dallas County Chapt.
Iowa Genealogical Society
Box 264, 50063

Davenport
Federation of Genealogical Societies
Box 220, 52808

Scott County Chapter
Iowa Genealogical Society
Box 3132, 52805

Scott County Iowa Genealogical Society
c/o Paul E. Bohnsack
1919 N. Ohio Blvd., 52804

Des Moines
Iowa Genealogical Society
Box 3815, 50322

Pioneer Sons & Daughter (Polk) Chapter
Iowa Genealogical Society
Box 2103, 50310

Tree Shakers (Polk) Chapter
Iowa Genealogical Society
Mary Dickey
1731 Searle St., 50317

Dubuque
Key City Chapter
Iowa Genealogical Society
Box 13, 52001

Fairfield
Jefferson County Genealogy Society
Mrs. Verda Baird
Correspondence Secretary
Rt. 1
Box 112, 52556

Forest City
Lime Creek Chapter
Iowa Genealogical Society
c/o Mrs. Forest Olson
435 S. 8th, 50436

Fort Dodge
Webster County Chapter
Iowa Genealogical Society
Box 1584, 50501

Gravity
Taylor County Genealogical Society
Box 8, 50848

Greenfield
Adair County Chapter
Iowa Genealogical Society
Mrs. Marvin McBride
311 West Iowa, 50849

Harlan
Nishnabotna Genealogical Society
Rt. 2
Box 129, 51537

Henderson
Mills County Genealogical Society
Beverly Boileau
Rt. 1, 51541

Independence
Buchanan County Chapter
Iowa Genealogical Society
Ellen Foland
408–3rd St.
N.W., 50644

Indianola
Warren County Genealogical Society
504 N. Buxton
Apt. 7, 50125

Iowa City
Iowa City Chapter
Iowa Genealogical Society
Box 822, 52244

Iowa City Genealogical Society
Box 822, 52244

Jamaica
Guthrie County Chapter
Iowa Genealogical Society
Box 96, 50128

Jefferson
Greene County Chapter
Iowa Genealogical Society
Mrs. Barbara Van Dyke
504 N. Elm, 50129

Keokuk
Lee County Genealogical Society of Iowa
Box 303, 52632

Knoxville
Marion County Genealogical Society
Box 385, 50138

Le Mars
Northwest Iowa Genealogy Society
Le Mars Public Library
46 - 1st St.
S.W., 51031

Linn Grove
Iowa Lakes Chapter
Iowa Genealogical Society
Janet Baisch
Rt. 1, 51033

Lucas
Lucas County Chapter
Iowa Genealogical Society
Wanda Willis
Rt. 1, 50151

Lytton
Sac County Genealogical Society
Box 234, 50561

Madrid
Boone County Chapter
Iowa Genealogical Society
Bonita Kingsbury
Rt. 1, 50156

Manchester
Delaware County Genealogical Society
Tim Tutton
200 E. Main St., 52057

Marshalltown
Central Iowa Chapter
Iowa Genealogical Society
Box 945, 50158

Mason City
North Central Iowa Genealogical Society
Box 237, 50401

Modale
Harrison County Genealogical Society
Judy White
Box 158, 51556

Montezuma
Poweshiek County Historical & Genealogical Society
Box 70 (114 S. 3rd St.), 50171

Mount Ayr
Ringgold County Chapter
Iowa Genealogical Society
Lena Saville
204 W. Jefferson St., 50854

New Hampton
Chickasaw County Chapter
Iowa Genealogical Society
Mrs. Willis Huffman
603 W. Hale, 50659

New Market
Southwest Iowa Genealogical Society
Box 93, 51646

Newton
Jasper County Chapter
Iowa Genealogical Society
Box 163, 50208

Oakland
Botna Valley Chapter
Iowa Genealogical Society
Dorothy Cain, President
839 Senic Circle, 51560

Oelwein
Fayette County/Oelwin Area Chapter
Iowa Genealogical Society
Dorothy Gosse
Rt. 2
Box 92A, 50663

Onawa
Monona County Chapter
Iowa Genealogical Society
c/o Emma Stanislav, 51040

Ottumwa
Wapello County Chapter
Iowa Genealogical Society
c/o Mrs. John D. Ware
Rt. 4
Four Winds, 52501

Red Oak
Montgomery County Chapter
Iowa Genealogical Society
Jean Schaffer
901 Washington Ave., 51566

Rockwell City
Calhoun County Chapter
Iowa Genealogical Society
c/o Rockwell City Public Library
425-5th St., 50579

Calhoun County Genies
c/o Judy Webb
Rt. 2, 50579

Sheffield
Franklin County Chapter
Iowa Genealogical Society
Mrs. Dorothy Davolt
Box 427, 50475

Shellrock
Bremer County Genealogical Society
c/o Thelma Richardson
Box 365, 50670

Sioux City
Woodbury County Chapter
Iowa Genealogical Society
Marjorie Ellis
4316 Orleans Ave., 51106

Thompson
Lime Creek/Winnebago Chapter
Iowa Genealogical Society
Box 252, 50478

Toledo
Tama County Tracers Genealogical Society
Box 84 (200 N. Broadway St.), 54342

Waterloo
Northeast Iowa Chapter
Iowa Genealogical Society
Mrs. Bert Medhaug
1236 Pleasant Valley Dr. 50701

Northeast Iowa Genealogical Society
c/o Grout Museum of History & Science
503 South St., 50701

Webster City
Hamilton County Chapter
Iowa Genealogical Society
Vivan W. Kalton
814 N. Terrace Dr., 50595

Winterset
Madison County Chapter
Iowa Genealogical Society
Box 26, 50237

Kansas

Belleville
Republic County Genealogical Society
Mrs. G. D. Strafford
810 Shady Lane, 66935

Brewster
Rawlins County Genealogical Society
c/o Mary Scott
Rt. 2
Box 41, 67732

Cawker City
North Central Kansas Genealogical Society & Library, Inc.
Box 251, 67430

Chanute
Chanute Genealogical Society
1000 S. Allen, 66720

Coffeyville
Montgomery County Genealogical Society
Box 444, 67337

Columbus
Cherokee County Genealogical Society of Southeast Kansas
205 N. Kansas, 66725

Concordia
Cloud County Genealogical Society
c/o Mrs. Ralph Chubbuck
Rt. 3, 66901

Dodge City
Kansas Genealogical Society, Inc.
Box 103, 67801

Emporia
Flint Hills Genealogical Society
Box 555, 66801

Fort Scott
Old Fort Genealogical Society
c/o Public Library
201 S. National, 66701

Garden City
Finney County Genealogical Society
Box 592, 67846

Goodland
Sherman County Historical & Genealogical Society
Box 684, 67335

Great Bend
Barton County Genealogical Society
Box 425, 67530

Harper
Harper County Genealogical Society
Rt. 2
Box 46 (1524 S. Ash), 67058

Hays
Ft. Hays Kansas Genealogical Society
c/o Forsyth Library, 67601

Hutchinson
Hutchinson Genealogical Society
c/o Garland Henson
510 E. 24th St., 67501

Reno County Genealogical Society
Box 5, 67501

Independence
Wheatland Genealogical Society
161 N. Irving, 67301

Iola
East Central Kansas Genealogical Society
Box 78, 66749

Kingman
Branches & Twigs Genealogical Society
Helen Gurtner
Rt. 2, 67068

Lawrence
Douglas County Genealogical Society
Box 3664, 66044

Leavenworth
Leavenworth County Genealogical Society
Box 362, 66048

Manhattan
Riley County Kansas Genealogical Society
2005 Claflin Rd., 66502

Marysville
Blue Valley Genealogical Society
Rev. Earl Underwood
809 N. Twelfth, 66508

Neodesha
The Heritage Genealogical Society
Box 73, 66575

Norton
Norton County Genealogical Society
c/o Peggy Kendall
Rt. 2
1012 West Ave., 67654

Olathe
Harlan County Genealogical Society of Kentucky
800 Sheridan Circle, 66061

Osborne
Osborne County Genealogical & Historical Society
Osborne Public Library, 67473

Oskaloosa
Jefferson County Genealogical Society
Box 174, 66066

Parsons
LaBette Genealogical Society
c/o Mrs. Tina Rice
Box 826, 67357

Phillipsburg
Phillips County Genealogical Society
Box 114, 67661

Pittsburg
Crawford County Genealogical Society
c/o Pittsburg Public Library
211 West 4th St., 66762

Pleasanton
Linn County Historical & Genealogical Society
Box 137, 66075

Salina
Smoky Valley Genealogical Society, Inc.
881 South 10th St., 66208

Shawnee Mission
Johnson County Genealogical Society & Library, Inc.
Box 8057, 66208

Syracuse
Santa Fe Trail Genealogical Society
Mrs. Karl Venneberg
North Rt.
Box 13A, 67878

Stafford
Stafford County Historical & Genealogical Society
Mrs. Marshall Gary Sr.
RFD
Box 84, 67578

Topeka
Kansas Council of Genealogical Societies
Box 8038, 66608

Topeka
Topeka Genealogical Society
Box 4048, 66604

Wichita
Midwest Historical & Genealogical Society, Inc.
Box 1121, 67201

Yates Center
East Central Kansas Genealogical Society
c/o Velva Hall
410 N. State St.,

Kentucky

Ashland
Eastern Kentucky Genealogical Society
Box 1544, 41101

Benton
Marshall County Genealogical Society
c/o Benton Public Library
Rt. 6
Box 67, 42025

Bowling Green
Southern Kentucky Genealogical Society
1425 Audubon Drive, 42101

Central City
Muhlenberg County Genealogical Society
Central City Public Library
Broad St., 42330

Corbin
Corbin Genealogical Society
c/o Reba Cummins
1506 Woodwind Ct., 40701

Frankfort
Kentucky Genealogical Society
Box 153, 40602

Fulton
Fulton County Genealogical Society
Box 31, 42041

Glasgow
Kentucky Cemetery Restoration Committee
c/o 108 W. Brown St., 42141

South Central Kentucky Historical & Genealogical Society
Box 80, 42141

Harrodsburg
Genealogy Committee
Harrodsburg Historical Society
Box 316, 40330

Hazard
Perry County Geneaalogical & Historical Society
301 Kentucky Blvd., 41701

Henderson
Henderson County Genealogical & Historical Society
Box 715, 42420

Hopkinsville
Christian County Genealogical Society
Attn: Mrs. Margaret P. Mason
1101 Bethel St., 42240

Louisville
Knox County Genealogical Society
Box 18414, 40128

Madisonville
Hopkins County Genealogical Society
Box 51, 42431

Mayfield
Graves County Genealogical Society
Box 245, 42066

Melber
Jackson Purchase Genealogical Society
c/o Don Simmons, President, 42069

Morehead
Dean & Creech Families of America
Rt. 6
Box 498, 40351

Dean and Creech Families of America
Lloyd Dean, Director
Rt. 6
Box 498, 40351

Rowan County Historical Society, Inc.
Lloyd Dean, President
Rt. 6
Box 498, 40351

Owensboro
West Central Kentucky Family Research Association
Box 1465, 42301

Paducah
Western Kentucky Genealogical Society
c/o Mrs. D. T. Cooper
3238 Madison St., 42001

Paintsville
Big Sandy Valley Genealogical Society
1215 Strafford Ave., 41240

Ravenna
Estill County Historical & Genealogical Society
Box 221, 40472

Russellville
Logan County Genealogical Society
c/o Logan County Library
201 W. 6th St., 42276

Vine Grove
Ancestral Trails Historical Society
Box 573, 40175

Louisiana

Alexandria
Alexandria Historical & Genealogial Society
c/o Constance Henderson
503 Washington St., 71301

Central Louisiana Genealogical Society
503 Washington St., 71301

Baton Rouge
Baton Rouge Genealogical & Historical Society
Box 80565 S.E. Station, 70808

Chalmette
St. Bernard Genealogical Society
Box 271, 70044

Destrehan
German-Acadian Coast Historical & Genealogical Society
Box 517, 70047

Houma
Terrebonne Parish Genealogical Society
c/o Mrs. Cap Kelly
200 Westview, 70360

Jennings
Jennings Genealogical Society
406 E. Norwood Dr., 70546

Lafayette
Attakapas Historical Association
Box 43010 U.S.L., 70504

Lake Charles
Southwest Louisiana Genealogical Society
Box 5652
Drew Station, 70606

Monroe
Northeast Louisiana Genealogical Society
Box 2743, 71201

New Orleans
Genealogical Research Society of New Orleans
Box 51751, 70151

Powhatan
Natchitoches Genealogical & Historical Association
Box 641, 71457

Shreveport
Ark-La-Tex Genealogical Association, Inc.
Box 4462, 71104

Southern Genealogical Institute, Inc.
9418 Shartel Dr. 71118

Ethnic International
Box 6403, 71106

Ville Platte
Evangeline Genealogical and Historical Society
Box 664, 70586

West Monroe
Ouitchita Genealogical Society
c/o Agatha Burkett
106 Laurel St., 71291

Maine

Augusta
Maine Old Cemetery Association
Box 324, 04330

Farmington
Maine Genealogical Society
Box 221, 04938

Lewiston
Begin Chapter
American-Canadian Genealogical Society
Normand L. Rioux, President
14 Tanglewood Dr.
Apt. 4, 04240

Machiasport
Sunrise Institute for Genealogy
Box 276, 04655

Maryland

Aberdeen
Harford County Genealogical Society
Box 15, 21001

Anneslie
Polish Nobility Association
Sovereign Hospitaller Order of St. John
Villa Anneslie
419 Dunkirk Rd., 211212

Baltimore
Genealogy Committee
Maryland Historical Society
201 W. Monument St., 21201

Maryland Genealogical Society
201 W. Monument St., 21201

Olde Town Genealogical Society
706 Park Ave., 21201

Bowie
Genealogical Council of Maryland
12511 Brewer Lane, 20715

Prince George's County Genealogical Society
Box 819, 20715-0819

Callaway
St. Mary's County Genealogical Society
Doris Bevan Jones, Editor
General Delivery, 20620

Catonsville
Genealogical Section
Catonsville Historical Society
1824 Frederisk Rd., 21228

Centreville
Genealogical Committee
Queen Anne's County Historical Society
Box 296, 21617

Charleston
Cecil County Genealogical Society
Box 11, 21914

Cockeysville
Unitarian & Universalist Genealogical Society
Willis Clayton Tull Jr., Director
10605 Lakespring Way, 21030

Columbia
Howard County Genealogical Society
10545 Rivulet Row, 21044

Cumberland
Genealogical Society of Allegany County Maryland
611 Washington St., 21502

Easton
Upper Shore Genealogical Society of Maryland
Box 275, 21601

Frederick
Frederick County Genealogical Society
c/o George Perry
1333 Apple Tree Ct., 21701

Hagerstown
Washington County Genealogical Society
J. Christopher Ramsay, President
1206 Oak Hill Ave., 21740

Pasadena
Anne Arundel Genealogical Society
Box 221, 21122

Potomac
Jewish Genealogical Society of Greater Washington
Aline Bohm Greif
18 Buckspark Ct., 20854

Rockville
Genealogy Club of Montgomery County Historical Society
103 W. Montgomery Ave., 20852

Hamilton National Genealogical Society
14326 Blackmon Dr., 20853

Salisbury
Lower Delmarva Genealogical Society
c/o Peggy Lauridsen
528 Druid Hill Ave., 21801

Towson
Baltimore County Genealogical Society
Box 10085, 21204

Westminster
Carroll County Genealogical Society
Carroll County Public Library
50 E. Main St. 21157

Massachusetts

Ashland
Massachusetts Society of Genealogists
Box 215, 01721

Boston
New England Historic Genealogical Society
101 Newbury St., 02116

Bridgewater
Ashleys of America, Inc.
68 Spring Hill Ave., 02324

Brockton
Worcester Chapter
Massachusetts Society of Genealogists
18 Denton St., 02401

Concord
Concord Genealogical Roundtable
Concord Public Library, 01742

Conway
Hampshire County Genealogical Society
c/o Wendell B. Cook Jr.
Rt. 1
Mathews Rd., 01341

Harwich Center
Cape Cod Genealogical Society
c/o Brooks Library, 02645

Holyoke
The Belgian Researchers
8 Wycoff Ave., 01040

Hampden Chapter
Massachusetts Society of Genealogists
c/o C. Leslie Hall
Box 388, 01040

Lynnfield
Essex Society of Genealogists
Lynnfield Public Library
18 Summer St., 01940

Newton
The Genealogists Lobby
173 Tremont St., 02158

The Irish Family History Society
173 Tremont St., 02158

Pittsfield
Berkshire Family History Association
Box 1437, 01201

Shelburne
Franklin Chapter
Massachusetts Society of Genealogists
c/o Wallace Trumper
Anderson Rd., 01370

Somerset
Bristol Chapter
Massachusetts Society of Genealogists
George H. Petrin, Secretary
71 Statler Ave., 02725

Springfield
Hampden Chapter
Massachusetts Society of Genealogists
c/o Fern E. Gibeau
42 Lanwood St., 01119

Western Massachusetts Genealogical Society
Box 206, 01108

Taunton
American-Portuguese Genealogical Society, Inc.
Box 644, 02780

Walpole
Norfolk Chapter
Massacussetts Society of Genealogists
c/o Paul Dingwell Jr.
Box 55, 02081

Wilmington
Middlesex North Chapter
Massachusetts Society of Genealogists
Hugh A. Forest, President
155 Lake St., 01887

Michigan

Adrian
Lenawee County Family Researchers
c/o Lenawee County Historical Museum, Inc.
Box 511, 49221

Alpena
Northeast Michigan Genealogical & Historical Society
Jessee Besser Museum
491 Johnson, 49707

Ann Arbor
American Association of University Women Genealogy Colloquium
1830 Washtenaw, 48104

Genealogical Society of Washtenaw County
Box 7155, 48107

Birmingham
Oakland County Genealogical Society
Box 1094, 48012

Boyne City
Antrim-Charlevoix-Emmet County Genealogical Society
c/o Boyne City Public Library, 49712

Bridgman
Jacobite Society Auxilliary
Box 151
California Rd., 49106

Cheboygan
Cheboygan County Genealogical Society
646 Old Mackinaw Rd., 49721

Coldwater
Branch County Genealogical Society
Box 443, 49036

Dearborn
Dearborn Genealogical Society
Box 1112, 48121

Detroit
The Detroit Society for Genealogical Research
c/o Burton Historical Collection
Detroit Public Library
5201 Woodward Ave., 48202

Fred Hart Williams Genealogical Society
5201 Woodward Ave., 48202

Polish Genealogical Society of Michigan
Burton Historical Collection
Detroit Pub. Lib.
5201 Woodward Ave., 48202

Edwardsburg
Genealogical Society of Cass County
c/o Edwardsburg Library
49112

Essexville
Bay County Genealogical Society
Box 27, 48732

Farmington
Farmington Genealogical Society
Farmington Public Library
23550 Liberty St., 48024

Fremont
Newaygo County Society of History & Genealogy
c/o Tom Kidder
314 E. Main, 49412

Flint
Flint Genealogical Society
Box 1217, 48501

Fulton
Searchers
Eva Henderson
Box 103, 49052

Grand Haven
Grand Haven Genealogical Society
c/o Loutit Library
707 Columbus, 49417

Grand Rapids
Western Michigan Genealogical Society
Grand Rapids Public Library
Library Plaza, 49502

Holland
Holland Genealogical Society
300 River Ave., 49423

Iron Mountain
Dickinson County Genealogical Society
c/o Dickinson County Public Library
401 Iron Mountain St., 49801

Kalamazoo
Kalamazoo Valley Genealogical Society
315 Rose St., 49007

Lake Orion
North Oakland Genealogical Society
845 S. Lapeer Rd., 48035

Lansing
French Canadian Heritage Society of Michigan
Box 15134, 48901

Mid-Michigan Genealogical Society
Michigan Unit
State Library
Dept. of Education
Box 30007
735 East Michigan Ave., 48909

Lapeer
Lapeer County Genealogical Society
c/o Lapeer City Branch Library
921 E. Nepessing St., 48446

Lincoln Park
Downriver Genealogical Society
1384 Cleophus, 48146

Litchfield
Southern Michigan Genealogical Society
c/o Eleanor Wildt
420 Jonesville St., 49252

Livonia
Western Wayne County Genealogical Society
Box 63, 48151

Ludington
Mason County Genealogical Society
Box 352, 49431

Midland
Midland County Genealogical Society
Grace A. Dow Library
1710 W. St. Andrews Dr., 48640

Monroe
Genealogical Society of Monroe County
Michigan
Monroe County Historical Society Museum
126 S. Monroe St., 48161

Mount Clemens
Macomb Genealogical Society
c/o Mt. Clemens Public Library
150 Cass Ave., 48043

Muskegon
Muskegon County Genealogical Society
c/o Hackley Public Library
316 W. Webster St., 49440

New Hudson
Lyon Township Genealogical Society
Kim S. Harison
55832 Pontiac Trail Ct., 48165

Niles
Four Flags Area Genealogical Society
Box 414, 49120

Owosso
Shiawassee County Genealogical Society
Box 145, 48867

Oxford
Slovak Cultural & Literary Center
775 W. Drahner Rd., 48051

Pontiac
Pontiac Area Historical & Genealogical
Society
Box 3571, 48059

Royal Oak
Oakland County Genealogical Society
c/o Royal Oak Public Library
211 East 11 Mile Rd., 48068

Saginaw
Saginaw Genealogical Society
Saginaw Public Library
505 Janes Ave., 48605

St. Johns
Clinton County Genealogical Society
110 Lewis St., 48879

St. Joseph
Genealogical Association of Southwestern
Michigan
Box 573, 49085

Spring Arbor
Jackson County Genealogical Society
Box 364, 49283

Sterling Heights
Sterling Heights Genealogy Club
Sterling Heights Public Library
40255 Dodge Park Rd., 48078

Sturgis
Tri-State Genealogical Society
30874–U.S. #12, 49091

Three Rivers
Three Rivers Genealogical Society
13724 Spence Rd., 49093

Traverse City
Grand Traverse Genealogical Society
c/o Traverse Public Library
49684

Union City
Union City Genealogical Club
Union Township Library
221 N. Broadway, 49094

Vicksburg
Vicksburg Area Genealogical Society
120 W. Maple St., 49097

Wayland
Wayland Tree Tracers Genealogy Society
Donna Benedict
Corr. Sec.
129 W. Cedar St., 49348

West Branch
Ogemaw Genealogical & Historical Society
West Branch Public Library
119 N. 4th St., 48661

Minnesota

Albert Lea
Freeborn County Genealogical Society
Box 403, 56007

Anoka
Anoka County Genealogical Society
1900 Third Ave.
So., 55303

Austin
Mower County Genealogical Society
Box 145, 55912

Bovey
Itasca County Genealogical Society
Box 130, 55709

Brainerd
Crow Wing County Genealogical Society
131 Belle Rae Circle, 56401

Breckenridge
Genealogy Guild of Wilkins (MN) &
Richland (ND) Counties
Box 330, 56520

Buffalo
Wright County Genealogical Society
911–2nd Ave.
S., 55313

Buhl
Range Genealogical Society, Inc.
Box 278, 55713

Cloquet
Genealogical Society of Carlton County
Box 204, 55720

Detroit Lakes
Heart O'Lakes Genealogical Society
Rt. 2
Box 420, 56501

Duluth
Twin Ports Genealogical Society
Box 3340, 55803

Edina
Edina Historical Society
Genealogical Roundtable
Village Hall
4801 West 50th St., 55424

Fergus Falls
Ottertail County Historical Society
1110 Lincoln Ave.
W., 56537

Lindstrom
Chisago Lakes Genealogical Society
Lindstrom High School Library, 55045

Mankato
Traverse-des-Sioux Genealogical Society
Box 315, 56001

Marshall
Prairieland Genealogical Society
703 North 6th St., 56258

Minneapolis
La Societe Canadienne-Francaise de
Minnesota
1401 Circle Terr., 55421

Northfield
Northfield-Rice County Genealogical
Society
411 East 6th St., 55057

Rochester
Olmstead County Genealogical Society
Box 6411, 55901

St. Cloud
St. Cloud Area Genealogical Society
Box 213, 56302

St. Louis Park
Northwest Territory French & Canadian
Heritage Institute
Box 26372, 55426

St. Paul
Minnesota Genealogical Society
Box 16069, 55116

North Star Chapter
American Historical Soc. of Germans from
Russia
Robert Hopkins President
1468 Carroll Ave., 55104

The Scandinavian-American Genealogical
Society
Chapter Minnesota Genealogical Society
Box 16006, 55105

White Bear Lake Genealogical Society
4107 White Bear Ave., 55110

Waseca
Waseca Area Genealogy Society
Box 314, 56039

Winona
Genealogy Roundtable
Box 644, 55987

Young America
Lower Minnesota Valley Genealogical Society
Box 99, 55397

Mississippi

Batesville
Panola Genealogical & Historical Society
210 Kyle St., 38606,

Jackson
Historical and Genealogical Association of Mississippi
618 Avalon Rd., 39026

Mississippi Genealogical Society
408 Dunbar St., 39205

Ocean Springs
Ocean Springs Genealogy Society
Box 300, 39564

Oxford
Skipwith Historical & Genealogical Society
c/o Mrs. Theron Bratton
R. 1
Box 76-J, 38655

Pascagoula
Jackson County Genealogical Society
815 Lake Ave., 39567

Ripley
Tippah County Historical & Genealogical Society
308 N. Commerce St., 38663

State College
Oktibbeha County Genealogical Society
Box 555, 39762

Tupelo
North East Mississippi Historical & Genealogical Society
Box 434, 38801

Washington
Genealogical Society of Adams County
c/o Mrs. V.L. Barker
Box 187, 39190

Missouri

Bethany
Harrison County Genealogical Society
515 N. 22nd St., 64424

Booneville
Santa Fe Researchers
c/o Joan Seevers
Box 319, 65233

Brookfield
Genealogical Researchers of Linn County, MO
Audrey Stigall President
771 Tomahawk, 64628

Cadet
Old Mines Historical Society
Kent Beauline
Box 300Z
Old Mines
Fertile, 63630

Carthage
Carthage Genealogical Society
c/o Joan Kunkel
Rt. 3, 64836

Missouri Genealogical Society
c/o Carthage Public Library
7th and Garrison St., 64836

Columbia
Genealogical Society of Central Missouri
Box 26, 65201

Excelsior Springs
Excelsior Springs Genealogical Society
Box 601, 64024

Farmington
St. Francois County Historical and Genealogical Society
c/o Farmington Public Library
114 W. Columbia, 63640

Florissant
Florissant Valley Historical and Genealogical Society
Box 298, 63032

Franklin
Santa Fe Trail Researchers Genealogical Society
c/o Karen Boggs
Rt. 1, 65250

Houston
Texas County Genealogical Society
Rt. 1
Box 41, 65483

Independence
Jackson County Genealogical Society
(formerly Gen. Soc. of Eastern Jackson Co. MO)
Box 471, 64051

Missouri Archives Genealogical Society
Robert L. Grover President
3929 Milton Dr., 64055

Jackson
Cape Girardeau County Genealogical Society
204 S. Union Ave., 63755

Jefferson City
Mid-Missouri Genealogical Society
Box 715, 65101

Missouri State Genealogical Association
Box 387, 65102

Kansas City
American Family Records Association
c/o Kansas City Public Library
311 East 12th St., 64106

Heart of America Genealogical Society & Library
Kansas City Public Library
311 E. 12th St., 64106

Kansas City Adult Adoptees Organization
Box 15225, 64106

Kennett
Genealogical Society of Dunklin County
c/o Dunklin County Library
226 N. Main St., 63857

Lawson
Lawson Tree Climbers
Box 58, 64062

Liberty
Genealogical Society of Liberty
Calvin W. Hawkins, Corresponding Secretary
Box 442, 64068

Marylville
Nodaway County Genealogical Society
Mrs. Mary Lou Sharr
Rt. 3
Box 228, 64468

O'Fallon
Lincoln County Genealogical Society
419 Wood Crest Blvd., 63366

Platte City
Platte County Genealogical Society
Box 103, 64079

Poplar Bluff
Genealogical Society of Butler County
320 N. Main St., 63901

St. Charles
St. Charles County Genealogical Society
Box 715, 63301

St. Joseph
Northwest Missouri Genealogical Society
Box 68
Station E., 64505

St. Louis
Missouri/Southern Illinois Chapter
Palatine to America
c/o R.R. Edleman
2800 Olive St. Apt. 6, 63103

St. Louis Genealogical Society
1695 S. Brentwood Blvd.
Suite 203, 63144

Springfield
Ozarks Genealogical Society, Inc.
Box 3494
Glenstone Station, 65808

Versailles
Morgan County Historical Society
William W. Williams
Genealogical Chairman
120 N. Monroe St., 65804

Warrensburg
West Central Missouri Genealogical Society & Library, Inc.
312 Johnson Ave., 64093

West Plains
South Central Missouri Genealogical Society
c/o Kimberlin Book Store, 65775

Montana

Billings
Yellowstone Genealogy Forum
Billings Parmly Library
510 N. 28th, 59101

Bozeman
Gallatin Genealogy Society
Box 2020, 59715

Chester
Broken Mountains Genealogical Society
Liberty Co. Public Library
Box 261, 59522

Great Falls
Great Falls Genealogy Society
Paris Gibson Square
1400–1st Ave.
North, 59401

Havre
Assiniboine Genealogical Society
Box 321, 59501

Kalispell
Flat Head Valley Genealogical Society
c/o O. A. Baugh
857–1st Ave.
E.N., 59901

Lewistown
Lewistown Genealogical Society
c/o Ruby E. Peccia, Librarian
312 Cook St., 59457

Nebraska

Alliance
Nebraska State Genealogical Society
Box 756, 69301

Northwest Genealogical Society
Box 6, 69301

Beatrice
Southeast Nebraska Genealogical Society
Box 562, 68310

Belvidere
Thayer County Genealogical Society
c/o Mrs. Kent Williamson
Box 388, 68315

Blair
Washington County Genealogical Soicety
c/o Blair Public Library
1665 Lincoln St., 68008

Cairo
Cairo Roots Historical & Genealogical Society
Box 404, 68824

Columbus
Platte Valley Kin Seekers
c/o Mrs. Gary Harkness
6411–65th St., 68601

Cozad
Cozad Genealogy Club
Box 253, 69130

Dawson County Genealogy Club
514 E. 8th St., 69130

Curtis
Frontier County Genealogical Society
Box 507, 69025

Dalton
Dalton Genies
Box 275, 69131

Enders
Chase County Genealogical Society
c/o Mrs. Gordon Luhrs, 69027

Fremont
Eastern Nebraska Genealogical Society
Box 541, 68025

Fullerton
Pawnee Genealogy Scouters
Box 397, 68638

Gering
Rebecca Winters Genealogical Society
c/o Shirley Weihing, President
1605 Holly, 69341

Grand Island
Prairie Pioneer Genealogical Society
Box 1122, 68802

Grant
Perkins County Genealogical Society
Box 418, 69140

Hastings
Adams County Genealogical Society
Box 424, 68901

Imperial
Chase County Genealogical Society
Box 303, 69033

Kearney
Ft. Kearney Genealogical Society
Box 22, 68847

Kimball
Plains Genealogical Society
c/o Kimball Public Library
69145

Lexington
Lexington Genealogy Club
Box 37, 68850

Lincoln
American Historical Society of Germans From Russia
631 D St., 68502

Lincoln-Lancaster Genealogical Society
Box 30055, 68503

Lyons
The Northeastern Nebraska Genealogical Society
c/o Maxine Sandquist
Box 249, 68038

McCook
Southwest Nebraska Genealogical Society
Box 6, 69001

Minden
South Central Genealogical Society
c/o Mrs. Haldine Johnson
Rt. 2
Box 57, 68959

Mullen
Hooker County Genealogical Society
Box 486, 69152

Norfolk
Madison County Genealogical Society
Box 615, 68701

North Platte
North Platte Genealogical Society
North Platte Public Library
120 West 4th St., 69101

Ogallala
Sandhills Seekers
c/o Mrs. Gene Casper
1110 Robin Lane, 69153

Omaha
Greater Omaha Genealogical Society
Box 4011, 68104

Orchard
Northern Antelope County Genealogical Society
Box 267, 68764

Ord
Valley County Genealogical Society
619 South 10th, 68862

O'Neill
Northern Nebraska Genealogical Society
Box 362, 68763

Plattsmouth
Cass County Genealogy Club
1116–3rd Ave., 68048

Ravenna
Ravenna Genealogical Society
Mrs. Lois Johnston
105 Alba, 68869

St. Paul
Howard County Kinquestors
Mrs. Emma Ostermann
317–7th St., 68873

Sidney
Cheyenne County Genealogical Society
Box 802, 69162

Thedford
Thomas County Genealogical Society
c/o Mrs. Calvin Jones
Box 136, 69166

Valentine
Cherry County Genealogical Society
Box 30, 69201

Wahoo
Genealogical Seekers
c/o Margaret Chisholm
Rt. 1
Box 41, 68066

York
Genealogical Society of York County
c/o Carol McKenzie
Rt. 1
Box 5, 68467

Greater York Area Genealogical Society
c/o Charles Baucom
Levitt Library
York College, 68467

Nevada

Carson City
Carson City Genealogical Society
c/o Michael Wittmuss
1509 Shoron Dr., 89701

Elko
Northeastern Nevada Genealogical Society
Box 1903, 89801

Las Vegas
Clark County Genealogical Society
c/o Barbara Brown
4333 El Cid Circle, 89121

Reno
Nevada State Genealogical Society
Box 20666, 89515

New Hampshire

Central Ossipee
Carroll County Chapter
New Hampshire Society of Genealogists
c/o Jeanne Oxandaburu
Box 488, 03814

Contoocook
Merrimack County Chapter
New Hampshire Society of Genealogists
c/o Priscilla Bohana
Rt. 1, 03229

Dover
Strafford County Chapter
New Hampshire Society of Genealogists
Box 322, 03820

Durham
New Hampshire Old Graveyard Association
c/o Philip A. Wilcox
Old Landing Rd., 03834

Exeter
New Hampshire Society of Genealogists
Box 633, 03833

Piscataqua Pioneers
c/o Edward G. Wood
71 High St. 03833

Rockingham County Chapter
New Hampshire Society of Genealogists
Box 81, 03833

Freedom
Carrol County Chapter
New Hampshire Society of Genealogists
Box 250, 03836

Lebanon
Grafton County Chapter
New Hampshire Society of Genealogists
Nancy Yacavone
15 School St., 03766

Manchester
Acadian Genealogical & Historical Association of New England
Box 668, 03105

American-Canadian Genealogical Society
Box 668, 03105

Federation of Franco-American Genealogical & Historical Societies
Box 668, 03105

Merrimack
Hillsboro County Chapter
New Hampshire Society of Genealogists
c/o Mrs. Joyce Bishop, President
Baboosic Lake Rd., 03054

Northfield
Belknap County Chapter
New Hampshire Society of Genealogists
c/o Mrs. Carol Twomey, President
Rt. 1
Shaker Rd., 03276

New Jersey

Belvidere
Warren County Historical and Genealogical Society
County Courthouse, 07823

Cape May Court House
Cape May County Historical & Genealogical Society
Rt. 9, 08210

Mt. Holly
The Burlington County Genealogy Club
E. Renee Heiss, President
Burlington County Library
Woodlane Rd., 08060

New Brunswick
Genealogical Society of New Jersey
Box 1291, 08930

Newark
Family History & Genealogy Club
New Jersey Historical Society
230 Broadway, 07104

Toms River
Ocean County Historical Society
Genealogy Committee
26 Hadley Ave., 08753

Westfield
Westfield Genealogy Club
c/o Westfield Memorial Library
425 E. Broad St., 07090

Westwood
Bergen County Genealogical Society
191 Fourth Ave., 07675

New Mexico

Albuquerque
Genealogy Club of the Albuquerque Public Library 423 Central Ave.
N.E., 87101

New Mexico Genealogy Society
Box 8330, 87198

Carlsbad
Eddy County Genealogical Society
Box 461, 88220

Farmington
Totah Tracers Genealogical Society
975 US Hwy 64, 87401

Hobbs
Southeastern New Mexico Genealogical Society
1607 Cobb Dr., 88240

Las Cruces
Southern New Mexico Genealogical Society
Thomas Branigan Memorial Library
200 E. Picacho Ave., 88001

Lovington
Lea County Genealogical Society
Box 1044, 88260

Roswell
Roswell Genealogical Society
Drawer 70, 88201

New York

Albany
Capitol District Genealogical Society
Box 2175
Empire State Plaza., 12220

Appleton
Niagara County Genealogical Society
c/o Nancy Balling Smith
2650 Hess Rd. Rural, 14008

Brooklyn
Genealogical and Heraldic Institute of America
c/o John N. LaCorte
111 Columbia Heights, 11201

Genealogical Workshop/Long Island Historical Society
128 Pierrepont St., 11201

Canadaigua
Canandaigua Genealogical Society
c/o Mrs. Mary Lapeer, President
96 Hubbell St., 14424

Carle Place
Genealogy Workshop
Port Washington Library
15 Titus Place, 11514

Dunkirk
Chautauqua Genealogical Society
Mrs. Mollie L. Smith
Box 97, 14048

Elmira
Twin Tier Genealogical Society
Box 763, 14902

Fairport
Tri-Town Genealogical and Historical Society
c/o Mrs. Robert Vogt
138 Roselawn Crescent, 14450

Flushing
The Ethnic Genealogy Center
Queens College
CUNY
House 37, 153-57 61st Rd., 11367

Fonda
Heritage & Genealogical Society of Montgomery County
Old Court House. 12068

Glens Falls
Northeastern New York Genealogical Society
Mrs. Pamela Vogel, Secretary
29 Garfield St., 12801

Goshen
Orange County Genealogical Society
101 main St., 10924

Hamburg
Western New York Genealogical Society
Box 338, 14075

Huntington
Genealogical Workshop
Huntington Historical Society
2 High St., 11743

New York
Alma (Adoptees Liberty Movement Association)
Box 154, 10033

Jewish Genealogical Society
300 East 71st St., 10021

New York Genealogical & Biographical Society
122 East 58th St., 10022

Russian Historical & Genealogical Society
971 First Ave., 10022

Society for the Promotion of Scholarship in Genealogy, Ltd.

Nunda
Livingston County Genealogical Society
c/o Mrs. Lyman F. Barry, President
Rt. 1
Box 313, 14517

Owego
Tioga Historical Society, Genealogical Committee
c/o Tioga Historical Society, 13827

Plattsburg
Genealogical Committee
Clinton County Historical Association
City Hall, 12901

Poughkeepsie
Dutchess County Genealogical Society
Box 708, 12602

Riverhead
Genealogy Section
Suffolk County Historical Society
300 W. Main St., 11901

Rochester
Genealogical Roundtable
Mrs. Harry F. Noble
130 Dale Rd., 14621

Kodak Genealogy Club
Dr. Stanley R. Ames, President
Box 1911, 14602

Rochester Genealogical Society
Doris J. Andrus, President
156 Nob Hill, 14617

Saranac Lake
Adriondack Genealogical-Historical Society
100 Main St., 12983

Seneca Falls
Finger Lakes Genealogical Society
Box 47, 13148

Stone Ridge
Ulster County Genealogical Society
Rt. Box 84, 12484

Syracuse
Central New York Genealogical Society
Box 104, Colvin Sta., 13205

Wayland
Livingston County Genealogical Society
c/o Mrs. Marion E. Scott
14 Pine St., 14572

North Carolina

Asheboro
Randolph County Genealogical Society
201 Worth St., 27203

Asheville
Old Buncombe County Genealogical Society
Box 2122, 28802

Charlotte
Mecklenburg County Genealogical Society
Box 32453, 28232

Dobson
Surry County Genealogical Society
Box 997, 27018

Durham
Kerr Family Association
North American Branch
201 Snow Bldg., 27701

Elizabeth City
Genealogy Committee
Pasquotank Historical Society
Box 523, 27909

Forest City
Genealogical Society of Old Tryon County
Box 938, 28043

Greensboro
Guilford County Genealogical Society
Box 9693, 27429-0693

Lenoir
Caldwell County Genealogical Society
Box 2476, 28645

Lexington
Genealogical Society of Davidson County
Box 1665, 27292

Monroe
Carolinas Genealogical Society
c/o Louis E. Hicks
407 S. Church, 28110

Murphy
Southwestern North Carolina Genealogical Society
101 Blumenthal, 28906

New Bern
Eastern North Carolina Genealogical Society
Box 395, 28560

North Wilkesboro
Wilkes County Genealogical Society
Box 1629, 28659

Raleigh
North Carolina Genealogical Society
Box 1492, 27604

Smithfield
Johnston County Genealogical Society
c/o Public Library
305 Market St., 27577

Statesville
Genealogical Society of Iredell, NC
Box 946, 28677

Swansboro
Coastal Genealogical Society
Box 1421, 28584

North Dakota

Bismarck
Bismarck-Mandan Historical & Genealogical Society
Box 485, 58501

Germans From Russia Heritage Society
Box 1671, 58502

Minot
Mouse River Loop Genealogy Society
Box 1391, 58701

Wahpeton
Genealogy Guild of Wilkin and Richland Counties
c/o Leach Public Library, 58075

West Fargo
Red River Valley Genealogical Society
626-22nd St.
East, 58078

Ohio

Akron
Summit County Chapter
Ohio Genealogical Society
Virginia Pickenpaugh, President
3842 Faith St., 44319

Ashland
Ashland County Chapter
Ohio Genealogical Society
Shirley Boyd, Corresponding Secretary
912 Claremont, 44805

Athens
Athens County Chapter
Ohio Genealogical Society
Beverly Schumacher, President
Rt 6
Box 67, 45701

Barnesville
Belmont County Chapter
Ohio Genealogical Society
Betsey Hartley, President
Rt. 2, 43713

Batavia
Clermont County Genealogical Society
180 S. 3rd St., 45103

Bellefontaine
Logan County Genealogical Society
Box 296, 43311

Bellville
Morrow County Chapter
Ohio Genealogical Society
Daniel L. Rhodebeck
7695 C.R. 97, 44813

Bowling Green
Wood County Chapter
Ohio Genealogical Society
Glen VanWormer, President
203 Biddle St., 43402

Wood County Genealogical Society
Paul W. Jones, President
217 N. Prospect, 43402

Brecksville
Cuyahoga-Brecksville County Chapter
Ohio Genealogical Society
c/o Dorothy Sutton
8410 Sunnydale Dr., 44141

Bryan
Definace County Chapter
Ohio Genealogical Society
Gladys Donson, Corresponding Secretary
Rt. 4
Beerbower Rd., 43506

Williams County Genealogical Society
Box 293, 43506

Burbank
Wayne County Chapter
Ohio Genealogical Society
Lovinia Parmenter, President
Parmeter Rd., 44214

Cambridge
Guernsey County Chapter
Ohio Genealogical Society
Kurt Tostenson, President
1211 Greenacre Dr., 43725

Canfield
Mahoning County Chapter
Ohio Genealogical Society
Jocelyn Wilms, Corresponding Secretary
3430 Rebecca Dr., 44406

Canton
Stark County Chapter
Ohio Genealogical Society
Hazel Murphy, Corresponding Secretary
2361 Ivy Way
N.E., 44705

Carrollton
Carroll County Chapter
Ohio Genealogical Society
Linda Houyouse, President
5321 Germano Rd.
S.E., 44615

Celina
Mercer County Chapter
Ohio Genealogical Society
Sue Miller, Receiving Secretary
3181 Mud Pike, 45822

Chardon
Geauga County Genealogical Society
c/o Geauga County Public Library
110 E. Park St., 44024

Chillicothe
Ross County Genealogical Society
Box 395, 45601

Cincinnati
Hamilton County Chapter
Ohio Genealogical Society
Box 15185, 45215

Cleveland
The American Heraldic Association
c/o A.W.C. Phelps
10109 Lake Ave., Apt. 304, 44102

Genealogy Club
Western Reserve Historical Society
10825 East Blvd., 44106

Greater Cleveland Genealogical Society
P.O. Box 40254, 44140

International Society for British Genealogy & Family History
Box 20425, 44120

Columbus
Franklin County Chapter
Ohio Genealogical Society
Box 09234, 43209

Coshocton
Coshocton County Chapter
Ohio Genealogical Society
Box 117, 43812

Dayton
Miami Valley Genealogical Society
Box 1364, 45401

Montgomery County Chapter
Ohio Genealogical Society
Box 1584, 45401

East Liverpool
Tri-State Genealogical Society
Box 1053, 43920

Elyria
Genealogical Workshop
Lorain County Historical Society
509 Washington Ave., 44039

Findlay
Hancock County Chapter
Ohio Genealogical Society
Anita J. Rush, Secretary/Treasurer
12500 TR 10, 45840

Fostoria
Tri-County Lineage Research Society
Kaubisch Library
205 Perry St., 44830

Fremont
Kin-Hunter Society (Branch of Sandusky Co. Historical Soc.)
Hayes Library
1337 Hayes Ave., 43420

Galion
Crawford County Genealogical Society
Box 523, 44820

Georgetown
Brown County Genealogical Society
Ohio Genealogical Society
Box 83, 54121

Greenville
Darke County Genealogical Society
c/o Toni Seiler
Garst Museum, 45331

Hillsboro
Southern Ohio Genealogical Society
Box 414, 45133

Jackson
Jackson County Chapter
Ohio Genealogical Society
Box 807, 45640

Jefferson
Ashtabula County Genealogical Society
Henderson Memorial Library
54 E. Jefferson St., 44047

Johnstown
The Johnstown Genealogy Society
Box 345, 43031

Kent
Portage county Chapter
Ohio Genealogical Society
Sadie Crabb, Secretary
790 Marilyn St., 44240

Kenton
Hardin County Genealogical Society
David Rish, President
15726 C.R. 209, 43326

Lakewood
West Cuyahoga Chapter
Ohio Genealogical Society
Helen Stieber, President
Shore House Apt. 200
12031 Edgewater Dr., 44107

Lancaster
Fairfield County Chapter
Ohio Genealogical Society
Patsy Kishler, President
407 W. Hubert Ave., 43130

Lebanon
Warren County Genealogical Society
12 W. South St., 45036

Lima
Allen County Chapter
Ohio Genealogical Society
Betty Hoehn, President
2065 University Blvd., 45805

London
Madison County Chapter
Ohio Genealogical Society
Elizabeth J. Russell, Receiving Secretary
165 N. Main St., 43140

Lorain
Black River Genealogists
351 Sixth St., 44052

Lucasville
Scioto County Chapter
Ohio Genealogical Society
Mrs. Robert Crabtree, President
Rt. 1
Box 207, 45648

Lyndhurst
Johannes Schwalm Historical Association, Inc.
4983 S. Sedgewick Rd., 44124

McConnelsville
Morgan County Genealogical Society
Ohio Genealogical Society
142 E. Main St., 43756

Mansfield
Ohio Genealogical Society
Box 2625, 44906

Richland County Chapter
Ohio Genealogical Society
Robert Cunning, President
993 W. Cook Rd., 44903

Marietta
Washington County Genealogical Society
401 Aurora St., 45750

Marion
Marion Area Chapter
Ohio Genealogical Society
Maxine Marshall, President
1067 Richmond Ave., 43302

Medina
Medina Genealogical Society
c/o George M. Gifford
4052 Smith Rd., 44256

Middletown
Butler County Chapter
Ohio Genealogical Society
Betty P. Evans, President
706–7th Ave., 45042

Mt. Vernon
Knox County Chapter
Ohio Genealogical Society
Richard DeLauder, Corresponding Secretary
648 Howard St., 43050

Newark
Licking County Genealogical Society
Box 215 (743 E. Main St.), 43055

New Philadelphia
Tuscarawas County Genealogical Society
Box 141, 44663

Norwalk
Kinologists of the Firelands Historical Society
4 Case Ave., 44857

Painesville
Lake County Chapter
Ohio Genealogical Society
Morley Public Library
184 Phelps St., 44077

Parma
Cuyahoga-Parma Chapter
Ohio Genealogical Society
Roy E. Christen, President
7935 Greenwood View Dr., 44129

Plain City
Union County Chapter
Ohio Genealogical Society
Dorothy Robinson, President
14125 Robinson Rd., 43064

Pomeroy
Meigs County Chapter
Ohio Genealogical Society
Keith D. Ashley
34465 Crew Rd., 45769

Port Clinton
Ottawa County Chapter
Ohio Genealogical Society
Franklin Ballard, President
1975 NE Catawba Rd., 43452

Richmond Heights
East Cuyahoga county Chapter
Ohio Genealogical Society
Florence Chambers, Corresponding Secretary
515 Trebesky Rd., 44143

Salem
Columbiana County Chapter
Ohio Genealogical Society
Mrs. Janet Borrelli, Corresponding Secretary
194 W. 7th St., 44460

Sandusky
Erie County Chapter
Ohio Genealogical Society
Box 1301, 44870

Sidney
Shelby County Genealogical Society
c/o Amos Memorial Library
230 E. North St., 45365

Springfield
Clark County Chapter
Ohio Genealogical Society
Mrs. Martha Evans, President
4463 Detrick–Jordan Pike, 45502

Strongsville
Southwest Cuyahoga Chapter
Ohio Genealogical Society
Carol Williams, President
18631 Howe Rd., 44136

Swanton
Fulton County Chapter
Ohio Genealogical Society
305 Chestnut St., 43558

Tiffin
Seneca County Chapter
Ohio Genealogical Society
Box 841, 44883

Toledo
Lucas County Chapter
Ohio Genealogical Society
Toledo-Lucas County Public Library
Local History & Genealogy Dept.
325 N. Michigan St., 43624

Northwestern Ohio Genealogical Society
4303 Willys Pkwy., 43612

Torch
Calhoun County (WV) Historical and Genealogical Society
Box 268, 45781

Van Wert
Van Wert County Chapter
Ohio Genealogical Society
c/o Helen L. Prill
Rt. 4
Box 126, 45891

Wapakoneta
Auglaize County Chapter
Ohio Genealogical Society
Box 2021, 45895

Warren
Trumbull County Chapter
Ohio Genealogical Society
Trissa haefling, Secretary
351 Bonnie Brae N.E., 44483

Washington Court House
Fayette County Genealogical Society
Ohio Genealogical Society
Box 342, 43160

Wauseon
The Family Tree Genealogical Society
450 Potter St., 43567

Waverly
Pke County Chapter
Ohio Genealogical Society
Box 224, 45690

West Alexandria
Preble County Genealogy Club
c/o Mrs. Joan B. Brubaker
Rt. 3
Box 159, 45381

West Union
Adams County Genealogical Society
Box 231, 45693

Wilminton
Clinton County Historical Society
Box 529 (140 E. Locust St.), 45177

Xenia
Greene County Chapter
Ohio Genealogical Society
Donna Randall, President
1171 Hook Rd., 45385

Zanesville
Muskingum County Chapter
Ohio Genealogical Society
Robert Price, Treasurer
845 Lenox Ave., 43701

Oklahoma

Ada
Pontotoc County Genealogical Society
Box 1646, 74820

Altus
Western Trails Historical and Genealogical Society
Box 574, 73521

Alva
Woods County Genealogists
Box 234, 73717

Bartlesville
Bartlesville Genealogical Society
O. Phillip Kent, President
3818 Wayside Dr., 74003

Broken Arrow
Broken Arrow Genealogical Society
c/o Edward S. Baker
717 S. Birch Pl., 74012

Coalgate
Coal County Historical & Genealogical Society
Box 322, 74538

Enid
Garfield County Genealogists
Box 427, 73701

Guthrie
Logan County Genealogical Society
Box 1419, 73044

Haskell
Rogers County Heritage Society
Box 284, 74436

Lawton
Southwest Oklahoma Genealogical Society
Box 5044, 73504

Marietta
Love County Heritage Society
Rt. 2
Box 55A, 73448

Miami
Ottawa County Genealogical Society
Box 1383, 74534

Moore
Cleveland County Genealogical Society
Box 6434, 73153

Oklahoma City
Oklahoma Genealogical Society
Box 314, 73101

Okmulgee
Okmulgee County Genealogical Society
1711 East 9th St., 74447

Pawhuska
Pawhuska Genealogical Society
301 East 6th, 74056

Ponca City
Pioneer Genealogical Society
Box 1839, 74601

Poteau
Poteau Valley Genealogical Society, Inc.
Box 1031, 74953

Tahlequah
Indian Territory Genealogical Society
309 West Kectoowah St., 74464

Tulsa
Heritage Society of America, Inc.
Box 35104

Tulsa Genealogical Society
Box 585, 74101

Vinita
Northeast Oklahoma Genealogical Society
Box 484, 74301

Wilburton
Kiamichi Genealogical Society
Rt. 3
Box 53, 74587

Wister
Leflore County Genealogists
c/o Gloryann Young
Box 21, 74966

Oregon

Albany
Linn Genealogical Society
520 Chicago
S.E., 97321

Bend
Central Oregon Chapter, End of Trail Researchers
Deschutes County Historical Society
Box 5252, 97708

Brownsville
Oregon Pioneer Research Bureau
c/o Mrs. D.F. Menefee
Box 366, 97327

Canyonville
Canyonville Genealogical Society
c/o Mrs. Wilma Jeffries
Stanton Rd., 97417

Corvallis
Mid-Valley Genealogical Society
3960 N.W. Elizabeth Place, 97330

Cottage Grove
Cottage Grove Genealogical Society
c/o W.A. Woodward Memorial Library
6th & Washington Sts., 97424

Eugene
Emerald Empire Genealogy Workshop
Mrs. Lorrain C. Secevicky, President
2494 Newcastle St., 97404

Oregon Genealogical Society
Box 1214, 97440

Gold Beach
Curry Genealogical Society
Box 1336, 97444

Grants Pass
Grants Pass Genealogical Society
Box 1834, 97526

Jefferson
Jefferson Chapter
End of Trail Researchers
c/o Mrs. Vera Swartz
Rt. 1
Box 96, 97352

McMinnville
Yamhill County Genealogical Society
Box 568, 97128

Medford
Rogue Valley Genealogical Society
643 Ipson St. 97501

Northbend
Coos Genealogical Forum
Box 1067, 97459

Oregon City
Mt. Hood Genealogical Forum
Box 208, 97045

Port Orford
Port Orford Genealogical Society
Box 138, 97465

Portland
Canadian Genealogical Interest Group
6036 S.W. Vermont, 97219

Genealogical Forum of Portland Oregon
Suite 812
1410 S.W. Morrison St., 97205

Redmond
Veitch Historical Society
6060 S.W. Coyote Ave., 97756

Roseburg
Genealogical Society of Douglas County
Box 579, 97470

Salem
End of Trail Researchers
145–24th St.
S.E., 97301

Willamette Valley Genealogical Society
Box 2083, 97308

The Dalles
Mid-Columbia Genealogical Society
The Dalles Public Library
722 Court St., 97058

Pennsylvania

Abington
Old York Road Genealogical Society
1030 Old York Rd., 19001

Altoona
Blair County Genealogical Society
Box 855, 16603

Beaver
Beaver County Genealogical Society
699–5th St., 15009

Broomall
Scottish Historical & Research Society of the Delaware Valley
2137 MacLarie Lane, 19008

Breinigsville
The Pennsylvania German Society
Rt. 1
Box 469, 18031

Brookville
Jefferson County Historical & Genealogical Society
236 Jefferson St., 15825

Camp Hill
National Society
Palatines to America
Dr. John A. Frithey II
President
106 November Dr., 17011

Doylestown
Bucks County Genealogical Society
Box 1092, 18901

Easton
Northampton Historical & Genealogical Society
101 S. 4th St., 18042

Erie
Erie Society for Genealogical Research
Box 1403, 16512

Harrisburg
Pennsylvania Chapter
Palatines To America
c/o Lt. Col. Oscar H. Stroh
Rt. 4
Box 295, 17112

Indiana
Historical & Genealogical Society of Indiana County
Silas M. Clark House
S. Sixth & Wayne Ave., 15701

Johnstown
Historical & Genealogical Society of Dale Borough
c/o Cecil K. Liberknight
715 Von Lunen Rd.–Dale, 15902

Lancaster
Lancaster Mennonite Historical Society
2215 Millstream Rd., 17602

Meadville
Crawford County Genealogical Society
848 N. Main St., 16335

Newport
The Perry Historians
Box 73, 17074

Oil City
Venango County Genealogical Club
Box 811, 16301

Philadelphia
Genealogical Society of Pennsylvania
1300 Locust St., 19107

Pittsburgh
Historical Society of Western Pennsylvania
4338 Bigelow Blvd., 15213

Western Pennsylvania Genealogical Society
4338 Bigelow Blvd., 15213

Sharon
Mercer County Genealogical Society
Box 812, 16146

Somerset
Historical & Genealogical Society of Somerset County
Rt. 2
Box 238, 15501

State College
Central Pennsylvania Genealogical Society & Library
c/o Mrs. Henry B. Harvey, Secretary
629 North Holmes St., 16801

Washington
Genealogical Society of Southwestern Pennsylvania
Box 894, 15301

Waynesburg
Cornerstone Genealogical Society
Box 547, 15370

Windber
Windber-Johnstown Area Genealogical Society
Mrs. Brenda Borski, President
#1, Mine 30, 15963

York
South Central Pennsylvania Genealogical Society
Box 1824, 17405

Zelienople
Zelienople Historical Society
Box 45 (243 S. Main St.), 16063

Rhode Island

Pawtucket
American French Genealogical Society
Box 2113, 02861

Warwick
Rhode Island Genealogical Society
Box 7618, 02887

South Carolina

Charleston
Charleston Chapter
South Carolina Genealogical Society
Harold W. Syfrett, President
Box 2266, 29403

South Carolina Genealogical Society
Box 2266, 29403

Chester
Chester County Genealogical Society
Box 808, 29706

Clemson
Pendleton District Chapter
South Carolina Genealogical Society
W. Carl Nettles, President
19 Folger St., 29631

Greenville
Greenville Chapter
South Carolina Genealogical Society
M. Gordon Thurston Jr., President
Rt. 2
Shannon Lake Circle, 29607

Greenwood
Greenwood Chapter
South Carolina Genealogical Society
Harry B. McGinn, President
Rt. 3
Box 344, 29646

Lexington
Columbia Chapter
South Carolina Genealogical Society
Melba P. Shealy, President
1609 S. Lake Dr., 29072

Marion
Pee Dee Chapter
South Carolina Genealogical Society
Mrs. Gretchen R. Clark, President
205 Warwick Dr., 29536

Orangeburg
Orangeburg Historical & Genealogical Society
Rt. 1
Box 1069-C, 29115

Spartanburg
Pinckney Chapter
South Carolina Genealogical Society
Mrs. Mary E.G. Wood, President
2352 Bruce St., 29302

Sumter
Sumter Chapter
South Carolina Genealogical Society
Mrs. Marilyn Ayers, President
7 Pickens St., 29150

South Dakota

Aberdeen
Aberdeen Area Genealogical Society
Alexander Mitchell Library
519 S. Kline St., 57401

Belle Fourche
Tri-State Genealogical Society
514 Third Ave., 57717

Brookings
Brookings Area Genealogical Society
524–4th St., 57006

Edgemont
Edgemont Genealogical Society
c/o Mary Lou Faulkner
Box 313, 57735

Highmore
Hyde County Historical & Genealogical Society
c/o Mrs. Birgit Hinkle 57345

Huron
East River Genealogical Forum
c/o Y.W.C.A.
17–5th St. S.W., 57305

Mitchell
Mitchell Area Genealogical Society
Betty Fillmore
Pres. 1004 W. Birch, 57301

Pierre
Pierre-Fort Pierre Genealogical Society
Box 925, 57501

Rapid City
Rapid City Society for Genealogical Research
Box 1495, 57701

Sioux Falls
Sioux Valley Genealogical Society
Box 655, 57101

Watertown
Watertown Genealogical Society
c/o Public Library, 57201

Tennessee

Brentwood
Brentwood Historical & Genealogical Society
Box 21, 37027

Middle Tennessee Society of Professional Genealogists
Box 21, 27027

Clinton
Pellissippi Genealogy Society
Clinton Library
118 Hicks St., 37716

Cookeville
Upper Cumberland Genealogical Association
Box 575, 38501

Fayetteville
Lincoln County Genealogical Society
c/o Mabel Tucker
Rt. 2
Box 170A, 37334

Jackson
Mid-West Tennessee Genealogical Society
Box 3343, 38301

Johnson City
Watauga Association of Genealogists
Box 117, 37601

Knoxville
East Tennessee Historical Society
Genealogical Committee
Lawson McGhee Library
37902

Memphis
The Tennessee Genealogical Society
Box 12124, 38112

Paris
Paris Area Genealogical Society
Box 726, 38242

Texas

Abilene
West Texas Genealogical Society
2825 South 11th St., 79605

Amarillo
Amarillo Genealogical Society
Amarillo Public Library
Box 2171, 79189

Arlington
Arlington Genealogical Society
c/o Arlington Pubic Library
101 E. Abram St., 76010

Athens
Athens Genealogical Organization
Box 1411, 75751

Austin
Austin Genealogical Society
Box 774, 78767

Balch Springs
Balch Springs Historical and Genealogical Society
c/o Mrs. Exa Thomas
2023 Hillcrest. Apt., 1087

Bay City
Matagorda County Genealogical Society
Box 264, 77414

Baytown
Baytown Genealogical Society1313 Towne Circle, 77520

Beaumont
Southeast Texas Genealogical & Historical Society
c/o Tyrell Historical Society
Box 3827, 77704

Bedford
Mid-Cities Genealogical Society
Box 171, 76021

Big Spring
Genealogical Society of Big Spring
c/o Howard County Library
4th & Scurry St., 79720

Boerne
Genealogical Society of Kendall County Texas
Box 623, 78006

Bonham
Fannin County Genealogical and Historical Society Bonham Public Library
City Hall, 75418

Borger
Hutchinson County Genealogical Society
Hutchinson County Library
625 Wetherly St., 79007

Bryan
Family History Foundation
Family & Local History Society
Box 4464, 77805
(811 East 29th St. 77801)

Buda
German-Texas Heritage Society
c/o Dona Reeves
Rt. 2
Box 239-A, 78610

Burnet
Burnet County Genealogical Society
c/o Herman Brown Free Library
100 E. Washington, 78611

Canadian
Hemphill County Historical and Genealogical Society
c/o John Ramp
Rt. 2, 79014

Canyon
High Plains Genealogical Society
c/o Cornette Library
Lecture Room
West Texas State University, 79105

Cleveland
Cleveland Area Genealogical Enterprises
c/o Austin Memorial Library
220 S. Bonham 77327

Conroe
Montgomery County Genealogical Society
Box 751, 77305

Corpus Christi
Coastal Bend Genealogical Society
Box 2711, 78403

Corsicana
Navarro County Genealogical Society
Box 821, 75110

Dallas
Dallas Genealogical Society
Box 12648, 75225

Irish Family Research Association, Inc.
Mrs. Richard G. Champ, President
9411 Hunters Creek Dr., 75243

Del Rio
Southwest Texas Genealogical Association
308 Ave. K, 78840

Denton
Denton County Genealogical Society
Box 23322 TWU Sta., 76204

Dimmitt
Dumas Genealogical and Historical Society
Box 911, 79027

Dumas
Dumas Genealogical and Historical Society
127 Oak Ave., 79029

El Paso
El Paso Genealogical Society
Box 12722, 79912

Southwestern Genealogical Society
5301 Hanawalt Dr., 79903

Fairfield
Freestone County Genealogical Society
Box 14, 75840

Gatesville
Coryell County Genealogical Society
c/o Gatesville Public Library
811 Main St., 76528

Gonzales
South Texas Genealogical and Historical Society
Box 40, 78629

Graham
Fort Belknap Genealogical Association
c/o Mrs. Barbara Ledbetter
Murray Rte., 76046

Grand Prairie
Grand Prairie Genealogical Society
c/o Grand Prairie Memorial Library
326 W. Main St., 75050

Harlingen
Tip-O-Texas Genealogical Society
c/o Harlingen Public Library
502 E. Taylor St., 78550

Henderson
Rusk County Genealogical Society
203 N. Van Buren, 75652

Hereford
Deaf Smith County Genealogical Society
c/o Deaf Smith County Library
211 E. 4th St., 79045

Houston
Bellaire Genealogical Society
c/o Margie Harris
6445 Sewanee, 77005

Committee for Advanced Genealogical Research
Box 55723, 77107

Houston Area Genealogical Association
2507 Tannehill, 78008

Huntsville
Walker County Genealogical Society
Box 1717, 77340

Jacksonville
Cherokee County Genealogical Society
409 N. Bolton St., 75766

Jayton
Kent County Genealogical & Historical Society
Box 344, 79528

Kountze
Piney Woods Pioneers Genealogy Club
Honey Island
Rt. 2
Box 1030, 77625

Lake Jackson
Brazosport Genealogical Society
Brazosport College Library
500 College Dr., 77566

Lamesa
Lamesa Area Genealogical Society
Box 1090, 79331

Lancaster
Lancaster Genealogical Society
Box 185, 75146

Lewisville
Lewisville Genealogical Society
Box 622, 75067

Littlefield
Llano Estacado Genealogical Society
1313 W. 9th St., 79339

Llano
Hill County Genealogical Society
c/o Evelyn Wade
Prairie Mt. Rt., 78643

Lubbock
South Plains Genealogical Society
Municipal Garden & Arts Center
4215 University Ave., 79413

West Texas Scottish Heritage Society
Box 1081, 79408

Madisonville
Madison County Genealogical Society
Box 26, 77864

Marquez
Leon County Genealogical Society
c/o Joyce D. Petty
Birch Creek Ranch, 77865

McAllen
McAllen Genealogical Society
Box 4714, 78501

Mesquite
Dallas County East Genealogical Society
c/o James P. Cummings
515 Freeman St., 75149

Mesquite Historical & Genealogical Society
Box 165, 75149

Midland
Midland Genealogical Society
Box 1191, 79702

Mineola
Northeast Texas Genealogical Society
Box 240, 75773

Mt. Pleasant
Cypress Basin Genealogical and Historical Society
Box 403, 75455

Nacogdoches
Nacogdoches Genealogical Society
Box 4634 S.F.A. Sta., 75962

Oakhurst
Walker County Genealogical Society
c/o Ynette Boyce
Rt. 1
Box 96, 77359

Odessa
Permian Basin Genealogical Society
c/o Ector County Library
622 N. Lee, 79761

Palestine
Anderson County Genealogical Society
502 N. Queen St., 75801

Pampa
Pampa Genealogical and Historical Society
420 N. Sumner St., 79065

Pasadena
Harris County Genealogical Society
Box 391, 77501

Plano
Collin County Genealogical Society
3724 Yosemite, 75023

Port Lavaca
Calhoun County Genealogical Society
Box 1150
77979

Rankin
Upton County Genealogical Society
Box 6, 79778

Richmond
Fort Bend County Genealogical Society
Fort Bend County Library
1601 Liberty, 77469

Round Rock
Williamson County Genealogical Society
Box 585, 78664

San Angelo
San Angelo Genealogical Society
Box 3453, 76902

San Antonio
San Antonio Genealogical and Historical Society
Box 5907, 78201

Southwest Genealogical Society
1300 San Pedro Ave., 78212

San Marcos
Hays County Historical and Genealogical Society, Inc.
Box 1387, 78666

Sherman
Grayson County Genealogical Society
c/o Library Dept.
City of Sherman
421 N. Travis, 75090

Snyder
West Texas Genealogical Society
c/o Mrs. John H. Boren
1807–38th St., 79549

Western Texas Genealogical Association
c/o Scurry County Library
1916–23rd St., 79549

Stephensville
Erath County Genealogical Society
Box 924, 76401

Sugarland
Sugarland Genealogical Society
c/o Mrs. L. Anhaiser
719 Borden St., 77478

Texas City
Galveston County Genealogical Society
c/o 1701–9th Ave. N., 77590

TomballChaparral Genealogical Society
Box 606, 77375

Tyler
East Texas Genealogical Society
Box 6967, 75711

Victoria
Victoria County Genealogical Society
302 N. Main St., 77901

Waco
Central Texas Genealogical Society
Waco McLennan County Library
1717 Austin Ave., 76701

Waxahachie
Ellis County Genealogical Society

Weatherford
Parker County Genealogical Society
1214 Charles St., 76086

Wharton
Wharton Genealogical Society
c/o Robert P. Story
604 N. Texas, 77488

Whitesboro
Grayson County Genealogical Society
c/o Mrs. F.R. Banfield
box 40, 76273

Wills Point
Van Zandt County Genealogical Society
Box 434, 75169

Winters
The Genealogical Club of Winters High School
Box 125, 79567

Utah

Brigham City
Golden Spike Chapter
Utah Genealogical Association
c/o Mrs. Jean M. Minert
821 Fairview Dr., 84302

Provo
Utah Valley Branch Genealogical Library
Room 4386 HBLL
Brigham Young University, 85602

Utah Valley Chapter
Utah Genealogical Association
c/o Ms. Helen Clegg
1785 North 1500 East St., 84601

St. George
St. George Genealogy Club
Box 184, 84770

Salt Lake City
Adoption Identity
Utah
Box 8124, 84108

American-German Genealogical Association
4246 South 3100 East 84117

Association of Professional Genealogists
19 W. South Temple
Suite 761
Box 11601, 84147

The Genealogical Society of Utah
50 East North Temple St., 84150
See Appendix D for branch addresses.

Great Salt Lake Chapter
Utah Genealogical Society
c/o Ms. Norma H. Lundberg
1208 Fenway Ave., 84110

Professional Genealogists Chapter
Utah Genealogical Society
Wilma Adkins, President
Box 1144, 84110

Progenitor Genealogical Society
Box 16422, 84115

Southern States Chapter
Utah Genealogical Society
c/o Gayle Ellis
1439 Stratford, 84106

Utah Genealogical Association
Box 1144, 84110

Vermont

Burlington
Vermont Old Cemetery Association
c/o Prof. Leon W. Dean
308 South Prospect St., 05401

Putney
Vermont Genealogical Society
c/o Mrs. Carol Church
Rt. 3, 05346

Virginia

Charlottesville
Central Virginia Genealogical Association
c/o J. Tracy Walker
Rt. 5
Box 258, 22901

Danville
VA-NC Piedmont Genelogical Society
Box 2272, 24541

Culpepper
Memorial Foundation Germanna Colonies, Inc.
Box 693, 22701

Hampton
Tidewater Genealogical Society
Box 29, 23669

Portsmouth
Portsmouth Genealogical Society
c/o Portsmouth Public Library
601 Court St., 23704

Richmond
Genealogical Research Institute of Virginia
Box 29178, 23229

Roanoke
Southwestern Virginia Genealogical Society
Box 4364, 24015

Springfield
Nation's Capitol Area Chapter
American Historical Society of Germans from Russia
c/o Emma Haynes
6949 Conservation Ave., 22153

Vienna
Fairfax Genealogy Club
Box 276, 22180

Virginia Beach
Norfolk Genealogical Society
Diane M. Gray, Treasurer
3281 Coldchester Rd., 23456

Winchester
Winchester-Frederick County Genealogical Society
c/o Handley Library
Box 58, 22601

Woodbridge
Prince William Genealogy Club
c/o Potomac Branch Library
2201 Opitz Blvd., 22191

Washington

Aberdeen
Grays Harbor Genealogy Club
308 W. 6th St., 98520

Bellingham
Whatcom Genealogical Society
Box 1493, 98225

Bremerton
Puget Sound Genealogical Society
(Formerly Olympic Genealogical Society)
Box 2146 Sheridan Sta., 98310

Chehalis
Genealogical Committee
Lewis County Historical Society
78 N.E. Washington Avenue, 98532

Dayton
Columbia County Genealogical & Historical Society
c/o Mrs. Nettie Lingrow
708 E. Main St., 99328

Ephrata
Grant County Genealogical Society
c/o Ephrata Public Library
339 First Ave.
S.W., 98823

Longview
Lower Columbia Genealogical Society
Box 472, 98632

Olympia
Olympia Genealogical Society
c/o Timberland Regional Public Library
8th & Franklin, 98501

Omak
Okanogan County Genealogical Society
c/o Lavon Mundinger
Rt. 2
Box 87E, 99841

Pomeroy
Garfield County Genealogy Club
c/o Mrs. Elaine Anderson Box 697, 99347

Port Angeles
Clallam County Genealogical Society
(formerly Olympic Penninsula Genealogical Society)
c/o Clallam County Museum Genealogy Library
223 E. Fourth St. 98362

Richland
The Tri-City Genealogical Society
c/o Mrs. J.W. Ehrig
Rt. 1
Box 5006, 99352

Seattle
Seattle Genealogical Society
Box 549, 98111

Spokane
Eastern Washington Genealogical Society
Box 1826, 99210

Metis Genealogical Society
Eastern Washington Genealogical Society
N. 6206 Washington, 99208

Sumner
Sumner – Puyallup Genealogical Society
c/o Sumner Public Library, 98390

Tacoma
Pierce County Genealogical Society
Box 99094, 98499

Tacoma-Pierce County Genealogical Society
Box 1592, 98401

Vancouver
Clark County Genealogical Society
Box 2728 (1511 Main St.), 98668

Walla Walla
Walla Walla Valley Genealogical Society
Box 115, 99362

Wenatchee
Genealogical Society of North Central Washington
Box 613, 98801

Yakima
Yakima Valley Genealogical Society
Box 445, 98907

West Virginia

Berkley Springs
Morgan County Historical and Genealogical Society
c/o Leonard Davis
Rt. 2
Box 27, 25411

Calhoun County
Calhoun County Historical and Genealogical Society
See entry under Torch, OH

Eklins
Randolph County Genealogical Society
Box 583, 26241

Fairview
Marion County Genealogy Club
c/o Mrs. Helen White, President
Jefferson St.
General Delivery, 26570

Griffithsville
Lincoln County Genealogical Society
Box 92, 25521

Hancock County
See listing under East Liverpool, OH

Harrisville Ritchie County Historical Society
200 S. Church St., 26362

Hewett
Boone County Genealogical Society
Box 10, 25108

Huntington
KYOWVA Genealogical Society
Box 1254, 25715

Logan
Logan County Genealogical Society
c/o Dr. Dana R. Dorsey
Box 783, 25601

New Martinsville
Wetzel County Genealogical Society
Box 464, 26155

South Charleston
Kanahwa Valley Genealogical Society
Att: Mrs. Genevieve B. McDaniel
Box 8765, 25303

Washington
West Augusta Historical & Genealogical Society
Rt. 1
Box 70C, 26181

Wheeling
Wheeling Area Genealogical Society
2237 Marshall Ave., 26003

Wisconsin

Appleton
Fox Valley Genealogical Society
Mrs. Beverly Bowen, President
725 Fernmeadow Dr., 54911

Baldwin
St. Croix Chapter
Wisconsin State Genealogical Society
Mrs. Kenneth Bjerkeset, Secretary
1190 Oak St., 54002

Black River Falls
Monroe
Juneau
Jackson County
WI Genealogical Workshop
Carolyn Habelman, President
Rt. 3
Box 253, 54615

Fond Du Lac
Wisconsin State Old Cemetery Association
Mrs. Jean R. Rentmeister
Regional Director
456–3rd St., 54935

Green Bay
Bay Area Genealogical Society
832 S. Quincy St., 54301

Hartford
Hartford Genealogical Society
105 Prospect Ave., 53027

Janesville
Rock County Genealogical Society
Beatrice W. Seitz
214 W. Van Buren St., 53545

Kenosha
Kenosha County Genealogical Society
4902–52nd St., 53142

LaCrosse
LaCrosse Area Chapter
Wisconsin State Genealogical Society
Box 1782, 54601

Lancaster
Grant County Group
Wisconsin State Genealogical Society
c/o Harriet Gehrke
Rt. 2
Box 102, 53813

Madison
South Central Chapter
Wisconsin State Genealogical Society
c/o Sharon Kampen
1914 Jefferson St., 53711

Vesterheim Genealogical Center
4909 Sherwood Rd., 53711

Manitowoc
Manitowoc County Genealogical Society
511 Waldo Blvd., 54220

Marinette
White Pine Genealogy Society
Box 512, 54143

Milwaukee
Milwaukee County Genealogical Society
916 E. Lyon St., 53202

Wisconsin State Old Cemetery Society
F. Winston Luck, President
4319 N. 70th St., 53216

Monroe
Wisconsin State Genealogical Society
2109 Twentieth Ave., 53566

North Fond Du Lac
Fond du Lac County Genealogical Society
Chapter Wisconsin State Genealogical Society
c/o Mrs. Lucille Le Mieux, Chairman
915 Wisconsin Ave., 54935

Oconomowoc
Oconomowoc Genealogy Club of Waukesha County c/o Kathryn Martin
107 Division St., 53066

Platteville
Grant County Genealogical Society
c/o Mrs. Gilbert Jentz
955 Williams St., 53818

Shawano
Northern Wisconsin Genealogists
Box 321 (910 Zingler Ave.), 54166

Sheboygan
Sheboygan County Genealogical Society
Bos 781, 53081

Spooner
Washburn County Genealogical Society
214 Elm St. 54801

Stevens Point
Stevens Point Area Genealogical Society
5569 Hwy 10, 54481

Waupaca
Waupaca County Chapter
Wisconsin State Old Cemetery Society
c/o Guyant
Rt. 1
Box 664, 54981

Wausau
Marathon County Genealogical Society
Box 1512, 54401

Wisconsin Rapids
Heart O'Wisconsin Genealogical Society
McMillan Memorial Library
490 East Grand Ave., 54494

Wyoming

Casper
Casper Amateur Genealogists c/o Casper College
Administration Bldg. Room 198
125 College Dr., 82601

Natrona County Society for Genealogical Research
Box 9244, 82609

Cheyenne
Cheyenne Genealogical Society
c/o Laramie Public Library
2800 Central Ave., 82001

Torrington
The Goshen County Genealogical Society
Box 491, 82240

GENEALOGY BOOK PUBLISHERS

A Press, Inc.
Box 8796
Greenville,SC 29604
(803) 233-8358
Southeastern States

ALA Publishing Services
50 E. Huron
Chicago, IL 60611

Accelerated Indexing Systems
70 E. South Temple
Salt Lake City, UT 84111

Aceto Bookmen
5721 Antietam Drive
Sarasota, FL 33581

Adams Press
30 W. Washington Street
Chicago, IL 60602

American Association for State and Local History
1400 Eighth Avenue S.
Nashville, TN 37203

American Reference Publishers Inc.
Green Oaks Inn
6901 W. Freeway
Fort Worth, TX 76116

Ancestor Publishers
Box 682
Arvada, CO 80001

Ancestors Unlimited, Inc.
1462 Shangrila Circle
Riverdale, GA 30296

Ancestral Routes
Box 11745
Salt Lake City, UT 84111

Ancestry Publishing Co.
Box 476
Salt Lake City, UT 84110
(801) 359-2000

Dr. William Anderson
2935 Cordell
Memphis, TN 38118
(901) 794-9566

Anundsen Publishing Co.
108 Washington Street
Decorah, IA 52101
(319) 382-4295

Arlington Century Printing
1111 West Abram
Citizen Journal Building
Arlington, TX 76013
(817) 277-7691

Banner Press, Inc.
Box 20180
Birmingham, AL 35216

Beehive Press
321 Bernard Street
Savannah, GA 31401

Berkley Publishing Co.
1050 Wall Street
W. Lyndhurst, NJ 07071

Bireline Publishing Co.
Box 415
Newell, IA 50568

Bond Wheelwright Co.
Freeport, ME
04032

Book Crafters, Inc.
Box 370
140 Buchanan Street
Chelsea, MI 48118
(313) 475-9145

The Bookmark
Box 74
Knightstown, IN 46148

Book Masters, Inc.
830 Claremont Ave.
Box 159
Ashland, OH 44805

Brevet Press
519 W. 10th Street
Sioux Falls, SD 57104

Briarwood Press
Specialty Publications
Rt. 1, Box 221
Hanceville, AL 35077
(205) 734-8662

Brigham Young University
205 University Press Bldg.
Provo, UT 84602

Marlin Brossart
20715 Viento Valle
Escondido, CA 92025

Car-del-Scribe
Box 73
Ludlow, MA 01056

Carothers Publishing Co.
1510 Cranwell Road
Lutherville, MD 21093

Catalogue B
Box 612
West Jordan, UT 84084

Centennial Press
Box 41134
Memphis, TN 38104

Channing Books
Box 552
Marion, MA 02738

Charles Scribner's Sons
Vreeland Ave.
Totowa, NJ 07512

Closson Press
RD Box 373
Apollo, PA 15613

College and University Press
263 Chapel Street
New Haven, CT 06513

Community Press
5600 North University Avenue
Provo, UT 84601
(801) 225-2293

Cook-McDowell Publications
1233 Sweeney Street
Owensboro, KY 42301

Country Squire
Granville, MA
01034

Mrs. Owen Crickard
Route 1, Box 218
Beverly, WV 26253

Dan Crowe
2361 Hiwassee Drive
Kingsport, TN 37664

David and Charles
Box 57
North Pomfret, VT 05053

Dean Publications
1005 Bryant Way
Sunnyvale, CA 94087

Decatur Publishing Co.
141 So. Second Street
Decatur, IN 46733

Phileas Diegh Corporation
Suite 321
600 Old Country Road
Garden City, NY 11530

Deseret Book Company
44 E. South Temple
Salt Lake City, UT 84111

Dillon Press
500 3rd Street
Minneapolis, MN 55413

Dorrance & Company
Cricket Terrace Road
Ardmore, PA 19003

Durant Publishing Company
1208 Tatum Drive
Alexandria, VA 22307

Edwards Letter Shop, Inc.
711 North University
Ann Arbor, MI 48108

EIG Publishing
Box 476
Salt Lake City, UT 84110
(801) 539-2000

Everton Publishers
Box 368
Logan, UT 84321
(801) 752-6022

Family Histories of America
Box 48, Dept. 101
Duarte, CA 91010

Family History World
57 W. South Temple
Suite 255
Salt Lake City, UT 84101
(801) 532-3327

Family Roots
RR 4
Crawfordsville, IN 47933

Family Tree
Box 9581
Madison, WI 53715

Farmer Genealogy Co.
Box 140880
Dallas, TX 75214

Fortress Press
2900 Queen Lane
Philadelphia, PA 19129

Friends United Press
101 Quaker Hill Drive
Richmond, IN 47374

Gale Research Company
Book Tower
Detroit, MI 48226
(313) 961-2242

Gateway Press, Inc.
111 Water Street
Baltimore, MD 21202

Gatewood Co.
Box 16128
Richmond, VA 23222

Genealogical Publishing Co.
1001 N. Calvert
Baltimore, MD 21202

Reprinted from *APG Newsletter* 5 (Jan. 1983)

Genealogical Research
and Productions
6619 Clayton Road
Suite 5A
St. Louis, MO 63117

Genealogical Researchers
206 Road 1
Washington, NJ 07882

Genealogy Today
2815 Clearview Place
Atlanta, GA 30340
(404) 457-7801

Genealogy Unlimited, Inc.
789 S. Buffalo Grove Road
Buffalo Grove, IL 60090
(312) 541-3175

George Shumway Publishers
Rural Delivery 7, Box 388
York, PA 17402

Great Bridge Books
404 Woodford Drive
Chesapeake, VA 23320

Greenwood Press, Inc.
51 Riverside Avenue
Westport, CT 06880

Gregath Company
Box 1045
Cullman, AL 35055
offset printing, binding

Harp and Thistle, Ltd.
Box 2072
Warner Robins, GA 31099

Hartwell Company
1617 W. 261st Street
Harbor City, CA 90710

Gary T. Hawbaker
Route 2, Box 409
Elizabethtown, PA 17022

Hawkes Publishing, Inc.
156 W. Utopia Ave.
Salt Lake City, UT 84115
(801) 487-1695

Byron Kennedy & Co.
Box 10937
St. Petersburg, FL 33733

Heart of the Lakes Publishers
Interlaken, NY
14847

Heritage Books
3602 Maureen Lane
Bowie, MD 20715

Heritage West
Box 50304
Palo Alto, CA 94303

History Publications, Inc.
RR 1
Pollock, MO 63560

Holbrook Research Institute
Oxford, MA
01540

Brent H. Holcomb
Box 21766
Columbia, SC 29221

Honford House Publishers
Box 7029
Arlington, VA 22207

Hoosier Heritage Press
520 N. Campbell Street
Indianapolis, IN 46219

Hope Farm Press & Bookshop
Strong Road
Cornwallville, NY 12418

Howe Brothers, Inc.
Box 6394
Salt Lake City, UT 84112
(801) 272-3330 or 272-5174

Hunterdon House
38 Swan Street
Lambertville, NJ 08530

Hunter Publishing Co.
Box 5867
Winston-Salem, NC 27113
(800) 334-1988

In-Print Books
3812 Lafayette
Fort Worth, TX 76107

Intercollegiate Press
835 Argonne Ave. #4
Atlanta, GA 30308
(404) 876-8505

Intercollegiate Press
6015 Travis Lane
Box 10
Shawnee Mission, KS 66201
(913) 432-8100

Jenny Martin Fagg Pub.
4314 Nenana
Houston, TX 77035

Jim-Mar Publications
Box 2161
Covina, CA 91722

Johnson Historical Publishers
2409 Gaboury Lane
Huntsville, AL 35811

KM Enterprises
351 N. Sernnado Street
Orange, CA 92669

Kenma Publishing
1911 Conlin Avenue
Evansville, IN 47714

Keyline Publishers
Box 98
Elizabeth, CO 80107

Kinforms
Box 11374
Salt Lake City, UT 84147
(801) 277-6796

Langdon Associates
41 Langdon Street
Cambridge, MA 02138

Leeran Publishers
Box 247
Burkesville, KY 42717

Liberty Bell Associates
Box 51
Franklin Park, NJ 08823

Libra Publications
Box 29
Linthicum Heights, MD 21090

Little, Brown & Co.
34 Beacon Street
Boston, MA 02106
(617) 227-0730

Littleshield Press
925 Flat Street N.E.
Grand Rapids, MI 49503

Louisiana State University
Baton Rouge
Louisiana 70803

Lucas Brothers Publishing
909 Lowry Street
Columbia, MO 65201

Magee Publications
611 Miller Valley Road
Suite 59
Prescott, AZ 86301

Magna Carta Book Co.
5502 Magnolia Avenue
Baltimore, MD 21215

Manor Publishing Co.
4021 Manor Drive
South Bend, IN 46614

Masspac Publishing Co.
48855 North Gratiot Avenue
Mount Clemens, MI 48045

McNally and Loftin Pub.
510 W. 4th Street
Charlotte, NC 28202

Meico Associates, Inc.
Box 119
South Prairie, WA 98385
(206) 897-8607

Mid-South Publishing Co.
Box 188
Amelia, VA 23002

Moench Printing
255 W. 800 South
Salt Lake City, UT 84101

Monocacy Book Co.
Box 765
Redwood City, CA 94064

W.E. Morrison & Co.
Ovid, NY
14521

Muleskinner Publishing
950 E. 1st Street
Peculiar, MO 64078

National Share Graphics
1949 Stemmons
Dallas, TX 75207
(214) 651-1025

Neal-Schuman Publishers
Sources
64 University Place
New York, NY 10003

Nevada Publications
Box 15444
Las Vegas, NV 89114

Ohio State University Press
Hitchcock Hall, Room 316
Columbus, OH 43210

Old Timer Press
Box 572
Ripley, MS 38663

Oxmoor House, Inc.
Book Division of the
Progressive Farmer
Box 2463
Birmingham, AL 35202

Palatine Transcripts
Box 129, RR 1
Rhinebeck, NY 12572

Pathways Publications
266 Moon Mt. Drive
Sonoma, CA 95476

Pelican Publishing Co.
Box 189
Gretna, LA 70053

Penns Valley Publishers
211 W. Beaver Avenue
State College, PA 16801

Pioneer Press
Newfane, VT
05345

Polyanthos
Drawer 51359
New Orleans, LA 70151

Porter Publishing Co.
Box 134
Center City, MN 55012

Potomac Books
Box 40604
Palisades Station
Washington, DC 20016

Prentice Hall, Inc.
Englewood Cliffs, NJ
07632

Printing by Faisal
Printing Impressions
365 So. Main Street
Bountiful, UT 84010
(801) 295-2060

Quarterman Publications
5 South Main Street
Lawrence, MS 01843

Quick-Scan
9033 Michigan Ave.
Sun Lakes, AZ 85224

Carole J. Reddock
Box 61
Bloomington, CA 92316

Mrs. Alvaretta K. Register
307 College Blvd.
Statesboro, TN 38080

Reprint Company Publishers
Box 5401
Spartanburg, SC 29304
(803) 582-0732

Roots International
3239 N. 58th Street
Milwaukee, WI 53216

Rose Publishing Co.
301 Louisiana
Little Rock, AR 72201

Russell and Russell
597 Fifth Avenue
New York, NY 10017

Salisbury Printing Co.
1717 W. Innes Street
Salisbury, NC 28144
(704) 633-9071

Sanders Historical Publishers
13603 Pebblebrook
Houston, TX 77079

W.M. Sanner Co.
Commerce and Water Streets
Baltimore, MD 21202

Scholarly Resources, Inc.
104 Greenhill Avenue
Wilmington, DE 19805
(302) 654-7713

George K. Schweitzer
7914 Gleason
Knoxville, TN 37919

Search-n-Print
Box 777
Farmersville, TX 75031

Selby Publishing & Printing
3405 W. Zartman
Kokomo, IN 46901

Sheffield Press
Box 366
Princeton, NJ 08540

Sims Publishing Co.
Box 9576
Sacramento, CA 95828

Southern Historical Press
Box 738
Easley, SC 29640

Southern Illinois University Press
Box 3697
Carbondale, IL 62901

Southwest Pennsylvania Genealogical Services
Box 253
Laughlintown, PA 15655

Stackpole Books
Cameron and Keller Streets
Harrisburg, PA 17103

State Printing Co.
1305 Sumter Street
Columbia, SC 29202

Stevenson's Genealogical Supply
230 W. 1230 North
Provo, UT 84601

Summit Publications
Box 222
Munroe Falls, OH 44262

S.W. Publishing Co.
5101 Madison Road
Cincinnati, OH 45227

Jim W. Tackitt
1830 Johnson Drive
Concord, CA 94520

Teachers College Press
81 Adams Drive
Totowa, NJ 07512

TLC Associates
639 Broad Acres Road
Narberth, PA 19072

Trinity University Press
715 Stadium Drive
San Antonio, TX 78284

Tuttle Antiquarian Books
Box 541
Rutland, VT 05701

Unigraphics
1401 N. Fares Avenue
Evansville, IN 47711
Indexes, reprints

University Microfilm
Box 1346
Ann Arbor, MI 48106

University of Alabama Press
Drawer 2877
University, AL 35486

University of California Press
2223 Fulton Street
Berkeley, CA 94720

University of Georgia
Athens, GA
30602

University of Nebraska
901 N. Seventeenth Street
Lincoln, NE 68588

University of Oklahoma
1005 Asp Street
Norman, OK 73019

University of Pittsburgh
127 N. Bellefield Avenue
Pittsburgh, PA 15213

University of Utah Press
Finding Aids Project
Salt Lake City, UT 84112

Valkyrie Press
2135 1st Ave. South
St. Petersburg, FL 33712

Verlene Publishing
915 E. Green
Gallup, NM 87301

Virginia Book Co.
Box 431
Berryville, VA 22611

Wentworth Press
26 Harriett Street
Marrickville, N.S.W. 2204
Australia

Westland Publications
Box 117
McNeal, AZ 85617

Whipporwill Publications
4400 Jackson Avenue
Evansville, IN 47715

Wilaine Books
Box 67
Wilmington, MA 01887

Wilson & Grover Publishing
571 Headden Drive
Ridgley, TN 38080

Winter Farm Books
Pittsfield, ME
04967

WH Wolfe Associates
Historical Publications Div.
Box 972
Roswell, GA 30077
(404) 475-6782

William A. Yates
Box 274
Ozark, MO 65721

Ye Old Genealogie Shoppe
Box 39128
Indianapolis, IN 46239

Yesterdesign
W. 628 Augusta, #1
Spokane, WA 99205

GLOSSARY

Most words used in the text with specialized or unfamiliar meanings are defined within the context of the chapters where they appear for the first time. Many of these words are also included in the subject index at the end of the volume. Some chapters also have glossaries for their own specialized subject matter like computer terminology or unusual occupations found in old documents.

The words selected for this glossary usually appear throughout the book often separated from their definitions. It is designed to be helpful to the beginning researcher as well as the experienced genealogist exploring new research tools.

For other specialized terms there are word books available in most research libraries or the serious genealogist may wish to acquire personal copies for convenient reference.

Black, Henry Campbell. *Black's Law Dictionary: Definitions of the Forms and Phrases of American and English Jurisprudence, Ancient and Modern.* St. Paul, Minn.: West Publishing Company, 1968. Standard legal reference.

Evans, Barbara Jean. *From A to Zax.* Available from Unigraphic, Inc., 1401 North Fares Ave., Evansville, IN 47711. Glossary of words, abbreviations, legal terms often encountered in genealogical research, especially compiled for genealogists.

Martin, Charles T. *The Legal Interpreter: A Collection of Abbreviations, Latin Words and Names Used in English Historical Manuscripts and Records.* London: Stevens and Sons, 1910. Facsimile reprint, Dorking, Surrey: Kohler & Coombes, 1976. The standard work for legal and historical documents.

Mills, Elizabeth Shown. "How to Understand Ethnic Terminology in Old Louisiana." *The Genealogical Helper,* Sept.-Oct., 1978, pp. 13-14. Very useful.

Some how-to books like Val Greenwood, *The Researcher's Guide to American Genealogy* (Baltimore: Genealogical Publishing Company 1973) include useful glossaries of legal or specialized terms the genealogist can expect to encounter in research.

ACC: American Computing Centers

AFRA: American Family Records Association.

AG: Accredited Genealogist

AGBI: The *American Genealogical-Biographical Index.*

AIS: Accelerated Indexing Systems.

APG: Association of Professional Genealogists

APJI: Association for Protection of Jewish Immigrants

ASG: American Society of Genealogists

AWOL: Absent without leave.

Abstract: Essential items selected from an original document—names, dates, places, relationships.

Acre rights: Rights of individuals in common lands.

Ad litem: For this case only. A guardian ad litem represents a minor or imcompetent person in this specific case only.

Administration: Settling an estate usually when there is no will. The term *administration* is associated almost exclusively with intestate estates. The only exceptions are: (1) cases where a will may have existed but was disallowed for some reason and what began as a testate case has changed to an administration (intestate), and (2) cases where the executor nominated by the deceased refuses to act and the court appoints an administrator (administration with will annexed).

Affidavit: A statement made under oath, usually in writing.

American: A person born within any territory subject to United States jurisdiction or born abroad of American parents. Excludes Canada (North America) and Latin America.

Anglo-American: English-American. In Louisiana, used to differentiate between Louisiana-born (Creole) and United States-born.

Archives: Either specific documents or volumes or the physical facility which houses documents. Sometimes used incorrectly to refer to compiled sources or indexes.

Area keys: Basic resource guides to Ohio, New York, Colorado, and Pennsylvania. Separate guides for each Pennsylvania county are also available. Published by Keyline Publishers. See Appendix H for address.

Assignment: Legal grant of a right, privilege, benefit, or property, usually conveyed by written document.

Assize: Special session of a law court, or (usually *assizes*) a court with capital jurisdiction for handling crime against the people or government.

Attest: To certify the authenticity of testimony, signature, or document.

Authenticate: To establish authorship, or prove that a document is real and not a forgery.

BCG: Board for Certification of Genealogists

BIA: Bureau of Indian Affairs

BLM: Bureau of Land Management.

Banns: Public announcement that a marriage is about to take place. Persons knowing any reason the marriage should not occur are encouraged to speak up or hold their peace thereafter. Usually "read" in church three consecutive weeks preceding the marriage.

Baseline: Specific survey line on which all latitude measurements are based.

Bastardy: Record of illegitimacy or an official attempt to identify the father of an illegitimate child.

Batch number: Reference to original input source for the International Genealogical Index.

Bishop's transcripts: Official copy of local church birth, marriage, and/or death registers submitted to the bishop.

Blood bands: Clans of persons biologically related, usually in Indian research. Specific degrees of kinship are required for citizenship to be acknowledged.

Blood-kin: Persons related by blood.

Bounty land: Land awarded as a bonus to attract soldiers to sign up or as payment in addition to or in lieu of wages for military service.

Brief: Written summary of evidence and points of law in a lawsuit, usually preprinted.

CALS: Certified American Lineage Specialist

CCC: Copyright Clearance Center.

CFI: Computer File Index, now the IGI or International Genealogical Index.

CG: Certified Genealogist

CGL: Computerized Genealogy Library

CGRS: Certified Genealogical Record Searcher

Cajun: Born in Louisiana of Acadian (French) ancestry.

Calendar: (1) Log of research steps showing each source consulted, whether it contained relevant information or not, how each record was searched, and what was found; (2) Summary of record contents; (3) System of dating used in specific areas.

Cartulary: A register of title deeds and charters. Also spelled chartulary.

Caveat: Literally "beware," a warning to investigate before action is taken.

Citation: Detailed description of specific records which document a pedigree, a genealogy, or a statement of fact. Often in specific format. Style manuals like Richard Lackey, *Cite Your Sources* (New Orleans: Polyanthos, 1980) outline such formats. Civil registration: Registration of births, marriages, deaths, and other vital events by a civil authority.

Clemency: Merciful or lenient moderation of a sentence or judgement.

Codicil: Section added to a will after it has been witnessed and signed which alters the provisions of the original will. Also applies to other legal documents.

Collateral: descended from a common ancestor, but through a different line; as a cousin, aunt, uncle, nephew, etc.

Common fields: Proportion of a town cultivated in common.

Common-law marriage: The union of a man and woman living together by personal agreement rather than legal action but legally recognized after a specific time period with neighborhood (or society) recognition of the relationship as marital. A live-together arrangement is not a common-law marriage.

Commoner: Legal term meaning proprietor. Those who have jurisdiction to act in common are called commoners.

Compiled source: A biography, pedigree, or family history compiled from a variety of record types representing conclusions of the compiler or data summarized and merged together.

Conciliation: Officially santioned method of settling a dispute out of court.

Conscript: To draft into the armed forces.

Consent affidavit: Written permission by parent or legal guardian for person underage to marry, buy property, drive a car, or serve in the military.

Consortium: Group of agencies united to fill a common purpose by pooling resources.

Consulate: Term of office of a foreign consul or the physical premises where the consul resided while in office.

Corroborate: Using the same or similar evidence recorded in two or more sources distinct and unrelated to each other to confirm a conclusion.

Court baron: Civil and administrative jurisdiction exercised by a lord over his subjects.

Court leet: Criminal and capital jurisdiction exercised by a lord over his subjects.

Covert: A married woman.

Creole: American-born children of European-born parents. In Louisiana, anyone born in Louisiana regardless of racial mix, except Cajuns (*q.v.*).

Curtesy: Life estate (usually one-third interest) husband has in property which is independently owned by his wife, provided they had at least one child born alive. Similar to dower rights (*g.v.*) of wife.

DAR: Daughters of the American Revolution.

Decedent: A deceased person; usually death is recent.

Decennial: Every ten years.

Defunct county: County no longer in existence. Many reference books do not list or describe them, yet they are essential knowledge for efficient use of local records and land patents.

Delayed birth record: Birth record created many years after the fact from eyewitnesses, or a record giving specific age at a particular period of time, like a census or school enrollment. This record has its own value separate from the birth data.

Delinquent lands: Lands on which payment of taxes, fees, or specific requirements of title become past due.

Demographics: Analysis of compiled population statistics dealing with births, deaths, disease, marriage rate, etc.

Denizen: A person given a form of citizenship permitting legal residence in a foreign country.

Deposition: Testimony of a witness, usually in writing, authenticated by court official.

Discrepancy: Two or more facts in conflict with each other. Some can be resolved, some cannot. Both can be shown on summary or research forms with footnotes documenting sources and explaining implications for research.

Distraint: Seizure of property for unpaid debts or to force appearance in court.

Dower: Life estate, (usually one-third interest) wife has in property of dead husband, to be used to support herself and her children. No dower in community-property states.

ERIC: Educational Resources Information Center.

Enrollment: An official list, register, or record.

Entailed: Entailed lands automatically descend to a specific person and his/her lineal descendents. Trigger phrase: "to x and the heirs of his/her body lawfully begotten." The phrase "to his heirs and assigns forever" is not an entail, it is a freehold.

Entryman: Legal claimant for a federal land grant.

Enumerator: Person who records census or tax assessment.

Escheat: Reversion of property title to the state, country, or lord of the manor when there are no legal hairs to inherit

Established church: Specific church officially supported by local taxes or government funds.

Ethnic: Relating to a group of people sharing specific language, customs, social viewpoints, or physical attributes.

Exhumation: to dig up a dead body by government order.

Extract: Brief verbatim quotation from original document.

Extralegal: Outside of the law, not covered by the law.

FARC: Federal Archives and Records Centers (branches of the National Archives).

FASG: Fellow, American Society of Genealogists

FGRA: Family Group Records Archives in the Genealogical Society of Utah.

FGS: Federation of Genealogical Societies

FR: Family registry (listing of family organization research efforts).

FSG: Fellow, Society of Genealogists (London)

Family group sheet: Genealogical form summarizing genealogical data for a single family unit-husband/father, wife/mother, children (eight to twelve per sheet).

Family tradition: Anecdotes, stories, bits of information, isolated facts passed from one generation to another.

Finding aid: Printed, manuscript, or microform material that provides information about the contents, use, or location of a source. Includes indexes, inventories, lists, calendars, etc.

Fraktur: An ornamental, elaborately decorated parchment document or printing style of German origin. May also refer specifically to birth certificate, marriage certificate, or death notice.

Free man of color: a black born free, or given freedom many years earlier.

Freedman: An emancipated slave.

Freehold: Land holdings which could be bought, sold, bequeathed by by will, or inherited according to law.

Freeholder: Owner of enough property to vote, serve on jury, and hold public office.

Freeman: Always a white man in legal sense. In New York, a citizen free to practice trade within city limits. In Pennsylvania, a single white man over twenty-one years of age. In Massachusetts, an adult male with enough property to vote.

Friendly society: Mutual benefit society organized around a mutual concern and pooling resources.

GIA: Genealogical Indexing Associates.

GLO: General Land Office. Merged with U.S. Grazing Service in 1946 to form the Bureau of Land Management.

GPAI: *Genealogical Periodical Annual Index.*

GS: Genealogical Society of Utah.

Gaol delivery: Court process to empty the jail of prisoners by hearing the cases. Imprisonment was originally until trial, not as punishment after being convicted.

Gazetteer: Descriptive guide to geographical features for a specific area. May or may not have accompanying maps.

Grantee: Buyer of land.

Grantor: Seller of land.

Grid: Two-dimensional graph that shows the relationship of two or more facts.

Griff: Mixed Indian and black ancestry.

HIAS: Hebrew Immigrant Aid Society

Half-blood: Biologically descended from one side of the family only. Such individuals have limited inheritance rights.

Headright: Specific number of acres (usually 50 acres) for importing oneself or an immigrant into the state/province. Pre-1860. Actual provisions vary from place to place.

Heir-at-law: During the colonial period the eldest son; if dead, to his heir-at-law; in absence of son, daughters inherit jointly as heirs-at-law. After 1790, all children inherited equally; other family members inherit as stipulated by law.

Heirship: Right of inheritance.

Historiographer: An historian *officially appointed* to write and interpret the history of specific institutions, laws, and practices. This position was a political appointment.

Homestead: (1) Place of residence (home) and small piece of land (usually one to five acres) reserved by law from creditors to insure family is not rendered destitute. (2) One hundred sixty acres acquired from the United States government under the Homestead Act of 1862 and subsequent land laws.

Hymnal: Music or verse books used in a church setting.

IGI: International Genealogical Index compiled by the Genealogical Society of Utah.

INS: Immigration and Naturalization Service.

Illegal: Forbidden by the law.

Impfschein: Vaccination certificate, usually in German.

Imprint: Book issued from a specific publisher or printed during a specific time period.

Indenture: A contract in two or more copies binding one person to labor for another and learn a specified trade during a specific period of time. During the colonial period, indentures allowed immigrants to trade their labor as payment for travel costs, maintenance, or training.

Independent city: City jurisdiction separate and independent from county authority with powers conferred by charter from state legislature.

Indiscriminate: Non-selective, including nearly all possibilities within the realm of choice.

Injunction: Official court order to do or stop doing something.

Intendant: A high-level administrative official under Spanish or French control.

International Reply Coupon: A coupon purchased at your local post office which can be exchanged for appropriate postage in any country of the world. Used with self-addressed, stamped envelope in non-U.S. countries.

Inventory: A descriptive list of records in a repository. Entries may be annotated and indexed.

Jurisdiction: The right to exercise power over a region or area; and the territory over which the power is exercised.

Kindred: Persons related by blood. May or may not mean children.

LC: Library of Congress

LDS: Church of Jesus Christ of Latter-day Saints, the "Mormons".

Land warrant: A government guarantee of authenticity and undisturbed possession.

Landsat map: Map of the entire global land surface based on satellite images on a scale and resolution of sufficient clarity to show specific geographical and cultural features which are recognizable to the naked eye. With special interpretive tools or film, you can use Landsat images to disclose the buildup of strategic weapons, the amassing of bodies of troops and vehicles, high concentrations of particular foodstuffs, etc.

Lien: Claim against property as security for payment of a debt including unpaid taxes. In most states mortgages are liens; they do not transfer title.

Lis pendens: Court action pending. Usually applies to land title claims.

Lis: a lawsuit.

Litigation: Lawsuit before the courts.

Loose papers: Unrecorded, unverified documents filed with a public official, including wills, deeds, powers of attorney, petitions, etc.

MCA: Microfilm Corporation of America.

Manifest: A detailed list of cargo, crew, and passengers on board a ship, signed and authenticated by a ship's officer.

Manumission: A formal, often written, act which frees a slave.

Manuscript: An *unpublished* record or volume containing handwritten material. Letters, diaries, and typed papers are manuscripts. A printed book with someone's handwritten notes interspersed through it can also be called a manuscript and filed with manuscript material in an archive.

Matriculation: Formal admittance into a school or institution of higher learning; formal registration as a student.

Memorial: An object or verse displayed to the public in memory of someone who has died.

Meridian: Line or circle of longitude from which map lines are projected.

Metes and Bounds: Property described by natural boundary markings like "meanderings of the creek," "along the brow of the hill," "adjoining Thomas Brown's south line," or "three notches on a white oak tree," rather than lineal measures.

Metizo: One parent Indian, one parent white.

Microform: Collective term for any storage film containing images that must be magnified to be read. Includes microfilm (roll film), microfiche (sheet film), ultrafiche (high-density sheet film reduced 90 times), micro-opaque cards (double-sided with different images on either side of sheet film), cassettes, and cartridges.

Military reserve: Tract of land set aside within specific state boundaries where military bounty land warrants could be assigned.

Miracode: Soundex index to 1910 census based on household number rather than enumeration district. Data is almost identical to Soundex.

Mortality schedule: Census of those who died within a specific period of time.

Mulatto: Mixed black and European ancestry. In Louisiana, one parent black, one parent white.

Muniment: Written evidence used to defend title to property. Term used more commonly in England where deed registries were not established until the twentieth century. Muniments are personal or family documents, not public records.

Muster: A periodic assembly to drill (usually) militia.

NARS: National Archives Records Services

NEH: National Endowment for the Humanities.

NEHGS: New England Historic Genealogical Society

NGS: National Genealogical Society

NUCMC: *National Union Catalog of Manuscript Collections*. A very useful multi-volume listing of manuscripts, what they contain, and where they can be found. Added to annually.

Née: Literally "born." "Nancy Johnson née Greenlee" means that Nancy's maiden name was Greenlee.

Necrology: Of or relating to the recently dead.

Notary: Public official who certifies and authenticates documents; an appointed official with probate and family law jurisdiction under French and Spanish control.

OCLC: Online Computer Library Center.

Octoroon: One-eighth black; one great-grandparent who is black.

Oral history: Collective term for oral interviews, folklore, family tradition, anecdotes, or life stories related orally, and usually recorded on tape.

Oyer and terminer: To hear and determine.

Palatinate: A region west of the Rhine River in West Germany.

Palatine: An official exercising royal rights in his own territory.

Pathology: An examination to determine if death is caused by disease.

Patronymics: Custom of using father's given name or some form of it as a surname for the children.

Pedigree chart: Genealogical form showing lines of ancestry generation by generation.

Pellon: Matted, nonwoven fabric available in most department or dry goods stores; used for interfacings in clothes and to make tombstone rubbings.

Perambulation: Literally "to walk around." Practice of walking the boundaries of local landowners in a group so every male over age eighteen knows the boundary lines of his neighbor's. Boundary markers obliterated or moved were repositioned. Prevented litigation and boundary disputes.

Performance bond: Posting a bond to guarantee performance of court order.

Periodical: A publication issued at regular intervals.

Personalty: Collective term meaning all kinds of personal or moveable property.

Pew rent: Payment made by a family for a specific seat assignment in the church. Can vary from a few pence to six-digit figures.

Pitch: Rights drawn in division of common land to lay out a specific portion.

Plat, Plot: A plat is a map. A plot is the territory or physical section shown on the plat.

Poll: A head of household over a specific age responsible for payment of taxes or someone eligible to vote. Usually a free white male.

"Pony": An answer sheet prepared in advance.

Poorhouse: A government-supported and -maintained place to house the poor and those physically or mentally unable to care for themselves.

Post mortem: Literally "after death" – examination of deceased person, usually to determine cause of death, or examination of deceased person's estate to assign portions/interest to heirs.

Preemption Rights: Right of squatters to first right to buy when lands became available for sale.

Prelimary inventory: Descriptive list of record holdings. May or may not be annotated.

Presentment: Statement of a criminal offence based on first-hand or eyewitness knowledge; an accusation of crime.

Primogeniture: Oldest son inherits specific portions of *landed* estate.

Processioning: *See* perambulation.

Proprietor: Those to whom a grant of land was given in common for settlement, part of a quasi-corporation.

Protocol: First page of a notarial document; document dealing with diplomatic relations or emigration across local and provincial boundaries.

Public domain: Land owned by the federal government.

Quadroon: One-fourth black, three-fourths white.

Quaker Dating System: Months are numbered and referred to as 11th mo. 10th [day] 1822, or 1st [day] of ye 6th [month] 1822. Requires careful analysis to copy them correctly.

Quitclaim: Release of all title, interest, or claim to ownership in specific property. May transfer title to someone else.

Quitman: Colonial tax official responsible to assess and collect quitrents.

Quitrent: Annual tax on land paid in New York and colonial South.

Quota/Nonquota: Number of immigrants from any one country allowed to enter the United States legally each year.

RG: Registered Genealogist

Recognizance: Binding a person to follow orders of the court or pay a fine.

Rectangular townships: Square townships six miles square with thirty-six sections each a mile square.

Redemptioner: An immigrant who redeems passage money by becoming a bond servant for a specific term of years. Differs from indentured servant in that the immigrant is sold to the highest bidder after arrival, rather than contracting labor before immigrating.

Register System: Numbering system by which generations in a genealogy are written down. Developed for, not by, the *New England Historical and Genealogical Register* and thus called the Register System.

Renunciation: Act of giving up title or claim to property.

Replevin: Law action to recover property unlawfully seized.

Repository: Place where records are physically stored.

Residencies: Territory in a protected area in which administrative powers are executed by a resident official.

Residency: Statement of residence requirement in force in a specific area (varies from 3 months to 3 years) before a specific legal action can take place.

Returns: Written acknowledgement that an action ordered or licensed has been performed. Requires date and signature to be legal.

SASE: Self-addressed, stamped envelope.

Sacrament certificate: Certificate given after person takes communion in established church to prove loyalty to government in power and refute belief in transubstantiation. Those refusing to take the sacrament are called recusants.

Serial: A publication issued in volumes or parts. May or may not be regular.

Sexton: Person responsible to bury the dead and keep a record of the burial.

Sibling: Brother or sister, first-generation relationship with one or both parents the same.

Soundex: Index which groups together names pronounced roughly alike.

Sovereignity: Autonomous and supreme political control over a specific geographic area.

Statement of settlers: Census of marketable commodities and other assets which local settlers have on hand. Taken by Holland Land Company to determine ability of settlers to pay for their land.

Statute: Law enacted by legislative body.

Stet: To remove a record no longer active but preserve for use.

Subpoena: Official written order to appear in court under penalty.

Substantiate: To prove that a fact, a statement, or a document is true by corroborating it from other sources or logically deducing the truth from the comfortable fit of many bits of evidence.

Taufschein: Baptismal certificate, usually in German.

TIB: Temple Records Index Bureau in the Genealogical Society of Utah.

TVA: Tennessee Valley Authority.

Tenement: Any property held by tenure, usually applies to buildings.

Tenure: Specific holding in land.

Topographical: Detailed drawings or written description of physical features for any given area.

Torrens: Land registration system based on tracts, showing all former owners, rights, interests, and liens, rather than alphabetical lists of buyer-seller. Used in about twenty states.

Toxology: An examination to determine if death is caused by poison.

Transcript: Verbatim copy of entire original document.

Typescript: A typewritten copy.

VIP: Very Important Person.

WPA: Works Progress Administration.

Ward: Administrative division of a city, or someone under guardianship.

Watch and ward: An old custom of patroling towns and cities watching for law breakers, fire, or other dangers to person and property. Forerunner of modern police force.

Whole-blood: Biologically descended from both sides of the family.

Writ: Official written order of the court issued under seal.

Yiddish: High German dialect combining Hebrew and/or Slavic elements, written in Hebrew characters, spoken by German Jews relocated in Russia.

BIBLIOGRAPHIC INDEX

A LIST OF AUTHORS AND TITLES NOT CITED IN CHAPTER BIBLIOGRAPHIES

A

A Bibliography of Iowa Newspapers, 1836-1976, 420
A Bibliography of Loyalist Source Material in the United States, Canada and Great Britain, 235
"A Bibliography of Nevada Newspapers, 1858-1875", 421
A Bibliography of Newspapers Published in Illinois Prior to 1860, 420
A Century of American Life Insurance: A History of the Mutual Life Insurance Company of New York 1843-1943, 341
A Check List of Western Newspapers in the Mills Collection, 419
"A Check-List of Extant Florida newspapers, 1845-1846", 420
A Genealogical Dictionary of the First Settlers of New England, 440
A Guide to Newspaper Indexes in New England, 423
A History of California Newspapers, 1846-1858, 419
A History of Family-Owned Newspapers in Hartford City, Indiana: 1852-1977, 420
A History of Printing in Colonial Maryland, 1686-1776, 421
A History of the Massachusetts Hospital Life Insurance Company The Whitesmiths of Taunton: A History of Reed and Baron, 1824-1943, 372
A History of the Newspapers of Ann Arbor, 1829-1920, 421
A History of the Public Land Policies, 224
"A List of Newspapers published in the District of Columbia, 1820-1850", 420
A List of Periodicals, Newspapers in Principal Libraries of Boston and Vicinity, 421
A Union List of Newspapers Published in Michigan Based on the Principal Newspaper Collections in the State with Notes Concerning Papers Not Located, 421
A Union List of Newspapers in Offices of Publishers in Libraries of Southern California, 419
Abbott, Martin, 581
Abel, Annie H., 538
"About Families", 688
Abstracts (mainly deaths) from the "Pennsylvania Gazette," 1725-1748, 425
Abstracts from Ben Franklin's Pennsylvania Gazette, 1728-1748, 425, 467
Abstracts of All Original Texas Land Titles, 250
Abstracts of Georgia Death Notices from the Southern Recorder, 1830-1855, 424
Abstracts of Georgia Marriages from the Southern Recorder, 1830-1955, 424
Abstracts of Marriage, Death, and Estate Notices from the "Oquawka Spectator, "Henderson County, Illinois, 1848-1852, 424
"Abstracts of Oregon Donation Land Claims, 1852-1903", 248
Abstracts of Vital Records From Raleigh, North Carolina Newspapers, 425
"Abstracts of Washington Donation Land Claims, 1855-1902", 252
"Academic Archives," 372
Accelerated Indexing System, 18
Access, rights of, 25-26
"Account of Servants Bound and Assigned before James Hamilton, Mayor of Philadelphia," 340, 341
"Account of the Invasion of South Carolina by the French andAckerman, Robert Kilgo, 249
"Activities of the Freedmen's Bureau in Southern Maryland 1865-70," 581
Adams, Arthur, 685
Adkins, Wilma, 432
"Administration and Sale of Public Land in Indiana 1800-1860", 241
Administration of the Public Domain in South Dakota, 249
Advancing the Frontier, 1830-1860, 535
"Afro-American Immigration to Liberia: An International Perspective on Black Genealogy," 593
Ahnenpass of Nazi Germany, 457
Ainsworth, Mary G., 198
Akagi, Roy Hidemichi, 222
Alaska Directory and Gazetteer for 1934-1935, 388
Albrecht, Abraham, 503
Allen, Cameron, 143
Allen, David Grayson, 222
Allen, Robert S., 235
Allis, Frederick S.,
Allison, William H., 139
Alphabetical Index of Revolutionary Pensioners Living in Maine,
Alter, J. Cecil, 422
American Advertising Directory Manufacturers and Dealers in American Goods for the Year 1831, 398
American Agricultural Press, 423
American Archivist, 370
American Banker. Index, 426
American Bibliography: A Chronological Dictionary of all Books, Pamphlets, and Periodical Publications Printed in the United States, 1639-1820, 408
American Blue Book of Funeral Directors, 400
American Congressional Records, 199
American Council for Nationalities Service, 423
American Courts: Their Organization and Procedures, 210
American Digest System, 193
American Family Laws: Comparative Study of the Forty-Eight American States, Alaska, District of Columbia, and Hawaii to 1 Jan. 1931, 186
American Genealogical Resources in German Archives (AGRIGA): A Handbook, 455, 457,504
American Genealogical-Biographical Index, 434, 449
American Genealogist, The, 176, 398, 437
American Indian Census Rolls, 1885-1940, 536
American Indian Policy in Crisis: Christian Reformers and the Indian, 1865-1900, 534
American Indian Policy in the Formative Years: The Indian Trade and Intercourse Acts, 1790-1834, 534
American Loyalist Claims. Vol. I: Abstracted from the Public Records Office, 257
American Loyalist Claims: Abstracted from the Public Record Office, Audit Series 13, Bundles 1-35 and 37, 235
American Medical Directory, 399, 400
American Newspapers, 407
"American Public Land History: A Review Essay," 224
"American Quaker Records and Family History," 146
American State Papers, Public Lands, 198, 230, 238, 239, 241, 243, 244, 252
Ames, Susie, 176
Anderson, George L., 240, 242
"Anguished Odyssey: The Flight of the Utes, 1906-08," 535
Annual Index to Genealogical Periodicals and Family Histories, 438
"Applicability of the Public Land System to Louisiana," 243
Architects and Builders, 400
"Archives of Coca-Cola Company", 374
Arkansas Military Bounty Grants (War of 1812), 239
Arndt, Karl J. R., 467, 504
Arts and Crafts in New York, 1777-1799: Advertisements and News Items from New York City Newspapers, 414
Ash, Lee, 370, 372, 530
Askin, Jayne, 212, 335, 468
Association for Gravestone Studies, 66
Association of American University Presses, resolutions on permissions, 27
Association of Professional Genealogists, 5
Atlas of the State of New York, 246
Authentic List of All Land Lottery Grants Made to Veterans of the Revolutionary War by the State of Georgia, 240
Avina, Rose H., 239
Ayers' Directory, 407, 418

B

Bailey, Rosalie Fellows, 519, 532, 594
Baird's Manual of American College Fraternities, 401
Baird, Charles W., 143
Ball, Walter V., 169
Balloting Book, and Other Documents Relating to Military Bounty Lands in the State of New York, New York Legislature, 246, 296
Banet, Charles, 417
"Bank of America's Archival Program", 373
Banker's Alamanac and Year Book, 400
Baptist Bibliography, Being A Register of Printed Material By and About Baptists, 141
"Baptist Records for Genealogy and History," 141
Barber, Gertrude, 417
Barker, Joel, 251
Barnet, Leroy, 244
Bartis, Peter, 464
Bartlett, John R., 249
Bason, William H., 478
Baum, Willa K., 580, 594
Becker, Robert A., 156
Beers, Henry Putney, 229, 559,
Beginnings of West Tennessee in the Land of the Chickasaws, 1541-1841, 535
"Beginnings of the United States Military Land Bounty Policy," 234
Beijbom, Ulf, 481

Bell, Carol Willsey. *See also* Flavell, 187,
Bell, Raymond M., 249, 252,
Benedict, Karen M., 372
"Benevolence in Emergent San Francisco: A Note on Immigrant Life in the Urban Far West," 468
"Benning Wentworth's Land Grant Policy: A Reappraisal," 245
Benson, Canville D., 244
Bergquist, James M., 248
Bibliographical Sketches of Knox County [Ohio] Writers, 330
Bibliography of American Directories Through 1860, 387, 403,
Bibliography of Loyalist Source Material in the United States, Canada, and Great Britain, 257,
Bibliography of Passenger Lists, 480
Bibliography of Research Project Reports, See also*WPA Bibliography*, 524
Bibliothek and Archiv, Katalog, 612
Bicentennial Supplement of the 1972 Register, 655
Bien, J. R., 246
Bigham, Barbara, 455
Billeter, Julius, 488
Billington, Ray Allen, 224
Biographical Dictionary of American Science, 446
Biographical Dictionary of Early Virginia, 1607-1660, 251
Biographical Dictionary of the Confederacy, 265
Biographical Directory of Railroad Officials of America, 338, 371
Biographical Directory of the American Congress, 1774-1971, 446
Biographical Directory of the Indiana General Assembly, 446
Biographical Register, Officers and Graduates of the U.S. Military Academy, West Point, New York, 265
Biographical Sketches of Loyalists of the American Revolution, 257, 675
Biography and Genealogy Master Index: A Consolidated Index to more than 3,200,000 Biographical Sketches in over 350 Current and Retrospective Biographical Dictionaries, 371,
Bitton, Davis, 456
"Black Monongolians: A Judicial View of Slavery and the Negro in Monongolia County, 1776-1865", 214
Black's Law Dictionary, 152, 163, 186, 217
Black, James M., 249
Blackstone, William, 253
Blake, Robert, 561
Blood, Martin H. 85
Bodge, George M., 295,
Bogue, Allan G., 242
Bonanza West: The Story of the Western Rushes, 1848-1900, The, 213
Bond, Beverley, W., Jr., 236, 243
Bond, C. T., 176
"Book Reviews," *Genealogical Journal*, 437
"Bounty Grants to Revolutionary Soldiers," 249
Bounty and Donation Land Grants of Texas 1835-1838, 250, 657
Bowden, J. J., 251
Bowen, Richard Le Baron, 253,
Bowman, Larry, 206
Boyd, Julian P., 247, 249
"Braun and Loesch Families: Neighbors in Germany and America," 476
Brennan, Patricia C., 241
Brewer, John M., 243
Brickford, Maynard, 372
Bridgham, Lawrence Donald, 243
Brief Guide to the Temple Records Index Bureau, 432
"Brief Notes on the Public Domain," 253
Brief Report on How Certain Germans Have Fared, Who Have Come to Pennsylvania, 456
Brigham, Clarence, 407,
British Immigration to North America, 457
Britzell, Edwin W., 297Brooke, N. M., 665
Brookes-Smith, Joan E., 242
Brower, Philip P., 229, 231, 238
Brown, Elizabeth Gaspar, 243
Brown, J., 387
Brown, Jean C., 248
Brown, Wallace, 257
Browning, James R., 194
Brownstone, David M, 337,
Bruce, R. M., 257
Brumbough, Gaius Marcus, 235, 595
Bryant, Pat, 240
Buchanan, John, 383
Buenker, John D., 492, 519, 530
Buffalo and Erie Historical Society, 246
Bundy, David A., 222, 253
Burlington Court Book, The, 176
Burness, Lawrence R., 500
Burns, Frances B., 243
Burrows, J. Lansing, 402
Burton, A. Agnes, 244
Burton, Clarence M., 244
Burton, William C., 152
Business History, 372
Business Incorporations in the United States, 1800-1943, 372
Business Organizations and Agencies Directory, 337,
Business Periodicals Index, 337,
"Bute Co., N.C.: 1771 Tax List", 253

C

CCC. *See* Copyright Clearance Center, 27-28
Calendar of Archives of the Pacific Coast Steamship Companies of Alaska and America, 457
Calendar of N.Y. Colonial Manuscripts, Endorsed Land Papers, in the Office of the Secretary of State of New York, 1643-1803, 246
Calendar of Records in the Office of the Secretary of State, 1664-1703, 245
"Calendar of the Letters of Antonio Martinez, Last Spanish Governor of Texas, 1817-1822", 558
Calendar of the Warrants for Land in Kentucky, Granted for Service in the French and Indian War, 242,
California Mining Town Newspapers, 1850-1880, 213
Callender, Clarence N., 210
"Campbell's (Law) List," 398-399
Campbell, Penelope, 593
Candler, Charles Howard, 374
Carbonate Camp Called Leadville, The, 213
Carleton, Mark T., 324
Carlson, Theodore L., 241
Carruth, Gordon, 337
Cartwright, Betty G.C., 249
Catalog of the United States Geological Survey Library, 224
Catalogue of Census 1790-1880, 393
Catalogue of Revolutionary Soldiers and Sailors of the Commonwealth of Virginia to Whom Land Bounty Warrants Were Granted, 242
Catholics in Colonial America, 146
Cavaliers and Pioneers, 251
Cavanaugh, Karen B., 212
Censuses of Nacogdoches, Tenehaw and Sabine, Bevil's Settlement, 561
Century of American Life Insurance: A History of the Mutual Life Company of New York, 1843-1943, 340, 343
"Certificate Book of the Virginia Land Commission, 1779-80", 242
Chandler, Marion C., 249
Change of Destination for Some 100 Emigrants from Virginia and Maryland to South Carolina, 465
Chapin, Bradley, 176, 209
Chapman, Berlin Basil, 248
Charters Granted by the State of Vermont, 251
Chaston, Gloria D., 141, 432, 433
Check List of Historical Records Survey Publications, 139
Checklist of Printed Maps of the Middle West to 1900, 229
"Cherokee Courts, The," 213
Childs, St. Julien R., 502
"Chimborazo Hospital and J. B. McCaw, Surgeon in Chief," 324
Chinen, Jon J., 241
"Choctaw-Chickasaw Court Citizens, The," 213
Christensen, Katheren, 239
Chronicles of the Pilgrim Fathers of the Colony of Plymouth from 1602-1625, 658
Church Records of St. John's Lutheran Church, Ruma, Illinois, 135
"Church Records of the United States: Jewish Synagogue Records," 143
"Church Records of the United States: Methodist Records," 145
"Church Records of the United States: Presbyterian," 145
"Church Records of the United States: Quaker Records in America: Records with an Extra Demension," 146
"Church Records of the United States: Roman Catholic Sacramental Records," 147
Church of Jesus Christ of Latter-day Saints, The, 13
"Civilian Defense in Baltimore, 1814-15: Minutes of the Committee of Vigilance and Safety," 206
"Claim Associations and Frontier Democracy in Early Minnesota," 244
Clarke, Janet R., 467
"Classification Scheme of the Nacogdoches Archives", 561
Clay, Robert Young, 252
Clint, Florence, 247
Clough, Shepard B., 340, 343
Cochran, Thomas Childs, 372
Cocke, William Ronald, Jr., 194
Coddington, John I., 457
"Code of Land Titles in Ohio: A Compilation from Official Records of All Charters, Indian Treaties, Grants...", 248
Coldham, Peter Wilson, 235
Coles, Harry L. Jr., 243
"Collecting Data on American Business Officials in the late Nineteenth and Early Twentieth Century," 371
Colonial Conveyances: Provinces of East and West New Jersey, 246
Colonial Justice in Western Massachusetts (1639-1702): The Pynchon Court Record, 176
"Colonial Land Conflicts in New Jersey," 246
"Colonial Law Governing the Distribution and Alienation of Land", 237
"Colonial and Commonwealth Land Records of Virginia," 252
Colonists in Bondage: Indentured Servants in America, 455
Colony of Massachusetts Loyalists at Bristol, England, The, 257
Columbia University Alumni Register, 401-402
Combs, Barry B., 245
"Comics and Cels," 382
Commentaries on the Laws of England, 253
Commercialism and Frontier: Perspectives on the Early Shenandoah Valley, 253
Committees of Safety of Westmoreland and Fincastle: Proceedings of the County Committees, 1774-1776, The, 207
Compiled Records Showing Service of Military Units in Confederate Organizations, 541
Compiled Service Records of Confederate General and Staff Officers and Nonregimental Enlisted Men, 541
Complement to Genealogies in the Library of Congress, 434

Comprehensive Dissertation Abstracts, 436, 663
Conant, H. J., 156, 210
Confederate States Army Casualties: Lists and Narrative Reports 1861-1865, 523
"Confirmation of Foreign Land Titles in Louisiana," 243
"Connecticut", 252
Consolidated Index of Claims Reported by the Commissioner of Claims to House of Representatives, 199
Constitution and Records of the Claim Association of Johnson County, Iowa, 242
Constitution and Register of Membership of the General Society of the War of 1812, The, 655
Conway, Roseanne, 472
Cook, Sylvia, 240
Cope, Giblert, 482
Corrigan, John, 417
Cottler, Susan M. 433
Coulter, E. Merton, 246
"Counties and Districts of South Carolina," 249
"County Committees of 1774-1775 in Virginia, The," 207
County Court Records of Accomack-Northampton, Virginia, 1632-40, 176
County Courthouses and Records of Maryland. Part 2: The Records, 218, 243
Craig, Tracy Linton, 338
"Credit Land Sales, 1811-1815: Mississippi Entries East of the Pearl, 244
"Credit Reports of R.G. Dun and Co., as Historical Sources," 340
Creek Frontier, 1540-1783, 535
Crouch, Barry A., 581
Crowl, Philip A., 176
Crown Lands of Hawaii, 241
"Crown versus Council in the Virginia Land Policy", 252
Cullum, George W., 265
Curren, George Barton, 330
Currer-Briggs, Noel, 251
Curtis, Carolyn, 340
"Custom-House Records in Massachusetts as a Source of History," 464

D

Damon, Allan L., 491
Daniels, Bruce C., 209
Daniels, Lorna M., 341, 372
Dargan-Carver Library, 13
Data Communications Buyers' Guide, 654
Data Transfer Associates, 654
Dataguide, 654
Datapro Directory of Microcomputer Software, 654
Datapro Reports, 654
Daughters of the American Revolution Magazine, 438
Davidson, Helen L., 376
Davis, J. C. Bancroft, 194
Davis, Robert Scott, Jr., 241, 529
Davisson, William I., 244
Debeau, Sharon, 257
"Debtors, Creditors, and the General Assembly in Colonial Maryland", 156
"Decline of Imprisonment for Debt in Kentucky, The," 156
Delaware's Fugitive Records: An Inventory of the Official Land Grant Records Relating to the Present State of Delaware, 240
Demaree, Albert L., 372
Demond, Robert O., 257
Denia, Herbert W., 251
Dental Register of the United States, 400
Dentist Register, 400
"Depreciation and Donation Lands", 249
Derning, Dorothy, 240
"Descriptive Inventory of the Archives of the City and County of Philadelphia", 331
Descriptive Inventory of the Archives of the State of Illinois, 241
Descriptive Inventory of the English Collection, 433
Descriptive Inventory of the New York Collection, 433
Desjardins, Bertrans, 661
Detroit Society for Genealogical Research Magazine, 438
Development of Virginia Taxation, 1775-1860, 251
"Development of a Land Registration System in New York," 246
Dewart, Franklin H., 251
Dice, Mrs. G., 251
Dickson, R. J., 455
Dictionary Catalog of the Local History and Genealogy Division, 435
Dictionary Catalog of the National Agriculture Library, 224
Dictionary of American Biography, 371, 445
"Directory Information Service", 398
Directory of Archives and Manuscript Repositories in the United States, 436, 541, 592
Directory of Business Archives in the United States and Canada, 369
Directory of Computer Software and Related Technical Reports, 654
Directory of Corporate Affiliations, 336, 371
Directory of Directories: An Annotated Guide to Business and Industrial Directories, Professional and Scientific Rosters, and Other Lists and Guides of All Kinds, 387, 398-399, 400, 654
Directory of Historical Societies and Agencies in U.S.A. and Canada, 140, 338, 416
Directory of Individuals Residing in Salt Lake City Wards 1854-1861, 658
Directory of Small Computers, 654
Directory of the Reformed Church in America, 1962-1965, 332
Directory of the United States, 400
Directory or List of Principal Traders in London, 387
Disciples of Christ, A History, 142
Disposal of Lands in Mississippi Territory, 244
"Disposal of the Public Domain in Illinois, 1848-1856," 241
Disposition of Loyalist Estates in the Southern District of the State of New Your, 259
"Disposition of the Public Domain in Oregon," 248
Distant Magnet: European Emigration to the U.S.A., 455, 491
"Distribution of the Public Domain in Dakota Territory," 247, 349
Divorces and Names Changed in Maryland By Act of the Legislature, 1634-1654, 190
Dobbert, G. A., 468
Documenting Your Four Generations, 432
Documents Relating to Colonial History of New Jersey, 340
Documents Relating to the Dutch and Swedish Settlements on the Delaware River, 240
Documents Relating to the History and Settlement of the Towns Along the Hudson and Mohawk Rivers (with the Exception of Albany) from 1630-1682, 246
Doggett's New York City Directories 1845-46 and 1846-47, 396
"Doing Business from the Source", 666
Dolan, Jay P., 503
Doll, Louis W., 421
"Domumentos para la historia de Mexico en los archivos de San Antonio, Texas", 576
Donaldson, Thomas, 224
Dorman, John Frederick, 237
Doster, James F., 239
Downes, Randolph Chandler, 247
Duckett, Kenneth, 248
Dugan, Dennis J., 244
Dumont, William H., 251
Dun's Marketing Services, 337
Dunlop, A.R., 240
Durham County; Lord Baltimore's Attepmt at Settlement of His Lands on the Delaware Bay, 1670-1685, 240
"Dutch Land System of New Netherland," 246
"Dutch and Swedish Land Records Relating to Delaware," 240

E

Eakle, Arlene H., 199, 236, 417, 418, 433, 457, 481, 491, 500, 666
Early 18th Century Palatine Emigration, 456
Early German-American Newspapers, 467
"Early New England Court Records: A Bibliography of Published Materials," 176
Early Ohioans Residences from the Land Grant Records, 248
Early Rehoboth: Documented Historical Studies of Families and Events in this Plymouth Colony Township, 253
Early Settlers of Maryland, an Index to Names of Immigrants Compiled from Records of Land Patents 1633-1680, 243
East Florida Land Commission: A Study in Frustration, 240
Edmonds, Henry E., 376
Eichholz, Alice, 579, 580
"El Paso Area in the Mexican Period, 1821-1848, The," 558
Elliot, Mary Q., 330
Elliott, Clark A., 446
Ellis, John Tracy, 146
Ellison, Joseph, 239
Emerson, Louis L., 526
Emigrant Sources for Tracing Pennsylvania German Ancestors, 457, 481
Emigrantinstitutet, Svensk-Amerikansha Kyrkoarkiv Med Canada, 481
Emigration and Disenchantment: Portraits of Englishmen Repatriated from the United States, 468
Emigration, Europe to U.S.A., 455
Encyclopedia Britannica, information on land practices in, 217
Encyclopedia of American Quaker Genealogy, 146
Encyclopedia of Associations, 372
Encyclopedia of German-American Genealogical Research, 478
Encyclopedia of World Methodism, 145
Encyclopedic Directory of Ethnic Newspapers and Periodicals in the United States, 467
Encyclopedica of Associations, 436
English Crown Grants, 1755-1775, 240
English Duplicates of Lost Virginia Records, 251
Entry Claims for Georgia Landholder, 1733-1775, 240
Epitaphs from Burial Hill, Plymouth, Massachusetts—1657-1892, 658
Ernst, Joseph W., 381
"Establishing and Maintaining Land Ownership in Utah Prior to 1869," 251
"European Religious and Spatial Origins of the Pennsylvania Dutch," 478
"Evaluation and Preservation of Business Archives," 372
Evans, George H., Jr., 372
Evans,Charles. 408
Everly, Elaine, 582
Everton, George B., Sr., 252
Every Name Index to Egle's Notes and Queries, 439
Everybody's Business: An Almanac, 336, 353
"Evolution of Ohio County Boundaries," 247
"Evolution of the Virginia Land Grant/System in the Eighteenth Century," 252
Ewing, John S., 372, 373
"Examination of Hospital Records," 324
Expansion and American Indian Policy, 1713-1812, 534

F

Fairburn, William Armstrong, 457
Familiengeschichtliche Quellen, 488
Family History for Fun and Profit, 266
"Family History in the Bible Belt: Southern U.S. Church Records," 141
"Family Records from County Court Order Books," 169
"Family of Conchelyne, etc., in America", 340
Fannin, ____________________, 521
Farnham, Charles W., 212
Federal Land Grants in the Territory of Orleans, the Delta parishes, 243
Federal Land Grants to the States with Special Reference to Minnesota, 244
"Federal Land Office Records," 226
Federal Land Series, 229, 233, 234, 247, 248
"Federal Management and Disposition of the Lands of Oklahoma Territory 1860-1907," 248
Fernow, B., 240, 246
Ferrell, J. T., 176
Few, Robert A., 156
Fifty Million Acres: Conflicts Over Kansas Land Policy, 1854-1890, 242
Filby, P. William, 457, 464, 468, 480
Finding Aids to the Microfilmed Manuscript Collections of the Genealogical Society of Utah, 433
Finding Aids to the Microfilmed Records of the Genealogical Society of Utah: Preliminary Survey of the German Collection, 619
Finding Our Fathers: A Guide to Jewish Genealogy, 143, 614
"Finding the Ancestral Home of a Palatine Forefather: The Case of Martin Zerbe," 476
Finns on the Delaware, 1638-1655, 501
Finster, Jerome, 464
"Firestone Archives and Library", 376
First Census of Texas, 1829-1836, to which are added Texas Citizenship Lists 1821-1835, and other early records of the Republic of Texas, 561
Fisher, Edgar J., 246
Fisher, Robert D., 371
Flavell, Carol Willsey, 247, 248
Flick, Roger, 435
Flinn, John J., 529
"Ford Motor Company Archives," 376
Foreign Versions of English Names, 478
Forrest, D., 251
Forsythe, Doll W., 253
Founders of Early American Families – Emigrants from Europe 1607-1657, 657
Fowler, Robert L., 246
Fox, Michael J., 229
Fox, Michael K., 252
"Franklin-Warren-Vance Cos. Area: Father-Son Relationships in 1771," 253
Franks, David, 387
Fraser, Alexander, 235
"Freedmen's Bureau in Tennessee," 581
Freund, Rudolf, 234
Friends Historicial Library, 146
From Generation to Generation: How to Trace Your Jewish Genealogy and Personal History, 143
"From Herrnhut to Hagerstown: Johann Cristoph Poet's Journal of His Trip from Hernnhut Down the Elbe and Thence to Haarlem," 456
From You to Your Ancestors, 432
"Frontier Land Business in Wisconsin," 252
Fry, Edward A., 190
Fundamentals of Genealogical Research, 433

G

Galena Lead District: Federal Policy and Practice, 1824-1847, 241
Gardiner, Lillian Johnson, 249
Gates, Paul W., 224, 230, 231, 234, 239, 241, 245, 252, 253
Gazetteer and Business Directory of Monroe County, New York for 1869-1870, 397
Genealogical Catalog, 435
Genealogical Computing, 654, 658
Genealogical Computing: The Beginning, 665
Genealogical Data Relating to the German Settlers of Pennsylvania from Advertisements in German Newspapers Published in Philadelphia and Germantown, in 1743-1800, 467
Genealogical Index of the Newberry Library, 437
Genealogical Journal, 176
Genealogical Material in Oregon Donation Land Claims, 248
"Genealogical Note from Supreme Court Reports", 194
Genealogical Periodical Annual Index, 140, 331
Genealogical Records of Utah, 141
Genealogical Research Methods and Sources, 252
Genealogical Research Standards, 141
"Genealogical Research in Massachusetts: A Survey and Bibliographical Guide", 253
Genealogical Research in the National Archives, 294, 463
"Genealogical Sources in Sweden," 514
"Genealogical Sources in the Province of Manitoba," 496
"Genealogical Systems Analysis," 667
"Genealogical Telecommunciations," 666
"Genealogical Uses of Computers," 667
Genealogical and Local History Books in Print, 435, 449
Genealogies in the Library of Congress: A Bibliography, 434
"Genealogist's First Look at Federal Land Records", 226
Genealogy and Local History Catalog, 435
Genealogy and Local History Guide, 435
"Genealogy's New Ancestral File," 432
Genealogy, Heraldry, Local History Catalogs, 435
Genealoigcal Periodical Annual Index, 438
Gentry, Daphne S., 252
"Geographical Aspects of Pennsylvania German Genealogical Study," 478,
George, Henry, 449
Georgia Land Lottery Papers, 1805-1914: Genealogical Data from the Loose Papers Filed in the Georgia Surveyor General Office Concerning the Lots Won in the State Land Lotteries and the People Who Won Them, 241
Georgia Surveyor General Department: A History and Inventory of Gerogia's Land Office, 240
German Immigration Diary: 1848, 456
"German Newspapers of Berks County," 467
German Pietists of Provincial Pennsylvania, 1694-1708, 504
"German Surnames in America," 478
German-American Newspapers and Periodicals 1732-1955, History and Bibliography. 467
German-American Newspapers and Perodicals, 1732-1955, 467
German-Language Press in America, 467
"German/Dutch Names," 478
Giddens, Paul H., 243
Gilroy, Marion, 257
Glaab, Charles N., 529
Glenn, Bess, 194
Glynn, Joseph Martin, Jr., 238
Gould, Clarence P., 243
Government Publications and Their Use, 195
Government and Labor in Early America, 455
Governor and Judges Journal: Proceedings of the Land Board of Detroit, 244
"Grants South of Green River", 242
Grassroots in America, 243, 244
Grassroots of America, 198, 230, 238, 241
Great Mahele: Hawaii's Land Division of 1848, 241
Green, Charles, L., 249
Greenlaw, William Prescott, 437
Greenwood, Val, 142, 143, 146, 217
Gregoria, Anne K., 176
Gubler, Greg, 599
Guertler, John, 468
Guide to American Indian Documents in the Congressional Serial
Guide to Business History, 372
Guide to Genealogical Records in the Pennsylvania State Archives, 340
Guide to Genealogical Research in the National Archives, 230, 234, 239, 248, 262, 443
Guide to Genealogical Sources at the Pennsylvania State Archives, 333
"Guide to Genealogy", 253
Guide to Manuscript Collections and Institutional Records in Ohio, 340
Guide to Microfilm Edition of Bexar Archives 1804-1821, 543
Guide to Microfilm of Bexar Archives 1717-1803, 543
Guide to New England Genealogy, 253
Guide to Records in the National Archives of the Unites States Relating to American Indians, 537
Guide to Records of the Illinois Central Railroad, 377
"Guide to the Counties of Virginia: Alexandria County (Arlington County)", 240
Guide to the Holdings at Hall of Records, 243
Guide to the Manuscript Collections of the Historical Philadelphia, 331
Guide to the Manuscript Collections of the Historical Society of Pennsylvania, 462
Guide to the Mariano Guadalupe Vallejo Documentos para la Historia de California, 1780-1875, A, 559
Guide to the Principal Sources for Early American History in the City of New York, A, 176
Guide to the manuscripts in the Eleutherian Mills Historical Library, 375
Gunn, Ray, 433

H

Hahn, Marilyn Davis, 239
Haigh, Roger M., 433
Half Century of Conflict: Queen Anne's War 1701-1714 and King George's War 1744-1748, 651
Hall, G. K., 435
Handbook of American Denominations, 139
Handy Book for Genealogists, 252
Handy Guide to Record Searching in the Larger Cities of the United States, 394, 521
Hanson, Edward W., 253
Harding, George Mark, 242
Hargrett, Lester, 551
Harland, Derek,
Harrell, Isaac Samuel, 257
Harris, Marshall, 222
Harrison, Fairfax, 252
Harsook, Elizabeth, 243
Harwell, Richard B., 207
Hathaway, Beverley West, 242
Haugen, Einar, 508
"Have You Overlooked Military Records?", 372
Haynes, Robert V., 244
"Headrights and Pitfalls", 251
Hefner, Loretta L., 139, 524
"Heirs in Court of Appeals Deeds", 242
Heiss, Willard, 146, 456
Heite, Edward F., 240
Helmbold, F. Wilbur, 141
Hemperley, Marion R., 240
Hereditary Register of the United States of America, 688
Hibbard, Benjamin Horace, 224

"Hidden Sources of Black History: The Texas Freedmen's Bureau Records as a Case Study," 581
Hill, Edward E., 537
Hillman Library, 12
Hilton, Ronald
Hinke, William J., 455, 466
Historical Abstract, 436, 663
Historical Foundation of the Presbyterian and Reformed Churches, 13
Historical Highlights of the Jamestowne Society's First Quarter of a Century–Roster of Members 1936-1971, 659
Historical Register of Officers of the Continental Army during the War of the Revolution, 1914, With Addenda by Robert H. Kelby, 1932, 654
Historical Sketch of the Catalogue of the Saint Andrews Society of Philadelphia with Biographical of Deceased Members 1749-1913, 661
Historical Sketch of the Saint Andrews Society of the City of Albany 1803-1903, 661
Historical Statistics of the United States Colonial Times to 1970, 340, 511
"Histories of the American Frontier: A Series", 224
History of Chicago Police, 529
History of Land Titles in Massachusetts, 243
History of Land Titles in Massachusetts, 244
History of Land Titles in Western North Carolina, 246
History of Macy's of New York, 1858-1929: Chapters in the History of a Department Store, 372, 378
History of New Hanover and the Lower Cape Fear, 206
History of Norwich from Its Possession by the Indians to the Year 1866, 658
History of Public Land Law Development, 253
History of Public Land Law Development, 224, 230-231, 245, 253
"History of Taxation in Colonial Virginia, 1607-1775", 251
History of Taxation in New Hampshire, 245
History of Urban America, 529
History of Western Maryland, 243
History of an Advertising Agency, 372
History of an Advertising Agency: N.X.W. Ayer & Son at Work, 1869-1949, 380
History of the Congregational Churches in the United States, 142
History of the Land Titles in Hudson County, N.Y., 1609-1871, 246
History of the Law of Real Property in New York, 246
History of the Massachusetts Hospital Life Insurance Company, 379
History of the Public Domain of Georgia, 241
History of the Saint Andrews Society of Charleston, South Carolina 1729-1929, 661
History of the United States Indian Factory System: 1795-1822, 535
"History, Jurisdiction and Practice of the Court of Claims of the United States", 197
Hitz, Alex M., 240
Hocker, Edward W., 417, 467
Hoffman, Margaret M., 246
Holbrook, Jay Mack, 251
Holmes, Dorothy P., 524
Holmes, Oliver Wendell, 372
"Homesteading in Zion", 251
Hoover, Roy Otto, 252
Hopple, Lee C., 478
Horwitz, Robert H., 241
House Index to Committee Reports, 230
House, Charles J., 243
Houts, Alice K., 296
"How Long Should You Keep Computers?" 666
"How Would You Spend $4,500?" 646
"How to Find Business and Employment Records", 336
How to Use the Freedom of Information Act: FOIA, 468
Howe, Irving, 603
Howe, Mark D., 244
"Howell on Numbering," 667
Hower, Ralph M., 372, 380
Hoyt, William D., Jr., 206, 593
"Hubbell's Legal Directory", 399
Hufford, Mary, 464
Hughes, Sarah S., 220, 252
Huse, Hiram A., 251
Hutchinson, William Thomas, 248

I

"IGI Instructions and Regions," 430
Illinois Military Tract: A Study of Land Occupation, Utilization and Tenure, 241
"Immigrant Aid Societies Before 1820," 468
Immigration and Colonization, 1841-1903, 455
"Imprisonment for Debt in Colonial Virginia", 156
"Imprisonment for Debt in Massachusetts", 156
"Imprisonment for Debt in Vermont: A History", 156, 210
"Imprisonment for Debt: Its Origin and Repeal", 156
In English Ways: The Movement of Societies and the Transferral of English Local Law and Custom to Massachusetts Bay in the Seventeenth Century, 222
Index for Old Kentucky Surveys and Grants [and Tellico Surveys and Grants] Microfilmed by Kentucky Historical Society, 242
Index of Obituaries of Boston Newspapers 1704-1800, 417
Index of Revolutionary War Pension Applications in the National Archives, 233, 273
Index to Changes of Name Under Authority of Act of Parliament 1760-1901, An, 190
Index to Compiled Service Records of Voluntter Union Soldiers Who Served with the United States Colored Troops, 580
Index to Deeds of the Province and State of South Carolina 1719-1785 and Charleston District 1785-1800, 249
"Index to El Archivo de Hidalgo del Parral, 1631-1821" 557
Index to Genealogical Periodical Literature, 439
Index to Genealogical Periodicals, 140, 437
"Index to Names of Irish Americans in Chicago Newspapers" 417
Index to Revolutionary War Pension Applications in the National Archives 233, 439
Index to Spanish and Mexican Land Grants in Texas, 250
Index to Vital Records from Chicago Newspapers, 417
Index to the Archives of Spanish West Florida, 1782-1810, 243
Index to the Headright and Bounty Grants of Georgia, 1756-1909, 241
Index to the Manuscript and Revised Printed Opinions of the Supreme Court of the United States in the National Archives, 1808-1873, 194
Indian Boundary in the Southern Colonies, 1763-1775, 535
Indian Papers of Texas and the Southwest, 1825-1916, 534
Indian Removal, 538
Indian Treaties, 1778-1883, 534
Institute for Scientific Information (ISI), 13, 28
"International Genealogical Index: A Tool to be Used with Understanding,"*Genealogical Magazine* 21 (June 1983): 60-63; (Sept. 1983): 165-70., 432
"International Genealogical Index"*New England Historical Genealogical Register* 87 (July 1983), guide to use of IGI, 430
International Genealogical Library Catalog, 142
International Institute Movement: A Guide to Records of Immigrant Society Agencies in the United States, 468
"Introduction to the IGI Batch Number Index," 430
"Inventory of All the Archives [of Yerba Buena] from the Foundation of the Ayuntamiento in 1835, to the End of the Present Year [1845], The", 558
Inventory of Federal Archives in the States, Series VIII, The Department of the Interior, No. 3, Arizona, No. 8, California, 558-559
Inventory of Unpublished Material for American Religious History in Protestant Church Archives and Other Repositories, 139
Inventory of the Church Archives of New York City, 138-139
"Iowa Claims Clubs: Symbols and Substance", 242
Irons, Victoria, 241
"Is Your Name Dutchified?" 478
"It All Started With a Mouse: The Walt Disney Archives", 382-383
Iten, Icko, 417

J

Jackson, Elisabeth C., 340
Jackson, Thonstina, 505
Jacob, Lance J., 432
Jacobus, Donald Lines, 140, 252, 430, 437
Jacques, Contstant H., 341
Jadques, Legore, 661
James, Colinr, 174
Jamestown Society–Roster of Members January 31, 1983, 659
Jarboe, Betty M., 416, 417
Jaussi, Laureen R., 141, 432, 433
Jednosc-Polonia, 417
Jenkins, William S., 561
Jensen, C. Russell, 433, 502
Jenson, Andrew, 446
Jesuit Relations and Allied Documents: Travels and Explorations of the Jesuit Missionaries in New France, 1610-1791, 534
"Jewish Migrations", 603
Jillson, Willard Rouse, 233, 242
Johnson, Arta F., 488
Johnson, Marion M., 194
Johnson, Maxine C., 245
Jones, D., 244
Jones, Henry Z., Jr., 476
Jones, Matt Bushnell, 249
Jones, Thomas B., 250
Jones, Vincent L., 416
Jordan, Weymouth T., 581
"Journal and Correspondence of the Maryland Council of Safety, 1775-1793", 206
Journal of American Legal History, 176
"Journal of Committee of Observation of the Middle District of Frederick County, Maryland", 206
Journal of the Hampshire Family History Society, 342

K

Kabakoff, Dr. Marvin H., 372
Kaminkow, Marion J., 434
Kay, Marvin L. Michael, 247
Kelby, William, 257
Kelener, W.A., 246
Kennebec Proprietors, 1749-1775, 243
Kentucky Genealogical Research Sources, 242
Kentucky Historical Society, 242
Kentucky Land Grants: A Systematic Index to All of the Land Grants Recorded in the State Land Office at Frankfort, Kentucky 1782-1924, 242
"Kentucky Land Warrants, 1816-73", 242
Kershaw, Gordon E., 243

Kezys, Alginantes, 525
Kielman, Chester V., 561
Kim, Sung Bok, 246
Kirkham, E. K., 226, 394, 521
Klingberg, Frank W., 199
Knight, Lois V., 432
Knittle, Walter A., 456
Know Your Ancestors, 146
Knowlton, Clark S., 230
Konig, David T., 177
Kranzler, David, 143
Krebs, Friedrick, 67
Kruzas, Anthony T., 337
Kuhns, Oscar, 504, 515
Kurzweil, Arthur, 143, 603, 608

L

LDS Biographical Encyclopedia, 441, 446
LDS Church Records and Research Aids, 141, 432, 433
LaPotin, Armand, 246
"Labor Union Records in the United States", 344
Lackey, Richard S., 226, 224
Lacy, Dan, 247
Lancour, Harold, 480
"Land Disposal in Nebraska, 1854-1906: The Homestead Story", 245
Land Grant Maps, 249
"Land Grant Policy of Colonial Virginia,1607-1774", 252
Land Granting in Colonial Georgia, 241
Land Grants for Service in the Revolution, 231, 232, 234
"Land Grants in Colonial North Carolina", 246
"Land Grants in New Mexico: A Selective Bibliography", 246
"Land Grants", *North Carolina Research: Genealogy and Local History*, 246
Land Office Business: The Settlement and Administration of American Public Lands, 224
Land Office and Prerogative Court Records of Colonial Maryland, 243
Land Ownership Maps, 229
"Land Policies and Administration in Colonial Maryland, 1753-1769", 243
"Land Policy in British East Florida", 240
"Land Precedents in Essex County, Massachusetts", 244
"Land Processing in Colonial Virginia," 252
Land Records of America and Their Genealogical Value, 226
"Land System of Colonial New York", 246
Land System of Provincial Pennsylvania, 249
"Land System of the Connecticut Towns", 240
"Land System of the New England Colonial Colonies", 253
"Land Systems and Land Policies in Nebraska", 245
Land Tenure in Proprietary North Carolina, 247
"Land Titles and Public Land Sales in Early Alabama", 239
Land in California, the Story of Mission Lands, Ranchos, Squatters Mining Claims, Railroad Grants, Land Scrip [and] Homestead, 239
Landlord and Tenant in Colonial New York: Manorial Society, 1664-1775, 246
Lane, George A., 525
Larkin, Harold F., 340
Larson, Henrietta, 372
Larson, Sarah, 199
"Law Lists", 398-399
"Law and Practice of Change of Name", 190
Law of Baron and Femme of Parent and Child, of Guardian and Ward, Master and Servant, and of the Powers of the Courts of Chancery; with an Essay on the Terms Heir, Heirs, Heirs of the Body, The, 186
"Law of the New Mexico Land Grant", 246
Laws and Rules of the Land Office of Maryland, 243
Laws of the State of Indiana...Tenth Session, 253
Laws of the United States of a Local or Temporary Character and Exhibiting the Entire Legislation of Congress upon Which the Public Land Titles in Each State and Territory Have Depended, 224
Leake, James M., 207
Leary, Helen F. M., 247
Lee, Lawrence B., 224, 251
"Legal Name Changes by Act of North Carolina Assembly, 1790-1799", 190
"Legal Systems in Conflict: Orleans Territory 1804-1812", 243
Legal Thesaurus, 152
Leng Tsun, 600
Leonard, Florence M., 132
Lest We Forget: A Guide to Genealogical Research in the Nations's Capital, 398
Levine, Gene N., 601
Lewinson, Paul, 344
Liberati Purges: Political Conflict in Early Yi Korea,, 600
Library Catalog, Volume One: Family Histories and Genealogies, 436
Library of Congress Index to Biographies in State and Local Histories, 437
Lichtenberg, C., 234
Lightner, David, 239
"Limit of 18th Century Sources in New York and New Jersey", 253
Lindgard, Elmer W., 464
"Lindsey's of Maury County, Tennessee", 253
Lineages of Members of the National Society of the Sons and Daughters of the Pilgrims to 1 January 1929, 658; *1920-1952*, 658
Linford, Lawrence, 251
Lingegren, A.M., 234
Lipscomb, Robert G., 241
List of Cartographic Records of the General Land Office (Record Group 49), 558
List of Churches: Official Forms of the Names for Denominational Bodies with Brief Description and Historical Notes, 525
"List of Documents Relating to Grants of Land by the Spanish and Mexican Governments in the Archives of the Office of the Surveyor-General of New Mexico, June 30, 1885", 559
List of Free Black Heads of Families in the First Census of the United States, 580
List of Geographical Atlases in the Library of Congress, 229
List of Persons Whose Names Have Been Changed in Massachusetts, 1780-1892, 190
List of Pioneers of 1847 with Biographical Notes from the Journal of the History of the Church 1847 and The Historical Record, 658
Little, Brooks R., 145
Lo, Hisang-lin, 600
Locating Your Immigrant Ancestors: A Guide to Naturalization Records, 472
Loe, Lola, 85
Lokken, Roscoe L., 242
"Look at the Records: The Facts Behind the Current Controversy Over Immigration," 491
Looney, John F., 245
"Lord Fairfax Rent Rolls", 251
"Lost Archives of the Cherokee Nation, 1763-1772", 536
Lowell, Waverly, 464
Lowery Collection: A Descriptive List of Maps of the Spanish Possessions within the Present Limits of the United States, 1502-1820, The, 558
Loyalism in Virginia, 257, 655
Loyalist Literature: An Annotated Bibliographic Guide to the Writings on the Loyalists of the American Revolution, 235
Loyalist Trail, 257
Loyalists and Land Settlement in Nova Scotia,257
Loyalists in North Carolina During the Revolution, 257
Loyalists in the American Revolution, 257 675
Loyalists of America and Their Time; 1620-1816, The, 257
Loyalists of East Florida 1774-1785, 257
Loyalists of Massachusetts and the Other Side of the American Revolution, The, 257
Loyalists of Ontario: Sons and Daughters of the American Loyalists of Upper Canada, The, 257
Lucas, Silas Emmett, Jr., 241, 249
Luck, Winston F. 66
Luckingham, Bradford, 468
Luebking, Sandra, 478
Luecker, Edwin L., 143
Lumpkin, Wilson, 553
Lutheran Church Directory for the United States, 144
Lutheran Cyclopedia, 143"Lutheran Family in North America", 143
Lutz, Paul V., 230, 232, 234
Lux, Leonard, 230, 241

M

MacPherson's Directory for the City and Suburbs of Philadelphia, 387
MacPherson, John, 387
Mackenzie, Janis, 383
Madison, James H., 340, 341
Madvell, Charles R., 243
"Main Depositories of Church History Material and Sources", 332
"Maine Public Lands 1781-1795: Claims, Trespassers and Sales", 243
Major Sources in Customs Bureau Records in Statistical Data on Exports and Imposts of the United States to 1900, 464
Making a State; Formation of West Virginia, Including Maps, Illustrations, Plats, Grants..., 252
"Management of Nevada's State Lands, 1864-1900", 245
Mann, Conklin, 340
Manual of Instructions for the Survey of the Public Lands of the United States, 225
Manual of Railroads, 371
Manual of Statistics, 371
Manual of Valuable and Worthless Securities, 371
Manuals, 371
Manuscripts Catalog of the American Jewish Archives, 612
Manuscripts of the Historical Society of Pennsylvania, 369
Maps and Atlases Showing Land Ownership in Wisconsin, 252
Marie Dickore, 417
Marriage Records of Early Texas 1824-1846, 657
Martin's Bench and Bar of Philadelphia, 332, 333
Martin, John Hill, 341
Martin, S. W., 240
Martin, T. P., 230
Martindale-Hubbell Law Directory, 332, 399
"Massachusetts Land Grants in Vermont", 251
Master Index: Virginia Surveys and Grants 1774-1791, 242
Mathews, Linda M., 374
Mathias, P., 457
Matkov, Albert, 190
Mayer, Lewis, 243
Mayflower Descendant, The, 438
Mayhew, Catherine, M., 438
McBee, May Wilson, 244
McBride, Ransom, 190, 465
McCall, Mrs. Howard H., 285

McClintock, Walter J., 249
McDonald, Norman, 455
McKee, T. H., 230
McKitrick, Reuben, 251
McLendon, Samuel Guyton, 241
McMullin, Philip W., 118, 230, 238, 241, 244, 243
McMullin, Ruth, 370
McWilliams, Jerry, 464
Mead, Frank, 139
Mead, Nelson P., 240
Means, David A., 249
Meckler, Alan M, 370
Medical and Surgical Register, 399
Meek, W. Frank, 226
Mennonite Encyclopedia: A Comprehensive Reference Work on the Anabaptist-Mennonite Movement, 144
Mennonites in Indiana and Michigan, 446
Mercer, James C., 447
Merchant Sail, 457
Meriwether, Robert L., 249
Methodist Union Catalog of History, Biography, Disciplines, and Hymnals, 145
Metropolitan areas, maps of, 16
"Mexican Land Grants in Colorado", 239
"Mexican Land Grants in the Arkansas Valley", 239
Meyer, Mary K., 190, 457, 464, 468, 480
Microfilm Card Catalog, 434
Microfilm of Censuses, 1828-1836, of Nacogdoches, Tenehaw, and Sabine, Bevil's Settlement (Jasper, Texas), William's Settlement, and San Augustine, 561
"Migration from East Anglia to New England before 1660," 500
Migration of New Englanders to England, 1640-1660, 468
Migration, Emigration, Immigration: Principally to the United States and in the United States, 457
"Milestones in Michigan Mapping", 244
"Military Bounty Land Policies", 234
"Military Bounty Land Warrants of the Mexican War", 234, 253
"Military Bounty Land and the Origins of the Public Domain", 234
"Military Bounty Lands of the American Revolution in Ohio", 248
"Military Land Bounties During the Revolutionary and Confederate Periods", 234
Military Records Register, Vol. II: Civil War, 257, 265
Military Records Register, 257
"Military Tract of Central N.Y.", 246
Miller, Daniel, 467
Miller, E. I., 207
Miller, G. J., 176
Miller, Olga K., 457
Miller, Thomas Lloyd, 250, 251
Miller, William B., 145
Million Dollar Directory, 337
Mills, Elizabeth Shown, 579
Mills, Gary B., 199, 527, 579
Milner, Anita C., 416
"Mineral Land Question in California, 1848-1866", 239
"Minisink Grant: Partnerships, Patents and Processing Fees in Eighteenth Century New York", 246
Minutes of the Pennsylvania Provincial Council, 206
"Miscellaneous Papers of the General Committee, Secret Committee, and Provincial Congress, 1775", 206
Mississippi Court Records 1799-1835, 659
Missoula City Directory., 334
"Missouri Public Domain: United States Land Sales, 1818-1922, 244
Mitchell, Robert D. K., 253
Mittlebeller, Emmet V., 156
Mohr, Carolyn Curtis, 340, 377
Montalto, Nicholas V., 468
Moody's Transportation Manual, 338
Moore, John W., 263
Morgan, Lawrence N., 247
Mormon Diaries and Autobiographies, 456
Morris, Richard B., 176, 237, 455
Morton Allan Directory of European Passenger Steamship Arrivals, 457
Mother Earth: Land Grants in Virginia, 1607-1699, 252 on death certificate, 53
"Mouse is Born", 383
Mullins, Marions D., 561
"Munsell Genealogical Indexes," 437
Murin, William J., 519
Muster Rolls of New York Provincial Troops, 1755-1764, 651
My Jewish Roots: A Practical Guide to Tracing and Recording Your Genealogy and Family History, 143

N

NUCMC.*See also National Union Catalog of Manuscript Collections*, 435
Naegles, James C., 472
Name Changes Granted by Indiana General Assembly to 1852, 190
Name Changes, Maryland, Finding Aids, 190
"Names Changed Legally in Georgia, 1800-1856," 190
"Names Changed in Maryland, 1855-1867: A Supplement to Divorces and Names Changed. . .," 190
Names and Numbers: A Journalist's Guide to the Most Needed Information Sources and Contacts, 371
Names of Soldiers of the American Revolution Who Applied for the State Bounty under Resolves of March 17, 1835, March 24, 1836 and March 20, 1836 as Appears of Record in Land Office, 243
Natchez Court Records, 1767-1805: Abstracts of Early Records, 244, 659
National Archives, 1-3
National Cyclopedia of American Biography, 371
National Directory of Addresses and Telephone Numbers, 371
National Directory of Morticians, 335, 336
National Endowment for the Humanities, 417
National Genealogical Society Newsletter, 688
National Genealogical Society Quarterly, 438
National Genealogical Society, 23, 273
National Index of Family Associations and Periodicals, 688
National Newspaper Index, 436
National Technical Information Service, 28
National Union Catalog of Manuscript Collections, ethnic collections, 3
National Union Catalog of Manuscript Collections, 369, 435-36, 612
Navajo Indians and Federal Indian Policy, 1900-1935, 535
Neagles, Lila Lee, 472
Neal, Colleen, 398
Necrology of Diocesan Priests of the Chicago Archdiocese 1837-1959 , 524
Neeley, Fredrick T., 251
Neible, George W., 340
Nelson, William, 245, 340
Ness, John, Jr., 145
New Brunswick Loyalists: A Bicentennial Tribute, 257
New England Historic Library, 1
New England Historical and Genealogical Register, 438, 443
New Hampshire Provincial Papers, 245
New Immigration, 491
New Jersey Genealogical Magazine, 438
New Mexico Business Directory, 398
New Orleans French 1720-1733, 659
New Sources of Indian History, 1850-1891, 534
New Urban History, 467
New World Atlas, 521
New York Alien Residents, 1825-1848, 472
New York Area Key, 529
New York Genealogical and Biographical Records, 438
New York Land Patents 1688-1786 Covering Land Now Included in the State of Vermont (Not Including Military Patents), 251
New York Legislature, 246
"New York-Vermont Land Dispute, 1749-1791", 251
Newberry Libary, 17
Newberry Library, 1,3
Newburger, Adele, 468
Newhard, Malinda E., 190
Newman, Debra L., 580
"Newspaper Project and NELINET: The American Antiquarian Society," 417
Newsletter of the International Society for British Genealogy and Family History, 688
"Newspaper Date Bank to be Developed", 417
Newspaper Genealogical Column Directory, 416
Newspapers of Berks County, Pennsylvania, 1789-1900, 422
Newspapers on Microfilm, 407
Nichols, Elizabeth L., 430
"Nicknaming in an Amish-Mennonite Community," 479
Nicolosi, Anthony S., 207
Nissinson, S.G., 246
Nordland, Rod, 371
"North American Business Archives: Results of a Survey," 372
North Carolina Genealogical Journal, 465
North Carolina Genealogy, 246
North Carolina Land Grants in Tennessee, 1778-1791, 249
North Carolina Lands: Ownership, Use and Management of Forest and Related Lands, 246
Norton, Nancy P., 372, 373
Note by the Commissioner on the Sources of Land Titles in Maine, 243
Notes and Queries Relating to Pennsylvania, 439
"Notes on the Preparation of Conveyances by Laymen in the Colony of Maryland," 244
Notice, of divorce, 85
"Notices by German and Swiss Settlers Seeking Information of Members of their Families, Kindred, and Friends Inserted between 1742-1761 in Pennsylvania Berichte and 1762-1779 in Pennsylvania Staatsbote," 467
Nugent, Nell Marion, 251
Nye, Mary Greene, 251

O

O'Callaghan, Jerry A., 248
OATS. *See* Original Article Text Service, 13
Oberly, James W., 234, 253
Obituaries from Tennessee Newspapers, 1851-1899, 426*Obituaries: A Guide to Sources*, 416, 523
Oczon, Annabelle M., 246
Office of Indian Afairs, 1824-1880: Historical Sketches, 534
Official Catholic Directory, 147, 402
Ohio Architects and Builders' Directory, 400
Ohio Area Key, 247
Ohio Genealogical Guide, 248
"Ohio Land Grants," 247
"Ohio Land Patents," 248
"Ohio Lands and Their History", 248
"Ohio Lands and Their Subdivision," 248
Ohio Wills and Estates to 1850: An Index, 187
Oklahoma Research: The Twin Territories, 248

Old Cahaba Land Office Records Military Warrants, 1817-1853, 239
Old Kentucky Entries and Deeds: A Complete Index to All of the Earliest Land Entries, Military Warrants, Deeds and Wills of Earliest Land Entries, Military Warrants, Deeds and Wills the Commonwealth of Kentucky, 235 of the Commonwealth of Kentucky, 242
"Old Records of Madison County, Alabama", 239
Old Sparta and Elba Land Office Records and Military Warrants, 1822-1860, 239
Old St. Stephen's Land Office Records and American State Papers, Public Lands, Vol. 1, 1768-1808, 239
Oldstone Enterprises, 69
Olson, May E., 467
"Omnes Unum Sint: The Rockefeller Archives", 381
"On-Line System for Processing Loosely Structured Records," 468
"Operation of the Land Laws in the Minnesota Iron District," 244
Oral History Collections, 370
Oral History for the Local Historical Society, 580 Membership Roster, 681
Orderly Book of the Three Battalions of Loyalists Commanded by Brigadier-General Oliver de Lancey, 257
"Oregon Donation Act and National Land Policy," 248
"Oregon and Washington Donation Land Files, 1851-1903", 248
"Oregon and Washington Donation Land Files, 1851-1903", 252
Orfield, Mattias N., 244
Origin of the Land Tenure System in the United States, 222
Original Article Text Service (OATS) 13-14
Original Land Titles in Hawaii, 241
Original Ohio Land Subdivisions, 247
Original Titles in Delaware Commonly Known as the Duke of York Record, 240
Oskam, Bob, 468
Our Landed Heritage: The Public Domain, 224
Outsen, Arvilla, 433
Overman, William, D., 376
Oxford English Dictionary, 387, 403

P

Page, Anne, 324
"Palatine Emigration Materials from the Nechan Valley, 1726-1766," 467 503
Palmer, Gregory, 235, 257
"Papers of the Maryland State Colonization Society," 593
Parker, J. Carlyle, 437
Passenger and Immigration Lists Bibliography, 1538-1900, 480
Passenger and Immigration Lists Index, 457, 464, 468, 480
Patents and Deeds and Other Early Records of New Jersey, 1664-1703, 246
"Patents and Tithables in Proprietary North Carolina, 1663-1729", 247
Pelzer, Louis, 230
Penn's Colony, Passengers and Ships Prior to 1684, 658
Penn, William, 248
Pennsylvania Architects and Builders' Directory, 400
Pennsylvania Evening Post, 417
Pennsylvania Folklife, 481
Pennsylvania German Pioneers, 1727-1808, 455, 466, 478, 488
Perkins, Carol A. 66
"Personal Indebtedness and the American Revolution in Maryland," 156 441
Peters, William E., 248
Peters, William S., 245
Petitions for Grants of Land 1778-1811, 251
Pfannkuche, Craig, 340
Phillimore, W. P. W., 190
Piepkopt, Arthur Carl, 141
Pioneer Families of the Oregon Territory, 1850, 658
Pioneers and Profits: Land Speculation on the Iowa Frontier, 242
Pioneers of Maine Rivers with Lists to 1651, 658
Pioneers of Maine and New Hampshire 1623-1660, 658
Pittsburgh, Allegheny City, and Allegheny County Business Directory for 1900, 394
Planters of Colonial Virginia, 251
Plymouth Colony Marriages to 1650, 658
Plymouth Court Records, 1686-1859, 177
Pocket Dictionary of Shoe Manufacturers, 372
Poet, Johann Cristoph, 456
"Policy of Land Distribution in Pennsylvania Since 1779," 249
Polk's World Bank Directory, 400
Pomeroy, Kenneth B., 246
Pomfret, John E., 246
Population Bibliography, 663
"Population of the El Paso Area – A Census of 1784, The", 558
Portrait and Biographical Album of Fond du Lac County, 449
Posey, Joanna W., 666
Powell, Sumner Chilton, 222, 476
Preliminary Guide to Church Records and Repositories, a Standard Reference of Denominational Archives; and, for Those with a Roman Catholic Interest, the Official Catholic Directory, 525
Preliminary Guide to Eighteenth-Century Records Held by the Georgia Department of Archives and History, 1976, 241
"Preliminary Inventory of the Cartographic Records of the Bureau Land Management (Record Group 49)," 558
Preliminary Inventory of the German Collection at the Genealogical Society of Utah, 456
Preliminary Inventory of the Land Entry Papers of the General Land Office, 229, 231, 238
Preliminary Inventory of the Records Bureau of Refugees, Freedmen, and Abandoned Lands, Washington Headquarters, 582
Preliminary Inventory of the Records of the Bureau of Indian Affairs, 537*Preliminary Inventory of the Records of the Bureau of Land Management – Utah*, 251, 558
Preliminary Inventory of the Records of the Supreme Court of the United States (Record Group 267), 558
Preliminary Survey of the French Collection, 433
Preliminary Survey of the Mexican Collection, 433
"Primitive Baptists of North America," 141
"Private Land Claims Against the Public Domain in New Mexico on File in the Office [of the] United States Surveyor-General for New Mexico, June 30, 1855", 559
"Private Land Claims in Alabama", 239
"Private Land Claims in Missouri", 230, 245
"Private Land Claims in the South", 230
"Private Land Claims of the the Old Northwest Territory", 230
Proceedings of the Maryland Court of Appeals, 176
"Processioning in the Southern States," 253
Promised Land; the History of the South Carolina Land Commission, 1869-1890, 249
Province of North Carolina, 1663-1729, Abstracts of Land Patents, 246
Psychological Abstracts, 663
"Public Domain in Territorial Florida," 240
Public Domain. It's History with Statistics, 224
Public Land Bibliography, 224
"Public Land Disposal in California," 239
"Public Land Disposal in Washington," 252
Public Land Policy in Hawaii: An Historical Analysis, 241
"Public Land Policy of Washington State: The Initial Period 1889-1912," 252
Public Land System of Texas 1823-1910, 251
Public Lands in Montana, Their History and Current Significance, 245
"Public Lands of Tennessee," 250
Public Lands of Texas 1519-1970, 251
Public Records Relating to Land in New York State, 246
Puritan Village: The Formation of a New England Town, 222, 476
Putnam, David W., Jr., 442

Q

"Quaker Records", 146
"Quit Rent System in South Carolina," 249
"Quit Rents in Colonial New Jersey," 246
"Quit-rent System in Maryland," 243

R

Radke, Michael Friedrich, 456
Radoff, Morris L., 243
Railroad Leaders, 1845-1980: The Business Mind in Action, 372
"Rand McNally List of Bank-Recommended Attorneys," 399
"Reconstructing Work Histories by Computer: Pullman Shop Workers", 380
"Record of Name Changes, 1866-1883 (California), 187
"Recording of Deeds in the Colony of Massachusetts Bay," 244
"Records in the Offices of Registers of Deeds in N.C.," 247
Records of Baltimore's Private Organizations: A Guide to Archival Resources, 468
Records of Plymouth Colony – Births, Marriages, Death, Burials, etc. 1633-1689, 658
Records of the Collector of Customs Puget Sound District in the Federal Records Center, 464
Records of the Colony of New Plymouth in the New England, 243
Records of the Colony of Rhode Island and Providence Plantations in New England, 249
Records of the Court of Chancery of South Carolina, 1671-1679, 176
Records of the Court of Prince Georges' County, 176
Records of the Court of Vice Admiralty of Rhode Island, 176
Records of the Governor and Company of the Massachusetts Bay in New England, 244
"Records of the Huguenots in the United States, Canada and the West Indies with Some Mention of Dutch and German Sources," 143
"Records of the Lutheran Church in America," 143-144
"Records of the Lutheran Church in America," 144
Records of the Moravians in North Carolina, 1752-1820, 534
"Records of the Southern Claims Commission","199
Records of the Suffolk County Court, 1671-1680, 176
Reed, H. Clay, 176
Reeder, Faye B., 252
Reeve, Judge Tapping, 186
Reference Directory of Booksellers, Stationers, and Printers in the U.S. and Canada, 372
Register of Commanderies and Members, Military Order of Foreign Wars of the United States 1894-1900, 655
Register of Genealogical Society Call Numbers, 432
Register of the Albemarle Parish Surrey and Sussex [Counties, Virginia], 1739-78, 132

Reid, William D., 257
Reiger, Morris, 344
"Report of the Classifier and Translator of Manuscripts in the Texas State Library," 561
Reports of the Committees on Private Land Claims of the Senate and House of Representatives, 230
Representative Men of Ohio, 447
Research in Georgia, 241, 529
"Research in Virginia's District of West Augusta," 249, 252
Researcher's Guide to American Genealogy, 143, 217
Researching European Origins of Pennsylvania German Families, 457
"Retention of Life Insurance Records," 340
"Revolutionary War Records in the Archives and Records Division of the Virginia State Library," 235
Revolutionary War Records – Virginia Army and Navy Forces with Bounty Land Warrants for Virginia Military Scrip from Federal and State Archives, 235
Reynolds, Francis J., 521
Rhode Island Land Evidences, Vol. 1, 1648-1696, Abstracts, 249
Richards, Gertrude, 132
Richardson, Lemont K., 230, 245
Richardson, William A., 197
Rider, Fremont, 434
Ridge, Martin, 224
Riegel, Mayburt Stephenson, 248
Rife, Edward K., 447
Riggs, John B., 375
Risch, Erna, 468
Rischin, Moses, 612
Rising Sun Times of Rising Sun, 417
Ritchey, C. J., 244
Roach, Hannah B., 456
Robbins, Roy Marvin, 224
Roberts, Peter, 491
Robinson, Maurice H., 245
Robinson, W. Stitt, 252
Robinson, William Wilcox, 239
Rohrbough, Malcolm J., 224, 241
"Roman Catholic Family in North America: Family History as Viewed Through Catholic Church Records," 147
Roots, 579
Rose, James, 579-580
Rose, Robert S., 246
Roster of North Carolina Troops in the War Between the States, 263
Roster of Revolutionary Soldiers in Georgia, 285
Rothrock, Carol K., 249
Rottenberg, Dan, 143, 614
Rowland, Arthur R., 190
Roy, William G., 371
"Royal Bastards from the Time of the Norman Conquest – The Consitiution, Annual Reports, Lineages of Descents of Members, Etc.", 688
Royal Land Grants of the Rio Grande 1777-1821, 657
Royce, Jack F., 242
Rubincam, Milton, 252, 457
Ruddy, Joseph C., 249
Rutherford, Homer Vincent, 253
Rutman, Anita H., 212
Ryan, Edward L., 156
Ryerson, Adolphus E., 257

S

Sabine, Lorenzo, 257
Sachse, William L., 468
Salley, Alexander S., 249
Salmon, John, 235
"Salus populi supreme lex: Public Peace and South Carolina Debtor Relief Laws," 156
Saretsky, Gary D., 372
Scanland, Roger, 437
Scharf, J. Thomas, 243
Schelbert, Leo, 478
Schick, Tom W., 593
Schlesinger, Keith, 522
Schmeckebier, Lawrence F., 195
Schnore, Leo F., 467
Schory, Eva D., 439
Schreiner-Yantis, Netti, 435,
Scotch-Irish Migration to South Carolina, 1772: Reverend William Martin and His Five Shiploads of Settlers, 467, 476
Scott, Florence Johnson, 251
Scott, Hattie, M., 242
Scott, Kenneth, 331, 417, 467
Search, 335
Search: A Handbook for Adoptees and Birthparents, 468
Seiler, William H., 252
Select Bibliography on Business Archives and Records Management, 372
Select Cases of the Mayor's Court of New York City, 176
Sequestration, Confiscation and Sale of [Loyalist] Estates, 251
Sessions Laws of American States and Territories Prior to 1900, 183
Settlement of the Connecticut Towns, 240
Severs, Frederick B., 541
Shawneetown Land District Records, 241
Sheldon, Addison Erwin, 245
Shellem, John J., 147
Shenefield, Hale T., 456
Sheperd, Rebecca A., compiler, 446
Shepherd, W.R., 249
Shepperson, Wilbur S., 468
Sherick, L. G., 468
Sherman, C.E., 247
Shinedling, Abraham I, 613*Shipping: A Survey of Historical Records,* 457
Shurtleff, Nathaniel B., 244
Siebert, Wilbur Henry, 257
Siegel, Steven W., 630
Silversmiths of Virginia from 1694 to 1850, 330
Sim's Index to Land Grants in West Virginia, 252
Sims, Edgar B., 252
Sinaloa Roots: An Account of the 1781 Expedition to Alta, California and Ancestral Records of Early California Settlers, 1723-1808, 559
Sinko, Peggy Tuck, 522
Skirven, Percy G., 240
Skordas, Gust, 243
Smelser, Ronald, 433, 456, 619
Smith, Anna P., 455, 457, 478
Smith, Clifford Neal, 229, 234, 247, 455, 457, 478
Smith, David R., 382
Smith, Jonathan, 245
Smith, Joseph H., 176
Smith, Warren B., 455
Society of Piscataqua Pioneers, Register of Members and Ancestors, 1905-1981, 658
Socolofsky, Homer, 245
Some Aspects of Italian Immigration to the United States, 454
Some Original Land Grant Surveys along Green River in Lincoln and Casey Counties, Kentucky (1781-1836), 253
South Carolina Archives: A Temporary Summary Guide, 249
"South Carolina Colonial Land Policies", 249
South Carolina Gazette, 1732-1775, 417
South Carolina Historical and Genealogical Magazine, 438
South Carolina Regulators, The, 204
South Carolina and Georgia Almanack, 387
Southern Baptist Convention, 13
Southern Claims Commission, 199
Southern Ute Lands, 1848-1899: The Creation of a Reservation, 535*Spanish Land Grants in Florida,* 240
"Spanish Land Grants in New Mexico and Colorado", 240, 246
"Spanish Land Laws of Louisiana", 243
Spanish West Florida. *See also* Mississippi, 244
Spanish and Mexican Land Grants in California, 239
Spanish and Mexican Land Grants in the Chihuahuan Acquisition, 251
"Spanish and Mexican Land Grants in the Southwest: A Symposium", 230
Spanish and Mexican Records of the American Southwest: A Bibliographical Guide to Archive and Manuscript Sources, 229, 559
Spaulding, Thomas Marshall, 241
Spear, Dorothea N., 387, 403
Spencer, Charles W., 246
Sperry, Kip, 253, 439
Spohr, Oswald, 488
Spouse, name of, on death certificate, 53
Spouses, names of, on monuments, 63
Stamm-und-Ahnentafelwerke (Pedigree and Ancestor Tables), 456
"Standard Guides to Church Archives," 332
Starke, James H., 257, 675
Starr, Edward Caryl, 141
State Papers of Vermont, 251 Results", 666
Stella, Antonia, 454
Stephenson, Jean, 465, 476
Stephenson, Richard W., 229
Stern, Malcolm H., 143, 603
Strassburger, Ralph B., 455, 466, 478, 488
Strausberg, Stephen Frederick, 241
Street Directory of the Prindipal Cities of the United States...to April 1908, 402 States Embracing Letter-Carrier Offices Established to April 30, 1908, 403
Stryker-Rodda, Kenn, 246, 252, 253, 330, 603
Subject Collections: A Guide to Special Book Collections and Subject Emphases as Reported by University, College, Public and Special Libraries and Museums in the United States and Canada, 370
Suelflow, August, 144, 525
Suffolk Deeds, 244
Sullivan, James, 243, 244
Superior Court Diary of William Samuel Johnson, The, 176
Supplement to the Preliminary Survey of the Mexican Collection, 433
"Supreme Court Collections at the National Archives, The," 194
Survey and Sale of the Public Land in Michigan, 1815-1862, 244
Survey of Federal Archives in Louisiana, Land Claims and Other Documents, 243
Surveyors and Statesmen, Land Measuring in Colonial Virginia, 220, 252
Susquehannah Company Papers, 247, 249
"Susquehannah Settlers, 1755-1796", 247, 249
Sutherland, Arthur E., 246
Sutherland, James Franklin, 253
Swathers, George Henry, 246
Swedish Settlers on the Delaware, 1638-65, 664
Swierenga, Robert P., 242
"Swiss Mennonite Family Names: An Annotated Checklist," 478
Szucs, Loretto Dennis, 529

T

Tabular Analysis of the Records of the U.S. Colored Troops and Their Predecessor Units in the National Archives of the United States, 580
Tax Records: A Common Source with Uncommon Value, 236
"Tax and Fiscal Records", 253
Taxation and Political Change in the Young Nation, 1781-1833, 253
Taylor, Philip, 454-455, 491

Taylor, Robert J., 247, 249
Taylor, Virginia H., 250
"Tellico Grants, 1803-53," 242
The Administration of Federal land Laws in Western Kansas, 1880-1890: A Factor in Adjustment to a New Environment, 242
The American Agricultural Press, 1819-1860, 372
The Boston Evening Post, 417
The History of Events Resulting in Indian Consolidation West of the Mississippi, 538
"The History of the Land Bonus of 1812," 234
The Movement for Indian Assimilation, 1860-90, 535
The National Land System, 1785-1820, 224, 253
The New Hampshire Grants, Being Transcripts of the Charters of Townships and Other Minor Grants of Land Made by the Provincial Government of New Hampshire Within the Present Boundaries of the State of Vermont from 1749-1754, 251
The New-York Directory of 1786, 387
The Nez Percés: Tribesmen of the Columbia Plateau, 535
The Philadelphia Directory, 387
The Preservation of Land Office Records, 242
The Public Domain in New Mexico, 1854-1981, 246
The Quit-Rent System in the American Colonies, 236
"The Recording of Land Titles in South America," 249
The Researcher's Guide to American Genealogy, 142, 146
The Silversmiths of Virginia from 1694 to 1850., 330
The Town Proprietors in Vermont: New England Town Proprietors In Decline, 251
"Thirty-three Years with Coca-Cola, 1890-1923," 374
"Thomas Stone and the Reorganization of the Maryland Council of Safety," 206
Thomas, N., 247, 249
Thomas, Robert C., 337
Thompson, Tommy R., 156
Thorndale, William, 253, 661
"Title Difficulties of the Holland Land Company in Northwestern Pennsylvania," 249
Toledot: The Journal of Jewish Genealogy, 619, 630, 643
Tompson, Richard S., 433
Toole, H. Greshaw, 246
Towle, Dorothy S., 176
Towle, Laird C., 438
"Town Patents under Belcher," 245
Town Proprietors of the New England Colonies; a Study of Their Development, Organization, Activities and Controversies, 1620-1770, 222
Town and Country: Essays on the Structure of Local Government in the American Colonies, 209
Tracing the Immigrant Ancestor, 453, 491
Treat, Payson Jackson, 224, 253
Triadoption Library, address of
"Tricks in Using Indexed Genealogical Books, 430
Trowbridge, Frederick N., 252
True, Ransome B., 251
Tuttle Antiquarian Books, 15
Twonley, John M., 245

U

U.S. Bureau of Census, 340, 529
U.S. Department of Labor, 340
U.S. Reports, 194, 196
Ulrich's International Periodicals Directory, 436
Ulster Emigration to Colonial America, 1718-1775, 455
"Uncertainty of Early Kentucky Land Titles," 242
Underground Railroad from Slavery to Freedom, The, 591
Union Catalog of Presbyterian Manuscripts, 145
"Union Pacific Railroad and the Early Settlement of Nebraska 1868-1880, 245
United Empire Loyalists Inquiry into the Losses of Services in Consequence of Their Loyalty. Evidence in the Canadian Claims 235
United Empire Loyalists, The. A Chronicle of the Great Migration, 257
"United States Court Records, Part II: Genealogical Data to be Found in Court Records", 174
United States Newspaper Project: A National Project, 417
"Urban Finding Aid for Manuscript Census Searches", 522
Urban History: A Guide to Information Sources, 519
"Using Computers to Reconstitute Families: French Canadian Seventeenty-Century Families as an Example", 661

V

Vallentine, John F., 224, 249, 252, 453, 491
Van Hook, Joseph O., 239
Van Tyne, Claude Halstead, 257
Vandenberge, Peter N., 332
Vault, 63
"Vehicles of Discontent: The Committees of Correspondence in the Southern Colonies, 1773-1776", 207
Vermont Old Cemetery Association, 66
Vermont in the Making, 251
Vermont's First Settler's, 251
Vernier, Chester G., 186
Vincennes Donation Lands, 230, 241
Virginia Committee System and the American Revolution, The, 207
"Virginia Committee of Correspondence, 1759-70, The," 207
"Virginia County Committees of Safety, 1774-1776, The," 206
"Virginia Expedition Against the Overhill Cherokee, 1776," 535
Virginia Genealogical Resources, 252
Virginia Genealogist, 438
"Virginia Land Grants in Kentucky and Ohio, 1784-1799", 235
"Virginia Land Grants in Pennsylvania", 249, 252
Virginia Land Grants: A Study of Conveyancing in Relation to Colonial Politics, 252
"Virginia Settlers Research Project," 661
Vivian, Jean H., 206. 234
Volkel, Lowell M., 241
Voorhis, Manning C., 252

W

WPA Bibliography, 524
WPA Historical Records Survey: A Guide to the Unpublished Inventories, Indexes and Transcripts, 139 *Inventories, Indexes, and Transcripts*, 524
Waddell, Alfred M., 206
Wade, Earl W., 249
Wagner, Edward, 600
Wakelyn, Jon L., 265
Waldenmaier, Inez B., 438
Wallace, W. Stewart, 257
War Department Collection of Revolutionary War Records, Special List 36, 562
War of 1812 Bounty Lands in Illinois, 241
War of 1812 Military Bounty Land Warrants, 1815-1858, 239, 241, 245
Ward's Directory of 55,000 Largest Corporations, 337
Warrants for Land in South Carolina, 1672-1711, 249
Water, Margaret R., 241
Watson, Alan D., 249
Weathers, Shirley A., 433
"Wells Fargo & Co.: Banking on the Past", 383
Were Your Ancesters Front-Page News?, 417
Wertenbaker, Thomas J., 251
West Virginia Jewry: Origins and History 1850-1958, 593
Westerberg, Frank B., 207
"Western Electric Historical Library," 383
"Western Lands, 1783-1789," 247
"Western Lands, 1783-89," 249
Western New York Architects and Builders' Directory, 400
Westphall, Victor, 246
Whatley, George C., 240
Where to Find Business Information, 337Whitaker, Bessie Lewis, 206
White Servitude in Colonial South Carolina, 455
White, Francis, 387
White, Gerald T., 379
Whitney, Henry D., 250
Who's Who in America, 445
Whyte, James H., 581
Wiebe, Robert, 529
Wilderness Politics and Indian Gifts, the Northern Colonial Frontier 1748-1761, 535
Willeston, Walker, 142
William Bingham's Maine Lands 1790-1820, 243
William F.J. Boardman Collection, 1661-1835, 240
Williams, Ethel W., 146
Wilson, O.G., 373
Wilson, Samuel M., 242
Winfield, Charles H., 246
Winks, Robin W., 592
Winner, John E., 249
Winslow, Raymond A., Jr., 253
Wisconsin State Old Cemetery Society, 66
Wittke, Carl F., 467
Wolf, Jacquelyn H., 247
Wolfe, Richard, 480
Woodward, Florence May, 251
World Conference on Records and Genealogical Seminar, 143
World of Our Fathers, 603
Worth, C.E., 244
Worthington, Dorothy, 249
Wright, James E., 241
Wyllys, Rufus Kay, 467
Wynar, Lubomar R., 529

X

Xerox University Microfilms, 15, 28

Y

Yearbook of American and Canadian Churches and Reformed Churches, 146, 140, 141-142, 332
Yearbook of the Society, Sons of the American Revolution in the Commonwealth of Kentucky, 242
Yoder, Don, 478, 481
Yoder, Eleanor, 479
Yoho, James G., 246
Yonce, Frederick Jay, 252
York Deeds, 243
Yoshpe, Harry P., 229, 231, 238 , 257

SUBJECT INDEX

A

Abdel Ross Wentz Library and archives of the Lutheran church in America, 144
Abigail O'Flyng Act of 1816, 234
Abjuration. *See* Oath of allegiance
Abolition societies, records *table*, 593
Acadians. *See* French immigrants, 501
Accelerated Indexing Systems (AIS), 18, 99
  1981-present, 441-442
  indexes censuses prior to 1850, 440
Access
  legally restricted to vital records, 60
  rights of, 25-26
Accounts books, of colonial period, 328, 330
Accuracy of indexes, 429
Acts of 1850-1855
  bounty land warrants for, 233
Adair, John H., collection of, 541
Address and street coordinates, in directories, 394
Address books, family information in, 40
Administration petitions, probate, 185
Administrative courts, *illus.*, 154
Administrator accounts, probate, 185
Administrator of probate. *See* Court records, probate
Admiralty, in court records, 194-197
Admission records of prisons, 173
admissions register, *illus.*, 304
Adoption
  birth certificates, 192
  case file contents, 192
  citizenship requirements, 192
  name changes in, 190
  petition for, 190-191
  records of, 190
  rights of inheritance, 192
  statutes governing, 190
Adoptions,
  in court records, 190-192
  records of, 25
Ads and newspaper indexes, 417
Adultery
  grounds for divorce, 84
  property rights, 88
Adventist archives, 141; *See also* Seventh-Day Adventists
Advertisements, in business directories, 397
Advertising directories, 397
Aerial photographs, National Cartographic Information Center, 16
African colonization records, 580
Afro-American. *See* Black research
AGBI. *See* Indexes, Rider's Index
Age of deceased
  in mortuary records, 311
  mortality schedules, 50
  on death certificate, 53
Age, patients
  in hospital records, 322
Agriculture
  in 1885 census, 103
Agriculture schedules
  1850-80, location *table*, 108-109
  censuses 1840-1910, 105
Ahnenpass, emigration records, 456-457
AIS. *See* Accelerated Indexing Systems
Alabama
  1860-1880 census, index to, *table*, 101
  access to adoption records in, 192
  Cherokees in, 535, 536
  city/town schedules, *table*, 120
  Confederate pensions for, 279
  Confederate volunteers from, *table*, 262
  correctional institutions in *table*, 302
  Federal census, 1790-1910, *table*, 94
  Freedmen's Bureau records, 581
  genealogical records of, 9
  indexes to land patents, 226
  Ku Klux Klan, records of, 209
  land records summary, 239
  military records, indexes, *table*, 261
  military records, microfilmed by Genealogical Society of Utah, *table*, 264
  mining district, extra-legal, 207
  mortality schedules, *table*, 104
  Perry County 1890 census, 101
  printed court records, 194
  state census schedules, 1623-1910, *table*, 113
  state laws, printed, 182
  Union volunteers, indexes, *table*, 262
  veterans' home in, 285
Alaska
  access to adoption records in, 192
  correctional institutions in, *table*, 302
  Federal census, 1790-1910,*table*, 94
  genealogical records of, 9
  indexes to land patents, 226
  jurisdictions in, 533
  land records summary, 239
  printed court records of, 194
  state census schedules, 1623-1910, *table*, 113
Alfred the Great, 685
Aliases, 185
Alien Registration Law (1940), 507
Alien registration, 468
Alimony, 87
Allen, Ethan, 219
Allodial ownership, of land, 237
Alpha Delta Phi Fraternity Alumni Association, 401
Altar pieces
  as memorials, 63
Amendment to petition, example of, 163
  See also Court records, 163
American Antiquarian Society, 387
  and newspaper index, 416
  city directories, 396
  indexed listings of card catalog, 435
American Association for State and Local History, photographing gravestones, 68
American Baptist Convention, records of, 141
American Bar Association, law directories, 399
American Evangelical Lutheran church (Danish-American), 144
American Immigration Library, access to, 492
American Indian. *See* Native American research
  naturalization of, 469
American Jewish Archives, 143
  610
American Legal Records Series, 176
American Lutheran church, 143
American Medical Association, medical directories, 399
American Officers of the Great War. *See* Military Order of the World Wars, 676
American Protestant confirmation records, 135
American State Papers, Public Lands, 244
Americanization. *See* Immigration records, 468-474
Amish, in Pennsylvania, 137
Amnesty act, for naturalization, 469
Anabaptists, 131
Analysis of data, 21-23
Ancestral File, in Family Group Record Archives, 432
Ancestral home, locating, 610-617
Ancestry, Inc., 128
Ancient and Honorable Artillery Company of Massachusetts, 671
Ancient and Honorable Order of the Jersey Blues, 674
Andover Newton Theological School, 141
Andrews University Library, 141
Animal brands, in deed books, 217
Anniversaries, wedding announcement of, in newspapers, 410
Annuals. *See* Directories, 387
Annuity roll, 1851, 518
Annulment of marriages, 84, 185
Anti-slavery groups and their records, 593
Apalachicola, removal records, 538
APG. *See* Association of Professional Genealogists
APJI. *See* Association for the Protection of Jewish Immigrants
Appeal bond, example of, 159
Appeal, in criminal case, 157
Appeals Court. *See also* Courts, appeals.
  probate court, 185
  records microfilmed, 194
  records of, 152, 157, 192-194, 2185
  relationship to trial courts, 152, 157, 185
Appellate Courts of Special Jurisdiction, *illus.*,154
applicant's genealogical chart, *illus.*, 682-683
Apprentice records, 185, 328
  in deed books, 217
  legal age of, *table*, 186
  regulated by local courts, 151
Archer family, 680
Architects, records of, 332
Archives of the American Lutheran church, 143, 144
Archives of the Mennonite Church, 144
Archives of the Moravian church, 145
Archives, 1-3
  denominational, 141-148
  Jewish, holdings of, *table*, 612
  municipal, 529
Arizona
  1860-1880 census, index to, *table*, 101
  1885 census, 102
  Catholic church records, 569
  Confederate volunteers from, *table*, 262
  correctional institutions in *table*, 302
  extra-legal courts, 204
  Federal census, 1790-1910,*table*, 94

genealogical records in. *See also* Spanish and Mexican American research, 559
indexes to land patents, 226
Japanese-Americans in, *table,* 200
land grants, 567
land records summary, 239
location of records, *listing,* 571
mining district, extra-legal, 207
mortality schedules, *table,* 104
printed court records, 194
Spanish records of, 229, 568-569
state census schedules, 1623-1910, *table,* 113
state laws, printed, 182
Union volunteers, indexes, *table,* 262
Arkansas
access to adoption records in, 192
black marriage records of, 582
Cherokees in, 536, 541
Confederate pensions for, 279
Confederate volunteers from, *table,* 262
correctional institutions in, *table,* 302
divorces in, 88
Federal census, 1790-1910,*table,* 94
Freedmen's Bureau records, 581
Fulton County, 1850 census, 18
genealogical records of, 9
Indians in, 54
Japanese-Americans in, *table,* 200
land records summary, 239
land taxes, 236
military land reserves, 231
mortality schedules, *table,* 104
Newspaper bibliography for, 419
printed court records of, 194
registers of blacks, 592
state census schedules, 1623-1910, *table,* 113
state laws, printed, 182
Union volunteers, indexes, *table,* 262
Arlington National Cemetery, records of, 280
Arrival lists. *See* passenger lists, 462-465
indexes, 440
Ashkenazic Jews, *See,* Jewish American research, 603
Asian American research, 597-601
1980 census figures, 577-578
Asia, sources in, 600
Chinese immigration, 597
historical and genealogical records, 600
East Indian immigration, 598
Filipino immigration, 598
Japanese American Citizens League, 598, 599
immigration, 597-598
newspapers, 599
records in Asia, 600
immigration, 598
National Association, 598
records in Asia, 600
Korean Christian churches, 598
Assignment of real estate, probate, 185
Association for Gravestone Studies, 66
Association for the Protection of Jewish Immigrants (APJI), 613, 615
Association of American University Presses,
resolution on permissions, 27
Association of Professional Genealogists (APG),
directory of members, 442
"Associators," extra-legal group, 207
Atlases, collections, 15-16
historical, 229
Attachment bond, 158, 185
See also Court records
Attorney in fact, 107
Augustana Evangelical Church (Swedish-American), 144
Augustana Synod records, 144
Austin, Stephen, 250
Australia,
research and bibliography, 492
Austria, Jewish records in, 616, 630, 643
Auxiliary to the Sons of the Union, 676
Awards, probates, 185
Aztec Club of 1847, 655

B

B'nai Jeshurun, 605
Baby books,
birth information in, 35
Bacon's Rebellion, 219
Bail, in criminal case procedure, 153
Balch Institute and foreign language newspapers, 416
Baltimore City Passenger Lists 1833-1866, 464
Baltimore, Baron, 681
Baltimore, Jews in, 613
colonial society of, 681
Hall of Records
special census in 1850-1880, *table,* 108
Balzekas Museum of Lithuanian Culture, 416
Bancroft Library, California
private land claims in, 239
California provincial records in, 569
Mexican records in, 569
San Antonio records in, 564
Bank records, of blacks, 582
Banns, marriage records, 76
Baptism records
certificate, 33, 53
illus., 133
infant, 140
records of, 131-133
registration required (1538), 131
witnesses, 140
Baptist
archives, 151
church records, 3, 131
in Pennsylvania, 137
Bar/Bat Mitzvah and confirmation records, 606
Barker History Center,
index to 1860 Texas census, 101
Baron of Arizona, court case of, 565
Baronial Order of Magna Charta, 685
Barons of Runnemede, 685
BASIC, 653
Bastardy papers, 185
Battle of Goliad, 250
Battle of Lexington, membership society for, 671
Battlefields, maps of, 16
Belgium immigrants,
Ahnenpass, 456
Bell and Howell
newspapers on microfilm, 408
Benevolent associations
membership lists of, 411
Bentley Historical Library, 244
Bethany Theological Seminary, 142
Bethel Seminary, 141
Better Business Bureau, 337
Bexar Archives, Texan records, 559
BIA. *See* Bureau of Indian Affairs, 535
Bible record
death records, 63
evidence of birth, 35, 53
marriage information in, 36, 83
Bibliographic Retrieval Services, 661
Bibliographic search networks, 436
Bibliographies
military records, 294-298
of newspapers, 417
Billop family, 680
Bills for provisions,
Passenger agreements, 462
Bills of sale. *See* Deeds
Biographic indexes. *See* Indexes, Biographic
Biographical dictionaries, 4
biographical register, *illus.,* 307
Biographies
how to evaluate, 448-449
in newspapers, 411-412
indexes to, 436-437
indexes, 449
local histories, *illus.,* 447
research problems in, 445
unpublished, 448
urban research, in, 525
Biographies, compiled, 445-446
bibliography of, 449
children in, 445
church affiliation in, 445
country, date of entry, in, 446
evaluation of, 449-450
local histories, in, 447-448
military service in, 447
occupational, 446
political party in, 445
political, 446
religious affiliation, 446
residences listed in, 447-448
ritual records, 446
unpublished, 448
women in, 445
Biographies, index to, 441
Biological parents, rights of, 25
Birth certificate, 31-33
delayed, 52-53
foreign-born children, 468
illus. of, 53
of adoptees, 192
Birth records, 32-35
and Social Security benefits, 52
christening certificate, 33
in business directories, 397
in newspapers, 35, 410, 411
Jewish American Research, 607
medical records, 33
modern and privacy laws, 52
modern, 52
of blacks, 50, 583
on death certificate, 53
on monuments, 60, 63
published, 60
requests for, 51
urban research, 522
Birth, place of
from church records, 140
on death certificate, 53
Birth
in biographies, 446
in medical directories, 399
in military pension files, 50
in orphanage records, 321
See also Vital records, 49-53
Birthdate. *See also* Age
in directories, 397
Birthplace
in biographies, 446
in directories, 397
in hospital records, 322
in military pension files, 50
in mortality schedules, 50
in mortuary records, 311
in obituaries, 409
in orphanage records, 321
Bishop Museum, 599
"Bishops' transcripts", 131, 477
Black American research, 579-595
abolition records, 593
African colonization records, 580
anti-slavery groups, records of, *table,* 593
bibliography, 594-595
case history, 583-591
census records, *illus.,* 584
census schedules, 580
court records, 583
estate records, 583
Freedmen's Bureau, 581-582
Freedmen's Savings and Trust Co., *table,* 582
freedmen, 580
indexes, usefulness, 579
local censuses, 123-124
manumission records, 591
marriage records, 581-582
military records, 580-581
oral tradition, history, 579
pension files, indexed, 580
petition for support, *illus.,* 590
plantation records, 583
regimental records, 581
registration of blacks, 592
slave declarations, 592
slave records, 583-591
slave sales, records of, 583
slave, advertisements for, *illus.,* 591
Underground Railroad, 591-592
vigilance committees, records of, 591
Blacks
1790 census, 124

and newspapers, 416
census of in New York, 124
in 1870 census, 99
in 1890 census, 100
in city directories, 388
in graveyards, 68
in Illinois, 593
in vigilante records, 207
manumission records of, 209
marriage records of, 209
naturalization of, 469
petition for freedom, 209
sales of, announced in newspapers, 416
ship's manifests, in, 416
special court records, 209
with Cherokees, 537
Blackstone, William, 237
Blake Collection, of Spanish records, 561
Blood heirs. *See* Probate, 187
Blood, Martin H. 85
"Blue laws," retained today, 155
Board for Certification of Genealogists, 442
Board of Trade minutes, divorce records in, 87
Bond, in probate, 185
Bondsmen, in probate, 177
Bookkeeping, double-entry, pre-1890, 369
Books on Demand, 15
Books, locations, 14-15
Borough courts, *illus.*, 153-154
Boston Atheneaum, indexed listings of card catalog, 435
Boston Public Library, 417
Boston Tea Party, 195
Bottomry. *See* Courts, admiralty
Boundary changes, of counties on computer, 17
Bounds, copying of, 220
Bounty land. *See* Land records, bounty land
Boy Scout troops, Tombstone inscriptions, 64, 66
Brenner Collection, *Ahnenpass*, 456
Brethren Historical Library and Archives, 142
Brethren in Christ Church archives, 141
Brief, example of, 162-163
See also Court records
Brigham Young University
computer index to microfilmed holdings, 434-435
index to DAR family Bible compilation, 50
Brooke family, 680
Brothers and sisters. *See* Siblings
Buddhist mortuary tablets, 600
death registers, 600
Buddhists, in census reports, 599
Buffalo and Erie Historical Society, 127
Bulgarian immigrants, research aids and bibliography, 498
Bureau of Immigration and Naturalization, 525
Bureau of Indian Affairs, 535
census, 109-112
land patents in, 217, 224-226
school census, 118
school records, 318
Bureau of Prisons, Washington, D.C., 302
Bureau of Refugees, Freedmen, and Abandoned Lands. *See* Black ancestral research
Bureau of Vital Statistics
marriage records, 75
Burial records, 60-73
Confederate soldiers, 263, 264
Jewish, 609
registration required (1538), 131
soldiers, 60, 280-281
Burial registers, 61, 63
and state health departments, 62
death certificate, 53
Burial-Transit Permit, *illus.*, of, 63
illus., of, 63
Business
50 largest, *listing*, 362
50 largest diversified finanacial, *listing*, 368
50 largest retailing companies, *listing*, 364
50 largest transportation, *listing*, 363
50 largest utilities, *listing*, 365
500 largest, *listing*, 354-361
Business and employment records, 327-383
colonial employment records, 327-331
account books, 330
apprentice, 327
indenture, 328-329
indenture, *illus.*, 328
locating, 330-331
pilot indenture book, *illus.*, 328
early American employment records, 331-333
finding aids, 369-370
how to locate, 527
modern employment records, 333-336
old trades and occupations, *listing*, 342
urban research in, 527
vital records in, 50
Business directories, guide to, 341, 397-398
Business licences, 335
Byron Sistler & Associates, 99
Byte, 652

C

C.S. Williams, directory publisher, 387
Calendar system of notekeeping, 21
Califonia
access to adoption records in, 192
Asian American immigration, 597
Catholic church records, in *listing*, 570-571
Cherokees in, 536
city directories, 441
city/town schedules, *table*, 120
correctional institutions in *table*, 302
court records of, 570
Federal census, 1790-1910,*table*, 94
genealogical records of, 9
Gold Rush, 229
Indexes and abstracts, 423
Indians in, 110
Japanese-Americans in *table*, 200
land records summary, 239
land records, under Spanish rule, 569-570
location of records, *listing*, 571-572
mining district, extra-legal, 207
Monterey Park, city directories, 397
mortality schedules, *table*, 104
name change, finding aids, 187
newspaper bibliography for, 419
printed court records of, 194
registration rolls, immigrants, 465
San Francisco, court records of, 570
San Francisco, election districts of, 388-393
San Francisco, jurisdiction of, 533
San Jose, court records of, 570
San Luis Obispo, court records of, 570
Santa Clara Catholic church, 571
Santa Cruz, court records of, 570
see also Spanish and Mexican American research
Society of Pioneers, 676-677
Spanish land system in, 229
Spanish sovereignty and Mexican national government, records under, 569-571
state census schedules, 1623-1910, *table*, 113
state laws, printed, 182
Union volunteers, indexes, *table*, 262
veterans' home in, 281
Calvert papers, 243
Calvert, George, 678
Calvinism, in Germany, 137
Cambodian refugees, 598
Canada,
finding aids and bibliography, 495-497; *map*, 496
loyalists in, 235
Canal Museum, holdings of, 12
in adoptions, 192
Case files, types of court, 170
attorney records, 171
coroners' records, 171-173
jury records, 170-171
sheriff records, 173-174
Catalogs. *See* directories of libraries, 1, 387
Catholic Archives of America, 147
Catholic Church records
burials, 68
confirmations, 135
for immigrant societies, 468
in California, 570-571
in Texas, 563-564
marriage registers, 134
orphanage records, 322
Cause of death,
on death certificate, 53
CCC. *See* Copyright Clearance Center, 27-28
Cemeteries
associations, 66
consolidation of, 66
deeds and plats, 61
descriptions of, in social schedules, 1850-80, 109
family, 64
hazards of, 68
illus. of, 67
in morticians' records, 313
inscriptions, 64, 66
maps of, 66
military, 66
on death certificates, 64
pauper, 68
plotting, 69
public, 60
religious sections, 68
relocated, 66-67
research preparation, 64-66
searching a, 68
sexton's record, 61
Swedish, 68
traffic pattern map, 67
types of, 60-61
cemeteries in, relocated, 66
Cemetery records, 60-73
birth and death dates, 60
Confederate soldiers, 263-264
Jewish, 605, 609
soldiers and veterans, 280
soldiers' headstones applications, 281
urban research in, 523
Census records
1790 *illus.*, 93, 124
1790-1910, 92-97, *table*, 94-97
1800 Pennsylvania, 91
1850, 93-99
1850-1910 contents of, *table*, 98
1850-1910, contents of, *table*, 98
1850-60 slave schedules, 103
1850-80 special schedules summarized, 108-9
1860 census wards, 388
1860 indexes, 99
1870 census wards, *table*, 390-393
1870 Pennsylvania, 395
1880 indexes, 99, 100-101
1890 census veterans' schedule, *illus.*, 107
1890 index to, 100-101
1890 schedule of Union veterans & widows of veterans, 105
1900 list of slaves, *illus.*, 565
1900 marriage information in, 84
1900 population, 525, *illus.*, 102
1900 Soundex, 102
1910, 102, 590
accuracy of, 91-92
agriculture schedules 1840-1910, 102, 105
bibliography of, 126
blacks in, 580
catalog of 1790-1880, 389
Cherokees, 518-519
church enumerations, 50, 121
cities and towns available, *table*, 120-121
directories with, 388
duplicate entries in, 91
England, 1851, 482
enumeration districts, 128

enumerator district maps, 522
estate values, 99
extracting information from, 92
federal census, 93-119
forms, addresses for producers of, 128-129
immigrants in, 99, 474, 590
indexes for, 91-92, 99
Indian schedules 1840-1942, 109-112, *table*, 110-112, 535-537, 546
industrial, 103
Jewish American Research, 610
legal age in, *table*, 186
local, 119-126
manufacturing schedules, 105, 109
microfilm catalogs of, 127
military, 285; *illus.*, 106
missing, 124-125
Mormon 1914, 123-124
mortality schedules (1850-1900) 50
mortality schedules, 103
of schools *illus.*, 122
only children under 10 in, 91
"padding the totes" 91
problems in, 91-92
See also, Native American research
slaves, *illus.*, 583-585
Soundex abbreviations, 99, 521
Spanish and Mexican American research, 561
special schedules 1850-1880, 102-119, *table*, 108-109
state schedules, 1623-1910, *table*, 113-118
state, 102-103, 119-126
substitute catalogs, 127
substitute census checklist of *illus.*, 126, 127
table, 101
Union veterans (1890) 105
urban research in, 521-522
veterans' schedules, 103, *table*, 105, 107
worksheets for, 128-129
Centennial histories, to locate businesses, 371
Central processing unit. *See* CPU, 652-653
Central Tracing Bureau. *See* International Tracing Service
Certificates of competency, 538
divize, probate, 185
of devize, probate, 185
of freedom, 185
Certified American Lineage Specialist, 689
Certiorari, in appeals court, 192
Ch'ing period, genealogical records from the, 600
Chamber of commerce, 338
Chancellor, equity proceedings, 161
Chancery courts, *illus.*, 154
Changes of name, in probate, 185
Chapman Roll, 1851-52, 518
Chapman, Alfred, 536
Charlemagne, Order of the Crown of in the United States of America, 685-688
Charles Muhls Bancroft Library, 46
Cherokee. *See also* Native American research
censuses, 517-535
Eastern band, 538-539
freedmen with, 580
in Confederacy, 541
Chicago Historical Society, map collection in, 521
Chickasaw, records of, 535-541
Chief justice courts, *illus.*, 153
Chihuahua Archives, Arizona records, 569
Children
evidence of in cemeteries, 60
in burial registers, 61
in compiled biographies, 445
in custody cases, 185
in divorce, 88
in newspapers, 411
in orphanage records, 321
Children of the Confederacy, 676
Chilton, James, 677
China, genealogical records in, 600
Chinese
in 1870 census, 99
in 1890 census, 100
Chinese in the U.S. *See* Asian American research, 597
Chinese Provincial Library of Guangdong, 600
Choctaws
in Confederacy, 541
records of, 535
Christening records, 33, 131-133
Christian Reformed Colonial Origins Collection, 146
Christian Scientist. *See* First Church of Christ, Scientist
Christian Theological Seminary, 142
Christmas cards, family information in, 40
Church of Christ, Scientist, archives, 142
Church of England
and Protestant Episcopal records, 146
in marriage annulments, 84
in southern colonies, 131
Church of God archives, 142
Church of Jesus Christ of Latter-Day Saints, The, (Mormons) archives, 142
Church of the Brethren archives, 142
Church records
archives and repositories, 141-148
Baptists, 131
Catholic, 140, 563-564, 568, 569
confirmation records, 135
death registers, 140
family registers, 135
how to locate, 135, 137-140, 525
immigrants, 131, 468
in city directories, 388
Lutheran, 131
marriage records, 75
minutes of the church council, 135
New Mexico, 568
pew rentals, 135
private ownership of, 140
repositories of, 141-148
Spanish and Mexican American research 563-564, 568, 569
synagogue records, 650-608, *See also* Jewish American research
transcriptions of, 140
translations of, 140
types of, 131-135
urban research for, 523-525
use of city directories with, 388, 396
vital records in, 49-53
Church records, 131-148
affiliation, 64, 69, 109, 135, 441, 445
burial registers, 60
census records, 50, 123
historical societies, 50
Churches of Christ archives, 142
Circuit courts of appeal, *illus.*, 153-155
Circuit courts, *illus.*, 155
Circumcision, record, *illus.*, 607
Citation, problems of, 23-24
Citizenship
for adopted people, 192
for soldiers, 472
in epitaphs, 69
in Soundex, 101
process of, 469-472
through territorial acquisition, 469
City censuses
See also local censuses
state-by-state listing of *table*, 120-121
City courts, *illus.*, 153
City directories, 137, 389-393
1870 census, use with, 388
1870 census, wards, *table*, 390-393
businesses, 388
children in, 388
how to use, 388-389
indexes, 440
organizations in, 388
place of birth and death in, 388
problems with, 388-397
City directories, 389-393
Civil cases, procedures in, 152-153
Civil courts of record, *illus.*, 153
Civil registration of vital records, 137
Civil service personnel, records of, 371
registers, 399-400
Civil War. *See also* military records
casualty lists, 416
claims for, *table*, 199
Confederate military academy records of, 265
criminal prosecutions, 151
lists and volunteers, 400
membership in societies of, 675-676
military government during, 204
military indexes of, 440
pension applications, 84
records relating to blacks, 580
veterans of, in 1890 census, 105
vintage assessments, 526
Civilization and Statistics Divison of BIA, 539
Claggett family, 680
Claim-jumping, 229
Claims club, extra-legal courts, 209
Claims courts, 197
Claims, against U.S., *table*, 198-200
Claims, dockets of, 167, 185
Claims, in court records, 197
Claims, in probate, 185
Claims, types of, *table*, 198-200
Clan genealogies, 600
Clemency files of prisoners
Clergy, lineal descendants of, 681
Clergyman, name of, on marriage records, 396
Code of Military Justice, 203
Collections, institutional, 12
Colleges and universities records of, 370-371
directories, 400
Colonial Assembly (court), *illus.*, 153
Colonial court system. *See* Courts, colonial
marriage records of, 75
Colonial Dames of America, 680
Colonial employment records, 327-331
Colonial Order of the Acorn, 680
Colonial societies, lists of, 679-680
Colonial Order of the Acorn, 680
Vermont Society of Colonial Dames, 680
Colonial Society of Pennsylvania, 680
Colonial tombstones, 60
Colonial wars (1675-1763). *See* Military records
Colonial Wars, General Society of, 671
Colonial, societies of descendants, 671-674, 677
Colonies
Commitees of Correspondence in, 205
extra-legal records of, 206
name changes, finding aids, 190
Colony of Virginia, 684
Color,
in mortality schedules, 50
Colorado
1860-1880 census, index to, *table*, 101
1870 wards, 388
1885 census, 102
Asian American immigration, 597
cemeteries in, relocated, 66
Cherokees in, 536
correctional institutions in *table*, 302
Denver, city directories, 397
federal census, 1790-1910, *table*, 94
indexes and abstracts, 423
jurisdiction of, 533
land grants, 567
land records summary, 239-240
location of records, *listing*, 572
marriage records in (1968), 75
mining district, extra-legal, 207
mortality schedules, *table*, 104
newspaper bibliography for, 419
printed court records of, 194

Spanish land system in, 229
state census schedules, 1623-1910, *table*, 113
state laws, printed, 182
Union volunteers, indexes, *table*, 262
Commercial banking companies, fifty largest, 366
Commericial memorial park, 61
Commission reports, probate, 185
Commissioner's report, in sample equity case, 164-165
Commitment register, in prisons, 173-174
Committee of Claims. *See* court *illus.*, 155
Committee of Pensions. *See* courts *illus.*, 155
Committees of Correspondence extra legal activities, 205
Committees of Safety, extralegal colonial courts, *illus.*, 153
Common law marriages, 83
Common law, *def.*, of, 151
Common Pleas, courts of, 192
Common pleas. *See* courts, *illus.*, 154
Commoners, land rights of in, 222
Communicant lists, 135
Community histories, Jewish, 608-609
Community property. states jurisdictions, 177
Compass, thirty-two-point card, 220
Compiled sources, limitations of, 4
Computer Card Catalog, family histories indexing, 434
Computer databases, bibliography of, 654-668
for emigrant/immigrant records, 481
Computer file index. *See* Indexes, Mormon.
Computer file, 651
Computer program, of Ancestral File, 432
Computer searches of online databases, 661-662
Computer, periodical queries, 441
Computers and genealogy, 651-668
buyer's guides, 654-655
databases and information sources, *listing*, 654-665
definition of terms and commands, 652
educational resources, information center, 662, 663
genealogical/computer publications, *listing*, 665
genealogy programs, *listing*, 655-658
glossary, 653-654
hardware, determining "what you need," 652-653
hardware, types of, 652-653
information services, on-line, *listing*, 662
languages, programming, 653
library catalogs, 664-665
networks, genealogical, *listing*, 664
operating systems, 652-653
reading list, 665-668
software, *listing*, 655-658
Concordia Historical Institute, 144
Concurrent jurisdiction. *See* Courts
Condemnations, dockets of, 167
Confederacy, Indian records of, 540-541
Confederate Army. *See* "war" societies, 676
Confederate records. *See* military records, 261-263
Confederate soldiers, claims of, *table*, 199
Confederation Congresses, records of, 442
Confessionals, as memorials gifts, 63
Confirmation records
American Protestant, 135
German-American Lutheran and Reformed, 135
register, *illus.*, 136
Scandinavian-American Lutheran, 135
Congregational Christian Churches (National Association), 142
Congregational Church in New England, 131
Congregational Church Library, 142, 147
Congressional petitions, 185
Connecticut
1790 census, 124
1790 census, 92
access to adoption records in, 192
admiralty court,*table*, 196
adoption in, 192
adoption jurisdiction in, *illus.*, 190
correctional institutions in, *table*, 302
deeds in, 222
direct tax list for, 236
divorce in, 86, 88, *illus.*, of, 85
early court system in, 192
Federal census, 1790-1910,*table*, 94
Founders of Hartford, 679
founders society of Norwich, 677
genealogical records of, 9
immigrants in, *table*, 453
Indexes and abstracts, 423
land records summary, 240
mortality schedules, *table*, 104
Newspaper Bibliography for, 420
no bounty land grants, 231
printed court records of, 194
published Committee of Safety records, 206
sheriff census 1669-70, *illus.*, 121
state census schedules, 1623-1910, *table*, 113
state laws, printed, 182
Union volunteers, indexes, *table*, 262
urban jurisdictions in, 533
volunteers in Revolutionary War, *table*, 256
Consent affidavits, marriage records, 76
Conservator accounts, probate, 185
Conservator. *See* Guardian
Constable census. *See* Sheriff census, 121
Constable records, 173-174
Continental Army, descendants of, 675
Continental Congress
extra-legal activities of, 206
papers of, black history, 580
records of, 442
Contracts. *See also* Deeds
legal age for signing, *table*, 186
Contributions, as memorial gifts, 63
Convict dockets, 306
Convicts, *See* Institutional Records, prison records records
Cooper, Adolph E., 614
Cooper, Douglas H., 541
Cooper, Samuel, Confederate Inspector General, 261
Copyright Clearance Center (CCC) 13-14, 27-28
Copyright, 26-28
1978 Law, 27
notices of, 27
violations of, 27
Cornell University Library, 126, 246
Coroner's courts, *illus.*, 153, 154
Coroner's jury, in court records, 170
Coroners' inquests, urban research in, 523
Coroners' records, 314-317
death certificate, 314
evidence book, *illus.*, 316
inquest report, *illus.*, 317
inquest testimony, 314
locating, 317
microfilmed by Genealogical Society of Utah, 314
See also Court records, coroners'
vital records in, 50
Corporations
Fortune 500, *listing*, 354-361
records of, 335
correctional institutions, listings, *Table*, 302-304
Correctional institutions. *See* Institutional records, prison
Correspondence log, in notekeeping, 21
Council of Trent, 131
"Counsil of Safty Minutes", 206
Counties,
locating of, 17
modern, surviving, 17
Country of origin,
census records, using, 474
from census, 474
from church records, 474
from homestead applications, 474
from voter registration, 474
how to research approaches, 474
migration patterns, using, 474
Country-by-country summary of research aids, 495-516
County and regional business directories, 397-398
County boundaries inclusive, boundary changes, changes in, 17
County coroners. *See* Coroners' records
County court records, orphanage records, 321
County courts, *illus.*, 153, 154
County governments, marriage records in, 75
County incorporation registers, 371
County or town histories, and buriel records, 64
County plat maps, residence in, 137
Court baron, *illus.*, 153
Court executive. *See* Court records, sheriff
Court leet, *illus.*, 153
Court minutes, vital records in, 55
Court of Appeals, *illus.*, 155
Court of Appeals. *See* Court Appeals
Court of Assistants. *See* Courts, appeals
Court of Claims
history of federal, 197
illus., 155
jurisdiction of, 197
location of records, 208-210
Court of common rights, *illus.*, 153
Court of customs, *illus.*, 155
Court of Inquiry. *See* Courts, courts-martial
Court of military appeals, *illus.*, 155
Court procedures, 152-165
Court records, 165-174
admiralty courts, 1776-89, *table*, 196
admiralty, 194-197
adoption, *illus.*, 191
adoptions in, 190
American law, 183-185
and memorials, 63
appeals courts records summarized, 193-194
appeals courts, 192-194
appointment of Guardian, 170
attorney records, 171
attorneys, rolls of, 171
bill of costs, example of, 163
case files, 170
civil case, example of, 157-159
claims against U.S. Government, *table*, 198-200
claims courts, 197
claims court
jurisdiction, 201
record locations *table*, 200
commissioner's report, 164-165
constable records, 173-174
coroners' records, 171-173
courts-martial in, 197-204
criminal case, 156
illus., 160-161
criminal case, appeal in, 157
decrees, example of, 161-162
deeds, 170
depositions, 156
difficulty in use of, 151
division documents, 183
dockets, 167-168
documents produced by, *table*, 185
equity proceedings, example of, 161-165
example of, 163
extra-legal court, 204-207
for witnesses, *illus.*,, 161

grand jury in, 154
guardian bond, *illus*, 180
guardianship, 177
how to find, 176-177
in America, 151-214
indexes, 165-167
Indians, related to, 540
intestate estates, 177
inventory of estate, *illus.*, 184
jail record, 173-174
jail record, *illus.*, 174
judgements, 165, 170
judicial jurisdiction in, 151
jury in, 156
jury records *illus.*, 172
jury records, 170-171, 173
jury summons, *illus.*, 160-161
laws, printed state by state, *table*, 182-183
laws, *table*, 182-183
legal ages, *table*, 186
local histories, 176
manumission, 209
Massachusetts State Archives, 167
memorials, 169
microfilm, 157, 175
minutes, 165, 168-169
minutes, *illus.*, 158
name changes in, 187-190
named all involved in case, 155
Native American research, for, 539
naturalization, 170, 187
of Indians. *See* Native American research
of sentence execution appeals, 157
petition of lands, *illus.*, 181
primogenture, 183
printed court records, 176
printed, 176-177
prior to World War I, 151
prisoners, 173
community property, 177
donor rights, 177
executor, 177-179
guardianship, 177
inventory of estate, *illus.*, 179
petition, *illus.*, 177
proceedings, 177-183
probate, 177-187
validity of will, 178
probates, testate/intestate, 237
published federal, 194
records published, *table*, 195
requests for, 175
searching of, 174-177
See also Spanish and Mexican American research, 562
sheriff records, 173-174
Spanish, 562
adoption, 190-192
name changes, 187-190
special court proceedings
special types, 187-209
subpoena of witnesses, 154
testate estates, 177
Texan, 562
transcripts, *illus.*, 175
types of *illus.*, 166-167
vigilante societies, 207-209
illus., 188-189
wills,
Spanish, *illus.*, 566
types of, 177
witness lists, 170
witness lists, *illus.*, 171
Court system, federal or state, 152
Courts
American court system, *illus.*, 154
appeals courts, 192-193
appelas in colonial times, 192
appellate jurisdiction of *def.* of 151
Black, 209
civil cases, 152-153
colonial court system, *illus.*, 153
colonial system explained, 152; *table*, 153
concurrent jurisdiction *def.* of 152
Confederates, 209
court dockets in urban research, 526
criminal cases, 153-154
divorce records in urban research, 526
English influence on, 151
exclusive jurisdiction *def.* of 151
Ku Klux Klan, 209
extra-legal, 204
vigilante societies 207-209
Extra-legal
committees of safety , *illus.*, 206
Mayflower Compact, 207
Mining Districts, 207
Mining Districts, *illus.*, 207
record, location, 205
Federal court files in urban research, 526
federal court system, *illus.*, 155
federal system explained, 152
Foreign powers, 209
general jurisdiction *def.* of 152
imprisonment for debt in, 156
Indians, 209
judgement enforcement of, 156
legal age for punishment, *table*, 186
def. of 152
limited jurisdiction *def.* of 152
magistrates, example of, 168
of arbitration, 153
original jurisdiction of *def.* of 151
pleadings, 152-154
Private land claims, court of, 567
probate records in urban research, 526
probate, use of directories with, 395
procedural rules of, 152
Slaves, 209
special courts, 209
special jurisdiction *def.* of 152
types of, *illus.*, 153-154
writ of summons, 152
Courts martial, *illus.*, 154, 155
Courts of Appeals, Indian records in, 540
Creek
census of 1833, 519
in Confederacy, 541
records of, 535
Cremated, ashes of the, 63
Crime. *See* Prison records, 301
Criminal actions, *def.* of, 152
Criminal case,
colonial law, 153
records of, 157
sample of, 160-161
Criminal courts of record, *illus.*, 153, 154
Culver-Stockton College Library, 142
Curator. *See* Guardian
Currey, Major Benjamin F., 535
Curtesy rights, probate, 185
Custody, of children in divorce, 88
Customary courts, *illus.*, 153
Customs and Patent appeals court, *illus.*, 155
Customs lists of aliens 1798-1800, 465
Customs passenger lists 1820-1905, 465
Customs passenger lists, computer databases of, 481
Customs records, emigration, 456
Cutter number, in call numbers, 2
Czechoslovakian immigrants, access to records, 492
Jewish records, 616, 643
research aids and bibliography, 515-516; *map*, 516

D

Daily roll of prisoners, 173
Dakota territory
1885 census, 102
Indians in, 110
state laws, printed, 182
Union volunteers, indexes, *table*, 262
Dames of the Loyal Legion of the United States, 676
Damrell & Moore, directory publisher, 387
Danish immigrants
finding aids and bibliography, 496-497; *map*, 497
Danish-American archives of the Lutheran church in America, 143, 144
DAR, 522
church records, 140
compilations of family Bible records, 140
index to military records, 294
indexed in Computer Card Catalog, 434
libary catalog, 436
marriage records collected by, 83
membership in, 674
mortality schedules in, 103
New Jersey 1783 taxlists, 125
Patriot Index, 294, 440
Revolutionary War indexes, 439-440
Dargan-Carver Library, 13
Database
for indexes, 436
in genealogy, 651
periodical queries 441
Dates of death on headstones, 68
Daughters of American Revolution. *See* DAR
Daughters of the Cincinnati, 674
Daughters of the Republic of Texas, 677
Daughters of Union Veterans of the Civil War 1816-1865, 656
Davis, Earl, case study, 551
Davis, Jefferson, 261
Dawes Commission, 118, 537
dBASE II, 652
de Lotbiniere family, 680
Death certificate, 137
coroners' records, 314
illus., of, 37, 59
in pension file, 279
information contained in, 53
modern, 57
names of cemeteries, 64
See also Institutional records, mortuary records
Death date
in bill of costs, 163
in mortality schedules, 50
mortuary records, 311
on cemetery records, 60
probate, 187
See also Court records, 163
Death lists, in newspapers *illus.*, 408
Death records, 36-37
and family traditions, 58
Asian American research, 600
cause of, in mortality schedules, 50
church, 140
civil, 137
Confederate soldiers, 263-264
contents of, 53-59
death certificate, 37
death notices, 37
funeral notices, 37
hospitals, 322
illus., of, 38
in newspapers, 408-409
Jewish American Research, 608-609
legal notices, 36
mortality schedules 1850-1885, 103
mortuary records, 311
nineteenth century, 53
of blacks, 583
of slaves, 53
place of, on death certificate, 53
published by genealogical societies, 60
registers, church, 140
registers, Manhattan, 396
See also Vital records, 53-60
soldiers, 280-281
urban research, 522
use of directory with, 388, 395
warrants, 309
Debt, imprisonment for, 173
Debtors, property auctioned, 156
Decennial Digest, 193
Declaration of Independence, Descendants of the Signers of the, 680
Declaration of Independence, index for signers, *table*, 442
Declaration of intention, 37, 472
Declarations of Intent (to marry) 76
Decree of heirship, probate, 185
Decrees of distribution, probate, 185
Decrees, probate court, 185
"Dedicated" computers, 652
Deeds, 185, 217-219
See also Land records

Defendant. *def.*, 152
 See also Courts
Defenders of Baltimore, 675
Defunct businesses, 337-338
Delaware
 1790 census, 124, 125
 access to adoption records in, 192
 admiralty court, *table*, 196
 adoption in, 192
 adoption jurisdiction in, *illus.*, 190
 correctional institutions in *table*, 302
 court records, 194
 direct tax list for, 236
 divorce in, 86, 88
 Federal census, 1790-1910,*table*, 94
 Freedmen's Bureau records, 581
 genealogical records of, 9
 land inheritance in, 238
 land records of, Land grants in New York, 240
 land records summary, 240
 mortality schedules, *table*, 104
 newspaper bibliography for, 420
 no bounty land grants, 231
 registers of blacks, 592
 state census schedules, 1623-1910, *table*, 113
 state laws, printed, 182
 Union volunteers, indexes, *table*, 262
 volunteers in Revolutionary War, *table*, 256
Demurrer, in equity proceeding, 161
Denominational archives, 141-148
Dental licenses, 333
Department of Archives and Manuscripts
 and Catholic records, 147
Department of Social and Welfare Services, 321
Deposition of witness, 158
 See also Court records, 158
Depositions
 in deed books, 217
Descendants of the Illegitimate Sons and Daughters of the Kings of Britain, 688
Descendants of the Signers of the Declaration of Independence, 680
Descendants, 678
Desert Land Act (1877), 225, 226
Detroit Society of Genealogical Research, 525
Dewey Decimal call numbers (over page) 2
Diaries,
 birth information in, 35
 illus., of, 34
 marriage information in, 36, 83
 vital records in, 50
Directories, 387-404
 1910 city atlas, 394
 address and street coordinates in, 394
 American Medical Directory, illus., 400
 blacks, 388
 business directories, county and regional, 397-398
 business directories
 dates of marriage, 397
 length of residence, 397
 names of children, 397
 business, rural areas, 397-398
 census, 388
 children, 388
 city directories, 396, 519
 civil and military, 399-400
 college-related, 400
 death and probate records, 395-396
 directories with church records, 396
 fraternity, 401
 history of, 387
 laborers in, 387
 law, 398-399
 maps, use of, 394-395
 medical, 399
 microfilmed, 397
 military, location of, 400
 miscellaneous professions, 400
 naturalization and land records, 396
 of genealogists, 442-443
 organizational, 400-402
 post office and street, 402-403
 private directories, libraries, *listing*, 397
 problems with, 388
 professional, 398-400
 publishers, 387
 religious, 402
 religious, *illus.*, 403
 schools, in, 321
 source locations, 396
 street directories, 393, 519-520
 telephone, 388
 transients in, 387
 types of, 387
 university alumni, 401
 use with censuses, 388
Disaster victims, list of, 409
Discharge book, of prisoners, 173-174
Discharge records, of wars, 265
Disciples of Christ archives, 142
Disinheritance, in English law, 238
Disk drives, computer, 653
Disqualification of voters, dockets of, 167
Dissertations Publishing, 15
Dissertations, available through University Microfilms, 3
Dissolved companies, registers of, 371
Distribution of National Groups in the Present United States, *table*, 453
District of Columbia
 1890 census, 101
 census, special schedules 1850-1880, *table*, 108
 Federal census, 1790-1910,*table*, 94
 Freedmen's Bureau records, 581
 Indexes and abstracts, 424
 land records summary, 240
 mortality schedules, *table*, 104
 newspaper bibliography for, 420
 records relating to slaves, 580
 Union volunteers, indexes, *table*, 262
Diversified financial companies, 50 largest, *listing*,, 368
Divinity Library and University Library
 and congregational records, 147
Divorce certificates, in New Hampshire, 85
Divorce courts, 86-87
Divorce meccas, 88
Divorce records, 75-88
Divorce, 75-88, 185
 alimony, 87
 American laws, 84
 civil, 85
 easy in some locations, 88
 English laws, 84, 87
 illus., of, 85
 in Hawaii, 84
 in Texas, 84
 Kentucky, 84
 Legislative Act, 85
 Maine, 84
 name changes in, 190
 New Jersey, 84
 New York, 84
 notice of in newspapers, 413
 notice of, 85
 Ohio, 84
 Pennsylvania, 84
 provisions for children, 88
 residency requirements for, 88
 role of courts, 84
 Southern states, 84
 Tennessee, 84
 Vermont, 84
 West Virginia, 84
Docket of sheriff, 173
Dockets, types of, 167-168
Documentation. *See* Proof and citation, 23-24
Domestic relations. *See* courts. *illus.*, 154
Donation Act for New Mexico (1854), 246
Donation Act of 1850, 250
Double-entry bookkeeping, pre-1890, 369
Dower rights, probate, 185
Dower rights. *See* Court records, Intestate
Dr. Linden J. Carter Library Adventist records, 141
Draper Manuscript Collection. *See* Oral interviews, historical collection of, 46
Drennen, John, 535
Drew Allis Company, 393
Duke University
 special census schedules in 1850-1880, *table*, 108-109
DUP. *See* Daughters of Utah Pioneers,
Durango Archives, Arizona records in, 569
Dutch Colonial Society of Delaware, application form, 682-683
Dutch immigrants, 1790, 453
 Ahnenpass, 456
 distribution of by state, *table*, 453
 research aids and bibliography, 507-508; *map*, 507
Dutch Reformed Church, in New Netherland (New York), 131, 146
Dutch Settlers Society of Albany, 684

E

Early American records (1760-1870), 331-333
Early settlers, societies of, 676, 679
Early immigration, 1607-1790, 453
East Asian Library of Columbia University, 600
East Germany, Jewish records in, 620-630
East Indians in the U.S. *See* Asian American research, 598
Eastern European research, 497-498
Eastern European immigrants finding aids and bibliography, 497; *map*, 498
Eastern Orthodox church archives, 143
Eastern state, church registers, 142
Eaton, Francis, 677
Eden Archives
 Evangelical and reformed records, 147
Education, handled by local courts, 151
Educational Resources Information Center (ERIC), 662, 663
Egle, William Henry, 248-249
Ehime prefecture, 599
"Elites and personalities," 600
Ellis Island, immigration screening, 462
Emigrant Roll, 1851, 518
Emigrants
 indentures, 455
 indentures, German origins for, *map*, 456
 listing or records by port of jurisdiction, *table*, 458-461
 See also Immigrants, 453-519
Emigration,
 agent, 455
 for Jews from Russia, 603
 registers, availability of, 474
 route from Germany, 455
Emigration records,
 Ahnenpass, containing German pedigree,456
 computer databases, 480
 court or council minute books, 454
 customs records, 456
 emigrant agents, Mormon, 491
 emigrant lists, 457
 emigration lists by port of jurisdiction, *table*, 458-461
 manumission, letter of, *illus.*, 456
 Passenger Lists, 462-465
 permit to emigrate, 454-455
 recommendation, letter of, 454
 registers, 454
 sale of property, 454
 See also Immigration records, 454-519
 shipping company records, 457
 travel documents, 455-456
Employment records, Asian genealogy, in, 599

Employment records, *See* Business and employment records, 327-383
Empressario contracts, in California, 569
Encyclopedias, biographical. *See* Biographies, compiled
Engagement information, in newspapers, 410
England,
 Almondbury, Yorkshire, 476
 immigrants, migration patterns, 474
 influenced American courts, 155
 nationality society for descendants of, 681
English immigrants,
 1790, 453
 distribution, *table*, 453
 indentured servants, 455
 migration patterns, 474
 research aids and bibliography, 498-500
 shipping company records, 457
English marriage indexes, 1837-1906, 481
English marriage laws, 84
English Mutiny Act in 1689, 197
English Privy Council, divorce laws in, 87
Enlarged Homestead Act (1909), 225
Enlistment papers, for Civil War, 259
Entailed property. *See* Court records, probate, 187
Enumeration districts, for locating census, 128
 for locating census, 128
Epitaphs, 69
Equity actions, *def.*, 152
Equity claims, in Court of claims, 197
Equity proceedings, example of, 161
ERIC. *See* Educational Resources Information ccenter, 662, 663
Estate docket, 185
Estate inventory, *See* court records, probate
Estate records, blacks in, 579, 583
Estate taxes, in probate, 185
Estate, values in federal census, 99
Estates,
 taxes, in probate, 185
 claims against, in newspapers *illus.*, 413
 claims against, in newspapers, 414
Ethnic,
 American Series, 492
 in newspapers, 416
 associations, 599
 collections of manuscripts, 3
 groups in the U.S., 597-598
 organizations in newspapers, 416
 research. *See* Urban ancestors, 519
 societies, 681-684
 sources, in urban research, 529
Europe, modern and sixteenth-century boundaries of, 477
European records, Jewish American Research, for, 603-562
Evangelical and Reformed Church archives, 147
Evangelical Congregational Church archives, 142
Evangelical Covenant Church of America, archives, 143, 144
Evangelical Free Church of America, 143, 144
Evangelical Lutheran church, 143
Evangelical United Brethren Church, records of, 143
Evans Early American Imprints, 408
Exclusive jurisdiction. *See* Courts
Executions, by sheriff, 173
Executions, lists of, 309
Executions, probate court, 185
Executor
 accounts, probate, 185
 approved by court, 1777
 legal age for acting as, *table*, 186
Expedientes, Spanish land records, 561
Expediente records, California, 569
Extra-legal courts, *See* Courts, extra-legal, 204-209

F

Fair use, definition of, 27
Fairfax Northern Neck Proprietary, 251
Family associations. *See* Family societies and organizations, 688
Family Bible records, compiled by DAR, 50
Family Bibles, vital records in, 50
 vital records in, 50
Family burial plot, 60
Family crests, Asian American research, 600
Family crests, Japanese, 600
Family Group Record Archives of the LDS church, 142
Family group sheet,
 in record keeping, 42; *illus.*, 44
Family group sheets, in Family Group Record Archives, 432
Family group sheets, in notekeeping, 32
Family histories
 adoptions in, 190
 and Goodspeeds Book Shop, 435
 books indexed, 435
 DAR index, 436
 in printed genealogies, 437
 indexes to, 433
 Jewish, 617
 problems of, 4
 publishers of, 435
Family History World, 128
Family Name Index, 4
Family organizations, locating, 688
Family organizations. *See* Hereditary societies, 684
Family records,
 discrepancies in, 59
 vital records in, 50
Family registers, church, 135
Family sources,
 business records as, 40
 land records as, 40
 legal records as, 40
 See also Home sources
Family traditions *see also*, home sources, 31-41, 46,
Family traditions, and death records, 58
Farmers, in business directories, 397
farming, 334
farming, records of, 334
Father of deceased,
 on death certificates, 53
Federal Aviation Agency. *See* courts
 illus. 155
Federal Bureau of Investigation. *See* courts.
 illus. 155
Federal Court System, explained, 151, 152
 1789-1891 *illus.* of, 155
 1891-1911 *illus.* of, 155
 1911-1952 *illus.* of, 155
Federal courts, procedural rules of, 152
Federal courts, published reports of *table*, 195
Federal township and Range System
 legal description in, 225
Federal township and range system, 219
Federation of Genealogical Societies, 1910 city atlas, 394
Fee tail, of land, 237
Felonies, 152
Femme sole, 187
Ferdinando Gorges proprietary, 243
FGRA. *See* Indexes, Mormon
FGS notekeeping,
 illus. of, 22
file, in Nacogdoches archives, 559
Filipinos in the U.S. *See* Asian American Research, 598
Final papers. *See* Petition, 472
Finance Division records, 539
Finding aids, 12-15
 finding books, 14
 guides and inventories, 12
 indexes, 15
 institutional and private collections, 12
 library holdings, 12
 name changes, 187-190
 periodicals, books, and book dealers, 13
Fingerprint file, 173
Finnish Evangelical Lutheran church (Finnish-American), 144
Finnish immigrants,
 finding aids and bibliography, 500-501; *map*, 500
Finnish-American archives of the Lutheran church in America, 144
Fire insurance maps, 521
Fire lands, Ohio, 231
Firemen, lists of, in newspapers, 411
First Church of Christ, Scientist, the, 142
First Families of Ohio, 679
 Howe Historical Collection for eighty-eight Ohio counties, 679
"First papers." *See* Naturalization and Declaration of Intention
"First Purchasers of Pennsylvania, 1681-1700", 248-249
First-title deed, *See also* Deeds
First-title grant, 217
Five Civilized Tribes, map of locations, 541
Flagon and Trencher/Descendants of Colonial Tavern-keepers, 681
Florida,
 1870 census, 388
 1885 census, 102
 Confederate pensions for, 279
 Confederate volunteers from, *table*, 262
 correctional institutions in *table*, 302
 divorces in, 88
 Duval County, jurisdiction of, 533
 Federal census, 1790-1910,*table*, 94
 Freedmen's Bureau records, 581
 genealogical records of, 9
 indexes to land patents, 226
 Jacksonville, jurisdiction of, 533
 land records summary, 240
 military records, indexes, *table*, 261
 military records, microfilmed by Genealogical Society of Utah, *table*, 264
 mortality schedules, *table*, 104
 newspaper bibliography for, 420
 printed court records, 194
 state census schedules, 1623-1910, *table*, 114
 state laws, printed, 182
 Union volunteers, indexes, *table*, 262
 veterans' home in, 285
Florida Armed Occupation Act (1842), 240
Foote notebooks, 46
Foreign countries, researcher, 614-617
Foreign genealogies, 4
Foreign language newspapers, 416
Foreign powers, court records, 209
Foreign wars, society of, 675
Foreman, Grant, collection of, 541
Forest, Nathan B., 209
Forman, Samuel I. and John S., 464
Fort McPherson National Cemetery, 66
Fort Wayne-Allen County Public Library, 417
Fort Worth Federal Record Center, Native American research, 535
Fortune 500, *listing*, 354-361
Founders societies, 686-689
Fourth of July claims, *table*, 199
France,
 Allsace, 40
 Colmar, 40
 territorial changes of, 478
France, Jewish records of, microfilmed, 615-616
Franciscan missions
 deceased members of, 409
 in California, 570

in New Mexico, 568
Fraternal organizations, in morticians' records, 313
Fraternity directories, 400-402
Fraudulent pedigrees, 23
Free men of color, 579
Free Methodist church, Historical Center, 145
Freedman's Bureaus, 580
illus., 155
records, state-by-state listing, 581
Freedmen's Savings and Trust Company, 582
Freedmen, 580
Freedom of Information Act, 25, 335, 371, 468
Freedom of Information Clearing House, 26
Freehold, 237
Freeholders. (Freeman), 205
Freeman of color, 580
French
and Indian War, 255, 259
and Indian War, Virginia Bounty Land Warrants for, 252
Huguenot immigrants, migration patterns, 474
marriage contracts, 78
Protestants, 143
French immigrants, 1790, 453
distribution of by state, *table*, 453
in Ohio in 1803, 453
in Vermont, 453
research aids and bibliography, 501-502; *map*, 501
societies for, 468
Frontiers. *See*, Courts, extra-legal courts
Fugitive Journals, of escaped slaves, 591
Fukuoka prefecture, 599
Fuller, Samuel, 677
Fun P'ing-shan Library, 600
Funeral homes, records of, 400
Funeral or death notices in newspapers, 409
Furniture, family information on, 40

G

Gadsden Treaty, purchase of Arizona, 568
Gardiner family, 680
Garrett Evangelical Theological Seminary Library, 145
Genealogical Books in Print, 128
Genealogical columns in current newspapers, 416
Genealogical databases, *listing*, 658-661
Genealogical Helper, census indexes announced in, 101
Genealogical Indexing Associates. *See* GIA
Genealogical Institute, cemetery records, 60
Genealogical networks, *listing*, 664
Genealogical periodicals
church records, 140
current index, 438
indexes to, 437-439
specialty, listing, 493
where listed, 443
Genealogical Publishing Company, lineage society sources at, 689
Genealogical societies
birth and death records published by, 60
directory of, 66
Mexican Southwest, 559-577
periodicals, local, 140
tombstone inscriptions, 64, 66
Genealogical Society of Utah
Brenner Collection, 456
business directories, 398
business records in, 331
cemetery projects, 66
church records in, 525
Church records, 142
city court records in, 526
city vital records in, 522
Confederate soldier card abstracts, index, 263
coroners' records microfilmed, 314
court records microfilmed, 175
eastern church registers, of microfiches, 141
emigration records in, 456
English vital records, 51-52
ethnic records in, 529
Family Registry, 432-433
finding aids, for immigrant records, 494-495
Hawaiian Asian records, 599
indexes 430-433
Jewish records in, 610
Jews in Poland, original records, 475
Korean records, microfilmed, 600
land records microfilmed, 217
largest genealogical collection in world, 13
local church records, 137
map collection, 394
maps with ward boundaries, 394
marriage records microfilmed in, 83
micfroform copies of directories, 397
microcards of the *Boston Transcript*, 417
microfilm collections, of immigrant records, 494
microfilmed birth records, 51
microfilmed church records, 140
microfilmed Civil War records of, 265
microfilmed passenger lists, 612
microfilms of DAR family Bible compilations, 50
microfilms of mortality schedules, 50
mortality schedules, *table*, 104-105
naturalization records on microfilm, 610
New Mexico church records in, 568
passenger lists microfilmed, 463
Pennsylvania prison records, microfilmed, 311
post office and street directories, 403
publishers' catalogs in, 435
records of black Union soldiers, 580
research aids, 8
Revolutionary War service records, 255
state by state listing of military records, *table*, 264
Genealogical user interest groups, *listing*, 664
Genealogical/computer serial publications, 665
Genealogies, printed, in the Library of Congress, by county, 4
Genealogists Bookshelf, 15
Genealogists, indexes to, 442
Genealogy and the computer, 667-668
Genealogy computer programs, *listing*, 655-658
Genealogy library catalogs, 434
Genealogy techniques, overview, 5
General Allotment Act, 1887, 520
General Conference of Seventh-day Adventists, 141
General Council of the Congregational Churches, 147
General Court, *See* Court Appeals
General jurisdiction. *See* Courts
General Land Office, records in, 226
General minute books, Jewish, 605, *Illus.*, 604
General Sessions. *See* courts, *illus*, 153, 154
General Society of Mayflower, 12
General Society of the War of 1812, membership in, 655
Geographical jurisdictions, how to identify, 15-16
Geography, in genealogy, 15-17
George Adams, directory publisher, 387
Georgetown University Catholic church records, 147
Georgia
1790 census, 125
admiralty court, *table*, 196
adoption in, 192
adoption jurisdiction in, *illus.*, 190
bigamy in, 87
bounty land grants, 231
census, special schedules 1850-1880, *table*, 108
cession of western lands, 222
Cherokees in, 535-536, 542
church records in, 131
Confederate pensions for, 279
Confederate volunteers from, *table*, 262
correctional institutions in *table*, 302
court records, microfilmed, 175
direct tax list for, 236
divorce in, 87
entailed lands in, 238
Federal census, 1790-1910,*table*, 94
Freedmen's Bureau records, 581
genealogical records of, 9
immigrants in, *table*, 453
indexes and abstracts, 424
Indians in, 551
inheritance by adoptees, 192
Ku Klux Klan in, 209
land lottery index, 441
land offices in, 219
land records summary, 240-241
lottery system for settlers, 125
military records, indexes, *table*, 261
military records, microfilmed by Genealogical Society of Utah, *table*, 264
mining district, extra-legal, 207
mortality schedules, *table*, 104
Muscogee County 1890 census, 101
name changes, finding aids, 190
newspaper bibliography for, 420
primogeniture in, 238
printed court records, 194
Revolutionary War land grants, *table*, 232
Savannah court records located at, 526
Savannah, Jews in, 603
second marriages in, 87
state archives located in, 240
State Archives, 236
state census schedules, 1623-1910, *table*, 114
state laws, printed, 182
Union volunteers, indexes, *table*, 262
volunteers in Revolutionary War, *table*, 256
German,
Baptist records, 141
immigrants, migration patterns, 474
German aliens, relocation of, *Table*, 200
German burial patterns, 68
German churches, marriage records in, 75
German Evangelical churches in America, 137
German genealogical words, *table*, 490-491
familiengesch ichfliche Quellen, 489
genealogical periodicals, specialty, *listing*, 493
health certificates, 462
immigrant registers, *listing*, 493
indentures, 467
indexes to, 480-481
land records, 469
letter of manumission, 454
letters of thanks, 467
merchants, records, 462
microfilm collections, Genealogical Society of Utah, 494
national source papers, *listing*, 493
nationality reference directory, 492
naturalization records, 469-472
naturalization, certificate of, *illus.*, 473
naturalization, summary of provisions, *table*, 470-472
newspaper and hospital accounts, 462

newspaper announcements, 466, 467
oaths of allegiance, 465; *illus.*, 466
overseas ancestors periodicals, 493
passenger lists, 462-465
alien identification, 468
Forman papers, 464
locating, 462, 464
ships, logs, repositories for, 464
types of, 462
"pest" hospital records, 462
printed sources, *table*, 485-488
research aids, speical, *listing*, 493
research approaches, 474-476
shipping company records, 457
ships' report and manifest, *illus.*, 463
sources, printed, *table*, 485-488
undertakers' and merchants' records, 462
German immigrants,
1790, 453
1820-1860, 453
Ahnenpass, 456
distribution of by state, *table*, 453
finding aids and bibliography, 502-504; *map*, 502
indentured servants, 455
links with American churches, Pennsylvania, 481
name changes, 478
newspaper announcements of emigration, index of, 457
societies for, 468
German Methodists, records of, 143
German pedigrees, published, 456-457
German records,
access to 2,000 family histories, 488
in Lutheran records, 143
in Pennsylvania, 488
searching them in American, 482-491
German Reformed churches in America, 137
German-American archives of the Lutheran church in America, 144
German-American congregations, 143
German-American Lutheran congregations, 144
German-American Lutheran, confirmation records, 135
German-American Pietist-Anabaptist, 142
German-Jewish Records microfilmed by Genealogical Society of Utah, 619-630
Germans, in Pennsylvania, 137
in Pennsylvania, 137
Germans, position of graves, 6464
Germany
church records, 131
Jewish records of, microfilmed, 615
Rhineland, *map* of, 456
sixteenth-and twentieth-century, *map*, 481
territorial changes of, 478
GIA, statewide index to local histories, 437
Glossary, computer, 653-654
Goal delivery. *See* courts. *illus.*, 154
Godparents
recorded on baptismal records, 133
Goodspeeds Book Shop, family histories, 435
lineage society sources at, 689
Gossip columns and newspaper indexes, 417
Government agencies, records of, 25
GPAI. *See* Genealogical Periodical Annual Index
Grand jury, in criminal case procedure, 154
Grant. *See also* Deeds
Grant/patent. *See* Land records, deeds, 219
Grantee. *See* Land records
Grantor. *See* Land records
Grave opening orders
illus. of, 62
Grave opening orders, 60
Graves
locating, 66-67
position of and family relationships, 63
positions of and national origins, 63
Gravestones,
chalking, 68
cleaning, 68
photographing, 68
reading, 68
See Tombstones, 68
special problems with, 69
Graveyards, ethnic, 68
Great Awakening, 131, 137
Great Depression, death notice during, 409
Great Depression, the and church records, 139
Greek immigrants,
research aids and bibliograhy, 498
Greek Orthodox Archdiocese of North America, records of, 143
Greenlaw Index, 437
Gregorian calendar, 133
"Gretna Green," marriage locales, 83
Guardian accounts, probate, 185
Guardian, legal age for choosing, *table*, 186
Guardians, appointed for orphans, 321
Guardianship docket, 185
Guardianship documents, 526
Guardianship, in probate, 177
Guides to,
library holdings, 12
See Directories, 387
to Genealogical Society of Utah, 433
Guion Miller Rolls, 538

H

Hamburg passenger lists, 612-613, *illus.*, 613
Hamilton, Alexander, 675
Hampshire Grants, 245
Hanranty, Peter, collection of, 541
"Hard copies." *See* printouts.
Harding Graduate School of Religion Library, 142
Hardware, computer, 652-653
Harland, Derek, 137
Harold B. Lee Library, genealogical holdings, 434-435
Hartford Theological Seminary Library and congregational records, 147
Harvard Divinity School Library and congregational records, 147
Harvard University, Baker Library, 332
Hawaii
adoption in, 192
adoption jurisdiction in, *illus.*, 190
city/town schedules, *table*, 120
correctional institutions in *table*, 302
divorce in, 84, 87
Federal census, 1790-1910, *table*, 94
genealogical records of, 9-10
Honolulu, city directories, 397
Honolulu, jurisdiction of, 533
Japanese-Americans in, *table*, 200
land records summary, 241
naturalization in, 469
Polynesian communal land customs in, 237
printed court records, 194
State Archives, 599
state census schedules, 1623-1910, *table*, 114
Hawkers, licenses, 1820-1838, 333
Headstones, applications for soldiers', 281
Health certificates, of immigrants, 462
Heathcote family, 680
Hebrew Immigration Aid Society (HIAS), records of, 613
Hebrew Sheltering Society, 613
Hebrew Union College Collection, 617
Hebrew University Campus, 615
Heirs,
listed in obituaries, 59
petitions, probate, 185
Henderson Roll, 1835, 518, 551
Henderson Roll, Cherokee Census of 1835, 517
Henderson, Daniel, 535
Heraldic devices
of the American Revolution, membership in, 674
on deeds, 218
Hereditary and lineage society records, 671-689
Colonial Societies, 679
Colonial Dames of America, 679
Colonial Order of the Acorn, 680
Colonial Society of Pennsylvania, 680
Daughters of the Republic of Texas, 677
Descendants of the Signers of the Declaration of Independence, 680
First Families of Ohio, 679
Flagon and Trencher–Descendants of Colonial Tavernkeepers, 681
General Society of Mayflower Descendents, 677
Hereditary Order of the Descendants of Colonial Governors, 680
Jamestowne Society, 679
Louisiana Colonials, 679
National Society of Colonial Dames of the XVII Century, 680
National Society of Dames of the Court of Honor, 681
National Society of Lords of the Maryland Manors, 681
National Society of the Children of the American Colonists, 681
National Society of the Colonial Dames of America, 680
National Society of the Colonial Daughters of the Seventeenth Century, 680
National Society of the Daughters of the American Colonists, 680
Order of Americans of Armorial Ancestry, 680
Order of Colonial Lords of Manors in America, 680
Order of Descendants of Colonial Physicians and Chirurgieons, 681
Society of Descendants of the Colonial Clergy, 681
Vermont Society of Colonial Dames, 680
Early Settler and Ship Societies, 676
National Society of New England Women, 677
National Society of the Daughters of Founders and Patriots of America, 677
National Society of the Daughters of Utah Pioneers, 677
National Society of the Old Plymouth Colony Descendants, 678
National Society of the Sons and Daughters of the Pilgrims, 678
Order of the First Families of Mississippi 1699-1817, 679
Order of the First Families of Virginia, 678
Order of the Founders and Patriots of America, 677
Piscataque Pioneers, 678
Saint Nicholas Society of

the City of New York, 676
Society of California Pioneers, 676
Society of Indiana Pioneers, 679
Society of the Ark and the Dove, 678
Society of the Descendants of the Founders of Hartford, 679
Society of the Founders of Norwich, Connecticut, 677
Sons and Daughters of Oregon Pioneers, 678 679
Sons and Daughters of the First Settlers of Newbury, Massachusetts,
Sons of the Republic of Texas, 677
Sons of Utah Pioneers, 678
Welcome Society of Pennsylvania, 678
Dutch Settlers Society of Albany, 684
Holland Society of New York, 684
Netherlands Society of Philadelphia, 684
Nationality (Ethnic) Societies, 681
Saint Andrew's Society, 681
Saint David's Society of the State of New York, 684
Saint George's Society, 681
Society of the Friendly Sons of Saint Patrick, 684
Swedish Colonial Society, 684
Welsh Society of Philadelphia, 681
Religious Societies, 684
Huguenot Society of America, 684
Huguenot Society of South Carolina, 684
Huguenot Society of the Founders of Manakin in the Colony of Virginia, 684
National Huguenot Society, 684
Baronial Order of Magna Charta, 685
Descendants of the Illegitimate Sons and Daughters of the Kings of Britain, 688
Military Order of the Crusades, 685
Royal and Baronial Societies, 685
National Society of Americans of Royal Descent, 685
National Society of Daughters of the Barons of Runnemede, 685
National Society of Magna Charta Dames, 685
Order of the Crown in America, 685, 685
Order of the Crown of Charlemagne in the United States of America,
Order of Three Crusades 1096-1192, 685
War Societies, 671
Ancient and Honorable Artillery Company of Massachusetts, 671
Ancient and Honorable Order of the Jersey Blues, 674
Auxiliary to the Sons of the Union Veterans of the Civil War, 676
1846-1848, 675
Aztec Club of 1847 – The Military Society of the Mexican War
Children of the Confederacy, 676
Dames of the Loyal Legion of the United States, 676
Daughters of the Cincinnati, 674
Daughters of Union Veterans of the Civil War 1861-65, 676
General Society of Colonial Wars, 671
General Society of the War of 1812, 675
General Society Sons of the Revolution, 674
Hereditary Order of Descendants of the Loyalists and Patriots of the American Revolution, 674
Ladies of the Grand Army of the Republic, 676
Military Order of Foreign Wars of the United States, 675
Military Order of the Loyal Legion of the United States, 675
Military Order of the World Wars, 676
National Society Children of the American Revolution, 674
National Society Daughters of Colonial Wars, 671
National Society Daughters of the American Revolution, 674
National Society Sons of the American Revolution, 674
National Society United States Daughters of 1812, 675
National Society Women Descendants of the Ancient and Honorable Artillery Company,671
Order of Stars and Bars, 676
Society of the Cincinnati, 674
Society of the Descendants of Washington's Army at Valley Forge, 675
Society of the Whiskey Rebellion of 1794, 675
Sons of Confederate Veterans, 676
Sons of the Union Veterans of the Civil War, 676
United Daughters of the Confederacy, 676
Hester Roll, 1882, 518
Hester, Joseph G., 536
HIAS. *See* Hebrew Immigration Aid Society
Highland Emigration Society, 463
Hillman Library, 12
Hiroshima prefecture, 599
Historical articles in current newpapers, 416
Historical atlases, 229
Historical business records, survival of, 369
Historical Commission of the United Church of Christ, 147
Historical Foundation of the Presbyterian and Reformed Churches, 13
historical information, 341
Historical Institute of the Wisconsin Evangelical Lutheran Church, 144
Historical maps, 16
Historical societies,
birth and death records published by, 60
family burial plots, 60
Historical Society of Pennyslvania, 240
immigrant records in, 462
undertaker's records, 462
Historical Society of the Evangelical Congregational Church, 142
Histories
congregational and community, 608-610
printed, 613, 617
local. *See* Local histories
History, in genealogy, 15
Holland Land Company, Pennsylvania
holdings of, 246, 249
Holland Society of New York, 146, 684
Holland. *See also* Netherlands
Holocaust survivors, *table*, 612, 617
Home sources, 30-47
declarations of intentions, 37, *illus.*, of 39
family Bible, 63
memorials in, 63
military discharge papers, 39
naturalization certificates, 35-37, *illus.* of, 38
Homestead Act (1862), 225, 226
Homestead applications, vital records in, 50
Homestead Case files, genealogical information found in, 226
Horn Papers, fraudulent, 23
Hospital and doctors' records, 137, 301, 306
birth information in, 35
vital records in, 50
House of Lords, in divorce cases, 84
How-to articles, 14
How-to books, bibliographies, 8
how to evaluate, 4-8
important elements *table*, 5
publications by region and state, 8-12
techniques covered *table*, 6
sources covered *table*, 7
Hubert Howe Bancroft Papers, 46
Huguenot archives, 143
Huguenot Historical Society, 143
Huguenot Society of America, 684-685
Huguenot Society of South Carolina, 684
Hungarian immigrants, research aids and bibliography, 498
Hungarian National Archives, 643
Hungarian-Austrian immigrants, 1880-1920, 454
Hungarian-Jewish records on microfilm, *Listing*, 643-649
Hungary, Jewish records in, microfilmed, 615, 643-649
Huntington Library
collections, 133
New Mexico church records, 568
noble family manuscripts, 475
quitrients for Virginia counties in, 251
Hutterites, 131

I

Icelandic immigrants, finding aids and bibliography, 504-505, *map*, 505
Idaho
cemeteries in, relocated, 66
correctional institutions in *table*, 302
divorces in, 88
Federal census, 1790-1910,*table*, 94
land records summary, 241
mortality schedules, *table*, 104
printed court records, 194
state census schedules, 1623-1910, *table*, 114
state laws, printed, 182
Union volunteers, indexes, *table*, 262
Yellowstone National Park, jurisdiction of, 533
IGI. *See* Indexes, Mormon.
Illegitimate persons
adoption proceedings, 190-192
inheritance by, 177
records of, 25
children of annulled marriages declared, 84
Illinois
1860-1880 census, index to, *table*, 101
1900 atlas for the city of, 394
blacks in, 592
census, special schedules 1850-1880, *table*, 108
Cherokees in, 536
city directories, 397
city/town schedules, *table*, 120
Confederate burials in, *table*, 264
correctional institutions in *table*, 302

divorces in, 88
Federal census, 1790-1910, *table*, 94-95
genealogical records of, 10
GIA index anticipated, 437
immigrants of, 468
indexes and abstracts, 424
land records in, Historical Survey Collection, 235
land records of, 229
land records summary, 241
land reserve, 231
maritime records of, 527
Mc Donough County 1890 census, 101
military land reserves, 231
mortality schedules, *table*, 104
Municipal Reference Library, 529
naturalization records, 525
naturalization records, 610
newspaper bibliography for, 420
parishes of, 525
plat maps and books, 229
printed court records, 194
railroad records for, 527
registers of blacks, 592
state census schedules, 1623-1910, *table*, 114
state laws, printed, 182
Union volunteers, indexes, *table*, 262
veterans' home in, 285
Soundex, 1880 ommissions, 100

Immigrants, 453-519
aid societies, 468
alien identification card, *illus.*, 468
archives, 416
Americanization, 468-474
churches, 131
emigrants, *See also*, 454-457
in 1870 census, 99
indentures, 467
indentures, German origins for, *map*, 456
Jewish, 614-616
list of, 465-466
nationality societies for, 681-684
nationality, percentages of by,453
numbers of by year, 453
origin, patterns of by time period, 453-454
photographs, use of, 468
research approaches, 474-476
residence of, 396
societies, location of records, 468
tombstones of, 60
urban centers, in, 454

Immigration Act of 1965, 578
Immigration Exclusion Act, 597
records of, 599
Immigration records, 454-516
Ahnenpass, containing German pedigree, 456
aid societies, 468
archives, 416
alien registration, identification card, *illus.*, 468
aliens naturalized, percentages by country, *table*, 469
American Immigration Collection, 492
arrival lists, 465
arrival, certificate of, *illus.*, 469
Australia, 495
bibliography, 492
bills for provisions and passenger agreements, 462
Bulgaria, 498
Canada, 495-496, *map*, 495
church records, and bibliographies, 495-516
country-by-country summary of research aids
customs list of aliens, 465
immigration passenger lists, 465
customs passenger lists, 465
declaration of intention, 472
Denmark, 496-497; *map*, 497
Eastern Europe, 497; *map*, 498
emigrant lists by port of jurisdiction, *table*, 458, 461
emigration, *See also*, 454, 457
England, 498-500
Ethnic American series
census, 1851, England, 482
computer databases, emigrant/immigrant, 481
English marriage indexes, *table*, 481
German sources, 482-491
International Genealogical Index, 476-480; *illus.*, 478 parish records, 476 provincial boundaries, 477 vital records, 476
Julius Billeter Swiss collection, 488
Pennsylvania County Historical Society, 488
Women Friends Petition, 1659, 481; *illus.*, 484
European/English sources, 476-491
immigration list indexes, 480-481
printed sources, *table*, 485-488
Finland, 500-501; *map*, 500
France, 501-502; *map*, 501
Germany, 502-504; *map*, 502
Greece, 498
Hungary, 498
Iceland, 504-505; *map*, 505
Immigration and Naturalization Service of the U.S., 599
in 1900 federal census, 102
indexes to, 440
Ireland, 505-506; *map*, 505
Italy, 506-507; *map*, 506
Netherlands, 507-508; *map*, 507
Norway, 508-509; *map*, 508
Phillipines, 509
Poland, 509-510; *map*, 509
Roumania, 498
Russia, 510; *map*, 510
Scotland, 510-511; *map*, 511
South Africa, 512
Spain, 512-513; *map*, 512
Sweden, 513-514; *map*, 513
Switzerland, 514-515; *map*, 514
Wales, 515; *map*, 515
World Conference on Records Papers, 492
Yugoslavia, 515-516; *map*, 516

Immigration, 453-516
Asian American research, *See also*, 597-598
bibliography, 492-516
early, 1607-1790, 453
emigration. *See also*, 454-457
Impfschein, *illus.*, 33
process of, the, 457-467
settlement patterns, by time period, *maps*, 453-454
Impressment. *See* Courts, admiralty,
Incorporation registers and files, 371
Indenture papers. *See* Deeds
indenture, 328-329; *illus.*, 329
Indentured servants
immigration of, 455
in newspapers, 416
of immigrants, 467
Indexes, 428-443
1860-80 federal censuses, 99, 101
1910 census, 102
abstracts, and, state-by-state listing of, 423-426
companies 15
contents of 15
genealogical societies 15
historical societies 15
how to use 15
individuals 15
of libraries 15
access to and use of, 15
accuracy, 429
American Genealogical-Biographical Index, 434
appeals courts records, 193
arrival lists, 440
Bexar archives, Texas, records of, 559
bibliographic search networks, 436
biographical indexes, 434-436
blacks omitted in, 579
bounty land records, 233, 234
card catalog listings, 435
census 1790-1850 99
census records, 92
census, by state, 440
Civil War pensions, 275
Civil War, 440
compiled or secondary sources, 429
computer file index, 430
Confederate soldier card abstracts, 263
court records. *See* court records, indexes
DAR family history index, 436
databases for, 436
Declaration of Independence, signers, *table*, 442
directories of genealogists, 442-443
English marriages, to, *table*, 489
family indexes, 434-436
GDAI, 328
genealogical library catalogs, 434
genealogical periodicals, 437-439
Genealogical Society of Utah, 434
genealogists, to, 442
Greenlaw Index, 437
Harold B. Lee Library, 434-435
immigration arrival lists, 440
Indian censuses 1898-1906
International Genealogical Index, 430-432
International Genealogical Index, *illus.*, 431
Jacobus's Index, 437, *illus.*, 438
Ku Klux Klans records, 209
language implications, 429-430
manuscript catalogs, 435-436
marriages in England, *table*, 481
Mexican War pension applications, 275
military records (1812-1848), 259
military, 439-440
Family Group Record Archives, (FGRA), microfilmed, 432
Family Registry, 432-433
International Genealogical Index, guides to, 430
Mormons, 433, 525
International Genealogical Index, 525
source of church registers, 525
Temple Records Index Bureau, 432
Munsell Index, 437
name indexes, 441-442
National Union Catalog of Manuscript Collections, *illus.*, 436
New York Public Libary card catalog, 435
newspapers, 416-417, 441
New York Times, 35, 59, 311, 409
parish and vital records listings, 432
pension records, Revolutionary War, 273
personal name, 429-430
primary or original sources, 429
printed genealogies, 436-437
probate court, 185
problems with, 429
publishers and booksellers catalogs, 435
regional, *listing*, 440-441
Revolutionary War service records, 255
Revolutionary War, 439
Rider's Index to family histories, 434
See also Court records, Dockets, 167
service records (1898-1902), 265
soldiers' headstones applications, (1870-1903), 281
subject index to, 439
surnames, 429
Temple Records Index Bureau, 432-433
to land patent records, 226
to land registrations, 218-219
Union Army in Civil War, 259
Waldenmaier, 438

Indian
1860 and 1870 censuses incomplete, 110

1910 census, partial, 102
allotment records, 248
census schedules 1840-1942 , *table*, 110-112
censuses 1910-1939, 118-19
claims in court of claims, 197
courts, state records of, 209
dissolution of Indian reservations, records of, 229
schools censuses 1910-1939, 118-19
scouts, 539-540
See also Native American research
Tennessee, lands in, 238
title to lands, 217
U.S. Court of Claims, records of, 540
U.S. Courts of Appeal, records of, 540
Veteran Administration, records of, 540
wars, 255, 259

Indian Claims Commission. *See* courts, *illus.*, 155
Indian Territories
land records of, 248
Union veterans census for, 105
Indiana
1860-1880 census, index to, *table*, 101
1870 census, 99
census, 109-112, 118-19
Confederate burials in, *table*, 264
correctional institutions in *table*, 302
court records, 209
divorces in, 88
Federal census, 1790-1910,*table*, 95
genealogical records of, 10
GIA indexes for, 437
graveyards, 68
indexes and abstracts, 424
Indianapolis, jurisdiction of, 533
land records summary, 241
Marion County, jurisdiction of, 533
marriage applications in, 80
marriage laws in, 83
military government of, 204
mortality schedules, *table*, 104
name changes, finding aids, 190
newspaper bibliography for, 420
plat maps and books, 229
printed court records, 194
Society of Pioneers, 679
Soundex, 100
state census schedules, 1623-1910, *table*, 114
state laws, printed, 182
tribal allotments for, 118
Union volunteers, indexes, *table*, 262
United Methodism archives, 145
veterans' home in, 281

Indictment for murder, example of, 160
See also court records, 160
Indictment jury. *See* Grand jury
Industry, in 1885 census, 103
Industry schedules, 1850-1880, location of, *table*, 109

Infant. *See* Orphan
Inferior Courts of Special Jurisdiction, *illus.*, 154
Inferior courts, colonial, *illus.*, 153
Inheritance,
in ecclesiastical courts, 237
laws of, 237
legal age, *table*, 186
of land, 237
Inquests. *See* Court records, Coroners'
Inscriptions, 68, 69
Insolvency, dockets of, 167
Inspection rolls, blacks in (1783), 562
Institute for Scientific Information (ISI), 13, 28
Institutional Records
biographical date form, *illus.*, 312
biographical information, 311, 313, 321
certificate of death form
convict dockets, 306
coroners', orphanage, and prison records, 301-325
Federal Agencies and Institutions, *table*, 302-304
fraternal organizations
hospital records registers, 322, *illus.*, 323
hospital records, immigrants, 462
indexing of, 321
list of survivors
locating, 322
matron's report, *illus.*, 321
microfilmed by the Genealogical Society of Utah, 322
mortician's records contain, 313
Mortuary, Jewish American Research, 608, 609
orphanage records, 321-322
Prison records, admission and discharge books, 301
prison records
availability, 311
death warrants, 309
list of executions, 311
pardon book, *illus.*, 310
reception descriptive lists of convicts, 306, 309
registers of prisoners, 301; *illus.*, 303
types of, 301, 306, 309
use and problems, 311
religious affiliation
residence of deceased, 311
See also, school, hospital, mortuary

Insurance companies, 50 largest, *listing*, 362
insurance records, 331-332
Intentions, marriage records *illus.*, 77
Interdecennial, 102-3
Interlibrary loan, 3, 14-15
Intermediary Court of Appeals, *illus.*, 153, 154
Internal Revenue Service. *See* IRS
International Genealogical Index (IGI), 2, 101, 123, 141
use of in British/European research, 476-480
International Ladies Garment Workers, 335

International Tracing Service, 617
Interviews, letter, 45-46
Intestate estates. *See* Court records, probate
Inventories
divorce case, 85
library holdings, 12
probate, 185
Iowa
bounty lands, 231
city directories index, 441
city/town schedules, *table*, 120
Confederate burials in, *table*, 264
correctional institutions in *table*, 302
county histories of, 441
Federal census, 1790-1910,*table*, 95
genealogical records of, 10
land records summary, 241-242
Mormon census for (1847, 1852), 123
mortality schedules, *table*, 104
Pilot Project, 407
plat maps and books, 229
printed court records, 194
records, index to, 441
state census schedules, 1623-1910, *table*, 114
state laws, printed, 182
Union Volunteers, indexes, *table*, 262
Irish immigrants,
1790, 453
1820-1860, 453
distribution of by state, *table*, 453
research aids and bibliographies, 505-506; *map*, 505
societies for, 468
IRS records, in urban research, 526
ISI. *See* Institute for Scientific Information, 28
Italian immigrants,
1880-1920, 454
Aryan descent, *Ahnenpass*, 456
migration patterns, 474
research aids and bibliography, 506-507; *map*, 506
relocation of, *table*, 453

J

JACL. *See* Japanese American Citizens League, 597
Jacobus's Index, to genealogical periodicals, 437
Jacobus, Donald Lines, 92, 216
Jail records
by Sheriff, 173
in court process, 173-174
Jamestowne, colonial society for descendants, 679
Janos Archives, Arizona records 1721-1900, 551
Japan Congress Library, 600
Japan, genealogical records in, 600
Japanese American Citizens League, 597

Japanese Canadian Citizens Association, 599
Japanese in the U.S. *See* Asian American research, 597-598
Japanese, in 1890 census, 100
Japanese-American relocations, *table*, 200
Jewelry,
birth information on, 35
family information in, 40
Jewish-American
aid societies, 613-614
American, Historical Society, collections of, 13
archives, 143
birth records, 606
burials, 68
circumcision records, 606
circumcision records, *illus.*, 609
congregational and community histories, Jewish, 608
death and cemetery records, 607, *illus.*, 609
Georgia, Savannah, 603
immigrants, from Poland, 475
immigration, after 1885, 454
locating, 608
marriage records, 606-607
marriage records, *illus.*, 608
migration patterns, 603
records, locating, 610
synagogue records in America, 605-608
tombstones
Jewish Child Care Association of New York, 13
Jewish Theological Seminary Library, 612
John Doggett Company, directory publisher, 387
John F. Trow, directory publisher, 387
Johnston, Zachariah, 436
Jonathan Sheppard Books, 15
Journals,
marriage records in, 83
vital records in, 50
Jubilee books, 524
Judah L. Magres Memorial Museum, 612
Judgements
example of, 165
lien, 157
probate court, 185
types of court, 165, 170
Judicial actions, in newspapers, 413
Judicial jurisdiction, *def.* of, 151
Julian calendar, 133
Juneau Indian Agency and school records, 318
Juniata College Library, 142
Jurisdictions, marriage records, 75-76
Jury of inquiry. *See* Court records, Coroner
Jury trial, in equity proceedings, 162
Jury, payroll, *illus.*, 172
Jury, record of, 156
Justice courts, *illus.*, 153, 154
Justice of the peace
marriage by, 137
marriage records, 75-76
Justice of the Peace Courts, *def.* of, 152
Juvenile courts, *illus.*, 154

K

Kansas
 1860-1880 census, index to, *table,* 101
 access to adoption records in, 192
 Cherokees in, 536
 claims of citizens against government, *table,* 200
 Confederate burials in, *table,* 264
 correctional institutions in *table,* 302
 Federal census, 1790-1910,*table,* 95
 Freedmen's Bureau records, 581
 land records summary, 242
 mortality schedules, *table,* 104
 newspaper bibliography for, 420
 plat maps and books, 229
 printed court records, 194
 state census schedules, 1623-1910, *table,* 115
 state laws, printed, 182
 Union Volunteers, indexes, *table,* 262
 veterans' home in, 281
Kates-Boylston Publications, 400
Kearny, General Steven W., 565
Kentucky
 1790 census, 125
 adoption in, 192
 adoption jurisidction in, *illus.,* 190
 Baptist records, 141
 black marriage records of, 582
 census, special schedules 1850-1880, *table,* 108
 Cherokees in, 536
 Confederate burials in, *table,* 264
 Confederate volunteers from, *table,* 262
 correctional institutions in *table,* 302
 courts of appeal, 192
 divorce in, 84, 87
 Federal census, 1790-1910,*table,* 95
 Freedmen's Bureau records, 581
 genealogical records of, 10
 Indexes and abstracts, 424
 land office in, 219
 land records summary, 242
 marriage laws in, 83
 marriage records in, 75
 military records, microfilmed by Genealogical Society of Utah, *table,* 264
 mortality schedules, *table,* 104
 newspaper bibliography for, 420
 poll tax in, 235
 printed court records of, 194
 registers of blacks, 592
 state census schedules, 1623-1910, *table,* 115
 state laws, printed, 182
 substitute for 1790 census schedule for, 125
 Union veterans census for, 105
 Union Volunteers, indexes, *table,* 262
Kentucky Cemetery Project, 66
Kickapoo, removal records, 538
Killinger Church, 70
Kilobytes. *See* Cg, 653
Kincaid Act (1904), 225
King George's War, 255
King Philip's War, 255
King William's War, 255
KKK. *See* Ku Klux Klans
Korean action, 255
Korean National Association, 598
Korean National Library and clan records, 600
Koreans in the U.S. *See* Asian American research, 598
Ku Klux Klan. *See* courts; *illus.,* 154
Ku Klux Klans, Congressional investigations of, 209

L

labor union records, 334-335
labor union records, *listing,* 344-352
Labor Unions, extra-legal activities of, 209
Laborers, included in directories, 387
Ladies Aid Society. *See* Auxiliary to the Sons of the Union, 676
Ladies of the Grand Army of the Republic, 676
Land and cattle companies, extra-legal activities of, 209
Land bank, federal and burial plots, 66
Land Claims Commissions. *See* courts
Land courts, *illus.,* 154
Land entry case files. *See* Land records
Land grants, 219-224
Land laws, history of, 224-225, 236, 238
Land offices, by state, 238-252
Land offices, records found in, 226
Land offices, survival of records, 219
Land and tax records, 216-253
 bounty land records,
  1812 war, 231
  abstracting, 218
  applications and warrants, 274
  deeds in fee simple, 217
  difficulty in finding, 219
  first title, 219
  indexes, 231
  late recording, 219
  locating records, 233
  map, 231
  Mexican war, 233
  military, 230-235
  patents for, 231
  scrip applic., 233
  signatures and seals on, 218-219
  types of, 237
  Virginia, 234-235
  warrant, *illus.,* 274
  warrants, available from NARS, 256-257
 directories, 396
 family information in, 40
 how to use, 236
 immigrant ownership, 469
 in county records, 217
 indexes to, 218-219, 441
 land claims, cancelled, 226
 land entry case files, 226
 land grant, *illus.,* 220
 land grants, New England systems of, 220-224
 land offices, 226
 Mexican national government, in, 561-562
 military bounty land, 230-235
 New England, jurisdiction in, 222
 patent, 217-226
 plat maps, 220
 plat maps, how to draw, *illus.,* 221
 private land claims, 229-230
 public domain states, 224-230
 residence in, 137
 southern land grants, 219-220
 Spanish and Mexican American research, 561-562, 565-567, 569-570
 state-by-state summary, 219-224, 238-252
 statute of frauds, 238
 survey field notes, 226
 taxes. *See* Taxes and tax records
 titles, 217-235
 township and range systems, *illus.,*225
 township plat map, 228
 tract book, *illus.,* 227
 tract books, 226
 under Spanish sovereignty, 561-562
 urban ancestors. *See also,* 521
 use of, 236-238
 use of, with city directories, 388
 western records of claims, 441
Land rushes, Oklahoma, 248
Land sold for back taxes, 185
Land titles, how to first acquire, 219
Land, grants and claims index, 441
Land, inheritance of, 237
Lands Mann Schaften. See memorial books
Landsat maps, National Cartographic Information Center, 16
Languages, programming, 653
Laotian refugees, 598
Laredo Archives, 562
Laws
 common, *def.* of, 151
 directories, 398-399
 enforcement records. *See* Court records, sheriff
 family relationships, 187
 list compilers, 399
 probate, published, 183
 regarding legal age, *table,* 186
 slaves, 187
Ledgers, probate, 185
Legal actions, types of, 152
Legal actions.
 See also Courts, 152
Legal age, by state, *table,* 186
Legal business, *See also* Courts and Courts records
Legal notices in newspapers, 413
Legal procedures. *See* Court procedures
Legal records, family information in, 40
Legal terms, 151-152
Legalities, 23-28
Legislative papers, 185
Legislatures. *See* Courts,appeals, 192
Legitimation, in probate, 185
Leo Baeck Institute, 612
Letters
 birth information in, 35
 recommendation, emigrant, 454
 thanks, from immigrants, 467
 testamentary, 185
 vital records in, 50
Levi, Levi Andrew, 248
Lewers, Eva, collection of, 541
Lexington Theological Seminary, 142
Libraries
 business directories, 398
 call numbers, 2
 church records in, 140
 city directories, 396
 civil and military service registers, 400
 collections of Bible records, 63
 directories, 387
 early professional directories, 400
 genealogical periodical indexes, 438
 guide to holdings, 12
 in urban research, 528
 index to local history biographies, 437
 inventories, 12
 libraries, medical and medical directories, 399
 library catalogs, 664-665
 manuscript collections of, 435
 map collection of, 16, 394, 521
 Martindale-Hubbell directory, 399
 newspaper files, 407
 newspaper indexes, 417
 organizational directories, 402
 post office and street directories, 403
 private computer systems, 436
 professional directories, 400
 Protestant Episcopal records, 146
 publisher's catalogs, 435
 railroad records, 339
 religious directories, 402
 religious directories, 402
 state and private, list of, 139
 Texan provincial records, 561
 union records, 339
Licenses,
 dental, 333
 illus., 79, 80
 Indiana, 80
 issued by local courts, 151
 marriage, 80
 medical, 333
 Utah, 80
 Wyoming, 80
Lien book, in sheriff records, 173
Liens, 185
Life estate, in land, 237
Life insurance companies, *listing,* 343
Lindsey, Isaac, 238
Lineage societies, records of. *See,* Hereditary and Lineage

Society records, 671-688
Lipe receipt roll, 1879-80, 518
Lis Pendens, 185
Litchfield Historical Society, 247
Lithuania, Jewish records of, microfilmed, 615
Lithuanian immigrants, research aids and bibliography, 498
Livery of seizen, of land, 237
Livingston family, 680
Lloyd family, 680
Lloyds registers, passenger list resource, 464
Local census
    1623-1918, 119-126
    by schools, 121
    churches, 121
    function different now, 151
    sheriff's data, 121
    social function of, 151
    units of governments, 151
Local histories,
    biographies in, 447
    Greenlaw Index, 437
    in Munsell Index, 437
    indexed by University of Michigan, 435
    indexes for, 436
Local History and Genealogy Room,
    Library of Congress, 4
Local scrapbooks, to locate businesses, 371
Los Angeles Public Library, indexed listings of card catalog, 435
Lottery, for land in Georgia, 125
Louisiana
    access to adoption records in, 192
    Baton Rouge, jurisdiction of, 533
    black families in, 579
    black marriage records of, 582
    census, special schedules 1850-1880, *table*, 108
    colonial society of, 679
    Confederate pensions for, 279
    Confederate volunteers from, *table*, 262
    correctional institutions in, 302
    divorces in, 88
    East Baton Rouge Parish, jurisdiction of, 533
    Federal census, 1790-1910,*table*, 95
    Freedmen's Bureau records, 581
    French land law in, 237
    Historical Center, 243
    indexes and abstracts, 424
    indexes to land patents, 226
    Indians in, 541
    land records summary, 242-243
    marriage contracts in, 78
    military records, indexes, *table*, 261
    military records, microfilmed by Genealogical Society of Utah, *table*, 264
    mortality schedules, *table*, 104
    New Orleans, registration of vital records in (1790), 49
        registration of vital records in (1790) 49
    newspaper bibliography for, 420
    printed court records, 194
    state census schedules, 1623-1910, *table*, 115
    state laws, printed, 182
    Union veterans census for, 105
    Union volunteers, indexes, *table*, 262
Loyal Ladies League. *See* Ladies of the Grand Army of the Republic
Loyalists, records of, 257, 259
Luck, Winston F. 66
Ludlow, Edwin, collection of, 541
Lunacy commitments, dockets of, 167
Lutheran
    Archives Center at Philadelphia, 144
    archives, 143
    baptisms, 131
    births, 131
    church in America, 143-144
    church records, 131, 143
    Council in the U.S., 144
    Free church, 143
    Southern Seminary, 144
Lutheran church-Missouri Synod, 144
Lutheran congregational records
    Swedish-American, 144

M

Magill Historical Library, 146
Magistrates' courts, *illus.*, 153, 154
Magna Charta, membership society, 685
Magres, Judah L., museum, 612
Maine
    York County, court records microfilmed, 175
    1790 census, 124
    adoption in, 192
    adoption jurisdiction in, *illus.*, 190
    bounty land grants, 231
    correctional institutions in *table*, 302
    direct tax list for, 236
    divorce in, 84, 86
    Federal census, 1790-1910,*table*, 95
    genealogical records of, 10
    inheritance by adoptees, 192
    land records summary, 243
    mortality schedules, *table*, 104
    newspaper bibliography for, 420
    Old Cemetery Association, 66
    Piscataqua Pioneers of, 678
    Portland, city directories, 397
    printed court records of, 194
    state census schedules, 1623-1910, *table*, 115
    state laws, printed, 182
    Union veterans census for, 105
    Union volunteers, indexes, *table*, 262
    veterans' home in, 281
Malcolm of Scotland, 685
Manifests. *See* passenger lists, 462-465
Manscript collections, Library of Congress, 435
Manufacture schedules, 1850-1880, location of, *table*, 109
Manumission, 185
    court records of, 209
    for emigrants, 454
    in deed books, 217
    papers, of black, 579
    records, 591
    Society of Guilford COunty, North Carolina, 593
manuscripts collections, 341
Manuscripts, permission to use, 28
Maps
    battlefields
    cemeteries of, 66
    cities available for, 521
    collections, locality, 15-16
    colonial roads, 16
    copying of, 521
    county boundaries, former, 16
    county or city, of cemeteries, 66
    eastern United States, 16
    fire insurance, 521
    historical, 15, 16
    land grant bounds, 16
    land ownership, 16
    metropolitan areas,
    national parks
    on microfilm, 16
    problems of, 15
    property tax, 16
    scales of, 16
    See also, plat maps
    See Directories, maps
    sheet maps, 15
    topographical, 15
    U.S. Geodetic Survey quad, 66
    U.S. territorial acquisitions, *illus.*, 560
    urban ancestors. *See also*, 521
    USGS, specialty, 16
    using with directories, 394
    western United States, 16
Marine Corps, register, 399
Marines, military records of, 267
Markers, buried and moved, 69
Marriage
    certificates, 35, 80
    contracts, 185
        French, 78
        Louisiana, 78
        Spanish, 78
    legal age for, *table*, 186
Marriage date
    Civil War pension applications, 84
    in biographies, 446
    in business directories, 397
    in estate records, *See also* court records, 164
Marriage information, from 1900 census, 84
Marriage laws, English, 84
Marriage license, 35; *illus.*, 79, 80; application for, *illus.*, 3 36
    of blacks, 581
    illus., 79, 80
    illus. of application for, 36
Marriage property settlements. *See* Deeds
Marriage records, 35-37, 75-88, 133-134
    banns, 76
    bonds, 77
    bond *illus.*, 77
    Catholic, 134
    certificates, 35, 80
    church, 140
    collected by,
        DAR, 83
        Genealogical Society of Utah, 83
        Works Progress Administration, 83
    consent affidavits, 76
    county, 137
    Declaration of Intent, *illus.*, 76
    found in, 83
    German Reformed, 134
    in court records, 83
    in New England, 75
    in newspapers, 83, 409, 410
    in Philadelphia, 396
    in the South, 75, 76
    intentions, 76
    Jewish American Research, 607-608
    jurisdictions, 75-76
    kept by churches, 75
    kept by colonial governors, 75
    kept by justices of the peace, 75-76
    kept by local governments, 75
    kept by military and naval personnel, 75
    kept by ministers, 75
    locating, 81, 83
    Lutheran, 134
    marriage licenses, of blacks, 581
    marriage registers and returns, 80-81
    marriage returns, *illus.*, 82
    of blacks, 209, 581, 583
    problems, 83
    registration required (1538), 131
    Spanish and Mexican American research, 563-564
    spelling variants, 84
    state boards of health, 75
    types of, 76-81
    urban research, 522
Marriage settlement, 177, 185
    in pension files for Civil War, 279
    notices of in newspapers, 409-410
Marriages, common law, 83
Marital status of deceased, on death certificate, 53
Maryland
    1790 census, 124
    admiralty court, *table*, 196
    adoption in, 192
    adoption jurisdiction in, *illus.*, 190
    appeals in Court of Delegates, 192
    Baltimore city archives, holdings of, 529
    Baltimore, ethnic and immigrant societies, 468
    Baltimore, jurisdiction of, 533
    bounty land grants, 231
    census, special schedules 1850-1880, *table*, 108
    Confederate burials in, *table*, 264

Confederate volunteers from, *table*, 262
copyhold in, 237
correctional institutions in *table*, 302
direct tax list for, 236
divorce in, 86
early court system in, 192
Federal census, 1790-1910,*table*, 95
Frederick County, 1850 census, 18
Freedmen's Bureau records, 581
genealogical records of, 10
index to wills, 441
indexes and abstracts, 424
land records summary, 243
mortality schedules, *table*, 104
newspaper bibliography for, 420-21
printed court records of, 194
published Committee of Safety records, 206
registers of blacks, 592
Revolutionary War land grants, *table*, 232
state census schedules, 1623-1910, *table*, 115
state laws, printed, 182
Union veterans census for, 105
Union volunteers, indexes, *table*, 262
volunteers in Revolutionary War, *table*, 256
Maryland Historical Society Hall of Records, 236
Masonian patent papers, 245
Masonic burials, 68
Massachusetts
1790 census, 124
admiralty court, *table*, 196
adoption in, 192
adoption jurisdiction in, *illus.*, 190
bounty land grants, 231
census, special schedules 1850-1880, *table*, 108
city directories, 397
city/town schedule, *table*, 121
Confederate burials in, *table*, 264
correctional institutions in *table*, 303
direct tax list for, 236
divorce in, 86, 88
early court system in, 192
Federal census, 1790-1910,*table*, 95
Freedman in, 580
genealogical records of, 10
indexes and abstracts, 424
Jews in, 613
land records summary, 244
maritime records of, 527
marriage records in, 75
Massachusetts Bay, deeds recorded, 222
mortality schedules, *table*, 104
name changes, finding aids, 190
Nantucket County, jurisdiction of, 533
naturalization records, 525
newspaper bibliography for, 421
Plymouth Colony, divorce in, 86
published Committee of Safety records, 206
records of, printed court, 194
Revolutionary War land grants, *table*, 232
settlement 1820-1860, 453
state census schedules, 1623-1910, *table*, 115
state laws, printed, 182
Suffolk County, jurisdiction of, 533
Union veterans census for, 105
Union volunteers, indexes, *table*, 262
volunteers in Revolutionary War, *table*, 256
Massachusetts State Archives, court record's index, 167
Mausoleum, 63
Mayflower Compact, extra-legal association, 207
Mayors' courts, *illus.*,153, 154
McCormick Theological Seminary, 145
Meadville Theological School of Lombard College, 147
Medical associations, local and state medical directories, 399
Medical directories, 399
Medical examiner. *See* Coroners' records
Medical licenses, 333
Medical records, 322
location of, 399
of prisoners, 173
medical/dental licenses, 333
Membership records, church, 135
Memorial books, 617
Memorials and monuments, 63
Mennonite church archives, 144
Mennonites, 131, 137
Mercantile Agency, R.G. Dun and Company, 332
Merriam, Grace, papers of, 541
Meserve, John, collection of, 541
Metes and bounds, Southern system of, 219
Methodist church archives, 144-145
Methodists, German pastors, 137
Metropolitan areas, maps of, 16
Mexican Archives (1833-45), 239
Mexican national government, California records under, 569-571
Mexican National Government, New Mexico records under, 565-568
Mexican War Military Society of 1846-1848, 655
Mexican War, 255, 259
bounty land warrants for, 233
claims for, *table*, 199
records of possession during, 562
Mexican. *See* Spanish and Mexican American research
Mexico, claims against by U.S. citizens, *table*, 200
Meyhew family, 680
Michigan
city/town schedule, *table*, 121
correctional institutions in *table*, 303
Detroit, city directories, 397
Federal census, 1790-1910,*table*, 95
genealogical records of, 10
indexes and abstracts, 424
land records summary, 244
maritime records of, 527
military records, indexes, *table*, 261
mortality schedules, *table*, 104
newspaper bibliography for, 421
plat maps and books, 229
state census schedules, 1623-1910, *table*, 115
state laws, printed, 182
Union veterans census for, 105
Union volunteers, indexes, *table*, 262
Micro-opaque, records on, 2
Microfiche, records on, 2
Microfilm
Confederate records, 265
family group sheets, 432
family histories, University of Michigan, 435
how to read, 92
indexes of Revolutionary War, 255
marriage registers
newspapers, 408, 416
of bound volumes, 2
printed books, 2
recorded deeds, 2
records on, 2
Microfilming Corporation of America, and local histories, 435
Microform
copies of original manuscripts, 3
newspapers on, 2, 408
obtaining through interlibrary loan, 2
telephone directories on, 2
Midwest, genealogical records of, 9
Midwest, settlement 1820-1860, 453
Midwestern Evangelical Synod of North America, 147
Midwife records, in urban research, 522
Migration patterns, 14, 16-17
Migration records, of slaves, 592
Migrations, tracing, in newspapers, 414
Military Bounty Land, *See* Land records, bounty land
Military government, of Indians, 204
Military homes, records of, *table*, 264
Military installations, in censuses, 91
Military land grants, Revolutionary War, *table*, 232
Military offenses, courts-martial for, 204
Military Order of Foreign Wars of the United States, 675
Military Order of the Crusades, 685
Military Order of the Loyal Legion of the United States, 675-676
Military Order of the World Wars, 676
Military records, 255-298
bibliography of, 294-298
blacks in 580-581
bounty land applications, 274
bounty land warrant, *illus.*, 274
Brigham Young University, index to Revolutionary War records, 294
burial records, 280-281
censuses 1840, 1890, 285
Civil War , 259-265
Civil War, pension application, *illus.*, 276-278
Civil War, pension records of, 275-280
Civil War, Union Army records of, 259
Colonial wars (1675-1763), 255
Confederate army volunteers, indexes, *table*, 262
Confederate military academy, 265
Confederate reconstruction court, 265
Confederate records, checklist of , *table*, 265, 266, 267
Confederate records, pensions, 279
Confederate records, soldiers' burials, 263
Confederate records, soldiers' burials, *table*, 264
Confederate war records, card abstracts 263-265
correspondence files of burials, 281
courts-martial, 197-204
Courts, Courts-martial
deserters list, *illus.*, 259
discharge records, 265, 267
draft records, modern, 265
headstone applications, 281
hereditary "war" societies, 671-676
indexes (1812-48), 259
indexes to, 439-440
indexes to, 439
Indian wars, *table*, 261, 175
Indians in Veterans Administration records, 540
Korean action, 255
local, 294
loyalist sources, 257, 259
marines, 267
Mexican war, *table*, 261, 275
microfilmed by Genealogical Society of Utah, *table*, 264
missing in action file, 281-282
muster lists, 202
muster rolls, 255; *illus.*, 260
NARS, *table* available from, 256-257
National Personnel Records Center, modern records, 265
pension application file, *illus.*, 285-291
pension records, (1789-1861), 274-275
pension records, of blacks, 580-581
periodical sources of, 294
personnel files of, 371
Philippine Insurrection, discharge records of, 265
printed sources, 285
private collections, 294
revolutionary pension file, *illus.*, 267-271
Revolutionary War pension application, *illus.*, 273

Revolutionary War, 255-267
Revolutionary War, DAR
Patriot Index, 294
Revolutionary War, index to, 256-257
Revolutionary War, pensions for, 267
see also courts, courts martial
Selective Service in urban research, 525
Spanish American war, 265-267
state military records, 294
Union army volunteers, indexes, *table*, 262
veteran's
biographical sketch, *illus.*, 292-293
homes, 281, 285
medical records, modern, 265
records of benefits, 267-294
schedules in 1890 census
Vietnam action, 255
War of 1812, *table*, 261, 274
World War I burial records, 281
World War I, 265-267
World War I, discharge records, 265
World War I, draft records of, 265
World War II, 265-267
World War II, discharge records, 267
Military reserve district, Virginia, 234
Military service
in 1890 census, 100
in biographies, 445
in epitaphs, 69
morticians' records, in, 313
register, 399
Militia court, for courts-martials, 197
Miller Roll, 1910, 518
Miller, Guion, 536
Milwaukee Public Library, mortality schedules for Wisconsin, *table*, 105
Mining Districts, records of, 207
Mining, schedule, 1870, location of, *table*, 109
Ministers
itinerant, 402
marriage records, 75
records of, 140, 332
Minnesota
1857 census falsified, 91
1860-1880 census, index to, *table*, 101
adoption records in, 192
census, special schedules 1850-1880, *table*, 108
correctional institutions in *table*, 303
court records, 194
Federal census, 1790-1910,*table*, 95
genealogical records of, 10
land records summary, 244
Minnesota Historical Society, 108
mortality schedules, *table*,104
newspaper bibliography for, 421
Rockford, 1890 census, 101
special census in 1850-1880, *table*, 108
St. Paul, city directories, 397
state census schedules, 1623-1910, *table*, 116
state laws, printed, 182
Union veterans census for, 105
Union volunteers, indexes, *table*, 262
Wright County 1890 census
Minors' estates, in probate, 185
Minute dockets, *See* also Court records, Dockets, 167
Minutes of the church council, 135
"Minutes of the Committee of Safety", 206
Minutes, probate court, 185
Minutes, types of court, 165, 168-169
Misdemeanors, 152
Missing censuses, listings of, 124-125
Missing persons, ads for, 414
Mississippi
adoption investigations, 192
black marriage records of, 582
census, special schedules 1850-1880, *table*, 108
city/town schedule, *table*, 121
Confederate pensions for, 279
Confederate volunteers from, *table*, 262
correctional institutions in *table*, 303
court records, 194
Federal census, 1790-1910,*table*, 95
Freedmen's Bureau records, 581
Indexes and abstracts, 424
Indians in, 541
land records summary, 244
military records, microfilmed by Genealogical Society of Utah, *table*, 264
mortality schedules, *table*, 104
newspaper bibliography for, 421
Order of the First Families of 1699-1817, 659
state census schedules, 1623-1910, *table*, 116
state laws, printed, 182
Union veterans census for, 105
Union volunteers, indexes, *table*, 262
veterans' home in, 285
Missouri
burial grounds, 66
Cherokees in, 536
city/town schedule, *table*, 121
Confederate burials in, *table*, 264
Confederate volunteers from, *table*, 262
correctional institutions in, *table*, 303
court records, 194
Federal census, 1790-1910,*table*, 95
Freedmen's Bureau records, 581
genealogical records of, 10
indexes and abstracts, 424
Indians in, 541
Kansas City, city directories, 397
land claims, 245
land records summary, 244-245
military land reserves, 231
military records, microfilmed by Genealogical Society of Utah, *table*, 264
mortality schedules, *table*, 104
newspaper bibliography for, 421
plat maps and books, 229
registers of blacks, 592
St. Louis, city directories, 397
St. Louis, jurisdiction of, 533
state census schedules, 1623-1910, *table*, 116
state laws, printed, 182
Union veterans census, 105
Union volunteers, indexes, *table*, 262
Mitchell, Katie Edward Bemo, collection of, 541
Modern American records, (1870-), 333-335
Mohel register, 606
Montana
1870 census, 388
adoption records in, 192
census, special schedules 1850-1880, *table*, 108
correctional institutions in *table*, 303
court records, 194
Federal census, 1790-1910,*table*, 95
genealogical records of, 10
land records summary, 245
mining district, extra-legal, 207
mortality schedules, *table*, 104
state census schedules, 1623-1910, *table*, 116
state laws, printed, 182
Union veterans census for, 105
Union volunteers, indexes, *table*, 262
Yellowstone National Park, 533
Montreal, Jews in, (1760s) 583
Montrose Genealogical Services, 660
Monument art, 63
illus., of, 63
inscriptions, 60, 63
Monument inscriptions, 60, 63
Monuments and memorials, *See also* Tombstones, 63
Moody's Investors Service, 340
Moravian church archives, 145
Mormons
census records of, 123
church archives, 142
land distribution of, 251
missionary program of, 137
Morris family, 680
Morristown National Historical Park, Revolutionary War Collection, 294
Mortality records
1890-1900 destroyed, 50
in 1885 census, 103
in decennial census, 50
state-by-state depositories for, 104-105
Mortgages. *See* Deeds
Mortician records
problems with, 313
vital records in, 50, 58, 301, 311-313, 335
mortuaries, 335
Mother of deceased on death certificate, 53
Mulatto
in 1870 census, 99
in 1890 census, 100
Mullay Roll
1848, 518
1858, 517
Multi-generation pedigrees, 14
Municipal archives
city vital records in, 522
holdings of, 529
Munsell Index, for printed genealogies, 437
Murder trial. *See* court records, criminal
Musicians, lists of, in newspapers, 411
Muslim burials, 68
Muster list, for military, 202

N

Nacogdoches Archives, Texan records, 559
Names
change of, 187-190
christian, of slaves, 579
spelling of in Soundex, 99-100
in mortality schedules, 50
in prison records, 301
Name index. *See* Soundex, 3
NARS. *See* National Archives, 257
National Archives
black records in, 580, 582
bounty land claims, 274
bounty land records, 231, 233
burial records, 66
California land records, 569-570
Cherokee census of 1835, 517-518
city censuses in, *table*, 120-121
civil and military service registers, 400
collections of Bible records, 63
Confederate records in, 263
histories of Confederate military units, 263
land patents, 224
maritime records, 527
microfilm catalogs of census, 127
mortality schedules, 103
mortality schedules, *table*, 104-105
Native American research, 535
passenger lists in, 463 , 612
records services, 139
Revolutionary War service records of, 257
Revolutionary War, pension applications, 273
Texas provincial records, 561
National Cartographic Information Center, 16
aerial photographs, 16
Landsat maps, colored, 16
topographical maps, color separates of, 16
National Directory of Local Researchers, 443

National Endowment for the Humanities newspaper project, 407
National Fire Protection Association, 372
National Genealogical Society, 23
National Historic Trust for Records Preservation, for private military collection, 294
National Huguenot Society, 684-685
National parks, maps of, 16
National Retail Dry Goods Association, 372
National societies, for immigrants, 681-684
National Society Children of the American Revolution, 674
National Society Daughters of Colonial Wars, 671
membership in. *See also* DAR, 674
National Society Daughters of the American Revolution, 677
National Society of Americans of Royal Descent, 685
National Society of Colonial Dames of the XVII Century, 660
National Society of Dames of the Court of Honor, 681
National Society of Daughters of the Barons of Runnemede, 685
National Society of Lords of the Maryland Manors, 681
National Society of Magna Charta Dames, 685
National Society of New England Women, membership in, 677
National Society of Old Plymouth Colony, 678
National Society of the Children of the American Colonists, 681
National Society of the Colonial Dames of America, 680
National Society of the Colonial Daughters of the of America, 677
National Society of the Daughters of Founders and Patriots of America, 677
National Society of the Daughters of the American Colonists, 680
National Society of the Daughters of Utah Pioneers, 677
National Society of Women Descendents of the Ancient and Honorable Artillery Company, 671
National Society Sons of the American Revolution, 674
National Society Southern Dames of America, 681
National Society United States Daughters of 1812, 655
National Technical Information Service, 28
Nationality (Ethnic) Societies, 681-684
Nationality reference directory, immigrant patterns in, 492
Native American Research, 535-557
1890 census, 100
1900 census Cherokee Nation, *illus.*, 528
Apache, Chiricahua, 539
Apache, Warm Springs, 539
Army records in National Archives, 540
BIA field office records, *table*, 554-557
Indian Civil War claims, 539
Indian removal records, 538
civilization division, 539
enrollment records, 538-539
finance division, 539
BIA records in National Archives, 537-540
land division records, 538
law and probate divisions, 539
statistics division, 539
Cantoment Agency, records of, *table*, 542
case studies, 542-551
census, 1900 Soundex, *illus.*, 525
Cherokee Commission on Citizenship, 536
1851 Drennen Roll, *illus.*, 533
application, *Illus.*, 548-550
census of 1835, 517
censuses, east of Mississippi, 535-536
censuses, west of Mississippi, 536-537
enrollment of, 538-539
finance division of BIA, 539
Henderson Roll, 535
land division records, 538
Cherokee records, 535-537, *table*, 542
Trail of Tears, 537
removal records, 538
Cherokee, census, 537
Chickasaw records, 535
in Civil War, 539
records of, *table*, 542
removal records, 538
in Civil War, 539
records of, *table*, 542
Choctaw records, 535
removal records, 538
Choctaw records,
census, enumerations, and indexes, 537
Confederate War Department records, 540-541
court records in National Archives, 540
in Civil War, 539
Creek records, 536, *table*, 542
removal records, 538
Delaware-Cherokee index, 536
Five Civilized Tribes, 537-542
index to, *illus.*, 544
map, 541
records of, *table*, 542
Indian pioneer history, sources, 541
Indians, intermarriage among, 541
Oklahoma Historical Society, 541
Oklahoma, Indians of, *map*, 542
records for, *table*, 542
repositories, 535
Seminole freedmen, 537
Seminole records, census and indexes, 537
Seminole, records, census and indexes, 537
records of, *table*, 542
scouts, 539
Shawnee, with Cheroke, 537
Naturalization
amnesty act, through, 469
in 1890 census, 100
legal age for, *table*, 186
on census, 474
on church records, 474
on homestead applications, 474
on voter registration records, 474
Virgin Islands in, 469
Naturalization Records, 37, 170, 469
birth information in, 35
certificates, 37-38; *illus.* of, 38
immigrants records, 469-472
summary of provisions, *table*, 470-472
use of, with city directories, 388
Naturalization records, 525
Naturalization records, 610
in New York City, 396
Naval personnel, marriage reocrds of, 75
marriage records of, 75
Naval service register, 399
Nebraska
1860-1880 census, index to, *table*, 101
1885 census, 102
adoption records in, 192
cemeteries in, relocated, 66
census, special schedules 1850-1880, *table*, 108
correctional institutions in, 303
court records, 194
Federal census, 1790-1910,*table*, 95
genealogical records of, 10
Indexes and abstracts, 424
land records summary, 245
mortality schedules, *table*, 104
newspaper bibliography for, 421
plat maps and books, 229
state census schedules, 1623-1910, *table*, 116
state laws, printed, 182
Union veterans census for, 105
Union volunteers, indexes, *table*, 262
Negroes. *See* Black research
Neighborhoods, in urban research, 528
Netherlands
church records, 131
Jewish records of, microfilmed, 616-617
Netherlands Society of Philadelphia, 684
Netherlands, The. *See* Dutch
Nevada
Carson City, jurisdiction of, 533
census, special schedules 1850-1880, *table*, 108
correctional institutions in, *table*, 303
court records of, 194
divorces in, 88
Federal census, 1790-1910,*table*, 95
genealogical records of, 10
indexes to land patents, 226
land records summary, 245
mining district, extra-legal, 207
mortality schedules, *table*, 104
newspaper bibliography for, 421
state census schedules, 1623-1910, *table*, 116
state laws, printed, 182
Union veterans census for, 105
Union volunteers, indexes, *table*. 262
New England
burial traditions, 68
church records from, 142
colonial land history of, 222
congregational records from, 142
divorce easy in, 88
Historic Genealogical Society Library (Boston),
and photographic and field notes archives, 66
land inheritance in, 238
land records, jurisdiction in, 222
marriage records in, 75
Methodist Historical Society Library, 145
National Society of Women, 677
newspaper indexes, 417
royal lineage in, 685
town system, 219
vital records in, 50
vital records of at Genealogical Society library, 51-52
New Hampshire
1790 census, 124
admiralty court, *table*, 196
adoption in, 192
adoption jurisdiction in, *illus.*, 190
border dispute of, 251
correctional institutions in, *table*, 303
court records of, 194
deserters in Revolutionary War, *illus.*, 259
direct tax list for, 236
divorce in, 85, 86
Federal census, 1790-1910,*table*, 95
genealogical records of, 10
immigrants in, *table*, 453
indexes and abstracts, 424
land records summary, 245
marriage records in (1640) 75
mortality schedules, *table*, 104
state census schedules, 1623-1910, *table*, 116
state laws, printed, 182
Union veterans census for, 105
Union volunteers, indexes, *table*, 262
volunteers in Revolutionary War, *table*, 256
New Jersey
1783 tax lists for, 125

1790 census, 125
admiralty court, *table*, 196
adoption in
adoption jurisdiction in, *illus.*, 190
appeals in Prerogative Court, 192
Cherokees in, 536
Confederate burials in, *table*, 264
correctional institutions in, *table*, 303
court records of, 194
divorce in, 86, 88
Federal census, 1790-1910,*table*, 95
genealogical records of, 10
Hudson County 1890 census, 101
index to records, 441
inheritance by adoptees, 192
Jersey City 1890 census, 101
land allotment in, 219
land records summary, 245-246
Monmouth Co., passenger lists, 464
Monmouth County, Historical Association, 464
mortality schedules, *table*, 104
newspaper bibliography for, 421
no bounty land grants, 231
primogeniture in, 238
proprietors and their lands, 1664-1776, 246
records, index to, 441
state census schedules, 1623-1910, *table*, 116
state laws, printed, 182
substitute for 1790 census schedule, 123
Union veterans census for, 105
Union volunteers, indexes, *table*, 262
vigilante records of, 207
volunteers in Revolutionary War, *table*, 256

New Mexico
1860-1880 census, index to, *table*, 101
1870 census, 388
1885 census, 102
church records of, 568
Confederate burials in, *table*, 264
correctional institutions in, *table*, 303
court records of, 194
federal census, 1790-1910,*table*, 95
genealogical records in, 559
land records of, 565-567
land records summary, 246
location of records, *listing*, 572
mining district, extra-legal, 207
mortality schedules, *table*, 104
newspaper bibliography for, 421
printed court records of, 194
private land, claims in, 567
Southwest Mexico, *See also*
Spanish land system in, 229
Spanish records of, 565-568
state census schedules, 1623-1910, *table*, 116
state laws, printed, 182
Union veterans census for, 105
Union volunteers, indexes, *table*, 262

New Netherland. *See* New Jersey, 245
New Orleans. *See* Louisiana
New Sweden. *See also* Delaware, 240
New York
1790 census, 124
admiralty court, *table*, 196
adoption jurisdiction in, *illus.*, 190
Albany, Dutch Settlers Society of, 684
Binghamton, city directories, 397
blacks in first census, 124
border dispute of, 251
bounty land grants, 231
Bronx, vital records in, 522
Brookhaven Township, 1890 census, 101
Brooklyn, vital records in, 522
city/town schedule, *table*, 121
Clinton county, 1880 census, 18
Colonial Order of the Acorn chapter, 680
Confederate burials in, *table*, 264
correctional institutions in, *table*, 303
court records, 176, 194
direct tax list for, 236
divorce in, 84, 86, 88
early court system in, 192
Eastchester, 1890 census, 101
election districts of, 388
Federal census, 1790-1910,*table*, 95
Freedman in, 580
genealogical records of, 11
Hastings, 402
Hebrew Immigration Aid Society, 613
immigrant population in 1910, 454
immigrants in, *table*, 453
indexes and abstracts, 424-425
Indian court records in, 209
Italian immigrants, 454
land allotment in, 219
land inheritance in, 238
land records summary, 246
Long Island, deeds recorded, 222
Manhattan
death regesters, 396
vital records in, 522
military records, indexes, *table*, 261
Morristown National Historical Park collections, 294
mortality schedules, *table*, 104
Municipal Archives of New York City, 529
naturalization records, 396, 525
New York City
city directories, 397
correctional institutions in, *table*, 303
directories for, 388
indexes of genealogy and local histories, 435
Jews in, 613
map collection in, 521
Municipal archives, 522
New York Historical Society, 387
newspapers indexes, 417
printed vital records, 522
urban jurisdictions of, 533
Bronx, 533 Kings (Brooklyn), 533 New York (Manhattan), 533
New York City, 533
newspaper bibliography for, 421
Queens, vital records in, 522
quitrient land taxes, 236
registration rolls, immigrants, 465
Revolutionary War land grants, *table*, 232
Richmond, vital records in, 522
Rochester city directory, 393
Russian immigrants, 454
Saint David's Society of the State of, 684
Saint Nicholas Society of the City of New York, 676
Schenectady, city directories, 397
settlement 1820-1860, 453
settlers in, censused (1806), 123
state census schedules, 1623-1910, *table*, 116
state laws, printed, 182
Staten Island, vital records in, 522
Suffolk County, 1890 census, 101
Sussex County, deeds in, 222
taxes in, 236
Union veterans census for, 105
Union volunteers, indexes, *table*, 262
veterans' home in, 285
volunteers in Revolutionary War, *table*, 256
Westchester County, 1890 census, 101
Westchester County, 402

New York Times Index, 416
New York Times obituary index, 409
Newberry Library, 17, 377, 417
atlas for the city of Chicago (1900), 394
church records source, 525
help in searching 1850-1900 censuses, 504
index to 1860 census, 101
local histories index, 437
plat books and land maps, 229
publishers' catalogs in, 435
railroad records in, 527
Newspapers, 407-426
accidental deaths reported in, 409
ads for missing people, 414
anniversary announcements of, 410
biographies in, 411-412, 417
birth announcements in, 140, 410
birth records in, 35, 411
blacks, 416
community, 410
death records in, 408-409
divorce proceedings, 413
divorce records in, 87
estate claims, 414
firemen, lists of, in, 411
foreign language in U.S., 416, 467
genealogical columns in, 416
historical artricles in current, 416
hospital reports published, 462
how to locate, 407
how to search inclusive, 408-416
illnesses announced in, 410
immigrant arrivals in, 466, 467
indentured servants, announcements of, 416
index by American Antiquarian Society, 416
indexes of, 416-417, 441
Japanese, 599
judicial actions in, 413
legal notices in, 413; *illus.*, 512
letter lists, 414; *illus.*, 414
list of war dead in, 409; *illus.*, 409
lists of disaster victims in, 409
local history in, 140
marriage announcements in, 83, 410
memorial gifts, accounts of, 63
microfilmed, 408, 416
migrations, 414
military casualty lists in, 408
murders reported in, 409
musicians, lists of, in, 411
notices of marriage, 409-410
obituaries in, 408-409
policemen, lists of, in, 411
political groups, lists of, in, 411
probate in, 413
probate, *illus.*, 413
problems with, 417
real estate transactions in, 407, 413
religious, 416
retirees, lists of, in, 411
school news in, 411
slaves, announcements of runaway, 415-416
suicides reported in, 409
vistors announced in, 410
vital records in, 50
wedding announcement of, 410
wills in, 413
women and children, data on, in local, 411

Newssheets, specialty, how to locate, 372
Niagara frontier, sheriff census in, 121
Night courts, *illus.*, 154
Non-commoners, land rights of in New England, 222
Non-Conformist, list of chapels, 477; *illus.*, 479
Non-parochial registers, list of, 479
North Carolina
1790 census, 124
admiralty court, *table*, 196
adoption in, 192

adoption jurisdiction in, *Illus*, 190
bounty land grants, 231
census, special schedules 1850-1880, *table*, 108
Cherokees in, 535-536
city/town schedule, *table*, 121
Cleveland County, 101
Confederate
military records of, 263, 279
Confederate volunteers from, *table*, 262
copyhold in, 237
correctional institutions in, *table*, 303
court records, 194
Court of Conference in, 192
divorce in, 87, 88
extra-legal courts, 204
federal census, 1790-1910,*table*, 96
Freedmen's Bureau records, 581
Gaston County, 1890 census, 101
genealogical records of, 11
immigrants and arrivals, list of, 465; *table*, 453
indexes and abstracts, 425
Indian court records in, 209
Lake Junaluska, 145
land records summary, 247
military records, indexes, *table*, 261
military records, microfilmed by Genealogical Society of Utah, *table*, 264
mortality schedules, *table*, 104
newspaper bibliography for, 421
poll taxes in, 235
primogeniture in, 238
regulator movement, 204
Revolutionary War land grants, *table*, 232
River Bend Township, 101
South Point Township, 1890 census, 101
state census schedules, 1623-1910, *table*, 117
state laws, printed, 182
Union veterans census for, 105
Union volunteers, indexes, *table*, 262
volunteers in Revolutionary War, *table*, 256
North Dakota
adoption records in, access to, 192
correctional institutions in, *table*, 303
court records, 194
federal census, 1790-1910,*table*, 96
land records summary, 247
mortality schedules, *table*, 104
newspaper bibliography for, 422
plat maps and books, 229
state census schedules, 1623-1910, *table*, 117
state laws, printed, 182
Union veterans census for, 105
Northern Baptist Convention, records of, 141
Northern Neck Proprietary, 252
Northern-Pacific Railroad, 334
Northwest Territory
immigrants in, *table*, 453
private land claims in, 229
state laws, printed, 182
Northwestern Historical Society, 340
Northwestern Memorial Hospital Archives, source of midwife records, 522
Norway, dominant religion of, 137
Norwegian immigrants, research aids and bibliography, 508-509;
map, 508
Norwegian records, 135
Norwegian-American Lutheran congregational records, 143
Notekeeping, 21-23
Notice of deposition, 158, 162
example of, 152
Notice, of divorce, 85
Nova Scotia, loyalists in, 235
Nuncupative will. *See* Court records, probate
Nuns
in Soundex, 100

O

Oath of allegiance, 472
OATS. *See* Original Article Text Service, 13
Obituaries
of biographical data in, 523
birthplace listed in, 409
Occupation
biographies, 446
death certificate, on, 53
deceased, of, in mortuary records, 311, 313
directories, 388
epitaphs in, 69
mortality schedules, 50
monuments, on, 63
OCLC, Online Computer Library Center, 436
Of Immigrant Ways Series, 492
Office of Indian Affairs. *See* Bureau of Indian Affairs
Official Catholic Directory, The, 402
Ohio
1860-1880 census, index to, *table*, 101
1890 census
adoption jurisdiction in, *illus.*, 190
Akron, city directories, 397
Ashtabula County, divorces in, 88
black censuses in, 123
Cincinnati
1890 census, 101
city directories, 397
German Obituaries, 468
Jewish records, 609
marriage records in 83
Cleveland, city directories, 397
Clinton County, 1890 census, 101
Columbus, city directories, 397
Confederate burials in, *table*, 264
correctional institutions in, *table*, 303
court records, 194
divorce in, 84, 87
federal census, 1790-1910,*table*, 96
fire lands in, 231
First Families of, 679
genealogical records of, 11
Hamilton County,
Hamilton County, 1890 census, 101
indexes and abstracts, 425
inheritance by adoptees, 192
land records summary, 247-248
maritime records of, 527
marriage laws in, 83
marriage license, 35-36
Meigs County, mortality schedules, *table*, 104
plat maps and books, 229
state census schedules, 1623-1910, *table*, 117
state laws, printed, 182
Union veterans census for, 105
Union volunteers, indexes, *table*, 262
veterans' home in, 281
Wayne Township, 1890 census, 101
will index, 441
Ohio Company, 231
Okayama prefecture, 599
Oklahoma
1860-1880 census, index to, *table*, 101
adoption investigations, 192
correctional institutions in, *table*, 303
court records of, 194
federal census, 1790-1910,*table*, 96
land records summary, 248
newspaper bibliography for, 422
state census schedules, 1623-1910, *table*, 117
state laws, printed, 182
Union veterans census for, 105
Union volunteers, indexes, *table*, 262
Oklahoma Historical Society, Native American research, 535, 541
Old Spanish Mission Historical Research Library, 573
Old trades, names of, 342
Oldstone Enterprises, 69
On-Line Databases, 662-664
Onate, Juan de, 568
Online Computer Library Center, how to use, 407, 436
Online, definition of, 663
Ontario, Canada, divorces in Ohio for, 88
Oral history, 41-47
in black research, 579
Oral interview,
Charles Muhls Bancroft Library,
notebooks 46
Chautauqqua Historical Society,
Draper Manuscript Collection, 46
equipment for, 46
how to conduct, 41-42
Hupert Howe Bancroft Papers, 46
Westfield, New York, papers, 46
Oral Roberts University Library, 146
Order of Americans of Armorial Ancestry, 680
Order of Colonial Lords of Manors in America, 680
Order of Descendants of Colonial Physicians and Chirurgieons, 681
Order of Stars and Bars, 676
Order of the Crown in America, 685
Order of the Crown of Charlemagne in the United States of America, 685, 688
Order of the First Families of Virginia, 678-679
Order of the Founders and Patriots of America, 677
Order of Three Crusades 1096-1192, 665
Orders, types of court, 165, 169-170
See also court records, 165, 169-170
Oregon
1870 census, 388
adoption investigations, 192
correctional institutions in, *table*, 303
court records, 194
draft records of, 265
federal census, 1790-1910,*table*, 96
genealogical records of, 11
indexes and abstracts, 425
land claim indexes, 441
land records summary, 248
mining district, extra-legal, 207
mortality schedules, *table*, 104
newspaper bibliography for, 422
Sons and Daughters of Pioneers, 678
state census schedules, 1623-1910, *table*, 117
state laws, printed, 182
Union veterans census for, 105
Union volunteers, indexes, *table*, 262
veterans, home in, 285
Organizational directories, 387, 400-402
Orientals. *See also* Asian American research
Soundex, 100
Original Article Text Service (OATS) 13-14
Original jurisdiction, *def.*, 151; *See also* Courts
Original manuscripts, on microform, 3
Ornaments, as memorial gifts, 63
Orphan, *def.*, 177; apprenticed, 321
Orphanagè records
Catholic Church, the, 322
court records, 185; *illus.*, 154
Osage, in Confederacy, 541
Ottawa, removal records, 538
Out-of-print books, University Microfilms, 3
Oyer and terminer. *See* courts. *illus.*, 154

P

Pacific School of Religion, 145
"Padding the totes," in census records, 91
Palatine
emigration, sources of, *map,* 456
immigrants, migration patterns, 474
passenger list order, 466
Palmer family, 680
Paper, for tombstone rubbing, 69
Pardons, *illus.*, 310
Parents
in biographies
on monuments, 63
orphanage records, 321
Parish and vital records listings, 476
Parish registers, vital records in, 50
Parish vestry courts, *illus.*, 153
Parliament, appeals to, 192
Partnerships. *See* Deeds
Passenger lists, 613; *illus.*, 614
newspaper indexes, 417
of immigrants, 462-465
retained by shipping companies, 457
See also immigration, indexes
ship's *illus.*, 612
Passport, as emigration records, 39, 454-455
Patent books. *See* Land records
Patent. *See* Deeds, land titles
Paupers, section of graveyards, 68
Payroll records, 335
Peabody Library, indexed listings of card catalog, 435
peddlers, licenses, 1750-1855, 333
Pedigree chart,
use in oral interviews, 42
illus., of 43
Pedigrees, fraudulent, 23
Peking University Library, 600
Pell family, 680
Penitentiaries, United States, *table,* 302
Penn, William, 240
Pennsylvania
1790 census, 124
access to adoption records in, 192
admiralty court, *table,* 196
adoption in, 192
adoption jurisdiction in, *illus.*, 190
Amish, 137
bounty land grants, 231
census, special schedules 1850-1880, *table,* 108
city/town schedule, *table,* 121
Colonial Society of, 680
Committee of Safety records, 206
Confederate burials in, *table,* 264
correctional institutions in, *table,* 303
court minutes, *illus.*, 168
court records, 194
direct tax list for, 236
directories, Pittsburgh, 388
divorce in, 84, 86, 88
Federal census, 1790-1910,*table,* 96
Freedman in, 580
genealogical records of, 11
German church records, 144
German emigrants, links with American churches, 481
German Reformed church records, 148
immigrants in, *table,* 453
indexes and abstracts, 425, 441
Jewish settlement of, 603
Lancaster County, 157
land allotment in, 219
land inheritance, 238
land records summary, 248-249
licenses, tavern, 1750-1855, 333
marriage records in, 74, 396
mining district, extra-legal, 207
mortality schedules, *table,* 104
newspaper bibliography for, 422
Philadelphia
1870 enumerations, 395
black censuses (1838, 1856, 1847), 124
census records of blacks, 593
city directories, 397
Eastern State Penitentiary, 301
immigrant index, 441
immigrants of, 468
Jewish Archives Center, 612
jurisdiction of, 533
licenses for peddlers and hawkers, 1820-1838, 333
marriage records in, 396
Pittsburgh
directories, 396; *illus.*, 393
marriage records in, 396
prison records, microfilmed, 311
Providence Island, hospital for diseased immigrants, 462
registration rolls, immigrants, 465
Revolutionary War land grants, *table,* 232
state census schedules, 1623-1910, *table,* 117
state laws, printed, 182
taxation censuses, 121
teaching certificates from 1866, 333
Union veterans census for, 105
Union volunteers, indexes, *table,* 262
volunteers in Revolutionary War, *table,* 256
Pennsylvania Abolition Society, 124
Pennsylvania Historical Society in Philadelphia, travel documents, 456
Pension Office, records of, *table,* 199
Pension records
1840 census, 103
applications, (1789-1861), 274-275
award to widow of veteran, 50
Civil War indexes, 440
Civil War, 275-280
Civil War, applications file, *Illus.*, 285-291
Confederate, 279
military records available from NARS, 256-257; (1774-1811), 267-274
Revolutionary war, 231, 439
Revolutionary War, application, *illus.*, 273,
Pensions, Bureau of, Special Examination Division, 540
Pentecostal Church records, 146
Performance bonds. *See* Deeds
Periodicals
genealogical church records, 140
genealogical, 13; list of, 438
of historical society, 140
specialty, how to locate, 372
University microfilms, 3
Perkins, Carol A. 66, 70
Permissions, resolution on, of Association of American University Presses, 27
Personal histories, marriage records in, 83
"Personal liberty laws", of northern states, 591
Personal name indexes, 429-430
"Pest" hospital records, 462
Petit jury, records of, 170
Petitions
for adoption, 190-191
for freedom, 185
for naturalization, 472
for support, 586
See Land grants
See Land records, 219
Pew rentals, 135
Phelps Gorham Collection, 251
Phelps Gorham Land Company, 246
Phelps Gorham Papers, 247
Philadelphia Free Library, 387
Philadelphia Insurance Company, records of, 331
Philadelphia, Jews in, 613
Philippine immigrants, research aids and bibliography, 509
Philips family, 680
Photograph archives, in urban resrach, 528-529
Photographs,
birth information in, 35
identification of, 39
in family records, to locate businesses, 371
in research, 468
Pike, Albert, 541
Pilgrim societies. *See* Early settlers societies, 686-689
Pilot indentures book, 328; *illus.*, 328
Pimeria Alta. *See* Arizona.
Pinkasim. 612
Pioneer Societies. *See* Lineage and heritage societies
Piscataqua Pioneers, 678
Pitts Theology Library, 145
Place-names,
how to identify, 15
Plaintiff's declaration, example of, 157
See also court records, 157
Plaintiff. *See* Courts
Plantation records, 583
Plaques or inscriptions, 63
Plat
books. *See* Land records
map, how to draw, *illus.*, 221
map, use of, 220
record, 61
See also Land grants
Pleadings.
See also Courts
Plot registers,
cemetery, 60
Poland
dominant religion of, 137
Jewish records in, 620
Jewish records in, microfilmed, 615, 630-645
Police census. *See* Sheriff census, 121
Policemen, lists of, in newspapers, 411
Polish Genealogical Society of Chicago, 417
Polish graveyards, 68
Polish immigrants,
research aids and bibliography, 509-510; *map,* 509
Polish-Jewish records on microfilm, *listing,* 510-623
Political groups
lists of in newspapers, 411
Political party, in biographies, 445
Polk, R.L., 387, 399-400
Poll tax. *See* Taxes
Polynesian customs, in Hawaii, 237
Pomfret, John E., 248
Poorhouse
1880 census, 100
in censuses, 91
Popular tribunals. *See* courts. *illus.*, 154
Post office and street directories, 402-403
Postcard photographs, 39
illus., of, 51
Postcards
family information in, 40
Potawatomi, removal records, 538
Powell Roll, 1867, 518
Powers of attorney. *See* Deeds
Precincts
1870 census, 388
Preemption rights, 229
Prefectural associations, 599
Preliminary hearing, in criminal case, 154
Prereogative courts, *illus.*, 154
Presbyterian, biographical index, 145
church archives, 145
church, records of, by country, 13
Historical Society, 145
Ministers Fund, (1759-), 331
Presentment, of criminal case, 153
Primogeniture, 237
Princeton Theological Seminary, 145
Printed genealogies, indexes to, 436-437
Printed Histories and Compiled Sources, 3-4, 613
Printouts, computer, 653
Prison records, 301
biographical registers, 301
hospital record books, 306

jurisdictions of, 301
See also Institutional Records
Prisoner's docket, 173
Prisoners, registers of, 301; *illus.*, 306
Prisons
in censuses, 91
Privacy laws, relating to divorce, 85
Privacy, rights of, 25-26
Privacy. *See* Right to Privacy laws
Private disbursement, probates, 185
Private land claims, location of, 229-230
Privy Council of the King, 192
Prize cases, appealed to Continental Congress, 194
Probate, 185
bonds. *See* Deeds
bondsmen, 187
court records, death date in, 187
executor, 187
femme sole, 187
guardians, 187
in newspapers *illus.*, 413
in newspapers, 413
Processioning, 219
Professional directories, 398-400
Professional genealogists. *See* genealogists, 442
Professional records. *See* Business records
professionals, 332-333
Programming languages, 653
Progressive movement, influence on vital records, 522
Proof, problems of, 23-24
Property
disputes. *See* court records equity
in divorce cases, 87
law, English, before 1860, 237
real/personal, 230
taxes. *See* Taxes
Proprietor, in land transactions, 219, 222
Prostitutes, registering of, *illus.*, 333
Protestant Episcopal church archives, 145-146
in southern colonies, 137
Protestant immigrants, societies for, 468
Providence Plantation, 249. *See also* Rhode Isalnd, 249
Provincil Congress, extra-legal activities of, 206
Prussia
Calvinism in, 137
church records, 131
territorial boundaries of, 478
Prussian immigrants
1820-1860, 453
Public domain states, 224-230
Public interests, in land, 237
Public lands,
vital records in applications for, 50
Public Record Office, divorce records in, 87
Public-domain states, 217
Published biographies. *See* Biographies, compiled, 448-449
Published local histories, vital records in, 50
Pueblo, land grants, 566
Puerto Rico
naturalization in, 469
Purisima Condeption de Acuna records, 563
Puritans, marriage records, 134

Q

Quaker records
archives, 146
gravestones, 68
in America before 1776, 481
monthly meetings, marriage records in, 75
Swarthmore College, 140
vital records in, 51
Women Friends Petition, 1659, 481
Quapaw, removal records, 538
Quarter Sessions, courts of, 192; *illus.*, 153
Quartermaster claims, *table*, 199
Queen Anne's War, 255
Quitclaim deeds. *See* Deeds
Quitrient, land taxes, 236

R

R.G. Dun and Company, 332
R.J. Taylor, Jr., Foundation, 241
R.L. Polk and Company, 397
Railroad archives, *table*, 340
Railroad employees, records of, 338-340
Newberry Library, 527
Retirement Board, 337,340
Random Access Memory. *See* RAM, 652
Ranger-Regulator court, 204
Real estate transactions in newspapers, 407, 413; *illus.*, 412
"Real" property, *def.*, 236-237
Reavis, James Addison, 565
Receiver. *See* Guardian
Reconstruction, land transference during, 249
Recorders courts. *See* Courts
Redemptioners, in immigration, 455
Redress petitions, probate, 185
Reform Judaism, 606
Reformed church archives, Dutch, 146
Refuge Tract, 248
Regimental records, of blacks, 580
Regional indexes, 440-441
Regional, business directories, 397-398
Register system of family relationships, how to use, 24-25
Registers
descriptive, of prisoners, 306
illus. of, 52
of births, 50-52
prisoners, 173
religious school, Jewish, 606
See also Directories, 387
Registration rolls for immigrants, 465
Registry of Black American Genealogy, for black records, 593
Registry of Jewish Ancestry, 617
Regular Army Mobile Units, 1821-1942, 521
Regulators, colonial courts, *illus.*, 153
Reinterment projects, 66
Relational databases, 651
Releases in probate, 185
Religion, in prison records, 301
Religious newspapers, 416
Religious affiliation of deceased, in mortician's records, 313
Religious affiliation, determining, 137-141
Religious directories, 402
Religious school registers, Jewish, 606; *illus.*, 606
Religious sections of graveyards, 68
Religious societies, 684-685
Removal records. *See* Native American research, 538
Renunciation petitions, probate, 185
Repositories, 1-3, 338-340, 612
church records, 141-148
Repositories, Jewish, *tables*, 612
Research and finding aids, 341
See also Spanish and Mexican American research, 561
Research calendar, in record keeping, 45; *illus.*, of 45
Research in foreign countries, 614-617
Research log, in notekeeping, 21
Research procedures, 31-47
Research Publications, Inc. and microfilmed directories, 397 404
Research skills, 21-23
family group sheets, 21
fraudulent pedigrees, 23
notekeeping, 21-23
tablet notes, 21, 22
Researchers. *See* Genealogists
Residence, in directories, 387
Residence licenses, of blacks, 579
Residence of deceased, on death certificate, 53
Residences in biographies, 445
Residency requirements in divorce cases, 88
Retailing companies, 50 largest, *listing*, 364
Review procedure, 204
Revolution
1776 census during, 119, 121
substitute censuses during, 125
Revolutionary War
Brigham Young University Library, card index to soldiers of, 294
Committees of Correspondence in, 205
courts in, 195
index to pension records of, 273
membership societies of, 674
military indexes, 439
military land grants, *table*, 232
pensioners in census, 103
Prize cases, 1776-1787, 194
records relating to blacks, 580
Sons of Liberty, 207
veterans indexed, *illus.*, 106
Rhenish Palatinate and Calvinism, 137
Rhode Island
1790 census, 124
1860-1880 census, index to, *table*, 101
admiralty court, *table*, 196
adoption jurisdiction in, *illus.*, 190
Confederate burials in, *table*, 264
correctional institutions in, *table*, 303
court records, 194
deeds in, 222
direct tax list for, 236
divorce in, 86, 88
draft records of, 265
early court system in, 192
Federal census, 1790-1910,*table*, 96
genealogical records of, 11
immigrants in, *table*, 453
inheritance by adoptees, 192
Jewish settlement of, 603
land records summary, 249
mortality schedules, *table*, 104
no bounty land grants, 231
primogeniture in, 238
state census schedules, 1623-1910, *table*, 117
state laws, printed, 182
Union veterans census for, 105
Union volunteers, indexes, *table*, 262
urban jurisdiction in, 533
volunteers in Revolutionary War, *table*, 256
Rider Index (AGBI), national 1790 census index, 434, 440
Right of Privacy Act of 1974, limitations of, 25
Right to know, 25
Right to Privacy Laws
relating to marrige records, 83
Right-of-Privacy laws, 25-26, 321
and social security number, 53
regarding military records, 265
Rights of access, 25-26
Rights of inheritance. *See* Adoption, 192
Robert C. Winthrop Collection, 1631-1794, 240
Robertson, Alice, papers of, 541
Robertson, Anna Eliza Worcester, papers of,541
Roman Catholic Church, 131; archives, 146-147
Romania, Jewish records in, 643
Rooting Treasures, 68
Rost, G. A., collection Oklahoma land rush, 542
Roumanian immigrants, research aids and bibliography, 498
Royal and Baronial Societies, 685; *illus.*, 686-687
Royal lineage, proof of, 685
Rubbings, tombstone, 68-69
Russia
immigrants, 1880-1920, 454
Jewish emigration routes from, 603
Jewish records in, 630
research aids and bibliography, 510; *map*, 510
Russian-American Company, control of Alaska, 239

S

Saint Andrew's Society, 681
Saint Augustin Church of Laredo, Spanish church records in, 565
Saint David's Society of the State of New York, 684
Saint George's Society, 681-684
Saint Nicholas Society of the City of New York, 676
Salvage. *See* Courts, admiralty
Salvation Army archives, 147
Samford University Library, and Baptist records, 141
Samplers,
  birth information on, 35
  marriage information in, 36
San Antonio Mission, records of, 563
San Felipe de Austin, Spanish court records of, 562
San Francisco, 1852 census falsified, 91
San Jacinto Descendants, 675
San Xavier del Bac Mission, Oblasser Library, 571
SAR. *See* National Society Sons of the American Revolution, 674
Scandinavian immigrants, diaries, 456
  Lutheran records, 135, 143
Scandinavians, positions of graves, 6363
Schlesinger, Keith, 521
School
  legal age, *table*, 186
School board minutes in community newspapers, 411
School board minutes, 317, 318
School census, *illus.*, 122
School news, in community newspapers, 411
School records, 301, 317-321
  admission application, *illus.*, 319
  Bureau of Indian Affairs, 318
  census of students, *illus.*, 320
  directories, 321
  evidence of birth, 53
  microfilmed by the Genealogical Society of Utah, 318
  poor children, list of, *illus.*, 319
  school board minutes, 317-318
  school board minutes, *illus.*, 318
  university and college, 321
School records, in Asian genealogy, 599
Schools, in prison records, 301
Schwenkfelder church archives, 147
Scotland
  dominant religion of, 137
  Dumfriesshire, 42
  church records, 131
Scots-Irish immigrants
  research aids and
    bibliography, 511-512;
    map, 512
Scottish immigrants, 1790, 453
  distribution of by state, *table*, 453
  migration patterns, 474
  research aids and
    bibliography, 510-511;
    map, 511
  societies for, 468
"Seals," 218, 252
Seaman records. *See* Courts, admiralty
Secretary of State, civil and military service registers, 400
  incorporation records of, 338
Selective Service Board of Registration.
  See Military records, draft records.
Seminoles
  in Confederacy, 541
  records of, 535
  removal records, 538
Seoul National University Library and clan records, 600
Sephardic Jews, *See also,* Jewish American Research, 603
Service companies, forty-five largest, 367
Service records, of Spanish American War, through modern wars, 265, 267
Setterdahl, Mrs. Lennart, 144
Settlement patterns, 16-17; process of, 467-468
  probate, 185
Settler and ship societies, 676-679
Seventh Day Baptist Library, 141
Seventh-day Adventist. *See* Adventist
Severs, Frederick B., collection of, 541
Sewell family, 680
Sex, in mortality schedules, 50
Sexton's records, 58-59, 60, 67; *illus.*, 62
Shakers archives, 147
Shakers, and alimony, 88
Shawnee, with Cherokee, 537
Sheriff census, examples of 1669-70, 121
Sheriff's sale, 218
Sheriff, docket of, 173
Sheriff. *See also* Court records, sheriff
Shiga prefecture, 599
Ship societies, membership in, 676-679
Ship's passenger lists, 612
Ship's records. *See* Courts, admiralty courts
Shipping companies, list of, 457
Ships
  in newspapers, 414
  logs, sources of, 464
  manifests, 416
Siblings, names of, on monuments, 63
Signers of the Declaration of Independence, 442
Silar, David W., 536
Simons Historical Library and Archives, 144
Sisters and brothers. *See* Siblings
Sistler, Byron & Associates, 99
Sixkiller, Samuel, case study, 542
Slattery, Thomas E., 248
Slave courts, *illus.*, 154
Slave declarations, 592
Slave schedules for Virginia, 1860, *table*, 109
Slavery, records of, 583-591
Slavery, shipping records of, 583
Slaves
  1840 census, 103
  census schedules of 1850-60, *illus.*, 105
  christening records of, 133
  death records of, 53
  in census records, 91
  in vigilante records, 207
  laws concerning property of, 187
  manumission records of, 591
  runaway, advertisements for, 415-416
  Underground Railroad, 591-592
Slovak Lutheran congregations, 144
Small business, 335
Small Claims courts, *illus.*, 154
Smith Tangier genealogies, 680
Social and welfare services, orphans, 321, 529
Social Security
  application for, evidence for birth certificate, 53
  area allocations, *table*, 337
  benefits and birth registration, 52
  records of, 335
Social Security number of deceased,
  on death certificate, 53
Social statistics (1850-80)
  cemetery descriptions, 109
  church memberships, 109
  social groups, 109
Social Statistics schedule, 1850-1880, location, *table*, 108-109
Society column, and birth notices, 410
Society of American Archivists Committee on Labor Records, 335
Society of American Archivists, 139, 369
Society of California Pioneers, 676-677
Society of Descendants of the Colonial Clergy, 681
Society of Friends. *See also* Quakers, 124
Society of Indiana Pioneers, 679
Society of the Ark and the Dove, 678
Society of the Cincinnati, 674
Society of the Descendants of Washington's Army at Valley Forge, 675
Society of the Founders of Norwich, Connecticut, 687-688
Society of the Friendly Sons of Saint Patrick, 684
Society of the Whiskey Rebellion of 1794, 655
Software, computer, 652-653
Software, genealogy programs, 655-658
Soldier Brides Bill, 598
Soldiers. *See* Military records, 439
Sons and Daughters of Oregon Pioneers, 678
Sons and Daughters of the First Settlers of Newbury, Massachusetts, 679
Sons of Confederate Veterans, 676
Sons of the American Revolution, indexes of, 442
Sons of the Republic of Texas, 677
Sons of the Union Veterans of the Civil War, 676
Sons of Utah Pioneers, 678
Soundex
  1880 limitations, 100
  1900 card file system, 101
  1910 federal census, 102
  family relationships in, 101
  household card, *illus.*, 102
  how to use of, 99
  in citizenship, 101
  index to federal census, 99, 101
  spelling system, 91
  use of with censuses, 521-522
  use of, 128
Soundex abbreviations, *table*, 101
South African immigrant, research aids and
    bibliography, 512
South Carolina
  1790 census, 92, 124
  admiralty court, *table*, 196
  adoption investigations, 192
  adoption jurisdiction in, *illus*, 190
  alimony in, 88
  black court records, 209
  bounty land grants, 231
  Charleston, Jews in, 603
  Cherokees in, 536
  church records in, 131
  Committee of Safety records, 206
  Confederate pensions for, 279
  Confederate volunteers from, *table*, 262
  copyhold in, 237
  correctional institutions in, *table*, 303
  court records, 194
  court laws for blacks in, 209
  divorce in, 87-88
  extra-legal courts, 204
  federal census, 1790-1910, *table*, 96
  genealogical records of, 11
  Huguenot Society of, 684
  immigrants and arrivals, list of, 465
  Indexes and abstracts, 425-426
  land records summary, 249
  marriage records in, 75
  mortality schedules, *table*, 104
  newspaper bibliography for, 422
  primogeniture in, 238
  ranger-regulator court unit, 204
  Revolutionary War land grants, *table*, 232
  separation from North Carolina, 249
  state census schedules, 1623-1910, *table*, 117
  state laws, printed, 182
  Union veterans census for, 105
  Union volunteers, indexes, *table*, 262
  volunteers in Revolutionary War, *table*, 256
  will abstracts, 187
South Dakota
  adoption records in, 192

correctional institutions, *table*, 303
court records, 194
federal census, 1790-1910,*table*, 96
Jefferson Township, 1890 census, 101
land records summary, 250
mortality schedules, *table*, 105
plat maps and books, 229
state census schedules, 1623-1910, *table*, 117
state laws, printed, 182
Union County, 1890 census, 101
Union veterans census for, 105
urban jurisdictions in, 533
veterans' home in, 285
Southeast Aisan immigration, 598
ethnic associations, 599
home sources, use in, 598
tracing Asian ancestry, 598-600
U.S. repositories, 599
vital records, for, 598-599
Southern Baptist Convention, 13
Southern Baptist Theological Seminary Library, 141
Southern Claims Commission, records of, 527
table, 199
illus., 155
Southern Lutheran church records, 144
Southern states
land allotment in, 219
Southern states records, index to, 441
divorce in, 84
Southwest Museum, 572
Southwest states, genealogical sources in, 559-577
Southwest Territory, immigrants in, *table*, 453
Southwestern Baptist Theological Seminary Library, 141
Soviet Union, Jewish records of, 617, 620
Spanish American War records, 265-267
Spanish and Mexican American research, 559-577
Arizona, records and archives, 568-569
baptism records, *illus.*, 564
Bexar archives, Texas, records of, 559
bibliography, 573-577
Calfornia, church records, *listing*, 570-571
California, court records, 570
California, land records, 569-570
California, provincial records, 569
Catholic church, records of, 563-564, 568, 569, 570-571
census records available, 561
court of private land claims, 567
court records, 562-563
empressario contracts, 561
land grants, 567
land records, 561-562, 565-567, 569-570; *table*, 544
Laredo Archives, 562
legal records, 562-563
marriage records, 563-564
Mexican national government, records of, 559-565
Nacogdoches archives, Texas, records of, 559
New Mexico, church records, *listing*, 568
New Mexico, provincial archives, records of, 565
repositories, *listing*, 571-573
Spanish sovereignty, records under, 559.571
territorial acquisitions by U.S., *illus.*, 560
Texas provincial records, 559-565
will and probate records, *illus.*, 566-567
Spanish Cabildo judicial records in Louisiana, 243
Spanish court records, 562
Spanish immigrants, 1790, 453
distribution of by state, *table*, 453
research aids and bibliography, 512-513; *map*, 512
Spanish land law, in the Southwest, 237
Spanish marriage contracts, 78
Spanish records, bibliography of, 573-577
Spanish, California records, 569-571
Spanish, genealogical sources, 559-567
genealogical sources, 559-577
Spanish-Portuguese Jews, 603
Special court proceedings, genealogical value in, 187-209
Special Examination Divison, Bureau of Pensions, 540
Special federal schedules cross-referenced, 102, 103. *See also* Federal schedules, 102-119
Special jurisdiction. *See* Courts
Special schedules
census 1850-1880, *table*, 108-109
See also Census
Spelling variants, 17-20, 59, 84, 99-100, 429
Spouse, name of,
on death certificate, 53
on monuments, 63
St. David's Reformed Church, 70
St. Francis River, Cherokees in, 536
St. John's Seminary Library, 571
St. Louis University
Catholic church records, 147
St. Mary's Seminary and University
Catholic church records, 147
Stained glass windows, as memorials, 63
Standing Committee on Law Lists, 398-399
Starr Roll, 1894, 518
State archives, extra-legal colonial records, 206
State bar associations and law directories, 399
State board of health, marriage records, 75
State census, 1623-1918, 119-126, 522
State court, system explained 1789-present *illus.*, of, 154
State health departments, and burial regulations, 62
State Historical Society of Wisconsin
records of the United Church of Christ, 137
State incorporation registers, 371
State medical examiners. *See* Coroners' records
State indexes of Civil War, 440
State military records, 294
State-by-state listing
city censuses, *table*, 120-121
Confederate volunteers, 262
correctional institutions, *table*, 302-304
Federal census, 1790-1910,*table*, 94-97
Freedmen's Bureau records, 581
indexes and abstracts, 423-26
indexes to 1860-1880 censuses, *table*, 101
land offices, 238-252
military records, Genealogical Society of Utah collection, *table*, 264
nationality, distribution of in 1790, *table*, 453
of divorce courts, 86
Social Security number allocations, 337
special census schedules 1850-1880, *table*, 108-109
state land records, 238-252
State-land states, 217, 219
Statues, as memorial gifts, 63
Statute. *See* Law
Statute of frauds, 238
Statute of uses, 237
Steamships, in city directories, 388
Stephen F. Austin State College Archive
Collection, Bexar records in, 559
Stets, dockets of, 167
Stock-Raising Homestead Act (1916), 225
Street directory, 393, 402-403
Subject encyclopedias, 4
Subpoena, in criminal case, 154
Suicide, example of inquest for, 172
Summary of aids, Eastern Europe, 497-498
Summary trial. *See also* Courts
Summons, by sheriff, 173
Sunday closing law, 151
Superior Courts of Special Jurisdiction, *table*, 153-154
Supreme Court
appeals to, 192
Indian records, in, 540
Supreme court of appeals, *table*, 154. *See* Courts appeals
Surname
common, 396
indexes, 13, 429
list, of U.S. Census Bureau, 18
listings of, 443
of immigrants on tombstones, 60
spelling sound patterns *table*, 19
Surrogate courts, *illus.*, 154
Survey plat. *See* Land records, titles
Sutro Library, California provincial records in, 569
Swarthmore College, Quaker records, 140
Sweden, society for immigrants from, 684
Swedish Baptist records, 141
Swedish burial patterns, 68
Swedish cemetery, 68
Swedish Colonial Society, 684
Swedish immigrants, 1790, 453
locating the immigrant ancestor, 481
research aids and bibliography, 513-514; *map*, 513
Swedish-American archives, of Lutheran Church, 143, 145
Swenson Swedish Immigration Research Center, 416
Swetland Roll, 1868, 518
Swetland, S. H., 536
Swiss immigrants
in Billeter collection, 488
Switzerland
church records, 131
Sylvester family, 680
Symmes Purchase, 247
Symmes, John Cleves, 231
Synagogue records, 604-608
account books, 606
minute books, 604-606; *illus.*, 604
religious school registers, 606
System Development Corporation, 661

T

Tangier *See* Smith, Tangier, 680
Taufschein See Birth records, 33
Tavern licenses, 1750-1855, 333
Tax lists, in deed books, 217
personal property in, 99
Tax roll (1764) 413
Taxation
census for, in Pennsylvania, 121
census records for, 91
legal age for, *table*, 186
Taxes and tax records, 235-236
assessed by local courts, 151
county lists, 235-236
direct federal, 236
genealogical information in, 235
head or poll taxes, 235
illus., 235
liens, 185
lists of, 236
property taxes, 235
quitrient, 236
See also Land records
use in replacing missing census, 236
Teachers, 333
Teaching certificates, 333
Teamsters Union, 335
Telegrams, birth information in, 35
Telephone directories, 388
Temple Records Index Bureau (TIB), 142
Tennessee
1790 census, 125
1860-1880 census, index to, *table*, 101
adoption jurisdiction in, *illus.*, 190

appeals in, 192
census, special schedules 1850-1880, *table*, 108
Cherokees in, 535-536
Civil War pensions applications of, 280
Confederate pensions for, 279
Confederate volunteers from, *table*, 262
correctional institutions in, *table*, 304
court records, 175, 194
direct tax list for, 236
divorce in, 84, 87-88
federal census, 1790-1910, *table*, 96
Freedmen's Bureau records, 581
genealogical records of, 11
indexes and abstracts, 426
inheritance by adoptees, 192
Ku Klux Klan in, 209
land office in, 219
land records summary, 250
military records, indexes, *table*, 261
military records, microfilmed by Genealogical Society of Utah, *table*, 264
mortality schedules, *table*, 105
newspaper bibliography for, 422
registers of blacks, 592
state census schedules, 1623-1910, *table*, 118
state laws, printed, 182
substitute for 1790 census schedule, 125
Union veterans census for, 105
Union volunteers, indexes, *table*, 262
veterans' home in, 285
Tennessee Valley Authority. *See also* courts
interments, 66
Tennessee, Watauga Association of extra-legal group, 207
Tenures, in land, 237
Territorial acquisitions, of U.S., 560
Territorial Courts, *illus.*, 155
Testate estate. *See* Court records, probate
Testify in court
legal age for, *table*, 186
Testimony at inquests, 314
Texas
1860-1880 census, index to, *table*, 101
access to adoption records in, 192
adoption jurisdiction in, *illus.*, 190
adoption records in, 192
Baptist records, 141
census, special schedules 1850-1880, *table*, 109
Confederate pensions for, 279
Confederate volunteers from, *table*, 262
correctional institutions, *table*, 304
court of claims, 1856-60, 250
court records of, 194, 562
courts of appeal, 192
Dallas, city directories, 397
Daughters of the Republic of, 677
divorce in, 84, 87
El Paso, city directories, 397
Ellis County, 1890 census, 101
extra-legal courts, 204
federal census, 1790-1910, *table*, 96
Freedmen's Bureau records, 581
genealogical records in. *See also* Spanish and Mexican American research, 559-568
genealogical records of, 11
Hood County, 1890 census, 101
Independence Day, society founded on, 675
indexes and abstracts, 426
Kaufman County, 1890 census, 101
land records of, 561
land records summary, 250
location of records, *listing*, 572 Society of Utah, *table*, 264
military records, microfilmed by Genealogical
mortality schedules, *table*, 105
naturalization in, 469
newspaper bibliography for, 422
provincial archives of, 559-561
Rusk County, 1890 census, 101
Spanish land system in, 229
Spanish records of, 562
state census schedules, 1623-1910, *table*, 118
state laws, printed, 182
Trinity Township, 1890 census, 101
Union veterans census for, 105
Union volunteers, indexes, *table*, 262
Texas Christian University, 142
Texas State Library, Nacogdoches Archives in, 559
Texas State University, Utah mortality *table*, 105
TIB. *See* Indexes, Mormon, Temple Index Bureau
Timber Act, 226
Tithingman, in criminal case procedure, 153
Title conveyance. *See* Deeds
Tokyo Bunko (Library), 600
Toledo Strip, 244
Tomahawk grant, 219
Tombs,
burial registers stored in, 63
Tombstones
birth and death dates, 60
colonial, 60
duplicate, 69
illus., of, 64-65
inscriptions, 60
inscriptions, Japanese, 600
rubbings, 68
soldier applications for, 281
See also Gravestones, 68
styles and materials of, 64-65
Tompkins Roll, 1867, 518
Topographical maps,
from National Cartographic Information Center, 16
Tories. *See* Loyalists
Torrens, land registry system, 218
Torts. *See also* Courts
Towns, marriage records of, 75
Towns, New England
history of, 220
land grants in, 220
Township plat, located, 226
Tract book, located, 226. *See also* Land records
Tract maps, drawing of, 220
Trade and Navigation Acts, *See* courts, admiralty
Transcript of case, example of sample equity case, 161-163
Transcripts, court records, 175
Transients, in directories, 387
Transition zone, in land grants, 219
Transportation companies, 50 largest, *listing*, 363
Transportation company records, 527
Travel documents, emigration records, 455-456
Treaty of 1817, 518
Treaty of Guadalupe Hidalgo, 569-570
Treaty of New Echota, 535-536
Trial briefs, in appeals courts, 193
Trial court, relationship to appeals
courts explained, 152
Trial courts, *def.* of, 152
Tribes. *See* Indians
Trophies,
family information in, 40
Trustee accounts, probate, 185
Tutor. *See* Guardian
Tuttle Antiquarian Books, 15

U

U. S. District Courts, records microfilmed, 194
U.S. Census Bureau, surname list of, 18, 403
U.S. census. *See* Census
U.S. Corps of Army Engineers, tombstone inscriptions, 66
U.S. Court of Claims, records of microfilmed, 194
U.S. Court of Customs and Patent Appeals, records of microfilmed, 194
U.S. Court of Military Appeals records of microfilmed, 194
U.S. Department of Agriculture, maps of, eastern U.S., western U.S., 17
U.S. Department of Energy, tombstone inscriptions, 66
U.S. Geodetic Survey quad map, 66
U.S. Geological Survey Maps (USGS) 15, 16
U.S. government, personnel records of, 371
U.S. ships and navy yards, in veterans census, 105
U.S. Soldiers Home Cemetery, 1861-68 registers of, 281
Ubanization, reasons for, 519
UDC. *See* United Daughters of the Confederacy, 676
Ultrafiche, records on, 2
UMI. *See* Xerox University Microfilms, 28
Underground Railroad, 1786-1860, *map*, 573
Undertaker, records of, 137, 464
Union lists and newspaper files
Union records, locating, 528
Unitarian Universalist Association, 142, 147
United Autombile Workers, 335
United Church of Christ, 137, 142, 147, 148
United Daughters of the Confederacy, 676
United Evangelical Lutheran church, 143-144
United Methodist Church, 137, 143, 145
United Mine Workers, 335
United States Congress, *See* Courts
United States Court of Claims, Indian records of, 539
United States Newspaper Project, 407
United States penitentiaries, *table*, 302
United States Regulatory Commission, *See* courts
illus., 155
United States settlement. *See* Immigration
United States Supreme Court, appeals to, 192
United States, territorial acquisitions of,
illus., 560
University alumni directories, 400-402
University Microfilms, 3, 14
dissertations, American and foreign, 3
out-of-print books, American and foreign, 3
periodicals, American and foreign, 3
theses, American and foreign
University of Hawaii, Japanese-American records, 599
University of Michigan, family histories, 435
University of Texas
and Protestant Episcopal records, 146
Bexar Arhives in, 559
University of Texas Library, Arizona records in, 569
University Press of Virginia, court records printed, 177
Unpublished genealogies, 4
Unrecorded wills, 185
Urban ancestors, sources for, 519-533
birth records, 522
business/occupational records, 527
cemetery records, 523
census records, 521-522
city directories, 519-520
coroners inquests, 523
court records, 526-527
death records, 522
enumerator district maps, 522
land indexes, 521
libraries and local archives, 529
maps, 521
marriage records, 522
naturalization records, 525
neighborhood sources, 528-529
printed sources, biographical, 525

religious sources, 523-524
Schlesinger, Keith, use of census, 521
selective service records, 525-526
street directories, 519-520
WPA inventory of records, 524
Urban jurisdictions, not subject to county authority, 533
Urban research, immigration patterns, 454
Used books, sources of, 15-16
USGS. *See* U.S. Geological Survey Maps, 16
Utah
1880 census falsified, 91
Asian American immigration, 597
census, special schedules 1850-1880, *table*, 109
correctional institutions in, *table*, 304
court records, 194
divorce in, 85, 88
draft records of, 265
genealogical records of, 11
indexes to land patents, 226
inheritance by adoptees, 192
land records summary, 250-251
marriage applications in, 78
mortality schedules, *table*, 105
newspaper bibliography for, 422
pioneer societies of, 677-678
Salt Lake City, city directories, 397
Sons of Pioneers, 678
state census schedules, 1623-1910, *table*, 118
state laws, printed, 182
Union veterans census for, 105
Union volunteers, indexes, *table*, 262
Utah Territory, divorces in, 88
Utilities, 50 largest, *listing*, 365, 368

V

Vaccination certificate, *illus.* of, 33
Van Courtlandt family, 680
van der Donck, family, 680
Van Rensselaer family, 680
Vault, 63
Velasco Treaty of 1836, territorial agreements after, 544
Vermont
1790 census, 124
1870 census, 388
adoption in, 192; *illus.*, 190
border dispute of, 251
census, special schedules 1850-1880, *table*, 109
correctional institutions, *table*, 304
court records of, 194
deeds in, 222
divorce in, 84, 86
draft records of, 265
extra-legal courts, 204
federal census, 1790-1910,*table*, 96
French immigrants, 453
immigrants in, *table*, 453
Indexes and abstracts, 426
inheritance by adoptees, 192
land records summary, 251
marriage records in (1770), 75
mortality schedules, *table*, 105
newspaper bibliography for, 422
Society of Colonial Dames, 680
state census schedules, 1623-1910, *table*, 118
state laws, printed, 182
Union veterans census for, 105
Union volunteers, indexes, *table*, 262
volunteers in Revolutionary War, *table*, 256
Vermont Old Cemetery Association, 66
Vermont Society of Colonial Dames, 680
Veterans
burial sites of, 60
census schedules, 1840, 1890, 103, 105
Civil War in 1890 census, 105
pensions of Civil War, 275-280
published names of, 103, 1105, 106
records of, *See* Military records
Revolutionary War indexed, 103, 105
Veterans Administration Computer database, for medical records, 265
Veterans' homes, records of, 281-285
Vietnam action, 255
Vietnam, officers, society, 675
Vigal, Donaciano, 565
Vigilante Committee of Philadelphia, slave records, 207
Vigilante committees. *See* also courts.
illus., 154
Vigilante records, of frontier, 207
Vigilante societies, extra-legal *See* courts
Viligance Committees, transported slaves, 591
Vintage assessments, Civil War, 526
Virgin Islands, naturalization in, 469
Virginia
admiralty court, *table*, 196
adoption in, 192; *illus.*, 190
appeals courts in, 192
birth records, of blacks, 583
bounty land grants, 231
burial traditions, 68
cemeteries in, Lexington, 69
census, special schedules 1850-1880, *table*, 109
Cherokees in, 536
church records in, 131
Committee of Safety reports, 206-207
Confederate pensions for, 279
Confederate volunteers from, *table*, 262
correctional institutions, *table*, 304
court records, 175, 194
divorce in, 86, 88
draft records of, 265
early court system in, 192
extra-legal courts, 204
federal census, 1790-1910,*table*, 96-97
Freedmen's Bureau records, 581
genealogical records of, 11-12
Huguenot Society of the Founders of Manakin in the Colony of, 684
index to printed genealogies, 441
indexes and abstracts, 426
land law in, 237
land records summary, 251-252
lineage in, 685
maps of, 16
marriage records in, 75
marriage registers in, 81
military district records, 234-235
mortality schedules, *table*, 105
newspaper bibliography for, 422
Order of the First Families of, 678-679
primogeniture in, 238
quitrient land taxes, 236
Revolutionary War land grants, *table*, 232
Richmond, city directories, 397
Richmond, Jews in, 603
society for early settlers of Jamestowne, 679
state census schedules, 1623-1910, *table*, 118
state laws, printed, 182
substitute for 1790 census schedule, 125
Union veterans census for, 105
Union volunteers, indexes, *table*, 262
urban jurisdiction in, 533
veterans' home in, 281
volunteers in Revolutionary War, *table*, 256
1790 census, 125
Virginia Company of London, 251
Visa, emigration, 454
Visiting rights, for children in divorce, 88
Vital records
duplicate copies of, 60
finding aids to, 60-73
in business and employment records, 50
in church records, 49-53
in coroners' reports, 50
in court minutes, 50
in diaries, 50
in family Bibles, 50
in family record books, 50
in homestead applications, 50
in hospital and doctors' records, 50
in journals, 50
in letters, 50
in local histories, 50
in Massachusetts, 49
in military pension files, 50
in morticians' records, 50
in New England town records, 50
in newspapers, 50, 417
in probate records, 50
in Quaker records, 51
in Virginia, 49-50
in West Virginia, 49
problems with completeness, 50, 59
restricted access, 59-60
state-by-state listing, 49
states registry prior to 1880, 49
urban research, 522
published local histories, 50
Vital statistics, church records, 131
church records, 131
Volunteer army in the Civil War, 400
Voting records, in cities, 525

W

Waiver, in probate, 185
Wakayama prefecture, 599
Wales, research, 515
Wales, society for descendants of, 681
Wales, society for immigrants from, 684
Wallenberg Foundation, 144
"War brides", 598
War dead, lists of, 409
lists of, 409
War of 1812, 127, 255
1790 census, 124
bounty land warrants, 233
census of New York victims
tax lists for, Civil War, tax lists, 236
War Records. *See* Military records
War Relocation Authority, *table*, 200
"War" societies, 671-676
Ward boundaries, on maps, 394
Ward. *See* Orphan
Warden's report of deaths, Congregation Bene Israel, 591
Warrant, example of, 160
See also court records, 160
Warrant, in criminal court procedure, 153, 173
See also Land records, titles
Warranty deed. *See* Deeds
Washington
1860-1880 census, index to, *table*, 101
correctional institutions, *table*, 304
court records, 194
draft records of, 265
federal census, 1790-1910,*table*,, 97
genealogical records of, 12
land records summary, 252
maps for Tacoma, 521
mortality schedules, *table*, 105
newspsper bibliography for, 422
Seattle, city directories, 397
state census schedules, 1623-1910, *table*, 118
state laws, printed, 182
Union veterans census for, 105
Union volunteers, indexes, *table*, 262
Washington National Records Service, 226, 394

Washington Territory
1870 census, 388
Indians in, 110
Washington, D.C.
city directories, 397
Confederate burials in, *table*, 264
correctional institutions in *table*, 302
courts, 155
direct tax list for, 236
Freedmen's Bureau records, 581
marriage records in (1811) 75
state census schedules, 1623-1910, *table*, 113
Union veterans census for, 105
urban jurisdiction of, 533
Washington, George, 675
Washington, Japanese-Americans in, *table*, 200
Watie, Stand, 541
WATTS line, to locate companies, 337
Waxes, for tombstone rubbing, 69
Wedding announcements, 137
Weddings, witnesses on church records,140
Weinburg, Andrew, 248
Welcome Society of Pennsylvania, 678
Welsh immigrants, 1790, 453
distribution, *table*, 453
research aids and bibliography, 515; *map*, 515
Welsh Society of Philadelphia, 681
West Florida archives, Alabama records in, 239
West Germany, Jewish records in, 620-630
West Jersey. *See also* New Jersey, 245
West Point, Civil War records of, 265
West Virginia
1860-1880 census, index to, *table*, 101
adoption in, 192
adoption jurisdiction in, *illus.*, 190
Confederate burials in, *table*, 264
correctional institutions in, *table*, 304
court records, 175, 194
divorce in, 84
divorce in, 87
federal census, 1790-1910, *table*, 97
Freedmen's Bureau records, 581
genealogical records of, 12
Kanawha County, 51
land office in, 219
land records summary, 252
marriage laws in, 83
marriage registers in, 81
mining district, extra-legal, 207
mortality schedules, *table*, 105
newspaper bibliography for, 422
state census schedules, 1623-1910, *table*, 118
state laws, printed, 182
Union veterans census for, 105
Union volunteers, indexes, *table*, 262
West Virginia University Library, manuscripts in, 12
Western Jewish History Center, 612
Western Michigan Genealogical Society, 129
Western Reserve Historical Society
and Shakers archives, 147
Who's Who. *See* Biographies, compiled, 445
Widows' allowances in probate, 185
William H. Boyd, directory publisher, 387
William R. Perkins Library, 145
Wills, 185
bequests in to maintain a graveyard, 64
blacks in, 583
date recorded, 187
example of, 175-176
in deed books
in deed volumes, 218
in equity case, 162
in newspapers, 413
legal age for writing, *table*, 186
omitted family members in, 187
See also Court records, probate
Winthrop, family, 680
Wisconsin
1860-1880 census, index to, *table*, 101
access to adoption records in, 192
census, special schedules 1850-1880, *table*, 109
church records, 137
Confederate burials in, *table*, 264
correctional institutions in, *table*, 304
court records of, 194
divorces in, 88
federal census, 1790-1910,*table*, 97
Fond du Lac County, biographics, 447
genealogical records of, 12
Indexes and abstracts, 426
land records summary, 252
marriage application in, 80
Milwaukee, city directories, 397
mortality schedules, *table*, 105
newspaper bibliography for, 422-423
plat maps and books, 229
state census schedules, 1623-1910, *table*, 118
state laws, printed, 182
Union veterans census for, 105
Union volunteers, indexes, *table*, 262
veterans' home in, 281
Wisconsin Evangelical Lutheran Church, archives of, 144
Wisconsin State Old Cemetery Society, 66
Wisconsin Synod, archives of, 144
Witnesses, legal age of, *table*, 186
Wollmershauser, Friedrich, 457
Women
data on, in local newspapers, 411
evidence of in cemeteries, 60, 67
in burial registers, 61
in compiled biographies, 445
locating graves of, 67
not included on tax lists, 235
omitted in indexes, 429
Women Friends Petitioners against Tithes, 1659, 481
Women immigrants, societies for, 468
Women's courts, *illus.*, 154
Word processing, 668
Workhouse records, paupers burials, 68
Works Progress Administration. *See* WPA, 167
Worksheets, for census records, 128-129
World War I, veterans records, 255, 265-267
World War II Exclusion Files, *table*, 200
World War II, veterans records, 255, 267
WPA
church and public records inventory, 524
court indexing projects by, 167
index to Chicago deaths, *illus.*, 523
marriage records collected by, 83
slave interviews, 593
Wright, Marcus J., 263
Writ of capias, in criminal court procedure.
example of, 160
See also Warrant
Writ of summons, example of, 157 , 159
See also Court records
Writs of court, 173
Wyandot, removal records, 538
Wyllys family, 680
Wyoming
1860-1880 census, index to, *table*, 101
cemeteries in, relocated, 66
census, special schedules 1850-1880, *table*, 109
correctional institutions in, *table*, 304
court records, 194
divorces in, 88
draft records of, 265
extra-legal courts, 204
federal census, 1790-1910, *table*, 97
jurisdiction of, 533
land records summary, 259
mortality schedules, *table*, 105
newspaper bibliography for, 423
state census schedules, 1623-1910, *table*, 118
state laws, printed, 182
Union veterans census for, 105
Union volunteers, indexes, *table*, 262

X

Xerox University Microfilms (UMI) 28

Y

Yad Vashem, 617
Yamaguchi prefecture, 599
Yearbooks. *See* Directories, 387
Yellowstone National Park, jurisdiction of, 533
YIVO Institute for Jewish Research, 612, 617
YIVO Institute for Jewish Research, 617
Yizkor books, Jewish holocaust survivors, 612
Young, Brigham, 123
Yugoslavia, Jewish records in, 643
Yugoslavian immigrants, research aids and bibliography, 515-516; *map*, 516
YWCA, and women immigrants, 468

Z

Zimmerman Library, University of New Mexico, Spanish records in, 565